# 2022 U.S. Master™ Depreciation Guide

**Wolters Kluwer Editorial Staff Publication**

***Access the Latest Tax Law Developments***

A special webpage created by CCH for the *U.S. Master Depreciation Guide®* will keep you up-to-date with late-breaking tax legislative and administrative developments occurring after publication of the 2022 edition. Visit *CCHCPELink.com/TaxUpdates* to find the information you'll need to keep *U.S. Master Depreciation Guide®* your first source for practical tax guidance.

Wolters Kluwer

ISBN: 978-0-8080-5370-5



2700 Lake Cook Road
Riverwoods, IL 60015
800 344 3734
CCHCPELink.com



Printed in the United States of America

FSC www.fsc.org MIX From responsible sources FSC® C099992

# Recent Developments

The Modified Accelerated Cost Recovery System (MACRS), introduced by the Tax Reform Act of 1986 and applicable to most tangible depreciable property placed in service after 1986, now dominates a stage formerly shared with both the Accelerated Cost Recovery System (ACRS), introduced by the Economic Recovery Tax Act of 1981, and the Treasury Department's Asset Depreciation Range (ADR) System, which was given a statutory basis by the Revenue Act of 1971.

Both MACRS and ACRS bear a special relationship to the ADR class life guidelines in that, under either system, property is generally classified by reference to class lives. Rev. Proc. 87-56, as modified by Rev. Proc. 88-22, prescribes class lives (and sets forth recovery periods) for MACRS property (¶ 191). Optional table percentages set forth in Rev. Proc. 87-57 and included in this publication may, with certain exceptions, be used to compute MACRS deductions.

Special rules apply to "listed property" which is defined to include automobiles and other types of business property particularly susceptible to personal use. These rules slow the recovery of the cost of cars and other "listed" property by requiring the use of the MACRS alternative depreciation system unless the listed property is used more than 50 percent for business (¶ 206). In addition, annual depreciation deductions for vehicles with a gross vehicle rating of 6,000 pounds or less are capped under the so-called "luxury car" rules regardless of the percentage of business use (¶ 200).

The *2022 U.S. Master™ Depreciation Guide*, covers all of these rules, including:

☐ recent legislation and administrative guidance (see 2022 Highlights on next page);

☐ depreciation fundamentals at ¶ 3–¶ 77;

☐ Code Sec. 197 intangibles at ¶ 12–¶ 64;

☐ Change of accounting rules when depreciation has not been claimed or incorrectly computed at ¶ 75;

☐ Change of accounting rules to comply with final MACRS general asset account, item/multiple asset account, and disposition regulations at ¶ 77;

☐ MACRS at ¶ 80–¶ 191;

☐ web site development costs at ¶ 125;

☐ bonus depreciation guidance at ¶ 127D–¶ 127J;

☐ MACRS general asset accounts under the final MACRS regulations at ¶ 128;

☐ MACRS dispositions including loss deductions for retired structural components under the final MACRS regulations at ¶ 162;

☐ passenger automobiles and other listed property at ¶ 200–¶ 214;

☐ cost segregation at ¶ 127–¶ 127C;

☐ ACRS at ¶ 220–¶ 290;

☐ the Code Sec. 179 expensing election at ¶ 300–¶ 307 and ¶ 487;

☐ the ADR system at ¶ 400–¶ 485;

☐ general (pre-1981) depreciation at ¶ 330–¶ 384; and

☐ planning for acquisitions and dispositions of depreciable property at ¶ 486–¶ 488.

Optional IRS tables for computing MACRS deductions (¶ 180) accompany the discussions of appropriate classes of property (¶ 100 and following), the alternative depreciation system (¶ 150), and the rules for recomputing allowances for purposes of the alternative minimum tax (¶ 170).

Selected regulations are reproduced beginning at ¶ 510.

## *Access the Latest Tax Law Developments*

A special webpage created by CCH for the *U.S. Master Depreciation Guide®* will keep you up-to-date with late-breaking tax legislative and administrative developments occurring after publication. Visit *CCHCPELink.com/TaxUpdates* to find the information you'll need to keep the *U.S. Master Depreciation Guide®* your first source for practical tax guidance.

---

## 2022 HIGHLIGHTS

### *IRS Rulings*

*Changes in computing certain residential rental property depreciation.* Rev. Proc. 2021-28 provides guidance explaining how taxpayers changes their method of computing depreciation for certain residential rental property. Automatic consent procedures for changing their accounting method are available for taxpayers adopting the depreciation method changes. The Tax Cuts and Jobs Act (P.L. 115-97) added residential rental property held by an electing real property trade or business to the list of property to which a 30 year recovery periods applies under the alternative depreciation system (ADS), thus changing the recovery period from 40 years to 30 years. The change applied to property placed in service after December 31, 2017, and therefore only to property newly place in service. The Taxpayer Certainty and Disaster Tax Relief Act (Taxpayer Certainly Act) (P.L. 116-260), extended the 30-year recovery period to apply to residential rental property held by certain electing real property trade or businesses and placed in service before January 1, 2018. To apply the 30-year recovery period to property already placed in service, taxpayers have to their change computation of depreciation for the property. See ¶ 152, "*Real property trade or business electing out of interest deduction limitation.*"

*Procedures provided for changing depreciation method* Rev. Proc. 2021-28 permits taxpayers who are affected by the Taxpayer Certainly Act's retroactive effective date to file an amended federal income tax return or information return, administrative adjustment request (AAR), or a Form 3115, Application for Change in Accounting Method, to change their method of computing depreciation of certain residential rental property held by an electing real property trade or business to use a 30-year ADS recovery period. If the property is included in a general asset account, it permits taxpayers to change their general asset account treatment for the property to comply with Reg. § 1.168(i)-1(h)(2). See ¶ 152, "*Real property trade or business electing out of interest deduction limitation.*"

*2021 and 2020 luxury car depreciation caps and lease inclusion tables.* The depreciation caps for cars and trucks placed in service in 2021 were announced in Rev. Proc. 2021-31 and for 2020 in Rev. Proc. 2020-37. See ¶ 200 for cap amounts and ¶ 205 for lease inclusion tables.

*Luxury car depreciation cap safe harbor for 100 percent bonus depreciation.* A safe harbor allows taxpayers to claim depreciation deductions in each year of a vehicle's depreciation period even though the 100 percent bonus deduction is claimed in the placed-in-service year. The first-year 100 percent bonus deduction is limited to the first-year cap ($18,200 for a vehicle placed in service in 2021 and $18,100 for a vehicle placed in service in 2020). No special statement is required (Rev. Proc. 2019-13). See ¶ 200, *1A. Safe Harbor for Vehicles Acquired after September 27, 2017 and placed in service before 2023 if 100 Percent Bonus Claimed.*

See ¶ 75 for a discussion of the change in accounting method rules.

*2020 and 2021 Code Sec. 179 limitations.* The section 179 dollar limits are $1,050,000 for a tax year beginning in 2021 (Rev. Proc. 2020-45) and $1,080,000 for a tax year beginning in 2022 (Rev. Proc. 2021-45). The investment limitation is $2,620,000 for 2021 and $2,700,000 for 2022.

*2021 and 2020 standard mileage rates.* The standard mileage rate for miles driven in 2022 is 58.5 cents per mile and in 2021 is 56 cents per mile (Notice 2022-3; Notice 2021-2). See ¶ 217.

*$25,000 SUV expensing limit adjusted for inflation.* The $25,000 section 179 expensing limit for SUV's, short-bed trucks, and vans seating 10 or more persons behind the driver's seat is increased to $26,200 for tax years beginning in 2021 (Rev. Proc. 2020-45) and $27,000 for 2022 (Rev. Proc. 2021-45). This limit applies if the vehicle is exempt from the luxury car depreciation limits because it exceeds 6,0000 pounds gross vehicle weight rating. See ¶ 201.

### *Updated Luxury Car Chart Listing Heavy Vehicles and Trucks with Short Bed Length*

The quick reference table that list trucks, vans, and SUVs with a gross vehicle weight rating (GVWR) in excess of 6,000 pounds is updated to include 2022 models. Pick-up trucks in excess of 6,000 pounds GVWR and a cargo bed length of less than 6 feet which are subject to a section 179 expensing limit of $26,200 for tax years beginning in 2021 ($27,000 in 2022) is included. See page 1295 in the Appendix.

**December 2021**

# TABLE OF CONTENTS

Paragraph

## Corporate Earnings and Profits



## Roundup of Selected Rules for Pre-1981 Property



## Class Life ADR System

# The Depreciation Story

## *Historical Background*

## ¶ 1

### From 1913 to Now

Until 1934, taxpayers were given broad leeway to estimate useful lives of their depreciable assets. Then—to help finance public works launched during the Great Depression—the Treasury stiffened its stance and required taxpayers to prove that the lives they selected were appropriate (T.D. 4422). Revenue goals were achieved, but problems of proof saddled taxpayers with unrealistically long useful lives for many of their depreciable assets.

*Bulletin F—1942*

The Treasury's conservative policy was further implemented in 1942 by the issuance of Bulletin F, an item-by-item listing of useful lives. The issuance of Bulletin F may have been precipitated by the Revenue Act of 1942, under which, for the first time, gain recognized from the sale of depreciable business property qualified as capital gain. Slowing depreciation reduced the amount of deductions against ordinary income that, upon sale of an asset, would be recoverable from the taxpayer only as capital gain.

In the 1954 Code, Congress authorized the use of accelerated methods of depreciation, including the 200-percent declining-balance and sum of the years-digits methods. This accelerated cost recovery considerably encouraged a number of taxpayers to buy or build new plants and equipment.

*Special guidelines—1962*

In 1962, the pendulum swung almost all the way back to where it had been before 1934. The IRS abandoned Bulletin F and adopted special guidelines under Rev. Proc. 62-21, 1962-2 CB 418, for examination of depreciation deductions. These guidelines were issued to reduce taxpayer-agent controversy over individual asset lives and to liberalize depreciation rates. This was done by replacing Bulletin F's item-by-item listing with broad industry classes of assets. To be assured that a deduction would not be challenged on audit, it was necessary to show that retirement and replacement policies for a class of assets were consistent with the class life used for that category of assets. This could have been done:

(1) by the use of the complicated reserve ratio test, or

(2) on the basis of all the facts and circumstances.

The guideline lives for machinery and equipment averaged 30 percent to 40 percent less than those previously suggested.

This more relaxed view, however, did not come about until it was reasonably certain that Congress would pass, in the 1962 Revenue Act, a provision taxing gain on the sale of depreciable personal property as ordinary income to the extent of depreciation taken. This eased IRS concern that a more liberal depreciation policy would permit wholesale conversion of ordinary income into capital gain.

For the first three years under the 1962 guidelines, taxpayers did not have to meet the reserve ratio test. Further, a transitional rule was initially granted which provided a period equal to the class guideline life to move toward and eventually meet the reserve ratio test. In spite of the three-year moratorium and the transitional rule, difficulties arose.

To cope with these difficulties, the IRS issued Rev. Proc. 65-13, 1965-1 CB 759, in which it offered a new form of the reserve ratio test, the guideline form, to overcome deficiencies of the initial form of the test, the tabular form. The guideline form of the test permitted the computation of the reserve ratio standard to be tailored to individual circumstances. Also, additional transitional rules were introduced in an attempt to make it possible for many taxpayers, who would otherwise be unable to do so, to pass the reserve ratio test.

*Class Life Asset Depreciation Range System (ADR)—1971*

When, in 1971, the guideline transitional allowances began running out, many taxpayers were expected to fail to meet the reserve ratio test. Moreover, in the IRS, it was a widely held view that the test was impracticable and unworkable. It was in this atmosphere that the new Class Life Asset Depreciation Range System (ADR) came into being. This system provided class lives for broad classes of assets and a range from which a life could be selected for depreciation purposes. Originally, the Treasury approved Regulations (June 1971) for an ADR System covering only machinery and equipment and excluding buildings and land improvements. Later, the 1971 Revenue Act gave the ADR System legal authority, expanded it to include buildings and land improvements, and made some changes. The Treasury approved amendments to the ADR Regulations reflecting this Act.

Further, the Treasury prescribed a Class Life System (CLS) under which a taxpayer could choose a class life for the post-1970 depreciation of assets placed in service before 1971. This system had class lives only, no ranges. As under ADR, the reserve ratio test did not apply.

However, certain buildings and Sec. 1250 property were temporarily removed from the ADR system under a transitional rule that provided an election to exclude such property from the less favorable ADR system even if this system was used for non-Sec. 1250 property. In such case, useful lives could be determined under Rev. Proc. 62-21, above.

In 1974, buildings and other Sec. 1250 property were withdrawn from the application of the ADR system until such time as Sec. 1250 property was explicitly included in ADR classes prescribed by the Treasury (P.L. 93-625 (1974), Act Sec. 5; S. Rept. 93-1357, 1975-1 CB 517, 523).

Thus, although the Treasury is authorized to include buildings and Sec. 1250 property in the ADR system, it generally has not done so except to the extent that Sec. 1250 property is included within a specific business activity class (Rev. Proc. 77-3, 1977-1 CB 535).

This was the posture of the rules prior to the Accelerated Cost Recovery System (ACRS) introduced by the Economic Recovery Tax Act of 1981 and the Modified Accelerated Cost Recovery System (MACRS) introduced by the Tax Reform Act of 1986. It continues to be the posture of the rules for property placed in service before 1981 and for some post-1980 property not qualifying for either of these systems.

*Accelerated Cost Recovery System (ACRS)—1981*

Along with simplifying cost recovery, the Accelerated Cost Recovery System (ACRS), introduced by the Economic Recovery Tax Act of 1981, was designed to stimulate capital formation.

By 1984, legislative concern had shifted to controlling the size of the deficit and curbing real estate tax shelters and tax-motivated real estate transactions. With the Tax Reform Act of 1984, Congress slowed down cost recovery for real property (other than low-income housing) placed in service after March 15, 1984, by increasing the minimum recovery period to 18 (from 15) years. Moreover, for 18-year property, a mid-month convention was adopted so that property placed in service (or disposed of) in any particular month was regarded as placed in service (or disposed of) in the middle (rather than at the start) of that month.

For property placed in service after May 8, 1985, and not subject to transitional rules and that otherwise would have been 18-year property, P.L. 99-121 (1985) increased the recovery period to 19 years.

The 1984 Act also slowed depreciation for "luxury" automobiles by capping annual cost recovery and deliberalized depreciation rules for Code Sec. 280F "listed" property (cars, home computers, and certain other property that lends itself to personal use), unless such property was used more than 50 percent for business.

*Modified Accelerated Cost Recovery System (MACRS)—1986*

The Modified Accelerated Cost Recovery System (MACRS), the latest major chapter in the ongoing depreciation story, applies to most tangible depreciable property placed in service after 1986 and could be elected for comparable property placed in service before 1987 but after July 31, 1986.

Although sharing the statutory designation of Accelerated Cost Recovery System with its statutory predecessor (ACRS), MACRS is an entirely new system. Classes of property are revised, and methods and conventions are prescribed (rather than embodied in specified recovery percentages). Perhaps the most dramatic change introduced by MACRS is the limiting of cost recovery to straight-line depreciation over 27.5 years for residential rental property and to straight-line depreciation over 31.5 or 39 years for most other depreciable real property.

MACRS includes an alternative system under which depreciation is deducted under the straight-line method over generally longer periods than under regular MACRS. This system is mandatory for tangible property used predominantly outside the United States, certain property leased to tax-exempt entities, property financed with tax exempt bonds, and, subject to various requirements, property imported from a country that the President determines to be maintaining certain trade restrictions or engaging in certain trade practices. A system is also provided for computing depreciation for purposes of minimum tax.

Since ACRS liberalized the rules for recovering the cost of most tangible depreciable property, special rules were included to prevent transfers between related parties or transactions in which users stayed the same from "churning" pre-1981 property into recovery (ACRS) property. Similar rules are included under MACRS but are modified so as not to shield otherwise qualifying property from the largely less generous treatment accorded under MACRS than under ACRS.

Some chapters of the depreciation story bear a special relationship to the repealed regular investment credit. As originally introduced, ACRS was supplementary to a general 10-percent credit for the cost of most tangible personal property and other categories of property (exclusive of buildings and their components). For property placed in service after 1982, the double benefit was reduced, and, for property placed in service after 1985, it was completely eliminated (to some extent retroactively) by the repeal of the credit. Thus, simply comparing the MACRS rules to the prior ACRS rules does not fully reflect the impact of the Tax Reform Act of 1986 on overall cost recovery.

Three major revenue procedures provided further guidance for depreciating MACRS property. Rev. Proc. 87-56, 1987-2 CB 674, sets forth the class lives to be used for purposes of MACRS. Rev. Proc. 87-57, 1987-2 CB 687, provides optional tables for computing recovery allowances and explains the basic operation of

MACRS. Rev. Proc. 89-15, 1989-1 CB 816, sets forth rules for short-year computations.

Despite the advent of these depreciation systems and class life tables, the depreciation Code provision ranks in the top 14 Code provisions causing disputes between taxpayers and the IRS, according to a 1993 study by the General Accounting Office.

## Historical Background from IRS Cost Segregation Audit Guide

The IRS audit guide for cost segregation provides the following historical background for depreciation.

[Beginning of IRS text—CCH.]

### *Early History of Depreciation*

For about 20 years after the introduction of our present income tax system in 1913, taxpayers were generally given freedom to determine depreciation allowances. Both individuals and corporations could claim a reasonable allowance for depreciation of property arising out of its use or employment in the business or trade. The deductions claimed were not challenged unless it could be shown by clear and convincing evidence that they were unreasonable. Prior to 1934, a taxpayer had wide leeway as to the amount which could be written off each year against current income as an allowance for the cost of machinery, equipment and buildings. As long as the taxpayer's policy was consistent and in accordance with sound accounting practice, the tax authorities raised little question, realizing that the cost could be written off only once. See Announcement 71-76, 1971-2 C.B. 503.

In 1934, the Treasury Regulations (Treas. Reg.) were amended to provide that the burden of proof would rest upon the taxpayer to sustain the depreciation deduction claimed. Taxpayers became responsible to furnish full and complete information with respect to the cost or other basis of the assets related to the claimed depreciation. The required information for each asset included the age, condition and remaining useful life, the portion of their cost or other basis, which had been recovered through depreciation allowances for prior taxable years, and any other information as the Commissioner may require in substantiation of the deduction claimed. Whatever plan or method of depreciation a taxpayer would choose to adopt, it "must be reasonable and must have due regard to operating conditions during the taxable period." T.D. 4422, 1934-1 C.B. 58."

### *Bulletin F*

The earliest edition of Bulletin "F" was a pamphlet issued in 1920, which contained no schedule of suggested average lives but defined depreciation as follows: "Depreciation means the gradual reduction in the value of property due to physical deterioration, exhaustion, wear, and tear through use in trade or business." Obsolescence was treated as a separate and supplemental factor in computing the depreciation allowance where the facts supported an additional amount. Bulletin "F" was first revised in 1931, at which time the first schedule of suggested lives was published as a separate pamphlet. The schedule provided useful lives for individual assets used by industry groups. In Bulletin "F", the Internal Revenue Service (Service) explicitly frowned on the use of a composite rate of depreciation; rather, the Service advocated depreciation by items or by groups of items having practically identical physical characteristics and length of life. In conjunction with the burden shifting from the Service to the taxpayer regarding depreciation deductions, useful life became largely determined by reference to standardized lives prescribed in Bulletin "F" and a taxpayer had a heavy burden of proof to sustain any shorter life for an individual asset.

Bulletin "F" underwent a second revision in 1942 and provided a useful life guide for various types of property based on the nature of a taxpayer's business or industry. Bulletin "F" identified over 5,000 assets used in 57 different industries and activities and described two procedures for computing depreciation for buildings:

**Composite Method:** A depreciation chart provided a composite rate for 14 different types of buildings, including all installed building equipment. The recommended rates ranged from 1.5% per year for good quality warehouses and grain elevators to 3.5% per year for lesser quality theaters. These composite depreciation rates correspond to useful lives ranging from 28.5 years to 66.7 years.

**Component Method:** Taxpayers could elect to depreciate building equipment separately from the structure. A list provided lives for various types of structures, ranging from 50 years for apartments, hotels and theaters, to 75 years for warehouses and grain elevators. A separate list provided lives for over 100 items of installed building equipment, ranging from 5 to 25 years, with certain installed building equipment listed as having the same life as the life of the building in which it was installed.

Bulletin "F" also allowed taxpayers to either depreciate individual items on a separate basis or to combine assets into composite, classified, or group accounts and depreciate the group account as a single asset. Historically, some taxpayers have interpreted this to mean that assets can be segregated into components and depreciated separately.

*Codification of Depreciation Changes*

In 1954, major changes were made to depreciation laws. Aside from the authorization of new methods of [accelerated] depreciation, § 167(d) was added which authorized written agreements between the Service and taxpayers specifically dealing with the useful life and rate of depreciation of any property.

In 1956, the ability to depreciate on an account basis (first allowed in Bulletin "F") was codified in Treas. Reg. § 1.167(a)-7(a). The regulations moved away from the concept of physical life, focusing instead on the period of time the property was used in the trade or business of the taxpayer. See Treas. Reg. § 1.167(a)-1(a). Also, as part of a policy designed to reduce administrative controversies, the Service codified a policy that it would only re-determine estimated useful life when the change in the useful life is significant and there is a clear and convincing basis for the redetermination. See Treas. Reg. § 1.167(a)-1(b).

In *Shainberg vs. Commissioner*, 33 T.C. 241 (1959), the Service challenged the taxpayer's method of depreciation of segregating buildings and the various items of equipment in the buildings into separate component groups. The Tax Court held that the taxpayer could calculate depreciation using a component grouping method as was their right under the regulations. In general, the courts have sustained the estimated useful lives assigned by taxpayers such as a 40-year life for the building structure, a 15-year life for the roofs, plumbing, wiring and elevators, and a 10-year life for the paving, ceilings, and heating and air conditioning systems.

*Guideline Life System*

Revenue Procedure (Rev. Proc.) 62-21, 1962-2 C.B. 418, superseded Bulletin "F". Instead of thousands of asset classifications, assets were grouped into approximately 75 broad industrial classifications and by certain broad general asset classifications, with a "Guideline Life" established for each of these classes. The guideline lives were about 30-40 percent shorter than Bulletin "F" lives and about 15 percent shorter than the lives in actual use by taxpayers. Use of the guideline lives required taxpayers to meet a reserve ratio test (complex provision). The Rev. Proc. represented a fundamental change by treating assets as a class rather than as individual assets; even though assets within a class were heterogeneous with respect to ages, useful lives and physical characteristics. The asset class for buildings included "the structural shell of the building and all integral parts thereof", as well as "equipment which services normal heating, plumbing, air conditioning, fire prevention and power requirements, and equipment such as elevators and escalators." The Rev. Proc. listed 13 different types of buildings, with guideline lives ranging from 40 years for apartments, hotels, and theaters, to 60 years for warehouses and grain elevators. The Guideline Life system did not address repair and maintenance expenditures.

Revenue Ruling (Rev. Rul.) 66-111, 1966-1 C.B. 46, addressed the use of component depreciation for used real property and distinguished its facts from those in *Shainberg*. Rev. Rul. 66-111 decided that "when a used building is acquired for a lump sum consideration, separate components are not bought; a unified structure is purchased" such that the value of components (e.g., ceilings, floors, electrical systems, etc.) of a used building cannot be separated from the value of the building as a whole. Thus, the cost basis of used real property cannot be allocated into separate component accounts for determining a composite life in computing depreciation; rather, an overall useful life for the building must be determined based upon the building as a whole. The ruling was later modified by Rev. Rul. 73-410, 1973-2 C.B. 53, which held that the component method of computing depreciation may be utilized for used real property if: 1) the cost of acquisition is properly allocated to the various components based on their value; and 2) useful lives are assigned to the component accounts based on the condition of such components at the time of acquisition. See also *Lesser v. Commissioner*, 352 F.2d 789 (9th Cir. 1965).

Rev. Rul. 68-4, 1968-1 C.B. 77, concluded that "it is not proper to use the component method of computing depreciation by assigning the guideline class life from Rev. Proc. 62-21 to the structural shell of a building and assign different useful lives to the other integral parts or components of the building. Rev. Proc. 62-21 may only be used where all the assets of the guideline class (building shell and its components) are included in the same guideline class for which one overall composite life is used for computing depreciation."

*Asset Depreciation Range (ADR) System*

Rev. Proc. 72-10, 1972-1 C. B. 721, superseded Rev. Proc. 62-21 and set forth the Class Life Asset Depreciation Range (ADR) system for tangible assets placed in service after 1970. The purpose of the ADR system was to minimize controversies about useful life, salvage value, and repair and maintenance expenditures. It also abolished the controversial reserve ratio test. Under the elective ADR system, all tangible assets were grouped into more than 100 asset guideline classes (generally corresponding to those set out in Rev. Proc. 62-21) based on the business and industry of the taxpayer. Each class of assets (other than land improvements and buildings) was given a class life as well as a range of years (called "asset depreciation range") that was approximately 20 percent above and below the class life. A taxpayer could select a depreciation period from this range and it would not be challenged by the Service. Thus, the ADR system disassociated an asset's depreciation period from its useful life, but treated it as the useful life for all income tax purposes, even though the depreciation period could be significantly shorter than the actual useful life. However, buildings were generally excluded from the ADR system (except for a 3-year transitional period). The ADR system served as a comprehensive scheme for dealing with property, including repair and maintenance expenditures (via an optional repair allowance) and salvage value. The asset guideline set forth in Rev. Proc. 72-10 was superseded by Rev. Proc. 77-10, 1977-1 C.B. 548, and served as an update to the asset guideline classes and class lives.

*Accelerated Cost Recovery System (ACRS)*

In 1981, Congress enacted the Accelerated Cost Recovery System (ACRS) to simplify the depreciation rules and to stimulate the economy by allowing greater deductions over shorter periods. ACRS eliminated salvage value, minimized exceptions and elections, and moved away from the useful life concept. ACRS allowed depreciation deductions (this term is used for convenience; since ACRS is not based on estimated useful lives, cost recovery under it may not technically qualify as depreciation) for recovery property over a predetermined recovery period by applying a statutory percentage to its basis (cost). These statutory percentages were set forth in a series of tables. In contrast to the elective ADR system, ACRS was mandatory and provided only five (later six) recovery periods. ACRS allowed for a faster cost recovery of assets than had been allowed under previous rules (e.g., the 40-year life for real property was reduced to a 15, 18, or 19-year recovery period, depending on the placed-in-service date of the property). ACRS was generally applicable for property placed in service from 1981 through 1986.

ACRS prohibited component depreciation as a method of computing depreciation for buildings. ACRS required the depreciation deduction for any component of a building to be computed in the same manner as the deduction allowable for the building, beginning on the later of the date the component is placed in service or the building is placed in service. See former § 168(f)(1); Proposed Treas. Reg. § § 1.168-2(e) and 1.168-6. The driving force behind this action was to eliminate controversies surrounding the determination of qualifying § 1245 property.

*Modified Accelerated Cost Recovery System (MACRS)*

In 1986, Congress enacted the Modified Accelerated Cost Recovery System (MACRS). Cost recovery was now based on the applicable depreciation method, the applicable recovery period, and the applicable convention, as outlined in § 168. MACRS provided two depreciation systems: the general depreciation system and the alternative depreciation system (applicable for property used outside the United States, tax-exempt use property, property for which an alternative depreciation system election has been made, and a couple of other finite categories not germane to this discussion). MACRS also required appropriate basis adjustments to compute subsequent year deductions and modified other ACRS provisions including property classifications. The recovery period for buildings and structural components increased dramatically. For example, the 15, 18, or 19-year recovery periods for real property became 39 years for nonresidential real property (31.5 years for nonresidential real property placed in service before May 13, 1993) and 27.5 years for residential rental property, under the general depreciation system. Both types of buildings have a 40-year recovery period under the alternative depreciation system. In Rev. Proc. 87-57, 1987-2 C.B. 687, the Service furnished optional tables to provide applicable deduction percentages under MACRS.

The classification of property under MACRS is important because it affects the applicable depreciation method, recovery period, and convention. Each item of property depreciated under MACRS is assigned to a property class, which establishes the item's recovery period. The applicable recovery periods for MACRS are determined by statute or by reference to class lives. Class lives for MACRS are set forth in Rev. Proc. 87-56, 1987-2 C. B. 674. This Rev. Proc. establishes two broad categories of depreciable assets: 1) asset classes 00.11 through 00.4 that consist of specific assets used in all business activities; and 2) asset classes 01.1 through 80.0 that consist of assets used in specific business activities. The same item of depreciable property can be described in both an asset category (asset classes 00.11 through 00.4) and an activity category (asset classes 01.1 through 80.0), in which case the item is classified in the asset category (unless it is specifically included in the activity category). See *Norwest Corp. & Subs. v. Commissioner*, 111 T.C. 105 (1998) (item described in both an asset and an activity category should be placed in the asset category).

MACRS continued the prohibition against the use of the component method of depreciation. Although MACRS repealed ACRS § 168(f)(1), which related specifically to components of § 1250 class property, it enacted § 168(i)(6), which provides that improvements made to real property are depreciated using the same recovery period applicable to the underlying property as if the underlying property were placed in service at the same time the improvements were made. Regarding improvements, the statute makes reference to § 1245 property and § 1250 property. § 168(i)(12) provides that the terms "§ 1245 property" and "§ 1250 property" have the meanings given such terms by § 1245(a)(3) and § 1250(c), respectively.

[End of IRS text—CCH]

# Fundamentals

## *Depreciation*

## ¶ 3

### Depreciable Property

Depreciation is a reasonable allowance for the exhaustion, wear and tear, and obsolescence on certain types of property used in a trade or business or for the production of income (Code Sec. 167(a)). Depreciation is an accounting concept that treats an allocable part of the cost of certain limited-life assets as an expense (return of capital) in determining taxable income. This expense is also deducted (matched against income) over the number of years that the asset is expected to be used or a specified recovery period rather than deducted all in one year.

Amortization is similar to depreciation but generally refers to the periodic recovery of the cost of an intangible asset. Amortization and depreciation are both authorized by Code Sec. 167(a).

Depreciation is considered an amount paid or incurred for purposes of the Internal Revenue Code. Thus, a medical marijuana dispensary could not deduct depreciation deductions by reason of Code Sec. 280E, which disallows deductions for amounts paid or incurred in the trade or business of trafficking controlled substances prohibited under federal or state law (*San Jose Wellness*, 156 T.C. No. 4, CCH Dec. 61,820).

*What is depreciable*

Property is depreciable if it (1) is used for business or held for the production of income; (2) has a useful life exceeding one year; and (3) wears out, decays, becomes obsolete, or loses value from natural causes. Depreciation does not apply to inventories or stock in trade, or to land apart from any land improvements added to it (Reg. § 1.167(a)-2).

*Assets acquired and sold in same tax year.* Depreciation generally should not be claimed on an asset that is acquired and disposed of in the same tax year. See ¶ 160.

*Useful life.* Useful life is determined by reference to the useful life of the asset in the taxpayer's trade or business (the period over which it will be used by the taxpayer) and not by its physical condition (Reg. § 1.162-3(c)(4)). Under ACRS and MACRS, assets are generally assigned a recovery (depreciation) period which applies regardless of an asset's actual useful life in a taxpayer's business. However, if the actual useful life is one year or less, then the cost of the asset can be expensed. This rule applied even before the IRS issued the regulations for materials and supplies. See "*Materials and supplies,*" below. For example, industrial garments and dust control items (e.g., mops, towels, mats) which were leased to a variety of customers had a useful life to an industrial laundry corporation of one year or less and could be currently expensed when placed in service (*Prudential Overall Supply*, TC Memo. 2002-103, Dec. 54,723(M)).

For ACRS and MACRS property, statutorily prescribed recovery periods are the deemed useful life of property and a definite useful life, item (2) above, need not be proved if the property is a wasting asset, according to the Tax Court (*R.L. Simon*, 103 TC 247, Dec. 50,059, aff'd, CA-2, 1995-2 USTC ¶ 50,552 (Nonacq. 1996-2 CB 2); *B.P. Liddle*, 103 TC 285, Dec. 50,060, aff'd, CA-3, 1995-2 USTC ¶ 50,488). The Court of Appeals for the Eighth Circuit, citing the *Liddle* and *Simon* cases, has indicated that even imperceptible physical damage to or impact upon a particular item of property during its usage is sufficient to qualify a property for depreciation (*R. O'Shaughnessy*, CA-8, 2003-1 USTC ¶ 50,522). Accordingly, even though they had no known or determinable useful life, nineteenth-century violin bows that were tangible property, used by professional violinists in their trade or business, and subject to wear and tear qualified as five-year ACRS recovery property (*Simon*). A similar result was reached regarding a seventeenth-century bass viol under similar circumstances (*Liddle*). See also ¶ 125. Under MACRS, a five-year recovery period applies to musical instruments used by professional musicians (Asset Class 57.0) (¶ 104).

The fact that the value of the bows as collectibles had appreciated was irrelevant because economic and statutory depreciation need not be coincident. Accounting for depreciation of assets is an annual offset to gross income by deductions that represent the exhaustion, wear and tear, or obsolescence of an income-producing asset. Accounting for changes in the value of depreciable property because of market conditions (such as inflation or scarcity) is reportable as gain or loss upon the sale of the depreciable asset.

Note that the IRS's official position continues to be that a determinable depreciation period is required. See, for example, Rev. Rul. 2015-11, relating to the depreciation of precious metals.

Vintage photographs, magazines, and newspapers acquired by a film maker in connection with an anticipated project regarding a famous personage were not depreciable without proof that the items were subject to wear and tear (*D. Rooney*, Dec. 58,517(M), TC Memo. 2011-14).

Show cars (exotic automobiles possessing state-of-the-art high technology) that would become obsolete over time were depreciable (*B. Selig*, 70 TCM 1125, Dec. 50,975(M)) even though a definite useful life could not be shown. The cars were not similar to antique cars placed in a museum which are nondepreciable because they do not deteriorate in a controlled environment (*Harrah's Club*, CtCls, 81-1 USTC ¶ 9466).

Note that intangible assets must have a determinable useful life in order to be amortized or depreciated unless a statutorily prescribed amortization period applies, such as the 15-year recovery period for section 197 intangibles and certain self-created intangibles. See ¶ 10.

*Idle assets.* Depreciation should be claimed on a business asset even when it is temporarily idle (not in use). Thus, the basis for gain or loss must be reduced by the depreciation allowable during a period of idleness, even though no depreciation was claimed (*P. Dougherty Co.*, CA-4, 47-1 USTC ¶ 9117; 159 F2d 269).

Unless an asset is permanently withdrawn from use in a business or income-producing activity through a sale, abandonment, retirement, or other disposition, it is considered temporarily idle and should be depreciated (*D.L. Hamby*, 56 TCM 783, CCH Dec. 45,204(M)). A taxpayer that has failed to claim depreciation on an idle asset should be able to file an application for a change in accounting method and deduct the unclaimed depreciation as a Code Sec. 481(a) adjustment. The application for a change in accounting method may be filed as late as three years after the tax year of the sale. See ¶ 75.

A building or other asset which is placed up for sale by a trade or business remains depreciable even though it is no longer actively used in the business so long as it has not been converted to personal use or otherwise retired or abandoned. Thus, a taxpayer that was discontinuing its poultry business was entitled to continue claiming depreciation deductions on poultry buildings which no longer housed poultry during the two-year period that the taxpayer was attempting to sell the building (*M.R. Lenington*, 25 TCM 1350, TC Memo. 1966-264, CCH Dec. 28,201(M)). A more common application of the principle likely involves unoccupied residential and commercial real estate which was formerly leased to tenants but is now held by the lessor for sale.

*Materials and supplies.* Materials and supplies may be deducted in the year used or consumed (nonincidental materials and supplies) or, if incidental, in the year paid or incurred. Among other items, materials and supplies include units of property (as determined under Reg. § 1.263(a)-3(e)) with an acquisition or production cost of $200 or less and units of property with an economic useful life of 12 months or less beginning when the property is used or consumed in the taxpayer's operations. The cost of a material or supply is deducted in the year used or consumed. However, incidental materials and supplies are deducted in the year their cost is paid or incurred. An incidental material or supply is a material or supply that is carried on hand and for which no record of consumption is kept or of which physical inventories at the beginning and end of the tax year are not taken (Reg. § 1.162-3).

The annually elected de minimis expensing safe harbor (Reg. § 1.263(a)-1(f)) may apply to allow the current deduction of materials and supplies in the year their cost is paid or incurred. Units of property and items of materials and supplies acquired or produced by a taxpayer costing $2,500 or less per unit or item ($5,000 for a taxpayer with an applicable financial statement) may also be deducted under the de minimis safe harbor. Depreciable MACRS property may also be expensed under Code Sec. 179. See ¶ 307 for a discussion of materials and supplies and the de minimis expensing safe harbor.

*When depreciation begins—placed in service requirement*

Depreciation may not be claimed until the tax year that the property is placed in service for either the production of income or use in a trade or business. A similar rule applies to the Code Sec. 179 deduction and to various amortization deductions as well as the investment tax credit.

Property is considered placed in service when it is in a condition or state of readiness and available for a specially assigned function (Prop. Reg. § 1.168-2(l)(2)); Reg. § 1.167(a)-11(e)(1)(i); Field Service Advice Memorandum 199916040, date not given; republished to include previously redacted information on April 29, 2005.

Generally, an asset cannot be placed in service until its construction is complete. An aircraft runway under construction which had a rock base was not in a condition or state of readiness for its specifically assigned function until it was paved even though aircraft occasionally landed on the rock surface. The rock surface could not be used on a permanent basis because pilots risked damaging their aircraft by landing and the landing area easily could be ruined by the weather (*M. Noell*, 66 TC 718, Dec. 33,927).

The principle of the *Noell* case was applied to a private jet aircraft that was delivered and flown for business purposes on December 30, 2003 and then returned to the manufacturer for installation of a conference table and monitors over a six week period at an additional $500,000 cost in accordance with a supplemental agreement to the purchase contract was not placed in service until the table and monitors were installed. Although the aircraft was fully functional for air transportation and used as such in 2003, the IRS successfully argued that in this particular case the aircraft's primary function was to serve as a meeting place with clients and, therefore, it was not "available for its specifically assigned function" until the conference table and monitors had been installed. This case hinged upon the taxpayer's testimony that it was essential to his insurance business that the airplane have a conference table and the monitors so he could make his Power Point presentations to clients and other agents. Since the plane wasn't fully functional for the very specific needs of the taxpayer's insurance business the court concluded that the plane wasn't placed in service until it had been properly outfitted in accordance with the purchase contract (*M. Brown*, 106 TCM 630, TC Memo. 2013-275, CCH Dec. 59,709(M)).

An asset can be considered placed in service prior to its actual use if it is in a state of readiness and availability for actual use (i.e., operational) and nothing within the taxpayer's control prevents its actual use. For example, an operational automobile was placed in service in the year purchased even though the taxpayer decided not to register and use the car until the following year when he returned from vacation because the decision not to register and use the car was within the taxpayer's control (*M. Giles*, 50 TCM 1342, TC Memo. 1985-543, Dec.42,455(M)).

> ***Example (1):*** James Elm is a building contractor that specializes in constructing office buildings. He bought a truck last year that had to be modified to lift materials to second-story levels. The installation of the lifting equipment was completed and James accepted delivery of the modified truck on January 10 of this year. The truck was placed in service on January 10, the date it was ready and available to perform the function for which it was bought even if it was not actually used until after January 10. The placed-in-service date is not the date of first use (IRS Publication 946 (How to Depreciate Property)).

However, if a taxpayer fails to take steps that are within its control to make a machine operational and capable of actual use, the asset cannot be considered placed in service until steps are taken to make the machine operational.

> ***Example (2):*** Donald Steep, a calendar-year taxpayer, bought a machine for his business in Year 1. The machine was delivered in Year 1. However, it was not installed and operational until Year 2. It is considered placed in service in Year 2 when Steep installed and made the machine operational and capable of actual use. If the machine had been ready and available for use (i.e., was operational) when it was delivered in Year 1, it would be considered placed in service in Year 1 even if it was not actually used until Year 2 (IRS Publication 946, How to Depreciate Property).

The definition of placed in service for purposes of the investment tax credit and depreciation are the same. The investment tax credit regulations set forth nonexclusive examples illustrating situations in which actual use is not required for an asset to be considered placed in service (Reg. § 1.46-3(d)).

- Parts are acquired and set aside during the tax year for use as replacements for a particular machine (or machines) in order to avoid operational time loss
- Operational farm equipment is acquired during the taxable year and it is not practicable to use such equipment for its specifically assigned function in the taxpayer's business of farming until the following year
- Equipment is acquired for a specifically assigned function and is operational but is undergoing testing to eliminate any defects

For example, a unit of a power plant wasn't available for use until it had completed all preoperational testing even though the generated electricity was sold to customers. Only after the unit had demonstrated that it was available for service on a regular basis was the unit in a state of readiness and availability for its specifically assigned function (*Consumers Power*, 89 TC 710, Dec. 44,250). See, also, the following factors cited in Rev. Rul. 76-428 and Rev. Rul. 76-256:

- approval of all required licenses and permits;
- passage of control of the facility to the taxpayer;

- completion of critical tests;
- commencement of daily or regular operations; and
- with respect to electric power plants, synchronization of the plant facility

The preceding factors were considered in determining placed in service dates for power plants and have been used for wind turbine generators, including foundations and tower, eligible for the Code Sec. 45 renewable electricity production credit (IRS Letter Ruling 201205005, February 3, 2012).

The investment tax credit regulations further provide that fruit-bearing trees and vines are not placed in service until they have reached an income-producing stage and that materials and parts to be used in the construction of an item of equipment are not considered placed in service merely by reason of their acquisition.

The depreciation regulations additionally provide (Prop. Reg. § 1.168-2(l)(2); Reg. § 1.167(a)(11)(e)(1)):

- In the case of a building which is intended to house machinery and equipment, readiness and availability is determined without regard to whether the housed machinery or equipment has been placed in service
- Where a building is essentially an item of machinery or equipment, or the use of the building is so closely related to the use of the machinery or equipment that it clearly can be expected to be replaced or retired when the property it initially houses is replaced or retired, the determination of readiness or availability of the building is made by taking into account the readiness and availability of such machinery or equipment

*Factors outside of taxpayer's control preventing actual use.* In some instances where depreciation has been allowed for property in a state of readiness but not yet placed into actual use, the taxpayer has done all that was in its power to make the property operational but due to circumstances outside of its control it is not possible to actually use the property. This rule is based on the operational farm equipment exception described above. Thus, if a farmer purchases an operational tractor in November but doesn't begin actual use until the next spring it is considered placed in service in November. The weather preventing actual and practicable use of the tractor is not within the farmer's control. In another case involving weather, barges were placed in service in December when they were ready for service even though they were frozen in the water and could not be actually used until the following May (*Sears Oil Co., Inc.*, CA-2, 66-1 USTC ¶ 9384, 359 F2d 191). Depreciation was allowable with respect to an air conditioner even though, because of weather conditions, the taxpayer did not actually use the air conditioner until the following year (*Schrader*, CA-6, 78-2 ustc ¶ 9824). A metal shredder was considered placed in service during the tax year of purchase even though it was not operational during that tax year because a power company was unable to install an overhead electrical connection to the plant due to litigation regarding an easement for the power lines. The installation of the electrical connection was not in the taxpayer's control (*SMC Corp.*, CA-6, 82-1 USTC ¶ 9309, 675 F2d 113). See, also, *Northern States Power*, CA-8, 98-2 USTC ¶ 50,671 and *Connecticut Yankee Atomic Power Company*, 97-2 USTC ¶ 50,693, 38 FedCl 721, discussed below.

*Newly constructed retail buildings.* A district court granted summary judgment and ruled that it is not necessary for a building to be open for business to the general public in order to be considered placed in service (*Stine, LLC*, DC, W.D. Louisiana, 2015-1 USTC ¶ 50,172, nonacq.). The case involved an existing building materials and supplies retailer that constructed two additional buildings. The buildings were considered placed in service when they were substantially complete (as evidenced by certificates of completion and limited occupancy issued by a state fire marshal which for a 30-day period permitted employees to install equipment, shelving, racks and stock merchandise) and, therefore, ready and available for their intended use to store and house equipment, racks, shelving, and merchandise. The court believed that the limited occupancy permit satisfied the requirements of Proposed Reg. § 1.168-2(e)(3) which provides that "a building shall be considered placed in service . . . only when a significant portion is made available for use in a finished condition (e.g. when a certificate of occupancy is issued with respect to such portion) . . .". The IRS failed to present any authority which required that a building must actually be open for business (here, open to the public) in order to be placed in service. The *Stine* case will not be appealed by the IRS. However, the IRS issued a nonacquiescence (2017-15 I.R.B. 107) (based on the reasoning in Action on Decision 2017-2, April 24, 2017) indicating it will continue to litigate this issue. The Action on Decision cites Reg. § 1.46-3(d)(1)(ii), which provides that property is placed in service when it is in a condition or state of readiness and available for its specifically assigned function (i.e., when it is ready and available for regular operation and income-producing use). Under Reg. § 1.46-3(d)(1)(ii), according to the Action on Decision, a retail store is available for its specifically assigned function when the building is ready and available to operate as a retail store not when ready for shelving and merchandise to be stocked. The store's ability to begin operations is determined by considering the five factors set forth in Rev. Rul. 76-428 and Rev. Rul. 76-256 and listed above which are used to determined whether an electric power facility has been placed in service.

Although the Action on Decision is somewhat unclear on this point, it appears that a building can be considered placed in service before the general public actually begins to use the facility. It appears sufficient that the facility is ready to be opened to the general public.

*Rental buildings.* As noted below (see "*Leased buildings and equipment*") the courts have held that a rental property is placed in service when it is made available for leasing. Thus, if the building in the *Stine* case was leased, availability to the general public would not be relevant in determining when the building was placed in service.

*Buildings placed in service in stages.* The proposed ACRS regulations recognize that a building (for example, a high-rise) may be placed in service in stages. These regulations provide that each significant portion of a building should be separately depreciated as it is placed in service. Placed in service means made available for use in a finished condition, for example, as when a certificate of occupancy is issued. However, the same recovery period and depreciation method must be used to depreciate the entire building. For example, this rule, when applied to MACRS residential rental property, would mean that a taxpayer could not depreciate one portion of the building over a 27.5 year period and elect ADS (40-year depreciation period) for another portion of the building. The ACRS regulations explain the allocation of basis among the completed portions and provide examples (Proposed Reg. § 1.168-2(e)(3) and (5)).

*Component parts and machinery used in single system.* The upper reservoir component of a pumped storage hydroelectric plant was not placed in service until the entire plant was placed in service. The reservoir and physical plant operated as one integrated unit to produce electrical power (*Consumers Power*, 89 TC 710, Dec.

44,250). Telephone switching equipment and toll carriers were not considered placed in service even though capable of performing individual functions because wiring for the systems in which they were to operate had not been completed and employees had not been trained to use the equipment (*Siskiyou Communications*, 60 TCM. 475, Dec. 46,797(M)). See also *Hawaiian Indep. Refinery, Inc.*, 83-1 USTC ¶ 9141, 697 F.2d 1063 (Fed. Cir.), cert. denied 464 U.S. 816 (1983) (two offsite components not considered separately from refinery in considering applicable construction date because all were designed as a single unit and together they functionally formed a single property).

*Equipment used in retail stores.* Equipment located in new retail stores, which is to be used in connection with the trade or business conducted in those stores, is placed in service upon the opening of the stores (assuming the equipment is otherwise installed and ready for use). If the equipments is installed, operating, and in use in an existing store that is being remodeled and the store remains open to the public depreciation begins when the equipment is installed (*Piggly Wiggly Southern, Inc.*, 84 TC 739, Dec. 42,039, aff'd on another issue, CA-11, 86-2 USTC ¶ 9789). See "*Taxpayer must be engaged in trade or business,*" below.

*Leased buildings and leased equipment.* Property which is held for leasing to others is considered placed in service when it is first held out for lease if it is otherwise ready for use (*W.R. Waddell*, 86 TC 848, Dec. 43,023 (electrocardiogram (ECG) terminals); *J.A. Helfand*, 47 TCM 1203, Dec. 41,030(M) (commercial real property); *M.H. Wood*, 61 TCM 2571, Dec. 47,334(M) (solar water-heating equipment)).

> ***Example (3):*** On April 6, Sue Thorn bought a house to use as residential rental property. She made several repairs and had it ready for rent on July 5. At that time, she began to advertise it for rent in the local newspaper. The house is considered placed in service in July when it was ready and available for rent. She can begin to depreciate it in July (IRS Publication 946 (How to Depreciate Property)).

This IRS example does not make it absolutely clear that depreciation begins when the property is first offered for lease. However, the case law cited above would require that the property actually be offered for lease. In the case of newly constructed nonresidential commercial buildings which are not leased, the courts have placed emphasis on the issuance of an occupancy permit. See "*Newly constructed buildings*, above.

Leased equipment which is returned after the termination or expiration of the lease may continue to be depreciated (even though it is generating no income) until it is permanently withdrawn from the leasing business, for example, by being sold or specifically identified as no longer available for leasing (IRS Letter Ruling 9811004, November 18, 1997). This can be viewed as an application of the "idle asset" rule which allows a taxpayer to claim depreciation on temporarily idle assets.

*Motion pictures, books, recordings, patents.* Motion picture rights, book manuscript rights, master recording rights, and patent rights are placed in service when the film, book, product or process is first released for exhibition, distribution and sale, or is used in a trade or business or for the production of income (Rev. Rul. 79-285, 1979-2 CB 91). However, patents are not placed in service before the issue date.

*Taxpayer must be engaged in trade or business.* The Tax Court has ruled that depreciation may start no sooner than the tax year that a taxpayer begins to engage in the trade or business in which the asset will be used (*Piggly Wiggly Southern, Inc.*, 84 TC 739, Dec. 42,039, aff'd on another issue, CA-11, 86-2 USTC 9789, 803 F2d 1572, holding that refrigeration units installed in the taxpayer's new grocery stores (the new stores were in addition to existing stores) were not placed in service until the stores opened to the public). Since depreciation may not be claimed prior to the tax year in which a trade or business is in operation, depreciation is not considered a start-up expense under Code Sec. 195 (IRS Letter Ruling 9235004, May 20, 1992). See, also, ¶ 132, "Application of short tax year rules to a new business."

*Relationship of placed in service date to depreciation conventions.* The date on which depreciation begins under a convention (¶ 86) or a particular method of depreciation does not determine the date on which the property is first placed in service (Reg. § 1.167(a)-11(e)(1)). Thus, the applicable convention specifies when the recovery period begins for depreciable property after it is determined when the property is first placed in service.

> ***Example (4):*** An existing calendar-year business purchased 5-year MACRS property that was in a state of readiness for a specially assigned function on August 1. The property was depreciated using the half-year convention. Although the property is considered placed in service on August 1, the recovery period for such property begins on July 1.

The depreciation of an asset ends when the asset is retired from service (by sale, exchange, abandonment, or destruction) (Reg. § 1.167(a)-10). Generally, depreciation for the year in which an asset is retires is computed by using the applicable depreciation convention (see ¶ 86 (MACRS), ¶ 160 (MACRS), ¶ 280 (ACRS), and ¶ 358 (pre-ACRS)).

*Placed-in-service-date incorrectly determined.* See ¶ 75 for handling depreciation calculations if the placed-in-service date was incorrectly determined.

## ¶ 5
## Tangible Property

For depreciation purposes, tangible property is divided into two basic types: real property (such as land, land improvements, buildings, and structural components of buildings) and personal property (such as business machinery and equipment, office furniture and fixtures, and appliances that are furnished to tenants).

See ¶ 116, ¶ 127, ¶ 127A, ¶ 127B, and ¶ 127C for a discussion of the definitions of buildings, structural components, and personal property.

### *Demolition of buildings or other property*

The adjusted basis of a "structure" that is demolished and the cost of demolition, including removal costs, (less any salvage) is capitalized and added to the basis of the land. The rule applies to the owner or lessee of the structure (Code Sec. 280B; Reg. § 1.263(a)-1(g)(2)). As explained below, this rule does not apply to a building that is placed in a MACRS general asset account.

The term structure only includes a building and its structural components as defined in Reg. § 1.48-1(e) (Reg. § 1.280B-1; Preamble to T.D. 8745). Thus, adjusted basis and demolition costs of a variety of otherwise inherently permanent structures that are not considered buildings, such as oil and gas storage tanks, blast furnaces, and coke ovens are not subject to Code Sec. 280B. See ¶ 162. Code Sec. 280B was designed to lay the thorny intent question to rest, at least in the case of buildings.

The regulations provide that if a building acquired with the intent to demolish is used for business or income-producing purposes for some time before it is demolished, a portion of the cost basis not to exceed the present value of the right to receive rentals during the period of its expected use may be allocated to the building and depreciated over that period (Reg. § 1.165-3(a)(2)(i)). Although intent is no longer relevant to the issue of the capitalization of building demolition costs, the IRS may contend that this portion of the regulation still applies. Where a building is not acquired with the intent of demolishing it, then depreciation should be calculated on the basis of the building (determined by allocating the purchase price between the land and the building in proportion to their fair market values), as in any other situation.

Special rules apply to the destruction or abandonment of leasehold improvements. See ¶ 126.

*Casualty losses.* If a casualty damages or destroys a structure, and the structure is then demolished, the basis of the structure must be reduced by the casualty loss allowable under Code Sec. 165 before the "loss sustained on account of" the demolition is determined (Notice 90-21, 1990-1 CB 332).

*Abnormal retirements.* The Tax Court has ruled that the exception for casualty losses above in Notice 90-21 also applies to a building that is retired because the usefulness to the taxpayer suddenly and unexpectedly terminates upon the discovery of latent defects (i.e., abnormal obsolescence) (*De Cou*, 103 TC 80, CCH Dec. 49,998). See ¶ 162.

*Rehabilitation v. demolition.* A modification or rehabilitation of a building will not be considered a demolition if the following conditions are satisfied (Rev. Proc. 95-27, 1995-1 CB 704):

(1) 75 percent or more of the existing external walls of the building are retained in place as internal or external walls and

(2) 75 percent or more of the existing internal structural framework of the building is retained in place.

If the building is a certified historic structure, the modification must also be part of a certified rehabilitation.

If these conditions are met, the costs of the modifications are generally added to the basis of the building and recovered through depreciation unless the costs are properly accountable for under some other Code provision, for example, as deductible repairs. In certain cases, the modification of a historic structure or, for expenditures paid or incurred before 2018, a building placed in service before 1936 may qualify for the rehabilitation credit under Code Sec. 47.

*Using general asset account to avoid capitalization of demolition loss on buildings.* Under final regulations, a taxpayer may place a building in a single asset general asset account (GAA) and continue to depreciate the building after its demolition rather than increasing the basis of the land by the adjusted depreciable basis of the building as otherwise required by Code Sec. 280B. There is no requirement that the taxpayer must terminate the GAA upon the disposition of the building and capitalize the loss under Code Sec. 280B. The regulations contain language which makes the termination of the account optional (i.e., elective) even in the case of a demolition of a building in a single asset GAA (Reg.§ 1.168(i)-1(e)(3)(i); Reg. § 1.168(i)-1(e)(3)(ii)(A)). However, an asset may not be placed in a GAA if it is acquired and disposed of in the same tax year (Reg. § 1.168(i)-1(c)(1)(i)). See, also, the anti-abuse rule (Reg. § 1.168(i)-1(e)(3)(vii)) which could possibly be interpreted by the IRS to prohibit avoidance of Code Sec. 280B in certain situations.

Code Sec. 280B requires that demolition removal costs also be capitalized to the basis of the land, in addition to the remaining basis of the building. However, a special rule provides that so long as the GAA account is not voluntarily terminated upon the disposition of the last asset in the account, removal costs associated with the disposed asset are currently deductible (Reg. § 1.263(a)-3(g)(2)(i), second sentence).

Rev. Proc. 2014-54 allows a taxpayer to file an accounting method change for a tax year beginning in 2012 or 2013 to make a late election to place assets that were placed in service prior to the 2012 tax year in a GAA. However, the time for filing this accounting method change has expired since the change must be filed by the extended due date of the 2013 return. This planning tip, therefore, is mainly available for buildings for which a timely current-year GAA election may be made (e.g., a building placed in service in the 2021 tax year for which a timely GAA election is made on the 2021 tax return). However, the remodel/refresh safe harbor for restaurants and retail buildings allows a taxpayer to make a late GAA election for a building previously placed in service in the first tax year that the safe harbor is elected as an accounting method. See Rev. Proc. 2015-56. Under the safe harbor, 75 percent or remodel/refresh costs are deducted and 25 percent of such costs are capitalized.

The downside to a GAA election for a building is that the partial disposition election, which allows a taxpayer to elect to claim a loss on the remaining basis of a building's structural components when they are replaced, is not available if a building is in a GAA. See ¶ 162.

The IRS has allowed a taxpayer to make a late election to place demolished buildings in separate GAAs in order to avoid the capitalization of demolition costs (IRS Letter Ruling 201626013, March 24, 2016). The taxpayer was not advised by the return preparer that the GAA election was available and the statute of limitations for filing an amended return had not expired prior to filing the letter ruling request. The facts also state that the taxpayer had not formed an intent to demolish the buildings when the buildings were purchased although the taxpayer considered this as a possibility. The buildings were placed in service in Tax Year 1 and demolished in Tax Year 3.

See ¶ 128 for rules concerning GAAs and the election procedure.

*Demolition of property other than buildings.* Code Sec. 280B only applies to the demolition of buildings. Reg. § 1.165-3, which was never updated to reflect amendments to Code Sec. 280(B) that made capitalization of demolition losses to the basis of land mandatory regardless of when the taxpayer formed the intention to demolish the building, has not been updated and continues to provide that demolition losses are capitalized only if the taxpayer had the intent to demolish a building at the time of acquisition. Although Reg. § 1.165-3 deals only with buildings, the courts have applied the intent rule to disallow demolition losses in situations where a taxpayer purchases property other than a building (e.g., a land improvement) with the intent to demolish it. See, for example, *A.M. Wilson*, 41 TCM 381, TC Memo. 1980-514, CCH Dec. 37,407(M) (value of an orchard which the taxpayer intended to destroy at the time the land was acquired had to be capitalized).

This case law, however, now seems to have been overturned by Reg. § 1.168(i)-8, which deals with dispositions of MACRS property and was issued as part of the "repair regulations." Reg. § 1.168(i)-8 specifically allows a taxpayer to claim a loss upon the disposition of an asset. Disposition for this purpose includes physical destruction of an asset (Reg. § 1.168(i)-8(b)(2)). Although the regulation specifically provides that the demolition loss rules of Code Sec. 280B take priority (i.e., no loss may be claimed on the demolition of a building), they provide that in other cases loss must be recognized upon a disposition that is an abandonment (Reg. § 1.168(i)-8(e)(2)) or, under a default rule, physical destruction (Reg. § 1.168(i)-8(e)(3)). Thus, it seems that a taxpayer is required to recognize a loss under these regulations on an asset other than a building that is physically destroyed (i.e., demolished) without regard to intent. Although, Reg. § 1.168(i)-8(e) only deals with the loss attributable to the basis of the disposed asset, related removal costs upon the demolition of an asset other than a building would also be deductible under the repair regulations if a gain or loss is realized upon the disposition (Reg. § 1.263(a)-1(g)(2)). This regulation also provides that removal costs of a demolished building are not deductible.

*Depreciation on machines and other assets used in self-construction project*

Depreciation on property used by a business to construct its own assets may not be currently deducted. Instead, the uniform capitalization rules require that such depreciation must be capitalized as part of the cost of the constructed assets and be deducted over the depreciation period for the constructed assets. Depreciation on assets used to manufacture a taxpayer's own inventory must also be capitalized under the uniform capitalization rules (Code Sec. 263A(a)). In effect, depreciation expense is reflected in the computation of cost of goods sold and is recovered as items are sold.

*Inventory and assets held for both sale and lease*

Inventory held for sale to customers is not depreciable (Reg. § 1.167(a)-2).

A "primary purpose" test is applied to determine whether property which is held for both sale or lease ("dual-use property") is considered inventory or depreciable property (*Latimer-Looney Chevrolet, Inc.*, 19 TC 120, CCH Dec. 19,280 (Acq. 1953-1 C.B. 5); CCA Letter Ruling 201025049, March 12, 2010).

IRS Notice 2013-13 (I.R.B. 2013-12, February 6, 2013) summarizes the issues involved and factors considered in determining whether dual-use property should be treated as depreciable property or as non-depreciable inventory. The Notice asks for comments on whether construction and agricultural equipment held simultaneously for sale or lease to customers (dual-use property) by an equipment dealer is properly treated as inventory or as depreciable property and whether, and under what circumstances, dual-use property may be eligible for like-kind exchange treatment under Code Sec. 1031. Inventory is not eligible for section 1031 like-kind exchange treatment. Code Sec. 1031 will generally only apply to exchanges of real property after 2017 (Code Sec. 1031(a), as amended by P.L. 115-97).

The Notice indicates that the IRS presumptively treats dual-use property held by a dealer as inventory (Rev. Rul. 75-538, 1975-2 C.B. 35). For example, a model home used by a developer is inventory. To rebut this presumption, the IRS has required the dealer to show that the property was actually used in the dealer's business and that the dealer looks to consumption through use of the property in the ordinary course of business operation to recover the dealer's cost (Rev. Rul. 75-538; Rev. Rul. 89-25, 1989-1 C.B. 79). As a factual matter, it can be difficult to discern whether dual-use property is held primarily for sale to customers in the ordinary course of business or as an asset used in a trade or business. For example, in *Latimer-Looney Chevrolet, Inc.*, 19 TC 120, CCH Dec. 19,280 (Acq. 1953-1 C.B. 5), new automobiles were "held for use in a trade or business" where the automobile dealer provided them to employees for use in the business prior to sale and in *Duval Motor Co.*, CA-5, 59-1 USTC ¶ 9280, 264 F.2d 548, aff'g 28 TC 42 and *Johnson-McReynolds Chevrolet Corporation*, 27 TC 300, new automobiles were "property held for sale to customers" where automobile dealer temporarily removed them from inventory for use by employees.

Factors cited in Notice 2013-13 as considered by the IRS in determining whether property held for sale and lease is depreciable include:

• The dealer's prior business experience with dual-use property, including the proportion of the dealer's total dual-use property that is leased and the number of times the same property is leased or re-leased by the dealer prior to disposition;

• Whether dual-use property may be leased (or held for subsequent lease) for a period exceeding its recovery period for depreciation purposes;

• The proportion of annual lease revenue to total revenue, the proportion of annual lease revenue to revenue from sales of leased property, and the proportion of revenue from sales of leased property to annual sales revenue;

• Whether lease agreements customarily allow the dealer to terminate the lease and reacquire the property at any time without penalty (and, if so, the frequency with which the dealer exercises this option);

• For lease agreements that provide a purchase option, the frequency with which the lessee exercises this option and whether the lessee receives a price reduction;

• The manner in which dual-use property is typically disposed of (e.g. sold to lessee, at auction, or through a third-party); and

• The dealer's initial classification of dual-use property (as inventory or depreciable property) for federal income tax and financial accounting purposes.

Residential property rented by a real estate developer prior to its sale is not depreciable if it is primarily held for sale (*J.P. Vidican*, 28 TCM 1099, CCH Dec. 29,773(M), TC Memo. 1969-207).

For rules relating to the depreciation period of leased property, see ¶ 190.

*Containers*

Containers that are part of inventory are not depreciable. Some durable containers used to ship products may be depreciated if they have a useful life longer than one year, qualify as property used in a trade or business, and title to them does not pass to the buyer. Factors considered in determining whether a container may be depreciated include: (1) whether the sales contract, sales invoice, or acknowledgment of order indicates that title is retained; (2) whether the invoice treats the containers as separate items; and (3) whether the taxpayer's records properly state the basis in such (Rev. Rul. 75-34, 1995-1 CB 271). Trailer mounted containers, if depreciable, are MACRS 5-year property (Asset Class 00.27). Leased containers that were moved from trailers to cargo ships and vice versa were Asset Class 00.27 assets (IRS Letter Ruling 7939004, May 30, 1979).

See also ¶ 152.

*Land and land improvements*

Unimproved, raw land is not depreciable (Reg. § 1.167(a)-2). The purchase price of land and a building must be allocated between the depreciable building and the nondepreciable land in proportion to their relative fair market values (Reg. § 1.167(a)-5; IRS Publication 551, Basis of Assets). If the land and building are part of the purchase of a trade or business subject to applicable asset acquisition rules of Code Sec. 1060 special rules apply. See below, "*Allocation of purchase price when business or multiple asset purchased.*"

The IRS has ruled that where a term interest in land and depreciable buildings are purchased and the remainder interest is held by an unrelated person the cost allocable to the term interest in the land may be amortized as an intangible asset over the term of the interest and the cost of the buildings are depreciated using the applicable MACRS recovery period (IRS Letter Ruling 200852013, September 24, 2008). See "*Term Interests*," at ¶ 74.

If depreciable, land improvements are usually treated as 15-year property under MACRS (Asset Class 00.3 of Rev. Proc. 87-56). In a few instances, land improvements are depreciable over a different recovery period if they are specifically included in the Asset Class that describes the business activity of the taxpayer. See ¶ 110. The following paragraphs discuss various types of land improvements. See ¶ 110 and ¶ 127C for additional discussion of land improvements.

*Apartment complex.* Sidewalks, concrete driveways, asphalt streets and concrete curbs, playground equipment, fencing, and landscaping constructed or installed in connection with an apartment complex were land improvements (IRS Letter Ruling 8848039, September 2, 1988). The ruling notes that certain portions of the costs may not qualify for depreciation because they might be considered land. For example, this might impact part of the costs of the streets and landscaping.

*Golf courses.* In general, a golf course consists of three types of components: the land, depreciable land improvements, and non-depreciable land improvements. Depreciable land improvements include bulkheads, cart paths, drainage systems, and irrigation systems.

IRS guidance allows land preparation costs related to land above subterranean drainage and irrigation systems to be depreciated as a land improvement over 15 years. Specifically, land preparation costs undertaken in the original construction or reconstruction of a golf course green, bunker, tee, fairway, or rough are depreciable to the extent attributable to the preparation of the area above a subterranean irrigation and/or sprinkler system or other depreciable asset. A taxpayer that purchases an existing golf course or constructs a new golf course may allocate a portion of the purchase or construction price to the value of such land preparation costs, as well as to the underlying irrigation and sprinkler systems, pursuant to the rules for cost segregation. Current owners may also conduct a cost segregation study to reclassify these assets as depreciable property. See ¶ 127.

Previously, it was unclear whether land preparation above a subterranean irrigation or sprinkler system was nondepreciable land or a depreciable land improvement. The IRS, however, ruled, with respect to golf course greens, in Rev. Rul. 2001-60, 2001-2 CB 587, that such costs are depreciable. As noted below, owners of golf courses are also applying the principles of Rev. Rul. 2001-60 to other types of golf course land improvements such as bunkers, tees, fairways, and roughs.

Rev. Rul. 2001-60 holds that the costs of land preparation undertaken in the original construction or reconstruction of traditional push-up or natural soil greens are inextricably associated with the land and, therefore, nondepreciable. This is the same position taken in Rev. Rul. 55-290, which is modified and superseded by Rev. Rul. 2001-60. Traditional greens are essentially landscaping that involves some reshaping or regrading of the land. The soil is pushed up or reshaped to form the green. A subsurface drainage system is not utilized (hoses and sprinklers, if any, are adjacent to the greens). See, also, *The Edinboro Company*, DC-Pa., 63-2 USTC ¶ 9759 (no depreciation on purchased golf course, including tees, greens, fairways, and traps); *Atlanta Athletic Club*, 61 TCM 2011, Dec. 47,195(M) (no depreciation or current deduction for golf course improvements required to host P.G.A. championship tournament); *University Country Club, Inc.*, 64 TC 460, Dec. 33,277 (no depreciation on golf course, grass, and driving range).

Significantly, Rev. Rul. 2001-60 allows depreciation on the portion of a "modern green" that is so closely associated with depreciable assets, such as a network of underground drainage tiles or pipes, that the land preparation will be retired, abandoned, or replaced contemporaneously with those depreciable assets. Specifically, depreciation may be claimed on the costs of land preparation above the drainage system, for example, a gravel and/or sand layer, rootzone layer, and turf grass. These costs of land preparation undertaken by a taxpayer in the original construction or reconstruction of modern greens may be capitalized and depreciated over the recovery period of the tiles, pipes, etc., with which the land is associated because the land preparation must be destroyed to replace the irrigation or sprinkler system. Drainage and sprinkler systems are land improvements (Asset Class 00.3) with a 15-year recovery period, according to the ruling; thus the associated land preparation costs are also 15-year property. General earthmoving, grading, and initial shaping of the area surrounding and underneath the modern green that occur before the construction are inextricably associated with the land and are nondepreciable, according to the ruling. Note that the cost of the land on which the modern green is built is not depreciable. The ruling limits depreciation to the cost of the land preparation *above* the drainage or sprinkler system.

The IRS has issued a "Field Directive on Depreciable Golf Course Land Improvements and the Impact of Rev. Rul. 2001-60" (February 7, 2002) which addresses the proper treatment of golf course land improvements other than greens in the light of the rationale of Rev. Rul. 2001-60. The Directive applies the principles of Rev. Rul. 2001-60 to bunkers, fees, fairways, and roughs.

The Field Directive provides that if a bunker contains depreciable assets such as a liner, and/or drain tiles or pipes the cost of improving the land above those items is depreciable.

If a tee contains underlying depreciable assets such as drain tiles or pipes, the cost of the land preparation above the underlying depreciable assets is also depreciable since the land preparation would have to be replaced if the drain tiles or pipes were replaced.

In the case of a fairway, a portion of the costs of final grading, preparation, seed (including any grow-out period costs), and sod are depreciable if the fairway has underlying depreciable irrigation and drainage pipes. The Directive provides the following example.

***Example (1):*** The removal of a 6-inch drainage pipe that carries runoff from a fairway would require a 12-inch wide ditch. Depreciation may be claimed on fairway land preparation costs attributable to 12 inches times the length of the pipe. Thus, if 30,000 feet of pipe are installed on a golf course, 30,000 square feet of land preparation costs are depreciable.

If there are drainage or irrigation pipes underlying a rough, land preparation costs are subject to depreciation to the extent the land preparation above the pipes would be replaced if the pipes were replaced.

As in Rev. Rul. 55-290, the new ruling allows a current deduction for operating expenses for sod, seed, soil, and other sundry maintenance costs.

Sec. 6.04 of Rev. Proc. 2019-43 contains automatic change of accounting method consent procedures for persons seeking to conform to the holding of Technical Advice Memorandum 2001-60. See ¶ 75. See, also, "IRS LMSB Industry Directive Issued on February 25, 2002: Audit Procedures for Golf Course Land Improvements –Change in Accounting Method, March 11, 2004," which provides general guidance to IRS personnel that review an application for an accounting method change.

In Chief Counsel Advice 200116043, February 13, 2001, which was issued prior to Rev. Rul. 2001-60, IRS auditors were advised to concentrate on "extreme" positions taken by taxpayers. These positions are cases in which a taxpayer:

(1) expensed, as an operating cost, reconstruction costs for greens, tees, and sand bunkers on an existing course;

(2) claimed depreciation on "push-up" or natural soil greens and tees;

(3) expensed or depreciated construction or reconstruction costs of fairways and roughs; and

(4) allocated golf course construction costs to residential building lots.

With the exception of fairways and roughs with irrigation or drainage pipes, these positions would still be considered extreme even after the issuance of Rev. Rul. 2001-60. However, the undepreciated cost of a depreciable golf course improvement may be deductible as an abandonment loss if the improvement is removed or replaced as part of a renovation prior to being fully depreciated. An abandonment loss may also be available with respect to a nondepreciable improvement that is removed or replaced if adequate records can substantiate the adjusted basis of the removed or replaced property. For example, if a nondepreciable push-up green is leveled, then the cost or other basis of the push-up green may be deductible as an abandonment loss (whether or not it is replaced with a new green). See ¶ 162 for a discussion of abandonment and retirement losses.

Golf courses (other than miniature golf courses) are specifically excluded from Asset Class 79.0 of Rev. Proc. 87-56 (Recreation). Rev. Proc. 87-56 does not otherwise mention golf courses. Rev. Proc. 72-10, 1972-1 CB 721, which sets forth the depreciation periods under the ADR depreciation system, specifically indicates in the text of the description for Asset Class 00.3 (Land Improvements) that the cost of general grading of land, "as in the case of cemeteries and golf courses," is not a land improvement and is not depreciable under any other class. The Rev. Proc. 62-21 depreciation period guideline (see ¶ 1), in its definition of land improvements, excluded "land improvements which are a major asset of a business, such as cemeteries or golf courses."

*Grading and land preparation costs.* Raw (unimproved) land is not depreciable (Reg. § 1.167(a)-2). Land preparation costs, however, may be depreciable if they are directly associated with the construction of a depreciable building (Rev. Rul. 65-265. 1965-2 CB 52). Thus, in Rev. Rul. 65-265, costs attributable to excavation, grading, and removing soil necessary to the proper setting of buildings were added to the depreciable basis of the buildings in an industrial complex. The cost of general grading, not directly associated with the construction of the building, however, was added to the basis of the land. See, also, for example, *Eastwood Mall Inc.*, DC Oh., 95-1 USTC ¶ 50,236 (aff'd, CA-6, unpublished opinion, 59 F3d 170 (1995)), which concludes that the cost of clearing, grubbing, blasting, filling, and grading 100 acres of uneven land into an earthen plateau used for the construction of a shopping mall was not depreciable since these improvements were permanent and would not be reincurred if the mall building was rebuilt or replaced. The IRS did not dispute the depreciability of the cost of digging spaces and trenches for the mall building's foundations and utilities and the cost of installing utilities and sewers and paving roads and parking lots.

The cost of clearing, grubbing, cutting, filling, and rough and finish grading necessary to bring land to a suitable grade for the development of a mobile home part was nondepreciable and added to the basis of the land. However, the cost of excavation and backfilling required for the construction of laundry facilities and a storm sewer system that would be destroyed when those assets were replaced was included in the depreciable basis of those assets (Rev. Rul. 80-93, 1980-1 CB 50).

Costs incurred for fill dirt that is used to raise the level of a building construction site are inextricably associated with the land and, therefore, are not depreciable. Costs incurred for fill dirt used to set the foundation of a building are depreciable, as are earth-moving costs incurred for digging spaces and trenches for a building's foundations and utilities (IRS Letter Ruling 200043016, July 14, 2000).

The cost of backfilling a lake to create additional land on which to expand a taxpayer's steel mill facilities was nondepreciable (Rev. Rul. 77-270, 1977-2 CB 79).

The initial grading and clearing costs related to the costs of acquiring right-of-way easements for electrical transmission and distribution lines are depreciable even though these costs are not necessarily incurred again when the lines are replaced on the same easements (Rev. Rul. 72-403, 1972-2 CB 102). These costs are specifically excluded from the definition of a land improvement by Asset Class 00.3 and Asset Class 49.14 (see ¶ 191). These costs were previously depreciated under MACRS as 7-year property (property without an assigned class life). Effective for property placed in service after October 22, 2004, this property is treated as MACRS 20-year property (Code Sec. 168(e)(3)(F), as added by the 2004 Jobs Act). See ¶ 112.

The cost of boundary and mortgage surveys are included in the basis of the land. The cost of percolation tests and contamination studies may be included in the basis of a building if these tests would have to be reperformed if the building was destroyed and reconstructed. This test is applied without regard to whether a local ordinance required such a survey to be reperformed (IRS Letter Ruling 200043016, July 14, 2000).

Staking costs should be allocated between depreciable and nondepreciable assets. For example, staking relating to sidewalks may be added to the basis of the sidewalk and depreciated. Staking relating to nondepreciable landscaping is added to the basis of the land, along with the landscaping costs (IRS Letter Ruling 200043016, July 14, 2000).

*Mobile home parks.* The cost of clearing, grading, terracing, and landscaping was an integral part of the construction and development of a taxpayer's mobile home park and depreciable over the same period as the related pads, patios, and other depreciable improvements (*Trailmont Park Inc.*, 30 TCM 871, Dec. 30,950(M)). The court concluded that the improvements in question were not an inextricable part of the land alone but were directly related to and a necessary part of the construction of the depreciable assets necessary to the operation of the park. Furthermore, any other use of the land would require its reshaping as the land configuration was usable only to support a park. See, also, *R.W. Tunnel*, DC Del., 74-1 USTC 9122, for a case involving a mobile home park (cost of clearing and thinning woods into a configuration suitable only for a mobile park was depreciable where clearing and thinning actually reduced value of land for residential construction purposes; landscaping, including gravel streets, were depreciable since they would have to be destroyed to put the land to any other use; general grading costs, including filling of marshland, which increased the value of the land, were nondepreciable).

Other improvements to land that may be depreciable include sidewalks, roads, canals, drainage facilities, waterways, sewers, wharves, docks, bridges, fences, and radio and television towers. See ¶ 110.

*Parking lots.* Parking lots are considered land improvements. Note, for example, that parking lots are specifically mentioned as a type of land improvement in

Rev. Proc. 87-56, Asset Class 80.0 (Theme and Amusement Parks). As to the depreciability of land preparation costs associated with a parking lot, see "*Roads,*" below. The IRS has ruled that an open-air parking structure is a building (39-year real property) and not a land improvement (Applicable Recovery Period Under Code Sec. 168(a) for Open-Air Parking Structures, Coordinated Issue Paper (LMSB4-0709-029) (Effective Date July 31, 2009)). See ¶ 127C.

The cost of resurfacing or applying sealcoat on a parking lot is a current expense (*Toledo Home Federal Savings and Loan Assn.*, DC Ohio, 62-1 USTC ¶ 9366, 203 FSupp 491; *W.K. Coors*, 60 TC 368, Dec. 32,003 (Acq.)).

A parking lot located at a steam production plant was 20-year property (Asset Class 49.13) since land improvements related to assets used in the steam power production of electricity are specifically included in Asset Class 49.13. Although land improvements are described in an asset category (Asset Class 00.3) as 15-year property, Asset Class 49.13 specifically includes land improvements related to assets used in the steam power production of electricity. However, a parking lot located 100 miles from the plant at the corporate headquarters was 15-year property (Asset Class 00.3) because in the IRS's view it "is not related to the plant that produces the electricity" as required by Asset Class 49.13 (Rev. Rul. 2003-81, 2003-2 CB 126). Apparently, the types of assets used in activities conducted at the corporate headquarters, even though connected with the business of producing electricity, are not considered by the IRS "as used" in the production of electricity within the meaning of Asset Class 49.13.

*Playground equipment.* Playground equipment located on an apartment complex and treated as a land improvement (15-year MACRS property under Asset Class 00.3) included swing sets, climbers, slides, see-saws, merry-go-rounds, picnic tables, pipe-frame park benches, basketball backboards, football/soccer goal posts, flag staffs or poles, softball backstops, jogging trails, and stationary aerobic equipment (IRS Letter Ruling 8848039, September 2, 1988).

The treatment of all types of playground equipment as a land improvement by IRS Letter Ruling 8848039 is not particularly well explained by the ruling and is probably unwarranted. Land improvements must be inherently permanent (see ¶ 127C). Picnic tables, aerobic equipment, and benches for example, do not appear to meet this requirement unless, possibly, they are cemented into the ground. Note that an LMSB directive on cost segregation in the restaurant industry dated December 8, 2003 categorizes "playground equipment" under the "Restaurant Decor Accessories" entry as 5-year property and not as a land improvement. The context of the "playground equipment" entry, however, could be interpreted to refer to playground equipment located within a restaurant building. By definition, land improvements do not include property located within or attached to a building. The 5-year recovery period applies because this is the period assigned to property (other than land improvements) used in the restaurant business (Asset Class 57.0 of Rev. Proc. 87-56 at ¶ 191).

*Roads.* Rev. Rul. 65-265 concludes that the cost of excavating, grading, and removing soil directly connected to the construction of roadways located between industrial buildings in an industrial park was depreciable. However, the ruling was subsequently clarified to indicate that this holding was premised upon the peculiar circumstances which would require regrading of the roads if the buildings were reconstructed. According to the clarification, the costs of grading roadways may be depreciable where it can be established that the grading is associated with a depreciable asset and the grading will be retired, abandoned, or replaced contemporaneously with the asset (Rev. Rul. 68-193, 1968-1 CB 79, *clarifying* Rev. Rul. 65-265). See, also, Rev. Rul. 88-99, 1988-2 CB 33, which hold that the cost of constructing a logging road (roadbeds, surfacing, bridges, culverts) that would be abandoned after four years when timber was harvested is depreciable; however, if the road will not be abandoned the cost of constructing the roadbed is not depreciable since its useful life is indeterminable. The IRS affirms the position taken in Rev. Rul. 88-99 in an Industry Specialization Program (ISP) Coordinated Issue Paper (Logging Truck Roads, October 31, 1991). The cost of temporary timber roads may be depreciated over 15 years as a land improvement or using the unit of production method in the proportion to the removal of the volume of timber for which the road was constructed. According to Rev. Rul. 68-281, 1968-1 C.B. 22, the total costs of a temporary road, including the costs of clearing, grubbing, rough cut, and fill grading, are recoverable (IRS Hardwood Timber Industry Audit Technique Guide (Dec. 2012)). Similarly, the cost of roads and trails that led to improvements on a ranch were depreciable because they would be abandoned if the improvements were abandoned (*Rudolph Investment Corp.*, 31 TCM 573, Dec. 31,421(M)).

If a taxpayer builds a permanent road that becomes the property of the landowner at the end of the agreement, the taxpayer may recover the depreciable portions of the road. On termination of the agreement, any remaining basis that the taxpayer has with respect to the depreciable portion of the road would be recoverable in that tax year. For the non-depreciable portion of the road, an equal part may be taken as a business deduction over the life of the agreement (IRS Hardwood Timber Industry Audit Technique Guide (Dec. 2012)).

An IRS Field Service Advice (FSA) provides additional clarification on the IRS position with respect to the depreciability of road building costs (Field Service Advice Memorandum 200021013). The depreciability of road building costs, under this ruling, hinges largely upon establishing that the road will have a limited or determinable useful life. For example, if the road will be abandoned when a related asset will be abandoned (as in the *Rudolph* case, above), then depreciation of all the capitalized road building costs is allowable. Certain of the roads involved in the FSA connected ski resort buildings and structures (such as ski lifts, a ski lodge, parking lots, restaurants, and snow grooming equipment). The FSA concluded that the roads would not be abandoned because the structures would not be abandoned, but rather, would be rebuilt, if they were to deteriorate. Also, if certain structures were abandoned the roads would continue to be used to service other facilities. Moreover, abandonment due to the expiration of lease permits with respect to the federal land on which the resort was built was unlikely since the permits were renewable for an indefinite period.

It is worth noting that the roads in *Rudolph* also led to improvements (specifically, residences, barns, corrals, chutes, fences, and pasture) which arguably would be replaced upon deterioration rather than abandoned. The court, however, unlike the FSA, did not discuss the probability of abandonment, simply finding that the roads were depreciable because they would be abandoned if the related improvements were abandoned. The FSA states that *Rudolph* is factually distinguishable because the types of improvements in *Rudolph* are different from those involved in the FSA. Presumably, the *Rudolph* improvements, in the IRS view, were more likely to be abandoned or would be abandoned over time.

The FSA provides that the costs directly related to surfacing (e.g., graveling or paving) a road are depreciable even if the particular circumstances do not allow depreciation of the costs related to clearing land, grading, and construction of the roadbed. This is so because surfacing needs to be replaced over time (i.e., has a definite or limited useful life).

A road is considered a land improvement and, if depreciable, usually would be recovered over a 15-year period under MACRS. See ¶ 110.

The taxpayer in the FSA argued that the IRS's requirement that a road have a determinable or limited useful life in order to be depreciable was inappropriate in the context of ACRS and MACRS because these systems assign recovery periods without regard to an asset's actual useful life. The IRS, however, rejected this view, stating that ACRS and MACRS simply provide the rules for determining the amount of a depreciation deduction and not the rules for determining the more fundamental question of whether an asset is depreciable. These rules, according to the IRS, are governed by Code Sec. 167 and the regulations thereunder which require that an asset must have a determinable useful life in a taxpayer's trade or business. Although not discussed in the FSA, the Tax Court has ruled in two decisions (which were also affirmed at the appellate level) that musical instruments that appreciate in value and have no determinable useful life are depreciable so long as they are subject to wear and tear because they are actually being used. These decisions may provide a basis for challenging the position taken by the IRS in this FSA and similar earlier rulings which hinge upon establishing a determinable useful life. See ¶ 3.

*Site utilities.* Site utilities at a hotel/casino complex were structural components (¶ 127) and not land improvements. Site utilities included underground piping that connected water, sewer, and gas services to the building and overground and underground lines that connected electric service to the building. These items were used to distribute city furnished utility services to the building and were not directly associated with specific items of machinery and equipment (IRS Field Service Advice 200203009, October 3, 2001).

However, various components of an electrical distribution system (pine poles, aerial lines, transformers, meters, street lighting) and water distribution system (valves, fire hydrants, fittings, tapping sleeves, PVC water pipe, water meters) that were installed and maintained by the taxpayer in connection with an apartment complex were depreciable land improvements. These items were not classified as Rev. Proc. 87-56 Asset Class 49.14, Electric Utility Transmission and Distribution Plant, and Asset Class 49.3, Water Utilities, because those classifications only apply to taxpayers that sell electricity and water (IRS Letter Ruling 8848039, September 2, 1988).

*Trees, shrubbery and other landscaping.* The IRS officially maintains that trees and shrubbery may be depreciated only if they would be destroyed upon the replacement of a depreciable asset such as a building at the end of their useful life.

> ***Example (2):*** A taxpayer constructs a new commercial building and incurs costs for clearing, general grading, top soil, seeding, finish grading, and planting perennial shrubbery and trees. Some bushes and trees are planted next to the building and other bushes and trees are planted around the perimeter of a parking lot. The IRS allows the bushes and trees planted next to the building to be depreciated because they have a determinable useful life that is closely associated with the building. All other costs are added to the basis of the land and are not depreciable because they have no determinable life (Rev. Rul. 74-265, 1974-1 CB 56; GCM 35693 (February 26, 1974); IRS Publication 946, How to Depreciate Property).

It appears that the IRS position is that the costs of clearing and general and finish grading in the immediate vicinity of the building is not depreciable since these costs would not be reincurred if the building is destroyed and replaced.

Although Rev. Rul. 74-265 (a pre-MACRS ruling) provides that the cost of the trees and shrubbery are recovered over the life of the related building, under MACRS the cost of depreciable shrubbery and trees should be recovered over 15 years as a land improvement. Depreciable shrubbery is specifically included in Asset Class 00.3 (Land Improvements). Asset Class 00.3 provides a 15-year MACRS recovery period. Also noteworthy is IRS Publication 527 (Residential Rental Property) which contains a table which indicates that depreciable shrubbery is recovered over 15-years and IRS Letter Ruling 8848039 (September 2, 1988) which allows a 15-year recovery period for depreciable trees and shrubs planted next to residential rental property.

Several cases (to which the IRS has not acquiesced) have held that an asset may be depreciable under MACRS even if it has no determinable useful life. This could be the basis for arguing that landscaping not located next to a building is deductible. See ¶ 3.

Trees and bushes planted on a farm to serve as a windbreak to prevent soil erosion and to conserve moisture in the fields, thus increasing farm production and revenue, were nondepreciable (*G. Everson*, CA-9, 97-1 USTC ¶ 50,258). Note, however, that windbreaks may be currently deductible as soil and water conservation expenditures under Code Sec. 175.

*Personal (nonbusiness) assets*

Personal assets, such as a residence used by an individual or an automobile used only for personal purposes are not depreciable (Reg. § 1.167(a)-2)). If an asset is used partly for personal purposes and partly for business or investment purposes, only the portion of the asset used for business or investment purposes is depreciable.

*Property subject to a lease*

Generally, for post-August 10, 1993, acquisitions of property subject to a lease, the purchaser must allocate the entire cost to the basis of the property. No portion of the cost may be allocated to the acquired leasehold interest (Code Sec. 167(c)(2); Reg. § 1.197-2(c)(8)).

***Example (3):*** A taxpayer purchases a shopping center that is under lease to tenants operating retail stores. The portion of the purchase price of the shopping center that is attributable to any favorable aspects of the leases is treated as part of the basis of the shopping center.

*Leasehold acquisition costs*

The cost of acquiring an interest as a lessee of tangible property is amortized over the term of the lease (Code Sec. 178; Reg. § 1.162-11(a); Reg. § 1.197-2(c)(8)(ii)). The regulations provide that where an interest as a lessee under a lease of tangible property is acquired in a transaction with any other intangible property, the portion of the total purchase price allocable to the interest as a lessee is based on all of the relevant facts and circumstances (Reg. § 1.197-2(c)(8)(ii)). However, the House Committee Report to P.L. 103-66 provided that the portion of the purchase price that may be allocated to a lessee's interest under a lease of tangible property in such a situation may not exceed the excess of:

(1) the present value of the fair market value rent for the tangible property for the term of the lease, over

(2) the present value of the rent reasonably expected to be paid over the term of the lease.

A taxpayer may pay to acquire an existing lease from a *lessee.* In general, the amount paid to the lessee for the leasehold interest is also amortized over the term of the lease.

Amounts paid by a lessor to terminate a lease contract are amortized over the remaining term of the lease (*Peerless Weighing and Vending Machine Corp.*, 52 T.C. 850, Dec. 29,713).

Leasehold acquisition costs are not amortizable under Code Sec. 197. See ¶ 52.

The term of the lease (i.e., amortization period) includes all renewal options and any other period that the lessor and lease purchaser expect the lease to be renewed if less than 75 percent of the cost is for the term of the lease remaining on the purchase date without regard to renewal options that the lease purchaser may exercise (Code Sec. 178; Reg. § 1.178-1(b)).

***Example (4):*** A taxpayer enters into a lease for $10,000. The lease term is 20 years with two options to renew for periods of five years each. If at least $7,500 of the acquisition cost is allocable to the 20-year original term of the lease, then the taxpayer may amortize the $10,000 cost over a 20-year period whether or not the lease will be renewed.

***Example (5):*** Same facts as *Example (4)*, except that $7,000 is allocable to the original term of the lease. Since less than 75% of the leasehold acquisition cost is allocable to the original term of the lease, the $10,000 acquisition cost is amortizable over 30 years (20-year original term plus 10-year renewal period). However, if the taxpayer can establish that it is more probable that the renewal options will not be exercised than that they will be exercised, the amortization period is limited to the 20-year original term of the lease.

An amortization period that does not include the period of a renewal option that is not expected to be exercised must be increased to include the renewal period in the tax year that a reasonable expectation that the renewal option will be exercised arises (Reg. § 1.178-3(b)).

In applying the 75-percent test, the lease cost is allocated between the original term and renewal periods based on the facts and circumstances. The allocation may, in certain circumstances, be based upon a present value computation (Reg. § 1.178-1(b)(5)).

*Repairs or improvements*

The cost of a repair is currently deductible (Reg. § 1.162-4). However, an improvement is capitalized and depreciated (Reg. § 1.263(a)-3). See ¶ 126.

## ¶ 10

## Intangible Property

In deciding how to recover the cost of intangible property, a determination must first be made as to whether the intangible property qualifies for an amortization deduction under Code Sec. 197 (¶ 12) or some other provision such as the 15-year safe harbor for self-created intangibles (¶ 66).

In order for Code Sec. 197 to apply a particular intangible property must constitute a section 197 intangible, and the section 197 intangible must be an amortizable section 197 intangible.

If a Code Sec. 197 amortization deduction is allowed on an intangible, no other depreciation or amortization deduction may be claimed on such property (Code Sec. 197(b)). Depreciation-amortization treatment under Code Sec. 167 may apply (if other requirements are met) to an intangible that is not amortizable under Code Sec. 197.

The capitalized costs of amortizable section 197 intangibles are ratably amortized over a 15-year period generally beginning with the month of acquisition regardless of their actual useful life (Code Sec. 197(a)). The section 197 amortization rules do not apply to intangible property for which a current business expense deduction may be claimed.

*Amortizable basis of section 197 intangible*

The amount amortized is the adjusted basis for purposes of determining gain (usually cost) of an amortizable section 197 intangible (Code Sec. 197(a)). See also ¶ 70.

Section 197 intangibles acquired pursuant to an asset acquisition to which Code Sec. 338 or Code Sec. 1060 applies should be treated as Class IV assets. Consequently, the purchase price of section 197 intangibles so acquired is the amount by which the total purchase price (as reduced by the Class I Assets) exceeds the value of assets included in Class II and Class III (Reg. § 1.197-2(f)(4)(ii)).

*Amortization deductions for other intangibles*

Intangible property that is not amortizable under Code Sec. 197 or another specific provision is amortizable if an ascertainable limited life can be determined (Reg. § 1.167(a)-3) and the property has an ascertainable value.

Both MACRS and ACRS are inapplicable to intangible assets (Code Sec. 168(a)) (see ¶ 140 and ¶ 228).

Depreciation of intangible assets under certain accelerated depreciation methods (including the declining-balance and the sum of the years-digits methods) was not permitted under former Code Sec. 167(c) (before repeal by the Omnibus Budget Reconciliation Act of 1990 (P.L. 101-508) to eliminate deadwood but not to change the rule of law).

Intangible assets may be depreciated under any reasonable method (Code Sec. 167(a)). The straight-line method must be used absent a different acceptable method (Reg. § 1.167(b)-1(a)).

A method other than the straight-line method is appropriate provided that, considering the facts of the case, it results in a fair allocation of the basis of the asset to periods in which income is realized (*Citizens & Southern Corp.*, 91 TC 463, Dec. 45,036, aff'd per curiam, CA-11, 91-1 USTC ¶ 50,043; *IT&S of Iowa, Inc.*, 97 TC 496, Dec. 47,735; *Computing & Software, Inc.*, 64 TC 223, Dec. 33,197, (Acq.) 1976-2 CB 1; *Trustmark Corp.*, 67 TCM 2764, Dec. 49,813(M), TC Memo. 1994-184). (See also ¶ 28.)

Other permissible methods for depreciating certain intangible assets include the income forecast method (Rev. Rul. 60-358, 1960-2 CB 68, amplified by Rev. Rul. 64-273, 1964-2 CB 62) (see also ¶ 364) and the sliding-scale method (*Kiro, Inc.*, 51 TC 155, Dec. 29,205 (Acq., 1974-2 CB 3)). See ¶ 364.

## ¶ 12

## Amortizable Section 197 Intangibles

A section 197 intangible is amortizable if it is acquired after August 10, 1993, and held in connection with a trade or business or in an activity engaged in for the production of income (Code Sec. 197(c)(1)). An irrevocable election allowed taxpayers to apply Code Sec. 197 to property acquired after July 25, 1991 (Temp. Reg. § 1.197-1T).

The standard for determining when an amortizable section 197 intangible is held in connection with the conduct of a trade or business is the standard under Code Sec. 162. This determination will depend on the facts of each case, in particular when the taxpayer began carrying on a trade or business within the meaning of Code Sec. 162 (CCA Letter Ruling 200137050, August 8, 2001).

*Amortization period*

Amortizable section 197 intangibles are amortized over 15 years beginning the later of the first day of the month of acquisition or, in the case of property held in connection with the conduct of a trade or business or an income-producing activity, the first day of the month in which the conduct of the trade or business or the activity begins (Reg. § 1.197-2(f)(1)). No amortization deduction is claimed in the month of disposition.

*Assets treated as section 197 intangibles*

The following assets are considered section 197 intangibles (Code Sec. 197(d); Reg. § 1.197-2(b)):

(1) goodwill (¶ 18);

(2) going concern value (¶ 20);

(3) workforce in place (¶ 22);

(4) information base (¶ 24);

(5) patent, copyright, formulas, process, design, pattern, know-how, format, or similar item (¶ 26);

(6) customer-based intangible (¶ 28);

(7) supplier-based intangible (¶ 30);

(8) government license or permit (¶ 32);

(9) covenant not to compete entered into in connection with the acquisition of an interest in a trade or business (¶ 34); and

(10) franchise, trademark, or trade-name (¶ 36).

Intangible property that is similar in all material respects to the property described in items (3) - (7) is a section 197 intangible (Reg.§ 1.197-2(b)(12)).

Any right under a license, contract, or other arrangement for the use of property that would be a section 197 intangible is generally treated as a section 197 intangible (Code Sec. 197(d)(1)(C)(vi); Reg. § 1.197-2(b)(11)).

A term interest in a section 197 intangible is treated as a section 197 intangible (Reg. § 1.197-2(b)(11)).

*Exclusions from definition of section 197 intangible*

The following assets are specifically excluded from the definition of a section 197 intangible and, therefore, are not amortizable under Code Sec. 197 under any circumstance (Code Sec. 197(e); Reg.§ 1.197-2(c)):

(1) any interest in a corporation, partnership, trust, or estate (¶ 42);

(2) any interest under an existing futures contract, foreign currency contract, notional principal contract, or other similar financial contract (¶ 44);

(3) any interest in land (¶ 46);

(4) off-the shelf computer software (¶ 48);

(5) any interest under an existing lease of tangible property (¶ 52) or any existing indebtedness (¶ 54);

(6) sport franchises acquired on or before October 22, 2004 (¶ 56);

(7) certain transaction costs incurred in connection with nonrecognition transactions (¶ 60 and ¶ 64).

*Exclusion for certain separately acquired intangibles*

The following assets are not section 197 intangibles unless acquired in a transaction or series of related transactions involving the acquisition of assets constituting a trade or business or substantial portion thereof (Code Sec. 197(e)(4)):

(1) any interest in a film, sound recording, video tape, book, or similar property (Reg.§ 1.197-2(c)(5));

(2) any right to receive tangible property or services under a contract or granted by a government (Reg.§ 1.197-2(c)(6)) (¶ 50);

(3) an interest in a patent or copyright (Reg.§ 1.197-2(c)(7)) (¶ 26);

(4) any right under a contract or granted by a government if the right has a fixed duration of less than 15 years, or is fixed as to amount and would be recoverable under a method similar to the unit-of-production method (Reg. § 1.197-2(c)(13))

(5) computer software that is not off-the shelf software (Code Sec. 197(e)(3)(A)(ii)); and

(6) certain mortgage servicing rights (Code Sec. 197(e)(6)) (¶ 58)

A covenant not to compete is a section 197 intangible only if it is entered in connection with the acquisition of an interest in a trade or business or substantial portion thereof (Code Sec. 197(d)(1)(E)). See ¶ 34.

Taxpayers must treat a right granted under a license, contract or other arrangement providing for use of an amortizable section 197 intangible as an amortizable section 197 intangible. Taxpayers must also treat term interests (whether outright or in trust) in an amortizable section 197 intangible like an amortizable section 197 intangible (Reg. § 1.197-2(b)(11)).

Although the preceding assets need to be acquired in connection with the acquisition of a trade or business or substantial portion thereof in order to be amortized under Code Sec. 197, all section 197 intangibles need to be used in connection with the conduct of a trade or business or an income-producing activity to be so amortized (Code Sec. 197(c)(1)).

As explained below, most types "self-created" section 197 intangibles are also not amortizable under section 197 unless *created* in connection with a transaction or series of related transactions involving the acquisition of the assets constituting a trade or business or substantial portion thereof (Code Sec. 197(c)(2)).

See ¶ 50 for details regarding the exclusion for separately acquired intangibles.

*Self-created intangibles*

Generally, amortization under Code Sec. 197 is not allowed in the case of a section 197 intangible created by the taxpayer ("self-created intangible"). Such intangibles, however, may be amortizable over 15 years under a separate safe-harbor provision described at ¶ 66. A self-created intangible, however, is amortizable under Code Sec. 197 if it is created in connection with a transaction or series of related transactions involving the acquisition of a trade or business (Code Sec. 197(c)(2); Reg. § 1.197-2(d)(2)).

A section 197 intangible is created by a taxpayer to the extent the taxpayer makes payments or otherwise incurs costs for its creation, production, development, or improvement. This also applies if the payment etc., is made to a third party to create the intangible for the taxpayer. For example, a taxpayer that pays a third party to develop a technological process that will be owned by the taxpayer may not treat the technological process as an amortizable section 197 intangible because it is self-created. However, a section 197 intangible is not self-created to the extent that it results from the entry into or renewal of a contract for the use of an existing section 197 intangible. For example, capitalized legal and professional fees incurred by a licensee in connection with the entry into or renewal of a contract for the use of know-how or similar property is not a self-created intangible (Reg. § 1.197-2(d)(2)).

Goodwill created through a taxpayer's own efforts in running a business is considered a self-created intangible and is not amortizable under any provision (Field Service Advice Memorandum 200106006, October 17, 2000).

This rule preventing a taxpayer from amortizing a self-created section 197 intangible under Code Sec. 197 unless it is created in connection with the acquisition of a trade or business does not apply to the following section 197 intangibles (Code Sec. 197)(c)(2)(A); Reg.§ 1.197-2(d)(2)):

(1) licenses, permits, or other rights granted by a governmental unit, agency, or instrumentality;

(2) a covenant not to compete entered into in connection with the acquisition of a business or substantial portion thereof; and

(3) a franchise, trademark, or tradename (¶ 36).

A license, permit, or other right granted by the government that is not acquired in connection with the acquisition of a trade or business is amortizable over its duration if such duration is fixed for a period of less than 15 years. See ¶ 32.

A covenant not to compete is amortizable under Code Sec. 197 only if it is entered into in connection with the acquisition of a trade or business (Code Sec. 197(d)(1)(E); Reg.§ 1.197-2(b)(9)). Thus, the cost of covenants entered into by an employer with departing employees or officers are recovered over the term of the agreement as under pre-Code Sec. 197 law. See ¶ 34.

*Loss disallowed on certain sales and dispositions*

No loss is recognized when a taxpayer disposes of an amortizable section 197 intangible if the taxpayer (or a related person) retains other section 197 intangibles that were acquired in the same transaction or series of related transactions. The disallowed loss is allocated among the adjusted bases of the retained intangibles (Code Sec. 197(f)(1); Reg. § 1.197-2(g)(1)). This rule also applies to abandoned and worthless amortizable section 197 intangibles.

*Recapture*

An amortizable section 197 intangible is treated as depreciable property for purposes of recapture (Code Sec. 197(f)(7); Reg. § 1.197-2(g)(8)). A special recapture rule applies if more than one amortizable section 197 intangible is sold in the same transaction. See also *"Dispositions of amortizable section 197 intangibles"* at ¶ 160 for a discussion of the section 197 recapture rules.

*Section 1231 asset*

If used in a trade or business and held for more than one year, gain or loss on the disposition of an amortizable section 197 asset generally qualifies as section 1231 gain or loss. Nonamortizable and nondepreciable intangibles generally qualify as capital assets under Code Sec. 1221 (IRS Letter Ruling 200243002, July 16, 2002).

## ¶ 14

## Anti-churning Rules for Section 197 Intangibles

Certain section 197 intangibles acquired in certain transactions do not qualify for an amortization deduction under Code Sec. 197 (Code Sec. 197(f)(9); Reg. § 1.197-2(d)(3)).

An amortization deduction is barred under anti-churning rules for a section 197 intangible that is goodwill, going-concern value, or that would not otherwise be depreciable or amortizable but for Code Sec. 197, if it is acquired after August 10, 1993, and the taxpayer:

(1) or a related person held or used the intangible at any time during the period beginning on July 25, 1991, and ending on August 10, 1993;

(2) acquired the intangible from a person that held it any time during the period beginning on July 25, 1991, and ending on August 10, 1993, and, as part of the transaction, the user of the intangible did not change; or

(3) grants the right to use the intangible to a person (or a person related to such person) that held or used the intangible at any time during the period beginning on July 25, 1991, and ending on August 10, 1993 (Code Sec. 197(f)(9)(A); Reg. § 1.197-2(h)(2)).

*Related persons*

For purposes of the anti-churning rules, related persons include (a) relationships similar to those indicated at ¶ 266 but applying 20-percent stock and partnership ownership percentage tests and (b) persons engaged in trades or businesses under common control. Persons are treated as related if the requisite relationship exists immediately before or after the acquisition of the intangible (Code Sec. 197(f)(9)(C); Reg.§ 1.197-2(h)(6)).

*Anti-abuse rule*

No section 197 amortization deduction is allowed if a section 197 intangible is acquired in a transaction, one of the principal purposes of which is to avoid the requirement that the intangible be acquired after August 10, 1993, or to avoid the anti-churning rules (Code Sec. 197(f)(9)(F); Reg.§ 1.197-2(j)).

*Partnerships*

In determining whether the anti-churning rules apply to an increase in the basis of partnership property under Code Sec. 732 (basis of distributed property other than money), Code Sec. 734 (optional adjustment to basis of undistributed partnership property), or Code Sec. 743 (optional adjustment to basis of partnership property), the determinations are made at the partner level. Each partner is treated as having owned or used the partner's proportionate share of the partnership property (Code Sec. 197(f)(9)(E); Reg. § 1.197-2(h)(12)(i)).

***Example:*** The anti-churning rules do not apply to any increase in the basis of partnership property that occurs upon the acquisition of an interest in a partnership that made a Code Sec. 754 election to utilize the optional adjustment to the basis of partnership property if the person acquiring the partnership interest is not related to the person selling the partnership interest (Reg. § 1.197-2(k), *Example 14*).

*Partnerships—contributions of anti-churning property to partnership with foreign related partners.* Unless a partnership adopts the "gain deferral method," the general rule that gain or loss is not recognized when property is contributed to a partnership in exchange for a partnership interest (Code Sec. 721(a)) does not apply to built-in gain property contributed by a U.S. transferor if after the contribution a foreign person related to the transferor is a direct or indirect partner and the transferor and related person or persons own 80 percent or more of the interests in partnership capital, profits, deductions, or losses (Temporary Reg. § 1.721(c)-1T through Temporary Reg. § 1.721(c)-7T, as added by T.D. 9814 (January 18, 2017)). Under the gain deferral method, a "modified" remedial allocation method applies with respect to allocations to a person related to the U.S. transferor in the case of built-in-gain property that is was not an amortizable section 197 intangible in the hands of the transferor due to application of the section 197 anti-churning rules (Temporary Reg. § 1.197-2T(h)(12)(vii)(C) and (l)(5), as added by T.D. 9814 (January 18, 2017); Temporary Reg. § 1.704-3T(d)(5)(iii), as added by T.D. 9814).

*Partial exception election*

A partial exception to the anti-churning rules is provided if these rules would not apply to an acquired intangible but for the 20-percent stock and partnership ownership percentage tests and if the person from whom the intangible is acquired elects to (1) recognize gain on the disposition and (2) pay a tax on the gain that, when added to any other federal income tax imposed on the gain, equals the product of the gain times the highest income tax rate applicable to such person. In this case, the anti-churning rules apply to the acquired intangible only to the extent that the adjusted basis of the acquirer in the intangible exceeds the recognized gain (Code Sec. 197(f)(9)(B); Reg. § 1.197-2(h)(9)).

*Franchises, trademarks, and trade names*

Deductible transferee payments made in connection with the transfer of a franchise, trademark, or trade name under Code Sec. 1253(d) are treated as an amortization deduction. Consequently, a franchise, trademark, or trade name for which such payments were made is not subject to the anti-churning rules (Code Sec. 197(f)(9)(A); Reg. § 1.197-2(h)(3)).

*Transfer from decedent*

Also, the anti-churning rules do not apply to intangibles acquired from a decedent if the acquiring taxpayer's basis in the intangible is determined under the stepped-up basis rules of Code Sec. 1014(a) (Code Sec. 197(f)(9)(D); Reg. § 1.197-2(h)(5)).

Under final regulations, which are effective on or after January 19, 2017, if a transferee's basis is determined under Code Sec. 1022 (relating to an election to use the gift tax rules to determine the basis of property acquired from certain decedents who died in 2010 (see ¶ 70) the anti-churning rules do not apply (Reg. § 1.197-2(h)(5)(i); Reg.§ 1.197-2(l)(5))).

*Purchase or acquisition of section 197 intangible in hands of seller*

The anti-churning rules do not apply to the acquisition of a section 197 intangible that was an amortizable section 197 intangible in the hands of the seller (or transferor), but only if the acquisition transaction and the transaction in which the seller (or transferor) acquired the intangible or interest therein are not part of a series of related transactions (Reg. § 1.197-2(h)(5)).

## ¶ 18
## Goodwill

*Section 197 treatment*

Goodwill is a section 197 intangible (Code Sec. 197(d)(1)(A)). It is defined as the value of a trade or business that is attributable to the expectancy of continued customer patronage, whether due to name or reputation of the trade or business or to any other factor (Reg. § 1.197-2(b)(1)).

Typically, amortizable goodwill and going concern value are acquired by a taxpayer who purchases an existing trade or business at a price in excess of the fair market value of all of its other assets, including other intangible assets. Goodwill and going concern value are Class VII assets for purposes of allocating the purchase price among the assets of an acquiring business using the residual method (Reg. § 1.338-6(b)). However, it may be possible that there is no sale of goodwill unless a covenant not to compete (also a section 197 intangible, see ¶ 34) is entered into with a key person who is responsible for generating the goodwill. See cases cited in Field Service Advice Memorandum 200106006, October 17, 2000.

Goodwill is not amortizable under Code Sec. 197 if it is created by the taxpayer unless is it created by the taxpayer in connection with a transaction of series of transactions involving the acquisition of assets constituting a trade or business or a substantial portion thereof (Code Sec. 197(c)(2);Reg.§ 1.197-2(d)(2)(iii)(B)). For example, a taxpayer who starts a business and creates goodwill over time cannot amortize the value of the goodwill. See, ¶ 12, "Self-created intangibles."

Goodwill and going concern value which are amortizable section 197 intangibles are not capital assets for purposes of Code Sec. 1221, but if used in a trade or business and held for more than one year, gain or loss upon their disposition generally qualifies as section 1231 gain or loss (IRS Letter Ruling 200243002, July 16, 2002).

*Depreciation if section 197 does not apply*

Goodwill which is not amortizable under section 197 is generally not depreciable because it has an indefinite useful life or, even if it is considered an asset that does waste, its useful life cannot be determined with reasonable accuracy (Reg. § 1.167(a)-3).

## ¶ 20

## Going-Concern Value

*Section 197 treatment*

Section 197 intangibles include going-concern value, which is the additional value that attaches to property because it is an integral part of a going concern. It includes the value attributable to the ability of a trade or business to continue to operate and generate income without interruption in spite of a change in ownership (Code Sec. 197(d)(1); Reg. § 1.197-2(b)(2)).

As in the case of goodwill, going concern value is not amortizable under Code Sec. 197 if it is created by the taxpayer unless is it created by the taxpayer in connection with a transaction of series of transactions involving the acquisition of assets constituting a trade or business or a substantial portion thereof (Code Sec. 197(c)(2); Reg. § 1.197-2(d)(2)(iii)(B)). For example, a taxpayer who starts a business or buys a business and creates going concern value over time cannot amortize the value of that going concern value. See, ¶ 12, "Self-created intangibles."

Goodwill and going concern value which are amortizable section 197 intangibles are not capital assets for purposes of Code Sec. 1221, but if used in a trade or business and held for more than one year, gain or loss upon their disposition generally qualifies as section 1231 gain or loss (IRS Letter Ruling 200243002, July 16, 2002).

*Depreciation if section 197 does not apply*

The depreciation rules applicable to going-concern value that is not amortizable under Code Sec. 197 are similar to the rules for goodwill (*Ithaca Industries, Inc.*, CA-4, 94-1 USTC ¶ 50,100, cert. denied taxpayer 10/3/94) (see ¶ 18). Thus, no depreciation is allowed on this asset unless it has an ascertainable value and a limited useful life that can be determined with reasonable accuracy.

## ¶ 22
## Work Force in Place

*Section 197 treatment*

Workforce in place is a section 197 intangible (Code Sec. 197(d)(1)). Workforce in place includes the composition of a work force (experience, education, or training), the terms and conditions of employment whether contractual or otherwise, and any other value placed on employees or their attributes. The amount paid or incurred for workforce in place includes, for example, any portion of the purchase price of an acquired trade or business attributable to the existence of a highly-skilled workforce, an existing employment contract (or contracts), or a relationship with employees or consultants (including, but not limited to, any key employee contract or relationship). Workforce in place does not include any covenant not to compete or other similar arrangement (Reg. § 1.197-2(b)(3)).

Workforce in place is not amortizable under Code Sec. 197 if it is created by the taxpayer unless is it created by the taxpayer in connection with a transaction of series of transactions involving the acquisition of assets constituting a trade or business or a substantial portion thereof (Code Sec. 197(c)(2); Reg. § 1.197-2(d)(2)(iii)(B)). For example, a taxpayer who starts a business or buys a business and creates a workforce in place over time cannot amortize the value of the workforce in place. However, a taxpayer who purchases an existing workforce in place separately or as part of the acquisition of a business may amortize this intangible under section 179. See, ¶ 12, "Self-created intangibles."

*Depreciation if section 197 does not apply*

If this intangible asset is not amortizable under Code Sec 197, the following rules apply. Generally, no depreciation is allowed on this intangible asset unless it has an ascertainable value and a limited useful life that can be determined with reasonable accuracy.

The mass-asset rule is often used to prohibit depreciation of a work force in place if this asset constitutes a self-regenerating asset that may change but never waste. This rule treats the individual employees comprising a work force as a single asset and, even though the individual components of the asset may rise or fall over time or expire or be replaced, there are only minimal fluctuations and no measurable loss in the value of the whole.

For purposes of the mass-asset rule, the distinguishing feature of a true mass asset is its ability to self-regenerate (the asset's maintenance is not accompanied by significant efforts of the owner other than those already expended in the initial formation or purchase of the asset).

An amortization deduction was denied for an acquired work force that was not subject to any predetermined contractual or other limit because it lacked a limited useful life and was not an amortizable intangible asset. However, it was not the mass-asset rule that barred the deduction because this company's work force was preserved only through the company's substantial training and recruiting efforts and it was not a self-regenerating asset (*Ithaca Industries, Inc.*, CA-4, 94-1 USTC ¶ 50,100, cert. denied taxpayer 10/3/94).

For a detailed discussion of the amortization of assembled workforce under the pre-Code Sec. 197 rules, see IRS Industry Specialization Program (ISP) Coordinated Issue Paper, Amortization of Assembled Workforce, (as revised February 19, 1996 and reproduced in full text in the CCH IRS POSITIONS Reporter at ¶ 80,115).

## ¶ 24
## Information Base

*Section 197 treatment*

Information base is a section 197 intangible. Business books and records; operating systems; customer lists; subscription lists; insurance expirations; patient or client files; the intangible value attributable to technical manuals, training manuals or programs, data files, and accounting or inventory control systems; and lists of newspaper, magazine, radio or television advertisers are included in this category (Code Sec. 197(d) (1); Reg. § 1.197-2(b) (4)).

Information base is not amortizable under Code Sec. 197 if it is created by the taxpayer unless is it created by the taxpayer in connection with a transaction of series of transactions involving the acquisition of assets constituting a trade or business or a substantial portion thereof (Code Sec. 197(c) (2);Reg. § 1.197-2(d) (2) (iii) (B)). For example, a taxpayer who starts a business or buys a business and creates an information base over time cannot amortize the value of the information base. However, a taxpayer who purchases an existing information base, either separately or as part of the acquisition of an existing business may amortize the information base. See, ¶ 12, "Self-created intangibles."

*Depreciation if section 197 does not apply*

If these intangible assets are not amortizable under Code Sec. 197, a depreciation deduction is allowed provided that they have an ascertainable value and a limited useful life that can be determined with reasonable accuracy.

## ¶ 26
## Patents, Copyrights, Formulas, Processes, Designs, Patterns, Know-How, Computer Software, Films, Recordings, Books, Etc.

*Section 197 treatment*

Section 197 intangibles include (Code Sec. 197(d) (1)):

- patents
- copyrights
- formulas
- processes
- designs
- patterns
- know-how
- formats
- similar items

This category also includes (Reg. § 1.197-2(b) (5)):

- package designs
- certain computer software
- interests in films, sound recordings, video tapes, books and similar property

If self-created, none of the above items above are considered section 197 intangibles unless created in connection with a transaction involving the acquisition of a trade or business or a substantial portion of a trade or business (Code Sec. 197(c)(2); Reg. § 1.197-2(d)(2)(iii)(B)). For example, a taxpayer who starts a business or buys a business and creates a formula cannot amortize the value of the formula under section 197. However, a taxpayer who purchases an existing formula, either separately or as part of the acquisition of an existing business may amortize the formula. See, ¶ 12, "Self-created intangibles."

Computer software is considered a section 197 intangible only if it is not "off-the-shelf" software and is acquired in a transaction involving the acquisition of a trade or business (Code Sec. 197(e)(3); Reg. § 1.197-2(c)(4)). See ¶ 48.

However, unless acquired in connection with the acquisition of a trade or business or a substantial portion thereof, an interest (such as a license) in a film, sound recording, video tape, book or similar property is not an amortizable section 197 intangible (Code Sec. 197(e)(4)(A); Reg. § 1.197-2(c)(5)). Similarly, patents and copyrights not acquired in connection with the acquisition of a trade or business are not amortizable under Code Sec. 197 (Code Sec. 197(e)(4)(B); Reg. § 1.197-2(c)(7)). Thus, even if such items are separately purchased or created in connection with the acquisition of a trade or business, they are not amortizable under section 197. See ¶ 50.

*Depreciation if section 197 does not apply*

*Computer software.* See ¶ 48.

*Patents and copyrights.* If an interest in a patent or copyright is not amortizable under Code Sec. 197 because it is separately acquired (¶ 50), the depreciation deduction for a tax year is equal to the amount of the purchase price paid during the tax year in situations where the purchase price is payable on an annual basis as either a fixed amount per use or a fixed percentage of the revenue derived from the use. Otherwise, the basis of the patent or copyright (or an interest therein) is depreciated ratably over its remaining useful life or under the income forecast method. If a patent or copyright becomes worthless in any year before its legal expiration, the adjusted basis may be deducted in that year (Reg. § 1.167(a)-6; Reg. § 1.167(a)-14(c)(4)).

Amortization on a patent or copyright that is not a section 197 intangible begins when it is placed in service (Reg. § 1.167(a)-14(c)(5)). Rev. Rul. 79-285 provides that rights to patents and master recordings are first placed in service when products or processes resulting from the these rights are first released for distribution and sale, or are used in the taxpayer's trade or business or for the production of income. The ruling states, however, that patents are not considered placed in service prior to the issue date. However, due to the law change described below, the ruling's reference to "issue date" should probably be changed to "application filing date."

The straight-line method may be used to depreciate the cost of a patent or copyright. For example, if a patent is acquired and placed in service by a calendar-year taxpayer on July 1 for $10,000 and its remaining useful life as of that date is 10 years, the straight-line deduction is $500 ($10,000 ÷ 10 × 6⁄12).

Prior to June 8, 1995, patents generally had a legal life of 17 years starting from the date the patent was issued. Patents granted on or after June 8, 1995, generally have a 20-year legal life measured from the date of the first filing of the patent application. Patents that were in force before June 8, 1995, or that result from an application filed before June 8, 1995, generally have a term that is the greater of (1) 20 years from the date the application was first filed or (2) 17 years from the date of grant (35 U.S.C. § 154).

For copyrighted material published before 1978, the U.S. copyright term was for 28 years, and copyrights could be renewed for a second term of 28 years.

For works created after 1977, the copyright term is for the life of the author plus 70 years. The copyright term for joint works created after 1977 is the life of the last surviving author plus 70 years. Where works made for hire are created after 1977, the copyright period is 95 years from the date of first publication or a term of 120 years from the year of creation, whichever expires first (17 USC § § 302, 303, and 304).

There must be a sale of the capital asset (the patent) rather than a license agreement (right to use the product) in order for the transferee to qualify as the owner for depreciation purposes. A sale exists if there is a transfer of the exclusive right to make, use, and sell a particular product in the United States for the full term of a patent because none of the attributes of ownership is retained (*Magee-Hale Park-O-Meter Co.*, 15 TCM 254, Dec. 21,616(M), TC Memo. 1956-57). However, a transfer of the attributes of ownership is not precluded by a security provision designed to protect the transferor's right to receive compensation under the sale agreement (*Newton Insert Co.*, 61 TC 570, Dec. 32,439, aff'd per curiam, CA-9, 77-1 USTC ¶ 9132, 545 F2d 1259).

*Package design costs.* Prior to the issuance of the final *INDOPCO* intangibles capitalization regulations (Reg. § 1.263(a)-4 and Reg. § 1.263(a)-5 as adopted by T.D. 9107, filed with the Federal Register on December 31, 2003), the cost of developing and designing product packages generally had to be capitalized. These regulations are generally effective for amounts paid or incurred on or after December 31, 2003.

Reg. § 1.263(a)-4(b)(3)(v) of the final *INDOPCO* regulations provides that amounts paid to develop a package design are treated as amounts that do not create a separate and distinct intangible asset. Thus, these amounts are not required to be capitalized and may be currently deducted.

The cost of purchasing an existing package design cost, however, continues to be subject to capitalization but typically may be amortized under Code Sec. 197 over 15 years.

If a package design cost is not deductible under the *INDOPCO* regulations or amortizable under Code Sec. 197, three alternative methods of accounting for package design costs are provided—the capitalization method, the design-by-design capitalization and 60-month amortization method, and the pool-of-cost capitalization and 48-month amortization method (Rev. Proc. 97-35, 1997-2 CB 448, as modified by Rev. Proc. 98-39, 1998-1 CB 1320).

Under the capitalization method, a package design with an ascertainable useful life is amortized using the straight-line method over its useful life, beginning with the month in which the package design is placed in service. If the package design has no ascertainable useful life, no depreciation or amortization deduction is allowed (Reg. § 1.167(a)-3), and package design costs may be deducted only upon the disposition, abandonment, or modification of the package design (Reg. § 1.165-2(a); Rev. Rul. 89-23, 1989-1 CB 85).

Under the design-by-design capitalization method, the basis of each package design is capitalized and amortized using the straight-line method over a 60-month period, beginning with the month the design is treated as placed in service using a half-year convention. This method applies to both an intangible asset with no ascertainable useful life and an intangible asset with an ascertainable useful life substantially exceeding one year. If the package design is disposed of or abandoned within the amortization period, the remaining unamortized basis of the design may be deducted in the tax year of disposition or abandonment.

Under the pool-of-cost capitalization method, all package design costs incurred during a tax year are capitalized and amortized using the straight-line method over a 48-month period, beginning with the month the costs are treated as incurred using a half-year convention. This method applies to all package design costs, regardless of whether they have an ascertainable useful life that extends substantially beyond the end of the tax year in which the costs are incurred. However, no deduction is allowed for the unamortized cost of a design that is (a) never placed in service or (b) disposed of or abandoned within the amortization period.

Capitalized costs under either of these three methods are determined by applying the capitalization rules of Code Sec. 263 in the case of package design costs incurred in tax years beginning after December 31, 1993. The uniform capitalization rules of Code Sec. 263A apply to costs incurred in tax years beginning after December 31, 1986 and before January 1, 1994 (Rev. Proc. 98-39, 1998-1 CB 1320, modifying Rev. Proc. 97-35, 1997-2 CB 448).

These three methods do not apply to package design costs that qualify as Code Sec. 197 intangibles (generally, package designs acquired by purchase) (Rev. Proc. 98-39).

Automatic consent to change to one of these three procedures is provided in Rev. Proc. 2019-43 (Section 11.01). Rev. Proc. 2019-43 does not apply to a taxpayer that wants to change to the capitalization method for costs of developing or modifying any package design cost that has an ascertainable useful life.

The following IRS Coordinated Issue Papers provide useful background on the treatment of package design costs: IRS Coordinated Issue Paper (Package Design Costs, October 31, 1991) reproduced in the CCH IRS POSITIONS REPORTER at ¶ 110,505 (decoordinated effective September 28, 2007, due to modification by Reg. § 1.263(a)-4 on capitalization of intangibles) and ISP Settlement Guidelines for Package Design Costs (September 21, 1992) reproduced in the CCH IRS POSITIONS REPORTER at ¶ 180,355.

*Graphic design costs.* Expenditures relating to the graphic design of cigarette packaging materials (cartons, soft-packs, and crush-proof boxes) and cigarette papers, tips, and other components of the cigarette product were currently deductible business expenses (*RJR Nabisco Inc.*, 76 TCM 71, CCH Dec. 52,786(M); Nonacq. I.R.B. 1999-40). Note that this case involved the 1984 tax year. Rev. Rul. 89-23, which defines package design costs for purposes of Rev. Proc. 97-35, above, appears to treat the types of expenditures considered in *RJR* as package design costs. See, also, FSA 200147035, August 15, 2001, which rejects the *RJR* case.

## ¶ 28

## Customer-Based Intangibles

### *Section 197 treatment*

A customer-based intangible is a section 197 intangible (Code Sec. 197(d)(1)). This category of section 197 intangibles encompasses the composition of market, market share, and any other value resulting from future provision of goods or services under relationships (contractual or otherwise) in the ordinary course of business with customers. It includes the portion of the purchase price of an acquired trade or business that is attributable to an existing customer base, circulation base, undeveloped market or market growth, insurance in force, the existence of a qualification to supply goods or services to a particular customer, mortgage servicing contracts (see ¶ 58), investment management contracts, or other relationships with customers that involve the future provision of goods or services (Code Sec. 197(d)(1) and (2); Reg. § 1.197-2(b)(6)).

For financial institutions, deposit base and similar items are also included in customer-based intangibles. Thus, the amount paid or incurred for customer-based intangibles also includes any portion of the purchase price of an acquired financial institution attributable to the value represented by existing checking accounts, savings accounts, escrow accounts, and other similar items of the financial institution. However, any portion of the purchase price of an acquired trade or business attributable to accounts receivable or other similar rights to income for goods or services provided to customers prior to the acquisition of a trade or business is not an amount paid or incurred for a customer-based intangible (Code Sec. 197(d)(2); Reg. § 1.197-2(b)(6)).

A customer-based intangible is not amortizable under Code Sec. 197 if it is created by the taxpayer unless is it created by the taxpayer in connection with a transaction of series of transactions involving the acquisition of assets constituting a trade or business or a substantial portion thereof (Code Sec. 197(c)(2); Reg. § 1.197-2(d)(2)(iii)(B)). For example, a taxpayer who starts a business or buys a business and creates a customer-based intangible over time cannot amortize the value of the customer-based intangible. See, ¶ 12, "Self-created intangibles." However, a taxpayer who separately purchases a customer-based intangible or acquires a trade or business which includes a customer based intangible may amortize the intangible under section 197. A customer-based intangible that is a residential mortgage servicing right must be acquired in connection with the acquisition of a trade or business or substantial portion thereof. See ¶ 58. Similarly any customer-based intangible relating to a right to receive tangible property or services or an interest under an existing lease of tangible property must be acquired in connection with the acquisition of a trade or business (Code Sec. 197(e)(4)). See ¶ 50 for these and other exceptions to the definition of a section 197 intangible.

*Depreciation if section 197 does not apply*

For those assets in this group that are not amortizable under Code Sec. 197, a depreciation deduction is allowed using the straight-line method over their respective useful lives, provided that they have (1) ascertainable values and (2) limited useful lives that can be ascertained with reasonable accuracy.

*Insurance expirations.* Purchased insurance expirations that were considered a mass (single) asset with an ascertainable value separate from goodwill and a useful life of not more than ten years from the date of purchase were depreciable (*Richard S. Miller & Sons, Inc.*, CtCls, 76-2 USTC ¶ 9481, 537 F2d 446). The principal value of this asset is in the information about the customer and the indication of the most advantageous time to solicit a policy renewal.

The mass-asset rule is often used to prohibit depreciation of certain customer-based intangibles because they constitute self-regenerating assets that may change but never waste. See the discussion of the mass-asset rule at ¶ 22.

*Bank core deposits.* An acquired bank deposit base was depreciable because it had an ascertainable value and a limited useful life that could be measured with reasonable accuracy (*Citizens & Southern Corp.*, 91 TC 463, aff'd CA-11, 91-1 USTC

¶ 50,043, 919 F2d 1492; *Colorado National Bankshares, Inc.*, 60 TCM 771, Dec. 46,875(M), aff'd CA-10, 93-1 USTC ¶ 50,077).

A bank deposit base is a purchased intangible asset which represents the present value of the future stream of income to be derived from employing the purchased core deposits. The value of the deposit base is the ascertainable probability that inertia will cause depositors to leave their funds on deposit for predictable periods. Depreciation was allowed on the portion of the purchase price attributable to the present value of the difference between the ongoing cost of maintaining the core deposits and the cost of the market alternative for funding loans and other investments. The fact that new accounts were opened as old accounts closed did not make the original purchased deposit base self-regenerating.

Because of discounting and the fact that it was shown that bank core deposits decline more quickly in the years immediately following acquisition, accelerated depreciation was allowed for a particular year representing that portion of the present value of the income stream (or cost savings) determined as of the date of acquisition of bank core deposits which was attributable to the current year (*Citizens & Southern Corp.*, supra; *IT&S of Iowa, Inc.*, 97 TC 496, Dec. 47,735).

For a detailed discussion of the tax treatment of bank core deposits under the pre-Code Sec. 197 rules, see IRS Industry Specialization Program (ISP) Coordinated Issue Paper, Core Deposit Intangibles (October 31, 1991) reproduced in full text in the CCH IRS POSITIONS Reporter at ¶ 165,050.

*Newspaper subscription list.* A purchased newspaper subscription list was depreciable where it met the two tests indicated above (*Donrey Inc.*, CA-8, 87-1 USTC ¶ 9143, 809 F2d 534). The value of the list was the present value of the difference in advertising revenues generated by the subscription list compared to the revenues of an equivalent paper without a subscription list.

An acquired intangible asset denominated "paid subscribers" (at-will subscribers, each of whom had requested that the paper be delivered regularly to a specified address in return for payment of the subscription price rather than subscribers that had paid in advance) had substantial value above that of a mere list of customers. The asset met the two tests indicated above and was depreciable using the straight-line method over stipulated useful lives (*Newark Morning Ledger Co.*, SCt, 93-1 USTC ¶ 50,228). The asset constituted a finite set of identifiable subscriptions, each of which had a limited useful life that could be measured with reasonable accuracy and was not self-regenerating. The value of the intangible asset was the present value of the after-tax subscription revenues to be derived from the paid subscribers, less the cost of collection, plus the present value of the tax savings resulting from the depreciation of the asset.

(Although the useful life of the asset was limited, an evidentiary concession apparently saved the deduction from failing the test that the asset's useful life must be measurable with reasonable accuracy. That is, the useful life of the pre-sale goodwill attributable to the subscribers' subscription habits (faithfulness) was not shown to be coextensive with the predicted life of the subscriptions, which was based on the assumption that the total number of subscribers would remain stable.)

For a detailed discussion of the tax treatment of customer subscription lists under the pre-Code Sec. 197 rules, see IRS Industry Specialization Program (ISP) Coordinated Issue Paper, Customer Subscription Lists (October 31, 1991) reproduced in full text in the CCH IRS POSITIONS Reporter at ¶ 135,825.

*Additional ISP papers*

For a detailed discussion of the amortization of market based intangibles under the pre-Code Sec. 197 rules, see IRS Industry Specialization Program (ISP) Coordinated Issue Paper, Amortization of Market Based Intangibles (as revised February 19, 1996) and reproduced in the CCH IRS Positions Reporter at ¶ 80,125.

For a detailed discussion of the amortization of order backlog (unfilled customer orders or contracts at the time of acquisition of a business) under the pre-Code Sec. 197 rules, see IRS Industry Specialization Program (ISP) Coordinated Issue Paper, Amortization of Order Backlog (as revised February 19, 1996) and reproduced in the CCH IRS Positions Reporter at ¶ 80,135.

For a detailed discussion of the amortization of customer-based intangibles under the pre-Code Sec. 197 rules, see IRS Industry Specialization Program (ISP) Coordinated Issue Paper, Customer Based Intangibles (as revised February 19, 1996) and reproduced in the CCH IRS Positions Reporter at ¶ 80,275.

## ¶ 30
## Supplier-Based Intangibles

*Section 197 treatment*

A supplier-based intangible is a section 197 intangible (Code Sec. 197(d)(1)). A supplier-based intangible is defined as the value resulting from the future acquisition of goods or services pursuant to relationships (contractual or otherwise) in the ordinary course of business with suppliers of goods or services to be used or sold by the taxpayer (Code Sec. 197(d)(3)). For example, the portion of the purchase price of an acquired business attributable to the existence of a favorable relationship with persons that provide distribution services such as favorable shelf or display space at a retail outlet, or the existence of favorable supply contracts are section 197 intangibles. The amount paid or incurred for supplier-based intangibles does not include any amount required to be paid for the goods or services themselves pursuant to the terms of the agreement or other relationship (Reg. § 1.197-2(b)(7)).

Additional exceptions to the definition of a section 197 intangible are described in Code Sec. 197(e) and Reg. § 1.197-2(c), including the exception in Reg. § 1.197-2(c)(6) for certain rights to receive tangible property or services from another person (Reg. § 1.197-2(b)(7)). See ¶ 12.

A supplier-based intangible is not amortizable under Code Sec. 197 if it is created by the taxpayer unless is it created by the taxpayer in connection with a transaction of series of transactions involving the acquisition of assets constituting a trade or business or a substantial portion thereof (Code Sec. 197(c)(2); Reg. § 1.197-2(d)(2)(iii)(B)). For example, a taxpayer who starts a business or buys a business and creates a supplier-based intangible over time cannot amortize the value of the supplier-based intangible. However, a taxpayer who separately purchases a supplier-based intangible or acquires a trade or business which includes such an intangible may amortize the intangible under section 197. See, ¶ 12, "Self-created intangibles."

*Favorable credit rating.* A favorable credit rating can constitute a supplier-based intangible. Reg. § 1.197-2(b)(7) was amended, effective for supplier-based intangibles acquired after July 6, 2011 (T.D. 9533; T.D. 9637, filed with the Federal Register on September 6, 2013) to remove a specific reference to favorable credit ratings. Previously, the amended sentence in Reg. § 1.197-2(b)(7) provided: "Thus, the amount paid or incurred for supplier-based intangibles includes, for example, any portion of the purchase price of an acquired trade or business attributable to the existence of a favorable relationship with persons providing distribution services (such as favorable shelf or display space at a retail outlet), *the existence of a favorable crediting rating,* or the existence of favorable supply contracts." The removal of the reference to a favorable credit rating was required by the Dodd-Frank Wall Street Reform and Consumer Protection Act which requires Federal agencies to remove any reference to, or requirement of reliance on, credit ratings in their regulations and to substitute a standard of credit-worthiness that the agency deems appropriate. Although the reference to a favorable credit rating as a supplier based intangible has been removed, the IRS indicated that no substantive change in the treatment of a favorable credit rating as a supplier-based intangible is intended (Preamble to T.D. 9533).

*Depreciation if section 197 does not apply*

If these intangibles are not amortizable under Code Sec. 197, they are depreciable provided that they have an ascertainable value and a limited useful life that can be determined with reasonable accuracy (*Ithaca Industries, Inc.*, 97 TC 253, Dec. 47,536, aff'd on another issue, CA-4, 94-1 USTC ¶ 50,100, cert. denied taxpayer 10/3/94).

## ¶ 32

## License, Permit, or Other Right Granted by the Government

*Section 197 treatment*

Subject to the exceptions described below, section 197 intangibles include licenses, permits, or other rights granted by a governmental unit, agency, or instrumentality (Code Sec. 197(d)(1)(D)). Liquor licenses, taxicab medallions, airport landing or takeoff rights, regulated airline routes, and television or radio broadcasting licenses are included in this category (Reg. § 1.197-2(b)(8)).

Amortization is allowed under section 197 whether such an intangible is separately acquired or acquired as part of a the acquisition of a trade or business or substantial portion thereof. The issuance of such an intangible by the government is considered an acquisition for this purpose (Reg. § 1.197-2(b)(8)). The rule which prohibits self-created intangibles from qualifying as an amortizable section 197 intangible does not apply (Code Sec. 197(c)(2)(A)).

Costs paid or incurred for the renewal of any amortizable section 197 license, permit, or other right granted by a government are amortized over the 15-year period that begins in the month of renewal (Reg. § 1.197-2(f)(3)(iv)(B)(4)).

In an IRS private letter ruling, apparently involving the liability of California public utilities for wildfires, the IRS ruled that a participating utility's payment of an initial contribution to a fund created pursuant to a state law resulted in an amortizable section 197 asset (i.e., a right granted by a governmental entity) and subsequent required annual payments to the fund are amortizable over the remaining 15-year section 197 amortization period. The fund granted the utility the right to reimbursement of eligible losses and a liability cap on a requirement to reimburse the fund if the utility is found to have acted imprudently. The utility was also subject to a new (favorable) standard of review for determining whether it acted prudently by participating in the fund (IRS Letter Ruling 202037001, September 17, 2020).

*Exceptions*

*Right to receive tangible property or services.* A right to receive tangible property or services that is granted by a government is not a section 197 intangible if the right is separately acquired (i.e., not acquired as part of the purchase of a trade or business) (Code Sec. 197(e)(4)(B); Reg. § 1.197-2(b)(8); Reg. § 1.197-2(c)(6)).

*Fixed duration of less than 15 years or recoverable under unit-of-production method.* Licenses, permits, or other rights granted by the government which are related to a trade or business (or the production of income) and which are not acquired in connection with the acquisition of a trade or business are not section 197 intangibles if they have a fixed duration of less than 15 years or are fixed in amount and would be recoverable under a method similar to the unit-of-production method. Taxpayers recover the cost over the fixed term of the license, permit, or right or by using the unit-of-production or similar method (Code Sec. 197(e)(4)(D); Reg.§ 1.197-2(c)(13); Reg.§ 1.167(a)-14(c)(2)). See ¶ 50.

In determining whether the license, permit, or other right granted by the government has a fixed duration of less than 15 years potential renewal periods are taken into account if based on all the facts and circumstances in existence at any time during the taxable year in which the right is acquired, the facts clearly indicate a reasonable expectancy of renewal (Reg. § 1.167(a)-14(c)(3)). For example, the IRS ruled that PCS licenses (personal communication system licenses issued to cell phone companies) issued by the FCC for a ten-year period were under the circumstances likely to be renewed and, therefore, were section 197 intangibles because they had a fixed duration in excess of 15 years (CCA Letter Ruling 200137050, August 8, 2001).

The rule for licenses, permits, or other rights granted by the government that have a fixed duration of less than 15 years or relate to a fixed amount recoverable under the unit-of-production method also applies to rights under a contract (whether or not a governmental contract) that have a fixed duration of less than 15 years or are related to a fixed amount that can be recovered under the unit-of-production or similar method (Code Sec. 197(e)(4)(D)).

This exception from treatment as a section 197 intangible does not apply if the government right or contract right otherwise qualifies for amortization under Code Sec. 197 as goodwill, going concern value, a covenant not to compete, a franchise, trademark, or tradename or is a customer-based intangible, customer-related information base, or any other similar item (Reg. § 1.197-2(c)(13)).

*Interests in land.* Section 197 intangibles do not include any interest in land (Code Sec. 197(e)(2)) (¶ 46). A license, permit, or other right granted by a government that represents an interest in land is not a section 197 intangible (Reg. § 1.197-2(b)(8)). An interest in land includes a fee interest, life estate, remainder, easement, mineral right, timber right, grazing right, riparian right, air right, zoning variance, and any other similar right, such as a farm allotment, quota for farm commodities, or crop acreage base. An interest in land does not include an airport landing or takeoff right, a regulated airline route, or a franchise to provide cable television service. The cost of acquiring a license, permit, or other land improvement right, such as a building construction or use permit, is taken into account in the same manner as the underlying improvement (Reg. § 1.197-2(c)(3)).

*Interest under a lease of tangible property or existing indebtedness.* A government-granted right in an interest under a lease of tangible property or under existing indebtedness is not a section 197 intangible (Code Sec. 197(e)(5); Reg. § 1.197-2(c)(8)). See ¶ 52.

*Depreciation if section 197 does not apply*

For these intangibles that are not amortizable under Code Sec. 197 , the value of a particular intangible is depreciable over the term of the license, permit or right.

However, an amortization deduction was denied for the cost of a liquor license and a taxicab license that represented a renewal privilege extending the existence of each for an indeterminable period because these privileges lacked a limited useful life (*Morris Nachman et al.*, CA-5, 51-2 USTC ¶ 9483; *W.K. Co.*, 56 TC 434, Dec. 30,798, aff'd CA-7 (unpublished order 5/21/73)).

Similarly, the cost of liquor license which is renewable is not amortizable because its life cannot be estimated with reasonable certainty (Rev. Rul. 70-248, 1970-1 CB 172).

For emission allowances see, ¶ 50.

## ¶ 34
## Covenants Not to Compete

*Section 197 treatment*

A covenant not to complete, or agreement having substantially the same effect is a section 197 intangible only if it is entered into in connection with an acquisition of an interest in a trade or business or substantial portion thereof (Code Sec. 197(d)(1)(E)). The exception from section 197 treatment for self-created intangibles does not apply to a covenant not to compete (Code Sec. 197(c)(2)). See ¶ 12. An agreement requiring the performance of services for the acquiring taxpayer or the provision of property or its use to the acquiring taxpayer does not have substantially the same effect as a covenant not to compete to the extent that the amount paid under the agreement represents reasonable compensation for the services actually rendered or for the property or use of the property actually provided (Reg. § 1.197-2(b)(9)).

For this purpose, an interest in the trade or business may be acquired in the form of an asset acquisition (including a qualified stock purchase that is treated as a purchase of assets under section 338), a stock acquisition or redemption, and the acquisition or redemption of a partnership interest (Reg. § 1.197-2(b)(9)).

In an issue of first impression, the Tax Court determined that the taxpayer's redemption of 75 percent of its stock was an acquisition of an interest in a trade or business within the meaning of Code Sec. 197(d)(1)(E). The covenant not to compete, entered into at the same time as the redemption, was, therefore, deemed a Code Sec. 197 intangible subject to amortization over 15 years, rather than the term of the covenant (60 months) (*Frontier Chevrolet Co.,* Dec. 54,336, aff'd by CA-9, 2003-1 USTC ¶ 50,490, 329 F3d 1131.

The Tax Court has provided further clarification of Code Sec. 197(d)(1)(E) by ruling that the acquisition of an interest in a trade or business encompasses the acquisition of any portion of the stock of a trade or business and that the reference in Code Sec. 197(d)(1)(E) to the acquisition of a "substantial portion thereof" refers to the acquisition of a substantial portion of the assets of a trade or business (*Recovery Group, Inc., et al.*, Dec. 58,184(M), TC Memo. 2010-76). The court also discusses what percentage of the assets must be acquired in order to satisfy the substantial standard.

*Capitalization of costs.* In general, all amounts that are required to be paid pursuant to an amortizable section 197 covenant not to compete must be capitalized whether or not some or all of the amount would be deductible under section 162 if the covenant were not a section 197 intangible (Code Sec. 197(f)(3); Reg. § 1.197-2(f)(3)(i); Reg. § 1.197-2(f)(3)(iv)(B)(4)(ii); Reg. § 1.197-2(k), Example 6).

*Deduction for worthlessness.* A special rule defers a loss upon the disposition or worthlessness of an amortizable covenant until the disposition or worthlessness of all trades or businesses acquired in connection with the covenant (Code Sec. 197(f)(1)(B); Reg. § 1.197-2(g)(1)(iii)).

*Related party rules.* Code Sec. 267(a)(2) may operate to defer otherwise allowable amortization deductions (whether or not claimed under Code Sec. 197) with respect to amounts owed to a related party until the related party includes the amount owed in income. For example, if the amount negotiated for a covenant not to complete is not payable to a related cash basis taxpayer until the end of the term of the covenant, no amortization deductions can be claimed prior to the tax year of payment (Temporary Reg. § 1.267(a)-2T(b)).

*Depreciation if section 197 does not apply*

A covenant not to compete that is not amortizable under Code Sec. 197 generally has a specified term and is, therefore, depreciable using the straight-line method.

A covenant not to compete was amortizable over the life of the covenant rather than a shorter period for which the payments were to be made because there was no evidence that the covenant was only enforceable for the shorter period (*Warsaw Photographic Associates, Inc.*, 84 TC 21, Dec. 41,822).

No current-year write-off was permitted for the remaining amounts owed under a covenant not to compete upon the death of the covenantor because no loss was incurred (*ABCO Oil Corp.*, 58 TCM 1280, Dec. 46,343(M), TC Memo. 1990-40).

No portion of the premium that a target corporation paid to two stockholders to repurchase its stock in order to avert a hostile takeover attempt was amortizable. The stock repurchase agreement allocated all of the financial consideration to stock and none to the non-stock items, such as a standstill covenant not to acquire any of the company's stock for a specified period (*Lane Bryant, Inc.*, CA-FC, 94-2 USTC ¶ 50,481).

A covenant not to compete is not amortizable under Code Sec. 197 or the pre-Code Sec. 197 rules unless (1) the covenant is genuine, i.e., it has economic significance apart from the tax consequences, (2) the parties intended to attribute some value to the covenant at the time they executed their formal buy-sell agreement, and (3) the covenant has been properly valued. For a detailed discussion of these requirements, see IRS Industry Specialization Program (ISP) Coordinated Issue Paper, Covenants Not to Compete (as revised September 1, 1998, and reproduced in full text in the CCH IRS POSITIONS Reporter at ¶ 80,245).

Income received pursuant to a covenant not to compete is treated as ordinary income. Such income should not be subject to self-employment tax since that tax applies to income derived from a "trade or business carried on" by a taxpayer. However, if the payment is actually for services rendered to the payor, for example, consulting services, then the self-employment tax applies (unless the services are performed as an employee) (*F.W. Steffens,* CA-11, 83-1 USTC ¶ 9425).

## ¶ 36

## Franchises, Trademarks or Trade Names

*Section 197 treatment*

Franchises, trademarks or trade names are section 197 intangibles (Code Sec. 197(d)(1); Reg. § 1.197-2(b)(10)). See ¶ 56 for sports franchises.

A franchise, trademark, or trade name is a section 197 intangible whether or not it is created by the taxpayer, acquired separately, or acquired in connection with the acquisition of a trade or business or substantial portion therefore (Code Sec. 197(c)(2); Code Sec. 197(e)(4)).

Any license, permit, or other right granted by a governmental unit that otherwise meets the definition of a franchise, such as an FCC broadcast license or cable television franchise, is treated as a franchise (Reg. § 1.197-2(b)(10)). Thus, these licenses are not subject to the rule which excludes rights granted by a governmental unit from the definition of a section 197 intangible unless acquired in a transaction involving the acquisition of assets constituting a trade or business or substantial portion thereof (Code Sec. 197(e)(4)).

A franchise includes any agreement that provides one of the parties to the agreement the right to distribute, sell, or provide goods, services, or facilities within a specified area (Reg. § 1.197-2(b)(10); Code Sec. 1253(b)(1)).

The term trademark includes any word, name, symbol, or device, or any combination thereof, adopted and used to identify goods or services and distinguish them from those provided by others. The term trade name includes any name used to identify or designate a particular trade or business or the name or title used by a person or organization engaged in a trade or business. A trademark or trade name includes any trademark or trade name arising under statute or applicable common law, and any similar right granted by contract (Reg. § 1.197-2(b)(10)).

The renewal of a franchise, trademark, or trade name that is a section 197 intangible is treated as an acquisition of the franchise, trademark, or trade name for those costs incurred in connection with the renewal and are amortized over the 15-year period that begins with the month of renewal (Code Sec. 197(f)(4)(B); Reg. § 1.197-2(b)(10)). Any costs paid or incurred for an earlier renewal, continue to be taken into account over the remaining portion of the amortization period that began at the time of the earlier renewal. Any amount paid or incurred for the protection, expansion, or defense of a trademark or trade name and chargeable to capital account is treated as an amount paid or incurred for a renewal (Reg. § 1.197-2(f)(3)(iv)(B)(4)).

Certain contingent payments (amounts dependent on productivity, use, or disposition) that are paid or incurred during the tax year regarding the transfer of a franchise, trademark, or trade name are deductible by the transferee as a trade or business expense provided that they are incurred in the conduct of a trade or business (Code Sec. 1253(d)(1)(A)). This deduction is restricted to payments that are (a) contingent amounts paid as part of a series of amounts payable at least annually throughout the term of the transfer agreement and (b) substantially equal in amount or to be paid under a fixed formula (Code Sec. 1253(d)(1)(B); Reg. § 1.197-2(b)(10)).

Contingent payments (deductible as a business expense within the above situation) are not charged to the capital account of the intangible, are excluded from the basis of the intangible asset acquired by the transferee, and do not qualify for amortization under Code Sec. 197 (Code Secs. 1253(d)(2) and 197(f)(4)(C)). All other amounts, whether fixed or contingent, that are paid on account of the transfer of a franchise, trademark, or trade name that are section 197 intangibles are chargeable to capital account and are ratably amortized over a 15-year period (Reg. § 1.197-2(g)(6)).

Contingent payments are discussed in more detail below.

*Depreciation if section 197 does not apply*

The rule that specifically prohibited the allowance of depreciation deductions regarding trademark or trade name expenditures was repealed for expenditures paid or incurred after October 2, 1989 (except for certain binding contracts) (former Code Sec. 167(r)) before repeal by the Omnibus Budget Reconciliation Act of 1989 (P.L. 101-239). Thus, expenditures for the acquisition of a new trademark or trade name may be amortizable under the general principles applicable to intangible assets.

Similar rules apply to the purchase of an existing trademark, trade name, or franchise; however, Code Sec. 1253 may allow more favorable treatment for certain transfers.

*Contingent payments.* Regarding the amortization aspects of such provision, the treatment of contingent serial payments made for the transfer, sale, or other disposition of a franchise, trademark, or trade name by a transferee that do not qualify for a business expense deduction (Code Sec. 1253(d)(1)) because they are not payable at least annually for the entire term of the transfer agreement or are not substantially equal in amount depends on when the intangible was acquired.

For franchises, trademarks or trade names generally acquired after August 10, 1993, contingent payments that are not deductible as business expenses are treated as amounts chargeable to a capital account (Code Sec. 1253(d)(2)). Consequently, they are includible in section 197 intangible property and are amortized under the straight-line method over a 15-year period beginning with the month in which the intangible was acquired (Code Sec. 197(a)).

For franchises, trademarks or trade names generally acquired before August 11, 1993, contingent payments that are not deductible as business expenses are also treated as an amount chargeable to a capital account (Code Sec. 1253(d)(3)(A), before amendment by the Omnibus Budget Reconciliation Act of 1993 (P.L. 103-66)). There are two choices for recovering this capital.

(1) An election could be made to amortize this amount under the straight-line method over a 25-year period beginning with the tax year in which the transfer occurred (Code Sec. 1253(d)(3)(B), before amendment by the Omnibus Budget Reconciliation Act of 1993 (P.L. 103-66)).

(2) The amount may be amortized under the general principles applicable to intangible property, provided that the asset has an ascertainable limited life which can be determined with reasonable accuracy and it has an ascertainable value (Reg. § 1.167(a)-3).

*Noncontingent payments.* Amounts not dependent upon productivity, use or disposition are noncontingent payments.

(A) The treatment of an initial fee paid by a transferee where the transferor retains no significant power, right, or continuing interest in the transferred intangible and the transfer is a sale or exchange qualifying for capital gain treatment depends on when the intangible was acquired.

(1) For franchises, trademarks and trade names generally acquired after August 10, 1993, an initial fee paid by a transferee in a sale or exchange of an intangible is an amount chargeable to a capital account (Code Sec. 1253(d)(2)). Consequently, it is includible in section 197 intangible property and is amortized under the straight-line method over a 15-year period beginning with the month in which the intangible was acquired (Code Sec. 197(a)).

(2) For these intangibles generally acquired before August 11, 1993, an initial fee paid by a transferee in a sale or exchange of an intangible is also an amount chargeable to a capital account (Code Sec. 1253(d)(3)(A), before amendment by the Omnibus Budget Reconciliation Act of 1993 (P.L. 103-66)). However, this capital may be recovered by an amortization deduction under

the general principles applicable to intangible property provided that the asset has a limited useful life that can be determined with reasonable accuracy and it has an ascertainable value (Reg. § 1.167(a)-3).

(B) The treatment of an initial fee paid by a transferee where the transferor retains a significant power, right, or continuing interest in the transferred intangible and the transfer is considered a license depends on when the intangible was acquired.

(1) For these intangibles generally acquired after August 10, 1993, an initial fee paid by a transferee in a license of an intangible is an amount chargeable to a capital account (Code Sec. 1253(d)(2)). Consequently, it is includible in section 197 intangible property and is amortized under the straight-line method over a 15-year period beginning with the month in which the intangible was acquired (Code Sec. 197(a)).

(2) For these intangibles generally acquired before August 11, 1993, an initial fee paid by a transferee in a license of an intangible that the transferee treats as an amount chargeable to a capital account is subject to the following deduction rules (Code Sec. 1253(d), before amendment by the Omnibus Budget Reconciliation Act of 1993 (P.L. 103-66)).

The transferee may amortize a single lump-sum noncontingent payment which is made in discharge of an initial fee that does not exceed $100,000 under the straight-line method over the shorter of 10 consecutive tax years or the term of the agreement (Code Sec. 1253(d)(2)(A)(i), before amendment by the Omnibus Budget Reconciliation Act of 1993 (P.L. 103-66)).

For transfers generally after October 2, 1989, and before August 11, 1993, this amortization deduction is not allowed if the single lump-sum payment is in discharge of an initial fee that is larger than $100,000 (Code Sec. 1253(d)(2)(B), before amendment by the Omnibus Budget Reconciliation Act of 1993 (P.L. 103-66)). In this situation, there are two choices for recovering capital:

(1) An election could be made to amortize this amount under the straight-line method over a 25-year period beginning with the tax year in which the transfer occurred (Code Sec. 1253(d)(3)(B), before amendment by the Omnibus Budget Reconciliation Act of 1993 (P.L. 103-66)).

(2) The amount may be amortized under the general principles applicable to intangible property, provided that the asset has a limited useful life that can be determined with reasonable accuracy and an ascertainable value (Reg. § 1.167(a)-3).

## ¶ 42

## Interests in a Corporation, Partnership, Trust, or Estate

The cost of acquiring an interest in a corporation , partnership, trust, or estate is not a Code Sec. 197 intangible whether or not the interest is regularly traded on an established market (Code Sec. 197(e)(1)(A); Reg. § 1.197-2(c)(1)).

Special rules apply to property of a partnership when a Code Sec. 754 election is in effect for the partnership. Any increase in the adjusted basis of a section 197 intangible under Code Sec. 732(b) or Code Sec. 732(d) (relating to a partner's basis in property distributed by a partnership), Code Sec. 734(b) (relating to the optional adjustment to the basis of undistributed partnership property after a distribution of property to a partner), or Code Sec. 743(b) (relating to the optional adjustment to the basis of partnership property after transfer of a partnership interest) is treated as a separate section 197 intangible. (Reg. § 1.197-2(g)(3)).

## ¶ 44

## Interests Under Certain Financial Contracts

An interest under an existing futures contract, foreign currency contract, notional principal contract, interest rate swap, or other similar financial contract is not a Section 197 intangible whether or not the interest is traded on an established securities market (Code Sec. 197(e)(1)(B); Reg. § 1.197-2(c)(2)).

An interest under a mortgage servicing contract, credit card servicing contract, or other contract to service indebtedness that was issued by another person, or any interest under an assumption reinsurance contract are not excluded from the definition of a section 197 intangible by reason of this exception (Reg. § 1.197-2(c)(2)).

See ¶ 58 for discussion of mortgage servicing rights secured by residential property.

Section 197 generally applies to insurance and annuity contracts acquired from another person through an assumption reinsurance transaction. See Code Sec. 197(f)(5) and Reg. § 1.197-2(g)(5) for the treatment of assumption reinsurance contracts.

## ¶ 46

## Interests in Land

An interest in land is not a section 197 intangible (Code Sec. 197(e)(2)). This exclusion includes a fee interest, life estate, remainder, easement, mineral rights, timber rights, grazing rights, riparian rights, air rights, zoning variances, and any other similar rights, such as a farm allotment, quota for farm commodities, or crop acreage base (Code Sec. 197(e)(2); Reg. § 1.197-2(c)(3)).

However, an airport landing or takeoff right, regulated airline route, and a franchise to provide cable television services are not excluded from the definition of section 197 intangible by reason of this exception (Reg. § 1.197-2(c)(3)).

The cost of acquiring a license, permit, or other land improvement right, such as a building construction permit or use permit, is taken into account in the same manner as the underlying improvement (Reg. § 1.197-2(c)(3)).

*Easements.* Right-of-way easements for oil pipelines, electric transmission lines, etc., are depreciable using the straight-line method if a useful life can be established. See also ¶ 5 as to grading and land preparation costs with respect to an easement.

## ¶ 48

## Computer Software

Computer software is considered a section 197 intangible only if acquired in a transaction involving the acquisition of assets constituting a trade or business or substantial portion thereof (Code Sec. 197(d)(1)(C)(iii); Code Sec. 197(e)(3); Reg. § 1.197-2(b)(5)). However, computer software that is readily available for purchase by the general public, is subject to a nonexclusive license, and has not been substantially modified (i.e., off-the-shelf computer software) is not a section 197 intangible even if acquired in connection with the acquisition of a trade or business (Code Sec. 197(e)(3); Reg. § 1.197-2(c)(4)). The definition of off-the-shelf computer software is detailed in Reg. § 1.197-2(c)(4)(i) and is not limited to software that is available through retail outlets. The definition of computer software is provided in Reg. § 1.197-2(c)(4)(ii).

*Three-year depreciation period.* Depreciable computer software generally acquired after August 10, 1993, that is not an amortizable section 197 intangible is depreciated using the straight-line method over a three-year period beginning on the first day of the month that the software is placed in service. Salvage value is considered zero. No amortization is allowed in the month of disposition. In a short tax year the amortization deduction is based on the number of months in the tax year (Code Sec. 167(f); Reg. § 1.167(a)-14; Rev. Proc. 2000-50).

Reg. § 1.263(a)-4(c)(1) requires a taxpayer to capitalize amounts paid to another party to acquire any intangible from that party in a purchase or similar transaction. Computer software is specifically listed as at type of acquired intangible that a taxpayer must capitalize (Reg. § 1.263(a)-4(c)(1)(xiv)).

The three-year amortization period applies to separately acquired computer software if the costs to acquire the software are separately stated and required to be capitalized (Reg. § 1.167(a)-14; Rev. Proc. 2000-50).

Computer software whose cost is included, without being separately stated, in the cost of the hardware or other tangible property is treated as part of the cost of the hardware or other tangible property (Reg. § 1.167(a)-14(b); Rev. Proc. 2000-50) and is not treated as a Code Sec. 197 intangible (Reg. § 1.197-2(g)(7)). For example, software programs loaded onto a computer and included in the price of the computer without being separately stated are depreciated as part of the cost of the computer, i.e., over five years under MACRS.

Acquired software is not currently deductible (unless section 179 applies). The treatment required for acquired (or developed) software by Rev. Proc. 2000-50 was not affected by the promulgation of Reg. § 1.263(a)-4 relating to amounts paid to acquire, create, or enhance intangible assets (CCA Letter Ruling 201549024, October 23, 2015).

*Section 179 allowance.* "Off-the-shelf" or "canned" computer software is eligible for expensing under Code Sec. 179 if placed in service in a tax year beginning after 2002 (Code Sec. 179(d)(1)(A)). See ¶ 302.

*Bonus depreciation.* The additional depreciation allowance (bonus depreciation) applies to computer software which is depreciated under Code Sec. 167(f) over three years using the straight-line method (Code Sec. 168(k)(2)(A)(i)(II)). In general, computer software is depreciable under Code Sec. 167(f) if it is not amortizable under Code Sec. 197 because it is either off-the-shelf computer software as defined in Code Sec. 197(e)(3)(A)(i) and Reg. § 1.197-2(c)(4)(i) or is not acquired as part of the acquisition of a trade or business (Code Sec. 197(e)(3)). Bonus depreciation can apply to acquired software and software developed by or for a taxpayer so long as it is depreciated over 3 years under Code Sec. 167(f) and all other requirements for claiming bonus depreciation are satisfied. See *"19. Computer Software"* at ¶ 127D for additional details.

*Useful life less than one year.* Computer software with a useful life of less than one year is currently deductible as a business expense.

*Computer software defined.* Computer software is defined broadly to include any program designed to cause a computer to perform a desired function. However, a database or similar item is not considered computer software unless it is in the public domain and is incidental to the operation of otherwise qualifying computer software (Code Sec. 197(e)(3)(B)).

Software includes computer programs of all classes (such as operating systems, executive systems, monitors, compilers, translators, assembly routines, utility programs, and application programs).

Refer to Reg. § 1.197-2(c)(4)(iv) and Rev. Proc. 2000-50 for additional details regarding the definition of computer software.

*Developed software.* Depreciable software programs developed by a taxpayer (for its own use or sale) are treated in a manner similar to that of research and development expenses under Code Sec. 174 (Rev. Proc. 2000-50, superseding Rev. Proc. 69-21). The cost may either be (1) deducted as a current expense under Code Sec. 162 or (2) capitalized and amortized using the straight-line method over a period of three years beginning in the month the software is placed in service (i.e., depreciated under Code Sec. 167(f), thereby also making it eligible for bonus depreciation) or over 60 months from the date of completion of development if a Code Sec. 174(b) election is made (Rev. Proc. 2000-50, Section 5; Reg. § 1.167(a)-14(b)(1)).

Research and experimental expenditures paid or incurred in tax years beginning after 2021 generally must be amortized ratably over five years beginning at the midpoint of tax year in which the expenditures are paid or incurred. Any amount paid or incurred in connection with the development of any software is treated as a research or experimental expenditure for purposes of this amortization provision. A 15-year amortization period applies to research or experimental expenditures attributable to foreign research (Code Sec. 174, as amended by the 2017 Tax Cuts Act (P.L. 115-97)).

*Rented software.* Rental payments for leased software programs that are not subject to Code Sec. 197 may be deductible as a business expense over the term of the lease as provided in Reg. § 1.162-11 (Reg. § 1.167(a)-14(b)(2)). Code Sec. 197 applies to certain costs incurred with respect to leased software (that is, costs to acquire a section 197 intangible that is a limited interest in software (T.D. 8865)).

*Licensing transactions.* Software costs are currently deductible if they are not chargeable to capital account under the Code Sec. 197 rules applicable to licensing transactions and are otherwise currently deductible. For this purpose, a payment described in Reg. § 1.162-11 is not currently deductible if, without regard to that regulation, the payment is properly chargeable to capital account (Reg. § 1.197-2(a)(3)). A proper and consistent practice of taking software costs into account under Reg. § 1.162-11 may, however, be continued if the costs are not subject to Code Sec. 197.

*Enterprise software.* An IRS letter ruling addresses in detail the proper tax treatment of various costs, including consulting costs, associated with a corporation's purchase, development, and implementation of Enterprise Resource Planning (ERP) software and related hardware (IRS Letter Ruling 200236028, June 4, 2002). ERP software is a shell that integrates different software modules for financial accounting, inventory control, production, sales and distribution, and human resources. Any taxpayer that has or intends to install ERP software (or any other major software) should carefully review this ruling.

The ruling concludes that:

(1) The cost of purchased ERP software (including sales tax) is amortized ratably over 36 months beginning in the month the software is placed in service;

(2) Employee training and related costs (maintenance, troubleshooting, running reports) are deductible as current expenses under Code Sec. 162 (pre-paid training expenses under a consulting contract are deductible in the year in which incurred under the requirements of Code Sec. 461);

(3) Separately stated computer hardware costs are depreciated as 5-year MACRS property;

(4) If the taxpayer is solely responsible for the creation and performance of the software project covered by its consulting contracts, the costs of writing machine readable code software (and an allocable portion of modeling and design of additional software) under the taxpayer's consulting contracts are treated as developed software and may be currently deducted in a manner similar to research and development expenditures pursuant to Section 5.01(1) of Rev. Proc. 2002-50. See "*Developed software,*" above; and

(5) The costs of option selection and implementation of existing embedded ERP templates (and an allocable portion of the costs of modeling and design of additional software) under the taxpayer's consulting contracts are installation/modification costs that are amortized as part of the purchased ERP software over 36 months beginning in the later of the month the purchased software is placed in service by the taxpayer or the month the template work is available for use by the taxpayer.

(6) Undefined miscellaneous costs under the consulting contracts are also capitalized as part of the underlying purchased ERP software and amortized over 36 months.

With respect to item four, treatment as developed software was predicated upon the fact that the taxpayer bore the risk of failure. Though not specifically stated in the ruling, if the consultant had guaranteed success, these costs would likely have been amortized over 36 months.

The principles and holdings in IRS Letter Ruling 200236028 are not affected by the subsequent promulgation of Reg. § 1.263(a)-4 relating to amounts paid to acquire, create, or enhance intangible assets (CCA Letter Ruling 201549024, October 23, 2015).

CCA Letter Ruling 201549024 indicates that the cost of the purchased ERP software (including the sales tax) are capital expenditures pursuant to Code Sec. 263(a) and Reg. § 1.263(a)-4(c)(1)(xiv). Because the ERP software is not usable to the taxpayer without the option selection and implementation of templates, the costs of option selection and implementation of templates (and its allocable portion of the costs of modeling and design of additional software) are capitalized as part of the purchased ERP software (citing Reg. § 1.263(a)-4(g)(1)). The preamble to the regulations (T.D. 9107) indicates that the treatment of computer software will likely be covered in separate guidance.

*Web site development costs and domain names.* See ¶ 125.

*Y2K expenses.* Costs incurred to convert or replace computer software to recognize dates beginning in the year 2000 (i.e., year 2000 costs) must be treated in accordance with the guidelines contained in Rev. Proc. 2000-50 (Rev. Proc. 97-50, as modified by Rev. Proc. 2000-50).

*Pre-Code Sec. 197 rules.* For depreciable computer software generally purchased before August 11, 1993, if the cost of the software is not separately stated but is included in the price of the computer hardware, the entire amount is treated as the cost of the hardware (tangible property) and is depreciable under MACRS over a five-year recovery period. If the cost of the purchased software (intangible property) is separately stated, the cost is amortized using the straight-line method over a period of five years (unless a shorter useful life is established) (Rev. Proc. 69-21, prior to being superseded by Rev. Proc. 2000-50).

The final regulations under Code Sec. 197 and 167(f) are generally effective for property acquired after January 25, 2000.

*Case law.* Purchased software may also involve the question of whether intangible computer program information is independent from the tangible medium used as a means of delivery. If it is independent, the software is intangible personal property (*Bank of Vermont*, DC Vt., 88-1 USTC ¶ 9169). If the medium is inherently connected to the existence of the computer program information itself, the software is tangible property (*Texas Instruments, Inc.*, CA-5, 77-1 USTC ¶ 9384, 551 F2d 576). Purchased computer program master source codes were inextricably connected with the medium (tapes and discs) because the investment could not be placed in a productive usable form without the tangible medium. The feasibility of receiving the data without the tapes and discs (via computer-to-computer telephone link and transfer of the data to tapes and discs by the taxpayer) was irrelevant (*Comshare Inc.*, CA-6, 94-2 USTC ¶ 50,318).

*Change in accounting method.* The IRS will grant automatic consent to change to a method of accounting for software costs that is described in Rev. Proc. 2000-50, as modified by Rev. Proc. 2007-16 (see Rev. Proc. 2019-43, Section 9).

## ¶ 50

## Separately Acquired Interests

The following interests and rights are not a section 197 intangible if they are not acquired in a transaction involving the acquisition of the assets of a trade or business or a substantial portion thereof (Code Sec. 197(e)(4)):

(1) an interest (such as a licensee) in a film, sound recording, video tape, book or similar property (including the right to broadcast or transmit a live event) (Reg. § 1.197-2(c)(5));

(2) a right to receive tangible property or services under a contract or granted by a governmental entity (Reg. § 1.197-2(c)(6));

(3) an interest in a patent or copyright (Reg. § 1.197-2(c)(7)); and

(4) a right received under a contract (or a license, permit, or other right granted by a governmental entity) if the right has a fixed duration of less than 15 years *or* is fixed in amount and would be recoverable under a method similar to the unit-of-production method (Reg. § 1.197-2(c)(15)).

Under a separate provision, a covenant not to compete is a section 197 intangible only if it is *entered into* in connection with an acquisition of an interest in a trade or business or substantial portion thereof (Code Sec. 197(d)(1); Reg. § 1.197-2(b)(9)). See ¶ 34. Similarly, computer software must be acquired in a transaction involving the acquisition of a trade or business or a substantial portion therefore in order to be considered a section 197 intangible (Code Sec. 197(e)(3); Reg. § 1.197-2(c)(4)(iii)). See ¶ 48.

The item (4) exclusion for contractual or governmental rights of a fixed duration of less than 15 years or rights that are fixed in amount does not apply to a right if the right relates to goodwill, going concern value, a covenant not to compete, a franchise, trademark, or tradename, a customer-based intangible, a customer-related information base, or any other similar item (Reg. § 1.197-2(c)(13)).

With respect to item (4), the basis of a right to an unspecified amount over a fixed duration of less than 15 years is amortized ratably over the period of the right. The basis of a right to a fixed amount is amortized for each tax year by multiplying the basis by a fraction. The numerator is the amount received during the tax year and the denominator is the total amount received or to be received (Reg. § 1.197-2(c)(2)).

The manner of recovering the cost of a right to receive tangible property or services described in item (2) is similar to the item (4) methodology (Reg. § 1.167(a)-14(c)(1)).

Only those costs incurred by a manufacturer in connection with acquisition of a manufacturing certificate (permit) issued by a government agency for a specific products which were required to be capitalized under Code Sec. 263(a) were amortizable under Code Sec. 197. Depending upon the development of additional facts and analysis, certain identified costs may be treated as pre-production costs of the product under Code Sec. 263A or, alternatively, allowable as a credit or deduction under Code Secs 41 and 174 (Field Service Advice Memorandum 200137023, June 13, 2001).

*Emission allowances.* The tax treatment of a sulfur dioxide emission allowance issued by the Environmental Protection Agency is detailed in Rev. Proc. 92-91, 1992-2 CB 503. The Committee Report for the Revenue Reconciliation Act of 1993 (P.L. 103-66) indicates that Code Sec. 197 is not intended "to disturb the result in Rev. Proc. 92-91." See footnote 144 of the report. As a result, it appears that such emission allowances do not need to be amortized under Code Sec. 197.

In general, Rev. Proc. 92-91 provides that emission allowances are not depreciable under any method, including the unit-of-production method, and that the cost of an allowance is recovered as sulfur dioxide is emitted. However, capitalization may be required in some instances and the cost of make-up allowances purchased at the end of the year are deducted under the taxpayer's method of accounting pursuant to Code Sec. 461.

## ¶ 52

## Interests Under Existing Leases of Tangible Property

The acquisition of an interest as a lessor or a lessee under an existing lease or sublease of tangible real or personal property is excluded from the definition of a section 197 intangible (Code Sec. 197(e)(5)(A); Reg. § 1.197-2(c)(8)). See also ¶ 5.

## ¶ 54

## Interests Under Existing Indebtedness

Creditor or debtor interests in an indebtedness that is in existence on the date the interest is acquired, except for a deposit base and other similar items of a financial institution specified in Code Sec. 197(d)(2)(B), are not section 197 intangibles (Code Sec. 197(e)(5)(B); Reg. § 1.197-2(c)(9)). Thus, the value of assuming an existing indebtedness with a below-market interest rate or the premium paid for acquiring a debt interest with an above-market interest rate is not amortizable under Code Sec. 197. Code Sec. 171 provides rules for amortizing bond premium.

Deposit base and similar items of a financial institution are considered customer-based section 197 intangibles (Code Sec. 197(d)(2)(B)). See ¶ 28.

Additionally, mortgage servicing rights, to the extent that they are stripped coupons within the meaning of Code Sec. 1286, are considered an interest under an existing indebtedness and, therefore, are not section 197 intangibles (Reg. § 1.197-2(c)(9)). See also ¶ 58.

## ¶ 56

## Sports Franchises

A franchise to engage in professional football, basketball, baseball, or any other professional sport, as well as any item acquired in connection with such a franchise, is not a section 197 intangible if it is acquired on or before October 22, 2004 (Code Sec. 197(e)(6), prior to being stricken by the American Jobs Creation Act of 2004 (P.L. 108-357); Reg. § 1.197-2(c)(10)).

The IRS has issued a comprehensive MSSP audit guide covering most tax issues involved in purchasing and operating a sports franchise (Market Segment Specialization Program (MSSP) Audit Technique Guide—Sports Franchises (8-99)). Among depreciation-related issued covered are depreciation of a sports stadium (including leasehold improvements) and amortization of player contracts and broadcasting rights.

## ¶ 58

## Residential Mortgage Servicing Rights

The right to service indebtedness that is secured by residential property is not a section 197 intangible unless it is acquired in a transaction or series of related transactions involving the acquisition of the assets (other than the mortgage servicing rights) of a trade or business or of a substantial portion of a trade or business (Code Sec. 197(e)(6); Reg. § 1.197-2(c)(11)).

Depreciable residential mortgage servicing rights generally acquired after August 10, 1993, that are not section 197 intangibles may be depreciated under the straight-line method over a nine-year period under Code Sec. 167(f) (Reg. § 1.167(a)-14(d)). Such rights generally acquired before August 11, 1993, were depreciated over their useful lives (Reg. § 1.167(a)-3). See also ¶ 10.

Mortgage servicing rights, to the extent that they are stripped coupons within the meaning of Code Sec. 1286, are considered an interest under an existing indebtedness (¶ 54) and, therefore, are not section 197 intangibles.

A mortgage servicing right that is treated as a stripped coupon under Code Sec. 1286 is not depreciable (Rev. Rul. 91-46, 1991-2 CB 358).

## ¶ 60

## Corporate Transaction Costs

Fees paid for professional services and other transactions incurred in a corporate organization or reorganization (Code Secs. 351-368) in which gain or loss is not recognized are not section 197 intangibles (Code Sec. 197(e)(7); Reg. § 1.197-2(c)(11)).

*Corporate charters.* Corporate charters generally are for indefinite periods and therefore are not depreciable. However, an election may be made to deduct the first $5,000 of organizational expenses (subject to a phase-out rule) and amortizing the remainder using the straight-line method over a 15-year period beginning with the month in which the corporation begins business (Code Sec. 248).

## ¶ 64

## Certain Nonrecognition Transfers

In certain exchanges of section 197 intangibles, a transferee is treated as the transferor with respect to the portion of adjusted basis which does not exceed the adjusted basis of the transferor. This step-into-the-shoes rule applies to a section 197 intangible acquired (Code Sec. 197(f)(2); Reg. § 1.197-2(g)(1)(C)):

(1) in any transaction between members of the same affiliated group during a tax year for which a consolidated return is filed, or

(2) in nonrecognition transactions under Code Secs. 332, 351, 361, 721, 731, 1031, or 1033

***Example:*** An individual amortized a section 197 intangible for five years, and the remaining unamortized basis of the asset is $300,000. In a like-kind exchange, the intangible and $100,000 are exchanged for another section 197 intangible. The adjusted basis of the acquired intangible is $400,000. Of such amount, $300,000 attributable to the basis of the old property is amortized over the remaining 10-year period attributable to the old property and $100,000 is amortized over a 15-year period.

Code Sec. 1031 will generally only apply to exchanges of section 1250 property after 2017 (Code Sec. 1031(a), as amended by P.L. 115-97).

## ¶ 66

## 15-Year Safe-Harbor for Self-Created Intangibles

Reg. § 1.167(a)-3(b) provides a safe harbor that allows a taxpayer to amortize certain created intangibles that do not have readily ascertainable useful lives over a 15-year period using the straight-line method and no salvage value. For example, amounts paid to acquire memberships or privileges of indefinite duration, such as a trade association membership, are covered by this safe harbor. The provision applies to intangibles created on or after December 31, 2003 (Reg. § 1.167(a)-3(b), as added by T.D. 9107). Change of accounting method procedures are described below.

Eligible intangibles are those not specifically excluded from the scope of the provision. The following intangibles, described in more detail below, are not eligible:

(1) Any intangible acquired from another person;

(2) Created financial interests;

(3) Any intangible that has a useful life that can be estimated with reasonable accuracy;

(4) Any intangible that has an amortization period or useful life that is specifically prescribed by the Code, regulations, or other published IRS guidance; or

(5) Any intangible for which an amortization period or useful life is specifically proscribed by the Code, regulations, or other published IRS guidance.

The safe-harbor also does not apply to any amount that is required to be capitalized by Reg. § 1.263(a)-5. In general, these are amounts paid to facilitate an acquisition of a trade or business, a change in the capital structure of a business entity, and certain other transactions.

*Intangibles acquired from another person.* The safe-harbor provision does not apply to intangibles described in Reg. § 1.263(a)-4(c) (Reg. § 1.167(a)-3(b)(1)(i)). This regulation requires the capitalization of amounts paid to another party to acquire any intangible from that party in a purchase or similar transaction. The regulation lists numerous examples (i.e., a nonexclusive list) of intangibles within the scope of the provision. The following intangibles are specifically listed:

(1) An ownership interest in a corporation, partnership, trust, estate, limited liability company, or other entity;

(2) A debt instrument, deposit, stripped bond, stripped coupon, regular interest in a REMIC or FASIT, or any other intangible treated as debt for federal income tax purposes;

(3) A financial instrument, such as a notional principal contract, foreign currency contract, futures contract, a forward contract, an option, and any other financial derivative;

(4) An endowment contract, annuity contract, or insurance contract;

(5) A lease;

(6) A patent or copyright;

(7) A franchise, trademark or tradename;

(8) An assembled workforce;

(9) Goodwill or going concern value;

(10) A customer list;

(11) A servicing right;

(12) A customer-based intangible or supplier-based intangible;

(13) Computer software; and

(14) An agreement providing either party the right to use, possess or sell the first five types of intangibles described above (certain ownership interests through nonfunctional currency).

Note that many of these intangibles may be amortized over 15 years under Code Sec. 197.

*Created financial interests.* The 15-year safe harbor amortization provision does not apply to a created financial interest described in Reg. § 1.263(a)-4(d)(2) (Reg. § 1.167(a)-3(b)(1)(ii)). The specified financial interests are:

(1) An ownership interest in a corporation, partnership, trust, estate, limited liability company, or other entity;

(2) A debt instrument, deposit, stripped bond, stripped coupon (including a servicing right treated for federal income tax purposes as a stripped coupon), regular interest in a REMIC or FASIT, or any other intangible treated as debt for federal income tax purposes;

(3) A financial instrument, such as a letter of credit, credit card agreement, notional principal contract, foreign currency contract, futures contract, forward contract, an option, and any other financial derivative;

(4) An endowment contract, annuity contract, or insurance contract that has or may have cash value;

(5) Non-functional currency; and

(6) An agreement that provides either party the right to use, possess or sell a financial interest described in items (1)-(5), above.

*Intangibles with reasonably certain useful life.* The safe harbor does not apply to created intangibles that have readily ascertainable useful lives on which amortization can be based. Taxpayers may amortize intangible assets with reasonably estimable useful lives in accordance with Reg. § 1.167(a)-3(a). For example, prepaid expenses, contracts with a fixed duration, and certain contract terminations have readily ascertainable useful lives. Prepaid expenses are amortized over the period covered by the prepayment. Amounts paid to induce another to enter into a contract with a fixed duration are amortized over the duration of the contract. Amounts paid by a lessor to terminate a lease contract are amortized over the remaining term of the lease (*Peerless Weighing and Vending Machine Corp.*, 52 T.C. 850, Dec. 29,713).

*Intangibles with assigned useful life.* The safe-harbor provision does not apply to any intangible that has an amortization period or useful life that is specifically prescribed by the Code, regulations, or other published IRS guidance. For example, an expense may not be amortized under this provision if it is amortizable under Code Sec. 167(f)(1)(A) (prescribing a 36-month life for certain computer software); Code Sec. 171 (prescribing rules for determining the amortization period for bond premium); Code Sec. 178 (prescribing the amortization period for costs to acquire a lease); Reg. § 1.167(a)-14(d)(1) (prescribing a 108-month useful life for mortgage servicing rights); Code Sec. 197 (prescribing a 15 year amortization period for amortizable section 197 intangibles); Code Sec. 195 (prescribing a 180 month amortization period for capitalized start-up expenses); Code Sec. 248 (prescribing a 180 month amortization period for capitalized organizational expenditures); or Code Sec. 709 (prescribing a 180 month amortization period for capitalized partnership organization and syndication fees).

*Amounts paid to facilitate an acquisition of a trade or business, a change in the capital structure of a business entity, and certain other transactions.* The 15-year safe harbor amortization provision does not apply to an amount that must be capitalized under Reg. § 1.263(a)-5 (Reg. § 1.167(a)-3(b)(2)). In general, Reg. § 1.263(a)-5 requires a taxpayer to capitalize an amount paid to facilitate each of the following transactions:

(1) An acquisition of assets that constitute a trade or business (whether the taxpayer is the acquirer in the acquisition or the target of the acquisition);

(2) An acquisition by the taxpayer of an ownership interest in a business entity if, immediately after the acquisition, the taxpayer and the business entity are related within the meaning of Code Sec. 267(b) or Code Sec. 707(b);

(3) An acquisition of an ownership interest in the taxpayer (other than an acquisition by the taxpayer of an ownership interest in the taxpayer, whether by redemption or otherwise);

(4) A restructuring, recapitalization, or reorganization of the capital structure of a business entity;

(5) A transfer described in Code Sec. 351 and Code Sec. 721 (whether the taxpayer is the transferor or transferee);

(6) A formation or organization of a disregarded entity;

(7) An acquisition of capital;

(8) A stock issuance;

(9) A borrowing. A borrowing means any issuance of debt, including an issuance of debt in an acquisition of capital or recapitalization and a debt issued in a debt for debt exchange under Reg. § 1.1001-3; and

(10) Writing an option.

*25-year amortization period for certain intangibles related to benefits arising from the provision, production, or improvement of real property.* A taxpayer must increase the 15-year safe-harbor amortization period to 25 years if the intangible asset is described in Reg. § 1.263(a)-4(d)(8) (Reg. § 1.167(a)-3(b)(1)(iv)).

Under Reg. § 1.263(a)-4(d)(8), a taxpayer must capitalize amounts paid for real property if the taxpayer transfers ownership of the real property to another person (except to the extent the real property is sold for fair market value) and if the real property can reasonably be expected to produce significant economic benefits to the taxpayer after the transfer.

The regulation also requires a taxpayer to capitalize amounts paid to produce or improve real property owned by another (except to the extent the taxpayer is selling services at fair market value to produce or improve the real property) if the real property can reasonably be expected to produce significant economic benefits for the taxpayer.

For purposes of this regulation, real property includes property indefinitely affixed to real property such as roads, bridges, tunnels, pavements, wharves and docks, breakwaters and sea walls, elevators, power generation and transmission facilities, and pollution control facilities.

> ***Example (1):*** A shipping company contributes a breakwater to a port authority to enable the authority to build a larger breakwater that will benefit the company by enabling it to unload its ships in bad weather. The adjusted basis of the breakwater at the time of contribution may be amortized over 25 years (Reg. § 1.263(a)-4(d)(8), Example 1).

> ***Example (2):*** A contribution of $100,000 to a city to structurally improve an existing bridge to enable the taxpayer's trucks to use the bridge is capitalized. The capitalized amount can be amortized over 25 years (Reg. § 1.263(a)-4(d)(8), Example 2).

Impact fees and dedicated improvements contributed by developers are not amortizable under this safe-harbor provision (Reg. § 1.263(a)-4(d)(8)(iv), and (v), Example 3). See ¶ 125 for treatment of impact fees.

*How to compute the safe harbor amortization deduction.* Amortization under this provision is determined by amortizing the basis of the intangible asset ratably over the 15 (or 25) year assigned useful life beginning on the first day of the month in which the intangible asset is placed in service by the taxpayer. No amortization deduction may be claimed in the month of disposition (Reg. § 1.167(a)-3(b)(3)).

*Changes in accounting method.* In conjunction with the issuance of T.D. 9107, the IRS has issued three revenue procedures that taxpayers must use to obtain automatic consent to change to a method of accounting provided for in Reg. § 1.167(a)-3(b).

The first revenue procedure applies to a taxpayer that makes the change in its first tax year ending on or after December 31, 2003 (Rev. Proc. 2004-23, 2004-1 CB 785, as modified by Rev. Proc. 2004-57, 2004-2 CB 498). The next revenue procedure applies to a taxpayer's second tax year ending on or after December 31, 2003 (Rev. Proc. 2005-9, 2005-1 CB 303, as modified by Rev. Proc. 2005-17, 2005-1 CB 797).

The third procedure applies to tax years ending on or after December 31, 2005 and for any earlier tax year that is after the taxpayer's second tax year ending on or after December 31, 2003 (Rev. Proc. 2006-12 , 2006-1 CB 310, superseding Rev. Proc. 2004-23, 2004-1 CB 785, and Rev. Proc. 2005-9, 2005-1 CB 303). This third procedure was modified to allow a taxpayer to utilize the advance consent procedures when seeking a change to a method of accounting provided in the final regulations in conjunction with a change for the same item to a method of accounting utilizing the 3 1/2 month rule authorized by Reg. § 1.461-4(d)(6)(ii) or the recurring item exception authorized by Reg. § 1.461-5 (Rev. Proc. 2006-37, 2006-2 CB 499, modifying Rev. Proc. 2006-12). For related automatic change in accounting method procedures, see Section 11.05 of Rev. Proc. 2019-43.

The IRS announced in the preamble to the related proposed regulations (REG-125638-01, 2003-1 C.B. 373) that it would not grant a request to change to a method of accounting provided for in T.D. 9107 for a tax year earlier than the effective date provided by the final regulations. These procedure contains special guidance for a taxpayer that made an unauthorized change in method of accounting.

## ¶ 67

## 15-year Safe-Harbor Amortization of Film Industry Creative Property Costs

The IRS has issued a safe-harbor method of accounting that allows taxpayers in the film industry to amortize creative property costs ratably over a 15-year period. The safe-harbor is effective for tax years ending *on or after* December 31, 2003 (Rev. Proc. 2004-36; Rev. Proc. 2019-43, Section 15.06).

The safe-harbor allows a taxpayer to amortize the cost of purchasing creative property, such as a film script or production rights to a book or play, in the tax year that the cost of the creative property is written off for financial accounting purpose in accordance with Statement of Position 00-2, as issued by the American Institute of Certified Public Accountants (AICPA) on June 12, 2000. Under these guidelines, a write-off is allowed if the property is not scheduled for production within three years of acquisition. (Only a small percentage of creative property is set for production within three years). If a taxpayer decides not to set the property for production at an earlier time, the write-off is allowed then.

Prior to issuance of this safe harbor, taxpayers were required (for tax purposes) to capitalize creative property costs and could not recover these costs through depreciation (e.g., under the income-forecast method) or amortization unless a film or similar property was actually produced.

In related guidance, the IRS ruled that a Code Sec. 165(a) loss for the capitalized costs of acquiring or developing a creative property may not be claimed unless the producer establishes an intention to abandon the property and an affirmative act of abandonment occurs, or there is an identifiable event that evidences a closed or completed transaction that establishes worthlessness (Rev. Rul. 2004-58, 2004-1 CB 1043). Since creative properties not set for production are generally retained indefinitely, Code Sec. 165(a) deductions are generally not available. Consequently, the safe-harbor method is of particular benefit to the film industry and should also encourage the acquisition of creative property from script writers, novelists, and playwrights.

*Creative property costs defined.* For purposes of the 15-year amortization safe harbor, creative property costs are costs to *acquire and develop* (for purposes of potential future film development, production, and exploitation):

(1) screenplays;

(2) scripts;

(3) story outlines;

(4) motion picture production rights to books and plays; and

(5) similar properties.

Costs that are written off under SOP 00-2 must be amortized under the safe-harbor ratably over 15 years beginning on the first day of the second half of the tax year in which the write-off occurs. All creative property costs that are written off in the same tax year for financial accounting purposes are aggregated and treated as a single asset for amortization purposes.

Once amortization with respect to a creative property cost begins, the taxpayer must continue amortizing the cost even if (1) the creative property is later set for production or (2) the creative property is disposed of in a sale, exchange, abandonment, or other disposition.

Upon a disposition, the basis of the creative property is considered zero. Thus, no loss is recognized upon the disposition and any gain is ordinary income.

However, if a taxpayer disposes of all of its creative property (e.g., through the sale of the taxpayer's entire trade or business), any gain attributable to the disposition of creative property costs that were amortized under the safe-harbor is ordinary income to the extent of the amortization allowed.

*Additional costs paid or incurred after amortization begins.* Additional costs may be paid or incurred with respect to a creative property in a tax year after amortization has begun with respect to the initial costs for that property. These additional costs are amortized over a 15-year period beginning on the first day of the second half of the tax year in which they are paid or incurred.

A taxpayer may set a creative property for production in a tax year after amortization of creative costs has begun (e.g., the taxpayer sets the property in production more than three years from the time of the first capitalization transaction). Creative costs paid or incurred after the property has been set for production must be capitalized and depreciated using an allowable depreciation method at the time the property is placed in service by the taxpayer. Costs for which amortization has begun are continued to be amortized over the remainder of the 15-year amortization period.

*Procedures for changing to safe-harbor method.* Taxpayers that wish to change to this safe-harbor method for amortizing qualifying creative property costs should follow the automatic consent procedures of Rev. Proc. 2019-43, Section 15.06.

*Audit protection.* Certain taxpayers may currently be using a method consistent with the safe-harbor method for a tax year that ends before December 31, 2003. The IRS will not challenge the use of such a consistent method in an audit. Similarly, if the issue is currently under examination, before an appeals office, or before the U.S. Tax Court for a tax year that ends before December 31, 2003, the issue will not be pursued by the IRS.

*Losses for abandonment or worthlessness of creative property.* In conjunction with issuance of the 15-year amortization safe-harbor, the IRS has issued a revenue ruling which holds that a taxpayer may not deduct the costs of acquiring and developing creative property as a loss under Code Sec. 165(a) unless the taxpayer (1) establishes an intention to abandon the property and there is an affirmative act of abandonment, or (2) there is an identifiable event or events that evidence a closed and completed transaction establishing worthlessness (Rev. Rul. 2004-58, 2004-1CB 1043).

The ruling effectively prevents a taxpayer from claiming a Code Sec. 165(a) loss deduction for most creative property costs because taxpayers typically retain rights to a creative property indefinitely even if a decision not to proceed to production has been made. The fact that a taxpayer writes off creative property costs under SOP 00-2 does not establish an abandonment loss or a loss for worthlessness.

The ruling described three fact situations:

In the first situation, a taxpayer purchases the exclusive rights to a script for the remainder of its copyright term. The taxpayer makes a decision not to set the script to production and writes the cost off for financial accounting purposes. The taxpayer, however, retains all rights to the script indefinitely. No Code Sec. 165(a) deduction may be claimed.

In the second situation, a taxpayer purchases limited exploitation rights to a screenplay. All rights in the screenplay expire after four years if it is not set into production. The screenplay is not set to production within four years. At the end of the third year the taxpayer may write the costs off for financial accounting purposes. However, a Code Sec. 165(a) deduction may not be claimed until the fourth year when all the rights tot he screenplay have expired.

In the third situation, a taxpayer purchases exclusive motion picture rights from the author of a novel. The fact that no other studio will purchase the rights from the taxpayer does not establish the worthlessness of those rights. So long as the taxpayer retains the rights, no Code Sec. 165(a) deduction may be claimed.

## ¶ 68

## Research and Experimental Expenditures

Research and experimental expenditures paid or incurred in connection with a trade or business may be treated as not chargeable to a capital account and currently deducted as a research expense instead of depreciated (Code Sec. 174(a)(1); Reg. § 1.174-3(a)). Depreciation deductions on property used in connection with research or experimentation are research expenditures (Code Sec. 174(c); Reg. § 1.174-2(b)(1)).

An election may be made to defer and amortize research and experimental expenditures chargeable to a capital account regarding property that has no determinable useful life and, therefore, is not depreciable (Code Sec. 174(b); Reg. § 1.174-4(a)(2)). These deferred expenses are amortized using the straight-line method over five years, beginning with the month in which benefits are first realized. If during the amortization period the deferred expenses result in the development of depreciable property, the unrecovered expenditures must be depreciated beginning with the time the asset becomes depreciable in character (Reg. § 1.174-4(a)(4)).

Expenditures that are neither treated as a currently deductible research expense nor deferred and amortized under Code Sec. 174(b) must be charged to a capital account (Reg. § 1.174-1). Depreciation of such assets would depend on whether there is a determinable useful life.

Research and experimental expenditures paid or incurred in tax years beginning after 2021 generally must be amortized ratably over five years beginning at the midpoint of tax year in which the expenditures are paid or incurred. Any amount paid or incurred in connection with the development of any software is treated as a research or experimental expenditure for purposes of this amortization provision. A 15-year amortization period applies to research or experimental expenditures attributable to foreign research (Code Sec. 174), as amended by the 2017 Tax Cuts Act (P.L. 115-97).

## ¶ 70

## Cost or Other Basis for Depreciation

For property depreciable under the Modified Accelerated Cost Recovery System, depreciation is computed using the table percentages on the unadjusted depreciable basis of the property (Reg. § 1.168(b)-1(a)(3); Reg. § 1.167(g)-1). See ¶ 180 for examples of table percentage computations. Unadjusted depreciable basis is the basis of property for purposes of Code Sec. 1011 (i.e., the basis of the property for purposes of determining gain or loss) without regard to any adjustments described in Code Sec. 1016(a)(2) and (3) (i.e., adjustments for depreciation, amortization, and depletion previously claimed). This basis reflects the reduction in basis for the percentage of the taxpayer's use of property for the taxable year other than in the taxpayer's trade or business (or for the production of income), for any portion of the basis the taxpayer properly elects to treat as an expense under Code Sec. 179, Code Sec. 179C (relating to the election to expense certain refineries), or any similar provision, and for any adjustments to basis provided by other provisions of the Code and the regulations under the Code (other than Code Sec. 1016(a)(2) and (3)) (for example, a reduction in basis by the amount of the disabled access credit pursuant to Code Sec. 44(d)(7)). See below.

Adjusted depreciable basis is the unadjusted depreciable basis of the property less the adjustments described in Code Sec. 1016(a)(2) and (3) for depreciation, amortization, and depletion. If the MACRS percentage tables are not used, depreciation is computed on the adjusted depreciable basis as of the close of the tax year. Under the *allowed or allowable rule*, the adjustment for depreciation is generally the greater of the amount of depreciation that was claimed or that should have been claimed. See ¶ 75. See ¶ 179 for examples of non-table MACRS depreciation computations.

The starting point for determining the unadjusted basis of an asset is typically the cost (e.g. invoice price). Special rules described below apply if the asset was not acquired by purchase (e.g., the asset was acquired in an exchange, by inheritance, as a gift, or converted from personal to business use). Where depreciable and nondepreciable property is purchased (e.g., a building and land) or multiple assets are purchased, cost, including transaction costs, need to be allocated. See *"Allocation of purchase price when business or multiple assets purchased,"* below.

Cost may be increased by amounts such as sales tax (if not separately deducted as an itemized deduction), freight charges, installation costs, and testing costs. In the case of real property, cost may be increased by settlement costs such as legal and recording fees, abstract fees, survey charges, owner's title insurance, and amounts owed by the seller but paid for by the buyer, such as back taxes or interest, recording or mortgage fees, charges for improvements or repairs, and sales commissions. It may be necessary to allocate these items between land (not depreciable) and a building located on the land (depreciable). See *"Allocation of purchase price,"* below.

*Transaction costs.* In addition to the invoice price, transaction costs described in Reg. § 1.263(a)-2(f) and costs for work performed prior to the date that the unit of property is placed in service by the taxpayer, such as installation costs, are included in basis (Reg. § 1.263(a)-2(d)(1); Reg. § 1.263(a)-2(d)(2), Example 11).

Transaction costs include (but are not limited to) cost of: (A) transporting the property (for example, shipping fees and moving costs); (B) securing an appraisal or determining the value or price of property; (C) negotiating the terms or structure of the acquisition and obtaining tax advice on the acquisition; (D) application fees, bidding costs, or similar expenses; (E) preparing and reviewing the documents that effectuate the acquisition of the property (for example, preparing the bid, offer, sales contract, or purchase agreement); (F) examining and evaluating the title of property; (G) obtaining regulatory approval of the acquisition or securing permits related to the acquisition, including application fees; (H) conveying property between the parties, including sales and transfer taxes, and title registration costs; (I) finders' fees or brokers' commissions, including amounts paid that are contingent on the successful closing of the acquisition; (J) architectural, geological, engineering, environmental, or inspection services pertaining to particular properties; or (K) services provided by a qualified intermediary or other facilitator of an exchange under Code Sec. 1031.

*Installation and removal costs.* The final repair regulations provide that the cost of removing a depreciable asset or a component of a depreciable asset does not need to be capitalized under Code Sec. 263(a) if the taxpayer realizes gain or loss on the removed asset or component, for example, by making a partial disposition election under Reg. § 1.168(i)-8(d) (¶ 162). The final regulations also provide that if a taxpayer disposes of a component of a unit of property and the disposal is not a disposition (e.g., because no partial disposition election was made to recognize a loss on the disposed of component), then the taxpayer must deduct or capitalize the costs of removing the component based on whether the removal costs directly benefit or are incurred by reason of a repair to the unit of property or an improvement to the unit of property (Reg. § 1.263(a)-3(g)(2)). See, for example, *Towanda Coke Corp*, 95 T.C. 124 CCH Dec. 46,793 (holding that costs of removing piping damaged in a fire and installing new pipe were capital expenditures); *Phillips Easton Supply Co.*, 20 T.C. 455, CCH Dec. 19,691 (holding that costs of removing a cement floor in a building and replacing it with a concrete floor were capital expenditures to improve the property); Rev. Rul. 2000-7 (2000-1 CB 712) (providing that the costs of removing a component of a depreciable asset are either capitalized or deducted based on whether the replacement of the component constitutes an improvement or a repair). As with other costs incurred during an improvement, a taxpayer may deduct the costs of removing a component if the taxpayer can demonstrate that such costs relate only to the disposition of the removed property and that the costs do not have the requisite relationship to any improvement (Preamble to T.D. 9564).

Amounts paid to move and reinstall a unit of property that has already been placed in service by the taxpayer are not required to be capitalized unless the costs of moving and reinstalling a unit of property directly benefit, or are incurred by reason of, an improvement to the unit of property that is moved and reinstalled (Preamble to T.D. 9564; Reg. § 1.263(a)-3(j)(3), Examples 9 and 10).

*Basis adjustments for first-year deductions and credits.* In many cases a downward basis adjustment is required in the tax year that a deduction or credit is claimed with respect to the property (usually in the tax year that the property is placed in service or acquired). Thus, before computing depreciation, cost or other basis (as increased by items similar to those above) is adjusted downward for any applicable items described in Code Sec. 1016 (other than depreciation) including but not limited to the following:

(1) 100 percent of the rehabilitation investment credit, 50 percent of the business energy credit, and 50 percent of the reforestation investment credit (Code Secs. 50(c) and 1016(a)(19));

(2) 100 percent of the deduction for clean-fuel vehicles and clean-fuel vehicle refueling property (for property placed in service after June 30, 1993, and before 2006) (Code Secs. 179A(e)(6)(A) and 1016(a)(24));

(3) 100 percent of the credit for qualified electric vehicles (for property placed in service after June 30, 1993, and before 2007) (Code Secs. 30(d)(1) and 1016(a)(25));

(4) 100 percent of the railroad tax maintenance credit (Code Secs. 45G(e)(3) and Code Sec. 1016(a)(29));

(5) 100 percent of the deduction for complying with EPA sulfur regulations (Code Sec. 179B(c) and Code Sec. 1016(a)(28));

(6) 100 percent of the deduction for energy efficient commercial buildings (Code Sec. 179D(e) and Code Sec. 1016(a)(31));

(7) 100 percent of the energy efficient home credit (Code Sec. 45L(e) and 1016(a)(32));

(8) 100 percent of the credit for nonbusiness energy property (Code Secs. 25C(f) and Code Sec. 1016(a)(33));

(9) 100 percent of the credit for residential energy efficient property (Code Secs. 25D(f) and 1016(a)(34));

(10) 100 percent of the alternative motor vehicle credit which consists of four component credits (Code Sec. 30B(h)(4) and Code Sec. 1016(a)(35)):

(a) qualified fuel cell motor vehicle credit

(b) advanced lean burn technology motor vehicle credit

(c) qualified hybrid motor vehicle credit

(d) qualified alternative fuel motor vehicle credit

(11) 100 percent of the alternative fuel refueling property credit (Code Sec. 30C(e) and Code Sec. 1016(a)(36));

(12) 100 percent of the gas guzzler excise tax imposed by Code Sec. 4064 on certain automobiles (Code Sec. 1016(d));

(13) 100 percent of the enhanced oil recovery credit but not in excess of basis increase that (Code Sec. 43(d)(1)); and

(14) 100 percent of the credit for new qualified electric drive motor vehicles (Code Sec. 30D(f)(1))

The amount of the disabled access credit reduces the basis of capitalized expenditures taken into account in computing the credit (Code Sec. 44(d)(7)). Expenditures to remove architectural and transportation barriers to the handicapped and elderly for which a deduction is allowed under Code Sec. 190 are excluded from basis (Code Sec. 190(a)(1)).

If property is not used 100 percent for production of income or business purposes, the basis on which depreciation is computed must be apportioned (Code Sec. 167(a); Reg. § 1.167(a)-5).

The adjusted basis of the property before computing depreciation (including the bonus depreciation allowance, see ¶ 127D) must be reduced for any cost recovered under cost recovery provisions other than depreciation (Rev. Proc. 87-57, 1987-2 CB 687). Thus, no depreciation is allowed on the portion of basis for which the following are claimed:

(1) amortization (see ¶ 10);

(2) depletion;

(3) Code Sec. 179 expense deduction (see ¶ 300);

The result is the unadjusted depreciable basis for depreciation purposes (the basis immediately before depreciation deductions) (Reg. § 1.168(b)-1(a)(3)).

The bonus depreciation allowance (¶ 127D) is computed on the unadjusted depreciable basis (Reg. § 1.168(k)-1(a)(2)(iii)). For example, if an item of property costs $100,000 and a taxpayer expensed $50,000 under Code Sec. 179, the first-year bonus depreciation allowance is $25,000 (($100,000 – $50,000) × 50%) assuming a 50 percent rate applies. The regular MACRS depreciation deductions are computed on the remaining basis of $25,000 ($100,000 – $50,000 – $25,000).

*Cars*

The depreciable basis of a car is its cost reduced by any credits and deductions (other than depreciation) claimed. Cost includes sales taxes, destination charges, and dealer preparation. The cost is reduced by the clean-fuel vehicle deduction, the qualified electric vehicle credit, and the alternative motor vehicle credit for vehicles, including hybrid vehicles, placed in service after December 31, 2005 (Code Sec. 30B).

For purposes of computing depreciation, the basis of a vehicle that is subject to the gas guzzler tax because it belongs to a model type whose fuel economy rating is less than 22.5 miles per gallon or is not otherwise exempt (Code Sec. 4064) must be reduced by the amount of the tax (Code Sec. 1016(d)).

Special rules apply to vehicle trade-ins (i.e., like-kind exchanges) before 2018. See ¶ 214. Code Sec. 1031 will generally only apply to exchanges of real property after 2017 (Code Sec. 1031(a), as amended by P.L. 115-97).

*Like-kind exchanges*

See ¶ 167.

*Property converted from personal to business use*

A special rule applies to property converted from personal to business or investment use, such as where a personal residence is converted into rental property (Reg. § 1.167(g)-1). In this case, the basis for depreciation is the lesser of the fair market value at the time of the conversion or the adjusted basis of the property at that time.

The basis for computing gain is the taxpayer's original cost adjusted for depreciation (and any other items since purchase) (Code Sec. 1011; Reg. § 1.1011-1). However, in the case of a converted residence, the basis for computing loss is the lesser of the original cost adjusted for depreciation (and any other items since purchase) or the fair market value at the time of conversion adjusted for depreciation (and any other items since the conversion) (Reg. § 1.165-9(b)).

See, also, ¶ 168.

*Gifts and Inherited Property*

If, at the time of a gift, the fair market value of the gifted property is equal to or exceeds the adjusted basis of the property in the hands of the donor, the donor's adjusted basis is used for purposes of computing depreciation, depletion, amortization and gain or loss. However, the donor's adjusted basis must be increased by the part of any gift tax paid with respect to the property that is attributable to the difference between the fair market value of the property and its adjusted basis (Code Sec. 1015(a), Code Sec. 1015(d)(1), and Code Sec. 1015(d)(6)). To determine this portion of the gift tax, the gift tax with respect to the property is multiplied by a fraction, the numerator of which is the difference between the fair market value of the property and its adjusted basis and the denominator of which is the value of the gift. The amount of gift tax deemed paid with respect to a gift is determined in accordance with the rules set forth in Code Sec. 1015(d)(2).

> ***Example (1):*** Tom Kline deeds John Jones a building as a gift. The building has an adjusted basis of $110,000 and a fair market value of $200,000. Tom pays a $50,000 gift tax with respect to the property. The gift tax that is attributable to the net increase in value of the gift is $22,500 ($50,000 × ($90,000/$200,000)).

In the case of a gift made before 1977, the gift tax basis adjustment is equal to the gift tax paid with respect to the gift except that the gift tax adjustment may not increase the adjusted basis of the property above its fair market value at the time of the gift (Code Sec. 1015(a); Code Sec. 1015(d)(1)).

*Adjusted basis exceeds fair market value.* If the donor's adjusted basis exceeds the fair market value of the gift, the donee's basis for purposes of determining depreciation, depletion, or amortization is also the donor's adjusted basis at the time of the gift. (As mentioned above, the same rule, applies if the fair market value exceeds the adjusted basis). The basis for determining gain is also the donor's adjusted basis; however the property's basis for purposes of determining loss is its fair market value at the time of the gift (Code Sec. 1015(a)). In the case of a gift made after 1976, it is not necessary to make an adjustment for any gift tax paid where the fair market value of the property is less than its adjusted basis since there is no net appreciation in the value of the gift (Code Sec. 1015(d)(6)). If the gift was made before 1977, the rules in the preceding paragraph apply to determine the adjustment to basis for the gift tax.

Special gift tax basis adjustment rules apply to property acquired by gift before September 2, 1958 (Code Sec. 1015(d)(1)(B)).

*Suspended passive activity losses increase donor's adjusted basis.* A taxpayer's gift of his entire interest in a passive activity does not trigger the deductibility of disallowed passive activity losses allocable to the activity because a gift is not a fully taxable transaction (Code Sec. 469(j)(6)(B); Senate Committee Report to P.L. 99-514 (1986), S. Rep. No. 99-313). The losses become nondeductible for any tax year and are added to the basis of the property immediately before the gift because the taxpayer can no longer make a taxable disposition of the interest (Code Sec. 469(j)(6)). If the taxpayer gives only a portion of an activity, a portion of the disallowed losses are allocated to the gift portion, which becomes nondeductible and is added to the donee's basis. However, for purposes of determining the donee's loss in a subsequent transaction, the donee's basis may not exceed the fair market value of the gift at the time he received it.

*Anti-churning rules.* Real property received as a gift should be depreciated using MACRS. However, if personal property received as a gift was owned by the donor in 1986, MACRS only applies if the first-year MACRS deduction (using the half-year convention) is equal to or smaller than the first-year deduction that would apply under ACRS. Most of the time the MACRS deduction will be less since MACRS recovery periods are generally longer. See discussion of MACRS anti-churning rules at ¶ 142.

*How to depreciate gifted property.* Assuming MACRS applies to gifted property and the property was being depreciated by the donor, it appears the donee should continue depreciating the adjusted basis of the gifted property over the remaining MACRS recovery period using the donor's method and convention. Normally, this is advantageous to the donee since the adjusted (carryover) basis will be recovered in a shorter period of time than if the depreciation period is restarted. Similarly, property with a carryover basis does not qualify for the section 179 allowance (Code Sec. 179(d)(2)(C)).

Although there are no MACRS regulations dealing specifically with the depreciation of gifted property, ACRS proposed regulations would have extended the step-in-the shoes rule for nonrecognition transactions described in former Code Sec. 168(f)(10) (current Code Sec. 168(i)(7)) to gifted recovery property (Proposed Reg. § 1.168-5(f)(3) at ¶ 540). Thus, under the proposed regulation, the donor's adjusted basis of gifted property immediately prior to the gift is depreciated using the remaining recovery period of the asset and same recovery period and convention. To the extent that the adjusted basis is increased, such as on account of the payment of gift tax, the increase is depreciated separately as newly acquired property. Some background information can be found in Field Service Advice Memorandum 0746, May 19, 1993.

Significant support for depreciating the carryover basis of gifted property using the donor's remaining recovery period is also found in the safe harbor guidance for executors that make an election under Code Sec. 1022 to treat property acquired from a decedent dying in 2010 as a gift (Rev. Proc. 2011-41). See below, "*Special rule for decedents dying in 2010 if Code Sec. 1022 election is made to treat transfer as gift.*"

*Inherited property*

The depreciable basis of property acquired by bequest, devise, inheritance, or by the decedent's estate from a decedent is its stepped-up basis (Code Sec. 1014(b)). Rcal and personal property received by bequest, etc., should be depreciated using MACRS even if the decedent owned the property in 1986.

If an election is made to value property includible in a decedent's gross estate as of the alternate valuation date for estate tax purposes (Code Sec. 2032(a)), that value relates back to the date of the decedent's death and is the basis upon which depreciation subsequent to the date of death is computed for income tax purposes (Rev. Rul. 63-223, 1963-2 CB 100).

The stepped-up basis rule of Code Sec. 1014(b) generally applies to the partnership interest acquired from a deceased partner and not the partnership assets themselves. The basis of the assets would typically be stepped-up by making a timely Code Sec.754 election. This rule also applied in a husband-wife partnership where the partnership was deemed to continue following the death of the husband for purposes of winding up its affairs (*Estate of Ernest Skaggs*, 75 TC 191, CCH Dec. 37,379).

*Special rule for decedents dying in 2010 if Code Sec. 1022 election is made to treat transfer as gift.* If the executor of an estate of a decedent that dies in 2010 makes a Code Sec. 1022 election described in Notice 2011-66 the property acquired from the decedent is generally treated as having been transferred by gift. If the decedent's adjusted basis is less than or equal to the property's fair market value determined as of the decedent's date of death, the recipient's basis is the adjusted basis of the decedent. If the decedent's adjusted basis is greater than that fair market value, the recipient's basis is limited to that fair market value (Code Sec. 1022(a)(2)). To the extent a recipient's basis in property is determined under Code Sec. 1022, the tax character of the property, as in the case of gifted property in general, is the same as it would have been in the hands of the decedent. Consequently, for property described in Code Sec. 1221 (capital assets) or Code Sec. 1231 (property used in a trade or business and involuntary conversions), and for property subject to the recapture provisions of Code Sec. 1245 or Code Sec. 1250, the tax character of the property described in these sections (the basis of which is determined under Code Sec. 1022) in the hands of the recipient is the same as it would have been in the hands of the decedent. For example, depreciation claimed by the decedent will be subject to the section 1245 and 1250 recapture rules when the recipient disposes of the property. However, the tax character of the property may be affected by a subsequent change in the recipient's use of the property (Rev. Proc. 2011-41).

A taxpayer may compute depreciation on property that is subject to a Code Sec. 1022 election using the safe-harbor method described in Section 4.06(3) of Rev. Proc. 2011-41.

Under the safe harbor, the recipient is treated for depreciation purposes as the decedent for the portion of the recipient's basis in the property that equals the decedent's adjusted basis in that property. Consequently, the recipient determines any allowable depreciation deductions for this carryover basis by using the decedent's depreciation method, recovery period, and convention applicable to the property. If the property is depreciable property in the hands of both the decedent and the recipient during 2010, the allowable depreciation deduction for 2010 for the decedent's adjusted basis in the property is computed by using the decedent's depreciation method, recovery period, and convention applicable to the property, and is allocated between the decedent and the recipient on a monthly basis. This allocation is made in accordance with the rules in Reg. § 1.168(d)-1(b)(7)(ii) for allocating the depreciation deduction between the transferor and the transferee. See ¶ 144.

The portion of the recipient's basis in the property that exceeds the decedent's adjusted basis in the property as of the decedent's date of death (for example, a the special basis increase described in Code Sec. 1022(b) and (c) which is allocated by the executor with respect to property that was acquired from and owned by the decedent) is treated for depreciation purposes as a separate asset that the recipient placed in service on the day after the date of the decedent's death. Accordingly, the recipient determines any allowable depreciation deductions for this excess basis by using the depreciation method, recovery period, and convention applicable to the property on its placed-in-service date or, if not held on that date as depreciable property by the recipient, on the date of the property's conversion to depreciable property. The special basis increase is computed on Form 8939 (Allocation of Increase in Basis for Property Acquired From a Decedent) and includes unused NOL carryforwards.

If an executor elects not to have the estate tax apply with respect to a decedent that died in 2010 the transfer of a passive activity by reason of the decedent's death will be treated as a gift and the carryover basis rules in Code Sec. 1022 will apply. Consequently, the rule for gifts (Code Sec. 469(j)(6)) rather than the rule for death (Code Sec. 469(g)(2)) applies and the decedent's adjusted basis in such property is increased by the amount of the suspended losses immediately before the transfer (Rev. Proc. 2011-41, Section 4.06). Thus, the suspended losses are taken into account as part of the decedent's adjusted basis that is recovered over the remaining recovery period of the property by the recipient of the property.

Under final regulations which are effective on or after January 19, 2017, if a transferee's basis is determined under Code Sec. 1022 (relating to the election discussed above to use the gift tax rules to determine the basis of property acquired from certain decedents who died in 2010) the property is not considered acquired by purchase and is not eligible for expensing under Code Sec. 179 (Reg.§ 1.179-4(c); Reg.§ 1.179-6(d)). Since the effective date does not apply to "property placed in service" on or after January 19, 2017, it appears that taxpayers who claimed the Section 179 deduction on such property would be considered to have adopted an impermissible accounting method by expensing the cost rather than depreciating it. The situation is similar to the "for tax years beginning on or after January 1, 2014" effective date provided in the repair regulations which resulted in requiring a taxpayer who, prior to the 2014 tax year, expensed an amount as a repair which should have been capitalized and depreciated (or vice versa) to file an accounting method change to correct the erroneous treatment through a Code Sec. 481(a) adjustment. The text of the Notice of Proposed Rulemaking (REG-107595-11, May 11, 2015) provides no additional information regarding the effective date.

### *Carryover Basis Transactions*

#### *Carryover basis transactions*

Code Sec. 168 contains only one provision which explicitly requires the recipient of property to continue depreciating the property using the method and remaining depreciation period of the transferor. Specifically, Code Sec. 168(i)(7) applies this rule to nonrecognition transactions described in Code Secs. 332, 351, 361, 721, and 731 (similarly to former Code Sec. 168(f)(10) under ACRS). See ¶144. In addition, the regulations allow a taxpayer to continue depreciating the carryover basis of property received in a like-kind exchange or involuntary conversion over the remaining recovery period of the property received in most circumstances (Reg.§1.168(i)-6). See ¶167.

The IRS has ruled that a carryover basis is generally depreciated over a new recovery period with the exception of the transactions described in Code Sec. 168(i)(7) and the related proposed regulation, Proposed Reg. §1.168-5(f)(3) (Field Service Advice Memorandum 0746 (CCH Field Service Advice Memorandum 1993-0519-2). The ruling specifically held that the purchaser of a depreciable asset to which a protective carryover election under former Temporary Reg.§1.338-4T(f)(6)(ii) applied did not step into the shoes of the seller to determine the purchaser's costs recovery deductions. In footnote 5 of the same ruling, the IRS similarly indicates that a beneficiary who receives a carryover basis in depreciable property distributed from a trust (Code Sec. 643(e)(1)) also depreciates the property over a new recovery period and not the remainder of the trust's recovery period.

*Allocation of purchase price when business or multiple assets purchased*

Where depreciable and nondepreciable properties are bought for a single price, the purchase price must be allocated between these depreciable and nondepreciable assets in proportion to their fair market values (Reg. §1.167(a)-5; IRS Publication 551, Basis of Assets).

If a building and land are purchased, the purchase price is allocated between the land and building based on their relative fair market values (Reg. §1.167(a)-5). Assets scheduled to be demolished should have no basis or value assigned to them. Any abandonment losses incurred in connection with a demolition should also be considered for capitalization to the land. See Technical Advice Memorandum 9131005 (Apr. 25, 1991) (IRS Audit Technique Guide For Cost Segregation, Chapter 4).

The IRS Audit Technique Guide For Cost Segregation, Chapter 5 provides that in applying Reg. §1.167(a)-5 to a land/building acquisition, the purchase price is first allocated to the fair market value of the land based on the land's highest and best use. Anything remaining is generally allocated to the building and land improvements. If, for example, nothing remains to be allocated to the building and improvements this simply means that the building and improvements have no fair market value. That is, they do not contribute to the value of the property. The guide notes that it is inappropriate to estimate the value of the land by subtracting the estimated value of the improvements from the lump real estate price. Basis assigned to land in this residual fashion may result in understating the appropriate basis in the land and overstating the appropriate basis in the depreciable improvements.

The Guide states:

"The fair market value of land should be based on the highest and best use of the land as though vacant, even if the land has improvements. The land value may equal the value of the total real estate even if the real estate has substantial improvements, when such improvements do not contribute value to the property. Whereas land has value, improvements contribute value. The value of the total real estate, less the value of the land, results in the value of the improvements. Accordingly, it is inappropriate to estimate the value of the land by subtracting the estimated value of the improvements from the lump real estate price. Basis assigned to land in this residual fashion may result in understating the appropriate basis in the land and overstating the appropriate basis in the depreciable improvements. Examiners should also be wary if a cost segregation study relies solely on local assessed values rather than appropriately determining fair market values."

If the fair market values of the properties are uncertain, costs may be allocated among them based on their assessed values for real estate tax purposes (*F Smith*, T.C. Memo. 2010-162, Dec. 58,283(M)). While (assessment) valuation for real estate tax purposes may not furnish correct value, such drawback will not cause it to be rejected for purposes of determining the *relative* value of land and a building for the purpose of allocating cost basis (*2554-58 Creston Corp.*, 40 TC 932, Dec. 26,294). However, an allocation of cost may not be made solely according to assessed values when better evidence (such as an engineering report) exists to determine fair market value (IRS Letter Ruling 9110001, August 2, 1990).

The Tax Court in a summary opinion approved the IRS's use of county assessment values to allocate the purchase price between land and rental real estate (*Neilson*, T.C. Summ. Op. 2017-31, May 8, 2017). The county assessment values were deemed more reliable than the "land sales method" and "insurance method" proposed by the taxpayer. Moreover, the county assessment values were in line with the results of a professional appraisal conducted for the taxpayer in the year of purchase.

Any transfer of a group of assets constituting a trade or business where the purchaser's basis is determined wholly by reference to the consideration paid for the assets is an applicable asset acquisition (Code Sec. 1060). A group of assets constitutes a trade or business if (a) the use of the assets would constitute an active trade or business under Code Sec. 355 (see Reg. § 1.355-3) or, (b) its character is such that goodwill or going concern value could under any circumstances attach to such group of assets. See Reg. § 1.1060-1(b)(2). In an applicable asset acquisition, the seller and the purchaser each must allocate the consideration among the assets transferred in the same manner as the amounts are allocated under the residual method (Code Sec. 338(b)(5)) relating to certain stock purchases treated as asset acquisitions (Code Sec. 1060(a)). Where the parties to an applicable asset acquisition agree in writing as to the allocation of any amount of consideration, or as to the fair market value of any of the assets transferred, that agreement is "binding" on the transferee and the transferor unless the Commissioner determines that the allocation (or fair market value) is not appropriate (Code Sec. 1060(a)(2)). Land and buildings are a Class V asset. Therefore, the purchase price is first allocated to Class I through IV assets in an amount equal to each asset's fair market value. Any remaining amount is allocated to Class V assets. If the combined fair market values of the Class IV assets exceed the remaining amount, then the remaining amount is allocated among them in proportion to their fair market values (Reg. § 1.338-6).

Regarding an acquisition of a combination of depreciable and nondepreciable assets for a lump sum in an applicable asset acquisition, the basis for depreciation of a depreciable asset cannot exceed the amount of consideration allocated to that asset under Code Sec. 1060 and Reg. § 1.1060-1 (Temp. Reg. § 1.167(a)-5T).

A sufficiently specific allocation of purchase price between buildings and section 1245 property in an applicable asset acquisition will prevent a taxpayer from using a cost segregation study subsequent to the purchase to change the original allocation (*Peco Foods, Inc.* TC Memo. 2012-18, Dec. 58,920(M), aff'd CA-11 (unpublished opinion) 2013-2 USTC 50,412, 522 FedAppx 840). See ¶ 127.

For a detailed description of the valuation of goodwill using the residual valuation method in a like-kind exchange of radio stations see *Deseret Management Corporation*, U.S. Court of Federal Claims, 2013-2 ustc ¶ 50,459 (Jul. 31, 2013).

*Qualified Joint Interests of Married Persons*

One half of the fair market value of property held by a married couple as tenants by the entirety or as joint tenants with right of survivorship is included in the decedent's gross estate, regardless of how much each spouse contributed towards the original purchase price (Code Sec. 2040(b)(1)). The surviving spouse's basis in the property equals one half of the original cost of the property, plus one half of the fair market value of the property on the decedent's death or alternate valuation date, less any depreciation or depletion allowed to the surviving spouse (Reg. §§ 1.1014-1(a), 1.1014-6(a)).

***Example:*** Mr. and Mrs. Albert purchased property for $40,000, of which Mr. Albert contributed $30,000 and Mrs. Albert contributed $10,000. The property is held as a qualified joint interest. The couple took $10,000 of depreciation deductions through Mr. Albert's death. On his death, the fair market value of the property was $70,000. Mrs. Albert's basis in the property is as follows:

| | | |
|---|---|---|
| One half of original cost | $20,000 | (1/2 of $40,000) |
| Interest acquired from husband | $35,000 | (1/2 of $70,000) |
| Less one half of depreciation | $ 5,000 | (1/2 of $10,000) |
| | $50,000 | |

The Sixth Circuit, however, has held that the rule requiring one half of the value of spousal joint property to be included in the decedent's gross estate applies only to joint interests created after 1976, regardless of the date of death of the first spouse to die. The court held that the full value of property acquired before 1976 and held jointly by the spouses was included in the decedent's estate because the decedent had furnished all of the consideration for the property. As a result, the surviving spouse received a step-up in basis for the full fair market value of the property at the date of the decedent's death (*M.L. Gallenstein v US*, CA-6, 92-2 USTC ¶ 60,114, 975 F2d 286).

The Sixth Circuit's decision in *Gallenstein* has been followed by the Fourth Circuit (*J.B. Patten v US*, CA-4, 97-2 USTC ¶ 60,279, 116 F3d 1029, aff'g, DC Va., 96-1 USTC ¶ 60,231) two US district courts (*M.H. Anderson v US*, DC Md., 96-2 USTC ¶ 60,235, and *E. Baszlo v US*, DC Fla., 98-1 USTC ¶ 60,305) and the Tax Court (*Hahn v Commr*, 110 TC 140, Dec. 52,606).

If a husband and wife hold property as joint tenants with right of survivorship, but the husband and wife are not the sole joint tenants, the ownership is not a qualified joint interest. The basis of the property to the surviving spouse reflects the portion of the property included in the decedent's estate (Reg. § 1.1014-2(b)(2)). Similarly, if spouses hold property as joint tenants with right of survivorship and the surviving spouse is not a U.S. citizen, the full value of the property, reduced by the proportionate value of the consideration deemed to have been paid by the surviving spouse, is included in the decedent's estate (Code Secs. 2040(a), 2056(d)(1)(B)). Special rules determine the amount of consideration treated as paid by the surviving spouse. The basis must then be reduced by any depreciation or depletion allowed to the surviving spouse (Rev. Rul. 56-519, 1956-2 CB 123, amplified by Rev. Rul. 58-130, 1958-1 CB 121). No adjustment is required for depreciation allowed to the decedent spouse before his death with respect to the interest in property that is acquired from him by reason of his death if it was not actually acquired before his death (Rev. Rul. 58-130, 1958-1 CB 121).

If the surviving spouse and the decedent filed joint income tax returns before the decedent's death, and claimed depreciation or depletion deductions, then the basis of the property to the surviving spouse must reflect the depreciation and depletion deductions claimed before the decedent's death in connection with her interest in the property. How much income each tenant is entitled to receive under local law determines a joint tenant's interest in jointly held property (Reg. § 1.1014-6(a)(2)). If all of the income is allocated under local law to the decedent, then the surviving spouse's basis in the property is the property's fair market value on the estate tax valuation date, without any reduction for depreciation or depletion deductions taken before the decedent's death (Reg. § 1.1014-6(a)(3), Ex 2.).

*Other rules*

*Assessments.* An assessment for improvements or other items that increase the value of a property are added to the basis of the property and not deducted as a tax. Such improvements may include streets, sidewalks, water mains, sewers, and public parking facilities. The amount of such an assessment may be a depreciable asset, for example, the cost of an assessment for sidewalks paid for by a business taxpayer. Assessments for maintenance or repair or meeting interest charges on the improvements are currently deductible as a real property tax (Code Sec. 164(c)(1), Reg. § 1.164-4, Rev. Proc. 73-188).

*Basis unknown.* No depreciation is allowed if the taxpayer is unable to establish basis. General ledger entries ordinarily are not acceptable evidence of cost for depreciation purposes unless supported by book entries or reliable secondary evidence.

*Casualty losses and similar basis adjustments that occur during depreciation period.* For the manner of computing depreciation if a mid-stream basis adjustment is required, see ¶ 179.

*Imputed interest.* Imputed interest costs are includible in depreciable basis (IRS Letter Ruling 9101001, September 11, 1990).

*Leased property.* For the basis of tangible leased property, see ¶ 5.

*Liens and contingent liabilities.* The basis of property was not reduced because it was subject to a lien or because only a part of the actual purchase price was paid (*B.B. Crane*, SCt, 47-1 USTC ¶ 9217, 331 US 1). No depreciation was allowed on that portion of basis which was attributable to contingent liabilities (costs that may never be incurred) (*W.R. Waddell*, 86 TC 848, Dec. 43,023, aff'd per curiam CA-9, 88-1 USTC ¶ 9192, 841 F2d 264).

*Nonrecourse debt.* In many tax shelter cases where the stated purchase price of an asset was grossly inflated over the asset's fair market value by purported nonrecourse debt, the nonrecourse debt was not considered a valid debt for income tax purposes and it was not includible in basis.

Whether a nonrecourse debt is a valid debt includible in basis depends on the validity of the repayment assumption. One approach for testing nonrecourse debt compares the fair market value of the property in relation to the stated purchase price and/or the principal amount of the indebtedness. A nonrecourse debt is treated as a valid debt only if the acquired property reasonably secures payment of the obligation. Another approach utilized in tax shelter cases involving nonrecourse debt where the principal was payable out of exploitation proceeds holds that an obligation, even if a recourse debt, will not be treated as a valid debt where payment, according to its terms, is too contingent. Under these circumstances, depreciable basis cannot exceed the fair market value of the property (*W.R. Waddell, supra; G.B. Lemmen*, 77 TC 1326, Dec. 38,510, (Acq.) 1983-2 CB 1).

*Partnership basis adjustment.* In the event that a partnership makes a Code Sec. 754 election and the basis of a partnership's recovery property is increased under Code Sec. 734(b) (relating to the optional adjustment to the basis of undistributed partnership property) or Code Sec. 743(b) (relating to the optional adjustment to the basis of partnership property) as a result of the distribution of property to a partner or the transfer of an interest in a partnership, the increased portion of the basis is taken into account as if it were newly purchased recovery property placed in service when the distribution or transfer occurs. No change is made for purposes of determining the depreciation allowance for the portion of the basis for which there is no increase (Reg. § 1.734-2(e)(1); Reg. § 1.743-1(j)(4)(i)).

If the basis of a partnership's recovery property is decreased under Code Sec. 734(b) or Code Sec. 743(b) as a result of the distribution of property to a partner or the transfer of a partnership interest, the decrease is taken into account over the remaining recovery period of the property (Reg. § 1.734-2(e)(2); Reg. § 1.743-1(j)(4)(ii)).

***Example (2):*** Anne owns a 20% interest in the Anzac Partnership and sells her entire interest to Brian for $600,000. The partnership makes or has a section 754 election in effect. The Anzac Partnership's sole asset is a nonresidential building (including the land on which is stands) that was placed in service after 1986. Assume that the portion of the Code Sec. 743(b) basis adjustment allocable to the building increases the basis of the building with respect to Brian from $100,000 to $300,000 and that the portion of the basis adjustment allocable to the land increases the basis of the land is from $100,000 to $300,000. The amount of the basis adjustment allocable to the building ($200,000) is taken into account as if it were newly purchased property placed in service on the date that Anne sold her interest in Anzac. This portion of the basis has a new 39-year recovery period that begins on the date of sale. No change is made with respect to the calculation of depreciation allowances for the portion of the basis of the building (i.e., $100,000) not affected by the basis adjustment under Code Sec. 743.

See ¶ 127 for partnership tax planning opportunities involving cost segregation studies.

Bonus depreciation only applies to an increase to the inside basis of a new partner's interest in partnership property when a Code Sec. 754 election is in effect. See ¶ 127D.

*State energy incentives.* State or third party incentives to purchase energy efficient property are generally taxed as income unless the incentive represents a price rebate, in which case the incentive reduces the basis of the energy property. Generally, a price rebate is only provided by the manufacturer or seller. States often mistakenly characterize incentive payments as price rebates (Notice 2013-70, Q&A 11; IRS Letter Ruling 8924002, February 27, 1989). Specific statutory exceptions may apply. For example, Code Sec. 136 excludes from income certain payments made by utilities to customers for the purchase of energy efficient equipment and requires a basis reduction.

*Taxes.* Any tax paid in connection with the acquisition of a property is included in the basis of the property. A tax paid in connection with the disposition of a property reduces the amount realized on the disposition (Code Sec. 164(a)).

## ¶ 74

## Who Is Entitled to the Depreciation Deduction?

The right to deduct depreciation is not predicated upon ownership of the legal title to property but upon capital investment in the property (*Gladding Dry Goods Co.*, 2 BTA 336, Dec. 642). The test is who bears the burden of exhaustion of the capital investment (*F. & R. Lazarus & Co.*, SCt, 39-2 USTC ¶ 9793, 308 US 252). Thus, a company had a capital investment in property and was entitled to depreciation because a transaction in which a bank held legal title to the property was a loan secured by the property involved rather than a sale and leaseback.

A farmer-stockholder in a nonprofit mutual corporation had no depreciable investment in a dam constructed for the corporation. Although he was assessed a pro-rata share of the cost of a loan obtained by the corporation to finance the dam, he was not personally liable on the debt and did not suffer the burden of exhaustion of the property (*R.L. Hunter*, 46 TC 477, Dec. 28,025).

Generally, the owner of the property makes the capital investment and claims the depreciation deduction. Factors considered in determining that has the benefits and burdens of ownership include: (1) whether legal title passes; (2) how the parties treat the transaction; (3) whether an equity was acquired in the property; (4) whether the contract creates a present obligation on the seller to execute and deliver a deed and a present obligation on the buyer to make payments; (5) whether the right of possession is vested in the buyer; (6) which party pays the property taxes; (7) which party bears the risk of loss or damage to the property; and (8) which party receives the profits from the operation and sale of the property (*Grodt and McKay Realty Inc.*, 77 TC 1221, Dec. 38,472). See, also, *E.R. Arevalo*, 124 TC 244, Dec. 56,026 (depreciation denied to taxpayer that invested in payphones and held legal title but did not receive benefits and burdens of ownership).

*Lease or purchase*

Whether a transaction is treated as a lease or as a purchase for tax purposes is important in determining that is entitled to a depreciation deduction. In determining whether a transaction is a lease or a purchase, judicially formulated standards consider whether the transaction (1) is genuinely a multiple party transaction, (2) has economic substance, (3) is compelled by business realities, and (4) is imbued with tax-independent considerations that are not shaped solely by tax-avoidance features.

For a nonleveraged lease or a real property lease transaction to be considered a lease under such rules, the lessee may not hold title to, or have an equity interest in, the property. The lessor must show that the transaction had a bona fide business purpose (the property was used for a business or other income-producing purpose) and that there is a reasonable expectation of profit from such transaction independent of tax benefits. In addition, the lessor must retain meaningful benefits and burdens of ownership that in turn consider whether (a) the lessee has an option to acquire the property at the end of the lease for a nominal amount, (b) the residual value of the property to the lessor is nominal, and (c) the lessor could force the lessee to purchase the property at the end of the lease.

For leveraged leases of equipment (property financed by a nonrecourse loan from a third party) the following criteria must be met in order for a transaction to be considered a lease for tax purposes: (1) the lessor must have at least a 20-percent at-risk investment in the property; (2) any lessee option to purchase the property at the end of the lease must be exercisable at fair market value; (3) the lessee must have no investment in the property; (4) the lessee must not loan money to the lessor (or guarantee a lessor loan) to enable the lessor to acquire such property; (5) the lessor must expect to receive a profit and a positive cash flow from the transaction exclusive of tax benefits; and (6) the fair market value of the property at the end of the lease term must equal at least 20 percent of the value when the lease was entered and the useful life of the property at the end of the lease must equal at least the longer of one year or 20 percent of the original useful life (Rev. Proc. 2001-28, 2001-1 CB 1156; Rev. Proc. 2001-29, 2001-1 CB 1160).

Where equipment or other depreciable property is leased with an option to buy, the lessor is allowed depreciation and the lessee deducts the rent paid. However, if the lease is in substance a sale of the property, the lessee is allowed to depreciate the leased property and may not deduct the payments as rent (Rev. Rul. 55-540, 1955-2 CB 39).

Factors implying that there was a sale rather than a lease include: (1) payments are specifically applicable to the purchase price if the option is exercised; (2) the lessee will acquire title upon payment of a stated amount of rentals; (3) the lessee is required to pay a substantial part of the purchase price in the early years of the asset's life; (4) the rental payments exceed a fair rental value; (5) the option purchase price is nominal compared with the expected value of the asset when the option is exercised; (6) some part of the payments is designated as interest; and (7) the lease may be renewed at nominal rentals over the useful life of the property.

*Leasehold acquisition costs*

See ¶ 5.

*Life tenant, trust and estate*

The holder of a life estate is allowed a depreciation deduction as if the life tenant were the absolute owner of the property (Code Sec. 167(d)). Thereafter, any remaining depreciation is allowed to the remainderman (Reg. § 1.167(h)-1(a)).

In computing depreciation, a life tenant must use the prescribed recovery period of an asset rather than a shorter life expectancy of the life tenant (*M. Penn*, CA-8, 52-2 USTC ¶ 9504, 199 F2d 210, cert. denied, 344 US 927). For example, the owner of a life estate in a rental property would depreciate the property over 27.5 years under MACRS.

A trust or estate must compute a depreciation deduction on properties it holds in its capacity as a separate tax entity before the deduction is apportioned between the trust and its beneficiaries or the estate and the estate heirs, legatees, and devisees. A trust or estate is allowed a depreciation deduction only to the extent that it is not allowable to beneficiaries (Code Sec. 642(e)).

For property held in trust, the depreciation deduction is apportioned between the income beneficiaries and the trustee on the basis of the trust income allocable to each, unless the governing instrument (or local law) requires or permits the trustee to maintain a reserve for depreciation (Reg. § 1.167(h)-1(b)). In the latter case, the deduction is first allocated to the trustee to the extent that income is set aside for a depreciation reserve. Any part of the deduction exceeding the income set aside for the reserve is apportioned between the income beneficiaries and the trustee on the basis of the trust income allocable to each.

For an estate, the depreciation allowance is apportioned on the basis of the income of the estate allocable to the estate heirs, legatees and devisees (Reg. § 1.167(h)-1(c)).

Although a depreciation deduction is apportioned on the basis of the income of the trust or the income of the estate allocable to each of the parties (without regard to the depreciation deduction allocable to them), the amount of a depreciation deduction allocated to a beneficiary may exceed the amount of the latter's pro rata share of such income (Rev. Rul. 74-530, 1974-2 CB 188).

If an election is made to value property includible in a decedent's gross estate as of the alternate valuation date for estate tax purposes (Code Sec. 2032(a)), that value relates back to the date of the decedent's death and is the basis upon which depreciation subsequent to the date of death is computed for income tax purposes (Rev. Rul. 63-223, 1963-2 CB 100).

*Term interests*

A "term interest in property" means a life interest in property, an interest in property for a term of years, or an income interest in a trust (Code Secs. 167(e)(5)(A) and 1001(e)(2)).

The purchaser of a term interest in property held for business or investment is generally entitled to amortize the cost of the term interest over its stated term or depreciate the cost over the applicable depreciation period. However amortization/depreciation may not be claimed if the holder of the remainder interest is a related person (Code Sec. 167(e)(1); *1220 Realty Corp.*, CA-6, 63-2 USTC ¶9703, 322 F2d 495). For this purpose, a related person is anyone bearing a relationship to the taxpayer that is described in Code Sec. 267(b) or (e) (Code Sec. 167(e)(5)(B)). The constructive ownership rules of Code Sec. 267(c) apply in determining whether persons are related.Code Sec. 167(e) applies to interests created or acquired after July 27, 1989, in tax years ending after that date (The Omnibus Budget Reconciliation Act of 1989, P.L. 101-239, Act §7645(b) (December 19, 1989)).

The holder of a life or terminable interest acquired by gift, bequest, or inheritance is not subject to the rule barring a depreciation or amortization deduction on the life or terminable interest where there is a related remainderman (Code Sec. 167(e)(2)(A)). Income from these term interests may not be reduced for shrinkage (i.e., amortization) in the value of such interests due to a lapse of time (Code Sec. 273). See "*Code Sec. 273,*" below.

This provision barring depreciation deductions on a term interest where there is a related remainderman does not affect a depreciation deduction that is not attributable to a term of years or a life estate (Code Sec. 167(e)(4)(B)). For example, the owner of a life estate in a building cannot amortize the term interest but may claim the depreciation deduction with respect to the building that is allowed for the owner of a life estate as described in "*Life tenant, trust and estate,*" above (House and Final Conference Committee Reports on P.L. 101-239 (Omnibus Budget Reconciliation Act of 1989)).

Applying Code Sec. 167(e), the IRS has held that where a taxpayer purchases a life estate in land and buildings and uses the property for business or investment purposes and the person holding the remainder interest is not related to the taxpayer, the taxpayer may amortize the cost of the term interest that is allocable to the land over the period of the term interest and depreciate the cost that is allocable to the buildings using the Modified Accelerated Cost Recovery System (MACRS) (IRS Letter Ruling 200852013, September 24, 2008). Although the taxpayers involved in the ruling were not related, the portion of the ruling which concludes that the buildings would not be depreciable by the life estate holder if the remainderman is related to the taxpayer who purchased the life estate appears to be incorrect insofar as it fails to take Code Sec. 167(e)(4)(B) and the related committee reports into consideration.

A taxpayer may claim a depreciation deduction on the amortized value of a purchased leasehold, even if the property underlying the leasehold is non-depreciable. See, e.g., *1220 Realty Co. v. Commissioner*, 322 F. 2d 495, 498 (6th Cir. 1965) (lease on vacant land is depreciable over unexpired term). The taxpayer in this situation claims a depreciation deduction for an estate for years.

A depreciable interest may not be created where none previously existed. Thus, no amortization or depreciation deduction is allowed on a term interest created by a taxpayer that divides or splits a fee interest in nondepreciable business property into a retained term interest and a transferred remainder interest (even if the remainderman that acquires the remainder interest is unrelated to the taxpayer) by reserving the term interest (*Lomas Santa Fe, Inc.*, 74 TC 662, Dec. 37,052, aff'd CA-9, 82-2 USTC ¶ 9658, 693 F2d 71); *Georgia Railroad and Banking Co*, CA-5, [65-2 ustc ¶ 9525, 348 F. 2d 278, cert. denied, 382 U. S. 973 (1966). A taxpayer who sells a remainder interest

A taxpayer may depreciate a term interest that is purchased subsequent to the taxpayer's acquisition of the remainder. See, e.g., Bell v. Harrison, CA-7, 54-1 ustc ¶ 9351, 212 F. 2d 253, 256; *Triangle Publications, Inc.*, 54 T. C. 158, Dec. 29,944; *Fry*, 31 T. C. 522, 527, Dec. 23,277, aff'd, CA-6, 60-2 ustc ¶ 9738, 283 F. 2d 869.

Prior to enactment of Code Sec. 167(e), a common method of deferring income tax was for two related persons to purchase jointly a term and remainder interest in property. Typically, a parent would purchase an income interest (e.g., in interest bearing bonds) for a term of years and the child would purchase the remainder interest. The parent would reduce taxable income from the term interest by claiming amortization deductions on the cost of the term interest.

> ***Example (1):*** John purchases for $435 a 6-year term interest in preferred stock that has a par value of $1,000 and pays dividends of 10 percent per year. John's son Joe purchases the remainder interest for $565. John receives $100 of dividend income per year but is allowed a $72.50 annual amortization deduction ($435/6). If the value of the preferred stock does not change, the Joe will recognize $435 ($1,000 - $565) on the sale or redemption of the stock. If John had purchased the preferred stock outright and given the remainder interest in the stock to Joe, John would have been taxed on $100 of dividend income without being able to claim any amortization deduction because a taxpayer may not divide an interest in property into two parts to create an amortizable asset where none previously existed, as noted below.

If the remainderman is a related person, the purchaser is required to reduce the basis of the property by the amortization or depreciation deduction disallowed solely by the related-remainderman rule (Code Sec. 167(e)(3)(A)). The remainderman's basis in the property is increased by the disallowed deductions (Code Sec. 167(e)(3)(B)). No increase in the remainderman's basis is made for disallowed deductions attributable to periods during which the term interest is held by (1) an exempt organization or (2) a nonresident alien individual or foreign corporation if income from the term interest is not effectively connected with the conduct of a trade or business in the United States (Code Sec. 167(e)(4)).

The holder of dividend rights that were separated from any Code Sec. 305(e) stripped preferred stock is not subject to the restrictions on depreciation deductions imposed where there is a related remainderman if the rights were purchased after April 30, 1993 (Code Sec. 167(e)(2)(B)).

*Code Sec. 273.* Amounts paid as income to the holder of a life or a terminable interest acquired by gift, bequest, or inheritance may not claim deductions for shrinkage (whether called by depreciation or any other name) in the value of such interest due to the lapse of time (Code Sec. 273; Reg. § 1.273-1). This provision does not operate to disallow depreciation deductions by a holder of a life estate in a depreciable building or other depreciable tangible property because depreciation deductions are not attributable to the lapse of time, but rather to wear and tear on the depreciating asset. Code Sec. 273, would operate, for example, to prevent the holder of a gifted life interest in dividend paying securities from offsetting the dividend income with deductions attributable to the life interest holder's basis in the securities. See also, *A. E. Jackson*, 72 T.C.M. 1102, Dec. 51,620(M), in which the holder of a life interest in the income of a trust received by gift could not amortize the value of the trust (reduced by the value of the remainderman's interest in the trust) over her life expectancy.

*Landlord and tenant*

A landlord can depreciate property already on the premises when the property is leased and any improvements constructed by the landlord during the term of the lease. A tenant can deduct depreciation for permanent improvements made to the leased property by the tenant (Code Sec. 168(i)(8); Temporary Reg. § 1.167(a)-4T). See also ¶ 126 and ¶ 258.

## ¶ 75

## Incorrect Depreciation Claimed/Accounting Method Changes

A taxpayer may not simply increase the depreciation deduction for the current tax year by the amount of depreciation allowable but not claimed in a previous tax year or years or decrease the current year depreciation deduction by the amount of excess depreciation claimed in a prior tax year or tax years (Reg. § 1.167(a)-10(a); Reg. § 1.1016-3(a)(1)(ii)). Nevertheless, the basis of the property is reduced by the greater of the amount of depreciation claimed or the amount of depreciation that should have been claimed (i.e., greater of amount "allowed or allowable"). See below, "*Basis Reduction—Allowed or Allowable Rule.*"

In general, if incorrect depreciation has been claimed the situation is corrected by filing an amended return if only one incorrect return was filed or by filing or an accounting method change on Form 3115 if two or more incorrect returns were filed. A taxpayer may also usually choose to file a Form 3115 instead of an amended return if only one incorrect return was filed.

If an accounting method change is filed a taxpayer will generally reduce or increase taxable income in the year of change (i.e., the tax year for which the Form 3115 is filed) by the amount of a "Code Sec. 481(a) adjustment" which represents the cumulative unclaimed or excess depreciation. The full amount of a negative (taxpayer favorable adjustment) reduces taxable income in the year the accounting method is changed. Positive adjustments which increase taxable income are taken into account over a four-year period. However, if the positive adjustment is less than $50,000, a taxpayer may elect to take it into account entirely in the year of change. See below, "*Code Sec. 481(a) Adjustment Periods.*"

These are the three most recent revenue procedures providing a list of all automatic accounting method changes allowed by the IRS:

- Rev. Proc. 2019-43 for changes filed on or after filed on or after November 8, 2019, for a year of change ending on or after March 31, 2019
- Rev. Proc. 2018-31 for changes filed on or after May 9, 2018, for a year of change ending on or after September 30, 2017
- Rev. Proc. 2017-30, for Forms 3115 filed on or after April 19, 2017 and before May 10, 2018 for a year of change ending on or after August 31, 2016

*Form 3115 filing requirements for automatic changes.* Generally, for automatic changes, Form 3115 must be attached to the taxpayer's original return for the year of change by the due date (including any extensions). A signed duplicate copy must also be filed with the IRS Ogden, Utah office no sooner than the first day of the tax year of change and no later than when the Form 3115 is filed with the taxpayer's original return (Instructions to Form 3115).

A taxpayer who fails to file Form 3115 with the original return, however, may filed Form 3115 with an amended return and the duplicate copy with the Ogden office within 6 months of the original due date (excluding extensions) if certain requirements are met (Rev. Proc. 2015-13, Sec. 6.03(4)(a); Reg. § 301.9100-2).

In addition, if the original copy of the Form 3115 was attached to the taxpayer's timely filed original federal income tax return, but the duplicate copy of the Form 3115 was not filed by the date the original Form 3115 was filed, the automatic 6-month extension applies to the duplicate copy of the Form 3115 (Office of Chief Counsel Internal Revenue Service Memorandum: AM 2020-002 (4/10/2020)).

Taxpayers who do not meet the filing deadlines must submit a letter ruling requesting an extension to file (Rev. Proc. 2015-13, Sec. 6.03(4)(a)). See, for example, IRS Letter Ruling 200334026, May 14, 2003, granting extension of time to file with the National Office.

*Advance consent procedure.* If the automatic consent procedures of Rev. Proc. 2019-43 do not apply to the type of accounting method change being made, then the advance consent accounting method change guidelines of Rev. Proc. 2015-13 should be followed. If the automatic consent procedures apply to a taxpayer's situation, the taxpayer may not use the advance consent procedures. The section 481(a) adjustment periods described below for automatic consent also apply to adjustments under the advance consent procedure. The IRS will formally approve or disapprove the requested change in a letter ruling. A substantial filing fee is required.

*When Is an Accounting Method Adopted?—Two Year Rule*

If a taxpayer has claimed an incorrect amount of depreciation (for example it has used the wrong MACRS depreciation period, MACRS depreciation method (e.g., straight-line instead of 150 percent declining balance) or failed to claim depreciation deductions because it erroneously believed the asset was not depreciable) and has only filed one return the taxpayer has not adopted an accounting method with respect to the manner in computing the depreciation deduction. In this case, the previously filed return can be amended to make the correction (Rev. Rul. 90-38, 1990-1 C.B. 570). However, even though the taxpayer has not adopted an accounting method because only one incorrect return was filed, the IRS will waive the "two-year rule" and allow a taxpayer to utilize the change of accounting method procedures for the types of changes described in section 6.01 of Rev. Proc. 2019-43 (relating to changes from impermissible to permissible method) by filing a Form 3115 with the current year's return (the return for the year following the year in which the property was placed in service and depreciation incorrectly computed) and claiming a Code Sec. 481(a) adjustment on the current year's return (Rev. Proc. 2007-16; Section 6.01(1)(b) of Rev. Proc. 2019-43).

If two or more incorrect returns have been filed a taxpayer has adopted an accounting method with respect to the incorrect manner in which the depreciation was claimed (Rev. Rul. 90-38). In this situation, a taxpayer may only file Form 3115 to change its accounting method.

> ***Example (1):*** XYZ corporation misclassifies an item of 5 year property as 10 year property on its 2020 tax return. It discovers the error when preparing its 2021 tax return. XYZ has not adopted a method of accounting because it has not filed two incorrect returns. Generally, this error would be fixed by filing an amended return for 2020. However, pursuant to Rev. Proc. 2007-16, XYZ may choose to fix the error by applying the change of accounting method procedures and make a Code Sec. 481(a) adjustment on its 2021 tax return because this change is described in Sec. 6.01 of Rev. Proc. 2019-43. It is not necessary to file an amended return for 2020.

If a return using a permissible accounting method has been filed, the permissible method is considered adopted after filing only one return. A taxpayer changing from one permissible method of accounting to another permissible method of accounting will generally need to file under the advance consent procedure. Certain exceptions described below may apply.

*What Types of Depreciation Changes Are Accounting Method Changes?*

Certain depreciation changes do not relate to an accounting method and may only be made on an amended return. For example, as explained below, the correction of a math or posting error may only be made on an amended return for open years (Rev. Proc. 2015-13, Section 2.02(2); Reg. § 1.446-1(e)(2)(ii)(b)).

Regulations describe in detail changes in depreciation that are considered changes in accounting method and changes that are not accounting method changes (Reg. § 1.446-1(e)(2)(ii)(d); Reg. § 1.167(e)-1).

The regulations apply to a change of accounting method made for a depreciable or amortizable asset placed in service in a tax year ending on or after December 30, 2003. With respect to a change in depreciation or amortization that is not a change in method of accounting, the regulations apply to a change made for assets placed in service in tax years ending on or after December 30, 2003 (Reg. § 1.446-1(e)(4); Reg. § 1.167(e)-1). A taxpayer may apply a special rule described below to assets placed in service in a tax year ending before December 30, 2003 which have not been fully depreciated. Application of this rule may produce favorable results if a taxpayer has adopted an accounting method that resulted in claiming excess depreciation.

The regulations generally provide that a change in the depreciation method, period of recovery, or convention of a depreciable or amortizable asset is a change in method of accounting (Reg. § 1.446-1(e)(2)(ii)(d)(2)(i)). Thus, a change from an improper depreciation period to a proper depreciation period is a change in accounting method if two or more returns have been filed. See *"Misclassified assets"* immediately below.

Changes in accounting method listed in the regulations include (Reg. § 1.446-1(e)(2)(ii)(d)(2)):

(1) A change in the depreciation or amortization method, period of recovery, or convention of a depreciable or amortizable asset;

(2) changing the treatment of an asset from depreciable to nondepreciable or vice versa (e.g., from an inventory item to a depreciable asset);

(3) a correction to require depreciation or amortization in lieu of a deduction for the cost of depreciable or amortizable assets that had been consistently treated as an expense in the year of purchase, or vice versa;

(4) change by a taxpayer that didn't elect out of bonus depreciation, from not claiming to claiming bonus depreciation and correcting depreciation deductions affected by such a change;

(5) change from incorrectly claiming bonus depreciation to not claiming bonus depreciation and correcting depreciation deductions affected by such a change;

(6) change from using an incorrect bonus depreciation rate and correcting depreciation deductions affected by such a change;

(7) change from incorrectly taking salvage value into account in computing depreciation deductions on assets for which salvage value should not be taken into account such as MACRS and ACRS assets;

(8) a change in the accounting for depreciable assets from single asset accounting to multiple asset accounting (pooling), or vice versa, or from one

type of multiple asset accounting to a different type of multiple asset accounting; and

(9) a change in the method of identifying which mass assets accounted for in multiple asset accounts or pools have been disposed of (e.g., from specific identification to a FIFO method).

A change from deducting an item of expenditure to capitalizing such item of expenditure (or vice versa) constitutes a change in method of accounting and a Code Sec. 481(a) adjustment should be recognized in connection with the change. The section 481(a) adjustment may reflect amounts previously deducted in closed tax years (CCA Letter Ruling 201231004, April 18, 2012).

*Misclassified assets.* The regulations resolve (in the IRS's favor) a conflict that has arisen between the courts regarding whether the reclassification of a misclassified MACRS asset is a change in accounting method (Reg. § 1.446-1(e)(2)(ii)(d)(2)(i); Field Service Advice Memorandum 001881).

By way of background, the Tenth Circuit first affirmed the long-standing IRS position that a taxpayer that misclassifies a MACRS asset and claims incorrect depreciation on two or more returns has adopted an accounting method (*S.M. Kurzet*, 2000-2 USTC ¶ 50,671) and, therefore, must take a Code Sec. 481(a) adjustment into account. The Fifth and Eighth Circuits, as well as the Tax Court, however, ruled that such a reclassification is not a change in accounting method by reason of former Reg. § 1.446-1(e)(2)(ii)(*b*) (*Brookshire Brothers Holding, Inc.*, CA-5, 2003-1 USTC ¶ 50,214; *R. O'Shaughnessy*, CA-8, 2003-1 USTC ¶ 50,522; and *Green Forest Manufacturing Inc.*, 85 TCM 1020, T.C. Memo. 2003-75, CCH Dec. 55,083(M)). That regulation provided that a change in method of accounting does not include an adjustment in the useful life of a depreciable asset. Traditionally, if there is no accounting method change under this regulation, depreciation is corrected by adjustments in current and future years.

The new regulations move the useful life exception in Reg. § 1.446-1(e)(2)(ii)(b) to Reg. § 1.446-1(e)(2)(ii)(d)(3)(i) and clarify that it only applies to property depreciated under Code Sec. 167 (i.e., not to property depreciated under MACRS or ACRS). However, a change to or from a useful life (or a recovery or amortization period) that is specifically assigned (e.g., 36 months for software under Code Sec. 167(f)(1)) is a change in accounting method (Reg. § 1.446-1(e)(2)(ii)(d)(3)(i)).

*Mathematical and posting errors.* The correction of a mathematical or posting error is not considered a change of accounting method and may only be corrected on an amended return for an open tax year (Rev. Proc. 2015-13 and predecessors, § 2.01(2); Reg. § 1.446-1(e)(2)(ii)(b)).

A posting error can occurs when an asset is omitted from a depreciation schedule or misclassified as the result of a data entry error. The Tax Court interpreted the term "posting error" to mean an error in "the act of transferring an original entry to a ledger" (*Wayne Bolt and Nut Co.*, 93 TC 500, Dec. 46,100).

The term mathematical error is not further defined in Rev. Proc. 2015-13, § 2.01(2) or Reg. § 1.446-1(e)(2)(ii)(b). However, a definition of the term "mathematical or posting error" is provided in Code Sec. 6213(g)(2) in the context of a the rule which allows the IRS to summarily assess additional tax in the case of a mathematical or clerical error without issuing a notice of deficiency. See "The Math or Clerical Error Exception", William D. Elliott, Journal of Tax Practice and Procedure®, July 2011 which discusses the mathematical error rule solely in the context of Code Sec. 6213(g)(2). In general, for purposes of Code Sec. 6213(g)(2) the term mathematical error has been defined to include only actual errors in arithmetic; i.e., an error in addition, subtraction, multiplication, or division. In *D.A. Huffman*, 126 T.C. 322, Dec. 56,523, the Tax Court accepted this definition for the purposes of Reg. § 1.446-1(e)(2)(ii)(b). The Sixth Circuit, 2008-1 USTC ¶ 50,210, 518 F3d 357, refused to either adopt or reject the Tax Court's definition. See, also, CCA Letter Ruling 201442051 and cases cited therein in which the IRS neither accepted nor rejected this definition of mathematical error for accounting method purposes.

*Correction of internal inconsistency.* The correction of an internal inconsistency is also not considered the adoption of an accounting method. For example, an internal inconsistency exists if identical assets are not depreciated similarly (*H.E. Butt Grocery Store Co.*, DC Tex. 2000-2 USTC ¶ 50,649)

*Other changes that are not accounting method changes.* Other changes that are not considered a change in accounting method include:

- a change in use (¶ 169) that causes a change in recovery period or method provided that the taxpayer does not file two or more returns without applying the change in use rule as required in the year the change in use occurs (Sec. 6.05 of Rev. Proc. 2019-43 and Rev. Proc. 2018-31, as amended by Rev. Proc. 2019-8)
- making a late depreciation or amortization election or revoking a timely made election unless otherwise provided in IRS guidance (permission is generally obtained by submitting a request for a private letter ruling)
- a change in salvage value (unless a salvage value of zero is expressly required, as in the case of ACRS, MACRS, and Section 197 assets)
- a change in the placed-in-service date of an asset

*Placed in service date changes.* If a taxpayer incorrectly determines that a depreciable or amortizable asset is nondepreciable property and later changes the treatment of the asset to depreciable property, such a change is not a change in the placed-in-service date of the asset and, therefore, is a change in method of accounting. Likewise, a change in the convention of a depreciable or amortizable asset is not a change in the placed-in-service date of the asset (Reg. § 1.446-1(e)(2)(ii)(d)(3)(v)).

The change in placed-in-service date, whether initiated by the IRS or a taxpayer, may be corrected by adjustments in the earliest tax year open under the period of limitation for assessment or the earliest tax year under examination by the IRS but in no event earlier than the placed-in-service year of the asset, and in subsequent taxable years. However, if a taxpayer initiates the change in placed-in-service date, in lieu of filing amended Federal tax returns, the taxpayer may correct the placed-in-service date by adjustments in the current and subsequent tax years (Reg. § 1.446-1(e)(2)(ii)(d)(5)(v)).

*Section 6 Automatic Accounting Method Changes*

Section 6 of Rev. Proc. 2019-43 provides various automatic accounting method changes related to depreciation. The most common change, from an impermissible depreciation method to a permissible depreciation method, is described in Sec. 6.01 and is assigned #7 as the designated account number change. Each type of change listed in section 6 (and the other sections of Rev. Proc. 2019-43) has its own designated accounting number. If the change which a taxpayer wants to make is not listed in section 6, then a taxpayer will need to use the non-automatic procedures (i.e., the "advance consent" procedure) described in Rev. Proc. 2015-13 and pay a significant filing fee. The IRS will send the taxpayer a letter ruling accepting or rejecting the requested change.

The following automatic accounting method changes related to depreciation are provided in Section 6 of Rev. Proc. 2019-43:

- 6.01 Impermissible to permissible method of accounting for depreciation or amortization
- 6.02 Permissible to permissible method of accounting for depreciation
- 6.03 Sale, lease, or financing transactions
- 6.04 Change in general asset account treatment due to a change in the use of MACRS property
- 6.05 Change in method of accounting for depreciation due to a change in the use of MACRS property (see below)
- 6.06 Depreciation of qualified non-personal use vans and light trucks (relating to exemption from annual depreciation limitations underCode Sec. 280F for passenger automobiles)
- 6.07 Impermissible to permissible method of accounting for depreciation or amortization for disposed depreciable or amortizable property
- 6.08 Tenant construction allowances
- 6.09 Safe harbor method of accounting under Rev. Proc. 2011-22 for determining the depreciation of certain tangible assets used by wireless telecommunications carriers
- 6.10 Partial dispositions of tangible depreciable assets to which an IRS's audit adjustment pertains under Reg. § 1.168(i)-8
- 6.11 A change described in Rev. Proc. 2014-17, 2014-12 I.R.B. 661 from improperly depreciating leasehold improvements over the term of a lease (including renewals) to depreciating the improvement over its proper recovery period (see ¶ 77)
- 6.12 Permissible to permissible method of accounting for depreciation of MACRS property (Reg. §§ 1.168(i)-1 (general asset accounts), 1.168(i)-7 (single asset and multiple asset accounts, and 1.168(i)-8) (dispositions) (see ¶ 77)
- 6.13 Disposition of a building or structural component (see ¶ 77)
- 6.14 Dispositions of tangible depreciable assets (other than a building or its structural components) (see ¶ 77)
- 6.15 Dispositions of tangible depreciable assets in a general asset account (see ¶ 77)
- 6.16 Summary of certain changes in methods of accounting related to dispositions of MACRS property (see ¶ 77)
- 6.17 Depreciation of fiber optic transfer node and fiber optic cable used by a cable system operator
- 6.18 Late elections or revocations for tax year that includes September 28, 2017 under Code Sec. 168(k)(5) (claiming bonus depreciation in year of planting or grafting), Code Sec. 168(k)(7) (election out of bonus depreciation), and Code Sec. 168(k)(10) (50 percent bonus rate in place of 100 percent rate) (relating to Rev. Proc. 2019-33) (see ¶ 127D)
- 6.19 Change from impermissible to permissible method of depreciating qualified improvement property placed in service after December 31, 2017 (relating to Rev. Proc. 2020-25; see ¶ 127D)

- 6.20 Late elections and revocations allowed for elections made or otherwise required in tax years ending in 2018, 2019, and 2020 if return for placed-in-service year filed on or before April 17, 2020: Code Sec. 168(k)(5) (claiming bonus depreciation in year of planting or grafting) and Code Sec. 168(k)(7) (election out of bonus depreciation). Also late election or revocation under Code Sec. 168(k)(10) (50 percent bonus rate in place of 100 percent rate) for tax years that include September 28, 2017 (relating to Rev. Proc. 2020-25, as modified by Rev. Proc. 2020-50; see ¶ 127D).

- 6.21 Change in depreciation as a result of applying the additional first year depreciation regulations. Provides guidance on retroactively applying 2020 final bonus regulations, 2019 final bonus regulations, or 2019 final and proposed regulations. Also allows late elections and revocation of certain elections for the 2017, 2018, 2019, and 2020 tax years. These elections include Code Sec. 168(k)(5), Code Sec. 168(k)(7), Code Sec. 168(k)(10), and the Reg.§ 1.168(k)-2(c) component election. Sec. 6.21 was added to Rev. Proc. 2019-43 by Rev. Proc. 2020-50. See ¶ 127D.

*Section 6.01—impermissible to permissible depreciation method.* The automatic consent procedure for taxpayers that have adopted an impermissible method of accounting for depreciation (or amortization) and have either claimed no allowable depreciation, less depreciation than allowable, or more depreciation than allowable is provided in Sec. 6.01 of Rev. Proc. 2019-43.

Section 6.01 does not apply unless the taxpayer owns the asset for which the change is made at the beginning of the tax year of change. However, Section 6.07, "Impermissible to permissible method of accounting for depreciation or amortization for disposed depreciable or amortizable property," provides automatic consent rules for an asset that is no longer owned if insufficient or no depreciation was claimed (see below).

A taxpayer may not change from an impermissible method of depreciation to a permissible method described in Section 6.01 if the taxpayer claimed any type of federal income tax credit on the property for which the change is being made (Section 6.01(1)(c)(xvi)). Prior to the issuance of Rev. Proc. 2016-29 this rule only applied if the taxpayer claimed the rehabilitation credit. The advance consent procedure (Rev. Proc. 2015-13) must be used in this situation.

In general, Section 6.01 of the automatic consent procedure applies to property which is owned by a taxpayer at the beginning of the year of change and for which depreciation is claimed under Code Secs. 56(a)(1) (AMT depreciation), 56(g)(4)(A) (AMT ACE depreciation), 167, 168 (ACRS and MACRS), 197 (15-year amortization), 1400I, 1400L(c) or under any type of additional first-year (bonus) depreciation provision such as Code Sec. 168(k), New York Liberty Zone property, Gulf Opportunity Zone property, and Kansas Disaster Area property. The procedure does not apply to specified property, including intangible property amortized under Code Sec. 167 (except for property excluded from Code Sec. 197 by Code Sec. 167(f)) and property depreciated under the Asset Depreciation Range (ADR) system.

Section 6.01 also does not apply if a taxpayer is seeking to change the useful life of an asset that is depreciated under Code Sec. 167 but does apply to a change in recovery period under ACRS or MACRS.

However, Section 6.01 does not apply if a taxpayer wants to reclassify section 1250 property to an asset class that does not explicitly include section 1250 property (Sec. 6.01(1) of Rev. Proc. 2017-30). For example, automatic consent is not available with respect to an item of a building, such as a wall or acoustical ceiling tile that a taxpayer has treated as *section 1250 property*, but now wishes to treat as 5-year *section 1250 property* under Asset Class 57.0 (Distributive Trades and Services) because this asset class does not include section 1250 property.

This rule is in response to the *Walgreen Co.* case, in which a taxpayer unsuccessfully argued that certain types of Section 1250 property are includible in Asset Class 57.0 (relating to retail trades, see ¶ 104) and, therefore, are depreciable as 5-year property (*Walgreen Co.*, 72 TCM 382, Dec. 51,503(M)). This rule does not prevent a taxpayer from using the automatic consent procedure to reclassify items that were incorrectly depreciated as Section 1250 (real) property as Section 1245 (personal) property. For example, a taxpayer may use Section 6.01 in connection with a cost segregation study that determines that certain items that were included in the basis of commercial or residential rental property should have been separately depreciated as personal property over a five- or seven-year period. However, a statement of law and facts supporting such a reclassification must be submitted (Rev. Proc. 2019-43, Sec. 6.01(3)(b)(vii)).

*Section 6.02 Permissible to permissible method under Code Sec. 167.* Sec. 6.02 of Rev. Proc. 2019-43 provides an automatic consent procedure for changing from a permissible depreciation method under Code Sec. 167 to another permissible method under Code Sec. 167. The procedure, for example, covers a change from the straight-line method to the sum-of-the-years digits method, the sinking fund method, the unit-of-production method, or the declining-balance method using any proper percentage of the straight-line method rate. If a change is made from one permissible method to another permissible method, there is no Code Sec. 481(a) adjustment and no change to the basis of an asset is made as the result of the change in accounting method (Reg. § 1.446-1(e)(2)(ii)(d)(5)(iii)).

*Permissible to permissible method under Code Sec. 168 (MACRS).* In order to change from one permissible method to another permissible method of depreciation under MACRS a taxpayer must generally file Form 3115 using the advance consent procedures of Rev. Proc. 2015-13. No Code Sec. 481(a) adjustment is made (Reg. § 1.446-1(e)(2)(ii)(d)(5)(iii)). However, see Sec. 6.12 of Rev. Proc. 2019-43 for certain permissible to permissible MACRS changes that may be made under the automatic consent procedures.

*Sections 6.04 and 6.05—Change in use.* Generally, a change in depreciation period or method required by the change in use rules (Reg. § 1.168(i)-4) is not an accounting method change provide the change in period or method is made in the year that the change in use occurs. However, if a taxpayer delays making the required change on two or more returns an improper method of accounting has been adopted and an accounting method change under Sec. 6.05 of Rev. Proc. 2019-43 is required. A Code Sec. 481(a) adjustment is required. See ¶ 168 and following for discussion of change in use rules.

Section 6.04 provides accounting method change procedures when there is a change in use of an asset in a general asset account.

*Sec. 6.07—Sales of property on which insufficient or no depreciation claimed.* A taxpayer that used an impermissible method of accounting and sold or disposed of a depreciable asset on which insufficient or no depreciation was claimed may file a Form 3115 to claim the depreciation through a Code Sec. 481(a) adjustment on an amended return for the year of sale filed within the limitations period for the year of the sale or on an original return for the year of the sale (Sec. 6.07 of Rev. Proc. 2019-43 which is based on Rev. Proc. 2007-16).

Exceptions apply to certain property held by tax-exempt organizations and property disposed of in any nonrecognition transactions, unless, in the case of a Code Sec. 1031 (like-kind exchange) or Code Sec. 1033 (involuntary conversion) the taxpayer elected to depreciate the entire basis of the replacement property as newly acquired property. See ¶ 167 for a description of this election.

*Code Sec. 481(a) Adjustment Periods*

The section 481(a) adjustment period for a change in method of accounting is generally one tax year (year of change) for a net negative adjustment (resulting in a decrease in taxable income) and four tax years (year of change and next three tax years) for a net positive adjustment (resulting in an increase to taxable income). A net positive adjustment is taken into account ratably over the 4-year adjustment period. A taxpayer, however, may elect to use a one-year adjustment period in lieu of the 4-year adjustment period for a positive adjustment if the net adjustment for the change is less than $50,000. To make this election, the taxpayer must complete the appropriate line on Form 3115 and take the entire adjustment into account in the year of change (Sec. 7.03(3)(c) of Rev. Proc. 2015-13).

Often a taxpayer will need to change its accounting method with respect to more than one asset. If a taxpayer has one or more assets on which too little depreciation was claimed resulting in a negative section 481(a) adjustment (resulting in a decrease in taxable income) and also one or more assets on which too much depreciation was claimed, resulting in a positive section 481(a) adjustment, two choices are available. First, the taxpayer may combine the negative and positive adjustment and report a single net negative or net positive section 481(a) adjustment. Alternatively, the taxpayer may report a separate positive adjustment and a separate negative adjustment (Sec. 6.01(8) of Rev. Proc. 2019-43).

***Example (2):*** A taxpayer files a single Form 3115 to change the MACRS depreciation methods, recovery periods, and/or conventions resulting from the reclassification of two computers from 39-year nonresidential real property to 5-year property, one office desk from 39-year nonresidential real property to 7-year property, and two office desks from 5-year property to 7-year property. On that Form 3115, the taxpayer must provide either (a) a single net § 481(a) adjustment that covers all the changes resulting from all of these reclassifications, or (b) a single negative § 481(a) adjustment that covers the changes resulting from the reclassifications of the two computers and one office desk from nonresidential real property to 5-year property and 7-year property, respectively, and a single positive § 481(a) adjustment that covers the changes resulting from the reclassifications of the two office desks from 5-year property to 7-year property.

***Example (3):*** Assume that in the preceding example the negative adjustment is $40,000 and the positive adjustment is $120,000. The taxpayer may either report a net positive adjustment of $80,000 ($120,000 - $40,000) and report that amount ratably as a positive adjustment over 4 years (i.e., $20,000 increase in taxable income per year assuming the taxpayer is a calendar year taxpayer and the change is effective January 1) or report a $10,000 decrease in taxable income in the first year ($40,000 negative adjustment + $30,000 positive adjustment) and a $30,000 positive adjustment in each of the three remaining years of the four-year adjustment period for positive adjustments ($120,000/4 = $30,000).

*Code Sec. 481(a) adjustment and statute of limitations.* The Code Sec. 481(a) adjustment reflects relevant amounts (e.g., net excess or unclaimed depreciation) from any tax year preceding the tax year of change even if such years are closed by the statute of limitations (CCA Letter Ruling 201231004, April 18, 2012 and cases cited therein; Rev. Proc. 2015-13, Section 2.06(1)).

*Reporting Code Sec. 481(a) adjustment.* Positive (unfavorable) adjustments are typically reported on the "other income" line of the income tax return and negative (favorable) adjustments are reported on the "other deductions" line (Form 1120 Instructions).

*Special Rules for Assets Placed in Service in Tax Years Ending Before December 30, 2003*

For property placed in service in a tax year ending before December 30, 2003 (i.e., the effective date of the final change in accounting method regulations), the IRS will not assert that a change in computing depreciation under Code Sec. 167, 168, 197, 1400I, 1400L(c), or ACRS for depreciable or amortizable property that is treated as a capital asset is a change in accounting method under Code Sec. 446(e) (IRS Chief Counsel Notice CC-2004-007, January 28, 2004, as clarified by Chief Counsel Notice 2004-024, July 14, 2004).

A service-initiated change in computing depreciation with respect to depreciable or amortizable property that is treated as a capital asset and placed in service in taxable years ending before 12/30/2003 is treated in a manner consistent with a taxpayer amending its returns. However, where the change is not initiated by the IRS, a taxpayer may either file an accounting method change or amended returns.

This means, with respect to an asset placed in service in a tax year ending before December 30, 2003 a taxpayer may choose to file amended returns in open tax years or file Form 3115 with the current tax year (year of change) in order to correct a depreciation period or some other change in computing depreciation that might otherwise be considered an accounting method change. If a taxpayer claimed too much depreciation and some of those years are closed, the amended return option will preserve the deduction claimed in the closed tax years. If too little depreciation was claimed in closed years, then a taxpayer will generally want to change its accounting method in order to report a negative (taxpayer favorable) Code Sec. 481(a) adjustment that reflects the unclaimed depreciation from all closed and open years. It is no longer possible for all tax years to be open for an asset placed in service in a tax year ending before December 30, 2003 assuming the regular limitations period for filing an amended return is applicable. In situations where all tax years were open the taxpayer had the choice of reporting the correct amount of depreciation on each return filed beginning with the tax year the asset was placed in service or taking the aggregate depreciation that was either underreported or overreported during those years into account as a Code Sec. 481(a) adjustment over the appropriate adjustment period beginning in the year of change.

In general, an amended return must be filed by the later of (1) three years from the date the original return which claimed the incorrect depreciation was filed or (2) two years from the date that the tax was paid for the year that the incorrect depreciation was claimed. For purposes of item (1), a return filed early is considered filed on the due date. A refund is limited to the amount of tax paid during the three-year period (plus any extension of time to file the original return) prior to filing the amended return.

The following example is based on an example appearing in Chief Counsel Notice CC-2004-007, January 28, 2004, as clarified by Chief Counsel Notice 2004-024, July 14, 2004:

> ***Example (4):*** A taxpayer conducts a cost segregation study in 2005 and reclassified building elements of 39-year property placed in service in 2002 as 5-year property. The taxpayer may file an amended return for 2002, 2003, and 2004 reporting depreciation as if the property had originally been classified as 5-year property or follow the change of accounting method procedures by filing Form 3115 and claiming a Code Sec. 481(a) adjustment in 2005 (the year of change).

If the cost segregation study had been conducted in 2021, the amended return option would be of no significance since the 5-year property would have been fully depreciated in 2007 which is a closed tax year. In this situation, a taxpayer will want to file a change in accounting method and claim a Code Sec. 481(a) adjustment (equal to the difference between the depreciation that could have been claimed on the 5-year property (i.e., its total cost since it would have been fully depreciated) less the depreciation that was actually claimed using the 39-year recovery period through the tax year immediately preceding the year of change).

The amended return option is beneficial if the taxpayer claimed excess depreciation in closed tax years (e.g., because it depreciated an asset over a shorter recovery period than was proper).

> ***Example (5):*** A taxpayer placed an item of 39-year commercial real property in service in 2002 but has been depreciating it using the 27.5 year recovery period applicable to residential rental property. Assume that the property cost $100,000 and that the taxpayer has been claiming $3,636 per year in depreciation for 19 years (2002 - 2020) for a cumulative amount of $69,084 ($3,636 × 19 = $69,084). Assume that the proper annual deduction computed as if the property were 39 year real property is $2,564 per year or $48,716 ($2,564 × 19 = $48,716).
>
> If a change of accounting method is filed for 2021, the taxpayer will report a positive Code Sec. 481(a) adjustment over the adjustment period that increases taxable income by the $20,368 ($69,084 – $48,716) excess depreciation. The undepreciated basis of $51,284 ($100,000 – $69,084 + $20,368 = $51,284) is recovered over the remaining 20 years in the recovery period at the rate of $2,564 ($51,284/20 = $2,564) per year. The net effect is an aggregate $100,000 deduction ($69,084 – $20,368 + $1,284 = $100,000) over 39 years.
>
> However, the amended return option is available because the building was placed in service in a tax year that ended before December 30, 2003. If an amended return is filed for the 3 open years the taxpayer will reduce the depreciation shown on each open-year return ($3,636) to reflect the correct amount of depreciation that should have been claimed computed using the basis of the building and remaining recovery period of the building as of the first open year. The basis of the building as of the beginning of the first open year (2018) is $41,824 ($100,000 - ($3,636 × 16 closed years)). Correct depreciation that should be claimed in each open year (and for the remainder of the 24-year recovery period) is $1,818 ($41,824/23 years in remaining recovery period as of first open year = $1,818) or $5,454 over 3 open years.
>
> Thus, each amended return must reduce the depreciation claimed by $1,818 ($3,636 – $1,818) or $5,454 over 3 open years. The $17,152 excess depreciation claimed in 16 closed years (($3,636 × 16) – ($2,564 × 16) = ($17,152)) is unaffected but does reduce basis for purposes of determining the recomputed basis as of the first open year. Total depreciation claimed over 39 years is $100,000 ($58,176 for first 16 years + $41,824 for the next 24 years = $100,000).
>
> When the amended return option is chosen the taxpayer only increases income by $5,454. If the fix is made as a change in accounting method, $20,368 is included in income as a positive section 481(a) adjustment.
>
> ***Example (6):*** Assume the same facts except that the taxpayer depreciated the 39-year property as 5 year property. In this case the taxpayer will have recovered the entire $100,000 cost over 6 tax years that are now closed. The IRS will not require a taxpayer to change its accounting method to make the correction because the asset was placed in service in a tax year ending before December 31, 2003 and under the IRS guidelines it is not necessary for the taxpayer to file amended returns since there no longer is a basis to recover in the open years.

The change in litigating position (i.e. amended return option) does not apply to (1) an adjustment in useful life under Code Sec. 167 (other than MACRS, Code Sec. 1400I, Code Sec. 14000L, or ACRS) if the useful life is not specifically assigned by the Code, regulations, or other IRS guidance; (2) to any adjustment to correct an incorrect classification or characterization of depreciable property under the class life asset depreciation range system (CLADR property); (3) or to a change in computing depreciation or amortization due to a posting error, a mathematical error, a change in underlying facts (other than a change in the placed-in-service date), a change in use of property in the hands of the same taxpayer, the making of a late election, or a revocation of an election. Items (1)-(3) are not changes in accounting method.

The change in litigating position doe not apply to a change in the treatment of property from a non-capital asset (e.g., inventory, materials and supplies) to a capital, depreciable or amortizable asset (or vice versa), or to a change from expensing the cost of depreciable or amortizable property to capitalizing and depreciating or amortizing the cost (or vice versa). These changes are a change in method of accounting.

The IRS has clarified the application of Chief Counsel Notice CC-2004-007 in a subsequently issued Chief Counsel Notice—Chief Counsel Notice CC-2004-024, July 14, 2004. CC-2004-024 provides that:

(1) A Code Sec. 481(a) adjustment is not required or permitted to be claimed on an amended return filed pursuant to CC-2004-007;

(2) A taxpayer may not file amended returns for some years and a Form 3115 for other tax years with respect to the same asset;

(3) Amended returns may be filed to "unwind" a Form 3115 that was filed under the automatic or advance consent change of accounting method procedures before the issuance of Chief Counsel Notice CC-2204-007. The year for which the change was effective, however, must still be an open tax year.

The rule in item (2) would prevent a taxpayer that placed an asset in service in a closed year from filing amended returns for open tax years and filing a Form 3115 to claim a Code Sec. 481(a) adjustment with respect to the depreciation that should have been claimed in the closed tax years.

*Change in Accounting Methods Initiated by IRS During Audit*

Under a general rule that applies to any type of automatic or non-automatic accounting method change, including those relating to depreciation, the IRS may require the taxpayer to change its method of accounting for the same item that is the subject of a Form 3115 filed under Rev. Proc. 2015-13 (relating to automatic and non-automatic changes) for tax years prior to the requested year of change if the taxpayer is under examination as of the date the taxpayer files the Form 3115 (Rev. Proc. 2015-13, Sec. 8.02(1)). A number of exceptions are listed in Sec. 8.02(1)(a) – (f).

Exception 8.02(1)(e) gives audit protection for filings that result in a negative (taxpayer favorable) Code Sec. 481(a) adjustment. Specifically, the exception provides that the rule denying audit protection for taxpayers under examination does not apply to a change in method of accounting for an item that:

- results in a negative §481(a) adjustment (taxpayer favorable) for that item *for the year of change*; and
- would have resulted in a negative §481(a) adjustment *in each tax year under examination* if the change in method of accounting for that item had been made in the tax year(s) under examination.

The Form 3115 must include a statement that the Form 3115 is filed under the provisions of SECTION 8.02(1)(e) of Rev. Proc. 2015-13.

***Example (7):*** Taxpayer is under audit for the 2018 tax year and files a Form 3115 for 2021 to correct the depreciation period of an asset that was placed in service in 2016. The IRS cannot require this change to be made effective for a tax year prior to the 2021 tax year (i.e., the 2018 audit year) if the 481 adjustment would have been negative if computed in the 2018 and 2021 tax years.

The IRS illustrates the exception with the following example:

> ***Example (8):*** A taxpayer placed Properties A and B in service in its 2017 tax year. In its 2017 through 2020 tax years, the taxpayer depreciated Property A using a 7-year recovery period instead of its correct 5-year recovery period and depreciated Property B using a 5-year recovery period instead of its correct 7-year recovery period. The taxpayer is under examination for its 2019 tax year. The taxpayer filed a Form 3115 to request a change in method of accounting for its 2021 tax year to change its methods of accounting for depreciation for Properties A and B. Under the general rule, the taxpayer generally does not receive audit protection for a change in method of accounting filed for its 2021 tax year. However, the taxpayer may receive audit protection for the change in method of accounting for depreciation for Property A because the § 481 (a) adjustment for that item required in its 2021 tax year, and that would have been required in its 2019 tax year, is negative. However, the taxpayer does not receive audit protection for the change in method of accounting for depreciation for Property B because the § 481 (a) adjustment for that item required in its 2021 tax year, and that would have been required in its 2019 tax year, is positive.

Where a taxpayer misclassified the recovery period of an asset by depreciating the asset over a longer recovery period than appropriate, the taxpayer will have a negative adjustment in each year of change unless the taxpayer also incorrectly claimed the section 179 allowance or bonus depreciation in the year the asset was placed in service. Note also that if an asset is fully depreciated taking into account the proper, longer recovery period, the section 481 (a) adjustment would be $0 which is not a negative adjustment. Therefore, it appears that the exception would not apply in this situation.

Generally, a taxpayer that is contacted for examination and required to change its method of accounting by the Service ("involuntary change") receives less favorable terms and conditions when the change results in a positive (unfavorable) section 481 (a) adjustment than the taxpayer would have received if it had filed an application to change its method of accounting ("voluntary change") before the taxpayer was contacted for examination. For example, in the absence of an agreement, the section 481 (a) adjustment is taken into account in computing taxable income completely in the year of change. However, Code Sec. 481 (b) may limit the amount of tax attributable to a substantial adjustment that increases taxable income (Rev. Proc. 2002-18).

An examining agent changing a taxpayer's method of accounting will make the change in a year under examination. Ordinarily, the change will be made in the earliest taxable year under examination, or, if later, the first taxable year the method is considered to be impermissible, although an examining agent may defer the year of change to a later taxable year in appropriate circumstances. An examining agent will not defer the year of change in order to reflect the hazards of litigation. Moreover, an examining agent will not defer the year of change to later than the most recent year under examination on the date of the agreement finalizing the change. (Rev. Proc. 2002-18, section 5.04 (1)).

A Code Sec. 481 (a) adjustment is mandatory in an accounting method change initiated by the taxpayer or the IRS to take into account adjustments that are necessary solely by reason of the method change to prevent amounts from being duplicated or omitted. However, no adjustment is necessary with respect to amounts that were taken into account in tax years prior to the enactment of Code Sec. 481 (i.e., tax years beginning before January 1, 1954) if the taxpayer initiates the accounting method change (Reg. § 1.481-1 (a)). As stated in CCA Letter Ruling 201231004, which involved an auditor initiated adjustment relating to a taxpayer who claimed a current deduction for amounts which should have been capitalized, "the computation and recognition of an appropriate adjustment under section 481(a) becomes mandatory to eliminate any distortions (duplications or omissions of income or deductions) caused by the [auditor's] accounting method change." Thus, it appears that the computation of an accurate adjustment is required whether it favors the IRS (positive adjustment) or the taxpayer (negative adjustment). For example, if a taxpayer capitalizes a repair expense that should have been deducted, the IRS-computed adjustment should be in the taxpayer's favor based on the difference between the repair expense and the amount of any depreciation actually claimed on the capitalized repair expense prior to the year of change. It would be inappropriate under the mandate of Code Sec. 481(a) to simply disallow all depreciation deductions in open tax years and allow no deduction at all for the repair expense. Conversely, if a taxpayer deducts as a repair expense an amount that should have been capitalized and depreciated (or just capitalized), the IRS should compute a positive section 481(a) adjustment equal to the difference between the erroneous repair expense and the amount of any depreciation, if any, that should have been claimed in the tax years prior to the year of change.

Note that accounting method changes involve the timing of a deduction which does not affect a taxpayer's "lifetime" income (Reg. § 1.446-1(e)(2)(ii)(a); Section 2.01 of Rev. Proc. 2015-13). For example, the capitalization of an amount that should have been claimed as a repair deduction is an improper accounting method (and requires an accounting method change to be filed) because a taxpayer claims the same deduction amount, either at one time through a repair expense deduction, or recovers the same amount through depreciation deductions over the life of the capitalized amount, and/or recovers the capitalized amount when the asset is disposed of through the recognition of less gain or a greater loss. However, if a taxpayer simply fails to claim a repair deduction without capitalizing and depreciating the repair expenditures the failure to claim the deduction is not an impermissible accounting method. The taxpayer needs to file an amended return within the limitations period or will lose the benefit of the deduction.

The failure to claim an allowable loss is likewise the adoption of an impermissible accounting method if the loss is required to reduce the basis an asset and the taxpayer does not reduce the basis for purposes of computing depreciation and determining gain or loss. For example a taxpayer may dispose of an asset at a loss and continue to depreciate it. As in the case of the capitalization of a permissible repair deduction, the failure to claim such a loss does not affect the "lifetime" income and therefor is an impermissible accounting method. The failure to claim a gambling loss, however, would affect lifetime income and, therefore, is not the adoption of permissible or impermissible accounting method. The taxpayer may only claim the disregarded gambling loss by filing an amended return within the limitations period.

Note that it is not likely that the IRS would exercise its authority to initiate a change in accounting method where a taxpayer capitalized an amount that should have been expensed or failed to claim a loss on basis that the taxpayer continues to depreciate because the taxpayer would be entitled to a favorable (negative) section 481(a) adjustment. The responsibility for making this type of change is usually left with the taxpayer. As discussed above, the IRS in fact allows a taxpayer under audit to initiate a method change where the Code Sec. 481(a) adjustment results in a negative § 481(a) adjustment (taxpayer favorable) for the year of change and would have resulted in a negative § 481(a) adjustment *in each tax year under examination* if the change in method of accounting for that item had been made in the tax year(s) under examination.

The IRS has issued guidance with respect to "involuntary" change-of-accounting methods under Code Sec. 446 and Code Sec. 481 in Rev. Proc. 2002-18, 2002-1 C.B. 678. In addition, the IRS has provided further guidance in Rev. Proc. 2002-19, 2002-1 CB 696, that permits taxpayers under examination that otherwise could not request a voluntary change in method of accounting under the advance consent revenue procedure or the automatic consent revenue procedure to do so prospectively without audit protection.

*Basis Reduction—Allowed or Allowable Rule*

The basis of depreciable property for purposes of determining gain or loss is reduced by the amount of allowable depreciation if this is greater than the amount of depreciation actually claimed (allowed depreciation) that resulted in a tax benefit (Code Sec. 1016(a)(2); Reg. § 1.1016-3(b)). Allowable deduction generally refers to a deduction which qualifies under a specific Code provision whereas allowed deduction refers to a deduction granted by the Internal Revenue Service which is actually taken on a return and will result in a reduction of the taxpayer's income tax (*Lenz*, 101 T.C. 260, 265, Dec. 49,315 (1993)). A depreciation deduction is considered to have resulted in a tax benefit if it was treated as part of an NOL and reduced taxes in an NOL carryback or carryforward year (Reg. § 1.1016-3(e)(2)).

***Example (9):*** Assume that a taxpayer determines the following allowed and allowable amounts with respect to an asset:

| *Year* | *Amount Allowed (which reduced taxes)* | *Amount Allowable* | *Greater of Allowed or Allowable* |
|---|---|---|---|
| 1 | $6,500 | $6,000 | $6,500 |
| 2 | 4,000 | 4,000 | 4,000 |
| 3 | 4,500 | 6,000 | 6,000 |
| | | | $16,500 |

The taxpayer should reduce the basis of the asset by $16,500 (Reg. § 1.1016-3(i), *Example (1)*).

Proposed Reg. § 1.1016-3 explains how to compute allowable depreciation on ACRS assets (i.e., assets placed in service after 1980 and before 1987). In general, if no depreciation deduction was claimed, the regular (i.e., non-elective recovery periods and methods) are applied. If depreciation was claimed under a proper method for one or more years but not claimed in other years, allowable depreciation is computed using the method chosen by the taxpayer. See, also, Sec. 6.01(7)(g) of Rev. Proc. 2019-43 and its predecessors, relating to automatic accounting method changes.

No MACRS regulations on this subject have been issued. However, Rev. Proc. 2019-43 provides that allowable depreciation is determined under the MACRS GDS (unless ADS is required or has been elected for a class of property (Sec. 6.01(7)(e))). Accordingly, if a taxpayer elected the GDS straight-line method or GDS 150-percent declining-balance method with respect to a class of property, allowable depreciation is computed using those elective methods for an item of property that falls within a property class to which the election applied. Otherwise, regular GDS method applies. See ¶ 84 for a discussion of GDS, ADS, etc.

Although Reg. § 1.1016-3(a)(2)(i) provides that depreciation on an asset for which no depreciation was claimed should be computed using the "straight-line" method, it appears that this rule was intended only to apply to pre-ACRS assets and should no longer apply to ACRS and MACRS assets.

In addition, allowable depreciation under MACRS includes any type of bonus depreciation that could have been claimed unless a valid election out was made.

> ***Example (10):*** A taxpayer makes an election to use the GDS 150% declining-balance method with respect to 5-year property placed in service in 2021. She later discovers that she failed to claim depreciation on an item of 5-year property placed in service in 2021. Assume that the ADS is not required for that property. Allowable depreciation should be computed using the GDS 150% declining-balance method.

Sec. 6.01(6) of Rev. Proc. 2019-43 also provides guidance on the definition of allowable depreciation under Code Sec. 56 (minimum tax), Code Sec. 167, Code Sec. 197 (amortizable section 197 intangibles), Code Sec. 1400I (qualified revitalization buildings), and Code Sec. 1400L (New York Liberty Zone leasehold improvement property) for purposes of determining gain or loss. Under this guidance, allowable depreciation does not include depreciation that is limited by other provisions of the Code, such as the luxury car rules of Code Sec. 280F. Another possible example of depreciation that is limited by a Code provision is depreciation that may not be claimed by reason of the 2 percent adjusted gross income floor for certain miscellaneous itemized deductions (Code Sec. 67(a)). However, depreciation deductions that are suspended under the passive loss rules constitute a reduction to basis (S. Rept. 99-313). The Tax Court has ruled that no basis adjustment is allowed with respect to suspended losses attributable to depreciation in a situation where there was a possibility, however remote, that the suspended losses could be claimed at a later date. Note that the Tax Court did not consider whether a basis adjustment could be made if the possibility of deducting suspended passive losses was entirely lost (*St. Charles Investment Co.,* 110 TC 46, Dec. 52,548, rev'd on another issue by CA-10, 2000-2 USTC 50,840).

*Ordinary income recapture not required on unclaimed depreciation.* The rule requiring basis reduction for unclaimed (allowable) depreciation applies for purposes of determining gain or loss. Note that when computing depreciation recapture, a taxpayer need not recapture as ordinary income unclaimed depreciation (Code Sec. 1245(a)(2)(B); Code Sec. 1250(b)(3)). See ¶ 488. Note also that unrecaptured section 1250 gain which is subject to a 25-percent capital gains rate (as opposed to the normally applicable 20-percent rate) does not include gain attributable to allowable depreciation. Only gain attributable to depreciation that was actually claimed and unrecaptured is subject to the 25-percent rate (Code Sec. 1(h)(7)(A)).

*Accounting method changes.* It is also important to understand the relationship between the accounting method change rules and the greater of the "allowed or allowable" depreciation rule of Reg. § 1.1016-3.

That regulation stands for the propositions that (1) the basis of an asset for purposes of determining gain or loss must be reduced by the greater of depreciation allowed (i.e., actually claimed) or allowable (the depreciation that should have been claimed) and (2) a taxpayer may not increase or decrease the depreciation deduction on a current year return to account for claiming too much or too little depreciation in a past year. If a taxpayer has failed to claim the proper amount of depreciation (too much or too little) and the failure to claim the correct depreciation is an improper accounting method the taxpayer must take corrective action by filing an accounting method change. Such change may even be filed after the asset is sold if the taxpayer claimed too little depreciation. See discussion above of Rev. Proc. 2007-16, "*Sales of property on which insufficient or no depreciation claimed.*" Note that if a taxpayer claims too much or too little depreciation because of a posting or mathematical error or some other reason that is not considered an accounting method, the taxpayer must file an amended return to make the correction, as explained above.

The following example, which appears in Reg. § 1.1016-3 is instructive.

> ***Example (11):*** On July 1, 2014, A, a calendar-year taxpayer, purchased and placed in service "off-the-shelf" computer software at a cost of $36,000. This computer software is not an amortizable section 197 intangible. Pursuant to section 167(f)(1), the amortization period of the computer software is 36 months. It has no salvage value. Computer software placed in service in 2014 is not eligible for the additional first year depreciation deduction provided by section 168(k). A did not deduct any depreciation for the computer software for 2014 and deducted depreciation of $12,000 for the computer software for 2015. As a result, the total amount of depreciation allowed for the computer software as of December 31, 2015, was $12,000. However, the total amount of depreciation allowable for the computer software as of December 31, 2015, is $18,000 ($6,000 for 2014 + $12,000 for 2015). As a result, the unrecovered cost of the computer software as of December 31, 2015, is $18,000 (cost of $36,000 less the depreciation allowable of $18,000 as of December 31, 2015). Accordingly, depreciation for 2016 for the computer software is $12,000 (unrecovered cost of $18,000 divided by the remaining useful life of 18 months as of January 1, 2016, multiplied by 12 full months in 2016).

First note that at the time this example was adopted, bonus depreciation had expired. It was later retroactively reinstated to apply to qualified property, including software depreciated under Code Sec. 167(f)(1), placed in service in 2014. Assume that bonus depreciation was not reinstated. The taxpayer failed to claim any depreciation in 2014 (i.e., failed to claim the $6,000 "allowable" depreciation). It claimed $12,000 in 2015, which is the correct amount using the 36-month amortization period under Code Sec. 167(f). The example indicates that the unclaimed $6,000 depreciation may not be added to the $12,000 of depreciation that is correctly allowed for 2016 using the 36-month amortization period. How may the taxpayer correct the situation? The example is silent on whether the taxpayer has adopted an accounting method or simply made a posting or math error. If the taxpayer's failure to claim the $6,000 depreciation is a posting or math error, or the result of an internal inconsistency (see discussions above) no accounting method has been adopted and the taxpayer must file an amended return for the 2014 tax year to claim the $6,000 depreciation in that year. The taxpayer would have until the expiration of the limitations period to do so. If an accounting method has been adopted, then, in addition to computing depreciation correctly for the 2016 tax year ($12,000) the taxpayer is required to file an accounting method change for the 2016 year. The accounting method change would reflect a negative (favorable) Code Sec. 481(a) adjustment equal to $6,000 ($18,000 total depreciation that should have been claimed in 2014 and 2015 less amount of depreciation actually claimed in 2014 and 2015 ($12,000)). If the taxpayer has adopted an impermissible accounting method, it should file the method change when the improper method is discovered in order to avoid any adverse audit consequences.

*Foreign sales corporation regime and extraterritorial income exclusion provisions: allowed or allowable rule.* Under the formerly applicable foreign sales corporation regime (repealed Code Sec. 921 - 927), 30 percent of depreciation deductions that are allocable to exempt foreign trade income and disallowed for purposes of computing taxable income are not considered "allowed or allowable" and, therefore, do not reduce the basis of the depreciated asset for purposes of computing gain or loss (*CBS Corporation*, FedCl, 2012-1 USTC ¶ 50,346, 105 FedCl 74). The IRS says this rule also applies to the 30 percent of depreciation deductions that may not be claimed against taxable income under the extraterritorial income (ETI) exclusion provisions of former Code Sec. 114 (CCA Letter Ruling 201625011, May 3, 2016).

The IRS has explained how to compute depreciation on an asset to which the 30 percent disallowance rules apply (1) using the optional percentage tables and (2) not using the optional percentage tables (CCA Letter Ruling 201625011, May 3, 2016). If tables are not used the applicable depreciation rate for the tax year is applied against the original cost of the asset as reduced by the 70 percent of depreciation allowed against taxable income in each prior tax year. 70 percent of each annual deduction is claimed against taxable income and the remaining 30 percent is allocated to exempt foreign trade income. However, if tables are used, the taxpayer computes depreciation on the original cost each tax year by applying the applicable table percentage for the tax year and claiming 70 percent of the resulting deduction for the year against taxable income and allocating the remaining 30 percent to exempt foreign trade income. The basis of the asset is reduced, in accordance with *CBS Corporation*, only by the depreciation deductions claimed against taxable income each tax year.

Detailed examples provided in CCA Letter Ruling 201625011 illustrate that if the percentage tables are not used, the total annual depreciation deductions allowed against taxable income during the asset's recovery period will be significantly greater than if the table percentages are used. Specifically, if the table percentages are not used and the FSC regime applies to all taxable years of the asset's recovery period the total depreciation deductions allowed against taxable income will equal the asset's original basis reduced only by 30 percent of the amount calculated as the final year's depreciation deduction. If the table percentages are used, then only 70 percent of the original basis will be allowed as depreciation deductions against taxable income throughout the asset's recovery period.

The IRS ruling provides that an accounting method change under the advance consent procedure (Rev. Proc. 2015-13) may be filed in situations where a taxpayer did not use the optional tables and has unrecovered basis that could have been depreciated if depreciation was computed properly.

## ¶ 77

## Accounting Method Changes to Comply with Final MACRS Item/ Multiple Asset Account, GAA, and Disposition Regulations

Accounting method changes filed on or after May 9, 2018, for a year of change ending on or after September 30, 2017, to comply with the final tangible property regulations dealing with MACRS general asset accounts (Reg. § 1.168(i)-1) (see ¶ 128), MACRS item and multiple asset accountReg. § 1.168(i)-7) (see ¶ 132), and MACRS dispositions (Reg. § 1.168(i)-8) (see ¶ 162) are governed by Sections 6.10 through 6.17 of Rev. Proc. 2019-43 which supersedes Rev. Proc. 2018-31, effective for a Form 3115 filed on or after November 8, 2019, for a year of change ending on or after March 31, 2019. Rev. Proc. 2018-31 superseded Rev. Proc. 2017-30 for a Form 3115 filed on or after May 9, 2018, for a year of change ending on or after September 30, 2017.

Accounting method changes filed on or after April 19, 2017 for a year of change ending on or after August 31, 2016 were governed by Sections 6.10 through 6.18 of Rev. Proc. 2017-30, which supersedes Rev. Proc. 2016-29.

The accounting method changes described in sections 6.10 through 6.17 of Rev. Proc. 2019-43 and Rev. Proc. 2018-31 are identical to those described in Rev. Proc. 2017-30. Section 6.18 of Rev. Proc. 2017-30 relating to the revocation of the partial disposition election under the remodel-refresh harbor were obsolete and removed from Rev. Proc. 2018-31. Rev. Proc. 2019-43 does not contain waiver of eligibility rules contained its predecessors which are not delete. See below.

This explanation will only refer to sections so the current automatic consent procedures in Rev. Proc. 2019-43. However, these sections are generally identical in number and content to the corresponding sections in its predecessors.

Accounting method changes filed on or after May 5, 2016 for a year of change ending on or after September 30, 2015 to comply with the final tangible property regulations were governed by Sections 6.10 through 6.20 of Rev. Proc. 2016-29, which updated and superseded Rev. Proc. 2015-14. See "Effective Date" section of Rev. Proc. 2016-29.

Taxpayers were required to comply with the final MACRS tangible property regulations in tax years beginning on or after January 1, 2014 (e.g., the 2014 tax year for a calendar year taxpayer). To the extent a taxpayer is not in compliance with an accounting method required by the final MACRS tangible property regulations, the taxpayer is using an impermissible accounting method and is subject to any adverse consequences of an IRS audit if the change to comply is not filed prior to notification of the audit.

A taxpayer who filed an accounting method change for a 2012 or 2013 tax year to adopt an accounting method permitted in the temporary or proposed MACRS tangible property regulations but not permitted by the final regulations is using an impermissible method if an accounting method change has not been filed to change to the method required by the final regulations. Again, taxpayers were expected to file these changes for their first tax year beginning on or after January 1, 2014 (i.e., the effective date of the final regulations) but may file these changes using the automatic procedures in a later tax year if not otherwise barred by the eligibility limitations. The advance consent (non-automatic) procedures of Rev. Proc. 2015-13 must be used to make automatic accounting method changes that are barred by the eligibility limitations. A change made under the advance consent procedure requires actual consent by the IRS and the payment of a significant filing fee.

*Waiver of eligibility limitations.* The 5-year eligibility rule in Sec. 5.01(1)(f) of Rev. Proc. 2015-13 is waved for the following accounting method changes filed under Rev. Proc. 2018-31 or Rev. Proc. 2017-30:

- Sec. 6.12, relating to a change from a permissible to another permissible method of accounting for depreciation of MACRS property under §§1.168(i)-1, 1.168(i)-7, and 1.168(i)-8;
- Sec. 6.13, relating to dispositions of a building or structural component under Reg. §1.168(i)-8;
- Sec. 6.14, relating to dispositions of tangible depreciable assets (other than a building or its structural components) under Reg. §1.168(i)-8; and
- Sec. 6.15, relating to dispositions of tangible depreciable assets in a general asset account under Reg. §1.168(i)-1;

The eligibility rule in Sec. 5.01(1)(f) of Rev. Proc. 2015-13 prevents a taxpayer from using the automatic consent procedure if the taxpayer has made or requested a change for the same specific item during any of the five tax years ending with the year of change. The advance consent procedures must be used if the eligibility rule prevents use of the automatic procedure.

*OVERVIEW OF CHANGES UNDER REV. PROC. 2019-43 and PREDECESSORS*

The following is a brief description of the accounting method changes to comply with the MACRS tangible property regulation allowed under Rev. Proc. 2019-43 and its predecessors. Certain obsolete changes are also discussed. A more detailed description of each section follows.

*Late Partial Disposition Election (Obsolete)*

Sec. 6.10 (Change #196) of Rev. Proc. 2016-29 allowed a taxpayer to file an accounting method change to make a late partial disposition election. This change is obsolete and was not included in Rev. Proc. 2017-30 or its successors. Section 6.10 allowed:

- A late partial disposition election under Reg. § 1.168(i)-8(d)(2)(i) for the disposition of a portion of an asset

- A late partial disposition election under Reg. § 1.168(i)-8(d)(2)(i) for the disposition of a portion of an asset that is made pursuant to Reg. § 1.168(i)-8(d)(2)(iv)(B) (relating to the option that allows a taxpayer who chose to apply to the provisions of Reg. § 1.168(i)-8 to a tax year beginning on or after January 1, 2012 and ending on or before July 19, 2013 to file an accounting method change to make a late partial disposition election for a portion of an asset that was disposed of in a tax year beginning on or after January 1, 2012 and ending on or before July 19, 2013). This option applies only if the taxpayer filed a timely original return (including extensions) for such tax year without making a partial disposition election.

The accounting method change to make a late partial disposition election offered taxpayers the opportunity to claim retirement losses on structural components of buildings and components of section 1245 property retired in prior tax years. This accounting method change may not be made in a tax year that begins on or after January 1, 2015. For any taxpayer that previously filed an accounting method change to apply the temporary regulations and claim retirement losses through a Code Sec. 481(a) adjustment for prior tax years it was necessary to file this change to "reconfirm" those losses. Taxpayers who did not file this change to reconfirm their losses before the expiration date, must file an accounting method change that recaptures the previously claimed losses as a Code Sec. 481(a) adjustment.

*A late partial disposition election could not be filed by a qualifying small business taxpayer that did not file Form 3115 in its 2014 tax year to change methods to comply with the Code Sec. 263 repair regulations because it was covered by the Form 3115 relief provision of Rev. Proc. 2015-20.*

See detailed discussion of Sec. 6.10 of Rev. Proc. 2016-29 below.

*General Asset Accounts: Revocation of Late GAA Elections and Certain Current GAA Elections (Obsolete)*

Sec. 6.11 (Change #197) of Rev. Proc. 2016-29 allowed a taxpayer to file an accounting method change to:

- revoke a late GAA election previously made by filing an accounting method change under Sec. 6.32 of Rev. Proc. 2015-14 (Change #180) for MACRS property that was placed in service in a tax year beginning before January 1, 2012

- revoke a timely GAA election that was made for MACRS property placed in service in a tax year beginning on or after January 1, 2012, and before January 1, 2014

This accounting method change to revoke certain GAA elections may not be filed in a tax year that begins on or after January 1, 2015. It is not included in Rev. Proc. 2017-30 and its successors because it is obsolete.

A revocation should have been made where a taxpayer filed an accounting method change to make a late GAA election for a building in order to avoid a rule in the temporary regulations, which has been eliminated by the final regulations, that allowed a taxpayer to choose whether or not to recognize a gain or loss on the retirement of a structural component only if the building was placed in a GAA. Under the final regulations a taxpayer may not recognize gain or loss on the retirement of a structural component if the building is in a GAA and may choose whether or not to recognize gain or loss only if the building is outside of a GAA. A similar consideration applied where a late GAA election was made to place section 1245 property in a GAA.

See detailed discussion of Sec. 6.11 of Rev. Proc. 2016-29 below.

*Late Partial Disposition Election Following IRS Audit*

Sec. 6.10 of Rev. Proc. 2019-43 (Change #198) allows a taxpayer to:

- make a late partial disposition election if the taxpayer deducted the amount paid for the replacement of a portion of an asset as a repair, the taxpayer did not make a timely partial disposition election for the disposed portion of that asset, and the IRS later applies the rules in the repair regulations and disallows the taxpayer's repair deduction and instead capitalizes it

See detailed discussion of Sec. 6.10 below.

*Change from Depreciating Leasehold Improvement Over Lease Term*

Sec. 6.11 (Change #200) of Rev. Proc. 2019-43 apply to a taxpayer that wants to change from improperly depreciating a leasehold improvement over the term of the lease (including renewals, if applicable) to depreciating the improvement over its assigned recovery period under Code Sec. 168, Code Sec. 167, or Code Sec. 197, as applicable.

See detailed discussion of Sec. 6.11 below.

*IRS Form 3115 filing relief allowed a qualifying small business taxpayer to change to the accounting methods required by the final repair regulations under Code Secs. 162, 164, and 263 without filing Form 3115 (Rev. Proc. 2015-20, I.R.B. 2015-9, February 13, 2015). The repair regulation accounting method changes covered by this relief at the time it was issued were described in Sec. 10.11(3) of Rev. Proc. 2015-14. Theses changes were considered made on a cut-off basis. Therefore, no Code Sec. 481(a) adjustment was required or allowed with respect to amounts paid or incurred in tax years beginning before January 1, 2014. If such a taxpayer accepted this relief by not filing a Form 3115 for its for its first tax year beginning on or after January 1, 2014 and later files a Form 3115 to comply with an accounting method required by the repair regulations in Sec. 10.11(3) of Rev. Proc. 2015-14 or the corresponding section of its successors (Sec. 11.08 of Rev. Proc. 2016-29 or Sec. 10.08 of Rev. Proc. 2017-30, Rev. Proc. 2018-31, or Rev. Proc. 2019-43), the change is made and the Sec. 481 adjustment is computed on a cut-off basis that only takes into account amounts paid or incurred in tax years beginning on or after January 1, 2014.*

*If a taxpayer accepted this filing relief, it was also treated as making accounting method changes required for its first tax year beginning in 2014 under Sec. 6.37(3)(a)(iv), (v), (vii), and (viii), Sec. 6.38, and Sec. 6.39 of Rev. Proc. 2015-14 on a cut-off basis that took into account dispositions that occurred in tax years beginning before January 1, 2014 (Rev. Proc. 2015-20, Section 5, I.R.B. 2015-9, February 13, 2015). No Form 3115 was required to make these changes with respect to dispositions that took place in tax years beginning before the taxpayer's first tax year beginning on or after January 1, 2014. If a taxpayer accepted the filing relief by not filing a Form 3115 for its for its first tax year beginning on or after January 1, 2014 and later files a Form 3115 to comply with an accounting method required by Sec. 6.37(3)(a)(iv), (v), (vii), and (viii), Sec. 6.38, and Sec. 6.39 of Rev. Proc. 2015-14 or the corresponding sections of its successors (Sec. 6.14(3)(a)(iv), (v), (vii), and (viii), Sec. 6.15, and Sec. 6.16 of Rev. Proc. 2016-29 and Sec. 6.12(3)(a)(iv), (v), (vii), and (viii), Sec. 6.13, and Sec. 6.14 of Rev. Proc. 2018-31 and Rev. Proc. 2017-30), the change is made and the Code Sec. 481(a) adjustment is computed on a cut-off basis that only takes into account dispositions occurring in tax years beginning on or after January 1, 2014 (Sec. 6.12(4)(f) of Rev. Proc. 2019-43; Rev. Proc. 2018-31; and Rev. Proc. 2017-30; Sec. 6.14(4)(f) of Rev. Proc. 2016-29; Sec. 6.37(4)(f) of Rev. Proc. 2015-14, as added by Rev. Proc. 2015-20). In addition, a taxpayer who accepted the filing relief may not make a late partial disposition election under Sec. 6.33 of Rev. Proc. 2015-14 or the corresponding section of its successors for dispositions that occurred prior to the taxpayer's first tax year beginning on or after January 1, 2014.*

*Audit protection does not apply to any changes made for the 2014 tax year under the relief provision that are considered made without filing a Form 3115.*

*Permissible to Permissible Method in Grouping Assets in GAA and Pools, Identifying Disposed Assets, Computing Unadjusted Basis of Disposed Asset*

Sec. 6.12 of Rev. Proc. 2019-43 (Change #200) relate to the following changes:

- Change from single item accounts to multiple asset accounts or vice versa
- Asset grouping changes within a multiple asset or general asset account
- Changes in identifying asset disposed of from multiple asset account or general asset account
- Change in determining unadjusted depreciable basis of disposed asset or portion of disposed asset from one reasonable method to another reasonable method (for assets in item, multiple asset or general asset accounts)

Sec. 6.12 changes all relate to changes from one permissible method of accounting under the final regulations to another permissible method under the final regulations. Consequently, these are not mandatory changes required to comply with the final MACRS item/multiple asset account, general asset account, or disposition regulations.

See detailed discussion of Sec. 6.12 below.

*Buildings not in GAA: Impermissible to Permissible Method: Definition of Asset, Recognition of Gain/Loss on Previously Disposed Asset, Identification of Disposed Asset, Computation of Unadjusted Depreciable Basis of Disposed Asset*

Sec. 6.13 of Rev. Proc. 2019-43 (Change #205) provide the following changes for buildings not in a general asset account:

- Change to treating building, condo, coop, or addition or improvement, including structural components thereof, as appropriate asset for disposition purposes

  Most often this change is filed by a taxpayer that treated a building as a separate asset and its structural components as a separate asset in accordance with temporary regulations, including a taxpayer that claimed a retirement loss on a structural component that was treated as a separate asset but does not file an accounting method change under Sec. 6.10 (Change #196) to make a late partial disposition election.

• Change to recognizing gain or loss on disposed building, condo, coop, addition or improvement, or portion thereof that continues to be depreciated

Most often this change requires a taxpayer to recognize gain or loss on the disposition of a portion of a building which under the final regulations is considered disposed of without making a partial disposition election (e.g., dispositions on account of a casualty event or sale). Another example this change applies to is a lessor or lessee that continues to depreciated a retired leasehold improvement.

• Change from improper to proper method of identifying building, condo, coop, addition or improvement disposed of from multiple asset account)

The final regulations specify allowable methods to identify an asset that is disposed of from a multiple asset account. This change is required by taxpayers that are using an impermissible method.

• Change from impermissible to permissible method to determine unadjusted depreciable basis of building, condo, cooperative, or addition or improvement disposed of from a multiple asset account or a portion of such an asset disposed of from an item or multiple asset account

The final regulations require a taxpayer to use its records if practicable to determine the unadjusted depreciable basis of a disposed asset or portion, thereof. If impracticable, any reasonable method may be used. Taxpayers that previously used the consumer price index rollback method (an unreasonable method under the final regulations) will need to file this change and switch to the producer price index rollback method or some other reasonable method. See discussion below, "SECTION 6.13: DISPOSITION OF BUILDING OR STRUCTURAL COMPONENT."

• In the case of a taxpayer that revoked a general asset account election by filing a change under Sec. 6.11 of Rev. Proc. 2016-29 (Change #197) (or its predecessor) and in a tax year prior to the revocation made a qualifying disposition election under the temporary regulations (including a late qualifying disposition election) to recognize gain or loss on a building, condo, coop, or addition or improvement under the temporary regulations, a change to recognizing gain or loss under the final regulations

See detailed discussion of Sec. 6.13 below.

*Section 1245 Property and Land Improvements not in GAA: Impermissible to Permissible Method: Definition of Asset, Recognition of Gain/Loss on Previously Disposed Asset, Identification of Disposed Asset, Computation of Unadjusted Depreciable Basis of Disposed Asset*

Sec. 6.14 of Rev. Proc. 2019-43 provides for the same type of changes for section 1245 property and land improvements not in a GAA that Sec. 6.13 of Rev. Proc. 2019-43 provides for buildings that are not in a GAA (including buildings removed from a GAA).

*Buildings and Section 1245 Property in a GAA: Impermissible to Permissible Method: Definition of Asset, Identification of Disposed Asset, Computation of Unadjusted Depreciable Basis*

Sec. 6.15 of Rev. Proc. 2019-43 (Change #207) contains four accounting method changes relating to dispositions of assets from GAAs that are similar to those allowed for buildings (Sec. 6.13 of Rev. Proc. 2019-43 and section 1245 property (Sec. 6.14 of Rev. Proc. 2019-43) that are not in a GAA:

- For purposes of determining the asset disposed of from a GAA, a change from an inappropriate asset to an appropriate asset

- A change in the method of identifying which assets or portions of assets in a GAA have been disposed of from an impermissible method to a permissible method

- A change in the method of determining the unadjusted depreciable basis of a disposed asset or disposed portion of an asset in a GAA from a method not using the taxpayer's records to a method using the taxpayer's records

- A change in the method of determining the unadjusted depreciable basis of a disposed asset or the disposed portion of an asset in a GAA from an unreasonable method (for example, the Consumer Price Index rollback method) to a reasonable method such as the Producer Price Index rollback method

*Late GAA Elections and Partial Disposition Election Revocations Under the Remodel/Refresh Safe Harbor*

Taxpayers who change accounting methods to use the remodel/refresh safe harbor described in Rev. Proc. 2015-56 are required to make a late GAA election for the building and amounts that are capitalized under the safe harbor. See below, "SECTION 11.10: Late General Asset Account Election for Buildings Subject to Remodel/Refresh Safe Harbor." In addition, the method cannot be applied to past remodeling projects unless the taxpayer revokes any partial disposition elections (including late partial disposition elections) previously made with respect to the building. This revocation under the automatic procedures is now obsolete. See below, "SECTION 6.18: Revocation of Partial Disposition Elections Under Remodel Refresh Safe Harbor."

The following table is based on Sec. 6.16 of Rev. Proc. 2019-43 summarizes the automatic accounting method changes that may be filed to comply with the final MACRS tangible property regulations relating to leasehold improvements (Reg. § 1.167(a)-4), MACRS item/multiple asset accounts (Reg. § 1.168(i)-7), general asset accounts (Reg. § 1.168(i)-1), and dispositions (Reg. § 1.168(i)-8).

| FINAL REGULATION SECTION | SECTION # in Rev. Proc. 2019-43 or predecessor | DESIGNATED CHANGE NUMBER (DCN) |
|---|---|---|
| § 1.167(a)-4, Depreciation of leasehold improvements | 6.11 | 199 |
| *General Asset Accounts*: | | |
| a. § 1.168(i)-1(c), Change in grouping assets | 6.12 | 200 |
| b. § 1.168(i)-1(e)(2)(viii), Change in determining asset disposed of | 6.15 | 207 |
| c. § 1.168(i)-1(j)(2), Change in method of identifying which assets or portions of assets have been disposed of from one method to another method specified in § 1.168(i)-1(j)(2) | 6.12 | 200 |

| FINAL REGULATION SECTION | SECTION # in Rev. Proc. 2019-43 or predecessor | DESIGNATED CHANGE NUMBER (DCN) |
|---|---|---|
| d. § 1.168(i)-1(j)(2), Change in method of identifying which assets or portions of assets have been disposed of from a method not specified in § 1.168(i)-1(j)(2) to a method specified in § 1.168(i)-1(j)(2) | 6.15 | 207 |
| e. § 1.168(i)-1(j)(3), Change in determining unadjusted depreciable basis of disposed asset or disposed portion of an asset from one reasonable method to another reasonable method when it is impracticable from the taxpayer's records to determine the unadjusted depreciable basis of disposed asset or disposed portion of asset | 6.12 | 200 |
| f. § 1.168(i)-1(j)(3), Change in determining unadjusted depreciable basis of disposed asset or disposed portion of an asset from not using to using the taxpayer's records when it is practicable from the taxpayer's records to determine the unadjusted depreciable basis of disposed asset or disposed portion of asset | 6.15 | 207 |
| g. § 1.168(i)-1(j)(3), Change in determining unadjusted depreciable basis of disposed asset or disposed portion of an asset from an unreasonable method to a reasonable method when it is impracticable from the taxpayer's records to determine the unadjusted depreciable basis of disposed asset or disposed portion of asset | 6.15 | 207 |
| *Single Asset Accounts or Multiple Asset Accounts for MACRS Property*: | | |
| a. § 1.168(i)-7, Change from single asset accounts to multiple asset accounts, or *vice versa* | 6.12 | 200 |
| b. § 1.168(i)-7(c), Change in grouping assets in multiple asset accounts | 6.12 | 200 |
| *Dispositions of MACRS Property (not in a general asset account)*: | | |
| a. § 1.168(i)-8(c)(4), Change in determining asset disposed of | 6.13 (Building or structural component)<br>6.14 (Property other than a building or structural component) | 205<br>206 |

| FINAL REGULATION SECTION | SECTION # in Rev. Proc. 2019-43 or predecessor | DESIGNATED CHANGE NUMBER (DCN) |
|---|---|---|
| b. § 1.168(i)-8(f)(2) or (3), Change in determining unadjusted depreciable basis of disposed asset in a multiple asset account or disposed portion of an asset from one reasonable method to another reasonable method when it is impracticable from the taxpayer's records to determine the unadjusted depreciable basis of disposed asset or disposed portion of asset | 6.12 | 200 |
| c. § 1.168(i)-8(f)(2) or (3), Change in determining unadjusted depreciable basis of disposed asset in a multiple asset account or disposed portion of an asset from not using to using the taxpayer's records when it is practicable from the taxpayer's records to determine the unadjusted depreciable basis of disposed asset or disposed portion of asset | 6.13 (Building or structural component) | 205 |
| | 6.14 (Property other than a building or structural component) | 206 |
| d. § 1.168(i)-8(f)(2) or (3), Change in determining unadjusted depreciable basis of disposed asset in a multiple asset account or disposed portion of an asset from an unreasonable method to a reasonable method when it is impracticable from the taxpayer's records to determine the unadjusted depreciable basis of disposed asset or disposed portion of asset | 6.13 (Building or structural component) | 205 |
| | 6.14 (Property other than a building or structural component) | 206 |
| e. § 1.168(i)-8(g), Change in method of identifying which assets in a multiple asset account or portions of assets have been disposed of from one method to another method specified in § 1.168(i)-8(g)(1) or (2) | 6.12 | 200 |
| f. § 1.168(i)-8(g), Change in method of identifying which assets in a multiple asset account or portions of assets have been disposed of from a method not specified in § 1.168(i)-8(g)(1) or (2) to a method specified in § 1.168(i)-8(g)(1) or (2) | 6.13 (Building or structural component) | 205 |
| | 6.14 (Property other than a building or structural component) | 206 |

| FINAL REGULATION SECTION | SECTION # in Rev. Proc. 2019-43 or predecessor | DESIGNATED CHANGE NUMBER (DCN) |
|---|---|---|
| g. § 1.168(i)-8(h)(1), Change from depreciating a disposed asset or disposed portion of an asset to recognizing gain or loss upon disposition when a taxpayer continues to depreciate the asset or portion that the taxpayer disposed of prior to the year of change | 6.13 (Building or structural component) | 205 |
| | 6.14 (Property other than a building or structural component) | 206 |
| h. § 1.168(i)-8(d)(2)(iii), Partial disposition election for the disposition of a portion of an asset to which the IRS's adjustment pertains | 6.10 | 198 |

(2) *Late elections or revocation of a general asset account election.* The following chart summarizes the late partial disposition election allowed under Rev. Proc. 2016-20 that was treated as a change in method of accounting for a limited period of time. The chart includes the revocation of a general asset account election that was also treated as a change in method of accounting for a limited period of time.

| ELECTION OR REVOCATION | TIME PERIOD FOR TREATING ELECTION OR REVOCATION AS A METHOD CHANGE | SECTION # IN REV. PROC. 2016-29, AND DCN |
|---|---|---|
| *General Asset Accounts*: | | |
| a. Revocation of a general asset account election made under § 1.168(i)-1, Prop. Reg. § 1.168(i)-1, or § 1.168(1)-1T, or made under section 6.32 in the APPENDIX of Rev. Proc. 2011-14 or section 6.32 in Rev. Proc. 2015-14, as applicable | Taxable year beginning on or after 1/1/2012 and beginning before 1/1/2015 | 6.11<br>DCN 197 |
| *Late Partial Disposition Election for MACRS Property (not in a general asset account)*: | | |
| a. Late partial disposition election made under § 1.168(i)-8(d)(2)(iv)(B) | First or second taxable succeeding the applicable taxable year as defined in § 1.168(i)-8(d)(2)(iv) | 6.10<br>DCN 196 |
| b. Other late partial disposition elections made under § 1.168(i)-8(d)(2)(i) | Taxable year beginning on or after 1/1/2012 and beginning before 1/1/2015 | 6.10<br>DCN 196 |

**SECTION 6.10 of Rev. Proc. 2016-29: LATE PARTIAL DISPOSITION ELECTION (Obsolete)**

*Unless, indicated otherwise references to Section 6 in this discussion of the late partial disposition election are to Section 6 of Rev. Proc. 2016-29.*

Sec. 6.10 of Rev. Proc. 2016-29 provided the following optional accounting method changes to make late partial disposition elections under the final regulations:

- A late partial disposition election under Reg. § 1.168(i)-8(d)(2)(i) for the disposition of a portion of an asset that was disposed of in a tax year that begins before January 1, 2014 (Sec. 6.10(1)(a)). This change had to be filed no later than a taxpayer's last tax year beginning in 2014.

• A late partial disposition election under Reg. § 1.168(i)-8(d)(2)(i) for the disposition of a portion of an asset that is made pursuant to Reg. § 1.168(i)-8(d)(2)(iv)(B). This change was allowed for a taxpayer who applied final Reg. § 1.168(i)-8 in a tax year beginning on or after January 1, 2012 and ending on or before July 19, 2013 and filed a timely (including extensions) original return without making the partial disposition election that occurred during the tax year that began on or after January 1, 2012 and ended on or before July 19, 2013. (Sec. 6.10(1)(a)).

These changes did not apply unless the taxpayer owned the asset of which the partial disposition was a part at the beginning of the tax year of change (Sec. 6.10(1)(b)(i)).

*Methods of computing retirement losses.* See ¶ 162 for a discussion of the methods allowed by the IRS for computing retirement losses on partial dispositions of assets when a partial disposition election is made. The IRS has ruled that a taxpayer making a late partial disposition election incorrectly applied a statistical sampling technique to determine losses on pre-2012 partial dispositions (Field Attorney Advice 20154601F, November 13, 2015).

*A late partial disposition election could not be filed by a qualifying small business taxpayer that did not file Form 3115 for its 2014 tax year to change methods to comply with the Code Sec. 263 repair regulations if it took advantage of the filing relief provision of Rev. Proc. 2015-20.*

*Deadline for filing late partial disposition election.* The accounting method change to make a late partial disposition election under Reg. § 1.168(i)-8(d)(2)(i) could have been made for any tax year beginning on or after January 1, 2012 and beginning before January 1, 2015 provided the change was filed with the original income tax return for the tax year of change by the extended due date of the income tax return. Consequently, a calendar-year taxpayer had to file this change no later than for the 2014 calendar tax year with respect to partial dispositions that took place prior to the year of change.

A Sec. 6.10(1)(a) change made under Reg. § 1.168(i)-8(d)(2)(iv)(B) for dispositions that occurred in a tax year beginning on or after January 1, 2012 and ending on or before July 19, 2013 had to be made for the first or second tax year following the tax year of disposition (Sec. 6.10(3)(b)). It was also possible to file an amended return to make a late partial disposition election for these partial dispositions. The amended return for the applicable tax year (tax year of disposition) was required to be filed on or before 180 days from the due date, including extensions, of the taxpayer's return for the applicable tax year, notwithstanding that the taxpayer may not have extended the due date (Reg. § 1.168(i)-8(d)(2)(iv)(A)).

*Certain eligibility rules inapplicable.* The eligibility limitations of Section 5.01(d) and (f) of Rev. Proc. 2015-13, which prevent a taxpayer from filing a method change in the last year of the trade or business or filing a method change for the same specific item during any of the five tax years ending with the year of change was inapplicable (Sec. 6.10(4)). Consequently, a taxpayer that previously filed this change (e.g., under the proposed or final regulations for the 2013 tax year), could file the change for the 2014 tax year to make partial disposition elections for additional assets.

*Who should have made this change.* This change should have been filed by taxpayers who wished to claim retirement losses on partial dispositions that occurred prior to the year of the method change.

This change should also have been filed by taxpayers that previously filed an accounting method change for a 2012 or 2013 tax year to recognize retirement losses for partial dispositions that occurred in an earlier tax year by applying the disposition rules that applied under the temporary regulations (see ¶ 162). Taxpayers that filed an accounting method change for a 2012 or 2013 tax year to make a late general asset account election for buildings or other assets placed in service before the 2012 tax year and a concurrent change to make a qualifying disposition election to claim retirement losses on previously retired components of the building or asset for which the late GAA election was made were required to file a method change to revoke the GAA election (Sec. 6.11 of Rev. Proc. 2016-29) and a late partial disposition election (Sec. 6.10 of Rev. Proc. 2016-29) if they wanted to preserve those losses. The deadline for revoking a GAA and making a late partial disposition election was for the taxpayer's last tax year beginning before January 1, 2015. See ¶ 128. A taxpayer that claimed a retirement loss on a portion of an asset under the temporary regulations (including retirements from a GAA as the result of a qualifying disposition election) and did not make these changes is required to file an accounting method change (Sec. 6.13 (non-GAA) or Sec. 6.15 (GAA) of Rev. Proc. 2019-43) to restore the loss.

***Example 2:*** A December 1 - November 30 taxpayer placed a building in service in 2000 and replaced the roof in 2010. In 2012 it applied the disposition rules under the temporary regulations and filed a Form 3115 to claim a loss equal to the $10,000 adjusted depreciable basis (remaining basis after prior years' depreciation) of the retired roof by filing accounting method changes to treat the building as an asset and each structural component of the building as a separate asset for disposition purposes (Sec. 6.29(3)(a) of Appendix of Rev. Proc. 2011-14 as added by Rev. Proc. 2012-20) and to change from depreciating the original roof to recognizing a loss upon its retirement (Sec. 6.29(3)(b) of Appendix of Rev. Proc. 2011-14, as added by Rev. Proc. 2012-20). In order to preserve this loss, for no later than its December 1, 2014 - November 30, 2015 tax year, the taxpayer must file Form 3115 and make a late partial disposition election (Sec. 6.10(1)(a) of Rev. Proc. 2016-29 (Change #196)), and treat for disposition purposes the original building and original roof (and all other original structural component of the building) as a separate asset and the replacement roof as a separate asset (Sec. 6.10(3)(b)(iii) of Rev. Proc. 2016-29), and recognize a loss upon the retirement of the original roof under Reg. § 1.168(i)-8 (Sec. 6.10(3)(b)(iii) of Rev. Proc. 2016-29). The Code Sec. 481(a) adjustment is $0 (the $10,000 loss claimed in 2012 reduced by the $10,000 loss that could have been claimed under the partial disposition rule under Reg. § 1.168(i)-8 in 2012 (Sec. 6.10(7)(b) of Rev. Proc. 2016-29, Example 2)).

If the taxpayer in the preceding example does not make the late partial disposition election for 2014, then it should have filed an accounting method change for 2014 under Sec. 6.15 to change its definition of the asset as the building including its structural components (Change #205), and report a positive Code Sec. 481(a) adjustment.

Specifically, although Sec. 6.15(3)(a) (Change #205) provides changes relating to the definition of an asset in the context of a building, dispositions that require a partial disposition election to recognize gain or loss are specifically excluded from the ambit of any change described in Sec. 6.15 (6.15(1)(b)(iv)). No concurrent Sec. 6.10 and Sec. 6.15 changes are listed in either Sec. 6.10 or Sec. 6.15. The change in asset definition and recognition of loss are included in the #196 filing. Nevertheless, as part of the late partial disposition Sec. 6.10(1)(a) (Change #196) filing documentation the taxpayer should specifically indicate that it is changing the definition of its asset (pursuant to Sec. 6.10(65)(b)(iii) and recognizing loss pursuant to Sec. 6.10(5)(b)(v)).

*Code Sec. 481(a) adjustment.* A taxpayer making any change described in Sec. 6.10 (Change #196) for more than one asset for the same tax year had to file a single Form 3115 for all assets. The taxpayer may compute a single net Code Sec. 481(a) adjustment for the 6.10(1)(a) method change by combining all negative and positive adjustments or net all negative adjustments separately. Alternatively, all negative adjustments may be added and reported as a single negative adjustment and all positive adjustments may be added and reported as a single positive adjustment. This option should be considered in connection with the rule which requires favorable (negative) adjustments to be reported in one year and positive (unfavorable adjustments) to be reported over four years. Note that a taxpayer could also elect to report a net positive (unfavorable) adjustment of less than $50,000 in a single year (Sec. 6.10(6)(b) of Rev. Proc. 2016-29). See ¶ 75.

*Concurrent filings.* A taxpayer that filed any change under Sec. 6.10(1) was required to include the following changes on the same Form 3115 if any of these changes was also made for the same tax year:

- Sec. 6.01 — Certain impermissible to permissible depreciation method changes
- Sec. 6.11 — Revocation of GAA election

*Public utilities.* Special filing rules apply to public utility property as defined in Code Sec. 168(i)(10) (Sec. 6.10(5)(b)(vi)).

*Streamlined Form 3115 filing.* Taxpayers with average annual gross receipts less than or equal to $10 million in the three tax years preceding the year of change qualify for simplified Form 3115 filing (Sec. 6.10(5)(a)).

*Covington filing of copy.* Taxpayers making this change filed a signed copy with IRS in Covington, Kentucky (Form 3115 Instructions).

**SECTION 6.11: REVOCATION OF GENERAL ASSET ACCOUNT ELECTION (Obsolete)**

*References to section 6 in this discussion of GAA revocations are to section 6 of Rev. Proc. 2016-29 unless otherwise indicated.*

Sec. 6.11 (Change #197) of Rev. Proc. 2016-29 allowed a taxpayer to file an accounting method change to:

- revoke a late GAA election made by filing an accounting method change under Sec. 6.32(1)(a)(i) of Rev. Proc. 2015-14 or the Appendix to Rev. Proc. 2011-14 (Change #180) for MACRS property that was placed in service in a tax year beginning before January 1, 2012 (Sec. 6.11(1)(a)(i))
- revoke a timely GAA election that was made for MACRS property placed in service in a tax year beginning on or after January 1, 2012, and before January 1, 2014 (Sec. 6.11(1)(a)(ii))

Some taxpayers may have made a timely GAA election for assets placed in service in a 2011 tax year in reliance on the GAA rules in Temp. Reg. 1.168(i)-1. Although it appears to be an oversight on the part of the IRS, these elections may not be revoked under Sec. 6.11. Note also that a taxpayer may not revoke previous timely GAA elections that were made for assets placed in service in a tax year beginning before 2012.

The change to revoke a GAA election only applies to the accounting method change to make a late election to place an asset placed in service in a tax year beginning on or before January 1, 2012 in a GAA or the timely GAA election for assets placed in service in the 2012 or 2013 tax year. The change does not specifically apply to any related late election allowed under 6.32(1)(a) of Rev. Proc. 2015-14 or the Appendix to Rev. Proc. 2011-14, for example, a late election to terminate a GAA upon the disposition of the last asset or the late qualifying disposition election (Sec. 6.32(1)(a)(ii) - (v)).

The revocation may be made for one or more GAA accounts. It does not need to be made for all accounts that qualify for revocation.

*Deadline for revoking election.* The revocation must be made for a tax year that begins on or after January 1, 2012 and begins before January 1, 2015 (Sec. 6.11(2)). Consequently, a calendar-year taxpayer had until the extended due date of its 2014 return to file Form 3115 to make a revocation effective for the 2014 tax year. If the revocation was not timely made, the GAA election will stand.

*Eligibility rules inapplicable.* The eligibility limitations of Section 5.01(d) and (f) of Rev. Proc. 2015-13, which prevent a taxpayer from filing a change in the last year of the trade or business or filing a change for the same specific item during any of the five tax years ending with the year of change, are inapplicable (Sec. 6.11(3)). Consequently, for example, a taxpayer may file more than one change under Sec. 6.11 to revoke a GAA election prior to the deadline (e.g., file a Form 3115 for 2013 revoking certain elections and another Form 3115 for 2014 revoking other elections).

*Ownership of property not required.* Sec. 6.11 does not require a taxpayer to own the property at the beginning of the tax year for which the accounting method change to revoke the election is made.

*Examples.* Sec. 6.11 illustrates the #197 changes with the following examples.

***Example 3:*** *GAA Election Revoked; No Dispositions.* A December 1 through November 30 fiscal-year taxpayer made a current GAA election for its tax year ending November 30, 2013 (the 2012 tax year) and placed a group of assets into the GAA account. None of the assets were disposed of during the 2012 tax year. Because of the change in the definition of a qualifying disposition made by the final regulations and the addition of the partial disposition election added by the final regulations, the taxpayer wants to revoke the GAA election. The taxpayer may revoke the GAA election by filing a #197 accounting method change for its 2014 tax year and include the assets in a single multiple asset account. No Code Sec. 481(a) adjustment is made because the adjusted depreciable basis of the assets does not change as a result of the revocation and transfer of the assets to the multiple asset account (Sec. 6.11(7)(a), Ex. 1).

***Example 4:*** *GAA Election Revoked; Loss on Qualifying Disposition Confirmed.*

A December 1 through November 30 fiscal-year taxpayer purchased three trucks in May of 2012 and sold one of the trucks, which cost $20,000, for $12,000 in June 2013 of its 2012 tax year. The other two trucks cost $30,000 each.

For the tax year ending November 30, 2013 (the 2012 tax year) the taxpayer files an accounting method change (Change #180) to make a late GAA election to place the three trucks in a single GAA. The truck that was sold may be placed in the GAA because it was owned at the beginning of the tax year for which the late election was made. Under the temporary regulations the sale of the truck was a qualifying disposition and the taxpayer elected to remove the truck from the GAA and claim an $800 loss deduction $12,000 sales proceeds less $12,800 adjusted depreciable basis for the truck ($20,000 cost less $7,200 depreciation for 2011 and 2012 tax years) under Temp. Reg. Sec. 1.168(i)-8T (the loss is recognized as a result of the sale under this provision since the truck is no longer in the GAA as a result of the qualifying disposition election). Note that it was not necessary to file an additional accounting method change to make a late qualifying disposition election (Change #180) because the disposition took place in the 2012 tax year and the election was timely made on the 2012 return. Nor was it necessary to file an accounting method change to recognize the loss in the 2012 tax year under Temp. Reg. Sec. 1.168(i)-8T.

The taxpayer decides to apply the final regulations to its 2014 tax year and revoke the late GAA election because a sales transaction is no longer a qualifying disposition under Reg. § 1.168(i)-1(e)(3)(iii)(B), which must be applied for the 2014 tax year to prior year dispositions.

As a result, the taxpayer files Form 3115 with its 2014 tax year return making a #197 change under Sec. 6.11(1)(a)(i) to revoke the general asset account for the three trucks and include the two unsold trucks in one multiple asset account in accordance with Reg. § 1.168(i)-7, and a concurrent #206 change under Sec. 6.16(3)(k) to recognize the loss of $800 upon the sale of the truck in the 2012 tax year under Reg. § 1.168(i)-8. There is no Code Sec. 481(a) adjustment because the loss that was allowed on the truck in the 2012 tax year under Temporary Reg. § 1.168(i)-8T ($800) is the same as the loss that would have been allowed in the 2012 tax year under Reg. § 1.168(i)-8 ($800) (Sec. 6.11(7)(b), Ex. 2).

In the preceding example, it is not necessary to place the two remaining trucks in a multiple asset account. They may each be placed in an item account. See Sec. 6.11(5)(b)(ii). There is no specific accounting method change for placing the trucks in a multiple asset account or item accounts in this situation. It appears that this requirement is simply an action that must be taken pursuant to Sec. 6.11(5)(b)(ii) if the #197 revocation is filed. However, it is advisable to specifically indicate on the Form 3115 whether the trucks are placed in item accounts or multiple assets accounts and to provide the additional information, specified in Sec. 6.11(5)(b)(ii), regarding beginning balance for unadjusted depreciable basis and depreciation reserve for the each item or multiple asset account. See, *"Manner of making change."*

The Sec. 6.16(3)(k) #206 accounting method change referred to in the example is a change from recognizing gain or loss under Temp. Reg. § 1.168(i)-8T upon the disposition of section 1245 property that was in a GAA where the taxpayer made a qualifying disposition election under the Temp. Reg. 1.168(i)-1T(e)(3)(iii) and the taxpayer files an accounting method change (Sec. 6.11(a)(1)(i) or (ii)) to revoke the GAA election. If this change is made, the taxpayer recognizes gain or loss under Reg. § 1.168(i)-8 instead of Temp. Reg. Sec. 1.168(i)-8T.

A #197 accounting method change to revoke a GAA election and #206 change should be filed concurrently on a single Form 3115.

In the preceding example it is not necessary to file an accounting method change to make a late partial disposition election (Sec. 6.11(1)(a), Change #197) to preserve the loss on the disposed truck because the truck is an entire asset. A partial disposition election would only be necessary if a portion of the truck was disposed of.

***Example 5:*** *Late GAA Election Revoked; Loss on Structural Component Subject to Late Qualifying Disposition Election Recaptured.* A December 1 through November 30 fiscal-year taxpayer placed a building in service in 2000 and replaced the roof in 2010. The taxpayer claimed no loss on the old roof and continued to depreciate the old roof in accordance with the then applicable rules. For the 2012 tax year the taxpayer applied the temporary regulations and filed change #180 on a Form 3115 to make a late GAA election to include the building in one GAA and the replacement roof in another GAA. The taxpayer also filed a concurrent accounting method change to make a late election on the Form 3115 to treat the disposition of the old roof as a qualifying disposition under the temporary regulations (Change #180). The old roof was removed from the GAA and a negative (favorable) $10,000 Code Sec. 481(a) adjustment equal to the adjusted depreciable basis of the roof as of the end of the 2011 tax year was reported on the 2012 tax year return.

For the 2014 tax year, the taxpayer files an accounting method change to revoke the GAA election for the building and for the replacement roof (Sec. 6.11(1)(a)(i), Change #197) and files a change to treat the building, including its structural components and the original roof, as a separate asset and the replacement roof as a separate asset using the method change for redefining an asset that is not in a GAA (Sec. 6.15(3)(a), Change #205).

Since the taxpayer does not file an accounting method change to make a late partial disposition election (Sec. 6.11(1)(a), Change #197) to preserve the loss that it previously claimed in 2012, the loss is recaptured as a Sec. 481(a) adjustment.

If the depreciation that could have been claimed on the $10,000 loss amount in the 2012 and 2013 tax years is $1,000, then the net positive Code Sec. 481(a) adjustment included in income for the 2014 tax year is $9,000 ($10,000 – $1,000) (Sec. 6.11(7)(c), Ex 3).

The #197 and #205 changes are filed concurrently on a single Form 3115 (Sec. 6.15(10)(c)).

If the taxpayer does not revoke the GAA election and does not make a late partial disposition election, it must redefine the building and structural components as a single asset in the 2014 tax year using the method change for redefining an asset that remains in a GAA (Sec. 6.17(3)(a), Change #207) and also recapture the earlier claimed loss as a section 481(a) adjustment. See *Sec. 6.17(6)(c), Example.*

Under the temporary regulations, which the taxpayer in Example 5 applied, each structural component is treated as a separate asset for disposition purposes whether the asset is in or outside of a GAA. Under the final regulations the asset is the entire building including its structural components. Sec. 6.15(3)(a) (Change #205) provides a method change to the appropriate asset for disposition purposes for assets that are not in a GAA. The revocation of the GAA results in the assets no longer being in the GAA. For assets that are in a GAA and are not properly defined, an accounting method change is provided in Sec. 6.17(a) (Change #207). An accounting method change wasn't necessary in Example 4 to redefine the asset because each truck was correctly treated as the asset for disposition purposes.

*Code Sec. 481(a) adjustment.* A taxpayer making a Sec. 6.11(a)(1) method change to revoke a GAA must take the entire Code Sec. 481(a) adjustment into account in the year of change (Sec. 6.11(4)).

*Manner of making change.* A taxpayer must attach to its Form 3115 a statement with a description of the asset(s) to which this change applies (for example, all general asset accounts established pursuant to a Form 3115 filed under Sec. 6.32(1)(a)(i) of Rev. Proc. 2011-14 for the year of change beginning December 1, 2012 (for a change to revoke an election for pre-2012 assets pursuant 6.11(1)(a)(i)); one desk costing $2,000 in 2012 General Asset Account #1 (for a change to revoke a current election pursuant to Sec. 6.11(1)(a)(ii) (Sec. 6.11(5)(b)(i))).

The asset(s) that were in the general asset account(s) at the end of the tax year immediately preceding the year of change must be placed in a single asset account or a multiple asset account. The single asset account or the multiple asset account must include a beginning balance for both the unadjusted depreciable basis and the depreciation reserve (Sec. 6.11(5)(b)(ii)).

For a single asset account, the beginning balance for the unadjusted depreciable basis is equal to the unadjusted depreciable basis as of the beginning of the year of change for the asset included in the single asset account and the beginning balance of the depreciation reserve of that single asset account is the greater of the depreciation allowed or allowable as of the beginning of the year of change for the asset included in that single asset account (Sec. 6.11(5)(b)(ii)).

For a multiple asset account, the beginning balance for the unadjusted depreciable basis is equal to the sum of the unadjusted depreciable bases as of the beginning of the year of change for all assets included in the multiple asset account and the beginning balance of the depreciation reserve is equal to the sum of the greater of the depreciation allowed or allowable as of the beginning of the year of change for all assets included in that multiple asset account (Sec. 6.11(5)(b)(ii)).

*Public utility property.* Special rules apply to public utility property as defined in Code Sec. 168(i)(10) (Sec. 6.11(5)(b)(iii)).

*Concurrent filings required.* A taxpayer making any Sec. 6.11(1)(a) change to revoke a GAA account for more than one asset for the same tax year of change must file a single Form 3115 for all assets and compute a single net Code Sec. 481(a) adjustment that is taken into account in a single year (Sec. 6.11(6)(a); Sec. 6.11(4)). A taxpayer that files any change under Sec. 6.11(1)(a) under the final regulations should include the following changes on the same Form 3115 if any of these changes are also made for the same tax year and the change is made for a tax year beginning on or after January 1, 2012 and beginning before January 1, 2015 (Sec. 6.11(6)(b)):

- Sec. 6.01 — Certain impermissible to permissible depreciation method changes
- Sec. 6.10 — Late partial disposition election
- Sec. 6.15 — Disposition of building or structural component not in GAA
- Sec. 6.16 — Disposition of section 1245 property or land improvement not in GAA

Similar concurrent filing requirements apply to revocations made under the temporary or proposed regulations for tax years beginning on or after January 1, 2012 and before January 1, 2014 (Sec. 6.11(6)(c)).

*Streamlined Form 3115 filing.* Taxpayers with average annual gross receipts less than or equal to $10 million in the three tax years preceding the year of change qualify for simplified Form 3115 filing (Sec. 6.11(5)(a)).

*Covington filing.* Taxpayers making this change file a signed copy with IRS in Covington, Kentucky (Form 3115 Instructions).

**SECTION 6.10: LATE PARTIAL DISPOSITION ELECTION - IRS AUDIT**

*References to section 6 in this discussion are to section 6 in Rev. Proc. 2019-43 and its predecessors.*

Sec. 6.10 (Change #198) allows a taxpayer to:

- make a late partial disposition election by filing an accounting method change if the taxpayer deducted the amount paid or incurred for the replacement of a portion of an asset as a repair, the taxpayer did not make a timely partial disposition election for the disposed portion of that asset, and as a result of a subsequent examination of the taxpayer's Federal tax return, the IRS disallows the taxpayer's repair deduction for the amount paid or incurred for the replacement of the portion of that asset and instead capitalizes the amount deducted pursuant to Reg. § 1.263(a)-2 or Reg. § 1.263(a)-3 (the repair regulations). This late election is described in Reg. § 1.168(i)-8(d)(2)(iii).

*Ownership of asset required.* The taxpayer must still own the asset with respect to which the disposed portion was a part at the beginning of the tax year of change (Sec. 6.10(1)(b)(i)).

*Who should make this change.* A taxpayer that claims a loss by making a partial disposition election for a portion of an asset (Reg. § 1.168(i)-8(d)(2)) is required under the repair regulations to capitalize the replacement costs as a restoration even if the replacement costs would otherwise be a currently deductible repair (Reg. § 1.263(a)-3(k)(1)(ii)). In most cases the tax benefit of claiming a repair expense is greater than the tax benefit of a loss deduction on the retired component. Accordingly, if a taxpayer foregoes a loss deduction in order to avoid the rule foreclosing the treatment of an expenditure as a repair and the IRS on audit determines that the expenditures must be capitalized (e.g., as a betterment) the taxpayer will have lost the chance to make a partial disposition election because the election was not timely made. This accounting method change gives such taxpayers a second chance to make the election.

Additional terms and conditions apply if the asset is public utility property as defined in Code Sec. 168(i)(10) (Sec. 6.10(4)(b)(v)).

*Deadline for making the change.* Sec. 6.10 and Reg. § 1.168(i)-8(d)(2)(iii) do not impose a deadline for making this change once the IRS capitalizes the previously deducted repair. Taxpayers are advised to make the change as soon as practicable following the IRS's capitalization of the previously deducted repair expense.

*Eligibility rules inapplicable.* The eligibility limitations of Section 5.01(d) and (f) of Rev. Proc. 2015-13, which prevent a taxpayer from filing a change in the last year of the trade or business or filing a change for the same specific item during any of the five tax years ending with the year of change are inapplicable (Sec. 6.10(3)).

*Manner of making change.* If this change is made a taxpayer will stop depreciating the disposed portion of the asset for which the late election is made and compute gain or loss which is reported as part of the Code Sec. 481(a) adjustment, as explained below. Stopping depreciation, correctly identifying the asset of which the partial disposition is a part, and recognizing gain or loss is done as part of the Sec. 6.10 change and not as a separate or concurrent accounting method change (Sec. 6.10(4)(b)(i)-(iv)). The taxpayer should specifically state the correct identification of the asset under Reg. § 1.168(i)-8(c)(4) (or state that its identification is correct) and a statement that depreciation is being stopped on its Form 3115. The loss is reported as a negative (favorable) Code Sec. 481(a) adjustment.

If the asset of which the disposed portion is a part is included in one of the asset classes 00.11 through 00.4 of Rev. Proc. 87-56, the replacement portion of the asset must be classified in the same asset class as the disposed portion (Sec. 6.10(4)(b)(ii)).

*Code Sec. 481(a) adjustment.* The computation of a Code Section 481(a) adjustment is required (Sec. 6.10(5)). The adjustment is equal to the amount of loss that could have been claimed if the partial disposition election was timely made reduced by the amount of depreciation that was claimed on the loss amount prior to the year of the accounting method change. This change is separate from the change which the auditor makes with respect to the erroneously deducted repair expense.

A taxpayer making any change described in Sec. 6.10 for more than one asset for the same tax year must file a single Form 3115 for all assets. The taxpayer may compute a single net Code Sec. 481(a) adjustment for all of the changes by combining all negative and positive adjustments. Alternatively, all negative adjustments may be added and reported as a single negative adjustment and all positive adjustments may be added and reported as a single positive adjustment. This option should be considered in connection with the rule which requires favorable (negative) adjustments to be reported in one year and positive (unfavorable adjustments) to be reported over four years (Sec. 6.10(5)). Note that a taxpayer may also elect to report a net positive (unfavorable) adjustment of less than $50,000 in a single year (Sec. 7.03(c) of Rev. Proc. 2015-13). See ¶ 75.

*Concurrent filings.* No concurrent filings with other types of accounting method changes are provided in Sec. 6.10.

*Streamlined Form 3115 filing.* Taxpayers with average annual gross receipts less than or equal to $10 million in the three tax years preceding the year of change qualify for simplified Form 3115 filing (Sec. 6.10(4)(a)).

*Covington filing of copy.* Taxpayers making this change file a signed copy with the IRS in Covington, Kentucky (Form 3115 Instructions).

## SECTION 6.11: LEASEHOLD IMPROVEMENTS - CHANGE FROM IMPROPERLY DEPRECIATING OVER TERM OF LEASE

*References to section 6 in this discussion are to section 6 in Rev. Proc. 2019-43 and its predecessors.*

Sec. 6.11 (Change #200) applies to a taxpayer that wants to change its method of accounting to comply with Reg. § 1.167(a)-4 for leasehold improvements in which the taxpayer has a depreciable interest at the beginning of the year of change:

- From improperly depreciating the leasehold improvements to which Code Sec. 168 applies over the term of the lease (including renewals, if applicable) to properly depreciating these improvements under Code Sec. 168 (Sec. 6.11(1)(a))
- From improperly amortizing leasehold improvements to which Code Sec. 197 applies over the term of the lease (including renewals, if applicable) to properly amortizing these improvements under Code Sec. 197 over 15 years (Sec. 6.11(1)(b))
- From improperly amortizing leasehold improvements to which Code Sec. 167(f)(1) applies (relating to computer software) over the term of the lease (including renewals, if applicable) to properly amortizing these improvements under Code Sec. 167(f)(1) (Sec. 6.11(1)(c)).

*Who should make this change.* Capital expenditures made by either a lessee or lessor for the erection of a building or for other permanent improvements on leased property are recovered by the lessee or lessor under the provisions of the Internal Revenue Code applicable to the cost recovery of the building or improvements, if subject to depreciation or amortization, without regard to the period of the lease. For example, if the building or improvement is property to which MACRS applies, the lessee or lessor determines the depreciation deduction for the building or improvement under MACRS (Code Sec. 168(i)(8)(A)). If the improvement is property to which Code Sec. 167 or Code Sec. 197 applies, the lessee or lessor determines the depreciation or amortization deduction for the improvement under Code Sec. 167 or Code Sec. 197, as applicable (Reg. § 1.167(a)-4). Some taxpayers, however, incorrectly depreciate leasehold improvements over the term of the lease. The accounting method change allowed by Sec. 6.11 (Change #200) is used by lessors or lessees to correct this situation.

*Code Sec. 481(a) adjustment.* A taxpayer making any change described in Sec. 6.11(1) for more than one asset for the same tax year must file a single Form 3115 for all assets. The taxpayer may compute a single net Code Sec. 481(a) adjustment for the 6.11(1) changes by combining all negative and positive adjustments. Alternatively, all negative adjustments may be added and reported as a single negative adjustment and all positive adjustments may be added and reported as a single positive adjustment (Sec. 6.11(4)(a)). This option should be considered in connection with the rule which requires favorable (negative) adjustments to be reported in one year and positive (unfavorable adjustments) to be reported over four years. Note that a taxpayer may also elect to report a net positive (unfavorable) adjustment of less than $50,000 in a single year (Sec. 7.03(c) of Rev. Proc. 2015-13).

*Public utilities.* Special filing rules apply to public utility property as defined in Code Sec. 168(i)(10) (Sec. 6.11(3)(b)).

*Concurrent filing.* A taxpayer that makes a change described in Sec. 6.11(1) and a change to a UNICAP method under Secs. 12.01, 12.02, 12.08, or 12.12 for the same tax year should file a single Form 3115 for all such changes (Sec. 6.11(4)(b)).

*Streamlined Form 3115 filing.* Taxpayers with average annual gross receipts less than or equal to $10 million in the three tax years preceding the year of change qualify for simplified Form 3115 filing (Sec. 6.11(3)(a)).

*Eligibility rules inapplicable.* The eligibility limitation of Section 5.01(d) of Rev. Proc. 2015-13, which prevent a taxpayer from filing a change in the last year of the trade or business is inapplicable. The eligibility limitation of Section 5.01(f) of Rev. Proc. 2015-13, which prevent a taxpayer from filing a change for the same specific item during any of the five tax year ending with the year of change does not apply to a taxpayer making this change for any tax year beginning on or after January 1, 2012 and before January 1, 2016 (Sec. 6.11(2) of Rev. Proc. 2017-30. The Section 5.01(f) waiver does not apply to changes filed under Rev. Proc. 2018-31 or Rev. Proc. 2019-43.

*Covington copy.* Taxpayers making this change file a signed copy with IRS in Covington, Kentucky (Form 3115 Instructions).

## SECTION 6.12: PERMISSIBLE TO PERMISSIBLE METHOD CHANGES FOR MACRS ITEM, MULTIPLE ASSET, AND GAA ACCOUNTS; GROUPING, ASSET IDENTIFICATION, AND COMPUTATION OF UNADJUSTED BASIS

*References to Section 6 in this discussion are to Section 6 of Rev. Proc. 2019-43 in and its predecessors unless otherwise stated.*

Sec. 6.12 (Change #200) lists more specific accounting method changes than any other section. These changes, however, all relate to changes from one permissible method of accounting under the final regulations to another permissible method under the final regulations. Consequently, these are not mandatory changes required to comply with the final MACRS item/multiple asset account, general asset account, or disposition regulations and would not ordinarily need to be filed for the 2014 tax year in which taxpayers must first apply the related final MACRS regulations. Changes from impermissible methods to permissible methods described below are generally covered in other sections of Rev. Proc. 2019-43.

Broadly speaking Sec. 6.12 deals with:

- Change from single item accounts to multiple asset accounts or vice versa
- Asset grouping changes within a multiple asset and general asset accounts
- Changes in identifying assets disposed of from multiple asset accounts and general asset accounts
- Change in determining unadjusted depreciable basis of disposed asset or portion of disposed asset from one reasonable method to another reasonable method (for assets in item, multiple asset or general asset accounts)

*Property must be owned at beginning of year.* The taxpayer must own the property at the beginning of the tax year of change. MACRS must apply to the property (Sec. 6.12(1)(a)).

*IRS Form 3115 filing relief allowed a qualifying small business taxpayer to change to the accounting methods required by the final repair regulations under Code Secs.*

*162, 164, and 263 without filing Form 3115 (Rev. Proc. 2015-20, I.R.B. 2015-9, February 13, 2015). The repair regulation accounting method changes covered by this relief at the time it was issued were described in Sec. 10.11(3) of Rev. Proc. 2015-14. Theses changes were considered made on a cut-off basis. Therefore, no Code Sec. 481(a) adjustment was required or allowed with respect to amounts paid or incurred in tax years beginning before January 1, 2014. If such a taxpayer accepted this relief by not filing a Form 3115 for its for its first tax year beginning on or after January 1, 2014 and later files a Form 3115 to comply with an accounting method required by the repair regulations in Sec. 10.11(3) of Rev. Proc. 2015-14 or the corresponding section of its successors (Sec. 11.08 of Rev. Proc. 2016-29 or Sec. 10.08 of Rev. Proc. 2018-31, Rev. Proc. 2017-30, or Rev. Proc. 2019-43), the change is made and the Sec. 481 adjustment is computed on a cut-off basis that only takes into account amounts paid or incurred in tax years beginning on or after January 1, 2014.*

*If a taxpayer accepted this filing relief, it was also treated as making accounting method changes required for its first tax year beginning in 2014 under Sec. 6.37(3)(a)(iv), (v), (vii), and (viii), Sec. 6.38, and Sec. 6.39 of Rev. Proc. 2015-14 on a cut-off basis that took into account dispositions that occurred in tax years beginning before January 1, 2014 (Rev. Proc. 2015-20, Section 5, I.R.B. 2015-9, February 13, 2015). No Form 3115 was required to make these changes with respect to dispositions that took place in tax years beginning before the taxpayer's first tax year beginning on or after January 1, 2014. If a taxpayer accepted the filing relief by not filing a Form 3115 for its for its first tax year beginning on or after January 1, 2014 and later files a Form 3115 to comply with an accounting method required by Sec. 6.37(3)(a)(iv), (v), (vii), and (viii), Sec. 6.38, and Sec. 6.39 of Rev. Proc. 2015-14 or the corresponding sections of its successors (Sec. 6.14(3)(a)(iv), (v), (vii), and (viii), Sec. 6.15, and Sec. 6.16 of Rev. Proc. 2016-29 and Sec. 6.12(3)(a)(iv), (v), (vii), and (viii), Sec. 6.13, and Sec. 6.14 of Rev. Proc. 2018-31, Rev. Proc. 2017-30, and Rev. Proc. 2019-43), the change is made and the Code Sec. 481(a) adjustment is computed on a cut-off basis that only takes into account dispositions occurring in tax years beginning on or after January 1, 2014 (Sec. 6.12(4)(f) of Rev. Proc. 2019-43, Rev. Proc. 2018-31 and Rev. Proc. 2017-30; Sec. 6.14(4)(f) of Rev. Proc. 2016-29; Sec. 6.37(4)(f) of Rev. Proc. 2015-14, as added by Rev. Proc. 2015-20). In addition, a taxpayer who accepted the filing relief may not make a late partial disposition election under Sec. 6.33 of Rev. Proc. 2015-14 or the corresponding section of its successors for dispositions that occurred prior to the taxpayer's first tax year beginning on or after January 1, 2014.*

*Audit protection does not apply to any changes made for the 2014 tax year under the relief provision that are considered made without filing a Form 3115.*

*Multiple Asset and Item Accounts - Permissible to Permissible Changes*

*Change from multiple asset accounting to item accounting or vice versa.* The first set of changes for multiple and item accounts are changes from accounting for an asset in an item account to accounting for the asset in a multiple asset account and vice versa and grouping changes within multiple asset account. These changes do not apply to assets that are in a general asset account. Specifically the change are:

- a change from single asset accounts (i.e., item accounts) for specific items of MACRS property to one or more multiple asset accounts (i.e., pool accounts) for the same assets, or vice versa, in accordance with Reg. § 1.168(i)-7 (Sec. 6.12(3)(a)(i))

- a change from one or more multiple asset accounts (i.e. pool accounts) to single asset accounts (i.e., item accounts), in accordance with Reg. § 1.168(i)-7 (Sec. 6.12(3)(a)(i))

- a change from grouping specific items of MACRS property in multiple asset accounts to a different grouping of the same assets in multiple asset accounts in accordance with Reg. § 1.168(i)-7(c) (Sec. 6.12(3)(a)(ii))

These three changes are made using a modified cut-off method under which the unadjusted depreciable basis and the depreciation reserve of the asset as of the beginning of the tax year of change are accounted for using the new method of accounting (Sec. 6.12(4)(a)).

If the change is a change from a multiple asset account to a single asset account (second change above), the new single asset account must include a beginning balance for both the unadjusted depreciable basis and the depreciation reserve of the asset included in that single asset account (Sec. 6.12(4)(a)(i)).

If the change is a change to a multiple asset account (either a new one or a different grouping (first and third changes above)), the multiple asset account must include a beginning balance for both the unadjusted depreciable basis and the depreciation reserve. The beginning balance for the unadjusted depreciable basis of each multiple asset account is equal to the sum of the unadjusted depreciable bases as of the beginning of the year of change for all assets included in that multiple asset account. The beginning balance of the depreciation reserve of each multiple asset account is equal to the sum of the greater of the depreciation allowed or allowable as of the beginning of the year of change for all assets included in that multiple asset account (Sec. 6.12(4)(a)(ii)).

*Changes in identifying asset disposed of from multiple asset account.* In the case of items other than mass assets accounted for in a multiple asset account, Sec. 6.12 applies to a change in the method of identifying which assets (or portions of assets) have been disposed of (relates to Reg. § 1.168(i)-8(g)):

- from the specific identification method to the FIFO method of accounting or the modified FIFO method of accounting (Sec. 6.12(3)(a)(iii))

- from the FIFO method of accounting or the modified FIFO method of accounting to the specific identification method (Sec. 6.12(3)(a)(iv))

- from the FIFO method of accounting to the modified FIFO method of accounting (Sec. 6.12(3)(a)(v))

- from the modified FIFO method of accounting to the FIFO method of accounting (Sec. 6.12(3)(a)(v))

A change from the specific identification method (first item) is made using a cut-off method and applies to dispositions occurring on or after the beginning of the year of change (Sec. 6.12(4)(b)).

A Code Sec. 481(a) adjustment is required for a change described in the second, third, and fourth items (Sec. 6.12(4)(c)).

*Changes in identifying mass asset disposed of from multiple asset account.* In the case of items of MACRS property that are mass assets (as defined Reg. § 1.168(i)-8(b)(3)) and accounted for in a multiple asset account, Sec. 6.12 applies to a change in the method of identifying which assets (or portions of assets) have been disposed of:

- from the specific identification method to a mortality dispersion table in accordance with Reg. § 1.168(i)-8(g)(2)(iii) (Sec. 6.12(3)(a)(vi))

- from the FIFO method of accounting or the modified FIFO method of accounting to a mortality dispersion table (Sec. 6.12(3)(a)(vii))

• from a mortality dispersion table to the specific identification method, the FIFO method of accounting, or the modified FIFO method of accounting in accordance with Reg. § 1.168(i)-8(g)(2)(iii) (Sec. 6.12(3)(a)(viii))

• from a mortality dispersion table in accordance with Reg. § 1.168(i)-8(g)(2)(iii) to the specific identification method, the FIFO method of accounting, or the modified FIFO method of accounting (Sec. 6.12(3)(a)(viii))

A change from the specific identification method to a mortality dispersion table (first item) is made using a cut-off method and applies to dispositions occurring on or after the beginning of the tax year of change (Sec. 6.12(4)(b)).

A Code Sec. 481(a) adjustment is required for a change described in the second and third items (Sec. 6.12(4)(b)).

A change from an impermissible method of identifying an asset disposed of from a multiple asset account to a permissible method is filed pursuant to Sec. 6.12(3)(d) (Change #205)

*Change in determining unadjusted depreciable basis of asset disposed of from multiple asset or item account.* The following method changes relate to a change in the method of determining the unadjusted depreciable basis of a disposed of asset or portion of an asset from one reasonable method to another reasonable method where the taxpayers books and records are inadequate to make the determination:

• If the taxpayer accounts for the asset disposed of in a multiple asset account or pool and it is impracticable from the taxpayer's records to determine the unadjusted depreciable basis of the asset disposed of, a change in the method of determining the unadjusted depreciable basis of all assets in the multiple asset account from one reasonable method to another reasonable method for purposes of determining the unadjusted depreciable basis of the disposed of asset

This change relates to Reg. § 1.168(i)-8(f)(2) (Sec. 6.12(3)(a)(ix)).

• If a taxpayer disposes of a portion of an asset (including an portion of an asset in a multiple asset account) in a disposition to which Reg. § 1.168(i)-8(f)(3) applies (i.e., a disposition described Reg. § 1.168(i)-8(d), generally in which gain or loss is recognized) and it is impracticable from the taxpayer's books and records to determine the unadjusted depreciable basis of the disposed portion, a change in the method of determining the unadjusted depreciable basis of all portions of the asset from one reasonable method to another reasonable method (Sec. 6.12(3)(a)(x))

These changes are applied using a cut-off method (i.e., no Code Sec. 481(a) adjustment is made) and apply to dispositions occurring on or after the beginning of the tax year of change (Sec. 6.12(4)(b)).

A taxpayer is required to determine unadjusted depreciable basis using its records if such are adequate to make the determination. Otherwise any reasonable method, including those described in Reg. § 1.168(i)-8(f)(3) may be used. A change to using a taxpayer's records or from an impermissible method to a permissible method is made using Sec. 6.13 (Change #205) for buildings and Sec. 6.14 (Change #206) for section 1245 property and land improvements.

*General Asset Accounts - Permissible to Permissible Changes*

The accounting method changes in Sec. 6.12 for general asset accounts parallel the preceding changes in Sec. 6.12 that apply to multiple asset accounts described above. The changes discussed below only apply if the taxpayer made a valid general asset account election and relate to permissible to permissible changes. Similar changes from an impermissible method to a permissible method are governed by Sec. 6.15 (Change #207).

*Change from one permissible grouping of assets in general asset account to a different permissible grouping.* The first change allows a taxpayer to:

- change from grouping specific items of MACRS property in general asset accounts to a different grouping of the same assets in general asset accounts in accordance with Reg. § 1.168(i)-1(c) (Sec. 6.12(3)(b)(i))

This change is made using a modified cut-off method under which the unadjusted depreciable basis and the depreciation reserve of the asset as of the beginning of the tax year of change are accounted for using the new method of accounting (Sec. 6.12(4)(a)). This change requires the general asset account to include a beginning balance for both the unadjusted depreciable basis and the depreciation reserve. The beginning balance for the unadjusted depreciable basis of each general asset account is equal to the sum of the unadjusted depreciable bases as of the beginning of the year of change for all assets included in that general asset account. The beginning balance of the depreciation reserve of each general asset account is equal to the sum of the greater of the depreciation allowed or allowable as of the beginning of the year of change for all assets included in that general asset account (Sec. 6.12(4)(a)(iii)).

*Change in identification of asset disposed of from GAA.* In the case of items of MACRS property that are not mass assets and are accounted for in a general asset account a change in the method of identifying which assets (or portions of assets) have been disposed of in accordance with Reg. § 1.168(i)-1(j)(2):

- from the specific identification method to the FIFO method or the modified FIFO method (Sec. 6.12(3)(b)(ii))
- from the FIFO method or the modified FIFO method to the specific identification method (Sec. 6.12(3)(b)(iii))
- from the FIFO method to the modified FIFO method (Sec. 6.12(3)(b)(iv))
- from the modified FIFO method to the FIFO method (Sec. 6.12(3)(b)(iv))

A change from the specific identification method (first method change) is made using a cut-off method and applies to dispositions occurring on or after the beginning of the year of change (Sec. 6.12(4)(b)).

A Code Sec. 481(a) adjustment is required for the second, third, and fourth method changes above. The adjustment, however, should be zero unless Reg. § 1.168(i)-1(e)(3) applies to the asset subject to the change as the result of the mandatory or elective termination of the general asset account (Sec. 6.12(4)(c)).

*Change in identification of mass asset disposed of from GAA.* In the case of items of MACRS property that are mass assets and are accounted for in a separate general asset account in accordance Reg. § 1.168-1(c)(2)(ii)(H), a change in the method of identifying which assets (or portions of assets) have been disposed of:

- from the specific identification method to a mortality dispersion table in accordance with Reg. § 1.168(i)-1(j)(2)(i)(D) (Sec. 6.12(3)(b)(v))
- from the FIFO method or the modified FIFO method to a mortality dispersion table Reg. § 1.168(i)-1(j)(2)(i)(D) (Sec. 6.12(3)(b)(vi))
- from a mortality dispersion table to the specific identification method, the FIFO method, or the modified FIFO method under Reg. § 1.168(i)-1(j)(2)(i)(A), (B), or (C) (Sec. 6.12(3)(b)(vii))

A change from the specific identification method to a mortality dispersion table (first method change) is made using a cut-off method and applies to dispositions occurring on or after the beginning of the year of change (Sec. 6.12(4)(b)).

A Code Sec. 481(a) adjustment is required for the second and third method changes. The adjustment, however, should be zero unless Reg. § 1.168(i)-1(e)(3) applies to the asset subject to the change as the result of the mandatory or elective termination of the general asset account (Sec. 6.12(4)(b)).

*Change in method of determining unadjusted depreciable basis of asset disposed of from GAA.* The final change relating to GAAs is made for purposes of determining the unadjusted depreciable basis of a disposed asset or a disposed portion of an asset in a general asset account when it is otherwise impracticable to do so from the taxpayer books and records. The change allows a taxpayer to:

- change the method of determining the unadjusted depreciable basis of all assets in the general asset account from one reasonable method to another reasonable method under Reg. § 1.168(i)-1(j)(3)(i) (Sec. 6.12(3)(b)(viii))

This change is made using a cut-off method and applies to dispositions occurring on or after the beginning of the year of change (Sec. 6.12(4)(b)).

*Additional Rules*

*Section 481(a) adjustment.* The taxpayer may compute a single net Reg. §481(a) adjustment for all changes that are not applied using a modified cut-off method by combining all negative and positive adjustments. Alternatively, all negative adjustments may be added and reported as a single negative adjustment and all positive adjustments added and reported as a single positive adjustment. This option should be considered in connection with the rule which requires favorable (negative) adjustments to be reported in one year and positive (unfavorable adjustments) to be reported over four years (Sec. 6.12(5)(a)). Note that a taxpayer may also elect to report a net positive (unfavorable) adjustment of less than $50,000 in a single year (Sec. 7.03(c) of Rev. Proc. 2015-13).

*Concurrent filings.* A taxpayer making any change described in Sec. 6.12 for more than one asset for the same tax year must file a single Form 3115 for all assets (Sec. 6.12(6)(a)).

A taxpayer making any change described in Sec. 6.12 and any of the following additional changes for the same tax year should file a single Form 3115 for the changes and include the designated accounting method change numbers on the appropriate line of Form 3115 (Sec. 6.12(6)(b)):

(1) Sec. 6.01 — Certain impermissible to permissible depreciation method changes

(2) Sec. 6.13—Disposition of building or structural component not in GAA

(3) Sec. 6.14—Disposition of section 1245 property or land improvement not in GAA

(4) Sec. 6.15—Dispositions of assets in GAA

*Public utilities.* Special filing requirements apply to public utility property as defined in Code Sec. 168(i)(10) (Sec. 6.12(4)(e)).

*Streamlined Form 3115 filing.* Taxpayers with average annual gross receipts less than or equal to $10 million in the three tax years preceding the year of change qualify for simplified Form 3115 filing (Sec. 6.12(4)(d)).

*Eligibility rules inapplicable.* The eligibility limitation of Section 5.01(d) of Rev. Proc. 2015-13, which prevents a taxpayer from filing a change using the automatic consent procedure in the last year of the trade or business is inapplicable (Sec. 6.12(2)).

*Covington filing of copy.* Taxpayers making this change file a signed copy with IRS in Covington, Kentucky (Form 3115 Instructions).

## SECTION 6.13: DISPOSITION OF BUILDING OR STRUCTURAL COMPONENT

*References to section 6 in this discussion are to section 6 in Rev. Proc. 2019-43 and its predecessors.*

Sec. 6.13 (Change #205) provides certain changes in methods of accounting for disposing of a building (including a condominium or cooperative unit) or a structural component, or disposing of a portion of a building (including its structural components) to which the mandatory partial disposition rule of Reg. § 1.168(i)-8(d)(1) applies.

*IRS Form 3115 filing relief allows a qualifying small business taxpayer to change to the accounting methods required by the final repair regulations under Code Secs. 162, 164, and 263 (Sec. 11.08(3) of Rev. Proc. 2019-43 and its predecessors; Sec. 10.11(3)) of Rev. Proc. 2015-14 for pre-May 5, 2016 filings) on a cut-off basis that only takes into account amounts paid or incurred in tax years beginning on or after January 1, 2014 (Rev. Proc. 2015-20). If this relief was chosen, the taxpayer did not need to file Form 3115 for these changes for its 2014 tax year. In addition, however, if the taxpayer accepted this filing relief, it is required to make accounting method changes under Sec. 6.12(3)(a)(iv), (v), (vii), and (viii), Sec. 6.13, and Sec. 6.14 of Rev. Proc. 2019-43, , Rev. Proc. 2018-31 and Rev. Proc. 2017-30 (or Sec. 6.14(3)(a)(iv), (v), (vii), and (viii), Sec. 6.15, and Sec. 6.16 of Rev. Proc. 2016-29 and Sec. 6.37(3)(a)(iv), (v), (vii), and (viii), Sec. 6.38, and Sec. 6.39 of Rev. Proc. 2015-14) on a cut-off basis that only takes into account dispositions that occur in tax years beginning on or after January 1, 2014. No Form 3115 is required to make these changes for a taxpayer's first tax year that begins on or after January 1, 2014 if the taxpayer calculates a section 481(a) adjustment that only takes into account dispositions in tax years beginning on or after January 1, 2014. Audit protection does not apply to any of these covered changes (Sec. 6.12(4)(4) of Rev. Proc. 2019-43, Rev. Proc. 2018-31 and Rev. Proc. 2017-30; Sec. 6.14(4)(f) of Rev. Proc. 2016-29; Sec. 6.37(4)(f) of Rev. Proc. 2015-14, as added by Rev. Proc. 2015-20). In addition, a taxpayer may not make a late partial disposition election under Sec. 6.11 of Rev. Proc. 2016-29 (Sec. 6.33 of Rev. Proc. 2015-14).*

Sec. 6.13 provides for the following changes, each of which is discussed in more detail below:

- Change to treating building, condo, coop, or addition or improvement, including structural components thereof, as appropriate asset for disposition purposes

  Most often this change is filed by a taxpayer that treated a building as a separate asset and its structural components as a separate asset in accordance with temporary regulations, including a taxpayer that claimed a retirement loss on a structural component that was treated as a separate asset but did not file a timely accounting method change under now obsoleted Sec. 6.10 of Rev. Proc. 2016-29 (or a predecessor) (Change #196) to make a late partial disposition election

- Change to recognizing gain or loss on disposed building, condo, coop, addition or improvement, or portion thereof that continues to be depreciated

Most often this change requires a taxpayer to recognize gain or loss on the disposition of a portion of a building which under the final regulations is considered disposed of without making a partial disposition election (e.g., dispositions on account of a casualty event or sale that are mandatory recognition events).

• Change from improper to proper method of identifying building, condo unit, coop unit, addition or improvement disposed of from multiple asset account

The final regulations specify allowable methods to identify an asset that is disposed of from a multiple asset account. This change is required by taxpayers that are using an impermissible method.

• Change from impermissible to permissible method to determine unadjusted depreciable basis of building, condominium unit, cooperative unit, or addition or improvement disposed of from a multiple asset account or a portion of such an asset disposed of from an item or multiple asset account

The final regulations require a taxpayer to use its records if practicable to determine the unadjusted depreciable basis of a disposed asset or portion, thereof. If impracticable, any reasonable method may be used. For example, taxpayers that used the consumer price index rollback method (an unreasonable method) will need to file this change and switch to a producer price index rollback method or some other reasonable method.

• In the case of a taxpayer that revoked a general asset account election by filing a change under now obsoleted Sec. 6.11 of Rev. Proc. 2016-29 (or a predecessor) (Change #197) and in a tax year prior to the revocation made a qualifying disposition election under the temporary regulations (including a late qualifying disposition election) to recognize gain or loss on a building, condo, coop, or addition or improvement under the temporary regulations, a change to recognizing gain or loss under the final regulations

This changes should be made, for example, if two buildings were placed in a general asset account (e.g., a late general asset account election was made), one building was sold, and the taxpayer made a qualifying disposition election under the temporary regulations with respect to the sale causing the building to be removed from the GAA and the recognition of gain or loss. If the taxpayer made a qualifying disposition election with respect to a structural component of a building in a GAA, the taxpayer should previously have filed Form 3115 to make a timely revocation the GAA election (obsoleted Sec. 6.11 of Rev. Proc. 2016-29 (or a predecessor)) and a concurrent partial disposition election (obsoleted Sec. 6.10 of Rev. Proc. 2016-29 (or a predecessor)).

Sec. 6.14 (Change #206) provides corresponding changes for dispositions of section 1245 property.

*Inapplicability.* Sec. 6.13 (Change #205) does not apply to the following (Sec. 6.13(1)(b)):

• Any asset not depreciated using MACRS under the taxpayer's present and proposed method of accounting

• Any asset subject to a general asset account election (Change #197)

Sec. 6.15 contains disposition-related changes for assets subject to a GAA election which is not revoked.

• Any multiple buildings, condominium units, or cooperative units that are treated as a single building under the taxpayer's present or proposed method of accounting pursuant to Reg. § 1.1250-1(a)(2)(ii)

• Any disposition of a portion of an asset for which a partial disposition election under Reg. § 1.168(i)-8(d)(2) is required but for which the taxpayer did not make the election

• Any demolition of a structure to which Code Sec. 280B and Reg. § 1.280B-1 apply

Although changes relating to demolition losses are in the list of changes "not covered," the list of "covered changes" below include certain changes related to demolition losses (see Sec. 6.13(3)(b)).

*Definition of Building (Including Structural Components) as Asset*

Sec. 6.13 applies to the following changes in methods of accounting for a building (including its structural components), condominium unit (including its structural components), cooperative unit (including its structural components), or an improvement or addition (including its structural components) thereto:

• For purposes of determining the asset disposed of a change to the appropriate asset as determined under Reg. § 1.168(i)-8(c)(4)(ii)(A) (which treats a building (including its structural components) as the asset, (B) (which treats a condominium or cooperative unit (including its structural components) as an asset, or (D) (which treats subsequent additions or improvement (including their structural components) as an asset (Sec. 6.13(3)(a))

A taxpayer making this change must attach a statement with a description of the asset for disposition purposes under the present and proposed method of accounting (Sec. 6.13(5)(a)(ii)).

The entire Code Sec. 481(a) adjustment must be taken into account in the year of change if this Sec. 6.13(3)(a) change is made and the taxpayer recognized gain or loss under Temp. Reg. Sec. 1.168(i)-8T on the disposition of the asset or a portion of the asset prior to the year of change (Sec. 6.13(8)(a)(i)).

***Example 6:*** ABC placed a building and its structural components in service in 2000. In 2005, ABC constructed and placed in service an addition to this building. A change by ABC to treating the original building (including its structural components) as a separate asset and the addition to the building (including the structural components of such addition) as a separate asset for disposition purposes is a change described in Sec. 6.13(3)(a) (Sec. 6.13(4)(a), Example 1).

This change, however, primarily affects a taxpayer that applied the rules in the temporary regulations and treated structural components of buildings, etc. as separate assets for which a loss could be recognized upon a retirement.

***Example 7:*** CAD placed a building in service in 2000 and replaced the original roof in 2010. CAD continued to depreciate the original roof and began to depreciate the replacement roof as a separate asset when it was placed in service. In 2012 CAD decided to apply the temporary regulations (Temp. Reg. 1.168(i)-8T) in order to claim a retirement loss on the original roof. A Form 3115 was filed with the 2012 return which made an accounting method change to treat the building as a separate asset and each structural component as a separate asset for disposition purposes and also to change from depreciating the original roof to claiming a loss on the original roof as a negative (favorable) Code Sec. 481(a) adjustment equal to the unadjusted depreciable basis of the original roof reduced by the total depreciation claimed on the original roof prior to the 2012 year of change (Sec. 6.29(3)(a) and (b) of Rev. Proc. 2015-14 (prior to being superseded by Rev. Proc. 2016-29), Change #177).

CAD could have filed an accounting method change to make the late partial disposition election to confirm the loss (Change #196) (the deadline for filing an accounting method change to make the late election was the extended due of income tax return for the 2014 tax year). If a timely late partial disposition election is not filed, CAD is still required to file a change to redefine the asset as the building, including its structural components, and report a positive Code Sec. 481(a) adjustment equal to the loss claimed in 2012 decreased by the depreciation that could have been claimed on the original roof prior to the year of change (Sec. 6.13(3)(a), Change #205). Beginning in year of change in which the positive adjustment is reported CAD will continue to depreciate the roof (Sec. 6.13(8)(c), Example). The Code Sec. 481(a) adjustment appears to flow from the redefinition of the asset and not from any additional or concurrent accounting method change.

The #196 change (i.e., late partial disposition election (Sec. 6.10(1)(a) of Rev. Proc. 2016-29 or a predecessor) to confirm the prior loss deduction must be filed no later than for the taxpayer's 2014 tax year (i.e., by the extended due date of the 2014 return)). See Sec. 6.10 late partial disposition discussion above.

*Change from Depreciating to Recognizing Gain or Loss on Disposed Building or Structural Component Disposed in a Mandatory Partial Disposition Transaction*

- If the taxpayer makes the preceding change to redefine the asset, and if the taxpayer disposed of the building, condo, etc. in a tax year prior to the year of change but under its present method of accounting continues to deduct depreciation for the disposed asset, a change from depreciating the disposed asset to recognizing gain or loss upon disposition or capitalizing the loss if the demolition loss rules of Code Sec. 280B or Reg.§ 1.280B-1 should have been applied to the disposition (Sec. 6.13(3)(b), Change #205)

- If the taxpayer makes the preceding change to redefine the asset, and if the taxpayer disposed of a portion of the building, condo, etc. in a tax year prior to the year of change in a transaction that is treated as a disposition under Reg.§ 1.168(i)-8(d)(1) (e.g., casualty loss or sale) but under its present method of accounting continues to deduct depreciation for the disposed portion of asset, a change from depreciating the disposed asset to recognizing gain or loss upon disposition or capitalizing the loss if the demolition loss rules of Code Sec. 280B or Reg.§ 1.280B-1 should have been applied to the disposition (Sec. 6.13(3)(c), Change #205)

- If the taxpayer's present method of accounting for its buildings (including their structural components), condominium units (including their structural components), cooperative units (including their structural components), and improvements or additions (including its structural components) that are depreciated under MACRS is in accord with Reg. § 1.168(i)-8(c)(4)(ii)(A), (B), and (D) (i.e., the taxpayer's present method of accounting correctly defines the asset), and if the taxpayer disposed of the correctly defined asset in a prior tax year but under its present method of accounting continues to deduct depreciation for the disposed asset, a change from depreciating the disposed asset to recognizing gain or loss upon disposition or capitalizing the loss if the demolition loss rules of Code Sec. 280B or Reg. § 1.280B-1 should have been applied to the disposition (Sec. 6.13(3)(d), Change #205)

- If the taxpayer's present method of accounting for its buildings (including their structural components), condominium units (including their structural components), cooperative units (including their structural components), and improvements or additions (including its structural components) that are depreciated under MACRS is in accord with Reg. § 1.168(i)-8(c)(4)(ii)(A), (B), and (D) (i.e., the taxpayer's present method of accounting correctly defines the asset), and if the taxpayer disposed of a portion of the correctly defined asset in a prior tax year in a transaction that is treated as a disposition under Reg.§ 1.168(i)-8(d)(1) (e.g., casualty loss or sale) but under its present method of accounting continues to deduct depreciation for the disposed portion, a change from depreciating the disposed asset or disposed portion to recognizing gain or loss upon disposition or capitalizing the loss if the demolition loss rules of Code Sec. 280B or Reg. § 1.280B-1 should have been applied to the disposition (Sec. 6.13(3)(e), Change #205)

> ***Example 8:*** YAK placed a building in service in 1990. In 2000, a tornado damaged the roof and YAK replaced it. YAK did not recognize a loss on the retirement of the original roof and continues to depreciate the original roof. YAK also capitalized the cost of the replacement roof and has been depreciating this roof since 2000. Because the original roof was disposed of as a result of a casualty event a mandatory partial disposition recognition event under the final regulations (Reg. § 1.168(i)-8(d)(1)), YAK must change from depreciating the original roof to recognizing a loss upon its retirement. This is a change described in Sec. 6.13(3)(e) (Sec. 6.13(4)(b), Example 2).

This change could also apply, for example, if a lessor or lessee continued to depreciate a leasehold improvement after it was retired or abandoned.

Note that under the final regulations the destruction of a portion of a building or other property in a casualty event is one type of mandatory disposition event (Reg. § 1.168(i)-8(d)(1)). The partial disposition election (Reg. § 1.168(i)(d)(2)), which gives a taxpayer the option to treat a transaction as a disposition does not apply.

The mandatory partial disposition rule of Reg. § 1.168(i)-8(d)(1) treats the following transactions as a partial disposition of an asset without making the partial disposition election specified in Reg. § 1.168(i)-8(d)(2):

- Disposition of a portion of an asset as a result of a casualty event described in Code Sec. 165
- Disposition of a portion of an asset for which gain, determined without regard to Code Sec. 1245 or Code Sec. 1250, is not recognized in full or in part under Code Sec. 1031 or Code Sec. 1033
- a transfer of a portion of an asset in a "step-in-the-shoes" transaction described in Code Sec. 168(i)(7)(B)
- Sale of a portion of an asset.

A taxpayer must file this accounting method change if the taxpayer is depreciating a portion of a building that is considered disposed of as a result of one of these four transactions.

Note also that when a taxpayer claims a retirement or casualty loss, whether mandatorily or by making a partial disposition election, otherwise deductible repair expenses (e.g., the cost of the replacement) must be capitalized even if such expenses would otherwise be currently deductible as a repair expense (Reg. § 1.263(a)-3(k)(1)(ii)). A special rule, however, may allow the deduction of repair expenses in the case of a casualty (Reg. § 1.263(a)-3(k)(4); Reg. § 1.263(a)-3(k)(7), Ex. 5).

> ***Example 9:*** Assume in the preceding example that the roof was replaced because it had aged and was leaking. In this case, YAK could claim a retirement loss on the replaced roof only if it files an accounting method change to make a timely late partial disposition election prior to its last tax year ending in 2014 (Change #196) (Reg. § 1.168(i)-8(d)(2)(i)) because the retirement of an aged roof is not a mandatory disposition event described in Reg. § 1.168(i)-8(d)(1).

Under the regulations the replacement roof is a separate depreciable asset because it was not placed in service at the same time as the building. If the replacement roof is itself replaced in its entirety the taxpayer is required to claim a retirement loss in the year of disposition without making a partial disposition election since there is no partial disposition of an asset. If the retirement of a replacement roof took place in a prior tax year then a taxpayer's current accounting method (claiming annual depreciation deductions) is incorrect and the taxpayer needs to file an accounting method change to claim a loss equal to the cost of the replacement roof less the depreciation claimed on replacement roof through the tax year of the change. This is a #205 change described in Sec. 6.13(3)(d).

*Change From Improper to Proper Method of Identifying Building, Condo/Coop Unit Disposed of From Multiple Asset Account*

Taxpayers that have identified a building, condo, or coop, or portion thereof, disposed of from a multiple asset account using an impermissible method must file:

- A change in the method of identifying which building, etc. in a multiple asset account or which portion of a building in a multiple asset account has been disposed of from a method of accounting not specified in Reg. § 1.168(i)-8(g)(1) or (2)(i), (ii), or (iii) (for example, the last-in, first-out (LIFO) method of accounting) to a method of accounting specified in Reg. § 1.168(i)-8(g)(1) or (2)(i), (ii), or (iii), as applicable (Sec. 6.13(3)(f))

A taxpayer making this change must attach to the Form 3115 a statement describing the methods of identifying which assets have been disposed of under the taxpayer's present and proposed methods of accounting (Sec. 6.13(5)(a)(iii)).

Changes from one permissible method to another permissible method of identifying assets or portions of assets disposed of from a multiple asset account are filed pursuant to Sec. 6.12 (Change #200).

*Determination of Unadjusted Depreciable Basis of Disposed Building or Portion of Disposed Building*

Taxpayers are required to determine the unadjusted depreciable basis of an asset disposed of from a multiple asset account or a portion of an asset disposed of from a multiple asset or item accounting using the taxpayer's records if it is practicable to do so. If it is not practicable, a reasonable method may be used. The following changes are provided by Sec. 6.13 to change to a taxpayer's records or a reasonable method in the case of a building, condo, coop, or a structural component:

- A change in the method of determining the unadjusted depreciable basis of a disposed asset to a method of using the taxpayer's records (relates to Reg. § 1.168(i)-8(f)(2)) (Sec. 6.13(3)(g))

- If it is impracticable from the taxpayer's records to determine the unadjusted depreciable basis of an asset disposed of from a multiple asset account, a change in the method of determining the unadjusted depreciable basis of all assets in the same multiple asset account from an unreasonable method (for example, discounting the cost of the replacement asset to its placed-in-service year cost using the Consumer Price Index) to a reasonable method (relates to Reg. § 1.168(i)-8(f)(2)) (Sec. 6.13(3)(h)).

  A taxpayer making this change must attach to the Form 3115 a statement describing the methods of determining the unadjusted depreciable basis of the disposed asset, or disposed portion of the asset, under the present and proposed method of accounting (Sec. 6.13(5)(a)(iv)).

- If a portion of an asset is disposed of (including a portion of an asset in a multiple asset account), and it is practicable to determine the unadjusted depreciable basis of the disposed asset, a change in the method of determining the unadjusted depreciable basis of the disposed portion of the asset to a method of using the taxpayer's records (relates to Reg. § 1.168(i)-8(f)(3)) (Sec. 6.13(3)(i))

Sec. 6.15 provides a similar change for an asset in a GAA.

• If it is impracticable from the taxpayer's records to determine the unadjusted depreciable basis of the disposed portion of an asset (including a disposition of a portion of an asset from a multiple asset account), a change in the method of determining the unadjusted depreciable basis of the disposed portion of the asset from an unreasonable method (for example, discounting the cost of the replacement portion of the asset to its placed-in-service year cost using the Consumer Price Index) to a reasonable method (relates to Reg. § 1.168(i)-8(f)(3)) (Sec. 6.15(3)(j), Change #205)

Sec. 6.15 provides a similar change for an asset in a GAA

A taxpayer making this change must attach to the Form 3115 a statement describing the methods of determining the unadjusted depreciable basis of the disposed asset, or disposed portion of the asset, under the present and proposed method of accounting (Sec. 6.13(5)(a)(iv)).

The references to "asset" in the preceding changes only refer to buildings, condos, co-ops, and additions and improvements thereto. Sec. 6.14 contains corresponding changes for section 1245 property and land improvements.

The proposed regulations provided that a taxpayer could use the CPI rollback method to determine the unadjusted depreciable basis of a disposed portion of an asset if it was impracticable to make the determination using the taxpayer's records (Proposed Reg. Sec. 1.168(i)-8(f)(3)). The final regulations replaced the CPI rollback method with the producer price rollback method because the IRS determined that the CPI rollback method could produce unreasonable results (Reg. § 1.168(i)-8(f)(3)). See ¶ 162. Consequently, taxpayers that used the CPI rollback method in reliance on the proposed or temporary regulations, will need to file an accounting method change to change to the PPI rollback method (or some other reasonable method) to correct Code Sec. 481(a) adjustments computed on any previously filed Form 3115s that used the CPI rollback method. However, this change cannot be made using the PPI rollback method and instead must be made using some other reasonable method if the replacement resulted in a capitalized betterment rather than a capitalized restoration of the asset to its original condition (Reg. § 1.168(i)-8(f)(3)). A betterment will generally cost more than a restoration and skew the rollback calculation.

If the taxpayer used the CPI rollback method to compute gain or loss on a disposition of a portion of an asset that was disposed of during a 2012 or 2013 tax year (i.e., the gain or loss was reported on the 2012 or 2013 return without filing Form 3115 to claim the gain or loss as a Code Sec. 481(a) adjustment), an amended return can be filed if no subsequent returns were filed because an accounting method has not been adopted until two returns are filed. See ¶ 75.

*General asset accounts: Revocation of late GAA election and confirmation of qualifying disposition election loss claimed on entire asset*

This accounting method change requires a taxpayer to confirm a previously recognized gain or loss on a building, condo, or coop that was removed from a GAA as a result of a qualifying disposition election made under the temporary regulations by revoking the GAA election. Specifically the change is:

• A change from recognizing gain or loss under Temp. Reg. § 1.168(i)-8T upon the disposition of an asset (as determined under Reg. § 1.168(i)-8(c)(4)(ii)(A) treating a building (including its structural components) as a separate asset, (B) (treating each condominium or cooperative unit (including its structural components) as a separate asset, or (D) (treating each addition or improvement (including its structural components) as a separate asset) included in a general asset account to recognizing gain or loss upon the disposition of the same asset under Reg. § 1.168(i)-8 if: (1) the taxpayer makes the accounting method change to revoke the GAA election (obsoleted Sec. 6.11(1)(a) of Rev. Proc. 2016-29, (Change #197)); (2) the taxpayer made a qualifying disposition election under § 1.168(i)-1T(e)(3)(iii) in a tax year prior to the year of change for the disposition of such asset; (3) the taxpayer's present method of accounting for such asset is in accord with Reg. § 1.168(i)-8(c)(4)(ii)(A), (B), or (D), as applicable; and (D) the taxpayer recognized a gain or loss under § 1.168(i)-8T upon the disposition of such asset in a tax year prior to the year of change (Sec. 6.13(3)(k), Change #205))

Note that the #197 and #205 changes were filed concurrently on the same Form 3115 (Sec. 6.11(6)(b)).

The entire Code Sec. 481(a) adjustment must be taken into account in the year of change if this Sec. 6.13(3)(k) change is made (Sec. 6.13(8)(a)(ii)).

This change will affect a taxpayer that placed more than one building, etc., in the same general asset account and then made a qualifying disposition election for a building other than the last building in the account applying the definition of a qualifying disposition contained in Temp. Reg. Sec. 1.168(i)-1T(e)(3)(iii). For example, the change should be made by a taxpayer that placed two buildings in the same GAA, sold one of the buildings at a gain or loss and made the qualifying disposition election under the temporary regulations, removed the building from the GAA, and consequently recognized a gain or loss on the building under Temp. Reg. Sec. 1.168(i)-8T.

A similar but more commonly used change is allowed where a taxpayer placed multiple items of section 1245 property in a GAA and made a qualifying disposition election under the temporary regulations. See discussion for Sec. 6.14.

If a taxpayer applied the temporary regulations and made a qualifying disposition election with respect to a structural component of an asset in a GAA (e.g., an original roof of a building that is replaced), it was necessary to revoke the GAA election (Sec. 6.11(1)(a)(i) of Rev. Proc. 2016-29 or a predecessor, Change #197) and make a late partial disposition election (Sec. 6.10(1)(a) Rev. Proc. 2016-29 or a predecessor, Change #196) in order to preserve the loss. See Example 5.

*Section 481(a) adjustment*

Accounting method changes under Sec. 6.13 generally require a Code Sec. 481(a) adjustment. Statistical sampling is permitted to determine the adjustment (Sec. 6.13(7)).

If a taxpayer makes a Sec. 6.13 change for more than one asset, the taxpayer may compute a single net Code Sec. 481(a) adjustment for all changes included on Form 3115 by combining all negative and positive adjustments. Alternatively, all negative adjustments may be added and reported as a single negative adjustment and all positive adjustments added and reported as a single positive adjustment. This option should be considered in connection with the rule which requires favorable (negative) adjustments to be reported in one year and positive (unfavorable adjustments) to be reported over four years (Sec. 6.13(10)(a)). Note that a taxpayer may also elect to report a net positive (unfavorable) adjustment of less than $50,000 in a single year (Sec. 7.03(c) of Rev. Proc. 2015-13). See ¶ 75. However, a taxpayer must take the entire Sec. 481(a) adjustment into account in the year of change if the taxpayer is making the change specified in Sec. 6.13(3)(a) (relating to definition of asset) and recognized a gain or loss under Temp. Reg. Sec. 1.168(i)-8T on the disposition of the asset or a portion of the asset in a tax year prior to the year of change (Sec. 6.13(8)(a)(i)). This rule also applies if the taxpayer is making the change specified in Sec. 6.13(3)(k) (relating to taxpayer that files a change to revoke a GAA and recognize gain or loss on an asset for which a qualifying disposition election was made under the temporary regulations) (Sec. 6.13(8)(a)(ii)).

*Concurrent filings*

A taxpayer making any change described in Sec. 6.13 for more than one asset for the same tax year should file a single Form 3115 for all assets (Sec. 6.13(10)(a)).

A taxpayer making any change described in Sec. 6.13 and any of the following additional changes for the same tax year should file a single Form 3115 for the changes and include the designated accounting method change numbers on the appropriate line of Form 3115 (Sec. 6.13(10)(b)):

- Sec. 6.01 — Certain impermissible to permissible depreciation method changes
- Sec. 6.12 — Permissible to permissible depreciation method changes for item, multiple asset, and GAAs
- Sec. 6.14 — Disposition of section 1245 property or land improvement not in GAA
- Sec. 6.15 — Dispositions of assets in GAA

*Public utilities*

Public utilities that make any change described in Sec. 6.13 are subject to special terms and conditions (Sec. 6.13(5)(a)(v)).

*Streamlined Form 3115 filing*

Taxpayers with average annual gross receipts less than or equal to $10 million in the three tax years preceding the year of change qualify for simplified Form 3115 filing (Sec. 6.13(5)(b)).

*Eligibility rules inapplicable*

The eligibility limitation of Section 5.01(d) of Rev. Proc. 2015-13, which prevent a taxpayer from filing a change using the automatic consent procedure in the last year of the trade or business is inapplicable (Sec 6.13(2) of Rev. Proc. 2019-43).

*Covington filing*

Taxpayers making this change file a signed copy with IRS in Covington, Kentucky (Form 3115 Instructions).

## SECTION 6.14: DISPOSITIONS OF SECTION 1245 PROPERTY AND LAND IMPROVEMENTS

*References to Section 6 in this discussion are to Section 6 in Rev. Proc. 2019-43.*

Sec. 6.14 (Change #206) provides accounting method changes for disposing of a section 1245 property or a depreciable land improvement, or disposing of a portion of a section 1245 property or land improvement to which the mandatory partial disposition rules in Reg. § 1.168(i)-8(d)(1) apply.

The accounting method changes in Sec. 6.14 for section 1245 property correspond to the similar changes provided in Sec. 6.13 for dispositions of buildings and structural components.

*IRS Form 3115 filing relief allows a qualifying small business taxpayer to change to the accounting methods required by the final repair regulations under Code Secs. 162, 164, and 263 (Sec. 11.08(3) of Rev. Proc. 2019-43 and its predecessors; Sec. 10.11(3) of Rev. Proc. 2015-14 for pre-May 5, 2016 filings) on a cut-off basis that only takes into account amounts paid or incurred in tax years beginning on or after January 1, 2014 (Rev. Proc. 2015-20). If this relief was chosen, the taxpayer did not need to file Form 3115 for these changes for its 2014 tax year. In addition, however, if the taxpayer accepted this filing relief, it is required to make accounting method changes under Sec. 6.12(3)(a)(iv), (v), (vii), and (viii), Sec. 6.13, and Sec. 6.14 of Rev. Proc. 2019-43, Rev. Proc. 2018-31 or Rev. Proc. 2017-30 (or Sec. 6.14(3)(a)(iv), (v), (vii), and (viii), Sec. 6.15, and Sec. 6.16 of Rev. Proc. 2016-29 and Sec. 6.37(3)(a)(iv), (v), (vii), and (viii), Sec. 6.38, and Sec. 6.39 of Rev. Proc. 2015-14) on a cut-off basis that only takes into account dispositions that occur in tax years beginning on or after January 1, 2014. No Form 3115 is required to make these changes for a taxpayer's first tax year that begins on or after January 1, 2014 if the taxpayer calculates a section 481(a) adjustment that only takes into account dispositions in tax years beginning on or after January 1, 2014. Audit protection does not apply to any of these covered changes (Sec. 6.12(4)(4) of Rev. Proc. 2019-43, Rev. Proc. 2018-31 and Rev. Proc. 2017-30; Sec. 6.14(4)(f) of Rev. Proc. 2016-29; Sec. 6.37(4)(f) of Rev. Proc. 2015-14, as added by Rev. Proc. 2015-20). In addition, a taxpayer was not allowed to make a late partial disposition election under Sec. 6.11 of Rev. Proc. 2016-29 (Sec. 6.33 of Rev. Proc. 2015-14).*

As described in detail below, Sec. 6.14 applies to the following changes in methods of accounting for a section 1245 property, depreciable land improvement, or addition or improvement to a section 1245 property or land improvement:

- Change to the appropriate asset for disposition purposes

- Change to recognizing gain or loss on disposed section 1245 property, depreciable land improvement, addition or improvement thereto, (or portion of such an asset treated as disposed of without making a partial disposition election) that continues to be depreciated

  Among other things, this change requires a taxpayer to recognize gain or loss on the disposition of a portion of a section 1245 property or land improvement which under the final regulations (Reg. § 1.168(i)-8(d)(1), see ¶ 162) is mandatorily considered disposed of without making a partial disposition election (e.g., dispositions on account of a casualty event or sale).

- Change from improper to proper method of identifying section 1245 property, depreciable land improvement, or addition or improvement thereto disposed of from multiple asset account

  The final regulations specify allowable methods to identify an asset that is disposed of from a multiple asset account. This change is required by taxpayers that are using an impermissible method.

- Change from impermissible to permissible method to determine unadjusted depreciable basis of section 1245 property, depreciable land improvement, or addition or improvement thereto disposed of from a multiple asset account, or a portion of such an asset disposed of from an item or multiple asset account

  The final regulations require a taxpayer to use its records if practicable to determine the unadjusted depreciable basis of a disposed asset or portion thereof. If impracticable, any reasonable method may be used. For example, taxpayers that used the consumer price index rollback method will need to file this change and switch to a producer price index rollback method or some other reasonable method.

- In the case of a taxpayer that revoked a general asset account election by filing a change under Sec. 6.11 of Rev. Proc. 2016-29 or a predecessor

(Change #197) and in a tax year prior to the revocation made a qualifying disposition election under the temporary regulations (including a late qualifying disposition election) to recognize gain or loss on a section 1245 property, depreciable land improvement, or addition or improvement thereto under the temporary regulations, a change to recognizing gain or loss under the final regulations

This change should be made, for example, if several items of section 1245 property were placed in a general asset account (e.g., a late general asset account election was made), one asset was sold, and the taxpayer made a qualifying disposition election under the temporary regulations with respect to the sale causing the asset to be removed from the GAA and the recognition of gain or loss. If the taxpayer made a qualifying disposition election with respect to a portion of a section 1245 property in a GAA, the taxpayer should have revoked the GAA election (Sec. 6.11 of Rev. Proc. 2016-29 or a predecessor, Change #197) and made a concurrent late partial disposition election (Sec. 6.10 of Rev. Proc. 2016-29 or a predecessor, Change #196). A GAA election, however, cannot be revoked any later than a taxpayer's last tax year beginning before January 1, 2015 and, therefore, has expired. A similar deadline applied to late partial disposition elections.

Each of these changes is discussed in greater detail below.

*Inapplicability.* Sec. 6.14 does not apply to (Sec. 6.14(1)(b)):

- Any asset not depreciated using MACRS under the taxpayer's present and proposed method of accounting

- Buildings, condominium and cooperative units, improvements and additions

  See Sec. 6.13 (Change #205) for disposition-related changes for these assets.

- Assets subject to a GAA election unless an accounting method change was filed to revoke the election prior to the taxpayers last tax year beginning before January 1, 2015 (Change #197)

  See Sec. 6.15 (Change #207) for disposition-related changes for assets in a GAA.

- Any disposition of a portion of an asset for which a partial disposition election under Reg. § 1.168(i)-8(d)(2) is required but for which the taxpayer did not make the election.

*Section 1245 Property or Land Improvement: Change to Appropriate Asset*

The first Sec. 6.14 method change allows a taxpayer using an incorrect asset definition with respect to section 1245 property, land improvements, or addition or improvements thereto to change to the appropriate asset as defined in the final regulations. Specifically, the change covers:

- For purposes of determining the asset disposed of, a change to the appropriate asset as determined under Reg. § 1.168(i)-8(c)(4)(i) (providing that a facts and circumstances test generally applies to determine the asset, except that items placed in service on different dates cannot constitute a single asset), (ii)(C) (providing the commonly used business items described in asset classes 00.11 through 00.4 of Rev. Proc. 87-56 (1987-2 CB 674) are separate assets, except for additions or improvements thereto), or (ii)(D) (providing that each addition or improvement is a separate asset) (Sec. 6.14(3)(a))

A taxpayer making a Sec. 6.14(3)(a) change is required to attach a statement to the Form 3115 describing the assets for disposition purposes under the taxpayer's present and proposed methods of accounting (Sec. 6.14(4)(a)(ii)).

> ***Example 10:*** ABC placed a machine in service in 2000. In 2005, ABC constructed and placed in service an addition to this machine. A change by ABC to treating the machine as a separate asset and the addition to the machine as a separate asset for disposition purposes is a change described in Sec. 6.14(3)(a) (Change #206).

This change primarily affects a taxpayer that applied the rules in the temporary regulations and treated original components of section 1245 property or components of improvements as separate assets (Temp. Reg. § 1.168(i)-8T(c)(4)(ii)(F)) and claimed a retirement loss upon the retirement under the temporary regulations by filing an accounting method change. Under the final regulations, original components of assets are generally not treated as separate assets (Reg. § 1.168(i)-8(c)). A taxpayer may, however, recognize a loss on the retirement of an original component of a depreciable asset (or component of a capitalized and separately depreciated replacement component) by making a partial disposition election (Reg. § 1.168(i)-8(d)(2)). The replacement component must be capitalized and treated as a separate depreciable asset if the partial disposition election is made. Where a component is replaced and no partial disposition election is made, the taxpayer will either claim a repair expense with respect to the replacement costs and continue to depreciate the replaced component as part of the original cost of the section 1245 property or, if the replacement is considered a capital expenditure, capitalize and depreciate the replacement component as a separate asset (Reg. § 1.263(a)-3(k)(1)(ii)).

Taxpayers that filed an accounting method change to claim retirement losses on components of a section 1245 property by applying the temporary regulations needed to file another accounting method change to preserve the earlier-claimed loss to make a late partial disposition election prior to their last tax year beginning before January 1, 2015. If this accounting method was not timely filed, such a taxpayer must file an accounting method change to recapture the prior claimed loss.

> ***Example 11:*** CAD placed an electronic billboard in service in the 2000 tax year (Asset Class 57.1 of Rev. Proc. 87-56) and replaced a major electronic component in 2010. CAD continued to depreciate the original component and capitalized and depreciated the cost of the replacement component. In 2012 CAD decided to apply the temporary regulations in order to claim a retirement loss on the original component. A Form 3115 was filed with the 2012 return which made an accounting method change to treat the original component as a separate asset for disposition purposes and also to change from depreciating the original component to claiming a loss on the original component as a negative Code Sec. 481(a) adjustment equal to the unadjusted depreciable basis of the original component reduced by the total depreciation claimed on the original component prior to the 2012 year of change (Sec. 6.30(3)(a) and (b), Change #178 in Rev. Proc. 2015-14 prior to being superseded by Rev. Proc. 2016-29).
>
> In the 2014 tax year CAD has two options. CAD could either file an accounting method change to make the late partial disposition election to confirm the loss and make no Code Sec. 481(a) adjustment (Change #196) (the deadline for the late election is the extended due date of the 2014 tax year return) or file a change to redefine the asset as the billboard including the original major component (Change #206) and report a positive Code Sec. 481(a) adjustment equal to the loss claimed in 2012 decreased by the depreciation that could have been claimed on the original component after the retirement in 2012 and 2013. If the latter option applied, beginning in 2014 CAD continues to depreciate the original component. If CAD waits until after the 2014 tax year to file Change #206, the adjustment is equal to the original loss less the depreciation that could have been claimed prior to the year of change (Sec. 6.13(8)(c), Example).

A taxpayer must take the entire Sec. 481(a) adjustment into account in the year of change if the taxpayer is making the change specified in Sec. 6.14(3)(a) (relating to definition of asset) and recognized a gain or loss under Temp. Reg. Sec. 1.168(i)-8T on the disposition of the asset or a portion of the asset in a tax year prior to the year of change (Sec. 6.14(7)(a)(i)).

The IRS on audit can force the preceding change to recapture the previously claimed retirement loss if the taxpayer failed to file the alternative change to make a late partial disposition election (Reg. §1.168(i)-8(d)) to confirm the previously recognized retirement loss. This change (i.e., late partial disposition election (Change #196)) to confirm the prior loss deduction had to be filed no later than for the taxpayer's last tax year beginning in 2014 (i.e., by the extended due date of the 2014 return). See discussion of the obsoleted version of Section 6.10 of Rev. Proc. 2016-29 above.

*Change to Recognizing Gain or Loss on Disposed Section 1245 Property or Land Improvement or Portion of Disposed Section 1245 Property or Land Improvement That Continues To Be Depreciated*

- If the taxpayer makes the preceding change to redefine the asset, and if the taxpayer disposed of the section 1245 property or land improvement in a tax year prior to the year of change but under its present method of accounting continues to deduct depreciation for the disposed asset, a change from depreciating the disposed asset to recognizing gain or loss upon the disposition (Sec. 6.14(3)(b), Change #206)

- If the taxpayer makes the preceding change to redefine the asset, and if the taxpayer disposed of portion of the section 1245 property or land improvement asset in a transaction that must be treated as a disposition under the partial disposition rules of Reg.§1.168(i)-8(d)(i) (e.g., a sale or casualty loss) in a tax year prior to the year of change but under its present method of accounting continues to deduct depreciation for the disposed portion of the asset, a change from depreciating the disposed portion of the asset to recognizing gain or loss upon the disposition (Sec. 6.14(3)(c), Change #206)

- If the taxpayer's present method of accounting for the section 1245 property, depreciable land improvement, addition or improvement correctly defines the asset in accordance with Reg. §1.168(i)-8(c)(4) and if the taxpayer disposed of the correctly defined asset in a prior tax year, but under its present method of accounting continues to deduct depreciation for the disposed asset, a change from depreciating the disposed asset to recognizing gain or loss upon disposition (Sec. 6.14(3)(d))

- If the taxpayer's present method of accounting for the section 1245 property, depreciable land improvement, addition or improvement correctly defines the asset in accordance with Reg. §1.168(i)-8(c)(4) and if the taxpayer disposed of a portion of such asset in a prior tax year in a transaction that must be treated as a disposition under the partial disposition rules of Reg.§1.168(i)-8(d)(i) (e.g., a sale or casualty loss), but under its present method of accounting continues to deduct depreciation for the disposed portion, a change from depreciating the disposed portion to recognizing gain or loss upon disposition (Sec. 6.14(3)(e))

***Example 12:*** YAK placed an electronic billboard in service in 2010. In 2012, a tornado damaged the billboard and YAK replaced a portion of the billboard. YAK did not recognize a loss on the retirement of the original portion and continues to depreciate the original portion. YAK also capitalized the cost of the replacement portion and has been depreciating this portion separately since 2012. Because the original portion was disposed of as a result of a casualty event (a mandatory partial disposition event under the final regulations (Reg. § 1.168(i)-8(d)(1))), YAK must file an accounting method change to change from depreciating the original portion of the replaced billboard to recognizing a loss upon its retirement. This is a change described in Sec. 6.14(3)(e) (Based on Sec. 6.13(4)(a), Example 2).

Note that under the final regulations the destruction of a portion of a building or other property in a casualty event is one type of mandatory disposition event (Reg. § 1.168(i)-8(d)(1)). The partial disposition election (Reg. § 1.168(i)(d)(2)), which gives a taxpayer the option to recognize gain or loss, is not applicable in this situation because gain or loss must be recognized.

The mandatory partial disposition rule of Reg. § 1.168(i)-8(d)(1) treats the following transactions as a partial disposition of an asset without making the partial disposition election specified in Reg. § 1.168(i)-8(d)(2):

- Disposition of a portion of an asset as a result of a casualty event described in Code Sec. 165
- Disposition of a portion of an asset for which gain, determined without regard to Code Sec. 1245 or Code Sec. 1250, is not recognized in full or in part under Code Sec. 1031 or Code Sec. 1033
- a transfer of a portion of an asset in a "step-in-the-shoes" transaction described in Code Sec. 168(i)(7)(B)
- Sale of a portion of an asset

Taxpayers who are currently depreciating portions of assets that are subject to one of these mandatory disposition events are using an improper depreciation method and should file an accounting method change.

Note also that when a taxpayer claims a retirement or casualty loss, whether mandatorily or by making a partial disposition election, otherwise deductible repair expenses (e.g., the cost of the replacement) must be capitalized even if such expenses would otherwise be currently deductible as a repair expense (Reg. § 1.263(a)-3(k)(1)(ii)). A special rule, however, may allow the deduction of repair expenses in the case of a casualty (Reg. § 1.263(a)-3(k)(4); Reg. § 1.263(a)-3(k)(7), Ex. 5).

***Example 13:*** Assume in the preceding example that a portion of the billboard was replaced in 2012 because it had aged and was leaking. In this case, YAK could claim a retirement loss on the replaced portion only if it filed an accounting method change to make a late partial disposition election (Reg. § 1.168(i)-8(d)(2)(i)) under Sec. 6.10 of Rev. Proc. 2016-29 or a predecessor (Change #196) no later than its last tax year beginning before January 1, 2015 because the retirement of an aged component is not a mandatory disposition event described in Reg. § 1.168(i)-8(d)(1).

*Change From Improper to Proper Method of Identifying Which Section 1245 Property or Land Improvement Disposed of From Multiple Asset Account*

Taxpayers that have identified an item of section 1245 property, land improvement, or portion thereof, disposed of from a multiple asset account using an *impermissible* method must file:

- A change in the method of identifying which section 1245 property, etc., in a multiple asset account or which portion of the section 1245 property, etc., in a multiple asset account has been disposed of from a method of accounting not specified in Reg. § 1.168(i)-8(g)(1) or (2)(i), (ii), or (iii) (for example, the last-in, first-out (LIFO) method of accounting) to a method of accounting specified in Reg. § 1.168(i)-8(g)(1) or (2)(i), (ii), or (iii), as applicable (Sec. 6.14(3)(f))

A taxpayer making a Sec. 6.14(3)(f) change must include a statement with the Form 3115 that identifies the methods of identifying which assets have been disposed of under the taxpayer's present and proposed methods of accounting (Sec. 6.14(4)(a)(iii)).

Changes from one permissible method to another permissible method of identifying assets or portions of assets disposed of from a multiple asset account are filed pursuant to Sec. 6.12 (Change #200).

*Determination of Unadjusted Depreciable Basis of Disposed Section 1245 property, Land Improvement, or Portion Thereof*

Taxpayers are required to determine the unadjusted depreciable basis of an asset disposed of from a multiple asset account or a portion of an asset disposed of from a multiple asset or item accounting using the taxpayer's records if it is practicable to do so. If it is not practicable, a reasonable method may be used. The following changes are provided by Sec. 6.14 to change to a taxpayer's records or a reasonable method in the case of a section 1245 property, depreciable land improvement, or portion thereof:

- If it is practicable to determine the adjusted basis of an asset disposed of from a multiple asset account, a change in the method of determining the unadjusted depreciable basis of the disposed asset to a method of using the taxpayer's records (relates to Reg. § 1.168(i)-8(f)(2)) (Sec. 6.14(3)(g))

A similar change is provided in Sec. 6.15 for assets in a general asset account.

- If it is impracticable from the taxpayer's records to determine the unadjusted depreciable basis of an asset disposed of from a multiple asset account, a change in the method of determining the unadjusted depreciable basis of all assets in the same multiple asset account from an unreasonable method (for example, discounting the cost of the replacement asset to its placed-in-service year cost using the Consumer Price Index) to a reasonable method (relates to Reg. § 1.168(i)-8(f)(2)) (Sec. 6.14(3)(h))

A taxpayer making a Sec. 6.14(3)(h) change is required to attach a statement to Form 3115 describing the methods of determining the unadjusted depreciable basis of the disposed asset under the present and proposed methods of accounting (Sec. 6.14(4)(a)(iv)).

A similar change is provided in Sec. 6.15 for assets in a general asset account.

- If a portion of an asset is disposed of (including a portion of an asset in a multiple asset account), and is practicable to determine the unadjusted depreciable basis of the disposed portion, a change in the method of determining the unadjusted depreciable basis of the disposed portion of the asset to a method of using the taxpayer's records (relates to Reg. § 1.168(i)-8(f)(3)) (Sec. 6.14(3)(i))

A similar change is provided in Sec. 6.15 for the disposition of a portion of an asset in a general asset account.

- If it is impracticable from the taxpayer's records to determine the unadjusted depreciable basis of the disposed portion of an asset (including a disposition of a portion of an asset from a multiple asset account), a change in the method of determining the unadjusted depreciable basis of the disposed portion of the asset from an unreasonable method (for example, discounting the cost of the replacement portion of the asset to its placed-in-service year cost using the Consumer Price Index) to a reasonable method (relates to Reg. § 1.168(i)-8(f)(3)) (Sec. 6.14(3)(j), Change #206)

A taxpayer making a Sec. 6.14(3)(j change is required to attach a statement to Form 3115 describing the methods of determining the unadjusted depreciable basis of the disposed asset or disposed portion of the asset under the taxpayers present and proposed methods of accounting (Sec. 6.14(4)(a)(iv)).

Sec. 6.15 provides a similar change for the disposition of a portion of an asset in a GAA.

The proposed regulations provided that a taxpayer could use the CPI rollback method to determine the unadjusted depreciable basis of a disposed portion of an asset if it was impracticable to make the determination using the taxpayer's records (Proposed Reg. Sec. 1.168(i)-8(f)(3)). The final regulations replaced the CPI rollback method with the producer price rollback method because the IRS determined that the CPI rollback method could produce unreasonable results (Reg. § 1.168(i)-8(f)(3)). Consequently, taxpayers that used the CPI rollback method in reliance on the proposed or temporary regulations will need to file an accounting method change to change to the PPI rollback method (or some other reasonable method) to correct Code Sec. 481(a) adjustments computed on any previously filed Form 3115s that used the CPI rollback method. However, this change cannot be made using the PPI rollback method and instead must be made using some other reasonable method if the replacement resulted in a capitalized betterment rather than a capitalized restoration of the asset to its original condition (Reg. § 1.168(i)-8(f)(3)). A betterment will generally cost more than a restoration and skew the rollback calculation. See ¶ 162.

If the taxpayer used the CPI rollback method to compute gain or loss on a disposition of a portion of an asset that was disposed of during a 2012 or 2013 tax year (i.e., the gain or loss was reported on the 2012 or 2013 return without filing Form 3115 to claim the gain or loss as a Code Sec. 481(a) adjustment), an amended return can be filed if no subsequent returns were filed because an accounting method has not been adopted until two returns are filed. See ¶ 75.

*General Asset Accounts: Recognition of Gain or Loss Previously Recognized on Qualifying Dispositions of Sec. 1245 Property or Land Improvement Other than Portions Thereof*

This accounting method change requires a taxpayer to confirm a previously recognized gain or loss on a section 1245 property, land improvement, or addition or improvement as a result of a qualifying disposition election made under the temporary regulations by revoking the GAA election and recognizing gain or loss under the final regulations. Specifically the change is:

- A change from recognizing gain or loss under Temp. Reg. § 1.168(i)-8T upon the disposition of a section 1245 property, land improvement, or addition or improvement thereto included in a GAA to recognizing gain or loss upon the disposition of the same asset under Reg. § 1.168(i)-8 if: (A) the taxpayer makes the accounting method change to revoke the GAA election specified in Sec. 6.11(1)(a)(i) of Rev. Proc. 2016-29 or a predecessor (Change #197); (B) the taxpayer made a qualifying disposition election under § 1.168(i)-1T(e)(3)(iii) in a tax year prior to the year of change for the disposition of such asset; (C) the taxpayer's present method of accounting for such asset is in accord with § 1.168(i)-8(c)(4)(i) or (ii) (i.e., the asset is properly defined), as applicable; and (D) the taxpayer recognized a gain or loss under § 1.168(i)-8T upon the disposition of such asset in a tax year prior to the year of change (Sec. 6.14(3)(k))

A taxpayer making this Sec. 6.14(3)(k) change must take the entire Code Sec. 481(a) adjustment into account in the year of change (Sec. 6.14(7)(a)(ii)).

A Sec. 6.11 revocation of a general asset account election must be made for a tax year beginning on or after January 1, 2012 and beginning before January 1, 2015.

This change will affect a taxpayer that placed more than item of section 1245 property or land improvement in the same general asset account and then made a qualifying disposition election for an asset other than the last asset in the account applying the definition of a qualifying disposition contained in Temp. Reg. Sec. 1.168(i)-1T(e)(3)(iii). For example, the change should be made by a taxpayer that placed two machines in the same GAA, sold one of the machines at a loss and made the qualifying disposition election under the temporary regulations, removed the building from the GAA, and consequently recognized a loss under Temp. Reg. Sec. 1.168(i)-8T.

If a taxpayer made a qualifying disposition on a component of an asset in a GAA, it was necessary to revoke the GAA election (Sec. 6.11(1)(a)(i) of Rev. Proc. 2016-29 or a predecessor) (Change #197) and make a late partial disposition election pursuant to Sec. 6.10(1)(a) of Rev. Proc. 2016-29 or a predecessor (Change #196) to confirm the loss under the final regulations. See Sec. 6.11 discussion above.

*Section 481(a) adjustment*

If a taxpayer makes a Sec. 6.14 change for more than one asset, the taxpayer should compute a single net Code Sec. 481(a) adjustment for all changes included on Form 3115 by combining all negative and positive adjustments. Alternatively, all negative adjustments may be added and reported as a single negative adjustment and all positive adjustments added and reported as a single positive adjustment. This option should be considered in connection with the rule which requires favorable (negative) adjustments to be reported in one year and positive (unfavorable adjustments) to be reported over four years (Sec. 6.14(9)(a)). Note that a taxpayer may also elect to report a net positive (unfavorable) adjustment of less than $50,000 in a single year (Sec. 7.03(c) of Rev. Proc. 2015-13). See ¶ 75.

However, a taxpayer must take the entire Sec. 481(a) adjustment into account in the year of change if the taxpayer is making the change specified in Sec. 6.14(3)(a) (relating to definition of asset) and recognized a gain or loss under Temp. Reg. Sec. 1.168(i)-8T on the disposition of the asset or a portion of the asset in a tax year prior to the year of change (Sec. 6.14(7)(a)(i)). This rule also applies if the taxpayer is making the change specified in Sec. 6.14(3)(k) (relating to taxpayer that files a change to revoke a GAA and recognize gain or loss on an asset for which a qualifying disposition election was made under the temporary regulations) (Sec. 6.14(7)(a)(ii)).

Statistical sampling as described in Rev. Proc. 2011-42, 2011-37 I.R.B. 318, may be used to determine a Sec. 6.14 (Change #206) method change (Sec. 6.14(6)).

*Concurrent filings*

A taxpayer making any change described in Sec. 6.14 for more than one asset for the same tax year should file a single Form 3115 for all assets (Sec. 6.14(9)(a)).

A taxpayer making any change described in Sec. 6.14 and any of the following additional changes for the same tax year should file a single Form 3115 for the changes and include all of the designated accounting method change numbers on the appropriate line of Form 3115 (Sec. 6.14(9)(b)):

- Sec. 6.01 — Certain impermissible to permissible depreciation method changes
- Sec. 6.12 — Permissible to permissible depreciation method changes for item, multiple asset, and GAAs
- Sec. 6.13 — Disposition of building or structural component not in GAA
- Sec. 6.15 — Dispositions of assets in GAA

*Public utilities*

Public utilities that make any change described in Sec. 6.14 are subject to special terms and conditions (Sec. 6.14(4)(a)(4)).

*Streamlined Form 3115 filing*

Taxpayers with average annual gross receipts less than or equal to $10 million in the three tax years preceding the year of change qualify for simplified Form 3115 filing (Sec. 6.14(4)(b)).

*Eligibility rules inapplicable*

The eligibility limitation of Section 5.01(d) of Rev. Proc. 2015-13, which prevents a taxpayer from filing a change using the automatic consent procedure in the last year of the trade or business is inapplicable (Sec. 6.14(2) of Rev. Proc. 2019-43).

*Covington filing*

Taxpayers making this change file a signed copy with IRS in Covington, Kentucky (Form 3115 Instructions).

### SECTION 6.15: GENERAL ASSET ACCOUNTS - CHANGE TO PROPER ASSET FOR DISPOSITION PURPOSES, PROPER METHOD OF IDENTIFYING DISPOSED OF ASSET, PROPER METHOD OF DETERMINING UNADJUSTED BASIS

*References to Section 6 in this discussion are to Section 6 in Rev. Proc. 2019-43 and its predecessors.*

Sec. 6.15 (Change #207) contains four accounting method changes relating to dispositions of assets from GAAs under the final regulations. These changes allow a taxpayer to change to an appropriate asset disposed of from a GAA, change from an improper to a proper method of identifying which asset is disposed of from the GAA, change to using the taxpayer's books and records to determine the unadjusted basis of an asset disposed of, and change from an improper to a proper method of determining the unadjusted depreciable basis of a disposed asset.

As discussed in detail below, the covered changes are:

- For purposes of determining the asset disposed of from a GAA, a change from an inappropriate asset to an appropriate asset as defined in Reg. § 1.168(i)-1(e)(2)(viii) (Sec. 6.15(3)(a))
- A change in the method of identifying which assets or portions of assets in a GAA have been disposed of from a method not specified in Reg. § 1.168(i)-1(j)(2) (e.g., LIFO method) to a method that is specified in Reg. § 1.168(i)-1(j)(2) (Sec. 6.15(3)(b))
- A change in the method of determining the unadjusted depreciable basis of a disposed asset or disposed portion of an asset in a GAA from a method not using the taxpayer's records to a method using the taxpayer's records when using the taxpayer's records is practicable as required by Reg. § 1.168(i)-1(j)(3) (Sec. 6.15(3)(c))

• A change in the method of determining the unadjusted depreciable basis of the disposed portion of an asset from an unreasonable method (for example, discounting the cost of the replacement portion of the asset to its placed-in-service year cost using the Consumer Price Index) to a reasonable method as required by Reg. § 1.1168(i)-1(j)(3) (Sec. 6.15(3)(d))

When making any of these changes a taxpayer is required to attach a description of the assets to which the change applies (Sec. 6.15(4)(a)(i)).

These changes all relate to a change from an impermissible method to a permissible method of accounting for assets disposed of from a GAA. For assets not in a GAA, changes from these impermissible to permissible methods are provided in Sec. 6.13 (Change # 205) for buildings and Sec. 6.14 (Change #206) for section 1245 property and land improvements. Similar changes for permissible to permissible methods (e.g., one permissible method for identifying an asset disposed of from a multiple asset account to another permissible method, or from one permissible method of computing unadjusted depreciable basis on an asset or portion of an asset in an item or multiple asset account) are provided for GAAs (as well as item and multiple asset accounts) in Sec. 6.12 (Change #200).

*Sec. 6.15(3)(a)(1) changes.* The first change is required if a taxpayer applied the temporary regulations and made a qualifying disposition election to claim a loss on a structural component of a building in a GAA or on a component of an item of section 1245 property in a GAA that was treated as an asset for disposition purposes (Temp. Reg. § 1.168(i)-8T(c)(4)). Under the final regulations a building including its original structural components is the asset and components of section 1245 property are not separate assets (assuming the structural component or section 1245 component is not placed in service separately from the building or section 1245 property). Similarly, a taxpayer could treat a component of section 1245 property as an asset for disposition purposes under the temporary regulations (Reg. § 1.168(i)-8(c)(4)).

This change is only for an asset in a GAA. It does not apply if a taxpayer filed a change to revoke the GAA election (Sec. 6.11 of Rev. Proc. 2016-29 or a predecessor, Change #197) because the revocation removes the asset from the GAA.

A taxpayer making a Sec. 6.15(3)(a)(1) change is required to include with Form 3115, a statement describing the assets for disposition purposes under the taxpayer's present and proposed methods of accounting (Sec. 6.15(3)(a)(ii)).

***Example 14:*** *Late GAA election not revoked: Loss recaptured on structural component for which late qualifying disposition election made by redefining asset properly.* TEB, a calendar year taxpayer, placed a building in service in 2000 and replaced the roof in 2010. TEB continued to depreciate the replaced roof. In 2012 TEB filed an accounting method change under the temporary regulations to make a late GAA election to place the building in one GAA and the replacement roof in another GAA (Sec. 6.32(1)(a)(i) under Rev. Proc. 2015-14, Change #180). TEB also filed a concurrent change to make a late qualifying disposition election for the original roof (Sec. 6.32(1)(a)(iv) under Rev. Proc. 2015-14, Change #180) and reported a $20,000 negative (favorable) Code Sec. 481(a) adjustment equal to the adjusted depreciable basis of the original roof ($30,000) reduced by $10,000 of depreciation claimed on the original roof from 2000 through 2011.

Assuming that TEB did not file an accounting method change to revoke the GAA election (Sec. 6.11(1)(a)(i), Change #197) no later than its last tax year beginning before January 1, 2015, TEB will file a change under Sec. 6.15(3)(a) to change to treating the building (including its original roof and other original structural components) placed in service in 2000 as an asset and the replacement roof as a separate asset for disposition purposes. As a result, TEB must include the original roof retired in 2010 in the GAA and report a positive (unfavorable) Code Sec. 481(a) adjustment.

> The positive Code Sec. 481(a) adjustment for 2016 (assuming the 6.15(3)(a) accounting method change is filed for the 2016 tax year) is equal to the $20,000 negative adjustment claimed in 2012 for the adjusted depreciable basis of the original roof as of the end of 2011 reduced by depreciation that could have been claimed on the roof in 2012 through 2015 (Sec. 6.15(6)(c), Example).

In order to comply with the final regulations for the 2014 tax year, which treat the original roof and the building as a single asset, TEB must either (1) revoke the GAA election by the deadline which is for no later than the last tax year beginning before January 1, 2015 (Sec. 6.11, Change #197) and file an accounting method change to redefine the building and its structural components as a single asset (Sec. 6.15(3)(a) of Rev. Proc. 2016-29 or a predecessor, Change #205) and not make the late partial disposition election (this also results in recapture of the previously claimed loss as a positive (unfavorable) Code Sec. 481(a) adjustment) (see Example 5); (2) revoke the GAA election (Sec. 6.11 of Rev. Proc. 2016-29 or a predecessor, Change #197) and make a late partial disposition election (Sec. 6.10 of Rev. Proc. 2016-29 or a predecessor, Change #196) no later than the last tax year beginning before January 1, 2015 (this preserves the loss; there is no Code Sec. 481(a) adjustment); or (3) not revoke the GAA election and change the improper definition of the asset from the structural component to the building including its structural component (Sec. 6.17(3)(a) of Rev. Proc. 2016-29 or a predecessor; Change #207) and recapture the prior loss as a Code Section 481(a) adjustment as illustrated in Example 14. The latter is the only choice currently available.

*481(a) adjustment period.* A positive or negative Code Sec. 481(a) adjustment must be taken into account in a single tax year if a taxpayer makes a change resulting from defining an asset properly pursuant to Sec. 6.15(3)(a) and the taxpayer recognized gain or loss on the disposition of a portion of the asset under the Temp. Reg. Sec. 1.168(i)-1T or -8T in a year prior to the year of change (Sec. 6.15(6)(a)(i)). The adjustment is also taken into account in a single tax year if the taxpayer is adopting the remodel/refresh safe harbor and because the taxpayer claimed a retirement loss under the temporary regulations is required to redefine the asset in accord with the final regulations and restore the previously claimed loss in income as a positive section 481(a) adjustment (Sec. 6.15(6)(a)(ii); Rev. Proc. 2015-56, Section 5.02).

*Concurrent filings.* A taxpayer making any change described in Sec. 6.15 for more than one asset for the same tax year of change should file a single Form 3115 for all assets (Sec. 6.15(7)(a)). If a taxpayer makes a Sec. 6.15 change for more than one asset, the taxpayer should compute a single net Code Sec. 481(a) adjustment for all changes included on Form 3115 by combining all negative and positive adjustments. Alternatively, all negative adjustments may be added and reported as a single negative adjustment and all positive adjustments added and reported as a single positive adjustment (Sec. 6.15(7)(b)). This option should be considered in connection with the rule which requires favorable (negative) adjustments to be reported in one year and positive (unfavorable adjustments) to be reported over four years. Note that a taxpayer may also elect to report a net positive (unfavorable) adjustment of less than $50,000 in a single year (Sec. 7.03(c) of Rev. Proc. 2015-13). See ¶ 75.

A taxpayer making any change described in Sec. 6.15 and any of the following additional changes for the same tax year should file a single Form 3115 for the changes and include all of the designated accounting method change numbers on the appropriate line of Form 3115 (Sec. 6.15(7)(b)):

- Sec. 6.01 — Certain impermissible to permissible depreciation method changes
- Sec. 6.12 — Permissible to permissible depreciation method changes for item, multiple asset, and GAAs

- Sec. 6.13 — Disposition of building or structural component not in GAA
- Sec. 6.14 — Disposition of section 1245 property or land improvement not in GAA

*Public utilities.* Public utilities that make any change described in Sec. 6.15 are subject to special terms and conditions (Sec. 6.15(4)(a)(v)).

*Streamlined Form 3115 filing.* Taxpayers with average annual gross receipts less than or equal to $10 million in the three tax years preceding the year of change qualify for simplified Form 3115 filing (Sec. 6.15(4)(b)).

*Eligibility rules inapplicable.* The eligibility limitation of Section 5.01(d) of Rev. Proc. 2015-13, which prevents a taxpayer from filing a change using the automatic consent procedure in the last year of the trade or business is inapplicable (Sec. 6.15(2)(b) of Rev. Proc. 2019-43).

*Covington filing.* Taxpayers making this change file a signed copy with IRS in Covington, Kentucky (Form 3115 Instructions).

**SECTION 6.18: REVOCATION OF PARTIAL DISPOSITION ELECTIONS UNDER REMODEL REFRESH SAFE HARBOR (Obsolete)**

*References to Section 6 in this discussion are to Section 6 in Rev. Proc. 2017-30, which is generally effective for Forms 3115 filed on or after April 19, 2017 for a year of change ending on or after August 31, 2016, unless otherwise noted. For changes filed on or after May 5, 2016 and before April 20, 2017, for a year of change ending on or after September 30, 2015, Section 6 of Rev. Proc. 2016-29 governs. Section 6.20 of Rev. Proc. 2016-29 is identical to Section 6.18 of Rev. Proc. 2017-30 discussed below. Section 6.18 was removed from the list of accounting method changes by Rev. Proc. 2018-31 because it is obsolete.*

Sec. 6.18 (Change # 221) provides an accounting method change which allows a qualified taxpayer who is filing an accounting method change to change to the remodel-refresh safe harbor of Rev. Proc. 2015-56 to revoke prior year partial disposition elections, including late elections previously filed as an accounting method change (see discussion of obsoleted Sec. 6.10 of Rev. Proc. 2016-29 above). Section 11.10 of Rev. Proc. 2017-30 provides procedures for filing an accounting method change to apply the remodel-refresh safe harbor described in Rev. Proc. 2015-56. Under this safe harbor, 25 percent of qualified remodeling costs of a retail store or restaurant building are capitalized and 75 of such costs are currently deducted.

A taxpayer that made partial disposition elections prior to the tax year it adopts the remodel refresh safe harbor must file this accounting method change to revoke those elections if the taxpayer does not want to apply the safe harbor on a cut-off basis (i.e., it was to apply the safe harbor to remodel/refreshes that occurred in tax years prior to the tax year of change). Taxpayers that applied the temporary regulations to claim a retirement loss on a structural component retired in a 2012 or 2013 tax year and/or filed an accounting method changes to claim such retirement loss for pre-2012 retirements and have not filed an accounting method change to include the retirement loss in income as a section 481(a) adjustment must also apply the safe-harbor on a cut-off basis. See Sec. 3.02(5) and (6) ofRev. Proc. 2015-56.

As explained above under the discussion for Sec. 6.10 taxpayers who applied the temporary regulations to claim retirement losses on structural components were required to file an accounting method to make a late partial disposition election to affirm the loss. If this option was filed the taxpayer now needs to revoke those partial disposition elections. If a timely late partial disposition election was not made and the taxpayer did not file an accounting method change to include the loss in income as a section 481 adjustment, the taxpayer must do so in order to apply the remodel-refresh safe harbor to tax years prior to the year of change.

*Deadline.* This accounting method change to revoke prior year disposition elections may only be made for a tax year beginning after December 31, 2013, and ending before December 31, 2016 (Sec. 6.18(3)). This is a modification of the original deadline set forth in Rev. Proc. 2015-56, which indicated that the change had to be filed with the timely filed original federal tax return for the taxpayer's first or second taxable year beginning after December 31, 2013 (Sec. 5.02(4)(b)(ii)(B) of Rev. Proc. 2015-56).

*Streamlined Form 3115 filing.* Taxpayers with average annual gross receipts less than or equal to $10 million in the three tax years preceding the year of change qualify for simplified Form 3115 filing.

*Eligibility rules inapplicable.* The eligibility rules in sections 5.01(1)(d) and (f) of Rev. Proc. 2015-13 do not apply to a qualified taxpayer making this change for any taxable year beginning after December 31, 2013, and ending before December 31, 2016. The eligibility limitation of Section 5.01(d) prevents a taxpayer from filing a change using the automatic consent procedure in the last year of a trade or business. The eligibility limitation of Section 5.01(f) prevents a taxpayer from filing a change using the automatic consent procedure for the same item during any of the five tax year ending with the year of change.

If a qualified taxpayer makes both a change under Sec. 6.18 and a change under section 11.10 for any tax year beginning after December 31, 2013, and ending before December 31, 2016, on a single Form 3115 for the same asset for the same year of change in accordance with Sec. 6.18(7)(b), the eligibility rules in sections 5.01(1)(d) and (f) of Rev. Proc. 2015-13 do not apply to the qualified taxpayer for either change.

*Section 481(a) adjustment period.* A qualified taxpayer making this change must take the entire § 481(a) adjustment into account in computing taxable income for the year of change.

*Concurrent changes.* A taxpayer making this change for more than one asset for the same year of change should file a single Form 3115 for all such assets. The single Form 3115 must provide a single net section 481(a) adjustment for all such changes. A taxpayer making this change and a change under section 11.10 for the same year of change should file a single Form 3115 for both changes.

*LATE GENERAL ASSET ACCOUNT ELECTIONS UNDER REMODEL REFRESH SAFE HARBOR*

A qualified taxpayer that changes to the remodel-refresh safe harbor method of accounting must make a late GAA election for the building which is the subject of the safe-harbor on its original federal tax return for the first tax year that the taxpayer uses the remodel-refresh safe harbor. The IRS treats the making of the late general asset account election as a change in method of accounting. The manner of making this change in method of accounting is described in section 11.10 of Rev. Proc. 2017-30 below.

### SECTION 11.10: LATE GENERAL ASSET ACCOUNT ELECTION FOR BUILDINGS SUBJECT TO REMODEL/REFRESH SAFE HARBOR

A qualified taxpayer that changes to the remodel-refresh safe harbor method of accounting (Sec. 11.10 of Rev. Proc. 2019-43) (Change # 222) must make a late GAA election for the building which is the subject of the safe-harbor on its original federal tax return for the tax year that the taxpayer changes to the remodel-refresh safe harbor. The IRS treats this late general asset account election as a change in method of accounting. This method change is provided in Sec. 11.10 as part of the remodel-refresh safe harbor method change. It does not have a separate change number. The remodel refresh safe harbor is described in detail in Rev. Proc. 2015-56.

In addition, the taxpayer must include the amount capitalized under the safe harbor in a general asset account. Where the remodel-refresh safe harbor is applied to a prior tax year, a late GAA election must be made for these expenditures as well as the building. Note that the building and capitalized expenditures cannot be placed in the same GAA because they were placed in service on different dates. See ¶ 128 for rules for grouping assets in GAAs.

It is also necessary to place prior-year improvements to a building in a GAA even if the improvements are not subject to the remodel-refresh safe harbor (Sec. 5.02(6)(a) of Rev. Proc. 2015-56).

Sec. 5.02(6)(a) only states that the building, improvements subject to the safe harbor, and prior-year improvements must be placed in a GAA. Presumably, future-year improvements which are not subject to the safe harbor must also be placed in a GAA. No partial disposition election may be made for any part of the building or its structural components. See Sec. 5.02(4) of Rev. Proc. 2015-56.

A late general asset account election change is made using a modified cut-off method under which the unadjusted depreciable basis and the depreciation reserve of the asset as of the beginning of the year of change are accounted for using the new method of accounting. The late general asset account election change requires the general asset account to include a beginning balance for both the unadjusted depreciable basis and the depreciation reserve. The beginning balance for the unadjusted depreciable basis of each general asset account is equal to the sum of the unadjusted depreciable bases as of the beginning of the year of change for all assets included in that general asset account. The beginning balance of the depreciation reserve of each general asset account is equal to the sum of the greater of the depreciation allowed or allowable as of the beginning of the year of change for all assets included in that general asset account (Sec. 11.10(4)(b)(i)).

The taxpayer must attach to its Form 3115 a statement providing that the qualified taxpayer agrees to the following additional terms and conditions: (A) The consents to, and agrees to apply, all of the provisions of Reg. § 1.168(i)-1 to the assets that are subject to the election and (B) except as provided in Reg.§ 1.168(i)-1(c)(1)(iii)(A), (e)(3), (g), or (h), the election made by the taxpayer is irrevocable and will be binding on the qualified taxpayer for computing taxable income for the year of change and for all subsequent tax years with respect to the assets that are subject to the election (Sec. 11.10(4)(b)(ii)).

If the taxpayer's present methods of accounting are not in accord with final general asset account regulations (Reg.§ 1.168(i)-1), the taxpayer must change to the methods of accounting permitted under § 1.168(i)-1 no later than the first tax year that the qualified taxpayer uses the remodel-refresh safe harbor. For example, if the taxpayer's present method of accounting is not in accord with Reg.§ 1.168(i)-1(e)(2)(viii) (determination of appropriate asset disposed of), the qualified taxpayer must change to the appropriate asset by making the change specified in Sec. 6.15 of Rev. Proc. 2018-31 or Rev. Proc. 2017-30 discussed above no later than the first tax year that the taxpayer uses the remodel-refresh safe harbor.

*Section 481(a) adjustment.* A section 481(a) adjustment is neither required nor permitted for the late general asset account election.

*Concurrent filings.* A taxpayer filing this method change to use the remodel-refresh safe harbor should file a single Form 3115 to report related changes under Sec. 6.13(3)(a) (determination of appropriate asset upon disposition of a structural component) or Sec. 6.18 (revocation of partial disposition election under remodel-refresh safe harbor), and any change listed in Sec. 6.12(3)(b) (permissible to permissible changes for items in a general asset account) or Sec. 6.15 (dispositions of assets in a general asset account) filed for the same year of change (Sec. 11.10(6)(b)).

## ¶79

## Reporting Depreciation and Amortization on Form 4562

Noncorporate taxpayers (including S corporations) are not required to file Form 4562, Depreciation and Amortization, for a current tax year unless any of the following deductions are claimed: or a deduction based on the standard mileage rate (which reflects an allowance for depreciation expense). Noncorporate taxpayers exempt from filing Form 4562 enter their depreciation deduction directly on the appropriate line of their return.

Form 4562 contains separate instructions;

- a depreciation or amortization deduction on an asset placed in service in the current tax year;
- a Sec. 179 expense deduction (including a carryover from a previous year);
- a depreciation deduction on any vehicle or other listed property (regardless of when the listed property was placed in service); and
- a deduction for any vehicle reported on a form other than Form 1040 Schedule C or Form 1040 Schedule C-EZ.

If a taxpayer is an employee deducting job-related vehicle expenses using either the standard mileage rate or actual expense method Form 2106, Employee Business Expenses or Form 2106-EZ, Unreimbursed Employee Business Expenses is used for this purpose.

If a taxpayer files Schedule C (Form 1040) or Schedule C-EZ (Form 1040) and claims the standard mileage rate or actual vehicle expenses (except depreciation), and the taxpayer is not required to file Form 4562 for any other reason, the taxpayer reports vehicle information in Part IV of Schedule C or in Part III of Schedule C-EZ and not on Form 4562.

A corporation (other than an S corporation) claiming depreciation or amortization on any asset, regardless of when placed in service, must file Form 4562.

A separateForm 4562 is required for each separate business or activity of a taxpayer. However, Part I, which is used to claim the Code Sec. 179 expense deduction, is completed in its entirety on only one form where multiple forms are filed.

A Form 4562 must be filed to claim an amortization deduction in the first year of an asset's amortization period. The first-year amortization deduction is reported in Part VI on line 42 (line reference to 2021 Form 4562). The amounts reported in Part VI are then transferred to the "Other Expenses" or "Other Deductions" line of the income tax return. A statement should be attached to the return in the first year of the amortization period. Required information includes the following: a description of the costs amortized, the date that the amortization period begins, the amortizable amount, the Code section under which amortization is claimed, the amortization period or percentage, and the amortization deduction for the year.

In a tax year after the first amortization deduction is reported on Form 4562, amortization deductions should be reported directly only on the "Other Expenses" or "Other Deductions" line of the income tax return *unless* the taxpayer is otherwise required to file Form 4562. If the taxpayer must file Form 4562, for example, because listed property is still in service or new property has been placed in service, then the amortization deduction for such year should also be reported on Part VI line 43 of Form 4562.

Expenses, including depreciation, related to the production of income under Code Sec. 212 or an activity not engaged in for a profit under Code Sec. 183 are miscellaneous itemized deductions subject to the 2-percent of adjusted gross income floor (Temporary Reg. § 1.67-1T(a)). Therefore, depreciation claimed on an asset used in a Code Sec. 212 activity or a Code Sec. 183 "hobby" activity not engaged in for a profit should be computed on Form 4562 and reported on the "other expenses" line on Form 1040 Schedule A.

# Modified ACRS (MACRS)

## *Modified Accelerated Cost Recovery System*

## ¶ 80

### Introduction

Notwithstanding some shared terminology, the Accelerated Cost Recovery System (ACRS) introduced by the Economic Recovery Tax Act of 1981 (ERTA) and the Modified Accelerated Cost Recovery System (modified ACRS, or MACRS) introduced by the Tax Reform Act of 1986 are intrinsically different systems for deducting the cost of tangible depreciable property.

ACRS (the discussion of which begins at ¶ 220) shuns the word "depreciation," providing instead a deduction "with respect to recovery property." MACRS abandons the concept of recovery property and prescribes its own methods for determining the depreciation deduction accorded under older rules that still apply to most nonrecovery property. MACRS, in contrast to ACRS, recognizes salvage value but assigns it a value of zero.

Although the two systems use some similar names to classify personal property, it should be noted that, pursuant to the applicable conventions (see ¶ 86), the cost of 3-year property, 5-year property, or 10-year property placed in service under MACRS generally must be recovered over one more tax year (four, six, or 11 years) as compared to the cost of similarly named classes of property placed in service under ACRS.

*Distinctions Between ACRS and MACRS*

One seemingly basic distinction is that, in contrast to ACRS, under which the annual deduction is generally a designated percentage of unadjusted basis, MACRS may require appropriate basis adjustments to compute second- and subsequent-year deductions. Optional MACRS tables furnished by the IRS provide percentages that are applied to the unadjusted basis of property in a manner similar to statutory percentages provided to compute ACRS deductions.

Other differences include depreciation methods; conventions; property classifications; short tax year rules; and rules for computing depreciation of personal property in the year of disposition.

The following table compares deductions that would be allowed for an item of personal property costing $10,000 and classified as 5-year property under ACRS with an item costing the same, classified as 5-year property under MACRS, and subject to the half-year convention:

| *Year* | *ACRS* | *MACRS* |
|---|---|---|
| 1 | $1,500 | $2,000 |
| 2 | 2,200 | 3,200 |
| 3 | 2,100 | 1,920 |
| 4 | 2,100 | 1,152 |
| 5 | 2,100 | 1,152 |
| 6 | ... | 576 |

(The computations disregard MACRS bonus depreciation.)

*Rounding*

In rounding applicable rates, a taxpayer may adopt any convention that is reasonable, consistent, and accurate to at least one-hundredth of one percent for recovery periods of less than 20 years and one-thousandth of one percent for longer recovery periods. No convention may be applied to recover more than 100 percent of the property's recoverable basis (Rev. Proc. 87-57, 1987-2 CB 687).

## ¶ 82

## Transitional Rules

Although, generally, MACRS applies to all otherwise eligible property placed in service after 1986, prior contracts and/or construction may render some post-1986 property still subject to ACRS. Property so affected, referred to as transition property, may include (1) property with a class life in the 7-to-19-year range and placed in service before 1989, and (2) property with a longer class life and real property placed in service before 1991.

Since transition property is subject to ACRS, it is more fully discussed at ¶ 228. So-called anti-churning rules, which may also require that the cost of some property placed in service after 1986 be recovered under ACRS (or a pre-ACRS method), are discussed at ¶ 142.

An irrevocable election, on an asset-by-asset basis, was available to apply the MACRS rules to property other than transition property that was placed in service after July 31, 1986, and before January 1, 1987.

# MACRS General Depreciation System (GDS)

## ¶ 84

## Applicable Depreciation Methods

There are two depreciation systems under MACRS, the MACRS general depreciation system (GDS) (discussed below) and the MACRS alternative depreciation system (ADS) (see ¶ 150).

The cost of most tangible depreciable property generally placed in service after 1986 is recovered using (1) the applicable depreciation method, (2) the applicable recovery period (see ¶ 100 –¶ 126), and (3) the applicable convention (see ¶ 86).

Under GDS, applicable depreciation methods are prescribed for each class of property. Applicable depreciation methods include the 200-percent declining-balance method, the 150-percent declining-balance method (which may be elected), and the straight-line method (which may be elected).

Under ADS (which may be elected) the applicable depreciation method is the straight-line method.

A half-year convention (¶ 88) applies in the tax year personal property is acquired unless the mid-quarter convention applies because 40 percent or more of the aggregate bases of MACRS personal property was placed in service in the last quarter of the tax year (¶ 92). A mid-month convention applies to MACRS real property (¶ 90).

*200-percent declining-balance method*

The 200-percent declining-balance method is used to depreciate 3-year, 5-year, 7-year, and 10-year property (other than crop bearing trees or vines). The cost of trees or vines placed in service after 1988 are recovered using the straight-line method (Code Sec. 168(b)(3)(E)). See ¶ 108. A switch is made to the straight-line method in the first tax year that the straight-line method, when applied to the adjusted basis remaining at the beginning of the year, results in a larger deduction. The table percentages take this switch into account.

*150-percent declining-balance method*

The 150-percent declining-balance method is used to depreciate 15- and 20-year property and 3-, 5-, 7-, and 10-year property for which an election is made (see below). As in the case of the 200-percent declining-balance method, a switch is made to the straight-line method in the tax year that the straight-line method results in a greater deduction.

The 150-percent declining-balance method also applies to 3-, 5-, 7-, and 10-year property used in a farming business and placed in service before 2018. See below.

*150-percent declining-balance method election*

A taxpayer may make an irrevocable election to use the 150-percent declining-balance method to depreciate 3-, 5-, 7-, or 10-year property (other than fruit- or nut-bearing trees or vines), as well as 15-or 20-year property (Code Sec. 168(b)(2); Code Sec. 168(b)(5)).

The election applies to all assets within a property class (including farm property within a property class) for which an election is made and which are placed in service during the tax year of the election. The election is made on Form 4562. No special election statement is attached to the return. See below for making the election on an amended return.

The applicable recovery period depends on the date that the property for which the election is made is placed in service. For property placed in service before January 1, 1999, the ADS recovery period for a property applies (¶ 150) (Code Sec. 168(c)(2), prior to being stricken by P.L. 105-206). For property placed in service after December 31, 1998, the regular recovery period for a property applies (¶ 100) (Code Sec. 168(c), as amended by P.L. 105-206). No alternative minimum tax depreciation adjustment is necessary with respect to a property for which this election is made since the applicable AMT depreciation method for 3-, 5-, 7-, 10-, 15-, and 20-year property is the 150-percent declining-balance method over the ADS recovery period (for property placed in service before 1999) or the regular recovery period (for property placed in service after 1998). See ¶ 170.

The effect of the election with respect to 15- and 20-year property placed in service before 1999 is to substitute the ADS recovery period for the regular 15- or 20-year recovery period. The 150-percent declining-balance method applies to such property whether or not the election is made. In the case of 15-and 20-year property placed in service after 1998, the election would have no impact since the regular 15- or 20-year tax recovery period will apply whether or not the election is made.

A half-year or mid-quarter convention (¶ 86) applies to property depreciated using the 150-percent declining-balance method.

*Straight-line method*

The straight-line method is mandatory for residential rental property (¶ 114), nonresidential real property (¶ 116), water utility property (¶ 113), railroad gradings and tunnel bores (¶ 120), certain fruit or nut bearing trees and vines (¶ 108), 15-year qualified improvement property (¶ 110), 15-year qualified leasehold improvement property (¶ 126), 15-year qualified restaurant property (¶ 110), and 15-year qualified retail improvement property (¶ 110). The straight-line method is applied over the GDS recovery periods (¶ 100 and following).

A mid-month convention applies to nonresidential real property, residential rental property, and railroad grading and tunnel bores. A half-year or mid-quarter convention applies to all other property depreciated using a straight-line method. See ¶ 86.

*Straight-line election*

For other property classes (i.e., 3-, 5-, 7-, 10-, 15-, and 20-year property), a taxpayer may elect the straight-line method over the GDS recovery periods. The election applies to all property within a class for which an election is made that is placed in service during the tax year. The election is irrevocable and is made on Form 4562 (Code Sec. 168(b)(3)(D); Code Sec. 168(b)(5)). No special election statement is attached to the return. See below for making the election on an amended return.

*MACRS Alternative Depreciation System (ADS)*

The straight-line method also applies to property depreciated using ADS. A taxpayer may make an irrevocable ADS election (Code Sec. 168(g)(7)). The ADS election differs from the straight-line election discussed above in that longer recovery periods are generally required under ADS. No special election statement is attached to the return. See below for making the election on an amended return.

*Farm property*

Farm business property in the 3-, 5-, 7-, and 10-year property classes placed in service after 1988 and before 2018 is depreciated using the 150-percent declining-balance method (instead of the 200-percent declining-balance method) (Code Sec.

168(b)(2)(B), prior to being stricken by the 2017 Tax Cuts Act (P.L. 115-97)). An exception to the required use of the 150-percent declining balance method is provided for property placed in service before July 1, 1989, if certain action (construction or binding contract) was taken on or before July 14, 1988 (Act Sec. 6028 of P.L. 100-647). The MACRS depreciation tables 14 through 18, at ¶ 180, that pertain to depreciation computations for the alternative minimum tax incorporate the 150-percent declining-balance method. Thus, depreciation for farm business property computed under the 150-percent declining-balance method may be determined under Table 14 if the half-year convention is used and under Tables 15 through 18 if the mid-quarter convention is used.

The 2017 Tax Cuts Act eliminated the requirement that farming property in the 3-, 5-, 7-, and 10-year property classes must be depreciated using the 150-percent declining balance method, effective for property placed in service after 2017 (Code Sec. 168(b)(2)(B), stricken by the 2017 Tax Cuts Act (P.L. 115-97)).

A farmer may make the straight-line and ADS elections described above for a class of property. After 2018, the 150 percent declining balance election described above may also be made for a class of 3-, 5-, 7-, and 10-year property.

If an election is made by the taxpayer or a related person (as defined in Code Sec. 263A(d)(3)) to deduct preproduction expenditures the MACRS alternative depreciation system (ADS) must be used (Code Sec. 263A(e)(2)).

See also ¶ 118 for rules relating to farmers.

*Straight-line, 150 DB, and ADS election on amended return*

Generally, these elections must be made by the due date of the return (including extensions) for the year that the property is placed in service. The election is made on Form 4562 by completing the form properly and applying the elected method. See IRS Publication 946 (How to Depreciate Property). If the election is not made on the original return, it can be made by filing an amended return within six months of the due date of the original return (excluding extensions). IRS Publication 946 says the following: "Attach the election to the amended return and write 'Filed pursuant to section 301.9100-2' on the election statement. File the amended return at the same address you filed the original return."

*Alternative minimum tax*

For rules explaining the allowable depreciation deduction for alternative minimum tax purposes see ¶ 170.

## ¶ 86

## Applicable Convention

In computing MACRS deductions for the tax year in which property is placed in service and the year of disposition, averaging conventions are used to establish when the recovery (depreciation) period begins and ends. After depreciation for a full tax year is computed using the appropriate method, the appropriate averaging convention is applied to arrive at the amount of deductible depreciation. IRS depreciation tables incorporate the appropriate convention (except for the year of an early disposition (see ¶ 180)). The applicable convention is not elective; but rather one of three conventions (half-year (¶ 88), mid-month (¶ 90), and mid-quarter (¶ 92)) applies to specified property (Code Sec. 168(d)).

These averaging conventions apply to depreciation computations whether made under the MACRS general depreciation system (GDS) (i.e., the regular MACRS method), the MACRS straight-line method, or the MACRS alternative depreciation system (ADS). The recovery period begins on the date specified under the applicable convention.

The same convention that is applied to depreciable property in the tax year in which it is placed in service must also be used in the tax year of disposition (Reg. § 1.168(d)-1(c)(1)).

No depreciation deduction is allowed for property placed in service and disposed of in the same tax year (Reg. § 1.168(d)-1(b)(3)).

No depreciation deduction is allowed for property purchased for business use and converted to personal use in the same tax year (Reg.§ 1.168(i)-4(c)).

See ¶ 160 for special rules that apply with respect to each convention in the year of a disposition.

See also ¶ 179 and ¶ 180 for sample calculations using the applicable conventions.

Special rules for applying averaging conventions in a short tax year are discussed at ¶ 132.

## ¶ 88

## Half-Year Convention

The half-year convention applies to property other than residential rental property, nonresidential real property, and railroad grading and tunnel bores (Code Sec. 168(d)(1)). Under this convention, the recovery period begins or ends on the midpoint of the tax year (Code Sec. 168(d)(4)(A)). Thus, one-half of the depreciation for the first year of the recovery period is allowed in the tax year in which the property is first placed in service, regardless of the date the property is placed in service during the tax year.

If property is held for the entire recovery period, a half-year of depreciation is allowable in the tax year in which the recovery period ends.

Generally, a half-year of depreciation is allowed in the tax year of disposition if there is a disposition of property before the end of the recovery period (an "early disposition"). A half-year of depreciation is allowed on an asset subject to the half-year convention in the last year of its recovery period whether or not it is disposed of.

See ¶ 160 for special rules that apply with respect to the half-year convention in the year of a disposition.

Once it is determined that this convention applies, it applies to all depreciable property (other than residential rental property, nonresidential real property, and railroad grading and tunnel bores) placed in service during the tax year.

## ¶ 90

## Mid-month Convention

The mid-month convention applies to residential rental property (including low-income housing), nonresidential real property, and railroad grading and tunnel bores (Code Sec. 168(d)(2)). Under this convention, the recovery period begins or ends on the midpoint of the month. The MACRS deduction is based on the number of months that the property was in service. Thus, one-half month of depreciation is allowed for the month that property is placed in service and for the month of disposition if there is a disposition of property before the end of the recovery period.

See ¶ 160 for special rules that apply with respect to the mid-month convention in the year of a disposition. See also ¶ 179 and ¶ 180.

## ¶ 92
## Mid-quarter Convention

The mid-quarter convention applies to all MACRS property placed in service during a tax year (other than MACRS residential rental property, nonresidential real property, and railroad grading and tunnel bores) if more than 40 percent of the aggregate bases of such property is placed in service during the last three months of the tax year even if the tax year is a short tax year (Code Sec. 168(d)(3); Reg. § 1.168(d)-1(b)). Under this convention, the recovery periods for all MACRS property (other than MACRS residential rental property, nonresidential real property, and railroad grading and tunnel bores) placed in service, or disposed of, during any quarter of a tax year begin or end on the midpoint of that quarter.

A quarter is a period of three months. The first, second, third, and fourth quarters in a tax year begin on the first day of the first month, the first day of the fourth month, the first day of the seventh month, and the first day of the tenth month of the tax year, respectively.

In determining whether the mid-quarter convention is applicable, the aggregate basis of property placed in service in the last three months of the tax year must be computed regardless of the length of the tax year. Thus, if a short tax year consists of three months or less, the mid-quarter convention applies regardless of when depreciable property is placed in service during the tax year (see ¶ 132).

In applying the 40-percent test, the following rules are utilized:

(1) The depreciable basis of property not subject to MACRS is disregarded (Code Sec. 168(d)(3)(A)).

(2) Amounts expensed under Code Sec. 179 are disregarded (Reg. § 1.168(d)-1(b)(4); IRS Letter Ruling 9126014, March 29, 1991).

(3) The depreciable basis of MACRS nonresidential real property, residential rental property, and railroad grading and tunnel bores is disregarded (Code Sec. 168(d)(3)(b)(i)).

(4) The depreciable basis of MACRS listed property is included (unless otherwise disregarded, for example, because it is expensed under Code Sec. 179) (Reg. § 1.168(d)-1(b)(2)).

(5) MACRS property placed in service and disposed of within the same tax year is disregarded (Code Sec. 168(d)(3)(B)(ii)). However, if such property is subsequently reacquired and again placed in service during the same tax year, depreciable basis as of the later of the dates placed in service is included (Reg.§ 1.168(d)-1(b)(3)).

(6) The portion of the basis of MACRS property that is attributable to personal use is disregarded (Reg. § 1.168(d)-1(b)(4)).

The first-year MACRS bonus depreciation allowance does not reduce depreciable basis for purposes of determining whether the mid-quarter convention applies (Rev. Proc. 2011-26; Reg.§ 1.168(k)-2(g)(11); Reg.§ 1.168(d)-1(b)(4)). For items that reduce basis for this purpose, see ¶ 70.

Property acquired and placed in service after September 27, 2017 and before 2023 qualifies for 100 percent bonus depreciation. Used property acquired and placed in service after September 27, 2017 generally qualifies for bonus depreciation. See ¶ 127D.

*Example (1):* A calendar year taxpayer places a $45,000 15-year land improvement in service in December 2021 and a $500 machine in service in January 2021. 100 percent bonus is claimed on the land improvement and no portion of the basis of the machine is expensed under section 179 or claimed as bonus depreciation. The mid-quarter convention applies to the machine even though the entire cost of the land improvement is deducted as bonus depreciation.

*Example (1A):* A calendar year taxpayer places a new machine that cost $100,000 in service in October 2021. An election out of bonus depreciation is made and no amount is expensed under section 179. The taxpayer also placed a used machine that cost $100,000 in service in January 2021. No portion of its cost is expensed under Code Sec. 179 or claimed as bonus depreciation. The mid-quarter convention applies to the new and used machines because more than 40% of the depreciable basis of property was placed in service in during the last 3 months of the tax year ($100,000/$200,000 = 50%).

By properly allocating the Code Sec. 179 deduction or timing purchases of depreciable property, a taxpayer may be able to trigger or avoid the mid-quarter convention. These and other mid-quarter convention planning opportunities are discussed at ¶ 486.

See ¶ 160 for special rules that apply with respect to the mid-quarter convention in the year of a disposition. See ¶ 179 and ¶ 180 for examples that illustrate the computation of depreciation using the mid-quarter convention.

*Example (1B):* In October, a calendar-year taxpayer purchases a truck and places it in service. There is no election to expense any part of the cost of the truck under Code Sec. 179, bonus depreciation is not claimed, and this is the only asset placed in service during the tax year. The more than 40% test is satisfied and the mid-quarter convention applies because 100% of the depreciable basis of property placed in service during the tax year is placed in service during the last three months of the tax year. Two years later, in April (before the end of the asset's recovery period), the truck is sold. The mid-quarter convention must be used in determining the depreciation deduction for the truck in the year of disposition.

*Example (2):* During the current tax year, a calendar-year taxpayer purchased and placed in service the following items:

January: A light general purpose truck that cost $8,000;

August: An office desk that cost $5,000 and a safe that cost $1,000;

November: A computer that cost $3,000.

No amount was expensed under Code Sec. 179 or claimed as bonus depreciation. In September, the truck and the desk are sold. Thus, the truck and desk were placed in service and disposed of in the same tax year. In determining whether the mid-quarter convention applies to depreciable property placed in service during the current tax year, the depreciable basis of the truck and the desk are not considered. For purposes of the 40% test, the amount of the aggregate bases of property placed in service during the current tax year is $4,000 ($1,000 safe + $3,000 computer). The depreciable basis of property placed in service during the last three months of the tax year is $3,000 (the computer), which exceeds $1,600 (40% of the $4,000 aggregate bases of property placed in service during the current tax year). Thus, the mid-quarter convention applies to the safe and the computer. No depreciation is allowed on the truck and desk because they were placed in service and disposed of in the same tax year.

*Example (3):* The facts are the same as in *Example (2)*, except that the truck is acquired in December for $7,000 and is not sold. The truck is considered placed in service in December and its basis is included in determining whether the mid-quarter convention applies. The amount of the aggregate bases of property placed in service during the current tax year is $11,000 ($1,000 safe + $3,000 computer + $7,000 truck). The depreciable basis of property placed in service during the last three months of the tax year is $10,000 ($3,000 computer + $7,000 truck), which exceeds $4,400 (40% of the $11,000 aggregate bases of property placed in service during the current tax year). Thus, the mid-quarter convention applies to the truck, safe, and computer.

*Election for tax year that includes September 11, 2001*

Taxpayers were permitted to elect to apply the half-year convention in a tax year that included September 11, 2001, in the third or fourth quarter to all property that would otherwise be subject to the mid-quarter convention (Notice 2001-70, 2001-2 CB 437; Notice 2001-74, 2001-2 CB 551).

The IRS stated its intention to amend its regulations under Code Sec. 168 to incorporate this guidance but has not followed through. The relief applied whether or not a taxpayer was directly affected by the terrorist attacks.

*Aggregate basis of property*

For purposes of the 40-percent test, the aggregate basis of property is the sum of the depreciable bases of all items of depreciable property that are considered in applying this test (Reg. § 1.168(d)-1(b)(4)).

*Like-kind exchanges and involuntary conversions*

Special rules apply if a taxpayer acquires property in a like-kind exchange or involuntary conversion (Reg. § 1.168-6(f)). See ¶ 167.

*Affiliated group*

If a taxpayer is a member of an affiliated group under Code Sec. 1504, without regard to Code Sec. 1504(b), all the members of the group that are included on the consolidated return are treated as one taxpayer for purposes of applying the 40-percent test. Thus, the depreciable bases of all property placed in service by members of a consolidated group during a consolidated return year are considered (unless otherwise excluded) in applying the 40-percent test to determine whether the mid-quarter convention applies to property placed in service by members during the consolidated return year. The test is applied separately to the depreciable bases of property placed in service by any member of an affiliated group that is not included in a consolidated return for the tax year during which the property is placed in service (Reg. § 1.168(d)-1(b)(5)).

For a subsidiary created by a member of an affiliated group during the consolidated return year that is itself a member of the group, the depreciable bases of property placed in service by the subsidiary during the consolidated return year of formation is included with the depreciable bases of property placed in service in such year by other members in applying the 40-percent test. The newly formed subsidiary is treated as being in existence for the entire consolidated return year for purposes of applying the applicable convention to determine when the recovery period begins (Reg. § 1.168(d)-1(b)(5)).

The depreciable bases of property placed in service by a corporation that joins or leaves a consolidated group during the portion of the consolidated return year that it is a member of the group is included with the depreciable bases of property placed in service during the consolidated return year by other members in applying the 40-percent test. For such property, the corporation is treated as being a member of the consolidated group for the entire consolidated return year for purposes of applying the applicable convention to determine when the recovery period begins. However, the depreciable bases of property placed in service while the corporation is not a member of the group is not considered by the affiliated group (Reg. § 1.168(d)-1(b)(5)).

For depreciable property placed in service by a corporation in the tax year ending immediately before it joins a consolidated group or beginning immediately after it leaves a consolidated group, the applicable convention is applied to such property under the rules applicable to either a full tax year or a short tax year, as appropriate (Reg. § 1.168(d)-1(b)(5)).

For purposes of the 40-percent test, depreciable basis does not include adjustments resulting from transfers of property between members of the same affiliated group filing a consolidated return. Accordingly, such property is considered as placed in service on the date that it is placed in service by the transferor-member (or first transferor-member to place such property in service if there are multiple transfers between members). The depreciable basis of such property for purposes of the 40-percent test is the depreciable basis of the transferor-member (or the first transferor-member to place such property in service if there are multiple transfers between members) (Reg. § 1.168(d)-1(b)(5)).

***Example (4):*** A new subsidiary is formed on August 1 of the current tax year by a member of a consolidated group that files a calendar-year consolidated return. The subsidiary places depreciable property in service on August 5. If the mid-quarter convention applies to property placed in service by the members of the consolidated group (including the newly formed subsidiary), the recovery period of the property placed in service by the subsidiary begins on the midpoint of the third quarter of the consolidated return year (August 15). If the half-year convention applies to such property, it begins on the midpoint of the consolidated return year (July 1).

***Example (5):*** A calendar-year corporation joins a consolidated group on July 1 of the current tax year and is included in a calendar-year consolidated return. For purposes of the 40% test, the amount of the depreciable bases of property placed in service before the corporation joined the group is not considered, but the amount of the depreciable bases of property placed in service during the period July 1 through December 31 is included with the amount of the depreciable bases of property placed in service by other members of the group during the entire consolidated return year.

However, in applying the applicable convention to determine when the recovery period begins for depreciable property placed in service for the period July 1 to December 31, the new member is treated as a member of the consolidated group for the entire consolidated return year. Thus, if the half-year convention applies to depreciable property placed in service by the group (including the depreciable basis of property placed in service after June 30 by the new member), the recovery period of the property begins on the midpoint of the consolidated return year (July 1).

***Example (6):*** A consolidated group files a calendar-year consolidated return. One member of the group purchases $50,000 of depreciable property and places it in service on January 5 of the current tax year. On December 1 of the current tax year, the property is transferred to another of the group for $75,000. For purposes of applying the 40% test to the group, the property is treated as placed in service on January 5, the date that the transferor placed the property in service, and the depreciable basis of the property is $50,000, the transferor's depreciable basis.

See also ¶ 132, for an additional discussion on the MACRS depreciation computation for short tax years of new subsidiaries.

*Partnerships and S corporations*

For property placed in service by a partnership or an S corporation, the 40-percent test is generally applied at the partnership or corporate level. However, such test is applied at the partner, shareholder, or other appropriate level if a partnership or an S corporation is formed or availed of for the principal purpose of either avoiding the application of the mid-quarter convention or having it apply where it otherwise would not apply (Reg. § 1.168(d)-1(b)(6)).

*Certain nonrecognition transactions*

Generally, the depreciable basis of transferred property in a nontaxable transfer under Code Sec. 332, 351, 361, 721, or 731 is not considered by the transferor in applying the 40-percent test if the property was placed in service in the year of transfer. Such property is deemed placed in service by the transferee on the date of transfer and must be considered by the transferee in applying the 40-percent test. These rules do not cover transfers between members of a consolidated group (Reg. § 1.168(d)-1(b)(7)).

However, the date that the transferor placed the property in service must be used in applying the applicable convention to determine when the recovery period for the transferred property begins. Thus, if the mid-quarter convention applies to property transferred in a nonrecognition transaction indicated above, the recovery period for the property begins on the midpoint of the quarter of the tax year that the transferor placed the property in service.

If the transferor placed the transferred property in service in a short tax year, the transferor is treated as having a 12-month tax year beginning on the first day of the short tax year for purposes of applying the applicable convention and allocating the depreciation deduction between the transferor and the transferee. The depreciation deduction is allocated based on the number of months in the transferor's tax year that each party held the property in service. The transferor would include the month that the property is placed in service and exclude the month in which the transfer occurs.

The balance of the depreciation deduction for the transferor's tax year in which the property was transferred is allocated to the transferee. For the remainder of the transferee's current tax year (if the transferee has a different tax year than the transferor) and for subsequent tax years, the depreciation deduction for the transferee is calculated by allocating to the transferee's tax year the depreciation attributable to each recovery year, or portion thereof, that falls within the transferee's tax year.

The transferor may use either the mid-quarter or the half-year convention in determining the depreciation deduction for the transferred property if the applicable convention is not determined by the time the income tax return for the year of transfer is filed because the transferee's tax year has not ended. However, the transferor must indicate such fact on the depreciation form. If the transferee determines that a different convention applies to the transferred property, the transferor should redetermine the depreciation deduction and file an amended return within the period of limitation (Reg. § 1.168(d)-1(b)(7)).

***Example (7):*** During the current tax year, a calendar-year taxpayer purchases \$100,000 of satellite equipment and \$15,000 of computer equipment. The former is placed in service in January and the latter is placed in service in February. On October 1, the computer equipment is transferred to a calendar-year partnership in a nontaxable transaction under Code Sec. 721. During the current tax year, the partnership purchases 30 office desks for a total of \$15,000 and places them in service in June.

In applying the 40% test, the computer equipment is treated as placed in service by the transferee-partnership on the date of transfer (October 1) because the equipment was transferred in a nontaxable transfer in the same tax year that it was placed in service by the transferor. The \$15,000 depreciable basis of the computer equipment that is placed in service during the last three months of the transferee's tax year exceeds \$12,000 (40% of the \$30,000 aggregate depreciable bases of property placed in service by the transferee during the tax year (\$15,000 desks + \$15,000 computer equipment)). Thus, the transferee satisfies the 40% test and the mid-quarter convention applies to the property placed in service by the transferee (including the transferred property).

In applying the mid-quarter convention to the computer equipment, the recovery period of the equipment begins on the mid-point of the first quarter of the transferor's tax year (February 15). The depreciation deduction allowable for the transferor's tax year is $5,250 ($15,000 × 35%) (Table 2 at ¶ 180, first-year table percentage for five year property subject to mid-quarter convention and placed in service in first quarter).

The depreciation deduction is allocated between the transferor and the transferee based on the number of months that each held the property in service. For this purpose, the computer equipment is treated as in service for 11 months (Feb.-Dec.) during the transferor's tax year and the transferor held it for 8 of the 11 months (Feb.-Sep.). Thus, the transferor's depreciation deduction on the computer equipment is $3,818 (8/11 × $5,250). The balance of the depreciation deduction on the computer equipment for the transferor's tax year, $1,432 (3/11 × $5,250), is allocated to the transferee.

In the following tax year, the transferee's depreciation deduction on the computer equipment is $3,900 ($15,000 × 26%) (second-year table percentage).

This example is based on the example in Reg. § 1.168(d)-1(b)(7).

# Classification and Recovery Period of Property

## ¶ 100

## MACRS Property Classes and Recovery Periods

***A "Quick-Reference" recovery-period chart is reproduced in the back of this book before the Case Table. This chart lists numerous types of assets and business activities, as well as the recovery period for these assets and the assets used in these business activities. If the particular asset or business activity is discussed in this book, a cross-reference is provided. A separate group of Quick Reference charts list structural components of a building generally depreciable over the recovery period of the building and section 1245 components which are generally depreciable over 5 or 7 years. Rev. Proc. 87-56, which provides a comprehensive table of depreciation periods is reproduced at ¶ 191.***

Each item of property depreciated under MACRS is assigned to a property class which establishes the number of years over which the basis of an asset is recovered (the recovery period). A comprehensive IRS table of these property classes and depreciation periods (including ADS recovery periods) for MACRS property is contained in Rev. Proc. 87-56, which is reproduced at ¶ 191. The explanations at ¶ 190 and ¶ 191 explain how to determine the recovery period of a particular asset.

Recovery periods are the same for new and used MACRS property.

Recovery years are 12-month periods. The 12-month period begins on the date that the property is considered placed in service under the applicable convention. For example, if an automobile with a five-year recovery period is placed in service in the 2021 calendar tax year and the half-year convention applies, the recovery period begins on July 1, 2021, and ends on June 30, 2026. Depreciation will be claimed in each of six tax years (2021, 2022, 2023, 2024, 2025, and 2026) even though the recovery period is only five years.

The applicable recovery periods are not elective but are prescribed for each property class. The specific recovery period will depend upon whether the property is being depreciated under the general MACRS depreciation rules (GDS) or the alternative MACRS depreciation system (ADS).

The following are the property classes and GDS recovery periods (Code Sec. 168(c)):

| *Property Class* | *Recovery Period* |
|---|---|
| 3-year property | 3-years (¶ 102) |
| 5-year property | 5-years (¶ 104) |
| 7-year property | 7-years (¶ 106) |
| 10-year property | 10-years (¶ 108) |
| 15-year property | 15-years (¶ 110) |
| 20-year property | 20-years (¶ 112) |
| Water utility property | 25-years (¶ 113) |
| Residential rental property | 27.5-years (¶ 114) |
| Nonresidential real property | 39 or 31.5 years (¶ 116) |
| Railroad grading and tunnel bores | 50-years (¶ 120) |

Longer recovery periods generally apply if the alternative MACRS depreciation system (ADS) is used (¶ 150).

Shorter recovery periods may apply to property used on an Indian reservation (¶ 124).

Property is classified based upon the property's class life (if any) unless a different recovery class is assigned under Code Sec. 168(e)(2) (residential rental and nonresidential real property), Code Sec. 168(e)(3) (property assigned to a recovery class notwithstanding the class life of the property, if any), or Code Sec. 168(e)(4) (railroad grading and tunnel bores).

Class lives and recovery periods for MACRS purposes are set forth in Rev. Proc. 87-56, 1987-2 CB 674, and vary in some respects from the class lives set forth in Rev. Proc. 83-35, 1983-1 CB 745, which is still effective for property depreciated under ACRS or the Class Life Asset Depreciation Range (CLADR) System. Class lives and recovery periods as prescribed under Rev. Proc. 87-56 are set forth at ¶ 190.

## ¶ 102

## 3-Year Property

Three-year property is defined as property with a class life of four years or less (Code Sec. 168(e)(1)), but also includes certain property specifically designated as 3-year property by Code Sec. 168(e)(3). The 200-percent declining-balance method applies (¶ 84).

Three-year property includes (but is not limited to):

(1) Tractor units for use over the road (Rev. Proc. 87-56 Asset Class 00.26).

Tractor units are not defined for depreciation purposes, but presumably the definition provided in Reg. § 145.4051-1(e)(1) for excise tax purposes would apply. In general, this regulation provides that a tractor is a highway vehicle primarily designed to tow a vehicle, such as a trailer or semitrailer, but which does not carry cargo on the same chassis as the engine. A vehicle equipped with air brakes and/or a towing package is presumed to be a tractor.

In contrast to a tractor unit, a truck (5-year property) is a highway vehicle primarily designed to transport its load on the same chassis as the engine even if it is also equipped to tow a vehicle, such as a trailer or semitrailer (Reg. § 145.4051-1(e)(2)).

Assets used in the commercial and contract carrying of freight by road, except transportation assets included in classes with prefix 00.2 are 5-year property (Rev. Proc. 87-56 Asset Class 42.0).

(2) Breeding hogs (Rev. Proc. 87-56 Asset Class 01.23).

(3) Any race horse placed in service after December 31, 2008 and before January 1, 2022 regardless of its age when placed in service (Code Sec. 168(e)(3)(A)(i)(I)).

(4) Any race horse placed in service after December 31, 2021 which is more than two years old when placed in service by the purchaser (Code Sec. 168(e)(3)(A)(i)(II)).

(5) Any horse other than a race horse that is more than 12 years old when placed in service (Code Sec. 168(e)(3)(A)(ii))

A race horse is generally considered placed in service when its training begins. This is usually at the end of its yearling year, which is typically less than two years after birth. A race horse that has previously raced is generally considered placed in service when purchased from the prior owner. A horse's age is measured by reference to its actual birth date rather than the racing industry's treatment of January 1 of the year of birth as the birth date (Prop. Reg. § 1.168-3(c)(iii) (ACRS); Rev. Proc. 87-56, 1987-2 CB 674, as clarified and modified by Rev. Proc. 88-22, 1988-1 CB 785).

Race horses that are two years or younger when placed in service are 7-year MACRS property if placed in service before January 1, 2009 or after December 31, 2021 (Asset Class 01.225 of Rev. Proc. 87-56 at ¶ 191).

Race horses have no class life. Therefore, the alternative depreciation system (ADS) recovery period of a race horse, regardless of age, is 12 years (Asset Class 01.223 and 01.225 of Rev. Proc. 87-56).

For additional information regarding race horses and other types of horses, see ¶ 118.

Reg. § 1.1231-2(c)(1) provides rules and examples for determining whether a horse is a race horse. Presumably, these guidelines may be used for depreciation classification purposes.

(5) Qualified rent-to-own property (Code Sec. 168(e)(3)(A)(iii)).

Qualified rent-to-own property is treated as 3-year property, effective for property placed in service after August 5, 1997 (Code Sec. 168(e)(3)(A)(iii)). A 4-year ADS period is assigned. In general, qualified rent-to-own property is property held by a rent-to-own dealer for purposes of being subject to a rent-to-own contract (Code Sec. 168(i)(14)). Previously, such property was classified as 5-year property (Asset Class 57.0, Distributive Trades and Services) (Rev. Rul. 95-52, 1995-2 CB 27; Rev. Proc. 95-38, 1995-2 CB 397). See, also, ¶ 364 for treatment of rent-to-own property under the income forecast depreciation method.

Purchased computer software that is not amortizable under Code Sec. 197 is generally amortized over a 3-year period using the straight-line method beginning in the month it is placed in service (Code Sec. 167(f)(1); Reg. § 1.167(a)-14). Purchased off-the-shelf computer software described in Code Sec. 197(e)(A)(3)(i) is also eligible for expensing under Code Sec. 179. See ¶ 48 for a discussion of the various treatments available for purchased and developed computer software.

See ¶ 191 for a table of Asset Classes and recovery periods.

## ¶ 104

## 5-Year Property

Property with a class life of more than four but less than 10 years is generally classified as 5-year property (Code Sec. 168(e)(1)). In addition, certain property is specifically categorized as 5-year property even though the class life does not fall within this class life range (Code Sec. 168(e)(3)(B)). The 200-percent declining-balance method applies (¶ 84).

Five-year property includes (but is not limited to):

(1) automobiles, light general purpose trucks, and (Code Sec. 168(e)(3)(B)(i)) as well as heavy general purpose trucks (Asset Classes 00.22, 00.241, and 00.242 of Rev. Proc. 87-56 at ¶ 191; Code Sec. 168(e)(3)(B)(i)).

*Trucks.* A truck is a highway vehicle primarily designed to transport its load on the same chassis as the engine even if it is also equipped to tow a vehicle, such as a trailer or semitrailer (Reg. § 145.4051-1(e)(2)).

A light general purpose truck includes trucks for use over the road with actual unloaded weight of less than 13,000 pounds. Heavy general purpose trucks are trucks for use over the road with actual unloaded weight of 13,000 pounds or greater.

Heavy general purpose trucks include concrete ready mix trucks and ore trucks. The distinction between light and heavy trucks, which are both 5-year property, is important if the MACRS alternative depreciation system (ADS) is used because a heavy truck has an ADS depreciation period of 6 years and a light truck has a 5-year ADS period. Automobiles also have a 5-year ADS recovery period.

Tractor units that pull trailers are 3-year property (Rev. Proc. 87-56 Asset Class 00.26). Tractor units are defined in Reg.§ 145.4051-1(e)(1)(i). See ¶ 102.

The IRS has ruled that a step truck (e.g., a UPS or FED EX delivery truck) is a heavy general purpose truck (CCA Letter Ruling 002524, January 31, 2004). The IRS in its market segmentation specialization program for the garden supplies industry classifies a dump truck as a heavy truck.

*Indy race car.* Indianapolis race cars are 7-year property (Rev. Proc. 87-56 Asset Class 79.0, relating to property used for recreation or entertainment on payment of a fee for admission) and not 5-year property (Asset Class 00.22, automobiles) (CCA Letter Ruling 200052019, September 27, 2000).

*Recreational vehicles.* A recreational vehicle, RV, or motor home is a light general purposes truck if its unloaded weight is less than 13,000 pounds. Otherwise an RV or motor home is a heavy general purpose truck (IRS Letter Ruling 8630022, April 25, 1986). This ruling was issued to an S corporation that owned and leased various types of RV vehicles pursuant to lease agreements. Note, also, that an RV or motor home would not be subject to the passenger automobile depreciation caps since it would be considered a truck with a (loaded) gross vehicle weight rating in excess of 6,000 pounds. See ¶ 208. As to the eligibility of an RV or motor home for the Code Sec. 179 deduction, see the discussion of "*Lodging facilities*" at ¶ 302.

The Tax Court has ruled that an RV or motor home is considered a dwelling unit for purposes of the vacation home rules of (Code Sec. 280A) (*D.R. Jackson*, 108 TCM 150, Dec. 59,986(M), TC Memo. 2014-160, aff'd, unpublished opinion, CA-9, 2017-1 USTC ¶ 50,121; *R.L. Haberkorn,* 75 TC 259, Dec. 37,392; *K. Dunford*, 106 TCM 130, Dec. 59,609(M), TC Memo. 2013-189; *C.H. Perry,* 71 TCM 2840, Dec. 51,308(M), TC Memo. 1996-194). Under these rules an individual or S corporation may not claim a business or income production deduction for the use of the dwelling unit if the dwelling unit is used for personal purposes for more than 14 days during the tax year. If the dwelling unit is rented the lessor- taxpayer may not use the dwelling unit for the greater of more than 14 days or 10 percent of the number of days during the tax year that the dwelling unit is rented at fair market value. According to the Jackson case, any personal use during the course of a day, such as "watching television," is counted as using the vehicle as a residence even if the predominant use of the vehicle during the day is for business. Consequently, in the Jackson case all depreciation and business interest deductions claimed by an individual taxpayer who attended rv rallies primarily for the purpose of selling insurance were disallowed. The case mentions no other deductions. In the *Perry* case, gas, depreciation and maintenance on a motor home were disallowed under Code Sec. 280A. However, in the Dunford case, the IRS did not contest the taxpayer's use of the standard mileage rate for the business use of a motor home even though the standard mileage rate reflects maintenance, gas, and depreciation. It should be noted that the Code Sec. 280A deduction limitation does not apply to business deductions which are otherwise allowable under Code Sec. 162(a)(2) ("traveling expenses (including amounts expended for meals and lodging other than amounts which are lavish or extravagant under the circumstances) while away from home in the pursuit of a trade or business") or any deduction which meets the tests of Code Sec. 162(a)(2) but is allowable under another provision (Code Sec. 280A(f)(4)). This exception does not apply if the taxpayer is away from home in the pursuit of the trade or business of renting dwelling units. This exception has not been discussed in the context of a motor home as a basis for deducting gas, maintenance, and depreciation for business mileage. In addition, otherwise allowable non-business deductions (e.g., taxes and qualified residence interest) may be claimed (Code Sec. 280A(e)(2)). See, *K. Dunford*, 106 TCM 130, Dec. 59,609(M), TC Memo. 2013-189, interest on debt secured by motor home used as a residence more than 14 days during the tax year was deductible underCode Sec. 163(h).

(2) taxis and buses (Rev. Proc. 87-56 Asset Classes 00.22 and 00.23);

(3) airplanes not used in commercial or contract carrying of passengers or freight; all helicopters (Rev. Proc. 87-56 Asset Class 00.21);

Commercial/contract airplanes are 7-year property (Rev. Proc. 87-56 Asset Class 45.0).

Planes used in a pilot school are 5-year property (Rev. Proc. 87-56 Asset Class 57.0).

(4) trailers and trailer-mounted containers (Rev. Proc. 87-56 Asset Class 00.27) (see ¶ 5);

(5) computers and peripheral equipment (Code Sec. 168(i)(2)(B)) (Rev. Proc. 87-56 Asset Class 00.12);

A computer is a programmable electronically activated device capable of accepting information, applying prescribed processes to the information, and supplying the results of these processes with or without human intervention. It usually consists of a central processing unit containing extensive storage, logic, arithmetic, and control capabilities (Code Sec. 168(i)(2)(B); Rev. Proc. 87-56 Asset Class 00.12 description).

Peripheral equipment consists of auxiliary machines designed to be placed under the control of the computer. Examples include: card readers, card punches, magnetic tape feeds, high speed printers, optical character readers, tape cassettes, mass storage units, paper tape equipment, keypunches, data entry devices, teleprinters, terminals, tape drives, disc drives, disc files, disc packs, visual image projector tubes, card sorters, plotters, and collators (Assets Class 00.12 description).

Peripheral equipment does not include (1) typewriters, calculators, adding and accounting machines, copiers, duplicating equipment, and similar equipment or (2) equipment of a kind used primarily for amusement or entertainment of the user.

Computers and peripheral equipment are one of three types of qualified technological equipment (see below) which are assigned a five-year GDS recovery period by Code Sec. 168(e)(3)(B)(iv). Rev. Proc. 87-56 Asset Class 00.12 is entitled "Information Systems" and consists entirely of computers and peripheral equipment.

In general, the definitions of computers and peripheral equipment contained in Code Sec. 168(i)(2) and Asset Class 00.12 are nearly identical. A five-year GDS and ADS recovery period applies in each case. One important difference, however, is that Asset Class 00.12 only applies to computers and peripheral equipment that are "used in administering normal business transactions and the maintenance of business records, their retrieval and analysis." No such requirement exists under the Code Sec. 168(i)(2) definition.

Peripheral equipment does not include any equipment which is an integral part of other property which is not a computer (Code Sec. 168(i)(2)(B)(iv)). In this regard, Asset Class 00.12 states that peripheral equipment "does not include equipment that is an integral part of other capital equipment that is included in other classes of economic activity, i.e., computers used primarily for process or production control, switching, channeling, and automating distributive trades and services such as point of sale (POS) computer systems."

In Chief Counsel Advice 200229021 (April 12, 2002), the IRS ruled that assets relating to hydroelectric and nuclear power plants such as control and/or monitoring systems, nuclear simulator complex, radiation measurement and detection equipment, dispatch boards, supervisory control units, relays and meters, training simulator, and pilot wire protection were not computer or peripheral equipment under Rev. Proc. 87-56 Asset Class 00.12 because the equipment was not used in administering normal business transactions and the maintenance of business records, their retrieval and analysis. In addition, these assets did not qualify under Asset Class 00.12 or Code Sec. 168(i)(2) because they are an integral part of property which is not a computer.

Computer software that is not a Code Sec. 197 intangible is generally amortized over 3 years beginning in the month it is placed in service. However, software that is part of the purchase price of a computer is depreciated over 5 years as part of the cost of the computer. Separately purchased off-the-shelf computer software is eligible for expensing under Code Sec. 179 (Code Sec. 179(d)(1)(A)).

See ¶ 48 for details concerning the depreciation of computer software.

Computers and peripheral equipment are no longer considered a category of listed property if placed in service after 2017 (Code Sec. 280F(d)(4)). See ¶ 208.

(6) data handling equipment other than computers, such as typewriters, calculators, adding and accounting machines, copiers, duplicating equipment, and similar equipment (Code Sec. 168(i)(2)(B)(iv); Rev. Proc. 87-56 Asset Class 00.13);

(7) semi-conductor manufacturing equipment (Code Sec. 168(e)(3)(B)(ii));

This category includes printed wiring board and printed wiring assembly production equipment.

(8) computer-based telephone central office switching equipment (Code Sec. 168(e)(3)(B)(iii); Rev. Proc. 87-56 Asset Class 48.121);

(9) qualified technological equipment, which is defined as computers and peripheral equipment (see above), high technology telephone station equipment installed on a customer's premises, and high technology medical equipment (Code Sec. 168(e)(3)(B)(iv); Code Sec. 168(i)(2));

Telephone station equipment (teletypewriters, telephones, booths, private exchanges, and comparable equipment described in Rev. Proc. 87-56 Asset Class 48.13) which is not considered qualified technological equipment is 7-year property.

High technology medical equipment means any electronic, electromechanical, or computer-based high technology equipment used in the screening, monitoring, observation, diagnosis, or treatment of patients in a laboratory, medical, or hospital environment (Code Sec. 168(i)(2)(C)). Property used in the provision of personal or professional services is classified as MACRS 5-year property by reason of its status as property described in Asset Class 57.0 of Rev. Proc. 87-56 at ¶ 191. Most high technology equipment appears to qualify as five-year property under Asset

Class 57.0 independently of its classification as five-year property by Code Sec. 168(e)(3)(B)(iv).

(10) section 1245 property used in connection with research and experimentation as that term is defined for purposes of Code Sec. 174 (Code Sec. 168(e)(3)(B)(v); Code Sec. 168(i)(11));

Under ACRS (pre-1986) proposed regulations, research and experimentation property is defined as section 1245 property *predominantly* used in connection with research and experimentation (as described in Code Sec. 174 and Reg. § 1.174-2(a)). The property must be used (A) by its owner to conduct research and experimentation in its owner's trade or business, (B) by its owner to conduct research and experimentation for another person, (C) by a lessee to conduct research and experimentation in its trade or business, or (D) by the lessee to conduct research and experimentation for another person (Prop. Reg. § 1.168-3(c)(iii)). No MACRS regulations defining research and experimentation property have yet been issued. The ACRS and MACRS Code definitions ("section 1245 property used in connection with research and experimentation expenditures . . . " etc.), however, are identical.

See ¶ 168 for depreciation computation if a property's use changes to or from research and experimentation during its recovery period.

See ¶ 68 regarding capitalization and expensing of research and experimentation expenditures under Code Sec. 174.

(11) Energy property described in Code Sec. 48(a)(3)(A) (Code Sec. 168(e)(3)(B)(vi)(I); see Reg.§ 1.48-9 for detailed definitions) and certain small power production biomass facilities (Code Sec. 168(e)(3)(B)(vi)(II));

*Energy property.* The following types of property are described in Code Sec. 48(a)(3)(A) and qualify for a 5-year recovery period under this category (even if the property would otherwise be treated as public utility property (Code Sec. 168(e)(3)(B), last sentence):

(a) equipment (excepting property used to generate energy for the purposes of heating a swimming pool) which uses solar (or wind (see below)) energy to (a) generate electricity (e.g., solar panels), (b) heat or cool (or provide hot water for use in) a structure, or (c) provide solar (or wind) process heat,

(b) equipment placed in service after December 31, 2005 that uses solar energy to illuminate the inside of a structure using fiber-optic distributed sunlight but only with respect to property the construction of which begins before January 1, 2022,

(c) equipment used to produce, distribute, or use energy derived from a geothermal deposit (within the meaning of Code Sec. 613(e)(2)), but only, in the case of electricity generated by geothermal power, up to (but not including) the electrical transmission stage,

(d) qualified fuel cell property or qualified microturbine property,

(e) combined heat and power system property,

(f) qualified small wind energy property, or

(g) equipment which uses the ground or ground water as a thermal energy source to heat a structure or as a thermal energy sink to cool a structure, but only with respect to property the construction of which begins before January 1, 2022.

Wind energy property qualifies as 5-year property if it would be described in Code Sec. 48(a)(3)(A)(i) (item (a) above) if the words "wind energy" are substituted for the words "solar energy" (Code Sec. 168(e)(3)(B)(vi)).

Note that if the Code Sec. 48 energy credit is claimed on the preceding property, the basis for purposes of determining gain or loss and depreciation deductions (including bonus depreciation and section 179 deductions) must be reduced by 50% of the energy credit claimed (Code Sec. 50(c)(3)(A)).

A technical correction made by the Energy Tax Incentives Act of 2005 (P.L. 109-58) clarifies that property described in items a - g may qualify for a five-year recovery period even though the property also qualifies for the Code Sec. 45 credit for electricity produced from renewable resources (Code Sec. 168(e)(3)(B)(vi)(I)).

In IRS Letter Ruling 201214007, January 3, 2012, the IRS ruled that pursuant to Code Sec. 167(c)(2) (which treats the basis of property purchased subject to a leasehold interest as including the value of the leasehold interest), the purchase price of a wind energy facility (i.e., windmill) that was subject to a favorable power purchase agreement (PPA) was entirely allocable to the facility, thereby making the portion of the purchase price allocable to the PPA eligible for accelerated depreciation as part of the adjusted basis of the facility (MACRS 5-year energy property). In addition, allocation to the adjusted basis of the facility would causes the available energy investment tax credit to be increased. Subsequently, the IRS without explanation, revoked the ruling as being inconsistent with "the current views of the Service" (IRS Letter Ruling 201249013, September 6, 2012). The revocation was not entirely unexpected insofar as the ruling in IRS Letter Ruling 201214007 was inconsistent with existing IRS guidance that excludes from basis the value of PPAs for purpose of computing the amount of a section 1603 energy grant that may be claimed in lieu of an energy credit (http://www.treasury.gov/initiatives/recovery/Pages/1603.aspx).

As to the placed-in-service date of a wind energy farm, see IRS Letter Ruling 200334031, May 19, 2003.

*Small power production facility.* Effective for property placed in service before March 24, 2018, MACRS 5-year property includes a qualifying small power production facility within the meaning of section 3(17)(C) of the Federal Power Act (16 U.S.C. 796(17)(C)), as in effect on September 1, 1986, which also qualifies as biomass property described in Code Sec. 48(l)(15), as in effect on the day before the date of the enactment of the Revenue Reconciliation Act of 1990 (Code Sec. 168(e)(3)(B)(vi)(II)). A qualifying small power production facility is defined as a facility with a power production capacity not greater than 80 megawatts and that is not owned more than 50 percent by an electric utility or any affiliate of an electric utility. The electric utility ownership limitation in section 3(17)(C) of the Federal Power Act was repealed by the Energy Policy Act of 2005 (P.L. 109-58) but continues to apply to property placed in service before March 24, 2018 for purposes of determining whether the 5-year recovery period is applicable. See IRS Letter Ruling 201539024, June 23, 2015.

Effective for property placed in service after March 23, 2018, the reference to the definition of a qualifying small power production facility within the meaning of section 3(17)(C) of the Federal Power Act is eliminated and replaced with a reference to property with a power production capacity of not greater than 80 megawatts. The rule that electric utilities owning more than a 50 percent interest in such a production facility are not entitled to depreciate the facility over a 5-year period is eliminated (Code Sec. 168(e)(3)(B)(vi)(II)). In addition, the 5-year recovery period applies even if the production facility is considered public utility property (Code Sec. 168(e)(3)(B), last sentence).

(12) breeding cattle and dairy cattle (Asset Class 01.21) and breeding sheep and breeding goats (Rev. Proc. 87-56 Asset Class 01.24);

Raised cattle usually have no depreciable basis because associated costs are currently deducted. See ¶ 118 for a discussion of farm property.

(13) assets used in construction by certain contractors, builders, and real estate subdividers and developers (Rev. Proc. 87-56 Asset Class 15.0);

(14) logging machinery and equipment and road building equipment used by logging and sawmill operators and pulp manufacturers for their own account (Rev. Proc. 87-56 Asset Class 24.1) (see Asset Classes 24.2 and 24.3 for sawmill equipment depreciation periods);

(15) assets used in the commercial and contract carrying of freight by road, except for transportation assets included in classes with the prefix 00.2 (Rev. Proc. 87-56 Asset Class 42.0, Motor Transport—Freight);

(16) assets used in the urban and interurban commercial and contract carrying of passengers by road, except for transportation assets included in classes with the prefix 00.2 (Rev. Proc. 87-56 Asset Class 41, Motor Transport—Passengers);

Transportation assets with prefix 00.2 generally include automobiles (5-year property), light and heavy trucks (5-year property), tractor units for use over-the road (three-year property), and trailers and trailer-mounted containers (five-year property);

(17) qualified New York Liberty Zone leasehold improvement property (see ¶ 124A);

(18) assets used in distributive trades and services, including assets used in wholesale and retail trade and personal and professional services and assets used in marketing petroleum and petroleum products (see below) (Rev. Proc. 87-56 Asset Class 57.0).

(19) new farm machinery or equipment (other than a grain bin, cotton ginning asset, fence or land improvement) placed in service in 2009 or after 2017 (Code Sec. 168(e)(3)(B)(vii), as added by P.L. 110-343 and Code Sec. 168(e)(3)(B)(vii)). See ¶ 118.

(20) assets used in offshore drilling for oil and gas (Asset Class 13.0) and onshore drilling of oil and gas wells (Rev. Proc. 87-56 Asset Class 13.1).

*Personal and professional services/retail and wholesale trades*

Rev. Proc. 87-56 Asset Class 57.0 encompasses a large number of taxpayers. As in the case of any business activity class (business activity classes are described in Table B-2 of Rev. Proc. 87-56 at ¶ 191), recovery periods for specific assets described in Table B-1 take precedence even if the asset is used in the Asset Class 57.0 activity. For example, office furniture used by a lawyer is considered 7-year property because it is listed in Table B-1 (Asset Class 00.11). However, professional reference books (e.g., a professional library purchased by a lawyer) used in the same office are 5-year property (Asset Class 57.0) because books are not described in Table B-1. However, if a specific asset listed in Table B-1 is also specifically listed in the Table B-2 business activity classification, then the recovery period for the business activity classification in Table B-2 governs. This situation, however, is rare and does not affect Asset Class 57.0 since no specific asset types are listed there. See ¶ 191 for additional discussion of these points.

Examples of personal and professional services are not specifically set forth in the description for MACRS Asset Class 57.0 contained in Rev. Proc. 87-56. However, Rev. Proc. 77-10 (1977-1 CB 548), which provided class lives for purposes of the ADR depreciation system, listed some examples of personal and professional services included within this classification. Rev. Proc. 77-10 specifically listed hotels and motels, laundry or laundromats, and dry cleaning establishments, beauty and barber shops, photographic studios and mortuaries as examples of personal service businesses. Examples of professional service businesses cited by Rev. Proc. 77-10 included services offered by doctors, dentists, lawyers, accountants, architects, engineers, and veterinarians. Assets used in the provision of repair and maintenance services, assets used in providing fire and burglary protection services are also included. Equipment or facilities used by a cemetery organization, news agency, teletype wire service, and frozen food lockers were included.

Rev. Proc. 77-10 also indicates that wholesale and retail trade includes activities of purchasing, assembling, storing, sorting, grading, and selling goods at the wholesale or retail level. Specific examples are restaurants, cafes, coin-operated dispensing machines, and the brokerage of scrap metal. A corporation engaged in the business of leasing warehouse space was engaged in an Asset Class 57.0 activity (IRS Letter Ruling 9411002, November 19, 1993).

Activities involving the sale of merchandise, food and other items to the general public for personal or household consumption, and the rendering of services incidental to the sale of goods are considered retail activities rather than manufacturing (Rev. Rul. 81-66, 1981 CB 19).

A manufacturer stored food and meat products that it manufactured in distribution centers before selling the products to others. Citing Rev. Rul. 77-476 (see ¶ 190), the IRS held that the taxpayer was not engaged in a wholesale distributive trade or business (Asset Class 57.0). Instead, assets related to the distribution centers were classified as seven-year property (Asset Class 20.4, Manufacture of Other Food and Kindred Products). Test kitchens were also included in Asset Class 20.4 (Chief Counsel Advice 200137026, June 14, 2001).

Rev. Proc. 77-10 listed glassware, silverware, crockery, china, linens, napkins, tablecloths, towels, sheets, pillowcases used by a restaurant or hotel or motel as falling within the retail/wholesale and personal/professional service category. However, the IRS has issued a procedure under which smallwares used by restaurants and bars can be deducted in the year of purchase. See ¶ 125.

*Rental businesses.* Taxpayers who rent consumer durables, other than pursuant to rent-to-own contracts, are engaged in an Asset Class 57.0 business activity, according to the IRS (Rev. Rul. 95-52, 1995-2 CB 27). Consumer durables rented pursuant to a rent-to-own contract were depreciated over five-years as Asset Class 57.0 property prior to enactment of Code Sec. 168(e)(3)(A)(iii), which now provides a three-year recovery period for such property. See ¶ 102.

Tuxedo rental is an Asset Class 57.0 activity.

The rental of furniture is generally considered an Asset Class 57.0 activity. However, if the furniture is used in an office, then the IRS may require that it be depreciated over seven years as office furniture. See "*Office furniture, fixtures, and equipment*," below.

Generally, the IRS will determine the depreciation period of an asset by reference to the use to which the lessee puts the property unless a separate Asset Class has been established for the lessor's business activity. See ¶ 191, "*Leased property.*"

*Property used in connection with residential rental property.* The IRS has ruled that the rental of MACRS 27.5-year residential rental property is an Asset Class 57.0 activity. As a result, free-standing property (e.g., appliances, such as stoves and refrigerators, and furniture in tenant apartments or a lobby) and items that are considered personal property components of the building under the cost segregation rules described at ¶ 127 and following, such as appliances (e.g., dishwashers and refrigerators), carpets, blinds, window treatments, and portable air conditioning units (see ¶ 127A) etc., are 5-year property (five-year GDS recovery period and nine-year ADS recovery period). IRS Publication 527 (Residential Rental Property) and Form 4562 (Depreciation and Amortization) which have consistently categorized this property as 7-year property, have been corrected (Announcement 99-82, 1999-2 CB 244).

Effective for property placed in service in tax years beginning after 2017, the rule which prevents the section 179 deduction from being claimed on property used in connection with lodging (e.g., residential rental units) is eliminated (Code Sec. 179(d)(1)). See ¶ 302.

Office furniture, fixtures, and equipment (Rev. Proc. 87-56 Asset Class 00.11) (Office furniture, fixtures, and equipment) (¶ 106) used in a manager's office is 7-year property because such property is described in the first part of the Rev. Proc. 87-56 Asset Classification table (see discussions and table at ¶ 190 and ¶ 191). Land improvements used in connection with residential rental property are 15-year property (Asset Class 00.3) (Land improvements) (¶ 110). The building itself and any structural components, such as a replacement HVAC, added to the building are depreciated as 27.5 year residential rental property using the straight-line method and a 27.5-year recovery period (see ¶ 114 and ¶ 126 and following). For the treatment of replacement roofs, see ¶ 125.

In a letter ruling that classified a wide variety of assets used in a residential rental complex the IRS ruled that: (1) heating/air conditioning equipment (HVAC); smoke detectors and water heaters were 27.5 year residential rental property; (2) walks; streets; driveways; electrical system; assets that are part of a water distribution system; playground equipment; fencing; and landscaping were 15-year property (land improvements - Asset Class 00.3); (3) a sewage treatment plant was 15-year property (municipal wastewater treatment plant - Asset Class 50.0); (4) assets that are part of a sanitary sewer system were 20-year property (municipal sewer - Asset Class 51.0) (IRS Letter Ruling 8848039, September. 02, 1988). Note that items included in Asset Class 51.0 now have a 25-year recovery period. See ¶ 113.

*Office furniture, fixtures, and equipment used in retail industry.* According to guidelines contained in the IRS Internal Revenue Manual, a common issue in the retail industry is whether furniture, fixtures, and equipment is 7-year property (Rev. Proc. 87-56 Asset Class 00.11 (Office furniture, fixtures, and equipment) (¶ 106) or 5-year property under MACRS Asset Class 57.0 (IRM 4.43.1.9.6.4 (07-23-2009))). The guidelines state: "The decision is based entirely on the asset's inherent nature. For example, if a table is used on the retail floor for display or for cutting material and can also be used in the store manager's office, then it is 7-year property under Class 00.11. However, if a table can only be used on the retail floor for display or cutting material, then it is 5-year property under Class 57.0."

*Norwest Corporation and Subsidiaries*, 70 TCM 416, Dec. 50,834(M) involved the depreciation of furniture and fixtures used in a bank. The IRS conceded that furniture which was only suitable for use in a bank (property unique to banks) was 5-year property (Asset Class 57.0). However, the IRS argued, and the court agreed, that furniture and fixtures that were suitable for use in a variety of businesses were not removed from Asset Class 00.11 (7-year property) to Asset Class 57.0 merely because they were used by a bank.

In a subsequent case involving the same taxpayer, the Tax Court delved into the issue in more detail and established a priority rule. If an asset is described in both an asset category (Asset Classes 00.11 through 00.4) and an activity category (Asset Classes 01.1 through 80.0), the asset category classification will prevail (*Norwest Corporation and Subsidiaries*, 111 TC 105, Dec. 52,830). See ¶ 190 for details.

It appears that this priority rule is causing problems for taxpayers in the short-term furniture rental business. This business involves the temporary rental of furniture for business or residential use. Taxpayers in this service industry have apparently depreciated all such furniture over a five-year period as Asset Class 57.0 property without objection from the IRS. In the wake of the *Norwest* decision, however, it has been reported that IRS auditors are taking the position that when such furniture is rented for office use the priority rule applies and it should be depreciated as 7-year property (Asset Class 00.11). While the IRS position may be correct, it can result in unfortunate complications when the same furniture is rented multiple times for office use and residential use. In such case, the furniture is reclassified in the year in which its use changes and special depreciation calculations are required (Code Sec. 168(i)(5); Prop. Reg. § 1.168(i)-4 (explaining the rule in the context of ACRS)). See ¶ 169 for computational details. It may be necessary to enact legislation similar to that which applies to rent-to-own property (Code Sec. 168(e)(3)(A); Code Sec. 168(i)(14)) to eliminate this problem. See, for example, H.R. 1597 (introduced April 3, 2003, in the first session of the 108th Congress), which would retroactively classify office furniture held by a rental dealer for short-term rentals of no longer than 18 months as five-year property.

IRS Asset Class descriptions are provided at ¶ 191.

## ¶ 106

## 7-Year Property

Property with a class life of at least 10 but less than 16 years or without any class life (and not classified as residential rental property or nonresidential real property) is generally classified as 7-year property (Code Sec. 168(e)(3)(C)). The 200-percent declining-balance method applies (¶ 84).

*Office furniture, fixtures, and equipment.* This class includes desks, files, safes, overhead projectors, cell phones or cellular phones, fax machines, and communications equipment not used included in other property classes (Rev. Proc. 87-56 Asset Class 00.11). Note that the heading for this Asset Class refers to "office" furniture and equipment. Thus, for example, furniture in a hotel or motel room does not fit into this classification, but rather would be considered property used in the provision of personal services (Asset Class 57.0) and have a five-year depreciation period. However, furniture used in the manager's office in a hotel or motel would be considered Asset Class 00.11 property. See ¶ 104 for additional information on office furniture and equipment, including office equipment held for rental or used in a retail store.

*Railroad assets.* Certain railroad asset are 7-year property. These include railroad machinery and equipment (Rev. Proc. 87-56 Asset Class 40.1), roadway accounts (Asset Class 40.1) and railroad track (Asset Class 40.4), and railroad cars and locomotives, except those owned by railroad transportation companies (Asset Class 00.25). Other railroad assets are given longer recovery periods. See Asset

Classes 40.1 through 40.54. Railroad grading and tunnel bores have a 50-year recovery period (see ¶ 120).

Subway cars were classified as personal property with no class life (IRS Letter Ruling 8711110, December 18, 1986). Under MACRS such property has a seven-year recovery period.

A Class II or Class III railroad may elect a safe-harbor procedure (the "track maintenance allowance method") for accounting for track structure expenditures (Rev. Proc. 2002-65, 2002-2 CB 700). Safe-harbor procedures that apply to a railroad that files (or is a member of a combined reporting group that files) a Railroad Annual Report R-1 ("Form R-1") with the Surface Transportation Board based on the same reporting period as the taxpayer's taxable year are provided in Rev. Proc. 2001-46, 2001-2 CB 263. A Class II or III railroad that is reclassified as a Class I railroad required to file a Form R-1 may be able to change to the safe-harbor procedure of Rev. Proc. 2001-46.

*Air transport.* Includes assets (except helicopters) used in commercial and contract carrying of passengers and freight by air. See Rev. Proc. 87-56 Asset Class 45.0 for details. Other aircraft and helicopters are 5-year property (Asset Class 00.21). See ¶ 104. For the treatment of maintenance costs, see ¶ 125.

*Livestock and horses.* Certain livestock, breeding or work horses 12 years old or less when placed in service, and other horses (Rev. Proc. 87-56 Asset Classes 01.1, 01.221, and 01.225) (see ¶ 191) are 7-year property. See ¶ 118.

*Plants bearing fruits and nuts.* A seven-year recovery period applies to plant bearing fruits and nuts as property without a prescribed class life (Code Sec. 168(e)(3)(C)(v); Committee Report for P.L. 114-113). For special rules related to bonus depreciation on plants, see ¶ 127D.

*Orchards and vines.* For depreciation, including bonus depreciation, on orchards and vines, see ¶ 108.

*Agricultural and horticultural structures.* Single-purpose agricultural or horticultural structures generally placed in service before 1989 are also 7-year property, but they are classified as 10-year property if placed in service after 1988 unless subject to transitional rules. See ¶ 118.

*Certain assets used in agricultural activities.* Any machinery or equipment (other than a grain bin, cotton ginning asset, fence, or land improvement), the original use of which begins with the taxpayer in 2009 or after 2017, and that is placed in service by the taxpayer in a farming business in 2009 or after 2017, has a recovery period of five years under GDS (Code Sec. 168(e)(3)(B)(vii), as added by the Emergency Economic Stabilization Act of 2008 (P.L. 110-343) and Code Sec. 168(e)(3)(B)(vii)). Subject to the preceding exception, depreciable assets used in agricultural activities are 7-year property under Asset Class 01.1 of Rev. Proc. 87-56. This category includes machinery, equipment, grain bins, and fences (but no other land improvements) used in the production of crops, plants, vines, and trees; livestock; the operation of farm dairies, nurseries, greenhouses, sod farms, mushroom cellars, cranberry bogs, apiaries (i.e., bee keeping activities), and farms; and the performance of agriculture, animal husbandry, and horticultural services. See ¶ 118.

*Fishing vessels and equipment.* A fishing vessel, does not have an assigned class life under MACRS and, therefore, is seven-year property (IRS Audit Technique Guide for the Fishing Industry (August 2011)). The guide notes that fishing vessels are not considered water transportation equipment (10-year property described in Asset Class 00.28 of Rev. Proc. 87-56).

The ADS period for personal property with no class life is 12 years.

However, according to the audit guide, fish tender vessels and fish processing vessels are generally considered water transportation equipment and have a 10-year depreciation period and 18-year ADS period (Rev. Proc. 87-56 Asset Class 00.28). See, also, IRS Letter Ruling 9502001 (June 30, 1994) which categorized a factory trawler which harvested and processed fish as an Asset Class 00.28 vessel even though the primary activity of the trawler was, according to the IRS, described in Asset Class 20.4 (Asset Class 20.4, Manufacture of Other Food and Kindred Products, 7-year MACRS recovery period). The trawler was removed from Asset Class 20.4 of Rev. Proc. 87-56 by virtue of being described as a specific asset type in Asset Class 00.28.

The guide appears to take the position that catcher/harvester vessels that have the capacity only to "head and gut" and freeze fish are not primarily engaged in a processing or transportation activity and, therefore, qualify as 7-year property (i.e., property without a class life).

The guide classifies nets, pots, and traps as MACRS 7-year property. If they do not last more than one year then their cost may be currently deducted.

Fish processing equipment (belts and screws, holding bins and tanks, washes, climate control devices, screens, separators, automatic deheaders/filleters, waste product recovery systems) that may be carried on fishing vessels, tender vessels or processing vessels have a 7-year MACRS recovery period (Asset Class 20.4 of Rev. Proc. 87-56 (food production and manufacturing equipment)). A three-year MACRS recovery period applies to returnable pallets, palletized containers or boxes, baskets, carts and flaking trays (Asset Class 20.5 (special handling devices)).

The cost of replacing netting on the same cork and lead line is a currently deductible repair provided the taxpayer does not make a partial disposition election (see ¶ 162) to claim a loss on the remaining basis of the replaced net and continues to depreciate the original net/cork/line.

Boats and equipment are tangible personal property that may qualify for expensing under Code Sec. 179 (¶ 300), as well as the bonus depreciation deduction (¶ 127D).

Fishing permits generally are considered an intangible asset and amortized over a 15-year period under Code Sec. 197, according to the audit guide. See ¶ 32.

The depreciable basis of a vessel does not include the amount of funds withdrawn from a capital construction fund established under Sec. 607 of the Merchant Marine Act (MMA) to pay for the vessel (Code Sec. 7518). Thus, no depreciation deductions are allowed in determining regular tax liability or net income from self-employment if a fishing vessel is purchased entirely with withdrawn amounts (IRS Letter Ruling 200022007, February 15, 2000).

See, also, "Vessels and barges" at ¶ 108.

*Ethanol plants.* The appropriate depreciation classification of tangible assets used in converting corn to fuel grade ethanol is Asset Class 49.5 of Rev. Proc. 87-56, Waste Reduction and Resource Recovery Plants, of Rev. Proc. 87-56 (MACRS 7-year property), and not Asset Class 28.0, Manufacture of Chemicals and Allied Products, of Rev. Proc. 87-56 (MACRS 5-year property). Asset Class 49.5 specifically applies to assets used in the conversion of biomass to a liquid fuel. For purposes of Asset Class 49.5, corn is a biomass and liquid grade ethanol is a liquid fuel. This ruling does not apply to assets that a taxpayer places in service before June 9, 2014 (Rev. Rul. 2014-17). The ruling was issued in proposed form in Notice 2009-64, I.R.B. 2009-36).

*Gathering systems (oil and gas)*. The Energy Tax Incentives Act of 2005 (P.L. 109-59) classifies a natural gas gathering line as 7-year MACRS property with a 14 year alternative depreciation system (ADS) recovery period if:

(1) the original use commenced with the taxpayer after April 11, 2005;

(2) the property was placed in service after April 11, 2005; and

(3) the taxpayer or a related party did not enter into a binding contract for the construction of the pipeline on or before April 11, 2005 (or, in the case of self-constructed property, the taxpayer or a related party did not start construction on or before that date) (Code Sec. 168(e)(3)(C)(iv); Act Sec. 1326(e) of P.L. 109-59 (relating to effective date)).

No alternative minimum tax adjustment is required if the natural gas gathering line qualifies for the 7-year recovery period under this provision (Code Sec. 56(a)(1)(B)).

A natural gas gathering line is defined to mean (1) the pipe, equipment, and appurtenances determined to be a gathering line by the Federal Energy Regulatory Commission (FERC) and (2) the pipe, equipment, and appurtenances used to deliver natural gas from the wellhead or a commonpoint to the point at which the gas first reaches a processing plant, an interconnection with a transmission pipeline for which a certificate as an interstate transmission pipeline has been issued by the FERC, an interconnection with an intrastate transmission pipeline, or a direct interconnection with a local distribution company, a gas storage facility, or an industrial consumer (Code Sec. 168(i)(17), as added by the Act).

The correct depreciation period for oil and gas pipeline gathering systems that do not qualify as MACRS property under the preceding rule (e.g., because placed in service before the effective date) is in dispute. The two possible classifications are: (1) Asset Class 13.2 of Rev. Proc. 87-56, which provides a 7-year recovery period for "assets used by petroleum and natural gas producers for drilling wells and the production of petroleum and natural gas, including gathering pipelines . . ." and (2) Asset Class 46.0 of Rev. Proc. 87-56, which provides a 15-year recovery period for "assets used in private, commercial, and contract carrying of petroleum, gas, and other products by means of pipes and conveyors."

The Tax Court has held that interconnected subterranean pipelines leading from wells to a processing plant and related compression facilities (gathering systems) were 15-year MACRS property (Asset Class 46.0—Pipeline Transportation) because the taxpayer was a nonproducer (*Duke Energy Natural Gas Corporation*, 109 TC 416, Dec. 52,395; similarly, *Clajon Gas Co., L.P.*, 119 TC 197, Dec. 54,919). However, the Tenth, Eighth, and Sixth Circuit Court of Appeals have classified such property as 7-year MACRS property.

The Court of Appeals for the Tenth Circuit reversed the Tax Court's decision in *Duke*, and ruled that the assets were 7-year MACRS property (Asset Class 13.2 of Rev. Proc. 87-56—Exploration for and Production of Petroleum and Natural Gas Deposits) because the pipelines were used for the benefit of the producer with whom the taxpayer contracted to transport the gas to production facilities (*Duke Energy Natural Gas Corporation*, CA-10, 99-1 USTC ¶ 50,449 (Nonacq. 1999-2 CB xvi)). In an action on decision (AOD 1999-017 (November 22, 1999)), the IRS Chief Counsel issued a recommendation of nonacquiescence to the Tenth Circuit's *Duke Energy* decision. Most recently, the Court of Appeals for the Eighth Circuit followed Tenth Circuit's reasoning and reversed the Tax Court's *Clajon* decision (*Clajon Gas Co. L.P.*, 2004-1 USTC ¶ 50,123). The Sixth Circuit has also determined that a natural gas pipeline gathering system owned by a nonproducing partnership engaged in the business of transporting natural gas to a processing plant was seven-year property (*Saginaw Bay Pipeline Co., et al.*, CA-6, 2003-2 USTC ¶ 50,592, rev'g DC Mich., 2001-2 USTC ¶ 50,642). In addition, a Wyoming district court has sided with the Tenth, Eighth, and Sixth Circuits (*J.D. True*, DC Wyo., 97-2 USTC ¶ 50,946).

An oil pipeline used by a utility to deliver fuel to a generating facility was not Asset Class 46.0 property. Asset Class 46.0 of Rev. Proc. 87-56 is not intended to cover private fuel systems (Rev. Rul. 77-476, 1977-2 CB 5).

*Alaska natural gas pipeline.* Alaska natural gas pipeline is 7-year MACRS property (Code Sec. 168(e)(3)(C)(iii)). Alaska natural gas pipeline is qualifying pipeline property placed in service in Alaska after December 31, 2013 or which is treated as placed in service on January 1, 2014, if the taxpayer who places the property in service after December 31, 2004 and before January 1, 2014, elects such treatment. Qualifying property includes the pipe, trunk lines, related equipment, and appurtenances used to carry natural gas, but does not include any gas processing plant. (Code Sec. 168(i)(16)). Election procedures are provided in Notice 2006-47.

*Assets used in recreation businesses.* Assets used in the provision of entertainment services for payment of a fee or admission charge are 7-year MACRS property with a 10-year ADS depreciation period (Asset Class 79.0 of Rev. Proc. 87-56). Examples include assets used in bowling alleys, billiard and pool halls, theaters, concert halls, and miniature golf courses. Specialized land improvements and structures such as golf courses, sports stadia, race tracks, and ski slopes are specifically excluded from this class. Buildings which house the assets used in providing the entertainment services are also excluded and treated as 39-year real property. See the description for Asset Class 80.0 of Rev. Proc. 87-56 at ¶ 191 and IRS Letter Ruling 200508015 which concludes that an outdoor music theatre was an Asset Class 79.0 activity and not a theme or amusement park (Asset Class 80.0 activity).

The IRS has ruled that slot machines and video terminals placed in casinos, bars, hotels, and restaurants pursuant to space leases (site owner leases space to machine owner in return for share of profits) are assets used in a recreation business. Similarly, slot machines, video lottery terminals, and supporting casino equipment, such as furniture and fixtures for slots, poker, roulette, blackjack, baccarat, bingo, and keno located within a taxpayer's casino/hotel are seven-year property. According to the IRS, this property does not qualify as five-year property as qualified technological equipment, an information system (Asset Class 00.12 of Rev. Proc. 87-56), or property used in a distributive trade or service (Asset Class 57.0 of Rev. Proc. 87-56) (Coordinated Issue Paper for the Gaming Industry, April 10, 2000; this Coordinated Issue Paper was updated in nearly identical form with an effective/reissue date of September 28, 2001).

For the classification of casino riverboats and barges, see ¶ 125.

*Assets used in theme and amusement parks.* These assets are also seven-year property but have an ADS period of 12.5 years (Asset Class 80.0 of Rev. Proc. 87-56 at ¶ 191). For example, VIP structures and smoking lounges, kiosks, and other structures from which concession sales at a theme or amusement park are made are Asset Class 80.0 assets (i.e., "appurtenances associated with a ride, attraction, amusement, or theme setting within the park", as described in Asset Class 80.0 of Rev. Proc. 87-56). A theme or amusement park is characterized by amusements, rides, or other attractions *permanently* situated on park land. See IRS Letter Ruling 200508015 which concludes that an outdoor music theatre is not a theme or amusement park.

Buildings other than warehouses, administration buildings, hotels and motels are listed in Asset Class 80.0 as eligible for a 7-year recovery period. However, the IRS has ruled that buildings that have been converted to theme park use by any person (including the person from whom a theme park is being acquired) are treated as nonresidential real property (IRS Letter Ruling 8928017, April 12, 1989).

*Motorsports entertainment complexes.* "Motorsports entertainment complexes" placed in service after October 22, 2004 and before January 1, 2026 are 7-year property (Code Sec. 168(e)(3)(C)(ii); Code Sec. 168(i)(15)).

A motorsports entertainment complex is defined as a racing track facility situated permanently on land and which hosts one or more racing events for automobiles, trucks, or motorcycles during the 36-month period following the first day of the month in which the facility is placed in service. The events must be open to the public for the price of admission. Specified ancillary and support facilities provided for the benefit of complex patrons are also treated as 7-year motorsports entertainment complex property if owned by the person who owns the complex (Code Sec. 168(i)(15)).

Historically, auto race tracks were treated by the IRS the same as theme or amusement parks and were thus depreciated over a seven-year period (Asset Class 80.0). However, the IRS challenged the seven-year period and would assign a depreciation period of 15 years or more. See, for example, Technical Advice Memorandum 200526019, March 10, 2005.

Race track facilities placed into service after October 22, 2004 may not be treated as 7-year property under Asset Class 80.0 of Rev. Proc. 87-56 (Act Sec. 704(e)(2) of P.L. 108-357). This provision is not part of the Code and does not have an expiration date. Thus, unless the preceding January 1, 2026, expiration date is extended, it appears that motorsports entertainment complexes placed in service after 2025 may once again be subject to treatment as 15-year property.

No inference should be drawn from this provision regarding the proper treatment of property placed in service on or before October 22, 2003 (the date of enactment of P.L. 108-357) (Act Sec. 704(e)(3) of P.L. 108-357).

Indianapolis racing cars are 7-year property (Rev. Proc. 87-56 Asset Class 79.0). The race cars were not 3-year property (Asset Class 00.22, automobiles) (CCA 200052019, September 27, 2000).

*Street lights.* Street lights have been classified as 7-year property (property with no class life) on the basis of being readily removable and also as 15-year land improvements. See ¶ 112.

*Property with no class life.* Personal property and section 1245 real property with no class life are categorized as 7-year property. Personal property is given a 12-year ADS period. A 40-year ADS period applies to section 1245 real property with no class life (Code Sec. 168(e)(3)(C), (g)(2)(C), and (g)(3)(E)). The definitions of personal and section 1245 real property are discussed at ¶ 127C.

## ¶ 108

## 10-Year Property

Property with a class life of at least 16 but less than 20 years is classified as 10-year property (Code Sec. 168(e)(3)(D)). The 200-percent declining-balance method generally applies (¶ 84). 10-year property includes (but is not limited to):

(1) vessels (e.g., yachts), barges, tugs, and similar means of water transportation, but not used in marine construction or as a fishing vessel (Asset Class 00.28 of Rev. Proc. 87-56);

(2) single-purpose agricultural or horticultural structures generally placed in service after 1988 (Asset Class 01.4 of Rev. Proc. 87-56) (150-percent declining balance method generally applies; see below);

(3) fruit- or nut-bearing trees or vines placed in service after 1988 (straight-line method may apply; see below); and

(4) smart electric meters and smart electric grid systems (150-percent declining balance method applies, see below)

*Vessels and barges*

Fishing vessels have no assigned class life and are considered 7-year property. See ¶ 106. Vessels used in marine construction are 5-year property (Asset Class 15.0 of Rev. Proc. 87-56). Assets used in the contract or commercial carrying of freight or passengers by water, except for assets included in classes which begin with the prefix 00.2 (e.g., a vessel), including land improvements, are 15-year property (Asset Class 44.0 of Rev. Proc. 87-56).

Although Asset Class 13.0 of Rev. Proc. 87-56, provides that support vessels such as tenders, barges, towboats, and crewboats used in offshore drilling for oil and gas are classified as 5-year property, the IRS has concluded that such vessels are 5-year property when used in any phase of offshore oil and gas operations, including exploration, development, and production. This classification also applies if the vessels are used by a contractor (Technical Advice Memorandum 201001018, September 8, 2009). See, also, "*Leased property*" at ¶ 190.

The depreciable basis of a vessel does not include the amount of funds withdrawn from a capital construction fund established under Sec. 607 of the Merchant Marine Act (MMA) to pay for the vessel (Code Sec. 7518).

Salvage value must be estimated for ships, barges, and other vessels placed in service before 1981 and depreciated under the pre-ACRS rules (IRS Industry Specialization Program (ISP) Coordinated Issue Paper, I.R.C. Section 167 Salvage Value (October 7, 1996), reproduced in the CCH IRS POSITIONS REPORTER at ¶ 172,490).

The IRS has ruled in a Field Service Advice (FSA) (Field Service Advice Memorandum 199922033, March 3, 1999) that a three-story entertainment facility built on a barge which was no longer capable of water transportation, was nonresidential real property. A later FSA dealing with a similar facility concluded that additional factual development was needed. However, based on the facts presented, the FSA tended toward the conclusion that the barge was nonresidential real property (Field Service Advice Memorandum 199950004, August 30, 1999). See, also, ¶ 125 (*Gambling Boats and Barges*).

A vessel includes every description of watercraft or other artificial contrivance used, or capable of begins used, as a means of transportation on water (Code Sec. 7701(m)(1)(7); 1 USC section 3; ISP Coordinated Issue Paper: Shipping and Gaming Industries: Class Life of Floating Gaming Facilities, March 12, 2001; reproduced in CCH IRS Positions Reporter (IRPO) at ¶ 173,155).

A barge is a non-self propelled vessel (46 USC section 2101(2); ISP Coordinated Issue Paper cited above).

See, also, "*Leased property*" at ¶ 191.

*Single purpose structures*

Single-purpose agricultural or horticultural structures (item 2) include:

(1) enclosures or structures specifically designed, constructed, and used to house, raise, and feed a particular type of livestock (including poultry but not horses) and to house related equipment;

(2) greenhouses specifically designed, built, and used for commercial production of plants; and

(3) structures specifically designed, constructed, and used for commercial production of mushrooms.

5-, 7-, and 10-year farm property placed in service after 1988 is generally depreciated using the 150 percent declining balance method. See ¶ 118 for a detailed discussion of single-purpose agricultural or horticultural structures.

*Trees and vines*

Fruit- or nut-bearing trees and vines (e.g., apples, avocadoes, grapes, pecans, pistachios, or walnuts) placed in service after 1988 must be depreciated using the straight-line method over the regular recovery period (10-years) unless ADS (straight-line method and 20-year recovery period) applies (Code Sec. 168(b)(3)(E)) because the taxpayer elected *not* to capitalize pre-productive expenditures (cost incurred during the development period of plants, such as costs to cultivate, spray, fertilize and irrigate the plants to their crop-producing stage) of the orchard (¶ 118).

Under a transitional rule, the straight-line method and 10-year recovery period do not apply to property acquired pursuant to a written contract which was binding on July 14, 1988, and placed in service before January 1, 1990 (Act Sec. 6027(c)(2) of P.L. 100-647).

As explained in the Conference Committee Report for the Technical and Miscellaneous Revenue Act of 1988 (P.L. 100-647), the IRS treats fruit or nut bearing trees or vines placed in service before 1989 as a land improvement (Asset Class 00.3 of Rev. Proc. 87-56) with a MACRS recovery period of 15 years (20 years under ADS). Some taxpayers, however, have asserted that such property is personal property with no class life, and, therefore, is depreciable over seven years (12 years under ADS).

The placed-in-service date occurs and depreciation on an orchard, grove, or vineyard begins in the tax year that the trees or vines reach the income-producing stage (i.e., bear fruit, nuts, or grapes in commercially viable quantities) (Rev. Rul. 80-25, 1980-1 CB 65; Rev. Rul. 69-249, 1969-1 CB 31; Reg.§ 1.46-3(d)(2)).

*Section 179.* Such property also qualifies for the Code Sec. 179 expense allowance (CCA Letter Ruling 201234024, May 9, 2012; IRS Market Segment Specialization Program (MSSP) Guide for Grain Farmers). If an orchard, grove, or vineyard is purchased prior to reaching the income-producing stage, the allowance should apparently be claimed in the tax year that the trees or vines reach the income-producing stage since Code Sec. 179(a) specifically provides that the deduction is claimed in the tax year that the acquired property is placed in service. See, also, ¶ 302.

*Fruit or nut-bearing trees, plants, and vines planted, grafted, or placed in service after 2015.* A taxpayer may elect the first-year bonus deduction for "specified plants" in the tax year of planting or grafting, effective for plantings or graftings after 2015 in lieu of claiming a bonus depreciation deduction in the year that the specified plant is placed in service (i.e., commercially productive) (Code Sec. 168(k)(5)). The rate is 50 percent for plantings and graftings after 2015 and before

September 28, 2017 and 100 percent for plantings and graftings after September 27, 2017 and before January 1, 2023. Beginning in 2023, the rate is reduced 20 percent annually.

A specified plant is any tree or vine which bears fruits or nuts or any other plant which will have more than one yield of fruits or nuts and which has a pre-productive period of more than two years from the time of planting or grafting to the time at which the plant begins bearing fruits or nuts.

Assuming this election is not made, a taxpayer may claim a bonus depreciation deduction on specified plants placed in service after 2015 (or other depreciable horticulture that is not a specified plant) in the year the tree, vine, etc., is placed in service (i.e., becomes commercially productive). Bonus depreciation in the year or planting or grafting or in the year placed in service does not apply to specified plants that must be depreciated using the alternative depreciation system (ADS).

See ¶ 127D, item #33B, for discussion of bonus depreciation on specified plants.

*Bonus depreciation on fruit or nut-bearing trees, plants, and vines placed in service before January 1, 2016.* Bonus depreciation on fruit or nut-bearing trees, plants, or vines (e.g., orchards) placed in service before January 1, 2016 may only be claimed in the placed in service year. A depreciable fruit or nut-bearing tree, plant, or vineyard that is planted by a taxpayer is considered placed in service when it becomes commercially productive. Bonus depreciation does not apply to property which must be depreciated under the MACRS alternative depreciation system (ADS) (e.g., if an election not to capitalize pre-productive period costs under Code Sec. 263A(d)(3) is made). The IRS has issued no specific bonus depreciation guidance with respect to trees, plants, and vines that bear fruit or nuts. See ¶ 127D, item #33B.

*Irrigation systems.* For depreciation of trellising and drip irrigation systems, see ¶ 118.

*Smart electric meters and grid systems*

A 10-year recovery period applies to qualified smart electric meters and qualified smart electric grid systems placed in service after October 3, 2008 (Code Sec. 168(e)(3)(D)(iii) and (iv)). The 150-percent declining balance method is assigned as the applicable depreciation method (Code Sec. 168(b)(2)(C)). Normally the 200-percent declining balance method is used to depreciate 10-year property.

A 30-year alternative depreciation system (ADS) period applies to qualified smart electric meters and grid systems.

A qualified smart electric meter is any time-based meter and related communication equipment placed in service by a taxpayer who is a supplier of electric energy or a provider of electric energy services, and which is capable of being used by the taxpayer as part of a system that:

(1) Measures and records electricity usage data on a time-differentiated basis in at least 24 separate time segments per day;

(2) Provides for the exchange of information between the supplier or provider and the customer's smart electric meter in support of time-based rates or other forms of demand response;

(3) Provides data to such supplier or provider so that the supplier or provider can provide energy usage information to customers electronically; and

(4) Provides net metering (Code Sec. 168(i)(18); Joint Committee on Taxation, Technical Explanation of H.R. 7060 (P.L. 110-343), the "Renewable Energy and Job Creation Tax Act of 2008" (JCX-75-08)).

No definition of net metering appears to be provided. However, previous versions of the provision have defined the term as the ability of the meter to provide a credit to the customer for providing electricity to the supplier or provider.

A qualified smart electric grid system is any smart grid property used as part of a system for electric distribution grid communications, monitoring, and management placed in service by a taxpayer who is a supplier of electric energy or a provider of electric energy services. Smart grid property includes electronics and related equipment that is capable of:

(1) Sensing, collecting, and monitoring data of or from all portions of a utility's electric distribution grid;

(2) Providing real-time, two-way communications to monitor to manage such grid; and

(3) Providing real-time analysis of an event prediction based upon collected data that can be used to improve electric distribution system reliability, quality, and performance (Code Sec. 168(i)(19)).

A technical correction retroactively clarifies that property that would otherwise have a class life of less than 16 years but 10 or more years does not qualify as a qualified smart electric meter or a qualified smart electric grid system (Code Sec. 168(i)(18)(A)(ii) and (19)(A)(ii), as amended by the Tax Increase Prevention Act of 2014 (P.L. 113-295)). Prior to amendment, only property with a class life of less than 10 years were not subject to the 10-year recovery period.

MACRS property with a class life of less than 16 years but 10 or more years is classified as seven-year property. If the class life is less than 10 years but more than 4 years it is classified as five-year property. Property with a class life of 4 years or less is considered three-year property (Code Sec. 168(e)(1)). The rule that property with a class life of less than 10 years does not qualify as a smart meter or smart electric grid system meant that the provision did not change the depreciation period of property that would otherwise qualify as 3-year or 5-year property. On the other hand, seven-year property would be depreciated as 10-year property under the provision because seven-year property has a class life of 10 years or more but less then 16 years. The technical correction was necessary because Congress did not intend to apply a longer recovery period to seven-year property insofar as the provision is intended to provide an energy incentive.

The legislative history indicates that, but for this provision, property which qualifies as a smart electric meter or a smart electric grid system would generally be treated as property described in Asset Class 49.14 of Rev. Proc. 87-56 at ¶ 191 (CCA Letter Ruling 200914062, March 10, 2009). Such property is MACRS 20-year property with a 30-year year class life (i.e., a 30-year alternative depreciation system (ADS) recovery period). No specific alternative depreciation system recovery period is assigned to qualified smart electric meters and smart electric grid systems that qualify for the regular 10-year recovery period. Generally, when an ADS recovery period is not specially assigned, the ADS recovery period is equal to the asset's class life as set forth in the table of assets in Rev. Proc. 87-56 at ¶ 191. This suggests that the ADS period should be based on the class life that would apply if the property was not specially assigned a regular ten-year recovery period. For example, if a smart electric meter or grid system that qualifies for a regular ten-year recovery period is described in Asset Class 49.14 of Rev. Proc. 87-56, the ADS recovery period would be 30 years.

The IRS has ruled that property which met the definition of a qualified smart electric meter was an information system described in Asset Class 00.12 of Rev. Proc. 87-56 with a 5-year recovery period. Since Asset Class 00.12 property has a class life of 6 years and the 10-year recovery period for smart electric meters does not apply if a class life of less than 10-years (now 16 years) would otherwise apply, the 5-year recovery period for information systems applied. Further, the associated equipment was peripheral equipment for purposes of Asset Class 00.12. Although the meter was also described in activity class (49.14, assets used in the transmission and distribution of electricity for sale, with a 30-year class life) the Asset Classification (00.12) took precedence under the general rule that when an asset is described in both an Asset Class and an activity class, the Asset Class classification controls (IRS Letter Ruling 201244015, September 16, 2011).

## ¶ 110

## 15-Year Property

Fifteen-year property includes property with a class life of at least 20 but less than 25 years (Code Sec. 168(e)(1)). Such property includes municipal wastewater plants, telephone distribution plant and comparable equipment, certain depreciable land improvements (such as sidewalks, walkways, roads, docks, bridges, fences, landscaping, and shrubbery), assets used in producing cement (but not cement products), water carrier assets not qualifying as 10-year property, pipelines, and service station buildings (Code Sec. 168(e)(3)(E)). Generally, 15-year property is depreciated using the 150 percent declining-balance method.

Fifteen-year property includes (but is not limited to):

(1) depreciable land improvements not specifically included in another Asset Class (Asset Class 00.3 of Rev. Proc. 87-56);

(2) qualified improvement property placed in service after 2017 (Code Sec. 168(e)(6); Code Sec. 168(e)(3)(E)(vii)). See below;

(3) qualified leasehold improvements to the interior portion of nonresidential real property that is at least three years old and which is placed in service by a lessor or lessee pursuant or under the terms of a lease after October 22, 2004 and before 2018 (Code Sec. 168(e)(3)(E)(iv), prior to being stricken by the Tax Cuts and Jobs Act (P.L. 115-97)). See "15-year qualified leasehold improvement property" at ¶ 126;

(4) qualified restaurant property placed in service after October 22, 2004 and before 2018 (Code Sec. 168(e)(3)(E)(v), prior to being stricken by the Tax Cuts and Jobs Act (P.L. 115-97)). See below;

(5) qualified retail improvement property placed in service after December 31, 2008 and before 2018 (Code Sec. 168(e)(3)(E)(ix), prior to being stricken by the Tax Cuts and Jobs Act (P.L. 115-97)). See "15-year qualified retail improvement property" at ¶ 126;

(6) municipal wastewater treatment plants (Code Sec. 168(e)(3)(E); Asset Class 50 of Rev. Proc. 87-56);

(7) telephone distribution plant and comparable equipment used for two-way exchange of voice and data communications (Code Sec. 168(e)(3)(E); Asset Class 48.14 of Rev. Proc. 87-56);

(8) assets used in producing cement (but not cement products) (Asset Class 32.2 of Rev. Proc. 87-56);

(9) water transportation assets used in the commercial and contract carrying of freight and passengers by water if not included in an Asset Class with the prefix 00.2 (Asset Class 44.0 of Rev. Proc. 87-56);

(10) certain pipeline transportation assets (¶ 106) (Asset Class 46.0 of Rev. Proc. 87-56);

(11) qualifying retail motor fuel outlets (Code Sec. 168(e)(3)(E));

(12) section 1250 assets, including service station buildings, and depreciable land improvements (whether section 1245 or section 1250 property), used in marketing petroleum and petroleum products (Asset Class 57.1 of Rev. Proc. 87-56);

(13) car wash buildings and related land improvements (Asset Class 57.1 of Rev. Proc. 87-56);

According to the IRS, a car wash tunnel is included in Asset Class 57.1 of Rev. Proc. 87-56 even if gasoline or petroleum products are not sold at the location. A 15-year depreciation period applied to the entire car wash structure, including office space which was separated from the car wash frame by a wall (IRS Audit Technique Guide for the Car Wash Industry, reproduced in the CCH IRS POSITIONS REPORTER at ¶ 202,950).

(12A) billboards (Asset Class 00.3 of Rev. Proc. 87-56 (Asset Class 57.1 if used in petroleum marketing) (see ¶ 127A, "*Signs*"));

(13) assets, including land improvements, used in electric utility nuclear power production (Asset Class 49.12 of Rev. Proc. 87-56);

The costs of constructing a spent nuclear fuel interim storage facility (SNFISF) to temporarily hold a utility's spent nuclear fuel were not currently deductible as business expenses (Code Sec. 162) or losses (Code Sec. 165). The SNFISF was depreciable over 15 years under Asset Class 49.12 of Rev. Proc. 87-56 (IRS Letter Ruling 9719007, January 17, 1997). The costs associated with the construction, operation, and decommissioning of an independent spent fuel storage installation (ISFSI) were, however, deductible as an abandonment loss (¶ 162) in the year paid or incurred where the related nuclear plant was abandoned and decommissioned (IRS Letter Ruling 200012082, December 22, 1999).

(14) Assets used in the commercial and contract carrying of freight and passengers by water except transportation assets included in classes with the prefix 00.2 (e.g., vessels) (Asset Class 44.0 of Rev. Proc. 87-56);

(15) Gas utility trunk pipelines and related storage facilities (Asset Class 49.24 of Rev. Proc. 87-56); and

(16) Initial clearing and grading land improvements pertaining to any gas utility property, effective for property placed into service after October 22, 2004 (Code Sec. 168(e)(3)(E)(vi)). The ADS period under the new provision is 20 years (Code Sec. 168(g)(3)(B)).

Initial clearing and grading costs are specifically excluded from Asset Class 49.24 of Rev. Proc. 87-56 (Gas Utility Trunk Pipelines and Related Storage) and Asset Class 00.3 of Rev. Proc. 87-56, relating to land improvements. Thus, according to the Conference Committee Report for the American Jobs Creation Act, they were depreciated as 7-year MACRS property (section 1245 real property for which no class life is provided).

(17) Natural gas distribution lines placed in service after April 11, 2005 and before January 1, 2011 (Code Sec. 168(e)(3)(E)(viii)).

The original use of the distribution line must commence with the taxpayer after April 11, 2005. The taxpayer or a related party may not have entered into a binding contract for construction of the property on or before April 11, 2005, or, in the case of self-constructed property, started construction on or before April 11, 2005 (Act Sec. 1325(c) of the Energy Tax Incentives Act of 2005 (P.L. 109-58)). A 35-year ADS recovery period is assigned (Code Sec. 168(g)(3)(B)). Natural gas distribution lines which do not qualify for a 15-year recovery period under this provision are treated as MACRS 20-year property under Asset Class 49.21 of Rev. Proc. 87-56 (Gas Utility Distribution Facilities) of Rev. Proc. 87-56.

(18) Section 1245 property used in the transmission at 69 or more kilovolts of electricity for sale, if placed in service after April 11, 2005 (Code Sec. 168(e)(3)(E)(vii)).

The original use must begin with the taxpayer after April 11, 2005. The taxpayer or a related party may not have entered into a binding contract for the construction on or before April 11, 2005, or, in the case of self-constructed property, have started construction on or before April 11, 2005 (Act Sec.1309(c) of the Energy Act). A 30-year ADS period applies. Property that qualifies under this provision was previously treated as 20-year MACRS property under Asset Class 49.14 of Rev. Proc. 87-56 (Electric Utility Transmission and Distribution Plant) of Rev. Proc. 87-56.

*15-year qualified leasehold improvement property*

See ¶ 126.

*15-year qualified retail improvement property*

See ¶ 126.

*15-year qualified improvement property*

A technical correction retroactively assigns a 15-year recovery period to qualified improvement property (QIP), effective for property placed in service after 2017 (Code Sec. 168(e)(3)(E)(vii)). A 20-year alternative depreciation system period applies (Code Sec. 168(g)(3)(B)). Because QIP is assigned a 15-year recovery period it also qualifies for bonus depreciation under the general rule that property with an MACRS recovery period of 20 years or less is eligible for bonus depreciation. See ¶ 127D item "*33A. Qualified improvement property placed in service after 2015.*" IRS guidance explains how to change accounting methods or file amended returns to reassign a 15-year recovery period and/or claim bonus depreciation on QIP which was depreciated over 39 years (Rev. Proc. 2020-25). See ¶ 127D *1A. CARES Act: Qualified improvement property placed in service after 2017—guidance for changing to 15-year recovery period and claiming bonus depreciation—guidance for making late elections and revoking prior elections.*

Qualified improvement property is defined as any improvement to an interior portion of a building which is nonresidential real property if the improvement is *made by the taxpayer* and placed in service after the date the building was first placed in service by any taxpayer. The improvement must be section 1250 property (Code Sec. 168(e)(6); Reg. § 1.168(b)-1(a)(5)). For additional details see ¶ 127D *33A. Qualified improvement property placed in service after 2015.*.

Qualified improvement property placed in service before 2018 is depreciated as 39-year nonresidential real property unless it qualifies for a 15-year recovery period by meeting the definition of 15-year qualified leasehold improvement property, 15-year qualified retail improvement property, or 15-year restaurant property.

*Recapture.* The Code Sec. 1250 recapture rules apply to 15-year qualified improvement property except to the extent expensed as qualified real property under section 179. Since such property is depreciated using the straight-line method, the regular depreciation deductions claimed on such property are not subject to recapture as ordinary income upon a sale or disposition under section 1250. However, any bonus depreciation in excess of straight-line depreciation that could have been claimed on the bonus deduction if the bonus had not been claimed is subject to recapture under section 1250 upon a sale or disposition. See instructions for line 26a of Form 4797. Also, if the Code Sec. 179 allowance is claimed on qualified improvement property, the section 179 allowance is subject to recapture as ordinary income under the section 1245 recapture rules (Code Sec. 1245(a)(3)(C)). Section 1245 recapture is limited to the gain that is allocable to the portion of the property expensed (Notice 2013-59). See ¶ 302 for recapture details.

*15-year qualified restaurant property*

The American Jobs Creation Act of 2004 (P.L. 108-357) created a new category of 15-year property called "qualified restaurant property." This category applies to property placed in service after October 22, 2004 and before 2018 (Code Sec. 168(e)(3)(E)(v), as added by P.L. 108-357 and prior to being stricken by the Tax Cuts and Jobs Act (P.L. 115-97)). The straight-line method applies to such property (Code Sec. 168(b)(3)(H), prior to being stricken by P.L. 115-97). If the MACRS alternative depreciation system (ADS) is elected or otherwise applies, the applicable MACRS recovery period is 39 years and the straight-line method applies (Code Sec. 168(g)(3)(B), prior to amendment by P.L. 115-97). Whether or not ADS is elected, the applicable convention is the half-year convention, unless the mid-quarter convention applies.

The 15-year recovery period is not elective. However, a taxpayer could effectively elect out by making an ADS election and depreciating the restaurant property using a 39-year recovery period. An ADS election, however, would apply to all types of MACRS 15-year property placed in service by the taxpayer during the tax year. See ¶ 150.

*Qualified restaurant property defined for property placed in service after October 22, 2004 and before January 1, 2009.* In the case of property placed in service after October 22, 2004 and before January 1, 2009, qualified restaurant property is any section 1250 property which is an improvement to a building if the improvement is placed in service more than three years after the date the building was first placed in service by any person and more than 50 percent of the building's square footage is devoted to preparation of and seating for on-premises consumption of prepared meals (Code Sec. 168(e)(7), prior to amendment by P.L. 110-343). The improvement may be on the inside or on the outside of the building.

The three-year period is measured from the date that the building was originally placed in service, whether or not it was originally placed in service by the taxpayer. For example, improvements to a restaurant building that is at least three years old at the time the taxpayer buys the building may qualify.

*Qualified restaurant property defined for property placed in service after December 31, 2008 and before 2018.* Restaurant improvements placed in service after December 31, 2008 and before 2018 continue to qualify as 15-year property. The same rules described above for restaurant improvements placed in service before 2009 continue to apply with the significant exception that an improvement will now qualify even if the improved restaurant building was not at least three years old when the improvement was made. The three-year requirement continues to apply to improvements placed in service in 2008 and earlier (Code Sec. 168(e)(7), prior to amendment by P.L. 115-97).

P.L. 110-343 also expands the definition of qualified restaurant property to include a building placed in service after December 31, 2008 and before 2018, if more than 50 percent of the building's square footage is devoted to preparation of, and seating for on-premises consumption of, prepared meals (Code Sec. 168(e)(7) and Code Sec. 168(e)(3)(E)(v), prior to amendment by P.L. 115-97). Such a building is depreciated similarly to an improvement to a restaurant building. Thus, the building is depreciated over 15 years (39 years under the MACRS alternative depreciation system (ADS) using the straight-line method and the half-year or mid-quarter convention).

The 15-year recovery period applies to a restaurant building placed in service after 2008 and before 2018 whether it is new construction or an existing structure.

*Bonus depreciation.* Effective for property placed in service after December 31, 2008 and before January 1, 2016, bonus depreciation under Code Sec. 168(k) may not be claimed on qualified restaurant property that is not also qualified leasehold improvement property as defined in Code Sec. 168(k)(3), prior to amendment by P.L. 114-113 (Code Sec. 168(e)(7)(B), prior to amendment by P.L. 114-113). Qualified restaurant property placed in service after 2015 and before 2018 only qualifies for bonus depreciation if it also qualifies as "qualified improvement property," as defined in Code Sec. 168(k)(3), prior to amendment by P.L. 115-97. In general, qualified improvement property is any improvement to the interior of nonresidential real property except improvements for the enlargement of a building, any elevator or escalator, or the internal structural framework of the building (Code Sec. 168(e)(6); Reg. § 1.168(b)-1(a)(5)). See ¶ 127D for discussion of bonus depreciation and the definitions of qualified leasehold improvement property and qualified improvement property.

These three categories of 15-year property are removed from the Code, effective for property placed in service after 2017. They are replaced by the generally more expansive category of 15-year qualified improvement property.

*Relationship to qualified leasehold improvement property.* A 15-year recovery period and straight-line depreciation method apply to "qualified leasehold improvement property" placed in service after the October 22, 2004 and before 2018 (Code Sec. 168(e)(6), prior to amendment by P.L. 115-97). Qualified leasehold improvement property is generally defined as section 1250 leasehold improvements made to commercial property by a lessor or lessee pursuant to a lease more than three years after the commercial property was placed in service. In certain circumstances, an improvement made by a lessor or lessee of a restaurant building could qualify for a 15-year recovery period either as qualified leasehold improvement property or as qualified restaurant property. The provision for qualified restaurant property, however, is much broader in that it is not limited to leasehold improvements or by other restrictions that apply to qualified leasehold improvement property. See ¶ 126 for a discussion of qualified leasehold improvement property.

The IRS retroactively clarified that a qualified restaurant improvement placed in service after 2008 and before 2016 that also meets the definition of a qualified leasehold improvement may qualify for bonus depreciation. Structural improvements to a restaurant placed in service in 2007 or after October 22, 2004 and before January 1, 2005 (bonus applied during these periods) that are depreciated over 15 years as qualified restaurant property may be able to qualify for bonus depreciation even if such property was not qualified leasehold improvement property (CCA Letter Ruling 201203014, December 14, 2011; Rev. Proc. 2011-26). As noted immediately above under "*Bonus depreciation,*" restaurant improvement property placed in service after 2015 and before 2018 only qualifies for bonus depreciation if it meets the definition of "qualified improvement property."

*Code Sec. 179.* The shortened depreciation period does not change the status of qualified restaurant property as section 1250 property. The Code Sec. 179 expense allowance generally only applies to section 1245 property (Code Sec. 179(d)(1)). However, for qualified real property placed in service in tax years beginning after 2009 and before 2016 up to $250,000 of the cost of the qualified real property may be expensed under Code Sec. 179 and applied toward the overall $500,000 dollar limitation. For tax years beginning after 2015, the $250,000 cap is eliminated (Act Sec. 124(c)(1) of P.L. 114-113). Qualified real property consists of 15-year restaurant property, 15-year leasehold improvement property, and 15-year retail improvement property. However, effective for property placed in service in tax years beginning after 2017, qualified real property is redefined to mean qualified improvement property (generally, improvements to the interior of nonresidential real property made by the taxpayer (Code Sec. 168(e)(6); Reg.§ 1.168(b)-1(a)(5))). See section 179 discussion at ¶ 302.

*Recapture.* The Code Sec. 1250 recapture rules apply to 15-year restaurant property except to the extent expensed as qualified real property under section 179. Since such property is depreciated using the straight-line method, the regular depreciation deductions claimed on such property are not subject to recapture as ordinary income upon a sale or disposition under section 1250. However, any bonus depreciation in excess of straight-line depreciation that could have been claimed on the bonus deduction if the bonus had not been claimed is subject to recapture under section 1250 upon a sale or disposition. See instructions for line 26a of Form 4797. Also, if the Code Sec. 179 allowance is claimed on restaurant property, the section 179 allowance is subject to recapture as ordinary income under the section 1245 recapture rules (Code Sec. 1245(a)(3)(C)). Section 1245 recapture is limited to the gain that is allocable to the portion of the property expensed (Notice 2013-59). See ¶ 302 for recapture details.

*Treatment of nonqualifying property.* Prior to enactment of the 15-year recovery period for qualified restaurant property, a section 1250 improvement to a restaurant building was depreciated over 39 years beginning in the month that it was placed in service using the mid-month convention. The 15-year recovery period did not change the current rule that allows an improvement to a restaurant that is section 1245 property (personal property) to be depreciated as MACRS five-year property (Rev. Proc. 87-56 Asset Class 57.0) under the MACRS cost segregation rules.

*Chart of section 1245 and section 1250 property used in restaurants.* The IRS issued an "Industry Directive" which contains a detailed chart that categorizes various original restaurant components as section 1250 property (depreciable over 39 years) or section 1245 property (depreciable over five years under the cost segregation rules) (LMSB Directive on Cost Segregation in the Restaurant Industry reproduced as a Quick Reference Table in the appendix of this guide). Items listed in this chart as section 1250 property and placed in service after October 22, 2004 and before 2018, as an improvement can qualify for 15-year depreciation period. Examples of such qualifying items include, electrical system components not dedicated to specific machinery or kitchen equipment, most interior and exterior lighting, elevators and escalators, fire protection systems, security systems, fireplaces, permanent floor coverings (other than carpeting), floors, most HVACs (heating ventilating and air conditioning units) unless dedicated solely to the kitchen, most plumbing unless dedicated to specific equipment, restroom accessories and partitions, walls, permanent wall coverings, and roofs.

The chart only applies to improvements to a building. Improvements that are not part of or attached to the restaurant building, for example, a detached sign supported on a concrete foundation, sidewalk or walkways, or depreciable landscaping, would generally constitute separately depreciable land improvements which also have a 15-year recovery period but may be depreciated using the 150-percent declining balance method. Other unattached improvements may qualify for a shorter recovery period if not considered a land improvement.

*Alternative minimum tax.* No AMT depreciation adjustment is required for 15-year restaurant property because the straight-line method applies. See ¶ 170.

*Land improvements*

Depreciable land improvements described in Asset Class 00.3 of Rev. Proc. 87-56 are 15-year property. In a few instances land improvements that would otherwise be considered 15-year property have a different recovery period because they are specifically included in a different Asset Class. See *"Land improvements included in a different Asset Class,"* below.

Land improvements include improvements made directly to or added to land, whether section 1245 or section 1250 property. A structure is not a land improvement unless it is inherently permanent. See ¶ 127C. However, buildings and their structural components as defined in Reg. § 1.48-1(e) do not qualify as land improvements. See ¶ 127 and ¶ 128.

Most land improvements are section 1250 property. Certain land improvements are section 1245 real property because described in Code Sec. 1245(a)(3)(B) (e.g., tangible property (other than buildings and structural components) used as an integral part of manufacturing, production, or extraction or of furnishing transportation, communications, electrical energy, gas, water, or sewage disposal services) (Reg. § 1.48-1(d)). See *"Property used in manufacturing, production, extraction, and certain other activities..."* below. Tangible personal property includes all property (other than structural components) contained in or attached to a building (Reg.§ 1.48-1(c)). In addition, property in the nature of machinery (other than structural components of a building or other inherently permanent structure) is considered tangible personal property even though located outside a building (Reg. § 1.48-1(c)). Thus, for example, a gasoline pump, hydraulic car lift, or automatic vending machine, although annexed to the ground, is considered tangible section 1245 personal property described in Code Sec. 1245(a)(3)(A).

Land improvements must qualify as a depreciable asset in order to be depreciated. See ¶ 5 for additional discussion of land improvements.

If a land improvement is section 1250 property an AMT adjustment is required unless the taxpayer elected ADS or the MACRS straight-line method, the property qualified for bonus depreciation and no election out was made, or in the case of property placed in service after 2015, the property qualified for bonus depreciation whether or not an election out was made. See ¶ 170. In addition, the section 1250 depreciation recapture rules apply. Under these rules, depreciation claimed (including bonus depreciation) in excess of straight-line depreciation is subject to recapture as ordinary income if an asset is disposed of at a gain. See ¶ 160.

Examples of land improvements include:

(1) sidewalks and walkways;

(2) roads (¶ 5);

(3) canals;

(4) waterways;

(5) drainage facilities;

(6) sewers (but not municipal sewers);

(7) wharves and docks (however, see Asset Class 44.0 of Rev. Proc. 87-56, below);

(8) bridges;

(9) fences (nonagricultural);

(10) landscaping (¶ 5);

(11) shrubbery (¶ 5);

(12) radio and television transmitting towers; and

(13) parking lots (¶ 5).

Sidewalks, concrete driveways, asphalt streets and concrete curbs, playground equipment, fencing, and landscaping constructed or installed in connection with an apartment complex were land improvements (IRS Letter Ruling 8848039, September 2, 1988). The ruling notes that certain portions of the costs may not qualify for depreciation because they might be considered land. For example, this might impact part of the costs of the streets and landscaping. See ¶ 5 for determining portion of road and landscaping costs that are considered depreciable.

Playground equipment treated as a land improvement included swing sets, climbers, slides, see-saws, merry-go-rounds, picnic tables, pipe-frame park benches, basketball backboards, football/soccer goal posts, flag staffs or poles, softball backstops, jogging trails, and stationary aerobic equipment. See, also, ¶ 5 for additional discussion of playground equipment.

In the same ruling, various components of an electrical distribution system (pine poles, aerial lines, transformers, meters, street lighting) and water distribution system (valves, fire hydrants, fittings, tapping sleeves, PVC water pipe, water meters) that were installed by the taxpayer were also land improvements. These items were not classified as Asset Class 49.14 of Rev. Proc. 87-56, Electric Utility Transmission and Distribution Plant, and Asset Class 49.3 of Rev. Proc. 87-56, Water Utilities, because those classifications only apply to taxpayers that *sell* electricity and water.

Parking lots are considered land improvements. Note, for example, that parking lots are specifically mentioned as a type of land improvement in Rev. Proc. 87-56 Asset Class 80.0 (Theme and Amusement Parks) at ¶ 191. See ¶ 5. The IRS has ruled that open-air parking structures are buildings (39-year property) and not land improvements (Applicable Recovery Period Under Code Sec. 168(a) for Open-Air Parking Structures, Coordinated Issue Paper (LMSB4-0709-029) (Effective Date July 31, 2009)). See ¶ 127C.

Specialized land improvements or structures such as golf courses (¶ 5), sports stadiums, race tracks, ski slopes, and buildings which house assets used in entertainment services are specifically excluded from Rev. Proc. 87-56 Asset Class 79.0 (Recreation) which has a seven-year recovery period.

It appears that a dam is generally considered a depreciable land improvement under MACRS with a 15-year recovery period under Rev. Proc. 87-56 Asset Class 00.3 (Land Improvements) unless described in another Asset Class (e.g., dams are described in Rev. Proc. 87-56 Asset Class 49.11 (Electric Utility Hydraulic Production Plant)). An earthen dam used by a farmer may qualify as a currently deductible soil and water conservation expenditure. In *R.L. Hunter*, 46 TC 477, Dec. 28,025, a dam was treated as a depreciable asset with a determinable useful life. See ¶ 118 for additional information concerning dams.

*Land improvements included in another Asset Class*

Land improvements specifically included in an Asset Class other than Rev. Proc. 87-56 Asset Class 00.3 (Land Improvements) are not treated as 15-year property described in Rev. Proc. 87-56 Asset Class 00.3. The depreciation period for the Asset Class in which the land improvement is mentioned governs. However, in applying this rule, the land improvement described in the business activity class must generally be directly related to the business activity. For example, depreciable landscaping is still subject to a 15-year recovery period under Asset Class 00.3 even if the term land improvement is mentioned in another Asset Class. See, also, Rev. Rul. 2003-81, discussed at ¶ 190. The following Rev. Proc. 87-56 Asset Classes include specific references to the treatment of land improvements (land improvements are either included or excluded):

(1) Asset Class 01.1 (Agriculture) (agricultural fences but no other land improvements are 7-year property);

(2) Asset Class 26.1 (Manufacture of Pulp and Paper);

(3) Asset Class 28.0 (Manufacture of Chemicals and Allied Products);

(4) Asset Class 33.3 (Manufacture of Foundry Products);

(5) Asset Class 33.4 (Manufacture of Primary Steel Mill Products);

(6) Asset Class 37.32 (Ship and Boat Building Dry Docks and Land Improvements);

(7) Asset Class 40.2 (Railroad Structures and Similar Improvements);

(8) Asset Class 44.0 (Water Transportation);

(9) Asset Class 46.0 (Pipeline Transportation);

(10) Asset Class 48.14 (Telephone Distribution Plant);

(11) Asset Class 48.2 (Telegraph, Ocean Cable, and Satellite Communications);

(12) Asset Class 49.11 (Electric, Gas, Water and Steam, Utility Services; Electric Utility Hydraulic Production Plant);

(13) Asset Class 49.12 (Electric Utility Nuclear Production Plant);

(14) Asset Class 49.13 (Electric Utility Steam Production Plant);

(15) Asset Class 49.14 (Electric Utility Transmission and Distribution Plant);

(16) Asset Class 49.15 (Electric Utility Combustion Turbine Production Plant);

(17) Asset Class 49.223 (Substitute Natural Gas-Coal Gasification);

(18) Asset Class 49.24 (Gas Utility Trunk Pipeline and Related Storage Facilities);

(19) Asset Class 49.25 (Liquefied Natural Gas Plant);

(20) Asset Class 49.5 (Waste Reduction and Resource Recovery Plants);

(21) Asset Class 57.1 (Distributive Trades and Services-Billboard, Service Station Buildings, and Petroleum Marketing Land Improvements);

(22) Asset Class 79.0 (Recreation); and

(23) Asset Class 80.0 (Theme and Amusement Parks).

*Property used in manufacturing, production, extraction, and certain other activities classified as section 1245 real property land improvements*

Section 5.05 of Rev. Proc. 87-56 provides that Asset Class 00.3 land improvements include "other tangible property" described in Reg. § 1.48-1(d). This is property which is not tangible personal property (within the meaning of Code Sec. 1245(a)(3)(A)) (¶ 127C) and which is used as an integral part of manufacturing, production, or extraction, or as an integral part of furnishing transportation, communications, electrical energy, gas, water, or sewage disposal services, or which constitutes a research or storage facility used in connection with any of these activities. However, section 5.05 further provides that a structure that is essentially an item of machinery or equipment, or a structure that houses property used as an integral part of any of these activities if the use of the structure is so closely related to the use of such property that the structure clearly can be expected to be replaced when the property it initially houses is replaced, is included in the asset guideline class appropriate to the equipment to which it is related.

Tangible personal property is property other than (1) a building and a structural component of a building, (2) an improvement to land, or (3) a inherently permanent structure or a structural component of an inherently permanent structure. See ¶ 116.

Reg. § 1.48-1(d) defines other tangible property as tangible property (other than a building and its structural components) used as an integral part of manufacturing, production, or extraction, or as an integral part of furnishing transportation, communications, electrical energy, gas, water, or sewage disposal services by a person engaged in a trade or business of furnishing any such service, or which constitutes a research or storage facility used in connection with any of the foregoing activities. The regulation further define the terms "manufacturing, production, and extraction," "research and storage facilities," "integral part,", and gives examples of transportation and communication businesses.

"Other tangible property" described in the regulation is the same property described in Code Sec. 1245(a)(3)(B). Thus, an item which is considered a land improvement under this rule is section 1245 real property for various purposes of the Code, including depreciation recapture and AMT calculations.

If an item of "other tangible property" is described in an Asset Class other than Rev. Proc. 87-56 Asset Class 00.3 or "land improvements" are included in an Asset Class other than Asset Class 00.3 then the depreciation period of the item of other tangible property should be determined by reference to that other Asset Class. See "Land improvements included in another Asset Class," above.

See ¶ 127C for a discussion of other tangible property and property in the nature of machinery.

A permanency test was applied to determine whether petroleum storage tanks, which both the IRS and taxpayer agreed were section 1245(a)(3)(E) property, should be treated as a land improvement (*PDV America, Inc. and Subsidiaries v Commr.*, Dec. 55,638(M), TC Memo. 2004-118). The court determined that the tanks were not permanent, based partly upon a history of past removals and relocations, and treated the tanks as five-year property under Rev. Proc. 87-56 Asset Class 57.0 ("section 1245 assets used in marketing petroleum") rather than 15-year property under Rev. Proc. 87-56 Asset Class 57.1 ("land improvements, whether section 1245 property or section 1250 property...used in the marketing of petroleum").

The IRS has ruled that a structure that housed equipment in a waste-treatment production facility was essentially an item of machinery or equipment and, therefore, was not a land improvement (or a building or structural component). The structure instead was classified as 7-year property under Rev. Proc. 87-56 Asset Class 49.5 (Waste Reduction and Resource Recovery Plants) (IRS Letter Ruling 200013038, December 27, 1999).

*Real estate developers*

The cost of improvements to subdivided real estate that is held for sale are not generally depreciable by a developer. Rather, these costs are capital expenditures, allocable to the basis of the developer in the subdivided lots (*W.C. & A.N. Miller Development Co.*, 81 TC 619, Dec. 40,486).

Streets, sewage, and utility systems built by a real estate developer were not depreciable as tangible property or amortizable as intangible property where the developer was required to dedicate the property to the city and the city was responsible for the cost of maintenance and reconstruction of the assets (IRS Letter Ruling 200017046, September 10, 1999). However, the transfer of the assets to the city in exchange for the proceeds of a bond sale was a disposition.

See, also, Reg.§ 1.263(a)-2, Reg.§ 1.263(a)-3, and Reg.§ 1.263(a)-4.

*Gasoline service stations and retail motor fuel outlets (convenience stores)*

Section 1250 property, including service station buildings and land improvements, whether section 1245 property or section 1250 property, primarily used in the marketing of petroleum and petroleum products is treated as 15-year property under MACRS (Rev. Proc. 87-56 Asset Class 57.1). Section 1245 property, not described above, which is primarily used for such a purpose is treated as five-year property under MACRS (Rev. Proc. 87-56 Asset Class 57.0).

The IRS determined that a multi-story (most likely two stories) industrial building structure that contained office space, restrooms, a work room, a mechanical room, a truck service center, and a truck wash was *primarily used* as a service station building and therefore qualified for a 15-year recovery period as property described in Rev. Proc. 87-56 Asset Class 57.1 (CCA Letter Ruling 201123001, February 24, 2011). The truck service center portion of the building possessed the features typically associated with a service station building in that the truck service center included service bays in which taxpayer provided maintenance services for trucks, such as, front-end alignments, oil changes, mechanical work, and other truck repair services. In addition, there a fuel island was located in the rear of the building. The taxpayer sold fuel, oil, lube and other petroleum products as part of its maintenance and repair business. The truck service center (including the service bay for the drive-through truck wash) comprises approximately 84 percent of the floor space of the Property building. Redactions in the ruling eliminated specific references to the amount of income derived from the sale of petroleum products. The office space was presumably used primarily in connection with the taxpayer's truck leasing activities.

The IRS has ruled that the sale of gasoline and/or diesel fuel is required in order to be a service station building within the meaning of Rev. Proc. 87-56 Asset Class 57.1 (CCA Letter Ruling 201509029, September 29, 2014.) Consequently, buildings used by a vehicle dealership engaged in the sale, service, and leasing of new and used heavy and medium-duty trucks and trailers were 39-year property where the only petroleum products marketed related to oil changes. Unlike CCA Letter Ruling 201123001 above, no fuel was sold.

See ¶ 125 for service station equipment and canopy depreciation.

*Convenience stores.* Effective for property placed in service after August 19, 1996, section 1250 property that qualifies as a "retail motor fuel outlet" is 15-year real property whether or not food or other convenience items are sold at the outlet (Code Sec. 168(e)(3)(E)(iii)). A 20-year ADS recovery period applies (Code Sec. 168(g)(3)(B)).

The definition of a retail motor fuels outlet is not provided in Code Sec. 168(e)(3)(E)(iii). The controlling committee report, however, provides a definition which is discussed at length in an IRS Coordinated Issue Paper for Petroleum and Retail Industries Convenience Stores, issued April 2, 1997. This paper modifies an earlier ISP paper, dated March 1, 1995, which outlines the treatment of convenience stores prior to enactment of Code Sec. 168(e)(3)(E)(iii).

The ISP paper, however, discusses the definition of a retail motor fuels outlet only in the context of a convenience store (C-store) even though the committee report and text of Code Sec. 168(e)(3)(E)(iii) apply the definition generally to "section 1250" property.

With respect to C-stores the ISP paper states:

> "A C-store contains none of the features typically associated with traditional service stations such as service bays, tiring changing and repair facilities, and car lifts. The C-store provides no services relating to the maintenance of automobiles and trucks and employs no mechanics or other personnel who specialize in caring for motor vehicles. The typical employee resembles an employee found in other consumer goods retail facilities. . . . Because a C-store does not provide the services offered by a traditional service station, we do not believe that a C-store building can be a 'service station building' within the meaning of Rev. Proc. 87-56 Asset Class 57.1. However, the building can still be treated as 15-year property if it is primarily used in petroleum marketing or is a retail motor fuels outlet."

According to the ISP paper, a C-store will qualify as a retail motor fuels outlet (15-year property) if one or more of the following tests are met:

(1) more than 50 percent of the gross revenues generated by the C-store are derived from gasoline sales (the committee report and other IRS guidance, including IRS Publication 946, use the phrase "petroleum sales," so that oil sales would be also be included); or

(2) 50 percent or more of the floor space in the building (including restrooms, counters, and other areas allocable to traditional service station "services") are devoted to the petroleum marketing activity (the committee report and, other IRS guidance, including IRS Publication 946, use the phrase "petroleum marketing sales" in place of "the petroleum marketing activity"); or

(3) the C-store building is 1400 square feet or less.

The earlier ISP Paper, which was issued on March 1, 1995, provided a similar definition except that a convenience store had to satisfy *both* tests (1) *and* (2) or be 1400 square feet or less in order to qualify as Rev. Proc. 87-56 Asset Class 57.1 property.

*Definition of gross revenues and floor space.* The background section of the April 2, 1997 ISP paper indicates that typically, only about 10 to 20 percent of a C-store's floor space is devoted to the marketing of petroleum products. "This includes facilities such as counters relating to the sale of gasoline dispensed from pump islands, as well as automobile supplies such as oil, anti-freeze, and window-washer fluid (which are marketed along with other consumer goods). The remainder of the C-store floor space is devoted to office area, storage, restrooms, food preparation, walk-in cooler, general sales area, and, in some cases, seating for customers." Thus, the paper appears to take the position that in addition to the space devoted to the sale of oil and gasoline, space devoted to the sale of car-related products, such as anti-freeze, oil filters, wiper blades, etc., is attributable to a petroleum marketing activity for purposes of item (2) in the preceding definition.

However, the IRS takes a more restrictive view in Sec. 6.01(1)(c)(3)(b)(vi) of Rev. Proc. 2019-43 which relates to automatic accounting method changes. This procedure requires a taxpayer who is changing the classification of an item of section 1250 property placed in service after August 19, 1996, to a retail motor fuels outlet, to include the following statement with Form 3115:

> "For purposes of § 168(e)(3)(E)(iii) of the Internal Revenue Code, the taxpayer represents that (A) 50 percent or more of the gross revenue generated from the item of § 1250 property is from the sale of petroleum products (not including gross revenue from related services, such as the labor cost of oil changes and gross revenue from the sale of nonpetroleum products such as tires and oil filters), (B) 50 percent or more of the floor space in the item of property is devoted to the sale of petroleum products (not including floor space devoted to related services, such as oil changes and floor space devoted to nonpetroleum products such as tires and oil filters), or (C) the item of § 1250 property is 1,400 square feet or less."

In response to a CCH query, a spokesperson from the examination division of the IRS confirmed that service bay areas are not treated as floor space devoted to a petroleum marketing activity because such space is used primarily to provide services and is not used primarily for the sale of petroleum products (oil and gas). (However, the Court of Appeals for the Eighth Circuit, has considered service bay and similar areas as floor space devoted to a petroleum marketing activity by applying a "traditional service station" standard. See discussion in "*Multiple Buildings*", below). With respect to the gross receipts test, the spokesperson indicated that only receipts from oil and gas sales are treated as receipts from a petroleum marketing activity.

The ISP paper indicates that gross revenue from petroleum sales should be compared to gross revenue from all other sources (e.g., food items, beverages, lottery, video rentals, etc.). Gross revenue includes all excise and sales taxes.

The IRS, however, has issued an audit technique guide for gas retailers under its market segment specialization program (MSSP Audit Technique Guide on Gas Retailers, March 23, 2003) which adds an arrow to the taxpayer's quiver. The guide now includes a description of the rules relating to qualification as a retail motor fuels outlet. The description of the gross receipts and floor space test treats floor space devoted to the sale of automotive related products and receipts from such products as floor space and gross receipts from petroleum products for purposes of the 50-percent tests.

> "The gross revenue attributable to the petroleum sales (motor fuel, lube oil, battery, tires, auto accessories and other traditional motor fuel retail outlet sales) should be compared to gross revenue from all other sources (for example, food items, beverages, lottery, video rentals, etc.). If the petroleum sales as reflected in (a) receipts or (b) floor space utilization, are greater than the non-petroleum sales receipts or floor use, the building qualifies as 15-year property."

The test should be applied on an annual basis. If the test is met (or not met) in one tax year and not met (or met) in another tax year the property must generally be reclassified. In other words, the property has undergone a change in use described in Code Sec. 168(i)(5). See ¶ 168 for change in use rules. Rev. Proc. 97-10 (1997-1 CB 680), however, citing legislative history, indicates that there is no change in use if the failure to meet (or not meet) the test is only "temporary." According to the Coordinated Issue Paper, a failure to meet (or not meet) the test is temporary if caused by a temporary fluctuation in revenue. For example, a special promotion which is run for six months could cause a temporary fluctuation in revenue. According to the legislative history, if a property is placed in service near the end of the tax year and the use of the property is not representative of the subsequent use of the property, the test may be applied in the subsequent tax year.

A building may qualify as a retail motor fuels outlet (15-year property) whether or not the taxpayer-owner is the operator of the motor fuels business. Also, in applying the gross revenue tests, the owner of a building must aggregate the gross revenues of all businesses operated in the building (such as a restaurant or video arcade) whether or not such businesses are operated by the owner (Rev. Rul. 97-29, I.R.B. 1997-28, 4).

A taxpayer could elect to apply this provision to property placed in service before August 20, 1996 (Act Sec. 1120(c) of P.L. 104-188). The election, however, was required to be made by July 14, 1997 (Rev. Proc. 97-10 describes the election procedure).

Taxpayers who depreciated a building placed in service before August 20, 1996 over 15-years are treated as having made the election if the property qualifies as a retail motor fuels outlet under these guidelines.

The recovery period for a retail motor fuels outlet is 20 years under the MACRS alternative depreciation system (Code Sec. 168(g)(3)(B)).

The fact that a building is considered a convenience store (i.e., fails the test) will not affect the treatment of other assets used in the business as property used to market petroleum. For example, adjacent car wash buildings and associated land improvements used for the marketing of petroleum products such as pump islands and canopies are considered Rev. Proc. 87-56 Asset Class 57.1 property eligible for a 15-year depreciation period. (Removable canopies may be considered 5-year property. See ¶ 125.) Tanks, pipelines, and pumps fall within Rev. Proc. 87-56 Asset Class 57.0 and may be depreciated over five years.

*Multiple buildings—revenues and floor space test applied.* The Court of Appeals for the Eight Circuit has affirmed a district court's ruling that the revenue and floor spaced tests are applied on a building by building basis (*Iowa 80 Group, Inc. & Subsidiaries*, CA-8, 2003-2 USTC ¶ 50,703, aff'g DC Iowa, 2002-2 USTC ¶ 50,474). Thus, the classifications of a main building, diesel fuel center, truckomat (truck wash), and service (repair) center at a truck stop had to be determined by applying the gross revenue test and floor space tests separately to each structure. The taxpayer lost its argument that the buildings should be treated as a single retail motor fuel "*outlet*." Apparently, the main building (presumably the most expensive) could only qualify for the 15-year recovery period if the revenue attributable to all of the buildings, including the main building, was aggregated.

The taxpayer's brief provides some additional details of interest. For example, the IRS applied the gross revenue test by taking into account the gross revenue earned by various lessees in the main building of the truck stop complex (e.g., a Wendy's restaurant and Dairy Queen). This is in accord with Rev. Rul. 97-29. It should be noted that the IRS did not include the lease payments to the taxpayer/owner as part of the gross revenue from the building.

If fuel was paid for within the main building, then those revenues were counted toward the gross revenue test as it applied to the main building. However, revenue from fuel paid for outside of the main building in a diesel fuel center was apparently only taken into account in determining the classification of the diesel fuel center.

For procedural reasons, the district court did not consider floor space allocation issues. The Eighth Circuit remanded the case to the district court to rule on these issues. Upon remand, the district court concluded that the floor space test was not satisfied and this conclusion was affirmed by the Eighth Circuit (*Iowa 80 Group Inc. & Subsidiaries*, CA-8, 2005-1 USTC ¶ 50,343, aff'g DC Iowa, 2005-1 USTC ¶ 50,342). The appellate court applied a "traditional service station" test. Floor space on the second floor of the building attributed to the movie theater, arcade, showers, laundromat, and TV lounge were not features normally associated with a traditional service station and, therefore, were not considered devoted to petroleum marketing sales. However, citing the 1995 and 1997 Coordinated Issue Papers discussed above, it concluded that service bays, tire changing and repair facilities, and car lifts are part of a traditional service station.

*AMT adjustment required.* An AMT depreciation adjustment is required on Section 1250 property, such as a retail motor fuel outlet, which is not depreciated using the straight-line method for regular tax purposes unless the bonus depreciation deduction is claimed on the property, or for property placed in service after 2015, the outlet qualified for bonus depreciation. See ¶ 170.

## ¶ 112

## 20-Year Property

Property with a class life of 25 or more years is classified as 20-year property (Code Sec. 168(e)(1)).

*Farm buildings.* Farm buildings, such as barns and machine sheds, are 20-year MACRS property (Asset Class 01.3 of Rev. Proc. 87-56). See ¶ 118 for a discussion of farm property.

*Municipal sewers.* Municipal sewers placed in service before June 13, 1996 are 20-year property (Code Sec. 168(e)(3)(F), prior to being stricken by P.L. 104-188). A 25-year recovery period now applies to municipal sewers. See ¶ 113.

*Property used by utility to gather, treat, and distribute water.* Twenty-year property also includes property placed in service before June 13, 1996, which is used by a utility in the gathering, treatment, and commercial distribution of water. See ¶ 113 for the treatment of such property placed in service after June 12, 1996.

*Assets used in the transmission and distribution of electricity.* Assets that are used in the transmission and distribution of electricity *for sale* are included in Asset Class 49.14 of Rev. Proc. 87-56 and have an MACRS recovery period of 20 years and an ADS recovery period of 30 years (IRS Letter Ruling 8848039, September 2, 1988). However, assets used in the transmission and distribution of electricity at 69 or more kilovolts for sale are treated as 15-year property if placed in service after April 11, 2005 and certain other requirements are met. See ¶ 110.

In IRS Letter Ruling 8848039, various components of an electrical distribution system (pine poles, aerial lines, transformers, meters, street lighting) and water distribution system (valves, fire hydrants, fittings, tapping sleeves, PVC water pipe, water meters) that were installed by the taxpayer were 15-year land improvements. These items were not classified as Rev. Proc. 87-56 Asset Class 49.14, Electric Utility Transmission and Distribution Plant, and Asset Class 49.3, Water Utilities, because those classifications only apply to taxpayers that *sell* electricity and water.

Street light assets owned by an electric utility were primarily used to make light for sale to public and private entities, not to distribute electricity for sale. The street lights were, therefore, not described in Rev. Proc. 87-56 Asset Class 49.14 with a 20-year recovery period. Furthermore, the street lights were not land improvements (15-year property) since they were readily removable. The street lights, accordingly, were property without a class life to which a 7-year recovery period applies (*PPL Corporation and Subsidiaries*, 135 TC —, No. 8, Dec. 58,286; *Entergy Corporation and Affiliated Subsidiaries*, Dec. 58,288(M), TC Memo. 2010-166).

Initial clearing and grading costs described in Rev. Rul. 72-403 are specifically excluded from Rev. Proc. 87-56 Asset Class 49.14 and from Asset Class 00.3 relating to land improvements. Taxpayers have been depreciating these costs as MACRS 7-year property (section 1245 real property for which no class life is provided). The recovery period for the cost of the initial clearing and grading land improvements pertaining to any electric utility transmission and distribution plant has been increased from seven years to 20 years, effective for property placed in service after October 22, 2004 (Code Sec. 168(e)(3)(F)). The ADS period is 25 years (Code Sec. 168(g)(3)(B)).

*Depreciation method and convention for 20-year property.* MACRS twenty-year property is depreciated for regular tax purposes over a 20-year recovery period using the 150-percent declining balance method with a switch to the straight-line method in the tax year that maximizes the deduction. The half-year or mid-quarter convention apply.

## ¶ 113

## 25 Year Water Utility Property

The cost of water utility property is recovered over a period of 25 years using the straight-line method (Code Sec. 168(b)(3) and Code Sec. 168(c), as amended by the Small Business Job Protection Act of 1996 (P.L. 104-188)). See ¶ 112 for the treatment of water utility property placed in service before June 13, 1996.

Water utility property is defined as (1) property that is an integral part of the gathering, treatment, or commercial distribution of water, and that, would have a 20-year recovery period if the 25-year recovery period was not assigned to it, and (2) any municipal sewer (Code Sec. 168(e)(5), as added by the Small Business Job Protection Act of 1996 (P.L. 104-188), effective for property placed in service after June 12, 1996, other than property placed in service pursuant to a binding contract in effect before June 10, 1996, and at all times thereafter before the property is placed in service). Water utility property is described in Asset Classes 49.3 and 51.0 of Rev. Proc. 87-56 (reproduced at ¶ 190).

## ¶ 114

## 27.5-Year Residential Rental Property

Residential rental property is depreciated over a 27.5 year recovery period using the straight-line method and the mid-month convention. A 40 years alternative depreciation system (ADS) recovery period applies to residential rental property placed in service before 2018. Effective for property placed in service after 2017, the ADS period is reduced to 30 years (Code Sec. 168(g)(2)(C)). Further, to the extent a real property trade or business that makes the election provided in Code Sec. 163(j)(7)(B) has residential rental property placed in service before 2018, such residential rental property is also recovered over a 30-year period for ADS purposes assuming that ADS was not otherwise required to be utilized (or elected into) separate and apart from the Code Sec. 163(j)(7)(B) election. The IRS has issued a depreciable table for residential rental property depreciated over 30 years under ADS (Rev. Proc. 2019-8; Table 12A at ¶ 180). Further, the IRS released Rev. Proc. 2021-28 to provide guidance on how an electing real property trade or business changes its method of depreciating residential rental property that may have been previously depreciated using an impermissible 40-year ADS recovery period. See ¶ 152.

See *"Property used in connection with residential property"* at ¶ 104 for the depreciation periods that apply to appliances and other property used in connection with residential rental property.

Residential rental property includes buildings or structures for which 80 percent or more of the gross rental income is rental income from dwelling units (Code Sec. 168(e)(2)(A)(i)). If any portion of the building or structure is occupied by the taxpayer, the gross rental income from the property includes the fair rental value of the unit occupied by the taxpayer (Code Sec. 168(e)(2)(A)(ii)(II)).

A dwelling unit is a house or apartment used to provide living accommodations in a building or other structure. A dwelling unit does not include a unit in a hotel, motel, or other establishment in which more than 50 percent of the units are used on a transient basis (Code Sec. 168(e)(2)(A)(ii)(I)). Thus, if a motel, etc., rents more than 50 percent of its units on a transient basis, it cannot be classified as residential rental property regardless of the amount of gross rental income derived from its permanently rented units.

The definition of residential rental property prior to enactment of ACRS was similar to the current MACRS definition and was provided in Reg. § 1.167(j)-3(b) (see T.D. 7166 for text). Although Reg. § 1.167(j)-3(b) was withdrawn by the IRS in 1993 (T.D. 8474, 1993-1 C.B. 242), it provides useful information concerning the manner in which residential rental property status is determined.

Reg. § 1.167(k)-3(c) (see T.D. 7167 for text), which was also withdrawn in 1993 (T.D. 8474) and (Code Sec. 167(k)(3)(C)) (repealed in 1990) provide that a dwelling unit is used on a transient basis if, for more than one-half of the days in which the unit is occupied on a rental basis during the taxpayer's tax year, it is occupied by a tenant or series of tenants each of whom occupies the unit for less than 30 days. If a dwelling unit is occupied subject to a sublease for any portion of the taxable year, the determination of whether the unit is occupied on a transient basis shall be made with respect to the sublessee who occupies the unit, not with respect to the lessee.

For purposes of computing the gross rental income from a building or structure, the rental at which a vacant unit is offered is not taken into account (Reg. 1.167(j)(3)(b)(4) (see T.D. 7166 for text)).

> ***Example (1):*** In May, Jones pays $240,000 for real property of which $40,000 is allocable to land and $200,000 is allocable to a building consisting of a single store front and 6 similar upper-story apartments. Jones, a calendar-year taxpayer, moves into one of the apartments and, pursuant to existing leases, receives $400 per month for each of the other 5 apartments and $700 per month for the store. Since the gross rental income from the apartments is less than 80% of the gross rental income from the building, the building is not 27.5-year rental property and must be depreciated over a 39-year recovery period as nonresidential real property (¶ 116).

> ***Example (2):*** The facts are the same as in *Example (1)*, except that each apartment rents for $500 per month. Since gross rental income from the apartments (counting $500 per month for the owner occupied unit) totals 80% or more of the gross rental income from the building, the building is 27.5-year residential rental property. Assuming depreciation is allocated in proportion to rents, Jones's depreciation deduc-

tion is \$3,931, which is computed as follows: \$200,000 adjusted basis of the building × .03636 (straight-line method rate determined by dividing 1 by 27.5 years in the recovery period) × 7.5/12 (to reflect the mid-month convention and the number of months that the building is deemed placed in service during the year) = \$4,545 depreciation if the building was used 100% for the production of income. Such amount, \$4,545, is multiplied by 32/37 (\$3,200/\$3,700) = \$3,931 in order to limit the claimed deduction to the portion of depreciation not allocable to personal use.

***Example (3):*** The facts are the same as in *Example (1)*. Since the property does not qualify as 27.5-year residential property, it is 39-year nonresidential property. Before any adjustment for personal use, depreciation for the year that the property is placed in service is \$3,205 (\$200,000 adjusted basis × .02564 (the MACRS straight-line rate is 1 divided by 39 years in the recovery period)) × 7.5/12 (to reflect the mid-month convention and the number of months the building is deemed placed in service during the year). The actual deduction is \$2,791 (27/31 × \$3,205, reflecting the ratio of rents (\$2,700 per month) to \$2,700 + the monthly rental value (\$400) of the owner-occupied apartment).

As the example indicates, the 11.5-year longer recovery period for nonresidential real property than for residential rental property reduces current depreciation deductions by about 29.5 percent ((1/27.5 – 1/39.0) / 1/27.5).

According to the Construction Industry Audit Techniques Guide (May 2009), the Regulations Policy Committee deleted a reference in the proposed version of Reg. 1.167(j)-3 that a dwelling unit must be self-contained with facilities generally found in a principal place of residence such as a kitchen. Deleting this reference indicates the intent to expand the scope of "dwelling unit" to include other living accommodations such as nursing homes, retirement homes, and college dormitories. Because nursing homes, retirement homes, and dormitories provide "living accommodations in a building or structure," they are dwelling units only if no more than one-half of the units are used for less than 30 days by the same tenant.

*Depreciation computation upon change in use from residential to nonresidential or vice versa.* If a building changes from a residential rental property to a noresidential real property or vice versa by reason of the 80 percent test (or some other reason) the change in use rules described at ¶ 169 apply (Reg.§ 1.168(i)-4). Under these rules if residential rental property becomes nonresidential real property, the remaining basis as of the beginning of the year of change is recovered using the straight line method over the number of years that would remain in the 39-year recovery period as of the beginning of the year of change if the property had been classified as nonresidential real property when placed in service. If nonresidential real property becomes residential real property, the remaining basis is depreciated over a 27.5 year recovery period beginning with the year of change as though the MACRS property was first placed in service in the year of change. However, if the number of years remaining in the 39-year recovery period is less than 27.5 years the taxpayer may elect to continue depreciating the property over the remaining 39-year recovery period. The election is made by computing depreciation on Form 4562 as if the change in use had not occurred. See ¶ 169.

*Condominiums and vacation properties.* A condominium or other vacation property that is only rented for more than 30 days at a time by the owner should be treated as residential rental property as such use is not considered transient. However, in many cases a condominium or other vacation property is rented one or two weeks at a time to different persons. It appears in this situation such property should be treated as nonresidential real property, assuming that condominiums and other vacation properties (such as a lakefront home) are considered a type of "structure" subject to the transient use limitation.

*Example (4):* A condominium is rented one week at a time to 12 different persons and is not used by the owner. In this case, there are 84 days of transient use (7 x 12) and no days of non-transient use. Since more than 50% of the total days of use is transient (100% are transient in this example), the condominium is considered rented on a transient basis and does not qualify as a residential rental building depreciable over 27.5 years.

Note that Code Sec. 168(e)(2)(A)(ii)(II) specifically provides that if any portion of the building or structure is occupied by the taxpayer, the gross rental income from the property includes the fair rental value of the unit occupied by the taxpayer for purposes of the rule which requires that 80 percent or more of the rental income must be from dwelling units. It does not appear, however, based on the wording of Reg. § 1.167(k)-3(a), above, that days of use by an owner are taken into account in determining whether a dwelling unit is used on a transient basis. The regulation states that: "a dwelling unit is used on a transient basis if, for more than one-half of the days in which the unit is occupied on a rental basis during the taxpayer's tax year, it is occupied by a tenant or series of tenants each of whom occupies the unit for less than 30 days." Thus, the test is apparently applied only by taking into account the days that the unit is rented by a paying tenant. This interpretation would mean that most vacation rental homes that are also used by an owner should be depreciated as nonresidential real property even though in actual practice it may be common to treat such property as residential rental property.

IRS Publication 946 (How to Depreciate Property) and IRS Publication 527 (Residential Rental Property (Including Rental of Vacation Homes) do not provide any guidance in this area. Nor does there appear to be any guidance in any court case or IRS document).

*Elevators and escalators.* Elevators and escalators located in a residential rental property are structural components of the building (section 1250 property) and, therefore, depreciated as 27.5-year residential rental property. P.L. 99-514 section 201(d)(11) removed elevators and escalators from the list of definitions of section 1245 property.

*Mobile homes, trailers, and manufactured homes.* Mobile homes, trailers, and manufactured homes that are permanently affixed to the ground are depreciated as 27.5-year residential rental property if rented by the owner. A mobile home, trailer, or manufactured home that is readily transportable, however, may be considered personal property even though it functions as a building. See ¶ 127C which also discusses the status of readily moveable mobile homes and trailers as personal property. The proper recovery period in such a case is not entirely clear. However, classification as MACRS 5-year property under Rev. Proc. 87-56 Asset Class 57.0 (relating to the provision of personal and professional services) based on Announcement 99-82) may be appropriate. This announcement treats a taxpayer who rents residential rental property as engaged in an Asset Class 57.0 activity and, therefore, classifies appliances and personal property used in a residential rental building as 5-year property. See ¶ 104. A taxpayer who rents residential living space should be considered engaged in an Asset Class 57.0 activity regardless of whether or not the living space is considered real or personal property. Alternatively, classification as personal property without a class life (i.e., property not described in Rev. Proc. 87-56) could be considered. Personal property without a class life is assigned a 7-year recovery period. See "*Property with no class life*" at ¶ 106. Classification of a moveable manufactured home, mobile home, or trailer as a 15-year land improvement is not appropriate because a land improvement must be affixed to land and does not include personal property. Furthermore, even if such property is affixed to the ground, buildings (defined at ¶ 127C) are specifically excluded from classification as land improvements. Hence a permanently affixed mobile home or trailer is depreciated as 27.5 year residential rental property or 39-year nonresidential real property. See ¶ 110 for a discussion of land improvements.

*Home office.* Generally, a home office is depreciated as nonresidential real property. See ¶ 116 for discussion of home offices.

*Appliances and property used in residential rental property.* Appliances and non-structural components used in residential rental property are 5-year property (Asset Class 57.0 of Rev. Proc. 87-56). See *"Property used in connection with residential property"* at ¶ 104 for the depreciation periods that apply to appliances and other property used in connection with residential rental property. Effective for property placed in service in tax years beginning after 2017, the section 179 allowance may be claimed on section 1245 property used in connection with residential rental property (Code Sec. 179(d)(1), last sentence). See ¶ 302.

*Nursing home.* It is possible for a nursing or retirement home to qualify as a residential rental property (IRS Letter Ruling 8239121, June 30, 1982; IRS Letter Ruling 9825024, March 20, 1998; IRS Letter Ruling 8240067, July 7, 1982; IRS Letter Ruling 7848036, August 30, 1978; CCA Letter Ruling 201147025, November 29, 2011).

Taxpayers who converted their personal residence into a 24-hour adult care business could claim depreciation for the portion of the house considered leased as dwelling units by adults to whom the taxpayer's provided care. Bedroom apartments (and associated common areas) used to provide living accommodations to the live-in adults were rental units within a building and were not used on a transient basis. The portion of the house that was considered owner-occupied was not depreciable (CCA Letter Ruling 201049026, September 23, 2010).

*Personal residence converted to residential rental property.* MACRS is used to depreciate a personal residence that is converted to rental property after 1986 regardless of the date that the personal residence was purchased (IRS Publication 946 (How To Depreciate Property); Reg.§ 1.168(i)-4(b) at ¶ 568).

*Building placed in service in stages.* Residential rental property, such as a high-rise, may be placed in service in stages, as occupancy certificates are issued. If so, each completed stage may be separately depreciated. See ¶ 226.

*Multiple buildings located on single tract or varied use units within same building.* Former Reg. § 1.167(j)-3(b)(1)(ii) provided that in any case where two or more buildings or structures on a single tract or parcel (or contiguous tracts or parcels) of land are operated as an integrated unit (as evidenced by their actual operation, management, financing, and accounting), they may be treated as a single building for purposes of determining whether the building or structure is residential rental property. Two buildings separated by a public street but connected by a skywalk were considered contiguous (IRS Letter Ruling 200947004, August 14, 2009; IRS Letter Ruling 200947005, August 14, 2009). In IRS Letter Ruling 200949019 (August 31, 2009), 3 separate buildings were treated as a single building for purposes of determining whether the buildings were residential rental property or nonresidential real property even though the buildings were not placed in service in the same month. The buildings were also treated as a single item of section 1250 property for recapture purposes pursuant to Reg.§ 1.1250-1(a)(2)(ii). The IRS has also applied this rule to treat five separate "condominium units" located within the same building as a single building for purposes of determining whether the building (and its structural components) is residential rental property or nonresidential real property under MACRS. Condominium units consisted of a (1) residential units and parking spaces; (2) commercial space in the cellar and first floor; (3) two community facility units on the first floor (each treated as a separate condominium unit); and (4) commercial space on the first floor (IRS Letter Ruling 201103006, October 05, 2010).

A building divided into two sections consisting of residential rental apartments and hotel rooms could be treated as a single item of property for purposes of determining whether the building was residential rental property or nonresidential real property under MACRS and for purposes of Code Sec. 1250 recapture because the apartments and rooms were on a single parcel of land and were operated as a single unit. The IRS considered actual operation, management, financing, and accounting as factors in making this determination (IRS Letter Ruling 201243003, Oct. 29, 2012).

*Allocate purchase price to land.* When computing depreciation on residential rental property and nonresidential real property, keep in mind that the portion of the purchase price allocable to land is not included in the depreciable basis of the building (Reg. § 1.167(a)-2; Reg. § 1.168(a)-1). See ¶ 70, "*Allocation of purchase price when realty purchased.*"

## ¶ 116

## 39-Year Nonresidential Real Property

MACRS nonresidential real property is section 1250 property which is not MACRS residential rental property (¶ 114) and which has a class life (i.e. as shown in Rev. Proc. 87-56 at ¶ 191) of 27.5 years or greater (Code Sec. 168(e)(2)(B)).

The cost of nonresidential real property is recovered under the straight-line method over a recovery period of 39 years for property generally placed in service after May 12, 1993. The ADS recovery period is 40 years.

The mid-month convention must be used to compute depreciation on nonresidential real property.

Nonresidential real property placed in service before May 13, 1993, is recovered under the straight-line method over a recovery period of 31.5 years. The ADS recovery period is 40 years.

Under a transitional rule, nonresidential real property placed in service before January 1, 1994, may be treated as 31.5-year property if the taxpayer or a qualified person (1) entered into a binding written contract to purchase or construct the property before May 13, 1993, or (2) construction began for these persons before such date (Omnibus Budget Reconciliation Act of 1993 (P.L. 103-66), Act Sec. 13151(b)(2)). A qualified person is a person who transfers his or her rights in such contract or property to the taxpayer before the property is placed in service.

When placing nonresidential real property in service, the taxpayer should keep in mind that the cost segregation rules allow section 1245 (personal) property components to be depreciated over a shortened recovery period (see ¶ 127 et seq.) and that a taxpayer's additions and improvements that are section 1250 property are depreciated over a 39-year recovery period beginning in the year the addition or improvement is placed in service by the taxpayer unless a 15-year recovery period applies because the addition or improvement was placed in service before 2018 and is qualified leasehold improvement property (generally, internal improvements and made under or pursuant to a lease more than three years after the building was placed in service by any person) (see ¶ 126), qualified retail improvement property (generally internal improvements made to a building used for retail sales more than three years after the building was placed in service by any person) (see ¶ 126), or qualified restaurant property (internal or external improvements to a restaurant building regardless of when the restaurant was placed in service if the improvement was placed in service by the taxpayer after 2008) (see ¶ 110). A restaurant building placed in service by a taxpayer after 2008 and before 2018 also qualifies for a 15-year recovery period (see ¶ 110). Qualified retail, leasehold, and restaurant improvements placed in service in a tax years beginning before 2018 may also qualify for expensing under Code Sec. 179 as qualified real property. Effective for property placed in service in tax years beginning after 2017, qualified improvement property qualifies for section 179 expensing. See ¶ 302. Further, improvements made to the interior of 39-year nonresidential real property previously qualified for bonus depreciation as "qualified improvement property" as defined in Code Sec. 168(e)(6) and Reg.§ 1.168(b)-1(a)(5). This rule applies to property placed in service on or after January 1, 2016 and before 2018. Prior to 2016 qualified leasehold improvement property, including retail and restaurant improvement property that also satisfied the definition of qualified leasehold improvement property, was eligible for bonus depreciation. See ¶ 127D.

Effective for property placed in service after 2017, qualified improvement property is removed by the 2017 Tax Cuts Act (P.L. 115-97) as a separate category of bonus depreciation property (Code Sec. 168(k)(3)), prior to removal by P.L. 115-97). Effective for property placed in service after 2017, qualified improvement property qualifies for bonus depreciation by reason of a technical correction (Code Sec. 168(e)(3)(E)(vii)) that retroactively assigns the intended 15-year recovery period to qualified improvement property. With a 15-year recovery period qualified improvement property qualifies for bonus depreciation under the generally applicable rule that bonus depreciation applies to property with an MACRS recovery period of 20 years or less (Rev. Proc. 2020-25). See ¶ 127D. Qualified improvement property placed in service before 2018 is depreciated as 39-year nonresidential real property unless it qualifies for a 15-year recovery period by meeting the definition of 15-year qualified leasehold, retail, or restaurant improvement property. These three categories of property are eliminated, effective for property placed in service after 2017.

Land is not usually depreciable. Accordingly, the depreciable basis of a commercial building does not include any cost allocable to the land. However, the cost of a term interest in land may be depreciated over the term of the interest. See "*Term interests*," at ¶ 74.

If a commercial building is placed in service in stages, each completed stage may be separately depreciated. See ¶ 226.

Even if a building is described in an Asset Class with a class life of 27.5 years or more, the applicable recovery period for that property is 39 years for purposes of the general depreciation system and 40 years for purposes of the alternative depreciation system, regardless of the applicable recovery periods set out for the Asset Class in the Rev. Proc. 87-56 tables (Section 5.02 of Rev. Proc. 87-56, as modified by Rev. Proc. 88-22). For example, although station and office buildings and roadway buildings are described in Rev. Proc. 87-56 Asset Class 40.2 (Railroad Structures and Similar Improvements) and Asset Class 40.2 has a class life of 30 years, such buildings have a 39-year recovery period even though Asset Class 40.2 provides for a 20-year recovery period (CCA Letter Ruling 200709063, November 21, 2006). The only other Rev. Proc. 87-56 Asset Class with a class life of 27.5 or more in which a building is described appears to be Asset Class 48.11, relating to Telephone Central Office Buildings.

Nonresidential real property includes elevators and escalators that are part of a building which is nonresidential real property as well as other structural components. Typical examples of nonresidential real property are office buildings, shopping malls, hotels and motels, and industrial buildings such as factories. In a rare circumstance a hotel or motel that rents 50 percent or more of its units on a non-transient basis classified is classified as 27.5 year residential rental property. See ¶ 114.

*Home office.* Generally, a home office is depreciated as nonresidential real property. The 80 percent residential rental property test discussed at ¶ 114 cannot be satisfied because no portion of the residential property in which the home office is located is generating rental income. In this situation, the home-owner's use is not treated as generating rental income for purposes of the 80 percent test. On the other hand, if a home office is located in an apartment occupied by the owner of a residential rental property with one or more additional units, the home office is depreciable as 27.5 year residential rental property (CCA Letter Ruling 200526002, May 9, 2005).

*Computation of depreciation under home office safe harbor.* Depreciation (including additional first-year depreciation and the Code Sec. 179 allowance) may not be claimed for the portion of a home that is used as a home office in a tax year in which the safe harbor method of computing the home office deduction is elected (Section 4.06 of Rev. Proc. 2013-13, I.R.B. 2013-6, January 15, 2013). In general, under the safe harbor a taxpayer deducts $5 per square foot of home office space up to a maximum of 300 square feet. The $5 is deemed to include depreciation and certain other expenses such as allocable taxes allowed by Code Sec. 280A.

A home office does not currently qualify for any type of bonus depreciation or section 179 allowance since it is nonresidential real property. There may be special situations, such as natural disasters, in which these deductions could be extended to real property.

If a taxpayer elects the safe harbor method for any tax year, then in any subsequent tax year in which the taxpayer reverts to the actual expense method of computing the home office deduction depreciation must be computed using the IRS table percentages provided in IRS Publication 946 (Depreciation and Amortization). The table percentages must be used even if the taxpayer was not previously using the table percentages to compute allowable depreciation deductions prior to the first tax year in which the safe harbor method was elected. Thus, generally, taxpayers will use the table percentages for MACRS 39-year real property to compute the depreciation deduction on the home office. These table percentages are applied against the "remaining adjusted depreciable basis" (as defined in Reg. § 1.168(k)-1(d)(2)(i)) of the home that was allocated to the home office. In the context of nonresidential real property, remaining adjusted depreciable basis is the original cost or other basis of the entire home that was allocated to the home office without reduction for any depreciation claimed on the home office. The applicable table percentage is the table percentage for the current tax year based on the placed in service year of the home office (Section 4.07 of Rev. Proc. 2013-13, I.R.B. 2013-6, January 15, 2013).

In any year in which the safe harbor is used, the deemed depreciation claimed in $0. Thus, the adjusted basis of the home office used for purposes of determining gain or loss is not reduced by any amount of depreciation in any year that the safe harbor applies.

> ***Example (1):*** Joe placed his home office in service in 2017. He elected the safe harbor method in 2020 but in 2021 he decides not to use the safe harbor method. Joe's depreciation deduction for 2021 must be computed using the optional MACRS table percentages for 39-year nonresidential real property. The fifth-year table percentage will apply since 2021 is the fifth year of the 39-year recovery period of the home office. The fifth year percentage from IRS Percentage Table 7A at ¶ 180 is 2.564%. Assuming that the original basis allocable to the home office is $10,000, Joe's depreciation deduction is $256 ($10,000 × 2.564%).

Any depreciation that is claimed on a home office is recaptured as section 1250 gain (subject to a 25 percent tax rate) to the extent of gain on the entire residence (Reg. § 1.121-1(e)). The remainder of the gain is eligible for the Code Sec. 121 exclusion for gain from the sale of a principle residence. The depreciation allowed or allowable reduces the basis of the home for purposes of computing gain. In tax years that the safe harbor method applies, however, it is not necessary to reduce the basis of the home by any amount of depreciation even though foregone depreciation arguably constitutes a portion of the safe harbor deduction. This treatment is in contrast, for example, to taxpayers who depreciate vehicles using the standard mileage rate. That method treats a specified portion of the standard mileage allowance as a depreciation deduction that reduces the basis of the vehicle.

For home office depreciation recapture rules, see *Sale of Residence* at ¶ 488.

*Buildings specifically described in an Asset Class in Rev. Proc. 87-56 with a class life of less than 27.5 years.* Buildings are described in the following Rev. Proc. 87-56 Asset Classes with a class life of less than 27.5 years and, therefore, are depreciable over shortened recovery periods:

(1) Asset Class 01.3 (Farm buildings) - 20 year recovery period

(2) Asset Class 01.4 (Single purpose agricultural or horticultural structures) - 10 year recovery period

(3) Asset Class 40.1 (Railroad Machinery and Equipment) -7 year recovery period

(4) Asset Class 57.1 (relating to service station buildings and car was buildings) - 15 year recovery period

(5) Asset Class 70.0 (Recreation) - 7 year recovery period

(6) Asset Class 80.0 (Theme and Amusement Parks) - 7 year recovery period

Buildings other than warehouses, administration buildings, hotels and motels are listed in Rev. Proc. 87-56 Asset Class 80.0 (Theme and Amusement Parts) as eligible for a 7-year recovery period. However, the IRS has ruled that buildings that have been converted to theme park use by any person (including the person from whom a theme park is being acquired) are treated as nonresidential real property (IRS Letter Ruling 8928017, April 12, 1989).

*Multiple buildings located on single tract or varied use units within same building.* Former Reg. § 1.167(j)-3(b)(1)(ii) provided that in any case where two or more buildings or structures on a single tract or parcel (or contiguous tracts or parcels) of land are operated as an integrated unit (as evidenced by their actual operation, management, financing, and accounting), they may be treated as a single building for purposes of determining whether the building or structure is residential rental property. Two buildings separated by a public street but connected by a skywalk were considered contiguous (IRS Letter Ruling 200947004, August 14, 2009; IRS Letter Ruling 200947005, August 14, 2009). In IRS Letter Ruling 200949019 (August 31, 2009), 3 separate buildings were treated as a single building for purposes of determining whether the buildings were residential rental property or nonresidential real property even though the buildings were not placed in service in the same month. The buildings were also treated as a single item of section 1250 property for recapture purposes pursuant to Reg.§ 1.1250-1(a)(2)(ii). The IRS has also applied this rule to treat five separate "condominium units" located within the same building as a single building for purposes of determining whether the building (and its structural components) is residential rental property or nonresidential real property under MACRS. Condominium units consisted of a (1) residential units and parking spaces; (2) commercial space in the cellar and first floor; (3) two community facility units on the first floor (each treated as a separate condominium unit); and (4) commercial space on the first floor (IRS Letter Ruling 201103006, October 05, 2010).

A building divided into two sections consisting of residential rental apartments and hotel rooms could be treated as a single item of property for purposes of determining whether the building was residential rental property or nonresidential real property under MACRS and for purposes of Code Sec. 1250 because the apartments and rooms were on a single parcel of land and were operated as a single unit. The IRS considered actual operation, management, financing, and accounting as factors in making this determination. Each section of the building was owned by a separate taxpayer; however, the taxpayers were owned 100% by the same entities and were controlled partnerships under Code Sec. 707(b)(1)(B), thereby supporting treating the separate sections as a single building (IRS Letter Ruling 201243003, Oct. 29, 2012).

*Definition of section 1250 property and section 1245 property*

Section 1250 property is defined as any real property (other than section 1245 property, as defined in Code Sec. 1245(a)(3)) which is or has been property of a character subject to the allowance for depreciation provided in Code Sec. 167 (Code Sec. 1250(c)).

Real property is defined by Reg. § 1.1250-1(e)(3) to mean any property which is not personal property within the meaning of Reg. § 1.1245-3(b). This regulation defines personal property by reference to the definition of tangible personal property within the meaning of investment tax regulation § 1.48-1(c).

In general, Reg. § 1.48-1(c) defines tangible personal property as any tangible property except:

(1) land;

(2) buildings and structural components of buildings (see ¶ 127); and

(3) land improvements (viz., inherently permanent structures (and their structural components) such as swimming pools, paved parking areas, wharves and docks, bridges, and fences (land improvements are generally assigned a 15-year depreciation period under MACRS (Rev. Proc. 87-56 Asset Class 00.3) (see ¶ 110));

Tangible personal property includes all property (other than structural components) which is contained in or attached to a building. Thus, such property as production machinery, printing presses, transportation and office equipment, refrigerators, grocery counters, testing equipment, display racks and shelves, and neon and other signs, which is contained in or attached to a building constitutes tangible personal property (§ 1.48-1(c)).

All property which is in the nature of machinery (other than structural components of a building or other inherently permanent structure) is considered tangible personal property even though located outside a building. Thus, for example, a gasoline pump, hydraulic car lift, or automatic vending machine, although annexed to the ground, shall be considered tangible personal property (§ 1.48-1(c)).

Section 1250 property does not include property that is described in Code Sec. 1245(a)(3). If an item of section 1245 real property is not assigned a class life in Rev. Proc. 87-56, then it is treated as section 1245 real property with no class life and is assigned a MACRS seven-year recovery period (40-year ADS recovery period) (Code Sec. 168(e)(3)(C); Code Sec. 168(g)(3)(E)). Note that any section property described in Code Sec. 1245(a)(3) which is not personal property is considered section 1245 real property. The section 1245 recapture rules apply to this property.

Code Sec. 1245(a)(3) covers the following depreciable property:

(1) personal property;

(2) tangible property (other than a building and its structural components) used as an integral part of manufacturing, production, or extraction or of furnishing transportation, communications, electrical energy, gas, water, or sewage disposal services; research facilities used in connection with any of these activities; facilities used in connection with any of these activities for the bulk storage of fungible commodities (including commodities in a liquid or gaseous state);

(3) real property (other than real property described in item (2)) to the extent that its adjusted basis reflects amortization deductions under Code Sec. 169 (relating to pollution control facilities), the expense allowance under Code Sec. 179, the expense allowance under Code Sec. 179A for qualified clean-fuel vehicle property (generally, certain storage and fuel dispensing facilities), the former amortization deduction for railroad grading and tunnel bores (Code Sec. 185); the former amortization deduction for child care facilities (Code Sec. 188); the deduction for expenditures to remove architectural and transportation barriers (Code Sec. 190); the deduction for qualified tertiary injectant expenses (Code Sec. 193); and the amortization deduction for reforestation expenditures (Code Sec. 194);

(4) single purpose agricultural and horticultural structures (10-year MACRS recovery period (¶ 108));

(5) a storage facility (not including a building or its structural components) used in connection with the distribution of petroleum or any primary product of petroleum; or

(6) any railroad grading or tunnel bore (MACRS assigns a 50-year recovery period (¶ 120)).

Section 5.05 of Rev. Proc. 87-56 provides that tangible property described in item (2) above (see Reg.§ 1.48-1(d)) is an Rev. Proc. 87-56 Asset Class 00.3 land improvement with a 15 year recovery period. However, a structure that is essentially an item of machinery or equipment or a structure that houses property used as an integral part of an activity described in item (2), if the use of the structure is so closely related to the use of the property that the structure clearly can be expected to be replaced when the property it initially houses is replaced, is included in the asset guideline class appropriate to the equipment to which it is related.

See ¶ 127 and following for additional details regarding the definition of tangible personal property, section 1245 real property, land improvements, buildings, and structural components.

## ¶ 118

## Farm Property

*1. 200-percent DB method prohibited on farm property before 2018*

*2. ADS mandatory if election made to deduct preproduction expenditures*

*2A. ADS mandatory if election out of interest limitation rules made after 2017*

*3. Depreciation periods for farm property*

*4. Farm machinery and equipment*

*5. Farm buildings*

*6. Livestock*

*7. Horses*

*8. Ratites (ostrich, emu, rhea)*

*9. Alternative livestock*

*10. Dogs*

*11. Irrigation systems and water wells*

*12. Dams, ponds, and terraces*

*13. Fruit and nut-bearing trees and vines*

*14. Plant bearing fruits and nuts*

*15. Property used in vineyards*

*16. Single purpose agricultural or horticultural structure*

*1. 200-percent DB method prohibited on farm property before 2018*

3-, 5-, 7-, and 10-year property placed in service before 2018 and used in a "farming business" as defined in Code Sec. 263A(e)(4) and Reg. § 1.263A-4(a)(4) may not be depreciated using the 200-percent DB method which is normally applicable to these property classes (the 150-percent DB method has always applied to 15-and 20-year property whether or not used in farming). Instead, farming property placed in service before 2018 in these classes is depreciated using the 150-percent DB method (unless the ADS or straight-line method is required or elected) (Code Sec. 168(b)(2)(B), prior to amendment by the Tax Cuts and Jobs Act (P.L. 115-97)). As a result, Depreciation Tables 1-5 at ¶ 180 do not apply to such property when placed in service before 2018. Instead, Tables 14-18 (the AMT tables because these tables incorporate the 150-percent DB method) are used in conjunction with the asset's regular (GDS) recovery period.

Farm property in the 3-, 5-, 7-, and 10-year classes is depreciated using the 200 percent declining balance method if placed in service after 2017 unless an election is made to use the 150 percent declining balance method, the straight-line method, or ADS (Code Sec. 168(b)(2)(B)).

As defined in Code Sec. 263A(e)(4) and Reg. § 1.263A-4(a)(4), the term "farming business" means a trade or business involving the cultivation of land or the raising or harvesting of any agricultural or horticultural commodity (e.g., the trade or business of operating a nursery or sod farm; the raising or harvesting of trees bearing fruit, nuts, or other crops; the raising of ornamental trees (other than evergreen trees that are more than six years old at the time they are severed from their roots); and the raising, shearing, feeding, caring for, training, and management of animals). A farming business includes processing activities that are normally incident to the growing, raising, or harvesting of agricultural or horticultural products. A farming business does not include contract harvesting of an agricultural or horticultural commodity grown or raised by another taxpayer, or merely buying and reselling plants or animals grown or raised by another taxpayer.

For additional information see ¶ 84.

*2. ADS mandatory if election made to deduct preproduction expenditures*

A farmer that elected not to apply the uniform capitalization rules to any plant produced in the farming business must use ADS for all property used predominantly in the farming business that is placed in service in any year that the election is in effect (Code Sec. 263A(e)(2)). Bonus depreciation does not apply to property which must be depreciated under ADS.

See ¶ 152 for details including rules for revoking the election if a farmer becomes exempt from the UNICAP rules by reason of having $25 million or less in average annual gross receipts.

*2A. ADS mandatory if election out of interest limitation rules made*

Any property with a regular recovery period of 10 years or greater owned by a farming business that makes an election out of new rules (Code Sec. 163(j)) disallowing the deduction for net interest expense in excess of 30 percent (50 percent for tax years beginning in 2019 and 2020) of a business' adjusted taxable income must be depreciated using the MACRS alternative depreciation system (ADS), effective for tax years beginning after 2017 (Code Sec. 168(g)(1)(G); Rev. Proc. 2019-8). Bonus depreciation does not apply to property placed in service in tax years beginning after 2017, if this election applies and ADS must be used. See ¶ 152 for details, including manner of changing to ADS for property placed in service in a tax year that began before 2018.

*3. Depreciation periods for farm property*

The following chart, which is adapted from the IRS Audit Technique Guide for Grain Farmers (July 1995) (reproduced in the CCH IRS Positions Reporter at ¶ 205,500), shows the MACRS depreciation period for various types of common farm assets. *However, note that new machinery and equipment (Asset Class 01.1 of Rev. Proc. 87-56) placed in service by a taxpayer engaged in a farming business is considered 5-year property if placed in service in 2009 or after 2017, as explained above.*

| *Asset* | *Rev. Proc. 87-56 Asset Class (¶ 191)* | *MACRS GDS* | *MACRS ADS* |
|---|---|---|---|
| Airplane | 00.21 | 5 | 6 |
| Auto | 00.22 | 5 | 5 |
| Calculators | 00.13 | 5 | 6 |
| Cattle (Dairy or Breeding) | 01.21 | 5 | 7 |
| Communications Equipment | 00.11 | 7 [3] | 10 |
| Computer and Peripheral Equipment | 00.12 | 5 | 5 |
| Copiers | 00.13 | 5 | 6 |
| Cotton Ginning Assets | 01.11 | 7 | 12 |
| Farm Buildings (General Purpose) | 01.3 | 20 | 25 |
| Farm Equipment and Machinery | 01.1 | 7 [4] | 10 |
| Fences (Agricultural) | 01.1 | 7 | 10 |
| Goats (Breeding or Milk) | 01.24 | 5 | 5 |
| Grain Bin | 01.1 | 7 | 10 |
| Greenhouse | 01.4 | 10 [1] | 15 |
| Helicopter | 00.21 | 5 | 6 |
| Hogs (Breeding) | 01.23 | 3 | 3 |
| Horses (Nonrace, < 12 yrs.) | 01.221 | 7 | 10 |
| Horses (Nonrace, 12 yrs. and older) | 01.222 | 3 | 10 |
| Logging Equipment | 24.1 | 5 | 6 |
| Machinery | 01.1 | 7 [4] | 10 |
| Mobile homes on permanent foundations (Farm tenants) | 00.3 | 15 [5] | 20 |
| Office equipment | 00.11 | 7 | 10 |

| Asset | Rev. Proc. 87-56 Asset Class (¶ 191) | MACRS GDS | MACRS ADS |
|---|---|---|---|
| Office fixtures and furniture | 00.11 | 7 | 10 |
| Orchards (Code Sec. 168(e)(3)(D)) | — | 10 [2] | 20 |
| Paved feedlots | 00.3 | 15 | 20 |
| Property with no class life (personal) | — | 7 | 12 |
| Property with no class life (real) | — | 7 | 40 |
| Pumps and irrigation equipment | 01.1 | 7 [4] | 10 |
| Sheep (breeding) | 01.24 | 5 | 5 |
| Single purpose agricultural or horticultural structure | 01.4 | 10 [1] | 15 |
| Solar property (Code Sec. 168(e)(3)(B)(vi)) | — | 5 | 12 |
| Tile (drainage), water wells | 00.3 | 15 | 20 |
| Tractor units (over-the-road) | 00.26 | 3 | 4 |
| Trailer for use over-the-road | 00.27 | 5 | 6 |
| Trees/vines (Code Sec. 168(e)(3)(D)) | — | 10 [2] | 20 |
| Truck (heavy duty, general purpose) | 00.242 | 5 | 6 |
| Truck (light, < 13,000 lbs.) | 00.241 | 5 | 5 |
| Underground pipe and well | 00.3 | 15 | 20 |
| Vineyard (Code Sec. 168(e)(3)(D)) | — | 10 [2] | 20 |
| Water wells | 00.3 | 15 | 20 |
| Wind energy property (Code Sec. 168(e)(3)(B)(vi)) | — | 5 | 12 |

[1] 7 years if green house or agricultural or horticultural structure placed in service before 1989.
[2] 15 years if orchard, trees, vines, or vineyard placed in service before 1989. See ¶ 108.
[3] Not including communications equipment listed in other Asset Classes.
[4] 5 years if new machinery or equipment placed in service in 2009 or after 2017.
[5] However, see comments at ¶ 127C under *"Mobile homes."*

*4. Farm machinery and equipment*

Machinery and equipment, grain bins, and fences used in agriculture are classified as 7-year MACRS property (Rev. Proc. 87-56, Asset Class 01.1). Agriculture is defined as the production of crops or plants, vines, and trees; livestock; the operation of farm dairies, nurseries, greenhouses, sod farms, mushroom cellars, cranberry bogs, apiaries (i.e., bee production activities), and fur farms; and the performance of agricultural, animal husbandry, and horticultural services (Asset Class 01.1). *However, any machinery or equipment (other than a grain bin, cotton ginning asset, fence, or land improvement), the original use of which begins with the taxpayer in 2009 or after 2017 (i.e., new property), and that is placed in service by the taxpayer in a farming business (as defined in Code Sec. 263A(e)(4) and discussed below) in 2009 or after 2017, has a recovery period of five years (i.e., is MACRS 5-year property) (Code Sec. 168(e)(3)(B)(vii), as added by the Emergency Economic Stabilization Act of 2008 (P.L. 110-343) and Code Sec. 168(e)(3)(B)(vii), as amended by the Tax Cuts and Jobs Act (P.L. 115-97)). Such property has a recovery period of 10 years under ADS (Code Sec. 168(g)(3)(B)).*

The term machinery is not limited to a complex machine such as a farm tractor but may be something as simple as a lever (*L. Trentadue*, 128 TC No. 8, Dec. 56,886, holding that vineyard trellising was 7-year property (Rev. Proc. 87-56 Asset Class 01.1) and not a land improvement).

*5. Farm buildings*

Farm buildings other than single purpose agricultural or horticultural structures are 20-year property (Asset Class 01.3 of Rev. Proc. 87-56). A machine shed would fall into this category (unless it is not a building because it could be categorized as section 1245 property by reason of being a removable structure). See

¶ 127C. Single purpose agricultural or horticultural structures (defined in Code Sec. 168(i)(13)) placed in service after 1988 are 10-year property (Asset Class 01.4). See detailed discussion of agricultural and horticultural structures below. Land improvements (other than machinery and equipment, grain bins, and fences) are 15-year property (Asset Class 00.3). See ¶ 110.

*6. Livestock*

Breeding and dairy cattle are five-year property (Rev. Proc. 87-56 Asset Class 01.21). Sheep and goats used for breeding are 5-year property (Asset Class 01.24). Breeding hogs are 3-year property (Asset Class 01.23).

Immature livestock acquired for draft, dairy, or breeding purposes is eligible for depreciation in the tax year it reaches maturity, i.e., when it reaches the age when it can be worked, milked, or bred. The basis for depreciation is the initial cost for the immature livestock plus freight and other costs related to the acquisition (IRS Market Segment Specialization Program Guide (MSSP) for Livestock (May 11, 2000); IRS Publication 225 (Farmer's Tax Guide); Reg. § 1.46-3(d)(2)(ii)).

The expenses of raising animals are currently deductible; therefore, raised animals have no depreciable basis.

Depreciable livestock (horses, cattle, hogs, sheep, goats, and mink and other furbearing animals) qualify for the Code Sec. 179 expense allowance (Reg. § 1.1245-3(a)(4); IRS Publication 225 (Farmer's Tax Guide)).

*7. Horses*

The depreciation period for a horse depends upon its age and use. A horse is more than 2 or 12 years old after the day that is 24 (or 144) months after its actual birthdate (Footnote 1 for Rev. Proc. 87-56 Asset Classes 01.222 - 01.224).

*Horse other than race horse more than 12 years old when placed in service.* Any horse *other than a race horse* which is more than 12 years old at the time it is placed in service is MACRS 3-year property (Code Sec. 168(e)(3)(A)(ii)). The alternative depreciation system (ADS) period for a breeding or work horse that is more than 12 years old when placed in service is 10 years (Rev. Proc. 87-56 Asset Class 01.222). A 12 year ADS period applies to other horses that are more than 12 years old (Asset Class 01.224).

*Horse other than race horse 12 years old or less when placed in service.* Any horse *other than a race horse* that is 12 years old or less when placed in service is MACRS 7-year property (Rev. Proc. 87-56 Asset Class 01.221 relating to breeding and work horses; Asset Class 01.225 relating to all other horses). The ADS period for a breeding or work horse that is 12 years old or less is 10 years (Asset Class 01.221). A 12 year ADS period applies to other horses that are 12 years old or less (Asset Class 01.225).

*Race horses.* Effective for race horses placed in service after December 31, 2008 and before January 1, 2022, all race horses are treated as three-year property (Code Sec. 168(e)(3)(A)(i)). Under prior law, race horses that were two years or younger when placed in service were depreciated as 7-year MACRS property and race horses that were more than two years old when placed in service were three-year property. The prior law rule is scheduled to be reinstated effective for race horses placed in service after December 31, 2021 (Code Sec. 168(e)(3)(A)(i)(II)). The ADS period for a race horse, regardless of age, is 12 years (Rev. Proc. 87-56 Asset Class 01.223 and 01.225).

A race horse is generally considered placed in service when its training begins. This is usually at the end of its yearling year, which is typically less than two years after birth. A race horse that has previously raced is generally considered placed in service when purchased from the prior owner. A horse's age is measured by reference to its actual birth date rather than the racing industry's treatment of January 1 of the year of birth as the birth date (Prop. Reg. § 1.168-3(c)(iii) (ACRS); Rev. Proc. 87-56, 1987-2 CB 674 (footnote 1 for Rev. Proc. 87-56 Asset Class 01.223)).

Reg. § 1.1231-2(c)(1) provides rules and examples for determining whether a horse is a race horse. Presumably, these guidelines may be used for depreciation classification purposes.

Geldings cannot be placed in service in a breeding operation except in working or "teasing" applications (IRS Market Segment Specialization Guide (MSSP) for Livestock (May 11, 2000)).

Prior to the extension of bonus depreciation to used property, a retired race horse purchased for breeding purposes did not qualify for bonus depreciation (Temp. Reg. § 1.168(k)-1T(b)(3)(v), *Example 3*). The example involves a race horse acquired by the racer on April 1, 2000 and then purchased by the taxpayer on October 1, 2003. The example simply says that the original use requirement is not satisfied. Under the original use requirement (as in effect at the time the regulations were issued), the original use must commence with the *taxpayer* after September 10, 2001. Since original use is defined as the first use to which the property is put whether or not that use commences with the taxpayer (see ¶ 127D for a discussion of the original use requirement), this example should not be read to mean that if the racer had acquired the horse after September 10, 2001, the original use requirement would have been satisfied. The original use requirement would not have been satisfied because the original use commenced with the racer and not the taxpayer. Another point worth noting is that the horse was a depreciable asset in the hands of the racer. If the horse was raised and held as nondepreciable inventory by the seller and sold to the taxpayer after September 10, 2001, then it seems that the original use requirement would be satisfied. This situation would be analogous to the sale of a new vehicle from a car dealership's inventory. Note that effective for property acquired and placed in service after September 27, 2017, used property may qualify for bonus depreciation. See ¶ 127D.

*8. Ratites (ostrich, emu, rhea)*

An IRS Market Segment Specialization Guide (MSSP) for Livestock (May 11, 2000) provides guidance concerning the tax treatment of persons engaged in the business of raising ostrich, emu, and rhea. These birds are members of the ratite family of birds. According to the guide, the birds are not considered livestock for purposes of Code Sec. 1231, and, therefore, are not considered section 1231 property for purposes of determining gain or loss upon their sale. However, it is the IRS position that ratites are livestock for other purposes of the Code.

Ratites are considered personal property with no class life and, therefore, by default have a seven-year depreciation period (12 years under ADS). Fences, rearing pens, incubators and hatchers are also 7-year property. A hatchery building may qualify as a single-purpose agricultural structure (10-year property). However, old barns, sheds, and the like which have been merely converted to hatchery facilities do not qualify.

Ratites purchased for breeding "probably" qualify for the Code Sec. 179 expense allowance, according to the MSSP which cites IRS Letter Ruling 8817003, holding that rare birds purchased for breeding purposes qualify for expensing under Code Sec. 179. However, ratites purchased for breeding may not be expensed until they are placed in service (presumably the year that they are capable of breeding, which is the rule applicable to livestock purchased for breeding).

The issue of the applicability of Code Sec. 195 (which allows five-year amortization of start-up costs beginning in the month a trade or business begins) to new ratite producers who were not previously in the business of farming is unsettled, according to the MSSP. Some authorities feel that a taxpayer is not yet engaged in the animal breeding business until the animals are placed in service as breeding stock. Thus, if a taxpayer acquires ratite chicks to be raised for breeding, farm expenses are capitalized until the animals are ready for breeding.

*9. Alternative livestock*

The IRS Market Segment Specialization Guide (MSSP) for Livestock (May 11, 2000) notes that taxpayers may raise miniature donkeys, miniature horses, llamas (including vicuna, guanaco, alpaca), deer, elk, reindeer, bison, miniature pigs, sport sheep, lemurs, big cats, wallabies, wallaroos, monkeys, parrots, alligators, and munchkin cats. If depreciable, these animals are 7-year property (12-year ADS period). Animals purchased for resale are not depreciable. Breeding animals qualify for the Code Sec. 179 expense allowance in the year that they are placed in service for breeding purposes (i.e., are capable of breeding).

*10. Dogs*

A farmer may use dogs to herd cattle, sheep, pigs, etc. or for some other farm-related use. If such a dog is purchased (and, therefore, has a basis), it is depreciable (*Rodgers Dairy Company*, 14 TC 66, Dec. 17,453 (show dogs used for advertising purposes by closely-held corporation are depreciable (pre-MACRS))); *P.P. Slawek*, 54 TCM 364, Dec. 44,160(M), TC Memo. 1987-438 (guard dog used by doctor to guard office is depreciable (pre-MACRS)).

It appears that a farm dog is property without a class life and, therefore, has a seven-year recovery period. See ¶ 106 for a discussion of property without a class life. Asset Class 01.1 of Rev. Proc. 87-56, relating to farm "machinery and equipment" also has a 7-year recovery period although it is not likely that a dog is an item of machinery or equipment within the meaning of Asset Class 01.1.

A five-year recovery period appears appropriate for a security dog if used by a security company (Rev. Proc. 87-56 Asset Class 57.0, assigns a 5-year recovery period to property used in the provision of professional or personal services (see ¶ 104) and a dog clearly falls within the ambit of "property"). However, where a taxpayer purchases a security dog for use in a business unrelated to the provision of security services the depreciation period will usually be the depreciation period stated for the taxpayer's business activity in Rev. Proc. 87-56. If the description of assets qualifying for the recovery period prescribed for the taxpayer's business activity appears to exclude dogs (or the taxpayer is engaged in a business activity that is not described in Rev. Proc. 87-56) then the dog is MACRS property with a class life (i.e., MACRS 7-year property).

*11. Irrigation systems and water wells*

IRS Publication 225 (Farmer's Tax Guide) states that farmers may depreciate irrigation systems and wells composed of masonry, concrete, tile, metal, or wood. The costs of moving dirt to make irrigation systems and water wells composed of these materials is also depreciable. The publication further provides that irrigation systems and waterwells are depreciable over 15 years as a land improvement. However, the IRS Audit Technique Guide for Grain Farmers listed "pumps and irrigation" systems as 7-year property. This Guide may be referring to above ground systems.

A drip irrigation system installed primarily underground in connection with a vineyard was a 15-year land improvement, according to the Tax Court (*L. Trentadue*, 128 TC No. 8, Dec. 56,886). If the system had been primarily installed above the ground the court indicated that it would likely be considered personal property depreciable over 7 years (Rev. Proc. 87-56 Asset Class 01.1). The court further indicated that if the issue had been presented it would have allowed certain above ground portions of the irrigation system such as tubing, emmiters, and the like to be separately depreciated as personal property. The court also concluded that a well was a 15-year land improvement.

Land preparation costs for center pivot irrigation systems are not depreciable (IRS Publication 225 (Farmer's Tax Guide)). These land preparation costs are also specifically excluded from qualification as deductible soil and water conservation expenditures (Code Sec. 175(c)(3)(B)).

*12. Dams, ponds, and terraces*

IRS Publication 225 further provides that, in general, earthen dams, ponds, and terraces are not depreciable unless the structures have a determinable useful life. See, however, ¶ 3, which discusses recent decisions that negate the determinable useful life requirement in the context of ACRS and MACRS. Note that the publication provides that expenditures for such assets may be deductible as soil and water conservation expenditures under Code Sec. 175. For additional information concerning dams, see "Land improvements" at ¶ 110.

*13. Fruit and nut-bearing trees and vines*

For depreciation, including bonus depreciation, on orchards and vines, see ¶ 108 and ¶ 127D.

*14. Plants bearing fruits and nuts*

A seven-year recovery period applies to plants bearing fruits and nuts (other than trees and vines described above) as property without a prescribed class life (Code Sec. 168(e)(3)(C)(v); Committee Report for P.L. 114-113). For special rules related to bonus depreciation on plants eligible for bonus depreciation, see ¶ 127D.

*15. Property used in vineyards*

A trellising system was agricultural machinery with a 7-year recovery period (Rev. Proc. 87-56 Asset Class 01.1). The components of the trellises could be moved and reused, the trellises were not designed to remain permanently in place, and the trellising posts were not set in concrete and could easily be removed from the ground (*L. Trentadue*, 128 TC No. 8, Dec. 56,886). The taxpayer used vertical shoot positioning (VSP) and T-trellis design systems.

A drip irrigation system was a 15-year land improvement. If the system had been primarily installed above the ground the court indicated that it would likely be considered personal property depreciable over 7 years (Rev. Proc. 87-56 Asset Class 01.1). Certain above-ground portions of the drip irrigation system could likely have been depreciated separately as personal property. A well was classified as a land improvement (*L. Trentadue*, 128 TC No. 8, Dec. 56,886).

See also, ¶ 108 for depreciation of vines.

*16. Single purpose agricultural or horticultural structure*

A single purpose agricultural or horticultural structure as defined in Code Sec. 168(i)(13) is considered section 1245 property and, therefore, qualifies for the Code Sec. 179 expense allowance (Code Sec. 1245(a)(3)(D)). The definition is borrowed from former Code Sec. 48(p). Such structures are 10-year property for purposes of

MACRS (Rev. Proc. 87-56 Asset Class 01.4) if placed in service after 1988. The ADS period is 15 years.

The detailed requirements for qualification are set forth in Reg. § 1.48-10.

In general, to qualify, a structure must either be a single purpose livestock structure or a single purpose horticultural structure.

*Specific design and use tests—single purpose livestock structure.* A single purpose livestock structure is defined as any enclosure or structure specifically designed and constructed exclusively to:

(1) house, raise, and feed a particular type of livestock (including poultry but not horses) and, at the taxpayer's option, their produce (e.g., milk and eggs held for sale); and

(2) house the equipment (including any replacements) necessary for the housing, raising, and feeding of livestock (or poultry) and their produce (Reg. § 1.48-10(b)).

The term "housing, raising, and feeding" includes the full range of livestock breeding and raising activities, including ancillary post-production activities.

The structure must be used exclusively for these purposes. The livestock structure may be used for storing feed or machinery (related to these purposes), but more than strictly incidental use for storing feed or machinery will disqualify the structure. The structure may not be used for processing or marketing. If more than one-third of a structure's total usable volume is devoted to storage (feed, for example), a rebuttable presumption arises that the storage function is not incidental. The feed stored must be for use by the type of livestock for which the structure was constructed (Reg. § 1.48-10(e)(1)).

The livestock structure must also house the equipment necessary to house, raise, and feed the livestock. For example, a structure with no equipment and used only to house feeder cattle while they are fed hay is not a qualifying livestock structure (Reg. § 1.48-10(b)(4)). The equipment must be an integral part of the structure (i.e., physically attached to or part of the structure). Examples are equipment that contains the livestock, provides them with food and water, or controls temperature, lighting, or humidity. Equipment, such as loading chutes, necessary to conduct ancillary post-production activities may be housed in the structure.

The structure must be designed, constructed, and used with respect to one particular type (species) of livestock. For example, a structure designed as a single purpose hog-raising facility will not qualify if it is used to raise dairy cows. A structure used to house more than one type of livestock also fails the exclusive use test. A structure which originally qualified as a single-purpose livestock structure is disqualified if it is placed in service and later modified to accommodate a different species of livestock (e.g., a hog-raising facility is placed in service and later modified to raise chickens) (Reg. § 1.48-10(b)(3)).

A structure used solely to house the produce of livestock or equipment is not a qualifying structure. For example, a structure used solely for storing milk will not qualify. Eggs held for hatching and newborn livestock are considered livestock and not the produce of livestock.

A dairy facility will qualify if it is used for activities consisting of the (1) production of milk or (2) of the production of milk and the housing, raising, or feeding of dairy cattle. In addition the facility must be used to house equipment (including replacements) necessary for these activities (Reg. § 1.48-10(b)(2)).

*Single purpose horticultural structure.* A single purpose horticultural structure is a:

(1) greenhouse specifically designed and constructed for the commercial production of plants (including plant products such as flowers, vegetables, or fruits); or

(2) a structure specifically designed and constructed for the commercial production of mushrooms (Reg. § 1.48-10(c)).

The structure must be used exclusively for these purposes.

A single purpose horticultural structure may, but is not required to, house equipment necessary to carry out the commercial production of plants or mushrooms.

The commercial production of plants and mushrooms includes ancillary post-production activities.

*Work space.* An enclosure or structure which contains work space may be treated as a single purpose agricultural or horticultural structure only if the work space is used for:

(1) the stocking, caring for, or collecting of livestock, plants, or mushrooms (as the case may be) or their produce;

(2) the maintenance of the structure; or

(3) the maintenance or replacement of the equipment or stock enclosed or housed therein (Reg. § 1.48-10(f)).

An agricultural or horticultural structure that contains an area to process or market the product is an impermissible use. For example, if a taxpayer sets up a sales counter within a greenhouse, the greenhouse will not qualify as a horticultural structure (Reg. § 1.48-10(j), *Example (2)*).

*Ancillary post-production activities.* Such activities include gathering, sorting, and loading livestock, plants, and mushrooms, and packing unprocessed plants, mushrooms, and the live offspring and unprocessed produce of the livestock. Ancillary post-production activities do not include processing activities, such as slaughtering or packing meat, or marketing activities (Reg. § 1.48-10(f)).

*Specifically designed and constructed requirement.* A structure is considered specifically designed and constructed for a qualifying purpose if it is not economical to design and construct the structure for the intended qualifying purpose and then use the structure for a different purpose (Reg. § 1.48-10(d)).

*Types of greenhouses.* The IRS has issued a market segment specialization guide for the garden supplies industry (February 1, 2000). The guide lists five common types of greenhouses which are all depreciable over a ten year period. These include:

(1) Detached A-frame truss greenhouse—This is a separate structure (as opposed to a lean-to next to a building) made from aluminum, iron, steel, or wood and covered with glass or plastic.

(2) Ridge and furrow A-frame truss greenhouse range—This is several A-frames side by side with no interior walls, same structure and coverings as above.

(3) Quonset style greenhouse—This is made from pipe arches and covered with plastic (looks like army barracks).

(4) Lath or shadehouse—Simply a roof made of fencing or fabric to provide shade on plants (no walls). Some garden centers set these up in parking lots.

(5) Brick cold frame or hotbed—This is made of concrete blocks or wood, covered with glass or plastic. Generally, low to the ground. A hotbed structure has heat on the floor.

*Demolition of greenhouse.* The cost of demolishing and preparing the land for a new greenhouse is added to the basis of the new greenhouse unless the greenhouse is accounted for in an MACRS general asset account. See ¶ 5.

*Depreciation method for operators of a greenhouse.* Generally, the operation of a greenhouse is considered a farming business. As such the 150-percent declining balance method is required in lieu of the 200-percent declining balance method unless the straight-line method is elected. See ¶ 84.

The uniform capitalization rules (Code Sec. 263A) do not generally apply to greenhouse operators because taxpayers not required to be on the accrual method are excepted if the plants being produced have a pre-productive period of two years or less. However, if the greenhouse grows plants with a pre-productive period of more than two years, it can elect to avoid the UNICAP rules. If the election is made, the taxpayer must use the MACRS alternative depreciation system (ADS).

## ¶ 120

## Railroad Grading and Tunnel Bores

Railroad grading and tunnel bores are included in a specially assigned recovery class with a 50-year recovery period. The MACRS straight-line method and the mid-month convention must be used to compute depreciation on this property (Code Sec. 168(c)(1)).

Railroad grading and tunnel bores include all improvements resulting from excavations (including tunneling), construction of embankments, clearings, diversions of roads and streams, sodding of slopes, and similar work necessary to provide, construct, reconstruct, alter, protect, improve, replace, or restore a roadbed or right-of-way for railroad track (Code Sec. 168(e)(4)).

See ¶ 106 for the depreciation period of other types of railroad assets.

## ¶ 124

## Qualified Indian Reservation Property

For qualified Indian reservation property that is placed in service after 1993 and before January 1, 2022, special MACRS recovery periods are provided that result in faster writeoffs (Code Sec. 168(j); Rev. Proc. 2017-33, Section 5). These recovery periods are in lieu of the generally applicable recovery periods provided in Code Sec. 168(c). No AMT depreciation adjustment is required if these recovery periods are used or the election out described below is made.

Although the recovery periods are shortened, no change is made to the depreciation method or convention that would otherwise apply. For example, if the alternative depreciation system (ADS) is elected for a class of property the straight-line method is used over the shorter recovery periods for Indian reservation property. The shorter recovery periods for Indian reservation property do not apply if ADS must be used to depreciate the property (Code Sec. 168(j)(4)(B)).

For tax years beginning after December 31, 2015, taxpayers are permitted to make an election out of the special rules. If the election out is made for any class of property for any tax year, the special rules will not apply to all property in that class placed in service during that tax year. The election is irrevocable (Code Sec. 168(j)(8)). AMT does not apply to Indian Reservation property even if the election out is made. See below.

| *Property Class* | *Recovery Period* |
|---|---|
| 3-year property | 2 years |
| 5-year property | 3 years |
| 7-year property | 4 years |
| 10-year property | 6 years |
| 15-year property | 9 years |
| 20-year property | 12 years |
| Nonresidential real property | 22 years |

IRS Publication 946 includes special Indian Reservation Depreciation Tables for property with a 2-, 4-, 6-, 9-, 12-, and 22-year recovery period. Regular IRS tables can be used for 5-year Indian reservation property with a three-year recovery period, 15-year Indian reservation property with a nine-year recovery period, and 20-year Indian reservation property with a 12-year recovery period. For example, the regular half-year and mid-quarter convention tables for 3-year property with a three-year recovery period may be used to compute depreciation on 5-year Indian reservation property with a three-year recovery period.

These tables are reproduced at ¶ 180. Refer to the index at that paragraph for the exact location.

Qualified Indian reservation property includes 3-, 5-, 7-, 10-, 15-, 20-year property and nonresidential real property that is:

(1) used predominantly in the active conduct of a trade or business within an Indian reservation;

(2) not used or located outside an Indian reservation on a regular basis;

(3) not acquired (directly or indirectly) from a related person (as defined in Code Sec. 465(b)(3)(C)); and

(4) not used for certain gaming purposes (Code Sec. 168(j)(4)(A)).

*Indian reservation defined.* The term Indian reservation is defined in section 3(d) of the Indian Financing Act of 1974 (25 U.S.C. 1452(d)) and section 4(10) of the Indian Child Welfare Act of 1978 (25 U.S.C. 1903(10)). For purposes of section 3(d) of the Indian Financing Act of 1974, the term Indian reservation includes *former* Indian reservations. The definition of a *former* Indian reservation contained in section 3(d), as it pertains to the State of Oklahoma, was modified by the Taxpayer Relief Act of 1997 (P.L. 105-34) to include only lands that are both within a jurisdictional area of an Oklahoma Indian tribe and eligible for trust land status under 25 CFR Part 151 (Code Sec. 168(j) (6)). The modified definition is generally effective for property placed in service after December 31, 1993. However, it does not apply to MACRS 10-year, 7-year, 5-year, or 3-year property with a recovery period of 6 years or less under Code Sec. 168(j) if a taxpayer claimed depreciation on the property using the applicable Code Sec. 168(j) recovery period in the year it was placed in service on an original return filed before March 18, 1997 (Act Sec. 1604(c)(2) of P.L. 105-34). For a specific description of the localities in Oklahoma that are considered former Indian reservations, see Notice 98-45, I.R.B. 1998-35, 7.

*Predominant and regular use tests: mobile assets.* The IRS has issued an internal technical assistance memorandum (Letter Ruling 199947026) which considers the predominant and regular use tests (items (1) and (2), above) in the context of mobile assets. Mobile assets include rolling stock, trucks, cars, airplanes, buses, and mobile heavy equipment, such as oil and gas drilling equipment, cranes, and gain combines.

For purposes of the requirement that the asset be used predominantly within an Indian reservation, the memorandum concludes that the asset must be used more than 50 percent of the time during the tax year in the active conduct of a trade or business within an Indian reservation. The standard does not necessarily require that the asset be used or physically located within the reservation more than 50 percent of the time. The ruling states in this regard:

> ". . . our view is that the standard requires a connection between the trade or business operated within an Indian reservation and the use of the property in carrying on that trade or business. For example, a car that is used in the trade or business of providing taxi service only within an Indian reservation and is also used for personal purposes, must be used more than 50 percent of the time during the taxable year in that taxi service to satisfy the requirement of section 168(j)(4)(A)(i). Further, for example, we believe that in those instances where a corporate taxpayer's headquarters are located off an Indian reservation but the taxpayer operates a manufacturing plant within the Indian reservation, the standard of section 168(j)(4)(A)(i) is satisfied."

With respect to the requirement that an asset may not be used or located outside an Indian reservation on a *regular* basis, the IRS concluded that this means that the asset may "not be used or located outside the Indian reservation on more than an occasional or incidental basis during the tax year."

The determination of whether these two tests are satisfied, according to the ruling, is made in light of all of the facts and circumstances and is made on an asset-by-asset basis.

*Change in use.* The technical advice memorandum discussed above also notes that if a mobile asset (or other Indian reservation property) meets the definition of qualified Indian reservation property in one tax year but does not meet the definition in a later tax year while it continues to be held by the same person, then a change in use has occurred and Code Sec. 168(i)(5) applies in determining depreciation in the year that the change in use occurs.

*Real property rental.* The rental of real property located within a reservation is treated as the active conduct of a trade or business within an Indian reservation. The classification of property as real or personal is based on federal income tax law and not local (state law) (IRS Letter Ruling 200601020, September 19, 2005).

*ADS.* Qualified property does not include any property that must be depreciated using the MACRS alternative depreciation system (ADS). The determination of whether property is qualified is made without regard to the election to use ADS (¶ 150) and after applying the special rules for listed property not used predominantly in a qualified business (¶ 206) (Code Sec. 168(j)(4)(B)); IRS Publication 946, How to Depreciate Property.

It appears that if the alternative depreciation system (ADS) is elected for a class of property, the regular ADS recovery periods applies to Indian reservation property within that class. Code Sec. 168(j) does not specifically address this issue.

*Qualified infrastructure property.* Qualified infrastructure property located outside an Indian reservation may be eligible for faster writeoffs provided that the purpose of such property is to connect with qualified infrastructure property located within the reservation. Qualified infrastructure property is property that is depreciable under MACRS, benefits the tribal infrastructure, is available to the general public, and is placed in service in connection with the taxpayer's active conduct of a trade or business within the reservation. Such property includes, but is not limited to, roads, power lines, water systems, railroad spurs, and communication facilities.

*Election out.* For tax years beginning after December 31, 2015, taxpayers are permitted to make an election out of the special depreciation periods for Indian reservation property. If the election is made for any class of property for any tax year, the special rules will not apply to all property in that class placed in service during that tax year. The election is irrevocable (Code Sec. 168(j)(8)).

The election must be made by the due date, including extensions, of the Federal tax return for the tax year in which the taxpayer places in service the qualified Indian reservation property. The election must be made in the manner prescribed on Form 4562, Depreciation and Amortization, and its instructions (Rev. Proc. 2017-33, Section 5). The Form 4562 instructions require a taxpayer to attach a statement to the timely filed return (including extensions) indicating the class or classes of property for which the election out is made and that the taxpayer is electing not to apply Code Sec. 168(j).

If a taxpayer makes an election out for a class of property by attaching the required statement, then the taxpayer computes depreciation using the GDS recovery periods appropriate to the class, or if ADS is elected for the class of property, the appropriate ADS recovery periods. As mentioned earlier, if ADS must be used for a class of property, then the property is excluded form the definition of qualified Indian reservation property.

A retroactive technical correction by the Tax Technical Corrections Act of 2018 (P.L. 115-141) clarifies that no alternative minimum tax (AMT) adjustment is required for MACRS Indian reservation property even if an election out of the shortened recovery period is made (Code Sec. 168(j)(3) and (j)(8), effective for tax years beginning after 2015).

*Deemed election out for 2016 short tax year.* A taxpayer with a short tax year that began in 2016 and also ended in 2016 and that did not make the election out in the time and manner required above will be treated as making a valid election out for a class of property that is qualified Indian reservation property if the taxpayer, on its timely filed Federal tax return for the short tax year, determined depreciation for that class of property under the MACRS general depreciation system by using the applicable recovery period for that class of property in accordance with the table contained in Code Sec. 168(c) (Rev. Proc. 2017-33, Section 5).

Code Sec. 168(c) describes the regular (GDS) recovery periods that apply under MACRS. As worded, the deemed election out for a 2016 short tax year would not apply if the taxpayer without filing the required election out statement elected the alternative depreciation system (ADS) for the Indian reservation property and used the ADS recovery periods (rather than the shorter periods prescribed for Indian reservation property) insofar as the ADS recovery periods are described in Code Sec. 168(g) and not in Code Sec. 168(c).

*GAO report.* The General Accounting Office has issued a report entitled "Available Data Are Insufficient to Determine the Use and Impact of Indian Reservation Depreciation" (GAO-08-731 (June 2008)) which provides insights on the impact of the reduced depreciation periods for Indian Reservation Property. See http://www.gao.gov/new.items/d08731.pdf

## ¶ 124A

## New York Liberty Zone Leasehold Improvement Property

Qualified New York Liberty Zone leasehold improvements to nonresidential real property that are placed in service after September 10, 2001, and before January 1, 2007, are classified as 5-year MACRS property unless an election out is made. The straight-line method must be used to depreciate this property. A nine-year ADS period applies (Code Sec. 1400L(c)(1)). The election out was retroactively provided by the Working Families Tax Relief Act of 2004 (P.L. 108-311). See below for details.

Because the Job Creation and Worker Assistance Act of 2002 (P.L. 107-147) was enacted after many taxpayers filed their 2000 or 2001 returns it is possible that qualifying New York Liberty Zone improvements were not properly classified and depreciated on those returns. The IRS has issued guidance (Rev. Proc. 2003-50) that allows a taxpayer to file an amended 2000 or 2001 return by December 31, 2003, to correct the problem or to file a Form 3115 with their 2003 return and claim a Code Sec. 481(a) adjustment.

Liberty Zone leasehold improvements that are eligible for a five-year recovery period are *not* also eligible for the 30- or 50-percent first-year bonus depreciation allowance under Code Sec. 168(k) or the 30-percent allowance under Code Sec. 1400L(b) (Code Sec. 168(k)(2)(C)(ii); Code Sec. 1400L(b)(2)(C)(iii)). See ¶ 127D and ¶ 127E for discussion of bonus depreciation.

*Definition of qualifying property*

The term "qualified New York Liberty Zone leasehold improvement property" means qualified leasehold improvement property as defined under new Code Sec. 168(k)(3) (see ¶ 127D) if:

(1) the building is located in the New York Liberty Zone;

(2) the qualifying improvement is placed in service after September 10, 2001, and before January 1, 2007; and

(3) no binding written contract for such improvement was in effect before September 11, 2001 (Code Sec. 1400L(c)(2)).

Qualified leasehold improvement property generally consists of interior improvements to nonresidential real estate. The term is defined in Code Sec. 168(k)(3) (see ¶ 127D). In general, qualified leasehold improvement property must satisfy the following requirements:

(1) the improvement must be to the interior portion of a building that is nonresidential real property;

(2) the improvement must be made under or pursuant to a lease by a lessee, sublessee, or lessor, or pursuant to a commitment to enter into a lease;

(3) the lessor and lessee may not be related persons;

(4) the portion of the building that is improved must be exclusively tenant-occupied (by a lessee or sublessee); and

(5) the improvement must be placed in service more than three years after the date that the building was first placed in service (Code Sec. 168(k)(3)).

Leasehold improvements to residential rental property, such as apartment buildings, are not considered qualified leasehold improvements. Exterior leasehold improvements to nonresidential real property, such as the addition of a roof, are also excluded from the definition.

The following improvements are specifically excluded from the definition of qualified leasehold improvement property:

(1) improvements that enlarge the building;

(2) elevators and escalators;

(3) any structural component benefiting a common area; and

(4) improvements to the internal structural framework of the building (Code Sec. 168(k)(3)(B)).

Improvements that do not qualify as New York Liberty Zone leasehold improvements may still be eligible for the 30-percent first-year bonus depreciation allowance under Code Sec. 168(k) or Code Sec. 1400L(b), according to the Joint Committee Explanation.

*Location of New York Liberty Zone*

The New York Liberty Zone is the area located on or south of Canal Street, East Broadway (east of its intersection with Canal Street), or Grand Street (east of its intersection with East Broadway) in the Borough of Manhattan in New York City (Code Sec. 1400L(h)).

*Straight-line method applies*

The MACRS straight-line method (and half-year or mid-quarter convention) must be used to depreciate qualified Liberty Zone leasehold improvement property (Code Sec. 1400L(c)(3)). Ordinarily, 5-year property is depreciated using a 200-percent declining-balance method switching to straight line in the year a larger deduction results.

*ADS recovery period*

A nine-year recovery period is assigned to qualified New York Liberty Zone leasehold improvement property for purposes of the MACRS alternative depreciation system (ADS) under Code Sec. 168(g) (Code Sec. 1400L(c)(4)).

*Alternative minimum tax*

No depreciation adjustment will be required on qualified Liberty Zone leasehold improvements for alternative minimum tax (AMT) purposes because the straight-line method is used for regular tax purposes. AMT depreciation will be computed in the same manner as regular tax depreciation (i.e., five-year recovery period and straight-line method).

*Code Sec. 179 expense deduction*

The Code Sec. 179 expense allowance (¶ 300) may only be claimed on tangible Sec. 1245 property as defined in Code Sec. 1245 (a)(3) (subject to an exception for qualified real property placed in service in tax years beginning after 2009 (Code Sec. 179(e)). See ¶ 116. Thus, a qualified New York Liberty Zone leasehold improvement should not qualify for the Code Sec. 179 expense allowance if it is a structural component (real property). The fact that the depreciation period for such an improvement is shortened by the new provision from 39 years (the depreciation period for structural components of nonresidential real property) to five years does not change an improvement's status as section 1250 real property.

Qualified leasehold improvement property status under former Code Sec. 168(k)(3) or Code Sec. 1400L(c) can only apply to section 1250 property (Reg. § 1.168(k)-1(c)(1)). Elements of a building that are personal property (section 1245 property), as opposed to structural components (section 1250 property), may be depreciated under cost segregation principles over shortened recovery periods and may qualify for bonus depreciation and the Code Sec. 179 expense allowance.

*Election out of New York Liberty Zone leasehold improvement property provision*

A taxpayer may elect out of the New York Liberty Zone leasehold improvement property provision (Code Sec. 1400L(c)(5); Rev. Proc. 2005-43). The election out may be made retroactively to apply to Liberty Zone leasehold improvement property placed in service after September 10, 2001. The election procedures are explained in Rev. Proc. 2005-43. An election out may only be revoked with IRS consent.

*Recovery period if election out made.* If an election out is made and the Liberty Zone leasehold improvement property was placed in service after October 22, 2004 and before January 1, 2006, the property is depreciated using a 15-year recovery period (9 years under ADS), the straight-line method, and the half-year or mid-quarter convention. In other words, it is depreciated as if it were 15-year qualified leasehold improvement property under Code Sec. 168(e)(3)(E)(iv) and (e)(6). See ¶ 126. If the Liberty Zone leasehold improvement property would not qualify for the 15-year recovery period because it was not placed in service after October 22, 2004 and before January 1, 2006, then it is depreciated as MACRS 39-year nonresidential real property (i.e., in the same manner as any other structural component) (Rev. Proc. 2005-43, Section 2.04; IRS Publication 946).

*Bonus depreciation.* Rev. Proc. 2005-43 states that no bonus depreciation may be claimed if the election out is made even if the 15-year recovery period applies (Rev. Proc. 2005-43, Sec. 2.04). In other words, it appears to be the IRS position that an election out does not transform the New York Liberty Zone leasehold improvement property into leasehold improvement property described in Code Sec. 168(k)(3) which does qualify for bonus depreciation if placed in service after September 10, 2001 and before January 1, 2005. The Committee Reports and Joint Committee Blue Book explanation for this provision do not mention bonus depreciation.

*Election procedures.* An election out applies to all Liberty Zone leasehold improvement property placed in service during the tax year of the election. In general, the election must be made by the due date (including extensions) of the return for the tax year the improvements were placed in service in the manner prescribed in the instructions for Form 4562 (Depreciation and Amortization). However, an automatic 6-month extension from the due date of the return (excluding extensions) is available if the requirements of Reg. § 301.9100-2(c) and (d) are satisfied. Additional extensions may be requested under the rules in Reg. § 301.9100-3. These procedure applies to any 2003 or 2004 return filed after June 29, 2005, except that additional extensions may be requested under Reg. § 301.9100-3 if the deadlines described below for returns filed on or before June 29, 2004 are not met.

*Special election procedures for 2000, 2001, 2002, 2003, and 2004 returns filed on or before June 29, 2004.* A taxpayer who did not make an election out on a return filed on or before June 29, 2004 for the 2000 through 2004 tax years may make the election out by filing amended returns for the placed in service year and subsequent affected years before expiration of the limitations period for filing any of the amended return(s). In no event may an amended return be filed after June 29, 2007.

Alternatively, Form 3115 (Application for Change in Accounting Method) may be filed with the return for the tax year that includes June 29, 2005 or with the return for the first tax year that follows the tax year that includes June 29, 2005. A

Code Sec. 481(a) adjustment for the excess depreciation claimed by using a 5-year recovery period would taken into account if this option is used.

*Deemed election out.* A taxpayer will be treated as having made an election out if the taxpayer failed to depreciate qualified Liberty Zone Leasehold improvement property placed in service during the 2000, 2001, 2002, 2003, or 2004 tax year using a 5-year recovery period and instead treated the property as 39-year nonresidential real property or 15-year qualified leasehold improvement property, as applicable.

## ¶ 125

## Miscellaneous Property

This paragraph ¶ 125 discusses the depreciation treatment of the following types of property:

*Apartment complex (reference to ¶ 5)*

*Art and décor*

*Bed and breakfasts*

*Breast implants of exotic dancer*

*Cars, antiques and show cars*

*Containers (reference to ¶ 5)*

*Dogs (reference to ¶ 118)*

*Domain names*

*Cellular telephone property*

*Forklifts and bobcats*

*Gambling boats and barges*

*Gasoline service stations and retail motor fuel outlets*

*Golf course (reference to ¶ 5)*

*Grading and land preparation costs (reference to ¶ 5)*

*Gym equipment*

*Impact fees*

*Intermodal facilities*

*Inventory and self-constructed assets (reference to ¶ 5)*

*ISO 9000 costs*

*Land and land improvements (reference to ¶ 5)*

*Leased property (reference to ¶ 190)*

*Leasehold acquisition costs (reference to ¶ 5)*

*Materials and supplies (reference to ¶ 307)*

*Mobile home parks (reference to ¶ 5)*

*Model homes and sales offices*

*Painting and remodeling*

*Parking lots (reference to ¶ 5)*

*Playground equipment (reference to ¶ 5)*

*Product samples*

*Professional library*

*Property subject to lease (reference to ¶ 5)*

*Roads (reference to ¶ 5)*

*Restaurants and taverns—smallwares*

*Roofs*

*Rotable spare parts*

*Slot Machines, Video Lottery Terminals And Gaming Furniture, Fixtures And Equipment*

*Site utilities (reference to ¶ 5)*

*Trees, shrubbery and other landscaping (reference to ¶ 5)*

*Tires and tubes*

*Tools, shop equipment, laboratory equipment*

*Uniforms*

*Website development costs*

*Zoning variance*

*Apartment complex*

See ¶ 5.

*Art and décor*

Artwork which is displayed for business purposes normally does not suffer from wear or tear or obsolescence, and, therefore, is not depreciable under ACRS (*W.C. Clinger*, 60 TCM 598, Dec. 46,832(M); Prop. Reg. § 1.168-3(a) (ACRS); Rev. Rul. 68-232, 1968-1 CB 79 ((pre-ACRS) artwork has no determinable useful life and, therefore is nondepreciable))). These cases and rulings, however, deal with valuable (appreciating) pieces of art and were decided prior to the enactment of ACRS and MACRS when an asset had to have a reasonably estimated useful life in order to depreciated. Logically, nonappreciating artwork, for which there is no incentive to protect from wear and tear, should be depreciable even if the wear and tear is essentially minuscule. Senate Report 95-1263, 1978-3 CB (Vol. 1) 315, 415, which accompanied the Revenue Act of 1978, states that tangible personal property for investment tax credit purposes includes small pictures of scenery, persons, and the like which are attached to walls or suspended from the ceiling. Note that tangible personal property was eligible for the investment credit only if it was depreciable. The Senate Report appears to have considered such "art" as a depreciable asset. The IRS Field Directive on the Planning and Examination of Cost Segregation Issues in the Restaurant Industry reproduced in the appendix of this guide specifically provides a 5-year recovery period for pictures and other decorative props but excludes appreciating artwork, such as a Persian rug that does not suffer wear and tear, from depreciation. The five-year recovery period applies because personal property used in a restaurant falls within Asset Class 57.0 of Rev. Proc. 87-56 relating to assets used in a retail trade or business.

*Bed and breakfasts*

Generally, the depreciable portion of a personal residence operated as a bed and breakfast is considered 39-year nonresidential real property because bed and breakfast rooms are rented on a transient basis, thus disqualifying the property as residential rental property. See ¶ 114 for the definition of residential rental property. According to an IRS audit guide, a frequent mistake of bed and breakfast owners is the deduction of depreciation for "common" areas (i.e., space used by the taxpayer's family and guests, such as the kitchen, living room dining, room, and den). Pursuant to Code Sec. 280A, depreciation may only be claimed for areas of the home (e.g., bedrooms) used exclusively for business purposes (IRS Audit Guide: Bed and Breakfasts: Market Segment Specialization Program (MSSP) (5-93), reproduced in the CCH IRS POSITIONS REPORTER at ¶ 202,101).

The IRS audit guide states that some taxpayers erroneously claim a current expense deduction for the entire cost of items such as kitchen cookware, appliances, tableware, linens, furniture, carpeting, and garden equipment. These costs should be capitalized (unless current expensing is allowed under Code Sec. 179) and depreciated. The guide does not indicate the proper depreciation period but presumably a bed and breakfast, like a hotel, is an Rev. Proc. 87-56 Asset Class 57.0 business activity (relating to the provision of personal services) (see ¶ 104) and a five-year recovery period applies.

Only the cost of items directly related to rooms related to business may be deducted. For example, the cost of antiques placed in common areas may not be depreciated. The depreciable basis of an antique includes shipping and other acquisition costs, according to the guide.

Expenses incurred to repair or restore portions of a bed and breakfast used as a taxpayer's personal residence or portions that are considered common areas not used exclusively for business purposes, such as expenses to restore the exterior of a home, are not currently deductible. Also, expenses incurred in maintaining common exterior areas, such as expenses for yard work or landscaping are also not deductible (IRS Letter Ruling 8732002, April 2, 1987).

The audit guide notes that if a bed and breakfast contains a large number of rental rooms (for example, 20 rooms) it is more like a hotel or motel business and the deductibility of expenses is generally governed by Code Sec. 162 rather than Code Sec. 280A (which deals with personal residences used for business purposes).

*Breast implants of exotic dancer*

An exotic dancer (a.k.a., "Chesty Love") was allowed to depreciate the cost of breast implants. Each implant weighed about 10 pounds and the court concluded that the dancer derived no personal benefit due to their large and cumbersome size (*Cynthia Hess*, Tax Court Summary Opinion). Presumably, the implants were treated as MACRS 5-year property (Rev. Proc. 87-56 Asset Class 57.0, property used in the provision of personal or professional services).

*Cars, antiques and show cars*

Show cars (exotic automobiles possessing state-of-the-art high technology) that would become obsolete over time were depreciable (*B. Selig*, 70 TCM 1125, Dec. 50,975(M)) even though a definite useful life could not be shown. The cars were not similar to antique cars placed in a museum which are nondepreciable because they do not deteriorate in a controlled environment (*Harrah's Club*, CtCls, 81-1 USTC ¶ 9677).

*Cellular telephone property*

The IRS has issued a revenue procedure that provides a safe harbor method of accounting for determining the MACRS recovery periods of tangible assets used by *wireless* telecommunications carriers. The revenue procedure also explains how a taxpayer may obtain automatic consent to change to the depreciation periods provided for in the procedure (Rev. Proc. 2011-22, I.R.B. 2011-18, April 4, 2011). The IRS has also provided two alternative safe harbor approaches that taxpayers may use to determine whether expenditures to maintain, replace or improve wireless network assets must be capitalized under Code Sec. 263(a) (Rev. Proc. 2011-28),

I.R.B. 2011-18, April 4, 2011. Similar safe harbors are provided for wireline (i.e., landline) network assets (Rev. Proc. 2011-27 , I.R.B. 2011-18, April 4, 2011).

In a letter ruling that interprets Rev. Proc. 2011-28, cell phone land towers, horizontal towers, and rooftop towers and their supporting foundations (i.e., concrete foundations for the land towers and steel platforms for the rooftop towers) were classified as 15-year land improvements because they were inherently permanent structures (IRS Letter Ruling 201216029, December 13, 2011).

The IRS provided MACRS recovery periods for various types of property used by cellular telephone companies in IRS Letter Ruling 9825003 (January 30, 1998). A useful reference is a study prepared by Ernst & Young LLP, "Federal Tax Depreciation of Cellular Assets: The Need for Clarification on Cellular Equipment" (November 10, 1999), which was submitted to the IRS and made available as an "incoming treasury letter."

The Tax Court has ruled that antenna support structures fall within Asset Class 48.14 with a recovery period of 15 years, as specified in Rev. Proc. 87-56. A computerized switch was depreciable over 5 years under Rev. Proc. 87-56 Asset Class 48.121. The remaining cell site equipment, including the base station, was covered by Asset Class 48.12, which has a recovery period of ten years (*R. Broz* 137 TC 46, CCH Dec. 58,693). Note that Rev. Proc. 2011-22 classifies a base station controller (or generational equivalent) and base transceiver station (or generational equivalent) in Asset Class 48.121 with a recovery period of five years. Taxpayers accordingly will prefer to apply the safe-harbor method depreciation periods rather than follow the Tax Court's ruling.

Cell phones are MACRS 7-year property. See ¶ 106.

*Containers*

See ¶ 5.

*Dogs*

See ¶ 118.

*Domain names*

A domain name serves as the website's address on the internet by providing a coded series of numbers that allows computers to locate the site. Some domain names are registered as trademarks or function as trademarks and for this reason qualify as an amortizable Code Sec. 197 intangible with a 15 year amortization period beginning in the month of acquisition (IRS Chief Counsel Advice 201543014, September 10, 2015). Generic and non-generic domain names acquired in the secondary market may also qualify for amortization under Code Sec. 197 as a customer-based intangible.

Many domain names are purchased in a secondary market from third parties who previously registered them but no longer need them for their own businesses, or who register names and resell them at a profit. These costs must be capitalized because the name will have a useful life of more than one year. The costs cannot be amortized over the name's useful life because a domain name has no useful life. However the IRS has ruled that domain names purchased in the secondary market may in the situations described below be amortizable under Code Sec. 197 as customer-based intangibles (IRS Chief Counsel Advice 201543014, September 10, 2015).

The IRS ruling considers the proper tax treatment of generic and non-generic domain names acquired in the secondary market which are not registered as trademarks (IRS Chief Counsel Advice 201543014, September 10, 2015). The ruling assumes that (1) each purchased domain name is associated with a web site already constructed and will be maintained by the acquiring taxpayer and (2) the taxpayer purchased the generic domain name for use in its trade or business either to generate advertising revenue by selling space on the website or to increase its market share by providing goods or services through the website.

The ruling first concludes that the cost of acquiring a non-generic or generic domain in the secondary market is capitalized. In some situations, the capitalized amount may be amortized as a section 197 intangible over 15 years beginning on the first day of the month in which acquired.

*Nongeneric domain names acquired from secondary market.* If a non-generic domain name is registered as a trademark or functions as a trademark, the capitalized costs of acquiring such a non-generic domain name from the secondary market for use in the acquiring taxpayer's trade or business meets the definition of a trademark in Reg. § 1.197-2(b)(10) and constitutes an amortizable section 197 intangible. Alternatively, if the non-generic domain name does not meet the definition of a trademark but will be used by the acquiring taxpayer in its trade or business to provide goods or services through a website that is already constructed and will be maintained by the acquiring taxpayer, the capitalized costs of acquiring such a non-generic domain name from the secondary market meets the definition of a customer-based intangible in Reg. § 1.197-2(b)(6) and constitutes an amortizable § 197 intangible which is amortized over 15 years beginning in the year of acquisition.

A non-generic domain name is usually a company or product name. Besides providing the domain name holder's internet address, a non-generic domain name actually is used to identify the particular good, service, and/or business that is associated with the website. If the non-generic domain name is used to identify goods or services *and* to distinguish them from those provided by others then it meets the definition of a trademark under Reg. § 1.197-2(b)(10) and is amortizable over 15 years.

*Generic domain names.* A generic domain name is not a company or product name, but rather describes a product or service using generic terms people associate with the topic. A generic domain name usually does not meet the definition of a trademark under Reg. § 1.197-2(b)(10).

However, a generic domain name acquired in the secondary market meets the definition of a customer-based intangible in Reg. § 1.197-2(b)(6) and is amortizable over 15 years under Code Sec. 197 if the generic domain name is associated with a website that is already constructed and will be maintained by the acquiring taxpayer, and the taxpayer acquired the generic domain name for use in its trade or business either to generate advertising revenue by selling space on the website or to increase its market share by providing goods or services through the website (IRS Chief Counsel Advice 201543014, September 10, 2015).

*Forklifts and bobcats*

No specific depreciation period is provided for a forklift or a bobcat in Rev. Proc. 87-56 (¶ 191). The applicable depreciation period will generally depend upon the business activity in which the taxpayer is engaged. For example, the IRS classified these assets when used by a nursery as 7-year property because a nursery is considered a farming business (Rev. Proc. 87-56 Asset Class 01.1 at ¶ 191) (IRS market segment specialization program audit guide for the garden supplies industry). Similarly, a chipper used by a nursery is 7-year property. However, if the chipper were used by a professional tree trimmer, it would presumably be classified as 5-year property (Asset Class 57.0, relating to assets used in the provision of personal or professional services).

*Gambling boats and barges*

A casino riverboat that is in operating condition and coast-guard certified is 10-year property with an 18-year ADS period (Rev. Proc. 87-56 Asset Class 00.28, Vessels, Barges, Tugs and Similar Water Transportation Equipment). If such a boat were to lose its certification or otherwise fail to be ready and available as an asset described in Asset Class 00.28 for any tax year, it would be subject to the change of use rules described in Code Sec. 168(i)(5) (ISP Coordinated Issue Paper: Shipping and Gaming Industries: Class Life of Floating Gaming Facilities, March 12, 2001; reproduced in CCH IRS Positions Reporter (IRPO) at ¶ 173,155).

Generally, a casino which is built on a barge (a vessel which is not self-propelled) is permanently moored and not ready and available for operation as water transportation equipment. Thus, it does not fall within Asset Class 00.28. The issue then becomes whether the casino is considered nonresidential real property (39-year recovery period) or is an asset described in Asset Class 79.0 (Recreation) with a 10-year recovery period. The fact that a gaming facility is permanently moored does not necessarily mean that it is an inherently permanent structure (i.e., a building) for depreciation purposes. The *Whiteco* case factors (see ¶ 127C) are applied to make this determination. For example, a multi-story barge that is permanently moored in a river canal which was dug, enclosed, and isolated from the river is 39-year real property. If upon application of the Whiteco factors, a particular gaming facility is determined to be impermanent then it falls within Asset Class 79.0 (ISP Coordinated Issue Paper referenced above).

Slot machines and other gambling devices are seven-year property. See ¶ 106.

*Gasoline service stations and retail motor fuel outlets*

The IRS has released a revised Market Segment Specialization Program (MSSP) Audit Guide for gas retailers (issued October 3, 2001). The guide now covers many depreciation issues.

Rev. Proc. 87-56 Asset Class 57.0 (5-year property) includes section 1245 property used in marketing petroleum and petroleum products.

Rev. Proc. 87-56 Asset Class 57.1 (15-year property) includes (1) section 1250 assets, including service station buildings and (2) depreciable land improvements, whether section 1245 property or section 1250 property, used in the marketing of petroleum and petroleum products, but does not include any facilities related to petroleum and natural gas trunk pipelines. Car wash buildings and related land improvements are included in Asset Class 57.1. All other land improvements, buildings, and structural components are excluded.

Modular (i.e., movable) service station buildings (e.g., a kiosk) and modular car wash buildings will generally qualify as five-year personal property (Rev. Proc. 87-56 Asset Class 57.0) because they are nonpermanent structures. Otherwise a service station building or car wash building that is a permanent structure is 15-year property (Asset Class 57.1).

A building in which nonpetroleum products are sold (e.g., a convenience store) is considered 39-year nonresidential real property unless it qualifies as a "retail motor fuels outlet" in which case a 15-year recovery period also applies. See ¶ 110.

Underground storage tanks, gasoline pumps, hydraulic car lifts, other mechanical equipment, piping, shelves, counters, refrigerators, neon and other signs (contained in or attached to a building), and vending machines are five-year property (Rev. Proc. 87-56 Asset Class 57.0).

With respect to underground storage tanks, the IRS has specifically considered and concluded that petroleum product storage tanks are land improvements described in Rev. Proc. 87-56 Asset Class 57.1. However, asphalt storage tanks are not related to petroleum marketing and, therefore, are 15-year land improvements described in Asset Class 00.3 (Field Service Advice Memorandum 001605, May 31, 1995).

A parking lot is 15-year property (Rev. Proc. 87-56 Asset Class 57.1). However, an outdoor parking structure is nonresidential real property. See ¶ 5.

A canopy falls within Rev. Proc. 87-56 Asset Class 57.1 with a 15-year depreciation period unless it qualifies under the *Whiteco* test (see ¶ 127C) as personal property because it is a nonpermanent structure. In *JFM, Inc.* (67 TCM 3020, CCH Dec. 49,871(M), TC Memo. 1994-239), canopies bolted down onto four to six special concrete footings were personal property (Asset Class 57.0) with a five-year recovery period. Some of the canopies in question had in fact been moved and reused. The audit guide notes that "the absence of a plan to move a modular structure is not critical, that is, indefinite installation does not taint the personal property characterization."

The IRS selected the recovery period for the depreciation of gasoline pump canopies as an issue for the 2002 Industry Resolution (IIR) program (IRS News Release IR-2002-89, July 10, 2002). In response, the IRS issued Rev. Rul. 2003-54 (I.R.B. 2003-23) in May of 2003. The IRS and taxpayers agree that a canopy which is considered a permanent structure is depreciated over 15 years as a land improvement and that a removable canopy is 5-year personal property (Rev. Proc. 87-56 Asset Class 57.0). The area of contention is the standard for determining whether a canopy is personal property or a land improvement. In the vast majority of cases, IRS auditors were taking the position that canopies are land improvements.

Rev. Rul. 2003-54 describes a typical stand-alone gasoline pump canopy in use by about 90 percent of service stations. The canopy can be removed cost effectively within a short period of time. The ruling concludes, on the basis of the *Whiteco* factors (¶ 127), that the canopy is tangible personal property and depreciable over five years (Rev. Proc. 87-56 Asset Class 57.0). However, the supporting concrete footings are inherently permanent structures and depreciable over 15 years (Asset Class 57.1). Rev. Rul. 2003-54 indicates that taxpayers who have been claiming depreciation deductions in any other manner for two or more tax years may receive automatic consent to change their accounting method pursuant to Section 6.01 of Rev. Proc. 2019-43 (see ¶ 75). If a taxpayer has been treating its gasoline canopies and footings in accordance with this ruling, the IRS will not raise the issue in an audit. If the issue is a matter under consideration in examination, in appeals, or before the Tax Court with respect to a tax year that ends before May 8, 2003, it will not be pursued further by the IRS.

*Golf courses*

See ¶ 5.

Grading and land preparation costs

See ¶ 5.

*Gym equipment*

Gymnasium equipment purchased by a taxpayer engaged in a health club or similar business is presumably 5-year property on the grounds that the taxpayer is providing professional or personal services to the persons who pay to use the equipment (Rev. Proc. 87-56 Asset Class 57.0) (see ¶ 104). The depreciation period for equipment purchased by a company for the use of its employees is based on the business activity of the company (assuming the activity is described in Rev. Proc. 87-56). For example, in a Chief Counsel Advice, the IRS ruled that unspecified equipment in a company's "wellness center" was seven-year property where the company was engaged in a farming business (Asset Class 01.1) or a food and meat manufacturing business (Asset Class 20.4) (Chief Counsel Advice 200137026). If the company's business activity is not described, then the equipment would have no class life and be treated as seven-year property (see ¶ 106).

*Impact fees*

The IRS has ruled that impact fees incurred by real property developers in connection with the construction of a new residential rental building are indirect costs that, pursuant to Code Secs. 263(a) and 263A, should be capitalized and added to the basis of the buildings constructed. Impact fees are one-time charges imposed by a state or local government to finance specific capital improvements, generally located offsite (e.g., schools, police, and fire buildings). If the residential buildings are depreciable the impact fees may be recovered through depreciation deductions when they are placed in service. No allocation to land is required under the facts of this ruling. Such fees may also be included in the eligible basis of the buildings for purposes of computing the low income housing credit (Rev. Proc. 2019-43, Sec. 12.03; IRS Letter Ruling 200916007) See, also Reg. § 1.263(a)-4(d)(8)(iv) which extends this rule for impact fees to dedicated improvements that are made by a developer and transferred to a governmental unit.

Rev. Rul. 2002-9 is an "about face." For example, in Technical Advice Memorandum 200043016 (July 14, 2000) local impact fees collected to pay for a variety of capital improvements could not be added to the basis of the constructed property and depreciated. The IRS concluded that the taxpayer merely acquired a business benefit (an intangible asset) with no determinable useful life. Technical Advice Memorandum 200043016 was subsequently modified to conform to Rev. Rul. 2002-9 (see TAM 200227009, March 11, 2002). TAM 200443016 contains a useful summary of case law and IRS rulings regarding the treatment of impact fees and dedicated improvements.

Taxpayers may use the automatic change of accounting method procedures of Section 12.03 of Rev. Proc. 2019-43 (¶ 75) to conform to Rev. Rul. 2009-9.

Impact fees, dedicated improvements, and payments made to improve real property that is owned by another person or to produce or improve real property that is owned by the taxpayer and then transferred to another person and which are not covered by the rule described above (e.g., there is no current development project to which the UNICAP rules apply) are generally capitalized as intangible assets if the taxpayer obtains a significant economic benefit that extends beyond one year. See Reg. § 1.263(a)-4(d)(8)(i). However, such an intangible asset may qualify for safe-harbor amortization over a period of 25 years if the intangible asset does not have an ascertainable useful life, as is often the case (Reg.§ 1.167(a)-3(b)). See ¶ 66.

*Intermodal facilities*

Assets used in a taxpayer's intermodal facilities and consisting of container handlers, load/unload ramps, straddle cranes, piggypacker side loaders, tire shredder passive and operative, truck scales, translift cranes, and crane pads were described in Rev. Proc. 87-56 Asset Class 40.2 (Railroad Structures and Similar

Improvements). Fences; paving; sewer, lighting, outside wiring, road crossings; and computerized access gates were described in Asset Class 40.1 (Railroad Machinery and Equipment). Buildings which were specifically described in Asset Class 40.2 were depreciable as 39-year nonresidential real property (CCA Letter Ruling 200709063, November 21, 2006). The taxpayer is a railroad company that owns intermodal terminals that transfer freight in containerized cargoes from one mode of transportation to another, i.e., from trucks to railcars and vice versa. The taxpayer's intermodal facilities include areas for railroad operations and truck terminal operations. The taxpayer argued that its assets were properly classified under Asset Class 42.0 (Motor Transport-Freight). See ¶ 152 for the treatment of intermodal containers.

*Inventory and self-constructed assets*

See ¶ 5.

*Land and land improvements*

See ¶ 5.

*Leased property*

See ¶ 190.

*Leasehold acquisition costs*

See ¶ 5.

*Materials and supplies*

See ¶ 307.

*Mobile home parks*

See ¶ 5.

*Model homes and sales offices*

Model homes built by a home builder which will be sold at the end of development are not subject to an allowance for depreciation. Sales offices in such a model home are also not depreciable. These items remain nondepreciable inventory (Rev. Rul. 89-25, 1989- 1 C.B. 79). However, furniture used in a model home is depreciable as 7-year property (office furniture (Asset Class 00.11 of Rev. Proc. 87-56) or property without a class life ( Code Sec. 168(e)(3)(C)(ii))) (IRS Construction Industry Audit Technique Guide (ATG)).

*Painting and remodeling*

The cost of painting the interior or exterior of an existing building is normally considered a deductible repair.

The "repair" regulations, which are generally effective for tax years beginning on or after January 1, 2014 (see ¶ 128) provide that repairs that are made at the same time as an improvement, but that do not directly benefit or are not incurred by reason of the improvement, are not required to be capitalized. If the repairs are required directly in connection with the improvement, they are capitalized (Reg.§ 1.263(a)-3(g)). This principle is illustrated in store "refresh" examples contained in the repair regulations. The repair regulations effectively obsolete the judicially-created plan of rehabilitation doctrine, particularly with regard to the assertion that the doctrine transforms otherwise deductible repair costs into capital improvement costs solely because the repairs are performed at the same time as an improvement, or are pursuant to a maintenance plan, even though the repairs do not improve the property (Preamble to T.D. 9564; Reg.§ 1.263(a)-3).

A taxpayer who is an individual may capitalize amounts paid for repairs and maintenance that are made at the same time as capital improvements to units of property not used in the taxpayer's trade or business or for the production of income if the amounts are paid as part of an improvement (for example, a remodeling) of the taxpayer's residence (Reg.§ 1.263(a)-3(g)).

*Parking lots*

See ¶ 5.

*Playground equipment*

See ¶ 5.

*Precious Metals*

The capitalized cost of unrecoverable precious metals that are used in a manufacturing process are depreciable. The capitalized cost of the recoverable portion of such metals, if any, is not depreciable (Rev. Rul. 2015-11, I.R.B. 2015-21, revoking Rev. Rul. 90-65, 1990-2 CB 41 and Rev. Rul. 75-491, 1975-2 CB 19).

> ***Example:*** A jeweler fabricated sample gold jewelry that was not held for sale. Every three years the jewelry was melted down and 100 percent of the gold was recovered for reuse in fabricating new sample jewelry. Since no portion of the gold was subject to exhaustion, wear and tear, or obsolescence depreciation could not be claimed.

> ***Example:*** A petroleum refiner used a catalyst that was made from platinum and certain chemicals. The cost of the platinum was capitalized. 10 percent of the platinum was lost over the course of the platinum's reasonably expected useful life in the refining process. The remaining 90 percent was recovered and became available for other purposes. The 10 percent of lost platinum undergoes exhaustion, wear and tear, or obsolescence over a determinable useful life and, therefore, is depreciable.

> ***Example:*** A taxpayer that capitalized molten tin used to manufacture flat glass. During the manufacturing process, the tin declined in purity and volume due to chemical reactions and vaporization. Additional tin was added, as needed, to maintain the amount required for the production of the glass. After seven years, all of the original tin was lost. The entire amount of original tin is depreciable because it is subject to exhaustion, wear and tear, or obsolescence over a determinable useful life.

The revoked guidance allowed the cost of recoverable precious metals to be depreciated if the total cost of all precious metals in the produced product was 50 percent or less of the cost of the produced product (Rev. Rul. 90-65, 1990-2 CB 41, prior to revocation by Rev. Rul. 2015-11). The new guidance does not allow the depreciation of recoverable metals regardless of the cost of the metal relative to the produced product.

*Product samples*

The IRS has ruled that where sample products are actually distributed to customers for free, they may be treated as materials and supplies. For example, a taxpayer's deduction for the costs of pharmaceutical product samples and starter packs were deferred until the time at which the samples and starter packs were distributed to licensed physicians or pharmacies. (Field Service Advice Memorandum 199925009). Note, however, that recently issued regulations define a material or supply as a unit of property costing $200 or less (Reg.§ 1.162-3). However, if the de minimis expensing rule (Reg.§ 1.263(a)-1(f)) is elected, a higher per unit of property limitation may apply. See ¶ 307.

*Professional library*

A professional library may be depreciated. A current business expense deduction is allowed for technical books, journals and business information services that have a useful life of one year or less.

Generally, books will fall within MACRS Asset Class 57.0 (¶ 190)—assets used in a wholesale or retail trade or in personal or professional services—and have a depreciation period of five years. For example, the IRS Market Segment Specialization Paper (MSSP) for attorneys indicates that permanent volumes used in a law library are 5-year property (Asset Class 57.0). Presumably, books used in connection with research and experimentation (as that term is used in Code Sec. 174, i.e., research and development costs in a laboratory or experimental sense) are also 5-year property (Item C of Rev. Proc. 87-56, relating to certain property for which recovery periods assigned; Code Sec. 168(e)(3)(B)(v); Code Sec. 168(i)(11)).

The cost of technical books and services which have a useful life of one year or less (including periodicals and loose-leaf services which are purchased on an annual basis), is deductible currently as a business expense.

*Property subject to lease*

See ¶ 5.

*Restaurants and taverns—smallwares*

Taxpayers engaged in the business of operating a restaurant or tavern may treat smallwares as nonincidental materials and supplies and, therefore, claim a current deduction in the year they are first used (Rev. Proc. 2002-12; Preamble to T.D. 9564). Smallwares purchased and stored at a warehouse or facility other than the restaurant where the smallwares will be used are not currently deductible until they are received by the restaurant or facility where they will be used and are available for use. This current deduction safe-harbor treatment does not apply to smallwares purchased by a start-up business.

Oddly, Rev. Proc. 2002-12 indicates that smallwares are start-up expenditures governed by Code Sec. 195 if a taxpayer purchases the smallwares prior to beginning a restaurant business and the taxpayer elects to apply Code Sec. 195. Under this provision a taxpayer may elect to deduct the first $5,000 of its start-up expenditures (Code Sec. 195(b)(3)). The remaining start-up expenditures are amortized over fifteen years beginning in the month in which an active trade or business begins. The $5,000 current deduction, however, is reduced one dollar for each dollar that total start-up expenditures exceed $50,000 ($60,000 if the $10,000 limit applies). Note that Code Sec. 195 does not apply to a taxpayer who is currently operating one or more restaurants and is opening a new restaurant. If a taxpayer treated smallwares as start-up expenditures it is not necessary to depreciate the smallwares over the full 15-year amortization period. A retirement loss could be claimed in the year that they are retired.

The problem with treating smallwares as start-up expenditures is that smallwares are depreciable assets (5-year recovery period under Rev. Proc. 87-56 Asset Class 57.0) because they have a useful life in excess of one year. Depreciable assets are excluded from the definition of a start-up expenditure (Code Sec. 195(c)(1)(B); IRS Letter Ruling 9235004, May 20, 1992.)

A taxpayer that is not engaged in a restaurant business and that does not elect Code Sec. 195, may claim depreciation beginning in the year the business begins. Property is not considered placed in service any sooner than the year the taxpayer engages in a trade or business. See ¶ 3, *"Taxpayer must be engaged in a trade or business."* A 5-year recovery period applies to smallwares (Rev. Proc. 87-56 Asset

Class 57.0 of Rev. Proc. 87-56). However, smallwares should also qualify for bonus deduction (100 percent if acquired after September 27, 2017) (¶ 127D) and expensing under section 179 (¶ 300) in the year the business begins since this is the year that the smallwares are considered placed in service.

Smallwares of an existing restaurant business continue to qualify as materials and supplies under Reg.§ 1.162-3 because the property is identified in published guidance as materials and supplies (Preamble to T.D. 9564). The final regulations do not supersede, obsolete, or replace Rev. Proc. 2002-12 to the extent it deems smallwares to constitute materials and supplies under Reg. § 1.162-3. These material and supplies regulations were issued as part of the IRS "repair" regulations. Reg.§ 1.162-3 is generally effective for amounts paid or incurred to acquire or produce property in tax years beginning on or after January 1, 2014 or, at a taxpayer's option, to tax years beginning on or after January 1, 2012.

Smallwares include (1) glassware and paper or plastic cups; (2) flatware (silverware) and plastic utensils; (3) dinnerware (dishes) and paper or plastic plates; (4) pots and pans; (5) table top items; (6) bar supplies; (7) food preparation utensils and tools; (8) storage supplies; (9) service items; and (10) small appliances costing no more than $500 each. Refer to Rev. Proc. 2002-12 for specific examples of these items.

The operation of a restaurant includes cafeterias, special food services, such as food service contractors, caterers, and mobile food services. The operation of a restaurant or tavern may also include food or beverage services at grocery stores, hotels and motels, amusement parks, theaters, casinos, country clubs, and similar social or recreational facilities.

Automatic change in accounting method procedures are provided in Section 3.03 of Rev. Proc. 2019-43. A taxpayer must change its accounting method under these procedures in order to take advantage of the rule provided in Rev. Proc. 2002-12.

Interior and exterior improvements to a restaurant placed in service after October 22, 2004 and before 2018 may qualify as 15-year MACRS property if specified requirements are satisfied. A restaurant building placed in service after 2008 and before 2018 may also be able to qualify as 15-year MACRS property. Interior improvements to a restaurant made by a taxpayer after 2018 may be depreciated over 15 years as qualified improvement property (Code Sec. 168(e)(6); Reg.§ 1.168(b)-1(a)(5)). Effective for property placed in service after 2017, exterior improvements to a restaurant and restaurant buildings are depreciated over 39 years since exterior improvements are not considered qualified improvement property. See ¶ 110.

*Remodel-refresh safe harbor for restaurant and retail buildings*

The remodel refresh safe harbor for restaurant and retail buildings allows a taxpayer with an applicable financial statement (generally, an audited financial statement) to elect to file a change in accounting method that enables the taxpayer to deduct 75 percent of remodel/refresh costs are capitalize 25 percent See Rev. Proc. 2015-56.

*Roads*

See ¶ 5.

*Roofs*

Effective for property placed in service in tax years beginning after 2017, capitalized replacement roofs for nonresidential real property are eligible for expensing under Code Sec. 179 as a category of qualified real property (Code Sec. 179(e)). See ¶ 302. Assuming a capitalized roofing cost may not be expensed under section 179 (e.g., section 179 investment limit applies), the cost is either depreciated as 39-year nonresidential real property or 27.5-year residential rental property under the rules for additional and improvements. See ¶ 126. However, a replacement roof for a restaurant building that is installed before 2018 may qualify as 15-year restaurant improvement property. See ¶ 110.

The IRS position regarding which expenses related to roofs are deductible and which must be capitalized are in final regulations (Reg. § 1.263(a)-3). Under the regulations, the replacement of an entire roof (including the sheathing and rafters) or a significant portion of a roof that has deteriorated overtime is a restoration that is capitalized as an improvement (Reg. § 1.263(a)-3(k)(7), Example 14). The replacement of a worn and leaking waterproof membrane on a roof comprised of structural elements, insulation, and a waterproof membrane with a similar but new membrane is not required to be capitalized so long as the membrane was not leaking when the taxpayer placed the building in service (Reg. § 1.263(a)-3(j)(3), Example 13, and (k)(7), Example 15). Likewise, the in example dealing with the treatment of removal costs, the IRS assumes that the cost of shingles that replaces similar shingles that became leaky while the taxpayer owned the building is not capitalized (Reg. § 1.263(a)-3(g)(2)(ii), Example 3).

Under the final regulations, a taxpayer must capitalize amounts paid to ameliorate a material condition or defect that existed prior to the taxpayer's acquisition of a unit of property (e.g., a building) whether or not the taxpayer was aware of the condition (Reg. § 1.263(a)-3(j)(1)(i)). The regulations do not provide an example of the repair of a building with a leaky roof at the time of purchase; however, it appears that generally such a repair would be capitalized.

An otherwise deductible repair expense (e.g., the cost of replacing a portion of a roof) must be capitalized if the taxpayer claims a retirement loss deduction on the portion of the roof that is retired (Reg. § 1.263(a)-3(k)(1)(i)). A taxpayer may make a partial disposition election to claim a loss on an original roof that is replaced. The replacement roof is a separately depreciable asset. Therefore, if a replacement roof is replaced, it is not necessary to make a partial disposition election to claim a retirement loss. The retirement loss must be claimed. However, if the shingles on the replacement roof are replaced, a partial disposition election is required to claim a loss on the remaining basis of the shingles. However, the election would prevent the taxpayer from claiming a repair expense. See ¶ 162.

Although a replacement roof is a separate asset, it remains part of the building unit of property for purposes of determining whether an expenditure is a repair or capitalized improvement because it is depreciated in the same manner as the building (i.e., over 39 years). Improvements to a unit of property that are depreciated using the same recovery period as the underlying property are not treated as separate units of property (Reg.§ 1.263(a)-3(e)(4) and (5)(i)).

The cost of a capitalized roof is treated as MACRS 27.5 year residential rental property if placed in service on residential rental property or as 39-year MACRS nonresidential real property if placed in service on commercial property. See ¶ 126.

Where a roof has been damaged or destroyed in a casualty event, special rules apply for determining the capitalized costs (Reg.§ 1.263(a)-3(k)(4)). See ¶ 179.

With respect to case law, in *Badger Pipeline Company*, 74 TCM 856, Dec. 52,292(M), the Tax Court indicated that it would treat the replacement of a few slate roof tiles as a repair, but the replacement of all of the roof tiles as a capital expenditure. In *Pierce Estates*, 16 TC 1020, Dec. 18,270, the Tax Court treated the cost of replacing a corrugated metal roof as a capital expenditure but the cost of patching leaks on an asphalt roof as currently deductible repairs. In *Oberman Manufacturing Co.*, 47 TC 471, Dec. 28,334, however, the cost of removing and replacing the entire perlite and asphalt and gravel covering on a roof (as well as replacing an expansion joint) was held to be a deductible repair. The court indicated that the work merely kept the building in operating condition and did not increase the useful life or the value of the building.

The *Oberman* decision was cited in a Tax Court small case summary opinion (these opinions are not reviewable and may not be cited as authority), which held that replacement of all of the "top layers" of the roof of a one-story residential rental house with fiberglass sheets and hot asphalt was a deductible repair (*N. Campbell*, T.C. Summary Opinion 2002-117). A subsequent Tax Court small case summary opinion, again citing *Oberman*, also allowed the current deduction of roof replacement costs (*T.J. Northen Jr.* and *S. Cox*, T.C. Summary Opinion 2003-113). The case involved a 26,000 square foot commercial building. The roof leaked in one location. Nevertheless, the roofing company removed all tar and gravel down to the plywood, replaced twenty-eight sheets of dry rotted plywood, and sprayed with a primer and a polyurethane foam coating before applying new tar and gravel. An air conditioning unit also had to be removed and reattached to repair the roof. The Court reasoned that the work was done to prevent leakage, keep the property in operating condition and did not prolong the life of the property, increase its value, or make it adaptable to another use.

A taxpayer may elect to have a case tried under the small tax case procedures if the deduction involves $50,000 or less (Code Sec. 7463). If the deficiency exceeds this amount, the taxpayer may obtain jurisdiction by conceding the excess. There is no appeal from a small tax case decision.

In *D.W. Stark* (77 TCM 1181, CCH Dec. 53,202(M)), "roofing material was removed down to the wooden structure of the building," a new roof drain was added, and a new roof was reapplied. These expenditures had to be capitalized. The *Oberman* decision was distinguished. The facts are unclear but in *Stark* perhaps the plywood covering on which a roof is placed may have been removed. Stark appears to be the only roofing case in which *Oberman* is cited by another court (other than the summary decisions mentioned above).

Another case that held that the cost of a new roof had to be capitalized is *C.E. Drozda*, T.C. Memo. 1984-19, CCH Dec. 40,926(M). This case, however, does not offer any particular insight into its reasoning.

In *Vanalco, Inc.*, 78 TCM 251, Dec. 53,493(M), the replacement of 10 percent of the roofing material and underlying decking on an industrial building to stop leaks was considered a deductible expense. The court ruled that there was no plan to replace the entire roof even though a substantial portion of the roof had been previously replaced in earlier tax years.

In *G.H. Hable*, 48 TCM 1079, Dec. 41,481(M), the IRS unsuccessfully argued that the replacement of barn shingles blown off during a storm was a capital expenditure (similarly, *G.W. Pontel*, 42 TCM 113, Dec. 37,988(M)).

For additional cases holding that the cost of a new roof is not deductible, see annotations at CCH Standard Federal Tax Reporter ¶ 8630.60 and following and ¶ 13,709.567.

*Rotable spare parts*

The treatment of rotable spare parts for amounts paid or incurred to acquire or produce property in tax years beginning on or after January 1, 2014 is governed by

Reg.§ 1.162-3 relating to materials and supplies (T.D. 9636 (September 19, 2013) (the final "repair" regulations)). Reg. § 1.162-3 may be applied to tax years beginning on or after January 1, 2012. Change in accounting method procedures for taxpayers applying the final regulations are provided in Section 11.08 of Rev. Proc. 2019-43 (automatic method changes). See ¶ 77.

Rotable spare parts are defined as materials and supplies described in Reg. § 1.162-3(c)(1)(i) (i.e., components of a unit of property) (see ¶ 307) that are acquired for installation on a unit of property, removable from that unit of property, generally repaired or improved, and either reinstalled on the same or other property or stored for later installation. Temporary spare parts are materials and supplies that are used temporarily until a new or repaired part can be installed and then are removed and stored for later (emergency or temporary) installation (Reg.§ 1.162-3(c)(2)).

Under the general rule, a taxpayer deducts the cost of a rotable spare part (or temporary spare part) when the part is discarded from the taxpayer's operations (i.e., when it is considered used or consumed) (Reg. § 1.162-3(a)(3)) or by electing to capitalize and depreciate the part over the part's applicable recovery period (Reg. § 1.162-3(d)). This rule treating a rotable as a deduction when discarded prevents taxpayers from prematurely deducting the cost of a unit of property by systematically replacing components with rotable spare parts. The IRS anticipates that taxpayers with rotable or temporary spare parts that are not discarded after their original use generally will prefer to capitalize their costs and treat those parts as depreciable assets.

An optional method of accounting for rotable or temporary spare parts allows a taxpayer to deduct the amount paid to acquire or produce the part in the tax year that the part is first installed on a unit of property for use in the taxpayer's operations (Reg. § 1.162-3(e)).

The final regulations also define standby emergency spare parts and limit the application of the election to capitalize materials and supplies to only rotable, temporary, and standby emergency spare parts (Reg. § 1.162-3(c)(3); Reg. § 1.162-3(d)).

If a taxpayer elects the de minimis expending rule (¶ 307) rotable, temporary, and standby emergency parts are deductible under that rule in the year their cost is paid or incurred unless the taxpayer makes the election to capitalize and depreciate or, in the case of rotable or temporary spare parts, the taxpayer elects the optional method (Reg.§ 1.263(a)-1(f)(1)(iii)).

In the preamble to T.D. 9564, the IRS states the previously issued safe harbor for rotables in Rev. Proc. 2007-48 may need to be revised. In addition, the final regulations modify Rev. Rul. 2003-37, Rev. Rul. 81-185, Rev. Rul. 69-200, and Rev. Rul. 69-201 to the extent that the final regulations characterize certain tangible properties addressed in these rulings as materials and supplies. However, the final regulations permit taxpayers to elect to treat these properties as assets subject to the allowance for depreciation consistent with the holdings in these revenue rulings.

In Rev. Proc. 2007-48, the IRS created a safe-harbor as a result of its ruling that it would allow taxpayers to treat rotable spare parts as a pool of depreciable capital assets in situations substantially similar to those of the *Hewlett-Packard* and *Honeywell* cases (Rev. Rul. 2003-37). In the *Hewlett-Packard* case, a computer maintenance business was conducted by the seller of the computers pursuant to standardized maintenance agreements (*Hewlett-Packard*, CA-FC, 96-1 USTC ¶ 50,046). Malfunctioning computer parts were replaced with spare parts from a rotable pool. The IRS contended had that each exchange of parts was a sale of inventory. The Appellate Court ruled that the parts were a depreciable capital asset. The Tax Court and the Eighth Circuit ruled similarly in *Honeywell* (*Honeywell Inc. and Subsidiaries*, 64 TCM 437, CCH Dec. 48,412(M), aff'd, CA-8 (unpublished opinion), 27 F3d 577).

The safe harbor allows a taxpayer to treat rotable spare parts as depreciable assets rather than as inventory and is generally effective for tax years ending on or after December 31, 2006. Taxpayers can obtain automatic consent to adopt the new safe harbor if they account for their rotable spare parts in accordance with specific provisions in Rev. Proc. 2007-48 (Rev. Proc. 2007-48, I.R.B. 2007-29; Rev. Proc. 2019-43, Section 11.06).

The safe harbor may be used by a taxpayer that has gross sales (less returns) of rotable spare parts from the taxpayer's maintenance operation that do not exceed 10 percent of the taxpayer's total gross revenues (less returns) from its maintenance operation for the taxable year. In addition, the taxpayer must:

(1) repair customer-owned (or customer-leased) equipment under warranty or maintenance agreements that are provided to the customer for either no charge or a predetermined fee that does not change during the term of the agreement (regardless of the taxpayer's costs to comply with the agreement);

(2) be obligated under the warranty or maintenance agreements to repair the customer's equipment (including all parts and labor related to the repair) for either no charge or a nominal service fee that is unrelated to the actual cost of parts and labor provided;

(3) maintain a pool or pools of spare parts that are used primarily in the taxpayer's maintenance operation of repairing customer-owned (or customer-leased) equipment under warranty or maintenance agreements, exchange the spare parts for defective parts in the customer-owned (or customer-leased) equipment, and generally repairs and reuse the defective parts in its pool of spare parts; and

(4) have a depreciable interest in the rotable spare parts and has placed in service the rotable spare parts after 1986.

A taxpayer using the safe harbor method of accounting for rotable spare parts must:

(1) capitalize the cost of the rotable spare parts under Code Sec. 263(a) and depreciate these parts using MACRS;

(2) establish one or more pools for the rotable spare parts;

(3) identify the disposed rotable spare parts; and

(4) determine a depreciable basis of the rotable spare parts.

Rev. Proc. 2007-48 explains how the parts are to be depreciated under MACRS and the manner in which the pools are established, the disposed parts are identified, and the basis of the parts determined.

A taxpayer that is not eligible to use the safe harbor method may request to change its method of accounting for treating rotable spare parts by filing a Form 3115 with the Commissioner in accordance with the requirements of Reg. § 1.446-1(e)(3)(i) and the advance consent procedures of Rev. Proc. 2015-13.

The IRS previously took the position that rotable spare parts maintained by a manufacturer to service *customer-owned* computer and data processing equipment are nondepreciable inventory. However, rotable spare parts held exclusively to service equipment *leased* to customers could be treated as depreciable capital assets. Rotable spare parts held both for servicing customer-owned equipment and leased equipment, according to the prior IRS position, were properly treated as inventory (IRS Industry Specialization Program (ISP) Coordinated Issue Paper, "Rotable" Spare Parts (as revised on July 31, 1992) and reproduced in the CCH IRS POSITIONS REPORTER at ¶ 100,575).

Many taxpayers currently treat rotable spare parts as capital expenditures depreciable beginning in the year of purchase over the depreciation period of the unit of property in which the rotables are used. See Rev. Rul. 69-200, 1969-1 CB 60 and Rev. Rul. 69-201, 1969-1 CB 60.

*Slot Machines, Video Terminals and Gaming Furniture, Fixtures And Equipment*

Slot machines, video terminals and gaming furniture, fixtures and equipment are includible in asset class 79.0 Recreation of Rev. Proc. 87-56 and depreciated using a 7-year recovery period. This class includes "assets used in the provision of entertainment services on payment of a fee or admission charge, as in the operation of bowling alleys, billiard and pool establishments, theaters, concert halls, and miniature golf courses." Slot machines etc., are not qualified technological equipment under Code Sec. 168(i)(2) entitled to a 5-year recovery period; information systems includible in asset class 00.12 Information Systems of Rev. Proc. 87-56, 1987-2 C.B. 674, entitled to a 5-year recovery period; "Distributive trades and services" property entitled to a five year recovery period (asset class 57.0) as defined in Rev. Proc. 87-56 (IRS Cash Intensive Businesses Audit Techniques Guide - Chapter 13 - Coin Operated Amusements). See, also, 106.

*Site utilities*

See ¶ 5.

*Timeshares*

The vacation home rules of Code Sec. 280A will in most cases prevent a taxpayer from claiming a loss deduction in excess of rental income, with respect to a timeshare. However, disallowed losses are carried forward and can be deducted in future years if sufficient rental income in excess of expenses is generated (Code Sec. 280A(c)(5)). Code Sec. 280A(a) states the general rule that no deductions (except for interest, taxes, etc. that are deductible as nonbusiness deductions) may be claimed for a dwelling unit used during the tax year by the taxpayer as a residence (Code Sec. 280A(d)(1)). Code Sec. 280A(c)(3) and Code Sec. 280A(e) provide an exception to the no deduction rule where the residence is rented, essentially limiting total deductions to an amount that can be no greater than the rents included in income. In order for Code Sec. 280A to apply the dwelling unit must be used as a residence. A dwelling unit is considered used as a residence if the taxpayer or any other person with an interest in the unit uses it for personal purposes more than 14 days during the year (Code Sec. 280A(d)(2)). For this purpose, each owner of the time share is considered to have an interest in the dwelling unit (*E. Fudim*, Dec. 49,867(M), 67 T.C.M. 3011, T.C. Memo. 1994-235, denying loss deduction to taxpayer who owned three rented time-share units). Therefore, the unit will be considered a residence by the taxpayer if the total amount of time spent for personal use during the tax year, taking into account all owners, exceeds 14 days. This situation will almost always exist, meaning that the limitations of Code Sec. 280A will apply. It also appears that Code Sec. 280A(g), which requires a taxpayer to exclude rental income from a dwelling unit used as a residence (as defined above) and claim no business related deductions attributable to the rental if the "dwelling unit is actually rented for less than 15 days during the taxable year..." will not apply. The rule does not say that the dwelling unit must be rented *by the taxpayer* for less than 15 days. Accordingly, it appears that all rental days by other owners should be taken into account in making this determination.

In one case, the court determined that a taxpayer who rented several time shares was not engaged in an activity for a profit, and, therefore limited deductions to income (*D. Rundlett*, Dec. 58,766(M), TC Memo. 2011-229). The court did not consider the application of Code Sec. 280A although it was one theory put forward by the IRS.

Even if a timeshare rental is not subject to the limitations of Code Sec. 280A because it is not considered used as a residence or subject to Code Sec. 183, the Code Sec. 469 passive loss rules do not treat an activity as a rental activity if the average period that the property is rented by a particular renter is seven days or less (Temporary Reg.§ 1.469-1T(e)(3)(ii)(A); IRS Letter Ruling 9505002). Accordingly, the less stringent active participation standard for rental real estate activities under the rule which permits up to $25,000 of passive losses to be deducted (Code Sec. 469(i)) does not apply in the typical situation where timeshare renters use the timeshare for only a week at a time. Instead material participation needs to be shown (IRS Letter Ruling 9505002, September 20, 1994).

For depreciation purposes a timeshare is 27.5 year MACRS residential rental property.

*Tires and tubes*

The IRS has issued Rev. Proc. 2002-27 which provides a method (the "original tire capitalization method") for accounting for the cost of original and replacement truck tires. Under the original tire capitalization method, a taxpayer:

(1) capitalizes the cost of the original tires of a qualifying vehicle (whether purchased separately or equipped on the vehicle when purchased) and depreciates those tires using the same depreciation method, recovery period, and convention applicable to the vehicle on which the tires are first installed;

(2) treats the original tires as disposed of when the vehicle is disposed of; and

(3) treats the cost of all replacement tires as a current deduction in the tax year the replacement tires are installed on the vehicle by the taxpayer regardless of their useful life.

Note that the cost of original tires must be depreciated over the depreciation period of the vehicle even if they have been disposed of. Furthermore, no current expense deduction can be claimed for original tires even if they wear out in one year or less.

If elected, the original tire capitalization method applies to all original and replacement tires mounted on all of a taxpayer's light general purpose trucks (Rev. Proc. 87-56 Asset Class 00.241 (5-year property)), heavy general purpose trucks (Asset Class 00.242 (5-year property)), tractor units for use over-the-road (Asset Class 00.26 (3-year property)), trailers (Asset Class 00.27 (5-year property)), and converter dollies (converter gears) (a converter dolly is an accessory used to convert a semitrailer to a full trailer (Reg. § 48.4061-(b)(2))). The procedures contained in Rev. Proc. 2002-27, therefore, do not apply to tires used on buses (Asset Class 00.23) or automobiles and taxis (Asset Class 00.22).

Rev. Proc. 2002-27 is generally effective for tax years ending on or after December 31, 2001. The ruling contains detailed guidance on automatic change of accounting method procedures. This guidance was last specifically incorporated into Section 6.05 of Rev. Proc. 2011-14 (the automatic accounting method change procedure). However, Rev. Proc. 2011-14 was superseded by Rev. Proc. 2015-14, effective for Forms 3115 filed on or after January 16, 2015, for a year of change ending on or after May 31, 2014. "Significant Changes," Section .01(23) of Rev. Proc. 2015-14 states that Section 6.05 was eliminated because taxpayers may file this change under the general rules of Sec. 6.01 of the applicable automatic consent procedure (currently Rev. Proc. 2019-43) relating to changes from an impermissible method of depreciation to a permissible method. The change is, therefore, still made under the applicable automatic procedure.

Rev. Proc. 2002-27 provides that a taxpayer that does not choose to use the original tire capitalization method on its qualifying vehicles must account for the cost of its original and replacement tires in accordance with the case law and rulings cited by the IRS in section 2.03 of the ruling. This precedent allows the cost of truck tires and tubes which are consumed within one year to be claimed as a current deduction. The depreciation period for other original and replacement truck tires, however, is determined by reference to the business activity of the taxpayer and not the depreciation period of the vehicle. The truck tires are considered an asset entirely separate from the vehicle to which they are attached. See, for example, IRS Field Service Advice 200122002, January 30, 2001.

In many instances if the original tire capitalization method is not used, the truck tires will be treated as 5-year property under Rev. Proc. 87-56 Asset Class 42.0 (Motor Transport-Freight, relating to assets (other than vehicles) used in the commercial and contract carrying of freight by road). Classification by reference to business activity rather than truck type may be disadvantageous in the case of tractor units for use over-the-road since these trucks are treated as 3-year property under MACRS (Asset Class 00.26).

Rev. Proc. 2002-27 is clearly disadvantageous to a taxpayer that consumes all of its tires (original and replacement) within one year since no expense deduction can be claimed on the original tires. In most other situations, Rev. Proc. 2002-27 seems preferable as it allows the cost of all replacement tires to be deducted in full in the year they are installed.

*Retreaded tires.* Following the release of Rev. Proc. 2002-27, the IRS clarified that a taxpayer who does not elect the OTC method should capitalize and depreciate the cost of retreaded tires as separate assets whether the retreaded tires are used as the original set of tires or as replacements. The cost may be deducted as a repair if the tire is consumed in less than one year (Chief Counsel Advice 200252091, October 31, 2002; clarified by Chief Counsel Advice 200307087, February 19, 2003).

The ruling further clarifies that a taxpayer who has elected the OTC method should treat retreaded tires that are acquired as the first set of tires on newly-acquired vehicles as "original tires" that are depreciated as part of the cost of the vehicle.

Retreads that are received in exchange for original or replacement tires should be considered "replacement tires" whose cost may be claimed as a current deduction. The ruling notes that a retread company may return the taxpayer's original tires or replace them with different tires. The conclusions reached by the ruling do not appear to depend on whether or not the taxpayer receives its original tires from the retreader.

*Treatment of tires under the MACRS disposition regulations and repair regulations if safe harbor is not used.* The preamble to a proposed version of the repair regulations indicates that a taxpayer that uses the safe harbor method of Rev. Proc. 2002-27, is bound by that method (NPRM REG-168745-03). A taxpayer who adopts or adopted the original tire capitalization method, is precluded from making the partial disposition election and must continue to depreciate the original tires when retired even if they are treated as part of the "vehicle asset" and would otherwise be eligible for the partial disposition election. As noted above, under the safe harbor method, the original tires are treated as disposed of when the vehicle is disposed of.

For taxpayers who do not use the safe harbor, under Reg.§ 1.168(i)-8(d), a taxpayer may elect to make a partial disposition election when a component of an asset is retired. This regulation is generally effective for tax years beginning on or after January 1, 2014. See ¶ 162 If the tires are treated as a separate depreciable asset or unit of property then it is not necessary to make a partial disposition election in order to claim a retirement loss. Recognition of the loss is mandatory when a separate asset is disposed of.

The repair regulations only contain one example dealing with tires.

> ***Example:*** R is engaged in the business of transporting freight throughout the United States. To conduct its business, R owns a fleet of truck tractors and trailers. Each tractor and trailer is comprised of various components, including tires. R purchased a truck tractor with all of its components, including tires. The tractor tires have an average useful life to R of more than one year. At the time R placed the tractor in service, it treated the original tractor tires as a separate asset for depreciation purposes. R properly treated the tractor (excluding the cost of the tires) as 3-year property and the tractor tires as 5-year property. Under the general rule of Reg. § 1.263(a)-3(e)(3)(i), the tractor and tires would be treated as a single unit of property because the tires and tractor are functionally independent (that is, the placing in service of the tires is dependent upon the placing in service of the tractor). Nevertheless, under an exception described in Reg. § 1.263(a)-3(e)(5)(i), R must treat the tractor and tires as separate units of property because R properly treated the tires as being within a different class of property than the tractors (Reg. § 1.263(a)-3(e)(6), Example 16).

Replacement tires may be considered materials and supplies under the materials and supplies regulations (Reg.§ 1.162-3) which are effective for amounts paid or incurred in tax years beginning on or after January 1, 2014. Non-incidental materials and supplies (i.e., materials and supplies for which records of consumption or beginning and ending inventories are kept) are deductible in the tax year in which the materials and supplies are first used in the taxpayer's operations or are consumed in the taxpayer's operations. Incidental materials and supplies are deductible in the tax year in which their cost is paid or incurred, provided taxable income is clearly reflected.

Materials and supplies include tangible property that is used or consumed in the taxpayer's operations that is not inventory and which is:

- A component acquired to maintain, repair, or improve a unit of tangible property (as determined under § 1.263(a)-3(e)) owned, leased, or serviced by the taxpayer and that is not acquired as part of any single unit of tangible property;

- Fuel, lubricants, water, and similar items, reasonably expected to be consumed in 12 months or less, beginning when used in the taxpayer's operations;

- A unit of property as determined under Reg.§ 1.263(a)-3(e) that has an economic useful life of 12 months or less, beginning when the property is used or consumed in the taxpayer's operations;

- A unit of property as determined under Reg.§ 1.263(a)-3(e) that has an acquisition cost or production cost (as determined under section Code Sec. 263A) of $200 or less; and

- Any other item tangible property that is used or consumed in the taxpayer's operations that is not inventory and which is identified in published guidance in the Federal Register or in the Internal Revenue Bulletin as materials and supplies.

*Standard mileage rate and actual expense method.* Certain taxpayers who use their cars for business purposes may either elect the standard mileage rate or use the actual expense method (¶ 217). No depreciation deduction is claimed if the standard mileage rate is used. It appears that most taxpayers who decide not to use the standard mileage rate recover the cost of the original equipment tires through depreciation deductions on the vehicle and then deduct the cost of replacement tires in full (IRS Publication 463; Form 2106 instructions). This treatment is consistent with the original tire capitalization method.

*Tools, shop equipment, laboratory equipment*

The IRS has ruled that tools, shop equipment, and laboratory equipment, such as lathes, bandsaws, hydraulic presses used by a utility involved in the generating, transmitting, and distributing of electricity were used in furtherance of its business activity and, therefore, includible in the business activity class of Rev. Proc. 87-56 in which they were primarily used. The tools were used in the following property class business activities: Rev. Proc. 87-56 Asset Class 49.13, Electric Utility Steam Production Plant; Asset Class 49.14, Electric Utility Transmission and Distribution Plant, and Asset Class 49.21, Gas Utility Distribution Facilities (CCA Letter Ruling 200246006, August 5, 2002). It is useful to note that the fact that these Asset Classes list specific types of assets did not preclude the inclusion of the tools etc., within the Asset Classification so long as the tools were used in the furtherance of the business activity described by the Asset Class. Thus, in general, it appears that a taxpayer should include tools etc. in the Asset Class for their business activity as described in Rev. Proc. 87-56. A tool may be deductible as a material or supply if it has an economic useful life of less than one year or costs $100 (potentially subject to inflation adjustment at the IRS's discretion) or less (Temporary Reg.§ 1.162-3T). Temporary Reg.§ 1.263A-1(e)(3)(ii)(R) requires taxpayers to capitalize the cost of tools and equipment allocable to property produced or property acquired for resale.

*Trees, shrubbery and other landscaping*

See ¶ 5.

*Uniforms*

Generally, uniforms would constitute MACRS 5-year property (Rev. Proc. 87-56 Asset Class 57.0, relating to property used in providing personal or professional services or property used in a distributive trade or business). See ¶ 104. However, units of property costing $200 or less may be deducted in the year first used as materials and supplies or, if applicable, under the elective de minimis expensing safe harbor if the cost does not exceed an applicable per item amount generally set at $500 per item of property ($2,500 in tax years beginning in 2016) or, for taxpayers with an applicable financial statement, $5,000 per item. Materials and supplies also include items of property, regardless of cost, which are consumed within a one-year period. See ¶ 307 for a discussion of materials and supplies and the de minimis safe harbor.

*Website development costs*

The tax treatment of the costs of developing and maintaining a web site has not been officially addressed by the IRS. Although some taxpayers have been deducting the entire cost of creating a website as an "advertising" expense, it seems clear that such a wholesale treatment is not acceptable to the IRS. Some of the cost of creating or purchasing a website, however, may be currently deductible as a software development cost. Rev. Proc. 2000-50 and Rev. Proc. 69-21 (prior to being superseded by Rev. Proc. 2000-50) allow taxpayers to currently deduct software development costs in the same manner as a research and development expenditure under Code Sec. 174.

Domain names are discussed separately above.

One important change to Rev. Proc. 69-21 made by Rev. Proc. 2000-50 should be noted. Rev. Proc. 2000-50 now states that, "[t]his revenue procedure does not apply . . . to costs that a taxpayer has treated as a research and experimentation expenditure under § 174." This change clarifies that amounts that a taxpayer deducts under the authority of Rev. Proc. 2000-50 are considered deducted by virtue of Code Sec. 162 and do not necessarily qualify as research and experimental expenditures under Code Sec. 174. Some taxpayers have interpreted Rev. Proc. 69-21 as meaning that all software expenditures qualify as research and experimental expenditures under Code Sec. 174 and are deductible under that section. The distinction is important for taxpayers who want to claim the research and development credit since only expenditures that are deductible under Code Sec. 174 can qualify for the credit. Also, for a start-up business, Code Sec. 195 requires the capitalization of ordinary and necessary business expenses incurred during the start-up period; this requirement, however, does not apply to amounts for which a deduction is allowable Code Sec. 174. Thus, software development costs cannot qualify for current deduction by a start-up company unless they also qualify for deduction under Code Sec. 174.

It should be noted that when an independent contractor is paid to develop software, software development costs are deductible under Code Sec. 174 only if the purchaser is at risk that the project will fail (Reg. § 1.174-2(b)(2)).

The following material regarding the tax treatment of website development costs appeared in the Spring 2000, *ISP Digest Data Processing*. This is an unofficial publication of the IRS's Data Processing ISP (Industry Specialization Program). It does not represent the IRS's official position (no official position has been taken as of press time). In addition, a related outline, is also reproduced below. Both items were drafted by Robert L. Rible, in his capacity as the Technical Advisor for the Data Processing Industry, within the Pre-filing and Technical Guidance Office of the Large and Mid-Size Business Division (Washington D.C.).

In short, the discussion strictly construes the types of expenses that qualify for a current deduction as software development or as a currently deductible advertising cost. It takes the position that a website should primarily be viewed as an item of software amortizable over three years when placed in service. The creation of website pages with a software tool would not be considered software development that is currently deductible as a software development cost. Software development costs that are eligible for current deduction under Rev. Proc. 2000-50 would relate to the cost of writing source code (i.e., programming) that enables a computer to perform a desired function. In most cases, according to the outline, direct HTML coding of a web page would not qualify as software development. Currently deductible advertising expenses would be limited to costs that relate to material that is changed or updated on a regular basis. Permanent elements of a cite which do not qualify as currently deductible software development expenditures would generally be amortized over three years by including such costs in the basis of the website and treating the website as if it were a software asset.

Arguably, the treatment of a website as amortizable three-year software seems favorable to the taxpayer in that costs capitalized into a website would likely not otherwise be recoverable because a website does not usually have a determinable useful life.

**Web Site Design Costs (Text from Spring 2000, ISP Digest Data Processing)**

Another issue arising in the area of software programs is the treatment of website design costs. In fact, during the last filing season there were a number of questions about this topic from the Taxpayer Service Division, as taxpayers were curious about how these costs should be treated. First, the same issue about who bears the economic risk for the work being done is present. If the taxpayer does not bear the risk, he is clearly getting purchased software, and it should be treated as the asset it is. For a good discussion of the "at risk" issue, see FSA 199930016 [Field Service Advice—Editor], issued on September [April—Editor.]27, 1999. But if he does bear the risk, then the same old question arises: does the work of designing the website constitute software development? Frequently, the process of making this design involves the use of purchased software, such as Adobe PageMill 3.0™, Microsoft FrontPage 2000™, or Macromedia's Dreamweaver 2™. Such software packages contain templates that enables one to configure the web page in any way that the designer wants. As with the ERP and CRM software [references are to discussion of Enterprise Resource Planning and Customer Relationship Management Software that appear earlier in the *Digest*—Editor.], using templates is not software development. So if the taxpayer or his outside consultant is designing the website using such software, it can be maintained that he is getting an asset with a useful life beyond the first taxable year.

One argument that some taxpayers may want to use is that the cost of the website design is deductible as an advertising expense. Advertising expenses usually get to be expensed currently, as per Reg. § 1.162(a). But the Service has argued—in the context of package design costs—that such "design costs more closely resemble nonrecurring promotional or advertising expenditures that result in benefits to the taxpayer which extend beyond the year in which the expenditures are incurred; such expenditures are a capital investment and are not currently deductible" (Rev. Rul. 89-23, 1989-1 CB 85). And more recently the Service has argued that, "Only in the unusual circumstance where advertising is directed toward obtaining future benefits significantly beyond those traditionally associated with ordinary product advertising or with institutional goodwill advertising, must the costs of that advertising be capitalized" (Rev. Rul. 92-80, I.R.B. 1992-39). In a recent court case, *RJR Nabisco Inc., et al., v. Commissioner*, TC Memo. 1998-252, the government lost its argument that such package design costs should be capitalized. But a nonacquiescence on this case was issued on October 4, 1999 (AOD/CC 1999-012), in which it is stated that, "The Service has expressly determined that package design costs are essentially different from deductible advertising costs." The situation involving a website design is very similar to the package design issue in the food and beverage industry. See the coordinated issue paper in this industry for a complete discussion of the issue. Even though there is an advertising aspect to both package designs and website designs, it can be argued that the costs of making these designs are capital expenditures under § 263.

A relevant court case is *Alabama Coca-Cola Bottling Co. v. Commissioner*, TC Memo. 1969-123. The taxpayer argued that billboards, signs and scoreboards were a current advertising expense. But the court concluded that they were assets with a life of more than one year, insofar as the structure of the items remained from year to year, even though their contents may change many times during a year. In the case of a website, there are going to be periodic changes to them, because of changes in products sold, changes in personnel, changing financial conditions, etc. The changes that are made on a monthly or other regular basis are clearly ordinary advertising expenses, but the basic website design that may endure over a longer period of time can easily be seen to be an asset. Again, as a form of purchased software, this asset should be given a three year life under § 167(f). Some companies are spending hundreds of thousands of dollars on these website designs, so its is an issue of some materiality. [end of IRS text—Editor]

The IRS outline below indicates that even the creation of a web page using HTML coding (as opposed to purchased software such as Microsoft FrontPage ™) is probably not software development for purposes of Rev. Proc. 2000-50 and its predecessor, Rev. Proc. 69-21. However, in fact, many taxpayers have been deducting the cost of directly coded HTML graphics related to the look and feel of a website such as borders, color, fonts, frames, background, toolbars, menubars, banners, logos, buttons, hyperlinks, and blank forms for ordering products or obtaining user information as a software development cost.

**Full Text IRS Outline**

- Most companies now have websites on the internet. They contain information about a company's products, personnel, services, and even its financials.

- These websites are frequently designed using purchased software, such a Adobe PageMill 3.0 ™, Microsoft FrontPage 2000 ™, or Macromedia's Dreamweaver 2 ™.

- Such software packages contain templates that enable one to design the web page in any way that the designer wants. Sometimes HTML code is directly integrated into the design project.

- In addition, sometimes HTML (hypertext markup language) code is used to create a web page. HTML is very simple code, and is not a classical programming language, such as COBOL, FORTRAN, or C++ etc.

- One common definition of an HTML document is that it is "simply a plain-text document that has HTML tags embedded in it."

- The definition of software contained in sections 167(f) and 197(e)(3)(B) of the Internal Revenue Code is that it is a "program designed to cause a computer to perform a desired function." Such programs are dynamic and can be used over and over again in various and different ways at various times.

• A web page is more of a fixed, static document that is just there. The internet browser on the computer and the software on the server computer feeding the system are what cause the computer to perform various functions.

• **Legally, a number of points can be made:**

• If the taxpayer does not bear the economic risk for the work being done to create the website, but is getting something from an outside contractor which is guaranteed to work, at a set dollar amount, it can be argued that he is buying an asset, not just paying for a service. See *FSA 199930016*, September [April—Editor.] 27, 1999, for a good discussion of the risk issue in relation to software projects.

• Even if he does bear the economic risk for the work done, it can still be questioned as to whether what he is paying for is software development or not. Using templates and even writing in HTML code may not constitute "software development." No source code is being written using a classical programming language. "Software" as the IRC defines it is not being created ("a program that causes a computer to perform a desired function").

• If such work does not constitute software development, it cannot be expensed under the provisions of Rev. Proc. 69-21 [now superseded by Rev. Proc. 2000-50—Editor.], which permits all true software development to be expensed, even if the work does not constitute actual research and development.

• To consider website design similar to research and development under section 174 is stretching the human imagination beyond its normal limits.

• Insofar as an asset with a life beyond one year is being acquired, the cost of creating it should be capitalized and amortized.

• Because a website is similar to software and is used in conjunction with software (the browser and the server's software), these costs of development should be amortized over 36 months under section 167(f), beginning with the day that it is placed on the world-wide web.

• Some may argue that website design costs should be deducted as advertising expenses under section 162-1(a) of the Income Tax Regulations.

• But a website may be considered analogous to a billboard. See *Alabama Coca-Cola Bottling Co. v. Comm.*, T.C. Memo. 1969-123. In this case the court decided that billboards were assets with a life beyond one taxable year, even though the contents may change periodically. The cost of the billboard structure itself could not be deducted as a current advertising expense. A website can be considered a similar asset, in that the basic website design may endure from year to year, even though the contents on the website may change weekly, monthly, or annually. [End of text of IRS outline—Editor]

*Impact of Code Sec. 195.* Code Sec. 195 requires taxpayers who create a website for the purpose of entering a new trade or business to capitalize the costs of creating a website that are paid or incurred before the day active conduct of the trade or business begins. The rule, however, only applies to costs that would otherwise be deductible in the year paid or incurred. An election may be made to amortize these costs over a five-year period (or a longer period selected by the taxpayer) beginning in the month that the active trade or business begins (Code Sec. 195(b) prior to amendment by the American Jobs Creation Act of 2004 (P.L. 108-357)). See below for rules that apply underP.L. 108-357.

Thus, for example, otherwise deductible consulting fees may be considered an amortizable start-up cost under Code Sec. 195 in the case of a taxpayer that is starting an on-line business (as opposed to an existing taxpayer that is expanding its current business to include an internet site).

Importantly, any costs that are deductible under Code Sec. 174 (e.g., software development costs), are not considered start-up costs and may be currently deducted (Code Sec. 195(c)).

The IRS has ruled that depreciation deductions are not Code Sec. 195 start-up costs because an asset is not considered placed in service until a trade or business activity begins (IRS Letter Ruling 9235004, May 20, 1992). Consequently, depreciation on hardware and software purchased by a start-up internet company cannot begin until the business activity commences (presumably when the website is up and running).

Effective for amounts paid or incurred after October 22, 2004, taxpayers may elect to deduct up to $5,000 of start-up expenditures in the tax year in which their trade or business begins (Code Sec. 195(b)). The $5,000 amount must be reduced (but not below zero) by the amount by which the start-up expenditures exceed $50,000. For tax years beginning in 2010, the $5,000 and $50,000 amounts are increased to $10,000 and $60,000. This increase does not apply to subsequent tax years. The remainder of any start-up expenditures, those that are not deductible in the year in which the trade or business begins, must be ratably amortized over the 180-month period (15 years) beginning with the month in which the active trade or business begins. A similar rule applies to the organizational expenditures of corporations and partnerships. The dollar amounts, however, are not increased for tax years beginning in 2010 (Code Sec. 248(a) and Code Sec. 709(b)).

*Financial accounting.* The Emerging Issues Task Force of the Financial Accounting Standards Board (FASB) reached a consensus on Issue No. 00-2, Accounting for Web Site Development Costs, at a March 16, 2000, meeting.

*Zoning variance*

The costs of obtaining zoning variations were added to the depreciable basis of buildings constructed by a developer where the variations related to the buildings themselves. However, the cost of obtaining zoning changes that related to the use of the land were added to the basis of the land (*Maguire/Thomas Partners Fifth & Grand, Ltd., Depreciation*, 89 TCM 799, Dec. 55,935(M)).

## ¶ 126

## Additions and Improvements

Additions or improvements made to property, including improvements made by a lessee or lessor to leased property, are treated as separate depreciable assets for MACRS depreciation purposes (Code Sec. 168(i)(6); Reg. § 1.168(i)-8). In general, depreciation on additions or improvements (whether to real or section 1245 property) is computed in the same way as depreciation would be computed on the property added to or improved if such property had been placed in service at the same time as the addition or improvement. However, a 15-year recovery period applies to (1) qualified restaurant property (¶ 110) and qualified leasehold improvement property placed into service after October 22, 2004 and before 2018, (2) qualified retail improvement property placed in service after December 31, 2008 and before 2018; and (3) qualified improvement property placed in service after 2017. See below.

Depreciation on an addition or improvement begins in the tax year that it is placed into service; however depreciation cannot begin before the tax year that the property to which the addition or improvement is made is placed into service (Code Sec. 168(i)(6)(B)).

> ***Example:*** In January of the current tax year, the deck of a residential rental property that is depreciated under the ACRS rules is replaced and placed in service. The deck must be depreciated under the MACRS rules and is considered 27.5-year residential rental property placed in service in January because the building would be 27.5-year residential rental property if it had been placed in service in January of the current tax year. Note that the deck does not satisfy the requirements for any of the types of 15-year property.

See ¶ 125 for a discussion of the treatment of roofs.

The additions and improvements covered by this rule include those that are in the nature of structural components which are considered section 1250 (real) property—for example, walls and partitions or certain wiring and plumbing. See ¶ 127 which discusses the difference between structural components and personal property which may be depreciated without reference to the depreciation period of the building.

*Section 179 expensing for certain improvements*

Qualified real property (Code Sec. 179(e)) may be expensed if the taxpayer is eligible to claim the section 179 deduction. In the case of property placed in service in tax years beginning after 2017, qualified real property general consists of qualified improvement property as defined in Code Sec. 168(e)(6) and Reg.§ 1.168(b)-1(a)(5) (generally, improvements to the interior of nonresidential real property) placed in service after the nonresidential real property is placed in service and the following structural components to nonresidential real property placed in service after the nonresidential real property is placed in service:

- Roofs
- Heating, ventilation, and air-conditioning property
- Fire protection and alarm systems
- Security systems

For tax years beginning before 2018, qualified real property eligible for expensing under section 179 consists of 15-year qualified leasehold improvement property, 15-year retail improvement property, and 15-year restaurant improvements and buildings.

See ¶ 302 for a detailed discussion of qualified real property under section 179.

*Treatment of retired structural component*

A taxpayer may continue depreciating or claim a loss on the remaining basis of a retired structural component of a building such as a roof (or a retired component of section 1245 property). The loss is claimed by making a partial disposition election (¶ 162) (Reg. § 1.168(i)-8(d)(2)). However, if a loss is claimed the cost of the replacement component must be capitalized as a restoration even if the cost would otherwise be a deductible repair expense (Reg. § 1.263(a)-3(k)). Under prior law rules, a taxpayer was required to continue depreciating a retired structural component and could not claim a loss deduction. A replacement roof (or other replacement component) that is being separately depreciated is a separate asset and its retirement results in a retirement loss without making a partial disposition election. See ¶ 162 for a detailed discussion of retired components.

*Recovery of leasehold improvements in general*

The cost of a leasehold improvement placed in service after 1986 is recovered by the lessor or lessee, as applicable, under MACRS without regard to the length of the lease (Code Sec. 168(i)(8)(A); Reg. § 1.167-4). (For leasehold improvements placed in service before January 1, 1987, see Reg. § 1.167(a)-4 as in effect prior to amendment by T.D. 9636). Taxpayers depreciating leasehold improvements over the lease term are required to file an accounting method change under Rev. Proc. 2019-43, Section 6.13, as discussed at ¶ 77.

The lessee claims depreciation deductions for improvements paid for by the lessee (if such payments are not in lieu of rent as explained below) even if the terms of the lease provide that legal title belongs to the lessor at the moment the improvements are made. Legal title is not necessary to claim depreciation deductions (Reg. § 1.162-11(b); Reg. § 1.167(a)-4, first sentence prior to amendment by T.D. 9564 (remaining portion of regulation is outdated); *M.A. McGrath*, T.C. Memo. 2002-231, Dec. 54,873(M), aff'd *per curiam*, CA-5 (unpublished opinion), 2003-2 USTC ¶ 50,663). If the lessor pays directly for the improvement, or indirectly through an improvement or construction allowance pursuant to the terms of the lease, the lessor depreciates the improvement and the lessee depreciates any portion of the cost of the improvement that is not reimbursed (e.g., the cost exceeds the construction allowance). The lessee may not claim a loss deduction (Technical Advice Memorandum 201027045, March 15, 2010).

Pursuant to Code Sec. 109, a lessor's gross income does not include the value of improvements made by a lessee on a lessor's property that become the lessor's property upon the termination or forfeiture of the lease. However, this rule does not apply to the extent that the improvements represent the liquidation of lease rentals. Nor does it apply with respect to improvements representing rental income during the period of the lease (Reg. § 1.109-1).

If a lessee makes a capital expenditure in lieu of rent, the lessee may claim a current deduction for rent. The lessor is treated as receiving rent (taxable income) in the amount of the expenditures for the improvements and then using the rent to make the improvements. Thus, the lessor reports rent income and claims depreciation deductions on the improvements. In order for this nonstatutory exception to apply, the lessor and lessee must clearly intend that some or all of the lessee's capital expenditures are rent (Reg. § 1.61-8(c); *M.A. McGrath*, T.C. Memo. 2002-231, Dec. 54,873(M), aff'd *per curiam*, CA-5 (unpublished opinion), 2003-2 USTC ¶ 50,663).

If upon termination of the lease, an improvement made and depreciated by the lessee is not retained by the lessee, the lessee may compute gain or loss on the improvement by reference to the remaining adjusted basis of the improvement (see the Joint Committee Blue Book for the 1986 Tax Reform Act, p. 108).

*Retirements and abandonments of leasehold improvements.* The IRS had contended that a lessor must continue to depreciate an improvement made by the lessor that is a structural component of a building even if the improvement is retired, abandoned, or destroyed at the end of the lease term. The IRS, however, allowed a lessee who abandoned a leasehold improvement that is a structural component to claim a loss deduction. To address the rule that applied to lessors, the 1996 Small Business Job Protection Act (P.L. 104-188) added Code Sec. 168(i)(8)(B), which provides that a lessor "shall" take the adjusted depreciable basis of an improvement made by the lessor for the lessee into account for purposes of determining gain or loss if the improvement is irrevocably disposed of or abandoned by the lessor at the termination of the lease.

The Conference Committee Report for P.L. 104-188 clarifies that the provision does not apply to the extent that Code Sec. 280B applies to the demolition of a building, a portion of which may include leasehold improvements. Code Sec. 280B requires the capitalization to the land of amounts expended by an owner or lessee for the demolition of a structure as well as losses sustained on account of such demolition. An exception to the demolition loss rule applies if a building is placed in an MACRS general asset account. See ¶ 5.

An abandonment loss claimed by a lessor or lessee with respect to a leasehold improvement is reported on Form 4797, Part II, line 10 along with ordinary gains and losses from other Section 1231 assets (IRS Publication 225).

Final MACRS disposition regulations incorporate the rule of Code Sec. 168(i)(8)(B) and the similar treatment for lessees by providing that the disposition or abandonment of a leasehold improvement by a lessor or lessee on or before the termination of a lease is a disposition that generates a loss deduction (Reg. § 1.168(i)-8(c)(3)). However, an addition or improvement to an existing asset, such as a building, is also defined as an asset for disposition purposes if the addition or improvement is placed in service after the improved asset was placed in service (Reg. § 1.168(i)-8(c)(4)(ii)(D)). Thus, the disposition of an addition or improvement made by a lessee or lessor to a leased building is the disposition of a separate asset and should generate a loss deduction upon its retirement regardless of the time of retirement. Note that a lessee would normally be deemed to abandon a leasehold improvement at the termination of the lease. Also, since an addition or improvement is a separate asset for disposition purposes, the *partial* asset disposition election described in Reg. § 1.168(i)-8(c)(4)(ii)(D) is not allowed upon the retirement or abandonment of an entire addition or improvement that is a separate asset. If the partial asset disposition election is not allowed then the taxpayer is required to claim gain or loss upon disposition of the asset. The partial disposition election does not override any treatment required for demolition losses of a building under Code Sec. 280B (Reg.§ 1.168(i)-8(e)). See ¶ 162 for a discussion of dispositions of structural components, the partial disposition election, and effective dates.

*Qualified lessee construction allowances.* Pursuant to a safe-harbor, a lessee of retail space who sells tangible personal property or services to the general public may exclude from income cash or rent reductions received from a lessor if the cash or reductions are used to construct or improve "qualified long-term real property," which reverts to the lessor at the termination of a lease with a term of 15-years or less. Such property is depreciable by the lessor as nonresidential real property. The lessor must claim gain or loss on the improvement in accordance with Code Sec. 168(i)(8)(B), as described above, if the improvement is disposed of or abandoned at the termination of the lease (Code Sec. 110, as added by the Taxpayer Relief Act of 1997 (P.L. 105-34), effective for leases entered into after August 5, 1997; Reg. § 1.110-1; Rev. Proc. 2009-39; Rev. Proc. 2019-43, Section 6.08, relating to accounting method changes).

The exclusion only applies to the extent that the construction allowance is used to construct or improve "qualified long-term real property." Qualified long-term real property is defined as nonresidential real property which is part of, or otherwise present at, the retail space and which reverts to the lessor at the termination of the lease (Code Sec. 110(c)(1)). Qualified long-term real property does not include personal property or any other property that qualifies as section 1245 property under Code Sec. 1245(a)(3) (Reg. § 1.110-1(b)(2)(i)). See ¶ 116 for a discussion of section 1245(a)(3) property. A reporting requirement ensures that a lessor and lessee consistently treat the property funded with the construction allowance as nonresidential real property owned by the lessor (Code Sec. 110(d)).

The lease agreement must provide that the construction allowance is for the purpose of constructing or improving qualified long-term real property. The agreement does not need to provide that the entire construction allowance must be devoted to this purpose. However, exclusion only applies to the portion of the construction allowance that is spent on qualified long-term real property (Rev. Rul. 2001-20, I.R.B. 2001-18, 1143).

Code Sec. 110 is a safe-harbor. The legislative history of Code Sec. 110 indicates that no inference is intended regarding the treatment of amounts not subject to the safe harbor.

*15-year qualified improvement property*

A 15-year recovery period is assigned to "qualified improvement property" (QIP), effective for property placed in service after 2017. A retroactive technical correction by the Coronavirus Aid, Relief, and Economic Security (CARES) Act (P.L. 116-136 clarifies that a 15-year recovery period applies to QIP placed in service after 2017 (Code Sec. 168(e)(3)(E)(vii)). QIP is depreciated using the straight-line method and the half-year convention unless the mid-quarter convention applies.

As defined by Code Sec. 168(e)(6) and Reg. § 1.168(b)-1(a)(5), qualified improvement property generally means an internal improvement to nonresidential real property made by a taxpayer after the real property was placed in service. QIP, however, does not include improvements related to elevators and escalators, the internal structural framework, or an enlargement of the building.

See ¶ 127D, discussion item *16. Qualified improvement property placed in service after 2015.*

*15-year qualified leasehold improvement property placed in service before 2018*

Qualified leasehold improvement property placed in service before 2018 qualifies for a 15-year recovery period. In order to qualify as "qualified leasehold improvement property" the improvement must be made to the interior portion of nonresidential real property and the improvement must be placed in service more than three years after it was first placed in service by any person. The applicable depreciation method is the MACRS straight-line method (Code Sec. 168(b)(3)(G), stricken by P.L. 115-97). If the MACRS alternative depreciation system (ADS) is elected or otherwise applies, the recovery period is 39 years and the recovery method is the straight-line method (Code Sec. 168(g)(3)(B), stricken by P.L. 115-97). Whether or not ADS is elected, the applicable convention for qualified leasehold improvement property that is depreciable over 15 years is the half-year convention unless the mid-quarter convention applies.

This provision was not elective. If the requirements for qualification are met, then the improvement must be depreciated over 15 years using the straight-line method. A taxpayer, however, could effectively avoid the provision by electing ADS and depreciating the improvements over 39 years. However, the ADS election would also apply to any other MACRS 15 year property that the taxpayer happened to place in service in the same tax year (Code Sec. 168(g)(7)).

15-year qualified leasehold improvement property is defined the same way as the term "qualified leasehold improvement property" was defined in Code Sec. 168(k)(3), prior to amendment by P.L. 114-113, for bonus depreciation purposes with certain additional minor restrictions contained in Code Sec. 168(e)(6), prior to amendment by P.L. 115-97 and discussed below. The amendment to Code Sec. 168(k)(3), replaced the bonus depreciation category of "qualified leasehold improvement property" with the broader "qualified improvement category," effective for property placed in service after 2015 and before 2018. See ¶ 127D, discussion item #15 and #16. The definition of "qualified leasehold improvement property" formerly contained in Code Sec. 168(k)(3) was transferred, without substantive change, to Code Sec. 168(e)(6). An improvement made by the person who was the lessor of the improvement when the improvement was placed in service, is 15-year qualified leasehold improvement property (if at all) only so long as the improvement is held by that person (Code Sec. 168(e)(6)). An exception to the rule applies in the case of death and the transactions listed in Code Sec. 168(e)(6). See below.

The IRS has issued bonus depreciation regulations which provide guidance concerning the definition of qualified leasehold improvement property under Code Sec. 168(k)(3), prior to removal by P.L. 115-97 (Reg.§ 1.168(k)-1(c)). These regulations should apply equally to the definition for purposes of qualifying for the 15-year recovery period.

Under the bonus depreciation provision, qualified leasehold improvement property is any improvement to an *interior portion* of nonresidential real property if the following requirements are satisfied:

(1) the improvement is made under or pursuant to a lease by the lessee, any sublessee, or the lessor (a commitment to enter into a lease is treated as a lease for this purpose);

(2) the lease is not between related persons;

(3) the building (or portion that the improvement is made to) is occupied exclusively by the lessee or sublessee;

(4) the improvement is section 1250 property (i.e., a structural component); and

(5) the improvement is placed into service more than 3 years after the date that the building was first placed into service by any person (Code Sec. 168(k)(3), prior to amendment by P.L. 114-113; Reg.§ 1.168(k)-1(c)).

HVAC units located on concrete pads adjacent to large stand-alone commercial building used for retail sales and on the store's roof were not qualified leasehold improvement property because they were not located in the interior of the building (CCA Letter Ruling 201310028, October 9, 2012).

Improvements to residential rental property do not qualify. The building must be nonresidential real property (section 1250 property with a class life of 27.5 years or greater that is not residential rental property (Code Sec. 168(e)(2)(B)), such as an office building, retail store, or industrial building).

A commitment to enter into a lease is treated as a lease, with the parties to the commitment treated as the lessor and lessee (Reg. § 1.168(k)-1(c)(3)(vi)).

The lease may not be between related persons. Members of an affiliated group (as defined in Code Sec. 1504) are related persons. Persons with a relationship described in Code Sec. 267(b)are related persons. However, the phrase "80 percent or more" is substituted in each place that the phrase "more than 50 percent" appears (Reg.§ 1.168(k)-1(c)(3)(vi)).

A leasehold improvement which is section 1245 property may be separately depreciated over a shorter recovery period (usually 5 or 7 years depending upon the business activity in which the improvement is primarily used) under the MACRS cost segregation rules. Examples of section 1245 leasehold improvements include removable carpeting and removable partitions. Qualified section 1250 leasehold improvements to nonresidential real property would normally be considered structural components depreciable over 39 years in the absence of this new provision.

Expenditures for the following are not qualified leasehold improvement property:

(1) the enlargement (as defined in Reg.§ 1.48-12(c)(10)) of the building;

(2) elevators and escalators;

(3) structural components (as defined in Reg.§ 1.48-1(e)(2)) that benefit a common area; and

(4) internal structural framework (as defined in Reg.§ 1.48-12(b)(3)(i)(D)).

The term "common area" generally refers to areas used by different lessees of a building, such as stairways, hallways, lobbies, common seating areas, interior and exterior pedestrian walkways and pedestrian bridges, loading docks and areas, and rest rooms (Reg.§ 1.168(k)-1(c)(3)(ii)).

*Limitations on subsequent owners with respect to improvements placed in service by original lessor.* An improvement made and depreciated by the lessor when the improvement is placed in service can be 15-year qualified leasehold improvement property only so long as the improvement is held by the lessor (Code Sec. 168(e)(6)(A), prior to amendment by P.L. 114-113; Code Sec. 168(e)(6)(D), effective for property placed in service after 2015). This limitation does not apply for purposes of determining whether property is qualified leasehold improvement property eligible for bonus depreciation as defined in Code Sec. 168(k)(3), prior to amendment by P.L. 114-113, if placed in service before 2016. Effective for property placed in service after 2015 and before 2018, the "qualified leasehold improvement" category of bonus depreciation property is replaced with the "qualified improvement" category (Code Sec. 168(k)(3), as amended by P.L. 114-113, prior to removal by P.L. 115-97). Property which meets the definition of 15-year qualified leasehold improvement property will necessarily meet the definition of qualified improvement property. The definition of qualified improvement property (Reg.§ 1.168(b)-1(a)(5)) is much broader than qualified leasehold improvement property. See ¶ 127D, discussion item #33 and #33A.

This limitation prevents a subsequent purchaser of a building from using the 15-year depreciation period on leasehold improvements placed in service by the prior lessor-owner. For example, a subsequent purchaser is not entitled to conduct a cost segregation study and depreciate prior leasehold improvements over 15 years.

This limitation, however, is not triggered if the leasehold improvement is acquired from the original lessor by reason of the lessor's death or in any of the following types of transactions that qualify for nonrecognition treatment (Code Sec. 168(e)(6)(B), prior to amendment by P.L. 114-113; Code Sec. 168(e)(6)(E), as amended by P.L. 114-113, and prior to removal by P.L. 115-97):

(1) transactions to which Code Sec. 381(a) applies (relating to corporate acquisitions in transactions involving the liquidation of subsidiaries or certain qualified reorganizations);

(2) a mere change in the form of conducting the trade or business so long as the property is retained in the trade or business as qualified leasehold improvement property and the taxpayer retains a substantial interest in the trade or business;

(3) a like-kind exchange (Code Sec. 1031), involuntary conversion (Code Sec. 1033), or the sale of real estate which is reacquired in partial or full satisfaction of debt on the property (Code Sec. 1038) to the extent that the basis in the acquired leasehold improvement property is a carryover basis; and

(4) a transaction described in Code Sec. 332 (complete liquidation of a subsidiary), Code Sec. 351 (transfers to controlled corporations), Code Sec. 361 (exchanges of property solely for corporate stock in a reorganization), Code Sec. 721 (contributions of property in exchange for a partnership interest), and Code Sec. 731 (distributions of property by partnerships to partners) to the extent that the basis of the leasehold improvement property in the hands of the taxpayer is determined by reference to its basis in the hands of the transferor or distributor. The acquisition of the leasehold improvement property from the transferee or acquiring corporation in one of these transactions also does not cause the property to cease to be leasehold improvement property to the extent that the basis of the property in the hands of the taxpayer is determined by reference to its basis in the hands of the transferor or distributor.

Similar limitations also apply to the transfer of 15-year qualified retail improvement property as discussed below (Code Sec. 168(e)(8)(B)).

*Section 179 expensing.* Qualified leasehold improvement property retains its status as section 1250 property even though its depreciation period is reduced to 15 years. Although the section 179 expense allowance may generally not be claimed on section 1250 property, 15-year qualified leasehold improvement property placed in service in a tax year that begins after 2009 and before 2018 is a category of "qualified real property" that may be expensed (Code Sec. 179(f), prior to amendment by P.L. 115-97). Qualified real property placed in service in a tax year beginning after 2017 is redefined to mean qualified improvement property (Reg.§ 1.168(b)-1(a)(5)) and certain other property types (Code Sec. 179(e)). See the discussion relating to "Qualified real property" at ¶ 302 for rules and limitations.

*Bonus depreciation.* In addition to the 15-year recovery period for qualified leasehold property, bonus depreciation was available for qualified leasehold improvement property placed in service before January 1, 2016 (Code Sec. 168(k)(3), prior to amendment by P.L. 114-113). Effective for property placed in service after 2015 and before 2018, the "qualified leasehold improvement" category of bonus depreciation property is replaced with the "qualified improvement" category (Code Sec. 168(k)(3), prior to amendment by P.L. 115-97). Property which meets the definition of 15-year qualified leasehold improvement property will necessarily meet the definition of qualified improvement property. In general, qualified improvement property consists of improvements to the interior of nonresidential real property (Code Sec. 168(e)(6); Reg.§ 1.168(b)-1(a)(5)).

Qualified improvement property was removed as a separate category of bonus depreciation property by the 2017 Tax Cuts Act (P.L. 115-97). Bonus depreciation continues to apply to qualified improvement property placed in service after 2017 because it has a 15-year recovery period as the result of a technical correction (Code Sec. 168(e)(3)(E)(vii)) enacted by the Coronavirus Aid, Relief, and Economic Security (CARES) Act (P.L. 116-136).

See ¶ 127D, *15. Qualified leasehold improvement property placed in service before 2016* and *16. Qualified improvement property placed in service after 2015*

*Section 1245 and section 1250 recapture.* Since qualified leasehold improvement property and qualified improvement property retain their status as section 1250 property and depreciation is computed using the straight-line method, no regular depreciation deductions are subject to ordinary income recapture upon a sale or disposition. Bonus depreciation, however, is considered an accelerated depreciation deduction (Reg.§ 1.168(k)-1(f)(3)). Consequently, if the leasehold improvement property or qualified improvement property on which bonus depreciation is claimed is disposed of prior to the expiration of its 15-year recovery period, the amount of the bonus depreciation deduction and regular depreciation deductions that exceed the amount of straight-line depreciation that would have been allowed if bonus depreciation had not been claimed on the property using the straight-line method through the year of disposition is subject to section 1250 recapture. The instructions for line 26a of Form 4797 treat the computation of additional depreciation on section 1250 bonus depreciation property in the manner described in the preceding sentence. In the case of individuals, estates, and trusts, if the 50 percent bonus deduction was claimed, the unrecaptured straight-line depreciation on the remaining 50 percent of the basis is treated as unrecaptured section 1250 gain in an amount that does not exceed 50 percent of the gain. Unrecaptured section 1250 gain is subject to a 25 percent tax rate, as described at ¶ 488.

The basis of section 1250 property which is reduced by a section 179 expense deduction is treated as section 1245 property. Thus, the amount expensed under Code Sec. 179 on section 1250 property is subject to recapture as ordinary income under the section 1245 recapture rules to the extent of gain allocable to the amount expensed (Code Sec. 1245(a)(3)(C)). The IRS has ruled that any reasonable allocation methodology may be used to allocate gain to the portion of the property treated as section 1245 property and the portion treated as section 1250 property (Notice 2013-59). See ¶ 302 for details.

*15-year qualified retail improvement property*

The Emergency Economic Stabilization Act of 2008 (P.L. 110-343) created a new category of MACRS property—"qualified retail improvement property"—effective for property placed in service after December 31, 2008 (Code Sec. 168(e)(3)(E)(ix), and Code Sec. 168(e)(8)).

The categories of 15-year qualified retail improvement property, 15-year qualified leasehold improvement property, and 15-year restaurant property were eliminated by the Tax Cuts and Jobs Act (P.L. 115-97), effective for property placed in service after 2017. In place of these categories, a 15-year recovery period was assigned to "qualified improvement property" (Code Sec. 168(e)(3)(E)(vii) as added by the Coronavirus Aid, Relief, and Economic Security (CARES) Act (P.L. 116-136)). The CARES Act provided the 15-year recovery period in a retroactive technical correction. As defined by Code Sec. 168(e)(6) and Reg. § 1.168(b)-1(a)(5), qualified improvement property generally means an internal improvement to nonresidential real property.

Qualified retail improvement property placed in service before 2018 is treated as MACRS 15-year property and, accordingly, has a 15-year recovery period. A 39-year MACRS alternative depreciation system (ADS) recovery period applies if ADS is elected or required. The straight-line method must be used to depreciate qualified retail improvement property (Code Sec. 168(b)(3)(I), stricken by P.L. 115-97). The half-year convention applies unless the mid-quarter convention is applicable because the taxpayer placed more than 40 percent of the total basis of its depreciable property (other than residential rental and nonresidential real property) in service in the last quarter of its tax year.

Qualified retail improvement property placed in service after 2017 is treated as nonresidential real property and depreciated over 39 years using the mid-month convention.

This provision is not elective. However, if a taxpayer elects to depreciate all types of 15-year MACRS property that it places in service during the tax year using the MACRS alternative depreciation system (ADS), it may depreciate its qualified retail improvement property using the straight-line method, a 39-year recovery period, and the half-year or mid-quarter convention. In effect, the ADS election operates as an election out of the provision.

*Qualified retail improvement property defined.* The following requirements must be met in order to meet the definition of a qualified retail improvement (Code Sec. 168(e)(8)(A) and (C)):

- the property must be an improvement to an interior portion of a building that is nonresidential real property;
- the interior portion of the building to which the improvement is made must be open to the general public and used in the retail trade or business of selling tangible personal property to the general public (e.g., stock room in back of retail space does not qualify because it is not open to the general public (Joint Committee on Taxation, Technical Explanation of the Revenue Provisions Contained in the "Tax Relief, Unemployment Insurance Reauthorization, and Job Creation Act of 2010" (JCX-55-10), December 10, 2010));
- the improvement must be placed in service more than three years after the building was first placed in service by any person; and
- the improvement must be placed in service after December 31, 2008 and before 2018.

The following improvements are specifically disqualified from the definition of qualified retail improvement property (Code Sec. 168(e)(8)(C), stricken by P.L. 115-97):

- elevators and escalators
- internal structural framework of a building
- structural components that benefit a common area
- improvements relating to the enlargement of a building

These types of improvements are also excluded from the definition of a qualified leasehold improvement which is eligible for a 15-year recovery period as discussed above (Code Sec. 168(k)(3)(B), prior to amendment by P.L. 114-113, Code Sec. 168(e)(6)(B), as amended by P.L. 114-113). Thus, the definition of these terms provided in Reg. § 1.168(k)-1(c)(3) for purposes of the qualified leasehold improvement provision should apply equally to qualified retail improvement property.

*Internal structural framework.* Internal structural framework is defined to include all load-bearing internal walls and any other internal structural supports, including the columns, girders, beams, trusses, spandrels, and all other members that are essential to the stability of the building (Reg. § 1.48-12(b)(3)(i)(d)(iii); Reg. § 1.168(k)-1(c)(3)(v)).

*Common area.* A common area means any portion of a building that is equally available to all users of the building on the same basis for uses that are incidental to the primary use of the building. For example, stairways, hallways, lobbies, common seating areas, interior and exterior pedestrian walkways and pedestrian bridges, loading docks and areas, and rest rooms generally are treated as common areas if they are used by different lessees of a building (Reg. § 1.168(k)-1(c)(3)(ii)).

*Enlargement.* A building is enlarged to the extent that the total volume of the building is increased. An increase in floor space resulting from interior remodelling is not considered an enlargement. The total volume of a building is generally equal to the product of the floor area of the base of the building and the height from the underside of the lowest floor (including the basement) to the average height of the finished roof (as it exists or existed). For this purpose, floor area is measured from the exterior faces of external walls (other than shared walls that are external walls) and from the centerline of shared walls that are external walls (Reg. § 1.168(k)-1(c)(3)(iv); Reg. § 1.48-12(c)(10)).

Presumably, qualified retail improvement property must be section 1250 property (i.e., a structural component) even though this requirements is not specifically stated. Improvements to retail property that are section 1245 property should, therefore, continue to be eligible for a shortened recovery period under the cost segregation rules. Note that the definition in Code Sec. 168(k)(3), prior to amendment by P.L. 114-113, and Code Sec. 168(e)(6), as amended by P.L. 114-113, of a qualified leasehold improvement also does not specifically limit that provision to section 1250 property. Reg. § 1.168(k)-1(c), however, does impose this requirement.

The Joint Committee on Taxation states that for purposes of qualifying for the 15-year recovery period for retail improvement property, it is generally intended businesses defined as a store retailer under the current North American Industry Classification System (NAICS) (industry sub-sectors 441 through 453) qualify while those in other industry classes do not qualify. See http://www.bls.gov/iag/tgs/iag_index_naics.htm for the list. This information does not appear to have been previously provided to taxpayers. Applying this standard, businesses primarily engaged in providing services, such as professional services, health services, and entertainment services will not qualify. Examples of qualifying businesses are grocery, hardware, convenience, and clothing stores (Joint Committee on Taxation, Technical Explanation of the Revenue Provisions Contained in the "Tax Relief, Unemployment Insurance Reauthorization, and Job Creation Act of 2010" (JCX-55-10), December 10, 2010). The same information is restated in the Joint Committee's "Blue Book" explanation (General Explanation of Tax Legislation Enacted in the 111th Congress" (JCS-2-11, March 2011)).

*Improvement must be made by owner.* Qualified retail improvement property retains its status only so long as the improvement is held by the owner that made the improvement. The exceptions relating to acquisitions in certain nonrecognition transactions or by reason of the death of the original owner that apply to qualified leasehold improvement property also apply to qualified retail improvement property (Code Sec. 168(e)(8)(B), stricken by P.L. 115-97). See the above discussion of this rule as it applies to 15-year leasehold improvement property.

> ***Example:*** John Johnston owns a retail established and places a qualified retail improvement in service in 2015. In a later tax year, Johnson sells the building with the improvement to Fred Jackson. Jackson may not separately depreciate the improvement as 15-year qualified retail improvement property.

*ADS recovery period.* The MACRS alternative depreciation system (ADS) recovery period for qualified retail improvement property is 39 years if ADS is elected or required (Code Sec. 168(g)(3)(b), stricken by P.L. 115-97). The half-year or mid-quarter convention applies even if ADS is used to depreciate the property over 39 years.

*Bonus depreciation.* The bonus depreciation deduction allowed by Code Sec. 168(k) may not be claimed on qualified retail improvement property placed in service before 2016 unless it also qualifies as 15-year qualified leasehold improvement property (Code Sec. 168(e)(8)(D), prior to amendment by P.L. 114-113; Rev. Proc. 2011-26; CCA Letter Ruling 201203014, December 14, 2011).

In most cases, a 15-year qualified retail improvement will also qualify as a 15-year qualified leasehold improvement if the improvement is placed in service by a lessor or lessee (or sublessee) pursuant to or under the terms of a lease with an unrelated person. See "*15-year qualified leasehold improvement property,*" above.

Effective for property placed in service after 2015 and before 2018, the "qualified leasehold improvement" category of bonus depreciation property is replaced with the "qualified improvement" category (Code Sec. 168(k)(3), as amended by P.L. 114-113 and prior to being stricken by P.L. 115-97). Qualified improvement property consists of any interior improvement to nonresidential real property other than expenditures which are attributable to the enlargement of a building, any elevator or escalator, or the internal structural framework of the building (Code Sec. 168(e)(6); Reg. § 1.168(b)-1(a)(5)). The qualified improvement property does not need to be placed in service more than three years after the property was placed in service by any person. Property which meets the definition of 15-year qualified retail improvement property will necessarily meet the definition of qualified improvement property and be eligible for bonus depreciation if placed in service after 2015 and before 2018. After 2017, qualified retail improvement property is removed as a category of property. A 15-year recovery period, however, applies to qualified improvement property placed in service after 2017 (Code Sec. 168(e)(3)(E)(vii); Rev. Proc. 2020-25).

Qualified improvement property was removed as a separate category of bonus depreciation property by the 2017 Tax Cuts Act effective for property placed in service after 2017 (P.L. 115-97). Bonus depreciation applies to qualified improvement property placed in service after 2017 because it has a recovery period of 20 years or less.

See ¶ 127D, *15. Qualified leasehold improvement property placed in service before 2016* and *16. Qualified improvement property placed in service after 2015*

*Alternative minimum tax.* The straight-line depreciation deduction claimed on 15-year qualified retail improvement property is allowed in full for alternative minimum tax (AMT) purposes (Code Sec. 56(a)(1)(A)). The corporate AMT is repealed effective for tax years beginning after 2017.

*Section 179 expensing.* Although a 15-year recovery period applies, qualified retail improvement property does not lose its status as section 1250 property. Furthermore, although the Code Sec. 179 expense allowance is generally limited to section 1245 property (Code Sec. 179(d)(1)) an exception allows up to $250,000 of the cost of qualified real property (which is defined to include qualified retail improvement property, qualified leasehold improvement property, and qualified restaurant property) placed in service in a tax year beginning after 2009 and before 2016 to be expensed under Code Sec. 179 and applied to the overall $500,000 section 179 expense limitation that applied in those years (Code Sec. 179(f)(1), prior to amendment by P.L. 114-113). In tax years beginning after 2015, the $250,000 restriction on qualified real property is eliminated. Effective for property placed in service in tax years beginning after 2017, qualified real property is redefined to include qualified improvement property (Code Sec. 179(e)). Section 179 expensing applies to qualified improvement property without regard to its recovery period. See discussion above.

See "*Qualified real property*" at ¶ 302 for a discussion of section 179.

*Section 1245 and section 1250 recapture.* Qualified retail improvement property retains its status as section 1250 property even though its depreciation period is reduced to 15 years. Thus, upon a sale or disposition, no regular depreciation deductions are subject to recapture, since the regular depreciation deductions are computed using the straight-line method. However, any section 179 expense allowance claimed on section 1250 property, including 15-year qualified retail improvement property, is subject to recapture as ordinary income (Code Sec. 1245(a)(3)(C)). Recapture is limited to the amount of gain that is allocable to the basis of the property that was expensed (Notice 2013-59). See ¶ 302 for a discussion of the recapture rules where a Code Sec. 179 allowance was claimed. In the case of individuals, estates, and trusts, the amount of depreciation that is not recaptured as ordinary income is treated as unrecaptured section 1250 gain to the extent of the gain allocable to the basis of the property that is not expensed under Code Sec. 179. For the recapture of bonus depreciation claimed on qualified real property see ¶ 302. See ¶ 488 for a discussion of unrecaptured section 1250 gain.

*15-year qualified restaurant property*

See ¶ 110.

## ¶ 127

## Cost Segregation: Distinguishing Structural and Personal Property Components of Buildings

*The IRS has issued a comprehensive Audit Techniques Guide (ATG) developed to assist IRS examiners in their review of cost segregation studies (Audit Technique Guide for Cost Segregation, revision date 10/2016). The guide explains why cost segregation studies are performed, how such studies are prepared and what to look for when reviewing these studies. Although it is not an official IRS pronouncement and may not be cited as authority, specialists who prepare these studies, as well as practitioners who hire such specialists for their clients, will undoubtedly want to review this IRS guidance. The guidance includes property classification lists (section 1245 personal property vs. section 1250 structural components) and supporting authority for the classifications. Separate classification lists are provided for the gambling, restaurant, retail business, pharmaceutical and biotechnology, and auto dealership and manufacturing industries. These lists were initially released in the form of IRS Field Directives.*

*Selected classification lists are reproduced in as a Quick Reference Table in the appendix of this book.*

*The complete text of the Cost Segregation Audit Guide is available on the IRS website at http://www.irs.gov.*

Although component depreciation is not allowed under MACRS or ACRS, the Tax Court has ruled that items in a building that qualify as tangible personal property under the former investment tax credit (ITC) rules (as defined in Reg. §1.48-1(c)) may be separately depreciated under MACRS and ACRS as personal property (*Hospital Corp. of America*, 109 TC 21, Dec. 52,163). See Field Service Advice Memorandum 001310, June 20, 1994, for an example of the IRS's earlier contrary view.

If a building component is not personal property under the former ITC rules, then it is considered a structural component. In the case of new construction, a building's structural components are part of the basis of the building and not depreciated separately. If a structural component is added to an existing building then it is depreciated separately using the same method and period that would apply to the building if the building were placed in service at the same time as the structural component (i.e., as 27.5-year residential rental property or 39-year nonresidential real property under MACRS). See ¶ 126.

Under the pre-ACRS (pre-1981) rules, taxpayers could generally depreciate structural components separately based on the useful life of the component. Personal property status was primarily important for purposes of qualifying for the investment tax credit.

Structural components of a building are specifically excluded from the definition of tangible personal property by the investment tax credit regulations.

Reg. § 1.48-1(e)(2) (which was adopted in 1964 by T.D. 6731) provides:

> "The term 'structural components' includes such parts of a building as walls, partitions, floors, and ceilings, as well as any permanent coverings therefor such as paneling or tiling; windows and doors; all components (whether in, on, or adjacent to the building) of a central air conditioning or heating system, including motors, compressors, pipes and ducts; plumbing and plumbing fixtures, such as sinks and bathtubs; electric wiring and lighting fixtures; chimneys; stairs, escalators, and elevators, including all components thereof; sprinkler systems; fire escapes; and other components relating to the operation or maintenance of a building. However, the term 'structural components' does not include machinery the sole justification for the installation of which is the fact that such machinery is required to meet temperature or humidity requirements which are essential for the operation of other machinery or the processing of materials or foodstuffs . . . ."

It is important to note an item is not a structural component (section 1250 property) even if it is listed unless the item relates to the operation or maintenance of the building. For example, plumbing or electrical wiring that services a machine that is not related to the operation or maintenance of a building is considered unrelated to the operation and maintenance of the building and, therefore, is considered personal property.

The regulations do not define the term "operation and maintenance." Instead, examples of items that are generally considered related to the operation and maintenance of a building are listed. See Reg. § 1.48-1(e)(2), above. The regulations also list items that are "accessory to a taxpayer's business" and, therefore, not considered related to the building's operation and maintenance. See Reg. § 1.48-1(c), discussed below. When the operation and maintenance issue is in doubt, the manner of attachment and the likelihood of removal are decisive factors in determining whether the asset relates to the operation and maintenance of the building. The Courts generally apply the *Whiteco* permanency test described below in making this decision.

In Rev. Rul. 75-178, 1975 CB 9, the IRS ruled that the classification of property should be based "on the manner of attachment to the land or the structure and how permanently the property is designed to remain in place." In Rev. Rul. 75-178, the IRS reversed its prior position (Rev. Rul. 69-14, 1969-1 CB 26) that movable partitions were the functional equivalent of walls and, therefore, were structural components. It is clearly not the intent of Rev. Rul. 75-178 to replace the operation and maintenance standard set forth in the regulations. For example, a hinged door, even though much more easily removable than the partitions described in Rev. Rul. 69-14, is still considered by the IRS as a structural component because it relates to the operation and maintenance of the building.

The Tax Court in a memorandum decision which considered a cost segregation study conducted on an apartment building recently ruled that the operation and maintenance standard is applied by taking into account the type of building under consideration rather than merely a generic or shell building. For example, under this standard, in the case of an apartment building, items related to the operation and maintenance of an apartment building would be classified as structural components (*Amerisouth XXXII Ltd.*, TC Memo. 2012-67, CCH Dec. 58,975(M), discussed at ¶ 127A). This interpretation is considered by many commentators to contradict the standard as applied by prior case law.

The Tax Court in *Whiteco Industries* (65 TC 664, CCH Dec. 33,594) (¶ 127C) lists six factors that should be taken into account in applying the permanency test in the context of determining whether a *structure* should be considered *personal property or a building* (see ¶ 127C). These factors, however, are often used by courts in determining whether property which is attached to a building is a structural component. The factors are:

(1) Is the property capable of being moved, and has it in fact been moved?

(2) Is the property designed or constructed to remain permanently in place?

(3) Are there circumstances which tend to show the expected or intended length of affixation, i.e., are there circumstances which show the property may or will have to be moved?

(4) How substantial a job is removal of the property and how time-consuming is it? Is it readily movable?

(5) How much damage will the property sustain upon its removal?

(6) What is the manner of affixation of the property to the land?

The manner in which the permanency test is applied varies among courts, with the result that many decisions are conflicting and cannot be reconciled. Many decisions, for example, place little weight on the fact that an item of property can be readily removed, causing little or no damage to either the removed item or the structure to which it is attached. Instead, greater significance is placed on the fact that the property is intended to remain in place permanently. For this reason, doors, windows, tiling, and paneling, although readily removable, are considered structured components.

The characterization of property as personal under local law does not control its characterization as personal property for depreciation and investment credit purposes (Reg. § 1.48-1(c)).

With respect to the definition of tangible personal property, Reg. § 1.48-1(c) provides:

> "The term tangible personal property means any tangible property except land and improvements thereto, such as buildings or other inherently permanent structures (including items which are structural components of such buildings or structures). Thus, buildings, swimming pools, paved parking areas, wharves and docks, bridges, and fences are not tangible personal property. Tangible personal property includes all property (other than structural components) which is contained in or attached to a building. Thus, such property as production machinery, printing presses, transportation and office equipment, refrigerators, grocery counters, testing equipment, display racks and shelves, and neon and other signs, which is contained in or attached to

a building constitutes tangible personal property for purposes of the credit allowed by section 38. Further, all property which is in the nature of machinery (other than structural components of a building or other inherently permanent structure) shall be considered tangible personal property even though located outside of a building. Thus, for example, a gasoline pump, hydraulic car lift, or automatic vending machine, although annexed to the ground, shall be considered tangible personal property."

The above regulation incorporates Congressional intent to treat property that relates to a taxpayer's specific business rather than being adaptable to most commercial uses as personal property even though contained in or attached to a building. A Senate Finance Committee Report provides that assets "accessory to the operation of a business such as machinery, printing presses, transportation or office equipment, refrigerators, individual air conditioning units, grocery counters, testing equipment, display racks, and shelves etc.," generally constitute tangible personal property even though treated as fixtures under local law (S. Rept. No. 1881, 87th Cong., 2d Sess. (1962), 1962-3 C.B. 707, 722). The regulation above qualifies the rule by providing that structural components of a building (i.e., components relating to the operation and maintenance of the building) do not qualify.

Senate Report 95-1263, 1978-3 CB (Vol. 1) 315, 415, which accompanied the Revenue Act of 1978, states that tangible personal property includes special lighting (including lighting to illuminate the exterior or a building or store, but not lighting to illuminate parking areas), false balconies, and other exterior ornamentation that have no more than an incidental relationship to the operation or maintenance of a building, and identity symbols that identify or relate to a particular retail establishment or restaurant such as special material attached to the exterior or interior of a building or store and signs (other than billboards). The Report further states that personal property includes floor coverings which are not an integral part of the floor itself, such as floor tile generally installed in a manner to be readily removed (that is not cemented, mudded, or otherwise permanently affixed to the building floor but, instead, has adhesives applied which are designed to ease its removal), carpeting, wall panel inserts such as those designed to contain condiments or to serve as a framing for pictures of the products of a retail establishment, beverage bars, ornamental fixtures (such as coat-of-arms), artifacts (if depreciable), booths for seating, movable and removable partitions, and large and small pictures of scenery, persons, and the like which are attached to walls or suspended from the ceiling.

Applying these investment tax credit standards, the court in the *Hospital Corp.* case treated as depreciable personal property electrical systems and wiring allocable to hospital equipment (based on electrical load), telephone and communications wiring and equipment, removable carpeting attached with a latex adhesive, vinyl wall and floor coverings, folding wall partitions, plumbing connections for equipment, kitchen water piping, kitchen steam lines, kitchen hoods and exhaust systems, special plumbing for x-ray machines, and patient handrails. Lights, bathroom accessories, acoustical ceilings, and boilers (where the amount of use for operating equipment was not shown) were structural components.

The depreciation period for the property categorized as personal property was five years under MACRS as it fell within Rev. Proc. 87-56 Asset Class 57.0, relating to assets used in wholesale and retail trade or personal and professional services. The taxpayer was a hospital which provided personal and professional services. See

¶ 104 for a discussion of Asset Class 57.0. See ¶ 127B for rules in determining the depreciation period of personal property components of a building.

Note that personal property with no class life and for which no recovery period is assigned is treated as 7-year property under MACRS.

The IRS has issued an internal legal memorandum (IRS Letter Ruling 199921045, April 1, 1999) which sets forth the response that examiners should take to the Tax Court's decision. The memorandum does not dispute the holding of the court but aptly notes that "the determination of whether an asset is a structural component or tangible personal property is a facts and circumstances assessment . . . no bright line test exists."

Subsequent to the issuance of this memorandum the IRS acquiesced to the Tax Court's finding that the ITC rules applied in determining whether an item is personal property or a structural component but nonacquiesced with respect to the Tax Court's application of these rules to the items in question (I.R.B. 1995-35, 314, as corrected by Announcement 99-116, I.R.B. 1999-52, 763).

*Cost segregation studies.* The memorandum notes that a taxpayer bears the burden of determining the depreciable basis of equipment or assets that are considered personal property and sets forth standards for cost segregation studies. Additionally it states that an "accurate cost segregation study may not be based on non-contemporaneous records, reconstructed data, or taxpayer's estimates or assumptions that have no supporting records." In other words, taxpayers who are constructing buildings and plan to take advantage of this exception to component depreciation will need to maintain accurate records (including presumably architectural and engineering reports) that establish the items that constitute personal property and that properly allocate costs to these depreciable items. The memorandum also notes, with respect to buildings that are already in service, that a change in depreciation method (including a change in depreciation periods) is a change in method of accounting and requires IRS consent. The automatic consent procedures of section 6.01 of Rev. Proc. 2019-43 will apply unless the taxpayer claimed a tax credit, such as the Code Sec. 47 rehabilitation credit, on the building. See ¶ 75. Note that Rev. Proc. 2019-43 specifically requires a taxpayer to attach a statement of the facts and law supporting the reclassification of assets from Sec. 1250 property to Sec. 1245 property (Section 6.01(3)(b)(vii)).

The *Boddie-Noel Enterprises, Inc.* case (CA-FC, 96-2 USTC ¶ 50,627) illustrates the importance of an adequately documented cost segregation study. Failure to meet cost substantiation requirements led to the denial of most ITC claims with respect to various elements of remodeled and newly constructed *Hardee's* restaurant buildings. Similarly, in *Deseret Management Corporation*, U.S. Court of Federal Claims, 2013-2 ustc ¶ 50,459 (Jul. 31, 2013), the failure to document detailed descriptions and identification of assets resulted in denial of their reclassification. See, also, detailed discussion of *Amerisouth* case at ¶ 127A for a discussion of a failed cost segregation study.

Scores of firms, often working with engineering and architectural consultants, specialize in the provision of cost segregation studies. (Use the search term "cost segregation" on any internet search engine and count the hits!) It is not unusual for these firms to classify 20 to 40 percent of the cost of new construction as personal property with a five- or seven-year recovery period and land improvements with a 15-year recovery period. Depending upon the size of the construction project, the federal tax savings can easily pay for the cost of the study. In addition, there are usually state and local tax benefits associated with the reclassification of real property as personal property. Many firms will make an initial determination as to whether a cost segregation study is warranted at no cost.

An IRS Chief Counsel Advice ruled that a penalty may be on a cost segregation firm under Code Sec. 6701 for aiding and abetting an income understatement where its cost segregation studies apparently intentionally or due to extreme negligence misclassified 39-year real property as 5-year property. The penalty was $1,000 for each return filed by noncorporate taxpayers and $10,000 for each return filed by a corporate taxpayers that underreported income in reliance on the faulty studies (CCA Letter Ruling 201805001).

*Cost segregation studies on existing buildings—effect of purchase price allocation agreements.* Cost segregation studies are typically conducted in connection with new construction projects; however, they are also available with respect to acquisitions of existing structures and can be used to justify depreciation reclassifications in the case of previously purchased structures.

A taxpayer may be bound by a purchase price allocation agreement entered into at the time of the purchase of a group of assets that constitute a business under the rules for an applicable asset acquisition. Code Sec. 1060(a) generally provides that the agreement allocating purchase price among assets in an applicable asset acquisition is binding on the seller and buyer. The agreement may be unenforceable due to mistake, fraud, duress. In *Peco Foods, Inc.* (TC Memo. 2012-18, Dec.58,920(M), aff'd CA-11 (unpublished opinion), 2013-2 USTC 50,412, 522 FedAppx 840) a taxpayer purchased two poultry processing plants. The allocation agreement included with Form 8594 specifically allocated separate amounts of the purchase price to "buildings" and to machinery, equipment, improvements, and other property with recovery periods shorter than 39-years. The allocation agreement further provided that it applied "for all purposes (including financial and tax purposes)" and that the contract, documents, ect., "constitute the entire agreement between" the parties. A subsequent cost segregation study attempted to allocate a portion of the purchase price that was allocated to the buildings to additional equipment but the taxpayer was bound by the written allocation agreement. The adverse decision could clearly have been avoided if the cost segregation study had been conducted at the time of purchase and its results incorporated into the allocation agreement. Alternatively, the buyer and purchaser exceeded the requirements of Code Sec. 1060 by allocating the purchase price between real and personal depreciable property. Under Code Sec. 1060 a taxpayer is only required to allocate a portion of the purchase price to all depreciation property (real and personal) as a lump sum as Class V assets. Such an allocation would likely not have prevented a subsequent allocation of the Class V assets in a cost segregation study between buildings (39-year property) and other depreciable property with a shorter depreciation period.

*Tax Benefits of Cost Segregation*

Classification of building components as personal property will save federal taxes and increase cash flow by accelerating depreciation deductions that reduce income taxes during the early years of a buildings recovery period. The tax savings are further enhanced if the personal property components also qualify for bonus depreciation under Code Sec. 168(k). See below.

If a cost segregation study is conducted on an existing building, the unclaimed depreciation on personal property components that were previously classified as real property can be deducted as a negative Code Sec. 481(a) adjustment in the year change. The automatic change of accounting method rules of Rev. Proc. 2019-43, described in detail at ¶ 75, apply. Note that Section 6.01(3)(b)(vii) of Rev.

Proc. 2019-43 requires that a statement of the law and facts supporting the reclassification of each property item from real property to personal property must be attached to Form 3115.

An amended return may be filed to claim the benefits of a cost segregation study only if the building was placed in service in the tax year for which the amended return is filed and no returns for subsequent years have been filed. A taxpayer may also file Form 3115 in such as case (Rev. Proc. 2007-16, Section 4). A taxpayer who has filed two returns may only file Form 3115 because an accounting method has been adopted. See ¶ 75.

*Partial disposition election to claim loss on retired building components.* In addition to determining the depreciable cost of personal property components of a building, cost segregation studies will now be used to determine the cost of structural components and sub-components of a building for which a retirement loss may be claimed by making a partial disposition election under Reg. § 1.168(i)-8(d). Previously, it was only important to determine the cost of the separately depreciable personal property elements. Going forward, the partial disposition election gives taxpayers the opportunity to claim a retirement loss on the undepreciated portion of the cost of any retired portion of a building. Thus, a cost segregation study will now need to determine the cost of any potentially replaceable part of a building, such as the roof, windows, doors, lighting, etc. This partial disposition election is quite favorable provided that the replacement costs must be capitalized and cannot be claimed as repair expenses. Claiming a retirement loss on a replaced component will convert an otherwise deductible repair expense into a capital expenditure. Thus, for example, claiming a retirement loss on the undepreciated basis of an entire roof that is replaced by making a partial disposition election makes sense because the cost of the new roof needs to be capitalized even if the election is not made. However, the election should not be made to claim a loss on the undepreciated basis of shingles that wore out while owned by a taxpayer because the otherwise deductible cost (i.e., repair expense) of replacing only the shingles will need to be capitalized if the election is made. For the treatment of roof repairs see ¶ 125.

See ¶ 162 for a detailed discussion of the partial disposition election.

Taxpayers were allowed file an accounting method change to make a late partial disposition election to claim retirement losses on structural components that were retired in tax years beginning before 2014. This accounting method change had to be made no later than for the taxpayer's last tax year beginning in 2014 and filed no later than the extended due date of the taxpayer's 2014 return. For post-May 5, 2016 filings this change was last described in Sec. 6.10 of Rev. Proc. 2016-29 (change # 196). The change, however, was removed from Rev. Proc. 2017-30, which superseded Rev. Proc. 2016-29, as obsolete. See ¶ 77.

*Code Sec. 179 expensing.* Personal property components of a commercial building can qualify for the Code Sec. 179 expense allowance (¶ 300). The maximum deductible amount (dollar limitation) under Code Sec. 179 is $1,050,000 for a tax year beginning in 2021 and $1,080,000 for 2022. The applicable dollar limit is reduced by one dollar for each dollar of qualifying expenditures in excess of $2,620,000 for a tax year beginning in 2021 and $2,700,000 for 2022 (investment limitation). See ¶ 302. This generous investment limitation means that a taxpayer may expense up to $1,050,000 of the personal property elements of a commercial building placed in service in a tax year beginning in 2021 provided the total dollar value of the personal property elements in the building (and any other qualifying section 179 property placed in service during the tax year) do not exceed $3,670,000.

Prior to 2018 personal property components of a residential rental property *generally* do not qualify for the Code Sec. 179 allowance because property used in the provision of lodging was excluded from the definition of section 179 property. This rule no longer applies, effective for property placed in service in tax years beginning after 2017 (Code Sec. 179(d)(1)). See ¶ 302.

*Bonus depreciation.* 15-year land improvements and personal property elements of a building may qualify for MACRS bonus depreciation under Code Sec. 168(k). Bonus depreciable may be claimed even if the cost segregation study is for a building that the taxpayer previously placed in service provided that the personal property elements would have qualified for bonus depreciation in the placed-in-service year. See ¶ 127D.

*Alternative minimum tax.* If a taxpayer changes its accounting method to reclassify building components as separately depreciable personal property, any Code Sec. 481(a) adjustment taken into account for regular tax purposes needs to be recomputed for AMT purposes. Thus, it is possible that the reclassification of components as personal property can trigger an AMT liability. Corporations, however, are not subject to AMT in tax years beginning after 2017.

*Depreciation recapture.* Depreciation recapture (¶ 160) does not apply to MACRS real property since it is depreciated using the straight-line method. However, if the section 179 expense allowance or bonus depreciation is claimed on section 1250 property, such as qualified real property, depreciation recapture is required. See ¶ 302 for the definition of qualified real property.

Recapture applies to MACRS section 1245 property (e.g., personal property). Under the Code Sec. 1245 recapture rules, the depreciation claimed on personal property components of a building is taxed as ordinary income to the extent of gain allocable from the sale of the building to the personal property (assuming the personal property has not been retired or replaced prior to the sale of the building). The remaining gain, if any, is treated as section 1231 gain. Thus, a taxpayer who uses cost segregation will lose the benefit of the capital gains tax rates on an amount of gain equal to the depreciation claimed on the components of the building that are classified as section 1245 property. The negative impact is mitigated the longer that a building is held before it is sold or if gain on the building will be deferred in a section 1031 like-kind exchange.

*Passive activity losses.* The benefits of a cost segregation study are adversely affected if a taxpayer is subject to the passive loss limitations and there is insufficient passive income to offset the additional depreciation deductions generated by the study.

*Partnerships and partners.* Cost segregation studies are a useful tax savings technique for a partnership and its partners. For example, assume that a partnership that owns a commercial building conducts a cost segregation study six years after its formation and the acquisition of the building. A large section 481(a) depreciation adjustment may be obtained and the basis of short lived assets is reduced to zero (assuming a five-year recovery period for the personal property components). Further, if a new partner later purchases a partnership interest in that partnership, the new partner benefits from the study if a section 754 election is made because the new partner's 743 adjustment is allocated among all of the assets, including the short-lived assets with a zero basis. Sometimes a cost segregation study is conducted in conjunction with the sale of a partnership interest solely in order to maximize the tax savings for the new partner. As an extreme example, suppose a partnership owns a residential rental property and the property is fully depreciated. Although a cost segregation study would not benefit existing partners because the property is fully depreciated, a new partner with a section 743 adjustment in hand could benefit from the study by being able to allocate the adjustment among the assets identified in the study, including the short-lived assets. Thus, much of the adjustment could be recovered through depreciation deductions over five years (again, assuming a five-year recovery period). However, as a result of the reclassification, the original partners may eventually be disadvantaged by the requirement of ordinary income depreciation recapture on the building components that are reclassified as personal property.

*Energy credits.* Costs segregation studies may also be useful for purposes of identifying prior and current expenditures relating to heating and cooling systems, lighting systems, and the building envelope that qualify for energy tax deductions under Code Sec. 179D. In addition, the cost of previously capitalized major components which are currently deductible under the routine maintenance safe harbor may be identified through a cost segregation study (Reg. § 1.263(a)-3(i)). Rev. Proc. 2014-16 provides an automatic change of accounting method procedure to change to the routine maintenance safe harbor method of accounting and claim a negative (favorable) Code Sec. 481(a) adjustment for any amounts that were capitalized in prior years but which may be expensed under the safe harbor.

*Identification of previously disposed assets.* A cost segregation study will usually involve a review of a taxpayer's records to determine whether depreciable assets have been disposed of but are still being carried and depreciated on the books (e.g., tenant improvements or factory machinery and equipment). The remaining undepreciated basis of such assets may be claimed as a negative Code Sec. 481(a) adjustment.

*Compliance with repair regulations.* A cost segregation study may be expanded to determine prior compliance with the repair regulations. Amounts that were capitalized and should have been deducted as repairs, and vice versa, may be identified. For example, the cost of previously capitalized major components which are currently deductible under the routine maintenance safe harbor may be identified through a cost segregation study (Reg. § 1.263(a)-3(i)). Rev. Proc. 2014-16 provides an automatic change of accounting method procedure to change to the routine maintenance safe harbor method of accounting and claim a negative (favorable) Code Sec. 481(a) adjustment for any amounts that were capitalized in prior years but which may be expensed under the safe harbor.

*State and local real property taxes.* Cost segregation may also result in the reduction of state and local real property taxes by reducing building costs allocable to real property. In addition, nearly half of all states provide sales and use tax exemptions for tangible personal property used in a manufacturing process or for research and development. A cost segregation study will identify such qualifying personal property. Note, however, that these tax savings will depend upon the classification of the property as real or personal by applying applicable state law.

## ¶ 127A

## Cost Segregation: Specific Examples of Structural Components and Personal Property Components of a Building

*The IRS has issued a cost segregation audit guide which categorizes an extensive list of building elements as either section 1245 personal property or section 1250 structural components. See ¶ 127.*

As explained at ¶ 127, components of a building which qualify as personal property under the former investment tax credit rules can be depreciated over a shorter depreciation as personal property rather than real property. In the case of nonresidential real property, the depreciation period of the personal property component will generally depend upon the business use of the property. In the case of residential rental property, the applicable depreciation period is generally five years (Asset Class 57.0 of Rev. Proc. 87-56; Announcement 99-82, 1999-2 CB 244). See ¶ 127B.

The Amerisouth case, in which the Tax Court reviewed a cost segregation study conducted on an apartment complex, is considered separately at the end of this paragraph (*Amerisouth XXXII Ltd.*, TC Memo. 2012-67, CCH Dec.58,975(M)).

For examples of costs that may be separately depreciable as land improvements see ¶ 5. Land improvements are generally depreciable over 15 years using the 150-percent declining-balance method. See ¶ 110.

Following are examples of particular building components and whether they are treated as personal property or structural components (real property).

*Air conditioning.* See "*HVAC and air conditioning units,*" below.

*Air filtration systems.* Mechanical devices contained in a manufacturing facility such as blowers, blower housings, dust collectors, exhaust equipment, and air washers used to remove fumes, smoke, dust, and heat, as well as air make-up units used to replace air and heat, were related to the operation of the building as a whole and, thus, were structural components. However, air handling equipment and safety equipment (fire curtains, detection equipment, and explosion hatches) necessary to and used directly with a single machine or process such as paint spraying or welding or which protects a particular area against a hazard created by a single machine or process is tangible personal property (Rev. Rul. 75-78, 1975-1 CB 8).

*Carpeting.* Wall-to-wall carpeting installed in guest rooms, office space, bar areas and dining rooms was personal property and not a structural component. The carpeting was attached to the floor by hooking it to wood strips that were nailed to the perimeter of the walls (Rev. Rul. 67-349, 1967-2 CB 48). Similarly, with respect to carpeting attached to a floor with an adhesive where the carpeting could be removed and cleaned without damage (IRS Letter Ruling 7847028, August 23, 1978). In the *Hospital Corp. of America* case (109 TC 21, Dec. 52,163) carpeting attached with a latex adhesive was considered removable and, therefore, was personal property.

The controlling Senate Finance Committee Report for the 1978 Revenue Act states that easily removable floor coverings should be considered an item of personal property. Interestingly, the Report could be read to provide a blanket rule that all carpeting is personal property (S. Rep. 95-1263, 1978-3 CB 415) Specifically, the report states: ". . . floor coverings which are not an integral part of the floor itself such as floor tile generally installed in a manner to be readily removed (that is not cemented, mudded, or otherwise permanently affixed to the building floor but, instead, has adhesives applied which are designed to ease its removal), carpeting, . . . are considered tangible personal property."

The *Hospital Corp. of America* case (109 TC 21, Dec. 52,163) cites the Committee Report, which in the taxpayer's view represented a per se rule that carpeting is personal property, but analyzed the treatment of the carpeting using the ease of removability standard.

The LMSB Directive on Cost Segregation in the Restaurant Industry (see the Quick Reference Tables of this book) indicates that for purposes of the restaurant industry all carpeting is treated as not permanently attached and not intended to be permanent. It does not appear that the IRS intends this rule to apply to all industries, as its Cost Segregation Audit Techniques Guide (which was issued after the LMSB) indicates that carpeting may or may not be section 1245 property depending upon the specific facts and circumstances. The audit guide, however, does list carpeting as section 1245 property (citing the Hospital Corporation case as authority) in a table which categorizes building components as section 1245 or section 1250 property.

*Ceilings: suspended, acoustical, decorative.* Suspended acoustical ceilings are, in the IRS view, structural components (IRS Policy Position Paper, ACRS and ITC Suspended Acoustical Ceilings, October 31, 1991, reproduced in CCH IRS Positions Reporter at ¶ 160,045). See, also, ISP Settlement Guidelines for ACRS and Investment Credit for Suspended Ceilings reproduced in the CCH IRS Positions Reporter at ¶ 181,385. Note that the Tax Court, in *Hospital Corp. of America* (109 TC 21, Dec. 52,163), also ruled that acoustical ceilings are nondepreciable structural components. In *Boddie-Noel Enterprises, Inc.*, (CA-FC, 96-2 USTC ¶ 50,627) suspended ceilings were structural components. The Tax Court held similarly in *Metro National Corporation* (52 TCM 1440, TC Memo. 1987-38, Dec. 43,649(M)) even though the court conceded that the acoustical tiles could be readily removed and replaced. The court in *Metro* also ruled that the fluorescent lighting (prefabricated fixtures in light metal housings) installed as part of the ceiling was a structural component.

Decorative ceilings in a hotel/casino complex were sufficiently integrated into the overall design of the buildings to be considered structural components even though they were capable of being moved (IRS Field Service Advice 200203009, October 3, 2001). The ceilings consisted of ornamental polished gold and copper panels suspended from the finished ceiling or glued to soffits or lowered drywall ceilings systems. Suspension grids were hung by hanger wires from hooks or eyes set in the floor above or bottom of the roof, and attached to walls with nails or screws. Components, including lighting fixtures and air conditioning registers were placed on the grid. The ceilings hid plumbing, wiring, sprinkler systems and air conditioning ducts. By serving as a channel for the return air, the ceilings also operated as a component of the heating and air conditioning system.

In the *Hospital Corp. of America* case (109 TC 21, Dec. 52,163) acoustical ceilings were structural components. In IRS Letter Ruling 8102012 (September 29, 1980) suspended ceilings which included panels that could be removed and replaced, were structural components.

The asset matrix for the Cost Segregation ATG Industry Specific Guidance Chapters 7.2 for Restaurant and Chapter 7.3 Retail Industry (see Quick Reference Tables—Cost Segregation Matrixes for Casinos, Restaurants, Retail Stores, and Auto Dealerships in the index) show the asset term "Ceilings" as including all interior ceilings regardless of finish or décor. The term "ceiling" includes, for example, drywall or plaster ceilings, acoustic ceilings, suspended ceilings (including all hangers, frames, grids, and tiles or panels), decorative metal or tin finishes, kitchen plastic panels, decorative panels, etc. These are all considered § 1250 property and are to be recovered as § 1250 property over the 39 year life of the building.

*Doors.* Reg. § 1.48-1(e)(2) provides that doors (related to the operation and maintenance of a building) are structural components. The Courts have generally deferred to the regulation's classification. The fact that a door is easily removable should not on its own accord result in personal property classification—otherwise almost all doors would qualify as personal property. Doors generally are intended to remain permanently in place and are considered related to the operation of maintenance of the building.

Hotel room doors and a keycard locking system were structural components (IRS Letter Ruling 199924044, March 24, 1999 (released as a Written Technical Assistance document); IRS Field Service Advice 200203009, October 3, 2001).

An Eliason (brand name) lightweight double-action door with a window installed to prevent accidents in a heavily trafficked area between a serving line and kitchen was tangible personal property (*Morrison Incorporated*, 51 TCM 748, TC Memo. 1986-129, Dec. 42,963(M)). The decision is best supported on the basis of the specialized business needs exception described above and on the grounds that the door did not relate to the operation and maintenance of the building. The court stated that doors constitute a structural component only if they are a permanent part of the cafeteria building, so that their removal would affect the essential structure of the building.

In *La Petite Academy* (DC Mo., 95-1 USTC ¶ 50,193, aff'd CA-8 (unpublished opinion), 96-1 USTC ¶ 50,020), however, a district court found that a kitchen pass-through door, bypass doors used between classrooms, and a Dutch door that separated an entrance/reception area from children's classroom areas were structural components even though they were specially designed. The taxpayer made several "specialized business needs" arguments but the court concluded that the doors related to the operation and maintenance of the building.

Forty foot folding doors on an aircraft hangar were structural components. The doors related to the operation of the hangar by providing protection from the elements and vandalism (*J. McManus*, CA-7, 88-2 USTC ¶ 9623, 863 F2d 491).

Bank vault doors and bank record doors were not structural components but qualified as "equipment" under Reg. § 1.48-1(e) which was accessorial to the conduct of the banking business (Rev. Rul. 65-79, 1965-1 CB 26).

*Energy maintenance system.* An energy maintenance system installed in a building by a service provider to control all energy using systems (e.g., heating, cooling, lighting) was a structural component even though many of the components of the system could be easily removed (IRS Letter Ruling 8501009, September 28, 1984). The system was considered a component of a central air conditioning or heating system within the meaning of Reg. § 1.48-1(e)(2) which is definitionally a structural component regardless of ease of removability.

*Electrical distribution systems.* Certain property may service dual purposes. For example, electrical distribution systems may provide for the general power needs of a building (i.e., relate to the operation and maintenance of the building) and also provide power for specialized equipment that is not a structural component. The IRS now allows a percentage allocation of the cost in such instances.

The IRS initially opposed percentage allocations but lost several key court decisions.

The Seventh Circuit Court of Appeals ruled that 95 percent of the electrical load that was processed by a permanent electrical distribution system contained within a separate room in a corn milling factory was used to power specialized machinery that was accessory to the taxpayer's business (*Illinois Cereal Mills, Inc.*, CA-7, 86-1 USTC ¶ 9371). Therefore, 95 percent of the cost of system, which consisted of circuit breakers, transformers, power panels, switchboards, motor control centers, and associated wiring qualified for the ITC. The remaining five percent of the cost was attributable to electricity used to meet the building's general needs and, therefore, related to the building's operation and maintenance. A similar allocation between electricity for machinery and general use was made by the Tax Court with respect to an electrical distribution system in *Scott Paper Company* (74 TC 137, Dec. 36,920 (1980)).

Later, the Eleventh Circuit affirmed another Tax Court decision which held that the portion (percentage) of the primarily electrical system that was allocable to electrical power used by a cafeteria's food preparation equipment and appliances was personal property (*Morrison, Inc.*, CA-11, 90-1 USTC ¶ 50,034, 891 F2d 857, aff'g, 51 TCM 748, Dec. 42,963(M), TC Memo. 1986-129).

In *A.C. Monk & Co.* (CA-4, 82-2 USTC ¶ 9551), however, the Fourth Circuit ruled that a percentage allocation was improper. It looked at each individual component of a distribution system and determined whether that component was generally adaptable to uses other than the machinery to which it was designed to serve. "An electrical system providing power to machinery is a structural component if the system can feasibly be adapted to uses other than the specific machine it was designed to serve."

However, in a revised Action on Decision relating to the *Illinois Cereal Mills, Inc.*, case, the IRS decided that it will no longer challenge the functional (i.e., percentage) approach set forth in the *Scott Paper Company* case (Action on Decision, File No.: AOD/CC-1991-019, October 22, 1991).

An IRS Industry Specialization Program (ISP) Coordinated Issue Paper (reproduced in the CCH IRS POSITIONS REPORTER at ¶ 160,705) adopted the approach taken by the *A.C. Monk & Co.*, case with respect to mechanical service systems (electrical and plumbing) embedded or embodied within walls. However, this issue paper, which was decoordinated on March 3, 1992, appears to have been written before the AOD which authorizes the functional allocation approach.

For a more detailed explanation of the functional allocation approach, please see Chapter 8.1 - Electrical Distribution Systems of the IRS cost segregation audit guide. Chapter 8.1 is reproduced in the appendix of this book as a Quick Reference Table.

In the *L.A. Duaine* case (49 TCM 588, TC Memo. 1985-39, Dec. 41,845(M)), the Tax Court ruled that electrical outlets and conduits providing localized power sources for specialized restaurant equipment was personal property. Similarly, with respect to kitchen equipment hookups of a hotel/casino complex (IRS Field Service Advice 200203009, October 3, 2001). It did not matter that the electrical kitchen components were of a standard design rather than specially designed. However, electrical outlets located in guest rooms and bathrooms that were not specifically associated with particular items of hotel equipment were structural components.

In IRS Letter Ruling 8848039, various components of an exterior electrical distribution system (pine poles, aerial lines, transformers, meters, street lighting) used in connection with a residential rental complex were 15-year land improvements. These items were not classified as Rev. Proc. 87-56 Asset Class 49.14, Electric Utility Transmission and Distribution Plant because those classifications only apply to taxpayers that *sell* electricity and water.

The following material relating to electrical distribution systems is from the IRS cost segregation audit guide:

> Pursuant to *HCA* [Hospital Corporation of America—CCH], cost segregation methodologies previously used to allocate the cost of a building between ITC property and structural components likewise can be used for segregating § 1245 property from § 1250 property. However, this does not necessarily mean that an asset is exclusively either § 1245 property or § 1250 property; certain assets can contain characteristics of both code sections. Regarding primary and secondary electrical distribution systems, the court in HCA concluded that the portion of the cost of the primary and secondary electrical distribution systems

corresponding to the percentage of the electrical load carried to the hospitals' equipment constituted as § 1245 property, whereas the portion corresponding to building operations constituted as § 1250 property. As a result of the ruling in HCA, the Tax Court followed its precedent in *Morrison, Inc. v. Commissioner*, T.C. Memo. 1986-129, and *Scott Paper Co. v. Commissioner*, 74 TC 137 (1980).

In *Scott Paper*, the court focused on the ultimate uses of power at the taxpayer's facility and distinguished the power used in the overall operation or maintenance such as lighting, heating, ventilation and air-conditioning of the building from the power used to operate the taxpayer's machinery. It held that items which occur in an unusual circumstance and do not relate to the operation or maintenance of a building should not be structural components despite being listed in Treas. Reg. § 1.48-1(e)(2). To the extent that the primary electric carried electrical loads to be used for the taxpayer's production processes or other such qualifying uses, the investment credit was allowed for the primary electric improvements; to the extent that the primary electric related to the overall operation or maintenance of buildings, they were structural components of such buildings such that they did not qualify as tangible personal property for purposes of the ITC. This became known as the functional allocation approach. Hence, the court made an allocation of the facility's primary electric between § 1245 property and § 1250 property.

In *Morrison*, the court followed the functional allocation approach from *Scott Paper* and held that the electrical distribution systems were not structural components to the extent of the load percentages that were carried to equipment (§ 1245 property). On appeal, 891 F.2d 857 (11th Cir. 1990), the Circuit Court affirmed the decision in the Tax Court. It also made three broad announcements with regard to the electrical distribution system issue. First, taxpayers can claim ITC on a percentage basis. Second, it adopted the Tax Court's method of focusing on the ultimate use of electricity distributed with regard to the electrical system. Third, the Tax Court's method is consistent with the ITC's purpose to provide an incentive for businesses to make capital contributions. Subsequent to the Eleventh Circuit's opinion in Morrison, the Service issued AOD 1991-019 in which it stated that the Service would not challenge the functional allocation approach set forth in *Scott Paper* to determine the eligibility of electrical systems of a building to qualify as § 38 property. For a more detailed explanation of the functional allocation approach, please see Chapter 8.1 - Electrical Distribution Systems." [Chapter 8.1 is reproduced in the appendix of this book as a Quick Reference Table—CCH.]

Case law has extended the reasoning of *Scott Paper* to such items as electrical wiring, outlet receptacles, electrical connectors, telephone connection equipment, fire protection systems, water piping and lines, drain lines, gas lines, and plumbing and gas connectors. See *Amerisouth*, supra, *HCA*, supra; *Morrison*, supra; *Texas Instruments, Inc. v. Commissioner*, T.C. Memo 1992-306; *Duaine v. Commissioner*, T.C. Memo.1985-39. Please note, however, that the functional allocation approach is only applied to a building's primary and secondary electrical distribution systems.

*Exterior ornamentation.* False balconies and other exterior ornamentation that has no more than an incidental relationship to the operation and maintenance of a building may qualify as personal property. However, a mansard roof system installed on a day care center was a structural component (*La Petite Academy*, DC Mo., 95-1 USTC ¶ 50,193, aff'd, CA-8 (unpublished opinion), 96-1 USTC ¶ 50,020). The mansard roof related to the operation and maintenance of the building because it protected various building components from water, snow, wind, and moisture damage.

Decorative facades placed around the entire exterior of a hotel/casino complex were structural components (IRS Field Service Advice 200203009, October 3, 2001). The facades consisted of a synthetic plaster, or stucco, that was cemented or bolted on in the form of a panel to the frames of the exterior walls of the buildings. They were not readily removable, designed to withstand an 85 mph wind load, and provided a barrier to the outside elements. Their removal would expose other building elements to degradation. The facades were designed and constructed with the expectation that they would remain in place indefinitely.

*Fire detection and security protection systems.* Fire protection systems are generally considered related to the operation and maintenance of a building and, accordingly, are section 1250 property. However, detachable smoke detectors and fire extinguishers are personal property.

Fire sprinklers and fire escapes are specifically categorized as structural components by Reg. § 1.48-1(e)(2), assuming they relate to the operation and maintenance of the building.

An automatic fire protection system which had a variety of components, each of which could be mechanically removed, was a structural component because it was designed to remain in place permanently and also because it was an integral part of the operation of the building. The system was viewed as including all component parts. Therefore, the computer which controlled the system was a structural component even though freestanding and transportable (Rev. Rul. 77-362, 1977-2 CB 8; G.C.M. 37070, March 30, 1977). Similarly, with respect to a fire detection system and security (burglary) detection system installed in the building of a service provider's customer even though the components of the systems, with the exception of wiring, were easily removed or detached from walls, ceilings, and other locations when a protection contract was terminated (IRS Letter Ruling 8501009, September 28, 1984). In spite of this private letter ruling, most cost segregation specialists treat security systems (e.g., cameras and other detachable or removable components) as personal property. Security systems are not considered related to the operation or maintenance of a building.

In *La Petite* (DC Mo., 95-1 USTC ¶ 50,193, aff'd, CA-8 (unpublished opinion), 96-1 USTC ¶ 50,020), the court ruled that a fire protection system consisting of horns, an alarm control panel, magnetic holder/closers on kitchen doors, emergency lighting fixtures, heat and smoke detectors, and exit light fixtures were structural components relating to the operation and maintenance of the building.

A fire protection system related to a single item of machinery or equipment, however, is personal property (Rev. Rul. 75-78, 1975-1 CB 8).

Section 1250 fire detection and security systems qualify for expensing under Code Sec. 179 as a type of "qualified real property" if placed in service in a tax year beginning after 2017 on nonresidential real property after the nonresidential real property is placed in service (Code Sec. 179(e)). See ¶ 302.

*Floors and foundations, concrete.* A concrete floor is generally a structural component. The Tax Court held that modifications to the slab behind restaurant counters in the form of a raised perimeter on which storage shelves were placed and sloped drainage basins were not personal property (*L.A. Duaine,* 49 TCM 588, TC Memo. 1985-39, Dec. 41,845(M)).

A 38-inch reinforced-concrete floor designed to withstand the weight of 50 to 2,000 ton stamping presses was considered personal property because it was considered a part of the machinery or equipment. Similarly, with respect to press rails and girders that supported the presses (Rev. Rul. 79-183, 1979-1 CB 44).

*Floors, raised.* A raised floor was a structural component. The floor was constructed when the building was constructed and stood about two feet above an unfinished floor. The space was used to facilitate the installation of wiring, plumbing, and ventilation for computers and other equipment. Removal of the raised floor would necessitate a major renovation of the interior of the building (IRS Field Service Advice 200110001, September 13, 2000, rev'g, upon reconsideration, IRS Field Service Advice 200033002, April 17, 2000). In contrast, a raised floor described in Rev. Rul. 74-391 (1974-2 CB 9) was personal property. There, the raised floor was installed over an existing floor. Its removal would have returned the building to its original condition and would not have necessitated extensive renovation.

*Generators, emergency power.* A casino's emergency power system which consisted of two emergency standby generators with associated fuel tanks, feeder lines, alternator and controls, and battery powered lighting for critical operations was personal property (Field Service Advice Memorandum 200203009, October 3, 2001). Apparently, the personal property classification applied because the systems operated the building's "emergency/safety features" and building equipment that was personal property. The IRS considered the systems as "accessory" to the conduct of the business and unrelated to the building's operation. However, the ruling takes the position that if a percentage of the power generators' output is attributable to building operations, then that percentage of the generators' cost is depreciable as a structural component.

In the *Hospital Corporation of America* case (109 TC 21, Dec. 52,163), the parties stipulated that emergency power generators were accessory to the conduct of the hospital's business and, therefore, were personal property.

*Handrails.* The IRS considers handrails and banisters as safety features related to the operation and maintenance of a building and, therefore, classifies these devices as structural components (IRS Letter Ruling 6612301720A, December 30, 1966). The Tax Court in the *Hospital Corp. of America* case (109 TC 21, Dec. 52,163), apparently agreed with this characterization but determined that handrails placed in corridors to assist hospital patients served a specialized business need and, therefore, constituted personal property.

*HVAC and air conditioning units.* All components (whether in, on, or adjacent to a building) of a central air-conditioning or heating system including motors, compressors, pipes and ducts are treated as structural components unless the sole justification for the installation is to meet the temperature or humidity requirements essential for the operation of other machinery or the processing of foodstuffs (Reg. § 1.48-1(e)(2)). For example, special air conditioning units which cool rooms dedicated to computer equipment should qualify for separate depreciation as personal property.

The sole justification test is narrowly construed. Air conditioning units installed by a grocery store did not satisfy the sole justification test even if the sole purpose of their installation was to protect foodstuffs from spoilage caused by high humidity because the store was not engaged in the processing of foodstuffs within the meaning of the regulation (*Circle K Corporation*, 43 TCM 1524, TC Memo. 1982-298, Dec. 39,058(M)).

The IRS maintains that HVAC units (heating, ventilating, and air conditioning systems) located in retail grocery stores or supermarkets that provide a comfortable temperature for customers as well meeting the temperature and humidity requirements of open front freezers are structural components of the building since they fail to meet the "sole justification" test of the regulations (IRS Policy Position Paper, Heating, Ventilating, and Air Conditioning (HVAC) Systems ITC, October 31, 1991, reproduced in CCH IRS POSITIONS REPORTER at ¶ 160,255). The IRS will not follow a Tax Court's contrary decision, which found that the test was satisfied where the HVACs had to be installed in order to maintain a building temperature that would allow the store's open front frozen food display cases to operate properly (*Piggly Wiggly Southern, Inc.*, 84 TC 739, Dec. 42,039, aff'd CA-11, 86-2 USTC ¶ 9789). In the *Boddie-Noel Enterprises* case (CA-FC, 96-2 USTC ¶ 50,627, no portion of the cost of a HVAC unit in a restaurant was eligible for the ITC. The taxpayer argued that the unit met the sole justification test with respect to cooling provided in the kitchen area but the court ruled that one of the primary purposes was to provide a comfortable working area for employees).

It is the IRS's position that HVAC units located in retail stores or supermarkets that serve the building and that do not exclusively serve the freezers and refrigerators within the store are structural components of the building depreciable over 39 years. However, the "sole justification" test specified in the regulations allows retailers to treat separate HVAC units that exclusively serve freezers and refrigerators as personal property depreciable over 5 years (IRS Retail Audit Technique Guide (3/5/21)).

The term "central air conditioning or heating system" is not restricted to mean a system that cools or heats an entire building. The term also includes any air conditioning or heating or combination system which consists of two or more units, having accessory ducts, connections and other equipment necessary to make the equipment functional, regardless of where located or the manner of attachment (Rev. Rul. 67-359, 1967-2 CB 9).

Portable window air conditioning units and portable plug-in heaters are section 1245 personal property (Rev. Rul. 75-77, 1975-1 CB 7). Effective for tax years beginning on or after January 1, 2016, portable air conditioning units and heaters qualify for the Code Sec. 179 expense allowance. However, portable units placed in service in residential rental property do not qualify for expensing unless placed in service in a tax year beginning after 2017. Portable units were previously excluded from expensing under section 179 (Code Sec. 179(d)(1), prior to amendment by P.L. 114-113). See "*Section 1245(a)(3) property defined*" at ¶ 302.

HVACs for nonresidential real property placed in service after the building is placed in service qualify for expensing under section 179 as qualified real property, effective for property placed in service in tax years beginning after 2017. See ¶ 302.

Interior portions of HVAC systems that are structural components (i.e., not five-year property under the sole justification test) are allowed a 15-year recovery period rather than a 39-year straight-line if they are qualified leasehold improvement property (for placed in service before 2018) (¶ 126) or qualified improvement property (for property placed in service after 2017) (¶ 126). HVAC units placed in service after 2015 may also be eligible for expensing under Code Sec. 179 as qualified real property (¶ 302).

*Keycard locking system.* A keycard door locking system installed to replace key locks on hotel doors was classified as a structural component depreciable over 39 years as nonresidential real property because the locking system was an integral part of a structural component (viz., the door) (IRS Letter Ruling 199924044, March 24, 1999 (released as a Written Technical Assistance document); IRS Field Service Advice 200203009, October 3, 2001).

*Lighting, interior and exterior.* Lighting fixtures relating to the operation and maintenance of a building are structural components (Reg. § 1.48-1(e)(2)). Security lighting mounted flush with a building's soffit, grow lights for plants mounted in the interior ceiling, and exterior pedestal lights mounted to a building's foundation to highlight landscaped areas and shrubbery or aid in the growth of plants were personal property since they only "incidentally" related to the operation of the building (*Metro National Corporation*, 52 TCM 1440, TC Memo. 1987-38, Dec. 43,649(M)).

The *Metro* decision relied on Senate Committee Report language which explains that personal property includes "special lighting (including lighting to illuminate the exterior of a building or store, but not lighting to illuminate parking areas), false balconies, and other exterior ornamentation that have no more than an incidental relationship to the operation and maintenance of a building . . . " (S. Rep. No. 95-1263 (1978), 1978-3 CB 315, 415).

With respect to the exterior security lighting, the Metro court provided as an additional reason for personal property classification, its belief that the lighting was "accessory to a business" since its purpose was to prevent unauthorized departures by psychiatric patients who resided in the building and reassure area residents with respect to security.

The court in *Metro*, however, also ruled that the fluorescent lighting (prefabricated fixtures in light metal housings) installed as part of an acoustical tile ceiling was a structural component.

If lighting serves both a decorative purpose and a function related to the operation and maintenance of the building it has been classified as a structural component. For example, in La Petite Academy, above, lighting which washed the exterior walls during the night time hours, thus making the building highly visible to passersby and, thereby providing passive advertising, was a structural component because the lighting was also used to "directly" light the walkways around the building. Lighting relating to building accessibility was, in the court's view, related to its operation and maintenance (*La Petite Academy*, DC Mo., 95-1 USTC ¶ 50,193, aff'd, CA-8 (unpublished opinion), 96-1 USTC ¶ 50,020).

In *L.A. Duaine* (49 TCM 588, TC Memo. 1985-39, Dec. 41,845(M)), interior and exterior ornamental lighting fixtures at a Taco Bell restaurant which provided the only artificial illumination in the customer eating area and along the walkways to the building related to the operation and maintenance of the building (i.e., were structural components).

Emergency lighting in a cafeteria that was required by state law and would enable customers to finish their meals in the event of a power outage was personal property (*Morrison Incorporated*, 51 TCM 748, Dec. 42,963(M) (1986)). The court characterized the emergency lighting as "special lighting" that was "accessory" to the taxpayer's business and, therefore, excepted from the general rule of the regulation which it deemed to apply to the cafeteria's "basic lighting." The lighting was also easily removable. The lighting consisted of ceiling and wall mounted fixtures, batteries, and connections to the electrical system that charged the batteries.

The court also ruled that chandeliers, decor wall lights, and dimmers were "special lighting," accessory to the cafeteria business, readily removable, and unrelated to the operation and maintenance of the building. The lighting was not a major source of lighting in the cafeteria (15-watt bulbs were used) and merely incorporated the taxpayer's decorative motif and complemented the interior design of the cafeteria.

In *Consolidated Freightways* (CA-9, 83-1 USTC ¶ 9420, 708 F2d 1385), the Ninth Circuit ruled that lighting fixtures were an integral part (structural component) of loading docks. The lighting was designed as a permanent feature and its removal would detract significantly from the usefulness of the dock's operations.

In an IRS Field Service Advice (IRS Field Service Advice 200203009, October 3, 2001), basic illumination in a hotel/casino complex was provided by recessed lighting (a structural component). However, decorative lighting fixtures, including chandeliers, wall sconces, track spot lighting, torch lighting, and wall wash fixtures were "special lighting" that was only incidental to the operation or maintenance of the building.

*Molding, millwork, trim, finish carpentry, paneling.* Detailed crown moldings for ceilings, ornate wall paneling systems, and lattice work for walls and ceilings which were manufactured for a hotel/casino complex were personal property (IRS Field Service Advice 200203009, October 3, 2001). This millwork easily removable and not integrated into the design or construction of the building in any way. Although its removal would affect the appearance of the buildings, it would not affect their operation in any way.

In the *Morrison* case (CA-11, 90-1 USTC ¶ 50,034, 891 F2d 857, aff'g, 51 TCM 748, TC Memo. 1986-129, Dec. 42,963(M)), lattice millwork and decor window treatments were personal property. These items served a decorative purpose and could be removed at little cost without permanently damaging the walls or ceilings.

*Partitions and walls.* In determining whether a partition is a structural component the courts generally focus on the issue of movability. The controlling Senate Finance Committee Report to the 1978 Revenue Act states that "movable and removable" partitions are personal property (S. Rep. No. 95-1263 (1978), 1978-3 CB 315, 415).

Movable partitions installed in an office building were personal property (*Minot Federal Savings & Loan Assn.*, CA-8, 71-1 USTC ¶ 9131, 435 F2d 1368). The partitions did not bear any structural load. They were installed by fastening a channel to the floor and ceiling, putting the partitions in and fastening them. They could be moved from floor to floor or building to building and stored when not in use.

A movable partition system consisting of ceiling height and glazed rail height partitions used to divide floor space into offices, rooms, and work areas was personal property (*King Radio Corporation, Inc.*, CA-10, 73-2 USTC ¶ 9766, 486 F2d 1091). These partitions were also fastened to floor and ceiling channels. The court ruled that Rev. Rul. 69-14 (1969-1 CB 26) incorrectly treated movable partitions as structural components.

In light of the preceding decisions, the IRS revoked its position with respect to movable partitions (Rev. Rul. 75-178, 1975-1 CB 9, revoking Rev. Rul. 69-14, 1969-2 CB 26).

However, "storefront partitions" which separated office space from an atrium were structural components even though the partitions could be rearranged. If the partitions were removed or eliminated, the offices of the tenant doctors and dentists on all three floors would open onto the atrium without any way of closing or otherwise securing the offices. Without the storefront partitions the building could not reasonably operate for its intended purpose as an office space rental property. There was an intention that the partitions remain permanently in place (although reconfigurations were possible) (*Metro National Corporation*, 52 TCM 1440, TC Memo. 1987-38, Dec. 43,649(M)).

A steel partition which separated two abutting metal aircraft hangars (i.e., in effect serving as the back wall of each hangar) was a structural component. Although removable, it added to the strength of the structure and, thus, related to the operation of the building (*J. McManus*, CA-7, 88-2 USTC ¶ 9623, 863 F2d 491).

Wall paneling, including gypsum board or dry wall, is normally considered a structural component. Alliance wall panels (a wall panel with a porcelain enamel surface laminated to gypsum board) used by a day care center in place of regular wall panels to take advantage of its qualities as a writing and magnetic surface were structural components because they could not be readily removed (*La Petite Academy*, DC Mo., 95-1 USTC ¶ 50,193, aff'd, CA-8 (unpublished opinion), 96-1 USTC ¶ 50,020).

Walls (ceiling height dry wall nailed or screwed on a frame of 2 × 4 studs) installed in shopping centers to meet the requirements of tenants were structural components. The walls were destroyed and not reusable when removed (*Dixie Manor, Inc.*, DC Ky., 79-2 USTC ¶ 9469, aff'd, per curiam, CA-6, 81-1 USTC ¶ 9332).

Zip type drywall partition systems were personal property. The partitions were designed and constructed to be movable. They also remained in substantially the same condition after removal as before and can be reused or stored. In addition, removal did not cause any substantial damage to the partition or to the building (IRS Letter Ruling 201404001, August 23, 2013).

*Plumbing and wiring.* Plumbing and wiring that relates to the operation and maintenance of a building is a structural component (Reg. § 1.48-1(e)(2)). Permanently installed plumbing that serviced a cafeteria's kitchen equipment and machinery did not relate to the operation and maintenance of the cafeteria building and, therefore, was personal property (*Morrison Incorporated*, 51 TCM 748, Dec. 42,963(M) (1986)).

Plumbing and wiring may relate to the general operation and maintenance of a building and also service specialized equipment. In this case, a percentage allocation of cost should be made. See "*Electrical Distribution Systems*," above. If plumbing or wiring only services specialty equipment or machinery, then the entire cost may be treated as personal property.

A sewage disposal system, including tanks and motors located some distance from a shopping center and connected to the building only with pipes, was a structural component of the building because it related to its operation and maintenance. The unit, although capable of being removed, was inherently permanent since it was installed underground (*C.C. Everhart*, 61 TC 328, Dec. 32,241 (1973)).

*Restrooms.* Restroom accessories have generally been considered structural components on the grounds that they relate to the operation of the building. Vanity cabinets, counters, paper towel dispensers, electrical hand dryers, cup dispensers, purse shelves, toilet tissue holders, stainless steel soap dispensers and holders, sanitary napkin dispensers, waste receptacles, coat hooks, grab bars for the handicapped, and framed mirrors with shelves and ashtrays in employee and customer cafeteria restrooms were structural components (*Morrison Incorporated*, 51 TCM 748, Dec. 42,963(M) (1986)). Similarly, in *La Petite Academy* (DC Mo., 95-1 USTC ¶ 50,193, aff'd, CA-8 (unpublished opinion), 96-1 USTC ¶ 50,020), the court based its decision on the absence of intent to remove the accessories, rather than the actual ease of removability or relationship to the operation of the building.

The *Hospital Corp. of America* case (109 TC 21, Dec. 52,163) also characterized bathroom accessories for bathrooms located in patient rooms as structural components, rejecting the argument that patient bathrooms were provided as a specialized business need.

Although easily removable, toilet partitions were structural components (*Metro National Corporation*, 52 TCM 1440, TC Memo. 1987-38, Dec. 43,649(M)). The Court focused on the fact that the partitions were not likely to be removed and related to the operation and maintenance of the building (the court noted that movability "is not the sole test").

Plumbing and plumbing fixtures, related to the operation and maintenance of a building, such as toilets, sinks, and bathtubs, are structural components (Reg. § 1.48-1(e)(2)).

*Security systems.* See "*Fire protection and security systems,*" above.

*Septic systems.* A septic system attached to a commercial building was classified as section 1250 real property depreciable over 15 years (the depreciation period of the building under ACRS) (*J. Miller*, TC Memo. 1989-66, 56 TCM 1242, Dec. 45,485(M)). See, also, "*Plumbing and wiring,*" above, and "*Site utilities,*" below.

*Signs, poles, pylons, and billboards.* Signs and lettering attached to the outside of a building to identify or advertise a business are personal property. Neon signs contained in or attached to a building are personal property (Reg. § 1.48-1(c)). However, the IRS has interpreted this rule to treat inherently permanent billboards that were attached to the walls or roofs of buildings and that advertised products and services unrelated to the business activity carried on within the building as section 1250 property (IRS Letter Ruling 6606309980A, June 30, 1966).

Whether billboards are an inherently permanent structure and, therefore, considered a land improvement with a 15-year recovery property (Rev. Proc. 87-56 Asset Class 00.3.) or section 1245 personal property, which is depreciable over a shorter period, generally depends upon application of the *Whiteco* tests dealing with the determination of permanency. The Whiteco case (Whiteco Industries, 65 T.C. 664, CCH Dec. 33,594), in fact, involved the classification of outdoor signs and concluded that a sign face, stringers, poles, and lights were personal property.

In Rev. Rul. 80-151, billboards erected on wooden support poles were personal property. Billboards erected on welded steel frames were not personal property (i.e. were permanent land improvements). In IRS Letter Ruling 200041027, July 10, 2000, both wooden and steel billboards were considered permanently affixed (i.e., land improvements).

If a billboard is used in connection with the marketing of petroleum or petroleum products, e.g., a sign at a service station, it falls within Rev. Proc. 87-56 Asset Class 57.1 of Rev. Proc. 87-56 whether the billboard is section 1245 property or section 1250 property. These billboards have a 15-year depreciation period under Asset Class 57.1. In IRS Letter Ruling 200041027, July 19, 2000, a taxpayer classified billboards used in connection with service stations as Asset Class 57.1 property and all other billboards as Asset Class 00.3 land improvements, also with a 15-year recovery period.

The treatment of a pole as personal property or a land improvement depends upon the manner in which the pole is attached to the ground. Poles bolted to concrete foundations that held signs (ranging from 15 to 17 feet and 90 to 110 feet) and lights were not land improvements since they could be easily removed. (*Standard Oil Company (Indiana)*, 77 TC 349, CCH Dec. 38,141). Similarly, street light poles owned by an electric utility were not land improvements since they were readily removable (*PPL Corporation and Subsidiaries*, 135 TC —, No. 8, Dec. 58,286; *Entergy Corporation and Affiliated Subsidiaries*, Dec. 58,288(M), TC Memo. 2010-166).

A cost segregation field directive for the restaurant industry, reproduced in the Appendix, treats light poles for parking areas and other poles poured in concrete footings or bolt-mounted for signage, flags, etc. as land improvements depreciable over 15 years. See "*Pole and pylons*" in the related chart. In certain cases, however, a pole, etc., may be easily removed and reused (in some cases even if imbedded in concrete) and, thus, arguably considered section 1245 personal property. It appears that the IRS is taking the position that taxpayers generally intend signage poles to remain permanently in place even if attached with bolts, and, therefore, the poles should be treated as land improvements (i.e., permanently affixed property). Note that although Rev. Proc. 87-56 Asset Class 00.3 states that a land improvement is 15 year property "whether or not the land improvement is section 1250 property or section 1245 property" the reference to section 1245 property in Asset Class 00.3 can only refer to section 1245 property described in Code Sec. 1245(a)(3)(B), which relates to permanent structures used as an integral part of manufacturing, production, or extraction or of furnishing transportation, communications, electrical energy, gas, water, or sewage disposal services (integral use property). Although section 1245 property also includes "personal property" (Code Sec. 1245(a)(3)(A)) personal property is by definition nonpermanent, with the exception of certain property in the nature of machinery (see Reg.§ 1.48-1(c) and (d)). Since a land improvement must be permanent it cannot include section 1245 that is "personal property" but may include permanently installed section 1245 integral use property. See section 5.05 of Rev. Proc. 87-56 which specifically provides that integral use property (i.e., section 1245 real property) is included in Asset Class 00.3. See ¶ 110 for additional discussion of land improvements.

The directives further provides that the sign face of a pylon sign is personal property and, in the case of the directive for the restaurant industry, assigns a 5-year recovery period to the sign face (Rev. Proc. 87-56 Asset Class 57.0 since a restaurant is a distributive trade or service). The treatment of the sign face as personal property is justified since a sign can be easily removed from the pole or pylon. The same logic could also apply to an electronic billboard or electronic sign that changes message or ad displays. As noted above, the treatment of the mounting mechanism (i.e., pole or pylon) should depend upon whether it is permanently attached to the ground. Generally, a concrete foundation into which a pole or pylon is set, however, should be considered a permanent land improvement since it isn't intended to be removed and reused.

Field directives for the gaming industry, retail industry, pharmaceutical industry, and auto dealerships also treat poles and pylons as 15-year property whether or not imbedded in concrete or attached with bolts. Signs are treated as 5-year property in the case of casinos and restaurants (Asset Class 57.0) and as 7-year property in the case of pharmaceutical companies (personal property without a class life). These field directives are reproduced in the cost segregation guide and in the Appendix.

A *large* outdoor pylon sign which advertised a 3,000 room hotel/casino complex and was not attached to a building was a land improvement (15-year property, Rev. Proc. 87-56 Asset Class 00.3) (IRS Field Service Advice 200203009, October 3, 2001). The taxpayer argued that the sign was personal property under the "sole justification" test. The IRS, however, *assumed* that under the *Whiteco* tests the sign was an inherently permanent structure and, therefore, excluded from the definition of personal property under Reg. § 1.48-1(c). Replaceable equipment and circuitry within the sign, however, could qualify as personal property. The IRS cited Rev. Rul. 69-170, 1969-1 CB 28) which held scoreboards and message boards, mounted on steel poles and attached to concrete foundations with steel bolts, were separate from a stadium structure and depreciable as land improvements. Replaceable equipment and circuitry within the sign could qualify as personal property. The IRS did not actually apply the Whiteco tests. This ruling seems at odds with the field directives discussed above that do not treat an attached sign as a 15-year land improvement. The ruling however was issued before the field directives were developed and released.

See, also, *Standard Oil Company (Indiana)*, 77 TC 349, CCH Dec. 38,141 and cases cited therein, which held that service station signs were personal property but imbedded poles and concrete foundations were land improvements.

Note that Code Sec. 1033(g) allows a taxpayer to elect to treat "outdoor advertising displays" as real property for purposes of Chapter 1 of the Code (e.g., Code Secs. 1031 and 1033). The election cannot be made with respect to any billboard for which the taxpayer has claimed a Code Sec. 179 expense deduction. The term outdoor advertising display is defined by the Code to mean: "a rigidly assembled sign, display, or device permanently affixed to the ground or permanently attached to a building or other inherently permanent structure constituting, or used for the display of, a commercial or other advertisement to the public" (Code Sec. 1033(g)(3)(C)). See Reg. § 1.1033(g)-1 for details.

In a recent IRS ruling, a taxpayer treated "permanently affixed digital LED displays" as 5-year personal (i.e., section 1245 property), made the Code Sec. 1033(g) election to treat the displays as real property, and changed its depreciation period in the year of the election and as a consequence of the election, to 15 years (i.e., a land improvement). The IRS ruled that it was not necessary to file an accounting method change as a result of the change in depreciation period. Instead, the IRS ruled that depreciation beginning in the year of election should be calculated by applying the change is use rules of Reg.§ 1.168(i)-4(d) (IRS Letter Ruling 201450001, August 18, 2014). The ruling specifically states that no opinion is expressed on whether the displays qualified for the Code Sec. 1033(g) election, whether the taxpayer's classification of the displays as 5-year property was correct, and whether the displays are inherently permanent structures (i.e., land improvements). If the taxpayer was incorrectly depreciating the displays as personal property rather than 15-year (section 1250) land improvements the taxpayer would be required to file an automatic change in accounting method to correct the depreciation period (see ¶ 75) under Section 6.01 of Rev. Proc. 2019-43 and the change in use rules would not apply.

Another recent ruling allowed the Code Sec. 1033(g) election to be made with respect to LED signage permanently affixed to roof buildings and exterior walls. The taxpayer stipulated that the signs would be difficult to remove and that there was no intention to ever remove the signs. The election also applied to permanently affixed ancillary equipment necessary to operate the signs (IRS Letter Ruling 201450004, September 2, 2014). See, also, IRS Letter Ruling 200041027, July 19, 2000, which allowed the election for permanently affixed signage.

It does not appear that there are any rulings that consider whether the Code Sec. 1033(g) election may be made for outdoor advertising displays (or portions of such displays) that are considered personal property under the investment tax credit or *Whiteco* standards. The following excerpt from T.D. 7758, however, explains the provision as follows:

*Section 2127 of the Act [Tax Reform Act of 1976] amended section 1033(g) by adding a new paragraph to allow for an election to treat certain outdoor advertising displays as real property. Prior to the amendment of section 1033 by the Act, the treatment of outdoor advertising displays for purposes of section 1033 was uncertain. The Service has treated outdoor advertising displays as section 1250 property and disallowed treatment of such property as section 1245 property. Rev. Rul. 68-62, 1968-1 C.B. 365. Several court cases, however, have held that certain outdoor advertising displays are tangible personal property for purposes of the investment credit. Alabama Displays, Inc. et. al. v. United States, 507 F.2d 844 (Ct. Cls. 1974), and Whiteco Industries, Inc. v. Commissioner, 65 T.C. 664 (1975). Section 1033(g)(3) eliminated this uncertainty by allowing taxpayers an election to treat property which constitutes certain outdoor advertising displays as real property.*

Thus, it appears that displays that are considered personal property under the investment tax regulations and *Whiteco* standards (which also apply for depreciation purposes) may qualify for the election provided that the signage meets the "permanent affixation" requirement of Code Sec. 1033(g) and Reg. § 1.1033(g)-1.

*Site utilities.* Site utilities at a hotel/casino complex were structural components and not land improvements. Site utilities included underground piping that connected water, sewer, and gas services to the building and overground and underground lines that connected electric service to the building. These items were used to distribute city furnished utility services to the building and were not directly associated with specific items of machinery and equipment (IRS Field Service Advice 200203009, October 3, 2001).

Systems used to distribute utility services from the property line to a restaurant building (including water, sanitary sewer, gas, and electrical services) are section 1250 property with a 39-year depreciation period (LMSB Directive on Cost Segregation in the Restaurant Industry; similarly, Field Directive on Asset Class and Depreciation for Casino Construction Costs and Field Directive on the Planning and Examination of Cost Segregation Issues in the Retail Industry). A Field Directive on the Planning and Examination of Cost Segregation Issues in the Biotech/Pharmaceutical Industry provides more specifically: "Site utilities begin where the responsibility rests with the taxpayer and not the utility company which is providing the service. Site utilities end at either a building or other permanent structure. Site utilities also include any distribution systems between buildings or other permanent structures. The cost of the site utilities would not have to be reincurred if the building or other permanent structure was repaired, rebuilt, or even torn down and replaced with some other type of building. Typically the utilities provided would be electricity, natural gas, water, sewer, and steam. See also Electrical, Plumbing, and Gas & Sewer." See full text of these Directives in "Quick Reference Tables—Cost Segregation for Restaurants, Casinos/Hotels, Retail Stores, and Pharmaceutical Companies" located in the Appendix.

Various components of an electrical distribution system (pine poles, aerial lines, transformers, meters, street lighting) and water distribution system (valves, fire hydrants, fittings, tapping sleeves, PVC water pipe, water meters) that were installed and maintained by the taxpayer in connection with an apartment complex were depreciable land improvements. These items were not classified as Rev. Proc. 87-56 Asset Class 49.14, Electric Utility Transmission and Distribution Plant, and Asset Class 49.3, Water Utilities, because those classifications only apply to taxpayers that sell electricity and water (IRS Letter Ruling 8848039, September 2, 1988).

*Swimming pools.* Swimming pools and pool equipment (and spas attached to the swimming pools) that are contained within, on, or attached to a building are 39-year real property if part of a nonresidential complex, such as a hotel. However, exterior swimming pools and pool equipment (and spas attached to the swimming pools) that are built on land are 15-year land improvements (IRS LMSB Industry Directive on Asset Class and Depreciation for Casino Construction Costs July 26, 2006).

*Wall and floor coverings.* Pursuant to Reg. § 1.48-1(e)(2), "permanent" coverings for walls, floors, and ceilings that are structural components are also considered structural components.

In *Hospital Corp. of America* (109 TC 21, Dec. 52,163), strippable vinyl wall coverings were personal property because the wall coverings were not considered permanent. The IRS has taken the position that such coverings are a permanent, integral part of the wall and, as such, are structural components (unless attached to a movable partition). See, for example, IRS Letter Ruling 8404007 (September 28, 1983) in which the IRS ruled that strippable, fabric-backed, vinyl-coated wall coverings used in a hotel were structural components. However, in IRS Field Service Advice 200203009 (October 3, 2001), the IRS held that strippable wall paper and vinyl wall coverings used in a hotel/casino complex were personal property. The wall coverings were installed using strippable adhesive and could be removed easily for repair work and renovation projects without damaging the walls. The ruling approves the conclusion of the *Hospital Corporation of America* case.

Permanently glued wall and floor tiling used in the kitchen and work areas of a Taco Bell restaurant was a structural component even though it was apparently selected for "special use" considerations such as ease of cleaning and was not of a decorative nature suitable for general business purposes (*L.A. Duaine*, 49 TCM 588, TC Memo. 1985-39, Dec. 41,845(M)).

See, also, "*Carpeting*," above.

*Water heaters and related equipment.* A water heater that services an entire building is a plumbing fixture and, therefore is considered a structural component.

A thermal recovery system that preheats water before its enters a water heater is, likewise, considered a structural component (*La Petite Academy*, DC Mo., 95-1 USTC ¶ 50,193, aff'd, CA-8 (unpublished opinion), 96-1 USTC ¶ 50,020).

*Water softener.* Water softeners have been classified as structural components (Rev. Rul. 83-146, 1983-2 CB 17).

*Windows.* Windows are generally categorized as structural components (Reg. § 1.48-1(e)(2)). However, window treatments are personal property.

A walk-up teller's window and drive-up teller's window installed in a bank building and a drive-up teller's booth, however, were specialized equipment accessorial to the conduct of the banking business and unrelated to the operation of the structures as buildings (Rev. Rul. 65-79, 1965-1 CB 26). Thus, these windows qualified as personal property.

APARTMENT BUILDING — AMERISOUTH CASE

In *Amerisouth XXXII Ltd.*, TC Memo. 2012-67, CCH Dec. 58,975(M), the Tax Court reclassified numerous items in an apartment complex as structural components although they were identified as personal property in a cost segregation study conducted by an expert firm. The study reclassified 3.4 million dollars as personal property (including land improvements). The taxpayer paid 10.25 million for the complex and immediately expended 2 million dollars for renovation costs. Assuming that the basis of the building was 12.25 million (i.e., no repair expenses or loss deductions were claimed as a result of renovation), the Amerisouth cost segregation study classified 28 percent (3.4/12.25 million) of basis as personal property. The typical reclassification percentage for an apartment building is approximately 20 percent. The study took unusually aggressive positions in certain instances and the situation was exacerbated by evidentiary failures that caused the reclassification of certain items as structural components. It is also important to note that after trial, if not before, Amerisouth essentially opted out of its defense by ceasing communications with the court and its own attorneys. The court allowed Amerisouth's attorneys to withdraw and the company ignored an order to file a post-trial brief. The court could stated it could have dismissed the case but instead issued its opinion.

The aggressiveness of the cost segregation study was more than countered by the IRS. The court indicates that the total depreciation claimed on property classified as personal property and land improvements (5-year and 15-year property) in the three years at issue was $397,000 in 2003, $640,000 in 2004, and $375,000 in 2005 and that the IRS disallowed $314,996 in 2003 (79%), $508,977 in 2004 (79%) and $255,778 in 2005 (69%).

One potentially significant finding by the court, which does not appear to be directly addressed in any other case, relates to the manner in which the operation and maintenance rule is applied. Under this rule items which relate to the "operation and maintenance of a building" are generally classified as structural components (Reg.§ 1.48-1(e)(2)). See ¶ 127. The court concluded that this standard is applied by taking into account the type of building under consideration rather than merely a generic or shell building. Thus, items related to the operation and maintenance of an *apartment* building should be classified as structural components. This interpretation of the standard, however, only appeared to impact one item under consideration. Gas lines that extended from the utility source to the buildings and the cost of trenching and backfill related to the operation and maintenance of an *apartment* building but not necessarily a commercial building. This standard could likely have been used with respect to other property, such as kitchen sinks and cabinets, which were classified as structural components because the taxpayer failed to show that they were not permanently affixed. Most cost segregation experts believe that the court's interpretation conflicts with the manner in which the operation and maintenance rule has been applied by the courts.

*Site Preparation.* Amounts allocated to depreciable site preparation costs for excavating, grading, stone bases and compaction needed to construct sidewalks, parking and driveways were reclassified as nondepreciable land improvements. Although the court agreed such site preparation costs are depreciable, it accepted the IRS's position that the amounts claimed actually related to initial clearing and grubbing (i.e., tree removal) of the land before the apartments' construction in 1970.

Due to the difficulty in allocating costs to depreciable site preparation at an existing structure, cost segregation studies often do not take into account such costs. In fact, site preparation costs are sometimes disregarded for newly constructed property. The IRS Audit Technique Guide for Cost Segregation provides the following information.

"Building and facility projects often require general grading, site preparation and other costs to make the site suitable for a proposed use. These costs, along with costs for stripping existing forest and vegetation, grading and compaction to provide a level site, and construction of site access roads, are generally non-depreciable costs allocable to the basis of land. A study may exclude these costs as being outside the scope of its work. In other instances, a study may argue that no costs are allocable to non-depreciable items. Whether these types of costs are included in the study or not, the examiner should determine all land shaping costs and allocate these costs to either non-depreciable land, to the building, and/or to land improvements. Before-and-after photographs may help with this determination. Also, the examiner should inspect the taxpayer's books and records to determine how these items were treated for financial and tax purposes."

*Water distribution system.* Water-distribution systems running from a municipal water main to the apartment buildings were related to the operation and maintenance of the buildings and not separately depreciable over 15 years as land improvements. The distribution systems included water and fire lines, fire hydrants, and "trenching and backfill " consisting of (1) excavating soil where the utility will lay water lines, (2) testing the soil and ensuring it was suitable, (3) laying the lines, and then (4) replacing the excavated soil. The water-distribution systems were an integral part of the buildings plumbing and air-conditioning systems and also served the buildings generally by providing potable water. The location outside of the buildings did not make it unrelated to the operation and maintenance of the building.

*Sewer system.* The sanitary-sewer system, which included sewer lines extending from the buildings to the municipal sewer, sewer manholes, and the trenching and backfill for those lines, were not depreciable land improvements. The sewer system was similar to the water distribution systems and related to the operation and maintenance of the buildings because it served the buildings generally by draining water entering the buildings.

*Gas lines.* Gas lines that extended from the utility source to the buildings and the cost of trenching and backfill related to the operation and maintenance of the building in a manner similar to the water distribution systems and sanitary sewer system. The Court noted that gas lines are not necessarily related to the operation or maintenance of a commercial building but are related to the operation and maintenance of an *apartment* building.

*Site electric (underground electric lines).* Underground electric lines (primary and secondary conduit and wire, including trenching and backfill), like the sewer system and gas lines, related to operation and maintenance of the buildings.

The IRS generally maintains and cost segregation experts agree that systems used to distribute utility services from the property line to a building (including water, sanitary sewers, gas and electrical services) are structural components. See entry for "Site utilties" in the LMSB Directives on Cost Segregation for the Gaming Industry and Retail Industries reproduced in the Appendix of this book. For example, site utilities at a hotel/casino complex were structural components and not land improvements. Site utilities included underground piping that connected water, sewer, and gas services to the building and overground and underground lines that connected electric service to the building. These items were used to distribute city furnished utility services to the building and were not directly associated with specific items of machinery and equipment (Field Service Advice Memorandum 200203009, October 3, 2001). However, in a private letter ruling that deviates significantly from the norm, various components of an electrical distribution system (pine poles, aerial lines, transformers, meters, street lighting) and water distribution system (valves, fire hydrants, fittings, tapping sleeves, PVC water pipe, water meters) that were installed and maintained by the taxpayer in connection with an apartment complex were depreciable land improvements. At best, some studies might successfully allocate a portion of site utility costs to special machinery and equipment that is unrelated to the operation and maintenance of a building.

*Clothes dryer vents and stove hoods and venting.* Special HVAC consisted of clothes dryer vents (four-inch metal pipes that extend from the back of clothes dryers to the outside of the buildings) and stove hood venting that extends from stove hoods and pulled smoke, humidity, and hot air out of the kitchens. The court agreed clothes-dryer vents were personal property because they served specific equipment to expel hot air and carbon monoxide and reduce humidity and had no connection to the apartments' general ventilation system, as contended by the IRS. However, the stove hoods and venting were classified as structural components because the taxpayer presented little or no evidence that the stove hoods and vents operated only to remove odors and heat from the stove and not also from beyond the stove, as contended by the IRS. The sole justification test which treats an item otherwise classified as a structural component as personal property if the sole justification for its installation is "to meet temperature or humidity requirements which are essential for the operation of other machinery or the processing of materials or foodstuffs" (Reg.§ 1.48-1(e)(2)) (see ¶ 127) was not satisfied.

*Special Plumbing*

*Sinks.* Kitchen sinks and plastic utility sinks were structural components even though they were easily removed. The IRS did not dispute the treatment of undersink garbage disposals as MACRS 5-year personal property.

The court conceded that the sinks were easily removable but noted that the taxpayer failed to present any evidence that it would ever replace the sinks. In several instances, when considering the issue of removability, the court may have placed undue significance on the future intent to remove or replace particular items. Future intent is only one of the six Whiteco factors (*Whiteco Industries, Inc.* 65 TC 664, Dec. 33,594 (1975)) taken into account in determining whether an item is permanent or removable. See ¶ 127.

Alternatively, the court took the position that the sinks are structural components because toilets, sinks, and bathtubs are listed as structural components related to the operation and maintenance of a building in Reg.§ 1.48-1(e)(2). The sinks referred to in this regulation, however, are bathroom sinks. Arguably, kitchen and utility sinks relate to the operation and maintenance of an *apartment* building and would be structural components under the court's version of the operation and maintenance standard discussed above. Cost segregation studies typically claim kitchen sinks and related plumbing as personal property on the basis of removability and because they are considered an accessory to the business of renting apartments. The business accessory rule (discussed at ¶ 127) classifies assets accessory to a business such as grocery store counters, printing presses, individual air-conditioning units, etc. as personal property, even though they are considered fixtures under local law.

*Waste piping.* Waste piping connected to the garbage disposals to carry away the water and waste coming from kitchen sinks and rough-water piping consisting of fittings that connect the straight pipes coming from the wall to the sinks were related to a structural component and an integral part of the buildings' plumbing and thus, were also structural components.

Waste-and-rough-water piping for clothes washers in individual apartments and shared laundry rooms were classified as structural components. The record did not clarify whether this category deals only with components visible from the apartment side of the wall or whether pipes behind the wall (or some part of them) are also included. Although the term "rough" or "rough-in" usually refers to the plumbing fittings (e.g., water and drain lines) that connect a specific component, such as a sink or other plumbing fixture, to a building's plumbing lines, the taxpayer provided no evidence that the piping in question ran from where clothes washers were connected to the building's plumbing lines in the wall.

*Gas lines for dryers.* Gas lines which ran from the primary gas lines to clothes dryers were personal property since they were secondary lines that only serviced the dryers and did not supply gas to the building as part of its general operation.

*Floor drains to protect building from flooding washers.* Drains and waste lines which ran from the drains to pipe water out if a pipe leading to the clothes washers broke were structural components. They were a permanent part of the building, did not appear necessary for the effective operation of the washers, and served to protect the apartments from flooding.

*Special Electric*

*Recessed lighting.* No evidence was provided that recessed lights served a decorative or security purpose, and, accordingly were treated as structural components. The case provides no specific information regarding the location or nature of this lighting.

*Wallpacks and timers.* Wall packs which illuminated the exterior of the apartments for the convenience and safety of the tenants related to the operation and maintains of the building. No evidence was provided that the wall packs served as specialized lighting. Timers for wallpacks (exterior lighting) were structural components since they are integral to operation of the wallpacks which themselves are structural components.

*Paddle fans with lighting.* Paddle vans with lighting located in the dining area of some apartments were treated as structural components. The taxpayer presented no evidence to show that the fans were decorative and only incidentally served as general lighting or that they would eventually be removed and replaced.

Cost segregation studies typically classify chandeliers and removable overhead lighting as personal property if such lighting does not provide the sole source of lighting. Exterior lighting is also often classified as personal property. See "*Lighting, interior and exterior,*" above.

*Flood light for sign and timer.* IRS conceded that a sign flood light and accompanying timer, were tangible personal property.

*Doorbells.* Taxpayers provided no evidence that doorbells should be classified as anything other than structural components.

*Sliding gate components.* IRS conceded that unspecified gate components are land improvements, depreciable over 15 years.

*Timer for ground watering system.* IRS conceded that a duplex outlet and timer relating to an exterior watering system were land improvements.

*Surveillance system.* IRS conceded that the surveillance components—consisting of a camera and TV—were personal property.

The IRS concession on these surveillance items disregards several of its own industry directives (reproduced in the back of this book) which stipulate that "security cameras, recorders, monitors and related equipment" are structural components.

*Electric outlets.* Electric outlets, including countertop outlets, were structural components. The fact that an electric outlet could be used to power special equipment such as a treadmill or copier does not establish that the outlet is for that specific use rather than the general operation or maintenance of the building.

Duplex outlets in kitchen areas clearly accommodated refrigerators (personal property) and thus were also personal property. Similarly with outlets used solely for powering stoves, washers, and dryers.

*Cable, telephone, data outlets.* Cable, telephone, and data outlets were used for items that are not structural components and therefore were considered part of those items (i.e., personal property).

*Electric wiring.* The court stated that wiring that is directly connected to special machinery is treated as personal property. Evidence showed that the wiring in question ran from a unit panel in each apartment through wall cavities to outlets that kitchen garbage disposals, dishwashers, and the hoods over the stoves property plug into. However, it was possible that the wiring also connected to other outlets. Since the taxpayer never showed that the wiring supplied power for these specific components the wiring was treated as a structural component. Presumably, certain 220 volt wiring involved in the case was in fact dedicated to specific appliances such as stoves, refrigerators, and washing machines was treated as personal property under the court's standard.

*Electric panels.* The court treated the entire cost of main and unit electric panels as a structural component. The taxpayer attempted to allocate a portion of the cost between use for specialized equipment (personal property) and general purpose use as is commonly done in cost segregation studies. However, the court did not find the taxpayer's substantiation credible. It, therefore, did not need to consider whether it would allow such an allocation even if the taxpayer had reliably substantiated the allocation.

*Finish Carpentry and Millwork*

*Shelving and closet rods.* Shelving in pantry closets and in the living-room-wall recesses, as well as closet rods, were structural components. Although the shelves and closet rods were moveable, the taxpayer failed to show that it actually moved or planned to remove and reuse the shelves or closet rods.

*Paneling, molding, chair rails.* Paneling, molding, and chair rails were structural components. Paneling is specifically mentioned in the regulations as a structural component (Reg.§ 1.48-1(e)(2)).

*Cabinets and countertops.* The court classified cabinets and countertops as structural components strictly on the basis of a permanence standard. The taxpayer failed to present any evidence that these items were not permanent.

Molding, millwork, trim, finish carpentry, and ornate paneling has generally been classified as personal property. See *"Molding, millwork, trim, finish carpentry, paneling, above."*

*Windows and Mirrors*

*Interior windows.* Interior windows in an apartment building office were classified as structural components. The cost segregation study stated that an interior window "is not an asset we would normally treat as 1245 property unless the wall itself was demountable or the window served another unique function." However, no evidence of removable walls or the uniqueness of the windows was presented to the court.

Windows are generally categorized as structural components (Reg.§ 1.48-1(e)(2)). However, window treatments are personal property.

*Mirrors.* Mirrors found on the walls of all apartment dining rooms were structural components. Although removable, no evidence was offered that the mirrors were not intended to remain permanently in place or merely served a decorative purpose.

*Special Painting*

*Paint.* The paint on shelves, wood base, chair rails, closet rods, and crown molding was a structural component because it covered items that were found to be structural components.

Paint is generally considered a permanent wall, floor, or ceiling covering and as such is a structural component. The court, however, appeared to agree with the logical proposition that the cost of painting personal property may be recovered as part of the cost of that property over a shortened recovery period. Here, however, the painted items were in the court's opinion structural components and not personal property.

**For additional building components see the IRS Audit Technique Guide for Cost Segregation at http://www.irs.gov and also the cost segregation tables from that Guide reproduced as a Quick Reference Table in the appendix of this guide.**

The summary table reproduced below is from the IRS cost segregation audit guide.

Cost Segregation studies are often organized following the Construction Specifications Institute (CSI) MasterFormat Division system. The CSI MasterFormat system is a master list of numbers and titles classified by construction trades (concrete, electrical, plumbing, mechanical, carpentry, masonry, steel, etc.) that was developed to simplify and facilitate communication within the construction industry. The inclusion of the CSI MasterFormat Divisions in these tables is for informational purposes only and is not an endorsement of either the Construction Specifications Institute or the MasterFormat system.

**Table 2: Case Law listed by CSI MasterFormat Division (both 2004 and 1995 divisions)**

| CSI Master Format 2004 Classification | CSI Master Format 95 Classification | Asset | IRC § 1245 Prop. | IRC § 1250 Prop. | Case Name |
|---|---|---|---|---|---|
| | | **Division 03 - Concrete** | | | |
| 030000 | 03000 | Concrete slab floor | | X | L.L. Bean |
| 030000 | 03000 | Concrete slab floor & wood deck | | X | Texas Instruments |
| 030000 | 03000 | Concrete floor & columns | X | | Texas Instruments |
| 030000 | 03000 | Waste treatment facilities | X | | Texas Instruments |
| 030000 | 03000 | Truck loading platform | | X | Munford |
| 030000 | 03000 | Truck loading dock | | X | Consol. Freight. |
| 030000 | 03000 | Truck apron (concrete pad) | X | | A.C. Monk |
| 030000 | 03000 | Railroad concrete platform | | X | A.C. Monk |
| 030000 | 03000 | Rail loading platform | | X | Munford |

| CSI Master Format 2004 Classification | CSI Master Format 95 Classification | Asset | IRC § 1245 Prop. | IRC § 1250 Prop. | Case Name |
|---|---|---|---|---|---|
| 030000 | 03000 | Floors - insulated (cooler, freezer, garbage room) | | X | Morrison |
| 030000<br>033000 | 03000<br>03300 | Serving line concrete curb | | X | Morrison |
| 031000 | 03100 | Concrete foundation slab | | X | Duaine |
| | | **Division 04 - Masonry** | | | |
| 042000 | 04200 | Car wash facility structure | | X | Schrum |
| 042000 | 04200 | Boiler structure (concrete) | | X | Samis |
| | | **Division 05 - Metals** | | | |
| 051000 | 05100 | Craneway structures | X | | Lukens |
| | | **Div. 06 - Wood, Plastics, & Comp.** | | | |
| 062000 | 06200 | Finish carpentry | | X | AmeriSouth |
| 064000 | 06400 | Millwork | | X | AmeriSouth |
| 064000 | 06400 | Millwork, metalwork, trimwork | | X | Walgreen |
| 064400 | 06440 | Lattice millwork | X | | Morrison |
| 066300 | 05720 | Patient corridor handrails | X | | HCA |
| | | **Div. 07 - Thermal & Moisture Prot.** | | | |
| 074000 | 13140 | Roof and wall panels | | X | L.L. Bean |
| 074000 | 06170 | Roof panels - Mansard | | X | Boddie-Noelle |
| 074000 | 06170 | Roof - Mansard | | X | La Petite Acad. |
| 074000 | 05100 | High bay portion of roof | | X | A.C. Monk |
| | | **Division 08 - Openings** | | | |
| 081000 | 08100 | Doors, framing | | X | Walgreen |

| CSI Master Format 2004 Classification | CSI Master Format 95 Classification | Asset | IRC § 1245 Prop. | IRC § 1250 Prop. | Case Name |
|---|---|---|---|---|---|
| 081000 | 08100 | Emergency Doors | | X | Texas Instruments |
| 081000 | 08000 | Doors (in partitions) | X | | King Radio |
| 083000 | 08300 | Doors - split (bypass) | | X | La Petite Acad. |
| 083300 | 08330 | Dock overhead doors | | X | Consol. Freight. |
| 083400 | 08344 | Hangar doors | | X | McManus |
| 083800 | 08380 | Eliason doors | X | | Morrison |
| 085000 | 08500 | Interior windows & mirrors | | X | AmeriSouth |
| 085600 | 08582 | Drive-thru window units | | X | Boddie-Noelle |
| 088300 | 08830 | Decorative mirror | | X | Boddie-Noelle |
| 0884426 | 08970 | Window wall partitions | | X | Texas Instruments |
| 0884426 | 08970 | Partitions - glass storefront | X | X | Metro Nat'l Corp. |
| 089100 | 15700 | Louvered wall | X | | A.C. Monk |
| | | **Division 09 - Finishes** | | | |
| 092000 | 09250 | Wall panels - magnetic | | X | La Petite Acad. |
| 092000 | 09250 | Walls (interior) | | X | Grinalds |
| 092000 | 09250 | Partitions | | X | Grinalds |
| 092000 | 09250 | Partitions (drywall, glass) | | X | Walgreen |
| 092000 | 09250 | Drywall partitions | | X | Texas Instruments |
| 092000 | 09250 | Partitions (gypsum drywall) | X | | Metro Nat'l Corp. |
| 092000 | 09250 | Partitions (gypsum drywall) | | X | Mallinckrodt |
| 092000 | 09250 | Partitions (drywall) | | X | Dixie Manor |
| 092000 | 09250 | Customer line screen | X | | Morrison |
| 093000 | 09300 | Kitchen walls and floor tiles | | X | Morrison |
| 093000 | 09300 | Kitchen wall and floor tiles | | X | Duaine |

| CSI Master Format 2004 Classification | CSI Master Format 95 Classification | Asset | IRC § 1245 Prop. | IRC § 1250 Prop. | Case Name |
|---|---|---|---|---|---|
| 095000 | 09510 | Acoustical ceilings | | X | HCA |
| 095000 | 09500 | Ceilings (drywall, acoustic) | | X | Walgreen |
| 095000 | 09500 | Suspended Ceilings | | X | Boddie-Noelle |
| 095000 | 09500 | Ceilings - suspended | | X | Texas Instruments |
| 095000 | 09510 | False ceilings with lighting | | X | Metro Nat'l Corp. |
| 096000 | 09680 | Floor coverings (carpet, vinyl, tile) | | X | Walgreen |
| 096000 | 09680 | Carpeting | X | | HCA |
| 096000 | 09680 | Vinyl Floor Covering | X | | HCA |
| 097000 | 09720 | Vinyl Wall Covering | X | | HCA |
| 099000 | 09900 | Special painting | | X | AmeriSouth |
| | | | | | |
| | | **Division 10 - Specialties** | | | |
| 101400 | 10426 | Outdoor signs (billboards) | X | | Whiteco |
| 102000 | 10800 | Restroom partition (metal) | | X | Walgreen |
| 102000 | 10800 | Partitions - toilet/ restroom | | X | Metro Nat'l Corp. |
| 102200 | 05300 | Metal partitions | | X | McManus |
| 102200 | 10650 | Partitions / Room dividers | X | | HCA |
| 102200 | 10630 | Partitions: movable system | X | | King Radio |
| 102200 | 10630 | Partitions (ceiling height) | X | | King Radio |
| 102200 | 10630 | Partitions (5'6" height) | X | | King Radio |
| 102200 | 10630 | Partitions: movable system | X | | Minot |
| 102800 | 10800 | Bathroom accessories | | X | HCA |
| 102800 | 10800 | Restroom accessories | | X | Morrison |
| 102800 | 10800 | Restroom furnishings | | X | A.C. Monk |

| CSI Master Format 2004 Classification | CSI Master Format 95 Classification | Asset | IRC § 1245 Prop. | IRC § 1250 Prop. | Case Name |
|---|---|---|---|---|---|
| 102813 | 10800 | Restroom accessories | | X | La Petite Acad. |
| 105600 | 13140 | Storage rack system (also supports roof and walls) | | X | L.L. Bean |
| 107316 | 10536 | Decorative finishes, canopies, signs, concrete piers | X | | Walgreen |
| | | **Division 11 - Equipment** | | | |
| 113113 | 11450 | Special HVAC - kitchen vent hoods | | X | AmeriSouth |
| | | **Division 12 - Furnishings** | | | |
| 122000 | 16500 | Décor window treatment | X | | Morrison |
| 123000 | 06400 | Cabinets and hardware | X | | Metro Nat'l Corp. |
| 123500 | 06400 | Vanity cabinets & counters | | X | Morrison |
| | | **Div. 13 - Special Construction** | | | |
| 132000 | 13030 | Garbage room | | X | Morrison |
| 132000 | 13030 | Sorting and boxing room | | X | Catron |
| 132000 | 13030 | Lab and special rooms | | X | Texas Instruments |
| 132000 | 13030 | Saw room | | X | Coors |
| 132000 | 13030 | Valve-testing room | | X | Coors |
| 132000 | 13030 | Green storage room | | X | A.C. Monk |
| 132000 | 13120 | Environmental control rooms | X | | A.C. Monk |
| 132000 | 13030 | Sweet rooms | X | | Central Citrus |
| 132126 | 13030 | Refrigerator area | X | | Munford |
| 132126 | 13030 | Refrigerated room | X | | Catron |
| 132126 | 13030 | Cold storage room | | X | Circle K |
| 133400 | 13120 | Mezzanine system | | X | L.L. Bean |
| 133400 | 13120 | Water pump structure | | X | Texas Instruments |

| CSI Master Format 2004 Classification | CSI Master Format 95 Classification | Asset | IRC § 1245 Prop. | IRC § 1250 Prop. | Case Name |
|---|---|---|---|---|---|
| 133400 | 13120 | Elec. switch gear structure | X | | Texas Instruments |
| 133419 | 13120 | Storage sheds | X | | A.C. Monk |
| 133419 | 13120 | Airplane hangar | | X | McManus |
| | | **Division 21 - Fire Suppression** | | | |
| 211100 | 15300 | Fire protection system | | X | L.L. Bean |
| 211100 | 15300 | Fire protection system | | X | La Petite Acad. |
| 211100 | 15300 | Fire hose wall stations | | X | A.C. Monk |
| 211100 | 15300 | Localized fire protection system | X | | Texas Instruments |
| 211100 | 15300 | Sprinkler heads | | X | Texas Instruments |
| 211100 | 15300 | Sprinkler system | | X | Ponderosa |
| | | **Division 22 - Plumbing** | | | |
| 220000 | 15400 | Kitchen water piping, grease trap system, and steam lines | X | | HCA |
| 220000 | 15400 | Kitchen hot water heater | X | | Morrison |
| 220000 | 15400 | Kitchen water piping | X | | Morrison |
| 220000 | 15400 | Kitchen drainage sys. (grease trap) | X | | Morrison |
| 220000 | 15400 | Kitchen hand sinks | | X | Morrison |
| 220000 | 15400 | Plumbing - restroom | | X | Grinalds |
| 220000 | 15780 | Thermal recovery system | | X | La Petite Acad. |
| 220000 | 15400 | Plumbing connected to equipment | | X | Boddie-Noelle |
| 220000 | 15400 | Plumbing for equipment | X | | Texas Instruments |
| 220000 | 15100 | Plumbing to equipment | X | | Duaine |
| 220000 | 15100 | Gas lines to equipment | X | | Duaine |

| CSI Master Format 2004 Classification | CSI Master Format 95 Classification | Asset | IRC § 1245 Prop. | IRC § 1250 Prop. | Case Name |
|---|---|---|---|---|---|
| 221100 | 15100 | Plumbing system | X | | Schrum |
| 221200 | 13200 | Water tanks | | X | Texas Instruments |
| 221300 | 11442 | Kitchen grease trap | | X | La Petite Acad. |
| 223000 | 15480 | Solar water-heating equipment | X | | Wood |
| 224000 | 15400 | Special plumbing - dryer gas lines | X | | AmeriSouth |
| 224000 | 15400 | Special plumbing - laundry drain and waste lines | | X | AmeriSouth |
| 224000 | 15400 | Special plumbing - sinks and garbage disposals | | X | AmeriSouth |
| 224700 | 15412 | Electric water coolers | | X | Morrison |
| | | | | | |
| | | **Division 23 - HVAC** | | | |
| 230000 | 15510 | Steam boilers | | X | HCA |
| 230000 | 15850 | Kitchen hoods & exhaust system | X | | HCA |
| 230000 | 15780 | Kitchen heat recovery unit | X | | Morrison |
| 230000 | 15850 | Kitchen air makeup unit | X | | Morrison |
| 230000 | 15700 | Kitchen HVAC | | X | Boddie-Noelle |
| 230000 | 15700 | Air conditioning in telephone room | X | | Texas Instruments |
| 230000 | 15764 | Heating/ventilation system | | X | L.L. Bean |
| 230000 | 15700 | Air conditioning units | | X | Grinalds |
| 230000 | 15700 | HVAC system | | X | Albertson's |
| 230000 | 15700 | HVAC system | | X | Publix |
| 230000 | 15700 | Air conditioning units (roof) | | X | Circle K |
| 230000 | 15700 | Air conditioning/ heating units (roof) | | X | Dixie Manor |
| 230000 | 15700 | HVAC units | X | | Piggly Wiggly |
| 230000 | 15700 | Blowers and coolers | X | | Central Citrus |

| CSI Master Format 2004 Classification | CSI Master Format 95 Classification | Asset | IRC § 1245 Prop. | IRC § 1250 Prop. | Case Name |
|---|---|---|---|---|---|
| 231300 | 13200 | Fuel oil tanks | | X | Texas Instruments |
| 233000 | 15800 | Special HVAC - dryer vents | X | | AmeriSouth |
| 233000 | 15800 | Duct work (filter system) | | X | Coors |
| 235000<br>236000 | 15500<br>15600 | Energy plant | | X | Samis |
| 236000 | 15600 | Refrigeration system | X | | SuperValu |
| 237000 | 15700 | Air conditioning/ heating system | | X | Samis |
| 237000 | 15700 | Air conditioning/ heating units (roof) | | X | Kramertown |
| 237000 | 15700 | Air conditioning/ heating system | | X | Fort Walton |
| | | | | | |
| | | **Division 26 - Electrical** | | | |
| 260000 | 16200 | TV equipment and wiring | X | | HCA |
| 260000 | 16140 | Electrical conduits to equipment | X | | Duaine |
| 260000 | 16140 | Electrical system | X | X | Central Citrus |
| 260000 | 16140 | Elec. panel and transformer | | X | Central Citrus |
| 260000 | 16140 | Electrical outlets | | X | Central Citrus |
| 260000 | 16200 | Kitchen electrical service | | X | La Petite Acad. |
| 260000 | 16200 | Elec. conduit - restroom | | X | Grinalds |
| 261000 | 16400 | Electrical system | | X | L.L. Bean |
| 261000 | 16400 | Primary & secondary elec. dist. sys. | X | X | HCA |
| 261000 | 16400 | Special elec. equip. & branch wiring | X | | HCA |
| 261000 | 16400 | Primary electric distribution system | X | X | Morrison |
| 261000 | 16400 | Kitchen electric panel boards | X | | Morrison |
| 261000 | 16400 | Electrical system | X | | Schrum |

| CSI Master Format 2004 Classification | CSI Master Format 95 Classification | Asset | IRC § 1245 Prop. | IRC § 1250 Prop. | Case Name |
|---|---|---|---|---|---|
| 261000 | 16400 | Electrical distribution sys. (95%/5%) | X | X | Ill. Cereal Mills |
| 261000 | 16400 | Primary electric distribution system | X | X | Scott Paper |
| 261000 | 16400 | Secondary electric distribution sys. | X | X | Scott Paper |
| 261000 | 16400 | Electrical connected to equipment | | X | Boddie-Noelle |
| 261000 | 16400 | Electrical distribution system | | X | A.C. Monk |
| 261000 | 16400 | Wiring for computer room | X | | A.C. Monk |
| 261000 | 16400 | Elec. distribution system: adapters, fuses, switches, relays | X | | Central Citrus |
| 261000 | 16400 | Electrical - systems dedicated to equipment (Cat. 4) | X | | Texas Instruments |
| 261000 | 16400 | Electrical - spare transformers, breakers, cable (Cat. 3) | | X | Texas Instruments |
| 261000 | 16400 | Electrical - high voltage system (Cat. 2) | | X | Texas Instruments |
| 261100 | 16360 | Electrical - substations and transformers (Cat. 1) | | X | Texas Instruments |
| 262000 | 16400 | Special electric | X | X | AmeriSouth |
| 263000 | 16220 | Electrical generating equipment | X | | Westroads |
| 265000 | 16500 | Lighting fixtures and wiring | | X | Walgreen |
| 265100 | 16510 | Over-bed fluorescent lights | | X | HCA |
| 265100 | 16510 | Int. & ext. ornamental light fixtures | | X | Duaine |
| 265100 | 16510 | Dock lighting | | X | Consol. Freight. |
| 265100 | 16510 | Exterior accent lighting | X | | Metro Nat'l Corp. |
| 265100 | 16510 | Interior grow lights | X | | Metro Nat'l Corp. |

| CSI Master Format 2004 Classification | CSI Master Format 95 Classification | Asset | IRC § 1245 Prop. | IRC § 1250 Prop. | Case Name |
|---|---|---|---|---|---|
| 265100 | 16510 | Chandeliers and dimmers | X | | Morrison |
| 265100 | 16510 | Chandeliers and lanterns | X | | Shoney's |
| 265100 | 16510 | Hanging lanterns | X | | Shoney's |
| 265100 | 16510 | Lights: fluorescent & moisture-proof | X | | Central Citrus |
| 265100 | 16510 | Lights: ballast and exterior | X | | Central Citrus |
| 265200 | 16530 | Emergency lighting | X | | Morrison |
| 265200 | 16530 | Emergency/exit lights | | X | La Petite Acad. |
| 265600 | 16520 | Exterior façade lighting | | X | La Petite Acad. |
| 265600 | 16520 | Exterior security lighting | X | | Metro Nat'l Corp. |
| 265600 | 16510 | Lights: spotlights and flood lamps | X | | Central Citrus |
| | | **Division 27 - Communication** | | | |
| 270000 | 16700 | Telephone equip., wiring, and jacks | X | | HCA |
| 270000 | 16700 | Intercom equip. and call system | X | | HCA |
| | | **Div. 28 - Elec. Safety & Security** | | | |
| 283100 | 15300 | Heat and smoke detectors | | X | La Petite Acad. |
| | | **Division 31 - Earthwork** | | | |
| 311000 | 02200 | Site prep and earthwork (nondep.) | | | AmeriSouth |
| | | **Division 32 - Ext. Improvements** | | | |
| 323000 | 02800 | Trellises (§ 1245) | X | | Trentadue |
| 323100 | 02825 | Security fencing | X | | Texas Instruments |

| CSI Master Format 2004 Classification | CSI Master Format 95 Classification | Asset | IRC § 1245 Prop. | IRC § 1250 Prop. | Case Name |
|---|---|---|---|---|---|
| 323100 | 02825 | Fencing - playground | | X | La Petite Acad. |
| 323100 | 02825 | Dumpster enclosure (fence & concrete pad) | | X | La Petite Acad. |
| 328000 | 02810 | Sprinkler heads | | X | Metro Nat'l Corp. |
| 328423 | 02810 | Underground irrigation system | | X | Trentadue |
| 329300 | 02930 | Exterior landscaping | | X | Texas Instruments |
| 329300 | 02930 | Interior landscaping | X | | Texas Instruments |
| | | **Division 33 - Utilities** | | | |
| 331116 | 02510 | Water distribution system | | X | AmeriSouth |
| 332100 | 02520 | Well | | X | Trentadue |
| 333000 | 02530 | Sewage disposal system | | X | Everhart |
| 333100 | 02530 | Sanitary sewer system | | X | AmeriSouth |
| 335100 | 02550 | Gas line | | X | AmeriSouth |
| 337100 | 02580 | Site electric | | X | AmeriSouth |

## ¶ 127B

## Cost Segregation: Determining Depreciation Period of Personal Property Components of a Building

Once an item is identified as a separately depreciable personal property component of a building rather than a structural component (see ¶ 127A) it must be assigned to the proper MACRS property class. MACRS property classes for personal property include 3-year, 5-year, 7-year, 10-year, 15-year, and 20-year property. The 200-percent declining-balance method is generally used to depreciate 3-, 5-, 7-, and 10-year property; the 150-percent declining-balance method applies to 15- and 20-year property.

*Personal property components of residential rental property.* The IRS has ruled that owners of residential rental property are considered engaged in a personal service activity (Announcement 99-82, 1999-2 CB 244). Thus, property used in connection with residential rental property, such as appliances, and personal property components of the building, such as carpeting and window treatments, is five-year property (Asset Class 57.0 of Rev. Proc. 87-56). See *"Property used in connection with residential property"* at ¶ 104 for details. Effective for property placed in service in tax years beginning after 2017, property used in connection with lodging, such as residential rental property, qualifies for section 179 expensing. See ¶ 302.

*Personal property components of nonresidential real property.* The property class and recovery period for most property is prescribed by the IRS in a table contained in Rev. Proc. 87-56, (1987-2 CB 674) (reproduced at ¶ 191). The first part of the table lists a few types of depreciable assets that are commonly used by most businesses (e.g., cars, computers, furniture). The second part of the table lists various business activities.

If a particular asset is not listed in the first part of the table, then its property class and recovery period are determined by reference to the business activity in which the assets are primarily used. The property class for building components of nonresidential real property identified as personal property in a cost segregation study or otherwise will usually depend upon the business activity of the taxpayer as identified in Rev. Proc. 87-56. If the business activity of the taxpayer is not listed in that revenue procedure or the assets listed for the particular business activity would not include personal property elements of a building, then the property is treated as 7-year MACRS property. This is the default classification for personal property with no class life (Code Sec. 168(e)(3)(C)). Note that the business activity is determined by reference to the person using the building, for example, by the tenant. See "Leased Property" at ¶ 190.

Many taxpayers will be conducting a business activity described in Asset Class 57.0 of Rev. Proc. 87-56. Asset Class 57.0 applies to "Distributive Trades and Services" and prescribes a 5-year recovery period. It includes assets used in wholesale and retail trade, and personal and professional services.

Wholesale and retail trade includes (but is not limited to) purchasing, assembling, storing, sorting, grading, and selling goods at the wholesale or retail level. Restaurants and cafes are included in this category (Rev. Proc. 77-10, 1977-1 CB 548).

Examples of personal service activities include: hotels and motels, laundry and dry cleaning establishments, beauty and barber shops, photographic studios and mortuaries (Rev. Proc. 77-10).

All of the personal property components of the hospital building in the Hospital Corporation of America case (¶ 127) were classified as five-year property because the hospital was considered an asset used in the provision of professional services.

See ¶ 190 for a detailed discussion of property classification rules.

For examples of particular types of separately depreciable personal property building components, see ¶ 127A.

For examples of particular types of separately depreciable land improvements, see ¶ 5 and ¶ 110. Land improvements are generally depreciated over 15 years using the 150-percent declining-balance method regardless of the taxpayer's business activity. See ¶ 110.

## ¶ 127C

## Cost Segregation: Determining Whether a Structure is Personal or Real Property

Often it may be unclear whether a particular structure is nonresidential real property (¶ 116) depreciable over 39 years, a land improvement depreciable over 15 years, or some other type of real or personal property depreciable over a shorter period under MACRS. See ¶ 127 for the distinction between personal property and a structural component of a building.

Code Sec. 168(e)(2)(B) defines nonresidential real property as section 1250 property that is neither residential rental property nor property with a class life of less than 27.5 years. Thus, if a particular structure is not section 1250 property or is identified in Rev. Proc. 87-56 (¶ 101) as having a class life of less than 27.5 years it is not nonresidential real property. For example, Rev. Proc. 87-56 Asset Class 80.0 (Theme and Amusement Parks) provides that certain buildings have a class life of 10 years and are depreciable over 7 years. These buildings are not 39-year nonresidential real property although they retain their status as section 1250 property.

All section 1250 property is considered real property. Section 1250 property consists of any property that is not section 1245 property. Section 1245 property includes personal property and certain types of real property described in Code Sec. 1245(a)(3). See ¶ 116.

The rules are set forth in the Code as follows.

Code Sec. 168(i)(12) defines section 1250 property by reference to the definition in Code Sec. 1250(c).

Code Sec. 1250(c) provides that section 1250 property is any real property (other than real property which is treated as section 1245 property because it is described in Code Sec. 1245(a)(3)) that is or has been property of a character subject to the allowance for depreciation. See ¶ 116.

Reg. § 1.1245-3(b) defines personal property by reference to Reg. § 1.48-1 (relating to the investment tax credit). Under this regulation personal property includes any tangible property other than land and improvements thereto, such as buildings or other inherently permanent structures, including structural components of such buildings and permanent structures (Reg. § 1.48-1(c)). Thus, buildings and their structural components are treated as section 1250 real property. Other "inherently permanent structures" and their components which are improvements to land are also section 1250 property unless described in Code Sec. 1245(a)(3) (i.e., the property is section 1245 real property as explained below).

In determining whether a structure is a building, the definition of a building, as contained in the investment tax credit regulations is applied (Reg. § 1.1245-3(c)(2); Reg. § 1.48-1). Thus, the multitude of cases and rulings which have addressed this issue in the context of eligibility for the former investment tax credit remain relevant for determining the proper depreciation treatment. Subscribers to the CCH STANDARD FEDERAL TAX REPORTER may wish to refer to the annotations at ¶ 4580.21 and following for a summary of these decisions.

In determining whether a structure is a building, the courts have developed two tests derived from the ITC regulations: (1) the inherent permanency test and (2) the appearance and function test. A structure is not considered a building by most courts if it fails either test. On the other hand, a structure will be considered a building if it satisfies both tests unless the structure is essentially an item of machinery or equipment or houses property used as an integral part of an activity specified in former Code Sec. 48(a)(1)(B)(i) if the use of the structure is so closely related to the use of such property that the structure can be expected to be replaced when the property it initially houses is replaced (Reg.§ 1.48-1(e)(1)). Included among the activities specified in former Code Sec. 48(a)(1)(B)(i) are manufacturing, production, and extraction. See below for a discussion of these two exceptions.

*Permanency test*

With respect to the permanency test, Reg. § 1.48-1(c) provides, in part, that:

> "For purposes of this section, the term 'tangible personal property' means any tangible property except land and improvements thereto, such as buildings or other inherently permanent structures (including items, which are structural components of such buildings or structures)."

Based on the preceding regulation, most courts will rule that a structure cannot be considered a building unless it is "inherently permanent." Thus, in general, if a structure can be readily disassembled and moved to a new location, it will be considered personal property and not a building (real property).

In applying the permanency test, the courts frequently consider the following factors which were developed by the Tax Court in the *Whiteco Industries* case (65 TC 664, CCH Dec. 33,594):

(1) Is the property capable of being moved, and has it in fact been moved?

(2) Is the property designed or constructed to remain permanently in place?

(3) Are there circumstances that tend to show the expected or intended length of affixation, i.e., are there circumstances that show that property may or will have to be moved?

(4) How substantial a job is removal of the property and how time-consuming is it? Is it readily movable?

(5) How much damage will the property sustain upon its removal?

(6) What is the manner of affixation of the property to the land?

The IRS cost segregation audit guide provides that examiners should consider the following additional factors when addressing permanency (some of which may overlap with the Whiteco factors):

- History of the item or similar items being moved;
- Manner in which an item is attached to a building or to the land;
- Weight and size of the item;
- Function and design of the item;
- Intent of the taxpayer in installing the item;
- Time, cost, manpower, and equipment required to move the components;
- Time, cost, manpower, and equipment required to reconfigure the existing space if the item is removed;
- Effect of the item's removal on the building; and
- Extent the item can be reused after removal.

For example, a small metal shed for storing tools which can be disassembled and reassembled at another location should be considered personal property under the permanency test. A yurt might also meet this test.

The storage shed example, however, is a simple case, easily resolved in a taxpayer's favor. The application of the rule to larger and more expensive structures, which are necessarily more permanent in nature, is more difficult and will be subject to closer IRS scrutiny.

For example, it is less clear whether self-storage units used in a storage business are depreciable as buildings (39 year property) or personal property. The answer will depend on the application of the five factors above. Factor (3) would generally work against personal property classification since the typical operator of a self-storage business does not ever intend to remove or relocate the units. Such intent could exist, however, if the owner will disassemble and sell or relocate the units at a new location if the business does not operate profitably. Taxpayers taking the position that self-storage units used in a storage business are personal property have generally used a 7-year recovery period that applies to personal property without a class life (see ¶ 106). However, see IRS Letter Ruling 8248003 (September 28, 1981) in which the IRS ruled that a mini-warehouse structure (and its garage style doors) used for self-service storage warehousing was not personal property. Interestingly, this IRS letter ruling does not discuss the Whiteco factors and, in light of subsequent case law, such as *Fox Photo*, below, a taxpayer is now in a stronger position to argue for personal property classification.

One leading case, which was resolved in the taxpayer's favor, involved prefabricated "one-hour photo labs" erected on mall parking lots. The labs were 24 feet wide, 28 feet long, and 12 feet high. Although the labs had all of the appearances of a building and were attached to a concrete foundation, they were designed to be moved from one location to another if necessary by transporting one-half of the structure at a time on a flat-bed truck. Some structures were in fact removed over a two-day to three-day period and the cost of removal and relocation was less than the cost of a new replacement. The concrete foundation, however, was determined to be an inherently permanent structure, and, therefore, was not personal property (*Fox Photo Inc.*, 60 TCM 85, CCH Dec. 46,709(M)).

A smaller photo-processing "hut" which could be loaded on a trailer along with its attached concrete base in less than an hour without disassembly has also been classified as personal property (*Film N' Photos*, 37 TCM 709, CCH Dec. 35,125(M)).

In contrast, a specially designed warehouse for storing bulk merchandise (500' × 190' and 57' high) was considered permanent even though the taxpayer produced evidence that a similar structure had been disassembled, moved approximately 350 feet, and reassembled over a period of 3 months by a different taxpayer involved in the book printing business (*L.L. Bean*, CA-1, 98-1 USTC ¶ 50,454). This case illustrates that even though a building or structure *can be* moved such is not necessarily conclusive evidence that it is not inherently permanent. As the court in *Bean* notes, the fact that the London Bridge was disassembled and moved from England to the United States does not negate the inherent permanency of that structure. In determining that the warehouse was inherently permanent the court focused on the improbability and expense of relocation. The warehouse was specifically designed as an addition to the taxpayer's distribution center, the foundation was specially designed to meet the requirements of forklifts and weight loads and could only be replaced at considerable expense, the material and method of construction indicated the permanent nature of the structure, and substantial time and effort would be required to remove and re-erect the structure.

In *J. McManus,* DC, 87-2 USTC ¶ 9618, an airplane hangar, which was 34 feet wide and 200 feet long, was considered inherently permanent even though it could be disassembled by a four-person crew in about seven days and reassembled in a shorter period. The court indicated that even if the hangar was not an inherently permanent structure it would still be considered a building because it satisfied the appearance and function test.

Examples of nonpermanent structures:

*Mobile homes* set on concrete blocks and capable at all times of being moved from their sites on their own wheels have been classified as personal property (*J.H. Moore*, 58 TC 1045, Dec. 31,554, aff'd *per curiam*, CA-5, 74-1 USTC ¶ 9146).

However, if a mobile home has been permanently affixed to the land, the mobile home may be "residential rental property" and depreciable under MACRS over 27.5 years (if the mobile home is rented for use as a residence by the lessee) or over 39-years as nonresidential real property (if the mobile home is rented for nonresidential use by the lessee) (*J. Rupert,* 82 TCM 197, Dec. 54,411(M), TC

Memo. 2001-179, aff'd per curiam, CA-5 (unpublished opinion), 2003-1 USTC ¶ 50,486, 57 FedAppx 21; *F.D. Smith*, Dec. 58,283(M), TC Memo. 2010-162).

Mobile homes on "permanent foundations" and used by "farm tenants" are listed in the IRS farm assets chart reproduced at ¶ 118 as Rev. Proc. 87-56 Asset Class 00.3 property (i.e. land improvements) with a 15-year recovery period. Presumably, the IRS considers such mobile homes as permanently affixed structures since land improvements do not include structures that are not permanently affixed. See *"Land Improvements"* at ¶ 110. Classification of a mobile home as a land improvement seems incorrect, however, since Asset Class 00.03 specifically excludes "buildings." A more appropriate classification, assuming the mobile homes are not rented directly to tenants thereby constituting 27.5-year residential rental property, may be Asset Class 01.3 relating to "farm buildings." The recovery period for this Asset Class is 20 years.

*Trailers used as offices* if not affixed to the land or designed to remain permanently in place are personal property (Rev. Rul. 77-8, 1977-1 CB 3); *F.D. Smith*, Dec. 58,283(M), TC Memo. 2010-162.

*Steel petroleum storage tanks* varying in size from 7,000 to 194,000 barrels were personal property (*PDV America, Inc*, 87 TCM 1330, TC Memo. 2004-118, Dec. 55,638(M)). See ¶ 110 for discussion of appropriate recovery period of tanks.

*Appearance and function test*

The appearance and function test is based on Reg. § 1.48-1(e), which provides:

> "The term 'building' generally means any structure or edifice enclosing a space within its walls, and usually covered by a roof, the purpose of which is, for example, to provide shelter or housing, or to provide working, office, parking, display, or sales space. The term includes, for example, structures such as apartment houses, factory and office buildings, warehouses, barns, garages, railway or bus stations, and stores. Such term includes any such structure constructed by, or for, a lessee even if such structure must be removed, or ownership of such structure reverts to the lessor, at the termination of the lease. Such term does not include (i) a structure which is essentially an item of machinery or equipment, or (ii) a structure which houses property used as an integral part of an activity specified in section 48(a)(1)(B)(i) [relating to property used as an integral part of manufacturing, production, or extraction or furnishing transportation, communications, electrical energy, gas, water, or sewage disposal services (see below)—Editor.]if the use of the structure is so closely related to the use of such property that the structure clearly can be expected to be replaced when the property it initially houses is replaced. Factors which indicate that a structure is closely related to the use of the property it houses include the fact that the structure is specially designed to provide for the stress and other demands of such property and the fact that the structure could not be economically used for other purposes. Thus, the term 'building' does not include such structures as oil and gas storage tanks, grain storage bins, silos, fractionating towers, blast furnaces, basic oxygen furnaces, coke ovens, brick kilns, and coal tipples."

The appearance test relates to whether the structure looks like a building and generally only requires that the structure enclose a space within its walls and usually be covered by a roof.

The second part of the test requires that the building function as a building. In applying the function test, the courts have primarily focused on whether the structure provides working space for employees that is more than merely incidental to the primary function of the structure. Both the quantity and quality of human activity inside of the structure may be considered in this regard.

For example, in *Munford Inc.*, CA-11, 88-2 USTC ¶ 9432, a 35,000 square foot refrigerated structure that was designed primarily to maintain sub-zero temperatures to prevent the spoilage of frozen foods prior to shipment to grocery stores was held not to be a building. Although employees routinely moved goods into and out of the structure, this activity was held to be incidental to the specialized purpose of the structure. Moreover, the activities of the employees were limited in both scope and duration due to the cold temperature of the structure. Similar holdings have applied to other refrigeration and specialized storage buildings (*Catron*, 50 TC 306, Dec. 28,960 (Acq. 1972-2 CB 1)) (refrigerated area of a large Quonset-like structure used for cold storage of apples); *Merchants Refrigerating Co.*, 60 TC 856, CCH Dec. 32,120, Acq. 1974-2 CB 3 (large freezer room used for the storage of frozen foods); *Central Citrus Co.*, 58 TC 365, CCH Dec. 31,403 (atmospherically controlled "sweet rooms" used to ripen fruit).

In *L.L. Bean, Inc.*, above, a specially designed warehouse for housing bulk merchandise in floor-to-ceiling storage racks that supported the frame and roof satisfied the function test because human activity was essential, rather than merely incidental, to the function of the facility. Moreover, the ITC regulations and legislative history specifically list a warehouse as an example of a building. The fact that the *Bean* facility was uniquely designed only enhanced its function as a warehouse; it did negate is classification as a warehouse.

In *G.G. Hart*, 78 TCM 114, Dec. 53,462(M), a tobacco barn was determined to be a building rather than section 1245 property described in Code Sec. 1245(a)(3)(B) (property other than a building used as an integral part of the manufacturing or production of tobacco). Although employees transported tobacco from the fields and hung the tobacco on racks over a six week period, this activity was only ancillary to the function of the structure as a curing facility and did not constitute the provision of working space. However, the use of the barn on a full time basis to prepare the tobacco for sale by stripping, grading, bailing, and boxing constituted the provision of working space that was more than incidental to the function of the structure as a curing facility. As a result the structure was a building (rather than section 1245 property) and did not qualify for the Code Sec. 179 expense allowance. Since the barn was classified as a building it could not be depreciated as a land improvement (Rev. Proc. 87-56 Asset Class 00.3) over 15 years. (Buildings and structural components are specifically excluded from the definition of land improvements (see ¶ 110).) Instead, it was classified as a farm building (Asset Class 01.3) depreciable over 20 years (see ¶ 118).

In contrast to the *Hart* case, a tobacco shed in *Brown & Williamson Tobacco Corp.*, DC-Ky., 73-1 USTC ¶ 9317, was not considered a building where employees only placed and removed tobacco from storage racks.

*Open-air parking structures.* The IRS has ruled that an open-air parking structure is a building and that taxpayer who maintain that such a parking lot is a land improvement are likely subject to the twenty percent-accuracy penalty (Code Sec. 6662(b)(1)) (Applicable Recovery Period Under Code Sec. 168(a) for Open-Air Parking Structures, Coordinated Issue Paper (LMSB4-0709-029) (Effective Date July 31, 2009)). The function test is met because Reg.§ 1.48-1(e) specifically provides that the provision of parking space is a building function. The appearance test is satisfied because the structure has a roof and encloses a space within its walls. It is not necessary that all walls extend to the ceiling. Furthermore, the structure provides shelter from the elements and has many components that commonly present in other types of buildings such as walls, floors, elevators, stairs, sprinkler systems, fire escapes, and electric wiring and lighting fixtures.

Chief Counsel concluded that it was appropriate to impose a negligence penalty on a taxpayer who classified an open-air parking structure as a 15-year land improvement even though the classification occurred prior to issuance of the LMSB. The reasonable/cause good faith exception under Code Sec. 6664 did not apply even though the taxpayer had acted upon the advice of a tax professional (Field Attorney Advice 20125201F, December 29, 2012).

Chapter 8.2 of the IRS Audit Technique Guide for Cost Segregation also contains a detailed analysis of the IRS position. The Guide also recommends that the accuracy-related penalty under Code Sec. 6662 for a substantial understatement (if applicable) and in the alternative for negligence or disregard of rules or regulations be strongly considered for taxpayers who treat these structures as 15-year land improvements. The Guide notes that taxpayers have not argued that an open air parking lot which is connected to a building is depreciable over 15-years as a land improvement.

*Structures housing property used as an integral part of a manufacturing, production, etc. activity.* The IRS has ruled that a structure that housed equipment in a waste-treatment production facility was not a land improvement or a building or structural component. The structure housed equipment that was used as an integral part of production and the structure itself was so closely related to the use of this equipment that the structure clearly could be expected to be replaced when the equipment was replaced. The structure instead was classified as 7-year property under Rev. Proc. 87-56 Asset Class 49.5 (Waste Reduction and Resource Recovery Plants) (IRS Letter Ruling 200013038, December 27, 1999).

See also, ¶ 110.

*Other examples of buildings*

The following structures have been classified as buildings:

*Prefabricated structures used to store onions.* 100 foot by 100 foot pre-fabricated shed used to store onions and which contained no specialized equipment was a building in the nature of a warehouse or garage (*G. Tamura*, CA-9, 84-2 USTC ¶ 9545, 734 F2d 470).

*Truck loading docks.* Truck loading docks that provided working space, had the appearance of a building, and were adaptable to other uses were buildings (*Consolidated Freightways*, CA-9, 83-1 USTC ¶ 9420, 708 F2d 1385). Similarly, *Yellow Freight System Inc.*, CA-8, 76-2 USTC ¶ 9478, 538 F2d 790; Rev. Rul. 71-203, 1971-1 CB 7.

*Property in the nature of machinery is personal property*

Property which is in the nature of machinery (other than structural components of a building or other inherently permanent structure) is considered tangible personal property even though located outside of a building (Reg. § 1.48-1(c)). The regulations, cite, by way of example, gasoline pumps, hydraulic car lifts, and automatic vending machines.

The regulations further provide that a structure which is essentially an item of machinery or equipment is not considered a building or structural component (Reg. § 1.48-1(e)). Although the IRS has taken the position that a structure which is in the nature of machinery is not personal property if that structure is inherently permanent (*B.R. Roberts*, 60 TC 861, CCH Dec. 32,121) it subsequently conceded that an inherently permanent structure in the nature of machinery may qualify as personal property (*J.B. Weirick*, 62 TC 446, CCH Dec. 32,668; *Munford*, 87 TC 463, Dec. 43,283). A structure which is essentially an item of machinery is depreciated as part of the machinery (i.e., over the same period as the machinery).

In *Weirick*, the Tax Court held that line towers whose sole function was to support cable pulley mechanisms and cables at a ski resort were so closely related to the function of the pulley mechanisms (machinery) that the towers were also considered part of the machinery even though the towers were permanently affixed to the land.

A specially engineered structure which supported an overhead crane was essentially a part of the crane and qualified as personal property. Any function it may have served as a building component was strictly incidental to its function as an essential part of the crane (Rev. Rul. 79-183, 1979-1 CB 44).

In dealing with structures housing certain industrial processes, the Tax Court stated that the machinery exception only applies if the structure is part of the industrial process (*Illinois Cereal Mills, Inc.*, 46 TCM 1001, CCH Dec. 40,342(M), aff'd CA-7, 86-1 USTC ¶ 9371).

In *Munford* (above), although the components of the 35,000 square foot refrigeration structure used to store frozen foods prior to shipment to grocery stores chains was property in the nature of machinery, the structural elements (foundation, walls, floor, roofing, supports, vapor barrier, insulation, and electrical components) were not in the nature of machinery because they were not so closely associated with the refrigeration system as to comprise an integral, single asset. In *Weirick* it was as cheap to replace the line towers and pulley mechanisms as a single unit as it was to replace the pulley mechanisms separately. In *Munford*, the refrigeration components would normally be replaced separately from the structural elements. The structural elements, according to the court, also served a function independent of the refrigeration machinery, such as keeping out humidity, reducing temperature migration, and providing an enclosed, protected space in which the frozen foods could be stored.

The regulations provide an exception from the definition of a *building* for a structure which is "essentially an item of machinery or equipment" (Reg. § 1.48-1(e)(1)(i)) (reproduced above). This exception, which encompasses equipment as well as machinery, is arguably broader than the Reg. § 1.48-1(c) exception discussed above. In , the court noted that property may be considered an "item of machinery or equipment" for purposes of the exclusion from the definition of a building without necessarily constituting "property which is in the nature of machinery" within the meaning of Reg. § 1.48-1(c).

A structure that housed equipment in a waste-treatment production facility was not in the nature of machinery or equipment. The structure itself must be a part of an industrial process and function as machinery or equipment. Here the perimeter walls did not aid in the processing of waste and did not act as a unitary mechanism with the equipment it houses. Although the structure was not considered machinery or equipment it was not considered a building under the second exception described in Reg. § 1.48-1(e)(1) for a structure which houses property used as an integral part of manufacturing, production, or extraction or furnishing transportation, communications, electrical energy, gas, water, or sewage disposal services if the use of the structure is so closely related to the use of such property that the structure clearly can be expected to be replaced when the property it initially houses is replaced (IRS Letter Ruling 200013038, December 27, 1999).

See also, ¶ 110.

*Certain real property described in Code Sec. 1245(a)(3)*

In addition to personal property, Code Sec. 1245 property includes other tangible property (other than a building or its structural components):

(1) used as an integral part of manufacturing, production, or extraction or as an integral part of furnishing transportation, communications, electrical energy, gas, water, or sewage disposal services;

(2) that is a research facility used in connection with any activity described in item (1); or

(3) that is a facility used in connection with any activity described in item (1) for the bulk storage of fungible commodities (including commodities in a liquid or gaseous state) (Code Sec. 1245(a)(3)(B); Reg. § 1.1245-3(c); Reg.§ 1.48-1(d)).

This property was described in former Code Sec. 48(a)(1)(B) as qualifying for the investment tax credit (ITC). This property cannot be considered nonresidential real property because it is specifically excluded from the definition of section 1250 property (see above).

The investment tax credit regulations detail the types of property that qualify under this exception (Reg. § 1.48-1(d)(2)). For example, the terms "manufacturing," "production," and "extraction" include the construction, reconstruction, or making of property out of scrap, salvage, or junk material, as well as from new or raw material, by processing, manipulating, refining, or changing the form of an article, or by combining or assembling two or more articles.

With respect to item (1), the ITC regulations provide that certain structures housing property used for those activities are not considered buildings. See above.

Code Sec. 1245(a)(3) property also includes single purpose agricultural and horticultural structures, storage facilities used in connection with the distribution of petroleum, and railroad gradings and tunnel bores. These items, however, are assigned specific Asset Classes and recovery periods under MACRS and Rev. Proc. 87-56.

Property described in items (1) through (3), above, is generally classified by Sec. 5.05 of Rev. Proc. 87-56 as a land improvement (Asset Class 00.3) for purposes of MACRS. The MACRS depreciation period is, therefore, 15 years unless the improvement in question is specifically included in another property class described in Rev. Proc. 87-56. However, Sec. 5.05 provides that a structure that is essentially an item of machinery or equipment or a structure that houses property used as an integral part of an activity specified in former section 48(a)(1)(B)(i) of the Code (i.e., property used as an integral part of manufacturing, production, or extraction or of furnishing transportation, communications, electrical energy, gas, water, or sewage disposal services) if the use of the structure is so closely related to the use of the property that the structure clearly can be expected to be replaced when the property it initially houses is replaced, is included in the asset guideline class appropriate to the equipment to which it is related. Thus, such property would generally have a shorter recovery period than 15 years. As noted above, such a structure is also specifically excluded from the definition of a building by Reg. § 1.48-1(e).

# MACRS Bonus Depreciation

## ¶ 127D

## Bonus Depreciation - First-Year Additional Depreciation Allowance

*Organization of Explanation*

This bonus depreciation discussion is organized as follows:

**RECENT DEVELOPMENTS**

*1. Recent legislation*

*1A. Qualified improvement property placed in service after 2017—guidance for changing to 15-year recovery period and claiming bonus depreciation—guidance for making late elections and revoking prior elections for 2018, 2019, and 2020 tax years*

*1B. Final regs on 100 percent bonus depreciation for property acquired after September 27, 2017*

*1C. Change in accounting method procedures to apply 2020 final, 2019 final, or 2019 final and proposed regulations retroactively to 2017, 2018, 2019, or 2020 tax year*

*1D. Late elections and revocations for 2017, 2018, 2019, and 2020 tax years for taxpayers applying 2020 final, 2019 final, or 2019 final and proposed regulations*

**BONUS RATES AND COMPUTATION**

*2. Bonus depreciation rates, including 100 percent rate for property acquired after September 27, 2017*

*3. Computation of bonus allowance*

*4. How bonus depreciation affects rate of recovery*

*5. Coordination with Code Sec. 179*

*6. Short tax year*

*7. Like-kind exchanges and involuntary conversions*

*8. Computation of bonus deduction when basis increases or decreases after property placed in service*

*9. Election out of bonus depreciation*

*10. Election to claim 50-percent bonus depreciation in place of 100-percent bonus depreciation during tax year that includes September 28, 2017*

*11. Special rules for making and revoking elections in tax year that includes September 28, 2017*

*11A. Special rules for 2014/2015 fiscal year returns and 2015 short year returns if no bonus claimed on 2015 property*

*11B. Special rules for 2013/2014 fiscal year returns and 2014 short year returns if no bonus claimed on 2014 property*

**QUALIFIED PROPERTY**

*12. Qualified property*

*13. Used property acquired after September 27, 2017 qualifies for bonus depreciation*

*14. Code Sec. 754 elections and other partnership transactions*

*15. Qualified leasehold improvement property placed in service before 2016*

*16. Qualified improvement property placed in service after 2015*

RECENT DEVELOPMENTS

*1. Legislation*

**Coronavirus Aid, Relief, and Economic Security (CARES) Act (P.L. 116-136) (March 27, 2020)**

A technical correction retroactively assigns a 15-year recovery period to qualified improvement property (QIP), effective for property placed in service after 2017 (Code Sec. 168(e)(3)(E)(vii), as added by the CARES Act (P.L. 116-136)). Because QIP is assigned a 15-year recovery period it also qualifies for bonus depreciation under the general rule that property with an MACRS recovery period of 20 years or less is eligible for bonus depreciation. See "*16. Qualified improvement property placed in service after 2015.*" IRS guidance explains how to change accounting methods or file amended returns to reassign a 15-year recovery period as well as claiming bonus depreciation on QIP which was placed in service after 2017 and depreciated over 39 years (Rev. Proc. 2020-25). See *1A. Qualified improvement property placed in service after 2017—guidance for changing to 15-year recovery period and claiming bonus depreciation—guidance for making late elections and revoking prior elections for 2018, 2019, and 2020 tax years.*

**Tax Cuts and Jobs Act (P.L. 114-113) (December 22, 2017)**

The Tax Cuts Act contains several significant provisions that affect bonus depreciation. Highlights reflected in this explanation include:

- For property acquired after September 27, 2017 and placed in service before 2023 the bonus rate is 100 percent, 80 percent for 2023, 60 percent for 2024, 40 percent for 2025, and 20% for 2026. See "*2. Bonus depreciation rates, including 100 percent rate for property acquired after September 27, 2017.*"

- A taxpayer may elect to apply the 50 percent rate for property placed in service during the taxpayer's first tax year ending after September 27, 2017. See "*2. Bonus depreciation rates, including 100 percent rate for property acquired after September 27, 2017.*"

- For property acquired before September 28, 2017, the bonus rate is 50 percent for property placed in service in 2017, 40 percent for 2018, and 30 percent for 2019. See "*2. Bonus depreciation rates, including 100 percent rate for property acquired after September 27, 2017.*"

- Qualified improvement property is removed as a separate category of bonus depreciation property effective for property placed in service after December 31, 2017. A technical correction (Code Sec. 168(e)(3)(E)(vii)) retroactively provides that QIP has a 15-year recovery period and qualifies for bonus depreciation if placed in service after 2017. See "*16. Qualified improvement property placed in service after 2015.*"

• Used property may qualify for bonus depreciation if acquired and placed in service after September 27, 2017. See "*13. Used property acquired after September 27, 2017 qualifies for bonus depreciation.*"

• Films, television shows, and live theatrical productions are eligible for bonus depreciation if acquired and placed in service after September 27, 2017. See "*17. Film and television productions and live theatrical productions acquired and placed in service after September 27, 2017.*"

• Property used by rate-regulated utilities is excluded from bonus depreciation if placed in service in tax years beginning after 2017. See "*23. Rate-regulated utility property does not qualify for bonus if placed in service in tax years beginning after 2017.*"

• Property of certain motor vehicle, boat, and farm machinery retail and lease businesses that use floor plan financing indebtedness is excluded from bonus depreciation if placed in service in tax year that a tax benefit is received from the interest deduction on such indebtedness (for property placed in service in tax years beginning after 2017). See "*22. Property used by certain motor vehicle, boat, farm machinery businesses that used floor plan financing indebtedness does not qualify for bonus depreciation if placed in service in tax years beginning after 2017.*"

• Corporate election to claim AMT credits in lieu of bonus depreciation is repealed (effective for tax years beginning after December 31, 2017) in conjunction with repeal of the corporate AMT. See "*53. Corporate election to claim accelerated AMT and research credits in lieu of bonus depreciation.*"

• Long-term accounting method relief from impact of bonus depreciation is extended through 2027. See "*45. Coordination with long-term contract method of accounting.*"

**The Tax Technical Corrections Act of 2018 (Division U of P.L. 115-141) (March 23, 2018)**

The Tax Technical Corrections Act of 2018 (Division U of P.L. 115-141) (March 23, 2018) makes the following retroactive clarifications:

• The phase-down rates for longer production property and certain-noncommercial aircraft acquired before September 28, 2017 are clarified to provide that a 50 percent rate applies to such property placed in service in 2017 or 2018, 40 percent if placed in service in 2019, and 30 percent if placed in service in 2020. 2021 progress expenditures of longer production property acquired before September 28, 2017 do not qualify for bonus depreciation (P.L. 115-141 amending Code Sec. 168(k)(6), as in effect before enactment of the Tax Cuts and Jobs Act of 2017 (P.L. 115-97)). See discussion "*2. Bonus depreciation rates, including 100 percent rate for property acquired after September 27, 2017.*"

• Written contracts for the acquisition of property with a longer production period and certain non-commercial aircraft must be binding in order for the extended placed-in-service deadlines to apply (Code Sec. 168(k)(2)(B)(i)(III), as amended by theP.L. 115-141). See "*34. Acquisition and placed-in-service date requirement for property acquired before September 28, 2017 and placed in service after 2015*" and "*32. Acquisition and placed-in-service date requirements for 100 percent bonus rate property acquired after September 27, 2017.*"

• Specified plants include plants that will have more than one crop. The two-year pre-productive period is measured from the time of planting or grafting to the time that the plant begins bearing a marketable crop or yield of fruits or nuts (Code Sec. 168(k)(5)(B)(ii), as amended by P.L. 115-141). See discussion "*18. Specified plants.*"

• If a corporation makes a regular election out of bonus depreciation under Code Sec. 168(k)(7), as in effect on the day prior to enactment of the 2017 Tax Cuts Act, for a particular class of property (e.g., all 5-year property), then an election under Code Sec. 168(k)(4) to claim unused alternative minimum tax credits in lieu of bonus depreciation does not apply to the class of property for which an election out of bonus depreciation is made (Act Sec. 101(d)(4) of P.L. 115-141). See "*53. Corporate election to claim accelerated AMT and research credits in lieu of bonus depreciation.*"

*1A. Qualified improvement property placed in service after 2017—guidance for changing to 15-year recovery period and claiming bonus depreciation—guidance for making late elections and revoking prior elections for 2018, 2019, and 2020 tax years*

As a result a technical correction in the Coronavirus Aid, Relief, and Economic Security (CARES) Act (P.L. 116-136) (March 27, 2020) that retroactively assigns a 15-year recovery period to qualified improvement property (QIP) placed in service after 2017 (Code Sec. 168(e)(3)(E)(vii)), a taxpayer must stop depreciating QIP as nonresidential real property over a 39-year recovery period (40 years under ADS). IRS guidance (Rev. Proc. 2020-25) provides the various options for QIP placed in service in tax years ending in 2018, 2019, or 2020 that is depreciated using a 39-year recovery period. Under this guidance taxpayers may file an amended return or change in accounting method to (a) claim 100 percent bonus depreciation on the QIP or (b) make a late election out of bonus depreciation for all 15-year property placed in service during the tax year, including QIP, and depreciate the QIP over 15 years (or 20 years if ADS is elected).

*Form 3115 and amended return options.* A taxpayer will need to file an amended return or file a change in accounting method to switch from the now incorrect 39-year recovery period. If more than one return has been filed depreciating the QIP over the incorrect depreciation period, the taxpayer is still allowed to make the change by filing amended returns for each incorrect year, provided the amended returns are filed no later than October 15, 2021 or, if earlier, by the expiration of the limitations period for assessment of tax for the year the QIP was placed in service.

See CCH AnswerConnect for an example of a filled-in Form 3115. Use as a search term, "Filled-in Form 3115 for qualified improvement property."

A taxpayer who has filed only one incorrect return may file an amended return (before filing a second incorrect return) or file a Form 3115 with the return for the year after the QIP was placed in service. A Form 3115 will reflect a negative (favorable) section 481(a) adjustment equal to the difference between the depreciation and/or bonus that should have been claimed prior to the tax year of change and the depreciation that was actually claimed using the 39-year recovery period.

Rev. Proc. 2020-25 adds new section 6.19 to Rev. Proc. 2019-43, "Qualified improvement property placed in service after December 31, 2017," for the purpose of changing from the 39-year recovery period and using the 15-year recovery period and/or claiming bonus depreciation.

A taxpayer may file a change in accounting method for qualified improvement property under Sec. 6.01 of Rev. Proc. 2019-43 instead of Section 6.19, if the original Form 3115 was filed before November 17, 2020 (Sec. 6.01(c)(xvii) of Rev. Proc. 2019-43 as added by Rev. Proc. 2020-25 and modified by Rev. Proc. 2020-50).

Taxpayers who change their method for accounting for QIP and also use the accounting change method procedures to make a late election or revoke an election for property placed in service in the same tax year as the QIP (see below) should file a single Form 3115.

*October 15, 2021 due date for amended return.* An amended income tax return or amended Form 1065 for the placed in service year of the QIP is due on or before October 15, 2021 but may be filed no later than the applicable period of limitations on assessment for the tax year for which the amended return is filed. Special deadlines apply to a partnership subject to the centralized partnership audit regime for tax years beginning in 2018 and 2019. See Rev. Proc. 2020-23.

*QIP acquired before September 28, 2017.* For QIP "acquired" before September 28, 2017 but placed in service in 2018 or 2019 the taxpayer may file an amended return(s) or Form 3115 to reflect bonus depreciation and the 15- year recovery period. A 40 percent bonus depreciation rate applies if the QIP was placed in service in 2018. The 40 percent rate is reduced to 30% for QIP acquired before September 28, 2017 placed in service in 2019. No bonus is allowed thereafter. Extended placed-in-service deadlines apply to QIP acquired before September 28, 2017 that is long production property. Generally, qualified improvement property is considered acquired when construction begins. See "*34. Acquisition and placed-in-service date requirement for property acquired before September 28, 2017 and placed in service after 2015*" and "*32. Acquisition and placed-in-service date requirements for 100 percent bonus rate property acquired after September 27, 2017.*"

*Expensed QIP does not qualify.* QIP which was expensed by the taxpayer is not within the scope of the IRS guidance. For example, a taxpayer may not file an amended return or Form 3115 under Rev. Proc. 2020-25 in order to claim bonus depreciation on the cost of QIP that was deducted as a repair expense under the tangible property regulations of Code Sec. 263. Similarly QIP that was expensed under section 179 as qualified real property does not qualify for bonus under this guidance.

However, it appears that a taxpayer could change or revoke its section 179 election with respect to the QIP by filing an amended return within the limitation period for assessment of tax under the rules that are generally applicable to Code Sec. 179 property in order to make the QIP eligible for bonus depreciation. Bonus depreciation would be claimed on the amended return that was filed to change or revoke the election. See ¶ 304 for a discussion of the change or revocation procedures. A reason for doing this is that amounts expensed under section 179 are subject to the section 1245 recapture rules. The section 1250 recapture rules apply to bonus depreciation property. See ¶ 300, *Recapture upon sale or disposition.*

*QIP depreciated by certain real property trade or businesses or farming businesses does not qualify.* The CARES Act allows a real property trade or business or a farming businesses to make a late election out of the business interest limitations (Code Sec. 163(j)) or withdraw a prior election out of the limitations for a tax year beginning in 2018, 2019, or 2020 by filing an amended federal income tax return, amended Form 1065, or AAR (Rev. Proc. 2020-22). The guidance under Rev. Proc. 2020-25 does not apply to depreciation changes relating to QIP that is affected by a revocation or late election under Rev. Proc. 2020-22. See ¶ 152.

*QIP is not a separate property class for bonus purposes.* QIP is not treated as a separate class of bonus property if placed in service after 2017. It is part of the 15-year property class. Therefore, a taxpayer must also claim 100 percent bonus depreciation on any other 15-year property (e.g., 15-year land improvements) placed in service during the tax year. If a taxpayer made a timely election out of bonus depreciation for 15-year property in the same year the QIP was placed in service, that election will retroactively apply to the QIP. However, as explained below, IRS guidance allows a taxpayer to *revoke* a prior election out of bonus depreciation for any class of property placed in service in a tax year ending in 2018, 2019, or 2020. Alternatively, a taxpayer may also make a late election out of bonus depreciation for 15-year property placed in service during these tax years if the taxpayer does not want to claim bonus on the QIP, including any other 15-year property, placed in service during the same tax year.

The IRS guidance allows a taxpayer to revoke a prior election out of bonus depreciation or make a late election out of bonus depreciation with respect to any class of property. The taxpayer is not required to have placed QIP in service during the tax year. See below.

*Automatic extension of time to file certain elections and to revoke certain prior elections for property placed in service tax years ending in 2018, 2019, and 2020.* Taxpayers are given until October 15, 2021 to make or revoke certain elections with respect to property placed in service in a tax year ending in 2018, 2019, and 2020 if the income tax return or Form 1065 for the tax year was timely filed on or before April 17, 2020, the date of publication of Rev. Proc. 2020-25 (Rev. Proc. 2020-25). For example, a calendar year taxpayer that filed an income tax return or Form 1065 for the 2019 tax year after April 17, 2020 may not make or revoke an election for property placed in service in 2019 under this procedure. However, it could make or revoke elections for the 2018 tax year.

A taxpayer may make or revoke an election under these rules even if it did not place qualified improvement property in service during the tax year for which the election or revocation is made.

The following elections may be made late or revoked for a tax year ending in 2018, 2019, or 2020:

- the election out of bonus depreciation for a class of property (Code Sec. 168(k)(7))
- the election to claim bonus depreciation on specified plants in the year of planting or grafting (Code Sec. 168(k)(5))
- the election to use the MACRS alternative depreciation system (Code Sec. 168(g)(7))

In addition the election to claim 50 percent bonus depreciation on all 100 percent bonus property placed in service (or planted or grafted in the case of specific plants subject to a 168(k)(5) election) in a tax year that includes September 28, 2017 may be made or revoked (Code Sec. 168(k)(10)).

Rev. Proc. 2020-50 also allows taxpayers to make late elections and revoke elections under Code Sec. 168(k)(5) and (k)(7) for 2016 and 2017 tax years that include September 28, 2017, as well as later tax years that end before 2021 and under Code Sec. 168(k)(10) for a tax year that includes September 28, 2017 if the taxpayer applies final bonus depreciation regulations during the placed-in-service tax year. See *1D. Late elections and revocations for 2017, 2018, 2019, and 2020 tax years for taxpayers applying 2020 final, 2019 final, or 2019 final and proposed regulations.*

For a tax year that includes September 28, 2017, Rev. Proc. 2019-33 also allows late elections and revocation of elections under Code Sec. 168(k)(5), (k)(7), and (k)(10). See *11. Special rules for making and revoking elections in tax year that includes September 28, 2017.*

*Election or revocation made on amended return or Form 3115.* A taxpayer may generally make or revoke the election on an amended income tax return or an amended Form 1065 for the placed-in-service year of the property filed by the October 15, 2021 deadline. However, the amended return cannot be filed later than the limitations period for assessment of tax for the tax year that the amended return is filed for. If an amended return is filed collateral adjustments are required for any subsequently filed return. Thus, a taxpayer may need to file two amended returns if a return has already been filed for the tax year that follows the tax year for which the late election or revocation is made.

The time to file an amended Form 1065 return by a partnership subject to the centralized partnership audit regime (BBA partnership) for tax year beginning in 2018 or 2019 is governed by Rev. Proc. 2020-23. A BBA partnership that chooses not file an amended Form 1065 as permitted under Rev. Proc. 2020-23 or that cannot file an amended Form 1065 because the placed in service year is a tax year not within the scope of Rev. Proc. 2020-23 may file an AAR for the placed in service year by October 15, 2021 but not later that the applicable period of limitations on making adjustments for the reviewed year.

*Using Form 3115 to make or revoke an election.* Instead of making or revoking the election on an amended return a taxpayer may make or revoke the election on a Form 3115 and take a section 481(a) adjustment into account. The Form 3115 must be filed with a taxpayer's timely filed original income tax return or Form 1065 for the taxpayer's first or second tax year following the tax year in which the property was placed in service or, if later, any tax year for which a taxpayer files an original income tax return or Form 1065, as applicable, on or after April 17, 2020 and on or before October 15, 2020 (Section 6.20 of Rev. Proc. 2019-43 as added by Rev. Proc. 2020-25 and modified by Rev. Proc. 2020-50).

*Special rule for revocation of ADS election.* The election to revoke an ADS election may only be made by filing an amended return (Rev. Proc. 2020-25, Section 5.02(3)).

*Only one revocation permitted.* A taxpayer may not revoke a Code Sec. 168(k)(7) election out of bonus depreciation or a Code Sec. 168(k)(5) election to claim bonus depreciation in the year of planting or grafting if the taxpayer previously revoked the election under Rev. Proc. 2020-25 or under Rev. Proc. 2020-50 (relating to accounting method changes to apply bonus depreciation regulations and to make or revoke certain elections) (Sec. 4.01 of Rev. Proc. 2020-25, as modified by Rev. Proc. 2020-50).

### *1B. Final and proposed regulations on 100 percent bonus depreciation for property acquired after September 27, 2017*

The Tax Cuts and Jobs Act (P.L. 114-113) (December 22, 2017) made several changes to the bonus depreciation rules. Most significantly it increased the bonus depreciation rate to 100 percent effective for property acquired and placed in service after September 27, 2017 and before 2023 and also made used property acquired and placed in service after September 27, 2017 eligible for bonus depreciation.

The IRS issued the following series of proposed and final regulations implementing these and other changes for property acquired and placed in service after September 27, 2017:

(1) *2018 Proposed Regulations.* Proposed Reg. § 1.168(k)-2 was published in the Federal Register on August 8, 2018 in Notice of Proposed Rulemaking REG-104397-18.

(2) *2019 Final and Proposed Regulations.* The 2018 proposed regulations were adopted as final regulations with modifications by T.D. 9874 as published on September 24, 2019. Additional regulations were simultaneously proposed (REG-106808-19).

(3) *2020 Final Regulations.* The 2019 proposed regulations were adopted by T.D. 9916 as final regulations with certain modifications. Certain additional modifications were also made to the 2019 final regulations. Provisions relating to consolidated groups were moved from Reg. § 1.168(k)-2 to Reg. § 1.1502-68.

The final regulations are comprehensive. In many respects they are similar to or identical to the current final regulations in Reg. § 1.168(k)-1 for property acquired before September 28, 2017. However, they incorporate detailed guidance on changes made by the Tax Cuts and Jobs Act (P.L. 115-97) (enacted December 22, 2017). The most important change (other than the bonus rate increase to 100 percent) allows bonus depreciation on used property acquired after September 27, 2017. As explained below, used property may not have been previously owned by the taxpayer within a 5-year lookback period and must be acquired by "purchase" within the meaning of Code Sec. 179(d).

A summary of the main differences between the 2020 final regulations and the earlier regulations is provided in Rev. Proc. 2020-50 Section 2.02.

Other subjects covered in the final regulations relate to:

- Qualified improvement property
- 15-year leasehold, retail, and restaurant improvements
- Qualified film, television, and theatrical productions
- Specified plants
- Determining the acquisition date
- Property, including components, constructed by or for a taxpayer
- Long production property and noncommercial aircraft extended placed in service date
- Consolidated groups and used property
- Partnerships transactions and used property
- Election to use 50 percent rate for tax year that includes September 28, 2017

*Effective Date of Final Regulations*

In general, the 2020 final regulations are mandatory for property acquired after September 27, 2017 and placed in service in tax years beginning after December 31, 2020 (Reg. § 1.168(k)-2(h)(1) and Reg. § 1.1502-68(e)(1)).

A taxpayer may choose to apply Reg. § 1.168(k)-2 and Reg. § 1.1502-68 of the 2020 final regulations, in their entirety, to depreciable property acquired and placed in service after September 27, 2017, during a tax year ending on or after September 28, 2017, provided the taxpayer consistently applies all rules in these final regulations. However, once the final regulations are applied for a tax year, the taxpayer must continue to apply the final regulations for subsequent tax years (Reg. § 1.168(k)-2(h)(3)).

The preamble to the 2020 final regulations (T.D. 9916) provides that a taxpayer may rely on the 2019 proposed regulations for depreciable property acquired and placed in service after September 27, 2017, during a tax year ending on or after September 28, 2017, and ending before the mandatory effective date of the final regulations (i.e., the taxpayer's first tax year that begins on or after January 1, 2021) if the taxpayer follows the proposed regulations in their entirety and in a consistent manner, except for withdrawn Proposed Reg. § 1.168(k)-2(b)(3)(iii)(B)(5) which treated property owned by a partnership as owned by the partners for purposes of the five-year lookback rule for used property.

The IRS has issued a revenue procedure which explains how a taxpayer may apply the 2020 final regulations or earlier final and proposed regulations retroactively. See discussion below at "*1C. Change in accounting method procedures to apply 2020 final, 2019 final, or 2019 final and proposed regulations retroactively to 2017, 2018, 2019, or 2020 tax year*".

*Qualified Improvement Property*

A retroactive technical correction (Code Sec. 168(e)(3)(E)(vii)) provides that qualified improvement property (QIP) placed in service after 2017 has a 15-year recovery period and, therefore, is eligible for bonus depreciation by reason of having a recovery period of 20 years or less.

QIP placed in service in 2016 or 2017 is a separate category of bonus depreciation property and qualifies for bonus depreciation regardless of the length of its recovery period.

QIP general consists of improvements made by the taxpayer to the interior of nonresidential real property (Code Sec. 168(e)(6) and Reg. § 1.168(b)-1(a)(5)).

QIP acquired after September 27, 2017 and placed in service before 2023 is eligible for the 100 percent bonus rate.

See "*16. Qualified improvement property placed in service after 2015.*"

*15-Year Qualified Leasehold, Retail, and Restaurant Property*

Qualified leasehold improvement property, qualified retail improvement property, and qualified restaurant property are removed as categories of 15-year property, effective for property placed in service after 2017. If acquired and placed in service after September 27, 2017 and before 2018 these types of property may qualify for the 100 percent rate (Reg. § 1.168(k)-2(b)(2); Proposed Reg. § 168(k)-2(b)(2) in REG-104397-18).

15-year qualified leasehold improvement property and 15-year qualified retail improvement property placed in service in 2016 and 2017 qualify for bonus depreciation by reason of having a recovery period of 20 years or less and also because such property necessarily meets all of the definitional requirements of qualified improvement property. Qualified improvement property is a separate category of bonus depreciation property if placed in service in 2016 or 2017. After 2017, qualified improvement property is removed as a separate category of bonus depreciation property and will qualify for bonus depreciation by reason of having an MACRS recovery period of 20 years or less.

Bonus depreciation may not be claimed on 15-year qualified restaurant property placed in service in 2016 and 2017 unless the restaurant property is qualified improvement property (Code Sec. 168(e)(7)(B), prior to being stricken by the Tax Cuts Act). Therefore, restaurant buildings and exterior improvements to restaurants placed in service during this period do not qualify for bonus depreciation even though a 15-year recovery period applies. Interior improvements do qualify. The 100 percent bonus rate applies 15-year restaurant improvement property that is qualified improvement property if acquired and placed in service after September 27, 2017 and before 2018 (Reg. § 1.168(k)-2(b)(2); Proposed Reg. § 168(k)-2(b)(2) in REG-104397-18).

See "*15. Qualified leasehold improvement property placed in service before 2016.*"

*Specified Plants*

A specified plant that is planted or grafted after September 27, 2017 is considered acquired and placed in service after September 27, 2017 and may qualify for the 100 percent bonus in the year planting or grafting (Code Sec. 168(k)(5); Reg. § 1.168(k)-2(b)(5)(vii); Proposed Reg. § 1.168(k)-2(b)(5)(vi) in REG-104397-18).

A taxpayer must make an election by the due date (including extensions) of the return for the year of planting or grafting in order to claim bonus in the year of planting or grafting. The election may be made for one or more specified plants by the person owning the plant. The taxpayer, therefore, may make the election on a selective basis (Reg. § 1.168(k)-2(f)(2); Proposed Reg. § 1.168(k)-2(e)(2) in REG-104397-18).

If the election is not made for a specified plant, bonus depreciation is claimed in the year of commercial production.

An election may be made to claim the 50 percent bonus rate on specified plants that are planted or grafted after September 27, 2017 during the tax year that includes September 28, 2017. The election applies to all specified plants for which the election to claim bonus in the year of planting or grafting is made and which are planted or grafted after September 27, 2017 (Reg. § 1.168(k)-2(f)(3); Proposed Reg. § 1.168(k)-2(e)(3) in REG-104397-18).

A taxpayer may make a late election to claim 100 percent bonus or 50 percent bonus in place of 100 percent bonus on specified plants planted or grafted after September 27, 2017 in a tax year that includes September 28, 2017. The election is made by filing an accounting method change for the first, second, or third tax year that follows the tax year that includes September 28, 2017. These elections may also be revoked by filing an accounting method change. An amended return may also be filed to make or revoke these elections if the taxpayer has not filed a return for the tax year that follows the tax year that includes September 28, 2017 (Rev. Proc. 2019-33). Late elections and revocations for the tax year that includes September 28, 2017 may also be available under Rev. Proc. 2020-25 and Rev. Proc. 2020-50.

See "*18. Specified plants.*"

*Qualified films, television, and live theatrical productions*

Production costs of a qualified film, television, or live theatrical production as defined in Code Sec. 181(d) and (e) acquired and placed in service after September 27, 2017 qualify for bonus depreciation (Reg. § 1.168(k)-2(b)(2)(i)(E)). The fact that the production costs exceeds the $15 million deduction Code Sec. 181 expensing limit (Code Sec. 181(a)(2)) or the production commences after the expiration date of Code Sec. 181 does not affect the allowable bonus deduction. Only the owner of the production may claim the deduction.

A qualified film or television production is acquired on the date principal photography begins and placed in service on the date of initial release or broadcast (Reg. § 1.168(k)-2(b)(4)(iii) and (b)(5)(vi); Proposed Reg. § 1.168(k)-2(b)(4)(iii) and (b)(5)(v) in REG-104397-18).

A qualified live theatrical production is acquired on the date all necessary elements for producing the production are secured and is placed in service on the date of the first commercial performance before a live audience. A performance primarily for publicity, the raising of funds to finish production, or to determine the need for further production activity is not the first commercial performance (Reg. § 1.168(k)-2(b)(4)(iii) and (b)(5)(vi); Proposed Reg. § 1.168(k)-2(b)(4)(iii) and (5)(v) in REG-104397-18).

See "*17. Film and television productions and live theatrical productions acquired and placed in service after September 27, 2017.*"

*Rate-Regulated Utilities and Floor Plan Financing Effective Date*

The regulations clarify that the rule in Code Sec. 168(k)(9) which prevents rate-regulated public utilities from claiming bonus depreciation is effective for property placed in service in tax years beginning after 2017 (Reg. § 1.168(k)-2(b)(2)(ii)(F); Proposed Reg. § 1.168(k)-2(b)(2)(ii)(F) in REG-104397-18).

The rule in Code Sec. 168(k)(9) that prevents motor vehicle, boat, and farm machinery businesses with average annual gross receipts exceeding $25 million from claiming bonus depreciation if the business deducts floor plan financing interest is also effective for property placed in service in tax year beginning after 2017 (Reg. § 1.168(k)-2(b)(ii)(2)(G); Proposed Reg. § 1.168(k)-2(b)(2)(ii)(G) in REG-104397-18).

Technically, the effective date for Code Sec. 168(k)(9) is for property acquired and placed in service after 2017 (§ 13201(d) of P.L. 115-97, adding Code Sec. 168(k)(9) and § 13201(h)(1)-(2) providing the effective date). The IRS, however, apparently decided to use the effective date for the interest deduction limitations under Code Sec. 163(j) because of the need to coordinate the timing of the two provisions.

Final regulations (T.D. 9916) adopt proposed regulations that clarify that the floor plan financing rule is applied on an annual basis and deny bonus depreciation only if a tax benefit is received from any interest deduction on floor plan financing indebtedness during the tax year that the bonus property is placed in service (Reg. § 1.168(k)-2(b)(2)(ii)(G); Proposed Reg. § 1.168(k)-2(b)(2)(ii)(G) in REG-104397-18).

See "*22. Property used by certain motor vehicle, boat, farm machinery businesses that used floor plan financing indebtedness does not qualify for bonus depreciation if placed in service in tax years beginning after 2017*" and "*23. Rate-regulated utility property does not qualify for bonus if placed in service in tax years beginning after 2017.*"

*General Requirements for Used Property*

Used property must be acquired by "purchase" within the meaning of Code Sec. 179(d) after September 27, 2017 in order to qualify for bonus depreciation (Code Sec. 168(k)(2)(E)(ii)(II); Reg. § 1.168(k)-2(b)(3)(iii)(A); Proposed Reg. § 1.168(k)-2(b)(3)(iii)(A) in REG-104397-18). This means that:

(1) The property may not be acquired from a related person or by one component member of a controlled group from another component member of the same controlled group;

(2) The basis of the property in the hands of a person acquiring the property may not be determined in whole or in part by reference to the adjusted basis of the property in the hands of the person transferring the property; and

(3) The property may not be transferred at death with a fair market value basis or other basis determined under Code Sec. 1014(a).

In addition, the portion of the basis of acquired property that is determined by reference to the basis of other property held at any time by the person acquiring such property (for example, in a like-kind exchange) does not qualify as used property eligible for bonus depreciation (Code Sec. 168(k)(2)(E)(ii)(II); Reg. § 1.168(k)-2(b)(3)(iii)(A); Proposed Reg. § 1.168(k)-2(b)(3)(iii)(A) in REG-104397-18).

*Property previously used by taxpayer.* Property used by a taxpayer or predecessor prior to its acquisition does not qualify for bonus depreciation (Code Sec. 168(k)(2)(E)(ii)(I)). Property was previously used by the taxpayer prior to its acquisition, however, only if the taxpayer or predecessor had a depreciable interest in the property during the five-calendar years prior to the placed in service year or in the placed-in-service year prior to the actual placed-in-service date (Reg. § 1.168(k)-2(b)(3)(iii)(B)(1); Proposed Reg. § 1.168(k)-2(b)(3)(iii)(B)(1) in REG-104397-18). Thus, a lessee may purchase leased property and qualify for bonus depreciation since the lessee did not have a depreciable interest.

If a taxpayer has a depreciable interest in a portion of a property and later acquires an additional depreciable interest, the additional interest is not tainted and may qualify for bonus depreciation. For example, if a lessee with a depreciable interest in a leasehold improvement acquires the entire leased property, the leasehold improvement does not qualify for bonus depreciation. However, the remainder of the property may qualify (Reg. § 1.168(k)-2(b)(3)(iii)(B)(1); Proposed Reg. § 1.168(k)-2(b)(3)(iii)(B)(1) in REG-104397-18).

If a taxpayer sells a portion of an interest in property and then later reacquires another portion of the same property, bonus depreciation only applies to the extent the newly acquired interest is greater than the original interest (Reg. § 1.168(k)-2(b)(3)(iii)(B)(2); Proposed Reg. § 1.168(k)-2(b)(3)(iii)(B)(2) in REG-104397-18).

A de minimis rule provides that a taxpayer does not have a prior depreciable interest in a property on account of previously placing it in service for 90 days or less (Reg. § 1.168(k)-2(b)(3)(iii)(B)(4); Proposed Reg. § 1.168(k)-2(b)(3)(iii)(B)(4) in REG-104397-18).

If a taxpayer substantially renovates previously owned property, the taxpayer does not have a prior depreciable interest in the substantially renovated property (Reg. § 1.168(k)-2(b)(3)(B)(3)).

*Partnership lookthrough rule withdrawn.* The IRS withdrew a proposed regulation that treated a partner as having a depreciable interest in a portion of property prior to the person's acquisition of the property if the person was a partner in a partnership at any time the partnership owned the property (Proposed Reg. § 1.168(k)-2(b)(3)(iii)(B)(5), withdrawn by NPRM REG-106808-19, published in the Federal Register on Nov. 10, 2020)). The withdrawn proposal provided that a partner has a depreciable interest in a portion of property equal to the partner's total share of depreciation deductions with respect to the property as a percentage of the total depreciation deductions allocated to all partners with respect to that property during the current calendar year and five calendar years immediately prior to the partnership's current placed-in-service year of the property. For this purpose, only the portion of the current calendar year and previous 5-year period during which the partnership owned the property and the person was a partner is taken into account. Thus if a taxpayer later acquires the property held by the partnership while the taxpayer was a partner, the partner has held a disqualifying prior interest in a portion of the property as so calculated.

If the partnership did not own the property for the entire period or the taxpayer was not a partner in the partnership for the entire period, only the period during which the partnership owned the property or the taxpayer was a partner is taken into account.

The proposal provided no illustrative examples.

IRS determined that the complexity of applying the partnership lookthrough rule would place a significant administrative burden on both taxpayers and the IRS. Therefore, under the final regulations, a partner is not be treated as having a depreciable interest in partnership property solely by virtue of being a partner in the partnership. The IRS further determined that a replacement rule that applies only to controlling partners is not necessary because the related party rule in Code Sec. 179(d)(2)(A) applies to a direct purchase of partnership property by a current majority partner, and the series of related transactions rules in Reg. § 1.168(k)-2(b)(3)(iii)(C) prevents avoidance of the related party rule through the use of intermediary parties (Preamble to T.D. 9916).

*Property transferred within consolidated groups.* Property acquired by a member of a consolidated group does not qualify for bonus depreciation if any prior or current member of the group had a depreciable interest in the property during a five-year lookback period while a member of the group (Reg. § 1.1502-68(b)(1)).

> ***Example (1):*** ABC and BCD are members of the same consolidated group. ABC sells machinery to BCD. BCD may not claim bonus depreciation because ABC is a current group member that held a depreciable interest in the property. Furthermore ABC and BCD are related parties (Reg. § 1.1502-68(d), Example (1)).

> ***Example (2):*** ABC and BCD are members of the same consolidated group. ABC sells equipment to U, an unrelated party. In a later tax year within the five-year lookback period, BCD purchases the equipment from U. The equipment does not qualify for bonus depreciation because ABC previously had a depreciable interest in the machinery. The equipment does not qualify even if ABC left the consolidated group prior to BCD's purchase (Reg. § 1.1502-68(d), Example 2).

*Property acquired from related parties.* Used property acquired from a related party does not qualify for bonus depreciation (Reg. § 1.168(k)-2(b)(3)(iii)(A)(2); Proposed Reg. § 1.168(k)-2(b)(3)(iii)(A)(2) in REG-104397-18). Related parties are defined in Code Sec. 267 and Code Sec. 707(b) which disallow losses created in transfers between related parties (Code Sec. 179(d)(2)(A)).

See "*13. Used property acquired after September 27, 2017 qualifies for bonus depreciation.*"

*Special Rules for Partnerships*

Bonus depreciation has not been allowed in most transactions involving transfers of property to or from partnerships or transfers of interests in partnership property in connection with the transfer of a partnership interest. The requirement that the original use of the property must begin with the taxpayer claiming bonus depreciation was not satisfied. Now that used property can qualify for bonus depreciation the IRS regulations reconsider whether bonus depreciation can be claimed in some partnership transactions.

*Code Sec. 754 elections.* Any increase in the basis of partnership property under Code Sec. 734(b) as the result of the distribution of property to a partner with respect to which a Code Sec. 754 election is in effect does not qualify for bonus depreciation (Reg. § 1.168(k)-2(b)(3)(iv)(C); Proposed Reg. § 1.168(k)-2(b)(3)(iv)(C) REG-104397-18).

However, an increase to the inside basis of a new partner's interest in partnership property under Code Sec. 743(b) pursuant to a partnership's Code Sec. 754

election may qualify for bonus depreciation (Reg. § 1.68(k)-2(b)(3)(iv)(D); Reg. § 1.168(k)-2(b)(3)(vii), Example 14; Proposed Reg. § 1.168(k)-2(b)(3)(iv)(D); Proposed Reg. § 1.168(k)-2(b)(3)(vi), Example 13 REG-104397-18). A new partner includes an existing partner who acquires an additional partnership interest. The basis increase is generally equal to the difference between the cost of the partnership interest and partnership's inside basis in the new partner's share of partnership property to which the new partnership interest relates.

The transferor partner and new partner may not be part of the same controlled group. The new partner's basis in the partnership property may not be determined in whole or in part by reference to the transferor's adjusted basis or under Code Sec. 1014. For example, a basis increase on account of a transfer at death does not qualify if the transferee takes a fair market value basis under Code Sec. 1014 (Reg. § 1.168(k)-2(b)(3)(vii), Example 16; Proposed Reg. § 1.168(k)-2(b)(3)(vi), Example 15 REG-104397-18). No bonus may be claimed if the new partner or any predecessor previously had a depreciable interest in the property deemed transferred (Reg. § 1.168(k)-2(b)(3)(vii), Example 17; Proposed Reg. § 1.168(k)-2(b)(3)(vi), Example 16 REG-104397-18). It does not matter that the partnership previously used the property. In addition, the transferor and new partner may not be related (Reg. § 1.168(k)-2(b)(3)(iv); Reg. § 1.168(k)-2(b)(3)(vii), Example 15; Proposed Reg. § 1.168(k)-2(b)(3)(iv); Proposed Reg. § 1.168(k)-2(b)(3)(vi), Example 14 REG-104397-18).

*Contributions to partnerships.* Contributions of property to a partnership do not qualify for bonus depreciation because the basis of the property in the hands of the partnership is determined by reference to the basis in the hands of the contributor (Code Sec. 723; Reg. § 1.168(k)-2(b)(3)(vii), Example 13; Proposed Reg. § 1.168(k)-2(b)(3)(vi), Example 12 REG-104397-18).

> ***Example (3):*** O and P form an equal partnership, OP. O contributes cash to OP, and P contributes equipment to OP. OP's basis in the equipment contributed by P is determined under section 723. Because OP's basis in such equipment is determined in whole or in part by reference to P's adjusted basis in such equipment, OP's acquisition does not satisfy the used property acquisition requirements.

*Remedial allocations.* Remedial allocations under Code Sec. 704(c) for contributions of property with an adjusted tax basis less than book basis do not qualify for bonus depreciation because the partnership's basis in the property is determined by reference to the contributing partner's basis in the property. In addition, the partnership has a depreciable interest in the contributed property at the time the remedial allocation is made (Reg. § 1.168(k)-2(b)(3)(iv)(A); Reg. § 1.704-3(d)(2); Proposed Reg. § 1.168(k)-2(b)(3)(iv)(A) REG-104397-18; Proposed Reg. § 1.704-3(d)(2) REG-104397-18).

*Distributions other than in liquidation.* No portion of the basis of distributed partnership property as determined under Code Sec. 732 qualifies for bonus depreciation (Reg. § 1.168(k)-2(b)(3)(iv)(B); Proposed Reg. § 1.168(k)-2(b)(3)(iv)(B) REG-104397-18). Because the partnership used the property prior to the distribution the original use requirement is not satisfied. The requirements for used property are not met because the basis is determined by reference to the distributee partner's basis in the partnership interest and the partnership's basis in the property.

*Book depreciation on contributed property.* Bonus depreciation does not apply for purposes of determining book depreciation on property contributed to a partnership with a zero adjusted tax basis (Reg. § 1.704-1(b)(2)(iv)(g)(3); Proposed Reg. § 1.704-1(b)(2)(iv)(g)(3) REG-104397-18).

See "*14. Code Sec. 754 elections and other partnership transactions.*"

*Acquisition Date Rules*

The 100 percent bonus rate applies to property acquired after September 27, 2017 and before 2023.

*Binding contracts.* Property acquired pursuant to a written binding contract entered into before September 28, 2017 does not qualify for the 100 percent bonus rate. The acquisition date is the later of the date that the contract was entered, the contract is enforceable under state law, all cancellation periods end, or all conditions subject to contingency clauses are satisfied (Reg. § 1.168(k)-2(b)(5)(ii)).

If property is acquired pursuant to a contract but the contract does not meet the definition of a written binding contract, the property is considered acquired when the taxpayer pays or incurs more than 10 percent of the cost of the property, excluding land and preliminary activities. Final regulations clarify that this rule also applies to property that is manufactured, constructed, or produced for the taxpayer by another person under a written contract that is not binding and which is entered into prior to the manufacture, construction, or production (Reg. § 1.168(k)-2(b)(5)(v); Proposed Reg. § 1.168(k)-2(b)(5)(v) in REG-104397-18). This rule is similar to the safe harbor for determining when self-constructed property is acquired and only applies if the property would otherwise be considered acquired on the date that a written binding contract became effective.

The new regulations for property acquired after September 27, 2017 retain the rules for earlier acquired property in Reg. § 1.168(k)-1(b)(4)(ii) defining a binding contract and provide additionally that a letter of intent for an acquisition is not a binding contract (Reg. § 1.168(k)-2(b)(v)(iii); Proposed Reg. § 1.168(k)-2(b)(5)(iii) in REG-104397-18).

The final regulations provide that property manufactured, constructed, or produced for a taxpayer by another person under a written binding contract entered into prior to manufacture, construction, or production is considered self-constructed and not acquired pursuant to a written binding contract (Reg. § 1.168(k)-2(b)(5)(iv)). Consequently, if construction of such property is considered to begin after September 27, 2017, it will qualify for bonus depreciation at the 100 percent rate even if the contract is entered into before September 28, 2017.

This is a major change from the proposed regulations which provided that property manufactured, constructed, or produced for a taxpayer by another person under a written binding contract entered into prior to manufacture, construction, or production is considered acquired pursuant to a written binding contract. Consequently, under the proposals if such a contract is entered into before September 28, 2017, the property does not qualify for the 100 percent rate (Proposed Reg. § 1.168(k)-2(b)(5)(iv) in REG-104397-18).

A binding contract to acquire components of a larger property is not considered a contract to acquire the larger property. If a written binding contract to acquire the components was entered into before September 28, 2017 (and the components are not considered self-constructed under the rule added by the final regulations (see above), the components do not qualify for the 100 percent rate, whether or not the larger property is constructed by or for the taxpayer (Reg. § 1.168k)-2(b)(5)(iii)(F); Reg. § 1.168(k)-2(b)(5)(iv)(C); Proposed Reg. § 1.168(k)-2(b)(5)(iii)(F); Proposed Reg. § 1.168(k)-2(b)(5)(iv)(C) in REG-104397-18).

See "*32. Acquisition and placed-in-service date requirement for 100 percent bonus rate property acquired after September 27, 2017*" and "*28. Binding contract defined,*"

*Self-constructed property.* Self-constructed property is acquired after September 27, 2017 if manufacture, construction, or production of the property for use in the taxpayer's trade or business begins after September 27, 2017 (Reg. § 1.168(k)-2(b)(5)(iv)(B); Proposed Reg. § 1.168(k)-2(b)(5)(iv)(B) in REG-104397-18).

If the manufacture, construction, or production of self-constructed property begins before September 28, 2017, the self-constructed property does not qualify for the 100 percent rate or the related phase out rates (Reg. § 1.168(k)-2(b)(5)(iv)(C)(1) and (2); Proposed Reg. § 168(k)-2(b)(5)(iv)(C)(2) in REG-104397-18; Reg. § 1.168(k)-2(b)(5)(viii), Example 8; Proposed Reg. § 1.168(k)-2(b)(5)(viii), Example 8 in REG-104397-18).

Under the proposed regulations, the 100 percent rate did not apply to property constructed for a taxpayer under a written binding contract entered into before September 28, 2017 (Proposed Reg. § 1.168(k)-2(b)(5)(iv)(A) in REG-104397-18). The final regulations, however, now provide that property constructed for a taxpayer under a written binding contract entered into before construction begins is considered self-constructed property (Reg. § 1.168(k)-2(b)(5)(iv)(A)). The acquisition date is, therefore, when construction begins and is determined without reference to the contract.

Manufacture, construction, or production begins when physical work of a significant nature begins or, under an elective safe harbor, when 10 percent or more of the cost of the property (excluding the cost of land and preliminary activities) is paid or incurred (Reg. § 1.168(k)-2(b)(5)(iv); Proposed Reg. § 1.168(k)-2(b)(5)(iv) in REG-104397-18). In the case of property that is constructed by a third party but which is treated as constructed by the taxpayer, rather than acquired pursuant to a written binding contract, the final regulations provide that the taxpayer must satisfy the 10 percent test of the safe harbor (Reg. § 1.168(k)-2(b)(5)(iv)(B)). Preliminary work does not constitute the beginning of construction. These are the same standards that apply under the original final regulations dealing with pre-100 percent bonus depreciation for property acquired before September 28, 2017.

See "*32. Acquisition and placed-in-service date requirements for 100 percent bonus rate property acquired after September 27, 2017.*"

*Components of self-constructed property.* Self-constructed components of a larger property do not qualify for the 100 percent rate (and related phase-down rates) if they are considered acquired before September 28, 2017 because construction of the component began before that date (Reg. § 1.168(k)-2(b)(5)(iv)(C)(2); Proposed Reg. § 1.168(k)-2(b)(5)(iv)(C)(2) in REG-104397-18). Under the final regulations, components constructed for a taxpayer under a binding contract entered into before construction began are considered self-constructed.

Components of a larger self-constructed property that are not self-constructed (i.e., acquired components) do not qualify for the 100 percent rate if acquired before September 28, 2017. Thus, if an acquired component is acquired before September 28, 2017 pursuant to a written binding contract it does not qualify for the 100 percent rate.

Taxpayers may elect to claim 100 percent bonus depreciation on a component of a larger self-constructed property even though construction of the larger property began before September 28, 2017 provided the component is constructed by or for the taxpayer after September 27, 2017 or the component is acquired by the taxpayer after September 27, 2017. Other requirements apply (Reg. § 1.168(k)-2(c); Proposed Reg. § 1.168(k)-2(c) in REG-106808-19).

See "*32. Acquisition and placed-in-service date requirements for 100 percent bonus rate property acquired after September 27, 2017.*"

*Long Production Property and Noncommercial Aircraft*

Although bonus depreciation generally expires after 2026, long production property (LPP) (Code Sec. 168(k)(2)(B)) and certain non-commercial aircraft (NCA) (Code Sec. 168(k)(2)(C)) may be placed in service in 2027. However, the extended deadline does not apply unless the property was acquired before January 1, 2027 or acquired pursuant to a binding written contract entered into before January 1, 2027. This extended deadline does not apply if the LPP or NCA is considered acquired before September 28, 2017 under the previously discussed rules. The pre-September 28, 2017 rules and deadlines for LPP and NCA would apply in that case.

In the case of self-constructed LPP or NCA, the taxpayer must begin manufacture, construction, or production before January 1, 2027. Property constructed for a taxpayer by another person under a written binding contract entered into prior to the construction of the property is considered constructed by the taxpayer. Nevertheless, the taxpayer is considered to meet the January 1, 2027 deadline even if construction begins after 2026 if a written binding contract to construct the property was entered into before January 1, 2027 (Reg. § 1.168(k)-2(d)(3)(i); Proposed Reg. § 1.168(k)-2(c)(3)(i) in REG-104397-18).

Construction begins when work of a significant nature begins or when the taxpayer pays or incurs more than 10 percent of the total cost of the property (excluding the cost of land and any preliminary activities).

When LPP or NCA is constructed for the taxpayer by another person, the 10 percent safe harbor test must be satisfied by the taxpayer (Reg. § 1.168(k)-2(d)(3)(ii)(B); Proposed Reg. § 1.168(k)-2 (c)(3)(ii)(B) in REG-104397-18).

The basis of LPP attributable to construction in 2027 is not taken into account in computing the bonus when the LPP is placed in service in 2027. In other words 2027 progress expenditures are ignored (Code Sec. 168(k)(2)(B)(ii); Reg. § 1.168(k)(2)-(e)(1)(iii); Proposed Reg. § 1.168(k)-2(d)(1)(iii) in REG-104397-18).

*Progress expenditures defined.* Progress expenditures are defined by reference to the definition in Notice 2007-36 used for qualified opportunity zone property (Reg. § 1.168(k)-2(e)(1)(iii); Proposed Reg. § 1.168(k)-2(e)(1)(iii) in REG-104397-18). See "*40. Progress expenditures of longer production period property*" for definition of progress expenditures.

*Acquired components of self-constructed LPP or NCA.* Components of self-constructed LPP or NCA that are acquired pursuant to a written binding contract entered into after 2026 do not qualify for the extended placed-in-service deadline. However, bonus depreciation may apply to the LPP or NCA without regard to the cost of those components. If a binding contract for a component is entered into before January 1, 2027 but construction of the LPP or NCA does not begin before January 1, 2027, the component qualifies for bonus depreciation, assuming all other requirements are met (Reg. § 1.168(k)-2(d)(3)(iii)(A); Proposed Reg. § 1.168(k)-2(c)(3)(iii)(A) in REG-104397-18).

See "*32. Acquisition and placed-in-service date requirements for 100 percent bonus rate property acquired after September 27, 2017.*"

*Self-constructed components of self-constructed LPP or NCA.* If construction of a self-constructed component does not begin before January 1, 2027, the component does not qualify for bonus depreciation. The LPP or NCA, however, may qualify for bonus depreciation if the construction of the LPP or NCA begins before January 1, 2027. A self-constructed component may qualify for bonus depreciation if its construction begins before January 1, 2027 even though construction of the LPP or NCA does not begin before January 1, 2027 (Reg. § 1.168(k)-2(d)(3)(iii)(B); Proposed Reg. § 1.168(k)-2(c)(3)(iii)(B) in REG-104397-18).

See "*32. Acquisition and placed-in-service date requirements for 100 percent bonus rate property acquired after September 27, 2017.*"

*Like-Kind Exchanges and Involuntary Conversions*

The regulations retain the rule that the exchanged basis and excess basis of the replacement property in a tax-free like-kind exchange or involuntary conversion is eligible for bonus depreciation if the replacement property is new. However, if the replacement property is used, bonus depreciation only applies to the excess basis, if any, of the replacement property (Reg. § 1.168(k)-2(g)(5); Proposed Reg. § 1.168(k)-2(f)(5) in REG-104397-18).

The tax-free like-kind exchange rules of Code Sec. 1031 only apply to real property, generally effective for exchanges completed after 2017 (Code Sec. 1031(a)).

***Example (4):*** ABC purchases an item of real property with a 15-year recovery period in 2016 for $100,000 and in a like-kind exchange in November 2018, pays $10,000 cash for new real property. The remaining "exchanged basis" (carryover basis) on the 2016 section 1250 property at the time of the exchange is $40,612 ($100,000 - $50,000 (2016 bonus) - $2,500 (2016 regular depreciation) - $4,750 (2017 regular depreciation) - $2,138 (2018 depreciation prior to exchange taking half-year convention into account). The "excess basis" is $10,000. Since the exchange took place after September 27, 2017 the 100 percent bonus rate applies and is equal to $51,612 ($40,612 + $10,000).

***Example (5):*** Assume the preceding facts, except that the replacement property is used. Bonus depreciation only applies to the $10,000 excess basis. The $40,612 exchanged (carryover) basis is depreciated over the remaining portion of the real property's recovery period.

If a taxpayer makes an election under Reg. § 1.168(i)-6(i) to treat the sum of the exchanged (carryover) basis and excess basis as a single asset placed in service at the time of the replacement, the entire basis (i.e., exchanged basis plus any excess basis) is depreciated as a single asset placed in service in the year of replacement and bonus depreciation only applies to the excess basis whether the replacement property is new or used.

***Example (6):*** Assume that ABC makes the election under Reg. § 1.168(i)-6(i). Bonus depreciation applies to the $10,000 excess basis, whether the replacement property is used or new. The exchanged basis is depreciated beginning in 2018 over a fifteen-year recovery period.

See "*7. Like-kind exchanges and involuntary conversions.*"

*Conversion from Personal to Business Use*

Used property converted by a taxpayer from personal use to business use is eligible for bonus depreciation. However, the 100 percent rate only applies if the used property is acquired for personal use after September 27, 2017 and converted to business use before 2023. Used property acquired for personal use before September 28, 2017 does not qualify for bonus depreciation upon later conversion to business use. Property converted from business use to personal use in the same tax year does not qualify for bonus depreciation (Reg. § 1.168(k)-2(g)(6); Proposed Reg. § 1.168(k)-2(f)(6) in REG-104397-18).

See "*24. Property converted from personal use to business use or from business use to personal use.*"

*Election Out of Bonus Depreciation*

The election out of bonus depreciation is made for each class of property. The regulations define a property class for this purpose as (Reg. § 1.168(k)-2(f)(1)(ii); Proposed Reg. § 1.168(k)-2(e)(1)(ii) in REG-104397-18):

(1) Each separate class of 3-, 5-, 7-, 10-, 15-, and 20-year MACRS property;

(2) 25-year water utility property (not primarily used by a rate-regulated utility);

(3) Computer software with a 3-year depreciation period under Code Sec. 167(f)(1);

(4) Qualified improvement property acquired after September 27, 2017 and placed in service before 2018;

(5) Each separate qualified film or television production;

(6) Each separate qualified theatrical production; and

(7) Each partner's Code Sec. 743(b) basis adjustment in partnership assets for each class of property described in (1) - (6) above when a Code Sec. 754 election is in effect.

The election out of bonus depreciation for the Code Sec. 743(b) basis adjustment class is made by the partnership (Reg. § 1.168(k)-2(f)(1)(iii); Proposed Reg. § 1.168(k)-2(e)(1)(iii) in REG-104397-18).

The election is made in the manner prescribed by the instructions for Form 4562.

*Failure to make election out.* Although the rule is not new, the regulations now specifically provide that a taxpayer must reduce the basis of an asset by the bonus amount if the bonus was not claimed and no timely election out was made. If the election out is not made by the due date of the return (including extensions) it may not be made by filing an accounting method change. The IRS may, however, issue guidance that creates exceptions to this rule (see discussions at 1C and 1D, for example) (Reg. § 1.168(k)-2(f)(1)(iv); Proposed Reg. § 1.168(k)-2(e)(1)(iv) in REG-104397-18).

A taxpayer computing depreciation on an asset without claiming bonus depreciation for two tax years has adopted an improper accounting method and should file an accounting method change on Form 3115 in order to claim the bonus amount (as reduced by regular depreciation claimed on the bonus amount) as a Code Sec. 481(a) adjustment.

*Revocation of election.* The election out of bonus depreciation is revocable only with IRS consent obtained by filing a letter ruling. However, a taxpayer may file an amended return within 6 months of the due date (excluding extensions) to change the election. Taxpayers are affected by the election change (e.g., partners) are also required to file amended returns (Reg. § 1.168(k)-2(f)(5); Proposed Reg. § 1.168(k)-2(e)(5) in REG-104397-18).

*Special rule for tax year that includes September 28, 2017.* A taxpayer may make a late election out of bonus depreciation for a class of property that was placed in service in the tax year that includes September 28, 2017. The taxpayer must have placed property within the class in service after September 27, 2017 and the election only applies to the property within the class that was acquired after September 27, 2017. The election is made by filing an accounting method change for the first, second, or third tax year that follows the tax year that includes September 28, 2017. An election out of bonus depreciation for a class of property that includes property acquired after September 27, 2017 and placed in service in a tax year that includes September 28, 2017 may also be revoked by filing an accounting method change. An amended return may also be filed to make or revoke the election out if the taxpayer has not filed a return for the tax year that follows the tax year that includes September 28, 2017 (Rev. Proc. 2019-33; Reg. § 1.168(k)-2(f)(6)). A late election out of bonus depreciation or revocation of an election for a tax year that includes September 28, 2017 (as well as subsequent tax years) may also be available under Rev. Proc. 2020-25 or Rev. Proc. 2020-50.

See "*9. Election out of bonus depreciation*" for a complete discussion of the election out.

*Election to Claim 50 Percent Rate for Tax Year that Includes September 28, 2017*

A taxpayer may elect to claim 50 percent bonus depreciation in place of 100 percent bonus depreciation for qualified property acquired after September 27, 2017 and placed in service during the tax year that includes September 28, 2017 (Code Sec. 168(k)(10)). The regulations clarify that the election applies to all qualified property placed in service during this period that is otherwise eligible for the 100 percent rate. The election is not made at the property class level. However, the election is made separately for specified plants. The election applies to all specified plants planted or grafted after September 27, 2017 in the tax year that includes September 28, 2017 (Reg. § 1.168(k)-2(f)(3); Proposed Reg. § 1.168(k)-2(e)(3)). Rev. Proc. 2019-33 clarifies that the 50 percent election only applies to specified plants for which an election was made to claim bonus depreciation in the year of planting or grafting is made and which otherwise qualify for the 100 percent rate (Rev. Proc. 2019-33, Section 6.01).

The election must generally be made by the due of the return (including extensions) for the tax year that includes September 28, 2017 (Reg. § 1.168(k)-2(f)(3)). However, a late election or revocation of an election is allowed as explained below.

The election is made in the manner prescribed by the instructions for Form 4562.

The election is made by the person owning the property, for example, by a partnership or S corporation and not a partner or S shareholder.

The election to claim the 50 percent rate is generally revocable only with IRS consent obtained by filing a letter ruling. However, a taxpayer may file an amended return within 6 months of the due date (excluding extensions) of the original return to change the election. Taxpayers who are affected by the election change (e.g., partners) are also required to file amended returns (Reg. § 1.168(k)-2(f)(5); Proposed Reg. § 1.168(k)-2(e)(5) in REG-104397-18).

A taxpayer may also be able to make a late election to claim 50 percent bonus depreciation in a tax year that includes September 28, 2017 or revoke a prior election under procedures provided in Rev. Proc. 2019-33 (see *10. Election to claim 50-percent bonus depreciation in place of 100-percent bonus depreciation during tax year that includes September 28, 2017* and *11. Special rules for making and revoking elections in tax year that includes September 28, 2017*); Rev. Proc. 2020-25 (see *1A. Qualified improvement property placed in service after 2017—guidance for changing to 15-year recovery period and claiming bonus depreciation—guidance for making late elections and revoking prior elections for 2018, 2019, and 2020 tax years*); or Rev. Proc. 2020-50 (see *1D. Late elections and revocations for 2017, 2018, 2019, and 2020 tax years for taxpayers applying 2020 final, 2019 final, or 2019 final and proposed regulations*).

*1C. Change in accounting method procedures to apply 2020 final, 2019 final, or 2019 final and proposed regulations retroactively to 2017, 2018, 2019, or 2020 tax year*

Rev. Proc. 2020-50 provides guidance explaining how taxpayers may change their accounting method by filing amended returns, administrative adjustment requests under Code Sec. 6227 (AAR) or accounting method changes on Form 3115 to retroactively apply the 2020 final regulations, the 2019 final regulations, or the 2019 final and 2019 proposed regulations to property acquired after September 27, 2017 and placed in service before the mandatory effective date of the 2020 final regulations (i.e. property acquired after September 27, 2017 and placed in service before the taxpayer's first tax year that begins after December 31, 2020). A taxpayer applying the 2019 proposed regulations should not apply withdrawn Prop. Reg. Sec. 1.168(k)-2(b)(3)(B)(5) which treats property owned by a partnership as owned by the partners for purposes of the five-year lookback rule for used property.

The IRS issued the following series of proposed and final regulations implementing changes for property acquired and placed in service after September 27, 2017:

(1) *2018 Proposed Regulations.* Proposed Reg. § 1.168(k)-2 was published in the Federal Register on August 8, 2018 in Notice of Proposed Rulemaking REG-104397-18.

(2) *2019 Final and Proposed Regulations.* The 2018 proposed regulations were adopted as final regulations with modifications by T.D. 9874 as published on September 24, 2019. Additional regulations under Reg. 1.168(k)-2 were simultaneously proposed (REG-106808-19).

(3) *2020 Final Regulations.* The 2019 proposed regulations were adopted as final regulations by T.D. 9916, published on November 10, 2020, with modifications and incorporated into the 2019 final regulations. Certain additional modifications not in the 2019 proposed regulations were also made to the 2019 final regulations. Provisions relating to consolidated groups were moved from Reg. § 1.168(k)-2 to Reg. § 1.1502-68. The 2020 final regulations, therefore, consist of the 2019 final regulations as ultimately modified.

Either the 2020 final regulations, 2019 final regulations, or both the 2019 final regulations and the 2019 proposed regulations may be applied to depreciable property placed in service in the same tax year. However, if the 2020 final regulations are applied to property placed in service during a tax year, then the 2020 final regulations must be applied for all subsequent tax years. For example, if a partnership applies the 2020 final regulations for its 2018 tax year, it must apply the 2020 final regulations for its 2019, 2020, and subsequent tax years (Sec. 4.02(1) of Rev. Proc. 2020-50; Sec 6.21(1) and (5) of Rev. Proc. 2019-43, as added by Rev. Proc. 2020-50).

A summary of the differences between the 2020 final regulations and the 2019 final and proposed regulations is provided in Section 2.02Rev. Proc. 2020-50.

*Rev. Proc. 2019-43 modified to reflect method changes.* Rev. Proc. 2019-43, which lists all automatic accounting method changes, is modified by Rev. Proc. 2020-50 to add new Section 6.21 for making an accounting method change to apply the 2020 final regulations, 2019 final regulations, or the 2019 final regulations and proposed regulations. Impermissible to permissible and permissible to permissible changes are covered.

Certain eligibility rules that prevent a taxpayer from using the automatic procedures are waived (Sec. 6.21(2) of Rev. Proc. 2019-43, as added by Rev. Proc. 2020-50).

A single net 481(a) adjustment should be shown on the Form 3115 for changes made under Sec. 6.21.

Changes made under Sec. 6.01, 6.19, and 6.20 of Rev. Proc. 2019-43 for a tax year should also be made concurrently on the Form 3115 filed for the Sec. 6.21 changes and included in the single net 481(a) adjustment shown on the Form 3115 (Rev. Proc. 2019-43, Sec. 6.21(7), as added by Rev. Proc. 2019-43).

*Impermissible to permissible change.* The first time a taxpayer changes its method of accounting to comply with the 2020 final regulations, the 2019 final regulations, or the 2019 final regulations and 2019 proposed regulations for property placed in service in a tax year, the change is considered a change from an impermissible to a permissible depreciation method and is therefore made with a Code Sec. 481(a) adjustment (Sec. 4.02(2) of Rev. Proc. 2020-50). Subsequent changes for the same property placed in service in the same tax year are considered a change from a permissible to a permissible method and are applied on a cut-off basis (Sec. 4.04). These changes are made under the automatic consent procedures as described in Rev. Proc. 2015-13. Rev. Proc. 2019-43 which lists all automatic accounting method changes is modified by Rev. Proc. 2020-50 to add new Sec. 6.21 to include the changes described in Rev. Proc. 2020-50.

> ***Example (1):*** A calendar year taxpayer changes its method of accounting in its 2020 tax year to comply with the 2019 final regulations for property acquired after September 17, 2017 and placed in service in 2017 and 2018. This change is from an impermissible to an permissible method of accounting. If the taxpayer changes its accounting method again in its 2021 tax year to comply with the 2020 final regulations for property acquired after September 17, 2017 and placed in service in 2017, 2018, and 2019, the changes for the same property placed in service in 2017 and 2018 are considered a change from a permissible method to a permissible method that is made on a cut-off basis because the taxpayer previously filed a change in accounting method for this property for those years. The change for property placed in service in 2020, however, is a change from an impermissible method to an impermissible method and requires a section 481(a) adjustment (Sec. 4.02(3) of Rev. Proc. 2020-50).

The Code Sec. 481(a) adjustment calculated for this change must be adjusted by taxpayers with floor plan financing to account for the proper amount of interest expense, taking into account the business interest limitation under Code Sec. 163(j) and the regulations thereunder, as of the beginning of the year of change (Sec. 6.21(4) of Rev. Proc. 2019-43, as added by Rev. Proc. 2020-50).

*Form 3115 allowed for property placed in service in the preceding tax year.* Generally, a taxpayer changes from an impermissible method of determining depreciation for property placed in service in the immediately preceding tax year by filing an amended return or AAR. Sec. 6.21(3)(b) of Rev. Proc. 2019-43, as added by Rev. Proc. 2020-50 also allows the taxpayer to file a change in accounting method for such "one-year" property to comply with the applicable bonus regulations. Also see Sec. 4.03 of Rev. Proc. 2020-50.

*Amended returns in lieu of Form 3115 for change from impermissible to permissible method.* If a taxpayer has filed two or more returns computing depreciation in an impermissible manner, amended returns are generally not allowed. Rev. Proc. 2020-50, however, dispenses with this rule and allows a taxpayer to file an amended income tax return or Form 1065 for the placed-in-service year on or before December 31, 2021 but not later than the limitations period for filing an amended return. A partnership subject to the centralized partnership and audit regime (a "BBA partnership) must file an AAR for the placed-in-service year on or before December 31, 2021 but no later than the limitations period on making adjustments for the reviewed year (Sec. 4.03(4) of Rev. Proc. 2020-50.

The amended return or AAR filed to change from an impermissible to permissible depreciation accounting method must take into account any additional collateral adjustments attributable to the depreciation adjustment that affect tax liability or taxable income. Amended returns and AARs for affected subsequent years must also be filed.

*Permissible to permissible method changes.* If a taxpayer files an accounting method change to apply the 2020 final regulations, 2019 final regulations, or 2019 final regulations and proposed regulations to property placed in service in the same tax year and files a subsequent method change for the same depreciable property the subsequent change is a permissible to permissible change made on a cut-off basis. Therefore, no section 481(a) adjustment is required or permitted (Section 4.04 of Rev. Proc. 2050-50; Sec. 6.21(4) of Rev. Proc. 2019-43, as added by Rev. Proc. 2050-50).

*Ordering rule for late elections/revocations and method changes.* Late elections and election revocations made under Rev. Proc. 2050-50 with respect to a property that is the subject of an accounting method change are considered made before the accounting method change (Sec. 4.02(4) of Rev. Proc. 2050-50). See item "*1D. Late elections and revocations for 2017, 2018, 2019, and 2020 tax years for taxpayers applying 2020 final, 2019 final, or 2019 final and proposed regulations*"

### *1D. Late elections and revocations for 2017, 2018, 2019, and 2020 tax years for taxpayers applying 2020 final, 2019 final, or 2019 final and proposed regulations*

Sections 5 and 6 of Rev. Proc. 2020-50 allow a taxpayer to make certain late elections or revoke certain prior elections in a tax year ending on or after September 28, 2017, and before the taxpayer's first tax year that begins on or after January 1, 2021. The late election or revocation only applies for a tax year in which the taxpayer properly applies the 2020 final regulations, 2019 final regulations, or 2019 final and proposed regulations on an original return or by changing its accounting method in accordance with Rev. Proc. 2020-50. See discussion above "*1C. Change in accounting method procedures to apply 2020 final, 2019 final, or 2019 final and proposed regulations retroactively to 2017, 2018, 2019, or 2020 tax year.*"

The following late elections may be made (Sec. 6 of Rev. Proc. 2020-50):

(1) Code Sec. 168(k)(7) election out of bonus depreciation for a class of property;

(2) Code Sec. 168(k)(5) election to claim bonus depreciation on specified plants in year of planting or grafting;

(3) Component election in final 2020 regs or proposed component election in 2019 proposed regs (Reg. § 1.168(k)-2(c); Prop. Reg. 1.168(k)-2(c)(4) (REG-106808-18);

(4) Designated transaction election under Reg. § 1.1502-68(c)(4) to not to apply the Consolidated Asset Acquisition Rule or the Consolidated Deemed Acquisition Rule; and

(5) Code Sec. 168(k)(10) election to claim 50 percent bonus depreciation on property acquired after September 27, 2017 and placed in service (or planted or grafted) in the tax year that includes September 28, 2017.

These late elections, other than the election to apply the 50 percent bonus rate in place of the 100 percent rate to property acquired after September 27, 2017 in a tax year that includes September 28, 2017, may be made for property placed in service (or specified plants planted or grafted) in a tax year ending on or after September 28, 2017, and before the taxpayer's first tax year that begins on or after January 1, 2021. The taxpayer must have timely filed its income tax return or Form 1065 for the placed-in-service year of the property to which the late election applies before November 17, 2020.

The taxpayer may not make a late election if it previously revoked the election in accordance with the rules in this guidance (i.e., Rev. Proc. 2020-50) described below or revoked the election after November 16, 2020 in accordance with prior guidance under Rev. Proc. 2020-25 (see *1A. Qualified improvement property placed in service after 2017—guidance for changing to 15-year recovery period and claiming bonus depreciation—guidance for making late elections and revoking prior elections for 2018, 2019, and 2020 tax years*) or Rev. Proc. 2019-33 (see *11. Special rules for making and revoking elections in tax year that includes September 28, 2017*).

The late Code Sec. 168(k)(10) election to apply the 50 percent bonus rate only applies to property placed in service (or specified plants planted or grafted) in a tax year that includes September 28, 2017. The taxpayer must have timely filed its income tax return for that tax year and not have previously revoked the election under Rev. Proc. 2020-50 or after November 16, 2020 under Rev. Proc. 2020-25 or Rev. Proc. 2019-33.

*Amended returns to make late elections.* These late elections may be made by filing an amended income tax return or amended Form 1065 for the placed-in-service year (or year of planting or grafting) on or before December 31, 2021 but no later than expiration of the limitations period for filing an amended return. A BBA partnership may file an AAR on or before December 31, 2021 but not later than the limitation period for making adjustments for the reviewed year. Amended returns for subsequent years may need to be filed to reflect adjustments made for the revocation year.

*Form 3115 to make late elections.* A late election may be made by filing Form 3115 in the first or second tax year following the year that the property was placed in service (or the specified plants were planted or grafted). If later, the Form 3115 may also be filed with a timely filed original income tax return or Form 1065 that is filed after November 5, 2020 and before January 1, 2022. A section 481(a) adjustment is required.

***Example (1):*** *Late component election.* Calendar year taxpayer placed a self-constructed property in service in 2018 that was not eligible for 100 percent bonus depreciation because construction began before September 28, 2017. Under the 2020 final regulations certain components of this property acquired after September 27, 2017 now qualify for the 100 percent rate. If taxpayer retroactively changes its accounting method to apply the 2020 final regulations in its 2018 and 2019 tax year and timely files its 2020 tax return for the 2020 tax year applying the final regulations, taxpayer may make a late component election for 2018 under the 2020 final regulations by filing an amended return for 2018 and 2019 (an affected tax year) or by filing a Form 3115 for the 2020 tax year to apply the final regulations to its 2018 and 2019 tax years (Sec. 5.03 Rev. Proc. 2020-50, Example 1).

***Example (2):*** *Late component election.* Assume the preceding facts except that the taxpayer filed amended returns for 2018 and 2019 to apply only the 2019 final regulations. Since the component election is not allowed under the 2019 final regulations, the taxpayer may not make the component election for 2018 (Sec. 5.03 Rev. Proc. 2020-50, Example 2).

***Example (3):*** *Late election out of bonus depreciation, regs not retroactively applied.* A calendar year taxpayer deducted 100 percent bonus depreciation for a class of property placed in service in 2018. Taxpayer is not applying the 2020 final regulations, 2019 final regulations, or 2019 final regulations and 2019 proposed regulations to its 2018 tax year. The election may not be revoked under Rev. Proc. 2020-50. Taxpayer must file a private letter ruling request (Sec. 5.03 Rev. Proc. 2020-50, Example 3).

*Revocation of Elections.* The following elections for property placed in service (or specified plants planted or grafted) in a tax year ending on or after September 28, 2017, and before the taxpayer's first tax year that begins on or after January 1, 2021 may be revoked if the taxpayer applies to the 2020 final regulations, 2019 final regulations, or 2019 final regulations and 2019 proposed regulations to the tax year for which the election applies:

(1) Code Sec. 168(k)(7) election out of bonus depreciation for a class of property;

(2) Code Sec. 168(k)(5) election to claim bonus depreciation on specified plants in year of planting or grafting;

(3) Code Sec. 168(k)(10) election to claim 50 percent bonus depreciation on property acquired after September 27, 2017 and placed in service (or planted or grafted) in the tax year that includes September 28, 2017;

(4) Proposed component election in 2019 proposed regs (Prop. Reg. 1.168(k)-2(c)(4) (REG-106808-18)).

The election being revoked (other than the Code Sec. 168(k)(10) election to use the 50 percent rate) must have been made on a timely filed original income tax return or Form 1065 for the placed-in-service year (or year of planting or grafting of the specified plant) which was filed before November 17, 2020.

A timely Code Sec. 168(k)(10) election, or late Code Sec. 168(k)(10) election made in accordance with Rev. Proc. 2019-33 or Rev. Proc. 2020-25 before November 17, 2020, to claim 50 percent bonus in a tax year that included September 28, 2017 may be revoked if the taxpayer applies the 2020 final regulations, 2019 final regulations, or 2019 final and 2019 proposed regulations to the tax year that includes September 28, 2017.

*Amended return or Form 3115 to revoke election.* These elections may be revoked on an amended return or by filing a Form 3115 subject to the same restrictions that apply when making a late election, as explained above.

*Accounting method change rules for late elections and revocations integrated with Rev. Proc. 2020-25 late elections and revocations.* Section 6.20 of Rev. Proc. 2019-43 was added by Rev. Proc. 2020-25 to allow an accounting method change to make certain late elections and revocations of elections for property placed in service in a tax year ending in 2018, 2019, and 2020. See *1A. Qualified improvement property placed in service after 2017—guidance for changing to 15-year recovery period and claiming bonus depreciation—guidance for making late elections and revoking prior elections for 2018, 2019, and 2020 tax years.* The rules for making late elections and revoking elections as provided in Rev. Proc. 2020-50 are incorporated into Section 6.20 (Section 6.20 of Rev. Proc. 2019-43, as added by Rev. Proc. 2020-25 and modified by Rev. Proc. 2020-50).

*Concurrent changes on same Form 3115 required.* All late elections and revocations made under Rev. Proc. 2020-25 and Rev. Proc. 2020-50 pursuant to Section 6.20 of Rev. Proc. 2019-43, as modified by Rev. Proc. 2019-43 are reported concurrently on the same Form 3115. In addition, the change in accounting method to apply the 2020 final regulations, 2019 final regulations, or 2019 final and proposed regulations is made concurrently on the same Form 3115 with the any late revocations and elections. A single net section 481(a) adjustment is computed (Sec. 6.20(5) of Rev. Proc. 2019-43 as modified by Rev. Proc. 2020-50 and Sec. 6.21(7) of Rev. Proc. 2019-43 as added by Rev. Proc. 2020-50).

## BONUS RATES AND COMPUTATION

### *2. Bonus depreciation rates, including 100 percent rate for property acquired after September 27, 2017*

The bonus depreciation rate depends upon the date of acquisition and date the asset is placed in service.

*100 percent bonus rate and phase down for property acquired after September 27, 2017.* The 50-percent bonus depreciation rate is increased to 100 percent for qualified property acquired and placed in service after September 27, 2017, and before January 1, 2023 (Code Sec. 168(k)(1)(A) and (6)(A), as amended by the Tax Cuts and Jobs Act of 2017 (P.L. 115-97); Reg. § 1.168(k)-2; Proposed Reg. § 1.168(k)-2 as proposed by REG-104397-18; Proposed Reg. § 1.168(k)-2 as proposed by REG-106808-19)). Property subject to a pre-September 28, 2017 binding written contract is considered acquired before September 28, 2017 (Act Sec. 13201(h)(1) of P.L. 115-97) and does not qualify for the 100 percent rate. Under the final regulations, an exception applies to property subject to a pre-September 28, 2017 contract that is constructed for a taxpayer if construction begins after September 27, 2017 (Reg. § 1.168(k)-2(b)(5)(iv)). See "*32. Acquisition and placed-in-service date requirements for 100 percent bonus rate property acquired after September 27, 2017 and before 2027*" for a discussion of the rule disqualifying property subject to a pre-September 28, 2017 binding written contract.

The 100-percent allowance for property acquired after September 27, 2017 is phased down by 20 percent per calendar year for property placed in service after 2022. The bonus depreciation phase-down rates for property acquired after September 27, 2017 are as follows:

- 80 percent for property placed in service after December 31, 2022, and before January 1, 2024;
- 60 percent for property placed in service after December 31, 2023, and before January 1, 2025;
- 40 percent for property placed in service after December 31, 2024, and before January 1, 2026;
- 20 percent for property placed in service after December 31, 2025, and before January 1, 2027;
- 0 percent (bonus expires) for property placed in service after December 31, 2026 (Code Sec. 168(k)(6)(A), as amended by the 2017 Tax Cuts Act).

*Election to claim 50 percent bonus depreciation in lieu of 100 percent rule.* A taxpayer may elect to apply the 50-percent rate instead of the 100-percent rate for all qualified property placed in service during the taxpayer's tax year that includes September 28, 2017 (Code Sec. 168(k)(10), as added by P.L. 115-97; Reg. § 1.168(k)-2(f)(3); Proposed Reg. § 1.168(k)-2(e)(3) in REG-104397-18). See "*10.*

*Election to claim 50-percent bonus depreciation in place of 100-percent bonus depreciation during tax year that includes September 28, 2017."*

*Property with longer production period and noncommercial aircraft acquired after September 27, 2017.* In the case of property with a longer production period (LPP) and noncommercial aircraft (NCA), the placed-in-service deadlines for property acquired after September 27, 2017 are extended for one year (Code Sec. 168(k)(6)(B), as amended by P.L. 115-97). Property subject to a pre-September 28, 2017 binding written contract is considered acquired before September 28, 2017 (Act Sec. 13201(h)(1) of P.L. 115-97).

The applicable bonus rates for LPP and NCA acquired after September 27, 2017 are as follows:

- 100 percent for property placed in service after September 27, 2017, and before January 1, 2024;
- 80 percent for property placed in service after December 31, 2023, and before January 1, 2025;
- 60 percent for property placed in service after December 31, 2024, and before January 1, 2026;
- 40 percent for property placed in service after December 31, 2025, and before January 1, 2027;
- 20 percent for property placed in service after December 31, 2026, and before January 1, 2028;
- 0 percent (bonus expires) for property placed in service after December 31, 2027

2027 production expenditures for LPP acquired after September 27, 2017 do not qualify for bonus depreciation (Code Sec. 168(k)(2)(B)(ii), as amended by P.L. 115-97; Reg. § 1.168(k)-2(e)(1)(iii)). This rule does not apply to NCA.

*Property acquired before September 28, 2017 and placed in service after September 27, 2017.* Property other than LPP and NCA acquired before September 28, 2017, is subject to the 50-percent rate if placed in service in 2017, a 40-percent rate if placed in service in 2018, and a 30-percent rate if placed in service in 2019. Property other than LPP and NCA acquired before September 28, 2017, and placed in service after 2019 is not eligible for bonus depreciation (Code Sec. 168(k)(8), as added by P.L. 115-97; Code Sec. 168(k)(6), as in effect on the day prior to amendment by P.L. 115-97 and as so in effect retroactively amended by the 2018 Tax Technical Corrections Act (Division U of P.L. 115-141)).

If a written binding contract for the acquisition of property is in effect prior to September 28, 2017, the property is not considered acquired after the date the contract is entered into (Act Sec. 13201(h)(1) of the 2017 Tax Cuts Act). Consequently, property subject to a binding written contract entered into before September 28, 2017, is not eligible for the 100-percent rate, and is subject to a 40-percent rate if placed in service in 2018 and a 30-percent rate if placed in service in 2019. The 50-percent rate applies if such property is placed in service in 2017. However, if a taxpayer enters into a pre-September 28, 2017 contract with a third party for the construction, manufacture, or production of property that will be used by the taxpayer, the property is considered self-constructed and may qualify for the 100 percent rate if construction begins after September 27, 2017 (Reg. § 1.168(k)-2(b)(5)). See *32. Acquisition and placed-in-service date requirements for 100 percent bonus rate property acquired after September 27, 2017 and before 2027.*

*Longer production property and non-commercial aircraft acquired before September 28, 2017 and placed in service after September 27, 2017.* Longer production period property (LPP) and noncommercial aircraft (NCA) acquired before September 28, 2017 need to be placed in service before January 1, 2021 in order to qualify for bonus depreciation (Code Sec. 168(k)(2)(B) and (C), prior to amendment by P.L. 115-97).

The bonus rates for LPP and NCA acquired before September 28, 2017 and placed in service after September 27, 2017 are (Code Sec. 168(k)(8), as added by P.L. 115-97; Code Sec. 168(k)(6), as in effect on the day prior to amendment by P.L. 115-97 and as so in effect retroactively amended by the 2018 Tax Technical Corrections Act (Division U of P.L. 115-141):

- 50 percent for property placed in service in 2017 and 2018
- 40 percent for property placed in service in 2019
- 30 percent for property placed in service in 2020
- 0 percent for property placed in service in 2021

2020 LPP progress expenditures on LPP acquired before September 28, 2017 do not qualify for bonus depreciation (Code Sec. 168(k)(2)(B)(ii), prior to amendment by P.L. 115-97).

The retroactive amendments made by the 2018 Tax Technical Corrections Act to Code Sec. 168(k)(6), as in effect on the day prior to amendment by P.L. 115-97, clarify that the preceding rates apply to LPP and NCA acquired before September 28, 2017. See Rev. Proc. 2017-33 Section 4.03(b) for a description of the erroneous rates that could have affected LPP and NCA placed in service in 2018, 2019, and 2020 if the technical correction had not been enacted.

*Property placed in service after 2007 and before September 28, 2017.* A 50 percent rate applies to property placed in service after December 31, 2007 and before September 28, 2017 (Code Sec. 168(k) prior to amendment by P.L. 115-97). However, a 100 percent rate applied to property acquired and placed in service after September 8, 2010 and before January 1, 2012 (before January 1, 2013 in the case of property with a long production period and certain noncommercial aircraft) (Code Sec. 168(k)(5), as added by P.L. 111-312 and prior to being stricken by P.L. 114-113).

*Property placed in service in 2001 through 2007.* In general, a 30-percent bonus depreciation rate applied to property placed in service after September 10, 2001, and before May 6, 2003.

A 50-percent rate applied to property placed in service after May 5, 2003, and before January 1, 2005. The placed-in-service deadline was before January 1, 2006, for certain property with a long production period and noncommercial aircraft.

Bonus depreciation did not apply to property placed in service in 2005, 2006, and 2007, except for certain long production period and noncommercial aircraft placed in service in 2005.

### *3. Computation of bonus allowance*

The additional allowance is equal to the applicable percentage (see "*2. Bonus depreciation rates, including 100 percent rate for property acquired after September 27, 2017*") of the "unadjusted depreciable basis" of the qualified property (Reg. § 1.168(k)-1(d)(1); Reg. § 1.168(k)-2(e)(1); Proposed Reg. § 1.168(k)-2(d)(1) in REG-104397-18). Unadjusted depreciable basis is the adjusted basis of the property for determining gain or loss reduced by any amount expensed under Code Sec.

179, and any adjustments to basis provided by the Code and regulations, other than depreciation deductions (Reg. § 1.168(k)-2(e)(2); Reg. § 1.168(k)-1(a)(2)(iii); Reg. § 1.168(b)-1(a)(3)). Typically the unadjusted depreciable basis will be the cost of the property (adjusted downward to reflect any personal use) reduced by any amount expensed under Code Sec. 179. The regular MACRS deductions are computed after reducing the unadjusted depreciable basis by any amount expensed under section 179 and claimed as an additional first-year bonus allowance.

Prior to a taxpayer computing the bonus deduction (or regular depreciation deductions), the basis of property is reduced by the amount of any credits claimed for the property that require an adjustment to basis such as the disabled access credit (Code Sec. 44), the energy credit (Code Sec. 48), or any payments received for specified energy property under Section 1603 of the American Recovery and Reinvestment Tax Act of 2009, Division B, Pub. L. 111-5, 123 Stat. 115 (Section 1603 payments) (Rev. Proc. 2011-26, Section 3.03(5)).

The bonus deduction is claimed in the tax year that the qualifying property is placed in service (not the year of acquisition or the signing of an acquisition contract). The full 50 percent rate must be claimed (unless an election out is made).

*Mid-quarter convention.* In determining whether the mid-quarter convention applies because more than 40 percent of the basis of certain depreciable property is placed in service in the last three months of the tax year, the basis of property is not reduced by the bonus deduction, including the 100 percent bonus deduction (Reg. § 1.168(k)-2(g)(11); Proposed Reg. § 1.168(k)-2(g)(11) in REG-104397-18; Reg. § 1.168(d)-1(b)(4)). See ¶ 92.

*Comparison to section 179.* Unlike the Code Sec. 179 expense allowance, there is no dollar limit on the total amount of bonus depreciation that may be claimed. There is no investment or taxable income limitation. The bonus deduction can create a net operating loss deduction. See ¶ 487 for a detailed discussion of bonus and section 179 differences.

*Short tax year.* A short tax year does not affect the amount of bonus depreciation that may be claimed. Nor is the bonus deduction subject to proration based on the date during the tax year that the qualifying property was placed in service. A decline in business use does not trigger recapture of the bonus deduction unless the bonus deduction was claimed on a listed property such a passenger car or pick-up truck for which business use falls to 50 percent or less during the property's MACRS alternative depreciation system (ADS) recovery period. However, bonus depreciation is subject to section 1245 and section 1250 recapture.

*Capitalization.* The additional allowance is subject to the general rules regarding whether an item is deductible under Code Sec. 162 or subject to capitalization under Code Sec. 263 or Code Sec. 263A (Conference Committee Report on the American Jobs Creation Act of 2004, P.L. 108-357, HR 4520, footnote 49). The section 179 deduction, however, is not subject to capitalization under Code Sec. 263 or the uniform capitalization rules (UNICAP) rules of Code Sec. 263A (Reg. § 1.179-1(j); Reg. § 1.263A-1(e)(3)(iii)).

The bonus deduction claimed on specified plants in the year of planting or grafting is not subject to capitalization under the UNICAP rules (Code Sec. 263A(c)(7)).

*Failure to claim bonus depreciation.* A taxpayer who fails to claim bonus depreciation on qualifying without making an election out is using an improper depreciation method if more than one return has been filed. An accounting method change should be filed on Form 3115 using designated change number (DCN) #7 as described in section 6.01 of the current list of accounting method changes (presently Sec. 6.01 of Rev. Proc. 2019-43). If only one return has been filed, a taxpayer may either file an amended return to make the correction or file a Form 3115 with the following year's return. See ¶ 75 for discussion of accounting method changes related to depreciation.

The following example illustrates the computation of the 50-percent bonus depreciation allowance.

***Example (1):*** Joseph Short purchases $100,000 of new machinery that is MACRS 5-year property on June 1, 2017. The half-year convention applies and no amount is expensed under Code Sec. 179. The property is purchased before September 28, 2017, and, therefore, qualifies for the 50% bonus depreciation rate. The 2017 bonus depreciation deduction is $50,000 ($100,000 cost × 50%). The depreciation table percentages for 5-year property (Table 1, below) are applied to a depreciable basis of $50,000 ($100,000 – $50,000).

| *Recovery Year* | | | *Deduction* |
|---|---|---|---|
| 2017 | bonus depreciation | | $50,000 |
| 2017 | $50,000 × | 20% = | $10,000 |
| 2018 | $50,000 × | 32% = | $16,000 |
| 2019 | $50,000 × | 19.20% = | $9,600 |
| 2020 | $50,000 × | 11.52% = | $5,760 |
| 2021 | $50,000 × | 11.52% = | $5,760 |
| 2022 | $50,000 × | 5.76% = | $2,880 |
| | | | $100,000 |

### *4. How bonus depreciation affects rate of recovery*

The following three depreciation tables may be used to compare the effect of claiming bonus depreciation on the rate of recovery over the applicable recovery period, assuming that the half-year convention applies. Table 1 is the official IRS table, which contains table percentages that do not reflect the bonus depreciation deduction. These table percentages are applied to the cost of an asset after reduction by any amount expensed under section 179 and deducted as bonus depreciation. Table 2 shows recovery percentages that apply when 30-percent bonus depreciation was claimed for property acquired after September 10, 2001 and placed in service before May 6, 2003. The Table 2 percentages are applied to the cost of the property less any amount deducted under section 179. Table 3 shows the percentages that apply when 50-percent bonus depreciation is claimed. These percentages are also applied to the cost of the property less any amount expensed under section 179. The first recovery year percentages in Tables 2 and 3 were increased (relative to the Table 1 percentages) to reflect the applicable bonus depreciation rate. The Table 2 and Table 3 percentages for subsequent recovery years were reduced (relative to the Table 1 percentages) to reflect the required reduction in basis by the bonus depreciation amount. The IRS will not be issuing revised tables similar to Table 2 and Table 3. This is because the bonus depreciation allowance must be calculated and reported separately on Form 4562. Tables 2 and 3 should not be used to prepare tax returns. They simply show the effect of claiming bonus depreciation on the rate of depreciation over the recovery period.

***The following is the official IRS table used for computing MACRS deductions on 3-, 5-, 7-, 10-, 15-, and 20-year MACRS property when the half-year convention applies.***

TABLE 1
General Depreciation System
Applicable Depreciation Method: 200- or 150-Percent
Declining Balance Switching to Straight Line
Applicable Recovery Periods: 3, 5, 7, 10, 15, 20 years
Applicable Convention: Half-Year

| If the Recovery Year is: | and the Recovery Period is: 3-year | 5-year | 7-year | 10-year | 15-year | 20-year |
|---|---|---|---|---|---|---|
| | the Depreciation Rate is: | | | | | |
| 1 | 33.33 | 20.00 | 14.29 | 10.00 | 5.00 | 3.750 |
| 2 | 44.45 | 32.00 | 24.49 | 18.00 | 9.50 | 7.219 |
| 3 | 14.81 | 19.20 | 17.49 | 14.40 | 8.55 | 6.677 |
| 4 | 7.41 | 11.52 | 12.49 | 11.52 | 7.70 | 6.177 |
| 5 | | 11.52 | 8.93 | 9.22 | 6.93 | 5.713 |
| 6 | | 5.76 | 8.92 | 7.37 | 6.23 | 5.285 |
| 7 | | | 8.93 | 6.55 | 5.90 | 4.888 |
| 8 | | | 4.46 | 6.55 | 5.90 | 4.522 |
| 9 | | | | 6.56 | 5.91 | 4.462 |
| 10 | | | | 6.55 | 5.90 | 4.461 |
| 11 | | | | 3.28 | 5.91 | 4.462 |
| 12 | | | | | 5.90 | 4.461 |
| 13 | | | | | 5.91 | 4.462 |
| 14 | | | | | 5.90 | 4.461 |
| 15 | | | | | 5.91 | 4.462 |
| 16 | | | | | 2.95 | 4.461 |
| 17 | | | | | | 4.462 |
| 18 | | | | | | 4.461 |
| 19 | | | | | | 4.462 |
| 20 | | | | | | 4.461 |
| 21 | | | | | | 2.231 |

***Caution: The following is an unofficial CCH prepared depreciation table that has adjusted percentages that reflect the 50-percent bonus depreciation deduction.***

**UNOFFICIAL CCH DEPRECIATION TABLE INCORPORATING 50-PERCENT BONUS DEPRECIATION**

TABLE 3
General Depreciation System
Applicable Depreciation Method: 200- or 150-Percent Declining Balance Switching to Straight Line
Applicable Recovery Periods: 3, 5, 7, 10, 15, 20 years
Applicable Convention: Half-Year

| If the Recovery Year is: | and the Recovery Period is: | | | | | |
|---|---|---|---|---|---|---|
| | 3-year | 5-year | 7-year | 10-year | 15-year | 20-year |
| | the Depreciation Rate is: | | | | | |
| 1 | 66.665 | 60.00 | 57.145 | 55.00 | 52.50 | 51.875 |
| 2 | 22.225 | 16.00 | 12.245 | 9.00 | 4.750 | 3.6095 |
| 3 | 7.405 | 9.60 | 8.745 | 7.20 | 4.275 | 3.3385 |
| 4 | 3.705 | 5.76 | 6.245 | 5.76 | 3.850 | 3.0885 |
| 5 | | 5.76 | 4.465 | 4.61 | 3.465 | 2.8565 |
| 6 | | 2.88 | 4.460 | 3.685 | 3.115 | 2.6425 |
| 7 | | | 4.465 | 3.275 | 2.950 | 2.444 |
| 8 | | | 2.23 | 3.275 | 2.950 | 2.261 |
| 9 | | | | 3.28 | 2.955 | 2.231 |
| 10 | | | | 3.275 | 2.950 | 2.2305 |
| 11 | | | | 1.640 | 2.955 | 2.231 |
| 12 | | | | | 2.950 | 2.2305 |
| 13 | | | | | 2.955 | 2.231 |
| 14 | | | | | 2.950 | 2.2305 |
| 15 | | | | | 2.955 | 2.231 |
| 16 | | | | | 1.475 | 2.2305 |
| 17 | | | | | | 2.231 |
| 18 | | | | | | 2.2305 |
| 19 | | | | | | 2.231 |
| 20 | | | | | | 2.2305 |
| 21 | | | | | | 1.1155 |

***Example (1):*** Three-year property costing $100,000 and subject to the half-year convention is purchased on September 9, 2017. The taxpayer claims the 50% bonus depreciation deduction. The combined first-year depreciation deduction and 50% bonus depreciation allowance is $66,665 ($100,000 × 66.665%). The second-year depreciation deduction is $22,225 ($100,000 × 22.225%). The third-year depreciation deduction is $7,405 ($100,000 × 7.405%). The fourth-year deduction is $3,705 ($100,000 × 3.705%). Table 3 is used.

***Caution: The following is an unofficial CCH prepared depreciation table that has adjusted percentages that reflect the 30-percent bonus depreciation deduction.***

**UNOFFICIAL CCH TABLE INCORPORATING 30-PERCENT BONUS DEPRECIATION**

TABLE 2
General Depreciation System
Applicable Depreciation Method: 200- or 150-Percent Declining Balance Switching to Straight Line
Applicable Recovery Periods: 3, 5, 7, 10, 15, 20 years
Applicable Convention: Half-Year

| If the Recovery Year is: | and the Recovery Period is: | | | | | |
|---|---|---|---|---|---|---|
| | 3-year | 5-year | 7-year | 10-year | 15-year | 20-year |
| | the Depreciation Rate is: | | | | | |
| 1 | 53.331 | 44.00 | 40.003 | 37.00 | 33.50 | 32.625 |
| 2 | 31.115 | 22.40 | 17.143 | 12.60 | 6.65 | 5.0533 |
| 3 | 10.367 | 13.44 | 12.243 | 10.08 | 5.985 | 4.6739 |
| 4 | 5.187 | 8.064 | 8.743 | 8.064 | 5.39 | 4.3239 |
| 5 | | 8.064 | 6.251 | 6.454 | 4.851 | 3.9991 |
| 6 | | 4.032 | 6.244 | 5.159 | 4.361 | 3.6995 |
| 7 | | | 6.251 | 4.585 | 4.13 | 3.4216 |
| 8 | | | 3.122 | 4.585 | 4.13 | 3.1654 |
| 9 | | | | 4.592 | 4.137 | 3.1234 |
| 10 | | | | 4.585 | 4.13 | 3.1227 |
| 11 | | | | 2.296 | 4.137 | 3.1234 |
| 12 | | | | | 4.13 | 3.1227 |
| 13 | | | | | 4.137 | 3.1234 |
| 14 | | | | | 4.13 | 3.1227 |
| 15 | | | | | 4.137 | 3.1234 |
| 16 | | | | | 2.065 | 3.1227 |
| 17 | | | | | | 3.1234 |
| 18 | | | | | | 3.1227 |
| 19 | | | | | | 3.1234 |
| 20 | | | | | | 3.1227 |
| 21 | | | | | | 1.5617 |

***Example (2):*** Three-year property costing $100,000 and subject to the half-year convention is purchased on May 1, 2003. The taxpayer claimed 30% bonus depreciation. The combined first-year depreciation deduction and 30% bonus depreciation allowance is $53,331 ($100,000 × 53.331%). The second-year depreciation deduction is $31,115 ($100,000 × 31.115%). The third-year depreciation deduction is $10,367 ($100,000 × 10.367%). The fourth-year deduction is $5,187 ($100,000 × 5.187%). Table 2 is used.

*5. Coordination with Code Sec. 179*

The Code Sec. 179 expense allowance is claimed prior to the additional depreciation allowance (Reg. § 1.168(k)-1(d); Reg. § 1.168(k)-2(e)(1); Proposed Reg. § 1.168(k)-2(d)(1) in REG-104397-18).

***Example (1):*** An item of 5-year property placed in service in January 2017 costs $100,000. The taxpayer expenses $20,000 of the cost under Code Sec. 179. The taxpayer's bonus depreciation is $40,000 ($80,000 × 50%). The depreciable basis after reduction by the Code Sec. 179 expense allowance and bonus depreciation is $40,000 ($100,000 – $20,000 – $40,000).

If the 100 percent bonus rate applies, the expense allowance is $20,000 and the bonus allowance is $80,000 ($100,000 – $20,000).

Note that the basis of an asset is reduced by the amount elected to be expensed even if a portion of the amount elected to be expensed is carried forward due to the section 179 taxable income limitation. When the section 179 property is disposed the basis of the property is increased by any unused carryforward (Reg. § 1.179-3(f)(1)).

This required order of allocation will reduce the size of the bonus depreciation claimed on an asset with respect to which a Code Sec. 179 expense allowance is claimed. If bonus depreciation could be calculated prior to reduction by any amount expensed under Code Sec. 179, the bonus depreciation would have been $50,000 ($100,000 × 50%) rather than $40,000.

Unlike the Code Sec. 179 expense allowance, there is no dollar limit on the total amount of bonus depreciation that may be claimed. There is no investment or taxable income limitation. The bonus deduction can create a net operating loss deduction. See, also, ¶ 487.

Where 50 percent bonus depreciation applies, taxpayers should expense assets with the longest recovery (depreciation) period in order to accelerate the recovery of their costs. For example, given the choice of expensing the cost of 20-year property or 3-year property, the Code Sec. 179 expense allowance should be allocated to the 20-year property since the full cost of the 3-year property will be recovered in three years. However, if the section 179 deduction is claimed on qualified real property (Code Sec. 179(e)) the section 1245 recapture rules apply (gain is ordinary income to extent of section 179 deduction) whereas bonus depreciation claimed on section 1250 property is subject to the section 1250 recapture rules (gain is ordinary income to extent bonus depreciation exceeds straight-line depreciation that would have been claimed on the bonus amount through disposition year). See "*43. Section 1245 and section 1250 depreciation recapture.*"

See ¶ 487 for discussion of distinctions between the Code Sec. 179 deduction and bonus depreciation.

*6. Short tax year*

The full bonus depreciation deduction may be claimed in a short tax year (Reg. § 1.168(k)-1(d)(1)(i); Reg. § 1.168(k)-2(e)(1)(ii); Proposed Reg. § 1.168(k)-2(d)(1)(ii) in REG-104397-18).

*7. Like-kind exchanges and involuntary conversions*

In general, the entire adjusted basis of property received in a like-kind exchange (Code Sec. 1031) or acquired in an involuntary conversion (Code Sec. 1033) (i.e., the carryover (exchanged) basis and any excess basis) qualifies for bonus depreciation in the year of replacement (which may be before the placed-in-service year) if the original use of the replacement property begins with the taxpayer (i.e., the replacement property is new) (Reg. § 1.168(k)-1(f)(5); Reg. § 1.168(k)-2(g)(5); Proposed Reg. § 1.168(k)-2(f)(5) in REG-104397-18). Although used property acquired and placed in service after September 27, 2017 may qualify for bonus depreciation, the carryover basis of used property does not qualify for bonus depreciation (Reg. § 1.168(k)-2(b)(3)(A)(3); Proposed Reg. § 1.168(k)-2(b)(3)(iii)(A)(3) in REG-104397-18; Code Sec. 179(d)(3)). Therefore, used property acquired in a like-kind exchange or involuntary conversion only qualifies for bonus depreciation to the extent of the used property's basis in excess of its carryover basis which is usually any additional cash paid (Reg. § 1.168(k)-2(g)(5)(iii)(A); Proposed Reg. § 1.168(k)-2(f)(5)(iii)(A) in REG-104397-18).

Effective for like-kind exchanges completed after December 31, 2017, the tax-deferred like-kind exchanges only apply to real property (Code Sec. 1033(a), as amended by the Tax Cuts and Jobs Act (P.L. 115-97). Under a transition rule that protected deferred exchanges, the like-kind exchange rules applied to personal property if the relinquished property was disposed of or the replacement property was received on or before December 31, 2017 (Act Sec. 13303(c)(2) of P.L. 115-97).

Bonus depreciation and regular depreciation may not be claimed on relinquished property that is placed in service and replaced in a like-kind exchange in the same tax year (Reg. § 1.168(k)-1(f)(5)(iii)(B); Reg. § 1.168(d)-1(b)(3)(ii)).

*Long production property.* If the replacement property is long production property (Code Sec. 168(k)(2)(B)) eligible for an extended placed in service date deadline, bonus depreciation may not be claimed on exchanged or excess basis attributable to the manufacture, production, or construction during the one-year extension period (during 2027 for long production property acquired and placed in service after September 27, 2017; during 2020 for long production property acquired before September 28, 2017) (Reg. § 1.168(k)-1(f)(5)(iii)(C); Reg. § 1.168(k)-2(g)(5)(iii)(C); Proposed Reg. § 1.168(k)-2(f)(5)(iii)(C) in REG-104397-18). Subject to this restriction, as in the case of other types of property, the carryover and excess basis qualify for the bonus deduction if the replacement property is new and only the excess basis qualifies if the replacement property is used.

*Alternative minimum tax.* Bonus depreciation claimed on the replacement property is claimed in full for AMT purposes (Reg. § 1.168(k)-1(f)(5)(iii)(E); Reg. § 1.168(k)-2(g)(5)(iii)(E); Proposed Reg. § 1.168(k)-2(f)(5)(iii)(E) in REG-104397-18). Any regular depreciation claimed on the basis of the replacement property that is taken into account in computing bonus depreciation should also be claimed in full for AMT purposes. For example, if 50 percent bonus is claimed on $1,000 excess basis, MACRS depreciation claimed on $500 should be allowed in full. See "*44. Alternative minimum tax.*"

***Example (1):*** ABC places a gas station canopy (five-year property) in service in January 2017 at a cost of $200,000. In 2021 the canopy is destroyed in a fire and ABC purchases and places in service a new canopy using the $160,000 of insurance proceeds. The adjusted basis of the original canopy at the time of involuntary conversion was $111,520 ($200,000 – $100,000 bonus (pre-September 28, 2017 50% bonus rate) – $20,000 depreciation (2017) – $32,000 depreciation (2018) – $19,200 depreciation (2019) – $11,520 2020 depreciation – $5,760 2021 depreciation (applying half-year convention). The basis of the new canopy is $11,520 and qualifies for the 100 percent bonus deduction (Reg. § 1.168(k)-2(g)(5)(v), Examples 1 and 2; Proposed Reg. § 1.168(k)-2(f)(5)(v), Examples 1 and 2 in REG-104397-18).

***Example (2):*** Assume the same facts as the preceding example except that ABC used the insurance proceeds to purchase a used canopy. Since the entire basis of the used canopy ($11,520) is a carryover basis no portion of the basis qualifies for bonus depreciation in 2020 (Reg. § 1.168(k)-2(g)(5)(v)(C), Example 3; Proposed Reg. § 1.168(k)-2(f)(5)(v), Example 3 in REG-104397-18).

***Example (3):*** ABC places new 15-year real property X costing $10,000 in service in 2019 and elected out of bonus depreciation. In 2021 ABC exchanges X for new real property Y and pays $1,000 additional cash. The basis of Y is $9,122 ($10,000 – $500 depreciation (2019) – $950 depreciation (2020) – $428 depreciation (2021) + $1,000 additional cash). ABC may claim a $9,122 bonus deduction in 2021 for the carryover basis in Y ($8,122) and the additional cash paid ($1,000) (Reg. § 1.168(k)-2(g)(5)(v)(D), Example 4; Reg. § 1.168(k)-2(g)(5)(v)(D), Example 4; Proposed Reg. § 1.168(k)-2(f)(5)(v), Example 4 in REG-104397-18).

***Example (4):*** ABC, a calendar-year taxpayer, pays $20,000 for 15-year real property X in January 1, 2021 and exchanges the real property for like-kind used real property Y in December 2021. ABC pays an additional $5,000 cash for Y. ABC may not claim bonus depreciation or regular depreciation on X in 2021 because X was acquired and disposed of in the same tax year. The $20,000 carryover basis in Y does not qualify for bonus depreciation because Y is used. However, the additional $5,000 cash paid does qualify for bonus depreciation (Reg. § 1.168(k)-2(g)(5)(v)(E), Example 5; Proposed Reg. § 1.168(k)-2(f)(5)(v), Example 5 in REG-104397-18).

*Example 4A:* Same facts as above except that ABC makes a Reg. § 1.168(i)-6(i)(1) election out of the like-kind exchange depreciation calculation rules. No bonus or regular depreciation is allowed on X in 2021 because X was placed in service and disposed of in the same tax year. ABC is treated as placing Y in service in December 2021 with a basis of $25,000 (the total of the carryover basis of $20,000 and the excess basis of $5,000 which is depreciated with a fresh-start 15-year depreciation period (¶ 167)). However, the 100-percent bonus is only allowable for the $5,000 excess basis. The $20,000 carryover basis of Y is not eligible for bonus depreciation because Y is used property (Reg. § 1.168(k)-2(g)(5)(v)(E), Example 6; Proposed Reg. § 1.168(k)-2(f)(5)(v), Example 6 in REG-104397-18).

See ¶ 167 for the computation of regular depreciation deductions in a like-kind exchange or involuntary conversion on the portion of the basis of property which is not claimed as bonus depreciation.

*8. Computation of bonus deduction when basis increases or decreases after property placed in service*

The basis of property which qualified for bonus depreciation may be subject to and upward or downward adjustment after the property has been placed in service. Such an adjustment could be caused, for example, by a contingent purchase price or a discharge of indebtedness.

If the basis of the property is redetermined on or before the last date that the property could have been placed in service and still qualify for the bonus deduction, then the bonus depreciation deduction must be redetermined. Under the current rules the last placed-in-service date is December 31, 2026 unless the extended December 31, 2027 deadline for longer production property or noncommercial aircraft applies. For property acquired before September 28, 2017, the last placed in service date is December 31, 2019 (December 31, 2020 for longer production property or noncommercial aircraft). If the basis adjustment occurs after these dates, the bonus deduction is not redetermined (Reg. § 1.168(k)-1(f)(2); Reg. § 1.168(k)-2(g)(2); Proposed Reg. § 1.168(k)-2(f)(2) in REG-104397-18).

The regulations also explain how to compute the regular MACRS deductions on the increased or decreased basis.

*Increase in basis.* If there is an increase in basis, the taxpayer claims a bonus deduction on the increased basis in the tax year that the increase occurs. The taxpayer uses the same rate that applied to the underlying property (Reg. § 1.168(k)-1(f)(2)(i); Reg. § 1.168(k)-2(g)(2)(i); Proposed Reg. § 1.168(k)-2(f)(2)(i) in REG-104397-18).

The amount allowable as a regular depreciation deduction for the increase in basis is determined by first reducing the increase in basis by the bonus deduction allowed on the increased basis. The remaining increase in basis (if any) is depreciated over the recovery period that remains as of the beginning of the tax year in which the increase in basis occurred. The same depreciation method and convention that applies to the underlying property is used (Reg. § 1.168(k)-1(f)(2)(i)(A); Reg. § 1.168(k)-2(g)(2)(i)(A); Proposed Reg. § 1.168(k)-2(f)(2)(i)(A) in REG-104397-18). If the 100 percent bonus rate applies, then there is no remaining basis. Any remaining increase in the basis of computer software is depreciated ratably over the remainder of the Code Sec. 168(f) 36-month depreciation period as of the beginning of the first day of the month in which the increase in basis occurs (Reg. § 1.168(k)-1(f)(2)(i)(B); Reg. § 1.168(k)-2(g)(2)(i)(B); Proposed Reg. § 1.168(k)-2(f)(2)(i)(B)).

*Example (1):* ABC purchases 5-year property in 2023 for $200,000 and agrees to pay seller 25 percent of gross profits from operation of the property beginning in 2024. Gross profits of $40,000 are paid in 2024. In 2023 bonus depreciation is $160,000 ($200,000 × 80% bonus rate for property placed in service in 2023). In 2024 bonus depreciation is $32,000 ($40,000 × 80% bonus rate for property placed in service in 2023).

Regular depreciation in 2023 is $8,000 ($40,000 remaining basis not claimed as bonus × 20% first-year table percentage). In 2024 depreciation on the $40,000 remaining basis is $12,800 ($40,000 × 32% second-year table percentage). In addition, in 2024 ABC begins to claim depreciation on the $8,000 portion of the $40,000 basis increase that is not claimed as bonus depreciation ($40,000 - $32,000 = $8,000). The 2024 deduction is equal to $889 (1/4.5 years (straight-line rate) × 2 to reflect 200 percent declining balance rate for 5-year property). 4.5 years is the remaining recovery period at the beginning of 2024 (5-year recovery period - 1/2 year depreciation for 2023 under the half-year convention) (Reg. § 1.168(k)-1(f)(2)(iv), *Example 1*; Reg. § 1.168(k)-2(g)(2)(iv)(A), *Example 1* and Proposed Reg. § 1.168(k)-2(f)(2)(iv) in REG-104397-18), *Example 1*).

*Decrease in basis.* If the basis of bonus depreciation property acquired before September 28, 2017 decreases in a tax year after it is placed in service, the taxpayer must include in income the excess amount of additional first year depreciation previously claimed. The excess amount is the decrease in basis times the applicable bonus rate. The taxpayer uses the same rate that applied to the underlying property. If the taxpayer did not previously claim the allowable amount of additional first year depreciation, the excess amount can be based on the amount actually claimed by the taxpayer. The actual amount can be used only if the taxpayer establishes the amount by adequate records or other sufficient evidence (Reg. § 1.168(k)-1(f)(2)(ii)).

To determine the amount includible in income for excess depreciation claimed (other than additional the first year allowance), the decrease in basis is first adjusted by the excess additional first year allowance. Then, the remaining amount of decrease in basis is included in income over the recovery period for that property remaining as of the beginning of the tax year that the decrease in basis occurs. The same depreciation method and convention that applies to the underlying property is used (Reg. § 1.168(k)-1(f)(2)(ii)(A)). In the case of computer software the amount is included in income over the remainder of the Code Sec. 167(f) 36-month depreciation period as of the beginning of the first day of the month in which the decrease in basis occurs (Reg. § 1.168(k)-1(f)(2)(ii)(B)).

Final regulations and proposed regulations for property acquired and placed in service after September 27, 2017, provide a similar rule for decreases in basis. The regulations, however, clarify that excess bonus depreciation and regular depreciation deductions attributable to a decrease in basis are included in income by reducing the total amount otherwise allowable as a depreciation deduction for all of the taxpayer's depreciable property during the tax year. If there is insufficient depreciation to offset the excess depreciation, then the remaining excess depreciation is treated as a negative depreciation deduction in computing taxable income (Reg. § 1.168(k)-2(g)(2)(ii); Proposed Reg. § 1.168(k)-2(f)(2)(ii) in REG-104397-18).

***Example (2):*** In 2023 ABC, a calendar-year taxpayer, placed 5-year property costing $400,000 in service. In 2024, a lender who financed the property forgives $50,000 of the debt. Although the debt was forgiven in 2024 the basis of the property is reduced on January 1, 2025 (see Code Sec. 108(b)(5) and Code Sec. 1017(a)).

For 2023 ABC claims a $320,000 bonus deduction ($400,000 × 80 percent bonus rate for 2023). A $16,000 first-year depreciation deduction is claimed on the remaining $80,000 basis ($80,000 × 20% first year table percentage for five-year property = $16,000).

For 2024 a $25,600 second-year depreciation deduction is claimed ($80,000 × 32% second year table percentage).

For 2025, ABC computes a $15,360 third-year deduction on the $80,000 basis ($80,000 × 19.2% third-year percentage).

ABC, however, must reduce the $15,360 deduction by the depreciation previously claimed on the $50,000 basis reduction that is made as of January 1, 2025.

The decrease attributable to 2023 bonus depreciation is $40,000 ($50,000 × 80).

The decrease attributable to regular depreciation claimed on the remaining $10,000 ($50,000 - $40,000) is taken into account over the 3.5 years remaining in the recovery period as of January 1, 2025. The 2025 decrease is $5,714 ($10,000 × 1/3.5 (straight line rate) × 2 to reflect 200 percent declining balance method).

The total decrease in depreciation for 2025 is $45,714 ($40,000 + $5,714). This amount is first applied against the $15,360 depreciation allowed for 2025 and then against any other depreciation deductions from other assets for 2025. If there are insufficient depreciation deductions to offset, the excess is a negative depreciation deduction that increases taxable income (Reg. § 1.168(k)-2(g)(2)(iv)(B), Example 2 and Proposed Reg. § 1.168(k)-1(f)(2)(iv), *Example 2* in REG-104397-18).

*9. Election out of bonus depreciation*

Bonus depreciation must be claimed unless a taxpayer makes an election out (Code Sec. 168(k)(7)). Once made, an election out cannot be revoked without IRS consent.

*Late election out and revocation of election out for tax years ending in 2018, 2019, and 2020.* A taxpayer is allowed to make a late election out of bonus depreciation for any class of property or revoke a prior election out that was made for any class of property for a tax year ending in 2018, 2019, and 2020 (Rev. Proc. 2020-25). See discussion at "*1A. Qualified improvement property placed in service after 2017—guidance for changing to 15-year recovery period and claiming bonus depreciation—guidance for making late elections and revoking prior elections for 2018, 2019, and 2020 tax years*" for details. In addition, a late election or revocation may be made under Rev. Proc. 2020-50 for the 2017 - 2020 tax years. See "*1D. Late elections and revocations for 2017, 2018, 2019, and 2020 tax years for taxpayers applying 2020 final, 2019 final, or 2019 final and proposed regulations.*"

*Election out procedure.* Taxpayers must make the election out in the manner described in the instructions for Form 4562, *Depreciation and Amortization* (Reg. § 1.168(k)-1(e)(3)(ii); Reg. § 1.167(k)-2(f)(1); Proposed Reg. § 1.168(k)-2(e)(1) in REG-104397-18). The instructions require taxpayers to attach a statement to a timely filed income tax return (including extensions) indicating the class or classes of property (e.g., property in the 3-year class, i.e., 3-year property) to which the election applies and that the taxpayer will not claim bonus depreciation on the elected class or classes. The election is made separately by each person owning qualified property (for example, by the partnership, by the S corporation, or by the common parent of a consolidated group) (Reg. § 1.168(k)-1(e)(3)(ii); Reg. § 1.168(k)-2(f)(1)(iii)(B); Reg. § 1.168(k)-2(e)(1)(iii)(B)). If a timely return was filed without making the election, the election may still be made by filing an amended return within six months of the due date of the return (not including extensions). Write "Filed pursuant to section 301.9100-2" on the amended return. It is not necessary to make a reference to the Code Section which authorizes the election out (Form 4562 instructions).

*Special rule for tax year that includes September 28, 2017.* A taxpayer may make a late election out of bonus depreciation for a class of property placed in service in a tax year that includes September 28, 2017. A taxpayer may also revoke an election out for a class of property placed in service during that tax year. If a taxpayer did not claim bonus depreciation on a class of property placed in service during the tax year that includes September 28, 2017, a valid election is deemed made even if an election statement was not filed. The deemed election may also be revoked. These rules only apply to a class of property if property within that class was acquired and placed in service after September 27, 2017 in the tax year that includes September 28, 2017. The election out for a class of property is made or revoked by filing an accounting method change for the first, second, or third tax year that follows the tax year that includes September 28, 2017. An amended return may also be filed if the taxpayer has not filed a tax return for the tax year that follows the tax year that includes September 28, 2017 (Rev. Proc. 2019-33). See "*11. Special rules for making and revoking elections in tax year that includes September 28, 2017*". This late election or revocation may also be available under Rev. Proc. 2020-25 or Rev. Proc. 2020-50. See discussion at "*1A. Qualified improvement property placed in service after 2017—guidance for changing to 15-year recovery period and claiming bonus depreciation—guidance for making late elections and revoking prior elections for 2018, 2019, and 2020 tax years*" (relating to Rev. Proc. 2020-25) and "*1D. Late elections and revocations for 2017, 2018, 2019, and 2020 tax years for taxpayers applying 2020 final, 2019 final, or 2019 final and proposed regulations.*" (relating to Rev. Proc. 2020-50).

*Election out applies separately to each property class.* The election out is made at the property class level. The election applies to all property in the class or classes for which the election out is made that is placed in service for the tax year of the election (Code Sec. 168(k)(2)(C)(iii), as added by P.L. 107-147; Reg. § 1.168(k)-1(e)(1); Reg. § 1.168(k)-1(e)(3)(ii); Reg. § 1.168(k)-2(f)(1)(i); Proposed Reg. § 1.168(k)-2(e)(1)(i) in REG-104397-18).

Property class refers to the 3-, 5-, 7-, 10-, 15-, 20-year asset classifications described in Code Sec. 168(e). However, water utility property as defined in Code Sec. 168(e)(5) and computer software as defined in Code Sec. 167(f)(1) are treated as separate property classes (Reg. § 1.168(k)-2(f)(1)(ii); Proposed Reg. § 1.168(k)-2(e)(1)(ii) in REG-104397-18; Reg. § 1.168(k)-1(e)(2)). Thus, for example, a taxpayer may make the election out for all 3-year property placed in service in the tax year. The election out cannot be made for some, but not all, 3-year property placed in service during the tax year. Similarly, the election out may be made for all qualifying software placed in service during a tax year or for all water utility property placed in service during a tax year.

Effective for property acquired and placed in service after September 27, 2017, the regulations treat the following as separate classes of property (Reg. § 1.168(k)-2(f)(1)(ii); Proposed Reg. § 1.168(k)-2(e)(1)(ii) in REG-104397-18):

- each class of 3-, 5-, 7-, 10-, 15-, and 20-year property;
- water utility property described in Code Sec. 168(e)(5);
- computer software amortized over 3 years under Code Sec. 167(f)(1);
- each separate production of a qualified film or television production as defined in Reg. § 1.181-3(b)
- each separate production of a qualified live theatrical production as defined in Code Sec. 181(e)(2);
- qualified improvement property (Code Sec. 168(e)(6)) acquired after September 27, 2017 and placed in service before January 1, 2018
- a partner's basis adjustment in partnership assets under Code Sec. 743(b) for each class of property described above

Qualified improvement property placed in service after 2017 qualifies for bonus depreciation by reason of having a 15-year recovery period. Consequently, qualified improvement property placed in service after 2017 is treated as part of the 15-year property class for purposes of the election out.

Qualified improvement property placed in service in 2016 and 2017 is a separate *category* of property that qualifies for bonus depreciation (Code Sec. 168(k)(2)(A)(i)(IV) and (k)(3), stricken by the Tax Cuts and Jobs Act (P.L. 115-97)). However, the final and proposed regulations only treat qualified improvement property acquired and placed in service after September 27, 2017 and before 2018 as a separate *class* of property for purposes of the election out (Reg. § 1.168(k)-2(f)(1)(ii)(D); Proposed Reg. § 1.168(k)-2(e)(1)(ii)(D) in REG-104397-18). The September 27, 2017 date for treatment of qualified improvement property as a separate class for bonus depreciation purposes was apparently chosen because the final and proposed regulations in general apply to property acquired after September 27, 2017 which may qualify for the 100 percent bonus rate.

There is no specific authority for treating qualified improvement property acquired before September 28, 2017 and placed in service in 2016 or 2017 as a separate class of property for purposes of the election out even though it was a separate category of bonus depreciation property.

The regulations for property acquired before September 28, 2017 do not treat qualified improvement property as a separate class of property for purposes of the election out (Reg. § 1.168(k)-1(e)(2)(iv)). However, these regulations were issued before qualified improvement property replaced qualified leasehold improvement property as a separate class for purposes of the election out.

Qualified leasehold improvement property as defined in Code Sec. 168(k)(3) (prior to amendment by P.L. 114-113) was also treated as separate property class under regulations in effect for property acquired before September 28, 2017 (Reg. § 1.168(k)-1(e)(2)). Qualified leasehold improvement property was removed as a separate category of bonus depreciation property, effective for property placed in service after 2015, and, therefore, after 2015 is no longer treated as a separate property class for purposes of the election out.

*Section 743 basis adjustment treated as separate property class.* A partner's basis adjustment in partnership assets under Code Sec. 743(b) for each class of property is a separate class of property for purposes of the election out (Reg. § 1.168(k)-2(f)(1)(ii)(G); Proposed Reg. § 1.168(k)-2(e)(1)(ii)(G) in REG-104397-18).

A partnership is allowed to claim bonus depreciation for an increase in the basis of qualified property made under Code Sec. 743(b) in a class of property even if the partnership made the election out for all other qualified property of the partnership in the same class of property. The partnership may also make an election out for an increase in the basis of qualified property under Code Sec. 743(b) in a class of property even if the partnership does not make that election for all other qualified property of the partnership in the same class of property. In this case, the section 743(b) basis adjustment must be recovered under a reasonable method (Reg. § 1.743-1(j)(4)(i)(B)(1); Proposed Reg. § 1.743-1(j)(4)(i)(B)(1) in REG-104397-18).

See "*14. Code Sec. 754 elections and other partnership transactions.*"

*Revocation of election out.* A taxpayer who made an election out may also revoke that election without IRS consent by filing an amended return within six months (excluding extensions) of the due date of the return on which the election out was made if the taxpayer's original return was timely filed. If this rule does not apply, revocation is available only with IRS consent obtained by filing a letter ruling request (Reg. § 1.168(k)-1(e)(7); Reg. § 1.168(k)-2(f)(5)).

*Failure to claim bonus depreciation if no election out is made.* If a taxpayer fails to make an election out, depreciation deductions on the qualifying property must be computed as if the bonus deduction had been claimed on the return, whether or not the bonus allowance was in fact claimed. A taxpayer cannot make an election out by filing a request to change accounting method (Reg. § 1.168(k)-1(e)(5); Reg. § 1.168(k)-2(f)(1)(iv)). A taxpayer that failed to claim bonus depreciation may amend the return on which the deduction should have been claimed if no additional returns were filed. If two or more returns have been filed, an accounting method change under Sec. 6.01 of Rev. Proc. 2019-43 must be filed and a negative (favorable) section 481(a) adjustment claimed. By filing two returns the taxpayer has adopted an impermissible method of accounting. See ¶ 75.

*Alternative minimum tax.* The bonus deduction is allowed in full for AMT purposes (Code Sec. 168(k)(2)(G)). No AMT adjustment is required on the regular income tax depreciation deductions claimed on property on which bonus depreciation is claimed unless the regular tax basis and AMT basis on which depreciation is computer differ (Reg. § 1.168(k)-1(d)(1)(iii); Reg. § 1.168(k)-2(e)(1)(iv)(B)).

For property placed in service after 2015, no AMT adjustment is required on depreciation claimed on property which qualifies for bonus depreciation even if the election out is made.

The corporate AMT is eliminated effective for tax years beginning after 2017. See discussion below, "*44. Alternative minimum tax.*"

For property placed in service before 2016 if the election out is made, there is no special exemption from the AMT depreciation adjustment. The election out may trigger an AMT adjustment if the property would otherwise be subject to an depreciation adjustment (Reg. § 1.168(k)-1(e)(6)). A depreciation adjustment for property placed in service before 2016 is generally required if an election out is made with respect to 3-, 5-, 7-, or 10-year property which is depreciated using the 200-percent declining-balance method. See ¶ 170. The IRS has allowed a taxpayer to revoke a bonus depreciation election out in reliance on a CPA's advice where the election caused an AMT liability (IRS Letter Ruling 200626038, March 3, 2006).

*Corporate election to claim unused AMT credit in lieu of bonus depreciation.* A technical correction clarifies that if a corporation makes a regular election out of bonus depreciation under Code Sec. 168(k)(7), as in effect on the day prior to enactment of the 2017 Tax Cuts Act, for a particular class of property (e.g., all 5-year property), then an election under former Code Sec. 168(k)(4) to claim unused alternative minimum tax credits in lieu of bonus depreciation does not apply to the class of property for which an election out of bonus depreciation is made (Act Sec. 101(d)(4) of the 2018 Technical Corrections Act). See "*53. Corporate election to claim accelerated AMT and research credits in lieu of bonus depreciation.*"

As a result of the technical correction, if the regular election out of bonus depreciation is made for a class of property and the corporation also makes the Code Sec. 168(k)(4) election, the bonus depreciation that could have been claimed on the class for which the election out is made is not taken into account in determining the amount of the AMT credit refund. Furthermore, it is not necessary to depreciate the class of property for which the election out was made using the straight-line method as otherwise required by Code Sec. 168(k)(4)(A)(ii).

The corporate election to claim unused AMT credits is repealed, effective for tax years beginning after 2017, in conjunction with the repeal of the AMT on corporations.

*Election out for 2015/2016 fiscal-year filers.* The IRS issued guidance on the election out which applies to 2015/2016 fiscal-year taxpayers (Section 4.04(3) of Rev. Proc. 2017-33). Although the election out is made under former Code Sec. 168(k)(2)(D)(iii), prior to amendment by P.L. 114-113, for property placed in service before 2016 and under Code Sec. 168(k)(7), as added by P.L. 114-113, effective for property placed in service after 2015, it appears that a 2015/2016 fiscal year taxpayer that made an "election out" on Form 4562 was not required to make two separate elections. A single election appears to apply to all property in the same class placed in service in the fiscal year. The IRS guidance does not specifically require two elections. The instructions to Form 4562, which describes the election out procedure, do not require any reference to the specific Code Section that the election out is being made under.

*Election out for 2014/2015 fiscal-year filers and certain other fiscal-years.* 2014/2015 fiscal year filers who failed to claim bonus depreciation on property placed in service in 2015 may in certain situations be deemed to have made an election out of bonus depreciation (Rev. Proc. 2016-48). See discussion #11A, "*Special rules for 2014/2015 fiscal-year returns and 2015 short year returns if no bonus claimed on 2015 property.*" A similar rule applies to 2013/2014 fiscal-year taxpayers who failed to claim bonus depreciation on property placed in service in 2014 (Rev. Proc. 2015-48) (see discussion #11B above, "*Special rules for 2013/2014 fiscal-year returns and 2014 short year returns if no bonus claimed on 2014 property.*" and 2009/2010 fiscal-year taxpayers who did not claim bonus depreciation on property placed in service in 2010 (Rev. Proc. 2011-26).

*10. Election to claim 50-percent bonus depreciation in place of 100-percent bonus depreciation during tax year that includes September 28, 2017*

A taxpayer may elect to apply the 50-percent rate instead of the 100-percent rate for "all" qualified property acquired after September 27, 2017 and placed in service during the taxpayer's tax year that includes September 28, 2017 (Code Sec. 168(k)(10), as added by P.L. 115-97; Reg. § 1.168(k)-2(f)(3); Proposed Reg. § 1.168(k)-2(e)(3) in REG-104397-18). For example, a calendar year taxpayer making this election can apply the 50-percent rate to all qualified property placed in service in 2017 and ignore the 100-percent rate that would otherwise apply to qualified property acquired and placed in service after September 27, 2017 and before January 1, 2018. The election is not made on a property class by property class basis. It applies to all qualified property placed in service during the tax year.

IRS guidance allows a taxpayer to make a late election or revoke a prior election to claim 50 percent bonus depreciation in lieu of the 100 percent rate for property placed in service in a tax year that includes September 28, 2017 (Rev. Proc. 2020-25 and Rev. Proc. 2020-50). For Rev. Proc. 2020-25, see discussion at "*1A. Qualified improvement property placed in service after 2017—guidance for changing to 15-year recovery period and claiming bonus depreciation—guidance for making late elections and revoking prior elections for 2018, 2019, and 2020 tax years.*" and for Rev. Proc. 2020-50 see *1D. Late elections and revocations for 2017, 2018, 2019, and 2020 tax years for taxpayers applying 2020 final, 2019 final, or 2019 final and proposed regulations.*

Earlier guidance also allows a taxpayer to make a late election to claim the 50 percent rate or revoke the election to claim the 50 percent rate for its tax year that includes September 28, 2017 by filing an accounting method change or an amended return. At this point in time, the election or revocation can only be made under this guidance by filing an accounting method change for the third tax year that follows tax year that includes September 28, 2017 (i.e., 2020 tax year for a calendar-year taxpayer). In addition, a taxpayer was deemed to have made the election to claim the 50 percent rate in place of the 100 percent rate even if an election statement was not filed provided the taxpayer claimed the 50 percent rate on all qualified property placed in service in the tax year. The deemed election may be revoked (Rev. Proc. 2019-33). See "*11. Special rules for making and revoking elections in tax year that includes September 28, 2017.*"

The following discussion explains the rules provided in final (and earlier proposed) regulations for making and revoking the election to claim 50 percent bonus depreciation in place of the 100 percent rate (Reg. § 1.168(k)-2(f)(3); Proposed Reg. § 1.168(k)-2(e)(3) in REG-104397-18).

Code Sec. 168(k)(10) states that the election is available for a taxpayer's first tax year ending after September 27, 2017 (Code Sec. 168(k)(10)). The final and earlier proposed regulations (as well as related IRS guidance in Rev. Proc. 2019-33 and Rev. Proc. 2020-25), however, provide that the election applies to the tax year that includes September 28, 2017. This change prevents a newly formed taxpayer from making the election in a phase-out tax year when the bonus rates are below 50 percent in order to claim a 50 percent rate. The election procedures in the Instructions to 2017 Form 4562 and IRS Pub. 946 (2017), which were issued before the proposals, indicate that the election is made for the first tax year ending after September 27, 2017.

A proposed technical correction provides that the election may only be made for a tax year ending after September 27, 2017 and beginning before January 1, 2018 ("Tax Technical and Clerical Corrections Act Discussion Draft" (U.S. House of Representatives Committee on Ways and Means Chairman Kevin Brady January 2, 2019); Technical Explanation of the House Ways and Means Committee Chairman's discussion draft of the "Tax Technical and Clerical Corrections Act" (JCX-1-19, January 2, 2019).

The election is made by attaching a statement to a timely filed return (including extensions) for the tax year that includes September 28, 2017 indicating that the taxpayer is "electing to claim a 50 percent special depreciation allowance on all qualified property."

The election must be made separately by each person owning qualified property (for example, by the partnership, by the S corporation, or for each member of a consolidated group by the common parent of the group) (Reg. § 1.168(k)-2(f)(3)(ii); Proposed Reg. § 1.168(k)-2(e)(3)(ii) in REG-104397-18).

If a taxpayer makes a separate election under Code Sec. 168(k)(5) for a tax year that includes September 28, 2017 to claim bonus depreciation on specified plants in the year of planting or grafting, a separate election to claim 50 percent bonus on those plants which were planted or grafted after September 27, 2017 may be made (Reg. § 1.168(k)-2(f)(3)(i); Proposed Reg. § 1.168(k)-2(e)(3)(i) in REG-104397-18).

Without regard to the special rules in Rev. Rul. 2019-33, Rev. Proc. 2020-25, and Rev. Proc. 2020-50 a taxpayer was allowed to file an amended return within 6 months of the due date (excluding extensions) of the original return to change the election. Taxpayers are affected by the election change (e.g., partners) are also required to file amended returns (Reg. § 1.168(k)-2(f)(5); Proposed Reg. § 1.168(k)-2(e)(5) in REG-104397-18).

*11. Special rules for making and revoking elections in tax year that includes September 28, 2017*

A taxpayer may make certain late elections or revocations for a tax year that includes September 28, 2017 under Rev. Proc. 2019-33 as discussed here. The following late elections may be made or revoked:

- the election out of bonus depreciation for any class of property if property within that class was placed in service after September 27, 2017;
- the election to claim bonus depreciation on all qualified property acquired after September 27, 2017 at the 50 percent rate in lieu of the 100 percent rate;
- the election to claim bonus depreciation on a specified plant planted or grafted after September 27, 2017 in the year of planting or grafting; and

- the election to claim bonus depreciation at the 50 percent rate on all specified plants planted or grafted after September 27, 2017 for which an election to claim bonus depreciation in the year of planting or grafting was made.

In order to make or revoke one or more of these elections, the taxpayer must have filed a timely return for the tax year that includes September 28, 2017. In addition, the taxpayer must have acquired property after September 27, 2017 and placed the property in service in its tax year that includes September 28, 2017. In the case of elections related to specified plants, the taxpayer musts have planted or grafted a specified plant after September 27, 2017 in a tax year that includes September 28, 2017.

These elections may be made or revoked by filing a change in accounting method in any of the first three tax years after the tax year that includes September 28, 2017. The method is filed under the automatic consent procedure described in Section 6.18 of Rev. Proc. 2019-43 (Rev. Proc. 2019-33). A Code Sec. 481(a) adjustment is required.

For a limited period of time an amended return was allowed to be filed instead of an accounting method change. The amended return had to be filed prior to filing the tax return for the tax year that immediately follows the tax year that includes September 28, 2017. A partnership subject to the centralized partnership audit regime had to file an administrative adjustment request before filing its return for the tax year that immediately follows its tax year that includes September 28, 2017.

*Deemed election out of bonus depreciation for tax year that includes September 28, 2017.* A taxpayer is deemed to have made a valid election out of bonus depreciation for a class of property for its tax year that includes September 28, 2017 if the taxpayer acquired and placed property in that class in service after September 27, 2017 and the taxpayer did not claim bonus depreciation for that class of property. Thus, the election out is valid even if a taxpayer did not provide a written statement with the tax return specifying the class of property to which the election out applied. This deemed election applies unless the taxpayer revokes the election by filing an amended return or an accounting method change as explained above.

*Deemed election to claim 50 percent bonus depreciation for tax year that includes September 28, 2017.* Similarly, an election to use the 50 percent rate in lieu of the 100 percent rate for a tax year that includes September 28, 2017 is deemed valid if the taxpayer used the 50 percent rate for all qualified property in all classes placed in service after September 27, 2017. Thus, the election is valid even though the taxpayer failed to attach an election statement to the return stating that the taxpayer elected the 50 percent rate in lieu of the 100 percent rate. A taxpayer may also revoke this deemed election by filing an amended return or accounting method change.

*Deemed elections for specified plants.* A taxpayer that claimed bonus depreciation at the 100 percent rate on a specified plant that was planted or grafted after September 27, 2017 in a tax year that includes September 28, 2017 is deemed to have made valid election to claim bonus depreciation on that plant in the year of planting or grafting even if a statement identifying the plant for which 100 percent bonus is claimed was not attached to the return. A taxpayer may also revoke this deemed election for a plant that was planted or grafted after September 27, 2017 by filing an amended return or an accounting method change as explained above.

A taxpayer that used the 50 percent rate for all specified plants planted or grafted after September 27, 2017 for which the taxpayer elected to claim bonus depreciation in the tax year of planting or grafting that included September 28, 2017 is deemed to have made a valid election to use the 50 percent rate in lieu of the 100 percent rate even if an election statement was not attached to the return.

These deemed elections may also be revoked by filing an amended return or filing an accounting method change as explained above.

Note that specified plants for which an election is not made to claim bonus depreciation in the year of planting or grafting are treated as eligible for bonus depreciation in the year they become commercially productive which is considered the placed in service year. These plants are treated as a separate class of property for purposes of the election out of bonus depreciation.

*Late elections or election revocations also allowed under Rev. Proc. 2020-25 and Rev. Proc. 2020-50.*

Rev. Proc. 2020-50 also allows taxpayers to make late elections and revoke elections under Code Sec. 168(k)(5) and (k)(7) for tax years that include September 28, 2017 and later tax years that begin before 2021 and under Code Sec. 168(k)(10) for a tax year that includes September 28, 2017 if the taxpayer applies final bonus depreciation regulations during the placed-in-service tax year. See *1D. Late elections and revocations for 2017, 2018, 2019, and 2020 tax years for taxpayers applying 2020 final, 2019 final, or 2019 final and proposed regulations.*

Rev. Proc. 2020-25 also allows taxpayers to make a late elections or revoke elections under Code Sec. 168(k)(5) and (k)(7) for tax years ending in 2018, 2019, and 2020 and under Code Sec. 168(k)(10) for a tax year that includes September 28, 2017. See *1A. Qualified improvement property placed in service after 2017—guidance for changing to 15-year recovery period and claiming bonus depreciation—guidance for making late elections and revoking prior elections for 2018, 2019, and 2020 tax years.*

*11A. Special rules for 2014/2015 fiscal year returns and 2015 short year returns if no bonus claimed on 2015 property*

The Protecting Americans from Tax Hikes Act (PATH Act) (P.L. 114-113), which was enacted on December 18, 2015, retroactively extended bonus depreciation to apply to property placed in service in 2015. Consequently, some 2014/2015 fiscal-year filers and taxpayers with short tax years that began and ended in 2015 did not claim bonus depreciation on property placed in service in 2015 on their tax return. The IRS has provided guidance to such taxpayers in Rev. Proc. 2016-48, I.R.B. 2016-36, September 15, 2015, which allows bonus depreciation to be claimed by filing an amended return if a 2015/2016 return has not been filed or by filing an accounting method change on Form 3115, Application for Change in Accounting Method if a 2015/2016 has been filed. This rule and rules relating to revocations of elections out of bonus depreciation and the making of elections out of bonus depreciation are covered in detail immediately below. This procedure only applies to taxpayers that placed property that qualifies for bonus depreciation in service in 2015 in a tax year beginning in 2014 and ending in 2015 (2014/2015 fiscal year taxpayer) or in a tax year of less than 12 months beginning and ending in 2015 (2015 short tax year).

If a qualifying taxpayer failed to claim bonus depreciation on a class of property placed in service during 2015 and did not make an election not to deduct bonus depreciation on that property class on its tax 2014/2015 fiscal year return or 2015 short year return, the taxpayer may file an amended return to claim bonus depreciation provided the taxpayer has not filed a tax return for the first tax year that follows the 2014/2015 fiscal year or 2015 short tax year. In addition, the

2014/2015 fiscal year or 2015 short tax year return must have been timely filed. As explained below, a prior election out for a class of property may be revoked.

If a taxpayer timely filed both a 2014/2015 fiscal year return and a 2015 short year return, amended returns for those years may be filed provided the taxpayer has not filed the return for the first tax year succeeding the 2015 short tax year.

***Example (1):*** ClayJars Inc. has a fiscal year beginning on June 1, 2014 and ending on May 31, 2015. It placed several vehicles (MACRS 5-year property) in service during the parts of 2014 and 2015 which fell within its fiscal year. It made no election out of bonus depreciation for 5-year property and did not claim bonus depreciation on the vehicles placed in service in 2015 on its 2014/2015 fiscal-year return. ClayJars may file an amended 2014/2015 fiscal year return to claim bonus depreciation on the vehicles placed in service in 2015 provided it has not filed its 2015/2016 fiscal-year return.

If a taxpayer timely filed both a 2014/2015 fiscal year return and a 2015 short year return, amended returns for those years may be filed provided the taxpayer has not filed the return for the first tax year succeeding the 2015 short tax year.

If the requirements for filing an amended return are not met or the taxpayer does not wish to file an amended return, the taxpayer may claim bonus depreciation by filing Form 3115, Application for Change in Accounting Method, under section 6.01 of the automatic change procedures (change #7) (see ¶ 75) with a timely filed return for the first or second tax year succeeding the 2014/2015 fiscal year or 2015 short tax year. The taxpayer must own the property as of the first day of the year of change and have timely filed its 2014/2015 fiscal year or 2015 short-year return. If a taxpayer has both a 2014/2015 fiscal tax year and a 2015 short tax year, and has timely filed returns for both years, the Form 3115 must be filed with the taxpayer's timely filed return for the first or second tax year succeeding the 2015 short tax year. Again, the taxpayer must own the property as of the year of the change.

***Example (2):*** Assume ClayJars filed its 2015/2016 fiscal year tax year return without first amending its 2014/2015 return to claim bonus depreciation on the vehicles placed in service in 2015. ClayJars may file an accounting method change for the 2016/2017 tax year (i.e., the return for the second tax year following the 2014/2015 tax year). A negative (favorable) Code Sec. 481(a) adjustment is reported on the 2016/2017 return. The adjustment is equal to the difference between the bonus depreciation deduction that should have been claimed on the 2014/2015 return and the depreciation that was claimed on the 2014/2015 and 2015/2016 returns on the amount that should have been claimed as bonus depreciation. ClayJars may be also be able to file the accounting method change for the 2015/2016 fiscal year even if it has already filed the 2015/2016 return. Generally, taxpayers are given an automatic 6-month extension from the due date (excluding any extension) of the federal income tax return to file Form 3115 in the case of automatic change requests. For details, see section 6.03 of Rev. Proc. 2015-13 and Reg. § 301.9100-2.

A taxpayer that made an election not to claim bonus depreciation for a class of property on a timely filed 2014/2015 fiscal year return or 2015 short tax year return is granted consent to revoke the election on an amended return filed by the later of November 11, 2016, or before filing the return for the first tax year succeeding the 2014/2015 fiscal year or 2015 short tax year. The revocation is made by claiming bonus depreciation on the amended return.

Any valid election that was made on a 2014/2015 fiscal year return or 2015 short tax year return not to claim bonus depreciation on a class of property will apply to all qualified property placed in service during that tax year unless the election is revoked as described above.

***Example (3):*** Assume ClayJars made a valid election not to claim bonus depreciation on 5-year property placed in service during its 2014/2015 fiscal year. ClayJars may revoke that election by filing an amended 2014/2015 fiscal year return that claims bonus depreciation on all 5-year property placed in service during the 2014/2015 fiscal year. The amended return, however, must be filed by the later of: (1) November 11, 2016 or (2) before filing the 2015/2016 fiscal-year return. The election will apply the all 5-year property placed in service during the 2014/2015 fiscal year unless the election is revoked.

A taxpayer that filed 2014/2015 fiscal year return or a 2015 short tax year return without claiming bonus depreciation for any property within a particular property class placed in service during the tax year is deemed to have made an election out of bonus depreciation for that property class if an amended return or Form 3115 is not filed to claim bonus depreciation for qualified property within the property class.

The deemed election out only applies if the taxpayer did not claim bonus depreciation on all property within the class that was placed in service during the 2014/2015 fiscal year or 2015 short tax year and claimed regular depreciation deductions on the property. For example, if a 2014/2015 fiscal year taxpayer claimed bonus depreciation on a particular item of MACRS 5-year property placed in service in 2014 but failed to claim bonus depreciation on an item of 5-year property placed in service in 2015, the deemed election out does not apply to the property placed in service in 2015. However, if the taxpayer only placed items of 5-year property in service in 2015 and does not file an amended return or Form 3115 to claim bonus depreciation, the deemed election out applies to the 5-year property (if regular depreciation was claimed on the property) since it comprises all of the property within the 5-year property class placed in service in the 2014/2015 tax year and bonus depreciation was not claimed.

*11B. Special rules for 2013/2014 fiscal year returns and 2014 short year returns if no bonus claimed on 2014 property*

The Tax Increase Prevention Act of 2014 (P.L. 113-295), which was enacted on December 14, 2014, extended bonus depreciation one full year to apply to property placed in service in 2014. Consequently, some 2013/2014 fiscal-year filers and taxpayers with short tax years that began and ended in 2014 did not claim bonus depreciation on property placed in service in 2014 on their tax return. The IRS has provided transitional guidance to such taxpayers in Rev. Proc. 2015-48, I.R.B. 2015-40, September 15, 2015. This guidance is similar to that provided in Rev. Proc. 2016-48 for 2014/2015 fiscal years and 2015 short tax years if bonus depreciation was not claimed for property placed in service in 2015. See discussion in #11A above, "*Special Rules for 2014/2015 Fiscal Year Returns and 2015 Short Year Returns if No Bonus Claimed on 2015 Property.*" For additional details see earlier editions of the U.S. Master Depreciation Guide.

QUALIFYING PROPERTY

*12. Qualified property*

The following types of property may qualify for the bonus deduction if all other requirements are satisfied (Code Sec. 168(k)(2)(A)(i); Reg. § 1.168(k)-1(b)(2; Reg. § 1.168(k)-2(b); Proposed Reg. § 1.168(k)-2(b) in REG-104397-18):

(1) MACRS property with a recovery period of 20 years or less;

(2) computer software as defined in, and depreciated under Code Sec. 167(f)(1) (Reg. § 1.168(k)-1(b)(2)(B); Reg. § 1.168(k)-2(b)(2)(i)(B); Proposed Reg. § 1.168(k)-2(b)(2)(i)(B) in REG-104397-18) (see "19. *Computer Software*");

(3) water utility property as defined in Code Sec. 168(e)(5) and depreciated under MACRS and which is not rate-regulated utility property;

(4) qualified leasehold improvement property (see "*15. Qualified leasehold improvement property placed in service before 2016*") depreciated under MACRS and placed in service before 2016;

(5) qualified improvement property placed in service after 2015 (generally, improvements to the interior of nonresidential real property as explained below at "*16. Qualified improvement property placed in service after 2015*); and

(6) films, television shows, and live theatrical productions acquired and placed in service after September 27, 2017. See "*17. Film and television productions and live theatrical productions acquired and placed in service after September 27, 2017.*"

The regular MACRS recovery period (i.e., the general depreciation system (GDS) recovery period) and not the ADS recovery period is used to determine if MACRS property has a 20-year or less recovery period even if ADS is elected (Reg. § 1.168(k)-1(b)(2)(i)(A); Reg. § 1.168(k)-2(b)(2)(i)(A); Proposed Reg. § 1.168(k)-2(b)(2)(i)(A) in REG-104397-18).

Code Sec. 1245 property (personal property) or Code Sec. 1250 property (real property) may qualify for bonus depreciation. 27.5 year residential rental property (¶ 114) and 39-year real property (¶ 116) do not qualify, however, because their recovery periods exceed 20 years.

*Qualified leasehold improvement property, retail improvement property, and restaurant property.* Although 15-year qualified retail improvement and 15-year qualified restaurant property placed in service before 2016 have a recovery period less than 20 years (see item (1)) the Code provided that this property only qualified for bonus depreciation if it also met the definition of qualified leasehold improvement property as defined for bonus depreciation purposes in former Code Sec. 168(k)(3) (Code Sec. 168(e)(7)(B), prior to amendment by P.L. 114-113 and Code Sec. 168(e)(8)(D), prior to being stricken by P.L. 114-113).

Effective for property placed in service in 2016 and 2017, 15-year leasehold improvement property and 15-year retail improvement property qualified for bonus depreciation for two separate reasons. First, such property has a 15-year recovery period (see item (1) above) and second, such property also meets the definition of qualified improvement property (item (5)).

Although 15-year qualified restaurant property placed in service in 2016 and 2017 has a recovery period of 15 years, the Code specifically provided that such property placed in service during this period only qualifies for bonus depreciation if it meets the definition of qualified improvement property (Code Sec. 168(e)(7)(B), as amended by P.L. 114-113). Therefore, bonus depreciation, generally only applied to improvements to the interior of a restaurant placed in service in 2016 and 2017.

See "*15. Qualified leasehold improvement property placed in service before 2016.*"

*Qualified improvement property.* Effective for property placed in service after 2017, the Tax Cuts Act (P.L. 115-97) removes qualified improvement property as a separate category of bonus depreciation property (Code Sec. 168(k)(3), as amended by P.L. 115-97). Qualified improvement property placed in service after 2017, however, qualifies for bonus depreciation because a retroactive technical correction (Code Sec. 168(e)(3)(E)(vii)) assigns a 15-year recovery period to such property. In addition, the categories of 15-year qualified leasehold improvement, retail improvement, and restaurant improvement property are eliminated after 2017 by the Tax Cuts Act. Qualified leasehold improvement property and qualified retail improvement property will qualify for bonus depreciation by reason of satisfying the definition of qualified improvement property. Internal improvements to a restaurant building will also qualify for bonus depreciation as qualified improvement property.

See "*16. Qualified improvement property placed in service after 2015.*"

*Original use property and used property.* Property acquired before September 28, 2017 qualifies for bonus depreciation only if the original use of the property begins with the taxpayer. In general, this means that only new property acquired before September 28, 2017 qualifies for bonus depreciation. See "*30. Original use requirement.*" Effective for property acquired after September 27, 2017, used property may also qualify for bonus depreciation. See "*13. Used property acquired after September 27, 2017 qualifies for bonus depreciation.*"

*Specified plants.* A taxpayer engaged in a farming business may elect to claim the bonus deduction on the cost of specified plants in the year of planting or grafting to a planted plant, effective for plantings and graftings after 2015 (Code Sec. 168(k)(5), as added by P.L. 114-113). A specified plant is any tree or vine which bears fruits or nuts and any other plant which will have more than one crop or yield of fruits or nuts and which generally has a pre-productive period of more than two years. This election is in place of the regular bonus deduction generally available when the specified plant becomes commercially productive. See "*18. Specified plants.*"

*Mandatory ADS property does not qualify.* Property required to be depreciated under the MACRS alternative depreciation system (ADS) does not qualify for bonus depreciation. Bonus depreciation may apply to property for which ADS is elected. See "*21. Mandatory ADS property does not qualify for bonus depreciation.*"

*Floor plan financing indebtedness.* Property used by certain motor vehicle, boat, and farm machinery businesses that use floor plan financing indebtedness does not qualify for bonus depreciation if placed in service in a tax year beginning after 2017 and the taxpayer benefited from an interest deduction on the indebtedness in the placed-in-service tax year (Reg. § 1.168(k)-2(B)(2)(ii)(G); Proposed Reg. § 1.168(k)-2(b)(2)(ii)(G) in REG-104397-18). See discussion "*22. Property used by certain motor vehicle, boat, farm machinery businesses that used floor plan financing indebtedness does not qualify for bonus depreciation if placed in service in tax years beginning after 2017.*"

*Regulated utility property.* Rate-regulated utility property does not qualify for bonus if placed in service in a tax year beginning after 2017 (Reg. § 1.168(k)-2(B)(2)(ii)(F)). See "*23. Rate-regulated utility property does not qualify for bonus if placed in service in tax years beginning after 2017.*"

*Intangible property.* With the limited exception of computer software that is depreciated over three years under Code Sec. 167(f)(1) (see "*19. Computer software,*") and qualified film, television, and live theatrical productions (see "*17. Film and television productions and live theatrical productions acquired and placed in service after September 27, 2017*"), the additional allowance only applies to property that is depreciated using MACRS (Code Sec. 168(k)(2)(A)(i)(I), as added by P.L. 107-147; Reg. § 1.168(k)-1(b)(2); Reg. § 1.168(k)-2(b); Proposed Reg. § 1.168(k)-2(b) in REG-104397-18). For example, intangibles amortized over 15 years under Code Sec. 197 do not qualify for the bonus allowance. Property described in Code Sec. 168(f) which is specifically excluded from MACRS does not qualify (e.g., property depreciated under a method not expressed in a term of years, films and video tape, sound recordings, and property subject to the anti-churning rules). Bonus depreciation does not apply to an automobile if the standard mileage rate is used.

*Corporate AMT credit election.* Any class of property for which a corporation elected to claim an AMT credit under former Code Sec. 168(k)(4) doe not qualify for bonus depreciation in the year of the election (Reg. § 1.168(k)-2(b)(2)(ii)(E)).

*Property placed in service and disposed of in same tax year.* Property placed in service and disposed of in the same tax year does not qualify for bonus depreciation. However, an exception applies to Code Sec. 168(i)(7) step-in-the-shoes transactions and partnership technical terminations. If such property is reacquired in a later tax year it may qualify for bonus depreciation as used property under the rules of Reg. § 1.168(k)-2(b)(3)(iii)(B) (Reg. § 1.168(k)-2(g)(1)(i)).

A parallel rule provides that MACRS depreciation deductions may not be claimed on property placed in service and disposed of in the same tax year (Reg. § 1.168(d)-1(b)(3)).

*Section 168(i)(7) transactions.* If any qualified property is transferred in a transaction described in Code Sec. 168(i)(7) in the same tax year that the qualified property is placed in service or planted or grafted, as applicable, by the transferor, the additional first year depreciation deduction is allowable for the qualified property (Reg. § 1.168(k)-2(g)(1)(iii)). However, the bonus depreciation will be allocated between the transferor and the transferee on a monthly basis. See *"51. Certain step-in-the-shoes transactions."*

*Section 743(b) basis adjustment.* If a partnership interest is acquired and disposed of during the same tax year, the bonus deduction is not allowed on any section 743(b) basis adjustment arising from the initial acquisition (Reg. § 1.168(k)-2(g)(1)(i)). However, if a partnership interest is purchased and disposed of in a section 168(i)(7) transaction in the same tax year, the Code Sec. 743(b) adjustment with respect to the initial acquisition is allowed as a bonus deduction. The adjustment is apportioned between the purchaser/transferor and the transferee on a monthly basis (Reg. § 1.168(k)-2(g)(1)(iii)). If a partnership interest is acquired and disposed of during the same tax year in a transaction not described in a Code Sec. 168(i)(7), the bonus deduction is not allowed for any section 743(b) adjustment arising from the initial acquisition.

### *13. Used property acquired after September 27, 2017 qualifies for bonus depreciation*

Effective for property acquired and placed in service after September 27, 2017, property previously used by an unrelated person may qualify for bonus depreciation if the taxpayer meets "acquisition requirements" (Code Sec. 168(k)(2)(A)(ii), as amended by the 2017 Tax Cuts and Jobs Act (P.L. 115-97); Reg. § 1.168(k)-2(b)(3)(iii); Proposed Reg. § 1.168(k)-2(b)(3)(iii) in REG-104397-18). Used property acquired before September 28, 2017 does not qualify for bonus depreciation and original use must commence with the taxpayer. See "*30. Original use requirement.*"

The used property acquisition requirements are met if:

- the taxpayer (including a taxpayer's predecessor) did not use the property (i.e., have a depreciable interest in the property) during a 5-year lookback period described below before acquiring it (a 90-day prior use exception described below may apply); and
- the taxpayer acquired the property by "purchase" within the meaning of Code Sec. 179(d)(2) (Code Sec. 168(k)(2)(E)(ii), as amended by the 2017 Tax Cuts Act).

***Example (1):*** JM, a calendar year taxpayer purchases a new machine on January 1, 2021. JM sells the machine to NO on March 1, 2023. NO, a calendar year taxpayer, sells the machine to JM on June 1, 2023. JM may claim bonus depreciation on the machine in 2021. NO may not claim bonus depreciation because it placed in service and sold the machine in the same tax year. JM may not claim bonus depreciation on the machine in 2023 because it held a prior to depreciable interest during the five-year lookback period (Reg. § 1.168(k)(2)-(b)(3)(vii), Example 25).

***Example (2):*** AB, a calendar-year taxpayer, purchases a new machine on December 1 of YEAR 1. On February 1 of YEAR 2 AB sells the machine to DF a calendar year taxpayer. On March 1 of YEAR 2 DF sells the machine back to AB. AB may claim bonus depreciation in YEAR 1 because the machine was not sold and disposed of in the same tax year. DF may not claim bonus depreciation in YEAR 2 because it was purchased and disposed of in the same tax year. AB may also claim bonus depreciation in YEAR 2. AB's prior interest is ignored because AB sold the machine within 90 days of its December 1 YEAR 1 purchase (Reg. § 1.168(k)(2)-(b)(3)(vii), Example 31).

*Predecessor defined.* The final regulations provide that a predecessor includes (for all bonus depreciation purposes) (Reg. § 1.168(k)-2(a)(2)(iv)):

- a transferor of an asset to a transferee in a transaction to which Code Sec. 381(a) applies;
- a transferor of an asset to a transferee in a transaction in which the transferee's basis in the asset is determined, in whole or in part, by reference to the basis of the asset in the hands of the transferor;
- a partnership that is considered as continuing under Code Sec. 708(b)(2); or
- the decedent in the case of an asset acquired by an estate;

An amendment made to the final regulations provides that a transferor of an asset to a trust is a predecessor only if the trust takes a carryover basis (1.168(k)-2(a)(iv)(E), removed by T.D. 9916). Prior to removal, all transferors to trusts were treated as predecessors.

***Example (3):*** J corporation owns equipment which it sells to K. One year later J merges into L in a Code Sec. 368(a)(1)(A)transaction and L purchases the equipment from K. Because J is considered the predecessor of L, L is considered to have owned a prior depreciable interest (within the 5-year lookback period) and L may not claim bonus depreciation on the used property (Reg. § 1.168(k)-2(b)(3)(vii), *Example 24*; Reg. § 1.168(k)-2(b)(3)(vii)(BB), Example 28).

***Example (4):*** In Year 1, Jack contributes property to PART in a Code Sec. 721 exchange for a partnership interest. In Year 2 Jack sells other depreciable property to Ron. In Year 3 PART purchases the depreciable property from Ron. Jack is not a predecessor of PART with respect to the property purchased by PART from Ron. Jack's ownership of the purchased property is not considered in the 5-year lookback period. PART may claim bonus depreciation on the used property purchased from RON (Reg. § 1.168(k)-2(b)(3)(vii), *Example 26*).

***Example (5):*** In Year 1, Fred contributes Property A to PART in a Code Sec. 721 exchange for a partnership interest. Part sells Property A to Mark in Year 1. In Year 3 PART reacquires Property A from Mark. PART may not claim bonus depreciation in YEAR 3 because PART owned Property A during the lookback period. In addition, Fred is a predecessor with respect to Property A and also owned a depreciable interest in Property A during the lookback period (Reg. § 1.168(k)-2(b)(3)(vii), *Example 27*).

Note that the related party rule in Code Sec. 179(d)(2)(A) applies to a direct purchase of partnership property by a current majority partner, and the series of related transactions rules in Reg. § 1.168(k)-2(b)(3)(iii)(C) prevents avoidance of the related party rule through the use of intermediary parties.

Proposed regulations treated a person is treated as having a depreciable interest in a portion of property prior to the person's acquisition of the property if the person was a partner in a partnership at any time the partnership owned the property (Proposed Reg. § 1.168(k)-2(b)(3)(iii)(B)(5) in REG-104397-18). The final regulations withdraw this blanket rule. Instead, a person who contributes property to a partnership in a section 721 transaction will be treated as a predecessor of the partnership with respect to the contributed property because the partnership takes a carryover basis in the property.

*Property used by taxpayer prior to acquisition—five-year lookback and depreciable interest rule.* Property used by a taxpayer or a predecessor (as defined in Reg. § 1.168(k)-2(a)(2)(iv)) prior to its acquisition does not qualify for bonus depreciation. However, property is not considered used by a taxpayer or predecessor prior to acquisition unless the taxpayer or predecessor had a depreciable interest in the property during the five calendar years preceding the placed-in-service year. If the taxpayer or a predecessor, or both, are not in existence for the full five years prior to the placed-in-service year only the period of actual existence of the taxpayer or predecessor, or both, as applicable, is taken into account (Reg. § 1.168(k)-2(b)(3)(iii)(B), as amended by T.D. 9916). Property is considered as previously used by the taxpayer if the taxpayer or a predecessor had a depreciable interest in the property prior to the acquisition. It does not matter whether the taxpayer or predecessor actually claimed depreciation so long as they were entitled to claim the depreciation.

Initially the final regulations did not specifically include within the look-back period the period from January 1 to the date in the calendar year that the property is placed in service. The look-back period only included the five calendar years preceding the calendar year in which the property is place in service. The final regulations, however, were amended to also include the portion of the placed-in-service year before the actual placed-in-service date (Reg. § 1.168(k)-2(b)(3)(iii)(B)(1), as amended by T.D. 9916).

The proposed regulations did not have a look-back period (Proposed Reg. § 1.168(k)-2(b)(3)(iii)(B)(1) in REG-104397-18). Therefore, property used by the taxpayer or predecessor with a depreciable interest in the property at any time prior to acquisition by the taxpayer did not qualify for bonus depreciation as used property.

If a lessee acquires leased property and the lessee was entitled to claim depreciation on improvements made to the leased property, the basis of the acquired property attributable to the improvements is not eligible for bonus depreciation even if the remaining basis does qualify for bonus depreciation (Reg. § 1.168(k)-2(b)(3)(iii)(B)(1); Proposed Reg. § 1.168(k)-2(b)(3)(iii)(B)(1) in REG-104397-18).

> ***Example (6):*** In June 2017 lessee of a machine spends $500 on an improvement for the machine. The $500 qualifies the 50% bonus rate since the improvements were place in service before September 28, 2017. The original use of the improvement begins with the lessee. In July 2018, lessee purchases the machine for $10,000. Although the machine was used (lessor owned and depreciated it), the $10,000 (reduced by any portion allocable to the $500 improvement) qualifies for 100 percent bonus depreciation if the lessor and lessee are unrelated because the used machine was acquired by the lessee after September 27, 2017 (Reg. § 1.168(k)-2(b)(3)(vii), Examples 6, 7, an 8; Proposed Reg. § 1.168(k)-2(b)(3)(vi), Examples 6, 7, and 8 in REG-104397-18).

If a taxpayer has a depreciable interest in a portion of a property and later acquires an additional interest in which it never had a depreciable interest, the additional interest is not tainted and may qualify for bonus depreciation. A taxpayer's portion of a property is the taxpayer's percentage interest in the property (Reg. § 1.168(k)-2(b)(3)(iii)(B)(2); Reg. § 1.168(k)-2(b)(3)(vii)(I), Examples 9, 10, and 11; Proposed Reg. § 1.168(k)-2(b)(3)(iii)(B)(2); Proposed Reg. § 1.168(k)-2(b)(3)(vi), Examples 9 and 10 in REG-104397-18).

***Example (7):*** Andrew and Brenda each buy a 50 percent interest in equipment in 2016. In 2019 Andrew purchases Brenda's 50 percent interest. Andrew does not have a prior depreciable interest in the 50 percent interest purchased from Brenda and may claim 100 percent bonus depreciation on the purchased 50 percent interest under the rules for used property.

If a taxpayer sells a portion of an interest in property and then reacquires another portion of the same property, bonus depreciation only applies to the extent the newly acquired interest is greater than the original interest (Reg. § 1.168(k)-2(b)(3)(iii)(B)(2); Reg. § 1.168(k)-2(b)(3)(vii), Example 11; Proposed Reg. § 1.168(k)-2(b)(3)(iii)(B)(2); Proposed Reg. § 1.168(k)-2(b)(3)(vi), Example 11 in REG-104397-18).

***Example (8):*** Andrew and Brenda each buy a 50 percent interest in equipment. In 2019 Andrew purchases Brenda's 50 percent interest and Brenda purchases Andrew's 50 percent interest. Neither Andrew nor Brenda may claim bonus depreciation because each is considered to have held a prior 50 percent depreciable interest in the property.

*Exception for property placed in service 90 days or less.* A de minimis rule applies if a taxpayer disposes of property within 90 days after placing it in service and then later reacquires it. Specifically, if:

(1) a taxpayer acquires and places in service property;

(2) the taxpayer or a predecessor did not previously have a depreciable interest in the property;

(3) the taxpayer disposes of the property to an unrelated party within 90 calendar days after the date the property was originally placed in service by the taxpayer (without taking into account the applicable convention); and

(4) the taxpayer reacquires and again places in service the property.

The taxpayer's depreciable interest in the property during that 90-day period is not taken into account for determining whether the property was used by the taxpayer or a predecessor at any time prior to its reacquisition by the taxpayer (Reg. § 1.168(k)-2(b)(3)(iii)(B)(4); Proposed Reg. § 1.168(k)-2(b)(3)(iii)(B)(4) in REG-104397-18).

To prevent the churning of assets, this rule does not apply if the taxpayer originally reacquired the property before September 28, 2017 and again places in service the property during the same tax year the taxpayer disposed of the property to the unrelated taxpayer.

***Example (9):*** X a calendar year taxpayer acquired and placed in service a machine on January 1 of Year 1. On February 1 of Year 1, X sells the property to Y. Because X acquired and sold the machine in the same tax year X may not claim bonus depreciation. Y, however, may claim the bonus. Y then leases the machine back to X for 3 years with an option to purchase the machine at the end of the lease term. If X reacquires the machine at the end of the lease term it will qualify for bonus depreciation. X's period of ownership in Year 1 is ignored because it lasted 90 days or less and did not occur in the same tax year that X disposed and reacquired the property (Reg. § 168(k)-2(b)(3)(vii), Example 30).

*Purchase requirement.* Under Code Sec. 179(d)(2), any acquisition is considered a purchase unless the property:

- is acquired from a person whose relationship to the taxpayer would bar recognition of a loss in any transaction between them under Code Sec. 267 (with the taxpayer's family limited to spouse, ancestors and lineal descendants) or Code Sec. 707(b)) (Code Sec. 179(d)(2)(A); Reg. § 1.179-4(c)(1)(ii));

• is acquired by one member of a controlled group of corporations from another member (substituting 50 percent for the 80 percent that would otherwise apply with respect to stock ownership requirements) (Code Sec. 179(d)(2)(B); Reg. § 1.179-4(c)(1)(iii));

• has a basis in the hands of the acquiring taxpayer determined in whole or in part by reference to the adjusted basis of the person from who the property was acquired (e.g., a gift or section 1022 basis property) (Code Sec. 179(d)(2)(C); Reg. § 1.179-4(c)(1)(iv)); or

• has a basis determined under Code Sec. 1014(a) relating to inherited or bequested property (Code Sec. 179(d)(2)(C); Reg. § 1.179-4(c)(2)).

The acquired by purchase requirement of Code Sec. 179(d)(2) is discussed at ¶ 302, "*4. Acquired by Purchase Requirement.*"

***Example (10):*** K buys a new machine and leases it to L in 2016. In 2021 L enters into a binding contract to purchase the machine. L may claim bonus depreciation on the used machine because it was acquired after September 27, 2017 provided that the lease was a true lease, L had no prior depreciable interest in the machine, and all other requirements are met. If K and L are related parties, the used machine does not qualify for bonus depreciation (Reg. § 1.168(k)-2(b)(3)(vii), Examples 6 and 7; Proposed Reg. § 1.168(k)-2(b)(3)(vi), *Examples 6 and 7* in REG-104397-18).

*Property acquired from related parties.* Used property acquired from a related party does not qualify for bonus depreciation since such property is not considered acquired by purchase under Code Sec. 179(d)(2)(A) (Reg. § 1.168(k)-2(b)(3)(iii)(A)(2) and Proposed Reg. § 1.168(k)-2(b)(3)(iii)(A)(2) in REG-104397-18 referencing Code Sec. 179(d)(2)(A)). Related parties are defined in Code Sec. 267 and Code Sec. 707(b) which disallow losses created in transfers between related parties (Code Sec. 179(d)(2)(A)).

*Final regulations: related party rules: series of related transactions.* The final regulation simplify the proposed rules for testing relationship in a series of transactions.

Each transferee in a series of related transactions tests its relationship (1) with the transferor from which the transferee directly acquires the depreciable property (immediate transferor) and (2) with the original transferor of the depreciable property in the series. The transferee is treated as related to the immediate transferor or the original transferor if the relationship exists either immediately before the first transfer of the depreciable property in the series or when the transferee acquires the property (Reg. § 1.168(k)-2(b)(3)(iii)(C)(1)).

Examples of series of related transactions may include:

• a transfer of partnership assets followed by a transfer of an interest in the partnership, and

• a disposition of property and the direct or indirect disposition of the transferor or transferee of the property.

A party in a series of related transactions that is neither the original transferor nor the ultimate transferee is disregarded in applying the relatedness test if the party placed in service and disposed of the property in the party's same tax year or did not place the property in service (Reg. § 1.168(k)-2(b)(3)(iii)(C)(2)(i)). Instead the party to which the disregarded party disposed of the property tests is relationship with the party from whom the disregarded party acquired the depreciable property and with the original transferor of the property. If the series has consecutive disregarded parties, the party to which the last disregarded party disposed of the depreciable property tests its relationship with the party from which the first disregarded party acquired the depreciable property and with the original transferor of the depreciable property in the series. The rules for testing the relationships continue to apply for the other transactions in the series.

The final regulations address a change in relationship during the course of a transaction. Any transferor in a series of related transactions that ceases to exist during the series is deemed to continue to exist for purposes of testing relatedness (Reg. § 1.168(k)-2(b)(3)(iii)(C)(2)(vi)).

If a transferee in a series of related transactions acquires depreciable property from a transferor that was not in existence immediately prior to the first transfer of the property in the series (new transferor), the transferee tests its relationship with the party from which the new transferor acquired the depreciable property and with the original transferor (Reg. § 1.168(k)-2(b)(3)(iii)(C)(2)(vii)).

If the series of transactions has consecutive new transferors, the party to which the last new transferor disposed of the depreciable property tests its relationship with the party from which the first new transferor acquired the depreciable property and with the original transferor of the depreciable property in the series. The rules for testing the relationships continue to apply for the other transactions in the series (Reg. § 1.168(k)-2(b)(3)(iii)(C)(2)(vii)).

The final regulations add a rule that disregards certain transitory relationships created pursuant to a series of related transactions. Specifically, if a party acquires depreciable property in a series of related transactions in which the acquiring party acquires stock, meeting the 80 percent stock ownership requirements of requirements of Code Sec. 1504(a)(2), of a corporation in a fully taxable transaction, followed by a liquidation of the acquired corporation under Code Sec. 331, any relationship created as part of this series of transactions is disregarded in determining whether any party is related to the acquired corporation for purposes of testing relatedness (Reg. § 1.168(k)-2(b)(3)(iii)(C)(2)(v)). This rule is similar to Reg. § 1.197-2(h)(6)(iii).

The related transactions rule does not apply when all transactions in the series are Code Sec. 168(i)(7) step-in-the shoes transactions in which the property is transferred in the same tax year that the property was placed in service by the transferor) (Reg. § 1.168(k)-2(b)(3)(iii)(C)(2)(ii)).

A step in a series of related transactions that is neither the original step nor the ultimate step is disregarded for purposes of testing relatedness if the step is a transfer of property in a transaction described in a step-in the shoes Code Sec. 168(i)(7) transaction in the same tax year that the property is placed in service by the transferor (Reg. § 1.168(k)-2(b)(3)(iii)(C)(2)(iii)). The relationship is tested between (a) the transferor in the disregarded step and the party to which the transferee in that disregarded step disposed of the property, (b) the transferee in the disregarded step and the party to which that transferee disposed of the party, and (c) the original transferor in the series and the party to which the transferee in the disregarded step disposed of the depreciable property.

If there are a series of consecutive disregarded Code Sec. 168(i)(7) steps, the relationship is tested between (a) the transferor in the first disregarded step and the party to which the transferee in the last disregarded step disposed of the depreciable property, (b) the transferee in the last disregarded step and the party to which the transferee in the last disregarded step disposed of the depreciable property, and (c) the original transferor in the series and the party to which the transferee in the last disregarded step disposed of the depreciable property. The rules for testing the relationships continue to apply for the other transactions in the series and for the last transaction in the series.

The related transactions rule does not apply to a syndication transaction described in Reg. § 1.168(k)-2(b)(3)(vi) (Reg. § 1.168(k)-2(b)(3)(iii)(C)(2)(iv)).

Examples illustrating these rules are provided in the final regulations (Reg. § 1.168(k)-2(b)(3)(iii)(C)(2)(viii), Examples 35 - 41).

Special rules apply when the transferor and transferee are members of the same consolidated group (Reg. § 1.1502-68).

*Proposed regulations: related party rules: series of related transactions* Under the proposed regulations, which the final regulations above modified before adopting, the relationship between the parties in a series of related transactions is tested immediately after each step in the series, and between the original transferor and the ultimate transferee immediately after the last transaction in the series (Proposed Reg. § 1.168(k)-2(b)(3)(iii)(C)(1) in REG-104397-18).

A party in a series of related transactions that is neither the original transferor nor the ultimate transferee is disregarded in applying the relatedness test if the party placed in service and disposed of the property in the party's same tax year or did not place the property in service (Proposed Reg. § 1.168(k)-2(b)(3)(iii)(C)(2)(i) in REG-104397-18). Instead the relationship is tested between the party from whom the disregarded party acquired the depreciable property and the party to which the disregarded party disposed of the property. A transaction may have consecutive disregarded parties.

These rules for determining relationships in a series of related transactions do not apply if all of the transactions are Code Sec. 168(i)(7) step-in the shoes transactions in which the property is transferred in the same tax year that the property is placed in service by the transferor (Proposed Reg. § 1.168(k)-2(b)(3)(iii)(C)(2)(ii) in REG-104397-18). In addition the rules do not apply to a syndication transaction (Proposed Reg. § 1.168(k)-2(b)(3)(iii)(C)(2)(iv) in REG-104397-18).

A step in a series of related transactions that is neither the original step nor the ultimate step is disregarded for purposes of testing relatedness if the step is a transfer of property in a transaction described in a step-in the shoes Code Sec. 168(i)(7) transaction in the same tax year that the property is placed in service by the transferor (Proposed Reg. § 1.168(k)-2(b)(3)(iii)(C)(2)(iii) in REG-104397-18). The relationship is tested between (a) the transferor in the disregarded step and the party to which the transferee in that disregarded step disposed of the property, and (b) the transferee in the disregarded step and the party to which that transferee disposed of the party. If there are a series of consecutive disregarded steps, the relationship is tested between (a) the transferor in the first disregarded step and the party to which the transferee in the last disregarded step disposed of the depreciable property, and (b) the transferee in the last disregarded step and the party to which the transferee in the last disregarded step disposed of the depreciable property. The rules for testing the relationships continue to apply for the other transactions in the series and for the last transaction in the series.

The related transactions rule does not apply when all transactions in the series are described in Reg. § 1.168(k)-2(g)(1)(iii) (Code Sec. 168(i)(7) step-in-the shoes transactions) or to a syndication transaction described in Reg. § 1.168(k)-2(b)(3)(vi).

*Property acquired by target in Code Sec. 338 or Code Sec. 336(e) election.* Property acquired by a new target corporation as the result of a Code Sec. 338 deemed asset election or a Code Sec. 336(e) election (relating to certain stock dispositions treated as asset transfers) made for a disposition described in Reg. § 1.336-2(b)(1) is considered acquired by purchase for purposes of Code Sec. 179

and, therefore, may qualify for bonus depreciation (Reg. § 1.168(k)-2(b)(3)(iii)(A)(2); Proposed Reg. § 1.168(k)-2(b)(3)(iii)(A)(2) in REG-104397-18; Reg. § 1.179-4(c)(2)). The final regulations clarify that the reference to Code Sec. 336(e) in Reg. § 1.179-4(c)(2) does not include dispositions described in Code Sec. 355(d)(2) or Code Sec. 355(e)(2). Therefore, assets deemed purchased in such a qualified stock disposition are not considered acquired by purchase (Preamble to T.D. 9874).

*Reconditioned and rebuilt property.* Reconditioned or rebuilt property acquired and placed in service after September 27, 2017 may qualify for bonus depreciation as used property. Note also that a safe harbor has provided that original use begins with a taxpayer (i.e., the property is considered new) if no more than 20 percent of the cost of property is attributable to used parts (Reg. § 1.168(k)-2(b)(3)(ii); Reg. § 1.168(k)-2(b)(3)(vii), Example 1; Proposed Reg. § 1.168(k)-2(b)(3)(ii); Proposed Reg. § 1.168(k)-2(b)(3)(vi), Example 1 in REG-104397-18). Since used property now qualifies for bonus depreciation, this safe harbor is no longer important. See discussion "*30. Original use requirement.*"

*Substantial renovation exception to prohibition on prior ownership of used property.* Substantially renovated property in which the taxpayer or a predecessor previously held a depreciable interest is eligible for bonus depreciation as used property. A property is a substantially renovated if the cost of the used parts is less than or equal to 20 percent of the total cost of the (post-renovation) property, whether acquired or self-constructed (Reg. § 1.168(k)-2(b)(3)(iii)(B); Reg. § 1.168(k)-2(b)(3)(vii), *Example 19*). The substantial renovation removes the taint of prior ownership. The provision which was not in the proposed regulations, applies, for example, when a taxpayer purchases substantially renovated property and held a prior depreciable interest in the pre-renovation property (Reg. § 1.168(k)-2(b)(3)(vii), *Example 19*, airplane sold, substantially renovated, and then reacquired qualified for bonus depreciation as used property).

*Used property received in carryover basis transactions such as like-kind exchanges and involuntary conversions.* The acquisition of used property is also subject to the cost requirements of Code Sec. 179(d)(3) (Code Sec. 168(k)(2)(E)(ii)(II), as added by the 2017 Tax Cuts Act). Code Sec. 179(d)(3) (see also Reg. § 1.179-4(d)) provides that the cost of property eligible for Code Sec. 179 expensing does not include the portion of the basis of property that is determined by reference to the basis of other property held at any time by the person acquiring the property (e.g., the carryover basis in a like-kind exchange or involuntary conversion does not qualify for expensing but any additional cash paid does) (Conference Report on H.R. 1, Tax Cuts and Jobs Act (H. Rept. 115-466)).

This limitation on a like-kind exchange or involuntary conversion only applies when the replacement property is used property. Bonus depreciation may be claimed on both the carryover and excess basis of new property acquired in a like-kind exchange or involuntary conversion if the property received in the exchange meets all other qualification requirements (Reg. § 1.168(k)-1(f)(5); Reg. § 1.168(k)-2(g)(5)(iii); Proposed Reg. § 1.168(k)-2(f)(5)(ii) in REG-104397-18). Bonus depreciation may not be claimed on the carryover basis (Reg. § 1.168(k)-2(b)(3)(vii), *Example 20*).

*Partnership transactions and used property.* Bonus depreciation has not been claimed in most transactions involving transfers of property to or from partnerships or transfers of interests in partnership property in connection with the transfer of a partnership interest. The requirement that the original use of the property must begin with the taxpayer claiming bonus depreciation is not satisfied. Now that used property can qualify for bonus depreciation the IRS proposed regulations reconsider whether bonus depreciation can be claimed in some partnership transactions. See "*14. Code Sec. 754 elections and other partnership transactions.*"

*Syndication transactions*. See "*37. Sale-leasebacks and syndication transactions.*"

*Consolidated Groups and Used Property*

*Group prior use rule*. Bonus depreciation does not apply to depreciable property acquired by a member of a consolidated group if the consolidated group had a depreciable interest in the property at any time during the 5-year lookback period. The consolidated group is considered to have had a depreciable interest in property during the time any current or previous member of the group had a depreciable interest in the property while a member of the group (Reg. § 1.1502-68(b)(1)).

***Example (11):*** ABC and BCD are members of the same consolidated group. ABC sells machinery to BCD. BCD may not claim bonus depreciation under the Group Prior Use Rule because ABC is a current group member that held a depreciable interest in the property during the lookback period. Furthermore ABC and BCD are related parties Reg. § 1.1502-68(d), Example 1).

***Example (12):*** ABC and BCD are members of the same consolidated group. ABC sells equipment to U, an unrelated party. In a later tax year within the lookback period, BCD purchases the equipment from U. The equipment does not qualify for bonus depreciation under the Group Prior Use Rule because ABC previously had a depreciable interest in the machinery. The equipment does not qualify even if ABC left the consolidated group prior to BCD's purchase. If BCD purchased the machinery after expiration of the lookback period, BCD may claim bonus depreciation (Reg. § 1.1502-68(d), Example 2).

The group prior use rule applies only to the acquisition of property by a member of a consolidated group. Thus, the group prior use rule applies only as long as the consolidated group remains in existence. For example, the prior use rule does not apply if a group terminates as a result of all of its members joining another consolidated group, including as a result of a reverse acquisition as defined in Reg. § 1.1502-75(d)(3) (Preamble to REG-106808-19).

When a member deconsolidates, it does not continue to be treated as having a depreciable interest in the property. Accordingly, a departing member does not continue to have a depreciable interest in the property unless it actually owned the property (Preamble to REG-106808-19).

***Example (13):*** In Year 1, S, a member of consolidated group P, sells equipment to U, and unrelated party. In Year 2, P is acquired by another consolidated group and terminates. Members of P become members of the acquiring consolidated group. In Year 3, in a transaction that is *not part of a series of related transactions*, B, a former member of the terminated consolidated group and now new member of the acquiring group, purchases the equipment from U. B does not have a prior depreciable interest in the machinery under the Group Use Rule because B is a member of the acquiring group and no member of the acquiring group had a depreciable interest in the machinery during the lookback period while a member of the acquiring group (Reg. § 1.1502-68(d), Example 4).

If S instead of B had repurchased the equipment in Year 3, S may not claim bonus depreciation because S had a prior depreciable interest during the lookback period (Reg. § 1.1502-68(d), Example 4).

If the acquisition of the Y consolidated group and B's subsequent acquisition of the machinery were part of a series of related transactions, then B will be treated as having a prior depreciable interest during the lookback period under the Stock and Asset Acquisition Rule described below and B may not claim bonus depreciation (Reg. § 1.1502-68(d), Example 4).

*Stock and asset acquisition rule.* Property acquired by a member of a consolidated group does not qualify for bonus depreciation if it was previously owned by a corporation that is acquired by any member of the consolidated group within the lookback period and the acquisition of the corporation and the property *are part of a series of related transactions* (Reg. § 1.1502-68(b)(2)).

The stock and asset acquisition rule applies only when the member whose stock is acquired had an actual depreciable interest in the property that also is acquired during the lookback period as part of the same series of related transactions. Accordingly, the acquired corporation must have had a depreciable interest without regard to the application of the group prior use rule.

***Example (14):*** G sells equipment to U an unrelated party in Year 1. In a series of related transactions that does not include the Year 1 sale, the Parent of a consolidated group acquires all of the stock of G in Year 2. Later in Year 2, B, a member of the consolidated group, purchases the equipment from U. Because G has a depreciable interest in the equipment during the lookback period B is treated as having a prior depreciable interest under the Stock and Asset Acquisition Rule and may not claim bonus depreciation. If B had acquired the property in Year 7 B is not treated under the Stock and Asset Acquisition Rule as having a prior depreciable interest because G did not have a depreciable interest during the lookback period. In addition B did not have a prior depreciable interest under the Group Prior Use Rule because neither G nor any other member of consolidated group had a depreciable interest within the lookback period. Further B did not have a depreciable interest during the lookback period. (Reg. § 1.1502-68(d), Example 3)

If B had acquired the property in Year 7 B is not treated under the Stock and Asset Acquisition Rule as having a prior depreciable interest because G did not have a depreciable interest during the lookback period. In addition B did not have a prior depreciable interest under the Group Prior Use Rule because neither G nor any other member of consolidated group had a depreciable interest within the lookback period. Further B did not have a depreciable interest during the lookback period. Consequently, B may claim bonus depreciation (Reg. § 1.1502-68(d), Example 3)

***Example (15):*** G sells equipment to U an unrelated party in Year 1. In a series of *unrelated* transactions, the Parent of a consolidated group acquires all of the stock of G in Year 2. Later in Year 2, B, a member of the consolidated group, purchases the equipment from U. The Stock and Asset Acquisition Rule does not apply because the Parent's acquisition of G stock and B's acquisition of the equipment were not part of a series of related transactions. B is not treated under the Group Use Rule as having a prior depreciable interest because neither G nor any other member of the consolidated group had a depreciable interest in the equipment while a member of the group during the lookback period (Reg. § 1.1502-68(d), Example 3).

*Consolidated acquisition rule.* A consolidated acquisition rule allows a former member of a consolidated group to claim bonus depreciation on eligible bonus depreciation property acquired from another member of the consolidated group after the member leaves the group pursuant to a series of related transactions (Reg. § 1.1502-68(c)(1)). Specifically, if the requirements below are met:

(1) the special rules that prevent bonus depreciation from being claimed on property acquired as part of a series of related transaction (Reg. § 1.168(k)-2(b)(3)(iii)(C)) do not apply;

(2) for all federal income tax purposes, the transferee member is treated as selling the eligible property to an unrelated person on the day after the deconsolidation date in exchange for cash equal to the deemed sale amount; and

(3) for all federal income tax purposes, immediately after the deemed sale the transferee member is treated as purchasing the deemed replacement property from an unrelated person for cash equal to the deemed sale amount.

The requirements are met if:

(1) the property meets the used property requirements for claiming bonus depreciation in Reg. § 1.168(k)-2(b)(3)(iii)(A) except for the prohibition against acquisitions from related parties and without regard to the Group Prior Use Rule described above;

(2) as a part of the series of related transactions, the transferee member ceases to be a member of the consolidated group and ceases to be related to the transferor member; and

(3) the eligible property continues to be eligible property on the deconsolidation date and the day after the deconsolidation date.

This rule does not apply if the transferee member disposes of the property following its acquisition as part of the same series of related transactions that includes acquisition of the property (Reg. § 1.1502-68(c)(3)).

***Example (16):*** *Facts*: On January 1 Year 1 S, a member of consolidated group Y, sells equipment to M another member of group Y and M places the property in service. On June 1, Year 1, the parent of Y sells all of the stock of M to another consolidated group Z. Thus, M leaves group Y on June 1 and is a member of group Z on June 2. The January 1 sale and June 1 deconsolidation of M are part of the same series of transactions.

The Group Prior Use Rule (which would prevent M from claiming from claiming bonus depreciation) does not apply because M's acquisition of the machinery satisfies the requirements of the Consolidated Acquisition Rule. The requirements are satisfied because:

- M's acquisition of the machinery satisfied the requirements of Reg. § 1.168(k)-2(b)(3)(iii)(A) without regard to the related party tests and the Group Prior Use Rule;
- As part of the same series of transactions, which includes M's acquisition of the machinery from S, M ceased to be a member of Y group an ceased to be related to S; and
- The equipment continued to be eligible property on the June 1 deconsolidation date

*Consequences*: M is treated as transferring the equipment to an unrelated person on June 2 in exchange for cash equal to a deemed sale amount and using the cash to purchase new machinery from an unrelated person. M therefore may claim bonus depreciation on the deemed sale amount (Reg. § 1.1502-68(d), Example 5).

If the Consolidated Acquisition Rule does not apply, for example, because the equipment is not eligible property on the June 1 deconsolidation date, M is treated as owning a prior depreciable interest under the Group Prior Use Rule and may not claim bonus depreciation on the equipment. M is treated as having a prior depreciable interest because M is member of the Y group and S, while a member of the Y group, had a depreciable interest within the lookback period.

***Example (17):*** Assume the preceding facts except that on June 1, Y distributed the stock of M to its shareholders that are not related to S in a nonrecognition transaction under Code Sec. 355(a). The Consolidated Acquisition Rule also applies in this situation and M may claim bonus depreciation on the deemed sale amount (Reg. § 1.1502-68(d), Example 5).

*Consolidated deemed acquisition rule.* A member of a consolidated group who receives the stock of a transferor member (target) in a qualified stock purchase for which a Code Sec. 338 election is made or in a qualified stock disposition described in Reg. § 1.336-2(b)(1) for which a Code Sec. 336(e) election is made may claim bonus depreciation on eligible property held by target member (Reg. § 1.1502-68(c)(2)). Specifically, if the requirements below are satisfied:

(1) the special rules that prevent bonus depreciation from being claimed on property acquired as part of a series of related transaction (Reg. § 1.168(k)-2(b)(3)(iii)(C)) do not apply;

(2) for all federal income tax purposes, the target is treated as selling the eligible property to an unrelated person on the day after the deconsolidation in exchange for cash equal to the deemed sale amount; and

(3) for all federal income tax purposes, immediately after the deemed sale the target is treated as purchasing deemed replacement property from an unrelated person for cash equal to the deemed sale amount.

The requirements are met if:

(1) the target's acquisition of the eligible property meets the used property requirements for claiming bonus depreciation in Reg. § 1.168(k)-2(b)(3)(iii)(A) and without regard to the Group Prior Use Rule described above;

(2) as a part of the series of related transactions that includes the qualified stock purchase or qualified stock disposition, the transferee member and target cease to be members of the consolidated group and cease to be related to the transferor member; and

(3) the target's eligible property on the acquisition date (Reg. § 1.338-2(c)-1) or the disposition date (Reg. § 1.336-1(b)(8)) continues to be eligible property on the deconsolidation date and the day after the deconsolidation date.

This rule does not apply if the target disposes of the property pursuant to the same series of transactions that includes the qualified stock purchase or stock disposition (Reg. § 1.1502-68(c)(3)).

***Example (18):*** S, T and B Corporations are members of a consolidated group, Parent 1. S owns the stock of T. T owns machinery. On January 1, Year 1 B corporation acquired all of the stock of T from S in a qualified stock purchase and a Code Sec. 338(h)(10) election is made. On June 1 Year 1 Parent sells all of B's stock to Parent X corporation. B and T, therefore, leave Parent 1 group on June 1 (Old T and Old B) and are part of Parent X group on June 2 (New T and New B). B's acquisition of T and the sale of B were all part of a series of related transactions. The requirement remained eligible property on June 1.

Pursuant to Code Sec. 338(h)(10) Old T transferred its assets to an unrelated person in exchange for consideration at the close of January 1 Year 1 and reacquired all of its assets from an unrelated person in exchange for the consideration.

But for application of the Consolidated Deemed Acquisition Rule, New T would be treated as having a prior depreciable interest under the Group Prior Use Rule when New T reacquired the assets from a related person because OLD T had a depreciable interest while a member of the Parent 1 within the lookback period and New T was also a member of Parent 1. However, New T's acquisition of the machinery satisfied the Consolidated Deemed Acquisition Rule because:

- New T's acquisition of the equipment meets the used property requirements for claiming bonus depreciation in Reg. § 1.168(k)-2(b)(3)(iii)(A) and without regard to the Group Prior Use Rule

- as a part of the series of related transactions that includes the qualified stock purchase of T's stock, the B and T cease to be members of the consolidated group and cease to be related to S; and

- the equipment remained eligible property on the June 1 deconsolidation date.

New T is treated for all Federal income tax purposes as transferring machinery to an unrelated person on June 2 in exchange for an amount of cash equal to the deemed sale amount and, immediately thereafter, acquiring deemed replacement property from an unrelated person for an amount of cash equal to the deemed sale amount. New T is eligible to claim the additional first year depreciation deduction for an amount equal to the deemed sale amount for the tax year in which it places the machinery in service (Reg. § 1.1502-68(d), Example 5).

For application of the Consolidated Deemed Acquisition Rule to a Code Sec. 355 transaction following a Code Sec. 338(h)(10) transaction see Example 7 of Reg. § 1.1502-68(d).

*Election out of consolidated acquisition or deemed acquisition rule.* If a transaction satisfies the requirements of either the consolidated asset acquisition rule or consolidated deemed acquisition rule, the transferee member or target may elect not to apply the rule to all eligible property that is acquired or deemed acquired in the transaction. If an election is made, it applies to all other transactions in the same series of related transactions that satisfy the consolidated acquisition or deemed acquisition rules. Specific election procedures are provided. A taxpayer may only revoke an election with permission of the IRS obtained by filing a letter ruling request (Reg. § 1.1502-68(c)(4)).

*14. Code Sec. 754 elections and other partnership transactions*

Bonus depreciation has not been claimed in most transactions involving transfers of property to or from partnerships or transfers of interests in partnership property in connection with the transfer of a partnership interest. The requirement that the original use of the property must begin with the taxpayer claiming bonus depreciation was not satisfied. Effective for property acquired and placed in service after September 27, 2017, however, used property may qualify for bonus depreciation. See "*13. Used property acquired after September 27, 2017 qualifies for bonus depreciation.*" IRS final regulations reconsider whether bonus depreciation can be claimed in some partnership transactions and conclude that bonus depreciation only applies to an increase to the inside basis of a new partner's interest in partnership property when a Code Sec. 754 election is in effect.

*Code Sec. 754 Elections.* Any increase in the basis of partnership property under Code Sec. 734(b) as the result of the distribution of property to a partner with respect to which a Code Sec. 754 election is in effect does not qualify for bonus depreciation (Reg. § 1.168(k)-2(b)(3)(iv)(C); Proposed Reg. § 1.168(k)-2(b)(3)(iv)(C) in REG-104397-18).

However, an increase to the inside basis of a new partner's interest in partnership property under Code Sec. 743(b) pursuant to a partnership's Code Sec. 754 election may qualify for bonus depreciation (Reg. § .168(k)-2(b)(3)(iv)(D); Proposed Reg. § 1.168(k)-2(b)(3)(iv)(D) in REG-104397-18; Reg. § 1.168(k)-2(b)(3)(vii), Example 14; Proposed Reg. § 1.168(k)-2(b)(3)(vi), Example 13 in REG-104397-18). A new partner includes an existing partner who acquires an additional partnership interest. The basis increase is generally equal to the difference between the cost of the partnership interest and partnership's inside basis in the new partner's share of partnership property to which the new partnership interest relates.

The transferor partner and new partner may not be part of the same controlled group. The new partner's basis in the partnership property may not be determined in whole or in part by reference to the transferor's adjusted basis or under Code Sec. 1014. For example, a basis increases on account of a transfer at death does not qualify if the transferee takes a fair market value basis under Code Sec. 1014 (Reg. § 1.168(k)-2(b)(3)(vii)(P), Example 16; Proposed Reg. § 1.168(k)-2(b)(3)(vi), Example 15 in REG-104397-18). No bonus may be claimed if the new partner or any predecessor previously had a depreciable interest in portion of the property deemed transferred (Reg. § 1.168(k)-2(b)(3)(vii)(Q), Example 17; Proposed Reg. § 1.168(k)-2(b)(3)(vi), Example 16 in REG-104397-18). It does not matter that the partnership previously used the property. In addition, the transferor and new partner may not be related (Reg. § 1.168(k)-2(b)(3)(vii)(O), Example 15; Proposed Reg. § 1.168(k)-2(b)(3)(vi), Example 14 in REG-104397-18).

A partner's basis adjustment in partnership assets under Code Sec. 743(b) for each class of property as a separate class of property for purposes of the election out of bonus depreciation (Reg. § 1.168(k)-2(f)(1)(ii)(G); Proposed Reg. § 1.168(k)-2(e)(1)(ii)(G) in REG-104397-18.

A partnership is allowed to claim bonus depreciation for an increase in the basis of qualified property made under Code Sec. 743(b) in a class of property even if the partnership made the election out for all other qualified property of the partnership in the same class of property. The partnership may also make an election out for an increase in the basis of qualified property under Code Sec. 743(b) in a class of property even if the partnership does not make that election for all other qualified property of the partnership in the same class of property. In this case, the section 743(b) basis adjustment must be recovered under a reasonable method (Reg. § 1.743-1(j)(4)(i)(B)(1); Proposed Reg. § 1.743-1(j)(4)(i)(B)(1) in REG-104397-18).

If a partnership interest is acquired and disposed of during the same tax year, the bonus deduction is not allowed on any section 743(b) basis adjustment arising from the initial acquisition (Reg. § 1.168(k)-2(g)(1)(i)). However, if a partnership interest is purchase and transferred in a section 168(i) step-in-the-shoes transaction in the same tax year, bonus depreciation may be allowed for a section 743(b) basis adjustment if certain requirements are met (Reg. § 1.168(k)-2(g)(1)(iii)). See "*51. Certain step-in-the-shoes transactions.*"

*Substantial basis reduction.* Bonus depreciation may not be claimed on an increase in the basis of partnership property when there is a substantial basis reduction under Code Sec. 734(d) (Reg. § 1.168(k)-2(b)(3)(iv)(C); Proposed Reg. § 1.168(k)-2(b)(3)(iv)(C) in REG-104397-18; REG-104397-18).

*Substantial built-in loss.* Bonus depreciation may be claimed on an increase in the basis of partnership property under Code Sec. 743(a) when the partnership has a substantial built-in loss immediately after the transfer of an interest in a partnership by sale or exchange or on the death of a partner (Reg. § 1.168(k)-2(b)(3)(iv)(D); Proposed Reg. § 1.168(k)-2(b)(3)(iv)(D) in REG-104397-18; REG-104397-18).

*Contributions to partnerships.* Contributions of property to a partnership do not qualify for bonus depreciation because the basis of the property in the hands of the partnership is determined by reference to the basis in the hands of the contributor (Code Sec. 723

> ***Example (1):*** O and P form an equal partnership, OP, in 2019. O contributes cash to OP, and P contributes equipment to OP. OP's basis in the equipment contributed by P is determined under Code Sec. 723. Because OP's basis in such equipment is determined in whole or in part by reference to P's adjusted basis in such equipment, OP's acquisition does not satisfy the used property acquisition requirements (Reg. § 1.168(k)-2(b)(3)(vi)(M), Example 13; Proposed Reg. § 1.168(k)-2(b)(3)(vi), Example 12 in REG-104397-18).

*Remedial allocations.* Remedial allocations under Code Sec. 704(c) for contributions of property with an adjusted tax basis less than book basis do not qualify for bonus depreciation because the partnership's basis in the property is determined by reference to the contributing partner's basis in the property. In addition, the partnership has a depreciable interest in the contributed property at the time the remedial allocation is made. The same rule applies to revaluations of partnership property (reverse section 704(c) allocations) (Reg. § 1.168(k)-2(b)(3)(iv)(A); Proposed Reg. § 1.704-3(d)(2); Proposed Reg. § 1.168(k)-2(b)(3)(iv)(A); Proposed Reg. § 1.704-3(d)(2) in REG-104397-18).

*Distributions other than in liquidation.* No portion of the basis of distributed partnership property as determined under Code Sec. 732 qualifies for bonus depreciation (Reg. § 1.168(k)-2(b)(3)(iv)(B); Proposed Reg. § 1.168(k)-2(b)(3)(iv)(B) in REG-104397-18). Because the partnership used the property prior to the distribution the original use requirement is not satisfied. The requirements for used property are not met because the basis is determined by reference to the distributee partner's basis in the partnership interest and the partnership's basis in the property.

*Book depreciation on contributed property with zero adjusted basis.* Bonus depreciation does not apply for purposes of determining book depreciation on property contributed to a partnership with a zero adjusted tax basis (Reg. § 1.704-1(b)(2)(iv)(g)(3); Proposed Reg. § 1.704-1(b)(2)(iv)(g)(3) in REG-104397-18).

### *15. Qualified leasehold improvement property placed in service before 2016*

Qualified leasehold improvement property placed in service before January 1, 2016 (during years that bonus depreciation is in effect) is eligible for bonus depreciation if the requirements in discussion at #36 below "*Acquisition and placed-in-service date requirement for property placed in service before 2016*" below are satisfied (Code Sec. 168(k)(3), prior to amendment by the Protecting Americans from Tax Hikes (PATH) Act of 2015 (Division Q of P.L. 114-113) (December 18, 2015)). See, also, discussion at #35 "*Property manufactured, constructed, or produced by or for taxpayer before September 28, 2017,*" below. The qualified leasehold improvement property category of bonus depreciation property is replaced with the "qualified improvement property" category, effective for property placed in service in 2016 and 2017 (Code Sec. 168(k)(3), as amended by P.L. 114-113). See "*16. Qualified improvement property placed in service after 2015.*"

Qualified leasehold improvement property is any section 1250 property which is an improvement to an interior portion of a building that is nonresidential real property (as defined in Code Sec. 168(e)(2)(B)) and which is made under or pursuant to a lease (as defined in Code Sec. 168(h)(7)) by the lessee, sublessee, or lessor. The improvement must be placed in service more than three years after the date the building was first placed in service by any person. In addition, the interior of the building must be occupied exclusively by the lessee or sublessee. The lease may not be between related persons (Code Sec. 168(k)(3), prior to amendment by P.L. 114-113).

Leasehold improvements which are section 1245 (personal property under the cost segregation rules) may qualify for bonus depreciation without regard to this provision for qualifying leasehold improvements that are section 1250 property.

Expenditures for (1) the enlargement (as defined in Reg. § 1.48-12(c)(10)) of a building (as defined in Reg. § 1.48-1(e)(1)), (2) any elevator or escalator (as defined in Reg. § 1.48-1(m)(2)), (3) any structural component (as defined in Reg. § 1.48-1(e)(2)) that benefits a common area, or (4) the internal structural framework (as defined in Reg. § 1.48-12(b)(3)(i)(D)(iii)) of a building are not considered qualified leasehold improvement property (Reg. § 1.168(k)-1(c)(2) and (3)).

The term "common area" generally refers to areas used by different lessees of a building, such as stairways, hallways, lobbies, common seating areas, interior and exterior pedestrian walkways and pedestrian bridges, loading docks and areas, and rest rooms (Reg. § 1.168(k)-1(c)(3)).

A commitment to enter into a lease is treated as a lease, with the parties to the commitment treated as the lessor and lessee (Reg. § 1.168(k)-1(c)(3)(vi)).

The lease may not be between related persons. Members of an affiliated group (as defined in Code Sec. 1504) are related persons. Persons with a relationship described in Code Sec. 267(b) are related persons. However, the phrase "80 percent or more" is substituted in each place that the phrase "more than 50 percent" appears (Reg. § 1.168(k)-1(c)(3)(vi)).

Qualified leasehold improvement property placed in service after October 22, 2004 and before 2018 is also depreciable under MACRS over 15-years using the straight-line method (subject to minor exceptions). The category of 15-year qualified leasehold property was eliminated by the Tax Cuts and Jobs Act (P.L. 115-97), effective for property placed in service after 2017. See ¶ 126. Qualified leasehold improvement property placed in service prior to October 23, 2004 was depreciated over 39 years.

Although bonus depreciation generally only applies to property with an MACRS depreciation period of 20 years or less, Code Sec. 168(k)(2)(A)(i)(IV), prior to amendment by P.L. 114-113, made an exception for qualified leasehold improvement property as defined in Code Sec. 168(k)(3), prior to amendment by P.L. 114-113, at the time a 39-year recovery period still applied. Technically, it is was longer necessary for Code Sec. 168(k)(2)(A)(i)(IV) to specifically provide that qualified leasehold improvement property may qualify for bonus depreciation since such property as of October 22, 2004 had a 15-year recovery period. Bonus depreciation generally only applies to property with an MACRS recovery period of 20 years or less. At the time bonus depreciation was enacted a 15-year year recovery period did not apply to qualified leasehold improvement property. Therefore, it was necessary to specifically provide that bonus depreciation could be claimed on qualified leasehold improvement property that would otherwise have a 39-year recovery period. Although qualified restaurant property (¶ 110) and qualified retail improvement property (¶ 126) have a 15-year recovery period if placed in service before 2018, such property when placed in service prior to 2016 only qualifies for bonus depreciation if it also qualifies for bonus depreciation by reason of also qualifying as qualified leasehold improvement property (Code Sec. 168(e)(7)(B) and (8)(D), prior to amendment by P.L. 114-113). Effective for property placed in service in 2016 and 2017, 15-year qualified leasehold improvement property, retail improvement property, and restaurant property will qualify for bonus depreciation if they satisfy the definition of "qualified improvement property" contained in Code Sec. 168(k)(3), prior to amendment by P.L. 115-97. 15-year leasehold improvement property and retail improvement property will always satisfy the definition of "qualified improvement property."

Effective for property placed in service in 2016 and 2017, the qualified leasehold improvement category of bonus depreciation property is replaced with the "qualified improvement property" category. Qualified improvement property placed in service after 2017 qualifies for bonus depreciation because it has a recovery period of 15 years.

See discussion #16 below for qualified improvement property.

In tax years that begin after 2009, the section 179 deduction may be claimed on qualified real property as defined in Code Sec. 179(e) (formerly Code Sec. 179(f)).

See ¶ 302. Qualified real property includes 15-year qualified leasehold improvement property placed in service before 2018 and qualified improvement property placed in service after 2017. Note that to the extent that the section 179 deduction is claimed on section 1250 property, such as 15-year qualified leasehold improvement property or qualified improvement property, it is subject to the section 1245 recapture rules (Code Sec. 1245(a)(3)(C)). Thus, the section 179 deduction is recaptured as ordinary income to the extent of gain. Special guidance in Notice 2013-59 applies to determine the recapture amount if only a portion of an item of qualified real property is expensed. See ¶ 302. The bonus deduction on the other hand is treated as an accelerated depreciation deduction subject to recapture under the section 1250 recapture rules if claimed on section 1250 leasehold improvement property that is depreciated over a 15-year period. Under the section 1250 recapture rules gain is treated as ordinary income to the extent that the regular depreciation deductions and bonus depreciation exceed the depreciation that would have been claimed under the straight-line method through the recapture year if bonus depreciation had not been claimed. For this reason it may be preferable to claim bonus depreciation on 15-year qualified leasehold improvement property. See ¶ 488 for a general discussion of the recapture rules.

> ***Example (1):*** A taxpayer places $100,000 of 15-year qualified leasehold improvement property in service in 2017. If the taxpayer expenses the entire amount as qualified real property under section 179 in 2017, the section 179 deduction is recaptured as ordinary income to the extent of gain upon its disposition regardless of the date of disposition. If the taxpayer claims the 50 percent bonus allowance and depreciates the remaining basis of the property using the required straight-line method for 15-year leasehold improvement property recapture applies to the extent the bonus deduction exceeds the straight-line depreciation that could have been claimed on the bonus deduction. Note that 15-year qualified leasehold improvement property placed in service in 2016 and 2017 qualifies for bonus depreciation by reason of meeting the definition of qualified improvement property. See below, "*16. Qualified improvement property placed in service after 2015.*"

### *16. Qualified improvement property placed in service after 2015*

Qualified improvement property (Code Sec. 168(e)(6)) placed in service after 2017 qualified for bonus depreciation. As a result of a retroactive technical correction (Code Sec. 168(e)(3)(E)(vii)) qualified improvement property placed in service after 2017 has a 15-year recovery period. Property with an MACRS recovery period of 20 years of less generally qualifies for bonus depreciation.

Qualified improvement property placed in service in 2016 and 2017 was a separate category of bonus depreciation property regardless of its recovery period (Code Sec. 168(k)(3), prior to being stricken by P.L. 115-97 (P.L. 115-97); Reg. § 1.168(k)(2)-(b)(2)(i)(D)). As a result of assigning a 15-year recovery period, effective for property placed in service after 2017, it was no longer necessary for qualified improvement property to be treated as a separate category of bonus property. Consequently, it was removed as a separate category after 2017.

The 100 percent bonus rate applies to qualified improvement property acquired after September 27, 2017 and placed in service before 2023.

Qualified improvement property is defined as any improvement to an interior portion of a building which is nonresidential real property if the improvement is *made by the taxpayer* and placed in service after the date the building was first placed in service by any taxpayer. The improvement must be section 1250 property (Code Sec. 168(e)(6); Reg. § 1.168(b)-1(a)(5)). An improvement is made by the taxpayer if the taxpayer makes, manufactures, constructs, or produces the improvement for itself or if the improvement is made, manufactured, constructed, or produced for the taxpayer by another person under a written contract. In contrast, if a taxpayer acquires nonresidential real property in a taxable transaction and such nonresidential real property includes an improvement previously placed in service by the seller of such nonresidential real property, the improvement is not made by the taxpayer (Preamble to T.D. 9916; Reg. § 1.168(k)-2(b)(2)(iii)(I), Example 9).

The preamble further states that if a transferee taxpayer acquires nonresidential real property in a transaction described in section Code Sec. 168(i)(7)(B) (for example, Code Sec. 351 or Code Sec. 721), any improvement that was previously made by, and placed in service by, the transferor or distributor of such nonresidential real property and that is qualified improvement property in the hands of the transferor or distributor is treated as being made by the transferee taxpayer, and thus is qualified improvement property in the hands of the transferee taxpayer, but only for the portion of its basis in such property that does not exceed the transferor's or distributor's adjusted depreciable basis of this property. However, because the basis is determined by reference to the transferor's or distributor's adjusted basis in the improvement, the transferee taxpayer's acquisition does not satisfy Code Sec. 179(d)(2)(C) and Reg. § 1.179-4(c)(1)(iv) and thus, does not satisfy the used property acquisition requirements of Reg. § 1.168(k)-2(b)(3)(iii). Accordingly, the qualified improvement property is not eligible for the additional first year depreciation deduction in the hands of the transferee taxpayer.

Expenditures attributable to the enlargement of a building, any elevator or escalator, or the internal structural framework of the building are excluded from the definition of qualified improvement property. This rule is identical to the rule that applied to qualified leasehold improvement property, discussed above (#15), except that qualified leasehold improvement property also does not include any structural component (as defined in Reg. § 1.48-1(e)(2)) that benefits a common area. This restriction for common areas does not apply to qualified improvement property. In addition, qualified improvement property does not need to be placed in service pursuant to the terms of a lease and does not need to be placed in service more than three years after the improved building was first placed in service by any person. Where applicable, rules similar to those found in Reg. § 1.168(k)-1(c), dealing with leasehold improvement property, apply to qualified improvement property (Rev. Proc. 2017-33, Section 4.02(3)).

The Tax Cuts and Jobs Act of 2017 (P.L. 115-97) removed qualified improvement property as a separate category of bonus depreciation, effective for property placed in service after 2017 (Code Sec. 168(k)(2)(A)(i)(IV) and Code Sec. 168(k)(3), stricken by P.L. 115-97). Congress intended to assign a 15-year recovery period to qualified improvement property, effective for property placed in service after 2017. With a 15-year recovery period, qualified improvement property would have qualified for bonus depreciation under the generally applicable rule that makes property with a recovery period of 20 years or less eligible for bonus depreciation. Accordingly, Code Sec. 168(k)(3) was stricken because it was deemed no longer necessary. The 2017 Act, however, inadvertently failed to include language assigning a 15-year recovery period to qualified improvement property. Therefore, a technical correction (Code Sec. 168(e)(3)(E)(vii)) assigning a 15-year recovery period to qualified improvement property was enacted by the Coronavirus Aid, Relief, and Economic Security (CARES) Act (P.L. 116-136) (March 27, 2020) in order to make qualified improvement property eligible for bonus depreciation if placed in service after 2017.

Qualified improvement property placed in service in 2016 and 2017 does not qualify for a 15-year recovery period unless it meets the definition of 15-year qualified leasehold improvement property (¶ 126), 15-year qualified retail improvement property (¶ 110), or 15-year qualified restaurant property (¶ 110). Qualified improvement property which does not qualify for a 15-year recovery period is depreciated over 39-years as nonresidential real property using a mid-month convention. The 15- or 39-year recovery period applies even if the improved building is not MACRS property (i.e., is or was depreciated under a system other than MACRS, such as the Accelerated Cost Recovery System (ACRS) for assets placed in service after 1980 and before 1987) (Code Sec. 168(i)(6)).

The 15-year qualified leasehold improvement property, 15-year qualified retail improvement property, and 15-year restaurant property classes are eliminated by P.L. 115-97 effective for property placed in service after 2017 and replaced by the 15-year qualified improvement property class.

Property placed in service in 2016 and 2017 which meets the definition of qualified retail improvement property or qualified leasehold improvement property for purposes of the 15-year recovery period necessarily meets the definition of qualified improvement property and, therefore, qualifies for bonus depreciation. Qualified restaurant property placed in service in 2016 and 2017 which is eligible for a 15-year recovery period does not qualify for bonus depreciation unless it meets the definition of qualified improvement property (Code Sec. 168(e)(7)(B), prior to being stricken by P.L. 115-97). Internal improvements to a restaurant building that qualify for a 15-year recovery period will necessarily meet the definition of qualified improvement property. However, 15-year qualified restaurant property also includes a restaurant building (e.g., a building purchased by a taxpayer) and improvements to the external portion of a restaurant building. A restaurant building and improvements to the external portion of a restaurant building placed in service in 2016 and 2017 are not eligible for bonus depreciation as qualified improvement property since only internal improvements can qualify as qualified improvement property. See. Rev. Proc. 2017-33, Section 4.02(5), Examples 5 and 6.

Note also, that qualified improvement property relates to improvements to any type of nonresidential real property whether or not the property is leased or the building is a restaurant or used for retail. Thus, it is a much broader category of property.

In some cases a leasehold improvement or improvement to a retail building placed in service in 2016 and 2017 may not qualify for a 15-year recovery period but may qualify for bonus depreciation as qualified improvement property. For example, an internal improvement (structural component) that benefits a common area does not qualify for a 15-year recovery period in the case of a leased building property or a retail building. However, qualified improvement property does not contain this restriction. Therefore, such an internal improvement to a common area may nevertheless qualify for bonus depreciation as qualified improvement property.

IRS guidance includes the following examples (Rev. Proc. 2017-33, Section 4.02(5)):

> ***Example (1):*** A purchases an office building in February 2017 from B. B placed the building in service in 2010. In March 2017 A begins to construct section 1250 improvements to the interior of the building and places them in service in December 2017. The improvements qualify for bonus depreciation as qualified improvement property.

> ***Example (2):*** A enters into a contract whereby B will construct a new building (office space). During construction A contracts with C for the construction of a private restroom in the building, the construction of which was not called for in the original contract with B. On May 27, 2017 the building is placed in service. On May 28, 2017 the restroom is placed in service. The parts of the restroom that are section 1250 property are qualified improvement property.

The IRS does not explain whether the restroom would be qualified improvement property if it was built pursuant to the original terms of the construction contract. However, even in this situation there does not appear to be any reason why the restroom would not meet the definitional requirements of qualified improvement property so long as it is placed in service after the building is placed in service.

> ***Example (3):*** The facts are the same as the preceding example, except that A enters into an amendment of the original contract with B, whereby B will construct the restroom. The building is placed in service on May 27, 2017 and the restroom is placed in service on May 28, 2017. The section 1250 components of the restroom are qualified improvement property.

> ***Example (4):*** Lessor contracts with B in March 2016 to construct a multi-story commercial building with a minimally finished interior that consists only of elevators, heating, ventilation, and air conditioning systems, plumbing, restrooms, and concrete floors. In December 2016 lessor and lessee enter into a lease agreement whereby lessee will build out one floor of the building to meet the lessee's business needs. The building is placed in service in February 2017. In June 2017, the lessee places the build-out in service. The assets of the build-out that are section 1250 property are qualified improvement property.

*Accounting method changes.* IRS guidance allows a taxpayer to file amended returns (administrative adjustment request (AAR) by a partnership subject to the centralized partnership audit regime) or a change of accounting method under the automatic change procedures using Form 3115 to correct depreciation claimed on qualified improvement property placed in service in tax years ending in 2018, 2019, or 2020 (Rev. Proc. 2020-25, adding Section 6.19 to Rev. Proc. 2019-43). Amended returns (or AARs) are due on or before October 15, 2021 (or expiration of limitations period if earlier). Special rules apply to BBA partnerships for tax years beginning in 2018 and 2019 (Rev. Proc. 2020-25, adding Section 6.19 to Rev. Proc. 2019-43).

A taxpayer may file a change in accounting method for qualified improvement property under Sec. 6.01 of Rev. Proc. 2019-43 instead of Section 6.19, if the Form 3115 was filed before November 17, 2020 (Sec. 6.01(c)(xvii) of Rev. Proc. 2019-43 as added by Rev. Proc. 2020-25 and modified by Rev. Proc. 2020-50.

See CCH AnswerConnect for an example of a filled-in Form 3115. Use as a search term, "Filled-in Form 3115 for qualified improvement property."

For additional information, see "*1A. Qualified improvement property placed in service after 2017—guidance for changing to 15-year recovery period and claiming bonus depreciation—guidance for making late elections and revoking prior elections for 2018, 2019, and 2020 tax years.*"

*17. Film and television productions and live theatrical productions acquired and placed in service after September 27, 2017*

Bonus depreciation is allowed on the production costs of a qualified film, television show, or live theatrical production acquired and placed in service after September 27, 2017 and placed in service before 2027, if it qualifies for the Code Sec. 181 expense election without regard to the $15 million expensing limit or the expiration date (Code Sec. 168(k)(2)(A)(i), as amended by the 2017 Tax Cuts and Jobs Act (P.L. 115-97; Reg. § 1.168(k)-2(b)(1)(i)(E) and (F); Proposed Reg. § 1.168(k)-2(b)(1)(i)(E) and (F) in REG-104397-18). A qualified film or television production is placed in service at the time of its initial release or broadcast as defined in Reg. § 1.181-1(a)(7) (Reg. § 1.168(k)-2(b)(4)(iii); Proposed Reg. § 1.168(k)-2(b)(4)(iii) in REG-104397-18). A qualified live theatrical production is placed in service at the time of its initial live staged performance (Code Sec. 168(k)(2)(H), as added by P.L. 115-97; Reg. § 1.168(k)-2(b)(4)(iii); Proposed Reg. § 1.168(k)-2(b)(4)(iii) in REG-104397-18).

Initial live staged performance is the first commercial exhibition of a production to an audience. However, the term does not include limited exhibition prior to commercial exhibition to general audiences if the limited exhibition is primarily for purposes of publicity, determining the need for further production activity, or raising funds for the completion of production. For example, an initial live staged performance does not include a preview of the production if the preview is primarily to determine the need for further production activity (Reg. § 1.168(k)-2(a)(2)(iii); Proposed Reg. § 1.168(k)-2(b)(4)(iii) in REG-104397-18).

The taxpayer placing the film or television production or theatrical production in service must be the owner (Reg. § 1.168(k)-2(b)(4)(iii)). For example, a taxpayer who acquires from another party all rights to a film after production by that party but before initial release or broadcast may claim bonus depreciation. However, if only a limited license or right of release is obtained from the party, the taxpayer is not the owner and may not clam the bonus (Reg. § 1.168(k)-2(b)(iii)(A) and (B), *Examples 1 and 2*). Similarly, the acquisition of a film library that of previously broadcast or released films does not qualify for bonus depreciation (Reg. § 1.168(k)-2(b)(iii)(C), *Example 3*).

If a film, television show, or theatrical production is acquired before September 28, 2017, bonus depreciation may not be claimed. The acquisition date of a film or television show is the date on which principal photography begins. A theatrical production is acquired on the date when all necessary elements for producing the production are secured. These elements may include a script, financing, actors, set, scenic and costume designs, advertising agents, music, and lighting (Reg. § 1.168(k)-2(b)(5)(vi); Proposed Reg. § 1.168(k)-2(b)(5)(v) in REG-104397-18).

The bonus allowance only applies to production costs paid or incurred by an owner of the qualified film or television production prior to its initial release or broadcast or by an owner of the qualified live theatrical production prior to its initial live staged performance (i.e., the costs eligible for 181 expensing) (Reg. § 1.168(k)-2(b)(1)(i)(E) and (F)). Production costs are defined in the Code Sec. 181 regulations (Reg. § 1.181-1(a)(3)).

Bonus depreciation does not apply to a used qualified film, television, or live theatrical production (that is, such production acquired after its initial release or broadcast, or after its initial live staged performance, as applicable) (preamble to T.D. 9874).

The Code Sec. 181 deduction expires effective for productions commencing after December 31, 2025 (Code Sec. 181(g)). In the case of a film or television show, a production commences on the date of first principal photography. A theatrical production commences on the date of the first public performance before a paying audience. If a Code Sec. 181 election is made, production costs are expensed in the tax year paid or incurred. If the production does not commence until after the December 31, 2017, expiration date, costs expensed under Code Sec. 181 are subject to recapture. Under the bonus depreciation rule, the bonus allowance for production costs will be deducted in the tax year the production is placed in service and without regard to the $15 million limit.

A taxpayer generally makes an election under Code Sec. 181 on the income tax return for the tax year in which production costs are first paid or incurred (Reg. § 1.181-2(b)) and not at the later time when the production is placed in service, as defined above for bonus depreciation purposes. A taxpayer that made a Code Sec.

181 election at the time a production commenced is prohibited from claiming bonus depreciation on the portion of the basis of the same production that is expensed under Code Sec. 181 unless the IRS grants permission to revoke the election (Code Sec. 181(b) and (c)). Automatic consent, however, will be granted without filing a letter ruling request if the taxpayer recaptures previously claimed deductions under Code Sec. 181 (Reg. § 181-2(d)(2)).

*18. Specified plants*

Effective for "specified plants" that are planted after 2015 and before 2027 or grafted after 2015 and before 2027 to a plant that is already planted, a taxpayer may elect to claim bonus depreciation on the applicable percentage of the adjusted basis of a specified plant in the tax year of planting or grafting to a plant that has already been planted. If this election is not made, bonus depreciation is claimed in the year the specified plant is placed in service (i.e., the year of commercial production). The planting or grafting must occur in the ordinary course of the taxpayer's farming business as defined in Code Sec. 263A(e)(4) (Code Sec. 168(k)(5), as added by P.L. 114-113; Reg. § 1.168(k)-2(b)(2)(i)(G); Proposed Reg. § 1.168(k)-2(b)(4); Reg. § 1.168(k)-2(e)(1)(i)(B); Proposed Reg. § 1.168(k)-2(d)(1)(i)(B) in REG-104397-18). As explained below, the election is made for one or more plants. It does not need to be made for all of a taxpayer's plants.

The deduction reduces the adjusted basis of the specified plant on which the section 179 allowance may be claimed in the placed-in-service year (Rev. Proc. 2017-33). If the deduction is claimed in the year or planting or grafted, the specified plant is not treated as qualified property in the year that it is placed in service and no bonus depreciation may be claimed in that year. The entire plant is disqualified property for purposes of bonus depreciation (Code Sec. 168(k)(5)(D), as added by P.L. 114-113). No bonus may be claimed in the tax year of the planting or grafting if the plant is disposed of in the same tax year as the planting or grafting (Reg. § 1.168(k)-2(g)(1)(i); Proposed Reg. § 1.168(k)-2(f)(1)(i) in REG-104397-18).

Presumably, the bonus allowance is computed on the specified plant's adjusted basis as of the date of planting or grafting and not on the adjusted basis as of the close of the tax year in which the planting or grafting occurs. Capital expenditures after planting or grafting would then be added to any remaining basis of the specified plant (e.g., the 50 percent not deducted as bonus depreciation if the 50 percent bonus rate applies) and depreciated beginning in the year the specified plant is placed in service. No bonus depreciation may be claimed on additions to basis after planting or grafting in the year the plant is placed in service since, as noted above, the entire specified plant is disqualified for bonus depreciation in the placed in service year (Code Sec. 168(k)(5)(D), as added by P.L. 114-113).

A depreciable tree, vine, or plant is considered placed in service in the tax year that it first becomes productive, i.e., bears fruit, nuts, etc. in a commercial quantity (Reg. § 1.46-3(d)(2)), flush language). This provision accelerates the bonus depreciation deduction that would otherwise apply in the year that the specified plant became commercially productive to the to the year of planting or grafting. Regular depreciation deductions on the portion of the adjusted basis that is not claimed as bonus depreciation under this provision (including any amounts that are capitalized into the basis after the planting or grafting) are claimed beginning in the year that the specified plant is placed in service (i.e., becomes productive).

A specified plant is defined as (Code Sec. 168(k)(5)(B), as added by P.L. 114-113):

(1) any tree or vine which bears fruits or nuts; and

(2) any other plant which will have more than one crop or yield of fruits or nuts and which has a pre-productive period of more than two years from the

time of planting or grafting to the time at which the plant begins bearing a marketable crop or yield of fruits or nuts.

The 2018 Technical Corrections Act clarifies that specified plants include plants that will have more than one *crop* and that the two-year pre-productive period is measured from the time of planting or grafting to the time that the plant begins bearing a *marketable* crop or yield of fruits or nuts (Code Sec. 168(k)(5)(B)(ii), as amended by the Tax Technical Corrections Act of 2018 (Division U of P.L. 115-141)).

The specified plant must be planted or grafted in the United States.

If the bonus deduction is claimed in the tax year or planting or grafting to a planted plant, the bonus deduction is not subject to an AMT adjustment (i.e., the deductions is claimed in full for AMT purposes) (Code Sec. 168(k)(5)(E), as added by P.L. 114-113; Rev. Proc. 2017-33, Section 4.05(1)(a); Reg. § 1.168(k)-2(f)(4); Proposed Reg. § 1.168(k)-2(e)(4) in REG-104397-18). Any regular depreciation deductions claimed beginning in the year the specified plant is placed in service are also exempt from an AMT adjustment.

The bonus deduction is not subject to capitalization under the uniform capitalization rules of Code Sec. 263A (Code Sec. 263A(c)(7), as added by P.L. 114-113).

*Election procedure to claim in year of planting or grafting.* The election must be made by the due date, including extensions, of the Federal tax return for the tax year in which the taxpayer plants or grafts the specified plant to a planted plant. However, late elections may be made under Rev. Proc. 2020-50, Rev. Proc. 2020-25, or Rev. Proc. 2019-33, as explained below. The election must be made in the manner prescribed on Form 4562, Depreciation and Amortization, and its instructions (Rev. Proc. 2017-33, Section 4.05(1)(b); Reg. § 1.168(k)-2(f)(2); Proposed Reg. § 1.168(k)-2(e)(2) in REG-104397-18). The election may be made for one or more specified plants. The instructions require that a taxpayer attach a statement to a timely filed (including extensions) return indicating that the taxpayer is electing to apply section Code Sec. 168(k)(5) and identifying the specified plant(s) for which the election is made. The election once made cannot be revoked without IRS consent except with the six-month period described below (Reg. § 1.168(k)-2(f)(5); Proposed Reg. § 1.168(k)-2(e)(5) in REG-104397-18).

The election is made separately by each person owning specified plants (for example, for each member of a consolidated group by the common parent of the group, by the partnership, or by the S corporation).

*Revocation of election.* The election is only revocable with IRS consent (Code Sec. 168(k)(5)(C), as added by P.L. 114-113; Reg. § 1.168(k)-2(f)(2); Proposed Reg. § 1.168(k)-2(e)(2) in REG-104397-18). However, if the taxpayer made the election on a timely filed return, the election may be revoked by filing an amended return within six months of the due date of the timely filed return (not including extensions). All taxpayers whose tax liability would be affected by the revocation must file an amended return within the six-month period to reflect the revocation (Reg. § 1.168(k)-2(f)(5); Proposed Reg. § 1.168(k)-2(e)(5) in REG-104397-18; Rev. Proc. 2017-33, Section 4.05).

Late revocations may be made under Rev. Proc. 2020-50, Rev. Proc. 2020-25, or Rev. Proc. 2019-33, as explained below.

*Interaction with Code Sec. 179.* The Code Sec. 179 deduction is claimed in the placed-in-service year on the adjusted basis of the plant as reduced by the amount claimed as a bonus deduction in the year of planting or grafting (Rev. Proc. 2017-33, Section 4.05).

*100 percent rate.* Specified plants planted or grafted to a planted plant after September 27, 2017 and before January 1, 2023 qualify for a 100 percent bonus rate. Beginning in 2024 and each year thereafter the 100 percent rate is reduced by 20 percent per year. See the chart at "*2. Bonus depreciation rates, including 100 percent rate for property acquired after September 27, 2017,*" except that the date the specified plant was planted or grafted replaces the placed in service date (Code Sec. 168(k)(5)(A) and (6)(C), as amended by P.L. 114-113). Unlike other property, the acquisition date is not relevant in determining whether specified plants qualify for the 100 percent rate in the year of planting or grafting (Act. Sec. 13201(h)(2) of the Tax Cuts and Jobs Act (P.L. 115-97); Reg. § 1.168(k)-2(b)(5)(vii); Proposed Reg. § 1.168(k)-2(b)(5)(vi) in REG-104397-18).

*Alternative minimum tax.* The bonus deduction claimed in the year of planting or grafting is allowed in full for AMT purposes except that the bonus deduction is computed on AMT basis if this is different than regular tax basis (Reg. § 1.168(k)-2(e)(1)(iv)(A)(ii); Proposed Reg. § 1.168(k)-2(d)(1)(iv)(A)(ii) in REG-104397-18).

*Late elections and revocations for tax years ending in 2018, 2019, and 2020.* IRS guidance allows a taxpayer to make a late election or revoke a prior election to claim bonus depreciation in the year of planting or grafting. This option only applies to tax years ending in 2018, 2019, or 2020 (Rev. Proc. 2020-25). See discussion at *1A. Qualified improvement property placed in service after 2017—guidance for changing to 15-year recovery period and claiming bonus depreciation—guidance for making late elections and revoking prior elections for 2018, 2019, and 2020 tax years.*

*Late election and revocations for pre-2021 tax year in which final regulations are applied.* Taxpayers may also be able to make a late election or revocation of the election to claim bonus depreciation on specified plants in the year of planting grafting under Rev. Proc. 2020-50 for a tax that includes September 28, 2017 and for later tax years that end before 2021 by retroactively applying final or proposed bonus regulations. See "*1D. Late elections and revocations for 2017, 2018, 2019, and 2020 tax years for taxpayers applying 2020 final, 2019 final, or 2019 final and proposed regulations.*"

*Special rule for making a late election and revoking an election in tax year that includes September 28, 2017.* The IRS allows a taxpayer to make a late election or revoke an election to claim bonus depreciation on a specified plant in the year of planting or grafting in a tax year that includes September 28, 2017 by filing an accounting method change or amended return (Rev. Proc. 2019-33). See *11. Special rules for making and revoking elections in tax year that includes September 28, 2017.* A late election or revocation may also be possible under Rev. Proc. 2020-25 or Rev. Proc. 2020-50 referenced immediately above.

*Election to use 50 percent rate for tax year that includes September 28, 2017.* An election may be made to claim the 50 percent bonus rate on specified plants in the year of planting or grafting with respect to specified plants that are planted or grafted to a planted plant during the tax year that includes September 28, 2017. The election applies to all specified plants for which an election to claim bonus depreciation in the year of planting or grafting is made (Reg. § 1.168(k)-2(f)(3); Proposed Reg. § 1.168(k)-2(e)(3) in REG-104397-18). Generally, revocation requires IRS consent (Reg. § 1.168(k)-2(f)(5); Proposed Reg. § 1.168(k)-2(e)(5) in REG-104397-18).

For a limited period of time a taxpayer may make a late election to use the 50 percent rate or revoke the election to use the 50 percent rate without IRS consent

(Rev. Proc. 2019-33 referenced above). This late election or revocation may also be available under Rev. Proc. 2020-25 or Rev. Proc. 2020-50 referenced above.

*Deemed election for tax year that includes September 28, 2017.* At taxpayer who claimed bonus depreciation at the 50 percent rate on all specified plant that were planted or grafted after September 27, 2017 in a tax year that includes September 28, 2017 is deemed to have made an election to use the 50 percent rate in lieu of the 100 percent rate unless the deemed election is revoke (Rev. Proc. 2019-33). See *11. Special rules for making and revoking elections in tax year that includes September 28, 2017.*

*Deemed election for 2015/2016 fiscal-year taxpayer.* A 2015/2016 fiscal-year taxpayer or a taxpayer with a short tax year beginning and ending in 2016, is deemed to have made a valid election for a specified plant planted or grafted after December 31, 2015 if the taxpayer deducted the 50-percent additional first year depreciation for the specified plant on its fiscal-year or short-year return and does not revoke the deemed election (Rev. Proc. 2017-33, Section 4.05(1)(b)).

*19. Computer software*

The additional depreciation allowance (bonus depreciation) applies to computer software which is depreciated under Code Sec. 167(f) over three years using the straight-line method (Code Sec. 168(k)(2)(A)(i)(II)). See ¶ 48. The regulations require that the computer software actually be depreciated under Code Sec. 167(f), not that it merely be eligible for depreciation under that section (Reg. § 1.168(k)-1(b)(2)(i)(B); Reg. § 1.168(k)-2(b)(2)(i)(B); Proposed Reg. § 1.168(k)-2(b)(2)(i)(B) in REG-104397-18). Nevertheless, it seems clear that this rule should not apply if 100 percent bonus depreciation is available and the software could otherwise be depreciated over 3 years under Code Sec. 167(f). In general, computer software is depreciable under Code Sec. 167(f) if it is not amortizable under Code Sec. 197 because it is either off-the-shelf computer software as defined in Code Sec. 197(e)(3)(A)(i) or is not acquired as part of the acquisition of a trade or business (Code Sec. 197(e)(3)). Accordingly, software developed for internal use may qualify if it is depreciated over 3 years under Code Sec. 167(f). It should also be noted that eligible taxpayers may expense, under Code Sec. 179, off-the-shelf computer software placed in service in a tax year beginning after 2002. See ¶ 302.

*20. Pollution control facilities*

The bonus depreciation allowance may be claimed on a pollution control facility even if a taxpayer elects to amortize the facility under Code Sec. 169 (Reg. § 1.168(k)-1(f)(4); Reg. § 1.168(k)-2(g)(4); Proposed Reg. § 1.168(k)-2(f)(4) in REG-104397-18). The amortizable basis of the facility is reduced by the allowed or allowable bonus deduction (Reg. § 1.169-3). It appears that a taxpayer must make an election out of bonus depreciation if the taxpayer does not want to claim bonus depreciation on a pollution control facility whether or not amortization is elected.

*21. Mandatory ADS property does not qualify for bonus depreciation*

Property which pursuant to any Code provision or regulation must be depreciated using the MACRS alternative depreciation system (ADS) in the year that it is placed in service does not qualify for bonus depreciation. However, property that a taxpayer elects to depreciate using ADS is not disqualified (Code Sec. 168(k)(2)(D); Reg. § 1.168(k)-1(b)(2)(ii)(A)(*2*) and (B)(*1*); Reg. § 1.168(k)-2(b)(2)(ii)(B); Proposed Reg. § 1.168(k)-2(b)(2)(ii)(B) in REG-104397-18).

The following property must be depreciated using ADS and, therefore, does not qualify for bonus depreciation (Code Sec. 168(g)(1)):

(1) tangible property used predominantly outside of the United States during the tax year placed in service;

(2) tax-exempt use property;

(3) tax-exempt bond-financed property;

(4) property imported from a foreign country for which an Executive Order is in effect because the country maintains trade restrictions or engages in other discriminatory acts;

(5) listed property used 50 percent or less in business and certain farming property if a Code Sec. 263A(d)(3) election is made, see below;

(6) residential rental property, nonresidential real property, and qualified improvement property owned by a real property trade or business that elects out of the new rules enacted by the 2017 Tax Cuts Act (P.L. 115-97) which disallow deduction for excess business interest expense, effective for tax years beginning after 2017 (Code Sec. 163(j)(7)(B)); Code Sec. 168(g)(1)(F)); and

(7) Any property with a recovery period of 10 years or greater which is held by an "electing farming business" that makes an election out of the new rules which disallow the deduction for net interest expense in excess of a specified percentage of the business' adjusted taxable income, effective for tax years beginning after 2017 (Code Sec. 168(g)(1)(G)).

A taxpayer may use the change of use rules to switch to ADS in the case of property described in items (6) and (7) that is placed in service in a tax year beginning before the election year (Rev. Proc. 2019-8). An accounting method change is not required if the switch to ADS is made in the election year. See ¶ 150.

If a property changes use in a tax year after it is placed in service, the bonus deduction may not be claimed in the year the use changes. For example the bonus deduction may not be claimed on property used predominantly outside of the United States in the tax year of acquisition and moved into the United States in a later tax year. Conversely, the bonus deduction is not disallowed or recaptured if property becomes ineligible for the bonus allowance in a tax year after it was placed in service because it is described in items (1) through (4). For example, the bonus deduction claimed on property used predominantly in the U.S. in the tax year of acquisition is not disallowed or recaptured if the property is later moved outside of the U.S. in a later tax year (Reg. § 1.168(k)-1(f)(6)(iv); Reg. § 1.168(k)-2(g)(6); Proposed Reg. § 1.168(k)-2(f)(6) in REG-104397-18).

Predominant use is determined by comparing the number of days during the tax year that the property is physically located in the U.S. to the number of days it is located outside of the U.S. (Reg. § 1.48-1(g)(1)).

*ADS used for purposes other than computing regular tax depreciation deduction.* In some cases ADS is required to compute depreciation for tax purposes other than the regular depreciation deduction that is claimed on Form 4562. The mandatory use of ADS in such a case does not disqualify the property from bonus depreciation so long as regular depreciation deductions are not required to be computed using ADS (Reg. § 1.168(k)-2(b)(2)(ii)(B)).

Examples of ADS used for purposes other than computing regular tax depreciation deductions include property for which the adjusted basis is required to be determined using the alternative depreciation system for purposes of computing:

- foreign-derived intangible income (Code Sec. 250(b)(2)(B))
- qualified business asset investment of a controlled foreign corporation (Code Sec. 951A(d)(3))

- the allocation of business interest expense between excepted and non-excepted trades or businesses (Code Sec. 163(j))

*Listed property.* If a listed property (¶ 208), such as a car, must be depreciated using ADS (¶ 150) in the year that it is placed in service because it is not predominantly (more than 50%) used in a qualified business use, then bonus depreciation may not be claimed (Code Sec. 168(k)(2)(D)(i)(II); Reg. § 1.168(k)-1(b)(2)(ii)(A)(2); Reg. § 1.168(k)-2(b)(2)(ii)(B); Proposed Reg. § 1.168(k)-2(b)(2)(ii)(B) in REG-104397-18). Because the additional depreciation allowance is treated as depreciation, it is subject to recapture under the listed property rules (¶ 210) if business use falls to 50 percent or less in a tax year after it is placed in service but within the applicable ADS recovery period that applies to the property (Code Sec. 168(k)(2)(F)(ii), as added by P.L. 107-147).

As defined in Code Sec. 280F(d)(4), listed property includes any passenger automobile, any other property used as a means of transportation, any property of a type generally used for purposes of entertainment, recreation, or amusement, any computer or peripheral equipment (placed in service before 2018), any cellular telephone or similar telecommunications equipment (for tax years beginning before January 1, 2010), and certain other property specified in regulations. Cell phones and similar telecommunications equipment are not considered listed property effective for tax years beginning after December 31, 2009. Computers and peripheral equipment are removed from listed property classification if placed in service after 2017. See ¶ 208 for a discussion of listed property.

*Farmers.* Farmers who elect under Code Sec. 263A(d)(3) not to have the uniform capitalization rules apply, are required to depreciate farm property placed in service during any tax year that the election is in effect using ADS. Such farm property does not qualify for bonus depreciation. The prohibition applies even if the election was made by a person related to the taxpayer (Reg. § 1.168(k)-1(b)(2)(ii)(A)(2); Reg. § 1.168(k)-2(b)(2)(ii)(B); Proposed Reg. § 1.168(k)-2(b)(2)(ii)(B) in REG-104397-18).

Farmers who qualify for exemption from the UNICAP rules by reason of having average annual gross receipts of $25 million or less may revoke an election not to capitalize pre-productive period expenditures (Rev. Proc. 2020-13). See ¶ 152.

*Tax-exempt use property of tax-exempt partner.* Property owned by a partnership with a tax exempt entity as a partner may be treated as tax-exempt use property in proportion to tax-exempt entity's partnership interest (Code Sec. 168(h)(6)(A)). The tax-exempt entity's proportionate share of the property is not eligible for bonus depreciation (Reg. § 1.168(k)-2(b)(2)(ii)).

*22. Property used by certain businesses that have floor plan financing indebtedness does not qualify for bonus depreciation if a benefit received from deducting interest on such indebtedness*

Property used in a trade or business that has floor plan financing indebtedness does not qualify for bonus depreciation if the floor plan financing interest on the indebtedness is taken into account under the new rules that limit the business interest deduction to a specified percentage of adjusted taxable income plus floor plan financing interest and business interest income if the taxpayer's average annual gross receipts for three years exceed $25 million (Code Secs. 168(k)(9) and 163(j)(9), as added by the 2017 Tax Cuts and Jobs Act (P.L. 115-97)). The provision is effective for property placed in service in tax years beginning after 2017 (Reg. § 1.168(k)-2(b)(ii)(G)).

Generally, the specified percentage of adjusted taxable income is 30 percent. The 30 percent limitation is increased to 50 percent for a tax year that begins in 2019 or 2020 unless an election to use the 30 percent rate is made. The increase does not apply to partnerships for a tax year beginning in 2019 (Code Sec. 163(j)(10), as added by the CARES Act (P.L. 116-136).

This rule is applied on an annual basis and bonus depreciation is denied only if a tax benefit is received from any interest deduction on floor plan financing indebtedness during the tax year that the bonus property is placed in service (Reg. § 1.168(k)-2(b)(2)(ii)(G), as amended by T.D. 9916 by adopting Proposed Reg. § 1.168(k)-2(b)(2)(ii)(G) in REG-104397-18).

Specifically, bonus depreciation may be claimed in a tax year if the sum of the amounts calculated under Code Sec. 163(j)(1)(A) (business interest income) and Code Sec. 163(j)(1)(B) (50 percent of adjusted taxable income for tax years beginning in 2019 and 2020; 30 percent thereafter) for the tax year exceeds business interest (including floor plan financing interest and carryforwards of disallowed business interest for the tax year).

In the following examples, assume the election to use the 30 percent taxable income limitation is made.

***Example (1):*** In 2021, F, an automobile dealer, buys new computers for $50,000. F has the following for 2021: $700 of adjusted taxable income, $40 of business interest income, $400 of business interest (which includes $100 of floor plan financing interest). The sum of the amounts calculated under section 163(j)(1)(A) and (B) for F for 2021 is $390 ($40 + ($700 x 50 percent)). F's business interest, which includes floor plan financing interest, for 2021 is $400. As a result, F's floor plan financing interest is taken into account by F for 2021. Accordingly, the computers do not qualify for bonus depreciation (1.168(k)-2(b)(2)(iii)(G), Example 7; Proposed Reg. § 1.168(k)-2(b)(2)(iii)(G), Example 7 in REG-104397-18).

***Example (2):*** In 2021, F in the example above buys new copiers for $30,000 For 2021 F has: $1,300 of adjusted taxable income, $40 of business interest income, $400 of business interest (which includes $100 of floor plan financing interest). The sum of the amounts calculated under section 163(j)(1)(A) and (B) for F for 2021 is $690 ($40 + ($1,300 x 50 percent)). F's business interest, which includes floor plan financing interest, for 2021 is $400. As a result, F's floor plan financing interest is not taken into account by F for 2021. The new copiers qualify for bonus depreciation (Reg. § 1.168(k)-2(b)(2)(iii)(H), Example 8; Proposed Reg. § 1.168(k)-2(b)(2)(iii)(H), Example 8 in REG-104397-18).

A taxpayer that leases property to a person with floor plan financing may claim bonus depreciation unless the lessor has floor plan financing in effect during the tax that precludes the lessor from claiming the bonus depreciation (Reg. § 1.168(k)-2(b)(2)(ii)(G); Proposed Reg. § 1.168(k)-2(b)(2)(ii)(G); Reg. § 1.168(k)-2(b)(2)(iii)(F), Example 6; Proposed Reg. § 1.168(k)-2(b)(2)(iii)(F), Example 6 in REG-104397-18).

The regulations do not prevent a related lessor from claiming bonus depreciation on property leased to a related party who may not claim the bonus because it has floor plan financing.

Floor plan financing indebtedness means indebtedness:

- used to finance the acquisition of motor vehicles held for sale or lease; and

- secured by the inventory acquired (Code Sec. 163(j)(9), as added by P.L. 115-97).

A motor vehicle means:

- any self-propelled vehicle designed for transporting persons or property on a public street, highway, or road;
- a boat; or
- farm machinery or equipment.

The interest deduction limitation does not apply in any tax year that a taxpayer meets the gross receipts test of Code Sec. 448(c) by having average annual gross receipts for the three-tax-year period ending with the prior tax year that do not exceed $25 million (as adjusted annually for inflation) (Code Sec. 163(j)(3), as added by the 2017 Tax Cuts Act).

*23. Rate-regulated utility property does not qualify for bonus if placed in service in tax years beginning after 2017*

Rate-regulated utilities are prevented from claiming bonus depreciation, effective for property placed in service in tax years beginning after 2017 (Code Secs. 168(k)(9) and 163(j)(7)(A)(iv), as added by the 2017 Tax Cuts and Jobs Act (P.L. 115-97); Reg. § 1.168(k)-2(b)(2)(ii)(F); Reg. § 1.168(k)-2(b)(5)(viii)(K), *Example 11* (property acquired by calendar year utility before 2018 but placed in service after 2017 does not qualify for bonus); Proposed Reg. § 1.168(k)-2(b)(2)(ii)(F) in REG-104397-18).

Specifically, property does not qualify for bonus depreciation if it is primarily used in a trade or business of furnishing or selling for regulated rates:

- electrical energy or water;
- sewage disposal services;
- gas or steam through a local distribution system; or
- transportation of gas or steam by pipeline.

Rates are regulated if established or approved by a state or political subdivision thereof, by any agency or instrumentality of the United States, by a public service or public utility commission or other similar body of any state or political subdivision thereof, or by the governing or ratemaking body of an electric cooperative.

Proposed regulations finalized by T.D. 9916 clarify that a lessor of property to a rate-regulated utility may claim bonus depreciation if the lessor is not a rate-regulated utility (Reg. § 1.168(k)-2(b)(2)(ii)(F); Proposed Reg. § 1.168(k)-2(b)(2)(ii)(F) in REG-104397-18).

The "primary use" of an item is determined in accordance with Reg. § 1.167(a)-11(b)(4)(iii)(b) and Reg. § 1.167(a)-11(e)(3)(iii) for classifying property (Reg. § 1.168(k)-2(b)(2)(ii)(F); Proposed Reg. § 1.168(k)-2(b)(2)(ii)(F)v).

25-year water utility property as defined in Code Sec. 168(e)(5) and depreciated under MACRS continues to qualify for bonus depreciation if the property is not acquired by a rate-regulated utility.

*24. Property converted from personal use to business use or from business use to personal use*

The bonus deduction is not allowed if a taxpayer converts business or production of income property to personal use in the same tax year that it is placed in service for business use (Reg. § 1.168(k)-1(f)(6)(ii); Reg. § 1.168(k)-2(g)(6)(ii); Proposed Reg. § 1.168(k)-2(f)(6)(ii) in REG-104397-18). Property may qualify for bonus depreciation, however, if it is converted from personal use to business or production of income use in the same tax year that it was acquired or in a later tax year (Reg. § 1.168(k)-1(f)(6)(iii); Reg. § 1.168(k)-2(g)(6)(iii); Proposed Reg. § 1.168(k)-2(f)(6)(iii) in REG-104397-18).

Property converted from personal use to business use by the same taxpayer will satisfy the original use requirement, assuming that the personal use was the first use of the property (i.e., the property was new when acquired by the taxpayer for personal use) (Reg. § 1.168(k)-1(b)(3)(ii); Reg. § 1.168(k)-2(b)(3)(ii)(B); Proposed Reg. § 1.168(k)-2(b)(3)(ii)(B) in REG-104397-18). The original use requirement is not satisfied if a taxpayer acquires personal-use property from another person for use in the taxpayer's business. Such used property if acquired after September 27, 2017, however, may qualify. See below.

To qualify for bonus depreciation, new personal use property acquired by a taxpayer before September 28, 2017 must be converted to business use and placed in service by the taxpayer before January 1, 2020 (Reg. § 1.168(k)-1(f)(6)(iii)). A 50 percent rate applies if the property is placed in service in 2016 or 2017. A 40 percent rate applies if such property placed in service in 2018, and a 30 percent rate if placed in service in 2019. Property acquired for personal use after September 27, 2017 and converted to business use before 2023 qualifies for a 100 percent rate. The 100 percent rate is decreased 20 percent per year beginning in 2023. The acquisition date is determined by reference to the date the property was acquired for personal use.

The basis for computing the bonus deduction on personal property converted to business use is the lesser of the fair market value at the time of conversion or the adjusted basis at the time of conversion (Reg. § 1.167(g)(1)) reduced by any amount expensed under Code Sec. 179.

> ***Example (1):*** Tom Jacobs, a calendar-year taxpayer, purchases a new machine on January 1, 2016 for personal use. He converts it to business use in June 2019. The machine may qualify for bonus depreciation at the 30 percent rate. If the new machine had been acquired before January 1, 2008 for personal use and then converted in 2015 for business use, it would not qualify for bonus depreciation because it was acquired before January 1, 2008 and placed in service before 2016. However, if the machine was converted to business use in 2019 it could qualify for bonus depreciation at the 30 percent rate because the rule proscribing original use before 2008 no longer applies to property placed in service after 2015. See "*30. Original use requirement.*"

*Used property acquired for personal use and converted to business use.* Used property acquired by a taxpayer after September 27, 2017, qualifies for bonus depreciation (Code Sec. 168(k)(2)(A)(ii), as amended by the 2017 Tax Cuts and Jobs Act (P.L. 115-97)). Therefore, if used property is acquired by a taxpayer for personal use after September 27, 2017 and then converted to business use by the taxpayer the property may qualify for bonus depreciation even though the original use did not begin with the taxpayer. The 100 percent rate applies if the used property is acquired after September 27, 2017 and converted to business use before 2023. Used personal property acquired by a taxpayer before September 28, 2017 for personal use does not qualify for bonus depreciation upon later conversion to business use (Reg. § 1.168(k)-2(g)(6); Proposed Reg. § 1.168(k)-2(f)(6) in REG-104397-18).

See also "*13. Used property acquired after September 27, 2017 qualifies for bonus depreciation.*"

### *25. Change in depreciable use after placed in service year*

The use of a property may change and as a consequence, depreciation on the property may have to be computed using ADS or the use of ADS may be discontinued. For example, property used by a taxpayer in the United States may be moved abroad or vice versa, requiring the use or discontinuance of ADS.

The bonus depreciation regulations provide that if a property does not qualify for bonus depreciation in the year that it is placed in service (for example, because it is used abroad and ADS applies) bonus depreciation is not allowed in a subsequent year if a change in use occurs. Conversely, if a property qualified for bonus depreciation in the year it was placed in service but would not qualify in a later tax year because of a change in use, the bonus deduction is not recaptured (Reg. § 1.168(k)-1(f)(6)(iv); Reg. § 1.168(k)-2(g)(6)(iv); Proposed Reg. § 1.168(k)-2(f)(6)(iv) in REG-104397-18). This rule applies to any change in use described in Code Sec. 168(i)(5) and the regulations thereunder. The IRS has issued change in use regulations (Reg. § 1.168(i)-(4) at ¶ 568). See ¶ 169 for a discussion of depreciation computations when a change in use results in a new depreciation period or method under MACRS.

Bonus depreciation may not be claimed if property is converted from business use to personal use in the same tax year (Reg. § 1.168(k)-2(g)(6)(ii)).

*26. Other types of bonus depreciation*

This paragraph ¶ 127D discusses the bonus depreciation provision of Code Sec. 168(k). Other bonus depreciation provisions include:

- The New York Liberty Zone bonus depreciation provision (Code Sec. 1400L(b)) is discussed at ¶ 127E.
- The Gulf Opportunity Zone bonus depreciation provision (Code Sec. 1400N(d)) at ¶ 127F.
- The Kansas Disaster Area bonus depreciation provision at ¶ 127G for certain Kansas counties affected by storms in May of 2007.
- Bonus depreciation for replacement property purchased in connection with a Presidentially declared disaster (Code Sec. 168(n)) at ¶ 127H.
- Bonus depreciation for second generation biofuel plant property (Code Sec. 168(l)) ¶ 127I.

If a property can qualify for bonus depreciation under Code Sec. 168(k) and also under one of these provisions, the taxpayer should claim bonus depreciation under Code Sec. 168(k). No double deduction is allowed.

ACQUISITION AND PLACED-IN-SERVICE DATE REQUIREMENTS

*27. Acquisition defined*

For purposes of determining whether property is acquired after September 27, 2017 and, therefore, subject to the amendments to Code Sec. 168(k) by the Tax Cuts and Jobs Act (P.L. 115-97), e.g., whether the 100 percent bonus rate applies, property acquired pursuant to a written binding contract before September 28, 2017 is considered acquired before September 28, 2017 (Act Sec. 13201(h)(1) of the 2017 Tax Cuts Act). Final regulations provide a definition of a binding contract and specific rules for determining the acquisition date of property acquired under a binding contract (Reg. § 1.168(k)(2)(B)(5)(B)). See "*28. Binding contract defined.*"

Self-constructed property is deemed acquired when construction begins. Construction begins when physical work of a significant nature begins or, under a safe harbor, 10 percent or more of the total cost of construction is paid or incurred by the taxpayer (Reg. § 1.168(k)(2)-(b)(5)(iv)). If property is constructed for a taxpayer pursuant to a binding written contract entered into before construction begins, the property is considered self-constructed and acquired when construction begins. If the 10 percent safe harbor is elected, the taxpayer must pay or incur more than 10 percent of the cost (not the person constructing the property). See "*32. Acquisition and placed-in-service date requirements for 100 percent bonus rate for property acquired after September 27, 2017.*"

*Acquisition of "off-the-shelf property."* The regulations do not provide the definition of acquisition for purposes of off-the-shelf purchases of property (i.e., property that is not acquired under a contract or constructed by or for the taxpayer). However, the investment tax credit regulations provide that property is deemed acquired when reduced to physical possession or control (Reg. § 1.48-2(b)(6)). A similar definition is provided in the Code Sec. 167 depreciation regulations (Reg. § 1.167(c)-1(a)(2)). Control for this purpose occurs when the burdens and benefits of ownership are transferred to the taxpayer (Rev. Rul. 79-98, 1979-1 CB 103; GCM 37585 (June 23, 1978)).

*Special paid or incurred rule for off-the-shelf property for purposes of 100 percent rate for property acquired after September 8, 2010, and before January 1, 2012.* Section 3.02(1)(a) of Rev. Proc. 2011-26 provides that solely for purposes of the 100 percent bonus depreciation rate for property acquired after September 8, 2010, and before January 1, 2012, a taxpayer acquires qualified property when the taxpayer pays (cash basis) or incurs (accrual basis) the cost of the property. The final regulations for the 100 percent rate for property acquired after September 27, 2017 do not contain this rule.

*Paid or incurred defined.* The principles of Code Sec. 461 apply for purposes of determining when an amount is paid or incurred. An accrual-basis taxpayer generally incurs the cost of property when the property is "provided" to the taxpayer and the cost of services as the services are provided (Reg. § 1.461-4(d)(2)(i)). Taxpayers usually consider property as "provided" when it is delivered or accepted. A taxpayer, however, is also permitted to treat property as provided when title to the property passes. The method used by the taxpayer to determine when property is provided is a method of accounting that must be used consistently from year to year and cannot be changed without IRS consent (Reg. § 1.461-4(d)(6)(iii); IRS Letter Ruling 201210004, November 22, 2011). The "3 ½ month rule," (Reg. § 1.461-4(d)(6)) which treats economic performance as occurring on the date of prepayment if provision of the property or services is expected within 3 ½ months of a pre-payment also applies for purposes of bonus depreciation if an accrual basis taxpayer has consistently used that rule as a method of accounting.

If a taxpayer enters into a contract for the construction of property, the contract should be deemed a contract for the provision of property if the party constructing the property retains the benefits and burdens of ownership (risk of loss) during the construction period as in the case of many "turnkey" projects. See, for example, IRS Letter Ruling 201210004, November 22, 2011. Consequently, assuming the "3 ½ month rule" does not apply, no costs would be deemed incurred with respect to such a property until the property has been delivered or accepted, or when title to the property passes, depending upon the taxpayer's method of accounting. See, also, IRS Letter Ruling 201214003, December 21, 2011, in which an accrual basis taxpayer contracted for construction of utility property. Taxpayer used a method of accounting that treated property as provided when accepted. The all events test was satisfied and economic performance occurred under a turnkey contract when turnover, as defined under the contract, occurred. Turnover occurred when commercial operation was reached which was also the date that the property was considered placed in service for depreciation purposes. At that time the liability was fixed, the amount of liability had been determined with reasonable accuracy, and the risk of loss passed to the taxpayer. Thus, for purposes of the safe harbor, no costs under the contract were considered incurred prior to turnover for purposes of the safe harbor. However, certain costs were incurred outside of the contract prior to turnover, including accrued interest capitalization costs, and these costs were taken into account in applying the safe-harbor.

Many construction contracts are not turnkey but rather "design-bid-build" method contracts. In the this case amounts can be incurred in stages and sometimes prior to progress payments. See Field Service Advice Memorandum 20140202F, January 16, 2014. This ruling illustrates the importance of keeping records that identify the acquisition dates of components of a larger property (e.g., building) that separately qualify for bonus depreciation. See also "*35. Property manufactured, constructed, or produced by or for taxpayer before September 28, 2017*" for a discussion of this ruling.

See "*35. Property manufactured, constructed, or produced by or for taxpayer before September 28, 2017*" for additional discussion of paid or incurred.

*28. Binding contract defined*

Property acquired pursuant to a written binding contract prior to September 28, 2017 does not qualify for 100 percent bonus depreciation (Act Sec. 13201(h)(1) of P.L. 115-97). However, property is not considered acquired pursuant to a binding contract if it is manufactured, constructed, or produced for the taxpayer by another person under a written binding contract entered into prior to manufacture, construction, or production. This property is considered self-constructed and acquired when construction begins (Reg. §1.168(k)-(2)(b)(5)(ii)(A)). See "*32. Acquisition and placed-in-service date requirements for 100 percent bonus rate property acquired after September 27, 2017 and before 2027.*"

Property acquired pursuant to contract that is not a written binding contract is acquired on the date a cash basis taxpayer pays or an accrual basis taxpayer incurs more than 10 percent of the cost of the property, excluding land and preliminary activities (Reg. §1.168(k)-(2)(b)(5)(v); Proposed Reg. §1.168(k)-2(b)(5)(v) in REG-104397-18).

For details, see "*32. Acquisition and placed-in-service date requirements for 100 percent bonus rate property acquired after September 27, 2017*"

*Acquisition date of property acquired under binding contract.* Assuming the acquisition date is determined by reference to a written binding contact, the final regulations provide that the acquisition date is the later of the date (Reg. §1.168(k)-2(b)(5)(ii)(B)):

- the contract is entered into;
- the contract is enforceable under State law;
- on which all penalty-free cancellation periods end; or
- all contingency clauses are satisfied.

A cancellation period is the number of days stated in the contract for any party to cancel the contract without penalty.

A contingency clause is one that provides for a condition (or conditions) or action (or actions) that is within the control of any party or a predecessor.

The proposed regulations simply provided that property is considered acquired on the date the contract was entered into if the contract states the date the contract was entered into and the closing date, delivery date, or other similar date (Proposed Reg. §1.168(k)-2(b)(5)(ii)(A) in REG-104397-18). The final regulations make no reference to closing date, delivery date or similar date (Reg. §1.168(k)-2(b)(5)(ii)(B)).

If property is received under a contract that is not binding, the acquisition date is the date that the taxpayer pays or incurs more than 10 percent of the cost (Proposed Reg. § 1.168(k)-2(b)(5)(v) in REG-104397-18). See "*32. Acquisition and placed-in-service date requirements for 100 percent bonus rate property acquired after September 27, 2017*".

*Binding contract defined.* The original final regulations provide fairly detailed guidance on the definition of a binding contract (Reg. § 1.168(k)-1(b)(4)(ii)). The proposed and final regulations, which apply to property acquired after September 27, 2017, use an identical definition, except that they clarify that a letter of intent is not a binding contract (Reg. § 1.168(k)-2(b)(5)(iii); Proposed Reg. § 1.168(k)-2(b)(5)(iii) in REG-104397-18).

A special rule applies in determining whether a contract to acquire a trade or business or an entity is binding (Reg. § 1.168(k)-2(b)(5)(iii)(G) issued in conjunction with the final regulations). See "*Acquisition of trade or business or an entity,*" below.

In general, a contract is binding if it is enforceable under state law against the taxpayer (e.g., the purchaser) or a predecessor and does not limit damages to a specified amount, for example, by use of a liquidated damages provision. A contract is not treated as limiting damages to a specified amount, however, if the contract limits damages to an amount that is at least equal to five percent of the total contract price. The final regulations provide that if a contract has multiple provisions that limit damages, only the provision with the highest damages is taken into account. A contract may be considered binding even if local law limits a seller's damages to the difference between the contract price of an asset and its fair market value and, as a result, there will be little or no damages (Reg. § 1.168(k)-1(b)(4)(ii)(A); Reg. § 1.168(k)-2(b)(5)(iii)(A); Proposed Reg. § 1.168(k)-2(b)(5)(iii)(A) in REG-104397-18).

The IRS has taken the position that a liquidated damages provision is tested on the day before any proscribed acquisition period begins (i.e., tested on December 31, 2007, for property placed in service before January 1, 2016) to determine if a written contract is binding. Thus, if a contract tested on that date is enforceable under state law and does limit damages to a specified amount that exceeds the 5-percent de minimis amount, the contract is a binding written contract in effect on December 31, 2007, and bonus depreciation may not be claimed on property subject to the contract if the property is placed in service before January 1, 2016 (CCA Letter Ruling 200629027, April 10, 2006). As explained above, in the case of property placed in service after December 31, 2015, a binding contract in effect before January 1, 2008, does not disqualify the property from bonus depreciation.

A contract may be binding even if it is subject to a condition, provided that the condition is not within the control of either of the parties or a predecessor. The fact that insubstantial terms remain to be negotiated does not prevent a contract that otherwise imposes significant obligations on a taxpayer from being considered binding. Binding contract status is not negated by the fact that the parties may make insubstantial changes to terms or conditions or that any term is to be determined by a standard beyond the control of either party (Reg. § 1.168(k)-1(b)(4)(ii)(B); Reg. § 1.168(k)-2(b)(5)(iii)(B); Proposed Reg. § 1.168(k)-2(b)(5)(iii)(B) in REG-104397-18).

An option to acquire or sell property is not a binding contract (Reg. § 1.168(k)-1(b)(4)(ii)(C); Reg. § 1.168(k)-2(b)(5)(iii)(C); Proposed Reg. § 1.168(k)-2(b)(5)(iii)(C) in REG-104397-18).

A letter of intent is not a binding contract (Reg. § 1.168(k)-2(b)(5)(iii)(D); Proposed Reg. § 1.168(k)-2(b)(5)(iii)(D) in REG-104397-18).

A 3.6 percent increase in the total costs of constructing a utility facility and the extension of turnover dates were insubstantial changes to the terms and conditions of a binding contract (IRS Letter Ruling 201214003, December 21, 2011).

A supply agreement is not a binding contract if the amount and design specifications of the property to be purchased have not been specified (Reg. § 1.168(k)-2(b)(5)(iii)(E); Reg. § 1.168(k)-2(b)(5)(viii)(A), Examples 1, 2, and 3; Proposed Reg. § 1.168(k)-2(b)(5)(iii)(E) in REG-104397-18; Reg. § 1.168(k)-1(b)(4)(ii)(D); Reg. § 1.168(k)-1(b)(4)(v), *Examples 1, 2, and 3*). Agreed pricing terms are not relevant in determining whether a supply agreement is a binding contract (Preamble to T.D. 9283, filed with the Federal Register on August 28, 2006).

A binding contract to acquire one or more components of a larger property is not considered a binding contract to acquire the larger property (Reg. § 1.168(k)-1(b)(4)(ii)(E); Reg. § 1.168(k)-2(b)(5)(iii)(F); Proposed Reg. § 1.168(k)-2(b)(5)(iii)(F) in REG-104397-18).

*Acquisition of trade or business or an entity.* A contract to acquire all or substantially all of the assets of a trade or business or a corporation, partnership, limited liability company or other entity is binding if it is enforceable under State law. A condition outside the control of the parties, including, for example, regulatory agency approval, the fact that insubstantial terms remain to be negotiated, or that unsatisfied customary conditions remain does not negate status as a binding contract. This rule also applies to a contract for the sale of corporate stock that is treated as an asset sale under Code Sec. 338 (Reg. § 1.168(k)-2(b)(5)(iii)(G); Proposed Reg. § 1.168(k)-2(b)(5)(iii)(G) in REG-104397-18). The final regulations additionally provide that the rule applies to a contract for the sale of stock of a corporation that is treated as an asset sale as a result of an election under Code Sec. 336(e) made for a disposition described in Reg. § 1.336-2(b)(1).

*Property acquired before 2016.* Subject to an exception for property manufactured, constructed, or produced for a taxpayer pursuant to a binding contract (see "*16. Acquisition and placed-in-service date requirements for property placed in service before 2016*", above), property placed in service before 2016 and acquired by a taxpayer pursuant to a binding contract in effect prior to January 1, 2008 does not meet the requirement that the property be acquired after 2007 and, therefore, does not qualify for bonus depreciation. Property acquired pursuant to a binding contract in effect after December 31, 2007 satisfies the requirement that property placed in service before 2016 must be acquired after 2007 (Code Sec. 168(k)(2)(A)(iii), prior to amendment by P.L. 114-113).

*Property acquired after September 8, 2010 and before 2012.* Code Sec. 168(k)(5), prior to being stricken as deadwood by P.L. 114-113, provides that a 100 percent bonus depreciation rate applies to property acquired after September 8, 2010 and which is placed in service before January 1, 2012 (before January 1, 2013 for property with a long production period and certain noncommercial aircraft). The Joint Committee on Taxation provides that the 100 percent rate may apply if a binding contract was in effect on or before September 8, 2010, as long as the contract was not in effect prior to January 1, 2008 (Joint Committee on Taxation, Technical Explanation of the Revenue Provisions Contained in the "Tax Relief, Unemployment Insurance Reauthorization, and Job Creation Act of 2010" (JCX-55-10), December 10, 2010). See *"36. Acquisition and placed-in-service date requirements for property placed in service before 2016,"* below for additional discussion.

*29. Binding contract rule as applied to 100-percent rate property acquired after September 27, 2017*

If a written binding contract (Reg. § 1.168(k)-2(b)(5)(iii); Proposed Reg. § 1.168(k)-2(b)(5)(iii) in REG-104397-18) for the acquisition of property is in effect prior to September 28, 2017, the property is considered acquired before September 28, 2017 and the property does not qualify for the 100 percent bonus rate (Act Sec. 13201(h) of the Tax Cuts and Jobs Act (P.L. 115-97) (Reg. § 1.168(k)-2(b)(5)(ii); Proposed Reg. § 1.168(k)-2(b)(5)(ii) in REG-104397-18). However, under the final regulations, if property is constructed for a taxpayer pursuant to a binding written contract entered into before construction begins, the property is considered self-constructed and acquired when construction begins (Reg. § 1.168(k)-2(b)(5)(iv)).

If property is acquired pursuant to a contract but the contract does not meet the definition of a written binding contract, under a proposed regulation issued in conjunction with the final regulations, the property is considered acquired when the taxpayer pays or incurs more than 10 percent of the cost of the property, excluding land and preliminary activities (Proposed Reg. § 1.168(k)-2(b)(5)(v) in REG-104397-18). The final regulations extend this rule to property constructed for a taxpayer pursuant to a non-binding written contract entered into before construction begins (Reg. § 1.168(k)-2(b)(5)(v)). This rule is similar to the safe harbor for determining when self-constructed property is acquired and only applies if the property would otherwise be considered acquired on the date that a written binding contract became effective.

For details, see "*32. Acquisition and placed-in-service date requirements for 100 percent bonus rate property acquired after September 27, 2017*"

*30. Original use requirement*

As noted below (see discussion #36), the original use of a property must commence with the taxpayer on or after January 1, 2007 in order to qualify for bonus depreciation if the property is placed in service before 2016. Original use essentially means that the property is new. For property placed in service after 2015 and acquired before September 28, 2017, it is only necessary that the original use commence with the taxpayer. The date of commencement of original use is no longer relevant (see discussion #34). For property acquired after September 27, 2017, original use must begin with the taxpayer or used property may also qualify for bonus depreciation (see discussion #13).

The original use requirement prevents used property acquired before September 28, 2017 from qualifying for bonus depreciation. Original use means the first use to which the property is put, whether or not that use corresponds to the use of the property by the taxpayer (Reg. § 1.168(k)-1(b)(3); Reg. § 1.168(k)-2(b)(3); Proposed Reg. § 1.168(k)-2(b)(3) in REG-104397-18). Original use begins when new property is first placed in service, whether for personal or business purposes (Preamble to T.D. 9283, filed with the Federal Register on August 28, 2006).

The Joint Committee on Taxation Explanation to P.L. 107-147 indicates that the factors used in determining whether property qualified as new section 38 property for purposes of the investment tax credit apply in determining whether the property is original use property. These factors are contained in Reg. § 1.48-2. The bonus depreciation regulations, however, contain no specific reference to the ITC regulations.

*Improvements to existing property.* Additional capital expenditures incurred by a taxpayer to recondition or rebuild property that is acquired or owned by the taxpayer satisfy the original use requirement.

*Reconditioned or rebuilt property.* The cost of reconditioned or rebuilt property does not satisfy the original use requirement. Property, whether acquired or self-constructed, which contains used parts is not treated as reconditioned or rebuilt if the cost of the used parts is not more than 20 percent of the total cost of the property (Reg. § 1.168(k)-1(b)(3)(i); Reg. § 1.168(k)-2(b)(3)(ii); Reg. § 1.168(k)-2(b)(3)(vii), *Example 18*; Proposed Reg. § 1.168(k)-2(b)(3)(ii) in REG-104397-18). The question of whether property is reconditioned or rebuilt property is a question of fact. The preceding 20-percent rule is a safe-harbor. See, also, Rev. Rul. 68-111; Rev. Rul. 94-32, and Notice 2008-60. This 80/20 rule is also used to determine an original use requirement for certain energy facilities for purposes of the Code Sec. 45 energy credit. See Notice 2016-31, as modified by Notice 2017-4.

***Example (1):*** ABC purchases a used airplane #1 and places it in service in YEAR 1. In YEAR 2 ABC contracts with DEF to renovate the plane. To renovate Airplane #1, the third party used mostly new parts but also used parts from Airplane #1. The cost of the used parts is not more than 20 percent of the total cost of the renovated airplane, Airplane #2. Although Airplane #2 contains used parts, the cost of the used parts is not more than 20 percent of the total cost of Airplane #2. As a result, Airplane #2 is not treated as reconditioned or rebuilt property, and W is considered the original user of Airplane #2. Therefore, the amount paid or incurred by W for Airplane #2 qualifies for the additional first year depreciation deduction. (Reg. § 1.168(k)-2(b)(3)(vii), *Example 18*).

***Example (2):*** Al Stevens, a taxpayer, purchases a used machine on September 1, 2017, for $50,000. Stevens then pays $20,000 to recondition the machine in 2017. No part of the $50,000 cost qualifies for bonus depreciation because it is attributable to used property acquired before September 28, 2017 and is more than 20 percent of the total $70,000 cost. However, the $20,000 expenditure (whether it is added to the basis of the machine or capitalized and treated as a separate asset) will qualify.

Since used property acquired after September 27, 2017 may qualify for bonus depreciation, if Stevens had purchased the used machine after September 27, 2017, the $50,000 would also qualify for bonus depreciation assuming the seller was an unrelated party and all other requirements were satisfied (Reg. § 1.168(k)-2(b)(3)(ii); Reg. § 1.168(k)-2(b)(3)(vii), Example 1; Proposed Reg. § 1.168(k)-2(b)(3)(ii); Proposed Reg. § 1.168(k)-2(b)(3)(vi), Example 1 in REG-104397-18).

*Property converted from personal to business use.* See "*24. Property converted from personal use to business use or from business use to personal use.*"

*Inventory.* A taxpayer who converts a new inventory item to business use is considered the original user of the inventory item. A taxpayer who purchases a new item of inventory from another person for use in a trade or business is considered the original user of the property. The original use of the property commences on the date the inventory item is used in the taxpayer's trade or business (Reg. § 1.168(k)-1(b)(3)(ii)(B); Reg. § 1.168(k)-2(b)(3)(ii)(B)(2); Proposed Reg. § 1.168(k)-2(b)(3)(ii)(B)(2) in REG-104397-18).

***Example (3):*** A tractor dealer buys new tractors on September 1, 2017, which are held as inventory. On October 15, 2017, he withdraws the tractors from inventory and begins using them in his trade or business of leasing tractors. The original use of the tractors commences on October 15, 2017 since the dealer did not have a depreciable interest in the inventory until their conversion to rental use. However, the tractors do not qualify for the 100 percent rate because they were acquired before September 28, 2017 (Reg. § 1.168(k)-2(b)(3)(vii), *Example 5*; Proposed Reg. § 1.168(k)-2(b)(3)(vi), *Example 5* in REG-104397-18).

*Demonstration assets.* Demonstration assets, such as a demonstrator vehicle held in inventory by an automobile dealer, may be considered as originally used by the purchaser (Reg. § 1.168(k)-1(b)(3)(v), *Example 2*; Reg. § 1.168(k)-2(b)(3)(vii), *Example 2*; Proposed Reg. § 1.168(k)-2(b)(3)(vi), *Example 2* in REG-104397-18). The original use requirement was not violated where a manufacturer's use of a plane for purposes other than demonstration was less than two percent of the estimated flight time over the aircraft's useful life, and the manufacturer continued to hold it for sale during times it loaned it out or used it as a demonstrator (IRS Letter Ruling 200502004 September 30, 2004).

*Sale-leasebacks and fractional interests.* Special original use and placed in service date rules apply to sale-leasebacks and sales of fractional interests. See discussion at #37 and #38 below.

*Horses.* A horse that is acquired for racing by one person and then acquired by the taxpayer before September 28, 2017 for breeding purposes does not qualify for bonus depreciation. The taxpayer is not considered the original user (Reg. § 1.168(k)-1(b)(3)(v), *Example 3*)). However, if the horse is acquired by a taxpayer after September 27, 2017 it may qualify as bonus depreciation as used property (Reg. § 1.168(k)-2(b)(3)(vii), *Example 3*; Proposed Reg. § 1.168(k)-2(b)(3)(vi), *Example 3* in REG-104397-18). See "*13. Used property acquired after September 27, 2017 qualifies for bonus depreciation.*"

*31. Placed-in-service date requirements*

In order to qualify for bonus depreciation, qualifying property acquired after September 27, 2017 must be placed in service before January 1, 2027 (before January 1, 2028 if the extended placed-in-service date for long production property (LPP) and certain noncommercial aircraft applies (NCA)) (Code Sec. 168(k)(2)(A), as amended by the Tax Cuts and Jobs Act (P.L. 115-97)). Property acquired before September 28, 2017 must be placed in service before January 1, 2020 (before January 1, 2021 for LPP and NCA) (Code Sec. 168(k)(2)(A), prior to amendment by P.L. 115-97).

For applicable bonus rates for LPP and NCA see discussion #2.

The placed-in-service date requirement is separate from the acquisition date requirement discussed above. The date of acquisition of a property is not necessarily the date it is placed in service. A property is considered placed in service for depreciation purposes when it is ready and available for use. See ¶ 3 for discussion of placed-in-service date.

The definition of LPP and NCA to which the extended placed in service dates apply are discussed at #39 and #41 below.

Property placed in service and disposed of in the same tax year generally does not qualify for bonus depreciation. If qualified property is placed in service and disposed of during the same tax year and then reacquired and again placed in service in any subsequent tax year, the bonus is not allowed in the subsequent tax year unless the requirements relating to used property are satisfied (Reg. § 1.168(k)-1(f)(1); Reg. § 1.168(k)-2(g)(1)(i); Proposed Reg. § 1.168(k)-2(f)(1)(i) in REG-104397-18). This is consistent with the rule which denies a depreciation deduction on property placed in service and disposed of in the same tax year (Reg. § 1.168(d)-1(b)(3)). However, property which is place-in-service, disposed of, and placed-in-service again in the same tax year is eligible for MACRS regular depreciation deductions. See Reg. § 1.168(d)-1(b)(3) which indicates such property is taken into account in determining whether the mid-quarter convention applies. See "*12. Qualified property.*"

Special rules, described at #37 and #38, apply for purposes of determining the original user of property in a sale-leaseback transaction or syndication transaction and when property involved in such transactions is considered placed in service.

*32. Acquisition and placed-in-service date requirements for 100 percent bonus rate property acquired after September 27, 2017*

Property acquired after September 27, 2017 (or acquired pursuant to a binding contract that is considered effective after September 27, 2017 (see below)) is subject to the bonus depreciation rules as amended by the Tax Cuts and Jobs Act of 2017 (P.L. 115-97). If a written binding contract for the acquisition of property is in effect prior to September 28, 2017, the property is considered acquired before September 28, 2017. Then the rules discussed below at "*34. Acquisition and placed-in-service date requirement for property acquired before September 28, 2017 and placed in service after 2015*" as in effect prior to the enactment of the 2017 Tax Cuts Act apply (Act Sec. 13201(h) of the Tax Cuts and Jobs Act (P.L. 115-97) providing effective date).

Property constructed, manufactured, or produced by a third-party pursuant to a written binding contract entered into before September 28, 2017 may qualify for the 100 percent rate (or applicable phase-out rate) if the construction, manufacture, or production begins after September 27, 2017. This property is not considered acquired pursuant to a written binding contract (Reg. § 1.168(k)-2(b)(5)(iv)(A)). Under proposed regulations, a pre-September 28, 2017 contract would have disqualified property constructed by a third-party from qualifying for the 100 percent rate (Proposed Reg. § 1.168(k)-2(b)(5)(iv)(A) in REG-104397-18).

The 100 percent bonus rate applies to property acquired after September 27, 2017 and placed in service before January 1, 2023 (before January 1, 2024 in the case of long production property (LPP) and certain noncommercial aircraft (NCA)). The 100 percent rate is reduced by 20 percent each year beginning in 2023 (2024 for LPP and NCA). The bonus depreciation rates for property acquired after September 27, 2017 are discussed at "*2. Bonus depreciation rates, including 100 percent rate for property acquired after September 27, 2017.*"

For property, other than long production property (LPP) and certain noncommercial aircraft (NCA), acquired and placed in service after September 27, 2017 (Code Sec. 168(k)(2)(A)(ii) and (iii), as amended by P.L. 115-97):

(1) The original use of the property must begin with the taxpayer or the property may be used if acquired by purchase as that term is defined for section 179 purposes; and

(2) The property must be placed in service before January 1, 2027.

In the case of LPP and NCA acquired after September 27, 2017 or acquired pursuant to a post-September 27, 2017 written binding contract (Code Sec. 168(k)(2)(B)(i) and Code Sec. 168(k)(2)(C)(i), as amended by P.L. 115-97):

(1) The original use of the property must begin with the taxpayer or the property may be used if acquired by purchase as that term is defined for section 179 purposes;

(2) The property must be acquired by the taxpayer before January 1, 2027 or acquired pursuant to a written binding contract entered into before January 1, 2027; and

(3) The property must be placed in service before January 1, 2028.

A retroactive technical correction clarifies that the written contract (item (2), above) must be binding (Code Sec. 168(k)(2)(B)(i)(III), as amended by the Tax Technical Corrections Act of 2018 (Division U of P.L. 115-141)).

Original use is discussed at "*30. Original use requirement*" and used property is discussed at "*13. Used property acquired after September 27, 2017 qualifies for bonus depreciation.*"

Bonus depreciation may not be claimed on 2027 progress expenditures of long production property acquired after September 27, 2017 and placed in service in 2027 (Code Sec. 168(k)(2)(B)(ii), as amended by P.L. 115-97; Reg. § 1.168(k)-2(e)(1)(iii); Proposed Reg. § 1.168(k)-2(d)(1)(iii) in REG-104397-18). This rule does not apply to 2027 progress expenditures of a non-commercial aircraft.

The definition of a binding written contract is discussed at "*28. Binding contract defined.*" (Reg. § 1.168(k)-2(b)(5)(iii); Proposed Reg. § 1.168(k)-2(b)(5)(iii) in REG-104397-18).

*Components acquired under binding contract.* A component of a larger property does not qualify for 100 percent bonus depreciation and the related phase-down rates if it is acquired pursuant to a written binding contract entered into before September 28, 2017. A binding contract to acquire one or more components is not considered a binding contract to acquire the larger property (Reg. § 1.168(k)-2(b)(iii)(F); Proposed Reg. § 1.168(k)-2(b)(5)(iii)(F) in REG-104397-18).

*Component defined.* The regulations do not define the term component. However, prior guidance relating to bonus depreciation states that the term is intended to refer to any part used in the manufacture, construction, or production of the larger self-constructed property, which may or may not be the same as the asset for depreciation purposes or the same as the unit of property for purposes of other code sections (Rev. Proc. 2011-26).

*Property constructed for a taxpayer.* The proposed regulations (prior to modification by the final regulations) provided that property that is constructed, manufactured, or produced for the taxpayer by another person under a written binding contract entered into prior to construction of the property for use by the taxpayer is acquired pursuant to a written binding contract. Therefore, if the contract was entered into before September 28, 2017, the property would not have qualified for the 100 percent rate and its related phase-out rates for property acquired after September 27, 2017 (i.e., the 50 percent rate and phaseout rates for pre-September 28, 2017 acquisitions apply) (Proposed Reg. § 1.168(k)-2(b)(5)(ii) in REG-104397-18).

The final regulations, however, provide that property constructed, manufactured, or produced for the taxpayer by another person under a written binding contract entered into prior to construction of the property for use by the taxpayer is treated as constructed by the taxpayer. Thus, the 100 percent or related phase-down rates for property acquired after September 27, 2017 may apply (Reg. § 1.168(k)-2(b)(5)(ii); Reg. § 1.168(k)-2(b)(5)(iv)(A)).

The acquisition date is determined by reference to the beginning of construction or the elective ten percent safe harbor. In applying the ten percent safe harbor, the taxpayer for whom the property is constructed must pay or incur more than ten percent of the total costs (Reg. § 1.168(k)-2(b)(5)(iv)(B)).

> ***Example (1):*** Lindberg Inc. enters into a written binding contract with Ryan Corp. to manufacture a noncommercial aircraft described in Code Sec. 168(k)(2)(C) on August 15, 2017. Manufacture begins on October 1, 2017 and the aircraft is placed in service on March 1, 2019. The aircraft qualifies for the 100 percent rate because it is considered manufactured by Lindberg and manufacturing began after September 27, 2017 (Reg. § 1.168(k)-2(b)(5)(viii)(F), Example 6).

Under the final regulations that apply to property acquired before September 28, 2017, property constructed under a contract entered into prior to the beginning of construction is also considered constructed by the taxpayer (Reg. § 1.168(k)-1(b)(4)(iii)(A)).

*Self-constructed property.* The acquisition date of property constructed, manufactured, or produced by the taxpayer for use in its trade or business is the date that the construction begins. If construction begins after September 27, 2017, the 100 percent rate may apply (Reg. § 1.168(k)-2(b)(5)(iv)(A); Reg. § 1.168(k)-2(b)(5)(viii)(D), *Examples 4 and 5*; Proposed Reg. § 1.168(k)-2(b)(5)(iv)(A) in REG-104397-18). The acquisition date of property constructed for a taxpayer under a written binding contract entered into prior to construction is not determined by reference to the date of the written binding contract. The property is considered constructed by the taxpayer and the acquisition date is determined by reference to the construction beginning date.

*Determining construction beginning date.* For purposes of determining whether self-constructed property is acquired after September 27, 2017, construction of a property begins on the date physical work of a significant nature begins, or under an optional safe harbor, when the taxpayer pays (if a on cash basis) or incurs (if on accrual basis) more than 10 percent of the total costs of the property (Reg. § 1.168(k)-2(b)(5)(iv)(B); Proposed Reg. § 1.168(k)-2(b)(5)(iv)(B) in REG-104397-18). If the taxpayer is treated as constructing the property because a written binding contract for the construction was entered into before construction began, the taxpayer must pay or incur more than 10 percent of the costs if the elective safe harbor is applied (Reg. § 1.168(k)-2(b)(5)(iv)(B)). The same physical work test and safe harbor also applied for purposes of determining the beginning of construction for property acquired before September 28, 2017 (Reg. § 1.168(k)-1(b)(4)(iii)(B)). See "*35. Property manufactured, constructed, or produced by or for taxpayer before September 28, 2017.*"

Physical work does not include preliminary *activities* such as planning or designing, financing, exploring, or researching. Preliminary *work*, such as clearing a site, test drilling to determine soil conditions, and changing the contour of the land also do not mark the beginning of construction. Physical work of a significant nature can commence at an off-site location. For example, if a retail motor fuels outlet is assembled by a taxpayer from modular units manufactured off-site by the taxpayer, manufacturing begins when physical work of a significant nature begins at the off-site location by the taxpayer.

In applying the 10 percent safe harbor, the cost of land and preliminary activities are not counted.

No special election to apply the safe harbor is required. The taxpayer simply files a return claiming bonus depreciation in the placed in service year that is consistent with using the 10 percent safe harbor.

*Components of self-constructed property acquired under a contract.* A component of a larger self-constructed property does not qualify for bonus depreciation at the 100 percent rate (or phase-out rates for property placed in service after 2022) if it is acquired pursuant to a binding written contract entered into before September 28, 2017 and the component is not considered self-constructed (Reg. § 1.168(k)-2(b)(5)(iv)(C)(1); Proposed Reg. § 1.168(k)-2(b)(5)(iv)(C)(1) in REG-104397-18). The larger self-constructed property, however, may still qualify for the 100 percent rate if construction of the larger property began after September 27, 2017.

> ***Example (2):*** ABC enters into a written binding contract to acquire a component of a larger property that ABC is self-constructing. The contact is entered into on June 1, 2017. The component does not qualify for bonus depreciation at the 100 percent or related phase-down rates regardless of when ABC begins self-constructing the larger property (Reg. § 1.168(k)-2(b)(5)(viii), Example 7; Proposed Reg. § 1.168(k)-2(b)(5)(vii), Example 7 in REG-104397-18).

Under a general rule if construction of the larger self-constructed property began before September 28, 2017, any components for that property that are acquired under a contract (or are self-constructed, see below) do not qualify for the 100 percent rate regardless of the date the components are considered acquired (Reg. § 1.168(k)-2(b)(5)(iv)(C). However, a taxpayer may elect to claim bonus depreciation at the 100 percent and related phase down rates on components acquired (or self-constructed) after September 27, 2017 by making the component election described at *33. Component election to claim 100 percent bonus for components of larger property for which construction begins before September 28, 2017* below (Reg. § 1.168(k)-2(c)).

*Self-constructed components of self-constructed property.* As in the case of acquired components, a general rule provides that self-constructed components (including components constructed for a taxpayer under a written binding contact) of a larger self-constructed property do not qualify for bonus depreciation at the 100 percent (or related phase down rates) if construction of the larger property begins before September 28, 2017 (i.e., the larger property is acquired before that date) (Reg. § 1.168(k)-2(b)(5)(iv)(C)(2)). However, a taxpayer may also make the component election describe at *33. Component election to claim 100 percent bonus for components of larger property for which construction begins before September 28, 2017* below to claim bonus depreciation on the components at the 100 percent or related phase-down rates) (Proposed Reg. § 1.168(k)-2(c) in REG-104397-18). See below.

*Special rules for long-production property and certain noncommercial aircraft.* The following rules apply to long production property (LPP) and noncommercial aircraft that is acquired after September 27, 2017 and placed in service before 2028 (Reg. § 1.168(k)-2(d); Proposed Reg. § 1.168(k)-2(c) in REG-104397-18).

Long production property is defined as property that (Code Sec. 168(k)(2)(B)):

(1) has a recovery period of at least 10 years or is transportation property;

(2) is subject to the uniform capitalization rules (Code Sec. 263A); and

(3) has a production period estimated to exceed one year and a cost exceeding $1 million.

See "*41. Noncommercial aircraft eligible for extended placed-in-service deadline*" for definition of LPP and NCA.

With the exception of LPP and NCA, property acquired after September 27, 2017 must be placed in service before 2027 in order to qualify for bonus depreciation. The placed-in-service deadline for LPP and NCA acquired after September 27, 2017, however, is extended one year. Therefore, LPP and NCA acquired after September 27, 2017 may qualify for bonus depreciation even if placed in service during 2027. In the case of LPP, progress expenditures attributable to 2027 (adjusted basis attributable to manufacture, construction, or production in 2027) do not qualify for bonus depreciation when the LPP is placed in service in 2027 (Code Sec. 168(k)(2)(B)(ii); Reg. § 1.168(k)(2)-(e)(1)(iii); Proposed Reg. § 1.168(k)-2(d)(1)(iii) in REG-104397-18). This progress expenditure rule does not apply to NCA placed in service in 2027. The definition of progress expenditures in Notice 2007-36 used for qualified opportunity zone property applies for this purpose (Reg. § 1.168(k)-2(e)(1)(iii); Proposed Reg. § 1.168(k)-2(e)(1)(iii) in REG-104397-18). See "*41. Noncommercial aircraft eligible for extended placed-in-service deadline*" for definition of progress expenditures.

The one-year extension of the placed-in-service deadline does not apply unless the LPP or NCA is acquired before 2027 or acquired pursuant to a written binding contract entered into before 2027 (Code Sec. 168(k)(2)(B)(i)(III);Code Sec. 168(l)(2)(C)). However, the LPP or NCA may not be acquired or acquired pursuant to written binding contract entered into before September 28, 2017. The rules for determining whether LPP or NCA is acquired before September 28, 2017 (discussed above) are separate from the rules for determining whether the LPP or NCA is acquired before January 1, 2027. Each acquisition date requirement must be separately satisfied (Reg. § 1.168(k)-2(d)(1); Proposed Reg. § 1.168(k)-2(c)(1) in REG-104397-18). If the LPP or NCA is acquired before September 28, 2017 then the rules in effect before enactment of the 100 percent rate apply.

LPP or NCA is considered acquired before January 1, 2027 if it is acquired pursuant to a written binding contract entered into before January 1, 2027 (Reg. § 1.168(k)-2(d)(1); Proposed Reg. § 1.168(k)-2(c)(1) in REG-104397-18). LPP or NCA which is constructed for a taxpayer under a written binding contract entered into prior to construction is considered constructed by the taxpayer. If the contract to construct the LLP or NCA was entered into before January 1, 2027, then it is considered acquired before January 1, 2027 (Reg. § 1.168(k)-2(d)(3)(i); Proposed Reg. § 1.168(k)-2(c)(3)(i) in REG-104397-18).

Property that is acquired pursuant to a contract that is not a written binding contract and property constructed for the taxpayer by a third party under a written nonbinding contract entered into before construction begins is acquired before January 1, 2027 if the taxpayer pays (cash basis) or incurs (accrual basis) more than 10 percent of the total cost of the property before January 1, 2027 excluding the cost of land and preliminary activities (Reg. § 1.168(k)-2(d)(3)(iv)).

> ***Example (3):*** QQ enters into a written binding contract with RR to manufacture a qualifying noncommercial aircraft on December 1, 2026. Manufacture begins on February 27, 2027 and the aircraft is placed in service on August 1, 2027. The aircraft qualifies for bonus depreciation because it was acquired pursuant to a pre-January 1, 2027 contract and was placed in service before January 1, 2028. The entire cost is eligible for bonus depreciation since 2027 progress expenditures are not excluded in the case of noncommercial aircraft (Reg. § 1.168(k)-2(d)(4), Example 3; Proposed Reg. § 1.168(k)-2(c)(3)(iv), Example 3 in REG-104397-18).

*Self-constructed LPP and NCA.* In the case of self-constructed LPP or NCA, property is considered acquired before January 1, 2027 if the taxpayer begins construction before January 1, 2027 (Reg. § 1.168(k)-2(d)(3)(i); Proposed Reg. § 1.168(k)-2(c)(3)(i) in REG-104397-18). Construction begins on the date on the date physical work of a significant nature begins, or under an optional safe harbor, when a cash basis taxpayer pays or an accrual basis taxpayer incurs more than 10 percent of the total costs of the property (Reg. § 1.168(k)-2(d)(3)(iii); Proposed Reg. § 1.168(k)-2(c)(3)(ii) in REG-104397-18). This rule is discussed in detail above. For purposes of determining whether the LPP or NCA is acquired before January 1, 2027 the 10 percent safe-harbor must be satisfied by the taxpayer even when the property is manufactured for the taxpayer by another person (Reg. § 1.168(k)-2(d)(3)(ii)(B); Proposed Reg. § 1.168(k)-2(c)(3)(ii)(B)). However, as noted above, if LPP or NCA is constructed by a third party pursuant to a binding written contract and the contract is entered into before construction begins, then the LPP or NCA is considered acquired before January 1, 2027 if the written binding contract was entered into before January 1, 2027 (Reg. § 1.168(k)-2(d)(3)(i); Proposed Reg. § 1.168(k)-2(c)(3)(i) in REG-104397-18).

*Acquired components of self-constructed LPP or NCA.* A component of self-constructed LPP or NCA does not qualify for bonus depreciation if the component was acquired pursuant to a binding written contract that was entered into after 2026 (Reg. § 1.168(k)-2(d)(3)(iii)(A); Proposed Reg. § 1.168(k)-2(c)(3)(iii)(A) in REG-104397-18). The larger self-constructed LPP or NCA, however, may still qualify for bonus depreciation even though some components were acquired under a post-2026 contract.

A component of a self-constructed LPP or NCA property that is acquired pursuant to a pre-January 1, 2027 binding written contract and placed in service in 2027 may qualify for bonus depreciation even if the larger self-constructed property is not considered acquired before January 1, 2027 thereby making the larger property ineligible for bonus depreciation.

*Self-constructed components of self-constructed LPP and NCA.* If a self-constructed component of self-constructed LPP or NCA does not qualify for the extended December 31, 2027 placed in service deadline because construction of the component did not begin before January 1, 2027 (i.e., the property is not considered acquired before that date), the larger self-constructed property may still qualify for bonus depreciation when placed in service in 2027 if construction began before 2027 (i.e., the larger property is considered acquired before 2027). If construction of the larger self-constructed LPP or NCA begins after 2026 (i.e., is considered acquired after 2026), the larger self-constructed does not qualify for bonus depreciation (Reg. § 1.168(k)-(2)(d)(3)(iii)(B); Proposed Reg. § 1.168(k)-2(c)(3)(iii)(B) in REG-104397-18).

If a taxpayer enters into a written binding contract with another person to manufacture LPP or NCA (or a component) before January 1, 2027 and construction begins after 2026, the LPP or NCA is considered acquired before January 1, 2027 (Reg. § 1.168(k)-2(d)(3)(i); Proposed Reg. § 1.168(k)-2(c)(3)(iii)(B) in REG-104397-18).

> ***Example (4):*** Turbo Corp. will self-construct long production property. One of the components must be manufactured by a third party. Turbo enters into a written binding contract on August 15, 2016 to acquire the component for $100,000. Manufacture of the component begins on November 1, 2016. The component is delivered on September 1, 2017 at which time the $100,000 cost is considered incurred. $100,000 represents 9% of the total cost of the LPP. Turbo began constructing the LPP property on October 15, 2017 and placed it in service, including the component part, on November 1, 2020. Turbo elects the 10% safe harbor for determining the acquisition date of the LPP. The cost of the LPP (excluding the cost of the component) qualifies for bonus depreciation at the 100 percent rate because under the safe harbor construction of the LPP began after September 27, 2017 and before January 1, 2027 (i.e., the LPP was acquired after September 27, 2017 and before January 1, 2027) and the LPP was placed in service before January 1, 2028. The component does not qualify for the 100 percent rate because it is considered self-constructed and manufacturing began before September 28, 2017 (i.e., the component was acquired before September 28, 2017) (Reg. § 1.168(k)-2(d)(4), Example 1).

The IRS example indicates that the cost of the $100,000 component was 9 percent of the total cost of the LPP. Consequently, under the 10 percent safe harbor, acquisition of the component on September 1, 2017 (the date the 9% of cost was incurred) does not mark the beginning of construction of the LPP.

***Example (5):*** Metro Corp. will self-construct long production property. One of the components must be manufactured by a third party. Turbo enters into a written binding contract on August 15, 2026 to acquire the component for $100,000. Manufacture of the component began on September 1, 2026 and the completed component was delivered on February 1, 2027 at which time Metro incurred the $100,000 cost. Metro began constructing the LPP on January 15, 2027 and placed the LPP, including the component, into service on November 1, 2027

The component qualifies for bonus depreciation because its construction began before 2027 and the LPP of which the component is a part was placed in service before 2028. The component is considered constructed by the taxpayer since the binding contract for its construction was entered into before construction began.

However, the self-constructed LPP (other than the component) does not qualify for bonus depreciation because construction of the LPP began after 2026. Because construction of the LPP began after 2026, the LPP (other than the component) is not considered acquired before January 1, 2027.

The IRS example indicates that the cost of the $100,000 component was 9 percent of the total cost of the LPP and that the cost was incurred in 2027. Consequently, METRO cannot elect the safe harbor to establish that construction of the LLP began before 2027 even if the cost had exceeded 10 percent of the cost of the LPP.

The component qualifies for bonus depreciation because manufacturing of the component began before January 1, 2027 and the component was placed in service in 2027 (Reg. § 1.168(k)-2(d)(4), Example 2; Proposed Reg. § 1.168(k)-2(c)(3)(iv), Example 2 in REG-104397-18).

*Acquisition date of off-the-shelf purchases without a contract.* See "*27. Acquisition defined*" for acquisition date of off-the-shelf purchases.

*Acquisition date if contract is not binding contract.* If property is acquired pursuant to a contract but the contract does not meet the definition of a written binding contract, the property is considered acquired when the taxpayer pays or incurs more than 10 percent of the cost of the property, excluding land and preliminary activities. The final regulations clarify that this rule also applies if the property is constructed for a taxpayer pursuant to a non-binding written contract entered into before construction begins. This rule is similar to the safe harbor for determining when self-constructed property is acquired and only applies if the property would otherwise be considered acquired on the date that a written binding contract became effective (Reg. § 1.168(k)-2(b)(5)(v); Proposed Reg. § 1.168(k)-2(b)(5)(v) in REG-104397-18).

This rule does not apply to a qualified film, television, or live theatrical production, or a specified plant.

This rule does not apply to a contract to acquire all or substantially all of the assets of a trade or business or to acquire an entity (for example, a corporation, a partnership, or a limited liability company).

### *33. Component election to claim 100 percent bonus for components of larger property for which construction begins before September 28, 2017*

A general rule provides that components of a larger property for which construction begins before September 28, 2017 do not qualify for the 100 percent bonus rate (or the phase down rates that apply after 2022) (Reg. § 1.168(k)-(2)(b)(5)(iv)(C)). However, final regulations allow a taxpayer to make an election (the "component election") to claim 100 percent bonus depreciation (or the related phase down rates) on some or all components of a larger constructed property that are acquired or constructed after September 27, 2017 if the taxpayer began construction of the larger property before September 28, 2017. Property constructed for a taxpayer pursuant to a written binding or written non-binding contract entered into before construction on the larger property begins is considered constructed by the taxpayer (Reg. § 1.168(k)-(2)(c)(2)(i)).

The larger self-constructed property must meet the following three requirements:

(1) The larger property must be:

(i) MACRS property with a recovery period of 20 years or less (including qualified improvement property placed in service after 2017);

(ii) 15-year qualified leasehold improvement property placed in service after September 27, 2017 and before 2018, 15-year retail improvement property placed in service after September 27, 2017 and before 2018, or 15-year restaurant property placed in service after September 27, 2017 and before 2018 that is qualified improvement property;

(iii) computer software depreciated over 5 years under Code Sec. 167(f)(1);

(iv) MACRS water utility property; or

(v) or qualified improvement property placed in service after September 27, 2017 and before 2018

(2) The property described in item (1) must qualify for bonus depreciation by satisfying the requirements for qualified property under Reg. § 1.168(k)-2(b), determined without regard to the post-September 27, 2017 acquisition date requirement in Reg. § 1.168(k)-2(b)(5); and

(3) The taxpayer must begin construction, manufacture, or production of the larger property before September 28, 2017.

The larger property may not be included in a class of property for which the taxpayer elected out of bonus depreciation (Reg. § 1.168(k)-(2)(c)(2)(iv)).

The component election can apply to components of a larger property that is acquired before September 28, 2017 and placed in service before 2027 (2028 in the case of longer production property) even though the larger property is not eligible for bonus depreciation because it is place in service after 2019 (2020 in the case of longer production property). See Code Sec. 168(k)(8) for bonus phase down rates for property acquired before September 28, 2017 and placed in service before 2020 (before 2021 in the case of longer production property).

*When does construction begin?* If the taxpayer constructs the larger property itself or a third party constructs the larger property pursuant to a written binding contract entered into prior to construction, the construction beginning date is the date on which physical work of a significant nature begins or, if the safe harbor is elected, the date the taxpayer pays (a cash basis taxpayer) or incurs (an accrual basis taxpayer) more than ten percent of the total cost of the larger property, excluding land and preliminary activities. These construction beginning date rules are described in Reg. § 1.168(k)-2(b)(5)(iv)(B). The component election does not apply if a written binding contract was entered into before September 28, 2017 and construction began after September 27, 2017 (Reg. § 1.168(k)-(2)(c)(2)(iii)).

If the property is constructed for a taxpayer pursuant to a written contract that is not binding and the contract is entered into before construction begins, the construction beginning date is the date he taxpayer pays (a cash basis taxpayer) or incurs (an accrual basis taxpayer) more than ten percent of the total cost of the larger property, excluding land and preliminary activities. This construction beginning date rule is described in Reg. § 1.168(k)-2(b)(5)(v). The component election does not apply if the written non-binding contract was entered into before September 28, 2017 and construction began after September 27, 2017 (Reg. § 1.168(k)-(2)(c)(2)(iii)).

*Components eligible for election.* An eligible component must qualify for bonus depreciation (i.e., meet the requirements in Code Sec. 168(k)(2) and Reg. § 1.168(k)(2)-(b). An acquired component must be acquired after September 27, 2017. Construction of self-constructed components (including components constructed for the taxpayer) must begin after September 27, 2017 (Reg. § 1.168(k)-2(c)(3)(i))).

The acquisition date of a component acquired pursuant to a written binding contract is determined pursuant to the rules described in Reg. § 1.168(k)-2(b)(5)(ii)(B). Generally, this is the date that the contract is signed and enforceable under state law.

If the component is acquired pursuant to a non-binding written contract, the acquisition date is the date that the taxpayer pays or incurs more than ten percent of the total cost of the component, excluding preliminary activities (Reg. § 1.168(k)-2(b)(5)(v)).

If the component is constructed by the taxpayer or constructed by a third party pursuant to a written binding contract entered into prior to the construction, the acquisition date is the date on which physical work of a significant nature begins or, if the safe harbor is elected, the date the taxpayer pays (a cash basis taxpayer) or incurs (an accrual basis taxpayer) more than ten percent of the total cost of the larger property, excluding land and preliminary activities. These construction beginning date rules are described in Reg. § 1.168(k)-2(b)(5)(iv)(B).

If the component is constructed by a third party pursuant to a nonbinding written contract entered into prior to construction the acquisition date is the date that the taxpayer pays or incurs more than ten percent of the total cost of the component, excluding preliminary activities (Reg. § 1.168(k)-2(b)(5)(v)).

*What is the larger self-constructed property?* All property that is constructed, manufactured, or produced as part of a residential rental property, nonresidential real property, or an improvement to such property and which is eligible for bonus depreciation is the larger self-constructed property for purposes of the component election (Reg. § 1.168(k)-2(c)(ii)). For example, the section 1245 components of a building eligible for bonus depreciation under the cost segregation rules are the larger self-constructed property. This means that the 10 percent safe harbor for determining the beginning of construction of the larger property (i.e., the acquisition date) is determined by reference to the total cost of the section 1245 components without regard to the cost of the remaining section 1250 building components (Reg. § 1.168(k)-2(c)(8)(iii), Example 4).

*Computation of bonus on qualifying components.* The bonus deduction on the components eligible for the election is determined by multiplying the basis of those components by the applicable bonus percentage for the placed-in-service year of the larger self-constructed property as described in Code Sec. 168(k)(6). The bonus deduction on the remaining basis of the larger property is equal to the applicable percentage for the placed-in-service year of the larger property that would apply using the rules in effect prior to enactment of the Tax Cuts Act as described in Code Sec. 168(k)(8) (Reg. § 1.168(k)-2(c)(5)).

The cost of installing a component (including labor costs) of larger self-constructed property is eligible for bonus depreciation if the component is eligible for component election (Reg. § 1.168(k)-2(c)(4)).

*Election not made*. If the component election for a larger constructed property that is considered acquired before September 28, 2017 is not made then the bonus deduction for the larger property and its components is computed under the rules that applied prior to the Tax Cuts Act, i.e., the rules that apply to property acquired before September 28, 2017 (Reg. § 1.168(k)-2(c)(5)(ii)). Thus a 40 percent rate applies if the larger property and its components are placed in service in 2018 and a 30 percent rate applies if placed in service in 2019. If the larger property is long production property, a 50 percent rate applies for 2018, 40 percent for 2019, and 20 percent for 2020 (Code Sec. 168(k)(8)).

*How to make the component election*. The component election must be made by the due date, including extensions, of the return for the year in which the larger constructed property is placed in service. A statement is attached to the return indicating that the election is being made and whether the election is made for some or all of the qualifying components. The election is made separately by each person owning qualified property. For example, the election is made by the partnership including a lower-tier partnership), S corporation, and for each member of a consolidated group, the group's agent (Reg. § 1.168(k)-2(c)(6)).

In general, the revocation is revocable only with IRS consent through a letter ruling. However, a taxpayer may file an amended return within six months of the original due date of election return, excluding extensions, to make a revocation (Reg. § 1.168(k)-2(c)(6)).

***Example (1):*** C constructs a locomotive for B pursuant to written binding contract entered into in August 2017. B incurred $500,000 for the cost of components acquired or constructed by C before September 28, 2017. In February 2019 B placed the locomotive in service. Additional costs incurred after September 27, 2017 amounted to $4,000,000. If B elects the 10 percent safe harbor for determining the construction beginning date the locomotive is considered acquired before September 28, 2017 because more than 10 percent of the total costs were incurred by B before September 28, 2017 and B may make the component election. Assume the locomotive is long production property. Under the election, the $4,000,000 cost of the components acquired and placed in service after September 27, 2017 qualify for bonus depreciation at a 100 percent rate. The remaining $500,000 incurred before September 28, 2017 qualifies for bonus depreciation at a 40 percent rate. This is the rate specified by Code Sec. 168(k)(8) for long production property acquired before September 28, 2017 and placed in service in 2019. (Reg. § 1.168(k)-2(c)(8)(iii), Example 2).

***Example (2):*** Cruise Line enters written binding contract with Builder in February 2016 for the construction of a vessel which qualifies as long production property. Cruise Line incurs $30 million component costs before September 28, 2017. After September 27, 2017 and before 2021 Cruise Line incurs an additional $15 million in costs. In February 2021, Builder delivers the vessel and Cruise Line places it in service. Assuming the safe harbor applies, construction of the vessel began before September 28, 2017 because Cruise Line incurred more than 10 percent of the total cost of the vessel before September 28, 2017. Cruise Line may make the component election and claim 100 percent bonus depreciation on the $15 million in post-September 28, 2017 costs. However, because the vessel was acquired before September 28, 2017 and placed in service after 2020 no portion of any costs paid or incurred before September 28, 2017 is eligible for bonus depreciation. (Reg. § 1.168(k)-2(c)(8)(iii), Example 3).

***Example (3):*** Retailer, an accrual basis taxpayer, enters into a nonbinding written contract with Builder for the construction of a retail store in March 2017. Prior to September 28, 2017, Retailer incurred $500,000 of costs for section 1245 property building components and $3,000,000 for section 1250 components. Costs incurred after September 27, 2017 are $2,500,000 for section 1245 property and $4,000,000 for section 1250 property. Total cost of the building was $10,000,000 consisting of $3,000,000 of section 1245 property and $7,000,000 of section 1250 property. The building was placed in service in September 2019.

Since the building is not eligible for bonus depreciation, the larger self-constructed property for purposes of bonus depreciation consists of all of the section 1245 property. Because the contract is nonbinding, construction begins when the taxpayer incurred more than 10 percent of the total costs (see Reg. § 1.168(k)-2(b)(5)(v)). Therefore, construction of the larger section 1245 property began before September 28, 2017 and the component election may be made. Retailer may claim the 100 percent bonus rate on $2,500,000 of the costs for section 1245 property incurred after September 27, 2017. The 30 percent rate allowed by Reg. § 168(k)(8) for long production property placed in service in 2019 applies to the remaining $500,000 of section 1245 property that was acquired before September 28, 2017. (Reg. § 1.168(k)-2(c)(8)(iii), Example 4).

*34. Acquisition and placed-in-service date requirements for property acquired before September 28, 2017 and placed in service after 2015*

Property acquired before September 28, 2017 is subject to the bonus depreciation rules as in effect prior to amendment by the Tax Cuts and Jobs Act of 2017 (P.L. 115-97). If a written binding contract for the acquisition of property is in effect prior to September 28, 2017, the property is considered acquired before September 28, 2017 and the rules discussed in this paragraph apply (Act Sec. 13201(h) of the Tax Cuts and Jobs Act (P.L. 115-97) providing effective date). However, an exception applies if the property was constructed for a taxpayer under a pre-September 28, 2017 contract. See discussion #32. Property acquired before September 28, 2017 is not eligible for the 100-percent bonus rate provided by the 2017 Tax Cuts Act, and is subject to a 40-percent rate if placed in service in 2018 (2019 in the case of long production property (LPP) and noncommercial aircraft (NCA)) and a 30-percent rate if placed in service in 2019 (2020 in the case of LPP and NCA). The 50-percent rate applies if the property is placed in service in 2017 (2017 or 2018 in the case of LPP and NCA). See "*2. Bonus depreciation rates, including 100 percent rate for property acquired after September 27, 2017.*"

For property, other than long production property (LPP) and certain noncommercial aircraft (NCA), acquired before September 28, 2017 (or acquired subject to a pre-September 28, 2017 written binding contract) and placed in service after 2015, the requirements for property placed in service before 2016 (item #36 below) are simplified as follows (Code Sec. 168(k)(2)(A)(iv), as amended by the Protecting Americans from Tax Hikes (PATH) Act of 2015 (P.L. 114-113) and prior to amendment by P.L. 115-97):

(1) The original use of the property must begin with the taxpayer; and

(2) The property must be placed in service before January 1, 2020.

The PATH Act eliminates as deadwood the rules preventing property acquired before 2008 or subject to a pre-2008 contract from qualifying for bonus depreciation.

In the case of LPP and NCA acquired before September 28, 2017 (or acquired subject to a pre-September 28, 2017 written binding contract) and placed in service after 2015 (Code Sec. 168(k)(2)(B)(i) and Code Sec. 168(k)(2)(C)(i), as amended by P.L. 114-113 and prior to amendment by P.L. 115-97):

(1) The original use of the property must begin with the taxpayer; and

(2) The property must be placed in service before 2021.

As explained above, however, if the LPP or NCA is acquired after September 27, 2017, the preceding pre-2017 Tax Cut Act (P.L. 115-97) rules do not apply and the rules described at "*32. Acquisition and placed-in-service date requirements for 100 percent bonus rate property acquired after September 27, 2017*" apply instead.

Bonus depreciation may not be claimed on 2020 progress expenditures of long production property acquired before September 28, 2017 and placed in service in

2020 (Code Sec. 168(k)(2)(B)(ii), as amended by P.L. 114-113 and prior to amendment by P.L. 115-97). This rule does not apply to 2020 progress expenditures of a non-commercial aircraft.

*35. Property manufactured, constructed, or produced by or for taxpayer before September 28, 2017*

The rules for property manufactured, constructed, or produced by or for a taxpayer after September 27, 2017 to which the 100 percent bonus rate may apply are discussed at "*32. Acquisition and placed-in-service date requirements for 100 percent bonus rate for property acquired after September 27, 2017.*"

Generally, self-constructed property is considered acquired when manufacture, construction, or production "begins" as determined using the rules below (Reg. § 1.168(k)-1(b)(4)(iii)). In the case of property placed in service before 2016, bonus depreciation does not apply if manufacture, construction, or production began before 2008 (i.e., the property was acquired before 2008) (Code Sec. 168(k)(2)(A), as amended by Act Sec. 143(a) of the Protecting Americans from Tax Hikes (PATH) Act of 2015 (Division Q of P.L. 114-113) (December 18, 2015)). This rule preventing a taxpayer from claiming bonus depreciation on property acquired before 2008 does not apply to property placed in service after 2015 (Code Sec. 168(k)(2)(A), as amended by Act Sec. 143(b) of P.L. 114-113). Due to the passage of time, the prohibition is now deemed unnecessary.

Bonus depreciation applies to property placed in service before 2016 even if constructed for a taxpayer pursuant to contract entered into prior to January 1, 2008 so as long as construction begins after 2007. See, for example, IRS Letter Ruling 201214003, December 21, 2011. See, also , discussion #36, "*Acquisition and placed-in-service date requirements for property placed in service before 2016.*"

Property acquired before September 28, 2017 is not eligible for the 100 percent bonus depreciation rate. Property subject to a pre-September 28, 2017 binding written contract is considered acquired before September 28, 2017 (Act Sec. 13201(h)(1) of P.L. 115-97) and does not qualify for the 100 percent rate. See discussion "*2. Bonus depreciation rates, including 100 percent rate for property acquired after September 27, 2017.*"

Long production property and non-commercial aircraft acquired after September 27, 2017 are entitled to an extended December 31, 2027 placed-in-service deadline. The regular placed-in-service deadline is December 31, 2026. However, in order for the extended deadline to apply the long production property or non-commercial aircraft must be acquired before January 1, 2027 or acquired pursuant to a binding contract entered into before January 1, 2027. See discussion #39. In the case of self-constructed long production property, this acquisition requirement is satisfied if the taxpayer begins manufacture, construction, or production before January 1, 2027 (Code Sec. 168(k)(2)(E)(i), as amended by P.L. 114-113).

In the case of long production property and non-commercial aircraft acquired before September 28, 2017, the extended placed-in-service deadline is December 31, 2020. The regular placed-in-service deadline is December 31, 2019. However, in order for the extended deadline to apply the long production property or non-commercial aircraft must be acquired before January 1, 2020 or acquired pursuant to a binding contract entered into before January 1, 2020. See discussion #39. In the case of self-constructed long production property, this acquisition requirement is satisfied if the taxpayer begins manufacture, construction, or production before January 1, 2020 (Code Sec. 168(k)(2)(E)(i), prior to amendment by P.L. 114-113).

***Example (1):*** A utility begins construction of an electric generation power plant on December 31, 2007, and completed construction on May 1, 2012. No portion of the costs qualify for bonus depreciation because construction began before January 1, 2008 and the property was placed in service before 2016 (Reg. § 1.168(k)-1(b)(4)(v), *Example 4*). If the property was placed in service after 2015, it would not matter that construction began (i.e., the property was acquired) before 2008. The entire cost of the plant will qualify for bonus depreciation. However, if the plant qualified for the extended December 31, 2020 placed in service deadline for long production property and was placed in service in 2020, 2020 progress expenditures would not qualify for bonus depreciation. See discussion #40 for discussion of progress expenditures rule.

Property that is manufactured, constructed, or produced for a taxpayer by another person under a written binding contract that is entered into prior to the manufacture, construction, or production of the property is considered manufactured, constructed, or produced by the taxpayer (Reg. § 1.168(k)-1(b)(4)(iii)(A), second sentence). See, also, discussion #36, *"Acquisition and placed-in-service date requirements for property placed in service before 2016."*

Bonus depreciation is claimed on each depreciable "asset" which in some cases is smaller than a "unit-of-property." Therefore, each depreciable asset must separately meet the acquisition and placed-in-service date requirements. For example, each replacement component of a machine is treated as a separately depreciable asset and needs to separately satisfy the acquisition and placed-in-service date requirements. For the definition of an asset, see Reg. § 1.168(i)(8)(c)(4) discussed at ¶ 162.

*Physical work of a significant nature and 10 percent safe harbor.* Manufacture, production, or construction of self-constructed property begins when physical work of a significant nature begins. This is a facts and circumstances test. Physical work does not include preliminary activities such as planning or designing, securing financing, exploring, or researching (Reg. § 1.168(k)-1(b)(4)(iii)(A)). Under a safe harbor, physical work of a significant nature begins when a cash basis taxpayer pays or an accrual basis taxpayer incurs more than 10 percent of the total cost of the property (excluding the cost of any land and preliminary activities). In applying this safe harbor, when another party manufactures, constructs, or produces property for the taxpayer pursuant to a contract entered into before the other party begins manufacturing, constructing, or production, the safe harbor test must be met by the taxpayer (i.e., the taxpayer must pay (cash basis) or incur (accrual basis) more than 10 percent of the total cost of the property before manufacturing, etc., is considered to begin). Thus, for an accrual basis taxpayer the acquisition date of the constructed property for bonus depreciation purposes is generally the date of acceptance under a turnkey contract as discussed below. The regulations provide that a taxpayer chooses the safe harbor by filing an income tax return for the placed-in-service year of the property that determines when physical work of a significant nature begins consistent with the safe harbor (Reg. § 1.168(k)-1(b)(4)(iii)(B)). Note that the non-safe harbor test makes no reference to a "paid or incurred" requirement.

*Preliminary activities excluded.* The bonus depreciation regulations only list planning or designing, securing financing, exploring, and researching as among possible examples of preliminary activities. Notice 2013-29, as modified and clarified by Notice 2013-60, Notice 2014-46, Notice 2015-25, Notice 2016-31, and Notice 2017-4, which deals with rules for determining whether construction begins on an energy facility before a particular required construction start date so as to qualify for the Code Sec. 45 renewable energy production credit, also provides that construction begins when physical work of a significant nature begins, excluding preliminary activities. An expanded list of preliminary activities, tailored for energy facilities is provided. In addition to planning and designing, securing financing, exploring, and researching, Notice 2013-29, as modified by Notice 2016-31 lists conducting geologic mapping and modeling, obtaining permits and licenses, conducting geophysical, gravity, magnetic, seismic and resistivity surveys, conducting environmental and engineering surveys, clearing a site, test drilling to determine soil condition, excavation to change the contour of the land, and removal of existing turbines, towers, solar panels, or components that will no longer be part of a facility as preliminary activities. These additional items should likewise be considered preliminary activities for purposes of bonus depreciation.

*Inventory rule for energy production credit.* Notice 2013-29, as clarified by Notice 2013-60 also provides an inventory rule, for which there is no specific counterpart in the bonus depreciation regulations, to prevent a taxpayer from entering into a construction contract to trigger a construction start date if the constructed parts could have been obtained from existing inventory through an acquisition contract. The inventory rule for the Code Sec. 45 credit states: "Physical work of a significant nature does not include work (performed either by the taxpayer or by another person under a written binding contract) to produce property that is either in existing inventory or is normally held in inventory by a vendor" (Section 4.02(2) of Notice 2013-29). Thus, the Code Sec. 45 credit rules (which do not specifically apply to bonus depreciation) appear to prevent a taxpayer from treating construction of a component part as physical work if the part could "normally" have been purchased from the inventory of a vendor other than the contracted party.

*Multiple facilities treated as single facility for purposes of energy production credit.* An additional rule which is unique to the Code Sec. 45 credit, allows a taxpayer to treat multiple qualified energy facilities (e.g., multiple wind turbines) that are part of a single project (e.g., windmill farm owned by the same entity) as a single facility. For example, this rule allows a taxpayer who begins construction on a few windmills on a windmill farm to treat construction of all windmills on the farm as beginning before the applicable construction start deadline (Section 4.04 of Notice 2013-29, as modified by Notice 2015-25 and Notice 2016-31) (i.e., the initial construction would be considered physical work of a significant nature with respect to all the windmills). Assuming each windmill is considered a separate depreciable asset for bonus depreciation purposes, this rule should have no application for purposes of qualifying for bonus depreciation.

*Continuous program of construction requirement for energy production credit.* Finally, the Code Sec. 45 credit rules require a taxpayer who initially satisfies the physical work test (or an alternative 5% pay or incur safe harbor test) to maintain a continuous program of construction, subject to exceptions for delaying events that are outside of a taxpayer's control (Section 4.06 and Section 5.02 of Notice 2013-29, as modified by Section 4.02 of Notice 2016-31). Again, there is no such requirement in the bonus depreciation regulations. The requirement is not necessary for bonus depreciation because there is a placed-in-service deadline for bonus depreciation, whereas a qualified facility may qualify for the energy production credit regardless of the date it is placed in service so long as construction begins before the applicable construction start date. A taxpayer that places a facility in service in a calendar year that is no more than four calendar years after the calendar year during which construction of the facility began is generally deemed to have satisfied the continuity requirement.

*Off-site construction of components.* The regulations provide little guidance on the extent to which off-site construction is taken into account in applying the physical work of a significant nature standards with respect to an asset that is being constructed on-site. An example is given which provides that if a retail motor fuels outlet (MACRS 15-year property) or other facility is constructed on-site, construction begins when physical work of a significant nature starts on site. However, if the retail motor fuel outlet or other facility is assembled on-site from "modular units" manufactured off-site, manufacturing begins when physical work of a significant nature begins at the off-site location.

*Meaning of "incurred" for purposes of safe harbor.* The term "incurred" is not specifically defined for purposes of bonus depreciation, including the 10 percent safe harbor, but the IRS has indicated it will apply the term in accord with Code Sec. 461 and the regulations thereunder (IRS Letter Ruling 201210004, November 22, 2011; IRS Letter Ruling 201214003, December 21, 2011). Thus, an accrual basis taxpayer determines when the costs of a project have been incurred by applying the all events test and the economic performance requirement of Code Sec. 461(h). Costs associated with the provision of services are incurred when all the events have occurred that establish the fact of liability and the amount of the liability can be determined with reasonable accuracy (the "all events" test), and the services are rendered to the taxpayer (the "economic performance" test). Costs associated with the provision of property are incurred when all the events have occurred that establish the fact of liability and the amount of the liability can be determined with reasonable accuracy (the "all events" test), and the property is provided to taxpayer (i.e., when the property is delivered, when it is accepted, or when title to the property passes, depending upon taxpayer's method of accounting for determining when property is provided) (the "economic performance" test). In the two rulings above, which dealt with the construction of expensive utility projects pursuant to a turnkey contract with a third party, the IRS applied the ten percent rule by treating the entire transaction as if it were a provision of property. No amount was accrued *under the contract* until the property was accepted. However, in IRS Letter Ruling 201214003, certain costs were incurred outside of the contract prior to turnover, including accrued interest capitalization costs (interest capitalized under the uniform capitalization rules), and these costs were taken into account in applying the safe-harbor. The accrued interest which was capitalized into the cost of the property resulted in more than 10 percent of the total cost of one unit of property to have been incurred prior to September 9, 2010 but not before January 1, 2007. Accordingly, this unit of property was considered acquired under the safe harbor after January 1, 2007 and before September 9, 2010 and if the safe harbor was elected would not qualify for bonus depreciation at the 100 percent rate. The ruling does not consider whether the property could qualify for the 100 percent rate if the general rule was applied (i.e., whether physical work of a significant nature began prior to September 9, 2010).

Most construction contracts for buildings are not turnkey contracts. Generally, in a turnkey contract, the turnkey contractor acts as the developer, designer, and contractor and agrees to design and construct a completed project for the owner. In construction involving a turnkey contract an accrual basis taxpayer applying the safe harbor treats acquisition as occurring upon economic performance when the contractor completes *all* work for acceptance or delivers legal title to the *entire* project. Thus, the acquisition date is delayed for the longest possible period. This delay could be critical for purposes of avoiding the rule which prohibited property from qualifying for bonus depreciation if acquired before 2008. See Field Attorney Advice 20140202F, January 1, 2014. This rule preventing property acquired before 2008 from qualifying for bonus depreciation, however, does not apply to property placed in service after 2015.

According to Field Attorney Advice 20140202F the most common form of construction project delivery method for a building construction project is the design-bid-build method (DBB method). In the design phase the owner engages an architect. When the construction design documents are complete, the owner then opens bidding and selects a contractor. This is the bid-phase. In the build or construction phase, the owner contracts with a general contractor to build the project. The contractor's role is limited solely to construction. There is no contractual relationship between the contractor and architect. The owner, through a representative, is usually responsible for administering the construction contract, reviewing work, approving pay applications, making decisions that affect construction, and approving and rejecting sub-contractors.

In a DDB method contract, an accrual basis taxpayer generally accrues construction costs over a period of time when work is accepted or title is received by making a progress payment that is requested in a pay application. Pay applications are the formal certification from a contractor which show the total contract amount, the amount of construction completed, and a completion figure. The taxpayer reviews the amount, ascertains that the work is completed per contractual standards, accepts the work and title thereto, and then releases the progress payment.

In Field Attorney Advice 20140202F, the IRS concluded that a building project relating to a hotel/casino complex was constructed using the DBB method. Since the pay applications were not broken down to specify the individual properties that were completed or to which title passed, it was not possible to determine when the costs of separate properties that could have qualified for bonus depreciation such as depreciable landscaping, business signage, and decorative items (i.e., separately depreciable assets typically identified in a cost seg study) were incurred (i.e., when economic performance occurred) for purposes of the 10 percent safe harbor. The cost segregation study conducted for the taxpayer also failed to identify when the specific costs for the property were incurred, although the cost of each item of property was specified. The taxpayer, therefore, failed to meet its burden of proving that the separately depreciable properties identified in the cost segregation study were not acquired before January 1, 2008, and thus, no bonus depreciation could be claimed.

If the arrangement in Field Attorney Advice 20140202F has been a turnkey contract, then the project, including the separate properties of the type qualifying for bonus depreciation, would have been considered acquired upon delivery of the entire project after completion or when title to the project passed (depending upon taxpayer's method of accounting). This occurred after 2007.

*Additional rule for purposes of energy production credit.* For purposes of the Code Sec. 45 energy production credit, if a taxpayer enters into a binding written contract for a specific number of components to be manufactured, constructed, or produced for the taxpayer by another person under a binding written contract (a "master contract") and then through a new binding written contract (a "project contract") the taxpayer assigns its rights to certain components to an affiliated special purpose vehicle that will own the facility for which such property is to be used, work performed with respect to the master contract may be taken into account in determining when physical work of a significant nature begins with respect to the facility (Section 4.03(2) of Notice 2013-29). The bonus depreciation regulations contain no similar provision.

*36. Acquisition and placed-in-service date requirements for property placed in service before 2016*

For property placed in service before 2016, property cannot qualify for bonus depreciation unless each of the following requirements are met (Code Sec.

168(k)(2)(A), as amended by Act Sec. 143(a) of the Protecting Americans from Tax Hikes (PATH) Act of 2015 (Division Q of P.L. 114-113), but prior to amendment by Act Sec. 143(b); Reg. § 1.168(k)-1(b)(4)(i)):

(1) The original use of the property (whether for personal or business use) must commence with the taxpayer after December 31, 2007;

(2) The taxpayer must either acquire the property after December 31, 2007 and before January 1, 2016 (and no written binding contract may be in effect prior to January 1, 2008), or acquire the property pursuant to a written binding contract that was entered into after December 31, 2007 and before January 1, 2016; and

(3) The taxpayer must place the property in service before January 1, 2016 (before January 1, 2017 in the case of long production property and certain non-commercial aircraft).

In the case of a taxpayer manufacturing, constructing, or producing property for the taxpayer's own use, the acquisition date requirement (item (2)) is treated as met if the taxpayer begins manufacturing, constructing, or producing the property after December 31, 2007, and before January 1, 2016 (Code Sec. 168(k)(2)(E)(i), as amended by Act Sec. 143(a) of P.L. 114-113), but prior to amendment by Act Sec. 143(b)). Property that is manufactured, constructed, or produced for the taxpayer by another person under a written binding contract that is entered into prior to the manufacture, construction, or production of the property for use by the taxpayer in its trade or business is considered to be manufactured, constructed, or produced by the taxpayer (Reg. § 1.168(k)-1(b)(4)(iii)(A), second sentence). So long as the date the written contract became binding is before manufacture, construction, or production begins, the date the contract became binding is not relevant. See, for example, IRS Letter Ruling 201214003, December 21, 2011 in which bonus depreciation applies to property constructed for a taxpayer pursuant to contract entered into prior to January 1, 2008. Manufacture, construction, or production of property begins when physical work of a significant nature begins. A taxpayer may apply a safe harbor rule that provides that physical work of a significant nature will not be considered to begin before the taxpayer pays (cash basis) or incurs (accrual basis) more than ten percent of the total cost of the property, excluding land and preliminary activities (Reg. § 1.168(k)-1(b)(4)(iii)(B)(2)). In applying the safe harbor where another person manufactures, constructs, or produces the property under a binding contract, it is the taxpayer who must pay or incur more than 10 percent of the costs. See *"35. Property manufactured, constructed, or produced by or for the taxpayer before September 28, 2017,"* above.

The rule in item (2) that treats property acquired pursuant to a written binding contract entered into after December 31, 2007 and before January 1, 2016 as meeting the acquisition requirement appears relevant only to long production property and noncommercial aircraft that are eligible for an extended before January 1, 2017 placed-in-service deadline. See the last sentence of Reg. § 1.168(k)-1(b)(4)(iii)(A) which restates the rule in terms that apply only to such property. Since property other than long production property and noncommercial aircraft must be placed in service before January 1, 2016 it necessarily follows that such property must also be acquired (i.e., physical possession taken) before that date. However, as explained below, for only purposes of the 100 percent bonus rate property is deemed acquired when its cost is paid (cash basis) or incurred (accrual basis) under the principles of Code Sec. 461.

Since the preceding rules apply to property placed in service before January 1, 2016, long production property and non-commercial aircraft placed in service in

2016 are actually subject to the rules immediately below that apply to property placed in service after 2015 even though the Code as in effect for property placed in service before 2016 contains a rule which provides an extended December 31, 2016 placed-in-service deadline for long production property and non-commercial aircraft.

*37. Sale-leasebacks and syndication transactions*

The following rules for sale-leasebacks apply to property acquired before September 28, 2017. The sale leaseback rule was eliminated by the Tax Cuts and Jobs Act (P.L. 115-97) since used property may qualify for bonus depreciation. The rules for pre-September 28, 2017 and post-September 27, 2017 syndication transactions are described separately below.

> ***Example (1):*** ABC acquires and placed equipment in service on September 1, 2017 and on February 1, 2018 sells the property to DEF and leases the property back. ABC may claimed bonus depreciation at the 50 percent rate for property acquired and placed in service prior to September 28, 2017 and DEF may claim bonus depreciation on the used property at the 100 percent rate (Reg. § 1.168(k)-2(b)(5)(viii)(I), Examples 9 and 10).

*Sale-leasebacks—property acquired before September 28, 2017.* A limited exception to the prior-law requirement that the original use must begin with the taxpayer applied to sale-leasebacks. The rule applies to new property that is originally placed in service after December 31, 2007, by a person who sells it to the taxpayer and then leases it from the taxpayer within three months after the date that the property was originally placed in service. In this situation, the property is treated as originally placed in service by the taxpayer-lessor and the taxpayer-lessor's placed-in-service date is deemed to occur no earlier than the date that the property is used by the lessee under the leaseback (Code Sec. 168(k)(2)(E)(ii), prior to amendment by P.L. 115-97; Reg. § 1.168(k)-1(b)(3)(iii)(A); Reg. § 1.168(k)-1(b)(5)(ii)(A); Reg. § 1.168(k)-1(b)(4)(v), *Example 11*).

> ***Example (2):*** On January 15, 2017, ABC acquired and placed a new machine in service. On March 15, 2017 DEF purchased the machine from ABC and leased it back to ABC. Under the sale-leaseback rule, DEF is considered the original user of the property since it was acquired and leased back within three months of the date that ABC originally placed the property in service. If DEF acquires the property after September 27, 2017, DEF qualifies for bonus depreciation, not as the original user, but because used property acquired from an unrelated party qualifies for bonus depreciation. In addition, unless the dates of ABC's original acquisition and sale fall within the same tax year (see Reg. § 1.168(k)-2(g)(1) and Proposed Reg. § 1.168(k)-2(f)(1) in REG-104397-18), ABC should be able to claim bonus depreciation as the original user if the sale-leaseback rule does not apply.

If the property was originally placed in service after May 5, 2003 and before January 1, 2005 by the person who sells it to the taxpayer, then the 50-percent bonus depreciation rate applied under this rule (Code Sec. 168(k)(4)(C), as added by P.L. 108-27; Reg. § 1.168(k)-1(b)(3)(iii)(A); Reg. § 1.168(k)-1(b)(5)(ii)(A)).

Note that for property placed in service before 2016, if the person who sells the property to the taxpayer had a binding contract in effect for its acquisition before January 1, 2008, acquired the property before January 1, 2008, or began construction on the property for its own use before January 1, 2008, bonus depreciation may not be claimed (Code Sec. 168(k)(2)(E)(ii), prior to amendment by P.L. 114-113: Reg. § 1.168(k)-1(b)(4)(v), Examples 11 and 12).

Similar rules apply in determining whether the former 100 percent bonus depreciation rate applies (Rev. Proc. 2011-26, Section 3.02(1)(b) and (c)).

*Syndication transactions—property acquired before September 28, 2017.* A rule similar to the sale-leaseback rule applies to syndication transactions, effective for property acquired before September 28, 2017 (Code Sec. 168(k)(2)(E)(iii), prior to amendment by the Tax Cuts and Jobs Act (P.L. 115-97); Reg. § 1.168(k)-1(b)(3)(iii)(B); Reg. § 1.168(k)-1(b)(5)(ii)(B))).

If:

(1) a lessor of property originally places the property in service (or is considered to have originally placed it in service by operation of the sale-leaseback rule described above);

(2) the property is sold by the lessor (or any subsequent purchaser) within three months after the lessor originally places the property in service (*or, in the case of multiple units of property subject to the same lease, within three months after the date the final unit is placed in service, so long as the period between the time the first unit is placed in service and the time the last unit is placed in service does not exceed 12 months*); and

(3) the user of the property after the last sale during the three-month period remains the same as when the property was originally placed in service by the lessor;

then the property is treated as originally placed in service not earlier than the date of the last sale within the three-month period and the purchaser of the property in the last sale during the three-month period is considered the original user of the property (Reg. § 1.168(k)-1(b)(3)(iii)(B); Reg. § 1.168(k)-1(b)(5)(ii)(B)).

For property placed in service before 2016, the original use of the property must begin after 2007 (Code Sec. 168(k)(2)(E)(iii), prior to amendment by P.L. 114-113).

If a sale-leaseback transaction described above is followed by a syndication transaction that satisfies the requirements in the immediately preceding paragraph, then the original user and placed-in-service date is determined in accordance with the rule for syndication transactions (Reg. § 1.168(k)-1(b)(3)(iii)(C); Reg. § 1.168(k)-1(b)(5)(ii)(C)).

***Example (3):*** ABC Manufacturing Corporation purchases a new cargo container on January 1, 2017. It sells the cargo container to SYND corporation and leases it back from SYND on March 1, 2017. If there are no further transactions, SYND is considered to have originally placed the container in service on March 1, 2017, and may claim bonus depreciation. However, if SYND resells the container to an investor within three months after March 1, 2017, and ABC continues to use the container, the investor is considered to have originally placed the container in service on the date of purchase from SYND and may claim the bonus depreciation deduction.

***Example (4):*** Assume the same facts above, except that the first investor sells the container to a second investor within three months after March 1, 2017. Assuming that ABC continues to use the container, the second investor is entitled to claim the bonus depreciation deduction.

Bonus depreciation is available to investors if a syndicator is the original purchaser of the equipment, leases the equipment, and then sells the equipment subject to the lease to investors.

***Example (5):*** SYND corporation purchases a new cargo vessel on January 1, 2017, from a ship manufacturer and leases it on the same date to GHI corporation. If SYND sells the vessel to one or more investors before April 1, 2017, and GHI is still the lessee, the investors may claim the bonus depreciation deduction. However, if any investor resells its interest in the vessel before April 1, 2017, and GHI continues to lease the vessel, then the subsequent purchaser is entitled to the bonus depreciation deduction.

Similar rules apply in determining whether the former 100 percent bonus depreciation rate applies (Rev. Proc. 2011-26, Section 3.02(1)(b) and (c)).

*Syndication transactions—Property acquired after September 27, 2017.* For property acquired after September 27, 2017, the following syndication rule applies (Code Sec. 168(k)(2)(E)(iii), as amended by the Tax Cuts and Jobs Act (P.L. 115-97). If:

(1) new property is acquired and placed in service by a lessor (or if used property is acquired and placed in service by the lessor and the lessor or any predecessor did not have a prior depreciable interest in the property);

(2) the property is sold by the lessor (or any subsequent purchaser) within three months after the lessor first places the property in service (*or, in the case of multiple units of property subject to the same lease, within three months after the date the final unit is placed in service, so long as the period between the time the first unit is placed in service and the time the last unit is placed in service does not exceed 12 months*); and

(3) the user (i.e., lessee) of the property after the last sale during the three-month period remains the same as when the property was first placed in service by the lessor;

then the purchaser of the property in the last sale during the three-month period is considered the original user of the property if the lessor acquired and placed in service new property. The purchaser is the taxpayer having a depreciable interest in the property if the lessor acquired and placed in service used property. Neither the lessor nor any intermediate purchaser is treated as previously having a depreciable interest in the property (Reg. § 1.168(k)-2(b)(3)(vi); Proposed Reg. § 1.168(k)-2(b)(3)(v) in REG-104397-18). Consequently, if the lessor or an intermediate purchaser reacquires the property, bonus may be available.

The placed in service date is no earlier than the date of the last sale (Reg. § 1.168(k)-2(b)(4)(iv); Proposed Reg. § 1.168(k)-2(b)(4)(iv) in REG-104397-18).

***Example (6):*** M Corp. acquires and places a used airplane in service on March 26, 2019. On the same date M leases the airplane to AirlineCo. On May 27, 2019, M sell the airplane subject to the lease to Z Corp. In this scenario, assuming M Corp. and Z Corp. never had a prior depreciable interest in the used airplane, Z Corp. is considered the taxpayer that acquired the used airplane for purposes of applying the used property acquisition requirements and the airplane is treated as originally placed in service by Z Corp. on May 27, 2019. Therefore Z Corp. qualifies for bonus depreciation at the 100 percent rate.

Furthermore, Z Corp. may claim the bonus deduction even if it is related to M Corp because Z Corp. is treated as acquiring the airplane (Reg. § 1.168(k)-2(b)(3)(vii)(U), Example 21; Proposed Reg. § 1.168(k)-2(b)(3)(vi), Example 24 in REG-104397-18).

***Example (7):*** Assume the same facts as in Example 5 and that Z Corp. is a calendar year taxpayer. On September 5, 2019 (more than 3 months after M Corp. originally placed the airplane in service), Z Corp. resells the airplane to Y Corp. Z Corp. may not claim bonus depreciation because Z Corp. sold the plane in the same tax year that it purchased the plane. Y Corp may claim bonus depreciation assuming it had no prior depreciable interest in the plane (Reg. § 1.168(k)-2(b)(3)(vii), Example 22; Proposed Reg. § 1.168(k)-2(b)(3)(vi), Example 25 in REG-104397-18).

***Example (8):*** Assume the same facts as in Example 5, except that the original lessor M and the last purchaser O are unrelated. Further assume that O sells the airplane back to M on March 26, 2020. Assuming all other requirements are met, M may claim bonus depreciation on the used airplane because M is not treated as having had a prior depreciable interest in the airplane (Reg. § 1.168(k)-2(b)(3)(vii), *Example 23*).

*Special rule for multiple unit leases in syndicated transactions.* Code Sec. 168(k)(2)(E)(iii) (also Code Sec. 168(k)(2)(E)(iii), prior to amendment by the Tax

Cuts and Jobs Act (P.L. 115-97) contains the italicized language relating to multiple unit leases in requirement (2), above (Reg. § 1.168(k)-1(b)(3)(iii)(B); Reg. § 1.168(k)-2(b)(3)(vi); Proposed Reg. § 1.168(k)-2(b)(3)(v) in REG-104397-18).

> ***Example (9):*** SYN Inc. is the syndicator of a leasing transaction involving 100 cargo containers which are to be leased to ABC. The first container is purchased by SYN and leased to ABC on November 1, 2018. The last container is purchased within the required one-year period and leased to ABC on June 10, 2019. A person who purchases interests in the containers from SYN (or a subsequent purchaser from SYN) within 3 months after June 10, 2019, is treated as having originally placed the containers in service on the date of purchase and may be able to claim the bonus depreciation deduction.

### *38. Fractional interests*

If in the ordinary course of its business a person sells fractional interests in new bonus depreciation property to unrelated third parties, each first fractional owner (i.e., each first unrelated third party purchaser) of the property is considered as the original user of its proportionate share of the property. Furthermore, if the person engaged in the business of selling fractional interests uses the property before all of the fractional interests are sold and the property continues to be held primarily for sale, the original use of any fractional interest sold to an unrelated third party subsequent to the fractional interest seller's use, begins with the first unrelated purchaser of that interest. Relationship is determined by reference to the rules in Code Sec. 267(b), Reg. § 1.267(b)-1, Code Sec. 707(b), and Reg. § 1.707-1.Reg. § 1.168(k)-1(b)(3)(iv); Reg. § 1.168(k)-2(b)(3)(ii)(C);Proposed Reg. § 1.168(k)-2(b)(3)(ii)(C) in REG-104397-18).

> ***Example (1):*** Fractional Seller Inc. holds out for sale 10 equal fractional interests in a new aircraft. Fractional sells five of the shares to A on January 1, 2018, and the remaining five shares to B on January 1, 2019. A and B are unrelated to Fractional Seller Inc. A may claim bonus depreciation in 2018 and B may claim bonus depreciation in 2019 assuming all other requirements are satisfied (Reg. § 1.168(k)-1(b)(3)(v), *Example 4*; Reg. § 1.168(k)-2(b)(3)(vii)(D), Example 4; Proposed Reg. § 1.168(k)-2(b)(3)(vi), Example 4).

Similar rules applied in determining whether the 100 percent bonus depreciation rate for property acquired after September 8, 2010 and placed in service before 2012 applies (Rev. Proc. 2011-26, Section 3.02(1)(b) and (c)).

The final and proposed regulations cited above discuss this rule in the context of new property acquired for fractional sale. Buyers of fractional interests in used property from unrelated parties after September 27, 2017 should also qualify for bonus depreciation. See "*13. Used property acquired after September 27, 2017 qualifies for bonus depreciation.*"

## PROPERTY WITH LONGER PRODUCTION PERIOD AND NONCOMMERCIAL AIRCRAFT

### *39. Property with longer production periods eligible for extended placed-in-service deadline*

Long production property (LPP) and certain non-commercial aircraft (NCA) acquired after September 27, 2017 only need to be placed in service before January 1, 2028, while other property acquired after September 27, 2017 must be placed in service before January 1, 2027 in order to qualify for bonus depreciation (Code Sec. 168(k)(2)(B) and (C), as amended by P.L. 115-97). LPP and NCA acquired before September 28, 2017 need to be placed in service before January 1, 2021, while other property acquired before September 28, 2017 must be placed in service before

January 1, 2020 in order to qualify for bonus depreciation (Code Sec. 168(k)(2)(B) and (C), prior to amendment by the Tax Cuts and Jobs Act (P.L. 115-97)).

Bonus depreciation rates for LPP and NCA are discussed at "*2. Bonus depreciation rates, including 100 percent rate for property acquired after September 27, 2017.*"

Acquisition date rule for long production property are discussed at "*32. Acquisition and placed-in-service date requirements for 100 percent bonus rate property acquired after September 27, 2017*" and "*34. Acquisition and placed-in-service date requirements for property acquired before September 28, 2017 and placed in service after 2015.*"

Long production property is defined as property that:

(1) has a recovery period of at least 10 years or is transportation property;

(2) is subject to the uniform capitalization rules (Code Sec. 263A); and

(3) has an estimated production period exceeding one year and a cost exceeding $1 million (Code Sec. 168(k)(2)(B); Code Sec. 263A(f)(1)(B)(iii); Code Sec. 263A(f)(5)(B); Reg. § 1.263A-12).

A technical correction in the Working Families Tax Relief Act of 2004 (P.L. 108-311) clarified that requirement (2), above, is satisfied, regardless of the reason that the property is subject to the UNICAP.

Progress expenditures of long production property are discussed at "*40. Progress expenditures of longer production period property,*" below. Noncommercial aircraft are not subject to the rule that excludes progress expenditures from bonus depreciation.

Transportation property is defined as tangible personal property used in the trade or business of transporting persons or property, for example, a commercial passenger aircraft (Code Sec. 168(k)(2)(B)(iii)).

*Production period defined.* LPP must have an estimated production period exceeding 1 year (Code Sec. 168(k)(2)(B)(i)(VI) incorporating by reference Code Sec. 263A(f)(1)(B)(iii) relating to the uniform capitalization rules). The definition of production period for purposes of the UNICAP rules is provided in Reg. § 1.263A-12. The bonus depreciation regulations do not indicate how the 1-year period is determined. Presumably, the period is based on the UNICAP rules. However, the bonus depreciation regulations do provide a rule for determining the beginning of construction (significant physical work and 10 percent safe harbor) but only for purposes of determining the acquisition date of self-constructed property. Generally, the beginning construction date under the bonus rules for purposes of determining the acquisition date falls at a later date than the beginning construction date under the UNICAP rules for purposes of determining the construction period.

*40. Progress expenditures of longer production period property*

Longer production period property (LPP) and noncommercial aircraft (NCA) acquired after September 27, 2017 must be placed in service before January 1, 2028 in order to qualify for bonus depreciation (Code Sec. 168(k)(2)(B) and (C), as amended by the Tax Cuts and Jobs Act (P.L. 115-97)). However, bonus depreciation does not apply to 2027 progress expenditures of LPP acquired after September 27, 2017 and placed in service in 2027 (Code Sec. 168(k)(2)(B)(ii), as amended by the Tax Cuts and Jobs Act (P.L. 115-97; Reg. § 1.168(k)-2(e)(1)(iii); Proposed Reg. § 1.168(k)-2(d)(1)(iii) in REG-104397-18). 2027 progress expenditures of NCA, however, do qualify.

Longer production property acquired before September 28, 2017 must be placed in service before January 1, 2021 in order to qualify for bonus depreciation (Code Sec. 168(k)(2)(B) and (C), prior to amendment by P.L. 115-97; Code Sec. 168(k)(8), as added by P.L. 115-97). 2020 progress expenditures of LPP acquired before September 28, 2017 do not qualify for bonus depreciation (Code Sec. 168(k)(2)(B)(ii), prior to amendment by P.L. 115-97; Reg. § 1.168(k)-1(d)(1)(ii)).

For bonus rates for LPP and NCA see discussion "*2. Bonus depreciation rates, including 100 percent rate for property acquired after September 27, 2017.*"

Qualifying progress expenditures only includes the property's unadjusted depreciable basis attributable to manufacture, construction, or production prior to January 1, 2027 (for property acquired after September 27, 2017) or before January 1, 2020 (for property acquired before September 28, 2017) (Reg. § 1.168(k)-2(e)(1)(iii); Proposed Reg. § 1.168(k)-2(d)(1)(iii) in REG-104397-18; Reg. § 1.168(k)-1(d)(1)(ii)). The Joint Committee on Taxation Explanation to P.L. 107-147 indicates that it is intended that rules similar to Code Sec. 46(d)(3) (relating the former investment tax credit) as in effect prior to the Tax Reform Act of 1986 (P.L. 99-514) will apply for purposes of determining the amount of progress expenditures.

Progress expenditures are defined similarly to the definition contained in Notice 2007-36 which provides rules for Gulf Opportunity Zone property (Reg. § 1.168(k)-2(e)(1)(iii)). The rules of Notice 2007-36 apply regardless of whether the property is constructed for the taxpayer under a written binding contract or under a written contract that is nonbinding. The following rules apply under Notice 2007-36.

(1) Progress expenditures for property that is manufactured, constructed, or produced generally is the amount paid or incurred that is properly chargeable to capital account with respect to the property. The amount that is properly chargeable to capital account also includes any other costs paid or incurred by the taxpayer, such as interest, or any other direct or indirect costs that are required to be capitalized under Code Sec. 263A(a) and the regulations thereunder with respect to the manufacture, construction, or production of the property.

(2) For property actually manufactured, constructed, or produced by the taxpayer, the amount paid or incurred by the taxpayer is properly chargeable to capital account at the time and to the extent that the amount is properly includible in computing basis of the property under the taxpayer's method of accounting, such as, for example, after the requirements of Code Sec. 461 (including the economic performance requirement of Code Sec. 461(h)) are satisfied.

(3) In the case of property that is manufactured, constructed, or produced for the taxpayer by another person under a written binding contract, the amount that is properly chargeable to capital account includes any payments by the taxpayer under the contract that represent part of the purchase price of the property but only to the extent progress is made in manufacture, construction, or production of the property, or, to the extent costs are incurred by the taxpayer earlier than payments are made (determined on a cumulative basis for the property), any part of that price for which the taxpayer has satisfied the requirements of Code Sec. 461 (including the economic performance requirement of Code Sec. 461(h)). In the case of an accrual method taxpayer, the taxpayer has made a payment if the transaction would be considered a payment by a taxpayer using the cash receipts and disbursements method of accounting. The written binding contract must be entered

into before the manufacture, construction, or production of the property to be delivered under the contract is completed.

(4) With respect to property that is manufactured, constructed, or produced by another person and is purchased by the taxpayer after the manufacture, construction, or production of the property is completed, only the part of the purchase price attributable to the cost of manufacture, construction, or production of the property before January 1, 2027, is eligible for the additional first year depreciation deduction.

Property with a longer production period is subject to the progress expenditures disallowance rule only if it qualifies for bonus depreciation (i.e., it is "qualified property") solely by reason of the extended placed-in-service date that applies to property with a longer production period (Code Sec. 168(k)(2)(B)(ii)).

*41. Noncommercial aircraft eligible for extended placed-in-service deadline*

An aircraft that is *not* used in the trade or business of transporting persons or property (other than for agricultural or fire fighting purposes) will qualify for a one year extension of the placed-in-service deadline if certain requirements are met.

*Non-commercial aircraft (NCA) acquired after September 27, 2017.* The placed-in service deadline is extended to December 31, 2027 for a NCA acquired after September 27, 2017. The following requirements apply:

(1) the original use of the aircraft commences with the taxpayer or the aircraft is used but is considered acquired by purchase (for rules allowing certain used property acquired after September 27, 2017 to qualify for bonus depreciation see "*13. Used property acquired after September 27, 2017 qualifies for bonus depreciation*");

(2) the aircraft is placed in service by the taxpayer before January 1, 2028;

(3) the aircraft is acquired by the taxpayer (or acquired pursuant to a written binding contract entered into) before January 1, 2027;

(4) the aircraft is purchased and the at the time of the contract for purchase, the purchaser made a nonrefundable deposit at least equal to 10 percent of the cost or $100,000; and

(5) the aircraft has an estimated production period exceeding four months and a cost exceeding $200,000 (Code Sec. 168(k)(2)(A)(iv) and (C)).

A retroactive technical correction clarifies that the written contract (item (3), above) must be binding (Code Sec. 168(k)(2)(B)(i)(III), as amended by the Tax Technical Corrections Act of 2018 (Division U of P.L. 115-141)).

The acquisition requirements are discussed at *32. Acquisition and placed-in-service date requirement for property acquired after September 27, 2017.*

For the bonus rates that apply to NCA acquired after September 27, 2017, see "*2. Bonus depreciation rates, including 100 percent rate for property acquired after September 27, 2017.*"

As explained at discussion #42 below, 2027 progress expenditures on non-commercial aircraft qualify for the bonus deduction (Code Sec. 168(k)(2)(B)(iv)).

*Non-commercial aircraft acquired before September 28, 2017.* The placed-in service deadline is extended to December 31, 2020 for a NCA acquired before September 28, 2017. Property subject to a written binding contract in effect prior to September 28, 2017 is considered acquired by the taxpayer before September 28, 2017 (Act Sec. 13201(h) of P.L. 115-97). The following requirements apply:

(1) the original use of the aircraft commences with the taxpayer

(2) the NCA is placed in service by the taxpayer before January 1, 2021;

(3) is acquired by the taxpayer (or acquired pursuant to a written binding contract entered into) before January 1, 2020;

(4) the aircraft is purchased and the at the time of the contract for purchase, the purchaser made a nonrefundable deposit at least equal to 10 percent of the cost or $100,000; and

(5) the aircraft has an estimated production period exceeding four months and a cost exceeding $200,000 (Code Sec. 168(k)(2)(A)(iv) and (C)).

A retroactive technical correction clarifies that the written contract (item (3), above) must be binding (Code Sec. 168(k)(2)(B)(i)(III), as amended by the Tax Technical Corrections Act of 2018 (Division U of P.L. 115-141)).

2020 progress expenditures of NCA acquired before September 28, 2017 and placed in service in 2020 will qualify for bonus depreciation.

For the bonus rates that apply to NCA acquired before September 28, 2017, see "*2. Bonus depreciation rates, including 100 percent rate for property acquired after September 27, 2017.*"

In the case of a taxpayer manufacturing, constructing, or producing property for the taxpayer's own use, the requirement that the aircraft be acquired before January 1, 2020 is met if the taxpayer begins manufacturing, constructing, or producing the property before January 1, 2020 (Code Sec. 168(k)(2)(E)(i)). Special rules apply for purposes of determining when construction begins and for construction on behalf of a taxpayer. See discussion at #35 entitled, "*Property manufactured, constructed, or produced by or for taxpayer.*"

*Purchase defined.* For purposes of requirement (4), the term "purchase" is intended to have the same meaning as used in Code Sec. 179(d)(2) (H.R. Conf. Rep. No. 108-755). See ¶ 302.

*Nonrefundable deposit requirement.* With respect to the nonrefundable deposits requirement above, Section 5.02 of Rev. Proc. 2008-54 provides that the nonrefundable deposit requirement is satisfied if the purchaser, at the time of the purchase contract, has made a nonrefundable deposit of at least the lesser of 10 percent of the cost of the aircraft or $100,000.

### *42. Progress expenditures of noncommercial aircraft*

The restriction contained in Code Sec. 168(k)(2)(B)(ii) and described above at discussion #40 which limits the basis of long production property eligible for the bonus depreciation deduction to pre-January 1, 2027 progress expenditures (pre-January 1, 2020, progress expenditures for aircraft acquired before September 28, 2017) does not apply to noncommercial aircraft eligible for an extended placed in service deadline (Code Sec. 168(k)(2)(B)(iv)).

***Example (1):*** ABC corporation enters into a binding written contract to purchase a corporate jet on June 1, 2017. It is deemed acquired on this date. See "*41. Noncommercial aircraft eligible for extended placed-in-service deadline.*" The purchase price is $2,000,000. A $100,000 nonrefundable deposit is made. Production begins on August 1, 2017. Assuming that the production period for the aircraft exceeds four months, the entire cost will qualify for bonus depreciation if production is completed before January 1, 2021 and the aircraft is placed in service before January 1, 2021. If the aircraft is placed in service after December 31, 2020, no portion of the cost qualifies for bonus depreciation.

## COORDINATION WITH OTHER PROVISIONS

### *43. Section 1245 and section 1250 depreciation recapture*

Since bonus depreciation is treated as a depreciation deduction, the entire deduction is potentially subject to recapture as ordinary income under Code Sec. 1245 when section 1245 property is sold at a gain. The Code Sec. 1250 recapture rules apply if the bonus allowance is claimed on section 1250 property.

For purposes of recapture under section 1250, bonus depreciation is considered an accelerated depreciation method (Reg. § 1.168(k)-2(g)(3); Proposed Reg. § 1.168(k)-2(f)(3) in REG-104397-18). For example, the difference between the bonus deduction plus regular depreciation claimed on 15-year qualified leasehold improvement property (see discussion #15 above) and the straight-line depreciation that would have been claimed on the property up to the time of disposition computed as if bonus depreciation had not been claimed is subject to recapture as ordinary income to the extent of gain realized on the disposition of the section 1250 property.

Examples of section 1250 property on which bonus depreciation is or was allowed include:

- leasehold improvement property (discussion #15) placed in service before 2016 (including 15-year retail improvement property and 15-year restaurant improvement property ¶ 110) that qualify as leasehold improvement property and are placed in service before 2016)
- 15-year restaurant property (¶ 110) placed in service before January 1 2009, whether or not it also qualifies as 15-year leasehold improvement property
- qualified improvement property placed in service after 2015 (discussion #16)
- section 1250 land improvements
- certain residential rental and nonresidential real property located in the New York Liberty Zone (¶ 127E), Gulf Opportunity GO Zone (¶ 127F), Kansas Disaster Area (¶ 127G), or a Federally Declared Disaster Area (¶ 127H)

In tax years that begin after 2009 the section 179 deduction may be claimed on qualified real property as defined in Code Sec. 179(e) (formerly, Code Sec. 179(f)). To the extent that the section 179 deduction is claimed on section 1250 property (i.e., qualified real property), it is subject to the section 1245 recapture rules (Code Sec. 1245(a)(3)(C)). Thus, the entire section 179 deduction is recaptured as ordinary income to the extent of gain. For this reason, it may be preferable to claim bonus depreciation and the first year regular depreciation allowance on section 1250 property that qualifies for either the section 179 allowance or bonus depreciation in situations where gain may recognized upon a disposition. Special rules are provided in Notice 2013-59 to determine the recapture amount when the section 179 allowance has been claimed on qualified real property (the only type of section 1250 property that qualified for expensing under section 179). See ¶ 302 for a discussion of qualified real property.

See ¶ 488 for a discussion of the recapture rules under Code Secs. 1245 and 1250.

Except for listed property (¶ 208), such as a car or pick-up truck, no recapture of the bonus depreciation deduction claimed under Code Sec. 168(k) is required upon a decline of business use. In the case of a listed property, recapture of the bonus deduction is required if business use declines to 50 percent of less. See discussion #21 above.

*44. Alternative minimum tax*

The regular tax bonus depreciation allowance may generally be claimed in full for alternative minimum tax purposes (Code Sec. 168(k)(2)(G)). However, if the unadjusted depreciable basis of the bonus depreciation property is different for AMT purposes than for regular tax purposes, the bonus deduction is the product of the applicable bonus depreciation rate and the AMT unadjusted depreciable basis (Reg. § 1.168(k)-1(d)(1)(iii); Reg. § 1.168(k)-2(e)(1)(iv); Proposed Reg. § 1.168(k)-2(d)(1)(iv) in REG-104397-18). In addition, the regular tax MACRS deductions on bonus depreciation property may be claimed in full for AMT purposes, except that AMT MACRS deductions are computed on the property's AMT unadjusted depreciable basis as reduced by the AMT bonus allowance if the AMT unadjusted depreciable basis is different than the regular tax unadjusted depreciable basis (Reg. § 1.168(k)-1(d)(2)(ii); Reg. § 1.168(k)-2(e)(2)(ii); Proposed Reg. § 1.168(k)-2(d)(2)(ii) in REG-104397-18).

Effective for property placed in service after 2015, the AMT adjustment does not apply to "qualified property" as defined in Code Sec. 168(k)(2) (Code Sec. 168(k)(2)(G) and Code Sec. 168(k)(7), as amended by P.L. 114-113). Generally, this means that there is no AMT adjustment on any MACRS property that qualifies for bonus depreciation even if an election out of bonus depreciation is made (Reg. § 1.168(k)-2(f)(4); Proposed Reg. § 1.168(k)-2(e)(4) in REG-104397-18). However, AMT depreciation is computed on the AMT basis of the qualified property if this is different that the regular tax basis (Reg. § 1.168(k)-1(d)(2)(ii); Reg. § 1.168(k)-2(e)(2)(ii); Proposed Reg. § 1.168(k)-2(d)(2)(ii) in REG-104397-18). See "*12. Qualified Property*" for a discussion of the definition of qualified property. In the case of property placed in service before 2016, an AMT adjustment could be required if an election out of bonus depreciation was made if the property would otherwise be subject to an AMT adjustment. For example, for property placed in service before 2016 which is depreciated using the 200 percent declining balance method (3-, 5-, 7-, and 10-year property) and qualifies for bonus depreciation, AMT depreciation is computed using the 150 percent declining balance method if an election out of bonus depreciation is made.

Property which does not qualify for bonus depreciation (e.g., used property acquired before September 28, 2017) may be subject to an AMT adjustment regardless of when placed in service.

The corporate AMT is repealed by the Tax Cuts and Jobs Act (P.L. 115-97) effective for tax years beginning after 2017 (Code Sec. 55(a), as amended by The Tax Cuts and Jobs Act (P.L. 115-97)). Therefore, a corporation is not required to compute AMT depreciation adjustments in a tax year beginning after 2017. An S corporation will continue to compute AMT depreciation adjustments which are passed through to S shareholders.

See ¶ 170 for a discussion of the AMT depreciation adjustment.

*45. Coordination with long-term contract method of accounting*

Solely for purposes of determining the percentage of completion under Code Sec. 460(b)(1)(A), the cost of property with an MACRS recovery period of 7 years or less that qualifies for bonus depreciation is taken into account as a cost allocated to the contract as if the bonus depreciation provision was not enacted. The provision applies to property placed in service (1) after December 31, 2009 and before January 1, 2011 (before January 1, 2012 in the case of property described in Code Sec. 168(k)(2)(B)) (i.e. property with a long production period) and (2) after December 31, 2012, and before January 1, 2027 (before January 1, 2028, in the case of property with a long production period) (Code Sec. 460(c)(6)(B), as amended by the 2017 Tax Cuts and Jobs Act of 2017 (P.L. 115-97)). This provision does not apply to qualifying property placed in service in 2011 (except for long production property eligible for an extended December 31, 2011 deadline) or in 2012.

> ***Example (1):*** Assume a calendar year taxpayer is required to use the percentage-of-completion method to account for a long-term contract. Assume further that the taxpayer purchases and places into service equipment with a cost basis of $500,000 and MACRS recovery period of 5-years. The taxpayer uses the equipment exclusively in performing its obligation under the contract. In computing the percentage of completion under Code Sec. 460(b)(1)(A), the depreciation on the equipment (assuming a half-year convention) taken into account as a cost allocated to the contract for the placed in service year is $200,000 ($1,000,000 × 20% first-year table percentage for five-year property). The amount of the depreciation deduction that may be claimed by the taxpayer in the placed-in-service year with respect to the equipment is $1,000,000 because the 100 percent bonus depreciation rate applies.

With the exception of transportation property, property with a longer production period that is described in Code Sec. 168(k)(2)(B) must have a recovery period of 10 years or greater. Thus, long-production property that is not transportation property does not qualify for the special treatment provided by this provision. Transportation property is defined as tangible personal property used in the trade or business of transporting persons or property and is not subject to the rule which requires an MACRS depreciation period of 10 years or greater in order to constitute long-production property (Code Sec. 168(k)(2)(B)(iii)). See discussion "*39. Property with longer production periods eligible for extended placed-in-service deadline,*" above for the rules under which transportation property may qualify as long-production property. Note that transportation property will need an MACRS recovery period of seven years or less to qualify for the special long-term contract accounting treatment, including the extended before January 1, 2012 and before January 1, 2021 placed-in-service deadlines for long production property under this provision.

*46. Earnings and profits*

The bonus allowance is not allowable for purposes of computing a corporation's earnings and profits (Reg. § 1.168(k)-1(f)(7); Reg. § 1.168(k)-2(g)(7); Proposed Reg. § 1.168(k)-2(f)(7) in REG-104397-18). See ¶ 310.

*47. Coordination with Code Sec. 47 rehabilitation credit*

A taxpayer may claim bonus depreciation on qualified rehabilitation expenditures (as defined in Code Sec. 47(c)(2)) that qualify for bonus deduction. However, assuming no election out of bonus depreciation is made, the rehabilitation credit may only be claimed on the cost (or other applicable basis) of the rehabilitation expenditures less the amount claimed or allowable as bonus depreciation. The credit however only applies if the taxpayer depreciates the remaining basis of the rehabilitation expenditures using an MACRS straight-line method (Reg. § 1.168(k)-1(f)(10); Reg. § 1.168(k)-2(g)(9); Proposed Reg. § 1.168(k)-2(f)(9) in REG-104397-18).

*48. Coordination with investment credit and section 1603 energy grants in lieu of Code Sec. 48 energy credit*

The energy credit (Code Sec. 48) applies to a variety of energy-production property including energy produced from solar, wind, and geothermal sources. The basis of property for which an energy credit is claimed is reduced by 50 percent of the credit (Code Sec. 50(c)(3)(A)). The basis reduction for any other component of the investment credit is equal to 100 percent of the credit (Code Sec. 50(c)(1)). The bonus deduction is computed after the basis reduction. However, a special rule applies to the rehabilitation credit, as described above.

If a taxpayer takes a section 1603 grant in lieu of an energy credit, the basis of the energy property is reduced by 50 percent of the grant before computing bonus depreciation and regular depreciation (Code Sec. 48(d)(3)(B); Rev. Proc. 2011-26).

*49. Coordination with Code Sec. 514 relating to debt-financed property*

The bonus depreciation deduction may not be claimed under Code Sec. 514(a)(3) on depreciable debt-financed property for purposes of determining the amount of unrelated business taxable income (Reg. § 1.168(k)-1(f)(11); Reg. § 1.168(k)-2(g)(10); Proposed Reg. § 1.168(k)-2(f)(10) in REG-104397-18).

*50. Technical termination of partnership*

The rule providing for technical termination of partnerships is repealed for partnership tax years beginning after December 31, 2017 (Code Sec. 708(b)(1)(B), as amended by P.L. 115-97).

If a partnership is technically terminated in a tax years beginning before 2018 (sale or exchange of 50 percent of more of partnership interests in 12-months), qualified bonus depreciation property placed in service during the tax year of termination by the terminated partnership is treated as originally placed in service by the new partnership on the date that the property is contributed by the terminated partnership to the new partnership (Code Sec. 708(b)(1)(B), prior to amendment by the Tax Cuts and Jobs Act (P.L. 115-97; Reg. § 1.168(k)-1(b)(5)(iii); Reg. § 1.168(k)-2(b)(4)(v); Proposed Reg. § 1.168(k)-2(b)(4)(v) in REG-104397-18).

The new partnership claims the bonus deduction for the qualified bonus depreciation property placed in service during the tax year of the termination by the terminating partnership. The deduction is claimed by the new partnership's in the new partnership's tax year in which the property was deemed contributed. However, if the terminated partnership placed the property in service in the same tax year it is deemed contributed to the new partnership and the new partnership disposes of the property in the same tax year that it received the property, no bonus depreciation deduction is allowed (Reg. § 1.168(k)-1(f)(1)(ii); Reg. § 1.168(k)-2(g)(1)(ii); Proposed Reg. § 1.168(k)-2(f)(1)(ii) in REG-104397-18).

> ***Example (1):*** Partnership AB, a calendar year entity, purchases qualifying bonus depreciation property on February 1, 2017. The partnership is technically terminated as a result of the sale of partnership interests on November 1, 2017. New partnership AB may claim bonus depreciation. The bonus rate is 100 percent because new partnership AB is deemed to have acquired and originally placed the property in service after September 27, 2017 (Reg. § 1.168(k)-2(g)(1)(iv), *Example 1*; Proposed Reg. § 1.168(k)-2(f)(1)(iv), *Example 1* in REG-104397-18).

The regulations cited above also apply these rules to specified plants for which an election is made to claim bonus in the year of planting or grafting.

If qualified bonus depreciation property is placed in service by a partnership in a tax year of a technical termination under Code Sec. 708(b)(1)(B), any increase in basis of the property due to a Code Sec. 754 election is eligible for bonus depreciation (Reg. § 1.168(k)-1(f)(9)).

Prior to the rule making acquisitions of used property after September 27, 2027 eligible for bonus depreciation, this was the only situation in which a basis increase attributable to a section 754 election was eligible for bonus depreciation (Preamble to T.D. 9283, filed with the Federal Register on August 29, 2006). See "*14. Code Sec. 754 elections and other partnership transactions*" for rules applicable to property acquired after September 27, 2017.

*51. Certain step-in-the-shoes transactions*

Qualified bonus property that is transferred in a Code Sec. 168(i)(7) transaction in the same tax year it is placed in service by the transferor remains eligible for bonus depreciation. The property is considered originally placed in service on the date the transferor placed the property in service. If there are multiple transfers in multiple Code Sec. 168(i)(7) transactions in the same tax year, the placed in service date of the transferred property is the date on which the first transferor placed the qualified property in service (Reg. § 1.168(k)-1(b)(5)(iv); Reg. § 1.168(k)-2(b)(4)(vi); Proposed Reg. § 1.168(k)-2(b)(4)(vi) in REG-104397-18).

A Code Sec. 168(i)(7) step-in-the-shoes transaction is one of the following:

- complete subsidiary liquidation (Code Sec. 332)
- transfer to a controlled corporation (Code Sec. 351)
- nonrecognition reorganization (Code Sec. 361)
- contribution to a partnership (Code Sec. 721)
- distribution by a partnership to a partner (Code Sec. 731)
- any transaction between members of the same affiliated group for any tax year a consolidated return is file

The bonus deduction is allocated between the transferor and the transferee based on the number of months that each party held the property in service during the transferor's tax year in accordance with the rules described in Reg. § 1.168(d)-1(b)(7)(ii) for allocating depreciation deductions. Under these rules, the transferor is treated as holding the property during the month of acquisition while the transferee takes the month of the transfer into account. No bonus deduction is allowed to either the transferor or the transferee if the property is disposed of by the transferee (other than in another Code Sec. 168(i)(7) transaction) in the same tax year that the transferee received the property from the transferor (Reg. § 1.168(k)-1(f)(1)(iii); Reg. § 1.168(k)-2(g)(1)(iii); Proposed Reg. § 1.168(k)-2(f)(1)(iii) in REG-104397-18).

> ***Example (1):*** John places a $9,000 machine in service on January 5, YEAR 1. On August 20, YEAR 1 he transfers the machine in a section 721(a) transaction to partnership ABC. No partner (other than John) has held a prior depreciable interest in the property. John and ABC are calendar year taxpayers. The $9,000 bonus deduction is allocated between John and the partnership. Under the allocation rules, John has held the property for 7 months (January through July) and ABC has held the property for 5 months (August through December). John is allocated $5,250 ($9,000 × 7/12) and ABC is allocated $3,750 ($9,000 × 5/12) (Reg. § 1.168(k)-2(g)(1)(iv), *Example 2*; Proposed Reg. § 1.168(k)-2(f)(1)(iv), *Example 2* in REG-104397-18).

Effective for property acquired and placed in service after September 27, 2017, the bonus is allocated entirely to the transferor if the qualified property is transferred in a Code Sec. 721(a) transaction to a partnership in the same tax year that it was acquired by the transferor and the partnership has a partner, other than the transferor, with a prior depreciable interest in the qualified property (Reg. § 1.168(k)-2(g)(1)(iii); Proposed Reg. § 1.168(k)-1(f)(1)(iii) in REG-104397-18).

If a partnership interest is purchased and transferred in a section 168(i)(7) transaction in the same tax year, any Code Sec. 743(b) adjustment arising on account of the purchase with respect to qualified property held by the partnership is allowed as a bonus deduction provided the requirements of Reg. § 1.168(k)-2(b)(3)(iv)(D), relating to used property and section 743 adjustments, are satisfied. The adjustment is apportioned between the transferor and the transferee on a monthly basis (Reg. § 1.168(k)-2(g)(1)(iii)). If a partnership interest is acquired and disposed of during the same tax year in a transaction not described in a Code Sec. 168(i)(7), the bonus deduction is not allowed for any section 743(b) adjustment arising from the initial acquisition.

No bonus depreciation is allowed if qualified property is placed in service and transferred in a Code Sec. 168(i)(7) transaction by the transferor in the same tax year, and the property is disposed of by the transferee in a transaction not described in Code Sec. 168(i)(7) during the same tax year the transferee received the property from the transferor (Reg. § 1.168(k)-1(f)(1)(iii); Reg. § 1.168(k)-2(g)(1)(iii); Proposed Reg. § 1.168(k)-1(f)(1)(iii) in REG-104397-18).

The regulations provide similar rules for specified plants for which bonus depreciation is claimed in the year of planting or grafting (Reg. § 1.168(k)-2(g)(1)(iii); Proposed Reg. § 1.168(k)-1(f)(1)(iii) in REG-104397-18).

*52. Increase in first-year luxury car depreciation caps*

Assuming that the election out of bonus depreciation is not made, the first-year Code Sec. 280F depreciation cap for passenger automobiles that qualify for bonus depreciation is increased by $8,000 (Code Sec. 168(k)(2)(F)). However, in the rare situation where a vehicle is acquired before September 28, 2017 and placed in service in 2018, the $8,000 cap is reduced to $6,400 and for vehicles placed in service in 2019 is reduced to $4,800 (Code Sec. 168(k)(2)(F)(iii), as added by P.L. 114-113).

Bonus depreciation must be claimed on the vehicle—the increase is not available if the election out is made (Code Sec. 168(k)(7)).

The bump-up amounts are not reduced in a short tax year. The Code Sec. 179 allowance may be applied against the bump-up amount (Preamble to T.D. 9283, filed with the Federal Register on August 28, 2006).

See ¶ 200 and following for a complete discussion of the depreciation cap rules.

*53. Corporate election to claim accelerated alternative minimum tax credit and research credit in lieu of bonus depreciation*

*The corporate AMT is repealed by the Tax Cuts and Jobs Act of 2017 (P.L. 115-97) effective for tax years beginning after December 31, 2017. Consequently, the Code Sec. 168(k)(4) election has also been repealed, effective for tax years beginning after December 31, 2017.*

If a corporation elects out of bonus depreciation for a class of property and makes an election to forgo bonus depreciation, the election to forgo bonus depreciation does not apply to the class or classes of property for which the election out was made (Act Sec. 101(d)(4) of the 2018 Tax Technical Corrections Act (P.L. 115-141), amending Code Sec. 168(k)(7) as in effect the day before enactment of the Tax Cuts Act).

Effective for tax years ending after 2015 and before 2018, the accelerated AMT credit rules are simplified and the limitations on the amount of unused AMT credits that may be freed up are revised to allow more unused credits to be claimed (Code Sec. 168(k)(4), as amended by Act Sec. 143(b)(3) of P.L. 114-113).

For rules in effect prior for tax years ending before 2016, see earlier versions of the US Master Depreciation Guide.

Corporations with a fiscal tax year beginning in 2015 and ending in 2016 are subject to a transitional limitation on the amount of the credit which may be claimed in the 2015/2016 fiscal year. See below.

Under the new rules, the provision is elected on an annual basis. For any tax year for which the election is made, bonus depreciation may not be claimed on qualified property eligible for bonus depreciation (as defined in Code Sec. 168(k)(2)) placed in service during the tax year (i.e., property for which bonus depreciation could otherwise be claimed) (Code Sec. 168(k)(4)(A), as amended by Act Sec. 143(b)(3) of P.L. 114-113). Thus, it is not necessary to determine which "round" of bonus depreciation property is placed in service during the tax year. The election for a tax year is revocable only with IRS consent (Code Sec. 168(k)(4)(D)(i), as amended by Act Sec. 143(b)(3) of P.L. 114-113).

Depreciation on the qualified property is computed using the straight-line method over the regular recovery period (Code Sec. 168(k)(4)(A)(ii), as amended by Act Sec. 143(b)(3) of P.L. 114-113). The higher depreciation cap (Code Sec. 168(k)(2)(F)) that applies to passenger automobiles on which bonus depreciation could have been claimed does not apply.

The Code Sec. 53(c) limitation on the amount of unused AMT credits that may be claimed in a tax year (i.e., the limitation that allows unused AMT credits to be claimed against regular tax liability in excess of tentative minimum tax liability) is increased by the bonus depreciation amount computed for the tax year (Code Sec. 168(k)(4)(A)(iii), as amended by Act Sec. 143(b)(3) of P.L. 114-113).

The calculation of the bonus depreciation amount remains the same as the computation in tax years ending before 2016 (Code Sec. 168(k)(4)(B)(i), as amended by Act Sec. 143(b)(3) of P.L. 114-113). Thus, the bonus depreciation amount, for each asset placed in service in a tax year, is 20 percent of the difference between (1) the first year depreciation (including bonus depreciation) that could be claimed on the asset if the bonus is claimed and (2) the first-year depreciation that could be claimed on the asset if bonus depreciation is not claimed. In the case of a passenger automobile subject to the Code Sec. 280F depreciation caps, item (1) is computed by taking into account the higher cap for vehicles on which the bonus deduction is claimed and item (2) is computed by taking into account the regular cap that applies if bonus is not claimed.

The bonus depreciation amount is computed using the regular depreciation method that would otherwise apply to the property (e.g., the 200% declining balance method for 3-, 5-, 7-, and 10-year property and the 150% declining balance method for 15- and 20-year property). Elections made to use the MACRS straight-line method, 150 percent declining balance method, and alternative depreciation system are ignored (Code Sec. 168(k)(4)(B), last sentence, as amended by Act Sec. 143(b)(3) of P.L. 114-113).

The "maximum increase amount" limitation on the bonus depreciation amount is removed effective for tax years ending after 2015. Under this limitation, the bonus amount could not exceed the lesser of $30 million or 6 percent of the taxpayer's unused AMT credits attributable to tax years beginning before 2006 (i.e., the "AMT credit increase amount").

The maximum increase amount is replaced with a new limitation on the bonus depreciation amount (Code Sec. 168(k)(4)(B)(ii), as amended by Act Sec. 143(b)(3) of P.L. 114-113).

Under the new limitation the bonus depreciation amount computed for a tax year may not exceed the lesser of:

(1) 50 percent of the corporation's minimum tax credit under Code Sec. 53(b) for the corporation's first tax year ending after December 31, 2015, or

(2) The minimum tax credit for the tax year, determined by taking into account only the adjusted net minimum tax (as defined in Code Sec. 53(d)) for tax years ending before January 1, 2016 (determined by treating credits as allowed on a first-in, first-out basis).

The limitation above is computed in a special way by a corporation with a fiscal tax year beginning before January 1, 2016 and ending after December 31, 2015. See below.

*Aggregation rule.* All corporations treated as a single employer under Code Sec. 52(a) are treated as a single taxpayer for purposes of the election. If any corporation in a group of corporations that are treated as a single employer makes the election all corporations in the group are treated as having made the election (Code Sec. 168(k)(4)(B)(iii), as amended by Act Sec. 143(b)(3) of P.L. 114-113). This rule also applied in tax years ending before 2016.

*Credit is refundable.* The aggregate increase in credits allowable by reason of the increased limitation resulting from the election is treated as refundable (Code Sec. 168(k)(4)(C), as amended by Act Sec. 143(b)(3) of P.L. 114-113). This rule applied in tax years ending before 2016.

*Electing corporations that are partners.* In the case of a corporation making an election which is a partner in a partnership, for purposes of determining the electing partner's distributive share of partnership items, bonus depreciation does not apply to any eligible qualified property and the straight line method is used with respect to that property (Code Sec. 168(k)(4)(D)(ii), as amended by Act Sec. 143(b)(3) of P.L. 114-113). This rule applied in tax years ending before 2016.

*Corporate partner owning majority of partnership.* In the case of a partnership having a single corporate partner owning (directly or indirectly) more than 50 percent of the capital and profits interests in the partnership, each partner takes into account its distributive share of partnership depreciation in determining its bonus depreciation amount (Code Sec. 168(k)(4)(D)(iii), as amended by Act Sec. 143(b)(3) of P.L. 114-113).

*Transitional rule for 2015/2016 fiscal-year corporations.* Corporations with a fiscal tax year beginning before January 1, 2016 and ending after December 31, 2015 are subject to a transitional rule which takes into account the maximum increase amount limitation that applied in tax years ending before January 1, 2016 and the revised limitation that applies in tax years ending after December 31, 2015 (Act Sec. 143(b)(7)(B) of P.L. 114-113).

In the case of a tax year that begins before January 1, 2016 and ends after December 31, 2015, the limitation on the bonus depreciation amount is the sum of:

(1) the maximum increase amount (defined above under the discussion for the rules that apply to tax years ending before 2016) multiplied by a fraction, the numerator of which is the number of days in the tax year before January 1, 2016, and the denominator of which is the number of days in the tax year; and

(2) the bonus depreciation limitation (defined above under the rules for tax years ending after 2015) multiplied by a fraction the numerator of which is the number of days in the tax year after December 31, 2015, and the denominator of which is the number of days in the tax year.

## ¶ 127E

## Bonus Depreciation for New York Liberty Zone Property

"Qualified New York Liberty Zone property" was eligible for an additional 30-percent first-year depreciation allowance (Code Sec. 1400L(b)(1)(A), as added by the Job Creation and Worker Assistance Act of 2002 (P.L. 107-147); Reg. § 1.1400L(b)-1 at ¶ 599).

Bonus depreciation under the Liberty Zone provision (Code Sec. 1400L(b)) may not be claimed on property that qualified for the 30-percent or 50-percent additional first-year depreciation allowance that is provided by Code Sec. 168(k) (the "Code Sec. 168(k) allowance") and described at ¶ 127D (Code Sec. 1400L(b)(2)(C)(i)). Property that qualified for bonus depreciation under Code Sec. 168(k) is specifically excluded from the definition of "qualified New York Liberty Zone property" even if the property is located in the New York Liberty Zone.

Most property located in the New York Liberty Zone qualified for bonus depreciation under Code Sec. 168(k) rather than Code Sec. 1400L(b). However, qualification for New York Liberty Zone bonus depreciation is more liberal in some respects and, therefore, will cover certain property that is not eligible for bonus depreciation under Code Sec. 168(k). Most importantly, property placed in service after December 31, 2004 and before January 1, 2007 may qualify for New York Liberty Zone bonus depreciation (Code Sec. 1400L(b)(2)(A)(v)). Property generally only qualified for bonus depreciation under Code Sec. 168(k) if placed in service before January 1, 2005. Also, unlike regular bonus depreciation under Code Sec. 168(k), New York Liberty Zone bonus depreciation is available for residential rental or nonresidential real property that replaces certain destroyed or condemned real property and which is placed in service before January 1, 2010 (Code Sec. 1400L(b)(2)(A)(i)(II)) and for used property so long as the taxpayer was the first person to use the property in the New York Liberty Zone (Code Sec. 1400L(b)(2)(A)(iii)).

Although the bonus depreciation rate was increased from 30 percent to 50 percent for property that qualifies for bonus depreciation under Code Sec. 168(k), the 30-percent rate for property placed in service in the New York Liberty Zone that only qualifies for bonus depreciation under Code Sec. 1400L(b) (e.g., used property, certain real property, and property placed in service after December 31, 2004, and before January 1, 2007) was not increased.

Qualifying property must be acquired by purchase, as defined in Code Sec. 179(d) (see below) after September 10, 2001, and placed in service by the taxpayer on or before the "termination date," which is December 31, 2006 (December 31, 2009, in the case of qualifying residential rental and nonresidential real property).

*Final regulations and change in accounting method*

Final bonus depreciation regulations adopted by T.D. 9283 (8/31/06) generally apply to qualified New York Liberty Zone property acquired by a taxpayer after September 10, 2001 (Reg. § 1.1400L(b)-1(g)).

A taxpayer that seeks a change in method of accounting to comply with the final regulations for either: (1) the taxpayer's last tax year ending before October 18, 2006, if the taxpayer timely files (including extensions) its Federal income tax return after October 18, 2006, for that last tax year; or (2) the taxpayer's first tax year ending on or after October 18, 2006 should follow the procedures in Rev. Proc. 2006-43, I.R.B. 2006-4. For subsequent tax years, the automatic change in method of accounting procedures in Rev. Proc. 2002-9 (or its successor Rev. Proc. 2008-52), if applicable, or the advance consent change in method of accounting procedures in

Rev. Proc. 97-27, 1997-1 C.B. 680 (as modified and amplified by Rev. Proc. 2002-19, and amplified, clarified, and modified by Rev. Proc. 2002-54) (or its successor) apply.

*Location of New York Liberty Zone*

The New York Liberty Zone is the area located on or south of Canal Street, East Broadway (east of its intersection with Canal Street), or Grand Street (east of its intersection with East Broadway) in the Borough of Manhattan in New York City (Code Sec. 1400L(h); Reg. § 1.1400L(b)-1(b)).

*Basis for computing additional allowance*

The basis for computing bonus depreciation on New York Liberty Zone property is determined in the same manner as for the bonus deduction under Code Sec. 168(k) (Reg. § 1.1400L(b)-1(d)). Thus, the 30-percent rate is generally applied to cost as reduced by any amount expensed under Code Sec. 179. See ¶ 127D.

*Code Sec. 179 expense allowance increased by $35,000*

The otherwise allowable Code Sec. 179 deduction is increased by an additional $35,000 for qualifying Liberty Zone property placed in service before January 1, 2007. See ¶ 305.

*Election out*

A taxpayer may elect out of the provision. Rules similar to those that apply under Code Sec. 168(k) apply under Code Sec. 1400L(b) (Code Sec. 1400L(b)(2)(C)(iv); Reg. § 1.1400L(b)-1(d)(3); Rev. Proc. 2002-33, as modified and amplified by Rev. Proc. 2003-50). Thus, the election out is made at the property class level. See ¶ 127D.

The final regulations, which apply retroactively, make it clear that if a taxpayer elects out of bonus depreciation under Code Sec. 168(k) with respect to a class of property, the taxpayer may claim bonus depreciation on Liberty Zone property that falls within the same class. See Rev. Proc. 2006-43, I.R.B. 2006-4, for change in accounting method procedures that a taxpayer must follow in order to claim bonus depreciation on New York Liberty Zone property which did not qualify under the temporary regulations.

*Types of qualifying New York Liberty Zone property*

The following types of property can qualify for the additional Liberty Zone depreciation allowance:

(1) property that is depreciable under MACRS and has a recovery period of 20 years or less;

(2) computer software which is depreciable under Code Sec. 167(f)(1)(B) using the straight-line method over 36 months;

(3) water utility property; and

(4) nonresidential real property or residential rental property that rehabilitates real property damaged, or replaces real property destroyed or condemned, as a result of the September 11, 2001, terrorist attack (Code Sec. 1400L(b)(2)(A)(i)).

The first three types of property are eligible for the Code Sec. 168(k) allowance described at ¶ 127D.

*Additional requirements*

The following additional requirements must also be met in order for property to qualify for the Code Sec. 1400L(b) bonus depreciation allowance:

(1) substantially all (80% or more) of the use of the property must be in the New York Liberty Zone (Code Sec. 1400L(b)(2)(A)(ii); Reg. § 1.1400L(b)-1(c)(3)).

(2) the property must be used in the active conduct of a trade or business by the taxpayer in the Liberty Zone (Code Sec. 1400L(b)(2)(A)(ii));

(3) the original use of the property in the Liberty Zone must commence with the taxpayer after September 10, 2001 (Code Sec. 1400L(b)(2)(A)(iii));

(4) the property must be acquired by purchase, as defined in Code Sec. 179(d)(2) (see below) after September 10, 2001 (Code Sec. 1400L(b)(2)(A)(iv)); and

(5) the property must be placed in service by the taxpayer on or before the "termination date," which is December 31, 2006 (December 31, 2009, in the case of nonresidential real property and residential rental property) (see below for further qualification requirements for eligible real property) (Code Sec. 1400L(b)(2)(A)(v); Reg. § 1.1400L(b)-1(c)(6)).

Property will not qualify if a binding written contract for the acquisition of the property was in effect before September 11, 2001 (Code Sec. 1400L(b)(2)(A)(iv)).

Property can qualify for the Code Sec. 168(k) allowance (¶ 127D) only if it is placed in service on or before December 31, 2004 (December 31, 2005, for certain property with a longer production period).

An active conduct of a trade or business use requirement does not apply to the Code Sec. 168(k) allowance. Depreciable investment property may qualify for bonus depreciation under Code Sec. 168(k), but does not qualify for the Liberty Zone bonus depreciation allowance.

*Substantially all requirement.* The 80 percent test must be satisfied in the year the asset is placed in service. If business use in the Zone falls below 80 percent in a later tax year no recapture of the bonus deduction is required. However, if the asset is a listed property, such as a car, the bonus deduction and any amount expensed under section 179 is subject to recapture under the listed property rules in the year of the asset's assigned MACRS ADS recovery period that business use drops to 50 percent or less. See ¶ 206.

*Related party use and binding contracts*

Property will not qualify for the Liberty Zone bonus depreciation deduction if any of the following persons had a written binding contract in effect for the acquisition of the property at any time on or before September 10, 2001: (1) the user of the property on the date that the property was originally placed in service; (2) a person related to the user of the property on the date that the property was originally placed in service; or (3) a person related to the taxpayer. Likewise, property will not qualify for the bonus depreciation if its manufacture, construction, or production began at any time on or before September 10, 2001, and the property was manufactured, constructed, or produced for the user or the related parties listed above (Code Sec. 1400L(b)(2)(D), as amended by the Working Families Tax Relief Act of 2004 (P.L. 108-311) and Code Sec. 168(k)(2)(D)(iv), as amended by P.L. 108-311; Reg. § 1.1400L(b)-1(c)(5)).

*Acquired by purchase requirement*

Property is considered acquired by purchase if it meets the requirements prescribed by Code Sec. 179(d) and Reg. § 1.179-4(c) (Code Sec. 1400L(2)(A)(iv); Reg. § 1.1400L(b)-1(c)(5)). Code Sec. 179(d)(2) defines "purchase" as any acquisition of property *except* property: (1) acquired from a person whose relationship to the taxpayer would bar recognition of a loss in any transaction between them under Code Sec. 267 or Code Sec. 707(b); (2) acquired from another member of a controlled group (substituting a more-than-50-percent ownership test for the at-least-80-percent ownership test in Code Sec. 1563(a)(1)); (3) the adjusted basis of which is determined in whole or in part by reference to the adjusted basis of the property in the hands of the person from whom the property was acquired (i.e., a substituted basis); or (4) acquired from a decedent with a fair-market value (stepped-up) basis.

The Code Sec. 168(k) allowance does not have an acquisition by purchase requirement.

*Original use requirement and used property*

Used property may qualify as long as it was not previously used in the Liberty Zone (Reg. § 1.1400L(b)-1(c)(4)). The original use of the property in the Liberty Zone must begin with the taxpayer after September 10, 2001. Additional capital expenditures incurred to recondition or rebuild property for which the original use in the Liberty Zone began with the taxpayer will also satisfy the original use requirement (Reg. § 1.1400L(b)-1(c)(4); Joint Committee on Taxation, *Technical Explanation of the "Job Creation and Worker Assistance Act of 2002"* (JCX-12-02), March 6, 2002).

Used property does not qualify for the Code Sec. 168(k) bonus allowance.

All other original use rules described in Reg. § 1.168(k)-1(b)(3) and applicable under Code Sec. 168(k) apply to Liberty Zone property. See "*Original use requirement*" at ¶ 127D.

*Sale-leasebacks, syndication transactions, and fractional interests*

The special rules for sale-leasebacks, syndication transactions, and sales of fractional interests that apply under Code Sec. 168(k) (¶ 127D) also apply to New York Liberty Zone Property (Code Sec. 1400L(b)(2)(D); Reg. § 1.1400L(b)-1(c)(4) and (6)).

*Self-constructed property*

Property manufactured, constructed, or produced by a taxpayer for the taxpayer's own use is treated as acquired after September 10, 2001, if the taxpayer began manufacturing, constructing, or producing the property after September 10, 2001 (Code Sec. 1400L(b)(2)(D) and Code Sec. 168(k)(2)(E)(i); Reg. § 1.1400L(b)-1(c)(5)). Property that is manufactured, constructed, or produced for the taxpayer by another person under a contract that is entered into prior to the manufacture, construction, or production of the property is considered manufactured, constructed, or produced by the taxpayer (Reg. § 1.1400L(b)-1(c)(5); Reg. § 1.168(k)-1(b)(4)(iii); Joint Committee on Taxation, *Technical Explanation of the "Job Creation and Worker Assistance Act of 2002"* (JCX-12-02), March 6, 2002).

*Eligible real property*

Eligible real property is nonresidential real property or residential rental property that rehabilitates real property damaged, or replaces real property destroyed or condemned, as a result of the September 11, 2001, terrorist attack (Reg. § 1.1400L(b)-1(c)(2)).

Property is treated as replacing real property destroyed or condemned if, as part of an integrated plan, the property replaces real property which is included in a continuous area which includes real property destroyed or condemned (Code Sec. 1400L(b)(2)(B); Reg. § 1.1400L(b)-1(c)(2)).

Real property destroyed or condemned only includes circumstances in which an entire building or structure was destroyed or condemned as a result of the terrorist attacks. Otherwise, the property is considered damaged real property. If structural components of a building (for example, walls, floors, or plumbing fixtures) are damaged or destroyed and the building is not destroyed or condemned, then only costs related to replacing the damaged or destroyed components qualify for the additional allowance (Reg. § 1.1400L-1(c)(2)(B); Joint Committee on Taxation, Technical Explanation of the "Job Creation and Worker Assistance Act of 2002" (JCX-12-02), March 6, 2002).

The *replaced temporary regulations* defined real property as a building or its structural components, or other tangible real property except: (1) property described in Code Sec. 1245(a)(3)(B) (relating to depreciable property used as an integral part of a specified activity or as a specified facility); (2) property described in section Code Sec. 1245(a)(3)(D) (relating to a single purpose agricultural or horticultural structure); and (3) property described in Code Sec. 1245(a)(3)(E) (relating to storage facility used in connection with the distribution of petroleum or any primary product of petroleum). Under the definition contained in the former temporary regulations, nonresidential real property or residential rental property that rehabilitates or replaces any of the excluded properties that were damaged, destroyed, or condemned did not qualify for bonus depreciation. These exclusions to the definition of real property were retroactively eliminated in the final regulations. See Rev. Proc. 2006-43, I.R.B. 2006-45 for change in accounting procedures to claim bonus depreciation on property that now qualifies under the final regulations.

*Rehabilitation credit.* The final regulations provide that if qualified rehabilitation expenditures are qualified property under Code Sec. 168(k), 50-percent bonus depreciation property, or Liberty Zone property, a taxpayer may claim the additional first year depreciation deduction for the unadjusted depreciable basis of the qualified rehabilitation expenditures and may claim the rehabilitation credit (provided the requirements of Code Sec. 47 are met) for the remaining basis of the qualified rehabilitation expenditures (unadjusted depreciable basis less the additional first year depreciation deduction allowed or allowable, whichever is greater) provided the taxpayer depreciates the remaining adjusted depreciable basis of such expenditures using the straight line method. The taxpayer may also claim the rehabilitation credit for the portion of the basis of the qualified rehabilitated building that is attributable to the qualified rehabilitation expenditures if the taxpayer elects not to deduct the additional first year depreciation for the class of property that includes the qualified rehabilitated expenditures (Reg. § 1.1400L(b)-1(f)(9); Reg. § 1.1400L(b)-1(g)(6)).

*Mandatory ADS property disqualified*

Property which must be depreciated under the MACRS alternative depreciation system (ADS) does not qualify for the Code Sec. 1400L(b) allowance or the Code Sec. 168(k) allowance (Code Sec. 1400L(b)(2)(C)(ii); Reg. § 1.1400L(b)-1(c)(2)(ii)(C)). Property for which ADS is elected does qualify, assuming all other requirements are satisfied. The same rule applies to bonus depreciation under Code Sec. 168(k). See ¶ 127D.

*Leasehold improvement property*

"Qualified New York Liberty Zone leasehold improvement property" does not qualify for the Code Sec. 1400L(b) allowance or the Code Sec. 168(k) allowance (Code Sec. 1400L(b)(2)(C)(iii); Reg. §1.1400L(b)-1(c)(2)(ii)(E)). This property, however, may be depreciated using the straight-line method over five years. See ¶ 124A.

*Alternative minimum tax*

The Code Sec. 1400L(b) allowance may be claimed against alternative minimum tax in the tax year that the qualifying property is placed in service. No AMT adjustment is made. Also, no AMT adjustment is required for the regular MACRS allowances claimed on qualifying property if no election out is made (Code Sec. 1400L(b)(2)(E); Reg. §1.1400L(b)-1(d)). The same rule applies to property for which the Code Sec. 168(k) allowance is claimed (Code Sec. 168(k)(2)(F)). If the bonus depreciation deduction is claimed, no AMT adjustments are required on any of the regular MACRS depreciation deductions computed during the recovery period of the Liberty Zone property. See ¶ 127D.

## ¶ 127F

## Bonus Depreciation for Gulf Opportunity Zone Property

Taxpayers were allowed to claim an additional first-year depreciation allowance equal to 50 percent of the adjusted basis of qualified Gulf Opportunity Zone (GO Zone) property acquired on or after August 28, 2005, and placed in service on or before December 31, 2007 (Code Sec. 1400N(d), as added by the Gulf Opportunity Zone Act of 2005 (P.L. 109-135); Notice 2006-77, as modified by Notice 2007-36 providing extensive regulatory type guidance). The place- in-service deadline was December 31, 2008 for nonresidential real property and residential rental property. However, if such real property was located in a country or parish within the GO Zone where more than 60 percent of the housing units were destroyed by hurricanes that occurred during 2005, the deadline was December 31, 2011, as explained below.

The GO Zone bonus allowance must be claimed unless an election out is made (Code Sec. 1400N(d)(2)(A)(iv)). Election procedures and a special deemed election out are described below. The deduction is subject to the general rules regarding whether an item is deductible under Code Sec. 162 or subject to the capitalization rules under Code Sec. 263 or Code Sec. 263A (Joint Committee on Taxation, Technical Explanation of the Gulf Opportunity Zone Act of 2005 (JCX-88-05)).

Generally, the GO Zone bonus deduction is equal to 50 percent of the cost of the property after reduction by any amount expensed under Code Sec. 179. MACRS depreciation deductions are then computed on the cost as reduced by the expensed amount and the bonus deduction. This is the same computational rule that applied under the Code Sec. 168(k) bonus depreciation provision described at ¶ 127D.

> ***Example (1):*** A taxpayer purchases $1,000 of qualifying Gulf Opportunity Zone property and places it in service in 2006. If the taxpayer claims a $200 Code Sec. 179 expense allowance on the property, the additional allowance is equal to $400 (($1,000 - $200) × 50%). The regular first-year MACRS depreciation deduction, assuming the property is 5-year MACRS property and the half-year convention applies, is $80 (($1,000 - $200 - $400) × 20% first year MACRS table percentage for 5-year property subject to half-year convention).

*Sec. 179 expense allowance increased.* The Code Sec. 179 allowance may be claimed on Gulf Opportunity Zone property that is also qualifying section 179 property. The new law increases the section 179 dollar limitation on section 179

Gulf Opportunity Zone property placed in service on or before December 31, 2007 by an additional $100,000 and the investment limitation by an additional $600,000 (Code Sec. 1400N(e), as added by the Gulf Zone Act). The placed-in-service deadline is extended one year if the section 179 property is located in a county or parish within the GO-Zone where more than 60 percent of the housing units were destroyed by hurricanes during 2005. See ¶ 306.

*Qualifying Property*

The GO Zone bonus allowance is claimed on "qualified Gulf Opportunity Zone property." Subject to the exceptions described below, qualified Gulf Opportunity Zone property is property:

(1) that is described in Code Sec. 168(k)(2)(A)(i) (i.e., property of a type that would qualify for bonus depreciation under Code Sec. 168(k)) or is new nonresidential real property or residential rental property;

(2) substantially all (80 percent or more) of the use of the property is in the Gulf Opportunity Zone (i.e., the GO Zone) and is in the active conduct of a trade or business by the taxpayer in the GO Zone;

(3) the original use of the property in the GO Zone commences with the taxpayer on or after August 28, 2005;

(4) the property is acquired by the taxpayer by purchase (within the meaning of Code Sec. 179(d) (see ¶ 302)) on or after August 28, 2005 and no written binding contract for the acquisition was in effect before August 28, 2005; and

(5) the property is placed in service by the taxpayer on or before December 31, 2007 (December 31, 2008 or December 31, 2011, as explained below, in the case of residential rental property or nonresidential real property).

*Property described in Code Sec. 168(k)(2)(A)(i).* In general, this is property with an MACRS recovery period of 20 years or less, computer software that is amortizable over 3 years under Code Sec. 167(f) (see ¶ 48), MACRS 25-year water utility property (see ¶ 113), and qualified leasehold improvement property as defined for purposes of the Code Sec. 168(k) bonus allowance (see "*Qualified leasehold improvement property*" at ¶ 127D).

*Gulf Opportunity Zone defined.* In general, the Gulf Opportunity Zone is the area of the Gulf Coast that was declared a disaster area by President Bush as a result of Hurricane Katrina and for which individual or public assistance is authorized (Code Sec. 1400M(1)). See IRS Publication 4492 (January 2006) for a list of counties located in Alabama, Louisiana, and Mississippi that are within the GO zone.

*Residential rental and nonresidential real property.*

Unlike the Code Sec. 168(k) bonus depreciation allowance (¶ 127D), the Gulf Zone bonus allowance may be claimed on residential rental and nonresidential real property. The property must be new because the original use within the zone must commence with the taxpayer. However, if used property located in the Zone is purchased and rehabilitated (e.g., first story water damage repaired), the cost of rehabilitation may qualify for the allowance. In addition, as explained under the *Original Use* discussion below, the cost of the damaged building may also qualify if its cost is not more than 20 percent of the total value of the property after it is rehabilitated.

The Gulf Zone bonus deduction is treated as an accelerated depreciation deduction for purposes of the section 1250 recapture rules. This treatment is also prescribed when the Code Sec. 168(k) bonus deduction (¶ 127D) is claimed on section 1250 property (Reg. § 1.168(k)-1(f)(3)).

Rehabilitations to residential rental or nonresidential real property that is not MACRS property (for example, because placed in service before 1986 by the taxpayer) qualify for the bonus deduction because the cost of rehabilitation is treated as MACRS residential rental or nonresidential real property regardless of the depreciation method used to depreciate the rehabilitated building. As discussed below, however, no bonus deduction is allowed for nonresidential real property or rehabilitations to nonresidential real property located in a renewal community if an election is made to claim a current expense or amortization deduction under Code Sec. 1400I on the cost of new nonresidential real property placed in service by the taxpayer in a renewal community.

Generally, residential rental or nonresidential real property must be placed in service on or before December 31, 2008 in order to qualify for the GO-Zone bonus allowance. However, this deadline is extended to December 31, 2011 in the case of "specified Gulf Opportunity Zone extension property." Specified Gulf Opportunity Zone extension property is residential rental or nonresidential real property located in a county or parish within the GO-Zone where more than 60 percent of the housing units were destroyed by any hurricanes during 2005 (Code Sec. 1400N(d)(6), as amended by the Tax Relief, Unemployment Insurance Reauthorization, and Job Creation Act of 2010 (P.L. 111-312)). These are the Louisiana parishes of Calcasieu, Cameron, Orleans, Plaquemines, St. Bernard, St. Tammany, and Washington, and the Mississippi counties of Hancock, Harrison, Jackson, Pearl River, and Stone (Notice 2007-36). *Prior to amendment by P.L. 111-312, the placed-in-service deadline for specified Gulf Opportunity Zone extension property was December 31, 2010 and only progress expenditures incurred through December 31, 2009 qualified for the deduction.* P.L. 111-312, however, has effectively eliminated the progress expenditures limitation by only disallowing progress expenditures for post-2011 construction (Code Sec. 1400N(d)(6)(D), as amended by P.L. 111-312).

Code Sec. 1400N(d)(6)(B)(ii)(II) provides that property described in Code Sec. 168(k)(2)(A)(i) that is located in a building within one of these qualifying counties or parishes will qualify for the bonus allowance as specified Gulf Opportunity Zone extension property if the property is placed in service within 90 days after the building is placed in service, provided that the building is placed in service by the December 31, 2011 placed-in-service deadline. Code Sec. 168(k)(2)(A)(i) describes property of the type that qualifies for bonus depreciation under the regular rules (generally, property with an MACRS recovery period of 20 years or less). However, if property qualifies for bonus depreciation under both Code Sec. 168(k)(2) and another provision it is treated as qualifying only under Code Sec. 168(k)(2). Since Code Sec. 168(k)(2) has been extended to apply to property placed in service before January 1, 2015, Code Sec. 1400N(d)(6)(B)(ii)(II) presently has no relevance.

*Active trade or business requirement*

As noted below, Gulf Zone bonus depreciation may not be claimed unless substantially all (80 percent or more) of the use of the property in the Gulf Zone is in the active conduct of a trade or business. The following question and answer from the IRS web site (https://www.irs.gov/businesses/small-businesses-self-employed/faqs-for-hurricane-victims-bonus-depreciation-including-go-zone) considers the active conduct of a trade or business requirement in the context of a residential rental property. Notice 2006-77 discussed below provides additional guidance.

*Q: Regarding rental property – three scenarios:*

(1) *A taxpayer operates multiple rental units. In November 2005, he acquires a new apartment house under construction and places it in service in February 2006. Does he qualify for the 50% bonus depreciation?*

(2) *A taxpayer had no rental property as of August 29, 2005. In December he acquires seven new houses (never previously placed in service) in the GO Zone, which he rents to displaced Katrina victims. Does he qualify for the 50% bonus depreciation?*

(3) *A taxpayer had no rental property as of August 29, 2005. In December, he acquires one new house (never previously placed in service) in the GO Zone, which he rents to a displaced business associate. Does he qualify for the 50% bonus depreciation? Is he engaged in an active trade or business?*

*A: Like the Liberty Zone bonus, the GO Zone bonus applies to nonresidential real property and residential rental property. One of the requirements to be GO Zone property is that the property is in the active conduct of a trade or business by the taxpayer in the GO Zone. This requirement is similar to the one in the Liberty Zone bonus. The Liberty Zone bonus regulations do not define "active conduct."*

*With respect to rental real estate, the hurdle to get over is this active conduct requirement. There are two components to satisfy –*

(1) *Trade or business – has the same meaning as in Code Sec. 162 and the regulations thereunder.*

(2) *Active conduct – where Congress intended to treat all real estate rental as a active conduct in a trade or business, Congress provided such a provision (e.g., see Code Sec. 168(j)(5)). Because Code Sec. 1400N(d) does not contain a provision similar to that in Code Sec. 168(j)(5), it appears that some real estate rentals may not be in the active conduct of a trade or business for purposes of Code Sec. 1400N(d). Neither the statute nor the legislative history provides guidance on what standard to consider for "active conduct." Other Code sections have a standard. For example, there is the material participation standard in section 469 and the meaningful participation standard in Reg. § 1.179-2(c)(6)(ii). Future guidance may be provided on what standard to apply for "active conduct."*

Guidance on the active trade or business requirement was provided by the IRS in Notice 2006-77. A taxpayer generally is considered to actively conduct a trade or business if the taxpayer meaningfully participates in the management or operations of the trade or business. A partner, member, or shareholder of a partnership, limited liability company, or S corporation, respectively, is considered to actively conduct a trade or business of the partnership, limited liability company, or S corporation if the partnership, limited liability company, or S corporation meaningfully participates (through the activities performed by itself, or by others on behalf of the partnership, limited liability company, or S corporation, respectively) in the management or operations of the trade or business. Similar rules apply to other pass-thru entities such as trusts or estates (Notice 2006-77).

Note that even if the active conduct standard that applies for purposes of the deduction is satisfied, the passive activity rules of Code Sec. 469 could operate to prevent the deduction if the Code Sec. 469 material participation standard is not satisfied by the partner or LLC member.

A triple-net lease in which the lessee is responsible for all of the costs relating to the building (for example, paying all taxes, insurance, and maintenance expenses) in addition to paying rent does not satisfy the active conduct standard (Notice 2006-77, Sec. 3.02(3)(c), Example (3)).

For additional discussion of the active trade or business requirement, see ¶ 302, "5. Active Conduct of Trade or Business Requirement."

*Substantially all requirement*

Substantially all of the use of the property (80 percent or more) must be in the GO Zone and in the active conduct of a trade or business by the taxpayer in the GO Zone. Thus, if more than 20 percent of the use of the property is either outside the counties and parishes designated as being part of the GO Zone or is not in the active conduct of a trade or business by the taxpayer in the GO Zone, then the property is not GO Zone property and is not eligible for the GO Zone additional first year depreciation deduction (Code Sec. 1400N(d)(2)(A); Notice 2006-77). This requirement is the same as the requirement in section Code Sec. 1400L(b)(2)(A)(ii) for the New York Liberty Zone bonus depreciation. Reg. § 1.1400L(b)-1(c)(3) defines "substantially all" as meaning 80 percent or more.

If the substantially all requirement is not satisfied in a tax year after the property is placed in service, the GO Zone bonus depreciation deduction must be recaptured as explained below.

Many vessels have a base of operations in the GO Zone but are used predominantly outside of the GO Zone. Apparently, taxpayers who purchase replacement vessels or repair damaged vessels will not qualify for the bonus allowance since 80 percent or more of the use is not within the GO-Zone.

The owner of a charter fishing company located in the Gulf Opportunity Zone (GO Zone) was not entitled to bonus depreciation for Go Zone property with respect to a luxury charter fishing boat that he purchased. For the tax year at issue, the boat was used for 74 days in the GO Zone. However, prior to being put into service in the GO Zone, the boat was in the Caribbean for several months undergoing repairs. During this time, even though the boat was not fully functional, it was used on 43 days for charters. Since the boat was only used 63 percent of the time in the GO Zone, the "substantially all" requirement for bonus depreciation was not met (*B.C. Blakeney*, TC Memo. 2012-289, Dec. 59,224(M)).

*Original use requirement*

Generally, only new property qualifies for the additional bonus allowance. However, used property may also qualify if it has not been previously used for personal or business purposes within the Gulf Opportunity Zone by any person (i.e., its first use in the Zone must commence with the taxpayer). As explained below, additional capital expenditures incurred to recondition or rebuild property that is currently located in the GO Zone will qualify for the bonus deduction (Notice 2007-36, clarifying, modifying, and amplifying Section 2.02(3) of Notice 2006-77).

The original use rules for Code Sec. 168(k) bonus depreciation relating to sale-leasebacks, syndications, fractional interests, and certain other transactions also apply to Go Zone bonus depreciation (Section 5 of Notice 2007-36). See below.

*Original use—rehabilitations of personal or real property.* The cost of rehabilitations to real or personal business property located in the GO Zone meet the original use requirement. However, the materials and components used in the rehabilitation cannot previously have been used in the GO-Zone as this would violate the original use requirement. Also, as discussed below, no deduction is allowed for nonresidential real property or rehabilitations to nonresidential real property if a deduction for qualified revitalization buildings and rehabilitation expenditures is claimed under Code Sec. 1400I.

Generally, no portion of the cost of an existing building located in the GO-Zone can qualify for the GO-Zone bonus allowance because its original use in the GO-Zone is not by the taxpayer. An important exception, however, can apply to a substantially damaged building. Recent IRS guidance provides that the cost of a damaged building qualifies for bonus depreciation if it is not more than 20 percent of the total cost of the property taking into account the rehabilitations. This rule also applies to personal property—for example, used machinery and equipment originally located in the GO Zone that is rebuilt or reconditioned. This rule applies whether the property is acquired or self-constructed (Section 5 of Notice 2007-36, clarifying, modifying, and amplifying Section 2.02(3) of Notice 2006-77).

***Example (2):*** John's rental unit is damaged in Hurricane Katrina. The cost of any rehabilitations made by John that are capitalized meet the original use requirement. John may claim the bonus deduction on the cost of the rehabilitations when he places them into service assuming all other requirements for claiming the bonus deduction are satisfied.

***Example (3):*** John's rental unit is badly damaged in Hurricane Katrina. John spends $4 million rehabilitating or improving the building and then sells it to Sam for $5 million before placing the building back in service. $1 million of the cost is attributed to the building and $4 million to the rehabilitation expenditures. Sam may claim bonus depreciation on the $1 million cost (as well as the $4 million cost of the rehabilitation expenditures), assuming all other requirements for the deduction are met since only 20 percent of the total amount expended by Sam ($5 million × 20 percent = $1 million) is attributable to the damaged building (the "used part"). In effect, the $1 million cost of the building is considered new property (Example 4 of Section 5 of Notice 2007-36). Presumably, if Sam had purchased the damaged building from John for $1 million and spent at least $4 million on capitalized rehabilitations, the $1 million cost of the building (as well as the $4 million rehabilitation expenditures) would qualify for bonus depreciation since the 20 percent rule applies to property that is self-constructed by a taxpayer as well as property that is acquired by a taxpayer.

The following Question & Answer relating to the original use requirement is from the IRS web site (Headliner Volume 149 at http://www.irs.gov/businesses/small/article/0,,id=154787,00.html).

*Q: A business's building is severely damaged by the storm. Can it claim the additional 50% depreciation in the following circumstances?*

(1) *Business spends $450,000 restoring the building it operated in before the storm and an additional $600,000 expanding it.*

(2) *Business buys another pre-existing building in New Orleans for $1 million and spends another $450,000 adapting this building to its needs.*

*A: These two questions deal with the original use requirement, which is one of the five requirements for satisfying the definition of GO Zone property. The original use rule for GO Zone property is similar to the original use rule for Liberty Zone property. See Temporary Reg. § 1.168(k)-1T(b)(3) (now a final regulation, Reg. § 1.168(k)-1(b)(3)—CCH) and Temporary Reg. § 1.1400L(b)-1T(c)(4) (now a final regulation, Reg. § 1.1400L(b)-1(c)(4)—CCH). (For these two questions, we have assumed the building is not rental property.)*

(1) *Yes, assuming the improvements comprising the $1,050,000 are GO Zone property (e.g., the improvements are new components or are used components that are used for the first time in the GO Zone).*

(2) *No for the $1 million cost of the building because it does not satisfy the original use requirement. Yes for the $450,000 of additional capital expenditures to rebuild or recondition the building, assuming the improvements comprising the*

*$450,000 are GO Zone property (e.g., the improvements are new components or are used components that are used for the first time in the GO Zone).*

*Excluded property not qualifying for GO Zone bonus depreciation*

The following property is not considered qualified Gulf Opportunity Zone property even if the preceding requirements are satisfied:

(1) property which must be depreciated under the MACRS alternative depreciation system;

(2) tax-exempt bond-financed property;

(3) qualified revitalization buildings with respect to which a deduction for revitalization expenditures is claimed under Code Sec. 1400I; and

(4) property used in connection with a private or commercial golf course, a country club, a massage parlor, a hot tub facility, a suntan facility, a liquor store, or a gambling or animal or racing property (Code Sec. 1400N(p)).

If specified Gulf Opportunity Zone extension property also qualifies for bonus depreciation under Code Sec. 168(k) (¶ 127D), the bonus depreciation is only claimed under the rules of Code Sec. 168(k) (Code Sec. 1400N(d)(6)(E)). The only property that could qualify under both provisions is new personal property acquired after 2007 and placed in service before 2011 in or on a building placed in service in a specified portion of the GO Zone (Section 6.01(2)(b) of Rev. Proc. 2008-54). See *Residential Rental and Nonresidential Real Property*, above.

*Mandatory ADS property.* Any property that must be depreciated using the MACRS alternative depreciation system (ADS), except by reason of an election to use ADS, does not qualify for the GO Zone bonus depreciation allowance. Thus, the GO Zone bonus depreciation allowance does not apply to tangible property used predominantly outside of the U.S., tax-exempt use property, tax-exempt bond financed property, and listed property, such as a car, not used more than 50 percent for business purposes. See "*Mandatory ADS property does not qualify for bonus depreciation*" at ¶ 127D for additional information.

*Tax-exempt bond-financed property.* If any portion of a property is financed with the proceeds of an obligation that pays interest that is exempt from tax under Code Sec. 103, no portion of the property qualifies for GO Zone bonus depreciation. Note that a new law provision of the Gulf Opportunity Zone Act authorizes the issuance of tax-exempt private activity bonds to finance the construction and rehabilitation of residential rental and nonresidential real property in the Gulf Opportunity Zone (Code Sec. 1400N(a)). Property financed to any extent under this provision will not qualify for the Gulf Zone bonus depreciation allowance.

*Qualified revitalization buildings.* Code Sec. 1400I allows a taxpayer to claim a current expense or amortization deduction on the cost of new nonresidential real property placed in service by the taxpayer in a renewal community (as defined in Code Sec. 1400E). The current expense or amortization deduction is also available for the cost of rehabilitating used nonresidential real property that is acquired by a taxpayer and placed in service in a renewal community. The current expense deduction is 50 percent of the qualified revitalization expenditures (i.e., 50 percent of the cost of a new building or 50 percent of the sum of the cost of rehabilitating an existing building plus a specified percentage of the cost of acquiring the existing building for rehabilitation). Alternatively, all expenditures that would be deductible without regard to the 50 percent limit may be amortized over a 120-month period. If a taxpayer elects to claim a current expense or amortization deduction, the GO Zone bonus allowance may not be claimed on the qualified revitalization building and, presumably, any rehabilitation expenditures.

The government has designated 40 renewal communities. These communities are listed at http://www.hud.gov/offices/cpd/economicdevelopment/programs/rc/index.cfm.

*Golf courses etc. (prohibited activities).* The deduction may not be claimed for any property used in connection with any private or commercial golf course, massage parlor, hot tub facility, suntan facility, or any store the principal business of which is the sale of alcoholic beverages for consumption off premises or any gambling or animal racing property (Code Sec. 1400N(p); Notice 2006-77).

If real property is used for both a prohibited activity and an non-prohibited activity, the portion of the real property (determined by square footage) that is not dedicated to the prohibited activity is eligible for the bonus deduction (assuming all other requirements are met).

A taxpayer's trade or business activity that has less than 10 percent of its total gross receipts derived from massages, tanning services, or a hot tub facility is not treated as, respectively, a massage parlor, a suntan facility, or a hot tub facility. For example, no portion of a physical therapy office or a beauty/day spa salon is treated as prohibited property if the taxpayer's gross receipts derived from massages, suntanning, and hot tub facilities are less than 10 percent of total gross receipts. Only gross receipts from the taxpayer's trade or business activity that includes the massages, tanning services, or hot tub facility are taken into account. If a taxpayer is a member of a consolidated group, only the gross receipts of the taxpayer (and not the consolidated group) are taken into account. Also, if the taxpayer is a partnership, S corporation, or other pass-thru entity, only the gross receipts of the pass-thru entity (and not the owners of the pass-thru entity) are taken into account (Notice 2006-77). Gross receipts are specially defined in Notice 2006-77. This exception does not apply to gambling and animal racing property.

*Gambling and animal racing property.* Gambling or racing property is any equipment, furniture, software, or other property used directly in connection with gambling, the racing of animals, or the on-site viewing of such racing, and the portion of any real property (determined by square footage) which is dedicated to gambling, animal racing, or the on-site viewing of such racing. The exclusion for real property does not apply if the dedicated portion is less than 100 square feet (Code Sec. 1400N(p), as added by the Gulf Zone Act). For example, no apportionment is required under this 100-square-foot de minimis rule in the case of a retail store that sells lottery tickets in a less than 100 square foot area (Notice 2006-77).

Hotels, restaurants, parking lots and other nongaming property that is attached to a gaming facility is eligible for the GO Zone additional first year depreciation deduction (assuming all other requirements under are met). For example, the GO Zone additional first year depreciation deduction for a building that is used as both a casino and a hotel is determined without regard to the portion of the building's unadjusted depreciable basis that bears the same percentage to the total unadjusted depreciable basis as the percentage of square footage dedicated to gambling (that is, the casino floor) bears to the total square footage of the building (Notice 2006-77).

*Other exclusions.* Property placed in service and disposed of during the same tax year does not qualify. However, rules similar to the rules in Reg. § 1.168(k)-1(f)(1)(ii) and (iii) (technical termination of a partnership under Code Sec. 708(b)(1)(B), prior to amendment by P.L. 115-97, or transactions described in Code Sec. 168(i)(7)) apply. Property converted from business or income-producing use to personal use in the same taxable year in which the property is placed in service by a taxpayer does not qualify. If depreciable property is not GO Zone property in the tax year in which the property is placed in service by the taxpayer, the GO Zone additional first year depreciation deduction is not allowable for the property even if a change in use of the property subsequent to the placed-in-service year of the property results in the property being GO Zone property. See Reg. § 1.168(k)-1(f)(6)(iv)(B) (Notice 2006-77).

If specified Gulf Opportunity Zone extension property also qualifies for bonus depreciation under Code Sec. 168(k) (¶ 127D), the bonus depreciation is only claimed under the rules of Code Sec. 168(k) (Code Sec. 1400N(d)(6)(E)). The only property that could qualify under both provisions is new personal property acquired after 2007 and placed in service before 2010 in or on a building placed in service in a specified portion of the GO Zone (Section 6.01(2)(b) of Rev. Proc. 2008-54). See *Residential Rental and Nonresidential Real Property,* above.

*First-year depreciation caps on passenger automobiles not increased*

The provision does not increase the first-year depreciation caps on passenger automobiles for which the additional depreciation allowance is claimed. A $7,650 bump-up was allowed if 50-percent bonus depreciation was claimed under Code Sec. 168(k) (Code Sec. 168(k)(2)(F)). Although new Code Sec. 1400N(d) incorporates certain rules contained in Code Sec. 168(k) by cross-reference (see, for example, Code Sec. 1400N(d)(3) and (4)), no cross reference incorporation to Code Sec. 168(k)(2)(F) is provided. It seems likely that the failure to increase in the first-year cap was intentional given that Congress did not provide for a bump-up in the cap for vehicles located in the New York Liberty Zone when it enacted the New York Liberty Zone bonus depreciation provision contained in Code Sec. 1400L(b). See "*Vehicles in the New York Liberty Zone*" at ¶ 200.

*Self-constructed property, sale-leasebacks, syndication transactions, and related parties*

Rules similar to those contained under the Code Sec. 168(k) bonus depreciation provision for self-constructed property in Code Sec. 168(k)(2)(E)(i), sale leasebacks in Code Sec. 168(k)(2)(E)(ii), syndication transactions in Code Sec. 168(k)(2)(E)(iii), and limitations related to users and related parties in Code Sec. 168(k)(2)(E)(iv) apply to qualified Gulf Opportunity Zone property by substituting August 27, 2005 for December 31, 2007 each place it appears and in the case of the self-constructed property rule without regard to the requirement contained in Code Sec. 168(k)(2)(E)(i) that manufacture, construction, or production must begin before January 1, 2009 (Code Sec. 1400N(d)(3), as added by the Gulf Opportunity Zone Act and amended by the Housing Assistance Act of 2008 (P.L. 110-289)).

Thus, under the self-constructed property rule as it applies to GO Zone property that is manufactured, constructed, or produced by a taxpayer for its own use qualifies for the additional allowance if the taxpayer begins the manufacture, construction, or production after August 27, 2005, and the property is placed in service before January 1, 2008 (January 1, 2009 in the case of residential rental and nonresidential real property) (January 1, 2011 in the case of such property located in a specified county) (Code Sec. 1400N(d)(3), as added by the Gulf Opportunity Zone Act and amended by the Housing Assistance Act (P.L. 110-289), Code Sec. 168(k)(2)(E)(i); Reg. § 1.168(k)-1(b)(4)(iii))). Prior to amendment by P.L. 110-289, manufacture, construction, or production had to start after August 27, 2005 and before January 1, 2008 (Code Sec. 1400N(d)(3), prior to amendment by P.L. 110-289). The amended law now allows a taxpayer to claim GO-Zone bonus depreciation on real property if manufacture, construction, or production starts after August 27, 2005 and the property is placed in service before January 1, 2009 (January 1, 2011 if the property is placed in service in a specified county but only pre-January 1, 2010 progress expenditures qualify). Property manufactured, constructed, or produced for a taxpayer by another person under a contract entered into before the manufacture, construction, or production of the property is considered to be manufactured, constructed, or produced by the taxpayer.

The limitation related to users and related parties will prevent property from qualifying for the additional allowance if the user of the property as of the date on which the property was originally placed in service, or a related party to the user, acquired, or had a written binding contract in effect for the acquisition of the property at any time on or before August 27, 2005. In addition, property manufactured, constructed, or produced for the taxpayer or a related party does not qualify for the additional allowance if the manufacture, construction, or production of the property for the taxpayer or a related party began at any time on or before August 27, 2005. Persons are related if they have a relationship specified in Code Sec. 267(b) or Code Sec. 707(b) (Code Sec. 1400N(d)(3), as added by the Gulf Opportunity Zone Act; Code Sec. 168(k)(2)(E)(iv); Reg. § 1.168(k)-1(b)(4)(iv)(A)).

For additional information see ¶ 127D, "*Self-constructed property*", "*Sale-leasebacks*", "*Syndication transactions* " under "*Sale-leasebacks*", and "*Binding contracts in effect with respect to original user or related party—disqualified transaction rule*" under "*Binding contracts defined*".

*Recapture upon decline in business use*

If GO Zone property is no longer GO Zone property in the hands of the same taxpayer at any time before the end of the GO Zone property's recovery period as determined under § 167(f)(1) or § 168, as applicable, then the taxpayer must recapture in the taxable year in which the GO Zone property is no longer GO Zone property (the recapture year) the benefit derived from claiming the GO Zone additional first year depreciation deduction for such property. The GO Zone bonus depreciation deduction may not be claimed unless substantially all (80 percent or more) of the property's use is in the taxpayer's trade or business in the GO Zone. Recapture rules similar to those that apply to property expensed under Code Sec. 179 apply if the qualified Gulf Opportunity Zone property ceases to be qualified Gulf Opportunity Zone property. Thus, if such property is used less than 80 percent in a trade or business activity within the GO-Zone during any year of the MACRS recovery period that applies for regular tax purposes, the benefit of the deduction will be recaptured (Code Sec. 1400N(d)(5), as added by the Gulf Zone Act; Notice 2008-25).

If there is a disposition to which the section 1245 or section 1250 recapture rules apply, then recapture under this provision is not required (Notice 2008-25, Section 3.02). However, if GO Zone property is transferred by a taxpayer in a like-kind exchange or as a result of an involuntary conversion (relinquished property) and the replacement property is not GO Zone property in the hands of the taxpayer and is not substantially used in the GO Zone or in the active conduct of a trade or business by the taxpayer in the GO Zone, there is recapture under this provision. The amount to be recaptured and the resulting increase in basis are determined before the application of Code Secs. 1031, 1033, 1245, or 1250. If GO Zone property is transferred by a taxpayer in a like-kind exchange or as a result of an involuntary conversion (relinquished property) and the replacement property is not GO Zone property in the hands of the taxpayer but is substantially used in the GO Zone and in the active conduct of a trade or business by the taxpayer in the GO Zone, there is no recapture under this provision. However, if after the acquisition of the replacement property, that property ceases to be substantially used in the GO Zone or in the active conduct of a trade or business by the taxpayer in the GO Zone, there is recapture under this provision. Similarly, there is recapture under this provision if, after the acquisition of the replacement property, that property is transferred by the taxpayer in another like-kind exchange or another involuntary conversion and the subsequent replacement property is not GO Zone property in the hands of the taxpayer and is not substantially used in the GO Zone or in the active conduct of a trade or business by the taxpayer in the GO Zone.

Notice 2008-25 contains examples of recapture calculations, including calculations for property that is relinquished in a like-kind exchange or as a result of an involuntary conversion.

The recaptured benefit derived from claiming the GO Zone additional first-year depreciation deduction for the property is equal to the excess of the total depreciation claimed (including the GO Zone additional first year depreciation deduction) for the property for the tax years before the recapture year over the total depreciation that would have been allowable for the tax years before the recapture year had the GO Zone additional first year depreciation deduction not been claimed (regardless of whether such excess reduced the taxpayer's tax liability). The amount recaptured is treated as ordinary income for the recapture year. For the recapture year and subsequent tax years, the taxpayer's depreciation deductions are determined as if no GO Zone additional first year depreciation deduction was claimed with respect to the property. If, subsequent to the recapture year, a change in the use of the property results in the property again being GO Zone property, then the GO Zone additional first year depreciation deduction is not allowable for the property (Notice 2008-25).

> ***Example (4):*** Five-year MACRS property costing $1,000 is placed in service in the Gulf Zone in 2006. A $500 bonus deduction is claimed. Regular depreciation is $100 (($1,000 - $500) × 20% regular first year table depreciation percentage). In 2007 business use in the Gulf Zone drops to 70 percent. Recapture in 2007 is the $400 difference between the depreciation, including bonus depreciation, claimed in 2006 ($600) and the depreciation that would have been allowed in 2006 without claiming the bonus deduction ($1,000 × 20% = $200). The 2007 depreciation deduction is $224 ($1,000 × 70% business use × 32% second-year table percentage).

The IRS has ruled that a restructuring transaction involving the transfer of Gulf Zone property from a single member LLC to an S corporation and the lease of the property back to the LLC, pursuant to an operating lease, did not result in recapture. The taxpayer was the sole shareholder of the S corporation and the single member of the LLC. The same taxpayer owned the property before and after the transaction (both the LLC and S corporation were disregarded entities) and the property was used in the active conduct of a trade or business by the S corporation and taxpayer before and after the restructuring transactions (IRS Letter Ruling 201618008, February 1, 2016).

*Coordination with section 179 recapture rules and listed property recapture rules.* As noted above, the section 179 allowance ($125,000 in 2007 and $250,000 in 2008 and 2009) is increased by an additional $100,000 for qualifying section 179 Gulf Opportunity Zone property placed in service before January 1, 2008 (before January 1, 2009 in certain counties and parishes). This additional increase is subject to recapture if the property ceases to be qualified GO Zone property because its business use in the GO Zone drops below 80 percent (Code Sec. 1400N(e)(4)). The entire section 179 deduction claimed on Gulf Zone property (e.g., the basic allowance of $125,000 in 2007 and the $100,000 increase for GO Zone property) is subject to recapture under the existing section 179 recapture rules (¶ 300) if combined business use within and outside of the Zone falls to 50 percent or less. Thus, if business use of Gulf Zone property within the Zone is below 80 percent and above

50 percent, the bonus deduction is subject to recapture and any section 179 expense claimed that is attributable to the $100,000 increase for GO Zone property is subject to recapture. However, if Gulf Zone bonus depreciation and the section 179 deduction is claimed on a listed property, as defined at ¶ 208 and business use falls to 50 percent or less during the alternative depreciation system (ADS) recovery period, the bonus deduction is subject to recapture and the listed property recapture rules (¶ 210) apply to determine the recaptured section 179 deduction amount. The recapture guidance provided in Notice 2008-25 does not explain how to coordinate the Gulf Zone bonus depreciation recapture rules with the section 179 recapture rules for listed and nonlisted property.

***Example (5):*** Assume the same facts as in *Example (4)* except that a $100 section 179 expense allowance was also claimed. No portion of the allowance is attributable to the extra section 179 allowance for GO Zone property. The section 179 expense is not recaptured because business use is above 50 percent. 2006 bonus depreciation is $450 (($1,000 − $100) × 50%). Regular depreciation is $90 (($1,000 − $100 − $450) × 20%). Bonus recapture in 2007 is the $360 difference between the depreciation, including the section 179 expense allowance and bonus depreciation, claimed in 2006 ($100 + $450 + $90 = $640) and the depreciation (including section 179 allowance) that would have been allowed in 2006 without claiming the bonus deduction ($100 + (($1,000 − $100) × 20%) = $280). The 2007 depreciation deduction is $202 (($1,000 − $100) × 70% business use × 32% second-year table percentage). Without using the table percentages 2007 depreciation is also calculated as $202 (($1,000 − $100 − $450 − $90 + $360) × 70% business use percentage × 40% DB rate for five-year property).

The recapture rule for Gulf Opportunity Zone bonus depreciation set forth in Notice 2008-25 is similar to the rule that applies under the listed property recapture rules (viz., recapture is the difference between total depreciation claimed in recovery years prior to the recapture year (including the section 179 expense allowance and bonus allowance) and the depreciation that would have been claimed if the section 179 allowance and bonus allowance had not been claimed). Note, however, that under the listed property recapture rules recapture of both the bonus deduction and section 179 deduction should be determined by using the alternative depreciation system (ADS). Furthermore, ADS must be used to compute depreciation throughout the remaining ADS recovery period of the asset beginning in the recapture year determined as if ADS had been used from the year that asset was placed in service and no bonus or section 179 deduction was ever claimed.

***Example (6):*** Assume the same facts as *Example (5)* except that the asset is a 5-year MACRS listed property (which also has a 5-year alternative depreciation system (ADS) recovery period) and that business use drops to 40 percent in 2007. Now the listed property recapture rule (¶ 210) applies because the property is a listed property and business use dropped to 50 percent or below during the asset's ADS recovery period. Under the listed property recapture rules, recapture is the $540 difference between the total depreciation/bonus/section 179 expense claimed in 2006 ($640) and the depreciation that would have been allowed in 2006 under the MACRS alternative depreciation system (ADS) without claiming the section 179 allowance and bonus depreciation ($1,000 × 10% first-year ADS table percentage = $100). 2007 depreciation is $80 ($1,000 × 40% business use percentage × 20% second-year ADS table percentage for property with a 5-year ADS period). Without using table percentages, 2007 depreciation is also $80 ($1,000 − $100 − $450 − $90 + $540 × 40% business use × 22.22% ADS SL rate (1/ 4.5 remaining years in recovery period = 22.22%)).

The manner of computing MACRS deductions without table percentages is explained at ¶ 179.

*Alternative minimum tax*

The 50-percent GO Zone bonus deduction may be claimed in full for alternative minimum tax purposes. The MACRS depreciation deductions computed for regular tax purposes on the adjusted basis of the qualified Gulf Opportunity Zone property that remains after reduction by the 50-percent allowance may also be claimed in full for AMT purposes (Code Sec. 1400N(d)(4), as added by Gulf Opportunity Zone Act). The AMT rules for qualified Gulf Opportunity Zone property are similar to those that apply under Code Sec. 168(k)(2)(G) of the Code Sec. 168(k) bonus depreciation provision. The related regulations issued under the Code Sec. 168(k) bonus depreciation provision are in Reg. § 1.168(k)-1(d)(1)(iii) and Reg. § 1.168(k)-1(d)(2)(ii). Note that an election out of GO-Zone bonus depreciation could trigger an AMT liability since depreciation deductions claimed on 3-, 5-, 7-, and 10-year MACRS property will generate an AMT depreciation adjustment if such property is depreciated using the 200 percent declining balance method, as is generally the case. See, also, "*Alternative minimum tax*" at ¶ 127D.

*Election out of GO Zone bonus depreciation*

The GO Zone bonus depreciation allowance must be claimed unless a taxpayer makes an election out. Revocation of an election out may only be made with IRS permission. An election out must be made separately for each class of property (Code Sec. 1400N(d)(2)(B)(iv)). Thus, for example, a taxpayer may elect out for all five-year MACRS property placed in service during the tax year. A separate election out would need to be made for other MACRS property classes. The election out only applies to property within an elected class that is placed in service during the tax year of the election

In the case of the MACRS residential rental and MACRS nonresidential real property classes, the election out also applies to all real property in the same property class (i.e., to all property in the residential rental class and to all property in the nonresidential real property class). For example, if a taxpayer places several MACRS nonresidential real property buildings in service during the tax year, the election out, if made, would apply to all of the buildings.

See Form 4562 instructions for election procedures.

The election is made by each person owning GO Zone property (for example, for each member of a consolidated group by the common parent of the group, by the partnership, or by the S corporation) (Notice 2006-77).

In general, the election is made by the due date (including extensions) of the federal income tax return for the tax year in which the GO Zone property is placed in service by the taxpayer. The election must be made in the manner prescribed on Form 4562, Depreciation and Amortization, and its instructions (Notice 2006-77). The election out requires the attachment of a statement to the taxpayer's timely filed return (including extensions) indicating the class of property for which the taxpayer is making the election and that, for such class of property, the taxpayer is electing not to claim the GO Zone additional first year depreciation deduction.

An election not to deduct the GO Zone additional first-year depreciation allowance is revocable only with the prior written consent of the Commissioner (Notice 2006-77, Sec. 4.04). Although a taxpayer may revoke an election to claim bonus depreciation under Code Sec. 168(k) (¶ 127D) (Reg. § 1.168(k)-1(e)(7)) or in the Kansas disaster area (127G) (Sec. 4.01 of Notice 2008-67) within 6 months after the original due date (excluding extensions) of the timely filed return on which the election was made, it does not appear that this option is available for the GO Zone bonus depreciation election (Section 4(04) of Notice 2006-77; Instructions to Form 4562).

If an election out is not made, depreciation is computed on the basis that remains taking into account the allowable GO-Zone allowance even if the allowance was not claimed (Notice 2006-77, Sec. 4.05).

*Deemed election out rule for 2004 or 2005 federal income tax return filed before September 13, 2006.* A taxpayer that files its 2004 or 2005 federal income tax return before September 13, 2006, is treated as having made a valid election out for a class of property that is GO Zone property placed in service by the taxpayer on or after August 28, 2005, during the taxpayer's 2004 or 2005 taxable year, if the taxpayer:

(1) on that return, did not claim the GO Zone additional first year depreciation deduction for that class of property but did claim depreciation; and

(2) does not file an amended federal tax return for the taxpayer's 2004 or 2005 taxable year on or before February 14, 2007, or a Form 3115, Application for Change in Accounting Method, with the taxpayer's federal tax return for the taxpayer's next succeeding taxable year, to claim the GO Zone additional first year depreciation deduction for that class of property (Notice 2006-77, Sec. 4.03(2)(b)).

Form 3115 is filed in accordance with the automatic change of accounting method procedures provided in Rev. Proc. 2002-9 (see ¶ 75) except that the scope limitations in section 4.02 of Rev. Proc. 2002-9 do not apply. A Code Sec. 481(a) adjustment is also required.

## ¶ 127G

## Bonus Depreciation for Qualified Recovery Assistance Property Located in Kansas Disaster Area

Taxpayers were permitted to claim an additional first-year depreciation allowance equal to 50 percent of the adjusted basis of qualified Recovery Assistance property acquired on or after May 5, 2007, and placed in service on or before December 31, 2008 in the Kansas disaster area (Act § 15345 of the Heartland, Habitat, Harvest and Horticulture Act of 2008, P.L. 110-246 (May 5, 2008), applying Code Sec. 1400N(d); Notice 2008-67, I.R.B. 2008-32, July 23, 2008, providing regulatory type guidance). The placed-in-service deadline was December 31, 2009 in the case of new nonresidential real property and residential rental property that is qualified Recovery Assistance property (Act § 15345 of P.L. 110-246, applying Code Sec. 1400N(d)).

For a detailed discussion, see earlier editions of the U.S. Master Depreciation Tax Guide.

*Recapture of Kansas disaster area bonus depreciation upon decline in business use*

The Kansas disaster area bonus depreciation deduction may not be claimed unless the property is used substantially in the taxpayer's trade or business in the Kansas disaster area (i.e., 80 percent or more). Recapture rules similar to those that apply to property expensed under Code Sec. 179 apply if the qualified Recovery Assistance property ceases to be qualified Recovery Assistance property. Thus, if such property is used less than 80 percent in a trade or business during any year of its recovery period, the benefit of the deduction will be recaptured (Act § 15345 of P.L. 110-246 applying Code Sec. 1400N(d)(5); Section 2.07 of Notice 2008-67, applying recapture rules for GO-Zone property contained in Section 3 of Notice 2008-25 in a similar manner to Recovery Assistance property). Note that if a property is not used predominantly (more than 50 percent) for business in the tax year it is placed in service then it cannot qualify for expensing under Code Sec. 179.

The benefit derived from claiming the Kansas disaster area additional first-year depreciation deduction for the property is equal to the excess of the total depreciation claimed (including the Kansas disaster area additional first year depreciation deduction) for the property for the tax years before the recapture year over the total depreciation that would have been allowable for the tax years before the recapture year as a deduction under Code Sec. 167(f)(1) or Code Sec. 168, as applicable, had the Kansas disaster area additional first year depreciation deduction not been claimed (regardless of whether such excess reduced the taxpayer's tax liability). The amount recaptured is treated as ordinary income for the recapture year. For the recapture year and subsequent tax years, the taxpayer's depreciation deductions are determined as if no Kansas disaster area additional first year depreciation deduction was claimed with respect to the property (Notice 2008-25). Notice 2008-25 contains example recapture calculations, including calculations related to property that is relinquished in a like-kind exchange or as a result of an involuntary conversion.

See ¶ 127F for discussion of GO Zone property recapture rules which apply in a similar manner to Recovery Assistance property.

## ¶ 127H

## Bonus Depreciation for Qualified Disaster Assistance Property

An additional depreciation allowance (bonus depreciation) was permitted for the tax year in which qualified disaster assistance property was placed in service (Code Sec. 168(n), as added by the Emergency Economic Stabilization Act of 2008 (P.L. 110-343)). The provision applied to property placed in service after December 31, 2007, with respect to federally (i.e., Presidentially) declared disasters declared after such date and occurring before January 1, 2010. The deadline discussed below for placing qualifying property in service, however, has expired.

Code Sec. 168(n) is stricken from the Code by the Tax Technical Corrections Act of 2018 (Act Sec. 401(b)(13)(A) of Division U of P.L. 115-141), effective for property placed in service after March 23, 2018. However, it continues to apply to property placed in service on or before March 23, 2018 (Act Sec. 401(b)(13)(B) of Division U of P.L. 115-141). For example, the recapture provision of Code Sec. 168(n)(4), continues to apply to property for which the deduction was previously claimed.

As explained below disaster assistance property is property (including real property) that rehabilitates or replaces property that is destroyed or damaged as the result of a Presidentially declared disaster.

The additional first-year depreciation deduction is equal to 50 percent of the adjusted basis of the qualified disaster assistance property. The adjusted basis of the property is reduced by the amount of the additional deduction before computing the amount otherwise allowable as a depreciation deduction for the tax year in which the property is placed in service and for any subsequent tax year (Code Sec. 168(n)(1), as added by P.L. 110-343).

Since the bonus allowance is computed on the property's adjusted basis, the basis of the property is first reduced by any Code Sec. 179 allowance claimed. For a special provision that increases the Code Sec. 179 allowance on disaster assistance property (Code Sec. 179(e), as added by P.L. 110-343), see ¶ 306B.

This provision is not elective. However, a taxpayer can make an election out on a property class by property class basis (Code Sec. 168(n)(2)(B)(v)).

*Qualified disaster assistance property defined*

Qualified disaster assistance property must meet all of the following tests:

- The property must be described in Code Sec. 168(k)(2)(A)(i) (i.e., MACRS recovery property with an recovery period of 20 years or less, computer software that is depreciable over three years, water utility property, or qualified leasehold improvement property) or be nonresidential real property or residential rental property.

- Substantially all (80 percent or more) of the use of the property must be in a disaster area with respect to a federally declared disaster occurring before January 1, 2010, and in the active conduct of the taxpayer's trade or business in that disaster area.

- The property must rehabilitate property damaged, or replace property destroyed or condemned, as a result of the disaster. Property is treated as replacing property destroyed or condemned if, as part of an integrated plan, it replaces property that is included in a continuous area that includes real property destroyed or condemned. The property must also be similar in nature to, and located in the same county as, the property being rehabilitated or replaced.

- The original use of the property in the disaster area must commence with an eligible taxpayer on or after the date on which the disaster occurs.

- The property must be acquired by the eligible taxpayer by purchase on or after the date on which the disaster occurs, but only if no written binding contract for the acquisition was in effect before that date. A purchase is defined by reference to the definition in Code Sec. 179(d) (¶ 302); therefore, it cannot be a transaction between related parties or members of the same controlled group, and the transferee's basis in the property cannot be determined by reference to the transferor's basis.

- The property must be placed in service by the eligible taxpayer on or before the date that is the last day of the third calendar year following the date on which the disaster occurs (or the fourth calendar year in the case of nonresidential real property and residential rental property) (Code Sec. 168(n)(2)(A), as added by P.L. 110-343).

Used property that is acquired outside of the disaster area may qualify, as long as its first original use in the disaster area is by an eligible taxpayer.

*Federally declared disaster defined.* An eligible taxpayer is a taxpayer who has suffered an economic loss attributable to a federally declared disaster (Code Sec. 168(n)(3)(D), as added by P.L. 110-343). A federally declared disaster is any disaster subsequently determined by the President of the United States to warrant assistance by the federal government under the Robert T. Stafford Disaster Relief and Emergency Assistance Act (see 42 U.S.C. §5121 et seq.) (Code Sec. 168(n)(3)(B), as added by P.L. 110-343). The disaster area is the area determined to warrant disaster assistance (Code Sec. 168(n)(3)(C), as added by P.L. 110-343).

*Exceptions.* Qualified disaster assistance property does not include:

- any property that is eligible for bonus depreciation under Code Sec. 168(k) (¶ 127D) (without regard to any election under Code Sec. 168(k)(4) to forgo bonus depreciation in favor of an accelerated research or AMT credit), cellulosic biomass ethanol plant property (Code Sec. 168(l)), and qualified refuse and recycling property (Code Sec. 168(m));

- property that qualifies for bonus depreciation under the special rules for the Gulf Opportunity (GO) Zone (¶ 127F) (Code Sec. 1400N(d));

- any property used in connection with any private or commercial golf course, country club, massage parlor, hot tub facility, or suntan facility; any store whose principal business is the sale of alcoholic beverages for consumption off premises; or any gambling or animal racing property (i.e., property described in Code Sec. 1400N(p)(3));
- property that must be depreciated under the MACRS alternative depreciation system (ADS) (not including property for which an ADS election is made);
- property financed by tax-exempt bonds;
- qualified revitalization buildings for which the taxpayer has elected the Code Sec. 1400I commercial revitalization deduction; and
- if the taxpayer elects out of this bonus depreciation with respect to any class of property for any tax year, all property in that class placed in service during that tax year (Code Sec. 168(n)(2)(B), as added by P.L. 110-343).

*Special rules*

Bonus depreciation for qualified disaster assistance property applies to the taxpayer's self-constructed property if the taxpayer begins manufacturing, constructing, or producing the property after the date on which the disaster occurs. Sale-leaseback property that a taxpayer places in service after the date on which the disaster occurs, and then sells and leases back within three months, is treated as originally placed in service no earlier than the date on which the property is used under the taxpayer's leaseback. If property is originally placed in service after the date on which the disaster occurs by a lessor, then is sold by the lessor or any subsequent purchaser within three months after being placed in service, and the user of the property after the last sale during that three-month period remains the same as when the property was originally placed in service, the property is treated as originally placed in service no earlier than the date of the last sale. Finally, property is not qualified disaster assistance property if the user or a related party has a pre-2008 contract to acquire or produce it (Code Sec. 168(n)(2)(B), as added by P.L. 110-343; see Code Sec. 168(k)(2)(E)).

*AMT*

As with regular Code Sec. 168(k) bonus depreciation (127D), the additional depreciation allowance for qualified disaster assistance property may be claimed for alternative minimum tax purposes in the tax year that qualifying property is placed in service. No AMT adjustment is required. Furthermore, no AMT adjustment is required on any regular depreciation deductions claimed on the property over its entire recovery period (Code Sec. 168(n)(2)(D), as added by P.L. 110-343; see Code Sec. 168(k)(2)(G) and Reg. § 1.168(k)-1(d)).

*Recapture*

The tax benefits of the bonus depreciation deduction must be recaptured as ordinary income in a tax year in which the qualified disaster assistance property ceases to be qualified disaster assistance property by applying rules similar to those contained in Code Sec. 179(d)(10) (Code Sec. 168(n)(2)(B), as added by P.L. 110-343). Thus, recapture is required if the property is removed from the disaster area or business use in the disaster area falls below 80 percent.

The 50-percent GO Zone bonus depreciation allowance (Code Sec. 1400N(d)) is also required to be recaptured by applying rules similar to those applicable to section 179 property. Under guidance issued by the IRS in Notice 2006-77, I.R.B. 2006-40, the benefit derived from claiming the GO Zone additional first year depreciation deduction for the property is equal to the excess of the total depreciation claimed (including the GO Zone additional first year depreciation deduction) for the property for the tax years before the recapture year over the total depreciation that would have been allowable for the tax years before the recapture year had the GO Zone additional first year depreciation deduction not been claimed. The amount recaptured is treated as ordinary income for the recapture year. For the recapture year and subsequent tax years, the taxpayer's depreciation deductions are determined as if no GO Zone additional first year depreciation deduction was claimed with respect to the property. See ¶ 127F.

*Effective date*

The provision applies to property placed in service after December 31, 2007, with respect to disasters declared after such date and occurring before January 1, 2010 (Division C, Act Sec. 710(b) of P.L. 110-343).

## ¶ 127I

## Bonus Depreciation for Second Generation Biofuel Plant Property

A 50-percent additional depreciation allowance may be claimed on the adjusted basis of certain plant property acquired and placed in service after December 20, 2006 and before January 1, 2021 that is used to produce certain qualified biofuels (Code Sec. 168(l), as amended by the Taxpayer Certainty and Disaster Tax Relief Act of 2019 (P.L. 116-94)). This deduction cannot be claimed on property which also qualifies for the regular Code Sec. 168(k) bonus deduction for MACRS property with a recovery period of 20 years or less described at ¶ 127D. Regular MACRS depreciation deductions are computed on the adjusted basis of the property after reduction by the 50 percent allowance (Code Sec. 168(l)(1)(B), as added by P.L. 109-432).

- Effective for property placed in service after January 2, 2013 (date of enactment of the American Taxpayer Relief Act of 2012 (P.L. 112-240), the provision applies to second-generation biofuel plant property).

- Effective for property placed in service after October 3, 2008 (date of enactment of the Emergency Economic Stabilization Act of 2008 (P.L. 110-343) and before January 3, 2013 the provision applies to cellulosic biofuel plant property).

- Effective for property placed in service after December 20 2006 (date of enactment of the, Tax Relief and Health Care Act (P.L. 110-343) and before October 4, 2008, the provision applies to qualified cellulosic biomass ethanol property.)

*Qualified second generation biofuel plant property defined*

Effective for property placed in service after January 2, 2013 and before January 1, 2021, the Code Sec. 168(l) bonus deduction applies to qualified second generation biofuel plant property (Code Sec. 168(l)(2)).

Second generation biofuel plant property is qualified if it meets the following requirements:

(1) the property must be depreciable and used in the United States solely to produce second generation biofuel as defined in Code Sec. 40(b)(6)(E);

(2) the taxpayer must acquire the property by purchase (within the meaning of Code Sec. 179(d); see ¶ 302) after December 20, 2006, the date of enactment of P.L. 109-432;

(3) no written binding contract for the purchase of the property may be in effect on or before December 20, 2006; and

(4) the original use of the property must commence with the taxpayer (see below for special rules relating to sale-leasebacks and syndicated leasing transactions) (Code Sec. 168(l)(2), as amended by P.L. 112-240);

Second generation biofuel is defined by Code Sec. 40(b)(6)(E) (as amended by P.L. 112-240) as any liquid fuel that is derived by, or from, qualified feedstocks, and meets the registration requirements for fuels and fuel additives established by the Environmental Protection Agency under section 211 of the Clean Air Act (42 U.S.C. 7545). Qualified feedstock means any lignocellulosic or hemicellulosic matter that is available on a renewable or recurring basis, and any cultivated algae, cyanobacteria, or lemna.

Second generation biofuel does not include any fuel if (a) more than 4 percent of such fuel (determined by weight) is any combination of water and sediment, (b) the ash content of such fuel is more than 1 percent (determined by weight), or (c) such fuel has an acid number greater than 25. Second generation biofuel does not include any alcohol with a proof of less than 150. The determination of the proof of any alcohol is be made without regard to any added denaturants (Code Sec. 40(b)(6)(E)(ii) and (iii)).

*Qualified cellulosic biofuel plant property (QCBPP) defined*

Effective for property placed in service after October 3, 2008 and before January 3, 2013, the Code Sec. 168(l) bonus deduction applied to qualified cellulosic biofuel plant property.

Cellulosic biofuel plant property is qualified if it meets the following requirements:

(1) the property must be depreciable and used in the United States solely to produce cellulosic biofuel;

(2) the taxpayer must acquire the property by purchase (within the meaning of Code Sec. 179(d); see ¶ 302) after December 20, 2006, the date of enactment of P.L. 109-432;

(3) no written binding contract for the purchase of the property may be in effect on or before December 20, 2006; and

(4) the original use of the property must commence with the taxpayer (see below for special rules relating to sale-leasebacks and syndicated leasing transactions) (Code Sec. 168(l)(2), as amended by P.L. 110-343 but prior to being amended by P.L. 112-240).

The term cellulosic biofuel means any liquid fuel which is produced from any lignocellulosic or hemicellulosic matter that is available on a renewable or recurring basis (Code Sec. 168(l)(3), as amended by the Emergency Economic Stabilization Act of 2008 (P.L. 110-343) and prior to being stricken by the American Taxpayer Relief Act of 2012 (P.L. 112-240)).

*Qualified cellulosic biofuel plant property (QCBPP) defined*

Effective for property placed in service after December 20, 2006 and before October 4, 2008, the Code Sec. 168(l) deduction applied to qualified cellulosic biomass ethanol property. To qualify as QCBEPP:

(1) the property must be depreciable and used in the United States solely to produce cellulosic biomass ethanol;

(2) the taxpayer must acquire the property by purchase (within the meaning of Code Sec. 179(d); see ¶ 302) after December 20, 2006, the date of enactment of P.L. 109-432;

(3) no written binding contract for the purchase of the property may be in effect on or before December 20, 2006 (Code Sec. 168(l)(2), as added by P.L. 109-432 and prior to amendment by P.L. 110-343 and P.L. 112-240).

(4) the original use of the property must commence with the taxpayer after December 20, 2006 (see below for special rules relating to sale-leasebacks and syndicated leasing transactions) (Code Sec. 168(l)(2), as added by P.L. 109-432but prior to amendment by P.L. 110-343 and P.L. 112-240).

Cellulosic biomass ethanol means ethanol produced by hydrolysis of any lignocellulosic or hemicellulosic matter that is available on a renewable or recurring basis (Code Sec. 168(l)(3), as added by P.L. 109-432 and amended by P.L. 110-172 and prior to being stricken by the American Taxpayer Relief Act of 2012). Lignocellulosic or hemicellulosic matter that is available on a renewable or recurring basis includes (but is not limited to) bagasse (from sugar cane), corn stalks, and switchgrass (Joint Committee on Taxation, Technical Explanation of the Tax Relief and Health Care Act of 2006 (P.L. 109-432) (JCX-50-06) at ¶ 11,279.049).

Prior to amendment by the Tax Technical Corrections Act of 2007 (P.L. 110-172), Code Sec. 168(l)(3) required that the ethanol had to be produced by *enzymatic* hydrolysis (Code Sec. 168(l)(3), prior to amendment by P.L. 110-172). This change eliminating the specific manner of hydrolysis is retroactively effective and, therefore, applies to property acquired and placed in service after December 20, 2006 in tax years ending after that date.

Since original use of the property must commence with the taxpayer, only new property may qualify as QCBEPP. See, also, the similar original use requirement under the Code Sec. 168(k) bonus depreciation provision, discussed in detail at ¶ 127D.

*Property manufactured, constructed, or produced by or for a taxpayer*

Property manufactured, constructed, or produced by the taxpayer for the taxpayer's own use may qualify for the Code Sec. 168(l) bonus deduction if the taxpayer begins the manufacture, construction, or production of the property after December 20, 2006, and the property is placed in service before January 1, 2021. Property manufactured, constructed, or produced for the taxpayer by another person under a contract that is entered into prior to the manufacture, construction, or production of the property is considered manufactured, constructed, or produced by the taxpayer (Code Sec. 168(l)(4)).

The requirement that manufacture, construction, production begin after December 20, 2006 is eliminated, effective for property placed in service after 2015 (Code Sec. 168(l)(4); Code Sec. 168(k)(2)(E)), as amended by the Protecting Americans from Tax Hikes (PATH) Act of 2015 (Division Q of P.L. 114-113) (December 18, 2015).

*Sale-leasebacks*

A limited exception to the original use requirement applied to sale-leasebacks for property acquired or placed in service before September 28, 2017 (Code Sec. 168(k)(2)(E)(ii), stricken by the Tax Cuts and Jobs Act of 2017 (P.L. 115-97) and cross referenced by Code Sec. 168(k)(2)(l)). This rule was stricken by the 2017 Tax Cuts Act because used property acquired and placed in service after September 27,

2017 now qualifies for bonus depreciation under Code Sec. 168(k) (Code Sec. 168(k)(2)(A)(ii) and Code Sec. 168(k)(2)(E)(ii), as amended by P.L. 115-97).

The rule applies to property originally placed in service after December 20, 2006, by a person who sells it to the taxpayer and then leases it from the taxpayer within three months after the date that the property was originally placed in service. In this situation, the property is treated as originally placed in service by the taxpayer (rather than the seller) and the placed-in-service date is deemed to occur no earlier than the date that the property is used under the leaseback (Code Sec. 168(l)(4)).

It is somewhat unclear whether the Code Sec. 168(l) deduction applies to used property placed in service after September 27, 2017 (and before the January 1, 2021 expiration date) as a result of the 2017 Tax Cuts Act amendments. Code Sec. 168(l)(4) incorporates by reference the definition of used property in Code Sec. 168(k)(2)(E)(ii) that can qualify for regular bonus depreciation and, therefore, an argument can be made that used property will qualify despite retention of the specific requirement in Code Sec. 168(l)(2)(B), that the original use must begin with the taxpayer.

*Syndication transactions*

The ultimate purchaser in a syndicated leasing transaction may be able to qualify for the 50-percent deduction. If property is originally placed in service by a lessor after December 20, 2006, and is sold by the lessor or any later purchaser within three months after the date the property was originally placed in service by the lessor, and the user of the property does not change during this three-month period, then the purchaser of the property in the last sale is considered to be the original user of the property and the property is treated as originally placed in service not earlier than the date of the last sale by the purchaser of the property in the last sale (Code Sec. 168(l)(4)).

*Limitation on certain users and related parties*

*Limitation on certain users and related parties.* Property placed in service before 2016 does not qualify for the bonus deduction under this provision if the user of the property (as of the date on which the property is originally placed in service) or a person related (within the meaning of Code Sec. 267(b) or Code Sec. 707(b)) to such user or to the taxpayer had a written binding contract in effect for the acquisition of the property at any time on or before December 20, 2006, or in the case of property manufactured, constructed, or produced for such user's or person's own use, the manufacture, construction, or production of the property began at any time on or before December 20, 2006 (Code Sec. 168(l)(4)). These are the same rules that apply to property on which the bonus depreciation deduction under Code Sec. 168(k) is claimed with adjustments for placed-in-service dates (see ¶ 127D)

The rules relating to manufactured, constructed, or produced property, sale leasebacks, syndication transactions, and limitations on certain users and related parties are borrowed directly from Code Sec. 168(k)(2)(E) (prior to amendment by the PATH Act) adjusted for acquisition and placed-in-service dates. Thus, taxpayers should be able to rely on the related regulations issued under Code Sec. 168(k) for additional guidance. See ¶ 127D.

The requirement relating to pre-December 20, 2006 binding contracts and construction is eliminated, effective for property placed in service after 2015 (Code Sec. 168(l)(4); Code Sec. 168(k)(2)(E)), as amended by the Protecting Americans from Tax Hikes (PATH) Act of 2015 (Division Q of P.L. 114-113) (December 18, 2015).

*Tax-exempt bond-financed property excluded*

Property financed with tax-exempt bonds cannot qualify as Code Sec. 168(l) property and, therefore, does not qualify for the additional deduction (Code Sec. 168(l)(3)(C)).

*Mandatory ADS property excluded*

Property required to be depreciated under the MACRS alternative depreciation system (ADS) does not qualify as Code Sec. 168(l) property. The deduction is not denied if a taxpayer merely elects to depreciate the Code Sec. 168(l) property using ADS (Code Sec. 168(l)(3)(B)). See ¶ 127D.

*Election out*

A taxpayer may elect not to claim the deduction with respect to any class of property for any tax year. The election out applies to all property in the class for which the election out is made and which is placed in service during the tax year.

Code Sec. 168(l) property placed in service during a tax year may consist of various MACRS property classes, e.g., 5-year property, 7-year property, 10-year property, etc. The election out is made at the property class level. A taxpayer may make an election out for some or all of the property classes (Code Sec. 168(l)(3)(D)).

*Recapture when property loses qualifying status*

Recapture of the deduction is required in a tax year in which qualified second generation biofuel property, QCBEPP, or QCBPP ceases to be qualified second generation biofuel property, QCBEPP, or QCBBP. The recapture amount is computed in a similar manner to the recapture of the Code Section 179 deduction when section 179 property ceases to be used more than 50 percent in the active conduct of a taxpayer's trade or business during any year of the section 179 property's MACRS recovery period (Code Sec. 168(l)(6)).

The 50-percent GO Zone bonus depreciation allowance (Code Sec. 1400N(d)) is also required to be recaptured by applying rules similar to those applicable to section 179 property. Under guidance issued by the IRS in Notice 2006-77, I.R.B. 2006-40, the benefit derived from claiming the GO Zone additional first year depreciation deduction for the property is equal to the excess of the total depreciation claimed (including the GO Zone additional first year depreciation deduction) for the property for the tax years before the recapture year over the total depreciation that would have been allowable for the tax years before the recapture year had the GO Zone additional first year depreciation deduction not been claimed. The amount recaptured is treated as ordinary income for the recapture year. For the recapture year and subsequent tax years, the taxpayer's depreciation deductions are determined as if no GO Zone additional first year depreciation deduction was claimed with respect to the property. See ¶ 127F.

*Coordination with Code Sec. 179C election to expense refineries*

The 50-percent deduction for qualified second generation biofuel plant property, QCBEPP, or QCBPP does not apply to property with respect to which the taxpayer claims the 50-percent deduction allowed by Code Sec. 179C for qualified refinery property (Code Sec. 168(l)(7)).

The potential for a duplicative deduction exists because qualified refinery property can include a facility that processes biomass via gas into a liquid fuel.

*No AMT adjustment required*

The deduction is claimed in full for purposes of determining alternative minimum tax liability. In addition, all MACRS depreciation deductions claimed on the qualified second generation biofuel plant property, QCBEPP and QCBPP are allowed in full in computing AMT (i.e., no depreciation adjustment is required) (Code Sec. 168(l)(5)).

These are the same rules that apply to property on which the 30- or 50-percent bonus depreciation deduction under Code Sec. 168(k) is claimed. The bonus deduction and regular MACRS deductions on bonus depreciation property are allowed in full under the AMT (Code Sec. 168(k)(2)(G)). See ¶ 127D.

*Effective date*

The provision applies to property placed in service after December 20, 2006 in tax years ending after December 20, 2006 (Act Sec. 209(b) of the Tax Relief and Health Care Act of 2006 (P.L. 109-432)).

## ¶ 127J

## Bonus Depreciation for Qualified Reuse and Recycling Property

A 50-percent additional depreciation allowance (bonus depreciation) may be claimed on the adjusted basis of *qualified reuse and recycling property* acquired and placed in service after August 31, 2008. The additional depreciation is claimed in the tax year the property is placed in service. The original use of the property must begin with the taxpayer after August 31, 2008 (i.e., the property must be new) (Code Sec. 168(m), as added by the Emergency Economic Stabilization Act of 2008 (P.L. 110-343)). Regular MACRS depreciation deductions are computed on the adjusted basis of the property beginning in the tax year the property is placed in service after reduction by the 50-percent allowance (Code Sec. 168(m)(1)(B), as added by P.L. 110-343).

Since this bonus depreciation deduction is computed on the adjusted basis of the property, it is computed after the original basis is reduced by any Code Sec. 179 allowance that is claimed. This is the same rule that applies when computing the bonus depreciation allowance under Code Sec. 168(k).

*No AMT adjustment required*

The bonus deduction is claimed in full for purposes of determining alternative minimum tax liability. In addition, all MACRS depreciation deductions claimed on the qualified reuse and recycling property are allowed in full in computing AMT (i.e., no depreciation adjustment is required) (Code Sec. 168(m)(2)(D), as added by P.L. 110-343).

*Qualified reuse and recycling property defined*

"Qualified reuse and recycling property" is reuse and recycling property that meets certain conditions. "Reuse and recycling property" is machinery and equipment (not including buildings, real estate, rolling stock or equipment used to transport reuse and recyclable materials) that is used exclusively to collect, distribute, or recycle qualified reuse and recyclable materials. Machinery and equipment include appurtenances such as software necessary to operate the equipment. "Qualified reuse and recyclable materials" are scrap plastic, glass, textiles, rubber, packaging, and metal, as well as recovered fiber and electronic scrap (Code Sec. 168(m)(3), as added by P.L. 110-343).

The term "recycle" or "recycling" means the process by which worn or superfluous materials are processed into materials for use in manufacturing consumer and commercial products, including packaging (Code Sec. 168(m)(3)(C), as added by P.L. 110-343).

"Electronic scrap" includes cathode ray tubes, flat panel screens or similar video display devices with screen sizes greater than 4 inches when measured diagonally, as well as central processing units (Code Sec. 168(m)(2)(A)(ii), as added by P.L. 110-343).

The original use of "qualified reuse and recycling property," must begin with the taxpayer after August 31, 2008. In addition, the property must either be acquired by purchase by the taxpayer after August 31, 2008 (but only if there is not written binding contract for the acquisition in effect before September 1, 2008), or acquired by the taxpayer pursuant to a written binding contract entered into after August 31, 2008 (Code Sec. 168(m)(2)(A), as added by P.L. 110-343).

"Purchase" for this purpose has the meaning given to such term in Code Sec. 179(d)(2), which defines the term as any acquisition of property, but excludes acquisitions from related parties, transfers of property from a decedent in which the acquirer takes a stepped-up basis in the property under Code Sec. 1014(a), or transfers in which the acquirer takes a substituted basis in the property, such as like-kind exchanges qualifying under Code Sec. 1031. In addition, property acquired by purchase will only be considered qualified reuse and recycling property if no written, binding contract for the acquisition was in effect before September 1, 2008 (Code Sec. 168(m)(2)(A)(i), as added by P.L. 110-343).

The requirement of an acquisition by purchase is not imposed on acquisitions pursuant to a written binding contract entered into after August 31, 2008 (Code Sec. 168(m)(2)(A)(iv), as added by the Emergency Economic Stabilization Act of 2008). Presumably, it was not the intent of Congress to eliminate the purchase requirement simply because the reuse or recycling property was acquired pursuant to a contract entered into after August 31, 2008. For example, as enacted, it appears that a taxpayer could enter into a post-August 31, 2008 contract for an acquisition from a related person and qualify for the deduction even though such an acquisition is not considered a purchase under Code Sec. 179(d)(2). A technical correction may be required.

Qualified reuse and recycling property must have a *useful life* of at least five years (Code Sec. 168(m)(2)(A)(ii), as added by P.L. 110-343). The term useful life is not defined. It appears in the context of this provision to refer to actual economic useful life to the taxpayer rather than the length of the assigned MACRS recovery period. The only MACRS recovery period which is less than five years is three years (i.e., three-year property). MACRS 3-year property does not include any type of property that would be considered qualified reuse or recycling property. Similar considerations prevent the term from being defined by reference to an asset's class life as set forth in Rev. Proc. 87-56, 1987-2 CB 674.

*Self-constructed property*

The special depreciation allowance may be claimed on qualified reuse and recycling property the taxpayer manufactures, constructs, or produces for its own use, if the taxpayer begins manufacturing, constructing, or producing the property after August 31, 2008 (Code Sec. 168(m)(2)(C), as added by P.L. 110-343).

*Exceptions*

A taxpayer cannot "double dip" and claim the special qualified reuse and recycling property depreciation allowance for any property for which it may claim bonus depreciation under Code Sec. 168(k). Thus, if bonus depreciation is available under either this new provision or Code Sec. 168(k) it must be claimed under Code

Sec. 168(k). In addition, a taxpayer cannot take the special depreciation allowance on property which it is required to depreciate under the MACRS alternative depreciation system (ADS). However, if a taxpayer is not required to depreciate property under ADS, but elects to do so under Code Sec. 168(g)(7), the taxpayer may still claim the special depreciation allowance (Code Sec. 168(m)(2)(B), as added by P.L. 110-343).

An enacted technical correction affects a corporation that elects under Code Sec. 168(k)(4) to forgo bonus depreciation that is available under Code Sec. 168(k) for qualified reuse and recycling property in order to claim an unused pre-2006 research or AMT credit. The technical correction clarifies that such a corporation may not claim bonus depreciation under Code Sec. 168(m) for the property to which Code Sec. 168(k) would have applied if the election had not been made (Code Sec. 168(m)(2)(B)(i), as amended by P.L. 113-295).

*Election out*

A taxpayer may elect not to claim the deduction with respect to any MACRS assigned class of property for any tax year. The election out applies to all qualified reuse and recycling property in the particular MACRS property class (e.g., 5-, 7-, 10-, or 15-year property) for which the election out is made and which is placed in service during the tax year for which the election is made (Code Sec. 168(m)(2)(B)(iii), as added by P.L. 110-343).

# MACRS General Asset Accounts

## ¶ 128

## General Asset Accounts

*Effective date of final GAA regulations*

The IRS issued Temporary Reg. § 1.168(i)-1T, relating to general asset accounts, as part of T.D. 9564 (December 23, 2011). These temporary regulations were withdrawn and reissued as proposed regulations (Proposed Reg. § 1.168(i)-1, NPRM REG-110732-13 (September 19, 2013)). The proposed regulations were adopted as final regulations with no significant changes (Reg. § 1.168(i)-1, adopted by T.D. 9689 (August 14, 2014)). The final regulations apply to tax years beginning on or after January 1, 2014, or optionally, to tax years beginning on or after January 1, 2012 (Reg. § 1.168(i)-1(m)).

*Using GAA to avoid capitalization of demolition costs*

A taxpayer may place a building in a single asset general asset account (GAA) and continue to depreciate the building after its demolition rather than increasing the basis of the land by the adjusted depreciable basis of the building as otherwise required by Code Sec. 280B. There is no requirement that the taxpayer must terminate the GAA upon the disposition of the building and capitalize the loss under Code Sec. 280B (Reg. § 1.168(i)-1(e)(3)(i); Reg. § 1.168(i)-1(e)(3)(ii)(A)). However, an asset may not be placed in a GAA if it is acquired and disposed of in the same tax year (Reg. § 1.168(i)-1(c)(1)(i)).

See, also, the anti-abuse rule (Reg. § 1.168(i)-1(e)(3)(vii)) which could be used by the IRS to prohibit avoidance of Code Sec. 280B in certain situations.

Code Sec. 280B requires that demolition removal costs also be capitalized to the basis of the land, in addition to the remaining basis of the building. However, a special rule provides that so long as the GAA account is not voluntarily terminated upon the disposition of the last asset in the account, removal costs associated with the disposed asset are currently deductible (Reg. § 1.263(a)-3(g)(2)(i), second sentence).

See ¶ 5 for a discussion of the demolition cost rule.

The downside to a GAA election for a building is that the partial disposition election, which allows a taxpayer to elect to claim a loss on the remaining basis of a building's structural components when they are replaced, is not available if a building is in a GAA. See ¶ 162 for a discussion of the partial disposition election.

Rev. Proc. 2014-54 allowed a taxpayer to file an accounting method change for a tax year beginning in 2012 or 2013 to make a late election to place assets that were placed in service prior to the 2012 tax year in a GAA. However, the time for filing this accounting method change has expired since the change must be filed by the extended due date of the 2013 return. See ¶ 77 for details. This planning tip, therefore, is mainly available for buildings for which a timely current-year GAA election may be made (e.g., a building placed in service in the 2021 tax year for which a timely GAA election is made on the 2021 tax return). However, the remodel/refresh safe harbor for restaurants and retail buildings allows a taxpayer to make a late GAA election for a building previously placed in service in the first tax year that the safe harbor is elected as an accounting method. See Rev. Proc. 2015-56. Under the safe harbor, 75 percent or remodel/refresh costs are deducted and 25 percent of such costs are capitalized.

The IRS has allowed a taxpayer to make a late election to place demolished buildings in separate GAAs in order to avoid the capitalization of demolition costs (IRS Letter Ruling 201626013, March 24, 2016). The taxpayer was not advised by the return preparer that the GAA election was available and the statute of limitations for filing an amended return had not expired prior to filing the letter ruling request. The facts also state that the taxpayer had not formed an intent to demolish the buildings when the buildings were purchased although the taxpayer considered this as a possibility. The buildings were placed in service in Tax Year 1 and demolished in Tax Year 3.

*General rules for GAA accounting*

*GAA election procedure.* A taxpayer may make an irrevocable election to include assets in an MACRS general asset account (GAA) (Code Sec. 168(i)(4)). The election is made separately by each person owning an asset to be placed in a GAA. For example, the election is made by each member of a consolidated group, each partnership, or each S corporation (Reg. § 1.168(i)-1(l)(1)). Partners and S shareholders do not make the election for property owned by the pass-through entity. The election is made by following the Form 4562 Instructions. The instructions simply require a taxpayer to check box 18 of Form 4562 to indicate that the election is being made. The election must be made by the due date (including extensions) for the return for the tax year in which the assets included in the GAA are placed into service.

The taxpayer must maintain records (for example, "General Asset Account #1—all 1995 additions in asset class 00.11 for Salt Lake City, Utah facility") that identify the assets included in each general asset account, that establish the unadjusted depreciable basis and depreciation reserve of the general asset account, and that reflect the amount realized during the taxable year upon dispositions from each general asset account (Reg. § 1.168(i)-1(l)(3)).

*Assets used for personal purposes or acquired and disposed in same tax year may not be accounted for in a GAA.* An asset used both for personal and business purposes at any time during the tax year in which the asset is placed in service may not be placed in a GAA. An asset may not be placed in a GAA if it is placed in service and disposed of during the same tax year (Reg. § 1.168(i)-1(c)(1)). In addition, if an asset is used entirely or partially for personal services in a tax year after it is placed in service it must be removed from the GAA (Reg. § 1.168(i)-1(h)(1)).

*Asset's unadjusted depreciable basis is included in GAA.* An asset is included in a general asset account only to the extent of the asset's unadjusted depreciable basis (Reg. § 1.168(i)-1(c)(1).

Unadjusted depreciable basis is the basis of property for purposes of determining gain or loss but without regard to depreciation deductions (including bonus depreciation). Unadjusted basis reflects the reduction in basis for any portion of the basis the taxpayer elects to treat as an expense under Code Sec. 179 or a similar provision, as well as any basis reductions required by reason of claiming a credit or deduction with respect to the property (Reg. § 1.168(i)-1(b)(1)).

***Example (1):*** Rainbow Inc. purchases a $500,000 machine and elects to expense $100,000 of its cost under Code Sec. 179. The machine is placed into a single item GAA account. The unadjusted depreciable basis of the account is $400,000 ($500,000 – $100,000) (Reg. § 1.168(i)-1(c)(3), Example 11).

***Example (2):*** Assume that Rainbow Inc. purchased two machines for $200,000 each and elected to expense $100,000 of the cost of the one of the machines. If Rainbow places both machines in the same GAA, the unadjusted depreciable basis of the GAA is $300,000.

*Rules for grouping assets in a GAA.* Assets that are subject to a GAA election are grouped into one or more general asset accounts. Assets that are eligible for grouping into a single general asset account may be divided in any manner and placed into more than one general asset account (Reg. § 1.168(i)-1(c)(1)). A taxpayer may create a separate general asset account for each item of property that could otherwise be grouped into a single account (i.e., create GAAs with only one asset) (Reg. § 1.168(i)-1(c)(3), Examples 2 and 3).

An asset may be placed in a GAA whether it is depreciated under the MACRS general depreciation system (GDS) (¶ 84) or the MACRS straight-line alternative depreciation system (ADS) (¶ 150) (Reg. § 1.168(i)-1(c)(1)).

In order to ensure that only assets that are depreciated in exactly the same way are placed in service in the same GAA, each GAA may only include assets that:

(1) Have the same MACRS depreciation method;

(2) Have the same MACRS recovery (depreciation) period;

(3) Have the same MACRS convention; and

(4) Are placed in service in the same tax year (Reg. § 1.168(i)-1(c)(2)(i)).

***Example (3):*** Rainbow Inc. purchases 100 machines in the same tax year. The machines are 5-year MACRS property depreciated using the 200 percent declining balance method and half-year convention. Rainbow may create as few as one GAA for all of the machines or as many as 100 GAAs if Rainbow decides to place each machine in its own GAA.

Assets that are subject to the mid-quarter convention (¶ 92) may only be placed in the same GAA account if they were placed in service in the same quarter of the tax year. This is because MACRS depreciation percentages (rates) are based on the quarter of the tax year in which an asset is placed in service if the asset is subject to the mid-quarter convention (Reg. § 1.168(i)-1(c)(2)(ii)(A)).

Similarly, buildings subject to the mid-month convention (¶ 90) may be placed in the same GAA account only if placed in service in the same month of the tax year since the depreciation rate is based on the month of the tax year in which such property is placed in service. Note that 39-year nonresidential real property and 27.5-year residential rental property are the only assets that are subject to the mid-month convention. However, 39-year nonresidential real property and 27.5-year residential rental property but may not be placed in the same GAA because they have different recovery periods (i.e., 39 years and 27.5 years, respectively) (Reg. § 1.168(i)-1(c)(2)(ii)(B)). Assuming a building is placed in a GAA, it is recommended that each building be placed in its own GAA so that the account may be terminated upon the disposition of the building. (GAA accounts cannot be terminated until disposition of the last asset in the GAA).

The following types of property must be placed in the same GAA because they are subject to special depreciation computation rules (Reg. § 1.168(i)-1(c)(2)(ii)(C)-(I)):

(1) Passenger automobiles subject to the luxury car depreciation limits of Code Sec. 280F (¶ 200) must be grouped in a separate GAA;

(2) Assets not eligible for any bonus depreciation deduction (¶ 127D et. seq.) (including assets for which the taxpayer elected not to deduct bonus depreciation) provided by, for example, Code Sec. 168(k) through (n), Code Sec. 1400L(b), or Code Sec. 1400N(d), must be grouped into a separate GAA;

(3) Assets for which bonus depreciation (¶ 127D et. seq.) was claimed may only be grouped into a GAA with assets for which a similar bonus depreciation rate applied (e.g., 30%, 50%, or 100%);

(4) Except for passenger automobiles subject to the luxury car depreciation limits (¶ 200) which must be placed together in a separate account, listed property (as defined in Code Sec. 280F(d)(4)) (¶ 208) must be grouped into a separate GAA;

(5) Assets for which the depreciation allowance for the placed-in-service year is not determined by using an optional depreciation table (¶ 179 et. seq.) must be grouped into a separate GAA;

(6) Mass assets identified by a mortality dispersion table when disposed of must be grouped into a separate GAA (see below); and

(7) Assets subject to a change in use that results in a shorter recovery period or a more accelerated depreciation method (see below) for which the depreciation allowance for the year of change (as defined in Reg. § 1.168(i)-4(a)) is not determined by using an optional depreciation table must be grouped into a separate GAA.

Items (2) - (6) are not found in the original GAA regulations for pre-2014 tax years (Reg. § 1.168(i)-1, prior to amendment by T.D. 9564 (December 23, 2011)). Taxpayers who combined incompatible assets in the same GAA will need to make an accounting method change to separate the assets into permissible groupings.

***Example (4):*** ABC purchases computers (listed property), automobiles subject to Code Sec. 280F (also listed property), and machinery. Even if all of the assets are MACRS 5-year property purchased in the same tax year and depreciated using the same method and convention, the computers, automobiles, and machinery must be placed in separate GAAs (Reg. § 1.168(i)-1(c)(3), Example 4).

***Example (6):*** GHI purchases 100 items of 5-year property subject to the 200 percent declining balance method and half-year convention in 2017. The property is eligible for bonus depreciation at the 50 percent rate. GHI establishes two GAA accounts and places 30 items in one account and 70 items in another account. GHI must claim bonus depreciation on all items in both accounts unless an election is made out of bonus depreciation for 5-year property in which case no bonus depreciation may be claimed on any of the items in either account. The election out of bonus depreciation applies on a property-class basis, i.e., to all property in the same class for which the election is made. See ¶ 127D. Thus, the election out would apply to all of the 5-year property placed in service during 2017 by GHI even though the property was not placed in the same GAA.

Under the original GAA rules, a GAA could only include assets that were in the same asset class as provided in Rev. Proc. 87-56 (Reg. § 1.168(i)-1(c)(2)(i), prior to amendment by T.D. 9564 (December 23, 2011)). For example, office furniture described in asset class 00.11 could not be placed in the same GAA as mining property described in asset class 10.0 even though the office furniture and mining assets are both MACRS 7-year property. The new GAA rules allow these items to be placed in the same GAA assuming all other requirements are satisfied.

The pre-2014 regulations did not specifically prohibit non-listed property from being placed in the same GAA account as listed property. However, since the pre-2014 regulations only allowed property with the same asset class number to be placed in a GAA this issue was not particularly important. The IRS has provided an automatic change of accounting method procedure that allows a taxpayer to change from one permissible method of grouping assets in a GAA to another permissible grouping. See Sec. 6.12 of Rev. Proc. 2019-43. Sec. 6.12 would not apply if a taxpayer needed to switch from an impermissible grouping (e.g., listed property mixed with non-listed property) to a permissible grouping. However, Sec. 6.01 governs impermissible to permissible changes. See ¶ 77 for a discussion of accounting method changes.

*Computing depreciation on asset in a GAA*

Depreciation allowances are determined for each general asset account (GAA) and must be recorded in a depreciation reserve account for each account (Reg. § 1.168(i)-1(d)(1)).

*No bonus claimed.* If the assets in a GAA are not eligible for bonus depreciation, the allowable depreciation deduction for the GAA for the placed-in-service year and any subsequent tax year is determined by using the applicable depreciation method, recovery period, and convention for the assets in the account (Reg. § 1.168(i)-1(d)(1)).

*Bonus depreciation claimed.* An asset for which bonus depreciation will be claimed may only be placed in a GAA with other assets for which bonus depreciation will be claimed. Furthermore, the same bonus rate must apply to all assets in the GAA (i.e., 30%, 50%, or 100%) (Reg. § 1.168(i)-1(c)(2)(ii)(E) and Reg. § 1.168(i)-1(c)(3), Example 5).

The bonus deduction for the general asset account is determined for the placed-in-service year. The regular depreciation deduction for the GAA for the placed-in-service year and any subsequent tax year is then determined. The bonus deduction is determined by multiplying the unadjusted depreciable basis of the GAA (cost less section 179) by the bonus percentage rate that applies to the assets in the GAA. The remaining adjusted depreciable basis of the GAA is then depreciated using the applicable depreciation method, recovery period, and convention for the assets in the account (Reg. § 1.168(i)-1(d)(2)).

Remaining adjusted depreciable basis of a GAA is the unadjusted depreciable basis of the general asset account (cost less section 179) less the amount of the additional first-year depreciation deduction allowed or allowable, whichever is greater, for the general asset account (Reg. § 1.168(i)-1(b)(8)). The optional MACRS table percentages are applied to the GAA's remaining adjusted depreciable basis.

> ***Example (7):*** ABC Inc. places two machines costing $100,000 each in the same general asset account. The machines are MACRS 3-year property depreciated using the 200 percent declining balance method and half-year convention. Assume that ABC claims a $50,000 section 179 deduction for one of the machines and bonus depreciation at a 50% rate (for both machines). The unadjusted depreciable basis of the account is $150,000 ($200,000 – $50,000). The bonus deduction is equal to $75,000 ($150,000 unadjusted depreciable basis × 50% bonus rate). The remaining adjusted depreciable basis is $75,000 ($150,000 unadjusted depreciable basis – $75,000 bonus). The Year 1 depreciation deduction for the GAA is $24,997.50 ($75,000 unadjusted depreciable basis × 33.33% first year table percentage); Year 2 = $33,337.5 ($75,000 × 44.45%); Year 3 = $11,107.50 ($75,000 × 14.81%); Year 4 = $5,557.50 ($75,000 × 7.41%).

*GAA accounts for passenger automobiles subject to depreciation caps.* The annual depreciation deduction for a general asset account established for passenger automobiles is limited to the applicable annual cap (¶ 200) multiplied by the excess of the number of automobiles originally included in the account over the number of automobiles disposed of during the tax year or in any prior tax year (Reg. § 1.168(i)-1(d)(4)).

For this purpose a disposition includes a disposition in a:

- qualifying disposition;
- Code Sec. 168(i)(7) transaction;

- Code Sec. 1031 or Code Sec. 1033 transaction;
- technical terminations of a partnership;
- transaction subject to the anti-abuse rule of Reg. § 1.168(i)-1(e)(vii); or
- transaction involving a conversion to any percentage of personal use.

***Example (8):*** A taxpayer purchases 3 cars and a pickup truck in 2017. The 3 cars and truck are MACRS 5-year property, subject to the half-year convention, and depreciated using the 200 percent declining balance method. The 3 cars may be placed in the same GAA. However, the truck may not be placed in the same GAA as the cars even though it shares the same depreciation period, method, and convention because the depreciation caps that apply to a truck placed in service in 2017 are different than the caps that apply to a car placed in service in 2017.

Assume each car cost $30,000 and a 50 percent bonus allowance was claimed. The unadjusted depreciable basis of the account is $90,000 (($30,000 × 3) – $0 section 179 expense). Bonus depreciation on the account is $45,000 ($90,000 × 50%). The remaining adjusted depreciable basis of the account to which the optional table percentages are applied is $45,000 ($90,000 – $45,000 bonus deduction). The first-year regular depreciation deduction on the account is $9,000 ($45,000 × 20% first-year table percentage for 5-year property). The total first-year deduction, including bonus depreciation, is $53,000 ($9,000 + $45,000). The first-year cap for a car placed in service in 2017 if bonus depreciation is claimed is $11,160. Since $53,000 is greater than $33,480 ($11,160 × 3 cars) the first year deduction is limited to $33,480. The $19,520 disallowed depreciation ($53,000 – $33,480) may be recovered at the end of the 5-year recovery period at the rate of $5,625 per year ($1,875 post-recovery period cap × 3).

The depreciation caps are identical for cars and trucks (including SUVs) placed in service in the same calendar year after 2017. Therefore, beginning in 2018 it is possible to place cars and trucks in the same GAA account. See ¶ 200.

*Disposition of an asset from a general asset account*

In general, upon the disposition of an asset from a GAA that is not the last asset in the GAA the following rules apply (Reg. § 1.168(i)-1(e)):

- immediately before the disposition the asset is treated as having an adjusted depreciable basis of zero
- no loss is realized
- the amount realized is recognized as ordinary income to the extent that the sum of the unadjusted depreciable basis of the GAA and any expensed cost (as defined below) of assets in the account exceeds amount previously recognized as ordinary income
- the unadjusted depreciable basis and depreciation reserve of the GAA are not affected by the disposition and, accordingly, a taxpayer continues to depreciate the GAA, including the asset disposed of, as if no disposition occurred

Upon the disposition of all of the assets or the last asset in a GAA, a taxpayer may make an election to terminate the account and recognize gain or loss by reference to the adjusted depreciable basis of the account (Reg. § 1.168(i)-1(e)(3)(ii)). If the disposition does not involve all of the assets in the GAA account or the last asset, an alternative election for "qualifying dispositions" allows a taxpayer to remove the disposed of asset from the GAA account and recognize gain or loss by reference to the asset's adjusted depreciable basis (Reg. § 1.168(i)-1(e)(3)(iii)). Only a few specified types of dispositions are treated as a qualifying disposition under the final regulations. See "Termination of general asset account treatment upon certain dispositions" below. Transactions involving Code Sec. 168(i)(7), a like-kind exchange (Code Sec. 1031), an involuntary conversion

(Code Sec. 1033), a technical termination of a partnership under Code Sec. 708(b)(1)(B), or an abusive transaction are subject to special rules described below.

*Disposition defined.* An asset in a GAA is considered disposed of when ownership of the asset is transferred or when the asset is permanently withdrawn from use in either a trade or business or the production of income.

Dispositions include (Reg. § 1.168(i)-1(e)(1)):

(1) the sale, exchange, retirement, physical abandonment, or destruction of an asset;

(2) the transfer of an asset to a supplies, scrap, or similar account; and

The disposition of a portion of an asset in a general asset account (e.g., a structural component or component of an item of section 1245 property such as machinery) is not a disposition except in the following limited circumstances (Reg. § 1.168(i)-1(e)(1)(ii)):

- a sale of a portion of an asset
- a disposition of a portion of an asset as a result of a casualty event
- a disposition of a portion of an asset for which gain (other than gain under Code Sec. 1245 or Code Sec. 1250) is not recognized in whole or in part under Code Sec. 1031 (like-kind exchanges) or Code Sec. 1033 (involuntary conversions)
- a transfer of a portion of an asset in a transaction described in Code Sec. 168(i)(7)(B)
- a disposition of a portion of an asset in a transaction subject to the anti-abuse rule of Reg. § 1.168(i)-1(e)(3)(vii)(B)
- a disposition of a portion of an asset if the taxpayer makes the election under Reg. § 1.168(i)-1(e)(3)(ii) to terminate the general asset account in which the disposed of portion is included when all of the assets or the last asset in the account is disposed of
- the disposition of the portion of the asset is a "*qualifying disposition*" and the taxpayer makes the qualifying disposition election to recognize gain or loss by reference to the adjusted basis of the asset

A *qualifying disposition* is a disposition that does not involve all the assets or the last asset remaining in the GAA and is any of the following (Reg. § 1.168(i)-1(e)(3)(iii)(B)):

- a direct result of a fire, storm, shipwreck, or other casualty, or from theft
- a charitable contribution for which a deduction is allowable
- a direct result of the termination of a business
- a nonrecognition transaction other than a transaction involving Code Sec. 168(i)(7), Code Sec. 1031, Code Sec. 1033, a technical termination of a partnership, or the anti-abuse rule

For an example of a partial disposition involving a casualty event, see Reg. § 1.168(i)-1(e)(3)(iii)(D), Example 2.

The manner of disposition of an asset in a GAA (for example, normal retirement, abnormal retirement, ordinary retirement, or extraordinary retirement) is not taken into account in determining whether a disposition occurs or gain or loss is recognized (Reg. § 1.168(i)-1(e)(2)(v)).

*Effect of disposition on unadjusted depreciable basis and depreciation reserve of GAA.* The disposition of an asset does not affect the unadjusted depreciable basis and the depreciation reserve of a GAA (Reg. § 1.168(i)-1(e)(2)(iii)). The disposition of a portion of an asset that is treated as a disposition (see above) also does not affect the unadjusted depreciable basis and depreciation reserve of a GAA (Reg. § 1.168(i)-1(e)(2)(iii)).

*Losses are not realized upon disposition of asset from GAA.* Unless an election to recognize gain or loss under the rules described below for a qualifying disposition or disposition of the last asset in a GAA is made, the adjusted depreciable basis of an asset in a GAA that is disposed of (including dispositions by transfer to a supplies, scrap, or similar account) is treated as zero immediately before the disposition. As a result, no loss is realized upon the disposition (Reg. § 1.168(i)-1(e)(2)(i)).A similar rule applies to a portion of an asset that is treated as disposed of (Reg. § 1.168(i)-1(e)(2)(i)).

> ***Example (8):*** DEF maintains one general asset account for one office building that cost $10 million. DEF replaces the entire roof. Under the final and proposed regulations, a taxpayer may not treat the retirement of a structural component as a qualifying disposition on which gain or loss is recognized by reference to adjusted basis. The entire building, including its structural components, is treated as the asset. Although the retirement of a portion of an asset, such as the roof of a building, may be treated as a disposition in certain specific circumstances, none of those circumstances apply here. As a result, DEF must continue to depreciate the $10 million cost of the general asset account and no loss is recognized. Assuming the cost of the replacement roof is capitalized the replacement roof is depreciated as a separate asset because additions and improvements to an asset are treated as separate assets (Reg. § 1.168(i)-1(e)(2)(ix), Example 1).

> ***Example (9):*** GHI maintains one general asset account for five commercial aircraft that cost a total of $500 million. The aircraft, including its components, is treated as the asset. The original aircraft engines may not be treated as separate assets. Furthermore, the retirement of the original engines is not a partial disposition of an asset and the retirement is not a qualifying disposition for which an election to recognize gain or loss may be made. Accordingly, no loss is recognized, no adjustments are made to the account, and GHI continues to depreciate the $500 million cost of the GAA. Replacement engines are separate assets and are separately depreciated assuming that their cost must be capitalized (Reg. § 1.168(i)-1(e)(2)(ix), Example 2).

*Treatment of amount realized upon disposition of asset from GAA as ordinary income.* Any amount realized on a disposition is recognized as ordinary income to the extent the sum of the unadjusted depreciable basis of the general asset account and any expensed cost for assets in the account exceeds any amounts previously recognized as ordinary income upon the disposition of other assets in the account. The recognition and character of any excess amount realized are determined under other applicable provisions of the Internal Revenue Code (other than Code Sec. 1245 and Code Sec. 1250 or provisions of the Internal Revenue Code that treat gain on a disposition as subject to Code Sec. 1245 or Code Sec. 1250) (Reg. § 1.168(i)-1(e)(2)(ii)).

"Unadjusted depreciable basis of the general asset account" is the sum of the unadjusted depreciable bases of all assets included in the general asset account (Reg. § 1.168(i)-1(b)(2)).

"Adjusted depreciable basis of the general asset account" is the unadjusted depreciable basis of the general asset account less prior depreciation, amortization, and depletion (the adjustments to basis provided in Code Sec. 1016(a)(2) and (3)) (Reg. § 1.168(i)-1(b)(3)).

The term "expensed cost" includes any allowable credit or deduction that is treated as a depreciation or amortization deduction under Code Sec. 1245 such as the credit for qualified electric vehicles (Code Sec. 30); the Code Sec. 179 expense deduction; the deductions for clean-fuel vehicles and certain refueling property (Code Sec. 179A); and deductions for expenditures to remove architectural and transportation barriers to the handicapped and elderly (Code Sec. 190) (Reg. § 1.168(i)-1(b)(5)).

> ***Example (10):*** In 2019, JKL, a calendar-year taxpayer, places 10 machines (5-year property) in a single GAA. The total cost of the machines is $10,000. No section 179 allowance or bonus deduction is claimed. 2019 depreciation is $2,000 ($10,000 × 20% first-year table percentage). Therefore, as of January 1, 2020, the depreciation reserve of the account is $2,000. On February 8, 2020, JKL sells a machine that cost $8,200 for $9,000. The disposed of machine has an adjusted depreciable basis of zero. On its 2020 tax return, JKL recognizes the amount realized of $9,000 as ordinary income because such amount does not exceed the unadjusted depreciable basis of the general asset account ($10,000), plus any expensed cost for assets in the account ($0), less amounts previously recognized as ordinary income ($0). Moreover, the unadjusted depreciable basis and depreciation reserve of the account are not affected by the disposition of the machine. Thus, the depreciation allowance for the account in 2020 is $3,200 ($10,000 × 32% second-year table percentage) (Reg. § 1.168(i)-1(e)(2)(ix), Example 3).

> ***Example (11):*** On June 4, 2021, JKL in the preceding example, sells seven machines for a total of $1,100. The disposed of machines have an adjusted depreciable basis of zero. On its 2021 tax return, JKL recognizes $1,000 as ordinary income (the unadjusted depreciable basis of $10,000, plus the expensed cost of $0, less the amount of $9,000 previously recognized as ordinary income). The recognition and character of the excess amount realized of $100 ($1,100 - $1,000) are determined under applicable provisions of the Internal Revenue Code other than Code Sec. 1245 (such as Code Sec. 1231). The unadjusted depreciable basis and depreciation reserve of the account are not affected by the disposition of the machines. The depreciation allowance for the account in 2021 is $1,920 ($10,000 × 19.2% (third-year table percentage)) (Reg. § 1.168(i)-1(e)(2)(ix), Example 4).

*Dispositions by transfer to supplies account.* Under the final repair regulations, an election may only be made to capitalize materials and supplies that are rotable spare parts, temporary spare parts, or standby emergency spare parts. The final regulations, therefore, provide that a taxpayer may dispose of such parts in a GAA by a transfer to a supplies account only if the taxpayer obtains permission to revoke the election in accordance with Reg. § 1.162-3(d) (Reg. § 1.168(i)-1(e)(2)(vi)).

This provision was not in the pre-2014 GAA regulations since the election to capitalize a material or supply or spare part was not then available.

*Dispositions of leasehold improvements in GAA.* The rules above related to the disposition of assets from a general asset account apply to a depreciable leasehold improvement made by a lessor or lessee who has elected to include the leasehold improvement in a general asset account (Reg. § 1.168(i)-1(e)(2)(vii)). This provision was not in the pre-2014 GAA regulations.

### *How to determine which GAA asset is disposed of*

*Definition of the "asset" disposed of for GAA purposes.* Each building, including its structural components, is the asset disposed of. Structural components of buildings and components of assets other than buildings may not be treated as separate assets for disposition purposes (Reg. § 1.168(i)-(e)(2)(viii)). However, as noted above, in a few limited circumstances the disposal of a portion of an asset in a GAA is treated as a disposition of an asset (Reg. § 1.168(i)-1(e)(1)(ii)).

The facts and circumstances of each disposition are considered in determining what is the appropriate asset disposed of. The asset may not consist of items placed in service on different dates without taking into account the appropriate MACRS convention. The unit of property concept is not considered in determining the asset disposed of. Likewise, the definition of a "distinct asset" for purposes of the like-kind exchange rules (see Reg. § 1.1031(a)-3(a)(4)) does not apply (Reg. § 1.168(i)-1(e)(2)(viii)(A)).

The regulations provide the following definitions of an asset disposed of for GAA purposes (Reg. § 1.168(i)-1(e)(2)(viii)(B)):

(1) Each building (including its structural components) is the asset disposed of unless more than one building is treated as the asset under Reg. § 1.1250-1(a)(2)(ii) (for example, if two or more buildings or structures on a single tract or parcel (or contiguous tracts or parcels) of land are operated as an integrated unit (as evidenced by their actual operation, management, financing, and accounting), and are treated as a single item of section 1250 property (see ¶ 116)). If a building includes two or more condominium or cooperative units, then each condominium or cooperative unit is the asset unless operated as an integrated unit. Each structural component (including components thereof) of a building, condominium unit, or cooperative unit is also an asset for disposition purposes.

(2) If the taxpayer places in service an improvement or addition to an asset (including a building) after the taxpayer placed the asset in service, the improvement or addition is a separate asset. Structural components to a building are treated like an addition or improvement.

(3) If a taxpayer properly includes an item in one of the asset classes 00.11 through 00.4 of Rev. Proc. 87-56 (1987-2 CB 674) (i.e., certain common assets, such as office equipment, computers, cars, and trucks that are depreciable without regard to the business activity of the taxpayer) or classifies an item in one of the categories under Code Sec. 168(e)(3) (other than a category that includes buildings or structural components; for example, retail motor fuels outlet and qualified leasehold improvement property), each item in the asset class or categorized under Code Sec. 168(e)(3) is the asset. For example, each item of office furniture is the asset, each computer is the asset, and each qualified smart electric meter (an item described in Code Sec. 168(e)(3)) is the asset.

(4) The final regulations do not allow a taxpayer to treat the component of an asset as a separate asset for disposition purposes unless a partial disposition election is made.

The following commonly used business assets are described in Asset Classes 00.11 through 00.4 of Rev. Proc. 87-56 and are treated as the asset disposed of from the GAA. A taxpayer may not treat components of an asset described in one of these asset classes as a separate "asset."

- office furniture fixtures, and equipment
- computers and peripheral equipment
- noncommercial airplanes
- automobiles, taxis, buses, and trucks (light and heavy)
- railroad cars and locomotives
- trailers and trailer-mounted containers
- vessels, barges, and tugs
- land improvements
- industrial steam and electric generation/distribution systems

*Example (13):* A taxpayer places a single automobile in a GAA. He then replaces a door on the vehicle. The taxpayer has not disposed of an asset and, therefore, may not elect to recognize a loss by treating the retirement of the door as a qualifying disposition.

Code Sec. 168(e)(3) lists specific types of assets that are subject to particular depreciation periods. They are:

- horses
- rent-to-own property
- automobiles or light general purpose trucks
- semi-conductor manufacturing equipment
- computer-based telephone central office switching equipment
- qualified technological equipment
- section 1245 property used in connection with research and experimentation
- certain types of energy producing property (e.g., solar and wind) specified in Code Sec. 168(e)(3)(B)(vi)
- railroad track
- motorsports entertainment complexes
- Alaska natural gas pipelines
- certain natural gas gathering lines
- single purpose agricultural or horticultural structures
- trees or vines bearing fruit or nuts
- qualified smart electric meters
- qualified smart electric grid systems
- municipal wastewater treatment plants
- telephone distribution plants and comparable equipment used for 2-way exchange of voice and data communications
- section 1245 property used in the transmission at 69 or more kilovolts of electricity for sale
- certain natural gas distribution lines

As in the case of property described in Asset Classes 00.11 through 00.4 of Rev. Proc. 87-56, a taxpayer may not treat components of assets described in Code Sec. 168(e)(3) as separate assets.

The pre-2014 GAA regulations contained no rules regarding the definition of an asset disposed of from a GAA except that the retirement of a structural component was not a disposition (Reg. § 1.168(i)-1, prior to amendment by T.D. 9564 (December 23, 2011)).

*Elective termination of general asset account treatment upon certain dispositions*

Upon the disposition of the last or all of the assets in a GAA a taxpayer may elect to terminate GAA treatment and recognize gain or loss (Reg. § 1.168(i)-1(e)(3)(ii)). See "*Optional termination of a general asset account upon disposition of last or all assets in GAA,*" below.

A taxpayer may also elect to terminate general asset account treatment for a particular asset in a general asset account and recognize gain or loss with respect to the asset by reference to its adjusted basis when the taxpayer disposes of the asset in a "qualifying disposition." If a taxpayer elects to terminate general asset account treatment for an asset disposed of in a qualifying disposition, the taxpayer must remove the asset disposed of from the general asset account and adjust the unadjusted depreciable basis and depreciation reserve of the account (Reg. § 1.168(i)-1(e)(3)(iii)). The definition of a qualifying disposition is limited to a few minor categories of asset dispositions under the final regulations (Reg. § 1.168(i)-1(e)(3)(iii)). See "*Qualifying dispositions—Optional determination of gain, loss, or other deduction,*" below.

A taxpayer must terminate general asset account treatment for assets in a general asset account that are disposed of in transactions subject to Code Sec. 167(i)(7)(B), Code Sec. 1031, or Code Sec. 1033, or in an abusive transaction. In addition, a partnership must terminate its general asset accounts upon the technical termination of the partnership under Code Sec. 708(b)(1)(B). See below.

*Optional termination of a general asset account upon disposition of last or all assets in GAA.* Upon the disposition of all of the assets, or the last asset in a GAA (including the remaining portion of an asset if this is the last item in the GAA), a taxpayer may elect to recover the adjusted depreciable basis of the general asset account. If this optional termination method is elected (Reg. § 1.168(i)-1(e)(3)(ii)):

- the GAA terminates
- the amount of gain or loss for the GAA is determined by taking into account the adjusted depreciable basis of the GAA at the time of the disposition (determined by using the applicable depreciation convention for the GAA)
- the recognition and character of the gain or loss are determined under other applicable provisions of the Internal Revenue Code, including the rules for demolition losses (Code Sec. 280B), except that (a) the amount of gain subject to ordinary income depreciation recapture under Code Sec. 1245 is limited to the excess of the depreciation allowed or allowable for the GAA, including any expensed cost over any amounts previously recognized as ordinary income upon the prior disposition of particular assets and (b) the amount of gain subject to section 1250 recapture is limited to the excess of the additional depreciation allowed or allowable for the general asset account (for example, bonus depreciation on real property in excess of straight-line depreciation) over any amounts previously recognized as ordinary income

The election is made by reporting the gain or loss, or other deduction, on the taxpayer's timely filed (including extensions) original return for the tax year in which the disposition occurs. The election may only be revoked with IRS consent upon a showing a good cause by filing a private letter ruling request (Reg. § 1.168(i)-1(e)(3)(i)). The final regulations clarify that if the election is based on a demolition loss (Code Sec. 280B), the election is made by ending depreciation for the structure at the time of the disposition of the structure (taking into account the applicable convention) a reporting the depreciation allowed for the year of the demolition on a timely filed original return (including extensions). The pre-2014 GAA regulations did not specifically refer to this optional method as an "election" (Reg. § 1.168(i)-1(e)(3)(ii), prior to amendment by T.D. 9564 (December 23, 2011)).

***Example (15):*** EFG, a calendar-year corporation, maintains a general asset account for 1,000 calculators (MACRS 5-year property subject to half-year convention). The calculators cost a total of $60,000 and are placed in service in YEAR 1. No amount is expensed or claimed as bonus depreciation. Depreciation claimed in YEAR 1 is $12,000 ($60,000 × 20% first-year table percentage). In YEAR 2, 200 of the calculators are sold for $10,000. In YEAR 2, EFG will recognize $10,000 as ordinary income. (The disposed of calculators have a deemed adjusted depreciable basis of zero). On its YEAR 2 tax return, EFG recognizes the amount realized of $10,000 as ordinary income because such amount does not exceed the unadjusted depreciable basis of the general asset account

($60,000), plus any expensed cost for assets in the account ($0), less amounts previously recognized as ordinary income ($0). The unadjusted depreciable basis and depreciation reserve of the account are not affected by the disposition of the calculators. YEAR 2 depreciation is $19,200 ($60,000 × 32% second-year table percentage).

In YEAR 3, EFG sells the remaining calculators in the GAA are sold for $35,000. EFG elects the optional termination method. As a result, the account terminates and gain or loss is determined for the account. Depreciation for YEAR 3 is $5,760 ($60,000 × 19.20% third-year table percentage × 50% to reflect half-year convention). On the date of disposition, the adjusted depreciable basis of the account is $23,040 (unadjusted depreciable basis of $60,000 less total depreciation of $36,960). Thus, in YEAR 3, EFG recognizes gain of $11,960 (amount realized of $35,000 less the adjusted depreciable basis of $23,040). The gain of $11,960 is subject to Code Sec. 1245 to the extent of the depreciation allowed or allowable for the account (plus the expensed cost for assets in the account if any amount had been expensed) less the amounts previously recognized as ordinary income ($36,960 + $0 - $10,000 = $26,960). As a result, the entire gain of $11,960 is subject to Code Sec. 1245 (Reg. § 1.168(i)-1(e)(3)(ii)(B), Example 1).

***Example (16):*** RST, a calendar-year corporation, maintains a GAA for one item of equipment that cost $2,000 and is placed in service in YEAR 1. No Code Sec. 179 or bonus deduction is claimed. The equipment is 5-year property subject to the half-year convention. In June YEAR 3, RST sells the equipment for $1,000 and elects the optional termination method. As a result, the account terminates and gain or loss is determined for the account. On the date of disposition, the adjusted depreciable basis of the account is $768 (unadjusted depreciable basis of $2,000 less the depreciation allowed or allowable of $1,232 ($400 + $640 + 192)). Thus, in YEAR 3, RST recognizes gain of $232 (amount realized of $1,000 less the adjusted depreciable basis of $768). The gain of $232 is subject to Code Sec. 1245 to the extent of the depreciation allowed or allowable for the account (plus the expensed cost for assets in the account) less the amounts previously recognized as ordinary income ($1,232 + $0 - $0 = $1,232). As a result, the entire gain of $232 is recaptured as ordinary income under Code Sec. 1245 (Reg. § 1.168(i)-1(e)(3)(ii)(B), Example 2).

*Qualifying dispositions—Optional determination of gain and loss by reference to adjusted basis.* In the case of a qualifying disposition (as defined below) of an asset, a taxpayer may elect to (Reg. § 1.168(i)-1(e)(3)(iii)(A)):

- terminate GAA treatment for the asset as of the first day of the tax year of disposition, and
- determine the amount of gain, loss, or other deduction for the asset by taking into account the asset's adjusted depreciable basis at the time of the disposition

The election is made by reporting the gain or loss, or other deduction, on the taxpayer's timely filed (including extensions) original return for the tax year in which the disposition occurs. The election may only be revoked with IRS consent upon a showing of good cause by filing a private letter ruling request (Reg. § 1.168(i)-1(e)(3)(i)). The final regulations clarify that if the election is based on a demolition loss (Code Sec. 280B), the election is made by ending depreciation for the structure at the time of the disposition of the structure (taking into account the applicable convention) and reporting the depreciation allowed for the year of the demolition on a timely filed original return (including extensions). The pre-2014 GAA regulations did not specifically refer to this optional method as an "election" (Reg. § 1.168(i)-1(e)(3)(iii), prior to amendment by T.D. 9564 (December 23, 2011)).

The adjusted depreciable basis of the asset at the time of the disposition (as determined under the applicable convention for the GAA in which the asset was included) equals the unadjusted depreciable basis of the asset less the depreciation allowed or allowable for the asset, computed by using the depreciation method, recovery period, and convention applicable to the GAA in which the asset was included and by including the portion of the additional first year depreciation deduction (bonus depreciation) claimed for the GAA that is attributable to the asset (Reg. § 1.168(i)-1(e)(iii)(A)).

The recognition and character of the gain, loss, or other deduction are determined under other applicable provisions of the Internal Revenue Code, including the demolition loss rules of Code Sec. 280B. However, the amount of gain subject to ordinary income depreciation recapture under Code Sec. 1245 or Code Sec. 1250 is limited to the lesser of (Reg. § 1.168(i)-1(e)(iii)(A)):

(1) The depreciation allowed or allowable for the asset, including any expensed cost (or, in the case of section 1250 property, additional depreciation allowed or allowable for the asset); or

(2) The excess of—

(a) The original unadjusted depreciable basis of the GAA plus, in the case of section 1245 property originally included in the GAA, any expensed cost; over

(b) The cumulative amounts of gain previously recognized as ordinary income upon the prior disposition of particular assets or under Code Sec. 1245 or Code Sec. 1250.

A qualifying disposition is a disposition that does not involve all the assets, the last asset, or the last remaining portion of the last asset remaining in a general asset account and that is the result of:

(1) A direct result of a fire, storm, shipwreck, or other casualty, or from theft (Reg. § 1.168(i)-1(e)(3)(iii)(D), Example 2);

(2) A charitable contribution for which a deduction is allowable;

(3) A direct result of a cessation, termination, or disposition of a business; and

(4) A transaction to which a nonrecognition provision of the Code applies, except for the transactions listed above relating to Code Sec. 168(i)(7), Code Sec. 1031, Code Sec. 1033, technical terminations, and the anti-abuse rule.

Special rules that apply to each of these dispositions are described below.

The pre-2014 GAA regulations limited the qualifying disposition election to only a few types of dispositions, such as casualty and theft loss, charitable contributions, dispositions in connection with business terminations, and certain nonrecognition transactions (Reg. § 1.168(i)-1(e)(3)(iii), prior to amendment by T.D. 9564 (December 23, 2011)).

If the taxpayer elects to terminate GAA treatment for an asset disposed of in a qualifying disposition (Reg. § 1.168(i)-1(e)(3)(iii)(C)):

(1) The asset is removed from the GAA as of the first day of the tax year in which the qualifying disposition occurs and placed in a single asset account;

(2) The unadjusted depreciable basis of the GAA is reduced by the unadjusted depreciable basis of the asset as of the first day of the tax year of disposition;

(3) The depreciation reserve of the GAA is reduced by the depreciation allowed or allowable for the asset as of the end of the tax year immediately preceding the tax year of disposition, computed by using the depreciation method, recovery period, and convention applicable to the GAA and by

including the portion of the bonus depreciation deduction claimed for the GAA that is attributable to the asset; and

(4) Any portion of the cost of the asset that was expensed is disregarded for purposes of determining the amount of gain realized on subsequent dispositions that is subject to ordinary income treatment under the rules generally applicable to the disposition of an asset in a GAA.

***Example (17):*** XYZ, a calendar-year corporation, maintains one general asset account for 12 machines. Each machine costs $15,000 and is placed in service in YEAR 1. Of the 12 machines, nine machines that cost a total of $135,000 are used in XYZ's Kentucky plant, and three machines that cost a total of $45,000 are used in XYZ's Ohio plant. No Code Sec. 179 or bonus deduction is claimed. As of January 1, YEAR 3, the depreciation reserve for the account is $93,600.

In YEAR 3, XYZ sells its entire manufacturing plant in Ohio. The sales proceeds allocated to each of the three machines at the Ohio plant is $5,000. XYZ elects to treat the disposition as a qualifying disposition.

Note that the disposition is a qualifying disposition under the temporary, final, and proposed regulations. A qualifying disposition under the temporary regulations and under the final and proposed regulations includes a disposition upon the termination of a business (provided the disposition is not a disposition of all of the asset or the last asset in the GAA).

For XYZ's YEAR 3 return, the depreciation allowance for the account is computed as follows. As of December 31, YEAR 2, the depreciation allowed or allowable for the three machines at the Ohio plant is $23,400. Thus, as of January 1, YEAR 3, the unadjusted depreciable basis of the account is reduced from $180,000 to $135,000 ($180,000 less the unadjusted depreciable basis of $45,000 for the three machines), and the depreciation reserve of the account is decreased from $93,600 to $70,200 ($93,600 less the depreciation allowed or allowable of $23,400 for the three machines as of December 31, YEAR 2). Consequently, the depreciation allowance for the account in YEAR 3 is $25,920 ($135,000 × 19.2 percent).

For XYZ's YEAR 3 return, gain or loss for each of the three machines at the Ohio plant is determined as follows. The depreciation allowed or allowable in YEAR 3 for each machine is $1,440 [($15,000 × 19.2 percent) / 2 (to reflect half-year convention)]. The adjusted depreciable basis of each machine is $5,760 (the adjusted depreciable basis of $7,200 removed from the account less the depreciation allowed or allowable of $1,440 in YEAR 3). The loss recognized in YEAR 3 for each machine is $760 ($5,000 - $5,760), which is subject to Code Sec. 1231 (Reg. § 1.168(i)-1(e)(3)(iii)(D), Example 1).

*Special rules for transactions subject to Code Sec. 168(i)(7), like-kind exchanges and involuntary conversions, technical terminations, and abusive transactions*

*Transfers of One or More Assets in a GAA in Nonrecognition Transactions Described in Code Sec. 168(i)(7).*

When an asset or assets (or portions of an asset) in a GAA are transferred by a taxpayer in a nonrecognition transaction described in Code Sec. 168(i)(7)(B) the transferee is bound by the taxpayer's GAA election to the extent that the transferee's basis in the asset that does not exceed the taxpayer's adjusted depreciable basis of the GAA or the taxpayer's adjusted depreciable basis in the asset, as applicable (Reg. § 1.168(i)-1(e)(3)(iv)(A)). These are nonrecognition transactions described in Code Sec. 332, Code Sec. 351, Code Sec. 361, Code Sec. 721, or Code Sec. 731. See ¶ 144.

*All assets in GAA transferred in Code Sec. 168(i)(7) nonrecognition transaction.* If a taxpayer transfers all the assets, or the last asset, in a GAA in a Code Sec. 168(i)(7)(B) transaction (Reg. § 1.168(i)-1(e)(3)(iv)(A)):

(1) The taxpayer's GAA account is terminated on the transfer date. The taxpayer's depreciation deduction for the GAA is computed by using the depreciation method, recovery period, and convention applicable to the GAA. This depreciation deduction is allocated between the taxpayer and the transferee on a monthly basis. This allocation is made in accordance with the rules in Reg. § 1.168(d)-1(b)(7)(ii) for allocating the depreciation deduction between the transferor and the transferee;

(2) The transferee must establish a new GAA for all the assets, or the last asset, in the tax year of the transfer for the portion of its basis in the assets that does not exceed the adjusted depreciable basis of the taxpayer's GAA account. The taxpayer's adjusted depreciable basis of this GAA is equal to the adjusted depreciable basis of the GAA as of the beginning of the taxpayer's tax year in which the transfer occurs, decreased by the amount of depreciation allocable to the taxpayer as determined in item (1). The transferee is treated as the transferor for purposes of computing the allowable depreciation deduction for the new GAA. The unadjusted depreciable bases of all the assets or the last asset, and the greater of the depreciation allowed or allowable for all the assets or the last asset (including the amount of depreciation for the transferred assets that is allocable to the transferor for the year of the transfer), are included in the newly established GAA. Consequently, this GAA in the year of the transfer will have a beginning balance for both the unadjusted depreciable basis and the depreciation reserve of the general asset account; and

(3) The transferee treats the portion of its basis in the assets that exceeds the taxpayer's adjusted depreciable basis of the GAA in which all the assets, or the last asset, were included as a separate asset that the transferee placed in service on the date of the transfer. The transferee accounts for this asset in a single asset or multiple asset account (see ¶ 130) or may make an election to include the asset in a GAA.

*Portion of assets in GAA transferred in Code Sec. 168(i)(7) nonrecognition transaction.* If a taxpayer does not transfer all of the assets or the last asset in a GAA in a Code Sec. 168(i)(7) nonrecognition transaction (Reg. § 1.168(i)-1(e)(3)(iv)(C)):

(1) The transferred asset is removed from the GAA in which the asset is included, as of the first day of the tax year in which the transfer occurs. In addition, the following adjustments to the GAA are made:

- The unadjusted depreciable basis of the GAA is reduced by the unadjusted depreciable basis of the asset as of the first day of the tax year of disposition;

- The depreciation reserve of the GAA is reduced by the depreciation allowed or allowable for the asset as of the end of the tax year immediately preceding the tax year of disposition, computed by using the depreciation method, recovery period, and convention applicable to the GAA and by including the portion of the bonus depreciation deduction claimed for the GAA that is attributable to the asset; and

- Any portion of the cost of the asset that was expensed is disregarded for purposes of determining the amount of gain realized on subsequent dispositions that is subject to ordinary income treatment under the rules generally applicable to the disposition of an asset in a GAA;

(2) The depreciation deduction for the asset for the taxpayer's tax year is computed by using the depreciation method, recovery period, and convention applicable to the GAA in which the asset was included. This depreciation deduction is allocated between the taxpayer and the transferee on a monthly basis in accordance with the rules in Reg. § 1.168(d)-1(b)(7)(ii);

(3) The transferee must establish a new GAA for the asset in the tax year of transfer for the portion of its basis in the asset that does not exceed the taxpayer's adjusted depreciable basis of the asset. The taxpayer's adjusted depreciable basis is equal to the adjusted depreciable basis of the asset as of the beginning of the taxpayer's tax year in which the transfer occurs, decreased by the amount of depreciation allocable to the transferor for the year of the transfer. The transferee is treated as the taxpayer for purposes of computing the depreciation deduction for the new GAA. The unadjusted depreciable basis of the asset, and the greater of the depreciation allowed or allowable for the asset (including the amount of depreciation for the transferred asset that is allocable to the taxpayer for the tax year of the transfer), are included in the newly established GAA. As a result, the new GAA will have a beginning balance for both the unadjusted depreciable basis and the depreciation reserve of the GAA; and

(4) The transferee treats the portion of its basis in the asset that exceeds the taxpayer's adjusted depreciable basis of the asset as a separate asset that the transferee placed in service on the date of the transfer. The transferee accounts for this asset in a single item account or a multiple asset account or may make an election to include the asset in a GAA.

*Transfers of One or More Assets in a GAA in a Like-Kind Exchange or Involuntary Conversion*

*All assets or last asset in GAA transferred in like-kind exchange or involuntary conversion.* If all the assets, or the last asset, in a GAA are transferred by a taxpayer in a like-kind exchange (Code Sec. 1031) or in an involuntary conversion (Code Sec. 1033) (Reg. § 1.168(i)-1(e)(3)(v)(A)):

(1) The GAA terminates as of the first day of the tax year of disposition;

(2) The amount of gain or loss for the GAA is determined by taking into account the adjusted depreciable basis of the GAA at the time of disposition. The depreciation allowance for the GAA in the year of disposition is determined in the same manner as the depreciation allowance for the relinquished MACRS property in the year of disposition is determined under Reg. § 1.168(i)-6. The recognition and character of gain or loss are determined in accordance with the optional rule discussed above for the termination of a GAA when all of the assets, or the last asset, of a GAA is disposed of (i.e., the rule in Reg. § 1.168(i)-1(e)(3)(ii)(A)); and

(3) The adjusted depreciable basis of the GAA at the time of disposition is treated as the adjusted depreciable basis of the relinquished MACRS property.

*Portion of assets in GAA transferred in like-kind exchange or involuntary conversion.* If not all of the assets in a GAA are transferred by a taxpayer in a like-kind exchange (Code Sec. 1031) or in an involuntary conversion (Code Sec. 1033) (Reg. § 1.168(i)-1(e)(3)(v)(B)):

(1) GAA treatment for the asset terminates as of the first day of the tax year of disposition;

(2) The adjusted depreciable basis equals the unadjusted depreciable basis of the asset less the depreciation allowed or allowable for the asset, computed by using the depreciation method, recovery period, and convention applicable to the GAA and by including the portion of the bonus depreciation deduction claimed for the GAA that is attributable to the asset. The depreciation allowance for the asset in the year of disposition is determined in the same manner as the depreciation allowance for the relinquished MACRS property in the year of disposition is determined under Reg. § 1.168(i)-6;

(3) As of the first day of the year of disposition, the taxpayer must remove the asset from the GAA;

(4) The unadjusted depreciable basis of the GAA is reduced by the unadjusted depreciable basis of the asset as of the first day of the tax year of disposition;

(5) The depreciation reserve of the GAA is reduced by the depreciation allowed or allowable for the asset as of the end of the tax year immediately preceding the tax year of disposition, computed by using the depreciation method, recovery period, and convention applicable to the GAA and by including the portion of the bonus depreciation deduction claimed for the GAA that is attributable to the asset; and

(6) Any portion of the cost of the asset that was expensed is disregarded for purposes of determining the amount of gain realized on subsequent dispositions that is subject to ordinary income treatment under the rules generally applicable to the disposition of an asset in a GAA.

*Technical termination of partnership*

When a partnership is technically terminated, all of the terminated partnership's general asset accounts terminate as of the date of partnership's termination. The terminated partnership computes the allowable depreciation deduction for each of its general asset accounts for the tax year of technical termination by using the depreciation method, recovery period, and convention applicable to the GAA. The new partnership is not bound by the terminated partnership's GAA elections (Reg. § 1.168(i)-1(e)(3)(vi)).

The rule providing for technical termination of partnerships is repealed for partnership tax years beginning after December 31, 2017 (Code Sec. 708(b)(1)(B)).

*Anti-abuse rule*

A taxpayer must terminate general asset account treatment for assets in a GAA that are disposed of in an "abusive transaction" on the first day of the tax year in which the disposition occurs. The taxpayer must determine the amount of gain, loss, or other deduction attributable to the disposition in accordance with the optional elective rule for qualifying dispositions discussed above (Reg. § 1.168(i)-1(e)(3)(iii)(A)) and must make the following adjustments to the GAA account (Reg. § 1.168(i)-1(e)(3)(vii)(A)):

(1) The asset is removed from the GAA as of the first day of the tax year in which the qualifying disposition occurs and placed in a single asset account;

(2) The unadjusted depreciable basis of the GAA is reduced by the unadjusted depreciable basis of the asset as of the first day of the tax year of disposition;

(3) The depreciation reserve of the GAA is reduced by the depreciation allowed or allowable for the asset as of the end of the tax year immediately preceding the tax year of disposition, computed by using the depreciation method, recovery period, and convention applicable to the GAA and by

including the portion of the bonus depreciation deduction claimed for the GAA that is attributable to the asset; and

(4) Any portion of the cost of the asset that was expensed is disregarded for purposes of determining the amount of gain realized on subsequent dispositions that is subject to ordinary income treatment under the rules generally applicable to the disposition of an asset in a GAA.

An abusive transaction is a transaction entered into, or made, with a principal purpose of achieving a tax benefit or result that would not be available absent a general asset account election. However, a transaction is not abusive if it is subject to the GAA rules that apply to transfers in a Code Sec. 168(i)(7) nonrecognition transaction, like-kind exchanges and involuntary conversions, and technical terminations of partnerships (Reg. § 1.168(i)-1(e)(3)(vii)(B)).

The regulations provide two nonexclusive examples of an abusive transaction (Reg. § 1.168(i)-1(e)(3)(vii)(B)(1) and (2)):

(1) A transaction entered into with a principal purpose of shifting income or deductions among taxpayers in a manner that would not be possible absent a GAA election in order to take advantage of differing effective tax rates among the taxpayers; and

(2) A GAA election made with a principal purpose of disposing of an asset from a GAA in order to utilize an expiring net operating loss or credit if the transaction is not a bona fide disposition. The fact that a taxpayer with a net operating loss carryover or a credit carryover transfers an asset to a related person or transfers an asset pursuant to an arrangement where the asset continues to be used (or is available for use) by the taxpayer pursuant to a lease (or otherwise) indicates, absent strong evidence to the contrary, that the transaction is abusive.

*Assets generating foreign source income*

Assets generating foreign source income may be included in a general asset account if there is no substantial distortion of income (Reg. § 1.168(i)-1(c)(ii)). If general asset account treatment is terminated by the IRS under this rule, the assets must be included in single asset accounts.

The regulations provide rules for determining the source of any income, gain or loss recognized, and the appropriate Code Sec. 904(d) separate limitation category or categories for any foreign source income, gain, or loss recognized on a disposition of an asset in a GAA account that consists of assets generating both United States and foreign source income (Reg. § 1.168(i)-1(f)).

These rules, however, only apply to GAA asset dispositions governed by (Reg. § 1.168(i)-1(f)):

(1) The general disposition rules of Reg. § 1.168(i)-1(e)(2);

(2) The optional elective rule for disposition of all assets, or the last asset (or last portion of the last asset), remaining in a general asset account (Reg. § 1.168(i)-1(e)(3)(ii));

(3) The optional elective rule for the disposition of fewer than all assets in a GAA account in a qualifying disposition (Reg. § 1.168(i)-1(e)(3)(iii));

(4) The mandatory rules for dispositions under Code Sec. 1031 or Code Sec. 1033 (Reg. § 1.168(i)-1(e)(3)(v)); and

(5) The mandatory anti-abuse rule (Reg. § 1.168(i)-1(e)(3)(vii)).

*Source of ordinary income, gain, or loss determined by allocation and apportionment of depreciation allowed.* The amount of any ordinary income, gain, or loss that is recognized on the disposition of an asset in a GAA must be apportioned between United States and foreign sources based on the allocation and apportionment of the (Reg. § 1.168(i)-1(f)(2)(i)):

(1) Depreciation allowed for the GAA *as of the end of the tax year* in which the disposition occurs if the dispositions is governed by the general disposition rules of Reg. § 1.168(i)-1(e)(2),;

(2) Depreciation allowed for the GAA *as of the time of disposition* if (a) the taxpayer applies the optional elective rule for the disposition of all assets, or the last asset, in the general asset account (Reg. § 1.168(i)-1(e)(3)(ii)), or (b) if all the assets, or the last asset, in the GAA are disposed of in a transaction governed by the GAA disposition rules described in Code Sec. 1031 or Code Sec. 1033 (Reg. § 1.168(i)-1(e)(3)(v)(A)); or

(3) Depreciation allowed for the asset disposed of *for only the tax year* in which the disposition occurs if (a) the optional elective rule for the disposition of fewer than all assets in a GAA account in a qualifying disposition applies (Reg. § 1.168(i)-1(e)(3)(iii)), (b) a portion of the assets in the GAA are disposed of in a transaction governed by the mandatory GAA disposition rules described in Code Sec. 1031 or Code Sec. 1033 (Reg. § 1.168(i)-1(e)(3)(v)(B)), or (c) the asset is disposed of in a transaction governed by the GAA anti-abuse rule (Reg. § 1.168(i)-1(e)(3)(vii)).

The amount of ordinary income, gain, or loss recognized on the disposition of an asset from a GAA that is treated as foreign source income, gain, or loss is equal to the product of (Reg. § 1.168(i)-1(f)(2)(ii)):

(1) Total ordinary income, gain, or loss from the disposition of an asset, and

(2) Allowed depreciation deductions (for the time period prescribed above) allocated and apportioned to foreign source income/total allowed depreciation deductions for the GAA or for the asset disposed of (as applicable).

If the assets in the GAA generate foreign source income in more than one separate category under Code Sec. 904(d)(1), another section of the Internal Revenue Code, or under a United States income tax treaty, the amount of foreign source income, gain, or loss from the disposition of an asset as determined above must be allocated and apportioned to the applicable separate category or categories. The foreign source income, gain, or loss in a separate category is equal to the product of (Reg. § 1.168(i)-1(f)(3)):

(1) Foreign source income, gain, or loss from the disposition of an asset, and

(2) Allowed depreciation deductions allocated and apportioned to a separate category total/allowed depreciation deductions and apportioned to foreign source income.

*Termination of GAA treatment for assets with basis increase as result of recapture of deduction or credit*

General asset account treatment for an asset terminates as of the first day of the tax year in which the basis of an asset in a GAA is increased as a result of the recapture of any allowable credit or deduction. The asset must be removed from the GAA and the following adjustments to the GAA are required (Reg. § 1.168(i)-1(g)):

(1) The unadjusted depreciable basis of the GAA is reduced by the unadjusted depreciable basis of the asset as of the first day of the tax year of disposition;

(2) The depreciation reserve of the GAA is reduced by the depreciation allowed or allowable for the asset as of the end of the tax year immediately preceding the tax year of disposition, computed by using the depreciation method, recovery period, and convention applicable to the GAA and by including the portion of the bonus depreciation deduction claimed for the GAA that is attributable to the asset; and

(3) Any portion of the cost of the asset that was expensed is disregarded for purposes of determining the amount of gain realized on subsequent dispositions that is subject to ordinary income treatment under the rules generally applicable to the disposition of an asset in a GAA.

The following nonexclusive list of recapture provisions may cause a basis adjustment to an asset in a GAA account:

- Code Sec. 30(e)(5) (recapture of plug-in vehicle credit for vehicles which cease to be eligible for the credit)
- Code Sec. 50(c)(2) (recapture of investment credit claimed under Code Sec. 38)
- Code Sec. 168(l)(7) (recapture of bonus depreciation on qualified cellulosic biofuel plant property which ceases to be qualifying property) (¶ 127I)
- Code Sec. 168(n)(4) (recapture of bonus depreciation on qualified disaster assistance property which ceases to be qualifying property) (¶ 127H)
- Code Sec. 179(d)(10) (recapture of Code Sec. 179 expense allowance on section 179 property used 50 percent or less for business purposes) (¶ 300)
- Code Sec. 179A(e)(4) (recapture of deduction for clean-fuel vehicles and certain refueling property which ceases to be qualifying property)
- Code Sec. 1400N(d)(5) (recapture of bonus depreciation on Gulf Opportunity Zone property which ceases to be Gulf Opportunity Zone property) (¶ 127F)

*Assets with basis redeterminations for reasons other than recapture of deductions and credits*

If, after the placed-in-service year, the unadjusted depreciable basis of an asset in a GAA is redetermined due to a transaction other than a basis adjustment required on account of the recapture of a deduction or credit (for example, due to contingent purchase price or discharge of indebtedness), the taxpayer's GAA election for the asset also applies to the increase or decrease in basis resulting from the redetermination. For the tax year in which the increase or decrease in basis occurs, the taxpayer must establish a new GAA for the amount of the increase or decrease in basis. The applicable recovery period for the increase or decrease in basis is the recovery period of the asset remaining as of the beginning of the tax year in which the increase or decrease in basis occurs, the applicable depreciation method and applicable convention are the same depreciation method and convention that applies to the asset for the tax year in which the increase or decrease in basis occurs, and the increase or decrease in basis is deemed placed in service in the same tax year as the asset (Reg. § 1.168(i)-1(i)).

*Change in use of asset in GAA: Conversion to personal use or change in depreciation method or period*

An asset in a general asset account becomes ineligible for general asset account treatment if the taxpayer uses the asset in any personal activity during the tax year. If the asset is used for any personal purposes, the taxpayer must remove the asset from the general asset account as of the first day of the tax year in which the change in use occurs (the year of change) and must make the following adjustments to the general asset account (Reg. § 1.168(i)-1(h)(1)):

(1) The unadjusted depreciable basis of the GAA is reduced by the unadjusted depreciable basis of the asset as of the first day of the tax year of disposition;

(2) The depreciation reserve of the GAA is reduced by the depreciation allowed or allowable for the asset as of the end of the tax year immediately preceding the tax year of disposition, computed by using the depreciation method, recovery period, and convention applicable to the GAA and by including the portion of the bonus depreciation deduction claimed for the GAA that is attributable to the asset; and

(3) Any portion of the cost of the asset that was expensed is disregarded for purposes of determining the amount of gain realized on subsequent dispositions that is subject to ordinary income treatment under the rules generally applicable to the disposition of an asset in a GAA.

Any personal use requires that the asset be removed from the GAA.

*Change in use results in a different recovery period or depreciation method: Removal of asset from and adjustments to GAA required.* When a change in use after the tax year in which a GAA asset is placed in service results in a different recovery period or depreciation method for the asset (see ¶ 169) it must be removed from the GAA unless the change in use results in a shorter recovery period and/or less accelerated depreciation method and the taxpayer elects under Reg. § 1.168(i)-4(d)(3)(ii) to continue to depreciate the asset without regard to the change in use (Reg. § 1.168(i)-1(h)(2)(ii)).

A change in use can be caused by using an asset in a different business of the taxpayer, thereby, changing the asset's Rev. Proc. 87-56 asset class, or by moving the asset from the U.S. to a country outside of the U.S., thereby requiring use of the MACRS straight-line alternative depreciation system (ADS) and a longer ADS recovery (depreciation) period. See Reg. § 1.168(i)-4(d)(1) and Reg. § 1.168(i)-4(d)(2) for the definition of a change in use, as discussed at ¶ 168 and following.

An asset is treated as removed from the GAA as of the first day of the tax year in which the change of use occurs and the following adjustments to the account are made (Reg. § 1.168(i)-1(h)(2)(ii)):

(1) The unadjusted depreciable basis of the GAA is reduced by the unadjusted depreciable basis of the asset as of the first day of the tax year of disposition;

(2) The depreciation reserve of the GAA is reduced by the depreciation allowed or allowable for the asset as of the end of the tax year immediately preceding the tax year of disposition, computed by using the depreciation method, recovery period, and convention applicable to the GAA and by including the portion of the bonus depreciation deduction claimed for the GAA that is attributable to the asset; and

(3) Any portion of the cost of the asset that was expensed is disregarded for purposes of determining the amount of gain realized on subsequent dispositions that is subject to ordinary income treatment under the rules generally applicable to the disposition of an asset in a GAA.

*New GAA must be established for asset removed from GAA on account of change of use.* If a change in use results in a shorter recovery period or a more accelerated depreciation method, the taxpayer must establish a new GAA for the asset in the year of change. The *adjusted* depreciable basis of the asset as of the first day of the year of change is included in the GAA. The applicable depreciation method, recovery period, and convention (for purposes of computing deductions and determining the assets which may be placed in the same GAA) are the method, period, and convention required by the change of use rules pursuant to Reg. § 1.168(i)-4(d)(3)(i).

If a change in use results in a longer recovery period or slower depreciation method, the taxpayer must establish a separate GAA for the asset in the year of change. The unadjusted depreciable basis of the asset and the greater of the depreciation of the asset allowed or allowable in accordance as of the first day of the tax year of change are included in the newly established general asset account. Consequently, this general asset account as of the first day of the year of change will have a beginning balance for both the unadjusted depreciable basis and the depreciation reserve of the GAA. The applicable depreciation method, recovery period, and convention are determined under Reg. § 1.168(i)-4(d)(4)(ii).

*Identification of disposed of or converted asset*

As explained below, the following methods may be used for purposes of identifying the asset disposed of from a general asset account (GAA): the specific identification method, the FIFO method, the modified FIFO method, a mortality dispersion table if the asset disposed of is a mass asset grouped in a GAA with other mass assets, or any method designated by the Secretary. The LIFO method is not permitted (Reg. § 1.168(i)-1(j)). The pre-2014 regulations did not provide these rules.

Once the asset disposed of is identified, any reasonable method consistently applied to all of the taxpayer's GAAs may be used to determined the unadjusted depreciable basis of the asset removed from the account (Reg. § 1.168(i)-1(j)(3)). The final regulations clarify that it must be impracticable from the taxpayer's records to determine the unadjusted depreciable basis of the disposed of asset (Reg. § 1.168(i)-1(j)(3)).

Reasonable methods include: (1) discounting the cost of the replacement asset to its placed-in-service year cost using the Producer Price Index for Finished Goods, or its successor, the Producer Price Index for Final Demand (the proposed and temporary regulations allowed use of the Consumer Price Index); (2) a pro rata allocation of the unadjusted depreciable basis of the general asset account based on the replacement cost of the disposed of asset and the replacement cost of all of the assets in the general asset account; and (3) a study allocating the cost of the asset to its individual components (Reg. § 1.168(i)-1(j)(3)).

The IRS believes that the Consumer Price Index provides a less accurate determination of basis than the Consumer Producer Index for Finished Goods and, therefore, the final regulations do not allow use of the Consumer Price Index (Preamble to T.D. 9689 (August 18, 2014)).

Under the final regulations (Reg. § 1.168(i)-1(j)(3)), indexed discounting (item (1)) only applies if the replacement asset is capitalized as a restoration (defined in

Reg. § 1.263(a)-3(k)) and is not a capitalized betterment or adaptation (defined in Reg. § 1.263(a)-3(j) and (l)).

The identification methods listed above (and described in more detail below) apply when an asset in a GAA is disposed of or converted in a transaction described in (Reg. § 1.168(i)-1(j)(1))

(1) Reg. § 1.168(i)-1(e)(3)(iii) (disposition other than all or the last asset in a GAA in a qualifying disposition in which taxpayer elects the optional determination of gain or loss);

(2) Reg. § 1.168(i)-1(e)(3)(iv)(B) (transfer of assets in nonrecognition transaction subject to Code Sec. 168(i)(7));

(3) Reg. § 1.168(i)-1(e)(3)(v)(B) (like-kind exchange (Code Sec. 1031) or involuntary conversion (Code Sec. 1033) of less than all assets in a GAA);

(4) Reg. § 1.168(i)-1(e)(3)(vii) (disposition of an asset in violation of anti-abuse rule);

(5) Reg. § 1.168(i)-1(g) (assets removed from GAA as a result of a basis adjustment due to recapture of a deduction or credit)

(6) Reg. § 1.168(i)-1(h)(1) (asset removed from GAA as a result of conversion to personal use).

For purposes of identifying which asset in a GAA is disposed of or converted, a taxpayer must identify the disposed of or converted asset by using one of the following methods.

*Specific identification method.* The specific identification method may be used if the taxpayer can determine the particular tax year in which the disposed of or converted asset was placed in service by the taxpayer (Reg. § 1.168(i)-1(j)(2)(i)(A)).

*First-in, first out (FIFO) method.* If the taxpayer can readily determine from its records the total dispositions of assets with the same recovery period during the tax year but cannot readily determine from its records the unadjusted depreciable basis of the disposed of or converted asset (i.e., cannot determine the placed-in-service year) a taxpayer may use a FIFO identification method. Under this method, the taxpayer identifies the GAA with the earliest placed-in service year that has the same recovery period as the disposed of or converted asset and that has assets at the beginning of the tax year of the disposition or conversion, and the taxpayer treats the disposed of or converted asset as being from that GAA. To determine which GAA has assets at the beginning of the tax year of the disposition or conversion, the taxpayer reduces the number of assets originally included in the account by the number of assets disposed of or converted in any prior tax year in a transaction subject to these identification rules (Reg. § 1.168(i)-1(j)(2)(i)(B)).

*Modified FIFO method.* If the taxpayer can readily determine from its records the total dispositions of assets with the same recovery period during the tax year and the unadjusted depreciable basis of the disposed of or converted asset the taxpayer may use the modified FIFO method. Under this method, the taxpayer identifies the GAA with the earliest placed-in-service year that has the same recovery period as the disposed of or converted asset and that has assets at the beginning of the tax year of the disposition or conversion with the same unadjusted depreciable basis as the disposed of or converted asset, and the taxpayer treats the disposed of or converted asset as being from that GAA. To determine which GAA has assets at the beginning of the tax year of the disposition or conversion, the taxpayer reduces the number of assets originally included in the account by the number of assets disposed of or converted in any prior tax year in a transaction subject to these identification rules (Reg. § 1.168(i)-1(j)(2)(i)(C)).

*Mortality dispersion table.* A mortality dispersion table may be used to identify disposed of or converted mass assets accounted for in a mass asset GAA (see Reg. § 1.168(i)-1(c)(2)(H)) if the taxpayer can readily determine the total dispositions of mass assets with the same recovery period during the tax year. The mortality dispersion table must be based upon an acceptable sampling of the taxpayer's actual disposition and conversion experience for mass assets or other acceptable statistical or engineering techniques. To use a mortality dispersion table, the taxpayer must adopt recordkeeping practices consistent with the taxpayer's prior practices and consonant with good accounting and engineering practices (Reg. § 1.168(i)-1(j)(2)(i)(D)).

*Other methods designated by IRS.* A taxpayer may use any other identification method designated by the IRS on or after December 23, 2011 (Reg. § 1.168(i)-1(j)(2)(i)(E)).

*Last-in, first-out method (LIFO) is not permissible identification method.* A last-in, first-out method of accounting may not be used to identify disposed or converted assets in a GAA. Under the LIFO method, for example, the taxpayer identifies the GAA with the most recent placed-in-service year that has the same recovery period as the disposed of or converted asset and that has assets at the beginning of the tax year of the disposition or conversion, and the taxpayer treats the disposed of or converted asset as being from that general asset account. Similarly, a taxpayer may not treated the disposed portion of an asset as being from the GAA with the most recent placed-in service year that has assets that are the same as the asset of which the disposed portion is a part (Reg. § 1.168(i)-1(j)(2)(iii)).

## ¶ 130

## MACRS Item and Multiple Asset (Pool) Accounting

Rules for establishing and maintaining MACRS item and multiple asset accounts are contained in Reg. § 1.168(i)-7 (T.D. 9636 (September 19, 2013)).Reg. § 1.168(i)-8 is effective for tax years beginning on or after January 1, 2014, or at a taxpayer's option, to tax years beginning on or after January 1, 2012. However, a taxpayer was allowed to apply Temporary Reg. § 1.168(i)-7T to tax years beginning on or after January 1, 2012 and before January 1, 2014 (Reg. § 1.168(i)-7(e)). It is not necessary to apply either the final regulations or the temporary regulations to a tax year beginning on or after January 1, 2012 and before January 1, 2014. Temporary Reg. § 1.168(i)-7T was adopted as a final regulation (i.e., as Reg. § 1.168(i)-7) without any substantive change. Rev. Proc. 2019-43 currently provides the automatic accounting method change procedures to change to a method that is permitted by the final regulations. See ¶ 77.

*Item and pool accounting rules in general*

A taxpayer may account for MACRS property by (Reg. § 1.168(i)-7):

(1) treating each individual MACRS asset as an account (a "single asset account" or an "item account");

(2) by combining two or more MACRS assets in a single account (a "multiple asset account" or a "pool"); or

(3) by establishing a general asset account (see ¶ 128).

For example, if a taxpayer purchases two business cars during the current tax year, the taxpayer may separately depreciate each car. If this choice is made, each car is treated as a single asset or item account. Assuming that certain requirements described below are satisfied and the cars are placed in the same account (i.e., in a multiple asset account or pool), depreciation is computed on the combined cost of the vehicles. If an asset in a multiple asset account is disposed of during a tax year special rules apply for purposes of identifying the disposed of asset and determining gain or loss. See ¶ 162.

A taxpayer may establish as many single asset accounts or multiple asset accounts for MACRS property as the taxpayer wants.

*Required use of single asset accounts*

An asset must be accounted for in a single asset account if (Reg. § 1.168(i)-7(b)):

(1) the asset is used partially in a trade or business (or for the production of income) and partially in a personal activity;

(2) the asset is placed in service and disposed of in the same tax year;

(3) general asset account treatment for an asset terminates;

(4) the taxpayer disposes of an asset accounted for in a multiple asset account or pool (the taxpayer must account for the asset in a single asset account beginning in the tax year of disposition). See ¶ 162.

(5) under the final regulations, the taxpayer disposes of a portion of an asset by making a partial disposition election or in a disposition of a portion of an asset for which gain, determined without regard to section 1245 or section 1250, is not recognized in whole or in part under Code Sec. 1031 or Code Sec. 1033, a transfer of a portion of an asset in a step-in-the shoes transaction described in Code Sec. 168(i)(7)(B), or a sale of a portion of an asset. See ¶ 162.

*Rules for combining assets into a multiple asset account or pool*

Assets may be placed in the same multiple asset account of pool only if (Reg. § 1.168(i)-7(c)(2)(i)):

(1) the assets are placed in service in the same tax year;

(2) the assets have same depreciation method;

(3) the assets have the same recovery period;

(4) the assets have the same depreciation convention; and

(5) if applicable, any additional special rules described below for certain property are satisfied.

For example, a pool may be established for MACRS 5-year property (i.e. MACRS property with a 5-year recovery period) even if the property is not of the same type, so long as the property is placed in service in the same tax year and is subject to the same depreciation method (e.g. 200 percent declining balance method, 150 percent declining balance method, or straight-line method) and convention (e.g., half-year or mid-quarter convention). If the mid-quarter convention applies, the property must have been placed in service in the same quarter of the tax year (Reg. § 1.168(i)-7(c)(2)(ii)). It is not necessary to place all the MACRS 5-year property with the same depreciation method, recovery period, and convention in the same pool (Reg. § 1.168(i)-7(c)(2)(i)). A taxpayer can divide the property among several pools and also treat some of the property as single item accounts if it desires.

Property subject to the mid-month convention (i.e., 39-year nonresidential real property and 27.5 year residential rental property) which is placed in service in the same month of the same tax year may be placed in the same pool or divided among several pools provided the property has the same recovery period. For example, a taxpayer may create a pool for nonresidential real property depreciated over 39 years and placed in service in the same month of the tax year. However, this pool cannot include nonresidential real property to which the MACRS straight-line alternative depreciation system (ADS) applies because the depreciation period under ADS for nonresidential real property is 40 years. Nor may the pool include any residential rental property.

*Special rules for combining assets into a multiple asset account or pool*

In addition to the requirement that only assets with the same depreciation method, recovery period, and convention may be placed in the same multiple asset account or pool, the following special rules apply to the following property as a result of factors that affect the computation of depreciation (Reg. § 1.168(i)-7(c)(2)(ii)):

(1) Passenger automobiles subject to the luxury car depreciation caps (Code Sec. 280F) must be grouped into a separate multiple asset account or pool;

(2) Assets not eligible for any additional first year depreciation deduction (bonus depreciation) (including assets for which the taxpayer elected not to deduct the additional first year depreciation) provided by, for example, Code Sec. 168(k) through (n), Code Sec. 1400L(b), or Code Sec. 1400N(d), must be grouped into a separate multiple asset account or pool;

(3) Assets eligible for bonus depreciation deduction may only be grouped into a multiple asset account or pool if the same bonus depreciation rate applied (for example, 30 percent, 50 percent, or 100 percent);

(4) Except for passenger automobiles subject to the luxury car depreciation caps, listed property (as defined in Code Sec. 280F(d)(4)) must be grouped into a separate multiple asset account or pool;

(5) Assets for which the depreciation allowance for the placed-in-service year is not determined by using an optional depreciation table must be grouped into a separate multiple asset account or pool; and

(6) Mass assets (as defined in Reg. § 1.168(i)-8(b)(3)) that are or will be subject to Reg. § 1.168(i)-8(g)(2)(iii) (disposed of or converted mass asset is identified by a mortality dispersion table) must be grouped into a separate multiple asset account or pool. See ¶ 162.

*Dispositions of property in single item and multiple asset accounts*

For the treatment of property that is disposed of from a single item or multiple asset account, see Reg. § 1.168(i)-8 discussed at ¶ 162.

*Record-keeping requirements*

A taxpayer is required to maintain the records described in Reg. § 1.167(a)-7(c) (Reg. § 1.168(i)-7(d)).

Reg. § 1.167(a)-7(c) provides that depreciation preferably should be recorded in a depreciation reserve account for each asset account maintained; however, in appropriate cases it may be recorded directly in the asset account. Where depreciation reserves are maintained, a separate reserve account must be maintained for each asset account. The regular books of account or permanent auxiliary records shall show for each account the basis of the property, including adjustments necessary to conform to the requirements of Code Sec. 1016 and other provisions of law relating to adjustments to basis, and the depreciation allowances for tax purposes. In the event that reserves for book purposes do not correspond with reserves maintained for tax purposes, permanent auxiliary records shall be maintained with the regular books of account reconciling the differences in depreciation for tax and book purposes because of different methods of depreciation, bases, rates, salvage, or other factors. Depreciation schedules filed with the income tax return shall show the accumulated reserves computed in accordance with the allowances for income tax purposes.

*Accounting for property not depreciated under ACRS or MACRS*

When depreciation was determined using the useful lives of assets and average useful lives were permitted for an account, the common multiple asset accounts were a group account (assets similar in kind with approximately the same useful lives), a classified account (assets based on use without regard to useful life), and a composite account (assets in the same account without regard to their character or useful lives). The final regulations (Reg. § 1.167(a)-7) provide that those rules (which were originally issued in 1956) apply only to property subject to Code Sec. 167 and not to MACRS property (generally property placed in service after 1986) or ACRS property (generally property placed in service after 1980 and before 1987).

# MACRS Short Tax Years

## ¶ 132

## Applicable Convention Refinements

MACRS deductions are determined on a tax-year basis. In contrast, the applicable recovery period of an asset consists of recovery (12-month) years without regard to the underlying tax year. Because of the applicable conventions, the recovery year of an asset generally does not coincide with the tax year. Depreciation attributable to a recovery year is consequently allocated to the tax years that include the recovery year.

The discussions in this ¶ 132 and ¶ 134 provide rules for determining MACRS deductions in the following situations:

(1) property is placed in service in a short tax year;

(2) a short tax year occurs during the recovery period of property; or

(3) a disposition of property occurs before the end of the recovery period (see also ¶ 160).

If any of the above situations exist, refinements are made to the use of the applicable conventions and the MACRS depreciation tables (¶ 180) may not be used.

*Detailed guidance regarding MACRS depreciation computations for short tax years is provided by the IRS in Rev. Proc. 89-15, 1989-1 CB 816.*

*Application of short tax year rules to a new business*

In some situations involving individuals who begin a new trade or business it may be unclear whether a short tax year exists. Rev. Proc. 89-15 does not specifically address this issue. All short tax year examples in that revenue procedure deal with corporations. Nor are there any relevant short tax year MACRS regulations. However, short tax year rules are included among the ACRS regulations issued by the IRS. See ACRS Proposed Reg. § 1.168-2(f)(2). Although proposed regulations are not required to be followed by a taxpayer, it should not be inappropriate to do so in the absence of any other specific guidance. However, as noted below, the proposed regulations will cause an individual who begins a sole-proprietorship and has not been engaged in another trade or business activity during the year to have a short tax year. An employee is not considered a trade or business for this purpose. Some fixed asset software programs take an aggressive position, and do not apply the short tax year rules in a situation where an individual begins a sole proprietorship (Example 2, below) or takes his or her first job (Example 4, below) since there is no separate legal entity involved other than an individual taxpayer whose tax year is a complete calendar year.

Under the ACRS proposed regulations, the tax year of a person placing depreciable property in service does not include any month before the month in which the person begins engaging in *any* trade or business or holding depreciable property for the production of income. In applying this rule, an employee is not considered engaged in a trade or business by virtue of employment, except that the tax year includes any month during which a person is engaged in trade or business as an employee regarding depreciable property used for purposes of employment.

***Example (1):*** An individual has a calendar tax year and was engaged in a trade of business since the beginning of the year. He starts a new sole proprietorship business (and acquires new depreciable property for use in the new business) at some point during the year. There is no short tax year for the depreciable property acquired for use in the new business because the tax year of the individual includes all months in which he was engaged in business. However, if the new business was formed as a separate legal entity, such as a partnership, C corporation, or S corporation, the new business (assuming that it adopts a calendar year) would have a short tax year.

***Example (2):*** An individual, who was an employee since the beginning of the year and has a calendar tax year, purchases a car in July for use in the performance of her employment. The car was not placed in service in a short tax year because it was used in her trade or business as an employee and her tax year includes all months that she was an employee.

In June of the following calendar tax year, the individual purchases a truck for use in a new sole proprietorship business. She holds no other depreciable property for the production of income in such calendar year. In determining when a tax year begins for property not used in the trade or business of employment, the truck is considered placed in service in a short tax year because an employee is not considered engaged in a trade or business by virtue of employment.

***Example (3):*** An individual has a calendar tax year and was actively engaged in a sole proprietorship trade or business since the beginning of the year. In July, he agrees to work for a corporation and purchases a new truck for use in the performance of his employment for the corporation. The truck is not placed in service in a short tax year because the tax year of the individual placing the truck in service includes all months during which he was engaged in a trade or business.

***Example (4):*** An individual has a calendar tax year and graduates from college. In July, he begins work for a business and buys a car for use in his employment for the business. He holds no other depreciable property for the production of income in such year. The car is considered placed in service in a short tax year because the individual did not begin his trade or business of being an employee until July and he was not engaged in any other trade or business and did not hold other depreciable property for the production of income for the period before he became an employee.

***Example (5):*** A corporation with a calendar tax year was engaged in one business from the beginning of the year and buys a restaurant business (and new depreciable property for use in the new business) in July. The corporation does not have a short tax year for the new depreciable property used in the new business because the tax year of the corporation placing the property in service includes all months during which it is engaged in a trade or business.

The IRS has applied pre-ACRS short tax year regulations (Reg.§ 1.167(a)-11(c)(2)(iv)) which are similar to the proposed ACRS regulations to ACRS property, noting that it was appropriate to do so since neither final nor temporary regulations had been issued under ACRS. Arguably, these pre-ACRS regulations could also be applied to MACRS property for the same reason. See, Technical Advice Memorandum 8935002 (May 12, 1989) and *R.A. McKnight*, 58 TCM 1390, CCH Dec. 46,374(M) in which the short tax year rules did not apply to an individual who began a business during the year but was also engaged for the entire year in the separate trade or business of being a corporate director. (The position of corporate director was not considered an employee for purposes of the short tax year rules).

*Application of short tax year rules to new subsidiary filing consolidated return*

A existing corporation may join a consolidated group or a consolidated group may form new corporation which joins the consolidated group. The following discussion considers how the MACRS rules for short tax years applies when the subsidiary files a consolidated return with the affiliated group. See also ¶ 92.

*New corporation formed by consolidated group.* MACRS regulations provide that all members of a consolidated group are treated as a single taxpayer for purposes of determining whether the mid-quarter or half-year convention applies to personal property placed in service by members of the consolidated group. If the group forms a new subsidiary, the subsidiary is treated as in existence for the entire tax year for this purpose (Reg. § 1.168(d)-1(b)(5)(i) and (ii)). An example in the regulation, illustrates that an asset purchased by a new subsidiary may be considered placed in service by the subsidiary before it is actually organized.

> ***Example (6):*** Assume a member of a consolidated group that files its return on a calendar-year basis forms a subsidiary on August 1. The subsidiary places depreciable property in service on August 5. If the mid-quarter convention applies to property placed in service by the members of the consolidated group (including the newly-formed subsidiary), the property placed in service by the subsidiary on August 5 is deemed placed in service on the mid-point of the third quarter of the consolidated return year (i.e., August 15). If the half-year convention applies, the property is deemed placed in service on the mid-point of the consolidated return year (i.e., July 1) (Reg. § 1.168(d)-1(b)(5)(iii), Example).

A strict reading of the regulation provides that the subsidiary is treated as in existence for the entire tax year only for purposes of determining the applicable convention. However, insofar as the example shows the depreciation period for the subsidiary's assets as potentially starting on July 1, which is before the new subsidiary's August 1 through December 31 short tax year begins, it seems to contemplate that the subsidiary may compute and claim depreciation for a full tax year. In fact, this is the conclusion reached by the IRS in Technical Advice Memorandum 9235004, May 20, 1992 and IRS Letter Ruling 199944006, July 20, 1999. See, also, the preamble to the proposed version of the regulations, which indicates that the rule was adopted for purposes of simplification even though a short tax year computation for such property would result in a more accurate reflection of the depreciation that should be claimed (PS-54-89, December 31, 1990).

In contrast, under the ACRS (pre-MACRS) method, a short tax-year computation was required on assets acquired by a new subsidiary while a member of the consolidated group during a short tax year (*Hamilton Industries Inc.*, 97 TC 120 (1991), CCH Dec. 47,501)

> ***Example (7):*** Hamilton Inc. is incorporated on May 12, 1982, as a subsidiary of Mayline. Mayline has a fiscal year ending on June 30. Hamilton commenced business on June 28, 1982 when it acquired depreciable assets. It has a short tax year (for depreciation purposes) running from June 28, 1982, to June 30, 1982. ACRS depreciation was allowed for 1/12 of a full tax year under the ACRS rules for calculating depreciation for a short tax year of one month or less.

IRS Technical Advice Memorandum 8424009 (March 19, 1984) reached similar results, holding that a subsidiary that was formed in December 1980, acquired assets in March 1981, and filed as a member of the consolidated group with a tax year ending in May 1981, was required to compute depreciation using the ACRS short tax year rules based on a short tax year that began in March 1981 when the assets were placed in service.

*Existing corporation acquired by consolidated group.* The MACRS regulations also deal with an existing target that joins a consolidated group on a day other than the first day of the consolidated group's tax year. The regulations provides that the target is treated as a member of the consolidated group for the entire year for purposes of determining the applicable convention with respect to property placed in service for the part of the tax year that the target is a member of the consolidated group (Reg. § 1.168(d)-1(b)(6)(vi)).

> ***Example (8):*** A calendar-year corporation (target) joins a calendar-year consolidated group on July 1. For purposes of determining whether the half-year or mid-month

convention applies to property placed in service by all members of the consolidated group, including the target while it is a member of the consolidated group, the consolidated group only takes into account property placed in service by the target after July 1 and before January 1 (Reg.§ 1.168(d)-1(b)(5)(viii), Example).

Presumably, the target then computes depreciation on assets placed in service after June 30 and before January 1 using the applicable convention as if the target's tax year was a full tax year even though these assets were placed in service in a short tax year that runs from July 1 through December 31.

In the case of property placed in service or already in service in the target's tax year that ends immediately before joining the consolidated group, the regulations provide that depreciation is computed under the full tax year rules or short tax year rules, as applicable (Reg.§ 1.168(d)-1(b)(6)(vii)). Thus, in the preceding example, it appears that two short tax year computations are required on assets placed in service by the subsidiary before July 1: first, for the short-tax year that ended upon the acquisition of the target (January 1 through June 30) and, second, for the short tax year that the target is a member of the consolidated group (July 1 through December 31).

This rule is accord with the manner in which ACRS deductions would have been computed.

See, for example, *J. Cooke Inc.*, DC Va., 96-2 USTC 50,483, aff'd, CA-4, per curiam, unpublished opinion, 97-2 USTC 50,511, in which ACRS depreciation on a corporation's existing assets were computed using the short-tax year rules after it became a member of a consolidated group.

***Example (9):*** On December 28, 1984, Cooke Inc., a calendar year corporation, acquires the common stock of another corporation which owns 350 horses. A consolidated return is filed. Based on the date of the transaction, the acquired subsidiary had a 1984 tax year beginning on December 29 and ending on December 31. Because of this short tax year, the acquired corporation was entitled to deduct only one-twelfth of the 1984 depreciation.

See also Technical Advice Memorandum 8424009 (March 19, 1984), in which ACRS short tax year computations were required on assets owned by a target prior to becoming a subsidiary for the short tax year that ended before it became a member of the consolidated group and for the short tax year that it was a member of the group.

*Effect of deemed asset acquisition election.* An IRS Field Service Advice considers depreciation computations on ACRS personal property when a deemed asset acquisition election (Code Sec. 338(g)) is made for a target that becomes a member of a consolidated group (Field Service Advice Memorandum 1993-0504-3, May 4, 1993).

In general, when a deemed asset election is made, a target is treated as selling all of its assets at the close of the acquisition date and as a new corporation that purchases all of its assets as of the beginning of the day after the acquisition date (Code Sec. 338(a)). The target's existing tax year ends at the close of the acquisition date and a new tax year begins on the day after the acquisition date (Reg. § 1.338-1(a)). A new depreciation period applies for the new tax year.

The FSA concludes that the consolidated group is entitled to one-month's depreciation for the short tax year that the target was considered a member of the consolidated group. No depreciation was allowed for the short tax year that closed upon the target's acquisition because the target's asset's were considered disposed of in that tax year and no ACRS deduction is allowed in the year of disposition of ACRS personal property. Note, however, that under MACRS depreciation is allowed in the tax year that personal property is disposed of by applying the applicable convention.

A similar result dealing with ACRS and a section 338 election was also reached in *Brunswick Corporation*, DC, 2009-1 USTC ¶ 51,131.

*Effect of conventions on short tax year computations*

How a short tax year affects MACRS computations depends on the nature of the property and the applicable convention. For property subject to the mid-month convention (residential rental property, nonresidential real property, and railroad grading and tunnel bores), allowances are determined without regard to short tax years.

The mid-month convention is applied without regard to the tax year (Code Sec. 168(d)(4)(B)) unlike the half-year and mid-quarter conventions which are applied to the tax year (Code Sec. 168(d)(4)(A) and (C)). Accordingly, consideration of the tax year is necessary in establishing when the recovery period begins and ends under the latter two conventions.

*Half-year convention*

Under the half-year convention, the recovery period of property placed in service or disposed of in a short tax year begins or ends on the midpoint of the short tax year, which always falls on either the first day or the midpoint of a month.

(1) For a short tax year that begins on the first day of a month or ends on the last day of a month, the length of the tax year is measured in months. The midpoint of the short tax year is determined by dividing the number of months in the tax year by two.

If such short tax year includes part of a month, that entire month is included in the number of months in the tax year. However, if there are successive short tax years, with one tax year ending and the following tax year beginning in the same calendar month, then the first short tax year does not include the month in which the first short tax year terminates.

> ***Example (10):*** Property subject to MACRS and the half-year convention is acquired in a short tax year that begins on June 20 and ends on December 31. Because the tax year ends on the last day of a month, the short tax year is measured in months. The short tax year consists of seven months (including the month of June) and the midpoint of the short tax year is seven divided by two, or 3.5 months. Thus, the recovery period of this property begins in the middle of September for purposes of allocating depreciation for the first recovery year to the short tax year.

> ***Example (11):*** A taxpayer has successive short tax years. The first short tax year begins on June 1 and ends on October 15. The second short tax year begins on October 16 and ends on May 31. Because the first short tax year begins on the first day of a month, the short tax year is measured in months. The first short tax year consists of four months (excluding the month of October) and the midpoint of such short tax year is four divided by two, or two months. The recovery period of property subject to MACRS and the half-year convention that is acquired in the first short tax year begins on August 1. The second short tax year consists of eight months (including the month of October) and the midpoint of such short tax year is eight divided by two, or four months. The recovery period of property subject to MACRS and the half-year convention that is acquired in the second short tax year begins on February 1.

Rev. Proc. 89-15 does not specifically address a situation in which the first short tax year consists of a period of less than a month and is followed by another short tax year. The guidelines if literally applied appear to require that the month in which the first short tax year occurs be taken into account in the following short tax year. In effect, this eliminates a depreciation deduction in the first short tax year since there are no longer any months in that year. For example, if a taxpayer has a short tax year beginning January 1, 2021 and ending January 25, 2021, and that short tax year is following by a short tax year beginning January 25, 2021 and ending December 31, 2021, January is pushed into the second short tax. The second short tax year consists of 12 full months (i.e., is in this situation converted to a full tax year for depreciation purposes) and 6 full months of depreciation is claimed taking into account the half-year convention (i.e., the asset is treated as placed in service on July 1, 2021). Note that the bonus depreciation allowance and Code Sec. 179 expense allowance are claimed without regard to the length of the short tax year (Reg.§ 1.168(k)-1(d)(1)(i); Reg.§ 1.168(k)-2(e)(1)(ii); Reg. § 1.179-1(c)(1)). Thus, it is unclear whether the more specific rule provided in Rev. Proc. 89-15 "for computing depreciation allowance under section 168 requires a taxpayer to take Code Sec. 168 bonus depreciation and the section 179 deduction into account in the second short tax year in this very narrow situation.

(2) For a short tax year that neither begins on the first day of a month nor ends on the last day of a month, the length of the tax year is measured in days. The midpoint of the short tax year is determined by dividing the number of days in the tax year by two. If the result is a day other than the first day or the midpoint of a month, the midpoint of the short tax year is shifted to the nearest preceding first day or midpoint of a month.

***Example (12):*** Property subject to MACRS and the half-year convention is disposed of in a short tax year that begins on March 6 and ends on July 19. Because the short tax year neither begins on the first day of a month nor ends on the last day of a month, the short tax year is measured in days. The short tax year consists of 136 days and the midpoint is 136 divided by 2, or 68 days (March 6 through May 12). However, since the arithmetical midpoint result is a day other than the first day or the midpoint of a month, the midpoint of the short tax year is shifted to May 1, the nearest preceding first day of a month. Thus, the recovery period of such property ends on May 1.

### *Mid-quarter convention*

Under the mid-quarter convention, property is deemed placed in service or disposed of on the midpoint of the quarter, which always falls on either the first day or the midpoint of a month, in the short tax year that it is placed in service or disposed of. A short tax year is divided into four quarters and then the midpoint of each quarter is determined.

In determining the applicability of the mid-quarter convention, the aggregate basis of property placed in service in the last three months of the tax year must be computed regardless of the length of the tax year. If a short tax year consists of three months or less, the mid-quarter convention applies regardless of when the depreciable property is placed in service during the tax year.

(1) For a short tax year that consists of four or eight full calendar months, the length of each quarter is measured in whole months.

***Example (13):*** Taxpayer has a short tax year from March 1 through June 30. Property subject to MACRS is acquired as follows: $1,000 in March and $4,000 in June. Because the short tax year consists of four full calendar months, the length of each quarter is measured in whole months. Each quarter consists of one month (a four month short tax year divided by four), and this result is divided by two to determine the midpoint of each quarter (the middle of the month, in this case). Because 80% ($4,000 divided by $5,000) of the aggregate bases of property placed in service in the short tax year was placed in service in the last three months of the short tax year, the mid-quarter convention applies. Thus, for MACRS purposes, the recovery period of $1,000 of property begins in the middle of March, and the recovery period of $4,000 of property begins in the middle of June.

(2) For a short tax year that consists of anything other than four or eight full calendar months, the length of the short tax year and each quarter are measured in days. The midpoint of each quarter is determined by dividing the number of days in the short tax year by four, and then by dividing the result by two. If the arithmetical midpoint of a quarter is a day other than the first day or midpoint of a month, the midpoint of the quarter is shifted to the nearest preceding first day or midpoint of the month.

***Example (14):*** Under the mid-quarter convention, the MACRS midpoints of quarters in a short tax year that begins on March 1 and ends on July 20 (144 days) are determined as follows: The number of days in the short tax year (144) is divided by 4 to find the length of each quarter (36 days). The number of days in each quarter (36) is divided by two to find the midpoint of each quarter (18 days).

| *Quarter* | *Arithmetical Midpoint* | *MACRS Midpoint of Quarter* |
|---|---|---|
| Mar. 1-Apr. 5 | Mar. 18 | Middle of March |
| Apr. 6-May 11 | Apr. 23 | Middle of April |
| May 12-Jun. 16 | May 29 | Middle of May |
| Jun. 17-Jul. 22 | July 4 | July 1 |

*Mid-month convention*

This convention is applied without regard to the tax year. The recovery period of property subject to the mid-month convention begins or ends on the midpoint of the calendar month in which the property is placed in service or disposed.

*Code Sec. 179 expense allowance and bonus depreciation*

The Code Sec. 179 expense allowance (¶ 300) is computed without regard to the length of the tax year (Reg. § 1.179-1(c)(1)). The first-year bonus-depreciation allowance (¶ 127D) is likewise claimed in full without regard to the length of the tax year (Reg.§ 1.168(k)-2(e)(1)(ii); Reg.§ 1.168(k)-1(d)(1)(i); IRS Publication 946).

## ¶ 134

## Tax Year Refinements

After considering the applicable convention refinements indicated at ¶ 132, certain tax year refinements are made depending on the situation in determining MACRS deductions.

*Detailed guidance regarding MACRS depreciation computations for short tax years is provided by the IRS in Rev. Proc. 89-15, 1989-1 CB 816.*

*First tax year in the recovery period*

Depreciation for the first recovery year in the recovery period is computed by multiplying the taxpayer's basis in the property by the applicable depreciation rate. The depreciation allowance allocable to the first tax year that includes a portion of the first recovery year is derived by multiplying the depreciation for the first recovery year by a fraction, the numerator of which is the number of months (including fractions of months) the property is deemed to be in service during the tax year under the applicable convention and the denominator of which is 12.

*Subsequent tax years in the recovery period*

The correlation of depreciation allowances between recovery years and tax years after the first tax year in the recovery period may be made under either the allocation method or the simplified method. The correlation manner adopted must be consistently used until the tax year that a switch to the MACRS straight-line method is required because it produces a larger depreciation allowance. Depreciation allowances for short tax years that are computed for alternative minimum tax purposes under Code Sec. 56 must also be determined in a manner consistent with these rules.

Usually, the allocation method and the simplified method result in the same depreciation allowances. However, if after the first tax year, but before the switch to the straight-line method, there is a short tax year or a disposition of property, then the depreciation allowance for that year under the simplified method is less than under the allocation method.

*(1) Allocation method.* The depreciation attributable to each recovery year, or portion thereof, that falls within a tax year, whether the tax year is a 12-month year or a short tax year, is allocated to such tax year. For each recovery year included, the depreciation attributable to such recovery year is multiplied by a fraction, the numerator of which is the number of months (including fractions of months) of the recovery year that falls within the tax year and the denominator of which is 12.

If there is a disposition of property before the end of the recovery period, the applicable convention determines the date of disposition.

*For the sake of simplification, it is assumed in the following examples that the taxpayer does not expense any amount under Code Sec. 179 and bonus depreciation is not claimed. As noted at ¶ 132, the expense allowance and bonus depreciation are claimed in full without regard to the length of the tax year. Regular depreciation deductions on the cost of an asset, after reduction by any amounts expensed and/or claimed as bonus depreciation, are affected by a short tax year, as illustrated in these examples.*

***Example (1): Initial short tax year***

A calendar-year corporation began business on March 15. During its first tax year, the corporation placed in service tangible personal property consisting of $100 of 5-year property subject to MACRS depreciation. Assume that there are no other short tax years during the recovery period, the half-year convention is the applicable convention for such property, and the corporation made no elections under Code Sec. 168.

The applicable recovery period, applicable depreciation method, depreciation for the first tax year in the recovery period, depreciation for subsequent tax years in the recovery period, and the tax year of the switch to the straight-line method for such property are determined as follows:

Because the short tax year ends on the last day of the month, the length of the tax year is measured in months. The short tax year consists of 10 months (including March) and, under the half-year convention, the five-year recovery period of this property begins on the midpoint of the short tax year (10 months divided by 2 equals 5 months) (August 1). Thus, the corporation is entitled to 5 months of depreciation for the first recovery year in its first tax year.

The applicable depreciation method for 5-year property is the 200% declining-balance method, with a switch to the straight-line method for the first tax year in which the latter method produces a larger depreciation allowance. The applicable depreciation rate for the property is 40% (200% divided by 5, the number of years in the recovery period).

In the second tax year depreciation is computed on $100 for 7 months (7/12) since only 5 months (5/12) depreciation was claimed on that amount in the first (short) tax year. Depreciation is computed on $60 for the remaining 5 months (5/12) in the second tax year. The $60 figure is the $100 cost reduced by the $16.67 depreciation claimed in the first tax year and $23.33 claimed on the $100 for the first 7 months of the second tax year (.40 × $100 × 7/12 = $23.33; $100 − $16.67 − $23.33 = $60). Similar methodology is used for succeeding tax years in the recovery period.

| Tax Yr. | Method | | Depreciation |
|---|---|---|---|
| 1 | DB | (.40 × $100 × 5/12) . . . . . . . . . . . . . . . . . . . . . = | $16.67 |
| 2 | DB | (.40 × $100 × 7/12) + (.40 × $60 × 5/12) . . . . . . . . . = | 33.33 |
| 3 | DB | (.40 × $60 × 7/12) + (.40 × $36 × 5/12) . . . . . . . . . = | 20.00 |
| 4 | DB | (.40 × $36 × 7/12) + (.40 × $21.60 × 5/12) . . . . . . . = | 12.00 |
| 5 | SL* | (1/(1 + 7/12) × $18 × 12/12) . . . . . . . . . . . . . . . . = | 11.37 |
| 6 | SL* | (1 × $6.63 × 12/12) . . . . . . . . . . . . . . . . . . . . . = | 6.63 |
| | | Total . . . . . . . . . . . . . . . . | $100.00 |

* **Note:** For the fifth tax year, a larger MACRS depreciation allowance is obtained by switching to the straight-line method because the allowance determined under the declining-balance method would be only $7.20 ((.40 × $21.60 × 7/12) + (.40 × $12.96 × 5/12)). Also, the rate under the straight-line method is determined at the beginning of a tax year and is applied to the unrecovered basis. For comparison purposes, depreciation under the straight-line method is computed as follows in determining the tax year of changeover to the straight-line method. The entire adjusted basis is recovered in the sixth tax year under the straight-line method since the remaining recovery period—7 months—is less than one year. See ¶ 179.

| Tax Yr. | Adjusted Basis | × | Straight-Line Rate | × | Short Yr. Adjustment | = | Depreciation |
|---|---|---|---|---|---|---|---|
| 1 | $100.00 | | 1/5 | | 5/12 | | $8.33 |
| 2 | 83.33 | | 1/(4 + 7/12) | | 12/12 | | 18.18 |
| 3 | 50.00 | | 1/(3 + 7/12) | | 12/12 | | 13.95 |
| 4 | 30.00 | | 1/(2 + 7/12) | | 12/12 | | 11.61 |
| 5 | 18.00 | | 1/(1 + 7/12) | | 12/12 | | 11.37 |
| 6 | 6.63 | | 1 | | 12/12 | | 6.63 |

Note that the figures in the adjusted basis column are determined by subtracting the total depreciation claimed in all earlier tax years under the 200% declining-balance method or straight-line method. For example, the $83.33 adjusted basis for tax year 2 is equal to the original cost ($100) reduced by the depreciation claimed in year 1 under the 200% declining-balance method ($16.67).

***Example (2): Subsequent short tax years***

A calendar-year corporation began business on May 1 of its first short tax year (May 1 through December 31). On that date, the corporation placed in service 5-year MACRS property acquired for $100. The property is depreciated under the declining-balance method using a half-year convention and the depreciation allowance for recovery years is correlated with tax years under the allocation method. In its second tax year, there is also a second short tax year (January 1 through June 30) because the corporation is acquired by a fiscal-year corporation with a June 30 year end and the corporations file a consolidated return. Depreciation for the first tax year in the recovery period, subsequent tax years, and the year of changeover to the straight-line method for such property is determined as follows:

Because the first short tax year ends on the last day of the month, the length of the tax year is measured in months. The short tax year consists of eight months, and under the half-year convention the five-year recovery period of this property begins at the midpoint of the short tax year (8 divided by 2 equals 4 months) (September 1). Thus, the corporation is entitled to four months of depreciation for the first recovery year in its first tax year.

The applicable depreciation method for 5-year property is the 200% declining-balance method, with a switch to the straight-line method for the first tax year in which the latter produces a larger depreciation allowance. The applicable depreciation rate for the property is 40% (200% divided by 5, the number of years in the recovery period).

The second tax year is also a short tax year consisting of six months and includes six months of depreciation for the first recovery year. The remaining two months of depreciation for the first recovery year and ten months of depreciation for the second recovery year are claimed in the third year.

| *Tax Yr.* | *Method* | | | *Depreciation* |
|---|---|---|---|---|
| 1 | DB | (.40 × $100 × 4⁄12) . . . . . . . . . . . . . . . . . . | = | $13.33 |
| 2 | DB | (.40 × $100 × 6⁄12) . . . . . . . . . . . . . . . . . . | = | 20.00 |
| 3 | DB | (.40 × $100 × 2⁄12) + (.40 × $60 × 10⁄12) . . . . | = | 26.67 |
| 4 | DB | (.40 × $60 × 2⁄12) + (.40 × $36 × 10⁄12) . . . . . | = | 16.00 |
| 5 | SL* | (1/(2 + 2⁄12) × $24 × 12⁄12) . . . . . . . . . . . . . | = | 11.08 |
| 6 | SL | (1/(1 + 2⁄12) × $12.92 × 12⁄12) . . . . . . . . . . . | = | 11.07 |
| 7 | SL | (1 × $1.85 × 12⁄12) . . . . . . . . . . . . . . . . . . | = | 1.85 |
| | | Total . . . . . . . . . . . . . . . . . . . . . . . . | | $100.00 |

* **Note:** For the fifth year, a larger MACRS depreciation allowance is obtained by switching to the straight-line method because the allowance determined under the declining-balance method would be $9.60 ((.40 × $36 × 2⁄12) + (.40 × $21.60 × 10⁄12)). Also, the rate under the straight-line method is determined at the beginning of a tax year and is applied to the unrecovered basis. For comparison purposes, depreciation under the straight-line method is computed as follows in determining the tax year in which to change to the straight-line method.

| *Tax Yr.* | *Adjusted Basis* | × | *Straight-Line Rate* | × | *Short Yr. Adjustment* | = | *Depreciation* |
|---|---|---|---|---|---|---|---|
| 1 | $100.00 | | 1⁄5 | | 4⁄12 | | $6.67 |
| 2 | 86.67 | | 1/(4 + 8⁄12) | | 6⁄12 | | 9.29 |
| 3 | 66.67 | | 1/(4 + 2⁄12) | | 12⁄12 | | 16.00 |
| 4 | 40.00 | | 1/(3 + 2⁄12) | | 12⁄12 | | 12.63 |
| 5 | 24.00 | | 1/(2 + 2⁄12) | | 12⁄12 | | 11.08 |
| 6 | 12.92 | | 1/(1 + 2⁄12) | | 12⁄12 | | 11.07 |
| 7 | 1.85 | | 1 | | 12⁄12 | | 1.85 |

***Example (3): Disposition before end of recovery period***

Assume the same facts as in Example (1), above, except that there is a disposition of property on December 28 of the second tax year. The depreciation allowance for the second tax year must reflect the premature end of the recovery period. Because the half-year convention applies to such property, the recovery period of the property ends on the midpoint (July 1) of the second tax year. Thus, six months of depreciation for the first recovery year is allowed in the second tax year (five months of depreciation for the first recovery year was allowed in the first short tax year). The depreciation allowance for the second tax year is $20 (.40 × $100 × 6⁄12).

*(2) Simplified method.* (a) The unrecovered basis of property at the beginning of the tax year is multiplied by the applicable depreciation rate.

(b) If the tax year is a short tax year, the product in (a) is multiplied by a fraction, the numerator of which is the number of months (including fractions of months) in the tax year and the denominator of which is 12, in order to determine the depreciation allowance for the tax year.

(c) If there is a disposition of property in the tax year, the product in (a) is multiplied by a fraction, the numerator of which is the number of months the property is deemed in service under the applicable convention during the tax year and the denominator of which is 12 in order to determine the depreciation allowance for the tax year.

***Example (4): Initial short tax year***

Assume the same facts as in Example (1), above. Under the simplified method, the depreciation allowance for the *first* tax year in the recovery period is calculated in the same manner as under the allocation method in Example (1).

Depreciation allowances for subsequent tax years are calculated under the declining balance method by applying the applicable depreciation rate (40%) to the unrecovered basis of the property as of the beginning of the tax year. This calculation is made instead of allocating a portion of the depreciation attributable to the recovery years that fall within a tax year. Assuming the same facts as in Example (1), above, depreciation allowances under the simplified method are determined as follows:

| *Tax Yr.* | *Method* | | | *Depreciation* |
|---|---|---|---|---|
| 1 | DB | (.40 × \$100 × 5⁄12) . . . . . . . . . . . . . . . . . . | = | \$16.67 |
| 2 | DB | (.40 × \$83.33 × 12⁄12) . . . . . . . . . . . . . . . . | = | 33.33 |
| 3 | DB | (.40 × \$50.00 × 12⁄12) . . . . . . . . . . . . . . . . | = | 20.00 |
| 4 | DB | (.40 × \$30.00 × 12⁄12) . . . . . . . . . . . . . . . . | = | 12.00 |
| 5 | SL* | (1/(1 + 7⁄12) × \$18.00 × 12⁄12) . . . . . . . . . . . | = | 11.37 |
| 6 | SL | (1 × \$6.63 × 12⁄12) . . . . . . . . . . . . . . . . . . | = | 6.63 |
| | | Total . . . . . . . . . . . . . . . . . . . . . . . . | | \$100.00 |

* **Note:** For the fifth tax year, a larger MACRS depreciation allowance is obtained by switching to the straight-line method because the allowance determined under the declining balance method would be \$7.20 (.40 × \$18). For comparison purposes, depreciation under the straight-line method is computed as indicated in Example (1), above, in determining the tax year of switch to the straight-line method.

***Example (5): Subsequent short tax year***

Assume the same facts as in Example (2), above, except that the simplified method is used. Under the simplified method, the depreciation allowance for the first tax year in the recovery period is calculated in the same manner as under the allocation method in Example (2), above.

Because the second tax year is also a short tax year, the depreciation allowance for such tax year is calculated by multiplying the unrecovered basis of the property at the beginning of such tax year by the applicable depreciation rate, and then multiplying the product by a fraction, the numerator of which is the number of months in the tax year and the denominator of which is 12.

| *Tax Yr.* | *Method* | | | *Depreciation* |
|---|---|---|---|---|
| 1 | DB | (.40 × \$100 × 4⁄12) . . . . . . . . . . . . . . . . . . | = | \$13.33 |
| 2 | DB | (.40 × \$86.67 × 6⁄12) . . . . . . . . . . . . . . . . . | = | 17.33 |
| 3 | DB | (.40 × \$69.34 × 12⁄12) . . . . . . . . . . . . . . . . | = | 27.74 |
| 4 | DB | (.40 × \$41.60 × 12⁄12) . . . . . . . . . . . . . . . . | = | 16.64 |
| 5 | SL* | (1/(2 + 2⁄12) × \$24.96 × 12⁄12) . . . . . . . . . . . | = | 11.52 |
| 6 | SL | (1/(1 + 2⁄12) × \$13.44 × 12⁄12) . . . . . . . . . . . | = | 11.52 |
| 7 | SL | (1 × \$1.92 × 12⁄12) . . . . . . . . . . . . . . . . . . | = | 1.92 |

* **Note:** For the fifth tax year, a larger MACRS depreciation allowance is obtained by switching to the straight-line method because the allowance determined under the declining-balance method would be \$9.98 (.40 × \$24.96 × 12⁄12). For comparison purposes, depreciation under the straight-line method is computed as follows in determining the tax year of switch to the straight-line method.

| *Tax Yr.* | *Adjusted Basis* | × | *Straight-Line Rate* | × | *Short Yr. Adjustment* | = | *Depreciation* |
|---|---|---|---|---|---|---|---|
| 1 | \$100.00 | | 1⁄5 | | 4⁄12 | | \$6.67 |
| 2 | 86.67 | | 1/(4 + 8⁄12) | | 6⁄12 | | 9.29 |
| 3 | 69.34 | | 1/(4 + 2⁄12) | | 12⁄12 | | 16.64 |
| 4 | 41.60 | | 1/(3 + 2⁄12) | | 12⁄12 | | 13.14 |
| 5 | 24.96 | | 1/(2 + 2⁄12) | | 12⁄12 | | 11.52 |
| 6 | 13.44 | | 1/(1 + 2⁄12) | | 12⁄12 | | 11.52 |
| 7 | 1.92 | | 1 | | 12⁄12 | | 1.92 |

***Example (6): Disposition before end of recovery period***

Assume the same facts as in Example (1) above, except that there is a disposition of property on December 28 of the second tax year and the simplified method is used. The depreciation allowance for the second tax year must reflect the premature end of the recovery period. Because the half-year convention applies to such property, the recovery period of the property ends on the midpoint (July 1) of the second tax year. The depreciation allowance for the second tax year is $16.67 (the unrecovered basis of the property at the beginning of the second tax year ($83.33) times the applicable rate (40%), and then multiplying the product by 6/12).

# Excluded Property

## ¶ 140

## Property Ineligible for MACRS

Most depreciable tangible property (see ¶ 3 and ¶ 5) placed in service after 1986 that is not otherwise excluded property must be depreciated under the MACRS rules. MACRS may be used to claim deductions on both new and used property. It does not apply to inventory, stock in trade, valuable works of art that are not considered subject to wear and tear (¶ 3), or land (as distinguished from the structures on it). However, apart from these rules of general application, various special rules exclude property from MACRS.

Certain categories of property are specifically excluded from eligibility for MACRS, even if they are placed in service after 1986 (Code Sec. 168(f)). These categories include:

(1) property for which an election was made to use a depreciation method not expressed in a term of years, such as the unit-of-production method (¶ 360), machine-hours method (¶ 360), operating-days method, or the income-forecast method (¶ 364). For this purpose, the retirement-replacement-betterment method or similar method is not considered a method that is not expressed in a term of years;

(2) public utility property, unless a normalization method of accounting is used;

(3) motion picture films, videotapes, and videocassette movies (Rev. Rul. 89-62, 1989-1 CB 78);

(4) sound recordings, such as discs, tapes, or other phonorecordings in which musical or other sounds are embodied; and

(5) intangible assets (see ¶ 10).

Because of the similarity and the largely identical language of the exclusionary rules under MACRS and those under ACRS, the following discussion focuses on the distinctions between the relevant MACRS rules and the ACRS rules discussed at ¶ 260 – ¶ 268.

*Methods not expressed in a term of years*

As under ACRS (see ¶ 260), a taxpayer may make an election out of MACRS by properly depreciating property under the unit-of-production method or any method not expressed in a term of years (see above and ¶ 364) in the first tax year that the property is placed in service *and* attaching the required statement to its return (Code Sec. 168(f)(1)). Recovering the cost of a car through the IRS prescribed standard mileage allowance or a mileage-based method is regarded as such an election (see ¶ 217).

The election is made by reporting the depreciation on line 15 of Form 4562 and attaching the election statement as described in the instructions for line 15 (viz., an attached sheet with a description of the property, its basis, and the depreciation method selected). The election must be made by the return due date (including extensions) for the tax year the property is placed in service or by filing an amended return within six months of the return due date (excluding extensions). The amended return election requires that the statement be attached to the amended return and "Filed pursuant to section 301.9100-2" written on it (IRS Publication 946 (How to Depreciate Property); Temporary Reg. § 301.9100-7T).

The election is not considered made if the required statement is not attached to the return (*New Gaming Systems, Inc.*, 82 TCM 794, Dec. 54,520(M)).

Prop. Reg. § 1.168-4(b) (¶ 535) provides, with respect to the similar ACRS (pre-1987) election, that the method elected must be a recognized method prior to 1981 within the particular industry for the type of property in question. The regulation also indicates that the election is made on an asset-by-asset basis and does not automatically apply to all property in the same recovery class placed in service in the same tax year.

The election out of MACRS election is irrevocable (Temporary Reg. § 301.9100-7T(i)). However, the election out of ACRS (Code Sec. 168(e)(2), prior to amendment by the 1986 Tax Reform Act) was revocable with IRS consent, although consent was granted only in extraordinary circumstances (Proposed Reg. § 1.168-5(e)(1)(iv) and Proposed Reg. § 1.168-5(e)(9)).

*Films and recordings*

Motion picture films, video tapes, and sound recordings are expressly excluded from MACRS (Code Sec. 168(f)(3) and (4)). The exclusion for sound recordings extends to discs, tapes, or other phonorecordings resulting from the fixation of a series of sounds. Such assets are depreciable under the income forecast method or another method that would provide a reasonable allowance under Code Sec. 167(a). See ¶ 364.

A qualified film or television production (as defined in Code Sec. 181(d)) acquired and placed in service after September 27, 2017 is eligible for the 100 percent bonus depreciation deduction (Code Sec. 168(k)(2)(A)(iv)). See ¶ 127D.

*Video cassettes*

Video cassettes such as those purchased by video stores for rental to the general public fall in the category of "motion picture film, video tape, or sound recording." The cost less salvage value of video cassettes that have a useful life over one year may be depreciated under either the straight-line method over the useful life of the video cassettes in the particular taxpayer's business or the income forecast method (see ¶ 364) (Rev. Rul. 89-62, 1989-1 CB 78). Use of the latter method requires asset-by-asset income projections, and video cassettes may not be grouped except under a single title.

Eligible taxpayers who are able to show that particular video-cassettes do not have a useful life in excess of a single year are entitled to deduct the cost of such video cassettes as a current business expense. Such circumstances may arise, for instance, where a video rental store buys 60 videotapes of a new movie and claims a write-off for 12 tapes over a three-year period and a business expense deduction for the balance of the tapes in a single year as viewer interest wanes.

*Public utility property*

For purposes of MACRS public utility property is defined as property predominantly used to furnish or sell (1) electricity, (2) water, (3) sewage disposal services, (4) gas or steam through a local distribution system, (5) telephone services, or other communication services if furnished or sold by Comsat, or (5) transportation of gas or steam by pipeline if the rates for such furnishing or selling have been established or approved by a State or political subdivision thereof (including a public service or public utility commission or similar body), or an agency or instrumentality of the United States (Code Sec. 168(i)(10)).

A taxpayer's rates are "regulated" if they are established or approved on a rate of return basis. Rates regulated on a rate of return basis are an authorization to collect revenues that cover the taxpayer's cost of providing goods or services, including a fair return on the taxpayer's investment in providing such goods or services, where the taxpayer's costs and investment are determined by the use of the uniform system of accounts prescribed by the regulatory body (Field Service Advice Memorandum 001336, Updated 2004 (Jan. 31, 2004)).

Public utility property does not qualify for MACRS unless the utility uses a normalization method of accounting as described in Code Sec. 168(f)(9) (Code Sec. 168(f)(2)).

Rate-regulated utility property does not qualify for bonus if placed in service in tax years beginning after 2017 (Code Sec. 168(k)(9)). See ¶ 127D, *"23. Rate-regulated utility property does not qualify for bonus if placed in service in tax years beginning after 2017."*

If a normalization method of accounting is not used, then public utility property is depreciated using the same method used for regulatory purposes and the same or a shorter depreciation period as used for regulatory purposes (Code Sec. 168(i)(9)(C)).

The IRS has issued a safe harbor for a utility which unintentionally or inadvertently uses a practice or procedure that is inconsistent with the investment tax credit or Modified Accelerated Cost Recovery System's normalization requirements. Under this safe harbor, if a utility takes action to totally reverse the effect of the inconsistent practice or procedure in accordance with the procedure the IRS will not deny the benefits of the investment tax credit or accelerated depreciation under MACRS (Rev. Proc. 2017-47).

The IRS has clarified that total reversal only requires only that the taxpayer change its inconsistent practice or procedure to a consistent practice or procedure on a going forward basis. It does not require reversal of the prior financial effects of the inconsistent practice or procedure, for example through retroactive ratemaking by the taxpayer's regulator (IRS Advice Memorandum AM 2018-001, (Feb. 27, 2018)).

The normalization method of accounting requires that a utility make adjustments to a reserve to reflect the difference between the deductions allowable under Code Sec. 168 (taking into account all elections made under Code Sec. 168) and the amount allowed under Code Sec. 167 using the method (including the period, first and last year convention, and salvage value) used to compute tax expense for rate making purposes if these two amounts differ (Code Sec. 168(i)(9)(A)(ii)). The IRS has ruled that a utility that did not maintain such a reserve account because it did not depreciate its assets under Code Sec. 168 was not utilizing a normalization method of accounting. Accordingly its public utility property was excluded from ACRS and permission could not be granted to change its method of accounting to ACRS (IRS Letter Ruling 9047005, (Aug. 21, 1990)). This ruling would apply under MACRS.

For taxpayers subject to the normalization method of accounting, the 2017 Tax Cuts and Jobs Act provides for the normalization of excess deferred tax reserves resulting from the reduction of corporate income tax rates (with respect to prior depreciation or recovery allowances taken on assets placed in service before the corporate rate reduction takes effect. Specifically, a taxpayer is not treated as using a normalization method of accounting with respect to any public utility property for purposes of Code Sec. 167 or 168, if the taxpayer, in computing its cost of service for ratemaking purposes and reflecting operating results in its regulated books of account, reduces the excess tax reserve more rapidly or to a greater extent than such reserve would be reduced under the average rate assumption method (Act Sec. 13001(d)(1) of P.L. 115-97).

Guidance on normalization requirements for public utilities arising due to the corporate tax rate decrease enacted by the Tax Cuts and Jobs Act is found in Rev. Proc. 2020-39.

MACRS assets used in the production, transmission, and distribution of electricity, gas, steam, or water for sale including related land improvements are described in Asset Classes 49.11 through 49.4 of Rev. Proc. 87-56 at ¶ 191. The depreciation period will depend upon the applicable Asset Class. However, water utility property as defined in Code Sec. 168(e)(5) has a 25-year recovery period and is recovered using the straight-line method (Code Sec. 168(b)(3); Code Sec. 168(c)). If these assets also meet the definition of MACRS public utility property, these recovery periods only apply if a normalization method of accounting is used.

The IRS has ruled on the proper classification of four assets used by a steam production plant that produces electricity for sale (Asset Class 49.13, 20-year property) (Rev. Rul. 2003-81, I.R.B. 2003-30). In making the classifications, the IRS applied the general rule that the depreciation period for an asset described in an "asset" category (Asset Classes 00.11 through 00.4) is applicable even if the asset is used in a "business" category (Asset Classes 01.1 and following) unless the asset is specifically described in the business category. See ¶ 190. Thus, a bookcase used to store training manuals and operation protocols in the plant supervisor's office is seven-year property because it is described in an asset category (Asset Class 00.11 relating to office furniture). A work bench used to repair plant machinery and equipment is 20-year property since it is not described in an asset category (Asset Class 49.13).

A parking lot located at the production plant is 20-year property (Asset Class 49.13) since land improvements related to assets used in the steam power production of electricity are specifically included in Asset Class 49.13. Although land improvements are described in an asset category (Asset Class 00.3) as 15-year property, Asset Class 49.13 specifically includes land improvements used in the steam power production of electricity. However, a parking lot located 100 miles from the plant at the corporate headquarters is 15-year property (Asset Class 00.3) because in the IRS's view it "is not related to the plant that produces the electricity" as required by Asset Class 49.13. Apparently, the types of activities conducted at the corporate headquarters, even though connected with the business of producing electricity, are not considered by the IRS "as used" in the production of electricity within the meaning of Asset Class 49.13.

The ruling indicates that the utility's non-tax categorizations such as FERC account practices are not controlling for purposes of federal depreciation classification.

The ruling also states the following under the heading "Audit Protection":

> "A utility taxpayer, which owns a steam production plant and engages in the production of electricity for sale, may continue to use its present method of treating the cost of depreciable property described in an asset category (asset classes 00.11 through 00.4) or a specific utility services activity class (asset classes 49.11 through 49.4) that was placed in service during any taxable year ending on or before June 27, 2003 if use of such method results in a longer recovery period than would be required by this revenue ruling."

Note that the audit "protection" only applies in situations where the taxpayer would be entitled to claim more depreciation if it changed its accounting method to comply with the ruling.

## ¶ 142

## Anti-churning Rules

Since ACRS is generally more favorable than older depreciation rules, the provisions that ushered it in were accompanied by special rules designed to prevent the "churning" of pre-1981 assets into recovery property without any significant change in either its ownership or use (see ¶ 264). Similar rules, adopted largely by reference, prevent the churning of pre-1981 assets into MACRS property (Code Sec. 168(f)(5)). With exceptions for (1) residential rental property, (2) nonresidential real property, and (3) any property for which the ACRS allowance for the first full taxable year in which the property is placed in service would be more generous[1] than the corresponding MACRS deduction (assuming the half-year convention), similarly borrowed rules prevent the conversion of recovery property into property that is depreciable under MACRS. Thus, under exception (3), a car (3-year property under ACRS but 5-year property under MACRS) purchased from a related taxpayer after 1986 would not be depreciable under ACRS if the related taxpayer owned the car in 1986.

Care must be exercised in comparing first-year percentages because classes of MACRS property are not identical to similarly named classes of ACRS property. Thus, under the following chart, the anti-churning rules would not prevent office furniture, 5-year property under ACRS, from becoming 7-year property under MACRS:

| | *MACRS* | *ACRS* |
|---|---|---|
| 3-year | 33.33% | 25% |
| 5-year | 20% | 15% |
| 7-year | 14.29% | ... |
| 10-year | 10% | 8% |

> ***Example (1):*** In June of 1986, Smith's brother buys a car. In June of 1989, Smith purchases the car from his brother for use in a business. The car is depreciable under MACRS (for which, under the half-year convention, first-year depreciation would be 20%) rather than under ACRS (for which first-year depreciation would be 25%) even though Smith's brother (a related party) owned it in 1986.

Subject to this more-generous test, personal property acquired after 1986 (after July 31, 1986, if MACRS was elected under transitional rules) is excluded from MACRS under the anti-churning rules if:

(1) it was owned or used by the taxpayer or a related party during 1986;

(2) it was acquired from a person owning it during 1986, and, as part of the transaction, the user of the property stays the same;

(3) it is leased to a person who owned or used it during 1986 (or a person related to such person); or

(4) the property was not MACRS property in the hands of the transferor due to the application of rules (1) or (3), and the user of the property does not change.

---

[1] A TAMRA amendment clarifies Congress's intention to compare first-year deductions irrespective of whether or not *full* taxable years are involved.

***Example (2):*** In 1989, Higgins purchases a computer from his sister, who had placed it in service in June of 1986. Since the computer was 5-year property under both ACRS and MACRS, first-year depreciation would be more generous under MACRS (20%, assuming the half-year convention) than under ACRS (15%). Higgins must use ACRS.

In general, real property, other than residential rental property or nonresidential real property, acquired after 1986 (after July 31, 1986 if MACRS was elected under transitional rules) is excluded from MACRS under the anti-churning rules if:

(1) the taxpayer or a party related to the taxpayer owned it in 1986, or

(2) the property is leased back to a party (or a person related to such party) who owned it during 1986.

The anti-churning rule also applies to real property (other than residential rental property and nonresidential real property) acquired after 1986 in a nontaxable exchange described in Code Sec. 1031, 1033, 1038 or 1039 for property that the taxpayer or a related person owned during 1986, but only to the extent of the substituted basis of the property received.

If, under the anti-churning rules, MACRS is precluded, the taxpayer must use ACRS (unless it is also precluded) or some other appropriate method.

Personal property and real property (including residential rental property and nonresidential real property) acquired after 1980 which is subject to the ACRS anti-churning rules described at ¶ 264 because of ownership, use, etc., in 1980 may not be depreciated under MACRS (Code Sec. 168(f)(5)(A)(i)).

The MACRS anti-churning rules do not apply to property transferred by reason of (a) the death of a taxpayer, or (b) the acquisition of more than 90 percent of a partnership interest by parties unrelated to the selling partner (Code Sec. 168(f)(5)(A) referring to former Code Sec. 168(e)(4)(H) and (D)), respectively (before repeal by the Tax Reform Act of 1986 (P.L. 99-514)).

## ¶ 144

## Step-In-The-Shoes Nonrecognition Transactions

The basis of property received by a transferee in certain nonrecognition transactions must be depreciated by the transferee as if the transfer did not take place to the extent of the transferor's adjusted basis immediately before the transfer. These transactions include distributions in complete liquidation of a subsidiary (under Code Sec. 332), transfers to controlled corporations (under Code Sec. 351), exchanges of property solely for corporate stock in a reorganization (under Code Sec. 361), contributions of property in exchange for a partnership interest (under Code Sec. 721), and partnership distributions of property (under Code Sec. 731). This "step-in-the-shoes" rule extends to members of an affiliated group filing a consolidated return, but it does not apply in the case of a partnership technical termination where 50 percent or more of the interest in partnership capital and profits is sold or exchanged within a 12-month period (Code Sec. 168(i)(7)). The technical termination rule no longer applies, effective for partnership tax years beginning after December 31, 2017 (Code Sec. 708(b)(1)).

Except for regulations relating to application of the mid-quarter convention (Reg.§ 1.168(d)-1(b)(7) at ¶ 560), the IRS has not issued MACRS regulations that cover this rule. However, ACRS Prop. Reg. § 1.168-5(b) (relating to pre-1987 Code Sec. 168(f)(10)) illustrates the application of a generally similar rule as it applies in the context of ACRS property transfers. The principles there should be equally applicable to MACRS property.

The IRS has issued regulations explaining the allocation of the bonus depreciation deduction in these Code Sec. 168(i)(7) step-in-the-shoes transactions (Reg. § 1.168(k)-1(f); Reg.§ 1.168(k)-2(g)(1)(iii); Reg.§ 1.168(k)-2(b)(4)(vi)). See ¶ 127D.

For like-kind exchanges (Code Sec. 1031) and involuntary conversions (Code Sec. 1033), see ¶ 167.

## ¶ 145

## Property Reacquired by a Taxpayer

Code Sec. 168(i)(7)(C) states: "Under regulations, property which is disposed of and then reacquired by the taxpayer shall be treated for purposes of computing the deduction allowable under subsection (a) [the MACRS deduction—CCH.] as if such property had not been disposed of."

No regulations relating to this rule have been issued under MACRS.

A similar rule was provided under ACRS (Code Sec. 168(f)(10)(C), prior to 1987) and explained in detail in proposed regulations (Prop. Reg. § 1.168-5(c)). Under these regulations the provision applies only to a taxpayer who, at the time of the disposition of the property, anticipates a reacquisition of the same property. It does not apply to property that is disposed of during the same tax year that the property is placed in service by the taxpayer and then reacquired in a later tax year (Proposed Reg. § 1.168-5(c)(3)(i)). Note that depreciation deductions are not claimed in the placed-in-service year if the property is disposed in that year. See ¶ 160.

In the absence of rules specifically issued under MACRS, it should be reasonable to apply the ACRS rules to MACRS.

Under the proposed rules, a taxpayer who can factually show that he did not anticipate reacquiring the property at the time of the earlier disposition may be able to avoid the application of this anti-abuse rule, but such a factual showing may be difficult if the reacquisition occurs within a relatively brief period of time or if the property was reacquired from a related party.

Only that portion of a taxpayer's adjusted basis in the reacquired property that does not exceed the taxpayer's adjusted basis at the time of disposition is subject to this rule (Proposed Reg. § 1.168-5(c)(1)). Taxpayers may recover any amount in excess of their original adjusted basis in the reacquired property (other than a building) as newly acquired property, using any appropriate MACRS recovery period and method applicable to the excess (Proposed Reg. § 1.168-5(c)(5)).

If the property is a building, taxpayers must use the same recovery period and method to recover the amount in excess of their original adjusted basis as are used for the building itself (Proposed Reg. § 1.168-5(c)(5)). If the excess of the taxpayer's adjusted basis in the building would qualify as a substantial improvement (Proposed Reg. § 1.168-2(e)(4)) if paid or incurred by the taxpayer had he continued to own the building, the taxpayer may select any applicable recovery period and method to compute the depreciation allowance for the excess (Proposed Reg. § 1.168-5(c)(5)).

If a taxpayer's unadjusted basis in reacquired property is less than his adjusted basis in the property at the time of disposition, the taxpayer must compute a redetermined adjusted basis and a redetermined applicable percentage before computing depreciation allowances for the property (Proposed Reg. § 1.168-5(c)(6)). The redetermined adjusted basis is the reacquisition cost of the property reduced by the depreciation allowances previously allowed or allowable to the taxpayer for the property. The redetermined applicable percentage is the percentage determined by dividing the applicable percentage otherwise provided for the recovery year by the amount of the unrecovered percentage (that is, 100 percent minus the applicable percentages for recovery years before the year in which the basis is redetermined). The decrease in basis is accounted for over the remaining recovery years beginning with the recovery year in which the basis is redetermined (Proposed Reg. § 1.168-2(d)(3)).

Reacquiring taxpayers resume computing their recovery allowances from the point at which the property was disposed of rather than from the date of reacquisition. Thus, while a reacquiring taxpayer must resume calculating recovery allowances using the percentage for the recovery year of disposition, the recovery allowance for the year of reacquisition must be adjusted to reflect the number of months under the applicable convention that the property was used as recovery property during that year. Any portion of the total depreciation allowance otherwise allowable for the year of disposition/reacquisition that is not recovered in that year may be recovered in the year following the last recovery year (Proposed Reg. § 1.168-5(f)(1)(ii)(B)(1), (2)). Any excess over the original adjusted basis in the property is recovered beginning on the date of reacquisition (Proposed Reg. § 1.168-5(c)(4)).

***Example:*** On March 15, 2017 taxpayer Smith, a calendar-year taxpayer, purchased and placed in service 10-year property for $30,000. Under regular MACRS, Smith's recovery allowance for 2017 is $3,000 (0.10 × $30,000). Smith then decides that he wants to use the ADS straight-line method. To effectuate this change, Smith sells the property to Franklin on February 15, 2019, anticipating that Franklin will sell the property back to him. Smith's recovery allowance for 2018 is $5,400 (0.18 × $30,000) and for 2019 (the third recovery year) is $2,160 (0.144 × $30,000 × 1/2). In July 2022, Smith reacquires the property from Franklin for $28,000. For that portion of Smith's unadjusted basis in the reacquired property that does not exceed his adjusted basis at the time of disposition ($19,440), Smith's recovery allowance for 2022 is determined as if Smith had not disposed of the property, that is, by applying the percentage (.144 percent) applicable to the third recovery year (year of disposition) to the original unadjusted basis ($30,000). Thus, Smith's recovery allowance for 2022 would be $2,160 (0.144 × $30,000 × 1/2). For that portion of Smith's unadjusted basis in the reacquired property that exceeds his adjusted basis at the time of disposition ($10,560), cost recovery will begin in 2022, the year of reacquisition. The excess basis is considered newly acquired property. The ADS straight-line method may be elected with respect to this excess (Proposed Reg. § 1.168-5(c)(7)).

# MACRS Alternative Depreciation System

## ¶ 150

### MACRS Alternative Depreciation System (ADS)

Under the MACRS alternative depreciation system (ADS), the applicable depreciation method for all property is the straight-line method (Code Sec. 168(g)(2)(A)). The deduction is computed by applying the straight-line method (without regard to salvage value), the applicable convention, and the applicable prescribed (generally longer) recovery period for the respective class of property.

ADS *must* be used for (Code Sec. 168(g)):

(1) tangible property used predominantly outside the United States (¶ 152);

(2) tax-exempt use property leased to a tax-exempt entity (¶ 152);

(3) tax-exempt bond-financed property (¶ 152);

(4) property imported from a foreign country for which an Executive Order is in effect because the country maintains trade restrictions or engages in other discriminatory acts (¶ 152);

(5) listed property, such as a car or truck, used 50 percent or less in a qualified business use (¶ 210).

(6) property of farmers who elect under Code Sec. 263A(d)(3) to deduct preproductive period costs of certain plants (not apply the uniform capitalization rules) (¶ 152)

(7) residential rental property, nonresidential real property, and qualified improvement property owned by a real property trade or business that elects out of the new rules enacted by the 2017 Tax Cuts and Jobs Act (P.L. 115-97) which disallows deduction of net interest expense in excess of a specified percentage of a business' adjusted taxable income, effective for tax years beginning after 2017 (Code Sec. 168(g)(8); Code Sec. 163(j)(7)(B); Rev. Proc. 2019-8) (see ¶ 152); and

(8) Any property with a recovery period of 10 years or greater which is held by an "electing farming business" that makes an election out of the new rules which disallow the deduction for net interest expense in excess of a specified percentage of the business' adjusted taxable income, effective for tax years beginning after 2017 (Code Sec. 168(g)(1)(G); Rev. Proc. 2019-8) (see ¶ 152).

Taxpayers making the election out of the interest limitation rule (items (7) and (8)) do not need to file accounting method changes in order to switch to using the ADS system for property placed in service in a tax year prior to the election year. Instead the change in use rules (Reg. § 1.168-4(d)) will apply in making this switch provided the switch to ADS is made in the tax year of the election. However, if the switch is not made in the election year a taxpayer will need to file and amended return if only one incorrect return is filed or a change in accounting method if two incorrect returns are filed (Rev. Proc. 2019-8). See ¶ 152.

A technical correction would clarify that an electing real property trade or business must also depreciate 15-year leasehold improvements, retail improvements, and restaurant property placed in service before 2018 using ADS. See ¶ 152.

Property which must be depreciated using ADS does not qualify for any of the various bonus depreciation deductions (¶ 127D through ¶ 127J). Property for which ADS is elected (see below), however, may qualify.

*Other uses*

The alternative depreciation system is used for purposes of computing the earnings and profits of foreign or domestic corporations (Code Sec. 312(k)(3)).

In computing depreciation for alternative minimum tax purposes on property placed in service before 1999, the alternative depreciation system must be used on certain property. See ¶ 170.

The allowable depreciation deductions for luxury cars (¶ 200) and other listed property (¶ 208) used 50 percent or less in business are also determined under the alternative depreciation system (Code Sec. 280F(b)(1)). See ¶ 206.

*ADS election*

Instead of using the MACRS general depreciation system (GDS), taxpayers may irrevocably elect to apply the alternative depreciation system to any class of property for any tax year (Code Sec. 168(g)(7)). If elected, the alternative depreciation system applies to all property in the MACRS class placed in service during the tax year. However, for residential rental property and nonresidential real property, the election may be made on a property-by-property basis.

This ADS election differs from the MACRS straight-line election (¶ 84) in that the ADS usually requires longer straight-line recovery periods.

The ADS election is made by completing Form 4562 Section C line 20 (Instructions for line 20).

*Late elections and revocations for 2018, 2019, and 2020 tax years.* IRS guidance allows a taxpayer to make a late ADS election or withdraw an ADS election made for a tax year ending in 2018, 2019, or 2020 if a timely filed return was filed for the year the property was placed in service and the timely return was filed on or before April 17, 2020 (Rev. Proc. 2020-25, as modified by Rev. Proc. 2020-50). The late election or revocation must be made on an amended return filed on or before October 15, 202,1 but no later than the applicable limitations period for assessment for the tax year for which the amended return is filed. The late election (but not a revocation) may also be made by filing a Form 3115, Change in Accounting Method, for the first or second tax year following the tax year in which the property was placed in service or on or after April 17, 2020 and on or before October 15, 2021. This relief is provided in connection with a technical correction by the CARES Act (P.L. 116-136) assigning a 15-year recovery period to qualified improvement property placed in service after 2017 but does not require that the late election or revocation relate to qualified improvement property.

## ¶ 152

## MACRS Alternative Depreciation System Property

A brief description of the categories of property for which the use of the MACRS alternative depreciation system (ADS) is mandatory (see ¶ 150) is provided below. Note that bonus depreciation may not be claimed on *mandatory* ADS property.

*Preproductive cost election of farmers*

Farmers who elect under Code Sec. 263A(d)(3) to deduct preproductive period costs of certain plants (not apply the uniform capitalization rules) for the first tax year during which plant costs are otherwise required to be capitalized must depreciate all property used predominantly in any of their farming businesses that is placed in service during any year that the election is in effect under the MACRS alternative depreciation system (Code Sec. 263A(e)(2); Notice 87-76, 1987-2 CB 384; Reg. § 1.263A-4(d)(4)(ii)). If the election is made persons related to the electing farmer are also required to use ADS to depreciate farming property predominantly used in their farming business. See also ¶ 84. If the election is made the plants are treated as section 1245 property (Reg. § 1.263A-4(d)(4)(i)). See ¶ 160.

*Interaction Between Gross Receipts UNICAP exemption and preproductive cost election*

For tax years beginning after December 31, 2017, a taxpayer is not required to apply the UNICAP rules for the tax year if it meets the $25 million average gross receipts test of Code Sec. 448(c), "gross receipts test", which is adjusted annually for inflation. (Code Sec. 263A(i)(1)).

IRS guidance allows a farmer to revoke a valid and properly implemented Code Sec. 263A(d)(3) election not capitalize preproductive costs if the farmer qualifies for exemption from the UNICAP rules under Code Sec. 263A(i) by reason of the gross receipts test (Code Sec. 448(c)), in the tax year of the revocation. The guidance also allows a farmer to make the Code Sec. 263A(d)(3) election not to capitalize preproductive expenditures in the first tax year in which the farmer no longer qualifies for the gross receipts test exemption from the UNICAP rules (Rev. Proc. 2020-13; Reg. § 1.263A-4(d)(5) and (6)).

The revocation of the Code Sec. 263A(d)(3) election because the taxpayer may claim gross receipts test exemption or the change from the gross receipts test exemption to the Code Sec. 263A(d)(3) election because the taxpayer no longer qualifies for the gross receipts exemption, is not a change in accounting method (Reg. § 1.263A-4(d)(5) and (6)).

The $25 million figure is adjusted annually for inflation ($26 million in 2021 and $27 million in 2022) (Rev. Proc. 2020-45; Rev. Proc. 2021-45).

*ADS required if related persons do not revoke election.* An eligible small business farmer that revokes the election not to capitalize preproductive period costs must continue to use ADS on property predominantly used in its farming business during tax years that a related person continues to have an election not to capitalize preproductive expenditures in effect. Thus, a farmer may make a valid revocation even though related taxpayers do not revoke their election. The farmer, however, must continue to use ADS on property predominantly used in the farming business if previously placed-in-service and on property that is placed in service in the year of the revocation and subsequent tax years.

*Revocation procedure.* The election is revoked on an original tax return (including extensions) for the revocation year by continuing not to capitalize preproductive expenditures, changing from ADS in the revocation year using the change-in-use rules of Reg. § 1.168(i)-4(d), and continuing to treat plants that are or have been treated as section 1245 property for prior tax years as section 1245 property. Small business farmers who want to revoke the election in their 2018 tax year follow the procedures below.

*Late revocation for 2018 on amended return or Form 3115.* Small business farmers who did not revoke their election for a tax year beginning in 2018 on a timely filed original income tax return may make a late revocation by filing an amended return (AAR for partnerships subject to the centralized audit regime) or a Form 3115. The amended return must be filed before filing the federal income tax return for the first tax year beginning after the 2018 tax year.

If a small business farmer revokes the election using an amended return, all related taxpayers affected by the revocation must also file amended returns to reflect the farmer's revocation.

Alternatively, a small business farmer may revoke the election by filing Form 3115 with a timely filed income tax return for the first, second, or third tax beginning after the tax year that begins in 2018. The automatic consent procedure described in Sec. 6.19 of Rev. Proc. 2019-43, as added by Rev. Proc. 2020-13 applies. If a taxpayer fails to meet this deadline, the election may not be revoked by filing an accounting method change on Form 3115 under either the automatic or nonautomatic procedures.

If a small business farmer revokes the election by filing Form 3115, all related taxpayers affected by the revocation must use Form 3115 to reflect the farmer's revocation.

*Changing from ADS after revocation.* If the revocation is made by the small business farmer, the farmer and related parties are no longer required to depreciate the property previously placed in service and predominantly uses in the trade or business of farming using the MACRS alternative depreciation system (ADS). Likewise, ADS does not apply to property placed in service in the revocation year and subsequent years that the revocation remains in effect.

Beginning in the revocation year, the switch from ADS for existing property is made by applying the change-in-use rules of Reg. § 1.168(i)-4(d). However, under the change-in-use rules a taxpayer may elect to continue using ADS. Bonus depreciation may not be claimed on property to which ADS mandatorily applied in the placed-in-service year. Thus, bonus depreciation is not retroactively claimed on this property even though a switch out of ADS is being made.

If a farmer revoking the election or related person fails to apply the change-in-use rules to previously acquired property in both the revocation year and the subsequent tax year, an impermissible method of accounting is adopted. The farmer or related person must file Form 3115, usually applying the automatic consent procedure contained in Section 6.05 of Rev. Proc. 2019-43 that relates to failure to follow the change-in-use-rules when required.

An adjustment to income in the year of the change, a section 481(a) adjustment, is computed as if the change-in-use rules had been properly applied in the revocation year. Thus, the section 481(a) adjustment is the difference between the depreciation actually claimed in the revocation year and each subsequent year prior to the year for which Form 3115 is filed and the depreciation that should have been claimed in those years under the change-in-use rules.

Similarly, if the farmer or related person depreciates property placed in service in the revocation year or subsequent tax years using ADS, an impermissible accounting method is adopted if at least two returns were filed and the farmer or related person was not otherwise required to use ADS or did not elect ADS. Form 3115 must also be filed and Section 6.01 of Rev. Proc. 2019-43 relating to changes from an impermissible to permissible depreciation method applies.

*Procedures for Former Small Business Farmer to Make Election to Deduct Preproductive Expenditures*

A farmer may make an election not to capitalize preproductive period expenditures (Code Sec. 263A(d)(3) election) in the first tax year that it loses its Code Sec. 263A(i) exemption from the UNICAP rules as a small business taxpayer because its average annual gross receipts exceed the gross receipts test amount. If this procedure is followed, the Code Sec. 263A(d)(3) election is not considered a change in accounting method.

The Code Sec. 263A(d)(3) election is made on the original filed federal tax return, including extensions, for the first tax year in which the farmer no longer qualifies for exemption as a small business taxpayer. The regular Code Sec. 263A(d)(3) election procedures as described in Reg. § 1.263A-4(d)(3) apply. In general, these procedures require the farmer to deduct otherwise capitalized preproduction expenses and the farmer and any related taxpayer to use the ADS depreciation system for property placed in service in the election year and subsequent years during which the election is in effect. See above.

The ADS property is not eligible for bonus depreciation. ADS is not required for property placed in service before the election year. These rules apply to a related taxpayer even if otherwise exempt from the UNICAP rules as small business taxpayer.

If an electing farmer does not use ADS to depreciate newly acquired property for the placed-in-service year and the subsequent tax year, the farmer has not made a valid Code Sec. 263A(d)(3) election. The farmer will need to obtain consent to make the election by filing Form 3115 in accordance with the non-automatic change procedures in Rev. Proc. 2015-13.

If a person related to the electing farmer does not use ADS then an impermissible method of accounting is adopted and Form 3115 must be filed, generally under Section 6.01 (change from impermissible to permissible method) of the automatic consent procedures.

*Farming business electing out of interest deduction limitation*

Any property with a recovery period of 10 years or greater which is held by an "electing farming business" that makes an election out of the business interest deduction limitations (Code Sec. 163(j)) must be depreciated using the MACRS alternative depreciation system (ADS) (Code Sec. 168(g)(1)(G); Code Sec. 163(j)). The provision applies to tax years beginning after December 31, 2017 (Act Sec. 13205(b) of P.L. 115-97). The interest deduction limitation does not apply to a farming business that does not exceed the Code Sec. 448(c) gross receipts limit during the preceding three tax years ($26 million in 2021 and $27 million in 2022) (Rev. Proc. 2020-45; Rev. Proc. 2021-45). If the election is made, it is irrevocable.

An electing farming business is a farming business that elects out of the interest deduction limitation, or any trade or business of a "specified agricultural or horticultural cooperative" (as defined in new Code Sec. 199A(g)(2)) with respect to which the cooperative makes an election out of the interest deduction limitation (Code Sec. 167(j)(7)(C)).

A specified agricultural or horticultural cooperative is an organization to which part I of subchapter T applies, and which is engaged in—

(1) the manufacturing, production, growth, or extraction in whole or significant part of any agricultural or horticultural product;

(2) the marketing of agricultural or horticultural products which its patrons have so manufactured, produced, grown, or extracted; or

(3) the provision of supplies, equipment, or services to farmers or to organizations in items (1) or (2) (Code Sec. 199A(g)).

Since the provision applies to tax years beginning after 2017 and not to *property placed in service* in tax years beginning after 2017, a taxpayer subject to this provision needs to depreciate affected property placed in service in a tax year beginning prior to the election year using ADS. Taxpayers making the election out of the interest limitation rule do not need to file accounting method changes in order to switch to using the ADS system for property previously placed in service. Instead, the change in use rules will apply in making this switch if the switch is made in the election year or on an amended return filed for the election year prior to filing a return for the subsequent tax year (Rev. Proc. 2019-8; Reg. § 1.168(i)-4(d)).

Under the change in use rules, the remaining basis of an asset is recovered using ADS over the remaining ADS recovery period determined as if ADS had applied to the property when it was originally placed in service. See Example (2) below. See ¶ 169 for change in use rules. Bonus depreciation is not subject to recapture. However, property which is placed in service during or after the election year does not qualify for bonus depreciation because the bonus allowance may not be claimed on property which is mandatorily subject to ADS in the year it is placed in service (Code Sec. 168(k)(2)(D)).

If a taxpayer makes the election out and then files two or more returns without using ADS on affected property an improper accounting method has been adopted (see ¶ 75) and the electing taxpayer must then file Form 3115 in order to make the required switch to ADS. A positive (unfavorable) section 481(a) adjustment must be computed and is measured by the difference between the depreciation claimed beginning in the year of the election and the amount of depreciation that should have been claimed using ADS beginning with the year of election. If the property subject to the accounting method change was placed in service prior to the election year the change is filed under the automatic accounting method procedures described in Section 6.05 of Rev. Proc. 2019-43, "Change in method of accounting for depreciation due to a change in the use of MACRS property." Otherwise the procedures describe in Section 6.01, relating to changes from an impermissible method to a permissible method apply.

> ***Example (1):*** Farmer A, a calendar year taxpayer, makes the irrevocable election out of the interest limitation rules in 2018. In 2018, farmer A should begin depreciating any property placed in service prior to 2018 with a recovery period of 10 years or greater using ADS. In addition, any property placed in service in 2018 or later with a recovery period of 10 years or greater must be depreciated using ADS. Assume farmer A does not begin to depreciate affected property placed in service prior to 2018 using ADS in accordance with the change in use rules but does depreciate property placed in service in 2018 or later using ADS. Farmer A files its 2018, 2019, and 2020 returns without using ADS on its pre-2018 property. In this situation, farmer A has adopted an impermissible depreciation method with respect to its pre-2018 property since it has filed three improper returns. Farmer A needs to file an accounting method change. If the method change is filed for the 2021 tax year, a positive section 481(a) adjustment equal to the difference between the MACRS depreciation claimed in 2018, 2019 and 2020 on the property with a depreciation period of 10 years or greater and the depreciation that should have been claim using ADS in 2018, 2019 and 2020 under the change in use rules is included in income in 2021.

*Real property trade or business electing out of interest deduction limitation*

The 2017 Tax Cuts and Jobs Act (P.L. 115-97) requires a real property trade or business that elects out of the business interest deduction cap (Code Sec. 163(j)(7)(B)) to use the MACRS alternative depreciation system (ADS) to depreciate any nonresidential real property, residential rental property, or qualified improvement property it holds (Code Sec. 168(g)(1)). The provision is effective for tax years beginning after December 31, 2017 (Act Sec. 13204(b)(2) of P.L. 115-97). The provision does not apply to a real property trade or business that does not exceed the Code Sec. 448(c) gross receipts limit during the preceding three tax years ($26 million in 2021 and $27 million in 2022) (Rev. Proc. 2020-45; Rev. Proc. 2021-45).

The Joint Committee on Taxation's Blue Book states that a technical correction may be necessary to reflect that an electing real property trade or business is also required to use ADS to depreciate its 15-year qualified leasehold improvement property, qualified restaurant property, and qualified retail improvement property that was placed in service prior to 2018 and is owned by the taxpayer as of the beginning of the year of the election out of the interest limitation (JCT General Explanation of Public Law 115-97, JCS-1-18,Congress (United States), footnote 636 ("Blue Book")). This technical correction is provided for in a proposed technical corrections bill ("Tax Technical and Clerical Corrections Act Discussion Draft" (U.S. House of Representatives Committee on Ways and Means Chairman Kevin Brady January 2, 2019); Technical Explanation of the House Ways and Means Committee Chairman's discussion draft of the "Tax Technical and Clerical Corrections Act" (JCX-1-19, January 2, 2019)).

"Real property trade or business" means any real property development, redevelopment, construction, reconstruction, acquisition, conversion, rental, operation, management, leasing, or brokerage trade or business (Code Sec. 469(c)(7)).

Since the provision applies to taxable years beginning after 2017 and not to property placed in service in tax years beginning after 2017, a taxpayer subject to this provision needs to depreciate affected property placed in service in a tax year beginning prior to the election year using ADS. As in the case of farmers making the election out, the change in use rules (Reg. § 1.168(i)-4(d)) will apply in making this switch. An accounting method change is not required unless two or more returns are filed without making the required switch to ADS (Rev. Proc. 2019-8). For example, if a calendar year real property trade or business makes the election for 2018 and filed a 2018 and 2019 return without switching to ADS using the change in use rules, the taxpayer may not file an amended return to make the switch to ADS.

> ***Example (2):*** ABC, a calendar-year real property trade or business, placed 39-year nonresidential real property costing $100,000 in service in January 2013 and makes an irrevocable election out of the business interest deduction limitation in 2020. The ADS recovery period for 39-year property is 40 years. As of December 31, 2020, the property has been depreciated for seven years and eleven and one-half months. Only eleven and one-half month's depreciation was allowed in 2013 under the mid-month convention. Depreciation claimed through December 31, 2020 is $20,406. Under the change-in-use regulations, ABC will depreciate the remaining $79,594 basis using the straight-line method over the remaining ADS recovery period of 32 years and one-half month beginning on January 1, 2021.

See the discussion immediately above regarding farmers making the election as it also applies to real property trades and businesses making the election.

A retroactive law change made by the Taxpayer Certainty and Disaster Tax Relief Act of 2020 (P.L. 116-260) (December 27, 2020) allows an electing real property trade or business to use a 30-year ADS recovery period to depreciate residential rental property placed in service before 2018 (Act Sec. 13204(b) of The Tax Cuts and Jobs Act P.L. 115-97, as amended by Act Sec. 202 of P.L. 116-260). Prior to this change, a 30-year ADS period only applied to residential rental property placed in service after 2017 and a 40-year period applied to residential rental property placed in service before 2018. This provision is mandatory. The IRS released Rev. Proc. 2021-28 to provide guidance on how an electing real property trade or business changes its method of depreciating residential rental property that may have been previously depreciated using an impermissible 40-year ADS recovery period. In addition, an alternative process is provided for eligible partnerships to file amended returns for tax years 2018, 2019, and 2020, as well as amended Schedule K-1s, for this purpose without filing an administrative adjustment request (AAR) ( Rev. Proc. 2021-29).

Under Rev. Proc. 2021-28, generally a taxpayer will file a change in method of accounting under the automatic accounting method change procedures specific to a change in use of the asset (Sec. 6.05 of Rev. Proc. 2019-43) to effectuate such change, although in certain instances (e.g., the real property trade or business election is made in the tax year preceding the potential year of change) an amended return may be utilized to effectuate such change.

The provision applies to residential rental property:

- placed in service before January 1, 2018;
- held by a real property trade or business that elects out of the business interest limitations in a tax year beginning after 2017; and
- which was not depreciated under ADS before January 1, 2018.

If a real property trade or business elected or was otherwise required to apply ADS to a residential rental property placed in service before 2018, the 40-year ADS period for such property is not reduced to 30-years on account of an election out of the interest limitations in a tax year beginning after 2017.

*Farmers and Real Property Businesses Making Late or Revoking Prior Business Interest Deduction Elections in 2018, 2019, and 2020*

A real property trade or business or a farming businesses may make a late election out of the business interest limitations (Code Sec. 163(j)) or withdraw a prior election out of the limitations for a tax year beginning in 2018, 2019, or 2020 by filing an amended federal income tax return, amended Form 1065, or AAR (Rev. Proc. 2020-22). The return must include an election statement or withdrawal statement, and any collateral adjustments to taxable income. This includes depreciation of property affected by making a late election or withdrawing the election. The amended federal income tax return, Form 1065, or AAR generally must be filed by October 15, 2021. The guidance under Rev. Proc. 2020-25 which explains how to claim bonus depreciation on QIP placed in service after 2017 on account of the retroactive assignment of a 15-year recovery period (see ¶ 127D item 1A) does not apply if a revocation or late election under Rev. Proc. 2020-22 is made. For example, if a farming business or real property trade or business revokes an election out of the interest limitations that was made for the 2018 tax year, bonus depreciation on the QIP is claimed on the amended return that revokes the election. If the 2019 return has also been filed, the 2019 return will also need to be amended to reflect the proper depreciation in light of the changes made on the amended 2018 return.

The change in use rules apply in switching to the ADS method if a late election out of the interest limitations is made (Rev. Proc. 2019-8). For example, if a real property business files a late election out of the limitations on an amended return for a tax years beginning in 2018, the change in use rules apply to compute ADS on the amended return for nonresidential, residential, and qualified improvement property held by the taxpayer in that year. If the election is withdrawn, the amended return will reflect the depreciation that would have been claimed during that tax year computed as if the election had not been made. If a 2019 return has also been filed, that return needs to be amended since it is affected by the depreciation changes made on the amended 2018 return.

*Foreign-use property*

Generally, this category includes property physically located outside the United States more than half of the taxable year or more than half of the year considering only that part beginning on the day on which the property is placed in service (Reg. § 1.48-1(g)(1)). It does not include property owned by a U.S. corporation or a U.S. citizen (other than a citizen entitled to the benefits of Code Sec. 931 or Code Sec. 933) and predominantly used in a U.S. possession (by such corporation or citizen or a corporation created under the laws of the possession) (Code Sec. 168(g)(4)(g)). Depreciable property located in Puerto Rico was not treated as used predominantly outside the United States as long as the partners of the domestic partnership that owned the property were domestic corporations or U.S. citizens not entitled to benefits under Code Sec. 931 or 933 (IRS Letter Ruling 201216008, January 9, 2012; IRS Letter Ruling 201136018, May 25, 2011). Similarly IRS Letter Ruling 201324005, March 19, 2013 and IRS Letter Ruling 201324006, March 19, 2013. Similarly, provided taxpayer is a domestic partnership where all of its partners are domestic corporations (other than a corporation which has an election in effect under section 936) or are United States citizens that are not entitled to the benefits of section 931 or 933, property was not treated as used predominantly outside the United States within the meaning ofCode Sec. 168(g)(4) (IRS Letter Ruling 201943021, July 22, 2019).

Corporations with an election in effect under former Code Sec. 936 were required to use ADS (Code Sec. 168(g)(4)(G), prior to amendment by the Tax Technical Corrections Act of 2018 (Division U of P.L. 115-114); Act § 401(e)(1)(B) of Division U of P.L. 115-114).

*Change in use.* Special rules apply when property formerly used in the U.S. is used predominantly outside the U.S. or when property formerly used predominantly outside of the U.S. is moved into the U.S. These rules are described at ¶ 169.

*Other foreign use exclusions.* Other exclusions include: communications satellites; any satellite or spacecraft launched from within the United States; certain aircraft, railroad rolling stock, vessels, motor vehicles, and containers used in transportation to and from the United States; submarine telephone cables, offshore drilling equipment, and certain other resource exploration property used in international waters (Code Sec. 168(g)(4)).

*Cargo containers used predominantly outside of the U.S.* Code Sec. 168(g)(4)(E), as amended by P.L. 101-508, provides that ADS does not apply to containers of a United States person which are used in the transportation of property to *and* from the United States. The IRS has interpreted the exception, as in effect prior to amendment by P.L. 101-508, to apply to containers used substantially in the *direct* transportation of property to *or* from the United States (Rev. Rul. 90-9, 1990-1 CB 46). Prior to P.L. 101-508, the exception was not specifically stated in Code Sec. 168, but rather, based on a cross reference to a similar definition contained in former Code Sec. 48(a)(2)(B)(v) (relating to the investment tax credit).

In Rev. Rul. 90-9, the IRS also ruled that a taxpayer must depreciate cargo containers using ADS (and may not claim the investment credit) if the taxpayer cannot document that its containers were used substantially in the direct transportation of property to *or* from the United States during the tax year. Documentation is required on a container-by-container basis for each year of the depreciation recovery period and investment tax credit recapture period. However, fall-back positions based on valid statistical sampling are acceptable. See, also, IRS Letter Ruling 9045001 (May 3, 1990) upon which the position of Rev. Rul. 90-9 is based. An irrevocable election is provided by Rev. Proc. 90-10, 1990-1 CB 467, to United States owners of qualifying intermodal cargo containers to treat 50 percent of containers placed in service during the election year as meeting the exception for direct transportation to or from the United States. If this election is made it is not necessary to maintain records that trace the usage of the containers as required by Rev. Rul. 90-9. The retroactive application of Rev. Rul. 90-9 and Rev. Proc. 90-10 was upheld in *Norfolk Southern Corp.*, CA-4, 98-1 USTC ¶ 50,273, 140 F3d 240.

An undated FSA (Field Service Advice) provides significant guidance with respect to the application of Rev. Rul. 90-9 and Rev. Proc. 90-10, including the use of statistical analysis to establish the use of intermodal containers (FSA 9999-9999-273; 99 ARD 210-12 (cite for location in CCH Advance Release Documents)).

See, also, ¶ 5.

*Maquiladora.* Tangible property transferred by a U.S. entity to a maquiladora located in Latin America and used predominantly outside of the U.S. during the tax year in an assembly process must be depreciated under ADS unless one of the preceding exclusions apply. If the transferred property was being depreciated under an accelerated method of accounting while located in the U.S. the switch to the straight-line method under ADS in the first year the property is used outside of the U.S. is not considered a change in accounting method for which a Code Sec. 481 adjustment is required (ISP Coordinated Issue Paper on the Maquiladora Industry, issued July 23, 1997).

The IRS has issued settlement guidelines confirming that a U.S. entity is required to use the MACRS ADS depreciation system in the year tangible property is transferred to a maquiladora if the property is located more than 50 percent during the tax year of transfer on the maquiladora (Appeals Industry Specialization Program Settlement Guidelines Industry: Maquiladora Issue: Section 168(g), April 8, 2005). The ADS deduction is determined by applying the MACRS change in use regulations (Reg.§ 1.168(i)-4(d) reproduced at ¶ 568 and discussed at ¶ 168 and ¶ 169).

However, the guidelines provide that if the property is transferred across the U.S. border in the tax year that the taxpayer places the property in service, the appropriate depreciation method for the first tax year is based on the primary use of the property for that tax year. In other words, the property will either be depreciated using ADS for the entire year or the MACRS general depreciation system for the entire year. The primary use of the property may be determined in any reasonable manner that is consistently applied to the taxpayer's property. See Reg.§ 1.168(i)-4(e).

The guidelines also discuss the application of the change in accounting method rules and provide that the failure to switch to the ADS method in the tax year required will trigger the change in accounting method rules (¶ 75) if the entity files two or more consecutive tax returns before switching to the ADS method.

*Regulations.* There are currently no MACRS regulations dealing with foreign-use property. However, ACRS has a rule which modifies the otherwise applicable recovery period for foreign-use property and this rule is discussed in Prop. Reg. § 1.168-2(g). A definition of foreign use property is also found in the investment tax credit regulations (Reg.§ 1.48-1(g)). Issues relating to the definition of foreign-use property contained in these regulations should also apply to MACRS property to the extent they do not conflict with Code Sec. 168(g)(4).

*Tax-exempt use property*

Tax-exempt use property leased to a tax-exempt entity must be depreciated using ADS. The recovery period of tax-exempt use property subject to a lease may in no event be less than 125 percent of the lease term (Code Sec. 168(g)(3)(A)).

Tax-exempt use property includes (Code Sec. 168(h)(1)):

(1) tangible property other than nonresidential real property leased to a tax-exempt entity; and

(2) that part of nonresidential real property leased to a tax-exempt entity under a disqualified lease if the portion of the property so leased is more than 35 percent of the property.

The IRS ruled that 15-year qualified leasehold improvement property is nonresidential real property within the meaning of the tax-exempt use property rules of Code Sec. 168(h) and, therefore, is depreciable using the 39-year ADS recovery period (i.e., class life) applicable to qualified leasehold improvement property if the qualified leasehold improvement property is leased to a tax-exempt entity in a disqualified lease (CCA Letter Ruling 201436048, April 29, 2014).

Generally effective for leases entered into after March 12, 2004, the American Jobs Creation Act of 2004 expands the definition of tax-exempt use property to include the following intangible property if it is leased to a tax-exempt entity and would otherwise be considered tax-exempt use property under Code Sec. 168(h):

(1) computer software, as described in Code Sec. 167(f)(1)(B) and otherwise amortizable over 36 months (¶ 48) (Code Sec. 167(f)(1)(C), as added by the 2004 Jobs Act);

(2) the following separately acquired interests and rights which are specifically excluded by Code Sec. 197(e)(4) from the definition of a section 197 intangible:

(a) patent or copyright interests, as described in Code Sec. 197(e)(4)(C) (¶ 26),

(b) a right held under a contract or granted by a governmental unit to receive tangible property or services, as described in Code Sec. 197(e)(4)(B) (¶ 32), and

(c) a right held under a contract or granted by a governmental unit that has a fixed duration of less than 15 years, or that is fixed as to amount and recoverable under a method similar to the unit-of-production method, as described in Code Sec. 197(e)(4)(D) (¶ 50) (Code Sec. 167(f)(2), as amended by the 2004 Jobs Act); and

(3) Code Sec. 197 intangibles (¶ 12) (Code Sec. 197(f)(10)).

Any grant of a right to use property to a tax-exempt entity is a disqualified lease if:

(1) any part of the property was financed with a tax-exempt obligation of a state or a political subdivision of a state, and the entity participated in the financing;

(2) it is coupled with an option to purchase involving the tax-exempt entity;

(3) its term exceeds 20 years; or

(4) it is a leaseback of property used by the entity more than three months before the lease.

A tax-exempt entity is defined as (Code Sec. 168(h)(2)):

(1) the United States, any State or political subdivision, any possession of the United States, or any agency or instrumentality of the preceding;

(2) any organization (other than a Code Sec. 521 farmer's cooperative) exempt from U.S. income tax; and

(3) any foreign person or entity unless more than half of the gross income derived from the use is taxable or passed through to a U.S. shareholder under Code Sec. 951 rules relating to controlled foreign corporations (Code Sec. 168(h)(2)).

For leases entered into after October 3, 2004, the definition of tax-exempt entity for purposes of Code Sec. 168 is expanded to include Indian tribal governments (Code Sec. 168(h)(2)(A)).

Any portion of property that is predominantly used in an unrelated trade or business from which the income is taxable under Code Sec. 511 is not tax-exempt use property or treated as property leased under a disqualified lease (Code Sec. 168(h)(1)(D)). Nor shall property be treated as tax-exempt use property merely because it is subject to a lease of less than three years and less than the greater of one year or 30 percent of the property's present class life (Code Sec. 168(h)(1)(C)). Subject to exceptions (such as where the property itself has been financed under tax-exempt obligations or a sale and leaseback are involved), qualified technological equipment leased to a tax-exempt entity for a term of no more than five years is not tax-exempt use property (Code Sec. 168(h)(3)). Generally effective for leases entered into after March 12, 2004, a renewal period (up to 24 months) under a lessee's option to renew at a fair market value rent is not treated as extending the term of the lease for such property (Code Sec. 168(h)(3)(A), as amended by the 2004 Jobs Act).

The tax-exempt use character of property leased to a partnership is determined at the partner level (Code Sec. 168(h)(5)). Thus, for purposes of the applicable rules, property leased to a partnership is treated as leased to the partners in proportions based on partnership rules for determining distributive shares of deductions and other items.

A special rule applies to like-kind exchanges after April 19, 1995, between related parties that are designed to circumvent the tax-exempt use property rules. Property received by a taxpayer from a related party in a like-kind exchange for tax-exempt use property that is made to avoid the application of the MACRS ADS must be depreciated by the taxpayer using the same method, convention, and the remaining recovery period as that of the transferred tax-exempt use property (Reg. § 1.168(h)-1).

This rule applies only to the portion of the taxpayer's basis in the tainted property that does not exceed the taxpayer's basis in the transferred tax-exempt use property or is not subject to the nonrecognition transaction rules provided in Code Sec. 168(i)(7) (see ¶ 144). For purposes of this rule, parties are deemed related if they bear a relationship specified in Code Sec. 267(b) or 707(b)(1).

The term of a lease includes options to renew (Code Sec. 168 (i)(3)(A)(i)). In determining the length of a lease term for leases executed after April 19, 1995, an additional period of time during which a tax-exempt lessee may not continue to be the lessee is included in the lease term if the lessee or a related party retains financial responsibility (Reg. § 1.168(i)-2). For this purpose, parties are deemed related if they bear a relationship specified in Code Sec. 168(h)(4).

*Tax-exempt bond-financed property*

This category generally includes any property placed in service after 1986 to the extent it is financed, directly or indirectly, by bonds (issued after March 1, 1986) on which income is exempt from tax under Code Sec. 103(a) (Code Sec. 168(g)(5)). The extent to which property is deemed financed by the proceeds of such bonds is determined on the basis of the order in which property is placed in service. Qualified residential projects—projects at all times meeting a median-income test for occupants—are excluded from the definition of tax-exempt bond-financed property. For purposes of this exception, the issuer must elect, at the time of the issuance of the bonds, which of two tests applies. Under one of the tests, at least 20 percent of the residential units must be occupied by individuals whose income is no more than half of the area median gross income. Under the alternate test, 40 percent is substituted for 20 percent, and 60 percent is substituted for 50 percent.

Transitional rules shield tax-exempt bond-financed facilities from the alternative depreciation system if certain action was taken before March 2, 1986.

*Imported property*

This category includes only property manufactured or produced in a foreign country and subject to an Executive Order (Code Sec. 168(g)(6)). The President may issue such an order pursuant to a determination that:

(1) such country maintains variable import fees or other burdensome nontariff trade restrictions inconsistent with trade agreements; or

(2) unjustifiably restricts U.S. commerce by, among other things, engaging in discriminatory acts or tolerating cartels. To be considered "imported," property must (1) be completed outside the United States, its possessions, and Puerto Rico or (2) less than 50 percent of its basis must be attributable to value added within the United States, its possessions, or Puerto Rico.

## ¶ 156

## MACRS Alternative Depreciation System Recovery Periods

This paragraph describes the applicable recovery periods under the MACRS alternative depreciation system (ADS). Recovery periods are 12-month periods that begin on the date the property is deemed placed in service under the applicable convention. These ADS recovery periods are reflected in detail in Rev. Proc. 87-56 at ¶ 191.

The following recovery periods generally apply for purposes of ADS (Code Sec. 168(g)(2) and Code Sec. 168(g)(3)):

| *In the case of* | *ADS Recovery Period* |
|---|---|
| Qualified technological equipment | 5 years |
| Automobile or light general purpose truck | 5 years |
| Personal property with no class life | 12 years |
| Sec. 1245 property which is real property with no class life | 40 years |
| Nonresidential real property | 40 years |
| Residential rental property (placed in service after 2017) | 30 years |
| Residential rental property (placed in service before 2018) | 40 years (30 years for real property trade or business electing out of interest limits) |
| Railroad grading and tunnel bores | 50 years |

| *In the case of* | *ADS Recovery Period* |
|---|---|
| Water utility property | 50 years |
| All other property | The class life |

Residential rental property has a 30 year ADS period, effective for property placed in service after 2017 (Code Sec. 168(g)(2)(C); Rev. Proc. 2019-8).

Municipal sewers placed in service before June 13, 1996 were assigned a class life of 50 years for ADS purposes.

The term "qualified technological equipment" includes computers and peripheral equipment, high technology medical equipment, and certain high-technology telephone station equipment. See Code Sec. 168(i)(2).

Subject to a binding contracts exception, the 50-year ADS recovery period for water utility property generally applies to property placed in service after June 12, 1996 (Code Sec. 168(g)(2)(C)(iv)). Water utility property is defined at ¶ 113.

Some property is assigned a special class life solely for ADS purposes (Code Sec. 168(g)(3)). This specially assigned class life is treated as the appropriate ADS recovery period. The following chart lists selected property with a specially assigned class life:

| *Property* | *ADS Class life/ADS Recovery period (in years)* |
|---|---|
| (1) Rent-to-own property | 4 |
| (2) Semi-conductor manufacturing equipment | 5 |
| (3) Computer-based telephone central office switching equipment | 9.5 |
| (4) New farm machinery or equipment (other than a grain bin, cotton ginning asset, fence or land improvement) placed in service in 2009 or after 2017 | 10 |
| (5) Railroad track | 10 |
| (6) Any natural gas gathering line the original use of which commences with the taxpayer after April 11, 2005 | 14 |
| (7) Single-purpose agricultural and horticultural structures | 15 |
| (8) Any tree or vine bearing fruit or nuts | 20 |
| (9) Retail motor fuels outlets | 20 |
| (10) Initial clearing and grading land improvements with respect to gas utility property, | 20 |
| (11) Alaska natural gas pipeline | 22 |
| (12) Telephone distribution plant and comparable equipment | 24 |
| (13) Municipal wastewater treatment plants | 24 |
| (14) Initial clearing and grading land improvements with respect to any electric utility transmission and distribution plant. | 25 |
| (15) Any section 1245 property (as defined in section 1245(a)(3)) used in the transmission at 69 or more kilovolts of electricity for sale and the original use of which commences with the taxpayer after April 11, 2005 | 30 |
| (16) Any natural gas distribution line the original use of which commences with the taxpayer after April 11, 2005, and which is placed in service before January 1, 2011 | 35 |

| Property | ADS Class life/ADS Recovery period (in years) |
|---|---|
| (17) Qualified improvement property placed in service after 2017 | 20 |
| (18) Qualified 15-year restaurant property, 15-year leasehold improvement property, and 15-year retail improvement property | 39 |

*Tax-exempt use property subject to a lease.* For tax-exempt use property subject to a lease, the ADS recovery period is the longer of the asset's class life or 125 percent of the lease term (Code Sec. 168(g)(3)(A)).

The ADS recovery periods for MACRS property can be found in Rev. Proc. 87-56, which is reproduced at ¶ 191.

# Dispositions of MACRS Property

## ¶ 160

## Early Dispositions: Computation of Deduction; Recapture

A disposition is the permanent withdrawal of property from use in a trade or business or in the production of income. A withdrawal may be made by sale, exchange, involuntary conversion, retirement, abandonment, or destruction. The adjusted depreciable basis of abandoned property is deductible as a loss. Effective for tax years beginning on or after January 1, 2014 (or optionally, to tax years beginning on or after January 1, 2012), a disposition includes the retirement of a structural component of a building (or the retirement of a portion of any other asset) if a taxpayer makes a partial disposition election. A taxpayer had a limited opportunity to make a late partial disposition election with respect to dispositions that took place in tax years that began before January 1, 2012 by filing an accounting method change no later than the taxpayer's last tax year beginning in 2014. See ¶ 162 for a discussion of dispositions and the partial disposition election.

A disposition of property before the end of its recovery period is referred to as an early disposition. A MACRS deduction is usually allowed in the year of disposition of personal or real property unless the asset is disposed of in the same tax year that it was placed in service. See *"Property placed in service and disposed of in the same tax year,"* below.

*Conventions*

The same MACRS depreciation convention that applied in the tax year that disposed of property was placed in service must also be used in the year of disposition to compute any allowable depreciation deduction.

For residential rental and nonresidential real property, the mid-month convention (¶ 90) must be used. Under the mid-month convention, property disposed of anytime during a month is treated as disposed of in the middle of that month. Thus, the month of disposition is treated as one-half month of use for purposes of prorating the depreciation calculated for a full tax year.

For property subject to the half-year convention (¶ 88), the deduction for the year of an early disposition is one-half the depreciation determined for the full tax year. However, as explained below, if property subject to the half-year convention is disposed of in the last year of the asset's recovery period the depreciation deduction is the same as if the asset had not been sold.

For property subject to the mid-quarter convention (¶ 92), depreciation determined for the full tax year is multiplied by the following percentages for the quarter of the tax year in which the disposition occurred: first quarter, 12.5 percent; second quarter, 37.5 percent; third quarter, 62.5 percent; and fourth quarter, 87.5 percent. However, if property subject to the mid-quarter convention is disposed of in the last year of the asset's recovery period, a special rules applies. See "Disposition in last year of recovery period," below.

*Short tax year*

For a disposition of property in a short tax year, the unrecovered basis of property is multiplied by the depreciation rate and then by a fraction the numerator of which is the number of months the property is considered in service and the denominator of which is 12. An allocation method may also be used. See ¶ 134 for short tax year computations.

*Property placed in service and disposed of in same tax year*

If MACRS property subject to the half-year or mid-quarter convention (i.e., section 1245 property) is placed in service and disposed of in the same tax year no MACRS deduction is allowed (IRS Publication 946 (How To Depreciation Property); Reg. § 1.168(d)-1(b)(3)). This rule is effective for property placed in service in tax years ending after January 30, 1991 (Reg. § 1.168(d)-1(d)(1)). For earlier tax years it was permissible (though not required) to claim a depreciation deduction on property subject to the mid-quarter convention and placed in service and disposed of in the same tax year. However, in the case of property subject to the half-year convention, it appears no deduction could be claimed because under the half-year convention the property would be treated as placed in service and disposed of on the same date. See the preamble to T.D. 8444 for additional details.

No bonus deduction (¶ 127D) or section 179 deduction (¶ 300) may be claimed on property placed in service and disposed of in the same tax year.

It appears that taxpayers were permitted to claim depreciation deductions on MACRS residential rental and nonresidential real property placed in service and disposed of in the same tax year if the acquisition and disposition occurred in a tax year ending on or before June 17, 2004 (Reg. § 1.168(i)-4(c) stating the rule and Reg. § 1.168(i)-4(g) providing the effective date). Although these regulations deal with changes in use of MACRS property (see ¶ 168), they specifically state that "No depreciation deduction is allowable for MACRS property placed in service and disposed of in the same taxable year." The rule is not limited to personal property. Compare Reg. § 1.168(d)-1(b)(3) and Reg. § 1.168(d)-1(d) which state the rule in the context of a discussion of the half-year and mid-quarter convention for personal property. Logically, the rule for real property should have been provided in MACRS regulations dealing with the application of the mid-month convention, rather than changes in use, but the IRS has not yet issued regulations dealing with the mid-month convention. However, ever since after the issuance of T.D. 8444, IRS Publication 946 states, without distinguishing between personal and real property, that depreciation may not be claimed on an asset placed in service and disposed of during the same tax year. Note that a long-standing depreciation recapture rule provides that all depreciation claimed on real property held for less than one year is subject to recapture as ordinary income (Code Sec. 1250(b)(1)). Thus, even if a taxpayer claims MACRS depreciation on real property sold and disposed of in the same tax year, the benefit of the deduction would be recaptured in the same tax year.

The cost of property placed in service and disposed of in the same tax year is not taken into account in determining whether the mid-quarter convention applies to other property placed in service during that tax year (Code Sec. 168(d)(3)(B)(ii)). However, if the property is reacquired and placed in service in the same tax year that it was previously placed in service and disposed of, the basis of the property is taken into account in determining whether the mid-quarter convention applies (Reg.§ 1.168(d)-1(b)(3)). This implies that the property is depreciable.

Bonus depreciation may not be claimed on property placed in service and disposed of in the same tax year. Moreover, if the property is reacquired and placed in service in a subsequent tax year bonus may not be claimed (Reg.§ 1.168(k)-2(g)(1)). In determining whether the mid-quarter convention applies (more than 40 percent of basis of specified property placed in service in last 3 months of tax year) the basis is not reduced by the bonus deduction. See ¶ 92.

No depreciation deduction is allowed if a property is purchased for business use and converted to personal use in the same tax year (Reg. § 1.168(i)-4(c)).

Property placed in service and disposed of in the same tax year may not be placed in a general asset account (Reg. § 1.168(i)-1(c)(1)(i)).

*Disposition in last year of recovery period*

*Half-year convention.* The disposition of property subject to the half-year convention at any time in the tax year in which the last recovery year ends is not an early disposition that would result in claiming only one-half of the depreciation otherwise allowed for that tax year.

> ***Example (1):*** MACRS 3-year property is placed in service in 2017 by a calendar-year taxpayer. The property cost $1,000. Bonus depreciation (¶ 127D) is $500 ($1,000 × 50%). Depreciable basis to which the regular table percentages are applied is $500 ($1,000 - $500). Under the half-year convention the recovery period begins on the midpoint of 2017 and ends on the midpoint of 2020. If the property is sold at any time during the 2020 tax year the half-year convention treats the property as if it was disposed of on the midpoint of 2020 (Code Sec. 168(d)(4)(A)). As a consequence there is no early disposition and the year 2020 depreciation deduction is not reduced. The deduction is equal to $37.05 ($500 × 7.41% (4th year recovery percentage from Table 1 at ¶ 180)).

*Mid-quarter convention.* However, if property subject to the mid-quarter convention is disposed of in the tax year in which the recovery period ends, an early disposition may occur.

> ***Example (2):*** MACRS 3-year property is placed in service in December 2017 (fourth quarter) by a calendar-year taxpayer. The property cost $2,000. Bonus depreciation (¶ 127D) is $1,000 ($2,000 × 50%). Depreciable basis to which the regular table percentages are applied is $1,000 ($2,000 – $1,000). (The full amount of bonus depreciation is allowed even if the mid-quarter convention applies). Under the mid-quarter convention the recovery period begins on the mid-point of November 2017 and ends on the mid-point of November 2020. If the property is sold in 2020 prior to the beginning of the fourth quarter, then it is considered sold prior to the end of the recovery period and an early disposition has taken place. For example, if the property is sold in the second quarter on June 10, 2020, the property is considered sold on the midpoint of May and only 4 ½ months depreciation (January through mid-May) may be claimed for the 2020 tax year. The fourth-year table depreciation percentage for 3-year property placed in service in the fourth quarter under the mid-quarter convention (10.19% (Table 5 at ¶ 180)) may not be used because it reflects depreciation for 10½ months (January through the mid-point of November) rather than 4½ months. Instead, depreciation for the 4½ month period may be determined by using the last-year table percentage to determine depreciation for the 10½ month period ($1,000 × 10.19% = $101.90) and claiming 42.86% (4.5 ÷ 10.5) of that amount or $43.67 ($101.90 × 42.86% = $43.67) to reflect depreciation for the 4 ½ month period that the property is considered placed in service in the year of disposition under the mid-quarter convention. Alternatively, depreciation could be determined for one month ($101.90 ÷ 10.5 = $9.705) and this amount multiplied by 4.5 ($9.705 × 4.5 = $43.67).

*Depreciation recapture rules*

If section 1245 property is disposed of at a gain during the tax year, a specified amount (the "recapture amount") to the extent of recognized gain is treated as ordinary income. This recapture amount is recognized notwithstanding any other Code provision. Recapture only applies to depreciation allowed or allowable for periods after December 31, 1961 (Code Sec. 1245; Reg. § 1.1245-1(a)(1)). See ¶ 488, "*Keep records to reduce depreciation recapture—allowed or allowable rule,*" for a rule that will usually limit recapture to depreciation actually claimed.

In the case of a sale, exchange, or involuntary conversion, the recapture amount is equal to the lower of:

(1) the recomputed basis of the property, or

(2) the amount realized

reduced by the adjusted basis of the property (Code Sec. 1245(a)(1); Reg. § 1.1245-1(b)).

The recomputed basis is the property's adjusted basis plus previously allowed or allowable depreciation or amortization (including the Code Sec. 179 expense deduction, the Code Sec. 190 deduction for expenditures to remove architectural and transportation barriers to the handicapped and elderly, the Code Sec. 193 deduction for tertiary injectants, and, for property generally acquired before August 11, 1993 (see ¶ 10 and ¶ 36)), deductions under Code Sec. 1253(d)(2) and (3) (before amendment by the Omnibus Budget Reconciliation Act of 1993 (P.L. 103-66)) regarding fixed sum amounts paid on the transfer of a franchise, trademark or trade name reflected in the adjusted basis (Code Sec. 1245(a)(2)).

***Example (3):*** A depreciable machine is sold for $100. Its adjusted basis is $20. It cost $30 and $10 of depreciation has been claimed. The recapture amount is $10. This is the excess of the lesser of (1) $80 (the amount realized) or (2) $30 (the recomputed basis ($20 adjusted basis + $10 depreciation claimed) over $20 (the adjusted basis)).

As can be seen in the preceding example, the rule for sales, exchanges, and involuntary conversions in effect provides that depreciation is recaptured to the extent of the lesser of the (1) depreciation claimed or the (2) gain recognized.

In the case of a disposition other than a sale, exchange, or involuntary conversion, the recapture amount is equal to the lower of:

(1) the recomputed basis of the property, or

(2) the fair market value of the property on the date of disposition

reduced by the adjusted basis of the property (Code Sec. 1245(a)(1); Reg. § 1.1245-1(c)).

***Example (4):*** A corporation distributes section 1245 property to its shareholders as a dividend. The property has a $2,000 adjusted basis, a recomputed basis of $3,300, and a fmv of $3,100. $1,100 ($3,100 − $2,000) is recognized by the corporation as ordinary income even though Code Sec. 311(a) would otherwise preclude recognition of gain to the corporation.

The recapture amount recognized by a transferor in a transaction to which Code Sec. 332, 351, 361, 721, or 731 applies may not exceed the amount of gain recognized by the transferor (Code Sec. 1245(b)(3)).

***Example (5):*** A taxpayer transfers depreciated property to a controlled corporation in exchange for stock (no boot received) in a transaction to which Code Sec. 351 applies. No gain or loss is recognized. Accordingly, no amount is recaptured.

The IRS and certain courts have ruled that the transfer of property by the owner of a wholly-owned corporation to that corporation is governed by Code Sec. 351 even though no stock is received (*S. Lessenger*, CA-2, 89-1 USTC ¶ 9254; Rev. Rul. 64-155, 1964-1 CB 138). Thus, if no gain is recognized (because no boot is received), there should be no depreciation recapture.

Depreciable real property, other than real property that is Code Sec. 1245 property (see ¶ 127C), is subject to depreciation recapture under Code Sec. 1250. Gain on the sale or other disposition of Code Sec. 1250 property is treated as ordinary income rather than capital gain to the extent of the excess of post-1969 depreciation allowances over the depreciation that would have been available under the straight-line method. However, if Code Sec. 1250 property is held for one year or less, all depreciation (and not just the excess over straight-line depreciation) is recaptured (Code Sec. 1250(b)(1)). Special phaseout rules reduce recapture for certain property. Certain amounts are excluded in determining the amount of additional depreciation taken before the disposition of Code Sec. 1250 property (Code Sec. 1250(b)).

For a disposal of recapture property in an installment sale, any recapture income (ordinary income under Code Sec. 1245 or 1250) is recognized in the year of disposition, and any gain in excess of the recapture income is reported under the installment method (Code Sec. 453(i)). See ¶ 488.

The reduction of the capital gains rates for individuals, estates, and trusts by the 1997 Taxpayer Relief Act (P.L. 105-34) does not affect the amount of depreciation on section 1250 property which is subject to recapture as ordinary income. However, gain to the extent of any unrecaptured depreciation on section 1250 property, is subject to the 25-percent capital gains rate if the gain is treated as capital gain under Code Sec. 1231. Gain in excess of unrecaptured section 1250 depreciation would be eligible for the lower 15-percent capital gains rate. See, also, ¶ 488.

*Sales or exchanges with related parties.* Any gain from the sale or exchange of depreciable property with certain related persons may be recaptured as ordinary income if the property is depreciable in the hands of the related transferee (Code Sec. 1239). This rule is not limited to MACRS property. See below.

*Depreciation subject to recapture*

Gain on the disposition of section 1245 property (¶ 116) is treated as ordinary income to the extent of previously allowed MACRS deductions. If property from a general asset account (¶ 128) is disposed of, the full amount of proceeds realized on the disposition is treated as ordinary income.

An expense deduction for property for which a Code Sec. 179 expense election was made is treated as depreciation for recapture purposes (Code Sec. 1245(a)). Thus, the entire amount expensed (not simply the amount expensed in excess of straight-line depreciation) is potentially subject to recapture. For the recapture of a Code Sec. 179 expense deduction where business use fails to exceed 50 percent, see ¶ 210 (listed property, such as cars and trucks) and ¶ 300. An expense deduction claimed on qualified real property is subject to ordinary income recapture under the rules that apply to section 1245 property (Code Sec. 1245(a)(3)(C)). See "*Recapture of certain deductions, including section 179 deduction, claimed on real property,*" below.

The amount of the investment credit downward basis adjustment is treated as a depreciation deduction for section 1245 recapture purposes and an accelerated depreciation deduction for section 1250 recapture purposes (Code Sec. 50(c)(4)).

Land improvements are generally section 1250 property; however in some instances a land improvement may be section 1245 property. See ¶ 110.

15-year qualified improvement property (¶ 110), 15-year qualified leasehold improvement property (¶ 126), 15-year restaurant property (¶ 110), and 15-year qualified retail improvement property (¶ 110) retain their status as section 1250 property even though they are assigned a 15-year MACRS recovery period. 15-year retail motor fuel outlets (¶ 110) are also section 1250 property.

MACRS residential rental property and nonresidential real property placed in service after 1986 must be depreciated under the straight-line MACRS method. Therefore, recapture of depreciation on such section 1250 property is not required, since no depreciation in excess of straight-line depreciation could have been claimed. However, as noted above, and also explained at ¶ 488, depreciation claimed on section 1250 property that is not recaptured as ordinary income may be subject to a 25 percent tax rate as section 1250 unrecaptured gain. Thus, in the case of MACRS real property, all depreciation claimed is potentially subject to tax at a 25 percent rate if the recognized gain is at least equal to the amount of depreciation claimed.

As noted above, gain on the sale or other disposition of depreciable realty subject to Code Sec. 1250 recapture is treated as ordinary income to the extent of the excess of depreciation claimed over straight-line depreciation and any remaining gain is treated as long-term capital gain under Code Sec. 1231. For corporations (but not S corporations), the amount treated as ordinary income on the sale or other disposition of Code Sec. 1250 property is increased by 20 percent of the additional amount that would be treated as ordinary income if the property were subject to recapture under the rules of Code Sec. 1245 property (Code Sec. 291(a)(1)). This rule does not apply to Code Sec. 1250 property that is part of a certified pollution control facility for which a rapid amortization election is made.

*Recapture of bonus depreciation*

Bonus depreciation (¶ 127D), including bonus depreciation claimed on New York Liberty Zone property (¶ 127E), Gulf Opportunity Zone property (¶ 127F), Kansas Disaster Area property (¶ 127G) and Disaster Assistance property (¶ 127H) is also subject to recapture under the section 1245 recapture rules when claimed on section 1245 property. If bonus depreciation is claimed on section 1250 property, it is treated as an accelerated depreciation deduction and is subject to recapture to the extent that it exceeds the straight-line depreciation that would have been allowed (Reg. § 1.168(k)-1(f)(3)).

*Recapture of certain deductions, including section 179 deduction, claimed on section 1250 property*

For recapture purposes, Code Sec. 1245(a)(3)(C) treats the portion of the basis of section 1250 property for which deductions have been claimed under past and present versions of Code Sec. 179 as section 1245 property. Thus, any section 179 deduction claimed on section 1250 property is recaptured as ordinary income to the extent that gain is allowable to the portion of the property expensed. This rule would apply to qualified real property described at ¶ 302 which has been expensed under section 179. Under present law, no other types of section 1250 property may be expensed under section 179. Notice 2013-59 explains the recapture rules that are applicable to qualified real property, including rules for allocating gain where only a portion of the qualified real property has been expensed. See ¶ 302. Code Sec. 1245(a)(3)(C) makes other types of deductions subject to the same rule. These are the deductions are under claimed under Code Sec. 169 (amortization of certified pollution control facilities), Code Sec. 179A (deduction for clean-fuel vehicles and certain refueling property), Code Sec. 179B (deduction to comply with EPA sulfur regulations), Code Sec. 179C (election to expense qualified liquid fuel refineries), Code Sec. 179D (efficient commercial buildings property deduction), Code Sec. 179E (expensing election for advanced mine safety equipment), Code Sec. 185 (amortization of railroad grading and tunnel bores), Code Sec. 188 (amortization of child care facilities) (as in effect before its repeal by the Revenue Reconciliation Act of 1990), Code Sec. 190 (deduction for cost of removing barriers to the handicapped and the elderly), Code Sec. 193 (deduction for certain tertiary injectants), and Code Sec. 194 (deductions for reforestation expenditures).

*De minimis safe harbor expensing recapture*

Amounts expensed under the de minimis safe harbor of Reg.§ 1.263(a)-1(f) are subject to recapture (Form 4797 Instructions). See ¶ 307 for discussion of de minimis safe harbor.

See ¶ 488 for depreciation recapture planning issues.

See ¶ 280 and ¶ 488 for ACRS recapture.

*Recapture of the Code Sec. 179A deduction*

Code Sec. 179A allows taxpayers to claim a current deduction for a specified amount of the cost of qualified clean-fuel vehicle property and qualified clean-fuel vehicle refueling property placed in service after June 30, 1993 and before January 1, 2006.

Separate recapture rules apply to each type of property. In computing the recapture amount, the deduction is only taken into account to the extent the taxpayer received a tax benefit (Reg. § 1.179A-1(d)). The recapture amount is added to the basis of the property.

Clean-fuel vehicle property is subject to recapture if, within three full years of the date the related vehicle is placed in service, the vehicle: (1) is modified so that it no longer runs on clean-burning fuel; (2) is used in a manner described in Code Sec. 50(b) (relating to predominant use outside the U.S., use by a tax-exempt organization, and use by governmental units or foreign persons or entities); or (3) otherwise ceases to meet the definitional requirements for qualified clean-fuel property (Reg. § 1.179A-1(b)(1)).

Refueling property is subject to recapture if, at any time before the end of the property's MACRS recovery period, the property: (1) ceases to meet the definitional requirements for qualified clean-fuel refueling property; (2) is not used at least 50 percent in the taxpayer's trade or business during the tax year; or (3) is used in a manner described in Code Sec. 50(b) (Reg. § 1.179A-1(b)(2)(i)).

Recapture also applies if a taxpayer sells clean fuel vehicle property or clean fuel vehicle refueling property knowing that the vehicle or property will be used in a manner that will trigger recapture. Otherwise a sale or disposition is not a recapture event.

In the case of clean-fuel vehicle property, 100 percent of the deduction that resulted in a tax benefit is recaptured if the date of the recapture event is within the first full year after the date that the vehicle was placed in service. The recapture percentage is 66⅔ percent if the recapture event occurs during the second full year of service and 33⅓ percent if the recapture event occurs during the third full year of service (Reg. § 1.179A-1(d)(1)).

The recapture amount in the case of refueling property is the amount of the allowable deduction that resulted in a tax benefit multiplied by the ratio of the remaining recovery period of the property to the total recovery period (Reg. § 1.179A-1(d)(2)).

A deduction claimed under Code Sec. 179A is treated as a depreciation deduction for purposes of the Code Sec. 1245 recapture rules if the underlying property is depreciable (Reg. § 1.179A-1(f)).

*Recapture of preproductive period plant cost deduction*

If a farmer elect under Code Sec. 263A(d)(3) to deduct preproductive period costs of certain plants instead of capitalizing them (see ¶ 150), the plants produced are treated as Code Sec. 1245 property even if they would not otherwise be so treated (Code Sec. 263A(e)(1)). Accordingly, any gain realized upon disposition is recaptured as ordinary income to the extent that the total amount of the deductions which, but for the election, would have been required to be capitalized. In calculating the amount of gain that is recaptured, either the farm-price or any other simplified method permitted under the UNICAP regs is used in determining the deductions that would otherwise have been capitalized (Reg. § 1.263A-4(d)(4)(i)).

*Dispositions of amortizable Sec. 197 intangibles*

An amortizable Sec. 197 intangible is treated as depreciable property for purposes of recapture (Code Sec. 197(f)(7)). Amortization deductions under Code Sec. 197 are recaptured as ordinary income under Code Sec. 1245 to the extent of gain upon the disposition of an amortizable Sec. 197 intangible.

If Sec. 197 intangibles are transferred in certain nonrecognition transfers, the transferee is treated as the transferor to the extent of the transferor's basis for purposes of determining subsequent Sec. 197 amortization deductions.

No loss is recognized upon the disposition (or worthlessness) of an amortizable Sec. 197 intangible acquired in a transaction if other amortizable Sec. 197 intangibles acquired in the transaction (or in a series of related transactions) are retained. Instead, the adjusted bases of the retained amortizable Sec. 197 intangibles are increased by the amount of the unrecognized loss.

A loss may be recognized on the disposition of a separately acquired Sec. 197 intangible.

A covenant not to compete may not be treated as disposed of or worthless prior to the disposition or determination of worthlessness of the entire interest in the trade or business for which the covenant not to compete was created.

Effective for dispositions after August 8, 2005, if more than one amortizable section 197 intangible is disposed of in a transaction or series of related transactions, all of the section 197 intangibles are treated as a single section 197 intangible for purposes of the depreciation recapture rules (Code Sec. 1245(b)(8)).

This rule does not apply to any section 197 intangible with an adjusted basis in excess of its fair market value (i.e., an intangible that will generate a loss deduction).

> ***Example (6):*** A taxpayer acquires two section 197 intangibles for $45,000. Asset A is assigned a cost basis of $15,000 and Asset B is assigned a cost basis of $30,000. The annual section 197 amortization deduction for Asset A is $1,000 ($15,000/15) and $3,000 for Asset B ($45,000/15). Assume the assets are sold three years later for $45,000. At the time of the sale the adjusted basis of Asset A is $12,000 ($15,000 - $3,000) and the adjusted basis of Asset B is $21,000 ($30,000 -$9,000). The total recapture potential is $12,000 ($3,000 + $9,000). Under prior law, the actual amount recaptured will depend upon how the $45,000 sales price is allocated between the two assets. For example, if $12,000 is allocated to Asset A and $33,000 is allocated to Asset B, no gain or loss is recognized on Asset A and $12,000 gain is recognized on Asset B. Only $9,000 of the gain is recaptured as ordinary income and the remaining $3,000 gain is section 1231 gain. Under the new law, $12,000 gain is recognized but all of that gain is recaptured as ordinary income.

## ¶ 162

## Gain or Loss on Sales, Exchanges, Abandonment, Retirement (Including Structural Components), Obsolescence, and Other Dispositions

*Dispositions*

MACRS disposition regulations apply to dispositions of MACRS property in item an multiple asset accounts and also to depreciable property that would be

MACRS property but for an election made by the taxpayer either to expense all or some of the property's cost under (Reg. § 1.168(i)-8(a)):

- Code Sec. 179 (general expensing provision)
- Code Sec. 179A (deduction for clean-fuel vehicles and certain refueling property)
- Code Sec. 179B (deduction to comply with EPA sulfur regulations)
- Code Sec. 179C (election to expense certain refineries)
- Code Sec. 179D (energy efficient commercial buildings deduction)
- any similar provision

The disposition regulations also apply to depreciable property that would be MACRS property but for an election made by the taxpayer amortize all or some of the property's cost under Code Sec. 1400I(a)(2) (commercial revitalization amortization deduction) or any similar provision (Reg. § 1.168(i)-8(a)).

*Disposition Defined*

A disposition of MACRS property occurs when ownership of the asset is transferred or when the asset is permanently withdrawn from use either in the taxpayer's trade or business or in the production of income. A disposition occurs when an asset is (Reg. § 1.168(i)-8(b)(2))

- sold
- exchanged
- retired
- physically abandoned
- destroyed
- transferred to a supplies, scrap, or similar account (however; see special rule for transfers of materials and supplies below)

The manner of disposition (for example, normal retirement, abnormal retirement, ordinary retirement, or extraordinary retirement) is not taken into account in determining whether a disposition occurs or gain or loss is recognized (Reg. § 1.168(i)-8(c)(1)).

Dispositions also include certain dispositions of a portion of an asset if a partial disposition election is made or dispositions of portions of assets in certain specified transactions such as a sale. See "*Partial Disposition Election*," below.

*Transfer of materials and supplies to supplies account.* Under final repair regulations, the election to treat materials and supplies as a depreciable capital expenditure is limited to rotable spare parts, temporary spare parts, and standby emergency parts (Reg. § 1.162-3(d)). The final disposition regulations provide that the transfer of such assets to a supplies account is a disposition only if the taxpayer has obtained the consent of the Commissioner to revoke the election (Reg. § 1.168(i)-8(c)(2).

*Dispositions of leasehold improvements.* A lessor that makes a leasehold improvement for the lessee, has a depreciable basis in the improvement, and disposes of the improvement before or upon the termination of the lease with the lessee is treated as having made a disposition upon which gain or loss is recognized. A similar rule applies to a lessee of leased property that makes an improvement to that property, has a depreciable basis in the improvement, and disposes of the improvement before or upon the termination of the lease. As in the case of other assets, a partial disposition election may be made to recognize gain or loss upon the retirement of a portion of a leasehold improvement. As in the case of other types of assets, certain types of dispositions of a portion of a leasehold improvement described in Reg. § 1.168(i)-8(d)(1) (e.g., a sale or casualty loss) trigger gain or loss without a partial disposition election (Reg. § 1.168(i)-8(c)(3)).

Code Sec. 168(i)(8)(B) provides that if a lessor of a building makes an improvement for a lessee and that improvement is irrevocably disposed of or abandoned by the lessor *at the termination* of the lease the lessor recognizes gain or loss upon the disposition or abandonment of the improvement. The same rule (although not based on a particular Code provision) has applied to a lessee who retires a leasehold improvement at the termination of a lease by vacating the premises. The regulations incorporate this current rule for leasehold improvements.

The regulations appear to expand Code Sec. 168(i)(8)(B) by treating a lessor's disposition of a leasehold improvement "before" as well as "upon" termination of the lease as a loss event although this change is more likely a clarification than a substantiative modification.

A lessor's retirement of a leasehold improvement after expiration of the lease (as opposed to before or upon termination of the lease) is also considered a loss event. Once the lease has expired the lessor is subject to the rule that is generally applicable to all taxpayers under the regulations, viz., an addition or improvement is a separate asset (Reg. § 1.168(i)-8(c)(4)(ii)(D)) and the retirement of a separate asset at any time is a disposition that generates a loss equal to the lessor's adjusted depreciable basis of the separate asset at the time of the retirement (assuming no amount is received for the retired asset).

Generally, an abandonment loss does not arise from a sale or exchange and therefore is not subject to the Code Sec. 267 limitations on related party losses. Therefore, absent special circumstances, a lessee should be entitled to deduct the cost of abandoned leasehold improvements even though the lessor is a related party. See *Standard Commodities Import and Export Corp.,* 44 TCM 513, Dec. 39,196(M), TC Memo. 1982-408.

See ¶ 126 for a detailed discussion of leasehold improvements.

*Determination of Asset Disposed of*

The facts and circumstances of each disposition are considered in determining what is the appropriate asset disposed of (Reg. § 1.168(i)-8(c)(4)(i)).

The definition of a unit of property is not taken into account in determining the asset disposed of. Likewise, the definition of a "distinct asset" for purposes of the like-kind exchange rules (see Reg. § 1.1031(a)-3(a)(4)) does not apply. In addition, an asset cannot be composed of items that were placed in service on different dates without taking into account the applicable MACRS depreciation convention (Reg. § 1.168(i)-8(c)(4)(i)).

*Determination of asset disposed of—special rules for buildings.* In general, each building (including its original structural components) is the asset disposed. However, more than one building may be treated as a single asset by reason of Reg. § 1.1250-1(a)(2)(ii) (for example, if two or more buildings or structures on a single tract or parcel (or contiguous tracts or parcels) of land are operated as an integrated unit (as evidenced by their actual operation, management, financing, and accounting), and are treated as a single item of section 1250 property for recapture purposes). See ¶ 114, "*Multiple buildings located on a single tract or varied use units within the same building.*" If a building includes two or more condominium or cooperative units, then each condominium or cooperative unit and its original structural components is the asset (Reg. § 1.168(i)-8(c)(4)(ii)(A) and (B)).

A taxpayer to make a "partial disposition election" to treat the retirement of an original structural component or portion of an original or replacement structural component as an asset disposed of (Reg. § 1.168(i)-8(d)). A structural component that is a replacement is a separately depreciated asset. The partial disposition election makes recognition of gain or loss on retirements of original structural components (or portions of original or replacement structural components) elective. No loss may be recognized on the retirement of an original structural component from a general asset account (GAA) (or a portion of a replacement structural component which was placed in a separate GAA), except in limited situations (Reg. § 1.168(i)-1(e)(1)(i), last sentence; Reg. § 1.168(i)-1(e)(1)(ii)).

***Example (1):*** A taxpayer owns an office building with four elevators. The elevators have not been replaced since the taxpayer placed the building in service. Therefore, the office building and the elevators are considered a single asset. The elevators are structural components of the building asset. The taxpayer replaces one of the elevators. The taxpayer does not recognize a loss and continues to depreciate the retired elevator unless a partial disposition election is made to treat the retirement of the elevator as a partial disposition of the building (Reg. § 1.168(i)-8(i), Ex. 1, 2, and 3).

The replacement elevator is a separate asset which is separately depreciated as 39-year real property. If it is replaced in the future, it is not necessary to make the partial disposition election to claim a retirement loss because the replacement elevator is a separate asset. Loss must be recognized upon its retirement since an entire asset has been disposed. However, the partial disposition election is necessary in order to recognize a loss if only a portion of the replacement elevator is replaced in the future. The election, however, is unfavorable if the taxpayer may claim a repair expense because the otherwise deductible repair expense must be capitalized if a loss is recognized (Reg. § 1.263(a)-3(k)(1)(i)).

*Determination of asset disposed of—special rules for commonly used assets and certain assets with specially assigned recovery period.* If a taxpayer properly includes an item in one of the asset classes 00.11 through 00.4 of Rev. Proc. 87-56 (1987-2 CB 674) (i.e., certain common assets, such as office equipment, computers, cars, trucks, noncommercial aircraft, and land improvements that are depreciable without regard to the business activity of the taxpayer) (see ¶ 191) or classifies an item in one of the categories under Code Sec. 168(e)(3) (other than a category that includes buildings or structural components; for example, retail motor fuels outlet, qualified leasehold, retail, or restaurant improvement property, and qualified improvement property), each item in the asset class or categorized under Code Sec. 168(e)(3) is the asset (Reg. § 1.168(i)-8(c)(4)(ii)(C)). For example, each item of office furniture is the asset, each computer is the asset, and each qualified smart electric meter (an item described in Code Sec. 168(e)(3)) is the asset.

Code Sec. 168(e)(3) lists specific types of assets that are subject to particular depreciation periods. They are:

- horses
- rent-to-own property
- automobile or light general purpose trucks,
- semi-conductor manufacturing equipment,
- computer-based telephone central office switching equipment,
- qualified technological equipment,
- section 1245 property used in connection with research and experimentation,

- certain types of energy producing property (e.g., solar and wind) specified in Code Sec. 168(e)(3)(B)(vi),
- railroad track,
- certain machinery and equipment used in a farming business and placed in service after 2017,
- motorsports entertainment complexes,
- Alaska natural gas pipelines,
- certain natural gas gathering lines
- single purpose agricultural or horticultural structures
- trees or vines bearing fruit or nuts,
- qualified smart electric meters
- qualified smart electric grid systems,
- municipal wastewater treatment plants,
- telephone distribution plants and comparable equipment used for 2-way exchange of voice and data communications,
- section 1245 property used in the transmission at 69 or more kilovolts of electricity for sale
- certain natural gas distribution lines
- water utility property
- railroad grading and tunnel bores

***Example (2):*** A company owns several trucks that are described in Asset Class 00.241 of Rev. Proc. 87-56. Since Asset Class 00.241 is one of the asset classes described in Asset Classes 00.11 through 00.4 of Rev. Proc. 87-56 each truck is a separate asset.

If the company replaces an original engine, the taxpayer is allowed to make a partial disposition election and claim a loss if it desires (Reg. § 1.168(i)-8(i), Example 6). If the replacement engine is a deductible repair expense, this election should not be made because a repair expense may not be claimed under the repair regulations if a loss deduction is claimed on a replaced component (Reg. § 1.263(a)-3(k)(1)(i)).

***Example (3):*** A commercial airline company, owns several aircraft that are used in the commercial carrying of passengers and described in Asset Class 45.0 of Rev. Proc. 87-56. The company chooses to treat the original aircraft engines as a separate asset. Note that a commercial aircraft is not an asset described in Asset Classes 00.11 through 00.4 of Rev. Proc. 87-56 or in Code Sec. 168(e)(3) which means that the company can adopt an accounting method which treats original components of the aircraft as separate assets. The company will recognize a loss upon the retirement of an original engine without making the partial disposition election. The partial disposition election does not apply because a portion of an asset is not disposed of. An entire asset is disposed. The new engine is capitalized and separately depreciated. The partial disposition election is also not needed to claim a retirement loss when a replacement engine is replaced because the replacement engine is also a separate asset (Reg. § 1.168(i)-8(i), Examples 4 and 5).

*Determination of asset disposed of—additions and improvements.* An improvement or addition to an asset after the taxpayer placed the asset in service (including the addition of a structural component of an asset) is a separate asset for depreciation purposes (Reg. § 1.168(i)-8(c)(4)(ii)(D)).

Since an addition or improvement is a separate asset, a loss must be recognized on the retirement of the addition or improvement. For example, if a roof is replaced and the replacement roof is considered an addition or improvement under this rule (i.e., a separate asset) the election for partial dispositions of assets (Reg.

§ 1.168-8(d) (1)) would not apply when the replacement roof is replaced because an entire asset has been disposed of. Instead, the retirement of the replacement roof would be a disposition of an asset on which loss is recognized. The partial disposition election, however, could apply to a portion of the replacement roof, such as its shingles if later replaced. However, if a loss is claimed on the shingles the cost of replacing the shingles may not be deducted as a repair expense (Reg.§ 1.263(a)-3(k) (1) (ii)).

*Partial Disposition Election*

> ***Comment:*** *IRS LB&I issues process (practice) unit on partial disposition losses (10/29/19).* A 64 page document issued by the IRS Large Business and International (LB&I) division concentrates on five steps involved in examining a taxpayer who has elected to claim a loss on a partial disposition of a building or its structural components. This process unit is designed to assist IRS examiners in verifying a taxpayer's compliance with the Code Sec. 168 disposition regulations. See IRS LB&I issues process (practice) unit "Examining a Taxpayer Electing a Partial Disposition of a Building," https://www.irs.gov/pub/irs-utl/dce_p_252_04_03.pdf.

A disposition of a portion of an asset depreciated under MACRS is treated as a disposition on which gain or loss is recognized only if the partial disposition election is made, except that the following dispositions of a portion of an asset must be treated as a disposition with gain or loss being recognized under the applicable Code provision (no election is required or allowed for these dispositions) (Reg. § 1.168(i)-8(d) (1)):

- a sale of a portion of an asset
- a disposition of a portion of an asset as the result of a casualty event described in Code Sec. 165
- a disposition of a portion of an asset for which gain (determined without regard to recapture under Code Sec. 1245 or Code Sec. 1250) is not recognized in whole or in part in a like kind exchange (Code Sec. 1031) or involuntary conversion (Code Sec. 1033)
- a transfer of a portion of an asset in step-in-the-shoes nonrecognition transactions described in Code Sec. 168(i) (7) (B) (¶ 144)

The partial disposition election may be made with respect to the disposed portion of any asset. The asset, however, must be depreciable under MACRS. The partial disposition election does not apply to a fully depreciated asset. If the modifications to a building arise to the level of a demolition under Code Sec. 280B, the partial disposition election does not apply.

A building (or any asset) not placed in service is not a MACRS asset and the disposition regulations are not applicable to non-MACRS assets. Therefore, a partial disposition cannot occur before a building or other asset is placed in service (IRS LB&I issues process (practice) unit "Examining a Taxpayer Electing a Partial Disposition of a Building," https://www.irs.gov/pub/irs-utl/dce_p_252_04_03.pdf).

> ***Example (4):*** A taxpayer acquires a restaurant building on Date 1. The taxpayer remodels the building before placing it in service on Date 2 and begins using it for its intended purpose as a restaurant. The building is not MACRS property until it is placed in service. The disposition regulations do not apply to any structural components disposed of before this building is placed in service (IRS LB&I issues process (practice) unit "Examining a Taxpayer Electing a Partial Disposition of a Building," page 17).

An "improvement" to an existing building or structural component may involve the replacement of a portion of the building or structural component for which a partial disposition election may be made. An "addition" to an existing building or structural component will generally not result in a partial disposition. However, there may be circumstances when an addition would involve the disposition and replacement of a structural component of a building. For example, a taxpayer may replace the entire Heating, Ventilation, Air Conditioning (HVAC) system to accommodate a new building addition rather than just adding to the existing HVAC system (IRS LB&I issues process (practice) unit "Examining a Taxpayer Electing a Partial Disposition of a Building," https://www.irs.gov/pub/irs-utl/dce_p_252_04_03.pdf).

A taxpayer must have a depreciable interest in the portion of the asset disposed. For example, a lessee cannot make a partial disposition election if it pays for the replacement of an old HVAC system which is owned and depreciated by the lessor. If the lessee has to replace or restore a portion of the HVAC years later, then the lessee can make a partial disposition election with respect to the replaced portion of the HVAC system, provided the replacement/restoration is capitalized.

If a taxpayer makes the election with respect to an asset described in MACRS asset classes 00.11 through 00.4 of Rev. Proc. 87-56 (i.e., certain types of assets used across all businesses and industries, such as cars, trucks, office furniture and equipment, and computers), the disposition election may be made only be made if the replaced portion of the asset is in the same asset class as the replaced asset and, therefore, has the same recovery period as the disposed asset (Reg. § 1.168(i)-8(d)(2)(i)). Because this rule only applies to MACRS asset classes 00.11 through 00.4, it would not apply to the replacement of the 39-year structural components on a commercial building with 15-year qualified improvement property.

*Limitations on partial disposition election related to remodel-refresh safe harbor.* A qualified taxpayer engaged in the trade or business of operating a retail establishment or a restaurant may adopt a safe harbor method of accounting under which 25 percent of qualified remodel/refresh costs are treated as capital expenditures under Code Sec. 263(a) and the uniform capitalization rules of Code Sec. 263A and 75 percent of such costs are currently deductible (Rev. Proc. 2015-56, effective for tax years beginning on or after January 1, 2014; Sec. 11.10 of Rev. Proc. 2019-43). This safe harbor may only be used by taxpayers with an applicable financial statement (AFS) as defined in Reg.§ 1.263(a)-1(f). In order to apply the safe harbor, the building and capitalized improvements must be placed in separate MACRS general asset accounts. A late election to place the building in a GAA may be made in the tax year that the safe harbor is first used as part of the safe harbor accounting method change. Improvements that are depreciable under MACRS and made prior to the year that the safe harbor is first used generally must also be placed in a GAA by making a late election if the safe harbor applies to those improvements. A taxpayer may not make a partial disposition election (¶ 162) to claim retirement losses on building components once this safe harbor is used. The safe harbor is applied on a cut-off basis unless the taxpayer revokes any prior year partial disposition elections on an amended return filed within the limitations period for the tax year for which the election was made or files an accounting method change to revoke any partial disposition elections that were made in prior tax years. The method change to revoke prior partial disposition elections is only allowed for a tax year beginning after December 31, 2013, and ending before December 31, 2016 (Rev. Proc. 2017-30, Sec. 6.18(3)) (see ¶ 77 for a description of this accounting method change). Taxpayers who applied Temporary Reg.§ 1.168(i)-8T (¶ 162) (or the GAA rules under Temporary Reg.§ 1.168(i)-1T (¶ 128)) in a tax year beginning before January 1, 2014 to claim losses on building components may not use the safe harbor until a method change is filed to comply with the final regulations (Sec. 6.13 of Rev. Proc. 2019-43 for a change under Reg.§ 1.168(i)-8 or Sec. 6.15 of Rev. Proc.

2019-43 for a change under Reg.§ 1.168(i)-1). The Code Sec. 481(a) adjustment related to the losses previously claimed under the temporary regulations or partial disposition losses under the final regulations is included in income in a single tax year (i.e., the year of change).

*Partial disposition election procedure.* The partial disposition election must be made by the due date (including extensions) of the original Federal tax return for the tax year in which the portion of the asset is disposed of. No formal election statement is required. The taxpayer simply reports the gain or loss on the disposed portion of the asset on the return. The replacement part for an asset in MACRS asset classes 00.11 through 00.4 must be classified in the same asset class as the asset of which the replacement part is a component. MACRS depreciation must be computed based on this classification beginning in the tax year the replacement part is placed in service (Reg. § 1.168(i)-8(d)(2)(ii)). No special election statement or form needs is attached to the return.

The election may only be revoked with IRS consent obtained by filing a letter ruling request (Reg. § 1.168(i)-8(d)(2)(v)).

*Late partial disposition election for disposition in tax years beginning before January 1, 2012 on Form 3115.* Taxpayers were allowed to make a late partial disposition election for partial dispositions of MACRS property that took placed in tax years beginning before January 1, 2012 by filing an accounting method change (Sec. 6.10 of Rev. Proc. 2016-29; Sec. 6.33 of Rev. Proc. 2015-14) no later than for the taxpayer's last tax year beginning in 2014. The retroactive election for post-May 4, 2016 filings is discussed at ¶ 77.

*Late partial disposition election allowed for dispositions in 2012 and 2013 tax year on amended returns or Form 3115.* A taxpayer was allowed to make a late partial disposition election for tax years beginning on or after January 1, 2012 and ending on or before September 19, 2013 on an amended return filing on or before 180 days from the due date of the return (including extensions even if no extension was filed for). Alternatively the taxpayer could make the election by filing an application for an accounting method change (Form 3115) with a timely filed original return for the first or second tax year succeeding the applicable tax year (Reg. § 1.168(i)-8(d)(2)(iv); Proposed Reg. § 1.168(i)-8(d)(2)(iv)). Sec. 6.10 of Rev. Proc. 2016-29 provided applicable filing procedures for post-May 4, 2016 filings. See ¶ 77.

*Late partial disposition election based on adverse audit result.* If the IRS audits a taxpayer and determines that an amount previously claimed as a repair deduction should have been capitalized, the final and proposed regulations allow the taxpayer to make a retroactive partial disposition election by filing an application for a change in accounting method and claim a loss on the portion of the asset that was disposed of. The taxpayer, however, must own the asset as of the beginning of the tax year of change (Reg. § 1.168(i)-8(d)(2)(iii)).

This accounting method change procedure is currently provided in Appendix Sec. 6.10 of Rev. Proc. 2019-43. See ¶ 77.

### *Computing Gain or Loss on Disposition*

The final MACRS regulations provide rules for determining gain or loss upon the disposition of MACRS property.

*Disposition by sale, exchange, or involuntary conversion.* If an asset is disposed of by sale, exchange, or involuntary conversion, gain or loss must be recognized under the applicable provisions of the Internal Revenue Code (Reg. § 1.168(i)-8(e)(1)).

*Disposition by physical abandonment.* If an asset is disposed of by physical abandonment, loss must be recognized in the amount of the adjusted depreciable basis (as defined in Reg. § 1.168(b)-1(a)(4)) of the asset at the time of the abandonment (taking into account the applicable convention). However, if the abandoned asset is subject to nonrecourse indebtedness, the rule above for determining gain on a disposition by sale, exchange, or involuntary conversion applies. An asset is not abandoned unless the taxpayer discards the asset irrevocably so that the taxpayer will neither use the asset again nor retrieve it for sale, exchange, or other disposition (Reg. § 1.168(i)-8(e)(2)). For example, loss was recognized when a taxpayer abandoned (i.e., junked) used racing car components that were separately depreciable assets (IRS Letter Ruling 201710006, December 9, 2016).

Abandonment losses are ordinary losses and not capital losses since there has been no sale or exchange of a capital asset (Code Sec. 1221). Similarly, a loss from the abandonment of a section 1231 property is not a section 1231 loss because there has been no sale or exchange (Code Sec. 1231(a)(3)(A)). The same rule should apply to retirement losses, including losses arising by making a partial disposition election.

An abandonment loss is claimed as an ordinary loss on line 10 Part II of Form 4797 (Form 4797 Instructions).

*Disposition by conversion to personal use.* If an asset is disposed of by conversion to personal use, no gain or loss is recognized (Reg. § 1.168(i)-4(c)).

The conversion of MACRS property from business or income-producing use to personal use during a tax year is treated as a disposition of the property in that tax year. However, upon the conversion to personal use, no gain, loss, or depreciation recapture under Code Sec. 1245 or Code Sec. 1250 is recognized. These recapture provisions apply to any disposition of the converted property by the taxpayer at a later date. The conversion of a listed property, such as a car (Code Sec. 280F(d)(4)), to personal use may trigger depreciation recapture.

*Other types of dispositions, including transfers to supply, scrap, or similar account.* If an asset is disposed of other than by sale, exchange, involuntary conversion, physical abandonment, or conversion to personal use (for example, the transfer of an asset to a supplies or scrap account), gain is not recognized. Loss is recognized in the amount of the excess of the adjusted depreciable basis of the asset at the time of the disposition (taking into account the applicable convention) over the asset's fair market value at the time of the disposition (taking into account the applicable convention) (Reg. § 1.168(i)-8(e)(3)).

For example, where components of race cars which were treated as separate assets were transferred to a supplies or scrap account loss (if any) was recognized in an amount equal to the difference between the excess of adjusted depreciable basis at the time of transfer (taking into account the applicable MACRS depreciation convention) and the fair market value at the time of transfer, taking into account the applicable convention, whether or not the components would be reused to build another race car. (IRS Letter Ruling 201710006, December 9, 2016). Any gain was not recognized. If gain was not recognized, the basis of a component upon transfer to the supplied or scrap account was its adjusted depreciable basis at the time of transfer. If loss was recognized, the basis of the component was its fair market value at the time of transfer.

*Identification of Asset Disposed of*

A taxpayer must use the specific identification method of accounting to identify which asset is disposed of. Under this method of accounting, the taxpayer can determine the particular tax year in which the asset disposed of was placed in service by the taxpayer (Reg. § 1.168(i)-8(g)(1)). Special rules apply to assets in a multiple asset account or pool if a taxpayer cannot identify the tax year in which the disposed asset was placed in service. See *Disposition of Assets in Multiple Account or Pool* below.

Depreciation ends for an asset at the time of the asset's disposition, as determined under the applicable depreciation convention for the asset. If the asset is in a single asset account, the single asset account terminates at the time of the asset's disposition (Reg. § 1.168(i)-8(h)(1)).

If a taxpayer disposes of a portion of an asset and the taxpayer made the partial disposition election with respect to that portion or the taxpayer disposes of a portion of an asset in a transaction considered a disposition under Reg. § 1.168(i)-8(h)(1) because it is a sale, a disposition as the result of a casualty event, an involuntary conversion or like-kind exchange, or a Code Sec. 168(i)(7)(B) nonrecognition transaction, the specific identification method also applies. The alternative simplified methods applicable to a multiple asset account or pool (discussed below) also apply if it is impracticable to determine the tax year in which the portion of a disposed of asset in a single asset account was placed in service (Reg. § 1.168(i)-8(g)(3)). Depreciation ends for the disposed of portion of the asset at the time of disposition of the disposed of portion, determined using the applicable depreciation convention for the asset (Reg. § 1.168(i)-8(h)(1)).

The term "impracticable" should be considered in light of the taxpayer's existing responsibility to maintain its records as set forth in Reg.§ 1.167(a)-7(c). In other words, the taxpayer cannot use the simplified methods provided in the regulations if the taxpayer lacks the records required under Reg.§ 1.167(a)-7(c). Merriam-Webster Dictionary defines impracticable as "incapable of being performed or accomplished by the means employed or at command (IRS LB&I issues process (practice) unit "Examining a Taxpayer Electing a Partial Disposition of a Building," https://www.irs.gov/pub/irs-utl/dce_p_252_04_03.pdf).

The following simplified methods (discussed below) are available:

(1) A first-in, first-out (FIFO) method of accounting if the unadjusted depreciable basis of the asset disposed of *cannot* be readily determined from the taxpayer's records.

(2) A modified first-in, first-out method of accounting if the unadjusted depreciable basis of the asset disposed of *can* be readily determined from the taxpayer's records.

(3) A mortality dispersion table if the asset disposed of is a mass asset.

(4) Any other method designated by the IRS.

The simplified methods are not used to identify the disposed portion of an asset, including a building or its structural components. The simplified methods are used to identify which asset was partially disposed of (IRS LB&I issues process (practice) unit "Examining a Taxpayer Electing a Partial Disposition of a Building," https://www.irs.gov/pub/irs-utl/dce_p_252_04_03.pdf).

***Example (5):*** Taxpayer owns a retail building. Taxpayer's tax depreciation schedules show a fixed asset line item labeled "Store Remodel" on 7/1/2021, as a new capitalized improvement. Taxpayer states that the remodeling project involved the removal and capitalized replacement of all the doors and windows in the building. However, taxpayer has no documentation such as work orders, etc., to show that any doors or windows were removed. The taxpayer cannot use any of the simplified methods to assume that the 7/1/2021 store remodel resulted in any disposition of doors and windows, even if the retail building and its improvements can be identified in the tax depreciation schedules. The taxpayer must substantiate the identity of any portion of the building that was disposed of in the remodel project in its books and records. Since the taxpayer cannot identify the doors and windows disposed of in their books and records, the taxpayer has not substantiated that a partial disposition occurred and cannot recognize a partial disposition (IRS LB&I issues process (practice) unit "Examining a Taxpayer Electing a Partial Disposition of a Building," https://www.irs.gov/pub/irs-utl/dce_p_252_04_03.pdf).

***Example (6):*** A taxpayer has replaced various sections of a building's original roof over multiple years. The taxpayer accounted for the original building, including its roof, as a separate asset and has been capitalizing the partial roof replacements over the years as separate assets in their own single asset accounts. When applying the disposition regulations to the replacement of a portion of the roof in 2021, it may be impracticable to specifically determine which assets contained the section of roof being disposed of because each section replaced is a separate asset and the building, and remaining original portion of the roof, is a separate asset. So, the taxpayer may use one of the simplified methods to identify the asset partially disposed of in 2021. For example, the taxpayer can use the FIFO method to identify the original building asset as the partially-disposed asset (IRS LB&I issues process (practice) unit "Examining a Taxpayer Electing a Partial Disposition of a Building," https://www.irs.gov/pub/irs-utl/dce_p_252_04_03.pdf). See example below.

***Example (7):*** D replaces 60% of the original roof of a retail building (39-year MACRS nonresidential real property subject to the mid-month convention). The retail building, including its original roof and other original structural components, is the asset for disposition purposes. Assume the expenditures must be capitalized. D may make the partial disposition election for 60% of the replaced roof. 60% of the roof ceases to be depreciated at the time of its retirement, taking into account the mid-month convention, and D recognizes a loss upon this retirement. The replacement 60% of the roof is a separate asset for disposition purposes and is separately depreciated under MACRS as a new asset.

Ten years after replacing 60% of the roof, D replaces 55% of the roof and capitalizes the costs. For disposition purposes, the retail building, including the remaining 40 percent portion of the original roof and other original structural components is a separate asset. Assume D makes the partial disposition election for the 55% of the replaced roof. However, D cannot determine from its records whether the replaced 55% is part of the 60% of the roof replaced ten years ago or whether the replaced 55% includes part or all of the remaining 40% of the original roof. D may identify the portion of the roof disposed of by using the first-in, first-out method of accounting. Under the FIFO method, D disposed of the remaining 40% of the original roof and 25% of the 60% of the roof replaced ten years ago (40% + (60 x 25%) = 55%)).

Thus, depreciation for the remaining 40% of the original roof ceases at the time of its retirement, taking into account the applicable mid-month convention, and D recognizes a loss upon this retirement. Further, depreciation for 25% of the 60% of the roof replaced ten years ago ceases at the time of its retirement, taking into account the applicable convention, and D recognizes a loss upon this retirement. The replacement 55% of the roof is a separate asset for disposition and depreciation purposes (Reg. § 1.168(i)-8(i), Examples 7 and 8).

***Example (8):*** Same facts as preceding example, but the building is pre-MACRS property because it was placed in service before 1986. The partial disposition election may not be made when the taxpayer replaced 60 percent of the roof because the original roof was not MACRS property. When the taxpayer replaces 55 percent of the roof ten years later, using the FIFO method, the taxpayer may not make a partial disposition election for the remaining 40 percent of the pre-MACRS roof but may make the election for the 25% of the 60 percent of the roof replaced ten years ago which has been depreciated under MACRS as a separate asset (IRS LB&I issues process (practice) unit "Examining a Taxpayer Electing a Partial Disposition of a Building,", p. 40 Example 2, https://www.irs.gov/pub/irs-utl/dce_p_252_04_03.pdf).

*Zero basis assets.* If a partially-disposed building or structural component is identified as an asset with zero adjusted basis remaining at the time of disposition, the simplified methods may not be used to identify another asset having adjusted basis remaining as the partially disposed asset (IRS LB&I issues process (practice) unit "Examining a Taxpayer Electing a Partial Disposition of a Building," https://www.irs.gov/pub/irs-utl/dce_p_252_04_03.pdf).

> ***Example (9):*** A taxpayer replaces a portion of a roof on a fully depreciated building which includes a portion of the roof treated as a separate asset that is not fully depreciated. The taxpayer cannot use the FIFO method to identify another roof replacement, or any other asset on the building in its books and records that has basis remaining at the beginning of the year of disposition as being partially disposed of (IRS LB&I issues process (practice) unit "Examining a Taxpayer Electing a Partial Disposition of a Building," https://www.irs.gov/pub/irs-utl/dce_p_252_04_03.pdf).

A change in accounting method from an impermissible to permissible identification method is governed by Sec. 6.13 (buildings) and Sec. 6.14 (section 1245 property and land improvements) of Rev. Proc. 2019-43. A change from a permissible to permissible identification method is governed by Sec. 6.12 for both buildings and section 1245 property. See ¶ 77.

*Adjusted Depreciable Basis of Asset Disposed of for Computing Gain or Loss*

The adjusted basis of an asset disposed of for computing gain or loss is its adjusted depreciable basis at the time of the asset's disposition (as determined under the applicable convention for the asset) (Reg. § 1.168(i)-8(f)(1)). Special rules below apply to assets disposed of in a multiple asset or pool account.

*Adjusted basis—partial dispositions under final regulations.* If a taxpayer makes the partial disposition election or the transaction is otherwise considered a disposition under Reg. § 1.168(i)-8(d)(1) because it is a sale, a disposition as the result of a casualty event, an involuntary conversion or like-kind exchange, or a Code Sec. 168(i)(7)(B) nonrecognition transactions the adjusted basis of the disposed of portion of the asset for computing gain or loss is its adjusted depreciable basis at the time of disposition, applying the applicable depreciation convention. If it is impracticable to determine the unadjusted depreciable basis from the taxpayer's records, any reasonable method may be used to determine the unadjusted depreciable basis of the disposed of portion, including the following (Reg. § 1.168(i)-8(f)(3)):

- discounting the cost of the replacement portion of the asset to its placed placed-in-service year cost using the Producer Price Index for Final Demand, or its predecessor used before 2016, the Producer Price Index for Finished Goods;

- a pro rata allocation of the unadjusted depreciable basis of the asset based on the replacement cost of the disposed portion of the asset and the replacement cost of the asset; or

- a cost segregation study allocating the cost of the asset to its individual components.

The IRS has ruled that a taxpayer making a late partial disposition election incorrectly applied a statistical sampling technique to determine losses on pre-2012 partial dispositions (Field Attorney Advice 20154601F, November 13, 2015).

*Indexed discounting using the producer price index.* Under the final regulations, indexed discounting may not be used unless the replacement portion is a capitalized restoration (as defined in Reg. § 1.263(a)-3(k) and is not a betterment Reg. § 1.263(a)-3(j) or adaptation (Reg. § 1.263(a)-3(l)). This limitation did not apply under the proposed regulations. Also, under the proposed regulations, indexed discounting was based on the Consumer Price Index. The final regulations replace the Consumer Price Index with the Producer Price Index because the latter results in a more accurate determination of basis (Preamble to T.D. 9689). Rev. Proc. 2019-43 (providing automatic accounting method changes) specifically characterizes the CPI rollback method as unreasonable. Taxpayers who used the consumer price index to compute unadjusted basis are required to make recomputations of the retirement loss using the producer price index (assuming the replacement is not a betterment or restoration) or some other reasonable method. This requires the filing of an accounting method change. See below.

As mentioned above, discounting the cost of the replacement portion of the asset to its placed placed-in-service year cost may be done using the Producer Price Index for Finished Goods or its successor the Producer Price Index for Final Demand. The PPI for Finished Goods has inflation adjustment factors from January 1970 through December 2015. The Producer Price Index for Final Demand has inflation adjusted figures beginning with November 2009. Therefore, where a structural component that was placed in service before November 2009 is retired in 2016 or later it is necessary to use the Producer Price Index for Finished Goods to compute a rollback cost measured from the original acquisition date through December 2015. This rollback cost is then adjusted using the Producer Price Index for Final Demand from January 2016 through the month of retirement. See Example 10, below.

The regulations also clarify that reasonable methods may only be used if it is impracticable to determine basis using the taxpayer's records.

The reasonable method used must be consistently applied to all portions of the same asset for purposes of determining the unadjusted depreciable basis of each disposed portion of the asset (Reg. § 1.168(i)-8(f)(3)). The regulations apply a similar consistency requirement when a portion of an asset in a multiple asset account is disposed (Reg. § 1.168(i)-8(f)(3)).

For purposes of computing the adjusted depreciable basis on the disposed of portion, the depreciation allowed or allowable is computed using the same method, recovery period, and convention that apply to the asset of which the disposed of portion is a part. The basis of the disposed of asset should also be reduced by an allocable share of any bonus depreciation (Reg. § 1.168(i)-8(f)(3)).

A change from an impermissible method of computing unadjusted depreciable basis (e.g., CPI rollback method) to a permissible method (e.g., PPI rollback method) is made by filing an accounting method change under Sec. 6.13 (buildings) or Sec. 6.14 (section 1245 property and land improvements) of Rev. Proc. 2019-43. Permissible to permissible method changes of computation require accounting method changes filed under Sec. 6.12 of Rev. Proc. 2019-43 for buildings and section 1245 property. See ¶ 77.

***The Producer Price Index for Finished Goods and Producer Price Index for Final Demand can be found at the following website: http://data.bls.gov/cgi-bin/surveymost?wp.***

The following example illustrates the rollback computation using the PPI for Finished Goods, Series ID WPUSOP3000 to compute the rollback cost through December 2015 (the last month this PPI is available) and the PPI for Final Demand, Series WPUFD4 for January 2016 through March 2020, if an original roof is retired in March 2020. A combination of the PPI for Finished Goods and the PPI for Final Demand is necessary because the PPI for Finished Goods was discontinued after

2015 and its successor, the PPI for Final Demand, has no data for the 2001 tax year in which the original roof was placed in service.

***Example (10):*** ABC, a calendar-year taxpayer, placed new 39-year real property with a basis of $1 million in service in September 2001 and replaced the roof in March 2020 at a cost of $100,000. ABC makes the partial disposition election. ABC cannot determine with practicality the original cost of the roof using its records. Since the roof was retired after December 2015 and the PPI for Finished Goods contains no adjustment figures for months after December 2015, the taxpayer will need to compute a rollback cost using the PPI for Finished Goods through December 2015 and then compute an additional adjustment for January 2016 through March 2020 using the PPI index for Final Demand. It is not correct to use an inflation adjustment figure from each index to compute a single rollback cost (eg., use the September 2001 PPI for Finished Goods for the year of acquisition and the March 2020 for PPI for Final Demand for the year of sale in the same calculation).

Using the PPI rollback method, the original basis of the old roof is computed as follows:

September 2001 PPI for Finished Goods: 141.6

December 2015 PPI for Finished Goods: 190.1

Original basis of old roof as of December 2015: $100,000 × 141.6/190.1 = $74,487

January 2016 PPI for Final Demand: 109.7

March 2020 PPI for Final Demand: 118.1

Original basis of old roof as of close of March 2020 used for computing retirement loss: $69,189 ($74,487 × 109.7/118.1).

If a partial disposition election is made, ABC may claim a deduction equal to the difference between the $69,189 cost of the roof and the depreciation that was claimed on the roof from September 2001 through March 2020. Taking into account the mid-month convention the roof was in service for 18 years and 6 months (2002 – 2019 = 18 full years, 3 1/2 months from mid-September 2001 through December 2001 (.292 years), and 2 1/2 months from January 2020 through mid-March 2020 (.208 years). Depreciation using the straight-line method and 39 year recovery period is $32,820 ($69,189/39 × 18.5 years). The retirement loss deduction is $36,369 ($69,189 – $32,820).

Note that in order to claim a retirement loss in this example, the partial disposition election must be made because this is an original roof which is part of the building asset. However, if this were a separately depreciated replacement roof, the replacement roof is a separate asset and the retirement loss is claimed without making the election.

The regulations do not define "cost" for purposes of computing the retirement loss using the PPI but given that there were no removal costs in connection with the cost of the original roof (only capitalized installation costs), the cost of the new roof for purposes of determining the cost of the old roof under the PPI method should logically exclude removal costs. Removal costs may be currently deducted if a partial disposition election is made (Reg.§ 1.263(a)-3(g)(2)) and do not need to be included in the basis of the new roof. See ¶ 70. Even if a taxpayer decides to include the removal costs in the basis of the new roof, however, they should be excluded for purposes of determining the cost of the old original roof under the PPI method. Assume in this example that the $100,000 replacement cost does not include removal costs. The new roof is capitalized as a restoration both because a loss is claimed on the retired roof and because a roof is major component of a building (Reg. § 1.263(a)-3(k)(1)). See ¶ 125.

***Example (11):*** *Depreciation computations after partial disposition election for current year disposition.* Assume the same facts as in the preceding example.

With respect to the 2020 depreciation deduction claimed on the building and original roof, the regulations require that the disposed of asset be placed in a separate account as of the first day of the tax year of disposition and that the unadjusted depreciable basis of the building be reduced by the unadjusted depreciable basis of the original roof (i.e., original cost determined using the PPI or other reasonable method). Thus, as of the beginning of the 2020 tax year the building and the original roof are in separate accounts and separately depreciated (Reg. § 1.168(i)-8(h)(3)).

*Depreciation on building prior to 2020 is computed as follows:*

*2001: $1,000,000/39 × .292 years . . . . . . . . . . . . . . . $ 7,487*

*2002 – 2019: $1,000,000/39 × 18 years . . . . . . . . . . . . $461,538*

*Total . . . . . . . . . . . . . . . . . . . . . . . . . . . . . . . . . . . $469,025*

In 2020, depreciation is allowed on the original roof for the period it was in service in 2020 prior to the disposition taking into account the mid-month convention. Therefore, the depreciation deduction is allowed for January through mid-March or .208 years (2.5 months/12).

2020 depreciation on the original roof is $369 ($69,189/39 ×.208 years).

Beginning in 2020 depreciation on the building (excluding the original roof) must be computed on the building's unadjusted depreciable basis as of the beginning of 2020. The unadjusted depreciable basis of the building as of the beginning of 2020 is equal to $930,811 ($1,000,000 original cost less $69,189 unadjusted depreciable basis of the roof, as determined using the PPI rollback method).

*Total depreciation for tax years 20 – 39 (20 tax years, 2020 – 2039):*

*$930,811/39 ×20= $477,339*

*Depreciation in final tax year in recovery period (2041):*

*$930,811/39 × .708 = $16,898*

The building is considered in service for 8.5 months (.708 years) in 2041 (January through mid-September).

*Total depreciation:*

*$477,339 + $16,898 = $494,237*

As expected the sum of (1) the depreciation claimed on the building (including original roof) prior to the 2020 disposition year ($469,025), (2) the depreciation claimed on the original roof in the 2020 disposition year ($369), (3) the retirement loss on the original roof ($36,369), (4) and the depreciation claimed on the building beginning in the 2020 disposition year through the end of the recovery period ($494,237) is equal to the $1,000,000 original cost of the building.

The new roof is depreciated separately as 39-year real property beginning in March 2020 and the removal costs may be deducted or included in the basis of the new roof (¶ 70).

The computations in the preceding examples could also have been made using table percentages for 39-year property.

*Potential problems with PPI method*

The IRS regulations allow the use of any reasonable method to determine the unadjusted depreciable basis of a disposed asset or portion of a disposed asset where it is impracticable to determine that information from the taxpayer's own records. Further, the regulations state that discounting the cost of the replacement asset or portion of the asset to its placed-in-service year cost using the Producer Price Index for Finished Goods or its successor, the Producer Price Index for Final Demand is a reasonable method but may not be used if the cost of the replacement component is capitalized as a betterment or adaptation (Reg. § 1.168(i)-8(f)(3)). This restriction is necessary because a betterment or adaptation generally involves replacing an existing asset or portion of the asset with a dissimilar and more expensive asset which offers an unfair price comparison to the replaced component. The sole example employing the method shows no calculations (Reg. § 1.168(i)-8(i), Example 9). The regulations provide no further guidance.

Presumably, the producer price index rollback method cannot be used if it produces an unreasonable result.

The producer price index rollback method can produce unreasonable results where a taxpayer has purchased an existing building with particular components near the end of their economic life. The PPI rollback method, without further adjustment, will overstate the retirement loss upon the retirement of such a component. Consider the following example.

> ***Example (12):*** A taxpayer buys a used building in 2014 for $1 million. The taxpayer replaces the roof for $200,000 in 2021 (excluding removal costs for the reasons stated in the example above). Assume the replacement roof is not considered a betterment (e.g., an expenditure that ameliorates a material condition or defect that existed prior to the taxpayer's acquisition (Reg. § 1.263(a)-3(j)(1)(i)) that precludes use of the PPI rollback method. Applying the PPI rollback method assume that the original roof is valued at $190,000. The $190,000 figure, however, actually reflects the value of a new roof in 2014; the roof, however, was nearing the end of its economic life. Consequently, a retirement loss based on a $190,000 unadjusted depreciable basis appears unreasonable in this circumstance. However, it may be reasonable to make the rollback computation based on the PPI for the year in which the building was originally placed in service (i.e., the year the replaced roof was originally placed in service).

Alternatively, a taxpayer may apply an additional discount factor that takes into account the actual economic life of the retired component. For example, if a roof has an expected economic life of 20 years and the roof in the prior example was 16 years old when purchased then the value of the replaced roof at the time it was acquired by the taxpayer using the PPI rollback method should be adjusted to reflect its remaining economic useful life. In the preceding example, one straightforward approach would be to limit to value of the roof to 20% (4 years remaining/20 years total) of the initial rollback calculation.

The following example is from the IRS LB&I issues process (practice) unit on partial disposition losses (https://www.irs.gov/pub/irs-utl/dce_p_252_04_03.pdf).

> ***Example (13):*** Taxpayer purchases a building on 1/1/2016, that has been in service for 15 years and has a roof that is original to the building. Ten years later, 1/1/2026, the taxpayer replaces the entire roof and identifies the building as the partially-disposed asset. Discounting the cost of the replacement roof to the building's placed in service date (1/1/2016) overstates the unadjusted basis of the replaced roof because it was not new when the building was placed in service. The taxpayer should reduce the discounted amount to take into account the age and condition of the roof when the building was placed in service (1/1/2016).

There are various sources for determining the useful life of building components and land improvements. These include:

- American Society of Heating, Refrigerating, and Air-Conditioning Engineers
- Fannie Mae expected useful life tables
- Marshall and Swift valuation service
- Actual taxpayer experience

The PPI method could also produce unreasonable results where a taxpayer purchases a new or existing building at a discount. For example, assume a taxpayer purchases a building in a distressed area of a city from a housing agency for $1,000 in 2012 pursuant to an agreement to improve the building. Assume that the cost of replacing the roof in 2020 is $10,000. The PPI method could unreasonably result in a preliminary basis calculation for the original roof that far exceeded the $1,000 cost of the building.

Even where a taxpayer purchases a new building the PPI rollback arguably produces a higher retirement loss than should be expected. A building or section 1245 asset manufacturer that constructs an asset or group of assets as part of a single project has advantages of efficiency and economy, including materials and labor pricing, that are unavailable to an owner replacing an existing component. For example, a car manufacture may be able to manufacture and install a hood on a new car on its assembly line for $500 and charge a slight premium to the purchaser (as reflected in the total retail price of the car). The same hood may cost $1,000 to replace at an auto body shop or dealership. It may be unreasonable to claim a retirement loss using the PPI rollback method based on the $1,000 replacement cost in this situation. Similar reasoning can be applied to the cost of replacing a structural component of a building that was constructed by a developer for a taxpayer.

*Disposition of Assets in Multiple Account or Pool*

It may be impracticable for a taxpayer that accounts for assets in multiple asset accounts to determine from the taxpayer's records the unadjusted depreciable basis of the asset disposed of. Accordingly, in this situation, the regulations provide that the taxpayer may use any reasonable, consistent method to make that determination. Similar rules, described below, are provided if the asset disposed of is a component of a larger asset (Reg. § 1.168(i)-8(f)(2).

Specifically, if an asset disposed of is in a multiple asset account or pool and it is impracticable from the taxpayer's records to determine the asset's *unadjusted* depreciable basis (as defined in Reg. § 1.168(b)-1(a)(3)), any reasonable method that is consistently applied to the taxpayer's multiple asset accounts or pools or to the taxpayer's larger assets may be used to determine the unadjusted depreciable basis of asset (Reg. § 1.168(i)-8(f)(2)).

The final regulations provide the following examples of reasonable methods (Reg. § 1.168(i)-8(f)(2)):

- discounting the cost of the replacement asset to its placed-in-service year cost using the Producer Price Index for Finished Goods or its successor the Producer Price Index for Final Demand (Consumer Price Index under proposed regulations)

- a pro rata allocation of the unadjusted depreciable basis of the multiple asset account or pool based on the replacement cost of the disposed of asset and the replacement cost of all of the assets in the multiple asset account or pool

- a study (e.g., cost segregation study) allocating the cost of the asset to its individual components

Under the final regulations, indexed discounting may not be used unless the replacement portion is a capitalized restoration (as defined in Reg. § 1.263(a)-3(k) and is not a betterment (Reg. § 1.263(a)-3(j) or adaptation (Reg. § 1.263(a)-3(l)). This limitation did not apply under the proposed regulations. Also, under the proposed regulations, indexed discounting was based on the Consumer Price Index. The final regulations replace the Consumer Price Index with the Producer Price Index (or its successor) because the latter results in a more accurate determination of basis (Preamble to T.D. 9689). Taxpayers who used the consumer price index to compute unadjusted basis are required to make recomputations of the retirement loss using the producer price index. This requires the filing of an accounting method change pursuant to Rev. Proc. 2019-43. See below.

To determine the *adjusted* depreciable basis of an asset disposed of in a multiple asset account or pool, the depreciation allowed or allowable for the asset disposed of is computed by using the depreciation method, recovery period, and convention applicable to the multiple asset account or pool in which the asset was included and by including the additional first year depreciation deduction (bonus depreciation) claimed for the asset (Reg. § 1.168(i)-8(f)(2)).

A change from an impermissible method of computing unadjusted depreciable basis (e.g., CPI rollback method) to a permissible method (e.g., PPI rollback method) is made by filing an accounting method change under Sec. 6.13 (buildings) or Sec. 6.14 (section 1245 property and land improvements) of Rev. Proc. 2019-43. Permissible to permissible method changes of computation require accounting method changes filed under Sec. 6.12 for buildings and section 1245 property. See ¶ 77.

*Identification of asset disposed of from multiple asset account or pool—tax year asset placed in service unknown.* If a taxpayer accounts for the asset disposed of in a multiple asset account or pool and the total dispositions of assets with the same recovery period during the tax year can be readily determined from the taxpayer's records but it is impracticable from the taxpayer's records to determine the particular tax year in which the asset disposed of was placed in service, the taxpayer may identify the asset disposed of by using (Reg. § 1.168(i)-8(g)(2)):

(1) A first-in, first-out (FIFO) method of accounting if the unadjusted depreciable basis of the asset disposed of *cannot* be readily determined from the taxpayer's records.

(2) A modified first-in, first-out method of accounting if the unadjusted depreciable basis of the asset disposed of *can* be readily determined from the taxpayer's records.

(3) A mortality dispersion table if the asset disposed of is a mass asset.

(4) Any other method designated by the IRS.

If a taxpayer disposes of a portion of an asset and makes the partial disposition election and it is impracticable to determine the particular year that the asset was placed in service, the preceding methods may also be used (Reg. § 1.168(i)-8(g)(3)).

Under the first-in, first-out (FIFO) method (item (1)) the taxpayer treats the asset disposed of as being from the multiple asset account with the earliest placed-in-service year that has assets with the same recovery period as the asset disposed of. However, if the taxpayer can readily determine from its records the unadjusted depreciable basis of the asset disposed of, it may use the modified FIFO method (item (2)) under which the asset disposed of is treated as being from the multiple asset account with the earliest placed-in-service year that has assets with the same recovery period as the asset disposed of and with the same unadjusted depreciable basis of the asset disposed of (Reg. § 1.168(i)-8(g)(2)(i) and (ii)).

A mortality dispersion table must be based upon an acceptable sampling of the taxpayer's actual disposition experience for mass assets or other acceptable statistical or engineering techniques. To use a mortality dispersion table, the taxpayer must adopt recordkeeping practices consistent with the taxpayer's prior practices and consonant with good accounting and engineering practices (Reg. § 1.168(i)-8(g)(2)(iii)). Mass assets are a mass or group of individual items of depreciable assets: (a) that are not necessarily homogenous; (b) each of which is minor in value relative to the total value of the mass or group; (c) numerous in quantity; (d) usually accounted for only on a total dollar or quantity basis; (e) with respect to which separate identification is impracticable; and (f) placed in service in the same taxable year (Reg. § 1.168(i)-8(b)(3)).

A last-in, last-out (LIFO) method may not be used to identify an asset disposed of from a multiple asset account or pool. Under the LIFO method, for example, the taxpayer treats the asset disposed of as being from the multiple asset account with the most recent placed-in-service year that has assets with the same recovery period as the asset disposed of or treats the disposed portion of an asset as being from an asset with the most recent placed-in-service year that is the same as the asset of which the disposed portion is a part (Reg. § 1.168(i)-8(g)(2)(iv); Reg. § 1.168(i)-8(g)(4)).

A change from an impermissible to permissible identification method is governed by Sec. 6.13 (buildings) and Sec. 6.14 (section 1245 property and land improvements) of Rev. Proc. 2019-43. A change from a permissible to permissible identification method is governed by Sec. 6.35 for both buildings and section 1245 property. See ¶ 77 for changes filed on or after May 4, 2016.

*Accounting for asset disposed of in a multiple asset account or pool.* When an asset is disposed of from a multiple account or pool:

(1) the asset is removed from the multiple asset account or pool and is placed into a single asset account on the first day of the tax year of the disposition;

(2) the unadjusted depreciable basis of the multiple asset account or pool is reduced by the unadjusted depreciable basis of the asset on the first day of the tax year in which the disposition occurs;

(3) the depreciation reserve of the multiple asset account or pool is reduced by the depreciation allowed or allowable for the asset as of the end of the tax year immediately preceding the tax year of disposition, computed by using the depreciation method, recovery period, and convention applicable to the multiple asset account or pool in which the asset was included and by including the additional first year depreciation deduction (bonus depreciation) claimed for the asset (Reg. § 1.168(i)-8(h)(2)).

*Unadjusted depreciable basis of an asset.* Unadjusted depreciable basis is the basis of property for purposes of determining gain or loss without regard to depreciation adjustments. This basis reflects the reduction in basis for the percentage of the taxpayer's personal (nonbusiness) use, for any portion of the basis the taxpayer properly elects to treat as an expense under Code Sec. 179, Code Sec. 179C, or any similar provision, and for any adjustments to basis provided by other provisions of the Code and the regulation (Reg. § 1.168(b)-1(a)(3)).

*Unadjusted depreciable basis of multiple assert account or pool.* Unadjusted depreciable basis of a multiple asset account or pool is the sum of the unadjusted depreciable bases of all assets included in the multiple asset account or pool (Reg. § 1.168(i)-8(b)(6)).

***Example (14):*** EFG, a calendar year taxpayer, accounts for items of MACRS property that are mass assets in pools. Each pool includes only the mass assets that have the same depreciation method, recovery period, and convention, and are placed in service in the same tax year. None of the pools are general asset accounts. EFG identifies any dispositions of these mass assets by specific identification.

During 2019, EFG sells 10 items of mass assets with a 5-year recovery period each for $100. Under the specific identification method, EFG identifies these mass assets as being from a pool of mass assets established in 2017 for mass assets with a 5-year recovery period. Assume EFG depreciates this pool using the table percentages that reflect the 200-percent declining balance method, a 5-year recovery period, and the half-year convention. Assume that EFG elected not to claim bonus depreciation on 5-year property placed in service in 2017 so that the 5-year pool for 2017 does not contain assets on which bonus depreciation was claimed. As of January 1, 2019, this pool contains 100 similar items of mass assets with a total cost of $25,000 and a total depreciation reserve of $13,000. Thus, EFG allocates a cost of $250 ($25,000 × (1/100)) to each disposed of mass asset and depreciation allowed or allowable of $130 ($13,000 × (1/100)) to each disposed of mass asset. The depreciation allowed or allowable in 2019 for each disposed of mass asset is $24 [($250 × 19.2 percent (third-year table percentage)) / 2 (to reflect half-year convention for disposed of assets)]. As a result, the adjusted depreciable basis of each disposed of mass asset is $96 ($250 - $130 - $24). Thus, EFG recognizes a gain of $4 ($100 – $96) for each disposed of mass asset in 2019, which is subject to ordinary income recapture under Code Sec. 1245.

Further, as of January 1, 2019, the unadjusted depreciable basis of the 2017 pool of mass assets with a 5-year recovery period is reduced from $25,000 to $22,500 ($25,000 less the unadjusted depreciable basis of $2,500 for the 10 disposed of items), and the depreciation reserve of this 2017 pool is reduced from $13,000 to $11,700 ($13,000 less the depreciation allowed or allowable of $1,300 for the 10 disposed of items as of December 31, 2018). Consequently, as of January 1, 2019, the 2017 pool of mass assets with a 5-year recovery period has 90 items with a total cost of $22,500 and a depreciation reserve of $11,700. Thus, the depreciation allowance for this pool for 2019 is $4,320 ($22,500 × 19.2 percent (third-year table percentage)) (Reg. § 1.168(i)-8(i), Example 10).

***Example (15):*** Assume that EFG's recordkeeping is changed in 2021, and is impracticable to continue to identify disposed of mass assets using specific identification and to determine the unadjusted depreciable basis of the disposed of mass assets. As a result, EFG files a Form 3115, Application for Change in Accounting Method, and receives consent to change to a first-in, first-out method beginning with the tax year beginning on January 1, 2021, on a modified cut-off basis. Under the first-in, first-out method, the mass assets disposed of in a tax year are deemed to be from the pool with the earliest placed-in-service year that has assets as of the beginning of the tax year of the disposition with the same recovery period as the asset disposed of.

During 2021, EFG sells 20 items of mass assets with a 5-year recovery period each for $50. As of January 1, 2021, a 2014 pool is the pool with the earliest placed in-service year for mass assets with a 5-year recovery period, and this pool contains 25 items of mass assets with a total cost of $10,000 and a total depreciation reserve of $10,000. Thus, EFG allocates a cost of $400 ($10,000 × (1/25)) to each disposed of mass asset and depreciation allowed or allowable of $400 to each disposed of mass asset. As a result, the adjusted depreciable basis of each disposed of mass asset is $0. Thus, EFG recognizes a gain of $50 for each disposed of mass asset in 2021, which is subject to ordinary income recapture under Code Sec. 1245.

Further, as of January 1, 2021, the unadjusted depreciable basis of the 2014 pool of mass assets with a 5-year recovery period is reduced from $10,000 to $2,000 ($10,000 less the unadjusted depreciable basis of $8,000 for the 20 disposed of items ($400 × 20)), and the depreciation reserve of this 2014 pool is reduced from $10,000 to $2,000 ($10,000 less the depreciation allowed or allowable of $8,000 for the 20 disposed of items as of December 31, 2020). Consequently, as of January 1, 2021, the 2014 pool of mass assets with a 5-year recovery period has 5 items with a total cost of $2,000 and a depreciation reserve of $2,000 (Reg. § 1.168(i)-8(i), Example 11).

## Effective Date of Disposition Regulations

Temporary regulations dealing with dispositions of property accounted for in item or multiple asset accounts (Temporary Reg. § 1.168(i)-8T) were reissued as proposed regulations (Proposed Reg. § 1.168-8; NPRM REG-110732-13 (September 19, 2013)). These proposed regulations were finalized without significant change (Reg. § 1.168(i)-8, as adopted by T.D. 9689 (August 18, 2014)). The final regulations are effective for tax years beginning on or after January 1, 2014 or, optionally, tax years beginning on or after January 1, 2012.

The primary difference between (a) the final and proposed disposition regulations and (b) the temporary disposition regulations is that the final and proposed regulations no longer treat the retirement of a structural component of a building that is not in a general asset account as a mandatory loss recognition transaction. Instead, a taxpayer may make an election to recognize loss on the disposition of a structural component or any part of a structural component (the "partial disposition" election described in Reg. § 1.168(i)-8(d) or Proposed Reg. § 1.168(i)-8(d)). Under the temporary regulations, the only way in which a taxpayer could avoid mandatory loss recognition was by placing the building in a general asset account. In light of this new election, the final and proposed GAA regulations (Reg. § 1.168(i)-1; Proposed Reg. § 1.168(i)-1) modified the temporary general asset account regulations (Temporary Reg. § 1.168(i)-1) to eliminate the ability to choose whether or not to recognize a loss on the disposition of a structural component. Instead, under the final and proposed GAA regulations, a taxpayer is generally not permitted to recognize a loss when a structural component of a building in a general asset account is disposed of. The IRS allowed the revocation of GAA elections made in reliance on the rules in the temporary regulations by filing an accounting method change pursuant to Section 6.34 of Rev. Proc. 2015-14 (Sec. 6.11 of Rev. Proc. 2016-29 for changes filed on or after May 5, 2016). This change was required, however, no later than for a taxpayer's last tax year beginning in 2014 and is now obsolete. See ¶ 77. See ¶ 128 for a discussion of general asset accounts.

Taxpayers had a one-time opportunity to file late partial disposition elections under the final regulations to claim losses on retired structural components, as well as components of other assets, by filing an accounting method change for a tax years beginning on or after January 1, 2012 and beginning before January 1, 2014 pursuant Appendix Sec. 6.33 of Rev. Proc. 2011-14, Sec. 6.33 of Rev. Proc. 2015-14, or, for filings on or after May 5, 2016 for a year of change ending on or after September 30, 2015, Sec. 6.10 of Rev. Proc. 2016-29. This accounting change, which is now obsolete, also had to be filed by taxpayers who previously claimed such losses in a 2012 or 2013 tax year under the temporary regulations by filing an accounting method change if those losses were to be preserved. See discussion of Sec. 6.10 accounting method change (previously Sec. 6.33) at ¶ 77.

*Disposition Rules In Tax Years Beginning Before 2014*

Proposed ACRS regulations summarize some general rules which apply for purposes of determining gain or loss on the disposition of ACRS recovery property that is not contained in a mass asset account (Prop. Reg. § 1.168-6 at ¶ 545). It is appropriate for taxpayers to apply these rules to MACRS property that is not governed by the final, proposed, or temporary repair regulations discussed above. Although proposed regulations are not binding on a taxpayer or the IRS (unless specifically labelled as reliance regulations), the Service will generally not challenge a taxpayer's reliance on a proposed regulation if the taxpayer's situation fits within the strict confines of that proposed regulation (IRS Field Service Advice 199937022, June 17, 1999, discussed below).

The term disposition is defined by ACRS Prop. Reg. § 1.168-2(l)(1) at ¶ 525 to mean the permanent withdrawal of property from use in the taxpayer's trade or business or use for the production of income. Dispositions include sales, exchanges, retirements, abandonments, or destruction. Transfers by gift or by reason of death are not dispositions.

In the case of a sale or exchange, recognized gain or loss is determined by applying the controlling Code provision (Prop. Reg. § 1.168-6(a)(1)).

If an asset is physically abandoned, a taxpayer may deduct a loss (the loss is ordinary since there is no sale or exchange of a capital asset) in the amount of the adjusted basis in the year of abandonment. The taxpayer must intend to discard the asset irrevocably, by not intending to use the asset again, nor intending to retrieve it for sale, exchange or other disposition (Prop. Reg. § 1.168-6(a)(2)). The loss deduction for an abandonment of nondepreciable property is authorized by Reg. § 1.165-2, as discussed below.

An abandonment loss is claimed as an ordinary loss on line 10 Part II of Form 4797 (IRS Publication 225).

Gain is not recognized if a taxpayer disposes of an asset other than by sale, exchange, or physical abandonment (for example, where the asset is transferred to a supplies or scrap account). Loss is recognized to the extent that the adjusted basis exceeds the fair market value at the time of the disposition. The transfer of an asset to a supplies or scrap account falls within this rule (Prop. Reg. § 1.168-6(a)(3)). Again, the loss is an ordinary loss.

The conversion of a depreciable asset to personal use is not a disposition that triggers a loss (Prop. Reg. § 1.168-6(a)(3)).

The IRS has ruled that a corporation that placed a manufacturing facility which it had closed down in an account labeled "Assets Held for Sale" could not deduct a retirement loss in the year the facility was placed in the account because the taxpayer intended and, in fact, accomplished a sale in a later tax year (Field Service Advice 199937022, June 17, 1999). The FSA, citing *B.R. Kittredge*, CA-2, 37-1 USTC ¶ 9165, indicates that the asset was still considered in business use although it was withdrawn from active use in the business.

*Retirement of structural components.* The ACRS regulations provide that the retirement (whether ordinary or abnormal) of a structural component of real property is not a disposition (Prop. Reg. § 1.168-2(l)(1)). By way of example, the regulations provide that if the roof on 15-year ACRS property is replaced, no gain or loss is recognized with respect to the replaced roof (Prop. Reg. § 1.168-6).

The IRS takes the position (based on Prop. Reg. § 1.168-2(l)(1)) that the retirement of a structural component does not trigger gain or loss even if the retired component was separately depreciated (e.g., a retired roof that previously replaced the original roof). In a Field Service Advice, the IRS states: "The abandonment or retirement of a structural component of a building generally does not constitute a disposition. Accordingly, no loss deduction is allowed on the retirement of such property. The taxpayer continues to recovery the cost of such property through ACRS or MACRS deductions" (IRS Field Service Advice 200001005, September 10, 1999).

For special rules that apply to retirements of structural components by a lessor or lessee, see ¶ 126.

Additions and improvements added after 1986 are treated as MACRS property. Thus, a new roof or other new addition/improvement/structural component would be treated as 39-year nonresidential real property (assuming the building is commercial property) and separately depreciated as such (see ¶ 126).

*Pre-ACRS rules*

The proposed ACRS regulations dealing with abandonments and retirements are essentially the same as regulations that apply to pre-ACRS property that is not in a multiple item account under the general depreciation rules. A multiple property account is one in which several items have been combined with a single rate of depreciation assigned to the entire account. (ADR has its own set of rules). Thus, these pre-ACRS regulations and the related case law are useful in understanding situations in which an asset will be considered abandoned or retired.

See ¶ 380 for rules regarding retirements of pre-ACRS property from item accounts and ¶ 382 for rules regarding retirements of pre-ACRS property from multiple-asset accounts.

Although the proposed ACRS regulations do not define the term "retirement" it is defined in Reg. § 1.167(a)-8(a) which provides:

> ". . . the term 'retirement' means the permanent withdrawal of depreciable property from use in the trade or business or in the production of income. The withdrawal may be made in several ways. For example, the withdrawal may be made by selling or exchanging the asset, or by actual abandonment. In addition, the asset may be withdrawn from such productive use without disposition as, for example, by being placed in a supplies or scrap account."

If an asset is permanently retired but is not disposed of or physically abandoned (as for example, when the asset is transferred to a supplies or scrap account) gain is not recognized. Loss is recognized to the extent of the adjusted basis of the asset over the greater of estimated salvage value or fair market value if the retirement is abnormal, the retirement is a normal retirement from a single asset account, or in the case of certain retirements from multiple asset accounts (Reg. § 1.167(a)-8(a)(3)).

The IRS has ruled that transfers of dismantled assets to a supplies account are considered retirements (Rev. Rul. 80-311, 1980-2 CB 5; IRS Letter Ruling 8646008, August 5, 1986).

As in the case of the proposed ACRS regulations, a physical abandonment requires an irrevocable intent to discard the asset so that it will neither be used again by the taxpayer nor retrieved for sale, exchange, or other disposition. The mere nonuse of property is not a physical abandonment (*Hillcone Steamship Company*, 22 TCM 1096, CCH Dec. 26,265(M)).

The regulations provide that retirements may be "normal" or "abnormal." Reg. § 1.167(a)-8(b) states:

> "In general, a retirement shall be considered a normal retirement unless the taxpayer can show that the withdrawal of the asset was due to a cause not contemplated in setting the applicable depreciation rate. For example, a retirement is considered normal if made within the range of years taken into consideration in fixing the depreciation rate and if the asset has reached a condition at which, in the normal course of events, the taxpayer customarily retires similar assets from use in his business. On the other hand, a retirement may be abnormal if the asset is withdrawn at an earlier time or under other circumstances, as, for example, when the asset has been damaged by casualty or has lost its usefulness suddenly as the result of extraordinary obsolescence."

Obsolescence is defined in Reg. § 1.167(a)-9. In general, that regulation allows a taxpayer to redetermine the useful life of an asset for purposes of computing depreciation if the useful life has been shortened by obsolescence greater than that assumed in determining the useful life. This aspect of the regulation is of no relevance under ACRS and MACRS since the depreciation period is statutorily set irrespective of the actual useful life of an asset to a taxpayer. However, if the usefulness of depreciable property is suddenly terminated as the result of obsolescence, then the taxpayer may be entitled to a loss deduction for extraordinary obsolescence if the asset is permanently withdrawn from use in the trade or business. Such a retirement is considered an abnormal retirement, as discussed in the paragraph above.

Extraordinary obsolescence occurred where a city refused to grant a health permit due to the discovery by the purchasing taxpayer of a building's structural defects and the permit was necessary to operate the building as a restaurant/bar (*De Cou*, 103 TC 80, CCH Dec. 49,998). The building was boarded up (i.e., permanently withdrawn from business) and subsequently demolished because it was more expensive to repair the building than replace it. Although the structural defects occurred over the course of several years (before the taxpayer purchased the building), the building's usefulness to the taxpayer suddenly and unexpectedly terminated upon the discovery of the defects and the subsequent suspension of the building's health permit. The taxpayer was entitled to an ordinary loss deduction equal to the building's adjusted basis (fair market and salvage value were zero, so no reduction was made to adjusted basis).

A loss sustained before a building's demolition (as a result, for example, of a building's abnormal retirement because of a casualty or extraordinary obsolescence), is not disallowed under Code Sec. 280B, which requires capitalization of losses sustained on account of the demolition of a structure (IRS Notice 90-21, 1990-1 CB 332; *De Cou*, above). However, the actual costs of demolition would be capitalized under Code Sec. 280B. See ¶ 5.

In contrast to *De Cou*, where the loss deduction was claimed in the same year that the structural defects were discovered, the health permit withdrawn, and the building retired, a loss deduction was denied where the loss was claimed in a tax year after the discovery of asbestos in a building allegedly caused a sudden and unexpected termination of its usefulness (*L. Gates*, DC Pa., 98-1 USTC 50,353, aff'd CA-3 (unpublished opinion), 98-2 USTC ¶ 50,814). Furthermore, in a footnote citing Code Sec. 1016, the court indicated that the taxpayer may not be allowed to include the unclaimed loss in the basis of the land when the building is demolished.

A threat of condemnation in which compensation would be given for damage cannot give rise to an obsolescence deduction (*Keller Street Development Company*, CA-9, 63-2 UTSC ¶ 9734).

A bank which vacated a building in which it operated computers and then sold the building in a later tax year was not entitled to an abandonment loss or an extraordinary obsolescence loss (measured by the difference between its fair market value and adjusted basis) in the tax year the building was vacated. Instead, depreciation deductions should have been claimed during that period it was unoccupied (Field Service Advice Memorandum 200141026, July 11, 2001). There was no abandonment because the taxpayer did not irrevocably discard the building in a manner that prevented it from selling the building. The ruling recognized that based on the particular circumstances the bank could argue that it withdrew the building as a result of new developments in the banking industry which rendered it economically worthless thereby resulting in an obsolescence deduction. However, the ruling concludes that the closing of the building was not unusual or unexpected in the industry.

There appear to be no cases which directly consider whether an item of property which is abandoned or retired prior to being placed in service (for depreciation purposes) can be considered depreciable property for purposes of Reg. § 1.167(a)-8. However, in the *Keller* case, an obsolescence deduction was allowed for specialized brewery machinery that had never been used and had become worthless due to a change in market conditions. It is unclear whether the machinery was considered placed in service.

*Abandonments of nondepreciable property*

The preceding discussion relates to abandonments of depreciable property. Abandonment losses for nondepreciable property are authorized under Reg. § 1.165-2. Although the regulation heading refers to "obsolescence of nondepreciable property," the term obsolescence is best construed to mean "abandonment." In other words, retirements of nondepreciable property which are not abandonments may not be deducted under Reg. § 1.165-2. The abandonment rule of Reg. § 1.165-2 for nondepreciable property differs somewhat from that provided in Reg. § 1.167-8 in that the abandonment must arise "from the sudden termination of the usefulness" of the asset. This distinction, however, appears to be generally disregarded by the case law (*Coors Porcelain Co.*, 52 TC 682, CCH Dec. 29,680, aff'd, CA-10, 70-2 USTC ¶ 9539).

*Abandonments and cancellation of debt*

Generally, ordinary income is realized if a debt for which a taxpayer is personally liable and secured by the abandoned property is canceled. Exceptions apply if the cancellation is intended as a gift, the debt is qualified farm debt (see IRS Pub. 225, *Farmer's Tax Guide*), the debt is qualified real property business debt (see IRS Pub. 334, *Tax Guide for Small Business* (chapter 5)), or the taxpayer is insolvent or bankrupt (see IRS Pub. 908, *Bankruptcy Tax Guide*) (Code Sec. 61; Code Sec. 108).

*Abandonments of leasehold improvements*

A lessor may claim an ordinary loss deduction with respect to improvements that the lessor abandons. A similar rule applies to lessees who abandon an improvement. See ¶ 126.

*Installation and removal costs*

See ¶ 70.

*Demolitions*

See ¶ 5.

# Like-Kind Exchanges and Involuntary Conversions

## ¶ 167

## Like–Kind Exchanges and Involuntary Conversions

This discussion of the depreciation computation of MACRS property received in a like-kind exchange or involuntary conversion is organized as follows.

*1. Background, and effective date of final regulations*

*1A. Like-kind exchange rules only apply to real property after 2017*

*1B. Accounting method changes.*

*2. Election out of final regulations*

*3. Replacement property and relinquished property must generally be MACRS property*

*4. Land is still not depreciable*

*5. Final regulations in general*

*6. Section 179 allowance and bonus depreciation*

*7. Luxury car rules (cross reference to ¶ 214)*

*8. Effect of like-kind exchange or involuntary conversion in determining whether the mid-quarter convention applies*

*9. Disposition of replacement property during same tax year relinquished property acquired*

**General Principles of Computation**

*10. How to make the MACRS depreciation computations on property received in a like-kind exchange or in an involuntary conversion*

*11. Depreciation computation on exchanged basis if recovery period and depreciation method of relinquished and replacement property are both the same*

*12. Depreciation computation on exchanged basis if recovery period and/or depreciation method are different*

*13. Applicable convention*

**Depreciation Deductions in Year of Disposition and Year of Replacement**

*14. Deduction on relinquished property in year of disposition*

*15. Deduction on replacement property in year of acquisition*

*16. Deferred-like-kind exchange transactions*

*17. Exchanges of multiple properties*

*18. Deduction on replacement property in year of exchange*

*19. Involuntary conversions: replacement property placed in service before disposition of relinquished property*

**Computations With Optional Depreciation Tables**

*20. Depreciation on relinquished property in year of disposition using tables.*

*21. Depreciation on excess basis using tables*

*22. Depreciation on exchanged basis using tables*

*23. Transaction coefficient when using tables*

*1. Background and effective date of final regulations.* Final regulations explain how to depreciate MACRS property acquired in a like-kind exchange Code Sec. 1031 or an involuntary conversion under Code Sec. 1033 provided that the relinquished or converted property was also depreciated under MACRS or the taxpayer made a valid election to exclude the relinquished property from MACRS pursuant to Code Sec. 168(f)(1) (relating to property depreciated under the unit-of-production method or any method of depreciation not expressed in a term of years (other than the retirement-replacement-betterment method or similar method) (T.D. 9314, filed in the Federal Register on February 27, 2007). The final regulations are generally effective for a like-kind exchange or an involuntary conversion for which the time of disposition and time of replacement both occur after February 27, 2004. However, if the relinquished property was excluded from MACRS under Code Sec. 168(f)(1), a special effective date applies (Reg. § 1.168(i)-6(k)).

The final regulations adopt temporary regulations (T.D. 9115, filed with the Federal Register on March 1, 2004) with a few minor clarifications. The temporary regulations were also generally effective for like-kind exchanges and involuntary conversions in which the time of disposition and the time of replacement both occur after February 27, 2004 (Temporary Reg. § 1.168(i)-6T(k)(1)).

The IRS first issued guidance in Notice 2000-4 (2000-1 CB 313). This notice generally provided that MACRS replacement property received in a Code Sec. 1031 like-kind exchange or a Code Sec. 1033 involuntary conversion is depreciated over the remaining recovery period of, and using the same depreciation method and convention as, the relinquished MACRS property. Any excess of the basis in the replacement MACRS property over the adjusted basis of the relinquished MACRS property is depreciated as newly purchased MACRS property. The Notice applied to replacement MACRS property placed in service after January 3, 2000 if the time of disposition of the relinquished property or the time of replacement occur on or before February 27, 2004 (i.e., effective date of the temporary regulations which replaced the Notice).

For property placed in service before January 3, 2000, some taxpayers depreciated replacement property in a manner consistent with the Notice by applying the methodology of ACRS Proposed Reg. § 1.168-5(f). This regulation provides rules for ACRS property received in a like-kind exchange or involuntary conversion as a replacement for ACRS property relinquished in a like-kind exchange or involuntarily converted. Other taxpayers depreciated the entire basis of replacement property as new MACRS property.

Notice 2000-4 provided that for acquired MACRS property placed in service before January 3, 2000 (in an exchange or involuntary conversion in which the relinquished property is depreciated under MACRS), the IRS will allow a taxpayer to continue to use a bifurcated basis methodology that is consistent with the Notice and the Proposed ACRS regulations or to treat the entire basis of the acquired property as new MACRS property. Taxpayer who treated the entire basis of acquired property as newly purchased MACRS property were allowed to change their accounting methods in their first or second taxable year ending after January 3, 2000 to comport with the bifurcated methodology prescribed by Notice 2000-4.

*1A. Like-kind exchange rules only apply to real property after 2017.* Like-kind exchanges under Code Sec. 1031 are allowed only for real property after 2017 (Code Sec. 1031(a)(1)).

Final regulations provide that for purposes of section 1031 real property means land and improvements to land, unsevered natural products of land, and water and air space superjacent to land. An interest in real property, including fee ownership, co-ownership, a leasehold, an option to acquire real property, an easement, or a similar interest, is real property for purposes of section 1031. Except for a state's characterization of shares in a mutual ditch, reservoir, or irrigation company, local law definitions are not controlling for purposes of determining the meaning of the term real property under this section (Reg.§ 1.1031(a)-3; T.D 9935 (11/30/2020); REG-117589-18 (6/12/20)). The regulations apply to exchanges of real property beginning after December 2, 2020 (Reg. § 1.1031(a)-3(c)).

The IRS previously discussed the definition of real property for purposes of section 1031 in detail in General Counsel Memorandum 201238027.

The provision applies to exchanges completed after December 31, 2017 (Act Sec. 13303(c)(1) of the Tax Cuts and Jobs Act (P.L. 115-97)). However, the provision does not apply to an exchange if (1) the property disposed of by the taxpayer in the exchange is disposed of on or before December 31, 2017; or (2) the property received by the taxpayer in the exchange is received on or before December 31, 2017 (Act Sec. 13303(c)(2) of P.L. 115-97).

*1B. Accounting method changes.* Taxpayers are allowed to apply the final regulations (or prior guidance) to pre-effective date exchanges. Taxpayers who filed returns on or before February 27, 2004 could change their accounting method to comply with the final regulations or earlier guidance (e.g., Notice 2000-4 (2001-1 CB 313)) by following the automatic consent procedures (Reg. § 1.168(i)-6(k)(2)(i) and (ii)). This accounting method change was last specifically listed in Appendix Section 6.18 of Rev. Proc. 2011-14. Rev. Proc. 2015-14 ("Significant Changes" Section .01(23)(e)) states that the change formerly made under Section 6.18 of Rev. Proc. 2011-14 may be made under Section 6.01 of Rev. Proc. 2015-14 relating to impermissible to permissible accounting method changes. This change is now filed under Section 6.01 of Rev. Proc. 2019-43.

Changes made from an impermissible depreciation method to a permissible depreciation method for disposed depreciable property may generally be made under Section 6.07 of Rev. Proc. 2019-43. However, Section 6.07 does not apply any property disposed of by the taxpayer in a transaction to which a nonrecognition section of the Code applies (for example, Code Sec. 1031 or Code Sec. 1033). Section 6.07 provides that this prohibition does not apply to property disposed of by the taxpayer in a Code Sec. 1031 or Code Sec. 1033 transaction if the taxpayer elects under Reg.§ 1.168(i)-6(i) and 1.168(i)-6(j) to treat the entire basis (that is, both the exchanged and excess basis of the replacement MACRS property) as property placed in service by the taxpayer at the time of replacement and treat the adjusted depreciable basis of the relinquished MACRS property as being disposed of by the taxpayer at the time of disposition. Therefore, unless a taxpayer makes this election, it appears that such a change needs to be made under the advance consent procedure.

*2. Election out of final regulations.* A taxpayer may elect as provided in the instructions to Form 4562 (Depreciation and Amortization) not to apply the final regulations to a post-effective date exchange or conversion. The election is made separately for each like-kind exchange or involuntary conversion by the due date (including extensions) of the taxpayer's return for the year of replacement. See Reg. § 1.168(i)-6(j) for election details. In general, this election should be considered if the recovery period of the replacement property is shorter than the remaining recovery period of the relinquished property or the depreciation method of the replacement property is more accelerated than the depreciation method of the relinquished property. The election is revocable only in extraordinary circumstances.

If the election is made, the sum of the exchanged basis and excess basis (if any) is treated as property placed in service at the time of replacement and the adjusted depreciable basis of the relinquished MACRS property is treated as disposed of at the time of disposition. The election not to apply the regulations does not affect the application of the depreciation recapture rules of Code Secs. 1245 and 1250 (Reg. § 1.168(i)-6(i)(1)).

*3. Replacement and relinquished property must generally be MACRS property.* The final regulations, Notice 2000-4, and the temporary regulations only apply if the replacement property received by a taxpayer is depreciated by the taxpayer using MACRS (the method used by any prior owner of the replacement property is irrelevant). Subject to the exception below, the relinquished property must also have been depreciated by the taxpayer using MACRS. For example, if a taxpayer exchanges a building that is depreciated under MACRS for a building that another person is depreciating under ACRS or a pre-ACRS method, the final regulations apply to the taxpayer (unless an election out is made) because the building given up by the taxpayer was depreciated using MACRS and the replacement building received by the taxpayer will be depreciated under MACRS (Reg. § 1.168(i)-6(c)(2)). However, the regulations would not apply to the person who relinquished the ACRS building since the building that person gave up was not depreciated under ACRS. See in this regard, IRS Letter Ruling 8929047, April 25, 1989, which concludes that the proposed ACRS regulations do not apply to the exchange of ACRS property for MACRS property. Therefore, the *entire basis* of an airplane received by a taxpayer in a post-1986 transaction for an airplane being depreciated by the taxpayer under ACRS had to be depreciated as new MACRS property.

The final regulations allow a taxpayer to elect to treat relinquished property which was excluded from MACRS by reason of an election under Code Sec. 168(f)(1) (relating to unit-of-production property and certain other methods not expressed in a term of years) as MACRS property (Reg. § 1.168(i)-6(i)(2)). This option was not provided in the temporary regulations. The election, however, applies to like-kind exchanges and involuntary conversions occurring on, after, or before February 26, 2007. A taxpayer who filed a return without making the election may make the change by filing for a change of accounting method pursuant to the automatic consent procedures of Rev. Proc. 2002-9 (Reg. § 1.168(i)-6(k)(3)). If this election is made the sum of the "exchanged basis" (carryover basis) and "excess basis" (any additional cash paid for replacement property) is treated as MACRS property placed in service at the time of the replacement.

*4. Land is still not depreciable.* Neither Notice 2000-4 nor the temporary and final regulations should be interpreted to allow a taxpayer to depreciate land received in a like-kind exchange or involuntary conversion (Preamble to T.D. 9115).

*5. Final regulations in general.* The regulations mainly focus on the computation of the depreciation deductions on the depreciable exchanged basis (carryover basis attributable to business/investment use) of the property received in a like-kind exchange or involuntary conversion. The excess basis is typically the amount of any additional cash or boot paid for the property received. The excess basis is simply depreciated as if it were new property separately acquired and placed in service in the year of replacement (Reg. § 1.168(i)-6(d)(1)).

*6. Section 179 allowance and bonus depreciation.* Although the Code Sec. 179 allowance (¶ 300) may be claimed on the excess basis (usually additional cash paid) of the replacement property (assuming all other requirements are met), it may not be claimed on the exchanged basis (carryover basis) of the replacement property even if nondepreciable property (e.g., land) is replaced with depreciable property (Reg. § 1.168(i)-6(g)). The bonus depreciation deduction (¶ 127D) (assuming all other requirements are met) may be claimed on both the exchanged and excess basis if the replacement property is new (Reg. § 1.168(k)-1(f)(5); Reg.§ 1.168(k)-2(g)(5); Proposed Reg.§ 1.168(k)-2(f)(5)). If the replacement property is used property the exchanged basis does not qualify for bonus depreciation but the excess basis does (Reg. § 1.168(k)-1(f)(5); Reg.§ 1.168(k)-2(g)(5); Proposed Reg. 1.168(k)-2(f)(5)). See ¶ 127D, discussion at *7. Like-kind exchanges and involuntary conversions.*

*7. Luxury car rules.* See ¶ 214 for a discussion of the application of these regulations to the luxury car depreciation caps under Code Sec. 280F when a car or other vehicle is involved in a trade-in in that is treated as a like-kind exchange.

*8. Effect of like-kind exchange or involuntary conversion in determining whether the mid-quarter convention applies.* In determining whether the mid-quarter convention applies to the excess basis (noncarryover/boot basis) of the replacement property (and to other property placed in service during the tax year the replacement property is placed in service), the excess basis of replacement property is always taken into account in the quarter that the replacement property is placed in service (Reg. § 1.168(i)-6(f)(2)). The exchanged (carryover) basis of the replacement property is not taken into account in determining whether the mid-quarter convention applies to the excess basis and to any other property placed in service during the tax year (Reg. § 1.168(i)-6(f)(1)(iii)). However, special rules apply if, in the same tax year (1) property is acquired (but not in a like-kind exchange or involuntary conversion) and (2) disposed of in a like-kind exchange or involuntary conversion (Reg. § 1.168(i)-6(f)(1)(i) and Reg. § 1.168(i)-6(f)(1)(ii)). See *"Applicable convention,"* below.

If depreciable property is acquired for nondepreciable property in a like-kind exchange or involuntary conversion, both the exchanged basis and excess basis of the replacement property is taken into account in the year of replacement in determining whether the mid-quarter convention applies (Reg. § 1.168(i)-6(f)(3)).

The exchanged (carryover basis) of the replacement property is generally depreciated using the convention that applies to the relinquished property. However, if the mid-month convention applies to either the relinquished or replacement property, the exchanged basis is depreciated using the mid-month convention.

*9. Disposition of replacement property during same tax year relinquished property acquired.* If replacement property is disposed of in the same tax year that the relinquished property was placed in service, no MACRS deduction may be claimed on either property (Reg. § 1.168(i)-6(d)).

**General Principles of Computation**

*10. How to make the MACRS depreciation computations on property received in a like-kind exchange or in an involuntary conversion.* The manner in which depreciation computations are computed on the exchanged (carryover) basis of property received in a like-kind exchange or involuntary conversion will depend upon whether the recovery period and depreciation method of the replacement property are the same or different than the recovery period and depreciation method of the relinquished property.

*11. Depreciation computation on exchanged basis if recovery period and depreciation method of relinquished and replacement property are both the same.* In most like-kind exchanges and involuntary conversions the replacement property will have the same depreciation period and depreciation method as the relinquished property because both items of property are identical and have the same MACRS recovery period. For example, a commercial building will replace a commercial building

(39-year recovery period and straight-line method), a residential rental property will replace a residential rental property (27.5 year recovery period and straight-line method), or similar types of personal property will be exchanged, such as an airplane for an airplane (seven-year recovery period and 200 percent declining-balance method).

If both the recovery period and depreciation method of the replacement property are the same as the recovery period and depreciation method of the relinquished property, the depreciable exchanged basis of the replacement property is depreciated over the remaining recovery period of the relinquished property using the same method and convention that applied to the relinquished property. Depreciation allowances for the depreciable exchanged basis are determined by multiplying the depreciable exchanged basis by the applicable depreciation rate for each year (Reg. § 1.168(i)-6(c)(3)(ii)).

***Example (1):*** Building A is acquired in March 2018 for $100,000 and relinquished in a deferred exchange in March 2021. It is replaced by Building B in May 2021. Building A and B are 39-year real property depreciated using the straight-line method. Thus, the depreciation period (39 years) and depreciation method (straight-line method) and convention (mid-month) for the buildings are the same.

Total depreciation claimed through March 2021 on Building A is $7,692 computed as follows:

| | Year | Deduction | |
|---|---|---|---|
| | 2018 | $2,030 | ($100,000/39 × 9.5 months/12 months) |
| | 2019 | 2,564 | ($100,000/39) |
| | 2020 | 2,564 | ($100,000/39) |
| | 2021 | 534 | ($100,000/39 × 2.5 months/12 months) |
| Total | | 7,692 | |

Beginning in May 2021, the depreciable exchanged basis of Building B is depreciated over the remaining recovery period of Building A. The remaining recovery period of Building A is 36 years immediately after the disposition (39 − 9.5/12 − 1 − 1 − 2.5/12). The depreciable exchanged basis is $92,308 ($100,000 − $7,692). Depreciation is computed as follows:

| | Year | Deduction | |
|---|---|---|---|
| | 2021 | $1,602 | ($92,308/36 × 7.5 months/12 months) |
| | 2022-2057 | 2,564 | ($92,308/36) |
| | 2058 | 962 | ($92,308/36 × 4.5 months/12 months) |
| Total | | $92,308 | |

Assume that $50,000 cash was also paid for Building B. The excess basis of Building B is $50,000 and this amount is depreciated over 39-years beginning in May 2021 using the mid-month convention.

See, also, Reg. § 1.168(i)-6(c)(6), Example 1.

*12. Depreciation computation on exchanged basis if recovery period and/or depreciation method are different.* The following rules apply if the recovery period of the replacement property is different than the recovery period of the relinquished property or the depreciation method of the replacement property is different than the depreciation method of the relinquished property or both the method and period are different (Reg. § 1.168(i)-6(c)(3)(iii) and Reg. § 1.168(i)-6(c)(4)).

If the recovery period for the replacement property is the same as the recovery period for the relinquished property, the depreciation allowances for the depreciable exchanged basis of the replacement property beginning in the year of replacement are determined using the recovery period of the relinquished property (Reg. § 1.168(i)-6(c)(3)(iii)).

If the recovery period prescribed for the replacement property is longer than the recovery period prescribed for the relinquished property, the depreciable exchanged basis of the replacement property is depreciated over the remaining recovery period of the replacement property (Reg. § 1.168(i)-6(c)(4)(i)).

If the recovery period prescribed for the replacement property is shorter than the recovery period prescribed for the relinquished property, the depreciable exchanged basis of the replacement property is depreciated over the remaining recovery period of the relinquished MACRS property (Reg. § 1.168(i)-6(c)(4)(ii)).

If the depreciation method for the replacement property is the same as the depreciation method for the relinquished property at the time of disposition, the depreciation allowances for the depreciable exchanged basis of the replacement property are determined using the depreciation method that applies to the relinquished property (Reg. § 1.168(i)-6(c)(3)(iii)).

If the depreciation method for the replacement property is less accelerated than the depreciation method for the relinquished property at the time of disposition, the depreciable exchanged basis is depreciated using the less accelerated depreciation method (Reg. § 1.168(i)-6(c)(4)(iii)(A)).

If the depreciation method for the replacement property is more accelerated than the depreciation method that applies to the relinquished property at the time of disposition, the depreciation allowances for the depreciable exchanged basis of the replacement property are determined using the method that applies to the relinquished property (Reg. § 1.168(i)-6(c)(4)(iv)(A)).

When comparing depreciation methods, in the case of the relinquished property, the method taken into consideration is the method that applies in the year of disposition. The method that applies to the replacement property is the method that would apply in the year of disposition of the relinquished property if the replacement property had been placed in service at the same time as the relinquished property (Reg. § 1.168(i)-6(c)(3)(i)).

***Example (2):*** An item of seven-year property that was depreciated using the 200 percent declining balance method is exchanged for an item of 15-year property that is depreciable using the 150 percent declining balance method, and in the year of disposition the seven-year property is depreciated using the straight-line method because of the required switch from the 200 percent declining balance method to the straight-line method in the year that the straight-line method produces a larger deduction. The depreciation method of the seven-year property is considered to be the straight-line method and not the 200 percent declining balance method. Thus, the 15-year property will be depreciated using the straight-line method over the recovery period that would remain if it had been placed in service at the same time as the seven-year property.

***Example (3):*** In the year of disposition, the 200 percent declining balance method applies to relinquished property and the 150 percent declining balance method would apply to the replacement property if it had been placed in service at the same time as the relinquished property. The switch to the straight-line method from either of the declining balance methods has not occurred. The 150 percent declining balance method applies to determine the applicable depreciation rate until the required switch to the straight-line method (i.e., in the tax year that the rate for the straight-line method produces a larger deduction than the rate for the 150 percent declining balance method) (Reg. § 1.168(i)-6(c)(4)(iii)(B)).

***Example (4):*** Assume that in the year of disposition in the preceding example, the straight-line depreciation method would apply to the replacement property if it had been placed in service at the same time as the relinquished property. In this situation, the depreciable exchanged basis is depreciated using a rate based on the straight-line method (Reg. § 1.168(i)-6(c)(4)(iii)(B)).

For purposes of determining whether the depreciation method or recovery period of the replacement property is the same or different than the depreciation method or recovery period of the relinquished property, any straight-line, 150% declining balance, or MACRS alternative depreciation system (ADS) election made with respect to the relinquished property is taken into account (Reg. § 1.168(i)-6(c)(3)(i)).

*13. Applicable convention.* The convention for depreciating the exchanged (carryover) basis of property received in a like-kind exchange or involuntary conversion is determined under the following rules if the recovery period or depreciation method of the exchanged assets differ.

The exchanged basis (carryover basis) is depreciated using the mid-month convention if either the replacement or relinquished property is subject to the mid-month convention (i.e., the replacement or relinquished property is MACRS residential rental property or MACRS nonresidential real property) (Reg. § 1.168(i)-6(c)(4)(v)(A)). In each of the examples below the mid-convention applies because either the exchanged or relinquished property is subject to the mid-month convention. Each example illustrates how to determined the length of the remaining recovery period over which the exchanged basis is depreciated by taking into account the applicable convention. Note that in each case the remaining recovery period is determined by reference to the recovery period of the property with the longest recovery period.

***Example (5):*** 27.5-year residential rental property placed in service in March 2018 is exchanged for 39-year real property in September 2021. Depreciation deductions on the exchanged basis of the 39-year real property are computed under the mid-month convention over the portion of the 39-year recovery period that would remain under the mid-month convention if the 39-year property had been placed in service in mid-March 2018 and disposed of in mid-September 2021.

***Example (6):*** 20-year real property subject to the mid-quarter convention is exchanged for 39-year real property in June 2021. The 20-year real property was placed in service in March 2017. Under the mid-quarter convention, the 20-year property is considered placed in service on the mid-point of February 2017 and disposed of on the mid-point of May 2021. The exchanged basis of the 39-year real property is depreciated using the mid-month convention over the portion of the 39-year recovery period that would remain under the mid-month convention if it had been placed in service in mid-February 2017 and disposed of in mid-May 2021.

***Example (7):*** 20-year real property subject to the half-year convention was placed in service in March 2016 and exchanged for 27.5-year real property on February 10, 2023. The exchanged basis of the 27.5-year real property is depreciated using the mid-month convention over the portion of the 27.5 year recovery period that would remain under the mid-month convention if it had been placed in service on July 1, 2016 (deemed placed-in-service date of 20-year property under half-year convention) and disposed of on July 1, 2023 (deemed disposition date of 20-year property under half-year convention) (viz., 21.5 years—27.5 years less 6 years depreciation that would have been claimed from mid-July 2016 through mid-July 2023 under the mid-month convention) (Reg. § 1.168(i)-6(c)(6), Example (2)).

***Example (8):*** 39-year real property placed in service in March 2016 is exchanged for 15-year real property subject to the half-year convention on June 3, 2021. The exchanged basis of the 15-year property is depreciated using the mid-month convention over the remaining recovery period of the building (Reg. § 1.168(i)-6(c)(6), Example (3)). However, note that in this situation an election out of the regulations should be considered so that the exchanged basis could be depreciated over 15 years.

In the all the examples above the straight-line method will be used to determined the applicable depreciation rate. In any like-kind exchange in which real property (or any other property depreciated under the straight-line method) is involved, the straight-line method will apply. Note, however, that the straight-line method will also apply if the relinquished property is being depreciated in the year of disposition using the straight-line method due to the required switch from a declining balance method to the straight-line method in the year that the straight-line method produces a larger deduction. Similarly, the straight-line method will apply if the straight-line method would have applied to the replacement property in the year of disposition of the relinquished property if it had been placed in service at the same time as the relinquished property.

The exchanged (carryover) basis of the replacement property is depreciated using the same convention that applied to the relinquished property if neither the replacement property nor the relinquished property is subject to the mid-month convention (i.e., is not 27.5 residential rental or 39-year nonresidential real property) and the relinquished property was not acquired and disposed of in the same tax year (Reg. § 1.168(i)-6(c)(4)(v)(B)).

***Example (9):*** 5-year property subject to the half-year convention is placed in service in March 2015 and exchanged for 7-year property in April 2017. The depreciable exchanged basis of the replacement property is depreciated using the half-year convention applicable to the relinquished property over the recovery period of the replacement property that would remain if it had been placed in service in 2015 since the recovery period of the replacement property is longer than the recovery period of the relinquished property. The remaining recovery period is 5 years (7 – ½ year depreciation in 2015 – 1 year depreciation in 2016 – ½ year depreciation in 2017).

***Example (10):*** Assume the same facts as in Example 9 except that 7-year property subject to the half-year convention was placed in service in March 2015 and exchanged for 5-year property in 2017. The depreciable exchanged basis of the 5-year replacement property is depreciated using the half-year convention applicable to the relinquished property. The depreciable exchanged basis is depreciated over the remaining recovery period of the 7-year property since the recovery period of the relinquished property (7 years) is longer than the recovery period of the replacement property (5 years). The remaining recovery period is 5 years (7 - ½ year depreciation in 2015 - 1 year depreciation in 2016 – ½ year depreciation in 2017).

***Example (11):*** 3-year property subject to the mid-quarter convention is placed in service in January 2015. It is exchanged for 10-year property in December 2017. The mid-quarter convention applies to the depreciable exchanged basis. The depreciable exchanged basis is depreciated over the recovery period of the replacement property that would remain under the mid-quarter convention if it had been placed in service in the first-quarter of 2015 and disposed of in the fourth quarter of 2017. The remaining recovery period is 8 years (10 – 10.5/12 year depreciation claimed in 2015 under mid-quarter convention – 1 year depreciation in 2016 and – 1.5 year depreciation claimed in 2017 under the mid-quarter convention) (Reg. § 1.168(i)-6(c)(6), Example (4)).

In determining whether the mid-quarter convention applies to the excess basis (noncarryover/boot basis) of the replacement property (and to other property placed in service during the tax year the replacement property is placed in service), the excess basis of replacement property is always taken into account in the quarter that the replacement property is placed in service (Reg. § 1.168(i)-6(f)(2)).

In determining under the 40 percent test whether the mid-quarter convention applies to property placed in service during a tax year in which replacement property is received, the exchanged basis of the property received is ignored if the relinquished property was acquired in an earlier tax year than the tax year in which the relinquished property is disposed of and the replacement property is received (i.e., acquisition of relinquished property occurs in one tax year and disposition of relinquished property and replacement of relinquished property occur in a later tax year(s)) (Reg. § 1.168(i)-6(f)(1)(iii)). However, if the replacement property is received in a tax year subsequent to the tax year that the relinquishment of property was acquired and disposed (i.e., acquisition and disposition of relinquished property occur in same tax year and replacement of relinquished property occurs in a later tax year), the exchanged basis of the replacement property (determined without any adjustments for depreciation deductions during the taxable year) is taken into account in the year of replacement in the quarter the replacement MACRS property was placed in service by the acquiring taxpayer (Reg. § 1.168(i)-6(f)(1)(ii)). If the relinquished property is disposed of and the replacement property is received in the same tax year that the relinquished property was acquired (i.e., acquisition, disposition, and replacement occur in same tax year), the exchanged basis of the replacement property (determined without any adjustments for depreciation deductions during the taxable year) is taken into account in the year of replacement in the quarter the relinquished MACRS property was placed in service by the acquiring taxpayer (Reg. § 1.168(i)-6(f)(1)(i)).

If depreciable property is acquired for nondepreciable property in a like-kind exchange or involuntary conversion, both the exchanged basis and excess basis of the replacement property is taken into account in the year of replacement in determining whether the mid-quarter convention applies (Reg. § 1.168(i)-6(f)(3)).

**Depreciation Deductions in Year of Disposition and Year of Replacement**

The following rules apply in determining the depreciation deduction on relinquished and acquired (replacement) property in the year of disposition and year of replacement.

*14. Deduction on relinquished property in year of disposition.* Generally, the depreciation allowance on relinquished property in the year of disposition is computed by multiplying the allowable depreciation deduction for the property for the full year by a fraction, the numerator of which is the number of months the property is deemed to be placed in service during the year of disposition (taking into account the applicable convention of the relinquished property), and the denominator of which is 12 (Reg. § 1.168(i)-6(c)(5)(i)(A)). See, for example, *Example (12)*, below.

However, if the remaining recovery period of the relinquished property as of the beginning of the tax year of disposition expires before the date of disposition the taxpayer may claim the remaining undepreciated basis of the relinquished property as a depreciation deduction in the year of disposition. In this case, no portion of the basis of the replacement property is treated as an exchanged basis (Reg. § 1.168(i)-6(c)(5)(i)(B); Reg. § 1.168(i)-6(c)(6), Example 5). This rule was not contained in the temporary regulations.

No depreciation deduction may be claimed on relinquished property that is placed in service and disposed of by a taxpayer or involuntarily converted in the same tax year. No depreciation deduction may be claimed by a taxpayer on relinquished or replacement property if the replacement property is disposed of by the taxpayer in the same tax year that the relinquished property was placed in service (Reg. § 1.168(i)-6(c)(5); Reg. § 1.168(i)-6(c)(6), Example 6).

*15. Deduction on replacement property in year of acquisition.* The date that the replacement property is treated as placed in service by a taxpayer is determined by reference to the convention that applies to the replacement property under the like-kind exchange rules (Reg. § 1.168(i)-6(c)(5)(ii)(A)). See "Applicable convention for exchanged basis," above.

The remaining recovery period of the replacement property at the time of replacement is the excess of the recovery period for the replacement property as determined under the like-kind exchange rules that remains after reduction by the period of time that the replacement property would have been in service if it had been placed in service when the relinquished property was placed in service and removed from service at the time of disposition of the relinquished property. This period of time is determined by using the convention that applied to the relinquished MACRS property for purposes of determining its deemed acquisition and disposition dates. The length of time the replacement MACRS property would have been in service is determined by using these dates and the convention that applies to the replacement MACRS property (Reg. § 1.168(i)-6(c)(5)(ii)(A)). See Examples (5) through (11), above for examples showing how to determine remaining recovery period of replacement property at time of replacement.

The depreciation allowance in the tax year of replacement for the depreciable exchanged basis of the replacement property is computed as follows:

(1) determine the depreciation rate as of the beginning of the tax year of the replacement by taking into account the remaining recovery period of the replacement property as of the beginning of the tax year of replacement and depreciation method prescribed for the depreciable exchanged basis of the replacement property;

(2) add the depreciation deduction claimed on the relinquished property in the year of the disposition to the depreciable exchanged basis; and

(3) the depreciable exchanged basis as increased is multiplied by the depreciation rate and the product is multiplied by a fraction, the numerator of which is the number of months that the replacement property is deemed to be in service in the year of replacement under the convention applicable to the exchanged basis and the denominator of which is 12 (Reg. § 1.168(i)-6(c)(5)(ii)(B)).

It is important to note that for purposes of computing the depreciation rate (item (1)), the rate is determined by taking into account the recovery period of the replacement property that would remain *as of the beginning of the year* of disposition of the relinquished property. For this purpose, the replacement property is deemed to have been originally placed in service under the convention applicable to the exchanged basis but at the time the relinquished MACRS property was deemed to be placed in service under the convention that applied to the relinquished property when it was placed in service (Reg. § 1.168(i)-6(c)(5)(v)).

***Example (12):*** A parking lot, 15-year real property depreciated using the half-year convention and 150 percent declining balance method, is placed in service on January 1, 2018. On April 1, 2021, the lot is exchanged for 39-year nonresidential real property for which the straight-line method and mid-month convention is prescribed. The exchanged basis will be depreciated using mid-month convention (the mid-month convention applies if either the replacement property or relinquished property is depreciated using the mid-month convention) and the straight-line method (since the straight-line method is less accelerated than the 150 percent declining balance method).

For purposes of determining the applicable depreciation rate under the straight-line method in the year of replacement, the building's remaining depreciation period *as of the beginning of 2021* is 36 years and 6.5 months. This is determined by assuming that the building is placed in service on the date that the parking lot was placed in service under the half-year convention. Under the half-year convention the parking lot was placed in service on July 1, 2018. If the building was placed in service on July 1, 2018, then under the mid-month convention (which applies to the building) 5½ month's depreciation would have been claimed in 2018 (½ month in July and 5 months in August through December) and an additional 2 year's depreciation would have been claimed in 2019 and

2020. Thus, as of January 1, 2021, the remaining recovery period is 36 years and 6.5 months (39 – 5.5/12 – 2) or 36.541 years. 6.5 month is equivalent to .541 years (6.5/12 = .541).

The straight-line depreciation rate for 2021 is therefore .027737 (1/36.541). This rate is applied to the exchanged basis (carryover basis) of the building increased by the amount of depreciation claimed on the parking lot in 2021. The rate for 2022 is .02814 (1/35.541). This amount is applied to the unrecovered basis at the beginning of 2022 (i.e., the basis to which the 2022 rate applied reduced by the amount of depreciation claimed in 2022) (Reg. § 1.168(i)-6(c)(6), Example 8).

***Example (13):*** A bridge (15-year real property) subject to the half-year convention and 150 percent declining balance method is placed in service in January 2016 at a cost of $1,000,000,000. It is exchanged for a residential rental building (subject to the mid-month convention) in January 2021. Since the recovery period of the residential rental building is longer than the recovery period of the bridge and the straight-line method is less accelerated than the 150 percent declining balance method, the building is depreciated using the straight-line method over the amount of its 27.5 year recovery period that would remain if it had been placed in service at the same time as the bridge (taking into account the convention that applies to the bridge in the year of acquisition and disposition). Since the half-year convention applied to the bridge, the remaining recovery period of the building is determined as if it had been placed in service on July 1, 2016 and disposed of on July 1, 2021. 5½ months depreciation would have been claimed on the building in 2016 (1/2 month in July and a full month in each month of August through December) and 6½ months depreciation would have been claimed on the building in 2021 (one full month for each month of January through June and ½ month in July). One full year would have been claimed in 2017, 2018, 2019, and 2020. Thus, the remaining recovery period at the time of replacement is 21.5 years (27.5 – 5.5/12 (2016) – 5 (2017 - 2020) – 6.5/12 (2021)). The remaining recovery period at the beginning of the tax year of replacement is 22.0417 years (21.5 + 6.5/12).

The applicable straight-line rate for the year of replacement is .0454 (1/22.0417). Assuming that the undepreciated basis of the bridge after its disposition in the trade is $626,400, the exchanged basis is also $626,400. In determining the depreciation deduction on the exchanged basis of the building in the year of replacement, the exchanged basis is increased by the depreciation claimed on the bridge in the year of disposition. Assume that the depreciation deduction on the bridge in 2021 taking into account the half-year convention was $29,500 ($1,000,000 × 5.9% table percentage × 50% to reflect half-year convention). The depreciation rate is therefore applied to $655,900 ($626,400 + $29,500). Thus, the depreciation deduction for 2021 on the replacement property, taking into account the period that the replacement property was in service in 2021 by applying the mid-month convention (i.e., from the midpoint of July 2021) is $14,648 ($655,900 × .0454 × 5.5/12). The depreciation rate for 2022 is .0475 (1/21.0417). The 2022 depreciation deduction is $30,459 ($655,900 – $14,648 × .0475) (Reg. § 1.168(i)-6(c)(6), Example 2).

***Example (14):***

| Asset | Method | Conv. | Rec. Per. | Acquired | Exchanged |
|---|---|---|---|---|---|
| Office Building | S/L | MM | 39 | 1-1-2013 | 1-15-2021 |
| Transmitting Tower | 150%DB | HY | 15 | 1-15-2021 | |

A taxpayer places an office building (39-year real property depreciated using the straight-line method and mid-month convention) in service in January 2013. On January 15, 2021, the real property is exchanged for a transmitting tower (15-year real property subject to 150% DB method). Since the depreciation period for the real property (39 years) is longer than the depreciation period for the tower (15-years), the depreciable exchanged basis of the tower is depreciated over the remaining recovery period of the building as of the January 15, 2021 date of the exchange. The mid-month convention applies to the tower since the mid-month convention applies if either the relinquished or replacement property is subject to the mid-month convention. Under the mid-month convention the office building has been in service 8 years up to the time of disposition taking into account the mid-month convention (mid-January 2013 through mid-January 2021) and 31 years remain in the recovery period (39 – 8). The straight-line method and mid-month convention apply to compute the deductions on the depreciable exchanged basis of the tower.

The office building cost $100,000 and $20,406 of depreciation was claimed through 2020. The 2021 deduction on the office building is $107 ($100,000 × 1/39) (this represents a full year's deduction) × 1/2 (number of months deemed in service under the mid-month convention in 2021)/12). The depreciable exchanged basis of the tower after the exchange is $79,487 ($100,000 – $20,406 – $107). The 2021 deduction for the tower is $2,457 ($79,487 × .03226 × 11.5/12). 11.5 is the number of months that the tower is in service in 2021 taking into account the mid-month convention.

The straight-line depreciation rate for the tower in the year of acquisition is based on the recovery period that would remain as of the beginning of the tax year of disposition (not the recovery period that remains as of the time of disposition) (Reg. § 1.168(i)-6(c)(5)(ii)(B)(1)). The remaining recovery period is 31.0417 years (39 – 7.9583 years depreciation claimed as of January 1, 2021 ((11.5 months (2013) + 7 years (2014 - 2020) = 7.9583)). The straight-line rate for the year of replacement is .0322 (1/31.0417). This rate is applied to $79,594 (the depreciable exchanged basis of the office building ($79,487) increased by the depreciation claimed on the building in the year of disposition ($107)) (Reg. § 1.168(i)-6(c)(5)(ii)(B)(2)). The depreciation deduction on the tower in 2021 is therefore $2,456 ($79,594 × .0322 × 11.5/12). 11.5 is the number of months the tower was in service under the mid-month convention.

In 2022 and each full recovery year during the remaining recovery period, the depreciation deduction on the exchanged basis of the tower is equal to $2,563 ($79,594 × .0322) (Reg. § 1.168(i)-6(c)(6), Example 3).

Note that in the preceding example, the taxpayer could maximize deductions on the tower by simply electing out of the regulations. If an election out is made, the tower could be depreciated over 15 years using the half-year convention and 150% DB method rather than over the 31 years that remain in the building's recovery period using the straight line method.

***Example (15):*** A tool, costing $60,000, is exchanged for equipment.

| Asset | Method | Conv. | Rec. Per. | Acquired | Exchanged |
|---|---|---|---|---|---|
| Tool | S/L (elective) | MQ | 3 | 2-1-2014 | 6-15-2016 |
| Equipment | 200 DB | HY | 7 | 6-15-2016 | |

Since the recovery period of the equipment (7 years) is longer than the recovery period of the tool (3) years, the equipment is depreciated as if it had originally been placed in service on 2-15-2014 (date tools were placed in service under mid-quarter convention) using a 7-year recovery period. Also since the recovery method of the equipment (200% DB method) is more accelerated than the recovery method of the tool (S/L) at the time of replacement (2016), the exchanged basis of the equipment is depreciated using the S/L method. Since the mid-quarter convention was used to depreciate the tools (relinquished property) and the replacement property is not real property, the mid-quarter convention is used to depreciate the exchanged basis (Reg. § 1.168(i)-6(c)(4)(v)(B)).

If the equipment had originally been placed in service on 2-15-2014 it would also be considered placed in service on the same date under the mid-quarter convention and its remaining recovery period at the time of the exchange would be 4.75 years (7 – .875 years (or 10.5/12 months) (2014) – 1 year (2015) – .375 years (or 4.5/12 months) (2016) = 4.75 years).

Depreciation on the tools, assuming they cost $60,000, through 2015 is computed as follows:

| Year | Deduction | |
|---|---|---|
| 2014 | $17,500 | ($60,000 × 1/3 × 10.5/12) |
| 2015 | 20,000 | ($60,000 × 1/3) |

The depreciation allowance on the tools in 2016 is computed by multiplying the allowable depreciation deduction for the tools for 2016 without regard to the exchange by a fraction, the numerator of which is the number of months the tools are deemed to be placed in service during 2016 (taking into account the mid-quarter convention and the disposition), and the denominator of which is 12 (Reg. § 1.168(i)-6(c)(5)(i)).

The regular depreciation deduction for the tools in 2016 without regard to the exchange is computed as follows:

| | | |
|---|---|---|
| 2016 | $7,500 | ($60,000 × 1/3 × 4.5/12) |

4.5 is the number of months that the tools are considered to be in service in 2016 if disposed of in June under the mid-quarter convention (January 1 — May 15 = 4.5 months).

The remaining recovery period of the depreciable exchanged basis (i.e., the equipment) as of the beginning of 2015 is determined by assuming (a) the equipment has a 7-year recovery period, (b) the mid-quarter convention applies, and (c) that the equipment was placed in service in the first-quarter of 2014. The remaining recovery period as of the beginning of 2016 is, therefore, deemed to be 5.125 years (7 - .875 years (or 10.5/12 months) (2014) - 1 year (2015) = 5.125 years).

The depreciation rate, which is determined by reference to the remaining recovery period as of the beginning of the tax year (Reg. § 1.168(i)-6(c)(5)(ii)(B)) is, therefore, 0.1951 (1/5.125). The exchanged basis is $15,000 ($60,000 cost of tools - $17,500 (2014 depreciation) - $20,000 (2015 depreciation) - $7,500 (2016 depreciation prior to exchange)). The exchanged basis is increased by $7,500 to $22,500 (Reg. § 1.168(i)-6(c)(5)(ii)(B)). The deduction on the replacement equipment in the replacement year is, therefore, $2,744 ($22,500 × 19.51% × 7.5/12). 7.5 is the number of months that the equipment is deemed in service under the mid-quarter convention if acquired in June, 2016 (i.e., May 15 through December 31) (Reg. § 1.168(i)-6(c)(6), Example 4).

***Example (16):*** The facts are the same as in Example above except that the exchange takes place in June 2017. Under these facts, the remaining recovery period of the tool at the beginning of 2017 is 1.5 months and, as a result, is less than the 5-month period between the beginning of 2017 (year of disposition) and June 2017 (time of disposition). As a result, the 2017 depreciation allowance for the tools is $2,500 ($2,500 adjusted depreciable basis at the beginning of 2017 ($60,000 original basis minus $17,500 depreciation deduction for 2014 minus $20,000 depreciation deduction for 2015 minus $20,000 depreciation deduction for 2016)). Because the exchanged basis of the equipment is $0.00 no depreciation is allowable for the equipment (Reg. § 1.168(i)-6(c)(5)(i)(B); Reg. § 1.168(i)-6(c)(6), Example 5).

*16. Deferred like-kind exchanges transactions.* No depreciation may be claimed on relinquished MACRS property during the period between the disposition of the relinquished property and acquisition of the replacement property in a deferred exchange (except to the extent that depreciation is allowed under the applicable convention). The regulations reserve the issue of whether an exchange accommodation titleholder (or other intermediary) may claim depreciation (Reg. § 1.168(i)-6(c)(5)(iv)).

*17. Exchanges of multiple properties.* The determination of the basis of property acquired in a like-kind exchange involving multiple properties is described in Reg. § 1.1031(j)-1 and the determination of the basis of multiple properties acquired as a result of an involuntary conversion is described in Reg. § 1.1033(b)-1. Once basis in property is determined or allocated is so determined, these depreciation regulations apply to compute the depreciation allowable with respect to such basis (T.D. 9314, preamble).

*18. Involuntary conversions: replacement property placed in service before disposition of relinquished property.* A taxpayer who places replacement property from an involuntary conversion in service before disposing of the involuntarily converted property (see Code Sec. 1033(a)(2)(B), relating to acquisitions under threat of condemnation) should compute depreciation on the unadjusted depreciation basis of the replacement property without regard to the special rules under these regulations. However, at the time the relinquished property is disposed of the taxpayer should determine the exchanged and excess basis of the replacement property and begin to compute depreciation in accordance with the regulations. Furthermore, in the tax year that the relinquished property is disposed, the excess of the depreciation deductions allowable on the unadjusted depreciable basis of the replacement property over the depreciation deductions that would have been allowable on the depreciable excess basis of the replacement property from the date that the replacement property was placed in service (under the applicable convention) to the time of disposition of the relinquished property is recaptured (i.e., included in taxable income). Special rules apply if bonus depreciation is claimed on the replacement property (Reg. § 1.168(I)-6(d)(4)).

**Computations Using the Optional Depreciation Tables**

A taxpayer may use the optional depreciation tables to compute depreciation on the replacement property, whether or not the tables were used on the relinquished property (Reg. § 1.168(i)-6(e)(1)).

*19. Depreciation on relinquished property in year of disposition using tables.* Using the optional tables, the depreciation deduction on the relinquished property in the year of disposition is determined by multiplying the cost of the property (as reduced by any amount expensed under section 179 and as bonus depreciation) by the appropriate table percentage. The product is then adjusted to take into account the applicable convention (Reg. § 1.168(i)-6(e)(2)(i)).

> ***Example (18):*** 7-year property purchased in 2017 for $100,000 and subject to the half-year convention is involuntarily converted in 2021. No amount was expensed or claimed as bonus depreciation. The 2021 deduction is $4,465 ($100,000 × .0893 (fifth year table percentage expressed as a decimal) × 6/12 to reflect the half-year convention).

*20. Depreciation on excess basis using tables.* Any excess basis in the replacement property (e.g., additional cash paid for the replacement property in a trade-in) is treated as property placed in service at the time of the replacement. The excess basis is depreciated using the applicable table for the property (Reg. § 1.168(i)-6(e)(3)). The excess basis may be eligible for the Code Sec. 179 expense allowance and bonus depreciation. See "*Section 179 allowance and bonus depreciation,*" above.

*21. Depreciation on exchanged basis using tables.* The depreciation allowances for the depreciable exchanged basis are determined by applying table percentages from the table that corresponds to the recovery period, depreciation method, and convention of the replacement property that is determined under the rules that apply when the tables are not used (Reg. § 1.168(i)-6(e)(2)(ii)(A)).

The following steps apply in determining the depreciation deduction for the exchanged basis during each year of its remaining recovery period:

(1) Determine the appropriate depreciation table;

(2) Determine the appropriate recovery year from the table;

(3) The applicable table percentage (expressed as a decimal) for that year is multiplied by a transaction coefficient;

(4) The applicable depreciation rate for the year, as determined in (3), is applied to the depreciable exchanged basis.

The appropriate recovery year for the year of replacement is always the same recovery year that applied to the relinquished property in the year of its disposition (Reg. § 1.168(i)-6(e)(2)(ii)(B)(1)).

In the year of replacement, the depreciation deduction on the depreciable exchanged basis is adjusted to reflect the applicable convention (i.e., multiplied by a fraction, the numerator of which is the number of months (or partial months) the replacement property is deemed to be in service under the applicable convention and the denominator of which is 12) (Reg. § 1.168(i)-6(e)(2)(ii)(B)(2)).

If the replacement property has unrecovered depreciable basis after the final recovery year (this might occur in a deferred exchange), the unrecovered basis is claimed as a depreciation deduction in the tax year that corresponds to the final recovery year (Reg. § 1.168(i)-6(e)(2)(iii)).

*22. Transaction coefficient when using tables.* The transaction coefficient is equal to the following formula:

1/(1-x)

x is equal to the sum of the annual depreciation rates from the appropriate depreciation table (item 1) expressed as a decimal for the tax years beginning with the placed-in-service year of the relinquished property through the tax year immediately prior to the year of disposition.

The transaction coefficient is not recomputed each year.

***Example (19):*** 5-year property placed in service in 2017 is exchanged in an involuntary conversion for 7-year property in 2019. Assume that the appropriate table for computing depreciation on the depreciable exchanged basis of the replacement property is the table that applies to 7-year property using the half-year convention and 200% DB method. The sum of the recovery percentages expressed as a decimal for the first two recovery years prior to the exchange in the third recovery year is .3878 (.1429 + .2449). The transaction coefficient is 1.6335 (1/(1 – .3878)).

***Example (20):*** 5-year property costing $10,000 is placed in service in 2018. The half-year convention and 200% DB method apply to the 5-year property. Table 1 for 5-year property is used to compute deductions. The property is exchanged in an involuntary conversion in 2019 for 7-year property.

Since the replacement property has a longer recovery period (7 years vs. 5 years) and the same depreciation method applies in the disposition year to both the 5-year year property (200% DB method) and to the 7-year property if it had been placed in service in 2018 (200% DB method), the appropriate depreciation table for depreciating the exchanged basis of the replacement property is the table that applies to 7-year property, subject to the 200% DB method and the half-year convention (Table 1 for 7-year property at ¶ 180). The half-year convention applies because the 5-year property was depreciated using the half-year convention and the replacement property is not real property subject to the mid-month convention.

The depreciable exchanged basis of the 7-year property is $3,840 ($10,000 – $2,000 depreciation claimed on the 5-year property in 2018 ($10,000 × 20%) – $3,200 claimed in 2019 ($10,000 × 32%), and – $960 claimed in 2021 ($10,000 × 19.2% × 6/12 to reflect half-year convention)).

The depreciation deduction on the depreciable exchanged basis in 2021 is determined by reference to the third-year table percentage (17.49% or .1749) since this is the recovery that would apply to the replacement property in 2021 if it had been placed in service in 2018.

The transaction coefficient is 1.6335 (1/(1 – (.1429 + .2449))).

The depreciation rate for 2021 is, therefore, .2857 (.1749 × 1.6335).

The depreciation deduction on the exchanged basis in 2021 is $549 ($3,840 × .2857 × 6/12 (to reflect half-year convention)).

The depreciation rate for 2022 is .2040 (.1249 (year 4 table rate) × 1.6335).

The depreciation deduction on the exchanged basis in 2022 is $783 ($3,840 × .2040). (Reg. § 1.168(i)-6(e)(4), Example 1).

***Example (21):*** 5-year property costing $100,000 is placed in service in 2015. This property is subject to the half year convention and is depreciated using the 200DB method. The table percentage from Table 1 ¶ 164.01 for five-year property is used.

In 2019 (the fifth recovery year) the 5-year property is involuntarily converted.

In 2022, the 5-year property is replaced with 7-year property that would have been depreciated using the 200% DB method and half-year convention if placed in service in 2015.

Depreciation claimed on the 5-year property through 2019 amounted to $88,480 ($100,000 - $20,000 ($100,000 x .20) - $32,000 ($100,000 x .32) - $19,200 ($100,000 x .1920) - $11,520 ($100,000 x .1152) - $5,760 ($100,000 x .1152 x 6/12)).

The adjusted depreciable basis of the 5-year property at the time of replacement was $11,520 ($100,000 - $88,480).

The appropriate depreciation table for the 7-year property is based on the depreciation method that was being used to compute depreciation on the 5-year property in the year of its disposition. Referring to Table 1 at ¶ 180 and the depreciation percentages for 5-year property, it can be seen that in the fifth recovery year a switch was made from the 200DB method to the straight-line method when the (straight-line) rate became 11.52%. (Note that the DB rate and straight-line rate were identical in the fourth recovery year, therefore, the switch was actually considered made under IRS guidelines in the fifth recovery year). Since the 5-year property was being depreciated using the straight-line rate at the time of its disposition in its fifth recovery year, the 7-year replacement property must be depreciated using the straight-line method. The appropriate table, therefore, is the straight-line table for 7-year property subject to the half-year convention. These percentages are located in Table 8 at ¶ 180. This table would presumably not have been used if the disposition had occurred in the fourth recovery year when the DB and SL rates were identical.

For purposes of computing depreciation deductions on the exchanged basis the transaction coefficient, as determined by reference to this table, is 2.00 (1/(1 -.0714 - .1429 - .1429 - .1428) = 2.00).

The depreciation deduction on the exchanged basis for 2022 is determined by reference to the fifth-year table percentage (14.29% or .1429) and taking into account the half-year convention. The 2022 deduction is $1,646 ($11,520 depreciable exchanged basis after the involuntary conversion x .1429 x 2.00 x 6/12).

The depreciation deduction for 2023 (the sixth recovery year) is $3,290 ($11,520 x .1428 x 2.00).

The depreciation deduction for 2024 (the seventh recovery year) is $3,292 ($11,520 x .1429 x 2.00).

In the last recovery year (the eighth recovery year), the depreciation deduction is $1,645 ($11,520 x .0714 x 2.00). However, since $1,645 is less than the unrecovered basis of $3,292 ($11,520 - $1,646 - $3,290 - $3,292), the entire unrecovered basis is deducted. (Reg. § 1.168(i)-6(e)(4), Example (2)).

***Example (22):*** A computer is purchased in 2017 for $5,000 and destroyed (involuntarily converted) in a fire in 2019. The computer was depreciated using the 200DB method and half-year convention (Table 1 (at ¶ 164.01) percentages for five-year property). The computer was replaced in 2019.

The depreciation claimed in 2017 through 2019 on the destroyed computer amounted to $3,080 ($5,000 – $1,000 ($5,000 × .20) – $3,200 ($5,000 × .32) – $480 ($5,000 × .1920 × 6/12)).

The exchanged basis of the replacement computer acquired in 2019 is $1,920 ($5,000 – $3,080).

The replacement computer will be depreciated using the same depreciation method, recovery period, and convention as the destroyed computer. The applicable table for computing depreciation deductions on the exchanged basis is the same table that applies to the destroyed computer.

The transaction coefficient is 2.08 (1/1 – .20 – .32).

The depreciation rate for computing depreciation on the exchanged basis in 2019 is .40 (.192 × 2.08). The 2019 deduction, taking into account the half-year convention, is $384 ($1,920 × .40 × 6/12).

Depreciation for 2020 and 2022 is $460 ($1,920 × .1152 × 2.08) each year.

Depreciation for 2023 (the last recovery year) is $230 ($1,920 × .0576 × 2.08). However, since the unrecovered basis of $616 ($1,920 – $384 – $460 – $460) is greater than $230, the entire unrecovered basis is claimed as a deduction (Reg. § 1.168(i)-6(e)(4), Example (3)).

# Change in Use

## ¶ 168

## MACRS Property Converted to Personal Use or Business Use

Special rules contained in IRS regulations may apply to determine MACRS depreciation when a taxpayer changes the use to which property is put (Reg. § 1.168(i)-4, as added by T.D. 9132).

Changes in use covered by the rules include a conversion of personal use property to business or income-producing use property and vice versa. Most significantly, a change in use includes a change in the taxpayer's use of MACRS property that causes the property to have a different recovery period, depreciation method, or both (¶ 169). For example, a change in use occurs if a taxpayer switches the business activity in which a property is used, causing it to have a new recovery period.

*Effective date of change in use regulations.* The change in use regulations generally apply to a change in use of MACRS property that occurs in a tax year ending on or after June 17, 2004. For a change in use of MACRS property after December 31, 1986, in a tax year ending before June 17, 2004, the IRS will allow any reasonable method that is consistently applied. A taxpayer may also choose, on a property-by-property basis, to apply the regulations to MACRS property placed in service before June 17, 2004 (Reg. § 1.168(i)-4(g), preamble to T.D. 9132).

*Changing accounting methods to conform to regulations.* A change to conform to the regulations due to a change in use of MACRS property in a tax year ending on or after December 30, 2003 is a change in method of accounting if the taxpayer has adopted a method of accounting (for example, by filing two or more returns using the nonconforming method). The regulations provide that taxpayer may (i.e., is not required to) treat a change to conform to the regulations due a change in use after December 31, 1986, in a tax year ending before December 30, 2003 as a change in method of accounting. Thus, an amended return may be filed for an open tax year in this situation. Procedures for obtaining consent to change accounting methods to conform to the regulations are provided in Reg. § 1.168(i)-4(g)(2). The automatic consent procedures of Sections 6.04 and 6.05 of Rev. Proc. 2019-43, superseding Rev. Proc. 2018-31 currently apply (see ¶ 75). Sec. 6.05 of Rev. Proc. 2018-31 was modified by Rev. Proc. 2019-8 to clarify that a Code Sec. 481(a) adjustment is required if a taxpayer has adopted an impermissible accounting method by failing to timely apply the change in use rules (i.e., by filing two or more improper returns). This change is reflected in the text of Sec. 6.05 of Rev. Proc. 2019-43.

### *Personal Property Converted to Business or Income-Producing Use*

Personal-use property converted to business or income-producing use is treated as placed in service by the taxpayer on the date of the conversion. This type of conversion includes property that was previously used by the taxpayer for personal purposes, including real property (other than land) that is acquired before 1987 and converted from personal use to business or income-producing use after 1986, and depreciable property that was previously used by a tax-exempt entity before it changed to a taxable entity (Reg. § 1.168(i)-4(b)).

Upon a conversion to business or income-producing use, the depreciation allowance for the tax year of change and any subsequent tax year is determined as though the property was placed in service by the taxpayer on the date on which the conversion occurs. Thus, the taxpayer may choose any applicable depreciation method, recovery period, and convention for the property in the year of change, consistent with any depreciation election made by the taxpayer for that year. The depreciable basis of the property for the year of change is the lesser of its fair market value or its adjusted depreciable basis (as defined in Reg. § 1.168(b)-1(a)(4)), as applicable, at the time of the conversion to business or income-producing use.

***Example (1):*** Anne Elyse, a calendar-year taxpayer, purchases a house in 1986 that she occupies as her principal residence. In February 2021, Ms. Elyse ceases to occupy the house and converts it to residential rental property. At the time of the conversion to residential rental property, the house's fair market value (excluding land) is $130,000 and the adjusted depreciable basis attributable to the house (excluding land) is $150,000. Ms. Elyse is considered to have placed in service MACRS 27.5-year residential rental property (¶ 114) in February 2021 with a depreciable basis of $130,000. Ms. Elyse depreciates the residential rental property under the general depreciation system by using the straight-line method, a 27.5-year recovery period, and the mid-month convention. Thus, the depreciation allowance for the house for 2021 is $4,137, after taking into account the mid-month convention (($130,000 adjusted depreciable basis multiplied by the applicable depreciation rate of 3.636% (1/27.5)) multiplied by the mid-month convention fraction of 10.5/12).

Property converted to business or income-producing use after 2015 qualifies for bonus depreciation even though it was originally acquired by the taxpayer before 2008. Property converted to business or income-producing use after 2007 and before 2016 does not qualify if it was acquired by the taxpayer before 2008 (Reg. § 1.168(k)-1(f)(6)(iii)). If the property was not new when acquired for personal use, it does not qualify for bonus depreciation upon conversion to business use unless the used property was acquired for personal use after September 27, 2017.

Property converted from personal use to business does not qualify for expensing under Code Sec. 179 because it was not acquired by the taxpayer for use in the active conduct of a taxpayer's trade or business as required by Code Sec. 179(d)(1).

*MACRS Property Converted to Personal Use*

A conversion of MACRS property from business or income-producing use to personal use is treated as a disposition of the property. Depreciation for the year of change is computed by taking into account the applicable convention. Existing IRS guidance (Rev. Rul. 69-487, 1969-2 C.B. 165) indicates that no gain, loss, or depreciation recapture is recognized upon the conversion (Reg. § 1.168(i)-4(c)).

The depreciation allowance for MACRS property for the year of change is determined by first multiplying the adjusted depreciable basis of the property (as defined in Reg. § 1.168(b)-1(a)(4)) as of the first day of the year of change by the applicable depreciation rate for that tax year. This amount is then multiplied by a fraction, the numerator of which is the number of months (including fractions of months) the property is deemed in service during the year of change (taking into account the applicable convention) and the denominator of which is 12. No depreciation deduction is allowable for MACRS property placed in service and disposed of in the same tax year. See ¶ 160. Upon the conversion to personal use, no gain, loss, or depreciation recapture is recognized. However, the recapture provisions apply to any disposition of the converted property by the taxpayer at a later date (Reg. § 1.168(i)-4(c)).

***Example (2):*** Seven-year property is placed in service in 2020 and used 100% for business. In 2021, the property is converted to personal use. The half-year convention applied in 2020. Assume that the property cost $100,000 and no amount was expensed under Code Sec. 179 or claimed as bonus depreciation. 2020 depreciation was $14,286 ($100,000 × 1/7 × 2 × 6/12 to reflect half-year convention). In 2021, the taxpayer is also entitled to one-half year's depreciation or $12,245 ($85,714 × 1/7 × 2 × 6/12 to reflect half-year convention that applies during the year of the deemed disposition).

If an amount has been expensed under Code Sec. 179, and a property which is not listed property is converted to personal use before the end of its recovery period, the Code Sec. 179 expense deduction (but not any bonus deduction) is subject to recapture under Code Sec. 179(d)(10) because business use has declined to 50 percent or less. See ¶ 300 for a discussion of this recapture rule.

If the property converted to personal use is a listed property (such as an automobile) the difference between the depreciation claimed (including any amount expensed under Code Sec. 179 or claimed as bonus depreciation) and the amount that would have been claimed using the alternative depreciation system is recaptured pursuant to Code Sec. 280F(b)(2) because business use has declined to 50 percent or less (Reg. § 1.168(i)-4(c)). See ¶ 210.

## ¶ 169

## Changes in MACRS Property Use Resulting in Different Recovery Period or Method

MACRS regulations provide the rules for determining the annual MACRS depreciation allowances if a change in use of a property results in a different recovery period, depreciation method, or both. Generally, the rules differ depending upon whether the use changes in the tax year in which the property is placed in service or after the tax year the property is placed in service (Reg. § 1.168(i)-4(d)).

A change in computing the depreciation allowance *in the tax year the use of the property changes* to comply with the change in use regulations is not a change in accounting method under Code Sec. 446(e) (Reg. § 1.168(i)-4(f)). If a taxpayer does not apply the regulations in the tax year that the change in use occurs and has filed two or more returns, then it may be necessary to obtain consent to change accounting methods. See, "*Effective date of change in use regulations,*" at ¶ 168 above.

If MACRS property is depreciated using the depreciation tables before the change in use, the taxpayer may continue to depreciate the property using the tables after the change in use. However, the taxpayer is not required to do so. A taxpayer who did not use the tables may only switch to the tables if the change in use results in a shorter recovery period or more accelerated depreciation method.

*MACRS Property Changes Use in Same Tax Year Placed in Service.* If the use of MACRS property changes during its placed-in-service year, the depreciation allowance is simply determined by reference to the primary use of the property during that tax year. However, in determining whether MACRS property is used within or outside the United States during the placed-in-service year, the predominant use, instead of the primary use, of the MACRS property governs. Further, in determining whether MACRS property is tax-exempt use property or imported property covered by an Executive order during the placed-in-service year, the use of the property at the end of the placed-in-service year governs. If property is so categorized at year-end, the ADS system would apply; otherwise the GDS system would apply. Moreover, MACRS property is tax-exempt bond financed property during the placed-in-service year if a tax-exempt bond for the MACRS property is issued during that year. Depreciation on MACRS property that changes to tax exempt bond financed property in the placed-in-service year is also determined under the ADS system (Reg. § 1.168(i)-4(e)).

*MACRS Property Changes Use in Tax Year After Placed in Service.* The regulations provide computation rules for MACRS property if a taxpayer changes the use of property after the property's placed-in-service year but the property continues to be MACRS property in the hands of the taxpayer. The rules apply if the property continues to be MACRS property owned by the same taxpayer and, as a result of the change in use, has a different recovery period, a different depreciation method, or both. For example, this rule applies to MACRS property that:

(1) Begins or ceases to be used predominantly outside the United States;

(2) Results in a change in the property class of the property (e.g., 3-year property converted to 5-year property) due to a change in the use of the property; or

(3) Begins or ceases to be tax-exempt use property (Reg. § 1.168(i)-4(d)).

In general, the regulations provide that a change in the use of MACRS property occurs when the primary use of the MACRS property in the tax year is different from its primary use in the immediately preceding tax year. If a change in the use of MACRS property has occurred, the depreciation allowance for the MACRS property for the year of change is determined as though the change in the use of the MACRS property occurred on the first day of the year of change (Reg. § 1.168(i)-4(d)(2)).

*Computation if change in use results in shorter recovery period or more accelerated depreciation method.* If a change in the use of MACRS property results in a *shorter* recovery period and/or a *more accelerated* depreciation method (for example, MACRS property ceases to be used predominantly outside the United States), the adjusted depreciable basis of the property (as defined in Reg. § 1.168(b)-1(a)(4)) as of the beginning of the year of change is depreciated over the shorter recovery period and/or by the more accelerated depreciation method beginning with the year of change as though the MACRS property was first placed in service in the year of change. Under certain circumstances, this rule may adversely affect taxpayers (Reg. § 1.168(i)-4(d)(3)).

For example, if a change in the use of MACRS property would result in a shorter recovery period, a taxpayer must depreciate that MACRS property over the new shorter recovery period even if the remaining portion of the original longer recovery period is less than the new shorter recovery period. To avoid this adverse effect, the regulations allow a taxpayer to elect to continue to depreciate the MACRS property for which the new recovery period is shorter or a more accelerated method is allowed as though the change in use had not occurred. The election is made by computing depreciation on Form 4562 as if the change in use had not occurred.

***Example (1):*** A taxpayer changes the use of 20-year property subject to the 150% DB method to a use which results in its conversion to 5-year property subject to the 200% DB method. Assume that the change in use occurs during the 18th year of the 20-year recovery period. If no election out of the regulations is made, the taxpayer will recover the remaining basis of the property by depreciating it as though it were five-year property placed in service in the year of the change in use. If an election out is made, the basis is recovered over the 2 remaining recovery years in the 20-year recovery period.

Assuming that the election out is not made, the depreciation allowances for the MACRS property for any 12-month taxable year beginning with the year of change are determined by multiplying the adjusted depreciable basis of the MACRS property as of the first day of each tax year by the applicable depreciation rate for each tax year. In determining the applicable depreciation rate for the year of change and subsequent tax years, the taxpayer may choose any applicable depreciation method and recovery period for the MACRS property in the year of change, consistent with any MACRS depreciation election made by the taxpayer for that year. If there is a change in the use of MACRS property, the applicable convention that applies to the MACRS property is the same as the convention that applied before the change in the use of the MACRS property. However, the depreciation allowance for the year of change for the MACRS property is determined without applying the applicable convention, unless the MACRS property is disposed of during the year of change. Special rules apply to the computation of the depreciation allowance under the optional depreciation tables as explained below. If the year of change or any subsequent tax year is less than 12 months, the depreciation allowance must be adjusted for a short taxable year (Reg. § 1.168(i)-4(d)(3)).

MACRS property which has a shorter or longer recovery period or a more or less accelerated depreciation method as a result of a change in use in a tax year after it was placed in service is not eligible in the year of change for (1) the election to depreciate under the unit-of-production method or any method of depreciation not expressed in a term of years, (2) the Code Sec. 179 expensing election or (3) the additional first-year depreciation deduction (bonus depreciation) (there is no affect, however, on previously claimed bonus depreciation). For purposes of determining whether the mid-quarter convention would apply to other MACRS property placed in service during the year of change, the basis of the MACRS property which changes use in a tax year after it was placed in service is not taken into account in applying the 40 percent mid-quarter convention test (Reg. § 1.168(i)-4(d)(3)(i)(C); Reg. § 1.168(i)-4(d)(4)(i)).

> ***Example (2):*** ABC Corp., a calendar-year corporation, places $100,000 of 7-year property in service in 2017. The property is subject to the half-year convention and depreciated using the 200% DB method. Depreciation claimed through 2020 amounted to $77,689. In 2021, the primary business use of the property changes, and, as a result, it is reclassified as 5-year property. As of January 1, 2021, the adjusted depreciable basis is $22,311 ($100,000 – $77,689). ABC may (1) elect to continue depreciating the property as 7-year property or (2) depreciate the property as 5-year property placed in service in 2021. 2021 depreciation, assuming option (2) is chosen, is $8,924 ($22,311 × 40% (1/5 × 2)). Note that although 2021 is considered the first-year of the five-year recovery period, no adjustment is made for the half-year convention.

*Computation if change in use results in longer recovery period or slower depreciation method.* If a change in the use of MACRS property (in a tax year after it has been placed in service) would result in a *longer* recovery period and/or *slower depreciation* method (for example, MACRS property begins to be used predominantly outside the United States), the adjusted depreciable basis of the property is depreciated over the longer recovery period and/or by the slower depreciation method beginning with the year of change as though the taxpayer originally placed the MACRS property in service with the longer recovery period and/or slower depreciation method. Accordingly, the adjusted depreciable basis of the MACRS property as of the beginning of the year of change is depreciated over the remaining portion of the new, longer recovery period as of the beginning of the year of change (Reg. § 1.168(i)-4(d)(4)).

The depreciation allowances for the MACRS property for any 12-month taxable year beginning with the year of change are determined by multiplying the adjusted depreciable basis of the MACRS property as of the first day of each tax year by the applicable depreciation rate for each taxable year. The applicable convention that applies to the MACRS property is the same as the convention that applied before the change in the use of the MACRS property. If the year of change or any subsequent tax year is less than 12 months, the depreciation allowance is adjusted for a short tax year (Reg. § 1.168(i)-4(d)(4)).

If a change in use results in a longer recovery period and/or a slower depreciation method, a taxpayer may choose to use the depreciation tables in the tax year of a change in use and the following years in the remaining recovery period only if the table percentages were used prior to the change-in-use year (Reg. § 1.168(i)-4(d)(5)(i)). See below.

Assuming that the optional tables are not used, the following rules apply for purposes of determining the applicable depreciation rate (which is based on the applicable method and recovery period) for the year of change and any subsequent tax years:

The applicable depreciation method in the year of change or a subsequent tax year is the method that would have applied in the year of change or the subsequent tax year if the taxpayer had used the longer recovery period and/or the slower depreciation method in the placed in service year of the property. For example, if the 200 percent or 150 percent declining balance method would have applied in the placed-in-service year but the method would have switched to the straight line method in the year of change (or any prior tax year) the applicable depreciation method in the year of change is the straight-line method (Reg. § 1.168(i)-4(d)(4)(ii)(A)).

The applicable recovery period is either (Reg. § 1.168(i)-4(d)(4)(ii)(B)):

(1) The longer recovery period resulting from the change in the use if the applicable depreciation method is the 200- or 150-percent declining balance method (as determined above) unless the recovery period did not change as a result of the change in the use, in which case the applicable recovery period is the same recovery period that applied before the change in the use; or

(2) The number of years remaining as of the beginning of each tax year (taking into account the applicable convention) had the taxpayer used the longer recovery period in the placed-in-service year of the property if the applicable depreciation method is the straight line method (as determined above) unless the recovery period did not change as a result of the change in the use, in which case the applicable recovery period is the number of years remaining as of the beginning of each taxable year (taking into account the applicable convention) based on the recovery period that applied before the change in the use.

***Example (3):*** International Corp. places $100,000 of property in service in 2019. The property has a five-year recovery period, is subject to the half-year convention, and the 200% declining-balance method applies. In 2021, the property is moved outside of the U.S. As a result of this change in use, ADS is required. Assume the ADS recovery period is nine years. The ADS system uses the straight-line method. Assume further that International Corp. claimed a total of $52,000 of depreciation in 2019 and 2020 and that the adjusted depreciable basis of the property is, therefore, $48,000 ($100,000 – $52,000) at the beginning of 2021. 2021 depreciation is computed on $48,000 as if the property had originally been placed in service outside of the U.S. in 2019. If the property had been placed in service outside of the U.S. in 2019, the remaining recovery period at the beginning of 2021 would have been 7.5 years (9 years less 1/2 year depreciation in 2019 (half-year convention applied) and 1 year depreciation in 2020). The straight-line rate for 2021 is 1/7.5 or 13.33%. 2021 depreciation is $6,398 ($48,000 × 13.33%). Depreciation for 2022 is $6,398 ($41,602 adjusted depreciable basis × 15.38% (1/6.5 years remaining in the recovery period)) (Reg. § 1.168(i)-4(d)(6)).

*Computing MACRS Deductions Upon Change in Use With Optional Depreciation Tables.* A taxpayer who used a depreciation table to compute depreciation prior to the change-in-use year may use a depreciation table in the change-in-use year and later years in the applicable recovery period. A taxpayer who previously used the table percentages is not required to continue using table percentages. If the taxpayer did not use table percentages before the change in use, table percentages may only be used (beginning in the year of change) if the change in use results in a shorter recovery period and/or a more accelerated depreciation method (Reg. § 1.168(i)-5(i)).

*Computation using tables when change in use results in shorter recovery period and/or more accelerated depreciation method.* Assuming that the change in use results in a shorter recovery period and/or a more accelerated depreciation method, a taxpayer has the option of using the table percentages whether or not the table percentages were being used before the change in use. The depreciation allowances using table percentages are determined by multiplying the adjusted depreciable basis of the asset as of the beginning of the tax year of the change by the first-year table percentage. The second year table percentage is applied in the following tax year and so on until the end of the new shorter recovery period. The appropriate percentage table is based on the depreciation system, depreciation method, and recovery period applicable to the MACRS property in the year of change, as discussed above. Note that the applicable convention is the same convention that applied to the property before the change in use (Reg. § 1.168(i)-5(ii)(A)).

> ***Example (4):*** Assume the same facts as in Example 2. Since the change in use results in a shorter recovery period, ABC Corporation may compute the deductions in the change of use and subsequent years using the optional table percentages. This choice is available whether or not the property was originally depreciated using the tables. Assuming the tables will be used, the appropriate table is the table that applies to 5-year property subject to the half-year convention. The 2021 deduction using this table is $4,462 ($22,311 × 20% (first-year table percentage for 5-year property subject to half-year convention)). Note that the first-year table percentage (20%) reflects the half-year convention.

Taxpayers should be aware that using the table percentages when the change in use results in a shorter recovery period or more accelerated depreciation method will result in less depreciation in the year of change in use because the applicable convention is factored into the first-year depreciation table percentage. If the table percentages are not used, the convention is not taken into account in the year of change, and a full year of depreciation may be claimed without regard to the convention, as illustrated in Example 2, above.

*Computation using tables when change in use results in longer recovery period and/or less accelerated depreciation method.* If a change in use results in a longer recovery period and/or less accelerated depreciation method, the table percentages may be used in the year of change and subsequent tax years only if the table percentages were already being used. If the table percentages were being used, however, it is not necessary to continue using table percentages (Reg. § 1.168(i)-5(i)). The applicable table is the one that corresponds to the depreciation method, recovery period, and convention that would have applied to the MACRS property in the placed-in-service year if the property had been originally placed in service by the taxpayer with the longer recovery period and/or slower depreciation method (Reg. § 1.168(i)-5(ii)(B)(1)).

> ***Example (5):*** Five-year property subject to the half-year convention is placed in service in 2015 and depreciated using the 200% DB method. The table percentages for 5 year property in Table 1 were used. In 2017, the property is converted to farm use. The 150 percent declining balance method must be used to depreciate 5-year farm property placed in service before 2018 (see ¶ 84). No change to the recovery period, however, is required. As a result, in computing depreciation in 2017, Table 14 percentages for 5-year property (¶ 180) are used if use of a table is chosen. Note that Table 14 reflects the 150% DB method and the half-year convention.

Once the appropriate table is determined, the taxpayer locates the table rate (percentage) that would have applied in the year of change if the table had been used when the property was originally placed in service. Thus, in the preceding example, the third-year percentage (17.85% or .1785) is used since the first-year percentage (15.00%) would have applied in 2015, the second-year percentage (25.50%) would have applied in 2016, and the third-year percentage (17.85%) in 2017.

Next, the applicable table depreciation rate (expressed as a decimal percentage) is multiplied by a transaction coefficient.

The transaction coefficient is equal to 1/(1 – x) where x is equal to the sum of the annual depreciation rates from the appropriate table from the year the property was originally placed in service through the year immediately prior to the year of change. For example, the transaction coefficient for the preceding example is 1.68 [1/(1 – (.15 + .2550))]. The depreciation rate for the third recovery year expressed as a decimal (.1785) is then multiplied by the transaction coefficient (1.68) (.1785 × 1.68 = .30). The product of the annual depreciation rate and the transaction coefficient is then multiplied by the adjusted depreciable basis of the asset.

> ***Example (6):*** Assume the same facts as in Example 3, above, except that International Corp. used the depreciation tables in 2019 and 2020. This gives International the option of electing to use depreciation tables in 2021. If this election is made, the applicable table is the ADS table for property with a 9-year recovery period subject to the half-year convention since the half-year convention applied in 2019 when the property was originally placed in service (Table 8 at ¶ 180). The third year table percentage for property with a 9-year ADS recovery period from Table 8 is 11.11. The adjusted depreciable basis is multiplied by this percentage and the product is then multiplied by the transactional coefficient [1/1 – (.0556 + .1111), which equals 1.200]. .0556 is the first-year percentage from Table 8 expressed as a decimal and .1111 is the second-year percentage from Table 8 expressed as a decimal. The 2021 depreciation allowance using the optional table is, therefore, $6,399) [$48,000 × (.1111 (third-year table percentage expressed as a decimal) × 1.200)].

In computing depreciation deductions during all years of the remaining depreciation period, the transaction coefficient and unadjusted depreciable basis do not change.

> ***Example (7):*** 2022 depreciation in the preceding example is also $6,399 [$48,000 × (.1111 (fourth-year table percentage) × 1.200)].

## ¶ 169A

## Increased Business Use After Recovery Period

Depreciation on MACRS property that is used only partially for business or investment purposes does not necessarily end upon expiration of an asset's recovery period. Additional depreciation may be claimed if the percentage of business or investment use in a tax year after the recovery period ends exceeds the average percentage of business or investment use during the recovery period (Code Sec. 168(i)(5); ACRS Prop. Reg. § 1.168-2(j)(2)).

No MACRS regulations have been issued detailing the computational rules. However, a similar rule applied under ACRS (Code Sec. 168(f)(13) (pre-1986)) and was explained in ACRS Prop. Reg. § 1.168-2(j)(2). This rule, however, does not apply to listed property described in Code Sec. 280F at ¶ 208 (Temporary Reg. § 1.280F-4T(a)).

Under Prop. Reg. § 1.168-2(j)(2), a taxpayer determines the average percentage of business/investment use during the recovery period. In the first post-recovery period year that the percentage of business/investment use is greater than the average percentage of business/investment use, a depreciation allowance is claimed as if the property were placed in service at the beginning of that year. The deduction is computed by multiplying the original cost as reduced by prior depreciation (or the fair market value at the beginning of the tax year if this is less than cost reduced by prior depreciation) by the first-year recovery percentage. This amount is then multiplied by the percentage by which business/investment use for that year increased over the average business/investment use during the prior recovery period. The same procedure is followed for each subsequent year in the "second" recovery period. For any year in the "second" recovery period that business/investment use does not exceed the average business/investment use for the first recovery period, no deduction is allowed. The total depreciation that a taxpayer may claim may not exceed the original cost of the property. If the original cost is not recovered during the "second" recovery period, then the process may be applied to a "third" recovery period. The average business/investment use, however, would be redetermined by taking into account all of the years in the first and second recovery periods.

***Example (1):*** A calendar-year taxpayer places an item of 5-year MACRS property costing $1,000 in service in 2015. The half-year convention applies. Assume that business use during each year of the recovery period (2015-2020) is 50% and that deductions were claimed as follows:

| *Year* | *Calculation* | *Deduction* |
|---|---|---|
| 2015 | $1,000 × 20% × 50% | $100.00 |
| 2016 | $1,000 × 32% × 50% | 160.00 |
| 2017 | $1,000 × 19.20% × 50% | 96.00 |
| 2018 | $1,000 × 11.52% × 50% | 57.60 |
| 2019 | $1,000 × 11.52% × 50% | 57.60 |
| 2020 | $1,000 × 5.76% × 50% | 28.80 |
| | Total | $500.00 |

Assume that business use is 60% in 2021, 40% in 2022, 60% in 2023, 70% in 2024, 60% in 2025, and 20% in 2026. Assume further that at the beginning of 2021, the fair market value of the machine is greater than the remaining $500 undepreciated basis ($1,000 – $500 depreciation = $500). Average business/investment use during the first recovery period was 50%. For each year in the second recovery period that business/investment use exceeds this percentage, the taxpayer may claim an additional depreciation deduction. The depreciation deductions in the second recovery period are computed as follows:

| *Year* | *Calculation* | *Deduction* |
|---|---|---|
| 2021 | $500 × 20% × 10% | $10.00 |
| 2022 | | 00.00 |
| 2023 | $500 × 19.20% × 10% | 9.20 |
| 2024 | $500 × 11.52% × 20% | 11.52 |
| 2025 | $500 × 5.76% × 10% | 2.88 |
| 2026 | | 00.00 |
| | Total | $33.60 |

This cycle would be repeated beginning in 2026 because the taxpayer has not recovered the total cost ($1,000) of the property. If the fair market value of the property in the beginning of 2026 is less than the undepreciated basis ($1,000 - $500 - 33.60 = $466.40), then the recovery percentages are applied against the fair market value.

See also *Example (2)* in ACRS Prop. Reg. § 1.168-2(j)(7).

# Alternative Minimum Tax

## ¶ 170
## Computing AMT Depreciation

*MACRS property*

*The corporate alternative minimum tax is repealed, effective for tax years beginning after 2017 (Code Sec. 55(a), as amended by the Tax Cuts and Jobs Act (P.L. 115-97)). Thus, the AMT and the AMT adjustment for depreciation is only applicable to individuals, estates, and trusts after 2017.*

In computing alternative minimum taxable income (AMTI) for alternative minimum tax (AMT) purposes, the depreciation allowed in a particular tax year for AMT purposes may be different than the depreciation allowed for regular tax purposes in certain cases (Code Sec. 56(a)(1)). If the amount allowed for AMT tax purposes and the amount allowed for regular tax purposes is not the same, the difference is an AMT depreciation "adjustment." The adjustment may be positive or negative. The adjustment is reported on the applicable AMT tax form and reduces or increases the regular taxable income reported on the form for purposes of computing alternative minimum taxable income. The adjustment in effects results in claiming the proper AMT depreciation deduction for AMT purposes.

> ***Example (1):*** A taxpayer's regular tax liability is $1,000. The taxpayer deducted $100 in depreciation. Using the prescribed AMT depreciation method for the property the depreciation is $90. The taxpayer, therefore, computes a positive $10 AMT depreciation adjustment ($100 - $90) which results in $1,010 of alternative minimum taxable income when added to the regular tax liability ($1,000 + $10).

See below, "*Reporting AMT adjustment on Form 4626 or Form 6251.*".

As explained below, no AMT adjustment is required on any MACRS property for which the bonus depreciation deduction has been claimed, regardless of the bonus depreciation rate. Effective for property placed in service after 2015, no AMT adjustment is required on a property that qualifies for bonus depreciation even if the election out is made.

Also, no adjustment is ever necessary if regular tax depreciation is computed using the MACRS alternative depreciation system (ADS).

Effective for property placed in service after December 31, 1998, an AMT adjustment for property depreciated under MACRS only applies to MACRS 3-, 5-, 7-, and 10-year section 1245 recovery property depreciated using the 200-percent declining-balance method or, regardless of the recovery period, section 1250 MACRS recovery property depreciated using a method other than the MACRS straight-line method or the MACRS straight-line ADS method (Code Sec. 56(a)(1)(A), as amended by the Taxpayer Relief Act of 1997 (P.L. 105-34)). However, no adjustment is required on property placed in service before 2016 if bonus depreciation is claimed or, for property placed in service after 2015, on any property which qualifies for bonus depreciation even if an election out of bonus depreciation is made. Regardless of the date placed in service, property depreciated using the alternative depreciation system (ADS) for regular tax purposes is not subject to an AMT adjustment whether or not it qualifies for bonus depreciation or an election out is made.

When the exemption for bonus depreciation does not apply, AMT depreciation on section 1245 property depreciated under MACRS for regular tax purposes using the 200-percent declining-balance method is computed using the 150-percent declining-balance method and the depreciation period used by the taxpayer for regular tax purposes. Note that under MACRS, the 200-percent declining-balance method applies to 3-, 5-, 7-, and 10-year property for which the 150-percent declining-balance method, MACRS straight-line method, or ADS method have not been elected. The 150-percent declining-balance method applies to 15- and 20-year property other than 15-year leasehold improvement, retail improvement, and restaurant property. Also, 3-, 5-, 7-, and 10-year farm property placed in service before 2018 is depreciated using the 150-percent declining-balance method. See ¶ 84 regarding depreciation methods used under MACRS.

> ***Example (1A):*** Ten-year MACRS property costing $1,000 is placed in service in 2021. Assume the property does not qualify for bonus depreciation. 2021 regular tax depreciation using the 200% declining-balance method, 10-year recovery period, and half-year convention is $100 ($1,000 × 10%) (Table 1 at ¶ 180). 2021 AMT depreciation using the 150% declining-balance method, 10-year recovery period, and half-year convention is $75 ($1,000 × 7.50%) (Table 14 at ¶ 180 (first-year recovery percentage for property with a 10-year recovery period)). The AMT depreciation adjustment is $25 ($100 – $75).

A taxpayer may avoid AMT depreciation adjustments on 3-, 5-, 7-, and 10-year section 1245 property placed in service after 1998 by electing to depreciate such property for regular tax purposes using the 150-percent declining-balance method, straight-line method, or ADS method. If one of these elections is made or otherwise applies to the 3-, 5-, 7-, or 10-year property, the depreciation deductions allowed for regular tax purposes will also be allowed for AMT purposes. (It is not necessary to make such an election to avoid an AMT adjustment if the taxpayer claims bonus depreciation or, in the case of property placed in service after 2015, the property qualifies for bonus depreciation).

*Section 1250 property.* MACRS residential rental property and MACRS nonresidential real property (two types of section 1250 property) are always depreciated using the straight-line method (or ADS method if elected). Therefore, no AMT adjustment is ever required for such property if placed in service after December 31, 1998. 15-year restaurant improvement property (¶ 110), 15-year qualified leasehold improvement property (¶ 126), and 15-year qualified retail improvement property (¶ 126) are also section 1250 property. No AMT adjustment is required, however, because this property is also depreciated under MACRS using the straight-line method (or the ADS method if elected). On the other hand, an adjustment is required for section 1250 property depreciated using the 150 percent declining balance method, such as 15-year retail motor fuel establishments (¶ 110) and 15-year section 1250 land improvements (¶ 110).

*Property depreciated using certain special methods.* No adjustment is required for property that is depreciated under a method such as the unit-of-production method or any other method that is not expressed in terms of years; certain public utility property; films and video tapes; and sound recordings (Code Sec. 56(a)(1)(B)).

*Indian reservation property.* The regular tax depreciation deduction claimed on Indian reservation property placed in service after 1993 and before 2022 which is based on shortened recovery periods is allowed for AMT purposes. Furthermore, the Technical Corrections Act of 2018 (Division U of P.L. 115-141 retroactively clarifies that if the election out of the shorter recovery periods for Indian reservation property is made no AMT adjustment is required (Code Sec. 168(j)(3), as amended by P.L. 115-141). This election out is only available for tax years beginning after 2015. The shortened recovery periods are scheduled to expire, effective for property placed in service after 2021. See ¶ 124 for special recovery periods that apply in computing MACRS depreciation on Indian reservation property.

*AMT gain or loss.* The basis of a property for determining AMT gain or loss is reduced by AMT depreciation and not regular tax depreciation. See ¶ 486.

*Code Sec. 179 deduction allowed in full.* The Code Sec. 179 expense deduction (¶ 300) is allowed in full for AMT purposes.

*Bonus depreciation.* Any bonus depreciation allowance claimed for regular tax purposes is allowed in full for alternative minimum tax purposes regardless of the bonus depreciation rate (Code Sec. 168(k)(2)(G), prior to and after amendment by P.L. 114-113; Reg.§ 1.168(k)-1(d)(1)(iii); Reg.§ 1.168(k)-2(e)(1)(iv); Proposed Reg.§ 1.168(k)-2(d)(1)(iv)).

Effective for property placed in service after 2015, no AMT adjustment is required on regular depreciation deductions on "qualified property" as defined in Code Sec. 168(k)(2) (Code Sec. 168(k)(2)(G); Form 4562 Instructions; Reg. § 1.168(k)-2(e)(2)(ii); Proposed Reg. § 1.168(k)-2(d)(2)(ii)). Qualified property as defined in Code Sec. 168(k)(2) is property which qualifies for the bonus depreciation deduction. Generally, this consists of property depreciated under MACRS, originally placed in service by the taxpayer, and which has a regular MACRS depreciation period of 20 years or less. See ¶ 127D "*12. Qualified property.*" The AMT adjustment is not required for qualified property placed in service after 2015 even if an election out is made because the election out does not change the status of the property as "qualified property" (Code Sec. 168(k)(7), as amended by P.L. 114-113).

For property placed in service before 2016, no AMT adjustment is required on regular depreciation deductions on property for which the taxpayer claimed bonus depreciation (Code Sec. 168(k)(2)(G), prior and after amendment by P.L. 114-113; Reg.§ 1.168(k)-1(d)(2)(ii)). If an election out of bonus depreciation was made for property placed in service before 2016 an AMT adjustment is required if the property is otherwise subject to an AMT adjustment (e.g., 3-, 5-, 7-, or 10-year property depreciated for regular tax purposes using the 200 percent declining balance method requires an AMT adjustment based on the 150 percent declining balance method if an election out is made for those classes) (Code Sec. 168(k)(2)(G) and Code Sec. 168(k)(2)(D)(iii), prior to amendment by P.L. 114-113; Reg.§ 1.168(k)-1(e)(6)).

Note that if a taxpayer did not claim bonus depreciation on property which qualified for bonus depreciation and did not elect out, the taxpayer is using an improper depreciation method and is not simply treated as if an election out was made. If only one return was filed, the taxpayer may file an amended return that properly computes regular and AMT depreciation or may file a Form 3115 (using accounting change #7) with the current year return. If two returns have been filed then Form 3115 must be filed with the current year return. If a Form 3115 is filed, a negative (favorable) adjustment equal to the amount of regular depreciation, including bonus deduction, that should have been claimed prior to the year of change and the depreciation that was actually claimed is reported on the income tax return for the year of change. The AMT depreciation adjustment reported on the original return must also be recomputed as if bonus depreciation had been claimed, resulting in favorable adjustment for AMT purposes. See ¶ 75 for a discussion of accounting method changes.

If the depreciable basis of the qualifying bonus depreciation property for AMT purposes is different than the regular tax depreciable basis (i.e., the basis of the property is affected by another type of AMT adjustment), the AMT bonus allowance is computed on the AMT basis (Reg.§ 1.168(k)-1(d)(1)(iii); Reg. § 1.168(k)-2(e)(1)(iv)(B); Proposed Reg.§ 1.168(k)-2(d)(1)(iv)(B)), and AMT depreciation deductions are computed on the AMT basis as reduced by the amount of bonus depreciation allowed for AMT purposes (Reg.§ 1.168(k)-1(d)(2)(ii); Reg.§ 1.168(k)-2(e)(2)(ii); Proposed Reg.§ 1.168(k)-2(d)(2)(ii)). AMT depreciation allowances are computed on AMT basis whether or not the property qualifies for bonus depreciation.

These AMT rules for bonus depreciation claimed under Code Sec. 168(k) apply equally to bonus depreciation that is claimed on New York Liberty Zone property (¶ 127E), Gulf Opportunity Zone property (¶ 127F), Kansas Disaster Area property (¶ 127G), and Presidentially Declared Disaster Area property (¶ 127H).

*Other exclusions.* No AMT adjustment is required for (Code Sec. 56(a)(1)(B)):

- any natural gas gathering line the original use of which commences with the taxpayer after April 11, 2005
- MACRS property that a taxpayer elected to depreciate under the unit-of-production method or any method of depreciation not expressed in a term of years (other than the retirement-replacement-betterment method or similar method)
- public utility property (within the meaning of Code Sec. 168(i)(10)) if the taxpayer does not use a normalization method of accounting.
- Any motion picture film or video tape
- Sound recordings (i.e., any works which result from the fixation of a series of musical, spoken, or other sounds, regardless of the nature of the material (such as discs, tapes, or other phonorecordings) in which such sounds are embodied).

*Reporting AMT adjustment on Form 4626 or Form 6251.* The MACRS depreciation "adjustment" is the difference between regular tax depreciation and AMT depreciation. To compute alternative minimum taxable income on Form 4626 (corporations, for tax years beginning before 2018) or Form 6251 (individuals), regular taxable income is increased by any positive depreciation adjustment (where regular tax MACRS depreciation exceeds AMT depreciation) and reduced by any negative adjustment (where AMT depreciation exceeds regular tax MACRS depreciation). After combining all positive and negative adjustments, the total net adjustment for post-1986 (MACRS) depreciation is entered on the appropriate line of the alternative minimum tax form (Form 6251 in the case of individuals and Form 4626 for corporations).

*AMT adjustments for MACRS property placed in service before 1999*

(1) For residential rental property and nonresidential real property placed in service before January 1, 1999, the allowable MACRS AMT deduction is computed under the alternative depreciation system (ADS) (i.e., straight-line method and 40-year recovery period). The AMT depreciation adjustment for MACRS residential and nonresidential real property, however, is repealed effective for property placed in service after December 31, 1998. The AMT deduction on other types of section 1250 property which is not depreciated using the straight-line method for regular tax purposes is computed using ADS if the property was placed in service before

1999 and the straight-line method and regular recovery period if the property was placed in service after 1998.

*Example (2):* A taxpayer places a 27.5-year residential rental building in service in May of 1998. The depreciable basis of the property is $100,000. MACRS depreciation for regular tax purposes in 2021 is $3,637 ($100,000 × 3.637%). ADS depreciation is $2,500 ($100,000 × 2.5%). The $1,137 difference is an AMT adjustment. If the building had been placed in service after 1998, regular tax and AMT depreciation would have been computed the same way and no AMT adjustment would have been required.

(2) For section 1245 property placed in service before January 1, 1999, and depreciated under the elective MACRS straight-line method for regular tax purposes, the MACRS deduction is recomputed under the alternative depreciation system (ADS) (i.e., by using the straight-line method over the ADS recovery period for the property). No AMT depreciation adjustment is made for section 1245 property depreciated for regular tax purposes using the elective MACRS straight-line method effective for property placed in service after December 31, 1998.

*Example (3):* A taxpayer places an asset (10-year section 1245 property) in service for business purposes on January 3, 1998. The asset cost $100,000. The taxpayer elects the straight-line MACRS method. Under this method, a 10-year recovery period applies. MACRS elective straight-line regular tax depreciation for 2021 is $0 since the barge is fully depreciated). Under the MACRS alternative depreciation system (ADS), assume a 30-year recovery period applies. Allowable AMT depreciation for 2021 is $3,333 ($100,000 × 3.33% (Table 8 at ¶ 180)). The 2021 AMT depreciation adjustment is ($3,333) (a negative or favorable AMT adjustment that reduces alternative minimum taxable income). If the asset had been placed in service after 1998 and either the MACRS straight-line method or ADS method had been elected for regular tax purposes, regular tax and AMT depreciation would have been computed the same way and no AMT adjustment would have been required.

(3) For section 1245 property placed in service before January 1, 1999, and depreciated using the nonelective MACRS 150-percent declining-balance method or 200-percent declining-balance method for regular tax purposes, the MACRS AMT deduction is computed by using the 150-percent declining-balance method over the ADS recovery period. Note that under MACRS, the 200-percent declining-balance method applies to 3-, 5-, 7-, and 10-year property that is not farming property and for which the 150-percent declining-balance method, MACRS straight-line method, or ADS method have not been elected. The 150-percent declining-balance method applies to 15- and 20-year property.

*Example (4):* Assume the same facts as in *Example 3*, except that the ten-year property was depreciated for regular tax purposes using the 200 percent declining balance method. In this case, AMT depreciation is computed using the 150% declining-balance method and the *ADS recovery period* rather than the regular tax recovery period. Assume that the ADS recovery period is 30 years. The 2021 regular tax depreciation is $0 since the asset is fully depreciated. AMT depreciation for 2021 would be $299 ($100,000 × 2.994%) (Table 14 at ¶ 180 (recovery percentage using 150% declining balance method and 30-year recovery period). This is a negative adjustment that reduces alternative minimum taxable income.

The following charts show how AMT tax depreciation is computed when regular tax depreciation is computed as shown.

## MACRS PROPERTY FOR WHICH QUALIFIES FOR BONUS DEPRECIATION

The bonus depreciation allowance is claimed in full for AMT purposes (no AMT adjustment required). If bonus depreciation is claimed or should have been claimed no AMT adjustment is required for depreciation deductions computed on the bonus depreciation property. For property placed in service after 2015, regular depreciation and AMT depreciation deductions on property which qualifies for bonus depreciation are computed the same way even if an election out of bonus depreciation is made (no AMT adjustment required). See *"Bonus depreciation"* discussion above.

## MACRS PROPERTY PLACED IN SERVICE AFTER 1998

| *MACRS Regular Tax Depreciation Method (¶ 84)* | *MACRS AMT Tax Depreciation Method* |
|---|---|
| 200-percent declining-balance method (*3-*, *5-*, *7-*, *10-*year property which is not section 1250 real property) | Use 150-percent declining-balance method and regular tax depreciation period) |
| 150-percent declining-balance method (*15-*, *20-*year property which is not section 1250 real property; farm property before 2018) | No adjustment required, compute AMT and regular tax depreciation the same way |
| 150-percent declining-balance method election (*3-*, *5-*, *7-*, *10-*year property which is not section 1250 property) | No adjustment required, compute AMT and regular tax depreciation the same way |
| Straight-line (*27.5-*year residential and *31.5-*or *39-*year nonresidential real property) | No adjustment required, compute AMT and regular tax depreciation the same way |
| Straight-line election (*3-*, *5-*, *7-*, *10-*, *15-*, *20-*year property) | No adjustment required, compute AMT and regular tax depreciation the same way |
| MACRS ADS method (elective or nonelective) | No adjustment required, compute AMT and regular tax depreciation the same way on real and personal property |
| Section 1250 Property if 150- or 200-percent declining balance method used | Compute AMT depreciation using straight-line method and regular tax depreciation period |

## MACRS PROPERTY PLACED IN SERVICE AFTER 1986 AND BEFORE 1999

| *MACRS Regular Tax Depreciation Method (¶ 84)* | *MACRS AMT Tax Depreciation Method* |
|---|---|
| 200-percent declining-balance method (*3-*, *5-*, *7-*, *10-*year property which is not section 1250 property) | Use 150-percent declining-balance method and ADS recovery period |
| 150-percent declining-balance method (*15-*, *20-*year property which is not section 1250 property; farm property) | Use 150-percent declining-balance method and ADS recovery period |
| 150-percent declining-balance method election (*3-*, *5-*, *7-*, *10-*year property) | No adjustment required, compute AMT and regular tax depreciation the same way |
| Straight-line (*27.5-*year residential real property and *31.5-*or *39-*year nonresidential real property) | Use ADS |
| Section 1250 Property if 150- or 200-percent declining balance method used | Use ADS |

| *MACRS Regular Tax Depreciation Method (¶ 84)* | *MACRS AMT Tax Depreciation Method* |
|---|---|
| Straight-line election (*3-, 5-, 7-, 10-, 15-, 20-*year property) | Use ADS |
| MACRS ADS method (elective or nonelective) | No adjustment required, compute AMT and regular tax depreciation the same way on real and personal property |

In applying these rules, the same convention must be used in computing the MACRS deduction for AMT purposes that is used for computing such deduction for regular tax purposes.

The above rules are also used to refigure depreciation for AMT purposes that is capitalized to inventory under the uniform capitalization rules of Code Sec. 263A.

*Pre-MACRS property*

The following items pertaining to depreciation constitute tax preference items that must be added to regular taxable income in computing AMTI. These preferences are measured in an item-by-item manner that ignores negative balances (where AMT depreciation exceeds the depreciation for regular tax purposes on an item of property). In other words, the adjustment is computed separately for each item of property and only positive (unfavorable) adjustments are taken into account.

(1) The excess of accelerated depreciation on nonrecovery (pre-ACRS/MACRS) real property over straight-line depreciation.

(2) For noncorporate taxpayers and personal holding companies only, the excess of accelerated depreciation on leased nonrecovery (pre-ACRS/MACRS) personal property over straight-line depreciation.

(3) The excess of the ACRS deduction for 15-, 18-, or 19-year property (whichever applies) or low-income housing over the straight-line deduction that is available if salvage value is not included and a 15-, 18-, or 19-year recovery period (whichever applies) for real property or a 15-year recovery period for low-income housing is used. There is no tax preference if the actual recovery period used for regular tax purposes is longer than 15, 18, or 19 years (whichever applies).

(4) For noncorporate taxpayers and personal holding companies only, the excess of the ACRS deduction for leased recovery property (excluding 15-, 18-, or 19-year real property and low-income housing) over the straight-line depreciation deduction that is available if a half-year convention is used, salvage value is not included, and the following recovery periods are used:

| *In the case of:* | *The recovery period is:* |
|---|---|
| 3-year property | 5 years |
| 5-year property | 8 years |
| 10-year property | 15 years |
| 15-year public utility property | 22 years |

However, there is no tax preference if the actual recovery period used for regular tax purposes is longer than that listed above.

*Depreciation claimed as employee business expense or other type of miscellaneous itemized deduction*

It is not necessary to make a depreciation adjustment for AMT purposes if the depreciation is claimed on Schedule A as a miscellaneous itemized deduction subject to the 2% of adjusted gross income (AGI) floor. This is because the entire deduction on Schedule A for miscellaneous itemized deductions is disallowed for AMT purposes. See also, the discussion of the allowed or allowable rules at ¶ 75.

## ¶ 172

## Corporate Adjusted Current Earnings Adjustment

*The corporate alternative minimum tax is repealed, effective for tax years beginning after 2017 (Code Sec. 55(a), as amended by the Tax Cuts and Jobs Act (P.L. 115-97)). Thus, the AMT Ace adjustment is not required after 2017).*

C corporations were required to adjust AMTI for adjusted current earnings (ACE). The ACE adjustment is reported on line 4(e) of Form 4626 (Alternative Minimum Tax - Corporations) and computed on a worksheet contained in the instructions for Form 4626.

ACE means the pre-adjustment AMTI reduced or increased by required adjustments, including an adjustment for ACE depreciation (Code Sec. 56(g)(4)); "pre-adjustment AMTI" means AMTI determined without the ACE adjustment and without the alternative tax net operating loss deduction.

Pre-adjustment AMTI is increased by 75 percent of any excess ACE over pre-adjustment AMTI and is decreased by 75 percent of any excess pre-adjustment AMTI over ACE. The decrease for any tax year is limited to the excess of the aggregate increases in AMTI for prior tax years over the aggregate decreases in AMTI for such prior years (Code Sec. 56(g)).

For purposes of computing ACE, the ACE depreciation expense is subtracted from the depreciation deductions already included in the pre-adjustment AMTI (the depreciation deduction claimed for regular tax purposes as modified by the AMT depreciation adjustments and the AMT accelerated depreciation tax preference items). The difference (which may represent a positive or negative amount) is the ACE depreciation adjustment component that is includible in ACE. The amount of allowable ACE depreciation depends mainly upon the method used and the date that an asset was placed in service.

(1) For property generally placed in service after 1993, depreciation for ACE purposes is determined in the same manner as for determining AMTI (¶ 170) (Code Sec. 56(g)(4), as amended by the Omnibus Budget Reconciliation Act of 1993 (P.L. 103-66)). Thus, the ACE depreciation component is in effect eliminated because there is no difference (between the depreciation deduction included in pre-adjustment AMTI and the depreciation deduction computed for ACE purposes) includible in ACE. See line 2(b)(1) worksheet instructions.

The bonus depreciation deduction is not allowed when computing earnings and profits (Reg. §1.168(k)-1(f)(7)). Generally, no deduction is allowed when computing ACE for items that are not deductible when computing earnings and profits. Such amounts are entered on line 4 of the ACE worksheet. However, it does not appear that bonus depreciation should be entered on line 4 because this rule only applies to deduction items that are permanently disallowed (see instructions to line 4). The bonus deduction is not permanently disallowed for earnings and profits purposes; it is deferred insofar as the disallowed bonus deduction will be recovered over the earnings and profits depreciation period for the asset. See ¶ 310 for rules regarding earnings and profits.

(2) For property placed in service before 1994 in a tax year that begins after 1989, ACE depreciation is computed under the alternative MACRS depreciation system (ADS) using the straight-line method over the ADS recovery period. The

ACE depreciation adjustment must continue to be determined in this manner for property subject to this adjustment.

(3) For MACRS property placed in service in a tax year beginning before 1990, ACE depreciation is computed on the adjusted basis of the property for AMTI purposes as of the close of the last tax year beginning before 1990 using the straight-line method over the remainder of the ADS recovery period. The same convention that applies for regular tax purposes must be used to determine the remaining ADS recovery period.

***Example (1):*** A calendar-year corporation purchased and placed in service on August 1, 1987, an electric utility transmission and distribution plant. This was the only depreciable property placed in service during 1987. Thus, the half-year convention is the applicable convention. The adjusted basis of the property at the close of December 31, 1989, for AMTI purposes is $2,750,000. The alternate MACRS recovery period that would have applied to such property is 30 years (from July 1, 1987, through June 30, 2018). Thus, the recovery period for ACE purposes begins on January 1, 1990, and ends on June 30, 2018. For ACE purposes, the depreciation deduction determined under the straight-line method over each of the remaining years of the 27 ½-year ACE recovery period is $100,000. No adjustment is required for tax years beginning after 2017.

(4) For ACRS recovery property placed in service in a tax year beginning before 1990, ACE depreciation is computed on the adjusted basis of the property for regular tax purposes as of the close of the last tax year beginning before 1990 using the straight-line method over the remainder of the ADS recovery period had such recovery period originally applied. The same convention that applies for regular tax purposes must be used to determine the remaining ADS recovery period, except that the mid-quarter convention does not apply.

***Example (2):*** A calendar-year corporation purchased and placed in service on December 1, 1986, an electric utility transmission and distribution plant. The applicable convention that would have applied to such property without regard to the mid-quarter convention is the half-year convention. The adjusted basis of the property on January 1, 1990, for regular tax purposes is $1,325,000. The alternative MACRS recovery period for such property is 30 years (from July 1, 1986, through June 30, 2017). Thus, the ACE recovery period begins on January 1, 1990, and ends on June 30, 2017. For ACE purposes, the depreciation deductions under the straight-line method over each of the remaining 26½ years of the ACE recovery period is $50,000.

(5) For property depreciated under a method of depreciation not expressed in a term of years, certain public utility property, films and video tapes, and sound recordings, ACE depreciation is determined by treating the depreciation allowed for regular tax purposes as the amount allowed under the alternative depreciation system without regard to when such property was placed in service.

(6) For pre-1981 property and property not subject to ACRS or MACRS because of the anti-churning rules, ACE depreciation is determined in the same manner as for regular tax purposes.

Basis in subsequent years for ACE computations is derived from the use of the ACE depreciation method.

The ACE adjustment for AMT purposes does not apply to S corporations, regulated investment companies, real estate investment trusts, or real estate mortgage investment conduits.

# MACRS Depreciation Calculations and Tables

## ¶ 179

### Computing MACRS Deductions Without Optional Tables

The MACRS deduction is computed without the optional percentage tables (¶ 180) by first determining the rate of depreciation (dividing the number one by the recovery period). This basic rate is multiplied by the declining-balance factor allowed for the class of property being depreciated (1.5 or 2 for the 150-percent or 200-percent declining-balance method, respectively, whichever is applicable). In general, the 200-percent DB method applies to 3-, 5-, 7-, and 10-year property unless the 150-percent DB method, ADS, or the straight-line method is applies or is elected. The 150-percent DB method applies to 15- and 20-year property unless ADS or the straight-line method is elected. See ¶ 84.

*The computation of MACRS deductions without the use of tables is discussed in detail by the IRS in Rev. Proc. 87-57, 1987-2 CB 687.*

The depreciation allowance for a full tax year (that is, a tax year of 12 full months) is computed by applying the applicable depreciation rate to the unrecovered basis of the property for each tax year. For this purpose, the unrecovered basis of the property is the cost or other basis of the property adjusted for depreciation previously allowed or allowable and for all other applicable adjustments under Code Sec. 1016 or any other provision of law (Section 6.03 of Rev. Proc. 87-57). In effect, unrecovered basis appears to have an identical meaning to the term "adjusted depreciable basis," as defined in Reg.§ 1.168(b)-1(a)(4) and Reg.§ 1.168(k)-1(a)(2)(iii).

Adjustments to unrecovered basis include the Code Sec. 179 expense allowance (¶ 300) and first-year bonus depreciation (¶ 127D), including bonus depreciation claimed on New York Liberty Zone property (¶ 127E), Gulf Opportunity Zone property (¶ 127F), Kansas Disaster Area property (¶ 127G), and Disaster Assistance Property (¶ 127H) (Reg. § 1.168(k)-1(a)(2)). For additional adjustments see ¶ 180. When computing bonus depreciation, the cost or other basis is first reduced by the section 179 allowance. For example, if an item of new machinery costs $2,000 and the taxpayer expenses $500 under Code Sec. 179, the cost is first reduced to $1,500. Bonus depreciation is then computed ($1,500 × 50% bonus rate = $750). The cost is then reduced by the bonus depreciation to $750 ($1,500 – $750) and the regular MACRS depreciation deductions are computed with reference to this amount (the unrecovered basis). See ¶ 127D for additional examples. If the 100 percent bonus rate applies because the property was acquired after September 27, 2017 there will be no regular depreciation deductions to compute.

In each tax year, the unrecovered basis of the property is multiplied by the declining-balance or straight-line rate and the applicable convention is applied in computing depreciation for the first tax year. (This discussion assumes that tax years are 12 months in duration; for short tax years, see ¶ 132.)

The depreciation rate (in percentage terms) may also be determined by dividing the specified declining-balance percentage (150 percent or 200 percent) by the applicable recovery period.

A depreciation rate based on the straight-line method is used beginning in the tax year in which the depreciation deduction is greater than the depreciation deduction that would result using the 150-percent or 200-percent declining-balance method (whichever is applicable for the property).

Under the MACRS straight-line method, a new applicable depreciation rate is determined for each tax year in the applicable recovery period. For any tax year, the applicable depreciation rate (in percentage terms) is determined by dividing one by the length of the applicable recovery period remaining as of the beginning of such tax year. The rate is applied to the unrecovered basis of such property in conjunction with the appropriate convention. If, as of the beginning of any tax year, the remaining recovery period is less than one year, the applicable depreciation rate under the straight-line method for that year is 100 percent.

*Example using 200-percent DB method and half-year convention*

***Example (1):*** An item of 7-year property is purchased for $10,000 and placed in service in the current tax year. No Code Sec. 179 expense allowance or bonus depreciation is claimed. The unrecovered basis of the property is $10,000. The basic rate is 1 divided by 7, or 14.285%. The 200% declining-balance method rate of 28.57% is determined by multiplying 14.285% by 2. The unrecovered basis of the property ($10,000) is multiplied by 28.57% to obtain $2,857, which is then divided by 2 (for the half-year convention) to arrive at the MACRS deduction of $1,429 for the first tax year.

For the second tax year, depreciation is computed by subtracting $1,429 from $10,000 to determine the $8,571 remaining unrecovered basis of the property. This amount ($8,571) is multiplied by 28.57% to determine the MACRS deduction of $2,449.

For the third tax year, a similar procedure is used to determine the MACRS deduction of $1,749 ($8,571 – $2,449 = $6,122 × 28.57%).

For the fourth tax year, the MACRS deduction is $1,249 ($6,122 – $1,749 = $4,373 × 28.57%).

For the fifth tax year, the MACRS deduction is $893 ($4,373 – $1,249 = $3,124 × 28.57%).

For the sixth tax year, depreciation under the 200% declining-balance method would be $637 ($3,124 – $893 = $2,231 × 28.57%). However, a larger MACRS deduction is obtained by switching to the straight-line method ($3,124 – $893 = $2,231 × 40% (the straight-line rate is 1 divided by the 2.5 years remaining in the recovery period at the beginning of the tax year) = $892).

For the seventh tax year, depreciation is computed under the same method as in the sixth year and is $893 ($2,231 – $892 = $1,339 × 66.67% (the straight-line rate is 1 divided by 1.5 years remaining in the recovery period at the beginning of the tax year)).

For the eighth tax year, the MACRS deduction is the remaining basis of the property ($1,339 – $893 = $446). The straight-line rate for such year is 100% because the remaining recovery period at the beginning of the tax year (one-half year) is less than one year ($446 × 1.00 = $446).

*Example using 150-percent DB method and half-year convention*

***Example (2):*** Depreciation on 5-year property purchased by a calendar-year taxpayer in January of the current tax year at a cost of $15,000 is computed under the elective MACRS 150% declining-balance method over a 5-year recovery period using the half-year convention. A $5,000 Code Sec. 179 expense allowance is claimed. No bonus depreciation is claimed. The unrecovered basis of the property is $10,000 ($15,000 – $5,000).

Depreciation computed without the use of the IRS tables is determined as follows: the declining-balance depreciation rate is determined and compared with the straight-line rate. A switch is made to the straight-line rate in the year depreciation equals or exceeds that determined under the declining-balance method. The applicable rate is applied to the unrecovered basis. The 150% declining-balance depreciation rate is 30% (1 ÷ 5 (recovery period) × 1.5). The straight-line rate (which changes each year) is 1 divided by the length of the applicable recovery period remaining as of the beginning of each tax year (after considering the applicable convention for purposes of determining how much of the applicable recovery period remains as of the beginning of the year).

The switch to the straight-line method is made in year 4 since this is the first year that the straight-line rate is greater than the 150% DB rate. For year 4, the straight-line rate is 40% (1 ÷ 2.5). For year 5, the straight-line rate is 66.67% (1 ÷ 1.5). For year 6, the straight-line rate is 100% because the remaining recovery period is less than one year.

| *Yr.* | *Method* | *Rate* | | *Unrecovered Depreciable Basis* | | *Depreciation* |
|---|---|---|---|---|---|---|
| 1 | DB | 30% | × | $10,000 × 30% × 50% . . . . . . . . . . . . . . . | = | $1,500 |
| 2 | DB | 30% | × | (10,000 – 1,500) = $8,500 . . . . . . . . . . . . | = | 2,550 |
| 3 | DB | 30% | × | (8,500 – 2,550) = 5,950 . . . . . . . . . . . . . . . | = | 1,785 |
| 4 | SL | 40% | × | (5,950 – 1,785) = 4,165 . . . . . . . . . . . . . . . | = | 1,666 |
| 5 | SL | 66.67% | × | (4,165 – 1,666) = 2,499 . . . . . . . . . . . . . . . | = | 1,666 |
| 6 | SL | 100% | × | (2,499 – 1,666) = 833 . . . . . . . . . . . . . . . . | = | 833 |
| | | | | Total . . . . . . . . . . . . | | $10,000 |

### *Example using straight-line method and half-year convention*

***Example (3):*** Five-year property is placed in service in March of the current tax year at a cost of $100. No Code Sec. 179 expense allowance or bonus depreciation is claimed. An election is made to depreciate the property under the MACRS straight-line method over a five-year recovery period using the half-year convention. The depreciation deduction for the first tax year is $10 ($100 × 20% (the straight-line rate is 1 ÷ 5) × ½ (to reflect the half-year convention)).

For the second tax year, depreciation is computed by subtracting $10 from $100 to arrive at the $90 remaining unrecovered basis of the property. Such amount ($90) is multiplied by 22.22% (the straight-line rate is 1/4.5 (the remaining recovery period at the beginning of the second tax year)) to determine the MACRS deduction of $20.

For the third tax year, the MACRS deduction is $20 (($90 – $20) × 28.57% (the straight-line rate is 1/3.5)).

For the fourth tax year, the MACRS deduction is $20 (($70 – $20) × 40% (the straight-line rate is 1/2.5)).

For the fifth tax year, the MACRS deduction is $20 (($50 – $20) × 66.67% (the straight-line rate is 1/1.5)).

For the sixth tax year, the MACRS deduction is $10, the remaining unrecovered basis of the property ($30 – $20 = $10). The straight-line rate for such tax year is 100% because the remaining recovery period at the beginning of the tax year (one-half year) is less than one year ($10 × 100% = $10).

### *Computation using mid-quarter convention*

The MACRS deduction for the first tax year for property subject to the mid-quarter convention (¶ 92) is computed by first determining the depreciation deduction for the full tax year and then multiplying it by the following percentages for the quarter of the tax year that the property is placed in service:

| *Quarter of acquisition* | |
|---|---|
| First quarter . . . . . . . . . . . . . . . . . . . . . . . . . . . . . . . . . . . . . . . . . . | 87.5% |
| Second quarter . . . . . . . . . . . . . . . . . . . . . . . . . . . . . . . . . . . . . . . . | 62.5% |
| Third quarter . . . . . . . . . . . . . . . . . . . . . . . . . . . . . . . . . . . . . . . . . | 37.5% |
| Fourth quarter . . . . . . . . . . . . . . . . . . . . . . . . . . . . . . . . . . . . . . . . | 12.5% |

The MACRS mid-quarter depreciation tables (see Tables 2, 3, 4, and 5 at ¶ 180) incorporate these percentages in the first year depreciation percentage. Thus, these percentages only need to be used if a taxpayer computes depreciation without the table percentages in the year the property is placed into service.

If property subject to the mid-quarter convention is disposed of prior to the end of its recovery period, then the property is considered disposed of at the midpoint of the quarter of the disposition. To compute the allowable depreciation deduction, multiply the depreciation deduction for a full year by the percentage from the table below for the quarter that the property is disposed in. These table percentages, however, should not be used if the property is disposed of in the tax year in which the recovery period ends. See ¶ 160.

| *Quarter of disposition* | |
|---|---|
| First quarter | 12.5% |
| Second quarter | 37.5% |
| Third quarter | 62.5% |
| Fourth quarter | 87.5% |

***Example (4):*** A calendar-year taxpayer made the following purchases during the tax year: a $4,000 machine that is placed in service in January; $1,000 of office furniture that is placed in service in September; and a $5,000 computer that is placed in service in October. No Code Sec. 179 deduction or bonus depreciation is claimed. The total of the bases of all property placed in service is $10,000. Because the basis of the computer ($5,000), which was placed in service during the last 3 months of the tax year, exceeds 40% of the total bases of all property ($10,000) placed in service during the tax year, the mid-quarter convention must be used for all 3 items. The machine and office furniture are 7-year property and the computer is 5-year property under MACRS.

Depreciation for the machine and furniture is computed by dividing 1 by 7 resulting in a rate of 14.285%. Since the 7-year property is depreciated using the 200% declining-balance method, 14.285% is multiplied by 2 to arrive at the declining-balance rate, 28.57%. The depreciable basis of the machine ($4,000) is multiplied by 28.57% to compute the depreciation, $1,143, for a full year. Since the machine was placed in service in the first quarter of the tax year, $1,143 is multiplied by 87.5% (the mid-quarter percentage for the first quarter) to arrive at the MACRS deduction of $1,000 for the machine for the tax year.

Depreciation for the furniture is determined by multiplying the basis of the furniture ($1,000) by 28.57% to arrive at the depreciation, $286, for the full year. Because the furniture was placed in service in the third quarter of the tax year, $286 is multiplied by 37.5% to arrive at the MACRS deduction of $107 for the furniture for the tax year.

Depreciation for the computer is computed by dividing 1 by 5 resulting in a rate of 20%. Because 5-year property is depreciated using the 200% declining-balance method, 20% is multiplied by 2 to arrive at the declining-balance rate of 40%. The depreciable basis of the computer ($5,000) is multiplied by 40%, resulting in depreciation of $2,000 for a full year. Because the computer was placed in service in the fourth quarter of the tax year, $2,000 is multiplied by 12.5% (mid-quarter percentage for the fourth quarter) to arrive at the MACRS deduction of $250 for the computer for the tax year.

In determining whether the mid-quarter convention applies, the cost of the property is reduced by any Code Sec. 179 expense deduction claimed but not by any bonus depreciation claimed (see ¶ 92). Also, the amount of Code Sec. 179 expense allowance (¶ 300) or bonus depreciation deduction (¶ 127D) to which a taxpayer is entitled is not affected by the mid-quarter convention. For example, if a taxpayer places a machine costing $540,000 in service in December 2016 and the mid-quarter convention applies, the taxpayer may expense $500,000 (the 2016 limit) under Code Sec. 179 and claim a $20,000 bonus deduction (($540,000 – $500,000) × 50%), assuming the property is eligible for a 50 percent bonus rate.

*Computing MACRS depreciation when there is a basis adjustment such as a casualty loss—Table computation not allowed*

When the basis of a depreciable property changes during its recovery period for a reason other than claiming depreciation deductions, the taxpayer must stop using the MACRS depreciation table percentages in the year of the basis adjustment (Rev. Proc. 87-57, Section 8.02). For example, if a taxpayer suffers a casualty loss, the basis of the property, as reduced by the deductible casualty loss, insurance reimbursement, and depreciation claimed in prior years, is multiplied by the applicable depreciation rate for the tax year of the casualty (Rev. Rul. 71-161; IRS Publication 946). The recomputed basis of the property is recovered over the remaining depreciation period. The cost of any *capitalized* repairs are treated as a new asset which is separately depreciated over a new recovery period, as in the case of any other addition or improvement (¶ 126).

The treatment of repair costs has been a subject of controversy. Some taxpayers have contended that repair costs on account of a casualty to business property should be separately deductible as a trade or business expense under Code Sec. 162. The temporary "repair" regulations issued under T.D. 9564, optionally effective for tax years beginning on or after January 1, 2012 and before January 1, 2014, would have formalized the IRS position (IRS Advice Memorandum AM 2006-006, April 16, 2007; Rev. Rul. 71-161) that repair expenditures are capitalized if a taxpayer claims a casualty loss or otherwise adjusts the basis of the property (e.g., on account of the receipt of insurance proceeds) (Temporary Reg. § 1.263(a)-3T(i)(1)). See preamble to T.D. 9564 for a discussion of the IRS position.

However, the IRS softened its stance somewhat in the final repair regulations in recognition of the fact that it is unfair to require a taxpayer to capitalize all of its repair expenses in a situation where the casualty loss is limited to the adjusted basis of the damaged property. Thus, under the final repair regulations, the amount paid for otherwise deductible repairs to damage to the property that must be capitalized is limited to the excess (if any) of (a) the adjusted basis of the property for determining the loss allowable on account of the casualty, over (b) the amount paid for restoration of the property that also constitutes an improvement. The amounts paid for repairs that exceed the limitation are deductible to the extent they would otherwise constitute a deductible repair expense (Reg. § 1.263(a)-3(k)(4)(i)). See preamble to T.D. 9636. The final repair regulations apply to tax years beginning on or after January 1, 2014, or at a taxpayer's option, to tax years beginning on or after January 1, 2012 (Reg.§ 1.263(a)-3(r)). However, taxpayers that previously treated casualty losses in a manner inconsistent with the final repair regulations (e.g., by deducting repair expenses that are capitalizable under the final repair regulations) are expected to file an accounting method change (change #184 described in Section 11.08 of Rev. Proc. 2019-43) to capitalize the erroneously deducted amount and report a positive (unfavorable) section 481(a) adjustment equal to the difference between (a) the repair expense claimed and (b) the amount of the repair expense that should have been capitalized reduced by the amount of depreciation that could have been claimed on the amount that should have been capitalized.

***Example (4A):*** A taxpayer determines that the cost of restoring its property after a casualty is $750,000. The casualty loss, however, is limited the adjusted basis of the building which is $500,000. The casualty loss reduces the basis in the building to $0. The taxpayer hires a contractor to replacing the entire roof of the building at a cost of $350,000 and pays $400,000 to pump water from the building, clean debris from the interior and exterior, and replace areas of damaged dry wall and flooring at a cost of $400,000. Although resulting from the casualty event, the cost of pumping, cleaning, and replacing damaged drywall and flooring, does not directly benefit and is not incurred by reason of the roof replacement and, therefore, are considered "repair" expenses rather than capital expenditures. The taxpayer must capitalize the cost of the new roof since it is a capital expenditure. $150,000 ($500,000 – $350,000) of the repair expenditures must also be capitalized. The remaining $250,000 of repair expenditures ($400,000 – $150,000) are deductible as a repair costs since they are not capital improvements to the building (Reg.§ 1.263(a)-3(k)(7), Example 5).

The new roof is separately depreciated as 39-year real property. The $150,000 of capitalized repair expenses are also separately depreciated as 39-year real property. These costs are not depreciated over the remaining recovery period of the building.

The following example illustrates how depreciation is computed on a property with a casualty loss basis adjustment.

***Example (5):*** A taxpayer purchased 7-year property in 2020 for $100,000. Assume that no bonus depreciation or Code Sec. 179 expense allowance was claimed. The first-year deduction, assuming that the half year convention applies, is $14,290 ($100,000 x 14.29% first-year table percentage). In 2021, the property is damaged in a hurricane. The deductible casualty loss was $10,000 (i.e., the reduction in the fmv of the 7-year property). $15,000 was spent to restore/repair the property. No insurance was received. The adjusted basis of the property at the end of 2021 but before computation of 2021 depreciation is $75,710 ($100,000 - $14,290 -$10,000).

The applicable 200 percent declining balance rate for 7-year property is 1/7 x 2 or 28.57%. The 2021 deduction is $21,630 ($75,710 x 28.57%).

Depreciation is computed over the remaining recovery period by applying the 200 percent declining balance rate to the basis that remains as of the beginning of each tax year during the remaining recovery period. As explained above, a switch is made to the straight-line percentage in the year that it produces a larger deduction than the 200 percent declining balance method.

| *Yr.* | *Method* | *Rate* | | *Unrecovered Depreciable Basis* | | *Depreciation* |
|---|---|---|---|---|---|---|
| 2020 | DB | 14.29% | × | $100,000 | = | $14,290 |
| 2021 | DB | 28.57% | × | $75,710 | = | $21,630 |
| 2022 | DB | 28.57% | × | $54,080 | = | $15,451 |
| 2023 | DB | 28.57% | × | $38,629 | = | $11,036 |
| 2024 | DB | 28.57% | × | $27,593 | = | $7,883 |
| 2025 | SL | 40% | × | $19,710 | = | 7,884 |
| 2026 | SL | 66.67% | × | $11,826 | = | $7,884 |
| 2027 | SL | 100% | × | $3,942 | = | $3,942 |
| | | | | Total | | $90,000 |

The total depreciation deductions are equal to the original cost ($100,000) less the deducted casualty loss ($10,000). The $15,000 repair/restoration costs are capitalized (they do not exceed the property's adjusted basis prior to the casualty (see above discussion)) and separately depreciated over 7-years beginning in 2020. Since the repair costs are treated as newly acquired property they are eligible for bonus depreciation (¶ 127D). In addition, the section 179 deduction (¶ 300) should be available since the property is section 1245 property.

If MACRS residential rental property or nonresidential real property is damaged in a casualty, a taxpayer should also decrease the basis of the property as of the beginning of the tax year of the casualty by the amount of any casualty loss and insurance reimbursement and separately depreciate any capitalized repair costs. The table percentages may not be used to compute depreciation for the tax year of the casualty and any subsequent tax year. Instead divide 1 by the number of years that remain in the recovery period as of the beginning of the tax year and apply this rate to the basis (after adjustment by the casualty loss and repair costs and all prior year depreciation) to determine the depreciation deduction.

***Example (6):*** A MACRS residential rental property (27.5-year recovery period) is placed in service in 2020 in March by a calendar year taxpayer. The building cost $100,000. The first-year deduction using the applicable table percentage was $2,879 ($100,000 × 2.879%). If the taxpayer deducts a $15,000 casualty loss in 2021, the basis of the property prior to computation of the 2021 depreciation deduction is $82,121 ($100,000 - $15,000 – $2,879). Under the mid-month convention 9.5 months depreciation were claimed in 2020 (mid-month of March through December). This is the equivalent of .79 years (9.5 months/12 months). The remaining recovery period as of the beginning of 2021 is 26.71 years (27.5 – .79). The table percentages may not be used in 2021 or subsequent years. The applicable straight-line rate for 2021 is 3.744% (1/26.71). The depreciation deduction for 2021 is $3,075 ($82,121 × 3.744 %). The applicable straight-line rate for 2021 is 3.890% (1/25.71). The deduction for 2022 is $3,075 (($82,121 – $3,075) × 3.890%). Assuming no further basis adjustments during the remainder of the recovery period, the annual deduction will remain $3,075 except for the last year of the recovery period. As explained above, any restoration costs are capitalized and depreciated as a separate asset and a similar treatment applies to repair costs unless the sum of restoration and repair costs exceeds the adjusted basis of the building.

The preceding computation rules also apply when there are other types of basis adjustments (other than for casualty loss deductions) to an MACRS property in a tax year after it is placed into service. For example, basis may be reduced or increased due to changes in a contingent sales price or forgiveness of debt (Proposed Reg. § 1.168-2(d)(3)).

The retirement of a structural component of a building for which a loss deduction equal to the remaining undepreciated basis of the component is claimed, for example by making a partial disposition election (Reg. § 1.168(i)-8(d)) described at ¶ 162, results in a mid-stream basis adjustment to the building. Nevertheless, an IRS example computes depreciation on a building following the partial disposition election by applying the remaining table percentages to the original basis of the building (39-year nonresidential real property) as reduced by the retirement loss beginning in the year of the retirement loss. This IRS methodology correctly results in the recovery of the original basis of the building over the applicable 39-year recovery period taking into account the amount of the retirement loss (Reg.§ 1.168(i)-8(i), *Example 9*). However, a taxpayer could also compute its remaining allowable depreciation deductions following the retirement loss basis adjustment without the table percentages. See Example (4C) at ¶ 162 for details.

*Computing MACRS deductions without tables when there is partial business use*

When computing MACRS deductions without tables on property which is not used 100 percent for business purposes and which is depreciated using an MACRS declining balance method, the unadjusted basis of the asset (generally cost) is multiplied by the business use percentage (BUP) for the tax year and then reduced by the amount of depreciation that was allowed or allowable in all preceding tax years (including any section 179 deduction or bonus deduction). This amount is multiplied by the applicable declining balance rate (or by the applicable straight-line rate beginning in the tax year that a switch to the straight-line rate is required because the straight-line rate is larger than the declining balance rate).

***Example (7):*** Five-year property costing $125 is placed in service in Year 1 and used 80 percent for business. The 200% declining balance method and half-year convention apply. The taxpayer claimed a $10 section 179 deduction and $45 bonus deduction (($125 × 80% BUP – $10) × 50% = $45). The Year 1 deduction is $9 (($125 × 80% BUP - $10 section 179 – $45 bonus) × 40% declining balance rate × 50% to reflect the half-year convention). The 200% declining balance rate is 1/5 × 2 = 40%. If BUP drops to 70% in Year 2, the depreciation deduction is $9.40 (($125 × 70% – $10 – $45 – $9) × 40%).

***Example (8):*** Five-year property costing $100 is placed in service in Year 1 and used 80 percent for business. The 200% declining balance method and half-year convention apply. No section 179 deduction or bonus deduction is claimed. The Year 1 deduction is $16 ($100 × 80% BUP × 40% declining balance rate × 50% to reflect half-year convention).

***Example (9):*** Assume the same facts as in Example 8 except that BUP drops to 70% in Year 2. Year 2 depreciation is $21.60 (($100 × 70% – $16 Year 1 depreciation) × 40% = $21.60). If business use drops to 10% in Year 3, Year 3 depreciation is $0 ($100 × 10% – $16 Year 1 depreciation – $21.60 Year 2 depreciation). Note that Year 3 depreciation is considered $0 because the depreciation computation resulted in a negative figure. If business use increases to 90% in Year 4, Year 4 depreciation is $20.96 ($100 × 90% – $16 Year 1 depreciation – $21.60 Year 2 depreciation – $0 Year 3 depreciation) × 40% declining balance rate). If business use drops to 70% in Year 5, the Year 5 depreciation deduction is $7.63 (($100 × 70% – $16 – $21.60 – $0 – $20.96) × 66.67% straight-line rate). The straight-line rate is equal to 1/1.5 years remaining in recovery period as of beginning of Year 5. Since the straight-line rate is greater than the 40% declining balance rate it is used to compute depreciation in Year 5. See discussion at the beginning of this paragraph ¶ 170.

When the business use percentage of an asset varies during its recovery period, the depreciation computed using the tables after the first year will be somewhat different than the depreciation computed without the tables.

***Example (10):*** Assume the same facts as in Example 8 and 9 except that the MACRS table percentages for 5-year property subject to the half-year convention are used (Table 1 at ¶ 180). Year 1 depreciation is $16 ($100 × 80% × 20% first-year table percentage). Year 2 depreciation is $22.40 ($100 × 70% x 32% second-year table percentage). Year 3 depreciation is $1.92 ($100 × 10% × 19.2% third-year table percentage). Year 4 depreciation is $10.37 ($100 × 90% × 11.52% fourth-year table percentage). Year 5 depreciation is $8.06 ($100 × 70% × 11.52% fifth-year table percentage).

It is technically possible to make depreciation computations without tables equal to the table results when computing MACRS deductions on property which has various business use percentages during the recovery period. To do so, the unadjusted basis (i.e., cost) of the asset (reduced by any section 179 deduction and bonus claimed) is multiplied by the business use percentage (BUP) for the tax year and then reduced by the amount of depreciation that would have been claimed in all preceding tax years if the BUP for each of those preceding tax years was the same as the BUP for the current tax year. This amount is multiplied by the applicable declining balance rate (or the applicable straight-line rate beginning in the tax year that a switch to the straight-line rate is required). Although the IRS has provided no specific IRS examples showing how to make non-table computations in situations where the business use percentage is less than 100 percent, its explanations in Publication 946, Rev. Proc. 87-57, and in the Form 4562 instructions make reference to reducing the basis by prior "depreciation allowed or allowable" and applying the applicable depreciation rate. Thus, reduction by an assumed amount for prior years computed using the current-year business use percentage is not appropriate.

*Straight-line computations without tables.* Straight-line computations under the MACRS straight-line (¶ 84) or ADS (¶ 150) methods without tables when there is partial business use during the recovery period are made by computing a new straight-line rate for each year in the recovery period (see Example 3, above). The product of the cost of the asset and the BUP for the current year is reduced by all depreciation previously allowed or allowable and then multiplied by the straight-line rate computed for the year. In contrast, when an asset is subject to a declining balance rate, the same declining balance rate is used in each year of the recovery period until the straight-line rate is greater, as illustrated in the examples immediately above.

***Example (11):*** MACRS 5-year property costing $100 is depreciation using the straight-line method and half-year convention. The first-year business use percentage is 90% and the second-year business use percentage is 95 percent. A 50 percent bonus depreciation allowance is claimed in Year 1. The bonus allowance is equal to $45 ($100 × 90% x 50%). The first-year depreciation deduction is $4.50 (($100 × 90%) – $45 (bonus) ×

1/5 (first-year straight-line rate) × 50% (to reflect half-year convention)). The second-year deduction is $10.11 (($100 × 95% – $45– $4.50) × 1/4.5 (second-year straight-line rate (4.5 is the number of years remaining in the recovery period as of the beginning of Year 2))).

## ¶ 180

## Computing MACRS Deductions With Tables

MACRS depreciation tables contain the annual depreciation percentage rates that are applied to the unadjusted basis of a depreciable asset in each year of its recovery (depreciation) period (Section 8 of Rev. Proc. 87-57, 1987-2 CB 687, as amplified and clarified by Rev. Proc. 89-15, 1989-1 CB 816).

For purposes of applying the table percentages, the "unadjusted basis" appears by the IRS to be used interchangeable with the term "unadjusted *depreciable* basis." Unadjusted depreciable basis is the adjusted basis of property for purposes of determining gain or loss under Code Sec. 1011 without regard to any adjustments described in Code Sec. 1016(a)(2) and (3) (i.e., depreciation deductions). This basis reflects the reduction in basis for the percentage of the taxpayer's personal use of the property, for any portion of the basis the taxpayer properly elects to treat as an expense under Code Sec. 179, Code Sec. 179C, or any similar provision, and for any adjustments to basis provided by other provisions of the Internal Revenue Code and the regulations under the Code (other than Code Sec. 1016(a)(2) and (3)) (for example, a reduction in basis by the amount of the disabled access credit pursuant under Code Sec. 44(d)(7)) (Reg.§ 1.168(b)-1(a)(3)). Other adjustments include the bonus depreciation deduction, any amortization claimed on the property, deductions for clean fuel vehicles or clean fuel refueling property placed in service before January 1, 2006, and any electric vehicle (IRS Publication 946).

Thus, in most cases unadjusted depreciable basis is generally equal to cost (adjusted for personal use) less any Code Sec. 179 allowance (¶ 300) and any bonus depreciation deduction (¶ 127D and following) claimed. Bonus depreciation is computed on the cost (adjusted for personal use) after reduction by any amount expensed under Code Sec. 179 Reg. § 1.168(k)-1(a)(2). The regular MACRS depreciation deductions are then computed on the adjusted depreciable basis (cost as reduced by the section 179 expense allowance and bonus depreciation).

Adjusted depreciable basis is the unadjusted depreciable basis of the property, as defined above, less the depreciation adjustments described in Code Sec. 1016(a)(2) and (3) (Reg.§ 1.168(b)-1(a)(4)).

The depreciation tables generally may be used to compute depreciation instead of the statutorily prescribed method and convention over the applicable recovery period. The tables incorporate the appropriate convention and the switch required by Code Sec. 168(b) from the declining-balance method to the straight-line method in the year that the straight-line method provides a depreciation allowance larger than the declining balance method. The tables may be used for any item of property (that otherwise qualifies for MACRS) placed in service in a tax year (Rev. Proc. 87-57, 1987-2 CB 687, as amplified and clarified by Rev. Proc. 89-15, 1989-1 CB 816).

*Exceptions*

If a table is used to compute the annual depreciation allowance for any item of property, it must be used throughout the entire recovery period of such property. However, a taxpayer may not continue to use a table if there are any adjustments to the basis of the property for reasons other than (1) depreciation allowances or (2) an addition or improvement to such property that is subject to depreciation as a separate item of property (Rev. Proc. 87-57, Section 8.02).

For example, if the basis of property is reduced as a result of a casualty to the property, or some other mid-stream basis adjustment, the tables may no longer be used and depreciation for the year of adjustment and the remainder of the recovery period is computed on the amount of adjusted basis of the property at the *end* of the tax year of adjustment and the remaining recovery period. See ¶ 179 for an example of the computation.

Although the retirement of a structural component of a building for which a loss deduction equal to the remaining undepreciated basis of the component is claimed, for example, by making a partial disposition election, results in a mid-stream basis adjustment to the building, an IRS example computes depreciation on the building following the partial disposition election by applying the remaining table percentages to the original basis of the building (39-year nonresidential real property) as reduced by the retirement loss. This IRS methodology correctly results in the recovery of the original basis of the building over the applicable 39-year recovery period (Reg.§ 1.168(i)-8(i), *Example 9*). However, a taxpayer could also compute its remaining allowable depreciation deductions following the retirement loss basis adjustment without the table percentages. See Example (4C) at ¶ 162 for details.

The MACRS depreciation tables may not be used to depreciate property in a short tax year or thereafter. See ¶ 132 and ¶ 134 for short tax year computations. The depreciation table percentages are also inapplicable if an asset is disposed of before the end of its recovery (depreciation) period. See ¶ 160. However, the examples below illustrate how to make adjust the table percentage result in the year of an early disposition.

*Application*

The appropriate table depends on the depreciation system (general MACRS (GDS) or alternative MACRS (ADS)), and the applicable method, convention and recovery period. The tables list the percentage depreciation rates to be applied to the unadjusted basis of property in each tax year.

Tables 1 through 13 may be used for any property placed in service during a tax year. Tables 14 through 18 must be used for the alternative minimum tax computation or if a taxpayer has elected the MACRS 150-percent declining-balance method for regular tax depreciation calculations.

For three-, five-, seven-, and ten-year farm business property generally placed in service after 1988 and before 2018, the 200-percent declining-balance method is not available. The 150-percent declining-balance method with a switch to the straight-line method must be used. Consequently, for such property, Tables 1-5 may not be used if the farm property is placed in service before 2018. Instead, Tables 14-18, which incorporate the 150-percent declining-balance method and the appropriate convention, may be used.

*Examples of calculations using MACRS percentage tables*

The following examples illustrate how to use the depreciation tables to calculate MACRS deductions.

***Example (1):*** An item of 5-year property costing $21,000 is placed in service in August 2017. If the taxpayer claims a $1,000 section 179 expense allowance, MACRS bonus depreciation is equal to $10,000 (($21,000 – $1,000) × 50%) and the basis, prior to the computation of the regular MACRS depreciation allowances is reduced to $10,000 ($21,000 – $1,000 – $10,000). Assume the half-year convention applies and GDS (200%

DB) is chosen. The Table 1 percentages for 5-year property are applied to the $10,000 adjusted depreciable basis as follows:

| *Year* | *Calculation* | | *Deduction* |
|---|---|---|---|
| 2017 | $10,000 × 20% | | $ 2,000 |
| 2018 | $10,000 × 32% | | 3,200 |
| 2019 | $10,000 × 19.20% | | 1,920 |
| 2020 | $10,000 × 11.52% | | 1,152 |
| 2021 | $10,000 × 11.52% | | 1,152 |
| 2022 | $10,000 × 5.76% | | 576 |
| | | Total | $10,000 |

***Example (2):*** Assume that the 5-year property in *Example (1)* was sold in 2021. Technically, the tables may not be used to compute the deduction since the year 4 percentage for 2021 (11.52%) does not reflect the half-year convention (which allows one-half of a full year's depreciation in the year of disposition). However, this problem can be circumvented by using the year 4 table percentage but only claiming one-half of the deduction so computed ($10,000 × 11.52% × 50% = $576).

***Example (3):*** Nonresidential real property is placed in service in March of 2021 by a calendar-year taxpayer. The cost of the building (excluding land) is $100,000. The taxpayer chooses to compute depreciation using the GDS percentages based on the straight-line method and 39-year recovery period. Accordingly, the Table 7A percentages are used. The column 3 percentages apply because the building was placed in service in the third month (March) of the tax year.

| *Year* | *Calculation* | | *Deduction* |
|---|---|---|---|
| 2021 | $100,000 × 2.033% | | $ 2,033 |
| 2022 - 2058 | $100,000 × 2.564% | | 2,564 |
| 2059 | $100,000 × 0.535% | | 535 |
| | | Total | $100,000 |

***Example (4):*** Assume the same facts as *Example (3)* except that the building was sold in December 2022. The property was in service for 11.5 months during the 2022 calendar tax year (January 1 through Mid-December). Note that the mid-month convention applies to real property; therefore, the building was considered sold in mid-December and one-half month's depreciation is allowed for that month. Depreciation for 2022 is computed as follows: $100,000 × 2.564% (column 3 percentage for property placed in service in March) × 11.5/12 (to reflect 11.5 months of a full year's deduction) = $2,457.

***Example (5):*** An item of construction equipment costing $10,000 is placed in service in December 2021 by a calendar year taxpayer. This is the only depreciable property placed in service during 2021. The equipment is five-year property with a MACRS alternative depreciation system (ADS) recovery period of 6 years (Asset Class 15.0 at ¶ 191). The Taxpayer elects ADS, does not expense any amount under Code Sec. 179 and does not claim first-year bonus depreciation. The mid-quarter convention applies since more than 40% of the bases of all personal property was placed in service in the last quarter of the tax year (¶ 92). Depreciation should be calculated using the 6-year column from Table 12 (ADS mid-quarter convention table for property placed in service in the fourth quarter). The calculations are as follows:

| *Year* | *Calculation* | *Deduction* |
|---|---|---|
| 2021 | $10,000 × 2.08% | $ 208 |
| 2022 | $10,000 × 16.67% | 1,667 |
| 2023 | $10,000 × 16.67% | 1,667 |

| *Year* | *Calculation* | *Deduction* |
|---|---|---|
| 2024 | $10,000 × 16.67% | 1,667 |
| 2025 | $10,000 × 16.66% | 1,666 |
| 2026 | $10,000 × 16.67% | 1,667 |
| 2027 | $10,000 × 14.58% | 1,458 |
| | Total | $10,000 |

***Example (6):*** Assume the same facts as in *Example (5)* except that the machinery is sold in January of 2023. Under the mid-quarter convention the property is treated as sold on the mid-point of the first quarter (i.e., mid-February) and one and one-half months of a full year's depreciation may be deducted. Depreciation for 2023 is, therefore, $208 ($10,000 × 16.67% × 1.5/12 (to reflect one and one-half months depreciation)).

*Disposition in last year of recovery period*

For rules regarding the computation of depreciation on an item of personal property disposed of in the last year of its recovery period see ¶ 160.

*Partial business use computation*

If a depreciable asset is only used partially for business/investment purposes, the cost of the asset is multiplied by the business/investment use percentage. Any amount expensed under Code Sec. 179 or claimed as bonus depreciation is then subtracted from this amount (IRS Form 4562 Instructions for line 19 column (c) and line 26 column (e)).

***Example (7):*** A new machine costing $100,000 is purchased on January 17, 2017. The machine is 5-year property and is used 80% for business in 2017. The taxpayer may elect to expense up to $80,000 of the cost ($100,000 × 80%). The taxpayer, however, elects to expense $40,000 of the cost and claim bonus depreciation. Bonus depreciation is $20,000 (($100,000 × 80% – $40,000) × 50%).

Regular first-year depreciation using the first-year table percentage (20%) is $6,000 computed as follows:

(($100,000 × 80%) – $40,000 – $20,000) × 20% = $4,000

***Example (8):*** Assume the same facts as in Example (7). Business use drops to 55% in 2020.

Regular first-year depreciation using the fourth-year table percentage (11.52%) is $0 because the $60,000 sum of the bonus depreciation ($20,000) and section 179 deduction ($40,000) claimed in the first year exceeds the $55,000 business use portion of the cost for 2020 ($100,000 × 55% = $55,000).

Since the depreciation calculation yields a negative result (–$576), depreciation allowed is considered $0 ((($100,000 × 55%) – $20,000 – $40,000) ×11.52% = –$576).

If the percentage of business use in a tax year after the recovery period ends exceeds the average percentage of business use during the recovery period a taxpayer may be entitled to claim additional depreciation deductions (Code Sec. 168(i)(5); ACRS Proposed Reg.§ 1.168-2(j)(2)). This rule does not apply to listed property (¶ 208) such as a car (Reg.§ 1.280F-4T(a)). See ¶ 169A for details.

For additional examples of partial business use computations with and without table percentages, see "*Computing MACRS deductions without tables when there is partial business use*" at ¶ 179.

*Electronic depreciation calculator*

*An interactive calculator for computing MACRS deductions and creating depreciation schedules is available on CCH IntelliConnect browse tree under All Content/ Federal Tax/Federal Tax Practice Tools/Depreciation Toolkit.*

**→*Caution: Tables 1-5 may not be used for three-, five-, seven-, or ten-year farm business property placed in service before 2018. Instead, Tables 14-18 may be used, depending on the appropriate depreciation convention.*←**

## INDEX TO MACRS PERCENTAGE TABLES

MACRS PERSONAL PROPERTY

*General Depreciation System (GDS)*

| *Recovery Period* | *Method* | *Convention* | *Table* | *Page* |
|---|---|---|---|---|
| 3, 5, 7, 10, 15, 20 | 200/150DB | Half-year | 1 | 621 |
| | | Mid-quarter 1st | 2 | 622 |
| | | Mid-quarter 2nd | 3 | 623 |
| | | Mid-quarter 3rd | 4 | 624 |
| | | Mid-quarter 4th | 5 | 625 |

*Straight-Line and Alternative Depreciation Systems (ADS)*

| *Recovery Period* | *Method* | *Convention* | *Table* | *Page* |
|---|---|---|---|---|
| 2.5 - 50 | S/L | Half-year | 8 | 631 |
| | | Mid-quarter 1st | 9 | 641 |
| | | Mid-quarter 2nd | 10 | 651 |
| | | Mid-quarter 3rd | 11 | 661 |
| | | Mid-quarter 4th | 12 | 671 |

MACRS RESIDENTIAL RENTAL AND NONRESIDENTIAL REAL PROPERTY

*General Depreciation System (GDS)*

| *Recovery Period* | *Method* | *Convention* | *Table* | *Page* |
|---|---|---|---|---|
| 27.5 | S/L | Mid-month | 6 | 626 |
| 31.5 | | | 7 | 628 |
| 39 | | | 7A | 630 |

*Alternative Depreciation System (ADS)*

| *Recovery Period* | *Method* | *Convention* | *Table* | *Page* |
|---|---|---|---|---|
| 30 | S/L | Mid-month | 12A | 681 |
| 40 | S/L | Mid-month | 13 | 681 |

MACRS ALTERNATIVE MINIMUM TAX TABLES*

| *Recovery Period* | *Method* | *Convention* | *Table* | *Page* |
|---|---|---|---|---|
| 2.5 - 50 | 150DB | Half-year | 14 | 682 |
| | | Mid-quarter 1st | 15 | 692 |
| | | Mid-quarter 2nd | 16 | 702 |
| | | Mid-quarter 3rd | 17 | 712 |
| | | Mid-quarter 4th | 18 | 722 |

* Use also for 150% DB election and for 3-, 5-, 7-, and 10-year farm property.

MACRS INDIAN RESERVATION PROPERTY TABLES (see ¶ 124)

| *Recovery Period* | *Method* | *Convention* | *Table* | *Page* |
|---|---|---|---|---|
| 2 years | 200DB | Half-year or mid-quarter | 19 | 732 |
| 3 years | 200DB | Half-year | 1 | 621 |
| | | Mid-quarter | 2-5 | 622-625 |
| 4 years | 200DB | Half-year or mid-quarter | 20 | 732 |
| 6 years | 200DB | Half-year or mid-quarter | 21 | 732 |
| 9 years | 150DB | Half-year | 14 | 682 |
| | | Mid-quarter | 15-18 | 692-722 |
| 12 years | 150DB | Half-year | 14 | 682 |
| | | Mid-quarter | 15-18 | 692-722 |
| 22 years | S/L | Mid-month | 22 | 733 |

***→Caution: Table 1, below, may not be used for three-, five-, seven-, or ten-year farm business property placed in service before 2018. Table 14, below, incorporates the 150-percent declining-balance method and a half-year convention that may be used for such property.←***

TABLE 1
General Depreciation System
Applicable Depreciation Method: 200- or 150-Percent
Declining Balance Switching to Straight Line
Applicable Recovery Periods: 3, 5, 7, 10, 15, 20 years
Applicable Convention: Half-Year

| If the Recovery Year is: | and the Recovery Period is: | | | | | |
|---|---|---|---|---|---|---|
| | 3-year | 5-year | 7-year | 10-year | 15-year | 20-year |
| | the Depreciation Rate is: | | | | | |
| 1 | 33.33 | 20.00 | 14.29 | 10.00 | 5.00 | 3.750 |
| 2 | 44.45 | 32.00 | 24.49 | 18.00 | 9.50 | 7.219 |
| 3 | 14.81 | 19.20 | 17.49 | 14.40 | 8.55 | 6.677 |
| 4 | 7.41 | 11.52 | 12.49 | 11.52 | 7.70 | 6.177 |
| 5 | | 11.52 | 8.93 | 9.22 | 6.93 | 5.713 |
| 6 | | 5.76 | 8.92 | 7.37 | 6.23 | 5.285 |
| 7 | | | 8.93 | 6.55 | 5.90 | 4.888 |
| 8 | | | 4.46 | 6.55 | 5.90 | 4.522 |
| 9 | | | | 6.56 | 5.91 | 4.462 |
| 10 | | | | 6.55 | 5.90 | 4.461 |
| 11 | | | | 3.28 | 5.91 | 4.462 |
| 12 | | | | | 5.90 | 4.461 |
| 13 | | | | | 5.91 | 4.462 |
| 14 | | | | | 5.90 | 4.461 |
| 15 | | | | | 5.91 | 4.462 |
| 16 | | | | | 2.95 | 4.461 |
| 17 | | | | | | 4.462 |
| 18 | | | | | | 4.461 |
| 19 | | | | | | 4.462 |
| 20 | | | | | | 4.461 |
| 21 | | | | | | 2.231 |

***→Caution: Table 2, below, may not be used for three-, five-, seven-, or ten-year farm business property placed in service before 2018. Table 15, below, incorporates the 150-percent declining-balance method and the mid-quarter convention that may be used for such property.←***

TABLE 2
General Depreciation System
Applicable Depreciation Method: 200- or 150-Percent Declining Balance Switching to Straight Line
Applicable Recovery Periods: 3, 5, 7, 10, 15, 20 years
Applicable Convention: Mid-quarter (property placed in service in first quarter)

| If the Recovery Year is: | and the Recovery Period is: 3-year | 5-year | 7-year | 10-year | 15-year | 20-year |
|---|---|---|---|---|---|---|
| | the Depreciation Rate is: | | | | | |
| 1 | 58.33 | 35.00 | 25.00 | 17.50 | 8.75 | 6.563 |
| 2 | 27.78 | 26.00 | 21.43 | 16.50 | 9.13 | 7.000 |
| 3 | 12.35 | 15.60 | 15.31 | 13.20 | 8.21 | 6.482 |
| 4 | 1.54 | 11.01 | 10.93 | 10.56 | 7.39 | 5.996 |
| 5 | | 11.01 | 8.75 | 8.45 | 6.65 | 5.546 |
| 6 | | 1.38 | 8.74 | 6.76 | 5.99 | 5.130 |
| 7 | | | 8.75 | 6.55 | 5.90 | 4.746 |
| 8 | | | 1.09 | 6.55 | 5.91 | 4.459 |
| 9 | | | | 6.56 | 5.90 | 4.459 |
| 10 | | | | 6.55 | 5.91 | 4.459 |
| 11 | | | | 0.82 | 5.90 | 4.459 |
| 12 | | | | | 5.91 | 4.460 |
| 13 | | | | | 5.90 | 4.459 |
| 14 | | | | | 5.91 | 4.460 |
| 15 | | | | | 5.90 | 4.459 |
| 16 | | | | | 0.74 | 4.460 |
| 17 | | | | | | 4.459 |
| 18 | | | | | | 4.460 |
| 19 | | | | | | 4.459 |
| 20 | | | | | | 4.460 |
| 21 | | | | | | 0.565 |

***→Caution: Table 3, below, may not be used for three-, five-, seven-, or ten-year farm business property placed in service before 2018. Table 16, below, incorporates the 150-percent declining-balance method and the mid-quarter convention that may be used for such property.←***

TABLE 3
General Depreciation System
Applicable Depreciation Method: 200- or 150-Percent Declining Balance Switching to Straight Line
Applicable Recovery Periods: 3, 5, 7, 10, 15, 20 years
Applicable Convention: Mid-quarter (property placed in service in second quarter)

| If the Recovery Year is: | and the Recovery Period is: | | | | | |
|---|---|---|---|---|---|---|
| | 3-year | 5-year | 7-year | 10-year | 15-year | 20-year |
| | the Depreciation Rate is: | | | | | |
| 1 | 41.67 | 25.00 | 17.85 | 12.50 | 6.25 | 4.688 |
| 2 | 38.89 | 30.00 | 23.47 | 17.50 | 9.38 | 7.148 |
| 3 | 14.14 | 18.00 | 16.76 | 14.00 | 8.44 | 6.612 |
| 4 | 5.30 | 11.37 | 11.97 | 11.20 | 7.59 | 6.116 |
| 5 | | 11.37 | 8.87 | 8.96 | 6.83 | 5.658 |
| 6 | | 4.26 | 8.87 | 7.17 | 6.15 | 5.233 |
| 7 | | | 8.87 | 6.55 | 5.91 | 4.841 |
| 8 | | | 3.34 | 6.55 | 5.90 | 4.478 |
| 9 | | | | 6.56 | 5.91 | 4.463 |
| 10 | | | | 6.55 | 5.90 | 4.463 |
| 11 | | | | 2.46 | 5.91 | 4.463 |
| 12 | | | | | 5.90 | 4.463 |
| 13 | | | | | 5.91 | 4.463 |
| 14 | | | | | 5.90 | 4.463 |
| 15 | | | | | 5.91 | 4.462 |
| 16 | | | | | 2.21 | 4.463 |
| 17 | | | | | | 4.462 |
| 18 | | | | | | 4.463 |
| 19 | | | | | | 4.462 |
| 20 | | | | | | 4.463 |
| 21 | | | | | | 1.673 |

***→Caution: Table 4, below, may not be used for three-, five-, seven-, or ten-year farm business property placed in service before 2018. Table 17, below, incorporates the 150-percent declining-balance method and the mid-quarter convention that may be used for such property.←***

TABLE 4
General Depreciation System
Applicable Depreciation Method: 200-or 150-Percent Declining Balance Switching to Straight Line
Applicable Recovery Periods: 3, 5, 7, 10, 15, 20 years
Applicable Convention: Mid-quarter (property placed in service in third quarter)

| If the Recovery Year is: | and the Recovery Period is: | | | | | |
|---|---|---|---|---|---|---|
| | 3-year | 5-year | 7-year | 10-year | 15-year | 20-year |
| | the Depreciation Rate is: | | | | | |
| 1 | 25.00 | 15.00 | 10.71 | 7.50 | 3.75 | 2.813 |
| 2 | 50.00 | 34.00 | 25.51 | 18.50 | 9.63 | 7.289 |
| 3 | 16.67 | 20.40 | 18.22 | 14.80 | 8.66 | 6.742 |
| 4 | 8.33 | 12.24 | 13.02 | 11.84 | 7.80 | 6.237 |
| 5 | | 11.30 | 9.30 | 9.47 | 7.02 | 5.769 |
| 6 | | 7.06 | 8.85 | 7.58 | 6.31 | 5.336 |
| 7 | | | 8.86 | 6.55 | 5.90 | 4.936 |
| 8 | | | 5.53 | 6.55 | 5.90 | 4.566 |
| 9 | | | | 6.56 | 5.91 | 4.460 |
| 10 | | | | 6.55 | 5.90 | 4.460 |
| 11 | | | | 4.10 | 5.91 | 4.460 |
| 12 | | | | | 5.90 | 4.460 |
| 13 | | | | | 5.91 | 4.461 |
| 14 | | | | | 5.90 | 4.460 |
| 15 | | | | | 5.91 | 4.461 |
| 16 | | | | | 3.69 | 4.460 |
| 17 | | | | | | 4.461 |
| 18 | | | | | | 4.460 |
| 19 | | | | | | 4.461 |
| 20 | | | | | | 4.460 |
| 21 | | | | | | 2.788 |

***→Caution: Table 5, below, may not be used for three-, five-, seven-, or ten-year farm business property placed in service before 2018. Table 18, below, incorporates the 150-percent declining-balance method and the mid-quarter convention that may be used for such property.←***

TABLE 5
General Depreciation System
Applicable Depreciation Method: 200- or 150-Percent
Declining Balance Switching to Straight Line
Applicable Recovery Periods: 3, 5, 7, 10, 15, 20 years
Applicable Convention: Mid-quarter (property placed in
service in fourth quarter)

| If the Recovery Year is: | and the Recovery Period is: 3-year | 5-year | 7-year | 10-year | 15-year | 20-year |
|---|---|---|---|---|---|---|
| | the Depreciation Rate is: | | | | | |
| 1 | 8.33 | 5.00 | 3.57 | 2.50 | 1.25 | 0.938 |
| 2 | 61.11 | 38.00 | 27.55 | 19.50 | 9.88 | 7.430 |
| 3 | 20.37 | 22.80 | 19.68 | 15.60 | 8.89 | 6.872 |
| 4 | 10.19 | 13.68 | 14.06 | 12.48 | 8.00 | 6.357 |
| 5 | | 10.94 | 10.04 | 9.98 | 7.20 | 5.880 |
| 6 | | 9.58 | 8.73 | 7.99 | 6.48 | 5.439 |
| 7 | | | 8.73 | 6.55 | 5.90 | 5.031 |
| 8 | | | 7.64 | 6.55 | 5.90 | 4.654 |
| 9 | | | | 6.56 | 5.90 | 4.458 |
| 10 | | | | 6.55 | 5.91 | 4.458 |
| 11 | | | | 5.74 | 5.90 | 4.458 |
| 12 | | | | | 5.91 | 4.458 |
| 13 | | | | | 5.90 | 4.458 |
| 14 | | | | | 5.91 | 4.458 |
| 15 | | | | | 5.90 | 4.458 |
| 16 | | | | | 5.17 | 4.458 |
| 17 | | | | | | 4.458 |
| 18 | | | | | | 4.459 |
| 19 | | | | | | 4.458 |
| 20 | | | | | | 4.459 |
| 21 | | | | | | 3.901 |

TABLE 6
General Depreciation
System—Residential Rental Property
Applicable Depreciation Method: Straight Line
Applicable Recovery Period: 27.5 years
Applicable Convention: Mid-month

| If the Recovery Year is: | and the Month in the First Recovery Year the Property is Placed in Service is: | | | | | | | | | | | |
|---|---|---|---|---|---|---|---|---|---|---|---|---|
| | 1 | 2 | 3 | 4 | 5 | 6 | 7 | 8 | 9 | 10 | 11 | 12 |
| | the Depreciation Rate is: | | | | | | | | | | | |
| 1 | 3.485 | 3.182 | 2.879 | 2.576 | 2.273 | 1.970 | 1.667 | 1.364 | 1.061 | 0.758 | 0.455 | 0.152 |
| 2 | 3.636 | 3.636 | 3.636 | 3.636 | 3.636 | 3.636 | 3.636 | 3.636 | 3.636 | 3.636 | 3.636 | 3.636 |
| 3 | 3.636 | 3.636 | 3.636 | 3.636 | 3.636 | 3.636 | 3.636 | 3.636 | 3.636 | 3.636 | 3.636 | 3.636 |
| 4 | 3.636 | 3.636 | 3.636 | 3.636 | 3.636 | 3.636 | 3.636 | 3.636 | 3.636 | 3.636 | 3.636 | 3.636 |
| 5 | 3.636 | 3.636 | 3.636 | 3.636 | 3.636 | 3.636 | 3.636 | 3.636 | 3.636 | 3.636 | 3.636 | 3.636 |
| 6 | 3.636 | 3.636 | 3.636 | 3.636 | 3.636 | 3.636 | 3.636 | 3.636 | 3.636 | 3.636 | 3.636 | 3.636 |
| 7 | 3.636 | 3.636 | 3.636 | 3.636 | 3.636 | 3.636 | 3.636 | 3.636 | 3.636 | 3.636 | 3.636 | 3.636 |
| 8 | 3.636 | 3.636 | 3.636 | 3.636 | 3.636 | 3.636 | 3.636 | 3.636 | 3.636 | 3.636 | 3.636 | 3.636 |
| 9 | 3.636 | 3.636 | 3.636 | 3.636 | 3.636 | 3.636 | 3.636 | 3.636 | 3.636 | 3.636 | 3.636 | 3.636 |
| 10 | 3.637 | 3.637 | 3.637 | 3.637 | 3.637 | 3.637 | 3.636 | 3.636 | 3.636 | 3.636 | 3.636 | 3.636 |
| 11 | 3.636 | 3.636 | 3.636 | 3.636 | 3.636 | 3.636 | 3.637 | 3.637 | 3.637 | 3.637 | 3.637 | 3.637 |
| 12 | 3.637 | 3.637 | 3.637 | 3.637 | 3.637 | 3.637 | 3.636 | 3.636 | 3.636 | 3.636 | 3.636 | 3.636 |
| 13 | 3.636 | 3.636 | 3.636 | 3.636 | 3.636 | 3.636 | 3.637 | 3.637 | 3.637 | 3.637 | 3.637 | 3.637 |
| 14 | 3.637 | 3.637 | 3.637 | 3.637 | 3.637 | 3.637 | 3.636 | 3.636 | 3.636 | 3.636 | 3.636 | 3.636 |
| 15 | 3.636 | 3.636 | 3.636 | 3.636 | 3.636 | 3.636 | 3.637 | 3.637 | 3.637 | 3.637 | 3.637 | 3.637 |
| 16 | 3.637 | 3.637 | 3.637 | 3.637 | 3.637 | 3.637 | 3.636 | 3.636 | 3.636 | 3.636 | 3.636 | 3.636 |
| 17 | 3.636 | 3.636 | 3.636 | 3.636 | 3.636 | 3.636 | 3.637 | 3.637 | 3.637 | 3.637 | 3.637 | 3.637 |
| 18 | 3.637 | 3.637 | 3.637 | 3.637 | 3.637 | 3.637 | 3.636 | 3.636 | 3.636 | 3.636 | 3.636 | 3.636 |
| 19 | 3.636 | 3.636 | 3.636 | 3.636 | 3.636 | 3.636 | 3.637 | 3.637 | 3.637 | 3.637 | 3.637 | 3.637 |
| 20 | 3.637 | 3.637 | 3.637 | 3.637 | 3.637 | 3.637 | 3.636 | 3.636 | 3.636 | 3.636 | 3.636 | 3.636 |
| 21 | 3.636 | 3.636 | 3.636 | 3.636 | 3.636 | 3.636 | 3.637 | 3.637 | 3.637 | 3.637 | 3.637 | 3.637 |

| If the Recovery Year is: | and the Month in the First Recovery Year the Property is Placed in Service is: | | | | | | | | | | | |
|---|---|---|---|---|---|---|---|---|---|---|---|---|
| | 1 | 2 | 3 | 4 | 5 | 6 | 7 | 8 | 9 | 10 | 11 | 12 |
| | the Depreciation Rate is: | | | | | | | | | | | |
| 22 | 3.637 | 3.637 | 3.637 | 3.637 | 3.637 | 3.637 | 3.636 | 3.636 | 3.636 | 3.636 | 3.636 | 3.636 |
| 23 | 3.636 | 3.636 | 3.636 | 3.636 | 3.636 | 3.636 | 3.637 | 3.637 | 3.637 | 3.637 | 3.637 | 3.637 |
| 24 | 3.637 | 3.637 | 3.637 | 3.637 | 3.637 | 3.637 | 3.636 | 3.636 | 3.636 | 3.636 | 3.636 | 3.636 |
| 25 | 3.636 | 3.636 | 3.636 | 3.636 | 3.636 | 3.636 | 3.637 | 3.637 | 3.637 | 3.637 | 3.637 | 3.637 |
| 26 | 3.637 | 3.637 | 3.637 | 3.637 | 3.637 | 3.637 | 3.636 | 3.636 | 3.636 | 3.636 | 3.636 | 3.636 |
| 27 | 3.636 | 3.636 | 3.636 | 3.636 | 3.636 | 3.636 | 3.637 | 3.637 | 3.637 | 3.637 | 3.637 | 3.637 |
| 28 | 1.970 | 2.273 | 2.576 | 2.879 | 3.182 | 3.485 | 3.636 | 3.636 | 3.636 | 3.636 | 3.636 | 3.636 |
| 29 | 0.000 | 0.000 | 0.000 | 0.000 | 0.000 | 0.000 | 0.152 | 0.455 | 0.758 | 1.061 | 1.364 | 1.667 |

TABLE 7
General Depreciation
System—Nonresidential Real Property
Placed in Service before May 13, 1993
Applicable Depreciation Method: Straight Line
Applicable Recovery Period: 31.5 years
Applicable Convention: Mid-month

| If the Recovery Year is: | and the Month in the First Recovery Year the Property is Placed in Service is: | | | | | | | | | | | |
|---|---|---|---|---|---|---|---|---|---|---|---|---|
| | 1 | 2 | 3 | 4 | 5 | 6 | 7 | 8 | 9 | 10 | 11 | 12 |
| | the Depreciation Rate is: | | | | | | | | | | | |
| 1 | 3.042 | 2.778 | 2.513 | 2.249 | 1.984 | 1.720 | 1.455 | 1.190 | 0.926 | 0.661 | 0.397 | 0.132 |
| 2 | 3.175 | 3.175 | 3.175 | 3.175 | 3.175 | 3.175 | 3.175 | 3.175 | 3.175 | 3.175 | 3.175 | 3.175 |
| 3 | 3.175 | 3.175 | 3.175 | 3.175 | 3.175 | 3.175 | 3.175 | 3.175 | 3.175 | 3.175 | 3.175 | 3.175 |
| 4 | 3.175 | 3.175 | 3.175 | 3.175 | 3.175 | 3.175 | 3.175 | 3.175 | 3.175 | 3.175 | 3.175 | 3.175 |
| 5 | 3.175 | 3.175 | 3.175 | 3.175 | 3.175 | 3.175 | 3.175 | 3.175 | 3.175 | 3.175 | 3.175 | 3.175 |
| 6 | 3.175 | 3.175 | 3.175 | 3.175 | 3.175 | 3.175 | 3.175 | 3.175 | 3.175 | 3.175 | 3.175 | 3.175 |
| 7 | 3.175 | 3.175 | 3.175 | 3.175 | 3.175 | 3.175 | 3.175 | 3.175 | 3.175 | 3.175 | 3.175 | 3.175 |
| 8 | 3.175 | 3.174 | 3.175 | 3.174 | 3.175 | 3.174 | 3.175 | 3.175 | 3.175 | 3.175 | 3.175 | 3.175 |
| 9 | 3.174 | 3.175 | 3.174 | 3.175 | 3.174 | 3.175 | 3.174 | 3.175 | 3.174 | 3.175 | 3.174 | 3.175 |
| 10 | 3.175 | 3.174 | 3.175 | 3.174 | 3.175 | 3.174 | 3.175 | 3.174 | 3.175 | 3.174 | 3.175 | 3.174 |
| 11 | 3.174 | 3.175 | 3.174 | 3.175 | 3.174 | 3.175 | 3.174 | 3.175 | 3.174 | 3.175 | 3.174 | 3.175 |
| 12 | 3.175 | 3.174 | 3.175 | 3.174 | 3.175 | 3.174 | 3.175 | 3.174 | 3.175 | 3.174 | 3.175 | 3.174 |
| 13 | 3.174 | 3.175 | 3.174 | 3.175 | 3.174 | 3.175 | 3.174 | 3.175 | 3.174 | 3.175 | 3.174 | 3.175 |
| 14 | 3.175 | 3.174 | 3.175 | 3.174 | 3.175 | 3.174 | 3.175 | 3.174 | 3.175 | 3.174 | 3.175 | 3.174 |
| 15 | 3.174 | 3.175 | 3.174 | 3.175 | 3.174 | 3.175 | 3.174 | 3.175 | 3.174 | 3.175 | 3.174 | 3.175 |
| 16 | 3.175 | 3.174 | 3.175 | 3.174 | 3.175 | 3.174 | 3.175 | 3.174 | 3.175 | 3.174 | 3.175 | 3.174 |
| 17 | 3.174 | 3.175 | 3.174 | 3.175 | 3.174 | 3.175 | 3.174 | 3.175 | 3.174 | 3.175 | 3.174 | 3.175 |
| 18 | 3.175 | 3.174 | 3.175 | 3.174 | 3.175 | 3.174 | 3.175 | 3.174 | 3.175 | 3.174 | 3.175 | 3.174 |
| 19 | 3.174 | 3.175 | 3.174 | 3.175 | 3.174 | 3.175 | 3.174 | 3.175 | 3.174 | 3.175 | 3.174 | 3.175 |
| 20 | 3.175 | 3.174 | 3.175 | 3.174 | 3.175 | 3.174 | 3.175 | 3.174 | 3.175 | 3.174 | 3.175 | 3.174 |

| If the Recovery Year is: | and the Month in the First Recovery Year the Property is Placed in Service is: | | | | | | | | | | | |
|---|---|---|---|---|---|---|---|---|---|---|---|---|
| | 1 | 2 | 3 | 4 | 5 | 6 | 7 | 8 | 9 | 10 | 11 | 12 |
| | the Depreciation Rate is: | | | | | | | | | | | |
| 21 | 3.174 | 3.175 | 3.174 | 3.175 | 3.174 | 3.175 | 3.174 | 3.175 | 3.174 | 3.175 | 3.174 | 3.175 |
| 22 | 3.175 | 3.174 | 3.175 | 3.174 | 3.175 | 3.174 | 3.175 | 3.174 | 3.175 | 3.174 | 3.175 | 3.174 |
| 23 | 3.174 | 3.175 | 3.174 | 3.175 | 3.174 | 3.175 | 3.174 | 3.175 | 3.174 | 3.175 | 3.174 | 3.175 |
| 24 | 3.175 | 3.174 | 3.175 | 3.174 | 3.175 | 3.174 | 3.175 | 3.174 | 3.175 | 3.174 | 3.175 | 3.174 |
| 25 | 3.174 | 3.175 | 3.174 | 3.175 | 3.174 | 3.175 | 3.174 | 3.175 | 3.174 | 3.175 | 3.174 | 3.175 |
| 26 | 3.175 | 3.174 | 3.175 | 3.174 | 3.175 | 3.174 | 3.175 | 3.174 | 3.175 | 3.174 | 3.175 | 3.174 |
| 27 | 3.174 | 3.175 | 3.174 | 3.175 | 3.174 | 3.175 | 3.174 | 3.175 | 3.174 | 3.175 | 3.174 | 3.175 |
| 28 | 3.175 | 3.174 | 3.175 | 3.174 | 3.175 | 3.174 | 3.175 | 3.174 | 3.175 | 3.174 | 3.175 | 3.174 |
| 29 | 3.174 | 3.175 | 3.174 | 3.175 | 3.174 | 3.175 | 3.174 | 3.175 | 3.174 | 3.175 | 3.174 | 3.175 |
| 30 | 3.175 | 3.174 | 3.175 | 3.174 | 3.175 | 3.174 | 3.175 | 3.174 | 3.175 | 3.174 | 3.175 | 3.174 |
| 31 | 3.174 | 3.175 | 3.174 | 3.175 | 3.174 | 3.175 | 3.174 | 3.175 | 3.174 | 3.175 | 3.174 | 3.175 |
| 32 | 1.720 | 1.984 | 2.249 | 2.513 | 2.778 | 3.042 | 3.175 | 3.174 | 3.175 | 3.174 | 3.175 | 3.174 |
| 33 | 0.000 | 0.000 | 0.000 | 0.000 | 0.000 | 0.000 | 0.132 | 0.397 | 0.661 | 0.926 | 1.190 | 1.455 |

TABLE 7A
General Depreciation
System—Nonresidential Real Property
Placed in Service after May 12, 1993
Applicable Depreciation Method: Straight Line
Applicable Recovery Period: 39 years
Applicable Convention: Mid-month

| If the Recovery Year is: | and the Month in the First Recovery Year the Property is Placed in Service is: | | | | | | | | | | | |
|---|---|---|---|---|---|---|---|---|---|---|---|---|
| | 1 | 2 | 3 | 4 | 5 | 6 | 7 | 8 | 9 | 10 | 11 | 12 |
| | the Depreciation Rate is: | | | | | | | | | | | |
| 1 | 2.461 | 2.247 | 2.033 | 1.819 | 1.605 | 1.391 | 1.177 | 0.963 | 0.749 | 0.535 | 0.321 | 0.107 |
| 2 - 39 | 2.564 | 2.564 | 2.564 | 2.564 | 2.564 | 2.564 | 2.564 | 2.564 | 2.564 | 2.564 | 2.564 | 2.564 |
| 40 | 0.107 | 0.321 | 0.535 | 0.749 | 0.963 | 1.177 | 1.391 | 1.605 | 1.819 | 2.033 | 2.247 | 2.461 |

[IRS Pub. 946]

TABLE 8
General and Alternative Depreciation Systems
Applicable Depreciation Method: Straight Line
Applicable Recovery Periods: 2.5 — 50 years
Applicable Convention: Half-year

| If the Recovery Year is: | and the Recovery Period is: 2.5 | 3.0 | 3.5 | 4.0 | 4.5 | 5.0 | 5.5 | 6.0 | 6.5 | 7.0 | 7.5 | 8.0 | 8.5 | 9.0 | 9.5 |
|---|---|---|---|---|---|---|---|---|---|---|---|---|---|---|---|
| | the Depreciation Rate is: | | | | | | | | | | | | | | |
| 1 | 20.00 | 16.67 | 14.29 | 12.50 | 11.11 | 10.00 | 9.09 | 8.33 | 7.69 | 7.14 | 6.67 | 6.25 | 5.88 | 5.56 | 5.26 |
| 2 | 40.00 | 33.33 | 28.57 | 25.00 | 22.22 | 20.00 | 18.18 | 16.67 | 15.39 | 14.29 | 13.33 | 12.50 | 11.77 | 11.11 | 10.53 |
| 3 | 40.00 | 33.33 | 28.57 | 25.00 | 22.22 | 20.00 | 18.18 | 16.67 | 15.38 | 14.29 | 13.33 | 12.50 | 11.76 | 11.11 | 10.53 |
| 4 | | 16.67 | 28.57 | 25.00 | 22.23 | 20.00 | 18.18 | 16.67 | 15.39 | 14.28 | 13.33 | 12.50 | 11.77 | 11.11 | 10.53 |
| 5 | | | | 12.50 | 22.22 | 20.00 | 18.19 | 16.66 | 15.38 | 14.29 | 13.34 | 12.50 | 11.76 | 11.11 | 10.52 |
| 6 | | | | | | 10.00 | 18.18 | 16.67 | 15.39 | 14.28 | 13.33 | 12.50 | 11.77 | 11.11 | 10.53 |
| 7 | | | | | | | | 8.33 | 15.38 | 14.29 | 13.34 | 12.50 | 11.76 | 11.11 | 10.52 |
| 8 | | | | | | | | | | 7.14 | 13.33 | 12.50 | 11.77 | 11.11 | 10.53 |
| 9 | | | | | | | | | | | | 6.25 | 11.76 | 11.11 | 10.52 |
| 10 | | | | | | | | | | | | | | 5.56 | 10.53 |

| If the Recovery Year is: | and the Recovery Period is: 10.0 | 10.5 | 11.0 | 11.5 | 12.0 | 12.5 | 13.0 | 13.5 | 14.0 | 14.5 | 15.0 | 15.5 | 16.0 | 16.5 | 17.0 |
|---|---|---|---|---|---|---|---|---|---|---|---|---|---|---|---|
| | the Depreciation Rate is: | | | | | | | | | | | | | | |
| 1 | 5.00 | 4.76 | 4.55 | 4.35 | 4.17 | 4.00 | 3.85 | 3.70 | 3.57 | 3.45 | 3.33 | 3.23 | 3.13 | 3.03 | 2.94 |
| 2 | 10.00 | 9.52 | 9.09 | 8.70 | 8.33 | 8.00 | 7.69 | 7.41 | 7.14 | 6.90 | 6.67 | 6.45 | 6.25 | 6.06 | 5.88 |
| 3 | 10.00 | 9.52 | 9.09 | 8.70 | 8.33 | 8.00 | 7.69 | 7.41 | 7.14 | 6.90 | 6.67 | 6.45 | 6.25 | 6.06 | 5.88 |
| 4 | 10.00 | 9.53 | 9.09 | 8.69 | 8.33 | 8.00 | 7.69 | 7.41 | 7.14 | 6.90 | 6.67 | 6.45 | 6.25 | 6.06 | 5.88 |
| 5 | 10.00 | 9.52 | 9.09 | 8.70 | 8.33 | 8.00 | 7.69 | 7.41 | 7.14 | 6.90 | 6.67 | 6.45 | 6.25 | 6.06 | 5.88 |
| 6 | 10.00 | 9.53 | 9.09 | 8.69 | 8.33 | 8.00 | 7.69 | 7.41 | 7.14 | 6.89 | 6.67 | 6.45 | 6.25 | 6.06 | 5.88 |
| 7 | 10.00 | 9.52 | 9.09 | 8.70 | 8.34 | 8.00 | 7.69 | 7.41 | 7.14 | 6.90 | 6.67 | 6.45 | 6.25 | 6.06 | 5.88 |
| 8 | 10.00 | 9.53 | 9.09 | 8.69 | 8.33 | 8.00 | 7.69 | 7.41 | 7.15 | 6.89 | 6.66 | 6.45 | 6.25 | 6.06 | 5.88 |

| If the Recovery Year is: | and the Recovery Period is: 10.0 | 10.5 | 11.0 | 11.5 | 12.0 | 12.5 | 13.0 | 13.5 | 14.0 | 14.5 | 15.0 | 15.5 | 16.0 | 16.5 | 17.0 |
|---|---|---|---|---|---|---|---|---|---|---|---|---|---|---|---|
| | the Depreciation Rate is: | | | | | | | | | | | | | | |
| 9 | 10.00 | 9.52 | 9.09 | 8.70 | 8.34 | 8.00 | 7.69 | 7.41 | 7.14 | 6.90 | 6.67 | 6.45 | 6.25 | 6.06 | 5.88 |
| 10 | 10.00 | 9.53 | 9.09 | 8.69 | 8.33 | 8.00 | 7.70 | 7.40 | 7.15 | 6.89 | 6.66 | 6.45 | 6.25 | 6.06 | 5.88 |
| 11 | 5.00 | 9.52 | 9.09 | 8.70 | 8.34 | 8.00 | 7.69 | 7.41 | 7.14 | 6.90 | 6.67 | 6.45 | 6.25 | 6.06 | 5.89 |
| 12 | | | 4.55 | 8.69 | 8.33 | 8.00 | 7.70 | 7.40 | 7.15 | 6.89 | 6.66 | 6.45 | 6.25 | 6.06 | 5.88 |
| 13 | | | | | 4.17 | 8.00 | 7.69 | 7.41 | 7.14 | 6.90 | 6.67 | 6.45 | 6.25 | 6.06 | 5.89 |
| 14 | | | | | | | 3.85 | 7.40 | 7.15 | 6.89 | 6.66 | 6.46 | 6.25 | 6.06 | 5.88 |
| 15 | | | | | | | | | 3.57 | 6.90 | 6.67 | 6.45 | 6.25 | 6.06 | 5.89 |
| 16 | | | | | | | | | | | 3.33 | 6.46 | 6.25 | 6.06 | 5.88 |
| 17 | | | | | | | | | | | | | 3.12 | 6.07 | 5.89 |
| 18 | | | | | | | | | | | | | | | 2.94 |

| If the Recovery Year is: | and the Recovery Period is: 17.5 | 18.0 | 18.5 | 19.0 | 19.5 | 20.0 | 20.5 | 21.0 | 21.5 | 22.0 | 22.5 | 23.0 | 23.5 | 24.0 | 24.5 |
|---|---|---|---|---|---|---|---|---|---|---|---|---|---|---|---|
| | the Depreciation Rate is: | | | | | | | | | | | | | | |
| 1 | 2.86 | 2.78 | 2.70 | 2.63 | 2.56 | 2.500 | 2.439 | 2.381 | 2.326 | 2.273 | 2.222 | 2.174 | 2.128 | 2.083 | 2.041 |
| 2 | 5.71 | 5.56 | 5.41 | 5.26 | 5.13 | 5.000 | 4.878 | 4.762 | 4.651 | 4.545 | 4.444 | 4.348 | 4.255 | 4.167 | 4.082 |
| 3 | 5.71 | 5.56 | 5.41 | 5.26 | 5.13 | 5.000 | 4.878 | 4.762 | 4.651 | 4.545 | 4.444 | 4.348 | 4.255 | 4.167 | 4.082 |
| 4 | 5.71 | 5.55 | 5.41 | 5.26 | 5.13 | 5.000 | 4.878 | 4.762 | 4.651 | 4.545 | 4.445 | 4.348 | 4.255 | 4.167 | 4.082 |
| 5 | 5.72 | 5.56 | 5.40 | 5.26 | 5.13 | 5.000 | 4.878 | 4.762 | 4.651 | 4.546 | 4.444 | 4.348 | 4.255 | 4.167 | 4.082 |
| 6 | 5.71 | 5.55 | 5.41 | 5.26 | 5.13 | 5.000 | 4.878 | 4.762 | 4.651 | 4.545 | 4.445 | 4.348 | 4.255 | 4.167 | 4.082 |
| 7 | 5.72 | 5.56 | 5.40 | 5.26 | 5.13 | 5.000 | 4.878 | 4.762 | 4.651 | 4.546 | 4.444 | 4.348 | 4.255 | 4.167 | 4.082 |
| 8 | 5.71 | 5.55 | 5.41 | 5.26 | 5.13 | 5.000 | 4.878 | 4.762 | 4.651 | 4.545 | 4.445 | 4.348 | 4.255 | 4.167 | 4.082 |
| 9 | 5.72 | 5.56 | 5.40 | 5.27 | 5.13 | 5.000 | 4.878 | 4.762 | 4.651 | 4.546 | 4.444 | 4.348 | 4.255 | 4.167 | 4.081 |
| 10 | 5.71 | 5.55 | 5.41 | 5.26 | 5.13 | 5.000 | 4.878 | 4.762 | 4.651 | 4.545 | 4.445 | 4.348 | 4.255 | 4.167 | 4.082 |
| 11 | 5.72 | 5.56 | 5.40 | 5.27 | 5.13 | 5.000 | 4.878 | 4.762 | 4.651 | 4.546 | 4.444 | 4.348 | 4.256 | 4.166 | 4.081 |
| 12 | 5.71 | 5.55 | 5.41 | 5.26 | 5.13 | 5.000 | 4.878 | 4.762 | 4.651 | 4.545 | 4.445 | 4.348 | 4.255 | 4.167 | 4.082 |

| If the Recovery Year is: | and the Recovery Period is: 17.5 | 18.0 | 18.5 | 19.0 | 19.5 | 20.0 | 20.5 | 21.0 | 21.5 | 22.0 | 22.5 | 23.0 | 23.5 | 24.0 | 24.5 |
|---|---|---|---|---|---|---|---|---|---|---|---|---|---|---|---|
| | the Depreciation Rate is: | | | | | | | | | | | | | | |
| 13 | 5.72 | 5.56 | 5.40 | 5.27 | 5.13 | 5.000 | 4.878 | 4.762 | 4.651 | 4.546 | 4.444 | 4.348 | 4.256 | 4.166 | 4.081 |
| 14 | 5.71 | 5.55 | 5.41 | 5.26 | 5.13 | 5.000 | 4.878 | 4.762 | 4.651 | 4.545 | 4.445 | 4.348 | 4.255 | 4.167 | 4.082 |
| 15 | 5.72 | 5.56 | 5.40 | 5.27 | 5.13 | 5.000 | 4.878 | 4.762 | 4.651 | 4.546 | 4.444 | 4.348 | 4.256 | 4.166 | 4.081 |
| 16 | 5.71 | 5.55 | 5.41 | 5.26 | 5.12 | 5.000 | 4.878 | 4.762 | 4.651 | 4.545 | 4.445 | 4.348 | 4.255 | 4.167 | 4.082 |
| 17 | 5.72 | 5.56 | 5.40 | 5.27 | 5.13 | 5.000 | 4.878 | 4.762 | 4.652 | 4.546 | 4.444 | 4.347 | 4.256 | 4.166 | 4.081 |
| 18 | 5.71 | 5.55 | 5.41 | 5.26 | 5.12 | 5.000 | 4.878 | 4.762 | 4.651 | 4.545 | 4.445 | 4.348 | 4.255 | 4.167 | 4.082 |
| 19 | | 2.78 | 5.40 | 5.27 | 5.13 | 5.000 | 4.878 | 4.761 | 4.652 | 4.546 | 4.444 | 4.347 | 4.256 | 4.166 | 4.081 |
| 20 | | | | 2.63 | 5.12 | 5.000 | 4.879 | 4.762 | 4.651 | 4.545 | 4.445 | 4.348 | 4.255 | 4.167 | 4.082 |
| 21 | | | | | | 2.500 | 4.878 | 4.761 | 4.652 | 4.546 | 4.444 | 4.347 | 4.256 | 4.166 | 4.081 |
| 22 | | | | | | | | 2.381 | 4.651 | 4.545 | 4.445 | 4.348 | 4.255 | 4.167 | 4.082 |
| 23 | | | | | | | | | | 2.273 | 4.444 | 4.347 | 4.256 | 4.166 | 4.081 |
| 24 | | | | | | | | | | | | 2.174 | 4.255 | 4.167 | 4.082 |
| 25 | | | | | | | | | | | | | | 2.083 | 4.081 |

| If the Recovery Year is: | and the Recovery Period is: 25.0 | 25.5 | 26.0 | 26.5 | 27.0 | 27.5 | 28.0 | 28.5 | 29.0 | 29.5 | 30.0 | 30.5 | 31.0 | 31.5 | 32.0 |
|---|---|---|---|---|---|---|---|---|---|---|---|---|---|---|---|
| | the Depreciation Rate is: | | | | | | | | | | | | | | |
| 1 | 2.000 | 1.961 | 1.923 | 1.887 | 1.852 | 1.818 | 1.786 | 1.754 | 1.724 | 1.695 | 1.667 | 1.639 | 1.613 | 1.587 | 1.563 |
| 2 | 4.000 | 3.922 | 3.846 | 3.774 | 3.704 | 3.636 | 3.571 | 3.509 | 3.448 | 3.390 | 3.333 | 3.279 | 3.226 | 3.175 | 3.125 |
| 3 | 4.000 | 3.922 | 3.846 | 3.774 | 3.704 | 3.636 | 3.571 | 3.509 | 3.448 | 3.390 | 3.333 | 3.279 | 3.226 | 3.175 | 3.125 |
| 4 | 4.000 | 3.922 | 3.846 | 3.774 | 3.704 | 3.636 | 3.571 | 3.509 | 3.448 | 3.390 | 3.333 | 3.279 | 3.226 | 3.175 | 3.125 |
| 5 | 4.000 | 3.922 | 3.846 | 3.774 | 3.704 | 3.636 | 3.571 | 3.509 | 3.448 | 3.390 | 3.333 | 3.279 | 3.226 | 3.175 | 3.125 |
| 6 | 4.000 | 3.921 | 3.846 | 3.774 | 3.704 | 3.636 | 3.571 | 3.509 | 3.448 | 3.390 | 3.333 | 3.279 | 3.226 | 3.175 | 3.125 |
| 7 | 4.000 | 3.922 | 3.846 | 3.773 | 3.704 | 3.636 | 3.572 | 3.509 | 3.448 | 3.390 | 3.333 | 3.279 | 3.226 | 3.175 | 3.125 |

| If the Recovery Year is: | 25.0 | 25.5 | 26.0 | 26.5 | 27.0 | 27.5 | 28.0 | 28.5 | 29.0 | 29.5 | 30.0 | 30.5 | 31.0 | 31.5 | 32.0 |
|---|---|---|---|---|---|---|---|---|---|---|---|---|---|---|---|
| | | | the Depreciation Rate is: | | | | | | | | | | | | |
| 8 | 4.000 | 3.921 | 3.846 | 3.774 | 3.704 | 3.636 | 3.571 | 3.509 | 3.448 | 3.390 | 3.333 | 3.279 | 3.226 | 3.175 | 3.125 |
| 9 | 4.000 | 3.922 | 3.846 | 3.773 | 3.704 | 3.637 | 3.572 | 3.509 | 3.448 | 3.390 | 3.333 | 3.279 | 3.226 | 3.175 | 3.125 |
| 10 | 4.000 | 3.921 | 3.846 | 3.774 | 3.704 | 3.636 | 3.571 | 3.509 | 3.448 | 3.390 | 3.333 | 3.279 | 3.226 | 3.174 | 3.125 |
| 11 | 4.000 | 3.922 | 3.846 | 3.773 | 3.704 | 3.637 | 3.572 | 3.509 | 3.448 | 3.390 | 3.333 | 3.279 | 3.226 | 3.175 | 3.125 |
| 12 | 4.000 | 3.921 | 3.846 | 3.774 | 3.704 | 3.636 | 3.571 | 3.509 | 3.448 | 3.390 | 3.333 | 3.279 | 3.226 | 3.174 | 3.125 |
| 13 | 4.000 | 3.922 | 3.846 | 3.773 | 3.703 | 3.637 | 3.572 | 3.509 | 3.448 | 3.390 | 3.334 | 3.279 | 3.226 | 3.175 | 3.125 |
| 14 | 4.000 | 3.921 | 3.846 | 3.773 | 3.704 | 3.636 | 3.571 | 3.509 | 3.448 | 3.390 | 3.333 | 3.279 | 3.226 | 3.174 | 3.125 |
| 15 | 4.000 | 3.922 | 3.846 | 3.774 | 3.703 | 3.637 | 3.572 | 3.509 | 3.449 | 3.390 | 3.334 | 3.278 | 3.226 | 3.175 | 3.125 |
| 16 | 4.000 | 3.921 | 3.846 | 3.773 | 3.704 | 3.636 | 3.571 | 3.509 | 3.448 | 3.390 | 3.333 | 3.279 | 3.226 | 3.174 | 3.125 |
| 17 | 4.000 | 3.922 | 3.846 | 3.774 | 3.703 | 3.637 | 3.572 | 3.509 | 3.449 | 3.390 | 3.334 | 3.278 | 3.226 | 3.175 | 3.125 |
| 18 | 4.000 | 3.921 | 3.846 | 3.773 | 3.704 | 3.636 | 3.571 | 3.508 | 3.448 | 3.390 | 3.333 | 3.279 | 3.226 | 3.174 | 3.125 |
| 19 | 4.000 | 3.922 | 3.846 | 3.774 | 3.703 | 3.637 | 3.572 | 3.509 | 3.449 | 3.390 | 3.334 | 3.278 | 3.226 | 3.175 | 3.125 |
| 20 | 4.000 | 3.921 | 3.847 | 3.773 | 3.704 | 3.636 | 3.571 | 3.508 | 3.448 | 3.390 | 3.333 | 3.279 | 3.226 | 3.174 | 3.125 |
| 21 | 4.000 | 3.922 | 3.846 | 3.774 | 3.703 | 3.637 | 3.572 | 3.509 | 3.449 | 3.389 | 3.334 | 3.278 | 3.225 | 3.175 | 3.125 |
| 22 | 4.000 | 3.921 | 3.847 | 3.773 | 3.704 | 3.636 | 3.571 | 3.508 | 3.448 | 3.390 | 3.333 | 3.279 | 3.226 | 3.174 | 3.125 |
| 23 | 4.000 | 3.922 | 3.846 | 3.774 | 3.703 | 3.637 | 3.572 | 3.509 | 3.449 | 3.389 | 3.334 | 3.278 | 3.225 | 3.175 | 3.125 |
| 24 | 4.000 | 3.921 | 3.847 | 3.773 | 3.704 | 3.636 | 3.571 | 3.508 | 3.448 | 3.390 | 3.333 | 3.279 | 3.226 | 3.174 | 3.125 |
| 25 | 4.000 | 3.922 | 3.846 | 3.774 | 3.703 | 3.637 | 3.572 | 3.509 | 3.449 | 3.389 | 3.334 | 3.278 | 3.225 | 3.175 | 3.125 |
| 26 | 2.000 | 3.921 | 3.847 | 3.773 | 3.704 | 3.636 | 3.571 | 3.508 | 3.448 | 3.390 | 3.333 | 3.279 | 3.226 | 3.174 | 3.125 |
| 27 | | | 1.923 | 3.774 | 3.703 | 3.637 | 3.572 | 3.509 | 3.449 | 3.389 | 3.334 | 3.278 | 3.225 | 3.175 | 3.125 |
| 28 | | | | | 1.852 | 3.636 | 3.571 | 3.508 | 3.448 | 3.390 | 3.333 | 3.279 | 3.226 | 3.174 | 3.125 |
| 29 | | | | | | | 1.786 | 3.509 | 3.449 | 3.389 | 3.334 | 3.278 | 3.225 | 3.175 | 3.125 |
| 30 | | | | | | | | | 1.724 | 3.390 | 3.333 | 3.279 | 3.226 | 3.174 | 3.125 |
| 31 | | | | | | | | | | | 1.667 | 3.278 | 3.225 | 3.175 | 3.125 |
| 32 | | | | | | | | | | | | | 1.613 | 3.174 | 3.125 |
| 33 | | | | | | | | | | | | | | | 1.562 |

| If the Recovery Year is: | and the Recovery Period is: 32.5 | 33.0 | 33.5 | 34.0 | 34.5 | 35.0 | 35.5 | 36.0 | 36.5 | 37.0 | 37.5 | 38.0 | 38.5 | 39.0 | 39.5 |
|---|---|---|---|---|---|---|---|---|---|---|---|---|---|---|---|
| | the Depreciation Rate is: | | | | | | | | | | | | | | |
| 1 | 1.538 | 1.515 | 1.493 | 1.471 | 1.449 | 1.429 | 1.408 | 1.389 | 1.370 | 1.351 | 1.333 | 1.316 | 1.299 | 1.282 | 1.266 |
| 2 | 3.077 | 3.030 | 2.985 | 2.941 | 2.899 | 2.857 | 2.817 | 2.778 | 2.740 | 2.703 | 2.667 | 2.632 | 2.597 | 2.564 | 2.532 |
| 3 | 3.077 | 3.030 | 2.985 | 2.941 | 2.899 | 2.857 | 2.817 | 2.778 | 2.740 | 2.703 | 2.667 | 2.632 | 2.597 | 2.564 | 2.532 |
| 4 | 3.077 | 3.030 | 2.985 | 2.941 | 2.899 | 2.857 | 2.817 | 2.778 | 2.740 | 2.703 | 2.667 | 2.632 | 2.597 | 2.564 | 2.532 |
| 5 | 3.077 | 3.030 | 2.985 | 2.941 | 2.899 | 2.857 | 2.817 | 2.778 | 2.740 | 2.703 | 2.667 | 2.632 | 2.597 | 2.564 | 2.532 |
| 6 | 3.077 | 3.030 | 2.985 | 2.941 | 2.899 | 2.857 | 2.817 | 2.778 | 2.740 | 2.703 | 2.667 | 2.632 | 2.597 | 2.564 | 2.532 |
| 7 | 3.077 | 3.030 | 2.985 | 2.941 | 2.898 | 2.857 | 2.817 | 2.778 | 2.740 | 2.703 | 2.667 | 2.632 | 2.597 | 2.564 | 2.532 |
| 8 | 3.077 | 3.030 | 2.985 | 2.941 | 2.899 | 2.857 | 2.817 | 2.778 | 2.740 | 2.703 | 2.667 | 2.631 | 2.597 | 2.564 | 2.532 |
| 9 | 3.077 | 3.030 | 2.985 | 2.941 | 2.898 | 2.857 | 2.817 | 2.778 | 2.740 | 2.703 | 2.667 | 2.632 | 2.597 | 2.564 | 2.532 |
| 10 | 3.077 | 3.030 | 2.985 | 2.941 | 2.899 | 2.857 | 2.817 | 2.778 | 2.740 | 2.703 | 2.667 | 2.631 | 2.598 | 2.564 | 2.532 |
| 11 | 3.077 | 3.030 | 2.985 | 2.941 | 2.898 | 2.857 | 2.817 | 2.778 | 2.740 | 2.703 | 2.667 | 2.632 | 2.597 | 2.564 | 2.532 |
| 12 | 3.077 | 3.030 | 2.985 | 2.941 | 2.899 | 2.857 | 2.817 | 2.778 | 2.740 | 2.703 | 2.667 | 2.631 | 2.598 | 2.564 | 2.532 |
| 13 | 3.077 | 3.030 | 2.985 | 2.941 | 2.898 | 2.857 | 2.817 | 2.778 | 2.740 | 2.703 | 2.667 | 2.632 | 2.597 | 2.564 | 2.532 |
| 14 | 3.077 | 3.030 | 2.985 | 2.941 | 2.899 | 2.857 | 2.817 | 2.778 | 2.740 | 2.703 | 2.667 | 2.631 | 2.598 | 2.564 | 2.531 |
| 15 | 3.077 | 3.031 | 2.985 | 2.941 | 2.898 | 2.857 | 2.817 | 2.778 | 2.740 | 2.703 | 2.666 | 2.632 | 2.597 | 2.564 | 2.532 |
| 16 | 3.077 | 3.030 | 2.985 | 2.941 | 2.899 | 2.857 | 2.817 | 2.778 | 2.740 | 2.703 | 2.667 | 2.631 | 2.598 | 2.564 | 2.531 |
| 17 | 3.077 | 3.031 | 2.985 | 2.941 | 2.898 | 2.857 | 2.817 | 2.778 | 2.740 | 2.703 | 2.666 | 2.632 | 2.597 | 2.564 | 2.532 |
| 18 | 3.077 | 3.030 | 2.985 | 2.941 | 2.899 | 2.857 | 2.817 | 2.778 | 2.740 | 2.702 | 2.667 | 2.631 | 2.598 | 2.564 | 2.531 |
| 19 | 3.077 | 3.031 | 2.985 | 2.941 | 2.898 | 2.857 | 2.817 | 2.778 | 2.739 | 2.703 | 2.666 | 2.632 | 2.597 | 2.564 | 2.532 |
| 20 | 3.077 | 3.030 | 2.985 | 2.941 | 2.898 | 2.857 | 2.817 | 2.778 | 2.740 | 2.702 | 2.667 | 2.631 | 2.598 | 2.564 | 2.531 |
| 21 | 3.077 | 3.031 | 2.985 | 2.941 | 2.899 | 2.857 | 2.817 | 2.778 | 2.739 | 2.703 | 2.666 | 2.632 | 2.597 | 2.564 | 2.532 |
| 22 | 3.077 | 3.030 | 2.985 | 2.941 | 2.898 | 2.857 | 2.817 | 2.777 | 2.740 | 2.702 | 2.667 | 2.631 | 2.598 | 2.564 | 2.531 |
| 23 | 3.077 | 3.031 | 2.985 | 2.941 | 2.899 | 2.857 | 2.817 | 2.778 | 2.739 | 2.703 | 2.666 | 2.632 | 2.597 | 2.564 | 2.532 |
| 24 | 3.077 | 3.030 | 2.985 | 2.941 | 2.898 | 2.857 | 2.817 | 2.777 | 2.740 | 2.702 | 2.667 | 2.631 | 2.598 | 2.564 | 2.531 |

| If the Recovery Year is: | 32.5 | 33.0 | 33.5 | 34.0 | 34.5 | 35.0 | 35.5 | 36.0 | 36.5 | 37.0 | 37.5 | 38.0 | 38.5 | 39.0 | 39.5 |
|---|---|---|---|---|---|---|---|---|---|---|---|---|---|---|---|
| | the Depreciation Rate is: | | | | | | | | | | | | | | |
| 25 | 3.077 | 3.031 | 2.985 | 2.942 | 2.899 | 2.857 | 2.817 | 2.778 | 2.739 | 2.703 | 2.666 | 2.632 | 2.597 | 2.564 | 2.532 |
| 26 | 3.077 | 3.030 | 2.985 | 2.941 | 2.898 | 2.857 | 2.817 | 2.777 | 2.740 | 2.702 | 2.667 | 2.631 | 2.598 | 2.564 | 2.531 |
| 27 | 3.077 | 3.031 | 2.985 | 2.942 | 2.899 | 2.857 | 2.817 | 2.778 | 2.739 | 2.703 | 2.666 | 2.632 | 2.597 | 2.564 | 2.532 |
| 28 | 3.077 | 3.030 | 2.985 | 2.941 | 2.898 | 2.858 | 2.817 | 2.777 | 2.740 | 2.702 | 2.667 | 2.631 | 2.598 | 2.564 | 2.531 |
| 29 | 3.077 | 3.031 | 2.985 | 2.942 | 2.899 | 2.857 | 2.817 | 2.778 | 2.739 | 2.703 | 2.666 | 2.632 | 2.597 | 2.564 | 2.532 |
| 30 | 3.077 | 3.030 | 2.985 | 2.941 | 2.898 | 2.858 | 2.817 | 2.777 | 2.740 | 2.702 | 2.667 | 2.631 | 2.598 | 2.564 | 2.531 |
| 31 | 3.076 | 3.031 | 2.986 | 2.942 | 2.899 | 2.857 | 2.817 | 2.778 | 2.739 | 2.703 | 2.666 | 2.632 | 2.597 | 2.564 | 2.532 |
| 32 | 3.077 | 3.030 | 2.985 | 2.941 | 2.898 | 2.858 | 2.816 | 2.777 | 2.740 | 2.702 | 2.667 | 2.631 | 2.598 | 2.564 | 2.531 |
| 33 | 3.076 | 3.031 | 2.986 | 2.942 | 2.899 | 2.857 | 2.817 | 2.778 | 2.739 | 2.703 | 2.666 | 2.632 | 2.597 | 2.565 | 2.532 |
| 34 | | 1.515 | 2.985 | 2.941 | 2.898 | 2.858 | 2.816 | 2.777 | 2.740 | 2.702 | 2.667 | 2.631 | 2.598 | 2.564 | 2.531 |
| 35 | | | | 1.471 | 2.899 | 2.857 | 2.817 | 2.778 | 2.739 | 2.703 | 2.666 | 2.632 | 2.597 | 2.565 | 2.532 |
| 36 | | | | | | 1.429 | 2.816 | 2.777 | 2.740 | 2.702 | 2.667 | 2.631 | 2.598 | 2.564 | 2.531 |
| 37 | | | | | | | | 1.389 | 2.739 | 2.703 | 2.666 | 2.632 | 2.597 | 2.565 | 2.532 |
| 38 | | | | | | | | | | 1.351 | 2.667 | 2.631 | 2.598 | 2.564 | 2.531 |
| 39 | | | | | | | | | | | | 1.316 | 2.597 | 2.565 | 2.532 |
| 40 | | | | | | | | | | | | | | 1.282 | 2.531 |

and the Recovery Period is:

| If the Recovery Year is: | 40.0 | 40.5 | 41.0 | 41.5 | 42.0 | 42.5 | 43.0 | 43.5 | 44.0 | 44.5 | 45.0 | 45.5 | 46.0 | 46.5 | 47.0 |
|---|---|---|---|---|---|---|---|---|---|---|---|---|---|---|---|
| | the Depreciation Rate is: | | | | | | | | | | | | | | |
| 1 | 1.250 | 1.235 | 1.220 | 1.205 | 1.190 | 1.176 | 1.163 | 1.149 | 1.136 | 1.124 | 1.111 | 1.099 | 1.087 | 1.075 | 1.064 |
| 2 | 2.500 | 2.469 | 2.439 | 2.410 | 2.381 | 2.353 | 2.326 | 2.299 | 2.273 | 2.247 | 2.222 | 2.198 | 2.174 | 2.151 | 2.128 |
| 3 | 2.500 | 2.469 | 2.439 | 2.410 | 2.381 | 2.353 | 2.326 | 2.299 | 2.273 | 2.247 | 2.222 | 2.198 | 2.174 | 2.151 | 2.128 |
| 4 | 2.500 | 2.469 | 2.439 | 2.410 | 2.381 | 2.353 | 2.326 | 2.299 | 2.273 | 2.247 | 2.222 | 2.198 | 2.174 | 2.151 | 2.128 |
| 5 | 2.500 | 2.469 | 2.439 | 2.410 | 2.381 | 2.353 | 2.326 | 2.299 | 2.273 | 2.247 | 2.222 | 2.198 | 2.174 | 2.151 | 2.128 |

| If the Recovery Year is: | 40.0 | 40.5 | 41.0 | 41.5 | 42.0 | 42.5 | 43.0 | 43.5 | 44.0 | 44.5 | 45.0 | 45.5 | 46.0 | 46.5 | 47.0 |
|---|---|---|---|---|---|---|---|---|---|---|---|---|---|---|---|
| | | | the Depreciation Rate is: | | | | | | | | | | | | |
| 6 | 2.500 | 2.469 | 2.439 | 2.410 | 2.381 | 2.353 | 2.326 | 2.299 | 2.273 | 2.247 | 2.222 | 2.198 | 2.174 | 2.151 | 2.128 |
| 7 | 2.500 | 2.469 | 2.439 | 2.410 | 2.381 | 2.353 | 2.326 | 2.299 | 2.273 | 2.247 | 2.222 | 2.198 | 2.174 | 2.150 | 2.128 |
| 8 | 2.500 | 2.469 | 2.439 | 2.410 | 2.381 | 2.353 | 2.326 | 2.299 | 2.273 | 2.247 | 2.222 | 2.198 | 2.174 | 2.151 | 2.128 |
| 9 | 2.500 | 2.469 | 2.439 | 2.410 | 2.381 | 2.353 | 2.325 | 2.299 | 2.273 | 2.247 | 2.222 | 2.198 | 2.174 | 2.150 | 2.128 |
| 10 | 2.500 | 2.469 | 2.439 | 2.410 | 2.381 | 2.353 | 2.326 | 2.299 | 2.273 | 2.247 | 2.222 | 2.198 | 2.174 | 2.151 | 2.128 |
| 11 | 2.500 | 2.469 | 2.439 | 2.410 | 2.381 | 2.353 | 2.325 | 2.299 | 2.273 | 2.247 | 2.222 | 2.198 | 2.174 | 2.150 | 2.128 |
| 12 | 2.500 | 2.469 | 2.439 | 2.410 | 2.381 | 2.353 | 2.326 | 2.299 | 2.273 | 2.247 | 2.222 | 2.198 | 2.174 | 2.151 | 2.128 |
| 13 | 2.500 | 2.469 | 2.439 | 2.410 | 2.381 | 2.353 | 2.325 | 2.299 | 2.273 | 2.247 | 2.222 | 2.198 | 2.174 | 2.150 | 2.128 |
| 14 | 2.500 | 2.469 | 2.439 | 2.409 | 2.381 | 2.353 | 2.326 | 2.299 | 2.273 | 2.247 | 2.222 | 2.198 | 2.174 | 2.151 | 2.128 |
| 15 | 2.500 | 2.469 | 2.439 | 2.410 | 2.381 | 2.353 | 2.325 | 2.299 | 2.273 | 2.247 | 2.222 | 2.198 | 2.174 | 2.150 | 2.128 |
| 16 | 2.500 | 2.469 | 2.439 | 2.409 | 2.381 | 2.353 | 2.326 | 2.299 | 2.273 | 2.247 | 2.222 | 2.198 | 2.174 | 2.151 | 2.128 |
| 17 | 2.500 | 2.469 | 2.439 | 2.410 | 2.381 | 2.353 | 2.325 | 2.299 | 2.273 | 2.247 | 2.222 | 2.198 | 2.174 | 2.150 | 2.127 |
| 18 | 2.500 | 2.469 | 2.439 | 2.409 | 2.381 | 2.353 | 2.326 | 2.299 | 2.273 | 2.247 | 2.222 | 2.198 | 2.174 | 2.151 | 2.128 |
| 19 | 2.500 | 2.469 | 2.439 | 2.410 | 2.381 | 2.353 | 2.325 | 2.299 | 2.273 | 2.247 | 2.222 | 2.198 | 2.174 | 2.150 | 2.127 |
| 20 | 2.500 | 2.469 | 2.439 | 2.409 | 2.381 | 2.353 | 2.326 | 2.299 | 2.273 | 2.247 | 2.222 | 2.198 | 2.174 | 2.151 | 2.128 |
| 21 | 2.500 | 2.469 | 2.439 | 2.410 | 2.381 | 2.353 | 2.325 | 2.299 | 2.273 | 2.247 | 2.222 | 2.198 | 2.174 | 2.150 | 2.127 |
| 22 | 2.500 | 2.469 | 2.439 | 2.409 | 2.381 | 2.353 | 2.326 | 2.299 | 2.273 | 2.247 | 2.222 | 2.198 | 2.174 | 2.151 | 2.128 |
| 23 | 2.500 | 2.469 | 2.439 | 2.410 | 2.381 | 2.353 | 2.325 | 2.299 | 2.272 | 2.247 | 2.222 | 2.198 | 2.174 | 2.150 | 2.127 |
| 24 | 2.500 | 2.469 | 2.439 | 2.409 | 2.381 | 2.353 | 2.326 | 2.299 | 2.273 | 2.247 | 2.222 | 2.198 | 2.174 | 2.151 | 2.128 |
| 25 | 2.500 | 2.469 | 2.439 | 2.410 | 2.381 | 2.353 | 2.325 | 2.299 | 2.272 | 2.247 | 2.222 | 2.198 | 2.174 | 2.150 | 2.127 |
| 26 | 2.500 | 2.469 | 2.439 | 2.409 | 2.381 | 2.353 | 2.326 | 2.299 | 2.273 | 2.247 | 2.222 | 2.198 | 2.174 | 2.151 | 2.128 |
| 27 | 2.500 | 2.469 | 2.439 | 2.410 | 2.381 | 2.353 | 2.325 | 2.299 | 2.272 | 2.247 | 2.223 | 2.198 | 2.174 | 2.150 | 2.127 |
| 28 | 2.500 | 2.469 | 2.439 | 2.409 | 2.381 | 2.353 | 2.326 | 2.299 | 2.273 | 2.247 | 2.222 | 2.198 | 2.174 | 2.151 | 2.128 |
| 29 | 2.500 | 2.469 | 2.439 | 2.410 | 2.381 | 2.353 | 2.325 | 2.299 | 2.272 | 2.247 | 2.223 | 2.198 | 2.174 | 2.150 | 2.127 |
| 30 | 2.500 | 2.469 | 2.439 | 2.409 | 2.381 | 2.353 | 2.326 | 2.299 | 2.273 | 2.248 | 2.222 | 2.197 | 2.174 | 2.151 | 2.128 |
| 31 | 2.500 | 2.469 | 2.439 | 2.410 | 2.381 | 2.353 | 2.325 | 2.299 | 2.272 | 2.247 | 2.223 | 2.198 | 2.174 | 2.150 | 2.127 |
| 32 | 2.500 | 2.470 | 2.439 | 2.409 | 2.381 | 2.353 | 2.326 | 2.299 | 2.273 | 2.248 | 2.222 | 2.197 | 2.174 | 2.151 | 2.128 |

| If the Recovery Year is: | 40.0 | 40.5 | 41.0 | 41.5 | 42.0 | 42.5 | 43.0 | 43.5 | 44.0 | 44.5 | 45.0 | 45.5 | 46.0 | 46.5 | 47.0 |
|---|---|---|---|---|---|---|---|---|---|---|---|---|---|---|---|
| | the Depreciation Rate is: | | | | | | | | | | | | | | |
| 33 | 2.500 | 2.469 | 2.439 | 2.410 | 2.381 | 2.353 | 2.325 | 2.298 | 2.272 | 2.247 | 2.223 | 2.198 | 2.174 | 2.150 | 2.127 |
| 34 | 2.500 | 2.470 | 2.439 | 2.409 | 2.381 | 2.353 | 2.326 | 2.299 | 2.273 | 2.248 | 2.222 | 2.197 | 2.174 | 2.151 | 2.128 |
| 35 | 2.500 | 2.469 | 2.439 | 2.410 | 2.381 | 2.353 | 2.325 | 2.298 | 2.272 | 2.247 | 2.223 | 2.198 | 2.174 | 2.150 | 2.127 |
| 36 | 2.500 | 2.470 | 2.139 | 2.409 | 2.381 | 2.353 | 2.326 | 2.299 | 2.273 | 2.248 | 2.222 | 2.197 | 2.174 | 2.151 | 2.128 |
| 37 | 2.500 | 2.469 | 2.439 | 2.410 | 2.381 | 2.353 | 2.325 | 2.298 | 2.272 | 2.247 | 2.223 | 2.198 | 2.174 | 2.150 | 2.127 |
| 38 | 2.500 | 2.470 | 2.439 | 2.409 | 2.381 | 2.353 | 2.326 | 2.299 | 2.273 | 2.248 | 2.222 | 2.197 | 2.174 | 2.151 | 2.128 |
| 39 | 2.500 | 2.469 | 2.439 | 2.410 | 2.381 | 2.353 | 2.325 | 2.298 | 2.272 | 2.247 | 2.223 | 2.198 | 2.174 | 2.150 | 2.127 |
| 40 | 2.500 | 2.470 | 2.439 | 2.409 | 2.381 | 2.353 | 2.326 | 2.299 | 2.273 | 2.248 | 2.222 | 2.197 | 2.173 | 2.151 | 2.128 |
| 41 | 1.250 | 2.469 | 2.439 | 2.410 | 2.380 | 2.352 | 2.325 | 2.298 | 2.272 | 2.247 | 2.223 | 2.198 | 2.174 | 2.150 | 2.127 |
| 42 | | | 1.220 | 2.409 | 2.381 | 2.353 | 2.326 | 2.299 | 2.273 | 2.248 | 2.222 | 2.197 | 2.173 | 2.151 | 2.128 |
| 43 | | | | | 1.190 | 2.352 | 2.325 | 2.298 | 2.272 | 2.247 | 2.223 | 2.198 | 2.174 | 2.150 | 2.127 |
| 44 | | | | | | | 1.163 | 2.299 | 2.273 | 2.248 | 2.222 | 2.197 | 2.173 | 2.151 | 2.128 |
| 45 | | | | | | | | | 1.136 | 2.247 | 2.223 | 2.198 | 2.174 | 2.150 | 2.127 |
| 46 | | | | | | | | | | | 1.111 | 2.197 | 2.173 | 2.151 | 2.128 |
| 47 | | | | | | | | | | | | | 1.087 | 2.150 | 2.127 |
| 48 | | | | | | | | | | | | | | | 1.064 |

and the Recovery Period is:

| If the Recovery Year is: | 47.5 | 48.0 | 48.5 | 49.0 | 49.5 | 50.0 |
|---|---|---|---|---|---|---|
| | | | the Depreciation Rate is: | | | |
| 1 | 1.053 | 1.042 | 1.031 | 1.020 | 1.010 | 1.000 |
| 2 | 2.105 | 2.083 | 2.062 | 2.041 | 2.020 | 2.000 |
| 3 | 2.105 | 2.083 | 2.062 | 2.041 | 2.020 | 2.000 |
| 4 | 2.105 | 2.083 | 2.062 | 2.041 | 2.020 | 2.000 |
| 5 | 2.105 | 2.083 | 2.062 | 2.041 | 2.020 | 2.000 |

| If the Recovery Year is: | 47.5 | 48.0 | 48.5 | 49.0 | 49.5 | 50.0 |
|---|---|---|---|---|---|---|
| | the Depreciation Rate is: | | | | | |
| 6 | 2.105 | 2.083 | 2.062 | 2.041 | 2.020 | 2.000 |
| 7 | 2.105 | 2.083 | 2.062 | 2.041 | 2.020 | 2.000 |
| 8 | 2.105 | 2.083 | 2.062 | 2.041 | 2.020 | 2.000 |
| 9 | 2.105 | 2.083 | 2.062 | 2.041 | 2.020 | 2.000 |
| 10 | 2.105 | 2.083 | 2.062 | 2.041 | 2.020 | 2.000 |
| 11 | 2.105 | 2.083 | 2.062 | 2.041 | 2.020 | 2.000 |
| 12 | 2.105 | 2.083 | 2.062 | 2.041 | 2.020 | 2.000 |
| 13 | 2.105 | 2.083 | 2.062 | 2.041 | 2.020 | 2.000 |
| 14 | 2.105 | 2.083 | 2.062 | 2.041 | 2.020 | 2.000 |
| 15 | 2.105 | 2.083 | 2.062 | 2.041 | 2.020 | 2.000 |
| 16 | 2.105 | 2.083 | 2.062 | 2.041 | 2.020 | 2.000 |
| 17 | 2.105 | 2.083 | 2.062 | 2.041 | 2.020 | 2.000 |
| 18 | 2.105 | 2.083 | 2.062 | 2.041 | 2.020 | 2.000 |
| 19 | 2.105 | 2.084 | 2.062 | 2.041 | 2.020 | 2.000 |
| 20 | 2.105 | 2.083 | 2.062 | 2.041 | 2.020 | 2.000 |
| 21 | 2.105 | 2.084 | 2.062 | 2.041 | 2.020 | 2.000 |
| 22 | 2.105 | 2.083 | 2.062 | 2.041 | 2.020 | 2.000 |
| 23 | 2.105 | 2.084 | 2.062 | 2.041 | 2.020 | 2.000 |
| 24 | 2.105 | 2.083 | 2.062 | 2.041 | 2.020 | 2.000 |
| 25 | 2.105 | 2.084 | 2.062 | 2.041 | 2.020 | 2.000 |
| 26 | 2.106 | 2.083 | 2.062 | 2.041 | 2.020 | 2.000 |
| 27 | 2.105 | 2.084 | 2.062 | 2.041 | 2.020 | 2.000 |
| 28 | 2.106 | 2.083 | 2.062 | 2.041 | 2.020 | 2.000 |
| 29 | 2.105 | 2.084 | 2.062 | 2.041 | 2.020 | 2.000 |
| 30 | 2.106 | 2.083 | 2.062 | 2.041 | 2.020 | 2.000 |
| 31 | 2.105 | 2.084 | 2.062 | 2.041 | 2.021 | 2.000 |
| 32 | 2.106 | 2.083 | 2.062 | 2.041 | 2.020 | 2.000 |

| If the Recovery Year is: | 47.5 | 48.0 | 48.5 | 49.0 | 49.5 | 50.0 |
|---|---|---|---|---|---|---|
| | | | the Depreciation Rate is: | | | |
| 33 | 2.105 | 2.084 | 2.062 | 2.041 | 2.021 | 2.000 |
| 34 | 2.106 | 2.083 | 2.062 | 2.040 | 2.020 | 2.000 |
| 35 | 2.105 | 2.084 | 2.062 | 2.041 | 2.021 | 2.000 |
| 36 | 2.106 | 2.083 | 2.062 | 2.040 | 2.020 | 2.000 |
| 37 | 2.105 | 2.084 | 2.061 | 2.041 | 2.021 | 2.000 |
| 38 | 2.106 | 2.083 | 2.062 | 2.040 | 2.020 | 2.000 |
| 39 | 2.105 | 2.084 | 2.061 | 2.041 | 2.021 | 2.000 |
| 40 | 2.106 | 2.083 | 2.062 | 2.040 | 2.020 | 2.000 |
| 41 | 2.105 | 2.084 | 2.061 | 2.041 | 2.021 | 2.000 |
| 42 | 2.106 | 2.083 | 2.062 | 2.040 | 2.020 | 2.000 |
| 43 | 2.105 | 2.084 | 2.061 | 2.041 | 2.021 | 2.000 |
| 44 | 2.106 | 2.083 | 2.062 | 2.040 | 2.020 | 2.000 |
| 45 | 2.105 | 2.084 | 2.061 | 2.041 | 2.021 | 2.000 |
| 46 | 2.106 | 2.083 | 2.062 | 2.040 | 2.020 | 2.000 |
| 47 | 2.105 | 2.084 | 2.061 | 2.041 | 2.021 | 2.000 |
| 48 | 2.106 | 2.083 | 2.062 | 2.040 | 2.020 | 2.000 |
| 49 | | 1.042 | 2.061 | 2.041 | 2.021 | 2.000 |
| 50 | | | | 1.020 | 2.020 | 2.000 |
| 51 | | | | | | 1.000 |

TABLE 9
General and Alternative Depreciation Systems
Applicable Depreciation Method: Straight Line
Applicable Recovery Periods: 2.5 — 50 years
Applicable Convention: Mid-quarter (properly placed in service in first quarter)

| If the Recovery Year is: | and the Recovery Period is: 2.5 | 3.0 | 3.5 | 4.0 | 4.5 | 5.0 | 5.5 | 6.0 | 6.5 | 7.0 | 7.5 | 8.0 | 8.5 | 9.0 | 9.5 |
|---|---|---|---|---|---|---|---|---|---|---|---|---|---|---|---|
| | the Depreciation Rate is: | | | | | | | | | | | | | | |
| 1 | 35.00 | 29.17 | 25.00 | 21.88 | 19.44 | 17.50 | 15.91 | 14.58 | 13.46 | 12.50 | 11.67 | 10.94 | 10.29 | 9.72 | 9.21 |
| 2 | 40.00 | 33.33 | 28.57 | 25.00 | 22.22 | 20.00 | 18.18 | 16.67 | 15.38 | 14.29 | 13.33 | 12.50 | 11.77 | 11.11 | 10.53 |
| 3 | 25.00 | 33.33 | 28.57 | 25.00 | 22.22 | 20.00 | 18.18 | 16.67 | 15.39 | 14.28 | 13.33 | 12.50 | 11.76 | 11.11 | 10.53 |
| 4 | | 4.17 | 17.86 | 25.00 | 22.23 | 20.00 | 18.18 | 16.67 | 15.38 | 14.29 | 13.33 | 12.50 | 11.77 | 11.11 | 10.53 |
| 5 | | | | 3.12 | 13.89 | 20.00 | 18.18 | 16.66 | 15.39 | 14.28 | 13.34 | 12.50 | 11.76 | 11.11 | 10.52 |
| 6 | | | | | | 2.50 | 11.37 | 16.67 | 15.38 | 14.29 | 13.33 | 12.50 | 11.77 | 11.11 | 10.53 |
| 7 | | | | | | | | 2.08 | 9.62 | 14.28 | 13.34 | 12.50 | 11.76 | 11.11 | 10.52 |
| 8 | | | | | | | | | | 1.79 | 8.33 | 12.50 | 11.77 | 11.12 | 10.53 |
| 9 | | | | | | | | | | | | 1.56 | 7.35 | 11.11 | 10.52 |
| 10 | | | | | | | | | | | | | | 1.39 | 6.58 |

| If the Recovery Year is: | and the Recovery Period is: 10.0 | 10.5 | 11.0 | 11.5 | 12.0 | 12.5 | 13.0 | 13.5 | 14.0 | 14.5 | 15.0 | 15.5 | 16.0 | 16.5 | 17.0 |
|---|---|---|---|---|---|---|---|---|---|---|---|---|---|---|---|
| | the Depreciation Rate is: | | | | | | | | | | | | | | |
| 1 | 8.75 | 8.33 | 7.95 | 7.61 | 7.29 | 7.00 | 6.73 | 6.48 | 6.25 | 6.03 | 5.83 | 5.65 | 5.47 | 5.30 | 5.15 |
| 2 | 10.00 | 9.52 | 9.09 | 8.70 | 8.33 | 8.00 | 7.69 | 7.41 | 7.14 | 6.90 | 6.67 | 6.45 | 6.25 | 6.06 | 5.88 |
| 3 | 10.00 | 9.52 | 9.09 | 8.70 | 8.33 | 8.00 | 7.69 | 7.41 | 7.14 | 6.90 | 6.67 | 6.45 | 6.25 | 6.06 | 5.88 |

| If the Recovery Year is: | 10.0 | 10.5 | 11.0 | 11.5 | 12.0 | 12.5 | 13.0 | 13.5 | 14.0 | 14.5 | 15.0 | 15.5 | 16.0 | 16.5 | 17.0 |
|---|---|---|---|---|---|---|---|---|---|---|---|---|---|---|---|
| | the Depreciation Rate is: | | | | | | | | | | | | | | |
| 4 | 10.00 | 9.53 | 9.09 | 8.69 | 8.33 | 8.00 | 7.69 | 7.41 | 7.14 | 6.90 | 6.67 | 6.45 | 6.25 | 6.06 | 5.88 |
| 5 | 10.00 | 9.52 | 9.09 | 8.70 | 8.33 | 8.00 | 7.69 | 7.41 | 7.14 | 6.90 | 6.67 | 6.45 | 6.25 | 6.06 | 5.88 |
| 6 | 10.00 | 9.53 | 9.09 | 8.69 | 8.34 | 8.00 | 7.69 | 7.41 | 7.14 | 6.90 | 6.67 | 6.45 | 6.25 | 6.06 | 5.88 |
| 7 | 10.00 | 9.52 | 9.09 | 8.70 | 8.33 | 8.00 | 7.69 | 7.41 | 7.14 | 6.90 | 6.67 | 6.45 | 6.25 | 6.06 | 5.88 |
| 8 | 10.00 | 9.53 | 9.09 | 8.69 | 8.34 | 8.00 | 7.69 | 7.41 | 7.15 | 6.89 | 6.66 | 6.45 | 6.25 | 6.06 | 5.88 |
| 9 | 10.00 | 9.52 | 9.09 | 8.70 | 8.33 | 8.00 | 7.70 | 7.40 | 7.14 | 6.90 | 6.67 | 6.45 | 6.25 | 6.06 | 5.88 |
| 10 | 10.00 | 9.53 | 9.10 | 8.69 | 8.34 | 8.00 | 7.69 | 7.41 | 7.15 | 6.89 | 6.66 | 6.45 | 6.25 | 6.06 | 5.88 |
| 11 | 1.25 | 5.95 | 9.09 | 8.70 | 8.33 | 8.00 | 7.70 | 7.40 | 7.14 | 6.90 | 6.67 | 6.45 | 6.25 | 6.06 | 5.88 |
| 12 | | | 1.14 | 5.43 | 8.34 | 8.00 | 7.69 | 7.41 | 7.15 | 6.89 | 6.66 | 6.45 | 6.25 | 6.06 | 5.89 |
| 13 | | | | | 1.04 | 5.00 | 7.70 | 7.40 | 7.14 | 6.90 | 6.67 | 6.46 | 6.25 | 6.06 | 5.88 |
| 14 | | | | | | | 0.96 | 4.63 | 7.15 | 6.89 | 6.66 | 6.45 | 6.25 | 6.06 | 5.89 |
| 15 | | | | | | | | | 0.89 | 4.31 | 6.67 | 6.46 | 6.25 | 6.06 | 5.88 |
| 16 | | | | | | | | | | | 0.83 | 4.03 | 6.25 | 6.07 | 5.89 |
| 17 | | | | | | | | | | | | | 0.78 | 3.79 | 5.88 |
| 18 | | | | | | | | | | | | | | | 0.74 |

and the Recovery Period is:

| If the Recovery Year is: | 17.5 | 18.0 | 18.5 | 19.0 | 19.5 | 20.0 | 20.5 | 21.0 | 21.5 | 22.0 | 22.5 | 23.0 | 23.5 | 24.0 | 24.5 |
|---|---|---|---|---|---|---|---|---|---|---|---|---|---|---|---|
| | the Depreciation Rate is: | | | | | | | | | | | | | | |
| 1 | 5.00 | 4.86 | 4.73 | 4.61 | 4.49 | 4.375 | 4.268 | 4.167 | 4.070 | 3.977 | 3.889 | 3.804 | 3.723 | 3.646 | 3.571 |
| 2 | 5.71 | 5.56 | 5.41 | 5.26 | 5.13 | 5.000 | 4.878 | 4.762 | 4.651 | 4.545 | 4.444 | 4.348 | 4.255 | 4.167 | 4.082 |
| 3 | 5.71 | 5.56 | 5.41 | 5.26 | 5.13 | 5.000 | 4.878 | 4.762 | 4.651 | 4.545 | 4.444 | 4.348 | 4.255 | 4.167 | 4.082 |
| 4 | 5.71 | 5.56 | 5.40 | 5.26 | 5.13 | 5.000 | 4.878 | 4.762 | 4.651 | 4.546 | 4.444 | 4.348 | 4.255 | 4.167 | 4.082 |
| 5 | 5.72 | 5.55 | 5.41 | 5.26 | 5.13 | 5.000 | 4.878 | 4.762 | 4.651 | 4.545 | 4.445 | 4.348 | 4.255 | 4.167 | 4.082 |
| 6 | 5.71 | 5.56 | 5.40 | 5.26 | 5.13 | 5.000 | 4.878 | 4.762 | 4.651 | 4.546 | 4.444 | 4.348 | 4.255 | 4.167 | 4.082 |
| 7 | 5.72 | 5.55 | 5.41 | 5.26 | 5.13 | 5.000 | 4.878 | 4.762 | 4.651 | 4.545 | 4.445 | 4.348 | 4.255 | 4.167 | 4.082 |
| 8 | 5.71 | 5.56 | 5.40 | 5.26 | 5.13 | 5.000 | 4.878 | 4.762 | 4.651 | 4.546 | 4.444 | 4.348 | 4.255 | 4.167 | 4.082 |

| If the Recovery Year is: | and the Recovery Period is: 17.5 | 18.0 | 18.5 | 19.0 | 19.5 | 20.0 | 20.5 | 21.0 | 21.5 | 22.0 | 22.5 | 23.0 | 23.5 | 24.0 | 24.5 |
|---|---|---|---|---|---|---|---|---|---|---|---|---|---|---|---|
| | the Depreciation Rate is: | | | | | | | | | | | | | | |
| 9 | 5.72 | 5.55 | 5.41 | 5.26 | 5.13 | 5.000 | 4.878 | 4.762 | 4.651 | 4.545 | 4.445 | 4.348 | 4.255 | 4.167 | 4.082 |
| 10 | 5.71 | 5.56 | 5.40 | 5.27 | 5.13 | 5.000 | 4.878 | 4.762 | 4.651 | 4.546 | 4.444 | 4.348 | 4.256 | 4.166 | 4.081 |
| 11 | 5.72 | 5.55 | 5.41 | 5.26 | 5.13 | 5.000 | 4.878 | 4.762 | 4.651 | 4.545 | 4.445 | 4.348 | 4.255 | 4.167 | 4.082 |
| 12 | 5.71 | 5.56 | 5.40 | 5.27 | 5.13 | 5.000 | 4.878 | 4.762 | 4.651 | 4.546 | 4.444 | 4.348 | 4.256 | 4.166 | 4.081 |
| 13 | 5.72 | 5.55 | 5.41 | 5.26 | 5.13 | 5.000 | 4.878 | 4.762 | 4.651 | 4.545 | 4.445 | 4.348 | 4.255 | 4.167 | 4.082 |
| 14 | 5.71 | 5.56 | 5.40 | 5.27 | 5.12 | 5.000 | 4.878 | 4.762 | 4.651 | 4.546 | 4.444 | 4.348 | 4.256 | 4.166 | 4.081 |
| 15 | 5.72 | 5.55 | 5.41 | 5.26 | 5.13 | 5.000 | 4.878 | 4.762 | 4.651 | 4.545 | 4.445 | 4.348 | 4.255 | 4.167 | 4.082 |
| 16 | 5.71 | 5.56 | 5.40 | 5.27 | 5.12 | 5.000 | 4.878 | 4.762 | 4.651 | 4.546 | 4.444 | 4.348 | 4.256 | 4.166 | 4.081 |
| 17 | 5.72 | 5.55 | 5.41 | 5.26 | 5.13 | 5.000 | 4.878 | 4.762 | 4.652 | 4.545 | 4.445 | 4.348 | 4.255 | 4.167 | 4.082 |
| 18 | 3.57 | 5.56 | 5.40 | 5.27 | 5.12 | 5.000 | 4.878 | 4.761 | 4.651 | 4.546 | 4.444 | 4.347 | 4.256 | 4.166 | 4.081 |
| 19 | | 0.69 | 3.38 | 5.26 | 5.13 | 5.000 | 4.878 | 4.762 | 4.652 | 4.545 | 4.445 | 4.348 | 4.255 | 4.167 | 4.082 |
| 20 | | | | 0.66 | 3.20 | 5.000 | 4.879 | 4.761 | 4.651 | 4.546 | 4.444 | 4.347 | 4.256 | 4.166 | 4.081 |
| 21 | | | | | | 0.625 | 3.049 | 4.762 | 4.652 | 4.545 | 4.445 | 4.348 | 4.255 | 4.167 | 4.082 |
| 22 | | | | | | | | 0.595 | 2.907 | 4.546 | 4.444 | 4.347 | 4.256 | 4.166 | 4.081 |
| 23 | | | | | | | | | | 0.568 | 2.778 | 4.348 | 4.255 | 4.167 | 4.082 |
| 24 | | | | | | | | | | | | 0.543 | 2.660 | 4.166 | 4.081 |
| 25 | | | | | | | | | | | | | | 0.521 | 2.551 |

| If the Recovery Year is: | and the Recovery Period is: 25.0 | 25.5 | 26.0 | 26.5 | 27.0 | 27.5 | 28.0 | 28.5 | 29.0 | 29.5 | 30.0 | 30.5 | 31.0 | 31.5 | 32.0 |
|---|---|---|---|---|---|---|---|---|---|---|---|---|---|---|---|
| | the Depreciation Rate is: | | | | | | | | | | | | | | |
| 1 | 3.500 | 3.431 | 3.365 | 3.302 | 3.241 | 3.182 | 3.125 | 3.070 | 3.017 | 2.966 | 2.917 | 2.869 | 2.823 | 2.778 | 2.734 |
| 2 | 4.000 | 3.922 | 3.846 | 3.774 | 3.704 | 3.636 | 3.571 | 3.509 | 3.448 | 3.390 | 3.333 | 3.279 | 3.226 | 3.175 | 3.125 |
| 3 | 4.000 | 3.922 | 3.846 | 3.774 | 3.704 | 3.636 | 3.571 | 3.509 | 3.448 | 3.390 | 3.333 | 3.279 | 3.226 | 3.175 | 3.125 |
| 4 | 4.000 | 3.922 | 3.846 | 3.774 | 3.704 | 3.636 | 3.571 | 3.509 | 3.448 | 3.390 | 3.333 | 3.279 | 3.226 | 3.175 | 3.125 |
| 5 | 4.000 | 3.922 | 3.846 | 3.774 | 3.704 | 3.636 | 3.571 | 3.509 | 3.448 | 3.390 | 3.333 | 3.279 | 3.226 | 3.175 | 3.125 |

| If the Recovery Year is: | and the Recovery Period is: 25.0 | 25.5 | 26.0 | 26.5 | 27.0 | 27.5 | 28.0 | 28.5 | 29.0 | 29.5 | 30.0 | 30.5 | 31.0 | 31.5 | 32.0 |
|---|---|---|---|---|---|---|---|---|---|---|---|---|---|---|---|
| | the Depreciation Rate is: | | | | | | | | | | | | | | |
| 6 | 4.000 | 3.922 | 3.846 | 3.774 | 3.704 | 3.636 | 3.572 | 3.509 | 3.448 | 3.390 | 3.333 | 3.279 | 3.226 | 3.175 | 3.125 |
| 7 | 4.000 | 3.921 | 3.846 | 3.773 | 3.704 | 3.636 | 3.571 | 3.509 | 3.448 | 3.390 | 3.333 | 3.279 | 3.226 | 3.175 | 3.125 |
| 8 | 4.000 | 3.922 | 3.846 | 3.774 | 3.704 | 3.636 | 3.572 | 3.509 | 3.448 | 3.390 | 3.333 | 3.279 | 3.226 | 3.174 | 3.125 |
| 9 | 4.000 | 3.921 | 3.846 | 3.773 | 3.704 | 3.636 | 3.571 | 3.509 | 3.448 | 3.390 | 3.333 | 3.279 | 3.226 | 3.175 | 3.125 |
| 10 | 4.000 | 3.922 | 3.846 | 3.774 | 3.704 | 3.637 | 3.572 | 3.509 | 3.448 | 3.390 | 3.333 | 3.279 | 3.226 | 3.174 | 3.125 |
| 11 | 4.000 | 3.921 | 3.846 | 3.773 | 3.704 | 3.636 | 3.571 | 3.509 | 3.448 | 3.390 | 3.333 | 3.279 | 3.226 | 3.175 | 3.125 |
| 12 | 4.000 | 3.922 | 3.846 | 3.774 | 3.704 | 3.637 | 3.572 | 3.509 | 3.448 | 3.390 | 3.333 | 3.279 | 3.226 | 3.174 | 3.125 |
| 13 | 4.000 | 3.921 | 3.846 | 3.773 | 3.703 | 3.636 | 3.571 | 3.509 | 3.448 | 3.390 | 3.334 | 3.278 | 3.226 | 3.175 | 3.125 |
| 14 | 4.000 | 3.922 | 3.846 | 3.774 | 3.704 | 3.637 | 3.572 | 3.509 | 3.448 | 3.390 | 3.333 | 3.279 | 3.226 | 3.174 | 3.125 |
| 15 | 4.000 | 3.921 | 3.846 | 3.773 | 3.703 | 3.636 | 3.571 | 3.509 | 3.449 | 3.390 | 3.334 | 3.278 | 3.226 | 3.175 | 3.125 |
| 16 | 4.000 | 3.922 | 3.846 | 3.774 | 3.704 | 3.637 | 3.572 | 3.509 | 3.448 | 3.390 | 3.333 | 3.279 | 3.226 | 3.174 | 3.125 |
| 17 | 4.000 | 3.921 | 3.846 | 3.773 | 3.703 | 3.636 | 3.571 | 3.509 | 3.449 | 3.390 | 3.334 | 3.278 | 3.226 | 3.175 | 3.125 |
| 18 | 4.000 | 3.922 | 3.846 | 3.774 | 3.704 | 3.637 | 3.572 | 3.508 | 3.448 | 3.390 | 3.333 | 3.279 | 3.226 | 3.174 | 3.125 |
| 19 | 4.000 | 3.921 | 3.847 | 3.773 | 3.703 | 3.636 | 3.571 | 3.509 | 3.449 | 3.390 | 3.334 | 3.278 | 3.226 | 3.175 | 3.125 |
| 20 | 4.000 | 3.922 | 3.846 | 3.774 | 3.704 | 3.637 | 3.572 | 3.508 | 3.448 | 3.390 | 3.333 | 3.279 | 3.225 | 3.174 | 3.125 |
| 21 | 4.000 | 3.921 | 3.847 | 3.773 | 3.703 | 3.636 | 3.571 | 3.509 | 3.449 | 3.390 | 3.334 | 3.278 | 3.226 | 3.175 | 3.125 |
| 22 | 4.000 | 3.922 | 3.846 | 3.774 | 3.704 | 3.637 | 3.572 | 3.508 | 3.448 | 3.389 | 3.333 | 3.279 | 3.225 | 3.174 | 3.125 |
| 23 | 4.000 | 3.921 | 3.847 | 3.773 | 3.703 | 3.636 | 3.571 | 3.509 | 3.449 | 3.390 | 3.334 | 3.278 | 3.226 | 3.175 | 3.125 |
| 24 | 4.000 | 3.922 | 3.846 | 3.774 | 3.704 | 3.637 | 3.572 | 3.508 | 3.448 | 3.389 | 3.333 | 3.279 | 3.225 | 3.174 | 3.125 |
| 25 | 4.000 | 3.921 | 3.847 | 3.773 | 3.703 | 3.636 | 3.571 | 3.509 | 3.449 | 3.390 | 3.334 | 3.278 | 3.226 | 3.175 | 3.125 |
| 26 | 0.500 | 2.451 | 3.846 | 3.774 | 3.704 | 3.637 | 3.572 | 3.508 | 3.448 | 3.389 | 3.333 | 3.279 | 3.225 | 3.174 | 3.125 |
| 27 | | | 0.481 | 2.358 | 3.703 | 3.636 | 3.571 | 3.509 | 3.449 | 3.390 | 3.334 | 3.278 | 3.226 | 3.175 | 3.125 |
| 28 | | | | | 0.463 | 2.273 | 3.572 | 3.508 | 3.448 | 3.389 | 3.333 | 3.279 | 3.225 | 3.174 | 3.125 |
| 29 | | | | | | | 0.446 | 2.193 | 3.449 | 3.390 | 3.334 | 3.278 | 3.226 | 3.175 | 3.125 |
| 30 | | | | | | | | | 0.431 | 2.118 | 3.333 | 3.279 | 3.225 | 3.174 | 3.125 |
| 31 | | | | | | | | | | | 0.417 | 2.049 | 3.226 | 3.175 | 3.125 |

| If the Recovery Year is: | 25.0 | 25.5 | 26.0 | 26.5 | 27.0 | 27.5 | 28.0 | 28.5 | 29.0 | 29.5 | 30.0 | 30.5 | 31.0 | 31.5 | 32.0 |
|---|---|---|---|---|---|---|---|---|---|---|---|---|---|---|---|
| | and the Recovery Period is: the Depreciation Rate is: | | | | | | | | | | | | | | |
| 32 | | | | | | | | | | | | | 0.403 | 1.984 | 3.125 |
| 33 | | | | | | | | | | | | | | | 0.391 |

| If the Recovery Year is: | 32.5 | 33.0 | 33.5 | 34.0 | 34.5 | 35.0 | 35.5 | 36.0 | 36.5 | 37.0 | 37.5 | 38.0 | 38.5 | 39.0 | 39.5 |
|---|---|---|---|---|---|---|---|---|---|---|---|---|---|---|---|
| | and the Recovery Period is: the Depreciation Rate is: | | | | | | | | | | | | | | |
| 1 | 2.692 | 2.652 | 2.612 | 2.574 | 2.536 | 2.500 | 2.465 | 2.431 | 2.397 | 2.365 | 2.333 | 2.303 | 2.273 | 2.244 | 2.215 |
| 2 | 3.077 | 3.030 | 2.985 | 2.941 | 2.899 | 2.857 | 2.817 | 2.778 | 2.740 | 2.703 | 2.667 | 2.632 | 2.597 | 2.564 | 2.532 |
| 3 | 3.077 | 3.030 | 2.985 | 2.941 | 2.899 | 2.857 | 2.817 | 2.778 | 2.740 | 2.703 | 2.667 | 2.632 | 2.597 | 2.564 | 2.532 |
| 4 | 3.077 | 3.030 | 2.985 | 2.941 | 2.899 | 2.857 | 2.817 | 2.778 | 2.740 | 2.703 | 2.667 | 2.632 | 2.597 | 2.564 | 2.532 |
| 5 | 3.077 | 3.030 | 2.985 | 2.941 | 2.899 | 2.857 | 2.817 | 2.778 | 2.740 | 2.703 | 2.667 | 2.632 | 2.597 | 2.564 | 2.532 |
| 6 | 3.077 | 3.030 | 2.985 | 2.941 | 2.898 | 2.857 | 2.817 | 2.778 | 2.740 | 2.703 | 2.667 | 2.632 | 2.597 | 2.564 | 2.532 |
| 7 | 3.077 | 3.030 | 2.985 | 2.941 | 2.899 | 2.857 | 2.817 | 2.778 | 2.740 | 2.703 | 2.667 | 2.632 | 2.597 | 2.564 | 2.532 |
| 8 | 3.077 | 3.030 | 2.985 | 2.941 | 2.898 | 2.857 | 2.817 | 2.778 | 2.740 | 2.703 | 2.667 | 2.631 | 2.597 | 2.564 | 2.532 |
| 9 | 3.077 | 3.030 | 2.985 | 2.941 | 2.899 | 2.857 | 2.817 | 2.778 | 2.740 | 2.703 | 2.667 | 2.632 | 2.597 | 2.564 | 2.532 |
| 10 | 3.077 | 3.030 | 2.985 | 2.941 | 2.898 | 2.857 | 2.817 | 2.778 | 2.740 | 2.703 | 2.667 | 2.631 | 2.598 | 2.564 | 2.532 |
| 11 | 3.077 | 3.030 | 2.985 | 2.941 | 2.899 | 2.857 | 2.817 | 2.778 | 2.740 | 2.703 | 2.667 | 2.632 | 2.597 | 2.564 | 2.532 |
| 12 | 3.077 | 3.030 | 2.985 | 2.941 | 2.898 | 2.857 | 2.817 | 2.778 | 2.740 | 2.703 | 2.667 | 2.631 | 2.598 | 2.564 | 2.532 |
| 13 | 3.077 | 3.030 | 2.985 | 2.941 | 2.899 | 2.857 | 2.817 | 2.778 | 2.740 | 2.703 | 2.667 | 2.632 | 2.597 | 2.564 | 2.532 |
| 14 | 3.077 | 3.030 | 2.985 | 2.941 | 2.898 | 2.857 | 2.817 | 2.778 | 2.740 | 2.703 | 2.667 | 2.631 | 2.598 | 2.564 | 2.531 |
| 15 | 3.077 | 3.030 | 2.985 | 2.941 | 2.899 | 2.857 | 2.817 | 2.778 | 2.740 | 2.703 | 2.666 | 2.632 | 2.597 | 2.564 | 2.532 |
| 16 | 3.077 | 3.031 | 2.985 | 2.941 | 2.898 | 2.857 | 2.817 | 2.778 | 2.740 | 2.703 | 2.667 | 2.631 | 2.598 | 2.564 | 2.531 |
| 17 | 3.077 | 3.030 | 2.985 | 2.941 | 2.899 | 2.857 | 2.817 | 2.778 | 2.740 | 2.702 | 2.666 | 2.632 | 2.597 | 2.564 | 2.532 |
| 18 | 3.077 | 3.031 | 2.985 | 2.941 | 2.898 | 2.857 | 2.817 | 2.778 | 2.740 | 2.703 | 2.667 | 2.631 | 2.598 | 2.564 | 2.531 |
| 19 | 3.077 | 3.030 | 2.985 | 2.941 | 2.899 | 2.857 | 2.817 | 2.778 | 2.739 | 2.702 | 2.666 | 2.632 | 2.597 | 2.564 | 2.532 |
| 20 | 3.077 | 3.031 | 2.985 | 2.941 | 2.898 | 2.857 | 2.817 | 2.778 | 2.740 | 2.703 | 2.667 | 2.631 | 2.598 | 2.564 | 2.531 |

| If the Recovery Year is: | 32.5 | 33.0 | 33.5 | 34.0 | 34.5 | 35.0 | 35.5 | 36.0 | 36.5 | 37.0 | 37.5 | 38.0 | 38.5 | 39.0 | 39.5 |
|---|---|---|---|---|---|---|---|---|---|---|---|---|---|---|---|
| | | | the Depreciation Rate is: | | | | | | | | | | | | |
| 21 | 3.077 | 3.030 | 2.985 | 2.941 | 2.899 | 2.857 | 2.817 | 2.777 | 2.739 | 2.702 | 2.666 | 2.632 | 2.597 | 2.564 | 2.532 |
| 22 | 3.077 | 3.031 | 2.985 | 2.941 | 2.898 | 2.857 | 2.817 | 2.778 | 2.740 | 2.703 | 2.667 | 2.631 | 2.598 | 2.564 | 2.531 |
| 23 | 3.077 | 3.030 | 2.985 | 2.941 | 2.899 | 2.857 | 2.817 | 2.777 | 2.739 | 2.702 | 2.666 | 2.632 | 2.597 | 2.564 | 2.532 |
| 24 | 3.077 | 3.031 | 2.985 | 2.941 | 2.898 | 2.857 | 2.817 | 2.778 | 2.740 | 2.703 | 2.667 | 2.631 | 2.598 | 2.564 | 2.531 |
| 25 | 3.077 | 3.030 | 2.985 | 2.942 | 2.899 | 2.857 | 2.817 | 2.777 | 2.739 | 2.702 | 2.666 | 2.632 | 2.597 | 2.564 | 2.532 |
| 26 | 3.077 | 3.031 | 2.985 | 2.941 | 2.898 | 2.857 | 2.817 | 2.778 | 2.740 | 2.703 | 2.667 | 2.631 | 2.598 | 2.564 | 2.531 |
| 27 | 3.077 | 3.030 | 2.985 | 2.942 | 2.899 | 2.858 | 2.817 | 2.777 | 2.739 | 2.702 | 2.666 | 2.632 | 2.597 | 2.564 | 2.532 |
| 28 | 3.077 | 3.031 | 2.985 | 2.941 | 2.898 | 2.857 | 2.817 | 2.778 | 2.740 | 2.703 | 2.667 | 2.631 | 2.598 | 2.564 | 2.531 |
| 29 | 3.077 | 3.030 | 2.985 | 2.942 | 2.899 | 2.858 | 2.817 | 2.777 | 2.739 | 2.702 | 2.666 | 2.632 | 2.597 | 2.564 | 2.532 |
| 30 | 3.076 | 3.031 | 2.986 | 2.941 | 2.898 | 2.857 | 2.816 | 2.778 | 2.740 | 2.703 | 2.667 | 2.631 | 2.598 | 2.564 | 2.531 |
| 31 | 3.077 | 3.030 | 2.985 | 2.942 | 2.899 | 2.858 | 2.817 | 2.777 | 2.739 | 2.702 | 2.666 | 2.632 | 2.597 | 2.564 | 2.532 |
| 32 | 3.076 | 3.031 | 2.986 | 2.941 | 2.898 | 2.857 | 2.816 | 2.778 | 2.740 | 2.703 | 2.667 | 2.631 | 2.598 | 2.564 | 2.531 |
| 33 | 1.923 | 3.030 | 2.985 | 2.942 | 2.899 | 2.858 | 2.817 | 2.777 | 2.739 | 2.702 | 2.666 | 2.632 | 2.597 | 2.564 | 2.532 |
| 34 | | 0.379 | 1.866 | 2.941 | 2.898 | 2.857 | 2.816 | 2.778 | 2.740 | 2.703 | 2.667 | 2.631 | 2.598 | 2.565 | 2.531 |
| 35 | | | | 0.368 | 1.812 | 2.858 | 2.817 | 2.777 | 2.739 | 2.702 | 2.666 | 2.632 | 2.597 | 2.564 | 2.532 |
| 36 | | | | | | 0.357 | 1.760 | 2.778 | 2.740 | 2.703 | 2.667 | 2.631 | 2.598 | 2.565 | 2.531 |
| 37 | | | | | | | | 0.347 | 1.712 | 2.702 | 2.666 | 2.632 | 2.597 | 2.564 | 2.532 |
| 38 | | | | | | | | | | 0.338 | 1.667 | 2.631 | 2.598 | 2.565 | 2.531 |
| 39 | | | | | | | | | | | | 0.329 | 1.623 | 2.564 | 2.532 |
| 40 | | | | | | | | | | | | | | 0.321 | 1.582 |

and the Recovery Period is:

| If the Recovery Year is: | 40.0 | 40.5 | 41.0 | 41.5 | 42.0 | 42.5 | 43.0 | 43.5 | 44.0 | 44.5 | 45.0 | 45.5 | 46.0 | 46.5 | 47.0 |
|---|---|---|---|---|---|---|---|---|---|---|---|---|---|---|---|
| | | | the Depreciation Rate is: | | | | | | | | | | | | |
| 1 | 2.188 | 2.160 | 2.134 | 2.108 | 2.083 | 2.059 | 2.035 | 2.011 | 1.989 | 1.966 | 1.944 | 1.923 | 1.902 | 1.882 | 1.862 |
| 2 | 2.500 | 2.469 | 2.439 | 2.410 | 2.381 | 2.353 | 2.326 | 2.299 | 2.273 | 2.247 | 2.222 | 2.198 | 2.174 | 2.151 | 2.128 |

| If the Recovery Year is: | and the Recovery Period is: 40.0 | 40.5 | 41.0 | 41.5 | 42.0 | 42.5 | 43.0 | 43.5 | 44.0 | 44.5 | 45.0 | 45.5 | 46.0 | 46.5 | 47.0 |
|---|---|---|---|---|---|---|---|---|---|---|---|---|---|---|---|
| | the Depreciation Rate is: | | | | | | | | | | | | | | |
| 3 | 2.500 | 2.469 | 2.439 | 2.410 | 2.381 | 2.353 | 2.326 | 2.299 | 2.273 | 2.247 | 2.222 | 2.198 | 2.174 | 2.151 | 2.128 |
| 4 | 2.500 | 2.469 | 2.439 | 2.410 | 2.381 | 2.353 | 2.326 | 2.299 | 2.273 | 2.247 | 2.222 | 2.198 | 2.174 | 2.151 | 2.128 |
| 5 | 2.500 | 2.469 | 2.439 | 2.410 | 2.381 | 2.353 | 2.326 | 2.299 | 2.273 | 2.247 | 2.222 | 2.198 | 2.174 | 2.150 | 2.128 |
| 6 | 2.500 | 2.469 | 2.439 | 2.410 | 2.381 | 2.353 | 2.326 | 2.299 | 2.273 | 2.247 | 2.222 | 2.198 | 2.174 | 2.151 | 2.128 |
| 7 | 2.500 | 2.469 | 2.439 | 2.410 | 2.381 | 2.353 | 2.326 | 2.299 | 2.273 | 2.247 | 2.222 | 2.198 | 2.174 | 2.150 | 2.128 |
| 8 | 2.500 | 2.469 | 2.439 | 2.410 | 2.381 | 2.353 | 2.326 | 2.299 | 2.273 | 2.247 | 2.222 | 2.198 | 2.174 | 2.151 | 2.128 |
| 9 | 2.500 | 2.469 | 2.439 | 2.410 | 2.381 | 2.353 | 2.325 | 2.299 | 2.273 | 2.247 | 2.222 | 2.198 | 2.174 | 2.150 | 2.128 |
| 10 | 2.500 | 2.469 | 2.439 | 2.410 | 2.381 | 2.353 | 2.326 | 2.299 | 2.273 | 2.247 | 2.222 | 2.198 | 2.174 | 2.151 | 2.128 |
| 11 | 2.500 | 2.469 | 2.439 | 2.410 | 2.381 | 2.353 | 2.325 | 2.299 | 2.273 | 2.247 | 2.222 | 2.198 | 2.174 | 2.150 | 2.128 |
| 12 | 2.500 | 2.469 | 2.439 | 2.410 | 2.381 | 2.353 | 2.326 | 2.299 | 2.273 | 2.247 | 2.222 | 2.198 | 2.174 | 2.151 | 2.128 |
| 13 | 2.500 | 2.469 | 2.439 | 2.410 | 2.381 | 2.353 | 2.325 | 2.299 | 2.273 | 2.247 | 2.222 | 2.198 | 2.174 | 2.150 | 2.128 |
| 14 | 2.500 | 2.469 | 2.439 | 2.410 | 2.381 | 2.353 | 2.326 | 2.299 | 2.273 | 2.247 | 2.222 | 2.198 | 2.174 | 2.151 | 2.128 |
| 15 | 2.500 | 2.469 | 2.439 | 2.409 | 2.381 | 2.353 | 2.325 | 2.299 | 2.273 | 2.247 | 2.222 | 2.198 | 2.174 | 2.150 | 2.128 |
| 16 | 2.500 | 2.469 | 2.439 | 2.410 | 2.381 | 2.353 | 2.326 | 2.299 | 2.273 | 2.247 | 2.222 | 2.198 | 2.174 | 2.151 | 2.128 |
| 17 | 2.500 | 2.469 | 2.439 | 2.409 | 2.381 | 2.353 | 2.325 | 2.299 | 2.273 | 2.247 | 2.222 | 2.198 | 2.174 | 2.150 | 2.127 |
| 18 | 2.500 | 2.469 | 2.439 | 2.410 | 2.381 | 2.353 | 2.326 | 2.299 | 2.273 | 2.247 | 2.222 | 2.198 | 2.174 | 2.151 | 2.128 |
| 19 | 2.500 | 2.469 | 2.439 | 2.409 | 2.381 | 2.353 | 2.325 | 2.299 | 2.273 | 2.247 | 2.222 | 2.198 | 2.174 | 2.150 | 2.127 |
| 20 | 2.500 | 2.469 | 2.439 | 2.410 | 2.381 | 2.353 | 2.326 | 2.299 | 2.273 | 2.247 | 2.222 | 2.198 | 2.174 | 2.151 | 2.128 |
| 21 | 2.500 | 2.469 | 2.439 | 2.409 | 2.381 | 2.353 | 2.325 | 2.299 | 2.272 | 2.247 | 2.222 | 2.198 | 2.174 | 2.150 | 2.127 |
| 22 | 2.500 | 2.469 | 2.439 | 2.410 | 2.381 | 2.353 | 2.326 | 2.299 | 2.273 | 2.247 | 2.222 | 2.198 | 2.174 | 2.151 | 2.128 |
| 23 | 2.500 | 2.469 | 2.439 | 2.409 | 2.381 | 2.353 | 2.325 | 2.299 | 2.272 | 2.247 | 2.222 | 2.198 | 2.174 | 2.150 | 2.127 |
| 24 | 2.500 | 2.469 | 2.439 | 2.410 | 2.381 | 2.353 | 2.326 | 2.299 | 2.273 | 2.247 | 2.222 | 2.198 | 2.174 | 2.151 | 2.128 |
| 25 | 2.500 | 2.469 | 2.439 | 2.409 | 2.381 | 2.353 | 2.325 | 2.299 | 2.272 | 2.247 | 2.222 | 2.198 | 2.174 | 2.150 | 2.127 |
| 26 | 2.500 | 2.469 | 2.439 | 2.410 | 2.381 | 2.353 | 2.326 | 2.299 | 2.273 | 2.247 | 2.223 | 2.198 | 2.174 | 2.151 | 2.128 |
| 27 | 2.500 | 2.469 | 2.439 | 2.409 | 2.381 | 2.353 | 2.325 | 2.299 | 2.272 | 2.247 | 2.222 | 2.198 | 2.174 | 2.150 | 2.127 |
| 28 | 2.500 | 2.469 | 2.439 | 2.410 | 2.381 | 2.353 | 2.326 | 2.299 | 2.273 | 2.247 | 2.223 | 2.198 | 2.174 | 2.151 | 2.128 |

| If the Recovery Year is: | and the Recovery Period is: 40.0 | 40.5 | 41.0 | 41.5 | 42.0 | 42.5 | 43.0 | 43.5 | 44.0 | 44.5 | 45.0 | 45.5 | 46.0 | 46.5 | 47.0 |
|---|---|---|---|---|---|---|---|---|---|---|---|---|---|---|---|
| | the Depreciation Rate is: | | | | | | | | | | | | | | |
| 29 | 2.500 | 2.469 | 2.439 | 2.409 | 2.381 | 2.353 | 2.325 | 2.299 | 2.272 | 2.248 | 2.222 | 2.198 | 2.174 | 2.150 | 2.127 |
| 30 | 2.500 | 2.470 | 2.439 | 2.410 | 2.381 | 2.353 | 2.326 | 2.299 | 2.273 | 2.247 | 2.223 | 2.197 | 2.174 | 2.151 | 2.128 |
| 31 | 2.500 | 2.469 | 2.439 | 2.409 | 2.381 | 2.353 | 2.325 | 2.299 | 2.272 | 2.248 | 2.222 | 2.198 | 2.174 | 2.150 | 2.127 |
| 32 | 2.500 | 2.470 | 2.439 | 2.410 | 2.381 | 2.353 | 2.326 | 2.299 | 2.273 | 2.247 | 2.223 | 2.197 | 2.174 | 2.151 | 2.128 |
| 33 | 2.500 | 2.469 | 2.439 | 2.409 | 2.381 | 2.353 | 2.325 | 2.298 | 2.272 | 2.248 | 2.222 | 2.198 | 2.174 | 2.150 | 2.127 |
| 34 | 2.500 | 2.470 | 2.439 | 2.410 | 2.381 | 2.353 | 2.326 | 2.299 | 2.273 | 2.247 | 2.223 | 2.197 | 2.174 | 2.151 | 2.128 |
| 35 | 2.500 | 2.469 | 2.439 | 2.409 | 2.381 | 2.353 | 2.325 | 2.298 | 2.272 | 2.248 | 2.222 | 2.198 | 2.174 | 2.150 | 2.127 |
| 36 | 2.500 | 2.470 | 2.439 | 2.410 | 2.381 | 2.353 | 2.326 | 2.299 | 2.273 | 2.247 | 2.223 | 2.197 | 2.174 | 2.151 | 2.128 |
| 37 | 2.500 | 2.469 | 2.439 | 2.409 | 2.381 | 2.353 | 2.325 | 2.298 | 2.272 | 2.248 | 2.222 | 2.198 | 2.174 | 2.150 | 2.127 |
| 38 | 2.500 | 2.470 | 2.439 | 2.410 | 2.381 | 2.353 | 2.326 | 2.299 | 2.273 | 2.247 | 2.223 | 2.197 | 2.174 | 2.151 | 2.128 |
| 39 | 2.500 | 2.469 | 2.439 | 2.409 | 2.381 | 2.352 | 2.325 | 2.298 | 2.272 | 2.248 | 2.222 | 2.198 | 2.174 | 2.150 | 2.127 |
| 40 | 2.500 | 2.470 | 2.440 | 2.410 | 2.380 | 2.353 | 2.326 | 2.299 | 2.273 | 2.247 | 2.223 | 2.197 | 2.173 | 2.151 | 2.128 |
| 41 | 0.312 | 1.543 | 2.439 | 2.409 | 2.381 | 2.352 | 2.325 | 2.298 | 2.272 | 2.248 | 2.222 | 2.198 | 2.174 | 2.150 | 2.127 |
| 42 | | | 0.305 | 1.506 | 2.380 | 2.353 | 2.326 | 2.299 | 2.273 | 2.247 | 2.223 | 2.197 | 2.173 | 2.151 | 2.128 |
| 43 | | | | | 0.298 | 1.470 | 2.325 | 2.298 | 2.272 | 2.248 | 2.222 | 2.198 | 2.174 | 2.150 | 2.127 |
| 44 | | | | | | | 0.291 | 1.437 | 2.273 | 2.247 | 2.223 | 2.197 | 2.173 | 2.151 | 2.128 |
| 45 | | | | | | | | | 0.284 | 1.405 | 2.222 | 2.198 | 2.174 | 2.150 | 2.127 |
| 46 | | | | | | | | | | | 0.278 | 1.373 | 2.173 | 2.151 | 2.128 |
| 47 | | | | | | | | | | | | | 0.272 | 1.344 | 2.127 |
| 48 | | | | | | | | | | | | | | | 0.266 |

| If the Recovery Year is: | and the Recovery Period is: 47.5 | 48.0 | 48.5 | 49.0 | 49.5 | 50.0 |
|---|---|---|---|---|---|---|
| | the Depreciation Rate is: | | | | | |
| 1 | 1.842 | 1.823 | 1.804 | 1.786 | 1.768 | 1.750 |
| 2 | 2.105 | 2.083 | 2.062 | 2.041 | 2.020 | 2.000 |

| If the Recovery Year is: | and the Recovery Period is: 47.5 | 48.0 | 48.5 | 49.0 | 49.5 | 50.0 |
|---|---|---|---|---|---|---|
| | the Depreciation Rate is: | | | | | |
| 3 | 2.105 | 2.083 | 2.062 | 2.041 | 2.020 | 2.000 |
| 4 | 2.105 | 2.083 | 2.062 | 2.041 | 2.020 | 2.000 |
| 5 | 2.105 | 2.083 | 2.062 | 2.041 | 2.020 | 2.000 |
| 6 | 2.105 | 2.083 | 2.062 | 2.041 | 2.020 | 2.000 |
| 7 | 2.105 | 2.083 | 2.062 | 2.041 | 2.020 | 2.000 |
| 8 | 2.105 | 2.083 | 2.062 | 2.041 | 2.020 | 2.000 |
| 9 | 2.105 | 2.083 | 2.062 | 2.041 | 2.020 | 2.000 |
| 10 | 2.105 | 2.083 | 2.062 | 2.041 | 2.020 | 2.000 |
| 11 | 2.105 | 2.083 | 2.062 | 2.041 | 2.020 | 2.000 |
| 12 | 2.105 | 2.083 | 2.062 | 2.041 | 2.020 | 2.000 |
| 13 | 2.105 | 2.083 | 2.062 | 2.041 | 2.020 | 2.000 |
| 14 | 2.105 | 2.083 | 2.062 | 2.041 | 2.020 | 2.000 |
| 15 | 2.105 | 2.083 | 2.062 | 2.041 | 2.020 | 2.000 |
| 16 | 2.105 | 2.083 | 2.062 | 2.041 | 2.020 | 2.000 |
| 17 | 2.105 | 2.083 | 2.062 | 2.041 | 2.020 | 2.000 |
| 18 | 2.105 | 2.084 | 2.062 | 2.041 | 2.020 | 2.000 |
| 19 | 2.105 | 2.083 | 2.062 | 2.041 | 2.020 | 2.000 |
| 20 | 2.105 | 2.084 | 2.062 | 2.041 | 2.020 | 2.000 |
| 21 | 2.105 | 2.083 | 2.062 | 2.041 | 2.020 | 2.000 |
| 22 | 2.105 | 2.084 | 2.062 | 2.041 | 2.020 | 2.000 |
| 23 | 2.105 | 2.083 | 2.062 | 2.041 | 2.020 | 2.000 |
| 24 | 2.106 | 2.084 | 2.062 | 2.041 | 2.020 | 2.000 |
| 25 | 2.105 | 2.083 | 2.062 | 2.041 | 2.020 | 2.000 |
| 26 | 2.106 | 2.084 | 2.062 | 2.041 | 2.020 | 2.000 |
| 27 | 2.105 | 2.083 | 2.062 | 2.041 | 2.020 | 2.000 |
| 28 | 2.106 | 2.084 | 2.062 | 2.041 | 2.020 | 2.000 |

| If the Recovery Year is: | and the Recovery Period is: 47.5 | 48.0 | 48.5 | 49.0 | 49.5 | 50.0 |
|---|---|---|---|---|---|---|
| | the Depreciation Rate is: | | | | | |
| 29 | 2.105 | 2.083 | 2.062 | 2.041 | 2.020 | 2.000 |
| 30 | 2.106 | 2.084 | 2.062 | 2.041 | 2.020 | 2.000 |
| 31 | 2.105 | 2.083 | 2.062 | 2.041 | 2.020 | 2.000 |
| 32 | 2.106 | 2.084 | 2.062 | 2.040 | 2.021 | 2.000 |
| 33 | 2.105 | 2.083 | 2.062 | 2.041 | 2.020 | 2.000 |
| 34 | 2.106 | 2.084 | 2.062 | 2.040 | 2.021 | 2.000 |
| 35 | 2.105 | 2.083 | 2.062 | 2.041 | 2.020 | 2.000 |
| 36 | 2.106 | 2.084 | 2.062 | 2.040 | 2.021 | 2.000 |
| 37 | 2.105 | 2.083 | 2.061 | 2.041 | 2.020 | 2.000 |
| 38 | 2.106 | 2.084 | 2.062 | 2.040 | 2.021 | 2.000 |
| 39 | 2.105 | 2.083 | 2.061 | 2.041 | 2.020 | 2.000 |
| 40 | 2.106 | 2.084 | 2.062 | 2.040 | 2.021 | 2.000 |
| 41 | 2.105 | 2.083 | 2.061 | 2.041 | 2.020 | 2.000 |
| 42 | 2.106 | 2.084 | 2.062 | 2.040 | 2.021 | 2.000 |
| 43 | 2.105 | 2.083 | 2.061 | 2.041 | 2.020 | 2.000 |
| 44 | 2.106 | 2.084 | 2.062 | 2.040 | 2.021 | 2.000 |
| 45 | 2.105 | 2.083 | 2.061 | 2.041 | 2.020 | 2.000 |
| 46 | 2.106 | 2.084 | 2.062 | 2.040 | 2.021 | 2.000 |
| 47 | 2.105 | 2.083 | 2.061 | 2.041 | 2.020 | 2.000 |
| 48 | 1.316 | 2.084 | 2.062 | 2.040 | 2.021 | 2.000 |
| 49 | | 0.260 | 1.288 | 2.041 | 2.020 | 2.000 |
| 50 | | | | 0.255 | 1.263 | 2.000 |
| 51 | | | | | | 0.250 |

TABLE 10
General and Alternative Depreciation Systems
Applicable Depreciation Method: Straight Line
Applicable Recovery Periods: 2.5 — 50 years
Applicable Convention: Mid-quarter (property placed in service in second quarter)

| If the Recovery Year is: | and the Recovery Period is: 2.5 | 3.0 | 3.5 | 4.0 | 4.5 | 5.0 | 5.5 | 6.0 | 6.5 | 7.0 | 7.5 | 8.0 | 8.5 | 9.0 | 9.5 |
|---|---|---|---|---|---|---|---|---|---|---|---|---|---|---|---|
| | the Depreciation Rate is: | | | | | | | | | | | | | | |
| 1 | 25.00 | 20.83 | 17.86 | 15.63 | 13.89 | 12.50 | 11.36 | 10.42 | 9.62 | 8.93 | 8.33 | 7.81 | 7.35 | 6.94 | 6.58 |
| 2 | 40.00 | 33.33 | 28.57 | 25.00 | 22.22 | 20.00 | 18.18 | 16.67 | 15.38 | 14.29 | 13.33 | 12.50 | 11.77 | 11.11 | 10.53 |
| 3 | 35.00 | 33.34 | 28.57 | 25.00 | 22.22 | 20.00 | 18.18 | 16.67 | 15.38 | 14.28 | 13.33 | 12.50 | 11.76 | 11.11 | 10.53 |
| 4 | | 12.50 | 25.00 | 25.00 | 22.22 | 20.00 | 18.18 | 16.66 | 15.39 | 14.29 | 13.34 | 12.50 | 11.77 | 11.11 | 10.53 |
| 5 | | | | 9.37 | 19.45 | 20.00 | 18.19 | 16.67 | 15.38 | 14.28 | 13.33 | 12.50 | 11.76 | 11.11 | 10.52 |
| 6 | | | | | | 7.50 | 15.91 | 16.66 | 15.39 | 14.29 | 13.34 | 12.50 | 11.77 | 11.11 | 10.53 |
| 7 | | | | | | | | 6.25 | 13.46 | 14.28 | 13.33 | 12.50 | 11.76 | 11.11 | 10.52 |
| 8 | | | | | | | | | | 5.36 | 11.67 | 12.50 | 11.77 | 11.12 | 10.53 |
| 9 | | | | | | | | | | | | 4.69 | 10.29 | 11.11 | 10.52 |
| 10 | | | | | | | | | | | | | | 4.17 | 9.21 |

| If the Recovery Year is: | and the Recovery Period is: 10.0 | 10.5 | 11.0 | 11.5 | 12.0 | 12.5 | 13.0 | 13.5 | 14.0 | 14.5 | 15.0 | 15.5 | 16.0 | 16.5 | 17.0 |
|---|---|---|---|---|---|---|---|---|---|---|---|---|---|---|---|
| | the Depreciation Rate is: | | | | | | | | | | | | | | |
| 1 | 6.25 | 5.95 | 5.68 | 5.43 | 5.21 | 5.00 | 4.81 | 4.63 | 4.46 | 4.31 | 4.17 | 4.03 | 3.91 | 3.79 | 3.68 |
| 2 | 10.00 | 9.52 | 9.09 | 8.70 | 8.33 | 8.00 | 7.69 | 7.41 | 7.14 | 6.90 | 6.67 | 6.45 | 6.25 | 6.06 | 5.88 |
| 3 | 10.00 | 9.52 | 9.09 | 8.70 | 8.33 | 8.00 | 7.69 | 7.41 | 7.14 | 6.90 | 6.67 | 6.45 | 6.25 | 6.06 | 5.88 |
| 4 | 10.00 | 9.53 | 9.09 | 8.70 | 8.33 | 8.00 | 7.69 | 7.41 | 7.14 | 6.90 | 6.67 | 6.45 | 6.25 | 6.06 | 5.88 |
| 5 | 10.00 | 9.52 | 9.09 | 8.69 | 8.33 | 8.00 | 7.69 | 7.41 | 7.14 | 6.90 | 6.67 | 6.45 | 6.25 | 6.06 | 5.88 |
| 6 | 10.00 | 9.53 | 9.09 | 8.70 | 8.33 | 8.00 | 7.69 | 7.41 | 7.14 | 6.90 | 6.67 | 6.45 | 6.25 | 6.06 | 5.88 |

| If the Recovery Year is: | 10.0 | 10.5 | 11.0 | 11.5 | 12.0 | 12.5 | 13.0 | 13.5 | 14.0 | 14.5 | 15.0 | 15.5 | 16.0 | 16.5 | 17.0 |
|---|---|---|---|---|---|---|---|---|---|---|---|---|---|---|---|
| | the Depreciation Rate is: | | | | | | | | | | | | | | |
| 7 | 10.00 | 9.52 | 9.09 | 8.69 | 8.34 | 8.00 | 7.69 | 7.41 | 7.15 | 6.89 | 6.66 | 6.45 | 6.25 | 6.06 | 5.88 |
| 8 | 10.00 | 9.53 | 9.09 | 8.70 | 8.33 | 8.00 | 7.69 | 7.41 | 7.14 | 6.90 | 6.67 | 6.45 | 6.25 | 6.06 | 5.88 |
| 9 | 10.00 | 9.52 | 9.09 | 8.69 | 8.34 | 8.00 | 7.69 | 7.40 | 7.15 | 6.89 | 6.66 | 6.45 | 6.25 | 6.06 | 5.88 |
| 10 | 10.00 | 9.53 | 9.09 | 8.70 | 8.33 | 8.00 | 7.70 | 7.41 | 7.14 | 6.90 | 6.67 | 6.45 | 6.25 | 6.06 | 5.88 |
| 11 | 3.75 | 8.33 | 9.10 | 8.69 | 8.34 | 8.00 | 7.69 | 7.40 | 7.15 | 6.89 | 6.66 | 6.45 | 6.25 | 6.06 | 5.88 |
| 12 | | | 3.41 | 7.61 | 8.33 | 8.00 | 7.70 | 7.41 | 7.14 | 6.90 | 6.67 | 6.46 | 6.25 | 6.06 | 5.89 |
| 13 | | | | | 3.13 | 7.00 | 7.69 | 7.40 | 7.15 | 6.89 | 6.66 | 6.45 | 6.25 | 6.06 | 5.88 |
| 14 | | | | | | | 2.89 | 6.48 | 7.14 | 6.90 | 6.67 | 6.46 | 6.25 | 6.06 | 5.89 |
| 15 | | | | | | | | | 2.68 | 6.03 | 6.66 | 6.45 | 6.25 | 6.06 | 5.88 |
| 16 | | | | | | | | | | | 2.50 | 5.65 | 6.25 | 6.06 | 5.89 |
| 17 | | | | | | | | | | | | | 2.34 | 5.31 | 5.88 |
| 18 | | | | | | | | | | | | | | | 2.21 |

and the Recovery Period is:

| If the Recovery Year is: | 17.5 | 18.0 | 18.5 | 19.0 | 19.5 | 20.0 | 20.5 | 21.0 | 21.5 | 22.0 | 22.5 | 23.0 | 23.5 | 24.0 | 24.5 |
|---|---|---|---|---|---|---|---|---|---|---|---|---|---|---|---|
| | the Depreciation Rate is: | | | | | | | | | | | | | | |
| 1 | 3.57 | 3.47 | 3.38 | 3.29 | 3.21 | 3.125 | 3.049 | 2.976 | 2.907 | 2.841 | 2.778 | 2.717 | 2.660 | 2.604 | 2.551 |
| 2 | 5.71 | 5.56 | 5.41 | 5.26 | 5.13 | 5.000 | 4.878 | 4.762 | 4.651 | 4.545 | 4.444 | 4.348 | 4.255 | 4.167 | 4.082 |
| 3 | 5.71 | 5.56 | 5.41 | 5.26 | 5.13 | 5.000 | 4.878 | 4.762 | 4.651 | 4.545 | 4.444 | 4.348 | 4.255 | 4.167 | 4.082 |
| 4 | 5.71 | 5.56 | 5.40 | 5.26 | 5.13 | 5.000 | 4.878 | 4.762 | 4.651 | 4.545 | 4.444 | 4.348 | 4.255 | 4.167 | 4.082 |
| 5 | 5.72 | 5.55 | 5.41 | 5.26 | 5.13 | 5.000 | 4.878 | 4.762 | 4.651 | 4.546 | 4.445 | 4.348 | 4.255 | 4.167 | 4.082 |
| 6 | 5.71 | 5.56 | 5.40 | 5.26 | 5.13 | 5.000 | 4.878 | 4.762 | 4.651 | 4.545 | 4.444 | 4.348 | 4.255 | 4.167 | 4.082 |
| 7 | 5.72 | 5.55 | 5.41 | 5.26 | 5.13 | 5.000 | 4.878 | 4.762 | 4.651 | 4.546 | 4.445 | 4.348 | 4.255 | 4.167 | 4.082 |
| 8 | 5.71 | 5.56 | 5.40 | 5.26 | 5.13 | 5.000 | 4.878 | 4.762 | 4.651 | 4.545 | 4.444 | 4.348 | 4.255 | 4.167 | 4.082 |
| 9 | 5.72 | 5.55 | 5.41 | 5.27 | 5.13 | 5.000 | 4.878 | 4.762 | 4.651 | 4.546 | 4.445 | 4.348 | 4.255 | 4.167 | 4.081 |
| 10 | 5.71 | 5.56 | 5.40 | 5.26 | 5.13 | 5.000 | 4.878 | 4.762 | 4.651 | 4.545 | 4.444 | 4.348 | 4.255 | 4.167 | 4.082 |

| If the Recovery Year is: | 17.5 | 18.0 | 18.5 | 19.0 | 19.5 | 20.0 | 20.5 | 21.0 | 21.5 | 22.0 | 22.5 | 23.0 | 23.5 | 24.0 | 24.5 |
|---|---|---|---|---|---|---|---|---|---|---|---|---|---|---|---|
| | the Depreciation Rate is: | | | | | | | | | | | | | | |
| 11 | 5.72 | 5.55 | 5.41 | 5.27 | 5.13 | 5.000 | 4.878 | 4.762 | 4.651 | 4.546 | 4.445 | 4.348 | 4.255 | 4.166 | 4.081 |
| 12 | 5.71 | 5.56 | 5.40 | 5.26 | 5.13 | 5.000 | 4.878 | 4.762 | 4.651 | 4.545 | 4.444 | 4.348 | 4.256 | 4.167 | 4.082 |
| 13 | 5.72 | 5.55 | 5.41 | 5.27 | 5.13 | 5.000 | 4.878 | 4.762 | 4.651 | 4.546 | 4.445 | 4.348 | 4.255 | 4.166 | 4.081 |
| 14 | 5.71 | 5.56 | 5.40 | 5.26 | 5.12 | 5.000 | 4.878 | 4.762 | 4.651 | 4.545 | 4.444 | 4.348 | 4.256 | 4.167 | 4.082 |
| 15 | 5.72 | 5.55 | 5.41 | 5.27 | 5.13 | 5.000 | 4.878 | 4.762 | 4.651 | 4.546 | 4.445 | 4.348 | 4.255 | 4.166 | 4.081 |
| 16 | 5.71 | 5.56 | 5.40 | 5.26 | 5.12 | 5.000 | 4.878 | 4.762 | 4.651 | 4.545 | 4.444 | 4.348 | 4.256 | 4.167 | 4.082 |
| 17 | 5.72 | 5.55 | 5.41 | 5.27 | 5.13 | 5.000 | 4.878 | 4.762 | 4.652 | 4.546 | 4.445 | 4.348 | 4.255 | 4.166 | 4.081 |
| 18 | 5.00 | 5.56 | 5.40 | 5.26 | 5.12 | 5.000 | 4.878 | 4.762 | 4.651 | 4.545 | 4.444 | 4.347 | 4.256 | 4.167 | 4.082 |
| 19 | | 2.08 | 4.73 | 5.27 | 5.13 | 5.000 | 4.878 | 4.761 | 4.652 | 4.546 | 4.445 | 4.348 | 4.255 | 4.166 | 4.081 |
| 20 | | | | 1.97 | 4.48 | 5.000 | 4.878 | 4.762 | 4.651 | 4.545 | 4.444 | 4.347 | 4.256 | 4.167 | 4.082 |
| 21 | | | | | | 1.875 | 4.269 | 4.761 | 4.652 | 4.546 | 4.445 | 4.348 | 4.255 | 4.166 | 4.081 |
| 22 | | | | | | | | 1.786 | 4.070 | 4.545 | 4.444 | 4.347 | 4.256 | 4.167 | 4.082 |
| 23 | | | | | | | | | | 1.705 | 3.889 | 4.348 | 4.255 | 4.166 | 4.081 |
| 24 | | | | | | | | | | | | 1.630 | 3.724 | 4.167 | 4.082 |
| 25 | | | | | | | | | | | | | | 1.562 | 3.571 |

and the Recovery Period is:

| If the Recovery Year is: | 25.0 | 25.5 | 26.0 | 26.5 | 27.0 | 27.5 | 28.0 | 28.5 | 29.0 | 29.5 | 30.0 | 30.5 | 31.0 | 31.5 | 32.0 |
|---|---|---|---|---|---|---|---|---|---|---|---|---|---|---|---|
| | the Depreciation Rate is: | | | | | | | | | | | | | | |
| 1 | 2.500 | 2.451 | 2.404 | 2.358 | 2.315 | 2.273 | 2.232 | 2.193 | 2.155 | 2.119 | 2.083 | 2.049 | 2.016 | 1.984 | 1.953 |
| 2 | 4.000 | 3.922 | 3.846 | 3.774 | 3.704 | 3.636 | 3.571 | 3.509 | 3.448 | 3.390 | 3.333 | 3.279 | 3.226 | 3.175 | 3.125 |
| 3 | 4.000 | 3.922 | 3.846 | 3.774 | 3.704 | 3.636 | 3.571 | 3.509 | 3.448 | 3.390 | 3.333 | 3.279 | 3.226 | 3.175 | 3.125 |
| 4 | 4.000 | 3.922 | 3.846 | 3.774 | 3.704 | 3.636 | 3.571 | 3.509 | 3.448 | 3.390 | 3.333 | 3.279 | 3.226 | 3.175 | 3.125 |
| 5 | 4.000 | 3.922 | 3.846 | 3.774 | 3.704 | 3.636 | 3.571 | 3.509 | 3.448 | 3.390 | 3.333 | 3.279 | 3.226 | 3.175 | 3.125 |
| 6 | 4.000 | 3.921 | 3.846 | 3.774 | 3.704 | 3.636 | 3.572 | 3.509 | 3.448 | 3.390 | 3.333 | 3.279 | 3.226 | 3.175 | 3.125 |
| 7 | 4.000 | 3.922 | 3.846 | 3.774 | 3.704 | 3.636 | 3.571 | 3.509 | 3.448 | 3.390 | 3.333 | 3.279 | 3.226 | 3.175 | 3.125 |

| If the Recovery Year is: | 25.0 | 25.5 | 26.0 | 26.5 | 27.0 | 27.5 | 28.0 | 28.5 | 29.0 | 29.5 | 30.0 | 30.5 | 31.0 | 31.5 | 32.0 |
|---|---|---|---|---|---|---|---|---|---|---|---|---|---|---|---|
| | the Depreciation Rate is: | | | | | | | | | | | | | | |
| 8 | 4.000 | 3.921 | 3.846 | 3.773 | 3.704 | 3.636 | 3.572 | 3.509 | 3.448 | 3.390 | 3.333 | 3.279 | 3.226 | 3.175 | 3.125 |
| 9 | 4.000 | 3.922 | 3.846 | 3.774 | 3.704 | 3.636 | 3.571 | 3.509 | 3.448 | 3.390 | 3.333 | 3.279 | 3.226 | 3.174 | 3.125 |
| 10 | 4.000 | 3.921 | 3.846 | 3.773 | 3.704 | 3.637 | 3.572 | 3.509 | 3.448 | 3.390 | 3.333 | 3.279 | 3.226 | 3.175 | 3.125 |
| 11 | 4.000 | 3.922 | 3.846 | 3.774 | 3.704 | 3.636 | 3.571 | 3.509 | 3.448 | 3.390 | 3.333 | 3.279 | 3.226 | 3.174 | 3.125 |
| 12 | 4.000 | 3.921 | 3.846 | 3.773 | 3.704 | 3.637 | 3.572 | 3.509 | 3.448 | 3.390 | 3.334 | 3.279 | 3.226 | 3.175 | 3.125 |
| 13 | 4.000 | 3.922 | 3.846 | 3.774 | 3.703 | 3.636 | 3.571 | 3.509 | 3.448 | 3.390 | 3.333 | 3.279 | 3.226 | 3.174 | 3.125 |
| 14 | 4.000 | 3.921 | 3.846 | 3.773 | 3.704 | 3.637 | 3.572 | 3.509 | 3.448 | 3.390 | 3.334 | 3.278 | 3.226 | 3.175 | 3.125 |
| 15 | 4.000 | 3.922 | 3.846 | 3.774 | 3.703 | 3.636 | 3.571 | 3.509 | 3.449 | 3.390 | 3.333 | 3.279 | 3.226 | 3.174 | 3.125 |
| 16 | 4.000 | 3.921 | 3.846 | 3.773 | 3.704 | 3.637 | 3.572 | 3.509 | 3.448 | 3.390 | 3.334 | 3.278 | 3.226 | 3.175 | 3.125 |
| 17 | 4.000 | 3.922 | 3.846 | 3.774 | 3.703 | 3.636 | 3.571 | 3.509 | 3.449 | 3.390 | 3.333 | 3.279 | 3.226 | 3.174 | 3.125 |
| 18 | 4.000 | 3.921 | 3.846 | 3.773 | 3.704 | 3.637 | 3.572 | 3.508 | 3.448 | 3.390 | 3.334 | 3.278 | 3.226 | 3.175 | 3.125 |
| 19 | 4.000 | 3.922 | 3.846 | 3.774 | 3.703 | 3.636 | 3.571 | 3.509 | 3.449 | 3.390 | 3.333 | 3.279 | 3.226 | 3.174 | 3.125 |
| 20 | 4.000 | 3.921 | 3.847 | 3.773 | 3.704 | 3.637 | 3.572 | 3.508 | 3.448 | 3.390 | 3.334 | 3.278 | 3.226 | 3.175 | 3.125 |
| 21 | 4.000 | 3.922 | 3.846 | 3.774 | 3.703 | 3.636 | 3.571 | 3.509 | 3.449 | 3.389 | 3.333 | 3.279 | 3.225 | 3.174 | 3.125 |
| 22 | 4.000 | 3.921 | 3.847 | 3.773 | 3.704 | 3.637 | 3.572 | 3.508 | 3.448 | 3.390 | 3.334 | 3.278 | 3.226 | 3.175 | 3.125 |
| 23 | 4.000 | 3.922 | 3.846 | 3.774 | 3.703 | 3.636 | 3.571 | 3.509 | 3.449 | 3.389 | 3.333 | 3.279 | 3.225 | 3.174 | 3.125 |
| 24 | 4.000 | 3.921 | 3.847 | 3.773 | 3.704 | 3.637 | 3.572 | 3.508 | 3.448 | 3.390 | 3.334 | 3.278 | 3.226 | 3.175 | 3.125 |
| 25 | 4.000 | 3.922 | 3.846 | 3.774 | 3.703 | 3.636 | 3.571 | 3.509 | 3.449 | 3.389 | 3.333 | 3.279 | 3.225 | 3.174 | 3.125 |
| 26 | 1.500 | 3.431 | 3.847 | 3.773 | 3.704 | 3.637 | 3.572 | 3.508 | 3.448 | 3.390 | 3.334 | 3.278 | 3.226 | 3.175 | 3.125 |
| 27 | | | 1.442 | 3.302 | 3.703 | 3.636 | 3.571 | 3.509 | 3.449 | 3.389 | 3.333 | 3.279 | 3.225 | 3.174 | 3.125 |
| 28 | | | | | 1.389 | 3.182 | 3.572 | 3.508 | 3.448 | 3.390 | 3.334 | 3.278 | 3.226 | 3.175 | 3.125 |
| 29 | | | | | | | 1.339 | 3.070 | 3.449 | 3.389 | 3.333 | 3.279 | 3.225 | 3.174 | 3.125 |
| 30 | | | | | | | | | 1.293 | 2.966 | 3.334 | 3.278 | 3.226 | 3.175 | 3.125 |
| 31 | | | | | | | | | | | 1.250 | 2.869 | 3.225 | 3.174 | 3.125 |
| 32 | | | | | | | | | | | | | 1.210 | 2.778 | 3.125 |
| 33 | | | | | | | | | | | | | | | 1.172 |

| If the Recovery Year is: | and the Recovery Period is: 32.5 | 33.0 | 33.5 | 34.0 | 34.5 | 35.0 | 35.5 | 36.0 | 36.5 | 37.0 | 37.5 | 38.0 | 38.5 | 39.0 | 39.5 |
|---|---|---|---|---|---|---|---|---|---|---|---|---|---|---|---|
| | the Depreciation Rate is: | | | | | | | | | | | | | | |
| 1 | 1.923 | 1.894 | 1.866 | 1.838 | 1.812 | 1.786 | 1.761 | 1.736 | 1.712 | 1.689 | 1.667 | 1.645 | 1.623 | 1.603 | 1.582 |
| 2 | 3.077 | 3.030 | 2.985 | 2.941 | 2.899 | 2.857 | 2.817 | 2.778 | 2.740 | 2.703 | 2.667 | 2.632 | 2.597 | 2.564 | 2.532 |
| 3 | 3.077 | 3.030 | 2.985 | 2.941 | 2.899 | 2.857 | 2.817 | 2.778 | 2.740 | 2.703 | 2.667 | 2.632 | 2.597 | 2.564 | 2.532 |
| 4 | 3.077 | 3.030 | 2.985 | 2.941 | 2.899 | 2.857 | 2.817 | 2.778 | 2.740 | 2.703 | 2.667 | 2.632 | 2.597 | 2.564 | 2.532 |
| 5 | 3.077 | 3.030 | 2.985 | 2.941 | 2.898 | 2.857 | 2.817 | 2.778 | 2.740 | 2.703 | 2.667 | 2.632 | 2.597 | 2.564 | 2.532 |
| 6 | 3.077 | 3.030 | 2.985 | 2.941 | 2.899 | 2.857 | 2.817 | 2.778 | 2.740 | 2.703 | 2.667 | 2.632 | 2.597 | 2.564 | 2.532 |
| 7 | 3.077 | 3.030 | 2.985 | 2.941 | 2.898 | 2.857 | 2.817 | 2.778 | 2.740 | 2.703 | 2.667 | 2.632 | 2.597 | 2.564 | 2.532 |
| 8 | 3.077 | 3.030 | 2.985 | 2.941 | 2.899 | 2.857 | 2.817 | 2.778 | 2.740 | 2.703 | 2.667 | 2.631 | 2.597 | 2.564 | 2.532 |
| 9 | 3.077 | 3.030 | 2.985 | 2.941 | 2.898 | 2.857 | 2.817 | 2.778 | 2.740 | 2.703 | 2.667 | 2.632 | 2.598 | 2.564 | 2.532 |
| 10 | 3.077 | 3.030 | 2.985 | 2.941 | 2.899 | 2.857 | 2.817 | 2.778 | 2.740 | 2.703 | 2.667 | 2.631 | 2.597 | 2.564 | 2.532 |
| 11 | 3.077 | 3.030 | 2.985 | 2.941 | 2.898 | 2.857 | 2.817 | 2.778 | 2.740 | 2.703 | 2.667 | 2.632 | 2.598 | 2.564 | 2.532 |
| 12 | 3.077 | 3.030 | 2.985 | 2.941 | 2.899 | 2.857 | 2.817 | 2.778 | 2.740 | 2.703 | 2.667 | 2.631 | 2.597 | 2.564 | 2.532 |
| 13 | 3.077 | 3.030 | 2.985 | 2.941 | 2.898 | 2.857 | 2.817 | 2.778 | 2.740 | 2.703 | 2.667 | 2.632 | 2.598 | 2.564 | 2.532 |
| 14 | 3.077 | 3.030 | 2.985 | 2.941 | 2.899 | 2.857 | 2.817 | 2.778 | 2.740 | 2.703 | 2.666 | 2.631 | 2.597 | 2.564 | 2.531 |
| 15 | 3.077 | 3.031 | 2.985 | 2.941 | 2.898 | 2.857 | 2.817 | 2.778 | 2.740 | 2.703 | 2.667 | 2.632 | 2.598 | 2.564 | 2.532 |
| 16 | 3.077 | 3.030 | 2.985 | 2.941 | 2.899 | 2.857 | 2.817 | 2.778 | 2.740 | 2.703 | 2.666 | 2.631 | 2.597 | 2.564 | 2.531 |
| 17 | 3.077 | 3.031 | 2.985 | 2.941 | 2.898 | 2.857 | 2.817 | 2.778 | 2.740 | 2.703 | 2.667 | 2.632 | 2.598 | 2.564 | 2.532 |
| 18 | 3.077 | 3.030 | 2.985 | 2.941 | 2.899 | 2.857 | 2.817 | 2.778 | 2.740 | 2.702 | 2.666 | 2.631 | 2.597 | 2.564 | 2.531 |
| 19 | 3.077 | 3.031 | 2.985 | 2.941 | 2.898 | 2.857 | 2.817 | 2.778 | 2.739 | 2.703 | 2.667 | 2.632 | 2.598 | 2.564 | 2.532 |
| 20 | 3.077 | 3.030 | 2.985 | 2.941 | 2.899 | 2.857 | 2.817 | 2.778 | 2.740 | 2.702 | 2.666 | 2.631 | 2.597 | 2.564 | 2.531 |
| 21 | 3.077 | 3.031 | 2.985 | 2.941 | 2.898 | 2.857 | 2.817 | 2.778 | 2.739 | 2.703 | 2.667 | 2.632 | 2.598 | 2.564 | 2.532 |
| 22 | 3.077 | 3.030 | 2.985 | 2.941 | 2.899 | 2.857 | 2.817 | 2.777 | 2.740 | 2.702 | 2.666 | 2.631 | 2.597 | 2.564 | 2.531 |
| 23 | 3.077 | 3.031 | 2.985 | 2.941 | 2.898 | 2.857 | 2.817 | 2.778 | 2.739 | 2.703 | 2.667 | 2.632 | 2.598 | 2.564 | 2.532 |
| 24 | 3.077 | 3.030 | 2.985 | 2.942 | 2.899 | 2.857 | 2.817 | 2.777 | 2.740 | 2.702 | 2.666 | 2.631 | 2.597 | 2.564 | 2.531 |
| 25 | 3.077 | 3.031 | 2.985 | 2.941 | 2.898 | 2.857 | 2.817 | 2.778 | 2.739 | 2.703 | 2.667 | 2.632 | 2.598 | 2.564 | 2.532 |

| If the Recovery Year is: | 32.5 | 33.0 | 33.5 | 34.0 | 34.5 | 35.0 | 35.5 | 36.0 | 36.5 | 37.0 | 37.5 | 38.0 | 38.5 | 39.0 | 39.5 |
|---|---|---|---|---|---|---|---|---|---|---|---|---|---|---|---|
| | the Depreciation Rate is: | | | | | | | | | | | | | | |
| 26 | 3.077 | 3.030 | 2.985 | 2.942 | 2.899 | 2.857 | 2.817 | 2.777 | 2.740 | 2.702 | 2.666 | 2.631 | 2.597 | 2.564 | 2.531 |
| 27 | 3.077 | 3.031 | 2.985 | 2.941 | 2.898 | 2.857 | 2.817 | 2.778 | 2.739 | 2.703 | 2.667 | 2.632 | 2.598 | 2.564 | 2.532 |
| 28 | 3.077 | 3.030 | 2.985 | 2.942 | 2.899 | 2.858 | 2.817 | 2.777 | 2.740 | 2.702 | 2.666 | 2.631 | 2.597 | 2.564 | 2.531 |
| 29 | 3.077 | 3.031 | 2.985 | 2.941 | 2.898 | 2.857 | 2.817 | 2.778 | 2.739 | 2.703 | 2.667 | 2.632 | 2.598 | 2.564 | 2.532 |
| 30 | 3.076 | 3.030 | 2.985 | 2.942 | 2.899 | 2.858 | 2.816 | 2.777 | 2.740 | 2.702 | 2.666 | 2.631 | 2.597 | 2.564 | 2.531 |
| 31 | 3.077 | 3.031 | 2.986 | 2.941 | 2.898 | 2.857 | 2.817 | 2.778 | 2.739 | 2.703 | 2.667 | 2.632 | 2.598 | 2.564 | 2.532 |
| 32 | 3.076 | 3.030 | 2.985 | 2.942 | 2.899 | 2.858 | 2.816 | 2.777 | 2.740 | 2.702 | 2.666 | 2.631 | 2.597 | 2.564 | 2.531 |
| 33 | 2.692 | 3.031 | 2.986 | 2.941 | 2.898 | 2.857 | 2.817 | 2.778 | 2.739 | 2.703 | 2.667 | 2.632 | 2.598 | 2.564 | 2.532 |
| 34 | | 1.136 | 2.612 | 2.942 | 2.899 | 2.858 | 2.816 | 2.777 | 2.740 | 2.702 | 2.666 | 2.631 | 2.597 | 2.565 | 2.531 |
| 35 | | | | 1.103 | 2.536 | 2.857 | 2.817 | 2.778 | 2.739 | 2.703 | 2.667 | 2.632 | 2.598 | 2.564 | 2.532 |
| 36 | | | | | | 1.072 | 2.464 | 2.777 | 2.740 | 2.702 | 2.666 | 2.631 | 2.597 | 2.565 | 2.531 |
| 37 | | | | | | | | 1.042 | 2.397 | 2.703 | 2.667 | 2.632 | 2.598 | 2.564 | 2.532 |
| 38 | | | | | | | | | | 1.013 | 2.333 | 2.631 | 2.597 | 2.565 | 2.531 |
| 39 | | | | | | | | | | | | 0.987 | 2.273 | 2.564 | 2.532 |
| 40 | | | | | | | | | | | | | | 0.962 | 2.215 |

and the Recovery Period is:

| If the Recovery Year is: | 40.0 | 40.5 | 41.0 | 41.5 | 42.0 | 42.5 | 43.0 | 43.5 | 44.0 | 44.5 | 45.0 | 45.5 | 46.0 | 46.5 | 47.0 |
|---|---|---|---|---|---|---|---|---|---|---|---|---|---|---|---|
| | the Depreciation Rate is: | | | | | | | | | | | | | | |
| 1 | 1.563 | 1.543 | 1.524 | 1.506 | 1.488 | 1.471 | 1.453 | 1.437 | 1.420 | 1.404 | 1.389 | 1.374 | 1.359 | 1.344 | 1.330 |
| 2 | 2.500 | 2.469 | 2.439 | 2.410 | 2.381 | 2.353 | 2.326 | 2.299 | 2.273 | 2.247 | 2.222 | 2.198 | 2.174 | 2.151 | 2.128 |
| 3 | 2.500 | 2.469 | 2.439 | 2.410 | 2.381 | 2.353 | 2.326 | 2.299 | 2.273 | 2.247 | 2.222 | 2.198 | 2.174 | 2.151 | 2.128 |
| 4 | 2.500 | 2.469 | 2.439 | 2.410 | 2.381 | 2.353 | 2.326 | 2.299 | 2.273 | 2.247 | 2.222 | 2.198 | 2.174 | 2.151 | 2.128 |
| 5 | 2.500 | 2.469 | 2.439 | 2.410 | 2.381 | 2.353 | 2.326 | 2.299 | 2.273 | 2.247 | 2.222 | 2.198 | 2.174 | 2.151 | 2.128 |
| 6 | 2.500 | 2.469 | 2.439 | 2.410 | 2.381 | 2.353 | 2.326 | 2.299 | 2.273 | 2.247 | 2.222 | 2.198 | 2.174 | 2.150 | 2.128 |
| 7 | 2.500 | 2.469 | 2.439 | 2.410 | 2.381 | 2.353 | 2.326 | 2.299 | 2.273 | 2.247 | 2.222 | 2.198 | 2.174 | 2.151 | 2.128 |

| If the Recovery Year is: | 40.0 | 40.5 | 41.0 | 41.5 | 42.0 | 42.5 | 43.0 | 43.5 | 44.0 | 44.5 | 45.0 | 45.5 | 46.0 | 46.5 | 47.0 |
|---|---|---|---|---|---|---|---|---|---|---|---|---|---|---|---|
| | the Depreciation Rate is: | | | | | | | | | | | | | | |
| 8 | 2.500 | 2.469 | 2.439 | 2.410 | 2.381 | 2.353 | 2.326 | 2.299 | 2.273 | 2.247 | 2.222 | 2.198 | 2.174 | 2.150 | 2.128 |
| 9 | 2.500 | 2.469 | 2.439 | 2.410 | 2.381 | 2.353 | 2.326 | 2.299 | 2.273 | 2.247 | 2.222 | 2.198 | 2.174 | 2.151 | 2.128 |
| 10 | 2.500 | 2.469 | 2.439 | 2.410 | 2.381 | 2.353 | 2.325 | 2.299 | 2.273 | 2.247 | 2.222 | 2.198 | 2.174 | 2.150 | 2.128 |
| 11 | 2.500 | 2.469 | 2.439 | 2.410 | 2.381 | 2.353 | 2.326 | 2.299 | 2.273 | 2.247 | 2.222 | 2.198 | 2.174 | 2.151 | 2.128 |
| 12 | 2.500 | 2.469 | 2.439 | 2.410 | 2.381 | 2.353 | 2.325 | 2.299 | 2.273 | 2.247 | 2.222 | 2.198 | 2.174 | 2.150 | 2.128 |
| 13 | 2.500 | 2.469 | 2.439 | 2.410 | 2.381 | 2.353 | 2.326 | 2.299 | 2.273 | 2.247 | 2.222 | 2.198 | 2.174 | 2.151 | 2.128 |
| 14 | 2.500 | 2.469 | 2.439 | 2.409 | 2.381 | 2.353 | 2.325 | 2.299 | 2.273 | 2.247 | 2.222 | 2.198 | 2.174 | 2.150 | 2.128 |
| 15 | 2.500 | 2.469 | 2.439 | 2.410 | 2.381 | 2.353 | 2.326 | 2.299 | 2.273 | 2.247 | 2.222 | 2.198 | 2.174 | 2.151 | 2.128 |
| 16 | 2.500 | 2.469 | 2.439 | 2.409 | 2.381 | 2.353 | 2.325 | 2.299 | 2.273 | 2.247 | 2.222 | 2.198 | 2.174 | 2.150 | 2.128 |
| 17 | 2.500 | 2.469 | 2.439 | 2.410 | 2.381 | 2.353 | 2.326 | 2.299 | 2.273 | 2.247 | 2.222 | 2.198 | 2.174 | 2.151 | 2.127 |
| 18 | 2.500 | 2.469 | 2.439 | 2.409 | 2.381 | 2.353 | 2.325 | 2.299 | 2.273 | 2.247 | 2.222 | 2.198 | 2.174 | 2.150 | 2.128 |
| 19 | 2.500 | 2.469 | 2.439 | 2.410 | 2.381 | 2.353 | 2.326 | 2.299 | 2.273 | 2.247 | 2.222 | 2.198 | 2.174 | 2.151 | 2.127 |
| 20 | 2.500 | 2.469 | 2.439 | 2.409 | 2.381 | 2.353 | 2.325 | 2.299 | 2.273 | 2.247 | 2.222 | 2.198 | 2.174 | 2.150 | 2.128 |
| 21 | 2.500 | 2.469 | 2.439 | 2.410 | 2.381 | 2.353 | 2.326 | 2.299 | 2.273 | 2.247 | 2.222 | 2.198 | 2.174 | 2.151 | 2.127 |
| 22 | 2.500 | 2.469 | 2.439 | 2.409 | 2.381 | 2.353 | 2.325 | 2.299 | 2.273 | 2.247 | 2.222 | 2.198 | 2.174 | 2.150 | 2.128 |
| 23 | 2.500 | 2.469 | 2.439 | 2.410 | 2.381 | 2.353 | 2.326 | 2.299 | 2.272 | 2.247 | 2.222 | 2.198 | 2.174 | 2.151 | 2.127 |
| 24 | 2.500 | 2.469 | 2.439 | 2.409 | 2.381 | 2.353 | 2.325 | 2.299 | 2.273 | 2.247 | 2.222 | 2.198 | 2.174 | 2.150 | 2.128 |
| 25 | 2.500 | 2.469 | 2.439 | 2.410 | 2.381 | 2.353 | 2.326 | 2.299 | 2.272 | 2.247 | 2.222 | 2.198 | 2.174 | 2.151 | 2.127 |
| 26 | 2.500 | 2.469 | 2.439 | 2.409 | 2.381 | 2.353 | 2.325 | 2.299 | 2.273 | 2.247 | 2.222 | 2.198 | 2.174 | 2.150 | 2.128 |
| 27 | 2.500 | 2.469 | 2.439 | 2.410 | 2.381 | 2.353 | 2.326 | 2.299 | 2.272 | 2.247 | 2.223 | 2.198 | 2.174 | 2.151 | 2.127 |
| 28 | 2.500 | 2.469 | 2.439 | 2.409 | 2.381 | 2.353 | 2.325 | 2.299 | 2.273 | 2.247 | 2.222 | 2.198 | 2.174 | 2.150 | 2.128 |
| 29 | 2.500 | 2.469 | 2.439 | 2.410 | 2.381 | 2.353 | 2.326 | 2.299 | 2.272 | 2.248 | 2.223 | 2.197 | 2.174 | 2.151 | 2.127 |
| 30 | 2.500 | 2.469 | 2.439 | 2.409 | 2.381 | 2.353 | 2.325 | 2.299 | 2.273 | 2.247 | 2.222 | 2.198 | 2.174 | 2.150 | 2.128 |
| 31 | 2.500 | 2.470 | 2.439 | 2.410 | 2.381 | 2.353 | 2.326 | 2.299 | 2.272 | 2.248 | 2.223 | 2.197 | 2.174 | 2.151 | 2.127 |
| 32 | 2.500 | 2.469 | 2.439 | 2.409 | 2.381 | 2.353 | 2.325 | 2.298 | 2.273 | 2.247 | 2.222 | 2.198 | 2.174 | 2.150 | 2.128 |
| 33 | 2.500 | 2.470 | 2.439 | 2.410 | 2.381 | 2.353 | 2.326 | 2.299 | 2.272 | 2.248 | 2.223 | 2.197 | 2.174 | 2.151 | 2.127 |
| 34 | 2.500 | 2.469 | 2.439 | 2.409 | 2.381 | 2.353 | 2.325 | 2.298 | 2.273 | 2.247 | 2.222 | 2.198 | 2.174 | 2.150 | 2.128 |

| If the Recovery Year is: | 40.0 | 40.5 | 41.0 | 41.5 | 42.0 | 42.5 | 43.0 | 43.5 | 44.0 | 44.5 | 45.0 | 45.5 | 46.0 | 46.5 | 47.0 |
|---|---|---|---|---|---|---|---|---|---|---|---|---|---|---|---|
| | the Depreciation Rate is: | | | | | | | | | | | | | | |
| 35 | 2.500 | 2.470 | 2.439 | 2.410 | 2.381 | 2.353 | 2.326 | 2.299 | 2.272 | 2.248 | 2.223 | 2.197 | 2.174 | 2.151 | 2.127 |
| 36 | 2.500 | 2.469 | 2.439 | 2.409 | 2.381 | 2.353 | 2.325 | 2.298 | 2.273 | 2.247 | 2.222 | 2.198 | 2.174 | 2.150 | 2.128 |
| 37 | 2.500 | 2.470 | 2.439 | 2.410 | 2.381 | 2.353 | 2.326 | 2.299 | 2.272 | 2.248 | 2.223 | 2.197 | 2.174 | 2.151 | 2.127 |
| 38 | 2.500 | 2.469 | 2.439 | 2.409 | 2.381 | 2.353 | 2.325 | 2.298 | 2.273 | 2.247 | 2.222 | 2.198 | 2.174 | 2.150 | 2.128 |
| 39 | 2.500 | 2.470 | 2.439 | 2.410 | 2.381 | 2.352 | 2.326 | 2.299 | 2.272 | 2.248 | 2.223 | 2.197 | 2.173 | 2.151 | 2.127 |
| 40 | 2.500 | 2.469 | 2.440 | 2.409 | 2.380 | 2.353 | 2.325 | 2.298 | 2.273 | 2.247 | 2.222 | 2.198 | 2.174 | 2.150 | 2.128 |
| 41 | 0.937 | 2.161 | 2.439 | 2.410 | 2.381 | 2.352 | 2.326 | 2.299 | 2.272 | 2.248 | 2.223 | 2.197 | 2.173 | 2.151 | 2.127 |
| 42 | | | 0.915 | 2.108 | 2.380 | 2.353 | 2.325 | 2.298 | 2.273 | 2.247 | 2.222 | 2.198 | 2.174 | 2.150 | 2.128 |
| 43 | | | | | 0.893 | 2.058 | 2.326 | 2.299 | 2.272 | 2.248 | 2.223 | 2.197 | 2.173 | 2.151 | 2.127 |
| 44 | | | | | | | 0.872 | 2.011 | 2.273 | 2.247 | 2.222 | 2.198 | 2.174 | 2.150 | 2.128 |
| 45 | | | | | | | | | 0.852 | 1.967 | 2.223 | 2.197 | 2.173 | 2.151 | 2.127 |
| 46 | | | | | | | | | | | 0.833 | 1.923 | 2.174 | 2.150 | 2.128 |
| 47 | | | | | | | | | | | | | 0.815 | 1.882 | 2.127 |
| 48 | | | | | | | | | | | | | | | 0.798 |

and the Recovery Period is:

| If the Recovery Year is: | 47.5 | 48.0 | 48.5 | 49.0 | 49.5 | 50.0 |
|---|---|---|---|---|---|---|
| | | | the Depreciation Rate is: | | | |
| 1 | 1.316 | 1.302 | 1.289 | 1.276 | 1.263 | 1.250 |
| 2 | 2.105 | 2.083 | 2.062 | 2.041 | 2.020 | 2.000 |
| 3 | 2.105 | 2.083 | 2.062 | 2.041 | 2.020 | 2.000 |
| 4 | 2.105 | 2.083 | 2.062 | 2.041 | 2.020 | 2.000 |
| 5 | 2.105 | 2.083 | 2.062 | 2.041 | 2.020 | 2.000 |
| 6 | 2.105 | 2.083 | 2.062 | 2.041 | 2.020 | 2.000 |
| 7 | 2.105 | 2.083 | 2.062 | 2.041 | 2.020 | 2.000 |
| 8 | 2.105 | 2.083 | 2.062 | 2.041 | 2.020 | 2.000 |
| 9 | 2.105 | 2.083 | 2.062 | 2.041 | 2.020 | 2.000 |

| If the Recovery Year is: | and the Recovery Period is: 47.5 | 48.0 | 48.5 | 49.0 | 49.5 | 50.0 |
|---|---|---|---|---|---|---|
| | the Depreciation Rate is: | | | | | |
| 10 | 2.105 | 2.083 | 2.062 | 2.041 | 2.020 | 2.000 |
| 11 | 2.105 | 2.083 | 2.062 | 2.041 | 2.020 | 2.000 |
| 12 | 2.105 | 2.083 | 2.062 | 2.041 | 2.020 | 2.000 |
| 13 | 2.105 | 2.083 | 2.062 | 2.041 | 2.020 | 2.000 |
| 14 | 2.105 | 2.083 | 2.062 | 2.041 | 2.020 | 2.000 |
| 15 | 2.105 | 2.083 | 2.062 | 2.041 | 2.020 | 2.000 |
| 16 | 2.105 | 2.083 | 2.062 | 2.041 | 2.020 | 2.000 |
| 17 | 2.105 | 2.083 | 2.062 | 2.041 | 2.020 | 2.000 |
| 18 | 2.105 | 2.084 | 2.062 | 2.041 | 2.020 | 2.000 |
| 19 | 2.105 | 2.083 | 2.062 | 2.041 | 2.020 | 2.000 |
| 20 | 2.105 | 2.084 | 2.062 | 2.041 | 2.020 | 2.000 |
| 21 | 2.105 | 2.083 | 2.062 | 2.041 | 2.020 | 2.000 |
| 22 | 2.105 | 2.084 | 2.062 | 2.041 | 2.020 | 2.000 |
| 23 | 2.105 | 2.083 | 2.062 | 2.041 | 2.020 | 2.000 |
| 24 | 2.105 | 2.084 | 2.062 | 2.041 | 2.020 | 2.000 |
| 25 | 2.106 | 2.083 | 2.062 | 2.041 | 2.020 | 2.000 |
| 26 | 2.105 | 2.084 | 2.062 | 2.041 | 2.020 | 2.000 |
| 27 | 2.106 | 2.083 | 2.062 | 2.041 | 2.020 | 2.000 |
| 28 | 2.105 | 2.084 | 2.062 | 2.041 | 2.020 | 2.000 |
| 29 | 2.106 | 2.083 | 2.062 | 2.041 | 2.020 | 2.000 |
| 30 | 2.105 | 2.084 | 2.062 | 2.041 | 2.020 | 2.000 |
| 31 | 2.106 | 2.083 | 2.062 | 2.041 | 2.020 | 2.000 |
| 32 | 2.105 | 2.084 | 2.062 | 2.040 | 2.021 | 2.000 |
| 33 | 2.106 | 2.083 | 2.062 | 2.041 | 2.020 | 2.000 |
| 34 | 2.105 | 2.084 | 2.062 | 2.040 | 2.021 | 2.000 |
| 35 | 2.106 | 2.083 | 2.062 | 2.041 | 2.020 | 2.000 |

| If the Recovery Year is: | and the Recovery Period is: 47.5 | 48.0 | 48.5 | 49.0 | 49.5 | 50.0 |
|---|---|---|---|---|---|---|
| | the Depreciation Rate is: | | | | | |
| 36 | 2.105 | 2.084 | 2.061 | 2.040 | 2.021 | 2.000 |
| 37 | 2.106 | 2.083 | 2.062 | 2.041 | 2.020 | 2.000 |
| 38 | 2.105 | 2.084 | 2.061 | 2.040 | 2.021 | 2.000 |
| 39 | 2.106 | 2.083 | 2.062 | 2.041 | 2.020 | 2.000 |
| 40 | 2.105 | 2.084 | 2.061 | 2.040 | 2.021 | 2.000 |
| 41 | 2.106 | 2.083 | 2.062 | 2.041 | 2.020 | 2.000 |
| 42 | 2.105 | 2.084 | 2.061 | 2.040 | 2.021 | 2.000 |
| 43 | 2.106 | 2.083 | 2.062 | 2.041 | 2.020 | 2.000 |
| 44 | 2.105 | 2.084 | 2.061 | 2.040 | 2.021 | 2.000 |
| 45 | 2.106 | 2.083 | 2.062 | 2.041 | 2.020 | 2.000 |
| 46 | 2.105 | 2.084 | 2.061 | 2.040 | 2.021 | 2.000 |
| 47 | 2.106 | 2.083 | 2.062 | 2.041 | 2.020 | 2.000 |
| 48 | 1.842 | 2.084 | 2.061 | 2.040 | 2.021 | 2.000 |
| 49 | | 0.781 | 1.804 | 2.041 | 2.020 | 2.000 |
| 50 | | | | 0.765 | 1.768 | 2.000 |
| 51 | | | | | | 0.750 |

TABLE 11
General and Alternative Depreciation Systems
Applicable Depreciation Method: Straight Line
Applicable Recovery Periods: 2.5 — 50 years
Applicable Convention: Mid-quarter (property placed in service in third quarter)

| If the Recovery Year is: | and the Recovery Period is: 2.5 | 3.0 | 3.5 | 4.0 | 4.5 | 5.0 | 5.5 | 6.0 | 6.5 | 7.0 | 7.5 | 8.0 | 8.5 | 9.0 | 9.5 |
|---|---|---|---|---|---|---|---|---|---|---|---|---|---|---|---|
| | the Depreciation Rate is: | | | | | | | | | | | | | | |
| 1 | 15.00 | 12.50 | 10.71 | 9.38 | 8.33 | 7.50 | 6.82 | 6.25 | 5.77 | 5.36 | 5.00 | 4.69 | 4.41 | 4.17 | 3.95 |
| 2 | 40.00 | 33.33 | 28.57 | 25.00 | 22.22 | 20.00 | 18.18 | 16.67 | 15.38 | 14.29 | 13.33 | 12.50 | 11.76 | 11.11 | 10.53 |
| 3 | 40.00 | 33.34 | 28.57 | 25.00 | 22.22 | 20.00 | 18.18 | 16.67 | 15.39 | 14.28 | 13.33 | 12.50 | 11.77 | 11.11 | 10.53 |
| 4 | 5.00 | 20.83 | 28.58 | 25.00 | 22.23 | 20.00 | 18.18 | 16.66 | 15.38 | 14.29 | 13.33 | 12.50 | 11.76 | 11.11 | 10.52 |
| 5 | | | 3.57 | 15.62 | 22.22 | 20.00 | 18.18 | 16.67 | 15.39 | 14.28 | 13.34 | 12.50 | 11.77 | 11.11 | 10.53 |
| 6 | | | | | 2.78 | 12.50 | 18.19 | 16.66 | 15.38 | 14.29 | 13.33 | 12.50 | 11.76 | 11.11 | 10.52 |
| 7 | | | | | | | 2.27 | 10.42 | 15.39 | 14.28 | 13.34 | 12.50 | 11.77 | 11.11 | 10.53 |
| 8 | | | | | | | | | 1.92 | 8.93 | 13.33 | 12.50 | 11.76 | 11.11 | 10.52 |
| 9 | | | | | | | | | | | 1.67 | 7.81 | 11.77 | 11.11 | 10.53 |
| 10 | | | | | | | | | | | | | 1.47 | 6.95 | 10.52 |
| 11 | | | | | | | | | | | | | | | 1.32 |

| If the Recovery Year is: | and the Recovery Period is: 10.0 | 10.5 | 11.0 | 11.5 | 12.0 | 12.5 | 13.0 | 13.5 | 14.0 | 14.5 | 15.0 | 15.5 | 16.0 | 16.5 | 17.0 |
|---|---|---|---|---|---|---|---|---|---|---|---|---|---|---|---|
| | the Depreciation Rate is: | | | | | | | | | | | | | | |
| 1 | 3.75 | 3.57 | 3.41 | 3.26 | 3.13 | 3.00 | 2.88 | 2.78 | 2.68 | 2.59 | 2.50 | 2.42 | 2.34 | 2.27 | 2.21 |
| 2 | 10.00 | 9.52 | 9.09 | 8.70 | 8.33 | 8.00 | 7.69 | 7.41 | 7.14 | 6.90 | 6.67 | 6.45 | 6.25 | 6.06 | 5.88 |
| 3 | 10.00 | 9.52 | 9.09 | 8.70 | 8.33 | 8.00 | 7.69 | 7.41 | 7.14 | 6.90 | 6.67 | 6.45 | 6.25 | 6.06 | 5.88 |
| 4 | 10.00 | 9.52 | 9.09 | 8.69 | 8.33 | 8.00 | 7.69 | 7.41 | 7.14 | 6.90 | 6.67 | 6.45 | 6.25 | 6.06 | 5.88 |
| 5 | 10.00 | 9.53 | 9.09 | 8.70 | 8.33 | 8.00 | 7.69 | 7.41 | 7.14 | 6.90 | 6.67 | 6.45 | 6.25 | 6.06 | 5.88 |
| 6 | 10.00 | 9.52 | 9.09 | 8.69 | 8.33 | 8.00 | 7.69 | 7.41 | 7.14 | 6.89 | 6.67 | 6.45 | 6.25 | 6.06 | 5.88 |

| If the Recovery Year is: | and the Recovery Period is: | | | | | | | | | | | | | | |
|---|---|---|---|---|---|---|---|---|---|---|---|---|---|---|---|
| | 10.0 | 10.5 | 11.0 | 11.5 | 12.0 | 12.5 | 13.0 | 13.5 | 14.0 | 14.5 | 15.0 | 15.5 | 16.0 | 16.5 | 17.0 |
| | the Depreciation Rate is: | | | | | | | | | | | | | | |
| 7 | 10.00 | 9.53 | 9.09 | 8.70 | 8.34 | 8.00 | 7.69 | 7.41 | 7.14 | 6.90 | 6.66 | 6.45 | 6.25 | 6.06 | 5.88 |
| 8 | 10.00 | 9.52 | 9.09 | 8.69 | 8.33 | 8.00 | 7.70 | 7.40 | 7.14 | 6.89 | 6.67 | 6.45 | 6.25 | 6.06 | 5.88 |
| 9 | 10.00 | 9.53 | 9.09 | 8.70 | 8.34 | 8.00 | 7.69 | 7.41 | 7.15 | 6.90 | 6.66 | 6.45 | 6.25 | 6.06 | 5.88 |
| 10 | 10.00 | 9.52 | 9.09 | 8.69 | 8.33 | 8.00 | 7.70 | 7.40 | 7.14 | 6.89 | 6.67 | 6.45 | 6.25 | 6.06 | 5.88 |
| 11 | 6.25 | 9.53 | 9.10 | 8.70 | 8.34 | 8.00 | 7.69 | 7.41 | 7.15 | 6.90 | 6.66 | 6.45 | 6.25 | 6.06 | 5.88 |
| 12 | | 1.19 | 5.68 | 8.69 | 8.33 | 8.00 | 7.70 | 7.40 | 7.14 | 6.89 | 6.67 | 6.45 | 6.25 | 6.06 | 5.89 |
| 13 | | | | 1.09 | 5.21 | 8.00 | 7.69 | 7.41 | 7.15 | 6.90 | 6.66 | 6.46 | 6.25 | 6.06 | 5.88 |
| 14 | | | | | | 1.00 | 4.81 | 7.40 | 7.14 | 6.89 | 6.67 | 6.45 | 6.25 | 6.06 | 5.89 |
| 15 | | | | | | | | 0.93 | 4.47 | 6.90 | 6.66 | 6.46 | 6.25 | 6.06 | 5.88 |
| 16 | | | | | | | | | | 0.86 | 4.17 | 6.45 | 6.25 | 6.07 | 5.89 |
| 17 | | | | | | | | | | | | 0.81 | 3.91 | 6.06 | 5.88 |
| 18 | | | | | | | | | | | | | | 0.76 | 3.68 |

| If the Recovery Year is: | and the Recovery Period is: | | | | | | | | | | | | | | |
|---|---|---|---|---|---|---|---|---|---|---|---|---|---|---|---|
| | 17.5 | 18.0 | 18.5 | 19.0 | 19.5 | 20.0 | 20.5 | 21.0 | 21.5 | 22.0 | 22.5 | 23.0 | 23.5 | 24.0 | 24.5 |
| | the Depreciation Rate is: | | | | | | | | | | | | | | |
| 1 | 2.14 | 2.08 | 2.03 | 1.97 | 1.92 | 1.875 | 1.829 | 1.786 | 1.744 | 1.705 | 1.667 | 1.630 | 1.596 | 1.563 | 1.531 |
| 2 | 5.71 | 5.56 | 5.41 | 5.26 | 5.13 | 5.000 | 4.878 | 4.762 | 4.651 | 4.545 | 4.444 | 4.348 | 4.255 | 4.167 | 4.082 |
| 3 | 5.71 | 5.56 | 5.40 | 5.26 | 5.13 | 5.000 | 4.878 | 4.762 | 4.651 | 4.545 | 4.444 | 4.348 | 4.255 | 4.167 | 4.082 |
| 4 | 5.72 | 5.56 | 5.41 | 5.26 | 5.13 | 5.000 | 4.878 | 4.762 | 4.651 | 4.545 | 4.444 | 4.348 | 4.255 | 4.167 | 4.082 |
| 5 | 5.71 | 5.55 | 5.40 | 5.26 | 5.13 | 5.000 | 4.878 | 4.762 | 4.651 | 4.546 | 4.444 | 4.348 | 4.255 | 4.167 | 4.082 |
| 6 | 5.72 | 5.56 | 5.41 | 5.26 | 5.13 | 5.000 | 4.878 | 4.762 | 4.651 | 4.545 | 4.445 | 4.348 | 4.255 | 4.167 | 4.082 |
| 7 | 5.71 | 5.55 | 5.40 | 5.26 | 5.13 | 5.000 | 4.878 | 4.762 | 4.651 | 4.546 | 4.444 | 4.348 | 4.255 | 4.167 | 4.082 |
| 8 | 5.72 | 5.56 | 5.41 | 5.26 | 5.13 | 5.000 | 4.878 | 4.762 | 4.651 | 4.545 | 4.445 | 4.348 | 4.255 | 4.167 | 4.081 |
| 9 | 5.71 | 5.55 | 5.40 | 5.27 | 5.13 | 5.000 | 4.878 | 4.762 | 4.651 | 4.546 | 4.444 | 4.348 | 4.255 | 4.166 | 4.082 |
| 10 | 5.72 | 5.56 | 5.41 | 5.26 | 5.13 | 5.000 | 4.878 | 4.762 | 4.651 | 4.545 | 4.445 | 4.348 | 4.255 | 4.167 | 4.081 |

| If the Recovery Year is: | and the Recovery Period is: 17.5 | 18.0 | 18.5 | 19.0 | 19.5 | 20.0 | 20.5 | 21.0 | 21.5 | 22.0 | 22.5 | 23.0 | 23.5 | 24.0 | 24.5 |
|---|---|---|---|---|---|---|---|---|---|---|---|---|---|---|---|
| | the Depreciation Rate is: | | | | | | | | | | | | | | |
| 11 | 5.71 | 5.55 | 5.40 | 5.27 | 5.13 | 5.000 | 4.878 | 4.762 | 4.651 | 4.546 | 4.444 | 4.348 | 4.256 | 4.166 | 4.082 |
| 12 | 5.72 | 5.56 | 5.41 | 5.26 | 5.13 | 5.000 | 4.878 | 4.762 | 4.651 | 4.545 | 4.445 | 4.348 | 4.255 | 4.167 | 4.081 |
| 13 | 5.71 | 5.55 | 5.40 | 5.27 | 5.13 | 5.000 | 4.878 | 4.762 | 4.651 | 4.546 | 4.444 | 4.348 | 4.256 | 4.166 | 4.082 |
| 14 | 5.72 | 5.56 | 5.41 | 5.26 | 5.13 | 5.000 | 4.878 | 4.762 | 4.651 | 4.545 | 4.445 | 4.348 | 4.255 | 4.167 | 4.081 |
| 15 | 5.71 | 5.55 | 5.40 | 5.27 | 5.12 | 5.000 | 4.878 | 4.762 | 4.651 | 4.546 | 4.444 | 4.348 | 4.256 | 4.166 | 4.082 |
| 16 | 5.72 | 5.56 | 5.41 | 5.26 | 5.13 | 5.000 | 4.878 | 4.762 | 4.652 | 4.545 | 4.445 | 4.348 | 4.255 | 4.167 | 4.081 |
| 17 | 5.71 | 5.55 | 5.40 | 5.27 | 5.12 | 5.000 | 4.878 | 4.762 | 4.651 | 4.546 | 4.444 | 4.348 | 4.256 | 4.166 | 4.082 |
| 18 | 5.72 | 5.56 | 5.41 | 5.26 | 5.13 | 5.000 | 4.878 | 4.762 | 4.652 | 4.545 | 4.445 | 4.347 | 4.255 | 4.167 | 4.081 |
| 19 | 0.71 | 3.47 | 5.40 | 5.27 | 5.12 | 5.000 | 4.878 | 4.761 | 4.651 | 4.546 | 4.444 | 4.348 | 4.256 | 4.166 | 4.082 |
| 20 | | | 0.68 | 3.29 | 5.13 | 5.000 | 4.879 | 4.762 | 4.652 | 4.545 | 4.445 | 4.347 | 4.255 | 4.167 | 4.081 |
| 21 | | | | | 0.64 | 3.125 | 4.878 | 4.761 | 4.651 | 4.546 | 4.444 | 4.348 | 4.256 | 4.166 | 4.082 |
| 22 | | | | | | | 0.610 | 2.976 | 4.652 | 4.545 | 4.445 | 4.347 | 4.255 | 4.167 | 4.081 |
| 23 | | | | | | | | | 0.581 | 2.841 | 4.444 | 4.348 | 4.256 | 4.166 | 4.082 |
| 24 | | | | | | | | | | | 0.556 | 2.717 | 4.255 | 4.167 | 4.081 |
| 25 | | | | | | | | | | | | | 0.532 | 2.604 | 4.082 |
| 26 | | | | | | | | | | | | | | | 0.510 |

| If the Recovery Year is: | and the Recovery Period is: 25.0 | 25.5 | 26.0 | 26.5 | 27.0 | 27.5 | 28.0 | 28.5 | 29.0 | 29.5 | 30.0 | 30.5 | 31.0 | 31.5 | 32.0 |
|---|---|---|---|---|---|---|---|---|---|---|---|---|---|---|---|
| | the Depreciation Rate is: | | | | | | | | | | | | | | |
| 1 | 1.500 | 1.471 | 1.442 | 1.415 | 1.389 | 1.364 | 1.339 | 1.316 | 1.293 | 1.271 | 1.250 | 1.230 | 1.210 | 1.190 | 1.172 |
| 2 | 4.000 | 3.922 | 3.846 | 3.774 | 3.704 | 3.636 | 3.571 | 3.509 | 3.448 | 3.390 | 3.333 | 3.279 | 3.226 | 3.175 | 3.125 |
| 3 | 4.000 | 3.922 | 3.846 | 3.774 | 3.704 | 3.636 | 3.571 | 3.509 | 3.448 | 3.390 | 3.333 | 3.279 | 3.226 | 3.175 | 3.125 |
| 4 | 4.000 | 3.922 | 3.846 | 3.774 | 3.704 | 3.636 | 3.571 | 3.509 | 3.448 | 3.390 | 3.333 | 3.279 | 3.226 | 3.175 | 3.125 |
| 5 | 4.000 | 3.921 | 3.846 | 3.774 | 3.704 | 3.636 | 3.571 | 3.509 | 3.448 | 3.390 | 3.333 | 3.279 | 3.226 | 3.175 | 3.125 |
| 6 | 4.000 | 3.922 | 3.846 | 3.774 | 3.704 | 3.636 | 3.572 | 3.509 | 3.448 | 3.390 | 3.333 | 3.279 | 3.226 | 3.175 | 3.125 |

| If the Recovery Year is: | and the Recovery Period is: 25.0 | 25.5 | 26.0 | 26.5 | 27.0 | 27.5 | 28.0 | 28.5 | 29.0 | 29.5 | 30.0 | 30.5 | 31.0 | 31.5 | 32.0 |
|---|---|---|---|---|---|---|---|---|---|---|---|---|---|---|---|
| | the Depreciation Rate is: | | | | | | | | | | | | | | |
| 7 | 4.000 | 3.921 | 3.846 | 3.773 | 3.704 | 3.636 | 3.571 | 3.509 | 3.448 | 3.390 | 3.333 | 3.279 | 3.226 | 3.175 | 3.125 |
| 8 | 4.000 | 3.922 | 3.846 | 3.774 | 3.704 | 3.636 | 3.572 | 3.509 | 3.448 | 3.390 | 3.333 | 3.279 | 3.226 | 3.175 | 3.125 |
| 9 | 4.000 | 3.921 | 3.846 | 3.773 | 3.704 | 3.636 | 3.571 | 3.509 | 3.448 | 3.390 | 3.333 | 3.279 | 3.226 | 3.175 | 3.125 |
| 10 | 4.000 | 3.922 | 3.846 | 3.774 | 3.704 | 3.636 | 3.572 | 3.509 | 3.448 | 3.390 | 3.333 | 3.279 | 3.226 | 3.174 | 3.125 |
| 11 | 4.000 | 3.921 | 3.846 | 3.773 | 3.704 | 3.637 | 3.571 | 3.509 | 3.448 | 3.390 | 3.333 | 3.279 | 3.226 | 3.175 | 3.125 |
| 12 | 4.000 | 3.922 | 3.846 | 3.774 | 3.704 | 3.636 | 3.572 | 3.509 | 3.448 | 3.390 | 3.334 | 3.279 | 3.226 | 3.174 | 3.125 |
| 13 | 4.000 | 3.921 | 3.846 | 3.773 | 3.703 | 3.637 | 3.571 | 3.509 | 3.448 | 3.390 | 3.333 | 3.278 | 3.226 | 3.175 | 3.125 |
| 14 | 4.000 | 3.922 | 3.846 | 3.774 | 3.704 | 3.636 | 3.572 | 3.509 | 3.448 | 3.390 | 3.334 | 3.279 | 3.226 | 3.174 | 3.125 |
| 15 | 4.000 | 3.921 | 3.846 | 3.773 | 3.703 | 3.637 | 3.571 | 3.509 | 3.449 | 3.390 | 3.333 | 3.278 | 3.226 | 3.175 | 3.125 |
| 16 | 4.000 | 3.922 | 3.846 | 3.774 | 3.704 | 3.636 | 3.572 | 3.509 | 3.448 | 3.390 | 3.334 | 3.279 | 3.226 | 3.174 | 3.125 |
| 17 | 4.000 | 3.921 | 3.846 | 3.773 | 3.703 | 3.637 | 3.571 | 3.508 | 3.449 | 3.390 | 3.333 | 3.279 | 3.226 | 3.175 | 3.125 |
| 18 | 4.000 | 3.922 | 3.846 | 3.774 | 3.704 | 3.636 | 3.572 | 3.509 | 3.448 | 3.390 | 3.334 | 3.279 | 3.226 | 3.174 | 3.125 |
| 19 | 4.000 | 3.921 | 3.846 | 3.773 | 3.703 | 3.637 | 3.571 | 3.508 | 3.449 | 3.390 | 3.333 | 3.279 | 3.226 | 3.175 | 3.125 |
| 20 | 4.000 | 3.922 | 3.847 | 3.774 | 3.704 | 3.636 | 3.572 | 3.509 | 3.448 | 3.390 | 3.334 | 3.279 | 3.226 | 3.174 | 3.125 |
| 21 | 4.000 | 3.921 | 3.846 | 3.773 | 3.703 | 3.637 | 3.571 | 3.508 | 3.449 | 3.390 | 3.333 | 3.278 | 3.225 | 3.175 | 3.125 |
| 22 | 4.000 | 3.922 | 3.847 | 3.774 | 3.704 | 3.636 | 3.572 | 3.509 | 3.448 | 3.389 | 3.334 | 3.279 | 3.226 | 3.174 | 3.125 |
| 23 | 4.000 | 3.921 | 3.846 | 3.773 | 3.703 | 3.637 | 3.571 | 3.508 | 3.449 | 3.390 | 3.333 | 3.278 | 3.225 | 3.175 | 3.125 |
| 24 | 4.000 | 3.922 | 3.847 | 3.774 | 3.704 | 3.636 | 3.572 | 3.509 | 3.448 | 3.389 | 3.334 | 3.279 | 3.226 | 3.174 | 3.125 |
| 25 | 4.000 | 3.921 | 3.846 | 3.773 | 3.703 | 3.637 | 3.571 | 3.508 | 3.449 | 3.390 | 3.333 | 3.278 | 3.225 | 3.175 | 3.125 |
| 26 | 2.500 | 3.922 | 3.847 | 3.774 | 3.704 | 3.636 | 3.572 | 3.509 | 3.448 | 3.389 | 3.334 | 3.279 | 3.226 | 3.174 | 3.125 |
| 27 | | 0.490 | 2.404 | 3.773 | 3.703 | 3.637 | 3.571 | 3.508 | 3.449 | 3.390 | 3.333 | 3.278 | 3.225 | 3.175 | 3.125 |
| 28 | | | | 0.472 | 2.315 | 3.636 | 3.572 | 3.509 | 3.448 | 3.389 | 3.334 | 3.279 | 3.226 | 3.174 | 3.125 |
| 29 | | | | | | 0.455 | 2.232 | 3.508 | 3.449 | 3.390 | 3.333 | 3.278 | 3.225 | 3.175 | 3.125 |
| 30 | | | | | | | | 0.439 | 2.155 | 3.389 | 3.334 | 3.279 | 3.226 | 3.174 | 3.125 |
| 31 | | | | | | | | | | 0.424 | 2.083 | 3.278 | 3.225 | 3.175 | 3.125 |

| If the Recovery Year is: | and the Recovery Period is: 25.0 | 25.5 | 26.0 | 26.5 | 27.0 | 27.5 | 28.0 | 28.5 | 29.0 | 29.5 | 30.0 | 30.5 | 31.0 | 31.5 | 32.0 |
|---|---|---|---|---|---|---|---|---|---|---|---|---|---|---|---|
| | the Depreciation Rate is: | | | | | | | | | | | | | | |
| 32 | | | | | | | | | | | | 0.410 | 2.016 | 3.174 | 3.125 |
| 33 | | | | | | | | | | | | | | 0.397 | 1.953 |

| If the Recovery Year is: | and the Recovery Period is: 32.5 | 33.0 | 33.5 | 34.0 | 34.5 | 35.0 | 35.5 | 36.0 | 36.5 | 37.0 | 37.5 | 38.0 | 38.5 | 39.0 | 39.5 |
|---|---|---|---|---|---|---|---|---|---|---|---|---|---|---|---|
| | the Depreciation Rate is: | | | | | | | | | | | | | | |
| 1 | 1.154 | 1.136 | 1.119 | 1.103 | 1.087 | 1.071 | 1.056 | 1.042 | 1.027 | 1.014 | 1.000 | 0.987 | 0.974 | 0.962 | 0.949 |
| 2 | 3.077 | 3.030 | 2.985 | 2.941 | 2.899 | 2.857 | 2.817 | 2.778 | 2.740 | 2.703 | 2.667 | 2.632 | 2.597 | 2.564 | 2.532 |
| 3 | 3.077 | 3.030 | 2.985 | 2.941 | 2.899 | 2.857 | 2.817 | 2.778 | 2.740 | 2.703 | 2.667 | 2.632 | 2.597 | 2.564 | 2.532 |
| 4 | 3.077 | 3.030 | 2.985 | 2.941 | 2.899 | 2.857 | 2.817 | 2.778 | 2.740 | 2.703 | 2.667 | 2.632 | 2.597 | 2.564 | 2.532 |
| 5 | 3.077 | 3.030 | 2.985 | 2.941 | 2.899 | 2.857 | 2.817 | 2.778 | 2.740 | 2.703 | 2.667 | 2.632 | 2.597 | 2.564 | 2.532 |
| 6 | 3.077 | 3.030 | 2.985 | 2.941 | 2.898 | 2.857 | 2.817 | 2.778 | 2.740 | 2.703 | 2.667 | 2.632 | 2.597 | 2.564 | 2.532 |
| 7 | 3.077 | 3.030 | 2.985 | 2.941 | 2.899 | 2.857 | 2.817 | 2.778 | 2.740 | 2.703 | 2.667 | 2.632 | 2.597 | 2.564 | 2.532 |
| 8 | 3.077 | 3.030 | 2.985 | 2.941 | 2.898 | 2.857 | 2.817 | 2.778 | 2.740 | 2.703 | 2.667 | 2.631 | 2.597 | 2.564 | 2.532 |
| 9 | 3.077 | 3.030 | 2.985 | 2.941 | 2.899 | 2.857 | 2.817 | 2.778 | 2.740 | 2.703 | 2.667 | 2.632 | 2.597 | 2.564 | 2.532 |
| 10 | 3.077 | 3.030 | 2.985 | 2.941 | 2.898 | 2.857 | 2.817 | 2.778 | 2.740 | 2.703 | 2.667 | 2.631 | 2.598 | 2.564 | 2.532 |
| 11 | 3.077 | 3.030 | 2.985 | 2.941 | 2.899 | 2.857 | 2.817 | 2.778 | 2.740 | 2.703 | 2.667 | 2.632 | 2.597 | 2.564 | 2.532 |
| 12 | 3.077 | 3.030 | 2.985 | 2.941 | 2.898 | 2.857 | 2.817 | 2.778 | 2.740 | 2.703 | 2.667 | 2.631 | 2.598 | 2.564 | 2.532 |
| 13 | 3.077 | 3.030 | 2.985 | 2.941 | 2.899 | 2.857 | 2.817 | 2.778 | 2.740 | 2.703 | 2.667 | 2.632 | 2.597 | 2.564 | 2.532 |
| 14 | 3.077 | 3.030 | 2.985 | 2.941 | 2.898 | 2.857 | 2.817 | 2.778 | 2.740 | 2.703 | 2.667 | 2.631 | 2.598 | 2.564 | 2.532 |
| 15 | 3.077 | 3.031 | 2.985 | 2.941 | 2.899 | 2.857 | 2.817 | 2.778 | 2.740 | 2.703 | 2.666 | 2.632 | 2.597 | 2.564 | 2.531 |
| 16 | 3.077 | 3.030 | 2.985 | 2.941 | 2.898 | 2.857 | 2.817 | 2.778 | 2.740 | 2.702 | 2.667 | 2.631 | 2.598 | 2.564 | 2.532 |
| 17 | 3.077 | 3.031 | 2.985 | 2.941 | 2.899 | 2.857 | 2.817 | 2.778 | 2.740 | 2.703 | 2.666 | 2.632 | 2.597 | 2.564 | 2.531 |
| 18 | 3.077 | 3.030 | 2.985 | 2.941 | 2.898 | 2.857 | 2.817 | 2.778 | 2.740 | 2.702 | 2.667 | 2.631 | 2.598 | 2.564 | 2.532 |
| 19 | 3.077 | 3.031 | 2.985 | 2.941 | 2.899 | 2.857 | 2.817 | 2.778 | 2.740 | 2.703 | 2.666 | 2.632 | 2.597 | 2.564 | 2.531 |
| 20 | 3.077 | 3.030 | 2.985 | 2.941 | 2.898 | 2.857 | 2.817 | 2.778 | 2.739 | 2.702 | 2.667 | 2.631 | 2.598 | 2.564 | 2.532 |

| If the Recovery Year is: | and the Recovery Period is: 32.5 | 33.0 | 33.5 | 34.0 | 34.5 | 35.0 | 35.5 | 36.0 | 36.5 | 37.0 | 37.5 | 38.0 | 38.5 | 39.0 | 39.5 |
|---|---|---|---|---|---|---|---|---|---|---|---|---|---|---|---|
| | the Depreciation Rate is: | | | | | | | | | | | | | | |
| 21 | 3.077 | 3.031 | 2.985 | 2.941 | 2.899 | 2.857 | 2.817 | 2.778 | 2.740 | 2.703 | 2.666 | 2.632 | 2.597 | 2.564 | 2.531 |
| 22 | 3.077 | 3.030 | 2.985 | 2.941 | 2.898 | 2.857 | 2.817 | 2.777 | 2.739 | 2.702 | 2.667 | 2.631 | 2.598 | 2.564 | 2.532 |
| 23 | 3.077 | 3.031 | 2.985 | 2.941 | 2.899 | 2.857 | 2.817 | 2.778 | 2.740 | 2.703 | 2.666 | 2.632 | 2.597 | 2.564 | 2.531 |
| 24 | 3.077 | 3.030 | 2.985 | 2.942 | 2.898 | 2.857 | 2.817 | 2.777 | 2.739 | 2.702 | 2.667 | 2.631 | 2.598 | 2.564 | 2.532 |
| 25 | 3.077 | 3.031 | 2.985 | 2.941 | 2.899 | 2.857 | 2.817 | 2.778 | 2.740 | 2.703 | 2.666 | 2.632 | 2.597 | 2.564 | 2.531 |
| 26 | 3.077 | 3.030 | 2.985 | 2.942 | 2.898 | 2.858 | 2.817 | 2.777 | 2.739 | 2.702 | 2.667 | 2.631 | 2.598 | 2.564 | 2.532 |
| 27 | 3.077 | 3.031 | 2.985 | 2.941 | 2.899 | 2.857 | 2.817 | 2.778 | 2.740 | 2.703 | 2.666 | 2.632 | 2.597 | 2.564 | 2.531 |
| 28 | 3.077 | 3.030 | 2.985 | 2.942 | 2.898 | 2.858 | 2.817 | 2.777 | 2.739 | 2.702 | 2.667 | 2.631 | 2.598 | 2.564 | 2.532 |
| 29 | 3.076 | 3.031 | 2.985 | 2.941 | 2.899 | 2.857 | 2.817 | 2.778 | 2.740 | 2.703 | 2.666 | 2.632 | 2.597 | 2.564 | 2.531 |
| 30 | 3.077 | 3.030 | 2.986 | 2.942 | 2.898 | 2.858 | 2.817 | 2.777 | 2.739 | 2.702 | 2.667 | 2.631 | 2.598 | 2.564 | 2.532 |
| 31 | 3.076 | 3.031 | 2.985 | 2.941 | 2.899 | 2.857 | 2.816 | 2.778 | 2.740 | 2.703 | 2.666 | 2.632 | 2.597 | 2.564 | 2.531 |
| 32 | 3.077 | 3.030 | 2.986 | 2.942 | 2.898 | 2.858 | 2.817 | 2.777 | 2.739 | 2.702 | 2.667 | 2.631 | 2.598 | 2.564 | 2.532 |
| 33 | 3.076 | 3.031 | 2.985 | 2.941 | 2.899 | 2.857 | 2.816 | 2.778 | 2.740 | 2.703 | 2.666 | 2.632 | 2.597 | 2.564 | 2.531 |
| 34 | 0.385 | 1.894 | 2.986 | 2.942 | 2.898 | 2.858 | 2.817 | 2.777 | 2.739 | 2.702 | 2.667 | 2.631 | 2.598 | 2.565 | 2.532 |
| 35 | | | 0.373 | 1.838 | 2.899 | 2.857 | 2.816 | 2.778 | 2.740 | 2.703 | 2.666 | 2.632 | 2.597 | 2.564 | 2.531 |
| 36 | | | | | 0.362 | 1.786 | 2.817 | 2.777 | 2.739 | 2.702 | 2.667 | 2.631 | 2.598 | 2.565 | 2.532 |
| 37 | | | | | | | 0.352 | 1.736 | 2.740 | 2.703 | 2.666 | 2.632 | 2.597 | 2.564 | 2.531 |
| 38 | | | | | | | | | 0.342 | 1.689 | 2.667 | 2.631 | 2.598 | 2.565 | 2.532 |
| 39 | | | | | | | | | | | 0.333 | 1.645 | 2.597 | 2.564 | 2.531 |
| 40 | | | | | | | | | | | | | 0.325 | 1.603 | 2.532 |
| 41 | | | | | | | | | | | | | | | 0.316 |

| If the Recovery Year is: | and the Recovery Period is: | | | | | | | | | | | | | | |
|---|---|---|---|---|---|---|---|---|---|---|---|---|---|---|---|
| | 40.0 | 40.5 | 41.0 | 41.5 | 42.0 | 42.5 | 43.0 | 43.5 | 44.0 | 44.5 | 45.0 | 45.5 | 46.0 | 46.5 | 47.0 |
| | the Depreciation Rate is: | | | | | | | | | | | | | | |
| 1 | 0.938 | 0.926 | 0.915 | 0.904 | 0.893 | 0.882 | 0.872 | 0.862 | 0.852 | 0.843 | 0.833 | 0.824 | 0.815 | 0.806 | 0.798 |
| 2 | 2.500 | 2.469 | 2.439 | 2.410 | 2.381 | 2.353 | 2.326 | 2.299 | 2.273 | 2.247 | 2.222 | 2.198 | 2.174 | 2.151 | 2.128 |
| 3 | 2.500 | 2.469 | 2.439 | 2.410 | 2.381 | 2.353 | 2.326 | 2.299 | 2.273 | 2.247 | 2.222 | 2.198 | 2.174 | 2.151 | 2.128 |
| 4 | 2.500 | 2.469 | 2.439 | 2.410 | 2.381 | 2.353 | 2.326 | 2.299 | 2.273 | 2.247 | 2.222 | 2.198 | 2.174 | 2.151 | 2.128 |
| 5 | 2.500 | 2.469 | 2.439 | 2.410 | 2.381 | 2.353 | 2.326 | 2.299 | 2.273 | 2.247 | 2.222 | 2.198 | 2.174 | 2.151 | 2.128 |
| 6 | 2.500 | 2.469 | 2.439 | 2.410 | 2.381 | 2.353 | 2.326 | 2.299 | 2.273 | 2.247 | 2.222 | 2.198 | 2.174 | 2.151 | 2.128 |
| 7 | 2.500 | 2.469 | 2.439 | 2.410 | 2.381 | 2.353 | 2.326 | 2.299 | 2.273 | 2.247 | 2.222 | 2.198 | 2.174 | 2.150 | 2.128 |
| 8 | 2.500 | 2.469 | 2.439 | 2.410 | 2.381 | 2.353 | 2.326 | 2.299 | 2.273 | 2.247 | 2.222 | 2.198 | 2.174 | 2.151 | 2.128 |
| 9 | 2.500 | 2.469 | 2.439 | 2.410 | 2.381 | 2.353 | 2.326 | 2.299 | 2.273 | 2.247 | 2.222 | 2.198 | 2.174 | 2.150 | 2.128 |
| 10 | 2.500 | 2.469 | 2.439 | 2.410 | 2.381 | 2.353 | 2.325 | 2.299 | 2.273 | 2.247 | 2.222 | 2.198 | 2.174 | 2.151 | 2.128 |
| 11 | 2.500 | 2.469 | 2.439 | 2.410 | 2.381 | 2.353 | 2.326 | 2.299 | 2.273 | 2.247 | 2.222 | 2.198 | 2.174 | 2.150 | 2.128 |
| 12 | 2.500 | 2.469 | 2.439 | 2.410 | 2.381 | 2.353 | 2.325 | 2.299 | 2.273 | 2.247 | 2.222 | 2.198 | 2.174 | 2.151 | 2.128 |
| 13 | 2.500 | 2.469 | 2.439 | 2.409 | 2.381 | 2.353 | 2.326 | 2.299 | 2.273 | 2.247 | 2.222 | 2.198 | 2.174 | 2.150 | 2.128 |
| 14 | 2.500 | 2.469 | 2.439 | 2.410 | 2.381 | 2.353 | 2.325 | 2.299 | 2.273 | 2.247 | 2.222 | 2.198 | 2.174 | 2.151 | 2.128 |
| 15 | 2.500 | 2.469 | 2.439 | 2.409 | 2.381 | 2.353 | 2.326 | 2.299 | 2.273 | 2.247 | 2.222 | 2.198 | 2.174 | 2.150 | 2.128 |
| 16 | 2.500 | 2.469 | 2.439 | 2.410 | 2.381 | 2.353 | 2.325 | 2.299 | 2.273 | 2.247 | 2.222 | 2.198 | 2.174 | 2.151 | 2.128 |
| 17 | 2.500 | 2.469 | 2.439 | 2.409 | 2.381 | 2.353 | 2.326 | 2.299 | 2.273 | 2.247 | 2.222 | 2.198 | 2.174 | 2.150 | 2.127 |
| 18 | 2.500 | 2.469 | 2.439 | 2.410 | 2.381 | 2.353 | 2.325 | 2.299 | 2.273 | 2.247 | 2.222 | 2.198 | 2.174 | 2.151 | 2.128 |
| 19 | 2.500 | 2.469 | 2.439 | 2.409 | 2.381 | 2.353 | 2.326 | 2.299 | 2.273 | 2.247 | 2.222 | 2.198 | 2.174 | 2.150 | 2.127 |
| 20 | 2.500 | 2.469 | 2.439 | 2.410 | 2.381 | 2.353 | 2.325 | 2.299 | 2.273 | 2.247 | 2.222 | 2.198 | 2.174 | 2.151 | 2.128 |
| 21 | 2.500 | 2.469 | 2.439 | 2.409 | 2.381 | 2.353 | 2.326 | 2.299 | 2.273 | 2.247 | 2.222 | 2.198 | 2.174 | 2.150 | 2.127 |
| 22 | 2.500 | 2.469 | 2.439 | 2.410 | 2.381 | 2.353 | 2.325 | 2.299 | 2.273 | 2.247 | 2.222 | 2.198 | 2.174 | 2.151 | 2.128 |
| 23 | 2.500 | 2.469 | 2.439 | 2.409 | 2.381 | 2.353 | 2.326 | 2.299 | 2.272 | 2.247 | 2.222 | 2.198 | 2.174 | 2.150 | 2.127 |
| 24 | 2.500 | 2.469 | 2.439 | 2.410 | 2.381 | 2.353 | 2.325 | 2.299 | 2.273 | 2.247 | 2.222 | 2.198 | 2.174 | 2.151 | 2.128 |
| 25 | 2.500 | 2.469 | 2.439 | 2.409 | 2.381 | 2.353 | 2.326 | 2.299 | 2.272 | 2.247 | 2.222 | 2.198 | 2.174 | 2.150 | 2.127 |
| 26 | 2.500 | 2.469 | 2.439 | 2.410 | 2.381 | 2.353 | 2.325 | 2.299 | 2.273 | 2.247 | 2.222 | 2.198 | 2.174 | 2.151 | 2.128 |

| If the Recovery Year is: | and the Recovery Period is: 40.0 | 40.5 | 41.0 | 41.5 | 42.0 | 42.5 | 43.0 | 43.5 | 44.0 | 44.5 | 45.0 | 45.5 | 46.0 | 46.5 | 47.0 |
|---|---|---|---|---|---|---|---|---|---|---|---|---|---|---|---|
| | the Depreciation Rate is: | | | | | | | | | | | | | | |
| 27 | 2.500 | 2.469 | 2.439 | 2.409 | 2.381 | 2.353 | 2.326 | 2.299 | 2.272 | 2.247 | 2.223 | 2.198 | 2.174 | 2.150 | 2.127 |
| 28 | 2.500 | 2.469 | 2.439 | 2.410 | 2.381 | 2.353 | 2.325 | 2.299 | 2.273 | 2.247 | 2.222 | 2.198 | 2.174 | 2.151 | 2.128 |
| 29 | 2.500 | 2.469 | 2.439 | 2.409 | 2.381 | 2.353 | 2.326 | 2.299 | 2.272 | 2.247 | 2.223 | 2.198 | 2.174 | 2.150 | 2.127 |
| 30 | 2.500 | 2.469 | 2.439 | 2.410 | 2.381 | 2.353 | 2.325 | 2.299 | 2.273 | 2.248 | 2.222 | 2.197 | 2.174 | 2.151 | 2.128 |
| 31 | 2.500 | 2.469 | 2.439 | 2.409 | 2.381 | 2.353 | 2.326 | 2.299 | 2.272 | 2.247 | 2.223 | 2.198 | 2.174 | 2.150 | 2.127 |
| 32 | 2.500 | 2.470 | 2.439 | 2.410 | 2.381 | 2.353 | 2.325 | 2.299 | 2.273 | 2.248 | 2.222 | 2.197 | 2.174 | 2.151 | 2.128 |
| 33 | 2.500 | 2.469 | 2.439 | 2.409 | 2.381 | 2.353 | 2.326 | 2.298 | 2.272 | 2.247 | 2.223 | 2.198 | 2.174 | 2.150 | 2.127 |
| 34 | 2.500 | 2.470 | 2.439 | 2.410 | 2.381 | 2.353 | 2.325 | 2.299 | 2.273 | 2.248 | 2.222 | 2.197 | 2.174 | 2.151 | 2.128 |
| 35 | 2.500 | 2.469 | 2.439 | 2.409 | 2.381 | 2.353 | 2.326 | 2.298 | 2.272 | 2.247 | 2.223 | 2.198 | 2.174 | 2.150 | 2.127 |
| 36 | 2.500 | 2.470 | 2.439 | 2.410 | 2.381 | 2.353 | 2.325 | 2.299 | 2.273 | 2.248 | 2.222 | 2.197 | 2.174 | 2.151 | 2.128 |
| 37 | 2.500 | 2.469 | 2.439 | 2.409 | 2.381 | 2.353 | 2.326 | 2.298 | 2.272 | 2.247 | 2.223 | 2.198 | 2.174 | 2.150 | 2.127 |
| 38 | 2.500 | 2.470 | 2.439 | 2.410 | 2.381 | 2.353 | 2.325 | 2.299 | 2.273 | 2.248 | 2.222 | 2.197 | 2.174 | 2.151 | 2.128 |
| 39 | 2.500 | 2.469 | 2.439 | 2.409 | 2.381 | 2.353 | 2.326 | 2.298 | 2.272 | 2.247 | 2.223 | 2.198 | 2.174 | 2.150 | 2.127 |
| 40 | 2.500 | 2.470 | 2.439 | 2.410 | 2.380 | 2.352 | 2.325 | 2.299 | 2.273 | 2.248 | 2.222 | 2.197 | 2.174 | 2.151 | 2.128 |
| 41 | 1.562 | 2.469 | 2.439 | 2.409 | 2.381 | 2.353 | 2.326 | 2.298 | 2.272 | 2.247 | 2.223 | 2.198 | 2.173 | 2.150 | 2.127 |
| 42 | | 0.309 | 1.525 | 2.410 | 2.380 | 2.352 | 2.325 | 2.299 | 2.273 | 2.248 | 2.222 | 2.197 | 2.174 | 2.151 | 2.128 |
| 43 | | | | 0.301 | 1.488 | 2.353 | 2.326 | 2.298 | 2.272 | 2.247 | 2.223 | 2.198 | 2.173 | 2.150 | 2.127 |
| 44 | | | | | | 0.294 | 1.453 | 2.299 | 2.273 | 2.248 | 2.222 | 2.197 | 2.174 | 2.151 | 2.128 |
| 45 | | | | | | | | 0.287 | 1.420 | 2.247 | 2.223 | 2.198 | 2.173 | 2.150 | 2.127 |
| 46 | | | | | | | | | | 0.281 | 1.389 | 2.197 | 2.174 | 2.151 | 2.128 |
| 47 | | | | | | | | | | | | 0.275 | 1.358 | 2.150 | 2.127 |
| 48 | | | | | | | | | | | | | | 0.269 | 1.330 |

| If the Recovery Year is: | and the Recovery Period is: 47.5 | 48.0 | 48.5 | 49.0 | 49.5 | 50.0 |
|---|---|---|---|---|---|---|
| | the Depreciation Rate is: | | | | | |
| 1 | 0.789 | 0.781 | 0.773 | 0.765 | 0.758 | 0.750 |
| 2 | 2.105 | 2.083 | 2.062 | 2.041 | 2.020 | 2.000 |
| 3 | 2.105 | 2.083 | 2.062 | 2.041 | 2.020 | 2.000 |
| 4 | 2.105 | 2.083 | 2.062 | 2.041 | 2.020 | 2.000 |
| 5 | 2.105 | 2.083 | 2.062 | 2.041 | 2.020 | 2.000 |
| 6 | 2.105 | 2.083 | 2.062 | 2.041 | 2.020 | 2.000 |
| 7 | 2.105 | 2.083 | 2.062 | 2.041 | 2.020 | 2.000 |
| 8 | 2.105 | 2.083 | 2.062 | 2.041 | 2.020 | 2.000 |
| 9 | 2.105 | 2.083 | 2.062 | 2.041 | 2.020 | 2.000 |
| 10 | 2.105 | 2.083 | 2.062 | 2.041 | 2.020 | 2.000 |
| 11 | 2.105 | 2.083 | 2.062 | 2.041 | 2.020 | 2.000 |
| 12 | 2.105 | 2.083 | 2.062 | 2.041 | 2.020 | 2.000 |
| 13 | 2.105 | 2.083 | 2.062 | 2.041 | 2.020 | 2.000 |
| 14 | 2.105 | 2.083 | 2.062 | 2.041 | 2.020 | 2.000 |
| 15 | 2.105 | 2.083 | 2.062 | 2.041 | 2.020 | 2.000 |
| 16 | 2.105 | 2.083 | 2.062 | 2.041 | 2.020 | 2.000 |
| 17 | 2.105 | 2.083 | 2.062 | 2.041 | 2.020 | 2.000 |
| 18 | 2.105 | 2.084 | 2.062 | 2.041 | 2.020 | 2.000 |
| 19 | 2.105 | 2.083 | 2.062 | 2.041 | 2.020 | 2.000 |
| 20 | 2.105 | 2.084 | 2.062 | 2.041 | 2.020 | 2.000 |
| 21 | 2.105 | 2.083 | 2.062 | 2.041 | 2.020 | 2.000 |
| 22 | 2.105 | 2.084 | 2.062 | 2.041 | 2.020 | 2.000 |
| 23 | 2.105 | 2.083 | 2.062 | 2.041 | 2.020 | 2.000 |
| 24 | 2.106 | 2.084 | 2.062 | 2.041 | 2.020 | 2.000 |
| 25 | 2.105 | 2.083 | 2.062 | 2.041 | 2.020 | 2.000 |
| 26 | 2.106 | 2.084 | 2.062 | 2.041 | 2.020 | 2.000 |

| If the Recovery Year is: | and the Recovery Period is: 47.5 | 48.0 | 48.5 | 49.0 | 49.5 | 50.0 |
|---|---|---|---|---|---|---|
| | the Depreciation Rate is: | | | | | |
| 27 | 2.105 | 2.083 | 2.062 | 2.041 | 2.020 | 2.000 |
| 28 | 2.106 | 2.084 | 2.062 | 2.041 | 2.020 | 2.000 |
| 29 | 2.105 | 2.083 | 2.062 | 2.041 | 2.020 | 2.000 |
| 30 | 2.106 | 2.084 | 2.062 | 2.041 | 2.020 | 2.000 |
| 31 | 2.105 | 2.083 | 2.062 | 2.041 | 2.020 | 2.000 |
| 32 | 2.106 | 2.084 | 2.062 | 2.041 | 2.020 | 2.000 |
| 33 | 2.105 | 2.083 | 2.062 | 2.041 | 2.021 | 2.000 |
| 34 | 2.106 | 2.084 | 2.062 | 2.040 | 2.020 | 2.000 |
| 35 | 2.105 | 2.083 | 2.062 | 2.041 | 2.021 | 2.000 |
| 36 | 2.106 | 2.084 | 2.062 | 2.040 | 2.020 | 2.000 |
| 37 | 2.105 | 2.083 | 2.061 | 2.041 | 2.021 | 2.000 |
| 38 | 2.106 | 2.084 | 2.062 | 2.040 | 2.020 | 2.000 |
| 39 | 2.105 | 2.083 | 2.061 | 2.041 | 2.021 | 2.000 |
| 40 | 2.106 | 2.084 | 2.062 | 2.040 | 2.020 | 2.000 |
| 41 | 2.105 | 2.083 | 2.061 | 2.041 | 2.021 | 2.000 |
| 42 | 2.106 | 2.084 | 2.062 | 2.040 | 2.020 | 2.000 |
| 43 | 2.105 | 2.083 | 2.061 | 2.041 | 2.021 | 2.000 |
| 44 | 2.106 | 2.084 | 2.062 | 2.040 | 2.020 | 2.000 |
| 45 | 2.105 | 2.083 | 2.061 | 2.041 | 2.021 | 2.000 |
| 46 | 2.106 | 2.084 | 2.062 | 2.040 | 2.020 | 2.000 |
| 47 | 2.105 | 2.083 | 2.061 | 2.041 | 2.021 | 2.000 |
| 48 | 2.106 | 2.084 | 2.062 | 2.040 | 2.020 | 2.000 |
| 49 | 0.263 | 1.302 | 2.061 | 2.041 | 2.021 | 2.000 |
| 50 | | | 0.258 | 1.275 | 2.020 | 2.000 |
| 51 | | | | | 0.253 | 1.250 |

TABLE 12
General and Alternative Depreciation Systems
Applicable Depreciation Method: Straight Line
Applicable Recovery Periods: 2.5 — 50 years
Applicable Convention: Mid-quarter (property placed in service in fourth quarter)

| If the Recovery Year is: | and the Recovery Period is: 2.5 | 3.0 | 3.5 | 4.0 | 4.5 | 5.0 | 5.5 | 6.0 | 6.5 | 7.0 | 7.5 | 8.0 | 8.5 | 9.0 | 9.5 |
|---|---|---|---|---|---|---|---|---|---|---|---|---|---|---|---|
| | the Depreciation Rate is: | | | | | | | | | | | | | | |
| 1 | 5.00 | 4.17 | 3.57 | 3.13 | 2.78 | 2.50 | 2.27 | 2.08 | 1.92 | 1.79 | 1.67 | 1.56 | 1.47 | 1.39 | 1.32 |
| 2 | 40.00 | 33.33 | 28.57 | 25.00 | 22.22 | 20.00 | 18.18 | 16.67 | 15.39 | 14.29 | 13.33 | 12.50 | 11.76 | 11.11 | 10.53 |
| 3 | 40.00 | 33.33 | 28.57 | 25.00 | 22.22 | 20.00 | 18.18 | 16.67 | 15.38 | 14.28 | 13.33 | 12.50 | 11.77 | 11.11 | 10.53 |
| 4 | 15.00 | 29.17 | 28.57 | 25.00 | 22.22 | 20.00 | 18.18 | 16.67 | 15.39 | 14.29 | 13.33 | 12.50 | 11.76 | 11.11 | 10.52 |
| 5 | | | 10.72 | 21.87 | 22.23 | 20.00 | 18.19 | 16.66 | 15.38 | 14.28 | 13.33 | 12.50 | 11.77 | 11.11 | 10.53 |
| 6 | | | | | 8.33 | 17.50 | 18.18 | 16.67 | 15.39 | 14.29 | 13.34 | 12.50 | 11.76 | 11.11 | 10.52 |
| 7 | | | | | | | 6.82 | 14.58 | 15.38 | 14.28 | 13.33 | 12.50 | 11.77 | 11.11 | 10.53 |
| 8 | | | | | | | | | 5.77 | 12.50 | 13.34 | 12.50 | 11.76 | 11.11 | 10.52 |
| 9 | | | | | | | | | | | 5.00 | 10.94 | 11.77 | 11.11 | 10.53 |
| 10 | | | | | | | | | | | | | 4.41 | 9.73 | 10.52 |
| 11 | | | | | | | | | | | | | | | 3.95 |

| If the Recovery Year is: | and the Recovery Period is: 10.0 | 10.5 | 11.0 | 11.5 | 12.0 | 12.5 | 13.0 | 13.5 | 14.0 | 14.5 | 15.0 | 15.5 | 16.0 | 16.5 | 17.0 |
|---|---|---|---|---|---|---|---|---|---|---|---|---|---|---|---|
| | the Depreciation Rate is: | | | | | | | | | | | | | | |
| 1 | 1.25 | 1.19 | 1.14 | 1.09 | 1.04 | 1.00 | 0.96 | 0.93 | 0.89 | 0.86 | 0.83 | 0.81 | 0.78 | 0.76 | 0.74 |
| 2 | 10.00 | 9.52 | 9.09 | 8.70 | 8.33 | 8.00 | 7.69 | 7.41 | 7.14 | 6.90 | 6.67 | 6.45 | 6.25 | 6.06 | 5.88 |
| 3 | 10.00 | 9.52 | 9.09 | 8.69 | 8.33 | 8.00 | 7.69 | 7.41 | 7.14 | 6.90 | 6.67 | 6.45 | 6.25 | 6.06 | 5.88 |
| 4 | 10.00 | 9.52 | 9.09 | 8.70 | 8.33 | 8.00 | 7.69 | 7.41 | 7.14 | 6.90 | 6.67 | 6.45 | 6.25 | 6.06 | 5.88 |
| 5 | 10.00 | 9.53 | 9.09 | 8.69 | 8.33 | 8.00 | 7.69 | 7.41 | 7.14 | 6.90 | 6.67 | 6.45 | 6.25 | 6.06 | 5.88 |

| If the Recovery Year is: | and the Recovery Period is: 10.0 | 10.5 | 11.0 | 11.5 | 12.0 | 12.5 | 13.0 | 13.5 | 14.0 | 14.5 | 15.0 | 15.5 | 16.0 | 16.5 | 17.0 |
|---|---|---|---|---|---|---|---|---|---|---|---|---|---|---|---|
| | the Depreciation Rate is: | | | | | | | | | | | | | | |
| 6 | 10.00 | 9.52 | 9.09 | 8.70 | 8.34 | 8.00 | 7.69 | 7.41 | 7.14 | 6.90 | 6.67 | 6.45 | 6.25 | 6.06 | 5.88 |
| 7 | 10.00 | 9.53 | 9.09 | 8.69 | 8.33 | 8.00 | 7.69 | 7.41 | 7.14 | 6.89 | 6.67 | 6.45 | 6.25 | 6.06 | 5.88 |
| 8 | 10.00 | 9.52 | 9.09 | 8.70 | 8.34 | 8.00 | 7.69 | 7.40 | 7.15 | 6.90 | 6.66 | 6.45 | 6.25 | 6.06 | 5.88 |
| 9 | 10.00 | 9.53 | 9.09 | 8.69 | 8.33 | 8.00 | 7.70 | 7.41 | 7.14 | 6.89 | 6.67 | 6.45 | 6.25 | 6.06 | 5.88 |
| 10 | 10.00 | 9.52 | 9.09 | 8.70 | 8.34 | 8.00 | 7.69 | 7.40 | 7.15 | 6.90 | 6.66 | 6.45 | 6.25 | 6.06 | 5.88 |
| 11 | 8.75 | 9.53 | 9.09 | 8.69 | 8.33 | 8.00 | 7.70 | 7.41 | 7.14 | 6.89 | 6.67 | 6.45 | 6.25 | 6.06 | 5.88 |
| 12 | | 3.57 | 7.96 | 8.70 | 8.34 | 8.00 | 7.69 | 7.40 | 7.15 | 6.90 | 6.66 | 6.45 | 6.25 | 6.06 | 5.89 |
| 13 | | | | 3.26 | 7.29 | 8.00 | 7.70 | 7.41 | 7.14 | 6.89 | 6.67 | 6.45 | 6.25 | 6.06 | 5.88 |
| 14 | | | | | | 3.00 | 6.73 | 7.40 | 7.15 | 6.90 | 6.66 | 6.46 | 6.25 | 6.06 | 5.89 |
| 15 | | | | | | | | 2.78 | 6.25 | 6.89 | 6.67 | 6.45 | 6.25 | 6.06 | 5.88 |
| 16 | | | | | | | | | | 2.59 | 5.83 | 6.46 | 6.25 | 6.06 | 5.89 |
| 17 | | | | | | | | | | | | 2.42 | 5.47 | 6.07 | 5.88 |
| 18 | | | | | | | | | | | | | | 2.27 | 5.15 |

| If the Recovery Year is: | and the Recovery Period is: 17.5 | 18.0 | 18.5 | 19.0 | 19.5 | 20.0 | 20.5 | 21.0 | 21.5 | 22.0 | 22.5 | 23.0 | 23.5 | 24.0 | 24.5 |
|---|---|---|---|---|---|---|---|---|---|---|---|---|---|---|---|
| | the Depreciation Rate is: | | | | | | | | | | | | | | |
| 1 | 0.71 | 0.69 | 0.68 | 0.66 | 0.64 | 0.625 | 0.610 | 0.595 | 0.581 | 0.568 | 0.556 | 0.543 | 0.532 | 0.521 | 0.510 |
| 2 | 5.71 | 5.56 | 5.41 | 5.26 | 5.13 | 5.000 | 4.878 | 4.762 | 4.651 | 4.545 | 4.444 | 4.348 | 4.255 | 4.167 | 4.082 |
| 3 | 5.71 | 5.56 | 5.40 | 5.26 | 5.13 | 5.000 | 4.878 | 4.762 | 4.651 | 4.545 | 4.444 | 4.348 | 4.255 | 4.167 | 4.082 |
| 4 | 5.72 | 5.56 | 5.41 | 5.26 | 5.13 | 5.000 | 4.878 | 4.762 | 4.651 | 4.546 | 4.444 | 4.348 | 4.255 | 4.167 | 4.082 |
| 5 | 5.71 | 5.55 | 5.40 | 5.26 | 5.13 | 5.000 | 4.878 | 4.762 | 4.651 | 4.545 | 4.444 | 4.348 | 4.255 | 4.167 | 4.082 |
| 6 | 5.72 | 5.56 | 5.41 | 5.26 | 5.13 | 5.000 | 4.878 | 4.762 | 4.651 | 4.546 | 4.445 | 4.348 | 4.255 | 4.167 | 4.082 |
| 7 | 5.71 | 5.55 | 5.40 | 5.26 | 5.13 | 5.000 | 4.878 | 4.762 | 4.651 | 4.545 | 4.444 | 4.348 | 4.255 | 4.167 | 4.082 |
| 8 | 5.72 | 5.56 | 5.41 | 5.26 | 5.13 | 5.000 | 4.878 | 4.762 | 4.651 | 4.546 | 4.445 | 4.348 | 4.255 | 4.167 | 4.082 |
| 9 | 5.71 | 5.55 | 5.40 | 5.26 | 5.13 | 5.000 | 4.878 | 4.762 | 4.651 | 4.545 | 4.444 | 4.348 | 4.255 | 4.167 | 4.081 |

| If the Recovery Year is: | and the Recovery Period is: 17.5 | 18.0 | 18.5 | 19.0 | 19.5 | 20.0 | 20.5 | 21.0 | 21.5 | 22.0 | 22.5 | 23.0 | 23.5 | 24.0 | 24.5 |
|---|---|---|---|---|---|---|---|---|---|---|---|---|---|---|---|
| | the Depreciation Rate is: | | | | | | | | | | | | | | |
| 10 | 5.72 | 5.56 | 5.41 | 5.27 | 5.13 | 5.000 | 4.878 | 4.762 | 4.651 | 4.546 | 4.445 | 4.348 | 4.255 | 4.166 | 4.082 |
| 11 | 5.71 | 5.55 | 5.40 | 5.26 | 5.13 | 5.000 | 4.878 | 4.762 | 4.651 | 4.545 | 4.444 | 4.348 | 4.256 | 4.167 | 4.081 |
| 12 | 5.72 | 5.56 | 5.41 | 5.27 | 5.13 | 5.000 | 4.878 | 4.762 | 4.651 | 4.546 | 4.445 | 4.348 | 4.255 | 4.166 | 4.082 |
| 13 | 5.71 | 5.55 | 5.40 | 5.26 | 5.13 | 5.000 | 4.878 | 4.762 | 4.651 | 4.545 | 4.444 | 4.348 | 4.256 | 4.167 | 4.081 |
| 14 | 5.72 | 5.56 | 5.41 | 5.27 | 5.13 | 5.000 | 4.878 | 4.762 | 4.651 | 4.546 | 4.445 | 4.348 | 4.255 | 4.166 | 4.082 |
| 15 | 5.71 | 5.55 | 5.40 | 5.26 | 5.12 | 5.000 | 4.878 | 4.762 | 4.651 | 4.545 | 4.444 | 4.348 | 4.256 | 4.167 | 4.081 |
| 16 | 5.72 | 5.56 | 5.41 | 5.27 | 5.13 | 5.000 | 4.878 | 4.762 | 4.652 | 4.546 | 4.445 | 4.348 | 4.255 | 4.166 | 4.082 |
| 17 | 5.71 | 5.55 | 5.40 | 5.26 | 5.12 | 5.000 | 4.878 | 4.762 | 4.651 | 4.545 | 4.444 | 4.348 | 4.256 | 4.167 | 4.081 |
| 18 | 5.72 | 5.56 | 5.41 | 5.27 | 5.13 | 5.000 | 4.878 | 4.762 | 4.652 | 4.546 | 4.445 | 4.347 | 4.255 | 4.166 | 4.082 |
| 19 | 2.14 | 4.86 | 5.40 | 5.26 | 5.12 | 5.000 | 4.878 | 4.762 | 4.651 | 4.545 | 4.444 | 4.348 | 4.256 | 4.167 | 4.081 |
| 20 | | | 2.03 | 4.61 | 5.13 | 5.000 | 4.878 | 4.761 | 4.652 | 4.546 | 4.445 | 4.347 | 4.255 | 4.166 | 4.082 |
| 21 | | | | | 1.92 | 4.375 | 4.879 | 4.762 | 4.651 | 4.545 | 4.444 | 4.348 | 4.256 | 4.167 | 4.081 |
| 22 | | | | | | | 1.829 | 4.166 | 4.652 | 4.546 | 4.445 | 4.347 | 4.255 | 4.166 | 4.082 |
| 23 | | | | | | | | | 1.744 | 3.977 | 4.444 | 4.348 | 4.256 | 4.167 | 4.081 |
| 24 | | | | | | | | | | | 1.667 | 3.804 | 4.255 | 4.166 | 4.082 |
| 25 | | | | | | | | | | | | | 1.596 | 3.646 | 4.081 |
| 26 | | | | | | | | | | | | | | | 1.531 |

| If the Recovery Year is: | and the Recovery Period is: 25.0 | 25.5 | 26.0 | 26.5 | 27.0 | 27.5 | 28.0 | 28.5 | 29.0 | 29.5 | 30.0 | 30.5 | 31.0 | 31.5 | 32.0 |
|---|---|---|---|---|---|---|---|---|---|---|---|---|---|---|---|
| | the Depreciation Rate is: | | | | | | | | | | | | | | |
| 1 | 0.500 | 0.490 | 0.481 | 0.472 | 0.463 | 0.455 | 0.446 | 0.439 | 0.431 | 0.424 | 0.417 | 0.410 | 0.403 | 0.397 | 0.391 |
| 2 | 4.000 | 3.922 | 3.846 | 3.774 | 3.704 | 3.636 | 3.571 | 3.509 | 3.448 | 3.390 | 3.333 | 3.279 | 3.226 | 3.175 | 3.125 |
| 3 | 4.000 | 3.922 | 3.846 | 3.774 | 3.704 | 3.636 | 3.571 | 3.509 | 3.448 | 3.390 | 3.333 | 3.279 | 3.226 | 3.175 | 3.125 |
| 4 | 4.000 | 3.922 | 3.846 | 3.774 | 3.704 | 3.636 | 3.571 | 3.509 | 3.448 | 3.390 | 3.333 | 3.279 | 3.226 | 3.175 | 3.125 |
| 5 | 4.000 | 3.922 | 3.846 | 3.774 | 3.704 | 3.636 | 3.571 | 3.509 | 3.448 | 3.390 | 3.333 | 3.279 | 3.226 | 3.175 | 3.125 |

| If the Recovery Year is: | and the Recovery Period is: 25.0 | 25.5 | 26.0 | 26.5 | 27.0 | 27.5 | 28.0 | 28.5 | 29.0 | 29.5 | 30.0 | 30.5 | 31.0 | 31.5 | 32.0 |
|---|---|---|---|---|---|---|---|---|---|---|---|---|---|---|---|
| | the Depreciation Rate is: | | | | | | | | | | | | | | |
| 6 | 4.000 | 3.921 | 3.846 | 3.773 | 3.704 | 3.636 | 3.572 | 3.509 | 3.448 | 3.390 | 3.333 | 3.279 | 3.226 | 3.175 | 3.125 |
| 7 | 4.000 | 3.922 | 3.846 | 3.774 | 3.704 | 3.636 | 3.571 | 3.509 | 3.448 | 3.390 | 3.333 | 3.279 | 3.226 | 3.175 | 3.125 |
| 8 | 4.000 | 3.921 | 3.846 | 3.773 | 3.704 | 3.636 | 3.572 | 3.509 | 3.448 | 3.390 | 3.333 | 3.279 | 3.226 | 3.175 | 3.125 |
| 9 | 4.000 | 3.922 | 3.846 | 3.774 | 3.704 | 3.636 | 3.571 | 3.509 | 3.448 | 3.390 | 3.333 | 3.279 | 3.226 | 3.174 | 3.125 |
| 10 | 4.000 | 3.921 | 3.846 | 3.773 | 3.704 | 3.636 | 3.572 | 3.509 | 3.448 | 3.390 | 3.333 | 3.279 | 3.226 | 3.175 | 3.125 |
| 11 | 4.000 | 3.922 | 3.846 | 3.774 | 3.704 | 3.637 | 3.571 | 3.509 | 3.448 | 3.390 | 3.333 | 3.279 | 3.226 | 3.174 | 3.125 |
| 12 | 4.000 | 3.921 | 3.846 | 3.773 | 3.704 | 3.636 | 3.572 | 3.509 | 3.448 | 3.390 | 3.333 | 3.279 | 3.226 | 3.175 | 3.125 |
| 13 | 4.000 | 3.922 | 3.846 | 3.774 | 3.703 | 3.637 | 3.571 | 3.509 | 3.448 | 3.390 | 3.334 | 3.279 | 3.226 | 3.174 | 3.125 |
| 14 | 4.000 | 3.921 | 3.846 | 3.773 | 3.704 | 3.636 | 3.572 | 3.509 | 3.448 | 3.390 | 3.333 | 3.278 | 3.226 | 3.175 | 3.125 |
| 15 | 4.000 | 3.922 | 3.846 | 3.774 | 3.703 | 3.637 | 3.571 | 3.509 | 3.449 | 3.390 | 3.334 | 3.279 | 3.226 | 3.174 | 3.125 |
| 16 | 4.000 | 3.921 | 3.846 | 3.773 | 3.704 | 3.636 | 3.572 | 3.509 | 3.448 | 3.390 | 3.333 | 3.278 | 3.226 | 3.175 | 3.125 |
| 17 | 4.000 | 3.922 | 3.846 | 3.774 | 3.703 | 3.637 | 3.571 | 3.508 | 3.449 | 3.390 | 3.334 | 3.279 | 3.226 | 3.174 | 3.125 |
| 18 | 4.000 | 3.921 | 3.846 | 3.773 | 3.704 | 3.636 | 3.572 | 3.509 | 3.448 | 3.390 | 3.333 | 3.278 | 3.226 | 3.175 | 3.125 |
| 19 | 4.000 | 3.922 | 3.846 | 3.774 | 3.703 | 3.637 | 3.571 | 3.508 | 3.449 | 3.390 | 3.334 | 3.279 | 3.226 | 3.174 | 3.125 |
| 20 | 4.000 | 3.921 | 3.846 | 3.773 | 3.704 | 3.636 | 3.572 | 3.509 | 3.448 | 3.390 | 3.333 | 3.278 | 3.226 | 3.175 | 3.125 |
| 21 | 4.000 | 3.922 | 3.847 | 3.774 | 3.703 | 3.637 | 3.571 | 3.508 | 3.449 | 3.389 | 3.334 | 3.279 | 3.226 | 3.174 | 3.125 |
| 22 | 4.000 | 3.921 | 3.846 | 3.773 | 3.704 | 3.636 | 3.572 | 3.509 | 3.448 | 3.390 | 3.333 | 3.278 | 3.225 | 3.175 | 3.125 |
| 23 | 4.000 | 3.922 | 3.847 | 3.774 | 3.703 | 3.637 | 3.571 | 3.508 | 3.449 | 3.389 | 3.334 | 3.279 | 3.226 | 3.174 | 3.125 |
| 24 | 4.000 | 3.921 | 3.846 | 3.773 | 3.704 | 3.636 | 3.572 | 3.509 | 3.448 | 3.390 | 3.333 | 3.278 | 3.225 | 3.175 | 3.125 |
| 25 | 4.000 | 3.922 | 3.847 | 3.774 | 3.703 | 3.637 | 3.571 | 3.508 | 3.449 | 3.389 | 3.334 | 3.279 | 3.226 | 3.174 | 3.125 |
| 26 | 3.500 | 3.921 | 3.846 | 3.773 | 3.704 | 3.636 | 3.572 | 3.509 | 3.448 | 3.390 | 3.333 | 3.278 | 3.225 | 3.175 | 3.125 |
| 27 | | 1.471 | 3.366 | 3.774 | 3.703 | 3.637 | 3.571 | 3.508 | 3.449 | 3.389 | 3.334 | 3.279 | 3.226 | 3.174 | 3.125 |
| 28 | | | | 1.415 | 3.241 | 3.636 | 3.572 | 3.509 | 3.448 | 3.390 | 3.333 | 3.278 | 3.225 | 3.175 | 3.125 |
| 29 | | | | | | 1.364 | 3.125 | 3.508 | 3.449 | 3.389 | 3.334 | 3.279 | 3.226 | 3.174 | 3.125 |
| 30 | | | | | | | | 1.316 | 3.017 | 3.390 | 3.333 | 3.278 | 3.225 | 3.175 | 3.125 |
| 31 | | | | | | | | | | 1.271 | 2.917 | 3.279 | 3.226 | 3.174 | 3.125 |

| If the Recovery Year is: | and the Recovery Period is: 25.0 | 25.5 | 26.0 | 26.5 | 27.0 | 27.5 | 28.0 | 28.5 | 29.0 | 29.5 | 30.0 | 30.5 | 31.0 | 31.5 | 32.0 |
|---|---|---|---|---|---|---|---|---|---|---|---|---|---|---|---|
| | the Depreciation Rate is: | | | | | | | | | | | | | | |
| 32 | | | | | | | | | | | | 1.229 | 2.822 | 3.175 | 3.125 |
| 33 | | | | | | | | | | | | | | 1.190 | 2.734 |

| If the Recovery Year is: | and the Recovery Period is: 32.5 | 33.0 | 33.5 | 34.0 | 34.5 | 35.0 | 35.5 | 36.0 | 36.5 | 37.0 | 37.5 | 38.0 | 38.5 | 39.0 | 39.5 |
|---|---|---|---|---|---|---|---|---|---|---|---|---|---|---|---|
| | the Depreciation Rate is: | | | | | | | | | | | | | | |
| 1 | 0.385 | 0.379 | 0.373 | 0.368 | 0.362 | 0.357 | 0.352 | 0.347 | 0.342 | 0.338 | 0.333 | 0.329 | 0.325 | 0.321 | 0.316 |
| 2 | 3.077 | 3.030 | 2.985 | 2.941 | 2.899 | 2.857 | 2.817 | 2.778 | 2.740 | 2.703 | 2.667 | 2.632 | 2.597 | 2.564 | 2.532 |
| 3 | 3.077 | 3.030 | 2.985 | 2.941 | 2.899 | 2.857 | 2.817 | 2.778 | 2.740 | 2.703 | 2.667 | 2.632 | 2.597 | 2.564 | 2.532 |
| 4 | 3.077 | 3.030 | 2.985 | 2.941 | 2.899 | 2.857 | 2.817 | 2.778 | 2.740 | 2.703 | 2.667 | 2.632 | 2.597 | 2.564 | 2.532 |
| 5 | 3.077 | 3.030 | 2.985 | 2.941 | 2.899 | 2.857 | 2.817 | 2.778 | 2.740 | 2.703 | 2.667 | 2.632 | 2.597 | 2.564 | 2.532 |
| 6 | 3.077 | 3.030 | 2.985 | 2.941 | 2.899 | 2.857 | 2.817 | 2.778 | 2.740 | 2.703 | 2.667 | 2.632 | 2.597 | 2.564 | 2.532 |
| 7 | 3.077 | 3.030 | 2.985 | 2.941 | 2.898 | 2.857 | 2.817 | 2.778 | 2.740 | 2.703 | 2.667 | 2.632 | 2.597 | 2.564 | 2.532 |
| 8 | 3.077 | 3.030 | 2.985 | 2.941 | 2.899 | 2.857 | 2.817 | 2.778 | 2.740 | 2.703 | 2.667 | 2.631 | 2.597 | 2.564 | 2.532 |
| 9 | 3.077 | 3.030 | 2.985 | 2.941 | 2.898 | 2.857 | 2.817 | 2.778 | 2.740 | 2.703 | 2.667 | 2.632 | 2.597 | 2.564 | 2.532 |
| 10 | 3.077 | 3.030 | 2.985 | 2.941 | 2.899 | 2.857 | 2.817 | 2.778 | 2.740 | 2.703 | 2.667 | 2.631 | 2.597 | 2.564 | 2.532 |
| 11 | 3.077 | 3.030 | 2.985 | 2.941 | 2.898 | 2.857 | 2.817 | 2.778 | 2.740 | 2.703 | 2.667 | 2.632 | 2.598 | 2.564 | 2.532 |
| 12 | 3.077 | 3.030 | 2.985 | 2.941 | 2.899 | 2.857 | 2.817 | 2.778 | 2.740 | 2.703 | 2.667 | 2.631 | 2.597 | 2.564 | 2.532 |
| 13 | 3.077 | 3.030 | 2.985 | 2.941 | 2.898 | 2.857 | 2.817 | 2.778 | 2.740 | 2.703 | 2.667 | 2.632 | 2.598 | 2.564 | 2.532 |
| 14 | 3.077 | 3.030 | 2.985 | 2.941 | 2.899 | 2.857 | 2.817 | 2.778 | 2.740 | 2.703 | 2.667 | 2.631 | 2.597 | 2.564 | 2.532 |
| 15 | 3.077 | 3.030 | 2.985 | 2.941 | 2.898 | 2.857 | 2.817 | 2.778 | 2.740 | 2.703 | 2.667 | 2.632 | 2.598 | 2.564 | 2.531 |
| 16 | 3.077 | 3.031 | 2.985 | 2.941 | 2.899 | 2.857 | 2.817 | 2.778 | 2.740 | 2.703 | 2.666 | 2.631 | 2.597 | 2.564 | 2.532 |
| 17 | 3.077 | 3.030 | 2.985 | 2.941 | 2.898 | 2.857 | 2.817 | 2.778 | 2.740 | 2.702 | 2.667 | 2.632 | 2.598 | 2.564 | 2.531 |
| 18 | 3.077 | 3.031 | 2.985 | 2.941 | 2.899 | 2.857 | 2.817 | 2.778 | 2.740 | 2.703 | 2.666 | 2.631 | 2.597 | 2.564 | 2.532 |
| 19 | 3.077 | 3.030 | 2.985 | 2.941 | 2.898 | 2.857 | 2.817 | 2.778 | 2.740 | 2.702 | 2.667 | 2.632 | 2.598 | 2.564 | 2.531 |
| 20 | 3.077 | 3.031 | 2.985 | 2.941 | 2.899 | 2.857 | 2.817 | 2.778 | 2.739 | 2.703 | 2.666 | 2.631 | 2.597 | 2.564 | 2.532 |

| If the Recovery Year is: | and the Recovery Period is: 32.5 | 33.0 | 33.5 | 34.0 | 34.5 | 35.0 | 35.5 | 36.0 | 36.5 | 37.0 | 37.5 | 38.0 | 38.5 | 39.0 | 39.5 |
|---|---|---|---|---|---|---|---|---|---|---|---|---|---|---|---|
| | the Depreciation Rate is: | | | | | | | | | | | | | | |
| 21 | 3.077 | 3.030 | 2.985 | 2.941 | 2.898 | 2.857 | 2.817 | 2.778 | 2.740 | 2.702 | 2.667 | 2.632 | 2.598 | 2.564 | 2.531 |
| 22 | 3.077 | 3.031 | 2.985 | 2.941 | 2.899 | 2.857 | 2.817 | 2.778 | 2.739 | 2.703 | 2.666 | 2.631 | 2.597 | 2.564 | 2.532 |
| 23 | 3.077 | 3.030 | 2.985 | 2.941 | 2.898 | 2.857 | 2.817 | 2.777 | 2.740 | 2.702 | 2.667 | 2.632 | 2.598 | 2.564 | 2.531 |
| 24 | 3.077 | 3.031 | 2.985 | 2.941 | 2.899 | 2.857 | 2.817 | 2.778 | 2.739 | 2.703 | 2.666 | 2.631 | 2.597 | 2.564 | 2.532 |
| 25 | 3.077 | 3.030 | 2.985 | 2.942 | 2.898 | 2.857 | 2.817 | 2.777 | 2.740 | 2.702 | 2.667 | 2.632 | 2.598 | 2.564 | 2.531 |
| 26 | 3.077 | 3.031 | 2.985 | 2.941 | 2.899 | 2.857 | 2.817 | 2.778 | 2.739 | 2.703 | 2.666 | 2.631 | 2.597 | 2.564 | 2.532 |
| 27 | 3.077 | 3.030 | 2.985 | 2.942 | 2.898 | 2.858 | 2.817 | 2.777 | 2.740 | 2.702 | 2.667 | 2.632 | 2.598 | 2.564 | 2.531 |
| 28 | 3.077 | 3.031 | 2.985 | 2.941 | 2.899 | 2.857 | 2.817 | 2.778 | 2.739 | 2.703 | 2.666 | 2.631 | 2.597 | 2.564 | 2.532 |
| 29 | 3.076 | 3.030 | 2.985 | 2.942 | 2.898 | 2.858 | 2.817 | 2.777 | 2.740 | 2.702 | 2.667 | 2.632 | 2.598 | 2.564 | 2.531 |
| 30 | 3.077 | 3.031 | 2.985 | 2.941 | 2.899 | 2.857 | 2.817 | 2.778 | 2.739 | 2.703 | 2.666 | 2.631 | 2.597 | 2.564 | 2.532 |
| 31 | 3.076 | 3.030 | 2.986 | 2.942 | 2.898 | 2.858 | 2.816 | 2.777 | 2.740 | 2.702 | 2.667 | 2.632 | 2.598 | 2.564 | 2.531 |
| 32 | 3.077 | 3.031 | 2.985 | 2.941 | 2.899 | 2.857 | 2.817 | 2.778 | 2.739 | 2.703 | 2.666 | 2.631 | 2.597 | 2.564 | 2.532 |
| 33 | 3.076 | 3.030 | 2.986 | 2.942 | 2.898 | 2.858 | 2.816 | 2.777 | 2.740 | 2.702 | 2.667 | 2.632 | 2.598 | 2.564 | 2.531 |
| 34 | 1.154 | 2.652 | 2.985 | 2.941 | 2.899 | 2.857 | 2.817 | 2.778 | 2.739 | 2.703 | 2.666 | 2.631 | 2.597 | 2.565 | 2.532 |
| 35 | | | 1.120 | 2.574 | 2.898 | 2.858 | 2.816 | 2.777 | 2.740 | 2.702 | 2.667 | 2.632 | 2.598 | 2.564 | 2.531 |
| 36 | | | | | 1.087 | 2.500 | 2.817 | 2.778 | 2.739 | 2.703 | 2.666 | 2.631 | 2.597 | 2.565 | 2.532 |
| 37 | | | | | | | 1.056 | 2.430 | 2.740 | 2.702 | 2.667 | 2.632 | 2.598 | 2.564 | 2.531 |
| 38 | | | | | | | | | 1.027 | 2.365 | 2.666 | 2.631 | 2.597 | 2.565 | 2.532 |
| 39 | | | | | | | | | | | 1.000 | 2.303 | 2.598 | 2.564 | 2.531 |
| 40 | | | | | | | | | | | | | 0.974 | 2.244 | 2.532 |
| 41 | | | | | | | | | | | | | | | 0.949 |

| If the Recovery Year is: | and the Recovery Period is: | | | | | | | | | | | | | | |
|---|---|---|---|---|---|---|---|---|---|---|---|---|---|---|---|
| | 40.0 | 40.5 | 41.0 | 41.5 | 42.0 | 42.5 | 43.0 | 43.5 | 44.0 | 44.5 | 45.0 | 45.5 | 46.0 | 46.5 | 47.0 |
| | the Depreciation Rate is: | | | | | | | | | | | | | | |
| 1 | 0.313 | 0.309 | 0.305 | 0.301 | 0.298 | 0.294 | 0.291 | 0.287 | 0.284 | 0.281 | 0.278 | 0.275 | 0.272 | 0.269 | 0.266 |
| 2 | 2.500 | 2.469 | 2.439 | 2.410 | 2.381 | 2.353 | 2.326 | 2.299 | 2.273 | 2.247 | 2.222 | 2.198 | 2.174 | 2.151 | 2.128 |
| 3 | 2.500 | 2.469 | 2.439 | 2.410 | 2.381 | 2.353 | 2.326 | 2.299 | 2.273 | 2.247 | 2.222 | 2.198 | 2.174 | 2.151 | 2.128 |
| 4 | 2.500 | 2.469 | 2.439 | 2.410 | 2.381 | 2.353 | 2.326 | 2.299 | 2.273 | 2.247 | 2.222 | 2.198 | 2.174 | 2.151 | 2.128 |
| 5 | 2.500 | 2.469 | 2.439 | 2.410 | 2.381 | 2.353 | 2.326 | 2.299 | 2.273 | 2.247 | 2.222 | 2.198 | 2.174 | 2.151 | 2.128 |
| 6 | 2.500 | 2.469 | 2.439 | 2.410 | 2.381 | 2.353 | 2.326 | 2.299 | 2.273 | 2.247 | 2.222 | 2.198 | 2.174 | 2.150 | 2.128 |
| 7 | 2.500 | 2.469 | 2.439 | 2.410 | 2.381 | 2.353 | 2.326 | 2.299 | 2.273 | 2.247 | 2.222 | 2.198 | 2.174 | 2.151 | 2.128 |
| 8 | 2.500 | 2.469 | 2.439 | 2.410 | 2.381 | 2.353 | 2.326 | 2.299 | 2.273 | 2.247 | 2.222 | 2.198 | 2.174 | 2.150 | 2.128 |
| 9 | 2.500 | 2.469 | 2.439 | 2.410 | 2.381 | 2.353 | 2.325 | 2.299 | 2.273 | 2.247 | 2.222 | 2.198 | 2.174 | 2.151 | 2.128 |
| 10 | 2.500 | 2.469 | 2.439 | 2.410 | 2.381 | 2.353 | 2.326 | 2.299 | 2.273 | 2.247 | 2.222 | 2.198 | 2.174 | 2.150 | 2.128 |
| 11 | 2.500 | 2.469 | 2.439 | 2.410 | 2.381 | 2.353 | 2.325 | 2.299 | 2.273 | 2.247 | 2.222 | 2.198 | 2.174 | 2.151 | 2.128 |
| 12 | 2.500 | 2.469 | 2.439 | 2.410 | 2.381 | 2.353 | 2.326 | 2.299 | 2.273 | 2.247 | 2.222 | 2.198 | 2.174 | 2.150 | 2.128 |
| 13 | 2.500 | 2.469 | 2.439 | 2.410 | 2.381 | 2.353 | 2.325 | 2.299 | 2.273 | 2.247 | 2.222 | 2.198 | 2.174 | 2.151 | 2.128 |
| 14 | 2.500 | 2.469 | 2.439 | 2.409 | 2.381 | 2.353 | 2.326 | 2.299 | 2.273 | 2.247 | 2.222 | 2.198 | 2.174 | 2.150 | 2.128 |
| 15 | 2.500 | 2.469 | 2.439 | 2.410 | 2.381 | 2.353 | 2.325 | 2.299 | 2.273 | 2.247 | 2.222 | 2.198 | 2.174 | 2.151 | 2.128 |
| 16 | 2.500 | 2.469 | 2.439 | 2.409 | 2.381 | 2.353 | 2.326 | 2.299 | 2.273 | 2.247 | 2.222 | 2.198 | 2.174 | 2.150 | 2.128 |
| 17 | 2.500 | 2.469 | 2.439 | 2.410 | 2.381 | 2.353 | 2.325 | 2.299 | 2.273 | 2.247 | 2.222 | 2.198 | 2.174 | 2.151 | 2.127 |
| 18 | 2.500 | 2.469 | 2.439 | 2.409 | 2.381 | 2.353 | 2.326 | 2.299 | 2.273 | 2.247 | 2.222 | 2.198 | 2.174 | 2.150 | 2.128 |
| 19 | 2.500 | 2.469 | 2.439 | 2.410 | 2.381 | 2.353 | 2.325 | 2.299 | 2.273 | 2.247 | 2.222 | 2.198 | 2.174 | 2.151 | 2.127 |
| 20 | 2.500 | 2.469 | 2.439 | 2.409 | 2.381 | 2.353 | 2.326 | 2.299 | 2.273 | 2.247 | 2.222 | 2.198 | 2.174 | 2.150 | 2.128 |
| 21 | 2.500 | 2.469 | 2.439 | 2.410 | 2.381 | 2.353 | 2.325 | 2.299 | 2.273 | 2.247 | 2.222 | 2.198 | 2.174 | 2.151 | 2.127 |
| 22 | 2.500 | 2.469 | 2.439 | 2.409 | 2.381 | 2.353 | 2.326 | 2.299 | 2.273 | 2.247 | 2.222 | 2.198 | 2.174 | 2.150 | 2.128 |
| 23 | 2.500 | 2.469 | 2.439 | 2.410 | 2.381 | 2.353 | 2.325 | 2.299 | 2.272 | 2.247 | 2.222 | 2.198 | 2.174 | 2.151 | 2.127 |
| 24 | 2.500 | 2.469 | 2.439 | 2.409 | 2.381 | 2.353 | 2.326 | 2.299 | 2.273 | 2.247 | 2.222 | 2.198 | 2.174 | 2.150 | 2.128 |
| 25 | 2.500 | 2.469 | 2.439 | 2.410 | 2.381 | 2.353 | 2.325 | 2.299 | 2.272 | 2.247 | 2.222 | 2.198 | 2.174 | 2.151 | 2.127 |
| 26 | 2.500 | 2.469 | 2.439 | 2.409 | 2.381 | 2.353 | 2.326 | 2.299 | 2.273 | 2.247 | 2.222 | 2.198 | 2.174 | 2.150 | 2.128 |

| If the Recovery Year is: | and the Recovery Period is: 40.0 | 40.5 | 41.0 | 41.5 | 42.0 | 42.5 | 43.0 | 43.5 | 44.0 | 44.5 | 45.0 | 45.5 | 46.0 | 46.5 | 47.0 |
|---|---|---|---|---|---|---|---|---|---|---|---|---|---|---|---|
| | the Depreciation Rate is: | | | | | | | | | | | | | | |
| 27 | 2.500 | 2.469 | 2.439 | 2.410 | 2.381 | 2.353 | 2.325 | 2.299 | 2.272 | 2.247 | 2.222 | 2.198 | 2.174 | 2.151 | 2.127 |
| 28 | 2.500 | 2.469 | 2.439 | 2.409 | 2.381 | 2.353 | 2.326 | 2.299 | 2.273 | 2.247 | 2.223 | 2.198 | 2.174 | 2.150 | 2.128 |
| 29 | 2.500 | 2.469 | 2.439 | 2.410 | 2.381 | 2.353 | 2.325 | 2.299 | 2.272 | 2.247 | 2.222 | 2.197 | 2.174 | 2.151 | 2.127 |
| 30 | 2.500 | 2.469 | 2.439 | 2.409 | 2.381 | 2.353 | 2.326 | 2.299 | 2.273 | 2.248 | 2.223 | 2.198 | 2.174 | 2.150 | 2.128 |
| 31 | 2.500 | 2.469 | 2.439 | 2.410 | 2.381 | 2.353 | 2.325 | 2.299 | 2.272 | 2.247 | 2.222 | 2.197 | 2.174 | 2.151 | 2.127 |
| 32 | 2.500 | 2.469 | 2.439 | 2.409 | 2.381 | 2.353 | 2.326 | 2.299 | 2.273 | 2.248 | 2.223 | 2.198 | 2.174 | 2.150 | 2.128 |
| 33 | 2.500 | 2.470 | 2.439 | 2.410 | 2.381 | 2.353 | 2.325 | 2.299 | 2.272 | 2.247 | 2.222 | 2.197 | 2.174 | 2.151 | 2.127 |
| 34 | 2.500 | 2.469 | 2.439 | 2.409 | 2.381 | 2.353 | 2.326 | 2.298 | 2.273 | 2.248 | 2.223 | 2.198 | 2.174 | 2.150 | 2.128 |
| 35 | 2.500 | 2.470 | 2.439 | 2.410 | 2.381 | 2.353 | 2.325 | 2.299 | 2.272 | 2.247 | 2.222 | 2.197 | 2.174 | 2.151 | 2.127 |
| 36 | 2.500 | 2.469 | 2.439 | 2.409 | 2.381 | 2.353 | 2.326 | 2.298 | 2.273 | 2.248 | 2.223 | 2.198 | 2.174 | 2.150 | 2.128 |
| 37 | 2.500 | 2.470 | 2.439 | 2.410 | 2.381 | 2.353 | 2.325 | 2.299 | 2.272 | 2.247 | 2.222 | 2.197 | 2.174 | 2.151 | 2.127 |
| 38 | 2.500 | 2.469 | 2.439 | 2.409 | 2.381 | 2.353 | 2.326 | 2.298 | 2.273 | 2.248 | 2.223 | 2.198 | 2.174 | 2.150 | 2.128 |
| 39 | 2.500 | 2.470 | 2.439 | 2.410 | 2.381 | 2.353 | 2.325 | 2.299 | 2.272 | 2.247 | 2.222 | 2.197 | 2.174 | 2.151 | 2.127 |
| 40 | 2.500 | 2.469 | 2.439 | 2.409 | 2.380 | 2.352 | 2.326 | 2.298 | 2.273 | 2.248 | 2.223 | 2.198 | 2.173 | 2.150 | 2.128 |
| 41 | 2.187 | 2.470 | 2.439 | 2.410 | 2.381 | 2.353 | 2.325 | 2.299 | 2.272 | 2.247 | 2.222 | 2.197 | 2.174 | 2.151 | 2.127 |
| 42 | | 0.926 | 2.135 | 2.409 | 2.380 | 2.352 | 2.326 | 2.298 | 2.273 | 2.248 | 2.223 | 2.198 | 2.173 | 2.150 | 2.128 |
| 43 | | | | 0.904 | 2.083 | 2.353 | 2.325 | 2.299 | 2.272 | 2.247 | 2.222 | 2.197 | 2.174 | 2.151 | 2.127 |
| 44 | | | | | | 0.882 | 2.035 | 2.298 | 2.273 | 2.248 | 2.223 | 2.198 | 2.173 | 2.150 | 2.128 |
| 45 | | | | | | | | 0.862 | 1.988 | 2.247 | 2.222 | 2.197 | 2.174 | 2.151 | 2.127 |
| 46 | | | | | | | | | | 0.843 | 1.945 | 2.198 | 2.173 | 2.150 | 2.128 |
| 47 | | | | | | | | | | | | 0.824 | 1.902 | 2.151 | 2.127 |
| 48 | | | | | | | | | | | | | | 0.806 | 1.862 |

| If the Recovery Year is: | and the Recovery Period is: 47.5 | 48.0 | 48.5 | 49.0 | 49.5 | 50.0 |
|---|---|---|---|---|---|---|
| | the Depreciation Rate is: | | | | | |
| 1 | 0.263 | 0.260 | 0.258 | 0.255 | 0.253 | 0.250 |
| 2 | 2.105 | 2.083 | 2.062 | 2.041 | 2.020 | 2.000 |
| 3 | 2.105 | 2.083 | 2.062 | 2.041 | 2.020 | 2.000 |
| 4 | 2.105 | 2.083 | 2.062 | 2.041 | 2.020 | 2.000 |
| 5 | 2.105 | 2.083 | 2.062 | 2.041 | 2.020 | 2.000 |
| 6 | 2.105 | 2.083 | 2.062 | 2.041 | 2.020 | 2.000 |
| 7 | 2.105 | 2.083 | 2.062 | 2.041 | 2.020 | 2.000 |
| 8 | 2.105 | 2.083 | 2.062 | 2.041 | 2.020 | 2.000 |
| 9 | 2.105 | 2.083 | 2.062 | 2.041 | 2.020 | 2.000 |
| 10 | 2.105 | 2.083 | 2.062 | 2.041 | 2.020 | 2.000 |
| 11 | 2.105 | 2.083 | 2.062 | 2.041 | 2.020 | 2.000 |
| 12 | 2.105 | 2.083 | 2.062 | 2.041 | 2.020 | 2.000 |
| 13 | 2.105 | 2.083 | 2.062 | 2.041 | 2.020 | 2.000 |
| 14 | 2.105 | 2.083 | 2.062 | 2.041 | 2.020 | 2.000 |
| 15 | 2.105 | 2.083 | 2.062 | 2.041 | 2.020 | 2.000 |
| 16 | 2.105 | 2.083 | 2.062 | 2.041 | 2.020 | 2.000 |
| 17 | 2.105 | 2.083 | 2.062 | 2.041 | 2.020 | 2.000 |
| 18 | 2.105 | 2.084 | 2.062 | 2.041 | 2.020 | 2.000 |
| 19 | 2.105 | 2.083 | 2.062 | 2.041 | 2.020 | 2.000 |
| 20 | 2.105 | 2.084 | 2.062 | 2.041 | 2.020 | 2.000 |
| 21 | 2.105 | 2.083 | 2.062 | 2.041 | 2.020 | 2.000 |
| 22 | 2.105 | 2.084 | 2.062 | 2.041 | 2.020 | 2.000 |
| 23 | 2.105 | 2.083 | 2.062 | 2.041 | 2.020 | 2.000 |
| 24 | 2.105 | 2.084 | 2.062 | 2.041 | 2.020 | 2.000 |
| 25 | 2.106 | 2.083 | 2.062 | 2.041 | 2.020 | 2.000 |
| 26 | 2.105 | 2.084 | 2.062 | 2.041 | 2.020 | 2.000 |

| If the Recovery Year is: | and the Recovery Period is: 47.5 | 48.0 | 48.5 | 49.0 | 49.5 | 50.0 |
|---|---|---|---|---|---|---|
| | the Depreciation Rate is: | | | | | |
| 27 | 2.106 | 2.083 | 2.062 | 2.041 | 2.020 | 2.000 |
| 28 | 2.105 | 2.084 | 2.062 | 2.041 | 2.020 | 2.000 |
| 29 | 2.106 | 2.083 | 2.062 | 2.041 | 2.020 | 2.000 |
| 30 | 2.105 | 2.084 | 2.062 | 2.041 | 2.020 | 2.000 |
| 31 | 2.106 | 2.083 | 2.062 | 2.041 | 2.020 | 2.000 |
| 32 | 2.105 | 2.084 | 2.062 | 2.041 | 2.020 | 2.000 |
| 33 | 2.106 | 2.083 | 2.062 | 2.041 | 2.021 | 2.000 |
| 34 | 2.105 | 2.084 | 2.062 | 2.040 | 2.020 | 2.000 |
| 35 | 2.106 | 2.083 | 2.062 | 2.041 | 2.021 | 2.000 |
| 36 | 2.105 | 2.084 | 2.061 | 2.040 | 2.020 | 2.000 |
| 37 | 2.106 | 2.083 | 2.062 | 2.041 | 2.021 | 2.000 |
| 38 | 2.105 | 2.084 | 2.061 | 2.040 | 2.020 | 2.000 |
| 39 | 2.106 | 2.083 | 2.062 | 2.041 | 2.021 | 2.000 |
| 40 | 2.105 | 2.084 | 2.061 | 2.040 | 2.020 | 2.000 |
| 41 | 2.106 | 2.083 | 2.062 | 2.041 | 2.021 | 2.000 |
| 42 | 2.105 | 2.084 | 2.061 | 2.040 | 2.020 | 2.000 |
| 43 | 2.106 | 2.083 | 2.062 | 2.041 | 2.021 | 2.000 |
| 44 | 2.105 | 2.084 | 2.061 | 2.040 | 2.020 | 2.000 |
| 45 | 2.106 | 2.083 | 2.062 | 2.041 | 2.021 | 2.000 |
| 46 | 2.105 | 2.084 | 2.061 | 2.040 | 2.020 | 2.000 |
| 47 | 2.106 | 2.083 | 2.062 | 2.041 | 2.021 | 2.000 |
| 48 | 2.105 | 2.084 | 2.061 | 2.040 | 2.020 | 2.000 |
| 49 | 0.790 | 1.823 | 2.062 | 2.041 | 2.021 | 2.000 |
| 50 | | | 0.773 | 1.785 | 2.020 | 2.000 |
| 51 | | | | | 0.758 | 1.750 |

TABLE 12A (Rev. Proc. 2019-8)
Alternative Depreciation System
Applicable Depreciation Method: Straight Line
Applicable Recovery Period: 30 years
Applicable Convention: Mid-month

| If the Recovery Year is: | and the Month in the First Recovery Year the Property is Placed in Service is: | | | | | | | | | | | |
|---|---|---|---|---|---|---|---|---|---|---|---|---|
| | 1 | 2 | 3 | 4 | 5 | 6 | 7 | 8 | 9 | 10 | 11 | 12 |
| | the Depreciation Rate is: | | | | | | | | | | | |
| 1 | 3.204 | 2.926 | 2.649 | 2.371 | 2.093 | 1.815 | 1.528 | 1.250 | 0.972 | 0.694 | 0.417 | 0.139 |
| 2 - 30 | 3.333 | 3.333 | 3.333 | 3.333 | 3.333 | 3.333 | 3.333 | 3.333 | 3.333 | 3.333 | 3.333 | 3.333 |
| 31 | 0.139 | 0.417 | 0.694 | 0.972 | 1.250 | 1.528 | 1.815 | 2.093 | 2.371 | 2.649 | 2.926 | 3.204 |

TABLE 13
Alternative Depreciation System
Applicable Depreciation Method: Straight Line
Applicable Recovery Period: 40 years
Applicable Convention: Mid-month

| If the Recovery Year is: | and the Month in the First Recovery Year the Property is Placed in Service is: | | | | | | | | | | | |
|---|---|---|---|---|---|---|---|---|---|---|---|---|
| | 1 | 2 | 3 | 4 | 5 | 6 | 7 | 8 | 9 | 10 | 11 | 12 |
| | the Depreciation Rate is: | | | | | | | | | | | |
| 1 | 2.396 | 2.188 | 1.979 | 1.771 | 1.563 | 1.354 | 1.146 | 0.938 | 0.729 | 0.521 | 0.313 | 0.104 |
| 2 - 40 | 2.500 | 2.500 | 2.500 | 2.500 | 2.500 | 2.500 | 2.500 | 2.500 | 2.500 | 2.500 | 2.500 | 2.500 |
| 41 | 0.104 | 0.312 | 0.521 | 0.729 | 0.937 | 1.146 | 1.354 | 1.562 | 1.771 | 1.979 | 2.187 | 2.396 |

TABLE 14
Alternative Minimum Tax (see section 7 of this revenue procedure)
Applicable Depreciation Method: 150-Percent Declining Balance Switching to Straight Line
Applicable Recovery Periods: 2.5 — 50 years
Applicable Convention: Half-year

| If the Recovery Year is: | and the Recovery Period is: 2.5 | 3.0 | 3.5 | 4.0 | 4.5 | 5.0 | 5.5 | 6.0 | 6.5 | 7.0 | 7.5 | 8.0 | 8.5 | 9.0 | 9.5 |
|---|---|---|---|---|---|---|---|---|---|---|---|---|---|---|---|
| | the Depreciation Rate is: | | | | | | | | | | | | | | |
| 1 | 30.00 | 25.00 | 21.43 | 18.75 | 16.67 | 15.00 | 13.64 | 12.50 | 11.54 | 10.71 | 10.00 | 9.38 | 8.82 | 8.33 | 7.89 |
| 2 | 42.00 | 37.50 | 33.67 | 30.47 | 27.78 | 25.50 | 23.55 | 21.88 | 20.41 | 19.13 | 18.00 | 16.99 | 16.09 | 15.28 | 14.54 |
| 3 | 28.00 | 25.00 | 22.45 | 20.31 | 18.52 | 17.85 | 17.13 | 16.41 | 15.70 | 15.03 | 14.40 | 13.81 | 13.25 | 12.73 | 12.25 |
| 4 | | 12.50 | 22.45 | 20.31 | 18.52 | 16.66 | 15.23 | 14.06 | 13.09 | 12.25 | 11.52 | 11.22 | 10.91 | 10.61 | 10.31 |
| 5 | | | | 10.16 | 18.51 | 16.66 | 15.23 | 14.06 | 13.09 | 12.25 | 11.52 | 10.80 | 10.19 | 9.65 | 9.17 |
| 6 | | | | | | 8.33 | 15.22 | 14.06 | 13.09 | 12.25 | 11.52 | 10.80 | 10.19 | 9.64 | 9.17 |
| 7 | | | | | | | | 7.03 | 13.08 | 12.25 | 11.52 | 10.80 | 10.18 | 9.65 | 9.17 |
| 8 | | | | | | | | | | 6.13 | 11.52 | 10.80 | 10.19 | 9.64 | 9.17 |
| 9 | | | | | | | | | | | | 5.40 | 10.18 | 9.65 | 9.17 |
| 10 | | | | | | | | | | | | | | 4.82 | 9.16 |

| If the Recovery Year is: | and the Recovery Period is: 10.0 | 10.5 | 11.0 | 11.5 | 12.0 | 12.5 | 13.0 | 13.5 | 14.0 | 14.5 | 15.0 | 15.5 | 16.0 | 16.5 | 17.0 |
|---|---|---|---|---|---|---|---|---|---|---|---|---|---|---|---|
| | the Depreciation Rate is: | | | | | | | | | | | | | | |
| 1 | 7.50 | 7.14 | 6.82 | 6.52 | 6.25 | 6.00 | 5.77 | 5.56 | 5.36 | 5.17 | 5.00 | 4.84 | 4.69 | 4.55 | 4.41 |
| 2 | 13.88 | 13.27 | 12.71 | 12.19 | 11.72 | 11.28 | 10.87 | 10.49 | 10.14 | 9.81 | 9.50 | 9.21 | 8.94 | 8.68 | 8.43 |
| 3 | 11.79 | 11.37 | 10.97 | 10.60 | 10.25 | 9.93 | 9.62 | 9.33 | 9.05 | 8.80 | 8.55 | 8.32 | 8.10 | 7.89 | 7.69 |
| 4 | 10.02 | 9.75 | 9.48 | 9.22 | 8.97 | 8.73 | 8.51 | 8.29 | 8.08 | 7.88 | 7.70 | 7.51 | 7.34 | 7.17 | 7.01 |
| 5 | 8.74 | 8.35 | 8.18 | 8.02 | 7.85 | 7.69 | 7.53 | 7.37 | 7.22 | 7.07 | 6.93 | 6.79 | 6.65 | 6.52 | 6.39 |
| 6 | 8.74 | 8.35 | 7.98 | 7.64 | 7.33 | 7.05 | 6.79 | 6.55 | 6.44 | 6.34 | 6.23 | 6.13 | 6.03 | 5.93 | 5.83 |

| If the Recovery Year is: | 10.0 | 10.5 | 11.0 | 11.5 | 12.0 | 12.5 | 13.0 | 13.5 | 14.0 | 14.5 | 15.0 | 15.5 | 16.0 | 16.5 | 17.0 |
|---|---|---|---|---|---|---|---|---|---|---|---|---|---|---|---|
| | and the Recovery Period is: | | | | | | | | | | | | | | |
| | the Depreciation Rate is: | | | | | | | | | | | | | | |
| 7 | 8.74 | 8.35 | 7.97 | 7.64 | 7.33 | 7.05 | 6.79 | 6.55 | 6.32 | 6.10 | 5.90 | 5.72 | 5.55 | 5.39 | 5.32 |
| 8 | 8.74 | 8.35 | 7.98 | 7.63 | 7.33 | 7.05 | 6.79 | 6.55 | 6.32 | 6.10 | 5.90 | 5.72 | 5.55 | 5.39 | 5.23 |
| 9 | 8.74 | 8.36 | 7.97 | 7.64 | 7.33 | 7.04 | 6.79 | 6.55 | 6.32 | 6.10 | 5.91 | 5.72 | 5.55 | 5.39 | 5.23 |
| 10 | 8.74 | 8.35 | 7.98 | 7.63 | 7.33 | 7.05 | 6.79 | 6.55 | 6.32 | 6.11 | 5.90 | 5.72 | 5.55 | 5.39 | 5.23 |
| 11 | 4.37 | 8.36 | 7.97 | 7.64 | 7.32 | 7.04 | 6.79 | 6.55 | 6.32 | 6.10 | 5.91 | 5.72 | 5.55 | 5.39 | 5.23 |
| 12 | | | 3.99 | 7.63 | 7.33 | 7.05 | 6.78 | 6.55 | 6.32 | 6.11 | 5.90 | 5.72 | 5.55 | 5.39 | 5.23 |
| 13 | | | | | 3.66 | 7.04 | 6.79 | 6.56 | 6.32 | 6.10 | 5.91 | 5.72 | 5.54 | 5.38 | 5.23 |
| 14 | | | | | | | 3.39 | 6.55 | 6.31 | 6.11 | 5.90 | 5.72 | 5.55 | 5.39 | 5.23 |
| 15 | | | | | | | | | 3.16 | 6.10 | 5.91 | 5.72 | 5.54 | 5.38 | 5.23 |
| 16 | | | | | | | | | | | 2.95 | 5.72 | 5.55 | 5.39 | 5.23 |
| 17 | | | | | | | | | | | | | 2.77 | 5.38 | 5.23 |
| 18 | | | | | | | | | | | | | | | 2.62 |

| If the Recovery Year is: | 17.5 | 18.0 | 18.5 | 19.0 | 19.5 | 20.0 | 20.5 | 21.0 | 21.5 | 22.0 | 22.5 | 23.0 | 23.5 | 24.0 | 24.5 |
|---|---|---|---|---|---|---|---|---|---|---|---|---|---|---|---|
| | and the Recovery Period is: | | | | | | | | | | | | | | |
| | the Depreciation Rate is: | | | | | | | | | | | | | | |
| 1 | 4.29 | 4.17 | 4.05 | 3.95 | 3.85 | 3.750 | 3.659 | 3.571 | 3.488 | 3.409 | 3.333 | 3.261 | 3.191 | 3.125 | 3.061 |
| 2 | 8.20 | 7.99 | 7.78 | 7.58 | 7.40 | 7.219 | 7.049 | 6.888 | 6.733 | 6.586 | 6.444 | 6.309 | 6.179 | 6.055 | 5.935 |
| 3 | 7.50 | 7.32 | 7.15 | 6.98 | 6.83 | 6.677 | 6.534 | 6.396 | 6.264 | 6.137 | 6.015 | 5.898 | 5.785 | 5.676 | 5.572 |
| 4 | 6.86 | 6.71 | 6.57 | 6.43 | 6.30 | 6.177 | 6.055 | 5.939 | 5.827 | 5.718 | 5.614 | 5.513 | 5.416 | 5.322 | 5.231 |
| 5 | 6.27 | 6.15 | 6.04 | 5.93 | 5.82 | 5.713 | 5.612 | 5.515 | 5.420 | 5.328 | 5.240 | 5.153 | 5.070 | 4.989 | 4.910 |
| 6 | 5.73 | 5.64 | 5.55 | 5.46 | 5.37 | 5.285 | 5.202 | 5.121 | 5.042 | 4.965 | 4.890 | 4.817 | 4.746 | 4.677 | 4.610 |
| 7 | 5.24 | 5.17 | 5.10 | 5.03 | 4.96 | 4.888 | 4.821 | 4.755 | 4.690 | 4.627 | 4.564 | 4.503 | 4.443 | 4.385 | 4.327 |
| 8 | 5.08 | 4.94 | 4.81 | 4.69 | 4.57 | 4.522 | 4.468 | 4.415 | 4.363 | 4.311 | 4.260 | 4.210 | 4.160 | 4.111 | 4.062 |
| 9 | 5.08 | 4.94 | 4.81 | 4.69 | 4.58 | 4.462 | 4.354 | 4.252 | 4.155 | 4.063 | 3.976 | 3.935 | 3.894 | 3.854 | 3.814 |
| 10 | 5.08 | 4.94 | 4.81 | 4.69 | 4.57 | 4.461 | 4.354 | 4.252 | 4.155 | 4.063 | 3.976 | 3.890 | 3.808 | 3.729 | 3.655 |

| If the Recovery Year is: | and the Recovery Period is: 17.5 | 18.0 | 18.5 | 19.0 | 19.5 | 20.0 | 20.5 | 21.0 | 21.5 | 22.0 | 22.5 | 23.0 | 23.5 | 24.0 | 24.5 |
|---|---|---|---|---|---|---|---|---|---|---|---|---|---|---|---|
| | the Depreciation Rate is: | | | | | | | | | | | | | | |
| 11 | 5.08 | 4.94 | 4.81 | 4.69 | 4.58 | 4.462 | 4.354 | 4.252 | 4.155 | 4.063 | 3.976 | 3.890 | 3.808 | 3.729 | 3.655 |
| 12 | 5.08 | 4.95 | 4.81 | 4.69 | 4.57 | 4.461 | 4.354 | 4.252 | 4.155 | 4.063 | 3.976 | 3.890 | 3.808 | 3.729 | 3.655 |
| 13 | 5.09 | 4.94 | 4.82 | 4.69 | 4.58 | 4.462 | 4.354 | 4.252 | 4.155 | 4.064 | 3.976 | 3.890 | 3.808 | 3.730 | 3.655 |
| 14 | 5.08 | 4.95 | 4.81 | 4.69 | 4.57 | 4.461 | 4.354 | 4.252 | 4.155 | 4.063 | 3.976 | 3.890 | 3.808 | 3.729 | 3.655 |
| 15 | 5.09 | 4.94 | 4.82 | 4.69 | 4.58 | 4.462 | 4.354 | 4.252 | 4.155 | 4.064 | 3.976 | 3.890 | 3.808 | 3.730 | 3.655 |
| 16 | 5.08 | 4.95 | 4.81 | 4.69 | 4.57 | 4.461 | 4.354 | 4.252 | 4.155 | 4.063 | 3.976 | 3.890 | 3.808 | 3.729 | 3.655 |
| 17 | 5.09 | 4.94 | 4.82 | 4.69 | 4.58 | 4.462 | 4.354 | 4.252 | 4.155 | 4.064 | 3.976 | 3.889 | 3.808 | 3.730 | 3.655 |
| 18 | 5.08 | 4.95 | 4.81 | 4.70 | 4.57 | 4.461 | 4.354 | 4.252 | 4.156 | 4.063 | 3.976 | 3.890 | 3.807 | 3.729 | 3.655 |
| 19 | | 2.47 | 4.82 | 4.69 | 4.58 | 4.462 | 4.353 | 4.251 | 4.155 | 4.064 | 3.976 | 3.889 | 3.808 | 3.730 | 3.655 |
| 20 | | | | 2.35 | 4.57 | 4.461 | 4.354 | 4.252 | 4.156 | 4.063 | 3.976 | 3.890 | 3.807 | 3.729 | 3.655 |
| 21 | | | | | | 2.231 | 4.353 | 4.251 | 4.155 | 4.064 | 3.976 | 3.889 | 3.808 | 3.730 | 3.655 |
| 22 | | | | | | | | 2.126 | 4.156 | 4.063 | 3.976 | 3.890 | 3.807 | 3.729 | 3.655 |
| 23 | | | | | | | | | | 2.032 | 3.976 | 3.889 | 3.808 | 3.730 | 3.654 |
| 24 | | | | | | | | | | | | 1.945 | 3.807 | 3.729 | 3.655 |
| 25 | | | | | | | | | | | | | | 1.865 | 3.654 |

| If the Recovery Year is: | and the Recovery Period is: 25.0 | 25.5 | 26.0 | 26.5 | 27.0 | 27.5 | 28.0 | 28.5 | 29.0 | 29.5 | 30.0 | 30.5 | 31.0 | 31.5 | 32.0 |
|---|---|---|---|---|---|---|---|---|---|---|---|---|---|---|---|
| | the Depreciation Rate is: | | | | | | | | | | | | | | |
| 1 | 3.000 | 2.941 | 2.885 | 2.830 | 2.778 | 2.727 | 2.679 | 2.632 | 2.586 | 2.542 | 2.500 | 2.459 | 2.419 | 2.381 | 2.344 |
| 2 | 5.820 | 5.709 | 5.603 | 5.500 | 5.401 | 5.306 | 5.214 | 5.125 | 5.039 | 4.955 | 4.875 | 4.797 | 4.722 | 4.649 | 4.578 |
| 3 | 5.471 | 5.374 | 5.280 | 5.189 | 5.101 | 5.016 | 4.934 | 4.855 | 4.778 | 4.704 | 4.631 | 4.561 | 4.493 | 4.427 | 4.363 |
| 4 | 5.143 | 5.057 | 4.975 | 4.895 | 4.818 | 4.743 | 4.670 | 4.599 | 4.531 | 4.464 | 4.400 | 4.337 | 4.276 | 4.216 | 4.159 |
| 5 | 4.834 | 4.760 | 4.688 | 4.618 | 4.550 | 4.484 | 4.420 | 4.357 | 4.297 | 4.237 | 4.180 | 4.124 | 4.069 | 4.016 | 3.964 |
| 6 | 4.544 | 4.480 | 4.417 | 4.357 | 4.297 | 4.239 | 4.183 | 4.128 | 4.074 | 4.022 | 3.971 | 3.921 | 3.872 | 3.824 | 3.778 |
| 7 | 4.271 | 4.216 | 4.163 | 4.110 | 4.059 | 4.008 | 3.959 | 3.911 | 3.864 | 3.817 | 3.772 | 3.728 | 3.685 | 3.642 | 3.601 |

| If the Recovery Year is: | and the Recovery Period is: 25.0 | 25.5 | 26.0 | 26.5 | 27.0 | 27.5 | 28.0 | 28.5 | 29.0 | 29.5 | 30.0 | 30.5 | 31.0 | 31.5 | 32.0 |
|---|---|---|---|---|---|---|---|---|---|---|---|---|---|---|---|
| | the Depreciation Rate is: | | | | | | | | | | | | | | |
| 8 | 4.015 | 3.968 | 3.922 | 3.877 | 3.833 | 3.790 | 3.747 | 3.705 | 3.664 | 3.623 | 3.584 | 3.545 | 3.506 | 3.469 | 3.432 |
| 9 | 3.774 | 3.735 | 3.696 | 3.658 | 3.620 | 3.583 | 3.546 | 3.510 | 3.474 | 3.439 | 3.404 | 3.370 | 3.337 | 3.304 | 3.271 |
| 10 | 3.584 | 3.515 | 3.483 | 3.451 | 3.419 | 3.387 | 3.356 | 3.325 | 3.294 | 3.264 | 3.234 | 3.204 | 3.175 | 3.146 | 3.118 |
| 11 | 3.583 | 3.515 | 3.448 | 3.383 | 3.321 | 3.262 | 3.205 | 3.150 | 3.124 | 3.098 | 3.072 | 3.047 | 3.022 | 2.996 | 2.971 |
| 12 | 3.584 | 3.515 | 3.448 | 3.383 | 3.321 | 3.262 | 3.205 | 3.150 | 3.096 | 3.044 | 2.994 | 2.945 | 2.899 | 2.854 | 2.832 |
| 13 | 3.583 | 3.515 | 3.448 | 3.383 | 3.321 | 3.262 | 3.205 | 3.150 | 3.096 | 3.044 | 2.994 | 2.945 | 2.899 | 2.854 | 2.809 |
| 14 | 3.584 | 3.515 | 3.448 | 3.383 | 3.321 | 3.262 | 3.205 | 3.150 | 3.096 | 3.044 | 2.994 | 2.945 | 2.899 | 2.854 | 2.809 |
| 15 | 3.583 | 3.515 | 3.448 | 3.383 | 3.321 | 3.262 | 3.205 | 3.150 | 3.096 | 3.044 | 2.994 | 2.945 | 2.899 | 2.854 | 2.809 |
| 16 | 3.584 | 3.515 | 3.448 | 3.383 | 3.322 | 3.262 | 3.205 | 3.150 | 3.096 | 3.044 | 2.994 | 2.945 | 2.899 | 2.854 | 2.809 |
| 17 | 3.583 | 3.515 | 3.448 | 3.383 | 3.321 | 3.262 | 3.205 | 3.150 | 3.096 | 3.044 | 2.994 | 2.945 | 2.899 | 2.854 | 2.809 |
| 18 | 3.584 | 3.516 | 3.448 | 3.383 | 3.322 | 3.262 | 3.205 | 3.150 | 3.096 | 3.044 | 2.994 | 2.946 | 2.899 | 2.854 | 2.809 |
| 19 | 3.583 | 3.515 | 3.448 | 3.383 | 3.321 | 3.262 | 3.205 | 3.150 | 3.096 | 3.044 | 2.994 | 2.945 | 2.899 | 2.854 | 2.809 |
| 20 | 3.584 | 3.516 | 3.447 | 3.384 | 3.322 | 3.262 | 3.205 | 3.150 | 3.096 | 3.044 | 2.993 | 2.946 | 2.899 | 2.854 | 2.809 |
| 21 | 3.583 | 3.515 | 3.448 | 3.383 | 3.321 | 3.262 | 3.205 | 3.150 | 3.096 | 3.044 | 2.994 | 2.945 | 2.899 | 2.854 | 2.809 |
| 22 | 3.584 | 3.516 | 3.447 | 3.384 | 3.322 | 3.262 | 3.205 | 3.150 | 3.096 | 3.044 | 2.993 | 2.946 | 2.898 | 2.854 | 2.809 |
| 23 | 3.583 | 3.515 | 3.448 | 3.383 | 3.321 | 3.262 | 3.205 | 3.150 | 3.096 | 3.044 | 2.994 | 2.945 | 2.899 | 2.854 | 2.809 |
| 24 | 3.584 | 3.516 | 3.447 | 3.384 | 3.322 | 3.262 | 3.205 | 3.151 | 3.096 | 3.044 | 2.993 | 2.946 | 2.898 | 2.854 | 2.809 |
| 25 | 3.583 | 3.515 | 3.448 | 3.383 | 3.321 | 3.262 | 3.205 | 3.150 | 3.096 | 3.044 | 2.994 | 2.945 | 2.899 | 2.854 | 2.810 |
| 26 | 1.792 | 3.516 | 3.447 | 3.384 | 3.322 | 3.262 | 3.205 | 3.151 | 3.096 | 3.044 | 2.993 | 2.946 | 2.898 | 2.853 | 2.809 |
| 27 | | | 1.724 | 3.383 | 3.321 | 3.262 | 3.205 | 3.150 | 3.096 | 3.044 | 2.994 | 2.945 | 2.899 | 2.854 | 2.810 |
| 28 | | | | | 1.661 | 3.263 | 3.205 | 3.151 | 3.096 | 3.044 | 2.993 | 2.946 | 2.898 | 2.853 | 2.809 |
| 29 | | | | | | | 1.602 | 3.150 | 3.095 | 3.044 | 2.994 | 2.945 | 2.899 | 2.854 | 2.810 |
| 30 | | | | | | | | | 1.548 | 3.043 | 2.993 | 2.946 | 2.898 | 2.853 | 2.809 |
| 31 | | | | | | | | | | | 1.497 | 2.945 | 2.899 | 2.854 | 2.810 |
| 32 | | | | | | | | | | | | | 1.449 | 2.853 | 2.809 |
| 33 | | | | | | | | | | | | | | | 1.405 |

| If the Recovery Year is: | and the Recovery Period is: 32.5 | 33.0 | 33.5 | 34.0 | 34.5 | 35.0 | 35.5 | 36.0 | 36.5 | 37.0 | 37.5 | 38.0 | 38.5 | 39.0 | 39.5 |
|---|---|---|---|---|---|---|---|---|---|---|---|---|---|---|---|
| | the Depreciation Rate is: | | | | | | | | | | | | | | |
| 1 | 2.308 | 2.273 | 2.239 | 2.206 | 2.174 | 2.143 | 2.113 | 2.083 | 2.055 | 2.027 | 2.000 | 1.974 | 1.948 | 1.923 | 1.899 |
| 2 | 4.509 | 4.442 | 4.377 | 4.314 | 4.253 | 4.194 | 4.136 | 4.080 | 4.025 | 3.972 | 3.920 | 3.869 | 3.820 | 3.772 | 3.725 |
| 3 | 4.301 | 4.240 | 4.181 | 4.124 | 4.068 | 4.014 | 3.961 | 3.910 | 3.860 | 3.811 | 3.763 | 3.717 | 3.671 | 3.627 | 3.584 |
| 4 | 4.102 | 4.048 | 3.994 | 3.942 | 3.892 | 3.842 | 3.794 | 3.747 | 3.701 | 3.656 | 3.613 | 3.570 | 3.528 | 3.488 | 3.448 |
| 5 | 3.913 | 3.864 | 3.815 | 3.768 | 3.722 | 3.677 | 3.634 | 3.591 | 3.549 | 3.508 | 3.468 | 3.429 | 3.391 | 3.353 | 3.317 |
| 6 | 3.732 | 3.688 | 3.645 | 3.602 | 3.560 | 3.520 | 3.480 | 3.441 | 3.403 | 3.366 | 3.329 | 3.294 | 3.259 | 3.225 | 3.191 |
| 7 | 3.560 | 3.520 | 3.481 | 3.443 | 3.406 | 3.369 | 3.333 | 3.298 | 3.263 | 3.229 | 3.196 | 3.164 | 3.132 | 3.100 | 3.070 |
| 8 | 3.396 | 3.360 | 3.325 | 3.291 | 3.258 | 3.225 | 3.192 | 3.160 | 3.129 | 3.099 | 3.068 | 3.039 | 3.010 | 2.981 | 2.953 |
| 9 | 3.239 | 3.208 | 3.177 | 3.146 | 3.116 | 3.086 | 3.057 | 3.029 | 3.001 | 2.973 | 2.946 | 2.919 | 2.893 | 2.867 | 2.841 |
| 10 | 3.090 | 3.062 | 3.034 | 3.007 | 2.980 | 2.954 | 2.928 | 2.903 | 2.877 | 2.852 | 2.828 | 2.804 | 2.780 | 2.756 | 2.733 |
| 11 | 2.947 | 2.923 | 2.898 | 2.875 | 2.851 | 2.828 | 2.804 | 2.782 | 2.759 | 2.737 | 2.715 | 2.693 | 2.671 | 2.650 | 2.629 |
| 12 | 2.811 | 2.790 | 2.769 | 2.748 | 2.727 | 2.706 | 2.686 | 2.666 | 2.646 | 2.626 | 2.606 | 2.587 | 2.567 | 2.548 | 2.529 |
| 13 | 2.766 | 2.725 | 2.685 | 2.646 | 2.608 | 2.590 | 2.572 | 2.555 | 2.537 | 2.519 | 2.502 | 2.485 | 2.467 | 2.450 | 2.433 |
| 14 | 2.766 | 2.725 | 2.685 | 2.646 | 2.608 | 2.571 | 2.535 | 2.500 | 2.466 | 2.434 | 2.402 | 2.386 | 2.371 | 2.356 | 2.341 |
| 15 | 2.766 | 2.725 | 2.685 | 2.646 | 2.608 | 2.571 | 2.535 | 2.500 | 2.466 | 2.434 | 2.402 | 2.370 | 2.340 | 2.310 | 2.281 |
| 16 | 2.766 | 2.725 | 2.685 | 2.646 | 2.608 | 2.571 | 2.535 | 2.500 | 2.466 | 2.434 | 2.402 | 2.370 | 2.340 | 2.310 | 2.281 |
| 17 | 2.766 | 2.725 | 2.685 | 2.646 | 2.608 | 2.571 | 2.535 | 2.500 | 2.467 | 2.434 | 2.402 | 2.370 | 2.340 | 2.310 | 2.281 |
| 18 | 2.766 | 2.725 | 2.685 | 2.646 | 2.609 | 2.571 | 2.535 | 2.500 | 2.466 | 2.434 | 2.402 | 2.370 | 2.340 | 2.310 | 2.281 |
| 19 | 2.766 | 2.725 | 2.685 | 2.646 | 2.608 | 2.571 | 2.535 | 2.500 | 2.467 | 2.434 | 2.402 | 2.370 | 2.340 | 2.310 | 2.281 |
| 20 | 2.766 | 2.725 | 2.685 | 2.646 | 2.609 | 2.571 | 2.535 | 2.500 | 2.466 | 2.434 | 2.402 | 2.370 | 2.340 | 2.310 | 2.281 |
| 21 | 2.766 | 2.725 | 2.685 | 2.646 | 2.608 | 2.571 | 2.535 | 2.500 | 2.467 | 2.434 | 2.402 | 2.370 | 2.340 | 2.310 | 2.281 |
| 22 | 2.767 | 2.725 | 2.685 | 2.646 | 2.609 | 2.571 | 2.535 | 2.500 | 2.466 | 2.434 | 2.402 | 2.370 | 2.340 | 2.310 | 2.281 |
| 23 | 2.766 | 2.725 | 2.685 | 2.646 | 2.608 | 2.571 | 2.535 | 2.500 | 2.467 | 2.433 | 2.402 | 2.370 | 2.340 | 2.310 | 2.281 |
| 24 | 2.767 | 2.724 | 2.685 | 2.646 | 2.609 | 2.571 | 2.535 | 2.500 | 2.466 | 2.434 | 2.402 | 2.370 | 2.340 | 2.310 | 2.281 |
| 25 | 2.766 | 2.725 | 2.684 | 2.646 | 2.608 | 2.571 | 2.535 | 2.500 | 2.467 | 2.433 | 2.402 | 2.370 | 2.339 | 2.310 | 2.281 |
| 26 | 2.767 | 2.724 | 2.685 | 2.646 | 2.609 | 2.571 | 2.535 | 2.500 | 2.466 | 2.434 | 2.402 | 2.370 | 2.340 | 2.310 | 2.281 |

| If the Recovery Year is: | and the Recovery Period is: | | | | | | | | | | | | | | |
|---|---|---|---|---|---|---|---|---|---|---|---|---|---|---|---|
| | 32.5 | 33.0 | 33.5 | 34.0 | 34.5 | 35.0 | 35.5 | 36.0 | 36.5 | 37.0 | 37.5 | 38.0 | 38.5 | 39.0 | 39.5 |
| | the Depreciation Rate is: | | | | | | | | | | | | | | |
| 27 | 2.766 | 2.725 | 2.684 | 2.646 | 2.608 | 2.571 | 2.536 | 2.500 | 2.467 | 2.433 | 2.402 | 2.370 | 2.339 | 2.310 | 2.281 |
| 28 | 2.767 | 2.724 | 2.685 | 2.646 | 2.609 | 2.572 | 2.535 | 2.501 | 2.466 | 2.434 | 2.402 | 2.370 | 2.340 | 2.310 | 2.281 |
| 29 | 2.766 | 2.725 | 2.684 | 2.646 | 2.608 | 2.571 | 2.536 | 2.500 | 2.467 | 2.433 | 2.402 | 2.370 | 2.339 | 2.310 | 2.281 |
| 30 | 2.767 | 2.724 | 2.685 | 2.646 | 2.609 | 2.572 | 2.535 | 2.501 | 2.466 | 2.434 | 2.402 | 2.371 | 2.340 | 2.310 | 2.281 |
| 31 | 2.766 | 2.725 | 2.684 | 2.646 | 2.608 | 2.571 | 2.536 | 2.500 | 2.467 | 2.433 | 2.401 | 2.370 | 2.339 | 2.310 | 2.281 |
| 32 | 2.767 | 2.724 | 2.685 | 2.646 | 2.609 | 2.572 | 2.535 | 2.501 | 2.466 | 2.434 | 2.402 | 2.371 | 2.340 | 2.310 | 2.281 |
| 33 | 2.766 | 2.725 | 2.684 | 2.646 | 2.608 | 2.571 | 2.536 | 2.500 | 2.467 | 2.433 | 2.404 | 2.370 | 2.339 | 2.310 | 2.281 |
| 34 | | 1.362 | 2.685 | 2.645 | 2.609 | 2.572 | 2.535 | 2.501 | 2.466 | 2.434 | 2.402 | 2.371 | 2.340 | 2.310 | 2.281 |
| 35 | | | | 1.323 | 2.608 | 2.571 | 2.536 | 2.500 | 2.467 | 2.433 | 2.401 | 2.370 | 2.339 | 2.310 | 2.281 |
| 36 | | | | | | 1.286 | 2.535 | 2.501 | 2.466 | 2.434 | 2.402 | 2.371 | 2.340 | 2.310 | 2.281 |
| 37 | | | | | | | | 1.250 | 2.467 | 2.433 | 2.401 | 2.370 | 2.339 | 2.310 | 2.281 |
| 38 | | | | | | | | | | 1.217 | 2.402 | 2.371 | 2.340 | 2.310 | 2.281 |
| 39 | | | | | | | | | | | | 1.185 | 2.339 | 2.309 | 2.282 |
| 40 | | | | | | | | | | | | | | 1.155 | 2.281 |

| If the Recovery Year is: | and the Recovery Period is: | | | | | | | | | | | | | | |
|---|---|---|---|---|---|---|---|---|---|---|---|---|---|---|---|
| | 40.0 | 40.5 | 41.0 | 41.5 | 42.0 | 42.5 | 43.0 | 43.5 | 44.0 | 44.5 | 45.0 | 45.5 | 46.0 | 46.5 | 47.0 |
| | the Depreciation Rate is: | | | | | | | | | | | | | | |
| 1 | 1.875 | 1.852 | 1.829 | 1.807 | 1.786 | 1.765 | 1.744 | 1.724 | 1.705 | 1.685 | 1.667 | 1.648 | 1.630 | 1.613 | 1.596 |
| 2 | 3.680 | 3.635 | 3.592 | 3.549 | 3.508 | 3.467 | 3.428 | 3.389 | 3.351 | 3.314 | 3.278 | 3.242 | 3.208 | 3.174 | 3.141 |
| 3 | 3.542 | 3.500 | 3.460 | 3.421 | 3.382 | 3.345 | 3.308 | 3.272 | 3.237 | 3.202 | 3.169 | 3.135 | 3.103 | 3.071 | 3.040 |
| 4 | 3.409 | 3.371 | 3.334 | 3.297 | 3.262 | 3.227 | 3.193 | 3.159 | 3.126 | 3.094 | 3.063 | 3.032 | 3.002 | 2.972 | 2.943 |
| 5 | 3.281 | 3.246 | 3.212 | 3.178 | 3.145 | 3.113 | 3.081 | 3.050 | 3.020 | 2.990 | 2.961 | 2.932 | 2.904 | 2.876 | 2.849 |
| 6 | 3.158 | 3.126 | 3.094 | 3.063 | 3.033 | 3.003 | 2.974 | 2.945 | 2.917 | 2.889 | 2.862 | 2.836 | 2.809 | 2.784 | 2.758 |
| 7 | 3.040 | 3.010 | 2.981 | 2.952 | 2.924 | 2.897 | 2.870 | 2.843 | 2.817 | 2.792 | 2.767 | 2.742 | 2.718 | 2.694 | 2.670 |
| 8 | 2.926 | 2.899 | 2.872 | 2.846 | 2.820 | 2.795 | 2.770 | 2.745 | 2.721 | 2.698 | 2.674 | 2.652 | 2.629 | 2.607 | 2.585 |

| If the Recovery Year is: | 40.0 | 40.5 | 41.0 | 41.5 | 42.0 | 42.5 | 43.0 | 43.5 | 44.0 | 44.5 | 45.0 | 45.5 | 46.0 | 46.5 | 47.0 |
|---|---|---|---|---|---|---|---|---|---|---|---|---|---|---|---|
| | and the Recovery Period is: | | | | | | | | | | | | | | |
| | the Depreciation Rate is: | | | | | | | | | | | | | | |
| 9 | 2.816 | 2.791 | 2.767 | 2.743 | 2.719 | 2.696 | 2.673 | 2.651 | 2.629 | 2.607 | 2.585 | 2.564 | 2.543 | 2.523 | 2.503 |
| 10 | 2.710 | 2.688 | 2.666 | 2.644 | 2.622 | 2.601 | 2.580 | 2.559 | 2.539 | 2.519 | 2.499 | 2.480 | 2.460 | 2.441 | 2.423 |
| 11 | 2.609 | 2.588 | 2.568 | 2.548 | 2.529 | 2.509 | 2.490 | 2.471 | 2.452 | 2.434 | 2.416 | 2.398 | 2.380 | 2.363 | 2.345 |
| 12 | 2.511 | 2.492 | 2.474 | 2.456 | 2.438 | 2.421 | 2.403 | 2.386 | 2.369 | 2.352 | 2.335 | 2.319 | 2.303 | 2.287 | 2.271 |
| 13 | 2.417 | 2.400 | 2.384 | 2.367 | 2.351 | 2.335 | 2.319 | 2.304 | 2.288 | 2.273 | 2.257 | 2.242 | 2.228 | 2.213 | 2.198 |
| 14 | 2.326 | 2.311 | 2.296 | 2.282 | 2.267 | 2.253 | 2.238 | 2.224 | 2.210 | 2.196 | 2.182 | 2.169 | 2.155 | 2.141 | 2.128 |
| 15 | 2.253 | 2.226 | 2.212 | 2.199 | 2.186 | 2.173 | 2.160 | 2.148 | 2.135 | 2.122 | 2.110 | 2.097 | 2.085 | 2.072 | 2.060 |
| 16 | 2.253 | 2.226 | 2.198 | 2.172 | 2.146 | 2.121 | 2.097 | 2.073 | 2.062 | 2.051 | 2.039 | 2.028 | 2.017 | 2.005 | 1.994 |
| 17 | 2.253 | 2.226 | 2.198 | 2.172 | 2.146 | 2.121 | 2.097 | 2.073 | 2.050 | 2.027 | 2.005 | 1.983 | 1.962 | 1.941 | 1.931 |
| 18 | 2.253 | 2.226 | 2.198 | 2.172 | 2.147 | 2.121 | 2.097 | 2.073 | 2.050 | 2.027 | 2.005 | 1.983 | 1.961 | 1.941 | 1.920 |
| 19 | 2.253 | 2.226 | 2.199 | 2.172 | 2.146 | 2.121 | 2.097 | 2.073 | 2.050 | 2.027 | 2.005 | 1.983 | 1.962 | 1.941 | 1.920 |
| 20 | 2.253 | 2.226 | 2.198 | 2.172 | 2.147 | 2.121 | 2.097 | 2.074 | 2.050 | 2.027 | 2.005 | 1.983 | 1.961 | 1.941 | 1.920 |
| 21 | 2.253 | 2.225 | 2.199 | 2.172 | 2.146 | 2.122 | 2.097 | 2.073 | 2.050 | 2.027 | 2.005 | 1.983 | 1.962 | 1.941 | 1.920 |
| 22 | 2.253 | 2.226 | 2.198 | 2.172 | 2.147 | 2.121 | 2.097 | 2.074 | 2.050 | 2.027 | 2.005 | 1.983 | 1.961 | 1.941 | 1.920 |
| 23 | 2.253 | 2.225 | 2.199 | 2.172 | 2.146 | 2.122 | 2.097 | 2.073 | 2.050 | 2.027 | 2.005 | 1.983 | 1.962 | 1.941 | 1.920 |
| 24 | 2.253 | 2.226 | 2.198 | 2.172 | 2.147 | 2.121 | 2.097 | 2.074 | 2.050 | 2.027 | 2.004 | 1.983 | 1.961 | 1.941 | 1.920 |
| 25 | 2.253 | 2.225 | 2.199 | 2.172 | 2.146 | 2.122 | 2.097 | 2.074 | 2.050 | 2.027 | 2.005 | 1.983 | 1.962 | 1.941 | 1.920 |
| 26 | 2.253 | 2.226 | 2.198 | 2.172 | 2.147 | 2.121 | 2.097 | 2.073 | 2.050 | 2.027 | 2.004 | 1.983 | 1.961 | 1.941 | 1.920 |
| 27 | 2.253 | 2.225 | 2.199 | 2.172 | 2.146 | 2.122 | 2.097 | 2.074 | 2.050 | 2.027 | 2.005 | 1.983 | 1.962 | 1.941 | 1.920 |
| 28 | 2.253 | 2.226 | 2.198 | 2.172 | 2.147 | 2.121 | 2.097 | 2.073 | 2.050 | 2.027 | 2.004 | 1.983 | 1.961 | 1.941 | 1.920 |
| 29 | 2.253 | 2.225 | 2.199 | 2.172 | 2.146 | 2.122 | 2.097 | 2.074 | 2.050 | 2.027 | 2.005 | 1.983 | 1.962 | 1.941 | 1.920 |
| 30 | 2.253 | 2.226 | 2.198 | 2.172 | 2.147 | 2.121 | 2.097 | 2.073 | 2.050 | 2.027 | 2.004 | 1.983 | 1.961 | 1.941 | 1.920 |
| 31 | 2.253 | 2.225 | 2.199 | 2.172 | 2.146 | 2.122 | 2.097 | 2.074 | 2.050 | 2.027 | 2.005 | 1.983 | 1.962 | 1.941 | 1.920 |
| 32 | 2.253 | 2.225 | 2.198 | 2.172 | 2.147 | 2.121 | 2.097 | 2.073 | 2.050 | 2.027 | 2.004 | 1.983 | 1.961 | 1.941 | 1.920 |
| 33 | 2.252 | 2.226 | 2.199 | 2.172 | 2.146 | 2.122 | 2.097 | 2.074 | 2.050 | 2.027 | 2.005 | 1.983 | 1.962 | 1.941 | 1.920 |
| 34 | 2.253 | 2.225 | 2.198 | 2.172 | 2.147 | 2.121 | 2.097 | 2.073 | 2.050 | 2.027 | 2.004 | 1.983 | 1.961 | 1.940 | 1.920 |

| If the Recovery Year is: | and the Recovery Period is: 40.0 | 40.5 | 41.0 | 41.5 | 42.0 | 42.5 | 43.0 | 43.5 | 44.0 | 44.5 | 45.0 | 45.5 | 46.0 | 46.5 | 47.0 |
|---|---|---|---|---|---|---|---|---|---|---|---|---|---|---|---|
| | the Depreciation Rate is: | | | | | | | | | | | | | | |
| 35 | 2.252 | 2.226 | 2.199 | 2.173 | 2.146 | 2.122 | 2.097 | 2.074 | 2.050 | 2.027 | 2.005 | 1.983 | 1.962 | 1.941 | 1.920 |
| 36 | 2.253 | 2.225 | 2.198 | 2.172 | 2.147 | 2.121 | 2.098 | 2.073 | 2.050 | 2.027 | 2.004 | 1.982 | 1.961 | 1.940 | 1.920 |
| 37 | 2.252 | 2.226 | 2.199 | 2.173 | 2.146 | 2.122 | 2.097 | 2.074 | 2.050 | 2.027 | 2.005 | 1.983 | 1.962 | 1.941 | 1.920 |
| 38 | 2.253 | 2.225 | 2.198 | 2.172 | 2.147 | 2.121 | 2.098 | 2.073 | 2.050 | 2.027 | 2.004 | 1.982 | 1.961 | 1.940 | 1.920 |
| 39 | 2.252 | 2.226 | 2.199 | 2.173 | 2.146 | 2.122 | 2.097 | 2.074 | 2.050 | 2.027 | 2.005 | 1.983 | 1.962 | 1.941 | 1.921 |
| 40 | 2.253 | 2.225 | 2.198 | 2.172 | 2.147 | 2.121 | 2.098 | 2.073 | 2.049 | 2.027 | 2.004 | 1.982 | 1.961 | 1.940 | 1.920 |
| 41 | 1.126 | 2.226 | 2.199 | 2.173 | 2.146 | 2.122 | 2.097 | 2.074 | 2.050 | 2.027 | 2.005 | 1.983 | 1.962 | 1.941 | 1.921 |
| 42 | | | 1.099 | 2.172 | 2.147 | 2.121 | 2.098 | 2.073 | 2.049 | 2.027 | 2.004 | 1.982 | 1.961 | 1.940 | 1.920 |
| 43 | | | | | 1.073 | 2.122 | 2.097 | 2.074 | 2.050 | 2.027 | 2.005 | 1.983 | 1.962 | 1.941 | 1.921 |
| 44 | | | | | | | 1.049 | 2.073 | 2.049 | 2.027 | 2.004 | 1.982 | 1.961 | 1.940 | 1.920 |
| 45 | | | | | | | | | 1.025 | 2.026 | 2.005 | 1.983 | 1.962 | 1.941 | 1.921 |
| 46 | | | | | | | | | | | 1.002 | 1.982 | 1.961 | 1.940 | 1.920 |
| 47 | | | | | | | | | | | | | 0.981 | 1.941 | 1.921 |
| 48 | | | | | | | | | | | | | | | 0.960 |

| If the Recovery Year is: | and the Recovery Period is: 47.5 | 48.0 | 48.5 | 49.0 | 49.5 | 50.0 |
|---|---|---|---|---|---|---|
| | the Depreciation Rate is: | | | | | |
| 1 | 1.579 | 1.563 | 1.546 | 1.531 | 1.515 | 1.500 |
| 2 | 3.108 | 3.076 | 3.045 | 3.014 | 2.984 | 2.955 |
| 3 | 3.010 | 2.980 | 2.951 | 2.922 | 2.894 | 2.866 |
| 4 | 2.915 | 2.887 | 2.860 | 2.833 | 2.806 | 2.780 |
| 5 | 2.823 | 2.797 | 2.771 | 2.746 | 2.721 | 2.697 |
| 6 | 2.734 | 2.709 | 2.685 | 2.662 | 2.639 | 2.616 |
| 7 | 2.647 | 2.625 | 2.602 | 2.580 | 2.559 | 2.538 |
| 8 | 2.564 | 2.543 | 2.522 | 2.501 | 2.481 | 2.461 |

| If the Recovery Year is: | and the Recovery Period is: 47.5 | 48.0 | 48.5 | 49.0 | 49.5 | 50.0 |
|---|---|---|---|---|---|---|
| | the Depreciation Rate is: | | | | | |
| 9 | 2.483 | 2.463 | 2.444 | 2.425 | 2.406 | 2.388 |
| 10 | 2.404 | 2.386 | 2.368 | 2.351 | 2.333 | 2.316 |
| 11 | 2.328 | 2.312 | 2.295 | 2.279 | 2.262 | 2.246 |
| 12 | 2.255 | 2.239 | 2.224 | 2.209 | 2.194 | 2.179 |
| 13 | 2.184 | 2.169 | 2.155 | 2.141 | 2.127 | 2.114 |
| 14 | 2.115 | 2.102 | 2.089 | 2.076 | 2.063 | 2.050 |
| 15 | 2.048 | 2.036 | 2.024 | 2.012 | 2.000 | 1.989 |
| 16 | 1.983 | 1.972 | 1.961 | 1.951 | 1.940 | 1.929 |
| 17 | 1.921 | 1.911 | 1.901 | 1.891 | 1.881 | 1.871 |
| 18 | 1.900 | 1.880 | 1.861 | 1.842 | 1.824 | 1.815 |
| 19 | 1.900 | 1.880 | 1.861 | 1.842 | 1.824 | 1.806 |
| 20 | 1.900 | 1.880 | 1.861 | 1.842 | 1.824 | 1.806 |
| 21 | 1.900 | 1.880 | 1.861 | 1.842 | 1.824 | 1.806 |
| 22 | 1.900 | 1.880 | 1.861 | 1.842 | 1.824 | 1.806 |
| 23 | 1.900 | 1.880 | 1.861 | 1.842 | 1.824 | 1.806 |
| 24 | 1.900 | 1.880 | 1.861 | 1.842 | 1.824 | 1.806 |
| 25 | 1.900 | 1.880 | 1.861 | 1.842 | 1.824 | 1.806 |
| 26 | 1.900 | 1.880 | 1.861 | 1.842 | 1.824 | 1.806 |
| 27 | 1.900 | 1.880 | 1.861 | 1.842 | 1.824 | 1.806 |
| 28 | 1.900 | 1.880 | 1.861 | 1.842 | 1.824 | 1.806 |
| 29 | 1.900 | 1.880 | 1.861 | 1.843 | 1.824 | 1.806 |
| 30 | 1.900 | 1.881 | 1.861 | 1.842 | 1.824 | 1.806 |
| 31 | 1.900 | 1.880 | 1.861 | 1.843 | 1.824 | 1.806 |
| 32 | 1.900 | 1.881 | 1.861 | 1.842 | 1.824 | 1.806 |
| 33 | 1.900 | 1.880 | 1.861 | 1.843 | 1.824 | 1.806 |
| 34 | 1.900 | 1.881 | 1.861 | 1.842 | 1.824 | 1.806 |

| If the Recovery Year is: | and the Recovery Period is: | | | | | |
|---|---|---|---|---|---|---|
| | 47.5 | 48.0 | 48.5 | 49.0 | 49.5 | 50.0 |
| | the Depreciation Rate is: | | | | | |
| 35 | 1.900 | 1.880 | 1.861 | 1.843 | 1.824 | 1.806 |
| 36 | 1.900 | 1.881 | 1.861 | 1.842 | 1.824 | 1.806 |
| 37 | 1.900 | 1.880 | 1.861 | 1.843 | 1.824 | 1.806 |
| 38 | 1.900 | 1.881 | 1.861 | 1.842 | 1.824 | 1.806 |
| 39 | 1.900 | 1.880 | 1.861 | 1.843 | 1.824 | 1.806 |
| 40 | 1.900 | 1.881 | 1.862 | 1.842 | 1.824 | 1.806 |
| 41 | 1.900 | 1.880 | 1.861 | 1.843 | 1.824 | 1.806 |
| 42 | 1.900 | 1.881 | 1.862 | 1.842 | 1.824 | 1.805 |
| 43 | 1.900 | 1.880 | 1.861 | 1.843 | 1.824 | 1.806 |
| 44 | 1.900 | 1.881 | 1.862 | 1.842 | 1.824 | 1.805 |
| 45 | 1.900 | 1.880 | 1.861 | 1.843 | 1.825 | 1.806 |
| 46 | 1.900 | 1.881 | 1.862 | 1.842 | 1.824 | 1.805 |
| 47 | 1.900 | 1.880 | 1.861 | 1.843 | 1.825 | 1.806 |
| 48 | 1.899 | 1.881 | 1.862 | 1.842 | 1.824 | 1.805 |
| 49 | | 0.940 | 1.861 | 1.843 | 1.825 | 1.806 |
| 50 | | | | 0.921 | 1.824 | 1.805 |
| 51 | | | | | | 0.903 |

TABLE 15
Alternative Minimum Tax (see section 7 of this revenue procedure)
Applicable Depreciation Method: 150-Percent Declining Balance Switching to Straight Line
Applicable Recovery Periods: 2.5 — 50 years
Applicable Convention: Mid-quarter (property placed in service in first quarter)

| If the Recovery Year is: | and the Recovery Period is: 2.5 | 3.0 | 3.5 | 4.0 | 4.5 | 5.0 | 5.5 | 6.0 | 6.5 | 7.0 | 7.5 | 8.0 | 8.5 | 9.0 | 9.5 |
|---|---|---|---|---|---|---|---|---|---|---|---|---|---|---|---|
| | the Depreciation Rate is: | | | | | | | | | | | | | | |
| 1 | 52.50 | 43.75 | 37.50 | 32.81 | 29.17 | 26.25 | 23.86 | 21.88 | 20.19 | 18.75 | 17.50 | 16.41 | 15.44 | 14.58 | 13.82 |
| 2 | 29.23 | 28.13 | 26.79 | 25.20 | 23.61 | 22.13 | 20.77 | 19.53 | 18.42 | 17.41 | 16.50 | 15.67 | 14.92 | 14.24 | 13.61 |
| 3 | 18.27 | 25.00 | 21.98 | 19.76 | 17.99 | 16.52 | 15.27 | 14.65 | 14.17 | 13.68 | 13.20 | 12.74 | 12.29 | 11.86 | 11.46 |
| 4 | | 3.12 | 13.73 | 19.76 | 17.99 | 16.52 | 15.28 | 14.06 | 13.03 | 12.16 | 11.42 | 10.77 | 10.20 | 9.89 | 9.65 |
| 5 | | | | 2.47 | 11.24 | 16.52 | 15.27 | 14.06 | 13.02 | 12.16 | 11.42 | 10.77 | 10.19 | 9.64 | 9.15 |
| 6 | | | | | | 2.06 | 9.55 | 14.06 | 13.03 | 12.16 | 11.41 | 10.76 | 10.20 | 9.65 | 9.15 |
| 7 | | | | | | | | 1.76 | 8.14 | 12.16 | 11.42 | 10.77 | 10.19 | 9.64 | 9.15 |
| 8 | | | | | | | | | | 1.52 | 7.13 | 10.76 | 10.20 | 9.65 | 9.15 |
| 9 | | | | | | | | | | | | 1.35 | 6.37 | 9.64 | 9.14 |
| 10 | | | | | | | | | | | | | | 1.21 | 5.72 |

| If the Recovery Year is: | and the Recovery Period is: 10.0 | 10.5 | 11.0 | 11.5 | 12.0 | 12.5 | 13.0 | 13.5 | 14.0 | 14.5 | 15.0 | 15.5 | 16.0 | 16.5 | 17.0 |
|---|---|---|---|---|---|---|---|---|---|---|---|---|---|---|---|
| | the Depreciation Rate is: | | | | | | | | | | | | | | |
| 1 | 13.13 | 12.50 | 11.93 | 11.41 | 10.94 | 10.50 | 10.10 | 9.72 | 9.38 | 9.05 | 8.75 | 8.47 | 8.20 | 7.95 | 7.72 |
| 2 | 13.03 | 12.50 | 12.01 | 11.56 | 11.13 | 10.74 | 10.37 | 10.03 | 9.71 | 9.41 | 9.13 | 8.86 | 8.61 | 8.37 | 8.14 |
| 3 | 11.08 | 10.71 | 10.37 | 10.05 | 9.74 | 9.45 | 9.18 | 8.92 | 8.67 | 8.44 | 8.21 | 8.00 | 7.80 | 7.61 | 7.42 |
| 4 | 9.41 | 9.18 | 8.96 | 8.74 | 8.52 | 8.32 | 8.12 | 7.93 | 7.74 | 7.56 | 7.39 | 7.23 | 7.07 | 6.92 | 6.77 |
| 5 | 8.71 | 8.32 | 7.96 | 7.64 | 7.46 | 7.32 | 7.18 | 7.04 | 6.91 | 6.78 | 6.65 | 6.53 | 6.41 | 6.29 | 6.17 |
| 6 | 8.71 | 8.32 | 7.96 | 7.64 | 7.33 | 7.04 | 6.78 | 6.53 | 6.31 | 6.10 | 5.99 | 5.89 | 5.80 | 5.71 | 5.63 |

| If the Recovery Year is: | and the Recovery Period is: 10.0 | 10.5 | 11.0 | 11.5 | 12.0 | 12.5 | 13.0 | 13.5 | 14.0 | 14.5 | 15.0 | 15.5 | 16.0 | 16.5 | 17.0 |
|---|---|---|---|---|---|---|---|---|---|---|---|---|---|---|---|
| | the Depreciation Rate is: | | | | | | | | | | | | | | |
| 7 | 8.71 | 8.32 | 7.96 | 7.64 | 7.33 | 7.04 | 6.77 | 6.54 | 6.31 | 6.11 | 5.90 | 5.72 | 5.54 | 5.38 | 5.23 |
| 8 | 8.71 | 8.32 | 7.96 | 7.64 | 7.33 | 7.04 | 6.78 | 6.53 | 6.31 | 6.10 | 5.91 | 5.72 | 5.54 | 5.38 | 5.23 |
| 9 | 8.71 | 8.32 | 7.96 | 7.64 | 7.33 | 7.04 | 6.77 | 6.54 | 6.31 | 6.11 | 5.90 | 5.72 | 5.54 | 5.38 | 5.23 |
| 10 | 8.71 | 8.31 | 7.97 | 7.63 | 7.32 | 7.04 | 6.78 | 6.53 | 6.31 | 6.10 | 5.91 | 5.71 | 5.54 | 5.38 | 5.23 |
| 11 | 1.09 | 5.20 | 7.96 | 7.64 | 7.33 | 7.04 | 6.77 | 6.54 | 6.31 | 6.11 | 5.90 | 5.72 | 5.54 | 5.38 | 5.23 |
| 12 | | | 1.00 | 4.77 | 7.32 | 7.03 | 6.78 | 6.53 | 6.31 | 6.10 | 5.91 | 5.71 | 5.54 | 5.38 | 5.22 |
| 13 | | | | | 0.92 | 4.40 | 6.77 | 6.54 | 6.32 | 6.11 | 5.90 | 5.72 | 5.54 | 5.38 | 5.23 |
| 14 | | | | | | | 0.85 | 4.08 | 6.31 | 6.10 | 5.91 | 5.71 | 5.55 | 5.38 | 5.22 |
| 15 | | | | | | | | | 0.79 | 3.82 | 5.90 | 5.72 | 5.54 | 5.38 | 5.23 |
| 16 | | | | | | | | | | | 0.74 | 3.57 | 5.55 | 5.37 | 5.22 |
| 17 | | | | | | | | | | | | | 0.69 | 3.36 | 5.23 |
| 18 | | | | | | | | | | | | | | | 0.65 |

| If the Recovery Year is: | and the Recovery Period is: 17.5 | 18.0 | 18.5 | 19.0 | 19.5 | 20.0 | 20.5 | 21.0 | 21.5 | 22.0 | 22.5 | 23.0 | 23.5 | 24.0 | 24.5 |
|---|---|---|---|---|---|---|---|---|---|---|---|---|---|---|---|
| | the Depreciation Rate is: | | | | | | | | | | | | | | |
| 1 | 7.50 | 7.29 | 7.09 | 6.91 | 6.73 | 6.563 | 6.402 | 6.250 | 6.105 | 5.966 | 5.833 | 5.707 | 5.585 | 5.469 | 5.357 |
| 2 | 7.93 | 7.73 | 7.53 | 7.35 | 7.17 | 7.008 | 6.849 | 6.696 | 6.551 | 6.411 | 6.278 | 6.150 | 6.026 | 5.908 | 5.794 |
| 3 | 7.25 | 7.08 | 6.92 | 6.77 | 6.62 | 6.482 | 6.347 | 6.218 | 6.094 | 5.974 | 5.859 | 5.748 | 5.642 | 5.539 | 5.440 |
| 4 | 6.63 | 6.49 | 6.36 | 6.23 | 6.11 | 5.996 | 5.883 | 5.774 | 5.669 | 5.567 | 5.469 | 5.374 | 5.282 | 5.193 | 5.107 |
| 5 | 6.06 | 5.95 | 5.85 | 5.74 | 5.64 | 5.546 | 5.453 | 5.362 | 5.273 | 5.187 | 5.104 | 5.023 | 4.945 | 4.868 | 4.794 |
| 6 | 5.54 | 5.45 | 5.37 | 5.29 | 5.21 | 5.130 | 5.054 | 4.979 | 4.905 | 4.834 | 4.764 | 4.696 | 4.629 | 4.564 | 4.500 |
| 7 | 5.08 | 5.00 | 4.94 | 4.87 | 4.81 | 4.746 | 4.684 | 4.623 | 4.563 | 4.504 | 4.446 | 4.389 | 4.333 | 4.279 | 4.225 |
| 8 | 5.08 | 4.94 | 4.81 | 4.69 | 4.57 | 4.459 | 4.354 | 4.293 | 4.245 | 4.197 | 4.150 | 4.103 | 4.057 | 4.011 | 3.966 |
| 9 | 5.08 | 4.95 | 4.81 | 4.69 | 4.57 | 4.459 | 4.354 | 4.252 | 4.154 | 4.061 | 3.972 | 3.888 | 3.808 | 3.761 | 3.723 |
| 10 | 5.08 | 4.94 | 4.81 | 4.69 | 4.57 | 4.459 | 4.354 | 4.252 | 4.154 | 4.061 | 3.972 | 3.888 | 3.808 | 3.729 | 3.654 |

| If the Recovery Year is: | and the Recovery Period is: 17.5 | 18.0 | 18.5 | 19.0 | 19.5 | 20.0 | 20.5 | 21.0 | 21.5 | 22.0 | 22.5 | 23.0 | 23.5 | 24.0 | 24.5 |
|---|---|---|---|---|---|---|---|---|---|---|---|---|---|---|---|
| | the Depreciation Rate is: | | | | | | | | | | | | | | |
| 11 | 5.08 | 4.95 | 4.81 | 4.69 | 4.57 | 4.459 | 4.354 | 4.252 | 4.154 | 4.061 | 3.973 | 3.888 | 3.808 | 3.729 | 3.654 |
| 12 | 5.09 | 4.94 | 4.81 | 4.69 | 4.57 | 4.460 | 4.354 | 4.252 | 4.154 | 4.061 | 3.972 | 3.888 | 3.808 | 3.730 | 3.654 |
| 13 | 5.08 | 4.95 | 4.81 | 4.69 | 4.57 | 4.459 | 4.355 | 4.252 | 4.154 | 4.061 | 3.973 | 3.888 | 3.808 | 3.729 | 3.654 |
| 14 | 5.09 | 4.94 | 4.81 | 4.69 | 4.57 | 4.460 | 4.354 | 4.252 | 4.154 | 4.061 | 3.972 | 3.888 | 3.808 | 3.730 | 3.654 |
| 15 | 5.08 | 4.95 | 4.82 | 4.68 | 4.57 | 4.459 | 4.355 | 4.252 | 4.154 | 4.061 | 3.973 | 3.888 | 3.808 | 3.729 | 3.654 |
| 16 | 5.09 | 4.94 | 4.81 | 4.69 | 4.57 | 4.460 | 4.354 | 4.252 | 4.154 | 4.061 | 3.972 | 3.888 | 3.808 | 3.730 | 3.654 |
| 17 | 5.08 | 4.95 | 4.82 | 4.68 | 4.57 | 4.459 | 4.355 | 4.252 | 4.153 | 4.061 | 3.973 | 3.889 | 3.808 | 3.729 | 3.654 |
| 18 | 3.18 | 4.94 | 4.81 | 4.69 | 4.58 | 4.460 | 4.354 | 4.251 | 4.154 | 4.061 | 3.972 | 3.888 | 3.808 | 3.730 | 3.654 |
| 19 | | 0.62 | 3.01 | 4.68 | 4.57 | 4.459 | 4.355 | 4.252 | 4.153 | 4.061 | 3.973 | 3.889 | 3.808 | 3.729 | 3.654 |
| 20 | | | | 0.59 | 2.86 | 4.460 | 4.354 | 4.251 | 4.154 | 4.060 | 3.972 | 3.888 | 3.808 | 3.730 | 3.654 |
| 21 | | | | | | 0.557 | 2.722 | 4.252 | 4.153 | 4.061 | 3.973 | 3.889 | 3.808 | 3.729 | 3.654 |
| 22 | | | | | | | | 0.531 | 2.596 | 4.060 | 3.972 | 3.888 | 3.808 | 3.730 | 3.654 |
| 23 | | | | | | | | | | 0.508 | 2.483 | 3.889 | 3.809 | 3.729 | 3.654 |
| 24 | | | | | | | | | | | | 0.486 | 2.380 | 3.730 | 3.654 |
| 25 | | | | | | | | | | | | | | 0.466 | 2.284 |

| If the Recovery Year is: | and the Recovery Period is: 25.0 | 25.5 | 26.0 | 26.5 | 27.0 | 27.5 | 28.0 | 28.5 | 29.0 | 29.5 | 30.0 | 30.5 | 31.0 | 31.5 | 32.0 |
|---|---|---|---|---|---|---|---|---|---|---|---|---|---|---|---|
| | the Depreciation Rate is: | | | | | | | | | | | | | | |
| 1 | 5.250 | 5.147 | 5.048 | 4.953 | 4.861 | 4.773 | 4.688 | 4.605 | 4.526 | 4.449 | 4.375 | 4.303 | 4.234 | 4.167 | 4.102 |
| 2 | 5.685 | 5.580 | 5.478 | 5.380 | 5.286 | 5.194 | 5.106 | 5.021 | 4.938 | 4.859 | 4.781 | 4.706 | 4.634 | 4.563 | 4.495 |
| 3 | 5.344 | 5.251 | 5.162 | 5.075 | 4.992 | 4.911 | 4.832 | 4.757 | 4.683 | 4.611 | 4.542 | 4.475 | 4.410 | 4.346 | 4.285 |
| 4 | 5.023 | 4.942 | 4.864 | 4.788 | 4.714 | 4.643 | 4.574 | 4.506 | 4.441 | 4.377 | 4.315 | 4.255 | 4.196 | 4.139 | 4.084 |
| 5 | 4.722 | 4.652 | 4.584 | 4.517 | 4.453 | 4.390 | 4.329 | 4.269 | 4.211 | 4.154 | 4.099 | 4.046 | 3.993 | 3.942 | 3.892 |
| 6 | 4.439 | 4.378 | 4.319 | 4.262 | 4.205 | 4.150 | 4.097 | 4.044 | 3.993 | 3.943 | 3.894 | 3.847 | 3.800 | 3.754 | 3.710 |
| 7 | 4.172 | 4.121 | 4.070 | 4.020 | 3.972 | 3.924 | 3.877 | 3.831 | 3.787 | 3.743 | 3.700 | 3.657 | 3.616 | 3.576 | 3.536 |

| If the Recovery Year is: | 25.0 | 25.5 | 26.0 | 26.5 | 27.0 | 27.5 | 28.0 | 28.5 | 29.0 | 29.5 | 30.0 | 30.5 | 31.0 | 31.5 | 32.0 |
|---|---|---|---|---|---|---|---|---|---|---|---|---|---|---|---|
| | and the Recovery Period is: | | | | | | | | | | | | | | |
| | the Depreciation Rate is: | | | | | | | | | | | | | | |
| 8 | 3.922 | 3.878 | 3.834 | 3.793 | 3.751 | 3.710 | 3.669 | 3.630 | 3.591 | 3.552 | 3.515 | 3.478 | 3.441 | 3.405 | 3.370 |
| 9 | 3.687 | 3.650 | 3.615 | 3.578 | 3.543 | 3.508 | 3.473 | 3.439 | 3.405 | 3.372 | 3.339 | 3.307 | 3.275 | 3.243 | 3.212 |
| 10 | 3.582 | 3.513 | 3.447 | 3.383 | 3.346 | 3.316 | 3.287 | 3.258 | 3.229 | 3.200 | 3.172 | 3.144 | 3.116 | 3.089 | 3.062 |
| 11 | 3.582 | 3.513 | 3.447 | 3.384 | 3.321 | 3.261 | 3.204 | 3.148 | 3.095 | 3.044 | 3.013 | 2.989 | 2.965 | 2.942 | 2.918 |
| 12 | 3.582 | 3.513 | 3.447 | 3.383 | 3.321 | 3.261 | 3.204 | 3.148 | 3.095 | 3.044 | 2.994 | 2.945 | 2.898 | 2.853 | 2.809 |
| 13 | 3.582 | 3.513 | 3.447 | 3.384 | 3.321 | 3.261 | 3.204 | 3.149 | 3.095 | 3.044 | 2.994 | 2.945 | 2.898 | 2.853 | 2.809 |
| 14 | 3.582 | 3.513 | 3.447 | 3.383 | 3.321 | 3.261 | 3.204 | 3.148 | 3.095 | 3.044 | 2.994 | 2.945 | 2.898 | 2.853 | 2.809 |
| 15 | 3.582 | 3.513 | 3.447 | 3.384 | 3.321 | 3.261 | 3.204 | 3.149 | 3.095 | 3.044 | 2.994 | 2.945 | 2.898 | 2.852 | 2.809 |
| 16 | 3.582 | 3.513 | 3.447 | 3.383 | 3.321 | 3.261 | 3.204 | 3.148 | 3.095 | 3.044 | 2.994 | 2.945 | 2.898 | 2.853 | 2.809 |
| 17 | 3.582 | 3.513 | 3.447 | 3.384 | 3.321 | 3.262 | 3.204 | 3.149 | 3.095 | 3.044 | 2.994 | 2.945 | 2.898 | 2.852 | 2.809 |
| 18 | 3.582 | 3.513 | 3.447 | 3.383 | 3.321 | 3.261 | 3.204 | 3.148 | 3.095 | 3.044 | 2.994 | 2.945 | 2.898 | 2.853 | 2.809 |
| 19 | 3.581 | 3.513 | 3.447 | 3.384 | 3.322 | 3.262 | 3.204 | 3.149 | 3.095 | 3.044 | 2.994 | 2.945 | 2.898 | 2.852 | 2.809 |
| 20 | 3.582 | 3.513 | 3.446 | 3.383 | 3.321 | 3.261 | 3.204 | 3.148 | 3.095 | 3.044 | 2.994 | 2.945 | 2.898 | 2.853 | 2.809 |
| 21 | 3.581 | 3.513 | 3.447 | 3.384 | 3.322 | 3.262 | 3.203 | 3.149 | 3.095 | 3.044 | 2.993 | 2.945 | 2.898 | 2.852 | 2.808 |
| 22 | 3.582 | 3.512 | 3.446 | 3.383 | 3.321 | 3.261 | 3.204 | 3.148 | 3.096 | 3.044 | 2.994 | 2.945 | 2.898 | 2.853 | 2.809 |
| 23 | 3.581 | 3.513 | 3.447 | 3.384 | 3.322 | 3.262 | 3.203 | 3.149 | 3.095 | 3.044 | 2.993 | 2.945 | 2.898 | 2.852 | 2.808 |
| 24 | 3.582 | 3.512 | 3.446 | 3.383 | 3.321 | 3.261 | 3.204 | 3.148 | 3.096 | 3.044 | 2.994 | 2.945 | 2.898 | 2.853 | 2.809 |
| 25 | 3.581 | 3.513 | 3.447 | 3.384 | 3.322 | 3.262 | 3.203 | 3.149 | 3.095 | 3.044 | 2.993 | 2.945 | 2.898 | 2.852 | 2.808 |
| 26 | 0.448 | 2.195 | 3.446 | 3.383 | 3.321 | 3.261 | 3.204 | 3.148 | 3.096 | 3.044 | 2.994 | 2.945 | 2.898 | 2.853 | 2.809 |
| 27 | | | 0.431 | 2.115 | 3.322 | 3.262 | 3.203 | 3.149 | 3.095 | 3.044 | 2.993 | 2.944 | 2.898 | 2.852 | 2.808 |
| 28 | | | | | 0.415 | 2.038 | 3.204 | 3.148 | 3.096 | 3.045 | 2.994 | 2.945 | 2.897 | 2.853 | 2.809 |
| 29 | | | | | | | 0.400 | 1.968 | 3.095 | 3.044 | 2.993 | 2.944 | 2.898 | 2.852 | 2.808 |
| 30 | | | | | | | | | 0.387 | 1.903 | 2.994 | 2.945 | 2.897 | 2.853 | 2.809 |
| 31 | | | | | | | | | | | 0.374 | 1.840 | 2.898 | 2.852 | 2.808 |
| 32 | | | | | | | | | | | | | 0.362 | 1.783 | 2.809 |
| 33 | | | | | | | | | | | | | | | 0.351 |

| If the Recovery Year is: | and the Recovery Period is: 32.5 | 33.0 | 33.5 | 34.0 | 34.5 | 35.0 | 35.5 | 36.0 | 36.5 | 37.0 | 37.5 | 38.0 | 38.5 | 39.0 | 39.5 |
|---|---|---|---|---|---|---|---|---|---|---|---|---|---|---|---|
| | the Depreciation Rate is: | | | | | | | | | | | | | | |
| 1 | 4.038 | 3.977 | 3.918 | 3.860 | 3.804 | 3.750 | 3.697 | 3.646 | 3.596 | 3.547 | 3.500 | 3.454 | 3.409 | 3.365 | 3.323 |
| 2 | 4.429 | 4.365 | 4.302 | 4.241 | 4.182 | 4.125 | 4.069 | 4.015 | 3.962 | 3.910 | 3.860 | 3.811 | 3.763 | 3.717 | 3.671 |
| 3 | 4.225 | 4.166 | 4.110 | 4.054 | 4.001 | 3.948 | 3.897 | 3.847 | 3.799 | 3.752 | 3.706 | 3.661 | 3.617 | 3.574 | 3.532 |
| 4 | 4.030 | 3.977 | 3.926 | 3.876 | 3.827 | 3.779 | 3.733 | 3.687 | 3.643 | 3.600 | 3.557 | 3.516 | 3.476 | 3.436 | 3.398 |
| 5 | 3.844 | 3.796 | 3.750 | 3.705 | 3.660 | 3.617 | 3.575 | 3.534 | 3.493 | 3.454 | 3.415 | 3.377 | 3.340 | 3.304 | 3.269 |
| 6 | 3.666 | 3.624 | 3.582 | 3.541 | 3.501 | 3.462 | 3.424 | 3.386 | 3.350 | 3.314 | 3.278 | 3.244 | 3.210 | 3.177 | 3.145 |
| 7 | 3.497 | 3.459 | 3.421 | 3.385 | 3.349 | 3.314 | 3.279 | 3.245 | 3.212 | 3.179 | 3.147 | 3.116 | 3.085 | 3.055 | 3.025 |
| 8 | 3.336 | 3.302 | 3.268 | 3.235 | 3.203 | 3.172 | 3.141 | 3.110 | 3.080 | 3.050 | 3.021 | 2.993 | 2.965 | 2.937 | 2.910 |
| 9 | 3.182 | 3.152 | 3.122 | 3.093 | 3.064 | 3.036 | 3.008 | 2.980 | 2.953 | 2.927 | 2.901 | 2.875 | 2.849 | 2.824 | 2.800 |
| 10 | 3.035 | 3.008 | 2.982 | 2.956 | 2.931 | 2.906 | 2.881 | 2.856 | 2.832 | 2.808 | 2.785 | 2.761 | 2.738 | 2.716 | 2.693 |
| 11 | 2.895 | 2.872 | 2.849 | 2.826 | 2.803 | 2.781 | 2.759 | 2.737 | 2.716 | 2.694 | 2.673 | 2.652 | 2.632 | 2.611 | 2.591 |
| 12 | 2.766 | 2.741 | 2.721 | 2.701 | 2.682 | 2.662 | 2.642 | 2.623 | 2.604 | 2.585 | 2.566 | 2.548 | 2.529 | 2.511 | 2.493 |
| 13 | 2.766 | 2.725 | 2.684 | 2.645 | 2.607 | 2.571 | 2.535 | 2.514 | 2.497 | 2.480 | 2.464 | 2.447 | 2.431 | 2.414 | 2.398 |
| 14 | 2.766 | 2.725 | 2.684 | 2.645 | 2.607 | 2.571 | 2.535 | 2.500 | 2.466 | 2.433 | 2.401 | 2.370 | 2.340 | 2.322 | 2.307 |
| 15 | 2.766 | 2.725 | 2.684 | 2.645 | 2.607 | 2.571 | 2.535 | 2.500 | 2.466 | 2.433 | 2.401 | 2.370 | 2.340 | 2.310 | 2.281 |
| 16 | 2.766 | 2.725 | 2.684 | 2.645 | 2.607 | 2.571 | 2.535 | 2.500 | 2.466 | 2.433 | 2.401 | 2.370 | 2.340 | 2.310 | 2.281 |
| 17 | 2.766 | 2.725 | 2.684 | 2.645 | 2.608 | 2.571 | 2.535 | 2.500 | 2.466 | 2.433 | 2.401 | 2.370 | 2.340 | 2.310 | 2.281 |
| 18 | 2.767 | 2.725 | 2.684 | 2.645 | 2.607 | 2.571 | 2.535 | 2.500 | 2.466 | 2.433 | 2.401 | 2.370 | 2.340 | 2.310 | 2.281 |
| 19 | 2.766 | 2.725 | 2.684 | 2.645 | 2.608 | 2.571 | 2.535 | 2.500 | 2.466 | 2.433 | 2.401 | 2.370 | 2.340 | 2.310 | 2.281 |
| 20 | 2.767 | 2.725 | 2.685 | 2.645 | 2.607 | 2.571 | 2.535 | 2.500 | 2.466 | 2.433 | 2.401 | 2.370 | 2.340 | 2.310 | 2.281 |
| 21 | 2.766 | 2.725 | 2.684 | 2.645 | 2.608 | 2.571 | 2.535 | 2.500 | 2.466 | 2.433 | 2.401 | 2.370 | 2.340 | 2.310 | 2.281 |
| 22 | 2.767 | 2.725 | 2.685 | 2.645 | 2.607 | 2.571 | 2.535 | 2.500 | 2.466 | 2.433 | 2.401 | 2.370 | 2.340 | 2.310 | 2.281 |
| 23 | 2.766 | 2.725 | 2.684 | 2.646 | 2.608 | 2.571 | 2.535 | 2.501 | 2.466 | 2.433 | 2.401 | 2.370 | 2.340 | 2.310 | 2.281 |
| 24 | 2.767 | 2.725 | 2.685 | 2.645 | 2.607 | 2.570 | 2.535 | 2.500 | 2.466 | 2.433 | 2.401 | 2.370 | 2.340 | 2.310 | 2.281 |
| 25 | 2.766 | 2.724 | 2.684 | 2.646 | 2.608 | 2.571 | 2.535 | 2.501 | 2.466 | 2.433 | 2.401 | 2.370 | 2.340 | 2.310 | 2.281 |
| 26 | 2.767 | 2.725 | 2.685 | 2.645 | 2.607 | 2.570 | 2.536 | 2.500 | 2.466 | 2.433 | 2.401 | 2.370 | 2.340 | 2.310 | 2.281 |

| If the Recovery Year is: | and the Recovery Period is: 32.5 | 33.0 | 33.5 | 34.0 | 34.5 | 35.0 | 35.5 | 36.0 | 36.5 | 37.0 | 37.5 | 38.0 | 38.5 | 39.0 | 39.5 |
|---|---|---|---|---|---|---|---|---|---|---|---|---|---|---|---|
| | the Depreciation Rate is: | | | | | | | | | | | | | | |
| 27 | 2.766 | 2.724 | 2.684 | 2.646 | 2.608 | 2.571 | 2.535 | 2.501 | 2.466 | 2.433 | 2.401 | 2.370 | 2.339 | 2.310 | 2.281 |
| 28 | 2.767 | 2.725 | 2.685 | 2.645 | 2.607 | 2.570 | 2.536 | 2.500 | 2.466 | 2.433 | 2.401 | 2.370 | 2.340 | 2.310 | 2.281 |
| 29 | 2.766 | 2.724 | 2.684 | 2.646 | 2.608 | 2.571 | 2.535 | 2.501 | 2.466 | 2.433 | 2.401 | 2.370 | 2.339 | 2.310 | 2.281 |
| 30 | 2.767 | 2.725 | 2.685 | 2.645 | 2.607 | 2.570 | 2.536 | 2.500 | 2.466 | 2.433 | 2.401 | 2.370 | 2.340 | 2.310 | 2.280 |
| 31 | 2.766 | 2.724 | 2.684 | 2.646 | 2.608 | 2.571 | 2.535 | 2.501 | 2.467 | 2.434 | 2.401 | 2.370 | 2.339 | 2.310 | 2.281 |
| 32 | 2.767 | 2.725 | 2.685 | 2.645 | 2.607 | 2.570 | 2.536 | 2.500 | 2.466 | 2.433 | 2.401 | 2.370 | 2.340 | 2.310 | 2.280 |
| 33 | 1.729 | 2.724 | 2.684 | 2.646 | 2.608 | 2.571 | 2.535 | 2.501 | 2.467 | 2.434 | 2.401 | 2.370 | 2.339 | 2.310 | 2.281 |
| 34 | | 0.341 | 1.678 | 2.645 | 2.607 | 2.570 | 2.536 | 2.500 | 2.466 | 2.433 | 2.402 | 2.370 | 2.340 | 2.310 | 2.280 |
| 35 | | | | 0.331 | 1.630 | 2.571 | 2.535 | 2.501 | 2.467 | 2.434 | 2.401 | 2.370 | 2.339 | 2.310 | 2.281 |
| 36 | | | | | | 0.321 | 1.585 | 2.500 | 2.466 | 2.433 | 2.402 | 2.370 | 2.340 | 2.310 | 2.280 |
| 37 | | | | | | | | 0.313 | 1.542 | 2.434 | 2.401 | 2.369 | 2.339 | 2.309 | 2.281 |
| 38 | | | | | | | | | | 0.304 | 1.501 | 2.370 | 2.340 | 2.310 | 2.280 |
| 39 | | | | | | | | | | | | 0.296 | 1.462 | 2.309 | 2.281 |
| 40 | | | | | | | | | | | | | | 0.289 | 1.425 |

| If the Recovery Year is: | and the Recovery Period is: 40.0 | 40.5 | 41.0 | 41.5 | 42.0 | 42.5 | 43.0 | 43.5 | 44.0 | 44.5 | 45.0 | 45.5 | 46.0 | 46.5 | 47.0 |
|---|---|---|---|---|---|---|---|---|---|---|---|---|---|---|---|
| | the Depreciation Rate is: | | | | | | | | | | | | | | |
| 1 | 3.281 | 3.241 | 3.201 | 3.163 | 3.125 | 3.088 | 3.052 | 3.017 | 2.983 | 2.949 | 2.917 | 2.885 | 2.853 | 2.823 | 2.793 |
| 2 | 3.627 | 3.584 | 3.541 | 3.500 | 3.460 | 3.420 | 3.382 | 3.344 | 3.307 | 3.271 | 3.236 | 3.202 | 3.168 | 3.135 | 3.102 |
| 3 | 3.491 | 3.451 | 3.412 | 3.374 | 3.336 | 3.300 | 3.264 | 3.229 | 3.195 | 3.161 | 3.128 | 3.096 | 3.065 | 3.034 | 3.003 |
| 4 | 3.360 | 3.323 | 3.287 | 3.252 | 3.217 | 3.183 | 3.150 | 3.118 | 3.086 | 3.055 | 3.024 | 2.994 | 2.965 | 2.936 | 2.908 |
| 5 | 3.234 | 3.200 | 3.167 | 3.134 | 3.102 | 3.071 | 3.040 | 3.010 | 2.981 | 2.952 | 2.923 | 2.895 | 2.868 | 2.841 | 2.815 |
| 6 | 3.113 | 3.082 | 3.051 | 3.021 | 2.991 | 2.963 | 2.934 | 2.906 | 2.879 | 2.852 | 2.826 | 2.800 | 2.774 | 2.749 | 2.725 |
| 7 | 2.996 | 2.967 | 2.939 | 2.912 | 2.885 | 2.858 | 2.832 | 2.806 | 2.781 | 2.756 | 2.732 | 2.708 | 2.684 | 2.661 | 2.638 |
| 8 | 2.884 | 2.857 | 2.832 | 2.806 | 2.782 | 2.757 | 2.733 | 2.709 | 2.686 | 2.663 | 2.640 | 2.618 | 2.596 | 2.575 | 2.554 |

| If the Recovery Year is: | and the Recovery Period is: 40.0 | 40.5 | 41.0 | 41.5 | 42.0 | 42.5 | 43.0 | 43.5 | 44.0 | 44.5 | 45.0 | 45.5 | 46.0 | 46.5 | 47.0 |
|---|---|---|---|---|---|---|---|---|---|---|---|---|---|---|---|
| | the Depreciation Rate is: | | | | | | | | | | | | | | |
| 9 | 2.776 | 2.752 | 2.728 | 2.705 | 2.682 | 2.660 | 2.638 | 2.616 | 2.594 | 2.573 | 2.552 | 2.532 | 2.512 | 2.492 | 2.472 |
| 10 | 2.671 | 2.650 | 2.628 | 2.607 | 2.586 | 2.566 | 2.546 | 2.526 | 2.506 | 2.487 | 2.467 | 2.448 | 2.430 | 2.411 | 2.393 |
| 11 | 2.571 | 2.552 | 2.532 | 2.513 | 2.494 | 2.475 | 2.457 | 2.439 | 2.421 | 2.403 | 2.385 | 2.368 | 2.351 | 2.334 | 2.317 |
| 12 | 2.475 | 2.457 | 2.440 | 2.422 | 2.405 | 2.388 | 2.371 | 2.354 | 2.338 | 2.322 | 2.306 | 2.290 | 2.274 | 2.258 | 2.243 |
| 13 | 2.382 | 2.366 | 2.350 | 2.335 | 2.319 | 2.304 | 2.288 | 2.273 | 2.258 | 2.243 | 2.229 | 2.214 | 2.200 | 2.186 | 2.171 |
| 14 | 2.293 | 2.278 | 2.264 | 2.250 | 2.236 | 2.222 | 2.209 | 2.195 | 2.181 | 2.168 | 2.154 | 2.141 | 2.128 | 2.115 | 2.102 |
| 15 | 2.252 | 2.225 | 2.198 | 2.172 | 2.156 | 2.144 | 2.132 | 2.119 | 2.107 | 2.095 | 2.083 | 2.071 | 2.059 | 2.047 | 2.035 |
| 16 | 2.252 | 2.225 | 2.198 | 2.172 | 2.147 | 2.121 | 2.097 | 2.073 | 2.050 | 2.027 | 2.013 | 2.002 | 1.992 | 1.981 | 1.970 |
| 17 | 2.253 | 2.225 | 2.198 | 2.172 | 2.146 | 2.121 | 2.097 | 2.073 | 2.050 | 2.027 | 2.005 | 1.983 | 1.961 | 1.940 | 1.920 |
| 18 | 2.252 | 2.225 | 2.198 | 2.172 | 2.147 | 2.121 | 2.097 | 2.073 | 2.050 | 2.027 | 2.005 | 1.983 | 1.961 | 1.940 | 1.920 |
| 19 | 2.253 | 2.225 | 2.198 | 2.172 | 2.146 | 2.121 | 2.097 | 2.073 | 2.050 | 2.027 | 2.005 | 1.983 | 1.961 | 1.940 | 1.920 |
| 20 | 2.252 | 2.225 | 2.198 | 2.172 | 2.147 | 2.121 | 2.097 | 2.073 | 2.050 | 2.027 | 2.005 | 1.983 | 1.961 | 1.940 | 1.920 |
| 21 | 2.253 | 2.225 | 2.198 | 2.172 | 2.146 | 2.121 | 2.097 | 2.073 | 2.050 | 2.027 | 2.005 | 1.983 | 1.961 | 1.940 | 1.920 |
| 22 | 2.252 | 2.225 | 2.198 | 2.172 | 2.147 | 2.121 | 2.097 | 2.073 | 2.050 | 2.027 | 2.005 | 1.983 | 1.961 | 1.940 | 1.920 |
| 23 | 2.253 | 2.225 | 2.198 | 2.172 | 2.146 | 2.121 | 2.097 | 2.073 | 2.050 | 2.027 | 2.005 | 1.983 | 1.961 | 1.940 | 1.920 |
| 24 | 2.252 | 2.225 | 2.198 | 2.172 | 2.147 | 2.121 | 2.097 | 2.073 | 2.050 | 2.027 | 2.005 | 1.983 | 1.961 | 1.940 | 1.920 |
| 25 | 2.253 | 2.225 | 2.198 | 2.172 | 2.146 | 2.121 | 2.097 | 2.073 | 2.050 | 2.027 | 2.004 | 1.983 | 1.961 | 1.940 | 1.920 |
| 26 | 2.252 | 2.225 | 2.198 | 2.172 | 2.147 | 2.121 | 2.097 | 2.073 | 2.050 | 2.027 | 2.005 | 1.982 | 1.961 | 1.940 | 1.920 |
| 27 | 2.253 | 2.225 | 2.198 | 2.172 | 2.146 | 2.122 | 2.097 | 2.073 | 2.049 | 2.027 | 2.004 | 1.983 | 1.961 | 1.940 | 1.920 |
| 28 | 2.252 | 2.225 | 2.199 | 2.172 | 2.147 | 2.121 | 2.097 | 2.073 | 2.050 | 2.027 | 2.005 | 1.982 | 1.961 | 1.940 | 1.920 |
| 29 | 2.253 | 2.225 | 2.198 | 2.172 | 2.146 | 2.122 | 2.097 | 2.073 | 2.049 | 2.027 | 2.004 | 1.983 | 1.961 | 1.941 | 1.920 |
| 30 | 2.252 | 2.225 | 2.199 | 2.172 | 2.147 | 2.121 | 2.097 | 2.073 | 2.050 | 2.027 | 2.005 | 1.982 | 1.961 | 1.940 | 1.920 |
| 31 | 2.253 | 2.225 | 2.198 | 2.172 | 2.146 | 2.122 | 2.097 | 2.073 | 2.049 | 2.027 | 2.004 | 1.983 | 1.961 | 1.941 | 1.920 |
| 32 | 2.252 | 2.225 | 2.199 | 2.172 | 2.147 | 2.121 | 2.096 | 2.073 | 2.050 | 2.027 | 2.005 | 1.982 | 1.961 | 1.940 | 1.920 |
| 33 | 2.253 | 2.225 | 2.198 | 2.172 | 2.146 | 2.122 | 2.097 | 2.073 | 2.049 | 2.027 | 2.004 | 1.983 | 1.961 | 1.941 | 1.920 |
| 34 | 2.252 | 2.225 | 2.199 | 2.173 | 2.147 | 2.121 | 2.096 | 2.073 | 2.050 | 2.027 | 2.005 | 1.982 | 1.961 | 1.940 | 1.920 |

| If the Recovery Year is: | 40.0 | 40.5 | 41.0 | 41.5 | 42.0 | 42.5 | 43.0 | 43.5 | 44.0 | 44.5 | 45.0 | 45.5 | 46.0 | 46.5 | 47.0 |
|---|---|---|---|---|---|---|---|---|---|---|---|---|---|---|---|
| | and the Recovery Period is: | | | | | | | | | | | | | | |
| | the Depreciation Rate is: | | | | | | | | | | | | | | |
| 35 | 2.253 | 2.225 | 2.198 | 2.172 | 2.146 | 2.122 | 2.097 | 2.073 | 2.049 | 2.027 | 2.004 | 1.983 | 1.961 | 1.941 | 1.920 |
| 36 | 2.252 | 2.225 | 2.199 | 2.173 | 2.147 | 2.121 | 2.096 | 2.073 | 2.050 | 2.027 | 2.005 | 1.982 | 1.962 | 1.940 | 1.920 |
| 37 | 2.253 | 2.225 | 2.198 | 2.172 | 2.146 | 2.122 | 2.097 | 2.073 | 2.049 | 2.027 | 2.004 | 1.983 | 1.961 | 1.941 | 1.920 |
| 38 | 2.252 | 2.225 | 2.199 | 2.173 | 2.147 | 2.121 | 2.096 | 2.073 | 2.050 | 2.027 | 2.005 | 1.982 | 1.962 | 1.940 | 1.920 |
| 39 | 2.253 | 2.225 | 2.198 | 2.172 | 2.146 | 2.122 | 2.097 | 2.073 | 2.049 | 2.027 | 2.004 | 1.983 | 1.961 | 1.941 | 1.920 |
| 40 | 2.252 | 2.225 | 2.199 | 2.173 | 2.147 | 2.121 | 2.096 | 2.073 | 2.050 | 2.027 | 2.005 | 1.982 | 1.962 | 1.940 | 1.920 |
| 41 | 0.282 | 1.390 | 2.198 | 2.172 | 2.146 | 2.122 | 2.097 | 2.073 | 2.049 | 2.027 | 2.004 | 1.983 | 1.961 | 1.941 | 1.920 |
| 42 | | | 0.275 | 1.358 | 2.147 | 2.121 | 2.096 | 2.073 | 2.050 | 2.027 | 2.005 | 1.982 | 1.962 | 1.940 | 1.920 |
| 43 | | | | | 0.268 | 1.326 | 2.097 | 2.073 | 2.049 | 2.027 | 2.004 | 1.983 | 1.961 | 1.941 | 1.920 |
| 44 | | | | | | | 0.262 | 1.295 | 2.050 | 2.027 | 2.005 | 1.982 | 1.962 | 1.940 | 1.920 |
| 45 | | | | | | | | | 0.256 | 1.267 | 2.004 | 1.983 | 1.961 | 1.941 | 1.920 |
| 46 | | | | | | | | | | | 0.251 | 1.239 | 1.962 | 1.940 | 1.920 |
| 47 | | | | | | | | | | | | | 0.245 | 1.213 | 1.919 |
| 48 | | | | | | | | | | | | | | | 0.240 |

| If the Recovery Year is: | 47.5 | 48.0 | 48.5 | 49.0 | 49.5 | 50.0 |
|---|---|---|---|---|---|---|
| | and the Recovery Period is: | | | | | |
| | the Depreciation Rate is: | | | | | |
| 1 | 2.763 | 2.734 | 2.706 | 2.679 | 2.652 | 2.625 |
| 2 | 3.071 | 3.040 | 3.009 | 2.979 | 2.950 | 2.921 |
| 3 | 2.974 | 2.945 | 2.916 | 2.888 | 2.861 | 2.834 |
| 4 | 2.880 | 2.853 | 2.826 | 2.800 | 2.774 | 2.749 |
| 5 | 2.789 | 2.763 | 2.738 | 2.714 | 2.690 | 2.666 |
| 6 | 2.701 | 2.677 | 2.654 | 2.631 | 2.608 | 2.586 |
| 7 | 2.615 | 2.593 | 2.572 | 2.550 | 2.529 | 2.509 |
| 8 | 2.533 | 2.512 | 2.492 | 2.472 | 2.453 | 2.433 |

| If the Recovery Year is: | and the Recovery Period is: 47.5 | 48.0 | 48.5 | 49.0 | 49.5 | 50.0 |
|---|---|---|---|---|---|---|
| | the Depreciation Rate is: | | | | | |
| 9 | 2.453 | 2.434 | 2.415 | 2.397 | 2.378 | 2.360 |
| 10 | 2.375 | 2.358 | 2.340 | 2.323 | 2.306 | 2.290 |
| 11 | 2.300 | 2.284 | 2.268 | 2.252 | 2.236 | 2.221 |
| 12 | 2.228 | 2.213 | 2.198 | 2.183 | 2.169 | 2.154 |
| 13 | 2.157 | 2.144 | 2.130 | 2.116 | 2.103 | 2.090 |
| 14 | 2.089 | 2.077 | 2.064 | 2.052 | 2.039 | 2.027 |
| 15 | 2.023 | 2.012 | 2.000 | 1.989 | 1.977 | 1.966 |
| 16 | 1.959 | 1.949 | 1.938 | 1.928 | 1.917 | 1.907 |
| 17 | 1.900 | 1.888 | 1.878 | 1.869 | 1.859 | 1.850 |
| 18 | 1.900 | 1.880 | 1.861 | 1.842 | 1.824 | 1.806 |
| 19 | 1.900 | 1.880 | 1.861 | 1.842 | 1.824 | 1.806 |
| 20 | 1.900 | 1.880 | 1.861 | 1.842 | 1.824 | 1.806 |
| 21 | 1.900 | 1.880 | 1.861 | 1.842 | 1.824 | 1.806 |
| 22 | 1.900 | 1.880 | 1.861 | 1.842 | 1.824 | 1.806 |
| 23 | 1.900 | 1.880 | 1.861 | 1.842 | 1.824 | 1.806 |
| 24 | 1.900 | 1.880 | 1.861 | 1.842 | 1.824 | 1.806 |
| 25 | 1.900 | 1.880 | 1.861 | 1.842 | 1.824 | 1.806 |
| 26 | 1.900 | 1.880 | 1.861 | 1.842 | 1.824 | 1.806 |
| 27 | 1.900 | 1.880 | 1.861 | 1.842 | 1.824 | 1.806 |
| 28 | 1.900 | 1.880 | 1.861 | 1.842 | 1.824 | 1.805 |
| 29 | 1.900 | 1.880 | 1.861 | 1.842 | 1.824 | 1.806 |
| 30 | 1.900 | 1.880 | 1.861 | 1.842 | 1.824 | 1.805 |
| 31 | 1.900 | 1.880 | 1.861 | 1.842 | 1.824 | 1.806 |
| 32 | 1.900 | 1.881 | 1.861 | 1.842 | 1.824 | 1.805 |
| 33 | 1.900 | 1.880 | 1.861 | 1.842 | 1.823 | 1.806 |
| 34 | 1.900 | 1.881 | 1.861 | 1.842 | 1.824 | 1.805 |

| If the Recovery Year is: | and the Recovery Period is: 47.5 | 48.0 | 48.5 | 49.0 | 49.5 | 50.0 |
|---|---|---|---|---|---|---|
| | the Depreciation Rate is: | | | | | |
| 35 | 1.900 | 1.880 | 1.861 | 1.842 | 1.823 | 1.806 |
| 36 | 1.900 | 1.881 | 1.861 | 1.842 | 1.824 | 1.805 |
| 37 | 1.900 | 1.880 | 1.861 | 1.842 | 1.823 | 1.806 |
| 38 | 1.900 | 1.881 | 1.861 | 1.842 | 1.824 | 1.805 |
| 39 | 1.900 | 1.880 | 1.861 | 1.842 | 1.823 | 1.806 |
| 40 | 1.900 | 1.881 | 1.861 | 1.842 | 1.824 | 1.805 |
| 41 | 1.900 | 1.880 | 1.861 | 1.842 | 1.823 | 1.806 |
| 42 | 1.900 | 1.881 | 1.861 | 1.842 | 1.824 | 1.805 |
| 43 | 1.900 | 1.880 | 1.861 | 1.843 | 1.823 | 1.806 |
| 44 | 1.901 | 1.881 | 1.861 | 1.842 | 1.824 | 1.805 |
| 45 | 1.900 | 1.880 | 1.861 | 1.843 | 1.823 | 1.806 |
| 46 | 1.901 | 1.881 | 1.862 | 1.842 | 1.824 | 1.805 |
| 47 | 1.900 | 1.880 | 1.861 | 1.843 | 1.823 | 1.806 |
| 48 | 1.188 | 1.881 | 1.862 | 1.842 | 1.824 | 1.805 |
| 49 | | 0.235 | 1.163 | 1.843 | 1.823 | 1.806 |
| 50 | | | | 0.230 | 1.140 | 1.805 |
| 51 | | | | | | 0.226 |

TABLE 16
Alternative Minimum Tax (see section 7 of this revenue procedure)
Applicable Depreciation Method: 150-Percent Declining Balance Switching to Straight Line
Applicable Recovery Periods: 2.5 — 50 years
Applicable Convention: Mid-quarter (property placed in service in second quarter

| If the Recovery Year is: | and the Recovery Period is: 2.5 | 3.0 | 3.5 | 4.0 | 4.5 | 5.0 | 5.5 | 6.0 | 6.5 | 7.0 | 7.5 | 8.0 | 8.5 | 9.0 | 9.5 |
|---|---|---|---|---|---|---|---|---|---|---|---|---|---|---|---|
| | the Depreciation Rate is: | | | | | | | | | | | | | | |
| 1 | 37.50 | 31.25 | 26.79 | 23.44 | 20.83 | 18.75 | 17.05 | 15.63 | 14.42 | 13.39 | 12.50 | 11.72 | 11.03 | 10.42 | 9.87 |
| 2 | 37.50 | 34.38 | 31.38 | 28.71 | 26.39 | 24.38 | 22.62 | 21.09 | 19.75 | 18.56 | 17.50 | 16.55 | 15.70 | 14.93 | 14.23 |
| 3 | 25.00 | 25.00 | 22.31 | 20.15 | 18.36 | 17.06 | 16.45 | 15.82 | 15.19 | 14.58 | 14.00 | 13.45 | 12.93 | 12.44 | 11.98 |
| 4 | | 9.37 | 19.52 | 20.15 | 18.36 | 16.76 | 15.26 | 14.06 | 13.07 | 12.22 | 11.49 | 10.93 | 10.65 | 10.37 | 10.09 |
| 5 | | | | 7.55 | 16.06 | 16.76 | 15.26 | 14.06 | 13.07 | 12.22 | 11.49 | 10.82 | 10.19 | 9.64 | 9.16 |
| 6 | | | | | | 6.29 | 13.36 | 14.07 | 13.07 | 12.22 | 11.49 | 10.82 | 10.19 | 9.65 | 9.16 |
| 7 | | | | | | | | 5.27 | 11.43 | 12.23 | 11.48 | 10.83 | 10.19 | 9.64 | 9.16 |
| 8 | | | | | | | | | | 4.58 | 10.05 | 10.82 | 10.20 | 9.65 | 9.17 |
| 9 | | | | | | | | | | | | 4.06 | 8.92 | 9.64 | 9.16 |
| 10 | | | | | | | | | | | | | | 3.62 | 8.02 |

| If the Recovery Year is: | and the Recovery Period is: 10.0 | 10.5 | 11.0 | 11.5 | 12.0 | 12.5 | 13.0 | 13.5 | 14.0 | 14.5 | 15.0 | 15.5 | 16.0 | 16.5 | 17.0 |
|---|---|---|---|---|---|---|---|---|---|---|---|---|---|---|---|
| | the Depreciation Rate is: | | | | | | | | | | | | | | |
| 1 | 9.38 | 8.93 | 8.52 | 8.15 | 7.81 | 7.50 | 7.21 | 6.94 | 6.70 | 6.47 | 6.25 | 6.05 | 5.86 | 5.68 | 5.51 |
| 2 | 13.59 | 13.01 | 12.47 | 11.98 | 11.52 | 11.10 | 10.71 | 10.34 | 10.00 | 9.68 | 9.38 | 9.09 | 8.83 | 8.57 | 8.34 |
| 3 | 11.55 | 11.15 | 10.77 | 10.42 | 10.08 | 9.77 | 9.47 | 9.19 | 8.92 | 8.67 | 8.44 | 8.21 | 8.00 | 7.80 | 7.60 |
| 4 | 9.82 | 9.56 | 9.31 | 9.06 | 8.82 | 8.60 | 8.38 | 8.17 | 7.97 | 7.78 | 7.59 | 7.42 | 7.25 | 7.09 | 6.93 |
| 5 | 8.73 | 8.34 | 8.04 | 7.88 | 7.72 | 7.56 | 7.41 | 7.26 | 7.12 | 6.97 | 6.83 | 6.70 | 6.57 | 6.44 | 6.32 |
| 6 | 8.73 | 8.34 | 7.98 | 7.64 | 7.33 | 7.04 | 6.78 | 6.55 | 6.35 | 6.25 | 6.15 | 6.05 | 5.95 | 5.86 | 5.76 |

| If the Recovery Year is: | 10.0 | 10.5 | 11.0 | 11.5 | 12.0 | 12.5 | 13.0 | 13.5 | 14.0 | 14.5 | 15.0 | 15.5 | 16.0 | 16.5 | 17.0 |
|---|---|---|---|---|---|---|---|---|---|---|---|---|---|---|---|
| | and the Recovery Period is: | | | | | | | | | | | | | | |
| | the Depreciation Rate is: | | | | | | | | | | | | | | |
| 7 | 8.73 | 8.34 | 7.98 | 7.64 | 7.33 | 7.04 | 6.79 | 6.55 | 6.32 | 6.10 | 5.91 | 5.72 | 5.55 | 5.38 | 5.25 |
| 8 | 8.73 | 8.34 | 7.98 | 7.64 | 7.33 | 7.05 | 6.78 | 6.55 | 6.32 | 6.11 | 5.90 | 5.72 | 5.55 | 5.39 | 5.23 |
| 9 | 8.73 | 8.34 | 7.99 | 7.64 | 7.33 | 7.04 | 6.79 | 6.54 | 6.32 | 6.10 | 5.91 | 5.72 | 5.55 | 5.38 | 5.23 |
| 10 | 8.73 | 8.35 | 7.98 | 7.63 | 7.33 | 7.05 | 6.78 | 6.55 | 6.32 | 6.11 | 5.90 | 5.72 | 5.54 | 5.39 | 5.23 |
| 11 | 3.28 | 7.30 | 7.99 | 7.64 | 7.33 | 7.04 | 6.79 | 6.54 | 6.32 | 6.10 | 5.91 | 5.72 | 5.55 | 5.38 | 5.23 |
| 12 | | | 2.99 | 6.68 | 7.32 | 7.05 | 6.78 | 6.55 | 6.32 | 6.11 | 5.90 | 5.72 | 5.54 | 5.39 | 5.23 |
| 13 | | | | | 2.75 | 6.16 | 6.79 | 6.54 | 6.32 | 6.10 | 5.91 | 5.72 | 5.55 | 5.38 | 5.24 |
| 14 | | | | | | | 2.54 | 5.73 | 6.33 | 6.11 | 5.90 | 5.72 | 5.54 | 5.39 | 5.23 |
| 15 | | | | | | | | | 2.37 | 5.34 | 5.91 | 5.72 | 5.55 | 5.38 | 5.24 |
| 16 | | | | | | | | | | | 2.21 | 5.00 | 5.54 | 5.39 | 5.23 |
| 17 | | | | | | | | | | | | | 2.08 | 4.71 | 5.24 |
| 18 | | | | | | | | | | | | | | | 1.96 |

| If the Recovery Year is: | 17.5 | 18.0 | 18.5 | 19.0 | 19.5 | 20.0 | 20.5 | 21.0 | 21.5 | 22.0 | 22.5 | 23.0 | 23.5 | 24.0 | 24.5 |
|---|---|---|---|---|---|---|---|---|---|---|---|---|---|---|---|
| | and the Recovery Period is: | | | | | | | | | | | | | | |
| | the Depreciation Rate is: | | | | | | | | | | | | | | |
| 1 | 5.36 | 5.21 | 5.07 | 4.93 | 4.81 | 4.688 | 4.573 | 4.464 | 4.360 | 4.261 | 4.167 | 4.076 | 3.989 | 3.906 | 3.827 |
| 2 | 8.11 | 7.90 | 7.70 | 7.51 | 7.32 | 7.148 | 6.982 | 6.824 | 6.673 | 6.528 | 6.389 | 6.256 | 6.128 | 6.006 | 5.888 |
| 3 | 7.42 | 7.24 | 7.07 | 6.91 | 6.76 | 6.612 | 6.472 | 6.337 | 6.207 | 6.083 | 5.963 | 5.848 | 5.737 | 5.631 | 5.528 |
| 4 | 6.78 | 6.64 | 6.50 | 6.37 | 6.24 | 6.116 | 5.998 | 5.884 | 5.774 | 5.668 | 5.565 | 5.467 | 5.371 | 5.279 | 5.189 |
| 5 | 6.20 | 6.08 | 5.97 | 5.86 | 5.76 | 5.658 | 5.559 | 5.464 | 5.371 | 5.281 | 5.194 | 5.110 | 5.028 | 4.949 | 4.872 |
| 6 | 5.67 | 5.58 | 5.49 | 5.40 | 5.32 | 5.233 | 5.152 | 5.073 | 4.996 | 4.921 | 4.848 | 4.777 | 4.707 | 4.639 | 4.573 |
| 7 | 5.18 | 5.11 | 5.04 | 4.98 | 4.91 | 4.841 | 4.775 | 4.711 | 4.648 | 4.586 | 4.525 | 4.465 | 4.407 | 4.349 | 4.293 |
| 8 | 5.08 | 4.94 | 4.81 | 4.69 | 4.57 | 4.478 | 4.426 | 4.375 | 4.324 | 4.273 | 4.223 | 4.174 | 4.126 | 4.078 | 4.030 |
| 9 | 5.08 | 4.94 | 4.81 | 4.69 | 4.57 | 4.463 | 4.354 | 4.252 | 4.155 | 4.063 | 3.975 | 3.902 | 3.862 | 3.823 | 3.784 |
| 10 | 5.08 | 4.95 | 4.81 | 4.69 | 4.57 | 4.463 | 4.354 | 4.252 | 4.155 | 4.063 | 3.975 | 3.890 | 3.808 | 3.729 | 3.655 |

| If the Recovery Year is: | and the Recovery Period is: 17.5 | 18.0 | 18.5 | 19.0 | 19.5 | 20.0 | 20.5 | 21.0 | 21.5 | 22.0 | 22.5 | 23.0 | 23.5 | 24.0 | 24.5 |
|---|---|---|---|---|---|---|---|---|---|---|---|---|---|---|---|
| | the Depreciation Rate is: | | | | | | | | | | | | | | |
| 11 | 5.08 | 4.94 | 4.81 | 4.69 | 4.57 | 4.463 | 4.354 | 4.252 | 4.155 | 4.062 | 3.975 | 3.890 | 3.808 | 3.729 | 3.655 |
| 12 | 5.09 | 4.95 | 4.82 | 4.69 | 4.57 | 4.463 | 4.355 | 4.252 | 4.155 | 4.063 | 3.975 | 3.891 | 3.808 | 3.729 | 3.654 |
| 13 | 5.08 | 4.94 | 4.81 | 4.69 | 4.58 | 4.463 | 4.354 | 4.252 | 4.155 | 4.062 | 3.975 | 3.890 | 3.808 | 3.730 | 3.655 |
| 14 | 5.09 | 4.95 | 4.82 | 4.69 | 4.57 | 4.463 | 4.355 | 4.252 | 4.155 | 4.063 | 3.975 | 3.891 | 3.808 | 3.729 | 3.654 |
| 15 | 5.08 | 4.94 | 4.81 | 4.69 | 4.58 | 4.462 | 4.354 | 4.252 | 4.155 | 4.062 | 3.975 | 3.890 | 3.808 | 3.730 | 3.655 |
| 16 | 5.09 | 4.95 | 4.82 | 4.69 | 4.57 | 4.463 | 4.355 | 4.252 | 4.154 | 4.063 | 3.975 | 3.891 | 3.808 | 3.729 | 3.654 |
| 17 | 5.08 | 4.94 | 4.81 | 4.69 | 4.58 | 4.462 | 4.354 | 4.252 | 4.155 | 4.062 | 3.975 | 3.890 | 3.808 | 3.730 | 3.655 |
| 18 | 4.45 | 4.95 | 4.82 | 4.69 | 4.57 | 4.463 | 4.355 | 4.251 | 4.154 | 4.063 | 3.975 | 3.891 | 3.808 | 3.729 | 3.654 |
| 19 | | 1.85 | 4.21 | 4.69 | 4.58 | 4.462 | 4.354 | 4.252 | 4.155 | 4.062 | 3.975 | 3.890 | 3.808 | 3.730 | 3.655 |
| 20 | | | | 1.76 | 4.00 | 4.463 | 4.355 | 4.251 | 4.154 | 4.063 | 3.974 | 3.891 | 3.808 | 3.729 | 3.654 |
| 21 | | | | | | 1.673 | 3.810 | 4.252 | 4.155 | 4.062 | 3.975 | 3.890 | 3.808 | 3.730 | 3.655 |
| 22 | | | | | | | | 1.594 | 3.635 | 4.063 | 3.974 | 3.891 | 3.808 | 3.729 | 3.654 |
| 23 | | | | | | | | | | 1.523 | 3.478 | 3.890 | 3.809 | 3.730 | 3.655 |
| 24 | | | | | | | | | | | | 1.459 | 3.332 | 3.729 | 3.654 |
| 25 | | | | | | | | | | | | | | 1.399 | 3.198 |

| If the Recovery Year is: | and the Recovery Period is: 25.0 | 25.5 | 26.0 | 26.5 | 27.0 | 27.5 | 28.0 | 28.5 | 29.0 | 29.5 | 30.0 | 30.5 | 31.0 | 31.5 | 32.0 |
|---|---|---|---|---|---|---|---|---|---|---|---|---|---|---|---|
| | the Depreciation Rate is: | | | | | | | | | | | | | | |
| 1 | 3.750 | 3.676 | 3.606 | 3.538 | 3.472 | 3.409 | 3.348 | 3.289 | 3.233 | 3.178 | 3.125 | 3.074 | 3.024 | 2.976 | 2.930 |
| 2 | 5.775 | 5.666 | 5.561 | 5.460 | 5.363 | 5.269 | 5.178 | 5.090 | 5.005 | 4.923 | 4.844 | 4.767 | 4.692 | 4.620 | 4.550 |
| 3 | 5.429 | 5.333 | 5.240 | 5.151 | 5.065 | 4.981 | 4.900 | 4.822 | 4.746 | 4.673 | 4.602 | 4.532 | 4.465 | 4.400 | 4.337 |
| 4 | 5.103 | 5.019 | 4.938 | 4.859 | 4.783 | 4.710 | 4.638 | 4.568 | 4.501 | 4.435 | 4.371 | 4.310 | 4.249 | 4.191 | 4.134 |
| 5 | 4.797 | 4.724 | 4.653 | 4.584 | 4.518 | 4.453 | 4.389 | 4.328 | 4.268 | 4.210 | 4.153 | 4.098 | 4.044 | 3.991 | 3.940 |
| 6 | 4.509 | 4.446 | 4.385 | 4.325 | 4.267 | 4.210 | 4.154 | 4.100 | 4.047 | 3.996 | 3.945 | 3.896 | 3.848 | 3.801 | 3.755 |
| 7 | 4.238 | 4.184 | 4.132 | 4.080 | 4.030 | 3.980 | 3.932 | 3.884 | 3.838 | 3.792 | 3.748 | 3.704 | 3.662 | 3.620 | 3.579 |

| If the Recovery Year is: | and the Recovery Period is: 25.0 | 25.5 | 26.0 | 26.5 | 27.0 | 27.5 | 28.0 | 28.5 | 29.0 | 29.5 | 30.0 | 30.5 | 31.0 | 31.5 | 32.0 |
|---|---|---|---|---|---|---|---|---|---|---|---|---|---|---|---|
| | the Depreciation Rate is: | | | | | | | | | | | | | | |
| 8 | 3.984 | 3.938 | 3.893 | 3.849 | 3.806 | 3.763 | 3.721 | 3.680 | 3.639 | 3.600 | 3.561 | 3.522 | 3.485 | 3.448 | 3.411 |
| 9 | 3.745 | 3.707 | 3.669 | 3.631 | 3.594 | 3.558 | 3.522 | 3.486 | 3.451 | 3.417 | 3.383 | 3.349 | 3.316 | 3.283 | 3.251 |
| 10 | 3.583 | 3.514 | 3.457 | 3.426 | 3.395 | 3.364 | 3.333 | 3.303 | 3.273 | 3.243 | 3.213 | 3.184 | 3.156 | 3.127 | 3.099 |
| 11 | 3.583 | 3.515 | 3.448 | 3.384 | 3.321 | 3.262 | 3.205 | 3.150 | 3.103 | 3.078 | 3.053 | 3.028 | 3.003 | 2.978 | 2.954 |
| 12 | 3.583 | 3.514 | 3.448 | 3.383 | 3.321 | 3.262 | 3.205 | 3.150 | 3.096 | 3.044 | 2.994 | 2.945 | 2.898 | 2.853 | 2.815 |
| 13 | 3.583 | 3.515 | 3.448 | 3.384 | 3.321 | 3.262 | 3.205 | 3.150 | 3.096 | 3.044 | 2.994 | 2.945 | 2.898 | 2.853 | 2.810 |
| 14 | 3.583 | 3.514 | 3.448 | 3.383 | 3.321 | 3.262 | 3.205 | 3.150 | 3.096 | 3.044 | 2.994 | 2.945 | 2.899 | 2.853 | 2.810 |
| 15 | 3.583 | 3.515 | 3.448 | 3.384 | 3.321 | 3.262 | 3.205 | 3.150 | 3.096 | 3.044 | 2.994 | 2.945 | 2.898 | 2.853 | 2.810 |
| 16 | 3.583 | 3.514 | 3.448 | 3.383 | 3.321 | 3.262 | 3.204 | 3.150 | 3.096 | 3.044 | 2.994 | 2.945 | 2.899 | 2.854 | 2.809 |
| 17 | 3.583 | 3.515 | 3.448 | 3.384 | 3.321 | 3.262 | 3.205 | 3.150 | 3.097 | 3.044 | 2.994 | 2.945 | 2.898 | 2.853 | 2.810 |
| 18 | 3.583 | 3.514 | 3.449 | 3.383 | 3.321 | 3.262 | 3.204 | 3.149 | 3.096 | 3.044 | 2.993 | 2.945 | 2.899 | 2.854 | 2.809 |
| 19 | 3.583 | 3.515 | 3.448 | 3.384 | 3.321 | 3.261 | 3.205 | 3.150 | 3.097 | 3.044 | 2.994 | 2.945 | 2.898 | 2.853 | 2.810 |
| 20 | 3.583 | 3.514 | 3.449 | 3.383 | 3.322 | 3.262 | 3.204 | 3.149 | 3.096 | 3.044 | 2.993 | 2.945 | 2.899 | 2.854 | 2.809 |
| 21 | 3.583 | 3.515 | 3.448 | 3.384 | 3.321 | 3.261 | 3.205 | 3.150 | 3.097 | 3.044 | 2.994 | 2.945 | 2.898 | 2.853 | 2.810 |
| 22 | 3.583 | 3.514 | 3.449 | 3.383 | 3.322 | 3.262 | 3.204 | 3.149 | 3.096 | 3.044 | 2.993 | 2.945 | 2.899 | 2.854 | 2.809 |
| 23 | 3.583 | 3.515 | 3.448 | 3.384 | 3.321 | 3.261 | 3.205 | 3.150 | 3.097 | 3.044 | 2.994 | 2.945 | 2.898 | 2.853 | 2.810 |
| 24 | 3.582 | 3.514 | 3.449 | 3.383 | 3.322 | 3.262 | 3.204 | 3.149 | 3.096 | 3.044 | 2.993 | 2.946 | 2.899 | 2.854 | 2.809 |
| 25 | 3.583 | 3.515 | 3.448 | 3.384 | 3.321 | 3.261 | 3.205 | 3.150 | 3.097 | 3.044 | 2.994 | 2.945 | 2.898 | 2.853 | 2.810 |
| 26 | 1.343 | 3.075 | 3.449 | 3.383 | 3.322 | 3.262 | 3.204 | 3.149 | 3.096 | 3.044 | 2.993 | 2.946 | 2.899 | 2.854 | 2.809 |
| 27 | | | 1.293 | 2.961 | 3.321 | 3.261 | 3.205 | 3.150 | 3.097 | 3.044 | 2.994 | 2.945 | 2.898 | 2.853 | 2.810 |
| 28 | | | | | 1.246 | 2.854 | 3.204 | 3.149 | 3.096 | 3.044 | 2.993 | 2.946 | 2.899 | 2.854 | 2.809 |
| 29 | | | | | | | 1.202 | 2.756 | 3.097 | 3.044 | 2.994 | 2.945 | 2.898 | 2.853 | 2.810 |
| 30 | | | | | | | | | 1.161 | 2.663 | 2.993 | 2.946 | 2.899 | 2.854 | 2.809 |
| 31 | | | | | | | | | | | 1.123 | 2.577 | 2.898 | 2.853 | 2.810 |
| 32 | | | | | | | | | | | | | 1.087 | 2.497 | 2.809 |
| 33 | | | | | | | | | | | | | | | 1.054 |

| If the Recovery Year is: | and the Recovery Period is: 32.5 | 33.0 | 33.5 | 34.0 | 34.5 | 35.0 | 35.5 | 36.0 | 36.5 | 37.0 | 37.5 | 38.0 | 38.5 | 39.0 | 39.5 |
|---|---|---|---|---|---|---|---|---|---|---|---|---|---|---|---|
| | | | the Depreciation Rate is: | | | | | | | | | | | | |
| 1 | 2.885 | 2.841 | 2.799 | 2.757 | 2.717 | 2.679 | 2.641 | 2.604 | 2.568 | 2.534 | 2.500 | 2.467 | 2.435 | 2.404 | 2.373 |
| 2 | 4.482 | 4.416 | 4.352 | 4.290 | 4.230 | 4.171 | 4.114 | 4.058 | 4.004 | 3.951 | 3.900 | 3.850 | 3.801 | 3.754 | 3.707 |
| 3 | 4.275 | 4.216 | 4.157 | 4.101 | 4.046 | 3.992 | 3.940 | 3.889 | 3.840 | 3.791 | 3.744 | 3.698 | 3.653 | 3.609 | 3.567 |
| 4 | 4.078 | 4.024 | 3.971 | 3.920 | 3.870 | 3.821 | 3.773 | 3.727 | 3.682 | 3.637 | 3.594 | 3.552 | 3.511 | 3.471 | 3.431 |
| 5 | 3.890 | 3.841 | 3.793 | 3.747 | 3.702 | 3.657 | 3.614 | 3.572 | 3.530 | 3.490 | 3.450 | 3.412 | 3.374 | 3.337 | 3.301 |
| 6 | 3.710 | 3.666 | 3.624 | 3.582 | 3.541 | 3.501 | 3.461 | 3.423 | 3.385 | 3.349 | 3.312 | 3.277 | 3.243 | 3.209 | 3.175 |
| 7 | 3.539 | 3.500 | 3.461 | 3.424 | 3.387 | 3.351 | 3.315 | 3.280 | 3.246 | 3.213 | 3.180 | 3.148 | 3.116 | 3.085 | 3.055 |
| 8 | 3.376 | 3.341 | 3.306 | 3.273 | 3.239 | 3.207 | 3.175 | 3.144 | 3.113 | 3.083 | 3.053 | 3.024 | 2.995 | 2.967 | 2.939 |
| 9 | 3.220 | 3.189 | 3.158 | 3.128 | 3.099 | 3.069 | 3.041 | 3.013 | 2.985 | 2.958 | 2.931 | 2.904 | 2.878 | 2.852 | 2.827 |
| 10 | 3.071 | 3.044 | 3.017 | 2.990 | 2.964 | 2.938 | 2.912 | 2.887 | 2.862 | 2.838 | 2.813 | 2.790 | 2.766 | 2.743 | 2.720 |
| 11 | 2.930 | 2.906 | 2.882 | 2.858 | 2.835 | 2.812 | 2.789 | 2.767 | 2.745 | 2.723 | 2.701 | 2.679 | 2.658 | 2.637 | 2.617 |
| 12 | 2.794 | 2.773 | 2.753 | 2.732 | 2.712 | 2.692 | 2.671 | 2.651 | 2.632 | 2.612 | 2.593 | 2.574 | 2.555 | 2.536 | 2.517 |
| 13 | 2.766 | 2.725 | 2.685 | 2.646 | 2.608 | 2.576 | 2.559 | 2.541 | 2.524 | 2.506 | 2.489 | 2.472 | 2.455 | 2.438 | 2.422 |
| 14 | 2.766 | 2.725 | 2.685 | 2.646 | 2.608 | 2.571 | 2.535 | 2.500 | 2.466 | 2.433 | 2.402 | 2.374 | 2.359 | 2.345 | 2.330 |
| 15 | 2.767 | 2.725 | 2.685 | 2.646 | 2.608 | 2.571 | 2.535 | 2.500 | 2.466 | 2.433 | 2.402 | 2.370 | 2.340 | 2.310 | 2.281 |
| 16 | 2.766 | 2.725 | 2.685 | 2.646 | 2.608 | 2.571 | 2.535 | 2.500 | 2.466 | 2.433 | 2.402 | 2.370 | 2.340 | 2.310 | 2.281 |
| 17 | 2.767 | 2.725 | 2.685 | 2.646 | 2.608 | 2.571 | 2.535 | 2.500 | 2.466 | 2.433 | 2.402 | 2.370 | 2.340 | 2.310 | 2.281 |
| 18 | 2.766 | 2.725 | 2.685 | 2.646 | 2.608 | 2.571 | 2.535 | 2.500 | 2.466 | 2.434 | 2.402 | 2.370 | 2.340 | 2.310 | 2.281 |
| 19 | 2.767 | 2.725 | 2.685 | 2.646 | 2.608 | 2.571 | 2.535 | 2.500 | 2.466 | 2.433 | 2.402 | 2.371 | 2.340 | 2.310 | 2.281 |
| 20 | 2.766 | 2.725 | 2.685 | 2.646 | 2.608 | 2.571 | 2.535 | 2.500 | 2.466 | 2.434 | 2.401 | 2.370 | 2.340 | 2.310 | 2.281 |
| 21 | 2.767 | 2.725 | 2.684 | 2.646 | 2.608 | 2.572 | 2.535 | 2.500 | 2.466 | 2.433 | 2.402 | 2.371 | 2.340 | 2.310 | 2.281 |
| 22 | 2.766 | 2.725 | 2.685 | 2.646 | 2.608 | 2.571 | 2.535 | 2.500 | 2.467 | 2.434 | 2.401 | 2.370 | 2.340 | 2.310 | 2.281 |
| 23 | 2.767 | 2.725 | 2.684 | 2.645 | 2.608 | 2.572 | 2.535 | 2.500 | 2.466 | 2.433 | 2.402 | 2.371 | 2.340 | 2.310 | 2.281 |
| 24 | 2.766 | 2.725 | 2.685 | 2.646 | 2.608 | 2.571 | 2.536 | 2.500 | 2.467 | 2.434 | 2.401 | 2.370 | 2.340 | 2.310 | 2.281 |
| 25 | 2.767 | 2.725 | 2.684 | 2.645 | 2.608 | 2.572 | 2.535 | 2.501 | 2.466 | 2.433 | 2.402 | 2.371 | 2.340 | 2.310 | 2.281 |

| If the Recovery Year is: | 32.5 | 33.0 | 33.5 | 34.0 | 34.5 | 35.0 | 35.5 | 36.0 | 36.5 | 37.0 | 37.5 | 38.0 | 38.5 | 39.0 | 39.5 |
|---|---|---|---|---|---|---|---|---|---|---|---|---|---|---|---|
| | the Depreciation Rate is: | | | | | | | | | | | | | | |
| 26 | 2.766 | 2.725 | 2.685 | 2.646 | 2.608 | 2.571 | 2.536 | 2.500 | 2.467 | 2.434 | 2.401 | 2.370 | 2.340 | 2.310 | 2.281 |
| 27 | 2.767 | 2.724 | 2.684 | 2.645 | 2.608 | 2.572 | 2.535 | 2.501 | 2.466 | 2.433 | 2.402 | 2.371 | 2.339 | 2.310 | 2.281 |
| 28 | 2.766 | 2.725 | 2.685 | 2.646 | 2.608 | 2.571 | 2.536 | 2.500 | 2.467 | 2.434 | 2.401 | 2.370 | 2.340 | 2.310 | 2.281 |
| 29 | 2.767 | 2.724 | 2.684 | 2.645 | 2.608 | 2.572 | 2.535 | 2.501 | 2.466 | 2.433 | 2.402 | 2.371 | 2.339 | 2.310 | 2.281 |
| 30 | 2.766 | 2.725 | 2.685 | 2.646 | 2.608 | 2.571 | 2.536 | 2.500 | 2.467 | 2.434 | 2.401 | 2.370 | 2.340 | 2.310 | 2.281 |
| 31 | 2.767 | 2.724 | 2.684 | 2.645 | 2.608 | 2.572 | 2.535 | 2.501 | 2.466 | 2.433 | 2.402 | 2.371 | 2.339 | 2.310 | 2.281 |
| 32 | 2.766 | 2.725 | 2.685 | 2.646 | 2.608 | 2.571 | 2.536 | 2.500 | 2.467 | 2.434 | 2.401 | 2.370 | 2.340 | 2.310 | 2.281 |
| 33 | 2.421 | 2.724 | 2.684 | 2.645 | 2.608 | 2.572 | 2.535 | 2.501 | 2.466 | 2.433 | 2.402 | 2.371 | 2.339 | 2.310 | 2.281 |
| 34 | | 1.022 | 2.349 | 2.646 | 2.608 | 2.571 | 2.536 | 2.500 | 2.467 | 2.434 | 2.401 | 2.370 | 2.340 | 2.309 | 2.281 |
| 35 | | | | 0.992 | 2.282 | 2.572 | 2.535 | 2.501 | 2.466 | 2.433 | 2.402 | 2.371 | 2.339 | 2.310 | 2.281 |
| 36 | | | | | | 0.964 | 2.219 | 2.500 | 2.467 | 2.434 | 2.401 | 2.370 | 2.340 | 2.309 | 2.281 |
| 37 | | | | | | | | 0.938 | 2.158 | 2.433 | 2.402 | 2.371 | 2.339 | 2.310 | 2.281 |
| 38 | | | | | | | | | | 0.913 | 2.101 | 2.370 | 2.340 | 2.309 | 2.280 |
| 39 | | | | | | | | | | | | 0.889 | 2.047 | 2.310 | 2.281 |
| 40 | | | | | | | | | | | | | | 0.866 | 1.995 |

and the Recovery Period is:

| If the Recovery Year is: | 40.0 | 40.5 | 41.0 | 41.5 | 42.0 | 42.5 | 43.0 | 43.5 | 44.0 | 44.5 | 45.0 | 45.5 | 46.0 | 46.5 | 47.0 |
|---|---|---|---|---|---|---|---|---|---|---|---|---|---|---|---|
| | the Depreciation Rate is: | | | | | | | | | | | | | | |
| 1 | 2.344 | 2.315 | 2.287 | 2.259 | 2.232 | 2.206 | 2.180 | 2.155 | 2.131 | 2.107 | 2.083 | 2.060 | 2.038 | 2.016 | 1.995 |
| 2 | 3.662 | 3.618 | 3.575 | 3.533 | 3.492 | 3.452 | 3.412 | 3.374 | 3.336 | 3.300 | 3.264 | 3.229 | 3.194 | 3.161 | 3.128 |
| 3 | 3.525 | 3.484 | 3.444 | 3.405 | 3.367 | 3.330 | 3.293 | 3.258 | 3.223 | 3.189 | 3.155 | 3.122 | 3.090 | 3.059 | 3.028 |
| 4 | 3.393 | 3.555 | 3.318 | 3.282 | 3.247 | 3.212 | 3.178 | 3.145 | 3.113 | 3.081 | 3.050 | 3.019 | 2.990 | 2.960 | 2.931 |
| 5 | 3.265 | 3.231 | 3.197 | 3.163 | 3.131 | 3.099 | 3.068 | 3.037 | 3.007 | 2.977 | 2.948 | 2.920 | 2.892 | 2.865 | 2.838 |
| 6 | 3.143 | 3.111 | 3.080 | 3.049 | 3.019 | 2.989 | 2.961 | 2.932 | 2.904 | 2.877 | 2.850 | 2.824 | 2.798 | 2.772 | 2.747 |
| 7 | 3.025 | 2.996 | 2.967 | 2.939 | 2.911 | 2.884 | 2.857 | 2.831 | 2.805 | 2.780 | 2.755 | 2.731 | 2.706 | 2.683 | 2.660 |

| If the Recovery Year is: | 40.0 | 40.5 | 41.0 | 41.5 | 42.0 | 42.5 | 43.0 | 43.5 | 44.0 | 44.5 | 45.0 | 45.5 | 46.0 | 46.5 | 47.0 |
|---|---|---|---|---|---|---|---|---|---|---|---|---|---|---|---|
| | | | the Depreciation Rate is: | | | | | | | | | | | | |
| 8 | 2.912 | 2.885 | 2.858 | 2.833 | 2.807 | 2.782 | 2.758 | 2.733 | 2.710 | 2.686 | 2.663 | 2.640 | 2.618 | 2.596 | 2.575 |
| 9 | 2.802 | 2.778 | 2.754 | 2.730 | 2.707 | 2.684 | 2.661 | 2.639 | 2.617 | 2.596 | 2.574 | 2.553 | 2.533 | 2.513 | 2.492 |
| 10 | 2.697 | 2.675 | 2.653 | 2.632 | 2.610 | 2.589 | 2.569 | 2.548 | 2.528 | 2.508 | 2.489 | 2.469 | 2.450 | 2.431 | 2.413 |
| 11 | 2.596 | 2.576 | 2.556 | 2.536 | 2.517 | 2.498 | 2.479 | 2.460 | 2.442 | 2.424 | 2.406 | 2.388 | 2.370 | 2.353 | 2.336 |
| 12 | 2.499 | 2.481 | 2.463 | 2.445 | 2.427 | 2.410 | 2.392 | 2.375 | 2.359 | 2.342 | 2.325 | 2.309 | 2.293 | 2.277 | 2.261 |
| 13 | 2.405 | 2.389 | 2.372 | 2.356 | 2.340 | 2.325 | 2.309 | 2.294 | 2.278 | 2.263 | 2.248 | 2.233 | 2.218 | 2.204 | 2.189 |
| 14 | 2.315 | 2.300 | 2.286 | 2.271 | 2.257 | 2.243 | 2.228 | 2.214 | 2.200 | 2.187 | 2.173 | 2.159 | 2.146 | 2.133 | 2.119 |
| 15 | 2.253 | 2.225 | 2.202 | 2.189 | 2.176 | 2.163 | 2.151 | 2.138 | 2.125 | 2.113 | 2.101 | 2.088 | 2.076 | 2.064 | 2.052 |
| 16 | 2.253 | 2.225 | 2.199 | 2.172 | 2.146 | 2.121 | 2.097 | 2.073 | 2.053 | 2.042 | 2.031 | 2.019 | 2.008 | 1.997 | 1.986 |
| 17 | 2.253 | 2.225 | 2.199 | 2.172 | 2.147 | 2.121 | 2.097 | 2.073 | 2.050 | 2.027 | 2.005 | 1.983 | 1.961 | 1.941 | 1.923 |
| 18 | 2.253 | 2.225 | 2.199 | 2.172 | 2.146 | 2.121 | 2.097 | 2.073 | 2.050 | 2.027 | 2.005 | 1.983 | 1.961 | 1.941 | 1.920 |
| 19 | 2.253 | 2.225 | 2.199 | 2.172 | 2.147 | 2.121 | 2.097 | 2.073 | 2.050 | 2.027 | 2.005 | 1.983 | 1.962 | 1.941 | 1.920 |
| 20 | 2.253 | 2.225 | 2.199 | 2.172 | 2.146 | 2.121 | 2.097 | 2.073 | 2.050 | 2.027 | 2.005 | 1.983 | 1.961 | 1.941 | 1.920 |
| 21 | 2.253 | 2.225 | 2.199 | 2.172 | 2.147 | 2.121 | 2.097 | 2.073 | 2.050 | 2.027 | 2.005 | 1.983 | 1.962 | 1.941 | 1.920 |
| 22 | 2.253 | 2.225 | 2.198 | 2.172 | 2.146 | 2.122 | 2.097 | 2.073 | 2.050 | 2.027 | 2.005 | 1.983 | 1.961 | 1.941 | 1.920 |
| 23 | 2.253 | 2.225 | 2.199 | 2.172 | 2.147 | 2.121 | 2.097 | 2.073 | 2.050 | 2.027 | 2.004 | 1.983 | 1.962 | 1.941 | 1.920 |
| 24 | 2.253 | 2.226 | 2.198 | 2.172 | 2.146 | 2.122 | 2.097 | 2.073 | 2.050 | 2.027 | 2.005 | 1.983 | 1.961 | 1.940 | 1.920 |
| 25 | 2.253 | 2.225 | 2.199 | 2.172 | 2.147 | 2.121 | 2.097 | 2.073 | 2.050 | 2.027 | 2.004 | 1.983 | 1.962 | 1.941 | 1.920 |
| 26 | 2.253 | 2.226 | 2.198 | 2.172 | 2.146 | 2.122 | 2.097 | 2.073 | 2.050 | 2.027 | 2.005 | 1.983 | 1.961 | 1.940 | 1.920 |
| 27 | 2.253 | 2.225 | 2.199 | 2.172 | 2.147 | 2.121 | 2.097 | 2.074 | 2.050 | 2.027 | 2.004 | 1.983 | 1.962 | 1.941 | 1.920 |
| 28 | 2.253 | 2.226 | 2.198 | 2.172 | 2.146 | 2.122 | 2.097 | 2.073 | 2.050 | 2.027 | 2.005 | 1.983 | 1.961 | 1.940 | 1.920 |
| 29 | 2.253 | 2.225 | 2.199 | 2.172 | 2.147 | 2.121 | 2.097 | 2.074 | 2.050 | 2.027 | 2.004 | 1.983 | 1.962 | 1.941 | 1.920 |
| 30 | 2.252 | 2.226 | 2.198 | 2.172 | 2.146 | 2.122 | 2.097 | 2.073 | 2.050 | 2.027 | 2.005 | 1.983 | 1.961 | 1.940 | 1.920 |
| 31 | 2.253 | 2.225 | 2.199 | 2.172 | 2.147 | 2.121 | 2.097 | 2.074 | 2.050 | 2.027 | 2.004 | 1.983 | 1.962 | 1.941 | 1.920 |
| 32 | 2.252 | 2.226 | 2.198 | 2.173 | 2.146 | 2.122 | 2.097 | 2.073 | 2.050 | 2.027 | 2.005 | 1.983 | 1.961 | 1.940 | 1.920 |
| 33 | 2.253 | 2.225 | 2.199 | 2.172 | 2.147 | 2.121 | 2.097 | 2.074 | 2.050 | 2.027 | 2.004 | 1.983 | 1.962 | 1.941 | 1.920 |
| 34 | 2.252 | 2.226 | 2.198 | 2.173 | 2.146 | 2.122 | 2.097 | 2.073 | 2.050 | 2.027 | 2.005 | 1.983 | 1.961 | 1.940 | 1.920 |

| If the Recovery Year is: | 40.0 | 40.5 | 41.0 | 41.5 | 42.0 | 42.5 | 43.0 | 43.5 | 44.0 | 44.5 | 45.0 | 45.5 | 46.0 | 46.5 | 47.0 |
|---|---|---|---|---|---|---|---|---|---|---|---|---|---|---|---|
| | | | the Depreciation Rate is: | | | | | | | | | | | | |
| 35 | 2.253 | 2.225 | 2.199 | 2.172 | 2.147 | 2.121 | 2.097 | 2.074 | 2.050 | 2.027 | 2.004 | 1.983 | 1.962 | 1.941 | 1.921 |
| 36 | 2.252 | 2.226 | 2.198 | 2.173 | 2.146 | 2.122 | 2.097 | 2.073 | 2.050 | 2.027 | 2.005 | 1.983 | 1.961 | 1.940 | 1.920 |
| 37 | 2.253 | 2.225 | 2.199 | 2.172 | 2.147 | 2.121 | 2.097 | 2.074 | 2.050 | 2.027 | 2.004 | 1.982 | 1.962 | 1.941 | 1.921 |
| 38 | 2.252 | 2.226 | 2.198 | 2.173 | 2.146 | 2.122 | 2.097 | 2.073 | 2.050 | 2.027 | 2.005 | 1.983 | 1.961 | 1.940 | 1.920 |
| 39 | 2.253 | 2.225 | 2.199 | 2.172 | 2.147 | 2.121 | 2.097 | 2.074 | 2.050 | 2.027 | 2.004 | 1.982 | 1.962 | 1.941 | 1.921 |
| 40 | 2.252 | 2.226 | 2.198 | 2.173 | 2.146 | 2.122 | 2.097 | 2.073 | 2.050 | 2.027 | 2.005 | 1.983 | 1.961 | 1.940 | 1.920 |
| 41 | 0.845 | 1.947 | 2.199 | 2.172 | 2.147 | 2.121 | 2.097 | 2.074 | 2.050 | 2.027 | 2.004 | 1.982 | 1.962 | 1.941 | 1.921 |
| 42 | | | 0.824 | 1.901 | 2.146 | 2.122 | 2.098 | 2.073 | 2.050 | 2.027 | 2.005 | 1.983 | 1.961 | 1.940 | 1.920 |
| 43 | | | | | 0.805 | 1.856 | 2.097 | 2.074 | 2.050 | 2.026 | 2.004 | 1.982 | 1.962 | 1.941 | 1.921 |
| 44 | | | | | | | 0.787 | 1.814 | 2.050 | 2.027 | 2.005 | 1.983 | 1.961 | 1.940 | 1.920 |
| 45 | | | | | | | | | 0.769 | 1.773 | 2.004 | 1.982 | 1.962 | 1.941 | 1.921 |
| 46 | | | | | | | | | | | 0.752 | 1.735 | 1.961 | 1.940 | 1.920 |
| 47 | | | | | | | | | | | | | 0.736 | 1.698 | 1.921 |
| 48 | | | | | | | | | | | | | | | 0.720 |

and the Recovery Period is:

| If the Recovery Year is: | 47.5 | 48.0 | 48.5 | 49.0 | 49.5 | 50.0 |
|---|---|---|---|---|---|---|
| | | | the Depreciation Rate is: | | | |
| 1 | 1.974 | 1.953 | 1.933 | 1.913 | 1.894 | 1.875 |
| 2 | 3.096 | 3.064 | 3.033 | 3.003 | 2.973 | 2.944 |
| 3 | 2.998 | 2.968 | 2.939 | 2.911 | 2.883 | 2.855 |
| 4 | 2.903 | 2.875 | 2.848 | 2.822 | 2.795 | 2.770 |
| 5 | 2.811 | 2.786 | 2.760 | 2.735 | 2.711 | 2.687 |
| 6 | 2.723 | 2.699 | 2.675 | 2.652 | 2.629 | 2.606 |
| 7 | 2.637 | 2.614 | 2.592 | 2.570 | 2.549 | 2.528 |
| 8 | 2.553 | 2.533 | 2.512 | 2.492 | 2.472 | 2.452 |

| If the Recovery Year is: | 47.5 | 48.0 | 48.5 | 49.0 | 49.5 | 50.0 |
|---|---|---|---|---|---|---|
| | | the Depreciation Rate is: | | | | |
| 9 | 2.473 | 2.453 | 2.434 | 2.415 | 2.397 | 2.378 |
| 10 | 2.395 | 2.377 | 2.359 | 2.341 | 2.324 | 2.307 |
| 11 | 2.319 | 2.302 | 2.286 | 2.270 | 2.254 | 2.238 |
| 12 | 2.246 | 2.230 | 2.215 | 2.200 | 2.185 | 2.171 |
| 13 | 2.175 | 2.161 | 2.147 | 2.133 | 2.119 | 2.106 |
| 14 | 2.106 | 2.093 | 2.080 | 2.068 | 2.055 | 2.042 |
| 15 | 2.040 | 2.028 | 2.016 | 2.004 | 1.993 | 1.981 |
| 16 | 1.975 | 1.964 | 1.954 | 1.943 | 1.932 | 1.922 |
| 17 | 1.913 | 1.903 | 1.893 | 1.884 | 1.874 | 1.864 |
| 18 | 1.900 | 1.880 | 1.861 | 1.842 | 1.824 | 1.808 |
| 19 | 1.900 | 1.880 | 1.861 | 1.842 | 1.824 | 1.806 |
| 20 | 1.900 | 1.880 | 1.861 | 1.842 | 1.824 | 1.806 |
| 21 | 1.900 | 1.880 | 1.861 | 1.842 | 1.824 | 1.806 |
| 22 | 1.900 | 1.880 | 1.861 | 1.842 | 1.824 | 1.806 |
| 23 | 1.900 | 1.880 | 1.861 | 1.842 | 1.824 | 1.806 |
| 24 | 1.900 | 1.880 | 1.861 | 1.842 | 1.824 | 1.806 |
| 25 | 1.900 | 1.880 | 1.861 | 1.842 | 1.824 | 1.806 |
| 26 | 1.900 | 1.881 | 1.861 | 1.842 | 1.824 | 1.806 |
| 27 | 1.900 | 1.880 | 1.861 | 1.842 | 1.824 | 1.806 |
| 28 | 1.900 | 1.881 | 1.861 | 1.842 | 1.824 | 1.806 |
| 29 | 1.900 | 1.880 | 1.861 | 1.842 | 1.824 | 1.806 |
| 30 | 1.900 | 1.881 | 1.861 | 1.842 | 1.824 | 1.806 |
| 31 | 1.900 | 1.880 | 1.861 | 1.842 | 1.824 | 1.806 |
| 32 | 1.900 | 1.881 | 1.861 | 1.843 | 1.824 | 1.806 |
| 33 | 1.900 | 1.880 | 1.861 | 1.842 | 1.824 | 1.806 |
| 34 | 1.900 | 1.881 | 1.861 | 1.843 | 1.824 | 1.806 |
| 35 | 1.900 | 1.880 | 1.861 | 1.842 | 1.824 | 1.806 |

| If the Recovery Year is: | 47.5 | 48.0 | 48.5 | 49.0 | 49.5 | 50.0 |
|---|---|---|---|---|---|---|
| | | | the Depreciation Rate is: | | | |
| 36 | 1.900 | 1.881 | 1.861 | 1.843 | 1.824 | 1.806 |
| 37 | 1.900 | 1.880 | 1.861 | 1.842 | 1.824 | 1.806 |
| 38 | 1.900 | 1.881 | 1.861 | 1.843 | 1.824 | 1.806 |
| 39 | 1.900 | 1.880 | 1.861 | 1.842 | 1.824 | 1.806 |
| 40 | 1.900 | 1.881 | 1.861 | 1.843 | 1.824 | 1.806 |
| 41 | 1.900 | 1.880 | 1.862 | 1.842 | 1.824 | 1.806 |
| 42 | 1.900 | 1.881 | 1.861 | 1.843 | 1.824 | 1.806 |
| 43 | 1.900 | 1.880 | 1.862 | 1.842 | 1.824 | 1.806 |
| 44 | 1.900 | 1.881 | 1.861 | 1.843 | 1.824 | 1.806 |
| 45 | 1.900 | 1.880 | 1.862 | 1.842 | 1.823 | 1.805 |
| 46 | 1.900 | 1.881 | 1.861 | 1.843 | 1.824 | 1.806 |
| 47 | 1.900 | 1.880 | 1.862 | 1.842 | 1.823 | 1.805 |
| 48 | 1.663 | 1.881 | 1.861 | 1.843 | 1.824 | 1.806 |
| 49 | | 0.705 | 1.629 | 1.842 | 1.823 | 1.805 |
| 50 | | | | 0.691 | 1.596 | 1.806 |
| 51 | | | | | | 0.677 |

TABLE 17
Alternative Minimum Tax (see section 7 of this revenue procedure)
Applicable Depreciation Method: 150-Percent Declining Balance Switching to Straight Line
Applicable Recovery Periods: 2.5 — 50 years
Applicable Convention: Mid-quarter (property placed in service in third quarter)

| If the Recovery Year is: | and the Recovery Period is: 2.5 | 3.0 | 3.5 | 4.0 | 4.5 | 5.0 | 5.5 | 6.0 | 6.5 | 7.0 | 7.5 | 8.0 | 8.5 | 9.0 | 9.5 |
|---|---|---|---|---|---|---|---|---|---|---|---|---|---|---|---|
| | the Depreciation Rate is: | | | | | | | | | | | | | | |
| 1 | 22.50 | 18.75 | 16.07 | 14.06 | 12.50 | 11.25 | 10.23 | 9.38 | 8.65 | 8.04 | 7.50 | 7.03 | 6.62 | 6.25 | 5.92 |
| 2 | 46.50 | 40.63 | 35.97 | 32.23 | 29.17 | 26.63 | 24.48 | 22.66 | 21.08 | 19.71 | 18.50 | 17.43 | 16.48 | 15.63 | 14.85 |
| 3 | 27.56 | 25.00 | 22.57 | 20.46 | 19.44 | 18.64 | 17.81 | 16.99 | 16.22 | 15.48 | 14.80 | 14.16 | 13.57 | 13.02 | 12.51 |
| 4 | 3.44 | 15.62 | 22.57 | 20.46 | 18.30 | 16.56 | 15.19 | 14.06 | 13.10 | 12.27 | 11.84 | 11.51 | 11.18 | 10.85 | 10.53 |
| 5 | | | 2.82 | 12.79 | 18.30 | 16.57 | 15.20 | 14.06 | 13.10 | 12.28 | 11.48 | 10.78 | 10.18 | 9.64 | 9.17 |
| 6 | | | | | 2.29 | 10.35 | 15.19 | 14.06 | 13.11 | 12.27 | 11.48 | 10.78 | 10.17 | 9.65 | 9.17 |
| 7 | | | | | | | 1.90 | 8.79 | 13.10 | 12.28 | 11.48 | 10.78 | 10.18 | 9.64 | 9.18 |
| 8 | | | | | | | | | 1.64 | 7.67 | 11.48 | 10.79 | 10.17 | 9.65 | 9.17 |
| 9 | | | | | | | | | | | 1.44 | 6.74 | 10.18 | 9.64 | 9.18 |
| 10 | | | | | | | | | | | | | 1.27 | 6.03 | 9.17 |
| 11 | | | | | | | | | | | | | | | 1.15 |

| If the Recovery Year is: | and the Recovery Period is: 10.0 | 10.5 | 11.0 | 11.5 | 12.0 | 12.5 | 13.0 | 13.5 | 14.0 | 14.5 | 15.0 | 15.5 | 16.0 | 16.5 | 17.0 |
|---|---|---|---|---|---|---|---|---|---|---|---|---|---|---|---|
| | the Depreciation Rate is: | | | | | | | | | | | | | | |
| 1 | 5.63 | 5.36 | 5.11 | 4.89 | 4.69 | 4.50 | 4.33 | 4.17 | 4.02 | 3.88 | 3.75 | 3.63 | 3.52 | 3.41 | 3.31 |
| 2 | 14.16 | 13.52 | 12.94 | 12.41 | 11.91 | 11.46 | 11.04 | 10.65 | 10.28 | 9.94 | 9.63 | 9.33 | 9.05 | 8.78 | 8.53 |
| 3 | 12.03 | 11.59 | 11.18 | 10.79 | 10.43 | 10.08 | 9.77 | 9.46 | 9.18 | 8.92 | 8.66 | 8.42 | 8.20 | 7.98 | 7.78 |

| If the Recovery Year is: | 10.0 | 10.5 | 11.0 | 11.5 | 12.0 | 12.5 | 13.0 | 13.5 | 14.0 | 14.5 | 15.0 | 15.5 | 16.0 | 16.5 | 17.0 |
|---|---|---|---|---|---|---|---|---|---|---|---|---|---|---|---|
| | the Depreciation Rate is: | | | | | | | | | | | | | | |
| 4 | 10.23 | 9.93 | 9.65 | 9.38 | 9.12 | 8.88 | 8.64 | 8.41 | 8.20 | 7.99 | 7.80 | 7.61 | 7.43 | 7.26 | 7.09 |
| 5 | 8.75 | 8.51 | 8.33 | 8.16 | 7.98 | 7.81 | 7.64 | 7.48 | 7.32 | 7.17 | 7.02 | 6.87 | 6.73 | 6.60 | 6.47 |
| 6 | 8.75 | 8.34 | 7.97 | 7.63 | 7.33 | 7.05 | 6.79 | 6.65 | 6.54 | 6.42 | 6.31 | 6.21 | 6.10 | 6.00 | 5.90 |
| 7 | 8.75 | 8.34 | 7.97 | 7.63 | 7.33 | 7.05 | 6.79 | 6.55 | 6.31 | 6.10 | 5.90 | 5.72 | 5.55 | 5.45 | 5.38 |
| 8 | 8.74 | 8.34 | 7.97 | 7.63 | 7.33 | 7.05 | 6.79 | 6.54 | 6.31 | 6.10 | 5.90 | 5.72 | 5.55 | 5.38 | 5.23 |
| 9 | 8.75 | 8.34 | 7.97 | 7.63 | 7.33 | 7.05 | 6.79 | 6.55 | 6.32 | 6.10 | 5.91 | 5.72 | 5.55 | 5.39 | 5.23 |
| 10 | 8.74 | 8.34 | 7.97 | 7.63 | 7.32 | 7.05 | 6.79 | 6.54 | 6.31 | 6.10 | 5.90 | 5.72 | 5.55 | 5.38 | 5.23 |
| 11 | 5.47 | 8.35 | 7.96 | 7.63 | 7.33 | 7.05 | 6.79 | 6.55 | 6.32 | 6.10 | 5.91 | 5.72 | 5.55 | 5.39 | 5.23 |
| 12 | | 1.04 | 4.98 | 7.64 | 7.32 | 7.04 | 6.80 | 6.54 | 6.31 | 6.10 | 5.90 | 5.72 | 5.55 | 5.38 | 5.23 |
| 13 | | | | 0.95 | 4.58 | 7.05 | 6.79 | 6.55 | 6.32 | 6.11 | 5.91 | 5.72 | 5.55 | 5.39 | 5.22 |
| 14 | | | | | | 0.88 | 4.25 | 6.54 | 6.31 | 6.10 | 5.90 | 5.72 | 5.55 | 5.38 | 5.23 |
| 15 | | | | | | | | 0.82 | 3.95 | 6.11 | 5.91 | 5.73 | 5.55 | 5.39 | 5.22 |
| 16 | | | | | | | | | | 0.76 | 3.69 | 5.72 | 5.55 | 5.38 | 5.23 |
| 17 | | | | | | | | | | | | 0.72 | 3.47 | 5.39 | 5.22 |
| 18 | | | | | | | | | | | | | | 0.67 | 3.27 |

and the Recovery Period is:

| If the Recovery Year is: | 17.5 | 18.0 | 18.5 | 19.0 | 19.5 | 20.0 | 20.5 | 21.0 | 21.5 | 22.0 | 22.5 | 23.0 | 23.5 | 24.0 | 24.5 |
|---|---|---|---|---|---|---|---|---|---|---|---|---|---|---|---|
| | the Depreciation Rate is: | | | | | | | | | | | | | | |
| 1 | 3.21 | 3.13 | 3.04 | 2.96 | 2.88 | 2.813 | 2.744 | 2.679 | 2.616 | 2.557 | 2.500 | 2.446 | 2.394 | 2.344 | 2.296 |
| 2 | 8.30 | 8.07 | 7.86 | 7.66 | 7.47 | 7.289 | 7.116 | 6.952 | 6.794 | 6.644 | 6.500 | 6.362 | 6.230 | 6.104 | 5.982 |
| 3 | 7.58 | 7.40 | 7.22 | 7.06 | 6.90 | 6.742 | 6.596 | 6.455 | 6.320 | 6.191 | 6.067 | 5.947 | 5.833 | 5.722 | 5.616 |
| 4 | 6.94 | 6.78 | 6.64 | 6.50 | 6.37 | 6.237 | 6.113 | 5.994 | 5.879 | 5.769 | 5.662 | 5.559 | 5.460 | 5.364 | 5.272 |
| 5 | 6.34 | 6.22 | 6.10 | 5.99 | 5.88 | 5.769 | 5.666 | 5.566 | 5.469 | 5.375 | 5.285 | 5.197 | 5.112 | 5.029 | 4.949 |
| 6 | 5.80 | 5.70 | 5.61 | 5.51 | 5.42 | 5.336 | 5.251 | 5.168 | 5.088 | 5.009 | 4.932 | 4.858 | 4.785 | 4.715 | 4.646 |
| 7 | 5.30 | 5.23 | 5.15 | 5.08 | 5.01 | 4.936 | 4.867 | 4.799 | 4.733 | 4.667 | 4.604 | 4.541 | 4.480 | 4.420 | 4.362 |

| If the Recovery Year is: | 17.5 | 18.0 | 18.5 | 19.0 | 19.5 | 20.0 | 20.5 | 21.0 | 21.5 | 22.0 | 22.5 | 23.0 | 23.5 | 24.0 | 24.5 |
|---|---|---|---|---|---|---|---|---|---|---|---|---|---|---|---|
| | | | the Depreciation Rate is: | | | | | | | | | | | | |
| 8 | 5.08 | 4.94 | 4.81 | 4.69 | 4.62 | 4.566 | 4.511 | 4.456 | 4.402 | 4.349 | 4.297 | 4.245 | 4.194 | 4.144 | 4.095 |
| 9 | 5.08 | 4.94 | 4.82 | 4.69 | 4.57 | 4.460 | 4.353 | 4.252 | 4.156 | 4.064 | 4.010 | 3.968 | 3.926 | 3.885 | 3.844 |
| 10 | 5.08 | 4.94 | 4.81 | 4.69 | 4.57 | 4.460 | 4.353 | 4.252 | 4.156 | 4.064 | 3.975 | 3.889 | 3.807 | 3.729 | 3.655 |
| 11 | 5.08 | 4.94 | 4.82 | 4.69 | 4.57 | 4.460 | 4.353 | 4.252 | 4.156 | 4.064 | 3.975 | 3.889 | 3.807 | 3.730 | 3.655 |
| 12 | 5.08 | 4.95 | 4.81 | 4.69 | 4.57 | 4.460 | 4.353 | 4.252 | 4.156 | 4.064 | 3.975 | 3.889 | 3.807 | 3.729 | 3.655 |
| 13 | 5.08 | 4.94 | 4.82 | 4.69 | 4.57 | 4.461 | 4.353 | 4.252 | 4.156 | 4.064 | 3.975 | 3.889 | 3.807 | 3.730 | 3.655 |
| 14 | 5.08 | 4.95 | 4.81 | 4.69 | 4.58 | 4.460 | 4.353 | 4.252 | 4.156 | 4.064 | 3.975 | 3.889 | 3.807 | 3.729 | 3.655 |
| 15 | 5.08 | 4.94 | 4.82 | 4.70 | 4.57 | 4.461 | 4.353 | 4.252 | 4.155 | 4.064 | 3.975 | 3.889 | 3.808 | 3.730 | 3.655 |
| 16 | 5.08 | 4.95 | 4.81 | 4.69 | 4.58 | 4.460 | 4.353 | 4.252 | 4.156 | 4.064 | 3.975 | 3.889 | 3.807 | 3.729 | 3.655 |
| 17 | 5.09 | 4.94 | 4.82 | 4.70 | 4.57 | 4.461 | 4.354 | 4.252 | 4.155 | 4.064 | 3.974 | 3.889 | 3.808 | 3.730 | 3.655 |
| 18 | 5.08 | 4.95 | 4.81 | 4.69 | 4.58 | 4.460 | 4.353 | 4.251 | 4.156 | 4.065 | 3.975 | 3.889 | 3.807 | 3.729 | 3.655 |
| 19 | 0.64 | 3.09 | 4.82 | 4.70 | 4.57 | 4.461 | 4.354 | 4.252 | 4.155 | 4.064 | 3.974 | 3.889 | 3.808 | 3.730 | 3.655 |
| 20 | | | 0.60 | 2.93 | 4.58 | 4.460 | 4.353 | 4.251 | 4.156 | 4.065 | 3.975 | 3.889 | 3.807 | 3.729 | 3.655 |
| 21 | | | | | 0.57 | 2.788 | 4.354 | 4.252 | 4.155 | 4.064 | 3.974 | 3.889 | 3.808 | 3.730 | 3.655 |
| 22 | | | | | | | 0.544 | 2.657 | 4.156 | 4.065 | 3.975 | 3.889 | 3.807 | 3.729 | 3.655 |
| 23 | | | | | | | | | 0.519 | 2.540 | 3.974 | 3.889 | 3.808 | 3.730 | 3.655 |
| 24 | | | | | | | | | | | 0.497 | 2.431 | 3.807 | 3.729 | 3.656 |
| 25 | | | | | | | | | | | | | 0.476 | 2.331 | 3.655 |
| 26 | | | | | | | | | | | | | | | 0.457 |

| | | | and the Recovery Period is: | | | | | | | | | | | | |
|---|---|---|---|---|---|---|---|---|---|---|---|---|---|---|---|
| If the Recovery Year is: | 25.0 | 25.5 | 26.0 | 26.5 | 27.0 | 27.5 | 28.0 | 28.5 | 29.0 | 29.5 | 30.0 | 30.5 | 31.0 | 31.5 | 32.0 |
| | | | the Depreciation Rate is: | | | | | | | | | | | | |
| 1 | 2.250 | 2.206 | 2.163 | 2.123 | 2.083 | 2.045 | 2.009 | 1.974 | 1.940 | 1.907 | 1.875 | 1.844 | 1.815 | 1.786 | 1.758 |
| 2 | 5.865 | 5.753 | 5.644 | 5.540 | 5.440 | 5.343 | 5.250 | 5.159 | 5.072 | 4.988 | 4.906 | 4.827 | 4.751 | 4.677 | 4.605 |
| 3 | 5.513 | 5.414 | 5.319 | 5.227 | 5.138 | 5.052 | 4.968 | 4.888 | 4.810 | 4.734 | 4.661 | 4.590 | 4.521 | 4.454 | 4.389 |
| 4 | 5.182 | 5.096 | 5.012 | 4.931 | 4.852 | 4.776 | 4.702 | 4.630 | 4.561 | 4.493 | 4.428 | 4.364 | 4.302 | 4.242 | 4.184 |

| If the Recovery Year is: | and the Recovery Period is: 25.0 | 25.5 | 26.0 | 26.5 | 27.0 | 27.5 | 28.0 | 28.5 | 29.0 | 29.5 | 30.0 | 30.5 | 31.0 | 31.5 | 32.0 |
|---|---|---|---|---|---|---|---|---|---|---|---|---|---|---|---|
| | the Depreciation Rate is: | | | | | | | | | | | | | | |
| 5 | 4.871 | 4.796 | 4.723 | 4.652 | 4.583 | 4.515 | 4.450 | 4.387 | 4.325 | 4.265 | 4.207 | 4.150 | 4.094 | 4.040 | 3.987 |
| 6 | 4.579 | 4.514 | 4.450 | 4.388 | 4.328 | 4.269 | 4.212 | 4.156 | 4.101 | 4.048 | 3.996 | 3.945 | 3.896 | 3.848 | 3.800 |
| 7 | 4.304 | 4.248 | 4.194 | 4.140 | 4.088 | 4.036 | 3.986 | 3.937 | 3.889 | 3.842 | 3.796 | 3.751 | 3.707 | 3.664 | 3.622 |
| 8 | 4.046 | 3.998 | 3.952 | 3.906 | 3.860 | 3.816 | 3.773 | 3.730 | 3.688 | 3.647 | 3.607 | 3.567 | 3.528 | 3.490 | 3.453 |
| 9 | 3.803 | 3.763 | 3.724 | 3.685 | 3.646 | 3.608 | 3.571 | 3.534 | 3.497 | 3.461 | 3.426 | 3.392 | 3.357 | 3.324 | 3.291 |
| 10 | 3.584 | 3.542 | 3.509 | 3.476 | 3.443 | 3.411 | 3.379 | 3.348 | 3.316 | 3.286 | 3.255 | 3.225 | 3.195 | 3.165 | 3.136 |
| 11 | 3.584 | 3.514 | 3.447 | 3.383 | 3.321 | 3.262 | 3.205 | 3.171 | 3.145 | 3.118 | 3.092 | 3.066 | 3.040 | 3.015 | 2.989 |
| 12 | 3.584 | 3.514 | 3.447 | 3.383 | 3.321 | 3.262 | 3.205 | 3.150 | 3.096 | 3.044 | 2.994 | 2.946 | 2.899 | 2.871 | 2.849 |
| 13 | 3.584 | 3.514 | 3.447 | 3.383 | 3.321 | 3.262 | 3.205 | 3.150 | 3.096 | 3.044 | 2.994 | 2.946 | 2.899 | 2.853 | 2.809 |
| 14 | 3.584 | 3.515 | 3.447 | 3.383 | 3.321 | 3.262 | 3.205 | 3.150 | 3.096 | 3.044 | 2.994 | 2.945 | 2.899 | 2.853 | 2.809 |
| 15 | 3.584 | 3.514 | 3.447 | 3.383 | 3.321 | 3.262 | 3.205 | 3.149 | 3.096 | 3.044 | 2.994 | 2.946 | 2.899 | 2.853 | 2.809 |
| 16 | 3.584 | 3.515 | 3.447 | 3.383 | 3.322 | 3.262 | 3.206 | 3.150 | 3.096 | 3.044 | 2.994 | 2.945 | 2.899 | 2.853 | 2.809 |
| 17 | 3.584 | 3.514 | 3.447 | 3.383 | 3.321 | 3.262 | 3.205 | 3.149 | 3.095 | 3.044 | 2.994 | 2.946 | 2.899 | 2.853 | 2.809 |
| 18 | 3.584 | 3.515 | 3.447 | 3.383 | 3.322 | 3.262 | 3.206 | 3.150 | 3.096 | 3.044 | 2.994 | 2.945 | 2.899 | 2.853 | 2.809 |
| 19 | 3.584 | 3.514 | 3.447 | 3.383 | 3.321 | 3.263 | 3.205 | 3.149 | 3.095 | 3.044 | 2.994 | 2.946 | 2.899 | 2.854 | 2.809 |
| 20 | 3.584 | 3.515 | 3.447 | 3.383 | 3.322 | 3.262 | 3.206 | 3.150 | 3.096 | 3.044 | 2.993 | 2.945 | 2.899 | 2.853 | 2.809 |
| 21 | 3.585 | 3.514 | 3.448 | 3.383 | 3.321 | 3.263 | 3.205 | 3.149 | 3.095 | 3.043 | 2.994 | 2.946 | 2.899 | 2.854 | 2.809 |
| 22 | 3.584 | 3.515 | 3.447 | 3.383 | 3.322 | 3.262 | 3.206 | 3.150 | 3.096 | 3.044 | 2.993 | 2.945 | 2.899 | 2.853 | 2.809 |
| 23 | 3.585 | 3.514 | 3.448 | 3.383 | 3.321 | 3.263 | 3.205 | 3.149 | 3.095 | 3.043 | 2.994 | 2.946 | 2.899 | 2.854 | 2.809 |
| 24 | 3.584 | 3.515 | 3.447 | 3.383 | 3.322 | 3.262 | 3.206 | 3.150 | 3.096 | 3.044 | 2.993 | 2.945 | 2.899 | 2.853 | 2.809 |
| 25 | 3.585 | 3.514 | 3.448 | 3.382 | 3.321 | 3.263 | 3.205 | 3.149 | 3.095 | 3.043 | 2.994 | 2.946 | 2.899 | 2.854 | 2.809 |
| 26 | 2.240 | 3.515 | 3.447 | 3.383 | 3.322 | 3.262 | 3.206 | 3.150 | 3.096 | 3.044 | 2.993 | 2.945 | 2.899 | 2.853 | 2.809 |
| 27 | | 0.439 | 2.155 | 3.382 | 3.321 | 3.263 | 3.205 | 3.149 | 3.095 | 3.043 | 2.994 | 2.946 | 2.899 | 2.854 | 2.809 |
| 28 | | | | 0.423 | 2.076 | 3.262 | 3.206 | 3.150 | 3.096 | 3.044 | 2.993 | 2.945 | 2.899 | 2.853 | 2.809 |
| 29 | | | | | | 0.408 | 2.003 | 3.149 | 3.095 | 3.043 | 2.994 | 2.946 | 2.900 | 2.854 | 2.809 |
| 30 | | | | | | | | 0.394 | 1.935 | 3.044 | 2.993 | 2.945 | 2.899 | 2.853 | 2.809 |

| If the Recovery Year is: | and the Recovery Period is: 25.0 | 25.5 | 26.0 | 26.5 | 27.0 | 27.5 | 28.0 | 28.5 | 29.0 | 29.5 | 30.0 | 30.5 | 31.0 | 31.5 | 32.0 |
|---|---|---|---|---|---|---|---|---|---|---|---|---|---|---|---|
| | the Depreciation Rate is: | | | | | | | | | | | | | | |
| 31 | | | | | | | | | | 0.380 | 1.871 | 2.946 | 2.900 | 2.854 | 2.810 |
| 32 | | | | | | | | | | | | 0.368 | 1.812 | 2.853 | 2.809 |
| 33 | | | | | | | | | | | | | | 0.357 | 1.756 |

| If the Recovery Year is: | and the Recovery Period is: 32.5 | 33.0 | 33.5 | 34.0 | 34.5 | 35.0 | 35.5 | 36.0 | 36.5 | 37.0 | 37.5 | 38.0 | 38.5 | 39.0 | 39.5 |
|---|---|---|---|---|---|---|---|---|---|---|---|---|---|---|---|
| | the Depreciation Rate is: | | | | | | | | | | | | | | |
| 1 | 1.731 | 1.705 | 1.679 | 1.654 | 1.630 | 1.607 | 1.585 | 1.563 | 1.541 | 1.520 | 1.500 | 1.480 | 1.461 | 1.442 | 1.424 |
| 2 | 4.535 | 4.468 | 4.402 | 4.339 | 4.277 | 4.217 | 4.158 | 4.102 | 4.046 | 3.992 | 3.940 | 3.889 | 3.839 | 3.791 | 3.743 |
| 3 | 4.326 | 4.265 | 4.205 | 4.147 | 4.091 | 4.036 | 3.983 | 3.931 | 3.880 | 3.831 | 3.782 | 3.735 | 3.690 | 3.645 | 3.601 |
| 4 | 4.127 | 4.071 | 4.017 | 3.964 | 3.913 | 3.863 | 3.814 | 3.767 | 3.721 | 3.675 | 3.631 | 3.588 | 3.546 | 3.505 | 3.465 |
| 5 | 3.936 | 3.886 | 3.837 | 3.790 | 3.743 | 3.698 | 3.653 | 3.610 | 3.568 | 3.526 | 3.486 | 3.446 | 3.408 | 3.370 | 3.333 |
| 6 | 3.754 | 3.709 | 3.665 | 3.622 | 3.580 | 3.539 | 3.499 | 3.459 | 3.421 | 3.383 | 3.346 | 3.310 | 3.275 | 3.240 | 3.206 |
| 7 | 3.581 | 3.541 | 3.501 | 3.463 | 3.425 | 3.387 | 3.351 | 3.315 | 3.280 | 3.246 | 3.213 | 3.180 | 3.147 | 3.116 | 3.085 |
| 8 | 3.416 | 3.380 | 3.345 | 3.310 | 3.276 | 3.242 | 3.209 | 3.177 | 3.146 | 3.115 | 3.084 | 3.054 | 3.025 | 2.996 | 2.967 |
| 9 | 3.258 | 3.226 | 3.195 | 3.164 | 3.133 | 3.103 | 3.074 | 3.045 | 3.016 | 2.988 | 2.961 | 2.934 | 2.907 | 2.881 | 2.855 |
| 10 | 3.108 | 3.080 | 3.052 | 3.024 | 2.997 | 2.970 | 2.944 | 2.918 | 2.892 | 2.867 | 2.842 | 2.818 | 2.794 | 2.770 | 2.746 |
| 11 | 2.964 | 2.940 | 2.915 | 2.891 | 2.867 | 2.843 | 2.820 | 2.796 | 2.774 | 2.751 | 2.729 | 2.707 | 2.685 | 2.663 | 2.642 |
| 12 | 2.828 | 2.806 | 2.784 | 2.763 | 2.742 | 2.721 | 2.700 | 2.680 | 2.660 | 2.639 | 2.619 | 2.600 | 2.580 | 2.561 | 2.542 |
| 13 | 2.766 | 2.725 | 2.685 | 2.646 | 2.623 | 2.605 | 2.586 | 2.568 | 2.550 | 2.532 | 2.515 | 2.497 | 2.480 | 2.462 | 2.445 |
| 14 | 2.766 | 2.725 | 2.685 | 2.646 | 2.608 | 2.571 | 2.535 | 2.500 | 2.467 | 2.434 | 2.414 | 2.399 | 2.383 | 2.368 | 2.352 |
| 15 | 2.766 | 2.725 | 2.685 | 2.646 | 2.608 | 2.571 | 2.535 | 2.500 | 2.467 | 2.434 | 2.402 | 2.370 | 2.340 | 2.310 | 2.281 |
| 16 | 2.766 | 2.725 | 2.685 | 2.646 | 2.608 | 2.571 | 2.535 | 2.500 | 2.466 | 2.434 | 2.402 | 2.370 | 2.339 | 2.310 | 2.281 |
| 17 | 2.766 | 2.725 | 2.685 | 2.646 | 2.608 | 2.571 | 2.535 | 2.500 | 2.467 | 2.434 | 2.402 | 2.370 | 2.340 | 2.310 | 2.281 |
| 18 | 2.766 | 2.725 | 2.685 | 2.646 | 2.608 | 2.571 | 2.535 | 2.500 | 2.466 | 2.434 | 2.402 | 2.370 | 2.339 | 2.310 | 2.281 |
| 19 | 2.766 | 2.725 | 2.685 | 2.646 | 2.608 | 2.571 | 2.535 | 2.500 | 2.467 | 2.434 | 2.401 | 2.370 | 2.340 | 2.310 | 2.281 |

| If the Recovery Year is: | and the Recovery Period is: 32.5 | 33.0 | 33.5 | 34.0 | 34.5 | 35.0 | 35.5 | 36.0 | 36.5 | 37.0 | 37.5 | 38.0 | 38.5 | 39.0 | 39.5 |
|---|---|---|---|---|---|---|---|---|---|---|---|---|---|---|---|
| | the Depreciation Rate is: | | | | | | | | | | | | | | |
| 20 | 2.766 | 2.725 | 2.685 | 2.646 | 2.608 | 2.571 | 2.535 | 2.500 | 2.466 | 2.434 | 2.402 | 2.370 | 2.339 | 2.310 | 2.281 |
| 21 | 2.766 | 2.725 | 2.685 | 2.646 | 2.608 | 2.571 | 2.535 | 2.500 | 2.467 | 2.434 | 2.401 | 2.370 | 2.340 | 2.310 | 2.281 |
| 22 | 2.766 | 2.725 | 2.685 | 2.646 | 2.608 | 2.571 | 2.535 | 2.500 | 2.466 | 2.434 | 2.402 | 2.370 | 2.339 | 2.310 | 2.281 |
| 23 | 2.766 | 2.725 | 2.685 | 2.646 | 2.608 | 2.571 | 2.535 | 2.500 | 2.467 | 2.434 | 2.401 | 2.370 | 2.340 | 2.310 | 2.281 |
| 24 | 2.766 | 2.725 | 2.685 | 2.646 | 2.608 | 2.571 | 2.535 | 2.500 | 2.466 | 2.434 | 2.402 | 2.370 | 2.339 | 2.310 | 2.281 |
| 25 | 2.766 | 2.724 | 2.685 | 2.646 | 2.608 | 2.571 | 2.535 | 2.501 | 2.467 | 2.434 | 2.401 | 2.370 | 2.340 | 2.310 | 2.281 |
| 26 | 2.767 | 2.725 | 2.685 | 2.646 | 2.608 | 2.571 | 2.535 | 2.500 | 2.466 | 2.434 | 2.402 | 2.370 | 2.339 | 2.310 | 2.281 |
| 27 | 2.766 | 2.724 | 2.685 | 2.646 | 2.608 | 2.571 | 2.535 | 2.501 | 2.467 | 2.434 | 2.401 | 2.370 | 2.340 | 2.310 | 2.281 |
| 28 | 2.767 | 2.725 | 2.685 | 2.646 | 2.608 | 2.571 | 2.535 | 2.500 | 2.466 | 2.434 | 2.402 | 2.370 | 2.339 | 2.310 | 2.281 |
| 29 | 2.766 | 2.724 | 2.685 | 2.646 | 2.608 | 2.571 | 2.535 | 2.501 | 2.467 | 2.434 | 2.401 | 2.370 | 2.340 | 2.310 | 2.281 |
| 30 | 2.767 | 2.725 | 2.684 | 2.647 | 2.608 | 2.571 | 2.535 | 2.500 | 2.466 | 2.434 | 2.402 | 2.370 | 2.339 | 2.310 | 2.281 |
| 31 | 2.766 | 2.724 | 2.685 | 2.646 | 2.608 | 2.571 | 2.535 | 2.501 | 2.467 | 2.434 | 2.401 | 2.370 | 2.340 | 2.310 | 2.281 |
| 32 | 2.767 | 2.725 | 2.684 | 2.647 | 2.608 | 2.571 | 2.535 | 2.500 | 2.466 | 2.434 | 2.402 | 2.370 | 2.339 | 2.310 | 2.281 |
| 33 | 2.766 | 2.724 | 2.685 | 2.646 | 2.608 | 2.571 | 2.536 | 2.501 | 2.467 | 2.434 | 2.401 | 2.370 | 2.340 | 2.310 | 2.281 |
| 34 | 0.346 | 1.703 | 2.684 | 2.647 | 2.608 | 2.571 | 2.535 | 2.500 | 2.466 | 2.434 | 2.402 | 2.370 | 2.339 | 2.309 | 2.281 |
| 35 | | | 0.336 | 1.654 | 2.609 | 2.571 | 2.536 | 2.501 | 2.467 | 2.433 | 2.401 | 2.370 | 2.340 | 2.310 | 2.281 |
| 36 | | | | | 0.326 | 1.607 | 2.535 | 2.500 | 2.466 | 2.434 | 2.402 | 2.370 | 2.339 | 2.309 | 2.282 |
| 37 | | | | | | | 0.317 | 1.563 | 2.467 | 2.433 | 2.401 | 2.371 | 2.340 | 2.310 | 2.281 |
| 38 | | | | | | | | | 0.308 | 1.521 | 2.402 | 2.370 | 2.339 | 2.309 | 2.282 |
| 39 | | | | | | | | | | | 0.300 | 1.482 | 2.340 | 2.310 | 2.281 |
| 40 | | | | | | | | | | | | | 0.292 | 1.443 | 2.282 |
| 41 | | | | | | | | | | | | | | | 0.285 |

| If the Recovery Year is: | 40.0 | 40.5 | 41.0 | 41.5 | 42.0 | 42.5 | 43.0 | 43.5 | 44.0 | 44.5 | 45.0 | 45.5 | 46.0 | 46.5 | 47.0 |
|---|---|---|---|---|---|---|---|---|---|---|---|---|---|---|---|
| | and the Recovery Period is: | | | | | | | | | | | | | | |
| | the Depreciation Rate is: | | | | | | | | | | | | | | |
| 1 | 1.406 | 1.389 | 1.372 | 1.355 | 1.339 | 1.324 | 1.308 | 1.293 | 1.278 | 1.264 | 1.250 | 1.236 | 1.223 | 1.210 | 1.197 |
| 2 | 3.697 | 3.652 | 3.608 | 3.565 | 3.524 | 3.483 | 3.443 | 3.404 | 3.366 | 3.328 | 3.292 | 3.256 | 3.221 | 3.187 | 3.153 |
| 3 | 3.559 | 3.517 | 3.476 | 3.437 | 3.398 | 3.360 | 3.323 | 3.286 | 3.251 | 3.216 | 3.182 | 3.149 | 3.116 | 3.084 | 3.053 |
| 4 | 3.425 | 3.387 | 3.349 | 3.312 | 3.276 | 3.241 | 3.207 | 3.173 | 3.140 | 3.108 | 3.076 | 3.045 | 3.014 | 2.984 | 2.955 |
| 5 | 3.297 | 3.261 | 3.227 | 3.193 | 3.159 | 3.127 | 3.095 | 3.064 | 3.033 | 3.003 | 2.973 | 2.944 | 2.916 | 2.888 | 2.861 |
| 6 | 3.173 | 3.141 | 3.109 | 3.077 | 3.047 | 3.016 | 2.987 | 2.958 | 2.929 | 2.902 | 2.874 | 2.847 | 2.821 | 2.795 | 2.770 |
| 7 | 3.054 | 3.024 | 2.995 | 2.966 | 2.938 | 2.910 | 2.883 | 2.856 | 2.830 | 2.804 | 2.778 | 2.754 | 2.729 | 2.705 | 2.681 |
| 8 | 2.940 | 2.912 | 2.885 | 2.859 | 2.833 | 2.807 | 2.782 | 2.757 | 2.733 | 2.709 | 2.686 | 2.663 | 2.640 | 2.618 | 2.596 |
| 9 | 2.829 | 2.804 | 2.780 | 2.756 | 2.732 | 2.708 | 2.685 | 2.662 | 2.640 | 2.618 | 2.596 | 2.575 | 2.554 | 2.533 | 2.513 |
| 10 | 2.723 | 2.700 | 2.678 | 2.656 | 2.634 | 2.613 | 2.591 | 2.571 | 2.550 | 2.530 | 2.510 | 2.490 | 2.471 | 2.451 | 2.433 |
| 11 | 2.621 | 2.600 | 2.580 | 2.560 | 2.540 | 2.520 | 2.501 | 2.482 | 2.463 | 2.444 | 2.426 | 2.408 | 2.390 | 2.372 | 2.355 |
| 12 | 2.523 | 2.504 | 2.486 | 2.467 | 2.449 | 2.431 | 2.414 | 2.396 | 2.379 | 2.362 | 2.345 | 2.329 | 2.312 | 2.296 | 2.280 |
| 13 | 2.428 | 2.411 | 2.395 | 2.378 | 2.362 | 2.346 | 2.330 | 2.314 | 2.298 | 2.282 | 2.267 | 2.252 | 2.237 | 2.222 | 2.207 |
| 14 | 2.337 | 2.322 | 2.307 | 2.292 | 2.277 | 2.263 | 2.248 | 2.234 | 2.220 | 2.206 | 2.192 | 2.178 | 2.164 | 2.150 | 2.137 |
| 15 | 2.253 | 2.236 | 2.223 | 2.209 | 2.196 | 2.183 | 2.170 | 2.157 | 2.144 | 2.131 | 2.118 | 2.106 | 2.093 | 2.081 | 2.068 |
| 16 | 2.253 | 2.225 | 2.198 | 2.172 | 2.146 | 2.122 | 2.097 | 2.083 | 2.071 | 2.059 | 2.048 | 2.036 | 2.025 | 2.014 | 2.002 |
| 17 | 2.253 | 2.225 | 2.198 | 2.172 | 2.146 | 2.122 | 2.097 | 2.073 | 2.050 | 2.027 | 2.005 | 1.983 | 1.962 | 1.949 | 1.938 |
| 18 | 2.253 | 2.225 | 2.198 | 2.172 | 2.146 | 2.121 | 2.097 | 2.073 | 2.050 | 2.027 | 2.005 | 1.983 | 1.962 | 1.941 | 1.920 |
| 19 | 2.253 | 2.226 | 2.198 | 2.172 | 2.147 | 2.122 | 2.097 | 2.073 | 2.050 | 2.027 | 2.005 | 1.983 | 1.962 | 1.941 | 1.920 |
| 20 | 2.253 | 2.225 | 2.198 | 2.172 | 2.146 | 2.121 | 2.097 | 2.073 | 2.050 | 2.027 | 2.005 | 1.983 | 1.962 | 1.941 | 1.920 |
| 21 | 2.253 | 2.226 | 2.198 | 2.172 | 2.147 | 2.122 | 2.097 | 2.073 | 2.050 | 2.027 | 2.005 | 1.983 | 1.962 | 1.941 | 1.920 |
| 22 | 2.253 | 2.225 | 2.198 | 2.172 | 2.146 | 2.121 | 2.097 | 2.073 | 2.050 | 2.027 | 2.005 | 1.983 | 1.962 | 1.941 | 1.920 |
| 23 | 2.253 | 2.226 | 2.198 | 2.172 | 2.147 | 2.122 | 2.097 | 2.073 | 2.050 | 2.027 | 2.005 | 1.983 | 1.962 | 1.941 | 1.920 |
| 24 | 2.253 | 2.225 | 2.198 | 2.172 | 2.146 | 2.121 | 2.097 | 2.073 | 2.050 | 2.027 | 2.005 | 1.983 | 1.961 | 1.941 | 1.920 |
| 25 | 2.253 | 2.226 | 2.198 | 2.172 | 2.147 | 2.122 | 2.097 | 2.073 | 2.050 | 2.027 | 2.004 | 1.983 | 1.962 | 1.940 | 1.920 |
| 26 | 2.253 | 2.225 | 2.198 | 2.172 | 2.146 | 2.121 | 2.097 | 2.073 | 2.050 | 2.027 | 2.005 | 1.983 | 1.961 | 1.941 | 1.920 |

| If the Recovery Year is: | and the Recovery Period is: 40.0 | 40.5 | 41.0 | 41.5 | 42.0 | 42.5 | 43.0 | 43.5 | 44.0 | 44.5 | 45.0 | 45.5 | 46.0 | 46.5 | 47.0 |
|---|---|---|---|---|---|---|---|---|---|---|---|---|---|---|---|
| | the Depreciation Rate is: | | | | | | | | | | | | | | |
| 27 | 2.253 | 2.226 | 2.199 | 2.172 | 2.147 | 2.122 | 2.097 | 2.073 | 2.050 | 2.027 | 2.004 | 1.983 | 1.962 | 1.940 | 1.920 |
| 28 | 2.253 | 2.225 | 2.198 | 2.172 | 2.146 | 2.121 | 2.097 | 2.073 | 2.050 | 2.027 | 2.005 | 1.983 | 1.961 | 1.941 | 1.920 |
| 29 | 2.253 | 2.226 | 2.199 | 2.172 | 2.147 | 2.122 | 2.097 | 2.073 | 2.050 | 2.027 | 2.004 | 1.983 | 1.962 | 1.940 | 1.920 |
| 30 | 2.253 | 2.225 | 2.198 | 2.172 | 2.146 | 2.121 | 2.097 | 2.073 | 2.050 | 2.027 | 2.005 | 1.983 | 1.961 | 1.941 | 1.920 |
| 31 | 2.253 | 2.226 | 2.199 | 2.172 | 2.147 | 2.122 | 2.097 | 2.073 | 2.050 | 2.027 | 2.004 | 1.983 | 1.962 | 1.940 | 1.920 |
| 32 | 2.253 | 2.225 | 2.198 | 2.172 | 2.146 | 2.121 | 2.098 | 2.074 | 2.050 | 2.027 | 2.005 | 1.983 | 1.961 | 1.941 | 1.920 |
| 33 | 2.253 | 2.226 | 2.199 | 2.172 | 2.147 | 2.122 | 2.097 | 2.073 | 2.050 | 2.027 | 2.004 | 1.983 | 1.962 | 1.940 | 1.920 |
| 34 | 2.253 | 2.225 | 2.198 | 2.172 | 2.146 | 2.121 | 2.098 | 2.074 | 2.049 | 2.027 | 2.005 | 1.983 | 1.961 | 1.941 | 1.920 |
| 35 | 2.253 | 2.226 | 2.199 | 2.172 | 2.147 | 2.122 | 2.097 | 2.073 | 2.050 | 2.027 | 2.004 | 1.983 | 1.962 | 1.940 | 1.920 |
| 36 | 2.253 | 2.225 | 2.198 | 2.172 | 2.146 | 2.121 | 2.098 | 2.074 | 2.049 | 2.027 | 2.005 | 1.982 | 1.961 | 1.941 | 1.920 |
| 37 | 2.253 | 2.226 | 2.199 | 2.172 | 2.147 | 2.122 | 2.097 | 2.073 | 2.050 | 2.027 | 2.004 | 1.983 | 1.962 | 1.940 | 1.920 |
| 38 | 2.254 | 2.225 | 2.198 | 2.172 | 2.146 | 2.121 | 2.098 | 2.074 | 2.049 | 2.027 | 2.005 | 1.982 | 1.961 | 1.941 | 1.920 |
| 39 | 2.253 | 2.226 | 2.199 | 2.173 | 2.147 | 2.122 | 2.097 | 2.073 | 2.050 | 2.027 | 2.004 | 1.983 | 1.962 | 1.940 | 1.920 |
| 40 | 2.254 | 2.225 | 2.198 | 2.172 | 2.146 | 2.121 | 2.098 | 2.074 | 2.049 | 2.027 | 2.005 | 1.982 | 1.961 | 1.941 | 1.920 |
| 41 | 1.408 | 2.226 | 2.199 | 2.173 | 2.147 | 2.122 | 2.097 | 2.073 | 2.050 | 2.027 | 2.004 | 1.983 | 1.962 | 1.940 | 1.920 |
| 42 | | 0.278 | 1.374 | 2.172 | 2.146 | 2.121 | 2.098 | 2.074 | 2.049 | 2.026 | 2.005 | 1.982 | 1.961 | 1.941 | 1.920 |
| 43 | | | | 0.272 | 1.342 | 2.122 | 2.097 | 2.073 | 2.050 | 2.027 | 2.004 | 1.983 | 1.962 | 1.940 | 1.920 |
| 44 | | | | | | 0.265 | 1.311 | 2.074 | 2.049 | 2.026 | 2.005 | 1.982 | 1.961 | 1.941 | 1.920 |
| 45 | | | | | | | | 0.259 | 1.281 | 2.027 | 2.004 | 1.983 | 1.962 | 1.940 | 1.920 |
| 46 | | | | | | | | | | 0.253 | 1.253 | 1.982 | 1.961 | 1.941 | 1.920 |
| 47 | | | | | | | | | | | | 0.248 | 1.226 | 1.940 | 1.921 |
| 48 | | | | | | | | | | | | | | 0.243 | 1.200 |

| If the Recovery Year is: | and the Recovery Period is: 47.5 | 48.0 | 48.5 | 49.0 | 49.5 | 50.0 |
|---|---|---|---|---|---|---|
| | the Depreciation Rate is: | | | | | |
| 1 | 1.184 | 1.172 | 1.160 | 1.148 | 1.136 | 1.125 |
| 2 | 3.121 | 3.088 | 3.057 | 3.026 | 2.996 | 2.966 |
| 3 | 3.022 | 2.992 | 2.962 | 2.933 | 2.905 | 2.877 |
| 4 | 2.927 | 2.898 | 2.871 | 2.844 | 2.817 | 2.791 |
| 5 | 2.834 | 2.808 | 2.782 | 2.757 | 2.732 | 2.707 |
| 6 | 2.745 | 2.720 | 2.696 | 2.672 | 2.649 | 2.626 |
| 7 | 2.658 | 2.635 | 2.613 | 2.590 | 2.569 | 2.547 |
| 8 | 2.574 | 2.553 | 2.532 | 2.511 | 2.491 | 2.471 |
| 9 | 2.493 | 2.473 | 2.453 | 2.434 | 2.415 | 2.397 |
| 10 | 2.414 | 2.396 | 2.378 | 2.360 | 2.342 | 2.325 |
| 11 | 2.338 | 2.321 | 2.304 | 2.288 | 2.271 | 2.255 |
| 12 | 2.264 | 2.248 | 2.233 | 2.217 | 2.202 | 2.187 |
| 13 | 2.192 | 2.178 | 2.164 | 2.150 | 2.136 | 2.122 |
| 14 | 2.123 | 2.110 | 2.097 | 2.084 | 2.071 | 2.058 |
| 15 | 2.056 | 2.044 | 2.032 | 2.020 | 2.008 | 1.996 |
| 16 | 1.991 | 1.980 | 1.969 | 1.958 | 1.947 | 1.937 |
| 17 | 1.928 | 1.918 | 1.908 | 1.898 | 1.888 | 1.878 |
| 18 | 1.900 | 1.880 | 1.861 | 1.842 | 1.831 | 1.822 |
| 19 | 1.900 | 1.880 | 1.861 | 1.842 | 1.824 | 1.806 |
| 20 | 1.900 | 1.880 | 1.861 | 1.842 | 1.824 | 1.806 |
| 21 | 1.900 | 1.880 | 1.861 | 1.842 | 1.824 | 1.806 |
| 22 | 1.900 | 1.880 | 1.861 | 1.843 | 1.824 | 1.806 |
| 23 | 1.900 | 1.880 | 1.861 | 1.842 | 1.824 | 1.806 |
| 24 | 1.900 | 1.880 | 1.861 | 1.843 | 1.824 | 1.806 |
| 25 | 1.900 | 1.880 | 1.861 | 1.842 | 1.824 | 1.806 |
| 26 | 1.900 | 1.880 | 1.861 | 1.843 | 1.824 | 1.806 |

| If the Recovery Year is: | and the Recovery Period is: 47.5 | 48.0 | 48.5 | 49.0 | 49.5 | 50.0 |
|---|---|---|---|---|---|---|
| | the Depreciation Rate is: | | | | | |
| 27 | 1.900 | 1.880 | 1.861 | 1.842 | 1.824 | 1.806 |
| 28 | 1.900 | 1.881 | 1.861 | 1.843 | 1.824 | 1.806 |
| 29 | 1.900 | 1.880 | 1.861 | 1.842 | 1.824 | 1.806 |
| 30 | 1.900 | 1.881 | 1.861 | 1.843 | 1.824 | 1.806 |
| 31 | 1.900 | 1.880 | 1.861 | 1.842 | 1.824 | 1.806 |
| 32 | 1.900 | 1.881 | 1.861 | 1.843 | 1.824 | 1.806 |
| 33 | 1.900 | 1.880 | 1.861 | 1.842 | 1.824 | 1.806 |
| 34 | 1.900 | 1.881 | 1.861 | 1.843 | 1.824 | 1.806 |
| 35 | 1.900 | 1.880 | 1.861 | 1.842 | 1.824 | 1.806 |
| 36 | 1.900 | 1.881 | 1.861 | 1.843 | 1.824 | 1.806 |
| 37 | 1.900 | 1.880 | 1.861 | 1.842 | 1.824 | 1.805 |
| 38 | 1.900 | 1.881 | 1.861 | 1.843 | 1.824 | 1.806 |
| 39 | 1.900 | 1.880 | 1.861 | 1.842 | 1.824 | 1.805 |
| 40 | 1.900 | 1.881 | 1.861 | 1.843 | 1.824 | 1.806 |
| 41 | 1.900 | 1.880 | 1.861 | 1.842 | 1.824 | 1.805 |
| 42 | 1.900 | 1.881 | 1.862 | 1.843 | 1.824 | 1.806 |
| 43 | 1.900 | 1.880 | 1.861 | 1.842 | 1.824 | 1.805 |
| 44 | 1.900 | 1.881 | 1.862 | 1.843 | 1.824 | 1.806 |
| 45 | 1.900 | 1.880 | 1.861 | 1.842 | 1.824 | 1.805 |
| 46 | 1.900 | 1.881 | 1.862 | 1.843 | 1.824 | 1.806 |
| 47 | 1.899 | 1.880 | 1.861 | 1.842 | 1.824 | 1.805 |
| 48 | 1.900 | 1.881 | 1.862 | 1.843 | 1.823 | 1.806 |
| 49 | 0.237 | 1.175 | 1.861 | 1.842 | 1.824 | 1.805 |
| 50 | | | 0.233 | 1.152 | 1.823 | 1.806 |
| 51 | | | | | 0.228 | 1.128 |

TABLE 18
Alternative Minimum Tax (see section 7 of this revenue procedure)
Applicable Depreciation Method: 150-Percent Declining Balance Switching to Straight Line
Applicable Recovery Periods: 2.5-50 years
Applicable Convention: Mid-quarter (property placed in service in fourth quarter)

| If the Recovery Year is: | and the Recovery Period is: 2.5 | 3.0 | 3.5 | 4.0 | 4.5 | 5.0 | 5.5 | 6.0 | 6.5 | 7.0 | 7.5 | 8.0 | 8.5 | 9.0 | 9.5 |
|---|---|---|---|---|---|---|---|---|---|---|---|---|---|---|---|
| | the Depreciation Rate is: | | | | | | | | | | | | | | |
| 1 | 7.50 | 6.25 | 5.36 | 4.69 | 4.17 | 3.75 | 3.41 | 3.13 | 2.88 | 2.68 | 2.50 | 2.34 | 2.21 | 2.08 | 1.97 |
| 2 | 55.50 | 46.88 | 40.56 | 35.74 | 31.94 | 28.88 | 26.34 | 24.22 | 22.41 | 20.85 | 19.50 | 18.31 | 17.26 | 16.32 | 15.48 |
| 3 | 26.91 | 25.00 | 23.18 | 22.34 | 21.30 | 20.21 | 19.16 | 18.16 | 17.24 | 16.39 | 15.60 | 14.88 | 14.21 | 13.60 | 13.03 |
| 4 | 10.09 | 21.87 | 22.47 | 19.86 | 17.93 | 16.40 | 15.14 | 14.06 | 13.26 | 12.87 | 12.48 | 12.09 | 11.70 | 11.33 | 10.98 |
| 5 | | | 8.43 | 17.37 | 17.93 | 16.41 | 15.14 | 14.06 | 13.10 | 12.18 | 11.41 | 10.74 | 10.16 | 9.65 | 9.24 |
| 6 | | | | | 6.73 | 14.35 | 15.13 | 14.06 | 13.10 | 12.18 | 11.41 | 10.75 | 10.16 | 9.65 | 9.17 |
| 7 | | | | | | | 5.68 | 12.31 | 13.10 | 12.19 | 11.41 | 10.74 | 10.16 | 9.64 | 9.17 |
| 8 | | | | | | | | | 4.91 | 10.66 | 11.41 | 10.75 | 10.16 | 9.65 | 9.17 |
| 9 | | | | | | | | | | | 4.28 | 9.40 | 10.17 | 9.64 | 9.17 |
| 10 | | | | | | | | | | | | | 3.81 | 8.44 | 9.18 |
| 11 | | | | | | | | | | | | | | | 3.44 |

| If the Recovery Year is: | and the Recovery Period is: 10.0 | 10.5 | 11.0 | 11.5 | 12.0 | 12.5 | 13.0 | 13.5 | 14.0 | 14.5 | 15.0 | 15.5 | 16.0 | 16.5 | 17.0 |
|---|---|---|---|---|---|---|---|---|---|---|---|---|---|---|---|
| | the Depreciation Rate is: | | | | | | | | | | | | | | |
| 1 | 1.88 | 1.79 | 1.70 | 1.63 | 1.56 | 1.50 | 1.44 | 1.39 | 1.34 | 1.29 | 1.25 | 1.21 | 1.17 | 1.14 | 1.10 |
| 2 | 14.72 | 14.03 | 13.40 | 12.83 | 12.31 | 11.82 | 11.37 | 10.96 | 10.57 | 10.21 | 9.88 | 9.56 | 9.27 | 8.99 | 8.73 |
| 3 | 12.51 | 12.03 | 11.58 | 11.16 | 10.77 | 10.40 | 10.06 | 9.74 | 9.44 | 9.16 | 8.89 | 8.64 | 8.40 | 8.17 | 7.96 |
| 4 | 10.63 | 10.31 | 10.00 | 9.70 | 9.42 | 9.15 | 8.90 | 8.66 | 8.43 | 8.21 | 8.00 | 7.80 | 7.61 | 7.43 | 7.25 |
| 5 | 9.04 | 8.83 | 8.63 | 8.44 | 8.24 | 8.06 | 7.87 | 7.69 | 7.52 | 7.36 | 7.20 | 7.04 | 6.90 | 6.75 | 6.61 |

| If the Recovery Year is: | and the Recovery Period is: 10.0 | 10.5 | 11.0 | 11.5 | 12.0 | 12.5 | 13.0 | 13.5 | 14.0 | 14.5 | 15.0 | 15.5 | 16.0 | 16.5 | 17.0 |
|---|---|---|---|---|---|---|---|---|---|---|---|---|---|---|---|
| | the Depreciation Rate is: | | | | | | | | | | | | | | |
| 6 | 8.72 | 8.32 | 7.95 | 7.63 | 7.33 | 7.09 | 6.96 | 6.84 | 6.72 | 6.60 | 6.48 | 6.36 | 6.25 | 6.14 | 6.03 |
| 7 | 8.72 | 8.31 | 7.96 | 7.63 | 7.33 | 7.05 | 6.78 | 6.53 | 6.31 | 6.10 | 5.90 | 5.75 | 5.66 | 5.58 | 5.50 |
| 8 | 8.72 | 8.32 | 7.95 | 7.62 | 7.33 | 7.05 | 6.78 | 6.53 | 6.31 | 6.10 | 5.90 | 5.72 | 5.54 | 5.38 | 5.22 |
| 9 | 8.72 | 8.31 | 7.96 | 7.63 | 7.33 | 7.05 | 6.78 | 6.53 | 6.31 | 6.10 | 5.90 | 5.72 | 5.54 | 5.38 | 5.23 |
| 10 | 8.71 | 8.32 | 7.95 | 7.62 | 7.32 | 7.05 | 6.78 | 6.54 | 6.31 | 6.10 | 5.91 | 5.72 | 5.54 | 5.38 | 5.22 |
| 11 | 7.63 | 8.31 | 7.96 | 7.63 | 7.33 | 7.05 | 6.78 | 6.53 | 6.31 | 6.10 | 5.90 | 5.72 | 5.54 | 5.38 | 5.23 |
| 12 | | 3.12 | 6.96 | 7.62 | 7.32 | 7.04 | 6.78 | 6.54 | 6.30 | 6.10 | 5.91 | 5.72 | 5.55 | 5.38 | 5.22 |
| 13 | | | | 2.86 | 6.41 | 7.05 | 6.78 | 6.53 | 6.31 | 6.09 | 5.90 | 5.72 | 5.54 | 5.38 | 5.23 |
| 14 | | | | | | 2.64 | 5.94 | 6.54 | 6.30 | 6.10 | 5.91 | 5.72 | 5.55 | 5.38 | 5.22 |
| 15 | | | | | | | | 2.45 | 5.52 | 6.09 | 5.90 | 5.73 | 5.54 | 5.37 | 5.23 |
| 16 | | | | | | | | | | 2.29 | 5.17 | 5.72 | 5.55 | 5.38 | 5.22 |
| 17 | | | | | | | | | | | | 2.15 | 4.85 | 5.37 | 5.23 |
| 18 | | | | | | | | | | | | | | 2.02 | 4.57 |

| If the Recovery Year is: | and the Recovery Period is: 17.5 | 18.0 | 18.5 | 19.0 | 19.5 | 20.0 | 20.5 | 21.0 | 21.5 | 22.0 | 22.5 | 23.0 | 23.5 | 24.0 | 24.5 |
|---|---|---|---|---|---|---|---|---|---|---|---|---|---|---|---|
| | the Depreciation Rate is: | | | | | | | | | | | | | | |
| 1 | 1.07 | 1.04 | 1.01 | 0.99 | 0.96 | 0.938 | 0.915 | 0.893 | 0.872 | 0.852 | 0.833 | 0.815 | 0.798 | 0.781 | 0.765 |
| 2 | 8.48 | 8.25 | 8.03 | 7.82 | 7.62 | 7.430 | 7.250 | 7.079 | 6.916 | 6.760 | 6.611 | 6.469 | 6.332 | 6.201 | 6.076 |
| 3 | 7.75 | 7.56 | 7.38 | 7.20 | 7.03 | 6.872 | 6.720 | 6.573 | 6.433 | 6.299 | 6.170 | 6.047 | 5.928 | 5.814 | 5.704 |
| 4 | 7.09 | 6.93 | 6.78 | 6.63 | 6.49 | 6.357 | 6.228 | 6.104 | 5.985 | 5.870 | 5.759 | 5.652 | 5.549 | 5.450 | 5.354 |
| 5 | 6.48 | 6.35 | 6.23 | 6.11 | 5.99 | 5.880 | 5.772 | 5.668 | 5.567 | 5.469 | 5.375 | 5.284 | 5.195 | 5.110 | 5.027 |
| 6 | 5.93 | 5.82 | 5.72 | 5.63 | 5.53 | 5.439 | 5.350 | 5.263 | 5.179 | 5.097 | 5.017 | 4.939 | 4.864 | 4.790 | 4.719 |
| 7 | 5.42 | 5.34 | 5.26 | 5.18 | 5.11 | 5.031 | 4.958 | 4.887 | 4.817 | 4.749 | 4.682 | 4.617 | 4.553 | 4.491 | 4.430 |
| 8 | 5.08 | 4.94 | 4.83 | 4.77 | 4.71 | 4.654 | 4.596 | 4.538 | 4.481 | 4.425 | 4.370 | 4.316 | 4.263 | 4.210 | 4.159 |
| 9 | 5.08 | 4.94 | 4.81 | 4.69 | 4.57 | 4.458 | 4.352 | 4.252 | 4.169 | 4.124 | 4.079 | 4.034 | 3.991 | 3.947 | 3.904 |

| If the Recovery Year is: | 17.5 | 18.0 | 18.5 | 19.0 | 19.5 | 20.0 | 20.5 | 21.0 | 21.5 | 22.0 | 22.5 | 23.0 | 23.5 | 24.0 | 24.5 |
|---|---|---|---|---|---|---|---|---|---|---|---|---|---|---|---|
| | and the Recovery Period is: | | | | | | | | | | | | | | |
| | the Depreciation Rate is: | | | | | | | | | | | | | | |
| 10 | 5.08 | 4.94 | 4.81 | 4.69 | 4.57 | 4.458 | 4.352 | 4.252 | 4.156 | 4.062 | 3.972 | 3.888 | 3.807 | 3.730 | 3.665 |
| 11 | 5.08 | 4.95 | 4.81 | 4.69 | 4.57 | 4.458 | 4.352 | 4.252 | 4.156 | 4.062 | 3.972 | 3.887 | 3.807 | 3.729 | 3.655 |
| 12 | 5.08 | 4.94 | 4.82 | 4.69 | 4.57 | 4.458 | 4.352 | 4.252 | 4.156 | 4.062 | 3.973 | 3.888 | 3.807 | 3.730 | 3.655 |
| 13 | 5.08 | 4.95 | 4.81 | 4.69 | 4.57 | 4.458 | 4.352 | 4.252 | 4.155 | 4.062 | 3.972 | 3.887 | 3.807 | 3.729 | 3.655 |
| 14 | 5.08 | 4.94 | 4.82 | 4.69 | 4.57 | 4.458 | 4.352 | 4.252 | 4.156 | 4.061 | 3.973 | 3.888 | 3.807 | 3.730 | 3.655 |
| 15 | 5.08 | 4.95 | 4.81 | 4.69 | 4.57 | 4.458 | 4.352 | 4.252 | 4.155 | 4.062 | 3.972 | 3.887 | 3.806 | 3.729 | 3.655 |
| 16 | 5.08 | 4.94 | 4.82 | 4.69 | 4.57 | 4.458 | 4.352 | 4.252 | 4.156 | 4.061 | 3.973 | 3.888 | 3.807 | 3.730 | 3.655 |
| 17 | 5.08 | 4.95 | 4.81 | 4.68 | 4.57 | 4.458 | 4.353 | 4.252 | 4.155 | 4.062 | 3.972 | 3.887 | 3.806 | 3.729 | 3.655 |
| 18 | 5.08 | 4.94 | 4.82 | 4.69 | 4.57 | 4.459 | 4.352 | 4.252 | 4.156 | 4.061 | 3.973 | 3.888 | 3.807 | 3.730 | 3.655 |
| 19 | 1.90 | 4.33 | 4.81 | 4.68 | 4.57 | 4.458 | 4.353 | 4.252 | 4.155 | 4.062 | 3.972 | 3.887 | 3.806 | 3.729 | 3.655 |
| 20 | | | 1.81 | 4.10 | 4.57 | 4.459 | 4.352 | 4.251 | 4.156 | 4.061 | 3.973 | 3.888 | 3.807 | 3.730 | 3.655 |
| 21 | | | | | 1.72 | 3.901 | 4.353 | 4.252 | 4.155 | 4.062 | 3.972 | 3.887 | 3.806 | 3.729 | 3.655 |
| 22 | | | | | | | 1.632 | 3.720 | 4.156 | 4.061 | 3.973 | 3.888 | 3.807 | 3.730 | 3.655 |
| 23 | | | | | | | | | 1.558 | 3.554 | 3.972 | 3.887 | 3.806 | 3.729 | 3.655 |
| 24 | | | | | | | | | | | 1.490 | 3.402 | 3.807 | 3.730 | 3.656 |
| 25 | | | | | | | | | | | | | 1.427 | 3.263 | 3.655 |
| 26 | | | | | | | | | | | | | | | 1.371 |

| If the Recovery Year is: | 25.0 | 25.5 | 26.0 | 26.5 | 27.0 | 27.5 | 28.0 | 28.5 | 29.0 | 29.5 | 30.0 | 30.5 | 31.0 | 31.5 | 32.0 |
|---|---|---|---|---|---|---|---|---|---|---|---|---|---|---|---|
| | and the Recovery Period is: | | | | | | | | | | | | | | |
| | the Depreciation Rate is: | | | | | | | | | | | | | | |
| 1 | 0.750 | 0.735 | 0.721 | 0.708 | 0.694 | 0.682 | 0.670 | 0.658 | 0.647 | 0.636 | 0.625 | 0.615 | 0.605 | 0.595 | 0.586 |
| 2 | 5.955 | 5.839 | 5.728 | 5.620 | 5.517 | 5.417 | 5.321 | 5.229 | 5.139 | 5.052 | 4.969 | 4.888 | 4.809 | 4.734 | 4.660 |
| 3 | 5.598 | 5.496 | 5.397 | 5.302 | 5.211 | 5.122 | 5.036 | 4.953 | 4.873 | 4.796 | 4.720 | 4.647 | 4.577 | 4.508 | 4.442 |
| 4 | 5.262 | 5.172 | 5.086 | 5.002 | 4.921 | 4.842 | 4.766 | 4.693 | 4.621 | 4.552 | 4.484 | 4.419 | 4.355 | 4.293 | 4.233 |
| 5 | 4.946 | 4.868 | 4.792 | 4.719 | 4.648 | 4.578 | 4.511 | 4.446 | 4.382 | 4.320 | 4.260 | 4.202 | 4.145 | 4.089 | 4.035 |

| If the Recovery Year is: | 25.0 | 25.5 | 26.0 | 26.5 | 27.0 | 27.5 | 28.0 | 28.5 | 29.0 | 29.5 | 30.0 | 30.5 | 31.0 | 31.5 | 32.0 |
|---|---|---|---|---|---|---|---|---|---|---|---|---|---|---|---|
| | and the Recovery Period is: | | | | | | | | | | | | | | |
| | the Depreciation Rate is: | | | | | | | | | | | | | | |
| 6 | 4.649 | 4.582 | 4.516 | 4.452 | 4.389 | 4.329 | 4.269 | 4.212 | 4.155 | 4.101 | 4.047 | 3.995 | 3.944 | 3.894 | 3.846 |
| 7 | 4.370 | 4.312 | 4.255 | 4.200 | 4.146 | 4.093 | 4.041 | 3.990 | 3.940 | 3.892 | 3.845 | 3.798 | 3.753 | 3.709 | 3.666 |
| 8 | 4.108 | 4.059 | 4.010 | 3.962 | 3.915 | 3.869 | 3.824 | 3.780 | 3.737 | 3.694 | 3.653 | 3.612 | 3.572 | 3.532 | 3.494 |
| 9 | 3.862 | 3.820 | 3.779 | 3.738 | 3.698 | 3.658 | 3.619 | 3.581 | 3.543 | 3.506 | 3.470 | 3.434 | 3.399 | 3.364 | 3.330 |
| 10 | 3.630 | 3.595 | 3.561 | 3.526 | 3.492 | 3.459 | 3.426 | 3.393 | 3.360 | 3.328 | 3.296 | 3.265 | 3.234 | 3.204 | 3.174 |
| 11 | 3.582 | 3.513 | 3.446 | 3.383 | 3.321 | 3.270 | 3.242 | 3.214 | 3.186 | 3.159 | 3.132 | 3.105 | 3.078 | 3.051 | 3.025 |
| 12 | 3.582 | 3.513 | 3.446 | 3.382 | 3.321 | 3.262 | 3.204 | 3.148 | 3.095 | 3.043 | 2.994 | 2.952 | 2.929 | 2.906 | 2.883 |
| 13 | 3.582 | 3.513 | 3.446 | 3.383 | 3.321 | 3.262 | 3.204 | 3.148 | 3.095 | 3.043 | 2.994 | 2.945 | 2.898 | 2.853 | 2.808 |
| 14 | 3.582 | 3.513 | 3.446 | 3.382 | 3.321 | 3.262 | 3.204 | 3.148 | 3.095 | 3.043 | 2.994 | 2.945 | 2.898 | 2.853 | 2.808 |
| 15 | 3.582 | 3.513 | 3.446 | 3.383 | 3.321 | 3.262 | 3.204 | 3.148 | 3.095 | 3.043 | 2.994 | 2.945 | 2.898 | 2.853 | 2.808 |
| 16 | 3.583 | 3.513 | 3.446 | 3.382 | 3.321 | 3.262 | 3.204 | 3.148 | 3.095 | 3.043 | 2.994 | 2.946 | 2.898 | 2.852 | 2.809 |
| 17 | 3.582 | 3.513 | 3.446 | 3.383 | 3.322 | 3.262 | 3.204 | 3.148 | 3.095 | 3.043 | 2.994 | 2.945 | 2.898 | 2.853 | 2.808 |
| 18 | 3.583 | 3.513 | 3.446 | 3.382 | 3.321 | 3.262 | 3.204 | 3.149 | 3.095 | 3.043 | 2.994 | 2.946 | 2.898 | 2.852 | 2.809 |
| 19 | 3.582 | 3.513 | 3.446 | 3.383 | 3.322 | 3.262 | 3.204 | 3.148 | 3.095 | 3.043 | 2.993 | 2.945 | 2.898 | 2.853 | 2.808 |
| 20 | 3.583 | 3.513 | 3.446 | 3.382 | 3.321 | 3.262 | 3.204 | 3.149 | 3.095 | 3.044 | 2.994 | 2.946 | 2.898 | 2.852 | 2.809 |
| 21 | 3.582 | 3.512 | 3.447 | 3.383 | 3.322 | 3.262 | 3.204 | 3.148 | 3.095 | 3.043 | 2.993 | 2.945 | 2.898 | 2.853 | 2.808 |
| 22 | 3.583 | 3.513 | 3.446 | 3.382 | 3.321 | 3.263 | 3.204 | 3.149 | 3.095 | 3.044 | 2.994 | 2.946 | 2.898 | 2.852 | 2.809 |
| 23 | 3.582 | 3.512 | 3.447 | 3.383 | 3.322 | 3.262 | 3.205 | 3.148 | 3.095 | 3.043 | 2.993 | 2.945 | 2.898 | 2.853 | 2.808 |
| 24 | 3.583 | 3.513 | 3.446 | 3.382 | 3.321 | 3.263 | 3.204 | 3.149 | 3.095 | 3.044 | 2.994 | 2.946 | 2.898 | 2.852 | 2.809 |
| 25 | 3.582 | 3.512 | 3.447 | 3.383 | 3.322 | 3.262 | 3.205 | 3.148 | 3.095 | 3.043 | 2.993 | 2.945 | 2.898 | 2.853 | 2.808 |
| 26 | 3.135 | 3.513 | 3.446 | 3.382 | 3.321 | 3.263 | 3.204 | 3.149 | 3.095 | 3.044 | 2.994 | 2.946 | 2.898 | 2.852 | 2.809 |
| 27 | | 1.317 | 3.016 | 3.383 | 3.322 | 3.262 | 3.205 | 3.148 | 3.095 | 3.043 | 2.993 | 2.945 | 2.898 | 2.853 | 2.808 |
| 28 | | | | 1.268 | 2.906 | 3.263 | 3.204 | 3.149 | 3.095 | 3.044 | 2.994 | 2.946 | 2.898 | 2.852 | 2.809 |
| 29 | | | | | | 1.223 | 2.804 | 3.148 | 3.094 | 3.043 | 2.993 | 2.945 | 2.899 | 2.853 | 2.808 |
| 30 | | | | | | | | 1.181 | 2.708 | 3.044 | 2.994 | 2.946 | 2.898 | 2.852 | 2.809 |
| 31 | | | | | | | | | | 1.141 | 2.619 | 2.945 | 2.899 | 2.853 | 2.808 |

| If the Recovery Year is: | and the Recovery Period is: 25.0 | 25.5 | 26.0 | 26.5 | 27.0 | 27.5 | 28.0 | 28.5 | 29.0 | 29.5 | 30.0 | 30.5 | 31.0 | 31.5 | 32.0 |
|---|---|---|---|---|---|---|---|---|---|---|---|---|---|---|---|
| | the Depreciation Rate is: | | | | | | | | | | | | | | |
| 32 | | | | | | | | | | | | 1.105 | 2.536 | 2.852 | 2.809 |
| 33 | | | | | | | | | | | | | | 1.070 | 2.457 |

| If the Recovery Year is: | and the Recovery Period is: 32.5 | 33.0 | 33.5 | 34.0 | 34.5 | 35.0 | 35.5 | 36.0 | 36.5 | 37.0 | 37.5 | 38.0 | 38.5 | 39.0 | 39.5 |
|---|---|---|---|---|---|---|---|---|---|---|---|---|---|---|---|
| | the Depreciation Rate is: | | | | | | | | | | | | | | |
| 1 | 0.577 | 0.568 | 0.560 | 0.551 | 0.543 | 0.536 | 0.528 | 0.521 | 0.514 | 0.507 | 0.500 | 0.493 | 0.487 | 0.481 | 0.475 |
| 2 | 4.589 | 4.520 | 4.453 | 4.387 | 4.324 | 4.263 | 4.203 | 4.145 | 4.088 | 4.034 | 3.980 | 3.928 | 3.877 | 3.828 | 3.779 |
| 3 | 4.377 | 4.314 | 4.253 | 4.194 | 4.136 | 4.080 | 4.025 | 3.972 | 3.920 | 3.870 | 3.821 | 3.773 | 3.726 | 3.680 | 3.636 |
| 4 | 4.175 | 4.118 | 4.063 | 4.009 | 3.956 | 3.905 | 3.855 | 3.807 | 3.759 | 3.713 | 3.668 | 3.624 | 3.581 | 3.539 | 3.498 |
| 5 | 3.982 | 3.931 | 3.881 | 3.832 | 3.784 | 3.738 | 3.692 | 3.648 | 3.605 | 3.563 | 3.521 | 3.481 | 3.441 | 3.403 | 3.365 |
| 6 | 3.798 | 3.752 | 3.707 | 3.663 | 3.620 | 3.578 | 3.536 | 3.496 | 3.457 | 3.418 | 3.380 | 3.343 | 3.307 | 3.272 | 3.237 |
| 7 | 3.623 | 3.582 | 3.541 | 3.501 | 3.462 | 3.424 | 3.387 | 3.350 | 3.315 | 3.280 | 3.245 | 3.212 | 3.178 | 3.146 | 3.114 |
| 8 | 3.456 | 3.419 | 3.382 | 3.347 | 3.312 | 3.278 | 3.244 | 3.211 | 3.178 | 3.147 | 3.115 | 3.085 | 3.055 | 3.025 | 2.996 |
| 9 | 3.296 | 3.263 | 3.231 | 3.199 | 3.168 | 3.137 | 3.107 | 3.077 | 3.048 | 3.019 | 2.991 | 2.963 | 2.936 | 2.909 | 2.882 |
| 10 | 3.144 | 3.115 | 3.086 | 3.058 | 3.030 | 3.003 | 2.976 | 2.949 | 2.923 | 2.897 | 2.871 | 2.846 | 2.821 | 2.797 | 2.773 |
| 11 | 2.999 | 2.974 | 2.948 | 2.923 | 2.898 | 2.874 | 2.850 | 2.826 | 2.802 | 2.779 | 2.756 | 2.734 | 2.711 | 2.689 | 2.668 |
| 12 | 2.861 | 2.838 | 2.816 | 2.794 | 2.772 | 2.751 | 2.729 | 2.708 | 2.687 | 2.666 | 2.646 | 2.626 | 2.606 | 2.586 | 2.566 |
| 13 | 2.766 | 2.725 | 2.690 | 2.671 | 2.652 | 2.633 | 2.614 | 2.595 | 2.577 | 2.558 | 2.540 | 2.522 | 2.504 | 2.486 | 2.469 |
| 14 | 2.766 | 2.725 | 2.685 | 2.646 | 2.608 | 2.570 | 2.535 | 2.500 | 2.471 | 2.455 | 2.439 | 2.423 | 2.407 | 2.391 | 2.375 |
| 15 | 2.766 | 2.725 | 2.685 | 2.646 | 2.607 | 2.571 | 2.535 | 2.500 | 2.467 | 2.433 | 2.401 | 2.370 | 2.339 | 2.310 | 2.285 |
| 16 | 2.766 | 2.725 | 2.685 | 2.645 | 2.608 | 2.570 | 2.535 | 2.500 | 2.467 | 2.433 | 2.401 | 2.370 | 2.339 | 2.310 | 2.281 |
| 17 | 2.766 | 2.725 | 2.685 | 2.646 | 2.607 | 2.571 | 2.535 | 2.500 | 2.467 | 2.433 | 2.401 | 2.370 | 2.339 | 2.310 | 2.281 |
| 18 | 2.766 | 2.725 | 2.685 | 2.645 | 2.608 | 2.570 | 2.535 | 2.500 | 2.467 | 2.433 | 2.401 | 2.370 | 2.339 | 2.310 | 2.281 |
| 19 | 2.766 | 2.725 | 2.685 | 2.646 | 2.607 | 2.571 | 2.535 | 2.500 | 2.466 | 2.433 | 2.401 | 2.370 | 2.340 | 2.310 | 2.281 |
| 20 | 2.766 | 2.725 | 2.685 | 2.645 | 2.608 | 2.570 | 2.535 | 2.500 | 2.467 | 2.433 | 2.401 | 2.370 | 2.339 | 2.310 | 2.281 |

| If the Recovery Year is: | and the Recovery Period is: 32.5 | 33.0 | 33.5 | 34.0 | 34.5 | 35.0 | 35.5 | 36.0 | 36.5 | 37.0 | 37.5 | 38.0 | 38.5 | 39.0 | 39.5 |
|---|---|---|---|---|---|---|---|---|---|---|---|---|---|---|---|
| | the Depreciation Rate is: | | | | | | | | | | | | | | |
| 21 | 2.766 | 2.725 | 2.685 | 2.646 | 2.607 | 2.571 | 2.535 | 2.500 | 2.466 | 2.433 | 2.401 | 2.370 | 2.340 | 2.310 | 2.281 |
| 22 | 2.766 | 2.725 | 2.685 | 2.645 | 2.608 | 2.570 | 2.535 | 2.500 | 2.467 | 2.433 | 2.401 | 2.370 | 2.339 | 2.310 | 2.281 |
| 23 | 2.766 | 2.725 | 2.685 | 2.646 | 2.607 | 2.571 | 2.535 | 2.501 | 2.466 | 2.433 | 2.401 | 2.370 | 2.340 | 2.310 | 2.281 |
| 24 | 2.766 | 2.725 | 2.685 | 2.645 | 2.608 | 2.570 | 2.535 | 2.500 | 2.467 | 2.433 | 2.401 | 2.370 | 2.339 | 2.310 | 2.281 |
| 25 | 2.766 | 2.725 | 2.685 | 2.646 | 2.607 | 2.571 | 2.535 | 2.501 | 2.466 | 2.433 | 2.401 | 2.370 | 2.340 | 2.310 | 2.281 |
| 26 | 2.766 | 2.725 | 2.685 | 2.645 | 2.608 | 2.570 | 2.535 | 2.500 | 2.467 | 2.433 | 2.401 | 2.370 | 2.339 | 2.310 | 2.281 |
| 27 | 2.766 | 2.725 | 2.685 | 2.646 | 2.607 | 2.571 | 2.535 | 2.501 | 2.466 | 2.434 | 2.401 | 2.369 | 2.340 | 2.310 | 2.281 |
| 28 | 2.766 | 2.725 | 2.685 | 2.645 | 2.608 | 2.570 | 2.535 | 2.500 | 2.467 | 2.433 | 2.401 | 2.370 | 2.339 | 2.310 | 2.281 |
| 29 | 2.766 | 2.724 | 2.685 | 2.646 | 2.607 | 2.571 | 2.535 | 2.501 | 2.466 | 2.434 | 2.401 | 2.369 | 2.340 | 2.310 | 2.281 |
| 30 | 2.766 | 2.725 | 2.684 | 2.645 | 2.608 | 2.570 | 2.535 | 2.500 | 2.467 | 2.433 | 2.401 | 2.370 | 2.339 | 2.310 | 2.281 |
| 31 | 2.766 | 2.724 | 2.685 | 2.646 | 2.607 | 2.571 | 2.535 | 2.501 | 2.466 | 2.434 | 2.401 | 2.369 | 2.340 | 2.310 | 2.281 |
| 32 | 2.766 | 2.725 | 2.684 | 2.645 | 2.608 | 2.570 | 2.535 | 2.500 | 2.467 | 2.433 | 2.401 | 2.370 | 2.339 | 2.310 | 2.281 |
| 33 | 2.766 | 2.724 | 2.685 | 2.646 | 2.607 | 2.571 | 2.535 | 2.501 | 2.466 | 2.434 | 2.401 | 2.369 | 2.340 | 2.310 | 2.281 |
| 34 | 1.037 | 2.384 | 2.684 | 2.645 | 2.608 | 2.570 | 2.535 | 2.500 | 2.467 | 2.433 | 2.401 | 2.370 | 2.339 | 2.310 | 2.281 |
| 35 | | | 1.007 | 2.315 | 2.607 | 2.571 | 2.534 | 2.501 | 2.466 | 2.434 | 2.402 | 2.369 | 2.340 | 2.309 | 2.281 |
| 36 | | | | | 0.978 | 2.249 | 2.535 | 2.500 | 2.467 | 2.433 | 2.401 | 2.370 | 2.339 | 2.310 | 2.281 |
| 37 | | | | | | | 0.950 | 2.188 | 2.466 | 2.434 | 2.402 | 2.369 | 2.340 | 2.309 | 2.281 |
| 38 | | | | | | | | | 0.925 | 2.129 | 2.401 | 2.370 | 2.339 | 2.310 | 2.281 |
| 39 | | | | | | | | | | | 0.901 | 2.073 | 2.340 | 2.309 | 2.282 |
| 40 | | | | | | | | | | | | | 0.877 | 2.021 | 2.281 |
| 41 | | | | | | | | | | | | | | | 0.856 |

| If the Recovery Year is: | and the Recovery Period is: 40.0 | 40.5 | 41.0 | 41.5 | 42.0 | 42.5 | 43.0 | 43.5 | 44.0 | 44.5 | 45.0 | 45.5 | 46.0 | 46.5 | 47.0 |
|---|---|---|---|---|---|---|---|---|---|---|---|---|---|---|---|
| | the Depreciation Rate is: | | | | | | | | | | | | | | |
| 1 | 0.469 | 0.463 | 0.457 | 0.452 | 0.446 | 0.441 | 0.436 | 0.431 | 0.426 | 0.421 | 0.417 | 0.412 | 0.408 | 0.403 | 0.399 |
| 2 | 3.732 | 3.687 | 3.642 | 3.598 | 3.556 | 3.514 | 3.473 | 3.433 | 3.395 | 3.357 | 3.319 | 3.283 | 3.248 | 3.213 | 3.179 |
| 3 | 3.592 | 3.550 | 3.509 | 3.468 | 3.429 | 3.390 | 3.352 | 3.315 | 3.279 | 3.243 | 3.209 | 3.175 | 3.142 | 3.109 | 3.077 |
| 4 | 3.458 | 3.419 | 3.380 | 3.343 | 3.306 | 3.270 | 3.235 | 3.201 | 3.167 | 3.134 | 3.102 | 3.070 | 3.039 | 3.009 | 2.979 |
| 5 | 3.328 | 3.292 | 3.257 | 3.222 | 3.188 | 3.155 | 3.122 | 3.090 | 3.059 | 3.028 | 2.998 | 2.969 | 2.940 | 2.912 | 2.884 |
| 6 | 3.203 | 3.170 | 3.137 | 3.105 | 3.074 | 3.043 | 3.013 | 2.984 | 2.955 | 2.926 | 2.898 | 2.871 | 2.844 | 2.818 | 2.792 |
| 7 | 3.083 | 3.053 | 3.023 | 2.993 | 2.964 | 2.936 | 2.908 | 2.881 | 2.854 | 2.828 | 2.802 | 2.776 | 2.751 | 2.727 | 2.703 |
| 8 | 2.968 | 2.939 | 2.912 | 2.885 | 2.858 | 2.832 | 2.807 | 2.782 | 2.757 | 2.732 | 2.708 | 2.685 | 2.662 | 2.639 | 2.617 |
| 9 | 2.856 | 2.831 | 2.805 | 2.781 | 2.756 | 2.732 | 2.709 | 2.686 | 2.663 | 2.640 | 2.618 | 2.596 | 2.575 | 2.554 | 2.533 |
| 10 | 2.749 | 2.726 | 2.703 | 2.680 | 2.658 | 2.636 | 2.614 | 2.593 | 2.572 | 2.551 | 2.531 | 2.511 | 2.491 | 2.471 | 2.452 |
| 11 | 2.646 | 2.625 | 2.604 | 2.583 | 2.563 | 2.543 | 2.523 | 2.504 | 2.484 | 2.465 | 2.447 | 2.428 | 2.410 | 2.392 | 2.374 |
| 12 | 2.547 | 2.528 | 2.509 | 2.490 | 2.472 | 2.453 | 2.435 | 2.417 | 2.400 | 2.382 | 2.365 | 2.348 | 2.331 | 2.315 | 2.298 |
| 13 | 2.451 | 2.434 | 2.417 | 2.400 | 2.383 | 2.367 | 2.350 | 2.334 | 2.318 | 2.302 | 2.286 | 2.271 | 2.255 | 2.240 | 2.225 |
| 14 | 2.359 | 2.344 | 2.328 | 2.313 | 2.298 | 2.283 | 2.268 | 2.253 | 2.239 | 2.224 | 2.210 | 2.196 | 2.182 | 2.168 | 2.154 |
| 15 | 2.271 | 2.257 | 2.243 | 2.230 | 2.216 | 2.203 | 2.189 | 2.176 | 2.162 | 2.149 | 2.136 | 2.123 | 2.110 | 2.098 | 2.085 |
| 16 | 2.253 | 2.225 | 2.198 | 2.172 | 2.146 | 2.125 | 2.113 | 2.101 | 2.089 | 2.077 | 2.065 | 2.053 | 2.042 | 2.030 | 2.019 |
| 17 | 2.253 | 2.225 | 2.198 | 2.172 | 2.146 | 2.122 | 2.097 | 2.073 | 2.050 | 2.027 | 2.005 | 1.986 | 1.975 | 1.965 | 1.954 |
| 18 | 2.253 | 2.225 | 2.198 | 2.172 | 2.147 | 2.122 | 2.097 | 2.073 | 2.050 | 2.027 | 2.005 | 1.983 | 1.961 | 1.940 | 1.920 |
| 19 | 2.253 | 2.225 | 2.198 | 2.172 | 2.146 | 2.121 | 2.097 | 2.073 | 2.050 | 2.027 | 2.005 | 1.983 | 1.961 | 1.940 | 1.920 |
| 20 | 2.253 | 2.225 | 2.198 | 2.172 | 2.147 | 2.122 | 2.097 | 2.073 | 2.050 | 2.027 | 2.005 | 1.983 | 1.961 | 1.940 | 1.920 |
| 21 | 2.253 | 2.225 | 2.198 | 2.172 | 2.146 | 2.121 | 2.097 | 2.073 | 2.049 | 2.027 | 2.005 | 1.983 | 1.961 | 1.940 | 1.920 |
| 22 | 2.253 | 2.225 | 2.198 | 2.172 | 2.147 | 2.122 | 2.097 | 2.073 | 2.050 | 2.027 | 2.005 | 1.983 | 1.961 | 1.940 | 1.920 |
| 23 | 2.253 | 2.225 | 2.198 | 2.172 | 2.146 | 2.121 | 2.097 | 2.073 | 2.049 | 2.027 | 2.005 | 1.983 | 1.961 | 1.940 | 1.920 |
| 24 | 2.253 | 2.225 | 2.198 | 2.172 | 2.147 | 2.122 | 2.097 | 2.073 | 2.050 | 2.027 | 2.005 | 1.983 | 1.961 | 1.940 | 1.920 |
| 25 | 2.253 | 2.225 | 2.198 | 2.172 | 2.146 | 2.121 | 2.097 | 2.073 | 2.049 | 2.027 | 2.005 | 1.983 | 1.961 | 1.940 | 1.920 |
| 26 | 2.252 | 2.225 | 2.198 | 2.172 | 2.147 | 2.122 | 2.097 | 2.073 | 2.050 | 2.027 | 2.005 | 1.983 | 1.961 | 1.940 | 1.920 |

| If the Recovery Year is: | 40.0 | 40.5 | 41.0 | 41.5 | 42.0 | 42.5 | 43.0 | 43.5 | 44.0 | 44.5 | 45.0 | 45.5 | 46.0 | 46.5 | 47.0 |
|---|---|---|---|---|---|---|---|---|---|---|---|---|---|---|---|
| | and the Recovery Period is: | | | | | | | | | | | | | | |
| | the Depreciation Rate is: | | | | | | | | | | | | | | |
| 27 | 2.253 | 2.225 | 2.198 | 2.172 | 2.146 | 2.121 | 2.097 | 2.073 | 2.049 | 2.027 | 2.004 | 1.983 | 1.961 | 1.940 | 1.920 |
| 28 | 2.252 | 2.225 | 2.198 | 2.172 | 2.147 | 2.122 | 2.097 | 2.073 | 2.050 | 2.027 | 2.005 | 1.983 | 1.962 | 1.940 | 1.920 |
| 29 | 2.253 | 2.225 | 2.198 | 2.172 | 2.146 | 2.121 | 2.097 | 2.073 | 2.049 | 2.027 | 2.004 | 1.983 | 1.961 | 1.940 | 1.920 |
| 30 | 2.252 | 2.225 | 2.198 | 2.172 | 2.147 | 2.122 | 2.097 | 2.073 | 2.050 | 2.027 | 2.005 | 1.983 | 1.962 | 1.941 | 1.920 |
| 31 | 2.253 | 2.225 | 2.198 | 2.172 | 2.146 | 2.121 | 2.097 | 2.073 | 2.049 | 2.027 | 2.004 | 1.983 | 1.961 | 1.940 | 1.920 |
| 32 | 2.252 | 2.225 | 2.198 | 2.172 | 2.147 | 2.122 | 2.097 | 2.073 | 2.050 | 2.027 | 2.005 | 1.983 | 1.962 | 1.941 | 1.920 |
| 33 | 2.253 | 2.225 | 2.198 | 2.172 | 2.146 | 2.121 | 2.097 | 2.073 | 2.049 | 2.027 | 2.004 | 1.983 | 1.961 | 1.940 | 1.920 |
| 34 | 2.252 | 2.225 | 2.198 | 2.172 | 2.147 | 2.122 | 2.097 | 2.073 | 2.050 | 2.027 | 2.005 | 1.983 | 1.962 | 1.941 | 1.920 |
| 35 | 2.253 | 2.225 | 2.198 | 2.172 | 2.146 | 2.121 | 2.097 | 2.073 | 2.049 | 2.027 | 2.004 | 1.983 | 1.961 | 1.940 | 1.920 |
| 36 | 2.252 | 2.225 | 2.198 | 2.172 | 2.147 | 2.122 | 2.097 | 2.073 | 2.050 | 2.027 | 2.005 | 1.983 | 1.962 | 1.941 | 1.920 |
| 37 | 2.253 | 2.225 | 2.198 | 2.172 | 2.146 | 2.121 | 2.097 | 2.073 | 2.049 | 2.027 | 2.004 | 1.983 | 1.961 | 1.940 | 1.920 |
| 38 | 2.252 | 2.224 | 2.199 | 2.172 | 2.147 | 2.122 | 2.097 | 2.073 | 2.050 | 2.027 | 2.005 | 1.983 | 1.962 | 1.941 | 1.920 |
| 39 | 2.253 | 2.225 | 2.198 | 2.172 | 2.146 | 2.121 | 2.097 | 2.073 | 2.049 | 2.027 | 2.004 | 1.983 | 1.961 | 1.940 | 1.920 |
| 40 | 2.252 | 2.224 | 2.199 | 2.172 | 2.147 | 2.122 | 2.097 | 2.073 | 2.050 | 2.027 | 2.005 | 1.983 | 1.962 | 1.941 | 1.920 |
| 41 | 1.971 | 2.225 | 2.198 | 2.171 | 2.146 | 2.121 | 2.097 | 2.072 | 2.049 | 2.027 | 2.004 | 1.982 | 1.961 | 1.940 | 1.919 |
| 42 | | 0.834 | 1.924 | 2.172 | 2.147 | 2.122 | 2.097 | 2.073 | 2.050 | 2.027 | 2.005 | 1.983 | 1.962 | 1.941 | 1.920 |
| 43 | | | | 0.814 | 1.878 | 2.121 | 2.097 | 2.072 | 2.049 | 2.026 | 2.004 | 1.982 | 1.961 | 1.940 | 1.919 |
| 44 | | | | | | 0.796 | 1.834 | 2.073 | 2.050 | 2.027 | 2.005 | 1.983 | 1.962 | 1.941 | 1.920 |
| 45 | | | | | | | | 0.777 | 1.793 | 2.026 | 2.004 | 1.982 | 1.961 | 1.940 | 1.919 |
| 46 | | | | | | | | | | 0.760 | 1.754 | 1.983 | 1.962 | 1.941 | 1.920 |
| 47 | | | | | | | | | | | | 0.743 | 1.716 | 1.940 | 1.919 |
| 48 | | | | | | | | | | | | | | 0.728 | 1.680 |

| If the Recovery Year is: | and the Recovery Period is: 47.5 | 48.0 | 48.5 | 49.0 | 49.5 | 50.0 |
|---|---|---|---|---|---|---|
| | the Depreciation Rate is: | | | | | |
| 1 | 0.395 | 0.391 | 0.387 | 0.383 | 0.379 | 0.375 |
| 2 | 3.145 | 3.113 | 3.081 | 3.050 | 3.019 | 2.989 |
| 3 | 3.046 | 3.016 | 2.986 | 2.956 | 2.927 | 2.899 |
| 4 | 2.950 | 2.921 | 2.893 | 2.866 | 2.839 | 2.812 |
| 5 | 2.857 | 2.830 | 2.804 | 2.778 | 2.753 | 2.728 |
| 6 | 2.767 | 2.742 | 2.717 | 2.693 | 2.669 | 2.646 |
| 7 | 2.679 | 2.656 | 2.633 | 2.610 | 2.588 | 2.567 |
| 8 | 2.595 | 2.573 | 2.552 | 2.531 | 2.510 | 2.490 |
| 9 | 2.513 | 2.492 | 2.473 | 2.453 | 2.434 | 2.415 |
| 10 | 2.433 | 2.415 | 2.396 | 2.378 | 2.360 | 2.342 |
| 11 | 2.356 | 2.339 | 2.322 | 2.305 | 2.289 | 2.272 |
| 12 | 2.282 | 2.266 | 2.250 | 2.235 | 2.219 | 2.204 |
| 13 | 2.210 | 2.195 | 2.181 | 2.166 | 2.152 | 2.138 |
| 14 | 2.140 | 2.127 | 2.113 | 2.100 | 2.087 | 2.074 |
| 15 | 2.073 | 2.060 | 2.048 | 2.036 | 2.023 | 2.011 |
| 16 | 2.007 | 1.996 | 1.984 | 1.973 | 1.962 | 1.951 |
| 17 | 1.944 | 1.933 | 1.923 | 1.913 | 1.903 | 1.893 |
| 18 | 1.900 | 1.880 | 1.864 | 1.854 | 1.845 | 1.836 |
| 19 | 1.900 | 1.880 | 1.861 | 1.842 | 1.824 | 1.806 |
| 20 | 1.900 | 1.880 | 1.861 | 1.842 | 1.824 | 1.806 |
| 21 | 1.900 | 1.880 | 1.861 | 1.842 | 1.824 | 1.806 |
| 22 | 1.900 | 1.880 | 1.861 | 1.842 | 1.824 | 1.806 |
| 23 | 1.900 | 1.880 | 1.861 | 1.842 | 1.824 | 1.806 |
| 24 | 1.900 | 1.880 | 1.861 | 1.842 | 1.824 | 1.805 |
| 25 | 1.900 | 1.880 | 1.861 | 1.842 | 1.824 | 1.806 |
| 26 | 1.900 | 1.880 | 1.861 | 1.842 | 1.824 | 1.805 |

| If the Recovery Year is: | and the Recovery Period is: 47.5 | 48.0 | 48.5 | 49.0 | 49.5 | 50.0 |
|---|---|---|---|---|---|---|
| | the Depreciation Rate is: | | | | | |
| 27 | 1.900 | 1.880 | 1.861 | 1.842 | 1.824 | 1.806 |
| 28 | 1.900 | 1.880 | 1.861 | 1.842 | 1.824 | 1.805 |
| 29 | 1.900 | 1.880 | 1.861 | 1.842 | 1.824 | 1.806 |
| 30 | 1.900 | 1.881 | 1.861 | 1.842 | 1.824 | 1.805 |
| 31 | 1.900 | 1.880 | 1.861 | 1.842 | 1.824 | 1.806 |
| 32 | 1.900 | 1.881 | 1.861 | 1.842 | 1.823 | 1.805 |
| 33 | 1.900 | 1.880 | 1.861 | 1.842 | 1.824 | 1.806 |
| 34 | 1.900 | 1.881 | 1.861 | 1.842 | 1.823 | 1.805 |
| 35 | 1.900 | 1.880 | 1.861 | 1.842 | 1.824 | 1.806 |
| 36 | 1.900 | 1.881 | 1.861 | 1.842 | 1.823 | 1.805 |
| 37 | 1.900 | 1.880 | 1.861 | 1.842 | 1.824 | 1.806 |
| 38 | 1.900 | 1.881 | 1.861 | 1.842 | 1.823 | 1.805 |
| 39 | 1.900 | 1.880 | 1.861 | 1.843 | 1.824 | 1.806 |
| 40 | 1.900 | 1.881 | 1.861 | 1.842 | 1.823 | 1.805 |
| 41 | 1.899 | 1.880 | 1.861 | 1.843 | 1.824 | 1.806 |
| 42 | 1.900 | 1.881 | 1.861 | 1.842 | 1.823 | 1.805 |
| 43 | 1.899 | 1.880 | 1.862 | 1.843 | 1.824 | 1.806 |
| 44 | 1.900 | 1.881 | 1.861 | 1.842 | 1.823 | 1.805 |
| 45 | 1.899 | 1.880 | 1.862 | 1.843 | 1.824 | 1.806 |
| 46 | 1.900 | 1.881 | 1.861 | 1.842 | 1.823 | 1.805 |
| 47 | 1.899 | 1.880 | 1.862 | 1.843 | 1.824 | 1.806 |
| 48 | 1.900 | 1.881 | 1.861 | 1.842 | 1.823 | 1.805 |
| 49 | 0.712 | 1.645 | 1.862 | 1.843 | 1.824 | 1.806 |
| 50 | | | 0.698 | 1.612 | 1.823 | 1.805 |
| 51 | | | | | 0.684 | 1.580 |

TABLE 19
Indian Reservation Property
3-year property
2-year recovery period
200-percent declining-balance method
Half-year and mid-quarter conventions

| Recovery year | Half-year convention | Midquarter Convention (use percentages in column for quarter that property was placed in service) Q-1 | Q-2 | Q-3 | Q-4 |
|---|---|---|---|---|---|
| 1 | 50 | 87.5 | 62.5 | 37.5 | 12.5 |
| 2 | 50 | 12.5 | 37.5 | 62.5 | 87.5 |

TABLE 20
Indian Reservation Property
7-year property
4-year recovery period
200-percent declining-balance method
Half-year and mid-quarter conventions

| Recovery year | Half-year convention | Midquarter Convention (use percentages in column for quarter that property was placed in service) Q-1 | Q-2 | Q-3 | Q-4 |
|---|---|---|---|---|---|
| 1 | 25 | 43.75 | 31.25 | 18.75 | 6.25 |
| 2 | 37.5 | 28.13 | 34.37 | 40.63 | 46.87 |
| 3 | 18.75 | 14.06 | 17.19 | 20.31 | 23.44 |
| 4 | 12.5 | 12.5 | 12.5 | 12.5 | 12.5 |
| 5 | 6.25 | 1.56 | 4.69 | 7.81 | 10.94 |

TABLE 21
Indian Reservation Property
10-year property
6-year recovery period
200-percent declining-balance method
Half-year and mid-quarter conventions

| Recovery year | Half-year convention | Midquarter Convention (use percentages in column for quarter that property was placed in service) Q-1 | Q-2 | Q-3 | Q-4 |
|---|---|---|---|---|---|
| 1 | 16.67 | 29.17 | 20.83 | 12.5 | 4.17 |
| 2 | 27.78 | 23.61 | 26.39 | 29.17 | 31.94 |
| 3 | 18.52 | 15.74 | 17.59 | 19.44 | 21.3 |
| 4 | 12.35 | 10.49 | 11.73 | 12.96 | 14.2 |
| 5 | 9.87 | 9.88 | 9.88 | 9.88 | 9.87 |
| 6 | 9.87 | 9.88 | 9.88 | 9.88 | 9.88 |
| 7 | 4.94 | 1.23 | 3.70 | 6.17 | 8.64 |

TABLE 22
Indian Reservation Property
Nonresidential Real Property
22-year recovery period
Straight-line method and mid-month convention

| If the Recovery Year is: | And the Month in the First Recovery Year the Property is Placed in Service is: 1 | 2 | 3 | 4 | 5 | 6 | 7 | 8 | 9 | 10 | 11 | 12 |
|---|---|---|---|---|---|---|---|---|---|---|---|---|
| | the Depreciation Rate is: | | | | | | | | | | | |
| 1 | 4.356 | 3.977 | 3.598 | 3.22 | 2.841 | 2.462 | 2.083 | 1.705 | 1.326 | 0.947 | 0.568 | 0.189 |
| 2 | 4.545 | 4.545 | 4.545 | 4.545 | 4.545 | 4.545 | 4.545 | 4.545 | 4.545 | 4.545 | 4.545 | 4.545 |
| 3 | 4.545 | 4.545 | 4.545 | 4.545 | 4.545 | 4.545 | 4.545 | 4.545 | 4.545 | 4.545 | 4.545 | 4.545 |
| 4 | 4.546 | 4.546 | 4.546 | 4.545 | 4.545 | 4.546 | 4.546 | 4.545 | 4.545 | 4.546 | 4.546 | 4.546 |
| 5 | 4.545 | 4.545 | 4.545 | 4.546 | 4.546 | 4.545 | 4.545 | 4.546 | 4.546 | 4.545 | 4.545 | 4.545 |
| 6 | 4.546 | 4.546 | 4.546 | 4.545 | 4.545 | 4.546 | 4.546 | 4.545 | 4.545 | 4.546 | 4.546 | 4.546 |
| 7 | 4.545 | 4.545 | 4.545 | 4.546 | 4.546 | 4.545 | 4.545 | 4.546 | 4.546 | 4.545 | 4.545 | 4.545 |
| 8 | 4.546 | 4.546 | 4.546 | 4.545 | 4.545 | 4.546 | 4.546 | 4.545 | 4.545 | 4.546 | 4.546 | 4.546 |
| 9 | 4.545 | 4.545 | 4.545 | 4.546 | 4.546 | 4.545 | 4.545 | 4.546 | 4.546 | 4.545 | 4.545 | 4.545 |
| 10 | 4.546 | 4.546 | 4.546 | 4.545 | 4.545 | 4.546 | 4.546 | 4.545 | 4.545 | 4.546 | 4.546 | 4.546 |
| 11 | 4.545 | 4.545 | 4.545 | 4.546 | 4.546 | 4.545 | 4.545 | 4.546 | 4.546 | 4.545 | 4.545 | 4.545 |
| 12 | 4.546 | 4.546 | 4.546 | 4.545 | 4.545 | 4.546 | 4.546 | 4.545 | 4.545 | 4.546 | 4.546 | 4.546 |
| 13 | 4.545 | 4.545 | 4.545 | 4.546 | 4.546 | 4.545 | 4.545 | 4.546 | 4.546 | 4.545 | 4.545 | 4.545 |
| 14 | 4.546 | 4.546 | 4.546 | 4.545 | 4.545 | 4.546 | 4.546 | 4.545 | 4.545 | 4.546 | 4.546 | 4.546 |
| 15 | 4.545 | 4.545 | 4.545 | 4.546 | 4.546 | 4.545 | 4.545 | 4.546 | 4.546 | 4.545 | 4.545 | 4.545 |
| 16 | 4.546 | 4.546 | 4.546 | 4.545 | 4.545 | 4.546 | 4.546 | 4.545 | 4.545 | 4.546 | 4.546 | 4.546 |
| 17 | 4.545 | 4.545 | 4.545 | 4.546 | 4.546 | 4.545 | 4.545 | 4.546 | 4.546 | 4.545 | 4.545 | 4.545 |
| 18 | 4.546 | 4.546 | 4.546 | 4.545 | 4.545 | 4.546 | 4.546 | 4.545 | 4.545 | 4.546 | 4.546 | 4.546 |
| 19 | 4.545 | 4.545 | 4.545 | 4.546 | 4.546 | 4.545 | 4.545 | 4.546 | 4.546 | 4.545 | 4.545 | 4.545 |
| 20 | 4.546 | 4.546 | 4.546 | 4.545 | 4.545 | 4.546 | 4.546 | 4.545 | 4.545 | 4.546 | 4.546 | 4.546 |
| 21 | 4.545 | 4.545 | 4.545 | 4.546 | 4.546 | 4.545 | 4.545 | 4.546 | 4.546 | 4.545 | 4.545 | 4.545 |

| If the Recovery Year is: | And the Month in the First Recovery Year the Property is Placed in Service is: | | | | | | | | | | | |
|---|---|---|---|---|---|---|---|---|---|---|---|---|
| | 1 | 2 | 3 | 4 | 5 | 6 | 7 | 8 | 9 | 10 | 11 | 12 |
| | the Depreciation Rate is: | | | | | | | | | | | |
| 22 | 4.546 | 4.546 | 4.546 | 4.545 | 4.545 | 4.546 | 4.546 | 4.545 | 4.545 | 4.546 | 4.546 | 4.546 |
| 23 | 0.189 | 0.568 | 0.947 | 1.326 | 1.705 | 2.083 | 2.462 | 2.841 | 3.220 | 3.598 | 3.977 | 4.356 |

# MACRS Recovery Periods

## ¶ 190

## How to Determine an MACRS Asset's Depreciation Period

For MACRS property, the asset class, assets included in each asset class, class life for each asset class, and recovery periods under the general depreciation system (GDS) and alternative depreciation system (ADS) for each asset class are prescribed by an IRS table in Rev. Proc. 87-56, 1987-2 CB 674 (as clarified and modified by Rev. Proc. 88-22, 1988-1 CB 785). The table is reproduced at ¶ 191. A similar table is reproduced in IRS Publication 946 (Depreciation and Amortization). The regular and ADS depreciation period for a few types of specific assets are only prescribed in the text of Code Section 168 and not in Rev. Proc. 87-56. For example, Code Sec. 168(e)(3)(D) prescribes a ten-year recovery period for smart electric meters and grid systems. The text of Rev. Proc. 87-56 has not been amended by the IRS to reflect depreciation periods that were statutorily prescribed after its issuance.

*See also ¶ 100 through ¶ 127C for discussion of specific MACRS property recovery periods and types of property falling within each recovery period. A Quick Reference Table in the Appendix also provides a list of recovery periods for various types of assets and includes cross references to related explanation discussions in this guide. The discussion in this paragraph explains how to use the IRS Rev. Proc. 87-56 table to determine the applicable recovery period.*

The GDS and ADS recovery periods for property within an asset class is generally determined by reference to the class life assigned to the asset class by Rev. Proc. 87-56. For example, property with a class life of more than 4 years but less than 10 years is assigned a GDS recovery period of 5 years (Code Sec. 168(e)(1)). The ADS recovery period is generally the same as the class life (Code Sec. 168(g)(2)(c)(i)). In certain cases Code Sec. 168 assigns a special GDS and/or ADS recovery period to specific assets. These specially assigned recovery periods will trump any different period provided in Rev. Proc. 87-56.

Code Sec. 168(i)(1) defines "class life" as that "which would be applicable with respect to any property as of January 1, 1986, under subsection (m) of section 167." Code Sec. 167(m) (now repealed) provided for depreciation according to "the class life prescribed by the Secretary which reasonably reflects the anticipated useful life of that class of property to the industry or other group." Code Sec. 167(m) codified the Asset Depreciation Range system described in Reg. § 1.167(a)-11, and in particular the system of asset guideline classes (now referred to as asset classes) and class lives found therein. See H. Rept. 92-533, at 30-35 (1971), 1972-1 C.B. 498, 514-516; S. Rept. 92-437, at 45-52 (1971), 1972-1 C.B. 559, 584-588. Rev. Proc. 72-10 was the first of several revenue procedures establishing asset guideline classes (now asset classes), each superseding its predecessor. Rev. Proc. 87-56, established the asset guideline classes (asset classes) in effect for purposes of determining the class life (and, therefore, recovery periods) of MACRS assets. Act Sec. 6253 of the Technical and Miscellaneous Revenue Act of 1988, (P.L. 100-647) revoked the authority of the IRS to prescribe any new asset class or class life.

Certain property with no class life for which recovery periods are assigned is described in items A-E following Asset Class 80.0 in the table in Rev. Proc. 87-56. Personal property with no class life and Section 1245 real property with no class life is assigned a seven-year GDS recovery period and a 12-year and 40-year ADS recovery period, respectively (item A). Property without a class life is sometimes referred to as "residual class" property.

The first section of the table in Rev. Proc. 87-56 (Asset Classes 00.1100.4 (Table B-1)) covers specific depreciable assets used in all business activities and the second section (Asset Classes 01.180.0 (Table B-2)) generally lists specific types of assets used in particular business activities, e.g., production machinery and equipment for specified industries.

For each asset class, the table provides the class life of the property, the MACRS GDS recovery/depreciation period, and the recovery period under the MACRS alternative depreciation system (ADS) for such property (which is the same as the class life for the property).

It is important to keep in mind when using Table B-2 that the classification of an asset is not based on the taxpayer's business activity but rather upon whether the particular asset is specifically described or considered used in furtherance of the particular business activity described. Thus, it is necessary to determine the specific function and use of the asset in the taxpayer's business activity.

Although a particular asset class may include a list of assets included in the asset class, that list is not necessarily exclusive. Assets used in furtherance of the particular business activity described by the asset class may be included in that asset class. (CCA Letter Ruling 200246006, August 15, 2002). See the discussion under "*Tools*" at ¶ 125.

In another example, the IRS ruled that a parking lot located at a steam production plant was a "related land improvement" within the meaning of Asset Class 49.13 and, therefore, had to be depreciated over the 20 year recovery period prescribed for that asset class (Rev. Rul. 2003-81, I.R.B. 2003-30). The wording of Asset Class 49.13 requires that the land improvement be related to assets used in the steam power production of electricity. According to the IRS, the parking lot was related to the plant that produced electricity. On the other hand, although a parking lot located at the company's office building 100 miles away was used in connection with the taxpayer's business activity of producing electricity, it is was not considered related to assets that produced electricity as required by Asset Class 49.13. The office parking lot was, therefore, depreciable over 15-years as a land improvement described in Table B-1 Asset Class 00.3 entitled "Land Improvements." See *Parking lots* at ¶ 5. Presumably, if a cost segregation study were conducted on the office building, the personal property components of the building would generally be classified as property without an assigned class life and would be depreciable over 7-years. On the other hand, if personal or professional services, or retail or wholesale services, are provided from a building, the personal property elements of the building would presumably be classified as 5-year property under Asset Class 57.0 because the building would be considered a necessary asset directly used in the provision of these services. For example, all the personal property elements of the hospital building in the Hospital Corporation of America case (¶ 127) were classified as 5-year property under Asset Class 57.0 because the building was considered an asset used to provide professional services.

*Residential rental property and nonresidential real property*

Residential rental property has a recovery period of 27.5 years and nonresidential real property has a recovery period of 39 years (31.5 years for property placed in service before May 13, 1993). For purposes of the alternative depreciation system (ADS), nonresidential real property each has a recovery period of 40 years. The ADS recovery period for residential rental property placed in service before 2018 is also 40 years but is reduced to 30, effective for property placed in service after 2017. This 30-year ADS recovery period for residential rental property also applies to residential rental property placed in service by an electing real property trade or business before 2018.

Nonresidential real property does not include any property described in an asset class with a class life of less than 27.5 years (Code Sec. 168(e)(2)(B)(ii)). Even if nonresidential real property is described in an asset class in Rev. Proc. 87-56 with a class life of 27.5 years or more, the applicable recovery period for that property is 39 years for purposes of the general depreciation system and 40 years for purposes of the alternative depreciation system, regardless of the applicable recovery periods set out for the asset class in the Rev. Proc. 87-56 (Section 5.02 of Rev. Proc. 87-56, as modified by Rev. Proc. 88-22).

Thus, if a building is specifically described in an Asset Class with a class life of less than 27.5 years, the building is not classified as nonresidential real property with a recovery period of 39 years. Instead, the recovery period assigned by the asset class to the building will apply. On the other hand, if a building is described in an asset class in Rev. Proc. 87-56 with a class life of 27.5 years or more, the applicable recovery period for that property is 39 years. For example, although station and office buildings and roadway buildings are described in Asset Class 40.2 (Railroad Structures and Similar Improvements), such buildings have a 39-year recovery period even though Asset Class 40.2 provides for a 20-year recovery period (CCA Letter Ruling 200709063, November 21, 2006). The only other Asset Class with a class life of 27.5 or more in which a building is described appears to be Asset Class 48.11, relating to Telephone Central Office Buildings.

See ¶ 114 for complete discussion of residential rental property and ¶ 115 for complete discussion of nonresidential real property.

*Assets described in more than one asset class*

If a specific asset, such as a land improvement, is listed in an Asset Class that appears in both the first section of the table (Asset classes 00.11 through 00.4 (Table B-1)) and the Asset Class that applies to the taxpayer's business activity in the second part of the table (Asset Classes 01.1 and following (Table B-2)) the depreciation period is determined by reference to the Asset Class in the second part of the table. Except for land improvements, very few assets are specifically described in both sections of the table. The rules are explained more fully at ¶ 191 but the following examples serve as good illustrations.

***Example (1):*** An accountant buys a desk for business use. The desk is specifically described in Table B-1 under Asset Class 00.11, Office Furniture, Fixtures, and Equipment. The accountant now needs to refer to the second part of the table (Table B-1) to determine whether desks are specifically listed in her business activity. Her business activity falls within Asset Class 57.0 which covers taxpayers who provide personal and professional services. Desks, however, are not specifically described in Asset Class 57.0. Consequently, the depreciation period is determined by reference to Asset Class 00.11. Under Asset Class 00.11 the desk is treated as 7-year property.

***Example (2):*** An accountant buys permanent hard covered reference books for his professional library. Books are not listed in the first part of the table (Table B-1) as a type of asset used in all business activities and are also not specifically listed in Asset Class 57.0 (the asset class for the accountant's business activity). In this instance, the depreciation period is determined by reference to Asset Class 57.0 and the books are, therefore, treated as 5-year property. If the taxpayer was not an accountant and was engaged in a another business activity that was not described in the second part of the table, the books would have been treated as personal property without a class life and, by default, would have been treated as 7-year property.

A fishing trawler was a specific asset classified in the first part of the Rev. Proc. 87-56 table as a vessel (Asset Class 00.28) and had a ten-year recovery period. This asset class controlled the depreciation period even though the trawler was used in a business activity described in Asset class 20.4 (Manufacture of Other Food and Kindred Products) because vessels are not specifically described in Asset Class 20.4 (IRS Letter Ruling 9502001, Jun. 30, 1994).

*Taxpayer with multiple business activities*

The ADR regulations provide that property is included in the asset guideline for the activity in which the property is primarily used. Property is classified according to the primary use even though the activity in which the property is primarily used is insubstantial in relation to all the taxpayer's activities (Reg. 1.167(a)-11(b)(4)(iii)(b)). In IRS Letter Ruling 9101003, September 25, 1990, the IRS states that this rule may be applied for MACRS purposes.

A limitation on the application of this rule is illustrated in Rev. Rul. 77-476 (1977-2 CB 5). In Rev. Rul. 77-476, a public utility owned a 50-mile pipeline through which it transported oil for use at its generating facility. The ruling holds that the pipeline is not Asset Class 46.0 property (relating to pipeline transportation) but is Asset Class 49.13 property (relating to electric utility steam production plants). Asset Class 46.0 was inapplicable because the utility did not have a separate business activity of transporting oil or other goods by pipeline.

In Chief Counsel Advice 200137026, the IRS states: "Where a taxpayer is engaged in more than one industrial or commercial activity, the cost of assets used in each activity are to be separated and depreciation deductions calculated separately for each activity. If an item of property is used in two industrial or commercial activities that correspond to two activities, depreciation deductions for the item are calculated based on the activity in which the item is primarily used. If two identical items (for example, two forklifts) are primarily used in each of two separate industrial or commercial activities of a taxpayer, depreciation deductions for each item are computed based on the activity in which the item is primarily used" (Chief Counsel Advice 200137026, June 14, 2001; IRS Letter Ruling 200203009, October 3, 2001).

If a particular asset is used in two activities, the cost of the asset is not allocated between the two activities. The total cost of the asset is classified according to the activity in which the asset is primarily used. This determination may be made in any reasonable manner (IRS Letter Ruling 200203009, October 3, 2001, relating to assets used in both casino and hotel operations). For example, in Rev. Proc. 97-10 (1997-1 C.B. 628), either a gross receipts test or a square foot test was used to determine whether a building is primarily used as a retail motor fuels outlet.

*Leased property*

Regulations, which were issued in the context of the Asset Depreciation Range System (ADR), provide that in the case of a lessor of property, unless there is an asset guideline class in effect for lessors of such property, the asset guideline class for the property shall be determined as if the property were owned by the lessee (Reg. 1.167(a)-11(e)(3)(iii)). *A.J. Hauptli, Jr.*, CA-10, 90-1 USTC 50,259, interpreted this rule to mean that where the lessee subleases the asset, the sublessee is the relevant reference point. Under the principal of this regulation, the depreciation period for MACRS property that is leased is also determined by reference to the lessee unless a separate asset class is in effect for the lessor.

The classification of vessels leased to a taxpayer's subsidiary which time chartered the vessels for use in offshore oil drilling activities was determined by reference to the subsidiary's use, rather than the time charterer's use, where the time charter was considered a service contract and not a sublease (FSA 200232012, April 26, 2002). In an earlier ruling involving the same taxpayer, if a time charter is considered a sublease, the classification of the vessels is determined by reference to the use to which the time-charter puts the vessel. Vessels chartered during the tax year to multiple time charterers engaged in different business activities were classified in accordance with the business activity in which they were primarily used during the tax year (FSA 200221016, February 13, 2002). See *"Taxpayer with multiple business activities"* at ¶ 190.

> ***Example:*** ABC corporation is in the business of leasing gas cylinders. It leases 1,000 cylinders to a manufacturer of grain and grain mill products (Asset Class 20.1 in Rev. Proc. 87-56). The cylinders are treated as 10-year property under Asset Class 20.1 because the leasing of gas cylinders is not an activity described in Rev. Proc. 87-56.

Under the ADR regulations, if an asset class is based upon the type of property, as distinguished from the activity in which it is used, for example trucks or railroad cars, the property is classified without regard to the activity of the lessee (Reg. 1.167(a)-11(e)(3)(iii)). See also *"Assets falling within more than one asset class"* above.

See also ¶ 5 under *"Inventory"* for leased property issues.

*Other federal laws*

A federal law other than the federal income tax law may not be used in determining the asset class in which a particular property falls unless it is specifically indicated in Code Sec. 168 or Rev. Proc. 87-56 (IRS Letter Ruling 9502001, Jun. 30, 1994).

## *Full Text Classification Guidelines from IRS Cost Segregation Audit Guide*

The following text from the IRS Cost Segregation Audit Guide provides basic principles for determining the proper Rev. Proc. 87-56 Asset Class (i.e., recovery period) for MACRS assets.

**Introduction**

**Chapter 6.3 - Depreciation Overview**

For purposes of either GDS or ADS, the applicable recovery period is determined by statute or by reference to class life.

The recovery period of residential rental property, nonresidential real property, and railroad grading and tunnel bore are established by statute. See § § 168(c) and 168(g)(2)(c).

- Residential rental property has a recovery period of 27.5 years for purposes of GDS and 40 years for purposes of ADS [30 years for property placed in service after 2017 as well as for residential rental property placed in service by an electing real property trade or business before 2018].

- § 168(e)(2)(A) defines "residential rental property" as any building or structure if 80 percent or more of the gross rental income is rental income from dwelling units.

• Nonresidential real property has a recovery period of 39 years (or 31.5 years if the property was placed in service before May 13, 1993) for purposes of GDS and 40 years for purposes of ADS.

• § 168(e)(2)(B) defines "nonresidential real property" as § 1250 property which is not residential rental property or property with a class life of less than 27.5 years.

• Railroad grading and tunnel bore have a recovery period of 50 years for purposes of both GDS and ADS. § § 168(c) and 168(g)(2)(c).

§ 168(i)(12) provides that the terms "§ 1245 property" and "§ 1250 property" have the meanings given such terms by § 1245(a)(3) and § 1250(c), respectively.

§ 1245(a)(3) provides that "§ 1245 property" is any property which is or has been subject to depreciation under § 167 and which is either personal property or other tangible property (not including a building or its structural components) that was used as an integral part of certain activities.

§ 1250(c) defines "§ 1250 property" as any real property, other than § 1245 property, which is or has been subject to an allowance for depreciation. In other words, § 1250 property encompasses all depreciable property that is not § 1245 property.

§ 1245(a)(3) provides that "§ 1245 property" is any property which is or has been subject to depreciation under § 167 and which is either personal property or other tangible property (not including a building or its structural components) that was used as an integral part of certain activities. Such activities include manufacturing, production, or extraction; furnishing transportation, communication, electrical energy, gas, water, or sewage disposal services. Certain other "special use" property also qualifies as § 1245 property, but is not relevant to this discussion. It is important to note that a building or its structural components is specifically excluded from the definition of § 1245 property.

Treasury Regulation (Treas. Reg.) § 1.1245-3 defines "tangible personal property," "other tangible property," "building," and "structural component" by reference to Treas. Reg. § 1.48-1. This regulation relates to former § 48 which was enacted in 1962 along with § § 1245 and 1250. § 48 allowed an investment tax credit (ITC) based on the "applicable percentage" of the investment in tangible depreciable property placed in service during the taxable year. The ITC (§ 48) was later repealed in 1986. See the previous chapter, Legal Framework, for a description of the provisions set forth in Treas. Reg. § 1.48-1.

**CLASS LIVES**

§ 168(i)(1) provides that the term "class life" means the class life (if any) that would be applicable with respect to any property as of January 1, 1986, under former § 167(m) as if it were in effect and the taxpayer were an elector. Prior to its revocation, former § 167(m) provided that in the case of a taxpayer who elected the asset depreciation range system of depreciation, the depreciation deduction would be computed based on the class life prescribed by the Secretary which reasonably reflects the anticipated useful life, and the anticipated decline in value over time, of the property to the industry or other group.

Treas. Reg. § 1.167(a)-11(b)(4)(iii)(b) sets out the method for asset classification under former § 167(m). Property is included in the asset guideline class for the activity in which the property is primarily used, regardless of whether the activity is insubstantial in relation to all the taxpayer's activities. Thus, for depreciation purposes, a taxpayer may be engaged in more than one activity. If a taxpayer uses assets in more than one activity, the cost of the asset is not allocated between the two activities; rather, the total cost of the asset will be classified for depreciation purposes according to the activity in which the asset is primarily used. This determination may be made in any reasonable manner. Note that in Revenue Procedure (Rev. Proc.) 97-10, 1997-1 C.B. 628, either a gross receipts test or a square footage test was used to determine whether a building was primarily used as a retail motor fuels outlet.

For example, assume that a taxpayer owns and operates a hotel/casino complex. The taxpayer is engaged in two business activities: casino operations and hotel operations. Assets used by the taxpayer in its casino operations are includible in the activity category that includes casino operations (asset class 79.0 Recreation of Rev. Proc. 87-56). Assets used in hotel operations are includible in the activity category that includes hotel operations (asset class 57.0 Distributive Trades and Services of Rev. Proc. 87-56). If a particular asset is used in both activities, the total cost of the asset will be classified for depreciation purposes according to the activity in which the asset is primarily used; the cost of the asset is not allocated between the two activities. The determination of primary use may be made in any reasonable manner. For additional information, see IRS FSA 200203009.

Asset classifications are based on how the asset is primarily used. In the case of a lessor of property, the asset class for such property is determined as if the property were owned by the lessee. See Treas. Reg. § 1.167(a)-11(e)(3)(iii) and the following court cases for additional information and consideration.

- *Clajon Gas Co. L.P. v. Commissioner*, 354 F.3d 786 (8th Cir. 2004), rev'g 119 T.C. 197 (2002): Pipelines leased to producers to transport natural gas fell under the asset class for producing natural gas regardless of ownership.

- *Saginaw Bay Pipeline Co. v. United States*, 338 F.3d 600 (6th Cir.2003), rev'g 124 F.Supp.2d 465 (E.D. Mich. 2001): Every natural gas carriage pipeline which functions as a gathering pipeline is in the methane gas production process irrespective of the primary business of the owner of that pipeline.

- *Duke Energy Natural Gas Corp. v. Commissioner*, 172 F.3d 1255 (10th Cir.1999), rev'g, 109 T.C. 416 (1997): Based on the asset's primary use, the classification of natural gas gathering systems constituted as assets used in the production of natural gas.

As stated earlier, GDS contains ten property classes, based on the recovery period of an asset. For those classes of property not established by statute, the applicable recovery period is determined by reference to class life. See § 168(e)(1). It is also worth noting that Qualified Indian reservation property, however; generally have shorter applicable recovery periods. See § 168(j)(1)-(2).

## REVENUE PROCEDURE 87-56

Revenue Procedure 87-56, 1987-2 C.B. 674, sets forth the class lives of property that are necessary to compute the depreciation allowances under § 168 (MACRS). The revenue procedure establishes two broad categories of depreciable assets:

- Asset classes 00.11 through 00.4 that consist of specific assets used in all business activities.

- Asset classes 01.1 through 80.0 that consist of assets used in specific business activities.

The same item of depreciable property can be described in both an asset category (asset classes 00.11 through 00.4) and an activity category (asset classes

01.1 through 80.0). In this situation, the item is classified to the asset category unless it is specifically excluded from the asset category or specifically included in the activity category. For additional guidance see below:

- *Norwest Corporation & Subsidiaries v. Commissioner*, 111 T.C. 105 (1998) (item described in both an asset and an activity category (furniture and fixtures) should be placed in the asset category)

- Rev. Rul. 2003-81, 2003-2 C.B. 126 (an asset included in both an asset category and an activity category is placed in the asset category, unless it is specifically excluded from the asset category or specifically included in the activity category).

Revenue Procedure 87-56 contains tables of class lives and recovery periods. To properly utilize Rev. Proc. 87-56, the following steps are suggested:

(1) Check Asset Classes 00.11 through 00.4 that consist of specific assets used in all business activities to see if it contains a description of the asset in question.

- Refer below to Step 2 (if the asset is described in an asset category) or to Step 3 (if the asset is not listed in an asset category).

(2) If the subject asset is described in one of the asset categories, then check asset classes 01.1 through 80.0 that consist of assets used in specific business activities to find the activity to which the property relates or in which it is primarily being used.

- If the activity is described in one of the activity categories, read the text (if any) under the title to determine if the property is specifically included in the activity category.

- If it is, then use the recovery period shown for the activity category following the description of that activity.

- If the property is not specifically included in the activity category, or if the property is specifically excluded from the activity category, then use the recovery period shown in the appropriate asset category.

(3) If the asset is not listed in an asset category, then find the activity to which the property relates or in which the property is primarily being used, and use the recovery period shown in the appropriate column following the activity category description.

- If the property is not listed in an asset category and the activity to which it relates is not included in one of the activity categories, then the property should be categorized in "Certain Property for which Recovery periods Assigned (Personal Property/§ 1245 Real Property With No Class Life)." Property in this category generally has a recovery period of 7 years for GDS or 12 years for ADS. Please note that there are very few assets that fall under this default category.

•

**EXAMPLES**

The following examples illustrate the use of Rev. Proc. 87-56 for determining the proper asset recovery period. See also Appendix B of IRS Publication 946.

***Example 1:*** Richard Green is a paper manufacturer. During the year, he made substantial improvements to the land on which his paper plant is located. Assume that these land improvements are depreciable property. He checks the asset categories and finds land improvements under Asset Class 00.3 Land Improvements. He then checks the activity categories and finds his activity, paper manufacturing, under Asset Class 26.1, Manufacture of Pulp and Paper.

If Richard had only looked at the asset categories, he would have erroneously selected Asset Class 00.3, Land Improvements, and would have incorrectly used a recovery period of 15 years for GDS or 20 years for ADS. However, Richard uses the recovery period under Asset Class 26.1 Manufacture of Pulp and Paper, because it specifically includes land improvements. Thus, the land improvements have a 13-year class life and a 7-year recovery period for GDS. If he elects to use ADS, the recovery period is 13 years.

[Note: It is presumed in this example that the subject land improvements are directly associated with the factory site or production process, for example, effluent ponds or canals necessitated by the production process, or parking lots utilized by employees directly involved with the production process. However, those land improvements that are more closely associated with non-production activities, such as administrative or retail activities of the taxpayer, would be categorized in Asset Class 00.3 Land Improvements and have a 15-year recovery period under GDS. See Rev. Rul. 2003-81, 2003-2 C.B. 126.]

***Example 2:*** Sam Plower produces rubber products. During the year, he made substantial improvements to the land on which his rubber plants are located. Assume that these land improvements are depreciable property. He checks the asset categories and finds land improvements under Asset Class 00.3. He then checks the activity categories and finds his activity, producing rubber products, under Asset Class 30.1, Manufacture of Rubber Products. Reading the headlines and descriptions under Asset Class 30.1, Sam finds that it does not specifically include land improvements. Therefore, Sam uses the recovery period for Asset Class 00.3 Land Improvements. Thus, the land improvements have a 20-year class life and a 15-year recovery period for GDS. If he elects to use ADS, the recovery period is 20 years.

***Example 3:*** Pam Martin owns a retail-clothing store. During the year, she purchased a desk and a cash register for use in her business. She checks the asset categories and finds office furniture under Asset Class 00.11 Office Furniture, Fixtures, and Equipment. Cash registers are not specifically listed in any of the asset categories. She then checks the activity categories and finds her activity, retail store, under Asset Class 57.0 Distributive Trades and Services, which includes assets used in wholesale and retail trade. The description for this asset class does not specifically list office furniture or a cash register.

She looks back at the asset categories and uses Asset Class 00.11 for the desk, since it constitutes office furniture. Thus, the desk has a 10-year class life and a 7- year recovery period for GDS. If she elects to use ADS, the recovery period is 10 years. For the cash register, Pam uses Asset Class 57.0 Distributive Trades and Services, because cash registers are not specifically listed in one of the asset categories but are assets used in retail business. Accordingly, the cash register has a 9-year class life and a 5-year recovery period for GDS. If she elects to use the ADS method, the recovery period is 9 years.

## ADDITIONAL REFERENCES FOR DETERMINING THE PROPER ACTIVITY CATEGORY FOR PROPERTY

The Standard Industrial Classification Manual (SIC) published by the Office of Management and Budget can provide insight into the content of the asset classes described in Rev. Proc. 87-56. Care must be exercised because SIC does not make use of the same classification techniques and depreciation concepts of Rev. Proc. 87-56. While SIC has precise categorization by primary business activity using language very similar to that found in Rev. Proc. 87-56, the revenue procedure departs dramatically from the categorization scheme of SIC by establishing two broad categories of depreciable assets: (1) asset classes 00.11 through 00.4 that consist of specific assets used in all business activities; and (2) asset classes 01.1 through 80.0 that consist of assets used in specific business activities. However, the asset class numbers for the specific business activities described in Rev. Proc. 87-56 are largely taken from SIC.

Additionally, it may be helpful to look at the North American Industry Classification System (NAICS). NAICS was introduced in 1997 to replace the SIC system and more closely reflects the many new industries that have propagated since the establishment of the SIC system in 1937, including many service industries currently under-represented in the SIC system. Although the manner of categorization is similar under both SIC and NAICS, the category codes are vastly different, which is why the Service generally does not look to NAICS for insight purposes. However, NAICS can be helpful (because of its expanded description of service industries) in determining in which one of two activity categories, a particular asset should be categorized.

## ¶ 191

## Rev. Proc. 87-56 (IRS Recovery Period Table for MACRS Assets)

The following text is from IRS Publication 946 (How to Depreciate Property) and explains how to use the table of class lives and recovery periods contained in Rev. Proc. 87-56. For additional information on how to determine an asset's recovery period under MACRS, see ¶ 190.

The *Table of Class Lives and Recovery Periods* has two sections. The first section, *Specific Depreciable Assets Used In All Business Activities, Except as Noted:*, generally lists assets used in all business activities. It is shown as Table B-1. The second section, *Depreciable Assets Used In The Following Activities:*, describes assets used only in certain activities. It is shown as Table B-2.

### How To Use the Tables

You will need to look at both Table B-1 and B-2 to find the correct recovery period. Generally, if the property is listed in Table B-1 you use the recovery period shown in that table. However, if the property is specifically listed in Table B-2 under the type of activity in which it is used, you use the recovery period listed under the activity in that table. Use the tables in the order shown below to determine the recovery period of your depreciable property.

**Table B-1.** Check Table B-1 for a description of the property. If it is described in Table B-1, also check Table B-2 to find the activity in which the property is being used. If the activity is described in Table B-2, read the text (if any) under the title to determine if the property is specifically included in that asset class. If it is, use the recovery period shown in the appropriate column of Table B-2 following the description of the activity. If the activity is not described in Table B-2 or if the activity is described but property either is not specifically included in or is specifically excluded from that asset class, then use the recovery period shown in the appropriate column following the description of the property in Table B-1.

**Table B-2.** If the property is not listed in Table B-1, check Table B-2 to find the activity in which the property is being used and use the recovery period shown in the appropriate column following the description.

**Property not in either table.** If the activity or the property is not included in either table, check the end of Table B-2 to find *Certain Property for Which Recovery Periods Assigned.* This property generally has a recovery period of 7 years for GDS or 12 years for ADS. For residential rental property and nonresidential real property see Appendix A, Chart 2 or *Which Recovery Period Applies* in chapter 4 for recovery periods for both GDS and ADS.

> ***Example (1):*** Richard Green is a paper manufacturer. During the year, he made substantial improvements to the land on which his paper plant is located. He checks Table B-1 and finds land improvements under asset class 00.3. He then checks Table B-2 and finds his activity, paper manufacturing, under asset class 26.1, *Manufacture of Pulp and Paper.* He uses the recovery period under this asset class because it specifically includes land improvements. The land improvements have a 13-year class life and a 7-year recovery period for GDS. If he elects to use ADS, the recovery period is 13 years. If Richard only looked at Table B 1, hc would select asset class 00.3 *Land Improvements* and incorrectly use a recovery period of 15 years for GDS or 20 years for ADS.

> ***Example (2):*** Sam Plower produces rubber products. During the year, he made substantial improvements to the land on which his rubber plant is located. He checks Table B-1 and finds land improvements under asset class 00.3. He then checks Table B-2 and finds his activity, producing rubber products, under asset class 30.1 *Manufacture of Rubber Products.* Reading the headings and descriptions under asset class 30.1, Sam finds that it does not include land improvements. Therefore, Sam uses the recovery period under asset class 00.3. The land improvements have a 20-year class life and a 15-year recovery period for GDS. If he elects to use the ADS method, the recovery period is 20 years.

> ***Example (3):*** Pam Martin owns a retail clothing store. During the year, she purchased a desk and a cash register for use in her business. She checks Table B-1 and finds office furniture under asset class 00.11. Cash registers are not listed in any of the asset classes in Table B-1. She then checks Table B-2 and finds her activity, retail store, under asset class 57.0, *Distributive Trades and Services,* which includes **assets used in wholesale and retail trade**. This asset class does not specifically list office furniture or a cash register. She looks back at Table B-1 and uses asset class 00.11 for the desk. The desk has a 10-year class life and a 7-year recovery period for GDS. If she elects to use ADS, the recovery period is 10 years. For the cash register, she uses asset class 57.0 because cash registers are not listed in Table B-1 but it is an **asset** used in her retail business. The cash register has a 9-year class life and a 5-year recovery period for GDS. If she elects to use the ADS method, the recovery period is 9 years.

> [End of IRS text.—Editor.]

The Tax Court has ruled (in accordance with the preceding IRS explanation) that the depreciation period of an asset that was specifically described in an asset group (Asset Classes 00.11 through 00.4, specific depreciable assets used in all business activities) but could also be included in an activity group (Asset Classes 01.1 through 80.0, depreciable assets used in specified activities), should be determined by reference to the asset group classification (*Norwest Corp. and Subsidiaries*, 111 TC 105, Dec. 52,830). The case involved office furniture used by a bank. Banking is an activity described in Asset Class 57.0. Asset Class 57.0 (five-year recovery period) includes "assets used in wholesale and retail trade, and personal and professional services." However, Asset Class 00.11 (seven-year recovery period) specifically includes "furniture and fixtures that are not a structural component of a building." Applying the priority rule, the furniture was classified as 7-year property (Asset Class 00.11). If the office furniture had also been specifically described as included in Asset Class 57.0, then it would have been treated as 5-year property, as the preceding IRS guidelines also dictate.

It is unclear from the decision whether any of the furniture involved was of a type suitable only for use in banks (for example, check writing stands). In an earlier decision involving the same taxpayer, the IRS conceded that this type of furniture was 5-year property (*Norwest Corp. and Subsidiaries*, 70 TCM 416, Dec. 50,834(M)). See ¶ 106.

*Predecessors to Rev. Proc. 87-56*

Useful insight into the development of the current asset classes contained in Rev. Proc. 87-56 may be obtained by referring to various predecessor revenue procedures and publications issued by the IRS.

Bulletin F (revised January 1942)—provides an asset-by-asset listing of useful lives;

Rev. Proc. 62-21, 1962-2 CB 418—provides useful lives ("guideline lives") for assets used by businesses in general and guideline lives for assets used in specified business activities ("guideline classes"). Supplement II, 1963-2 CB 744, which consists of Questions and Answers, was published to assist taxpayers in applying Rev. Proc. 62-21;

Rev. Proc. 71-25, 1971-2 CB 553—sets forth asset guideline classes, asset guideline periods, and asset depreciation ranges for purposes of the Asset Depreciation Range System (ADR);

Rev. Proc. 72-10, 1972-1 CB 721—supersedes Rev. Proc. 71-25 and updates asset guideline classes, asset guideline periods, and asset depreciation ranges. Also supersedes Rev. Proc. 62-21;

Rev. Proc. 77-10, 1977-1 CB 548—updates and supersedes Rev. Proc. 72-10; and

Rev. Proc. 83-35, 1983-1 CB 745—updates and supersedes Rev. Proc. 77-10. The asset guideline periods (midpoint class lives) set forth in Rev. Proc. 83-35 are also used in defining the classes of recovery property under the Accelerated Cost Recovery System (i.e., pre-MACRS Code Sec. 168 property).

Rev. Proc. 87-56 and its predecessors are based in large part on the Standard Industrial Classification Manual (SIC) published by the Office of Management and Budget. SIC has precise categorization by primary business activity using language very similar to that found in Rev. Proc. 87-56. The asset class numbers for the particular business activities described in Rev. Proc. 87-56 are largely taken from SIC. For example, in ruling that gaming devices such as slot machines are 7-year property (Asset Class 79.0 (relating to assets used in the provision of entertainment services)), the IRS cited the SIC classification numbers for operators of coin operated amusement devices and casino operations which fell within SIC asset class 79 (IRS Coordinated Issue Paper for the Gaming Industry, April 10, 2000). The SIC manual (1987 version) is reproduced at the following government web site:

http://www.osha.gov/oshstats

While SIC has precise categorization by primary business activity using language very similar to that found in Rev. Proc. 87-56, that revenue procedure departs dramatically from the categorization scheme of SIC by establishing the two broad categories of depreciable assets (viz., assets used in all business activities (Table B-1) and assets used in particular business activities (Table B-2). The asset class numbers for specific business activities, however, are largely taken from SIC.

*Full Text of Rev. Proc. 87-56 Recovery Period Tables*

| *Asset class* | *Description of assets included* | *Class Life (in years)* | *Recovery Periods (in years)* General Depreciation System | Alternative Depreciation System |
|---|---|---|---|---|
| | [Table B-1] | | | |
| | SPECIFIC DEPRECIABLE ASSETS USED IN ALL BUSINESS ACTIVITIES, EXCEPT AS NOTED: | | | |
| 00.11 | **Office Furniture, Fixtures, and Equipment:** Includes furniture and fixtures that are not a structural component of a building. Includes such assets as desks, files, safes, and communications equipment. Does not include communications equipment that is included in other classes . . . . . . . . . . . . | 10 | 7 | 10 |
| 00.12 | **Information Systems:** Includes computers and their peripheral equipment used in administering normal business transactions and the maintenance of business records, their retrieval and analysis. Information systems are defined as: 1) Computers: A computer is a programmable electronically activated device capable of accepting information, applying prescribed processes to the information, and supplying the results of these processes with or without human intervention. It usually consists of a central processing unit containing extensive storage, logic, arithmetic, and control capabilities. Excluded from this category are adding machines, electronic desk calculators, etc. and other equipment described in class 00.13. 2) Peripheral equipment consists of the auxiliary machines which are designed to be placed under control of the central processing unit. Nonlimiting examples are: Card readers, card punches, magnetic tape feeds, high speed printers, optical character readers, tape cassettes, mass storage units, paper tape equipment, keypunches, data entry devices, teleprinters, terminals, tape drives, disc drives, disc files, disc packs, visual image projector tubes, card sorters, plotters, and collators. Peripheral equipment may be used on-line or off-line. Does not include equipment that is an integral part of other capital equipment that is included in other classes of economic activity, i.e., computers used primarily for process or production control, switching, channeling, and automating distributive trades and services such as point of sale (POS) computer systems. Also, does not include equipment of a kind used primarily for amusement or entertainment of the user . . | 6 | 5 | 5 |
| 00.13 | **Data Handling Equipment, except Computers:** Includes only typewriters, calculators, adding and accounting machines, copiers, and duplicating equipment . . . . . . . . . . . . . . . | 6 | 5 | 6 |

| Asset class | Description of assets included | Class Life (in years) | Recovery Periods (in years) General Depreciation System | Alternative Depreciation System |
|---|---|---|---|---|
| 00.21 | **Airplanes (airframes and engines), except those used in commercial or contract carrying of passengers or freight, and all helicopters (airframes and engines)** . . . | 6 | 5 | 6 |
| 00.22 | **Automobiles, Taxis** . . . . . . . . . . . . . . . . | 3 | 5 | 5 |
| 00.23 | **Buses** . . . . . . . . . . . . . . . . . . . . . . . . . | 9 | 5 | 9 |
| 00.241 | **Light General Purpose Trucks:** Includes trucks for use over the road (actual unloaded weight less than 13,000 pounds) . | 4 | 5 | 5 |
| 00.242 | **Heavy General Purpose Trucks:** Includes heavy general purpose trucks, concrete ready mix-truckers, and ore trucks, for use over the road (actual unloaded weight 13,000 pounds or more) . . . . . . . . . . . . . . | 6 | 5 | 6 |
| 00.25 | **Railroad Cars and Locomotives, except those owned by railroad transportation companies** . . . . . . . . . . . . . . . . . . . . . | 15 | 7 | 15 |
| 00.26 | **Tractor Units For Use Over-The-Road** . . | 4 | 3 | 4 |
| 00.27 | **Trailers and Trailer-Mounted Containers** . . . . . . . . . . . . . . . . . . . . . . . . . . . . . . | 6 | 5 | 6 |
| 00.28 | **Vessels, Barges, Tugs, and Similar Water Transportation Equipment, except those used in marine construction** . . . . . . . . . | 18 | 10 | 18 |
| 00.3 | **Land Improvements:** Includes improvements directly to or added to land, whether such improvements are section 1245 property or section 1250 property, provided such improvements are depreciable. Examples of such assets might include sidewalks, roads, canals, waterways, drainage facilities, sewers (not including municipal sewers in Class 51), wharves and docks, bridges, fences, landscaping, shrubbery, or radio and television transmitting towers. Does not include land improvements that are explicitly included in any other class, and buildings and structural components as defined in section 1.48-1(e) of the regulations. Excludes public utility initial clearing and grading land improvements as specified in Rev. Rul. 72-403, 1972-2 C.B. 102 . . . . . . . . . . . . . . . . . . . . . . . . . . . . . . | 20 | 15 | 20 |

| Asset class | Description of assets included | Class Life (in years) | Recovery Periods (in years) General Depreciation System | Alternative Depreciation System |
|---|---|---|---|---|
| 00.4 | **Industrial Steam and Electric Generation and/or Distribution Systems:** Includes assets, whether such assets are section 1245 property or 1250 property, providing such assets are depreciable, used in the production and/or distribution of electricity with rated total capacity in excess of 500 Kilowatts and/or assets used in the production and/or distribution of steam with rated total capacity in excess of 12,500 pounds per hour for use by the taxpayer in its industrial manufacturing process or plant activity and not ordinarily available for sale to others. Does not include buildings and structural components as defined in section 1.48-1(e) of the regulations. Assets used to generate and/or distribute electricity or steam of the type described above but of lesser rated capacity are not included, but are included in the appropriate manufacturing equipment classes elsewhere specified. Also includes electric generating and steam distribution assets, which may utilize steam produced by a waste reduction and resource recovery plant, used by the taxpayer in its industrial manufacturing process or plant activity. Steam and chemical recovery boiler systems used for the recovery and regeneration of chemicals used in manufacturing, with rated capacity in excess of that described above, with specifically related distribution and return systems are not included but are included in appropriate manufacturing equipment classes elsewhere specified. An example of an excluded steam and chemical recovery boiler system is that used in the pulp and paper manufacturing industry . . . . . . . . . . . . . . . . . . . . . . . . | 22 | 15 | 22 |

[Table B-2]

| Asset class | Description of assets included | Class Life (in years) | General Depreciation System | Alternative Depreciation System |
|---|---|---|---|---|
| DEPRECIABLE ASSETS USED IN THE FOLLOWING ACTIVITIES: | | | | |
| 01.1 | **Agriculture:** Includes machinery and equipment, grain bins, and fences but no other land improvements, that are used in the production of crops or plants, vines, and trees; livestock; the operation of farm dairies, nurseries, greenhouses, sod farms, mushrooms cellars, cranberry bogs, apiaries, and fur farms; the performance of agriculture, animal husbandry, and horticultural services [new farm machinery and equipment placed in service in 2009 or after 2017 may qualify for a 5-year recovery period (Code Sec. 168(e)(3)(B)(vii)). See ¶ 118—Editor.] . . . | 10 | 7 | 10 |
| 01.11 | **Cotton Ginning Assets** . . . . . . . . . . . . . | 12 | 7 | 12 |
| 01.21 | **Cattle, Breeding or Dairy** . . . . . . . . . . . | 7 | 5 | 7 |
| 01.221 | **Any breeding or work horse that is 12 years old or less at the time it is placed in service**[1] . . . . . . . . . . . . . . . . . . . . . . | 10 | 7 | 10 |

| Asset class | Description of assets included | Class Life (in years) | Recovery Periods (in years) General Depreciation System | Alternative Depreciation System |
|---|---|---|---|---|
| 01.222 | **Any breeding or work horse that is more than 12 years old at the time it is placed in service**[1] | 10 | 3 | 10 |
| 01.223 | **Any race horse that is more than 2 years old at the time it is placed in service**[Any race horse placed in service after December 31, 2008 and before January 1, 2021 is three-year property (Code Sec. 168(e)(3)(A)(i)). See ¶ 103—Editor.][1] | [2] | 3 | 12 |
| 01.224 | **Any horse that is more than 12 years old at the time it is placed in service and that is neither a race horse nor a horse described in class 01.222**[1] | [2] | 3 | 12 |
| 01.225 | **Any horse not described in classes 01.221, 01.222, 01.223, or 01.224** | [2] | 7 | 12 |
| 01.23 | **Hogs, Breeding** | 3 | 3 | 3 |
| 01.24 | **Sheep and Goats, Breeding** | 5 | 5 | 5 |
| 01.3 | **Farm buildings except structures included in Class 01.4** | 25 | 20 | 25 |
| 01.4 | **Single purpose agricultural or horticultural structures (within the meaning of section 168(i)(13) of the Code)** | 15 | 10 [3] | 15 |
| 10.0 | **Mining:** Includes assets used in the mining and quarrying of metallic and nonmetallic minerals (including sand, gravel, stone, and clay) and the milling, beneficiation and other primary preparation of such materials | 10 | 7 | 10 |
| 13.0 | **Offshore Drilling:** Includes assets used in offshore drilling for oil and gas such as floating, self-propelled and other drilling vessels, barges, platforms, and drilling equipment and support vessels such as tenders, barges, towboats and crewboats. Excludes oil and gas production assets | 7.5 | 5 | 7.5 |
| 13.1 | **Drilling of Oil and Gas Wells:** Includes assets used in the drilling of onshore oil and gas wells and the provision of geophysical and other exploration services; and the provision of such oil and gas field services as chemical treatment, plugging and abandoning of wells and cementing or perforating well casings. Does not include assets used in the performance of any of these activities and services by integrated petroleum and natural gas producers for their own account | 6 | 5 | 6 |

| Asset class | Description of assets included | Class Life (in years) | Recovery Periods (in years) General Depreciation System | Alternative Depreciation System |
|---|---|---|---|---|
| 13.2 | **Exploration for and Production of Petroleum and Natural Gas Deposits:** Includes assets used by petroleum and natural gas producers for drilling wells and production of petroleum and natural gas, including gathering pipelines and related storage facilities. Also includes petroleum and natural gas offshore transportation facilities used by producers and others consisting of platforms (other than drilling platforms classified in Class 13.0), compression or pumping equipment, and gathering and transmission lines to the first onshore transshipment facility. The assets used in the first onshore transshipment facility are also included and consist of separation equipment (used for separation of natural gas, liquids, and solids), compression or pumping equipment (other than equipment classified in Class 49.23), and liquid holding or storage facilities (other than those classified in Class 49.25). Does not include support vessels . . . . . . . . . . . . . . | 14 | 7[3A] | 14 |
| 13.3 | **Petroleum Refining:** Includes assets used for the distillation, fractionation, and catalytic cracking of crude petroleum into gasoline and its other components . . . . . . . . . . . . . . . . . . . . . . | 16 | 10 | 16 |
| 15.0 | **Construction:** Includes assets used in construction by general building, special trade, heavy and marine construction contractors, operative and investment builders, real estate subdividers and developers, and others except railroads . . . . . . . . . . . . . . . . . . . | 6 | 5 | 6 |
| 20.1 | **Manufacture of Grain and Grain Mill Products:** Includes assets used in the production of flours, cereals, livestock feeds, and other grain and grain mill products . . . . . . . . . . | 17 | 10 | 17 |
| 20.2 | **Manufacture of Sugar and Sugar Products:** Includes assets used in the production of raw sugar, syrup, or finished sugar from sugar cane or sugar beets . . . . . . . . . . . . . . . . | 18 | 10 | 18 |
| 20.3 | **Manufacture of Vegetable Oils and Vegetable Oil Products:** Includes assets used in the production of oil from vegetable materials and the manufacture of related vegetable oil products . . . . . . . . . . . . . . . . . . . . . . . . . . . . . . | 18 | 10 | 18 |
| 20.4 | **Manufacture of Other Food and Kindred Products:** Includes assets used in the production of foods and beverages not included in classes 20.1, 20.2 and 20.3 . . . . . . . . . . . . . . . . . | 12 | 7 | 12 |

| Asset class | Description of assets included | Class Life (in years) | Recovery Periods (in years) General Depreciation System | Alternative Depreciation System |
|---|---|---|---|---|
| 20.5 | **Manufacture of Food and Beverages—Special Handling Devices:** Includes assets defined as specialized materials handling devices such as returnable pallets, palletized containers, and fish processing equipment including boxes, baskets, carts, and flaking trays used in activities as defined in classes 20.1, 20.2, 20.3 and 20.4. Does not include general purpose small tools such as wrenches and drills, both hand and power-driven, and other general purpose equipment such as conveyors, transfer equipment, and materials handling devices | 4 | 3 | 4 |
| 21.0 | **Manufacture of Tobacco and Tobacco Products:** Includes assets used in the production of cigarettes, cigars, smoking and chewing tobacco, snuff, and other tobacco products | 15 | 7 | 15 |
| 22.1 | **Manufacture of Knitted Goods:** Includes assets used in the production of knitted and netted fabrics and lace. Assets used in yarn preparation, bleaching, dyeing, printing, and other similar finishing processes, texturing, and packaging, are elsewhere classified | 7.5 | 5 | 7.5 |
| 22.2 | **Manufacture of Yarn, Thread, and Woven Fabric:** Includes assets used in the production of spun yarns including the preparing, blending, spinning, and twisting of fibers into yarns and threads, the preparation of yarns such as twisting, warping, and winding, the production of covered elastic yarn and thread, cordage, woven fabric, tire fabric, twisted jute for packaging, mattresses, pads, sheets, and industrial belts, and the processing of textile mill waste to recover fibers, flocks, and shoddies. Assets used to manufacture carpets, man-made fibers, and nonwovens, and assets used in texturing, bleaching, dyeing, printing, and other similar finishing processes, are elsewhere classified | 11 | 7 | 11 |

| Asset class | Description of assets included | Class Life (in years) | Recovery Periods (in years) General Depreciation System | Alternative Depreciation System |
|---|---|---|---|---|
| 22.3 | **Manufacture of Carpets, and Dyeing, Finishing, and Packaging of Textile Products and Manufacture of Medical and Dental Supplies:** Includes assets used in the production of carpets, rugs, mats, woven carpet backing, chenille, and other tufted products, and assets used in the joining together of backing with carpet yarn or fabric. Includes assets used in washing, scouring, bleaching, dyeing, printing, drying, and similar finishing processes applied to textile fabrics, yarns, threads, and other textile goods. Includes assets used in the production and packaging of textile products, other than apparel, by creasing, forming, trimming, cutting, and sewing, such as the preparation of carpet and fabric samples, or similar joining together processes (other than the production of scrim reinforced paper products and laminated paper products) such as the sewing and folding of hosiery and panty hose, and the creasing, folding, trimming, and cutting of fabrics to produce nonwoven products, such as disposable diapers and sanitary products. Also includes assets used in the production of medical and dental supplies other than drugs and medicines. Assets used in the manufacture of nonwoven carpet backing, and hard surface floor covering such as tile, rubber, and cork, are elsewhere classified . | 9 | 5 | 9 |
| 22.4 | **Manufacture of Textured Yarns:** Includes assets used in the processing of yarns to impart bulk and/or stretch properties to the yarn. The principal machines involved are falsetwist, draw, beam-to-beam, and stuffer box texturing equipment and related highspeed twisters and winders. Assets, as described above, which are used to further process man-made fibers are elsewhere classified when located in the same plant in an integrated operation with man-made fiber producing assets. Assets used to manufacture man-made fibers and assets used in bleaching, dyeing, printing, and other similar finishing processes, are elsewhere classified . . . . . . . . . . . . . . . . | 8 | 5 | 8 |

| Asset class | Description of assets included | Class Life (in years) | Recovery Periods (in years) General Depreciation System | Alternative Depreciation System |
|---|---|---|---|---|
| 22.5 | **Manufacture of Nonwoven Fabrics:** Includes assets used in the production of nonwoven fabrics, felt goods including felt hats, padding, batting, wadding, oakum, and fillings, from new materials and from textile mill waste. Nonwoven fabrics are defined as fabrics (other than reinforced and laminated composites consisting of nonwovens and other products) manufactured by bonding natural and/or synthetic fibers and/or filaments by means of induced mechanical interlocking, fluid entanglement, chemical adhesion, thermal or solvent reaction, or by combination thereof other than natural hydration bonding as occurs with natural cellulose fibers. Such means include resin bonding, web bonding, and melt bonding. Specifically includes assets used to make flocked and needle punched products other than carpets and rugs. Assets, as described above, which are used to manufacture nonwovens are elsewhere classified when located in the same plant in an integrated operation with man-made fiber producing assets. Assets used to manufacture man-made fibers and assets used in bleaching, dyeing, printing, and other similar finishing processes, are elsewhere classified . . . . . . | 10 | 7 | 10 |
| 23.0 | **Manufacture of Apparel and Other Finished Products:** Includes assets used in the production of clothing and fabricated textile products by the cutting and sewing of woven fabrics, other textile products, and furs; but does not include assets used in the manufacture of apparel from rubber and leather . . . . . . . . | 9 | 5 | 9 |
| 24.1 | **Cutting of Timber:** Includes logging machinery and equipment and roadbuilding equipment used by logging and sawmill operators and pulp manufacturers for their own account . . . . . | 6 | 5 | 6 |
| 24.2 | **Sawing of Dimensional Stock from Logs:** Includes machinery and equipment installed in permanent or well established sawmills . | 10 | 7 | 10 |
| 24.3 | **Sawing of Dimensional Stock from Logs:** Includes machinery and equipment installed in sawmills characterized by temporary foundations and a lack, or minimum amount, of lumberhandling, drying, and residue disposal equipment and facilities . . . . . . . . | 6 | 5 | 6 |
| 24.4 | **Manufacture of Wood Products, and Furniture:** Includes assets used in the production of plywood, hardboard, flooring, veneers, furniture, and other wood products, including the treatment of poles and timber . . . . . . . | 10 | 7 | 10 |

| Asset class | Description of assets included | Class Life (in years) | Recovery Periods (in years) General Depreciation System | Alternative Depreciation System |
|---|---|---|---|---|
| 26.1 | **Manufacture of Pulp and Paper:** Includes assets for pulp materials handling and storage, pulp mill processing, bleach processing, paper and paperboard manufacturing, and on-line finishing. Includes pollution control assets and all land improvements associated with the factory site or production process such as effluent ponds and canals, provided such improvements are depreciable but does not include buildings and structural components as defined in section 1.48-1(e)(1) of the regulations. Includes steam and chemical recovery boiler systems, with any rated capacity, used for the recovery and regeneration of chemicals used in manufacturing. Does not include assets used either in pulpwood logging, or in the manufacture of hardboard . . . . . . . . . . . . | 13 | 7 | 13 |
| 26.2 | **Manufacture of Converted Paper, Paperboard, and Pulp Products:** Includes assets used for modification, or remanufacture of paper and pulp into converted products, such as paper coated off the paper machine, paper bags, paper boxes, cartons and envelopes. Does not include assets used for manufacture of nonwovens that are elsewhere classified . . . . . . . . . . . | 10 | 7 | 10 |
| 27.0 | **Printing, Publishing, and Allied Industries:** Includes assets used in printing by one or more processes, such as letter-press, lithography, gravure, or screen; the performance of services for the printing trade, such as bookbinding, typesetting, engraving, photo-engraving, and electrotyping; and the publication of newspapers, books, and periodicals . . . . . . | 11 | 7 | 11 |

| Asset class | Description of assets included | Class Life (in years) | Recovery Periods (in years) General Depreciation System | Alternative Depreciation System |
|---|---|---|---|---|
| 28.0 | **Manufacture of Chemicals and Allied Products:** Includes assets used to manufacture basic organic and inorganic chemicals; chemical products to be used in further manufacture, such as synthetic fibers and plastics materials; and finished chemical products. Includes assets used to further process man-made fibers, to manufacture plastic film, and to manufacture nonwoven fabrics, when such assets are located in the same plant in an integrated operation with chemical products producing assets. Also includes assets used to manufacture photographic supplies, such as film, photographic paper, sensitized photographic paper, and developing chemicals. Includes all land improvements associated with plant site or production processes, such as effluent ponds and canals, provided such land improvements are depreciable but does not include buildings and structural components as defined in section 1.48-1(e) of the regulations. Does not include assets used in the manufacture of finished rubber and plastic products or in the production of natural gas products, butane, propane, and by-products of natural gas production plants . . . . . . . . . . . . . . . . . . | 9.5 | 5 | 9.5 |
| 30.1 | **Manufacture of Rubber Products:** Includes assets used for the production of products from natural, synthetic, or reclaimed rubber, gutta percha, balata, or gutta siak, such as tires, tubes, rubber footwear, mechanical rubber goods, heels and soles, flooring, and rubber sundries, and in the recapping, retreading, and rebuilding of tires . . . . . . . . . . . . . . . . . . . . . . . . | 14 | 7 | 14 |
| 30.11[4] | **Manufacture of Rubber Products—Special Tools and Devices:** Includes assets defined as special tools, such as jigs, dies, mandrels, molds, lasts, patterns, specialty containers, pallets, shells; and tire molds, and accessory parts such as rings and insert plates used in activities as defined in class 30.1. Does not include tire building drums and accessory parts and general purpose small tools such as wrenches and drills, both power and hand-driven, and other general purpose equipment such as conveyors and transfer equipment . . . . . . . | 4 | 3 | 4 |
| 30.2 | **Manufacture of Finished Plastic Products:** Includes assets used in the manufacture of plastics products and the molding of primary plastics for the trade. Does not include assets used in the manufacture of basic plastics materials nor the manufacture of phonograph records . . . . . . . . . . . . . . . . . . . . . . . . | 11 | 7 | 11 |

| Asset class | Description of assets included | Class Life (in years) | Recovery Periods (in years) General Depreciation System | Alternative Depreciation System |
|---|---|---|---|---|
| 30.21 | **Manufacture of Finished Plastic Products—Special Tools:** Includes assets defined as special tools, such as jigs, dies, fixtures, molds, patterns, gauges, and specialty transfer and shipping devices, used in activities as defined in class 30.2. Special tools are specifically designed for the production or processing of particular parts and have no significant utilitarian value and cannot be adapted to further or different use after changes or improvements are made in the model design of the particular part produced by the special tools. Does not include general purpose small tools such as wrenches and drills, both hand and power-driven, and other general purpose equipment such as conveyors, transfer equipment, and materials handling devices . . . . . . . . . . . . | 3.5 | 3 | 3.5 |
| 31.0 | **Manufacture of Leather and Leather Products:** Includes assets used in the tanning, currying, and finishing of hides and skins; the processing of fur pelts; and the manufacture of finished leather products, such as footwear, belting, apparel, and luggage . . . | 11 | 7 | 11 |
| 32.1 | **Manufacture of Glass Products:** Includes assets used in the production of flat, blown, or pressed products of glass, such as float and window glass, glass containers, glassware and fiberglass. Does not include assets used in the manufacture of lenses . . | 14 | 7 | 14 |
| 32.11 | **Manufacture of Glass Products—Special Tools:** Includes assets defined as special tools such as molds, patterns, pallets, and specialty transfer and shipping devices such as steel racks to transport automotive glass, used in activities as defined in class 32.1. Special tools are specifically designed for the production or processing of particular parts and have no significant utilitarian value and cannot be adapted to further or different use after changes or improvements are made in the model design of the particular part produced by the special tools. Does not include general purpose small tools such as wrenches and drills, both hand and power-driven, and other general purpose equipment such as conveyors, transfer equipment, and materials handling devices . . . . . . . . . . . . | 2.5 | 3 | 2.5 |
| 32.2 | **Manufacture of Cement:** Includes assets used in the production of cement, but does not include any assets used in the manufacture of concrete and concrete products nor in any mining or extraction process . . . . . . . . . . . . . . . . . . . . . . . . | 20 | 15 | 20 |

| Asset class | Description of assets included | Class Life (in years) | Recovery Periods (in years) General Depreciation System | Alternative Depreciation System |
|---|---|---|---|---|
| 32.3 | **Manufacture of Other Stone and Clay Products:** Includes assets used in the manufacture of products from materials in the form of clay and stone, such as brick, tile, and pipe; pottery and related products, such as vitreous-china, plumbing fixtures, earthenware and ceramic insulating materials; and also includes assets used in manufacture of concrete and concrete products. Does not include assets used in any mining or extraction processes . . . . . . . . . | 15 | 7 | 15 |
| 33.2 | **Manufacture of Primary Nonferrous Metals:** Includes assets used in the smelting, refining, and electrolysis of nonferrous metals from ore, pig, or scrap, the rolling, drawing, and alloying of nonferrous metals; the manufacture of castings, forgings, and other basic products of nonferrous metals; and the manufacture of nails, spikes, structural shapes, tubing, wire, and cable . . . . . . . . . | 14 | 7 | 14 |
| 33.21 | **Manufacture of Primary Nonferrous Metals—Special Tools:** Includes assets defined as special tools such as dies, jigs, molds, patterns, fixtures, gauges, and drawings concerning such special tools used in the activities as defined in class 33.2, Manufacture of Primary Nonferrous Metals. Special tools are specifically designed for the production or processing of particular products or parts and have no significant utilitarian value and cannot be adapted to further or different use after changes or improvements are made in the model design of the particular part produced by the special tools. Does not include general purpose small tools such as wrenches and drills, both hand and power-driven, and other general purpose equipment such as conveyors, transfer equipment, and materials handling devices. Rolls, mandrels and refractories are not included in class 33.21 but are included in class 33.2 . . . . . . | 6.5 | 5 | 6.5 |
| 33.3 | **Manufacture of Foundry Products:** Includes assets used in the casting of iron and steel, including related operations such as molding and coremaking. Also includes assets used in the finishing of castings and patternmaking when performed at the foundry, all special tools and related land improvements . . . . . . . . . . . . . . . . . . . . | 14 | 7 | 14 |

| Asset class | Description of assets included | Class Life (in years) | Recovery Periods (in years) General Depreciation System | Alternative Depreciation System |
|---|---|---|---|---|
| 33.4 | **Manufacture of Primary Steel Mill Products:** Includes assets used in the smelting, reduction, and refining of iron and steel from ore, pig, or scrap; the rolling, drawing and alloying of steel; the manufacture of nails, spikes, structural shapes, tubing, wire, and cable. Includes assets used by steel service centers, ferrous metal forges, and assets used in coke production, regardless of ownership. Also includes related land improvements and all special tools used in the above activities . | 15 | 7 | 15 |
| 34.0 | **Manufacture of Fabricated Metal Products:** Includes assets used in the production of metal cans, tinware, fabricated structural metal products, metal stampings, and other ferrous and nonferrous metal and wire products not elsewhere classified. Does not include assets used to manufacture non-electric heating apparatus . . . . . . . . . . . . | 12 | 7 | 12 |
| 34.01 | **Manufacturer of Fabricated Metal Products—Special Tools:** Includes assets defined as special tools such as dies, jigs, molds, patterns, fixtures, gauges, and returnable containers and drawings concerning such special tools used in the activities as defined in class 34.0. Special tools are specifically designed for the production or processing of particular machine components, products, or parts, and have no significant utilitarian value and cannot be adapted to further or different use after changes or improvements are made in the model design of the particular part produced by the special tools. Does not include general purpose small tools such as wrenches and drills, both hand and power-driven, and other general purpose equipment such as conveyors, transfer equipment, and materials handling devices . . . . . . . . . . . . | 3 | 3 | 3 |

| Asset class | Description of assets included | Class Life (in years) | Recovery Periods (in years) General Depreciation System | Recovery Periods (in years) Alternative Depreciation System |
|---|---|---|---|---|
| 35.0 | **Manufacture of Electrical and Non-Electrical Machinery and Other Mechanical Products:** Includes assets used to manufacture or rebuild finished machinery and equipment and replacement parts thereof such as machine tools, general industrial and special industry machinery, electrical power generation, transmission, and distribution systems, space heating, cooling, and refrigeration systems, commercial and home appliances, farm and garden machinery, construction machinery, mining and oil field machinery, internal combustion engines (except those elsewhere classified), turbines (except those that power airborne vehicles), batteries, lamps and lighting fixtures, carbon and graphite products, and electromechanical and mechanical products including business machines, instruments, watches and clocks, vending and amusement machines, photographic equipment, medical and dental equipment and appliances, and ophthalmic goods. Includes assets used by manufacturers or rebuilders of such finished machinery and equipment in activities elsewhere classified such as the manufacture of castings, forgings, rubber and plastic products, electronic subassemblies or other manufacturing activities if the interim products are used by the same manufacturer primarily in the manufacture, assembly, or rebuilding of such finished machinery and equipment. Does not include assets used in mining, assets used in the manufacture of primary ferrous and nonferrous metals, assets included in class 00.11 through 00.4 and assets elsewhere classified . . . . . . . . . | 10 | 7 | 10 |

| Asset class | Description of assets included | Class Life (in years) | Recovery Periods (in years) General Depreciation System | Alternative Depreciation System |
|---|---|---|---|---|
| 36.0 | **Manufacture of Electronic Components, Products, and Systems:** Includes assets used in the manufacture of electronic communication, computation, instrumentation and control system, including airborne applications, also includes assets used in the manufacture of electronic products such as frequency and amplitude modulated transmitters and receivers, electronic switching stations, television cameras, video recorders, record players and tape recorders, computers and computer peripheral machines, and electronic instruments, watches, and clocks; also includes assets used in the manufacture of components, provided their primary use is in products and systems defined above such as electron tubes, capacitors, coils, resistors, printed circuit substrates, switches, harness cables, lasers, fiber optic devices, and magnetic media devices. Specifically excludes assets used to manufacture electronic products and components, photocopiers, typewriters, postage meters and other electromechanical and mechanical business machines and instruments that are elsewhere classified. Does not include semiconductor manufacturing equipment included in class 36.1 . . . . . . . . . . . . . . . | 6 | 5 | 6 |
| 36.1 | **Manufacture of Semiconductors:** Any Semiconductor Manufacturing Equipment . . . . . . . . . . . . . . . . . . . . . . | 5 | 5 | 5 |

| Asset class | Description of assets included | Class Life (in years) | Recovery Periods (in years) General Depreciation System | Alternative Depreciation System |
|---|---|---|---|---|
| 37.11 | **Manufacture of Motor Vehicles:** Includes assets used in the manufacture and assembly of finished automobiles, trucks, trailers, motor homes, and buses. Does not include assets used in mining, printing and publishing, production of primary metals, electricity, or steam, or the manufacture of glass, industrial chemicals, batteries, or rubber products, which are classified elsewhere. Includes assets used in manufacturing activities elsewhere classified other than those excluded above, where such activities are incidental to and an integral part of the manufacture and assembly of finished motor vehicles such as the manufacture of parts and subassemblies of fabricated metal products, electrical equipment, textiles, plastics, leather, and foundry and forging operations. Does not include any assets not classified in manufacturing activity classes, e.g., does not include any assets classified in asset guideline classes 00.11 through 00.4. Activities will be considered incidental to the manufacture and assembly of finished motor vehicles only if 75 percent or more of the value of the products produced under one roof are used for the manufacture and assembly of finished motor vehicles. Parts that are produced as a normal replacement stock complement in connection with the manufacture and assembly of finished motor vehicles are considered used for the manufacture and assembly of finished motor vehicles. Does not include assets used in the manufacture of component parts if these assets are used by taxpayers not engaged in the assembly of finished motor vehicles . . . | 12 | 7 | 12 |
| 37.12 | **Manufacture of Motor Vehicles—Special Tools:** Includes assets defined as special tools, such as jigs, dies, fixtures, molds, patterns, gauges, and specialty transfer and shipping devices, owned by manufacturers of finished motor vehicles and used in qualified activities as defined in class 37.11. Special tools are specifically designed for the production or processing of particular motor vehicle components and have no significant utilitarian value, and cannot be adapted to further or different use, after changes or improvements are made in the model design of the particular part produced by the special tools. Does not include general purpose small tools such as wrenches and drills, both hand and powerdriven, and other general purpose equipment such as conveyors, transfer equipment, and materials handling devices . | 3 | 3 | 3 |

| Asset class | Description of assets included | Class Life (in years) | Recovery Periods (in years) General Depreciation System | Alternative Depreciation System |
|---|---|---|---|---|
| 37.2 | **Manufacture of Aerospace Products:** Includes assets used in the manufacture and assembly of airborne vehicles and their component parts including hydraulic, pneumatic, electrical, and mechanical systems. Does not include assets used in the production of electronic airborne detection, guidance, control, radiation, computation, test, navigation, and communication equipment or the components thereof . . . . | 10 | 7 | 10 |
| 37.31 | **Ship and Boat Building Machinery and Equipment:** Includes assets used in the manufacture and repair of ships, boats, caissons, marine drilling rigs, and special fabrications not included in asset classes 37.32 and 37.33. Specifically includes all manufacturing and repairing machinery and equipment, including machinery and equipment used in the operation of assets included in asset class 37.32. Excludes buildings and their structural components . . . . . . . . . . . . . . . . . . . . . . | 12 | 7 | 12 |
| 37.32 | **Ship and Boat Building Dry Docks and Land Improvements:** Includes assets used in the manufacture and repair of ships, boats, caissons, marine drilling rigs, and special fabrications not included in asset classes 37.31 and 37.33. Specifically includes floating and fixed dry docks, ship basins, graving docks, shipways, piers, and all other land improvements such as water, sewer, and electric systems. Excludes buildings and their structural components . . . . . . . . . . . . . . . . . . . . . . | 16 | 10 | 16 |
| 37.33 | **Ship and Boat Building—Special Tools:** Includes assets defined as special tools such as dies, jigs, molds, patterns, fixtures, gauges, and drawings concerning such special tools used in the activities defined in classes 37.31 and 37.32. Special tools are specifically designed for the production or processing of particular machine components, products, or parts, and have no significant utilitarian value and cannot be adapted to further or different use after changes or improvements are made in the model design of the particular part produced by the special tools. Does not include general purpose small tools such as wrenches and drills, both hand and power-driven, and other general purpose equipment such as conveyors, transfer equipment, and materials handling devices . . . . . . . . . . . . . . . . . . | 6.5 | 5 | 6.5 |
| 37.41 | **Manufacture of Locomotives:** Includes assets used in building or rebuilding railroad locomotives (including mining and industrial locomotives). Does not include assets of railroad transportation companies or assets of companies which manufacture components of locomotives but do not manufacture finished locomotives . . . . . . . | 11.5 | 7 | 11.5 |

| Asset class | Description of assets included | Class Life (in years) | Recovery Periods (in years) General Depreciation System | Alternative Depreciation System |
|---|---|---|---|---|
| 37.42 | **Manufacture of Railroad Cars:** Includes assets used in building or rebuilding railroad freight or passenger cars (including rail transit cars). Does not include assets of railroad transportation companies or assets of companies which manufacture components of railroad cars but do not manufacture finished railroad cars . . . . . . . . . . . . . . . . | 12 | 7 | 12 |
| 39.0 | **Manufacture of Athletic, Jewelry and Other Goods:** Includes assets used in the production of jewelry; musical instruments; toys and sporting goods; motion picture and television films and tapes; and pens, pencils, office and art supplies, brooms, brushes, caskets, etc. | 12 | 7 | 12 |
| | **Railroad Transportation:** Classes with the prefix 40 include the assets identified below that are used in the commercial and contract carrying of passengers and freight by rail. Assets of electrified railroads will be classified in a manner corresponding to that set forth below for railroads not independently operated as electric lines. Excludes the assets included in classes with the prefix beginning 00.1 and 00.2 above, and also excludes any non-depreciable assets included in Interstate Commerce Commission accounts enumerated for this class. | | | |
| 40.1 | **Railroad Machinery and Equipment:** Includes assets classified in the following Interstate Commerce Commission accounts:<br>**Roadway accounts:**<br>(16) Station and office buildings (freight handling machinery and equipment only)<br>(25) TOFC/COFC terminals (freight handling machinery and equipment only)<br>(26) Communication systems<br>(27) Signals and interlockers<br>(37) Roadway machines<br>(44) Shop machinery<br>Equipment Accounts:<br>(52) Locomotives<br>(53) Freight train cars<br>(54) Passenger train cars<br>(57) Work equipment . . . . . . . . . . . . . . . | 14 | 7 | 14 |

| Asset class | Description of assets included | Class Life (in years) | Recovery Periods (in years) General Depreciation System | Alternative Depreciation System |
|---|---|---|---|---|
| 40.2 | **Railroad Structures and Similar Improvements:** Includes assets classified in the following Interstate Commerce Commission road accounts: (6) Bridges, trestles, and culverts (7) Elevated structures (13) Fences, snowsheds, and signs (16) Station and office buildings (stations and other operating structures only)[4A] (17) Roadway buildings[4A] (18) Water stations (19) Fuel stations (20) Shops and enginehouses (25) TOFC/COFC terminals (operating structures only) (31) Power transmission systems (35) Miscellaneous structures (39) Public improvements construction . . . | 30 | 20 | 30 |
| 40.3 | **Railroad Wharves and Docks:** Includes assets classified in the following Interstate Commerce accounts: (23) Wharves and docks (24) Coal and ore wharves . . . . . . . . . . . . | 20 | 15 | 20 |
| 40.4 | **Railroad Track** . . . . . . . . . . . . . . . . . . | 10 | 7 | 10 |
| 40.51 | **Railroad Hydraulic Electric Generating Equipment** . . . . . . . . . . . . . . . . . . . . . | 50 | 20 | 50 |
| 40.52 | **Railroad Nuclear Electric Generating Equipment** . . . . . . . . . . . . . . . . . . . . . | 20 | 15 | 20 |
| 40.53 | **Railroad Steam Electric Generating Equipment** . . . . . . . . . . . . . . . . . . . . . | 28 | 20 | 28 |
| 40.54 | **Railroad Steam, Compressed Air, and Other Power Plant Equipment** . . . . . . . | 28 | 20 | 28 |
| 41.0 | **Motor Transport-Passengers:** Includes assets used in the urban and interurban commercial and contract carrying of passengers by road, except the transportation assets included in classes with the prefix 00.2 . . . . . . . . . . . . . . . . . . . . | 8 | 5 | 8 |
| 42.0 | **Motor Transport-Freight:** Includes assets used in the commercial and contract carrying of freight by road, except the transportation assets included in classes with the prefix 00.2 . . . . . . . . . . . . . . . . | 8 | 5 | 8 |
| 44.0 | **Water Transportation:** Includes assets used in the commercial and contract carrying of freight and passengers by water except the transportation assets included in classes with the prefix 00.2. Includes all related land improvements . . . | 20 | 15 | 20 |

| Asset class | Description of assets included | Class Life (in years) | Recovery Periods (in years) General Depreciation System | Alternative Depreciation System |
|---|---|---|---|---|
| 45.0 | **Air Transport:** Includes assets (except helicopters) used in commercial and contract carrying of passengers and freight by air. For purposes of section 1.167(a)-11(d)(2)(iv)(*a*) of the regulations, expenditures for "repair, maintenance, rehabilitation, or improvement" shall consist of direct maintenance expenses (irrespective of airworthiness provisions or charges) as defined by Civil Aeronautics Board uniform accounts 5200, maintenance burden (exclusive of expenses pertaining to maintenance buildings and improvements) as defined by Civil Aeronautics Board uniform accounts 5300, and expenditures which are not "excluded additions" as defined in section 1.167(a)-11(d)(2)(vi) of the regulations and which would be charged to property and equipment accounts in the Civil Aeronautics Board uniform system of accounts ...... | 12 | 7 | 12 |
| 45.1 | **Air Transport (restricted):** Includes each asset described in the description of class 45.0 which was held by the taxpayer on April 15, 1976, or is acquired by the taxpayer pursuant to a contract which was, on April 15, 1976, and at all times thereafter, binding on the taxpayer. This criterion of classification based on binding contract concept is to be applied in the same manner as under the general rules expressed in section 49(b)(1), (4), (5) and (8) of the Code (as in effect prior to its repeal by the Revenue Act of 1978, section § 12(c)(1), (d), 1978-3 C.B. 1, 60) .................. | 6 | 5 | 6 |
| 46.0 | **Pipeline Transportation:** Includes assets used in the private, commercial, and contract carrying of petroleum, gas and other products by means of pipes and conveyors. The trunk lines and related storage facilities of integrated petroleum and natural gas producers are included in this class. Excludes initial clearing and grading land improvements as specified in Rev. Rul. 72-403, 1972-2 C.B. 102, but includes all other related land improvements .................... | 22 | 15[4B] | 22[4B] |
| | **Telephone Communications:**[5] Includes the assets identified below and that are used in the provision of commercial and contract telephonic services such as: | | | |
| 48.11 | **Telephone Central Office Buildings:** Includes assets intended to house central office equipment, as defined in Federal Communications Commission Part 31 [32—Editor.]Account No. 212 whether section 1245 or section 1250 property .......... | 45 | 20[5A] | 45[5A] |

| Asset class | Description of assets included | Class Life (in years) | Recovery Periods (in years) General Depreciation System | Alternative Depreciation System |
|---|---|---|---|---|
| 48.12 | **Telephone Central Office Equipment:** Includes central office switching and related equipment as defined in Federal Communications Commission Part 31 [32—Editor.] Account No. 221. Does not include computer-based telephone central office switching equipment included in class 48.121. Does not include private branch exchange (PBX) equipment . . . . . . | 18 | 10 | 18 |
| 48.121 | **Computer-based Telephone Central Office Switching Equipment:** Includes equipment whose functions are those of a computer or peripheral equipment (as defined in section 168(i)(2)(B) of the Code) used in its capacity as telephone central office equipment. Does not include private branch exchange (PBX) equipment. | 9.5 | 5 | 9.5 |
| 48.13 | **Telephone Station Equipment:** Includes such station apparatus and connections as teletypewriters, telephones, booths, private exchanges, and comparable equipment as defined in Federal Communications Commission Part 31 [32—Editor.]Account Nos. 231, 232, and 234 . . . | 10 | 7 [6] | 10 [6] |
| 48.14 | **Telephone Distribution Plant:** Includes such assets as pole lines, cable, aerial wire, underground conduits, and comparable equipment, and related land improvements as defined in Federal Communications Commission Part 31 [32—Editor.]Account Nos. 241, 242.1, 242.2, 242.3, 242.4, 243, and 244 . . . . . . . . . . . . . . . . | 24 | 15 | 24 |
| 48.2 | **Radio and Television Broadcasting:** Includes assets used in radio and television broadcasting, except transmitting towers . . | 6 | 5 | 6 |
| | **Telegraph, Ocean Cable, and Satellite Communications (TOCSC)** includes communications-related assets used to provide domestic and international radio-telegraph, wire-telegraph, ocean-cable, and satellite communications services; also includes related land improvements. If property described in Classes 48.31—48.45 is comparable to telephone distribution plant described in Class 48.14 and used for 2-way exchange of voice and data communication which is the equivalent of telephone communication, such property is assigned a class life of 24 years under this revenue procedure. Comparable equipment does not include cable television equipment used primarily for 1-way communication. | | | |
| 48.31 | **TOCSC-Electric Power Generating and Distribution Systems:** Includes assets used in the provision of electric power by generation, modulation, rectification, channelization, control, and distribution. Does not include these assets when they are installed on customers' premises . . . . . . . . . . . . . . . . . . . . . . . | 19 | 10 | 19 |

| Asset class | Description of assets included | Class Life (in years) | Recovery Periods (in years) General Depreciation System | Alternative Depreciation System |
|---|---|---|---|---|
| 48.32 | **TOCSC-High Frequency Radio and Microwave Systems:** Includes assets such as transmitters and receivers, antenna supporting structures, antennas, transmission lines from equipment to antenna, transmitter cooling systems, and control and amplification equipment. Does not include cable and long-line systems . . . | 13 | 7 | 13 |
| 48.33 | **TOCSC-Cable and Long-line Systems:** Includes assets such as transmission lines, pole lines, ocean cables, buried cable and conduit, repeaters, repeater stations, and other related assets. Does not include high frequency radio or microwave systems . . . | 26.5 | 20 | 26.5 |
| 48.34 | **TOCSC-Central Office Control Equipment:** Includes assets for general control, switching, and monitoring of communications signals including electromechanical switching and channeling apparatus, multiplexing equipment, patching and monitoring facilities, in-house cabling, teleprinter equipment, and associated site improvements . . . . . . . . . . . . . . . . . . . | 16.5 | 10 | 16.5 |
| 48.35 | **TOCSC-Computerized Switching, Channeling, and Associated Control Equipment:** Includes central office switching computers, interfacing computers, other associated specialized control equipment, and site improvements . . . . . . . . . . . . . . . . . . . | 10.5 | 7 | 10.5 |
| 48.36 | **TOCSC-Satellite Ground Segment Property:** Includes assets such as fixed earth station equipment, antennas, satellite communications equipment, and interface equipment used in satellite communications. Does not include general purpose equipment or equipment used in satellite space segment property . . . . . . . . . . . . . . . . . . . . . . . | 10 | 7 | 10 |
| 48.37 | **TOCSC-Satellite Space Segment Property:** Includes satellites and equipment used for telemetry, tracking, control, and monitoring when used in satellite communications . . . | 8 | 5 | 8 |
| 48.38 | **TOCSC-Equipment Installed on Customer's Premises:** Includes assets installed on customer's premises, such as computers, terminal equipment, power generation and distribution systems, private switching center, teleprinters, facsimile equipment, and other associated and related equipment . . . | 10 | 7 | 10 |
| 48.39 | **TOCSC-Support and Service Equipment:** Includes assets used to support but not engage in communications. Includes store, warehouse and shop tools, and test and laboratory assets . . . . . . . . . . . . . . . . . | 13.5 | 7 | 13.5 |

| Asset class | Description of assets included | Class Life (in years) | Recovery Periods (in years) General Depreciation System | Alternative Depreciation System |
|---|---|---|---|---|
| | **Cable Television (CATV):** Includes communications-related assets used to provide cable television [(]community antenna services). Does not include assets used to provide subscribers with two-way communications services. | | | |
| 48.41 | **CATV-Headend:** Includes assets such as towers, antennas, preamplifiers, converters, modulation equipment, and program non-duplication systems. Does not include headend buildings and program origination assets . . . . . . . . . | 11 | 7 | 11 |
| 48.42 | **CATV-Subscriber Connection and Distribution Systems:** Includes assets such as trunk and feeder cable, connecting hardware, amplifiers, power equipment, passive devices, directional taps, pedestals, pressure taps, drop cables, matching transformers, multiple set connector equipment, and converters . . . . | 10 | 7 | 10 |
| 48.43 | **CATV-Program Origination:** Includes assets such as cameras, film chains, video tape recorders, lighting, and remote location equipment excluding vehicles. Does not include buildings and their structural components . . . . . . . . . . . . . . . . . . . . . . | 9 | 5 | 9 |
| 48.44 | **CATV-Service and Test:** Includes assets such as oscilloscopes, field strength meters, spectrum analyzers, and cable testing equipment, but does not include vehicles . . . . . . . . . . . . . . . . . . . . . . . . | 8.5 | 5 | 8.5 |
| 48.45 | **CATV-Microwave Systems:** Includes assets such as towers, antennas, transmitting and receiving equipment, and broad band microwave assets if used in the provision of cable television services. Does not include assets used in the provision of common carrier services . . . . . . . . . . . . . | 9.5 | 5 | 9.5 |
| | **Electric, Gas, Water and Steam, Utility Services:** Includes assets used in the production, transmission and distribution of electricity, gas, steam, or water for sale including related land improvements. | | | |
| 49.11 | **Electric Utility Hydraulic Production Plant:** Includes assets used in the hydraulic power production of electricity for sale, including related land improvements, such as dams, flumes, canals, and waterways . . . . . . . . . | 50 | 20 | 50 |
| 49.12 | **Electric Utility Nuclear Production Plant:** Includes assets used in the nuclear power production and electricity for sale and related land improvements. Does not include nuclear fuel assemblies . . . . . . . . . . . . . . . . . . . | 20 | 15 | 20 |

| Asset class | Description of assets included | Class Life (in years) | Recovery Periods (in years) General Depreciation System | Alternative Depreciation System |
|---|---|---|---|---|
| 49.121 | **Electric Utility Nuclear Fuel Assemblies:** Includes initial core and replacement core nuclear fuel assemblies (i.e., the composite of fabricated nuclear fuel and container) when used in a boiling water, pressurized water, or high temperature gas reactor used in the production of electricity. Does not include nuclear fuel assemblies used in breeder reactors | 5 | 5 | 5 |
| 49.13 | **Electric Utility Steam Production Plant:** Includes assets used in the steam power production of electricity for sale, combustion turbines operated in a combined cycle with a conventional steam unit and related land improvements. Also includes package boilers, electric generators and related assets such as electricity and steam distribution systems as used by a waste reduction and resource recovery plant if the steam or electricity is normally for sale to others | 28 | 20 | 28 |
| 49.14 | **Electric Utility Transmission and Distribution Plant:** Includes assets used in the transmission and distribution of electricity for sale and related land improvements. Excludes initial clearing and grading land improvements as specified in Rev. Rul. 72-403, 1972-2 C.B. 102 | 30 | 20 [6A] | 30 [6A] |
| 49.15 | **Electric Utility Combustion Turbine Production Plant:** Includes assets used in the production of electricity for sale by the use of such prime movers as jet engines, combustion turbines, diesel engines, gasoline engines, and other internal combustion engines, their associated power turbines and/or generators, and related land improvements. Does not include combustion turbines operated in a combined cycle with a conventional steam unit | 20 | 15 | 20 |
| 49.21 | **Gas Utility Distribution Facilities:** Includes gas water heaters and gas conversion equipment installed by utility on customers' premises on a rental basis | 35 | 20[6B] | 35 |
| 49.221 | **Gas Utility Manufactured Gas Production Plants:** Includes assets used in the manufacture of gas having chemical and/or physical properties which do not permit complete interchangeability with domestic natural gas. Does not include gas producing systems and related systems used in waste reduction and resource recovery plants which are elsewhere classified | 30 | 20 | 30 |
| 49.222 | **Gas Utility Substitute Natural Gas (SNG) Production Plant (naphtha or lighter hydrocarbon feedstocks):** Includes assets used in the catalytic conversion of feedstocks or naphtha or lighter hydrocarbons to a gaseous fuel which is completely interchangeable with domestic natural gas | 14 | 7 | 14 |

| *Asset class* | *Description of assets included* | *Class Life (in years)* | *Recovery Periods (in years) General Depreciation System* | *Recovery Periods (in years) Alternative Depreciation System* |
|---|---|---|---|---|
| 49.223 | **Substitute Natural Gas-Coal Gasification:** Includes assets used in the manufacture and production of pipeline quality gas from coal using the basic Lurgi process with advanced methanation. Includes all process plant equipment and structures used in this coal gasification process and all utility assets such as cooling systems, water supply and treatment facilities, and assets used in the production and distribution of electricity and steam for use by the taxpayer in a gasification plant and attendant coal mining site processes but not for assets used in the production and distribution of electricity and steam for sale to others. Also includes all other related land improvements. Does not include assets used in the direct mining and treatment of coal prior to the gasification process itself . . . . . . . . . . . . . . . . . . . . . | 18 | 10 | 18 |
| 49.23 | **Natural Gas Production Plant** . . . . . . . . | 14 | 7 | 14 |
| 49.24 | **Gas Utility Trunk Pipelines and Related Storage Facilities:** Excluding initial clearing and grading land improvements as specified in Rev. Rul. 72-403 . . . . . . . . . . . . . . . . . . . . . . . . . . . . | 22 | 15 | 22 |
| 49.25 | **Liquefied Natural Gas Plant:** Includes assets used in the liquefaction, storage, and regasification of natural gas including loading and unloading connections, instrumentation equipment and controls, pumps, vaporizers and odorizers, tanks, and related land improvements. Also includes pipeline interconnections with gas transmission lines and distribution systems and marine terminal facilities . . . . . . . . . . | 22 | 15 | 22 |
| 49.3 | **Water Utilities:** Includes assets used in the gathering, treatment, and commercial distribution of water . . . . . . . . . . . . . . . . . . . . . . . . . . | 50 | 20 or 25 [7] | 50 |
| 49.4 | **Central Steam Utility Production and Distribution:** Includes assets used in the production and distribution of steam for sale. Does not include assets used in waste reduction and resource recovery plants which are elsewhere classified . . . . . . . . . . . . . . . . | 28 | 20 | 28 |

| Asset class | Description of assets included | Class Life (in years) | Recovery Periods (in years) General Depreciation System | Alternative Depreciation System |
|---|---|---|---|---|
| 49.5 | **Waste Reduction and Resource Recovery Plants:** Includes assets used in the conversion of refuse or other solid waste or biomass to heat or to a solid, liquid, or gaseous fuel. Also includes all process plant equipment and structures at the site used to receive, handle, collect, and process refuse or other solid waste or biomass to a solid, liquid, or gaseous fuel or to handle and burn refuse or other solid waste or biomass in a waterwall combustion system, oil or gas pyrolysis system, or refuse derived fuel system to create hot water, gas, steam and electricity. Includes material recovery and support assets used in refuse or solid refuse or solid waste receiving, collecting, handling, sorting, shredding, classifying, and separation systems. Does not include any package boilers, or electric generators and related assets such as electricity, hot water, steam and manufactured gas production plants classified in classes 00.4, 49.13, 49.221, and 49.4. Does include, however, all other utilities such as water supply and treatment facilities, ash handling and other related land improvements of a waste reduction and resource recovery plant . . . . . . . . . . . . . . | 10 | 7 | 10 |
| 50.0 | **Municipal Wastewater Treatment Plant** . | 24 | 15 | 24 |
| 51.0 | **Municipal Sewer** . . . . . . . . . . . . . . . . . | 50 | 20 or [7] 25 | 50 |
| 57.0 | **Distributive Trades and Services:** Includes assets used in wholesale and retail trade, and personal and professional services. Includes section 1245 assets used in marketing petroleum and petroleum products . . . . . . . . . . . . . . . . . . . . . . . . . . . | 9 | 5 | 9 [8] |
| 57.1 | **Distributive Trades and Services-Billboard, Service Station Buildings and Petroleum Marketing Land Improvements:** Includes section 1250 assets, including service station buildings [See ¶ 110—Editor.]and depreciable land improvements, whether section 1245 property or section 1250 property, used in the marketing of petroleum and petroleum products, but not including any of these facilities related to petroleum and natural gas trunk pipelines. Includes car wash buildings and related land improvements. Includes billboards, whether such assets are section 1245 property or section 1250 property. Excludes all other land improvements, buildings and structural components as defined in section 1.48-1(e) of the regulations . . . . . . . . . . . . . . . . . . . . | 20 | 15 | 20 |

| Asset class | Description of assets included | Class Life (in years) | Recovery Periods (in years) General Depreciation System | Alternative Depreciation System |
|---|---|---|---|---|
| 79.0 | **Recreation:** Includes assets used in the provision of entertainment services on payment of a fee or admission charge, as in the operation of bowling alleys, billiard and pool establishments, theaters, concert halls, and miniature golf courses. Does not include amusement and theme parks and assets which consist primarily of specialized land improvements or structures, such as golf courses, sports stadiums, race tracks, ski slopes, and buildings which house the assets used in entertainment services . . . . . . . . . | 10 | 7 | 10 |
| 80.0 | **Theme and Amusement Parks:** Includes assets used in the provision of rides, attractions, and amusements in activities defined as theme and amusement parks, and include appurtenances associated with a ride, attraction, amusement or theme setting within the park such as ticket booths, facades, shop interiors, and props, special purpose structures, and buildings other than warehouses, administration buildings, hotels, and motels. Includes all land improvements for or in support of park activities, (e.g., parking lots, sidewalks, waterways, bridges, fences, landscaping, etc.) and support functions (e.g., food and beverage retailing, souvenir vending and other nonlodging accommodations) if owned by the park and provided exclusively for the benefit of park patrons. Theme and amusement parks are defined as combinations of amusements, rides, and attractions which are permanently situated on park land and open to the public for the price of admission. This guideline class is a composite of all assets used in this industry except transportation equipment (general purpose trucks, cars, airplanes, etc., which are included in asset guideline classes with the prefix 00.2), assets used in the provision of administrative services (asset classes with the prefix 00.1), and warehouses, administration buildings, hotels and motels [Race track facilities have been specifically excluded from Asset Class 80.0 (Act Sec. 704(e)(2) of P.L. 108-357). See ¶ 106. Buildings which are not originally used as theme park structures are depreciated over 39 years as nonresidential real property (IRS Letter Ruling 8928017, April 12, 1989) See ¶ 106.—Editor.] . . . . . . . . . . . . . . . . . . . | 12.5 | 7 | 12.5 |
| | **Certain Property for Which Recovery Periods Assigned** | | | |
| | A. Personal Property With No Class Life . . | | 7 | 12 |
| | Section 1245 Real Property With No Class Life . . . . . . . . . . . . . . . . . . . . . . . . . . . | | 7 | 40 |
| | B. Qualified Technological Equipment, as defined in section 168(i)(2) . . . . . . . . . . . | [9] | 5 | 5 |

| Asset class | Description of assets included | Class Life (in years) | Recovery Periods (in years) General Depreciation System | Alternative Depreciation System |
|---|---|---|---|---|
| | C. Property Used in Connection with Research and Experimentation referred to in section 168(e)(3)(B) . . . . . . . . . . . . . . . . | [9] | 5 | class life if no class life—12 |
| | D. Alternative Energy Property described in section[s] 48(l)(3)(A)(ix) (as in effect on the date before the date of enactment (11/5/90) of the Revenue Reconciliation Act of 1990) . | [9] | 5 | class life if no class life—12 |
| | E. Biomass property described in section 48(l)(15) (as in effect on the date before the date of enactment (11/5/90) of the Revenue Reconciliation Act of 1990) and is a qualifying small production facility within the meaning of section 3(17)(c) of the Federal Power Act, (16 U.S.C. 796(17)(C)), as in effect on September 1, 1986 . . . . . . . . . . . . . . . . . . | [9] | 5 | class life if no class life—12 |
| | F. Energy property described in section 48(a)(3)(A) (or would be described if "solar or wind energy" were substituted for "solar energy" in section 48(a)(3)(A)(i)). . . . . . . | [9] | 5 | class life if no class life—12 |

[1] A horse is more than 2 (or 12) years old after the day that is 24 (or 144) months after its actual birthdate.

[2] Property described in asset classes 01.223, 01.224, and 01.225 are assigned recovery periods under either section 168(e)(3)(A) or section 168(g)(2)(C) but have no class lives.

[3] 7 if property was placed in service before 1989.

[3A] [New natural gas gathering gas gathering lines are 7-year MACRS property with a 14-year ADS recovery period if placed in service after April 11, 2005 (Code Secs. 168(e)(3)(C)(iv), (g)(3)(B); and (i)(17)). See ¶ 106.—Editor.]

[4] [Asset Class 30.11 includes general rebuilding or rehabilitation costs for the special tools defined in class 30.11 that have been traditionally capitalized as the cost of a new asset, according to Rev. Proc. 87-56, section .05. This rule was incorporated from section 2.02 of Rev. Proc. 83-35.—CCH.]

[4A] [Buildings described in Asset Class 40.2 are 39-year nonresidential real property (CCA Letter Ruling 200709063, November 21, 2006)). See ¶ 190.—Editor.]

[4B] [New natural gas gathering gas gathering lines are 7-year MACRS property with a 14-year ADS recovery period if placed in service after April 11, 2005 (Code Secs. 168(e)(3)(C)(iv), (g)(3)(B); and (i)(17)). See ¶ 106.—CCH.]

[5] [References to Part 31 in Asset Classes 48.11—48.14 are to Vol. 47 Part 31 of the Code of Federal Regulations (CFR). However, Part 31 was replaced by Part 32, effective 1-1-88. See Vol. 52 Federal Register p. 43,499. Part 32 may be accessed through the FCC web site (www.fcc.gov).—Editor.]

[5A] [Buildings described in Asset Class 48.11 appear to be classified as 39-year nonresidential real property because the class life for Asset Class 48.11 is not less than 27.5 years (CCA Letter Ruling 200709063, November 21, 2006). See ¶ 190.—CCH.]

[6] Property described in asset guideline class 48.13 which is qualified technological equipment as defined in section 168(i)(2) is assigned a 5-year recovery period for both the general and alternative depreciation systems.

[6A] [Section 1245 property used in the transmission at 69 or more kilovolts of electricity for sale, if placed in service after April 11, 2005 is classified as 15-year property (Code Sec. 168(e)(3)(E)(vii)) with a 30-year ADS recovery period (Code Sec. 168(g)(3)(B)). See ¶ 110. Smart electric meters and grid systems placed in service after October 3, 2008 are 10-year property (Code Sec. 168(e)(3)(D)). See ¶ 108.—Editor.]

[6B] [New natural gas distribution lines placed in service after April 11, 2005 and before January 1, 2011 are 15-year MACRS property with a 35 year ADS recovery period (Code Secs. 168(e)(3)(E)(viii) and (g)(3)(B)). See ¶ 108.—CCH.]

[7] [A 25-year recovery period applies to property placed in service after June 12, 1996. See ¶ 113.—Editor.]

[8] Any high technology medical equipment as defined in section 168(i) (2) (C) which is described in asset guideline class 57.0 is assigned a 5-year recovery period for the alternative depreciation system.

[9] The class life (if any) of property described in classes B, C, D, E, or F is determined by reference to the asset guideline classes in this revenue procedure. If an item of property described in paragraphs B, C, D, E, or F is not described in any asset guideline class, such item of property has no class life.

Rev. Proc. 87-56, 1987-2 CB 674, as clarified and modified by Rev. Proc. 88-22, 1988-1 CB 785.

# Passenger Automobiles and Other Listed Property

## *Limitations on Depreciation Deductions*

### ¶ 200

### Passenger Automobiles

This discussion is organized as follows:



*Safe Harbor Method for Vehicles on Which 100 Percent Bonus Was Claimed in 2010 or 2011—See ¶ 200A.*

*$25,000 Expensing Limit on Certain Heavy SUVs, Trucks, and Vans—¶ 201*

*Post-Recovery Period Deductions—¶ 202*

*Leased Automobiles and Other Listed Property—See ¶ 204*

*Automobiles Lease Inclusion Tables—See ¶ 205*

*Consequences of Listed Property Classification—See ¶ 206*

*Categories of Listed Property—See ¶ 208*

*Qualified Business Use—See ¶ 210*

*Lessee's Inclusion Amount for Listed Property Other Than Passenger Automobiles—¶ 212*

### *1. In general*

Specific dollar amount limits apply to annual depreciation deductions that may be claimed for "passenger automobiles" (Code Sec. 280F(a)). These caps are often referred to as the "luxury car caps" even though they can apply to modestly priced vehicles.

For purposes of the caps, the Code Sec. 179 expense deduction (see ¶ 300) and the bonus depreciation allowance (see ¶ 127D) are treated as a depreciation deduction for the tax year in which a car is placed in service. Thus, the combined Code Sec. 179 deduction, bonus deduction, and regular first-year depreciation deduction is limited to the applicable first-year depreciation cap. Depreciation deductions is subsequent years of the vehicle's recovery period are limited to the cap for the applicable year in the recovery period. See Example (2), below. Any deductions that are disallowed by reason of the caps are deducted annually, at a specified rate, until the disallowed deductions are recovered. See *"13. Post-recovery period deductions,"* below.

### *1A. Safe harbor for vehicles acquired after September 27, 2017 and placed in service before 2023 if 100 percent bonus claimed*

An owner of a vehicle that is subject to the annual luxury car depreciation caps may adopt a safe harbor method of accounting to claim depreciation deductions during each year of the vehicle's regular recovery period even though the 100 percent bonus depreciation deduction is claimed in the year the vehicle is placed in service (Rev. Proc. 2019-13). If the safe harbor is adopted, a taxpayer's first-year deduction is limited to the applicable first-year cap ($18,200 for a vehicle placed in service in 2021). The depreciation deduction for each remaining tax year in the recovery period is equal to the lesser of (1) the applicable depreciation cap for the recovery year or (2) the depreciation deduction computed by applying the applicable table percentage for the tax year to the cost of the vehicle as reduced by the first-year cap. The disallowed depreciation (i.e., the unrecovered basis) is recovered beginning with the first tax year after the end of the recovery period at the regularly prescribed rate ($5,860 per year for a vehicle placed in service in 2021).

In order to adopt the safe harbor:

- The vehicle must cost at least as much as the first-year cap ($18,200 if placed in service in 2021);
- The taxpayer may not claim the section 179 expense allowance on any portion of the vehicle's cost;
- The 100 percent bonus must be claimed on the vehicle (i.e., no election out of bonus depreciation and no election to claim 50 percent rate on a vehicle placed in service in a tax year that includes September 28, 2017); and
- The taxpayer must use the optional depreciation table percentages to compute the safe harbor deductions.

If a taxpayer has already filed a return that claimed a section 179 expense deduction (e.g., a 2017 calendar-year return for a vehicle acquired after September 27, 2017 and before January 1, 2018) and wishes to adopt the safe harbor it is first necessary to file an amended return and revoke the section 179 election, see ¶ 304 for rules regarding the revocation of a section 179 election. If a taxpayer elected out of bonus depreciation for a tax year that includes September 28, 2017 and wishes to adopt the safe harbor for a vehicle placed in service in that year, the election out of bonus depreciation must also be revoked by filing an amended return or an automatic accounting method change in accordance with the procedures provided in Rev. Proc. 2019-33. See ¶ 127D, *"9. Election out of bonus depreciation."* Similarly, if an election to use the 50 percent rate in place of the 100 percent rate for property acquired in a tax year that includes September 28, 2017 was made a taxpayer may revoke the election and claim the 100 percent rate by filing an accounting method change. See *"49A. Election to claim 50-percent bonus depreciation in place of 100-percent bonus depreciation during tax year that includes September 28, 2017."* With the exception for a tax year that includes September 28, 2017, an election out of bonus depreciation may only be revoked with IRS consent obtained through a letter ruling request.

A vehicle used 50 percent or less for business purposes in the year it is placed in service must be depreciated using ADS and, therefore, does not qualify for bonus depreciation. Consequently, the safe harbor cannot be adopted in this situation. If business use drops to 50 percent or less during the recovery period, the taxpayer must cease using the safe harbor and recapture is required based on the difference between the depreciation deductions previously claimed (including bonus) and the depreciation that would have been allowed if ADS had applied beginning in the placed-in-service year and no bonus was claimed. See *"9. 50 percent or less business use: No bonus, ADS required, recapture required."*

The safe harbor method of accounting is adopted by computing allowable deductions in the tax year following the placed-in-service year using the safe harbor rules. No election statement is required. The safe harbor is a method of accounting, not an election.

Without the safe harbor the cost of a vehicle in excess of the first-year cap ($18,200 for a vehicle placed in service in 2021) is recovered at the prescribed rate ($5,860 per year for a vehicle placed in service in 2021) beginning in the first tax year after the end of the vehicle's regular recovery period. This is because (1) the basis of the vehicle is reduced by the full amount of bonus without regard to the caps, and (2) recovery of the portion of the 100 percent bonus deduction that is disallowed by the first-year depreciation cap is deferred until after the end of the vehicle's recovery period (Code Sec. 280F(a)(1)(B)).

The following example illustrates how depreciation is computed if the 100 percent bonus is claimed and the safe harbor is not adopted.

***Example (1):*** A car (5-year MACRS property) costing $60,000 that is subject to the luxury car limitations is placed in service in February 2021 by a calendar-year taxpayer. The taxpayer claims 100-percent bonus depreciation on its 5-year property, including the vehicle. The 100-percent rate applies to property acquired and placed in service after September 27, 2017 and before 2023. However, because the first-year depreciation cap for a vehicle placed in service in 2021 is $18,200, the bonus deduction that may be deducted is limited to $18,200. If the taxpayer does not apply the safe harbor method, the $41,800 excess ($60,000 - $18,200) may only be recovered at the rate of $5,860 per year beginning in 2027, which is the first year after the end of the vehicle's recovery period. No regular depreciation deductions are allowed after the first year of the vehicle's regular recovery period because the vehicle's basis for computing depreciation deductions is reduced to $0 by the entire amount of the bonus depreciation allowable without regard to the first-year depreciation cap. The table percentages when applied to a depreciable basis of $0 are equal to $0 in each year of the vehicle's regular 5-year recovery period.

| *Year* | *Regular Deduction* | *Luxury Car Cap* | *Allowable Depreciation* |
|---|---|---|---|
| 2021 | $60,000 | $18,200 | $18,200 |
| 2022 | $0 | $16,400 | $0 |
| 2023 | $0 | $9,800 | $0 |
| 2024 | $0 | $5,860 | $0 |
| 2025 | $0 | $5,860 | $0 |
| 2026 | $0 | $5,860 | $0 |
| | | TOTAL | $18,200 |

The unrecovered basis is $41,800 ($60,000 - $18,200). Assuming 100 percent business use continues, the taxpayer deducts $5,860 per year beginning in 2027 until the $41,800 is recovered.

If the safe harbor method of accounting is adopted by the taxpayer in the preceding example, depreciation deductions are computed as shown in this example.

***Example (2):***

| *Year* | *Regular Deduction* | *Luxury Car Cap* | *Allowable Depreciation* |
|---|---|---|---|
| 2021 | $60,000 | $18,200 | $18,200 |
| 2022 | $13,408 | $16,400 | $13,408 |
| 2023 | $8,045 | $9,800 | $8,045 |
| 2024 | $4,827 | $5,860 | $4,827 |
| 2025 | $4,827 | $5,860 | $4,827 |
| 2026 | $2,413 | $5,860 | $2,413 |
| | | TOTAL | $51,720 |

The unrecovered basis is $8,280 ($60,000 – $51,720). The taxpayer deducts $5,860 in 2027 and $2,420 in 2028.

The amounts shown in the "Regular Deduction" column for each year after 2021 are computed by applying the applicable first-year table percentages for each year in the recovery period to $41,800 ($60,000 vehicle cost reduced by $18,200 first-year cap). The 2021 regular depreciation deduction is the $60,000 cost of the vehicle since 100 percent bonus applies in that year. In each year, the actual deduction is limited to the smaller of the regular deduction or the applicable depreciation cap.

*Partial business use.* The safe harbor guidance does not specifically discuss or illustrate computations if business/investment use of the vehicle is less than 100 percent. Applying generally applicable rules, however, if the vehicle is used for personal purposes, the first-year deduction should equal to the product of the first-year cap and the percentage of business/investment use. Deductions in later years of the recovery period should equal the lesser of (1) the product of the applicable depreciation cap and the business/investment use percentage or (2) the depreciation deduction computed by applying the applicable depreciation table percentage to (a) the product of the original cost and the business-investment percentage reduced by (b) the allowable first-year deduction (i.e., the product of the first-year cap and the business/investment use percentage). As noted below, the safe harbor does not apply if business use is 50 percent or less.

***Example (3):*** Assume that the business use of the vehicle in the preceding example is 80 percent throughout its recovery period and post-recovery period years. The basis of the vehicle eligible for 100 percent bonus depreciation is $48,000 ($60,000 × 80%). However the bonus deduction for 2021 is limited to $14,560 ($18,200 × 80%) since this is less than $48,000. In 2022, the depreciation deduction is limited to $10,701—the lesser of $10,701 (($60,000 × 80%) - $14,560) × 32% second-year table percentage) or $13,120 ($16,400 second-year cap × 80%). 2023 depreciation is $6,420—the lesser of $6,420 (($60,000 × 80%) - $14,560) × 19.2% third-year table percentage) or $7,840 ($9,800 third-year cap × 80%). 2024 and 2025 depreciation is $3,852—the lesser of $3,852 (($60,000 × 80%) - $14,560) × 11.52 % fourth- and fifth-year table percentage) or $4,688 ($5,860 fourth- and fifth-year cap × 80%). 2029 depreciation (last year of recovery period) is $1,926 —the lesser of $1,926 (($60,000 × 80%) - $14,560) × 5.76% sixth-year table percentage) or $4,688 ($5,860 sixth-year cap × 80%).

The recovery period depreciation for 2021 through 2026 is computed as follows:

| *Year* | *80% Business-Use MACRS Depreciation* | *80% Luxury Car Limit* | *Lesser of Col. 2 or 3* | *Section 280F Unrecovered Basis* |
|---|---|---|---|---|
| 2021 . . . . . . . | $48,000 | $14,560 | $14,560 | 41,800 |
| 2022 . . . . . . . | 10,701 | 13,120 | 10,701 | 28,492 |
| 2023 | 6,420 | 7,840 | 6,420 | 20,447 |
| 2024 . . . . . . . | 3,852 | 4,688 | 3,852 | 15,620 |
| 2025 . . . . . . . | 3,852 | 4,688 | 3,852 | 10,793 |
| 2026 . . . . . . . | 1,926 | 4,688 | 1,926 | 8,280 |

*Unrecovered basis.* In determining the amount of unrecovered basis that is available for deduction after the end of the recovery period, the generally applicable rule applies. Under this rule, the unrecovered basis at the end of the recovery period is computed as if business use was 100 percent throughout the recovery period. That is, the original cost is reduced by the depreciation deductions that would have been allowed if business use was 100 percent taking into account the annual caps. See ¶ 202. Therefore, the unrecovered basis at the end of the recovery period in this example is $8,280 ($60,000 – $51,620) as computed in Example (2).

Assuming business use continues at 80 percent, the taxpayer may deduct $4,688 ($5,860 × 80%) in 2026. The remaining unrecovered basis in 2027 is computed as if business use was 100 percent in 2026. The unrecovered basis in 2027 is therefore $2,420 ($8,280 – $5,860). The 2027 deduction is $1,936 ($2,420 × 80%) since this is less than $4,688 ($5,860 × 80%). See ¶ 202 for additional examples illustrating the computation and recovery of unrecovered basis when business/investment use is less than 100 percent.

*Similar safe harbor for vehicles placed in service in 2010 and 2011.* When Congress last enacted a 100-percent bonus rate in the Tax Relief, Unemployment Insurance Reauthorization, and Job Creation Act of 2010 (P.L. 111-312), for property acquired after September 8, 2010, and placed in service before January 1, 2012, the IRS provided a safe harbor method that allowed a taxpayer to compute depreciation as if a 50-percent bonus rate applied, so that depreciation deductions could be claimed during the entire recovery period of the vehicle (Rev. Proc. 2011-26, § 3.03(5)(c), 2011-16 I.R.B. 664). This safe harbor is discussed at ¶ 200A.

*2. Determining proper 179 deduction if first-year depreciation does not exceed first-year cap*

Generally, the first-year cap is exceeded by regular and/or bonus depreciation even if the section 179 allowance is not claimed. In this situation it is not necessary to claim any section 179 allowance (assuming the taxpayer is eligible to expense assets under section 179).

If the 100 percent bonus rate is claimed on a vehicle it is not necessary to elect the section 179 expense allowance. Also, the safe harbor described at *1A. Safe harbor for vehicles acquired after September 27, 2017 and placed in service before 2023 if 100 percent bonus claimed* for vehicles subject to the luxury car caps will not apply and the taxpayer will not be able to claim depreciation deductions until after the end of the recovery period.

If a vehicle is placed in service in calendar-year 2021 and no bonus is claimed, and the 200 percent declining balance method and half-year convention apply (typical situation), the regular depreciation deduction is less than the first-year cap and a section 179 allowance should be claimed if the vehicle (car, truck (including SUV), and van) costs less than $51,000 ($51,000 × 20% first-year table percentage = $10,200 first-year cap).

If a vehicle is placed in service in calendar-year 2020 or 2019 and no bonus is claimed, and the 200 percent declining balance method and half-year convention apply (typical situation), the regular depreciation deduction is less than the first-year cap and a section 179 allowance should be claimed if the vehicle (car, truck (including SUV), and van) costs less than $50,500 ($50,500 × 20% first-year table percentage = $10,100 first-year cap).

If a vehicle is placed in service in calendar-year 2018 and no bonus is claimed, and the 200 percent declining balance method and half-year convention apply (typical situation), the regular depreciation deduction is less than the first-year cap and a section 179 allowance should be claimed if the vehicle (car, truck (including SUV), and van) costs less than $50,000 ($50,000 × 20% first-year table percentage = $10,000 first-year cap).

If a vehicle is placed in service in calendar year 2017 and the 200 percent declining balance method and half-year convention apply, the regular depreciation deduction (including any 50 percent bonus allowance) is less than the first-year cap and a section 179 allowance should be claimed (assuming the taxpayer qualifies) if the vehicle costs less than the following amount, as applicable: (1) car and no bonus: $15,800; (2) car and 50 percent bonus: $18,600; (3) truck or van (including SUV) and no bonus: $17,800; (4) truck or van (including SUV) and 50 percent bonus: $19,267.

For vehicles to which the midquarter convention applies or which are not depreciated using the 200 percent declining balance method, see table at ¶ 487. ¶ 487 also includes worksheets for determining the amount to expense under Code Sec. 179 if the regular first-year deduction (plus any bonus deduction) does not exceed the applicable first-year cap.

*3. Interactive Computation Tools*

The section 179 deduction to claim, if any, may be determined by using the CCH interactive tool entitled "Reconciling Luxury Auto Depreciation With Section 179 Deduction Interactive Example." The tool takes into account personal use of a vehicle in the placed-in-service year.

Another tool computes a depreciation schedule for a vehicle, including vehicles subject to the luxury car caps. This tool is entitled "Auto Depreciation Interactive Example." The tool takes into account personal use of a vehicle at any point in the regular or post-recovery period.

Locate theses tools on CCH IntelliConnect or AnswerConnect by using the search box.

*4. Trucks, vans, and SUVs in excess of 6,000 pounds GVWR are not subject to caps—Listing of heavy vehicles provided*

The annual limitations apply to "passenger automobiles". In general, all passenger cars are "passenger automobiles" and subject to the depreciation caps. Passenger automobiles do not include (and, therefore, the caps do not apply to) trucks (including SUVs that are considered trucks) and vans with a gross vehicle weight rating (GVWR) (i.e., loaded weight rating) in excess of 6,000 pounds. According to informal guidance provided by the IRS, an SUV (including an SUV on a unibody rather than a truck chassis) that is categorized by its manufacturer as a truck pursuant to Department of Transportation regulations is considered a truck. See ¶ 208 for a definition of passenger automobile.

See Quick Reference Chart section at end of this book (Tables I, II, and III) for a list of trucks, SUVs, and vans exempt under this rule. Online users may use search term "GVWR Exceeding 6,000."

*5. Exclusion from caps for trucks and vans unsuitable for personal use*

Certain trucks and vans (including SUVs) placed in service after July 6, 2003, are not subject to the caps if, because of their design, they are not likely to be used for personal purposes. See ¶ 208.

*6. Car rental businesses are not subject to caps*

Taxpayers who are regularly engaged in the business of leasing automobiles are not subject to the annual caps. See ¶ 204.

*7. Section 179 expensing limit on SUVs and certain vans in excess of 6,000 pounds and trucks in excess of 6,000 pounds with a bed length under six feet*

If a sports utility vehicle has a GVWR in excess of 6,000 pounds and is therefore, exempt from the annual depreciation caps, it is subject to a Code Sec. 179 sports utility vehicle expensing limit (Code Sec. 179(b)(5)). This rule also applies to pick-up trucks with a GVWR in excess of 6,000 pounds and an interior cargo bed length of less than six feet as well as to *certain* vans with a GVWR in excess of 6,000 pounds. This limit applies to vehicles placed in service after October 22, 2004 and is adjusted for inflation ($26,200 for vehicles placed into service in 2021 and $27,000 for vehicles placed into service in 2022) (Rev. Proc. 2020-45 and Rev. Proc. 2021-45). See ¶ 201 for a discussion of the provision. See Table IV in the Quick Reference Chart section for a list of trucks exceeding 6,000 pounds with a bed length under 6 feet. Online users may use search term "GVWR Exceeding 6,000."

*8. Trade-ins and involuntary conversions*

For the application of the luxury car caps on a vehicle relinquished or received in a trade-in before 2018 or involuntarily converted, see ¶ 214.

*9. 50 percent or less business use—No bonus deduction, ADS required, recapture required*

The MACRS alternative depreciation system (ADS) must be used to depreciate a "passenger automobile" or other listed property if its business use is 50 percent or less. No Code Sec. 179 expense allowance or bonus depreciation (including New York Liberty Zone (¶ 127E), GO-Zone bonus depreciation (¶ 127F), Kansas Disaster Area bonus depreciation (¶ 127G), or Disaster Area bonus depreciation (¶ 127H)) may be claimed. If business use falls to 50 percent or less after the first tax year, depreciation recapture (including the section 179 allowance and bonus depreciation) is required. See ¶ 210. These rules also apply to trucks (including SUVs that are considered trucks) and vans that are not considered passenger automobiles and are exempt from the luxury car caps as a result of having a GVWR in excess of 6,000 pounds because such vehicles are still considered a type of listed property—specifically, they are considered a property used as a means of transportation. See ¶ 208.

*10. Determining which set of caps applies*

The applicable set of annual dollar amount limits depends on the calendar year in which the vehicle is placed in service for use in a trade or business or for the production of income. Thus, if a car is converted from personal use to business use, the dollar limits are those that are in effect in the calendar year that the car is placed in service for business use.

> ***Example (1):*** Assume that a car is placed in service for business purposes on June 1, 2021 and no bonus depreciation is claimed. Based on Table I below, the dollar limits for a vehicle placed in service in 2021 for the vehicle's five-year recovery period are $10,200 (first-year cap if bonus depreciation is not claimed), $16,400 (second year), $9,800 (third year), and $5,860 (subsequent years).

*Fiscal-year taxpayers.* The appropriate limitation is determined by reference to the *calendar year* that the vehicle is first placed in service. For example, a corporation with a 2020-2021 fiscal year would apply the 2020 limitations to a vehicle placed in service in the 2020 calendar year and the 2021 limitations to a vehicle placed in service in the 2021 calendar year.

*Election to claim 50 percent bonus.* The election to claim a 50 percent bonus depreciation rate in place of the 100 percent rate for property placed in service in a tax year that includes September 27, 2017 (¶ 127D) does not affect the applicable caps. The caps are based on the placed in service year regardless of the bonus rate in this situation.

*11. Improvements to a Vehicle*

A taxpayer may make a capitalized improvement to a vehicle (e.g., replace the engine). The improvement is depreciated as a separate asset (using the same depreciation period that applies to the vehicle) beginning in the tax year the improvement is placed in service. However, the sum of the depreciation claimed on the vehicle and the improvement may not exceed the applicable cap for the vehicle. A single cap applies (Temporary Reg.§ 1.280F-2T(f)).

The cost of an improvement made before the vehicle is placed in service, for example, an improvement made by the dealer at the purchaser's request, should be added the depreciable basis of the vehicle.

*12. Vehicle basis amount*

See ¶ 70 for calculation of the depreciable basis of a car.

*13. Post-recovery period deductions*

The portion of a depreciation deduction that is disallowed during a particular year in a vehicle's recovery period because the cap for that year is smaller than the otherwise allowable depreciation deduction is combined with any disallowed deductions from all other recovery years. The combined amount is then deducted at an annual rate equal to the applicable "Year 4 and later" cap amount (for example $5,860 per year for a car placed in service in 2021 assuming 100-percent business use) beginning with the first year following the end of the recovery period. See ¶ 202.

*14. Separate depreciation caps for trucks and van placed in service before 2018*

If a truck or van (including an SUV) is placed in service before 2018 and the truck or van is subject to the annual caps (generally, because it has a gross vehicle weight rating of 6,000 pounds or less), the taxpayer must use a separate set of annual limitations that are somewhat higher than those that apply to cars. The caps for trucks and vans placed in service before 2018 are reproduced in Table III below. The caps for cars placed in service before 2018 are in Table II.

For vehicles placed in service in 2018 and thereafter, however, the caps for cars, trucks, and vans are identical and a same caps (inflation-adjusted each year beginning in 2019) apply. See Table I below.

*15. Annual lease inclusion amounts for lessees of cars, trucks, and vans*

See ¶ 204 for rules requiring lessees of cars, trucks, and vans that have a gross vehicle weight rating of 6,000 pounds or less to include an annual "lease inclusion amount" in income during the recovery period of the vehicle.

Separate lease inclusion tables are provided for trucks and vans (including SUVs that are considered trucks) first leased before 2018. However, for leases beginning in 2018 the same lease inclusion table applies to leased cars, trucks, and vans. Each year the table is inflation-adjusted for leases that begin in that calendar year. The inflation-adjusted lease inclusion amounts for vehicles first leased in 2019 are provided in Rev. Proc. 2019-26, for 2020 in Rev. Proc. 2020-37 and for 2021 in Rev. Proc. 2021-31.

*16. Luxury car depreciation limit amounts for cars and trucks and vans*

Table I below shows the depreciation limits for cars, trucks (including SUVs), and vans placed in service after 2017. Table II below shows the depreciable limits for cars placed in service before 2018. Table III shows the limits for trucks and vans, including SUVs, placed in service before 2018.

The caps for cars, trucks (including SUVs), and vans placed in service after 2017 are identical. Separate tables are no longer necessary. Each year, beginning in 2019, a new inflation-adjusted table is issued for these vehicles. The inflation-adjusted caps for vehicles placed in service in 2019, 2020 and 2021 are provided in Rev. Proc. 2019-26, Rev. Proc. 2020-37 and Rev. Proc. 2021-31 respectively.

**TABLE I**

*Depreciation Limits on Cars, Trucks, Suvs, and Vans Placed in Service After 2017*

| *For Cars, trucks, and vans Placed in Service* | | *Depreciation Allowable in—* | | | | |
|---|---|---|---|---|---|---|
| *After* | *Before* | *Year 1* | *Year 2* | *Year 3* | *Year 4, etc.* | *Authority* |
| 12/31/20 | 1/1/22 | 18,200*<br>10,200* | 16,400 | 9,800 | 5,860 | Rev. Proc. 2021-31 |
| 12/31/19 | 1/1/21 | 18,100*<br>10,100* | 16,100 | 9,700 | 5,760 | Rev. Proc. 2020-37 |
| 12/31/18 | 1/1/20 | 18,100*<br>10,100*<br>14,900** | 16,100 | 9,700 | 5,760 | Rev. Proc. 2019-26 |
| 12/31/17 | 1/1/19 | 18,000*<br>10,000*<br>16,400*** | 16,000 | 9,600 | 5,760 | Rev. Proc. 2018-25 |

* The higher limit applies if the vehicle qualifies for bonus depreciation and no election out is made.

** The $14,900 limit only applies if bonus depreciation is claimed in 2019 on a vehicle acquired before September 28, 2017. Otherwise, the $18,100 limit applies if the bonus is claimed on a vehicle placed in service in 2019.

*** The $16,400 limit only applies if bonus depreciation is claimed in 2018 on a vehicle acquired before September 28, 2017. Otherwise, the $18,000 limit applies if the bonus is claimed on a vehicle placed in service in 2018.

**TABLE II**

*Depreciation Limits on Cars Placed in Service Before 2018*

| *For Cars Placed in Service* | | *Depreciation Allowable in—* | | | | |
|---|---|---|---|---|---|---|
| *After* | *Before* | *Year 1* | *Year 2* | *Year 3* | *Year 4, etc.* | *Authority* |
| 12/31/03 . | | 10,610* | 4,800 | 2,850 | 1,675 | Rev. Proc. 2004-20 |
| | . 1/1/05 | 2,960* | | | | |
| 12/31/04 . | | 2,960 | 4,700 | 2,850 | 1,675 | Rev. Proc. 2005-13 |
| | . 1/1/06 | | | | | |
| 12/31/05 . | | 2,960 | 4,800 | 2,850 | 1,775 | Rev. Proc. 2006-18 |
| | . 1/1/07 | | | | | |
| 12/31/06 . | | 3,060 | 4,900 | 2,850 | 1,775 | Rev. Proc. 2007-30 |
| | . 1/1/08 | | | | | |
| 12/31/07 . | | 10,960* | 4,800 | 2,850 | 1,775 | Rev. Proc. 2008-22 |
| | . 1/1/09 | 2,960* | | | | |
| 12/31/08 . | | 10,960* | 4,800 | 2,850 | 1,775 | Rev. Proc. 2009-24 |
| | . 1/1/10 | 2,960* | | | | |
| 12/31/09 . | | 11,060* | 4,900 | 2,950 | 1,775 | Rev. Proc. 2010-18, as modified by Rev. Proc. 2011-21 |
| | . 1/1/12 | 3,060* | | | | |
| | | | | | | Rev. Proc. 2011-21 |
| 12/31/11 . | | 11,160* | 5,100 | 3,050 | 1,875 | Rev. Proc. 2012-23 |
| | . 1/1/13 | 3,160* | | | | |
| 12/31/12 . | | 11,160* | 5,100 | 3,050 | 1,875 | Rev. Proc. 2013-21 |
| | . 1/1/14 | 3,160* | | | | |
| 12/31/13 . | | 11,160* | 5,100 | 3,050 | 1,875 | Rev. Proc. 2014-21, as modified by Rev. Proc. 2015-19 |
| | . 1/1/15 | 3,160* | | | | |
| 12/31/14 . | | 11,160* | 5,100 | 3,050 | 1,875 | Rev. Proc. 2015-19, as modified by Rev. Proc. 2016-23 |
| | . 1/1/16 | 3,160* | | | | |
| 12/31/15 . | | 11,160* | 5,100 | 3,050 | 1,875 | Rev. Proc. 2016-23 |
| | . 1/1/17 | 3,160* | | | | |
| 12/31/16 . | | 11,160* | 5,100 | 3,050 | 1,875 | Rev. Proc. 2017-29 |
| | . 1/1/18 | 3,160* | | | | |

* The higher limit applies if the vehicle qualifies for bonus depreciation and no election out is made.

**TABLE III**

*Depreciation Limits on Trucks, SUVs, and Vans Placed in Service before 2018*

| *For Trucks/ Vans Placed in Service* | | *Depreciation Allowable in—* | | | | |
|---|---|---|---|---|---|---|
| *After* | *Before* | *Year 1* | *Year 2* | *Year 3* | *Year 4, etc.* | *Authority* |
| . | | 11,560* | | | | |
| 12/31/16 | . 1/1/18 | 3,560* | 5,700 | 3,450 | 2,075 | Rev. Proc. 2017-29 |
| . | | 11,560* | | | | |
| 12/31/15 | . 1/1/17 | 3,560* | 5,700 | 3,350 | 2,075 | Rev. Proc. 2016-23 |
| . | | 11,460* | | | | Rev. Proc. 2015-19, as modified by Rev. Proc. |
| 12/31/14 | . 1/1/16 | 3,460* | 5,600 | 3,350 | 1,975 | 2016-23 |

| *For Trucks/ Vans Placed in Service* | | *Depreciation Allowable in—* | | | | |
|---|---|---|---|---|---|---|
| *After* | *Before* | *Year 1* | *Year 2* | *Year 3* | *Year 4, etc.* | *Authority* |
| 12/31/13 | 1/1/15 | 11,460*<br>3,460* | 5,500 | 3,350 | 1,975 | Rev. Proc. 2014-21, as modified by Rev. Proc. 2015-19 |
| 12/31/12 | 1/1/14 | 11,360*<br>3,360* | 5,400 | 3,250 | 1,975 | Rev. Proc. 2013-21 |
| 12/31/11 | 1/1/13 | 11,360*<br>3,360* | 5,300 | 3,150 | 1,875 | Rev. Proc. 2012-23 |
| 12/31/10 | 1/1/12 | 11,260*<br>3,260* | 5,200 | 3,150 | 1,875 | Rev. Proc. 2011-21 |
| 12/31/09 | 1/1/11 | 11,160*<br>3,160* | 5,100 | 3,050 | 1,875 | Rev. Proc. 2010-18, as modified by Rev. Proc. 2011-21 |
| 12/31/08 | 1/1/10 | 11,060*<br>3,060* | 4,900 | 2,950 | 1,775 | Rev. Proc. 2009-24 |
| 12/31/07 | 1/1/09 | 11,160*<br>3,160* | 5,100 | 3,050 | 1,875 | Rev. Proc. 2008-22 |
| 12/31/06 | 1/1/08 | 3,260 | 5,200 | 3,050 | 1,875 | Rev. Proc. 2007-30 |
| 12/31/05 | 1/1/07 | 3,260 | 5,200 | 3,150 | 1,875 | Rev. Proc. 2006-18 |
| 12/31/04 | 1/1/06 | 3,260 | 5,200 | 3,150 | 1,875 | Rev. Proc. 2005-13 |
| 12/31/03 | 1/1/05 | 10,910*<br>3,260* | 5,300 | 3,150 | 1,875 | Rev. Proc. 2004-20 |
| 12/31/02 | 1/1/04 | $11,010*<br>7,960*<br>3,360* | $5,400 | $3,250 | $1,975 | Rev. Proc. 2003-75 |

* The higher limit applies if the vehicle qualifies for bonus depreciation and no election out is made.

### *17. Sample computations with bonus depreciation and without bonus depreciation*

For vehicles acquired and placed in service after September 27, 2017 on which 100 percent bonus is claimed see explanation and examples at *1A. Safe Harbor for Vehicles Acquired after September 27, 2017 and placed in service before 2023 if 100 Percent Bonus Claimed.*

***Example (1):*** *50 percent bonus claimed.* A car costing $25,000 is placed in service on August 1, 2017. No amount is expensed under Code Sec. 179. The 50% bonus depreciation allowance is claimed. The car is used 100% for business and the half-year convention applies. Bonus depreciation is $12,500. The adjusted depreciable basis to which the table percentages (20%, 32%, 19.20%, 11.52%, 11.52%, and 5.76%) are applied is $12,500 ($25,000 – $12,500 bonus deduction). Allowable depreciation deductions during the recovery period are as follows:

| *Year* | *Regular Deduction* | *Luxury Car Cap* | *Allowable Depreciation* |
|---|---|---|---|
| 2017 | $15,000 | $11,160 | $11,160 |
| 2018 | $4,000 | $5,100 | $4,000 |
| 2019 | $2,400 | $3,050 | $2,400 |
| 2020 | $1,440 | $1,875 | $1,440 |

| Year | Regular Deduction | Luxury Car Cap | Allowable Depreciation |
|---|---|---|---|
| 2021 | $1,440 | $1,875 | $1,440 |
| 2022 | $720 | $1,875 | $720 |
| | | TOTAL | $21,160 |

The $15,000 regular deduction for 2017 is the sum of the $12,500 bonus deduction and the $2,500 first-year depreciation deduction ($12,500 × 20%). 2017 is the only year during the recovery period that allowable depreciation is limited to the luxury car cap. The disallowed amount ($15,000 – $11,160) is $3,840. $1,875 (the cap for the fourth and succeeding years in the recovery period) of this amount may be deducted in 2023, $1,875 in 2024, and the remaining $90 may be deducted in 2025. See ¶ 202 for a discussion of post-recovery period deductions.

***Example (2):*** *Bonus not claimed.* A car costing $60,000 is placed in service on September 15, 2021. Bonus depreciation is not claimed. No amount is expensed under Code Sec. 179. The car is used 100% for business and the half-year convention applies. The adjusted depreciable basis to which the table percentages (20%, 32%, 19.20%, 11.52%, 11.52%, and 5.76%) are applied is $60,000. Allowable depreciation deductions during the recovery period are as follows:

| Year | Regular Deduction | Luxury Car Cap | Allowable Depreciation |
|---|---|---|---|
| 2021 | $12,000 | $10,200 | $10,200 |
| 2022 | $19,200 | $16,400 | $16,400 |
| 2023 | $11,520 | $9,800 | $9,800 |
| 2024 | $6,912 | $5,860 | $5,860 |
| 2025 | $6,912 | $5,860 | $5,860 |
| 2026 | $3,456 | $5,860 | $5,860 |
| | | TOTAL | $51,576 |

The disallowed depreciation deduction is $8,424 ($60,000 – $51,576). This amount is deducted at the rate of $5,860 (the cap used for the fourth and succeeding years in the recovery period) per year beginning in 2027 until used up.

See ¶ 202 for additional examples, including determining post-recovery period deductions.

### *18. Electric vehicles*

The annual depreciation caps are tripled for automobiles produced by an original equipment manufacturer to run primarily on electricity and placed in service after August 5, 1997, and before January 1, 2007 (Code Sec. 280F(a)(1)(C)). These are so-called "purpose built passenger vehicles" as defined in Code Sec. 4001(a)(2)(C)(ii). The IRS has announced the following depreciation caps are applicable for electric vehicles placed in service after August 5, 1997 and before January 1, 2007. For electric vehicles placed in service after 2006, the caps in Table I, Table II, or Table III above, as appropriate, are used.

**TABLE IV**
*Depreciation Caps for Electric Cars*

| *For Electric Cars Placed in Service* | | *Depreciation Allowable in—* | | | | |
|---|---|---|---|---|---|---|
| *After* | *Before* | *Year 1* | *Year 2* | *Year 3* | *Year 4, etc.* | *Authority* |
| 8/5/97 . . | 1/1/98 | $9,480 | $15,100 | $9,050 | $5,425 | Rev. Proc. 98-24 |
| 12/31/97 . . | 1/1/99 | $9,380 | $15,000 | $8,950 | $5,425 | Rev. Proc. 98-30 |
| 12/31/98 . . | 1/1/00 | $9,280 | $14,900 | $8,950 | $5,325 | Rev. Proc. 99-14 |
| 12/31/99 . . | 1/1/01 | $9,280 | $14,800 | $8,850 | $5,325 | Rev. Proc. 2000-18 |
| 12/31/00 . . | 9/11/01 | $9,280 | $14,800 | $8,850 | $5,325 | Rev. Proc. 2001-19 |

| *For Electric Cars Placed in Service* | | *Depreciation Allowable in—* | | | | |
|---|---|---|---|---|---|---|
| *After* | *Before* | *Year 1* | *Year 2* | *Year 3* | *Year 4, etc.* | *Authority* |
| 9/10/01 . . | 1/1/02 | $23,080* $9,280* | $14,800 | $8,850 | $5,325 | Rev. Proc. 2003-75 |
| 12/31/01 . . | 1/1/03 | $22,980* $9,180* | $14,700 | $8,750 | $5,325 | Rev. Proc. 2003-75 |
| 12/31/02 . . | 5/6/03 | $22,880* $9,080* | $14,600 | $8,750 | $5,225 | Rev. Proc. 2003-75 |
| 5/5/03 . . | 1/1/04 | $32,030* $9,080* | $14,600 | $8,750 | $5,225 | Rev. Proc. 2003-75 |
| 12/31/03 . . | 1/1/05 | $31,830* $8,880* | $14,300 | $8,550 | $5,125 | Rev. Proc. 2004-20 |
| 12/31/04 . . | 1/1/06 | $8,880 | $14,200 | $8,450 | $5,125 | Rev. Proc. 2005-13 |
| 12/31/05 . . | 1/1/07 | $8,980 | $14,400 | $8,650 | $5,225 | Rev. Proc. 2006-18 |

* The higher figure applies if the car qualifies for the additional bonus depreciation allowance and no election out is made. Otherwise, the lower limit is used.

### *19. Bonus depreciation and $8,000 bump-up in first-year cap*

The otherwise applicable first-year depreciation cap for a vehicle is increased by $8,000 if bonus depreciation is claimed under Code Sec. 168(k) on the vehicle (Code Sec. 168(k)(2)(F)). The $8,000 bump-up applies whether the bonus rate is 100 percent or 50 percent. For example the first-year cap for a car placed in service in 2021 if no bonus depreciation is claimed is $10,200. If bonus depreciation is claimed the $10,200 cap is increased by $8,000 to $18,200. If a car is placed in service in 2017, the first-year cap is $3,160 if bonus is not claimed and is increased by $8,000 to $11,160 if bonus is claimed. The $11,160 cap applies even if the 100 percent rate applied because the vehicle was acquired after September 27, 2017 and placed in service before 2018.

For vehicles that are acquired before September 28, 2017 and placed in service in 2018 or 2019 (a rare situation), the $8,000 cap increase is reduced to $6,400 for passenger automobiles placed in service in 2018 and to $4,800 for passenger automobiles placed in service in 2019 (Code Sec. 168(k)(2)(F)(iii), as amended by the Tax Cuts and Jobs Act (P.L. 115-97)). These decreases correspond to the scheduled decreases in the bonus depreciation rate from 50 percent to 40 percent in 2018 and to 30 percent in 2019 for property acquired before September 28, 2017 and placed in service in 2018 or 2019. See ¶ 127D. The 2019 first-year cap for a vehicle acquired before September 27, 2017 and placed in service in 2019 is $14,900 ($10,100 + $4,800) if the 30 percent bonus is claimed. The 2018 first-year cap for a vehicle acquired before September 27, 2017 and placed in service in 2018 is $16,400 ($10,000 + $6,400) if the 40 percent bonus is claimed.

*New York Liberty Zone*. Special rules applied to used vehicles placed in service in the New York Liberty Zone. See discussion #23 below.

### *20. Partial business use*

The maximum caps listed above apply when business/investment use is 100 percent and theses amounts must be reduced to reflect the personal use of a vehicle in any tax year. The limit imposed on the maximum amount of depreciation deduction is redetermined by multiplying the amount of the limitation by the percentage of business/investment use (determined on an annual basis) during the tax year (Temporary Reg.§ 1.280F-2T(i)).

See discussion *1A. Safe Harbor for Vehicles Acquired after September 27, 2017 and placed in service before 2023 if 100 Percent Bonus Claimed* for an example with partial business use where the 100 percent bonus rate applies.

***Example (3):*** A calendar-year taxpayer purchases a car for $40,000 in August 2017 and uses it 60% for business. Before consideration of the Code Sec. 280F limitations, the 2017 basis of the vehicle is $24,000 ($40,000 × 60% business use percentage for 2017). Bonus depreciation is $12,000 ($24,000 × 50% bonus depreciation rate). Regular first-year depreciation is $2,400 (($24,000 - $12,000) × 20% first-year table percentage from Table 1 at ¶ 180 for 5-year property). Total depreciation (including bonus depreciation) for 2017 is $14,400. However, the maximum MACRS deduction allowed for 2017 under the Code Sec. 280F luxury car limitations is $6,696 ($11,160 maximum limit for car placed in service in 2017 × 60% business use). The 2018 deduction, assuming 60% business use and without regard to the second-year cap, is $3,840 ($40,000 original cost × 60% business use in 2018 - $12,000 bonus deduction (bonus allowed without regard to first-year cap) × 32% second-year table percentage). The 2018 deduction, however, is limited to $3,060 ($5,100 second-year cap for car placed in service in 2017 × 60%).

See ¶ 202 for additional examples.

### *21. Short tax year*

The limitation imposed upon the maximum amount of allowable depreciation deductions (including any Code Sec. 179 expense deduction) must be adjusted if there is a short tax year. The limitation is reduced by multiplying the dollar amount that would have applied if the tax year were not a short tax year by a fraction, the numerator of which is the number of months and partial months in the short tax year and the denominator of which is 12 (Temp. Reg. § 1.280F-2T(i) (2)).

***Example (4):*** In August 2021, a corporation purchased and placed in service a passenger automobile and used it 100% for business. Bonus depreciation is not claimed. The corporation's 2021 tax year is a short tax year consisting of six months. The maximum amount that the corporation may claim as a depreciation deduction for the 2021 short tax year is $5,100 ($10,200 × 6/12). $10,200 is the first-year cap for a passenger car placed in service in 2021 for which bonus depreciation is not claimed. See Table I, above.

*Bonus deduction in short tax year.* The Code Sec. 168(k) bonus depreciation deduction (¶ 127D) is allowed in full in a short tax year (Rev. Proc. 2002-33; Reg.§ 1.168(k)-1(d)(1)). The $8,000 bump-up in the first-year depreciation cap for vehicles on which bonus depreciation is claimed is not reduced in a short tax year (Premable to T.D. 9283, filed with the Federal Register on August 28, 2006). This is consistent with the fact that the bonus deduction is allowed in full in a short tax year. The basic cap, however, is subject to the general rule which requires reduction in a short tax year.

***Example (5):*** Assume the same facts as in the preceding example, except that the car is new and 100 percent bonus depreciation is claimed. The first-year depreciation cap for the short tax year is $13,100 (full $8,000 bump-up + reduced $5,100 basic cap).

### *22. Deduction in year of disposition*

The applicable depreciation limit is not reduced in the year that a vehicle is placed in service or disposed of, except to reflect personal use, if necessary. Thus, even though only one-half of a full year's depreciation may be claimed in the year disposition (assuming the half-year convention applies and the disposition occurs during the recovery period), no similar reduction is made to the depreciation cap. If the mid-quarter convention applies, depreciation is allowed from the beginning of the year through the mid-point of the quarter of disposition if the recovery period has not ended.

If the 100 percent bonus rate applies, under the safe harbor the first-year deduction is limited to the first-year cap ($18,100 for a vehicle placed in service in 2020 or 2019). See *1A. Safe Harbor for Vehicles Acquired after September 27, 2017 and placed in service before 2023 if 100 Percent Bonus Claimed.* In the year of disposition, the depreciation deduction is equal to the lesser of (1) the applicable depreciation cap for the year of disposition or (2) the depreciation deduction computed by applying the applicable table percentage for the tax year to the cost of the vehicle as reduced by the first-year cap ($18,100 for a vehicle placed in service in 2020 or 2019) with an adjustment for the half-year or mid-quarter convention as applicable.

> ***Example 5A:*** A car (5-year MACRS property) costing $60,000 that is subject to the luxury car limitations is placed in service in February 2021 by a calendar-year taxpayer. The taxpayer claims 100-percent bonus depreciation on its 5-year property, including the vehicle. Under the safe harbor, the first-year deduction is limited to the 2021 first-year cap of $18,200 and depreciation in each subsequent year is equal to the product of the applicable table percentage and $41,800 ($60,000 – $18,200). If the car is sold in 2022 and the half-year convention applies, depreciation in the year of the disposition is $6,688, the lesser of (1) $16,400 second-year cap or (2) $6,688 ($41,800 × 32% × 50%).

> ***Example (6):*** A new car costing $50,000 was purchased on January 1, 2017, and disposed of in 2020. Bonus depreciation ($25,000) was claimed. However, the total depreciation deduction for 2017 was limited to the first-year cap of $11,160 for a vehicle placed in service in 2017. The allowable depreciation deduction in 2020 without regard to the third-year cap is $1,440 ($25,000 depreciable basis × 11.52% third year table percentage × 50% (to reflect half-year convention for year of sale)). The $25,000 depreciable basis is equal to the cost ($50,000) reduced by the bonus deduction ($25,000) determined without regard to the first-year cap. Since $1,440 does not exceed the $1,875 fourth-year depreciation cap for a car placed in service in 2017, the allowable 2020 depreciation deduction is $1,440.

> ***Example (7):*** Assume the same facts as in *Example (6)*, except that the business use percentage for 2020 is 80%. In this case, the allowable depreciation deduction without regard to the cap is $864 ((($50,000 cost × 80%) - $25,000 bonus) × 11.52% × 50%). The depreciation cap, as reduced to reflect personal use, is $1,500 ($1,875 × 80%). The taxpayer may claim $864 depreciation in 2020, since this is less than the adjusted $1,500 cap.

### *23. Vehicles in the New York Liberty Zone*

A new or used vehicle placed in service in the NYLZ after December 31, 2004, and before January 1, 2007, can only qualify for bonus depreciation at a 30-percent rate. The basic first-year luxury car cap amount, however, is not increased by any bump-up.

*Used vehicles.* A used vehicle placed in service in the NYLZ did not qualify for bonus depreciation unless substantially all of the use of the vehicle was in the New York Liberty Zone (NYLZ) in the active conduct of a trade or business by the taxpayer in the NYLZ and the first use of the vehicle in the NYLZ commenced with the taxpayer (Code Sec. 1400L(b)(2)(A)). A used vehicle placed in service in the NYLZ can only qualify for bonus depreciation at a 30-percent rate even if it is placed in service after May 5, 2003 when the rate under Code Sec. 168(k) increased to 50 percent. The $4,600 increase in the first-year basic cap that applies when bonus depreciation is claimed at the 30-percent rate does not apply to used vehicles placed in service in the NYLZ. Thus, the first-year cap for a *qualifying* used vehicle placed in service in the NYLZ in 2004, 2005, or 2006 is $2,960 in the case of a nonelectric car placed (Table I) and $3,260 in the case of a truck or van (Table II). The cap on a used electric vehicle placed in service in the NYLZ in 2004 and 2005 is $8,880 and in 2006 is $8,980 (Table III).

*New vehicles.* New vehicles placed in service in the NYLZ qualify for bonus depreciation at the 30-percent rate if placed in service after September 10, 2001, and before May 6, 2003. The 50-percent rate applies if the new vehicle is placed in service after May 5, 2003, and before January 1, 2005. The bump-ups ($4,600 if the 30-percent bonus rate applies and $7,650 if the 50-percent rate applies) to the basic first-year cap apply to these new vehicles.

A new or used vehicle placed in service in the NYLZ after December 31, 2004, and before January 1, 2007, only qualifies for bonus depreciation at the 30-percent rate. The basic luxury car cap amount for the first year, however, is not increased by any bump-up.

*Termination date for NYLZ bonus depreciation.* New or used vehicles placed in service in the NYLZ after 2006 do not qualify for NYLZ bonus depreciation. However, bonus allowance is available under the general bonus depreciation rules

*24. Vehicles in Gulf Opportunity GO-Zone, Kansas Disaster Area, or Presidentially Declared Disaster Area*

The regular luxury car depreciation caps apply to a vehicle that is placed in service in the Gulf Opportunity Zone (i.e., the GO-Zone) even if the 50 percent GO-Zone bonus deduction is claimed. There is no bump-up in the caps on account of the GO-Zone additional depreciation allowance available for qualifying property acquired after August 27, 2005 and placed in service before January 1, 2008. See ¶ 127F for a discussion of the Go-Zone bonus allowance.

There is also no bump-up if 50% bonus depreciation is claimed under Act § 15345 of the Heartland, Habitat, Harvest and Horticulture Acts of 2008 (P.L. 110-246) on a vehicle acquired on or after May 5, 2007 and placed in service in the Kansas Disaster Area on or before December 31, 2008. See ¶ 127G. Likewise, the otherwise allowable first-year cap is not increased if a vehicle qualifies for 50% bonus depreciation under Code Sec. 168(n) as qualified disaster assistance property placed in service after December 31, 2007, with respect to a federal disaster declared after that date and occurring before January 1, 2010. See ¶ 127H.

## ¶ 200A

## Safe Harbor Method for Vehicles on Which 100 Percent Bonus Was Claimed in 2010 or 2011

Section 3.03(5)(c) of Rev. Proc. 2011-26 provides a safe harbor method of accounting which addresses an anomalous result caused by the interaction of the 100 percent bonus depreciation rate for new vehicles acquired after September 8, 2010 and placed in service before January 1, 2012 and the Code Sec. 280F luxury car depreciation caps. As explained below, if the safe harbor method is not adopted a taxpayer will deduct an amount equal to the first-year cap in the year that the 100 percent-rate vehicle is placed in service and the remainder of the cost of the vehicle will only be recovered after the end of the vehicle's regular six-tax year depreciation period.

*Vehicles acquired after September 27, 2017 are also eligible for a 100 percent bonus rate. A separate safe harbor was issued for these vehicles (Rev. Proc. 2019-13). See discussion at ¶ 200, "1A. Safe Harbor for Vehicles Acquired after September 27, 2017 and placed in service before 2023 if 100 Percent Bonus Claimed."*

The first-year caps are $11,060 for a car placed in service in 2010 or 2011, $11,160 for a truck or van placed in service in 2010, and $11,260 for a truck or van placed in service in 2011. A comprehensive chart of depreciation caps is located above.

If the safe harbor method is adopted, a taxpayer will generally compute its depreciation deductions as if a 50 percent bonus depreciation rate applied to the vehicle. Consequently, the taxpayer will claim a first-year deduction equal to the applicable first-year cap and additional depreciation deductions will be claimed in each of the five remaining years of the vehicle's regular depreciation period as if a 50 percent bonus rate applied but in an amount no greater than the cap that applies for the year.

According to the General Explanation of Tax Legislation Enacted in the 111th Congress (JCS-2-11) (i.e., the "Blue Book" explanation) Congress intended that a 50 percent bonus depreciation rate apply to vehicles that are eligible for a 100 percent rate and subject to the Code Sec. 280F depreciation limitations. The report further states that a technical correction may be necessary to accomplish this result (Footnote 1597 of JCS-2-11). The IRS safe harbor in effect accomplishes this result.

*Vehicles that qualify for the safe harbor.* The safe harbor method may be used for vehicles placed in service in 2010 and 2011 to which a 100 percent bonus rate applies. The 100 percent rate applies to new vehicles acquired after September 8, 2010 and placed in service before January 1, 2012 (Code Sec. 168(k)(5), as added by the Tax Relief, Unemployment Insurance Reauthorization, and Job Creation Act of 2010 (P.L. 111-312)). The 100 percent bonus depreciation rate is discussed at ¶ 127D.

*How to adopt the safe harbor method.* The safe harbor method is adopted by using the safe-harbor computational method on the tax return for the tax year following the tax year in which the vehicle is placed in service (Rev. Proc. 2011-26, Section 3.03(5)(c)(ii)). No special election is required. Thus, a calendar-year taxpayer that claimed bonus depreciation on its 2011 return at the 100 percent rate adopts the safe harbor method by computing second-year depreciation in 2012 in the manner provided under the safe harbor. For a taxpayer who claimed a 100 bonus deduction on a vehicle acquired after September 8, 2010 and placed in service in 2010 but prior to issuance of the safe harbor method it is not necessary to amend the 2010 return (i.e., recompute the depreciation claimed on the 2010 return) since depreciation claimed on that return will have been computed correctly under the safe harbor method.

The safe harbor method may be used for none, some, or all of a taxpayer's eligible vehicles.

*How depreciation is computed if the safe harbor method is not adopted.* Without regard to the safe harbor relief, a taxpayer who claims a 100-percent bonus depreciation deduction on a new vehicle acquired after September 8, 2010, and placed in service before January 1, 2012 and that is used 100 percent for business purposes must deduct any cost in excess of the applicable first-year cap after the end of the vehicle's recovery period at the specified annual post-recovery period rate. In the case of a vehicle placed in service in 2010 and 2011, the post-recovery period rate is $1,775 for cars and $1,875 for trucks and vans. The first-year deduction claimed on the return is limited to the first-year cap. No deductions are allowed on the return during the remaining five years of the vehicle's regular recovery period (e.g., 2011 through 2015 if the vehicle is placed in service in 2010) because the 100 percent bonus deduction decreases the basis of the vehicle to $0 and, accordingly no regular depreciation may be claimed in the subsequent years of the vehicle's regular recovery period (Section 3.03(5)(c)(i) of Rev. Proc. 2011-26, 2011-12 I.R.B 560, amplifying Rev. Proc. 2011-21, 2011-12 I.R.B. 560).

The following example illustrates in detail how depreciation is computed if the safe harbor method of accounting is *not* adopted.

*Example (1):* A car costing $35,000 that is subject to the luxury car limitations is placed in service in November 2011 and used 100 percent for business purposes. The 100-percent bonus depreciation rate applies. However, because the first-year luxury car cap for the vehicle is $11,060, the bonus deduction that may be claimed is limited to $11,060. If the safe harbor method of accounting is not adopted, the $23,940 excess ($35,000 - $11,060) may only be recovered at the rate of $1,775 per year beginning in 2017, which is the first year after the end of the vehicle's depreciation period. No regular depreciation deductions are allowed after the first year of the vehicle's regular depreciation period because the vehicle's basis for computing depreciation deductions is reduced to $0 by the entire amount of the bonus depreciation allowed without regard to the first-year cap. The table percentages when applied to a depreciable basis of $0 are equal to $0.

| *Year* | *Regular Deduction* | *Luxury Car Cap* | *Allowable Depreciation* |
|---|---|---|---|
| 2011 | $35,000 | $11,060 | $11,060 |
| 2012 | $0 | $4,900 | $0 |
| 2013 | $0 | $2,950 | $0 |
| 2014 | $0 | $1,775 | $0 |
| 2015 | $0 | $1,775 | $0 |
| 2016 | $0 | $1,775 | $0 |
| | | TOTAL | $11,060 |

If a vehicle is used less than 100 percent for business in the placed-in-service year, the 100 percent bonus deduction applies, and the safe-harbor method is not adopted then a depreciation deduction will be allowed in any subsequent tax year of the regular recovery period in which the business use percentage exceeds the business use percentage in the placed-in-service year. However, the safe harbor method will still result in greater depreciation deductions as illustrated further below.

*Example (2):* A car costing $35,000 that is subject to the luxury car limitations is placed in service in November 2011 and used 75 percent for business purposes. Assume that the car is subject to the mid-quarter convention. The 100-percent bonus depreciation rate applies. The bonus depreciation deduction is $26,250 ($35,000 × 75%). However, because the first-year luxury car cap for the vehicle is $8,295 ($11,060 × 75%), the bonus deduction that may be claimed on the return is limited to $8,295. Assume that the business use percentage in 2012 increases to 90%. The depreciable basis of the car is equal to $5,250 ($35,000 × 90% – $26,250 bonus). The depreciation deduction without regard to the second-year cap is $1,995 ($5,250 × 38% second year table percentage for a vehicle subject to the mid-quarter convention and placed in service in the fourth quarter). Since the second-year cap of $4,410 ($4,900 × 90%) is greater than $1,995 depreciation computed without regard to the cap, the taxpayer may claim a $1,995 depreciation deduction on its tax return in 2012. If business use percentage drops to 75 percent or below in 2013, the depreciable basis of the vehicle is $0 ($35,000 ×75% – $26,250 bonus) and no depreciation may be claimed.

*How depreciation is computed if the safe harbor method is adopted.* If the safe harbor method is adopted depreciation on a 100 percent-rate vehicle is computed as follows (Rev. Proc. 2011-26 Section 3.02(5) (c) (ii)):

(1) In the placed-in-service year, the taxpayer will deduct the first-year limitation amount on its return.

(2) Next, the taxpayer will determine the unrecovered basis of the passenger automobile. The unrecovered basis is equal to the excess (if any) of (a) the depreciation (including bonus deduction) that would be allowed for the passenger automobile if the 50-percent bonus rate applied over (b) the first-year cap.

(3) If there is any unrecovered basis the taxpayer will determine the depreciation deductions for the passenger automobile for the tax years in the recovery period subsequent to the placed-in-service year as though the taxpayer claimed the 50-percent, instead of the 100-percent, bonus allowance in the placed-in-service year. The lesser of the deduction so computed for the tax year or the applicable cap for the tax year is claimed on the return.

(4) If there is no unrecovered basis in the placed-in-service year, the taxpayer *may not use the optional table percentages* and will determine the depreciation deduction for the passenger automobile for any 12-month tax year subsequent to the placed-in-service year by multiplying the adjusted depreciable basis of the passenger automobile (i.e., cost less depreciation deducted in prior years) by the applicable depreciation rate for each tax year. Depreciation rates are discussed at ¶ 179. If any tax year is less than 12 months, the depreciation deduction must be adjusted for a short tax year. For short tax year computations see "Short tax year," below, and ¶ 132 and following.

If the safe harbor method of accounting is adopted for a vehicle eligible for the 100 percent bonus rate, a taxpayer will deduct the amount of the first-year cap on the return (e.g. $11,060 for a car placed in service in 2011 assuming 100 percent business use) (Rev. Proc. 2011-26, Section 3.02(5) (c) (ii) (A)) whether or not there is an unrecovered basis.

The unrecovered basis attributable to the first recovery year (i.e., the placed-in-service year) and which is deductible beginning in the first post-recovery year at the specified rate ($1,775 for a car placed in service in 2011 assuming 100 business use and $1,885 for a truck or van), is equal to the excess (if any) of the depreciation that would have been claimed if a 50 percent bonus depreciation rate had applied (i.e., 50 percent bonus depreciation plus regular depreciation) over the applicable first-year cap.

If there is an unrecovered basis, depreciation deductions in each subsequent year of the recovery period are then determined as if bonus depreciation had been claimed at the 50 percent rate in the first-year of the recovery period. The deduction claimed on the return in each year after the placed-in-service year is the lesser of the depreciation cap for that year or the depreciation that would be allowed for that year if a 50 percent bonus had been claim in the placed-in-service year. As explained and illustrated below, use of the optional table percentages is not permitted if there is no unrecovered basis in the placed-in-service year because the first-year cap is greater than the sum of the deemed 50 percent bonus deduction and deemed regular first-year depreciation deduction.

*Practical effect of safe harbor.* The practical effect of the safe harbor is that if the sum of bonus depreciation and the regular first-year depreciation deduction, computed as if a 50 percent bonus rate apply, exceed the first-year cap, the taxpayer will claim exactly the same amount of depreciation during each of the six tax years of the vehicle's recovery period as would have been allowed if a 50 percent bonus depreciation rate had originally applied. If the deemed first-year deduction does not exceed the first-year cap, the taxpayer will claim a first-year deduction equal to the first-year cap and generally be able to deduct the entire amount of the remaining cost of the vehicle over the next five years of the regular six year recovery period.

In either situation, the first-year deduction is equal to the first-year cap (e.g., $11,060 for a car placed in service in 2010 or 2011). Thus, unless a taxpayer has a compelling reason to defer depreciation on the vehicle into post-recovery years, the safe harbor method should be adopted. In such a situation a taxpayer should consider an election out of bonus depreciation, as described at ¶ 127D.

*Relation of safe harbor to election to claim 50 percent bonus rate in lieu of 100 percent rate.* A taxpayer may elect a 50 percent bonus depreciation rate in lieu of the 100 percent rate for any class of MACRS property in a tax year that includes September 8, 2010 (Rev. Proc. 2011-26). See, *"Election to claim 50-percent bonus depreciation in place of 100-percent bonus depreciation for tax year that includes September 9, 2010"* at ¶ 127D. Thus, a taxpayer may make this election for five-year property (the property class of a car, truck, or van) to avoid the anomalous interaction between the 100 percent bonus rate and the caps. However, the election to use a 50 percent rate in lieu of the 100 percent rate would apply to all five-year property placed in service by the taxpayer—not simply its vehicles. Further, since the safe-harbor method generally provides a result equivalent to or better than the computation using a 50 percent bonus rate, the election to use the 50 percent rate in lieu of the 100 percent rate provides no benefit.

*Relation of safe-harbor to Section 179 allowance.* A taxpayer should not claim the section 179 allowance on a vehicle that is eligible for the 100 percent bonus depreciation rate. Since the entire cost of the vehicle can be claimed as a bonus deduction (subject to the first-year cap) no benefit would be derived by electing to expense any portion of the vehicle's cost. For a detailed discussion of the interrelationship of the Code Sec. 179 deduction and the Code Sec. 280F depreciation caps, see ¶ 487.

*Exception for trucks and vans with GVWR over 6,000 pounds.* Trucks and vans (including SUVs) with a gross vehicle rate rating (GVWR) in excess of 6,000 pounds are not subject to the Code Sec. 280F caps. See the first Quick Reference Table for a list of vehicles with a GVWR exceeding 6,000 pounds. Online users can use the search term "GVWR Exceeding 6,000." Thus, a taxpayer may avoid the caps and the necessity of utilizing the safe-harbor by purchasing a heavy vehicle.

*New vehicles costing less than first-year cap.* In the unlikely event that a new vehicle costs less than the applicable first-year cap it would not be necessary to adopt the safe harbor method of accounting since the entire cost could be claimed as a bonus deduction in the year of purchase. Used vehicles are not eligible for bonus depreciation. See 127D.

*Examples of safe harbor computations using table percentages when vehicle has unrecovered basis.* The following example illustrates how depreciation is computed if the safe harbor method of accounting is used in a situation where the sum of the deemed 50 percent bonus deduction and deemed regular first-year deduction exceed the first-year cap (i.e., there is an unrecovered basis).

> ***Example (3):*** A car costing $35,000 that is subject to the luxury car limitations is placed in service in November 2011 and used 100 percent for business purposes. The 200 percent declining balance method and mid-quarter convention apply. Because the first-year luxury car cap for the vehicle is $11,060, the 100 percent bonus deduction that may be claimed on the 2011 return is limited to $11,060. Next, the taxpayer computes the amount of depreciation that would have been allowed in 2011 without regard to the first-year cap if a 50 percent bonus rate applied. This amount is $18,375 (($35,000 × 50% = $17,500 deemed bonus deduction) + ($17,500 depreciable basis ($35,000 cost – $17,500 bonus deduction) × 5% = $875)). 5% is the first-year table percentage for assets placed in service in the fourth quarter if the mid-quarter convention applies. The unrecovered basis with respect to 2011 which may be deducted beginning in 2017 as a post-recovery period deduction at the rate of $1,775 per year is $7,315 ($18,375 – $11,060). In each

subsequent recovery year, the deduction for the tax year is the lesser of (1) the depreciation deduction computed as if bonus depreciation was claimed at the 50 percent rate in the first recovery year or (2) the applicable cap for the year. For example, in 2012, the depreciation deduction computed as if bonus depreciation had been claimed at the 50 percent rate is $6,650 ($17,500 depreciable basis × 38% second-year mid-quarter convention table percentage). Since this amount exceeds the second-year cap ($4,900) the taxpayer may claim a $4,900 deduction on his return. The $1,750 excess ($6,650 – $4,900) is the unrecovered basis for the year that is treated as a post-recovery period deduction. The 2013 return deduction is $2,950: the lesser of $3,990 ($17,500 × 22.80%) or the $2,950 third year cap. The unrecovered basis is $1,040 ($3,990 – $2,950). The 2014 return deduction is $1,775: the lesser of $2,394 ($17,500 × 13.68%) or $1,775 fourth year cap. The unrecovered basis is $619 ($2,394 – $1,775). The 2015 return deduction is $1,775: the lesser of $1,915 ($17,500 × 10.94%) or $1,775 fifth year cap. The unrecovered basis is $140 ($1,915 – $1,775). The 2016 return deduction is $1,677: the lesser of $1,677 ($17,500 × 9.58%) or $1,775 sixth year cap.

| *Year* | *Safe-Harbor Deduction* | *Luxury Car Cap* | *Allowable Safe-Harbor Depreciation* |
|---|---|---|---|
| 2011 | $18,375 | $11,060 | $11,060 |
| 2012 | $6,650 | $4,900 | $4,900 |
| 2013 | $3,990 | $2,950 | $2,950 |
| 2014 | $2,394 | $1,775 | $1,775 |
| 2015 | $1,915 | $1,775 | $1,775 |
| 2016 | $1,677 | $1,775 | $1,677 |
| | | TOTAL | $24,137 |

By adopting the safe harbor method of accounting, the taxpayer will claim a total of $24,137 ($11,060 + $4,900 + $2,950 + $1,775 + $1,775 + $1,677 = $24,137) in depreciation deductions on its return over the vehicle's regular recovery period and its unrecovered basis, recoverable at the rate of $1,775 per year beginning in 2017, is $10,863 ($7,315 + $1,750 + $1,040 + $619 + $140). The total deductions equal $35,000 ($24,137 + $10,863). The same annual amounts of depreciation would have been deducted if the vehicle had simply been eligible for a 50 percent bonus depreciation deduction.

See also Example 5 in Section 3.04 of Rev. Proc. 2011-26.

***Example (4):*** A car costing $35,000 that is subject to the luxury car limitations is placed in service in November 2011 and used 75 percent for business purposes. Assume that the car is subject to the mid-quarter convention. The safe harbor method is adopted. The bonus depreciation deduction is $26,250 ($35,000 × 75% business use percentage × 100% bonus rate). However, because the first-year luxury car cap for the vehicle is $8,295 ($11,060 × 75%), the bonus deduction that may be claimed on the return in 2011 is limited to $8,295. If the 50 percent bonus rate had applied bonus depreciation in 2011 would have been $13,125 ($35,000 ×75% × 50%). The basis to which the first-year table percentage is applied is $13,125 ($35,000 × 75% business use percentage – $13,125 bonus deduction). The regular first-year depreciation deduction would have been $656 ($13,125 × 5% first-year mid-quarter table percentage). If the 50 percent rate had applied in the first-year the deduction claimed on the return would have been limited to the first-year cap of $8,295 since this is less than the $13,781 sum of the bonus depreciation ($13,125) and regular depreciation ($656) computed as if the 50 percent rate applied. The unrecovered basis of the vehicle attributable to 2011 is $5,486 ($13,781 – $8,295) and will be recovered as a post-recovery period deduction. Assume that the business use percentage in 2012 increases to 90%. The depreciable basis of the car is deemed equal to $18,375 ($35,000 × 90% – $13,125 bonus). The depreciation deduction without regard to the second-year cap on the deemed basis is $6,983 ($18,375 × 38% second year table percentage for a vehicle subject to the mid-quarter convention and placed in service in the fourth quarter). Since the second-year cap of $4,410 ($4,900 × 90%) is less than $6,983, the taxpayer may claim a $4,410 depreciation deduction on its tax return in 2012. The unrecovered basis that may be deducted in post-recovery period years is $2,573 ($6,983 – $4,410). If business use drops to 60 percent in 2013, the deemed basis is $7,875 ($35,000 × 60% - $13,125 bonus). The depreciation deduction without regard to the third-year cap is $1,796 ($7,875 × 22.8%). Since this is greater than the third-year cap of $1,770 ($2,950 × 60%), the taxpayer may claim a $1,770 depreciation deduction on its tax return in 2013. The unrecovered basis that may be deducted in post-recovery years is $26 ($1,796 – $1,770).

| Year | *Safe-Harbor Deduction* | *Luxury Car Cap* | *Allowable Safe-Harbor Depreciation* |
|---|---|---|---|
| 2011 | $13,781 | $8,295 | $8,295 |
| 2012 | $6,983 | $4,410 | $4,410 |
| 2013 | $1,796 | $1,770 | $1,770 |
| | | TOTAL | $14,475 |

*Examples of safe harbor computations without using table percentages when vehicle has no unrecovered basis.* If there is no unrecovered basis for a passenger automobile in its placed-in-service year (i.e. the deemed bonus depreciation deduction computed at a 50% rate plus the deemed depreciation deduction for the placed-in-service year are less than the first-year cap), the optional table percentages may not be used after the year in which the vehicle is placed in service (Section 3.03(5)(c)(ii)(D) of Rev. Proc. 2011-26). Depreciation must be computed "long hand" using the applicable depreciation rate for the vehicle taking into account the depreciation method that applies to it. See ¶ 179 for rules relating to computations using rates in lieu of table percentages.

If the safe harbor method of accounting is adopted for a car placed in service after September 8, 2010 or in 2011 and the 200 percent declining balance method applies (the usual situation), the table percentages may not be used if a car costs less than the following amounts as shown for the applicable convention (half-year (HY) or mid-quarter (MQ)): $18,433.33—HY; $16,385.19—MQ1; $17,696.00—MQ2; $19,234.78—MQ3; $21,066.67—MQ4. In the case of a truck or van placed in service in 2010, the table percentages may not be used if the cost of the vehicle is the same or less than the following amounts: $18,600.00—HY; $16,533.33—MQ1; $17,856.00—MQ2; $19,408.70—MQ3; $21,257.14—MQ4. For trucks and vans placed in service after September 8, 2010 or in 2011 or vehicles not depreciated using the 200 percent declining balance method and half-year convention, refer to the Table A or B, as appropriate, below.

***Example (5):*** A car costing $20,000 that is subject to the luxury car limitations is placed in service by a calendar-year taxpayer in November 2011 and used 100 percent for business purposes. The 200 percent declining balance method and mid-quarter convention apply. Because the first-year luxury car cap for the vehicle is $11,060, the 100 percent bonus deduction that may be claimed on the 2011 return is limited to $11,060. Next, the taxpayer computes the amount of depreciation (including bonus) that would have been allowed in 2011 without regard to the first-year cap if a 50 percent bonus rate applied. This amount is $10,500 (($20,000 × 50% = $10,000 deemed bonus deduction) + ($10,000 depreciable basis ($20,000 cost – $10,000 bonus deduction) × 5% = $500 deemed depreciation deduction)). 5% is the first-year table percentage for assets placed in service in the fourth quarter if the mid-quarter convention applies. Under the mid-quarter convention the vehicle is deemed placed in service at the mid-point of the fourth quarter (October - December) or mid-November. Since $10,500 is less than the $11,060 first-year cap, there is no unrecovered basis and the optional table percentages may not be used to compute depreciation deductions subsequent to the 2011 placed-in-service year.

In 2012, depreciation is equal to $3,576 (($20,000 – $11,060) × 40%). 40% is the 200 percent double declining balance rate (1/5 (the recovery period for a vehicle) × 2) (see ¶ 179). Since $3,576 is less than the $4,900 second-year cap, the taxpayer may deduct $3,576 on its 2012 return. In 2013, depreciation without regard to the caps is $2,146 (($20,000 – $11,060 – $3,576) × 40%). Since this amount is less than the $2,950 third-year cap the taxpayer may deduct $2,146. In 2014, depreciation without regard to the caps is $1,287 (($20,000 – $11,060 – $3,576 – $2,146) × 40%). $1,287 is deducted since $1,287 is smaller than the $1,775 fourth-year cap. In 2015, the straight-line rate is 53.33 percent (1.875/1). Since the straight-line rate exceeds the 40 percent double declining balance rate, a switch to the straight-line method/rate applies. 1.875 is the number of years remaining in the 5-year recovery period as of the beginning of 2015 (1 full year in 2015 and .875 years in 2016 (i.e., January 1 through mid-November)). In 2015 depreciation claimed on the return is $1,030 (($20,000 – $11,060 – $3,576 – $2,146 – $1,287) × 53.33%) since this amount is less than the $1,775 fifth-year cap. In 2016, the straight-line rate is considered 100 percent and depreciation claimed on the return is $901 (($20,000 – $11,060 – $3,576 – $2,146 – $1,287 – $1,030) × 100%) since this amount is less than the $1,775 sixth-year cap. Total depreciation claimed is $20,000 ($11,060 + $3,576 + $2,146 + $1,287 + $1,030 + $901).

| *Year* | *Safe-Harbor Deduction* | *Luxury Car Cap* | *Allowable Safe-Harbor Depreciation* |
|---|---|---|---|
| 2011 | $11,060 | $11,060 | $11,060 |
| 2012 | $3,576 | $4,900 | $3,576 |
| 2013 | $2,146 | $2,950 | $2,146 |
| 2014 | $1,287 | $1,775 | $1,287 |
| 2015 | $1,030 | $1,775 | $1,030 |
| 2016 | $901 | $1,775 | $901 |
| | | TOTAL | $20,000 |

***Example (6):*** A new car costing $17,000 is placed in service in November 2011. Assume the vehicle is depreciated using the 200 percent declining balance method and the half-year convention applies. Business use in 2011 is 75% and in 2012 is 80 percent. Bonus depreciation computed using a deemed 50 percent bonus rate is $6,375 ($17,000 × 75% × 50% bonus rate). Deemed depreciation is $1,275 (($17,000 × 75% – $6,375) × 20% (first-year table percentage)). The sum of the deemed bonus depreciation and regular depreciation is $7,650 ($6,375 + $1,275). Since $7,650 is less than the $8,295 adjusted cap ($11,060 × 75% = $8,295) there is no unrecovered basis and the taxpayer may claim a $8,295 bonus deduction in 2011. In 2012 and subsequent years the optional table percentages may no longer be used. 2012 depreciation without regard to the caps is $2,122 (($17,000 × 80% – $8,295 accumulated depreciation) × 40% rate). The adjusted 2012 cap is $3,920 ($4,900 × 80%). The 2012 depreciation deduction is $2,122, since $2,122 is less than the $3,920 cap. If business use is 80% in 2013, the deduction is $1,273—the lesser of $2,360 ($2,950 × 80%) or $1,273 (($17,000 × 80% – $8,295 – $2,122) × 40%).

See also Example 6 in Section 3.04 of Rev. Proc. 2011-26. For partial business use computations without table percentages see ¶ 179.

See ¶ 179 for examples showing how to compute depreciation on an asset without tables when business use varies from year to year.

## ¶ 201
## $25,000 Expensing Limit on Certain Heavy SUVs, Trucks, and Vans

Taxpayers who purchased and placed a sport utility vehicle that was exempt from the luxury car depreciation limitations because it had a gross vehicle weight rating (GVWR) in excess of 6,000 pounds were allowed to claim the Code Sec. 179 expense deduction without restriction in the case of vehicles placed in service before October 23, 2004. For example, for tax years beginning in 2004 up to $102,000 of the cost of such a vehicle purchased before October 23, 2004 could be deducted, assuming the vehicle otherwise qualified for expensing under Code Sec. 179 and that the investment and taxable income limitations described at ¶ 300 did not limit the deduction.

The American Jobs Creation Act of 2004 (P.L. 108-357), however, limited the cost of an SUV that may be taken into account under Code Sec. 179 to $25,000 if the SUV is exempt from the Code Sec. 280F depreciation limitations, for example, because it has a gross vehicle weight rating in excess of 6,000 pounds or is a vehicle used in the trade or business of transporting persons or property for hire. The provision is effective for vehicles placed in service after October 22, 2004 (Code Sec. 179(b)(5), as added by the 2004 Jobs Act and redesignated by the Hiring Incentives to Restore Employment Act of 2010 (P.L. 111-147)). The limitation also applies to heavy pick-up trucks with a cargo bed under six feet that are exempt from the depreciation caps and certain heavy vans that are exempt from the depreciation caps.

The Code Sec. 179 SUV expense limit is inflation-adjusted annually, effective for tax years beginning after 2018 (Code Sec. 179(b)(6)). The inflation-adjusted limit for tax years beginning in 2022 is $27,000 (Rev. Proc. 2021-45), 2021 is $26,200 (Rev. Proc. 2020-45), $25,900 in 2020 (Rev. Proc. 2019-44), and $25,500 in 2019 (Rev. Proc. 2018-57).

The provision does not eliminate the exemption from the Code Sec. 280F luxury car depreciation limitations for sport utility vehicles that are considered trucks and have a gross vehicle weight rating in excess of 6,000 pounds (see ¶ 200). It simply prevents a taxpayer from expensing the entire cost of the vehicle under Code Sec. 179 if the vehicle is exempt. Consequently, owners of heavy sport utility vehicles that are considered trucks are still be able to claim a significantly higher first-year depreciation deduction than owners of lighter vehicles that are not exempt from the limitations.

*Partial business use.* Code Sec. 179(b)(5) states: "The cost of any sport utility vehicle for any taxable year which may be taken into account under this section shall not exceed $25,000." The limitation applies after the determination of the vehicle cost that is attributable to business use. Form 4562 and the instructions to Form 4562 (Depreciation and Amortization) do not require reduction for nonbusiness use.

> ***Example 1:*** An SUV that is exempt from the luxury car depreciation caps cost $100,000 in 2021 and is used 51% for business. Basis attributable to business use is $51,000 ($100,000 × 51%). Since this amount exceeds $26,200, a $26,200 expensing deduction is allowed. Note, that the section 179 allowance may not be claimed if business use is 50 percent or less.

*Interaction of SUV expensing limit with Code Sec. 179 investment limitation.* It appears that only the SUV expensing limit ($27,000 in tax years beginning in 2022, $26,200 in tax years beginning in 2021, and $25,900 in 2020) portion of the cost of a sport utility vehicle that is exempt from the caps should be taken into account in applying the Code Sec. 179(b)(2) investment limitation. This limitation reduces the maximum dollar amount ($1,050,000 in 2021) and $1,080,000 in 2022) by the excess of the amount invested in all section 179 property over the investment limitation for the tax year ($2,620,000 in 2021 and $2,700,000 in 2022). See ¶ 300 for discussion of the investment limitation. Code Sec. 179(b)(5) simply states: "The cost of any sport utility vehicle for any taxable year which may be taken into account under 'this section' shall not exceed $25,000." Since the Code Sec. 179(b)(2) investment limitation is a part of "this section" (i.e., Code Sec. 179) no more than the SUV expense limitation ($26,200 in 2021 and $27,000 in 2022) of the cost of an SUV should be taken into account under the Code Sec. 179(b)(2) investment limitation.

> ***Example 2:*** In the 2021 tax year, Tony places in service a heavy $100,000 sport utility vehicle and $2,650,000 of other section 179 property. The $1,050,000 dollar limitation is reduced by $56,200 (($26,200 + $2,650,000) – $2,620,000).

*Multiple vehicles purchased in single tax year.* The inflation-adjusted SUV expense limit applies to each separate vehicle (Code Sec. 179(b)(5)(A))

*Sport utility vehicle defined.* For purposes of the new provision, a "sport utility vehicle" is broadly defined as any four-wheeled vehicle:

> (1) primarily designed or which can be used to carry passengers over public streets, roads, or highways (except any vehicle operated exclusively on a rail or rails);
>
> (2) which is not subject to the Code Sec. 280F depreciation caps (i.e., the vehicle is considered a truck and has a GVWR in excess of 6,000 pounds or is otherwise exempt); and
>
> (3) which has a GVWR of not more than 14,000 pounds (Code Sec. 179(b)(5)(B)(i)).

Because this definition would include all heavy pickup trucks, vans, and small buses in addition to sport utility vehicles that are considered trucks, the term "sport utility vehicle" is further defined to exclude any of the following vehicles:

> (1) a vehicle designed to have a seating capacity of more than nine persons behind the driver's seat;
>
> (2) a vehicle equipped with a cargo area of at least six feet in interior length that is an open area and is not readily accessible directly from the passenger compartment;
>
> (3) a vehicle equipped with a cargo area of at least six feet in interior length that is designed for use as an open area but is enclosed by a cap and is not readily accessible directly from the passenger compartment; or
>
> (4) a vehicle with an integral enclosure, fully enclosing the driver compartment and load carrying device, does not have seating rearward of the driver's seat, and has no body section protruding more than 30 inches ahead of the leading edge of the windshield (Code Sec. 179(b)(5)(B)(ii)).

Under this definition, the inflation-adjusted SUV expensing limit ($27,000 for tax years beginning in 2021 and $26,200 for tax years beginning in 2021) applies to a passenger van with a GVWR in excess of 6000 pounds but which does not seat at least 10 persons behind the driver. Cargo vans are not subject to the limit if the requirements of item (4) are satisfied.

A few heavy pickup trucks with extended, quad, or crew cabs have a cargo bed shorter than six feet and, therefore, are subject to the $25,000 limit. ***A list of trucks with short beds is provided in Quick Reference Tables along with lists of SUVS, trucks, and vans that have a GVWR in excess of 6,000 pounds and***

***are exempt from the depreciation caps***. Online users may use search term "GVWR Exceeding 6,000."

Although the definition of an SUV for purposes of the SUV expensing limitation does not apply to a vehicle that weighs 6,000 pounds or less and is subject to the depreciation limitations, a taxpayer is already effectively prevented from claiming any expense allowance in most cases because regular first-year depreciation exceeds the first-year luxury car cap. See ¶ 200.

## ¶ 202

## Post-Recovery Period Deductions

If there is continued use of a vehicle for business purposes after expiration of the MACRS recovery period, a limited deduction (treated as a depreciation deduction) of the unrecovered basis resulting from application of the luxury car limits (¶ 200) is authorized by Code Sec. 280F(a)(1)(B). The authorized deduction may be claimed beginning in the first tax year after the tax year in which the recovery period ends. It would usually first be claimed in the seventh tax year after the vehicle is placed in service since the recovery period of most vehicles extends over six tax years. The limited deduction is claimed annually after the recovery period ends until the unrecovered basis of the car is considered fully recovered. A vehicle must continue to qualify as depreciable property in any year that a post-recovery period deduction is claimed.

The maximum post-recovery period deduction in each tax year after the tax year in which the recovery period ends is the same as the depreciation cap used for the vehicle in the fourth and succeeding years of the recovery period. Refer to the applicable annual dollar limits for the vehicle in the applicable table at ¶ 200 for the vehicle.

The maximum deduction must be reduced for personal use and is subject to the short tax year adjustments indicated at ¶ 200.

*Section 280F unrecovered basis*

In determining how much post-recovery period basis remains available for deduction, the basis of a passenger automobile is reduced by the maximum allowable deduction, taking into account the caps, computed as if the automobile were used 100 percent for business/investment use (Code Sec. 280F(d)(8)). Thus, the term "unrecovered basis" means the adjusted basis of the passenger automobile after reduction by the lesser of the amount of the full luxury car specific dollar limit or the depreciation deduction (assuming 100-percent business use even where, because of personal use, a smaller deduction was actually allowed).

There is currently no IRS guidance on the subject, but it appears based on the language of Code Sec. 280F(d)(8) that, for purposes of computing unrecovered basis in situations where business use is less than 100 percent in the placed-in-service year, the bonus depreciation deduction should be recomputed as if business use was 100 percent. See *Example 3*, below.

***Example (1):*** On April 5, 2021, a calendar-year taxpayer purchased a car for $70,000 and placed it in service. No amount is expensed under Code Sec. 179 or claimed as bonus depreciation. Business use of the car each year for the life of the car is 80%. Depreciation is computed under the general MACRS 200% declining-balance method over a 5-year recovery period using a half-year convention subject to limitation by Code Sec. 280F.

The recovery period depreciation for 2021 through 2026 is computed as follows:

| *Year* | *80% Business-Use MACRS Depreciation* | *80% Luxury Car Limit* | *Lesser of Col. 2 or 3* | *Section 280F Unrecovered Basis* |
|---|---|---|---|---|
| 2021 . . . . . . | $11,200 | $8,160 | $8,160 | See below |
| 2022 . . . . . . | 17,920 | 13,120 | 13,120 | See below |
| 2023 | 10,752 | 7,840 | 7,840 | See below |
| 2024 . . . . . . | 6,451 | 4,688 | 4,688 | See below |
| 2025 . . . . . . | 6,451 | 4,688 | 4,688 | See below |
| 2026 . . . . . . | 3,226 | 4,688 | 3,226 | See below |

The depreciation deduction for each year of the recovery period is the lesser of: (1) the depreciation deduction computed without regard to the luxury cap based on the percentage of business use for each year in the recovery period (80% in this example) or (2) the depreciation cap, as adjusted for the percentage of business use in each year of the recovery period (here 80%). For example, in 2021, regular depreciation assuming 80 percent business use is $11,200 ($70,000 cost × 80% business use × 20% first-year table percentage). The first-year cap as adjusted for personal use is $8,160 ($10,200 × 80% business use). The first-year deduction is limited to the smaller of the two amounts or $8,160.

The unrecovered basis during the regular recovery period of the car is computed by reducing the original basis ($70,000) in each year of the regular recovery period by the lesser of: (1) depreciation computed without regard to the annual depreciation caps as if business use is 100% or (2) the applicable depreciation cap determined as if business use is 100%.

| *Year* | *100% Business-Use MACRS Depreciation* | *100% Luxury Car Limit* | *Lesser of Col. 2 or 3* | *Section 280F Unrecovered Basis* |
|---|---|---|---|---|
| 2021 . . . . . | $14,000 | $10,200 | $10,200 | $59,800 |
| 2022 . . . . . | 22,400 | 16,400 | 16,400 | 43,400 |
| 2023 . . . . . | 13,440 | 9,800 | 9,800 | 33,600 |
| 2024 . . . . . | 8,064 | 5,860 | 5,860 | 27,740 |
| 2025 . . . . . | 8,064 | 5,860 | 5,860 | 21,880 |
| 2026 . . . . . | 4,032 | 5,860 | 4,032 | 17,848 |

The Sec. 280F unrecovered basis (Column 5) for each year in the recovery period is the original cost of the vehicle ($70,000) reduced by the accumulated depreciation that could have been claimed if business use for each year had been 100% (i.e., for each year, the lesser of Column 2 or Column 3). For example, 2021 unrecovered basis is $59,800 ($70,000 – $10,200). 2022 unrecovered basis is $43,400 ($70,000 – $10,200 – $16,400).

The $17,848 Section 280F unrecovered basis at the end of 2026 may be recovered in the post-recovery period years beginning in 2027. The allowable deduction for each post recovery period year is the lesser of: (1) the depreciation cap for post-recovery period years multiplied by the percentage of business use for the year ($4,688 ($5,860 × 80%)) or (2) the remaining Section 280F unrecovered basis at the beginning of the year multiplied by the percentage of business use. Section 280F unrecovered basis in each post-recovery year is reduced by the lesser of the full amount of the post-recovery period depreciation cap as if business use had been 100% or the Section 280F unrecovered basis at the beginning of the year.

Depreciation allowances for the years 2027 through 2030 after application of the luxury car limits are as follows, assuming 80% business use continues:

| *Year* | *Section 280F Unrecovered Basis at Beginning of Year* | *Luxury Car Limit* | *80% of Lesser* | *Section 280F Unrecovered Basis at End of Year* |
|---|---|---|---|---|
| 2027 . . . . . . . | $17,848 | $5,860 | $4,688 | $11,988 |
| 2028 . . . . . . . | 11,988 | 5,860 | 4,688 | 6,128 |
| 2029 . . . . . . . | 6,128 | 5,860 | 4,688 | 268 |
| 2030 . . . . . . . | 268 | 5,860 | 214 | 0 |

The total depreciation claimed by the taxpayer from 2021 through 2030 is $56,000 (the sum of Column 4 figures in the first and third tables in this example). This is the same amount of depreciation that would have been claimed during the regular recovery period (2020 - 2025) if the luxury car limits did not apply ($70,000 × 80%).

At first glance, one might conclude that the luxury car limits do not reduce overall depreciation (i.e., the depreciation that would be claimed if there were no luxury car caps) but rather simply increases the period over which otherwise allowable depreciation is claimed. However, this is not necessarily the case. For example, if the car in the preceding example had been converted to personal use for all of 2027 (the first post recovery period year), no additional depreciation deductions would be allowed and no portion of the disallowed deductions attributable to application of the depreciation caps during the earlier years would be recovered (Code Sec. 280F(a)(1)(B)(iii), indicating that post-recovery period deductions are not allowed unless the property is depreciable). Similarly, as illustrated in the example below, less than 80 percent of total cost will be deducted in the preceding example if the post-recovery business deductions drop below 80 percent.

***Example (2):*** Assume the same facts as in *Example (1)*, except that the business use percentages are 60% in 2027, 50% in 2028, 60% in 2029, and 80% in 2030. The post-recovery deductions would be computed as follows:

| *Year* | *Section 280F Unrecovered Basis at Beginning of Year* | *Luxury Car Limit* | *Business % of Lesser* | *Section 280F Unrecovered Basis at End of Year* |
|---|---|---|---|---|
| 2027 . . . . . . . | $17,848 | $5,860 | $3,516 | $11,988 |
| 2028 . . . . . . . | 11,988 | 5,860 | 2,930 | 6,128 |
| 2029 . . . . . . . | 6,128 | 5,860 | 3,516 | 268 |
| 2030 . . . . . . . | 268 | 5,860 | 214 | 0 |

In this example (which modifies Example (1), above) the total depreciation claimed on the vehicle (the sum of the Column 4 figures for 2021-2030) is $51,898. If there were no luxury car caps the taxpayer could have claimed $56,000 ($70,000 × 80% business use for the regular recovery 2020 - 2025 recovery period).

The following example shows how the first-year 50 percent bonus depreciation allowance is treated under the luxury car rules. See ¶ 200 *1A. Safe Harbor for Vehicles Acquired after September 27, 2017 and placed in service before 2023 if 100 Percent Bonus Claimed* for computations if the 100 percent bonus rate applies.

***Example (3):*** On April 5, 2017, a calendar-year taxpayer purchased a new car for $30,000 and claimed the 50% bonus depreciation allowance under Code Sec. 168(k). The 200 percent declining balance method and half-year convention apply. The vehicle is used 80% for business purposes during all years. 2017 bonus depreciation taking into account 80% business use but without regard to the first-year cap is $12,000 ($30,000 × 80% ×50%). Regular depreciation is $2,400 (($30,000 × 80% – $12,000) × 20%). The sum of regular and bonus depreciation taking into account 80% business use is $14,400 ($12,000 + $2,400). Depreciation in 2018, taking into account 80% business use is $3,840 (($30,000 × 80% - $12,000 bonus) ×32%). Depreciation is 2019 is $2,304 (($30,000 × 80% - $12,000 bonus) ×19.2%). Depreciation is 2020 and 2021 is $1,382 (($30,000 × 80% - $12,000 bonus) ×11.52%). Depreciation is 2022 is $691 (($30,000 × 80% - $12,000 bonus) ×5.76%).

The allowable recovery period depreciation for 2017 through 2022 taking into account the applicable depreciation caps is the lesser of: (1) the depreciation deduction for the year (based on 80% business use) computed without regard to the caps or (2) the caps (adjusted to reflect 80 percent business use).

| *Year* | *80% Business-Use MACRS Depreciation* | *80% Luxury Car Limit* | *Lesser of Col. 2 or 3* | *Section 280F Unrecovered Basis* |
|---|---|---|---|---|
| 2017 ....... | $14,400 | $8,928 | $8,928 | See below |
| 2018 ....... | 3,840 | 4,080 | 3,840 | See below |
| 2019 ....... | 2,304 | 2,440 | 2,304 | See below |
| 2020 ....... | 1,382 | 1,500 | 1,382 | See below |
| 2021 ....... | 1,382 | 1,500 | 1,382 | See below |
| 2022 ....... | 691 | 1,500 | 691 | See below |

The unrecovered basis during the regular recovery period of the car is computed by reducing the original basis ($30,000) in each year of the regular recovery period by the lesser of: (1) depreciation computed without regard to the annual depreciation caps as if business use is 100% or (2) the applicable depreciation cap determined as if business use is 100%.

| *Year* | *100% Business-Use MACRS Depreciation* | *100% Luxury Car Limit* | *Lesser of Col. 2 or 3* | *Section 280F Unrecovered Basis* |
|---|---|---|---|---|
| 2017 .................. | $18,000 | $11,160 | $11,160 | $18,840 |
| 2018 .................. | 4,800 | 5,100 | 4,800 | 14,040 |
| 2019 .................. | 2,880 | 3,050 | 2,880 | 11,160 |
| 2020 .................. | 1,728 | 1,875 | 1,728 | 9,432 |
| 2021 .................. | 1,728 | 1,785 | 1,728 | 7,704 |
| 2022 .................. | 864 | 1,875 | 864 | 6,840 |

The $6,840 unrecovered basis at the end of 2022 may be recovered in the post-recovery period years beginning in 2023 at the rate of $1,500 ($1,875 × 80%) per year, assuming business use continues at 80 percent. However, the unrecovered basis is reduced by $1,875 in each post recovery year. See Example (2).

## ¶ 204

## Leased Automobiles and Other Listed Property

*Lessors*

Listed property (¶ 208) leased or held for leasing by a person regularly engaged in the business of leasing listed property is not subject to the listed property rules of Code Sec. 280F (Code Sec. 280F(c)(1)). A person is considered to be regularly engaged in the business of leasing cars (or other listed property) only if contracts to lease cars (or other listed property) are made with some frequency over a continuous period. Occasional or incidental leasing is not considered leasing activity. An employer that allows an employee to use the employer's car for personal purposes and charges the employee for such use is not regularly engaged in the business of leasing (Temp. Reg. § 1.280F-5T(c)).

Listed property leased or held for leasing by a person not regularly engaged in the business of leasing listed property is subject to the listed property rules of Code Sec. 280F.

A car manufacturer that leased several thousand vehicles per year to its employees at reduced rates pursuant to a bona fide employee leasing program was considered regularly engaged in the business of leasing listed property. It was not necessary to show that the leasing program operated at a profit. It was sufficient that the leasing activity is substantial with a reasonable connection to the overall business activities of the taxpayer (Technical Advice Memorandum 200841037, May 30, 2008). A husband and wife formed two entities for the purpose of leasing one or two aircraft at a time to three lessees owned primarily by the husband and wife. Most of the use of the airplanes was by the husband and wife for personal purposes. Based on the totality of the circumstances, including the limited number of leased aircraft, the fact that the lessors and lessees were related, and the personal use of the aircraft, the IRS ruled that the lessor entities were not regularly engaged in the business of leasing listed property (Technical Advice Memorandum 200945037, July 29, 2009).

*Leases of Listed Property for 30 Days or More*

To prevent avoidance of the "listed property" luxury car rules (¶ 200) and the "listed property" business use rules (¶ 206 and ¶ 210) that apply to owned passenger automobiles and other listed property, a parallel system of limitations applies to leased passenger automobiles (discussed below) and to other leased listed property (see ¶ 212). The system applies to all lessees of passenger automobiles and other listed property regardless of whether the lessor is regularly engaged in the business of leasing.

The mechanics of providing comparable limitations on purchased property and leased property are accomplished by reducing the lessee's rental deductions by inclusion amounts. No inclusion amount is required if the lease term is less than 30 days (Code Sec. 280F(c)(2)).

Note that the lessee inclusion amounts that were included in income over the term of the lease are *not* deductible at the end of the lease term.

Under this system, a lessee who leases a passenger automobile for business may be required to include an amount in gross income, based on the price of the car, to offset rental deductions.

The inclusion amount is entered on Schedule C (Form 1040) by the self-employed, Form 2106 by employees, and on Schedule F (Form 1040) by farmers. On these forms, the inclusion amount is in effect included in gross income by reducing rental expense.

*Lease inclusion tables for passenger automobiles*

*Lease inclusion tables for passenger automobiles are reproduced at ¶ 205.*

*AnswerConnect and IntelliConnect subscribers have access to an interactive calculator which will compute a lease inclusion schedule..*

If a taxpayer leases a passenger automobile after 1986 for 30 days or more, the inclusion amount for each tax year that the automobile is leased is determined by referring to the appropriate table based on the calendar-year in which the lease term begins. The term "passenger automobile" cars and also pick-up trucks, SUVs, and vans with a gross vehicle weight rating (GVWR) of 6,000 pounds or less (see ¶ 208). The lease inclusion tables are only used if the vehicle would be subject to the depreciation caps if the lessee owned it. Thus, a taxpayer who leases a truck, SUV, or van with a GVWR in excess of 6,000 pounds is not required to compute an inclusion amount. In 2003, the IRS began to issue separate lease inclusion tables for trucks (including SUVs that are considered trucks) and vans.

To figure the lease inclusion amount for a leased passenger automobiles, from the appropriate table:

(1) Locate the dollar amounts for the years of the lease term based on the fair market value of the vehicle on the first day of the lease term.

(2) Select the dollar amount for the tax year in which the automobile is used under the lease.

(3) Prorate the dollar amount for the number of days of the lease term included in the tax year.

(4) Multiply the prorated dollar amount by the business/investment use for the tax year (Reg. § 1.280F-7(a)).

*Dollar amount for last tax year.* For the last tax year during any lease that does not begin and end in the same tax year, the dollar amount for the preceding year is used.

*Lease term.* The rules of Code Sec. 168(i)(3)(A) apply in determining the length of the term of a lease (Temporary Reg.§ 1.280F-5T(h)(2)).

*Fair market value.* With respect to fair market value, if the lease agreement provides a capitalized cost of the vehicle, that cost should be used as the fair market value. Otherwise, fmv is determined on the basis of what would be paid in an arms-length transaction on the first day of the lease term (Temporary Reg.§ 1.280F-5T(h)(2)). Similar sales at the time of the lease may be useful in determining fair market value.

*Fiscal-year taxpayer.* A fiscal-year taxpayer uses the table that applies based on the calendar year in which the vehicle is first leased. See *Example (12)* at ¶ 205.

*Partial business use.* The inclusion amount that applies for the tax year is multiplied by the percentage of business/investment use for the tax year. See *Example (13)* at ¶ 205.

*Business car converted to personal use.* If a leased business car is converted to personal use, the dollar amount for the tax year in which business use ceases is the dollar amount for the preceding tax year. See *Example (14)* at ¶ 205.

*Personal car converted to business use.* If a car leased for personal purposes is later converted to business use, the fair market value is determined on the date of the conversion to business use. See *Example (15)* at ¶ 205.

*FMV trigger points.* Lease inclusion amounts are required in the case of leased vehicles if the fair market value on the first day of the lease exceeds the amount listed in the appropriate table. Table I is for cars, trucks (including SUVS), and vans first leased after 2017. Table II is for cars first leased before 2018. Table III is for trucks (including SUVs) and vans leased before 2018.

Table I

*Cars, Trucks (Including SUVs), and Vans leased after 2017*

| *Calendar year first leased* | *FMV Over* | *Authority* |
|---|---|---|
| 2021 . . . . . . . . . . | $51,000 | Rev. Proc. 2021-31 |
| 2020 . . . . . . . . . . | $50,000 | Rev. Proc. 2020-37 |
| 2019 . . . . . . . . . . | $50,000 | Rev. Proc. 2019-26 |
| 2018 . . . . . . . . . . | $50,000 | Rev. Proc. 2018-25 |

Table II

*Vehicles (Other Than Trucks and Vans) First Leased Before 2018*

| *Calendar year first leased* | *FMV Over* | *Authority* |
|---|---|---|
| 2017 . . . . . . . . . . . . . . | $19,000 | Rev. Proc. 2017-29 |
| 2016 . . . . . . . . . . . . . . | $19,000 | Rev. Proc. 2016-23 |
| 2015 . . . . . . . . . . . . . . | $19,000 | Rev. Proc. 2015-19, as modified by Rev. Proc. 2016-23 |
| 2014 . . . . . . . . . . . . . . | $19,000 | Rev. Proc. 2014-21, as modified by Rev. Proc. 2015-19 |

*Vehicles (Other Than Trucks and Vans) First Leased Before 2018*

| *Calendar year first leased* | *FMV Over* | *Authority* |
|---|---|---|
| 2013 . . . . . . . . . . . . . . | $19,000 | Rev. Proc. 2013-21 |
| 2012 . . . . . . . . . . . . . . | $18,500 | Rev. Proc. 2012-23 |
| 2011 . . . . . . . . . . . . . . | $18,500 | Rev. Proc. 2011-21 |
| 2010 . . . . . . . . . . . . . . | $18,500 | Rev. Proc. 2010-18, as modified by Rev. Proc. 2011-21 |
| 2009 . . . . . . . . . . . . . . | $18,500 | Rev. Proc. 2009-24 |
| 2008 . . . . . . . . . . . . . . | $18,500 | Rev. Proc. 2008-22 |
| 2007 . . . . . . . . . . . . . . | $15,500 | Rev. Proc. 2007-30 |
| 2006 . . . . . . . . . . . . . . | $15,200 | Rev. Proc. 2006-18 |
| 2005 . . . . . . . . . . . . . . | $15,200 | Rev. Proc. 2005-13 |
| 2004 . . . . . . . . . . . . . . | $17,500 | Rev. Proc. 2004-20 |
| 2003 . . . . . . . . . . . . . . | $18,000 | Rev. Proc. 2003-75 |
| 2002 . . . . . . . . . . . . . . | $15,500 | Rev. Proc. 2002-14 |
| 2001 . . . . . . . . . . . . . . | $15,500 | Rev. Proc. 2001-19 |

### *Trucks and vans first leased before 2018*

A separate lease inclusion table is provided for trucks (including SUVs that are considered trucks) and vans that are leased before 2018. A lease inclusion amount using this table is only required if the truck or van would be subject to the annual depreciation caps if it was owned by the lessee. Thus, no inclusion amount is required if the leased truck or van has a loaded gross vehicle weight of more than 6,000 pounds.

Table III

*Trucks and Vans leased before 2018*

| *Calendar year first leased* | *FMV Over* | *Authority* |
|---|---|---|
| 2017 . . . . . . . . . . . . . . | $19,500 | Rev. Proc. 2017-29 |
| 2016 . . . . . . . . . . . . . . | $19,500 | Rev. Proc. 2016-23 |
| 2015 . . . . . . . . . . . . . . | $19,500 | Rev. Proc. 2015-19, as modified by Rev. Proc. 2016-23 |
| 2014 . . . . . . . . . . . . . . | $19,500 | Rev. Proc. 2014-21, as modified by Rev. Proc. 2015-19 |
| 2013 . . . . . . . . . . . . . . | $19,000 | Rev. Proc. 2013-21 |
| 2012 . . . . . . . . . . . . . . | $19,000 | Rev. Proc. 2012-23 |
| 2011 . . . . . . . . . . . . . . | $19,000 | Rev. Proc. 2011-21 |
| 2010 . . . . . . . . . . . . . . | $19,000 | Rev. Proc. 2010-18, as modified by Rev. Proc. 2011-21 |
| 2009 . . . . . . . . . . . . . . | $18,500 | Rev. Proc. 2009-24 |
| 2008 . . . . . . . . . . . . . . | $19,000 | Rev. Proc. 2008-22 |
| 2007 . . . . . . . . . . . . . . | $16,400 | Rev. Proc. 2007-30 |
| 2006 . . . . . . . . . . . . . . | $16,700 | Rev. Proc. 2006-18 |
| 2005 . . . . . . . . . . . . . . | $16,700 | Rev. Proc. 2005-13 |
| 2004 . . . . . . . . . . . . . . | $18,000 | Rev. Proc. 2004-20 |
| 2003 . . . . . . . . . . . . . . | $18,500 | Rev. Proc. 2003-75 |

### *Electric vehicles*

Separate inclusion amount tables are provided for clean-air vehicles (see ¶ 200) first leased after August 5, 1997 and before 2007. For such vehicles first leased in 2007 and thereafter, the appropriate lease inclusion table above is used.

The lease inclusion amounts are required if the fair market value of the vehicle on the date of lease exceeds the following amounts:

*Electric Vehicles first leased before 2007*

| *Calendar year first leased* | *FMV Over* | *Authority* |
|---|---|---|
| after 2006 | Refer to tables above | |
| 2006 | $45,000 | Rev. Proc. 2006-18 |
| 2005 | $45,000 | Rev. Proc. 2005-13 |
| 2004 | $53,000 | Rev. Proc. 2004-20 |
| 2003 | $53,000 | Rev. Proc. 2003-75 |
| 2002 | $46,000 | Rev. Proc. 2002-14 |
| 2001 | $47,000 | Rev. Proc. 2001-19 |
| 2000 | $47,000 | Rev. Proc. 2000-18 |
| 1999 | $47,000 | Rev. Proc. 99-14 |
| 1998 | $47,000 | Rev. Proc. 98-30 |
| 8/5/97 - 12/31/97 | $47,000 | Rev. Proc. 98-24 |

*Reporting the inclusion amount*

Employees who lease a vehicle report the inclusion amount on Form 2106, Section C. The self-employed use Schedule C (Form 1040), and farmers use Schedule F (Form 1040).

## ¶ 205

## Automobile Lease Inclusion Tables

**Lease Inclusion Table Index**



Lease inclusion tables not reproduced in full text in this paragraph can be found in the applicable annual IRS revenue procedure referenced in the tables at ¶ 204.

## VEHICLE LEASE INCLUSION AMOUNTS AFTER 2017

*Inclusion Amounts for Vehicles First Leased in 2021*

The following table from Rev. Proc. 2021-31 governs computation of includible amounts for passenger automobiles with a fair market value exceeding $51,000 and first leased in 2021. This table also applies to trucks and vans (including SUVs) with a fair market value exceeding $51,000 first leased in 2021.

**REV. PROC. 2021-** TABLE 3 DOLLAR AMOUNTS FOR PASSENGER AUTOMOBILES WITH A LEASE TERM BEGINNING IN CALENDAR YEAR 2021**

| Fair Market Value of Passenger Automobile | | Tax Year During Lease | | | | |
|---|---|---|---|---|---|---|
| Over | Not Over | 1st | 2nd | 3rd | 4th | 5th & later |
| $51,000 | $52,000 | 0 | 0 | 1 | 0 | 1 |
| 52,000 | 53,000 | 1 | 1 | 1 | 2 | 2 |
| 53,000 | 54,000 | 1 | 2 | 2 | 3 | 4 |
| 54,000 | 55,000 | 1 | 3 | 3 | 5 | 5 |
| 55,000 | 56,000 | 2 | 3 | 5 | 6 | 6 |
| 56,000 | 57,000 | 2 | 4 | 6 | 7 | 8 |
| 57,000 | 58,000 | 2 | 5 | 7 | 8 | 10 |
| 58,000 | 59,000 | 3 | 5 | 8 | 10 | 11 |
| 59,000 | 60,000 | 3 | 6 | 9 | 11 | 13 |
| 60,000 | 62,000 | 3 | 7 | 11 | 13 | 15 |
| 62,000 | 64,000 | 4 | 9 | 13 | 15 | 18 |
| 64,000 | 66,000 | 5 | 10 | 15 | 18 | 21 |
| 66,000 | 68,000 | 5 | 12 | 17 | 21 | 24 |
| 68,000 | 70,000 | 6 | 13 | 20 | 23 | 27 |
| 70,000 | 72,000 | 7 | 14 | 22 | 26 | 30 |
| 72,000 | 74,000 | 7 | 16 | 24 | 29 | 33 |
| 74,000 | 76,000 | 8 | 18 | 26 | 31 | 36 |
| 76,000 | 78,000 | 9 | 19 | 28 | 34 | 39 |
| 78,000 | 80,000 | 9 | 21 | 30 | 37 | 42 |
| 80,000 | 85,000 | 11 | 23 | 34 | 41 | 48 |
| 85,000 | 90,000 | 12 | 27 | 40 | 47 | 55 |
| 90,000 | 95,000 | 14 | 30 | 45 | 55 | 62 |
| 95,000 | 100,000 | 16 | 34 | 50 | 61 | 70 |
| 100,000 | 110,000 | 18 | 40 | 58 | 71 | 81 |
| 110,000 | 120,000 | 21 | 47 | 70 | 83 | 97 |
| 120,000 | 130,000 | 25 | 54 | 81 | 96 | 112 |
| 130,000 | 140,000 | 28 | 62 | 91 | 110 | 127 |
| 140,000 | 150,000 | 31 | 69 | 103 | 123 | 141 |
| 150,000 | 160,000 | 35 | 76 | 114 | 136 | 157 |
| 160,000 | 170,000 | 38 | 84 | 124 | 149 | 172 |
| 170,000 | 180,000 | 41 | 91 | 135 | 163 | 187 |
| 180,000 | 190,000 | 45 | 98 | 146 | 176 | 202 |
| 190,000 | 200,000 | 48 | 106 | 157 | 188 | 218 |
| 200,000 | 210,000 | 51 | 113 | 168 | 202 | 232 |
| 210,000 | 220,000 | 55 | 120 | 179 | 215 | 247 |
| 220,000 | 230,000 | 58 | 128 | 190 | 227 | 263 |
| 230,000 | 240,000 | 61 | 135 | 201 | 241 | 278 |
| 240,000 | and over | 65 | 142 | 212 | 254 | 293 |

***Example (1):*** A car costing $61,000 is leased for four years by a calendar-year taxpayer beginning on April 1, 2021, and is used 100 percent for business. The annual dollar amounts from the table for leases beginning in 2021 are: $3 for the first tax year during the lease, $7 for the second tax year, $11 for the third tax year, $13 for the fourth tax year, and $15 for the fifth and following tax years. In 2021, the inclusion amount is $2.26 (275/365 × $3). The inclusion amounts for 2022, 2023, and 2024 are $7, $11, and $13, respectively, since the vehicle is leased for the entire year during these tax years. In 2025, the inclusion amount is $3.21 (90/365 × $13 (the dollar amount for 2024, the preceding tax year, is used in the last year of the lease)).

*Inclusion Amounts for Vehicles First Leased in 2020*

The following table from Rev. Proc. 2020-37 governs computation of includible amounts for passenger automobiles with a fair market value exceeding $50,000 and first leased in 2020. This table also applies to trucks and vans (including SUVs) with a fair market value exceeding $50,000 first leased in 2020.

Rev. Proc. 2020-37 TABLE 4 DOLLAR AMOUNTS FOR PASSENGER AUTOMOBILES WITH A LEASE TERM BEGINNING IN CALENDAR YEAR 2020

| Fair Market Value of Passenger Automobile | | Tax Year During Lease | | | | |
|---|---|---|---|---|---|---|
| Over | Not Over | 1st | 2nd | 3rd | 4th | 5th & later |
| $50,000 | $51,000 | 0 | 1 | 0 | 2 | 2 |
| 51,000 | 52,000 | 2 | 6 | 9 | 10 | 13 |
| 52,000 | 53,000 | 5 | 11 | 17 | 20 | 24 |
| 53,000 | 54,000 | 7 | 17 | 24 | 30 | 35 |
| 54,000 | 55,000 | 10 | 22 | 32 | 39 | 46 |
| 55,000 | 56,000 | 12 | 27 | 41 | 48 | 57 |
| 56,000 | 57,000 | 15 | 32 | 49 | 58 | 68 |
| 57,000 | 58,000 | 17 | 38 | 56 | 68 | 79 |
| 58,000 | 59,000 | 19 | 44 | 64 | 77 | 90 |
| 59,000 | 60,000 | 22 | 49 | 72 | 87 | 100 |
| 60,000 | 62,000 | 26 | 56 | 84 | 102 | 117 |
| 62,000 | 64,000 | 30 | 68 | 99 | 121 | 139 |
| 64,000 | 66,000 | 35 | 78 | 116 | 139 | 161 |
| 66,000 | 68,000 | 40 | 89 | 131 | 159 | 183 |
| 68,000 | 70,000 | 45 | 99 | 148 | 177 | 205 |
| 70,000 | 72,000 | 50 | 110 | 163 | 197 | 227 |
| 72,000 | 74,000 | 55 | 121 | 179 | 215 | 249 |
| 74,000 | 76,000 | 60 | 131 | 195 | 235 | 271 |
| 76,000 | 78,000 | 64 | 142 | 211 | 254 | 293 |
| 78,000 | 80,000 | 69 | 153 | 227 | 272 | 315 |
| 80,000 | 85,000 | 78 | 172 | 254 | 306 | 353 |
| 85,000 | 90,000 | 90 | 198 | 295 | 353 | 408 |
| 90,000 | 95,000 | 102 | 225 | 334 | 401 | 463 |
| 95,000 | 100,000 | 114 | 252 | 373 | 449 | 518 |
| 100,000 | 110,000 | 133 | 292 | 433 | 520 | 600 |
| 110,000 | 120,000 | 157 | 345 | 513 | 615 | 710 |
| 120,000 | 130,000 | 181 | 399 | 592 | 710 | 820 |
| 130,000 | 140,000 | 206 | 452 | 671 | 805 | 931 |
| 140,000 | 150,000 | 230 | 506 | 750 | 901 | 1,040 |
| 150,000 | 160,000 | 254 | 559 | 830 | 996 | 1,150 |
| 160,000 | 170,000 | 279 | 612 | 909 | 1,091 | 1,260 |
| 170,000 | 180,000 | 303 | 666 | 988 | 1,186 | 1,370 |

Rev. Proc. 2020-37 TABLE 4 DOLLAR AMOUNTS FOR PASSENGER AUTOMOBILES WITH A LEASE TERM BEGINNING IN CALENDAR YEAR 2020

| Fair Market Value of Passenger Automobile | | Tax Year During Lease | | | | |
|---|---|---|---|---|---|---|
| Over | Not Over | 1st | 2nd | 3rd | 4th | 5th & later |
| 180,000 | 190,000 | 327 | 720 | 1,067 | 1,281 | 1,480 |
| 190,000 | 200,000 | 351 | 773 | 1,147 | 1,377 | 1,589 |
| 200,000 | 210,000 | 376 | 826 | 1,227 | 1,471 | 1,700 |
| 210,000 | 220,000 | 400 | 880 | 1,306 | 1,566 | 1,810 |
| 220,000 | 230,000 | 424 | 934 | 1,385 | 1,661 | 1,920 |
| 230,000 | 240,000 | 449 | 987 | 1,464 | 1,757 | 2,029 |
| 240,000 | and over | 473 | 1,040 | 1,544 | 1,852 | 2,139 |

***Example (1A):*** A car costing $61,000 is leased for four years by a calendar-year taxpayer beginning on April 1, 2020, and is used 100 percent for business. The annual dollar amounts from the table for leases beginning in 2020 are: $26 for the first tax year during the lease, $56 for the second tax year, $84 for the third tax year, $102 for the fourth tax year, and $117 for the fifth and following tax years. In 2020, the inclusion amount is $19.59 (275/365 × $26). The inclusion amounts for 2021, 2022, and 2023 are $56, $84, and $102, respectively, since the vehicle is leased for the entire year during these tax years. In 2024, the inclusion amount is $25.15 (90/365 × $102 (the dollar amount for 2023, the preceding tax year, is used in the last year of the lease)).

### *Inclusion Amounts for Vehicles First Leased in 2019*

The following table from Rev. Proc. 2019-26 governs computation of includible amounts for passenger automobiles with a fair market value exceeding $50,000 and first leased in 2019. This table also applies to trucks and vans (including SUVs) with a fair market value exceeding $50,000 first leased in 2019.

REV. PROC. 2019-26 TABLE 4 DOLLAR AMOUNTS FOR PASSENGER AUTOMOBILES WITH A LEASE TERM BEGINNING IN CALENDAR YEAR 2019

| Fair Market Value of Passenger Automobile | | Tax Year During Lease | | | | |
|---|---|---|---|---|---|---|
| Over | Not Over | 1st | 2nd | 3rd | 4th | 5th & later |
| $50,000 | $51,000 | 0 | 1 | 1 | 3 | 3 |
| 51,000 | 52,000 | 4 | 11 | 15 | 20 | 23 |
| 52,000 | 53,000 | 9 | 20 | 30 | 36 | 43 |
| 53,000 | 54,000 | 13 | 30 | 44 | 53 | 63 |
| 54,000 | 55,000 | 17 | 40 | 58 | 70 | 83 |
| 55,000 | 56,000 | 22 | 49 | 72 | 88 | 102 |
| 56,000 | 57,000 | 26 | 59 | 86 | 105 | 122 |
| 57,000 | 58,000 | 31 | 68 | 101 | 122 | 142 |
| 58,000 | 59,000 | 35 | 78 | 115 | 139 | 161 |
| 59,000 | 60,000 | 39 | 88 | 129 | 156 | 181 |
| 60,000 | 62,000 | 46 | 102 | 151 | 181 | 211 |
| 62,000 | 64,000 | 55 | 121 | 179 | 216 | 250 |
| 64,000 | 66,000 | 63 | 140 | 208 | 251 | 289 |
| 66,000 | 68,000 | 72 | 160 | 236 | 284 | 329 |
| 68,000 | 70,000 | 81 | 179 | 265 | 318 | 369 |
| 70,000 | 72,000 | 90 | 198 | 293 | 353 | 408 |
| 72,000 | 74,000 | 98 | 217 | 322 | 387 | 448 |
| 74,000 | 76,000 | 107 | 236 | 351 | 421 | 487 |

REV. PROC. 2019-26 TABLE 4 DOLLAR AMOUNTS FOR PASSENGER AUTOMOBILES WITH A LEASE TERM BEGINNING IN CALENDAR YEAR 2019

| Fair Market Value of Passenger Automobile | | Tax Year During Lease | | | | |
|---|---|---|---|---|---|---|
| Over | Not Over | 1st | 2nd | 3rd | 4th | 5th & later |
| 76,000 | 78,000 | 116 | 255 | 379 | 456 | 526 |
| 78,000 | 80,000 | 125 | 275 | 407 | 489 | 567 |
| 80,000 | 85,000 | 140 | 308 | 458 | 549 | 635 |
| 85,000 | 90,000 | 162 | 356 | 529 | 635 | 734 |
| 90,000 | 95,000 | 184 | 404 | 600 | 720 | 833 |
| 95,000 | 100,000 | 206 | 452 | 671 | 806 | 931 |
| 100,000 | 110,000 | 238 | 525 | 778 | 934 | 1,079 |
| 110,000 | 120,000 | 282 | 621 | 920 | 1,105 | 1,277 |
| 120,000 | 130,000 | 326 | 717 | 1,063 | 1,276 | 1,474 |
| 130,000 | 140,000 | 370 | 812 | 1,206 | 1,447 | 1,672 |
| 140,000 | 150,000 | 413 | 909 | 1,348 | 1,618 | 1,869 |
| 150,000 | 160,000 | 457 | 1,005 | 1,491 | 1,788 | 2,067 |
| 160,000 | 170,000 | 501 | 1,101 | 1,633 | 1,960 | 2,264 |
| 170,000 | 180,000 | 545 | 1,197 | 1,776 | 2,130 | 2,461 |
| 180,000 | 190,000 | 588 | 1,293 | 1,919 | 2,301 | 2,659 |
| 190,000 | 200,000 | 632 | 1,389 | 2,061 | 2,473 | 2,856 |
| 200,000 | 210,000 | 676 | 1,485 | 2,204 | 2,643 | 3,053 |
| 210,000 | 220,000 | 720 | 1,581 | 2,346 | 2,815 | 3,250 |
| 220,000 | 230,000 | 763 | 1,677 | 2,489 | 2,986 | 3,448 |
| 230,000 | 240,000 | 807 | 1,773 | 2,632 | 3,156 | 3,645 |
| 240,000 | and over | 851 | 1,869 | 2,774 | 3,328 | 3,842 |

***Example (1B):*** A car costing $61,000 is leased for four years by a calendar-year taxpayer beginning on April 1, 2019, and is used 100 percent for business. The annual dollar amounts from the table for leases beginning in 2019 are: $46 for the first tax year during the lease, $102 for the second tax year, $151 for the third tax year, $181 for the fourth tax year, and $211 for the fifth and following tax years. In 2019, the inclusion amount is $34.66 (275/365 × $46). The inclusion amounts for 2020, 2021, and 2022 are $102, $151, and $181, respectively, since the vehicle is leased for the entire year during these tax years. In 2023, the inclusion amount is $44.63 (90/365 × $181 (the dollar amount for 2022, the preceding tax year, is used in the last year of the lease)).

### *Inclusion Amounts for Vehicles First Leased in 2018*

The following table from Rev. Proc. 2018-25 governs computation of includible amounts for passenger automobiles with a fair market value exceeding $50,000 and first leased in 2018. This table also applies to trucks and vans (including SUVs) with a fair market value exceeding $50,000 first leased in 2018.

REV. PROC. 2018-25 DOLLAR AMOUNTS FOR PASSENGER AUTOMOBILES WITH A LEASE TERM BEGINNING IN CALENDAR YEAR 2018

| Fair Market Value of Passenger Automobile | | Tax Year During Lease | | | | |
|---|---|---|---|---|---|---|
| Over | Not Over | 1st | 2nd | 3rd | 4th | 5th & later |
| $50,000 | $51,000 | 1 | 3 | 5 | 5 | 6 |
| 51,000 | 52,000 | 4 | 9 | 13 | 16 | 19 |
| 52,000 | 53,000 | 7 | 15 | 22 | 27 | 31 |

REV. PROC. 2018-25 DOLLAR AMOUNTS FOR PASSENGER AUTOMOBILES WITH A LEASE TERM BEGINNING IN CALENDAR YEAR 2018

| Fair Market Value of Passenger Automobile | | Tax Year During Lease | | | | |
|---|---|---|---|---|---|---|
| Over | Not Over | 1st | 2nd | 3rd | 4th | 5th & later |
| 53,000 | 54,000 | 10 | 21 | 31 | 37 | 44 |
| 54,000 | 55,000 | 12 | 27 | 40 | 48 | 56 |
| 55,000 | 56,000 | 15 | 33 | 49 | 59 | 68 |
| 56,000 | 57,000 | 18 | 39 | 58 | 69 | 81 |
| 57,000 | 58,000 | 20 | 45 | 67 | 80 | 93 |
| 58,000 | 59,000 | 23 | 51 | 76 | 91 | 105 |
| 59,000 | 60,000 | 26 | 57 | 85 | 101 | 117 |
| 60,000 | 62,000 | 30 | 66 | 98 | 118 | 135 |
| 62,000 | 64,000 | 36 | 78 | 116 | 139 | 160 |
| 64,000 | 66,000 | 41 | 90 | 134 | 160 | 185 |
| 66,000 | 68,000 | 46 | 102 | 152 | 181 | 210 |
| 68,000 | 70,000 | 52 | 114 | 169 | 203 | 235 |
| 70,000 | 72,000 | 57 | 126 | 187 | 225 | 259 |
| 72,000 | 74,000 | 63 | 138 | 205 | 246 | 284 |
| 74,000 | 76,000 | 68 | 150 | 223 | 267 | 309 |
| 76,000 | 78,000 | 74 | 162 | 241 | 288 | 333 |
| 78,000 | 80,000 | 79 | 174 | 259 | 310 | 357 |
| 80,000 | 85,000 | 89 | 195 | 290 | 347 | 401 |
| 85,000 | 90,000 | 102 | 225 | 335 | 400 | 463 |
| 90,000 | 95,000 | 116 | 255 | 379 | 454 | 525 |
| 95,000 | 100,000 | 130 | 285 | 423 | 508 | 586 |
| 100,000 | 110,000 | 150 | 330 | 491 | 587 | 679 |
| 110,000 | 120,000 | 178 | 390 | 579 | 695 | 802 |
| 120,000 | 130,000 | 205 | 450 | 669 | 801 | 926 |
| 130,000 | 140,000 | 232 | 510 | 758 | 908 | 1,049 |
| 140,000 | 150,000 | 260 | 570 | 847 | 1,015 | 1,172 |
| 150,000 | 160,000 | 287 | 630 | 936 | 1,122 | 1,296 |
| 160,000 | 170,000 | 314 | 691 | 1,024 | 1,230 | 1,419 |
| 170,000 | 180,000 | 342 | 750 | 1,114 | 1,336 | 1,543 |
| 180,000 | 190,000 | 369 | 810 | 1,204 | 1,442 | 1,666 |
| 190,000 | 200,000 | 396 | 871 | 1,292 | 1,550 | 1,789 |
| 200,000 | 210,000 | 424 | 930 | 1,382 | 1,656 | 1,913 |
| 210,000 | 220,000 | 451 | 991 | 1,470 | 1,764 | 2,036 |
| 220,000 | 230,000 | 478 | 1,051 | 1,559 | 1,871 | 2,159 |
| 230,000 | 240,000 | 505 | 1,111 | 1,649 | 1,977 | 2,283 |
| 240,000 | and over | 533 | 1,171 | 1,738 | 2,084 | 2,406 |

***Example (1C):*** A car costing $61,000 is leased for four years by a calendar-year taxpayer beginning on April 1, 2018, and is used 100 percent for business. The annual dollar amounts from the table for leases beginning in 2018 are: $30 for the first tax year during the lease, $66 for the second tax year, $98 for the third tax year, $118 for the fourth tax year, and $135 for the fifth and following tax years. In 2018, the inclusion amount is $22.60 (275/365 × $30). The inclusion amounts for 2019, 2020, and 2021 are $66, $98, and $118, respectively, since the vehicle is leased for the entire year during these tax years. In 2022, the inclusion amount is $29.10 (90/365 × $118 (the dollar amount for 2021, the preceding tax year, is used in the last year of the lease)).

## PRE-2018 LEASE INCLUSION TABLES FOR VEHICLES OTHER THAN TRUCKS AND VANS

*January 1, 2017 to December 31, 2017 Leases of Vehicles Other than Trucks and Vans*

The following table from Rev. Proc. 2017-29 governs computation of includible amounts for passenger automobiles (that are not trucks (including SUVs that are considered trucks) or vans) with a fair market value exceeding $19,000 and first leased in 2017. This table also applies to electric vehicles first leased in 2017 that are not a truck or van.

Dollar Amounts for Passenger Automobiles
(That Are Not Trucks or Vans)
With a Lease Term Beginning in Calendar Year 2017
[Rev. Proc. 2017-29]

| *Fair Market Value of Passenger Automobile* | | *Tax Year During Lease* | | | | |
|---|---|---|---|---|---|---|
| *Over* | *Not Over* | *1st* | *2nd* | *3rd* | *4th* | *5th & later* |
| $19,000 | $19,500 | 6 | 14 | 20 | 23 | 27 |
| 19,500 | 20,000 | 7 | 16 | 23 | 27 | 31 |
| 20,000 | 20,500 | 8 | 18 | 26 | 30 | 35 |
| 20,500 | 21,000 | 9 | 20 | 28 | 35 | 39 |
| 21,000 | 21,500 | 10 | 21 | 32 | 38 | 44 |
| 21,500 | 22,000 | 11 | 23 | 35 | 42 | 47 |
| 22,000 | 23,000 | 12 | 27 | 39 | 47 | 53 |
| 23,000 | 24,000 | 14 | 31 | 45 | 54 | 62 |
| 24,000 | 25,000 | 16 | 34 | 52 | 61 | 70 |
| 25,000 | 26,000 | 18 | 38 | 58 | 68 | 78 |
| 26,000 | 27,000 | 19 | 43 | 63 | 75 | 87 |
| 27,000 | 28,000 | 21 | 47 | 69 | 82 | 95 |
| 28,000 | 29,000 | 23 | 51 | 75 | 89 | 103 |
| 29,000 | 30,000 | 25 | 55 | 80 | 97 | 112 |
| 30,000 | 31,000 | 27 | 58 | 87 | 104 | 120 |
| 31,000 | 32,000 | 29 | 62 | 93 | 111 | 128 |
| 32,000 | 33,000 | 30 | 67 | 99 | 118 | 136 |
| 33,000 | 34,000 | 32 | 71 | 104 | 126 | 144 |
| 34,000 | 35,000 | 34 | 75 | 110 | 133 | 152 |
| 35,000 | 36,000 | 36 | 79 | 116 | 140 | 160 |
| 36,000 | 37,000 | 38 | 82 | 123 | 147 | 169 |
| 37,000 | 38,000 | 40 | 86 | 129 | 154 | 177 |
| 38,000 | 39,000 | 41 | 91 | 134 | 161 | 186 |
| 39,000 | 40,000 | 43 | 95 | 140 | 168 | 194 |
| 40,000 | 41,000 | 45 | 99 | 146 | 175 | 202 |
| 41,000 | 42,000 | 47 | 103 | 152 | 182 | 210 |
| 42,000 | 43,000 | 49 | 106 | 159 | 189 | 218 |
| 43,000 | 44,000 | 50 | 111 | 164 | 197 | 226 |
| 44,000 | 45,000 | 52 | 115 | 170 | 204 | 234 |
| 45,000 | 46,000 | 54 | 119 | 176 | 211 | 243 |
| 46,000 | 47,000 | 56 | 123 | 182 | 218 | 251 |
| 47,000 | 48,000 | 58 | 127 | 187 | 225 | 260 |
| 48,000 | 49,000 | 60 | 130 | 194 | 232 | 268 |
| 49,000 | 50,000 | 61 | 135 | 200 | 239 | 276 |
| 50,000 | 51,000 | 63 | 139 | 206 | 246 | 284 |
| 51,000 | 52,000 | 65 | 143 | 211 | 254 | 292 |

Dollar Amounts for Passenger Automobiles
(That Are Not Trucks or Vans)
With a Lease Term Beginning in Calendar Year 2017
[Rev. Proc. 2017-29]

| *Fair Market Value of Passenger Automobile* | | *Tax Year During Lease* | | | | |
|---|---|---|---|---|---|---|
| *Over* | *Not Over* | *1st* | *2nd* | *3rd* | *4th* | *5th & later* |
| 52,000 | 53,000 | 67 | 147 | 217 | 261 | 301 |
| 53,000 | 54,000 | 69 | 151 | 223 | 268 | 309 |
| 54,000 | 55,000 | 70 | 155 | 229 | 275 | 318 |
| 55,000 | 56,000 | 72 | 159 | 235 | 282 | 326 |
| 56,000 | 57,000 | 74 | 163 | 241 | 289 | 334 |
| 57,000 | 58,000 | 76 | 167 | 247 | 296 | 342 |
| 58,000 | 59,000 | 78 | 171 | 253 | 303 | 350 |
| 59,000 | 60,000 | 80 | 174 | 260 | 310 | 359 |
| 60,000 | 62,000 | 82 | 181 | 268 | 321 | 371 |
| 62,000 | 64,000 | 86 | 189 | 280 | 335 | 387 |
| 64,000 | 66,000 | 90 | 197 | 292 | 349 | 404 |
| 66,000 | 68,000 | 93 | 205 | 304 | 364 | 420 |
| 68,000 | 70,000 | 97 | 213 | 315 | 379 | 436 |
| 70,000 | 72,000 | 101 | 221 | 327 | 393 | 453 |
| 72,000 | 74,000 | 104 | 229 | 339 | 407 | 470 |
| 74,000 | 76,000 | 108 | 237 | 351 | 421 | 486 |
| 76,000 | 78,000 | 111 | 245 | 363 | 436 | 502 |
| 78,000 | 80,000 | 115 | 253 | 375 | 450 | 518 |
| 80,000 | 85,000 | 122 | 267 | 396 | 474 | 548 |
| 85,000 | 90,000 | 131 | 287 | 425 | 511 | 588 |
| 90,000 | 95,000 | 140 | 307 | 455 | 546 | 630 |
| 95,000 | 100,000 | 149 | 327 | 485 | 581 | 671 |
| 100,000 | 110,000 | 162 | 357 | 530 | 635 | 733 |
| 110,000 | 120,000 | 181 | 397 | 589 | 706 | 815 |
| 120,000 | 130,000 | 199 | 437 | 649 | 777 | 898 |
| 130,000 | 140,000 | 217 | 477 | 708 | 849 | 980 |
| 140,000 | 150,000 | 235 | 517 | 768 | 920 | 1,062 |
| 150,000 | 160,000 | 254 | 557 | 827 | 991 | 1,145 |
| 160,000 | 170,000 | 272 | 597 | 887 | 1,062 | 1,227 |
| 170,000 | 180,000 | 290 | 637 | 946 | 1,134 | 1,309 |
| 180,000 | 190,000 | 308 | 677 | 1,006 | 1,205 | 1,391 |
| 190,000 | 200,000 | 326 | 718 | 1,064 | 1,277 | 1,473 |
| 200,000 | 210,000 | 345 | 757 | 1,124 | 1,348 | 1,556 |
| 210,000 | 220,000 | 363 | 797 | 1,184 | 1,419 | 1,638 |
| 220,000 | 230,000 | 381 | 837 | 1,244 | 1,490 | 1,721 |
| 230,000 | 240,000 | 399 | 878 | 1,302 | 1,562 | 1,803 |
| 240,000 | and over | 418 | 917 | 1,362 | 1,633 | 1,885 |

***Example (2):*** A car costing \$25,500 is leased for four years by a calendar-year taxpayer beginning on April 1, 2017, and is used 100 percent for business. The annual dollar amounts from the table for leases beginning in 2017 are: \$18 for the first tax year during the lease, \$38 for the second tax year, \$58 for the third tax year, \$68 for the fourth tax year, and \$78 for the fifth and following tax years. In 2017, the inclusion amount is \$13.56 (275/365 × \$18). The inclusion amounts for 2018, 2019, and 2020 are \$38, \$58, and \$68, respectively, since the vehicle is leased for the entire year during these tax years. In 2021, the inclusion amount is $16.77 (90/365 × $68 (the dollar amount for 2020, the preceding tax year, is used in the last year of the lease)).

*January 1, 2016 to December 31, 2016 Leases of Vehicles Other than Trucks and Vans*

The following table from Rev. Proc. 2016-23 governs computation of includible amounts for passenger automobiles (that are not trucks (including SUVs that are considered trucks) or vans) with a fair market value exceeding $19,000 and first leased in 2016. This table also applies to electric vehicles first leased in 2016 that are not a truck or van.

Dollar Amounts for Passenger Automobiles
(That Are Not Trucks or Vans)
With a Lease Term Beginning in Calendar Year 2016
[Rev. Proc. 2016-23]

| *Fair Market Value of Passenger Automobile* | | *Tax Year During Lease* | | | | |
|---|---|---|---|---|---|---|
| *Over* | *Not Over* | *1st* | *2nd* | *3rd* | *4th* | *5th & later* |
| $19,000 | $19,500 | 6 | 13 | 20 | 23 | 27 |
| 19,500 | 20,000 | 7 | 15 | 23 | 27 | 30 |
| 20,000 | 20,500 | 8 | 17 | 26 | 30 | 35 |
| 20,500 | 21,000 | 9 | 19 | 29 | 33 | 39 |
| 21,000 | 21,500 | 10 | 21 | 31 | 38 | 42 |
| 21,500 | 22,000 | 11 | 23 | 34 | 41 | 47 |
| 22,000 | 23,000 | 12 | 26 | 39 | 46 | 53 |
| 23,000 | 24,000 | 14 | 30 | 44 | 54 | 60 |
| 24,000 | 25,000 | 16 | 34 | 50 | 60 | 69 |
| 25,000 | 26,000 | 17 | 38 | 56 | 67 | 78 |
| 26,000 | 27,000 | 19 | 42 | 62 | 74 | 85 |
| 27,000 | 28,000 | 21 | 46 | 68 | 81 | 93 |
| 28,000 | 29,000 | 23 | 50 | 73 | 89 | 101 |
| 29,000 | 30,000 | 25 | 53 | 80 | 95 | 110 |
| 30,000 | 31,000 | 26 | 58 | 85 | 102 | 118 |
| 31,000 | 32,000 | 28 | 62 | 91 | 109 | 126 |
| 32,000 | 33,000 | 30 | 65 | 98 | 116 | 134 |
| 33,000 | 34,000 | 32 | 69 | 103 | 123 | 142 |
| 34,000 | 35,000 | 34 | 73 | 109 | 130 | 150 |
| 35,000 | 36,000 | 35 | 77 | 115 | 137 | 158 |
| 36,000 | 37,000 | 37 | 81 | 121 | 144 | 166 |
| 37,000 | 38,000 | 39 | 85 | 127 | 151 | 174 |
| 38,000 | 39,000 | 41 | 89 | 132 | 158 | 183 |
| 39,000 | 40,000 | 42 | 93 | 138 | 166 | 190 |
| 40,000 | 41,000 | 44 | 97 | 144 | 172 | 199 |
| 41,000 | 42,000 | 46 | 101 | 150 | 179 | 207 |
| 42,000 | 43,000 | 48 | 105 | 155 | 187 | 215 |
| 43,000 | 44,000 | 50 | 109 | 161 | 193 | 223 |
| 44,000 | 45,000 | 51 | 113 | 167 | 201 | 231 |
| 45,000 | 46,000 | 53 | 117 | 173 | 207 | 239 |
| 46,000 | 47,000 | 55 | 121 | 179 | 214 | 247 |
| 47,000 | 48,000 | 57 | 124 | 185 | 222 | 255 |
| 48,000 | 49,000 | 59 | 128 | 191 | 228 | 264 |
| 49,000 | 50,000 | 60 | 133 | 196 | 236 | 271 |
| 50,000 | 51,000 | 62 | 136 | 203 | 242 | 280 |
| 51,000 | 52,000 | 64 | 140 | 209 | 249 | 288 |

Dollar Amounts for Passenger Automobiles
(That Are Not Trucks or Vans)
With a Lease Term Beginning in Calendar Year 2016
[Rev. Proc. 2016-23]

| *Fair Market Value of Passenger Automobile* | | *Tax Year During Lease* | | | | |
|---|---|---|---|---|---|---|
| *Over* | *Not Over* | *1st* | *2nd* | *3rd* | *4th* | *5th & later* |
| 52,000 | 53,000 | 66 | 144 | 214 | 257 | 295 |
| 53,000 | 54,000 | 68 | 148 | 220 | 263 | 304 |
| 54,000 | 55,000 | 69 | 152 | 226 | 271 | 312 |
| 55,000 | 56,000 | 71 | 156 | 232 | 277 | 320 |
| 56,000 | 57,000 | 73 | 160 | 238 | 284 | 328 |
| 57,000 | 58,000 | 75 | 164 | 243 | 292 | 336 |
| 58,000 | 59,000 | 77 | 168 | 249 | 298 | 345 |
| 59,000 | 60,000 | 78 | 172 | 255 | 306 | 352 |
| 60,000 | 62,000 | 81 | 178 | 264 | 316 | 364 |
| 62,000 | 64,000 | 85 | 185 | 276 | 330 | 381 |
| 64,000 | 66,000 | 88 | 194 | 287 | 344 | 397 |
| 66,000 | 68,000 | 92 | 201 | 299 | 358 | 413 |
| 68,000 | 70,000 | 95 | 209 | 311 | 372 | 430 |
| 70,000 | 72,000 | 99 | 217 | 322 | 387 | 445 |
| 72,000 | 74,000 | 102 | 225 | 334 | 400 | 462 |
| 74,000 | 76,000 | 106 | 233 | 346 | 414 | 478 |
| 76,000 | 78,000 | 110 | 241 | 357 | 428 | 494 |
| 78,000 | 80,000 | 113 | 249 | 369 | 442 | 510 |
| 80,000 | 85,000 | 120 | 262 | 390 | 467 | 538 |
| 85,000 | 90,000 | 128 | 282 | 419 | 502 | 579 |
| 90,000 | 95,000 | 137 | 302 | 448 | 537 | 620 |
| 95,000 | 100,000 | 146 | 322 | 477 | 572 | 660 |
| 100,000 | 110,000 | 160 | 351 | 521 | 625 | 721 |
| 110,000 | 120,000 | 178 | 390 | 580 | 695 | 801 |
| 120,000 | 130,000 | 196 | 430 | 638 | 765 | 882 |
| 130,000 | 140,000 | 214 | 469 | 697 | 835 | 963 |
| 140,000 | 150,000 | 232 | 508 | 755 | 906 | 1,044 |
| 150,000 | 160,000 | 249 | 548 | 814 | 975 | 1,126 |
| 160,000 | 170,000 | 267 | 588 | 872 | 1,045 | 1,207 |
| 170,000 | 180,000 | 285 | 627 | 930 | 1,116 | 1,288 |
| 180,000 | 190,000 | 303 | 666 | 989 | 1,186 | 1,368 |
| 190,000 | 200,000 | 321 | 706 | 1,047 | 1,256 | 1,449 |
| 200,000 | 210,000 | 339 | 745 | 1,106 | 1,326 | 1,530 |
| 210,000 | 220,000 | 357 | 784 | 1,165 | 1,396 | 1,611 |
| 220,000 | 230,000 | 375 | 824 | 1,223 | 1,466 | 1,692 |
| 230,000 | 240,000 | 393 | 863 | 1,281 | 1,537 | 1,773 |
| 240,000 | and over | 411 | 902 | 1,340 | 1,607 | 1,854 |

***Example (3):*** A car costing $25,500 is leased for four years by a calendar-year taxpayer beginning on April 1, 2016, and is used 100 percent for business. The annual dollar amounts from the table for leases beginning in 2016 are: $17 for the first tax year during the lease, $38 for the second tax year, $56 for the third tax year, $67 for the fourth tax year, and $78 for the fifth and following tax years. In 2016, the inclusion amount is $12.81 (275/365 × $17). The inclusion amounts for 2017, 2018, and 2019 are $38, $56, and $67, respectively, since the vehicle is leased for the entire year during these tax years. In 2020, the inclusion amount is $16.52 (90/365 × $67 (the dollar amount for 2019, the preceding tax year, is used in the last year of the lease)).

### *January 1, 2015 to December 31, 2015 Leases of Vehicles Other than Trucks and Vans*

The following table from Rev. Proc. 2015-19, as modified by Rev. Proc. 2016-23, governs computation of includible amounts for passenger automobiles (that are not trucks (including SUVs that are considered trucks) or vans) with a fair market value exceeding $19,000 and first leased in 2015. This table also applies to electric vehicles first leased in 2015 that are not a truck or van. Rev. Proc. 2016-23 modified Rev. Proc. 2015-19 by removing the first three lines of inclusion amounts from the table for vehicles costing over $17,500 but not over $19,000.

Dollar Amounts for Passenger Automobiles
(That Are Not Trucks or Vans)
With a Lease Term Beginning in Calendar Year 2015
[Rev. Proc. 2015-19, modified by Rev. Proc. 2016-23]

| *Fair Market Value of Passenger Automobile* | | *Tax Year During Lease* | | | | |
|---|---|---|---|---|---|---|
| *Over* | *Not Over* | *1st* | *2nd* | *3rd* | *4th* | *5th & later* |
| 19,000 | 19,500 | 5 | 11 | 15 | 19 | 21 |
| 19,500 | 20,000 | 6 | 12 | 18 | 22 | 24 |
| 20,000 | 20,500 | 6 | 14 | 20 | 25 | 27 |
| 20,500 | 21,000 | 7 | 15 | 23 | 27 | 31 |
| 21,000 | 21,500 | 8 | 17 | 25 | 30 | 34 |
| 21,500 | 22,000 | 9 | 18 | 28 | 32 | 38 |
| 22,000 | 23,000 | 10 | 21 | 31 | 37 | 42 |
| 23,000 | 24,000 | 11 | 24 | 36 | 42 | 49 |
| 24,000 | 25,000 | 12 | 27 | 41 | 48 | 55 |
| 25,000 | 26,000 | 14 | 30 | 45 | 54 | 62 |
| 26,000 | 27,000 | 15 | 34 | 49 | 60 | 68 |
| 27,000 | 28,000 | 17 | 37 | 54 | 65 | 75 |
| 28,000 | 29,000 | 18 | 40 | 59 | 71 | 81 |
| 29,000 | 30,000 | 20 | 43 | 64 | 76 | 87 |
| 30,000 | 31,000 | 21 | 46 | 69 | 81 | 95 |
| 31,000 | 32,000 | 23 | 49 | 73 | 88 | 100 |
| 32,000 | 33,000 | 24 | 52 | 78 | 93 | 107 |
| 33,000 | 34,000 | 25 | 56 | 82 | 99 | 114 |
| 34,000 | 35,000 | 27 | 59 | 87 | 104 | 120 |
| 35,000 | 36,000 | 28 | 62 | 92 | 110 | 126 |
| 36,000 | 37,000 | 30 | 65 | 96 | 116 | 133 |
| 37,000 | 38,000 | 31 | 68 | 102 | 121 | 139 |

Dollar Amounts for Passenger Automobiles
(That Are Not Trucks or Vans)
With a Lease Term Beginning in Calendar Year 2015
[Rev. Proc. 2015-19, modified by Rev. Proc. 2016-23]

| *Fair Market Value of Passenger Automobile* | | *Tax Year During Lease* | | | | |
|---|---|---|---|---|---|---|
| *Over* | *Not Over* | *1st* | *2nd* | *3rd* | *4th* | *5th & later* |
| 38,000 | 39,000 | 33 | 71 | 106 | 127 | 146 |
| 39,000 | 40,000 | 34 | 75 | 110 | 132 | 153 |
| 40,000 | 41,000 | 35 | 78 | 115 | 138 | 159 |
| 41,000 | 42,000 | 37 | 81 | 120 | 143 | 166 |
| 42,000 | 43,000 | 38 | 84 | 125 | 149 | 172 |
| 43,000 | 44,000 | 40 | 87 | 129 | 155 | 179 |
| 44,000 | 45,000 | 41 | 90 | 134 | 161 | 185 |
| 45,000 | 46,000 | 43 | 93 | 139 | 166 | 191 |
| 46,000 | 47,000 | 44 | 97 | 143 | 172 | 198 |
| 47,000 | 48,000 | 45 | 100 | 148 | 177 | 205 |
| 48,000 | 49,000 | 47 | 103 | 153 | 183 | 210 |
| 49,000 | 50,000 | 48 | 106 | 158 | 188 | 218 |
| 50,000 | 51,000 | 50 | 109 | 162 | 194 | 224 |
| 51,000 | 52,000 | 51 | 112 | 167 | 200 | 230 |
| 52,000 | 53,000 | 53 | 115 | 172 | 205 | 237 |
| 53,000 | 54,000 | 54 | 119 | 176 | 211 | 243 |
| 54,000 | 55,000 | 56 | 122 | 180 | 217 | 250 |
| 55,000 | 56,000 | 57 | 125 | 186 | 222 | 256 |
| 56,000 | 57,000 | 58 | 128 | 191 | 227 | 263 |
| 57,000 | 58,000 | 60 | 131 | 195 | 234 | 269 |
| 58,000 | 59,000 | 61 | 135 | 199 | 239 | 276 |
| 59,000 | 60,000 | 63 | 137 | 205 | 244 | 283 |
| 60,000 | 62,000 | 65 | 142 | 212 | 253 | 292 |
| 62,000 | 64,000 | 68 | 149 | 220 | 265 | 304 |
| 64,000 | 66,000 | 71 | 155 | 230 | 275 | 318 |
| 66,000 | 68,000 | 73 | 162 | 239 | 287 | 331 |
| 68,000 | 70,000 | 76 | 168 | 249 | 298 | 343 |
| 70,000 | 72,000 | 79 | 174 | 258 | 309 | 357 |
| 72,000 | 74,000 | 82 | 180 | 268 | 320 | 370 |

Dollar Amounts for Passenger Automobiles
(That Are Not Trucks or Vans)
With a Lease Term Beginning in Calendar Year 2015
[Rev. Proc. 2015-19, modified by Rev. Proc. 2016-23]

| *Fair Market Value of Passenger Automobile* | | *Tax Year During Lease* | | | | |
|---|---|---|---|---|---|---|
| *Over* | *Not Over* | *1st* | *2nd* | *3rd* | *4th* | *5th & later* |
| 74,000 | 76,000 | 85 | 186 | 277 | 332 | 383 |
| 76,000 | 78,000 | 88 | 193 | 286 | 343 | 396 |
| 78,000 | 80,000 | 91 | 199 | 296 | 354 | 408 |
| 80,000 | 85,000 | 96 | 210 | 312 | 374 | 431 |
| 85,000 | 90,000 | 103 | 226 | 335 | 402 | 464 |
| 90,000 | 95,000 | 110 | 242 | 359 | 430 | 496 |
| 95,000 | 100,000 | 117 | 258 | 382 | 458 | 529 |
| 100,000 | 110,000 | 128 | 281 | 418 | 500 | 577 |
| 110,000 | 120,000 | 142 | 313 | 464 | 556 | 643 |
| 120,000 | 130,000 | 157 | 344 | 511 | 613 | 707 |
| 130,000 | 140,000 | 171 | 376 | 558 | 668 | 772 |
| 140,000 | 150,000 | 185 | 408 | 604 | 725 | 837 |
| 150,000 | 160,000 | 200 | 439 | 651 | 781 | 902 |
| 160,000 | 170,000 | 214 | 470 | 699 | 837 | 966 |
| 170,000 | 180,000 | 228 | 502 | 745 | 894 | 1,031 |
| 180,000 | 190,000 | 243 | 533 | 792 | 950 | 1,096 |
| 190,000 | 200,000 | 257 | 565 | 839 | 1,006 | 1,161 |
| 200,000 | 210,000 | 271 | 597 | 886 | 1,061 | 1,226 |
| 210,000 | 220,000 | 286 | 628 | 933 | 1,118 | 1,290 |
| 220,000 | 230,000 | 300 | 660 | 979 | 1,174 | 1,356 |
| 230,000 | 240,000 | 315 | 691 | 1,026 | 1,231 | 1,420 |
| 240,000 | and over | 329 | 723 | 1,073 | 1,286 | 1,485 |

***Example (4):*** A car costing $25,500 is leased for four years by a calendar-year taxpayer beginning on April 1, 2015, and is used 100 percent for business. The annual dollar amounts from the table for leases beginning in 2015 are: $14 for the first tax year during the lease, $30 for the second tax year, $45 for the third tax year, $54 for the fourth tax year, and $62 for the fifth and following tax years. In 2015, the inclusion amount is $10.55 (275/365 × $14). The inclusion amounts for 2016, 2017, and 2018 are $30, $45, and $54, respectively, since the vehicle is leased for the entire year during these tax years. In 2019, the inclusion amount is $13.32 (90/365 × $54 (the dollar amount for 2018, the preceding tax year, is used in the last year of the lease)).

*January 1, 2014 to December 31, 2014 Leases of Vehicles Other than Trucks and Vans*

The following table from Rev. Proc. 2014-21, as modified by Rev. Proc. 2015-19 to remove the first row of inclusion amounts for vehicles with a fair market value more than $18,500 but not more than $19,000, governs computation of includible amounts for passenger automobiles (that are not trucks (including SUVs that are considered trucks) or vans) with a fair market value exceeding $19,000 and first leased in 2014. This table also applies to electric vehicles first leased in 2014 that are not a truck or van.

**Dollar Amounts for Passenger Automobiles (Other than Trucks or Vans) First Leased in 2014**

| *Fair Market Value of Automobile* | | *Tax Year During Lease&ast* | | | | |
|---|---|---|---|---|---|---|
| *Over* | *Not Over* | *1st* | *2nd* | *3rd* | *4th* | *5th and Later* |
| 19,000 | 19,500 | 3 | 6 | 10 | 11 | 13 |
| 19,500 | 20,000 | 3 | 8 | 11 | 13 | 14 |
| 20,000 | 20,500 | 4 | 8 | 13 | 14 | 17 |
| 20,500 | 21,000 | 4 | 9 | 14 | 17 | 18 |
| 21,000 | 21,500 | 5 | 10 | 15 | 18 | 21 |
| 21,500 | 22,000 | 5 | 11 | 17 | 20 | 22 |
| 22,000 | 23,000 | 6 | 13 | 18 | 23 | 25 |
| 23,000 | 24,000 | 7 | 14 | 22 | 26 | 29 |
| 24,000 | 25,000 | 8 | 16 | 25 | 29 | 33 |
| 25,000 | 26,000 | 8 | 19 | 27 | 32 | 38 |
| 26,000 | 27,000 | 9 | 20 | 31 | 35 | 42 |
| 27,000 | 28,000 | 10 | 22 | 33 | 40 | 45 |
| 28,000 | 29,000 | 11 | 24 | 36 | 43 | 49 |
| 29,000 | 30,000 | 12 | 26 | 39 | 46 | 53 |
| 30,000 | 31,000 | 13 | 28 | 41 | 50 | 57 |
| 31,000 | 32,000 | 14 | 30 | 44 | 53 | 61 |
| 32,000 | 33,000 | 14 | 32 | 47 | 56 | 65 |
| 33,000 | 34,000 | 15 | 34 | 50 | 59 | 69 |
| 34,000 | 35,000 | 16 | 36 | 52 | 64 | 72 |
| 35,000 | 36,000 | 17 | 38 | 55 | 67 | 76 |
| 36,000 | 37,000 | 18 | 39 | 59 | 70 | 80 |
| 37,000 | 38,000 | 19 | 41 | 61 | 74 | 84 |
| 38,000 | 39,000 | 20 | 43 | 64 | 77 | 88 |
| 39,000 | 40,000 | 21 | 45 | 67 | 80 | 92 |
| 40,000 | 41,000 | 21 | 47 | 70 | 84 | 96 |
| 41,000 | 42,000 | 22 | 49 | 73 | 87 | 100 |

**Dollar Amounts for Passenger Automobiles (Other than Trucks or Vans) First Leased in 2014**

| *Fair Market Value of Automobile* | | *Tax Year During Lease&ast* | | | | |
|---|---|---|---|---|---|---|
| *Over* | *Not Over* | *1st* | *2nd* | *3rd* | *4th* | *5th and Later* |
| 42,000 | 43,000 | 23 | 51 | 75 | 91 | 104 |
| 43,000 | 44,000 | 24 | 53 | 78 | 94 | 108 |
| 44,000 | 45,000 | 25 | 55 | 81 | 97 | 112 |
| 45,000 | 46,000 | 26 | 56 | 84 | 101 | 116 |
| 46,000 | 47,000 | 27 | 58 | 87 | 104 | 120 |
| 47,000 | 48,000 | 28 | 60 | 90 | 107 | 124 |
| 48,000 | 49,000 | 28 | 62 | 93 | 111 | 127 |
| 49,000 | 50,000 | 29 | 64 | 96 | 114 | 131 |
| 50,000 | 51,000 | 30 | 66 | 98 | 118 | 135 |
| 51,000 | 52,000 | 31 | 68 | 101 | 121 | 139 |
| 52,000 | 53,000 | 32 | 70 | 104 | 124 | 143 |
| 53,000 | 54,000 | 33 | 72 | 106 | 128 | 147 |
| 54,000 | 55,000 | 34 | 74 | 109 | 131 | 151 |
| 55,000 | 56,000 | 34 | 76 | 112 | 135 | 155 |
| 56,000 | 57,000 | 35 | 78 | 115 | 138 | 159 |
| 57,000 | 58,000 | 36 | 80 | 118 | 141 | 163 |
| 58,000 | 59,000 | 37 | 81 | 121 | 145 | 167 |
| 59,000 | 60,000 | 38 | 83 | 124 | 148 | 171 |
| 60,000 | 62,000 | 39 | 86 | 128 | 153 | 177 |
| 62,000 | 64,000 | 41 | 90 | 134 | 159 | 185 |
| 64,000 | 66,000 | 43 | 94 | 139 | 167 | 192 |
| 66,000 | 68,000 | 44 | 98 | 145 | 173 | 201 |
| 68,000 | 70,000 | 46 | 102 | 150 | 180 | 209 |
| 70,000 | 72,000 | 48 | 105 | 156 | 188 | 216 |
| 72,000 | 74,000 | 50 | 109 | 162 | 194 | 224 |
| 74,000 | 76,000 | 51 | 113 | 168 | 200 | 232 |
| 76,000 | 78,000 | 53 | 117 | 173 | 208 | 239 |
| 78,000 | 80,000 | 55 | 120 | 179 | 215 | 247 |
| 80,000 | 85,000 | 58 | 127 | 189 | 226 | 261 |
| 85,000 | 90,000 | 62 | 137 | 203 | 243 | 281 |
| 90,000 | 95,000 | 67 | 146 | 217 | 260 | 301 |
| 95,000 | 100,000 | 71 | 156 | 231 | 277 | 320 |

**Dollar Amounts for Passenger Automobiles (Other than Trucks or Vans) First Leased in 2014**

| *Fair Market Value of Automobile* | | *Tax Year During Lease&ast* | | | | |
|---|---|---|---|---|---|---|
| *Over* | *Not Over* | *1st* | *2nd* | *3rd* | *4th* | *5th and Later* |
| 100,000 | 110,000 | 77 | 170 | 253 | 303 | 349 |
| 110,000 | 120,000 | 86 | 189 | 281 | 337 | 389 |
| 120,000 | 130,000 | 95 | 208 | 310 | 370 | 428 |
| 130,000 | 140,000 | 103 | 228 | 337 | 405 | 467 |
| 140,000 | 150,000 | 112 | 247 | 366 | 438 | 507 |
| 150,000 | 160,000 | 121 | 266 | 394 | 473 | 545 |
| 160,000 | 170,000 | 130 | 284 | 423 | 507 | 585 |
| 170,000 | 180,000 | 138 | 304 | 451 | 541 | 624 |
| 180,000 | 190,000 | 147 | 323 | 479 | 575 | 663 |
| 190,000 | 200,000 | 156 | 342 | 507 | 609 | 703 |
| 200,000 | 210,000 | 164 | 361 | 536 | 643 | 742 |
| 210,000 | 220,000 | 173 | 380 | 565 | 676 | 781 |
| 220,000 | 230,000 | 182 | 399 | 593 | 710 | 821 |
| 230,000 | 240,000 | 190 | 418 | 622 | 744 | 860 |
| 240,000 | and over | 199 | 437 | 650 | 778 | 899 |

* For the last tax year of the lease, use the dollar amount for the preceding year.

***Example (5):*** A car with a fair market value of $34,500 is leased for a term of 3 years beginning on April 1, 2014. Assuming full business use by a calendar-year taxpayer, the includible amount for 2014 is $12.05 (275/365 × $16). The includible amount for 2015 is $36. The includible amount for 2016 is $52. The includible amount for 2017 is $12.82 ($52 × 90/365) (the dollar amount for the preceding tax year is used for the last tax year of the lease).

## PRE-2018 LEASE INCLUSION TABLES FOR TRUCKS, VANS, OR SUVs THAT ARE CONSIDERED TRUCKS

### *January 1, 2017 to December 31, 2017 Leases of Trucks or Vans*

The following table from Rev. Proc. 2017-29, governs computation of includible amounts for trucks (including SUVs that are considered trucks) or vans with a GVWR of 6,000 pounds or less, a fair market value exceeding $19,500, and which are first leased in calendar-year 2017. This table should also be used for electric vehicles that are trucks or vans first leased in calendar-year 2017.

**Dollar Amounts for Trucks or Vans First Leased in 2017**

| *Fair Market Value of Automobile* | | *Tax Year During Lease** | | | | |
|---|---|---|---|---|---|---|
| *Over* | *Not Over* | *1st* | *2nd* | *3rd* | *4th* | *5th and Later* |
| $19,500 | $20,000 | 4 | 8 | 11 | 13 | 16 |
| 20,000 | 20,500 | 4 | 10 | 14 | 17 | 20 |
| 20,500 | 21,000 | 5 | 12 | 17 | 21 | 23 |
| 21,000 | 21,500 | 6 | 14 | 20 | 24 | 28 |
| 21,500 | 22,000 | 7 | 16 | 23 | 28 | 32 |

**Dollar Amounts for Trucks or Vans First Leased in 2017**

| *Fair Market Value of Automobile* | | *Tax Year During Lease** | | | | |
|---|---|---|---|---|---|---|
| *Over* | *Not Over* | *1st* | *2nd* | *3rd* | *4th* | *5th and Later* |
| 22,000 | 23,000 | 9 | 19 | 27 | 33 | 38 |
| 23,000 | 24,000 | 10 | 23 | 34 | 40 | 46 |
| 24,000 | 25,000 | 12 | 27 | 39 | 48 | 54 |
| 25,000 | 26,000 | 14 | 31 | 45 | 55 | 62 |
| 26,000 | 27,000 | 16 | 35 | 51 | 62 | 71 |
| 27,000 | 28,000 | 18 | 39 | 57 | 69 | 79 |
| 28,000 | 29,000 | 19 | 43 | 63 | 76 | 88 |
| 29,000 | 30,000 | 21 | 47 | 69 | 83 | 96 |
| 30,000 | 31,000 | 23 | 51 | 75 | 90 | 104 |
| 31,000 | 32,000 | 25 | 55 | 81 | 97 | 112 |
| 32,000 | 33,000 | 27 | 59 | 87 | 104 | 120 |
| 33,000 | 34,000 | 29 | 63 | 93 | 111 | 129 |
| 34,000 | 35,000 | 30 | 67 | 99 | 119 | 136 |
| 35,000 | 36,000 | 32 | 71 | 105 | 126 | 145 |
| 36,000 | 37,000 | 34 | 75 | 111 | 133 | 153 |
| 37,000 | 38,000 | 36 | 79 | 117 | 140 | 161 |
| 38,000 | 39,000 | 38 | 83 | 122 | 148 | 169 |
| 39,000 | 40,000 | 40 | 87 | 128 | 155 | 177 |
| 40,000 | 41,000 | 41 | 91 | 135 | 161 | 186 |
| 41,000 | 42,000 | 43 | 95 | 141 | 168 | 194 |
| 42,000 | 43,000 | 45 | 99 | 146 | 176 | 203 |
| 43,000 | 44,000 | 47 | 103 | 152 | 183 | 211 |
| 44,000 | 45,000 | 49 | 107 | 158 | 190 | 219 |
| 45,000 | 46,000 | 50 | 111 | 165 | 196 | 228 |
| 46,000 | 47,000 | 52 | 115 | 170 | 204 | 236 |
| 47,000 | 48,000 | 54 | 119 | 176 | 211 | 244 |
| 48,000 | 49,000 | 56 | 123 | 182 | 218 | 252 |
| 49,000 | 50,000 | 58 | 127 | 188 | 225 | 261 |
| 50,000 | 51,000 | 60 | 131 | 194 | 232 | 269 |
| 51,000 | 52,000 | 61 | 135 | 200 | 240 | 277 |
| 52,000 | 53,000 | 63 | 139 | 206 | 247 | 285 |
| 53,000 | 54,000 | 65 | 143 | 212 | 254 | 293 |
| 54,000 | 55,000 | 67 | 147 | 218 | 261 | 301 |
| 55,000 | 56,000 | 69 | 151 | 224 | 268 | 309 |
| 56,000 | 57,000 | 70 | 155 | 230 | 275 | 318 |
| 57,000 | 58,000 | 72 | 159 | 236 | 282 | 326 |
| 58,000 | 59,000 | 74 | 163 | 242 | 289 | 335 |
| 59,000 | 60,000 | 76 | 167 | 248 | 296 | 343 |
| 60,000 | 62,000 | 79 | 173 | 256 | 308 | 355 |
| 62,000 | 64,000 | 82 | 181 | 269 | 321 | 372 |
| 64,000 | 66,000 | 86 | 189 | 280 | 336 | 388 |
| 66,000 | 68,000 | 90 | 197 | 292 | 350 | 404 |
| 68,000 | 70,000 | 93 | 205 | 304 | 365 | 420 |
| 70,000 | 72,000 | 97 | 213 | 316 | 379 | 437 |
| 72,000 | 74,000 | 101 | 221 | 328 | 393 | 453 |
| 74,000 | 76,000 | 104 | 229 | 340 | 407 | 470 |
| 76,000 | 78,000 | 108 | 237 | 352 | 421 | 487 |
| 78,000 | 80,000 | 111 | 245 | 364 | 436 | 503 |
| 80,000 | 85,000 | 118 | 259 | 384 | 461 | 532 |

**Dollar Amounts for Trucks or Vans First Leased in 2017**

| *Fair Market Value of Automobile* | | *Tax Year During Lease** | | | | |
|---|---|---|---|---|---|---|
| *Over* | *Not Over* | *1st* | *2nd* | *3rd* | *4th* | *5th and Later* |
| 85,000 | 90,000 | 127 | 279 | 414 | 497 | 573 |
| 90,000 | 95,000 | 136 | 299 | 444 | 532 | 614 |
| 95,000 | 100,000 | 145 | 319 | 474 | 567 | 656 |
| 100,000 | 110,000 | 159 | 349 | 518 | 621 | 717 |
| 110,000 | 120,000 | 177 | 389 | 578 | 692 | 800 |
| 120,000 | 130,000 | 195 | 429 | 637 | 764 | 882 |
| 130,000 | 140,000 | 213 | 470 | 696 | 835 | 964 |
| 140,000 | 150,000 | 232 | 509 | 756 | 906 | 1,047 |
| 150,000 | 160,000 | 250 | 549 | 816 | 977 | 1,129 |
| 160,000 | 170,000 | 268 | 589 | 875 | 1,049 | 1,211 |
| 170,000 | 180,000 | 286 | 630 | 934 | 1,120 | 1,293 |
| 180,000 | 190,000 | 305 | 669 | 994 | 1,191 | 1,376 |
| 190,000 | 200,000 | 323 | 709 | 1,054 | 1,262 | 1,458 |
| 200,000 | 210,000 | 341 | 750 | 1,112 | 1,334 | 1,540 |
| 210,000 | 220,000 | 359 | 790 | 1,172 | 1,405 | 1,623 |
| 220,000 | 230,000 | 377 | 830 | 1,231 | 1,477 | 1,705 |
| 230,000 | 240,000 | 396 | 870 | 1,290 | 1,548 | 1,787 |
| 240,000 | and over | 414 | 910 | 1,350 | 1,619 | 1,870 |

* For the last tax year of the lease, use the dollar amount for the preceding tax year.

***Example (8):*** An SUV with a GVWR of 6,000 pounds or less and with a fair market value of $34,500 is leased for a term of 3 years beginning on April 1, 2017. The SUV is considered a truck. Assuming full business use by a calendar-year taxpayer, the includible amount for 2017 is $22.60 (275/365 × $30). The includible amount for 2018 is $67. The includible amount for 2019 is $99. The includible amount for 2020 is $24.61 ($99 × 91/366) (the dollar amount for the preceding tax year is used for the last tax year of the lease).

### *January 1, 2016 to December 31, 2016 Leases of Trucks or Vans*

The following table from Rev. Proc. 2016-23, governs computation of includible amounts for trucks (including SUVs that are considered trucks) or vans with a GVWR of 6,000 pounds or less, a fair market value exceeding $19,500, and which are first leased in calendar-year 2016. This table should also be used for electric vehicles that are trucks or vans first leased in calendar-year 2016.

**Dollar Amounts for Trucks or Vans First Leased in 2016**

| *Fair Market Value of Automobile* | | *Tax Year During Lease** | | | | |
|---|---|---|---|---|---|---|
| *Over* | *Not Over* | *1st* | *2nd* | *3rd* | *4th* | *5th and Later* |
| $19,500 | $20,000 | 3 | 8 | 12 | 14 | 16 |
| 20,000 | 20,500 | 4 | 10 | 15 | 17 | 20 |
| 20,500 | 21,000 | 5 | 12 | 17 | 21 | 25 |
| 21,000 | 21,500 | 6 | 14 | 20 | 25 | 28 |
| 21,500 | 22,000 | 7 | 16 | 23 | 28 | 32 |
| 22,000 | 23,000 | 8 | 19 | 28 | 33 | 38 |
| 23,000 | 24,000 | 10 | 23 | 33 | 41 | 46 |
| 24,000 | 25,000 | 12 | 26 | 40 | 47 | 55 |
| 25,000 | 26,000 | 14 | 30 | 46 | 54 | 63 |
| 26,000 | 27,000 | 16 | 34 | 51 | 62 | 70 |
| 27,000 | 28,000 | 17 | 38 | 58 | 68 | 79 |
| 28,000 | 29,000 | 19 | 42 | 63 | 76 | 86 |

**Dollar Amounts for Trucks or Vans First Leased in 2016**

| *Fair Market Value of Automobile* | | *Tax Year During Lease** | | | | |
|---|---|---|---|---|---|---|
| *Over* | *Not Over* | *1st* | *2nd* | *3rd* | *4th* | *5th and Later* |
| 29,000 | 30,000 | 21 | 46 | 69 | 82 | 95 |
| 30,000 | 31,000 | 23 | 50 | 75 | 89 | 103 |
| 31,000 | 32,000 | 25 | 54 | 80 | 97 | 111 |
| 32,000 | 33,000 | 26 | 58 | 86 | 104 | 119 |
| 33,000 | 34,000 | 28 | 62 | 92 | 111 | 127 |
| 34,000 | 35,000 | 30 | 66 | 98 | 117 | 136 |
| 35,000 | 36,000 | 32 | 70 | 104 | 124 | 143 |
| 36,000 | 37,000 | 34 | 73 | 110 | 132 | 151 |
| 37,000 | 38,000 | 35 | 78 | 115 | 139 | 160 |
| 38,000 | 39,000 | 37 | 82 | 121 | 146 | 167 |
| 39,000 | 40,000 | 39 | 85 | 128 | 152 | 176 |
| 40,000 | 41,000 | 41 | 89 | 133 | 160 | 184 |
| 41,000 | 42,000 | 42 | 94 | 139 | 166 | 192 |
| 42,000 | 43,000 | 44 | 97 | 145 | 174 | 200 |
| 43,000 | 44,000 | 46 | 101 | 151 | 181 | 208 |
| 44,000 | 45,000 | 48 | 105 | 157 | 187 | 217 |
| 45,000 | 46,000 | 50 | 109 | 162 | 195 | 224 |
| 46,000 | 47,000 | 51 | 113 | 169 | 201 | 233 |
| 47,000 | 48,000 | 53 | 117 | 174 | 209 | 240 |
| 48,000 | 49,000 | 55 | 121 | 180 | 216 | 248 |
| 49,000 | 50,000 | 57 | 125 | 186 | 222 | 257 |
| 50,000 | 51,000 | 59 | 129 | 191 | 230 | 265 |
| 51,000 | 52,000 | 60 | 133 | 197 | 237 | 273 |
| 52,000 | 53,000 | 62 | 137 | 203 | 244 | 281 |
| 53,000 | 54,000 | 64 | 141 | 209 | 250 | 290 |
| 54,000 | 55,000 | 66 | 144 | 216 | 257 | 298 |
| 55,000 | 56,000 | 68 | 148 | 221 | 265 | 305 |
| 56,000 | 57,000 | 69 | 153 | 226 | 272 | 314 |
| 57,000 | 58,000 | 71 | 156 | 233 | 279 | 321 |
| 58,000 | 59,000 | 73 | 160 | 239 | 285 | 330 |
| 59,000 | 60,000 | 75 | 164 | 244 | 293 | 338 |
| 60,000 | 62,000 | 77 | 170 | 253 | 304 | 350 |
| 62,000 | 64,000 | 81 | 178 | 265 | 317 | 366 |
| 64,000 | 66,000 | 85 | 186 | 276 | 331 | 383 |
| 66,000 | 68,000 | 88 | 194 | 288 | 345 | 399 |
| 68,000 | 70,000 | 92 | 202 | 299 | 360 | 414 |
| 70,000 | 72,000 | 95 | 210 | 311 | 374 | 431 |
| 72,000 | 74,000 | 99 | 217 | 324 | 387 | 447 |
| 74,000 | 76,000 | 102 | 226 | 335 | 401 | 463 |
| 76,000 | 78,000 | 106 | 233 | 347 | 415 | 480 |
| 78,000 | 80,000 | 110 | 241 | 358 | 430 | 495 |
| 80,000 | 85,000 | 116 | 255 | 379 | 454 | 524 |
| 85,000 | 90,000 | 125 | 274 | 409 | 489 | 564 |
| 90,000 | 95,000 | 134 | 294 | 437 | 525 | 605 |
| 95,000 | 100,000 | 143 | 314 | 466 | 560 | 645 |
| 100,000 | 110,000 | 156 | 344 | 510 | 612 | 706 |
| 110,000 | 120,000 | 174 | 383 | 569 | 682 | 787 |
| 120,000 | 130,000 | 192 | 422 | 628 | 752 | 868 |
| 130,000 | 140,000 | 210 | 462 | 685 | 823 | 949 |

**Dollar Amounts for Trucks or Vans First Leased in 2016**

| *Fair Market Value of Automobile* | | *Tax Year During Lease** | | | | |
|---|---|---|---|---|---|---|
| *Over* | *Not Over* | *1st* | *2nd* | *3rd* | *4th* | *5th and Later* |
| 140,000 | 150,000 | 228 | 501 | 744 | 893 | 1,030 |
| 150,000 | 160,000 | 246 | 540 | 803 | 963 | 1,111 |
| 160,000 | 170,000 | 264 | 580 | 861 | 1,033 | 1,192 |
| 170,000 | 180,000 | 282 | 619 | 920 | 1,102 | 1,274 |
| 180,000 | 190,000 | 300 | 658 | 979 | 1,172 | 1,354 |
| 190,000 | 200,000 | 318 | 698 | 1,036 | 1,243 | 1,435 |
| 200,000 | 210,000 | 335 | 738 | 1,095 | 1,313 | 1,516 |
| 210,000 | 220,000 | 353 | 777 | 1,154 | 1,383 | 1,597 |
| 220,000 | 230,000 | 371 | 816 | 1,212 | 1,454 | 1,678 |
| 230,000 | 240,000 | 389 | 856 | 1,270 | 1,524 | 1,759 |
| 240,000 | and over | 407 | 895 | 1,329 | 1,594 | 1,839 |

* For the last tax year of the lease, use the dollar amount for the preceding tax year.

***Example (9):*** An SUV with a GVWR of 6,000 pounds or less and with a fair market value of $34,500 is leased for a term of 3 years beginning on April 1, 2016. The SUV is considered a truck. Assuming full business use by a calendar-year taxpayer, the includible amount for 2016 is $22.60 (275/365 × $30). The includible amount for 2017 is $66. The includible amount for 2018 is $98. The includible amount for 2019 is $24.16 ($98 × 90/365) (the dollar amount for the preceding tax year is used for the last tax year of the lease).

*January 1, 2015 to December 31, 2015 Leases of Trucks or Vans*

The following table from Rev. Proc. 2015-19, as modified by Rev. Proc. 2016-23, governs computation of includible amounts for trucks (including SUVs that are considered trucks) or vans with a GVWR of 6,000 pounds or less, a fair market value exceeding $19,500, and which are first leased in calendar-year 2015. This table should also be used for electric vehicles that are trucks or vans first leased in calendar-year 2015. Rev. Proc. 2016-23 modified Rev. Proc. 2015-19 by removing the first two lines of the table which provided inclusion amounts for vehicles costing over $18,500 but not over $19,500.

**Dollar Amounts for Trucks or Vans First Leased in 2015**

| *Fair Market Value of Automobile* | | *Tax Year During Lease** | | | | |
|---|---|---|---|---|---|---|
| *Over* | *Not Over* | *1st* | *2nd* | *3rd* | *4th* | *5th and Later* |
| 19,500 | 20,000 | 4 | 7 | 11 | 13 | 16 |
| 20,000 | 20,500 | 4 | 9 | 13 | 16 | 19 |
| 20,500 | 21,000 | 5 | 11 | 15 | 19 | 22 |
| 21,000 | 21,500 | 6 | 12 | 18 | 22 | 25 |
| 21,500 | 22,000 | 6 | 14 | 20 | 25 | 28 |
| 22,000 | 23,000 | 7 | 16 | 24 | 29 | 33 |
| 23,000 | 24,000 | 9 | 19 | 29 | 34 | 40 |
| 24,000 | 25,000 | 10 | 23 | 33 | 40 | 46 |
| 25,000 | 26,000 | 12 | 25 | 38 | 46 | 53 |
| 26,000 | 27,000 | 13 | 29 | 42 | 51 | 60 |
| 27,000 | 28,000 | 15 | 32 | 47 | 57 | 65 |

**Dollar Amounts for Trucks or Vans First Leased in 2015**

| *Fair Market Value of Automobile* | | *Tax Year During Lease** | | | | |
|---|---|---|---|---|---|---|
| *Over* | *Not Over* | *1st* | *2nd* | *3rd* | *4th* | *5th and Later* |
| 28,000 | 29,000 | 16 | 35 | 52 | 62 | 73 |
| 29,000 | 30,000 | 18 | 38 | 56 | 68 | 79 |
| 30,000 | 31,000 | 19 | 41 | 61 | 74 | 85 |
| 31,000 | 32,000 | 20 | 45 | 66 | 79 | 91 |
| 32,000 | 33,000 | 22 | 48 | 70 | 85 | 98 |
| 33,000 | 34,000 | 23 | 51 | 75 | 91 | 104 |
| 34,000 | 35,000 | 25 | 54 | 80 | 96 | 111 |
| 35,000 | 36,000 | 26 | 57 | 85 | 101 | 118 |
| 36,000 | 37,000 | 28 | 60 | 89 | 108 | 124 |
| 37,000 | 38,000 | 29 | 63 | 94 | 113 | 131 |
| 38,000 | 39,000 | 30 | 67 | 98 | 119 | 137 |
| 39,000 | 40,000 | 32 | 70 | 103 | 124 | 144 |
| 40,000 | 41,000 | 33 | 73 | 108 | 130 | 150 |
| 41,000 | 42,000 | 35 | 76 | 113 | 135 | 157 |
| 42,000 | 43,000 | 36 | 79 | 118 | 141 | 163 |
| 43,000 | 44,000 | 38 | 82 | 122 | 147 | 169 |
| 44,000 | 45,000 | 39 | 85 | 127 | 153 | 176 |
| 45,000 | 46,000 | 40 | 89 | 131 | 158 | 183 |
| 46,000 | 47,000 | 42 | 92 | 136 | 163 | 189 |
| 47,000 | 48,000 | 43 | 95 | 141 | 169 | 195 |
| 48,000 | 49,000 | 45 | 98 | 145 | 175 | 202 |
| 49,000 | 50,000 | 46 | 101 | 151 | 180 | 208 |
| 50,000 | 51,000 | 48 | 104 | 155 | 186 | 215 |
| 51,000 | 52,000 | 49 | 108 | 159 | 192 | 221 |
| 52,000 | 53,000 | 51 | 110 | 165 | 197 | 228 |
| 53,000 | 54,000 | 52 | 114 | 169 | 203 | 234 |
| 54,000 | 55,000 | 53 | 117 | 174 | 208 | 241 |
| 55,000 | 56,000 | 55 | 120 | 178 | 214 | 248 |
| 56,000 | 57,000 | 56 | 123 | 183 | 220 | 254 |
| 57,000 | 58,000 | 58 | 126 | 188 | 225 | 261 |
| 58,000 | 59,000 | 59 | 130 | 192 | 231 | 267 |
| 59,000 | 60,000 | 61 | 133 | 197 | 236 | 273 |

**Dollar Amounts for Trucks or Vans First Leased in 2015**

| *Fair Market Value of Automobile* | | *Tax Year During Lease** | | | | |
|---|---|---|---|---|---|---|
| *Over* | *Not Over* | *1st* | *2nd* | *3rd* | *4th* | *5th and Later* |
| 60,000 | 62,000 | 63 | 137 | 204 | 245 | 283 |
| 62,000 | 64,000 | 66 | 144 | 213 | 256 | 296 |
| 64,000 | 66,000 | 68 | 150 | 223 | 268 | 308 |
| 66,000 | 68,000 | 71 | 157 | 232 | 278 | 322 |
| 68,000 | 70,000 | 74 | 163 | 241 | 290 | 335 |
| 70,000 | 72,000 | 77 | 169 | 251 | 301 | 348 |
| 72,000 | 74,000 | 80 | 175 | 261 | 312 | 361 |
| 74,000 | 76,000 | 83 | 182 | 269 | 324 | 374 |
| 76,000 | 78,000 | 86 | 188 | 279 | 335 | 386 |
| 78,000 | 80,000 | 89 | 194 | 288 | 346 | 400 |
| 80,000 | 85,000 | 94 | 205 | 305 | 366 | 422 |
| 85,000 | 90,000 | 101 | 221 | 328 | 394 | 455 |
| 90,000 | 95,000 | 108 | 237 | 351 | 422 | 488 |
| 95,000 | 100,000 | 115 | 253 | 375 | 450 | 519 |
| 100,000 | 110,000 | 126 | 276 | 410 | 492 | 569 |
| 110,000 | 120,000 | 140 | 308 | 457 | 548 | 633 |
| 120,000 | 130,000 | 155 | 339 | 504 | 604 | 698 |
| 130,000 | 140,000 | 169 | 371 | 551 | 660 | 763 |
| 140,000 | 150,000 | 183 | 403 | 597 | 717 | 827 |
| 150,000 | 160,000 | 198 | 434 | 644 | 773 | 893 |
| 160,000 | 170,000 | 212 | 466 | 691 | 829 | 957 |
| 170,000 | 180,000 | 226 | 497 | 738 | 885 | 1,023 |
| 180,000 | 190,000 | 241 | 528 | 785 | 942 | 1,087 |
| 190,000 | 200,000 | 255 | 560 | 832 | 997 | 1,152 |
| 200,000 | 210,000 | 269 | 592 | 878 | 1,054 | 1,217 |
| 210,000 | 220,000 | 284 | 623 | 925 | 1,110 | 1,282 |
| 220,000 | 230,000 | 298 | 655 | 972 | 1,166 | 1,346 |
| 230,000 | 240,000 | 312 | 687 | 1,019 | 1,222 | 1,411 |
| 240,000 | and over | 327 | 718 | 1,066 | 1,278 | 1,476 |

* For the last tax year of the lease, use the dollar amount for the preceding tax year.

***Example (10):*** An SUV with a GVWR of 6,000 pounds or less and with a fair market value of $34,500 is leased for a term of 3 years beginning on April 1, 2015. The SUV is considered a truck. Assuming full business use by a calendar-year taxpayer, the includible amount for 2015 is $18.84 (275/365 × $25). The includible amount for 2016 is

$54. The includible amount for 2017 is $80. The includible amount for 2018 is $19.73 ($80 × 90/365) (the dollar amount for the preceding tax year is used for the last tax year of the lease).

*January 1, 2014 to December 31, 2014 Leases of Trucks or Vans*

The following table from Rev. Proc. 2014-21, as modified by Rev. Proc. 2015-19 to remove the first row for vehicles with a fair market value of more than $19,000 but not more than $19,500, governs computation of includible amounts for trucks (including SUVs that are considered trucks) or vans with a GVWR of 6,000 pounds or less, a fair market value exceeding $19,500, and which are first leased in calendar-year 2014. This table should also be used for electric vehicles that are trucks or vans first leased in calendar-year 2014.

**Dollar Amounts for Trucks or Vans First Leased in 2014**

| *Fair Market Value of Automobile* | | *Tax Year During Lease** | | | | |
|---|---|---|---|---|---|---|
| *Over* | *Not Over* | *1st* | *2nd* | *3rd* | *4th* | *5th and Later* |
| 19,500 | 20,000 | 2 | 5 | 7 | 8 | 10 |
| 20,000 | 20,500 | 3 | 6 | 8 | 10 | 12 |
| 20,500 | 21,000 | 3 | 7 | 10 | 11 | 14 |
| 21,000 | 21,500 | 3 | 8 | 11 | 14 | 15 |
| 21,500 | 22,000 | 4 | 9 | 12 | 15 | 18 |
| 22,000 | 23,000 | 5 | 10 | 15 | 17 | 21 |
| 23,000 | 24,000 | 5 | 12 | 18 | 21 | 24 |
| 24,000 | 25,000 | 6 | 14 | 20 | 25 | 28 |
| 25,000 | 26,000 | 7 | 16 | 23 | 28 | 32 |
| 26,000 | 27,000 | 8 | 18 | 26 | 31 | 36 |
| 27,000 | 28,000 | 9 | 20 | 28 | 35 | 40 |
| 28,000 | 29,000 | 10 | 21 | 32 | 38 | 44 |
| 29,000 | 30,000 | 11 | 23 | 35 | 41 | 48 |
| 30,000 | 31,000 | 11 | 26 | 37 | 45 | 52 |
| 31,000 | 32,000 | 12 | 27 | 41 | 48 | 56 |
| 32,000 | 33,000 | 13 | 29 | 43 | 52 | 60 |
| 33,000 | 34,000 | 14 | 31 | 46 | 55 | 64 |
| 34,000 | 35,000 | 15 | 33 | 49 | 58 | 68 |
| 35,000 | 36,000 | 16 | 35 | 51 | 62 | 72 |
| 36,000 | 37,000 | 17 | 37 | 54 | 65 | 76 |
| 37,000 | 38,000 | 18 | 38 | 58 | 69 | 79 |
| 38,000 | 39,000 | 18 | 41 | 60 | 72 | 83 |
| 39,000 | 40,000 | 19 | 43 | 63 | 75 | 87 |
| 40,000 | 41,000 | 20 | 44 | 66 | 79 | 91 |

**Dollar Amounts for Trucks or Vans First Leased in 2014**

| *Fair Market Value of Automobile* | | *Tax Year During Lease** | | | | |
|---|---|---|---|---|---|---|
| *Over* | *Not Over* | *1st* | *2nd* | *3rd* | *4th* | *5th and Later* |
| 41,000 | 42,000 | 21 | 46 | 69 | 82 | 95 |
| 42,000 | 43,000 | 22 | 48 | 72 | 85 | 99 |
| 43,000 | 44,000 | 23 | 50 | 74 | 89 | 103 |
| 44,000 | 45,000 | 24 | 52 | 77 | 93 | 106 |
| 45,000 | 46,000 | 24 | 54 | 80 | 96 | 111 |
| 46,000 | 47,000 | 25 | 56 | 83 | 99 | 115 |
| 47,000 | 48,000 | 26 | 58 | 86 | 102 | 119 |
| 48,000 | 49,000 | 27 | 60 | 88 | 106 | 123 |
| 49,000 | 50,000 | 28 | 62 | 91 | 109 | 127 |
| 50,000 | 51,000 | 29 | 63 | 95 | 113 | 130 |
| 51,000 | 52,000 | 30 | 65 | 97 | 117 | 134 |
| 52,000 | 53,000 | 31 | 67 | 100 | 120 | 138 |
| 53,000 | 54,000 | 31 | 69 | 103 | 123 | 142 |
| 54,000 | 55,000 | 32 | 71 | 106 | 126 | 146 |
| 55,000 | 56,000 | 33 | 73 | 108 | 130 | 150 |
| 56,000 | 57,000 | 34 | 75 | 111 | 133 | 154 |
| 57,000 | 58,000 | 35 | 77 | 114 | 137 | 157 |
| 58,000 | 59,000 | 36 | 79 | 116 | 141 | 161 |
| 59,000 | 60,000 | 37 | 80 | 120 | 144 | 165 |
| 60,000 | 62,000 | 38 | 84 | 123 | 149 | 172 |
| 62,000 | 64,000 | 40 | 87 | 130 | 155 | 180 |
| 64,000 | 66,000 | 41 | 91 | 136 | 162 | 187 |
| 66,000 | 68,000 | 43 | 95 | 141 | 169 | 195 |
| 68,000 | 70,000 | 45 | 99 | 146 | 176 | 203 |
| 70,000 | 72,000 | 47 | 102 | 153 | 182 | 211 |
| 72,000 | 74,000 | 48 | 107 | 158 | 189 | 219 |
| 74,000 | 76,000 | 50 | 110 | 164 | 196 | 227 |
| 76,000 | 78,000 | 52 | 114 | 169 | 203 | 235 |
| 78,000 | 80,000 | 54 | 118 | 175 | 209 | 243 |
| 80,000 | 85,000 | 57 | 124 | 185 | 222 | 256 |
| 85,000 | 90,000 | 61 | 134 | 199 | 239 | 276 |
| 90,000 | 95,000 | 65 | 144 | 213 | 256 | 295 |

**Dollar Amounts for Trucks or Vans First Leased in 2014**

| *Fair Market Value of Automobile* | | *Tax Year During Lease** | | | | |
|---|---|---|---|---|---|---|
| *Over* | *Not Over* | *1st* | *2nd* | *3rd* | *4th* | *5th and Later* |
| 95,000 | 100,000 | 70 | 153 | 227 | 273 | 315 |
| 100,000 | 110,000 | 76 | 168 | 248 | 298 | 345 |
| 110,000 | 120,000 | 85 | 187 | 277 | 332 | 383 |
| 120,000 | 130,000 | 93 | 206 | 305 | 366 | 423 |
| 130,000 | 140,000 | 102 | 225 | 334 | 400 | 462 |
| 140,000 | 150,000 | 111 | 244 | 362 | 434 | 501 |
| 150,000 | 160,000 | 120 | 263 | 390 | 468 | 541 |
| 160,000 | 170,000 | 128 | 282 | 419 | 502 | 580 |
| 170,000 | 180,000 | 137 | 301 | 447 | 536 | 619 |
| 180,000 | 190,000 | 146 | 320 | 475 | 571 | 658 |
| 190,000 | 200,000 | 154 | 339 | 504 | 604 | 698 |
| 200,000 | 210,000 | 163 | 358 | 532 | 639 | 736 |
| 210,000 | 220,000 | 172 | 377 | 561 | 672 | 776 |
| 220,000 | 230,000 | 180 | 397 | 589 | 706 | 815 |
| 230,000 | 240,000 | 189 | 416 | 617 | 740 | 854 |
| 240,000 | and over | 198 | 435 | 645 | 774 | 894 |

* For the last tax year of the lease, use the dollar amount for the preceding tax year.

***Example (11):*** An SUV with a GVWR of 6,000 pounds or less and with a fair market value of $34,500 is leased for a term of 3 years beginning on April 1, 2014. The SUV is considered a truck. Assuming full business use by a calendar-year taxpayer, the includible amount for 2014 is $11.30 (275/365 × $15). The includible amount for 2015 is $33. The includible amount for 2016 is $49. The includible amount for 2017 is $12.08 ($49 × 90/365) (the dollar amount for the preceding tax year is used for the last tax year of the lease).

## APPLICATION OF LEASE INCLUSION TABLES

### *Full business use by fiscal-year taxpayer*

A fiscal-year taxpayer uses the table that applies based on the calendar year that the vehicle is first leased.

***Example (12):*** A car with a fair market value of $60,600 is leased for a term of 4 years beginning on February 14, 2021, by a February 1 through January 31 fiscal-year taxpayer. Since the vehicle is a car first leased in the 2021 calendar year the table for vehicles first leased in 2021 is used. Assuming full business use, the includible amounts from the table for vehicles first leased in 2021 are:

| *Tax Year* | *Dollar Amount* | *Proration* | *Business Use* | *Inclusion Amount* |
|---|---|---|---|---|
| 2021/2022 . . . | $ 3 | 353/366 | 100% | $ 2.90 |
| 2022/2023 . . . | $ 7 | 365/365 | 100% | $ 7 |
| 2023/2024 . . . | $ 11 | 365/365 | 100% | $ 11 |
| 2024/2025 . . . | $13 | 365/365 | 100% | $13 |
| 2025/2026 . . . | $13 | 13/366 | 100% | $ 0.46 |

353 is the number of days the car was leased in FY 2021/2022 (February 14–January 31). 13 is the number of days the car was leased in the FY 2025/2026 tax year (February 1–February 13). In the last tax year in which the car is leased, the dollar amount for the preceding tax year is used.

*Partial business use*

The inclusion amount that is applicable if 100 percent business use applies is multiplied by the percentage of business use during the tax year if the vehicle is only used partly for business purposes.

***Example (13):*** Same facts as above except the taxpayer is a calendar-year taxpayer and business use each year is 70%. The includible amounts are:

| *Tax Year* | *Dollar Amount* | *Proration* | *Business Use* | *Inclusion Amount* |
|---|---|---|---|---|
| 2021 ....... | $3 | 322/366 | 70% | $1.85 |
| 2022 ....... | $7 | 365/365 | 70% | $4.90 |
| 2023 ....... | $11 | 365/365 | 70% | $7.70 |
| 2024 ....... | $13 | 365/365 | 70% | $9.10 |
| 2025 ....... | $13 | 44/366 | 70% | $1.09 |

322 is the number of days the car was leased in the 2021 calendar tax year (February 14–December 31). 44 is the number of days the car was leased in the 2025 calendar tax year (January 1–February 13). In the last tax year in which the car is leased, the dollar amount for the preceding tax year is used.

*Vehicle converted to business use after lease term begins*

If a car leased for personal purposes is later converted to business use, the fair market value is determined on the date of the conversion to business use. Use the lease inclusion table for the year in which the vehicle was converted to business use. That year is treated as the first year of the lease.

***Example (14):*** A car is leased for 4 years for personal purposes by a calendar-year taxpayer in December 2018. On March 1, 2021, the car was converted to business use. The business-use percentage for the period March 1, 2021, through December 31, 2021, was 70%. The fair market value of the vehicle on March 1, 2021, was $70,200. The inclusion amount for 2021 is computed as follows:

| *Tax Year* | *Dollar Amount* | *Proration* | *Business Use* | *Inclusion Amount* |
|---|---|---|---|---|
| 2021 ....... | $7 | 306/366 | 70% | $4.10 |

306 is the number of days in the tax year that the car was leased (March 1–December 31). The 2021 lease inclusion table is used and $7 is the dollar amount for the first year of a lease.

*Vehicle converted from business use to personal use*

If a leased business car is converted to personal use, the dollar amount for the tax year in which business use ceases is the dollar amount for the preceding tax year.

***Example (15):*** A car with a fair market value of $78,600 is leased on September 1, 2020, by a calendar-year taxpayer and used exclusively for business purposes. On March 1, 2021, the taxpayer's business operations are terminated and the car is used exclusively for personal purposes as of that date. The inclusion amounts are computed as follows:

| *Tax Year* | *Dollar Amount* | *Proration* | *Business Use* | *Inclusion Amount* |
|---|---|---|---|---|
| 2020 ....... | $69 | 122/366 | 100% | $23 |
| 2021 ....... | $69 | 31/365 | 100% | $5.86 |

122 is the number of days the car was leased and used for business in the 2020 tax year (September 1–December 31). 31 is the number of days the car was leased and used for business in the 2021 tax year (January 1–January 31). $69 is the first-year dollar

amount from the lease inclusion table for cars placed in service in 2020. The $69 lease inclusion amount from 2020 also applies for 2021 because 2021 is the last year the lease applies for business purposes.

## ¶ 206

## Consequences of Listed Property Classification

Unless the qualified business use of an asset classified as listed property exceeds 50 percent, certain deductions for listed property are limited (Code Sec. 280F(b)(1)). Listed property that fails to meet this requirement in the year that it is placed in service does not qualify for the Code Sec. 179 expense deduction (¶ 302) or bonus depreciation (¶ 127D), including New York Liberty Zone bonus depreciation (¶ 127E) and Gulf Opportunity Zone bonus depreciation (127F), Kansas Disaster Area bonus depreciation (¶ 127G), or Presidentially-declared disaster area bonus depreciation (¶ 127H).

Listed property subject to MACRS that fails to meet this requirement in the year placed in service also must be depreciated under the alternative depreciation system (ADS) (¶ 150) for that tax year and all succeeding tax years. Further, failure to continuously meet this requirement during each year of the asset's ADS recovery period (which is usually longer than the regular recovery period) triggers the recapture of the amount by which the depreciation claimed prior to the recapture year (including the section 179 allowance and bonus depreciation) exceeded the amount that would have been allowable under ADS (without claiming the section 179 allowance or bonus depreciation) during the period prior to the recapture year. The recaptured amount is added back to the property's adjusted basis (Code Sec. 280F(b)(2)) and depreciation is computed using ADS during the recapture year and the remaining ADS recovery period as if ADS had been used since the asset was first placed in service. See ¶ 210 for examples of the required calculations.

Listed property subject to ACRS that fails to meet the business use requirement during any tax year must be depreciated under the ACRS straight-line method generally over the earnings and profits life (see ¶ 310) of the property for such year and all succeeding tax years (former Code Sec. 280F(b)(4)) (before repeal by the Tax Reform Act of 1986 (P.L. 99-514), which remains in effect for ACRS property). Depreciation claimed in previous tax years that exceeds the amount that would have been allowed under this method is recaptured.

The listed property limitations generally apply to property placed in service or leased after June 18, 1984, except for certain transitional property.

## ¶ 208

## Categories of Listed Property

Code Sec. 280F(d)(4) sets forth the following specific categories of listed property which are discussed in more detail below:

(1) passenger automobiles,

(2) any other property used as a means of transportation, such as an airplane (for exceptions relating to vehicles that are unlikely to be used for personal purposes, see discussion below),

(3) property of a type generally used for purposes of entertainment, recreation, or amusement (unless used either exclusively at the taxpayer's regular business establishment or in connection with the taxpayer's principal trade or business),

(4) for property placed in service before 2018, computers or peripheral equipment (unless used exclusively at a regular business establishment and owned or leased by the operator of the establishment), and

(5) for tax years beginning before January 1, 2010, cellular telephones or other similar telecommunications equipment.

The definition of listed property potentially extends to other types of property specified by the regulations, but, under the caption *"Other property,"* Reg.§ 1.280F-6(b)(4) has, so far, merely been reserved.

Improvements to listed property that must be capitalized are treated as new items of listed property.

*Passenger automobiles, including trucks, vans, and SUVs*

The luxury car depreciation caps only apply to a listed property that is a "passenger automobile." If any type of listed property, including a passenger automobile, is not used more than 50 percent for business, depreciation deductions must be computed under the MACRS alternative depreciation system (ADS) and recapture is required if the business use requirement is not satisfied after the first tax year that the property was placed in service. See ¶ 210.

For luxury car limitation and listed property purposes, a passenger automobile includes any four-wheeled vehicle manufactured primarily for use on public streets, roads, and highways that has an *unloaded gross* vehicle weight of 6,000 pounds or less (Code Sec. 280F(d)(5)(A)). A truck or van is included in such classification if it has a *gross* vehicle weight rating (GVWR) of 6,000 pounds or less. A recreational vehicle, also referred to as an RV or motor home, is considered a truck. See ¶ 104.

Ambulances or hearses used directly in a trade or business and vehicles (such as a taxi or limo) used directly in the trade or business of transporting persons or property for hire are not "passenger automobiles" and, therefore, are not subject to the depreciation caps (Code Sec. 280F(d)(5)(B)(iii); Reg.§ 1.280F-6(c)(3)).

*Treatment of sport utility vehicles as trucks.* Beginning in 2003, the IRS indicated in its annual revenue procedure which updates of the annual depreciation caps for luxury automobiles that an SUV is considered a truck if it is built on a truck chassis (Rev. Proc. 2003-75, Section 2.01). Thus, if an SUV, was built on a unibody platform it could not qualify as a truck. Although the definition was applied in the context of qualification for the higher depreciation limits that apply to trucks and vans, this definition was subsequently used in various IRS publications and the instructions for Form 4562 in the context of the exemption from the depreciation caps for trucks and vans that have a gross vehicle weight rating in excess of 6,000 pounds. In its update of the depreciation caps for 2008 (Rev. Proc. 2008-22) the language defining an SUV built on a truck chassis as a truck was dropped. Informally, the IRS indicated that this definition was intended as a safe harbor and not to exclude all unibody vehicles from truck classification. The determination of whether an SUV is a truck should be based on the manufacturer's classification of the vehicle in accordance with applicable Department of Transportation Standards.

Sport utility vehicle purchasers should check the manufacturer's specifications for their vehicle to determine if its gross vehicle weight exceeds 6,000 pounds and if it is classified as a truck by its manufacturer.

The fact that an SUV or other vehicle may not be subject to the passenger automobile caps because its GVWR exceeds 6,000 pounds does not mean that the vehicle is not a listed property. This is because listed property includes property used as a means of transportation (see immediately below) whether or not the depreciation caps apply. An SUV, therefore, as a listed property, is subject to the listed property limitations discussed at ¶ 206 if qualified business use does not exceed 50 percent. Thus, if qualified business use falls to 50 percent or lower, depreciation must be computed using ADS and depreciation recapture applies.

***LIST OF TRUCKS, VANS, AND SUVS WITH GROSS VEHICLE WEIGHT RATINGS IN EXCESS OF 6,000 POUNDS. SEE THE QUICK REFERENCE TABLE IN APPENDIX.*** Online users may use search term "GVWR Exceeding 6,000."

*Web site for locating vehicle weights* The following web site contains specifications and vehicle weight information for most vehicles:

http://www.carsdirct.com

*Qualified nonpersonal use trucks and vans placed in service after July 6, 2003.* Effective for trucks (including SUVs that are considered trucks) and vans placed in service on or after July 7, 2003, any truck or van that is a qualified nonpersonal use vehicle as defined in Reg.§ 1.274-5(k) is not considered a passenger automobile subject to the luxury car depreciation caps (Reg. § 1.280F-6(c)(3)(iii) and Reg.§ 1.280F-6(f)). These are trucks and vans that have been modified in such a way that they are not likely to be used more than a de minimis amount for personal purposes (Code Sec. 274(i)). The regulation can also apply to trucks and vans placed in service before July 7, 2003. See Reg.§ 1.280F-6(f)(2).

Reg.§ 1.274-5(k)(7) only provides one example of a specially modified truck or van that is not likely to be used more than a de minimus amount for personal purposes. That regulation describes a van that has a front bench for seating, has permanent shelving that fills most of the cargo area, constantly carries merchandise or equipment, and is specially painted with advertising or a company name. Other specially modified vans, however, should be able to qualify as nonpersonal use vehicles if they are not likely to be used more than a de minimis amount for personal purposes.

Reg.§ 1.274-5(k)(2)(ii) also provides a list of qualified nonpersonal use vehicles. Certain trucks or vans that could otherwise be considered passenger automobiles may be described in this list. These include a clearly marked police or fire vehicle, a clearly marked public safety officer vehicle (effective for uses after May 19, 2010), a delivery truck with seating only for the driver or only for the driver plus a folding jump seat, a flatbed truck, a refrigerated truck, and an unmarked vehicle used by law enforcement officers. In most cases, however, these vehicles would have a gross vehicle weight rating in excess of 6,000 pounds, and, therefore, not be considered a passenger automobile subject to the luxury car depreciation caps. See, "Property used for transportation below," for details.

A vehicle that is either a passenger automobile or a property used as a means of transportation is considered a listed property. As noted immediately below, qualified nonpersonal use vehicles described in Reg.§ 1.274-5(k)(2)(ii) are not considered property used as a means of transportation (Reg.§ 1.280F-6(b)(2)(ii)). Thus, trucks and vans that are qualified nonpersonal use vehicles and that are placed in service on or after July 7, 2003 (or are used after May 19, 2010 in the case of a public safety officer vehicle) are no longer considered listed property because they are neither a passenger automobile nor a means of transportation. Consequently, in addition to being exempt from the depreciation caps applicable to passenger automobiles, such trucks and vans are not subject to the rules requiring the use of the MACRS alternative depreciation system (ADS) if business use of a listed property falls to 50 percent or less or the recapture of depreciation claimed in excess of the amount that would have been allowed under ADS. See ¶ 210 for rules regarding 50 percent or less business use. However, any Code Sec. 179 deduction remains subject to recapture under the rules described at ¶ 300 if business use drops to 50 percent or less during the regular recovery period of the vehicle.

*Property used for transportation*

The term listed property includes "property used as a means of transportation" (Code Sec. 280F(d)(4)(A)(ii)). Trucks, vans, buses, trains, boats, airplanes, motorcycles, and any other vehicles used for transporting persons or goods are generally regarded as other property used as a means of transportation (Reg.§ 1.280F-6(b)(2)(i)), but exceptions are recognized for qualified nonpersonal use vehicles, which are defined as vehicles which by their nature are unlikely to receive more than minimal personal use (Reg.§ 1.280F-6(b)(2)(ii); Code Sec. 274(i)). Qualified nonpersonal use vehicles include clearly marked police and fire vehicles, ambulances and hearses used as such, any vehicle with a loaded gross vehicle weight over 14,000 pounds that is designed to carry cargo, bucket trucks ("cherry pickers"), cement mixers, combines, cranes, derricks, delivery trucks seating only the driver (except for one folding jump seat), dump trucks (garbage trucks included), flatbed trucks, forklifts, school buses, other buses that are used as buses and accommodate 20 or more passengers, qualified moving vans and specialized utility repair trucks, refrigerated trucks, tractors and other special purpose farm vehicles, and (subject to their authorized use) unmarked police cars (Reg.§ 1.274-5(k)).

Effective for uses occurring after May 19, 2010, a clearly marked public safety officer vehicle is a qualified nonpersonal use vehicle (Reg.§ 1.274-5(k)(2)(ii)(A) and Reg.§ 1.274-5(m), last sentence).

The definition of a clearly marked police, fire, and public safety officer vehicle is provided in Reg.§ 1.274-5(k)(3). The vehicle must be owned or leased to a governmental unit and personal use other than for commuting must be prohibited. Similar restrictions apply to unmarked law enforcement vehicles (Reg. § 1.274-5(k)(6)).

Except to the extent provided in regulations, property used as a means of transportation does not include any property substantially all of the use of which is in a trade or business of providing unrelated persons services consisting of the transportation of persons or property *for compensation or hire* (Code Sec. 280F(d)(4)(B), as redesignated). This exception was carved out by the 1986 Tax Reform Act (Code Sec. 280F(d)(4)(C), as added by P.L. 99-514). The regulations defining property used as a means of transportation treat trucks, buses, trains, boats, airplanes, motorcycles, and any other vehicle for transporting persons or goods as a means of transportation without providing an exception for vehicles used to transport people or property for hire or compensation. However, these regulations were adopted before enactment of the 1986 Act. Thus, a taxicab or limo should not be considered a means of transportation.

Although a heavy truck (including a heavy SUV that is considered a truck) or van is not a "passenger automobile," it may be a "means of transportation" and, therefore, a listed property. Thus, although the depreciation caps do not apply, depreciation recapture is required in a tax year that business use of a large truck, van, or SUV falls to 50 percent or less. Further, the MACRS alternative depreciation system (ADS) must be used if business use of such a vehicle is 50 percent or less (¶ 210). Also, if such a vehicle is leased, a lease inclusion amount is required in the tax year that business use is 50 percent or less (see ¶ 212). As noted above, however, trucks and vans that are not likely to be used for personal purposes are not considered a means of transportation and, therefore, would not be subject to these rules.

*Property used for entertainment, including photographic, phonographic, communication, and video recording equipment*

Photographic, phonographic, communication, and video recording equipment exemplifies property generally regarded as used for purposes of entertainment, recreation, or amusement. However, such equipment is not considered listed property if it is used either exclusively at a regular business establishment or in connection with a principal trade or business. A regular business establishment includes a home office for which home office deductions may be claimed (Reg. § 1.280F-6(b)(3)).

The IRS audit technique guide for the entertainment industry (April 1995) (reproduced at ¶ 204,500 in the CCH IRS POSITIONS REPORTER) indicates that horses may be listed property, apparently on the grounds that a horse is generally used for entertainment, recreation, or amusement.

*Computers*

The Tax Cuts and Jobs Act (P.L. 115-97 c)omputers and related peripheral equipment are removed as a listed property category, effective for property placed in service after 2017 (Code Sec. 280F(d)(4)(A)).

As defined under Code Sec. 168(i)(2)(B), a "computer" is a programmable electronically activated device that is capable of accepting information, applying prescribed processes to such information, and supplying the results of these processes (with or without human intervention) and that consists of a central processing unit containing extensive storage, logic, arithmetic, and control capabilities. Related peripheral equipment is any auxiliary machine (either on-line or off-line) designed to be placed under the control of a computer's central processing unit. Typewriters, adding machines, copiers, duplicating equipment, and similar equipment, as well as equipment of a kind used primarily for the user's amusement or entertainment, are not regarded as computers or peripheral equipment.

The exception for computers and peripheral equipment used exclusively at a regular business establishment can extend to the use of such property at a portion of a dwelling unit, provided such an area meets the Code Sec. 280A(c)(1) requirements for home-office deductions.

Employees must meet the convenience-of-the-employer and the conditions-of-employment tests for listed property to be treated as used in a trade or business (Code Sec. 280F(d)(3)). See ¶ 210.

> ***Example:*** An aerospace engineer uses his home computer exclusively for job-related research and development. The computer was placed in service before 2018 and is, therefore, a listed property. He bought the computer because he needed one for his job and the computers provided at work were frequently unavailable because of their use by others. According to the IRS (Rev. Rul. 86-129, 1986-2 CB 48), he cannot deduct depreciation on the computer even though it enables him to do his job more efficiently and his employer states in writing that purchasing the home computer was a condition of employment. Under the same rules that apply to employer-provided lodging (Code Sec. 119), this falls short of the requisite clear showing that he could not perform his job with the computers at his workplace.

*Cellular telephones*

In tax years that began before January 1, 2010 cellular telephones were classified as listed property and, if business use exceeded 50 percent, were depreciable over seven years (cell phones are considered MACRS 7-year property (Asset Class 00.11)). A 10-year recovery period and straight-line method applied under ADS if business use did not exceed 50 percent. See ¶ 206. As listed property, cell phones were subject to the stringent record keeping and substantiation requirements of Code Sec. 274(d). In tax years beginning after December 31, 2009, cell phones are no longer considered listed property and are not subject to these record keeping requirements. Note that the effective date is *not* phrased in terms of property placed in service after December 31, 2009; therefore, the provision applies to any cell phone regardless of the date placed in service but is effective for tax years beginning after December 31, 2009.

## ¶ 210

## Qualified Business Use

The MACRS alternative depreciation system (ADS) is used to depreciate a listed property use 50 percent of less for business purposes. As explained below, if business use exceeds 50 percent in the placed-in service year depreciation recapture is required if business use falls to 50 percent or less during the ADS recovery period and ADS must be used beginning in the year business use falls below the 50 percent threshhold.

Only trade or business use is counted toward the more-than-50-percent-business-use test (Code Sec. 280F(d)(6)(B); Reg. § 1.280F-6(d)(2)).

In determining whether listed property has a business-use percentage in excess of 50 percent (and, thus, may qualify for regular (accelerated) MACRS deductions, bonus depreciation, and the section 179 expensing allowance (see ¶ 206)), use of an automobile or other means of transportation is allocated on the basis of mileage, and use of other listed property is allocated on the basis of time of actual use, as measured in terms of the most appropriate unit of time (Reg.§ 1.280F-6(e)). For photographic equipment, for example, the qualified business-use percentage is hours of business use divided by total hours of use. For special rules that apply to aircraft, see below.

> ***Example (1):*** Andrew uses a personal computer placed in service before 2018 150 hours in his part-time business operated out of his home, 100 hours in managing his investments, and 75 hours for his personal entertainment. Since his business use of the computer is only 46% (150/325), he must use the MACRS alternative depreciation system (i.e., straight-line method over ADS recovery period) in computing the depreciation allocable to his 77% (250/325) business/investment use of his computer.

Computers placed in service after 2017 are no longer considered listed property (Code Sec. 280F(d)(4)(A)).

*Special rule for determining qualified business use of an employee.* Any employee's use of listed property, such as a car or computer, is not treated as use in a trade or business for purposes of determining the amount of any depreciation deduction allowable to the employee (or the amount of any deduction allowable to the employee for rentals or other payments under a lease of listed property) unless the use is for the convenience of the employer and required as a condition of employment. The term employee use means any use in connection with the performance of services as an employee (Code Sec. 280F(d)(3)(b)). For example, in Rev. Rul. 86-129, an engineer (employee) who purchased a computer for exclusive use in his home in connection with his employment could not treat any use of the computer as business use for purposes of computing a depreciation deduction even though he had a written statement from his employer that the computer was a condition of employment because under the facts the engineer could have accomplished his job by using employer-provided computers at the workplace. The use of a listed property must be required in order for an employee to properly perform the duties of his employment. This requirement is not satisfied merely by an employer's statement that the property is required as a condition of employment. The standard is objective and an employer's subjective requirement is not controlling.

Although Code Sec. 280F(d) uses the phrase *"For purposes of this section . . . "*, Rev. Rul. 86-129 further clarifies that the business use of an employee is not counted toward computing any depreciation deduction, including under the alternative depreciation system, unless the convenience of the employer and condition of employment requirements are met. Thus, the engineer could claim no depreciation deduction. The language of Reg.§ 1.280F-6(a)(1) also appears to adopt the absolute proscription.

This special rule for employees only prevents the deduction of depreciation deductions on listed property and the deduction of rental/lease fees paid for the use of listed property. It does not appear to apply to a monthly service charge, such as cell phone bills, since these charges are not for the lease of a listed property or a payment under a lease of a listed property.

*Special rules for five-percent owners and related persons.* The following uses of listed property by five-percent owners and related persons are not qualified business use (Code Sec. 280F(d)(6)(C)(i); Reg. § 1.280F-6(d)(2)(ii)(A)):

(A) The use of listed property that is leased to a five-percent owner or related person;

(B) The use of listed property was provided as compensation for the performance of services by a five-percent owner or related person; or

(C) The use of listed property is provided as compensation for the performance of services by any person not described in (B), above, unless an amount is reported as income to such person and taxes are withheld.

Qualified business use does not include leasing property to any 5-percent owner or related person (item A). The regulations clarify that this rule only applies to the extent that the use of the listed property is by an individual who is a related party or a 5-percent owner with respect to the owner or lessee of the property (Reg. § 1.280F-6(d)(2)(A)(ii), last sentence). In other words, where the lessee of listed property is a related person or a 5-percent owner with respect to the owner or the lessee of the property, any use of the listed property by an individual who is a related person or a 5-percent owner with respect to either the owner or the lessee of the property is not qualified business use of the property for purposes of determining whether the owner of the property has satisfied the more than 50 percent business use requirement. Use of the leased listed property by persons other than a related person or a 5-percent owner with respect to the owner or the lessee of the property is not excluded from qualified business use under this rule, but might be excluded under items B or C (Technical Advice Memorandum 200945037, July 29, 2009).

***Example (2):*** Husband and Wife are the owners of Lessor LLC which leases an aircraft to Lessee LLC which is also owned by Husband and Wife. Lessee LLC is a related person with respect Lessor LLC. Since the airplane is leased to a related person exclusion A applies. Therefore, to the extent that an individual that is a 5-percent owner or a related person with respect the Lessor LLC or the Lessee LLC (e.g., Husband, Wife, and their children, etc.) uses the aircraft either for personal or business use, the allocable amount of their use must be excluded from the qualified business use of the aircraft by the Lessor LLC.

***Example (3):*** Assume that the above aircraft is used to transport legislative representatives or competitors to various destinations, sometimes without any employees of the Lessee LLC. While these flights are likely personal in nature with respect to the Lessee LLC, they represent qualified business use (leasing) with respect to the Lessor LLC unless it is determined that one of the exclusions (A, B, or C, above) applies to the flight. For instance, if it is determined that a particular flight had no connection to the business activities of Lessee LLC and was essentially a favor done at the behest of Husband and Wife or one of their family members for a passenger on the flight, then, taking into account the commonality of ownership between the Lessee and Lessor LLCs, the flight arguably may be excluded from qualified business use as use by a 5-percent owner or related person without regard to whether a 5-percent owner or related person was physically present on the flight (Technical Advice Memorandum 200945037, July 29, 2009).

*Allocation when aircraft or other listed property concurrently transports qualified and disqualified persons.* A reasonable allocation must be performed when an aircraft flight transports both (1) a person described in A, B, or C above and (2) one or more other persons. A reasonable allocation may be made on the basis of the occupied seat hours or miles method described in Proposed Reg.§ 1.274-10(e) and Notice 2005-45, 2005-1 C.B. 1228. This method is designed for determining the amount of entertainment use of an aircraft by a particular individual, but is equally applicable to determining the amount of use by a particular individual for purposes of the listed property rules. Qualified business use must be reduced by any occupied seat hours or miles allocable to use by any 5-percent owner, related person, or employee described in A, B, or C, above. Occupied seat hours or miles related to business use on the same flight by persons not so described are considered qualified business use for purposes of the listed property rules (Technical Advice Memorandum 200945037, July 29, 2009).

*Allocation of aircraft maintenance flights.* Maintenance flights must be allocated between flight hours or miles that are for qualified business use and flight hours or miles that are not for qualified business use, taking into account the preceding exclusions for 5 percent owners and related persons. For example, if 40 percent of the flight hours (or miles) of an aircraft (other than maintenance flights) are qualified business use, then only 40 percent of maintenance flight hours (or miles) may be taken into account as qualified business use (Technical Advice Memorandum 200945037, July 29, 2009).

*Special rule for leased aircraft.* If the property involved is an airplane, the above-mentioned business use by five-percent owners and related persons (items A, B, and C) is qualified business use if at least 25 percent of the total use during the tax year consists of other types of qualified business use (Code Sec. 280F(d)(6)(C)(ii); Reg. § 1.280F-6(d)(2)(ii)(B)). Thus, if the 25 percent threshold is satisfied, trade or business use otherwise excluded under A, B, and C are counted in determining whether more than 50 percent of total use of the aircraft is qualified business use.

*Five-percent owner defined.* For a corporation, a five-percent owner is any person who owns, or is considered to own, more than five percent of the outstanding stock of the corporation or stock possessing more than five percent of the total combined voting power of all stock in the corporation. For other types of business, a five-percent owner is a person who owns more than five percent of the capital or profits interest in the business (Code Sec. 280F(d)(6)(D)(i); Code Sec. 416(i)(1)(B)(i)).

*Related person defined.* A related person is any person related to the taxpayer within the meaning of Code Sec. 267(b) (Code Sec. 280F(d)(6)(D)(ii)).

*Commuting is not qualified business use.* Commuting is not a qualified business use even if accompanied by a business meeting in the car, a business call from the car, or an advertising display. However, commuting (and other personal use) by employees in employer-owned cars used for business is a qualified business use if reported as income on which taxes are withheld. A similar rule applies to other types of listed property such as an aircraft.

***Example (4):*** A corporation owns several automobiles used by its employees for business purposes. The employees are allowed to take the automobiles home at night. However, the fair market value of the use of an automobile for any personal purpose, such as commuting to work, is reported by the corporation as income to the respective employee and taxes are withheld. The use of the automobiles by the employees, even for personal purposes, is a qualified business use provided that the employees are not 5% owners of the corporation.

***Example (5):*** The owner of a business allows his employee-brother to use one of the company automobiles for personal use as part of his compensation. The employee-brother's use of the company automobile is not a qualified business use because the owner and his brother are related parties.

***Example (6):*** Assume the owner in *Example (5)*, above, allowed an unrelated employee to use a company automobile as part of his compensation, but he neither includes the value of such use in the gross income of the employee nor withholds any tax. The unrelated employee's use of the company automobile is not business/investment use.

*MACRS/section 179 listed property recapture*

If a listed property such as a car satisfies the qualified business use test (more than 50-percent business use) in the tax year in which it is placed in service but fails to meet the test in a later tax year that would fall within the asset's recovery period under the MACRS alternative depreciation system (ADS), the MACRS deductions (including any Code Sec. 179 expense allowance and first-year bonus deduction under Code Sec. 168(k) (¶ 127D), the New York Liberty Zone provision (¶ 127E), the Gulf Opportunity Zone provision(¶ 127F), the Kansas Disaster Area provision (¶ 127G), or the Presidentially declared disaster area provision (¶ 127H)) are subject to recapture in the later year (Code Sec. 280F(b)(2); Reg.§ 1.280F-3T(c); Code Sec. 168(k)(2)(F)(ii)). The MACRS deductions for tax years preceding the tax year in which business use fell to 50 percent or less are recaptured to the extent that the MACRS deductions (including any Code Sec. 179 expense allowance and bonus deduction) for these years exceed the depreciation that would have been allowed under ADS (without claiming any section 179 deduction or bonus depreciation) (Code Sec. 280F(b)(2)(B); Reg.§ 1.280F-3T(d)).

For the year of recapture and subsequent tax years during the asset's ADS recovery period, depreciation must be computed using ADS. ADS depreciation during the remaining ADS recovery period is computed as if it was originally elected and no amount was expensed under section 179 or claimed as bonus depreciation.

No Code Sec. 179 allowance or bonus depreciation deduction of any type is allowed in the tax year that a listed property is placed in service if the 50 percent or greater qualified business use requirement is not satisfied in that year. The listed property must be depreciated beginning in the tax year that it is placed in service using ADS (Code Sec. 280F(b)(1)). The Code Sec. 179 deduction does not apply to property used 50 percent or less in the conduct of an active trade or business (Code Sec. 179(d)(1)); Reg.§ 1.179-1(e)(1)) and bonus depreciation does not apply to property that must be depreciated using ADS (Code Sec. 168(k)(2)(D)(i)(II)).

The section 179 allowance claimed on a property that is *not* a listed property is subject to recapture if business use falls to 50 percent or less during the regular MACRS recovery period. See ¶ 300. The bonus deduction on a non-listed property is not subject to recapture upon a decline in business use.

The amount recaptured is added back to the property's adjusted basis for the first tax year in which the property is not predominantly used in a qualified business use (Temp. Reg. § 1.280F-3T(d)(1)). Property is predominantly used in a qualified business use if the percentage of its use in a trade or business exceeds 50 percent (Reg. § 1.280F-6T(d)(4)).

The listed property recapture rules only apply if the business use test is failed during the ADS recovery period that applies to the asset. There is no excess depreciation/section 179 expense to recapture under the listed property rules if the applicable ADS recovery period has expired.

If a taxpayer elects to depreciate a listed property using ADS for regular tax purposes, there is no recapture if business use drops to 50 percent or less during the ADS recovery period after the placed-in-service year unless a Code Sec. 179 expense allowance or bonus depreciation allowance was also claimed.

> ***Example (7):*** In June 2021, a calendar-year taxpayer purchases a used airplane for $50,000 and uses it for business. Assume that the airplane is considered listed property. The airplane has a regular 5-year recovery period and a 6-year alternative depreciation system recovery period (Asset Class 00.21 of Rev. Proc. 87-56). The taxpayer recovers the cost of the airplane under the general MACRS 200% declining-balance method using a half-year convention. Assume that no amount is expensed or claimed as bonus depreciation. The MACRS depreciation claimed for 2021 is $10,000 ($50,000 × 40% × ½). If the business use of the airplane drops to 40% in 2022, a portion of the 2021 MACRS deduction claimed must be recaptured because the computer is listed property. The amount of the 2021 MACRS deduction that must be recaptured in 2022 is $5,835, the excess of $10,000 over $4,165 (what would have been allowed under the alternative depreciation system if such system had been used in 2021 ($50,000 × 8.33% × ½)).
>
> Beginning in 2022, and for all later tax years, depreciation is computed using ADS. The 2022 ADS deduction is $8,335 ($50,000 (original table basis) × 40% business use × 16.67% (second-year table percentage for 6-year property using ADS)).

In the above example, the bonus deduction would have been recaptured if it had been claimed. Bonus depreciation is subject to recapture if business use of a listed property falls to 50 percent or below (Code Sec. 168(k)(2)(F)(ii)). Bonus depreciation is not subject to recapture if business use of a non-listed property falls to 50 percent or below. The Code Sec. 179 deduction is subject to recapture if business use falls to 50 percent or less whether or not the expensed property is a listed property (Code Sec. 179(d)(10)).

*ACRS listed property recapture*

If ACRS recovery property that is also listed property satisfies the qualified business use test (more than 50-percent business use) in the tax year in which it is placed in service but fails to meet the test in a later tax year, ACRS deductions are subject to recapture in the later year. Depreciation deductions for tax years preceding the tax year in which business use fell to 50 percent or less are recaptured to the extent that the ACRS deductions for these years exceed the depreciation that would have been allowed under the straight-line method (with a half-year convention for personal recovery property) over the earnings and profits life of the property. For subsequent tax years, depreciation must be computed under the straight-line method over the earnings and profits life.

For ACRS purposes, the earnings and profits life recovery periods to be used under Code Sec. 280F where the business use of recovery property that is also listed property does not exceed 50 percent are at ¶ 310.

The table below shows the applicable percentages to be used under Code Sec. 280F for listed property that is recovery property other than 18- or 19-year real property where business use does not exceed 50 percent (Temp. Reg. § 1.280F-3T(e)).

**Table A1**

| *If the recovery year is:* | *And the recovery period is (in yrs.):* | | | |
|---|---|---|---|---|
| | *5* | *12* | *25* | *35* |
| 1 | 10 % | 4 % | 2 % | 1 % |
| 2 - 5 | 20 | 9 | 4 | 3 |
| 6 | 10 | 8 | 4 | 3 |
| 7 - 12 | | 8 | 4 | 3 |
| 13 | | 4 | 4 | 3 |
| 14 - 25 | | | 4 | 3 |
| 26 | | | 2 | 3 |
| 27 - 31 | | | | 3 |
| 32 - 35 | | | | 2 |
| 36 | | | | 1 |

The table below shows the applicable percentages to be used under Code Sec. 280F for listed property that is 18- or 19-year recovery real property where business use does not exceed 50 percent (IRS Pub. 534).

**Table A2**

*Month Placed in Service*

| *Year* | *1* | *2* | *3* | *4* | *5* | *6* | *7* | *8* | *9* | *10* | *11* | *12* |
|---|---|---|---|---|---|---|---|---|---|---|---|---|
| 1st | 2.4 | 2.2 | 2.0 | 1.8 | 1.6 | 1.4 | 1.1 | 0.9 | 0.7 | 0.5 | 0.3 | 0.1 |
| 2 - 40th | 2.5 | 2.5 | 2.5 | 2.5 | 2.5 | 2.5 | 2.5 | 2.5 | 2.5 | 2.5 | 2.5 | 2.5 |
| 41st | 0.1 | 0.3 | 0.5 | 0.7 | 0.9 | 1.1 | 1.4 | 1.6 | 1.8 | 2.0 | 2.2 | 2.4 |

## ¶ 212

## Lessee's Inclusion Amount for Listed Property Other Than Passenger Automobiles

Lessees of listed property are required to add a one-time an inclusion amount to gross income in the first tax year (and only in that year) during the lease term in which qualified business use fails to exceed 50 percent (Reg.§ 1.280F-7(b)). This rule does not apply to leased "passenger automobiles" for which inclusion amounts are required during each year of the lease term. This one-time inclusion amount rule would apply to a leased truck, van, or SUV that has a gross vehicle weight rating in excess of 6,000 pounds. Although such an SUV is not a "passenger automobile," it is a listed property because it is a "means of transportation" (see ¶ 208).

This particular lease inclusion rule is designed to place lessees on par with *owners* of listed property who are subject to depreciation recapture and required to use the MACRS alternative depreciation system (ADS) when business use falls to 50 percent or less (see ¶ 210).

The inclusion amount may not exceed the sum of all deductions related to the use of the listed property properly allocable to the lessee's tax year in which the inclusion amount is added to gross income (Temp. Reg. § 1.280F-5T(g) (3)).

Where a lease term begins within nine months of the end of the lessee's tax year, qualified business use is 50 percent or less, and the lease term continues into the next tax year, the inclusion amount is added to gross income in the lessee's subsequent tax year in an amount based on the average of the business/investment use for both tax years and the applicable percentage for the tax year in which the lease term begins (Temp. Reg. § 1.280F-5T(g) (1)).

If the lease term is for less than one year, the amount that must be added to gross income is an amount that bears the same ratio to the inclusion amount as the number of days in the lease term bears to 365 (Temp. Reg. § 1.280F-5T(g) (2)).

*Post-1986 leases*

The lessee's inclusion amount for listed property (other than passenger automobiles) leased after 1986 is the sum of the following (Reg. § 1.280F-7(b) (2)):

> (1) the fair market value of the property on the first day of the lease term × the business/investment use for the first tax year in which the business use percentage is 50 percent or less × the applicable percentage from Table I, below; and
>
> (2) the fair market value of the property on the first day of the lease term × the average business/investment use for all tax years in which the property is leased before the tax year in which the business use percentage is 50 percent or less × the applicable percentage from Table II, below.

**Table I**

| Type of Property | First Taxable Year During Lease in Which Business Use Percentage Is 50% or Less | | | | | | | | | | | |
|---|---|---|---|---|---|---|---|---|---|---|---|---|
| | 1 | 2 | 3 | 4 | 5 | 6 | 7 | 8 | 9 | 10 | 11 | 12 & Later |
| Property with a Recovery Period of Less Than 7 Years under the Alternative Depreciation System (Such as Computers, Trucks and Airplanes) | 2.1% | −7.2% | −19.8% | −20.1% | −12.4% | −12.4% | −12.4% | −12.4% | −12.4% | −12.4% | −12.4% | −12.4% |
| Property with a 7- to 10-Year Recovery Period under the Alternative Depreciation System (Such as Recreation Property) | 3.9% | −3.8% | −17.7% | −25.1% | −27.8% | −27.2% | −27.1% | −27.6% | −23.7% | −14.7% | −14.7% | −14.7% |

**Table I**

| Type of Property | First Taxable Year During Lease in Which Business Use Percentage Is 50% or Less | | | | | | | | | | | |
|---|---|---|---|---|---|---|---|---|---|---|---|---|
| | 1 | 2 | 3 | 4 | 5 | 6 | 7 | 8 | 9 | 10 | 11 | 12 & Later |
| Property with a Recovery Period of More Than 10 Years under the Alternative Depreciation System (Such as Certain Property with No Class Life) | 6.6% | −1.6% | −16.9% | −25.6% | −29.9% | −31.1% | −32.8% | −35.1% | −33.3% | −26.7% | −19.7% | −12.2% |

**Table II**

| Type of Property | First Taxable Year During Lease in Which Business Use Percentage Is 50% or Less | | | | | | | | | | | |
|---|---|---|---|---|---|---|---|---|---|---|---|---|
| | 1 | 2 | 3 | 4 | 5 | 6 | 7 | 8 | 9 | 10 | 11 | 12 & Later |
| Property with a Recovery Period of Less Than 7 Years under the Alternative Depreciation System (Such as Computers, Trucks and Airplanes) | 0.0% | 10.0% | 22.0% | 21.2% | 12.7% | 12.7% | 12.7% | 12.7% | 12.7% | 12.7% | 12.7% | 12.7% |
| Property with a 7- to 10-Year Recovery Period under the Alternative Depreciation System (Such as Recreation Property) | 0.0% | 9.3% | 23.8% | 31.3% | 33.8% | 32.7% | 31.6% | 30.5% | 25.0% | 15.0% | 15.0% | 15.0% |

Table II

| Type of Property | First Taxable Year During Lease in Which Business Use Percentage Is 50% or Less | | | | | | | | | | | |
|---|---|---|---|---|---|---|---|---|---|---|---|---|
| | 1 | 2 | 3 | 4 | 5 | 6 | 7 | 8 | 9 | 10 | 11 | 12 & Later |
| Property with a Recovery Period of More Than 10 Years under the Alternative Depreciation System (Such as Certain Property with No Class Life) | 0.0% | 10.1% | 26.3% | 35.4% | 39.6% | 40.2% | 40.8% | 41.4% | 37.5% | 29.2% | 20.8% | 12.5% |

***Example:*** On February 1, 2019, a calendar-year taxpayer leased and placed in service an SUV with a fair market value of $32,000. Assume that the SUV is listed property (a "means of transportation," ¶ 208) and the lease term is two years. The SUV is not a "passenger automobile" because its gross vehicle weight rating is in excess of 6,000 pounds and it is considered a truck. Qualified business use is 80% in 2019 and 40% in 2020. The lessee must add an inclusion amount to gross income for 2020, which was the first tax year in which qualified business use of the SUV did not exceed 50%. Since 2020 is the second tax year of the lease and the SUV has a 5-year recovery period, the applicable percentage from Table I is −7.2%, and the applicable percentage from Table II is 10%. The 2020 inclusion amount is $1,638, which is the sum of the amounts determined under the tables. The amount determined under Table I is $922 ($32,000 × 40% × (−7.2%)), and the amount determined under Table II is $2,560 ($32,000 × 80% × 10%). As noted above, the amount of the $1,638 inclusion amount that is actually included in income is limited to a smaller amount if the business deductions (such as the deductible portion of the lease payment and deductible gas and insurance expenses) related to the vehicle in 2020 are less than $1,638 (Temp. Reg. § 1.280F-5T(g)(2)). If the SUV had a gross vehicle weight rating of 6,000 pounds or less, it would be a "passenger automobile" and annual lease inclusion amounts would be required regardless of the percentage of business use. These inclusion amounts would be computed annually using the lease inclusion tables at ¶ 204.

### *Pre-1987 leases*

The lessee's inclusion amount for recovery property that is also listed property (other than passenger automobiles) leased after June 18, 1984, and before 1987 is the product of: the fair market value of the property on the first day of the lease term × the average business/investment use × the applicable percentage from the tables below.

The average business/investment use is the average of the combined business/investment use of the listed property for the first tax year in which the qualified business use percentage is 50 percent or less (see ¶ 210) and all previous tax years in which the property is leased (Temp. Reg. § 1.280F-5T(h)(3)). The following IRS tables provide the applicable percentages for five- and ten-year recovery property. The table for three-year recovery property is not reproduced because the applicable percentage is zero if business use fails to exceed 50 percent in the sixth tax year of the lease term or succeeding tax years.

5-year recovery property:
For the first tax year in which the business use percentage is 50 percent or less, the applicable percentage for such tax year is:

| Tax year during lease term | 1 | 2 | 3 | 4 | 5 | 6 | 7 | 8 | 9 | 10 | 11 | 12 |
|---|---|---|---|---|---|---|---|---|---|---|---|---|
| For a lease term of: | | | | | | | | | | | | |
| 1 year | 2.7 % | | | | | | | | | | | |
| 2 years | 5.3 | 1.2 % | | | | | | | | | | |
| 3 years | 9.9 | 6.1 | 1.6 % | | | | | | | | | |
| 4 years | 14.4 | 11.1 | 7.3 | 2.3 % | | | | | | | | |
| 5 years | 18.4 | 15.7 | 12.4 | 8.2 | 3.0 % | | | | | | | |
| 6 or more years | 21.8 | 19.6 | 16.7 | 13.5 | 9.6 | 5.25 % | 4.4 % | 3.6 % | 2.8 % | 1.8 % | 1.0 % | 0 % |

10-year recovery property:
For the first tax year in which the business use percentage is 50 percent or less, the applicable percentage for such tax year is:

| Tax year during lease term | 1 | 2 | 3 | 4 | 5 | 6 | 7 | 8 | 9 | 10 | 11 | 12 | 13 | 14 | 15 |
|---|---|---|---|---|---|---|---|---|---|---|---|---|---|---|---|
| For a lease term of: | | | | | | | | | | | | | | | |
| 1 year | 2.5 % | | | | | | | | | | | | | | |
| 2 years | 5.1 | .6 % | | | | | | | | | | | | | |
| 3 years | 9.8 | 5.6 | 1.0 % | | | | | | | | | | | | |
| 4 years | 14.0 | 10.3 | 6.2 | 1.4 % | | | | | | | | | | | |
| 5 years | 17.9 | 14.5 | 10.9 | 6.7 | 1.8 % | | | | | | | | | | |
| 6 years | 21.3 | 18.3 | 15.1 | 11.4 | 7.1 | 2.1 % | | | | | | | | | |
| 7 years | 21.9 | 19.0 | 15.9 | 12.4 | 8.4 | 3.9 | 2.4 % | | | | | | | | |
| 8 years | 22.4 | 19.6 | 16.7 | 13.4 | 9.7 | 5.5 | 4.5 | 2.7 % | | | | | | | |
| 9 years | 22.9 | 20.2 | 17.4 | 14.3 | 10.9 | 7.0 | 6.4 | 5.1 | 3.0 % | | | | | | |
| 10 years | 23.5 | 20.9 | 18.2 | 15.2 | 11.9 | 8.3 | 8.1 | 7.2 | 5.7 | 3.3 % | | | | | |
| 11 years | 23.9 | 21.4 | 18.8 | 16.0 | 12.8 | 9.3 | 9.4 | 8.9 | 7.7 | 5.9 | 3.1 % | | | | |
| 12 years | 24.3 | 21.9 | 19.3 | 16.5 | 13.4 | 10.1 | 10.3 | 10.0 | 9.3 | 7.8 | 5.5 | 2.9 % | | | |
| 13 years | 24.7 | 22.2 | 19.7 | 16.9 | 14.0 | 10.7 | 11.1 | 11.0 | 10.4 | 9.2 | 7.4 | 5.2 | 2.7 % | | |
| 14 years | 25.0 | 22.5 | 20.1 | 17.3 | 14.4 | 11.1 | 11.6 | 11.7 | 11.3 | 10.3 | 8.8 | 6.9 | 4.8 | 2.5 % | |
| 15 or more years | 25.3 | 22.8 | 20.3 | 17.5 | 14.7 | 11.5 | 12.0 | 12.2 | 11.9 | 11.1 | 9.8 | 8.2 | 6.5 | 4.5 | 2.3 % |

## ¶ 214

## Depreciation of Cars Involved in Trade-Ins or Involuntary Conversions

Special rules govern the depreciation deductions claimed on a business vehicle received in a tax-deferred like-kind exchange (trade-in) under Code Sec. 1031 or involuntarily conversion under Code Sec. 1033 after January 2, 2000. Like-kind exchanges are reported on Form 8824 (Like-Kind Exchanges).

*Like-kind exchange rules only apply to real property after 2017.* Like-kind exchanges under Code Sec. 1031 are allowed only for real property after 2017 (Code Sec. 1031(a)(1), as amended by the Tax Cuts and Jobs Act (P.L. 115-9)). See ¶ 167.

The provision generally applies to exchanges completed after December 31, 2017 (Act Sec. 13303(c)(1) of P.L. 115-97). However, the provision does not apply to an exchange if (1) the property disposed of by the taxpayer in the exchange is disposed of on or before December 31, 2017; or (2) the property received by the taxpayer in the exchange is received on or before December 31, 2017 (Act Sec. 13303(c)(2) of P.L. 115-9).

As a result of the law change, gain on vehicle trade-ins may not be deferred under Code Sec. 1031 after 2017. Gain or loss will be recognized. However, the deferral rules under Code Sec. 1033 for involuntary conversions will continue to apply.

*Most vehicles are like-kind.* Cars, light general purpose trucks (for use over the road having actual unloaded weight of less than 13,000 pounds) and vehicles that share characteristics of both cars and light general purpose trucks (e.g., crossovers, sport utility vehicles, minivans, cargo vans and similar vehicles) are of like-kind for purposes of Code Sec. 1031 (IRS Letter Ruling IRS Letter Ruling 200912004, December 2, 2008). Prior to this ruling the IRS had maintained that cars and trucks were not like-kind property.

*Like-kind exchange rules are not elective.* If the requirements for a like-kind exchange have been satisfied a taxpayer is required to apply the Code Sec. 1031 like-kind exchange rules. Prior to 2018, in most situations a taxpayer was considered to have engaged in a like-kind exchange of a vehicle if the used vehicle was sold to a dealership and a new vehicle was acquired from the same dealership as part of the same transaction. The following example from IRS Publication 544 (Sales and Other Dispositions of Assets for 2017 returns) illustrates this point.

> ***Example (1):*** You used your car in your business for 2 years. Its adjusted basis is \$3,500 and its trade-in value is \$4,500. You are interested in a new car that costs \$20,000. Ordinarily, you would trade your old car for the new one and pay the dealer \$15,500. Your basis for depreciation of the new car would then be \$19,000 (\$15,500 plus \$3,500 adjusted basis of the old car).
>
> You want your new car to have a larger basis for depreciation, so you arrange to sell your old car to the dealer for \$4,500. You then buy the new one for \$20,000 from the same dealer. However, you are treated as having exchanged your old car for the new one because the sale and purchase are reciprocal and mutually dependent. Your basis for depreciation for the new car is \$19,000, the same as if you traded the old car.

*Initial IRS guidance in Notice 2000-4.* Pursuant to IRS Notice 2000-4 and subsequently issued regulations which implement the principles of that notice (which has been declared obsolete, effective February 27, 2004), depreciation on the carryover portion of the adjusted basis of the acquired automobile (the "exchanged basis"), is separately depreciated from the noncarryover basis ("excess basis"). The "excess basis" (e.g., cash paid) is depreciated as if it is newly acquired property. The exchanged basis and excess basis each qualify for bonus depreciation if the trade-in occurs during a tax year that bonus depreciation is available and the vehicle received otherwise qualifies for bonus depreciation. See 127D for a discussion of bonus depreciation. This bifurcated treatment only applies if the taxpayer used MACRS to depreciate the relinquished vehicle and will use MACRS to depreciate the replacement vehicle.

Notice 2000-4 did not explain the interplay with the Code Sec. 280F luxury car depreciation caps. The IRS did not issue any formal guidance on this point until temporary regulations (now finalized) were released on February 27, 2004 (T.D. 9115, filed with the Federal Register on February 27, 2004).

*Effective date of regulations and transitional rules.* Final regulations apply to like-kind exchanges and involuntary conversions of MACRS property for which the time of disposition and time of replacement both occur after February 27, 2004 (Reg. § 1.168(i)-6(k)(1)). A taxpayer may apply the final regulations to pre-February 27, 2004 transactions or rely on prior guidance issued by the IRS (e.g., Notice 2000-4) (Reg. § 1.168(i)-6(k)(2)).

*Election not to apply trade-in regulations.* A taxpayer may elect not to apply the final regulations to a transaction occurring on or after the effective date (Reg. § 1.168(i)-6(i)(1)).

If the election not to apply the regulations is made, the exchanged (carryover) basis and excess basis (additional cash paid) in the acquired vehicle are treated as placed in service at the time of replacement and the adjusted depreciable basis (generally cost less depreciation claimed (including amounts expensed under section 179 and bonus depreciation)) of the relinquished vehicle is treated as disposed of by the taxpayer at the time of disposition.

Bonus depreciation may be claimed on both the exchanged and excess basis of the acquired vehicle assuming the vehicle otherwise qualifies for bonus depreciation. The Code Sec. 179 deduction is only available for the excess basis (additional cash paid).

*How to make election not to apply trade-in regulations.* To make the election out for a vehicle that is not employee-owned, compute the deduction without applying the regulations and enter the deduction on Part V of Form 4562. Attach a statement indicating "Election made under section 1.168(i)-6(i)" and identify the vehicle to which the election applies (Form 4562 instructions). An employee makes the election out by completing Form 2106, Part II, Section D, instead of Form 4562. If no election out is made the employee must use Form 4562 instead of Form 2106 to claim depreciation (Form 2106 instructions).

The election must be made by the due date (including extensions) of the tax return for the year of replacement. Once made, the election may only be revoked in extraordinary circumstances with IRS consent (Reg. § 1.168(i)-6(j)).

*Depreciation computations if election out of regulations is not made.* If no election out is made, a vehicle acquired in a like-kind exchange or involuntary conversion is treated as comprised of two separate components. The first component is the exchanged basis (generally, the adjusted basis of the relinquished vehicle immediately prior to the trade-in or involuntary conversion (computed as if business use was 100 percent throughout the recovery period)) and the second component is the excess basis (generally, the cash paid for the new vehicle, if any).

The exchanged basis in the acquired vehicle is determined after determining the depreciation deduction on the relinquished vehicle in the trade-in year.

Adjusted depreciable basis is the basis for determining gain or loss. This basis reflects basis reductions for the Code Sec. 179 expense allowance, bonus depreciation, and regular depreciation deductions previously claimed (taking into account any personal use).

Excess basis in the case of a vehicle trade-in is the additional cash paid by the buyer.

In the year of disposition the sum of the depreciation deductions for the relinquished MACRS passenger automobile and the replacement MACRS passenger automobile may not exceed the replacement automobile Section 280F limit (Reg. § 1.168(i)-6(d)(3)(i)).

Depreciation deductions on the relinquished car in the year of disposition and the replacement car in the year of replacement (*and each subsequent tax year*) are allowed in the following order (Reg. § 1.168(i)-6(d)(3)(ii)):

(1) The depreciation deduction on the relinquished car (prior to the trade-in) in the year of disposition is allowed to the extent of the smaller of (a) the relinquished car's 280F limit (for the year of disposition) or (b) the replacement car's 280F limit for the year of disposition.

(If the replacement vehicle is not acquired in the year of trade-in or involuntary conversion, the depreciation deduction on the relinquished vehicle is limited solely by the relinquished car's 280F limit).

(2) Bonus depreciation on the remaining exchanged basis of the replacement vehicle (i.e., the carryover basis of replacement car) is allowed to the extent of the replacement car's 280F limit reduced by the depreciation claimed on the relinquished car prior to the trade-in (item 1). Thus, the bonus deduction on the remaining exchanged basis can be claimed without regard to the 280F cap for the relinquished vehicle. It is only limited by the 280F cap for the replacement vehicle as reduced by depreciation claimed on the relinquished vehicle prior to the trade in the trade-in year.

(3) The depreciation deduction on the depreciable exchanged basis of the replacement vehicle is allowed to the extent of the smaller of the replacement car's 280F limit (i.e., first-year cap) or the relinquished car's 280F limit (i.e., cap for trade-in year), as reduced by items (1) and (2).

(4) Any section 179 deduction claimed on the excess basis of the replacement vehicle is allowed to the extent of the 280F limit for the replacement car as reduced by items (1), (2), and (3) above.

(5) The bonus deduction on the remaining excess basis of the replacement vehicle is allowed to the extent of the 280F limit for the replacement car as reduced by items (1), (2), (3), and (4), above.

(6) The depreciation deduction on the depreciable excess basis is allowed to the extent of the 280F limit for the replacement car as reduced by items (1), (2), (3), (4), and (5), above.

These ordering rules only apply in situations where both the relinquished vehicle and the replacement vehicle are "passenger automobiles" subject to the Code Sec. 280F luxury car caps. A truck or van (including an SUV) in excess of 6,000 pounds is not a passenger automobile and is not subject to the caps (Code Sec. 280F(d)(5)). See ¶ 208. The regulations contain no specific guidance or examples showing depreciation computations where one or both vehicles are not subject to the caps. Nevertheless it seems clear that where neither vehicle is subject to the caps, depreciation on the exchanged basis is simply computed over the remaining recovery period of the exchanged basis and the excess basis is treated as a newly acquired vehicle placed in service in the year of the trade in and depreciated over the replacement vehicle's five-year recovery period. If only one of the vehicles is subject to the caps then the depreciation on the exchanged basis is limited by the caps if the relinquished vehicle is subject to the caps or, alternatively, depreciation on the excess basis is limited by the caps if the replacement vehicle is subject to the caps. Depreciation claimed on the portion of the basis of the replacement vehicle that is not subject to the caps would not be limited in any way by the caps nor reduce the caps that apply to the portion of the basis that is subject to the caps.

Where the exchanged basis is subject to the caps and the excess basis is not subject to the caps it is unclear how bonus depreciation should be limited on the exchanged basis in the trade-in year. One possibility is that the bonus deduction plus regular deduction is limited to the cap that applies in the year of the trade-in. For example, if the vehicle is traded-in in the third tax year after being placed in service, the third-year limit would apply even though the limit is much smaller than the first-year cap that takes into account bonus depreciation. An equally reasonable approach would be to increase the third-year cap by $8,000 as provided in Code Sec. 168(k)(2)(F)(i).

> ***Example (2):*** Justin Hawleski purchases a Chevy Malibu (MACRS 5-year property) in 2014 for $30,000. The half-year convention and 200 percent declining balance method apply. The 200 percent depreciation rate for 5-year property is 40% with a switch to the straight-line method in the fifth tax year that the vehicle is in service. Alternatively, table percentages may be used. In 2017 he exchanges the Impala plus $15,000 cash for a new Chevy Impala which costs $35,000. No bonus deduction or section 179 allowance was claimed on the relinquished vehicle in 2014. However, bonus depreciation will be claimed on the replacement vehicle which is also depreciated using the half-year convention and 200 percent declining balance method. The vehicles are used 100 percent for business.

The table below shows how depreciation is computed on the traded-in Malibu through the year of the trade-in. Example 2A shows how depreciation is computed on the Impala received in the trade-in.

Note that trade-ins after 2017 are not governed by these rules. Gain or loss is separately computed and recognized on the exchanged vehicle unless the transaction involves an involuntary conversion.

| *Year Purchased* | *Price* | *Bonus* | *Sec. 179* | *Method* | *Convention* | *Trade-in Year* |
|---|---|---|---|---|---|---|
| 2014 | $30,000 | $0 | $0 | 200DB | Half-Year | 2017 |

| *Year* | *Annual Limit* | *Deduction** | *Lesser* |
|---|---|---|---|
| 2014 . . . . . . . . . . . . . | $3,160 | $6,000 | $3,160 |
| 2015 . . . . . . . . . . . . . | $5,100 | $9,600 | $5,100 |
| 2016 . . . . . . . . . . . . . | $3,050 | $5,760 | $3,050 |
| 2017 . . . . . . . . . . . . . | $1,875** | $1,728 | $1,728 |

* $30,000 × 40% × 6/12 = $6,000 (or $30,000 × 20% first-year table percentage)
($30,000 – $6,000) × 40% = $9,600 (or $30,000 × 32% second-year table percentage)
($30,000 – $6,000 – $9,600) × 40% = $5,760 (or $30,000 × 19.2% third-year table percentage)
($30,000 – $6,000 – $9,600 – $5,760) × 40% × 6/12 = $1,728 (or $30,000 × 11.52% fourth-year table percentage × 6/12 = $1,728)
6/12 is used to reflect half-year convention in the acquisition year and trade-in year.

** The 280F limit for the relinquished vehicle ($1,875) is used because it is smaller than the 280F limit for the replacement vehicle (i.e., $11,160) (ordering rule 1).

> ***Example 2A:*** Assume the same facts as Example 2. The exchanged basis of the replacement vehicle (Impala) is calculated by reducing the original cost of the relinquished Malibu ($30,000) by the depreciation (including any section 179 expense and bonus allowance) actually allowed on the replacement vehicle prior to the trade-in.

The exchanged basis is, therefore, $16,962 ($30,000 – $3,160 – $5,100 – $3,050 – $1,728 = $16,962).

Bonus depreciation and regular first-year deduction are then computed on the exchanged basis without regard to any 280F limit. Note that exchanged basis (i.e., carryover basis) never qualifies for expensing under Code Sec. 179.

Bonus depreciation on the exchanged basis is $8,481 ($16,962 × 50% = $8,481). The taxpayer should not use the table percentages to compute the regular depreciation deduction on the exchanged basis after the trade-in. Regular depreciation is $1,696 (($16,962 – $8,481) × 40% double declining balance rate for five year property × 6/12 = $1,696).

Under the second ordering rule, the bonus deduction ($8,481) may be claimed in full because it does not exceed $9,432. $9,432 is the replacement car's 280F limit ($11,160) reduced by the depreciation claimed on the relinquished car in 2017 prior to the trade-in ($1,728).

Under the third ordering rule, the $1,696 regular depreciation deduction on the remaining exchanged basis of the replacement car is allowed only to the extent of the lesser of: (a) $951 (the replacement car's 280F limit ($11,160)) reduced by the depreciation allowed on the relinquished car in 2017 prior to the trade in ($1,728) and the bonus depreciation allowed on the exchanged basis after the trade in ($8,481) or (b) $0 (the relinquished car's 280F limit ($1,875) reduced by the sum of the depreciation allowed on the relinquished car in 2017 prior to the trade in ($1,728) and the bonus depreciation allowed on the exchanged basis after the trade in ($8,481). Consequently, no regular depreciation deduction may be claimed on the remaining exchanged basis in 2017.

Next, the Code Sec. 179 allowance, bonus allowance, and regular first-year deduction are computed on the excess basis ($15,000 additional cash) without regard to any cap. This amount is depreciated as a separate item of new property placed in service in 2017. Assume that no amount is expensed under Code Sec. 179.

The bonus deduction is $7,500 ($15,000 × 50%). The regular first-year deduction is $1,500 (($15,000 – $7,500) × 40% × 6/12) or (($15,000 – $7,500) × 20% first-year table percentage).

The ordering rules are then applied.

The fourth ordering rule is not applicable since no Code Sec. 179 expense allowance is claimed on the excess basis.

Under the fifth ordering rule, the bonus deduction on the excess basis of the replacement vehicle may only be claimed to the extent that the bonus deduction does not exceed the 280F limit for the replacement car ($11,160) as reduced by the regular depreciation deduction on the relinquished vehicle ($1,728), bonus depreciation on the exchanged basis ($8,481), depreciation on the exchanged basis ($0), and any amount of the excess basis that is expensed under Code Section 179 ($0).

The bonus deduction, is therefore limited to $951 ($11,160 – $1,728 – $8,481). Since the first-year cap is now used up, no amount of the regular depreciation ($1,500) may be claimed (ordering rule 6).

> ***Example 3:*** Max Snider purchases a vehicle costing $30,000 in 2016. The vehicle is exchanged in 2017 with an additional $15,000 cash paid for the acquired vehicle. No section 179 expense allowance is claimed on either vehicle and an election out of bonus depreciation was made for both vehicles.

Depreciable allowed in 2016 on the relinquished automobile (the year prior to trade-in) is $3,160 (2016 first-year cap) since this is less than the regular first-year deduction of $6,000 ($30,000 × 40% × 6/12).

In determining the depreciation allowed on the relinquished vehicle in 2017 prior to the trade-in, the applicable cap is $3,160. This cap is the smaller of the second-year cap for a vehicle placed in service in 2016 ($5,100) or the first-year cap for the acquired vehicle placed in service in 2017 ($3,160 since no bonus is claimed on the acquired vehicle) (ordering rule 1).

The regular deduction on the relinquished automobile in 2017 prior to the trade-in, without regard to the $3,160 cap, is $4,800 ($30,000 – $6,000 × 40% × 6/12) or ($30,000 × 32% second year table percentage × 6/12). Since $4,800 exceeds the applicable cap of $3,160, the depreciation deduction is limited to $3,160.

In determining the depreciation allowed on the exchanged basis after the trade in, the applicable cap is $3,160 (the lesser of the second-year cap on the relinquished car ($5,100) or the first-year cap on the acquired car ($3,160)). Since no portion of the $3,160 first-year cap remains, no regular depreciation on the exchanged basis may be claimed (ordering rule 3).

Similarly, no regular depreciation deduction may be claimed on the excess basis ($15,000). The applicable cap for the excess basis is $3,160 (the first-year cap for the acquired vehicle placed in service in 2017). This cap has already been reduced to zero (ordering rule 6).

***Example 4:*** A used vehicle costing $10,000 is purchased is 2014 and traded in August 2017. An additional $14,000 cash is paid for a new vehicle. The 200 percent declining balance method and half-year convention apply to both vehicles.

*Deductions on relinquished vehicle prior to trade-in.*
*No bonus claimed.*

| *Year* | *Annual Limit* | *Deduction** | *Lesser* |
|---|---|---|---|
| 2014 . . . . . . . . . . | $3,160 | $2,000 | $2,000 |
| 2015 . . . . . . . . . . | $5,100 | $3,200 | $3,200 |
| 2012 . . . . . . . . . . | $3,050 | $1,920 | $1,920 |
| 2017 . . . . . . . . . . | $1,875** | $576*** | $576*** |
| Total depreciation allowed . . . . . . . . . . . . . . . . . . . . . . . . | | | $7,696 |

* ($10,000 × 40% × 6/12) or ($10,000 × 20% first-year table percentage) = $2,000
($10,000 – $2,000) × 40% or ($10,000 × 32% second-year table percentage) = $3,200
($10,000 – $2,000 – $3,200) × 40% or ($10,000 × 19.2 % third-year table percentage) = $1,920
*** ($10,000 – $2,000 – $3,200 – $1,920) × 40% × 6/12 or ($10,000 × 11.52% fourth-year table percentage × 6/12) = $576

** The annual limit for 2017 is the lesser of the 2017 limit for the relinquished vehicle ($1,875) or the $11,160 first-year limit for the acquired vehicle (ordering rule 1).

Depreciation on the exchanged and excess basis of the acquired vehicle is computed as follows.

First, bonus depreciation is computed on the exchanged basis of $2,304 ($10,000 – $7,696). The bonus deduction is $1,152 ($2,304 × 50%) and may be claimed in full since it does not exceed $10,584 (the first-year depreciation cap for the acquired vehicle ($11,160) reduced by the depreciation claimed on the relinquished vehicle in 2017 prior to the trade-in ($576)) (ordering rule 2).

Next regular depreciation is computed without using table percentages on the depreciable exchanged basis of $1,152 ($2,304 exchanged basis - $1,152 bonus deduction). The regular depreciation deduction is $230 ($1,152 × 40% × 6/12). Since the 2017 $1,875 cap for the relinquished vehicle is the less than the $11,160 cap for the acquired vehicle, the depreciation deduction cannot exceed $147 ($1,875 – $576 – $1,152) and, therefore, is limited to $147 (ordering rule 3).

The next step is to compute the Code Sec. 179 expense deduction, bonus deduction, and regular depreciation deduction that may be claimed on the excess basis (i.e., $14,000 cash paid). These three items are first figured without regard to the cap. Assume that the taxpayer expenses $1,400. Bonus depreciation is $6,300 ($14,000 - $1,400) × 50%). Regular first-year depreciation is $1,260 ($14,000 – $1,400 – $6,300) × 40% × 6/12) or ($14,000 – $1,400 – $6,300) × 20% first-year table percentage).

The applicable first-year cap for a vehicle placed in service in 2017 on which 50% bonus depreciation is claimed is $11,160. However, the cap must first be reduced by the amount of regular depreciation actually claimed on the relinquished vehicle in 2017 prior to the trade-in and the amount of bonus and regular depreciation claimed on the exchanged basis after the trade-in. The cap is, therefore, reduced to $9,285 ($11,160 - $576 - $1,152 - $147). Note that the deductions claimed on the relinquished vehicle and exchanged basis after the trade-in were limited to the $1,875 cap ($576 + $1,152 + $147 = $1,875).

The reduced cap ($9,285) is applied in the following order: First to any amount expensed under Code Sec. 179, then to any bonus deduction, then to the regular depreciation deduction (ordering rules 4, 5, and 6).

The $1,400 Code Sec. 179 deduction may be claimed in full ($9,285 - $1,400 = $7,885). The $6,300 bonus deduction is allowed in full ($7,885 - $6,300 = $1,585). The $1,260 regular first-year deduction may be claimed in full since it does not exceed the remaining $1,585 cap.

The regulations provide that the ordering rules are used to determine deductions allowed on the exchanged and excess basis in years after the trade-in (Reg. § 1.168(i)-6(d)(3)(ii), second sentence). However, the ordering rules only address the trade-in year and no examples of depreciation calculations on the exchanged and excess basis in the tax years after the trade-in year are provided. It appears, however, that the depreciation computed on the exchanged basis is limited to the applicable cap for the exchanged basis. The depreciation deduction on the excess basis is limited to the applicable cap for the excess basis reduced by the depreciation claimed on the exchanged basis. The regulations make it clear that a taxpayer may not claim depreciation both on the exchanged basis in an amount equal to the applicable exchanged basis cap and depreciation on the excess basis in an amount equal to the applicable excess basis cap as if the exchanged basis and excess were separate vehicles subject to separate caps.

***Example 5:*** Assume the same facts as in *Example 4*. The depreciation deduction in 2018 on the exchanged basis is limited to the $1,875 (fifth year cap for a vehicle placed in service in 2014). The depreciation deduction on the excess basis is limited to $5,100 (second-year cap for a vehicle placed in service in 2017) minus any depreciation allowed on the exchanged basis taking into account the $1,875 cap.

2018 depreciation on the $2,304 exchanged basis without regard to the first- or second-year caps is $615 (($2,304 - $1,152 bonus in 2017 - $230 depreciation in 2017) × 66.67%). Although the 200 percent declining balance rate for 5-year property is 40% (1/5 × 2) a switch to the straight-line method is required in 2018 because the straight-line rate is greater than the 40% declining balance rate. Since 1.5 years remain in the 5-year recovery period of the exchanged basis as of the beginning of 2018 the straight-line rate is 66.67% (1/1.5 × 1). See Example at DEPR: 3,204.052. Since $615 is less than the $1,875 fifth-year cap the $615 may be claimed as the regular 2018 depreciation deduction on the exchanged basis.

2018 depreciation on the $14,000 excess basis without regard to the first- and second-year caps is $2,016 ($14,000 - $1,400 179 deduction - $6,300 bonus deduction - $1,260 2017 regular first-year deduction × 40 percent double declining balance rate). Since $2,016 does not exceed the remaining 2018 cap of $4,485 ( $5,100 second-year cap - $615 depreciation actually claimed on the exchanged basis in 2018), the 2018 depreciation deduction on the excess basis is $2,016.

2019 depreciation on the $2,304 exchanged basis is $307. This is the lesser of the $1,875 sixth-year cap or depreciation computed on the $2,304 exchanged basis without regard to any caps (($2,304 - $1,152 bonus in 2017 - $230 depreciation in 2017 - $615 depreciation in 2018) × 100% straight-line rate for last year of recovery period = $307). Since the total actual depreciation claimed on the $2,304 exchanged basis is $2,140 ($1,152 + $143 + $230 + $615 = $2,140), the $164 excess ($2,304 -$2,140) will be claimed as a post-recovery period deduction in 2020 since $164 is less than the $1,875 post-recovery period cap for a vehicle placed in service in 2014. The $164, however, will reduce the $1,875 fourth year cap that applies to the depreciation computed on the excess basis in 2020.

2019 depreciation on the $14,000 excess basis without regard to the first-, second-, and third-year caps is $1,210 ($14,000 - $1,400 179 deduction - $6,300 bonus deduction - $1,260 2017 regular first-year deduction - $2,016 2018 regular depreciation deduction × 40% double declining balance rate = $1,210). Since $1,210 does not exceed the remaining 2019 cap of $2,743 ($3,050 third-year cap - $307 depreciation actually claimed on the exchanged basis in 2019) the 2019 depreciation deduction on the excess basis is $1,210.

*Partial business use.* The exchanged (carryover) basis of the relinquished automobile immediately after the trade-in for purposes of computing depreciation must be determined as if business use was 100 percent if the vehicle was only used partially for business purposes at any time prior to the trade-in. This rule applies even if the taxpayer elects not to apply the final trade-in regulations (Temporary Reg. § 1.280F-2T(g)(2)(ii)(A)) The basis adjustment does not apply for purposes of determining realized/recognized gain or loss on the trade-in, as reported on Form 8824 (Like-Kind Exchanges).

***Example 6:*** On January 1, 2016, Lily Landers, a calendar-year taxpayer, bought and placed in service a $30,000 car. The car was used 80% for business purposes each year. No Code Sec. 179 election was made. Lily elected out of bonus depreciation. The car was depreciated under the general MACRS 200% declining balance method over a five-year recovery period using the half-year convention. In August 2017, Lily purchased a new car for $31,000 consisting of a $7,000 cash payment plus a trade-in allowance of $24,000 on the old car. MACRS deductions allowed on the old car for 2016 and 2017 are $2,528 ($3,160 first-year cap × .8) for 2016 since this is less than $4,800 ($30,000 × 80% × 20% first-year table percentage) and $3,840 ($30,000 × 80% × 32% second-year table percentage × 6/12) for 2017 since $3,840 does not exceed the $4,080 ($5,100 × .8) second-year depreciation cap for a car placed in service in 2016 as adjusted for business use. (Note: In the tax year of disposition of a vehicle subject to the half-year convention, one-half of the MACRS deduction computed in the regular manner for a full tax year as adjusted for business use is compared with the full year Code Sec. 280F limit adjusted for business use.) No Code Sec. 179 election is made with respect to the excess basis of the new car and the new car is depreciated under the general MACRS 200% declining balance method over a five-year recovery period using the half-year convention. Lily elects not to take the additional 50% first-year depreciation under Code Sec. 168(k). The new car is used 100% for business purposes each year. The depreciable basis of the new car is determined as follows:

| | | |
|---|---|---|
| Original basis of old car | | $30,000 |
| Less: MACRS deductions allowed: | | |
| 2016 | $2,528 | |
| 2017 | 3,840 | 6,368 |
| Adjusted basis of old car | | $23,632 |
| New car: | | |
| Adjusted basis of old car | | $23,632 |
| Plus: Additional amount paid | | 7,000 |
| Total | | $30,632 |
| Less: Depreciation allowable assuming 100% business use: | | |
| For 2016 and 2017 ($3,160 + $4,800*) | $8,260 | |
| Less: MACRS deductions actually allowed | 6,368 | 1,892 |
| Depreciable basis of new car | | $28,740 |

* The $4,800 figure is equal to $30,000 cost × 32% (second-year table percentage) × 6/12 (to take into account half-year convention). Since $4,800 does not exceed the $5,100 second-year depreciation cap for a car placed in service in 2016, $4,800 is treated as the 2017 deduction, assuming 100% business use.

Although the total depreciable basis of the new car is $28,740, the basis must be separated into two parts. The noncarryover basis (excess basis) ($7,000 cash paid) is treated as newly purchased MACRS property. The carryover basis (exchanged basis) $21,740 ($28,740 - $7,000) (which is an adjusted amount that reflects 100 percent business use) is depreciated over the remaining recovery period using the same MACRS depreciation method.

***Example 7:*** Assume the same facts as in Example 2 except that the relinquished Chevy Malibu was used 75 percent of the time during each tax year. The total allowable depreciation claimed on the relinquished auto is $9,778.50 ($2,370 for 2014 ($3,160 limit × 75%), $3,825 for 2015 ($5,100 limit × 75%), $2,287.50 for 2016 ($3,050 limit × 75%), and $1,296 for 2017 ($30,000 × 75% × 11.52% (fourth-year table percentage) × 6/12). However, the exchanged basis is reduced by the excess (if any) of the depreciation that would have been allowable if the exchanged automobile had been used solely for business over the depreciation that was allowable in those years. Thus, the exchanged basis for purposes of computing depreciation for the replacement vehicle is $16,962 ($30,000 - $3,160 - $5,100 - $3,050 - 1,728 ($30,000 × 11.52% (fourth-year table percentage) × 6/12) which is the same amount as if the vehicle had been used 100% for business purposes as shown in Example 2 (Reg. § 1.168(i)-6(d)(3)(iii)).

# Mileage Allowances

## ¶ 217

## Standard Mileage Rates, FAVR Allowances, and Mileage-Based Methods

Mileage allowance methods may be grouped into three categories: the standard mileage rate, the fixed and variable rate allowance (FAVR), and other mileage allowances that meet specified requirements.

*Standard mileage rate*

The standard mileage rate is adjusted annually by the IRS generally in November or December in an IRS Notice. Rev. Proc. 2019-46, superseding Rev. Proc. 2010-51 currently contains the operative rules regarding the standard mileage allowance and will be modified or superseded to reflect any rule changes.

*Standard Mileage Rate*

| *Miles Driven During* | *Rate Per Mile* | *Source* |
|---|---|---|
| 1/1/22 - 12/31/2022 | 58.5 cents | Notice 2022-3 |
| 1/1/21 - 12/31/2021 | 56 cents | Notice 2021-2 |
| 1/1/20 - 12/31/2020 | 57.5 cents | Notice 2020-5 |
| 1/1/19 - 12/31/2019 | 58 cents | Notice 2019-2 |
| 1/1/18 - 12/31/2018 | 54.5 cents | Notice 2018-3 |
| 1/1/17 - 12/31/2017 | 53.5 cents | Notice 2016-79 |
| 1/1/16 - 12/31/2016 | 54 cents | Notice 2016-1 |
| 1/1/15 - 12/31/2015 | 57.5 cents | Notice 2014-79 |
| 1/1/14 - 12/31/2014 | 56 cents | Notice 2013-80 |
| 1/1/13 - 12/31/2013 | 56.5 cents | Notice 2012-72 |
| 1/1/12 - 12/31/2012 | 55.5 cents | Notice 2012-1 |
| 7/1/11 - 12/31/2011 | 55.5 cents | Notice 2010-88, as modified by Announcement 2011-40 |
| 1/1/11 - 6/30/11 | 51 cents | Notice 2010-88, as modified by Announcement 2011-40 |

Employees (in tax years beginning before 2018) and self-employed individuals who use their own or leased cars (including vans, pickups, and panel trucks) cars for business may determine deductible car expenses under the standard mileage rate for estimating expenses based on the number of business miles that a car is driven. A deduction computed using the standard mileage rate for business miles is in place of operating and fixed costs of the automobile allocable to business (including depreciation or lease payments, tires, gas, and taxes thereon, oil, insurance, and license and registration fees. Parking fees, tolls, interest, and state and local taxes are separately deductible.

The standard mileage rate may not be used to compute deductible automobile expenses of postal employees in connection with the collection and delivery of mail on a rural route if the employee receives qualified reimbursements. These reimbursements are considered as equivalent to such an employee's expenses (Code Sec. 162(o)).

Self-employed individuals may use the standard mileage rate to compute a deduction for expenses of operating a car in their business in arriving at adjusted gross income.

Employees claim vehicle expenses, whether or not computed using the standard mileage rate , as a miscellaneous itemized deduction. Form 2106, Employee Business Expenses, is used to compute the allowable deduction. However, in tax years beginning after 2017 and before 2026 (suspension period), the miscellaneous itemized deduction for employee business expenses, including vehicle expenses, is temporarily suspended (Code Sec. 67(g), as added by the 2017 Tax Cuts and Jobs Act (P.L. 115-97). The suspension does not apply to employees who may claim vehicle expenses as an adjustment to gross income. For example, members of a reserve component of the Armed Forces of the United States, state or local government officials paid on a fee basis, and certain performing artists are entitled to deduct unreimbursed employee travel expenses as an adjustment to total income on line 24 of Form 1040 Schedule 1 and therefore may continue to use the standard mileage rate.

The standard mileage rate is not allowable if five or more cars are used simultaneously in the same trade or business (for example, fleet operations); a depreciation method other than the straight-line method has been used; the taxpayer claimed a Code Sec. 179 expense deduction; or the car has been depreciated under ACRS or MACRS.

Vehicles used for hire, such as a taxicab, may qualify for the standard mileage rate.

An employee may deduct business expenses the employee pays or incurs in performing services as an employee under a reimbursement or other expense allowance arrangement with a payor against gross income (Code Sec. 62(a)(2)(A)). A taxpayer who pays or incurs unreimbursed employee travel expenses during the suspension period that are deductible by the taxpayer in computing adjusted gross income may use the business standard mileage rate to compute the adjustment to gross income.

An election to use the standard mileage allowance to figure the actual expenses of operating a passenger car (including a van, pickup, or panel truck) is considered an election under Code Sec. 168(f)(1) to exclude the automobile from MACRS by using a method not based on a term of years in the first year that an asset is placed in service. An election under Code Sec. 168(f)(1) to exclude property from MACRS is irrevocable. See ¶ 140. Nevertheless, a taxpayer may switch from the standard mileage rate in a subsequent tax year to the actual cost method and depreciate the vehicle over the remaining useful life of the vehicle using the straight-line method. This is a non-MACRS method and, therefore, its use apparently is not considered to violate the rule that an election out of MACRS under Code Sec. 168(f)(1) is irrevocable.

The election must be made in the year that such vehicle is first placed in service. Thereafter, an annual election may be made to compute deductible transportation expenses by using the standard mileage rate allowance or actual costs. However, if the car is leased the election to use the standard mileage rate applies for the entire lease term. The election to use the standard mileage allowance precludes a Code Sec. 179 expense deduction and bonus depreciation deduction in the year that a car is placed in service as well as the use of MACRS or ACRS in such year and subsequent years. Rev. Proc. 2019-46, as well as IRS Publication 463, (Travel, Entertainment, Gift, and Car Expenses), provide that in the event of a subsequent-year switch from the standard mileage rate allowance to the actual cost method for determining allowable expenses by an owner, depreciation is computed under the straight-line method over the car's remaining estimated useful life (subject to the Code Sec. 280F depreciation limits (i.e. luxury car depreciation cap limits) for passenger automobiles).

*FAVR (Fixed or Variable Rate) allowances*

Employers having five or more employees who each drive cars, which they either own or lease, on company business for 5,000 or more miles (or if greater, 80 percent of the business miles projected by the employer for purposes of computing the FAVR variable mileage rate) may set up a FAVR allowance to reimburse employees (Rev. Proc. 2019-46). This method may not be established by employees or self-employed individuals, although employees may be covered by the method if a FAVR allowance is established by their employers.

An employer must designate a standard automobile (i.e., a car of specific make, model and year) and standard automobile cost for each FAVR that it sets up. The standard automobile cost may not exceed 95 percent of the sum of the retail dealer invoice cost of the standard automobile and any state and local sales or use taxes applicable on the purchase of the vehicle. The standard automobile cost is adjusted annually by the IRS in November or December in an IRS Notice. Rev. Proc. 2019-46 currently contains the operative rules regarding the FAVR allowance.

*Standard Automobile Cost*

| *Year* | *Cost* | *Source* |
|---|---|---|
| 2022 | $56,100 ($56,100 also for trucks and vans) | Notice 2022-3 |
| 2021 | $51,100 ($51,100 also for trucks and vans) | Notice 2021-2 |
| 2020 | $50,400 ($50,400 also for trucks and vans) | Notice 2020-25 |
| 2019 | $50,400 ($50,400 also for trucks and vans) | Notice 2019-2 |
| 2018 | $50,000 ($50,000 also for trucks and vans) | Notice 2018-42 |
| 2017 | $27,900 ($31,300 for trucks and vans) | Notice 2016-79 |
| 2016 | $28,000 ($31,000 for trucks and vans) | Notice 2016-1 |
| 2015 | $28,200 ($30,800 for trucks and vans) | Notice 2014-79 |
| 2014 | $28,200 ($30,400 for trucks and vans) | Notice 2013-80 |
| 2013 | $28,100 ($29,900 for trucks and vans) | Notice 2012-72 |
| 2012 | $28,000 ($29,300 for trucks and vans) | Notice 2012-1 |
| 2011 | $26,900 ($28,200 for trucks and vans) | Notice 2010-88 |

An employee may not participate in a particular FAVR if the cost of his vehicle when new is less than 90 percent of the cost of the standard automobile. The employee's car does not have to be the same make and model as the standard automobile. However the employee's car may not be older than the number of calendar years that the employer determines that a standard automobile will be driven in connection with the performance of services as an employee before being replaced (i.e., the "retention period").

Amounts reimbursed under a FAVR arrangement are considered transportation expenses of the employer and are deductible as such. The allowance, which is determined by each employer using statistical methods based on local retail costs, consists of two component payments.

(1) Fixed payment. Projected fixed costs (including depreciation) for a standard automobile's projected retention period are prorated over the projected retention period and multiplied by the car's projected business use percentage (which may not exceed 75 percent). This amount must be paid to covered employees at least quarterly.

(2) Variable payment. This is a mileage allowance also paid at least quarterly to cover the operating costs for substantiated business miles. The mileage rate is the projected operating costs of a standard automobile for a computation period divided by projected miles driven for the period.

For purposes of (1), above, an employer may determine the projected business use percentage based on the following table instead of using other data.

| *(Projected) Annual business mileage* | *(Projected) Business use percentage* |
|---|---|
| 6,250 or more but less than 10,000 | 45% |
| 10,000 or more but less than 15,000 | 55% |
| 15,000 or more but less than 20,000 | 65% |
| 20,000 or more | 75% |

*Limits on depreciation component.* The total amount of the depreciation component of the fixed payments for the retention period may not exceed the excess of the standard automobile cost over the residual value of the standard automobile at the end of the projected retention period. Residual value may be determined by the employer or may be determined by multiplying the standard automobile cost by one of the following percentages.

| *Retention period* | *Residual value* |
|---|---|
| 2 years | 70% |
| 3 years | 60% |
| 4 years | 50% |

Also, in no event may the total amount of the depreciation component exceed the sum of the annual Code Sec. 280F limits on depreciation (in effect at the beginning of the retention period) that apply to the standard automobile during the retention period.

An exception to these two limitations on the depreciation component of the fixed payments made to an employee has been added, effective for reimbursements for 1999 expenses. The exception takes the form of a business standard mileage test and is available to an employee who drives at least 80 percent of the "annual business mileage" of their standard automobile (Rev. Proc. 2019-46, section 6.04(3)). The annual business mileage of a standard automobile is the mileage that the employer projects that a standard automobile will be driven for business purposes during the calendar year. The exception applies in any year during which the total annual amount of the fixed and variable payments made to the qualifying employee do not exceed the amount obtained by multiplying 80 percent of the annual business mileage of the standard automobile by the applicable standard mileage rate for that year.

### *Adjustments to basis*

Employees and self-employed individuals whose car expenses are determined under one of the foregoing mileage allowances (whether in computing their own deductions or in determining the amount of a reimbursement) are required to reduce the basis of their cars as follows:

(1) *Standard mileage rate basis adjustment.* For each year the standard mileage rate has been used, the basis of an owned vehicle is reduced (not below zero) as follows:

| *Year method used* | *Amount of adjustment (cents per mile)* |
|---|---|
| 2007 | 19.0 |
| 2008 - 2009 | 21.0 |
| 2010 | 23.0 |
| 2011 | 22.0 |
| 2012-2013 | 23.0 |
| 2014 | 22.0 |
| 2015 | 24.0 |

| *Year method used* | *Amount of adjustment (cents per mile)* |
|---|---|
| 2016 | 24.0 |
| 2017 | 25.0 |
| 2018 | 25.0 |
| 2019 | 26.0 |
| 2020 | 27.0 |
| 2021 | 26.0 |
| 2022 | 26.0 |

Pre-1990 use of the car in excess of 15,000 miles in one year is disregarded for the purposes of basis adjustment, even if the actual business mileage was higher.

(2) *FAVR method.* The basis of a car subject to a FAVR allowance is reduced (not below zero) by the depreciation component of the periodic fixed payment, which the employer is required to report to the employee.

(3) *Other mileage allowances.* The basis of a car covered under an accountable plan by another type of permitted mileage allowance is reduced by the standard-mileage-rate basis adjustment (item (1), above) or, if the employee claims expenses on Form 2106 (Employee Business Expenses) in excess of reimbursement, basis is adjusted in accordance with the method used on Form 2106.

*Mileage-based depreciation method*

The IRS has approved a mileage based depreciation method used by a corporation which leased fleets of vehicles to corporate clients. The lessor was allowed to make an election out of MACRS pursuant to Code Sec. 168(f)(1) which allows the use of a permissible method not based on a term of years (IRS Letter Ruling 200046020, August 17, 2000).

The leases were for a term of one year with automatic monthly renewals after the first year. The average lease lasted 32 months and the average mileage logged per vehicle was 67,000 miles. Upon termination of a lease, the leased vehicle was sold. Based on historical information, the lessor determined the average mileage life of the leased vehicles and the average salvage (resale) value at the end of the lease term. The average mileage life and salvage value were reviewed annually and adjusted for any significant changes. The annual depreciation deduction was determined by multiplying a vehicle's cost (less salvage value) by a fraction, the numerator of which was the actual number of miles the vehicle was driven during the year and the denominator of which was the average mileage life of the vehicle. Depreciation was not claimed below salvage value.

For a similar ruling under ACRS, see IRS Letter Ruling 8725004, March 5, 1987.

# ACRS

# *Accelerated Cost Recovery System*

## ¶ 220

### Rules for ACRS Recovery Property

The original version of the Accelerated Cost Recovery System (ACRS) (Code Sec. 168, prior to amendment by the 1986 Tax Reform Act (P.L. 99-514)), generally applicable to most tangible depreciable property placed in service after 1980 and before 1987, was born out of a consensus that further incentives were needed to stimulate capital investment. Inflation had diminished the value of previous depreciation allowances, and the need to upgrade technology had further increased the cost of replacing older equipment. The approach, as embodied in the Economic Recovery Tax Act of 1981, moved away from the useful-life concept and minimized exceptions and elections.

By 1984, economic priorities had changed, and the Tax Reform Act of 1984 increased the recovery period for what otherwise would have been 15-year real property to 18 years and introduced supplementary rules (see ¶ 200–214) for so-called mix-use property—cars and other specified kinds of property by their nature lending themselves to both business and personal use. P.L. 99-21 further increased the recovery period for what formerly would have been 15-year real property or 18-year property to 19 years, but the big overhaul was left to the Tax Reform Act of 1986, which, under the old system's name (the Accelerated Cost Recovery System), in effect, introduced a new system. The "old" system (ACRS) is discussed below. For an explanation of Modified ACRS (MACRS), see the discussion beginning at ¶ 80.

Since ACRS is not based on estimated useful lives, cost recovery under it may not, in a strict dictionary sense, qualify as depreciation. The ACRS rules are careful in this regard, defining "recovery property" as property that, among other things, is "of a character subject to the allowance for depreciation." Although the term "of a character subject to the allowance for depreciation" is undefined, the word depreciation means exhaustion or wear and tear (including a reasonable allowance for obsolescence). Thus, property must suffer exhaustion, wear and tear, or obsolescence in order to be depreciated (*R.L. Simon*, 103 TC 247, aff'd, CA-2, 95-2 USTC ¶ 50,552 (Nonacq., I.R.B. 1996-29, 4)). As a matter of convenience and practice, ACRS is considered a system of depreciation, but, given two similarly named systems, "recovery property" becomes a particularly useful term for purposes of distinguishing property subject to ACRS from MACRS property.

Just as the rules discussed at ¶ 264 prevent the "churning" of pre-1981 assets into recovery property, more recent anti-churning rules may thwart the churning of some recovery property into MACRS property. Thus, property placed in service after 1986 may still be recovery property. However, the latter rules are considerably narrower in scope than those fashioned for ACRS because, generally, MACRS is less generous than ACRS and the rules are, of course, not designed to benefit transferees of property from related taxpayers. Rules under which property placed in service after 1986 must be treated as recovery property are more fully discussed at ¶ 142.

## ¶ 222
## Computation of ACRS Allowances

Under pre-1981 rules, basis, salvage value, and useful life were the three essential elements for computing depreciation. Under ACRS, only basis is essential. Salvage value is no longer a factor, and assets may be "depreciated" over periods considerably shorter than their estimated useful lives. In contrast to methods prescribed under Modified ACRS (see ¶ 80), recovery percentages are applied to unadjusted basis.

The unadjusted basis to which recovery percentages are applied does not include any portion of the basis of an asset for which there is an election to amortize or to rapidly depreciate (¶ 320–326), or to expense under Code Sec. 179 (¶ 300). For property placed in service after 1982 and before 1986, unadjusted basis may reflect a reduction for an investment tax credit.

Once basis has been determined, it is necessary to identify the class to which the asset belongs (see ¶ 230). A recovery period is prescribed for each class, and statutory recovery percentages are assigned for each year of the recovery period.

Then, the ACRS allowance is determined by multiplying the unadjusted basis of the asset by the appropriate recovery percentage for the tax year. Except for 15-year real property, 18-year real property, or 19-year real property, the same recovery percentage applies to all recovery property in the same class placed in service in the same tax year, and the applicable recovery percentage may be applied to the total unadjusted basis of such property.

No short tax year adjustment (¶ 290) is made merely because real recovery property is placed in service during a tax year, even if such tax year is a short tax year (Prop. Reg. § 1.168-2(f)(1)).

> ***Example:*** A corporation is formed on February 10, 1985, and engages in the rental real estate business. It acquires and places in service on March 31, 1985, 18-year real recovery property that has an unadjusted basis of $100,000. No optional ACRS straight-line method election is made. The corporation's normal tax year is a calendar-year tax year so it has a short tax year for the first recovery year. The recovery allowance for 1985, the year that the property is placed in service, is computed as though it were a full tax year. Because the recovery property would have been deemed placed in service in the third month of the corporation's normal calendar-year tax year, the corporation is entitled to a recovery deduction for the short tax year computed as if the 18-year property had been placed in service in the third month of a 12-month tax year. The ACRS deduction is $8,000 ($100,000 unadjusted basis × 8% (third month of year one ACRS percentage)).

*Applicable recovery methods*

As the names of the property classes indicate, the cost of ACRS property is generally recoverable in 3, 5, 10, 15, 18, or 19 years (¶ 230). Most personal property is 3-year or 5-year property. However, taxpayers who elect straight-line ACRS allowances may elect to recover their costs over specified longer periods (¶ 254). Except for 15-year real property, 18-year real property, or 19-year real property, the straight-line method is elected on a class-by-class basis (for any tax year), and the half-year convention applies (thus spreading the recovery of basis over one more tax year). These optional longer periods are also available to taxpayers restricted to the straight-line method because the property was financed with the proceeds of industrial development bonds (¶ 256).

If, under the rules discussed at ¶ 206 – ¶ 214, property is classified as listed and not used more than 50 percent for business, straight-line depreciation is mandated over generally longer periods.

*Half-year convention*

Under the regular method (for other than 15-year real property, 18-year real property, or 19-year real property), the half-year convention is mandatory and built into the applicable tables. For 5-year property, for example, 15 percent of the cost is recoverable in the first year irrespective of the day of the year in which it is placed in service. No deduction is allowed for the year of disposition. Recovery percentages for tangible personal property are designed to approximate the effect of the use of the 150-percent declining-balance method with a later-year switch to straight-line recovery.

*Months*

If 15-year real property, 18-year real property, or 19-year real property is involved, months figure in computations, both in years of acquisition and in years of disposition (¶ 242–246). The recovery percentages for such property other than low-income housing approximate the use of the 175-percent declining-balance method with an eventual switch to the straight-line method. The recovery percentages for low-income housing provide 200-percent declining-balance recovery with a switch to the straight-line method. Fifteen-year property is regarded as placed in service on the first day of the month, and a mid-month convention applies to 18-year real property placed in service after June 22, 1984, and to 19-year real property. Thus, in the case of 15-year real property, a full month's depreciation is allowed for the month that the property is placed in service and no depreciation is allowed for the month that the property is disposed of. In the case of 18- and 19-year real property subject to the mid-month convention, one-half month's depreciation is allowed for both the month that the property is placed in service and the month that the property is disposed of. The table percentages for the year that the property is placed in service reflect the applicable convention. However, the table percentages must be adjusted for the year that a property is disposed of.

> ***Example:*** ACRS 19-year real property with a depreciable basis of $100,000 is placed in service in February 1986 and disposed of in April of 1999 by a calendar-year taxpayer. 1999 is the 14th year of the recovery period. The 14th year recovery percentage for 19-year real property placed in service in February is 4.2%. The taxpayer is allowed to claim 3½ months depreciation in 1999 as the property is considered in service during January, February, March, and one-half of April under the mid-month convention. The allowable deduction for 1999 is $1,225 ($100,000 × 4.2% × 3.5/12). If the property was 15-year real property, it would be considered in service only during the months of January, February, and March. No depreciation would be allowed for the month of disposition under the applicable convention.

Component depreciation is eliminated (¶ 242). The recovery period and method used for such items as wiring and plumbing are the same as are used for the building (or the shell, as it sometimes is called), unless the recovery period is longer because the dates of placing the building in service and of placing components in service straddle the effective date of one of the increases in the generally applicable period for recovering the cost of real property.

Consistent with prior-law treatment, costs recovered under ACRS or expensed under Code Sec. 179 are not the costs that are used in computing earnings and profits available for dividend payments. The relevant rules are discussed at ¶ 310.

## ¶ 226

## Property Placed in Service

Since property had to be placed in service after 1980 to be classified as recovery property, it is important to know when property has been placed in service. The IRS considers property to be placed in service when it is ready and available for a specifically assigned function (Prop. Reg. § 1.168-2(l)(2)). No distinction is drawn between readiness and availability for use in a trade or business or for the production of income and readiness and availability for use in a personal or tax-exempt activity. Depreciation, on the other hand, begins when the property becomes ready for service in a trade or business or for the production of income.

The IRS illustrates the distinction with the simple example of a taxpayer who buys a house in 1975, lives in it until 1981, and then begins renting the home out. Having been placed in service in 1975, the residence is not recovery property. It should be noted, however, that a statutory exception to this general principle requires that real property used by a taxpayer for personal purposes prior to 1987 and converted to business use after 1986 be depreciated using MACRS (Act Sec. 1002(c)(3) of the Technical and Miscellaneous Revenue Act of 1988 (P.L. 100-647)).

Since property may be placed in service after use by a prior owner, specific rules prevent the conversion of pre-1981 property into recovery property through transfers to related parties. These so-called anti-churning rules are discussed at ¶ 264.

*Changes in use*

The recovery allowance for property converted from personal (or tax-exempt) use to business (or investment) use is computed as if the property is placed in service as recovery property as of the date of conversion. To the extent of an increase in business (or investment) use, an allowance becomes available as if property is placed in service in the year of the increase. For purposes of applying these rules, the basis of any such property may not exceed fair market value.

> ***Example (1):*** In 1983, Harper purchases a car for $9,000 and, through 1985, uses it 80% for business. The car is 3-year property, and, for each of the three years included in the regular recovery period, he deducts recovery allowances based on the cost of the car, the applicable percentages, and his 80% business use. Beginning in 1986, his business use of the car, now worth $4,500, increases to 100%. Harper's allowable deduction for 1986 is $225, based on the car's fair market value at the beginning of the year ($4,500), 20% business use (the excess of 100% over 80%), and the applicable first-year percentage (25%). For 1987, the second-year percentage (38%) applies, and the allowable deduction is $342.

> ***Example (2):*** The facts are the same as in Example (1) except that all the dates of all relevant facts are advanced by one year. The question that this variance presents is whether the deduction of the "post-recovery period" year is computed under ACRS or MACRS. Since the governing date of placement in service may relate to placement in service for personal (not just business) use, the car was deemed placed in service in 1986, and ACRS should be used to compute additional depreciation.

At the option of the taxpayer, similar treatment is available where property is reassigned to a class with a shorter recovery period or property ceases to be used outside the United States. However, if property is reassigned to a class with a longer recovery period (as, for example, where property ceases to be predominantly used in connection with research and experimentation), ceases to be low-income housing, or starts being used predominantly outside the United States, deductions are computed as if allowances had always been computed on the basis of present status, and not only must current deductions be determined under these principles, but the taxpayer must account for prior-year excess allowances. The following example is adapted from proposed regulations:

> ***Example (3):*** A taxpayer pays $20,000 for property that, in the year of its purchase, is predominantly used for research and experimentation and qualifies as 3-year property. For the year it is placed in service, he deducts $5,000 (25% of $20,000). In the

following year, the property ceases to be used for research and development and is treated as 5-year property. Not only is the second-year deduction limited to 22% (the applicable second-year percentage for 5-year property) of $20,000, but it is further reduced by the allocable portion of the prior year excess allowance. The excess first-year allowance is $2,000 (the excess of 25% of $20,000 over 15% of $20,000), and the portion of this amount allocable to the second recovery year is $518, determined by multiplying $20,000 by .15 (the first-year percentage for 5-year property) and dividing by .85 (the remaining unused applicable percentages). Thus, the second-year deduction is $3,882 (the excess of the regular allowance (22% of $20,000) over $518 (the allowable portion of the first-year excess allowance)).

*Building placed in service in stages*

The proposed ACRS regulations recognize that a building (for example, a high-rise) may be placed in service in stages. These regulations provide that each significant portion of a building should be separately depreciated as it is placed in service. Placed in service means made available for use in a finished condition, for example, as when a certificate of occupancy is issued. However, the same depreciation method must be used to depreciate the entire building. For example, this rule, when applied to MACRS residential rental property, would mean that a taxpayer could not depreciate one portion of the building over a 27.5 year period and elect ADS (40-year depreciation period if placed in service prior to 2018, or 30-year depreciation period if placed in service in 2018 or future periods generally) for another portion of the building. The regulations explain the allocation of basis among the completed portions and provides examples (Prop. Reg. § 1.168-2(e)(3) and (5)).

The definition of "placed in service" is also discussed at ¶ 3.

## ¶ 228

## What Is ACRS Recovery Property?

Property to which ACRS applies is called recovery property. Except as indicated below, recovery property is tangible property that is:

(1) of a depreciable character;

(2) placed in service after 1980 and before 1987; and

(3) used in a trade or business or held for the production of income.

Property may be new or used, but, as subsequently discussed, special rules are designed to thwart the conversion of pre-1981 property into recovery property through various kinds of transactions involving related parties.

Intangible depreciable property cannot be recovery property, and land is, of course, not depreciable. Consistent with a pre-ACRS revenue ruling that a work of art is generally nondepreciable even though its physical condition may influence its valuation (Rev. Rul. 68-232, 1968-1 CB 79; Reg. § 1.168-3(a)(1)), the IRS has ruled that an old and valuable cello of a Professor of Cello and a concert performer did not qualify as recovery property (IRS Letter Ruling 8641006, July 1, 1986). However, the courts have said otherwise with respect to valuable instruments that are used in a musician's trade or business and are subject to wear and tear. See ¶ 3.

Exceptions to the rules under which tangible depreciable property placed in service after 1980 and before 1987 is regarded as recovery property fall into the following categories:

(1) property depreciated under methods not based on a term of years and, at the election of the taxpayer, excluded from ACRS;

(2) certain public utility property;

(3) property that was pre-1981 property in the hands of a related owner or user;

(4) property acquired in any of various enumerated transactions in which no gain or loss is recognized;

(5) property placed in service after July 31, 1986, and before 1987 and, pursuant to the taxpayer's election, depreciated under MACRS (see ¶ 228); and

(6) some post-1986 property not qualifying for MACRS under rules similar to those (see ¶ 264) that prevent some post-1980 property from qualifying for ACRS.

Recovery property for which an expensing election is made under Code Sec. 179 (see ¶ 302) is, to the extent of that election, effectively removed from the general ACRS rules.

Property that is properly amortized pursuant to a valid election is also effectively removed from the general ACRS rules, see ¶ 320–¶ 326.

A video tape is not recovery property; nor is any motion picture film not created primarily for use as public entertainment or for educational purposes and not (1) placed in service before March 15, 1984, and treated as recovery property on a return filed before March 16, 1984, or (2) placed in service before 1985, treated as recovery property, and produced at a cost of which at least 20 percent was incurred before March 16, 1984.

Sound recordings placed in service after March 15, 1984, could, at the election of a taxpayer with whom the original use began, be treated as 3-year recovery property.

Property predominantly used outside the United States qualifies as recovery property, but separate rules apply for determining recovery periods. See ¶ 252.

*Transitional rules*

Although MACRS governs property generally placed in service after 1986, certain property placed in service before 1991 is governed by ACRS under transitional rules if certain action was taken by March 1, 1986.

# Classes of ACRS Recovery Property

## ¶ 230

## Relationship to "Present Class Life"

ACRS recovery property must be classified. Most qualifying personal property falls into the 5-year class, but cars, light-duty trucks, research and experimentation equipment, and certain other items are classified as 3-year property. Except for property used in connection with research or experimentation, a "present class life" of no more than four years is a prerequisite for qualifying as 3-year property. Except for low-income housing (see ¶ 248), manufactured homes, and railroad tank cars, real property with a "present class life" of more than 12.5 years is 15-year real property, 18-year real property, or 19-year real property. Certain variations apply to public utility property.

"Present class life" is a statutory term used to key recovery periods to prior-law asset guideline periods. It refers to the class life that would have applied to property had there been no ACRS rules and had an ADR election been made under former Code Sec. 167(m). Thus, the guideline classes provided in Rev. Proc. 83-35, 1983-1 CB 745, for ADR property still play a continuing role in classifying ACRS recovery property even though obsoleted for MACRS property.

As hereafter used with respect to the ACRS rules, "ADR class life" means the same as "present class life."

As originally conceived, the classes of recovery property were entirely governed by the nature of the property, and naming the classes by reference to the length of recovery periods clarified application of the rules. Subsequent legislation lengthened recovery periods for real property placed in service after specified dates, and, thus, under ACRS, the date of placement in service generally governs whether a building is 15-year real property, 18-year real property, or 19-year real property.

Notwithstanding some similar names, classes of recovery property must be distinguished from classes of property established under Modified ACRS (MACRS). For example, under ACRS, an automobile is 3-year property but, under MACRS, an automobile is 5-year property.

## ¶ 240

## ACRS Personal Property

The ACRS classes for personal property are 3-year property, 5-year property, and 10-year property. (This property should be fully depreciated by now.)

In general, 3-year property included all Sec. 1245 class property with an ADR class life of no more than four years and machinery and equipment used in connection with research and experimentation.

Tangible personal property that was not 3-year property, 10-year property, or 15-year public utility property was included in the category of 5-year property.

Ten-year property includes.

(1) public utility property (that is not Sec. 1250 class property or property that is 3-year property by reason of its use in connection with research and experimentation) with an "ADR class life" of more than 18 but not more than 25 years and

(2) Sec. 1250 class property with a "present class life" of not more than 12.5 years.

Theme and amusement park structures, manufactured (including mobile) homes, railroad tank cars, and qualified coal utilization property that would otherwise be 15-year public utility property are 10-year property. Under a special rule for theme parks, a building and its structural components with a present class life of no more than 12.5 years will not become 10-year or 15-year property by reason of conversion to a use other than its original use.

Assuming no straight-line election, recovery percentages for 10-year property are as follows:

| *Property* | *Percentage* |
|---|---|
| Year 1 | 8 |
| Year 2 | 14 |
| Year 3 | 12 |
| Year 4 - 6 | 10 |
| Year 7 - 10 | 9 |

## ¶ 242

## ACRS 15-Year Real Property

Subject to when placed in service and the applicable transitional rules, Sec. 1250 class property with an "ADR class life" of more than 12.5 years is 15-year real property. Low-income housing must be distinguished from other 15-year real property because, in the early years, its costs are recoverable at a slightly faster rate. Separate tables are provided.

In general, 15-year real property must have been placed in service before March 16, 1984. However, otherwise eligible property qualified as 15-year real property if:

(1) it was purchased or constructed under a contract entered into before March 16, 1984, or construction began by that date; and

(2) the taxpayer placed the property in service before 1987.

This applied to a subsequent transferee so long as a qualified transferor had not yet placed the property in service.

Elevators and escalators are treated as 15-year real property even though they were also eligible for the investment credit.

Since the recovery percentages depend on the month on which an asset is placed in service, separate items of 15-year real property may be grouped together only if they are placed in service in both the same month and the same year.

The following recovery percentages were prescribed by the IRS for 15-year real property other than low-income housing:

| *If the Recovery Year Is* | *The applicable percentage is (use the column representing the month in the first tax year the property is placed in service):* | | | | | | | | | | | |
|---|---|---|---|---|---|---|---|---|---|---|---|---|
| | *1* | *2* | *3* | *4* | *5* | *6* | *7* | *8* | *9* | *10* | *11* | *12* |
| 1 | 12 | 11 | 10 | 9 | 8 | 7 | 6 | 5 | 4 | 3 | 2 | 1 |
| 2 | 10 | 10 | 11 | 11 | 11 | 11 | 11 | 11 | 11 | 11 | 11 | 12 |
| 3 | 9 | 9 | 9 | 9 | 10 | 10 | 10 | 10 | 10 | 10 | 10 | 10 |
| 4 | 8 | 8 | 8 | 8 | 8 | 8 | 9 | 9 | 9 | 9 | 9 | 9 |
| 5 | 7 | 7 | 7 | 7 | 7 | 7 | 8 | 8 | 8 | 8 | 8 | 8 |
| 6 | 6 | 6 | 6 | 6 | 7 | 7 | 7 | 7 | 7 | 7 | 7 | 7 |
| 7 | 6 | 6 | 6 | 6 | 6 | 6 | 6 | 6 | 6 | 6 | 6 | 6 |

| *If the Recovery Year Is* | | *The applicable percentage is (use the column representing the month in the first tax year the property is placed in service):* | | | | | | | | | | | |
|---|---|---|---|---|---|---|---|---|---|---|---|---|---|
| | | *1* | *2* | *3* | *4* | *5* | *6* | *7* | *8* | *9* | *10* | *11* | *12* |
| 8 | ....... | 6 | 6 | 6 | 6 | 6 | 6 | 5 | 6 | 6 | 6 | 6 | 6 |
| 9 | ....... | 6 | 6 | 6 | 6 | 5 | 6 | 5 | 5 | 5 | 6 | 6 | 6 |
| 10 | ....... | 5 | 6 | 5 | 6 | 5 | 5 | 5 | 5 | 5 | 5 | 6 | 5 |
| 11 - 15 | ....... | 5 | 5 | 5 | 5 | 5 | 5 | 5 | 5 | 5 | 5 | 5 | 5 |
| 16 | ....... | — | — | 1 | 1 | 2 | 2 | 3 | 3 | 4 | 4 | 4 | 5 |

*Additions and improvements*

Substantial improvements to a building are treated as a separate building under ACRS. This, for example, means that a new roof may qualify as recovery property even though the building itself may have to be depreciated under pre-1981 rules. (Note that this discussion relates to improvements placed in service after 1980 and before 1987. Additions and improvements placed in service after 1986 are depreciated using MACRS regardless of the depreciation system used to depreciate the building. See ¶ 126 for the applicable rules).

Two requirements must be met for an improvement to be "substantial":

(1) it must have been made three or more years after the building is placed in service; and

(2) the addition to the capital account for the building and its components during any 24-month period must be at least 25 percent of the building's adjusted basis (ignoring any adjustments for depreciation and amortization).

The 25-percent test is applied to the building's adjusted basis as of the first day of the 24-month period.

The general rule that the cost of a building's components—plumbing, wiring, storm windows, etc.—must be recovered in the same manner as the cost of the building itself is complicated by changes in the law that extended recovery periods and, eventually, replaced ACRS. Under a special transitional rule, applicable to the first component placed in service after 1980 on a building that was placed in service before 1981, the first such component was treated as a separate building. Thus, for components placed in service before March 16, 1984, either the statutory ACRS percentages for 15-year realty or straight-line ACRS allowances (¶ 254) had to be elected, and the method elected was mandatory for other components placed in service before March 16, 1984.

Consistent with this approach and subject to transitional rules, the first component placed in service after March 18, 1984, and before May 9, 1985, is treated as a separate building and classified as 18-year real property, and the first component placed in service after May 9, 1985, and not subject to MACRS is treated as a separate building and classified as 19-year real property. With regard to additions or improvements placed in service after July 31, 1986, and before 1987, a taxpayer could elect MACRS and treat what would otherwise be 19-year real property as, depending on which was applicable, 27.5-year residential rental property or 31.5-year nonresidential real property. Unless shielded by transitional rules, post-1986 improvements are MACRS property. See ¶ 126.

***Example:*** In September of 1985, a new roof is placed in service for a pre-1985 office building. The new roof is treated as a new building, and is classified as 19-year real property.

# ¶ 244

## ACRS 18-Year Real Property

Eighteen-year real property is real property placed in service after March 15, 1984, and before May 9, 1985. Eighteen-year real property also includes real property placed in service before 1987 if either purchased or constructed under a binding contract entered into before May 9, 1985 or construction of the property began before May 9, 1985 (Act Sec. 105(b)(2), P.L. 99-121).

A variation in the applicable convention for such real property, in effect, creates two subclasses of 18-year real property. Eighteen-year real property placed in service before June 23, 1984, is regarded as placed in service on the first day of the month, and 18-year real property placed in service after June 22, 1984, is regarded as placed in service on the midpoint of the month. Therefore, separate recovery percentages are prescribed for each "subclass."

The following recovery percentages, assuming no mid-month convention, apply to 18-year real property placed in service before June 23, 1984.

| *If the Recovery Year Is:* | *The applicable percentage is (use the column representing the month in the first tax year the property is placed in service):* | | | | | | | | | | | |
|---|---|---|---|---|---|---|---|---|---|---|---|---|
| | *1* | *2* | *3* | *4* | *5* | *6* | *7* | *8* | *9* | *10* | *11* | *12* |
| 1 . . . . . . . . . . . . | 10 | 9 | 8 | 7 | 6 | 6 | 5 | 4 | 3 | 2 | 2 | 1 |
| 2 . . . . . . . . . . . . | 9 | 9 | 9 | 9 | 9 | 9 | 9 | 9 | 9 | 10 | 10 | 10 |
| 3 . . . . . . . . . . . . | 8 | 8 | 8 | 8 | 8 | 8 | 8 | 8 | 9 | 9 | 9 | 9 |
| 4 . . . . . . . . . . . . | 7 | 7 | 7 | 7 | 7 | 7 | 8 | 8 | 8 | 8 | 8 | 8 |
| 5 . . . . . . . . . . . . | 6 | 7 | 7 | 7 | 7 | 7 | 7 | 7 | 7 | 7 | 7 | 7 |
| 6 . . . . . . . . . . . . | 6 | 6 | 6 | 6 | 6 | 6 | 6 | 6 | 6 | 6 | 6 | 6 |
| 7 . . . . . . . . . . . . | 5 | 5 | 5 | 5 | 6 | 6 | 6 | 6 | 6 | 6 | 6 | 6 |
| 8 - 12 . . . . . . . . . . . . | 5 | 5 | 5 | 5 | 5 | 5 | 5 | 5 | 5 | 5 | 5 | 5 |
| 13 . . . . . . . . . . . . | 4 | 4 | 4 | 5 | 5 | 4 | 4 | 5 | 4 | 4 | 4 | 4 |
| 14 - 18 . . . . . . . . . . . . | 4 | 4 | 4 | 4 | 4 | 4 | 4 | 4 | 4 | 4 | 4 | 4 |
| 19 . . . . . . . . . . . . | | | 1 | 1 | 1 | 2 | 2 | 2 | 3 | 3 | 3 | 4 |

The following recovery percentages, reflecting the mid-month convention, apply to 18-year real property placed in service after June 22, 1984.

| *If the Recovery Year Is:* | *The applicable percentage is (use the column representing the month in the first tax year the property is placed in service):* | | | | | | | | | | | |
|---|---|---|---|---|---|---|---|---|---|---|---|---|
| | *1* | *2* | *3* | *4* | *5* | *6* | *7* | *8* | *9* | *10* | *11* | *12* |
| 1 . . . . . . . . . . | 9 | 9 | 8 | 7 | 6 | 5 | 4 | 4 | 3 | 2 | 1 | 0.4 |
| 2 . . . . . . . . . . | 9 | 9 | 9 | 9 | 9 | 9 | 9 | 9 | 9 | 10 | 10 | 10.0 |
| 3 . . . . . . . . . . | 8 | 8 | 8 | 8 | 8 | 8 | 8 | 8 | 9 | 9 | 9 | 9.0 |
| 4 . . . . . . . . . . | 7 | 7 | 7 | 7 | 7 | 8 | 8 | 8 | 8 | 8 | 8 | 8.0 |
| 5 . . . . . . . . . . | 7 | 7 | 7 | 7 | 7 | 7 | 7 | 7 | 7 | 7 | 7 | 7.0 |
| 6 . . . . . . . . . . | 6 | 6 | 6 | 6 | 6 | 6 | 6 | 6 | 6 | 6 | 6 | 6.0 |
| 7 . . . . . . . . . . | 5 | 5 | 5 | 5 | 6 | 6 | 6 | 6 | 6 | 6 | 6 | 6.0 |
| 8 - 12 . . . . . . . . . . | 5 | 5 | 5 | 5 | 5 | 5 | 5 | 5 | 5 | 5 | 5 | 5.0 |
| 13 . . . . . . . . . . | 4 | 4 | 4 | 5 | 4 | 4 | 5 | 4 | 4 | 4 | 5 | 5.0 |
| 14 - 17 . . . . . . . . . . | 4 | 4 | 4 | 4 | 4 | 4 | 4 | 4 | 4 | 4 | 4 | 4.0 |
| 18 . . . . . . . . . . | 4 | 3 | 4 | 4 | 4 | 4 | 4 | 4 | 4 | 4 | 4 | 4.0 |
| 19 . . . . . . . . . . | | 1 | 1 | 1 | 2 | 2 | 2 | 3 | 3 | 3 | 3 | 3.6 |

## ¶ 246

## ACRS 19-Year Real Property

Real property placed in service after May 8, 1985 and before 1987 is generally classified as 19-year real property. Real property placed in service before 1991 may qualify as 19-year real property under transitional rules for binding contracts (Act Sec. 203(b)(1)(A) of P.L. 99-514) and self-constructed property (Act Sec. 203(b)(1)(B) of P.L. 99-514). The following recovery percentages, reflecting a mid-month convention, are prescribed for 19-year real property:

| *If the Recovery Year Is:* | *The applicable percentage is (use the column representing the month in the first tax year the property is placed in service):* | | | | | | | | | | | |
|---|---|---|---|---|---|---|---|---|---|---|---|---|
| | *1* | *2* | *3* | *4* | *5* | *6* | *7* | *8* | *9* | *10* | *11* | *12* |
| 1 .......... | 8.8 | 8.1 | 7.3 | 6.5 | 5.8 | 5.0 | 4.2 | 3.5 | 2.7 | 1.9 | 1.1 | 0.4 |
| 2 .......... | 8.4 | 8.5 | 8.5 | 8.6 | 8.7 | 8.8 | 8.8 | 8.9 | 9.0 | 9.0 | 9.1 | 9.2 |
| 3 .......... | 7.6 | 7.7 | 7.7 | 7.8 | 7.9 | 7.9 | 8.0 | 8.1 | 8.1 | 8.2 | 8.3 | 8.3 |
| 4 .......... | 6.9 | 7.0 | 7.0 | 7.1 | 7.1 | 7.2 | 7.3 | 7.3 | 7.4 | 7.4 | 7.5 | 7.6 |
| 5 .......... | 6.3 | 6.3 | 6.4 | 6.4 | 6.5 | 6.5 | 6.6 | 6.6 | 6.7 | 6.8 | 6.8 | 6.9 |
| 6 .......... | 5.7 | 5.7 | 5.8 | 5.9 | 5.9 | 5.9 | 6.0 | 6.0 | 6.1 | 6.1 | 6.2 | 6.2 |
| 7 .......... | 5.2 | 5.2 | 5.3 | 5.3 | 5.3 | 5.4 | 5.4 | 5.5 | 5.5 | 5.6 | 5.6 | 5.6 |
| 8 .......... | 4.7 | 4.7 | 4.8 | 4.8 | 4.8 | 4.9 | 4.9 | 5.0 | 5.0 | 5.1 | 5.1 | 5.1 |
| 9 .......... | 4.2 | 4.3 | 4.3 | 4.4 | 4.4 | 4.5 | 4.5 | 4.5 | 4.5 | 4.6 | 4.6 | 4.7 |
| 10 - 19 .......... | 4.2 | 4.2 | 4.2 | 4.2 | 4.2 | 4.2 | 4.2 | 4.2 | 4.2 | 4.2 | 4.2 | 4.2 |
| 20 .......... | 0.2 | 0.5 | 0.9 | 1.2 | 1.6 | 1.9 | 2.3 | 2.6 | 3.0 | 3.3 | 3.7 | 4.0 |

## ¶ 248

## ACRS Low-Income Housing

The cost of low-income housing is recovered in the same manner as the cost of ordinary real property except that recovery percentages are based on the use of the 200-percent declining-balance method. Property in this category includes federally assisted housing projects in which the mortgage is insured under the National Housing Act; housing financed or assisted under similar local law provisions; low-income rental housing for which rehabilitation expenditures qualified for depreciation deductions; low-income rental housing held for occupancy by families or persons who qualify for subsidies under the National Housing Act or local law that authorize similar subsidies; or housing that is insured or directly assisted under Title V of the Housing Act of 1949.

The IRS has prescribed the following recovery percentages:

(1) for low-income housing placed in service before May 9, 1985; and

(2) for low-income housing placed in service after May 8, 1985, and for which allowances are determined without regard to the mid-month convention.

| *If the Recovery Year Is:* | *For low-income housing placed in service before May 9, 1985, the applicable percentage is (use the column representing the month in the first tax year the property is placed in service):* | | | | | | | | | | | |
|---|---|---|---|---|---|---|---|---|---|---|---|---|
| | *1* | *2* | *3* | *4* | *5* | *6* | *7* | *8* | *9* | *10* | *11* | *12* |
| 1 | 13 | 12 | 11 | 10 | 9 | 8 | 7 | 6 | 4 | 3 | 2 | 1 |
| 2 | 12 | 12 | 12 | 12 | 12 | 12 | 12 | 13 | 13 | 13 | 13 | 13 |
| 3 | 10 | 10 | 10 | 10 | 11 | 11 | 11 | 11 | 11 | 11 | 11 | 11 |
| 4 | 9 | 9 | 9 | 9 | 9 | 9 | 9 | 9 | 10 | 10 | 10 | 10 |
| 5 | 8 | 8 | 8 | 8 | 8 | 8 | 8 | 8 | 8 | 8 | 8 | 9 |
| 6 | 7 | 7 | 7 | 7 | 7 | 7 | 7 | 7 | 7 | 7 | 7 | 7 |
| 7 | 6 | 6 | 6 | 6 | 6 | 6 | 6 | 6 | 6 | 6 | 6 | 6 |
| 8 | 5 | 5 | 5 | 5 | 5 | 5 | 5 | 5 | 5 | 5 | 6 | 6 |
| 9 | 5 | 5 | 5 | 5 | 5 | 5 | 5 | 5 | 5 | 5 | 5 | 5 |
| 10 | 5 | 5 | 5 | 5 | 5 | 5 | 5 | 5 | 5 | 5 | 5 | 5 |
| 11 | 4 | 5 | 5 | 5 | 5 | 5 | 5 | 5 | 5 | 5 | 5 | 5 |
| 12 | 4 | 4 | 4 | 5 | 4 | 5 | 5 | 5 | 5 | 5 | 5 | 5 |
| 13 | 4 | 4 | 4 | 4 | 4 | 4 | 5 | 4 | 5 | 5 | 5 | 5 |
| 14 | 4 | 4 | 4 | 4 | 4 | 4 | 4 | 4 | 4 | 5 | 4 | 4 |
| 15 | 4 | 4 | 4 | 4 | 4 | 4 | 4 | 4 | 4 | 4 | 4 | 4 |
| 16 | — | — | 1 | 1 | 2 | 2 | 2 | 3 | 3 | 3 | 4 | 4 |

| *If the Recovery Year Is:* | *For low-income housing placed in service after May 8, 1985, and before 1987, the applicable percentage is (use the column representing the month in the first tax year the property is placed in service):* | | | | | | | | | | | |
|---|---|---|---|---|---|---|---|---|---|---|---|---|
| | *1* | *2* | *3* | *4* | *5* | *6* | *7* | *8* | *9* | *10* | *11* | *12* |
| 1 | 13.3 | 12.2 | 11.1 | 10 | 8.9 | 7.8 | 6.6 | 5.6 | 4.4 | 3.3 | 2.2 | 1.1 |
| 2 | 11.6 | 11.7 | 11.9 | 12 | 12.1 | 12.3 | 12.5 | 12.6 | 12.7 | 12.9 | 13 | 13.2 |
| 3 | 10 | 10.1 | 10.2 | 10.4 | 10.5 | 10.7 | 10.8 | 10.9 | 11.1 | 11.2 | 11.3 | 11.4 |
| 4 | 8.7 | 8.8 | 8.9 | 9 | 9.1 | 9.2 | 9.3 | 9.5 | 9.6 | 9.7 | 9.8 | 9.9 |
| 5 | 7.5 | 7.6 | 7.7 | 7.8 | 7.9 | 8 | 8.1 | 8.2 | 8.3 | 8.4 | 8.5 | 8.6 |
| 6 | 6.5 | 6.6 | 6.7 | 6.8 | 6.9 | 6.9 | 7 | 7.1 | 7.2 | 7.3 | 7.4 | 7.4 |
| 7 | 5.7 | 5.7 | 5.8 | 5.9 | 5.9 | 6 | 6.1 | 6.1 | 6.2 | 6.3 | 6.4 | 6.5 |
| 8 | 4.9 | 5 | 5 | 5.1 | 5.2 | 5.2 | 5.3 | 5.3 | 5.4 | 5.5 | 5.5 | 5.6 |
| 9 | 4.6 | 4.6 | 4.6 | 4.6 | 4.6 | 4.6 | 4.6 | 4.6 | 4.6 | 4.7 | 4.8 | 4.8 |
| 10 | 4.6 | 4.6 | 4.6 | 4.6 | 4.6 | 4.6 | 4.6 | 4.6 | 4.6 | 4.6 | 4.6 | 4.6 |
| 11 | 4.6 | 4.6 | 4.6 | 4.6 | 4.6 | 4.6 | 4.6 | 4.6 | 4.6 | 4.6 | 4.6 | 4.6 |
| 12 | 4.5 | 4.6 | 4.6 | 4.6 | 4.6 | 4.6 | 4.6 | 4.6 | 4.6 | 4.6 | 4.6 | 4.6 |
| 13 | 4.5 | 4.5 | 4.6 | 4.5 | 4.6 | 4.6 | 4.6 | 4.6 | 4.6 | 4.5 | 4.6 | 4.6 |
| 14 | 4.5 | 4.5 | 4.5 | 4.5 | 4.5 | 4.5 | 4.5 | 4.6 | 4.6 | 4.5 | 4.5 | 4.5 |
| 15 | 4.5 | 4.5 | 4.5 | 4.5 | 4.5 | 4.5 | 4.5 | 4.5 | 4.5 | 4.5 | 4.5 | 4.5 |
| 16 | | 0.4 | 0.7 | 1.1 | 1.5 | 1.9 | 2.3 | 2.6 | 3 | 3.4 | 3.7 | 4.1 |

***Example:*** In May 1986, a calendar-year taxpayer purchases and places in service some property that qualifies as low-income rental housing. The purchase price is $80,000, of which $20,000 is allocable to land. For 1986, his deduction is $5,340 (8.9% of $60,000). For 1987, his deduction is $7,260 (12.1% of $60,000). If the property had not qualified as low-income property, his deductions are $3,480 for 1986 and $5,220 for 1987.

## ¶ 250

## ACRS 15-Year Public Utility Property

Public utility property that is not Sec. 1250 class property or 3-year property and that has an ADR class life of more than 25 years is classified as 15-year public utility property. It includes electric utility steam production plants, gas utility manufactured gas production plants, water utility property, and telephone distribution plants.

Except for the recovery period, 15-year public utility property is treated like 3-year, 5-year, or 10-year property rather than like 15-year real property. Recovery percentages are statutory, and the particular month in which property is placed in service does not affect computations.

Recovery percentages are as follows for 15-year public utility property:

| *Property* | *Percentage* |
|---|---|
| Year 1 | 5 |
| Year 2 | 10 |
| Year 3 | 9 |
| Year 4 | 8 |
| Year 5 | 7 |
| Year 6 | 7 |
| Year 7 - 15 | 6 |

## ¶ 252

## ACRS Property Used Outside the Country

Rules are modified for ACRS property that is predominantly used outside the United States. The cost of personal property is generally recoverable over its ADR class life. Absent such class life, a 12-year period applies. The cost of real property used predominantly outside the United States is generally recoverable over a 35-year period.

Property is regarded as used predominantly outside the United States if it is located outside the United States for more than 50 percent of the tax year or, if placed in service during the tax year, more than 50 percent of the period beginning on the day in which the property is placed in service and ending on the last day of the tax year. For a discussion of the effect of subsequent-year change of use, see ¶ 104.

The following tables, extracted from proposed regulations or Rev. Proc. 86-14, 1986-1 CB 542, provide recovery percentages for property predominantly used outside the United States.

**Property Used Predominantly Outside The United States**
**Other Than 15-, 18- or 19-Year Real Property**

**Accelerated Cost Recovery System**

*(200% Declining Balance)*
*(Half-Year Convention)*

**Recovery Period**

| *Year* | *2.5* | *3* | *3.5* | *4* | *5* | *6* | *6.5* | *7* | *7.5* | *8* | *8.5* | *9* | *9.5* | *10* | *10.5* | *11* | *11.5* | *12* | *12.5* | *13* | *13.5* | *14* | *15* |
|---|---|---|---|---|---|---|---|---|---|---|---|---|---|---|---|---|---|---|---|---|---|---|---|
| 1 | 40 | 33 | 29 | 25 | 20 | 17 | 15 | 14 | 13 | 13 | 12 | 11 | 11 | 10 | 10 | 9 | 9 | 8 | 8 | 8 | 7 | 7 | 7 |
| 2 | 48 | 45 | 41 | 38 | 32 | 28 | 26 | 25 | 23 | 22 | 21 | 20 | 19 | 18 | 17 | 17 | 16 | 15 | 15 | 14 | 14 | 13 | 12 |
| 3 | 12 | 15 | 17 | 19 | 19 | 18 | 18 | 17 | 17 | 16 | 16 | 15 | 15 | 14 | 14 | 13 | 13 | 13 | 12 | 12 | 12 | 11 | 11 |
| 4 | | 7 | 13 | 12 | 12 | 12 | 13 | 13 | 13 | 12 | 12 | 12 | 12 | 12 | 11 | 11 | 11 | 11 | 10 | 10 | 10 | 10 | 9 |
| 5 | | | | 6 | 12 | 10 | 10 | 9 | 9 | 9 | 9 | 9 | 9 | 9 | 9 | 9 | 9 | 9 | 9 | 9 | 8 | 8 | 8 |
| 6 | | | | | 5 | 10 | 9 | 9 | 9 | 8 | 8 | 8 | 7 | 7 | 7 | 7 | 7 | 7 | 7 | 7 | 7 | 7 | 7 |
| 7 | | | | | | 5 | 9 | 9 | 8 | 8 | 8 | 7 | 7 | 7 | 7 | 7 | 6 | 6 | 6 | 6 | 6 | 6 | 6 |
| 8 | | | | | | | | 4 | 8 | 8 | 7 | 7 | 7 | 7 | 7 | 6 | 6 | 6 | 6 | 6 | 6 | 5 | 5 |
| 9 | | | | | | | | | | 4 | 7 | 7 | 7 | 7 | 6 | 6 | 6 | 6 | 6 | 5 | 5 | 5 | 5 |
| 10 | | | | | | | | | | | | 4 | 6 | 6 | 6 | 6 | 6 | 6 | 6 | 5 | 5 | 5 | 5 |
| 11 | | | | | | | | | | | | | | 3 | 6 | 6 | 6 | 5 | 5 | 5 | 5 | 5 | 5 |
| 12 | | | | | | | | | | | | | | | | 3 | 5 | 5 | 5 | 5 | 5 | 5 | 5 |
| 13 | | | | | | | | | | | | | | | | | | 3 | 5 | 5 | 5 | 5 | 5 |
| 14 | | | | | | | | | | | | | | | | | | | | 3 | 5 | 5 | 4 |
| 15 | | | | | | | | | | | | | | | | | | | | | | 3 | 4 |
| 16 | | | | | | | | | | | | | | | | | | | | | | | 2 |

**Property Used Predominantly Outside The United States Other Than 15-, 18- or 19-Year Real Property**

**Accelerated Cost Recovery System**

*(200% Declining Balance)*
*(Half-Year Convention)*

**Recovery Period**

| *Year* | *16* | *16.5* | *17* | *18* | *19* | *20* | *22* | *25* | *26.5* | *28* | *30* | *35* | *45* | *50* |
|---|---|---|---|---|---|---|---|---|---|---|---|---|---|---|
| 1 | 6 | 6 | 6 | 6 | 5 | 5 | 5 | 4 | 4 | 4 | 3 | 3 | 2 | 2 |
| 2 | 12 | 11 | 11 | 10 | 10 | 10 | 9 | 8 | 7 | 7 | 6 | 6 | 4 | 4 |
| 3 | 10 | 10 | 10 | 9 | 9 | 9 | 8 | 7 | 7 | 6 | 6 | 5 | 4 | 4 |
| 4 | 9 | 9 | 9 | 8 | 8 | 8 | 7 | 6 | 6 | 6 | 6 | 5 | 4 | 4 |
| 5 | 8 | 8 | 8 | 7 | 7 | 7 | 6 | 6 | 6 | 6 | 5 | 5 | 4 | 3 |
| 6 | 7 | 7 | 7 | 7 | 6 | 6 | 6 | 6 | 5 | 5 | 5 | 4 | 4 | 3 |
| 7 | 6 | 6 | 6 | 6 | 6 | 6 | 5 | 5 | 5 | 5 | 5 | 4 | 3 | 3 |
| 8 | 5 | 5 | 5 | 5 | 5 | 5 | 5 | 5 | 5 | 4 | 4 | 4 | 3 | 3 |
| 9 | 5 | 5 | 5 | 5 | 5 | 4 | 4 | 4 | 4 | 4 | 4 | 4 | 3 | 3 |
| 10 | 5 | 5 | 4 | 4 | 4 | 4 | 4 | 4 | 4 | 4 | 4 | 3 | 3 | 3 |
| 11 | 5 | 4 | 4 | 4 | 4 | 4 | 4 | 4 | 4 | 4 | 3 | 3 | 3 | 3 |
| 12 | 4 | 4 | 4 | 4 | 4 | 4 | 4 | 3 | 3 | 3 | 3 | 3 | 3 | 3 |
| 13 | 4 | 4 | 4 | 4 | 4 | 4 | 4 | 3 | 3 | 3 | 3 | 3 | 3 | 2 |
| 14 | 4 | 4 | 4 | 4 | 4 | 4 | 3 | 3 | 3 | 3 | 3 | 3 | 3 | 2 |
| 15 | 4 | 4 | 4 | 4 | 4 | 3 | 3 | 3 | 3 | 3 | 3 | 3 | 2 | 2 |
| 16 | 4 | 4 | 4 | 4 | 4 | 3 | 3 | 3 | 3 | 3 | 3 | 3 | 2 | 2 |

**Accelerated Cost Recovery System**

**Recovery Period**

| *Year* | *16* | *16.5* | *17* | *18* | *19* | *20* | *22* | *25* | *26.5* | *28* | *30* | *35* | *45* | *50* |
|---|---|---|---|---|---|---|---|---|---|---|---|---|---|---|
| 17 | 2 | 4 | 3 | 4 | 3 | 3 | 3 | 3 | 3 | 3 | 3 | 2 | 2 | 2 |
| 18 | | | 2 | 3 | 3 | 3 | 3 | 3 | 3 | 3 | 3 | 2 | 2 | 2 |
| 19 | | | | 2 | 3 | 3 | 3 | 3 | 3 | 3 | 3 | 2 | 2 | 2 |
| 20 | | | | | 2 | 3 | 3 | 3 | 3 | 3 | 3 | 2 | 2 | 2 |
| 21 | | | | | | 2 | 3 | 3 | 3 | 3 | 3 | 2 | 2 | 2 |
| 22 | | | | | | | 3 | 3 | 3 | 2 | 2 | 2 | 2 | 2 |
| 23 | | | | | | | 2 | 3 | 3 | 2 | 2 | 2 | 2 | 2 |
| 24-25 | | | | | | | | 2 | 2 | 2 | 2 | 2 | 2 | 2 |
| 26 | | | | | | | | 1 | 2 | 2 | 2 | 2 | 2 | 2 |
| 27 | | | | | | | | | 1 | 2 | 2 | 2 | 2 | 2 |
| 28 | | | | | | | | | | 2 | 2 | 2 | 2 | 2 |
| 29 | | | | | | | | | | 1 | 2 | 2 | 2 | 2 |
| 30 | | | | | | | | | | | 2 | 2 | 2 | 2 |
| 31 | | | | | | | | | | | 1 | 2 | 2 | 2 |
| 32-35 | | | | | | | | | | | | 2 | 2 | 2 |
| 36 | | | | | | | | | | | | 1 | 2 | 1 |
| 37-46 | | | | | | | | | | | | | 1 | 1 |
| 47-51 | | | | | | | | | | | | | | 1 |

**Low-Income Housing Used Predominantly Outside the United States (placed in service after December 31, 1980 and before May 9, 1985)**
**15-Year Real Property Used Predominantly Outside the United States (placed in service after December 31, 1980 and before March 16, 1984)**
**18-Year Real Property Used Predominantly Outside the United States (placed in service after March 15, 1984 and before June 23, 1984)**

*(35-Year 150% Declining Balance)*
*(Assuming No Mid-Month Convention)*

| | Month Placed in Service | | | | |
|---|---|---|---|---|---|
| **Year** | **1** | **2-3** | **4-6** | **7-8** | **9-12** |
| 1 | 4 % | 4 % | 3 % | 2 % | 1 % |
| 2 - 5 | 4 | 4 | 4 | 4 | 4 |
| 6 | 3 | 3 | 3 | 4 | 4 |
| 7 - 24 | 3 | 3 | 3 | 3 | 3 |
| 25 | 3 | 2 | 3 | 2 | 3 |
| 26 - 35 | 2 | 2 | 2 | 2 | 2 |
| 36 | . | 1 | 1 | 2 | 2 |

**18-Year Real Property Used Predominantly Outside the United States (placed in service after June 22, 1984 and before May 9, 1985)**

*(35-Year 150% Declining Balance)*
*(Assuming Mid-Month Convention)*

| | Month Placed in Service | | | | | | |
|---|---|---|---|---|---|---|---|
| **Year** | **1** | **2** | **3** | **4-5** | **6-8** | **9-11** | **12** |
| 1 | 4 % | 4 % | 3 % | 3 % | 2 % | 1 % | 0.2 % |
| 2 - 5 | 4 | 4 | 4 | 4 | 4 | 4 | 4.0 |
| 6 | 3 | 3 | 3 | 3 | 4 | 4 | 4.0 |
| 7 | 3 | 3 | 3 | 3 | 3 | 3 | 3.8 |
| 8 - 24 | 3 | 3 | 3 | 3 | 3 | 3 | 3.0 |
| 25 | 3 | 2 | 3 | 2 | 2 | 3 | 3.0 |
| 26 - 35 | 2 | 2 | 2 | 2 | 2 | 2 | 2.0 |
| 36 | . | 1 | 1 | 2 | 2 | 2 | 2.0 |

**19-Year Real Property Used Predominantly Outside the United States (placed in service after May 8, 1985 and before 1987)**

*(35-Year 150% Declining Balance)*
*(Assuming Mid-Month Convention)*

| | Month Placed in Service | | | | | | | | | | | |
|---|---|---|---|---|---|---|---|---|---|---|---|---|
| **Year** | **1** | **2** | **3** | **4** | **5** | **6** | **7** | **8** | **9** | **10** | **11** | **12** |
| 1 | 4.1 | 3.7 | 3.4 | 3.0 | 2.7 | 2.3 | 2.0 | 1.6 | 1.3 | 0.9 | 0.5 | 0.2 |
| 2 | 4.1 | 4.1 | 4.1 | 4.2 | 4.2 | 4.2 | 4.2 | 4.2 | 4.2 | 4.3 | 4.3 | 4.3 |
| 3 | 3.9 | 4.0 | 4.0 | 4.0 | 4.0 | 4.0 | 4.0 | 4.0 | 4.1 | 4.1 | 4.1 | 4.1 |
| 4 | 3.8 | 3.8 | 3.8 | 3.8 | 3.8 | 3.8 | 3.9 | 3.9 | 3.9 | 3.9 | 3.9 | 3.9 |

**19-Year Real Property Used Predominantly Outside the United States (placed in service after May 8, 1985 and before 1987)**

*(35-Year 150% Declining Balance)*
*(Assuming Mid-Month Convention)*

| | Month Placed in Service | | | | | | | | | | | |
|---|---|---|---|---|---|---|---|---|---|---|---|---|
| Year | 1 | 2 | 3 | 4 | 5 | 6 | 7 | 8 | 9 | 10 | 11 | 12 |
| 5 ...... | 3.6 | 3.6 | 3.6 | 3.6 | 3.7 | 3.7 | 3.7 | 3.7 | 3.7 | 3.8 | 3.7 | 3.7 |
| 6 ...... | 3.5 | 3.5 | 3.5 | 3.5 | 3.5 | 3.5 | 3.5 | 3.5 | 3.5 | 3.6 | 3.6 | 3.6 |
| 7 ...... | 3.3 | 3.3 | 3.3 | 3.3 | 3.3 | 3.4 | 3.4 | 3.4 | 3.4 | 3.4 | 3.4 | 3.4 |
| 8 ...... | 3.2 | 3.2 | 3.2 | 3.2 | 3.2 | 3.2 | 3.2 | 3.2 | 3.3 | 3.3 | 3.3 | 3.3 |
| 9 ...... | 3.0 | 3.0 | 3.0 | 3.1 | 3.1 | 3.1 | 3.1 | 3.1 | 3.1 | 3.1 | 3.1 | 3.1 |
| 10 ...... | 2.9 | 2.9 | 2.9 | 2.9 | 2.9 | 2.9 | 3.0 | 3.0 | 3.0 | 3.0 | 3.0 | 3.0 |
| 11 ...... | 2.8 | 2.8 | 2.8 | 2.8 | 2.8 | 2.8 | 2.8 | 2.8 | 2.9 | 2.9 | 2.9 | 2.9 |
| 12 ...... | 2.6 | 2.7 | 2.7 | 2.7 | 2.7 | 2.7 | 2.7 | 2.7 | 2.7 | 2.7 | 2.8 | 2.8 |
| 13 - 29 ... | 2.6 | 2.6 | 2.6 | 2.6 | 2.6 | 2.6 | 2.6 | 2.6 | 2.6 | 2.6 | 2.6 | 2.6 |
| 30 - 35 ... | 2.5 | 2.5 | 2.5 | 2.5 | 2.5 | 2.5 | 2.5 | 2.5 | 2.5 | 2.5 | 2.5 | 2.5 |
| 36 ...... | 0.0 | 0.2 | 0.5 | 0.7 | 0.9 | 1.2 | 1.3 | 1.7 | 1.7 | 1.8 | 2.2 | 2.5 |

**Low-Income Housing Used Predominantly Outside the United States (placed in service after May 8, 1985 and before 1987)**

*(35-Year 150% Declining Balance)*
*(Assuming No Mid-Month Convention)*

| | Month Placed in Service | | | | | | | | | | | |
|---|---|---|---|---|---|---|---|---|---|---|---|---|
| Year | 1 | 2 | 3 | 4 | 5 | 6 | 7 | 8 | 9 | 10 | 11 | 12 |
| 1 ...... | 4.2 | 3.9 | 3.6 | 3.2 | 2.8 | 2.5 | 2.1 | 1.8 | 1.4 | 1.1 | 0.7 | 0.4 |
| 2 ...... | 4.1 | 4.1 | 4.1 | 4.2 | 4.2 | 4.2 | 4.2 | 4.2 | 4.2 | 4.2 | 4.3 | 4.3 |
| 3 ...... | 3.9 | 3.9 | 4.0 | 4.0 | 4.0 | 4.0 | 4.0 | 4.0 | 4.0 | 4.1 | 4.1 | 4.1 |
| 4 ...... | 3.8 | 3.8 | 3.8 | 3.8 | 3.8 | 3.8 | 3.8 | 3.8 | 3.9 | 3.9 | 3.9 | 3.9 |
| 5 ...... | 3.6 | 3.6 | 3.6 | 3.6 | 3.7 | 3.7 | 3.7 | 3.7 | 3.7 | 3.7 | 3.7 | 3.7 |
| 6 ...... | 3.4 | 3.5 | 3.5 | 3.5 | 3.5 | 3.5 | 3.5 | 3.5 | 3.5 | 3.6 | 3.6 | 3.6 |
| 7 ...... | 3.3 | 3.3 | 3.3 | 3.3 | 3.3 | 3.4 | 3.4 | 3.4 | 3.4 | 3.4 | 3.4 | 3.4 |
| 8 ...... | 3.2 | 3.2 | 3.2 | 3.2 | 3.2 | 3.2 | 3.2 | 3.2 | 3.3 | 3.3 | 3.3 | 3.3 |
| 9 ...... | 3.0 | 3.0 | 3.0 | 3.1 | 3.1 | 3.1 | 3.1 | 3.1 | 3.1 | 3.1 | 3.1 | 3.1 |
| 10 ...... | 2.9 | 2.9 | 2.9 | 2.9 | 2.9 | 2.9 | 3.0 | 3.0 | 3.0 | 3.0 | 3.0 | 3.0 |
| 11 ...... | 2.8 | 2.8 | 2.8 | 2.8 | 2.8 | 2.8 | 2.8 | 2.8 | 2.8 | 2.8 | 2.9 | 2.9 |
| 12 ...... | 2.6 | 2.7 | 2.7 | 2.7 | 2.7 | 2.7 | 2.7 | 2.7 | 2.7 | 2.7 | 2.7 | 2.8 |
| 13 - 28 ... | 2.6 | 2.6 | 2.6 | 2.6 | 2.6 | 2.6 | 2.6 | 2.6 | 2.6 | 2.6 | 2.6 | 2.6 |
| 29 ...... | 2.6 | 2.5 | 2.5 | 2.5 | 2.6 | 2.6 | 2.6 | 2.6 | 2.6 | 2.6 | 2.6 | 2.6 |
| 30 - 35 ... | 2.5 | 2.5 | 2.5 | 2.5 | 2.5 | 2.5 | 2.5 | 2.5 | 2.5 | 2.5 | 2.5 | 2.5 |
| 36 ...... | 0.0 | 0.2 | 0.4 | 0.6 | 0.8 | 1.0 | 1.3 | 1.6 | 1.8 | 1.9 | 2.1 | 2.3 |

# Straight-Line ACRS

## ¶ 254

### Straight-Line Elections

Taxpayers who may prefer slower recovery of the cost of ACRS property are not locked into the generally prescribed recovery percentages or the generally applicable recovery periods. They may elect a straight-line recovery method over the following optional recovery periods. For the classes of property indicated, straight-line recovery periods are elected in accordance with the following table:

| | |
|---|---|
| 3-year property | 3, 5, or 12 years |
| 5-year property | 5, 12, 25 years |
| 10-year property | 10, 25, or 35 years |
| 15-year real property (or low-income housing) | 15, 35, or 45 years |
| 15-year public utility property | 15, 35, or 45 years |
| 18-year real property | 18, 35, or 45 years |
| 19-year real property | 19, 35, or 45 years |

For real property in general, a straight-line election averted ordinary income recapture treatment if the property is subsequently sold at a gain. However, for residential real property, this is less of a consideration because the recapture rules limit ordinary income treatment to the excess of ACRS deductions over costs that would have been recovered under the straight-line method based on the applicable recovery period.

Except for most real property, a taxpayer may not pick and choose. An election must apply to all property of the same class placed in service in the same year. Property of a separate class or placed in service in a separate year qualifies for separate treatment. In the case of 15-year, 18-year, or 19-year real property, any election is made on an asset-by-asset basis.

For other than most real property, the half-year convention applies if the straight-line method is elected. Thus, in the case of 5-year property, the taxpayer may claim a half year's recovery in the first year, a full year's recovery in the next four years, and a half year's recovery in the sixth year. Straight-line percentages for property other than most real property are as follows for the recovery periods indicated:

| *Recovery Period* | *First Year* | *Annual Percentage* | *Last Year* |
|---|---|---|---|
| 3 Years | 16.667 | 33.333 | 16.667 |
| 5 Years | 10.000 | 20.000 | 10.000 |
| 10 Years | 5.000 | 10.000 | 5.000 |
| 12 Years | 4.167 | 8.333 | 4.170 |
| 15 Years | 3.333 | 6.667 | 3.329 |
| 25 Years | 2,000 | 4.000 | 2.000 |
| 35 Years | 1.429 | 2.857 | 1.433 |
| 45 Years | 1.111 | 2.222 | 1.121 |

Consistent with the general ACRS rules applying to most real property, computations must reflect the number of months in which such property is in service during the tax year. The annual percentages for 15, 35 and 45 years as well as the first year and last year percentages based on the month the real property is placed in service are provided in decimal form at ¶ 610.

In the case of property used outside the United States, straight-line recovery periods may be elected in accordance with the following table:

| *In the case of* | *The taxpayer may elect a recovery period of* |
|---|---|
| 3-year property | The ADR class life, 5 or 12 years |
| 5-year property | The ADR class life, 12 or 25 years |
| 10-year property | The ADR class life, 25 or 35 years |
| 15-year, 18-year, or 19-year real property | The ADR class life, 35 or 45 years |
| 15-year public utility property | The ADR class life, 35 or 45 years |

The annual percentages and the first-year and last-year percentages for 5, 12, 25, 35, and 45 years for property other than 15-year real property can be obtained from the above table of percentages for such property. If the applicable ADR class life is not included in the above table of percentages, the annual percentage and the first year and last-year percentages can be found in decimal form in the tables at ¶ 610 by using the "S-L" and the 6-month columns (half-year convention applies). The annual percentages for 35 and 45 years are provided in decimal form at ¶ 610.

An election is made on the return for the year in which the property is placed in service. Once made, it may not be revoked without IRS consent.

To the same extent that a tax-free exchange, a transfer between related parties, or a leaseback may not convert pre-1981 property into recovery property, such a transaction may not free recovery property from the consequences of a straight-line election. The transferee inherits the transferor's accounting method and recovery period. For the effect of "boot," see Example (2) at ¶ 264.

*15-Year Real Property*
*(Placed in Service After December 31, 1980, and Before March 16, 1984)*
*and Low-Income Housing For Which Alternate ACRS Method*
*Over a 15-Year Period Is Elected*
*(No Mid-Month Convention)*

| *Year* | *Month Placed in Service* | | | | | | |
|---|---|---|---|---|---|---|---|
| | *1* | *2–3* | *4* | *5–6* | *7–8* | *9–10* | *11–12* |
| 1st | 7% | 6% | 5% | 4% | 3% | 2% | 1% |
| 2–10th | 7% | 7% | 7% | 7% | 7% | 7% | 7% |
| 11–15th | 6% | 6% | 6% | 6% | 6% | 6% | 6% |
| 16th | | 1% | 2% | 3% | 4% | 5% | 6% |

*15-Year Real Property, 18-Year Real Property*
*(Placed in Service After March 15, 1984 and Before June 23, 1984),*
*and Low-Income Housing (Placed in Service Before May 9, 1985)*
*For Which Alternate ACRS Method Over a 35-Year Period Is Elected*
*(No Mid-Month Convention)*

| | *Month Placed in Service* | | |
|---|---|---|---|
| *Year* | *1–2* | *3–6* | *7–12* |
| 1st | 3% | 2% | 1% |
| 2–30th | 3% | 3% | 3% |
| 31–35th | 2% | 2% | 2% |
| 36th | | 1% | 2% |

*15-Year Real Property, 18-Year Real Property (Placed in Service After March 15, 1984 and Before June 23, 1984), and Low-Income Housing Placed in Service After December 31, 1980 For Which Alternate ACRS Method Over a 45-Year Period Is Elected (No Mid-Month Convention)*

| | *Month Placed in Service* | | | | | | | | | | | |
|---|---|---|---|---|---|---|---|---|---|---|---|---|
| *Year* | *1* | *2* | *3* | *4* | *5* | *6* | *7* | *8* | *9* | *10* | *11* | *12* |
| 1st | 2.3% | 2% | 1.9% | 1.7% | 1.5% | 1.3% | 1.2% | 0.9% | 0.7% | 0.6% | 0.4% | 0.2% |
| 2–10th | 2.3% | 2.3% | 2.3% | 2.3% | 2.3% | 2.3% | 2.3% | 2.3% | 2.3% | 2.3% | 2.3% | 2.3% |
| 11–45th | 2.2% | 2.2% | 2.2% | 2.2% | 2.2% | 2.2% | 2.2% | 2.2% | 2.2% | 2.2% | 2.2% | 2.2% |
| 46th | | 0.3% | 0.4% | 0.6% | 0.8% | 1% | 1.1% | 1.4% | 1.6% | 1.7% | 1.9% | 2.1% |

*18-Year Real Property (Placed in Service After March 15 and Before June 23, 1984) For Which Alternate ACRS Method Over an 18-Year Period Is Elected (No Mid-Month Convention)*

| | *Month Placed in Service* | | | | | | |
|---|---|---|---|---|---|---|---|
| *Year* | *1* | *2–3* | *4–5* | *6–7* | *8–9* | *10–11* | *12* |
| 1st | 6% | 5% | 4% | 3% | 2% | 1% | 0.5% |
| 2–10th | 6% | 6% | 6% | 6% | 6% | 6% | 6% |
| 11th | 5% | 5% | 5% | 5% | 5% | 5% | 5.5% |
| 12–18th | 5% | 5% | 5% | 5% | 5% | 5% | 5% |
| 19th | | 1% | 2% | 3% | 4% | 5% | 5% |

*Low-Income Housing (Placed in Service After May 8, 1985) For Which Alternate ACRS Method Over a 35-Year Period Is Elected (No Mid-Month Convention)*

| | *Month Placed in Service* | | | | | | | | | | | |
|---|---|---|---|---|---|---|---|---|---|---|---|---|
| *Year* | *1* | *2* | *3* | *4* | *5* | *6* | *7* | *8* | *9* | *10* | *11* | *12* |
| 1st | 2.9% | 2.6% | 2.4% | 2.1% | 1.9% | 1.7% | 1.4% | 1.2% | 1.0% | 0.7% | 0.5% | 0.2% |
| 2–20th | 2.9% | 2.9% | 2.9% | 2.9% | 2.9% | 2.9% | 2.9% | 2.9% | 2.9% | 2.9% | 2.9% | 2.9% |
| 21–35th | 2.8% | 2.8% | 2.8% | 2.8% | 2.8% | 2.8% | 2.8% | 2.8% | 2.8% | 2.8% | 2.8% | 2.8% |
| 36th | | 0.3% | 0.5% | 0.8% | 1.0% | 1.2% | 1.5% | 1.7% | 1.9% | 2.2% | 2.4% | 2.7% |

The following straight-line recovery percentages are provided for real property subject to the mid-month convention.

*18-Year Real Property (Placed in Service After June 22, 1984)*
*For Which Alternate ACRS Method Over an*
*18-Year Period Is Elected*
*(Mid-Month Convention)*

| Year | Month Placed in Service | | | | | |
|---|---|---|---|---|---|---|
| | 1–2 | 3–4 | 5–7 | 8–9 | 10–11 | 12 |
| 1st | 5% | 4% | 3% | 2% | 1% | 0.2% |
| 2–10th | 6% | 6% | 6% | 6% | 6% | 6% |
| 11th | 5% | 5% | 5% | 5% | 5% | 5.8% |
| 12–18th | 5% | 5% | 5% | 5% | 5% | 5% |
| 19th | 1% | 2% | 3% | 4% | 5% | 5% |

*18-Year Real Property*
*(Placed in Service After June 22, 1984)*
*For Which Alternate ACRS Method Over a*
*35-Year Period Is Elected*
*(Mid-Month Convention)*

| Year | Month Placed in Service | | | | |
|---|---|---|---|---|---|
| | 1–2 | 3–6 | 7–10 | 11 | 12 |
| 1st | 3% | 2% | 1% | 0.4% | 0.1% |
| 2–30th | 3% | 3% | 3% | 3% | 3% |
| 31st | 2% | 2% | 2% | 2.6% | 2.9% |
| 32–35th | 2% | 2% | 2% | 2% | 2% |
| 36th | | 1% | 2% | 2% | 2% |

*18-Year Real Property*
*(Placed in Service After June 22, 1984)*
*19-Year Real Property*
*For Which Alternate ACRS Method Over a*
*45-Year Period Is Elected*
*(Mid-Month Convention)*

| Year | Month Placed in Service | | | | | | | | | | | |
|---|---|---|---|---|---|---|---|---|---|---|---|---|
| | 1 | 2 | 3 | 4 | 5 | 6 | 7 | 8 | 9 | 10 | 11 | 12 |
| 1st | 2.1% | 1.9% | 1.8% | 1.6% | 1.4% | 1.2% | 1% | 0.8% | 0.6% | 0.5% | 0.3% | 0.1% |
| 2–11th | 2.3% | 2.3% | 2.3% | 2.3% | 2.3% | 2.3% | 2.3% | 2.3% | 2.3% | 2.3% | 2.3% | 2.3% |
| 12–45th | 2.2% | 2.2% | 2.2% | 2.2% | 2.2% | 2.2% | 2.2% | 2.2% | 2.2% | 2.2% | 2.2% | 2.2% |
| 46th | 0.1% | 0.3% | 0.4% | 0.6% | 0.8% | 1% | 1.2% | 1.4% | 1.6% | 1.7% | 1.9% | 2.1% |

The following table provides the general straight-line recovery percentages for 19-year real property.

*19-Year Real Property*
*For Which Alternate ACRS Method Over a 19-Year Period Is Elected*
*(Mid-Month Convention)*

| Year | Month Placed in Service | | | | | | | | | | | |
|---|---|---|---|---|---|---|---|---|---|---|---|---|
| | *1* | *2* | *3* | *4* | *5* | *6* | *7* | *8* | *9* | *10* | *11* | *12* |
| 1st | 5.0% | 4.6% | 4.2% | 3.7% | 3.3% | 2.9% | 2.4 | 2.0% | 1.5% | 1.1% | 0.7% | 0.2% |
| 2–13th | 5.3% | 5.3% | 5.3% | 5.3% | 5.3% | 5.3% | 5.3% | 5.3% | 5.3% | 5.3% | 5.3% | 5.3% |
| 14–19th | 5.2% | 5.2% | 5.2% | 5.2% | 5.2% | 5.2% | 5.2% | 5.2% | 5.2% | 5.2% | 5.2% | 5.2% |
| 20th | 0.2% | 0.6% | 1.0% | 1.5% | 1.9% | 2.3% | 2.8% | 3.2% | 3.7% | 4.1% | 4.5% | 5.0% |

If, for 19-year real property, a 45-year period is elected, the recovery percentages are the same as they are for 18-year real property placed in service after June 22, 1984. If a 35-year period is elected, the following percentages apply:

*19-Year Real Property*
*For Which Alternate ACRS Method Over a 35-Year Period Is Elected*
*(Mid-Month Convention)*

| Year | Month Placed in Service | | | | | | | | | | | |
|---|---|---|---|---|---|---|---|---|---|---|---|---|
| | *1* | *2* | *3* | *4* | *5* | *6* | *7* | *8* | *9* | *10* | *11* | *12* |
| 1st | 2.7% | 2.5% | 2.3% | 2.0% | 1.8% | 1.5% | 1.3 | 1.1% | 0.8% | 0.6% | 0.4% | 0.1% |
| 2–20th | 2.9% | 2.9% | 2.9% | 2.9% | 2.9% | 2.9% | 2.9% | 2.9% | 2.9% | 2.9% | 2.9% | 2.9% |
| 21–35th | 2.8% | 2.8% | 2.8% | 2.8% | 2.8% | 2.8% | 2.8% | 2.8% | 2.8% | 2.8% | 2.8% | 2.8% |
| 36th | 0.2% | 0.4% | 0.6% | 0.9% | 1.1% | 1.4% | 1.6% | 1.8% | 2.1% | 2.3% | 2.5% | 2.8% |

## ¶ 256

## ACRS Property Financed with Tax-Exempt Bonds

To the extent that property placed in service after 1983 was financed by the proceeds from the issue of post-October 18, 1983, tax-exempt industrial development bonds, the straight-line ACRS method was required to be used to recover cost (or other basis). However, residential rental projects for low-or-moderate-income individuals were not subject to this restriction.

The cost of low-income housing financed with IDBs is recoverable over 15 years under regular ACRS with the month of placement in service counting as one full month. The cost of residential rental projects that are financed with IDBs but are not low-income housing are recovered under the ACRS straight-line method over a 19-year recovery period (instead of the former 15-year recovery period) for property placed in service after May 8, 1985, and before 1987.

The cost of tax-exempt financed ACRS 3-, 5-, 10-, and 15-year public utility property is recoverable over 3-, 5-, 10-, and 15-year recovery periods.

Taxpayers required to use the straight-line method for property that was financed with industrial development bonds were not precluded from using the longer optional recovery periods available to those who elect straight-line ACRS.

# ACRS Leasehold Improvements

## ¶ 258

### Lessee's and Lessor's ACRS Deductions

An improvement made by a lessee after 1980 and before 1987 is depreciated under ACRS if the recovery period of the improvement is less than the remaining term of the lease when the improvement is placed in service (former Code Sec. 168(f)(6); Prop. Reg. § 1.168-5(d)). In determining the length of the lease term, the rules of Code Sec. 178 (prior to amendment by the 1986 Tax Reform Act (P.L. 99-514)) apply.

If the statutory recovery period is shorter than the lease term, ACRS allowances should be claimed over the recovery period. If the lease term is shorter, amortization should be claimed over the lease term.

If the statutory recovery period is shorter than the lease term, the taxpayer may elect a longer recovery period in connection with a straight-line ACRS election (¶ 254) if he wishes to claim amortization over the lease term or cost recovery over a longer period.

If, after the improvements are completed, the term remaining on the lease (excluding renewal periods) is less than 60 percent of the recovery period (former Code Sec. 178), and it cannot be shown that the lease will not be renewed, renewal periods must be counted in determining the term of the lease.

> ***Example:*** In 1985, a lessee put up a building on land on which his lease would expire in 1993. He also had an option to renew the lease for five additional years. The building is 15-year property. Since the eight years remaining on the lease were less than 60% of the 15-year recovery period, the renewal period must be counted as time remaining on the lease. Thus, the cost of the building is amortized over a period extending into 1998.

An improvement made by (i.e., owned by) the lessor is depreciated using ACRS regardless of the term of the lease (Prop. Reg. § 1.168-5(d)).

See ¶ 126 for leasehold improvements under MACRS.

# Excluded Property

## ¶ 260

## Specially Depreciated Property

If the taxpayer elects to depreciate property under the unit-of-production method (¶ 360), an income forecast method (¶ 364), or any other method not expressed in a term of years, the property will be excluded from ACRS. The election must be made for the first taxable year for which an ACRS deduction for the property would otherwise be allowable.

## ¶ 262

## Certain Public Utility Property Under ACRS

Subject to general requirements, public utility property qualifies as ACRS recovery property only if accounting is normalized for purposes of setting rates and reflecting operating results in regulated books of account. In theory, regulatory agencies set utility rates at levels that permit a fair rate of return on investments, and normalization (as opposed to "flow-through" accounting) limits the conversion of ACRS benefits into rate reductions for customers. Prior law imposed a similar limitation with respect to the accelerated depreciation methods and the 20-percent ADR useful life variance available to certain utilities.

As under prior law, regulatory agencies may treat any taxes deferred as zero-cost capital or as reductions in the rate base. Amounts so treated, however, may not exceed the amount of the taxes deferred as a result of the methods and recovery periods that were actually used to compute recovery allowances.

Post-1980 property that does not qualify as recovery property due to lack of normalization is not depreciated under the rules that apply to pre-1981 property. Depreciation must be based on the method used by the regulatory agency for rate-making purposes. Any averaging conventions and salvage value limitations are part of the regulatory agency's method. Useful lives must be at least as long as those used by the regulatory agency.

## ¶ 264

## The ACRS Anti-churning Rules

Two sets of rules—one for Sec. 1245 class property (generally, all personal property) and one for Sec. 1250 class property—prevent transfers, *other than by reason of death,* to related persons from "churning" pre-1981 assets into ACRS recovery property.

The first set of rules denies ACRS treatment to Sec. 1245 class property acquired by a taxpayer after 1980 if the property was:

(1) owned or used by the taxpayer or a related person at any time during 1980;

(2) acquired from a person who owned it at any time during 1980, and, as part of the transaction, the user remains the same;

(3) leased by the taxpayer to a person (or a person related to such person) who owned or used it at any time during 1980; or

(4) acquired in a transaction in which the user does not change and in which, due to (2) or (3), above, the property was not recovery property in the hands of the transferor.

*Example (1):* Smith rents a computer in 1980 and buys it in 1986. It is not ACRS property because he used it in 1980.

The second set of rules denies ACRS treatment to Sec. 1250 class property that was acquired by a taxpayer after 1980 if the property was:

(1) owned by the taxpayer (or a party related to the taxpayer) during 1980;

(2) leased back to a person that owned the property (or a person related to such person) during 1980; or

(3) acquired in certain like-kind exchanges and reacquisitions.

The exchanges and reacquisitions referred to in (3), above, are like-kind exchanges of property held for productive use in a trade or business or for investment (under Code Sec. 1031), involuntary conversions (under Code Sec. 1033), repossessions (under Code Sec. 1038), and rollovers of low-income housing (under Code Sec. 1039, repealed effective November 5, 1990). However, ACRS treatment is denied (and the old depreciation rules govern) only to so much of the basis of the property acquired as represents the basis of the property exchanged. To the extent of any "boot" (money or other property) that is given, ACRS applies.

*Example (2):* In 1986, a taxpayer exchanges an office building acquired before 1981 plus $120,000 for another office building. The office building exchanged had an adjusted basis of $180,000. To the extent that the basis of the building acquired is attributable to the adjusted basis ($180,000) of the building exchanged, ACRS is inapplicable. To the extent of the "boot" ($120,000), ACRS applies.

Pre-1981 ownership of property under construction will not bar ACRS treatment. For anti-churning rule purposes, the property is not treated as owned until it is placed in service.

Sec. 1245 class property transferred incidentally to the transfer of Sec. 1250 class property will be subject to the rules for the latter class of property. However, committee reports indicate that a transfer is not incidental if the Sec. 1245 class property is a "significant portion" of the transferred property.

## ¶ 266

## Related Persons Under ACRS Anti-Churning Rules

For purposes of the ACRS anti-churning rules (¶ 264), related persons are:

(1) brothers and sisters (half or full), spouses, ancestors, and lineal descendants;

(2) a corporation and an individual owning more than 10 percent of the value of the corporation's outstanding stock;

(3) two corporations if the same individual owns more than 10 percent of the value of each corporation's outstanding stock, if either corporation was a personal holding company for the preceding tax year;

(4) a grantor and a fiduciary of any trust;

(5) fiduciaries of separate trusts if the trusts have the same grantor;

(6) a fiduciary and a beneficiary of the same trust;

(7) a fiduciary of one trust and a beneficiary of another if the trusts have the same grantor;

(8) a fiduciary of a trust and a corporation of which more than a specified value of the outstanding stock is owned by or for the trust or for the grantor of the trust;

(9) certain tax-exempt educational or charitable organizations and a controlling individual or a member of a controlling family;

(10) a partnership and partner owning more than 10 percent of the partnership capital or profits;

(11) two partnerships if the same person owns (directly or indirectly) more than 10 percent of each partnership's capital or profits; and

(12) organizations engaged in trades or businesses under common control ("organization" here means a sole proprietorship, a partnership, a trust, an estate, or a corporation).

Where a partnership is considered terminated by reason of a sale or exchange within a 12-month period of at least 50 percent of an interest in partnership capital and profits, the relationship of an acquiring partnership is determined as of immediately before the terminating event. Thus, the antichurning rules are inapplicable to the acquisition of more than 90 percent of partnership interests by parties unrelated to the selling partners.

Relationships are determined as of the date of acquisition of the property, and ex-spouses are not related parties. These rules benefited a taxpayer who, under a settlement agreement, obtained a half interest in a condominium (*J.H. Drake II,* DC Ill., 86-2 USTC ¶ 9746).

## ¶ 268

## Nonrecognition Transactions Under ACRS

As might be expected, there are rules to prevent tax-free exchanges from conferring ACRS benefits on pre-1981 property (Code Sec. 168(f)(10)). These rules list the following categories of nonrecognition transactions by reference to the Code Secs. indicated:

(1) complete liquidations of subsidiaries (Code Sec. 332);

(2) transfers to controlled corporations (Code Sec. 351);

(3) exchanges, pursuant to plans of reorganization, solely for stock or securities of other corporations (Code Sec. 361);

(4) reorganizations in certain bankruptcy and receivership proceedings (Code Sec. 371, repealed effective November 5, 1990);

(5) certain railroad reorganizations (Code Sec. 374, repealed effective November 5, 1990);

(6) contributions to partners in exchange for partnership interests (Code Sec. 721); and

(7) distributions by partnerships to partners (Code Sec. 731).

As in the case of a leaseback or an acquisition from a related party, a transferee in a tax-free exchange is generally bound by the transferor's method and period of depreciation. If "boot" is involved, however, ACRS may apply to the same extent as explained at ¶ 264 with respect to the anti-churning rules.

For property placed in service after 1985, the "step-in-the-shoes rules" have been shored up for property acquired from related parties (other than in nonrecognition transactions) or leased back to transferors. To the extent of the transferor's adjusted basis in the hands of the transferee, the transferee is bound by a transferor's election of straight-line depreciation and, if applicable, longer recovery periods (however, so much of the basis of 15-year real property subject to the technically corrected rules would be recoverable over the applicable longer period). Furthermore, such basis is recovered over a new recovery period.

# Safe-Harbor Leases

## ¶ 278

## Transitional Rules

So-called safe-harbor leasing rules—under which transactions meeting certain requirements were assured of being treated as leases—proved controversial and were repealed for "leases" entered into after 1983. Moreover, for agreements entered into or property placed in service after July 1, 1982 (except where the lessee had already acquired, commenced to construct, or contracted to acquire or commence to construct the property), some safe-harbor requirements were stiffened, and, for safe-harbor leases, some tax benefits were reduced. Some of the tax benefit reductions are related to ACRS. Leases created during the period the safe harbor lease rules apply and for which the safe harbor lease election was made are controlled by such rules for the duration of the lease.

*Recovery periods and percentages*

Under safe-harbor leases subject to the more stringent rules, recovery periods were extended and recovery percentages were based on the 150-percent declining-balance method with an appropriately timed switch to the straight-line method. The cost of three-year property was recoverable over a five-year period, the cost of five-year property was recoverable over an eight-year period, and the cost of 10-year property was recoverable over a 15-year period. The recovery percentages for three-year and five-year property subject to safe-harbor leases (which are fully depreciated) are not reproduced. For 10-year property still subject to these more stringent rules, the recovery percentage is six percent for recovery years 7 through 15.

*Lessor's tax liability*

Under safe-harbor leases subject to the more stringent rules, a lessor could not reduce liability for federal income tax (corporate minimum tax included) by more than 50 percent through the use of safe-harbor lease benefits. Application of this limitation requires computation of tax liability without regard to the relevant rental income, interest and ACRS deductions, and investment tax credits.

> ***Example:*** A lessor's tax liability is $100,000 if rental income, deductions for interest and depreciation, and investment credit from safe-harbor leases are excluded but is $30,000 if such leasing benefits are included. The 50% limit would apply in such case, and the lessor's liability would be $50,000 (50% of $100,000).

Safe-harbor lease deductions and credits that are not utilized in the current tax year because of such limitation on tax liability may only be carried forward.

Although the 50-percent limitation does not apply to safe-harbor leases not subject to the new rules (generally leases covering property placed in service before July 2, 1982), those leases must be taken into account in computing the limitation.

*Finance leases*

The repeal of the safe-harbor lease rules was accompanied by the enactment of a new set of rules that, for post-1983 leases qualifying as "finance leases," would likewise entitle third parties to qualify as lessors and deduct ACRS allowances. These new rules were subsequently deferred and eventually repealed, so that, with exceptions for transition property, "true" leases are once again distinguishable from mere tax-motivated arrangements under the same nonstatutory rules that apply to pre-ACRS property. Transition property is:

(1) new investment credit farming-use property leased under qualifying arrangements entered into after July 1, 1982, and before 1988 (provided that the aggregate cost for a taxable year of all such farming-use property subject to a finance lease entered into by a lessee does not exceed $150,000);

(2) up to $150 million of qualifying automobile manufacturing property; and

(3) property that a lessee was bound to acquire or construct, or had acquired, or on which construction had begun by or for the lessee, before March 7, 1984.

# Dispositions of ACRS Recovery Property

## ¶ 280

## Early Dispositions

The treatment of the early disposition of ACRS recovery property to a large extent flows from the general rules for such property. Thus, dispositions of real property, for which computations must reflect actual months in service, must be distinguished from dispositions of other classes of recovery property. A disposition is the permanent withdrawal of property from use in a trade or business or in the production of income, and a disposition is early if it precedes the end of the applicable recovery period. An early disposition may arise from the sale, exchange, retirement, abandonment, or destruction of the property. The adjusted basis of abandoned property is deductible.

Generally, no part of the cost of 3-year, 5-year or 10-year property, or 15-year public utility property is recovered in the year of disposition or retirement. The relevant basis for determining gain or loss is the basis of the property as of the first day of the year in which disposition occurs.

> ***Example (1):*** In May of 1986, a construction contractor places in service an electric saw for which he paid $180. The saw was 5-year property, and, for 1986, the contractor deducts $27 (15% of $180). No other 5-year property was placed in service during 1986. For 1987, he deducts $40 (22% of $180), and, for 1988, he deducts $38 (21% of $180). In 1989, the contractor sells the saw. For 1989, there is no ACRS deduction for the saw, and $75 ($180 – $27 – $40 – $38) is the basis of the saw for determining gain or loss.

> ***Example (2):*** The facts are the same as in Example (1) except that the contractor (1) purchased several other items of 5-year property in 1986 at a total cost of $500 and (2) sold the saw in 1987 (rather than in 1989). For 1987, there was no deduction for the saw, the basis for determining gain or loss on the sale of the saw was $153 ($180 – $27), and (assuming no election to depreciate any eligible 1986 property under MACRS) $110 (22% of the unadjusted basis of all the 5-year property other than the saw placed in service in 1986) was deductible as depreciation. Assuming no dispositions, his deduction for either 1988 or 1989 is $105 (21% of $500).

Cost recovery would be computed in a similar manner (substituting the appropriate percentages) even if the taxpayer had elected to recover the cost of the property under the straight-line method.

If 15-year, 18-year, or 19-year real property is sold, there will probably be no need for the kind of adjustment illustrated in Example (2) (because separate items of such property may not be grouped together unless they are placed in service in both the same month and year). However, months in service are taken into account.

A partial recovery of the cost of 15-year, 18-year, or 19-year real recovery property is permitted in the year of disposition before the end of the recovery period (Prop. Reg. § 1.168-2(a)(3)).

*(1) Disposition in first recovery year*

The recovery allowance for real recovery property in this situation is determined for a full year and then prorated based on the number of months of business use divided by the number of months in the taxpayer's tax year after the recovery property was placed in service (including the month that the property was placed in service). This rule is applied in conjunction with the mid-month convention, if applicable.

*(2) Disposition in year other than first recovery year*

The recovery allowance for real recovery property in this situation is determined for a full year and then prorated based on the number of months of business use divided by 12. This rule is applied in conjunction with the mid-month convention, if applicable.

> ***Example (3):*** In May of 1986, a taxpayer purchases an office building for $150,000 (exclusive of the cost of the land) and immediately places it in service as 19-year real property. He does not elect the straight-line method, and, for 1986, the ACRS deduction is $8,700 (5.8% of $150,000—see the table at ¶ 246). The deduction for 1987 is $13,050 (8.7% of $150,000), for 1988 it is $11,850 (7.9% of $150,000), for 1989 it is $10,650 (7.1% of $150,000), for 1990 it is $9,750 (6.5% of $150,000), for 1991 it is $8,850 (5.9% of $150,000), for 1992 it is $7,950 (5.3% of $150,000), for 1993 it is $7,200 (4.8% of $150,000), for 1994 it is $6,600 (4.4% of $150,000), and for each year 1995—1998 it is $6,300 (4.2% of $150,000). He sells the building in September 1999, and his deduction for that year is $4,463. This represents 4.2% (the fifth-month percentage for the fourteenth year of service) of $150,000 with a proration (multiplying by 8.5/12) to reflect 1999 months of service.

Computations for 18-year real property placed in service after June 22, 1984, or as in the above example, 19-year real property, vary slightly from computations for 15-year real property or 18-year real property placed in service before June 23, 1984, to reflect the mid-month convention.

> ***Example (4):*** The facts are the same as in *Example (3)* except that the property was purchased in May of 1984 and is classified as 18-year property. Since the property was placed in service before June 22, 1984, the appropriate table (at ¶ 244) does not reflect the mid-month convention, and 8/12 (rather than 8.5/12) is the appropriate fraction for computing year-of-disposition recovery.

*(3) Disposition in short tax year*

Although a disposition of real recovery property occurs in a short tax year, no ACRS short tax year adjustment is made because the short tax year rule (¶ 290) does not apply to the year of disposition of real recovery property. The ACRS deduction is determined under (2), above.

In situations where a short tax year arises because, for example, the taxpayer dies or is a corporation that becomes a member or ceases being a member of an affiliated group filing a consolidated return, the ACRS deduction on real recovery property disposed of in the short tax year is determined under (2), above, but the denominator is modified to represent the number of months in the taxpayer's tax year (Prop. Reg. § 1.168-2(a)(3)).

> ***Example (5):*** An individual, who is a calendar-year taxpayer, acquired 18-year real recovery property for $100,000 in March 1985. The property is sold in February 1999, and the individual dies in March 1999. The 1999 short tax year recovery allowance for such property is $2,000 ($100,000 unadjusted basis × 4% (fifteenth-year percentage for 18-year real property placed in service in the third month of a full tax year) × 1.5 ÷ 3).

Provision is made under which, pursuant to regulations, year-of-disposition recovery is permissible with respect to transactions in which gain or loss is not recognized or to certain related-party transfers, sale-leasebacks, and tax-free transfers in which a transferee is bound by the transferor's recovery period and method of depreciation.

In the event of recapture of a basis-reducing credit, basis for gain or loss is correspondingly adjusted.

*Recapture*

Gain on the disposition of Sec. 1245 recovery property is recaptured as ordinary income to the extent of all ACRS deductions. Gain on the disposition of nonresidential real recovery property is recaptured to the extent of all ACRS deductions, but there is no recapture if the straight-line ACRS method was elected. Gain on the disposition of recovery property that is residential rental property, is recaptured to the extent of the excess of accelerated depreciation over straight-line depreciation. If there is a disposition of recovery property before it is held more than one year, all ACRS allowances are recaptured to the extent of gain. See also ¶ 488.

## ¶ 282

## ACRS Mass Asset Accounts

As an alternative to calculating gain on each disposition of an item of ACRS property from a mass asset account, a taxpayer may elect to recognize gain on the entire proceeds and recover the cost of the item in the same manner as if it still remained in the account. This may be practical for dispositions of a few of the items in a large group of items that are relatively minor in value and burdensome to identify separately. Candidates for such treatment might include minor fixtures or items of furniture. Such treatment is elected by reporting the total disposition proceeds (on Form 4797, Supplemental Schedule of Gains and Losses) as ordinary income and recovering the cost of the item or items, together with the cost of all the other items in the mass asset account, over the appropriate recovery period.

Items in any mass asset account need not be homogeneous, but they must have the same present class life, and they must be placed in service in the same taxable year. The election is made for the year in which the assets are placed in service. It is binding with respect to those assets, but has no bearing on similar assets placed in service in other years.

If an early disposition of an item in a mass asset account triggers a recapture of an investment credit, then any basis adjustment (generally 50 percent of the amount recaptured) is added to the account. However, if records are consistent with prior practice and good accounting and engineering practices, proposed regulations indicate that a taxpayer may construct a mortality dispersion table for identifying dispositions. Alternatively, the proposed regulations provide a standard table.

## ¶ 284

## ACRS Recordkeeping

Although 2014 Form 4562, Depreciation and Amortization, provides only line 16 for "ACRS and other depreciation" (including depreciation of pre-ACRS assets), and no attachments are necessary, the basis and amounts claimed for depreciation should be part of your permanent books and records. A sample Depreciation Summary contained in IRS Publication 534, Depreciation (and a substantially similar Depreciation Record from IRS Publication 583, Taxpayers Starting a Business), provides headings for the following information: "Description of Property," "Date Placed in Service," "Cost or Other Basis," "Business Use%," "Section 179 Deduction," "Depreciation for Prior Years," "Basis for Depreciation," "Depreciation Method/Convention," "Recovery Period or Useful Life," "Rate or Table Percentage," and "Depreciation Deduction for Current Year."

With regard to listed property, any deduction for a year beginning after 1985 is contingent on substantiation by adequate records or sufficient evidence corroborating a taxpayer's statement. However, for any listed property, records must be maintained for any year in which recapture may still occur. For example, in the case of a car (3-year property) depreciated under ACRS and placed in service after June

18, 1984, but before 1985, records must be kept for six years even if the full cost of the car is recovered in only three.

Maintaining adequate records means keeping an account book, diary, log, statement of expense, trip sheet, or similar record and documentary evidence. Information reflected on receipts need not be entered in such records so long as the records and receipt complement each other in an orderly manner.

# ACRS Short Tax Year

## ¶ 290

## ACRS Short Tax Year

In computing an ACRS recovery allowance for a tax year of less than 12 months, certain adjustments must be made depending on whether property is personal recovery property or 15-year, 18-year, or 19-year real recovery property. Recovery allowances for years in a recovery period following a short tax year are determined without regard to the short tax year.

*Personal recovery property*

For other than 15-year, 18-year, or 19-year real recovery property, the recovery allowance for a short tax year is determined by multiplying the deduction that would have been allowable if the recovery year was not a short tax year by a fraction the numerator of which is the number of months and part-months in the short tax year and the denominator of which is 12 (Prop. Reg. § 1.168-2(f)(1)).

Any unrecovered allowance (the difference between the recovery allowance properly allowed for the short tax year and the recovery allowance that would have been allowable if such year were not a short tax year) is claimed in the tax year following the last year in the recovery period (Prop. Reg. § 1.168-2(f)(3)). However, there is a maximum limitation on the amount of an unrecovered allowance that may be claimed in a tax year. The unrecovered allowance claimed as a recovery allowance in the tax year following the last year of the recovery period may not exceed the amount of the recovery allowance permitted for the last year of the recovery period, assuming that such year consists of 12 months. Any remaining unrecovered allowance is carried forward to the following tax years until the allowance is exhausted.

> ***Example (1):*** In January 1986, a calendar-year corporation purchases a railroad tank car (10-year ACRS recovery property). For 1986, the corporation deducts $8,000 (8% of $100,000) and, for 1987, the corporation deducts $14,000 (14% of $100,000). Pursuant to a change in accounting period, the corporation files a return for a short tax year ending October 31, 1988. But for the short tax year, the third-year recovery allowance would have been $12,000 (12% of $100,000). To reflect the short tax year, the corporation must multiply this regular third-year amount by a fraction of which the numerator is the number of months in the year (10) and the denominator is 12. Thus, for the short tax year, the corporation deducts $10,000 (10⁄12 of $12,000). Assuming no dispositions or further short tax years, the corporation deducts $10,000 (10% of $100,000) for each of the tax years ending October 31, 1989 through 1991, and $9,000 (9% of $100,000) for each of the tax years ending October 31, 1992 through 1995. The remaining $2,000 ($100,000 – $98,000 depreciation deducted) is recoverable for the tax year ending October 31, 1996.

In the case of automobiles depreciated under ACRS subject to the luxury car rules (see ¶ 200), ceilings must be similarly scaled down.

For depreciation purposes, a year does not begin until the first month in which a person engages in a trade or business or holds property for the production of income. An employee may be regarded as engaging in a trade or business merely by reason of his employment—but only with regard to recovery property used for purposes of employment.

For purposes of depreciating property, a taxable year may commence before a business is acquired if the taxpayer is already engaged in a trade or business. Moreover the trade or business in which the taxpayer was engaged need not be the same trade or business in which the property is used—or even the same kind of trade or business.

***Example (2):*** A calendar-year corporation engaged in selling appliances purchases a fast food restaurant. No short-year computation is required in depreciating the restaurant's assets irrespective of the month in which the restaurant is acquired.

According to the IRS, the benefit of the rule that is illustrated in the above example does not extend to a person engaging in a small amount of trade or business activity if:

(1) this activity is conducted to avoid the short-year requirements, and

(2) the subsequent placing in service of the assets in issue represents a substantial increase in the level of business activity.

Corresponding rules apply with regard to depreciating property held for the production of income.

*Real recovery property*

If ACRS 15-year, 18-year, or 19-year real recovery property is placed in service or disposed of during a short tax year, the cost recovery deduction for the short tax year is computed as if the property was placed in service or disposed of during a full calendar year. See ¶ 222 and ¶ 280 for rules explaining the manner of computing recovery allowances on real property acquired or disposed of during a tax year.

If the short tax year occurs after real recovery property is placed in service, recovery allowances for the short tax year and subsequent tax years during the recovery period are computed in the same manner applicable to personal recovery property.

***Example (3):*** A calendar-year taxpayer acquires and places in service 18-year real recovery property in March 1985. The taxpayer changes to a June through May fiscal year beginning June 1, 2000. As a result there is a short tax year beginning January 1, 1999 and ending May 31, 2000. Assuming the unadjusted basis of the property is \$100,000, depreciation for the short tax year is \$1,667 (\$100,000 × 4%) (fifteenth-year percentage for 18-year real property placed in service in the third month of a full tax year) × 5/12 (reflecting the number of months in the short tax year). The sixteenth-year table percentage (4%) is used to compute depreciation for the 2000-2001 fiscal year.

The unrecovered basis of the property (\$100,000 × 4% × 7/12) is recovered beginning in the tax year after the end of the recovery period as explained under the rules for personal property.

# Special Expensing Election (Code Sec. 179)

## Annual Expensing Election

¶ 300

### Code Sec. 179 Expensing Alternative

Organization of Explanation

***1. Legislative Changes***

***2. Overview***

*In general*

*Dollar and investment limitations*

*Basis reduction*

*Taxable income limitation and carryforwards*

*Expensing limitation for certain suvs, trucks, and vans*

*Recapture upon sale or disposition*

*Recapture upon decline in business use*

*Section 179 property defined*

*Purchase defined*

*Qualified real property*

*Married taxpayers*

*Partnerships and S corporations*

*Controlled groups*

*Noncorporate lessors.*

*Exemption from UNICAP and section 263 capitalization*

*Empowerment zones and renewal communities*

*Expired provisions for certain disaster areas*

*De minimis expensing rule under repair regs*

***3. Section 179 Interaction With Bonus Allowance and Depreciation***

*In general*

*Partial business use computations*

*Property acquired and disposed of in same tax year*

***4. Dollar Limitation***

*In general*

*Expensing limit on heavy short-bed trucks and vans*

*Short tax year and period of time in service in placed-in-service year*

***5. Investment Limitation***

*In general*

*Investment limitation of partners and S shareholders*

***6. Taxable Income Limitation***

*In general*

*1. Legislative Changes*

Recent legislation has made the following changes to Code Sec. 179:

- **Dollar and investment limitation.** The Tax Cuts and Jobs Act (P.L. 115-97) increased the Code Sec. 179 dollar limitation to $1,000,000 and the Code Sec. 179 investment limitation is increased to $2.5 million, effective for property placed in service in tax years beginning in 2018 (Code Sec. 179(b)(1) and (2)). These limitations are adjusted for inflation in tax years beginning after 2018 (Code Sec. 179(b)(6)). For 2021, the limitations are $1,050,000 and $2,620,000, and, for 2022, the limitations are $1,080,000 and $2,700,000. See "*4. Dollar Limitation*" and "*5. Investment Limitation.*"

• **Qualified real property.** Effective for property placed in service in tax years beginning after December 31, 2017, the definition of qualified real property which a taxpayer may elect to treat as section 179 property is changed to mean "qualified improvement property" and any of the following improvements made by the taxpayer to nonresidential real property that are placed in service after the nonresidential real property was first placed in service: roofs; heating, ventilation, and air-conditioning property; fire protection and alarm systems; and security systems (Code Sec. 179(e)). Qualified improvement property is generally defined to mean internal improvements to nonresidential real property made by the taxpayer after the nonresidential real property is placed in service. For tax years beginning before 2018 qualified real property consisted of 15-year qualified leasehold improvement property, 15-year qualified retail improvement property, and 15-year qualified restaurant property. These three categories of 15-year property are eliminated, effective for property placed in service after 2017.

The rules for qualified real property were formerly contained in Code Sec. 179(f). Code Sec. 179(f), however, was redesignated as Code Sec. 179(e) by the Tax Technical Corrections Act of 2018 (Division U of P.L. 115-141), effective March 23, 2018. Former Code Sec. 179(e), relating to an increased section 179 deduction for qualified disaster assistance property was stricken as deadwood.

See "*6. Qualified Real Property*" at ¶ 302.

• **Property used in connection with the furnishing of lodging.** Effective for property placed in service in tax years beginning after December 31, 2017, property used predominantly to furnish lodging or predominantly in connection with the furnishing of lodging (e.g., section 1245 property used in connection with residential rental units) qualifies for Code Sec. 179 expensing (Code Sec. 179(d)(1)). See "*3. Excluded Property*" at ¶ 302.

• **Expensing limit on certain vehicles adjusted for inflation**. The $25,000 maximum Code Sec. 179 deduction that may be claimed on SUVS, short-bed trucks, and certain passenger vans that are exempt from the luxury car depreciation caps because they have a GVWR in excess of 6,000 pounds will be adjusted for inflation effective for property placed in service in tax years beginning after 2018 (Code Sec. 179(b)(6)). The inflation-adjusted amount is $25,500 for tax years beginning in 2019, $25,900 for 2020, $26,200 for 2021, and $27,000 for 2022. See ¶ 201.

• **Empowerment Zones.** Empowerment zone designations have been extended through December 31, 2025 (Code Sec. 1391(d)(1), as amended by the Taxpayer Certainty and Tax Relief Act of 2020 (P.L. 116-260)). However, the rule which increases the otherwise applicable expensing limit by an additional $35,000 for property placed in an empowerment zone by an enterprise zone business was not extended and no longer applies to property placed in service after December 31, 2020. See ¶ 304A.

*2. Overview*

*In general.* Taxpayers other than estates, trusts, and certain noncorporate lessors may elect to expense and deduct the cost of qualifying section 179 property placed in service during the tax year rather than treating the cost as a capital expenditure (Code Sec. 179). The election is made on Form 4562. A taxpayer may also make, revoke, or change an election without IRS consent on an amended return filed during the period prescribed for filing an amended return (Code Sec. 179(c)(2); Reg. § 1.179-5). See ¶ 304 for election and revocation procedures.

*Dollar and investment limitations.* The amount which a taxpayer may elect to expense in a tax year is limited to the applicable dollar limitation for the tax year ($1,050,000 for tax years beginning in 2021 and $1,080,000 for 2022) after reduction, if necessary, by the cost of section 179 property placed in service in the tax year in excess of the investment limitation for the tax year ($2,620,000 for tax years beginning in 2021 and $2,700,000 for 2022 (Rev. Proc. 2020-45; Rev. Proc. 2021-45; Code Sec. 179(b)(1)). The reduction in the dollar limitation on account of the investment limitation is not carried back or forward. A taxpayer may not elect to expense an amount in excess of the cost of the section 179 property placed in service during the tax year. A taxpayer may allocate the maximum possible expense election among the section 179 property it purchased during the tax year in any manner desired. A taxpayer may elect to expense less than the maximum amount it is entitled to expense. Generally, a taxpayer will want to expense section 179 property with the longest recovery (depreciation) periods.

The dollar limitation and taxable income limitations apply to each taxpayer and not to each trade or business in which the taxpayer has an interest (Reg. § 1.179-2(a)).

See below, "*4. Dollar Limitation.*"

*Taxable income limitation and carryforwards.* The amount which a taxpayer elects to expense after applying the dollar limitation is deducted in full in the year of election provided that the taxpayer's taxable income from the active conduct of all of its trades and businesses in the year of election is at least equal to the elected amount. If the taxable income is less than the elected amount, the deduction is limited to the taxable income. Thus, the deduction for a tax year may be less than the amount which is elected to be expensed. Any amount that a taxpayer elects to expense and which is disallowed by the taxable income limitation is carried forward (Code Sec. 179(b)(3)).

See below, "*6. Taxable Income Limitation*" and "*7. Carryforwards of Section 179 Deductions.*"

*Basis reduction.* A taxpayer must reduce the depreciable basis of the section 179 property by the amount of the section 179 expense deduction, including any deduction deferred on account of the taxable income limitation (Reg. § 1.179-1(f)(1)). For special rules that apply to partner and partnerships, see *11. Partnerships and S Corporations*, below.

*Expensing limitation for certain suvs, trucks, and vans.* The expense deduction that may be claimed on SUVs, trucks with cargo beds less than six-feet long, and certain vans is limited if the vehicle is exempt from the luxury car depreciation limits, for example, because it has a gross vehicle weight rating in excess of 6,000 pounds (Code Sec. 179(b)(5)). The limitation is adjusted for inflation effective for property placed in service in tax years beginning after 2018. The inflation-adjusted limit is $25,500 for tax years beginning in 2019 (Rev. Proc. 2018-57), $25,900 for 2020 (Rev. Proc. 2019-44), $26,200 for 2021 (Rev. Proc. 2020-45), and $27,000 for 2022 (Rev. Proc. 2021-45). See ¶ 201.

*Recapture upon sale or disposition.* The Code Sec. 179 expense deduction is treated as depreciation for recapture purposes. Thus, gain on a disposition of section 179 property that is section 1245 property is treated as ordinary income to the extent of the Code Sec. 179 expense allowance claimed plus any depreciation claimed. A section 179 expense deduction for qualified real property is subject to recapture as ordinary income under the rules that apply to section 1245 property (Code Sec. 1245(a)(3)(C)).

See below, "*8. Section 179 Recapture Upon Sale or Disposition.*"

*Recapture upon decline in business use.* If business use of section 179 property does not exceed 50 percent during any year of the property's depreciation period, a portion of the amount expensed is recaptured as ordinary income (Code Sec. 179(d)(10); Reg. § 1.179-1(e)). If business use is not at least 50 percent in the tax year that the property is placed in service no section 179 deduction is allowed (the property is not section 179 property). The section 179 expense deduction may not be claimed even if business use increases in a later tax year.

The recapture amount is the difference between the expense claimed and the depreciation that would have been allowed on the expensed amount for prior tax years and the tax year of recapture. However, in the case of a listed property, such as passenger automobile used less than 50 percent for business the Code Sec. 280F recapture rules apply. Recapture is reported on Form 4797.

See below, "*9. Section 179 Recapture Upon Decline in Business Use.*"

*Section 179 property defined.* To qualify as section 179 property, the property must be tangible section 1245 property (new or used), depreciable under the Modified Accelerated Cost Recovery System (MACRS), and acquired by purchase for use in a trade or business (Code Sec. 179(d)). Property used predominantly outside of the United States and property used by tax-exempt organizations (unless the property is used predominantly in connection with an unrelated business income activity) do not qualify as section 179 property (Code Sec. 179(d)(1); Code Sec. 50(b)).

Property not predominantly used for business purposes (i.e., more than 50 percent) in the year it is placed in service does not qualify for expensing.

In tax years beginning before January 1, 2018, property used predominantly to furnish lodging or predominantly in connection with the furnishing of lodging (e.g., section 1245 property used in connection with residential rental units but not hotels and motels) does not qualify for Code Sec. 179 expensing. This rule no longer applies to property placed in service in tax years beginning after 2017 (Code Sec. 179(d)(1)). See "*3. Excluded Property*" at ¶ 302.

A taxpayer may also make an election to treat qualified real property as section 179 property (Code Sec. 179(d)(1)(B)(ii); Code Sec. 179(e)).

Off-the shelf computer software also qualifies as section 179 property (Code Sec. 179(d)(1)).

The definition of section 179 property eligible for expensing is covered in detail beginning at ¶ 302.

*Purchase defined.* Property is acquired by purchase unless it (1) is acquired from certain related persons, (2) is acquired by one member of a controlled group from another member, (3) has a substituted basis in whole or in part, or (4) is acquired from a decedent and has a basis determined under Code Sec. 1014(a) (generally, a fair-market value basis) (Code Sec. 179(d)(2); Reg. § 1.179-4(c)). See ¶ 302.

*Qualified real property.* A taxpayer may elect to treat the cost of qualified real property placed in service in a tax year that begins after 2009 as section 179 property (Code Sec. 179(d)(1)(B)(ii); Code Sec. 179(e); Notice 2013-59). The maximum amount of qualified real property that may be expensed in a tax year beginning in 2010 through 2015 was limited to $250,000. The expensed amount is counted toward the overall $500,000 annual expensing limit for those years. The

$250,000 limitation is eliminated in tax years beginning in 2016 and later (Code Sec. 179(f)(3), stricken by P.L. 114-113).

Effective for property placed in service in tax years beginning after 2017, qualified real property (Code Sec. 179(e)) is defined as:

(1) qualified improvement property (most internal improvements made to nonresidential real property by a taxpayer after the nonresidential real property was placed in service) (Code Sec. 168(e)(6); Reg. § 1.168(b)-1(a)(5)); and

(2) any of the following improvements to nonresidential real property placed in service after the date such property was first placed in service:

- roofs;
- heating, ventilation, and air-conditioning property;
- fire protection and alarm systems; and
- security systems.

In the case of tax years beginning before 2018, qualified real property is defined as:

(1) qualified leasehold improvement property, described in Code Sec. 168(e)(6), prior to amendment by P.L. 115-97 (¶ 126);

(2) qualified restaurant property (i.e., a restaurant building or improvement described in Code Sec. 168(e)(7), prior to amendment by P.L. 115-97 (¶ 110)); and

(3) qualified retail improvement property, described in Code Sec. 168(e)(8), prior to amendment by P.L. 115-97 (¶ 126).

See ¶ 302 for a discussion of qualified real property.

*Married taxpayers.* Married taxpayers filing jointly are treated as one taxpayer for purposes of applying the dollar, investment, and taxable income limitations regardless of which spouse placed the qualifying property in service (Reg. § 1.179-2(b)(5)(i); Reg. § 1.179-2(c)(7)(i)).

Married taxpayers filing separate returns may allocate the dollar limitation ($1,050,000 for tax years beginning in 2021 and $1,080,000 for tax years beginning in 2022) after any reduction by the investment limitation between themselves or, in the absence of an allocation agreement, divide it equally. Married taxpayers filing separate returns aggregate section 179 property for purposes of applying the investment limitation. The taxable income limitation is applied individually to separate filers.

See below, "*10. Married Taxpayers.*"

*Partnerships and S corporations.* The maximum dollar limit ($1,050,000 for tax years beginning in 2021 and $1,080,000 for 2022), investment limitation ($2,620,000 for tax years beginning in 2021 and $2,700,000 for 2022), and taxable income limitation are applied separately at the partnership and partner levels (Reg. § 1.179-2(b)(3)(i) and (4); Reg. § 1.179-2(c)(2)(i) and (c)(3)(i); *D.L. Hayden v Commr*, 112 TC 115, Dec. 53,293 (1999), aff'd CA-7, 2000-1 USTC ¶ 50,219, 204 F3d 772). A similar rule applies to an S corporation and its shareholders.

In applying the investment limitation, the cost of section 179 property placed in service by the partnership is not attributed to any partner (Reg. § 1.179-2(b)(3)). A similar rule applies to S shareholders) (Reg. § 1.179-2(b)(4)).

For purposes of applying the taxable income limitation at the partnership or S corporation level, taxable income (or loss) derived by a partnership or S corporation from the active conduct of a trade or business is computed by aggregating the net income (or loss) from all the trades or businesses actively conducted by the entity during the tax year (Reg. § 1.179-2(c)(1)).

A partner's or S shareholder's taxable income includes net distributable profit or loss from the pass-through entity in which the taxpayer is an active participant (Reg. § 1.179-2(c)(2)(v); IRS Letter Ruling 9126014, March 29, 1991).

Partners and S corporation shareholders are required to reduce the basis of their partnership or S corporation interest by the full amount of an expense deduction allocated to them by the respective entity even if part of the deduction must be carried over because of the partner or S corporation shareholder's taxable income limitation or the deduction is disallowed at the partnership or S shareholder level because of the dollar limitation (Rev. Rul. 89-7, 1989-1 CB 178; Reg. § 1.179-3(h)(1)).

See below, "*11. Partnerships and S Corporations.*"

The partnership or S corporation is required to reduced the basis of its partnership or S corporation property to reflect the amount of section 179 expense elected by the partnership or S corporation except for allocations attributable to partners or shareholders that are estates or trusts. This reduction must be made in the basis of partnership or S corporation property even if dollar or investment limitation prevents a partner in a partnership or a shareholder in an S corporation from deducting all or a portion of the amount of the section 179 expense allocated by the partnership or S corporation (Reg. § 1.179-1(f)(2)).

A partner or S corporation shareholder that is a trust or estate may not deduct its allocable share of the section 179 expense elected by the partnership or S corporation. The partnership's or S corporation's basis in section 179 property is not reduced to reflect any portion of the section 179 expense that is allocable to the trust or estate. The partnership or S corporation may claim a depreciation deduction with respect to any depreciable basis resulting from the trust or estate's inability to claim its allocable portion of the section 179 expense (Reg. § 1.179-1(f)(3)).

*Controlled groups.* Members of a controlled group on December 31 are treated as a single taxpayer for purposes of the dollar, investment, and taxable income limitation even if a consolidated return is not filed (Code Sec. 179(d)(9)). The allowable expense deduction may be allocated among members in any manner. However, the amount allocated to any member may not exceed the cost of section 179 property actually purchased and placed in service during the tax year by the member (Reg. § 1.179-2(b)(7)). See below, "*12. Controlled Groups.*"

*Noncorporate lessors.* A lessor, other than a corporation, may not claim the section 179 deduction on leased property unless the property was manufactured or produced by the lessor, or the term of the lease is less than one-half of the property's class life (¶ 180) and for the 12-month period following the date that the leased property is transferred to the lessee, the total Code Sec. 162 business deductions allowed to the lessor for the property exceed 15 percent of the rental income produced by the property (Code Sec. 179(d)(5); Reg. § 1.179-1(i)(2)). See below, "*13. Noncorporate Lessors.*"

*Exemption from UNICAP and section 263 capitalization.* The section 179 deduction is an indirect cost that is not required to be capitalized under the Code Sec. 263A uniform capitalization (UNICAP) rules (Reg.§ 1.179-1(j); Reg. § 1.263A-1(e)(3)(iii)). Amounts expensed under Code Sec. 179 are also not capitalized under Code Sec. 263 (Code Sec. 263(a)(1)(g); Reg. § 1.179-1(j).

*Interaction with alternative minimum tax and general business credit.* The section 179 deduction is allowed for both regular tax and the alternative minimum tax (See the Senate Finance Committee Report to Accompany H.R. 3838, Tax Reform Act of 1986, S. Rep. No. 99-313, May 29, 1985, p. 522. See also the Instructions for Form 6251, Alternative Minimum Tax - Individuals (2018), p. 6.) No general business credit under section 38 is allowed with respect to any amount for which a deduction is allowed under section 179 (Code Sec. 179(d)(9); Reg.§ 1.179-1(g)).

*Earnings and profits computation.* If a corporation makes an election under section 179 to deduct expenditures, the full amount of the deduction does not reduce earnings and profits. Rather, the expenditures that are deducted under section 179 reduce corporate earnings and profits ratably over a five-year period (Code Sec. 312(k)(3)(B)).

*Empowerment zones and renewal communities.* In tax years beginning before 2021, an enterprise zone business (as defined in Code Sec. 1397C) located within a government-designated empowerment zone (as defined in Code Sec. 1391(b)(2)) may increase the applicable annual dollar limitation ($1,040,00 for tax years beginning in 2020) by the lesser of $35,000 or the cost of Sec. 179 property that is qualified zone property (as defined in Code Sec. 1397D) and is placed in service before January 1, 2021 (Code Sec. 1397A). For tax years beginning after 2020, the increased $35,000 allowance is not available ( Code Secs. 1397A(c)). See ¶ 304A.

Rules that apply to an enterprise zone business also applied to a renewal community business (as defined in Code Sec. 1400G) that acquired qualified renewal property (as defined in Code Sec. 1400J(b)) by purchase and placed the property in service in a renewal community (as defined in Code Sec. 1400E(a)(1)) (Code Sec. 1400J). The property had to be acquired after December 31, 2001 and before January 1, 2010 (Code Sec. 1400J(b)(1)(A)), or, if earlier, before the day after the date that the designation of renewal community status was terminated (Code Sec. 1400E(b)(3)). See ¶ 304A.

*Expired provisions for certain disaster area.* Enhanced section 179 deductions for the New York Liberty Zone (¶ 305), Gulf Opportunity Zone (¶ 306), Kansas Disaster Area (¶ 306A), and Federally Declared Disaster Areas (¶ 306B) have expired. Recapture rules continue to apply to property on which an enhanced deduction was claimed unless the recovery period for the property has expired.

*De minimis expensing rule under repair regs.* A taxpayer may also be able to elect to write-off the acquisition or production cost of units of property, as well as materials and supplies which would otherwise be deductible in the tax year used or consumed, under a de minimis safe harbor established by the repair regulations (Reg. § 1.263(a)-1(f)). An annual election statement is required. See ¶ 307 for a discussion of the de minimis expensing rule.

*Section 179 tax planning.* See ¶ 487 for Code Sec. 179 tax planning strategies.

### *3. Section 179 Interaction With Bonus Allowance and Depreciation*

*In general.* The depreciable basis of a property is reduced by the amount of the property's cost which is elected to be expensed. No depreciation deduction may be claimed for this amount.

The amount of the Code Sec. 179 expense elected for a property reduces the basis before the Code Sec. 168(k) bonus depreciation deduction is computed on the property. See ¶ 127D. The table percentages are then applied.

***Example (1):*** A taxpayer purchases new 5-year property that qualifies for 50 percent bonus depreciation. The machine cost $100 and the taxpayer elected to expense $10. Bonus depreciation is $45 ($90 × 50%). First-year depreciation is $9 (($100 – $10 – $45) × 20% first-year table percentage). Second year depreciation is $14 (($100 – $10 – $45) × 32% second-year table percentage).

The basis of an expensed property for purposes of computing depreciation is reduced by the full amount elected to be expensed even if a portion of the elected amount is disallowed under the taxable income limitation and must be carried forward. If the property is sold, disposed of, or transferred in a nonrecognition transaction (including transfers at death) before the carryforward can be deducted, the basis of the property is increased by the carryforward attributable to the property that was not deducted (Reg. § 1.179-3(f)(1)).

See *"7. Carryforwards of Section 179 Deductions."*

*Partial business use computations.* If there is partial business use during any year of the recovery period, the original cost unreduced by the section 179 expense allowance and bonus deduction is multiplied by the business use percentage for the tax year and then reduced (but not below zero) by the section 179 allowance and bonus depreciation claimed or previously claimed, if any. The table percentage is then applied to this amount (Reg. § 1.179-1(d); IRS Form 4562 Instructions for line 19 column (c) and line 26 column (e)).

> ***Example (2):*** Assume that business use in the first example is 80 percent in the placed in service tax year. The starting basis of the asset is $80 ($100 × 80%). If the taxpayer claims a $10 expense deduction (up to $80 may be claimed) the bonus deduction is $35 (($80 − $10) × 50%) and first-year depreciation using the table percentages is $7 (($100 × 80% – $10 – $35) × 20% first-year table percentage)).

> ***Example (3):*** Assume that business use in the preceding example is 80% in Year 3 and 10% in Year 4. Year 3 depreciation is $6.72 (($100 × 80% – $10 – $35) × 19.2%). Year 4 depreciation is $0 (($100 × 10% – $10 – $35) × 11.52%).

See ¶ 180, "*Partial business use computation*" for detailed discussion of partial business use computations using the percentage tables and ¶ 179, "*Computing MACRS deductions without tables when there is partial business use.*"

If the percentage of business use in a tax year after the recovery period ends exceeds the average percentage of business use during the recovery period a taxpayer may be entitled to claim additional depreciation deductions (Code Sec. 168(i)(5); ACRS Proposed Reg. § 1.168-2(j)(2)). This rule does not apply to listed property (¶ 208) such as a car (Reg. § 1.280F-4T(a)). See ¶ 169A for details.

*Property acquired and disposed of in same tax year.* The section 179 expense allowance may not be claimed on property acquired and sold in the same tax year because such property is not depreciable under MACRS and, therefore, is not section 179 property. See ¶ 487, *"Self-employment tax savings"*.

*4. Dollar Limitation*

The following chart summarizes the maximum allowable Code Sec. 179 deduction for tax years since 1982 (Code Sec. 179(b)(1); Reg. § 1.179-2(b)(1)).

| *Maximum expense deduction for tax years beginning in:* | |
|---|---|
| 1982–1986 | $5,000 |
| 1987–1992 | $10,000 |
| 1993–1996 | $17,500 |
| 1997 | $18,000 |
| 1998 | $18,500 |
| 1999 | $19,000 |
| 2000 | $20,000 |
| 2001 or 2002 | $24,000 |
| 2003 | $100,000 |
| 2004 | $102,000 |
| 2005 | $105,000 |
| 2006 | $108,000 |

| *Maximum expense deduction for tax years beginning in:* | |
|---|---|
| 2007 | $125,000 |
| 2008 and 2009 | $250,000 |
| 2010 - 2015 | $500,000 |
| 2016 (Rev. Proc. 2016-14) | $500,000 |
| 2017 (Rev. Proc. 2016-55) | $510,000 |
| 2018 (Code Sec. 179(b)) | $1,000,000 |
| 2019 (Rev. Proc. 2018-57) | $1,020,000 |
| 2020 (Rev. Proc. 2019-44) | $1,040,000 |
| 2021 (Rev. Proc. 2020-45) | $1,050,000 |
| 2022 (Rev. Proc. 2021-45) | $1,080,000 |
| 2023 and thereafter | $1,080,000 to be adjusted annually for inflation |

*Expensing limit on heavy short-bed trucks and vans.* The expense deduction that may be claimed on SUVs, trucks with cargo beds less than six-feet long, and certain vans is limited to $26,200 for tax years beginning in 2021 and $27,000 for tax years beginning in 2022 if the vehicle is exempt from the luxury car depreciation limits (Code Sec. 179(b)(5)). See ¶ 201.

*Short tax year and period of time in service in placed-in-service year.* A taxpayer with a short tax year is entitled to claim the full maximum deduction (subject to the investment and taxable income limitations described below). Similarly, the period of time during the tax year in which the section 179 was in service is not relevant. For example, the full section 179 deduction may be claimed even if the section 179 property was placed in service on December 31, by a calendar-year taxpayer (Reg. § 1.179-1(c)(1)).

*5. Investment Limitation*

*In general.* The following chart summarizes the Code Sec. 179 investment limitation for tax years since 1987 (Code Sec. 179(b)(2)).

| *Maximum investment limitation for tax years beginning in:* | |
|---|---|
| 1987–2002 | $200,000 |
| 2003 | $400,000 |
| 2004 | $410,000 |
| 2005 | $420,000 |
| 2006 | $430,000 |
| 2007 | $500,000 |
| 2008 and 2009 | $800,000 |
| 2010 - 2015 | $2,000,000 |
| 2016 (Rev. Proc. 2016-14) | $2,010,000 |
| 2017 (Rev. Proc. 2016-55) | $2,030,000 |
| 2018 (Code Sec. 179(b)) | $2,500,000 |
| 2019 (Rev. Proc. 2018-57) | $2,550,000 |
| 2020 (Rev. Proc. 2019-44) | $2,590,000 |
| 2021 (Rev. Proc. 2020-45) | $2,620,000 |
| 2022 (Rev. Proc. 2021-45) | $2,700,000 |
| 2023 and thereafter | $2,700,000 to be adjusted annually for inflation |

The maximum annual dollar limitation for the tax year is reduced (but not below zero) by the excess of the cost of qualified Sec. 179 property placed in service during the tax year over the investment limitation above that applies to the tax year. Any amount of the dollar limitation ($1,050,000 for tax years beginning in 2021 and $1,080,000 for 2022) disallowed under this rule is lost and may not be carried over to another tax year.

> ***Example (4):*** A taxpayer places $2,900,000 of section 179 property in service in a tax year beginning in 2021. The maximum dollar limitation for 2021 ($1,050,000) must be reduced by $280,000 ($2,900,000 – $2,620,000) to $770,000. The $280,000 disallowed is not carried forward for deduction in later tax years.

| *Tax year beginning in:* | *Phaseout begins:* | *Phaseout ends:* |
|---|---|---|
| 2022 | $2,700,000 | $3,780,000 |
| 2021 | $2,620,000 | $3,670,000 |
| 2020 | $2,590,000 | $3,630,000 |
| 2019 | $2,550,000 | $3,570,000 |
| 2018 | $2,500,000 | $3,500,000 |
| 2017 | $2,030,000 | $2,540,000 |
| 2016 | $2,010,000 | $2,510,000 |
| 2010 - 2015 | $2,000,000 | $2,500,000 |

*Effect of qualified real property election on investment limitation.* If a taxpayer elects to treat qualified real property as section 179 property, the cost of all qualified real property is taken into account in determining the investment limitation (Code Sec. 179(f)(1), prior to amendment byP.L. 115-97; Section 3.01 of Rev. Proc. 2017-33; Code Sec. 179(d)(1)(B)(ii)). See ¶ 302, "*6. Qualified Real Property.*"

*Investment limitation of partners and S shareholders.* In applying the investment limitation, the cost of section 179 property placed in service by the partnership (or LLC treated as partnership) is not attributed to any partner (or LLC member) (Reg. § 1.179-2(b)(3)). A similar rule applies to S shareholders (Reg. § 1.179-2(b)(4)).

> ***Example (5):*** ABC partnership places $500,000 of section 179 property in service in 2021. No other section 179 property is placed in service. ABC elects to expense $500,000. Assume ABC's taxable income exceeds $500,000 and ABC is not required to make any reduction on account of the investment limitation. ABC passes $250,000 of the deduction through to partner John. In applying the investment limitation at the partner level, John is not considered to have purchased any of the property acquired by ABC.

### *6. Taxable Income Limitation*

*In general.* The expense deduction may not exceed the total amount of taxable income that is derived from the active conduct of all of the trades or businesses that a taxpayer engaged in during the tax year. This rule is applied after application of the investment limitation (Code Sec. 179(b)(3); Reg. § 1.179-2(c)). As explained below, amounts disallowed under the taxable income limitation are carried forward.

Taxable income is computed without regard to the expense deduction, any net operating loss carryback or carryforward, the deduction against gross income for one-half of self-employment tax liability for the self-employed, and deductions suspended under any Code provision (such as the limitation on a partner's share of partnership loss under Code Sec. 704(d)) (Reg. § 1.179-2(c)(1)). However, income items derived from the active conduct of a trade or business include Code Sec. 1231 gains or losses and interest from working capital of a trade or business.

Taxable income attributable to services performed by an employee is considered taxable income from the active conduct of a trade or business (Reg. § 1.179-2(c)(6)(iv)). Thus, wages, salaries, tips, and other compensation (not reduced by unreimbursed employee business expenses) derived as an employee are included in taxable income.

Computation of the aggregate amount of taxable income derived from the active conduct of any trade or business during the tax year includes the following: wages and salaries derived as an employee; net profit or loss from a sole proprietorship in which the taxpayer's involvement constitutes the active conduct of a trade or business; net profit or loss from the active conduct of rental real estate activities; and net distributable profit or loss from pass through entities (such as a partnership or S corporation) in which the taxpayer is an active participant (IRS Letter Ruling 9126014, March 29, 1991).

*Taxable income of S corporations and partnerships.* The taxable income (or loss) derived by a partnership or S corporation from the active conduct of a trade or business is computed by aggregating the net income (or loss) from all the trades or businesses actively conducted by the entity during the tax year (Reg. § 1.179-2(c) (2) (iv); Reg.§ 1.179-2(c) (3) (ii)).

Partnership net income is generally defined for this purpose as the aggregate amount of the partnership items of income and expense described in Code Sec. 702(a), other than credits, tax-exempt income, the section 179 expense deduction, and guaranteed payments under Code Sec. 707(c) (Reg. § 1.179-2(c) (2) (iv)).

S corporation net income is generally defined for this purpose as the aggregate amount of the S corporation items of income and expense described in Code Sec. 1366(a) (i.e., pass-thru items), other than credits, tax-exempt income, the section 179 expense deduction, and deductions for compensation paid to an S corporations shareholder-employees (Reg.§ 1.179-2(c) (3) (ii); Reg. § 1.1366-1).

The taxable income limitation is applied separately at the partner and partnership level and separately at the S shareholder and S corporation level, as explained below under the heading "*Partnerships and S corporations*" (Reg. § 1.179-2(c) (2) (i) and Reg. § 1.179-2(c) (3) (i)).

A taxpayer who is a partner in a partnership and is engaged in the active conduct of at least one of the partnership's trades or businesses includes as taxable income for purposes of the taxable income limitation the amount of the taxpayer's allocable share of taxable income (as defined above for purposes of a partnership) derived from the active conduct by the partnership of all of its trades or businesses (Reg. § 1.179-2(c) (2) (v)). A similar rule applies to S shareholders (Reg. § 1.179-2(c) (3) (iii)).

A partner's distributive share of a partnership's taxable income for a partnership's tax year is taken into account in the partnership's tax year that ends with or within the partner's tax year in accordance with Code Sec. 706 and the regulations thereunder (Reg. § 1.179-3(c) (2) (ii)). The same rule applies to an S corporation and its shareholders (Reg. § 1.179-3(c) (3) (i)).

> ***Example (5A):*** AB partnership has a tax year ending January 31, 2021. A, a partner of AB, has a tax year ending December 31. AB has taxable income from the active conduct of its trade or business of $100,000, $90,000 of which was earned during 2020. A includes A's entire share of partnership taxable income in computing A's taxable income limitation for A's tax year ending December 31, 2021.

A partnership or S corporation may not allocate an expense deduction deferred and carried forward at the partnership or S corporation level on account of the taxable income limitation until a tax year in which the partnership or S corporation has sufficient taxable income to allow use of the carryforward amount (Reg. § 1.179-3(g)).

*Taxable income of C corporations.* C corporation taxable income is generally defined for purposes of the taxable income limitation as the aggregate amount of taxable income before the section 179 expense deduction, net operating loss deduction and special deductions, (excluding items of income or deduction that were not derived from a trade or business actively conducted by the corporation during the tax year) (Reg. § 1.179-2(c)(4)).

*Taxable income of husband and wife.* The taxable income limitation is applied to a husband and wife who file a joint return by aggregating the taxable income of each spouse (Reg. § 1.179-2(c)(7)). Even though an individual has a loss from a sole proprietorship, a Sec. 179 expense deduction may be claimed for property place in service in that business if a joint return is filed and there is sufficient taxable income from all combined active trades or businesses of the couple.

*Taxable income computation when another deduction is based on taxable income.* If the amount of a deduction other than the section 179 allowance is determined by reference to taxable income (e.g., the charitable contribution deduction) the regulations provide an ordering rule for purposes of determining the taxable income used to compute the section 179 allowance and the taxable income used to compute the other deduction. First, compute taxable income without regard to the section 179 allowance or the other deduction (preliminary taxable income). Next, the other deduction is determined after reducing preliminary taxable income by the amount of the section 179 deduction that would be allowed if the other deduction did not reduce preliminary taxable income. The other deduction so computed then reduces preliminary taxable income for purposes of determining the actual section 179 allowance that may be claimed under the taxable income limitation. The other deduction is then computed by reducing the preliminary taxable income as reduced by the actual section 179 expense deduction allowed. The other deduction so computed is claimed on the tax return (Reg. § 1.179-2(c)(5)(i)).

> ***Example (6):*** X corporation elects to expense $10,000 of the cost of qualifying property placed in service in the current tax year. X also makes a charitable contribution of $5,000. X's taxable income is $11,000 without regard to the section 179 and charitable contribution deductions. X's charitable contribution deduction is limited to 10 percent of its taxable income (Code Sec. 170(b)(2)). Under the above ordering rule, X first computes a hypothetical contribution deduction by reducing its $11,000 preliminary taxable income by the section 179 allowance that could be claimed against the preliminary taxable income ($11,000 – $10,000 expense deduction = $1,000). The hypothetical charitable contribution deduction is $100 (10% of $1,000). The taxable income limitation for purposes of determining the allowable expense deduction is $10,900 ($11,000 – $100 hypothetical contribution deduction). Therefore, X's actual expense deduction is $10,000 for all purposes of the Code, including computation of the actual contribution deduction. The actual charitable contribution deduction, therefore, is $100 (10% of ($11,000 – $10,000) expense deduction) (Reg. § 1.179-2(c)(v)(ii)).

### *7. Carryforwards of Section 179 Deductions*

*In general.* The amount disallowed as a result of the taxable income limitation is carried forward to succeeding tax years (Code Sec. 179(b)(3); Reg. § 1.179-3). In a carryforward year, the taxpayer first determines, without regard to any carryforward, the maximum possible section 179 deduction (maximum limitation) taking into account the dollar, investment limitation, and taxable income limitation. The taxpayer then elects to expense section 179 property placed in service in the carryforward year subject to the maximum limitation. If the taxpayer elects to expense less than the maximum limitation, then the unused carryfoward must be applied against the amount of the unused maximum limitation (Reg. § 1.179-3(b)).

> ***Example (7):*** ABC has a $400,000 section 179 carryforward from 2020. In 2021 ABC places $900,000 of section 179 property in service. The maximum dollar amount for 2021 is $1,050,000. This amount is not reduced on account of the investment limitation since ABC has not placed more than $2,620,000 of section 179 property in service in 2021. If ABC's taxable income from the conduct of active trades and businesses for 2021

is at least $1,050,000, the maximum limitation is $1,050,000. If an election is made to expense the full $900,000 of section 179 property placed in service in 2021, ABC must claim an additional $150,000 section 179 carrryforward expense leaving a $250,000 ($400,000 – $150,000) unused carryforward. If ABC only elected to expense $700,000 of the $900,000 of section 179 property placed in service in 2021, then ABC must claim an additional $350,000 section 179 carryforward expense from 2020 ($700,000 + $350,000 = $1,050,000 maximum limitation).

*Ordering rule for carryforwards.* Carryforwards are considered used from the earliest year in which a carryforward arose. To the extent a carryforward is attributable to multiple properties placed in service in the same tax year, a taxpayer may select the properties and apportionment of cost for purposes of determining the source of the carryforward. This selection, however, must be recorded on the taxpayer's books and records in the tax year the property was placed in service and followed consistently in subsequent tax years. If no selection is made the carryover is apportioned "*equally*" among the items of section 179 property that were expensed in the tax year that carryforward arose. For this purpose, allocations of a section 179 expense from a partnership or S corporation are treated as a single item of section 179 property (Reg. § 1.179-3(e)).

The use of the word "equally" by the regulations appears to mean that an equal amount of the carryover is attributed to each separate property for which an expense election was made in the tax year to which the carryforward is attributed. Commentators, however, have noted that this interpretation is problematic in situations where the expensed cost of an item of section 179 property is less than the amount of carryforward allocated to that property. To avoid this problem, taxpayers should keep records that identify the property to which the carryforward is attributed.

***Example (8):*** A taxpayer has a $500 carryforward attributable to three items of property place in service in 2021. Property A cost $50 and properties B and C cost $1,000 each. The full cost of these properties were expensed. No records for purposes of apportioning carryforwards attributable to 2021 were kept. An even apportionment of the $500 carryforward would require that $50 of the carryforward first be attributed to A, B, and C. The remaining $350 of carryforward would be divided evenly between B and C ($175 to each property).

*Basis adjustment.* The basis of an expensed property for purposes of computing depreciation is reduced by the full amount elected to be expensed even if a portion of the elected amount is disallowed under the taxable income limitation and must be carried forward. If the property is sold, disposed of, or transferred in a nonrecognition transaction (including transfers at death) before the carryforward can be deducted, the basis of the property is increased immediately before the transfer by the carryforward attributable to the property that was not deducted. The unused carryforward may not be deducted by the transferor or transferee (Reg. § 1.179-3(f)(1)).

***Example (9):*** ABC purchases an item of section 179 property in 2020 for $100,000 and elects to expense the entire amount. Assume no amount may be deducted on account of the taxable income limitation and the entire $100,000 is a carryforward. In 2021 ABC sells the property for $200,000. No depreciation is claimed in 2021 because the basis of the property was $0 ($100,000 cost – $100,000 expense carryforward) as of 2020. For purposes of determining gain in 2021, however, ABC's basis is increased by the disallowed $100,000 carryforward. ABC's gain in 2021, therefore, is $100,000 ($200,000 received from the sale – $100,000 basis attributable to unused carryforward). None of this gain is subject to section 1245 recapture as no section 179 deductions or depreciation deductions were actually claimed.

*8. Section 179 Recapture Upon Sale or Disposition*

*In general.* The section 179 deduction is treated like a depreciation deduction, and, therefore is subject to the section 1245 recapture rules that apply upon the disposition of a depreciable property (Code Sec. 1245(a)(2)(C)). A separate recapture rule applies if business use falls to 50 percent or less. This recapture rule is discussed at #9 below.

Under the section 1245 recapture rules, gain on the disposition of property on which a Code Sec. 179 expense deduction was claimed is generally recaptured as ordinary income to the extent of the regular depreciation deductions (including bonus depreciation) and the amount expensed under section 179. This recapture rule has priority over the recapture rule discussed at #9 below for 50 percent or less business use (Reg. § 1.179-1(e)(3)).

The Code Sec. 1245 recapture rules apply not only to sales but to other types of dispositions including like-kind exchanges and involuntary conversions.

Unused section 179 carryforwards are not subject to recapture. Unused carryforwards are added to the basis of the property immediately prior to the sale or disposition of the property of the property or in a transfer of section 179 property in a transaction in which gain or loss is not recognized in whole or in part, including transfers at death (Reg. § 1.179-3(f)).

Generally only section 1245 property qualifies for expensing under Code Sec. 179. However, "qualified real property," placed in service in tax years that begin after 2009 also qualifies for expensing under section 179 even though such property is section 1250 property. Disposition of qualified real property on which the section 179 expense was claimed will trigger section 179 recapture under the section 1245 recapture rules (Code Sec. 1245(a)(3)(c)) (e.g., the 179 deduction is recaptured to the extent of gain if the entire property was expensed). However, bonus depreciation claimed on qualified real property is considered an accelerated deduction which is subject to recapture under the section 1250 recapture rules to the extent in excess of straight-line depreciation that could have been claimed on the bonus deduction through the recapture year (Reg. § 1.168(k)-1(f)(3)). See ¶ 302 for recaptures rules that apply to qualified real property. These rules require an allocation of gain between the portion of a qualified real property that is expensed and the portion that is depreciated if the entire cost of the property is not expensed.

See ¶ 160 and ¶ 488 for additional discussion of the 179 recapture rules that apply when section 179 property is sold or disposed of.

*9. Section 179 Recapture Upon Decline in Business Use*

*In general.* A portion of the Code Sec. 179 expense deduction is recaptured as ordinary income in any tax year of any asset's recovery period that business use fails to exceed 50 percent (Code Sec. 179(d)(10); Reg. § 1.179-1(e)). For listed property (defined at ¶ 208), such as a car, the applicable recapture rule is provided in Code Sec. 280F(b)(2) and takes precedence over the recapture rule discussed here (Reg. § 1.179-1(d)(3); Code Sec. 280F(d)(1)). The recapture rule for listed property is discussed at ¶ 210, "*MACRS/Section 179 Listed Property Recapture.*"

The recapture amount included in ordinary income is the difference between the Code Sec. 179 expense allowance claimed and the depreciation (including Code Sec. 168(k) bonus depreciation if applicable (see *Example 5*, below)) that would have been allowed on the Code Sec. 179 amount for prior tax years and the tax year of recapture (Reg. § 1.179-1(e)).

The recaptured amount increases the basis of the property (Reg. § 1.179-1(e)(3)).

The Code Sec. 179 expense subject to recapture does not include any amount not allowed as a deduction because of the dollar limitation or the investment limitation. A basis increase is allowed in the recapture year for unused deductions remaining deferred under the investment limitation. See *"Treatment of unused section 179 expense carryforwards upon decline in business use"* below.

In the case of an individual who does not itemize deductions in the tax year of recapture, the depreciation that would have been allowed in the tax year of recapture is determined by treating property used in the production of income (other than rents or royalties) as property used for personal purposes.

This recapture rule does not apply in a tax year in which Code Sec. 1245(a) applies to a disposition of the property (i.e., the property is disposed of in a transaction, such as a sale, and the section 179 allowance is subject to recapture as ordinary income under section 1245(a) (Reg. § 1.179-1(e) (3))). This recapture rules does apply if a taxpayer disposed of a property in a disposition to which Code Sec. 1245(a) does not apply (Reg. § 1.179-1(e) (2)).

A change from trade or business use to production of income use is treated as a change to personal use for purposes of the section 179 recapture rules and can trigger recapture (Reg. § 1.179-1(e) (2)).

The basis of the property is increased by any amount recaptured on account of a decline in business use (Reg. § 1.179-1(e) (3)). See "*Basis add-back*," below.

The Code Sec. 179 expense deduction on non-listed property is recaptured as ordinary income in the tax year during the recovery period that business use fails to exceed 50 percent.

The recapture amount is computed in Part IV of Form 4797. Any amount of the section 179 deduction recaptured by reason of a decline in business use to 50 percent or less is included on Schedule C in the case of a sole proprietor or Schedule F in the case of a farmer. The recaptured amount, accordingly, increases self-employment income. Although section 1245 recapture is not subject to self-employment tax (Code Sec. 1402(a) (3) (C)), an amount of the section 179 deduction recaptured upon a decline in business use is not treated as a section 1245 recapture amount since there has been no disposition as required by Code Sec. 1245(a) (1).

Although Code Sec. 179(d) (10) provides that the IRS shall issue regulations to provide for recapture with respect to any property which is not used predominantly in a trade or business at *any* time, Reg. § 1.179-1(e) (1) only requires recapture if the predominant business use test is not met during an asset's recovery (i.e., depreciation) period (e.g., GDS recovery period unless an election was made to depreciate the asset under the MACRS alternative depreciation period (ADS) which generally provides for a longer recovery period than GDS). Note that when an asset is disposed of through a sale or otherwise, the section 179 deduction is recaptured in full to the extent of gain along with other depreciation deductions.

The IRS provides no examples in its regulations, Publication 946, or elsewhere on how to compute MACRS depreciation in and after the section 179 recapture year. Following the tax year of recapture, MACRS deductions are computed as if the 179 election was not made (Reg. § 1.179-1(e) (1)).

***Example (10):*** Sam Jones bought an item of 7-year MACRS property (not a listed property) in 2018 that cost $22,000. He expensed $10,000 of the cost and used the property in his trade or business (100% business use) and claimed no bonus deduction. In 2021, he converted the property to Code Sec. 212 production of income use. This triggers the recapture of the Code Sec. 179 expense allowance.

To determine the recapture amount, Sam must subtract from the expense allowance claimed ($10,000), the amount of depreciation that could have been claimed on the amount expensed during 2018, 2019, 2020, and 2021.

| | | |
|---|---|---|
| Section 179 deduction claimed (2018) | | $10,000 |
| Allowable depreciation deduction on $10,000 expensed amount: | | |
| 2018 = $10,000 × 14.29% | $1,429 | |
| 2019 = $10,000 × 24.49% | 2,449 | |
| 2020 = $10,000 × 17.49% | 1,749 | |
| 2021 = $10,000 × 12.49% | 1,249 | 6,876 |
| 2021 recapture amount | | $3,124 |

The depreciation deductions for the years 2018 through 2021 are computed on $12,000 (the $22,000 cost of the property as reduced by the $10,000 expense deduction) using the table percentages for 7-year property.

| | |
|---|---|
| MACRS deductions through recapture year: | |
| 2018 = $12,000 × 14.29% | $1,715 |
| 2019 = $12,000 × 24.49% | 2,939 |
| 2020 = $12,000 × 17.49% | 2,098 |
| 2021 = $12,000 × 12.49% | $1,499 |

Beginning in 2022, depreciation is computed as if the 179 election had not been made. Thus, the table percentages are applied to the original $22,000 cost. For example, 2022 depreciation is $1,964 ($22,000 × 8.93% (5th year table percentage)); 2023 depreciation is $1,962 ($22,000 × 8.92% (6th year table percentage)); 2024 depreciation is $1,964 ($22,000 × 8.93% (7th year table percentage)); and 2025 depreciation is $980 ($22,000 × 4.46% (8th year table percentage)). The sum of all depreciation deductions claimed during the 7-year recovery period (which is spread over 8 tax years) is equal to the $22,000 purchase price ($6,876 depreciation allowed on expensed amount + ($1,715 + $2,939 + $2,098 + $1,499 depreciation claimed on unexpensed $12,000 amount in 2018 - 2021) + $1,964 + $1,962 + $1,964 + $980 depreciation on $22,000 claimed in 2022 through 2025)). See ¶ 179 for examples of computations without tables.

***Example (11):*** Donald Reed purchased 5-year property (not a listed-property) in April 2019 for $22,000. He expensed $10,000. No bonus deduction was claimed. In 2021, business use declined to 40%.

The recapture amount is computed as follows:

| | | |
|---|---|---|
| Section 179 deduction claimed (2019) | | $10,000 |
| Allowable depreciation deduction on $10,000 expensed amount: | | |
| 2019 = $10,000 × 20% | $2,000 | |
| 2020 = $10,000 × 32% | 3,200 | |
| 2021 = $10,000 × 40% × 19.2% | 768 | 5,968 |
| 2021 recapture amount | | $4,032 |

| | |
|---|---|
| MACRS deductions through recapture year: | |
| 2019 = $12,000 × 20% | $2,400 |
| 2020 = $12,000 × 32% | 3,840 |
| 2021 = $12,000 ×40% × 19.2% | 922 |

Beginning in 2022, depreciation is computed as if the section 179 allowance had not been claimed. Assuming business use continues at 40%, 2022 depreciation is $1,014 ($22,000 ×40% ×11.52% (fourth year table percentage)).

***Example (12):*** Assume the same facts as in the preceding example except that the property was converted to 100% personal use as of January 1, 2021. In this case, $4,800 ($10,000 – $2,000 – $3,200) is recaptured in 2021. No depreciation is allowed in 2021 or thereafter assuming that the asset continues to be used only for personal purposes.

*Treatment of unused section 179 expense carryforwards upon decline in business use.* The amount of an unused section 179 carryforward is not subject to recapture upon a decline in business use because no benefit was derived from the carryforward. The taxpayer makes the recapture computation as if the carryforward amount was never expensed (Reg. § 1.179-3(f)(1) and (2)). Although the regulations do not appear to specifically address the issue, the unused carryforward should be added to the basis of the property. Depreciation is not allowed on the unused carryforward until the tax year following the tax year in which the business use falls to 50 percent or below. Reg. § 1.179-1(e)(1) states: "For taxable years *following* the year of recapture, the taxpayer's deductions under Code Sec. 168(a) shall be determined as if no section 179 election with respect to the property had been made." Since the addition to basis is a mid-stream basis adjustment, the taxpayer must cease to use the depreciation tables (if they are being used) and compute remaining depreciation without table percentages. This allows the entire basis to be recovered during the remainder of the regular recovery period. If the tables are not being used, the recapture amount and carryforward are simply added to the basis. See ¶ 179, *Computing MACRS depreciation when there is a basis adjustment such as a casualty loss.*

*Interaction of bonus depreciation with section 179 recapture.* The bonus deduction that would have been allowed on the expensed amount should be taken into account in computing the section 179 recapture upon a decline in business use to 50 percent or less unless an election out of bonus depreciation was made in the year the asset was placed in service. If Gulf Zone bonus depreciation (¶ 127F), Kansas Disaster Area bonus depreciation (¶ 127G), or Disaster Area Assistance property (¶ 127H) was claimed the bonus depreciation is also subject to recapture under the rule unique to these provisions that requires bonus depreciation recapture if business use within the zone or area drops to less than 80 percent (i.e. the property ceases to be qualified GO Zone property, qualified Kansas Disaster Assistance property, or qualified Disaster Area Assistance property). A decline in business use does not trigger recapture of the Code Sec. 168(k) bonus allowance (¶ 127D) unless the decline is to 50 percent or less and the property is a listed property such as a car (Code Sec. 168(k)(2)(F)(ii)). For section 179 and bonus depreciation recapture rules that apply to listed property, see ¶ 210.

***Example (13):*** A calendar-year taxpayer places 5-year property (not a listed property) costing $150,000 in service on August 1, 2017, and uses it 100% for business purposes. She expenses $100,000 of the cost and claims a bonus depreciation deduction under Code Sec. 168(k) (¶ 127D) of $25,000 (($150,000 - $100,000) × 50%). In 2020, business use drops to 40%. The recapture amount is the difference between the $100,000 expensed and the depreciation (including bonus depreciation) that could have been claimed on that amount during 2017 through 2020. Bonus depreciation for 2017 on the expensed amount would have been $50,000 ($100,000 × 50%). 2017 regular depreciation would have been $10,000 (($100,000 – $50,000 bonus) × 20% first-year table percentage). 2018 depreciation would have been $16,000 ($100,000 - $50,000 bonus × 32% second-year table percentage). 2019 depreciation would have been $9,600 ($100,000 - $50,000 bonus × 19.2% third-year table percentage). 2020 depreciation would have been $0 (($100,000 × 40% BUP) - $50,000) × 11.52% fourth-year table percentage). The 2020 recapture amount is $14,400 ($100,000 – $50,000 – $10,000 – $16,000 – $9,600 – $0).

If, in the preceding example, the asset had cost $100,000 and the entire amount had been expensed, depreciation recapture should be computed by taking bonus depreciation into account, assuming no formal election out of bonus depreciation was made for 5-year property placed in service in 2017.

*Basis add-back.* The basis of property on which the Code Sec. 179 expense deduction is recaptured under the 50 percent or less business use recapture rule provided in Code Sec. 179(d)(10) is increased immediately before the recapture event by the amount recaptured (Reg. § 1.179-1(e)(3)).

See, also, related discussion at ¶ 487.

*10. Married Taxpayers*

*Joint return filed.* For taxpayers filing jointly, the dollar amount before reduction by the investment limitation is $1,050,000 for tax years beginning in 2021 ($1,080,000 for 2022). Married taxpayers who file a joint return are treated as a single taxpayer for purposes applying the investment limitation on the dollar amount (Reg. § 1.179-2(b)(5)(i)). The taxable income limitation is determined by aggregating the taxable income of each spouse (Reg. § 1.179-2(c)(7)(i)).

*Separate return filed.* Married persons filing separate returns are treated as one taxpayer for purposes of the dollar limitation ($1,050,000 for tax years beginning in 2021 and $1,080,000 for 2022) and any reduction to the dollar limitation required by the investment limitation ($2,620,000 for tax years beginning in 2021 and $2,700,000 for 2022). The cost of all section 179 property purchased by each spouse is aggregated to determine the maximum amount for which an election to expense may be made (Code Sec. 179(b)(4); Reg. § 1.179-2(b)(6)). However, the rule limiting the actual Sec. 179 expense deduction to taxable income from active trades or businesses is applied separately to each spouse (i.e., without regard to the other spouse's taxable income) (Reg. § 1.179-2(c)(8)). Once the maximum amount for which an election to expense may be made is determined, the spouses may allocate that amount between themselves in any manner. If either the taxpayer or the taxpayer's spouse does not make an election to allocate a percentage of the maximum amount or the sum of the percentages elected does not equal 100 percent, the IRS will allocate 50 percent to each spouse. (Code Sec. 179(b)(4); Reg. § 1.179-2(b)(6)). The allocation election is simply made by entering the taxpayer's share of the elected amount on line 5 of Form 4562 ("Dollar limit for the tax year").

> ***Example 14:*** John and Mary file separate returns in 2021. Their combined purchases of section 179 property in 2021 equal $3,000,000. The maximum amount for which an election to expense may be made computed jointly and without regard to the taxable income limitation is $670,000 ($1,050,000 – ($3,000,000 – $2,620,000)). Unless an election is made to allocate this amount differently, John and Mary are each entitled to elect to expense $335,000. The actual deduction claimed by each spouse, however, may be limited by the taxable income limitation which is computed separately by each spouse after the allocation.

Although the preceding regulations allow the allocation of the maximum expensing amount between spouses filing separate returns they do not appear to change the rule that an election to expense may only be made with respect to property actually placed in service by a taxpayer. Thus, in Example 14 above, if John only placed $10,000 of section 179 property in service in 2021, he could only elect to expense $10,000 even if he received a $335,000 expense allocation. Furthermore, in order to claim a $10,000 deduction in 2021 John's taxable income from active trades or businesses would need to be at least $10,000.

*Joint return filed after separate returns.* If married taxpayers who filed separately elect to file jointly within three years of the due date (excluding extensions) of the separate returns (see Code Sec. 6013(b)), the dollar limitation for the joint return is equal to the aggregate cost of section 179 property that was elected to be expensed on the separate returns if this amount is less than the dollar limitation as reduced by the investment limitation determined by taking into account all section 179 property placed in service by the husband and wife during the tax year (Reg. § 1.179-2(b)(5)(ii)). The taxable income limitation is determined under the regular rule above for married taxpayers filing jointly (Reg. § 1.179-2(c)(7)(ii)).

***Example (15):*** Hawthorne and Williams, calendar-year taxpayers, purchased and placed in service $10,000 worth of property qualifying for the section 179 expense deduction. Hawthorne and Williams filed separate income tax returns. Hawthorne elected to expense $3,000 of the qualifying property on his separate return, and Williams elected to expense $2,000 on her return. After the due date of the returns had passed, Hawthorne and Williams elected to refile as married, filing jointly. Hawthorne and Williams may only elect to expense $5,000 on their joint return since this is less than the aggregate cost elected to be expensed on their separate returns (Reg. § 1.179-2(b)(5)(iii)).

Note that the amount elected to be expensed on a return is determined without regard to the taxable income limitation. A taxpayer determines the maximum allowable expense election by taking into account the dollar and investment limitations and then makes the election to expense particular items of section 179 property placed in service during the tax year subject to the maximum allowable. The taxable income limitation may then result in a carryover of some or all of the amount elected to be expensed. See Form 4562, lines 1 -13.

*11. Partnerships and S corporations*

*In general.* The maximum dollar limit ($1,050,000 for tax years beginning in 2021 and $1,080,000 for 2022), investment limitation ($2,620,000 for tax years beginning in 2021 and $2,700,000 for 2022), and taxable income limitation are applied separately at the partnership and partner levels (Reg. § 1.179-2(b)(3)(i) and (4); Reg. § 1.179-2(c)(2)(i) and(c)(3)(i)). Thus, a partnership may elect to expense up to the maximum annual dollar cost limitation of the cost of qualifying property (assuming the taxable income and investment limitations as applied at the partnership level do not reduce the ceiling). The partner may not claim an expense deduction in excess of the maximum annual dollar cost limitation, taking into account his allocated share of the amount expensed by the partnership. The partner is also separately subject to the taxable income and investment limitations. A similar rule applies to S corporations and S shareholders.

A partner's distributive share of a partnership's Code Sec. 179 expenses for a partnership's tax year (as well as the partnership's taxable income that is attributable to a partner) is taken into account in the partnership's tax year that ends with or within the partner's tax year (Reg. § 1.179-2(b)(3)(iv); Reg.§ 1.179-3(c)(2)(ii)). The same rule applies to an S corporation and its shareholders (Reg. § 1.179-2(b)(4)). Thus, when the tax years of a pass-thru and its owners differ, each may be subject to a different dollar and investment limitation (Rev. Proc. 2008-54).

***Example (15A):*** ABC partnership has a fiscal year beginning on June 1, 2020. A is a calendar-year partner. ABC is subject to the $1,040,000 dollar limit that applies to tax years beginning in 2020 with respect to property placed in service in its 2020/2021 fiscal year and A is subject a $1,050,000 limit that applies to tax years beginning in 2021. ABC may expense no more than $1,040,000 of property in its 2020/2021 fiscal year. A's distributive share of the amount expensed by ABC in its 2020/2021 fiscal year is taken into account in A's 2021 calendar year because ABC's 2020/2021 fiscal year ends in A's 2021 calendar year. Thus, A's distributive share of ABC's 2020/2021 fiscal-year expense amount is applied toward A's 2021 calendar year limit of $1,050,000.

A partnership or S corporation may not allocate an expense deduction deferred and carried forward at the partnership level on account of the taxable income limitation until a tax year in which the partnership or S corporation has sufficient taxable income to allow use of the carryforward amount (Reg. § 1.179-3(g)). See "*6. Taxable Income Limitation*" discussion above for discussion of taxable income limitation in context of partnerships and S corporations.

No portion of the cost of section 179 property acquired by a partnership or S corporation is attributed to a partner or an S shareholder in applying the investment limitation at the partner level or S shareholder level. See *"5. Investment Limitation."*

The amount of section 179 deduction allocated by a partnership to a partner (or allocated by an S corporation to an S shareholder) is not considered in determining whether the partner (or S shareholder) placed more than the applicable investment limit of qualifying property into service during the tax year (Reg. § 1.179-2(b)(3) and Reg. § 1.179-2(b)(4)).

In the case of property acquired by purchase and placed in service by a partnership or S corporation the determination of whether the property is section 179 property is made solely at the entity level (Reg. § 1.179-1(h)(1)). For example, this means that the partnership must use the property in the active conduct of a trade or business. It is not necessary for a partner to actively participate in the conduct of the partnership's trade or business in order to receive an allocation of the section 179 deduction available to the partnership (Reg. § 1.179-1(h)(2), Example). The partnership must actively conduct a trade or business to treat purchased property as section 179 property. The partner, however, is separately subject to the dollar, investment, and taxable income limitations. In addition, when a section 179 deduction is passed through to a partner, (e.g., a limited partner) the deduction may be suspended under the passive activity rules of Code Sec. 469 if the partner has insufficient income from passive activities to offset the deduction.

Code Sec. 704 and the regulations thereunder govern the determination of a partner's share of a partnership's section 179 expenses for the tax year. No partnership allocation of the section 179 expenses may be modified after the due date of the partnership return (without regard to extensions of time) (Reg. § 1.179-2(b)(3)(ii)). Each shareholder's share of the section 179 expenses of an S corporation is determined under Code Sec. 1366 (Reg. § 1.179-2(b)(4)).

Partners and S corporation shareholders are required to reduce the basis of their partnership or S corporation interest by the full amount of an expense deduction allocated to them by the respective entity even though part of the deduction must be carried over because of the partner or S corporation shareholder's taxable income limitation or is disallowed because of the dollar limitation (Rev. Rul. 89-7, 1989-1 CB 178; Reg. § 1.179-3(h)(1)).

A partner who disposes of a partnership interest, or transfers a partnership interest in a transaction in which gain or loss is not recognized in whole or in part (including transfers of a partnership interest at death), may have an outstanding carryover of disallowed deduction of section 179 expenses allocated from the partnership. Immediately before the transfer the partner's basis in the partnership interest is increased by the amount of the partner's outstanding carryover of disallowed deduction with respect to the partnership interest. Similar rules apply to S corporation shareholders (Reg. § 1.179-3(h)(2)).

***Example 16:*** S is a 50% calendar-year partner in three separate calendar-year partnerships, A, B, and C. In 2021, S received a $500,000 share of a Code Sec. 179 expense deduction from each partnership ($1,500,000 total) that satisfied the $1,050,000 dollar limit, the $2,620,000 investment limit, and the aggregate taxable income limit at the partnership level. In 2021, S is engaged in other business activities that generate losses and has a total aggregate taxable income for the year, including the partnership income allocations, of $15,000.

For 2021, S's expense deduction is limited to the aggregate taxable income of $15,000 and there is a $1,035,000 ($1,050,000 – $15,000) carryover. Although S received a total allocation of $1,500,000 from the three partnerships, only $1,050,000 (subject to the taxable income limitation) may be taken into account. The $450,000 in excess of $1,050,000 is disregarded, and this amount may not be carried over.

*Example (16A):* ABC, a calendar-year partnership, owns and operates a restaurant business. During the current tax year, ABC purchases and places in service two items of section 179 property—a cash register costing $4,000 and office furniture costing $6,000. ABC elects to expense the full cost of the cash register and the office furniture. For the current tax year, ABC has $6,000 of taxable income derived from the active conduct of its restaurant business. Therefore, ABC may deduct only $6,000 of section 179 expenses and must carry forward the remaining $4,000 of section 179 expenses at the partnership level. ABC must reduce the adjusted basis of the section 179 property by the full amount elected to be expensed. However, ABC may not allocate to its partners any portion of the carryover of disallowed deduction until a carryforward year in which ABC satisfies the taxable income limitation.

*Limited liability companies.* The section 179 rules for partnerships and partner members also apply to a limited liability company and its members if the limited liability company is treated as a partnership under the check-in-the box rules. Otherwise, the rules applicable to corporations and individuals will apply. Under the check-in-the box rules of Reg. § 301.7701-3, a domestic LLC with two or more members that does not file an election to be treated as a corporation has a default classification of partnership. A domestic entity with one member that does not elect to be taxed as a corporation is considered a disregarded entity—i.e., it is ignored, and the taxpayer is treated as a sole proprietorship. Thus, a domestic LLC will be taxed as a partnership or disregarded entity unless it files an election to be taxed as a corporation.

### *12. Controlled Groups*

*In general.* All component members of a controlled group of corporations on a December 31 are treated as a single taxpayer for purposes of the maximum annual dollar cost limitation, the investment limitation, and the taxable income limitation (Code Sec. 179(d)(6)). "Controlled group" is defined by reference to the definition at Code Sec. 1563(a) and (b), relating to consolidated returns; however, the phrase "more than 50 percent" is substituted for the phrase "at least 80 percent" that would otherwise apply with respect to stock ownership requirements (Reg. § 1.179-4(f)).

The section 179 regulations for controlled groups (Reg. § 1.179-2(b)(7)) do not directly refer to the application of the taxable income limitation. However, Code Sec. 179(d)(6) specifically provides that all the limitations contained in Code Sec. 179(b) (i.e., dollar, investment, and taxable income limitations) are applied to component members of the group as if the controlled group is a single taxpayer. Since the taxable income limitation is in Code Sec. 179(b)(3) the taxable income limitation is also applied at an aggregate level to components members whether or not a consolidated return is filed.

*Allocation of deduction.* The expense deduction so computed may be allocated to one or more component members of the consolidated group or allocated among the component members of the group in any manner. If a consolidated return is filed for all component members, the common parent determines the allocation. If separate returns are filed, the amount must be allocated by agreement among the component members (or by agreement among the parent of component members filing a consolidated return and component members that file separately). The amount allocated to any component member may not exceed the cost of the qualifying property placed in service by that component member (Reg. § 1.179-2(b)(7)(i)).

A statement must be attached to the consolidated return and/or the return of any component member that does not file a consolidated return. The statement must include the name, address, employer identification number, and the tax year of each component member of the controlled group, a copy of the allocation agreement signed by persons duly authorized to act on behalf of the component members, and a description of the manner in which the deduction under section 179 has been divided among the component members (Reg. § 1.179-2(b)(7)(ii)).

The regulations provide that if a consolidated return is filed for all component members, an allocation among the members may not be revoked after the due date of the return (including extensions of time) of the common parent corporation. If some or all of the component members file separate returns for tax years including a particular December 31 for which an election to take the expense deduction is made, the allocation as to all members of the component group may not be revoked after the due date of the return (including extensions of time) of the component member of the controlled group whose tax year that includes such December 31 ends on the latest date (Reg. § 1.179-2(b)(7)(iii)).

This regulation was published prior to enactment of the rule which allows taxpayers to make, change, or revoke a section 179 election prior to expiration of the limitations period for filing an amended return (Code Sec. 179(c)(2)). See ¶ 304. If a parent or component member of a consolidated group can change an election pursuant to Code Sec. 179(c)(2), then it follows that a prior allocation may need to be changed if an election is made for additional property or revoked for some property.

*Property transferred between controlled group members.* Property acquired from a component member of a controlled group of corporations by another component member of the controlled group is not considered acquired by purchase and, therefore, is not eligible for expensing (Code Sec. 179(d)(2); Reg. § 1.179-4(c)).

*S corporations.* The IRS has ruled that an S corporation that is a member of a controlled group it is not considered a "component" member of the group. Therefore, the election is made separately by an S corporation that is a member of a controlled group and the limitations described in Code Sec. 179(b) (i.e., the dollar, investment, and taxable income limitations) are applied separately to an S corporation (IRS Information Letter INFO 2013-0016, Internal Revenue Service (Jul. 3, 2013)).

*13. Noncorporate Lessors*

A lessor, other than a corporation, may not claim the section 179 deduction on leased property unless the property was manufactured or produced by the lessor, or the term of the lease is less than one-half of the property's class life (¶ 180) and for the 12-month period following the date that the leased property is transferred to the lessee, the total Code Sec. 162 business deductions allowed to the lessor for the property exceed 15 percent of the rental income produced by the property (Code Sec. 179(d)(5); Reg. § 1.179-1(i)(2); *R. Thomann,* T.C. Memo. 2010-241, Dec. 58,378(M)). These conditions for exception to the rule are imposed to insure that the transaction is a normal business transaction of the lessor rather than a passive investment entered into for the purposes of sheltering other income. A similar exception applies to the current and former investment tax credit (Code Sec. 50(e)(1) incorporating the rules of former Code Sec. 46(e)(3)). Thus, Reg. § 1.46-4(d) and cases and rulings under Code Sec. 50(e)(1) and former Code Sec. 46(e)(3) may remain relevant for purposes of interpreting Code Sec. 179(d)(5).

It appears that an S corporation is treated as a noncorporate lessor (i.e., a lessor other than a corporation) for purposes of the noncorporate lessor rule. Code Sec. 1363(b) provides that an S corporation must compute its taxable income in the same manner as an individual. Consequently, an S corporation should treat itself as an individual when applying the noncorporate lessor rule of Code Sec. 179(d)(5). This treatment comports with the undisputed rule that applied prior to amendment of Code Sec. 179(d)(5) by the 1990 Revenue Reconciliation Act (P.L. 101-508). Prior to amendment by P.L. 101-508, Code Sec. 179(d)(5) provided: "This section shall not apply to any section 179 property purchased by any person described in section 46(e)(3) unless the credit under section 38 is allowable with respect to such person for such property (determined without regard to this section)." Former Code Sec. 46(e)(3)(B) specifically provided that an S corporation is not treated as a corporation. The amendment to Code Sec. 179(d)(5), however, did not specifically incorporate this rule.

*14. Farmers*

The section 179 deduction is an indirect cost that is not required to be capitalized under the Code Sec. 263A uniform capitalization (UNICAP) rules (Reg. § 1.263A-1(e)(3)(iii)).

Farmers who elect to deduct preproductive period costs of certain plants rather than capitalize them under Code Sec. 263A(d)(3) are required to depreciate farm property placed in service during the year of the election under the MACRS alternative depreciation system (ADS) (see ¶ 150). This election does not preclude a farmer from claiming a Code Sec. 179 expense deduction (Reg. § 1.263A-4(d)(4)(ii)).

## ¶ 302
## Code Sec. 179 Property Defined

***1. Overview***

*In general*

*Computer software*

*Qualified real property placed in service in tax years beginning after 2009*

*Excluded property*

*Used property*

*Predominant business use required*

*Investment use*

*Property acquired and disposed of in same tax year*

*Property converted from personal to business use*

***2. Sec. 1245 Property Defined***

*In general*

*Section 1245 personal property*

*Other section 1245 tangible property*

*Section 1245 and section 1250 land improvements*

*Vineyards and orchards*

*Livestock*

*Using former investment tax rulings to determine eligibility as section 1245 property*

***3. Excluded Property***

*In general*

*Property used predominantly outside of the United States*

*Property used by tax-exempt organizations*

*Property used by governments and foreign persons*

*Air conditioning and heating units*

*1. Overview*

*In general.* Only "section 179 property" is eligible for expensing under Code Sec. 179. Section 179 property is defined as property which is (Code Sec. 179(d)(1); Reg. § 1.179-4(a)):

- tangible Sec. 1245 property as defined in Code Sec. 1245(a)(3),
- depreciable under Code Sec. 168 (MACRS), and
- acquired by purchase for use in the active conduct of the taxpayer's trade or business

In addition, section 179 property includes (Code Sec. 179(d)(1)(A); Code Sec. 179(e)):

- off-the shelf computer software acquired by purchase for the use in the active conduct of a taxpayer's trade or business, and
- qualified real property acquired by purchase for use in the active conduct of a taxpayer's trade or business

New or used property can qualify for expensing.

*Computer software.* Off-the-shelf computer software placed in service in tax years beginning after 2002 may be expensed under Code Sec. 179 (Code Sec. 179(d)(1)(A); Reg. § 1.179-4(a)). Off-the-shelf computer software is software that is readily available for purchase by the general public, is subject to a nonexclusive license, and has not been substantially modified (Code Sec. 197(e)(3)(A)(i) and (e)(3)(B)). The definition of off-the-shelf computer software is detailed in Reg. § 1.197-2(c)(4)(i). Off-the-shelf software is amortizable over three years under Code Sec. 167(f). See ¶ 48. This rule is an exception to the requirement that only tangible property which is depreciable under MACRS may be expensed under section 179.

*Qualified real property placed in service in tax years ending after 2017.* The provision allowing taxpayers to elect to treat all qualified real property as section 179 property has been permanently extended.

Effective for property placed in service in tax years beginning after 2017, qualified real property is defined to mean "qualified improvement property" and any of the following improvements to nonresidential real property that are placed in service after the nonresidential real property was first placed in service: roofs; heating, ventilation, and air-conditioning property; fire protection and alarm systems; and security systems (Code Sec. 179(e)). Qualified improvement property is generally defined to mean internal improvements to nonresidential real property made by a taxpayer after the nonresidential real property is placed in service (Code Sec. 168(e)(6); Reg. § 1.168(b)-1(a)(5)).

See "*Qualified Real Property,*" below.

*Qualified real property placed in service in tax years beginning after 2009 and before 2018.* In tax years beginning before 2018, qualified real property generally consists of qualified leasehold improvements, qualified retail improvement property, and qualified restaurant property that qualify for a 15-year recovery period. These three categories of 15-year property are eliminated, effective for property placed in service after 2017.

In tax years that begin in 2010 through 2015, a taxpayer could elect to treat all qualified real property as section 179 property but could only elect to expense up to $250,000 of the cost of qualified real property. The $250,000 counted toward the $500,000 annual dollar limitation that applied to tax years beginning after 2009 and before 2016. In tax years beginning after 2015, the $250,000 limitation no longer applies. For example, for tax years beginning in 2021, up to $1,050,000 of the cost of qualified real property may be expensed and applied toward the overall $2,620,000 limitation that applies in 2021 (Notice 2013-59).

*Excluded property.* The following property which is described in Code Sec. 50(b) is excluded from the definition of section 179 property:

- property used predominantly outside of the US which must be depreciated using MACRS ADS
- property predominantly used to furnish lodging or predominantly in connection with furnishing of lodging (applies to property placed in service in tax years beginning before 2018)

• property used by tax-exempt organizations unless used in connection with the production of income that is subject to the tax on unrelated business income

• property used by governments and foreign persons

• portable air conditioning and heating units placed in service in tax years beginning before 2016

See below, *"3. Excluded Property."*

*Used property.* Section 179 property may be new or used.

*Predominant business use required.* The section 179 expense allowance may not be claimed on section 179 property which is not used in the conduct of a trade or business more than 50 percent during the tax year it is placed in service (Reg. § 1.179-1(d)).

The section 179 regulations do not explain how predominant business use is determined in the first year but it appears that typically a taxpayer would only take into account the period from the day of the tax year that the property was placed in service to the last day of the tax year. See Reg. § 1.48-1(g)(1) and Reg. § 1.168-2(g).

If business use falls to 50 percent or less in a later tax year during the recovery (depreciation) period for the property section 179 recapture is required (Code Sec. 179(d)(10); Reg. § 1.179-1(e)). These rules do not apply to bonus depreciation except in the case of listed property, such as a vehicle used for transportation. See ¶ 300, *"9. Section 179 Recapture Upon Decline in Business Use"*.

*Investment use.* The basis of section 179 property attributable to investment use does not qualify for expensing and is not taken into account in determining whether the predominant business use requirement is satisfied. In applying the dollar and investment limitations, only the cost of the portion of the basis of the property attributable to business use is taken into account (Reg. § 1.179-1(d)). See ¶ 300. Bonus depreciation, however, may be claimed on basis attributable to investment use.

Unlike bonus depreciation, property which must be depreciated under the MACRS alternative depreciation system (ADS), remains eligible for the section 179 expense allowance except that foreign use property generally does not qualify for expensing (Code Sec. 179(d)(1) referencing Code Sec. 50(b)). For a discussion of differences between bonus depreciation and the section 179 expense allowance, see ¶ 487.

*Property acquired and disposed of in same tax year.* The section 179 expense allowance may not be claimed on property acquired and sold in the same tax year because such property is not depreciable under MACRS (see ¶ 160) and, therefore, is not section 179 property.

*Property converted from personal to business use.* Property which is not acquired for use in a trade or business is excluded from the definition of section 179 property (Code Sec. 179(d)(1)(C)).

> ***Example:*** A car purchased for personal use in Year 1 is converted to business use in Year 2. Since the car was not acquired for use in a trade or business it does not qualify for expensing when converted to business use.

### *2. Sec. 1245 Property Defined*

*In general.* With the exception of qualified real property, only property that is section 1245 property as defined in *Section 1245(a)(3)* may qualify for expensing under section 179.

*Section 1245 personal property.* In general, property described in Code Sec. 1245(a)(3) is tangible personal property and "other tangible property" described below. Reg. §1.1245-3(b) defines tangible personal property by cross reference to the definition contained in Reg. §1.48-1(c) of the investment tax credit regulations. See ¶116, ¶127 and ¶127C for a detailed discussion of the definition of tangible personal property. Personal property elements of a building qualify may qualify for section 179 expensing. See ¶127 and following. However, property used in the provision of lodging (e.g., in a residential rental building) generally does not qualify for expensing if placed in service in a tax year beginning before 2018. See the heading "*Property used in connection with lodging.*" in "*3. Excluded Property.*" below.

*Other section 1245 tangible property.* In addition to tangible personal property, section 1245 property eligible for expensing includes "other tangible property" that is not personal property (Code Sec. 1245(a)(3)(B) - (F); Reg. §1.1245-3; Reg. §1.48-1(d)). Other tangible property is defined as:

- tangible property (other than a building and structural components) used as an integral part of manufacturing, production, or extraction or of furnishing transportation, communications, electrical energy, gas, water, or sewage disposal services (Reg. §1.48-1(d));
- research facilities (not including a building or its structural components) used in connection with any of the preceding activities;
- facilities (not including a building or it structural components) used in connection with any of the preceding activities for the bulk storage of fungible commodities (including commodities in a liquid or gaseous state);
- storage facilities (not including a building or its structural components) used in connection with the distribution of petroleum or any primary product of petroleum;
- single purpose livestock or horticultural structures (¶108); and
- railroad gradings and tunnel bores as defined in Code Sec. 168(e)(4)

The terms "manufacturing," "production," and "extraction" include the construction, reconstruction, or making of property out of scrap, salvage, or junk material, as well as from new or raw material, by processing, manipulating, refining, or changing the form of an article, or by combining or assembling two or more articles, and include the cultivation of the soil, the raising of livestock, and the mining of minerals. Thus, section 38 property would include, for example, property used as an integral part of the extracting, processing, or refining of metallic and nonmetallic minerals, including oil, gas, rock, marble, or slate; the construction of roads, bridges, or housing; the processing of meat, fish or other foodstuffs; the cultivation of orchards, gardens, or nurseries; the operation of sawmills, the production of lumber, lumber products or other building materials; the fabrication or treatment of textiles, paper, leather goods, or glass; and the rebuilding, as distinguished from the mere repairing, of machinery (Reg. §1.48-1(d)(2)).

Other portions of Reg. §1.48-1 expand upon the definition of personal tangible property and "other tangible property."

The definition of other tangible property is discussed at ¶110 and ¶127C.

*Section 1245 and section 1250 land improvements.* Generally, land improvements are section 1250 property and do not qualify for section 179 expensing. However, many land improvements fall within the definition of section 1245 property above as "other tangible property" and qualify for expensing. For example, agricultural fences and agricultural drain or drainage tiles are land improvements that fall within this category (Publication 225). Orchard trees and vines, as discussed below, also fall within this category.

*Vineyards and orchards.* Grape vines and trees of a fruit orchard or grove are considered property used as an integral part of a production activity and, thus, are eligible for expensing under Code Sec. 179 if the trees or vines are depreciable and acquired by purchase (CCA Letter Ruling 201234024, May 9, 2012). As noted at ¶ 108 vineyards and fruit/nut trees are generally depreciable over ten years (Code Sec. 168(e)(3)(D)). Further a vineyard (or orchard) which is planted by a taxpayer is considered acquired by purchase for purposes of Code Sec. 179 (CCA Letter Ruling 201234024, May 9, 2012). Costs eligible for expensing in the case of a vineyard which is planted by a taxpayer include capitalized land preparation, labor, rootstock, and planting costs. Land costs are nondepreciable and do not qualify for expensing. Rev. Rul. 67-51, 1967-1 CB 68, which holds that fruit trees are not eligible for expensing was based on a prior-law definition of section 179 property that did not include property held for manufacturing, production, or extraction and will not be followed. The IRS Audit Guide for Farmers (July 2006) erroneously indicates, based on this ruling, that fruit trees are not eligible section 179 property. Grape vines and fruit trees are considered placed in service when they bear fruit in commercial quantities. However, a taxpayer that acquires an existing commercially viable orchard is considered to have placed the orchard trees or vines in service in the year of acquisition. If the trees or vines have been planted but are not commercially viable when purchased then they are considered placed in service when they begin to produce fruit in commercial quantities. See ¶ 108, "*Trees and Vines,*" for additional information, including rules regarding depreciation.

*Livestock.* Other tangible property includes livestock. The term livestock includes horses, cattle, hogs, sheep, goats, mink, and other furbearing animals (Reg. § 1.1245-3(a)(4)). Thus, livestock may be expensed under Code Sec. 179 if all depreciable under MACRS and acquired by purchase.

*Using former investment tax rulings to determine eligibility as section 1245 property.* Generally, the former investment tax credit for "section 38 property" was only available for property that was similarly (but not identically) defined as section 1245 property (Reg. § 1.48-1(a)). Therefore, when researching whether a property is section 1245 property, it is often useful to consider cases and rulings that dealt with eligibility for the investment tax credit taking into account the unusual situation in which there is a difference between the current law definition of section 1245 property above and the definition of section 38 property provided in Reg. § 1.48-1(a). Annotations listing property which qualified for the investment tax credit can be found in the CCH Standard Federal Tax Reporter beginning at ¶ 4580.21. These annotations are listed under Code Sec. 46.

### *3. Excluded Property*

*In general.* The following property does not qualify for the Code Sec. 179 expense deduction (Code Sec. 179(d)(1)):

(1) the following property described in Code Sec. 50(b), relating to the investment tax credit:

- property used predominantly outside of the U.S.;
- subject to an exception for leases of property of less than six months, property used by certain tax-exempt organizations unless used in connection with the production of income subject to the tax on unrelated trade or business income;
- subject to an exception for leases of property for less than six months, property used by the United States, any State or political subdivi-

sion thereof, any possession of the United States, or any agency or instrumentality of any of the foregoing, and certain foreign persons or entities months; and

• in tax years beginning before 2018, property used predominantly to furnish lodging or used predominantly in connection with the furnishing of lodging (

(2) Permanent air conditioning units, such as HVACs, that are section 1250 property (structural components), unless falling within the exception for "qualified real property" (see "*Air conditioning and heating units*" below);

(3) in service in tax years beginning before January 1, 2016, portable air conditioning units (e.g., window air conditioners that are section 1245 property) (Code Sec. 179(d)(1), prior to amendment by P.L. 114-113); and

(4) in service in tax years beginning before January 1, 2016, portable heating units (e.g., plug-in space heaters that are section 1245 property) (Code Sec. 179(d)(1), prior to amendment by P.L. 114-113).

*Property used predominantly outside of the United States.* Property used predominantly outside of the United States is excluded from the definition of section 179 property unless the property is described in Code Sec. 168(g)(4) (Code Sec. 179(d)(1); Code Sec. 50(b)(1); Reg. § 1.48-1(g) (investment tax regulation); Reg. § 1.168-2(g) (ACRS regulation). Property used predominantly outside of the U.S. must be depreciated using the MACRS alternative (straight-line) depreciation system (ADS) except for the limited exceptions described in Code Sec. 168(g)(4)). These exceptions are for: communications satellites; any satellite or spacecraft launched from within the United States; certain aircraft, railroad rolling stock, vessels, motor vehicles, and containers used in transportation to and from the United States; submarine telephone cables, offshore drilling equipment, and certain other resource exploration property used in international waters. Similar exceptions are detailed in Reg. § 1.48-1(g) (investment tax regulation); Reg. § 1.168-2(g) (ACRS regulation).

Property owned by a U.S. corporation (other than a corporation which has an election in effect under Code Sec. 936) or a U.S. citizen (other than a citizen entitled to the benefits of Code Sec. 931 or Code Sec. 933) and predominantly used in a U.S. possession (by such corporation or citizen or a corporation created under the laws of the possession) is not foreign-use property (Code Sec. 168(g)(4)(g)).

Predominant use means more than half the tax-year considering only the part of the tax year beginning on the date that the asset was placed in service. The definition of the United States is defined by reference to Code Sec. 7701(a)(9) (Reg. § 1.48-1(g)(1); Reg. § 1.168-2(g)).

See ¶ 152 for additional details.

If the predominant use of a property outside of the United States begins in a tax year after it is placed in service it is not necessary to recapture the section 179 deduction. However, a taxpayer must begin depreciating the asset using the ADS method under the change in use rules described at ¶ 169.

*Property used by tax-exempt organizations.* Section 179 property does not include property used by a tax-exempt organization (other than a cooperative described in Code Sec. 521) unless the property is used predominantly in an unrelated trade or business the income of which is subject to tax as unrelated business income (Code Sec. 179(d)(1); Code Secs. 50(b)(3)).

Property used by a tax-exempt organization means:

- property owned by the tax-exempt organization whether or not leased to another person; and
- property leased to the tax-exempt organization (Reg. § 1.48-1(j)).

When a person leases property to a tax-exempt organization or when tax-exempt organization leases property to another person, the lessor may not treat the leased property as section 179 property unless the property is used predominantly in an unrelated trade or business with respect to the exempt organization (Reg. § § 1.48-1(j), 1.48-4).

Property leased on a casual or short-term basis (six months or less) to a tax-exempt organization does not come under this exclusion (Reg. § 1.48-1(j)).

The amount of qualified investment attributable to debt-financed property (Code Sec. 514(b)) is taken into account for purposes of determining the section 179 expense deduction is computed by using the same percentage as the exempt organization uses to compute gross income from that property for purposes of determining unrelated business income. The exempt organization must apply that percentage to the basis or cost of debt-financed property to determine the amount that may be expensed (Code Sec. 50(b)(3)).

*Property used by governments and foreign persons.* Section 179 property does not include property used by the United States, any state or political subdivision thereof, any international organization (as defined in section Code Sec. 7701(a)(18)) (other than the International Telecommunications Satellite Consortium or any successor organization), or any agency or instrumentality of these entities (Code Sec. 179(d)(1); Code Sec. 50(b)(4); Reg. § 1.48-1(k)).

Property used by the United States means (Reg. § 1.48-1(k)):

- property owned by any governmental unit, whether or not leased to another person; and
- property leased to the governmental unit.

Section 179 property also does not include property used by any foreign person or entity unless Code Sec. 168(h)(2)(B) applies, i.e., more than 50 percent of the gross income for tax year derived by the foreign person or entity from the use of the property is subject to U.S. income tax or included underCode Sec. 951 in the gross income of a U.S. shareholder of a controlled foreign corporation (Code Sec. 50(b)(4)(A)(ii)).

"Foreign person or entity" means any foreign government, any international organization, or any agency or instrumentality of any of the foregoing, and any person who is not a United States person. The term does not include any foreign partnership or other foreign pass-thru entity (Code Sec. 168(h)(2)(C)).

Property that is used under a lease with a term of less than six months (as determined under Code Sec. 168(i)(3)) is not excluded from the definition of section 179 property (Code Sec. 50(b)(4)(B)).

Special rules apply to property leased to or owned by partnerships and pass-thru entities (Code Sec. 50(b)(4)(D); Code Sec. 168(h)(5), (6)).

*Property used in connection with lodging.* In tax years beginning before 2018, property which is used predominantly to furnish lodging or predominantly in connection with the furnishing of lodging is excluded from the definition of section 179 property (Code Sec. 179(d)(1), prior to amendment by the Tax Cuts and Jobs Act (P.L. 115-97), referencing Code Sec. 50(b)).

Effective for property placed in service in tax years beginning after 2017, this exclusion is eliminated and property used predominantly to furnish lodging or predominantly in connection with the furnishing of lodging can qualify for expensing (Code Sec. 179(d)(1), as amended by P.L. 115-97, by eliminating exclusion referred to in Code Sec. 50(b)(2))

Property used in the living quarters of a lodging facility, including beds and other furniture, refrigerators, ranges, and other equipment is considered as used predominantly to furnish lodging. Property used in furnishing (to the management of a lodging facility or its tenants) electrical energy, water, sewage disposal services, gas, telephone service or similar services is not treated as used in connection with the furnishing of lodging (Reg. § 1.48-1(h)(1)).

Property which is used predominantly in the operation of a lodging facility or in serving tenants is considered used in connection with the furnishing of lodging, whether furnished by the owner of the lodging facility or another person. For example, lobby furniture, office equipment, and laundry and swimming pool facilities used in the operation of an apartment house or in serving tenants is considered used predominantly in connection with the furnishing of lodging (Reg. § 1.48-1(h)(1)).

The term lodging facility includes an apartment building or house (i.e., residential rental property), hotel, motel, dormitory, or (subject to certain exceptions) any other facility or part of a facility where sleeping accommodations are provided and let (Reg. § 1.48-1(h)(1)). However, property used by a hotel, motel, inn, or other similar establishment is not considered used in connection with the furnishing of lodging if more than half of the living quarters are used to accommodate tenants on a transient basis (rental periods of 30 days or less) (Code Sec. 50(b)(2)(B); Reg. § 1.48-1(h)(1)).

Commercial facilities, such as grocery stores, drug stores, and restaurants, that are located within a lodging facility are not considered lodging facilities if nontenants have equal access. Thus, section 1245 property used within such commercial facilities can qualify for the expensing allowance. Similarly, vending machines that are equally available to nontenants can qualify for expensing (Reg. § 1.48-1(h)(2)(i)).

Coin-operated vending machines, washers, and dryers described in Code Sec. 50 are not considered property used in lodging (Reg. § 1.48-1(h)(2)(iii)).

A lodging facility does not include a facility used primarily as a means of transportation (such as an aircraft, a vessel, or a railroad car) or used primarily to provide medical or convalescent services, even though sleeping accommodations are provided (Reg. § 1.48-1(h)(1)(i)).

The IRS has ruled that furniture rented directly to owners of apartment buildings, duplex houses, and similar establishments that lease to tenants for periods of more than 30 days was considered property used in connection with the furnishing of lodging and was not eligible for the investment tax credit. However, if the furniture had been leased directly to the tenants instead, it would not have been considered used in connection with the furnishing of lodging because the tenants did not furnish lodging to themselves (Rev. Rul. 81-133, 1981-1 CB 21).

A pickup truck used predominantly for hauling trash, carrying materials and equipment for repairs and maintenance, and for snow removal at a taxpayer's apartment complex that rents to tenants for periods of more than 30 days is property used in connection with the furnishing of lodging (Rev. Rul. 78-439). Similarly, a new car used by the owner of rental properties to inspect and repair the properties was property used in connection with the furnishing of lodging (*D. LaPoint*, 94 T.C. 733, Dec. 46,595).

Energy property (as defined in Code Sec. 48(a)(3)) is not disqualified even though used in connection with the furnishing of lodging (Code Sec. 50(b)(2)(D); IRS Publication 946). However, such property would also need to qualify as section 1245 property to be eligible for expensing under section 179 even if it is used in connection with lodging. For example, the IRS has ruled that an active solar energy system that supplemented an existing oil-fired hot water system of a manufacturing plant was not section 1245 property because it was a structural component of the building (Rev. Rul. 82-207). The system, which supplied heated water to restrooms and a cafeteria, was permanently installed and composed of roof-mounted solar collectors, a heat exchanger, pumps, a hot water storage tank, thermostats, electrical controls and associated piping and wiring.

The IRS has ruled that a motor home (recreational vehicle or RV) used by a railroad employee in connection with traveling to and lodging at temporary duty stations for as short as one week and as long as several months was used predominantly for lodging (Technical Advice Memorandum 8546005, August 20, 1985; GCM 39443, November 12, 1985; *Union Pacific Corporation*, 91 TC 771, CCH Dec. 44,886). The IRS stated that if a motor home is used at least as many days for lodging as it is for transportation, its predominant use is for lodging, particularly where the mileage driven is relatively low.

A motor home rented by taxpayers as part of their trade or business qualified as Section 179 property where all of the motor homes used in the trade or business and taken into consideration as a whole were typically used for less than 30 days by a renter. The court did not apply the test at the individual vehicle level although only one vehicle was at issue. It was not necessary to determine whether the motor homes were used primarily for transportation or for lodging since the transient exception applied even if the court were to determine that the motor homes were used primarily for lodging. The court noted that various tests could be used to determine the predominant use of the vehicle (e.g., time driving v. lodging time) but found it unnecessary to consider this issue (*R.D. Shirley*, 88 TCM 140, Dec. 55,724(M), TC Memo. 2004-188). In another case, a married couple's construction company was allowed to expense the costs of a motor home which was apparently used entirely for business purposes. The motor home was used primarily to transport the son and his motorcycles to races and was customized to serve as a repair facility. The court concluded the vehicle was not used primarily for lodging even though the son and his repair team slept in the vehicle (*W.D. Evans*, Dec. 60,081(M), TC Memo. 2014-237).

The IRS argued and the tax court agreed that mileage driven should be used to determine the percentage of personal and business use in a case involving a medical doctor who lived in a motor home that he parked in a hospital parking lot for 3-day periods while on duty and call (*J.C. Cartwright*, Dec. 60,440(M), TC Memo. 2015-212). The prohibition on property used for lodging was not considered. The IRS also overlooked the rule which prevents property used 50 percent or more for nonbusiness purposes from qualifying for the section 179 deduction insofar as the business use was determined to be 19.42% and 22.23% of the total mileage for 2008 and 2009. The effect of Code Sec. 280A was also not considered. See ¶ 104.

An RV is 5-year MACRS property (see ¶ 104) but is exempt from the luxury car depreciation caps since its GVWR exceeds 6,000 pounds. It, however, remains subject to any other limitations applicable to listed property. See ¶ 208.

A recreational vehicle park was not a lodging facility. The term "lodging facility" was intended to include only facilities with living accommodations contained within a building or structure (IRS Letter Ruling 200320018, February 4, 2003).

The IRS and courts have not ruled whether a taxpayer who rents space for mobile homes is engaged in the furnishing of lodging. However, see *J. Johnston*, DC MT, 85-1 USTC ¶ 9192, 605 FSupp 26 in which the IRS was estopped from claiming that the owner of a mobile home park was engaged in furnishing lodging when it took an inconsistent position earlier. See ¶ 114 for a discussion of the depreciation of mobile homes.

*Air conditioning and heating units.* The last sentence of Code Sec. 179(d), prior to being stricken by P.L. 114-113 (PATH Act), effective for tax years beginning after 2015, provided that Code Sec. 179 expensing did not apply to "air conditioning and heating units." Even without regard to this exclusion, section 179 expensing does not apply to air conditioning and heating units that are structural components, i.e., section 1250 property such as an HVAC unit. Code Sec. 179 generally only applies to section 1245 property. Thus, even though the Code Sec. 179(d)(1) exclusion for air conditioning and heating units has been removed, air conditioning and heating units that are section 1250 property continue to be disqualified from expensing subject to the exception described below for qualified real property and HVAC units used to meet temperature and humidity requirements for machinery and processed goods such as food..

Note that property used in connection with the provision of lodging that is not provided on a transient basis may not be expensed if placed in service in a tax year beginning before 2018. Thus, portable air conditioning units and heating units used in connection with a residential rental property may not be expensed if placed in service in a tax year beginning before 2018. See above, *"Property used in connection with lodging"*.

The IRS discusses the effect of the PATH Act amendment on air conditioning and heating units in Section 3.03 of Rev. Proc. 2017-33. The procedure states that an air conditioning or heating unit placed in service in a tax year beginning after 2015 may be expensed if the unit is section 1245 property and all other definitional requirements for section 179 property are met (e.g., the property is acquired by purchase, depreciable under MACRS, and used in the active conduct of a trade or business). Examples that qualify as section 179 property are portable air conditioners, such as window air conditioning units, and portable heaters, such as portable plug-in units. Citing Reg. § 1.48-1(e)(2), the IRS states that an example of an air conditioning or heating unit that does not qualify as section 179 property is any component of a central air conditioning or heating system of a building, including motors, compressors, pipes, and ducts, whether the component is in, on, or adjacent to a building. Such property is section 1250 property. However, the IRS qualifies this by indicating that a component of a central air conditioning or heating system that is section 1250 property can qualify for the section 179 allowance if it meets the definition of "qualified real property" in Code Sec. 179(f)(2) (prior to amendment by the Tax Cuts and Jobs Act (P.L. 115-97)) *and* (emphasis added) the component is placed in service in a tax year beginning after 2015. Consequently, it appears the IRS position is that non-portable air conditioning and heating units or components thereof that meet the definition of qualified real property do not qualify for the section 179 allowance if placed in service in a tax year beginning before 2016.

> ***Example:*** A calendar-year taxpayer installs an HVAC on the exterior of a restaurant in 2017. Since an interior or exterior improvement to a restaurant building is qualified real property if placed in service in a tax year beginning before 2018, the HVAC can qualify for expensing if the taxpayer elects to treat all of its qualified real property placed in service in 2017 as section 179 property.

Non-portable air conditioners primarily used to meet the temperature and humidity requirements of machinery, equipment or the processing of materials and foodstuffs are considered section 1245 property (Reg. § 1.48-1(e)(2); Senate Report No. 94-938 94th Congress 2d Session, 1976-3 CB 49). Consequently, such air conditioners should qualify for section 179 expensing regardless of the year placed in service. See *"HVAC and air conditioning units"* at ¶ 127A.

In tax years beginning after 2018, the definition of qualified real property is redefined to include heating, ventilation, and air-conditioning property installed on nonresidential real property after the nonresidential real property is placed in service (Code Sec. 179(e). Thus, at least in the case of nonresidential real property, the eligibility for section 179 expensing of HVAC units is resolved if the taxpayer elects to treat all of its qualified real property as section 179 property.

*4. Acquired by Purchase Requirement*

*In general.* Property does not qualify for expensing unless it is acquired by purchase (Code Sec. 179(d)(1)(C)). Property is not considered acquired by purchase if it (Code Sec. 179(d)(2); Reg. § 1.179-4(c)):

(1) is acquired from a person whose relationship to the taxpayer would bar recognition of a loss in any transaction between them under Code Sec. 267 or 707(b) (see below);

(2) is acquired by one member of a controlled group of corporations from another member (substituting 50 percent for the 80 percent that would otherwise apply with respect to stock ownership requirements);

(3) has a basis in the hands of the acquiring taxpayer determined in whole or in part by reference to the adjusted basis of the person from who the property was acquired (e.g., a gift or section 1022 basis property (see below));

(4) has a basis determined under Code Sec. 1014(a) relating to inherited or bequested property;

(5) is received in a corporate distribution the basis of which is determined under Code Sec. 301(d)(2)(B)

(6) is acquired by a corporation in a transaction to which Code Sec. 351 applies;

(7) is acquired by a partnership through a Code Sec. 723 contribution; or

(8) is acquired from a partnership in a distribution which has a carryover basis under Code Sec. 732(a)(1).

*Code Sec. 338 deemed asset acquisition.* Property acquired by a new target corporation as the result of a Code Sec. 338 deemed asset acquisition election is considered acquired by purchase and may qualify for section 179 expensing (Reg. § 1.179-4(c)(2); Premable T.D. 9874).

*Code Sec. 336(e) election.* Property deemed to have been acquired by a new target corporation as a result of a Code Sec. 336(e) election is considered acquired by purchase for purposes of section 179. This rule does not apply to a section 336(e) election made with respect to a qualified stock disposition described, in whole or in part, in Code Sec. 355(d)(2) or (e)(2) (Reg. § 1.179-4(c)(2)). Although this rule was only recently provided in the final and proposed version of the final regulation, the IRS noted that it considers this final regulation and the proposed version (Proposed Reg.§ 1.179-4(c)(2)) before finalization as a reaffirmation of existing law (Preamble to REG-104397-18).

If a Code Sec. 336(e) election is made with respect to a qualified stock disposition that is described, in whole or in part, in Code Sec. 355(d)(2) or (e)(2), old target is treated as selling its assets to an unrelated person but then purchasing the assets back (sale-to-self model) (Reg. § 1.336-2(b)(2)). Because the sale-to-self model does not deem a new target corporation to acquire the assets from an unrelated person, assets deemed purchased in such a qualified stock disposition are not considered acquired by purchase and do not qualify for expensing (Preamble to T.D. 9874).

*Carryover basis in trade-ins and involuntary conversions.* The portion of the basis of property that is attributable to the basis of property that was previously held by the taxpayer (e.g., carryover basis in a Code Sec. 1033 like-kind exchange/trade-in or Code Sec. 1034 involuntary conversion) does not qualify for the expense deduction (Code Sec. 179(d)(3); Reg. § 1.179-4(d)).

***Example (2):*** In 2017, ABC corporation purchases a new drill press for $10,000 and receives a trade-in allowance of $2,000 on an old press. The remaining basis of the old press was $1,200. The basis of the new press is $9,200 ($8,000 cash paid plus $1,200 basis of old press). Only $8,000 of the cost qualifies for section 179 expensing.

Like-kind exchanges are allowed only for real property, effective for exchanges completed after 2017 (Code Sec. 1031(a)(1)). However, a transition rule allowing like-kind exchange treatment applies to an exchange if (1) the property disposed of by the taxpayer in the exchange is disposed of on or before December 31, 2017; or (2) the property received by the taxpayer in the exchange is received on or before December 31, 2017 (Act Sec. 13303(c)(2) of the 2017 Tax Cuts Act). Real property is defined in such as way that section 1245 real property does not qualify for a like-kind exchange (Proposed Reg. § 1.1031(a)-3).

*Property acquired from a related party.* Property is not acquired by purchase if it is acquired from a person whose relationship to the taxpayer would result in the disallowance of losses under Code Sec. 267 or Code Sec. 707(b). Code Sec. 267 is applied by treating the family of the taxpayer as including only a spouse, ancestors, and lineal descendants (Reg. § 1.179-4(c)(1)).

***Example (3):*** Husband and wife acquire property jointly from the husband's father. The property is treated as purchased for purposes of section 179 only to the extent of the wife's interest in the property.

***Example (4):*** Frank owns, directly and indirectly, more than 50 percent in value of the stock of ABC corporation. An acquisition of property from ABC is not considered a purchase for purposes of section 179.

***Example (5):*** Frank acquires property from his wife and property from his sister. The acquisition from Frank's wife is not a purchase for purposes of section 179; however, the acquisition from his sister is a purchase for purposes of section 179.

*Code Sec. 1022 basis property for decedents dying in 2010.* Under final regulations, which are effective on or after January 19, 2017, if a transferee's basis is determined under Code Sec. 1022 (relating to an election to use the gift tax rules to determine the basis of property acquired from certain decedents who died in 2010 (see ¶ 70) the property is not considered acquired by purchase and is not eligible for expensing under Code Sec. 179 (Reg. § 1.179-4(c)(1)(iv); Reg. § 1.179-6(d); T.D. 9811 (January 19, 2017); REG-107595-11 (May 11, 2015)). Since the effective date does not apply to "property placed in service" on or after the date of publication as a final regulation, it appears that taxpayers who claimed the Section 179 deduction on such property would be considered to have adopted an impermissible accounting method by expensing the cost rather than depreciating it. The situation is similar to the effective date provided in the repair regulations (effective, generally, for tax years ending on or after January 1, 2014) which resulted in requiring a taxpayer who, prior to the 2014 tax year, expensed an amount as a repair which should have been capitalized and depreciated (or vice versa) to file an accounting method change to correct the erroneous treatment through a Code Sec. 481(a) adjustment.

*5. Active Conduct of Trade or Business Requirement*

*In general.* Property must be acquired by purchase for use in the active conduct of a trade or business in order to qualify as section 179 property (Code Sec. 179(d)(1)(C)). The regulations provide that the property must be acquired by purchase for use in the active conduct of the *taxpayer's* trade or business in order to qualify as section 179 property (Reg. § 1.179-4(a); Reg. § 1.179-2(c)(6)) More than 50 percent of the property's use in the tax year that it is placed in service must be for business purposes (Reg. § 1.179-1(d)(1)). Also, as discussed ¶ 300, *"9. Section 179 Recapture Upon Decline in Business Use,"* if business use of a property in a trade or business declines to 50 percent or below during the recovery period of an asset recapture of a portion of the section 179 allowance previously claimed is required (Code Sec. 179(d)(10); Reg. § 1.179-1(e)(1)).

An amount elected to be expensed under Code Sec. 179 is only deductible to the extent of a taxpayer's taxable income derived from the *active conduct* of the taxpayer's trades and businesses (Code Sec. 179(b)(3); Reg. § 1.179-2(c)(1); Reg. § 1.179-2(c)(6)). For example, net income distributions received as a passive partner are not taken into account when applying the taxable income limitation at the partnership level (Reg. § 1.179-2(c)(6)(iii)).

Thus, an active trade or business requirement applies for purposes of the taxable income limitation and for purposes of the requirement that the property be used in the active conduct of a trade or business. The predominant use rule makes no reference to an *active* trade or business requirement.

The determination of whether property is section 179 property is only made at the partnership or S corporation level (Reg. § 1.179-1(h)(1) and (2)). The partnership or S corporation must use the property in the active conduct of a trade or business. It is not necessary for the partner or S shareholder to actively participate in the conduct of the partnership's or S corporation's trade or business. However, for purposes of applying the taxable income limit, income from the partnership or S corporation is not taken into account by the partner or S shareholder unless the partnership or S shareholder actively participates in the trade or business. This active participation standard is different from the Note, however, even if the partner or S shareholder does not actively participate, taxable income from other businesses in which the taxpayer actively participates, including W-2 wage income, may be taken into account. However, when a section 179 deduction is passed through to a partner, (e.g., a limited partner) the deduction may be suspended under the passive activity rules of Code Sec. 469 if the partner has insufficient income from passive activities to offset the deduction.

*Investment use.* The trade or business limitation makes it clear that there is no expensing allowance for property that is passive loss standard. See below. Section 179 does not apply to property held merely for the production of income. To qualify for expensing, property must be used more than 50 percent in the conduct of a trade or business and cannot qualify by reason of being held for the production of income (Reg. § 1.179-2(c)(6)). If a property is used more than 50 percent for business and also for investment, the investment portion still does not qualify for the expensing allowance.

*Trade or business defined.* For all purposes of Code Sec. 179 the term "trade or business" has the same meaning as in Code Sec. 162 and the regulations thereunder. Thus, property held merely for the production of income or used in an activity not engaged in for profit does not qualify as section 179 property (Reg. § 1.179-2(c)(6)(i)).

*Active conduct defined.* The regulations provide that the determination of whether a trade or business is actively conducted by a taxpayer *for purposes of the taxable income limitation* is based on all the facts and circumstances. The purpose of the active conduct requirement is to prevent a passive investor in a trade or business from deducting section 179 expenses against taxable income derived from that trade or business. Consistent with this purpose, a taxpayer generally is considered to actively conduct a trade or business if the taxpayer meaningfully participates in the management or operations of the trade or business. Generally, a partner is considered to actively conduct a trade or business of the partnership if the partner meaningfully participates in the management or operations of the trade or business. A mere passive investor in a trade or business does not actively conduct the trade or business (Reg. § 1.179-2(c)(6)(ii)).

*Employees.* Employees are considered engaged in the active conduct of the trade or business of their employment (Reg. § 1.179-2(c)(6)(iv)). Therefore, taxable income from W-2 wages are counted toward the section 179 taxable income limitation.

Although not stated in the Code Sec. 179 regulations, the preamble to the regulations (T.D. 8455 indicates that the terms "active" and "passive" do not have the same meaning as in Code Sec. 469 (relating to passive activity losses) and that the definition of the Code Sec. 179 active conduct standard is different than the material participation standard of Code Sec. 469. Thus, it appears likely that a taxpayer can take rental activities into account in determining the taxable income limitation if the actively conducted standard of Code Sec. 179 is satisfied even though rental activities are generally considered *per se* passive under Code Sec. 469. The rule is a double-edged sword, however, insofar as losses from rental activities that are treated as a active trade or business income will reduce taxable income from other sources limitation.

Presumably, in determining whether property qualifies as section 179 by being used more than 50 percent in the conduct of an active trade or business, the same facts and circumstances standards apply for purposes of the taxable income limitation.

An IRS Notice relating to the GO-Zone bonus deduction sheds more light an the meaning of the active conduct of a trade or business (Notice 2007-36). The bonus deduction was available for property (including real estate) which a taxpayer predominantly used in the active conduct of a trade or business (Code Sec. 1400N(d)(2)(A)(ii)). The IRS appears to adopt the section 179 definition for his purpose.

Section 3.02, as in the case of the section 179 regulations, indicates that the definition of trade or business for purposes of Code Sec. 162 applies for purposes of Code Sec. 1400N(d)(2)(A)(ii). Section 3.02 in addition applies the same "meaningful participation" standard of the section 179 regulations for purposes of the active trade or business. However, Section 3.02 specifically provides that a partnership, limited liability company, or S corporation may meaningfully participate through the activities it performs itself *or through the activities others perform on behalf of* the partnership, limited liability company, or S corporation in the management or operations of the trade or business. The section 179 regulations do not mention the attribution of activities performed by others on behalf of a partnership, S corporation, or limited liability company.

Section 3.02 also contains some specific examples of the conduct of an active trade or business. In Example 2 below, an individual who does little more than review the activities of its management company is considered to actively conduct a restaurant operation. However, in *A.H. Jafarpour*, 103 TCM 1880, Dec.59,087(M), TC Memo. 2012-165, an individual who purchased three residential rental properties (apparently single family homes) in the GO-Zone and hired a management company did not actively participate in a conduct of a trade or business where there activity appears to be limited to approving tenants and rent prices. In, Example 3 below, a partnership is not considered actively engaged in a business activity with respect to a rental building because it is subject to a triple net lease. In IRS Letter Ruling 201618008 the sole owner of a limited liability company who actively managed and operated nonresidential real property which was leased conducted an active trade or business where the lease was an operating lease and not a triple net lease.

See, also, FAQs for Hurricane Victims - Bonus Depreciation (including GO Zone) on the IRS website at https://www.irs.gov/businesses/small-businesses-self-employed/faqs-for-hurricane-victims-bonus-depreciation-including-go-zone.

***Example (1):*** MNO, a limited liability company, constructs and places in service a new apartment building in the GO Zone. B, a member in MNO, manages and operates this apartment building for MNO. Because B manages and operates the apartment building for MNO, MNO meaningfully participates in the management and operations of the apartment building. Consequently, all of the use of the apartment building is in the GO Zone and in the active conduct of a trade or business by MNO in the GO Zone.

***Example (2):*** C, an individual, places in service a new restaurant in the GO Zone and employs D to operate it. During 2006, C periodically met with D to review operations relating to the restaurant. C also approved the restaurant's budget for 2006 that was prepared by D. D performs all the necessary operating functions, including hiring chefs, acquiring the necessary food and restaurant supplies, and writing the checks to pay all bills and the chefs' salaries. Based on these facts and circumstances, C meaningfully participates in the management of the restaurant.

***Example (3):*** PRS, a partnership, constructs and places in service a new small commercial building in the GO Zone and leases it to E, an unrelated party, who uses the building as a fast food restaurant. This building is the only property owned by PRS. The lease agreement between PRS and E is a triple net lease under which E is responsible for all of the costs relating to the building (for example, paying all taxes, insurance, and maintenance expenses) in addition to paying rent. Because of the triple net lease, PRS does not meaningfully participate in the management or operations of the building and the building is not used in the active conduct of a trade or business by PRS in the GO Zone.

***Example (4):*** Same facts as above, except that PRS constructs and places in service two other new commercial buildings in the GO Zone and leases these buildings to F, an unrelated party, who uses the two other buildings as office space. The lease agreement between PRS and F is not a triple net lease. G, a partner in PRS, manages and operates the two office buildings for PRS. Because G manages and operates the two office buildings for PRS, PRS meaningfully participates in the management and operations of the two office buildings. Consequently, these two office buildings are used in the active conduct of a trade or business by PRS in the GO Zone.

### *6. Qualified Real Property*

*In general.* For any tax year beginning after 2009 a taxpayer can elect to treat qualified real property as section 179 property if the qualified real property is depreciable and acquired by purchase for use in the active conduct of a trade or business (Code Sec. 179(d)(1)(B)(ii); Code Sec. 179(f), prior to amendment by P.L. 115-97). The exclusions described in the last sentence of Code Sec. 179(d)(1) also apply (Code Sec. 179(d)(1), last sentence; Code Sec. 179(f)(1)(C), prior to amendment by P.L. 115-97). Thus, qualified real property does not include property described in Code Sec. 50(b) (generally, property used predominantly outside of the United States, property used predominantly to furnish lodging or used predominantly in connection with furnishing lodging (this restriction only applies to tax years beginning before 2018), property used by certain tax-exempt organizations unless used in connection with the production of income subject to the tax on unrelated trade or business income, property used by governments and foreign persons, and, for tax years beginning prior to 2016, air conditioning and heating units) (Rev. Proc. 2017-33 (relating to air conditioning and heating units)).

For property placed in service in tax years beginning prior to 2018, property used predominantly in furnishing lodging was excluded from the definition of section 179 property (Code Sec. 179(d)(1), last sentence, prior to amendment by P.L. 115-97. Thus, section 1245 property used in connection with residential rental units did not qualify for expensing. The removal of this prohibition by P.L. 115-97 (Code Sec. 179(d)(1), last sentence as amended by P.L. 115-97) will have little or no impact in the context of qualified real property since residential rental property is excluded from the definition of qualified real property.

*Definition of qualified real property.* Effective for property placed in tax years beginning after 2017, qualified real property (Code Sec. 179(e)) is defined as:

(1) qualified improvement property; and

(2) any of the following improvements to nonresidential real property placed in service after the date such property was first placed in service:

- roofs;
- heating, ventilation, and air-conditioning property;
- fire protection and alarm systems; and
- security systems.

Heating, ventilation, and air-conditioning property includes all components (whether in, on, or adjacent to the building) of a central air conditioning or heating system, including motors, compressors, pipes and ducts (Reg.§ 1.48-1(e)(2); Rev. Proc. 2019-8).

A technical correction may be necessary to clarify that the improvements (items (1) and (2) above) must be made by the taxpayer in order to qualify for expensing (JCT General Explanation of Public Law 115-97, JCS-1-18, Congress (United States), footnote 421 ("Blue Book")). For example, a taxpayer cannot purchase an existing building and treat these types of section 1250 property as section 179 property even though the improvements were made by the seller after the building was placed in service by the seller.

The term "qualified improvement property" means any improvement to an interior portion of a building which is nonresidential real property if the improvement is placed in service by the taxpayer after the date such building was first placed in service. Qualified improvement property does not include any improvement for which expenditures are attributable to the enlargement of the building, any elevator or escalator, or the internal structural framework of the building (Code Sec. 168(e)(6); Reg. § 1.168(b)-1(a)(5)). Qualified improvement property only consists of section 1250 property. See ¶ 126 for a discussion of qualified improvement property.

In the case of property placed in service in tax years beginning before 2018, "qualified real property" Code Sec. 179(f)(2), prior to amendment by P.L. 115-97) is defined as:

- qualified leasehold improvement property as described in Code Sec. 168(c)(6), stricken by P.L. 115-97 (see ¶ 126 for a discussion of qualified leasehold improvement property);
- qualified restaurant property (i.e., restaurant buildings and improvements to restaurants) as described in Code Sec. 168(e)(7), P.L. 115-97 (see ¶ 110 for a discussion of qualified restaurant property); and

- qualified retail improvement property as described in Code Sec. 168(e)(8), P.L. 115-97 (see ¶ 126 for a discussion of qualified retail improvement property)

These categories of qualified real property only includes section 1250 property (the definitions of qualified leasehold improvement property, qualified retail improvement property, and qualified restaurant property exclude section 1245 property).

These categories of qualified real property are depreciable over a 15-year MACRS recovery period if placed in service before 2018. Effective for property placed in service after 2017, all three of these categories of 15-year real property are eliminated and replaced with the "qualified improvement property" category of property. Qualified improvement property has been retroactively assigned a 15-year recovery period, effective for property placed in service after 2017 (Code Sec. 168(e)(3)(E)(vii)). See ¶ 126.

*Manner of making qualified real property election.* The provision to treat qualified real property as section 179 property is described as an election by Code Sec. 179(f)(1), prior to amendment byP.L. 115-97 and Code Sec. 179(d)(1)(B)(ii). The manner of making the election is provided in the Form 4562 instructions which require the attachment of an election statement. This election is separate from the election to expense property that is section 179 property. For example, a taxpayer must first elect to treat its qualified real property as section 179 property. Then a taxpayer makes an election to expense a particular amount of its qualified real property.

It appears that a taxpayer may make or revoke the election to treat qualified real property as section 179 on an amended return filed within the limitations period. In addition, it appears that taxpayer can make, revoke, or change an election to expense qualified real property on an amended return in accordance with the procedures in Reg. § 1.179-5(c) in the same manner as other types of section 179 property (Rev. Proc. 2019-8, Sec. 2.01(5) and Sec. 3.02; Rev. Proc. 2017-33, Sec. 3.02; Rev. Proc. 2013-59, Section III; Rev. Proc. 2008-54, Sec. 3;. See ¶ 304.

*Effect of qualified real property election on investment limitation.* The provision provides that if the election is made, the "term section 179 property includes **any** qualified real property" which is depreciable, acquired by purchase, and not described in Code Sec. 50(b) (Code Sec. 179(f)(1), as in effect for tax years beginning prior to 2018 (i.e., prior to amendment by P.L. 115-97)). Thus, if the election to treat qualified real property as section 179 property is made the election applies to all qualified real property placed in service during the tax year and, therefore, should be taken into account in applying the investment limitation described at ¶ 300 (Rev. Proc. 2017-33, Section 3.01).

Code Sec. 179(d)(1)(B)(ii), effective for tax years beginning after 2017, slightly rewords the provision by providing that at the election of the taxpayer, section 179 property means property which is qualified real property. Thus, it appears that if the election is made after 2017 it will also apply to all of the taxpayer's qualified real property placed in service during the tax year.

***Example (6):*** A calendar-year taxpayer places $50,000 of section 179 machinery and $4 million of qualified improvement property in service in 2021. If the taxpayer makes the election to treat qualified real property as section 179 property, the taxpayer may not make an election to expense any amount because the $1,050,000 annual limitation for 2021 would be reduced to $0 by reason of the investment limitation which reduces the annual limitation by the amount of section 179 property placed in service in excess of $2,620,000. In this situation, the taxpayer should not make the election to treat qualified real property as section 179 property.

*Path Act amendments—overview*. The Protecting Americans from Tax Hikes (PATH) Act of 2015 (Division Q of P.L. 114-113 (enacted December 18, 2015)) amended Code Sec. 179(f), relating to qualified real property, in a two-step process. First, Act Sec. 124(c)(1) of the PATH Act extended the provision, which was scheduled to expire in tax years beginning after 2014, one year to expire in tax years beginning after 2015 (Code Sec. 179(f)(1), as amended by Act Sec. 124(c)(1)). The rule which prohibited carryovers to a tax year beginning in 2015 was also extended one year to prevent carryovers to a tax year beginning in 2016 (Code Sec. 179(f)(4), as amended by Act Sec. 124(c)(1)). These changes are effective for tax years beginning after December 31, 2014 and before January 1, 2016. Next, Act Sec. 124(c)(2) of the PATH Act amended Code Sec. 179(f)(1) again to extend the provision permanently and struck the $250,000 limitation contained in Code Sec. 179(f)(3), effective for tax years beginning after December 31, 2015. Also, effective for tax years beginning after December 31, 2015, the rule limiting carryforwards was eliminated (Code Sec. 179(f)(4), as stricken by the PATH Act). As explained below, these effective dates mean that taxpayers must still treat amounts that could be carried forward to 2016 as placed in service in their last tax year beginning in 2015 since the rules of Code Sec. 179(f) as amended by Act Sec. 124(c)(1) continue to apply to tax years beginning before 2016. Carryforwards attributable to qualified real property placed in service in tax years beginning after 2015 may be carried forward indefinitely, as in the case of other carryforwards attributable to other types of section 179 property. All carryforward rules that apply to other types of section 179 property apply to qualified real property placed in service in tax years beginning after 2015. See ¶ 300 for a discussion of carryforward rules.

*2010 - 2015 elections only apply to $250,000 of qualified real property.* For purposes of applying the dollar limitation described in Code Sec. 179(b)(1)(B) which limits the maximum annual section 179 election amount to $500,000 in tax years beginning after 2009 and before 2016, no more than $250,000 of the $500,000 cap may be attributable to qualified real property for any election made in a tax year beginning in 2010 through 2015 (Code Sec. 179(f)(1), as amended by P.L. 114-113).

> ***Example (7):*** A taxpayer places $700,000 of section 179 property in service in 2015. $300,000 of the property is section 179 property other than qualified real property and $400,000 is qualified real property. The taxpayer may make an election to expense up to $500,000. Of this amount no more than $250,000 of the expense election can be allocated to qualified real property assuming that the taxpayer makes the additional election to treat its qualified real property as section 179 property. If the taxpayer does not make the election to treat its qualified real property as section 179 property, then the maximum expense election is limited to $300,000.

The $250,000 limitation no longer applies to qualified real property placed in service in a tax year beginning after 2015. Thus, up to $510,000 of the cost of qualified real property may be expensed in a tax year beginning in 2017 and applied toward the overall $510,000 dollar limit that applies to tax years beginning in 2017. The maximum section 179 dollar amount increases to $1,000,000 in tax years beginning in 2018. Therefore, up to $1,000,000 of qualified real property placed in service in a tax year beginning in 2018 may be expensed. The expensed amount, however, remains subject to the generally applicable investment and taxable income limitations.

*Application of carryforward rules to qualified real property in tax years beginning before 2016.* Under the general rule, when the amount of section 179 property placed in service in a tax year that a taxpayer elects to expense is in excess of the taxpayer's taxable income from the active conduct of its trades or businesses, the section 179 deduction for the tax year is limited to such taxable income and the excess amount of the expense election is a carryover to future years with no limitation on the carryforward period. If an item of section 179 property is sold or disposed before the carryforward allocable to the item of section 179 property is deducted, the basis of the property is increased immediately before the disposition by the amount of the carryforward. See ¶ 300 for a discussion of the carryforward rules.

Under a special rule for qualified real property, the amount of a carryforward that it attributable to qualified real property may not be carried forward to a tax year that begins after 2015 (Code Sec. 179(f) (4) (A), as amended by P.L. 114-113 effective for tax years beginning after 2014 and prior to being stricken by P.L. 114-113, effective for tax years beginning after 2015; Notice 2013-59). Prior to amendment of Code Sec. 179(f) (4) (A) by the PATH Act, the rule prohibited a carryforward to a tax year beginning after 2014. IRS guidance in Rev. Proc. 2016-48, described below, allows a taxpayer to apply the former rule or to amend its 2014 and subsequent affected returns to apply the current rule which only prevents deductions of carryforwards attributable to qualified real property to tax years beginning after 2015.

> ***Comment:*** IRS guidance confirms that qualified real property which is section 179 property and placed in service in tax years beginning after 2015 is subject to the same carryover rules that apply to other types of section 179 property (Rev. Proc. 2017-33, Section 3.01).

If a carryforward attributable to qualified real property to 2016 is not allowed, then the Internal Revenue Code is applied as if the election to expense the qualified real property had not been made with respect to the disallowed amount. If the carryover is attributable to qualified real property placed in service in any tax year *other than the taxpayer's last tax year beginning in 2015*, the taxpayer is treated as having placed property in service on the first day of the taxpayer's last tax year beginning in 2015 (e.g., January 1, 2015 in the case of a calendar year taxpayer). Any disallowed carryover attributable to qualified real property placed in service in the taxpayer's last tax year beginning in 2015 is treated as if placed in service on the actual placed-in-service date (Code Sec. 179(f) (4) (B) and (C), as amended by P.L. 114-113, effective for tax years beginning after 2014 and prior to being stricken effective for tax years beginning after 2015).

> ***Caution:*** IRS guidance dealing with qualified real property misinterprets Code Sec. 179(f) by indicating that disallowed carryovers that would otherwise be carried to a tax year beginning in 2016 and which are attributable to qualified real property placed in service in the taxpayer's last tax year beginning in 2015 are also treated as qualified real property placed in service on the first day of the taxpayer's last tax year beginning in 2015 (Section 2.01(5) of Rev. Proc. 2016-48, 2016-37 I.R.B. __). The 2015 instructions to Form 4562 and Publication 946 (2015) repeat the error. Code 179(f) (4) (C), as amended by Act Sec. 124(c) (1) of the PATH Act prior to being stricken by Act Sec. 124(c) (2) of the PATH Act, specifically excludes carryovers attributable to qualified real property placed in service in a taxpayer's last tax year beginning in 2015 from being treated as placed in service on the first day of the taxpayer's last tax year beginning in 2015. Code Sec. 179(f) (4) (C) states: "If subparagraph (B) applies to any amount (or portion of an amount) which is carried over from a taxable year *other than the taxpayer's last taxable year beginning in 2015*, such amount (or portion of an amount) shall be treated for purposes of this title as attributable to property placed in service on the first day of the taxpayer's last taxable year beginning in 2015." Code Sec. 179(f) (4) (B), as amended by Act Sec. 124(c) (1) of the PATH Act (P.L. 114-113) prior to being stricken by Act Sec. 124(c) (2) of the PATH Act provides: "Except as provided in subparagraph (C), to the extent that any amount is not allowed to be carried over to a taxable year beginning after 2015 by reason of subparagraph (A), this title shall be applied as if no election under this section had been made with respect to such amount." Consequently, the carryover attributable to qualified real property placed in service in a taxpayer's last tax year

beginning in 2015 is ignored (i.e., taxpayer is treated as if no section 179 election had been made with respect to such property) and the qualified real property is treated as placed in service on the actual placed in service date rather than the first day of the taxpayer's last tax year beginning in 2015. The IRS took a similar erroneous position with respect to prior versions of Code Sec. 179(f) which reflected earlier termination dates for the election to expense qualified real property. See Notice 2013-39 and Rev. Proc. 2015-48 as well as versions of the instructions to Form 4562 and IRS Publication 946 for tax years earlier than 2015.

This issue (the actual placed in service date) is primarily important for purposes of determining whether the half-year or mid-quarter convention applies to property placed in service during the 2015 tax year.

***Example (8):*** A calendar year taxpayer has a $100,000 section 179 carryforward to 2015 attributable to qualified real property placed in service in 2014. The taxpayer has no taxable income in 2015, and, therefore may not deduct the $100,000 carryforward in 2015. Nor may the taxpayer carry the $100,000 carryforward to 2016, because the rule in effect for tax years beginning before 2016 applies and prohibits this treatment. Under the rule in effect for the 2015 tax year, the $100,000 must be treated as property placed in service on January 1, 2015. Effective for tax years beginning after 2015, there are no limitations on the period that a carryforward attributable to qualified real property placed in service in tax years beginning after 2015 may be carried forward.

***Example (9):*** A calendar year taxpayer elects to expense $100,000 of qualified real property placed in service in December 2015. This is the only depreciable property placed in service in 2015. If the taxpayer has no taxable income, the $100,000 expensed amount may not be carried forward. The election is ignored and the taxpayer is treated as having placed the property in service in December 2015 for depreciation purposes. The mid-quarter convention (¶ 92) will apply since more than 40 percent of the taxpayer's depreciable property other than residential rental and nonresidential real property was placed in service in the last three months of the tax year.

*Effect of qualified real property on taxable income limitation in tax years beginning before 2016.* When computing taxable income for purposes of the Code Sec. 179 taxable income limit (Code Sec. 179(b)(3)) (see ¶ 300) depreciation deductions reduce taxable income (Reg. § 1.179-2(c)). However, a technical correction made by the American Taxpayer Relief Act of 2012 (P.L. 112-240) clarifies that depreciation (including bonus depreciation) on qualified real property attributable to an unused carryforward that is considered placed in service in a taxpayer's last tax year beginning in 2015 does not reduce taxable income for this purpose (Code Sec. 179(f)(4)(C), last sentence as added by P.L. 112-240 and amended by P.L. 113-295 but prior to being stricken by P.L. 114-113).

***Example (10):*** A calendar-year taxpayer places $1 million of qualified real property in service on October 1, 2014 and elects to expense $250,000. The taxpayer has no taxable income in 2014 and the $250,000 deduction is carried over to 2015. In 2015, the taxpayer has $50,000 of taxable income and on September 1, 2015, places $250,000 of qualified real property in service. The taxpayer elects to expense $50,000 of the $250,000 of the qualified real property placed in service in 2015. The total carryover for 2016 attributable to qualified real property is $250,000 and this amount is solely attributable to the qualified real property placed in service in 2014. However, no amount may be carried over to 2016. The taxpayer is treated as having placed $250,000 of qualified real property in service on January 1, 2015 and may depreciate such amount. Depreciation on this amount does not reduce taxable income for purposes of the Code Sec. 179 taxable income limitation.

***Example (11):*** A calendar year taxpayer places $11,000 of qualified real property in service in 2014. He elects to expense the entire amount but no amount is deductible because he has no taxable income from a trade or business. His carryover to 2015 is $11,000. Assume that the taxpayer has $1,000 of taxable income in 2015 and makes no election to expense any property placed in service in 2015. $1,000 of the $11,000 carryover is deductible in 2015. Since no portion of the remaining $10,000 carryover may be carried over to 2016, the taxpayer is treated as if the election to expense $10,000 of the cost of the qualified real property had not been made in 2014 and the taxpayer had placed $10,000 of qualified real property in service on January 1, 2015. The taxpayer, therefore, may claim a depreciation deduction in 2015 determined as if he had placed the $10,000 of qualified real property in service on January 1, 2015. The amount claimed as depreciation on this amount does not reduce taxable income in 2015 for purposes of the section 179 taxable income limitation. Assuming that the half-year convention (¶ 88) applies to the qualified real property, the 2015 depreciation deduction is ($10,000 × 3.33% first-year table percentage for 15-year property subject to straight-line method and half-year convention (Table 8 at ¶ 180)). The mid-quarter convention and straight-line method would apply if more than 40 percent of the cost of all property (other than 39-year non-residential or 27.5-year residential property) placed in service in 2015 was placed in service in the last 3 months of the 2015 tax year (¶ 92). In making this determination, the qualified real property is treated as placed in service on January 1, 2015. Consequently if the mid-quarter convention applied, for example, because $50,000 of other property was placed in service in the last 3 months of 2015, the qualified real property would be depreciated using 5.83%—the first-year percentage for 15-year property from Table 9 at ¶ 180 for property subject to the straight-line method and mid-quarter convention which is placed in service in the first-quarter of the tax year.

The Code also appears to allow a taxpayer to disregard the depreciation deduction claimed on qualified real property acquired and placed in service in a taxpayer's last tax year beginning in 2015 in computing the section 179 taxable income limitation in a situation where the qualified real property real property placed in service in such tax year generates a carryforward to 2016 which is disallowed. The last sentence of Subparagraph (C) of Code Sec. 179(f)(4) (i.e., Code Sec. 179(f)(4)(C), as amended by P.L. 114-113 and prior to being stricken by P.L. 114-113) states: "For the last taxable year beginning in 2015, the amount determined under subsection (b)(3)(A) [editor: the taxable income limitation amount] for such taxable year shall be determined without regard to this paragraph [editor; i.e., paragraph (f) of Code Sec. 179]." Strictly interpreted, a taxpayer is not required to take the depreciation deduction on such property into account in determining the taxable income limitation amount since the depreciation deduction on a disallowed carryover attributable to qualified real property acquired and placed in service in a taxpayer's last tax year beginning in 2015 is allowed by reason of the operation of paragraph (f) of Code Sec. 179. If the last sentence had stated "...without regard to this subparagraph" then the rule would only apply to property described in Code Sec. 179(f)(4)(C), i.e., qualified real property placed in service in a tax year other than a taxpayer's last tax year ending in 2015 which generated a carryforward and is treated as placed in service on the taxpayer's first day of its last tax year beginning in 2015.

As noted above, the last sentence of Subparagraph (C) was originally added as a technical correction by the American Taxpayer Relief Act of 2012 (P.L. 112-240). There is no related committee report. The Blue Book (JCT General Explanation of Tax Legislation Enacted in the 112th Congress, JCS-2-13) states: "The provision makes a technical drafting correction by clarifying that for the last taxable year beginning in 2013, the taxable income limitation is computed without regard to any additional depreciation expense resulting from the application of the carryover limitation of section 179(f)(4)." Since the Joint Committee refers to section 179(f)(4) in its entirety rather than section 179(f)(4)(B) in which the technical correction language was placed, the Joint Committee explanation also appears to support the interpretation that depreciation claimed with respect to a carryover attributable to qualified real acquired and placed in service in a taxpayer's last tax year beginning in 2015 does not reduce taxable income for purposes of the taxable income limitation. Note that, at the time the technical correction was enacted carryforwards attributable to qualified real property could not be carried forward to tax years beginning after 2013.

*Section 1245 recapture of Code Sec. 179 deduction claimed on qualified real property upon sale or disposition.* Although qualified real property is section 1250 property, the amount expensed under Code Sec. 179 is treated as section 1245 property and is subject to the section 1245 recapture rules (Code Sec. 1245(a)(3)(C)). The remaining cost is treated as section 1250 property and is subject to the section 1250 recapture rules. Under the section 1245 recapture rules all depreciation claimed is subject to recapture as ordinary income to the extent of gain. Under the section 1250 recapture rules, ordinary income recapture applies to the extent that the depreciation claimed is in excess of the amount allowed using the straight-line method to the extent of gain. Since the portion of the cost of qualified real property which is not expensed under Code Sec. 179 must be depreciated using the straight-line method (over a 15-year recovery period (qualified leasehold, retail, or restaurant property placed in service before 2018 and 15-year qualified improvement property placed in service after 2017)), no amount is recaptured under section 1250 on qualified real property *unless* bonus depreciation was claimed. Generally, for property placed in service before 2016, bonus depreciation may only be claimed on qualified real property that is qualified leasehold improvement property, including restaurant improvement property and retail improvement property that also meets the requirements of qualified leasehold improvement property (see ¶ 110). For property placed in service after 2015 bonus depreciation applies to qualified real property that meets the definition of "qualified improvement property" as currently defined in Code Sec. 168(e)(6) and Reg. § 1.168(b)-1(a)(5). 15-year qualified retail improvement property and 15-year qualified leasehold improvement property placed in service after 2015 and before 2018 will always meet the definition of qualified improvement property. See ¶ 127D. Bonus depreciation is treated as an accelerated depreciation deduction (see ¶ 127D) and, therefore, the difference between the bonus deduction and the amount of straight-line depreciation that could have been claimed on the bonus deduction through the year of disposition is subject to ordinary income recapture under Code Sec. 1250 to the extent of gain. For a general discussion of the recapture rules see ¶ 160 and ¶ 488.

Notice 2013-59 explains how to allocate gain between the portion of qualified real property that has been expensed under Code Sec. 179 and the portion that has been depreciated using the straight-line method (Notice 2013-59). These rules do not specifically cover a situation in which a section 179 deduction, bonus deduction, and straight-line depreciation have been claimed. The principles of the ruling should, however, be equally applicable to this situation.

The ruling provides that a taxpayer may use any reasonable allocation methodology for determining the portion of the gain that is attributable to section 1245 property. The remaining portion of gain, if any, is attributable to section 1250 property.

Two examples of acceptable methods are provided: (1) the pro rata allocation methodology and (2) the gain allocation methodology.

***Example (12):*** *Pro-rata allocation method.* A calendar-year taxpayer places an item of qualified real property costing $20,000 in service in 2014. An election to expense $20,0000 is made; however, due to the taxable income limitation only $12,000 is deducted and $8,000 is a carryforward. Assume the carryforward cannot be deducted in 2015 due to the taxable income limit. The $8,000 carryforward is treated as placed in service on January 1, 2015 under the rule that prevents carryforwards attributable to qualified real property from being carried forward to tax years beginning after 2015. Depreciation claimed on the $8,000 in 2015 is $266.66 ($8,000 × 1/15 × 50% to reflect half-year convention in placed-in-service year). In 2016 the qualified real property is sold for $15,000. Depreciation claimed in 2016 is also $266.66 ($8,000 × 1/15 × 50% to reflect half-year convention in disposition year).

$12,000 of the original $20,000 basis is treated as section 1245 property. The remaining $8,000 is section 1250 property. On the sale date the adjusted basis of the section 1245 property is $0 ($12,000 – $12,000 179 expense). The adjusted basis of the section 1250 property is $7,467 ($8,000 – $266.66 – $266.66).

The $15,000 sales price is allocated pro rata between the section 1245 and section 1250 property as follows:

Section 1245: $15,000 × 12,000/$20,000 = $9,000.

Section 1250: $15,000 × 8,000/$20,000 = $6,000.

The gain allocable to the section 1245 and section 1250 property is computed as follows:

Section 1245: $9,000 – $0 = $9,000 gain.

Section 1250: $6,000 – $7,467 = ($1,467 loss).

The $12,000 section 179 expense deduction is recaptured as ordinary income to the extent of $9,000. The $1,467 loss is treated as a section 1231 loss.

***Example (13):*** Assume that qualified real property costing $20,000 was placed in service in 2020. $12,000 is expensed and the remaining $8,000 is depreciated as section 1250 property. The property is sold in 2021 for $15,000. The adjusted basis of the section 1250 property is $7,467 ($8,000 – $266.66 2020 depreciation – $266.66 2021 depreciation).

The $15,000 sales price is allocated pro rata between the section 1245 and section 1250 property as follows:

Section 1245: $15,000 × 12,000/$20,000 = $9,000.

Section 1250: $15,000 × 8,000/$20,000 = $6,000.

The gain allocable to the section 1245 and section 1250 property is computed as follows:

Section 1245: $9,000 – $0 = $9,000 gain.

Section 1250: $6,000 – $7,467 = ($1,467 loss).

The $12,000 section 179 expense deduction is recaptured as ordinary income to the extent of $9,000. The $1,467 loss is treated as a section 1231 loss.

***Example (14):*** *Gain allocation method.* Assume the same facts as in either Example 12 or 13. The gain from the sale of the property is $7,533 ($15,000 – $0 adjusted basis in section 1245 property – $7,467 adjusted basis in section 1250 property = $7,533). Under the gain allocation method, the gain allocated to the section 1245 property is the lesser of: (1) the amount of gain ($7,533) or (2) the amount of the unadjusted basis of the qualified real property that is treated as section 1245 property ($12,000). Therefore, the entire $7,533 gain is allocated to the section 1245 property and $7,533 is recaptured as ordinary income since $7,533 is less than the $12,000 amount expensed. No gain is allocated to the section 1250 property.

***Example (15):*** *Pro rata allocation method.* Again assume the same facts as in either Example 12 or 13. Assume that the property was sold for $25,000 rather than $15,000.

The $25,000 sales price is allocated pro rata between the section 1245 and section 1250 property as follows:

Section 1245: $25,000 × 12,000/$20,000 = $15,000.

Section 1250: $25,000 × 8,000/$20,000 = $10,000.

The gain allocable to the section 1245 and section 1250 property is computed as follows:

Section 1245: $15,000 – $0 = $15,000 gain.

Section 1250: $10,000 – $7,467 = $2,533 gain.

The $12,000 section 179 expense deduction is recaptured as ordinary income to the extent of $12,000. The remaining $3,000 of gain is section 1231 gain. The $2,533 gain on the section 1250 property is also section 1231 gain.

***Example (16):*** *Gain allocation method.* Assume the same facts as Example (15). The total gain from the sale of the property is $17,533 ($25,000 - $0 adjusted basis in section 1245 property - $7,467 adjusted basis in section 1250 property = $17,533). Under the gain allocation method, the gain allocated to the section 1245 property is the lesser of: (1) the amount of gain ($17,533) or (2) the amount of the unadjusted basis of the qualified real property that is treated as section 1245 property ($12,000). Therefore, $12,000 of gain is allocated to the section 1245 property and the entire amount expensed is recaptured as ordinary income. The remaining $5,533 of gain is allocated to the section 1250 property and is treated as section 1231 gain.

*Determining carryforward attributable to qualified real property placed in service in tax years beginning before 2016.* For purposes of applying the special carryforward rules that apply to qualified real property under former Code Sec. 179(f) and the general rules for determining the amount of a section 179 expense election that is disallowed and carried forward in any tax year under Code Sec. 179(b)(3)(B), the total carryforward for a tax year is allocated pro rata between the qualified real property and all other section 179 properly. Specifically, the amount which is disallowed and treated as a carryforward attributed to qualified real property is equal to the total amount of the section 179 expense election on qualified real property and other section 179 property that is disallowed in the tax year multiplied by a fraction—

(1) the numerator of which is the aggregate amount attributable to qualified real property placed in service during the tax year, increased by the portion of any amount carried over to such tax year from a prior tax year which is attributable to qualified real property, and

(2) the denominator of the total amount of section 179 property placed in service during the tax year, increased by the aggregate amount carried over to the tax year from any prior tax year ((Code Sec. 179(f)(4)(D), as added by the Creating Small Business Jobs Act of 2010 (P.L. 111-240) prior to being stricken by P.L. 114-113, effective for tax years beginning after 2015); (Notice 2013-59, Section V).

In making this calculation, only section 179 property (including qualified real property that is treated as section 179 property) for which an election to expense is made is taken into account. For this purpose, the rule above which treats a taxpayer as having made no section 179 expense election with respect to the amount of a section 179 carryforward to 2016 that is attributable to qualified real property is disregarded (Last sentence of Code Sec. 179(f)(4)(D), prior to being stricken by P.L. 114-113, effective for tax years beginning after 2015).

***Example (17):*** During its 2014 tax year, Stone Corporation purchased equipment costing $50,000 and qualified real property costing $150,000. No disallowed section 179 expense allowance was carried forward to 2014. Stone Corporation's taxable income for 2014, computed without regard to any Code Sec. 179 deduction, was $25,000. Stone Corporation can make an election to expense $200,000 in 2014 but the expense deduction is limited to $25,000 and $175,000 is carried forward to 2015. $131,250 of the $175,000 carryover is allocated to the qualified real property ($175,000 total disallowed carryover × ($150,000 qualified real property placed in service/$200,000 aggregate section 179 property placed in service = $131,250)) (Notice 2013-59, Section V(3)(a), Example 1).

***Example (18):*** Assume the same facts in the preceding example and that Stone Corporation places no section 179 property in service in 2015 and has no taxable income in 2015. No portion of the total $175,000 2014 carryover may be deducted in 2015 and the $131,250 portion of the carryover attributable to the qualified real property may not be carried forward to 2016. Stone is treated as if it had placed $131,250 of qualified real property in service on January 1, 2015 purposes since the carryforward is attributable to property placed in service in a taxpayer year that began before 2015. Stone is entitled to depreciate this property (Notice 2013-59, Section V(3)(a), Example 2).

***Example (19):*** A calendar-year taxpayer placed $250,000 of qualified real property in service in June 2015 and $250,000 of other section 179 property in service in January 2015. The taxpayer elected to expense $50,000 of qualified real property and $250,000 of other section 179 property. Assume the 2015 taxable income limitation is $0 and the entire $300,000 is a carryforward to 2016. The carryforward attributable to qualified real property is $50,000 ($50,000/$300,000) × $300,000)). The remaining $250,000 of the carryforward is attributable to the other section 179 property for which an expense election was made. Because no carryforward attributable to qualified real property may be carried forward to a tax year beginning in 2016 and the carryforward is attributable to qualified real property placed in service in 2015, the election for the qualified real property is ignored and it is treated as property placed in service in June 2015. This property is eligible for depreciation.

Effective for tax years beginning in 2016, the amount of a carryforward attributable qualified real property is determined under the rules that apply generally to all section 179 property. See ¶ 300.

*Special rules for 2014 returns which treated unused carryforwards as placed in service in 2014.* As explained above, the Protecting Americans from Tax Hikes Act of 2015 (P.L. 114-113), which was enacted on December 18, 2015, prohibits taxpayer's from carrying any unused section 179 carryforward attributable to qualified real property to a tax year beginning after 2015. Prior to the extension, taxpayers were prohibited from carrying the portion of a section 179 deduction attributable to qualified real property to tax years beginning after 2014 (Code Sec. 179(f)(4), prior to amendment by P.L. 114-113). Unused carryforwards attributable to property placed in service in tax years beginning before a taxpayer's last tax year beginning in 2014 were required to be treated as property placed in service on the first day of the taxpayer's last tax year beginning in 2014 and unused carryovers attributable to property placed in service in the taxpayer's last tax year beginning in 2014 were treated as property placed in service on the actual date that the property was placed in service in the last tax year beginning in 2014. A taxpayer who filed a 2014 calendar year return or a 2014/2015 fiscal year return may have treated an unused Code Sec. 179 carryover attributable to qualified real property as property placed in service in its 2014 tax year. To remedy this situation, the IRS allows a taxpayer that treated an unused carryover of a Code Sec. 179 deduction on qualified real property as property placed in service in the taxpayer's last tax year beginning in 2014 to continue that treatment or amend its 2014 return and subsequent affected returns to carryforward the disallowed deduction to its 2015 tax year. The option to carryforward to the 2015 tax year is only available so long as the limitations period (Code Sec. 6501(a)) for assessing tax for the 2014 tax year and all affected subsequent tax years remains open (Rev. Proc. 2016-48, I.R.B. 2015-40, September 15, 2015).

It appears that a taxpayer who did not make an election to treat section qualified real property placed in service in its 2014 tax year as section 179 property may file an amended return and make the election under the rules of Code Sec. 179(c)(2) and Reg. § 1.179-5 which allow a taxpayer to make, change, or revoke a Code Sec. 179 election for property by filing an amended return for the year the property was placed in service. See 2014 instructions to Form 4562.

***Example (20):*** XYZ is a calendar year taxpayer which had an unused section 179 allowance of $100,000 attributable to qualified real property placed in service in 2013. XYZ filed its 2014 return and treated the portion of the carryforward which remained after applying it against 2014 taxable income as property placed in service on January 1,

2014 and claimed depreciation on that property. Under the guidance, XYZ may continue that treatment. Alternatively, XYZ may amend its 2014 return by increasing its taxable income by the amount of depreciation claimed in 2014 on the carryover treated as property treated as placed in service in 2014 and making adjustments for any other items affected by this adjustment. Assuming XYZ has already filed its 2015 tax return it must amend that return to increase its taxable income by depreciation claimed in 2015 on the carryover treated as property placed in service on January 1, 2014 and to deduct any unused portion of carryforward to the extent allowable in 2015. Other items may need to be adjusted to reflect these adjustments to taxable income. Any remaining carryforward to 2016 would then be treated as placed in service on January 1, 2015 insofar as the current rules do not allow carryforwards to the 2016 tax year. The amended 2015 return would also reflect depreciation allowed on this amount for 2015.

*Special rules for 2013 returns which treated unused carryforwards as placed in service in 2013.* The Tax Increase Prevention Act of 2014 (P.L. 113-295), which was enacted on December 14, 2014, extended the expensing deduction for qualified real property one year to apply to property placed in service in tax years beginning in 2014. Prior to the extension, taxpayers were prohibited from carrying the portion of a section 179 deduction attributable to qualified real property to tax years beginning after 2013 (Code Sec. 179(f)(4), prior to amendment by P.L. 113-295). Unused carryforwards attributable to qualified real property placed in service in tax years beginning before a taxpayer's last tax year beginning in 2013 were required to be treated as property placed in service on the first day of the last tax year beginning in 2013 and unused carryovers attributable to qualified real property placed in service in the last tax year beginning in 2013 were treated as property placed in service on the actual date that the property was placed in service in the last tax year beginning in 2013. A taxpayer who filed a 2013 calendar year return or a 2013/2014 fiscal year return may have treated an unused Code Sec. 179 carryover attributable to qualified real property as property placed in service in its last tax year beginning in 2013 in accordance with Code Sec. 179(f)(4), prior to amendment by P.L. 113-295. To remedy this situation, the IRS allowed a taxpayer that treated an unused carryover of a Code Sec. 179 deduction on qualified real property as property placed in service in the taxpayer's last tax year beginning in 2013 to continue that treatment or amend its 2013 return and subsequent affected returns to carryforward the disallowed deduction to its 2014 tax year. The option to carryforward to the 2014 tax year is only available so long as the Code Sec. 6501(a) limitations period for assessing tax for the 2013 tax year and all affected subsequent tax years remains open (Rev. Proc. 2015-48).

*Special rules for taxpayers who treated 2010 or 2011 carryover as qualified real property placed in service in 2011.* The American Taxpayer Relief Act of 2012 (P.L. 112-240) retroactively extended the election to expense qualified real property to qualified real property placed in service in 2012 and 2013. Some taxpayers who filed their 2011 return prior to the enactment of P.L. 112-240 may have treated carryovers attributable to qualified real property that was placed in service in a tax year beginning in 2010 or 2011 as not allowed to be carried forward to 2012 in accordance with the rules than in effect. Such disallowed carryovers would have been treated as qualified real property placed in service in the 2011 tax year and depreciated. The IRS will allow such a taxpayer to (1) continue that treatment or (2) amend its return for 2011 to carryforward the disallowed amounts to tax years beginning in 2012 and 2013. However, the amended 2011 return would need to make adjustments for collateral adjustments to taxable income or tax liability (e.g., on account of the depreciation claimed on the qualified real property treated as placed in service in the 2011 tax year). In addition, similar adjustment would need to be made on amended returns for subsequent tax years for which a return was filed. If the 2011 tax year or any subsequent affected tax year is closed by the statute of limitations the taxpayer may not amend its return(s) and must continue to depreciate the disallowed carryover that was treated as placed in service in the 2011 tax year (Notice 2013-59, Section IV).

*Increase in basis for unused carryover upon sale or disposition or transfer in nonrecognition transaction.* The basis of qualified real property which is disposed of in a tax year beginning before the taxpayer's last tax year beginning in 2015 or is transferred during such a year in a transaction in which gain or loss is not recognized in whole or part, including transfers at death should be increased by the amount of any unused section 179 carryforward attributable to the property. If such a disposition occurs in the taxpayer's last tax year beginning in 2015, no basis increase is necessary because the carryforward is treated as property placed in service in the last tax year beginning in 2015 with the basis being treated as equal to the unused carryforward, as explained above. For dispositions, etc., of qualified real property placed in service in tax years beginning after 2015, the basis of the disposed qualified real property is also increased by any section 179 carryforward attributable to the property as is the case for other types of section 179 property (Notice 2013-59, Section VI(1); Reg. § 1.179-3(f)).

In addition, no adjustment should be required in a tax year in which a taxpayer applied one of the transitional rules above to treat unused carryovers as property placed in service in a tax year other than the taxpayer's last tax year beginning in 2015. For example, no adjustment should be required if a taxpayer treated an unused carryforward as property placed in service in the last tax year beginning in 2014 under the authority of Rev. Proc. 2016-48 and the property was disposed of in that tax year.

By way of background, after the extension of the election to expense qualified real property to apply to such property placed in service in tax years beginning in 2012 and 2013, the IRS released guidance which clarified that the basis of qualified real property is increased by the amount of an unused section 179 carryforward attributable to the property if the property is sold or disposed of in a tax year that begins in 2010, 2011, or 2012, or a tax year other than the last tax year beginning in 2013 or is transferred during those years in a transaction in which gain or loss is not recognized in whole or part, including transfers at death. The basis is increased immediately before the disposition or transfer. The guidance provided that the rule did not apply to the last tax year beginning in 2013. For example, the rule would apply to a short tax year beginning on January 1, 2013 and ending on March 31, 2013 but not to a succeeding tax year that begins on April 1, 2013 and ends on March 31, 2014. The rule would not apply to a tax year beginning on January 1, 2013 and ending on December 31, 2013 in the case of a calendar year taxpayer (Notice 2013-59, Section VI(1)).

The rule did not apply to the taxpayer's last tax year beginning in 2013 because, at the time Notice 2013-59 was issued any section 179 carryforward attributable to qualified real property could not be carried forward to a tax year beginning in 2014 and was treated as depreciable property placed in service in the taxpayer's last tax year ending in 2013. Consequently, there was no need to increase the basis of the disposed property by the unused carryover because the unused carryover was treated as a separate item of property placed in service in the disposition year.

The rule provided in Notice 2013-59 in the preceding paragraph does not reflect the subsequent extension of the qualified real property provision to qualified real property placed in service in tax years beginning in 2014 by the Tax Increase Prevention Act of 2014 (P.L. 113-295) or the permanent extension by the Protecting Americans from Tax Hikes Act of 2015 (P.L. 114-113. Therefore, now the basis increase should not apply to dispositions in the last tax year beginning in 2015 of qualified real property that generated a section 179 carryforward because, as previously explained, no amount of a section 179 carryforward may be deducted after the last tax year beginning in 2015 and the carryforward is treated as property placed in service in the last tax year beginning in 2015. In tax years beginning in 2016 and later, unused carryforwards attributable to qualified real property placed in service in tax years beginning after 2015 should be increased upon a disposition by reason of the general rule that applies to other types of section 179 property (Reg. § 1.179-3(f)).

*Interaction between qualified real property and empowerment zone property.* As explained at ¶ 304A, the dollar limitation is increased by the lesser of $35,000 or the cost of qualified empowerment zone property placed in service by an enterprise zone business before 2021. In addition only one-half of the cost of qualified zone property is taken into account in applying the investment limitation discussed at ¶ 300. Qualified real property (for which an election to treat as section 179 property is made) can also meet the definition of empowerment zone property, as discussed at ¶ 300. The $250,00 limit on the maximum amount of qualified real property that may be expensed in a tax year beginning after 2009 and before 2016 is affected by the property's dual status.

***Example (21):*** During its 2015 calendar tax year, XYZ placed $535,000 of qualified real property in service and elected to treat this property as section 179 property. $35,000 of this property was placed in service in an empowerment zone and met the definition of qualified zone property. Although the maximum dollar limit is increased to $535,000, XYZ may expense no more than $250,000 of the $535,000 cost of the qualified real property. The investment limitation for 2015 ($2,000,000) is increased by $17,500 to $2,017,500.

***Example (22):*** During its 2015 calendar tax year, XYZ placed $45,000 of qualified real property in service in an empowerment zone and elected to treat this property as section 179 property. Assume this property is qualified empowerment zone property. XYZ also placed $600,000 of section 179 property that is not qualified real property in service outside of the zone. The maximum dollar limit is increased to $535,000. XYZ may elect to expense the entire $45,000 of the cost of the qualified real property since this is less than the $250,000 maximum for qualified real property. The difference between $535,000 and the cost of the qualified real property which XYZ elects to expense (if any) may also be expensed. The investment limitation for 2015 ($2,000,000) is increased by $22,500 to $2,022,500.

*Interaction of qualified real property and disaster assistance property.* As explained at ¶ 306B, the dollar limitation ($500,000) was allowed for certain prior tax years to be increased by the lesser of $100,000 or the cost of qualified disaster assistance property placed in service during the tax year. The investment limitation was increased by the lesser of $600,000 or the cost of qualified disaster assistance property placed in service during the tax year.

Qualified disaster assistance property only included section 179 property as "defined in subsection [179](d)" (Code Sec. 179(e)(2)). Since qualified real property is not considered section 179 property by reason of Code Sec. 179(d) (see former Code Sec. 179(f)(1)), it does not appear that qualified real property could also constitute qualified disaster assistance property.

## ¶ 304

## Code Sec. 179 Making, Changing, and Revoking Elections

*In general.* A Code Sec. 179 election to expense the cost of qualifying property must specify the items of property to which the election applies and the portion of the cost of each of these items to be deducted currently. The election is made on

Form 4562 (Depreciation and Amortization) by claiming the expense allowance. The specification of property for which the election is made is made on line 6 of Form 4562. For partnerships and S corporations—which, up to the annual ceiling, may expense qualifying property and pass the deduction through to their partners or shareholders—the total amount expensed is carried to Schedules K and K-1 of Form 1065 or 1120S.

*Time for making, changing. and revoking an election for property placed in service in tax years beginning after 2002.* Any election or specification made for property placed in service in a tax year beginning after 2002 may be revoked by a taxpayer without IRS consent. The revocation, once made, is irrevocable (Code Sec. 179(c)(2); Reg. § 1.179-5(c)(1); Rev. Proc. 2017-33, Sec. 3.02; Rev. Proc. 2019-8). The provision was schedule to expire in tax years beginning after 2014 but was permanently extended by the Protecting Americans from Tax Hikes (PATH) Act of 2015 (P.L. 114-113) (enacted December 18, 2015).

Although Code Sec. 179(c)(2) only refers to the "revocation" of a Code Sec. 179 election without IRS consent, the related committee report states that a taxpayer may also "make" an election on an amended return without IRS consent under the provision. Final and temporary regulations which explain the provision adopt this position and clarify that the particular amount that a taxpayer elected to expense with respect to an item of property may be increased or decreased (T.D. 9209, filed with the Federal Register on July 12, 2005; Reg. § 1.179-5; T.D. 9146, filed with the Federal Register on August 4, 2004; Temporary Reg. § 1.179-5T). The IRS will follow these regulations for any tax year which Code Sec. 179(c)(2) allows a revocation on an amended return (i.e., for property placed in service in tax years beginning after 2002). The IRS intends to update the regulations to reflect the PATH Act's permanent extension of Code Sec. 179(c)(2) (Rev. Proc. 2017-33, Section 3.02).

The amended return must be filed before expiration of the applicable limitations period for filing an amended return for the tax year that the property was placed in service (Reg. § 1.179-5(c)(1)). The amended return must include the adjustment to taxable income caused by the election or revocation of the expense deduction as well as any collateral adjustments to taxable income or tax liability. Amended returns must also be filed for any subsequent affected tax years for which a return has been filed (Reg. § 1.179-5(c)(2)(i) and (c)(3)(i)).

Taxpayers should include a statement on the amended return which specifies the property or portion of the property for which the election, revocation, or change is made.

Generally, an amended return must be filed within three years from the date the original return was filed or within 2 years after the date the date tax was paid, whichever is later. For this purpose, a return that is filed early is considered filed on the due date. However, where a filing extension was received and the return was filed after the regular due date and before the extended due date, the three-year period runs from the date of filing. See instructions for Form 1040-X.

An election on an amended return to expense the entire cost of an asset or any portion of an asset that was not expensed on the original return is not considered a revocation of a Code Sec. 179 election (Reg. § 1.179-5(c)(2)(i)). Thus, the rule which prohibits the revocation of a revocation (Code Sec. 179(c)(2); Reg. § 1.179-5(c)(3)(ii)) is not applicable and a taxpayer may revoke an election made on an original or amended return (if the period for filing an amended return to make the revocation has not expired).

If a taxpayer elects to expense a portion of the cost of an item of section 179 property placed in service in a tax year beginning after 2002, the taxpayer may file an amended return (within the limitations period) to expense any or all of the cost basis that was not expensed. If no election was made to expense a particular item of property placed in service in a tax year beginning after 2002, an amended return may be filed (within the limitations period) to expense any portion or all of its cost basis (Reg. § 1.179-5(c)(2)(ii)).

A revocation may be made with respect to any portion of an election to expense an item of section 179 property placed in service in a tax year beginning after 2002 within the limitation period whether the election was made on an original or an amended return. The revocation may be made without IRS consent by filing an amended return within the limitations period and designating the dollar amount that the revocation applies to. The revocation is irrevocable. Thus, to the extent that a revocation applies to the cost basis of an item of property, no new election may be made to expense that property (Reg. § 1.179-5(c)(3)).

***Example (1):*** John Adams purchases a table saw in 2018 for $5,000. He only elects to expense $3,000 of its cost on the 2018 tax return filed on April 15, 2019. In November 2020, he decides to revoke the 2018 election. John may file an amended 2018 return to revoke the election since 2018 is still an open year under the statute of limitations. This election is irrevocable. He will also need to file an amended 2019 return since this is an affected year (he has to claim second-year depreciation on the $3,000 and make any other necessary adjustments). In June 2021, after filing his 2020 return, John decides that he wants to make an election to expense the $2,000 portion of the machine's cost that was not expensed in 2018. John may make the election on an amended 2018 return. He will also need to file amended returns for 2019 and 2020 since these are affected tax years. John may later revoke the election to expense the $2,000 (or any portion of the $2,000) by filing an amended 2018 return (and amended returns for subsequent affected tax years) before the expiration of the statute of limitations for amending the 2018 return.

The election/revocation process allows small businesses more time to consider whether making the section Code Sec. 179 election is to their advantage. For example, because an election to expense reduces adjusted gross income and taxable income it may also reduce exemptions and deductions, social security coverage of the self-employed, and certain tax credits.

An election out of bonus depreciation cannot be made without IRS consent. See ¶ 127D. Thus, if a taxpayer revokes a Code Sec. 179 expense election, bonus depreciation may not be claimed on the revoked amount if an election out of bonus depreciation applied to the property in the year it was placed in service.

***Example (2):*** Jack placed office furniture (seven-year MACRS property) in service in 2021 and expensed the entire cost. The furniture cost $100,000. He also placed other seven-year property in service in 2021 and made an election out of bonus depreciation for seven-year property. If Jack files an amended 2021 return to revoke the Code Sec. 179 expense election he may not claim a bonus depreciation deduction on the office furniture. The amended return will reflect the addition of a depreciation deduction of $1,429 ($100,000 × 14.29% first-year table percentage) and the elimination of the $100,000 expense deduction. Note that revocation is not considered a change in accounting method and no Code Sec. 481(a) adjustment is made.

*Manner of making qualified real property election.* The provision to treat qualified real property as section 179 property is described as an election by Code Sec. 179(f)(1), prior to amendment byP.L. 115-97 and Code Sec. 179(d)(1)(B)(ii). The manner of making the election is provided in the Form 4562 instructions which require the attachment of an election statement. This election is separate from the election to expense property that is section 179 property. For example, a taxpayer must first elect to treat its qualified real property as section 179 property. Then a taxpayer makes an election to expense a particular amount of its qualified real property. Code Sec. 179(c)(2) arguably allows a taxpayer to revoke (within the limitations period for filing an amended return) an election to treat qualified real property as section 179 property. That section, which was enacted to allow a taxpayer to revoke an election to expense section 179 property, states that it applies to "Any election made under this section" (i.e., section 179). Since the election to treat qualified real property as section 179 property is made under section 179, the language in Code Sec. 179(c)(2) appears to encompass the election.

*Court decisions relating to elections.*The Tax Court determined that the IRS did not abuse its discretion when it refused to allow a taxpayer to claim the Code Sec. 179 expense allowance on property which, as the result of an audit, was reclassified as depreciable (*S.H. Patton*, 116 TC 206, CCH Dec. 54,307). Similarly, *M.A. McGrath*, T.C. Memo. 2002-231, CCH Dec. 54,873(M), aff'd per curiam on another issue, CA-5, 2003-2 USTC ¶ 50,663).

The inclusion of property in cost of goods sold is not the equivalent of an election under section 179 (*M. Visin*, 86 TCM 279, T.C. Memo. 2003-246, Dec. 55,269(M), aff'd, CA-9 (unpublished opinion), 2005-1 USTC ¶ 50,199).

## ¶ 304A

## Code Sec. 179 Empowerment Zone Property

In a tax year beginning before 2021, an enterprise zone business (as defined in Code Sec. 1397C) located within a government-designated empowerment zone (as defined in Code Sec. 1391(b)(2)) may increase the applicable annual dollar limitation ($1,040,000 for tax years beginning in 2020) by the lesser of $35,000 or the cost of Sec. 179 property that is qualified zone property (as defined in Code Sec. 1397D) that is placed in service before January 1, 2021 (Code Sec. 1397A). See www.hud.gov/crlocator for a list of empowerment zones. This maximum amount is reduced (but not below zero) by the excess investment over the applicable investment limitation ($2,590,000 for tax years beginning in 2020). However, in applying this investment limitation, only one-half of the cost of qualified zone property is taken into account (the full cost of Code Sec. 179 property that is not qualified zone property is taken into account) (Code Sec. 1397A(a)(2)). This maximum amount is also subject to the taxable income limitation discussed below. If the property ceases to be used in an empowerment zone by the enterprise zone business, the benefit of the increased portion of the section 179 allowance is subject to recapture under the rules described below (Code Sec. 1397A(b)). The standard allowance remains subject to recapture if business use in or outside of the zone decreases to 50 percent or less.

Although empowerment zone designations were extended through December 31, 2025 (Code Sec. 1391(d)(1)), the rule allowing for a $35,000 increase in the expensing limitation was eliminated effective for tax years beginning after 2020 (Code Sec. 1397A(c)).

Farm businesses in an empowerment zone do not qualify as enterprise zone businesses and are ineligible for this increased Code Sec. 179 annual dollar limitation if the aggregate unadjusted bases (or, if greater, the fair market value) of the assets owned by the taxpayer which are used in the farm business and the aggregate value of assets leased by the taxpayer which are used in the farm business exceed $500,000 (Code Sec. 1397C(d)(5)). This $500,000 amount is not adjusted for inflation.

### *Qualified zone property defined*

Qualified zone property is defined as section 179 property (see ¶ 302) which also meets the following requirements (Code Sec. 1397D). The property must be depreciable under MACRS. The original use of the property in the empowerment zone must begin with the taxpayer. The property must be acquired by the taxpayer by purchase (as defined in Code Sec. 179(d)(2)) after the date on which the designation of the empowerment zone took effect. Substantially all of the use of the property must be in an empowerment zone and in the active conduct of a qualified business by the taxpayer in the zone. In the case of certain property which is substantially renovated by the taxpayer, the original use and purchase requirements are treated as satisfied (Code Sec. 1397D(a)(2)). For purposes of the original use requirement, if property is sold and leased back by the taxpayer within 3 months after the date such property was originally placed in service, the property is treated as originally placed in service not earlier than the date on which such property is used under the leaseback (Code Sec. 1397D(a)(3)).

Computer software which is section 179 property (see Code Sec. 179(d)(1)(A)(ii)) is not qualified zone property because it is depreciable over three years under Code Sec. 167(f) and empowerment zone property only includes property which is eligible for depreciation under Code Sec. 168 (see ¶ 48 for a discussion of computer software).

*District of Columbia enterprise zone*

The District of Columbia enterprise zone is treated as an empowerment zone through December 31, 2011 for purposes of the additional section 179 deduction (Code Sec. 1400). See www.hud.gov/crlocator for a list of areas within the District of Columbia that are treated as empowerment zones.

*Renewal communities*

Rules that apply to an enterprise zone business also apply to a renewal community business (as defined in Code Sec. 1400G) that acquires qualified renewal property (as defined in Code Sec. 1400J(b)) by purchase (as defined in Code Sec. 179(d)(2)) and places the property in service in a renewal community (as defined in Code Sec. 1400E(a)(1)) (Code Sec. 1400J). See www.hud.gov/crlocator for a list of renewal communities. The property must be acquired after December 31, 2001 and before January 1, 2010 (Code Sec. 1400J(b)(1)(A)), or, if earlier, before the day after the date that the designation of renewal community status is terminated (Code Sec. 1400E(b)(3)). The investment limit is also applied by only taking one-half of qualified renewal community property into account (Code Sec. 1400J(a); Code Sec. 1397A(a)(2)). The IRS has issued a revenue procedure that explains how a taxpayer may make a retroactive election to deduct the increased section 179 expensing allowance for qualified renewal property that is placed in service in an expanded area of a renewal community (i.e., a contiguous tract to a renewal community based on 2000 census data) that is authorized by Code Sec. 1400E(g) (Rev. Proc. 2006-16, I.R.B. 2006-9)).

## ¶ 305

## Code Sec. 179 New York Liberty Zone Property

The maximum dollar limitation on Code Sec. 179 property ($125,000 in 2007) was increased by an amount equal to $35,000 for Code Sec. 179 property which is "qualified New York Liberty Zone property" (as defined below) (Code Sec. 1400L(f), as amended by the Working Families Tax Relief Act of 2004 (P.L. 108-311)). The $35,000 increase applied to qualified NYLZ property acquired after September 10, 2001 and placed into service before January 1, 2007.

The amendment made by the Working Families Tax Relief Act retroactively clarifies that the term qualified New York Liberty Zone Property for purposes of the additional $35,000 expense allowance includes property which would be NYLZ property for purposes of the Code Sec. 1400L(b) NYLZ bonus depreciation allowance but for the fact that it qualifies for the 30-percent or 50-percent bonus depreciation allowance under Code Sec. 168(k). The amendment is particularly significant because most property placed in service in the NYLZ qualifies for bonus depreciation under Code Sec. 168(k)rather than Code Sec. 1400L(b) and, therefore, is not considered qualified New York Liberty Zone property. This point is discussed at ¶ 127E.

Taking the $35,000 increase into account, the maximum amount of qualified NYLZ property placed in service before January 1, 2007 that may be expensed is $143,000 for tax years beginning in 2006 ($108,000 (inflation-adjusted dollar limit) + $35,000) and $140,000 for tax years beginning in 2005 ($105,000 (inflation-adjusted dollar limit) + $35,000). The $35,000 bump-up is not adjusted for inflation. The $35,000 increase does not apply to property placed in service after December 31, 2006.

In addition to the increased expensing allowance, the deduction phaseout rule based on a taxpayer's total investments (the "investment limitation") for the tax year is modified to take into account only 50 percent of the taxpayer's investment in Code Sec. 179 property that qualifies (or would qualify) as New York Liberty Zone property (Code Sec. 1400L(f)(1)(B)). See "*Investment limitation modified,*" below.

Because the $35,000 bump-up provision was enacted after many taxpayers had already filed their 2000 (fiscal-year) or 2001 return, some taxpayers may not have claimed the additional section 179 allowance on qualifying Liberty Zone property. These taxpayers were directed to file an amended return by December 31, 2003 (Rev. Proc. 2003-50, I.R.B. 2003-29).

*Qualified New York Liberty Zone property*

The additional expensing allowance is limited to the cost of qualified New York Liberty Zone property placed in service during the tax year. Qualified New York Liberty Zone property has the same meaning as the definition used for purposes of the 30-percent additional first-year depreciation allowance (bonus depreciation allowance) for qualified New York Liberty Zone property provided for in Code Sec. 1400L(b)(2). However, the requirement in Code Sec. 1400L(b)(2)(C)(i) that the property not be eligible for expensing under the more general bonus depreciation provision of Code Sec. 168(k)(2) does not apply (Code Sec. 1400L(f)(2), as amended by the Working Families Tax Relief Act of 2004 (P.L. 108-311)). The definition of qualified New York Liberty Zone property for bonus depreciation purposes is described at ¶ 127E.

In addition to being qualified NYLZ property, the property must also qualify as Section 179 property (i.e., it must be the type of property that the Section 179 expense allowance can be claimed on without regard to the provision which increases the expense amount by $35,000). Thus, for example, section 1250 property which is eligible for bonus depreciation does not qualify for either the $35,000 increase or the $100,000 basic section 179 allowance.

Other requirements for claiming the additional Liberty Zone expensing allowance are:

(1) the property must have an MACRS recovery period of 20 years or less;

(2) the property must be acquired by the taxpayer by purchase (within the meaning of Code Sec. 179(d)(2)) after September 10, 2001, and placed in service before January 1, 2007;

(3) the original use of the property in the Liberty Zone must commence with the taxpayer after September 10, 2001; and

(4) substantially all (80 percent or more) of the use of the property must be in the New York Liberty Zone in the active conduct of a trade or business by the taxpayer in the Zone (Code Sec. 1400L(f)(2); Code Sec. 1400L(b)(2)).

*Mandatory ADS property does not qualify*

Property for which the MACRS alternative depreciation system (ADS) is mandatory (¶ 152) does not qualify for the increased Code Sec. 179 allowance (Code Sec. 1400L(f)(2); Code Sec. 1400L(b)(2)(C)(ii)).

*Leasehold improvements*

New York Liberty Zone leasehold improvement property (see ¶ 124A) does not qualify for the $35,000 increased expensing allowance (Code Sec. 1400L(f)(2); Code Sec. 1400L(b)(2)(C)(iii)). Furthermore, leasehold improvement property that is a structural component (Section 1250 real property) does not qualify for the basic $100,000 Code Sec. 179 deduction amount. See ¶ 124A.

*New York Liberty Zone defined*

The New York Liberty Zone is the area located on or south of Canal Street, East Broadway (east of its intersection with Canal Street), or Grand Street (east of its intersection with East Broadway) in the Borough of Manhattan in New York City (Code Sec. 1400L(h)).

*Acquisition by purchase after September 10, 2001*

The property must be acquired by purchase within the meaning of Code Sec. 179(d)(2) after September 10, 2001 and placed in service before January 1, 2007 (Code Sec. 1400L(b)(2)(A)(iv)). Under Code Sec. 179(d)(2), property is not considered purchased by the taxpayer if it is acquired from a related party or by a member of a controlled group, has a substituted basis or is acquired from a decedent with a fair market value basis. See ¶ 302. Property will not qualify if a binding written contract for the acquisition of the property was in effect before September 11, 2001.

*Self-constructed property*

Property manufactured, constructed, or produced by a taxpayer for the taxpayer's own use is treated as acquired after September 10, 2001, if the taxpayer began manufacturing, constructing, or producing the property after September 10, 2001 (Code Sec. 1400L(b)(2)(D)). The Joint Committee Explanation states that property manufactured, constructed, or produced for the taxpayer by another person under a contract entered into prior to the manufacture, construction, or production of the property is considered manufactured, constructed, or produced by the taxpayer (Joint Committee on Taxation, *Technical Explanation of the "Job Creation and Worker Assistance Act of 2002"* (JCX-12-02), March 6, 2002).

*Original use requirement*

The original use of the property in the New York Liberty Zone must commence with the taxpayer after September 10, 2001 (Code Sec. 1400L(b)(2)(A)(iii)). The Joint Committee Explanation indicates that used property may qualify as long as it was not previously used in the Liberty Zone. The Explanation further states that additional capital expenditures incurred to recondition or rebuild property for which the original use in the Liberty Zone began with the taxpayer will also satisfy the original use requirement (Joint Committee on Taxation, *Technical Explanation of the "Job Creation and Worker Assistance Act of 2002"* (JCX-12-02), March 6, 2002).

*Investment limitation modified*

For qualifying Liberty Zone property, the dollar limitation for the tax year (as increased by $35,000) is reduced by the excess of (1) 50 percent of the cost of Code Sec. 179 property that is qualified Liberty Zone property placed in service during the tax year plus the total amount of any other Code Sec. 179 property placed in service during the tax year, over (2) the applicable investment limitation for the tax year ($410,000 in 2004, $420,000 in 2005, and $430,000 in 2006). For Liberty Zone property placed in service in a tax year that begins in 2004, the dollar limit will be completely phased out once the section 179 property placed in service in the Liberty Zone equals or exceeds $1,094,000 ($1,094,000/2 - $410,000 = the increased dollar limit of $137,000). The phaseout is reached at $1,120,000 ($1,120,000/2 - $420,000 = the increased dollar limit of $140,000) in 2005 and at $1,146,000 ($1,146,000/2 - $430,000 = the increased dollar limit of $143,000) in 2006.

*Other Code Sec. 179 provisions apply*

Other than the increased dollar amount limitation and increased investment limitation phaseout range, the provisions of Code Sec. 179 are applied to Liberty Zone property in the same manner as they are applied to other businesses.

*Recapture*

The $35,000 additional section 179 dollar amount for New York Liberty Zone property is subject to recapture if the qualified New York Liberty Zone property ceases to be used during the asset's recovery period in the New York Liberty Zone 80 percent or more of the time in the active conduct of a trade or business. Rules similar toCode Sec. 179(d)(10) (relating to recapture when business use of section 179 property drops to 50 percent or less) apply (Code Sec. 1400L(f)(3)). See ¶ 300 for a discussion of these recapture rules.

For example, removal of the property from the Liberty Zone for continued business use outside of the Zone would result in recapture with respect to the $35,000 additional Code Sec. 179 allowance but not the standard Code Sec. 179 allowance ($108,000 is 2006). If the recovery period has not expired, the sum of both components of the allowance, however, would be subject to recapture in the year that the property is not used predominantly for business purposes (i.e., more than 50 percent) even if the property remains in the Zone.

The Code Sec. 179 expense allowance (including the increased section 179 allowance for qualifying New York Liberty Zone property) is treated as a depreciation deduction for section 1245 recapture purposes upon the disposition of the property. See ¶ 300.

*Expiration date*

Property placed in service after December 31, 2006, does not qualify for the additional $35,000 expense allowance (Code Sec. 1400L(b)(2)(A)(v)).

## ¶ 306

## Code Sec. 179 Gulf Opportunity Zone Property

The maximum allowable Code Sec. 179 expense allowance ($125,000 dollar limit for tax years beginning in 2007 and $250,000 for tax years beginning in 2008) was increased by the lesser of $100,000 or the cost of qualified section 179 Gulf Opportunity Zone property placed in service in the tax year. The investment limit ($500,000 for tax years beginning in 2007 and $800,000 for tax years beginning in 2008) was increased by the lesser of $600,000 or the amount of qualified section 179 Gulf Opportunity Zone property placed in service during the tax year (Code Sec. 1400N(e), as added by the Gulf Opportunity Zone Act of 2005 (P.L. 109-135);

Section 6.01(1) of Rev. Proc. 2008-54). The $100,000 increase in the dollar limitation and the $600,000 increase in the investment limitation are not adjusted for inflation.

The increases in the dollar and investment limits applied to qualified section 179 Gulf Opportunity Zone property acquired on or after August 28, 2005, and placed in service before January 1, 2008 (Code Sec. 1400N(d)(2)(A), (e)(2)). However, the placed-in-service deadline was extended an additional year for section 179 Gulf Opportunity Zone property placed in service in certain specified counties and parishes within the Gulf Opportunity Zone where more than 60 percent of the housing was destroyed by hurricanes in 2005 (Code Sec. 1400N(e)(2)(B)). Thus, the qualifying property located in one of these parishes or counties must be placed in service before January 1, 2009. These counties and parishes are referred to as "specified portions" of the GO Zone. This is the only type of GO Zone property placed in service in 2008 that qualifies for an increased section 179 allowance (Rev. Proc. 2008-54).

See ¶ 127F for a discussion of the Gulf Opportunity Go Zone 50 percent bonus depreciation deduction.

The specified portions of the GO Zone are (Notice 2007-36, I.R.B. 2007-17):

- **Alabama**: No counties.
- **Louisiana**: The parishes of Calcasieu, Cameron, Orleans, Plaquemines, St. Bernard, St. Tammany, and Washington.
- **Mississippi**: The counties of Hancock, Harrison, Jackson, Pearl River, and Stone.

Note that property may be acquired before it is considered placed in service. For example, a machine may be acquired before it is completely assembled and integrated into a manufacturing process for use in its assigned function (i.e., placed in service). See ¶ 3.

Taking into account these increases, the maximum dollar amounts for qualifying section 179 Gulf Opportunity Zone property acquired on or after August 28, 2005 and placed in service within a particular tax year are:

- $205,000 ($105,000 + $100,000) for property acquired on or after August 28, 2005 and placed in service in tax years beginning in 2005.
- $208,000 ($108,000 + $100,000) for property placed in service in tax years beginning in 2006.
- $225,000 ($125,000 + $100,000) for property placed in service before January 1, 2008 in tax years beginning in 2007.
- $350,000 ($250,000 + $100,000) for property placed in service before January 1, 2009 in tax years beginning in 2008 (in a specified portion of the GO Zone).

The dollar amount begins to be reduced by reason of the investment limitation (if at least $600,000 of qualifying zone property is placed in service) at:

- $1,020,000 ($420,000 + $600,000) for property acquired on or after August 28, 2005 and placed in service in tax years beginning in 2005.
- $1,030,000 ($430,000 + $600,000) for property placed in service in tax years beginning in 2006.
- $1,100,000 ($500,000 + $600,000) for property placed in service before January 1, 2008 in tax years beginning in 2007.
- $1,400,000 ($800,000 + $600,000) for property placed in service before January 1, 2009 in tax years beginning in 2008 (applies to specified portions of the GO Zone)

The dollar amount is completely phased out by reason of the investment limitation at:

- $1,225,000 ($205,000 – ($1,225,000 – ($420,000 + $600,000)) = $0) for property acquired on or after August 28, 2005 and placed in service in tax years beginning in 2005.
- $1,238,000 ($208,000 – ($1,238,000 – ($430,000 + $600,000)) = $0) for property placed in service in tax years beginning in 2006.
- $1,325,000 ($225,000 – ($1,325,000 – ($500,000 + $600,000)) = $0) for property placed in service before January 1, 2008 in tax years beginning in 2007.
- $1,750,000 ($350,000 – ($1,750,000 – ($800,000 + $600,000)) = $0) for property placed in service before January 1, 2009 in tax years beginning in 2008 (applies to specified portions of the GO Zone)

***Example (1):*** In 2008, a calendar-year taxpayer places $500,000 of qualified section 179 Gulf Opportunity Zone property in service in a specified county and $950,000 of other qualifying section 179 property in service. The dollar limitation is $350,000 ($250,000 + $100,000). The investment limitation is $1,300,000 ($800,000 basic limit + $500,000 amount of qualified section 179 Gulf Opportunity Zone property placed in service since this is less than $600,000). Because the total amount of section 179 property placed in service ($1,450,000) exceeds the investment limit by $150,000 ($1,450,000 – $1,300,000), the dollar limit is reduced to $200,000 ($350,000 - $150,000) and this amount is claimed as the deduction under Code Sec. 179 subject to the taxable income limitation.

***Example (2):*** XYZ corporation, a calendar-year taxpayer, places $1,200,000 of new machinery in service in 2007. The machinery is qualified section 179 Gulf Opportunity Zone property. XYZ places no other section 179 property in service in 2007. Under the dollar limitation, only $225,000 ($125,000 basic limit + $100,000 bump-up for section 179 Gulf Opportunity Zone property) of the total $1,200,000 of machinery placed in service may be expensed. The investment limit is $1,100,000 ($500,000 basic limit + $600,000 maximum increase since this is less than the cost of qualifying section 179 zone property placed in service). The dollar limit must be reduced by $100,000 ($1,200,000 cost of section 179 property placed in service – $1,100,000 investment limit). Thus, XYZ's section 179 deduction for 2007 is $125,000 ($225,000 dollar limit – $100,000), assuming that XYZ's taxable income is at least $125,000.

### *Property must be both section 179 property and qualified zone property*

For the increased limits to apply, the property must be both section 179 property and qualified Gulf Opportunity Zone property. If the property is not section 179 property, then no amount may be expensed under Code Sec. 179. To qualify as section 179 property, the property must be new or used tangible section 1245 property that is depreciable under MACRS (subject to an exception for off-the-shelf computer software) and used predominantly (more than 50 percent) in the active conduct of a trade or business. In addition, the property must be acquired by "purchase" from an unrelated person (Code Sec. 179(d)(2)). See ¶ 302 for a discussion of the definition of qualifying section 179 property.

Certain qualified Gulf Opportunity Zone property, most notably, residential rental and nonresidential real property will not qualify for any expensing under Code Sec. 179 because section 1250 property is not section 179 property. Most used property will not qualify for the increase in the dollar amount because such property cannot be qualified zone property unless the original use in the zone commences with the taxpayer. Used property, however, may constitute section 179 property and qualify for the basic section 179 allowance.

*Qualifying Gulf Opportunity Zone property*

Property that otherwise qualifies for expensing under Code Sec. 179 (i.e., section 179 property as defined in Code Sec. 179(d); see ¶ 302) will qualify for the increased section 179 limitations if it is Gulf Opportunity Zone property as defined for purposes of the 50-percent additional depreciation allowance (see ¶ 127F). In general, property is Gulf Opportunity Zone property if (Code Sec. 1400N(d)(2)):

- It is depreciable under MACRS and has a recovery period of 20 years or less.
- Substantially all (80 percent or greater) of the property is used in the active conduct of a trade or business by the taxpayer within the Gulf Opportunity Zone (as defined in Code Sec. 1400M(1))
- The original use of the property within the zone commences with the taxpayer on or after August 28, 2005, and the property is placed in service before January 1, 2008 (January 1, 2009 in specified areas of the GO Zone, as previously explained)
- It acquired by purchase (within the meaning of Code Sec. 179(d)(2); see ¶ 302) on or after August 28, 2005.
- No written binding contract for the acquisition of the property was in effect before August 28, 2005

If the first use of used property within the Gulf Opportunity Zone commences with the taxpayer, then the used property may qualify for the increased allowance. If the section 179 property was previously used by another taxpayer within the Zone, it will only remain eligible for the standard section 179 allowance ($105,000 in tax years beginning in 2005, $108,000 in 2006, and $125,000 in 2007, and $250,000 in 2008).

Gulf Opportunity Zone property does not include property that must be depreciated using the MACRS alternative depreciation system (ADS) (see ¶ 152) or property financed to any extent with state and local tax-exempt bonds that generate tax-exempt interest under Code Sec. 103 (Code Sec. 1400N(d)(2)(B)). Property which a taxpayer elects to depreciate under ADS may qualify.

The additional section 179 allowance may not be claimed on property used in connection with: a private or commercial golf course, a country club, a massage parlor, a hot tub facility, a suntan facility, a liquor store, or a gambling or animal racing property (Code Sec. 1400N(p); see ¶ 127F).

*Recapture if business use declines to less than 80 percent*

Code Sec. 1400N(e)(4) provides that: "For purposes of this subsection, rules similar to the rules under section 179(d)(10) shall apply with respect to any qualified section 179 Gulf Opportunity Zone property which ceases to be qualified section 179 Gulf Opportunity Zone property." Thus, recapture of the additional section 179 expense allowance allowed by Code Sec. 1400N(e) is required if the property ceases to be substantially used for business in the GO Zone (i.e., business use in the Zone is not 80 percent or greater or the property is removed from the zone) prior to the end of it recovery period since this would cause the property to lose its status as Gulf Opportunity Zone property. The standard section 179 deduction ($125,000 in 2007 and $250,000 in 2008) (as well as the additional section 179 deduction) is subject to recapture under the generally applicable rule if business use, whether in or outside the GO Zone, drops to 50 percent or less before the expiration of its recovery period. The recapture rules of Code Sec. 179(d)(10) are described at ¶ 300.

*Recapture upon disposition*

The Code Sec. 179 expense allowance (including the increased section 179 allowance for qualifying Gulf Zone property) is treated as a depreciation deduction for section 1245 recapture purposes upon the disposition of the property. See ¶ 300.

*Coordination with increased expense allowance for empowerment zones and renewal communities*

If qualifying section 179 Gulf Opportunity Property is placed in service within an empowerment zone or renewal community located within the Gulf Opportunity Zone, a taxpayer may not also claim the benefit of the additional $35,000 expense allowance provided for qualifying property placed in service in an empowerment zone (Code Sec. 1397A or a renewal community Code Sec. 1400J; see ¶ 304A) unless the taxpayer elects not to claim the additional $100,000 allowance provided for section 179 Gulf Opportunity Zone property (Code Sec. 1400N(e)(3)).

Generally, it will be preferable to take advantage of the $100,000 bump-up provided for qualified section 179 Gulf Opportunity Zone property since the additional allowance for empowerment zone and renewal community property is only $35,000 (e.g., $160,000 total in 2007 ($125,000 + $35,000)) as compared to $100,000 for Gulf Opportunity Zone property (e.g., $225,000 total in 2007 ($125,000 + $100,000)).

## ¶ 306A

## Code Sec. 179 Kansas Disaster Area Property

Taxpayers other than estates, trusts, and certain noncorporate lessors may elect to claim a Code Sec. 179 expense deduction on the cost of qualifying section 179 property acquired by purchase (see ¶ 302). The maximum allowable Code Sec. 179 expense allowance ($125,000 for tax years beginning in 2007 and $250,000 for tax years beginning in 2008) was increased by the lesser of $100,000 or the cost of qualified section 179 Recovery Assistance property placed in service in the tax year. The investment limit ($500,000 for tax years beginning in 2007 and $800,000 for tax years beginning in 2008) was increased by the lesser of $600,000 or the amount of qualified section 179 Recovery Assistance property placed in service during the tax year (Act Sec. 15345(d)(2) of the Heartland, Habitat, Harvest, and Horticulture Act of 2008 (P.L. 110-246), applying Code Sec. 1400N(e), as added by the Gulf Opportunity Zone Act of 2005 (P.L. 109-135); Section 6.01(1)(a) of Rev. Proc. 2008-54). The $100,000 increase in the dollar limitation and the $600,000 increase in the investment limitation are not adjusted for inflation.

The increases in the dollar and investment limits applied to qualified section 179 Recovery Assistance property acquired on or after May 5, 2007, and placed in service before January 1, 2009 in the Kansas disaster area (Act Sec. 15345(d)(1) and (2) of the Heartland, Habitat, Harvest, and Horticulture Act of 2008 (P.L. 110-246), applying Code Sec. 1400N(e)(2) and Code Sec. 1400N(d)(2)(A), (e)(2)).

The Kansas disaster area is an area with respect to which a major disaster has been declared by the President under section 401 of the Robert T. Stafford Disaster Relief and Emergency Assistance Act (FEMA-1699-DR, as in effect on the date of the enactment (May 5, 2008) by reason of severe storms and tornados beginning on May 4, 2007, and determined by the President to warrant individual or individual and public assistance from the Federal Government under such Act with respect to damages attributable to such storms and tornados (Act § 15345 of the Heartland, Habitat, Harvest and Horticulture Act of 2008, P.L. 110-246)). The Kansas disaster area is comprised of the following counties: Barton, Clay, Cloud, Comanche, Dickinson, Edwards, Ellsworth, Kiowa, Leavenworth, Lyon, McPherson, Osage,

Osborne, Ottawa, Phillips, Pottawatomie, Pratt, Reno, Rice, Riley, Saline, Shawnee, Smith, and Stafford (Notice 2008-67, I.R.B. 2008-32).

Note that property may be acquired before it is considered placed in service. For example, a machine may be acquired before it is completely assembled and integrated into a manufacturing process for use in its assigned function (i.e., placed in service). See ¶ 3.

Taking into account these increases, the maximum dollar amounts for qualifying section 179 Recovery Assistance property acquired on or after May 5, 2007 are:

- $208,000 ($108,000 + $100,000) for property placed in service in tax years beginning in 2006.
- $225,000 ($125,000 + $100,000) for property placed in service in tax years beginning in 2007.
- $350,000 ($250,000 + $100,000) for property placed in service before January 1, 2009 in tax years beginning in 2008.

The dollar amount begins to be reduced by reason of the investment limitation (if at least $600,000 of qualifying Recovery Assistance property is placed in service) at:

- $1,030,000 ($430,000 + $600,000) for tax years beginning in 2006.
- $1,100,000 ($500,000 + $600,000) for property placed in service in tax years beginning in 2007.
- $1,400,000 ($800,000 + $600,000) for property placed in service before January 1, 2009 in tax years beginning in 2008.

The dollar amount is completely phased out by reason of the investment limitation (assuming at least $100,000 of Recovery Assistance property is placed in service during the tax year) at:

- $1,238,000 ($208,000 – ($1,238,000 – ($430,000 + $600,000)) = $0) for tax years beginning in 2006
- $1,325,000 ($225,000 – ($1,325,000 – ($500,000 + $600,000)) = $0) for property placed in service in tax years beginning in 2007
- $1,750,000 ($350,000 – ($1,750,000 – ($800,000 + $600,000)) = $0) for property placed in service before January 1, 2009 in tax years beginning in 2008

***Example (1):*** In 2007, a calendar-year taxpayer places $200,000 of qualified section 179 Recovery Assistance property in service after May 5, 2007 and $550,000 of other qualifying section 179 property in service during 2007. The dollar limitation is $225,000 ($125,000 for 2007 + $100,000). The investment limitation is $700,000 ($500,000 basic limit + $200,000 amount of qualified section 179 Recovery Assistance property placed in service since this is less than $600,000). Because the total amount of section 179 property placed in service ($750,000) exceeds the investment limit by $50,000 ($750,000 - $700,000), the dollar limit is reduced to $175,000 ($225,000 - $50,000) and this amount is claimed as the deduction under Code Sec. 179 subject to the taxable income limitation. The 50% bonus depreciation is $12,500 (($200,000 - $175,000) × 50%) (see ¶ 125G).

***Example (2):*** XYZ corporation, a calendar-year taxpayer, places $1,500,000 of new machinery in service in 2008. The machinery is qualified section 179 Recovery Assistance property. XYZ places no other section 179 property in service in 2008. Under the dollar limitation, only $350,000 ($250,000 basic limit for 2008 + $100,000 bump-up for section 179 Recovery Assistance property) of the total $1,500,000 of machinery placed in service may be expensed. The investment limit is $1,400,000 ($800,000 basic limit for 2008 + $600,000). The dollar limit must be reduced by $100,000 ($1,500,000 cost of section 179 property placed in service - $1,400,000 investment limit). Thus, XYZ's section 179 deduction for 2008 is $250,000 ($350,000 dollar limit - $100,000), assuming that XYZ's taxable income is at least $250,000. XYZ's 50-percent additional depreciation allowance is $625,000 (($1,500,000 - $250,000) × 50%).

*Property must be both section 179 property and qualified Recovery Assistance property*

For the increased limits to apply, the property must be both section 179 property and qualified Recovery Assistance property. If the property is not section 179 property, then no amount may be expensed under Code Sec. 179. To qualify as section 179 property, the property must be new or used tangible section 1245 property that is depreciable under MACRS (subject to an exception for off-the-shelf computer software) and used predominantly (more than 50 percent) in the active conduct of a trade or business. In addition, the property must be acquired by "purchase" from an unrelated person (Code Sec. 179(d)(2)). See ¶ 302 for a discussion of the definition of qualifying section 179 property.

Certain qualified Recovery Assistance property, most notably, residential rental and nonresidential real property will not qualify for any expensing under Code Sec. 179 because section 1250 property is not section 179 property. Most used property will not qualify for the increase in the dollar amount because such property cannot be qualified Recovery Assistance property unless the original use in the zone commences with the taxpayer. Used property, however, may constitute section 179 property and qualify for the basic allowance.

*Qualifying Recovery Assistance property*

Property that otherwise qualifies for expensing under Code Sec. 179 (i.e., section 179 property as defined in Code Sec. 179(d); see ¶ 302) will qualify for the increased section 179 limitations if it is Recovery Assistance Property as defined for purposes of the 50-percent additional depreciation allowance for Recovery Assistance Property (see ¶ 127G). In general, property is Recovery Assistance property if:

- It is depreciable under MACRS and has a recovery period of 20 years or less.
- Substantially all (80 percent or greater) of the property is used in the active conduct of a trade or business by the taxpayer within the Kansas disaster area.
- The original use of the property commences with the taxpayer in the Kansas disaster area on or after May 5, 2007, and the property is placed in service before January 1, 2009.
- It acquired by purchase (within the meaning of Code Sec. 179(d)(2); see ¶ 302) on or after May 5, 2007.
- No written binding contract for the acquisition of the property was in effect before May 5, 2007.

If the first use of used property within the Kansas disaster area commences with the taxpayer, then the used property may qualify for the increased allowance. If the section 179 property was previously used by another taxpayer within the disaster area, it will only remain eligible for the standard section 179 allowance ($125,000 in 2007 and $250,000 in 2008).

Recovery Assistance property does not include property that must be depreciated using the MACRS alternative depreciation system (ADS) (see ¶ 152) (including listed property (¶ 208), such as a vehicle, used less than 50 percent for business purposes) or property financed to any extent with state and local tax-exempt bonds that generate tax-exempt interest under Code Sec. 103 (Code Sec.

1400N(d)(2)(B)). Property which a taxpayer elects to depreciate under ADS may qualify.

It appears that property used in connection with: a private or commercial golf course, a country club, a massage parlor, a hot tub facility, a suntan facility, a liquor store, or a gambling or animal racing property may qualify as Recovery Assistance property; see ¶ 127G.

*Recapture if business use declines 80 percent or less*

Rules similar to the rules Code Sec. 179(d)(10) apply with respect to any qualified section 179 Recovery Assistance property which ceases to be qualified section 179 Recovery Assistance Property (Act Sec. 15345(d)(2) of the Heartland, Habitat, Harvest, and Horticulture Act of 2008 (P.L. 110-246), applying Code Sec. 1400N(e)(4)). Thus, recapture of the $100,000 additional section 179 expense allowance is required if the property ceases to be substantially used in the Kansas disaster area prior to the expiration of its recovery period (i.e., business use in the disaster area is not 80 percent or greater or the property is removed from the disaster area) since this would cause the property to lose its status as Recovery Assistance property. Both the standard section 179 deduction ($125,000 in 2007 and $250,000 in 2008) and additional section 179 deduction for recovery assistance property are subject to recapture under the generally applicable section 179 recapture rule if business use, whether inside or outside the Kansas disaster area, drops to 50 percent or less prior to the expiration of the recovery period. The generally applicable recapture rules of Code Sec. 179(d)(10) are described at ¶ 300.

*Recapture upon disposition*

The Code Sec. 179 expense allowance (including the increase for qualifying Recovery Assistance property) is treated as a depreciation deduction for section 1245 recapture purposes upon the disposition of the property. See ¶ 300.

*Coordination with increased expense allowance for empowerment zones and renewal communities*

If qualifying section 179 Recovery Assistance property is placed in service within an empowerment zone or renewal community located within the Kansas Disaster Area, a taxpayer may not also claim the benefit of the additional $35,000 expense allowance provided for qualifying property placed in service in an empowerment zone (Code Sec. 1397A) or a renewal community (Code Sec. 1400J) (see ¶ 304A) unless the taxpayer elects not to claim the additional $100,000 allowance provided for section 179 Recovery Assistance property (Act Sec. 15345(d)(2) of the Heartland, Habitat, Harvest, and Horticulture Act of 2008 (P.L. 110-246), applying Code Sec. 1400N(e)(3)).

Generally, it will be preferable to take advantage of the $100,000 bump-up provided for qualified section 179 Recovery Assistance property since the additional allowance for empowerment zone and renewal community property is only $35,000 (e.g., $285,000 total in 2008 ($250,000 + $35,000)) as compared to $350,000 for Recovery Assistance property (e.g., $375,000 total in 2008 ($250,000 + $100,000)).

## ¶ 306B

## Code Sec. 179 Disaster Assistance Property

The Code Sec. 179 expense dollar limitation and investment limitation (¶ 300) were increased for section 179 property (i.e., eligible property as defined at ¶ 302) that is "qualified disaster assistance property" placed in service after December 31, 2007, with respect to disasters declared after December 31, 2007 and occurring before January 1, 2010 (Code Sec. 179(e), as added by the Emergency Economic

Stabilization Act of 2008 (P.L. 110-343)). For the 2014 tax year and later, the provision is in effect inapplicable because the disaster assistance property had to be placed in service by the end of the third calendar year following the applicable disaster date, as noted below.

The increases are as follows:

- The Code Sec. 179 expense deduction ($250,000 dollar limit for tax years beginning in 2008 and 2009, and $500,000 in 2010, 2011, 2012, 2013, 2014, and 2015) is increased by the lesser of $100,000 or the cost of qualified section 179 disaster assistance property placed in service during the tax year (Code Sec. 179(e)(1)(A), as added by P.L. 110-343).

- The amount of the investment limitation ($800,000 for tax years beginning in 2008 and 2009, and $2,000,000 for tax years beginning in 2010, 2011, 2012, 2013, 2014, and 2015) is increased by the lesser of $600,000 or the cost of qualified section 179 disaster assistance property placed in service during the tax year (Code Sec. 179(e)(1)(B), as added by P.L. 110-343).

These increases mean that for qualified Section 179 disaster assistance property placed in service during 2008 or 2009, the maximum allowable Code Sec. 179 expense deduction (dollar limit) is $350,000 ($250,000 + $100,000), and the investment limitation is $1,400,000 ($800,000 + $600,000). For qualified Section 179 disaster assistance property placed in service in a tax year beginning in 2010 through 2015, the dollar limit is $600,000 ($500,000 + $100,000) and the investment limit is $2,600,000 ($2,000,000 + $600,000).

*Eligible property*

Qualified Section 179 disaster assistance property is Section 179 property (as defined at ¶ 302) that is qualified disaster assistance property (Code Sec. 179(e)(2), as added by P.L. 110-343).

*Qualified disaster assistance property defined*

Qualified disaster assistance property is defined by reference to a bonus depreciation provision and must meet all of the following tests:

- The property must be described in Code Sec. 168(k)(2)(A)(i) (i.e., MACRS recovery property with an recovery period of 20 years or less, computer software that is depreciable over three years, water utility property, or qualified leasehold improvement property) or be nonresidential real property or residential rental property (note: Code Sec. 179 applies to section 1245 property and does not apply to section 1250 (i.e. real) property).

- Substantially all (80 percent or more) of the use of the property must be in a disaster area with respect to a federally declared disaster occurring before January 1, 2010, and in the active conduct of the taxpayer's trade or business in that disaster area.

- The property must rehabilitate property damaged, or replace property destroyed or condemned, as a result of the disaster. Property is treated as replacing property destroyed or condemned if, as part of an integrated plan, it replaces property that is included in a continuous area that includes real property destroyed or condemned. The property must also be similar in nature to, and located in the same county as, the property being rehabilitated or replaced.

- The original use of the property in the disaster area must commence with an eligible taxpayer on or after the applicable disaster date.

• The property must be acquired by the eligible taxpayer by purchase on or after the applicable disaster date, but only if no written binding contract for the acquisition was in effect before that date. A purchase is defined by reference to the definition in Code Sec. 179(d); therefore, it cannot be a transaction between related parties or members of the same controlled group, and the transferee's basis in the property cannot be determined by reference to the transferor's basis.

• The property must be placed in service by the eligible taxpayer on or before the date that is the last day of the third calendar year following the applicable disaster date (or the fourth calendar year in the case of nonresidential real property and residential rental property) (Code Sec. 168(n) (2) (A), as added by the Emergency Economic Act of 2008).

Qualified disaster assistance property does not include (Code Sec. 168(n) (2) (B), as added by P.L. 110-343):

• any property that is eligible for bonus depreciation under Code Sec. 168(k) (without regard to any election under Code Sec. 168(k) (4) to forgo bonus depreciation in favor of an accelerated research or AMT credit), cellulosic biomass ethanol plant property (Code Sec. 168(l)), and qualified refuse and recycling property (Code Sec. 168(m));

• property that qualifies for bonus depreciation under the special rules for the Gulf Opportunity (GO) Zone (Code Sec. 1400N(d));

• any property used in connection with any private or commercial golf course, country club, massage parlor, hot tub facility, or suntan facility; any store whose principal business is the sale of alcoholic beverages for consumption off premises; or any gambling or animal racing property (i.e., property described in Code Sec. 1400N(p) (3));

• property that must be depreciated under the MACRS alternative depreciation system (ADS) (not including property for which an ADS election is made);

• property financed by tax-exempt bonds;

• qualified revitalization buildings for which the taxpayer has elected the Code Sec. 1400I commercial revitalization deduction; and

*Federally declared disaster*

The term federally declared disaster means any disaster subsequently determined by the President of the United States to warrant assistance by the Federal Government under the Robert T. Stafford Disaster Relief and Emergency Assistance Act. The term disaster area means the area so determined to warrant such assistance (Code Sec. 165(h) (3) (C)).

*Recapture*

If any qualified Section 179 disaster assistance property ceases to be qualified Section 179 disaster assistance property prior to the end of its recovery period, then recapture of the tax benefit received is required under the section Code Sec. 179(d) (10) recapture rules described at ¶ 300 (Code Sec. 179(e) (4), as added by P.L. 110-343; see Code Sec. 179(d) (10)). Thus, in the tax year that property ceases to be qualified Section 179 disaster assistance property, the taxpayer must generally include in income the amount of tax benefit derived from the additional amount of the Code Sec. 179 deduction claimed in the year that the property was placed in service (i.e. the additional section 179 allowance less the amount of depreciation that could have been claimed on the allowance through the tax year that disaster assistance property status is lost). In general, property will lose its status as disaster assistance property if it is removed from the disaster zone or it is not used 80 percent or more for business purposes within the zone. Both the standard section 179 deduction ($250,000 for 2008 and 2009, and $500,000 for 2010 through 2016) and additional section 179 allowance for disaster assistance property are recaptured if business use (whether inside or outside of the disaster zone) drops to 50 percent or less prior to the end of the recovery period. See ¶ 300.

*Limitations*

Qualified Section 179 disaster assistance property cannot be treated as qualified zone property for purposes of the empowerment zone rules in Code Sec. 1397A, or as qualified renewal property for purposes of the renewal community rules in Code Sec. 1400J, unless the taxpayer elects not to take qualified section 179 disaster assistance property into account for purposes of the increased expensing amount and investment limitation (Code Sec. 179(e)(3), as added by P.L. 110-343).

## ¶ 307

## De Minimis Safe Harbor Election

Under the "repair" regulations (T.D. 9636 (September 19, 2013)), a taxpayer who meets certain requirements may make an annual de minimis safe harbor expensing election. The de minimis rule is a safe harbor that is elected annually by the extended due date of the income return. A statement described in Reg. § 1.263(a)-1(f)(5) must be attached to the return for the year of election. The election is irrevocable (Reg. § 1.263(a)-1(f)(5)). The de minimis safe harbor election is not an accounting method. Therefore, taxpayers who elect it for the first time do not file Form 3115 (Reg. § 1.263(a)-1(g)).

If the election is made, then the taxpayer may not capitalize amounts paid (cash basis taxpayer) or incurred (accrual basis taxpayer) for the acquisition or production of a unit of tangible property nor treat as a material or supply amounts paid or incurred for tangible property if the amount paid for the property costs no more than a specified amount that will be expensed for financial accounting or book purposes. If the taxpayer's financial or book policy sets expensing limits that are higher than $5,000 (for taxpayers with an applicable financial statement (AFS) or $2,500 for taxpayers without an AFS, as applicable, only items that cost $5,000 or $2,500 or less, as applicable, may be expensed for tax purposes and remain protected by the safe harbor (Reg. § 1.263(a)-1(f)(1)). IRS examples illustrate that if lower per-item limits are set for financial or book accounting purposes then the tax deduction under the safe harbor is limited to the lower amount. If higher limits are set, then the maximum $5,000 or $2,500 limit applies (Reg. § 1.263(a)-1(f)(7)).

An amount paid for property to which a taxpayer properly applies the de minimis safe harbor is not treated as a capital expenditure under Reg. § 1.263(a)-2(d)(1) (relating to amounts paid to acquire or produce a unit of property) or Reg. § 1.263(a)-3(d) (relating to amounts paid to improve a unit of property) or as a material and supply under Reg. § 1.162-3, and may be deducted under Reg. § 1.162-1 in the tax year the amount is paid provided the amount otherwise constitutes an ordinary and necessary expense incurred in carrying on a trade or business (Reg. § 1.263(a)-1(f)(3)(iv)).

The $2,500 threshold for taxpayers without an AFS, is effective for tax years beginning on or after January 1, 2016. Previously, a $500 threshold applied to taxpayers without an AFS. No change is made to the $5,000 threshold for taxpayers with an AFS. Audit protection is provided for taxpayers who qualified for the safe harbor and used a $2,500 threshold in a tax year beginning before January 1, 2016 (Notice 2015-82). The safe harbor in the final regulations was effective for amounts paid or incurred in tax years beginning on or after January 1, 2014, or alternatively, to amounts paid or incurred in tax years beginning on or after January 1, 2012 (Reg. § 1.263(a)-1(j)).

*Recapture rules apply.* Amounts expensed under the de minimis safe harbor are subject to recapture as ordinary income if the expensed property is sold for a gain and reported in Part II of Form 4797 (Form 4797 instructions).

*Applicable financial statement defined.* The term applicable financial statement is defined as (Reg. § 1.263(a)-1(f)(4)):

(1) A financial statement required to be filed with the Securities and Exchange Commission (SEC) (the 10-K or the Annual Statement to Shareholders);

(2) A certified audited financial statement that is accompanied by the report of an independent certified public accountant (or in the case of a foreign entity, by the report of a similarly qualified independent professional) that is used for (a) credit purposes; (b) reporting to shareholders, partners, or similar persons; or (c) any other substantial non-tax purpose; or

(3) A financial statement (other than a tax return) required to be provided to the federal or a state government or any federal or state agency (other than the SEC or the Internal Revenue Service).

A taxpayer may have more than one of the preceding applicable financial statements. For purposes of applying the de minimis rule the statement in the highest category (i.e., item (1) being the highest) is treated as the AFS.

*Taxpayers with applicable financial statements.* A taxpayer with an AFS that elects the safe harbor may deduct the cost qualifying property under the safe harbor if (Reg. § 1.263(a)-1(f)(1)(i)):

- The taxpayer has at the beginning of the tax year *written* accounting procedures that treat as an expense for non-tax purposes (a) amounts paid for property costing less than a specified dollar amount or (b) amounts paid for property with an economic useful life of 12 months or less;
- The taxpayer treats the amount paid for the property as an expense on its applicable financial statement in accordance with its written accounting procedures; and
- The amount paid for the property does not exceed $5,000 per invoice (or per item as substantiated by the invoice).

*Taxpayers without applicable financial statements.* A taxpayer without an AFS that elects the safe harbor may deduct the cost qualifying property under the safe harbor if (Reg. § 1.263(a)-1(f)(1)(ii)):

- The taxpayer has at the beginning of the tax year accounting procedures (whether or not written) that treat as an expense for non-tax purposes (a) amounts paid for property costing less than a specified dollar amount or (b) amounts paid for property with an economic useful life of 12 months or less;
- The taxpayer treats the amount paid for the property as an expense on its books and records in accordance with its accounting procedures; and
- The amount paid for the property does not exceed $2,500 per invoice (or per item as substantiated by the invoice) ($500 per invoice or item in tax years beginning before January 1, 2016).

Note that it is not necessary for a taxpayer without an AFS to have a *written* accounting policy. A policy, however, needs to be in place at the beginning of the tax year and should be communicated to appropriate employees.

If the taxpayer's financial results are reported on the applicable financial statement for a group of entities then the group's applicable financial statement may be treated as the applicable financial statement of the taxpayer and the written accounting procedures provided for the group and utilized for the group's applicable financial statement may be treated as the written accounting procedures of the taxpayer (Reg. § 1.263(a)-1(f)(3)(vi)).

A taxpayer with an AFS may only qualify for the de minimis safe harbor under the first set of rules that specifically apply to taxpayers with an AFS (Reg. § 1.263(a)-1(f)(1)). Thus, if such a taxpayer does not have a *written* accounting procedure in place at the beginning of the tax year it may not qualify for the $2,500 per item de minimis safe harbor for taxpayers without an AFS even though such a taxpayer's accounting procedure does not need to be written.

The de minimis rule can be elected even if the taxpayer's financial accounting procedure does not limit the amount expensed for non-tax purposes to the $5,000/$2,500 tax deduction limit. For example, the accounting procedure of a taxpayer with an AFS could provide that amounts not in excess of $10,000 are deducted for financial accounting purposes. However, only items costing no more than $5,000 could be deducted for tax purposes and receive audit protection under the de minimis safe harbor.

> ***Example (1):*** A calendar-year taxpayer without an AFS has an accounting procedure in place at the beginning of the tax year to expense amounts costing $3,000 or less and treats such amounts as current expenditures on its books and records. The taxpayer purchases a $2,600 computer. Although the taxpayer must expense the $2,600 on its books it may not deduct the $2,600 on its tax return and receive safe harbor protection for tax purposes because $2,600 exceeds the $2,500 limit (Reg. § 1.263(a)-1(f)(7), Examples 2 and 4). If the taxpayer deducts $2,600 on its tax return that amount is not protected from IRS review by the safe harbor. However, any items costing $2,500 or less and deducted on the tax return are protected by the safe harbor and may not be disallowed on audit.

A taxpayer who deducts amounts that are not protected by the safe harbor is allowed on audit to demonstrate that its accounting policy clearly reflects income.

The preamble to T.D. T.D 9636 states:

"Finally, for both taxpayers with applicable financial statements and taxpayers without applicable financial statements, the de minimis safe harbor is not intended to prevent a taxpayer from reaching an agreement with its IRS examining agents that, as an administrative matter, based on risk analysis or materiality, the IRS examining agents will not review certain items. It is not intended that examining agents must now revise their materiality thresholds in accordance with the de minimis safe harbor limitations provided in the final regulation. Thus, if examining agents and a taxpayer agree that certain amounts in excess of the de minimis safe harbor limitations are not material or otherwise should not be subject to review, that agreement should be respected, notwithstanding the requirements of the de minimis safe harbor. However, a taxpayer that seeks a deduction for amounts in excess of the amount allowed by the safe harbor has the burden of showing that such treatment clearly reflects income."

*Property with an economic useful life of 12 months or less.* The regulations allow an accounting policy that only provides for the expensing of property with an economic useful life of 12 months or less (Reg. § 1.263(a)-1(f)(i)(B)(ii); Reg. § 1.263(a)-1(f)(ii)(B)(ii)) even though a taxpayer would not likely adopt an accounting policy that omitted the permitted provision for the expensing of property costing less than a specified dollar amount (Reg. § 1.263(a)-1(f)(i)(B)(i); Reg. § 1.263(a)-1(f)(ii)(B)(i)). If a taxpayer's policy only provides for the expensing of property with an economic life of 12 months or less, examples in the regulations (see Example (3) below), illustrate that such property may not be expensed under the protection of the de minimis rule if its cost exceeds the maximum $2,500 ($500 before 2016) cap for taxpayers without an AFS or $5,000 cap for taxpayers with an AFS. In the much more likely scenario of an accounting policy which contains a provision for the expensing of property with an economic useful life of 12 months or less and a provision for property costing less than a stated dollar amount (not to exceed the $2,500 or $5,000 limit), the taxpayer must apply the de minimis safe harbor to amounts qualifying under either accounting procedure (Reg. § 1.263(a)-1(f)(3)(vii)). In this situation, the property with an economic useful life of 12 months or less is subject to the $2,500 or $5,000 limit without regard to the limit set for the other property. It is not necessary for the accounting procedure to specify a cost limit on property with a short economic useful life. However, the accounting procedure must specify a limit for other types of property. If an accounting policy only provides for the deduction of property costing less than a specified dollar amount (not to exceed the $2,500 or $5,000 cap) and makes no specific mention of the treatment of property with an economic useful life of 12 months or less, it also appears that a unit of property with an economic useful life of 12 months or less should still be expensed under the de minimis rule if its costs is less than the specified dollar amount (not to exceed the $2,500 or $5,000 cap). See Reg. § 1.263(a)-1(f)(7), Example 7, in which a hand-held point- of-service device with a useful economic life of less than 12 months is deductible because its cost was equal to the $300 limit set for property in general and not because its economic life was less than 12 months.

> ***Example (2):*** In 2021, a calendar-year taxpayer ABC does not have an applicable financial statement but does have accounting procedures in place that requires the expensing of tangible property costing $2,000 or less and property with an economic useful life of less than 12 months. The policy does not specifically limit the cost of items with a short economic life. ABC purchases a point of service device costing $2,500 and a computer costing $6,000. Both items have an economic useful life of less than 12 months. ABC must deduct the cost of the point of service device because its economic useful life is 12 months or less and its cost does not exceed the generally applicable $2,500 per item limit that applies in 2021. The cost of the $6,000 computer may not be deducted under the safe harbor even though it has an economic useful life of 12 months or less because its cost exceeds $2,500 If the point of service device cost $2,000 or less it would also be deductible under the accounting policy as an item of tangible property costing $2,000 or less (Reg. § 1.263(a)-1(f)(7), Examples 7 and 8).

*Materials and supplies.* If a taxpayer elects the safe harbor, it applies to materials and supplies (Reg. § 1.263(a)-1(f)(3)(ii)). Thus, the cost of materials and supplies which do not exceed the $5,000/$2,500 ($500 before 2016) limit (or any lower limit set by the accounting policy) are currently deducted for tax purposes in the tax year paid or incurred, rather than in the tax year used or consumed as is usually required for materials and supplies.

Materials and supplies are defined as (Reg. § 1.162-3(c)(1)):

- A component acquired (or produced) to maintain, repair, or improve a unit of tangible property owned, leased, or serviced by the taxpayer and that is not acquired as part of any single unit of tangible property;

- Fuel, lubricants, water, and similar items, reasonably expected to be consumed in 12 months or less, beginning when used in the taxpayer's operations;

• A unit of property that has an economic useful life of 12 months or less, beginning when the property is used or consumed in the taxpayer's operations;

• A unit of property that has an acquisition cost or production cost (as determined under Code Sec. 263A) of $200 or less; or

• Property identified in published guidance by the IRS as materials and supplies.

***Example (3):*** In 2021, calendar-year ABC corporation has no AFS but has an accounting policy in effect at the beginning of the tax year requiring the expensing for book purposes amounts paid for property costing $2,500 or less. ABC elects the de minimis safe harbor. ABC purchases 100 chairs which cost $100 each. The chairs are materials and supplies because they do not cost more than $200. The cost of the chairs is currently deductible for tax purposes under the de minimis rule in the year paid or incurred assuming the amounts are expensed for book purposes in accordance with ABC's accounting policy. If the chairs cost more than $200, they are not materials and supplies as defined for tax purposes; however, they remain deductible and protected under the de minimis rule because the de minimis rule also allows ABC to deduct acquisitions of units of property that cost $2,500 or less even if they are not materials and supplies for tax purposes (Reg. § 1.263(a)-1(f)(7), Example 9).

Materials and supplies as defined above that are "incidental" are deductible in the year paid or incurred provided that taxable income is clearly reflected. Incidental materials and supplies are defined as materials and supplies that are carried on hand and for which no record of consumption is kept or of which physical inventories at the beginning and end of the taxable year are not taken (Reg. § 1.162-3(a)(2)). If the de minimis safe harbor is elected it applies to all materials and supplies including incidental materials and supplies. If the de minimis safe harbor is elected incidental materials and supplies are deductible in the year paid or incurred whether or not their deduction affects the clear reflection of income. If the safe harbor is not elected, then a deduction is allowed in the year of payment or accrual only if income is clearly reflected.

*Inventory treated as non-incidental material and supplies.* Proposed regulations clarify that inventory which is treated by a taxpayer with average annual receipts of $25 million or less as a non-incidental material and supplies cannot be expensed under the de minimis rule (Proposed Reg.§ 1.471-1(b)(4)(i); Preamable to NPRM REG-132766-18).

*Materials and supplies used to improve property.* The de minimis safe harbor applies to materials and supplies. Materials and supplies are defined to include components used to improve a unit of property and, therefore, appear to be deductible under the safe harbor if the applicable dollar limitation (e.g., $5,000 maximum per item of property for a taxpayer with an AFS) is not exceeded. However, the cost of materials and supplies used to improve a property must be capitalized under the uniform capitalization rules of Code Sec. 263A if the taxpayer is subject to the UNICAP rules even if they are otherwise deductible under the safe harbor. See "*Coordination with UNICAP rules.*"

With respect to the safe-harbor deductibility of materials and supplies used to improve property, the de minimis safe harbor regulations provide that an amount paid for property to which a taxpayer properly applies the de minimis safe harbor is not treated as a capital expenditure under Reg. § 1.263(a)-3(d) (relating to amounts paid to improve a unit of property) (Reg. § 1.263(a)-1(f)(3)(iv)). This rule appears to trump Reg. § 1.263(a)-3(c)(2), which provides that a material or supply that is acquired and used to improve a unit of tangible property is subject to capitalization and is not treated as a material or supply under Reg. § 1.162-3. Former Temporary Reg. § 1.263(a)-3T(c)(3) (see T.D. 9564 for text) included a provision which provided that the de minimis safe harbor took precedence over the rule for materials and supplies in Reg. § 1.263(a)-3(c)(2) ("A taxpayer is not required to capitalize amounts paid to acquire or produce units of property used in improvements under paragraph (d) of this section... (including materials and supplies used in improvements) if these amounts are properly deducted under the de minimis rule.". Although the final regulations do not include this rule, it appears that it was excluded as unnecessary in light of the addition of the language cited in Reg. § 1.263(a)-1(f)(3)(iv) above by the final regulations added by T.D. 9636. Again, as noted above, the UNICAP rules trump the de minimis safe harbor and require the capitalization of improvements if a taxpayer is subject to the UNICAP rules.

*Exceptions to de minimis safe harbor.* The de minimis safe harbor does not apply to amounts paid for (Reg. § 1.263(a)-1(f)(1)(iii)):

- property that is or is intended to be included in inventory property;
- land;
- rotable, temporary, and standby emergency parts that a taxpayer elects to capitalized and depreciate under Reg. § 1.162-3(d);
- rotable and temporary spare parts accounted for under the optional method of accounting for rotable and temporary spare parts under Reg. § 1.162-3(e)

*Costs included in property.* Additional costs, such as delivery fees and installation services, are included in the cost of tangible property for purposes of the $5,000/$2,500 ($500 before 2016) threshold if such costs are included on the same invoice as the tangible property (Reg. § 1.263(a)-1(f)(3)(i); Reg. § 1.263(a)-1(f)(7), Example 5). The taxpayer may use any reasonable method to allocate these costs among multiple items of tangible property that are on the same invoice. If additional costs are not stated on the same invoice as the tangible property then the taxpayer may, but is not required to, treat the additional costs as part of the cost of the tangible property. Additional costs consist of the costs of facilitating the acquisition or production of the tangible property (Reg. § 1.263(a)-2(f)) and the costs for work performed prior to the date that the tangible property is placed in service (Reg. § 1.263(a)-2(d)). See Reg. § 1.263(a)-1(f)(7), Example 6.

*Coordination with UNICAP rules.* An amount that is deductible under the de minimis safe harbor may nevertheless need to be capitalized under the Code Sec. 263A uniform capitalization rules if the amount paid is a direct or allocable indirect cost of other property produced by the taxpayer or of property acquired for resale (Reg. § 1.263(a)-1(f)(3)(v)). For example, the cost of tools and equipment allocable to property produced or property acquired for resale must be capitalized (Reg. § 1.263A-1(e)(3)(ii)(R)). See, also, Reg. § 1.263(a)-1(f)(7), Example 10 (jigs, dies, molds, and patterns with useful life of less than one year and deductible under de minimis rule required to be capitalized).

If the cost of a component part is otherwise eligible for the safe harbor, but the part is installed (or expected to be installed) in manufacturing equipment that the taxpayer uses to produce property for sale, the cost of the part must be capitalized under Code Sec. 263A as an indirect cost of property produced by the taxpayer. However, if the taxpayer elects and properly applies the de minimis rule to property that it does not expect to use it in production, Code Sec. 263A does not require capitalization even if expectations change in a subsequent tax year and the taxpayers ends up using the property in production (Preamble to T.D. 9636 (September 19, 2013)).

For purposes of Code Sec. 263A, produce includes the following: construct, build, install, manufacture, develop, *improve*, create, raise, or grow (Code Sec.

263A(g)(1)). Therefore, if a component that would otherwise qualify as a material or supply is used to improve property, the cost of the component while technically qualifying for deduction under the de minimis rule is required to be capitalized under the UNICAP rules assuming the taxpayer expected to use the component to improve the property and is subject to the UNCAP rules.

For tax years beginning after 2017, a taxpayer is not required to apply the UNICAP rules for the tax year if it meets the gross receipts test of Code Sec. 448(c) by having average annual gross receipts during the prior three tax years that is less than the threshold amount ($26 million for 2021 and $27 million for 2022) (Code Sec. 263A(i)(1)). The expanded exception to the UNICAP rules applies to any producer or reseller, other than a tax shelter, that meets the $25 million gross receipts test (Conference Report on H.R. 1, Tax Cuts and Jobs Act (H. Rept. 115-466)). Therefore, most taxpayers will not be subject to the UNICAP rules after 2017 and may deduct materials and supplies used for improvements under the de minimis safe harbor.

*Treatment of property expensed under de minimis rule upon sale or disposition.* Property expensed under the de minimis rule is not treated upon sale or other disposition as a capital asset under Code Sec. 1221 or as property used in the trade or business Code Sec. 1231 (Reg. § 1.263(a)-1(f)(3)(iii)).

DE MINIMIS RULES FOR AMOUNTS PAID OR INCURRED TO ACQUIRE OR PRODUCE PROPERTY IN TAX YEARS BEGINNING BEFORE EFFECTIVE DATE OF FINAL REGULATIONS.

Strictly speaking, prior to the issuance of the de minimis rule in the final regulations discussed above, other than Code Sec. 179, there was no authority for immediately expensing or writing off the cost of assets which meet the criteria for depreciation. For example, in a Chief Counsel Advice (IRS Letter Ruling 199952010, September 29, 1999), the IRS rejected a taxpayer's request to change its method of accounting for assets such as machinery, equipment, furniture, and fixtures. The taxpayer's present method of accounting was not to capitalize and depreciate such assets if an asset was valued at $1,000 or less. The taxpayer requested to increase the minimum threshold amount to $2,000. The request was denied and the taxpayer informed that its present method of accounting was unacceptable. Said the IRS: "All property used in a trade or business (except land and inventory) that has a useful life of more than one year must be capitalized and depreciated. Taxpayers are not permitted to treat such items as current expenses simply because the particular item has a certain minimum value or less."

Nevertheless, the IRS recognizes and approves a practice by its auditors that allows taxpayers to write-off the cost of low-cost depreciable assets on the basis of relative immateriality. Certain court cases, discussed below, also lend support to taxpayers who expense immaterial amounts.

This unofficial de minimis rule applied by IRS auditors was described in the preamble to proposed regulations issued under Code Sec. 263. The relevant portion of the preamble is quoted in italics below (NPRM REG-168745-03, published in the Federal Register on August 21, 2006). These proposed regulations did not include a de minimis rule. The August 2006 proposals were withdrawn and reissued (NPRM REG-168745-03, published in the Federal Register on March 10, 2008). The reissued proposed regulations included a proposed de minimis rule (Proposed Reg. § 1.263(a)-2(d)(4)) which was adopted with certain modifications by T.D. 9564 in Temporary Reg. § 1.263(a)-2T(g) as discussed above. The proposed de minimis rule described in the proposed regulations could not be relied upon.

***De minimis rule as described in August 2006 preamble of withdrawn proposed regulations***

*"In Notice 2004-6, the IRS and Treasury Department requested comments on whether the regulations should provide a de minimis rule. Because the notice refers to the application of section 263(a) to amounts paid to repair, improve, or rehabilitate tangible property, most commentators focused on a de minimis rule for the cost of repairs rather than the cost to acquire property. However, one commentator requested that the regulations specifically provide a de minimis rule for acquisition costs, but allow taxpayers to continue to use their current method if they have reached a working agreement with their IRS examining agent regarding a de minimis rule.*

*The IRS and Treasury Department recognize that for regulatory or financial accounting purposes, taxpayers often have a policy for deducting an amount paid below a certain dollar threshold for the acquisition of tangible property (de minimis rule). For Federal income tax purposes, the taxpayer generally would be required to capitalize the amount paid if the property has a useful life substantially beyond the taxable year. However, in this context some courts have permitted the use of a de minimis rule for Federal income tax purposes. See Union Pacific R.R. Co. v. United States, 524 F.2d 1343 (Ct. Cl. 1975) (permitting the use of the taxpayer's $500 de minimis rule, which was in accordance with the Interstate Commerce Commission (ICC) minimum rule and generally accepted accounting principles); Cincinnati, N.O. & Tex. Pac. Ry. v. United States, 424 F.2d 563 (Ct. Cl. 1970) (same). But see Alacare Home Health Services, Inc. v. Commissioner, T.C. Memo 2001-149 (disallowing the taxpayer's use of a $500 de minimis rule because it distorted income).*

*The proposed regulations do not include a de minimis rule for acquisition costs. However, the IRS and Treasury Department recognize that taxpayers often reach an agreement with IRS examining agents that, as an administrative matter, based on risk analysis and/or materiality, the IRS examining agents do not select certain items for review such as the acquisition of tangible assets with a small cost. This often is referred to by taxpayers and IRS examining agents as a de minimis rule. The absence of a de minimis rule in the proposed regulations is not intended to change this practice.*

*The IRS and Treasury Department considered including a de minimis rule in the proposed regulations. The de minimis rule considered would have provided that taxpayers are not required to capitalize certain de minimis amounts paid for the acquisition or production of a unit of property. Under the rule considered, if a taxpayer had written accounting procedures in place treating as an expense on its applicable financial statement (AFS) amounts paid for property costing less than a certain dollar amount, and treated the amounts paid during the taxable year as an expense on its AFS in accordance with those written accounting procedures, the taxpayer would not have been required to capitalize those amounts if they did not exceed a certain dollar threshold. A taxpayer that did not meet these criteria (for example, a taxpayer that did not have an AFS) would not have been required to capitalize amounts paid for a unit of property that did not exceed the established dollar threshold. Because taxpayers without an AFS generally are smaller than taxpayers with an AFS, the dollar threshold for the de minimis rule that would have applied to them would have been lower than the threshold for taxpayers with an AFS (although the de minimis rule for taxpayers with an AFS also would have been limited to the amount treated as an expense on their AFS). The de minimis rule considered by the IRS and Treasury Department would not have applied to inventory property, improvements, land, or a component of a unit of property.*

*The de minimis rule considered also would have provided that property to which a taxpayer applies the de minimis rule is treated upon sale or disposition similar to section 179 property. Thus, de minimis property would have been property of a character subject to depreciation and amounts paid that were not capitalized under the de minimis rule would have been treated as amortization subject to recapture under section 1245. Thus, gain on disposition of the property would have been ordinary income to the taxpayer to the extent of the amount treated as amortization for purposes of section 1245.*

*The IRS and Treasury Department decided to not include a de minimis rule in the proposed regulations but instead to request comments on whether such a rule should be included in the final regulations or whether to continue to rely on the current administrative practice of IRS examining agents. Therefore, the IRS and Treasury Department request comments on whether a de minimis rule for acquisition costs should be included in the final regulations, and, if so, whether the de minimis rule should be the rule described above and what dollar thresholds are appropriate.*

*The IRS and Treasury Department also request comments on the scope of costs that should be included in a de minimis rule if one is provided in the final regulations and on the character of de minimis rule property. For example, the de minimis rule considered by the IRS and Treasury Department would have applied to the aggregate of amounts paid for the acquisition or production (including any amounts paid to facilitate the acquisition or production) of a unit of property and including amounts paid for improvements prior to the unit of property being placed in service. If a de minimis rule should be provided in the final regulations, the IRS and Treasury Department request comments on what, if any, type of rule should be provided to prevent a distortion of income when taxpayers acquire a large number of assets, each of which individually is within the de minimis rule (for example, the purchase by a taxpayer of 2,000 personal computers).*

*If a de minimis rule for acquisition costs should be provided in the final regulations, the IRS and Treasury Department request comments on whether the rule should permit IRS examining agents and taxpayers to agree to the use of higher de minimis thresholds on the basis of materiality and risk analysis and, if so, under what circumstances a higher threshold should be allowed. The IRS and Treasury Department also request comments on whether, if a de minimis rule should be provided in the final regulations, changes to begin using a de minimis rule or changes to a higher dollar amount within a de minimis rule should be treated as changes in a method of accounting."*

***Courts' position on de minimis expensing***

Courts that have considered the issue have rejected the hard-line IRS position taken in Chief Counsel Advice (IRS Letter Ruling 199952010, September 29, 1999 (discussed above), instead relying on a clear reflection of income standard set forth in Code Sec. 446(a) and (b)). In general, the amount expensed is compared to other significant income and balance sheet figures to determine whether an expensing policy distorts or does not clearly reflect income. These court decisions remain relevant for expenditures that are not subject to the temporary regulations (i.e., amounts paid or incurred in tax years ending before January 1, 2012).

In *Alacare Home Health Services Inc.*, 81 TCM 1794, TC Memo 2001-149, Dec. 54,378(M), a Medicare-certified home health care agency capitalized office and computer items costing less than $500. This treatment was permitted for non-tax purposes under the accounting guidelines contained in the Medicare Provider Reimbursement Manual (HCFA Publication 15-1) issued by the Federal Health Care Financing Administration (HCFA). The court, however, concluded that the taxpayer's treatment did not clearly reflect income for tax purposes. In making this determination, the court compared the ratios of the expensed items to various other balance sheet and income tax figures. In the two tax years at issue, the expensed items amounted to 165 percent and 83.5 percent of taxable income; 288 percent and 189 percent of its total depreciation deductions; .85 percent and .71 percent of its gross receipts; and .84 percent and 1.12 percent of total operating expenses.

The taxpayer in *Alacare* relied upon *Cincinnati, New Orleans & Tex. Pac. Ry. Co.*, CtCls, 70-1 USTC ¶ 9344, 424 F2d 563. In the *Cincinnati* case (which involved three tax years), the railroad followed the Interstate Commerce Commission's prescribed financial accounting convention which required the current deduction of equipment costing less than $500 (the "minimum rule"). The expensed items were less than one percent of the taxpayer's net income each year; less than two percent of total depreciation claimed year; .04 percent, .03 percent, and .07 percent of gross receipts; and .06 percent, .04 percent, and .01 percent of total operating expenses. These ratios were substantially lower than those in *Alacare*.

The *Alacare* court noted several additional factors that favored the taxpayer in the *Cincinnati* case. The taxpayer in *Cincinnati* presented 17 years of data (only two years were presented in *Alacare*) for the court's consideration and presented evidence that the Interstate Commerce Commission adopted an expensing policy only after specifically concluding that it would not cause a railroad's financial statement to not clearly reflect income. The taxpayer in *Cincinnati* also presented evidence that its expensing method complied with generally accepted accounting principles (GAAP). The *Alacare* taxpayer presented no evidence on these points.

The court also placed significance on the fact that the ICC required railroads to comply with its expensing policy for regulatory accounting purposes. The HCFA's expensing policy was not mandatory. In this regard the court cited *Idaho Power Co.*, SCt, 74-2 USTC ¶ 9521, 418 US 1 (where a taxpayer's generally accepted method of accounting is made compulsory by a regulatory agency and that method clearly reflects income, it is almost presumptively controlling for Federal tax purposes (depreciation on equipment used by a utility to build capital improvements had to be capitalized)).

Five years following its decision in the *Cincinnati* case, the Court of Claims allowed another railroad to expense items under $500 pursuant to the same ICC accounting standards at issue in the *Cincinnati* decision (*Union Pacific Railroad Co., Inc.*, CtCls, 75-2 USTC ¶ 9800, rehearing denied 76-1 USTC ¶ 9308, 524 F2d 1343, cert. denied 429 US 827). The ratio of expensed items to total investment account was .026 percent (compared to .014 percent for *Cincinnati*) and the ratio of expensed items to total operating expense was .052 percent (.059 percent for *Cincinnati*).

In *R.G. Galazin*, 38 TCM 851, TC Memo. 1979-206, Dec. 36,094(M), the Tax Court allowed a salesman to claim a current deduction for a calculator costing $52.45 and with an agreed upon useful life of two years. The court noted that the *Cincinnati* case did not sanction a blanket rule for the expensing of low-cost items but rather applied in situations involving a large number of expensed items that are relatively inexpensive. Nevertheless, the court, allowed the deduction of the calculator on the basis of Reg. § 1.162-6 (adopted by T.D. 6291, 4-3-58) which provides that "Amounts currently paid or accrued for books, furniture, and professional instruments and equipment, the useful life of which is short, may be deducted." An interesting contrast to the puzzling *Galazin* decision, is the Tax Court's decision in *G.O. Klutz* (38 TCM 724, TC Memo. 1979-169, Dec. 36,043(M)) in which a used adding machine costing $75 was required to be depreciated over five years.

# Corporate Earnings and Profits

## *Effect of Depreciation*

## ¶ 310

### Depreciation: Corporate Earnings and Profits

The straight-line method is required for computing corporate earnings and profits. This prevents rapid cost recovery from converting what would otherwise be taxable dividends (payable only out of earnings and profits) into nontaxable distributions or capital gain.

*MACRS property*

The MACRS alternative (straight-line) depreciation system (ADS) (¶ 150) must be used to depreciate MACRS property for purposes of computing corporate earnings and profits (Code Sec. 312(k)(3) and (4)).

*Bonus depreciation*

Bonus depreciation is not allowed in computing earnings and profits (Reg. § 1.168(k)-1(f)(7)).

*Sec. 179 expense allowance*

In figuring earnings and profits, any amount deducted under Code Sec. 179 in computing taxable income is considered deducted ratably over a five-year period beginning with the tax year that the cost is expensed (Code Sec. 312(k)(3)(B)). The amount deducted under Code Sec. 179 for taxable income purposes reduces the basis of the asset for purposes of computing the depreciation allowable under ACRS or MACRS for earnings and profits purposes.

*Other expense allowances and deductions*

In addition to the Code Sec. 179 expense allowance, for purposes of the earnings and profits computation, the following expense deductions are considered deducted ratably over five years beginning with the tax year the cost is expensed (Code Sec. 312(k)(3)(B)):

- environmental expenses deducted under Code Sec. 179B
- the cost of refinery property deducted under Code Sec. 179C
- the cost of energy-efficient property deducted under Code Sec. 179D
- and the cost of advanced mine safety equipment deducted under Code Sec. 179E

*ACRS recovery property*

A corporation's depreciation on ACRS recovery property is computed using the straight-line method over the earnings and profits recovery period. In the case of personal recovery property, a half-year convention applies. In the case of real property, the full-month or mid-month convention applies depending upon whether the property is 15-year, 18-year, or 19-year real property. Salvage value is disregarded in making the earnings and profits straight-line depreciation computation.

The following recovery periods are prescribed for making the straight-line depreciation computation unless a longer period was elected under the ACRS optional straight-line method for regular tax purposes:

| *In the case of:* | *E & P recovery period:* |
|---|---|
| 3-year recovery property | 5 years |
| 5-year recovery property | 12 years |
| 10-year recovery property | 25 years |
| 15-year real property | 35 years |
| 18-year real property | 35 or 40 years |
| 19-year real property | 40 years |
| 15-year public utility property | 35 years |

A 35-year earnings and profits recovery period applies to 18-year real property placed in service after March 15, 1984, in a tax year beginning before October 1, 1984 (Act Secs. 61(b) and 111(e)(5) of P.L. 98-369 (Tax Reform Act of 1984)).

The earnings and profits recovery period for low-income housing (recovery property) placed in service in tax years beginning after September 30, 1984 is 40 years. A 35-year recovery period applies to low-income housing placed in service after March 15, 1984 in a tax year beginning before October 1, 1984.

If a corporation elects to depreciate an item of recovery property for regular tax purposes using the ACRS optional straight-line method (¶ 254) or elects one of the optional recovery periods prescribed for property used predominantly outside of the U.S. (¶ 252) and the elected recovery period is longer than the recovery period that would otherwise apply for earnings and profits purposes, earnings and profits are computed using the longer optional recovery period (Code Sec. 312(k)(3)(C) (before repeal by the Tax Reform Act of 1986 (P.L. 99-514))).

No ACRS depreciation is claimed on personal recovery property for earnings and profits purposes in the year the property is disposed of. The full-month or mid-month convention is used to determine the allowable deduction for ACRS real property (including low-income housing) in the year of disposition.

The table below shows the applicable percentages (ACRS straight-line method over the earnings and profits life recovery period using a half-year convention) for Code Sec. 280F listed property that is ACRS recovery property (other than 18- or 19-year real property) where business use does not exceed 50 percent (Reg. § 1.280F-3T(e)).

| *If the recovery year is:* | *And the recovery period is (in yrs.):* | | | |
|---|---|---|---|---|
| | 5 | 12 | 25 | 35 |
| 1 | 10 % | 4 % | 2 % | 1% |
| 2-5 | 20 | 9 | 4 | 3 |
| 6 | 10 | 8 | 4 | 3 |
| 7-12 | | 8 | 4 | 3 |
| 13 | | 4 | 4 | 3 |
| 14-25 | | | 4 | 3 |
| 26 | | | 2 | 3 |
| 27-31 | | | | 3 |
| 32-35 | | | | 2 |
| 36 | | | | 1 |

The table below shows the applicable percentages (ACRS straight-line method over a 40-year earnings and profits life recovery period using a mid-month convention) for Code Sec. 280F listed property that is ACRS 18- or 19-year recovery real property where business use does not exceed 50 percent.

| | Month Placed in Service | | | | | | | | | | | |
|---|---|---|---|---|---|---|---|---|---|---|---|---|
| *Year* | *1* | *2* | *3* | *4* | *5* | *6* | *7* | *8* | *9* | *10* | *11* | *12* |
| 1st | 2.4% | 2.2% | 2.0% | 1.8% | 1.6% | 1.4% | 1.1% | 0.9% | 0.7% | 0.5% | 0.3% | 0.1% |
| 2-40th | 2.5% | 2.5% | 2.5% | 2.5% | 2.5% | 2.5% | 2.5% | 2.5% | 2.5% | 2.5% | 2.5% | 2.5% |
| 41st | 0.1% | 0.3% | 0.5% | 0.7% | 0.9% | 1.1% | 1.4% | 1.6% | 1.8% | 2.0% | 2.2% | 2.4% |

*Assets placed in service before 1981*

The straight-line method is used to compute depreciation or amortization on an asset placed in service by a corporation before 1981 in a tax year beginning after June 30, 1972 (Code Sec. 312(k)(1)). The straight-line method also applies to an asset placed in service after 1980 but which is not depreciable under ACRS or MACRS.

If an ADR election was made, straight-line depreciation is computed in accordance with ADR Reg. § 1.167(a)-11(g)(3). The provisions of Reg. § 1.167(b)-1 control the manner of computing straight-line depreciation on property not depreciable under ADR.

Any election to reduce salvage value or any convention adopted under ADR or the general pre-1981 rules with respect to additions or retirements from multiple-asset accounts for purposes of computing taxable income apply in computing straight-line earnings and profits depreciation.

*Method not based on a term of years*

A corporation that uses a method not based on a term of years (for example, the unit-of-production method) to compute depreciation for income tax purposes must also use that method for earnings and profits purposes (Code Sec. 312(k)(2); Reg. § 1.167-1(b)).

*ITC basis adjustment*

The depreciation allowance computed for earnings and profits purposes is determined without regard to any investment tax credit basis reduction required under Code Sec. 50(c) (formerly Code Sec. 48(q)) to the depreciated property (Code Sec. 312(k)(5)).

# Roundup of Selected Rules for Pre-1981 Property

## *Elements Needed to Compute Depreciation*

### ¶ 330

### Basis, Salvage Value, Useful Life

Under the rules that apply to property placed in service before 1981 (and post-1980 assets that do not qualify for ACRS or MACRS), three items are essential for computing depreciation. These are the basis of the asset for depreciation purposes, the estimated salvage value at the end of the useful life of the asset, and the estimated useful life of the asset. The basis reduced by salvage value is the amount to be depreciated. The useful life determines the period over which the asset is depreciated.

### ¶ 332

### Basis for Depreciation

The basis for depreciation is the same as the adjusted basis for determining gain on the sale or other disposition of the asset (see ¶ 70).

### ¶ 336

### Salvage Value

Salvage value is the amount a taxpayer expected to receive in cash or trade-in allowance upon disposition of an asset at the end of its useful life. This could be a large amount for property customarily disposed of while still in good operating condition. Or it could be junk value if the asset is used until it is worn out.

Under the straight-line and sum of the years-digits methods, salvage value is subtracted from the depreciation basis before applying the depreciation rate. See ¶ 346 and ¶ 352. This is not so under the declining-balance method (¶ 348). In any event, no asset may be depreciated below its salvage value.

Net salvage is salvage value minus the cost of removal and disposition. Either salvage or net salvage could have been used in figuring depreciation allowances, but the practice had to be consistent and the treatment of the costs of removal had to be consistent with the practice adopted.

### ¶ 338

### Election of Salvage Reduction Increases Depreciation

The salvage value of personal property (other than livestock) with a useful life of at least three years may, at the taxpayer's election, be reduced by an amount not exceeding 10 percent of the original depreciation basis (Code Sec. 167(f) before repeal by the Omnibus Budget Reconciliation Act of 1990 (P.L. 101-508)). This is 10 percent of the basis, which, for pre-1981 property, was before reduction for additional first-year depreciation.

As already noted at ¶ 336, no asset may be depreciated below its salvage value. This election to reduce salvage also applies for this purpose. Thus, the election increased the total depreciation that can be deducted. If the salvage value of an asset costing $10,000 is $800, salvage value can be completely ignored if the election was made. Depreciation deductions totaling $10,000 can be claimed (including additional first-year depreciation). Without the election, the maximum depreciation that could be claimed would be $9,200 ($10,000 – $800 salvage value).

If a change is made from the declining-balance method (in which salvage is not taken into account) to the straight-line method (in which salvage is taken into account), the election to reduce salvage may be made in the changeover year. If the estimated useful life (see ¶ 340) is redetermined, the salvage value may also be redetermined at the same time.

Of course, the reduction in salvage value reduces the basis at the end of useful life and increases the gain (or decreases the loss) upon disposition of the asset.

If a taxpayer elected ADR or CLS depreciation of equipment, salvage value is not considered in the computation of depreciation since the ADR and CLS rates were set up by taking salvage value into account. Also, salvage value for ADR purposes is gross salvage, not net salvage (¶ 446).

## ¶ 340

## Estimated Useful Life

The rate of depreciation depends upon the estimated useful life of the property. This is the period over which the asset may reasonably be expected to be useful *in the taxpayer's trade or business* or in the production of income. It is not necessarily its expected physical life.

Here are some factors affecting useful life:

(1) wear, tear, decay or decline from natural causes;

(2) the normal progress of the art, economic changes, inventions, and current developments within the industry and the taxpayer's trade or business;

(3) the effect of climate and other local conditions peculiar to the taxpayer's trade or business; and

(4) the taxpayer's policy as to repairs, renewals, and replacements.

If a taxpayer's experience was inadequate for determining useful life, it was permissible to use the general experience in the industry.

# Methods of Computing Depreciation

## ¶ 344

## Consistent Method Required

Any reasonable method of computing depreciation was permissible, so long as that method was used consistently. This means only that the method has to be consistent for the specific item (or items in a group account) being depreciated. It does not mean that the same method has to be used for all assets. Nor does a method chosen for depreciation of property in one year have to be adopted for similar property acquired in a later year.

Generally, the depreciation method for an asset may not be changed without the Commissioner's consent. However, a change from an acceptable declining-balance method to the straight-line method may be made without consent (Reg. § 1.167(e)-1(b)). Also, a number of other depreciation method changes will be automatically permitted if the change meets the conditions in Rev. Proc. 2015-14 (Section 6). See ¶ 75.

There are three primary methods: straight-line, declining-balance, and sum of the years-digits.

## ¶ 346

## Straight-Line Method

The depreciation deduction under this method is calculated by reducing the basis by the salvage value and either dividing the remainder by the useful life or multiplying it by the straight-line rate (Reg.§ 1.167(b)-1).

***Example:*** An asset costing $10,000 had a 20-year useful life with an expected $500 salvage value at the end of that period. If the taxpayer elected to reduce salvage by up to 10% of cost, annual depreciation allowances would be $500 ($10,000 ÷ 20). The deduction could also have been figured by multiplying the $10,000 by the 5% straight-line rate (1 ÷ 20).

If there was no election to ignore salvage, annual deductions would be $475—5% of $9,500 ($10,000 cost less $500 salvage value).

## ¶ 348

## Declining-Balance Method

The deduction under this method is determined by reducing the basis by any previously deducted depreciation and multiplying the balance by the declining-balance rate (Reg.§ 1.167(b)-2).

New tangible assets acquired after 1953 (and placed in service before 1981) qualified for rates up to twice the straight-line rates (double declining-balance method). Rates not in excess of one and one-half the straight-line rates (150-percent declining-balance method) were permissible for used assets acquired after 1953 and for new and used assets acquired before 1954. Special limitations applied in the case of real estate depreciation (Reg.§ 1.167(c)-1).

An asset was treated as new if its original use began with the taxpayer. An asset's original use was the first use to which it was put, whether or not that use corresponded to the use to which the taxpayer put it (Reg. § 1.167(c)-1(a)(2)).

***Example:*** New farm machinery with a 10-year useful life was bought for $100,000. Under the 200% declining-balance method, the first five years' depreciation at the 20% rate (twice the 10% straight-line rate) is calculated as follows:

| Year | Remaining Basis | Declining-Balance Rate | Depreciation Allowance |
|---|---|---|---|
| First . . . . . . . . . . . . . . . . . | $100,000 | 20% | $20,000 |
| Second . . . . . . . . . . . . . . | 80,000 | 20% | 16,000 |
| Third . . . . . . . . . . . . . . . . | 64,000 | 20% | 12,800 |
| Fourth . . . . . . . . . . . . . . | 51,200 | 20% | 10,240 |
| Fifth . . . . . . . . . . . . . . . . . | 40,960 | 20% | 8,192 |

The declining-balance method applies only to tangible assets with a useful life of three or more years. Although salvage value is not taken into account in determining the deduction under this method, an asset may not be depreciated below its salvage value.

## ¶ 350

## Declining-Balance Method with Change to Straight-Line

If the declining-balance method were followed throughout the life of an asset, the asset would in many cases not be fully depreciated down to salvage value. As a result, it is a common practice to change over to the straight-line method at the point where this method would give a larger deduction than the declining-balance method.

The straight-line rate in the changeover year is based on the remaining useful life at the beginning of the year and is applied to the adjusted basis at the beginning of the year (cost or other basis less depreciation deducted) reduced by salvage value.

> ***Example:*** After depreciating the farm machinery for the first 5 years of the 10-year life in the example at ¶ 348, above, under the double declining-balance method, the farmer had a remaining adjusted basis of $32,768 ($40,960 basis at the beginning of the fifth year minus $8,192 depreciation for that year). The straight-line rate based on the remaining useful life of five years is 20%. Assuming that salvage value is less than $10,000 (10% of $100,000) and the farmer elects to ignore it, straight-line depreciation for the sixth year is $6,554 (20% of $32,768).

## ¶ 352

## Sum of the Years-Digits Method

Under this method, the years of useful life are numbered and these numbers are totaled. The result is the sum of the years-digits. The deduction under this method is figured by reducing the basis by the salvage value and multiplying the remainder by a fraction. The fraction has the remaining useful life at the beginning of the year as its numerator and the sum of the years-digits as its denominator (Reg.§ 1.167(b)-3).

> ***Example:*** An automobile with a three-year life to a calendar-year taxpayer was bought for $3,600 and placed in service on January 1. Salvage value was estimated to be $300. The sum of the years-digits is 6 (1 + 2 + 3).

His deductions would be—

| | |
|---|---|
| 1st year ($3,300 × 3/6) . . . . . . . . . . . . . . . . . . . | $1,650 |
| 2nd year ($3,300 × 2/6) . . . . . . . . . . . . . . . . . . . | 1,100 |
| 3rd year ($3,300 × 1/6) . . . . . . . . . . . . . . . . . . . | 550 |
| Total . . . . . . . . . . . . . . . . . . . . . . . . . . . | $3,300 |

A speedy way to find the sum of the years-digits for an asset with a long useful life is to square the useful life, add the useful life to the result, and divide by two. Thus, the sum of the years-digits for an asset with a 40-year life would be 820—the sum of 1,600 (40 × 40) and 40 divided by 2.

The sum of the years-digits method was applicable only to new tangible assets with a useful life of three years or more.

See Reg. § 1.167(b)-3 for computational rules that apply if asset is not deemed placed in service on the first day of the tax year.

## ¶ 354

## Sum of the Years-Digits Remaining Life Method

Another way to compute years-digits depreciation was by applying rates based on the remaining life to the undepreciated basis at the beginning of the year (cost minus salvage value minus depreciation previously deducted). A remaining life rate is equal to the remaining life divided by the sum of the years-digits for the remaining life (Reg. § 1.167(b)-3).

> ***Example:*** In the example at ¶ 352, above, the computation of the first year's depreciation would be the same under the remaining life method. For the second year, the remaining life is 2 years and the sum of the years-digits for that life is 3 (1 + 2). The deduction for the second year would be ⅔ of the $1,800 undepreciated basis ($3,600 cost less $1,800 first year's depreciation), or $1,200.

## ¶ 356

## Other Consistent Methods

In addition to the straight-line, declining-balance, and the sum of the years-digits methods, any other method was permissible for new assets so long as it was consistently applied as explained at ¶ 344 and the accumulated allowances at the end of any tax year during the first two-thirds of the useful life are not more than those that would accumulate under the 200-percent declining-balance method (Reg. § 1.167(b)-4).

## ¶ 358

## Depreciation in Year of Purchase or Sale

If an asset was bought or sold during the year, only a fractional part of a year's depreciation was deducted, depending on the number of months the asset was held during the year.

In determining depreciation in the year of acquisition, it was proper to treat an asset as having been held a full month if it was acquired on or before the 15th of the month. If it was acquired after the 15th, the month was not counted. Consistently, it was proper to count the disposition month only if the asset was disposed of after the 15th of the month. Thus, an asset bought on May 14 by a calendar year taxpayer would get 8 months' first year depreciation (8/12 of first full year's depreciation). If acquired on May 17, only 7 months' depreciation was allowed.

Another possible way to handle this was to count the month of acquisition and exclude the month of disposition (regardless of the day acquired or disposed of).

Also, the taxpayer could compute the exact amount of depreciation on the basis of the number of days held during the year.

If the sum of the years-digits method was used, allocations must be made throughout the useful life of the asset. Thus, if an asset was held three months in the year it was bought, 3/12 of the first full year's depreciation was deductible in that year. In the second taxable year held, 9/12 of the first full year's depreciation and 3/12 of the second full year's depreciation were deductible. This procedure must be followed for the asset's entire useful life.

## ¶ 360

## Methods Keyed to Production

There are several depreciation methods which prorate the cost over an asset's production life.

Under the machine-hour method, the useful life is estimated in machine hours. An hourly rate is then found by dividing the depreciable cost by the total hours of useful life. The deduction is equal to the total hours of use times the rate.

Similar to this is the operating-day method, except that the life is estimated in days.

The unit-of-production method is mainly for equipment used in exploiting natural resources (mines, wells, etc.). This method prorates the cost according to the ratio of the units produced for the year to the total expected units to be produced. The space above a landfill or dump may be depreciated using the unit-of-production method (*H.K. Sanders*, 75 TC 157, CCH Dec. 37,348).

It should be noted that property depreciable under the unit-of-production method (or any other method not expressed in a term of years) may, if the taxpayer elects, be depreciated under this method even if it was placed in service after 1980. See ¶ 140 (MACRS) and ¶ 264 (ACRS).

## ¶ 364

## Income Forecast Method

The usefulness of certain tangible or intangible assets used in a trade or business is more accurately measured by the stream of income produced rather than over the passage of time. An irrevocable election may be made to depreciate these assets using the income forecast method. Under this method, which has been allowed since the early 1960s, the depreciable basis of a property is recovered over the anticipated income to be earned from the property. The depreciation deductions follow the uneven flow of income in order to avoid a distortion of income.

> ***Comment:*** *Taxpayers may elect to treat the cost of any qualified film or television production commencing before January 1, 2026 as a currently deductible expense (Code Sec. 181, as amended by the Taxpayer Certainty and Tax Relief Act of 2020 (P.L. 116-260)). A qualified live theatrical production of a play (with or without music) in venues of 3,000 persons or less derived from a written book or script and commencing after 2015 will also qualify. A theatrical production commences production on the date of the first public performance of the production for a paying audience (Act Sec. 169(d)(3) of the Protecting Americans from Tax Hikes Act of 2015 (December 18, 2015)). In the case of a film production commencing after December 31, 2007 or a live theatrical production commencing after 2015, the election applies regardless of the cost of the production and the first $15 million or $20 million of production costs are deductible. The election must be made by the due date (including extensions) for filing the taxpayer's tax return for the tax year in which costs of the production are first incurred. Once the election is made, the election may not be revoked without IRS consent. Election guidance is provided in Reg. § 1.181-2.*
>
> *100 percent bonus depreciation is allowed for a qualified film, television show, or theatrical production acquired and placed in service after September 27, 2017, if it would have qualified for the Code Sec. 181 expense election without regard to the $15 million expensing limit or the expiration date (Code Sec. 168(k)(2)(A)(i), as amended by the*

*2017 Tax Cuts Act). See ¶ 127D, 17. Film and television productions and live theatrical productions acquired and placed in service after September 27, 2017.*

*See also ¶ 67 for rules allowing 15-year amortization of film industry creative property costs.*

This depreciation method was developed by the IRS in response to a determination that a distortion of income occurred where producers of motion picture and television films did not report taxable income until the income from these assets exceeded costs incurred.

For tangible property, an election to depreciate property under the income forecast method (a method not expressed in a term of years) constitutes an election to exclude such property from MACRS (Code Sec. 168(f)(1)) (see also ¶ 140). This election must be made in the year that the property is placed in service (IRS Letter Ruling 9323007, March 8, 1993). The election to use the income forecast method is made on a property-by-property basis. Income forecast method depreciation is entered on line 16 ("Other depreciation") of Form 4562 (line reference to 2018 Form).

*Property eligible for income forecast method.*

Effective for property placed in service after August 5, 1997, the income forecast method (or any similar method) may only be used with respect to film, video tape, sound recordings, copyrights, books, patents, and other property to be specified in IRS regulations (Code Sec. 167(g)(6), as added by the Taxpayer Relief Act of 1997 (P.L. 105-34)). This provision essentially codifies the previous IRS position.

The income forecast method may not be elected to depreciate intangible assets that are amortizable Sec. 197 intangibles (Code Sec. 197(b); Code 167(g)(6)).

Prior to the 1997 Act, use of the income forecast method of depreciation was approved by the IRS for the following property: television films (Rev. Rul. 60-358, 1960-2 CB 68); motion picture films and video tapes (Rev. Rul. 64-273, 1964-2 CB 62; Code Sec. 168(f)(3)); sound recordings (Rev. Rul. 60-358, 1960-2 CB 680; Code Sec. 168(f)(4)); book manuscript rights, patents, and master recordings (Rev. Rul. 79-285, 1979-1 CB 91); copyrighted musical works (IRS Letter Ruling 8501006, 9-24-84); rental videocassettes (Rev. Rul. 89-62, 1989-1 CB 78 (see also ¶ 140)); video game machines (IRS Letter Ruling 9323007, 3-8-93), and other property of a similar character.

*Musical compositions and copyrights thereto.* A taxpayer may elect five-year amortization of capitalized expenses paid or incurred in creating or acquiring a musical composition (including the accompanying words) or a copyright to a musical composition if the expenses could otherwise be recovered using the income forecast method (Code Sec. 167(g)(8), as added by the Tax Increase Prevention and Reconciliation Act of 2005 (P.L. 109-222)).

*Rent-to-own property.* The Tax Court had ruled that the income forecast method may not be used to depreciate consumer durables (appliances, furniture, televisions, stereos, and video cassette recorders) leased under rent-to-own contracts (*ABC Rentals of San Antonio, Inc.*, 68 TCM 1362, TC Memo. 1994-601, CCH Dec. 50,278(M), affirmed *per curiam* under the name *El Charo TV Rentals*, CA-5, 97-1 USTC ¶ 50,140; Rev. Rul. 95-52, 1955-2 CB 27) because the property had a determinable useful life. The Tax Court decision, however, was also appealed by certain petitioners to the Court of Appeals for the Tenth Circuit, which held that the income forecast method could apply to the rented consumer durables (and presumably to other types of property) if the method meets certain standards of reasonableness set forth in Code Sec. 167 and the regulations. Since the IRS conceded that the income forecast method was a reasonable method, the taxpayers were entitled to use that method provided that the proper procedures were followed in electing out of MACRS under Code Sec. 168(f)(1) and the method was properly applied to produce reasonable allowances (*ABC Rentals of San Antonio, Inc.*, CA-10, 98-1 USTC ¶ 50,340). The case was remanded to the Tax Court to determine these two issues (see *ABC Rentals of San Antonio, Inc.*, et al., 77 TCM 1229, TC Memo. 1999-14, CCH Dec. 53,217(M) which found in favor of certain taxpayers and against others on these issues).

The 1997 Taxpayer Relief Act (P.L. 105-34), added a provision which treats rent-to-own property (property held by a rent-to-own dealer for purposes of being subject to a rent-to-own contract) as 3-year MACRS property, effective for property placed in service after August 5, 1997. Such property is assigned a four-year recovery period under the alternative depreciation system (ADS). (Code Sec. 168(e)(3); Code Sec. 168(g)(3); and Code Sec. 168(i)(14), as amended by P.L. 105-34). Rent-to-own property placed in service before August 6, 1997, was treated by the IRS as 5-year MACRS property.

*Formula for computing income forecast depreciation.*

Under the income forecast method, the cost of an asset placed in service after September 13, 1995, is multiplied by a fraction, the numerator of which is the net income from the asset for the tax year, and the denominator of which is the total net income to be derived from the asset before the close of the tenth tax year *following* the tax year in which the asset is placed in service (Code Sec. 167(g)(1)(A), as added by the Small Business Job Protection Act of 1996 (P.L. 104-188)). The unrecovered adjusted basis of the property as of the beginning of the tenth tax year is claimed as a depreciation deduction in the tenth tax year after the year in which the property is placed in service (Code Sec. 167(g)(1)(C), as added by P.L. 104-188).

If, in a later year, the outlook for the income forecast changes, the formula for computing depreciation would be as follows: the unrecovered depreciable cost of the asset at the beginning of the tax year of revision multiplied by a fraction, the numerator of which is the net income from the asset for the tax year of revision and the denominator of which is the revised forecasted total net income from the asset for the year of revision and the remaining years before the close of the tenth tax year following the tax year in which the asset was placed in service.

*Denominator of formula.* For purposes of the denominator in the formula, the total forecasted net income from the asset is based on the conditions known to exist at the end of the current tax year (Rev. Rul. 60-358, 1960-2 CB 68). There must be evidence to support the forecast of total net income from the asset or a depreciation deduction will be denied (*E.D. Abramson*, 86 TC 360, CCH Dec. 42,919). The amount of the denominator cannot be less than any nonrecourse loan secured by the asset (Rev. Rul. 78-28, 1978-1 CB 61).

Income projections must be made for each asset subject to this method. Videocassettes and video game machines may be grouped by title (but not by a broader grouping) for income projection purposes (Rev. Rul. 89-62, 1989-1 CB 78; IRS Letter Ruling 9323007, 3-8-93).

The types of income taken into account in the income forecast depreciation formula were significantly expanded by the Small Business Job Protection Act (P.L. 104-188), effective for property placed in service after September 13, 1995. Estimated income from films and TV shows include, but is not limited to, estimated income from foreign and domestic sources, theatrical releases, television releases and syndications, and video tape releases, sales, rentals and syndications. Estimated income also includes amounts derived from unrelated taxpayers with respect to the financial exploitation of characters, designs, scripts, scores, and other incidental income associated with the films (Code Sec. 167(g)(5)(C)).

When a taxpayer produces a TV series and initially does not anticipate syndicating the series, the forecasted income for the episodes of the first three years of the series need not take into account any future syndication fees. This rules does not apply if the taxpayer enters into a syndication agreement for the shows during the three-year period (Code Sec. 167(g)(5)(B)).

*Numerator of formula.* For purposes of the numerator in the formula, income from the asset means the actual net income from the asset determined without considering depreciation expense (Rev. Rul. 60-358, 1960-2 CB 68; *L. Greene*, 81 TC 132, CCH Dec. 40,390). No depreciation is allowed if there is no income from the asset during the tax year.

Income utilized in the numerator used to compute depreciation must reflect the same gross income used to compute taxable income from the asset for the same period under the taxpayer's method of accounting (Rev. Rul. 78-28, 1978-1 CB 61). Thus, a cash-basis entity could not include an accrued income amount in the numerator for depreciation purposes because the amount was not received before the end of the tax year and was not includible in gross income or taxable income for such year (Rev. Rul. 78-28, 1978-1 CB 61; *L. Greene*, 81 TC 132, CCH Dec. 40,390).

The new law also clarifies that the term "income from the property" is the taxpayer's gross income from the property (Code Sec. 167(g)(5)(E), as added by the American Jobs Creation Act of 2004 (P.L. 108-357)). This definition precludes taxpayers from taking distribution costs into account for purposes of determining current (numerator of formula) and total forecasted income (denominator of the formula) with respect to a property (Conference Committee Report (H.R. Conf. Rep. No. 108-755)).

*Cost basis under income forecast method—participations and residuals.*

The cost basis of an asset depreciated under the income forecast method is determined in a unique manner. Because forecasted total net income is used in the formula, the Ninth Circuit has ruled that estimated costs dependent on such amount are includible in cost basis (*Transamerica Corp.*, CA-9, 93-2 USTC ¶ 50,388). This is necessary so that all costs are included and spread evenly over the flow of income derived from the asset. Thus, estimated percentages (participations) to be paid based on the forecasted future gross receipts and net profits from a motion picture as well as percentages (residuals) to be paid stemming from forecasted future revenue received from the movie's television exhibition were includible in the cost basis of the property for purposes of computing depreciation under the income forecast method.

Since the *Transamerica* decision was decided prior to the enactment of the economic performance rules of Code Sec. 461(h), it has been unclear what effect the economic performance rules would have had on its outcome since the payments involved were contingent on the occurrence of future events. The Small Business Job Protection Act of 1996, however, specifically provides that the basis of a film or other property depreciated under the income forecast method only includes amounts that satisfy the economic performance standard of Code Sec. 461(h) (Code Sec. 167(g)(1)(B), as added by P.L. 104-188, generally effective for property placed in service after September 13, 1995). The IRS has taken the position in its proposed regulations, discussed below, that the economic performance requirement precludes the inclusion of contingent expenses in the basis of income forecast property.

Effective for property placed in service after October 22, 2004, a taxpayer may include participations and residuals in the basis of a film in the tax year that it is placed in service, but only to the extent that the participations and residuals relate to income estimated to be earned in connection with the film before the close of the tenth tax year after the tax year the property was placed in service (Code Sec. 167(g)(7)(A), as added by the American Jobs Creation Act of 2004 (P.L. 108-357)). This provision is not intended to create an inference regarding the proper treatment of participations and residuals paid in connections with films placed in service before the effective date.

As an alternative to including such participations and residuals in the basis of the film and recovering their cost over a 10-year period, a taxpayer may exclude the participations and residuals from basis and deduct them in full in the year that they are actually paid (Code Sec. 167(g)(7)(D)(i), as added by the 2004 Jobs Act). The Conference Committee Report (H.R. Conf. Rep. No. 108-755) states that the decision to currently deduct these expenses may be made on a property-by-property basis but must be applied consistently with respect to a given property thereafter.

The method of treating participations and residuals is considered an election. The election must be made by the due date (including extensions) for filing the return for the taxable year the income forecast property is placed in service. Election procedures (including rules for taxpayers who filed returns before June 15, 2006 for a tax year ending after October 22, 2004 without making the election) are provided in Notice 2006-47, I.R.B. 2006-20.

The Large and Mid-Size Business (LMSB) Division of the IRS has issued guidance regarding issues raised during examinations of taxpayers using the income forecast method (IRS LMSB Memo on Disposition of Income Forecast Method Issues, January 6, 2005). The most common issues during examination are net versus gross and participation/residuals. The net versus gross issue concerns whether income in the income forecast fraction includes distribution costs. Taxpayers using the net method could exclude distribution costs under Rev. Rul. 60-358, 1960-2 CB 68. However, under Code Sec. 167(g)(5)(E), as amended by the American Jobs Creation Act of 2004 (P.L. 108-357), taxpayers must use the gross method and include distribution costs in the income forecast fraction.

The participation/residual issue concerns the proper time for adding these payments to a film's basis. The IRS had taken the position that participations/residuals are deferred compensation under Code Sec. 404 and may not be added to a film's basis until the recipient includes the payment in income. Changes to Code Sec. 167(g)(7)(A), however, permit a taxpayer to include participations/residuals in basis for the tax year in which the property is placed in service for purposes of determining depreciation under the income forecast method. Alternatively, Code Sec. 167(g)(7)(D)(i) allows a taxpayer to claim a deduction for depreciation of the participations/residuals in the tax year in which they are paid. The memo further details how examining agents should deal with net versus gross and participations/residuals issues that arise during an examination in light of the recent changes to Code Sec. 167.

*Interest computation under look-back rule.*

Effective for property placed in service after September 13, 1995, taxpayers that claim depreciation under the income-forecast method are required to pay (or may be entitled to receive) interest based on the recalculation of depreciation using actual income figures. This look-back calculation is required during a recomputation year. In general, a recomputation year is the third and tenth tax years beginning after the tax year in which the film or other property was placed in service (Code Sec. 167(g)(2)). The look-back rule does not apply to property that had a cost basis of $100,000 or less or if the taxpayer's income projections were within 10 percent of the income actually earned (Code Sec. 167(g)(3)).

*Form 8866 for look-back interest computation.* The IRS released Form 8866 (Interest Computation Under the Look-Back Method for Property Depreciated Under the Income Forecast Method) in early 1999 to compute the interest due or owed during a recomputation year.

### *Proposed income forecast depreciation regulations*

The IRS has issued proposed income forecast depreciation regulations which reflect the addition of Code Sec. 167(g) by the Small Business Job Protection Act of 1996 (P.L. 104-188) and the amendment of Code Sec. 167(g) by the Taxpayer Relief Act of 1997 (P.L. 105-34) to limit the use of the income forecast method to specified types of property (Prop. Reg. § 1.167(n)-1 through 7).

The proposed regulations will apply to property placed in service on or after the date that final regulations are published in the Federal Register (Prop. Reg. § 1.167(n)-7).

#### *Property eligible for the income forecast method*

Under the proposed regulations, the following property is the only property eligible for the income forecast method (Prop. Reg. § 1.167(n)-5(a)):

(1) film, video tape, and sound recordings (property described in Code Sec. 168(f)(3) and (4));

(2) copyrights;

(3) books;

(4) patents;

(5) theatrical productions; and

(6) any other property designed by the IRS in published guidance.

With the exception of theatrical productions, these are the same items listed in Code Sec. 167(g)(6).

The income forecast method does not apply to any amortizable section 197 intangible as defined in Code Sec. 197(c) and Reg. § 1.197-2(d) (Code Sec. 167(g)(6); Prop. Reg. § 1.167(n)-5(b)).

#### *Computation*

Under Code Sec. 167(g) the depreciable basis of an income forecast property is generally recovered over an 11-year period beginning in the year that the income forecast property is placed in service.

The income-forecast method depreciation deduction is generally equal to:

$$\frac{\text{depreciable basis} \times \text{current year income}}{\text{forecasted total income}}$$

***Example (1):*** Income forecast property with a depreciable basis of $100,000 is placed in service in Year 1. Current-year income is $30,000. Forecasted total income to be received from the property before the close of the tenth tax year after the year the asset is placed in service is estimated at the end of Year 1 to be $200,000. Year 1 depreciation is $15,000 ($100,000 × $30,000/$200,000). If current-year income in Year 2 is $25,000, the depreciation deduction for Year 2 is $12,500 ($100,000 × $25,000/$200,000).

As explained below, in tax years after the tax year that the income forecast method property is placed in service it may be necessary to compute income forecast depreciation deductions using revise forecasted total income if the original estimate of forecasted income changes sufficiently. Revised forecasted total income for a tax year is the sum of current-year income for the tax year and all prior tax years, plus all income from the income forecast method property that the taxpayer reasonably believes will be included in current-year income in tax years after the current tax year up to and including the tenth tax year after the tax year in which the income forecast method property was placed in service.

In a tax year in which forecasted total income is revised, the income forecast method deduction is equal to the product of the unrecovered depreciable basis and the following fraction (Proposed Reg.§ 1.167(n)-4(b)):

$$\frac{\text{current year income}}{\text{revised forecasted total income} - \text{current year income from prior years}}$$

*Safe harbor.* The revised computation may be used in any year that revised forecasted total income differs from forecasted total income. However, a taxpayer is *required* to use the revised computation if forecasted total income (revised forecasted total income if the taxpayer previously revised its income projections) in the immediately preceding tax year is either:

(1) Less than 90 percent of revised forecasted total income for the tax year; or

(2) Greater than 110 percent of revised forecasted total income for the tax year (Prop. Reg. § 1.167(n)-4(b)(2)).

***Example (2):*** Assume same facts as in *Example (1)*, except that at the end of Year 3 the taxpayer estimates that $210,000 of income will be recognized over the remaining 8 years in the 11-year depreciation period. Assuming the current-year income for Year 3 is $35,000, the revised forecasted income is $300,000 ($30,000 + $25,000 + $35,000 + $210,000). The safe harbor does not apply because the taxpayer's original forecasted total income ($200,000) is less than 90% of the revised forecasted total income for Year 3 ($300,000). The taxpayer, therefore, must compute the Year 3 and later deductions based on the revised forecasted income amount. Revised forecasted income less actual income from years prior to the revision year is $245,000 ($300,000 – $30,000 – $25,000). The undepreciated basis at the beginning of Year 3 is $72,500 ($100,000 – $15,000 – $12,500). The Year 3 income forecast depreciation deduction is $10,357 ($72,500 × $35,000/$245,000). If Year 4 current income is $40,000, the Year 4 depreciation deduction is $11,837 ($72,500 × $40,000/$245,000).

*Computation if basis of property increases.* The depreciable basis of an income forecast method property is increased by capital expenses paid or incurred with respect to the property in a tax year after it is placed in service (Prop. Reg. § 1.167(n)-2(a)(2)). The increased basis is referred to as the "redetermined basis." The amount of the increase is referred to as the "basis redetermination amount."

In the tax year that the basis is redetermined, a taxpayer is entitled to an additional depreciation deduction (a "catch-up" deduction) equal to the portion of the basis increase (the basis redetermination amount) that would have been recovered in prior tax years if the redetermination amount had originally been included in depreciable basis (Prop. Reg. § 1.167(n)-4(c)(1)).

In the tax year that the basis is increased and in subsequent tax years, the redetermined basis is used to determine the regular income forecast depreciation deductions (Prop. Reg. § 1.167(n)-2(b)).

The catch up deduction is not allowed with respect to basis increases that occur in the last tax year of the depreciation period (i.e., the tenth tax year following the tax year that the income forecast method property was placed in service). Instead, the full amount of the basis increase is deducted, as explained below.

***Example (3):*** A movie producer agrees to pay a book author 5% of a movie's income in excess of $500,000. Forecasted total income is $1 million. The basis of the film is $500,000. The payments will be determined and made within one month after the end of each tax year.

| *Year* | *Current Year Income* | *Regular Deduction* |
|---|---|---|
| 1 | $300,000 | $150,000 (500,000 × 300,000/1,000,000) |
| 2 | $150,000 | $ 75,000 (500,000 × 150,000/1,000,000) |
| 3 | $100,000 | $ 50,000 (500,000 × 100,000/1,000,000) |

In the first month of Year 4, the producer pays the author $2,500 ($50,000 earnings in excess of $500,000 at end of Year 3 × 5%). Beginning in Year 4 the basis of the film is increased by $2,500 (see timing rule for deferred compensation payments under the heading "*Determining depreciable basis,*" below.).

| *Year* | *Current Year Income* | *Regular Deduction* |
|---|---|---|
| 4 | $90,000 | $45,225 (502,500 × 90,000/1,000,000) |

| *Year* | *Additional Deduction* |
|---|---|
| 4 | $ 750 (2,500 × 300,000/1,000,000) |
| | 375 (2,500 × 150,000/1,000,000) |
| | 250 (2,500 × 100,000/1,000,000) |
| | $1,375 |

The additional deduction can also be determined by multiplying the basis redetermination amount ($2,500) by the ratio of the $550,000 cumulative prior-year incomes ($300,000 + $150,000 + $100,000) to $1,000,000 forecasted total income ($2,500 × $550,000/$1,000,000 = $1,375).

In the first month of Year 5, the producer pays the author an additional $4,500 ($90,000 × 5%). In Year 5, the basis of the film is increased by $4,500 to $507,000 ($502,500 + $4,500). An additional depreciation deduction of $2,970 can be claimed.

| *Year* | *Current Year Income* | *Regular Deduction* |
|---|---|---|
| 5 | $110,000 | $55,770 (507,000 × 110,000/1,000,000) |

| *Year* | *Additional Deduction* |
|---|---|
| 5 | $1,350 (4,500 × 300,000/1,000,000) |
| | 675 (4,500 × 150,000/1,000,000) |
| | 450 (4,500 × 100,000/1,000,000) |
| | 495 (4,500 × 110,000/1,000,000) |
| | $2,970 |

The same computational process would be followed for each subsequent year of the 11-year depreciation period other than the final year.

Certain significant basis increases may be treated as a separate item of income forecast property. See "*Costs treated as separate property,*" below.

*Undepreciated basis recovered in final year.* The depreciation period for an item of income forecast property is generally 11 years—the tax year that the property is placed in service and ten additional tax years. Thus, the final year that a depreciation deduction is claimed is usually the tenth tax year following the tax year that the property is placed in service. The entire undepreciated basis of the property can be claimed in this year. However, if in an earlier tax year, a taxpayer reasonably believes, based on the conditions known to exist at the end of the earlier tax year, that no additional income will be earned in the remaining years of the 11-year depreciation period, the remaining basis (including any basis redetermination amount for that year (i.e., basis increase)) may be deducted in that year (Prop. Reg. § 1.167(n)-4(d)(1) and (2)).

A taxpayer may pay or incur expenses with respect to an income forecast property in a tax year after the final depreciation deduction is claimed. These expenses may be deducted in full as depreciation in the year paid or incurred if they would have constituted a basis redetermination amount (Prop. Reg. § 1.167(n)-4(d)(2)). If the additional expense will generate significant income, then it may be necessary to depreciate the expense as a separate item of income forecast property. See "*Costs treated as separate property,*" below.

*Depreciation in year of disposition.* If an income forecast property is sold or otherwise disposed of prior to the end of the 11-year recovery period, the depreciation allowance for the year of disposition is equal to the product of the depreciable or redetermined basis and the following fraction: (Prop. Reg. § 1.167(n)-4(d)(3)):

$$\frac{\text{current year income}}{\text{amount realized + current year income + current year income from all prior years}}$$

The rule allowing the deduction of the full amount of the remaining basis in the final year of depreciation does not apply in this situation.

See "*Income from dispositions,*" below.

*Determining depreciable basis*

The starting basis used to compute depreciation under the income forecast method is the basis for determining gain or loss under Code Sec. 1011 (Prop. Reg. § 1.167(n)-2(a)(1)).

*Salvage value.* Although Rev. Rul. 60-358, which had governed the computation of income forecast depreciation prior to the enactment of Code Sec. 167(g) required the reduction of basis by salvage value, the proposed regulations contain no such requirement. The introduction to the proposed regulations explains this change by concluding that Congress intended to allow the recovery of the *entire* basis of income forecast method property within ten tax years after the income forecast method property is placed in service.

*All events tests.* In the case of an accrual method taxpayer, costs are included in basis in the tax year that all events have occurred that establish the fact of the liability, the amount of the liability can be determined with reasonable accuracy, and economic performance (within the meaning of Code Sec. 461(h)) has occurred (Code Sec. 167(g)(1)(B); Prop. Reg. § 1.167(n)-2(a)(2)). These three requirements are referred to as the all events test. The basis of income forecast property produced by a taxpayer is determined under the uniform capitalization rules of Code Sec. 263A. Amounts are not taken into account under the UNICAP rules until the preceding all events test is satisfied (Reg. § 1.263A-1(c)(2)(ii)).

If any Code Section requires a liability of an accrual method taxpayer to be deducted later than the time that the all events test would otherwise be considered satisfied, then the depreciable basis is not increased until that later time (Reg. § 1.461-1(a)(2)(iii)(A)).

*Contingent payments.* Under the all events tests, contingent payments are not included in the basis of income forecast property until the tax year they are actually paid or incurred even if it is nearly certain that the forecasted total income used in the income forecast method computation method will be sufficient to satisfy the contingency (Prop. Reg. § 1.167(n)-2(a)(2)). However, participations and residuals may be included in basis or currently deducted, effective for films placed in service after October 22, 2004.

*Deferred compensation payments.* Deferred compensation payments which are subject to Code Sec. 404 (relating to employer contributions to a plan of deferred compensation) do not satisfy the economic performance requirement and, therefore, are not included in basis of income forecast method property, until the amount is deductible under Code Sec. 404 (Reg. § 1.461-1(a)(2)(3)(D)).

> ***Example (4):*** An accrual method studio contracts to pay an actor 5% of gross movie income in excess of $20 million. At the end of the third tax year after the movie is placed in service cumulative gross film revenue reaches $21 million. The studio makes a $50,000 payment to the actor 20 days after the end of the third tax year. The studio may increase the film's basis in the fourth tax year when the $50,000 is paid. Although the studio had a fixed liability to pay the actor $50,000 in the third tax year, the requirements for deductibility under Code Sec. 404 were not satisfied until the liability was actually paid.

*Separate property.* Certain amounts paid or incurred in a tax year after income forecast method property is placed in service are treated as separate items of property which are separately depreciated using the income forecast method (Prop. Reg. § 1.167(n)-5(c)). See "*Costs treated as separate property,*" below.

*Basis redeterminations.* Assuming that a capitalizable amount paid or incurred in a tax year after the income forecast property is placed in service is not treated as a separate property, the basis of the income forecast property is increased by the additional capitalizable amount (Prop. Reg. § 1.167(n)-2(b)).

The redetermined basis is used to computed the income forecast method deduction in the tax year that the basis is redetermined and in later tax years. However, an additional "catch up" deduction is allowed in the tax year that the basis of income forecast property is redetermined (Reg. § 1.167(n)-4(c)). See "*Computation if basis of property increases,*" above.

*Unrecovered depreciable basis.* The unrecovered depreciable basis of an item of income forecast property for any tax year is the depreciable basis of the property less prior depreciation deductions (Reg. § 1.167(n)-2(c)).

*Income from the property*

Under the income forecast method the depreciation allowance is generally computed by multiplying the basis of the income forecast method property by the ratio of current-year income to forecasted total income.

Forecasted total income (computed in the tax year the property is placed in service) and revised forecasted total income (computed in later tax years) are determined based on conditions known to exist at the end of the tax year of the computation.

*Current-year income.* Generally, current-year income is all income from the income forecast method property for the current year determined in accordance with the taxpayer's method of accounting. Current-year income may be reduced by any distribution costs for the year (Prop. Reg. § 1.167(n)-3(a)(1)). However, a new rule applies to films placed in service after October 22, 2004. See "*Distribution costs*" below.

In the tax year that an income forecast method property is placed in service, current-year income includes any amount connected with the property that was included in gross income in a prior tax year (i.e., advance payments) (Prop. Reg. § 1.167(n)-3(a)(2)).

*Films, television shows, and similar property.* The proposed regulations provide that current-year income includes (but is not limited to) (Prop. Reg. § 1.167(n)-3(a)(1)):

(1) Income from foreign and domestic theatrical, television, and other releases and syndications;

(2) Income from releases, sales, rentals, and syndications of video tape, DVD, and other media; and

(3) Incidental income associated with the property.

Incidental income includes, but is not limited to, income from the financial exploitation of characters, designs, titles, scripts, and scores provided the income is not received from a related person within the meaning of Code Sec. 267(b).

The proposed regulations provide a special rule for income from the syndication of a television series produced for distribution on television networks. The rule provides that syndication income does not need to be included in current-year income, forecasted total income, or revised forecasted total income until the earlier of the fourth tax year beginning after the date that the first episode is placed in service or the earliest tax year in which the taxpayer has an arrangement relating to the syndication of the series. An arrangement relating to the syndication of a series means any arrangement other than the first run exhibition agreement (Prop. Reg. § 1.167(n)-3(d)(2)).

*Forecasted total income.* Forecasted total income is sum of the current-year income for the year that the income forecast method property is placed in service and the total amount of current-year income that the taxpayer reasonably believes will be included in current-year income for the next 10 tax years. Forecasted total income includes any amounts that will be earned by any subsequent owner during the 11-year depreciation period (Prop. Reg. § 1.167(n)-3(b)).

*Revised forecasted total income.* A taxpayer must recompute forecasted total income in any tax year that information reveals that forecasted total income is inaccurate. However, a taxpayer is not required to actually use revised forecasted income in making the depreciation calculations unless the forecasted total income in the immediately preceding tax year is less than 90 percent or greater than 110 percent of the revised forecasted income (Prop. Reg. § 1.167(n)-4(b)(2)).

If revised forecasted total income was used to compute income forecast depreciation in the immediately preceding tax year, revised forecasted total income for the preceding year is compared to revised forecasted income for the current tax year for purposes of the 90/110 percent test.

Revised forecasted total income for a tax year is the sum of current-year income for the tax year of revision and all prior tax years, plus all income from the income forecast property that the taxpayer reasonably believes will be included in current-year income through the end of the tenth tax year following the tax year that the income forecast property was placed in service (Prop. Reg. § 1.167(n)-3(c)).

Special rules for the computation of the income forecast deduction apply if forecasted total income is revised. See *Example (2)*, above.

*Distribution costs.* Effective for films placed in service after October 22, 2004, distribution costs are not taken into account in computing current year and total forecasted income (Code Sec. 167(g)(5)(E), as added by the American Jobs Creation Act of 2004 (P.L. 108-357)). For the treatment of distribution costs prior to this provision see IRS Letter Ruling 200252028, August 7, 2002.

*Income from dispositions.* Income from the sale or other disposition of income forecast property is not included in current-year income. Anticipated income from the future sale of income forecast property is not included in forecasted total income. Such income is included in revised forecasted total income in the year of sale for purposes of computing depreciation in the year of disposition and for purposes of applying the look-back rule discussed below. When computing forecasted total income or revised forecasted total income, the entire anticipated income for the 11-year depreciation period (the tax year the income forecast depreciation property is placed in service plus the next 10 years) is taken into account even if a sale prior to the close of the depreciation period is reasonably anticipated (Prop. Reg. § 1.167(n)-3(d)(1)).

***Example (5):*** Art Tistick produces a feature film that is placed in service in 2009. Art reasonably anticipates selling the film on the last day of 2016 for $2 million. Income earned in 2009 is $5 million. Art estimates that $15 million will be earned in 2009 through 2016. Estimated income from 2017 through 2019 is $3 million. Therefore, in computing depreciation for 2009, forecasted total income is $23 million ($5M + $15M + $3M) and does not include the estimated sales proceeds. In computing depreciation for 2016 (year of the sale), revised forecasted total income is equal to the amounts actually earned through 2016 plus the sales proceeds. The sales proceeds, however, are not included in current-year income in 2016 when making the 2016 depreciation calculation. See, also, Prop. Reg. § 1.167(n)-3(d)(4), *Example 2.*

*Apportionment of income.* Income from a particular source may relate to more than one income forecast property. For example, income from the sale or license of merchandise that features the image of a movie character may relate to more than one film. The regulations require a reasonable allocation of the income among the income forecast properties based on all relevant factors (Prop. Reg. § 1.167(n)-3(d)(3)).

*Costs treated as separate property*

Any amount paid or incurred after an income forecast property is placed in service (but before the property is fully depreciated) must be treated as a separate item of income forecast property rather than an increase in basis (basis redetermination amount) if the cost is:

(1) significant and

(2) gives rise to an increase in income that is significant and which was not included in either forecasted total income or revised forecasted total income in a prior tax year (Code Sec. 167(g)(5)(A)(ii); Prop. Reg. § 1.167(n)-5(c)).

An amount treated as a separate item of income forecast property is considered placed in service in the year the amount is paid or incurred.

For purposes of item (1), a cost is not significant if it less than the lesser of five percent of depreciable basis (as of the date the cost is paid or incurred) or $100,000.

For purposes of item (2), whether an increase in income is significant is determined by comparing the amount that would be considered revised forecasted total income from the amounts treated as separate property to the most recent estimate of forecasted total income or revised forecasted total income used in calculating an allowance for depreciation with respect to the income forecast property.

***Example (6):*** A film which was released in 2006 is prepared in 2009 for future rerelease as a DVD. The costs attributable to rerelease as a DVD exceed $100,000 and 5% of the film's depreciable basis. Assuming that no amount of the anticipated DVD revenue was originally included in the prior-year income projections (assume the DVD release was unanticipated) and that the DVD release income will be significant in relation to the forecasted total income used in calculating the 2008 depreciation allowance on the film, the additional expenditures are treated as a separate item of income forecast depreciation property beginning in 2009 when the expenditures are paid or incurred.

Any amount paid or incurred with respect to an income forecast property in a tax year after the tax year in which a final-year income forecast depreciation allowance has been claimed (see above) is deductible when paid or incurred as a basis redetermination amount unless the amount is expected to give rise to a significant increase in current-year income in any tax year (Prop. Reg. § 1.167(n)-5(c)(3)).

***Example (7):*** Assume the same facts as in *Example (6)*, except that the DVD preparation costs are in incurred in 2023 and that the film was fully depreciated under the income forecast method in 2016. If income from the DVD release will be significant in relation to the revised forecasted total income used in calculating depreciation in 2016, the cost of preparing the release is separately depreciated as an income forecast property. If the anticipated income is not significant, the cost is fully deductible in 2023.

*Permissible aggregations of multiple properties*

The proposed regulations only allow aggregations of multiple properties as a single item of income forecast property in the following four situations (Prop. Reg. § 1.167(n)-5(d)):

(1) Multiple episodes of a single television series produced in the same tax year;

(2) Multiple episodes of a single television series that are produced as a single season of episodes and placed in service over a period not in excess of twelve consecutive calendar months;

(3) Multiple interests in specifically identified income forecast properties acquired for broadcast pursuant to a single contract; and

(4) Multiple copies of the same title of videocassettes and DVDs purchased or licensed in the same tax year for rental to the public.

If a taxpayer chooses one of these aggregations, the additional depreciation allowance provided in Prop. Reg. § 1.167(n)-4(c)(1) for a basis redetermination (basis increase) in a tax year after the property is placed in service and before the tenth tax year following the tax year that the property was placed in service is not allowed. Thus, the amount of depreciation that would have been recovered if the basis redetermination amount had originally been included in the depreciable basis of the property when it was placed in service may not be claimed.

The aggregation of multiple properties is considered an adoption of an accounting method that can only be changed with IRS permission.

*Look back method*

Effective for property placed in service after September 13, 1995, taxpayers that claim depreciation under the income-forecast method are required to pay (or may be entitled to receive) interest based on hypothetical increases and decreases in tax liability attributable to the recalculation of depreciation using actual income figures (Code Sec. 167(g)(2); Prop. Reg. § 1.167(n)-6).

A look-back calculation is required during each recomputation year. In general, a recomputation year is the third and tenth tax years beginning after the tax year in which the film or other property was placed in service. The look-back method also applies in the tax-year income from the income forecast property ceases with respect to a taxpayer (Code Sec. 167(g)(4); Prop. Reg. § 1.167(n)-6(e)).

The computation of look-back interest is made on Form 8866 (Interest Computation Under the Look-Back Method for Property Depreciated Under the Income Forecast Method (January 1999)).

The look-back rule does not apply to property that had a cost basis (unadjusted basis) of $100,000 or less at the end of the recomputation year or the taxpayer's income projections for each year before the recomputation year were within 10 percent of the income actually earned (Code Sec. 167(g)(3) and (4)). See "*De minimus exceptions to look-back rule*," below.

The look-back method applies separately to each income forecast property or group of properties which were aggregated pursuant to the special rules described above in Prop. Reg. § 1.167(n)-5(d).

Pass-thru entities are required to use a simplified look-back method. See "*Simplified look-back method for certain pass-thru entities*," below.

*Computational steps*

A taxpayer is entitled to receive interest if total income expected to be earned with respect to a property was overestimated, thereby causing a reduction in the depreciation allowances that should have been claimed and an increased tax liability. Interest is owed if total income was underestimated.

The following computational steps apply (Prop. Reg. § 1.167(n)-6(b)(1)):

(1) Recompute depreciation allowances for each year prior to the recomputation year using revised forecasted total income (i.e., the sum of current-year income for the recomputation year and all prior tax years plus a reasonable estimate of current-year income for future tax years through the end of the tenth tax year following the tax year that the income forecast property was placed in service).

(2) Substituting the recomputed depreciation allowances for the allowances allowed (or allowable), redetermine the tax liability for each prior year. The redetermined tax liability for each prior year is a "hypothetical" tax liability used only for purposes of computing whether interest is paid (too much depreciation was claimed) or received (too little depreciation was claimed).

(3) For each prior year, compare the hypothetical tax liability with the actual tax liability and compute the interest on the difference as explained below.

*Syndication income from television series.* Syndication income from a television series that was excluded from forecasted total income (or revised forecasted total income) in any prior tax year is excluded from revised forecasted total income for purposes of computing look-back interest (Prop. Reg. § 1.167(n)-6(c)(2)(ii)).

*Look-back computation in year of disposition.* Look-back interest must be computed in the year that an income forecast property is sold or otherwise disposed of if the disposition occurs prior to the end of the tenth tax year after the property is placed in service. Income from the disposition of income forecast property is included in the revised forecasted total income amount used in computing look-back interest. Thus, revised forecasted total income is the sum of the amount realized on the disposition plus all amounts included in current-year income in the year of disposition and prior years (Prop. Reg. § 1.167(n)-6(c)(2)(iii)).

*Treatment of basis redetermination amounts.* An amount paid or incurred after the property was placed in service which increased the basis of the property (i.e., a basis redetermination amount) may be taken into account by discounting the basis redetermination amount to its value as of the date the property was placed in service. The discounted basis redetermination amount is computing using the Federal mid-term rate (determined under Code Sec. 1274(d)) at the time the cost was paid or incurred. A taxpayer may elect not to discount the basis redetermination amount simply by making the look-back calculation without a discount (Prop. Reg. § 1.167(n)-6(c)).

*Computation of hypothetical overpayment or underpayment of tax*

For each prior year, a taxpayer must calculate a hypothetical overpayment or underpayment of tax by comparing the actual tax liability (as originally reported or subsequently adjusted on examination or by amended return) and hypothetical tax liability for the prior year (Prop. Reg. § 1.167(n)-6(d)(2)(i)). A hypothetical income tax liability must be determined for any prior tax year that income tax liability would be affected by a recalculated depreciation allowance. This rule includes changes in net operating losses that would be affected by a recalculated depreciation allowance. For example, if a recalculated depreciation allowance in the year that the income forecast property was placed in service reduces, increases, or results in a net operating loss carryforward in the following year, a hypothetical income tax liability must be recomputed for the following year that takes into account the change in the NOL carryforward.

The hypothetical tax liability for each prior year must be computed by taking into account all applicable additions to tax, credits, and net operating loss carrybacks and carryforwards. Any alternative minimum tax must also be taken into account.

The hypothetical tax liability for each prior year is compared to the actual tax liability for the prior year determined as of the latest of the following dates:

(1) The original due date of the return (including extensions);

(2) The date of a subsequently amended return;

(3) The date a return is adjusted by examination; or

(4) The date of the previous application of the look-back method.

When the look-back method is used for a second time (e.g., in the tenth tax year following the year the income forecast property was placed in service), the hypothetical tax liability for each prior tax year is compared to the hypothetical tax liability previously computed for those years the first time that the look-back method was applied.

*Computation of interest*

The adjusted overpayment rate under (Code Sec. 460(b)(7)), compounded daily, is applied to the overpayment or underpayment for each prior tax year for the period beginning with the due date of the return (excluding extensions) for the prior year and ending on the earlier of the due date of the return (excluding extensions) for the recomputation year or the first date by which both the income tax return for the recomputation year is filed and the tax for that year has been paid in full (Prop. Reg. § 1.167(n)-6(d)(2)(ii)).

The amounts of interest on overpayments are then netted against interest on underpayments to arrive at the look-back interest payable or receivable.

*Measurement of interest if recomputed depreciation changes net operating loss carryback or carryforward.* If a recomputation of income forecast depreciation results in an increase or decrease to a net operating loss carryback, the interest a taxpayer is entitled to receive or required to pay must be computed on the decrease or increase in tax attributable to the change to the carryback only from the due date (not including extensions) of the return for the prior tax year that generated the carryback (Prop. Reg. § 1.167(n)-6(d)(2)(iii)).

In the case of a change in the amount of a carryforward, interest is computed from the due date of the return for the years in which the carryforward was absorbed.

*Measurement of interest if prior-year tax liability was refunded as the result of a loss or credit carryback.* A special rule applies if the hypothetical tax liability for a prior tax year is less than the amount of the actual tax liability for the prior year and any portion of the prior-year tax liability was refunded as the result of a loss or credit carryback that arose in a later tax year. In this situation, interest is computed on the amount of any refund in excess of the hypothetical income tax liability for the prior year only until the due date (not including extensions) of the return for the year in which the carryback arose (Prop. Reg. § 1.167(n)-(6)(d)(iv)).

***Example (8):*** Assume that Year 3 is a recomputation year. In Year 1 actual tax liability before an NOL carryback from Year 2 is $1,000. The tax liability after an NOL carryback from Year 2 is $800 and the taxpayer receives a $200 refund for Year 1 taxes paid in Year 2. If the hypothetical tax liability for Year 1 is $850, the taxpayer has made a hypothetical overpayment of $150 ($1,000 less $850). Since the $200 refund does not exceed the $850 hypothetical tax liability, interest is credited on the $150 hypothetical overpayment from the due date of the Year 1 return to the due date of the Year 3 return for the recomputation year.

***Example (9):*** Assume the same facts as in *Example (8)* except that the taxpayer received a $1,000 refund in Year 1. Since the amount of the refund ($1,000), exceeds the hypothetical tax liability for Year 1 ($850) by $150, the taxpayer is only entitled to interest on the $150 hypothetical overpayment from the due date of the Year 1 return to the due date of the Year 2 return.

***Example (10):*** Assume the same facts as in *Example (8)*, except that the taxpayer received a $950 refund in Year 1. Since the amount of the refund ($950) exceeds the hypothetical tax liability ($850) by $100, interest is credited to the taxpayer on $100 of the hypothetical overpayment from the due date of the Year 1 return to the due date of the Year 2 return. Interest is credited on the remaining $50 of the hypothetical overpayment from the due date of the Year 1 return to the due date of the Year 3 return.

### *Simplified look-back method for certain pass-thru entities*

Pass-thru entities that are not closely-held must use a simplified method to compute their hypothetical overpayment or underpayment for each prior year in which depreciation deductions were claimed. The pass-thru entity applies the simplified method at the entity level and the owners do not calculate look-back interest (Reg. § 1.167(n)-(d)(3)). A pass-thru entity only includes a partnership, S corporation, estate, or trust. A closely-held pass-thru entity is one that, at any time during any year for which depreciation is recomputed, 50 percent or more (by value) of the beneficial interests in the entity are held (directly or indirectly) by or for five or fewer persons (Prop. Reg. § 1.167(n)-(d)(4)).

The proposed regulations do not require or allow other taxpayers to use the simplified method. However, the IRS requests comments on whether the method should be extended to other taxpayers.

Under the simplified method, look-back interest is computed for each prior year by applying a set tax rate to the net change in the depreciation allowance for that year.

Depreciation allowances are recomputed in the same manner as they are using the nonsimplified method described above. The recomputed depreciation allowances are compared with the depreciation allowances allowed (or allowable) for each prior tax year. For each prior tax year, the net change is multiplied by the highest rate in effect for corporations under Code Sec. 11 (35 percent) to arrive at the hypothetical underpayment or overpayment of tax for that year. The highest tax rate imposed on individuals under Code Sec. 1 (35 percent in 2003) is used if, at all times during all prior tax years more than 50 percent of the interests in the entity were held by individuals directly or through one or more pass-thru entities. The highest rate of tax imposed on individuals is determined without regard to any additional tax imposed for the purpose of phasing out multiple tax brackets or exemptions.

When multiple properties are subject to the look-back method in any prior year, the changes in depreciation allowances attributable to each income forecast property are cumulated or netted against one another to arrive at a net change in income forecast depreciation for purposes of computing the hypothetical overpayment or underpayment attributable to the year.

*Look-back recomputation years*

There are a maximum of two recomputation years. Generally, these are the third and tenth tax years beginning after the tax year that the income forecast property is placed in service. However, if income from the income forecast property ceases with respect to the taxpayer before the tenth tax year after the property is placed in service, the tax year the income ceases is a recomputation year. For example, if the taxpayer sells the property in the first or second tax year after the property is placed in service, then that second tax year is the only recomputation year. If the property is sold after the third tax year and before the tenth tax year, then the third tax year and the tax year that the income ceases are the computation years (Prop. Reg. § 1.167(n)-(e)(1)).

In determining whether income from a property has ceased, the income must cease with respect to all persons treated a single taxpayer under rules similar to Code Sec. 41(f)(1) (relating to single taxpayer treatment of members of controlled groups and trades or businesses under common control for purposes of the research credit).

*De minimis exceptions to look-back rule*

No look-back interest calculation is required in any tax year that would otherwise be a recomputation year if one of two de minimus exceptions apply in the recomputation year.

Under the first exception, the look-back method does not apply to any income forecast property with a basis of $100,000 or less in a look-back (recomputation) year. The basis is determined without reduction for prior depreciation allowed or allowable (Code Sec. 167(g)(3); Prop. Reg. § 1.167(n)-6(f)).

The second exception requires that the taxpayer's income projections be within 10 percent of the income actually received (Code Sec. 167(g)(4); Prop. Reg. § 1.167(n)-6(e)(2)). Specifically, the 10-percent test is met if forecasted total income (and revised forecasted total income, if applicable) for each year prior to the look-back (recomputation) year is:

(1) greater than 90 percent of revised forecasted total income for the look-back year; and

(2) less than 110 percent of revised forecasted total income for the look-back year.

If the look-back method applied in the first recomputation year (i.e., third tax year after the income forecast property was placed in service) the amount of the forecasted total income or the revised forecasted total income for each tax year up to and including the third tax year after the year the property was placed in service is deemed equal to the revised forecasted total income that was used for purposes of applying the look-back rule in the third tax year.

*Treatment of look-back interest*

A taxpayer who fails to report look-back interest when due is subject to any penalties imposed under Subtitle F of the Internal Revenue Code (other than estimated tax penalties) attributable to the failure to report and pay a tax liability (Prop. Reg. § 1.167(n)-6(g)(1)).

Look-back interest is treated as interest arising from an underpayment of income tax under Subtitle A of the Internal Revenue Code, even though it is treated as an income tax liability for penalty purposes. Thus, look-back interest that is paid by an individual (or by a pass-thru entity on behalf of an individual owner under the simplified method) is nondeductible personal interest.

The determination of whether look-back interest is treated as an income tax under Subtitle A, is determined on a net basis for each look-back (recomputation) year. Thus, in the recomputation year, the taxpayer nets the deemed overpayments or underpayments that are computed for each of the prior tax years, taking into account all income forecast property for which the look-back method is required in the recomputation year.

Interest received is treated as taxable interest rather than a reduction in tax liability.

Interest determined at the entity level is allocated among the owners (or beneficiaries) for reporting purposes in the same manner that interest income and interest expense are allocated to owners (or beneficiaries). The allocation rules generally applicable to the entity also apply.

*Interest on look-back payments*

Look-back interest is computed on the hypothetical increase or decrease in the liability only until the initial due date of the return (without regard to extensions) for the look-back year. Interest is charged on the amount of look-back interest payable by a taxpayer from the initial due date of the return (without regard to extensions) for the look-back year through the date the return is actually filed unless the taxpayer has a refund that fully offsets the amount of interest due. If look-back interest is refundable to the taxpayer, interest on the look-back amount is credited to the taxpayer from the initial due date of the return through the date the return is filed (Prop. Reg. § 1.167(n)-6(g)(2)).

# Computing Depreciation on Multiple-Asset Accounts

## ¶ 370

### Group, Classified and Composite Accounts

A group account is one that includes assets that are similar in kind and have roughly the same useful lives. The classified and composite accounts segregate assets without regard to useful lives—the classified account covering specific classes of assets (such as machinery and equipment or furniture and fixtures) and the composite account including more than one class of assets (such as all the assets of a business in one account).

Group, classified or composite accounts could be either open-end or year's acquisition accounts. An open-end account is one to which additions and from which retirements are made as they occur—a feature now substantially restricted since most property placed in service after 1980 must be treated as ACRS recovery property or MACRS property. An account that includes all the assets acquired in a year for a group or class of assets is a year's acquisition account.

## ¶ 372

### Averaging Conventions

Where many assets are acquired or disposed of during a taxable year, depreciation may be computed on an average balance, unless the deduction is materially distorted for a particular year.

One popular averaging convention assumes that additions and retirements occur uniformly during the year so that depreciation is computed on the average of the beginning and ending balances of the asset account. This is the same as the "half-year" convention under ADR at ¶ 428.

Another permissible averaging convention assumes that additions and retirements in the first half of the year occur on the first day of that year and that second-half additions and retirements occur on the first day of the next year. Thus, a full year's depreciation is taken on first-half additions and second-half retirements. No depreciation is taken on first-half retirements and second-half additions.

A different version of this convention, called the "modified half-year convention," is available under ADR, as explained at ¶ 428.

Of course, there can no longer be additions to such pre-1981 multiple-asset accounts. Only retirements will affect computations under these conventions.

## ¶ 374

### Straight-Line Depreciation on Multiple-Asset Account

Since useful lives of assets in a group account are roughly the same, the straight-line rate can be determined by averaging the useful lives of the assets.

In a classified or composite account, however, assets are grouped without regard to useful lives. To find the straight-line rate, one year's straight-line depreciation on each asset in the account is computed and the total annual depreciation is divided by the total basis of those assets. The average rate so obtained may continue to be used as long as the relative proportions of different types of assets in the account remain the same.

If an averaging convention was used that assumed uniform additions and retirements throughout the year, straight-line depreciation on an open-end, multiple-asset account may be computed by applying the average rate, adjusted for salvage, to the average of the beginning and ending balances of the asset account for the year.

## ¶ 376

## Declining-Balance Depreciation on Multiple-Asset Account

The deduction under this method may be computed by applying 200 percent (or, for used assets, 150 percent) of the straight-line rate, *not* adjusted for salvage, to the average balance in the account reduced by the average reserve (before depreciation for the year).

## ¶ 378

## Sum of the Years-Digits Depreciation on Multiple-Asset Account

The deduction under this method for an open-end account may be computed by using the complex remaining life plan prescribed by Reg. § 1.167(b)-3. Two rates are required, a years-digits rate based on the estimated *remaining* useful life of the account and a years-digits rate based on the *average* useful lives of the assets in the account. Here is a simplified explanation and illustration of how to compute the deduction:

(1) Multiply the *remaining life* rate by the beginning asset balance as adjusted for salvage and reduced by the beginning reserve.

(2) Multiply the rate based on *average life* by one-half of the additions during the year, adjusted for salvage.

(3) The sum of (1) and (2) is the deduction.

The sum of the years-digits deduction for a year's acquisition account can be determined by executing step (1) only of the remaining life plan, since there are no additions to the account after the first year, only retirements.

# Retirement of Depreciated Property

## ¶ 380

## Retirements from Item Accounts

Where depreciable property is retired from an item account through a sale, any gain or loss will be recognized to the extent of the difference between the selling price and the adjusted basis of the asset (Reg. § 1.167(a)-8).

Where the retirement is through an exchange, recognition of any gain or loss will depend on whether the exchange is wholly or partially "tax-free." If a gain or loss is recognized, it is the difference between the fair market value of the property received and the adjusted basis of the asset given in exchange.

If an asset is retired through actual physical abandonment, any loss will be recognized and it is measured by the adjusted basis of the asset at the time of abandonment. To qualify for a recognition of the loss, however, the taxpayer must intend to irrevocably abandon or discard the asset so that he will not use it again or retrieve it for sale or other disposition.

A depreciable asset may be withdrawn from productive use without a disposition. For instance, it could be placed in a supplies or scrap account. If a depreciated asset is retired from an item account without any disposition, any gain will not be recognized at that time. A loss, however, will be recognized to the extent of the excess of the adjusted basis of the asset at the time of retirement over the estimated salvage value. But if the fair market value of the retired asset is greater than the estimated salvage value, then the loss deduction is limited to the excess of the adjusted basis at retirement over the fair market value.

*Special rule for item accounts*

A loss on the normal retirement of an asset in a multiple asset account is not allowable where the depreciation rate is based upon the average useful life of the assets in the account. See ¶ 382. A taxpayer who sets up single item accounts for a few depreciable assets which cover a relatively narrow range of useful lives and which use an average useful life for such assets will generally not be treated as if a multiple-asset account has been set up (Reg. § 1.167(a)-8(d)).

*ACRS and MACRS*

See ¶ 162 for a rules regarding retirements and abandonments of ACRS and MACRS property, as well as a general discussion of what constitutes a retirement or abandonment.

*ADR*

For treatment of retirements from item vintage accounts under the ADR System, see ¶ 480.

## ¶ 382

## Retirements from Multiple-Asset Accounts

Where depreciable property is retired from a multiple-asset account because of a sale, exchange, or abandonment, the rules for recognition of gain or loss are basically the same as those for retirements from an item account.

If an asset is retired from a multiple-asset account without disposing of it, any gain will not be recognized at that time. And a loss will be recognized only on abnormal retirements. Losses on such abnormal retirements are computed in the same way as losses on retirements (without disposition) from an item account, as discussed at ¶ 380.

The adjusted basis for determining a gain or loss on any type of retirement from a multiple-asset account, however, depends on whether the retirement is normal or abnormal. A normal retirement is one which occurs within the normal range of years considered in fixing the depreciation rate. The condition of the retired asset should be similar to that of assets customarily retired from use in the business.

If the retirement is a normal one, the adjusted basis for gain or loss purposes is the amount of the estimated salvage value.

> ***Example (1):*** A machine in a multiple-asset account is sold for $35. The sale is a normal retirement. The original cost of the asset was $1,000 and estimated salvage value is $50. A loss of $15 is recognized on the sale—$50 adjusted basis (the estimated salvage value) minus $35 selling price.

If the retirement is an abnormal one, the adjusted basis for gain or loss is the original cost of the asset minus the depreciation which would have been proper had the asset been depreciated in an item account at the rate used for the multiple-asset account.

> ***Example (2):*** A machine costing $1,000 was recorded in a multiple-asset account with an average life of 10 years and a 10% salvage factor. The straight-line method was used to compute depreciation. After the asset is held 3 years, it is accidentally damaged beyond repair. The machine is sold as scrap for $50. If the machine had been depreciated in an item account using the multiple-asset account rates, annual depreciation would have been $90 ($1,000 − $100 salvage (10%) × 10%). The adjusted basis of the machine for gain or loss purposes is $730—$1,000 cost minus $270 depreciation ($90 × 3)—and a $680 loss is recognized on the sale ($730 − $50 scrap proceeds).

Where acquisitions and retirements are numerous, accounting for individual retirements becomes quite detailed. In such cases, the Internal Revenue Service permits taxpayers to handle retirements in either of the following ways, provided that the one used is consistently followed and income is clearly reflected:

(1) Charge the full cost of retirements and credit the salvage proceeds to the reserve.

(2) Reduce both the asset and the reserve accounts by the cost of retirements and report all receipts from salvage as ordinary income.

See ¶ 380 for rules regarding retirements from item accounts.

See ¶ 162 for rules regarding retirements and abandonments of ACRS and MACRS property, as well as a general discussion of what constitutes a retirement or abandonment.

For rules under the ADR System for retirements from multiple-asset vintage accounts, see ¶ 462–¶ 478.

## ¶ 384

## Item Accounts Treated as Multiple-Asset Accounts

The Regulations provide that if a separate account is set up for each asset and the depreciation rate is based on the average useful life of the assets (so that the same life is used for each account), the taxpayer may be subject to the rules governing losses on retirement from multiple-asset accounts.

# Class Life ADR System

## ADR System for Classes of Assets

### ¶ 400

### ADR System Grew Out of Guidelines

The Class Life Asset Depreciation Range System (ADR), effective for assets placed in service after 1970 (but inapplicable to most property placed in service after 1980) was a direct offshoot of the depreciation guidelines in Rev. Proc. 62-21,[1] 1962-2 CB 418 (Code Sec. 167(m), prior to repeal by P.L. 101-508). The ADR System was similarly intended to minimize conflict over individual asset lives and to liberalize depreciation rates.

The ADR System is also based on broad industry classes of assets. Basically, the Rev. Proc. 62-21 guideline classes for which guideline lives were specified were used initially under ADR (¶ 406).

In the case of classes for land improvements, a class life is given (called an "asset guideline period" (¶ 420)). For all other classes of assets, a range of years (called "asset depreciation range" (¶ 422)) is given in addition to the class life. The upper and lower limits of the range are about 20 percent above and below the class life. For each asset in a class that has a range in effect, the taxpayer could select a depreciation period from that range.

The ADR regulations refer to the "asset depreciation period" rather than the "useful life" in explaining how to compute ADR depreciation. This is because such depreciation period can be shorter than the actual useful life. However, the depreciation period is treated as the useful life for all income tax purposes (with a few exceptions), including the computation of depreciation (¶ 424).

A taxpayer using the ADR System does not have to justify his retirement and replacement policies. A depreciation period selected for an asset cannot be changed by either the taxpayer or the IRS during the remaining period of use of the asset.

The election to use the ADR System is an annual one (Reg. § 1.167(a)-11(a)(1)). If made it applies to all eligible assets placed in service in the trade or business during the year of election. The ADR System does not apply to assets first placed in service before 1971 (or to property placed in service after 1980 if depreciable under ACRS or MACRS) or in a year in which an ADR election was not made (Reg. § 1.167(a)-11(a)(1)). See ¶ 406–412 as to the eligibility of assets for ADR depreciation and ¶ 442 for a discussion of when an asset is first placed in service.

### ¶ 402

### A Survey of the ADR System

For land improvements, the class life is treated as the useful life for computing depreciation. For assets in other classes, the depreciation period selected by the taxpayer from the appropriate range is used to compute depreciation. Permissible depreciation methods under ADR include the straight-line, declining-balance and sum of the years-digits methods, with a special exception (¶ 426).

---

[1] As amplified by Rev. Proc. 68-27, 1968-2 CB 911, and supplemented by Rev. Procs. 65-13, 1965-1 CB 795; 66-18, 1966-1 CB 646; 66-39, 1966-2 CB 1244; and 68-35, 1968-2 CB 921.

ADR requires the use of either of two first-year averaging conventions (¶ 428). One is the half-year convention, in which a half year's depreciation can be taken on all assets first placed in service during the tax year. The other is the modified half-year convention, which allows a full year's depreciation on first-half additions and no depreciation on second-half additions. Any period prior to the month in which the taxpayer begins engaging in a trade or business or holding depreciable property for the production of income is not part of the taxable year for purposes of either convention. Employees by virtue of employment or, to a limited extent, persons engaging in a small amount of trade or business activity are not regarded as engaged in a trade or business. The latter limitation applies only so far as it prevents a small amount of trade or business from justifying a disproportionately large depreciation deduction for the year of the placing in service of assets that substantially increase the level of the taxpayer's business activity.

Assets must be accounted for in item accounts or multiple-asset accounts by year placed in service. These accounts by year placed in service are called "vintage accounts" (see ¶ 440).

Salvage value under the ADR System is gross salvage value, unreduced by the cost of removal, dismantling, demolition, or similar operations (¶ 446). These costs are currently deductible under the ADR System.

Generally, gain or loss on retirement from multiple-asset vintage accounts is not recognized under ADR unless the retirement is an "extraordinary" one—that is, a retirement because of casualty or because of discontinuance or curtailment of a sizable part of a business operation (¶ 462 – ¶ 466). Ordinary retirements are handled by adding the retirement proceeds to the depreciation reserve. These and other adjustments to the reserve may possibly result in the realization of gain during the life of the vintage account (¶ 476) or loss upon the termination of the account when the last asset is retired (¶ 478).

# Assets Eligible for ADR Depreciation

## ¶ 406

## Assets Generally Eligible Under ADR System

The ADR System may be elected for all Code Sec. 1245 and Code Sec. 1250 property that was first placed in service after 1970 (and that is not ACRS recovery property or depreciable under MACRS) for which a class and class life were in effect for the year of election. The classes and class lives are determined generally under Rev. Proc. 77-10, 1977-1 CB 548 (superseded by Rev. Proc. 83-35, 1983-1 CB 745) for applicable years ending after March 20, 1977, and under Rev. Proc. 72-10, 1972-1 CB 721 for applicable years ending before March 21, 1977 (superseded by Rev. Proc. 77-10).

Eligible property includes Sec. 1245 or 1250 property that was new property, used property (see ¶ 408), a property improvement (Reg. § 1.167(a)-11(d)(2)(vii)(a)), or an excluded addition (Reg. § 1.167(a)-11(d)(2)(vi)). Further, property qualified even if depreciation on it had to be capitalized, such as property used for self-construction of fixed assets.

If the ADR System is elected for any year, the election covers all eligible property first placed in service in that year by the taxpayer (Reg. § 1.167(a)-11(b)(5)(ii)). This is so whether the assets are used in a trade or business or held for the production of income. Thus, except as indicated at ¶ 408, the election cannot be made for all the assets put into operation in one trade or business for a year without making the election for those placed in service in any other trade or business of the same taxpayer or for those placed in service and held by him for the production of income in that same year.

Property received from a related person in a transfer that did not trigger an investment credit recapture and was not described in Code Sec. 381(a) (carryovers in certain corporate acquisitions) may have been ineligible for ADR depreciation. In the case of such a transfer, the transferred property was not eligible for the ADR election if the depreciation period used by the transferor in computing his investment credit is not within the range for the class in which the transferred asset falls. The question of whether a person is related is determined under Code Sec. 267 (disallowance of losses, etc., between related persons), except that brothers and sisters are not considered related. This rule also applies to transfers between controlled partnerships (or a partnership and its controlling partner) under Code Sec. 707(b) and transfers between corporate members of the same affiliated group (affiliation determined on the basis of a 50-percent rather than an 80-percent stock ownership test). However, if property was ineligible under this rule, the transferor may have recomputed any investment credit for the year the transferred asset was placed in service, using a depreciation period within the range for the class (this would be beneficial only if the initial depreciation period is below the range) (Reg. § 1.167(a)-11(e)(3)(iv)).

## ¶ 408

## Used Assets and the 10-Percent Rule

The ADR System applies to used assets as well as new assets. But if the unadjusted basis of used Sec. 1245 property first placed in service in a trade or business during the tax year for which there is no specific used property asset guideline class in effect is over 10 percent of the unadjusted basis of all the Sec. 1245 property placed in service in that year, the taxpayer can elect to apply ADR to only the new Sec. 1245 property and determine the useful lives of the used Sec. 1245 property by other means (Reg. § 1.167(a)-11(b)(5)(iii)(*a*)).

This same 10-percent rule applies separately in the case of used Sec. 1250 property (Reg. § 1.167(a)-11(b)(5)(iii)(*b*)).

The "unadjusted basis" means the cost or other basis of an asset without adjustment for regular depreciation or amortization, but with other adjustments required under Code Sec. 1016 or other applicable provisions. Thus, the cost or other basis of a Sec. 1245 asset had to be reduced by any 20-percent additional first-year depreciation claimed for property placed in service before 1981 to arrive at its unadjusted basis (Reg. § 1.167(a)-11(c)(1)(v)(*a*)).

An election may be made for either the Sec. 1245 or Sec. 1250 category to have the lives of both new and used assets determined under ADR even though over 10 percent of the assets placed in service in that category during the year were used.

Used assets are those whose original use did not begin with the taxpayer (Reg. § 1.167(a)-11(b)(5)(iii)(*c*)). This means that assets transferred in a tax-free transaction (such as a transfer to a controlled corporation) must be treated as used assets (but the transferred assets do not qualify for ADR if they were placed in service by the transferor before 1971 or are recovery property). Thus, the manner in which the transferred assets are depreciated depends on whether the transferee elected ADR for the year it placed the transferred assets in service and whether it elected the 10-percent used asset rule for either the Sec. 1245 or the Sec. 1250 property.

If Code Sec. 381(a) applied to a transfer, however, the transferee is bound by the transferor's election or failure to elect the ADR System for assets placed in service in pre-transfer years. See ¶ 450.

For the purpose of determining whether the used assets are more than 10 percent of the total assets placed in service during the year, any assets subject to special depreciation or amortization provisions (see ¶ 410) and any assets acquired in a transaction to which Sec. 381(a) applies are treated as used assets (Reg. § 1.167(a)-11(b)(5)(iii)(*c*)).

## ¶ 410

## Property Subject to Special Amortization or Depreciation

The ADR System does not apply to certain assets that are given special depreciation or amortization treatment.

If ADR was claimed in the first year an asset was placed in service, the ADR election for that asset was subject to termination at the beginning of any later year in which the taxpayer elected one of these special provisions (Reg. § 1.167(a)-11(b)(5)(v)). See ¶ 452 on how to account for such a termination.

## ¶ 412

## Public Utilities

The use of accelerated depreciation and the 20-percent ADR useful life variance by most public utilities (electric, water, sewage, gas distribution or pipeline, steam, or telephone companies) is conditioned on "normalized" accounting in setting the rates charged to customers. Rate-fixing generally reflects straight-line depreciation and ADR midpoint lives. The effect of these rules may be viewed as interest-free loans to utilities, but regulatory bodies are not prevented from passing through the tax benefits to customers by treating some capital as cost-free or by excluding some assets from a utility's rate base. This is distinguishable from "flow-through" accounting, under which the benefits are passed through in the form of accelerated methods and shorter useful lives.

A failure to "normalize" accounting in setting utility rates may terminate an ADR election. See ¶ 452 on how to account for any such termination.

For the treatment of public utility property under ACRS, see ¶ 262.

# Computation of ADR Depreciation

## ¶ 418

## Classifying Assets Under the ADR System

ADR elections cover all eligible property placed in service by the taxpayer during the taxable year. Computations reflect guideline classes into which such property falls. An asset guideline is an ADR class of assets for which a separate class life is in effect under Rev. Proc. 83-35, superseding Rev. Proc. 77-10. An asset for which no separate class life is provided is ineligible for ADR treatment and must be depreciated under the general depreciation rules.

Omission of classes pertaining to buildings in Rev. Proc. 77-10 (superseded by Rev. Proc. 83-35), which reorganized and reclassified assets that qualified for the ADR System, made buildings placed in service for certain relevant years subject to depreciation under the general rules. However, P.L. 93-625 provided transitional rules under which taxpayers electing ADR could determine the class life of Sec. 1250 property either under the guidelines in effect on December 31, 1970, or on the basis of facts and circumstances. A represcribed guideline brought land improvements under ADR.

Property is classified according to the activity in which it is primarily used (Reg. § 1.167(a)-11(b)(4)(iii)(*b*)). This is the case even though the primary activity is insubstantial in relation to all the taxpayer's activities. Once classified, an asset stays in the same class even if there is a change in its primary use after the ADR election year. This includes a change in primary use that causes Sec. 1250 property to become Sec. 1245 property.

Similarly, leased property is classified as if it were owned by the lessee (unless there is a class in effect for lessors of such property) (Reg. § 1.167(a)-11(e)(3)(iii)). However, property is classified without regard to the lessee's activity if the class covers property based upon type (trucks or railroad cars) as distinguished from the activity in which used.

An incorrect classification of property does not revoke an ADR election for an asset. The classification is corrected. See ¶ 448.

## ¶ 420

## Class Life (Asset Guideline Period)

The average class life given for each class is called an "asset guideline period" in the ADR Regulations and applicable revenue procedures. Herein, however, it is referred to as the "class life." Where a class has a class life in effect for the tax year but does not have a range (¶ 422) in effect for that year, depreciation is computed on the assets in that class by using the class life as the depreciation period (¶ 424). (Reg. § 1.167(a)-11(b)(4)(i)(*a*).) ("Present class life" under ACRS and the streamlined but similarly defined "class life" under Modified ACRS are statutory terms having particular meaning under the rules that apply to the classification of most property placed in service after 1980. See ¶ 230).

The class lives are set forth in applicable revenue procedures.

The class life for an ADR election year is the one that was in effect on the last day of the year. But it cannot be longer than it was on the first day of the tax year (or later date during the year when a class was first established). Thus, a taxpayer can take advantage of changes during a tax year resulting in a shorter class life but will not have a class life lengthened because of changes during the year (Reg. § 1.167(a)-11(b)(4)(ii)).

A change in the length of a class life after the year in which a vintage account is established is not effective for that account unless the supplement or revision making the change expressly permits change for the revision and succeeding years.

Assets used predominantly outside the United States in the year first placed in service were treated as if they were in separate classes from the assets used predominantly within the United States. Consequently, each class was divided into a class for assets used predominantly within the U.S. and a class for those used predominantly outside the U.S. Each class that includes only assets used predominantly outside the U.S. is treated as if the class life for the class is in effect but the range is not in effect. Depreciation on the assets in such a class is computed by using the class life as the depreciation period (¶ 424). And the depreciation period will not be changed in any later year because of a change in predominant use after the close of the ADR election tax year.

## ¶ 422

## Asset Depreciation Range

The asset depreciation range for a class is a range of years from 20 percent below to 20 percent above the class life (¶ 420), rounded to the nearest whole or half year. The lower limit of the range is 80 percent and the upper limit is 120 percent of the class life. The ranges for the various classes are set forth in Rev. Proc. 83-35. From the range for a class, the taxpayer selects a depreciation period (¶ 424) over which depreciation for an asset or group of assets in the class would be claimed.

The range for an ADR election year is the one that is in effect on the last day of the year. But the lower limit of the range cannot be longer than it was on the first day of the tax year (or later date during the year when a class was first established). This means that the taxpayer can take advantage of changes during a tax year resulting in shorter lower limits but cannot have a lower limit lengthened because of changes during the year (Reg. § 1.167(a)-11(b)(4)(ii)).

A change in the limits of a range after the year in which a vintage account is established is not effective for that account unless the supplement or revision making the change expressly permits change for the revision and succeeding years.

Lessors figuring ADR depreciation on leased property determine the range and the depreciation period without regard to the period for which the property is leased, including any extensions or renewals (Reg. § 167(a)-11(e)(3)(iii)).

## ¶ 424

## Asset Depreciation Period

The asset depreciation period is the period over which the taxpayer depreciates an asset. If the asset is in a class with a class life but no range in effect, the depreciation period is equal to the class life (¶ 420). If it is in a class with a range in effect, it is the period for depreciation selected from the range (¶ 422).

Any period which is a whole number of years or a whole number of years plus a half year may be selected (Reg. § 1.167(a)-11(b)(4)(i)(*b*)). If property is transferred from a related person in a transfer that does not trigger an investment credit recapture and is not described in Code Sec. 381(a) (see ¶ 406), however, the period selected by the transferee may not be shorter than the period used by the transferor in computing his investment credit (Reg. § 1.167(a)-11(e)(3)(iv)). (This interpretation is reached in spite of an ambiguous reference to the word "taxpayer" in the first sentence of subdivision (iv). In the first part of the sentence, "taxpayer" refers to the transferor. In the latter part of the sentence, it appears that the "taxpayer" means the transferee.) See ¶ 142 and ¶ 264 for rules that prevent transfers between related parties or tax-free exchanges from bringing pre-1987 property under the Modified Accelerated Cost Recovery System (MACRS) and pre-1981 property under the Accelerated Cost Recovery System (ACRS).

The depreciation period is used as if it were the useful life. Depreciation is then computed on the basis of that period, which may actually be shorter than the useful life.

Generally, the depreciation period must be treated as if it were the useful life for all other income tax purposes (Reg. § 1.167(a)-11(g)(1)) (for exceptions, such as the period used in estimating salvage value, see Reg. § 1.167(a)-11(g)(1)(ii)).

For example, if the depreciation period is less than six years, additional first-year depreciation may not have been claimed. If it is less than three years, accelerated depreciation could not be claimed and salvage value may not be ignored to the extent of 10 percent of the basis of the asset. If ADR is elected, the depreciation period chosen for improvements to leased assets is compared to the lease term in determining whether the lessee deducts depreciation based on the depreciation period or amortization based on the lease term (Reg. § 1.162-11). If the appropriate range lower limit is equal to or less than the lease term, it would seem to be advisable to select a depreciation period equal to or shorter than the lease term, if possible. If amortization is based on the lease term, an accelerated method of depreciation is not available.

If accelerated depreciation is taken under the ADR System on personal property subject to a lease, straight-line depreciation based on the depreciation period selected and computed according to ADR rules is subtracted from the ADR depreciation deducted for the asset in determining the minimum tax preference item (¶ 170) for noncorporate taxpayers and personal holding companies (see the example at Reg. § 1.167(a)-11(g)(3)(ii)).

The following three determinations are made, however, without regard to the depreciation period (Reg. § 1.167(a)-11(g)(1)(ii)):

(1) determination of the anticipated period of use for estimating salvage value at the end of the vintage year;

(2) determination of whether an expense prolongs the life of an asset (this is to be done on the basis of the anticipated period of use, estimated at the close of the vintage year); and

(3) determination of whether a transaction is a sale or a lease.

## ¶ 426

## Depreciation Methods Under ADR

If ADR is elected, the straight-line, the sum of the years-digits, or any acceptable declining-balance method must be applied to each asset properly included in the ADR election (Reg. § 1.167(a)-11(b)(5)(v)(*a*)). Thus, for new eligible property, the straight-line, the 200-percent declining-balance or the sum of the years-digits method may be used. For used eligible property, the straight-line or the 150-percent declining balance method may be used. Accelerated depreciation on realty is limited.

There is an exception, however. A taxpayer has the option of using a different method or methods for assets consisting of 75 percent or more of the unadjusted basis of all assets placed in service during the tax year in a class and excluding all the assets in that class from the ADR election. The different method must be continued for these excluded assets unless the Commissioner consents to a change.

Use of an ineligible method for an asset cancels the privilege of making the ADR election for all the assets in the same class unless there was a good faith misclassification (see ¶ 448).

The ADR System assumes that the depreciation period chosen already takes salvage value into account (Reg. § 1.167(a)-11(c)(1)(i)), just as did the depreciation guideline lives in Rev. Proc. 62-21, 1962-2 CB 418. Accordingly, the straight-line and sum of the years-digits depreciation computations under ADR do not take salvage value into account.

Straight-line ADR depreciation is computed by dividing the unadjusted basis of the asset (unreduced by salvage value) by the number of years in the depreciation period (Reg. § 1.167(a)-11(c)(1)(i)(*b*)). Alternatively, the unadjusted basis may be multiplied by a straight-line rate based on the depreciation period.

Sum of the years-digits ADR depreciation is calculated by multiplying the unadjusted basis of the asset (unreduced by salvage value) by a sum of the years-digits fraction (or its decimal equivalent) based on the depreciation period.

***Example (1):*** An item of equipment cost $10,000 and had an estimated salvage value of $900. A depreciation period of 5 years was selected for the determination of ADR depreciation. Straight-line depreciation under ADR for the first year the asset was placed in service (assuming a full year's depreciation) was $2,000 ($10,000 unadjusted basis either divided by 5 or multiplied by 20%). If the sum of the years-digits method was elected, the first year's depreciation was $3,333—5/15 of $10,000 unadjusted basis. The numerator of the fraction is the number of years remaining in the 5-year depreciation period at the beginning of the tax year. The denominator is the sum of the years-digits for a depreciation period of 5 years.

Where the depreciation period is a whole number of years plus a half year, the sum of the years-digits is the sum of the remaining depreciation periods at the beginning of each year of the period. Thus, the sum of the years-digits for a 5.5-year period is 18 (5.5 + 4.5 + 3.5 + 2.5 + 1.5 + .5). A quick way to determine the sum of the years-digits where the depreciation period is a whole number of years plus a half year is to square the next higher whole number and divide the result by two. Thus, the sum of the years-digits for the 5.5-year period could have been found by squaring six (36) and dividing by two (18).

The unadjusted basis of an asset had to be reduced by any 20-percent bonus depreciation before computing the straight-line or sum of the years-digits depreciation.

The 200-percent declining-balance rate under ADR is double the straight-line rate based on the depreciation period. The 150-percent declining-balance rate is 1½ times the straight-line rate based on the depreciation period. To compute depreciation under either the 150-percent or 200-percent declining-balance method, the proper rate is applied to the adjusted basis of the asset. The adjusted basis is the excess of the unadjusted basis over the depreciation reserve. In essence, this excess is the undepreciated basis of the asset.

***Example (2):*** If 200% declining-balance depreciation were claimed under ADR for the asset described in Example (1), the amount of the deduction would have been $4,000 for the first year ($10,000 × 40% (double the 20% straight-line rate based on the 5-year depreciation period)) and $2,400 for the next year (40% of the $6,000 adjusted basis (unadjusted basis of $10,000 minus $4,000 depreciation reserve)).

Where the tax year is less than 12 months, ADR depreciation is allowed only for the actual number of months in the tax year. In such a case, a full year's depreciation should be first computed and then prorated according to the percentage that the actual number of months during the year is of 12. (Reg. § 1.167(a)-11(c)(2)(iv).) The Tax Court has ruled that this does not bar a taxpayer commencing activity after the beginning of the month (and, in this case, electing the modified half-year convention discussed at ¶ 428) from treating the commencement month as a full month for purposes of computing depreciation in a short taxable year (*L.D. Greenbaum,* 53 TCM 708, Dec. 43,884(M)).

In no instance, however, may an asset be depreciated below salvage value (Reg. § 1.167(a)-11(d)(1)(iv)). Accordingly, depreciation for any tax year under ADR may not be greater than the excess at the beginning of the tax year of the unadjusted basis of the account over the sum of the depreciation reserve and the salvage value of the account (Reg. § 1.167(a)-11(c)(1)(i)(*a*)). For the determination of salvage value under ADR, see ¶ 446.

Post-1980 improvements to pre-1981 property are generally subject to ACRS or MACRS rules. However, the original property and pre-1981 improvements remain subject to ADR elections. Thus, improved property may be only partially subject to the Class Life ADR System.

## ¶ 428

## First-Year Convention Required Under ADR

In computing ADR depreciation, the taxpayer must use one of two first-year conventions:

*Half-year convention*

Under this convention, a half year's depreciation is taken on all assets put in service during the year. This is done on the assumption that all property is placed in service on the first day of the second half of the tax year (July 1 of a calendar year) (Reg. § 1.167(a)-11(c)(2)(iii)).

The consumption of only a half year's depreciation in the first tax year does not affect the computation of the straight-line and declining-balance depreciation in succeeding tax years. Under the straight-line method, the full ADR rate is applied to the unadjusted basis of the account. Declining-balance depreciation is computed by applying the full declining-balance ADR rate to the adjusted basis of the account (total unadjusted basis less depreciation previously deducted).

However, the using up of a half year's depreciation in the first tax year affects the sum of the years-digits computation for the second and following years. This is because it is necessary that the years-digits rate reflect the proration required where only a partial year's depreciation was allowed in the first year. See ¶ 358. Thus, the second tax year's fraction would be set up to provide half of the first full year's depreciation and half of the second full year's depreciation. This could be done conveniently by averaging the years-digits fractions for the two tax years involved. Accordingly, the fractions for the first two full depreciation years of a 10-year depreciation period would be 10/55 and 9/55. The fraction for the first tax year would be 5/55, half of the first year's fraction. The fraction for the second tax year would be 9.5/55, the average of 10/55 and 9/55. The third tax year's fraction would be 8.5/55, etc. The fraction for the second or later year is applied to the total unadjusted basis of the account.

*The modified half-year convention*

If the taxpayer elects this convention, it is assumed that first-half additions are made on the first day of the year and second-half additions are made on the first day of the succeeding year. Thus, depreciation for the first year is computed by applying the full ADR rate (straight-line, declining-balance or sum of the years-digits) to the first-half additions. This has the effect of giving a full year's depreciation on first-half additions and no depreciation on second-half additions.

In determining the second and following years' depreciation, it is assumed that a half year's depreciation has been allowed for the first tax year (full rate applied to only first-half additions obviously is considered the equivalent of a half year's depreciation). Consequently, the second tax year's depreciation is computed in basically the same manner as under the half-year convention. The full straight-line ADR rate is applied to the total unadjusted basis of the account. The full declining-balance ADR rate is applied to the adjusted basis of the account. The years-digits fraction for the second or later tax year (determined by averaging the fractions for the two tax years involved, as above) is applied to the total unadjusted basis of the account.

*Each of these two conventions applies* to both item and multiple-asset vintage accounts.

If one of these two conventions was elected under ADR for any year, it must be used for all eligible assets (see ¶ 406 – ¶ 412) placed in service in that year. However, the other convention may be elected for another ADR election year.

> ***Example (1):*** Of $80,000 of production machinery and equipment placed in service in 1980, $50,000 was charged to a multiple-asset vintage account and $30,000 was the cost of one piece of equipment recorded in an item account. From the range of eight to 12 years, the taxpayer selected an 8-year depreciation period for the $50,000 multiple-asset account and a 10-year period for the $30,000 item account. The assets in the $50,000 account were placed in service on January 15, 1980. The equipment in the item account was installed and began operating on August 15, 1980. The taxpayer elected ADR and the modified half-year convention for 1980, the double declining-balance method for the multiple-asset account, and the sum of the years-digits method for the item account.
>
> The 200% declining-balance ADR rate for the multiple-asset account is 25%, double the 12.5% straight-line ADR rate (based on an 8-year depreciation period). Depreciation on this account for 1980 is $12,500—25% of $50,000—since a full year's depreciation was allowed under the modified half-year convention (put in service in the first half of 1980).
>
> No depreciation was allowed on the item account for 1980 since the equipment was placed in service in the second half of the year.
>
> ***Example (2):*** If the taxpayer in *Example (1)* had chosen the half-year convention for 1980, only a half year's depreciation would have been allowable on the assets in the $50,000 account which were placed in service in the first half of the year. Depreciation on this account for 1980 under the half-year convention would have been $6,250 ($50,000 × 25% × ½). Likewise, a half year's depreciation was allowable on the $30,000 item account for 1980. This amounted to $2,727: 18.181% (10/55) × $30,000 × ½.
>
> ***Example (3):*** Double declining-balance depreciation for 1981 on the $50,000 multiple-asset account in *Example (1)* under the modified half-year convention would have been $9,375: $37,500 adjusted basis ($50,000 unadjusted basis – $12,500 first-year deduction) × 25% double declining-balance ADR rate. Thus, assuming no intervening shift to straight-line depreciation, the deduction for 1982 would have been $7,031 (25% of $28,125) and for 1983 would be $5,274 (25% of $21,094).
>
> Sum of the years-digits depreciation for 1981 on the $30,000 item account in *Example (1)* under the modified half-year convention would have been $5,182: $30,000 unadjusted basis × 9.5/55.

***Example (4):*** Double declining-balance depreciation for 1981 on the $50,000 multiple-asset account in *Example (2)* under the half-year convention would have been $10,938: $43,750 adjusted basis ($50,000 unadjusted basis – $6,250 first-year deduction) × 25% double declining-balance ADR rate. Thus, assuming no intervening switch to straight-line depreciation, the deduction for 1982 would have been $8,203 (25% of $32,812) and for 1983 would be $6,152 (25% of $24,609).

Sum of the years-digits depreciation for 1981 on the $30,000 item account in *Example (2)* under the half-year convention would have been $5,182, computed the same way as in *Example (3)* ($30,000 unadjusted basis × 9.5/55).

In applying these two half-year conventions, the first half of the year was considered as expiring at the close of the last day of a calendar month which was the closest such last day to the middle of the tax year. The second half of the year begins the day after the expiration of the first half of the tax year. (Reg. § 1.167(a)-11(c)(2)(iv).)

***Example (5):*** A taxpayer has a short tax year beginning February 1 and ending December 31. There are 334 days in this tax year and the midpoint is midnight of the 167th day. The 30th of June is the 150th day and the 31st of July is the 181st day of the tax year. July 31 is the day on which the first half of the tax year expires since it is closer to the middle of the year (13 days) than June 30 (17 days). Accordingly, the second half of the year begins on August 1.

In applying the above rule, however, there may be instances in which the middle of the tax year is exactly equidistant from the last day of the two calendar months.

***Example (6):*** If a year begins May 1 and ends November 30, the tax year consists of 214 days. The midpoint of the year is 12:00 midnight of the 107th day, which is August 15. This is exactly 15 days apart from both July 31 and August 31. The ADR regulations do not address this problem, although Reg. § 1.1250-5(f)(1), dealing with an analogous problem under the realty depreciation recapture rules, arbitrarily selects the earliest of two such days that are equidistant from the middle of the year.

If a taxable year consisted of only one calendar month, the first day of the second half of the taxable year begins on the fifteenth day of a 28-day month, the sixteenth day of a 29-day or 30-day month, and the seventeenth day of a 31-day month (Reg. § 1.167(a)-11(c)(2)(iv)).

## ¶ 430

## Effect of Retirements on Depreciation Computation

In the case of an ordinary retirement (see ¶ 462), the retired asset is not removed from a multiple-asset vintage account. Instead, the retirement proceeds are added to the depreciation reserve. See ¶ 464. Accordingly, the computation of straight-line and sum of the years-digits depreciation on the account from which the asset was retired is unaffected by the retirement except to the extent that the increase in the depreciation reserve limits the amount of depreciation that can be deducted. Since the increase in the depreciation reserve by the retirement proceeds decreases the adjusted basis of the account, declining-balance depreciation is reduced by an ordinary retirement.

An extraordinarily retired asset (see ¶ 462), however, is removed from a multiple-asset vintage account. See ¶ 466. Consequently, the amount of depreciation deductible in the retirement year is affected in a majority of cases. Whether and how much it is affected depends on which first-year convention was elected for the year the vintage account was established.

*Under the half-year convention,* extraordinary retirements are considered as occurring on the first day of the second half of the year. Hence, a half year's depreciation is allowed in the year of retirement.

*Under the modified half-year convention,* an extraordinary retirement gets a full year's depreciation, a half year's depreciation or no depreciation, depending on the time of year when the asset was acquired and retired. A first-half addition that is retired in the first half of the year gets no depreciation (assumption that the retirement occurred on the first day of the year). A half year's depreciation is allowed if a first-half addition is retired in the second half of the year or a second-half addition is retired in the first half of the year (assumption that the retirement occurred on the first day of the second half of the year). A full year's depreciation is granted if a second-half addition is retired in the second half of the year (assumption that the retirement occurred on the first day of the next tax year).

## ¶ 432

## Depreciation of Mass Assets

It may not have been practical to maintain records as to the vintage of mass assets or the time of the year in which such assets were placed in service. In such an instance, the computation of the first tax year's depreciation could have been based on the amount spent on such mass assets during the year under the half-year convention. Under the modified half-year convention, the calculation could have been based on the amount spent during the first half of the year.

If an ordinary retirement of mass assets occurs, there is no problem in computing depreciation since the retirement proceeds are simply added to the related depreciation reserve.

In the case of an extraordinary retirement, however, it becomes necessary to determine the vintage of the retired assets so as to figure out the vintage account and related reserve from which the assets and accumulated depreciation are to be removed. The vintage of the retired assets is also necessary in order to calculate the amount of accumulated depreciation.

If a taxpayer adopted reasonable recordkeeping practices for mass assets, their vintage may be determined upon retirement by an appropriate mortality dispersion table (Reg. § 1.167(a)-11(d)(3)(v)*(d)*). It may be based on an acceptable sampling of the taxpayer's experience or other acceptable statistical or engineering techniques. Or, a standard table prescribed by the Commissioner may be used, but the table must continue to be used in later years unless consent to change is obtained.

Where the allocation is apportioned to a year in which the half-year convention was elected, a half-year's depreciation is allowed for the retirement year as indicated at ¶ 430.

In order to compute depreciation in the retirement year for mass assets allocated to a year in which the modified half-year convention was elected, they must be separated into first-half and second-half retirements. The first-half retirements are then divided into first-half additions and second-half additions of the allocation year. This apportionment is made according to the respective percentages that the actual first-half additions and second-half additions are of the total actual additions for the allocation year (Reg. § 1.167(a)-11(c)(2)(v)). Next, the same type of apportionment is made for the second-half retirements. With the resulting information, depreciation for the retirement year is computed in accordance with the rules at ¶ 430.

***Example (1):*** Two years after electing the modified half-year convention, a taxpayer has mass asset extraordinary retirements from a class. By means of an appropriate mortality dispersion table, he determines that $9,000 of these retirements are allocable to the year of the election. Of this amount, $4,000 were first-half retirements and the remaining $5,000 were second-half retirements. In the election year, there were actual mass asset additions of $10,000 in the first half of the year and $15,000 in the second half of the year.

Of the $4,000 first-half retirements allocated to the election year, $1,600 is treated as first-half additions ($10,000/$25,000 × $4,000) and the remaining $2,400 balance is treated as second-half additions. Of the $5,000 second-half retirements so allocated, $2,000 is treated as first-half additions ($10,000/$25,000 × $5,000) and the remaining $3,000 balance is treated as second-half additions.

Accordingly, no depreciation is taken for the post-retirement year on the $1,600 first-half retirements treated as first-half additions. A half-year's depreciation is claimed on the $2,400 of first-half retirements treated as second-half additions and the $2,000 of second-half retirements treated as first-half additions. A full-year's depreciation may be deducted for the $3,000 of second-half retirements treated as second-half additions.

***Example (2):*** If the taxpayer in *Example (1)* had elected the half-year convention in the election year, a half-year's depreciation would be claimed on the post-retirement year on the $9,000 of the mass asset retirements in that were allocated to the year of the election.

## ¶ 434

## Depreciation Method Changes Under ADR Without Consent

Consent of the Commissioner is not needed under the ADR System to change from the declining-balance method to the sum of the years-digits method and from either a declining-balance method or the sum of the years-digits method to the straight-line method (Reg. § 1.167(a)-11(c)(1)(iii)). Although the Regulation does not specifically state that more than one change can be made without consent for the same vintage account, it appears that a taxpayer could start depreciating a vintage account with the 200-percent declining-balance method, change to the sum of the years-digits method, and change again to the straight-line method.

A statement must be furnished with the income tax return for the year of change setting forth the vintage accounts for which change is made.

As to public utility property, any changes required or permitted under Sec. 167(l) (prior to repeal by P.L. 101-508) are permissible under ADR rules.

Further, where changes are required or allowed because realty does or does not qualify as residential rental property, these changes are likewise permissible under ADR. Such a change causes a removal of the asset to a separate vintage account, however (see ¶ 440).

The above changes are the only ones available under ADR for which the Commissioner's consent is not necessary.

In determining the remaining portion of a depreciation period at the beginning of the year of change, it will be assumed that a half year's depreciation was taken in the year the asset was first placed in service regardless of which first-year convention was adopted by the taxpayer.

*Where the change is to the straight-line method,* the annual depreciation allowance beginning with the year of change is determined by dividing the adjusted basis (unadjusted basis less depreciation reserve) of the vintage account (unreduced by salvage value) by the number of years remaining in its depreciation period as of the beginning of the year of change. Or the adjusted basis could be multiplied by a straight-line rate based on the remaining depreciation period.

***Example (1):*** An item of equipment costs $10,000, has an estimated salvage value of $900, and is placed in service in the first half of the tax year. The taxpayer elects the modified half-year convention and selects a 5-year depreciation period. Double declining-balance depreciation is $4,000 for the first year (40% ADR double declining-balance rate × $10,000) and $2,400 for the second year (40% × $6,000 adjusted basis ($10,000 – $4,000 depreciation reserve)). If the taxpayer changes to the straight-line method in the third year, the asset will be treated as having a 3.5-year remaining depreciation period even though two full years' depreciation has been deducted under the modified half-year convention. Thus, depreciation for the year of change under the straight-line method would be $1,029: $3,600 adjusted basis/3.5.

If it is assumed that the above item of equipment is placed in service in the second half of the tax year, no depreciation is deductible in the year placed in service and $4,000 is deductible in the second year under the modified half-year convention. If the taxpayer changes to the straight-line method in the third year, the asset will be treated as having a 3.5-year remaining depreciation period even though only one full year's depreciation has been deducted. Depreciation for the year of change would be $1,714: $6,000 adjusted basis/3.5.

The amount of straight-line depreciation allowable after such a change may not be more than the annual ADR straight-line allowance based on the original depreciation period (unadjusted basis of account, without reduction for salvage value, divided by the number of years in the original depreciation period).

*Where the change is from a declining-balance method to the sum of the years-digits method,* depreciation for the year of change would be computed by applying a sum of the years-digits fraction or rate based on the remaining depreciation period to the adjusted basis of the asset at the beginning of the year of change.

***Example (2):*** Assume that depreciation on the asset placed in service in the first half of the year in *Example (1)* is changed to the sum of the years-digits method (instead of to the straight-line method) in the third year. The sum of the years-digits for the remaining 3.5-year depreciation period is 8 ($4^2 \div 2$) (see ¶ 426). The depreciation allowance for the year of change under the sum of the years-digits method is $1,575 – 3.5/8 × $3,600 adjusted basis. The years-digits fraction for the following years would be 2.5/8, 1.5/8 and .5/8.

# Depreciation Accounting Under ADR

## ¶ 440

## Vintage Accounts Required

As already observed at ¶ 400, a taxpayer electing ADR for any tax year must include all eligible assets (¶ 406 – ¶ 412) first placed in service in that year in either item or multiple-asset accounts by the year placed in service. These accounts by the year placed in service are called "vintage accounts." (Reg. § 1.167(a)-11(b)(3))

Each vintage account must include only assets within a single class (¶ 418). It may not include assets from more than one class. However, more than one account of the same vintage (for the same tax year) may be established for different assets of the same class.

Certain kinds of assets may not be included in the same vintage account. Sec. 1245 and 1250 property may not be placed in the same account. New and used assets require separate accounts. Where Code Sec. 381(a) applies to transferred assets, see ¶ 450. (Reg. § 1.167(a)-11(b)(3)(ii))

If a change in depreciation method is required for realty because it does or does not qualify as residential rental property, the realty must be removed from the vintage account and placed in a separate item vintage account (Reg. § 1.167(a)-11(b)(4)(iii)(*e*)). Similarly, accumulated depreciation allowances on the property must be subtracted from the related depreciation reserve and placed in a separate reserve. The amount accumulated is figured by using the method, rate and averaging convention selected, in the same way as accumulated depreciation is computed on extraordinary retirements, illustrated in the example at ¶ 466.

Also, salvage value for the multiple-asset vintage account may be decreased by the salvage value of the removed property. If separate salvage value was not otherwise established for the removed property, the amount of salvage value for it may be determined by multiplying the total salvage value for the account by the ratio of the unadjusted basis of the removed property to the unadjusted basis of the entire vintage account (before removal). (Reg. § 1.167(a)-11(d)(3)(vii)(*c*) and (*e*))

## ¶ 442

## Determining the Vintage of an Asset

The vintage account in which an asset is recorded depends on the vintage of the asset. That vintage depends on when the taxpayer first placed the asset in service.

An asset is first placed in service when it is first placed in a condition or state of readiness and availability for a specifically assigned function. This definition applies whether the asset is used in a trade or business, in the production of income, in a tax-exempt activity, or in a personal activity (Reg. § 1.167(a)-11(e)(1)).

The determination of the date on which property was first placed in service is not influenced by the date on which depreciation was treated as beginning under a first-year convention or a particular method of depreciation, such as the unit of production method or the retirement method.

The time when an asset was first placed in service is also significant in determining ADR depreciation under the modified half-year convention (¶ 428). The amount of depreciation in the first year depended on the half of the year in which the asset was first placed in service. The time during the year in which the asset was first placed in service does not affect depreciation computations under the half-year convention.

In the case of mass assets where it is impracticable to keep track of each individual asset, it is necessary to determine the vintage of these assets upon their retirement. If a taxpayer has followed reasonable recordkeeping practices, he may determine their vintage by means of an appropriate mortality dispersion table. See ¶ 432.

## ¶ 444

## Depreciation Reserve for Vintage Account

Each vintage account under ADR must have a depreciation reserve. The amount of the reserve for each vintage account must be stated on each income tax return on which ADR depreciation is claimed on that vintage account (Reg. § 1.167(a)-11(c)(1)(ii)).

The balance in a depreciation reserve is affected by a number of retirement adjustments on which gain (¶ 476) or loss (¶ 478) may be recognized. Moreover, this balance must be reduced by accumulated depreciation on an asset that must be removed from the related vintage account if a change in depreciation method is required for realty because it does or does not qualify as residential rental property. Termination of an ADR election for an asset upon election of rapid amortization or depreciation may also require or have required an adjustment.

## ¶ 446

## Salvage Value Under ADR

Many of the general depreciation rules apply in determining salvage value for a vintage account under ADR. Salvage value must be determined for each vintage account upon the basis of all the facts and circumstances existing at the close of the ADR election year. The estimated salvage value will not be redetermined merely because of price level fluctuations. Estimated salvage proceeds are the approximate amount that the taxpayer can be expected to receive on the disposition of an asset that is no longer useful in the taxpayer's trade or business and is to be disposed of or retired. This means that the resale value may be more than mere junk value if the asset would be relatively new at the time it is expected to be retired. (Reg. § 1.167(a)-11(d)(1)(i) and (iii).)

In the case of an ADR vintage account, however, *net* salvage value may not be used. Salvage value of a vintage account is its *gross* salvage value unreduced by the cost of removal, dismantling, demolition, or similar operations (Reg. § 1.167(a)-11(d)(1)(i) and (ii)). These costs are deductible as current expenses in the year paid or incurred (¶ 482).

## ¶ 448

## Correction of Asset Misclassification

Where an asset has been placed in the wrong class or has not been placed in a vintage account because of an incorrect classification or characterization, the classification or characterization shall be corrected. The asset shall be placed in a proper vintage account. A depreciation period is to be selected from the range for the proper class. The new depreciation period is to be specified on the return for the tax year in which the improper classification or characterization is found. (Reg. § 1.167(a)-11(b)(4)(iii)(*c*))

Adjustments will be made to correct the unadjusted basis, adjusted basis, salvage value, and depreciation reserve of all vintage accounts affected and the amount of the depreciation deductions for all open tax years involved.

***Example (1):*** An asset costing $10,000 but not qualifying as ACRS recovery property was placed in service in 1981. It was included in class 24.3 with a range of 5 to 7 years. Depreciation for 1981 and 1982 of $2,000 per year was claimed, based on a 5-year depreciation period and the straight-line method. As of January 1, 1983, the adjusted basis of the asset was $6,000—$10,000 unadjusted basis less $4,000 depreciation reserve. It was discovered in a 1983 IRS audit that the proper classification for the asset is class 24.4 with a depreciation range of 8 to 12 years. For 1983, the asset is included in class 24.4 and an 8-year depreciation period is selected by the taxpayer. The depreciation deductions for 1981 and 1982 are each reduced by $750 ($2,000 annual deduction based on 5-year depreciation period minus $1,250 deduction based on 8-year depreciation period). The depreciation reserve is decreased by the $1,500 total adjustment for the 2 years. The adjusted basis, accordingly, is increased by $1,500, to $7,500 (as of January 1, 1983). Depreciation for 1983 is $1,250.

Further, if this asset is included in a multiple-asset vintage account in class 24.4, the estimated salvage value for that vintage account is increased by the estimated salvage value for that asset.

Where an ineligible depreciation method is applied to an asset, all the assets in the same class become ineligible for ADR depreciation (Reg. § 1.167(a)-11(b)(4)(iii)(*d*)). But if the taxpayer can show that the use of the ineligible method is the result of a good faith misclassification, he can save the ADR election for that class. The asset can be reclassified and adjustments made to reflect the new depreciation period selected by the taxpayer from the correct range.

***Example (2):*** A taxpayer depreciated property included in one class on the machine-hour basis. He depreciated property included in another class under the ADR System using the sum of the years-digits method. One asset was depreciated under the machine-hour method because of a good faith misclassification of the asset in the former class. In the year the erroneous classification is brought to light, the taxpayer may include the asset in the latter class, depreciate the asset under the sum of the years-digits method using a depreciation period selected from the range for that class, and make adjustments for prior open years as explained above.

If the misclassified assets for which an ineligible method was used have a combined unadjusted basis that is at least 75 percent of the total unadjusted basis of all the assets in the class in which they belong (including the unadjusted basis of the misclassified assets), however, the taxpayer may elect to condone the use of the ineligible method for the misclassified assets and exclude the remaining assets in that same class from the ADR election. See ¶ 410 and ¶ 426.

## ¶ 450

## Successor Corporation Subject to Predecessor's Elections

Where depreciable property is received by a successor corporation in a transfer to which Code Sec. 381(a) applies, the successor must follow the depreciation elections of its predecessor. Thus, ADR depreciation cannot be claimed on the transferred assets unless the predecessor elected ADR for those assets (Reg. § 1.167(a)-11(e)(3)(i)).

The receiving corporation must separate the eligible property (for which the predecessor elected ADR depreciation) into vintage accounts as nearly coextensive as possible with the predecessor's vintage accounts identified by the year originally placed in service. The depreciation period for each vintage account of the predecessor must be used by the successor. Similarly, the same method of depreciation used by the predecessor must be continued by the successor unless the Commissioner's consent is obtained or a change is permissible (see ¶ 434).

See ¶ 142 and ¶ 264 – ¶ 268 for comparable rules de signed to prevent various transactions between related taxpayers or tax-free exchanges from bringing pre-1981 property under the Accelerated Cost Recovery System (ACRS) or Modified ACRS (MACRS).

## ¶ 452

## Termination of ADR Election for an Asset

An ADR election for an asset will be terminated if rapid amortization or depreciation is elected (¶ 410) and is subject to termination if the property is public utility property and the utility fails to normalize any tax deferral resulting from the ADR election (¶ 412). Termination of an election for an asset requires the removal of the asset's unadjusted basis from the vintage account in which it was recorded.

The depreciation reserve for the vintage account must also be reduced by the depreciation attributable to the terminated asset. The depreciation attributable to the terminated asset is computed by applying the method and rate used for the vintage account to the unadjusted basis of the asset for the number of depreciation periods the vintage account has been depreciated before the beginning of the year of termination (Reg. § 1.167(a)-11, subsections (b)(5)(v)(*b*), (b)(6)(iii), and (c)(1)(v)(*b*)).

The ADR election for a property improvement (Reg. § 1.167(a)-11(d)(2)(vii)(*a*)) is apparently not terminated just because the related asset's ADR election is terminated. Termination occurs if the reason for termination applies to the property improvement.

Where an ADR election is terminated for an asset and it is removed from its vintage account, the salvage value for the account may be decreased by the salvage value for the removed asset. If separate salvage value was not otherwise established for the removed asset, the salvage value for it may be determined by multiplying the total salvage value for the vintage account by the ratio of the unadjusted basis of the removed asset to the unadjusted basis of the entire vintage account. (Reg. § 1.167(a)-11(d)(3)(vii)(*c*) and (*e*)).

# Retirements Under ADR

## ¶ 460

### Retirements from Multiple-Asset or Item Accounts

While the rules on retirements from vintage accounts under Reg. § 1.167(a)-11(d)(3) are designed primarily for multiple-asset vintage accounts, pertinent portions of these rules also apply to item vintage accounts.

The more complex rules for retirements from multiple-asset vintage accounts are explained at ¶ 462 – ¶ 478. The easier rules for retirements from item vintage accounts are covered at ¶ 480.

## ¶ 462

### Ordinary and Extraordinary Retirements Distinguished

Generally, a retirement is defined the same way for ADR purposes as it is under the regular depreciation provisions in Reg. § 1.167(a)-8. An asset is treated as retired when it is permanently withdrawn from use in the business or the production of income. This can be accomplished by a sale or exchange of the asset, physical abandonment of it, or transfer of it to supplies or scrap. Aside from these similarities, however, ADR retirements have a completely different set of rules. The requirements of Reg. § 1.167(a)-8 do not apply.

Under ADR, retirements are separated into two categories—ordinary retirements and extraordinary retirements.

All retirements other than extraordinary retirements are ordinary retirements. Extraordinary retirements include—

(1) retirements of Sec. 1250 property;

(2) retirements of Sec. 1245 property as a direct result of fire, storm, shipwreck or other casualty where the taxpayer chooses to consistently treat such retirements as extraordinary;

(3) retirements of Sec. 1245 property as a direct result of the cessation, termination, curtailment or disposition of a business, manufacturing, or other income-producing process, operation, facility or unit; or

(4) retirements after 1980 of Sec. 1245 property by means of a charitable contribution for which a deduction is allowable.

A type (3) retirement event will result in extraordinary retirements, however, only if the unadjusted basis of the assets retired from a vintage account because of such an event is greater than 20 percent of the entire unadjusted basis of the account immediately before the event. Accounts from which type (3) retirements are made are grouped together and treated as a single vintage account for this 20-percent determination to the extent that they are in the same class and have the same vintage (Reg. § 1.167(a)-11(d)(3)(ii)).

***Example:*** A taxpayer has a type (3) retirement event. He has eight accounts from which retirements are made as a result of this event. Six of them are four-year-old accounts and two are three-year-old accounts. For purposes of the 20% test, there are two combined vintage accounts—one for the six four-year-old accounts and one for the two three-year-old accounts. Thus, if the total unadjusted basis of the retirements from the four-year-old accounts is more than 20% of the total unadjusted basis of those six accounts, the retirements from the four-year-old accounts are extraordinary. The retirements from the four-year-old accounts are ordinary if their total unadjusted basis is 20% or less of the total unadjusted basis of the six accounts. A similar comparison would be made for the three-year-old accounts.

Further, a type (3) retirement must be made other than by a transfer to supplies or scrap (sale, exchange, or other disposition, or physical abandonment of the asset would qualify).

A type (4) retirement removes the unadjusted basis of the contributed property from the vintage account, and the depreciation reserve is adjusted.

The transfer of property to a related person in the tax year in which it is first placed in service is treated as an extraordinary retirement regardless of the above rules. This exception applies to transfers between persons who would have losses, etc. disallowed under Code Sec. 267 (except for brothers and sisters), transfers between controlled partnerships or a partner and its controlling partner under Code Sec. 707(b), and transfers between corporate members of the same affiliated group (affiliation determined on the basis of a 50-percent rather than an 80-percent stock ownership test). (Reg. § 1.167(a)-11(d)(3)(v)(*c*).)

## ¶ 464

## Ordinary Retirements Handled Through Reserve

Generally, gain or loss is not recognized upon an ordinary retirement. The retirement proceeds are added to the depreciation reserve of the vintage account from which the asset is retired (Reg. § 1.167(a)-11(d)(3)(iii)). However, gain may be recognized if the depreciation reserve after adjustment exceeds the unadjusted basis of the vintage account (see ¶ 476).

Additions to the depreciation reserve for ordinary retirements made during the tax year are effective as of the beginning of that year (Reg. § 1.167(a)-11(c)(1)(ii)). See ¶ 430 for the effect this has on the computation of depreciation for the retirement year.

## ¶ 466

## Extraordinary Retirements Removed from Accounts

Unless a nonrecognition provision of the Code applies (see ¶ 474), gain or loss is recognized on an extraordinary retirement (Reg. § 1.167(a)-11(d)(3)(iv)). The gain or loss is recognized in the year of retirement.

The nature of the gain or loss depends on the type of retirement event involved. A sale or exchange could bring Code Sec. 1231 and either Code Sec. 1245 or Code Sec. 1250 into play. Any casualty loss would be determined under Code Sec. 165.

Where the asset extraordinarily retired is the only or the last asset in a vintage account, the account is terminated. Where the retirement is from a multiple-asset vintage account and the asset retired is not the last asset in the account, the unadjusted basis of the retired asset must be removed from the vintage account in which it was included. The accumulated depreciation allowances must be subtracted from the related depreciation reserve. The amount of accumulated depreciation for an asset is determined by applying the depreciation method, the ADR rate, and the ADR averaging convention selected (Reg. § 1.167(a)-11(c)(1)(v)(*b*)). Extraordinary retirements are considered made on the date specified by the averaging convention (¶ 428) adopted (see Reg. § 1.167(a)-11(c)(1)(ii)).

***Example:*** An asset in a 1985 vintage account has an unadjusted basis of $50,000. The account contains assets which were excluded from ACRS by reason of the anti-churning rules. The 200% declining-balance method, the half-year convention, and a 20-year depreciation period were chosen for the account. The asset is sold for $16,000 in an extraordinary retirement in 2002. Depreciation accumulated for the asset upon retirement is determined to be $41,639, as follows:

| Depreciation for— | |
|---|---|
| 1985 ($50,000 × 10% ADR DDB method rate × one-half) | $2,500 |
| 1986 ($47,500 adjusted basis × 10% rate) | 4,750 |
| 1987 ($42,750 adjusted basis × 10% rate) | 4,275 |
| 1988 ($38,475 adjusted basis × 10% rate) | 3,848 |
| 1989 ($34,627 adjusted basis × 10% rate) | 3,463 |
| 1990 ($31,164 adjusted basis × 10% rate) | 3,116 |
| 1991 ($28,048 adjusted basis × 10% rate) | 2,805 |
| 1992 ($25,243 adjusted basis × 10% rate) | 2,524 |
| 1993 ($22,719 adjusted basis × 10% rate) | 2,272 |
| 1994 ($20,447 adjusted basis × 10% rate) | 2,045 |
| 1995 ($18,402 adjusted basis × 10% rate) | 1,840 |
| 1996 ($16,562 adjusted basis × 10% rate) | 1,656 |
| 1997 ($14,906 adjusted basis × 10% rate) | 1,491 |
| 1998 ($13,415 adjusted basis × 10% rate) | 1,342 |
| 1999 ($12,073 adjusted basis × 10% rate) | 1,207 |
| 2000 ($10,866 adjusted basis × 10% rate) | 1,087 |
| 2001 ($ 9,779 adjusted basis × 10% rate) | 978 |
| 2002 ($ 8,801 adjusted basis × 10% rate × one-half) | 440 |
| Total depreciation accumulated | $41,639 |

Accordingly, the adjusted basis of the asset is $8,361 ($50,000 unadjusted basis less $41,639 depreciation accumulated), a $7,639 ($16,000 - $8,361) Sec. 1245 gain is recognized, and a $440 depreciation expense is deductible for 2002. The $50,000 unadjusted basis is removed from the vintage account, and the $41,639 depreciation accumulated is removed from the reserve for the vintage account.

Also, accumulated depreciation includes, to the extent identifiable, the amount added to the depreciation reserve for the proceeds from a previous ordinary retirement of a part of the asset extraordinarily retired.

## ¶ 468

## Salvage Value May Be Decreased by Retirements

When retirements are made from a vintage account, there are three choices as to the effect the retirement has on the estimated salvage value for the account (Reg. § 1.167(a)-11(d)(3)(vii)(*a*) and (*b*)):

(1) Leave salvage value as it is and not reduce it.

(2) Diminish salvage value by the portion related to each retired asset (for both ordinary and extraordinary retirements).

(3) Decrease salvage value by the portion related to each extraordinary retirement (and not ordinary retirements).

The salvage option chosen for a vintage account must be consistently followed. Since the Regulations require consistent treatment "for a vintage account," it appears that different options may be selected for different vintage accounts.

If option (1) above is selected for a vintage account and does not reduce salvage value, there may be a loss deduction when the last asset is retired from the account. See ¶ 478. The same would be true if option (3) is selected and salvage value is not reduced for ordinary retirements.

If salvage for a vintage account is reduced under option (2) or (3) for a retired asset, the amount of salvage value for the asset may be calculated as a pro rata portion of the total salvage for the account or by any other method consistently applied that reasonably reflects the original salvage related to the retired asset (Reg. § 1.167(a)-11(d)(3)(vii)(*c*)). The pro rata allocation is made by multiplying the total salvage value for the vintage account by the ratio of the unadjusted basis of the retired asset to the total unadjusted basis for the account. Thus, if an account has a total salvage value of $1,000 and a total unadjusted basis of $10,000, the pro rata reduction for retirement of an asset with a $500 unadjusted basis would be $50—$500/$10,000 × $1,000. Of course, if salvage is determined on an asset-by-asset basis, no allocation method is necessary.

Further, where adjustments to the depreciation reserve for ordinary retirements increase it to an amount greater than the depreciable basis of the account (unadjusted basis less salvage value), salvage value is reduced by the excess of the reserve over such depreciable basis (Reg. § 1.167(a)-11(d)(3)(iii)).

> ***Example:*** A multiple-asset vintage account has an unadjusted basis of $1,000 and estimated salvage value of $100. If ordinary retirement proceeds increase the depreciation reserve above $900, the excess over $900 reduces the salvage value. If the reserve is increased to $1,000, the salvage value is reduced to zero.

For special rules on ordinary retirements made by transfers to supplies or scrap accounts, see ¶ 472.

## ¶ 470

## How to Account for Retirements from Casualties

A retirement resulting from a fire, storm, shipwreck or other casualty is an ordinary retirement unless an election is made to treat it as an extraordinary retirement (¶ 462). In such case the casualty loss rules apply in determining the amount of deductible loss or, possibly, taxable gain (Reg. § 1.167(a)-11(d)(3)(iv)).

If the asset is transferred to a supplies or scrap account (see ¶ 472) after the casualty, its tax basis in that account for later sale, exchange, other disposition, or physical abandonment is also determined under the casualty loss rules.

For purposes of the casualty loss rules, the adjusted basis of the retired asset just before the casualty is the excess of its unadjusted basis over its accumulated depreciation (computed as explained at ¶ 466).

If an election is made to treat casualty losses as ordinary retirements, any salvage proceeds are added to the depreciation reserve (¶ 464).

## ¶ 472

## How to Handle Ordinary Retirements to Supplies or Scrap Account

As already explained at ¶ 464, gain or loss is not recognized on an ordinary retirement. If the ordinary retirement is the result of a transfer to a supplies or scrap account, the basis of the asset in that account depends on whether an election was made to reduce the salvage value of the vintage account as ordinary retirements occur (see ¶ 468).

*If there was no election to reduce salvage value,* it would appear that the asset would have a zero basis in the supplies account since the salvage value would be recovered through a possible loss when the last asset in the vintage account is retired (see ¶ 478). Any amount realized on a later disposition from the supplies account would seem to be fully taxable.

*If an election was made to reduce salvage value,* one of three consistent practices may be followed (Reg. § 1.167(a)-11(d)(3)(vii)(*d*) and (viii)):

(1) Reduce the salvage value of the vintage account by the retired asset's salvage value (as illustrated at ¶ 468). Nothing is added to the depreciation

reserve as in practices (2) and (3) below. The basis of the asset in the supplies account is zero. Any proceeds of a later sale of the asset are fully taxable.

(2) Reduce the salvage value of the vintage account by the retired asset's salvage value and add the amount of the reduction to the depreciation reserve. The basis of the asset in the supplies account is the amount of the reserve addition. Under this practice, the reserve may not be increased above an amount equal to the unadjusted basis of the vintage account. Accordingly, if the reserve addition is less than the salvage value reduction or is zero because of this limitation, the basis of the asset in the supplies account is the lesser amount or zero. Gain or loss is recognized on any later disposition to the extent of the difference between the amount realized and the asset's basis in that account.

(3) Determine the value of the retired asset by any reasonable method consistently applied, add that value to the depreciation reserve, and subtract that value from the salvage value of the vintage account (to the extent thereof). (Although the Regulations state that the reserve addition should be the greater of the salvage value reduction or the retired asset's value, it appears that, as a practical matter, the retired asset's value will never be smaller than the salvage value reduction.) Acceptable valuation methods include average cost, conditioned cost, or fair market value. The method used must be adequately identified in the books and records. The basis of the asset in the supplies account is the amount added to the reserve. Under this practice, the reserve may exceed the unadjusted basis of the vintage account. If this happens, gain is recognized to the extent of the excess and the reserve is reduced by such excess (¶ 476). Again, gain or loss is recognized on any later disposition to the extent of the difference between the amount realized and the asset's basis in that account.

Any depreciation reserve adjustments made under practice (2) or (3) are considered made as of the beginning of the tax year in which the ordinary retirement is made (Reg. § 1.167(a)-11(c)(ii)). This may possibly affect the amount of the retirement year's depreciation deduction. See ¶ 430.

## ¶ 474

## Nonrecognition of Gain or Loss on Retirements

Where gain or loss on a retirement is not recognized in whole or in part because of a special Code provision, such as like-kind exchanges under Code Sec. 1031, the retirement is treated as an extraordinary retirement (Reg. § 1.167(a)-11(d)(3)(iv) and (v)). No portion of the retirement proceeds is to be added to the depreciation reserve for the vintage account.

The retired asset's unadjusted basis is removed from the vintage account. The depreciation reserve is decreased by the asset's accumulated depreciation. The amount of an asset's accumulated depreciation is calculated in the same way as for an extraordinary retirement. See ¶ 466.

***Example:*** Corporation X has a 1980 vintage account consisting of machines A, B and C. Each has an unadjusted basis of $1,000. The unadjusted basis of the account is $3,000. Depreciation accumulated on the account at the end of 1982 is $2,100. At the beginning of 1987, machine A is transferred to wholly owned Corporation Y for stock of Y valued at $1,200 and $200 in cash.

The transaction qualifies as a transfer to a controlled corporation under Code Sec. 351. Gain of $1,100 is realized: $1,400 realized − $300 adjusted basis ($1,000 unadjusted basis − $700 depreciation). However, gain is recognized only to the extent of the $200 cash received.

> Although this was an ordinary retirement, it is handled as an extraordinary retirement. The proceeds are not added to the depreciation reserve. The $1,000 unadjusted basis of machine A is removed from the vintage account and the $700 accumulated depreciation is taken out of the depreciation reserve.

If a depreciable asset is received in exchange, for the retired asset and its basis is determined by reference to the retired asset (such as in a like-kind exchange), it would appear that the basis for the asset received in exchange, as determined under the nonrecognition provision, would be the unadjusted basis of the asset for ADR purposes and could be recorded in a vintage account for the year of exchange if ADR is elected for that year.

If a depreciable asset is not received in exchange, it would seem that the taxpayer would simply record the nonrecognized (and any recognizable) gain or loss on the retirement.

Where a retirement results because of a transaction between affiliated corporations, the retirement is treated as extraordinary and handled separately under the provisions of Reg. § 1.1502-13. No proceeds are added to the depreciation reserve of the vintage account from which the asset was retired. (Reg. § 1.167(a)-11(d)(3)(v)(*b*).)

## ¶ 476

## Gain May Result from Adjustments to Reserve

A number of retirement and other adjustments affect the balance in a depreciation reserve for a multiple-asset vintage account for Sec. 1245 property. The reserve must be—

(1) increased by the proceeds of ordinary retirements (see ¶ 464);

(2) increased by adjustments for reduction of the salvage value of a vintage account because of ordinary retirements to a supplies or scrap account (see practices (2) and (3) at ¶ 472);

(3) decreased by any adjustments for extraordinary retirements (see ¶ 466) and retirements on which gain or loss is fully or partially not recognized (see ¶ 474); and

(4) decreased by depreciation attributable to an asset removed from a vintage account because it is no longer eligible for ADR depreciation (see ¶ 452).

For a depreciation reserve regarding Sec. 1250 property, adjustment (3) applies. Also, the reserve is decreased by depreciation accumulated for residential rental property that must be placed in a separate vintage account (see ¶ 440).

The reserve may not be decreased below zero.

Where retirement adjustments (1) and (2) above for Sec. 1245 property increase the reserve to an amount in excess of the depreciable basis (unadjusted basis minus estimated salvage value) of the account, the salvage value is reduced by the excess of the reserve over such depreciable basis (see ¶ 468). If the reserve is increased to an amount in excess of the unadjusted basis of the vintage account, that excess is recognized as gain during the tax year (Reg. § 1.167(a)-11(d)(3)(ix)). The gain is treated as Sec. 1245 ordinary income to the extent of depreciation allowances accumulated in the reserve, reduced by any Code Sec. 1245 ordinary income previously recognized for that account.

Where gain results because retirement adjustments increase the reserve to an amount in excess of the unadjusted basis, the reserve is then reduced by the gain recognized (Reg. § 1.167(a)-11(c)(1)(ii)). This brings the reserve back to an amount equal to the unadjusted basis of the vintage account.

> ***Example:*** A multiple-asset vintage account has an unadjusted basis of $1,000 and an estimated salvage value of $100. If the depreciation reserve for that vintage account is increased by proceeds of ordinary retirements to $1,100, salvage will be decreased to zero (see example at ¶ 468) and a $100 gain will be recognized. The reserve will then be decreased by the $100 gain back to a $1,000 balance.
>
> If the ordinary retirement proceeds increase the reserve to $1,800 (instead of $1,100) and it is assumed that $600 of the reserve balance represents depreciation allowances, a gain of $800 would be recognized, $600 of which would be a Code Sec. 1245 gain and $200 of which would be a Code Sec. 1231 gain. The reserve would then be reduced by $800 back to a $1,000 balance.

## ¶ 478

## Loss May Result on Retirement of Last Asset in Vintage Account

When the last asset in a vintage account for Sec. 1245 property is retired, any excess of the unadjusted basis of the account over the depreciation reserve is deductible as a loss under Code Sec. 165 or as depreciation under Code Sec. 167. If the retirement is a sale or exchange on which gain or loss is recognized, the excess is a Code Sec. 1231 loss. (Reg. § 1.167(a)-11(d)(3)(ix)(*b*).)

Upon retirement of the last asset, the vintage account terminates.

## ¶ 480

## Simplified Rules for Retirements from Item Vintage Accounts

The rules explained at ¶ 462–478 are for retirements from multiple-asset vintage accounts. The rules for retirements from item vintage accounts are less complex.

A retirement from an item vintage account results in recognition of gain or loss to the extent of the difference between the unadjusted basis of the vintage account and the depreciation reserve balance.

If it is an extraordinary retirement, gain or loss is specifically recognized unless a nonrecognition provision applies (¶ 474). If the extraordinary retirement is by transfer to a supplies or scrap account as a result of a casualty loss, the casualty loss rules apply in determining the amount of deductible casualty loss (or possibly taxable gain) and the basis of the asset in the supplies account.

Although gain or loss is not recognized on ordinary retirements (¶ 464), gain is recognized if the addition of the retirement proceeds to the depreciation reserve makes it larger than the unadjusted basis of the asset (¶ 476). Also, since the retirement of the asset is from an item vintage account, it is the last asset in the account. Therefore, any excess of the unadjusted basis of the account over the depreciation reserve (as adjusted by retirement proceeds) is recognized as a loss or an additional depreciation deduction (¶ 478). If the ordinary retirement is the result of a transfer to a supplies or scrap account, the asset has a zero basis in that account since the excess of the unadjusted basis of the asset over the reserve is recognized as a loss upon retirement. The proceeds of a later sale of the asset are fully taxable.

Where a taxpayer uses item accounts for Sec. 1245 property as if they were a multiple-asset account by assigning the same depreciation period and method to each asset in the same class with the same vintage, these item accounts would be treated like a multiple-asset vintage account for purposes of determining loss upon retirement of the last asset from a vintage account (Reg. § 1.167(a)-11(d)(3)(xi)).

This has the effect of recognizing gains from retirement as they occur and of deferring losses until the last of those assets is retired.

## ¶ 482

## Cost of Dismantling, Demolishing or Removing Asset

When an asset is retired from a vintage account, the cost of dismantling, demolishing or removing it is deductible as a current expense. This cost is not subtracted from the depreciation reserve for a multiple-asset vintage account. (Reg. § 1.167(a)-11(d)(3)(x).) Therefore, a taxpayer should maintain adequate records of these costs and carefully distinguish them from costs of maintenance and repair.

# ADR Elections

## ¶ 483

### How the System Is Elected

Elections to use ADR are made on an annual basis and apply only to eligible assets first placed in service in the election year. Subject to certain options, provisions of the system are available on an all or nothing basis (Reg. § 1.167(a)-11(a)(1)). For assets included in the election, vintage accounts must be established and depreciation periods selected. The first-year convention to be used also has to be selected.

Taxpayers who elect ADR must maintain books and records that specify the information required under Reg. § 1.167(a)-11(f)(4) and any other required information. Failure to do so will not render an election invalid where the taxpayer has in good faith substantially complied with requirements.

Any election becomes irrevocable after the last day for filing it (Reg. § 1.167(a)-11(a)(1), (b)(5)(i), and (f)(3)). Different vintage accounts, different depreciation periods, or different first-year conventions may not thereafter be used for assets to which it applies. Thus, a lessor could not retreat from the selection of the lower asset depreciation range for a ship even though subsequent legislation made the depreciation resulting from the difference between the lower range and the middle range a tax preference item subject to the minimum tax (Rev. Rul. 82-22, 1982-1 CB 33). However, provision is made for correcting misclassifications (see ¶ 448).

A taxpayer electing the Class Life Asset Depreciation Range System for assets that do not qualify for ACRS or MACRS (and filing Form 4562) must attach a statement to timely (extensions included) returns that specifies the still applicable items from Reg. § 1.167(a)-11(f)(2). In addition to the taxpayer's consent to the general regulatory requirements, required information includes the asset guideline class for each vintage account, the first-year convention adopted, and whether any specially amortized or depreciated property was excluded from the election.

## ¶ 484

### ADR Strategy

Present recovery of cost under the ADR System may reflect prior ADR strategy. Insofar as this strategy centered on such items as depreciation periods or half-year conventions, it has no current application. However, for property subject to an ADR election, it remains important to maximize tax deferral by appropriate changes in methods of depreciating ADR property.

The ADR Regulations permit automatic changes (1) from a break method to the sum of the years-digits method or (2) from a break method or the sum of the years-digits method to the straight-line method.

To maximize the depreciation tax deferral, the 200-percent declining-balance method should be used for the first two years with a change to the sum of the years-digits method in the third year. This is true whether the half-year convention or the modified half-year convention is used.

Although the Regulations do not specifically say that two depreciation method changes can be made for the same vintage account, it would appear that this can be done. See Reg. § 1.167(a)-11(c)(1)(iii). Thus, a taxpayer who has changed from the 200-percent declining-balance method to the sum of the years-digits method could probably change again in a later year to the straight-line method. This might be advisable if he is trying to level out the latter years' deductions and avoid very small deductions in the final years.

## ¶ 485

## Class Life System for Pre-1971 Assets

Along with the Class Life ADR System for post-1970 assets, the Treasury Department provided an elective class life system (CLS) for post-1970 depreciation on pre-1971 assets. The classes were the same as initially set forth for post-1970 assets except that no ranges were specified. Class lives were as originally set forth in Rev. Proc. 72-10 unless shorter lives were prescribed in revisions or supplements and expressly made applicable to pre-1971 assets.

Under CLS, property could be depreciated under the straight-line, declining-balance, or sum of the years-digits method. Assets could be accounted for in any number of item or multiple-asset accounts. Salvage value had to be established for all assets for which CLS was elected. The rules for retirement of assets were generally the same as under ADR.

# Depreciation Planning

## *Acquisitions and Dispositions*

## ¶ 486

### Choosing the Best MACRS Depreciation Method and Period

A taxpayer has some flexibility in choosing a depreciation method and recovery period under MACRS. Generally, these choices allow the selection of a slower recovery method (such as the straight-line method) and/or a longer recovery period than would otherwise apply. These choices may offer certain tax planning opportunities as discussed below.

*Overview of MACRS methods and periods*

Under the MACRS general depreciation system (GDS) the 200-percent declining-balance method is used to depreciate MACRS 3-, 5-, 7-, and 10-year property over their respective 3-, 5-, 7-, and 10-year recovery periods. However, the 150-percent declining-balance method applies to 3-, 5-, 7-, and 10-year farm property placed in service before 2018.

The 150-percent declining-balance method also applies to MACRS 15-and 20-year property over their respective 15- and 20-year recovery periods under GDS. The straight-line method is used to depreciate residential rental property over a 27.5-year recovery period and nonresidential real property over a 39-year recovery period (31.5 years for property placed in service before May 13, 1993).

MACRS offers four elections that can defer depreciation deductions into later tax years. Situations in which depreciation deferral could be beneficial are discussed below.

First, a taxpayer may make an irrevocable election to use the 150-percent declining-balance method to depreciate 3-, 5-, 7-, or 10-year property that would otherwise be depreciable using the 200-percent declining-balance method (Code Sec. 168(b)(2)(D)). The election is made on a property class by property class basis. If the election is made for property placed in service after December 31, 1998, the recovery period for a particular property within a property class is the regular recovery period that applies under GDS. For property placed in service before January 1, 1999, the recovery period is the same period that would apply if the property was depreciated under the MACRS alternative depreciation system (ADS). In general, the ADS recovery period is equal to the Class Life of the property (or a specially assigned recovery period) which is longer than the regular period that applies under the GDS 200-percent declining-balance method.

The 150-percent declining-balance method and the ADS recovery period are used to compute AMT depreciation on MACRS section 1245 property placed in service before January 1, 1999. The 150-percent declining-balance method and depreciation period used for regular tax purposes applies for AMT purposes to section 1245 property placed in service after December 31, 1998 (Code Sec. 56(a)(1)(A)). As a result, a taxpayer making the 150-percent election for regular income tax purposes would not need to make an AMT depreciation adjustment for the property to which the election applies. If a taxpayer claims bonus depreciation (¶ 127D) then the bonus depreciation deduction and regular depreciation deductions are allowed in full for AMT purposes. Effective for property placed in service after 2015, no AMT adjustments are required on property which qualifies for bonus depreciation, even if an election out of bonus depreciation is made. See ¶ 170.

A taxpayer may also make an irrevocable election to depreciate 3-, 5-, 7-, 10-, 15-, or 20-year property classes using the straight-line method over the regularly applicable 3-, 5-, 7-, 10-, 15-, or 20-year recovery period (¶ 84). This election, which is also made on a property class by property class basis, does not apply to residential and nonresidential real property since the straight-line method is always used to depreciate such property (Code Sec. 168(b)(3)(D)). If a taxpayer makes this election, allowable AMT depreciation is computed using the straight-line method and applicable ADS recovery period for property placed in service before January 1, 1999. No AMT adjustment is required on property for which the straight-line election is made and which is placed in service after December 31, 1998 (Code Sec. 56(a)(1)(A)).

A taxpayer may elect the MACRS alternative depreciation system (ADS) (¶ 150). This irrevocable election applies to all property within the same class for which an election is made and which is placed in service during the tax year of the election. However, in the case of residential rental and nonresidential real property, the election is made on an asset-by-asset basis. The cost of property depreciated under ADS is recovered using the straight-line method over the class life of the asset or an assigned recovery period. ADS provides the slowest cost recovery under MACRS (Code Sec. 168(g)(7)). ADS is used to compute allowable AMT depreciation on MACRS Code Sec. 1250 real property placed in service before January 1, 1999. No AMT adjustment is required for Code Sec. 1250 real property which is depreciated using the straight-line method and placed in service after December 31, 1998. Thus, no AMT adjustment is required on MACRS residential rental and nonresidential real property placed in service after 1998 and depreciated over the regular 27.5 or 39-year recovery periods or the 40-year period prescribed under ADS for such property (30 years ADS period for residential rental property placed in service after 2017) (Code Sec. 56(a)(1)(A)(i)).

Most tangible depreciable property placed in service after 2007 with a recovery period of 20 years or less is eligible for a Code Sec. 168(k) bonus depreciation allowance. A 100 percent rate applies to property acquired after September 27, 2017 and placed in service before 2023. Used property acquired after September 27, 2017 now qualifies for bonus depreciation. The applicable rate is applied to the cost of the property after reduction by any amount expensed under Code Sec. 179. See ¶ 127D. If it makes tax sense to defer depreciation deductions then an election out of bonus depreciation should be made (and no amount should be expensed under Code Sec. 179 if the property qualifies for expensing). However, the election out for property placed in service prior to 2016 may trigger an AMT liability. After 2016, there is no AMT adjustment for property that qualifies for bonus depreciation even if an election out is made. In tax years beginning after 2017, the corporate AMT is repealed (¶ 170). To further minimize depreciation deductions claimed in the early years of the recovery period (and avoid an AMT depreciation adjustment), the taxpayer may also make the ADS, straight-line, or 150-percent declining-balance elections described above in conjunction with an election out of bonus depreciation.

*Planning considerations in choosing a recovery period*

In most instances, taxpayers will reap the greatest tax benefit by recovering the cost of their depreciable MACRS property as quickly as possible. Thus, the election of the 150-percent declining-balance method, MACRS straight-line method or the ADS method in lieu of GDS is generally not advisable since these methods delay cost recovery when compared to GDS. Similarly, an election out of bonus depreciation is generally not advantageous, since the amount of bonus depreciation that could otherwise be claimed in the first year of the recovery period will be deducted over the entire recovery period.

***Example (1):*** An individual taxpayer purchases machinery (5-year property) costing $100,000. Assume that the ADS recovery period is 10 years and that the half-year convention applies. The taxpayer will deduct $100,000 over six years using GDS. Without regard to bonus depreciation, if the taxpayer elects ADS the taxpayer will only deduct $55,000 under ADS during the same period. The remaining $45,000 will be deducted over an additional 5 years.

Some factors, however, may result in a greater tax savings by delaying the rate at which depreciation deductions are claimed. Most notably, a taxpayer may be in a low tax bracket during the first years after an asset is placed in service but expect to be in a higher tax bracket in the later years of the asset's recovery period. Deferring depreciation deductions to later years to offset ordinary income subject to higher tax rates by electing out of bonus depreciation (if available), not claiming a section 179 expense allowance (if available), and electing the MACRS straight-line method or ADS could make sense in this situation. For example, if the individual in the preceding example is in the 15-percent tax bracket during the first six years and is in a higher tax bracket during the next five years, the ADS election could result in a greater overall tax savings.

Another wrinkle that could work in favor of deferring depreciation deductions to high-bracket years is that recaptured depreciation that is claimed against ordinary income in low-bracket years could be taxed as ordinary income at a higher rate in the year of disposition if the asset is sold at a gain. As a result, the tax paid on the ordinary income recapture could exceed the tax saved when the depreciation was claimed against ordinary income in the low-bracket years. See ¶ 487.

*MACRS mid-quarter convention planning*

The mid-quarter convention (¶ 92) treats property placed in service during any quarter of the tax year (or disposed of during any quarter of the tax year) as placed in service (or disposed of) at the midpoint of the quarter. Thus, one and one-half months' depreciation is allowed for the quarter in which an MACRS asset subject to this convention is placed in service or disposed of.

The mid-quarter convention applies if the sum of the aggregate basis of MACRS property placed in service during the last three months (i.e., quarter) of the tax year is more than 40 percent of the sum of the total bases of all MACRS property placed in service during the entire tax year. The mid-quarter convention, however, does not apply to residential rental property and nonresidential real property. Furthermore, this property is not taken into account in determining whether the 40-percent test is met. Any amount expensed under Code Sec. 179 is also excluded from the calculation of total bases. However, amounts claimed as bonus depreciation (including 100 percent bonus) are included in the total bases that is taken into account in applying the 40 percent test (Reg.§ 1.168(k)-2(g)(11)).

***Example (1A):*** A calendar-year taxpayer places $100 of office furniture (7-year property) in service in January 2017 and $100 of machinery (5-year property) in service in December 2017. The 50 percent bonus allowance is claimed on the machinery placed in service in December and an election out was made for 7-year property. The mid-quarter convention will apply to the office furniture and machinery because 50 percent of the total bases of the machinery was placed in service in December. However, if the machinery had been expensed under section 179, the mid-quarter convention would not apply because the amount expensed is not included in total bases when applying the 40 percent test.

***Example (1AB):*** If the property in the preceding example is placed in service during the same months of 2021 and the taxpayer claims the 100 percent bonus allowance on the machinery the mid-quarter convention applies to the office furniture. If the machinery is expensed under section 179, the mid-quarter convention does not apply.

As a rule of thumb, a taxpayer is subject to the mid-quarter convention if more than 66.66 percent of the aggregate basis of all property placed in service in the first three quarters is placed in service in the fourth quarter. For example, if the property placed in service during the first three quarters has an aggregate basis of $100, fourth quarter additions must be no more than $66.66 ($166.66 × 40% = $66.66).

The MACRS deduction for property subject to the mid-quarter convention may be determined by figuring depreciation for a full tax year and then multiplying that amount by the following percentages for the quarter of the tax year in which the property is placed in service:

| *Quarter of tax year* | *Percentage* |
|---|---|
| First | 87.5% |
| Second | 62.5% |
| Third | 37.5% |
| Fourth | 12.5% |

A taxpayer may be able to control whether the mid-quarter convention applies in a particular tax year by taking the 40-percent test into consideration when timing the purchases of depreciable property. The Code Sec. 179 expense allowance can also provide an excellent tool for avoiding the mid-quarter convention. Since amounts expensed under Code Sec. 179 are not taken into account in determining whether the convention applies, it may be possible to avoid the convention by expensing assets placed in service in the fourth quarter. Conversely, it may be possible to trigger its application by expensing assets placed in service in the first, second, or third quarters. This planning technique does not apply to the bonus depreciation deduction. Unlike the Code Sec. 179 expense allowance, the bonus depreciation allowance (¶ 127D) does not reduce the basis of an asset for purposes of applying the 40-percent test regardless of the bonus depreciation rate (Reg.§ 1.168()-2(g) (11)).

It is not always desirable, however, to avoid the mid-quarter convention. When several assets are placed in service in the same tax year, the mid-quarter convention can produce an overall first-year depreciation deduction that is larger than the aggregate depreciation deduction that would otherwise result if the half-year convention applied.

***Example (2):*** Three-year MACRS property costing $550 is placed in service in the first quarter of the tax year. Ten-year MACRS property costing $450 is placed in service in the fourth quarter. Since the mid-quarter convention applies, total depreciation (assuming no bonus depreciation is claimed) is $332 (($550 × 66.67% × 87.5%)+ ($450 × 20% × 12.5%)).

However, if the half-year convention had applied, total depreciation would be $228 (($550 × 66.67% × 50%) + ($450 × 20% × 50%)).

Since the amount of bonus depreciation that a taxpayer may claim is not affected by application of the mid-quarter convention, the bonus deduction somewhat diminishes the potential acceleration of depreciation that the mid-quarter convention can sometimes offer.

***Example (3):*** Assume the same facts as in *Example (2)*, except that 50% bonus depreciation is claimed. Bonus depreciation on the 3-year property is $275 ($550 × 50%). The basis of the 3-year property for purposes of computing the regular depreciation deductions under either the half-year or mid-quarter convention is reduced to $275 ($550 – $275). Bonus depreciation on the 10-year property is $225 ($450 × 50%) and the basis is reduced to $225 ($450 – $225). If the mid-quarter convention applies, total depreciation (including bonus depreciation) is $666 ($275 + $225 + ($275 × 66.67% × 87.5%) + ($225 × 20% × 12.5%)). If the half-year convention had applied, total depreciation (including bonus depreciation) would be $615 ($275 + $225 + ($275 × 66.67% × 50%) + ($225 × 20% × 50%)).

The mid-quarter convention produces the best potential for tax savings when assets with the shortest recovery periods and highest costs (but not in excess of 60 percent of the total cost of all assets placed in service during the tax year) are placed in service during the first quarter. This can readily be seen by examining the applicable table percentages for the mid-quarter convention at ¶ 180 (Tables 2 through 5). For example, in the case of 5-year property subject to the mid-quarter convention, 35 percent of depreciable basis is recovered if the property is placed in service in the first quarter, 25 percent if placed in service in the second quarter, 15 percent if placed in service in the third quarter, and five percent if placed in service in the fourth quarter. Under the half-year convention, 20 percent of depreciable basis is recovered regardless of the quarter the property is placed in service.

For further discussion of mid-quarter convention planning opportunities, see ¶ 487.

*Planning for sales of depreciable business property at a loss*

Differences between the ordinary income and capital gains tax rates may play a role in deciding whether to depreciate an asset using GDS or an elective MACRS method. If nonrecaptured gains from Sec. 1231 assets exceed the losses from Sec. 1231 assets sold or disposed of during the tax year, the net gain (gains in excess of the losses) is treated as a long-term capital gain. In general, section 1231 assets are nondepreciable real property held for more than one year and depreciable property held for more than one year which are used in a trade or business or for the production of rents or royalties. When losses from Sec. 1231 assets exceed the gains from Sec. 1231 assets, the net loss is treated as an ordinary loss which is deductible in full against ordinary income. However, net gain is treated as ordinary income to the extent of any unrecaptured net loss incurred in the five preceding tax years.

***Example (4):*** An individual taxpayer in the highest tax bracket purchases machinery costing $100,000 and sells it in the third-year of the recovery period. An election out of bonus depreciation was made. Assume that the taxpayer remains in the highest tax bracket and that the straight-line ADS recovery period is 10 years. Using the MACRS GDS (200% declining-balance method, 5-year recovery period, and half-year convention), the taxpayer's total depreciation deductions are $61,600 ($20,000 for year 1, $32,000 for year 2 and $9,600 for year 3). Using the ADS depreciation system (straight-line method, 10-year recovery period, and half-year convention), the taxpayer's total depreciation deductions are $20,000 ($5,000 for year 1, $10,000 for year 2, and $5,000 for year 3).

Assume that the taxpayer sells the machinery for $38,400 in year 3. Under GDS, no gain or loss is recognized, and no depreciation deductions are recaptured as ordinary income because the taxpayer's adjusted basis is also $38,400 ($100,000 – $61,600). Under ADS, the taxpayer's adjusted basis is $80,000 ($100,000 – $20,000). Therefore, the taxpayer has a $41,600 ($80,000 – $38,400) Sec. 1231 loss and no depreciation recapture. This loss, assuming that there are no Sec. 1231 gains to offset, is deductible in full against ordinary income. However, the benefit of the ordinary income offset is subject to recapture if the taxpayer has net Sec. 1231 gains during the next five tax years. Disregarding this possibility, the benefit of GDS is limited to the increased depreciation deductions claimed in the tax years prior to the disposition.

***Example (5):*** Assume that the taxpayer in the preceding *Example* also had $41,600 in Sec. 1231 gains. This situation tips the scales a bit further against the ADS election. Instead of deducting the $41,600 Sec. 1231 loss against an equal amount of ordinary income taxed at the highest individual rate, the taxpayer is required to offset the Sec. 1231 gain, which would otherwise be taxed at the lower maximum capital gains rate for individuals.

*Planning for building demolitions*

A taxpayer intending to demolish a building in a tax year after it is acquired may elect to place the building in a general asset account and continue to depreciate the building after it is demolished provided the taxpayer does not elect to terminate the account. This strategy avoids the rule in Code Sec. 280B requiring the adjusted basis of the building to be capitalized into the land. See ¶ 5 for details.

*Planning for sales of depreciable business property at a gain*

In the case of the sale of Sec. 1245 property, depreciation is recaptured as ordinary income to the extent of any gain. The remaining gain is treated as Sec. 1231 gain. Gain from the sale of Sec. 1250 property is generally subject to recapture as ordinary income to the extent of accelerated depreciation in excess of straight-line depreciation.

When selling depreciable business property at a gain, taxpayers need to consider that Sec. 1231 gains generated by the sale will offset Sec. 1231 losses that might otherwise be deductible against ordinary income. Sec. 1231 gains, however, could be beneficial if they can be used to offset capital losses which would otherwise go unused during the tax year.

See ¶ 488, for additional details.

*Planning for the alternative minimum tax*

The tax benefits of depreciation deductions claimed in computing a taxpayer's regular income tax liability can be effectively reduced or eliminated if a taxpayer is subject to the alternative minimum tax. The alternative minimum tax depreciation adjustments and preferences currently apply to noncorporate taxpayers. Corporations are no longer subject to AMT in tax years beginning after 2017.

Briefly, in the case of MACRS residential rental and nonresidential real property placed in service after 1986 and before January 1, 1999, MACRS depreciation is a minimum tax *adjustment* to the extent it exceeds the depreciation that would have been claimed under the MACRS (straight-line) alternative depreciation system (ADS). Section 1250 property, other than residential rental and nonresidential real property, that is not depreciated using the straight-line method for regular tax purposes is also depreciated using ADS. In the case of MACRS section 1245 property placed in service after 1986 and before January 1, 1999 the AMT adjustment is the excess of the depreciation claimed over the amount of depreciation that would have been claimed using the 150-percent declining-balance method over the recovery period that would have applied under ADS. However, if an item of MACRS section 1245 property is depreciated for regular tax purposes using the MACRS straight-line method over the regular MACRS recovery period or using ADS, then AMT depreciation for that asset is computed using ADS (i.e., the straight-line method over the ADS recovery period) (Code Sec. 56(a)(1)).

In the case of MACRS property placed in service *after December 31, 1998*, the following rules apply. No AMT adjustment is required for MACRS residential rental and nonresidential real property and, if the straight-line method was used for regular depreciation purposes, any other type of section 1250 property. No AMT adjustment is required for MACRS section 1245 property depreciated using the straight-line method, ADS, or the 150-percent declining-balance method for regular tax purposes. An AMT adjustment will continue to be computed on MACRS 3-, 5-, 7-, and 10-year section 1245 property which is depreciated by a taxpayer using the

200-percent declining-balance method for regular tax purposes. For AMT purposes, such property must be depreciated using the 150-percent declining-balance method and the recovery period used by the taxpayer for regular tax purposes. AMT depreciation on any section 1250 property which is not depreciated for regular tax purposes using the straight-line method (e.g., certain land improvements) must be computed using the straight-line method and the depreciation period that applied for regular tax purposes (Code Sec. 56(a)(1), as amended by the Taxpayer Relief Act of 1997 (P.L. 105-34)).

If bonus depreciation under Code Sec. 168(k) was claimed on any asset, or, effective for property placed in service after 2015, the property qualifies for bonus depreciation (including property for which an election out is made), then AMT and regular tax depreciation are the same throughout the asset's recovery period provided the depreciable basis of the asset is the same for AMT and regular tax purposes, as is usually the case. No AMT adjustment is required (Code Sec. 168(k)(2)(F)). See ¶ 127D. The bonus deduction is also allowed in full for AMT purposes. These rules also apply if bonus depreciation is claimed on New York Liberty Zone Property (¶ 127E), Gulf Opportunity Zone Property (¶ 127F), Kansas Disaster Area Property (¶ 127G), and Disaster Assistance Property (¶ 127H).

The following charts show how AMT tax depreciation is computed when regular tax depreciation is computed as shown.

### MACRS PROPERTY WHICH QUALIFIES FOR BONUS DEPRECIATION

The bonus depreciation allowance is allowed in full for AMT purposes. If bonus depreciation is claimed in the first year of an asset's recovery period then regular tax depreciation and AMT depreciation is computed in the same manner throughout the asset's recovery period. For property placed in service after 2015, if property qualifies for bonus depreciation, regular and AMT depreciation deductions are computed in the same manner even if an election out of bonus depreciation is made. Corporations are not subject to the AMT in tax years beginning after 2017.

### MACRS PROPERTY PLACED IN SERVICE AFTER 1998

| *MACRS Regular Tax Depreciation Method (¶ 84)* | *MACRS AMT Tax Depreciation Method* |
|---|---|
| 200-percent declining-balance method (*3-*, *5-*, *7-*, *10-*year property that is not section 1250 property) | Use 150-percent declining-balance method and regular tax depreciation period |
| 150-percent declining-balance method (*15-*, *20-*year property that is not section 1250 property; farm property before 2018) | No adjustment required, compute AMT and regular tax depreciation the same way |
| 150-percent declining-balance method election (*3-*, *5-*, *7-*, *10* -year property that is not section 1250 property) | No adjustment required, compute AMT and regular tax depreciation the same way |
| Straight-line (*27.5-*year residential rental and *31.5-* or *39-*year nonresidential real property and other section 1250 property) | No adjustment required, compute AMT and regular tax depreciation the same way |
| Straight-line election (*3-*, *5-*, *7-*, *10-*, *15-*, *20-*year property) | No adjustment required, compute AMT and regular tax depreciation the same way |

| *MACRS Regular Tax Depreciation Method (¶ 84)* | *MACRS AMT Tax Depreciation Method* |
|---|---|
| MACRS ADS method (elective or nonelective) | No adjustment required, compute AMT and regular tax depreciation the same way on real and personal property |
| Section 1250 property if straight-line method not used. If ADS applies see above. | Compute AMT depreciation using straight-line method and regular tax depreciation period |

**MACRS PROPERTY PLACED IN SERVICE AFTER 1986 AND BEFORE 1999**

| *MACRS Regular Tax Depreciation Method (¶ 84)* | *MACRS AMT Tax Depreciation Method* |
|---|---|
| 200-percent declining-balance method (*3-*, *5-*, *7-*, *10-*year property that is not section 1250 property) | Use ADS |
| 150-percent declining-balance method (*15-*, *20-*year property that is not section 1250 property; farm property) | Use 150-percent declining-balance method and ADS recovery period |
| 150-percent declining-balance method election (*3-*, *5-*, *7-*, *10-*year property that is not section 1250 property) | No adjustment required, compute AMT and regular tax depreciation the same way |
| Straight-line (*27.5-*year residential rental property and *31.5-* or *39-*year nonresidential real property) | Use ADS |
| Section 1250 property not depreciated using straight-line | Use ADS |
| Straight-line election (*3-*, *5-*, *7-*, *10-*, *15-*, *20-*year property) | Use ADS |
| MACRS ADS method (elective or nonelective) | No adjustment required, compute AMT and regular tax depreciation the same way on section 1250 and section 1245 property |

Accelerated depreciation in excess of straight-line depreciation claimed on ACRS real property or pre-ACRS real property is an item of AMT *tax preference*. Accelerated depreciation in excess of straight-line depreciation claimed on section 1245 property which is placed in service before 1987 and depreciated under ACRS or a pre-ACRS method is generally not an item of tax preference unless the property is leased (Code Sec. 57(a)(7); Code Sec. 57(a)(3) and (12) (prior to amendment by the 1986 Tax Reform Act)).

Taxpayers with the option of electing out of MACRS by adopting a depreciation method not expressed in a term of years, such as the unit-of-production method, should consider in making the decision, that these methods do not give rise to AMT adjustments (Code Sec. 56(a)(1)(B)).

In most instances a taxpayer will have more than one item of MACRS property on which to compute the required AMT adjustment. The AMT adjustment is the difference between the total amount of MACRS depreciation claimed on all MACRS assets for regular tax purposes and the total amount of depreciation allowed on all MACRS assets for AMT purposes.

The allowable AMT deduction for a particular item of property may exceed the depreciation claimed for regular tax purposes. In this case, the difference is taken into account as a negative adjustment in computing the AMT adjustment and will reduce alternative minimum taxable income. This benefit only applies to property depreciated under MACRS. AMT depreciation in excess of ACRS or pre-ACRS depreciation may not be used to offset ACRS or pre-ACRS depreciation in excess of allowable AMT depreciation when computing the AMT depreciation preference for such property.

In the case of MACRS real property placed in service before 1999, allowable AMT depreciation will only exceed regular tax depreciation beginning with the final year of the applicable 27.5-, 31.5-, or 39-year recovery period and extending through the 40-year AMT (i.e., ADS) recovery period for such property. However, in the case of section 1245 property, AMT depreciation can begin to exceed regular tax depreciation well prior to the end of the standard recovery period.

> ***Example (6):*** A sole proprietor purchases equipment for $100,000 and places it in service in 2017. Assume the equipment does not qualify for bonus depreciation. The equipment is 7-year MACRS property. The half-year convention applies. Regular MACRS depreciation using the 200% DB method and 7-year recovery period for 2021 is $8,930 ($100,000 × 8.93%). Allowable, AMT depreciation using the 150% DB method and 7-year recovery period is $12,250 ($100,000 × 12.25%). The taxpayer is entitled to a negative (favorable) AMT depreciation adjustment in 2021 (assuming that it has no other depreciable MACRS property) of $3,320 ($12,250 – $8,930).
>
> Although the taxpayer is benefiting from the negative adjustment, if it sells or disposes of the property in a later tax year, the benefit would in effect be recaptured. This is because the amount of gain or loss recognized for AMT purposes is determined using the basis of the asset as adjusted for AMT depreciation. See, below.
>
> If the equipment qualified for bonus depreciation, there is no AMT adjustment even if an election out is made. Effective for property placed in service after 2015, it is not necessary to claim bonus depreciation in order to avoid an AMT adjustment. It is only necessary that the property qualify for bonus depreciation.

A taxpayer can avoid keeping two sets of depreciation records and calculating MACRS AMT depreciation adjustments by electing the applicable AMT method for regular tax purposes when an asset is placed in service. Except for residential rental and nonresidential real property, however, an election applies to all property in the same property class placed in service during the tax year.

In the case of section 1250 property placed in service after December 31, 1998, on which bonus depreciation is not claimed, record-keeping for AMT purposes will generally only be a concern with respect to 3-, 5-, 7-, and 10-year section 1245 property which is depreciated using the 200-percent declining-balance method for regular tax purposes because the MACRS method and depreciation period used for regular tax purposes for all other section 1245 property is the same method and period used for AMT purposes. In the case of 3-, 5-, 7-, and 10-year section 1245 property on which bonus depreciation is not claimed (for property placed in service before 2016) or does not qualify for bonus depreciation (for property placed in service after 2015), the 150-percent declining-balance method and depreciation period that apply for regular tax purposes (i.e., 3-, 5-, 7-, and 10-years) will be used for AMT purposes if the 200-percent declining-balance method is used for regular tax purposes. If the taxpayer elects the straight-line method, ADS method, or 150-percent declining-balance method for such property, a taxpayer claims the same amount of AMT depreciation as claimed for regular tax purposes whether or not bonus depreciation is claimed. Effective for property placed in service after 2015, no AMT adjustment is required if the property qualifies for bonus depreciation, even if an election out is made. Previously, the AMT adjustments were waived if the property qualified for bonus depreciation and no election out was made.

Notwithstanding potential savings in record-keeping costs, the decision to elect an AMT depreciation method for regular tax purposes would normally be made by comparing the additional regular income tax savings (if any) with the additional AMT liability resulting from the use of an MACRS method that results in an AMT depreciation adjustment. To the extent possible, the decision should take into account not only the impact of the AMT depreciation adjustment in the tax year that an asset is placed in service but also on the AMT impact in future years.

For example, while use of the 200-percent declining-balance method for MACRS section 1245 property not exempt from the AMT under the rules described above that apply to bonus depreciation property could trigger or increase AMT liability in the tax year the depreciable assets are placed in service, a taxpayer may anticipate claiming a Code Sec. 53 credit for prior-year AMT tax liability in the following year and having no additional AMT liability during the remaining GDS recovery period of the assets. In this situation, an election to depreciate using an allowable AMT method could result in a taxpayer claiming reduced depreciation deductions against regular tax liability in the immediately succeeding years when the 200-percent declining-balance method would not cause or increase AMT tax liability. Here, the additional AMT liability paid in one year as the result of using the 200-percent declining-balance method could be less than the value of income tax savings attributable to accelerated deductions claimed in succeeding non-AMT years against taxable income.

At the other extreme, a taxpayer may be in a "permanent" state of AMT liability and unable to recover its tax credit for prior-year AMT liability within the foreseeable future. Here, an election to depreciate using the applicable AMT method for regular tax purposes would allow the taxpayer to claim the entire cost of the depreciable assets against regular taxable income (if any) without increasing AMT tax liability. Note that a special election (Code Sec. 168(k)(4)) allows a corporation to forgo bonus depreciation in order to release locked up AMT and research credits. This election no longer applies in tax years beginning after 2017 due to repeal of the corporate alternative minimum tax. See ¶ 127D.

### *Adjusted AMT gain or loss*

When depreciated property is sold or exchanged the amount of gain or loss recognized for regular tax purposes must be redetermined for AMT purposes. The difference between the regular tax gain or loss and AMT gain or loss is taken into account as a positive or negative adjustment. The AMT gain or loss is determined by reducing the adjusted basis of the property by the amount of allowable AMT depreciation (and any other AMT basis adjustments) (Code Sec. 56(a)(7)). If the total amount of AMT depreciation allowed is less than the total depreciation claimed for regular tax purposes, the gain recognized for AMT purposes will be less than the regular tax gain, thereby reducing alternative minimum tax liability. However, the gain recognized for AMT purposes will be increased if the depreciation allowed under the AMT exceeds the depreciation claimed for regular tax purposes.

***Example (7):*** MACRS machinery is purchased for $10,000. Assume that its adjusted basis as the result of claiming MACRS depreciation is $4,000. Assume that for AMT purposes, the machinery's adjusted basis is $6,000, taking into account allowable AMT depreciation. If the machinery is sold for $7,000, the gain for regular tax purposes is $3,000 ($7,000 - $4,000) but its gain for AMT purposes is $1,000 ($7,000 - $6,000). Since the AMT gain is less than the regular tax gain, the difference ($2,000) is a negative AMT adjustment in favor of the taxpayer.

## ¶ 487

## Code Sec. 179 Expense and Bonus Depreciation Planning

Code Sec. 179 provides an election to treat a specified amount of new or used qualifying property ("section 179 property") as a current expense in the tax year that the section 179 property is placed in service. See, also, ¶ 300.

For tax years beginning in 2022, the limitation is $1,080,000. For tax years beginning in 2021, the limitation is $1,050,000. For tax years beginning in 2020, the limitation is $1,040,000. See ¶ 300. 100 percent bonus depreciation applies to property acquired after September 27, 2017 and before 2023. 50 percent bonus depreciation applies to property acquired before September 28, 2017. The rate is reduced to 40 percent if property acquired before September 28, 2017 is placed in service in 2018 and to 30 percent if placed in service in 2019. A 100 percent bonus rate applies to property acquired after September 27, 2017 and placed in service before 2023. The rate is reduced by 20 percent each year beginning in 2023. See ¶ 127D.

In general, section 179 property is section 1245 property as defined in Code Sec. 1245(a)(3) (i.e., personal property and certain types of real property described in Code Sec. 1245(a)(3)(B) - (F)) acquired by purchase from an unrelated party for use in the active conduct of a trade or business (Code Sec. 179(d)(1)). See ¶ 302 for a discussion of section 1245 property. Property held for personal use or for the production of income does not qualify as section 179 property. Property owned by a taxpayer and used for personal purposes does not qualify if it is converted to business use since it was not acquired for use in a trade or business (Code Sec. 179(d)(1)(C)).

A taxpayer may elect to treat "qualified real property" (QRP) as section 179 property.

Qualified real property for section 179 deduction purposes is defined, effective for property placed in service in tax years beginning after 2017, to mean qualified improvement property and also roofs, heating, ventilation, and air-conditioning property, fire protection and alarm systems, and security systems placed in service on nonresidential real property after the nonresidential real property is placed in service (Code Sec. 179(e), as amended by P.L. 115-97).

In tax years beginning before 2018, QRP consists of qualified leasehold improvements, qualified retail improvements, and qualified restaurant property that qualify for a 15-year recovery period (Code Sec. 179(f), prior to amendment by P.L. 115-97).

Qualified improvement property generally consists of internal improvements to nonresidential real property placed in service after the building is placed in service (Code Sec. 168(e)(6)). See ¶ 110. Qualified leasehold improvement property and retail improvement property will always meet the definition of qualified improvement property. Qualified improvement property placed in service after 2017 is retroactively assigned a 15-year recovery period (Code Sec. 168(e)(3)(E)(vii)). See ¶ 127D.

The election to treat qualified real property as section 179 property applies to all qualified real property placed in service during the tax year of the election. Accordingly, before making the election, a taxpayer should consider whether it will cause an adverse phaseout of the dollar limit under the investment limitation which requires the dollar limit ($1,080,000 for tax years beginning in 2022, $1,050,000 for tax years beginning in 2021, and $1,040,000 for tax years beginning in 2020) to be reduced by the amount of section 179 property in excess of the investment limit ($2,700,000 for tax years beginning in 2022, $2,620,000 for tax years beginning in 2021, and $2,590,000 for tax years beginning in 2020) that is placed in service during the tax year. See ¶ 302 and following for a detailed discussion of the rules applicable to qualified real property. For property placed in service before 2016, bonus depreciation may be claimed on qualified leasehold improvements but not on qualified retail improvement property or qualified restaurant property unless such property also meets the requirements for qualified leasehold improvement status. For property placed in service after 2015 and before 2018, bonus depreciation applies to qualified leasehold improvement property, retail improvement property, or restaurant property that meets the definition of "qualified improvement property." See ¶ 127D.

A taxpayer can allocate the maximum allowable expense deduction ($1,050,000 in 2021 and $1,080,000 in 2022, reduced if necessary to reflect investment limitation) to a single qualifying section 179 property or among several qualifying section 179 properties placed in service during the same tax year. The amount by which an item is expensed reduces its basis for depreciation, as well as for determining gain or loss. In general, the greatest benefit is derived by allocating the deduction to qualifying property with the longest recovery period. However, as noted below, amounts expensed under Code Sec. 179 are subject to recapture if business use of the property during a tax year falls to 50 percent or less (assuming that the MACRS recovery period for the asset has not ended). Thus, it is unwise to expense an asset if it is likely that it will be used 50 percent or less during the asset's recovery period if a different asset can be expensed.

> ***Example (1):*** Wanda Williams purchases qualifying 3-year property costing $1,050,000 and qualifying 10-year property costing $1,050,000 in 2021. Assume bonus depreciation is not claimed. If she expenses the 10-year property in 2021, she will have deducted $1,050,000 in regular depreciation deductions by 2024 (the last year of the recovery period for the 3-year property). If Williams elects to expense the cost of the 3-year property in 2021, she will not recover the $1,050,000 cost of the machinery through depreciation deductions until 2031 (the last year of the recovery period for the 10-year property).

Unless an election out is made, bonus depreciation applies to all qualifying property within an MACRS asset class (e.g., all 5-year property). Section 179 is elective and far more "targeted" since a taxpayer may elect to expense particular qualifying assets and is not even required to expense the entire cost of a qualifying asset.

For acquisitions of property prior to September 28, 2017, in order to maximize the 50 percent Code Sec. 168(k) first-year bonus depreciation allowance (¶ 127D), a taxpayer who has purchased new and used property should first allocate the section 179 expense allowance to the used property because the bonus allowance is only available for new property and in computing the bonus allowance, cost is first reduced by any amount expensed under Code Sec. 179.

> ***Example (1A):*** A calendar-year taxpayer purchases $500,000 of new property and $500,000 of used property in August 2017. The used property does not qualify for the bonus deduction. If the taxpayer expenses $500,000 of new property, no bonus depreciation may be claimed. If the used property is expensed, the bonus allowance on the new property is $250,000.

Effective for acquisitions after September 27, 2017, bonus depreciation applies to used property and the bonus rate is 100 percent. See ¶ 127D.

*Additional differences between bonus depreciation and the section 179 allowance*

The Code Sec. 179 expense deduction and bonus allowance are not prorated on the basis of the length of time that a qualifying asset is in service during the tax year. For example, up to $1,050,000 of the cost of a qualifying asset placed in service on the last day of a tax year beginning in 2021 can be deducted under Code Sec. 179. Also, no proration of the section 179 allowance or bonus deduction is required on account of a short tax year (Reg. § 1.179-1(c)(1); Reg. § 1.168(k)-1(d)(1)). MACRS depreciation allowances (other than the first-year bonus depreciation allowance), however, are prorated in a short tax year. Thus, the section 179 allowance and bonus depreciation deduction can be particularly beneficial in comparison to a regular depreciation deduction in a short tax year.

Unlike the Code Sec. 179 allowance, there is no taxable income or investment income limitation on the amount of additional first year depreciation claimed. The Code Sec. 179 allowance may only be claimed on property that is used more than 50 percent for business purposes. Even if this threshold is satisfied, investment/production of income may not be taken into account in determining the Code Sec. 179 allowance. The additional first year depreciation allowance applies to eligible property whether it is used for trade or business purposes or investment/production of income purposes. The percentage of business use is not relevant unless the property is a listed property, such as a passenger automobile, in which case the additional first year depreciation may not be claimed if business use is 50 percent or less or, if previously claimed, must be recaptured when business use falls to 50 percent or less. The Code Sec. 179 expensing election may not be claimed by estates and trusts and certain noncorporate lessors. This rule does not apply to the additional first year depreciation. Used and new MACRS property qualifies for the Code Sec. 179 expense allowance without regard to the recovery period. Only new MACRS property qualifies for additional first year depreciation if the property is acquired before September 28, 2017. New or used property purchased from a related party does not qualify for expensing. Used property purchased from a related party after September 27, 2017 does not qualify for bonus depreciation. The additional first year depreciation may be claimed on new assets purchased from a related party.

Some states have decoupled from federal bonus depreciation but not Section 179. In this situation it may be advantageous to claim a Section 179 deduction in lieu of bonus depreciation.

The Section 179 deduction is limited to the amount of taxable income derived from all of a taxpayer's active trades and businesses (including wages from employment). There is no taxable income limitation on the bonus deduction. Therefore, unlike the Section 179 deduction, a bonus deduction can create or increase a net operating loss. However, any Section 179 allowance that is disallowed on account of the taxable income limitation may be carried forward indefinitely (with the exception of a Section 179 carryforward attributable to qualified real property) until the taxpayer has sufficient taxable income to offset the carryforward.

The section 179 deduction is not subject to capitalization underCode Sec. 263A. There is no similar exemption for bonus depreciation.

The Section 179 expense deduction and bonus deduction are subject to recapture as ordinary income to the extent of gain when a Section 1245 asset is sold or otherwise disposed. Bonus depreciation claimed on an item of section 1250 property is treated as an accelerated deduction and is subject to section 1250 recapture to the extent in excess of straight-line depreciation (Reg. § 1.168(k)-1(f)(3)). The entire amount of section 179 claimed on an item of section 1250 property (e.g., qualified real property placed in service after 2009 (see ¶ 300)) is subject to recapture as ordinary income (Code Sec. 1245(a)(3)(C)). For this reason, it is more preferable to claim bonus depreciation on qualified real property that is otherwise eligible for expensing under section 179 (see above).

Generally, only section 1245 property qualifies for expensing. However, "qualified real property" also may be expensed (¶ 302). Both section 1245 and section 1250 property are eligible for bonus depreciation if the property has a recovery period of 20 years or less. However, "qualified improvement property" (Code Sec. 179(f), as in effect prior to 2018; Code Sec. 168(e)(6)) placed in service after 2015 and before 2018 qualifies for bonus depreciation as a separate category of bonus depreciation property even if it has a 39-year recovery period (see ¶ 127D). As a result of a technical correction that retroactively assigns a 15-year recovery period, qualified improvement property qualifies for bonus depreciation if placed in service after 2017. See ¶ 127D.

A final distinction between the bonus deduction and the Section 179 allowance is that the Section 179 deduction reduces the basis of property for purposes of determining whether the mid-quarter convention applies. The bonus deduction does not. Thus, a taxpayer may be able to avoid the mid-quarter convention by expensing property placed in service in the final quarter instead of claiming the bonus allowance or, alternatively, trigger the mid-quarter convention by expensing property placed in service in the first three quarters. See ¶ 486.

*Like-kind exchanges and involuntary conversions*

The portion of the basis of property received in a Code Sec. 1031 like-kind exchange (for example, a purchase involving a "trade-in") or acquired as replacement property in a Code Sec. 1033 involuntary conversion that is determined by reference to the basis of the property given in the exchange or replaced does not qualify for the Code Sec. 179 expense allowance (Code Sec. 179(d)(3)).

Like-kind exchanges under Code Sec. 1031 are allowed only for real property after 2017 (Code Sec. 1031(a)(1), as amended by the Tax Cuts and Jobs Act (P.L. 115-97)).

The provision generally applies to exchanges completed after December 31, 2017 (Act Sec. 13303(c)(1) of P.L. 115-97). However, the provision does not apply to an exchange if (1) the property disposed of by the taxpayer in the exchange is disposed of on or before December 31, 2017; or (2) the property received by the taxpayer in the exchange is received on or before December 31, 2017 (Act Sec. 13303(c)(2) of P.L. 115-97).

Regulations provide that for purposes of section 1031 real property means land and improvements to land, unsevered natural products of land, and water and air space superjacent to land. An interest in real property, including fee ownership, co-ownership, a leasehold, an option to acquire real property, an easement, or a similar interest, is real property for purposes of section 1031. Except for a state's characterization of shares in a mutual ditch, reservoir, or irrigation company, local law definitions are not controlling for purposes of determining the meaning of the term real property under this section (Reg. § 1.1031(a)-3; T.D. 9935 (11/30/2020); REG-117589-18 (6/12/20)). The regulations apply to exchanges of real property beginning after December 2, 2020 (Reg.§ 1.1031(a)-3(c)).

> ***Example (2):*** In a like-kind exchnage, John Jones purchases section 1250 property costing $20,000 for use in his business but is granted a $5,000 trade-in allowance so his cash outlay is $15,000. The old section 1250 property has an adjusted basis of $3,000. The adjusted basis of the new section 1250 property is $18,000 ($20,000 - $5,000 + $3,000). However, only $15,000 of the adjusted basis may be expensed under Code Sec. 179 since $3,000 of the $18,000 adjusted basis is determined by reference to the adjusted basis of the old machinery (i.e., is a carryover basis).

Although the carryover basis of property received in a like-kind exchange or involuntary conversion cannot be expensed under Code Sec. 179, bonus depreciation may be claimed on the entire adjusted basis of the property received (i.e., on both the carryover and noncarryover basis) in a like-kind exchange or involuntary conversion (Reg. § 1.168(k)-1(f)(5)). However, if property is acquired and exchanged or involuntarily converted in the same tax year, no depreciation or bonus deduction may be claimed on the originally acquired property (Reg. § 1.168(k)-1(f)(5)(iii)(B)). In addition, if the property received in a post-September 27, 2017 exchange is used, the carryover basis does not qualify for bonus depreciation (Reg. § 1.168(k)-2(g)(5)).

Often taxpayers restructure the sale of a depreciated asset having a low basis as a like-kind exchange in order to defer the gain that would otherwise be recognized upon the sale. The federal tax benefit associated with a like-kind exchange, however, may be effectively eliminated if the exchange takes place after September 27, 2017, when the bonus rate is 100 percent.

> ***Example (2A):*** In 2021, taxpayer Joan Simmons exchanges section 1245 real property with a fair market value of $10,000 and an adjusted basis of $4,000 for new like-kind property that has a $22,000 fair market value. She pays an additional $12,000 cash for the new property. The adjusted basis of the new property is $16,000 ($4,000 + $12,000). The bonus depreciation rules allow bonus depreciation to be claimed on both the carryover basis ($4,000) and the boot ($12,000). Thus, Joan claims a $16,000 bonus deduction and the basis of the new property for purposes of determining future gain is $0.
>
> If she simply sold the old property and purchased the new property, Joan would have been taxed on $6,000 gain ($10,000 – $4,000) as ordinary income depreciation recapture and claimed a $22,000 bonus deduction against ordinary income. The basis of the new property is $0 because Joan claimed its entire cost as a bonus deduction. Thus, $6,000 of the $22,000 bonus deduction offsets the $6,000 ordinary income recapture, leaving Joan a net $16,000 bonus deduction. The net tax benefit is the same with or without a like-kind exchange.

Many states have partially or completely decoupled from the federal system's bonus depreciation. Thus, a like-kind exchange may continue to save taxes at the state level even though federal bonus depreciation is claimed. Furthermore, because individual taxpayers are not allowed to claim state taxes in computing federal alternative minimum tax liability, an increased state tax liability (attributable to failure to structure a like-kind exchange) can trigger or increase the taxpayer's AMT liability.

See ¶ 167 for rules concerning the depreciation of property received in a like-kind exchange or an involuntary conversion.

*Bonus depreciation and long-term contract method of accounting*

A provision enacted by the Small Business Jobs Act (P.L. 111-240) allows taxpayers to compute depreciation as if bonus depreciation had not been enacted when determining the percentage of completion under a long-term contract (Code Sec. 460(c)(6)(B), as amended by the Tax Cuts and Jobs Act (P.L. 115-97)). Initially, the provision only applied to property with a recovery period of 7 years or less that was placed in service in 2010 (2011 in the case of longer production property that is section 1245 tangible personal property used in the trade or business of transporting persons or property). Due to various extensions of the provision it now applies to property with a recovery period of 7 years or less that is placed in service after December 31, 2012, and before January 1, 2027 (before January 1, 2028, in the case of longer production property that is used in the trade or business of transporting persons or property).

See ¶ 127D, discussion #49.

*Alternative minimum tax and uniform capitalization rules*

The Code Sec. 179 expense allowance is not an item of alternative minimum tax adjustment or preference. Depreciation deductions in excess of allowable AMT depreciation increase alternative minimum taxable income.

The section 179 deduction is an indirect cost that is not required to be capitalized under the Code Sec. 263A uniform capitalization (UNICAP) rules (Reg. § 1.179-1(j); Reg. § 1.263A-1(e)(3)(iii)). Amounts expensed under Code Sec. 179 are also not capitalizable under Code Sec. 263 (Code Sec. 263(a)(1)(g); Reg. § 1.179-1(j)).

Bonus depreciation is allowed for AMT purposes. However, if the AMT basis of the asset on which bonus depreciation is claimed is different than the regular tax basis, the AMT bonus deduction is the applicable percentage (i.e., 50 or 100 percent) of the AMT basis (Reg. § 1.168(k)-1(d)(2)).

The additional allowance is subject to the general rules regarding whether an item is deductible under Code Sec. 162 or subject to capitalization under Code Sec. 263 or Code Sec. 263A.

*Net operating losses*

The Section 179 deduction is also limited to the amount of taxable income derived from all of a taxpayer's active trades and businesses (including wages from employment). There is no taxable income limitation on the bonus deduction. Therefore, unlike the Section 179 deduction, a bonus deduction can create or increase a net operating loss. However, any Section 179 allowance that is disallowed on account of the taxable income limitation may be carried forward indefinitely until the taxpayer has sufficient taxable income to offset the carryforward.

A 2-year carryback and 20-year carryforward generally apply to NOLs arising in tax years beginning before 2018. A 5-year carryback and unlimited carryforward apply to NOLs arising in tax years beginning in 2018, 2019, and 2020. No carryback and an unlimited carryforward period apply to NOLs arising in tax years beginning after 2020.

Except for farmers, the carryback period for NOLs is eliminated, effective for NOLs arising in tax years beginning after 2020. This eliminates an important advantage of bonus depreciation over the section 179 allowance. In addition, effective for NOLs arising in tax years beginning after 2020, an NOL may only offset 80 percent of taxable income in a carryforward year. Thus, the section 179 deduction may be able to offset more taxable income in carryforward years since the 80 percent taxable income limitation does not apply to the section 179 allowance. See discussion of taxable income limitation below.

*Investment limitation*

The maximum expense deduction ($1,080,000 for tax years beginning in 2022, $1,050,000 for tax years beginning in 2021, and $1,040,000 for tax years beginning in 2020) is reduced by the amount that the cost of all qualifying property placed in service during the tax year exceeds the investment limit ($2,700,000 for 2022, $2,620,000 for 2021, and $2,590,000 for 2020). No amount may be expensed for a tax year beginning in 2022 if the aggregate cost of qualifying property placed in service is $3,780,000 or greater ($3,780,000 - $2,700,000 = $1,080,000). The cap is $3,670,000 or greater in 2021 ($3,670,000 - $2,620,000 = $1,050,000). The cap is $3,630,000 or greater in 2020 ($3,630,000 – $2,590,000 = $1,040,000). The cap is $3,570,000 or greater in 2019 ($3,570,000 – $2,550,000 = $1,020,000). The amount by which the Code Sec. 179 expense deduction is reduced under this "investment limitation" rule is lost and may not be carried forward and deducted in later tax years (Code Sec. 179(b)(2)). Thus, if possible, a taxpayer should attempt to time the placing of property in service in such a way as to avoid the investment limitation.

> ***Example (3):*** A calendar-year corporation purchases various machinery costing $3,670,000 in 2021 and places the machinery in service in the same year. The corporation may not claim a Code Sec. 179 expense allowance. If possible, the corporation should have delayed placing $1,040,000 of the machinery in service until 2022 so that its investment in section 179 property in 2021 would not have exceeded $2,620,000. If only $2,620,000 of equipment had been placed in service in 2021, the full $1,050,000 expense allowance could have been claimed in 2021.

*Taxable income limitation*

The "taxable income limitation" may also reduce the maximum expense deduction allowed for the tax year. Under this limitation, the total cost of section 179 property deducted in a tax year may not exceed the total amount of the taxable income of the taxpayer that is derived during the year from the active conduct of any trade or business. Taxable income for this purpose is determined without regard to the section 179 expense deduction, the Code Sec. 164(f) deduction for one-half of self-employment taxes paid, net operating loss carrybacks and carryforwards, and deductions suspended under other provisions of the Code. The taxable income limitation is applied after the "investment limitation" discussed above (Code Sec. 179(b)(3); Reg. § 1.179-2(c)(1); Reg. § 1.179-2(c)(6)).

A taxpayer whose Sec. 179 expense allowance would be reduced by the taxable income limitation should consider the possible advantage of accelerating the recognition of income in order to avoid the limitation.

Because amounts disallowed under the taxable income limitation may be carried forward indefinitely (Code Sec. 179(b)(3); Reg. § 1.179-2(c)(1)), it can be beneficial to elect the expense deduction even if no amount is currently deductible. In deciding whether to create a Sec. 179 carryforward, however, a taxpayer needs to consider the possibility that the taxable income limitation and dollar limitation can prevent its deduction in carryforward years. Note that a section 179 deduction disallowed by reason of the taxable income limitation is carried forward. It may not be carried back, either separately or as part of a NOL sustained during the tax year.

> ***Example (4):*** Acme Inc., expenses $500,000 in 2020 but the entire deduction is carried forward to 2021 due to the taxable income limitation. In 2021, Acme places $1,400,000 of depreciable property in service. Assume that Acme's 2021 taxable income is $1,100,000. Acme's Code Sec. 179 expense deduction is limited to $1,050,000 (the dollar limitation for 2021) and it continues to have a carryforward from 2020 to 2022 of $500,000. The $350,000 in excess of the $1,050,000 2021 dollar limit may not be expensed or carried forward.
>
> If Acme's taxable income had been $100,000 in 2021, its carryforward to 2022 would have been $1,450,000 ($500,000 from 2020 + $950,000 ($1,050,000 - $100,000) from 2021).
>
> If Acme had placed $3,670,000 of qualifying property in service in 2021, its dollar limitation for 2021 would have been reduced to zero ($3,670,000 - $2,620,000 = $1,050,000). It would not have been able to deduct any amount in 2021 and its carryforward to 2022 would have been $500,000 (from 2020).

Taxable income from the active conduct of a trade or business is determined by aggregating the net income (or loss) from all of the trades or businesses actively conducted by the taxpayer during the tax year. Sec. 1231 gains (or losses) from an actively conducted trade or business and interest from working capital of an actively conducted trade or business are taken into account in computing taxable income from the active conduct of the trade or business (Reg. § 1.179-2(c)(1)). Wages, salaries, tips, and other compensation (not reduced by unreimbursed employee business expenses) are treated as taxable income from the active conduct of a trade or business (Reg.§ 1.179-2(c)(6)(iv)).

*Dollar limitation and pass-thru entities*

Amounts that are disallowed as the result of the dollar limitation ($1,080,000 for tax years beginning in 2022, $1,050,000 for tax years beginning in 2021, and $1,040,000 for tax years beginning in 2020) and may not be carried forward and deducted in future years. This rule has particular relevance in the case of a taxpayer with an interest in more than one flow-through entity such as an S-corporation, partnership, or limited liability company. The dollar limitation applies at both the entity level and the flow-through owner's level. Thus, in determining whether the dollar limitation is exceeded, a taxpayer must aggregate the amounts received from each flow-through entity as well as any amounts elected by the taxpayer, for example, with respect to assets purchased through a business operation run as a sole proprietorship. If a taxpayer anticipates that the dollar limitation will be exceeded as a result of amounts received through flow-through entities, it may be possible for the taxpayer to convince one or more of the entities to reduce the amount that it elects to expense so as to avoid exceeding the limitation. It should also be noted that the owner's basis in a flow-through entity is reduced by the amount of the expense allocated to the owner even if the expense cannot be deducted by the owner because of the dollar limitation. This means that the owner will recognize increased gain (or reduced loss) upon the sale of the interest even though no benefit was derived from the Code Sec. 179 deduction which was passed through.

*Taxable income limitation and pass-thru entities*

In the case of a partner, taxable income (for purposes of the taxable income limitation) includes the partner's allocable share of taxable income derived from the active conduct by the partnership of any trade or business if the partner actively conducts a trade or business of the partnership by meaningfully participating in the management or operations of at least one of the partnership's trades or businesses (Reg. § 1.179-2(c)(2)(v); Reg. § 1.179-2(c)(6)(ii)). A similar standard applies to S shareholders in determining whether income or loss from an S corporation is included in the S shareholder's taxable income for purposes of the taxable income limitation (Reg. § 1.179-2(c)(3)).

*Investment limitation and pass-thru entities*

In determining the excess section 179 property placed in service by a partner in a tax year, the cost of section 179 property placed in service by the partnership is not attributed to any partner (Reg. § 1.179-2(b)(3)(i)). A similar standard applies to S shareholders (Reg. § 1.179-2(b)(4)).

*What is the active conduct of a trade or business?*

The determination of whether a trade or business is actively conducted by a taxpayer for purposes of the taxable income limitation and the requirement that the property be acquired for use in the active conduct of a trade or business is based on all of the facts and circumstances. The purpose of the standard is to prevent a passive investor in a trade or business from deducting section 179 expenses against taxable income derived from that trade or business (Reg. § 1.179-2(c)(6)(ii)). Although not stated in the Code Sec. 179 regulations, the preamble to the regulations T.D. 8455 indicates that the terms "active" and "passive" do not have the same meaning as in Code Sec. 469 (relating to passive activity losses) and that the definition of the Code Sec. 179 active conduct standard is different than the material participation standard of Code Sec. 469. Thus, it appears likely that a taxpayer can take rental activities into account in determining the taxable income limitation if the actively conducted standard of Code Sec. 179 is satisfied even though rental activities are generally considered *per se* passive under Code Sec. 469. The rule is a double-edged sword, however, insofar as losses from rental activities could reduce the taxable income limitation.

The active conduct of a trade or business requirements is discussed in detail at ¶ 302. See *5. Active Conduct of Trade or Business Requirement.*

*Mid-quarter convention planning*

Generally, MACRS section 1245 property is deprecated using the half-year convention. However, the mid-quarter convention applies to all property placed in service during the year if more than 40 percent of the aggregate adjusted bases of all assets (other than residential rental and nonresidential real property) placed in service during the year are placed in service during the last quarter of the year. The mid-quarter convention usually decreases the overall depreciation that would otherwise be claimed if the half-year convention applied but may, in some instances, result in an increased overall depreciation deduction. This point is discussed at ¶ 486.

Since the adjusted basis of an asset taken into account in determining whether the mid-quarter convention applies does not include amounts expensed under Code Sec. 179, a taxpayer may be able to avoid the mid-quarter depreciation convention by expensing assets placed in service in the fourth quarter of the tax year or, conversely, trigger the convention by expensing assets placed in service in the first three quarters.

> ***Example (5):*** John Jefferson, a calendar-year taxpayer, purchases MACRS 5-year property costing $1,000,000 and places it in service in January 2021 (quarter one). Jefferson also places 5-year property costing $1,000,000 in service in December 2021

(quarter four). If Jefferson expenses $400,000 of the cost of the 5-year property placed in service in December and $600,000 of the property placed in service in January, the mid-quarter convention will not apply since only 40% of the adjusted bases of all assets placed in service during the year were placed in service in quarter four. If John allocates more than $400,000 of the elected $1,000,0000 Sec. 179 expense allowance to the 5-year property placed in service in January, the mid-quarter convention would apply.

In determining whether the mid-quarter convention applies, the amount of bonus depreciation that may be claimed on an asset is not a factor in applying the 40-percent test (Reg.§ 1.168(k)-2(g)(11)). Note also that the full amount of bonus depreciation may be claimed on any asset subject to the mid-quarter convention.

***Example (5A):*** Cal Roberts, a calendar year taxpayer, placed a car costing $40,000 in service in June 2021 and furniture costing $60,000 in service in November 2021. Assume the car does not qualify for bonus depreciation. Even though Cal claimed 100% of the cost of the furniture as a bonus deduction, more than 40 percent of the total basis of the property (computed without reducing basis by bonus depreciation) was placed in service in the last quarter ($60,000 ÷ $100,000 = 60%). Therefore, the mid-quarter convention applies and the car must be depreciated using the mid-quarter convention.

If the mid-quarter convention applies, the greatest benefit from the Code Sec. 179 expense allowance is obtained by allocating the allowance to assets placed in service in the fourth quarter when all of the assets placed in service in the fourth quarter have recovery periods equal to or longer than the recovery period of any asset placed in service in prior quarters.

***Example (6):*** Assume that 3-year property costing $100,000 is placed in service in January 2021 (quarter one) and $1,500,000 of 3-year property is placed in service in the fourth quarter. Assume that bonus depreciation does not apply to the 3-year property. In this case, the mid-quarter convention will apply even if the $1,050,000 section 179 expense allowance is allocated to all the assets placed in service in the fourth quarter.

Under the mid-quarter convention, 58.33% of the depreciable basis of the 3-year property placed in service in the first quarter is claimed as a depreciation deduction in the year placed in service (Table 2 at ¶ 180). However, for 3-year property placed in service in the fourth quarter, the applicable table percentage is only 8.33% (Table 5 at ¶ 180). Therefore, the section 179 expense deduction should be allocated entirely to the property placed in service in the fourth quarter.

The tax benefit of expensing assets placed in service in the fourth quarter is maximized if the allowance is allocated to assets with long recovery periods because the applicable fourth quarter recovery percentage becomes smaller as the recovery period for the property increases. For example, if one of the assets placed in service in the fourth quarter in the preceding example was 20-year property, the first-year recovery percentage is only 0.938 percent.

Allocating the expense deduction to fourth quarter assets will not necessarily produce the greatest overall tax savings if the allowance can be allocated to property placed in service in an earlier quarter with a longer recovery period than any of the fourth quarter assets. For example, suppose 20-year property is placed in service in the first quarter and 3-year property is placed in service in the fourth quarter. Here, the allocation of the expense allowance to the 20-year property will produce the greatest overall tax savings. The difference between the first-year recovery percentages for the 3- and 20-year property (8.33 percent for 3-year property placed in service in the fourth quarter and 6.563 percent for 20-year property placed in service in the first quarter) is not nearly significant enough justify allocation to the 3-year property the cost of which will be recovered over three years.

*State tax considerations*

Some states have decoupled from federal bonus depreciation but not Section 179. In this situation it may be advantageous to claim a Section 179 deduction in lieu of bonus depreciation.

*Earned income credit, social security coverage, exemptions and deductions*

The election to expense under Code Sec. 179 (or not elect out of bonus depreciation) can reduce a taxpayer's earned income credit, reduce coverage under social security, and reduce exemptions and deductions that are based on adjusted gross income or taxable income.

On the other hand, reduction of adjusted gross income or taxable income can prevent the phase-out of certain deductions, exemptions, and credits.

*Self-employment tax savings*

The Code Sec. 179 expense deduction provides a self-employed person with the double benefit of reducing income tax liability and self-employment tax liability assuming that the deduction offsets self-employment income below the applicable base amount ($147,000 for 2022, $142,800 for 2021, and $137,700 for 2020) on which the tax (15.3 percent) is imposed. However, if a loss is reported on Schedule C (without regard to Code Sec. 179), the benefit of the section 179 election with respect to a Schedule C asset is limited to a reduction in income tax liability (assuming the taxpayer has taxable income from non-Schedule C sources). If the self-employed person anticipates being subject to SE tax in subsequent years, it may be preferable to depreciate rather than expense because the depreciation deductions claimed in later years could reduce both income tax and self-employment tax liability. On the other hand, if the taxable income limitation prevents the self-employed person from claiming an expense deduction, a Code Sec. 179 election made for the purpose of obtaining a section 179 carryforward could be even more beneficial assuming that the carryforward can be quickly deducted.

> ***Example (7):*** Joan Jackson, a sole proprietor, places 3-year property costing $25,000 into service in during the tax year. She reports a Schedule C loss without regard to the depreciable property and has no self-employment tax liability. Assume that the taxable income limitation is satisfied because Joan's spouse has significant wage income. If Joan makes the Code Sec. 179 election, the $25,000 expense deduction will reduce the taxable income on the couple's joint return but will not save self-employment taxes. In this case, it may be preferable to not elect to claim the section 179 expense allowance and to minimize depreciation deductions in the tax year by electing ADS or the MACRS straight-line method to depreciate the asset in order to reduce both income and self-employment taxes during the immediately following years if Joan will be subject to SE tax in those years.

> ***Example (8):*** Assume the same facts as in the preceding *Example* except that the taxable income limitation cannot be satisfied. Joan elects to expense the 3-year property and, as a result, has a $25,000 section 179 carryforward. Assume that Joan will have $100,000 of self-employment income in the following carryforward year (without regard to the carryforward) and will not place any additional depreciable assets in service in the carryforward year. In this case, Joan benefits by making the Code Sec. 179 election, since the entire carryforward can be deducted in the carryforward year and will reduce both taxable income and self-employment income. However, Joan may still want to elect the MACRS straight-line or ADS in order to defer first-year depreciation deductions into later years of the recovery period.

Depreciation recapture (including section 179 recapture) upon a sale or disposition does not increase self-employment income (Code Sec. 1402(a)(3)). The IRS maintains that the section 179 allowance may not be claimed on property placed in service and disposed of in the same tax year because section 179 property only includes property which is eligible for MACRS (Code Sec. 179(d)(1)(A)) and MACRS does not apply to property placed in service and disposed of in the same tax year (see ¶ 160). Accordingly, a taxpayer may not avoid self-employment tax by purchasing an asset, expensing its cost, and then selling it in the same tax year. However, this rule does not apply if the asset is purchased in one tax year and sold in the following tax year (e.g. an asset acquired in December and sold in January by a calendar-year taxpayer).

Section 179 deductions recaptured by reason of a decline in business use to 50 percent or less (¶ 300) are reported as self-employment income. The same rule applies to depreciation that is recaptured when a listed property such as a car is not used more than 50 percent in a trade or business (¶ 210). The Code Sec. 1402(a)(3) exemption from self-employment income does not apply because there has been no disposition.

*Collateral impact on AGI based items*

Code Sec. 179 expense deductions or first-year bonus depreciation allowances that reduce an individual's adjusted gross income may allow an individual to claim increased deductions, exclusions, credits, and other tax benefits that are tied to a taxpayer's adjusted gross income level (e.g., casualty losses, medical expense deductions, individual retirement account contributions, miscellaneous itemized deductions, itemized deductions of high-income taxpayers, savings bond interest exclusion, adoption credit, child credit, and dependent care credit).

*Recapture upon decline in business use*

The tax benefit received from the Sec. 179 expense deduction claimed on property placed in service after 1986 is recaptured as ordinary income during any tax year in which the trade or business use of the property falls to 50 percent or less prior to the end of the property's regular recovery period (ADS recovery period if ADS is used). Except as indicated below, the bonus depreciation is not recaptured upon a decline in business use unless the property is Code Sec. 280F listed property. The recapture amount included in income is the difference between the Sec. 179 expense deduction claimed and the depreciation that would have been allowed on the Sec. 179 amount for prior tax years and the year of recapture (Code Sec. 179(d)(10); Reg. § 1.179-1(e)). See ¶ 300 for examples of the calculation.

The additional portion of the section 179 allowance allowed for qualifying section 179 Gulf Opportunity Zone property (¶ 306), Kansas Disaster Area property (¶ 306A), and Disaster Assistance Property (¶ 306B) are also subject to recapture in a tax year during the property's recovery period that it is no longer substantially used in a trade or business in the Gulf Zone, Kansas Disaster Area, or Presidentially-declared disaster area (i.e., business use in the zone or area falls below 80 percent). The additional section 179 allowance that may be claimed on qualifying section 179 New York Liberty Zone property (see¶ 305) is subject to recapture if the property ceases to be used in the New York Liberty Zone regardless of the percentage of business use. Note that these section 179 bump-ups are also subject to recapture along with the standard section 179 deduction if business use within or outside the zone or area fall to 50 percent or less.

> ***Example (8A):*** A taxpayer claims a $350,000 section 179 expense allowance for a section 179 property placed in service in a Presidentially declared disaster area in 2009 ($250,000 standard section 179 allowance for 2009 plus $100,000 bump-up for Disaster Assistance Property). If business use in the disaster area falls below 80 percent during the expensed asset's recovery period but remains above 50 percent, only the $100,000 bump-up is subject to section 179 recapture. If business use in the disaster area falls to 50 percent or lower, the entire $350,000 section 179 expense allowance is subject to recapture.

The bonus depreciation deduction on Gulf Opportunity Zone property is subject to recapture in a tax year during an asset's recovery period that business use in the Gulf Zone is not 80 percent or greater (¶ 127F). A similar rule applies to Kansas disaster area bonus depreciation (¶ 127G) and bonus depreciation for disaster assistance property (¶ 127H). A decline in business use does not trigger bonus depreciation recapture in the case of New York Liberty Zone property (¶ 127E) or bonus depreciation claimed under Code Sec. 168(k) (¶ 127D).

In the case of a listed property such as a car or truck (¶ 200 and following), bonus depreciation claimed under Code Sec. 168(k) is subject to recapture (along with any amount expensed under section 179) if business use during the asset's recovery period under ADS does not exceed 50 percent (Code Sec. 168(k)(2)(F)(ii)). The recapture amount is the difference between the amount of bonus depreciation, section 179 expense, and regular depreciation deductions that exceed that amount of depreciation that would have been allowed under the MACRS alternative depreciation system. See Example (5) at ¶ 300.

Recapture amounts are added to the basis of the property. No recapture for decline in business use is required if the property is sold or disposed of in a transaction that triggers Sec. 1245 recapture. However, amounts expensed under Code Sec. 179 are treated as depreciation for purposes of Code Sec. 1245 recapture (Reg. § 1.179-1(e)(3)).

If a taxpayer expenses the entire cost of a property, the amount of depreciation that would have been allowed is computed using the MACRS method that would have applied if the asset had not been expensed. This will usually be the MACRS general depreciation system (GDS) (i.e., regular table percentages). However, if an election is made to depreciate other property in the same class as the property expensed using an alternate method (e.g., the MACRS straight-line method, the MACRS 150-percent DB method, or MACRS alternative straight-line method (ADS), that method is used to compute recapture since it would have applied to the property if it had not been expensed). Furthermore, the applicable recovery period during which recapture could be triggered is presumably the recovery period that would have applied under the elective method.

These rules dictate that when claiming a Code Sec. 179 expense allowance, a taxpayer should consider that allocation to an asset that is depreciated (or would be depreciated if the entire cost is expensed) under an elective MACRS depreciation system that uses a longer recovery period than applies under GDS will result in a longer recapture period.

> ***Example (9):*** A taxpayer expensed the entire cost of an item of 5-year property placed in service and elected the MACRS alternative straight-line system (ADS) for all other 5-year property placed in service that tax year. The ADS recovery period for the expensed asset is 10 years. If business use of the expensed property falls to 50% or less after expiration of the 5-year GDS recovery period but prior to the expiration of the 10-year ADS recovery period, recapture is computed using ADS even though no recapture would apply under GDS.

Code Sec. 179 recapture amounts are computed on Part IV of Form 4797. The recapture amount is reported as "other income" on the same form or schedule on which the deduction was claimed. Thus, for example, if the deduction was claimed on Form 1040 Schedule C by a sole proprietor, the recapture would be entered on that form and increase the amount of the sole proprietor's self-employment income. In contrast, amounts recaptured under Code Sec. 1245 are reported directly by individuals on Form 1040 as "other income" and are not subject to self-employment tax (Code Sec. 1402(a)(3)).

*Relationship of section 179 deduction to luxury car depreciation caps*

The Code Sec. 179 expense deduction is treated as a depreciation deduction for purposes of the depreciation caps imposed by the Code Sec. 280F luxury car rules (Code Sec. 280F(d)(1)). Consequently, the sum of the regular first-year depreciation deduction (including bonus allowance) and the Code Sec. 179 expense allowance may not exceed the applicable first-year depreciation cap. See ¶ 200 for applicable caps.

A 100 bonus depreciation rate applies to new vehicles acquired after September 27, 2017 and placed in service before 2023. Consequently, it is not necessary to expense any portion of a vehicle which is eligible for 100 percent bonus. In fact, if the section 179 allowance is elected for any portion of the vehicle's cost, the safe harbor depreciation calculation described in Rev. Proc. 2019-13 may not be used and the taxpayer may only claim a depreciation deduction (including elected section 179 allowance) during the first year of the recovery period that is not in excess of the applicable first-year cap. See ¶ 200, *"1A. Safe harbor for vehicles acquired after September 27, 2017 and placed in service before 2023 if 100 percent bonus claimed."*

If the first-year depreciation deduction (including bonus) on a car is less than the applicable first-year depreciation cap, the expense deduction may be claimed only to the extent necessary to reach the first-year cap. The instructions for Part V of Form 4562, on which passenger automobile depreciation is reported, indicate that the sum of the depreciation deduction entered on line 26, and the expense deduction elected and entered on line 26 may not exceed the applicable first-year cap.

If a taxpayer were allowed to expense an amount in excess of the cap, the section 179 expense allowance to the extent in excess of the cap cannot be recovered until after the end of the vehicle's recovery period. Thus, it is important not to claim an excess expense deduction in the first year.

> ***Example (9A):*** A car costing \$25,000 is subject to a first-year cap of \$10,200 in 2021 if bonus depreciation is not claimed. However, if the taxpayer expenses \$25,000, the first year expense deduction is limited to \$10,200. No amount of the \$14,800 unused expense deduction (\$25,000 - \$10,200 = \$14,800) may be deducted until after the recovery (i.e., depreciation) period ends. Furthermore, since the basis of the vehicle has been reduced to \$0, no regular depreciation deductions may be claimed during any years of the vehicle's recovery period. At the end of the recovery period, the taxpayer may begin to recover the \$14,800 unused expense deduction at the rate of \$5,860 per year assuming 100 percent business use in the post-recovery period years.

> ***Example (9B):*** On the other hand, if the taxpayer in the preceding example only expenses \$6,375, the sum of the \$3,725 regular first year depreciation deduction (\$25,000 – \$6,375) × .20 (Table 1 at ¶ 180)) and section 179 deduction will exactly equal the \$10,000 first year cap.

The following paragraphs explain how to compute the amount to expense under section 179 so that the sum of the section 179 allowance, and bonus deduction (if claimed and the 50% rate applies), and regular first-year depreciation deduction are exactly equal to the first year cap.

*An interactive tool is available to most users AnswerConnect and IntelliConnect for purposes of determining the proper Code Sec. 179 allowance to claim. IntelliConnect* users will find the tool under *Federal Tax/Federal Tax Practice Tools/Interactive Research Aids/Interactive Research Aids/Business/Depreciation/Reconciling*

*Luxury Auto Depreciation With Section 179 Deduction. AnswerConnect* subscribers may find the tool in the Tools section of the explanations for Code Sec. 179 and 280F. The tool also computes the first year depreciation deduction, including any bonus depreciation. A second interactive tool located in the same places will compute a complete schedule of depreciation deductions for a vehicle taking into account the luxury caps if they apply. This tool is entitled "*Automobile Depreciation Calculator Interactive Example.*"

*Formula for determining appropriate section 179 expense deduction on cars if bonus depreciation not claimed*

In many situations the first-year depreciation (including any bonus deprecia tion) on a car will exceed the applicable first-year cap that applies to cars on which bonus depreciation is not claimed. (Bonus depreciation may not be claimed on used property or if an election out is made). Thus, generally it is not necessary to elect to expense any portion under Code Sec. 179. If the 100 percent bonus rate applies it is never necessary to expense a vehicle under section 179.

However, if the cost of the vehicle is less than the amount shown in the applicable charts below for 2016 - 2018 purchases for the type of vehicle (car v. truck or van), placed in service year, depreciation method and convention, and whether or not 50 percent bonus is claimed, then regular depreciation plus any bonus will be less than the first-year cap. In this situation, a section 179 allowance should be claimed.

For a vehicle (car, truck, or van) placed in service in calendar-year 2021 on which no bonus depreciation is claimed, the first-year depreciation deduction (assuming half-year convention, 200-percent declining-balance method, five-year recovery period) will equal or exceed the $10,200 first-year cap if the vehicle costs at least $51,000 ($51,000 × 20% first-year depreciation percentage under half-year convention = $10,200). See ¶ 200 for applicable first-year caps.

If the mid-quarter convention and 200 percent declining balance method apply and bonus depreciation is not claimed, a vehicle placed in service in 2021 must cost less than the following amounts before any amount of the vehicle's cost needs to be expensed under section 179:

- First quarter $29,143 ($29,143 × 35% = $10,200)
- Second quarter $40,800 ($40,800 × 25% = $10,200)
- Third quarter $68,000 ($68,000 × 15% = $10,200)
- Fourth quarter $204,000 ($204,000 × 5% = $10,200)

See comprehensive charts below for 2016 - 2020 thresholds based on all MACRS depreciation methods and conventions.

If the cost of a car is less than the threshold amount shown in the applicable table below, a formula may be used to determine the amount to expense under Code Sec. 179 so that the sum of the regular depreciation allowance and the amount expensed under Code Sec. 179 is exactly equal to the applicable first-year cap. Note that if a taxpayer has placed other property in service that qualifies for the Code Sec. 179 expense allowance, the tax savings will be greater if the allowance is first allocated to other property with a recovery period that is longer than the five-year recovery period applicable to a vehicle. See comments at the beginning of this explanation paragraph.

Assuming that a vehicle is depreciated using MACRS, and no bonus deprecia- tion is claimed, the amount of Sec. 179 expense allowance to claim is determined by (1) reducing the amount of the first-year cap by the product of (a) the cost or other depreciable basis of the vehicle (determined without regard to the expense deduction) and (b) the applicable first-year depreciation table percentage, and then (2) dividing the amount determined in (1) by the difference between the number 1 and the first-year table percentage.

This formula works regardless of whether the half-year or mid-quarter convention applies and regardless of the MACRS depreciation method (i.e., regardless of whether the 200 percent declining balance method, 150 percent declining balance method, straight-line method, or ADS method applies). When applying the formula to a car that is used in part for personal purposes, the depreciation cap and cost or depreciable basis of the vehicle should be adjusted to reflect only business/investment use (i.e., multiply the full cap and cost by the business/investment use percentage).

Note that if the cost of a vehicle (adjusted to reflect only business/investment use) is equal to or less than the applicable depreciation cap (adjusted to reflect only business/investment use), the preceding formula is inapplicable. In such a case a taxpayer should expense the entire cost of the car if possible, subject to the proviso that a greater tax savings is derived when an asset with a longer recovery period (i.e., a recovery period in excess of 5 years) is expensed.

The above formula for computing the section 179 allowance when no bonus is claimed can be restated as follows:

(1) Determine the first-year depreciation cap.

(2) Multiply the first-year cap by the business/investment use percentage.

(3) Determine the cost or other depreciable basis of the vehicle unreduced by any amount to be expensed under Code Sec. 179.

(4) Multiply the cost or other depreciable basis determined in item 3 by the business/investment use percentage.

(5) Multiply the amount determined in item 4 by the applicable first-year table percentage (e.g. multiply by .20 if the 200 percent declining balance method and half-year convention apply).

(6) Reduce the amount determined in item 2 by the amount determined in item 5. If this results in a negative number, the first-year depreciation deduction exceeds the first-year cap and no amount needs to be expensed under section 179.

(7) Determine the difference between the number 1 and the first year table percentage (e.g., .80 (1 - .20) if the 200 percent declining balance method and half-year convention apply).

(8) Divide the amount determined in item 6 by the amount determined in item 7.

***Example (10):*** Assume that a car cost $12,000. The car is used 100% for business purposes and is placed in service in August 2021. The 200 percent declining balance method and half-year convention apply. An election out of bonus depreciation is made. The first-year table percentage for five-year property is 20% or .20 if the 200 percent declining balance method and half-year convention apply. See Table 1 at ¶ 180. The applicable first-year depreciation cap for 2021 is $10,200. The purchaser should expense $9,750 (($10,200 – ($12,000 × .20))/(1 – .20)). If the purchaser expenses $9,750, the sum of the $450 first year depreciation allowance plus the expensed amount will exactly equal the applicable first-year cap (($12,000 – $9,750) × .20 + $9,750 = $10,200)).

***Example (11):*** Assume the same facts as in the preceding *Example*, except that the mid-quarter convention applies and the car is placed in service in the fourth quarter of 2020. The mid-quarter depreciation table percentage for 5-year property placed in service in the fourth quarter is 5% or .05 if the 200 percent declining balance method applies. The purchaser in this case should expense $10,105.25 (($10,200 - ($12,000 × .05))/(1 - .05)). If the purchaser expenses $10,105.25, the sum of the $94.75 first year depreciation allowance plus the expensed amount will equal the applicable first-year cap (($12,000 – $10,000) × .05 + $10,105 = $10,200).

*Formula for determining appropriate section 179 expense deduction on cars if 50% bonus depreciation is claimed*

In most situations the first-year depreciation on a car on which 50 percent bonus depreciation is claimed will exceed the applicable first-year cap. Thus, it is usually not necessary to elect to expense any portion of the cost under Code Sec. 179.

Generally, a 100 percent bonus rate applies to vehicles placed in service in 2018. However, a fiscal-year 2017 - 2018 taxpayer that made an election to apply a 50 percent rate in lieu of the 100 percent rate for its tax year that includes September 27, 2017 will apply a 50 percent rate to vehicles placed in service during the part of 2018 that falls within the 2017 - 2018 fiscal year. See ¶ 127D discussion at item #49A.

If the 50 percent rate applies to a vehicle placed in service in 2018 by an electing 2017 - 2018 fiscal-year taxpayer, the first-year depreciation deduction and 50 percent bonus allowance on a vehicle that costs at least $30,000 will equal or exceed the $18,000 first-year cap ($15,000 bonus depreciation + $3,000 first-year depreciation deduction (($30,000 - $15,000) × 20% first-year depreciation percentage) = $18,000 first-year cap) assuming the 200 percent declining balance method and half-year convention apply (typical situation). See ¶ 200 for applicable first-year caps.

If the mid-quarter convention applies and 50 percent bonus depreciation is claimed, a car, truck, or van placed in service in 2018 on which 50 percent bonus is claimed by an electing 2017 - 2018 fiscal-year taxpayer must cost no more than the following amounts to make it necessary to claim a section 179 deduction.

- First quarter $26,667 (($26,667 × 50%) + ($13,334 × 35%) = $18,000)
- Second quarter $28,800 (($28,800 × 50%) + (14,400 × 25%) = $18,000)
- Third quarter $31,304 (($31,304 × 50%) + ($15,662 × 15%) = $18,000)
- Fourth quarter $34,286 (($34,286 × 50%) + ($17,143 × 5%) = $18,000)

See comprehensive charts below for 2016 - 2018 thresholds based on all MACRS depreciation methods and conventions.

The section 179 allowance to claim such that sum of the section 179 allowance, first-year depreciation deduction, and 50 percent bonus depreciation deduction are exactly equal to the first-year depreciation cap is determined by (1) reducing the amount of the first-year cap by the product of (a) the cost or other depreciable basis of the vehicle (determined without regard to the expense deduction) and (b) the sum of .50 and one-half of the applicable first-year depreciation table percentage, and then (2) dividing the amount determined in (1) by the difference between (a) the number 1 and (b) the sum of .50 and one-half of the first-year table percentage.

Note that if the cost of a vehicle (adjusted to reflect only business/investment use) is equal to or less than the applicable depreciation cap (adjusted to reflect only business/investment use), the preceding formula is inapplicable. In such a case a taxpayer should expense the entire cost of the car.

This formula works regardless of whether the half-year or mid-quarter convention applies and regardless of the MACRS depreciation method (i.e., regardless of whether the 200 percent declining balance method, 150 percent declining balance method, straight-line method, or ADS method applies). When applying the formula to a car that is used in part for personal purposes, the depreciation cap and cost or depreciable basis of the vehicle should be adjusted to reflect only business/ investment use (i.e., multiply the full cap and cost by the business/investment use percentage).

The above formula for computing the section 179 allowance when the bonus deduction is claimed can be restated as follows:

(1) Determine the first-year depreciation cap.

(2) Multiply the first-year cap by the business/investment use percentage.

(3) Determine the cost or other depreciable basis of the vehicle unreduced by any amount to be expensed under Code Sec. 179 or claimed as bonus depreciation.

(4) Multiply the cost or other depreciable basis determined in item 3 by the business/investment use percentage.

(5) Determine the sum of .50 and one-half of the applicable depreciation table percentage (e.g. .60 (.50 + .10 (.20 table percentage x .1/2)) if the 200 percent declining balance method and half-year convention apply)).

(6) Multiply the amount determined in item 4 by the amount determined in item 5.

(7) Reduce the amount determined in item 2 by the amount determined in item 6. If this results in a negative number, the first-year depreciation deduction (including bonus depreciation) exceeds the first-year cap and no amount needs to be expensed under section 179.

(8) Reduce the number 1 by the amount determined in item 5 (e.g., .40 (1 - .60) if the 200% declining balance method and half-year convention apply).

(9) Divide the amount determined in item 7 by the amount determined in item 8.

***Example (12):*** A car is purchased for $25,000 in January 2018 by a fiscal-year that payer that make the election to claim 50 percent bonus for its fiscal year that includes September 28, 2017. The half-year convention and 200 percent declining balance method apply. The applicable first-year cap is $18,000. The purchaser should expense $7,500 (($18,000 – ($25,000 × .60))/(1 – .60)). The .60 figure is the sum of .50 and .10 ( 1/2 of the first year table percentage (.20 × 1/2 = .10)). If the purchaser expenses $7,500, the sum of the expensed amount (7,500), bonus depreciation deduction ($8,750) (($25,000 – $7,500) × 50%), and regular first-year depreciation deduction ($1,750) (($25,000 – $7,500 – $8,750) × .20) will exactly equal the $18,000 cap.

***Example (13):*** Instead, the car was purchased in the first quarter of 2018 for $20,000. The mid-quarter convention and 200 percent declining balance method apply. The applicable first-year cap is $18,000. The first-year table percentage is .35. The purchaser should expense $13,846 ($18,000 – ($20,000 × .675%)/(1 – .675). The .675 figure is the sum of .50 and .175 ( 1/2 of the first year table percentage (.35 × 1/2 = .175)). If the purchaser expenses $13,846, the sum of the expensed amount ($13,846, bonus depreciation deduction ($3,077) ($20,000 – $13,846 × 50%), and regular first-year depreciation deduction ($1,077) ($20,000 – $13,846 – $3,077 × 35% (table percentage for 5-year property placed in service in first quarter)) is equal to the $18,000 cap.

Note that if the taxpayer in *Example (13)* placed other qualifying bonus depreciation property in service in later quarters of the tax year for which the first-year table percentage is lower than 35 percent, the section 179 allowance could produce greater tax savings if allocated to that property. If a taxpayer placed property in service which does not qualify for bonus depreciation and property which does qualify, it is also generally preferable to allocate the section 179 deduction to the nonqualifying property in order to maximize depreciation, bonus, and section 179 deductions claimed during the tax year.

*Chart of Purchase Prices Below Which Section 179 Allowance Should Be Computed on a Vehicle Subject to Annual Depreciation Caps*

If the purchase price of a vehicle that is placed in service in 2021 and is subject to the luxury car caps is less than the applicable amount shown in the chart below a taxpayer should compute a Code Sec. 179 allowance for the vehicle using the formulas above assuming the vehicle qualifies for expensing. No section 179 expense should be claimed on a vehicle placed service in 2021 if the 100 percent bonus rate applies.

| *Depreciation Method and Convention* | *Cars-No Bonus Claimed* | *Trucks and Vans-No Bonus Claimed* | *Cars-100% Bonus Claimed* | *Trucks and Vans-100% Bonus Claimed* |
|---|---|---|---|---|
| 200DBHY | $51,000.00 | $51,000.00 | N/A | N/A |
| 200DBMQ1 | $29,142.85 | $29,142.85 | N/A | N/A |
| 200DBMQ2 | $40,800.00 | $40,800.00 | N/A | N/A |
| 200DBMQ3 | $68,000.00 | $68,000.00 | N/A | N/A |
| 200DBMQ4 | $204,000.00 | $204,000.00 | N/A | N/A |
| 150DBHY | $68,000.00 | $68,000.00 | N/A | N/A |
| 150DBMQ1 | $38,857.14 | $38,857.14 | N/A | N/A |
| 150DBMQ2 | $54,400.00 | $54,400.00 | N/A | N/A |
| 150DBMQ3 | $90,666.67 | $90,666.67 | N/A | N/A |
| 150DBMQ4 | $272,000.00 | $272,000.00 | N/A | N/A |
| SLHY | $102,000.00 | $102,000.00 | N/A | N/A |
| SLMQ1 | $58,285.71 | $58,285.71 | N/A | N/A |
| SLMQ2 | $81,600.00 | $81,600.00 | N/A | N/A |
| SLMQ3 | $136,000.00 | $136,000.00 | N/A | N/A |
| SLMQ4 | $408,000.00 | $408,000.00 | N/A | N/A |
| ADSHY | $102,000.00 | $102,000.00 | N/A | N/A |
| ADSMQ1 | $58,285.71 | $58,285.71 | N/A | N/A |
| ADSMQ2 | $81,600.00 | $81,600.00 | N/A | N/A |
| ADSMQ3 | $136,000.00 | $136,000.00 | N/A | N/A |
| ADSMQ4 | $408,000.00 | $408,000.00 | N/A | N/A |

If the purchase price of a vehicle that is placed in service in 2019 or 2020 and is subject to the luxury car caps is less than the applicable amount shown in the chart below a taxpayer should compute a Code Sec. 179 allowance for the vehicle using the formulas above assuming the vehicle qualifies for expensing. No section 179 expense should be claimed on a vehicle placed service in 2019 or 2020 if the 100 percent bonus rate applies.

The chart below does not apply to a vehicle acquired before September 28, 2017 and placed in service in 2019 if bonus depreciation is claimed. These vehicles are subject to a 30 percent bonus rate (see ¶ 127D) and a special first-year cap for 2019 of $14,900 that is not taken into account by this chart (see ¶ 200, *19. Bonus depreciation and bump-up in first-year cap*).

**Purchase Price at Which Luxury Caps Apply in First Year of Recovery Period to Vehicles Placed in Service in 2019 or 2020**

| *Depreciation Method and Convention* | *Cars- No Bonus Claimed* | *Trucks and Vans- No Bonus Claimed* | *Cars- 100% Bonus Claimed* | *Trucks and Vans- 100% Bonus Claimed* |
|---|---|---|---|---|
| 200DBHY | $50,500.00 | $50,500.00 | N/A | N/A |
| 200DBMQ1 | $28,857.14 | $28,857.14 | N/A | N/A |
| 200DBMQ2 | $40,400.00 | $40,400.00 | N/A | N/A |
| 200DBMQ3 | $67,333.33 | $67,333.33 | N/A | N/A |
| 200DBMQ4 | $202,000.00 | $202,000.00 | N/A | N/A |
| 150DBHY | $67,333.33 | $67,333.33 | N/A | N/A |
| 150DBMQ1 | $38,476.19 | $38,476.19 | N/A | N/A |
| 150DBMQ2 | $53,866.67 | $53,866.67 | N/A | N/A |
| 150DBMQ3 | $89,777.78 | $89,777.78 | N/A | N/A |
| 150DBMQ4 | $269,333.33 | $269,333.33 | N/A | N/A |
| SLHY | $101,000.00 | $101,000.00 | N/A | N/A |
| SLMQ1 | $57,714.29 | $57,714.29 | N/A | N/A |
| SLMQ2 | $80,800.00 | $80,800.00 | N/A | N/A |
| SLMQ3 | $134,666.67 | $134,666.67 | N/A | N/A |
| SLMQ4 | $404,000.00 | $404,000.00 | N/A | N/A |
| ADSHY | $101,000.00 | $101,000.00 | N/A | N/A |
| ADSMQ1 | $57,714.29 | $57,714.29 | N/A | N/A |
| ADSMQ2 | $80,800.00 | $80,800.00 | N/A | N/A |
| ADSMQ3 | $134,666.67 | $134,666.67 | N/A | N/A |
| ADSMQ4 | $404,000.00 | $404,000.00 | N/A | N/A |

If the purchase price of a vehicle that is placed in service in 2018 and is subject to the luxury car caps is less than the applicable amount shown in the chart below a taxpayer should compute a Code Sec. 179 allowance for the vehicle using the formulas above assuming the vehicle qualifies for expensing. No section 179 expense should be claimed on a vehicle acquired for which the 100 percent bonus deduction is claimed. The 50 percent rate, however, continues to apply to vehicles placed in service in 2018 during a fiscal year that includes September 28, 2017 if the fiscal year taxpayer elected to claim the 50 percent rate in place of the 100 percent rate (see ¶ 127D, discussion item #49A.).

The chart below does not apply to a vehicle acquired before September 28, 2017 and placed in service in 2018 if bonus depreciation is claimed. These vehicles are subject to a 40 percent bonus rate (see ¶ 127D) and a special first-year cap for 2018 of $16,400 that is not taken into account by this chart (see ¶ 200, *19. Bonus depreciation and bump-up in first-year cap*).

**Purchase Price at Which Luxury Caps Apply in First Year of Recovery Period to Vehicles Placed in Service in 2018**

| *Depreciation Method and Convention* | *Cars- No Bonus Claimed* | *Trucks and Vans- No Bonus Claimed* | *Cars- 50% Bonus Claimed* | *Trucks and Vans- 50% Bonus Claimed* |
|---|---|---|---|---|
| 200DBHY | $50,000.00 | $50,000.00 | $30,000.00 | $30,000.00 |
| 200DBMQ1 | $28,571.43 | $28,571.43 | $26,666.67 | $26,666.67 |
| 200DBMQ2 | $40,000.00 | $40,000.00 | $28,800.00 | $28,800.00 |
| 200DBMQ3 | $66,666.67 | $66,666.67 | $31,304.35 | $31,304.35 |
| 200DBMQ4 | $200,000.00 | $200,000.00 | $34,285.71 | $34,285.71 |
| 150DBHY | $66,666.67 | $66,666.67 | $31,304.35 | $31,304.35 |
| 150DBMQ1 | $38,095.24 | $38,095.24 | $28,514.85 | $28,514.87 |

| *Depreciation Method and Convention* | *Cars- No Bonus Claimed* | *Trucks and Vans- No Bonus Claimed* | *Cars- 50% Bonus Claimed* | *Trucks and Vans- 50% Bonus Claimed* |
|---|---|---|---|---|
| 150DBMQ2 | $53,333.33 | $53,333.33 | $30,315.79 | $30,315.79 |
| 150DBMQ3 | $88,888.89 | $88,888.89 | $32,359.55 | $32,359.55 |
| 150DBMQ4 | $266,666.67 | $266,666.67 | $34,698.80 | $34,698.80 |
| SLHY | $100,000.00 | $100,000.00 | $32,727.27 | $32,727.27 |
| SLMQ1 | $57,142.86 | $57,142.86 | $30,638.30 | $30,638.30 |
| SLMQ2 | $80,000.00 | $80,000.00 | $32,000.00 | $32,000.00 |
| SLMQ3 | $133,333.33 | $133,333.33 | $33,488.37 | $33,488.37 |
| SLMQ4 | $400,000.00 | $400,000.00 | $35,121.95 | $35,121.95 |
| ADSHY | $100,000.00 | $100,000.00 | $32,727.27 | $32,727.27 |
| ADSMQ1 | $57,142.86 | $57,142.86 | $30,638.30 | $30,638.30 |
| ADSMQ2 | $80,000.00 | $80,000.00 | $32,000.00 | $32,000.00 |
| ADSMQ3 | $133,333.33 | $133,333.33 | $33,488.37 | $33,488.37 |
| ADSMQ4 | $400,000.00 | $400,000.00 | $35,121.95 | $35,121.95 |

## ¶ 488
## Planning for Depreciation Recapture

When acquiring or disposing of a depreciable asset, taxpayers need to consider that some or all of the depreciation claimed or allowable on the asset may be recaptured as ordinary income.

Recapture may be limited to actual depreciation claimed if adequate records are maintained. See "*Keep records to reduce depreciation recapture—allowed or allowable rule,*" below.

The amount of depreciation subject to recapture depends primarily on the type of asset (for example, real (Sec. 1250) or personal (Sec. 1245) property), the depreciation system used to depreciate the asset (MACRS, ACRS, or pre-ACRS), and the depreciation method used under that system (declining-balance or straight-line). Recapture is reported on Form 4797.

Generally, depreciation recapture is associated with the sale or exchange of a depreciable property. However, depreciation recapture can also apply to other types of dispositions in which no gain is recognized. For example, a corporation that transfers depreciable property as a dividend may need to recognize recapture income even though the transfer would otherwise be tax-free. See ¶ 160.

*Overview of recapture rules*

*MACRS.* In general, all gain from the sale, exchange, or involuntary conversion of Sec. 1245 property that is depreciated under MACRS is recaptured as ordinary income to the extent of previously allowed or allowable depreciation deductions (including the Code Sec. 179 expense deduction and bonus depreciation deduction) regardless of whether the cost of the property is recovered using the MACRS general depreciation system (GDS) or an elective MACRS method which slows the rate of cost recovery (Code Sec. 1245(a)). Depreciation recapture, however, is not required with respect to MACRS residential rental property or MACRS nonresidential real property held for more than one year. See ¶ 160. However, all MACRS depreciation deductions claimed on Sec. 1250 real property are subject to recapture if the property is held for one year or less (Code Sec. 1250(b)(1); Reg. § 1.1250-4).

See ¶ 160 for a discussion of the MACRS recapture rules.

*De minimis safe harbor expensing.* Amounts expensed under the de minimis safe harbor of Reg.§ 1.263(a)-1(f) are subject to recapture (Form 4797 Instructions). See ¶ 307 for discussion of de minimis safe harbor.

*Bonus depreciation on real property.* Bonus depreciation claimed on section 1250 property (e.g., section 1250 land improvements, MACRS qualified 15-year leasehold improvement property and qualified improvement property (¶ 127D)) is treated as accelerated depreciation for purposes of the section 1250 recapture rules. Thus, the difference between the bonus deduction and straight-line depreciation is subject to recapture to the extent of gain. See ¶ 160.

*Certain deductions, including section 179 deduction, claimed on real property.* For recapture purposes, Code Sec. 1245(a)(3)(C) treats the portion of the basis of real property (i.e., section 1250 property) for which deductions have been claimed under past and present versions of Code Sec. 179 as section 1245 property. Thus, any section 179 deduction claimed on section 1250 real property is recaptured as ordinary income to the extent of gain. This rule would apply to qualified real property which has been expensed under section 179. Recapture rules for qualified real property have been prescribed in Notice 2013-59. See ¶ 302 for recapture rules on qualified real property. Under present law, no other types of section 1250 property may be expensed under section 179. Code Sec. 1245(a)(3)(C) makes other types of deductions subject to the same rule. These are the deductions are under claimed under Code Sec. 169 (amortization of certified pollution control facilities), Code Sec. 179A (deduction for clean-fuel vehicles and certain refueling property), Code Sec. 179B (deduction to comply with EPA sulfur regulations), Code Sec. 179C (election to expense qualified liquid fuel refineries), Code Sec. 179D (efficient commercial buildings property deduction), Code Sec. 179E (expensing election for advanced mine safety equipment), Code Sec. 185 (amortization of railroad grading and tunnel bores), Code Sec. 188 (amortization of child care facilities) (as in effect before its repeal by the Revenue Reconciliation Act of 1990), Code Sec. 190 (deduction for cost of removing barriers to the handicapped and the elderly), Code Sec. 193 (deduction for certain tertiary injectants), and Code Sec. 194 (deductions for reforestation expenditures).

*ACRS.* Gain recognized on the sale of ACRS Sec. 1245 property is subject to recapture as ordinary income to the extent of previously claimed depreciation regardless of whether the property was depreciated using an accelerated or straight-line method. ACRS real property is treated as Sec. 1245 property for recapture purposes. However, ACRS 15-, 18-, and 19-year property that is residential rental property, any 15-, 18-, or 19-year nonresidential property that is depreciated under the ACRS straight-line method, and any low-income housing is treated as Sec. 1250 property for purposes of recapture (Code Sec. 1245(a)(5), prior to amendment by the 1986 Tax Reform Act). Gain on the sale or disposition of Sec. 1250 ACRS property is recaptured to the extent that the depreciation allowed exceeds the amount allowable under the ACRS straight-line method using the applicable 15-, 18-, or 19-year recovery period.

The recapture of gain on the sale of ACRS 15-year low-income housing is phased out after the property has been held for a prescribed number of months, at the rate of one percentage point per month (Code Sec. 168(c)(2)(F) (prior to amendment by the 1986 Tax Reform Act); Code Sec. 1250(a)(1)(B)).

*Pre-ACRS property.* Gain on the sale of Sec. 1245 property placed in service before 1981 is treated as ordinary income to the extent of prior depreciation allowed or allowable. Gain on the disposition of nonresidential real property is generally recaptured only to the extent that the depreciation claimed after 1969 exceeds the amount that would have been allowed after 1969 under the straight-line method. Gain on residential rental property is subject to recapture to the extent that accelerated depreciation claimed after 1975 exceeds straight-line depreciation. Special recapture rules apply to low-income housing.

*Additional corporate real property recapture*

A corporation (other than an S corporation) which disposes of Sec. 1250 property at a gain may be required to recapture up to 20 percent of its previously claimed depreciation even though recapture is not otherwise required. Specifically, in the case of section 1250 property which is disposed of during the tax year, 20 percent of the excess (if any) of the amount that would be treated as ordinary income if the property was Section 1245 property over the amount (if any) recaptured as ordinary income under Code Sec. 1250 is treated as ordinary income (Code Sec. 291(a)).

> ***Example (1):*** A corporation places MACRS residential real property costing $100,000 in service in 2010 and sells the property in 2020 for $130,000. Assume $40,000 of depreciation was claimed on the property. The depreciation is not subject to recapture under Code Sec. 1250. However, if the property was Code Sec. 1245 property the $40,000 of depreciation claimed would have been subject to recapture as ordinary income since the gain on the sale $70,000 ($130,000 amount realized – $60,000 adjusted basis) exceeded the depreciation claimed ($40,000). Thus, under Code Sec. 291, $8,000 (20% × $40,000) is recaptured as ordinary income.

Code Sec. 291(a) recapture is in addition to any recapture otherwise required under Code Sec. 1250, for example, with respect to ACRS real property depreciated using an accelerated method.

*Purpose of recapture*

The recapture provisions were enacted to prevent taxpayers from obtaining favorable capital gains tax rates on gain attributable to depreciation deductions which were used to offset ordinary income.

*Unrecaptured section 1250 gain—25-percent capital gains rate*

In the case of individuals, estates, and trusts, a maximum 25-percent capital gains tax rate applies to "unrecaptured section 1250 gain" (Code Sec. 1(h)(1)(E) and (6)(A)). A lower rate applies if the taxpayer's ordinary income tax bracket is lower than 25 percent. In general, unrecaptured section 1250 gain is the amount of depreciation claimed on section 1250 property which is not recaptured as ordinary income. Unrecaptured depreciation taken into account in computing unrecaptured section 1250 gain cannot exceed the amount of gain recognized on the property after the gain is reduced by any ordinary income recapture. Any gain in excess of the amount treated as unrecaptured section 1250 gain is eligible for the lower capital gains rates.

Since MACRS residential rental and nonresidential real property is not subject to ordinary income recapture, all depreciation on such property, to the extent of gain, is potentially characterized as unrecaptured section 1250 gain.

It should be kept in mind that depreciable property and nondepreciable real property (e.g., land) used in a trade or business and held for more than one year is section 1231 property. As a result, unrecaptured section 1250 gain is not subject to the maximum 25-percent rate unless a taxpayer has a net section 1231 gain for the year—that is, gains in excess of ordinary income depreciation recapture from section 1231 real and personal property must exceed losses from such property. Moreover, unrecaptured section 1250 gain cannot exceed net section 1231 gain. If a taxpayer has a net section 1231 gain, each section 1231 gain and loss is treated as a long-term capital gain and loss and is combined with any other capital gains and losses for the year in accordance with prescribed capital gain and loss netting rules. A net section 1231 loss, on the other hand, is deductible in full against ordinary income.

***Example (2):*** Sam Jones receives $150,000 for depreciable MACRS real estate acquired for $100,000. He has claimed $30,000 of depreciation on the property. His total gain is $80,000 ($150,000 – ($100,000 – $30,000)). Sam also receives $7,000 for a fully depreciated machine, which cost $5,000. Both properties have been held for more than a year. The $5,000 depreciation claimed on the machine is recaptured as ordinary income under Code Sec. 1245. Sam has a net section 1231 gain of $82,000 ($80,000 gain from the real estate plus $2,000 unrecaptured gain from the machine). $30,000 is taxed as unrecaptured section 1250 gain. The remaining $52,000 of section 1231 gain is treated as long-term capital gain and will be combined with any other capital gains and losses for the year in accordance with the capital gain and loss netting rules.

The recapture provisions can have an adverse impact on individuals or corporations even when there is no differential between ordinary income and capital gains rates. The following paragraphs point out possible pitfalls associated with the recapture provisions and techniques for avoiding them.

*Sell recapture assets in low-bracket tax year*

Recaptured depreciation is taxed at the ordinary income tax rate in effect in the year of recapture. The recapture provisions can operate as a penalty against taxpayers who offset ordinary income in low-bracket tax years (or have an operating loss) and then dispose of the asset in a high-bracket tax year.

***Example (3):*** Melinda Jones is in the 12% tax bracket in the year she purchases 5-year MACRS property for $20,000. Assume that she sells the property for $20,000 in the third year of the recovery period when she is in the 35% tax bracket. Under GDS, Jones would claim $4,000 ($20,000 × 20%) depreciation in Year 1 and $6,400 ($20,000 × 32%) in Year 2. The tax benefit of the deductions, without regard to present value considerations, is $1,248 ($10,400×12%). In Year 3, when the asset is sold, the $10,400 of depreciation is recaptured as ordinary income and an additional tax of $3,640 is imposed ($10,400 × 35% rate).

Note: Year 3 depreciation is not considered in the example since it will offset ordinary income taxed at a 35% tax rate and is subject to recapture as ordinary income at a 35% tax rate in the same year.

The result in the preceding example could have been avoided if the taxpayer had delayed the sale to a low-bracket tax year or a tax year in which a net operating loss was sustained. Another possibility, which could have mitigated the result somewhat, would have been to elect the MACRS alternative depreciation system (ADS), so that less depreciation would have been claimed in the earlier years when the benefit of the deductions were minimal. Also, it may have been possible to avoid immediate recapture by disposing of the asset in a Code Sec. 1031 like-kind exchange. However, section 1031 exchanges only apply to real property after 2017 (Code Sec. 1031(a)).

*Maximizing capital loss deductions*

In general, noncorporate taxpayers deduct capital losses to the extent of capital gains. Capital losses in excess of capital gains can offset up to $3,000 ($1,500 for a married person filing separately) of ordinary income per year. The nondeductible portion of the loss can be carried forward indefinitely (Code Sec. 1211(b)). Corporations may only deduct capital losses against capital gains (Code Sec. 1211(a)).

Even where there is no tax rate differential between a taxpayer's ordinary income tax rate and capital gains tax rate, the conversion of Sec. 1231 gain (see ¶ 496) to ordinary income under the recapture provisions can be significant for purposes of planning the deduction of capital losses. For example, the Sec. 1231 capital gain available for offset against capital losses may be reduced or eliminated.

***Example (4):*** John Jones recognizes a short-term capital loss of $15,000 on the sale of XYZ stock. He also sells depreciable Sec. 1245 business property at a gain of $15,000.

Assume that he has claimed $15,000 of depreciation on the property and that the entire amount is recaptured as ordinary income. If Jones has no other capital gains or losses, he may only deduct $3,000 of the short-term capital loss against ordinary income. The remaining $12,000 of the short-term capital loss must be carried forward. If the recapture provisions did not apply, the entire $15,000 of Sec. 1231 gain would have been treated as long-term capital gain and would have offset the entire short-term capital loss.

Note that if the taxpayer in the preceding example were a corporation, then the entire short-term capital loss would have been carried forward since a corporation may only deduct capital gains against capital losses (Code Sec. 1211(a)).

*Utilize net operating losses*

In general, net operating losses that arose in tax years ending before 2018 can be carried forward for 20 years (15 years for NOLs arising in tax years beginning before August 6, 1997). Rather than lose the tax benefit of an expiring NOL, a taxpayer who owns a depreciated asset which can readily be sold at a gain may be able to use the NOL to absorb ordinary income recapture that would otherwise be subject to tax in a later year. An unlimited NOL carryforward period applies to NOLs arising in tax years ending after 2017 (Code Sec. 172, as amended by the Tax Cuts and Jobs Act (P.L. 115-97)).

*Anticipate installment sale recaptures*

The recapture provisions are important to a taxpayer selling depreciable property (or a partnership interest in a partnership with depreciable property) and reporting income using the installment method because all depreciation recapture is reported as ordinary income *in the year of sale* (Code Sec. 453(i)). As a result, it may be advisable that the seller receives an initial payment in the year of sale sufficient to satisfy the additional tax liability caused by recapture.

This rule is not a concern with respect to the disposition of MACRS real property, as MACRS real property is not subject to depreciation recapture. However, special rules apply in determining what portion of an installment payment is considered attributable to the 25-percent capital-gains rate on unrecaptured section 1250 gain. See Reg. § 1.453-12.

***Example (5):*** John sells his raised dairy cows, machinery, and equipment to Jake for $260,000. The cows are valued at $120,000 and the machinery at $140,000. Jake pays $20,000 down and $80,000 plus interest annually for 3 years. John's machinery and equipment have an adjusted basis of $64,000; its original cost was $200,000. John's gain on the sale of the machinery and equipment is $76,000 ($140,000 – $64,000). The entire gain is recaptured as ordinary income under Code Sec. 1245 in the year of sale because the gain is less than the $136,000 ($200,000 – $64,000) of depreciation claimed in prior years. John will report the $120,000 cattle sale on the installment method.

If John and Jake are related and Jake resells the cattle within two years of the initial sale, then John may be required to recognized all of the gain from the cattle sale in the resale year. See Code Sec. 453(e)(1) and (2).

It should also be noted that the installment method generally does not apply to sales of depreciable property between related persons unless the taxpayer can show that tax avoidance is not one of the principal purposes of the transaction (i.e., there are no significant tax deferral benefits) (Code Sec. 453(g)).

*Delay sale of MACRS real property held for one year or less*

Depreciation recapture on Sec. 1250 real property is generally limited to the difference between accelerated depreciation claimed and straight-line depreciation. However, if the Sec. 1250 real property is held for one year or less all depreciation is subject to recapture (up to the amount of gain realized from the sale or disposition) (Code Sec. 1250(b)(1)). Although MACRS residential rental and nonresidential real property is not normally subject to recapture because it is depreciated using the straight-line method, all MACRS deductions on such property are subject to recapture if the property is not held for more than one year prior to the date of sale or disposition. Moreover, any gain not recaptured as ordinary income, would also not qualify for favorable treatment as Sec. 1231 gain. Thus, where possible, it may be advantageous to delay the sale of MACRS real property which would otherwise be sold within one year.

Since a taxpayer may not claim MACRS on a property that is acquired and disposed of in the same tax year (Reg. § 1.168(d)-1(b)(3)(ii)), the full recapture rule for property held for one year or less only has implications where the property is acquired in one tax year, disposed of in the following tax year, and held for one year of less.

*Allocate purchase price favorably*

When a taxpayer sells a group of assets (or a business) for a single price certain allocations of the purchase price may prove advantageous. For example, to the extent that the fair market value of assets are unclear or otherwise subject to negotiation, a seller may be able to allocate the purchase price to those assets that are not subject to depreciation recapture, such as MACRS real property or nondepreciable property. Allocations causing ordinary gain (recapture gain, for example) should be minimized if possible. This strategy could maximize capital gains recognition (generally taxable at a favorable rate) and reduce ordinary income recapture.

On the other hand, a purchaser may benefit by maximizing allocation of the purchase price to depreciable property with the shortest recovery periods in order to obtain larger depreciation deductions during the early years of the asset's recovery period. The present value of the tax-benefit of the current write-off will normally offset the negative impact of any future ordinary income recapture upon the sale of the depreciable asset if it is sold at a gain. A purchaser, however, also needs to consider whether the tax benefit of its depreciation deductions could be negatively impacted by an alternative minimum tax liability arising from accelerated depreciation on Sec. 1245 property or whether it may be in a higher income tax bracket in later tax years, in which case reduced depreciation deductions in earlier tax years may be warranted.

*Related party recapture trap*

When an asset is sold to a related party at a loss, Code Sec. 267 generally disallows the loss but allows the related purchaser to reduce the amount of gain otherwise recognizable on a subsequent sale by the amount of the previously disallowed loss. The reduction in subsequent gain is authorized by Code Sec. 267(d). However, the recapture regulations for Code Sec. 1245 and Code Sec. 1250 specifically override Code Sec. 267(d) (Reg. § 1.1245-6(b) and Reg. § 1.1250-1(c)(2)). Thus, the full amount of the subsequent gain without reduction for the disallowed loss is subject to recapture as ordinary income.

> ***Example (6):*** John James sells Sec. 1245 machinery to his wholly-owned corporation for $100,000. His basis in the machinery is $120,000. Since he is related to the corporation the $20,000 loss is disallowed. Assume that the corporation claims $40,000 of depreciation on the asset and then sells it to an unrelated party for $90,000. The corporation's gain is $30,000 ($90,000 - ($100,000 - $40,000)). If Code Sec. 267(d) applied, the corporation's gain would be reduced by $20,000 and only $10,000 would be recaptured as ordinary income. However, because Code Sec. 267(d) does not apply, the entire $30,000 gain is recaptured as ordinary income.

*Recapture on sales to or by controlled entities and certain other related persons*

All gain on the sale or exchange of property that is depreciable in the hands of certain related transferees is taxed as ordinary income to the transferor (Code Sec. 1239). In general, the following transferors and transferees are related for purposes of this rule:

(1) a person and a person's controlled entity;

(2) a taxpayer and a trust in which the taxpayer (or the taxpayer's spouse) is a beneficiary (other than a beneficiary with a remote contingent interest);

(3) an employer and the employer's controlled welfare benefit fund (Code Sec. 1239(d)); and

(4) an executor and a beneficiary of an estate, unless the sale or exchange is in satisfaction of a pecuniary bequest.

A corporation is controlled for purposes of this rule if a person owns (directly or indirectly) more than 50 percent of the value of its stock. A partnership is controlled if a person owns (directly or indirectly) more than 50 percent of the capital or profits interest in the partnership.

The rule also applies to two corporations that are members of the same controlled group (certain modifications apply to the Code Sec. 1563(a) definition of a controlled group); two S corporations, if the same persons own more than 50 percent in value of the outstanding stock of each corporation; and two corporations, one of which is an S corporation, if the same persons own more than 50 percent in value of the outstanding stock of each corporation.

A patent application is treated as depreciable property for purposes of this recapture rule (Code Sec. 1239(e)).

*Retired structural components and MACRS general asset accounts*

The sale or retirement of ACRS 15-, 18-, or 19-year real property can trigger depreciation recapture (often ordinary section 1245 recapture as explained above). Accordingly, retirement and replacement of a defective or worn component of ACRS property may be preferable to the sale of the entire structure where ordinary recapture income or Sec. 1231 gain would be recognized upon a sale. This strategy applies to MACRS residential rental and nonresidential real property insofar as it would defer the recognition of Sec. 1231 gain or the maximum 25 percent capital gain tax rate that applies to unrecaptured section 1250 gain of individuals, estates, and trusts discussed above. Depreciation on MACRS residential rental and nonresidential real property is not subject to ordinary income recapture because such MACRS property is not depreciated using an accelerated method.

ACRS proposed regulations provide that the retirement of a structural component of ACRS real property is not considered a disposition (Code Sec. 168(d)(2)(C) (prior to amendment by the 1986 Tax Reform Act); Prop. Reg. § 1.168-2(l)(1)). Thus, a loss (equal to the adjusted depreciable basis of the retired structural component at the time of retirement) may not be recognized and a taxpayer is required to continue depreciating the retired structural component. This rule applied to MACRS real property until the issuance of temporary regulations which expanded the definition of a disposition to include the retirement of a structural component (Temporary Reg.§ 1.168(i)-8T(b); Temporary Reg.§ 1.168(i)-8T(b)) (see T.D. 9564). Under the temporary regulations recognition of loss upon the retirement of a structural component was mandatory unless the taxpayer placed the building in a general asset account. Once in a general asset account, a taxpayer could decide on a case-by-case basis whether to claim a loss on a retirement by making a qualifying disposition election (see ¶ 128). In response to criticism of this rule, the IRS replaced the temporary regulations with proposed reliance regulations that allow a taxpayer to claim a loss if a partial disposition election is made (Proposed Reg.§ 1.168(i)-8 (see REG-110732-13). The proposed regulations were finalized without change (Reg. § 1.168(i)-8 (T.D. 9689)). Thus, under the final/proposed regulations, a taxpayer may decide on a case-by-case basis whether to recognize a loss upon the retirement of a structural component without placing the building in a general asset account. The final regulations apply to tax years beginning on or after January 1, 2014 but may be applied to tax years beginning on or after January 1, 2012.

Taxpayers that placed a building in a GAA in reliance on the temporary regulations (either by making a retroactive GAA election by filing an accounting method change pursuant to Section 6.32 of the Appendix of Rev. Proc. 2011-14 (prior to be superseded by Rev. Proc. 2015-14), as added by Rev. Proc. 2012-20 or a current GAA election for the 2012 or 2013 tax year) were allowed to revoke those elections by filing an accounting method change pursuant to Sec. 6.11 of Rev. Proc. 2016-29 for post-May 5, 2016 filings for tax years ending on or after September 30, 2015, and for earlier filings Section 6.34 of Rev. Proc. 2015-14 or Appendix Section 6.34 of Rev. Proc. 2011-14, as added by Rev. Proc. 2014-17 and modified by Rev. Proc. 2014-54. In order to preserve the losses claimed by making a qualifying disposition election on retired structural components of a building placed in a GAA, the taxpayer was required to file an accounting method change to revoke the GAA election and make a late partial disposition election. See Sec. 6.11(7)(c), Example 3 of Rev. Proc. 2016-29, effective for Form 3115s filed on or after May 5, 2016. See ¶ 77 and ¶ 128. The revocation of a GAA election and late partial disposition election was required to be made no later than a taxpayer's last tax year beginning in 2014 and is now obsolete.

The following points regarding late partial disposition elections are critical. First, a taxpayer was allowed to file an amended return (or Form 3115) to make a late partial disposition election for dispositions that occurred during the 2012 tax year (and, for certain fiscal-year taxpayers, dispositions that occurred during the 2013 tax year). Special time limits applied for filing the amended return or Form 3115 for these tax years (Reg. § 1.168(i)-8(d)(2)(iv)). See ¶ 162. Second, a taxpayer was allowed to file an accounting method change pursuant to Section 6.10 of Rev. Proc. 2016-29 for filings on or after May 5, 2016 for tax years ending on or after September 30, 2015 (or its predecessor) to make a late partial disposition election for dispositions of MACRS property that occurred in tax years beginning before January 1, 2012. The accounting method change to make a late partial disposition election had to be made no later than for a taxpayer's last tax year beginning in 2014. Third, a taxpayer that filed an accounting method change to claim a loss deduction on previously retired structural components in reliance of the disposition rules in the temporary regulations had to file another accounting method change to preserve those losses by making the late partial disposition election. If this accounting change was not filed such a taxpayer continues to be required to file an accounting method change to change its definition of an asset and restore the previously claimed loss through a Code Sec. 481(a) adjustment. Currently, the latter option is only available since the period for making a late partial disposition election has expired. These accounting method changes are described at ¶ 77.

See ¶ 128 for a detailed discussion of general asset account rules under the temporary and final and proposed regulations and ¶ 162 for rules regarding retirements of structural components of buildings outside of general assets accounts under the temporary and final and proposed regulations.

Under both temporary and final repair regulations, taxpayers may not claim a repair expense for replacing a component of real or personal property if a loss deduction is claimed on the retired component even though a repair deduction would otherwise be allowed (Temporary Reg. § 1.263(a)-3T(i)(1)(i) (T.D. 9564); Reg. § 1.263(a)-3(k)(1)(i)). For a special rule under the final repair regulations (Reg. § 1.263(a)-3(k)(4)) that may limit this rule where a casualty loss is claimed, see ¶ 179. The temporary and final repair regulations also provide that the replacement of a major component or a substantial structural part of a unit of property must be capitalized (Temporary Reg. § 1.263(a)-3T(i)(1)(vi) (T.D. 9564); Reg. § 1.263(a)-3(k)(1)(vi)). Thus, under the temporary and final regulations, if a taxpayer replaces a major structural component (such as an entire roof of a building) of a building no repair deduction may be claimed and a taxpayer will not be negatively affected by claiming a loss deduction on the retired structural component. See ¶ 162.

*Gift and death transfer exceptions to recapture*

Certain types of dispositions and transfers will not cause depreciation recapture or will at least result in a limitation on the amount otherwise recaptured.

Recapture can be avoided if a depreciable property is disposed of by gift or transferred on account of death (Code Sec. 1245(b)(1) and Code Sec. 1245(b)(2); Code Sec. 1250(d)(1) and (2); Reg.§ 1.1250-3; Reg.§ 1.1245-4). Thus, if a taxpayer plans on making a death or gift transfer and has the choice between transferring recapture property or nonrecapture property, it may be advantageous to transfer the recapture property. However, as noted below, the donee of a gift may be required to recognize recapture on a later sale or disposition of the property.

The exception from recapture for transfers at death does not apply to income in respect of a decedent (Code Sec. 1245(b)(2) and Code Sec. 1250(d)(2)). Thus, when a decedent sells property under the installment method prior to death, all recapture income would be reported in the year of the disposition (for example, on the decedent's final return) (Code Sec. 453(i)). The basis of the installment obligation, however, is stepped up to reflect the recapture income reported by the decedent.

It should be noted that in the case of a gift, the donee generally takes the donor's adjusted basis for purposes of computing gain (see ¶ 70). If the donee later sells the property in a disposition that is subject to recapture (e.g., sells the property at a gain), the donee must determine ordinary income recapture as if he had claimed the depreciation deducted by the donor (Code Sec. 1015). If the transfer of the depreciable property is for less than its fair market value, the transfer is considered part sale and part gift. The transferor will recognize gain to the extent that the amount realized exceeds the adjusted basis of the property. Prior depreciation on Sec. 1245 property (accelerated depreciation in excess of straight-line in the case of Sec. 1250 property) is subject to recapture to the extent of the gain. If the gain is not sufficient to offset the full amount of the otherwise recapturable depreciation, the balance must be taken into account by the transferee upon any later disposition (Reg. § 1.1001-1(e); Reg. § 1.1015-4; Reg. § 1.1245-4(a)(3); Reg. § 1.1250-3(a)(2)).

***Example (7):*** Joan Dilliard transfers depreciable personal property with a fair market value of $10,000 to her son for $6,500. She has claimed $7,000 of depreciation on the property which has an adjusted basis of $2,000. Joan is considered to have made a gift of $3,500 ($10,000 - $6,500). Her taxable gain on the transfer is $4,500 ($6,500 - $2,000). This gain is recaptured as ordinary income. The unrecaptured depreciation ($2,500 ($7,000 - $4,500)) is "carried over" to the son and is subject to recapture if he sells or disposes of the property at a gain.

In the case of a gift of depreciable real or personal property to a charity, the fair market value of the property for purposes of determining the amount of the contribution is reduced by the amount of depreciation that would have been recaptured if the property had been sold at its fair market value. The fair market value may also have to be reduced by any Sec. 1231 gain that would have resulted if the property had been sold (Code Sec. 170(e)(1); Reg. § 1.170A-1(c); Reg. § 1.170A-4(a) and (b)).

Special rules apply to bargain sales to charity (Reg. § 1.1011-2(a)(1)).

Transfers to a spouse (if an election was made) or former spouse incident to a divorce are treated as gifts under Code Sec. 1041 (Code Sec. 1041(b)). Code Sec. 1041 is generally effective for property received after July 18, 1984, under a divorce or separation instrument in effect after that date. It also applies to all other property received after 1983 if an election was made (Temp. Reg. § 1.1041-1T(g)).

The basis to the recipient spouse for determining gain or loss is the adjusted basis of the transferor. This basis applies regardless of the fair market value at the time of the transfer or any consideration paid (Temp. Reg. § 1.1041-1T(d), Q&A-11).

The transfer does not trigger depreciation recapture. However, depreciation claimed by the transferor is subject to recapture when the transferee disposes of the property.

Although the regulations under Code Sec. 1041 provide for the recapture of the investment tax credit if, upon or after the transfer, the property is disposed of by, or ceases to be Code Sec. 38 property with respect to, the transferee (Temp. Reg. § 1.1041-1T). The regulations under Code Secs. 179 and 1041 do not provide for a recapture of the Code Sec. 179 expense allowance if the transferee spouse uses the property 50 percent or less for business purposes. Presumably, therefore, no recapture is required. The IRS Publications also make no mention of this issue.

Since a Code Sec. 1041 transfer is treated as a gift, the transferee should compute depreciation as if the property were newly acquired, by reference to the carryover basis. However, no Code Sec. 179 expense allowance is permitted because only property acquired by purchase qualifies for the expense deduction. Property with a carryover basis is specifically disqualified. See ¶ 302.

*Like-kind exchange and involuntary conversion exception*

Like-kind exchanges under Code Sec. 1031 are allowed only for real property after 2017 (Code Sec. 1031(a)(1), as amended by the Tax Cuts and Jobs Act (P.L. 115-97)).

The provision generally applies to exchanges completed after December 31, 2017 (Act Sec. 13303(c)(1) of P.L. 115-97). However, the provision does not apply to an exchange if (1) the property disposed of by the taxpayer in the exchange is disposed of on or before December 31, 2017; or (2) the property received by the taxpayer in the exchange is received on or before December 31, 2017 (Act Sec. 13303(c)(2) of P.L. 115-97).

Proposed regulations provide that for purposes of section 1031 real property means land and improvements to land, unsevered natural products of land, and water and air space superjacent to land. An interest in real property, including fee ownership, co-ownership, a leasehold, an option to acquire real property, an easement, or a similar interest, is real property for purposes of section 1031. Except for a state's characterization of shares in a mutual ditch, reservoir, or irrigation company, local law definitions are not controlling for purposes of determining the meaning of the term real property under this section (Proposed Reg. § 1.1031(a)-3; REG-117589-18 (6/12/20)). The proposed regulations would apply to exchanges of real property beginning on or after the date of finalization (Proposed Reg. § 1.1031(a)-3(c)).

Depreciation recapture is not triggered in a like-kind exchange (Code Sec. 1031) or an involuntary conversion (Code Sec. 1033) unless (1) gain is recognized because money or property other than like-kind (Code Sec. 1031) or similar or related (Code Sec. 1033) property was also received or (2) the like-kind, similar, or related property given up and acquired are not both section 1245 property or both section 1250 real property (Code Sec. 1245(b)(4); Code Sec. 1250(d)(4)).

The recapture potential, however, attaches to the acquired property. For example, if a fully depreciated machine with a $0 basis that cost $100 and has a fair market value of $1,000 is traded for another machine with a fair market value of $1,000, the basis of the acquired machine is also $0. However, $100 of any gain recognized upon its subsequent sale is recaptured as ordinary income (Reg. § 1.1245-2(c)(4)).

Like-kind exchanges are reported on Form 8824. The amount recaptured as ordinary income is carried over from line 21 of Form 8824 to line 16 of Form 4797. Involuntary conversions are reported directly on Form 4797.

*Section 1245 property exchanged.* In the case of a like-kind exchange (Code Sec. 1031) or an involuntary conversion (Code Sec. 1033) of depreciated Sec. 1245 property, the amount of depreciation subject to recapture as ordinary income is limited to the sum of:

(1) the gain (if any) recognized under Code Sec. 1031 or Code Sec. 1033 because money or property other than like-kind, similar, or related property was also received; plus.

(2) the fair market value of like-kind, similar, or related property acquired in the transaction which is Sec. 1250 property (Code Sec. 1245(b)(4)).

***Example (8):*** Prior to 2018, a taxpayer exchanges MACRS machinery with an original cost of $2,000, an adjusted (depreciated) basis of $200 and a fmv of $1,000 for another new machine with a fmv of $800 and $200 cash. Gain of $800 is *realized* ($1,000 ($800 fmv of machine received + $200 cash) – $200 adjusted basis of machine given up) but *recognized gain* is limited to the $200 cash received. The recognized gain is treated as ordinary income under the recapture rules. The taxpayer's basis in the machine received is $400 ($200 adjusted basis + $200 recognized gain). Under the rules explained at ¶ 167, the taxpayer will continue to depreciate $200 of the $400 adjusted basis of the acquired property as if the exchange had not taken place. This $200 carryover basis does not qualify for the section 179 expense allowance but does qualify for bonus depreciation if the exchange took place during a tax year in which bonus depreciation applies). The additional $200 noncarryover basis is treated as newly purchased MACRS property for purposes of computing MACRS depreciation and qualifies for the Code Sec. 179 expense allowance (and bonus depreciation).

Summary of section 1245 for section 1245 exchange.

| Machinery Exchanged | | | Machinery Received | Cash Received |
|---|---|---|---|---|
| *Cost* | *Adjusted Basis* | *FMV* | *FMV* | |
| $2,000 | $200 | $1,000 | $800 | $200 |

*Amount realized:* $800 ($800 + $200 cash – $200 adjusted basis)
*Amount recognized:* $200 (cash received) (recaptured as ordinary income)
*Basis of machine received:* $400 ($200 adjusted basis + $200 cash)

ACRS real property, other than residential rental property and low-income housing, for which accelerated depreciation has been claimed is treated as section 1245 property for purposes of depreciation recapture. See "*Overview of recapture rules*" above. If such ACRS section 1245 property is exchanged for or involuntarily converted into MACRS real property which is section 1250 property, then item (2), above, would appear to require the recapture of the depreciation claimed on the ACRS property to the extent of the fair market value of the MACRS real property acquired.

Another situation in which item (2) would apply is an involuntary conversion in which the qualifying replacement property is stock (i.e., nondepreciable personal property).

***Example (9):*** ACRS commercial property (Section 1245 recapture property) that cost $1.5 million has an adjusted basis of $100,000 and a fair market value of $1 million is exchanged for MACRS commercial property with a fair market value of $1 million. The taxpayer will recognize $1 million of ordinary income recapture (an amount equal to the fair market value of the section 1250 property received in exchange for the ACRS Sec. 1245 recapture property). The remaining $400,000 of unrecaptured ordinary income ($1.5 million cost – $100,000 adjusted basis – $1 million recaptured ordinary income) attaches to the MACRS property and will be recaptured as ordinary income to the extent of gain recognized on its later disposition. The basis of the MACRS property received in the exchange is $1,100,000 ($100,000 carryover basis + $1 million recapture gain). The entire basis is depreciated as newly acquired MACRS commercial real property since this is an ACRS for MACRS property exchange and is not covered by the rule described at ¶ 167.

Summary of section 1245 for section 1250 exchange.

| 1245 Property Exchanged | | | 1250 Property Received |
|---|---|---|---|
| *Cost* | *Adjusted Basis* | *FMV* | *FMV* |
| $1.5M | $100,000 | $1M | $1M |

*Recapture Potential:* $1.4M ($1.5 – $100,000)
*Recapture Required:* $1.0M (FMV of Sec. 1250 property received)
*Basis of Section 1250 Property:* $1.1M ($100,000 + $1M recaptured gain)

The taxpayer could have avoided the recapture by exchanging the ACRS property for MACRS Sec. 1245 property. Note, however, that the like-kind exchange rules of Code Sec. 1031 do not apply to exchanges of section 1245 personal property after 2017 (see above). This, however, may not be a practical solution if the taxpayer wishes to trade for real property since real property is generally Sec. 1250 property under MACRS.

*Section 1250 property exchanged.* In the case of a like-kind exchange or an involuntary conversion of Sec. 1250 real property depreciated under an accelerated ACRS or pre-ACRS method, the amount of accelerated depreciation in excess of straight-line depreciation subject to recapture as ordinary income is limited to the larger of:

(1) the gain (if any) recognized under Code Sec. 1031 or Code Sec. 1033 because money or property other than like-kind, similar, or related property was also received; or

(2) the gain that would have been reported as ordinary income because of the depreciation recapture provisions if the transaction had been a cash sale, *less* (in the case of an involuntary conversion) the cost of the depreciable property acquired or (in the case of a like-kind exchange) the fair market value of the depreciable real property received (Code Sec. 1250(d)(4); Reg. § 1.1250-3(d)).

For purposes of item (1) gain is increased by the fair market value of stock purchased as replacement property in acquiring control of a corporation.

***Example (10):*** A taxpayer exchanges section 1250 real property placed in service in 1980 (land and a building) plus $300,000 cash for other section 1250 real property (land and a building) in a qualifying like-kind exchange. The adjusted basis of the land is $50,000 and its fair market value is $100,000. The building has a depreciated basis of $250,000 and a fair market value of $500,000. Additional depreciation subject to recapture is $150,000. The fair market value of the building acquired is $50,000, while the fair market value of the land acquired is $850,000.

Since the taxpayer received no cash or other boot, no gain is recognized under the like-kind exchange provisions of Code Sec. 1031. However, ordinary income that must be recaptured is the larger of (1) the gain that must be reported under the Code Sec. 1031 rules (but only to the extent attributable to the structure) ($0) or (2) the ordinary income depreciation that would have been recaptured ($150,000) if this had been a cash sale *less* the fair market value of the depreciable real property acquired ($50,000). Thus, $100,000 ($150,000 – $50,000) is recaptured as ordinary income.

If this had been a cash sale, the taxpayer would have received $500,000 for the structure. The adjusted basis of the structure is $250,000. The recognized gain would have been $250,000 ($500,000 – $250,000 adjusted basis). Since the potential recognized gain exceeds the $150,000 subject to recapture, the entire $150,000 would have been recaptured as ordinary income.

Ordinary income recapture which is not required to be reported in the year of the disposition is carried over as additional depreciation to the depreciable real property acquired in the like-kind exchange or involuntary conversion and may be taxed as ordinary income on a later disposition (Code Sec. 1250(d)(4)(E)).

If the ordinary income reported as additional depreciation is limited, the basis of the property acquired is its fair market value (its cost if purchased to replace property involuntarily converted to cash), minus the gain postponed.

If MACRS Sec. 1250 property is replaced or exchanged before it has been held for one year, then the entire amount of MACRS depreciation claimed is subject to recapture as ordinary income to the extent of the larger of (1) or (2). See Reg. § 1.1250-4 for rules regarding the determination of the holding period.

*Sale of principal residence*

Code Sec. 121 allows qualifying taxpayers to exclude up to $500,000 gain ($250,000 for taxpayers who do not file jointly) when a principal residence is sold. The exclusion, however, does not apply to the extent of any depreciation claimed or allowable on the residence that is attributable to periods after May 6, 1997 (Code Sec. 121(d)(6)). For example, the rule applies to depreciation claimed with respect to a home office, day care business, or the rental of the property.

> ***Example (11):*** John sells his residence for a $30,000 gain in 2021. He used the residence as a home office starting in 2016 and claimed $1,500 of depreciation. The maximum amount that John may exclude is $28,500. The remaining $1,500 gain is taxable at rates that apply to section 1250 unrecaptured gain (see above, "Unrecaptured section 1250 gain—25-percent capital gains rate"). The depreciation is not subject to ordinary income recapture since it was claimed at a straight-line rate on section 1250 property. Note that the IRS formerly did not allow any portion of gain attributable to a home office to be excluded under Code Sec. 121. Gain was computed separately on the home office and the remaining portion of the residence (Reg. § 1.121-1(e)).

A significant planning consideration may affect a taxpayer whose spouse has died where a house that was held jointly has significantly appreciated. In order to take advantage of the $500,000 exclusion, the requirements for qualifying for the $500,000 exclusion must have been satisfied before the death of the spouse and the taxpayer must sell the residence within two years of the date of the death. If the house is not sold within this period, the exclusion drops to $250,000 (Code Sec. 121(b)(4)). To determine whether a sale is worthwhile, however, consideration must be given to the step-up basis rules.

For joint interests acquired after 1976, (property held in joint tenancy by a married couple with a right of survivorship or as tenants by the entirety) the basis of one-half of the property is stepped-up to its fair market value regardless of the amount contributed by either spouse toward the purchase price since only one-half of the property is included in the deceased spouse's gross estate (Code Sec. 2040(b)). The surviving spouse's basis of the remaining half is the amount contributed by him or her toward the purchase price. Until recently, the IRS position was that the same rule applies to joint interests acquired before 1977. However, all courts that considered the issue, including the Tax Court (*T. Hahn,* 110 TC 140, CCH Dec. 52,606 (Acq.)), have rule that the amount of pre-1977 jointly held property included in a deceased spouse's estate is based on the decedent's contribution. See, also, *L. Gallenstein*, 92-2 USTC ¶ 61,114 and *J.B. Patten*, CA-4, 97-2 USTC ¶ 60,279. Thus, if the deceased spouse is considered to have paid for 100 percent of the property, the entire value is included in his or her gross estate. Due to the unlimited marital deduction, this is of no particular significance from an estate tax perspective. However, if 100 percent is included in the gross estate, then the surviving spouse is entitled to a full basis step-up. Conversely, if the surviving spouse contributed 100 percent of the cost, no amount is included in the deceased spouse's estate and there is no basis-step up for the survivor. The IRS has now acquiesced to the Hahn decision. Thus, taxpayers may no longer to whipsaw the

IRS by choosing the rule (former IRS position prior to its acquiescence or court positions) which best suits their situation.

*Keep records to reduce depreciation recapture—allowed or allowable rule*

Generally, recapture is based on the amount of allowable depreciation even though a taxpayer actually claimed less than the full amount of depreciation to which the taxpayer was entitled. Recapture can be limited to the actual amount of depreciation claimed on Sec. 1245 property, however, if the taxpayer can establish by adequate records or other sufficient evidence that the amount claimed was less than the amount allowable (Code Sec. 1245(a)(2)(B); Reg. § 1.1245-2(a)(7)). Recordkeeping requirements are set forth in (Reg. § 1.1245-2(b)). A similar rule applies in the case of Sec. 1250 property (Reg. § 1.1250-2(d)(4)). The allowed or allowable rule is less important now because the IRS will permit a taxpayer who has sold an asset without claiming the full amount of depreciation to request an accounting method change on Form 3115 and claim an adjustment on the return for the year of sale, as noted immediately below.

***Example 12:*** In 2018, Cash placed an item of section 1245 property costing $1,000 in service. The property was MACRS 5-year property subject to the half-year convention. First-year depreciation was not claimed and should have been $200 ($1,000 × 20% first year table percentage which reflects half-year convention for place in service year). 2019 depreciation was $320 ($1,000 × 32% second year table percentage). The property was sold in 2020 for $6,000. 2020 depreciation was $96 ($1,000 × 19.2% third year table percentage × 50% to reflect half-year convention). Although section 1245 depreciation recapture would normally equal $616, Cash's ordinary income recapture is limited to $416 if books and records show that 2018 depreciation was not claimed.

***Example 13:*** In 2018, Cash placed in service a section 1250 land improvement (MACRS 15-year property) which cost $1,000 but failed to claim depreciation. The 2018 depreciation deduction should have been $50 (i.e., allowable depreciation using the 150 percent declining balance method and half-year convention). Allowable and claimed 2019 depreciation was $95. The land improvement was sold in 2020 for $2,000. Allowable and claimed depreciation for 2020 was $42.75 (taking into account the half-year convention for the year of sale). Total depreciation allowable was $187.75. Straight-line depreciation for 2018 and 2020, taking into account the half-year convention, is $33.33 for each year. For 2019 straight-line depreciation is $66.66. Total straight-line depreciation allowable was $133.32. Total recapture is $54.43 ($187.75 - $133.32). However, since Cash did not claim depreciation in 2018 and has books and records establishing the amount that should have been claimed, the ordinary income recapture amount can be reduced by $50 to $4.43. The recapture amount could also be computed as the difference between the excess depreciation for 2019 and 2020 ($37.76) and the straight-line depreciation which was not claimed in 2018 ($33.33) (Reg. § 1.1250-2(d)(4)(ii)).

*Computing gain or loss on dispositions—greater of allowed or allowable depreciation rule*

Gain on the sale or disposition of a depreciable asset is equal to its cost reduced by the greater of the depreciation actually claimed or the depreciation actually allowable (Reg. § 1.1016-3(a)(1)). Thus, the rule in the preceding paragraph does not reduce the amount of gain recognized; it only reduces the amount of gain that is subject to recapture as ordinary income.

Previously, a taxpayer who sold a depreciable asset without having claimed the full amount of allowable depreciation could not request an accounting method change in order to claim the full amount of allowable depreciation unless the taxpayer owned the property at the beginning of the year of change. The IRS, however, now allows a taxpayer in certain circumstances to file a request for a change in accounting method on an original or amended return for the disposition year any time prior to expiration of the Code Sec. 6501(a) limitations period for assessments for the tax year of the disposition (Rev. Proc. 2019-43, Sec. 6.07; Rev. Proc. 2007-16). The revenue procedure generally applies to a taxpayer that is changing from an impermissible to a permissible method of accounting in situations where no depreciation or insufficient depreciation was claimed. Note that a math or posting error is not considered an accounting method (ee ¶ 75. Thus, this change of accounting method procedure does not apply to posting and math errors.

Exceptions apply to certain property held by tax-exempt organizations and property disposed of in any nonrecognition transactions, unless, in the case of a Code Sec. 1033 (involuntary conversions) or Code Sec. 1031 (like-kind exchanges) transaction, the taxpayer elected to depreciate the entire basis of the replacement property as newly acquired property. See ¶ 167 for a description of this election.

Originally, the effective date for this change was generally for Forms 3115 filed for tax years ending on or after December 30, 2003. However, the original procedure was revised to also extend its application to dispositions of depreciable property occurring in tax years ending before December 30, 2003. An additional change clarifies that the change in accounting method may also be made by filing Form 3115 with a timely filed original return for the year of disposition. The entire Code Sec. 481 adjustment for the unclaimed depreciation is taken into account on the original or amended return filed for the year of the disposition (Rev. Proc. 2007-16, modifying and superseding Rev. Proc. 2004-11, and modifying and amplifying Rev. Proc. 2002-9).

# Appendices of Selected Final, Temporary, and Proposed Regulations

# Code Sec. 167 Regulations

## ¶ 509

### Reg. § 1.167(a)-3

§ 1.167(a)-3. **Intangibles.**— (a) *In general* .—If an intangible asset is known from experience or other factors to be of use in the business or in the production of income for only a limited period, the length of which can be estimated with reasonable accuracy, such an intangible asset may be the subject of a depreciation allowance. Examples are patents and copyrights. An intangible asset, the useful life of which is not limited, is not subject to the allowance for depreciation. No allowance will be permitted merely because, in the unsupported opinion of the taxpayer, the intangible asset has a limited useful life. No deduction for depreciation is allowable with respect to good will. For rules with respect to organizational expenditures, see section 248 and the regulations thereunder. For rules with respect to trademark and trade name expenditures, see section 177 and the regulations thereunder. See sections 197 and 167(f) and, to the extent applicable, § § 1.197-2 and 1.167(a)-14 for amortization of goodwill and certain other intangibles acquired after August 10, 1993, or after July 25, 1991, if a valid retroactive election under § 1.197-1T has been made.

(b) *Safe harbor amortization for certain intangible assets* .—(1) *Useful life* .—Solely for purposes of determining the depreciation allowance referred to in paragraph (a) of this section, a taxpayer may treat an intangible asset as having a useful life equal to 15 years unless—

(i) An amortization period or useful life for the intangible asset is specifically prescribed or prohibited by the Internal Revenue Code, the regulations thereunder (other than by this paragraph (b)), or other published guidance in the Internal Revenue Bulletin (see § 601.601(d)(2) of this chapter);

(ii) The intangible asset is described in § 1.263(a)-4(c) (relating to intangibles acquired from another person) or § 1.263(a)-4(d)(2) (relating to created financial interests);

(iii) The intangible asset has a useful life the length of which can be estimated with reasonable accuracy; or

(iv) The intangible asset is described in § 1.263(a)-4(d)(8) (relating to certain benefits arising from the provision, production, or improvement of real property), in which case the taxpayer may treat the intangible asset as having a useful life equal to 25 years solely for purposes of determining the depreciation allowance referred to in paragraph (a) of this section.

(2) *Applicability to acquisitions of a trade or business, changes in the capital structure of a business entity, and certain other transactions* .—The safe harbor useful life provided by paragraph (b)(1) of this section does not apply to an amount required to be capitalized by § 1.263(a)-5 (relating to amounts paid to facilitate an acquisition of a trade or business, a change in the capital structure of a business entity, and certain other transactions).

(3) *Depreciation method* .—A taxpayer that determines its depreciation allowance for an intangible asset using the 15-year useful life prescribed by paragraph (b)(1) of this section (or the 25-year useful life in the case of an intangible asset described in § 1.263(a)-4(d)(8)) must determine the allowance by amortizing the basis of the intangible asset (as determined under section 167(c) and without regard to salvage value) ratably over the useful life beginning on the first day of the month in which the intangible asset is placed in service by the taxpayer. The intangible asset is not eligible for amortization in the month of disposition.

(4) *Effective date* .—This paragraph (b) applies to intangible assets created on or after December 31, 2003. [Reg. § 1.167(a)-3.]

**.01 Historical Comment:** Proposed 11/11/55. Adopted 6/11/56 by T.D. 6182. Amended 2/3/60 by T.D. 6452, 1/20/2000 by T.D. 8865 and 12/31/2003 by T.D. 9107.

## ¶ 510

## Reg. § 1.167(a)-14

§ 1.167(a)-14. **Treatment of certain intangible property excluded from section 197** .—(a) *Overview* .—This section provides rules for the amortization of certain intangibles that are excluded from section 197 (relating to the amortization of goodwill and certain other intangibles). These excluded intangibles are specifically described in § 1.197-2(c)(4), (6), (7), (11), and (13) and include certain computer software and certain other separately acquired rights, such as rights to receive tangible property or services, patents and copyrights, certain mortgage servicing rights, and rights of fixed duration or amount. Intangibles for which an amortization amount is determined under section 167(f) and intangibles otherwise excluded from section 197 are amortizable only if they qualify as property subject to the allowance for depreciation under section 167(a).

(b) *Computer software* .—(1) *In general* .—The amount of the deduction for computer software described in section 167(f)(1) and § 1.197-2(c)(4) is determined by amortizing the cost or other basis of the computer software using the straight line method described in § 1.167(b)-1 (except that its salvage value is treated as zero) and an amortization period of 36 months beginning on the first day of the month that the computer software is placed in service. Before determining the amortization deduction allowable under this paragraph (b), the cost or other basis of computer software that is section 179 property, as defined in section 179(d)(1)(A)(ii), must be reduced for any portion of the basis the taxpayer properly elects to treat as an expense under section 179. In addition, the cost or other basis of computer software that is qualified property under section 168(k)(2) and § 1.168(k)-1 or § 1.168(k)-2, as applicable, 50-percent bonus depreciation property under section 168(k)(4) or § 1.168(k)-1, or qualified New York Liberty Zone property under section 1400L(b) or § 1.1400L(b)-1, must be reduced by the amount of the additional first year depreciation deduction allowed or allowable, whichever is greater, under section 168(k) or section 1400L(b) for the computer software. If costs for developing computer software that the taxpayer properly elects to defer under section 174(b) result in the development of property subject to the allowance for depreciation under section 167, the rules of this paragraph (b) will apply to the unrecovered costs. In addition, this paragraph (b) applies to the cost of separately acquired computer software if the cost to acquire the software is separately stated and the cost is required to be capitalized under section 263(a).

(2) *Exceptions* .—Paragraph (b)(1) of this section does not apply to the cost of computer software properly and consistently taken into account under § 1.162-11. The cost of acquiring an interest in computer software that is included, without being separately stated, in the cost of the hardware or other tangible property is treated as part of the cost of the hardware or other tangible property that is capitalized and depreciated under other applicable sections of the Internal Revenue Code.

(3) *Additional rules* .—Rules similar to those in § 1.197-2(f)(1)(iii), (f)(1)(iv), and (f)(2) (relating to the computation of amortization deductions and the treatment of contingent amounts) apply for purposes of this paragraph (b).

(c) *Certain interests or rights not acquired as part of a purchase of a trade or business* .—(1) *Certain rights to receive tangible property or services* .—The amount of the deduction for a right (other than a right acquired as part of a purchase of a trade or business) to receive tangible property or services under a contract or from a governmental unit (as specified in section 167(f)(2) and § 1.197-2(c)(6)) is determined as follows:

(i) *Amortization of fixed amounts* .—The basis of a right to receive a fixed amount of tangible property or services is amortized for each taxable year by multiplying the basis of the right by a fraction, the numerator of which is the amount of tangible property or services received during the taxable year and the denominator of which is the total amount of tangible property or services received or to be received under the terms of the contract or governmental grant. For example, if a taxpayer acquires a favorable contract right to receive a fixed amount of raw materials during an unspecified period, the taxpayer must amortize the cost of acquiring the contract right by multiplying the total cost by a fraction, the numerator of which is the amount of raw materials received under the contract during the taxable year and the denominator of which is the total amount of raw materials received or to be received under the contract.

(ii) *Amortization of unspecified amount over fixed period* .—The cost or other basis of a right to receive an unspecified amount of tangible property or services over a fixed period is amortized ratably over the period of the right. (See paragraph (c)(3) of this section regarding renewals).

(iii) *Amortization in other cases* .—[Reserved]

(2) *Rights of fixed duration or amount* .—The amount of the deduction for a right (other than a right acquired as part of a purchase of a trade or business) of fixed duration or amount received under a contract or granted by a governmental unit (specified in section 167(f)(2) and § 1.197-2(c)(13)) and not covered by paragraph (c)(1) of this section is determined as follows:

(i) *Rights to a fixed amount* .—The basis of a right to a fixed amount is amortized for each taxable year by multiplying the basis by a fraction, the numerator of which is the amount received during the taxable year and the denominator of which is the total amount received or to be received under the terms of the contract or governmental grant.

(ii) *Rights to an unspecified amount over fixed duration of less than 15 years* .—The basis of a right to an unspecified amount over a fixed duration of less than 15 years is amortized ratably over the period of the right.

(3) *Application of renewals* .—(i) For purposes of paragraphs (c)(1) and (2) of this section, the duration of a right under a contract (or granted by a governmental unit) includes any renewal period if, based on all of the facts and circumstances in existence at any time during the taxable year in which the right is acquired, the facts clearly indicate a reasonable expectancy of renewal.

(ii) The mere fact that a taxpayer will have the opportunity to renew a contract right or other right on the same terms as are available to others, in a competitive auction or similar process that is designed to reflect fair market value and in which the taxpayer is not contractually advantaged, will generally not be taken into account in determining the duration of such right provided that the bidding produces a fair market value price comparable to the price that would be obtained if the rights were purchased immediately after renewal from a person (other than the person granting the renewal) in an arm's-length transaction.

(iii) The cost of a renewal not included in the terms of the contract or governmental grant is treated as the acquisition of a separate intangible asset.

(4) *Patents and copyrights* .—If the purchase price of a interest (other than an interest acquired as part of a purchase of a trade or business) in a patent or copyright described in section 167(f)(2) and § 1.197-2(c)(7) is payable on at least an

annual basis as either a fixed amount per use or a fixed percentage of the revenue derived from the use of the patent or copyright, the depreciation deduction for a taxable year is equal to the amount of the purchase price paid or incurred during the year. Otherwise, the basis of such patent or copyright (or an interest therein) is depreciated either ratably over its remaining useful life or under section 167(g) (income forecast method). If a patent or copyright becomes valueless in any year before its legal expiration, the adjusted basis may be deducted in that year.

(5) *Additional rules* .—The period of amortization under paragraphs (c)(1) through (4) of this section begins when the intangible is placed in service, and rules similar to those in § 1.197-2(f)(2) apply for purposes of this paragraph (c).

(d) *Mortgage servicing rights* .—(1) *In general* .—The amount of the deduction for mortgage servicing rights described in section 167(f)(3) and § 1.197-2(c)(11) is determined by using the straight line method described in § 1.167(b)-1 (except that the salvage value is treated as zero) and an amortization period of 108 months beginning on the first day of the month that the rights are placed in service. Mortgage servicing rights are not depreciable to the extent the rights are stripped coupons under section 1286.

(2) *Treatment of rights acquired as a pool* .—(i) *In general* .—Except as provided in paragraph (d)(2)(ii) of this section, all mortgage servicing rights acquired in the same transaction or in a series of related transactions are treated as a single asset (the pool) for purposes of determining the depreciation deduction under this paragraph (d) and any gain or loss from the sale, exchange, or other disposition of the rights. Thus, if some (but not all) of the rights in a pool become worthless as a result of prepayments, no loss is recognized by reason of the prepayment and the adjusted basis of the pool is not affected by the unrecognized loss. Similarly, any amount realized from the sale or exchange of some (but not all) of the mortgage servicing rights is included in income and the adjusted basis of the pool is not affected by the realization.

(ii) *Multiple accounts* .—If the taxpayer establishes multiple accounts within a pool at the time of its acquisition, gain or loss is recognized on the sale or exchange of all mortgage servicing rights within any such account.

(3) *Additional rules* .—Rules similar to those in § 1.197-2(f)(1)(iii), (f)(1)(iv), and (f)(2) (relating to the computation of amortization deductions and the treatment of contingent amounts) apply for purposes of this paragraph (d).

(e) *Effective dates* .—(1) *In general* .—This section applies to property acquired after January 25, 2000, except that § 1.167(a)-14(c)(2) (depreciation of the cost of certain separately acquired rights) and so much of § 1.167(a)-14(c)(3) as relates to § 1.167(a)-14(c)(2) apply to property acquired after August 10, 1993 (or July 25, 1991, if a valid retroactive election has been made under § 1.197-1T).

(2) *Change in method of accounting* .—See § 1.197-2(l)(4) for rules relating to changes in method of accounting for property to which § 1.167(a)-14 applies. However, see § 1.168(k)-1(g)(4) or 1.1400L(b)-1(g)(4) for rules relating to changes in method of accounting for computer software to which the third sentence in § 1.167(a)-14(b)(1) applies.

(3) *Qualified property, 50-percent bonus depreciation property, qualified New York Liberty Zone property, or section 179 property* .—This section also applies to computer software that is qualified property under section 168(k)(2) or qualified New York Liberty Zone property under section 1400L(b) acquired by a taxpayer after September 10, 2001, and to computer software that is 50-percent bonus depreciation property under section 168(k)(4) acquired by a taxpayer after May 5, 2003. This section also applies to computer software that is section 179 property

placed in service by a taxpayer in a taxable year beginning after 2002. The language "or § 1.168(k)-2, as applicable," in the third sentence in paragraph (b)(1) of this section applies to computer software that is qualified property under section 168(k)(2) and placed in service by a taxpayer during or after the taxpayer's taxable year that includes September 24, 2019. However, a taxpayer may choose to apply the language "or § 1.168(k)-2, as applicable," in the third sentence in paragraph (b)(1) of this section for computer software that is qualified property under section 168(k)(2) and acquired and placed in service after September 27, 2017, by the taxpayer during taxable years ending on or after September 28, 2017. A taxpayer may rely on the language "or § 1.168(k)-2, as applicable," in the third sentence in paragraph (b)(1) of this section in regulation project REG-104397-18 (2018-41 I.R.B. 558) (see § 601.601(d)(2)(ii)( *b*) of this chapter) for computer software that is qualified property under section 168(k)(2) and acquired and placed in service after September 27, 2017, by the taxpayer during taxable years ending on or after September 28, 2017, and ending before the taxpayer's taxable year that includes September 24, 2019. [Reg. § 1.167(a)-14.]

**.01 Historical Comment:** Proposed 1/16/97. Adopted 1/20/2000 by T.D. 8865. Amended 9/5/2003 by T.D. 9091, 8/28/2006 by T.D. 9283 and 9/17/2019 by T.D. 9874.

# MACRS Regulations

## ¶ 550

### Reg. § 1.168(a)-1

§1.168(a)-1. **Modified accelerated cost recovery system .**—(a) Section 168 determines the depreciation allowance for tangible property that is of a character subject to the allowance for depreciation provided in section 167(a) and that is placed in service after December 31, 1986 (or after July 31, 1986, if the taxpayer made an election under section 203(a)(1)(B) of the Tax Reform Act of 1986; 100 Stat. 2143). Except for property excluded from the application of section 168 as a result of section 168(f) or as a result of a transitional rule, the provisions of section 168 are mandatory for all eligible property. The allowance for depreciation under section 168 constitutes the amount of depreciation allowable under section 167(a). The determination of whether tangible property is property of a character subject to the allowance for depreciation is made under section 167 and the regulations under section 167.

(b) This section is applicable on and after February 27, 2004. [Reg. §1.168(a)-1.]

**.01 Historical Comment:** Proposed 3/1/2004. Adopted 2/26/2007 by T.D. 9314.

## ¶ 551

### Reg. § 1.168(b)-1

1.168(b)-1. **Definitions .**—(a) *Definitions .*—For purposes of section 168 and the regulations under section 168, the following definitions apply:

(1) *Depreciable property* is property that is of a character subject to the allowance for depreciation as determined under section 167 and the regulations under section 167.

(2) *MACRS property* is tangible, depreciable property that is placed in service after December 31, 1986 (or after July 31, 1986, if the taxpayer made an election under section 203(a)(1)(B) of the Tax Reform Act of 1986; 100 Stat. 2143) and subject to section 168, except for property excluded from the application of section 168 as a result of section 168(f) or as a result of a transitional rule.

(3) *Unadjusted depreciable basis* is the basis of property for purposes of section 1011 without regard to any adjustments described in section 1016(a)(2) and (3). This basis reflects the reduction in basis for the percentage of the taxpayer's use of property for the taxable year other than in the taxpayer's trade or business (or for the production of income), for any portion of the basis the taxpayer properly elects to treat as an expense under section 179, section 179C, section 181, or any similar provision, and for any adjustments to basis provided by other provisions of the Internal Revenue Code and the regulations under the Code (other than section 1016(a)(2) and (3)) (for example, a reduction in basis by the amount of the disabled access credit pursuant to section 44(d)(7)). For property subject to a lease, see section 167(c)(2).

(4) *Adjusted depreciable basis* is the unadjusted depreciable basis of the property, as defined in §1.168(b)-1(a)(3), less the adjustments described in section 1016(a)(2) and (3).

(5) *Qualified improvement property .*—(i) Is any improvement that is section 1250 property to an interior portion of a building, as defined in §1.48-1(e)(1), that is nonresidential real property, as defined in section 168(e)(2)(B), if the improvement is placed in service by the taxpayer after the date the building was first placed in service by any person and if—

(A) For purposes of section 168(e)(6), the improvement is made by the taxpayer and is placed in service by the taxpayer after December 31, 2017;

(B) For purposes of section 168(k)(3) as in effect on the day before amendment by section 13204(a)(4)(B) of the Tax Cuts and Jobs Act, Public Law 115-97 (131 Stat. 2054 (December 22, 2017)) ( "Act"), the improvement is acquired by the taxpayer before September 28, 2017, the improvement is placed in service by the taxpayer before January 1, 2018, and the improvement meets the original use requirement in section 168(k)(2)(A)(ii) as in effect on the day before amendment by section 13201(c)(1) of the Act; or

(C) For purposes of section 168(k)(3) as in effect on the day before amendment by section 13204(a)(4)(B) of the Act, the improvement is acquired by the taxpayer after September 27, 2017; the improvement is placed in service by the taxpayer after September 27, 2017, and before January 1, 2018; and the improvement meets the requirements in section 168(k)(2)(A)(ii) as amended by section 13201(c)(1) of the Act; and

(ii) Does not include any qualified improvement for which an expenditure is attributable to—

(A) The enlargement, as defined in § 1.48-12(c)(10), of the building;

(B) Any elevator or escalator, as defined in § 1.48-1(m)(2); or

(C) The internal structural framework, as defined in § 1.48-12(b)(3)(iii), of the building.

(b) *Applicability date* .—(1) *In general* .—Except as provided in paragraph (b)(2) of this section, this section is applicable on or after February 27, 2004.

(2) *Application of paragraph (a)(5) of this section and addition of "section 181" in paragraph (a)(3) of this section* .—(i) *In general* .—Except as provided in paragraphs (b)(2)(ii) through (iv) of this section, paragraph (a)(5) of this section and the language "section 181," in the second sentence in paragraph (a)(3) of this section are applicable on or after September 24, 2019.

(ii) *Early application of paragraph (a)(5) of this section and addition of "section 181" in paragraph (a)(3) of this section* .—A taxpayer may choose to apply paragraph (a)(5) of this section and the language "section 181," in the second sentence in paragraph (a)(3) of this section for the taxpayer's taxable years ending on or after September 28, 2017.

(iii) *Early application of regulation project REG-104397-18* .—A taxpayer may rely on the provisions of paragraph (a)(5) of this section in regulation project REG-104397-18 (2018-41 I.R.B 558) (see § 601.601(d)(2)(ii)( *b*) of this chapter) for the taxpayer's taxable years ending on or after September 28, 2017, and ending before the taxpayer's taxable year that includes September 24, 2019.

(iv) *Addition of language in paragraph (a)(5)(i)(A) of this section* .—The language "is made by the taxpayer and" in paragraph (a)(5)(i)(A) of this section applies to property placed in service by the taxpayer after December 31, 2017. [Reg. § 1.168(b)-1.]

**.01 Historical Comment:** Proposed 3/1/2004. Adopted 2/26/2007 by T.D. 9314. Amended 9/17/2019 by T.D. 9874 and 11/5/2020 by T.D. 9916.

## ¶ 559

## Reg. § 1.168(d)-0

§ 1.168(d)-0. **Table of contents for the applicable convention rules.**—This section lists the major paragraphs in § 1.168(d)-1.

(b) Additional rules for determining whether the mid-quarter convention applies and for applying the applicable convention.

(1) Property described in section 168(f).

(2) Listed property.

(3) Property placed in service and disposed of in the same taxable year.

(4) Aggregate basis of property.

(5) Special rules for affiliated groups.

(6) Special rule for partnerships and S corporations.

(7) Certain nonrecognition transactions.

(c) Disposition of property subject to the half-year or mid-quarter convention.

(1) In general.

(2) Example.

(d) Effective date. [Reg. § 1.168(d)-0.]

**.01 Historical comment:** Proposed 12/31/90. Adopted 10/28/92 by T.D. 8444.

## ¶ 560

## Reg. § 1.168(d)-1

§ 1.168(d)-1. **Applicable conventions—Half-year and mid-quarter conventions.**— (a) *In general* .—Under section 168(d), the half-year convention applies to depreciable property (other than certain real property described in section 168(d)(2)) placed in service during a taxable year, unless the mid-quarter convention applies to the property. Under section 168(d)(3)(A), the mid-quarter convention applies to depreciable property (other than certain real property described in section 168(d)(2)) placed in service during a taxable year if the aggregate basis of property placed in service during the last three months of the taxable year exceeds 40 percent of the aggregate basis of property placed in service during the taxable year ( "the 40-percent test"). Thus, if the depreciable property is placed in service during a taxable year that consists of three months or less, the mid-quarter convention applies to the property. Under section 168(d)(3)(B)(i), the depreciable basis of nonresidential real property, residential rental property, and any railroad grading or tunnel bore is disregarded in applying the 40-percent test. For rules regarding property that is placed in service and disposed of in the same taxable year, see paragraph (b)(3) of this section. For the definition of "aggregate basis of property," see paragraph (b)(4) of this section.

(b) *Applicable conventions—half-year and mid-quarter conventions* .—(1) *Property described in section 168(f)* .—In determining whether the 40-percent test is satisfied for a taxable year, the depreciable basis of property described in section 168(f) (property to which section 168 does not apply) is not taken into account.

(2) *Listed property* .—The depreciable basis of listed property (as defined in section 280F(d)(4) and the regulations thereunder) placed in service during a taxable year is taken into account (unless otherwise excluded) in applying the 40-percent test.

(3) *Property placed in service and disposed of in the same taxable year* .—(i) Under section 168(d)(3)(B)(ii), the depreciable basis of property placed in service and disposed of in the same taxable year is not taken into account in determining whether the 40-percent test is satisfied. However, the depreciable basis of property placed in service, disposed of, subsequently reacquired, and again placed in service, by the taxpayer in the same taxable year must be taken into account in applying the 40-percent test, but the basis of the property is only taken

into account on the later of the dates that the property is placed in service by the taxpayer during the taxable year. Further, see §§1.168(i)-6(c)(4)(v)(B) and 1.168(i)-6(f) for rules relating to property placed in service and exchanged or involuntarily converted during the same taxable year.

(ii) The applicable convention, as determined under this section, applies to all depreciable property (except nonresidential real property, residential rental property, and any railroad grading or tunnel bore) placed in service by the taxpayer during the taxable year, excluding property placed in service and disposed of in the same taxable year. However, see §§1.168(i)-6(c)(4)(v)(A) and 1.168(i)-6(f) for rules relating to MACRS property that has a basis determined under section 1031(d) or section 1033(b). No depreciation deduction is allowed for property placed in service and disposed of during the same taxable year. However, see §1.168(k)-1(f)(1) for rules relating to qualified property or 50-percent bonus depreciation property, and §1.1400L(b)-1(f)(1) for rules relating to qualified New York Liberty Zone property, that is placed in service by the taxpayer in the same taxable year in which either a partnership is terminated as a result of a technical termination under section 708(b)(1)(B) or the property is transferred in a transaction described in section 168(i)(7). Further, see §1.168(k)-2(g)(1) for rules relating to qualified property under section 168(k), as amended by the Tax Cuts and Jobs Act, Public Law 115-97 (131 Stat. 2054 (December 22, 2017)), that is placed in service by the taxpayer in the same taxable year in which either a partnership is terminated as a result of a technical termination under section 708(b)(1)(B) or the property is transferred in a transaction described in section 168(i)(7).

(4) *Aggregate basis of property* .—For purposes of the 40-percent test, the term "aggregate basis of property" means the sum of the depreciable bases of all items of depreciable property that are taken into account in applying the 40-percent test. "Depreciable basis" means the basis of depreciable property for purposes of determining gain under sections 1011 through 1024. The depreciable basis for the taxable year the property is placed in service reflects the reduction in basis for—

(i) Any portion of the basis the taxpayer properly elects to treat as an expense under section 179;

(ii) Any adjustment to basis under section 48(q); and

(iii) The percentage of the taxpayer's use of property for the taxable year other than in the taxpayer's trade or business (or for the production of income), but is determined before any reduction for depreciation under section 167(a) for that taxable year.

(5) *Special rules for affiliated groups* .—(i) In the case of a consolidated group (as defined in §1.1502-1(h)), all members of the group that are included on the consolidated return are treated as one taxpayer for purposes of applying the 40-percent test. Thus, the depreciable bases of all property placed in service by members of a consolidated group during a consolidated return year are taken into account (unless otherwise excluded) in applying the 40-percent test to determine whether the mid-quarter convention applies to property placed in service by the members during the consolidated return year. The 40-percent test is applied separately to the depreciable bases of property placed in service by any member of an affiliated group that is not included in a consolidated return for the taxable year in which the property is placed in service.

(ii) In the case of a corporation formed by a member or members of a consolidated group and that is itself a member of the consolidated group ("newly-formed subsidiary"), the depreciable bases of property placed in service by the newly-formed subsidiary in the consolidated return year in which it is formed is included with the depreciable bases of property placed in service during the consolidated return year by the other members of the consolidated group in applying the 40-percent test. If depreciable property is placed in service by a newly-formed subsidiary during the consolidated return year in which it was formed, the newly-formed subsidiary is considered as being in existence for the entire consolidated return year for purposes of applying the applicable convention to determine when the recovery period begins.

(iii) The provisions of paragraph (b)(5)(ii) of this section are illustrated by the following example.

*Example.* Assume a member of a consolidated group that files its return on a calendar-year basis forms a subsidiary on August 1. The subsidiary places depreciable property in service on August 5. If the mid-quarter convention applies to property placed in service by the members of the consolidated group (including the newly-formed subsidiary), the property placed in service by the subsidiary on August 5 is deemed placed in service on the mid-point of the third quarter of the consolidated return year ( *i.e.,* August 15). If the mid-quarter convention does not apply, the property is deemed placed in service on the mid-point of the consolidated return year ( *i.e.,* July 1).

(iv) In the case of a corporation that joins or leaves a consolidated group, the depreciable bases of property placed in service by the corporation joining or leaving the group during the portion of the consolidated return year that the corporation is a member of the consolidated group is included with the depreciable bases of property placed in service during the consolidated return year by the other members in applying the 40-percent test. The depreciable bases of property placed in service by the joining or leaving member in the taxable year before it joins or after it leaves the consolidated group is not taken into account by the consolidated group in applying the 40-percent test for the consolidated return year. If a corporation leaves a consolidated group and joins another consolidated group, each consolidated group takes into account, in applying the 40-percent test, the depreciable bases of property placed in service by the corporation while a member of the group.

(v) The provisions of paragraph (b)(5)(iv) of this section are illustrated by the following example.

*Example.* Assume Corporations A and B file a consolidated return on a calendar-year basis. Corporation C, also a calendar-year taxpayer, enters the consolidated group on July 1 and is included on the consolidated return for that taxable year. The depreciable bases of property placed in service by C during the period of July 1 to December 31 is included with the depreciable bases of property placed in service by A and B during the entire consolidated return year in applying the 40-percent test. The depreciable bases of property placed in service by C from January 1 to June 30 is not taken into account by the consolidated group in applying the 40-percent test. If C was a member of another consolidated group during the period from January 1 to June 30, that consolidated group would include the depreciable bases of property placed in service by C during that period.

(vi) A corporation that joins or leaves a consolidated group during a consolidated year is considered as being a member of the consolidated group for the entire consolidated return year for purposes of applying the applicable convention to determine when the recovery period begins for depreciable property placed in service by the corporation during the portion of the consolidated return year that the corporation is a member of the group.

(vii) If depreciable property is placed in service by a corporation in the taxable year ending immediately before it joins a consolidated group or beginning immediately after it leaves a consolidated group, the applicable convention is applied to the property under either the full taxable year rules or the short taxable year rules, as applicable.

(viii) The provisions of paragraphs (d)(5)(vi) and (vii) of this section are illustrated by the following example.

*Example.* Assume that on July 1, C, a calendar-year corporation, joins a consolidated group that files a return on a calendar-year basis. The short taxable year rules apply to C for the period of January 1 to June 30. However, in applying the applicable convention to determine when the recovery period begins for depreciable property placed in service for the period of July 1 to December 31, C is considered as being a member of the consolidated group for the entire consolidated return year. Thus, if the half-year convention applies to depreciable property placed in service by the consolidated group (taking into account the depreciable bases of property placed in service by C after June 30), the property is deemed placed in service on the mid-point of the consolidated return year ( *i.e.*, July 1, if the group did not have a short taxable year).

(ix) In the case of a transfer of depreciable property between members of a consolidated group, the following special rules apply for purposes of applying the 40-percent test. Property that is placed in service by one member of a consolidated group and transferred to another member of the same group is considered as placed in service on the date that it is placed in service by the transferor member, and the date it is placed in service by the transferee member is disregarded. In the case of multiple transfers of property between members of a consolidated group, the property is considered as placed in service on the date that the first member places the property in service, and the dates it is placed in service by other members are disregarded. The depreciable basis of the transferred property that is taken into account in applying the 40-percent test is the depreciable basis of the property in the hands of the transferor member (as determined under paragraph (b)(4) of this section), or, in the case of multiple transfers of property between members, the depreciable basis in the hands of the first member that placed the property in service.

(x) The provisions of paragraph (b)(5)(ix) of this section are illustrated by the following example.

*Example.* Assume the ABC consolidated group files its return on a calendar-year basis. A, a member of the consolidated group, purchases depreciable property costing $50,000 and places the property in service on January 5, 1991. On December 1, 1991, the property is transferred for $75,000 to B, another member of the consolidated group. In applying the 40-percent test to the members of the consolidated group for 1991, the property is considered as placed in service on January 5, the date that A placed the property in service, and the depreciable basis of the property that is taken into account is $50,000.

(6) *Special rule for partnerships and S corporations* .—In the case of property placed in service by a partnership or an S corporation, the 40-percent test is generally applied at the partnership or corporate level. However, if a partnership or an S corporation is formed or availed of for the principal purpose of either avoiding the application of the mid-quarter convention or having the mid-quarter convention apply where it otherwise would not, the 40-percent test is applied at the partner, shareholder, or other appropriate level.

(7) *Certain nonrecognition transactions* .—(i) Except as provided in paragraph (b)(6) of this section, if depreciable property is transferred in a transaction described in section 168(i)(7)(B)(i) (other than in a transaction between members of a consolidated group) in the same taxable year that the property is placed in service by the transferor, the 40-percent test is applied by treating the transferred property as placed in service by the transferee on the date of transfer. Thus, if the aggregate basis of property (including the transferred property) placed in service by the transferee during the last three months of its taxable year exceeds 40 percent of the aggregate basis of property (including the transferred property) placed in service by the transferee during the taxable year, the mid-quarter convention applies to the transferee's depreciable property, including the trans-

ferred property. The depreciable basis of the transferred property is not taken into account by the transferor in applying the 40-percent test for the taxable year that the transferor placed the property in service.

(ii) In applying the applicable convention to determine when the recovery period for the transferred property begins, the date on which the transferor placed the property in service must be used. Thus, for example, if the mid-quarter convention applies, the recovery period for the transferred property begins on the mid-point of the quarter of the taxable year that the transferor placed the property in service. If the transferor placed the transferred property in service in a short taxable year, then for purposes of applying the applicable convention and allocating the depreciation deduction between the transferor and the transferee, the transferor is treated as having a full 12-month taxable year commencing on the first day of the short taxable year. The depreciation deduction for the transferor's taxable year in which the property was placed in service is allocated between the transferor and the transferee based on the number of months in the transferor's taxable year that each party held the property in service. For purposes of allocating the depreciation deduction, the transferor takes into account the month in which the property was placed in service but does not take into account the month in which the property was transferred. The transferee is allocated the remaining portion of the depreciation deduction for the transferor's taxable year in which the property was transferred. For the remainder of the transferee's current taxable year (if the transferee has a different taxable year than the transferor) and for subsequent taxable years, the depreciation deduction for the transferee is calculated by allocating to the transferee's taxable year the depreciation attributable to each recovery year, or portion thereof, that falls within the transferee's taxable year. However, see § 1.168(k)-2(g)(1)(iii) for a special rule regarding the allocation of the additional first year depreciation deduction in the case of certain contributions of property to a partnership under section 721.

(iii) If the applicable convention for the transferred property has not been determined by the time the transferor files its income tax return for the year of transfer because the transferee's taxable year has not ended, the transferor may use either the mid-quarter or the half-year convention in determining the depreciation deduction for the property. However, the transferor must specify on the depreciation form filed for the taxable year that the applicable convention has not been determined for the property. If the transferee determines that a different convention applies to the transferred property, the transferor should redetermine the depreciation deduction on the property, and, within the period of limitation, should file an amended income tax return for the taxable year and pay any additional tax due plus interest.

(iv) The provisions of this paragraph (b)(7) are illustrated by the following example.

*Example.* (i) During 1991, C, a calendar-year taxpayer, purchases satellite equipment costing $100,000, and computer equipment costing $15,000. The satellite equipment is placed in service in January, and the computer equipment in February. On October 1, C transfers the computer equipment to Z Partnership in a transaction described in section 721. During 1991, Z, a calendar-year partnership, purchases 30 office desks for a total of $15,000. The desks are placed in service in June. These are the only items of depreciable property placed in service by C and Z during 1991.

(ii) In applying the 40-percent test, because C transferred the computer equipment in a transaction described in section 168(i)(7)(B)(i) in the same taxable year that C placed it in service, the computer equipment is treated as placed in service by the transferee, Z, on the date of transfer, October 1. The 40-percent test is satisfied with respect to Z, because the computer equipment is placed in service during the last three months of Z's taxable year and its basis ($15,000) exceeds 40 percent of the aggregate basis of property placed in service by Z during the taxable year (desks and computer equipment with an aggregate basis of $30,000).

(iii) In applying the mid-quarter convention to determine when the computer equipment is deemed to be placed in service, the date on which C placed the property in service is used. Accordingly, because C placed the computer equipment in service during the first quarter of its taxable year, the computer equipment is deemed placed in service on February 15, 1991, the mid-point of the first quarter of C's taxable year. The depreciation deduction allowable for C's 1991 taxable year, $5,250 ($15,000 × 40 percent × 10.5⁄12), is allocated between C and Z based on the number of months in C's taxable year that C and Z held the property in service. Thus, because the property was in service for 11 months during C's 1991 taxable year and C held it for 8 of those 11 months, C is allocated $3,818 ( 8⁄11 × $5,250). Z is allocated $1,432, the remaining 3⁄11 of the $5,250 depreciation deduction for C's 1991 taxable year. For 1992, Z's depreciation deduction for the computer equipment is $3,900, the sum of the remaining 1.5 months of depreciation deduction for the first recovery year and 10.5 months of depreciation deduction for the second recovery year (($15,000 × 40 percent × 1.5⁄12) + ($9,000 × 40 percent × 10.5/12)).

(c) *Disposition of property subject to the half-year or mid-quarter convention .*—(1) *In general .*—If depreciable property is subject to the half-year (or mid-quarter) convention in the taxable year in which it is placed in service, it also is subject to the half-year (or mid-quarter) convention in the taxable year in which it is disposed of.

(2) *Example .*—The provisions of paragraph (c)(1) of this section are illustrated by the following example.

*Example.* In October 1991, B, a calendar-year taxpayer, purchases and places in service a light general purpose truck costing $10,000. B does not elect to expense any part of the cost of the truck, and this is the only item of depreciable property placed in service by B during 1991. The 40-percent test is satisfied and the mid-quarter convention applies, because the truck is placed in service during the last three months of the taxable year and no other assets are placed in service in that year. In April 1993 (prior to the end of the truck's recovery period), B sells the truck. The mid-quarter convention applies in determining the depreciation deduction for the truck in 1993, the year of disposition.

(d) *Effective dates .*—(1) *In general .*—This section applies to depreciable property placed in service in taxable years ending after January 30, 1991. For depreciable property placed in service after December 31, 1986, in taxable years ending on or before January 30, 1991, a taxpayer may use a method other than the method provided in this section in applying the 40-percent test and the applicable convention, provided the method is reasonable and is consistently applied to the taxpayer's property.

(2) *Qualified property, 50-percent bonus depreciation property, or qualified New York Liberty Zone property .*—This section also applies to qualified property under section 168(k)(2) or qualified New York Liberty Zone property under section 1400L(b) acquired by a taxpayer after September 10, 2001, and to 50-percent percent bonus depreciation property under section 168(k)(4) acquired by a taxpayer after May 5, 2003. The last sentences in paragraphs (b)(3)(ii) and (b)(7)(ii) of this section apply to qualified property under section 168(k)(2) placed in service by a taxpayer during or after the taxpayer's taxable year that includes September 24, 2019. However, a taxpayer may choose to apply the last sentences in paragraphs (b)(3)(ii) and (b)(7)(ii) of this section to qualified property under section 168(k)(2) acquired and placed in service after September 27, 2017, by the taxpayer during

taxable years ending on or after September 28, 2017. A taxpayer may rely on the last sentences in paragraphs (b)(3)(ii) and (b)(7)(ii) of this section in regulation project REG-104397-18 (2018-41 I.R.B. 558) (see §601.601(d)(2)(ii)(*b*) of this chapter) for qualified property under section 168(k)(2) acquired and placed in service after September 27, 2017, by the taxpayer during taxable years ending on or after September 28, 2017, and ending before the taxpayer's taxable year that includes September 24, 2019.

(3) *Like-kind exchanges and involuntary conversions* .—(3) Like-kind exchanges and involuntary conversions.—The last sentence in paragraph (b)(3)(i) and the second sentence in paragraph (b)(3)(ii) of this section apply to exchanges to which section 1031 applies, and involuntary conversions to which section 1033 applies, of MACRS property for which the time of disposition and the time of replacement both occur after February 27, 2004. [Reg. 1.168(d)-1.]

**.01 Historical Comment:** Proposed 12/31/90. Adopted 10/28/92 by T.D. 8444. Amended 9/5/2003 by T.D. 9091, 2/27/2004 by T.D. 9115, 8/28/2006 by T.D. 9283, 2/26/2007 by T.D. 9314 and 9/17/2019 by T.D. 9874.

## ¶ 562

## Reg. § 1.168(h)-1

§1.168(h)-1. **Like-kind exchanges involving tax-exempt use property.**— (a) *Scope* .—(1) This section applies with respect to a direct or indirect transfer of property among related persons, including transfers made through a qualified intermediary (as defined in §1.1031(k)-1(g)(4)) or other unrelated person, (a transfer) if—

(i) Section 1031 applies to any party to the transfer or to any related transaction; and

(ii) A principal purpose of the transfer or any related transaction is to avoid or limit the application of the alternative depreciation system (within the meaning of section 168(g)).

(2) For purposes of this section, a person is related to another person if they bear a relationship specified in section 267(b) or section 707(b)(1).

(b) *Allowable depreciation deduction for property subject to this section* .—(1) *In general* .—Property (tainted property) transferred directly or indirectly to a taxpayer by a related person (related party) as part of, or in connection with, a transaction in which the related party receives tax-exempt use property (related tax-exempt use property) will, if the tainted property is subject to an allowance for depreciation, be treated in the same manner as the related tax-exempt use property for purposes of determining the allowable depreciation deduction under section 167(a). Under this paragraph (b), the tainted property is depreciated by the taxpayer over the remaining recovery period of, and using the same depreciation method and convention as that of, the related tax-exempt use property.

(2) *Limitations* .—(i) *Taxpayer's basis in related tax-exempt use property* .—The rules of this paragraph (b) apply only with respect to so much of the taxpayer's basis in the tainted property as does not exceed the taxpayer's adjusted basis in the related tax-exempt use property prior to the transfer. Any excess of the taxpayer's basis in the tainted property over its adjusted basis in the related tax-exempt use property prior to the transfer is treated as property to which this section does not apply. This paragraph (b)(2)(i) does not apply if the related tax-exempt use property is not acquired from the taxpayer (e.g., if the taxpayer acquires the tainted property for cash but section 1031 nevertheless applies to the related party because the transfer involves a qualified intermediary).

(ii) *Application of section 168(i)(7)* .—This section does not apply to so much of the taxpayer's basis in the tainted property as is subject to section 168(i)(7).

(c) *Related tax-exempt use property* .—(1) For purposes of paragraph (b) of this section, related tax-exempt use property includes—

(i) Property that is tax-exempt use property (as defined in section 168(h)) at the time of the transfer; and

(ii) Property that does not become tax-exempt use property until after the transfer if, at the time of the transfer, it was intended that the property become tax-exempt use property.

(2) For purposes of determining the remaining recovery period of the related tax-exempt use property in the circumstances described in paragraph (c)(1)(ii) of this section, the related tax-exempt use property will be treated as having, prior to the transfer, a lease term equal to the term of any lease that causes such property to become tax-exempt use property.

(d) *Examples* .—The following examples illustrate the application of this section. The examples do not address common law doctrines or other authorities that may apply to recharacterize or alter the effects of the transactions described therein. Unless otherwise indicated, parties to the transactions are not related to one another.

*Example 1.* (i) X owns all of the stock of two subsidiaries, B and Z. X, B and Z do not file a consolidated federal income tax return. On May 5, 1995, B purchases an aircraft ( *FA*) for $1 million and leases it to a foreign airline whose income is not subject to United States taxation and which is a tax-exempt entity as defined in section 168(h)(2). On the same date, Z owns an aircraft ( *DA*) with a fair market value of $1 million, which has been, and continues to be, leased to an airline that is a United States taxpayer. Z's adjusted basis in DA is $0. The next day, at a time when each aircraft is still worth $1 million, B transfers FA to Z (subject to the lease to the foreign airline) in exchange for DA (subject to the lease to the airline that is a United States taxpayer). Z realizes gain of $1 million on the exchange, but that gain is not recognized pursuant to section 1031(a) because the exchange is of like-kind properties. Assume that a principal purpose of the transfer of DA to B or of FA to Z is to avoid the application of the alternative depreciation system. Following the exchange, Z has a $0 basis in FA pursuant to section 1031(d). B has a $1 million basis in DA.

(ii) B has acquired property from Z, a related person; Z's gain is not recognized pursuant to section 1031(a); Z has received tax-exempt use property as part of the transaction; and a principal purpose of the transfer of DA to B or of FA to Z is to avoid the application of the alternative depreciation system. Accordingly, the transaction is within the scope of this section. Pursuant to paragraph (b) of this section, B must recover its $1 million basis in DA over the remaining recovery period of, and using the same depreciation method and convention as that of, FA, the related tax-exempt use property.

(iii) If FA did not become tax-exempt use property until after the exchange, it would still be related tax-exempt use property and paragraph (b) of this section would apply if, at the time of the exchange, it was intended that FA become tax-exempt use property.

*Example 2.* (i) X owns all of the stock of two subsidiaries, B and Z. X, B and Z do not file a consolidated federal income tax return. B and Z each own identical aircraft. B's aircraft ( *FA*) is leased to a tax-exempt entity as defined in section 168(h)(2) and has a fair market value of $1 million and an adjusted basis of $500,000. Z's aircraft (DA) is leased to a United States taxpayer and has a fair market value of $1 million and an adjusted basis of $10,000. On May 1, 1995, B and Z exchange aircraft, subject to their respective leases. B realizes gain of $500,000 and Z realizes gain of $990,000, but neither person recognizes gain because of the operation of section 1031(a). Moreover, assume that a principal purpose of the transfer of DA to B or of FA to Z is to avoid the application of the alternative depreciation system.

(ii) As in *Example 1*, B has acquired property from Z, a related person; Z's gain is not recognized pursuant to section 1031(a); Z has received tax-exempt use property as part of the transaction; and a principal purpose of the transfer of DA to B or of FA to Z is to avoid the application of the alternative depreciation system. Thus, the transaction is within the scope of this section even though B has held tax-exempt use property for a period of time and, during that time, has used the alternative depreciation system with respect to such property. Pursuant to paragraph (b) of this section, B, which has a substituted basis determined pursuant to section 1031(d) of $500,000 in DA, must depreciate the aircraft over the remaining recovery period of FA, using the same depreciation method and convention. Z holds tax-exempt use property with a basis of $10,000, which must be depreciated under the alternative depreciation system.

(iii) Assume the same facts as in paragraph (i) of this *Example 2*, except that B and Z are members of an affiliated group that files a consolidated federal income tax return. Of B's $500,000 basis in DA, $10,000 is subject to section 168(i)(7) and therefore not subject to this section. The remaining $490,000 of basis is subject to this section. But see § 1.1502-80(f) making section 1031 inapplicable to intercompany transactions occurring in consolidated return years beginning on or after July 12, 1995.

(e) *Effective date* .—This section applies to transfers made on or after April 20, 1995. [Reg. § 1.168(h)-1.]

**.01 Historical Comment:** Proposed 4/21/95. Adopted 4/26/96 by T.D. 8667.

## ¶ 564

## Reg. § 1.168(i)-0

§ 1.168(i)-0. **Table of contents for the general asset account rules.**—This section lists the major paragraphs contained in Reg. § 1.168(i)-1.

*§ 1.168(i)-1. General asset accounts.*

(a) Scope.

(b) Definitions.

(1) Unadjusted depreciable basis.

(2) Unadjusted depreciable basis of the general asset account.

(3) Adjusted depreciable basis of the general asset account.

(4) Building.

(5) Expensed cost.

(6) Mass assets.

(7) Portion of an asset.

(8) Remaining adjusted depreciable basis of the general asset account.

(9) Structural component.

(c) Establishment of general asset accounts.

(1) Assets eligible for general asset accounts.

(i) General rules.

(ii) Special rules for assets generating foreign source income.

(2) Grouping assets in general asset accounts.

(i) General rules.

(ii) Special rules.

(3) Examples.

(d) Determination of depreciation allowance.
(1) In general.
(2) Assets in general asset account are eligible for additional first year depreciation deduction.
(3) No assets in general asset account are eligible for additional first year depreciation deduction.
(4) Special rule for passenger automobiles.
(e) Dispositions from a general asset account.
(1) Scope and definition.
(i) In general.
(ii) Disposition of a portion of an asset.
(2) General rules for a disposition.
(i) No immediate recovery of basis.
(ii) Treatment of amount realized.
(iii) Effect of disposition on a general asset account.
(iv) Coordination with nonrecognition provisions.
(v) Manner of disposition.
(vi) Disposition by transfer to a supplies account.
(vii) Leasehold improvements.
(viii) Determination of asset disposed of.
(ix) Examples.
(3) Special rules.
(i) In general.
(ii) Disposition of all assets remaining in a general asset account.
(iii) Disposition of an asset in a qualifying disposition.
(iv) Transactions subject to section 168(i)(7).
(v) Transactions subject to section 1031 or 1033.
(vi) Technical termination of a partnership.
(vii) Anti-abuse rule.
(f) Assets generating foreign source income.
(1) In general.
(2) Source of ordinary income, gain, or loss.
(i) Source determined by allocation and apportionment of depreciation allowed.
(g) Assets subject to recapture.
(h) Changes in use.
(1) Conversion to any personal use.
(2) Change in use results in a different recovery period and/or depreciation method.
(i) No effect on general asset account election.
(ii) Asset is removed from the general asset account.
(iii) New general asset account is established.
(i) Redetermination of basis.
(j) Identification of disposed or converted asset.
(k) Effect of adjustments on prior dispositions.
(l) Election.
(1) Irrevocable election.
(2) Time for making election.
(3) Manner of making election.
(m) Effective/applicability dates.

[Reg. § 1.168(i)-0.]

**.01 Historical Comment:** Proposed 8/31/92. Adopted 10/7/94 by T.D. 8566. Amended 2/27/2004 by T.D. 9115, 6/16/2004 by T.D. 9132, 2/26/2007 by T.D. 9314, 12/23/2011 by T.D. 9564 (corrected 12/18/2012) and 8/14/2014 by T.D. 9689.

## ¶ 565

### Reg. § 1.168(i)-1

§ 1.168(i)-1. **General asset accounts.**— (a) *Scope* .—This section provides rules for general asset accounts under section 168(i)(4). The provisions of this section apply only to assets for which an election has been made under paragraph (l) of this section.

(b) *Definitions* .—For purposes of this section, the following definitions apply:

(1) *Unadjusted depreciable basis* has the same meaning given such term in § 1.168(b)-1(a)(3).

(2) *Unadjusted depreciable basis of the general asset account* is the sum of the unadjusted depreciable bases of all assets included in the general asset account.

(3) *Adjusted depreciable basis of the general asset account* is the unadjusted depreciable basis of the general asset account less the adjustments to basis described in section 1016(a)(2) and (3).

(4) *Building* has the same meaning as that term is defined in § 1.48-1(e)(1).

(5) *Expensed cost* is the amount of any allowable credit or deduction treated as a deduction allowable for depreciation or amortization for purposes of section 1245 (for example, a credit allowable under section 30 or a deduction allowable under section 179, section 179A, or section 190). Expensed cost does not include any additional first year depreciation deduction.

(6) *Mass assets* is a mass or group of individual items of depreciable assets—

(i) That are not necessarily homogenous;

(ii) Each of which is minor in value relative to the total value of the mass or group;

(iii) Numerous in quantity;

(iv) Usually accounted for only on a total dollar or quantity basis;

(v) With respect to which separate identification is impracticable; and

(vi) Placed in service in the same taxable year.

(7) *Portion of an asset* is any part of an asset that is less than the entire asset as determined under paragraph (e)(2)(viii) of this section.

(8) *Remaining adjusted depreciable basis of the general asset account* is the unadjusted depreciable basis of the general asset account less the amount of the additional first year depreciation deduction allowed or allowable, whichever is greater, for the general asset account.

(9) *Structural component* has the same meaning as that term is defined in § 1.48-1(e)(2).

(c) *Establishment of general asset accounts* .—(1) *Assets eligible for general asset accounts* .—(i) *General rules* .—Assets that are subject to either the general depreciation system of section 168(a) or the alternative depreciation system of section 168(g) may be accounted for in one or more general asset accounts. An asset is included in a general asset account only to the extent of the asset's unadjusted depreciable basis. However, an asset is not to be included in a general asset account if the asset is used both in a trade or business or for the production of income and in a personal activity at any time during the taxable year in which the asset is placed in service by the taxpayer or if the asset is placed in service and disposed of during the same taxable year.

(ii) *Special rules for assets generating foreign source income* .—(A) Assets that generate foreign source income, both United States and foreign source income, or combined gross income of a foreign sales corporation (as defined in former section 922), domestic international sales corporation (as defined in section 992(a)), or possession corporation (as defined in section 936) and its related supplier may be included in a general asset account if the requirements of paragraph (c)(2)(i) of this section are satisfied. If, however, the inclusion of these assets in a general asset account results in a substantial distortion of income, the Commissioner may disregard the general asset account election and make any reallocations of income or expense necessary to clearly reflect income.

(B) A general asset account shall be treated as a single asset for purposes of applying the rules in § 1.861-9T(g)(3) (relating to allocation and apportionment of interest expense under the asset method). A general asset account that generates income in more than one grouping of income (statutory and residual) is a multiple category asset (as defined in § 1.861-9T(g)(3)(ii)), and the income yield from the general asset account must be determined by applying the rules for multiple category assets as if the general asset account were a single asset.

(2) *Grouping assets in general asset accounts* .—(i) *General rules* .—If a taxpayer makes the election under paragraph (l) of this section, assets that are subject to the election are grouped into one or more general asset accounts. Assets that are eligible to be grouped into a single general asset account may be divided into more than one general asset account. Each general asset account must include only assets that—

(A) Have the same applicable depreciation method;

(B) Have the same applicable recovery period;

(C) Have the same applicable convention; and

(D) Are placed in service by the taxpayer in the same taxable year.

(ii) *Special rules* .—In addition to the general rules in paragraph (c)(2)(i) of this section, the following rules apply when establishing general asset accounts—

(A) Assets subject to the mid-quarter convention may only be grouped into a general asset account with assets that are placed in service in the same quarter of the taxable year;

(B) Assets subject to the mid-month convention may only be grouped into a general asset account with assets that are placed in service in the same month of the taxable year;

(C) Passenger automobiles for which the depreciation allowance is limited under section 280F(a) must be grouped into a separate general asset account;

(D) Assets not eligible for any additional first year depreciation deduction, including assets for which the taxpayer elected not to deduct the additional first year depreciation, provided by, for example, section 168(k), section 168(l), section 168(m), section 168(n), section 1400L(b), or section 1400N(d), must be grouped into a separate general asset account;

(E) Assets eligible for the additional first year depreciation deduction may only be grouped into a general asset account with assets for which the taxpayer claimed the same percentage of the additional first year depreciation (for example, 30 percent, 50 percent, or 100 percent);

(F) Except for passenger automobiles described in paragraph (c)(2)(ii)(C) of this section, listed property (as defined in section 280F(d)(4)) must be grouped into a separate general asset account;

(G) Assets for which the depreciation allowance for the placed-in-service year is not determined by using an optional depreciation table (for further guidance, see section 8 of Rev. Proc. 87-57, 1987-2 CB 687, 693 (see § 601.601(d)(2) of this chapter)) must be grouped into a separate general asset account;

(H) Mass assets that are or will be subject to paragraph (j)(2)(i)(D) of this section (disposed of or converted mass asset is identified by a mortality dispersion table) must be grouped into a separate general asset account; and

(I) Assets subject to paragraph (h)(2)(iii)(A) of this section (change in use results in a shorter recovery period or a more accelerated depreciation method) for which the depreciation allowance for the year of change (as defined in § 1.168(i)-4(a)) is not determined by using an optional depreciation table must be grouped into a separate general asset account.

(3) *Examples*.—The following examples illustrate the application of this paragraph (c):

*Example 1.* In 2014, J, a proprietorship with a calendar year-end, purchases and places in service one item of equipment that costs $550,000. This equipment is section 179 property and also is 5-year property under section 168(e). On its Federal tax return for 2014, J makes an election under section 179 to expense $25,000 of the equipment's cost and makes an election under paragraph (l) of this section to include the equipment in a general asset account. As a result, the unadjusted depreciable basis of the equipment is $525,000. In accordance with paragraph (c)(1) of this section, J must include only $525,000 of the equipment's cost in the general asset account.

*Example 2.* In 2014, K, a proprietorship with a calendar year-end, purchases and places in service 100 items of equipment. All of these items are 5-year property under section 168(e), are not listed property, and are not eligible for any additional first year depreciation deduction. On its Federal tax return for 2014, K does not make an election under section 179 to expense the cost of any of the 100 items of equipment and does make an election under paragraph (l) of this section to include the 100 items of equipment in a general asset account. K depreciates its 5-year property placed in service in 2014 using the optional depreciation table that corresponds with the general depreciation system, the 200-percent declining balance method, a 5-year recovery period, and the half-year convention. In accordance with paragraph (c)(2) of this section, K includes all of the 100 items of equipment in one general asset account.

*Example 3.* The facts are the same as in *Example 2*, except that K decides not to include all of the 100 items of equipment in one general asset account. Instead and in accordance with paragraph (c)(2) of this section, K establishes 100 general asset accounts and includes one item of equipment in each general asset account.

*Example 4.* L, a calendar-year corporation, is a wholesale distributer. In 2014, L places in service the following properties for use in its wholesale distribution business: computers, automobiles, and forklifts. On its Federal tax return for 2014, L does not make an election under section 179 to expense the cost of any of these items of equipment and does make an election under paragraph (l) of this section to include all of these items of equipment in a general asset account. All of these items are 5-year property under section 168(e) and are not eligible for any additional first year depreciation deduction. The computers are listed property, and the automobiles are listed property and are subject to section 280F(a). L depreciates its 5-year property placed in service in 2014 using the optional depreciation table that corresponds with the general depreciation system, the 200-percent declining balance method, a 5-year recovery period, and the half-year convention. Although the computers, automobiles, and forklifts are 5-year property, L cannot include all of them in one general asset account because the computers and automobiles are listed property. Further, even though the computers and automobiles are listed property, L cannot include them in one general asset account because the automobiles also are subject to section 280F(a). In accordance with paragraph (c)(2) of this section, L establishes three general asset accounts: one for the computers, one for the automobiles, and one for the forklifts.

*Example 5.* M, a fiscal-year corporation with a taxable year ending June 30, purchases and places in service ten items of new equipment in October 2014, and purchases and places in service five other items of new equipment in February 2015. On its Federal tax return for the taxable year ending June 30, 2015, M does not make an election under section 179 to expense the cost of any of these items of equipment and does make an election under paragraph (l) of this section to include all of these items of equipment in a general asset account. All of these items of equipment are 7-year property under section 168(e), are not listed property, and are property described in section 168(k)(2)(B). All of the ten items of equipment placed in service in October 2014 are eligible for the 50-percent additional first year depreciation deduction provided by section 168(k)(1). All of the five items of equipment placed in service in February 2015 are not eligible for any additional first year depreciation deduction. M depreciates its 7-year property placed in service for the taxable year ending June 30, 2015, using the optional depreciation table that corresponds with the general depreciation system, the 200-percent declining balance method, a 7-year recovery period, and the half-year convention. Although the 15 items of equipment are depreciated using the same depreciation method, recovery period, and convention, M cannot include all of them in one general asset account because some of items of equipment are not eligible for any additional first year depreciation deduction. In accordance with paragraph (c)(2) of this section, M establishes two general asset accounts: one for the ten items of equipment eligible for the 50-percent additional first year depreciation deduction and one for the five items of equipment not eligible for any additional first year depreciation deduction.

(d) *Determination of depreciation allowance*.—(1) *In general*.—Depreciation allowances are determined for each general asset account. The depreciation allowances must be recorded in a depreciation reserve account for each general asset account. The allowance for depreciation under this section constitutes the amount of depreciation allowable under section 167(a).

(2) *Assets in general asset account are eligible for additional first year depreciation deduction*.—If all the assets in a general asset account are eligible for the additional first year depreciation deduction, the taxpayer first must determine the allowable additional first year depreciation deduction for the general asset account for the placed-in-service year and then must determine the amount otherwise allowable as a depreciation deduction for the general asset account for the placed-in-service year and any subsequent taxable year. The allowable additional first year depreciation deduction for the general asset account for the placed-in-service year is determined by multiplying the unadjusted depreciable basis of the general asset account by the additional first year depreciation deduction percentage applicable to the assets in the account (for example, 30 percent, 50 percent, or 100 percent). The remaining adjusted depreciable basis of the general asset account then is depreciated using the applicable depreciation method, recovery period, and convention for the assets in the account.

(3) *No assets in general asset account are eligible for additional first year depreciation deduction*.—If none of the assets in a general asset account are eligible for the additional first year depreciation deduction, the taxpayer must determine the

allowable depreciation deduction for the general asset account for the placed-in-service year and any subsequent taxable year by using the applicable depreciation method, recovery period, and convention for the assets in the account.

(4) *Special rule for passenger automobiles* .—For purposes of applying section 280F(a), the depreciation allowance for a general asset account established for passenger automobiles is limited for each taxable year to the amount prescribed in section 280F(a) multiplied by the excess of the number of automobiles originally included in the account over the number of automobiles disposed of during the taxable year or in any prior taxable year in a transaction described in paragraph (e)(3)(iii) (disposition of an asset in a qualifying disposition), paragraph (e)(3)(iv) (transactions subject to section 168(i)(7)), paragraph (e)(3)(v) (transactions subject to section 1031 or section 1033), paragraph (e)(3)(vi) (technical termination of a partnership), paragraph (e)(3)(vii) (anti-abuse rule), paragraph (g) (assets subject to recapture), or paragraph (h)(1) (conversion to any personal use) of this section.

(e) *Dispositions from a general asset account* .—(1) *Scope and definition* .—(i) *In general* .—This paragraph (e) provides rules applicable to dispositions of assets included in a general asset account. For purposes of this paragraph (e), an asset in a general asset account is disposed of when ownership of the asset is transferred or when the asset is permanently withdrawn from use either in the taxpayer's trade or business or in the production of income. A disposition includes the sale, exchange, retirement, physical abandonment, or destruction of an asset. A disposition also occurs when an asset is transferred to a supplies, scrap, or similar account, or when a portion of an asset is disposed of as described in paragraph (e)(1)(ii) of this section. If a structural component, or a portion thereof, of a building is disposed of in a disposition described in paragraph (e)(1)(ii) of this section, a disposition also includes the disposition of such structural component or such portion thereof.

(ii) *Disposition of a portion of an asset* .—For purposes of applying paragraph (e) of this section, a disposition includes a disposition of a portion of an asset in a general asset account as a result of a casualty event described in section 165, a disposition of a portion of an asset in a general asset account for which gain, determined without regard to section 1245 or section 1250, is not recognized in whole or in part under section 1031 or section 1033, a transfer of a portion of an asset in a general asset account in a transaction described in section 168(i)(7)(B), a sale of a portion of an asset in a general asset account, or a disposition of a portion of an asset in a general asset account in a transaction described in paragraph (e)(3)(vii)(B) of this section. For other transactions, a disposition includes a disposition of a portion of an asset in a general asset account only if the taxpayer makes the election under paragraph (e)(3)(ii) of this section to terminate the general asset account in which that disposed portion is included or makes the election under paragraph (e)(3)(iii) of this section for that disposed portion.

(2) *General rules for a disposition* .—(i) *No immediate recovery of basis* .—Except as provided in paragraph (e)(3) of this section, immediately before a disposition of any asset in a general asset account or a disposition of a portion of such asset as described in paragraph (e)(1)(ii) of this section, the asset or the portion of the asset, as applicable, is treated as having an adjusted depreciable basis (as defined in § 1.168(b)-1(a)(4)) of zero for purposes of section 1011. Therefore, no loss is realized upon the disposition of an asset from the general asset account or upon the disposition of a portion of such asset as described in paragraph (e)(1)(ii) of this section. Similarly, where an asset or a portion of an asset, as applicable, is disposed of by transfer to a supplies, scrap, or similar account, the basis of the asset

or the portion of the asset, as applicable, in the supplies, scrap, or similar account will be zero.

(ii) *Treatment of amount realized* .—Any amount realized on a disposition is recognized as ordinary income, notwithstanding any other provision of subtitle A of the Internal Revenue Code (Code), to the extent the sum of the unadjusted depreciable basis of the general asset account and any expensed cost (as defined in paragraph (b)(5) of this section) for assets in the account exceeds any amounts previously recognized as ordinary income upon the disposition of other assets in the account or upon the disposition of portions of such assets as described in paragraph (e)(1)(ii) of this section. The recognition and character of any excess amount realized are determined under other applicable provisions of the Code other than sections 1245 and 1250 or provisions of the Code that treat gain on a disposition as subject to section 1245 or section 1250.

(iii) *Effect of disposition on a general asset account* .—Except as provided in paragraph (e)(3) of this section, the unadjusted depreciable basis and the depreciation reserve of the general asset account are not affected as a result of a disposition of an asset from the general asset account or of a disposition of a portion of such asset as described in paragraph (e)(1)(ii) of this section.

(iv) *Coordination with nonrecognition provisions* .—For purposes of determining the basis of an asset or a portion of an asset, as applicable, acquired in a transaction, other than a transaction described in paragraph (e)(3)(iv) (pertaining to transactions subject to section 168(i)(7)), paragraph (e)(3)(v) (pertaining to transactions subject to section 1031 or section 1033), and paragraph (e)(3)(vi) (pertaining to technical terminations of partnerships) of this section, to which a nonrecognition section of the Code applies, determined without regard to this section, the amount of ordinary income recognized under this paragraph (e)(2) is treated as the amount of gain recognized on the disposition.

(v) *Manner of disposition* .—The manner of disposition (for example, normal retirement, abnormal retirement, ordinary retirement, or extraordinary retirement) is not taken into account in determining whether a disposition occurs or gain or loss is recognized.

(vi) *Disposition by transfer to a supplies account* .—If a taxpayer made an election under § 1.162-3(d) to treat the cost of any rotable spare part, temporary spare part, or standby emergency spare part (as defined in § 1.162-3(c)) as a capital expenditure subject to the allowance for depreciation and also made an election under paragraph (l) of this section to include that rotable, temporary, or standby emergency spare part in a general asset account, the taxpayer can dispose of the rotable, temporary, or standby emergency spare part by transferring it to a supplies account only if the taxpayer has obtained the consent of the Commissioner to revoke the § 1.162-3(d) election. If a taxpayer made an election under § 1.162-3T(d) to treat the cost of any material and supply (as defined in § 1.162-3T(c)(1)) as a capital expenditure subject to the allowance for depreciation and also made an election under paragraph (l) of this section to include that material and supply in a general asset account, the taxpayer can dispose of the material and supply by transferring it to a supplies account only if the taxpayer has obtained the consent of the Commissioner to revoke the § 1.162-3T(d) election. See § 1.162-3(d)(3) for the procedures for revoking a § 1.162-3(d) or a § 1.162-3T(d) election.

(vii) *Leasehold improvements* .—The rules of paragraph (e) of this section also apply to—

(A) A lessor of leased property that made an improvement to that property for the lessee of the property, has a depreciable basis in the improvement, made an election under paragraph (l) of this section to include the improvement in a general asset account, and disposes of the improvement, or disposes of a portion of the improvement as described in paragraph (e) (1) (ii) of this section, before or upon the termination of the lease with the lessee. See section 168(i) (8) (B); and

(B) A lessee of leased property that made an improvement to that property, has a depreciable basis in the improvement, made an election under paragraph (l) of this section to include the improvement in a general asset account, and disposes of the improvement, or disposes of a portion of the improvement as described in paragraph (e) (1) (ii) of this section, before or upon the termination of the lease.

(viii) *Determination of asset disposed of* .—(A) *General rules* .—For purposes of applying paragraph (e) of this section to the disposition of an asset in a general asset account, instead of the disposition of the general asset account, the facts and circumstances of each disposition are considered in determining what is the appropriate asset disposed of. The asset for disposition purposes may not consist of items placed in service by the taxpayer on different dates, without taking into account the applicable convention. For purposes of determining what is the appropriate asset disposed of, the unit of property determination under § 1.263(a)-3(e) or in published guidance in the Internal Revenue Bulletin under section 263(a) (see § 601.601(d) (2) of this chapter) and the distinct asset determination under § 1.1031(a)-3(a) (4) do not apply.

(B) *Special rules* .—In addition to the general rules in paragraph (e) (2) (viii) (A) of this section, the following rules apply for purposes of applying paragraph (e) of this section to the disposition of an asset in a general asset account instead of the disposition of the general asset account:

*(1)* Each building, including its structural components, is the asset, except as provided in § 1.1250-1(a) (2) (ii) or in paragraph (e) (2) (viii) (B) ( *2*) or ( *4*) of this section.

*(2)* If a building has two or more condominium or cooperative units, each condominium or cooperative unit, including its structural components, is the asset, except as provided in § 1.1250-1(a) (2) (ii) or in paragraph (e) (2) (viii) (B) ( *4*) of this section.

*(3)* If a taxpayer properly includes an item in one of the asset classes 00.11 through 00.4 of Rev. Proc. 87-56 (1987-2 CB 674) (see § 601.601(d) (2) of this chapter) or properly classifies an item in one of the categories under section 168(e) (3), except for a category that includes buildings or structural components (for example, retail motor fuels outlet, qualified leasehold improvement property, qualified restaurant property, and qualified retail improvement property), each item is the asset, provided that paragraph (e) (2) (viii) (B) ( *4*) of this section does not apply to the item. For example, each desk is the asset, each computer is the asset, and each qualified smart electric meter is the asset.

*(4)* If the taxpayer places in service an improvement or addition to an asset after the taxpayer placed the asset in service, the improvement or addition and, if applicable, its structural components are a separate asset.

(ix) *Examples* .—The following examples illustrate the application of this paragraph (e) (2):

*Example 1.* A, a calendar-year partnership, maintains one general asset account for one office building that cost $10 million. A discovers a leak in the roof of the building and decides to replace the entire roof. The roof is a structural component of the building. In accordance with paragraph (e) (2) (viii) (B) ( *1*) of this section, the office building, including its structural components, is the asset for disposition purposes. The retirement of the replaced roof is not a disposition of a portion of an asset as described in paragraph (e)(1)(ii) of this section. Thus, the retirement of the replaced roof is not a disposition under paragraph (e)(1) of this section. As a result, A continues to depreciate the $10 million cost of the general asset account. If A must capitalize the amount paid for the replacement roof pursuant to § 1.263(a)-3, the replacement roof is a separate asset for disposition purposes pursuant to paragraph (e)(2)(viii)(B)( *4*) of this section and for depreciation purposes pursuant to section 168(i)(6).

*Example 2.* B, a calendar-year commercial airline company, maintains one general asset account for five aircraft that cost a total of $500 million. These aircraft are described in asset class 45.0 of Rev. Proc. 87-56. B replaces the existing engines on one of the aircraft with new engines. Assume each aircraft is a unit of property as determined under § 1.263(a)-3(e)(3) and each engine of an aircraft is a major component or substantial structural part of the aircraft as determined under § 1.263(a)-3(k)(6). Assume also that B treats each aircraft as the asset for disposition purposes in accordance with paragraph (e)(2)(viii) of this section. The retirement of the replaced engines is not a disposition of a portion of an asset as described in paragraph (e)(1)(ii) of this section. Thus, the retirement of the replaced engines is not a disposition under paragraph (e)(1) of this section. As a result, B continues to depreciate the $500 million cost of the general asset account. If B must capitalize the amount paid for the replacement engines pursuant to § 1.263(a)-3, the replacement engines are a separate asset for disposition purposes pursuant to paragraph (e)(2)(viii)(B)( *4*) of this section and for depreciation purposes pursuant to section 168(i)(6).

*Example 3.* (i) R, a calendar-year corporation, maintains one general asset account for ten machines. The machines cost a total of $10,000 and are placed in service in June 2014. Of the ten machines, one machine costs $8,200 and nine machines cost a total of $1,800. Assume R depreciates this general asset account using the optional depreciation table that corresponds with the general depreciation system, the 200-percent declining balance method, a 5-year recovery period, and a half-year convention. R does not make a section 179 election for any of the machines, and all of the machines are not eligible for any additional first year depreciation deduction. As of January 1, 2015, the depreciation reserve of the account is $2,000 ($10,000 × 20%).

(ii) On February 8, 2015, R sells the machine that cost $8,200 to an unrelated party for $9,000. Under paragraph (e)(2)(i) of this section, this machine has an adjusted depreciable basis of zero.

(iii) On its 2015 tax return, R recognizes the amount realized of $9,000 as ordinary income because such amount does not exceed the unadjusted depreciable basis of the general asset account ($10,000), plus any expensed cost for assets in the account ($0), less amounts previously recognized as ordinary income ($0). Moreover, the unadjusted depreciable basis and depreciation reserve of the account are not affected by the disposition of the machine. Thus, the depreciation allowance for the account in 2015 is $3,200 ($10,000 × 32%).

*Example 4.* (i) The facts are the same as in *Example 3.* In addition, on June 4, 2016, R sells seven machines to an unrelated party for a total of $1,100. In accordance with paragraph (e)(2)(i) of this section, these machines have an adjusted depreciable basis of zero.

(ii) On its 2016 tax return, R recognizes $1,000 as ordinary income (the unadjusted depreciable basis of $10,000, plus the expensed cost of $0, less the amount of $9,000 previously recognized as ordinary income). The recognition and character of the excess amount realized of $100 ($1,100-$1,000) are determined under applicable provisions of the Code other than section 1245 (such as section 1231). Moreover, the unadjusted depreciable basis and depreciation reserve of the account are not affected by the disposition of the machines. Thus, the depreciation allowance for the account in 2016 is $1,920 ($10,000 × 19.2%).

(3) *Special rules* .—(i) *In general* .—This paragraph (e)(3) provides the rules for terminating general asset account treatment upon certain dispositions. While the rules under paragraphs (e)(3)(ii) and (iii) of this section are optional rules, the rules under paragraphs (e)(3)(iv), (v), (vi), and (vii) of this section are mandatory rules. A taxpayer elects to apply paragraph (e)(3)(ii) or (iii) of this section by reporting the gain, loss, or other deduction on the taxpayer's timely filed original Federal tax return, including extensions, for the taxable year in which the disposition occurs. However, if the loss is on account of the demolition of a structure to which section 280B and § 1.280B-1 apply, a taxpayer elects to apply paragraph (e)(3)(ii) or (iii) of this section by ending depreciation for the structure at the time of the disposition of the structure, taking into account the convention applicable to the general asset account in which the demolished structure was included, and reporting the amount of depreciation for that structure for the taxable year in which the disposition occurs on the taxpayer's timely filed original Federal tax return, including extensions, for that taxable year. A taxpayer may revoke the election to apply paragraph (e)(3)(ii) or (iii) of this section only by filing a request for a private letter ruling and obtaining the Commissioner's consent to revoke the election. The Commissioner may grant a request to revoke this election if the taxpayer acted reasonably and in good faith, and the revocation will not prejudice the interests of the Government. See generally § 301.9100-3 of this chapter. The election to apply paragraph (e)(3)(ii) or (iii) of this section may not be made or revoked through the filing of an application for change in accounting method. For purposes of applying paragraphs (e)(3)(iii) through (vii) of this section, see paragraph (j) of this section for identifying an asset disposed of and its unadjusted depreciable basis. Solely for purposes of applying paragraphs (e)(3)(iii), (e)(3)(iv)(C), (e)(3)(v)(B), and (e)(3)(vii) of this section, the term *asset* is:

(A) The asset as determined under paragraph (e)(2)(viii) of this section; or

(B) The portion of such asset that is disposed of in a disposition described in paragraph (e)(1)(ii) of this section.

(ii) *Disposition of all assets remaining in a general asset account* .—(A) *Optional termination of a general asset account* .—Upon the disposition of all of the assets, the last asset, or the remaining portion of the last asset in a general asset account, a taxpayer may apply this paragraph (e)(3)(ii) to recover the adjusted depreciable basis of the general asset account rather than having paragraph (e)(2) of this section apply. Under this paragraph (e)(3)(ii), the general asset account terminates and the amount of gain or loss for the general asset account is determined under section 1001(a) by taking into account the adjusted depreciable basis of the general asset account at the time of the disposition, as determined under the applicable convention for the general asset account. Whether and to what extent gain or loss is recognized is determined under other applicable provisions of the Code, including section 280B and § 1.280B-1. The character of the gain or loss is determined under other applicable provisions of the Code, except that the amount of gain subject to section 1245 is limited to the excess of the depreciation allowed or allowable for the general asset account, including any expensed cost, over any amounts previously recognized as ordinary income under paragraph (e)(2) of this section, and the amount of gain subject to section 1250 is limited to the excess of the additional depreciation allowed or allowable for the general asset account, over any amounts previously recognized as ordinary income under paragraph (e)(2) of this section.

(B) *Examples* .—The following examples illustrate the application of this paragraph (e)(3)(ii):

*Example 1.* (i) T, a calendar-year corporation, maintains a general asset account for 1,000 calculators. The calculators cost a total of $60,000 and are placed in service in 2014. Assume T depreciates this general asset account using the optional depreciation table that corresponds with the general depreciation system, the 200-percent declining balance method, a 5-year recovery period, and a half-year convention. T does not make a section 179 election for any of the calculators, and all of the calculators are not eligible for any additional first year depreciation deduction. In 2015, T sells 200 of the calculators to an unrelated party for a total of $10,000 and recognizes the $10,000 as ordinary income in accordance with paragraph (e)(2) of this section.

(ii) On March 26, 2016, T sells the remaining calculators in the general asset account to an unrelated party for $35,000. T elects to apply paragraph (e)(3)(ii) of this section. As a result, the account terminates and gain or loss is determined for the account.

(iii) On the date of disposition, the adjusted depreciable basis of the account is $23,040 (unadjusted depreciable basis of $60,000 less the depreciation allowed or allowable of $36,960). Thus, in 2016, T recognizes gain of $11,960 (amount realized of $35,000 less the adjusted depreciable basis of $23,040). The gain of $11,960 is subject to section 1245 to the extent of the depreciation allowed or allowable for the account, plus the expensed cost for assets in the account, less the amounts previously recognized as ordinary income ($36,960 + $0 - $10,000 = $26,960). As a result, the entire gain of $11,960 is subject to section 1245.

*Example 2.* (i) J, a calendar-year corporation, maintains a general asset account for one item of equipment. This equipment costs $2,000 and is placed in service in 2014. Assume J depreciates this general asset account using the optional depreciation table that corresponds with the general depreciation system, the 200-percent declining balance method, a 5-year recovery period, and a half-year convention. J does not make a section 179 election for the equipment, and it is not eligible for any additional first year depreciation deduction. In June 2016, J sells the equipment to an unrelated party for $1,000. J elects to apply paragraph (e)(3)(ii) of this section. As a result, the account terminates and gain or loss is determined for the account.

(ii) On the date of disposition, the adjusted depreciable basis of the account is $768 (unadjusted depreciable basis of $2,000 less the depreciation allowed or allowable of $1,232). Thus, in 2016, J recognizes gain of $232 (amount realized of $1,000 less the adjusted depreciable basis of $768). The gain of $232 is subject to section 1245 to the extent of the depreciation allowed or allowable for the account, plus the expensed cost for assets in the account, less the amounts previously recognized as ordinary income ($1,232 + $0 - $0 = $1,232). As a result, the entire gain of $232 is subject to section 1245.

(iii) *Disposition of an asset in a qualifying disposition* .—(A) *Optional determination of the amount of gain, loss, or other deduction* .—In the case of a qualifying disposition (described in paragraph (e)(3)(iii)(B) of this section) of an asset, a taxpayer may elect to apply this paragraph (e)(3)(iii) rather than having paragraph (e)(2) of this section apply. Under this paragraph (e)(3)(iii), general asset account treatment for the asset terminates as of the first day of the taxable year in which the qualifying disposition occurs, and the amount of gain, loss, or other deduction for the asset is determined under §1.168(i)-8 by taking into account the asset's adjusted depreciable basis at the time of the disposition. The adjusted depreciable basis of the asset at the time of the disposition, as determined under the applicable convention for the general asset account in which the asset was included, equals the unadjusted depreciable basis of the asset less the greater of the depreciation allowed or allowable for the asset. The allowable depreciation is computed by using the depreciation method, recovery period, and convention applicable to the general asset account in which the asset was included and by including the portion of the additional first year depreciation deduction claimed for the general asset account that is attributable to the asset disposed of. Whether and to what extent gain, loss, or other deduction is recognized is determined under other applicable provisions of the Code, including section 280B and § 1.280B-1. The character of the gain, loss, or other deduction is determined under other applicable provisions of the Code, except that the amount of gain subject to section 1245 or section 1250 is limited to the lesser of—

*(1)* The depreciation allowed or allowable for the asset, including any expensed cost or, in the case of section 1250 property, the additional depreciation allowed or allowable for the asset; or

*(2)* The excess of—

*(i)* The original unadjusted depreciable basis of the general asset account plus, in the case of section 1245 property originally included in the general asset account, any expensed cost; over

*(ii)* The cumulative amounts of gain previously recognized as ordinary income under either paragraph (e)(2) of this section or section 1245 or section 1250.

(B) *Qualifying dispositions* .—A *qualifying disposition* is a disposition that does not involve all the assets, the last asset, or the remaining portion of the last asset remaining in a general asset account and that is—

*(1)* A direct result of a fire, storm, shipwreck, or other casualty, or from theft;

*(2)* A charitable contribution for which a deduction is allowable under section 170;

*(3)* A direct result of a cessation, termination, or disposition of a business, manufacturing or other income producing process, operation, facility, plant, or other unit, other than by transfer to a supplies, scrap, or similar account; or

*(4)* A transaction, other than a transaction described in paragraph (e)(3)(iv) (pertaining to transactions subject to section 168(i)(7)), paragraph (e)(3)(v) (pertaining to transactions subject to section 1031 or section 1033), paragraph (e)(3)(vi) (pertaining to technical terminations of partnerships), or paragraph (e)(3)(vii) (anti-abuse rule) of this section, to which a nonrecognition section of the Internal Revenue Code applies (determined without regard to this section).

(C) *Effect of a qualifying disposition on a general asset account* .—If the taxpayer elects to apply this paragraph (e)(3)(iii) to a qualifying disposition of an asset, then—

*(1)* The asset is removed from the general asset account as of the first day of the taxable year in which the qualifying disposition occurs. For that taxable year, the taxpayer accounts for the asset in a single asset account in accordance with the rules under § 1.168(i)-7(b);

*(2)* The unadjusted depreciable basis of the general asset account is reduced by the unadjusted depreciable basis of the asset as of the first day of the taxable year in which the disposition occurs;

*(3)* The depreciation reserve of the general asset account is reduced by the greater of the depreciation allowed or allowable for the asset as of the end of the taxable year immediately preceding the year of disposition. The allowable depreciation is computed by using the depreciation method, recovery period, and convention applicable to the general asset account in which the asset was included and by including the portion of the additional first year depreciation deduction claimed for the general asset account that is attributable to the asset disposed of; and

*(4)* For purposes of determining the amount of gain realized on subsequent dispositions that is subject to ordinary income treatment under

paragraph (e)(2)(ii) of this section, the amount of any expensed cost with respect to the asset is disregarded.

(D) *Examples* .—The following examples illustrate the application of this paragraph (e)(3)(iii):

*Example 1.* (i) Z, a calendar-year corporation, maintains one general asset account for 12 machines. Each machine costs $15,000 and is placed in service in 2014. Of the 12 machines, nine machines that cost a total of $135,000 are used in Z's Kentucky plant, and three machines that cost a total of $45,000 are used in Z's Ohio plant. Assume Z depreciates this general asset account using the optional depreciation table that corresponds with the general depreciation system, the 200-percent declining balance method, a 5-year recovery period, and the half-year convention. Z does not make a section 179 election for any of the machines, and all of the machines are not eligible for any additional first year depreciation deduction. As of December 31, 2015, the depreciation reserve for the account is $93,600.

(ii) On May 27, 2016, Z sells its entire manufacturing plant in Ohio to an unrelated party. The sales proceeds allocated to each of the three machines at the Ohio plant is $5,000. This transaction is a qualifying disposition under paragraph (e)(3)(iii)(B)( *3*) of this section, and Z elects to apply paragraph (e)(3)(iii) of this section.

(iii) For Z's 2016 return, the depreciation allowance for the account is computed as follows. As of December 31, 2015, the depreciation allowed or allowable for the three machines at the Ohio plant is $23,400. Thus, as of January 1, 2016, the unadjusted depreciable basis of the account is reduced from $180,000 to $135,000 ($180,000 less the unadjusted depreciable basis of $45,000 for the three machines), and, as of December 31, 2015, the depreciation reserve of the account is decreased from $93,600 to $70,200 ($93,600 less the depreciation allowed or allowable of $23,400 for the three machines as of December 31, 2015). Consequently, the depreciation allowance for the account in 2016 is $25,920 ($135,000 × 19.2%).

(iv) For Z's 2016 return, gain or loss for each of the three machines at the Ohio plant is determined as follows. The depreciation allowed or allowable in 2016 for each machine is $1,440 (($15,000 × 19.2%)/ 2). Thus, the adjusted depreciable basis of each machine under section 1011 is $5,760 (the adjusted depreciable basis of $7,200 removed from the account less the depreciation allowed or allowable of $1,440 in 2016). As a result, the loss recognized in 2016 for each machine is $760 ($5,000 - $5,760), which is subject to section 1231.

*Example 2.* (i) A, a calendar-year partnership, maintains one general asset account for one office building that cost $20 million and was placed in service in July 2011. A depreciates this general asset account using the optional depreciation table that corresponds with the general depreciation system, the straight-line method, a 39-year recovery period, and the mid-month convention. As of January 1, 2014, the depreciation reserve for the account is $1,261,000.

(ii) In May 2014, a tornado occurs where the building is located and damages the roof of the building. A decides to replace the entire roof. The roof is replaced in June 2014. The roof is a structural component of the building. Because the roof was damaged as a result of a casualty event described in section 165, the partial disposition rule provided under paragraph (e)(1)(ii) of this section applies to the roof. Although the office building, including its structural components, is the asset for disposition purposes, the partial disposition rule provides that the retirement of the replaced roof is a disposition under paragraph (e)(1) of this section. This retirement is a qualifying disposition under paragraph (e)(3)(iii)(B)( *1*) of this section, and A elects to apply paragraph (e)(3)(iii) of this section for the retirement of the damaged roof.

(iii) Of the $20 million cost of the office building, assume $1 million is the cost of the retired roof.

(iv) For A's 2014 return, the depreciation allowance for the account is computed as follows. As of December 31, 2013, the depreciation allowed or allowable for the retired roof is $63,050. Thus, as of January 1, 2014, the unadjusted depreciable basis of the account is reduced from $20,000,000 to $19,000,000 ($20,000,000 less the unadjusted depreciable basis of $1,000,000 for the retired roof), and the depreciation reserve of the account is decreased from $1,261,000 to $1,197,950 ($1,261,000 less the depreciation allowed or allowable of $63,050 for the retired roof as of December 31, 2013). Consequently, the depreciation allowance for the account in 2014 is $487,160 ($19,000,000 × 2.564%).

(v) For A's 2014 return, gain or loss for the retired roof is determined as follows. The depreciation allowed or allowable in 2014 for the retired roof is $11,752 (($1,000,000 × 2.564%) × 5.5/12). Thus, the adjusted depreciable basis of the retired roof under section 1011 is $925,198 (the adjusted depreciable basis of $936,950 removed from the account less the depreciation allowed or allowable of $11,752 in 2014). As a result, the loss recognized in 2014 for the retired roof is $925,198, which is subject to section 1231.

(vi) If A must capitalize the amount paid for the replacement roof under § 1.263(a)-3, the replacement roof is a separate asset for depreciation purposes pursuant to section 168(i)(6). If A includes the replacement roof in a general asset account, the replacement roof is a separate asset for disposition purposes pursuant to paragraph (e)(2)(viii)(B)(*4*) of this section. If A includes the replacement roof in a single asset account or a multiple asset account under § 1.168(i)-7, the replacement roof is a separate asset for disposition purposes pursuant to § 1.168(i)-8(c)(4)(ii)(D).

(iv) *Transactions subject to section 168(i)(7)*.—(A) *In general*.—If a taxpayer transfers one or more assets, or a portion of such asset, in a general asset account in a transaction described in section 168(i)(7)(B) (pertaining to treatment of transferees in certain nonrecognition transactions), the taxpayer (the transferor) and the transferee must apply this paragraph (e)(3)(iv) to the asset or the portion of such asset, instead of applying paragraph (e)(2), (e)(3)(ii), or (e)(3)(iii) of this section. The transferee is bound by the transferor's election under paragraph (l) of this section for the portion of the transferee's basis in the asset or the portion of such asset that does not exceed the transferor's adjusted depreciable basis of the general asset account or the asset or the portion of such asset, as applicable, as determined under paragraph (e)(3)(iv)(B)(*2*) or (C)(*2*) of this section, as applicable.

(B) *All assets remaining in general asset account are transferred*.—If a taxpayer transfers all the assets, the last asset, or the remaining portion of the last asset in a general asset account in a transaction described in section 168(i)(7)(B)—

*(1)* The taxpayer (the transferor) must terminate the general asset account on the date of the transfer. The allowable depreciation deduction for the general asset account for the transferor's taxable year in which the section 168(i)(7)(B) transaction occurs is computed by using the depreciation method, recovery period, and convention applicable to the general asset account. This allowable depreciation deduction is allocated between the transferor and the transferee on a monthly basis. This allocation is made in accordance with the rules in § 1.168(d)-1(b)(7)(ii) for allocating the depreciation deduction between the transferor and the transferee;

*(2)* The transferee must establish a new general asset account for all the assets, the last asset, or the remaining portion of the last asset, in the taxable year in which the section 168(i)(7)(B) transaction occurs for the portion

of its basis in the assets that does not exceed the transferor's adjusted depreciable basis of the general asset account in which all the assets, the last asset, or the remaining portion of the last asset, were included. The transferor's adjusted depreciable basis of this general asset account is equal to the adjusted depreciable basis of that account as of the beginning of the transferor's taxable year in which the transaction occurs, decreased by the amount of depreciation allocable to the transferor for the year of the transfer, as determined under paragraph (e)(3)(iv)(B)( *1*) of this section. The transferee is treated as the transferor for purposes of computing the allowable depreciation deduction for the new general asset account under section 168. The new general asset account must be established in accordance with the rules in paragraph (c) of this section, except that the unadjusted depreciable bases of all the assets, the last asset, or the remaining portion of the last asset, and the greater of the depreciation allowed or allowable for all the assets, the last asset, or the remaining portion of the last asset, including the amount of depreciation for the transferred assets that is allocable to the transferor for the year of the transfer, are included in the newly established general asset account. Consequently, this general asset account in the year of the transfer will have a beginning balance for both the unadjusted depreciable basis and the depreciation reserve of the general asset account; and

*(3)* For purposes of section 168 and this section, the transferee treats the portion of its basis in the assets that exceeds the transferor's adjusted depreciable basis of the general asset account in which all the assets, the last asset, or the remaining portion of the last asset, were included, as determined under paragraph (e)(3)(iv)(B)( *2*) of this section, as a separate asset that the transferee placed in service on the date of the transfer. The transferee accounts for this asset under §1.168(i)-7 or may make an election under paragraph (l) of this section to include the asset in a general asset account.

(C) *Not all assets remaining in general asset account are transferred* .—If a taxpayer transfers an asset in a general asset account in a transaction described in section 168(i)(7)(B) and if paragraph (e)(3)(iv)(B) of this section does not apply to this asset—

*(1)* The taxpayer (the transferor) must remove the transferred asset from the general asset account in which the asset is included, as of the first day of the taxable year in which the section 168(i)(7)(B) transaction occurs. In addition, the adjustments to the general asset account described in paragraphs (e)(3)(iii)(C)( *2*) through ( *4*) of this section must be made. The allowable depreciation deduction for the asset for the transferor's taxable year in which the section 168(i)(7)(B) transaction occurs is computed by using the depreciation method, recovery period, and convention applicable to the general asset account in which the asset was included. This allowable depreciation deduction is allocated between the transferor and the transferee on a monthly basis. This allocation is made in accordance with the rules in §1.168(d)-1(b)(7)(ii) for allocating the depreciation deduction between the transferor and the transferee;

*(2)* The transferee must establish a new general asset account for the asset in the taxable year in which the section 168(i)(7)(B) transaction occurs for the portion of its basis in the asset that does not exceed the transferor's adjusted depreciable basis of the asset. The transferor's adjusted depreciable basis of this asset is equal to the adjusted depreciable basis of the asset as of the beginning of the transferor's taxable year in which the transaction occurs, decreased by the amount of depreciation allocable to the transferor for the year of the transfer, as determined under paragraph (e)(3)(iv)(C)( *1*) of this section. The transferee is treated as the transferor for purposes of computing the allowable depreciation deduction for the new general asset account under section 168. The new general asset account must be established in accordance with the rules in paragraph (c) of this section, except that the unadjusted depreciable basis of the

asset, and the greater of the depreciation allowed or allowable for the asset, including the amount of depreciation for the transferred asset that is allocable to the transferor for the year of the transfer, are included in the newly established general asset account. Consequently, this general asset account in the year of the transfer will have a beginning balance for both the unadjusted depreciable basis and the depreciation reserve of the general asset account; and

*(3)* For purposes of section 168 and this section, the transferee treats the portion of its basis in the asset that exceeds the transferor's adjusted depreciable basis of the asset, as determined under paragraph (e)(3)(iv)(C)(*2*) of this section, as a separate asset that the transferee placed in service on the date of the transfer. The transferee accounts for this asset under § 1.168(i)-7 or may make an election under paragraph (l) of this section to include the asset in a general asset account.

(v) *Transactions subject to section 1031 or section 1033*.—(A) *Like-kind exchange or involuntary conversion of all assets remaining in a general asset account*.—If all the assets, the last asset, or the remaining portion of the last asset in a general asset account are transferred by a taxpayer in a like-kind exchange (as defined under § 1.168-6(b)(11)) or in an involuntary conversion (as defined under § 1.168-6(b)(12)), the taxpayer must apply this paragraph (e)(3)(v)(A) instead of applying paragraph (e)(2), (e)(3)(ii), or (e)(3)(iii) of this section. Under this paragraph (e)(3)(v)(A), the general asset account terminates as of the first day of the year of disposition (as defined in § 1.168(i)-6(b)(5)) and—

*(1)* The amount of gain or loss for the general asset account is determined under section 1001(a) by taking into account the adjusted depreciable basis of the general asset account at the time of disposition (as defined in § 1.168(i)-6(b)(3)). The depreciation allowance for the general asset account in the year of disposition is determined in the same manner as the depreciation allowance for the relinquished MACRS property (as defined in § 1.168(i)-6(b)(2)) in the year of disposition is determined under § 1.168(i)-6. The recognition and character of gain or loss are determined in accordance with paragraph (e)(3)(ii)(A) of this section, notwithstanding that paragraph (e)(3)(ii) of this section is an optional rule; and

*(2)* The adjusted depreciable basis of the general asset account at the time of disposition is treated as the adjusted depreciable basis of the relinquished MACRS property.

(B) *Like-kind exchange or involuntary conversion of less than all assets remaining in a general asset account*.—If an asset in a general asset account is transferred by a taxpayer in a like-kind exchange or in an involuntary conversion and if paragraph (e)(3)(v)(A) of this section does not apply to this asset, the taxpayer must apply this paragraph (e)(3)(v)(B) instead of applying paragraph (e)(2), (e)(3)(ii), or (e)(3)(iii) of this section. Under this paragraph (e)(3)(v)(B), general asset account treatment for the asset terminates as of the first day of the year of disposition (as defined in § 1.168(i)-6(b)(5)), and—

*(1)* The adjusted depreciable basis of the asset at the time of disposition equals the unadjusted depreciable basis of the asset less the greater of the depreciation allowed or allowable for the asset. The allowable depreciation is computed by using the depreciation method, recovery period, and convention applicable to the general asset account in which the asset was included and by including the portion of the additional first year depreciation deduction claimed for the general asset account that is attributable to the relinquished asset.

*(2)* As of the first day of the year of disposition, the taxpayer must remove the relinquished asset from the general asset account and make the adjustments to the general asset account described in paragraphs (e)(3)(iii)(C)(*2*) through (*4*) of this section.

(vi) *Technical termination of a partnership* .—In the case of a technical termination of a partnership under section 708(b)(1)(B), the terminated partnership must apply this paragraph (e)(3)(vi) instead of applying paragraph (e)(2), (e)(3)(ii), or (e)(3)(iii) of this section. Under this paragraph (e)(3)(vi), all of the terminated partnership's general asset accounts terminate as of the date of its termination under section 708(b)(1)(B). The terminated partnership computes the allowable depreciation deduction for each of its general asset accounts for the taxable year in which the technical termination occurs by using the depreciation method, recovery period, and convention applicable to the general asset account. The new partnership is not bound by the terminated partnership's election under paragraph (l) of this section.

(vii) *Anti-abuse rule* .—(A) *In general* .—If an asset in a general asset account is disposed of by a taxpayer in a transaction described in paragraph (e)(3)(vii)(B) of this section, general asset account treatment for the asset terminates as of the first day of the taxable year in which the disposition occurs. Consequently, the taxpayer must determine the amount of gain, loss, or other deduction attributable to the disposition in the manner described in paragraph (e)(3)(iii)(A) of this section, notwithstanding that paragraph (e)(3)(iii)(A) of this section is an optional rule, and must make the adjustments to the general asset account described in paragraphs (e)(3)(iii)(C)( *1*) through ( *4*) of this section.

(B) *Abusive transactions* .—A transaction is described in this paragraph (e)(3)(vii)(B) if the transaction is not described in paragraph (e)(3)(iv), (e)(3)(v), or (e)(3)(vi) of this section, and if the transaction is entered into, or made, with a principal purpose of achieving a tax benefit or result that would not be available absent an election under this section. Examples of these types of transactions include—

*(1)* A transaction entered into with a principal purpose of shifting income or deductions among taxpayers in a manner that would not be possible absent an election under this section to take advantage of differing effective tax rates among the taxpayers; or

*(2)* An election made under this section with a principal purpose of disposing of an asset from a general asset account to utilize an expiring net operating loss or credit if the transaction is not a bona fide disposition. The fact that a taxpayer with a net operating loss carryover or a credit carryover transfers an asset to a related person or transfers an asset pursuant to an arrangement where the asset continues to be used or is available for use by the taxpayer pursuant to a lease or otherwise indicates, absent strong evidence to the contrary, that the transaction is described in this paragraph (e)(3)(vii)(B).

(f) *Assets generating foreign source income* .—(1) *In general* .—This paragraph (f) provides the rules for determining the source of any income, gain, or loss recognized, and the appropriate section 904(d) separate limitation category or categories for any foreign source income, gain, or loss recognized on a disposition (within the meaning of paragraph (e)(1) of this section) of an asset in a general asset account that consists of assets generating both United States and foreign source income. These rules apply only to a disposition to which paragraph (e)(2) (general disposition rules), paragraph (e)(3)(ii) (disposition of all assets remaining in a general asset account), paragraph (e)(3)(iii) (disposition of an asset in a qualifying disposition), paragraph (e)(3)(v) (transactions subject to section 1031 or section 1033), or paragraph (e)(3)(vii) (anti-abuse rule) of this section applies. Solely for purposes of applying this paragraph (f), the term *asset* is:

(i) The asset as determined under paragraph (e)(2)(viii) of this section; or

(ii) The portion of such asset that is disposed of in a disposition described in paragraph (e)(1)(ii) of this section.

(2) *Source of ordinary income, gain, or loss* .—(i) *Source determined by allocation and apportionment of depreciation allowed* .—The amount of any ordinary income, gain, or loss that is recognized on the disposition of an asset in a general asset account must be apportioned between United States and foreign sources based on the allocation and apportionment of the—

(A) Depreciation allowed for the general asset account as of the end of the taxable year in which the disposition occurs if paragraph (e)(2) of this section applies to the disposition;

(B) Depreciation allowed for the general asset account as of the time of disposition if the taxpayer applies paragraph (e)(3)(ii) of this section to the disposition of all assets, the last asset, or the remaining portion of the last asset, in the general asset account, or if all the assets, the last asset, or the remaining portion of the last asset, in the general asset account are disposed of in a transaction described in paragraph (e)(3)(v)(A) of this section; or

(C) Depreciation allowed for the asset disposed of for only the taxable year in which the disposition occurs if the taxpayer applies paragraph (e)(3)(iii) of this section to the disposition of the asset in a qualifying disposition, if the asset is disposed of in a transaction described in paragraph (e)(3)(v)(B) of this section (like-kind exchange or involuntary conversion), or if the asset is disposed of in a transaction described in paragraph (e)(3)(vii) of this section (anti-abuse rule).

(ii) *Formula for determining foreign source income, gain, or loss* .—The amount of ordinary income, gain, or loss recognized on the disposition that shall be treated as foreign source income, gain, or loss must be determined under the formula in this paragraph (f)(2)(ii). For purposes of this formula, the allowed depreciation deductions are determined for the applicable time period provided in paragraph (f)(2)(i) of this section. The formula is:

| | | | | |
|---|---|---|---|---|
| Foreign Source Income, Gain, or Loss from The Disposition of an Asset | = | Total Ordinary Income, Gain, or Loss from the Disposition of an Asset | × | Allowed Depreciation Deductions Allocated and Apportioned to Foreign Source Income/Total Allowed Depreciation Deductions for the General Asset Account or for the Asset Disposed of (as applicable) |

(3) *Section 904(d) separate categories* .—If the assets in the general asset account generate foreign source income in more than one separate category under section 904(d)(1) or another section of the Code (for example, income treated as foreign source income under section 904(g)(10)), or under a United States income tax treaty that requires the foreign tax credit limitation to be determined separately for specified types of income, the amount of foreign source income, gain, or loss from the disposition of an asset, as determined under the formula in paragraph (f)(2)(ii) of this section, must be allocated and apportioned to the applicable separate category or categories under the formula in this paragraph (f)(3). For purposes of this formula, the allowed depreciation deductions are determined for the applicable time period provided in paragraph (f)(2)(i) of this section. The formula is:

| | | | | |
|---|---|---|---|---|
| Foreign Source Income, Gain, or Loss in a Separate Category | = | Foreign Source Income, Gain, or Loss from The Disposition of an Asset | × | Allowed Depreciation Deductions Allocated and Apportioned to a Separate Category/Total Allowed Depreciation Deductions and Apportioned to Foreign Source Income |

(g) *Assets subject to recapture* .—If the basis of an asset in a general asset account is increased as a result of the recapture of any allowable credit or deduction (for example, the basis adjustment for the recapture amount under section 30(e)(5), 50(c)(2), 168(l)(6), 168(n)(4), 179(d)(10), 179A(e)(4), or 1400N(d)(5)), general asset account treatment for the asset terminates as of the first day of the taxable year in which the recapture event occurs. Consequently, the taxpayer must remove the asset from the general asset account as of that day and must make the adjustments to the general asset account described in paragraphs (e)(3)(iii)(C)( *2*) through ( *4*) of this section.

(h) *Changes in use* .—(1) *Conversion to any personal use* .—An asset in a general asset account becomes ineligible for general asset account treatment if a taxpayer uses the asset in any personal activity during a taxable year. Upon a conversion to any personal use, the taxpayer must remove the asset from the general asset account as of the first day of the taxable year in which the change in use occurs (the year of change) and must make the adjustments to the general asset account described in paragraphs (e)(3)(iii)(C)( *2*) through ( *4*) of this section.

(2) *Change in use results in a different recovery period and/or depreciation method* .—(i) *No effect on general asset account election* .—A change in the use described in § 1.168(i)-4(d) (change in use results in a different recovery period or depreciation method) of an asset in a general asset account shall not cause or permit the revocation of the election made under this section.

(ii) *Asset is removed from the general asset account* .—Upon a change in the use described in § 1.168(i)-4(d), the taxpayer must remove the asset from the general asset account as of the first day of the year of change (as defined in § 1.168(i)-4(a)) and must make the adjustments to the general asset account described in paragraphs (e)(3)(iii)(C)( *2*) through ( *4*) of this section. If, however, the result of the change in use is described in § 1.168(i)-4(d)(3) (change in use results in a shorter recovery period or a more accelerated depreciation method) and the taxpayer elects to treat the asset as though the change in use had not occurred pursuant to § 1.168(i)-4(d)(3)(ii), no adjustment is made to the general asset account upon the change in use.

(iii) *New general asset account is established* .—(A) *Change in use results in a shorter recovery period or a more accelerated depreciation method* .—If the result of the change in use is described in § 1.168(i)-4(d)(3) (change in use results in a shorter recovery period or a more accelerated depreciation method) and adjustments to the general asset account are made pursuant to paragraph (h)(2)(ii) of this section, the taxpayer must establish a new general asset account for the asset in the year of change in accordance with the rules in paragraph (c) of this section, except that the adjusted depreciable basis of the asset as of the first day of the year of change is included in the general asset account. For purposes of paragraph (c)(2) of this section, the applicable depreciation method, recovery period, and convention are determined under § 1.168(i)-4(d)(3)(i).

(B) *Change in use results in a longer recovery period or a slower depreciation method* .—If the result of the change in use is described in § 1.168(i)-4(d)(4) (change in use results in a longer recovery period or a slower depreciation method), the taxpayer must establish a separate general asset account for the asset in the year of change in accordance with the rules in paragraph (c) of this section, except that the unadjusted depreciable basis of the asset, and the greater of the depreciation of the asset allowed or allowable in accordance with section 1016(a)(2), as of the first day of the year of change are included in the newly established general asset account. Consequently, this general asset account as of the first day of the year of change will have a beginning balance for both the unadjusted depreciable basis and the depreciation reserve of the general asset account. For purposes of paragraph (c)(2) of this section, the applicable depreciation method, recovery period, and convention are determined under § 1.168(i)-4(d)(4)(ii).

(i) *Redetermination of basis* .—If, after the placed-in-service year, the unadjusted depreciable basis of an asset in a general asset account is redetermined due to a transaction other than that described in paragraph (g) of this section (for example, due to contingent purchase price or discharge of indebtedness), the taxpayer's election under paragraph (l) of this section for the asset also applies to the increase or decrease in basis resulting from the redetermination. For the taxable year in which the increase or decrease in basis occurs, the taxpayer must establish a new general asset account for the amount of the increase or decrease in basis in accordance with the rules in paragraph (c) of this section. For purposes of paragraph (c)(2) of this section, the applicable recovery period for the increase or decrease in basis is the recovery period of the asset remaining as of the beginning of the taxable year in which the increase or decrease in basis occurs, the applicable depreciation method and applicable convention for the increase or decrease in basis are the same depreciation method and convention applicable to the asset that applies for the taxable year in which the increase or decrease in basis occurs, and the increase or decrease in basis is deemed to be placed in service in the same taxable year as the asset.

(j) *Identification of disposed or converted asset* .—(1) *In general* .—The rules of this paragraph (j) apply when an asset in a general asset account is disposed of or converted in a transaction described in paragraph (e)(3)(iii) (disposition of an asset in a qualifying disposition), paragraph (e)(3)(iv)(B) (transactions subject to section 168(i)(7)), paragraph (e)(3)(v)(B) (transactions subject to section 1031 or section 1033), paragraph (e)(3)(vii) (anti-abuse rule), paragraph (g) (assets subject to recapture), or paragraph (h)(1) (conversion to any personal use) of this section.

(2) *Identifying which asset is disposed of or converted* .—(i) *In general* .—For purposes of identifying which asset in a general asset account is disposed of or converted, a taxpayer must identify the disposed of or converted asset by using—

(A) The specific identification method of accounting. Under this method of accounting, the taxpayer can determine the particular taxable year in which the disposed of or converted asset was placed in service by the taxpayer;

(B) A first-in, first-out method of accounting if the taxpayer can readily determine from its records the total dispositions of assets with the same recovery period during the taxable year but the taxpayer cannot readily determine from its records the unadjusted depreciable basis of the disposed of or converted asset. Under this method of accounting, the taxpayer identifies the general asset account with the earliest placed-in-service year that has the same recovery period as the disposed of or converted asset and that has assets at the beginning of the taxable year of the disposition or conversion, and the taxpayer treats the disposed of or converted asset as being from that general asset account. To determine which general asset account has assets at the beginning of the taxable year of the disposition or conversion, the taxpayer reduces the number of assets originally included in the account by the number of assets disposed of or converted in any prior taxable year in a transaction to which this paragraph (j) applies;

(C) A modified first-in, first-out method of accounting if the taxpayer can readily determine from its records the total dispositions of assets with the same recovery period during the taxable year and the unadjusted depreciable basis of the disposed of or converted asset. Under this method of accounting, the taxpayer identifies the general asset account with the earliest placed-in-service year that has the same recovery period as the disposed of or converted asset and that has assets at the beginning of the taxable year of the disposition or conversion with the same unadjusted depreciable basis as the disposed of or converted asset, and the taxpayer treats the disposed of or converted asset as being from that general asset account. To determine which general asset account has assets at the beginning of the taxable year of the disposition or conversion, the taxpayer reduces the number of assets originally included in the account by the number of assets disposed of or converted in any prior taxable year in a transaction to which this paragraph (j) applies;

(D) A mortality dispersion table if the asset is a mass asset accounted for in a separate general asset account in accordance with paragraph (c)(2)(ii)(H) of this section and if the taxpayer can readily determine from its records the total dispositions of assets with the same recovery period during the taxable year. The mortality dispersion table must be based upon an acceptable sampling of the taxpayer's actual disposition and conversion experience for mass assets or other acceptable statistical or engineering techniques. To use a mortality dispersion table, the taxpayer must adopt recordkeeping practices consistent with the taxpayer's prior practices and consonant with good accounting and engineering practices; or

(E) Any other method as the Secretary may designate by publication in the **Federal Register** or in the Internal Revenue Bulletin (see §601.601(d)(2) of this chapter) on or after September 19, 2013. See paragraph (j)(2)(iii) of this section regarding the last-in, first-out method of accounting.

(ii) *Disposition of a portion of an asset* .—If a taxpayer disposes of a portion of an asset and paragraph (e)(1)(ii) of this section applies to that disposition, the taxpayer may identify the asset by using any applicable method provided in paragraph (j)(2)(i) of this section, after taking into account paragraph (j)(2)(iii) of this section.

(iii) *Last-in, first-out method of accounting* .—For purposes of paragraph (j)(2) of this section, a last-in, first-out method of accounting may not be used. Examples of a last-in, first-out method of accounting include the taxpayer identifying the general asset account with the most recent placed-in-service year that has the same recovery period as the disposed of or converted asset and that has assets at the beginning of the taxable year of the disposition or conversion, and the taxpayer treating the disposed of or converted asset as being from that general asset account, or the taxpayer treating the disposed portion of an asset as being from the general asset account with the most recent placed-in-service year that has assets that are the same as the asset of which the disposed portion is a part.

(3) *Basis of disposed of or converted asset* .—(i) Solely for purposes of this paragraph (j)(3), the term *asset* is the asset as determined under paragraph (e)(2)(viii) of this section or the portion of such asset that is disposed of in a disposition described in paragraph (e)(1)(ii) of this section. After identifying which asset in a general asset account is disposed of or converted, the taxpayer must determine the unadjusted depreciable basis of, and the depreciation allowed or allowable for, the disposed of or converted asset. If it is impracticable from the taxpayer's records to determine the unadjusted depreciable basis of the disposed of or converted asset, the taxpayer may use any reasonable method that is consistently applied to all assets in the same general asset account for purposes of determining the unadjusted depreciable basis of the disposed of or converted asset in that general asset account. Examples of a reasonable method include, but are not limited to, the following:

(A) If the replacement asset is a restoration (as defined in §1.263(a)-3(k)), and is not a betterment (as defined in §1.263(a)-3(j)) or an adaptation to a new or different use (as defined in §1.263(a)-3(l)), discounting the cost of the replacement asset to its placed-in-service year cost using the Producer Price Index for Finished Goods or its successor, the Producer Price Index for Final

Demand, or any other index designated by guidance in the Internal Revenue Bulletin (see § 601.601(d)(2) of this chapter) for purposes of this paragraph (j)(3);

(B) A pro rata allocation of the unadjusted depreciable basis of the general asset account based on the replacement cost of the disposed asset and the replacement cost of all of the assets in the general asset account; and

(C) A study allocating the cost of the asset to its individual components.

(ii) The depreciation allowable for the disposed of or converted asset is computed by using the depreciation method, recovery period, and convention applicable to the general asset account in which the disposed of or converted asset was included and by including the additional first year depreciation deduction claimed for the disposed of or converted asset.

(k) *Effect of adjustments on prior dispositions* .—The adjustments to a general asset account under paragraph (e)(3)(iii), (e)(3)(iv), (e)(3)(v), (e)(3)(vii), (g), or (h) of this section have no effect on the recognition and character of prior dispositions subject to paragraph (e)(2) of this section.

(l) *Election* .—(1) *Irrevocable election* .—If a taxpayer makes an election under this paragraph (l), the taxpayer consents to, and agrees to apply, all of the provisions of this section to the assets included in a general asset account. Except as provided in paragraph (c)(1)(ii)(A), (e)(3), (g), or (h) of this section or except as otherwise expressly provided by other guidance published in the Internal Revenue Bulletin (see § 601.601(d)(2) of this chapter), an election made under this section is irrevocable and will be binding on the taxpayer for computing taxable income for the taxable year for which the election is made and for all subsequent taxable years. An election under this paragraph (l) is made separately by each person owning an asset to which this section applies (for example, by each member of a consolidated group, at the partnership level and not by the partner separately, or at the S corporation level and not by the shareholder separately).

(2) *Time for making election* .—The election to apply this section shall be made on the taxpayer's timely filed (including extensions) income tax return for the taxable year in which the assets included in the general asset account are placed in service by the taxpayer.

(3) *Manner of making election* .—In the year of election, a taxpayer makes the election under this section by typing or legibly printing at the top of the Form 4562, "GENERAL ASSET ACCOUNT ELECTION MADE UNDER SECTION 168(i)(4)," or in the manner provided for on Form 4562 and its instructions. The taxpayer shall maintain records (for example, "General Asset Account #1—all 1995 additions in asset class 00.11 for Salt Lake City, Utah facility") that identify the assets included in each general asset account, that establish the unadjusted depreciable basis and depreciation reserve of the general asset account, and that reflect the amount realized during the taxable year upon dispositions from each general asset account. (But see section 179(c) and § 1.179-5 for the recordkeeping requirements for section 179 property.) The taxpayer's recordkeeping practices should be consistently applied to the general asset accounts. If Form 4562 is revised or renumbered, any reference in this section to that form shall be treated as a reference to the revised or renumbered form.

(m) *Effective/applicability dates* .—(1) *In general* .—Except as provided in paragraph (m)(5) of this section, this section applies to taxable years beginning on or after January 1, 2014. Except as provided in paragraphs (m)(2), (m)(3), and (m)(4) of this section, § 1.168(i)-1 as contained in 26 CFR part 1 edition revised as of April 1, 2011, applies to taxable years beginning before January 1, 2014.

(2) *Early application of this section* .—A taxpayer may choose to apply the provisions of this section to taxable years beginning on or after January 1, 2012.

(3) *Early application of regulation project REG-110732-13* .—A taxpayer may rely on the provisions of this section in regulation project REG-110732-13 (2013-43 IRB 404) (see § 601.601(d)(2) of this chapter) for taxable years beginning on or after January 1, 2012. However, a taxpayer may not rely on the provisions of this section in regulation project REG-110732-13 for taxable years beginning on or after January 1, 2014.

(4) *Optional application of TD 9564.* .—A taxpayer may choose to apply § 1.168(i)-1T as contained in 26 CFR part 1 edition revised as of April 1, 2014, to taxable years beginning on or after January 1, 2012. However, a taxpayer may not apply § 1.168(i)-1T as contained in 26 CFR part 1 edition revised as of April 1, 2014, to taxable years beginning on or after January 1, 2014.

(5) *Application of paragraph (e)(2)(viii)(A)* .—The language "and the distinct asset determination under § 1.1031(a)-3(a)(4) do not apply." in the last sentence of paragraph (e)(2)(viii)(A) of this section applies on or after December 2, 2020. Paragraph (e)(2)(viii)(A) of this section as contained in 26 CFR part 1 edition revised as of April 1, 2020, applies before December 2, 2020.

(6) *Change in method of accounting* .—A change to comply with this section for depreciable assets placed in service in a taxable year ending on or after December 30, 2003, is a change in method of accounting to which the provisions of section 446(e) and the regulations under section 446(e) apply. A taxpayer also may treat a change to comply with this section for depreciable assets placed in service in a taxable year ending before December 30, 2003, as a change in method of accounting to which the provisions of section 446(e) and the regulations under section 446(e) apply. This paragraph (m)(5) does not apply to a change to comply with paragraph (e)(3)(ii), (e)(3)(iii), or (l) of this section, except as otherwise expressly provided by other guidance published in the Internal Revenue Bulletin (see § 601.601(d)(2) of this chapter). [Reg. § 1.168(i)-1.]

**.01 Historical Comment:** Proposed 8/31/92. Adopted 10/7/94 by T.D. 8566 (corrected 12/15/94). Amended 2/27/2004 by T.D. 9115, 6/16/2004 by T.D. 9132, 2/26/2007 by T.D. 9314, 12/23/2011 by T.D. 9564 (corrected 12/18/2012), 8/14/2014 by T.D. 9689 (corrected 12/30/2014) and 11/30/2020 by T.D. 9935.

## ¶ 566

## Reg. § 1.168(i)-2

§ 1.168(i)-2. **Lease term.**— (a) *In general* .—For purposes of section 168, a lease term is determined under all the facts and circumstances. Paragraph (b) of this section and § 1.168(j)-1T, Q&A 17, describe certain circumstances that will result in a period of time not included in the stated duration of an original lease (additional period) nevertheless being included in the lease term. These rules do not prevent the inclusion of an additional period in the lease term in other circumstances.

(b) *Lessee retains financial obligation* .—(1) *In general* .—An additional period of time during which a lessee may not continue to be the lessee will nevertheless be included in the lease term if the lessee (or a related person)—

(i) Has agreed that one or both of them will or could be obligated to make a payment of rent or a payment in the nature of rent with respect to such period; or

(ii) Has assumed or retained any risk of loss with respect to the property for such period (including, for example, by holding a note secured by the property).

(2) *Payments in the nature of rent*.—For purposes of paragraph (b)(1)(i) of this section, a payment in the nature of rent includes a payment intended to substitute for rent or to fund or supplement the rental payments of another. For example, a payment in the nature of rent includes a payment of any kind (whether denominated as supplemental rent, as liquidated damages, or otherwise) that is required to be made in the event that—

(i) The leased property is not leased for the additional period;

(ii) The leased property is leased for the additional period under terms that do not satisfy specified terms and conditions;

(iii) There is a failure to make a payment of rent with respect to such additional period; or

(iv) Circumstances similar to those described in paragraph (b)(2)(i), (ii), or (iii) of this section occur.

(3) *De minimis rule*.—For the purposes of this paragraph (b), obligations to make de minimis payments will be disregarded.

(c) *Multiple leases or subleases*.—If property is subject to more than one lease (including any sublease) entered into as part of a single transaction (or a series of related transactions), the lease term includes all periods described in one or more of such leases. For example, if one taxable corporation leases property to another taxable corporation for a 20-year term and, as part of the same transaction, the lessee subleases the property to a tax-exempt entity for a 10-year term, then the lease term of the property for purposes of section 168 is 20 years. During the period of tax-exempt use, the property must be depreciated under the alternative depreciation system using the straight line method over the greater of its class life or 25 years (125 percent of the 20-year lease term).

(d) *Related person*.—For purposes of paragraph (b) of this section, a person is related to the lessee if such person is described in section 168(h)(4).

(e) *Changes in status*.—Section 168(i)(5) (changes in status) applies if an additional period is included in a lease term under this section and the leased property ceases to be tax-exempt use property for such additional period.

(f) *Example*.—The following example illustrates the principles of this section. The example does not address common law doctrines or other authorities that may apply to cause an additional period to be included in the lease term or to recharacterize a lease as a conditional sale or otherwise for federal income tax purposes. Unless otherwise indicated, parties to the transactions are not related to one another.

*Example. Financial obligation with respect to an additional period*—(i) *Facts*. X, a taxable corporation, and Y, a foreign airline whose income is not subject to United States taxation, enter into a lease agreement under which X agrees to lease an aircraft to Y for a period of 10 years. The lease agreement provides that, at the end of the lease period, Y is obligated to find a subsequent lessee (replacement lessee) to enter into a subsequent lease (replacement lease) of the aircraft from X for an additional 10-year period. The provisions of the lease agreement require that any replacement lessee be unrelated to Y and that it not be a tax-exempt entity as defined in section 168(h)(2). The provisions of the lease agreement also set forth the basic terms and conditions of the replacement lease, including its duration and the required rental payments. In the event Y fails to secure a replacement lease, the lease agreement requires Y to make a payment to X in an amount determined under the lease agreement.

(ii) *Application of this section*. The lease agreement between X and Y obligates Y to make a payment in the event the aircraft is not leased for the period commencing after the initial 10-year lease period and ending on the date the replacement lease is scheduled to end. Accordingly, pursuant to paragraph (b) of this section, the term of the lease between X and Y includes such additional period, and the lease term is 20 years for purposes of section 168.

(iii) *Facts modified.* Assume the same facts as in paragraph (i) of this *Example*, except that Y is required to guarantee the payment of rentals under the 10-year replacement lease and to make a payment to X equal to the present value of any excess of the replacement lease rental payments specified in the lease agreement between X and Y, over the rental payments actually agreed to be paid by the replacement lessee. Pursuant to paragraph (b) of this section, the term of the lease between X and Y includes the additional period, and the lease term is 20 years for purposes of section 168.

(iv) *Changes in status.* If, upon the conclusion of the stated duration of the lease between X and Y, the aircraft either is returned to X or leased to a replacement lessee that is not a tax-exempt entity as defined in section 168(h)(2), the subsequent method of depreciation will be determined pursuant to section 168(i)(5).

(g) *Effective date* .—(1) *In general* .—Except as provided in paragraph (g)(2) of this section, this section applies to leases entered into on or after April 20, 1995.

(2) *Special rules* .—Paragraphs (b)(1)(ii) and (c) of this section apply to leases entered into after April 26, 1996. [Reg. § 1.168(i)-2.]

**.01 Historical Comment:** Proposed 4/21/95. Adopted 4/26/96 by T.D. 8667.

## ¶ 568

## Reg. § 1.168(i)-4

§ 1.168(i)-4. **Changes in use.**— (a) *Scope* .—This section provides the rules for determining the depreciation allowance for MACRS property (as defined in § 1.168(b)-1T(a)(2)) for which the use changes in the hands of the same taxpayer (change in the use). The allowance for depreciation under this section constitutes the amount of depreciation allowable under section 167(a) for the year of change and any subsequent taxable year. For purposes of this section, the year of change is the taxable year in which a change in the use occurs.

(b) *Conversion to business or income-producing use* .—(1) *Depreciation deduction allowable* .—This paragraph (b) applies to property that is converted from personal use to use in a taxpayer's trade or business, or for the production of income, during a taxable year. This conversion includes property that was previously used by the taxpayer for personal purposes, including real property (other than land) that is acquired before 1987 and converted from personal use to business or income-producing use after 1986, and depreciable property that was previously used by a tax-exempt entity before the entity changed to a taxable entity. Except as otherwise provided by the Internal Revenue Code or regulations under the Internal Revenue Code, upon a conversion to business or income-producing use, the depreciation allowance for the year of change and any subsequent taxable year is determined as though the property is placed in service by the taxpayer on the date on which the conversion occurs. Thus, except as otherwise provided by the Internal Revenue Code or regulations under the Internal Revenue Code, the taxpayer must use any applicable depreciation method, recovery period, and convention prescribed under section 168 for the property in the year of change, consistent with any election made under section 168 by the taxpayer for that year (see, for example, section 168(b)(5)). See § 1.168(k)-1(f)(6)(iii) or 1.168(k)-2(g)(6)(iii), as applicable, and § 1.1400L(b)-1(f)(6) for the additional first year depreciation deduction rules applicable to a conversion to business or income-producing use. The depreciable basis of the property for the year of change is the lesser of its fair market value or its adjusted depreciable basis (as defined in

§ 1.168(b)-1T(a)(4)), as applicable, at the time of the conversion to business or income-producing use.

(2) *Example* .—The application of this paragraph (b) is illustrated by the following example:

*Example. A*, a calendar-year taxpayer, purchases a house in 1985 that she occupies as her principal residence. In February 2004, *A* ceases to occupy the house and converts it to residential rental property. At the time of the conversion to residential rental property, the house's fair market value (excluding land) is $130,000 and adjusted depreciable basis attributable to the house (excluding land) is $150,000. Pursuant to this paragraph (b), *A* is considered to have placed in service residential rental property in February 2004 with a depreciable basis of $130,000. *A* depreciates the residential rental property under the general depreciation system by using the straight-line method, a 27.5-year recovery period, and the mid-month convention. Pursuant to §§ 1.168(k)-1T(f)(6)(iii)(B) or 1.1400L(b)-1T(f)(6), this property is not eligible for the additional first year depreciation deduction provided by section 168(k) or section 1400L(b). Thus, the depreciation allowance for the house for 2004 is $4,137, after taking into account the mid-month convention (($130,000 adjusted depreciable basis multiplied by the applicable depreciation rate of 3.636% (1/27.5)) multiplied by the mid-month convention fraction of 10.5/12). The amount of depreciation computed under section 168, however, may be limited under other provisions of the Internal Revenue Code, such as, section 280A.

(c) *Conversion to personal use* .—The conversion of MACRS property from business or income-producing use to personal use during a taxable year is treated as a disposition of the property in that taxable year. The depreciation allowance for MACRS property for the year of change in which the property is treated as being disposed of is determined by first multiplying the adjusted depreciable basis of the property as of the first day of the year of change by the applicable depreciation rate for that taxable year (for further guidance, for example, see section 6 of Rev. Proc. 87-57 (1987-2 C. B. 687, 692) (see § 601.601(d)(2)(ii)( *b*) of this chapter)). This amount is then multiplied by a fraction, the numerator of which is the number of months (including fractions of months) the property is deemed to be placed in service during the year of change (taking into account the applicable convention) and the denominator of which is 12. No depreciation deduction is allowable for MACRS property placed in service and disposed of in the same taxable year. See § 1.168(k)-1(f)(6)(ii) or 1.168(k)-2(g)(6)(ii), as applicable, and § 1.1400L(b)-1(f)(6) for the additional first year depreciation deduction rules applicable to property placed in service and converted to personal use in the same taxable year. Upon the conversion to personal use, no gain, loss, or depreciation recapture under section 1245 or section 1250 is recognized. However, the provisions of section 1245 or section 1250 apply to any disposition of the converted property by the taxpayer at a later date. For listed property (as defined in section 280F(d)(4)), see section 280F(b)(2) for the recapture of excess depreciation upon the conversion to personal use.

(d) *Change in the use results in a different recovery period and/or depreciation method* .—(1) *In general* .—This paragraph (d) applies to a change in the use of MACRS property during a taxable year subsequent to the placed-in-service year, if the property continues to be MACRS property owned by the same taxpayer and, as a result of the change in the use, has a different recovery period, a different depreciation method, or both. For example, this paragraph (d) applies to MACRS property that—

(i) Begins or ceases to be used predominantly outside the United States;

(ii) Results in a reclassification of the property under section 168(e) due to a change in the use of the property; or

(iii) Begins or ceases to be tax-exempt use property (as defined in section 168(h)).

(2) *Determination of change in the use* .—(i) *In general* .—Except as provided in paragraph (d)(2)(ii) of this section, a change in the use of MACRS property occurs when the primary use of the MACRS property in the taxable year is different from its primary use in the immediately preceding taxable year. The primary use of MACRS property may be determined in any reasonable manner that is consistently applied to the taxpayer's MACRS property.

(ii) *Alternative depreciation system property* .—(A) *Property used within or outside the United States* .—A change in the use of MACRS property occurs when a taxpayer begins or ceases to use MACRS property predominantly outside the United States during the taxable year. The determination of whether MACRS property is used predominantly outside the United States is made in accordance with the test in § 1.48-1(g)(1)(i) for determining predominant use.

(B) *Tax-exempt bond financed property* .—A change in the use of MACRS property occurs when the property changes to tax-exempt bond financed property, as described in section 168(g)(1)(C) and (g)(5), during the taxable year. For purposes of this paragraph (d), MACRS property changes to tax-exempt bond financed property when a tax-exempt bond is first issued after the MACRS property is placed in service. MACRS property continues to be tax-exempt bond financed property in the hands of the taxpayer even if the tax-exempt bond (including any refunding issue) is no longer outstanding or is redeemed.

(C) *Other mandatory alternative depreciation system property* .—A change in the use of MACRS property occurs when the property changes to, or changes from, property described in section 168(g)(1)(B) (tax-exempt use property) or (D) (imported property covered by an Executive order) during the taxable year.

(iii) *Change in the use deemed to occur on first day of the year of change* .—If a change in the use of MACRS property occurs under this paragraph (d)(2), the depreciation allowance for that MACRS property for the year of change is determined as though the use of the MACRS property changed on the first day of the year of change.

(3) *Change in the use results in a shorter recovery period and/or a more accelerated depreciation method* .—(i) *Treated as placed in service in the year of change* .—(A) *In general* .—If a change in the use results in the MACRS property changing to a shorter recovery period and/or a depreciation method that is more accelerated than the method used for the MACRS property before the change in the use, the depreciation allowances beginning in the year of change are determined as though the MACRS property is placed in service by the taxpayer in the year of change.

(B) *Computation of depreciation allowance* .—The depreciation allowances for the MACRS property for any 12-month taxable year beginning with the year of change are determined by multiplying the adjusted depreciable basis of the MACRS property as of the first day of each taxable year by the applicable depreciation rate for each taxable year. In determining the applicable depreciation rate for the year of change and subsequent taxable years, the taxpayer must use any applicable depreciation method and recovery period prescribed under section 168 for the MACRS property in the year of change, consistent with any election made under section 168 by the taxpayer for that year (see, for example, section

168(b)(5)). If there is a change in the use of MACRS property, the applicable convention that applies to the MACRS property is the same as the convention that applied before the change in the use of the MACRS property. However, the depreciation allowance for the year of change for the MACRS property is determined without applying the applicable convention, unless the MACRS property is disposed of during the year of change. See paragraph (d)(5) of this section for the rules relating to the computation of the depreciation allowance under the optional depreciation tables. If the year of change or any subsequent taxable year is less than 12 months, the depreciation allowance determined under this paragraph (d)(3)(i) must be adjusted for a short taxable year (for further guidance, for example, see Rev. Proc. 89-15 (1989-1 C.B. 816) (see § 601.601(d)(2)(ii)(*b*) of this chapter)).

(C) *Special rules* .—MACRS property affected by this paragraph (d)(3)(i) is not eligible in the year of change for the election provided under section 168(f)(1), 179, or 1400L(f), or for the additional first year depreciation deduction provided in section 168(k) or 1400L(b). See § 1.168(k)-1(f)(6)(iv) or 1.168(k)-2(g)(6)(iv), as applicable, and § 1.400L(b)-1(f)(6) for other additional first year depreciation deduction rules applicable to a change in the use of MACRS property subsequent to its placed-in-service year. For purposes of determining whether the mid-quarter convention applies to other MACRS property placed in service during the year of change, the unadjusted depreciable basis (as defined in § 1.168(b)-1T(a)(3)) or the adjusted depreciable basis of MACRS property affected by this paragraph (d)(3)(i) is not taken into account.

(ii) *Option to disregard the change in the use* .—In lieu of applying paragraph (d)(3)(i) of this section, the taxpayer may elect to determine the depreciation allowance as though the change in the use had not occurred. The taxpayer elects this option by claiming on the taxpayer's timely filed (including extensions) Federal income tax return for the year of change the depreciation allowance for the property as though the change in the use had not occurred. See paragraph (g)(2) of this section for the manner for revoking this election.

(4) *Change in the use results in a longer recovery period and/or a slower depreciation method* .—(i) *Treated as originally placed in service with longer recovery period and/or slower depreciation method* .—If a change in the use results in a longer recovery period and/or a depreciation method for the MACRS property that is less accelerated than the method used for the MACRS property before the change in the use, the depreciation allowances beginning with the year of change are determined as though the MACRS property had been originally placed in service by the taxpayer with the longer recovery period and/or the slower depreciation method. MACRS property affected by this paragraph (d)(4) is not eligible in the year of change for the election provided under section 168(f)(1), 179, or 1400L(f), or for the additional first year depreciation deduction provided in section 168(k) or 1400L(b). See § 1.168(k)-1(f)(6)(iv) or 1.168(k)-2(g)(6)(iv), as applicable, and § 1.400L(b)-1(f)(6) for other additional first year depreciation deduction rules applicable to a change in the use of MACRS property subsequent to its placed-in-service year.

(ii) *Computation of the depreciation allowance* .—The depreciation allowances for the MACRS property for any 12-month taxable year beginning with the year of change are determined by multiplying the adjusted depreciable basis of the MACRS property as of the first day of each taxable year by the applicable depreciation rate for each taxable year. If there is a change in the use of MACRS property, the applicable convention that applies to the MACRS property is the same as the convention that applied before the change in the use of the MACRS property. If the year of change or any subsequent taxable year is less than 12 months, the depreciation allowance determined under this paragraph (d)(4)(ii) must be adjusted for a short taxable year (for further guidance, for example, see Rev. Proc. 89-15 (1989-1 C.B. 816) (see § 601.601(d)(2)(ii)(*b*) of this chapter)). See paragraph (d)(5) of this section for the rules relating to the computation of the depreciation allowance under the optional depreciation tables. In determining the applicable depreciation rate for the year of change and any subsequent taxable year—

(A) The applicable depreciation method is the depreciation method that would apply in the year of change and any subsequent taxable year for the MACRS property had the taxpayer used the longer recovery period and/or the slower depreciation method in the placed-in-service year of the property. If the 200- or 150-percent declining balance method would have applied in the placed-in-service year but the method would have switched to the straight line method in the year of change or any prior taxable year, the applicable depreciation method beginning with the year of change is the straight line method; and

(B) The applicable recovery period is either—

*(1)* The longer recovery period resulting from the change in the use if the applicable depreciation method is the 200- or 150-percent declining balance method (as determined under paragraph (d)(4)(ii)(A) of this section) unless the recovery period did not change as a result of the change in the use, in which case the applicable recovery period is the same recovery period that applied before the change in the use; or

*(2)* The number of years remaining as of the beginning of each taxable year (taking into account the applicable convention) had the taxpayer used the longer recovery period in the placed-in-service year of the property if the applicable depreciation method is the straight line method (as determined under paragraph (d)(4)(ii)(A) of this section) unless the recovery period did not change as a result of the change in the use, in which case the applicable recovery period is the number of years remaining as of the beginning of each taxable year (taking into account the applicable convention) based on the recovery period that applied before the change in the use.

(5) *Using optional depreciation tables* .—(i) *Taxpayer not bound by prior use of table* .—If a taxpayer used an optional depreciation table for the MACRS property before a change in the use, the taxpayer is not bound to use the appropriate new table for that MACRS property beginning in the year of change (for further guidance, for example, see section 8 of Rev. Proc. 87-57 (1987-2 C.B. 687, 693) (see § 601.601(d)(2)(ii)(*b*) of this chapter)). If a taxpayer did not use an optional depreciation table for MACRS property before a change in the use and the change in the use results in a shorter recovery period and/or a more accelerated depreciation method (as described in paragraph (d)(3)(i) of this section), the taxpayer may use the appropriate new table for that MACRS property beginning in the year of change. If a taxpayer chooses not to use the optional depreciation table, the depreciation allowances for the MACRS property beginning in the year of change are determined under paragraph (d)(3)(i) or (4) of this section, as applicable.

(ii) *Taxpayer chooses to use optional depreciation table after a change in the use* .—If a taxpayer chooses to use an optional depreciation table for the MACRS property after a change in the use, the depreciation allowances for the MACRS property for any 12-month taxable year beginning with the year of change are determined as follows:

(A) *Change in the use results in a shorter recovery period and/or a more accelerated depreciation method* .—If a change in the use results in a shorter recovery period and/or a more accelerated depreciation method (as described in paragraph (d)(3)(i) of this section), the depreciation allowances for the MACRS property for any 12-month taxable year beginning with the year of change are determined by multiplying the adjusted depreciable basis of the MACRS property as of the first day of the year of change by the annual depreciation rate for each recovery year (expressed as a decimal equivalent) specified in the appropriate optional depreciation table. The appropriate optional depreciation table for the MACRS property is based on the depreciation system, depreciation method, recovery period, and convention applicable to the MACRS property in the year of change as determined under paragraph (d)(3)(i) of this section. The depreciation allowance for the year of change for the MACRS property is determined by taking into account the applicable convention (which is already factored into the optional depreciation tables). If the year of change or any subsequent taxable year is less than 12 months, the depreciation allowance determined under this paragraph (d)(5)(ii)(A) must be adjusted for a short taxable year (for further guidance, for example, see Rev. Proc. 89-15 (1989-1 C.B. 816) (see §601.601(d)(2)(ii)(*b*) of this chapter)).

(B) *Change in the use results in a longer recovery period and/or a slower depreciation method*.—*(1) Determination of the appropriate optional depreciation table*.—If a change in the use results in a longer recovery period and/or a slower depreciation method (as described in paragraph (d)(4)(i) of this section), the depreciation allowances for the MACRS property for any 12-month taxable year beginning with the year of change are determined by choosing the optional depreciation table that corresponds to the depreciation system, depreciation method, recovery period, and convention that would have applied to the MACRS property in the placed-in-service year had that property been originally placed in service by the taxpayer with the longer recovery period and/or the slower depreciation method. If there is a change in the use of MACRS property, the applicable convention that applies to the MACRS property is the same as the convention that applied before the change in the use of the MACRS property. If the year of change or any subsequent taxable year is less than 12 months, the depreciation allowance determined under this paragraph (d)(5)(ii)(B) must be adjusted for a short taxable year (for further guidance, for example, see Rev. Proc. 89-15 (1989-1 C.B. 816) (see §601.601(d)(2)(ii)(*b*) of this chapter)).

*(2) Computation of the depreciation allowance*.—The depreciation allowances for the MACRS property for any 12-month taxable year beginning with the year of change are computed by first determining the appropriate recovery year in the table identified under paragraph (d)(5)(ii)(B)(*1*) of this section. The appropriate recovery year for the year of change is the year that corresponds to the year of change. For example, if the recovery year for the year of change would have been Year 4 in the table that applied before the change in the use of the MACRS property, then the recovery year for the year of change is Year 4 in the table identified under paragraph (d)(5)(ii)(B)(*1*) of this section. Next, the annual depreciation rate (expressed as a decimal equivalent) for each recovery year is multiplied by a transaction coefficient. The transaction coefficient is the formula (1 / (1 - x)) where x equals the sum of the annual depreciation rates from the table identified under paragraph (d)(5)(ii)(B)(*1*) of this section (expressed as a decimal equivalent) for the taxable years beginning with the placed-in-service year of the MACRS property through the taxable year immediately prior to the year of change. The product of the annual depreciation rate and the transaction coefficient is multiplied by the adjusted depreciable basis of the MACRS property as of the beginning of the year of change.

(6) *Examples*.—The application of this paragraph (d) is illustrated by the following examples:

*Example 1. Change in the use results in a shorter recovery period and/or a more accelerated depreciation method and optional depreciation table is not used*—(i) *X*, a calendar-year corporation, places in service in 1999 equipment at a cost of

$100,000 and uses this equipment from 1999 through 2003 primarily in its *A* business. *X* depreciates the equipment for 1999 through 2003 under the general depreciation system as 7-year property by using the 200-percent declining balance method (which switched to the straight-line method in 2003), a 7-year recovery period, and a half-year convention. Beginning in 2004, *X* primarily uses the equipment in its *B* business. As a result, the classification of the equipment under section 168(e) changes from 7-year property to 5-year property and the recovery period of the equipment under the general depreciation system changes from 7 years to 5 years. The depreciation method does not change. On January 1, 2004, the adjusted depreciable basis of the equipment is $22,311. *X* depreciates its 5-year recovery property placed in service in 2004 under the general depreciation system by using the 200-percent declining balance method and a 5-year recovery period. *X* does not use the optional depreciation tables.

(ii) Under paragraph (d)(3)(i) of this section, *X*'s allowable depreciation deduction for the equipment for 2004 and subsequent taxable years is determined as though *X* placed the equipment in service in 2004 for use primarily in its *B* business. The depreciable basis of the equipment as of January 1, 2004, is $22,311 (the adjusted depreciable basis at January 1, 2004). Because *X* does not use the optional depreciation tables, the depreciation allowance for 2004 (the deemed placed-in-service year) for this equipment only is computed without taking into account the half-year convention. Pursuant to paragraph (d)(3)(i)(C) of this section, this equipment is not eligible for the additional first year depreciation deduction provided by section 168(k) or section 1400L(b). Thus, *X*'s allowable depreciation deduction for the equipment for 2004 is $8,924 ($22,311 adjusted depreciable basis at January 1, 2004, multiplied by the applicable depreciation rate of 40% (200/5)). *X*'s allowable depreciation deduction for the equipment for 2005 is $5,355 ($13,387 adjusted depreciable basis at January 1, 2005, multiplied by the applicable depreciation rate of 40% (200/5)).

(iii) Alternatively, under paragraph (d)(3)(ii) of this section, *X* may elect to disregard the change in the use and, as a result, may continue to treat the equipment as though it is used primarily in its *A* business. If the election is made, *X*'s allowable depreciation deduction for the equipment for 2004 is $8,924 ($22,311 adjusted depreciable basis at January 1, 2004, multiplied by the applicable depreciation rate of 40% (1/2.5 years remaining at January 1, 2004)). *X*'s allowable depreciation deduction for the equipment for 2005 is $8,925 ($13,387 adjusted depreciable basis at January 1, 2005, multiplied by the applicable depreciation rate of 66.67% (1/1.5 years remaining at January 1, 2005)).

*Example 2. Change in the use results in a shorter recovery period and/or a more accelerated depreciation method and optional depreciation table is used*—(i) Same facts as in *Example 1*, except that *X* used the optional depreciation tables for computing depreciation for 1999 through 2003. Pursuant to paragraph (d)(5) of this section, *X* chooses to continue to use the optional depreciation table for the equipment. *X* does not make the election provided in paragraph (d)(3)(ii) of this section to disregard the change in use.

(ii) In accordance with paragraph (d)(5)(ii)(A) of this section, *X* must first identify the appropriate optional depreciation table for the equipment. This table is table 1 in Rev. Proc. 87-57 because the equipment will be depreciated in the year of change (2004) under the general depreciation system using the 200-percent declining balance method, a 5-year recovery period, and the half-year convention (which is the convention that applied to the equipment in 1999). Pursuant to paragraph (d)(3)(i)(C) of this section, this equipment is not eligible for the additional first year depreciation deduction provided by section 168(k) or section 1400L(b). For 2004, *X* multiplies its adjusted depreciable basis in the equipment as of January 1, 2004, of $22,311, by the annual depreciation rate in table 1 for recovery year 1 for a 5-year recovery period (.20), to determine the depreciation allowance of $4,462. For

2005, *X* multiplies its adjusted depreciable basis in the equipment as of January 1, 2004, of $22,311, by the annual depreciation rate in table 1 for recovery year 2 for a 5-year recovery period (.32), to determine the depreciation allowance of $7,140.

*Example 3. Change in the use results in a longer recovery period and/or a slower depreciation method*—(i) *Y*, a calendar-year corporation, places in service in January 2002, equipment at a cost of $100,000 and uses this equipment in 2002 and 2003 only within the United States. *Y* elects not to deduct the additional first year depreciation under section 168(k). *Y* depreciates the equipment for 2002 and 2003 under the general depreciation system by using the 200-percent declining balance method, a 5-year recovery period, and a half-year convention. Beginning in 2004, *Y* uses the equipment predominantly outside the United States. As a result of this change in the use, the equipment is subject to the alternative depreciation system beginning in 2004. Under the alternative depreciation system, the equipment is depreciated by using the straight line method and a 9-year recovery period. The adjusted depreciable basis of the equipment at January 1, 2004, is $48,000.

(ii) Pursuant to paragraph (d)(4) of this section, *Y*'s allowable depreciation deduction for 2004 and subsequent taxable years is determined as though the equipment had been placed in service in January 2002, as property used predominantly outside the United States. Further, pursuant to paragraph (d)(4)(i) of this section, the equipment is not eligible in 2004 for the additional first year depreciation deduction provided by section 168(k) or section 1400L(b). In determining the applicable depreciation rate for 2004, the applicable depreciation method is the straight line method and the applicable recovery period is 7.5 years, which is the number of years remaining at January 1, 2004, for property placed in service in 2002 with a 9-year recovery period (taking into account the half-year convention). Thus, the depreciation allowance for 2004 is $6,398 ($48,000 adjusted depreciable basis at January 1, 2004, multiplied by the applicable depreciation rate of 13.33% (1/7.5 years)). The depreciation allowance for 2005 is $6,398 ($41,602 adjusted depreciable basis at January 1, 2005, multiplied by the applicable depreciation rate of 15.38% (1/6.5 years remaining at January 1, 2005)).

*Example 4. Change in the use results in a longer recovery period and/or a slower depreciation method and optional depreciation table is used*—(i) Same facts as in *Example 3*, except that *Y* used the optional depreciation tables for computing depreciation in 2002 and 2003. Pursuant to paragraph (d)(5) of this section, *Y* chooses to continue to use the optional depreciation table for the equipment. Further, pursuant to paragraph (d)(4)(i) of this section, the equipment is not eligible in 2004 for the additional first year depreciation deduction provided by section 168(k) or section 1400L(b).

(ii) In accordance with paragraph (d)(5)(ii)(B) of this section, *Y* must first determine the appropriate optional depreciation table for the equipment pursuant to paragraph (d)(5)(ii)(B)(*1*) of this section. This table is table 8 in Rev. Proc. 87-57, which corresponds to the alternative depreciation system, the straight line method, a 9-year recovery period, and the half-year convention (because *Y* depreciated 5-year property in 2002 using a half-year convention). Next, *Y* must determine the appropriate recovery year in table 8. Because the year of change is 2004, the depreciation allowance for the equipment for 2004 is determined using recovery year 3 of table 8. For 2004, *Y* multiplies its adjusted depreciable basis in the equipment as of January 1, 2004, of $48,000, by the product of the annual depreciation rate in table 8 for recovery year 3 for a 9-year recovery period (.1111) and the transaction coefficient of 1.200 [1/(1-(.0556 (table 8 for recovery year 1 for a 9-year recovery period) +.1111 (table 8 for recovery year 2 for a 9-year recovery period)))], to determine the depreciation allowance of $6,399. For 2005, *Y* multiplies its adjusted depreciable basis in the equipment as of January 1, 2004, of $48,000, by the product of the annual depreciation rate in table 8 for recovery year 4 for a 9-year recovery period (.1111) and the transaction coefficient (1.200), to determine the depreciation allowance of $6,399.

(e) *Change in the use of MACRS property during the placed-in-service year* .—(1) *In general* .—Except as provided in paragraph (e)(2) of this section, if a change in the use of MACRS property occurs during the placed-in-service year and the property continues to be MACRS property owned by the same taxpayer, the depreciation allowance for that property for the placed-in-service year is determined by its primary use during that year. The primary use of MACRS property may be determined in any reasonable manner that is consistently applied to the taxpayer's MACRS property. For purposes of this paragraph (e), the determination of whether the mid-quarter convention applies to any MACRS property placed in service during the year of change is made in accordance with § 1.168(d)-1.

(2) *Alternative depreciation system property* .—(i) *Property used within and outside the United States* .—The depreciation allowance for the placed-in-service year for MACRS property that is used within and outside the United States is determined by its predominant use during that year. The determination of whether MACRS property is used predominantly outside the United States during the placed-in-service year shall be made in accordance with the test in § 1.48-1(g)(1)(i) for determining predominant use.

(ii) *Tax-exempt bond financed property* .—The depreciation allowance for the placed-in-service year for MACRS property that changes to tax-exempt bond financed property, as described in section 168(g)(1)(C) and (g)(5), during that taxable year is determined under the alternative depreciation system. For purposes of this paragraph (e), MACRS property changes to tax-exempt bond financed property when a tax-exempt bond is first issued after the MACRS property is placed in service. MACRS property continues to be tax-exempt bond financed property in the hands of the taxpayer even if the tax-exempt bond (including any refunding issue) is not outstanding at, or is redeemed by, the end of the placed-in-service year.

(iii) *Other mandatory alternative depreciation system property* .—The depreciation allowance for the placed-in-service year for MACRS property that changes to, or changes from, property described in section 168(g)(1)(B) (tax-exempt use property) or (D) (imported property covered by an Executive order) during that taxable year is determined under—

(A) The alternative depreciation system if the MACRS property is described in section 168(g)(1)(B) or (D) at the end of the placed-in-service year; or

(B) The general depreciation system if the MACRS property is not described in section 168(g)(1)(B) or (D) at the end of the placed-in-service year, unless other provisions of the Internal Revenue Code or regulations under the Internal Revenue Code require the depreciation allowance for that MACRS property to be determined under the alternative depreciation system (for example, section 168(g)(7)).

(3) *Examples* .—The application of this paragraph (e) is illustrated by the following examples:

*Example 1.* (i) *Z*, a utility and calendar-year corporation, acquires and places in service on January 1, 2004, equipment at a cost of $100,000. *Z* uses this equipment in its combustion turbine production plant for 4 months and then uses the equipment in its steam production plant for the remainder of 2004. *Z*'s combustion turbine production plant assets are classified as 15-year property and are depreciated by *Z* under the general depreciation system using a 15-year recovery period and the 150-percent declining balance method of depreciation. *Z*'s steam production plant assets are classified as 20-year property and are depreciated by *Z* under the general depreciation system using a 20-year recovery period and the 150-percent declining balance method of depreciation. *Z* uses the optional depreciation tables. The equipment is 50-percent bonus depreciation property for purposes of section 168(k).

(ii) Pursuant to this paragraph (e), *Z* must determine depreciation based on the primary use of the equipment during the placed-in-service year. *Z* has consistently determined the primary use of all of its MACRS properties by comparing the number of full months in the taxable year during which a MACRS property is used in one manner with the number of full months in that taxable year during which that MACRS property is used in another manner. Applying this approach, *Z* determines the depreciation allowance for the equipment for 2004 is based on the equipment being classified as 20-year property because the equipment was used by *Z* in its steam production plant for 8 months in 2004. If the half-year convention applies in 2004, the appropriate optional depreciation table is table 1 in Rev. Proc. 87-57, which is the table for MACRS property subject to the general depreciation system, the 150-percent declining balance method, a 20-year recovery period, and the half-year convention. Thus, the depreciation allowance for the equipment for 2004 is $51,875, which is the total of $50,000 for the 50-percent additional first year depreciation deduction allowable (the unadjusted depreciable basis of $100,000 multiplied by .50), plus $1,875 for the 2004 depreciation allowance on the remaining adjusted depreciable basis of $50,000 [(the unadjusted depreciable basis of $100,000 less the additional first year depreciation deduction of $50,000) multiplied by the annual depreciation rate of .0375 in table 1 for recovery year 1 for a 20-year recovery period].

*Example 2. T*, a calendar year corporation, places in service on January 1, 2004, several computers at a total cost of $100,000. *T* uses these computers within the United States for 3 months in 2004 and then moves and uses the computers outside the United States for the remainder of 2004. Pursuant to § 1.48-1(g)(1)(i), the computers are considered as used predominantly outside the United States in 2004. As a result, for 2004, the computers are required to be depreciated under the alternative depreciation system of section 168(g) with a recovery period of 5 years pursuant to section 168(g)(3)(C). *T* uses the optional depreciation tables. If the half-year convention applies in 2004, the appropriate optional depreciation table is table 8 in Rev. Proc. 87-57, which is the table for MACRS property subject to the alternative depreciation system, the straight line method, a 5-year recovery period, and the half-year convention. Thus, the depreciation allowance for the computers for 2004 is $10,000, which is equal to the unadjusted depreciable basis of $100,000 multiplied by the annual depreciation rate of .10 in table 8 for recovery year 1 for a 5-year recovery period. Because the computers are required to be depreciated under the alternative depreciation system in their placed-in-service year, pursuant to section 168(k)(2)(C)(i) and § 1.168(k)-1T(b)(2)(ii), the computers are not eligible for the additional first year depreciation deduction provided by section 168(k).

(f) *No change in accounting method* .—A change in computing the depreciation allowance in the year of change for property subject to this section is not a change in method of accounting under section 446(e). See § 1.446-1(e)(2)(ii)( *d*)( *3*)( *ii*).

(g) *Effective dates* .—(1) *In general* .—Except as provided in paragraph (g)(2) of this section, this section applies to any change in the use of MACRS property in a taxable year ending on or after June 17, 2004. For any change in the use of MACRS property after December 31, 1986, in a taxable year ending before June 17, 2004, the Internal Revenue Service will allow any reasonable method of depreciating the property under section 168 in the year of change and the subsequent taxable years that is consistently applied to any property for which the use changes in the hands of the same taxpayer or the taxpayer may choose, on a property-by-property basis, to apply the provisions of this section.

(2) *Qualified property under section 168(k) acquired and placed in service after September 27, 2017* .—(i) *In general* .—The language "or § 1.168(k)-2(g)(6)(iii), as applicable" in paragraph (b)(1) of this section, the language "or § 1.168(k)-2(g)(6)(ii), as applicable" in paragraph (c) of this section, and the language "or § 1.168(k)-2(g)(6)(iv), as applicable" in paragraphs (d)(3)(i)(C) and (d)(4)(i) of this section applies to any change in use of MACRS property, which is qualified property under section 168(k)(2), by a taxpayer during or after the taxpayer's taxable year that includes September 24, 2019.

(ii) *Early application* .—A taxpayer may choose to apply the language "or § 1.168(k)-2(g)(6)(iii), as applicable" in paragraph (b)(1) of this section, the language "or § 1.168(k)-2(g)(6)(ii), as applicable" in paragraph (c) of this section, and the language "or § 1.168(k)-2(g)(6)(iv), as applicable" in paragraphs (d)(3)(i)(C) and (d)(4)(i) of this section for any change in use of MACRS property, which is qualified property under section 168(k)(2) and acquired and placed in service after September 27, 2017, by the taxpayer during taxable years ending on or after September 28, 2017.

(iii) *Early application of regulation project REG-104397-18* .—A taxpayer may rely on the language "or § 1.168(k)-2(f)(6)(iii), as applicable" in paragraph (b)(1) of this section, the language "or § 1.168(k)-2(f)(6)(ii), as applicable" in paragraph (c) of this section, and the language "or § 1.168(k)-2(f)(6)(iv), as applicable" in paragraphs (d)(3)(i)(C) and (d)(4)(i) of this section in regulation project REG-104397-18 (2018-41 I.R.B. 558) (see § 601.601(d)(2)(ii)(*b*) of this chapter) for any change in use of MACRS property, which is qualified property under section 168(k)(2) and acquired and placed in service after September 27, 2017, by the taxpayer during taxable years ending on or after September 28, 2017, and ending before the taxpayer's taxable year that includes September 24, 2019.

(3) *Change in method of accounting* .—(i) *In general* .—If a taxpayer adopted a method of accounting for depreciation due to a change in the use of MACRS property in a taxable year ending on or after December 30, 2003, and the method adopted is not in accordance with the method of accounting for depreciation provided in this section, a change to the method of accounting for depreciation provided in this section is a change in method of accounting to which the provisions of sections 446(e) and 481 and the regulations under sections 446(e) and 481 apply. Also, a revocation of the election provided in paragraph (d)(3)(ii) of this section to disregard a change in the use is a change in method of accounting to which the provisions of sections 446(e) and 481 and the regulations under sections 446(e) and 481 apply. However, if a taxpayer adopted a method of accounting for depreciation due to a change in the use of MACRS property after December 31, 1986, in a taxable year ending before December 30, 2003, and the method adopted is not in accordance with the method of accounting for depreciation provided in this section, the taxpayer may treat the change to the method of accounting for depreciation provided in this section as a change in method of accounting to which the provisions of sections 446(e) and 481 and the regulations under sections 446(e) and 481 apply.

(ii) *Automatic consent to change method of accounting* .—A taxpayer changing its method of accounting in accordance with this paragraph (g)(2) must follow the applicable administrative procedures issued under § 1.446-1(e)(3)(ii) for obtaining the Commissioner's automatic consent to a change in method of accounting (for further guidance, for example, see Rev. Proc. 2002-9 (2002-1 C.B. 327) (see § 601.601(d)(2)(ii)(*b*) of this chapter)). Any change in method of accounting made under this paragraph (g)(2) must be made using an adjustment under section

481(a). For purposes of Form 3115, *Application for Change in Accounting Method*, the designated number for the automatic accounting method change authorized by this paragraph (g)(2) is "88." If Form 3115 is revised or renumbered, any reference in this section to that form is treated as a reference to the revised or renumbered form. [Reg. § 1.168(i)-4.]

**.01 Historical Comment:** Proposed 7/21/2003. Adopted 6/16/2004 by T.D. 9132. Amended 12/22/2006 by T.D. 9307 and 9/17/2019 by T.D. 9874.

## ¶ 568A

## Reg. § 1.168(i)-5

§ 1.168(i)-5. **Table of contents .**—This section lists the major paragraphs contained in § 1.168(i)-6.

*§ 1.168(i)-6 Like-kind exchanges and involuntary conversions.*

(a) Scope.

(b) Definitions.

(1) Replacement MACRS property.

(2) Relinquished MACRS property.

(3) Time of disposition.

(4) Time of replacement.

(5) Year of disposition.

(6) Year of replacement.

(7) Exchanged basis.

(8) Excess basis.

(9) Depreciable exchanged basis.

(10) Depreciable excess basis.

(11) Like-kind exchange.

(12) Involuntary conversion.

(c) Determination of depreciation allowance.

(1) Computation of the depreciation allowance for depreciable exchanged basis beginning in the year of replacement.

(i) In general.

(ii) Applicable recovery period, depreciation method, and convention.

(2) Effect of depreciation treatment of the replacement MACRS property by previous owners of the acquired property.

(3) Recovery period and/or depreciation method of the properties are the same, or both are not the same.

(i) In general.

(ii) Both the recovery period and the depreciation method are the same.

(iii) Either the recovery period or the depreciation method is the same, or both are not the same.

(4) Recovery period or depreciation method of the properties is not the same.

(i) Longer recovery period.

(ii) Shorter recovery period.

(iii) Less accelerated depreciation method.

(iv) More accelerated depreciation method.

(v) Convention.

(A) Either the relinquished MACRS property or the replacement MACRS property is mid-month property.

(B) Neither the relinquished MACRS property nor the replacement MACRS property is mid-month property.

(5) Year of disposition and year of replacement.

(i) Relinquished MACRS property.

(A) General rule.

(B) Special rule.

(ii) Replacement MACRS property.

(A) Remaining recovery period of the replacement MACRS property.

(B) Year of replacement is 12 months.

(iii) Year of disposition or year of replacement is less than 12 months.

(iv) Deferred transactions.

(A) In general.

(B) Allowable depreciation for a qualified intermediary.

(v) Remaining recovery period.

(6) Examples.

(d) Special rules for determining depreciation allowances.

(1) Excess basis.

(i) In general.

(ii) Example.

(2) Depreciable and nondepreciable property.

(3) Depreciation limitations for automobiles.

(i) In general.

(ii) Order in which limitations on depreciation under section 280F(a) are applied.

(iii) Examples.

(4) Involuntary conversion for which the replacement MACRS property is acquired and placed in service before disposition of relinquished MACRS property.

(e) Use of optional depreciation tables.

(1) Taxpayer not bound by prior use of table.

(2) Determination of the depreciation deduction.

(i) Relinquished MACRS property.

(ii) Replacement MACRS property.

(A) Determination of the appropriate optional depreciation table.

(B) Calculating the depreciation deduction for the replacement MACRS property.

(iii) Unrecovered basis.

(3) Excess basis.

(4) Examples.

(f) Mid-quarter convention.

(1) Exchanged basis.

(2) Excess basis.

(3) Depreciable property acquired for nondepreciable property.

(g) Section 179 election.

(h) Additional first year depreciation deduction.

(i) Elections.

(1) Election not to apply this section.

(2) Election to treat certain replacement property as MACRS property.

(j) Time and manner of making election under paragraph (i)(1) of this section.

(1) In general.

(2) Time for making election.

(3) Manner of making election.

(4) Revocation.

(k) Effective date.

(1) In general.

(2) Application to pre-effective date like-kind exchanges and involuntary conversions.

(3) Like-kind exchanges and involuntary conversions where the taxpayer made the election under section 168(f)(1) for the relinquished property. [Reg. § 1.168(i)-5.]

**.01 Historical Comment:** Proposed 3/1/2004. Adopted 2/26/2007 by T.D. 9314.

## ¶ 568B

## Reg. § 1.168(i)-6

§ 1.168(i)-6. **Like-kind exchanges and involuntary conversions .**—(a) *Scope* .—This section provides the rules for determining the depreciation allowance for MACRS property acquired in a like-kind exchange or an involuntary conversion, including a like-kind exchange or an involuntary conversion of MACRS property that is exchanged or replaced with other MACRS property in a transaction between members of the same affiliated group. The allowance for depreciation under this section constitutes the amount of depreciation allowable under section 167(a) for the year of replacement and any subsequent taxable year for the replacement MACRS property and for the year of disposition of the relinquished MACRS property. The provisions of this section apply only to MACRS property to which § 1.168(h)-1 (like-kind exchanges of tax-exempt use property) does not apply. Additionally, paragraphs (c) through (f) of this section apply only to MACRS property for which an election under paragraph (i) of this section has not been made.

(b) *Definitions* .—For purposes of this section, the following definitions apply:

(1) *Replacement MACRS property* is MACRS property (as defined in § 1.168(b)-1(a)(2)) in the hands of the acquiring taxpayer that is acquired for other MACRS property in a like-kind exchange or an involuntary conversion.

(2) *Relinquished MACRS property* is MACRS property that is transferred by the taxpayer in a like-kind exchange, or in an involuntary conversion.

(3) *Time of disposition* is when the disposition of the relinquished MACRS property takes place under the convention, as determined under § 1.168(d)-1, that applies to the relinquished MACRS property.

(4) *Time of replacement* is the later of—

(i) When the replacement MACRS property is placed in service under the convention, as determined under this section, that applies to the replacement MACRS property; or

(ii) The time of disposition of the exchanged or involuntarily converted property.

(5) *Year of disposition* is the taxable year that includes the time of disposition.

(6) *Year of replacement* is the taxable year that includes the time of replacement.

(7) *Exchanged basis* is determined after the depreciation deductions for the year of disposition are determined under paragraph (c)(5)(i) of this section and is the lesser of—

(i) The basis in the replacement MACRS property, as determined under section 1031(d) and the regulations under section 1031(d) or section 1033(b) and the regulations under section 1033(b); or

(ii) The adjusted depreciable basis (as defined in § 1.168(b)-1(a)(4)) of the relinquished MACRS property.

(8) *Excess basis* is any excess of the basis in the replacement MACRS property, as determined under section 1031(d) and the regulations under section 1031(d) or section 1033(b) and the regulations under section 1033(b), over the exchanged basis as determined under paragraph (b)(7) of this section.

(9) *Depreciable exchanged basis* is the exchanged basis as determined under paragraph (b)(7) of this section reduced by—

(i) The percentage of such basis attributable to the taxpayer's use of property for the taxable year other than in the taxpayer's trade or business (or for the production of income); and

(ii) Any adjustments to basis provided by other provisions of the Internal Revenue Code (Code) and the regulations under the Code (including section 1016(a)(2) and (3), for example, depreciation deductions in the year of replacement allowable under section 168(k) or 1400L(b)).

(10) *Depreciable excess basis* is the excess basis as determined under paragraph (b)(8) of this section reduced by—

(i) The percentage of such basis attributable to the taxpayer's use of property for the taxable year other than in the taxpayer's trade or business (or for the production of income);

(ii) Any portion of the basis the taxpayer properly elects to treat as an expense under section 179; and

(iii) Any adjustments to basis provided by other provisions of the Code and the regulations under the Code (including section 1016(a)(2) and (3), for example, depreciation deductions in the year of replacement allowable under section 168(k) or 1400L(b)).

(11) *Like-kind exchange* is an exchange of property in a transaction to which section 1031(a)(1), (b), or (c) applies.

(12) *Involuntary conversion* is a transaction described in section 1033(a)(1) or (2) that resulted in the nonrecognition of any part of the gain realized as the result of the conversion.

(c) *Determination of depreciation allowance* .—(1) *Computation of the depreciation allowance for depreciable exchanged basis beginning in the year of replacement* .—(i) *In general* .—This paragraph (c) provides rules for determining the applicable recovery period, the applicable depreciation method, and the applicable convention used to determine the depreciation allowances for the depreciable exchanged basis beginning in the year of replacement. See paragraph (c)(5) of this section for rules relating to the computation of the depreciation allowance for the year of disposition and for the year of replacement. See paragraph (d)(1) of this section for rules relating to the computation of the depreciation allowance for depreciable excess basis. See paragraph (d)(4) of this section if the replacement MACRS property is acquired before disposition of the relinquished MACRS property in a transaction to which section 1033 applies. See paragraph (e) of this section for rules relating to the computation of the depreciation allowance using the optional depreciation tables.

(ii) *Applicable recovery period, depreciation method, and convention* .—The recovery period, depreciation method, and convention determined under this paragraph (c) are the only permissible methods of accounting for MACRS property within the scope of this section unless the taxpayer makes the election under paragraph (i) of this section not to apply this section.

(2) *Effect of depreciation treatment of the replacement MACRS property by previous owners of the acquired property* .—If replacement MACRS property is acquired by a taxpayer in a like-kind exchange or an involuntary conversion, the

depreciation treatment of the replacement MACRS property by previous owners has no effect on the determination of depreciation allowances for the replacement MACRS property in the hands of the acquiring taxpayer. For example, a taxpayer exchanging, in a like-kind exchange, MACRS property for property that was depreciated under section 168 of the Internal Revenue Code of 1954 (ACRS) by the previous owner must use this section because the replacement property will become MACRS property in the hands of the acquiring taxpayer. In addition, elections made by previous owners in determining depreciation allowances for the replacement MACRS property have no effect on the acquiring taxpayer. For example, a taxpayer exchanging, in a like-kind exchange, MACRS property that the taxpayer depreciates under the general depreciation system of section 168(a) for other MACRS property that the previous owner elected to depreciate under the alternative depreciation system pursuant to section 168(g)(7) does not have to continue using the alternative depreciation system for the replacement MACRS property.

(3) *Recovery period and/or depreciation method of the properties are the same, or both are not the same* .—(i) *In general* .—For purposes of paragraphs (c)(3) and (c)(4) of this section in determining whether the recovery period and the depreciation method prescribed under section 168 for the replacement MACRS property are the same as the recovery period and the depreciation method prescribed under section 168 for the relinquished MACRS property, the recovery period and the depreciation method for the replacement MACRS property are considered to be the recovery period and the depreciation method that would have applied under section 168, taking into account any elections made by the acquiring taxpayer under section 168(b)(5) or 168(g)(7), had the replacement MACRS property been placed in service by the acquiring taxpayer at the same time as the relinquished MACRS property.

(ii) *Both the recovery period and the depreciation method are the same* .—If both the recovery period and the depreciation method prescribed under section 168 for the replacement MACRS property are the same as the recovery period and the depreciation method prescribed under section 168 for the relinquished MACRS property, the depreciation allowances for the replacement MACRS property beginning in the year of replacement are determined by using the same recovery period and depreciation method that were used for the relinquished MACRS property. Thus, the replacement MACRS property is depreciated over the remaining recovery period (taking into account the applicable convention), and by using the depreciation method, of the relinquished MACRS property. Except as provided in paragraph (c)(5) of this section, the depreciation allowances for the depreciable exchanged basis for any 12-month taxable year beginning with the year of replacement are determined by multiplying the depreciable exchanged basis by the applicable depreciation rate for each taxable year (for further guidance, for example, see section 6 of Rev. Proc. 87-57 (1987-2 CB 687, 692) and §601.601(d)(2)(ii)( *b*) of this chapter).

(iii) *Either the recovery period or the depreciation method is the same, or both are not the same* .—If either the recovery period or the depreciation method prescribed under section 168 for the replacement MACRS property is the same as the recovery period or the depreciation method prescribed under section 168 for the relinquished MACRS property, the depreciation allowances for the depreciable exchanged basis beginning in the year of replacement are determined using the recovery period or the depreciation method that is the same as the relinquished MACRS property. See paragraph (c)(4) of this section to determine the depreciation allowances when the recovery period or the depreciation method of the replacement MACRS property is not the same as that of the relinquished MACRS property.

(4) *Recovery period or depreciation method of the properties is not the same* .—If the recovery period prescribed under section 168 for the replacement MACRS property (as determined under paragraph (c)(3)(i) of this section) is not the same as the recovery period prescribed under section 168 for the relinquished MACRS property, the depreciation allowances for the depreciable exchanged basis beginning in the year of replacement are determined under this paragraph (c)(4). Similarly, if the depreciation method prescribed under section 168 for the replacement MACRS property (as determined under paragraph (c)(3)(i) of this section) is not the same as the depreciation method prescribed under section 168 for the relinquished MACRS property, the depreciation method used to determine the depreciation allowances for the depreciable exchanged basis beginning in the year of replacement is determined under this paragraph (c)(4).

(i) *Longer recovery period* .—If the recovery period prescribed under section 168 for the replacement MACRS property (as determined under paragraph (c)(3)(i) of this section) is longer than that prescribed for the relinquished MACRS property, the depreciation allowances for the depreciable exchanged basis beginning in the year of replacement are determined as though the replacement MACRS property had originally been placed in service by the acquiring taxpayer in the same taxable year the relinquished MACRS property was placed in service by the acquiring taxpayer, but using the longer recovery period of the replacement MACRS property (as determined under paragraph (c)(3)(i) of this section) and the convention determined under paragraph (c)(4)(v) of this section. Thus, the depreciable exchanged basis is depreciated over the remaining recovery period (taking into account the applicable convention) of the replacement MACRS property.

(ii) *Shorter recovery period* .—If the recovery period prescribed under section 168 for the replacement MACRS property (as determined under paragraph (c)(3)(i) of this section) is shorter than that of the relinquished MACRS property, the depreciation allowances for the depreciable exchanged basis beginning in the year of replacement are determined using the same recovery period as that of the relinquished MACRS property. Thus, the depreciable exchanged basis is depreciated over the remaining recovery period (taking into account the applicable convention) of the relinquished MACRS property.

(iii) *Less accelerated depreciation method* .—(A) If the depreciation method prescribed under section 168 for the replacement MACRS property (as determined under paragraph (c)(3)(i) of this section) is less accelerated than that of the relinquished MACRS property at the time of disposition, the depreciation allowances for the depreciable exchanged basis beginning in the year of replacement are determined as though the replacement MACRS property had originally been placed in service by the acquiring taxpayer at the same time the relinquished MACRS property was placed in service by the acquiring taxpayer, but using the less accelerated depreciation method. Thus, the depreciable exchanged basis is depreciated using the less accelerated depreciation method.

(B) Except as provided in paragraph (c)(5) of this section, the depreciation allowances for the depreciable exchanged basis for any 12-month taxable year beginning in the year of replacement are determined by multiplying the adjusted depreciable basis by the applicable depreciation rate for each taxable year. If, for example, the depreciation method of the replacement MACRS property in the year of replacement is the 150-percent declining balance method and the depreciation method of the relinquished MACRS property in the year of replacement is the 200-percent declining balance method, and neither method had been switched to the straight line method in the year of replacement or any prior taxable year, the applicable depreciation rate for the year of replacement and subsequent taxable years is determined by using the depreciation rate of the replacement MACRS property as if the replacement MACRS property was placed in service by the acquiring taxpayer at the same time the relinquished MACRS property was placed in service by the acquiring taxpayer, until the 150-percent declining balance method has been switched to the straight line method. If, for example, the depreciation method of the replacement MACRS property is the straight line method, the applicable depreciation rate for the year of replacement is determined by using the remaining recovery period at the beginning of the year of disposition (as determined under this paragraph (c)(4) and taking into account the applicable convention).

(iv) *More accelerated depreciation method* .—(A) If the depreciation method prescribed under section 168 for the replacement MACRS property (as determined under paragraph (c)(3)(i) of this section) is more accelerated than that of the relinquished MACRS property at the time of disposition, the depreciation allowances for the replacement MACRS property beginning in the year of replacement are determined using the same depreciation method as the relinquished MACRS property.

(B) Except as provided in paragraph (c)(5) of this section, the depreciation allowances for the depreciable exchanged basis for any 12-month taxable year beginning in the year of replacement are determined by multiplying the adjusted depreciable basis by the applicable depreciation rate for each taxable year. If, for example, the depreciation method of the relinquished MACRS property in the year of replacement is the 150-percent declining balance method and the depreciation method of the replacement MACRS property in the year of replacement is the 200-percent declining balance method, and neither method had been switched to the straight line method in the year of replacement or any prior taxable year, the applicable depreciation rate for the year of replacement and subsequent taxable years is the same depreciation rate that applied to the relinquished MACRS property in the year of replacement, until the 150-percent declining balance method has been switched to the straight line method. If, for example, the depreciation method is the straight line method, the applicable depreciation rate for the year of replacement is determined by using the remaining recovery period at the beginning of the year of disposition (as determined under this paragraph (c)(4) and taking into account the applicable convention).

(v) *Convention* .—The applicable convention for the exchanged basis is determined under this paragraph (c)(4)(v).

(A) *Either the relinquished MACRS property or the replacement MACRS property is mid-month property* .—If either the relinquished MACRS property or the replacement MACRS property is property for which the applicable convention (as determined under section 168(d)) is the mid-month convention, the exchanged basis must be depreciated using the mid-month convention.

(B) *Neither the relinquished MACRS property nor the replacement MACRS property is mid-month property* .—If neither the relinquished MACRS property nor the replacement MACRS property is property for which the applicable convention (as determined under section 168(d)) is the mid-month convention, the applicable convention for the exchanged basis is the same convention that applied to the relinquished MACRS property. If the relinquished MACRS property is placed in service in the year of disposition, and the time of replacement is also in the year of disposition, the convention that applies to the relinquished MACRS property is determined under paragraph (f)(1)(i) of this section. If, however, relinquished MACRS property was placed in service in the year of disposition and the time of replacement is in a taxable year subsequent to the year of disposition, the convention that applies to the exchanged basis is the convention that applies in that subsequent taxable year (see paragraph (f)(1)(ii) of this section).

(5) *Year of disposition and year of replacement* .—No depreciation deduction is allowable for MACRS property disposed of by a taxpayer in a like-kind exchange or involuntary conversion in the same taxable year that such property was placed in service by the taxpayer. If replacement MACRS property is disposed of by a taxpayer during the same taxable year that the relinquished MACRS property is placed in service by the taxpayer, no depreciation deduction is allowable for either MACRS property. Otherwise, the depreciation allowances for the year of disposition and for the year of replacement are determined as follows:

(i) *Relinquished MACRS property* .—(A) *General rule* .—Except as provided in paragraphs (c)(5)(i)(B), (c)(5)(iii), (e), and (i) of this section, the depreciation allowance in the year of disposition for the relinquished MACRS property is computed by multiplying the allowable depreciation deduction for the property for that year by a fraction, the numerator of which is the number of months (including fractions of months) the property is deemed to be placed in service during the year of disposition (taking into account the applicable convention of the relinquished MACRS property), and the denominator of which is 12. In the case of termination under § 1.168(i)-1(e)(3)(v) of general asset account treatment of an asset, or of all the assets remaining, in a general asset account, the allowable depreciation deduction in the year of disposition for the asset or assets for which general asset account treatment is terminated is determined using the depreciation method, recovery period, and convention of the general asset account. This allowable depreciation deduction is adjusted to account for the period the asset or assets is deemed to be in service in accordance with this paragraph (c)(5)(i).

(B) *Special rule* .—If, at the beginning of the year of disposition, the remaining recovery period of the relinquished MACRS property, taking into account the applicable convention of such property, is less than the period between the beginning of the year of disposition and the time of disposition, the depreciation deduction for the relinquished MACRS property for the year of disposition is equal to the adjusted depreciable basis of the relinquished MACRS property at the beginning of the year of disposition. If this paragraph applies, the exchanged basis is zero and no depreciation is allowable for the exchanged basis in the replacement MACRS property.

(ii) *Replacement MACRS property* .—(A) *Remaining recovery period of the replacement MACRS property* .—The replacement MACRS property is treated as placed in service at the time of replacement under the convention that applies to the replacement MACRS property as determined under this paragraph (c)(5)(ii). The remaining recovery period of the replacement MACRS property at the time of replacement is the excess of the recovery period for the replacement MACRS property, as determined under paragraph (c) of this section, over the period of time that the replacement MACRS property would have been in service if it had been placed in service when the relinquished MACRS property was placed in service and removed from service at the time of disposition of the relinquished MACRS property. This period is determined by using the convention that applied to the relinquished MACRS property to determine the date that the relinquished MACRS property is deemed to have been placed in service and the date that it is deemed to have been disposed of. The length of time the replacement MACRS property would have been in service is determined by using these dates and the convention that applies to the replacement MACRS property.

(B) *Year of replacement is 12 months* .—Except as provided in paragraphs (c)(5)(iii), (e), and (i) of this section, the depreciation allowance in the year of replacement for the depreciable exchanged basis is determined by—

(1) Calculating the applicable depreciation rate for the replacement MACRS property as of the beginning of the year of replacement taking

into account the depreciation method prescribed for the replacement MACRS property under paragraph (c)(3) of this section and the remaining recovery period of the replacement MACRS property as of the beginning of the year of disposition as determined under this paragraph (c)(5)(ii);

(2) Calculating the depreciable exchanged basis of the replacement MACRS property, and adding to that amount the amount determined under paragraph (c)(5)(i) of this section for the year of disposition; and

(3) Multiplying the product of the amounts determined under paragraphs (c)(5)(ii)(B)( *1*) and (B)( *2*) of this section by a fraction, the numerator of which is the number of months (including fractions of months) the property is deemed to be in service during the year of replacement (in the year of replacement the replacement MACRS property is deemed to be placed in service by the acquiring taxpayer at the time of replacement under the convention determined under paragraph (c)(4)(v) of this section), and the denominator of which is 12.

(iii) *Year of disposition or year of replacement is less than 12 months* .—If the year of disposition or the year of replacement is less than 12 months, the depreciation allowance determined under paragraph (c)(5)(ii)(A) of this section must be adjusted for a short taxable year (for further guidance, for example, see Rev. Proc. 89-15 (1989-1 CB 816) and § 601.601(d)(2)(ii)( *b*) of this chapter).

(iv) *Deferred transactions* .—(A) *In general* .—If the replacement MACRS property is not acquired until after the disposition of the relinquished MACRS property, taking into account the applicable convention of the relinquished MACRS property and replacement MACRS property, depreciation is not allowable during the period between the disposition of the relinquished MACRS property and the acquisition of the replacement MACRS property. The recovery period for the replacement MACRS property is suspended during this period. For purposes of paragraph (c)(5)(ii) of this section, only the depreciable exchanged basis of the replacement MACRS property is taken into account for calculating the amount in paragraph (c)(5)(ii)(B)( *2*) of this section if the year of replacement is a taxable year subsequent to the year of disposition.

(B) *Allowable depreciation for a qualified intermediary* .—[Reserved].

(v) *Remaining recovery period* .—The remaining recovery period of the replacement MACRS property is determined as of the beginning of the year of disposition of the relinquished MACRS property. For purposes of determining the remaining recovery period of the replacement MACRS property, the replacement MACRS property is deemed to have been originally placed in service under the convention determined under paragraph (c)(4)(v) of this section but at the time the relinquished MACRS property was deemed to be placed in service under the convention that applied to it when it was placed in service.

(6) *Examples* .—The application of this paragraph (c) is illustrated by the following examples:

*Example 1.* A1, a calendar-year taxpayer, exchanges Building M, an office building, for Building N, a warehouse in a like-kind exchange. Building M is relinquished in July 2004 and Building N is acquired and placed in service in October 2004. A1 did not make any elections under section 168 for either Building M or Building N. The unadjusted depreciable basis of Building M was $4,680,000 when placed in service in July 1997. Since the recovery period and depreciation method prescribed under section 168 for Building N (39 years, straight line method) are the same as the recovery period and depreciation method prescribed under section 168 for Building M (39 years, straight line method), Building N is depreciated over the remaining recovery period of, and using the same depreciation method and convention as that of, Building M. Applying the applicable convention, Building M is deemed disposed of on July 15, 2004, and Building N is placed in service on October 15, 2004. Thus, Building N will be depreciated using the straight line method over a remaining recovery period of 32 years beginning in October 2004 (the remaining recovery period of 32 years and 6.5 months at the beginning of 2004, less the 6.5 months of depreciation taken prior to the disposition of the exchanged MACRS property (Building M) in 2004). For 2004, the year in which the transaction takes place, the depreciation allowance for Building M is ($120,000) (6.5/12) which equals $65,000. The depreciation allowance for Building N for 2004 is ($120,000) (2.5/12) which equals $25,000. For 2005 and subsequent years, Building N is depreciated over the remaining recovery period of, and using the same depreciation method and convention as that of, Building M. Thus, the depreciation allowance for Building N is the same as Building M, namely $10,000 per month.

*Example 2.* B, a calendar-year taxpayer, placed in service Bridge P in January 1998. Bridge P is depreciated using the half-year convention. In January 2004, B exchanges Bridge P for Building Q, an apartment building, in a like-kind exchange. Pursuant to paragraph (k) (2) (i) of this section, B decided to apply § 1.168(i)-6 to the exchange of Bridge P for Building Q, the replacement MACRS property. B did not make any elections under section 168 for either Bridge P or Building Q. Since the recovery period prescribed under section 168 for Building Q (27.5 years) is longer than that of Bridge P (15 years), Building Q is depreciated as if it had originally been placed in service in July 1998 and disposed of in July 2004 using a 27.5 year recovery period. Additionally, since the depreciation method prescribed under section 168 for Building Q (straight line method) is less accelerated than that of Bridge P (150-percent declining balance method), then the depreciation allowance for Building Q is computed using the straight line method. Thus, when Building Q is acquired and placed in service in 2004, its basis is depreciated over the remaining 21.5 year recovery period using the straight line method of depreciation and the mid-month convention beginning in July 2004.

*Example 3.* C, a calendar-year taxpayer, placed in service Building R, a restaurant, in January 1996. In January 2004, C exchanges Building R for Tower S, a radio transmitting tower, in a like-kind exchange. Pursuant to paragraph (k) (2) (i) of this section, C decided to apply § 1.168(i)-6 to the exchange of Building R for Tower S, the replacement MACRS property. C did not make any elections under section 168 for either Building R or Tower S. Since the recovery period prescribed under section 168 for Tower S (15 years) is shorter than that of Building R (39 years), Tower S is depreciated over the remaining recovery period of Building R. Additionally, since the depreciation method prescribed under section 168 for Tower S (150% declining balance method) is more accelerated than that of Building R (straight line method), then the depreciation allowance for Tower S is also computed using the same depreciation method as Building R. Thus, Tower S is depreciated over the remaining 31 year recovery period of Building R using the straight line method of depreciation and the mid-month convention. Alternatively, C may elect under paragraph (i) of this section to treat Tower S as though it is placed in service in January 2004. In such case, C uses the applicable recovery period, depreciation method, and convention prescribed under section 168 for Tower S.

*Example 4.* (i) In February 2002, D, a calendar-year taxpayer and manufacturer of rubber products, acquired for $60,000 and placed in service Asset T (a special tool) and depreciated Asset T using the straight line method election under section 168(b) (5) and the mid-quarter convention over its 3-year recovery period. D elected not to deduct the additional first year depreciation for 3-year property placed in service in 2002. In June 2004, D exchanges Asset T for Asset U (not a special tool) in a like-kind exchange. D elected not to deduct the additional first year depreciation for 7-year property placed in service in 2004. Since the recovery period prescribed under section 168 for Asset U (7 years) is longer than that of

Asset T (3 years), Asset U is depreciated as if it had originally been placed in service in February 2002 using a 7-year recovery period. Additionally, since the depreciation method prescribed under section 168 for Asset U (200-percent declining balance method) is more accelerated than that of Asset T (straight line method) at the time of disposition, the depreciation allowance for Asset U is computed using the straight line method. Asset U is depreciated over its remaining recovery period of 4.75 years using the straight line method of depreciation and the mid-quarter convention.

(ii) The 2004 depreciation allowance for Asset T is $7,500 ($20,000 allowable depreciation deduction for 2004) × 4.5 months ÷ 12).

(iii) The depreciation rate in 2004 for Asset U is 0.1951 (1 ÷ 5.125 years (the length of the applicable recovery period remaining as of the beginning of 2004)). Therefore, the depreciation allowance for Asset U in 2004 is $2,744 (0.1951 × $22,500 (the sum of the $15,000 depreciable exchanged basis of Asset U ($22,500 adjusted depreciable basis at the beginning of 2004 for Asset T, less the $7,500 depreciation allowable for Asset T for 2004) and the $7,500 depreciation allowable for Asset T for 2004) × 7.5 months ÷ 12).

*Example 5.* The facts are the same as in *Example 4* except that D exchanges Asset T for Asset U in June 2005, in a like-kind exchange. Under these facts, the remaining recovery period of Asset T at the beginning of 2005 is 1.5 months and, as a result, is less than the 5-month period between the beginning of 2005 (year of disposition) and June 2005 (time of disposition). Accordingly, pursuant to paragraph (c)(5)(i)(B) of this section, the 2005 depreciation allowance for Asset T is $2,500 ($2,500 adjusted depreciable basis at the beginning of 2005 ($60,000 original basis minus $17,500 depreciation deduction for 2002 minus $20,000 depreciation deduction for 2003 minus $20,000 depreciation deduction for 2004)). Because the exchanged basis of asset U is $0.00 no depreciation is allowable for asset U.

*Example 6.* On January 1, 2004, E, a calendar-year taxpayer, acquired and placed in service Canopy V, a gas station canopy. The purchase price of Canopy V was $60,000. On August 1, 2004, Canopy V was destroyed in a hurricane and was therefore no longer usable in E's business. On October 1, 2004, as part of the involuntary conversion, E acquired and placed in service new Canopy W with the insurance proceeds E received due to the loss of Canopy V. E elected not to deduct the additional first year depreciation for 5-year property placed in service in 2004. E depreciates both canopies under the general depreciation system of section 168(a) by using the 200-percent declining balance method of depreciation, a 5-year recovery period, and the half-year convention. No depreciation deduction is allowable for Canopy V. The depreciation deduction allowable for Canopy W for 2004 is $12,000 ($60,000 × the annual depreciation rate of .40 × ½ year). For 2005, the depreciation deduction for Canopy W is $19,200 ($48,000 adjusted basis × the annual depreciation rate of .40).

*Example 7.* The facts are the same as in *Example 6,* except that E did not make the election out of the additional first year depreciation for 5-year property placed in service in 2004. E depreciates both canopies under the general depreciation system of section 168(a) by using the 200-percent declining balance method of depreciation, a 5-year recovery period, and the half-year convention. No depreciation deduction is allowable for Canopy V. For 2004, E is allowed a 50-percent additional first year depreciation deduction of $30,000 for Canopy W (the unadjusted depreciable basis of $60,000 multiplied by .50), and a regular MACRS depreciation deduction of $6,000 for Canopy W (the depreciable exchanged basis of $30,000 multiplied by the annual depreciation rate of .40 × ½ year). For 2005, E is allowed a regular MACRS depreciation deduction of $9,600 for Canopy W (the depreciable exchanged basis of $24,000 ($30,000 minus regular 2003 depreciation of $6,000) multiplied by the annual depreciation rate of .40).

*Example 8*. In January 2001, F, a calendar-year taxpayer, places in service a paved parking lot, Lot W, and begins depreciating Lot W over its 15-year recovery period. F's unadjusted depreciable basis in Lot W is $1,000x. On April 1, 2004, F disposes of Lot W in a like-kind exchange for Building X, which is nonresidential real property. Lot W is depreciated using the 150 percent declining balance method and the half-year convention. Building X is depreciated using the straight-line method with a 39-year recovery period and using the mid-month convention. Both Lot W and Building X were in service at the time of the exchange. Because Lot W was depreciated using the half-year convention, it is deemed to have been placed in service on July 1, 2001, the first day of the second half of 2001, and to have been disposed of on July 1, 2004, the first day of the second half of 2004. To determine the remaining recovery period of Building X at the time of replacement, Building X is deemed to have been placed in service on July 1, 2001, and removed from service on July 1, 2004. Thus, Building X is deemed to have been in service, at the time of replacement, for 3 years (36 months=5.5 months in 2001 + 12 months in 2002 + 12 months in 2003 + 6.5 months in 2004) and its remaining recovery period is 36 years (39 - 3). Because Building X is deemed to be placed in service at the time of replacement, July 1, 2004, the first day of the second half of 2004, Building X is depreciated for 5.5 months in 2004. However, at the beginning of the year of replacement the remaining recovery period for Building X is 36 years and 6.5 months (39 years - 2 years and 5.5 months (5.5 months in 2001 + 12 months in 2002 + 12 months in 2003)). The depreciation rate for building X for 2004 is 0.02737 (= 1/(39-2-5.5/12)). For 2005, the depreciation rate for Building X is 0.02814 (= 1/(39-3-5.5/12)).

*Example 9*. The facts are the same as in *Example 8*. F did not make the election under paragraph (i) of this section for Building Y in the initial exchange. In January 2006, F exchanges Building Y for Building Z, an office building, in a like-kind exchange. F did not make any elections under section 168 for either Building Y or Building Z. Since the recovery period prescribed for Building Y as a result of the initial exchange (39 years) is longer than that of Building Z (27.5 years), Building Z is depreciated over the remaining 33 years of the recovery period of Building Y. The depreciation methods are the same for both Building Y and Building Z so F's exchanged basis in Building Z is depreciated over 33 years, using the straight-line method and the mid-month convention, beginning in January 2006. Alternatively, F could have made the election under paragraph (i) of this section. If F makes such election, Building Z is treated as placed in service by F when acquired in January 2006 and F would recover its exchanged basis in Building Z over 27.5 years, using the straight line method and the mid-month convention, beginning in January 2006.

(d) *Special rules for determining depreciation allowances* .—(1) *Excess basis* .—(i) *In general* .—Any excess basis in the replacement MACRS property is treated as property that is placed in service by the acquiring taxpayer in the year of replacement. Thus, the depreciation allowances for the depreciable excess basis are determined by using the applicable recovery period, depreciation method, and convention prescribed under section 168 for the property at the time of replacement. However, if replacement MACRS property is disposed of during the same taxable year the relinquished MACRS property is placed in service by the acquiring taxpayer, no depreciation deduction is allowable for either MACRS property. See paragraph (g) of this section regarding the application of section 179. See paragraph (h) of this section regarding the application of section 168(k) or 1400L(b).

(ii) *Example* .—The application of this paragraph (d)(1) is illustrated by the following example:

*Example*. In 1989, G placed in service a hospital. On January 16, 2004, G exchanges this hospital plus $2,000,000 cash for an office building in a like-kind exchange. On January 16, 2004, the hospital has an adjusted depreciable basis of $1,500,000. After the exchange, the basis of the office building is $3,500,000. Pursuant to paragraph (k)(2)(i) of this section, G decided to apply § 1.168(i)-6 to the exchange of the hospital for the office building, the replacement MACRS property. The depreciable exchanged basis of the office building is depreciated in accordance with paragraph (c) of this section. The depreciable excess basis of $2,000,000 is treated as being placed in service by G in 2004 and, as a result, is depreciated using the applicable depreciation method, recovery period, and convention prescribed for the office building under section 168 at the time of replacement.

(2) *Depreciable and nondepreciable property*.—(i) If land or other nondepreciable property is acquired in a like-kind exchange for, or as a result of an involuntary conversion of, depreciable property, the land or other nondepreciable property is not depreciated. If both MACRS and nondepreciable property are acquired in a like-kind exchange for, or as part of an involuntary conversion of, MACRS property, the basis allocated to the nondepreciable property (as determined under section 1031(d) and the regulations under section 1031(d) or section 1033(b) and the regulations under section 1033(b)) is not depreciated and the basis allocated to the replacement MACRS property (as determined under section 1031(d) and the regulations under section 1031(d) or section 1033(b) and the regulations under section 1033(b)) is depreciated in accordance with this section.

(ii) If MACRS property is acquired, or if both MACRS and nondepreciable property are acquired, in a like-kind exchange for, or as part of an involuntary conversion of, land or other nondepreciable property, the basis in the replacement MACRS property that is attributable to the relinquished nondepreciable property is treated as though the replacement MACRS property is placed in service by the acquiring taxpayer in the year of replacement. Thus, the depreciation allowances for the replacement MACRS property are determined by using the applicable recovery period, depreciation method, and convention prescribed under section 168 for the replacement MACRS property at the time of replacement. See paragraph (g) of this section regarding the application of section 179. See paragraph (h) of this section regarding the application of section 168(k) or 1400L(b).

(3) *Depreciation limitations for automobiles*.—(i) *In general*.—Depreciation allowances under section 179 and section 167 (including allowances under sections 168 and 1400L(b)) for a passenger automobile, as defined in section 280F(d)(5), are subject to the limitations of section 280F(a). The depreciation allowances for a passenger automobile that is replacement MACRS property (replacement MACRS passenger automobile) generally are limited in any taxable year to the replacement automobile section 280F limit for the taxable year. The taxpayer's basis in the replacement MACRS passenger automobile is treated as being comprised of two separate components. The first component is the exchanged basis and the second component is the excess basis, if any. The depreciation allowances for a passenger automobile that is relinquished MACRS property (relinquished MACRS passenger automobile) for the taxable year generally are limited to the relinquished automobile section 280F limit for that taxable year. In the year of disposition the sum of the depreciation deductions for the relinquished MACRS passenger automobile and the replacement MACRS passenger automobile may not exceed the replacement automobile section 280F limit unless the taxpayer makes the election under § 1.168(i)-6(i). 6(i). For purposes of this paragraph (d)(3), the following definitions apply:

(A) *Replacement automobile section 280F limit* is the limit on depreciation deductions under section 280F(a) for the taxable year based on the time of replacement of the replacement MACRS passenger automobile (including the effect of any elections under section 168(k) or section 1400L(b), as applicable).

(B) *Relinquished automobile section 280F limit* is the limit on depreciation deductions under section 280F(a) for the taxable year based on when the relinquished MACRS passenger automobile was placed in service by the taxpayer.

(ii) *Order in which limitations on depreciation under section 280F(a) are applied* .—Generally, depreciation deductions allowable under section 280F(a) reduce the basis in the relinquished MACRS passenger automobile and the exchanged basis of the replacement MACRS passenger automobile, before the excess basis of the replacement MACRS passenger automobile is reduced. The depreciation deductions for the relinquished MACRS passenger automobile in the year of disposition and the replacement MACRS passenger automobile in the year of replacement and each subsequent taxable year are allowable in the following order:

(A) The depreciation deduction allowable for the relinquished MACRS passenger automobile as determined under paragraph (c)(5)(i) of this section for the year of disposition to the extent of the smaller of the replacement automobile section 280F limit and the relinquished automobile section 280F limit, if the year of disposition is the year of replacement. If the year of replacement is a taxable year subsequent to the year of disposition, the depreciation deduction allowable for the relinquished MACRS passenger automobile for the year of disposition is limited to the relinquished automobile section 280F limit.

(B) The additional first year depreciation allowable on the remaining exchanged basis (remaining carryover basis as determined under § 1.168(k)-1(f)(5), § 1.168(k)-2(g)(5), or § 1.1400L(b)-1(f)(5), as applicable) of the replacement MACRS passenger automobile, as determined under § 1.168(k)-1(f)(5), § 1.168(k)-2(g)(5), or § 1.1400L(b)-1(f)(5), as applicable, to the extent of the excess of the replacement automobile section 280F limit over the amount allowable under paragraph (d)(3)(ii)(A) of this section.

(C) The depreciation deduction allowable for the taxable year on the depreciable exchanged basis of the replacement MACRS passenger automobile determined under paragraph (c) of this section to the extent of any excess over the sum of the amounts allowable under paragraphs (d)(3)(ii)(A) and (B) of this section of the smaller of the replacement automobile section 280F limit and the relinquished automobile section 280F limit.

(D) Any section 179 deduction allowable in the year of replacement on the excess basis of the replacement MACRS passenger automobile to the extent of the excess of the replacement automobile section 280F limit over the sum of the amounts allowable under paragraphs (d)(3)(ii)(A), (B), and (C) of this section.

(E) The additional first year depreciation allowable on the remaining excess basis of the replacement MACRS passenger automobile, as determined under § 1.168(k)-1(f)(5), § 1.168(k)-2(g)(5), or § 1.1400L(b)-1(f)(5), as applicable, to the extent of the excess of the replacement automobile section 280F limit over the sum of the amounts allowable under paragraphs (d)(3)(ii)(A), (B), (C), and (D) of this section.

(F) The depreciation deduction allowable under paragraph (d) of this section for the depreciable excess basis of the replacement MACRS passenger automobile to the extent of the excess of the replacement automobile section 280F limit over the sum of the amounts allowable under paragraphs (d)(3)(ii)(A), (B), (C), (D), and (E) of this section.

(iii) *Examples* .—The application of this paragraph (d)(3) is illustrated by the following examples:

*Example 1.* H, a calendar-year taxpayer, acquired and placed in service Automobile X in January 2000 for $30,000 to be used solely for H's business. In December 2003, H exchanges, in a like-kind exchange, Automobile X plus

$15,000 cash for new Automobile Y that will also be used solely in H's business. Automobile Y is 50-percent bonus depreciation property for purposes of section 168(k)(4). Both automobiles are depreciated using the double declining balance method, the half-year convention, and a 5-year recovery period. Pursuant to §1.168(k)-1(g(3)(ii) and paragraph (k)(2)(i) of this section, H decided to apply §1.168(i)-6 to the exchange of Automobile X for Automobile Y, the replacement MACRS property. The relinquished automobile section 280F limit for 2003 for Automobile X is $1,775. The replacement automobile section 280F limit for Automobile Y is $10,710. The exchanged basis for Automobile Y is $17,315 ($30,000 less total depreciation allowable of $12,685 (($3,060 for 2000, $4,900 for 2001, $2,950 for 2002, and $1,775 for 2003)). Without taking section 280F into account, the additional first year depreciation deduction for the remaining exchanged basis is $8,658 ($17,315 × 0.5). Because this amount is less than $8,935 ($10,710 (the replacement automobile section 280F limit for 2003 for Automobile Y) - $1,775 (the depreciation allowable for Automobile X for 2003)), the additional first year depreciation deduction for the exchanged basis is $8,658. No depreciation deduction is allowable in 2003 for the depreciable exchanged basis because the depreciation deductions taken for Automobile X and the remaining exchanged basis exceed the exchanged automobile section 280F limit. An additional first year depreciation deduction of $277 is allowable for the excess basis of $15,000 in Automobile Y. Thus, at the end of 2003 the adjusted depreciable basis in Automobile Y is $23,379 comprised of adjusted depreciable exchanged basis of $8,657 ($17,315 (exchanged basis) — $8,658 (additional first year depreciation for exchanged basis)) and of an adjusted depreciable excess basis of $14,723 ($15,000 (excess basis) - $277 (additional first year depreciation for 2003)).

*Example 2.* The facts are the same as in *Example 1,* except that H used Automobile X only 75 percent for business use. As such, the total allowable depreciation for Automobile X is reduced to reflect that the automobile is only used 75 percent for business. The total allowable depreciation of Automobile X is $9,513.75 ($2,295 for 2000 ($3,060 limit × .75), $3,675 for 2001 ($4,900 limit × .75), $2,212.50 for 2002 ($2,950 limit × .75), and $1,331.25 for 2003 ($1,775 limit × .75). However, under §1.280F-2T(g)(2)(ii)(A), the exchanged basis is reduced by the excess (if any) of the depreciation that would have been allowable if the exchanged automobile had been used solely for business over the depreciation that was allowable in those years. Thus, the exchanged basis, for purposes of computing depreciation, for Automobile Y is $17,315.

*Example 3.* The facts are the same as in *Example 1,* except that H placed in service Automobile X in January 2002, and H elected not to claim the additional first year depreciation deduction for 5-year property placed in service in 2002 and 2003. The relinquished automobile section 280F limit for Automobile X for 2003 is $4,900. Because the replacement automobile section 280F limit for 2003 for Automobile Y ($3,060) is less than the relinquished automobile section 280F limit for Automobile X for 2003 and is less than $5,388 (($30,000 (cost) - $3,060 (depreciation allowable for 2002)) × 0.4 × 6/12), the depreciation that would be allowable for Automobile X (determined without regard to section 280F) in the year of disposition, the depreciation for Automobile X in the year of disposition is limited to $3,060. For 2003 no depreciation is allowable for the excess basis and the exchanged basis in Automobile Y.

*Example 4.* AB, a calendar-year taxpayer, purchased and placed in service Automobile X1 in February 2000 for $10,000. X1 is a passenger automobile subject to section 280F(a) and is used solely for AB's business. AB depreciated X1 using a 5-year recovery period, the double declining balance method, and the half-year convention. As of January 1, 2003, the adjusted depreciable basis of X1 was $2,880 ($10,000 original cost minus $2,000 depreciation deduction for 2000, minus $3,200 depreciation deduction for 2001, and $1,920 depreciation deduction for

2002). In November 2003, AB exchanges, in a like-kind exchange, Automobile X1 plus $14,000 cash for new Automobile Y1 that will be used solely in AB's business. Automobile Y1 is 50-percent bonus depreciation property for purposes of section 168(k)(4) and qualifies for the expensing election under section 179. Pursuant to paragraph § 1.168(k)-1(g)(3)(ii) and paragraph (k)(2)(i) of this section, AB decided to apply § 1.168(i)-6 to the exchange of Automobile X1 for Automobile Y1, the replacement MACRS property. AB also makes the election under section 179 for the excess basis of Automobile Y1. AB depreciates Y1 using a five-year recovery period, the double declining balance method and the half-year convention. For 2003, the relinquished automobile section 280F limit for Automobile X1 is $1,775 and the replacement automobile section 280F limit for 2003 for Automobile Y1 is $10,710.

(i) The 2003 depreciation deduction for Automobile X1 is $576. The depreciation deduction calculated for X1 is $576 (the adjusted depreciable basis of Automobile X1 at the beginning of 2003 of $2,880 × 40% × ½ year), which is less than the relinquished automobile section 280F limit and the replacement automobile section 280F limit.

(ii) The additional first year depreciation deduction for the exchanged basis is $1,152. The additional first year depreciation deduction of $1,152 (remaining exchanged basis of $2,304 ($2,880 adjusted basis of Automobile X1 at the beginning of 2003 minus $576) × 0.5)) is less than the replacement automobile section 280F limit minus $576.

(iii) AB's MACRS depreciation deduction allowable in 2003 for the remaining exchanged basis of $1,152 is $47 (the relinquished automobile section 280F limit of $1,775 less the depreciation deduction of $576 taken for Automobile X1 less the additional first year depreciation deduction of $1,152 taken for the exchanged basis) which is less than the depreciation deduction calculated for the depreciable exchanged basis.

(iv) For 2003, AB takes a $1,400 section 179 deduction for the excess basis of Automobile Y1. AB must reduce the excess basis of $14,000 by the section 179 deduction of $1,400 to determine the remaining excess basis of $12,600.

(v) For 2003, AB is allowed a 50-percent additional first year depreciation deduction of $6,300 (the remaining excess basis of $12,600 multiplied by .50).

(vi) For 2003, AB's depreciation deduction for the depreciable excess basis is limited to $1,235. The depreciation deduction computed without regard to the replacement automobile section 280F limit is $1,260 ($6,300 depreciable excess basis × 0.4 × 6/12). However the depreciation deduction for the depreciable excess basis is limited to $1,235 ($10,710 (replacement automobile section 280F limit) - $576 (depreciation deduction for Automobile X1) - $1,152 (additional first year depreciation deduction for the exchanged basis) - $47 (depreciation deduction for exchanged basis) $1,400 (section 179 deduction) - $6,300 (additional first year depreciation deduction for remaining excess basis)).

(4) *Involuntary conversion for which the replacement MACRS property is acquired and placed in service before disposition of relinquished MACRS property .—* If, in an involuntary conversion, a taxpayer acquires and places in service the replacement MACRS property before the date of disposition of the relinquished MACRS property, the taxpayer depreciates the unadjusted depreciable basis of the replacement MACRS property under section 168 beginning in the taxable year when the replacement MACRS property is placed in service by the taxpayer and by using the applicable depreciation method, recovery period, and convention prescribed under section 168 for the replacement MACRS property at the placed-in-service date. However, at the time of disposition of the relinquished MACRS property, the taxpayer determines the exchanged basis and the excess basis of the replacement MACRS property and begins to depreciate the depreciable exchanged basis of the replacement MACRS property in accordance with paragraph (c) of this

section. The depreciable excess basis of the replacement MACRS property continues to be depreciated by the taxpayer in accordance with the first sentence of this paragraph (d)(4). Further, in the year of disposition of the relinquished MACRS property, the taxpayer must include in taxable income the excess of the depreciation deductions allowable on the unadjusted depreciable basis of the replacement MACRS property over the depreciation deductions that would have been allowable to the taxpayer on the depreciable excess basis of the replacement MACRS property from the date the replacement MACRS property was placed in service by the taxpayer (taking into account the applicable convention) to the time of disposition of the relinquished MACRS property. However, see § 1.168(k)-1(f)(5)(v) for replacement MACRS property that is qualified property or 50-percent bonus depreciation property and § 1.1400L(b)-1(f)(5) for replacement MACRS property that is qualified New York Liberty Zone property. Further, see § 1.168(k)-2(g)(5)(iv) for replacement MACRS property that is qualified property under section 168(k), as amended by the Tax Cuts and Jobs Act, Public Law 115-97 (131 Stat. 2054 (December 22, 2017)).

(e) *Use of optional depreciation tables* .—(1) *Taxpayer not bound by prior use of table* .—If a taxpayer used an optional depreciation table for the relinquished MACRS property, the taxpayer is not required to use an optional table for the depreciable exchanged basis of the replacement MACRS property. Conversely, if a taxpayer did not use an optional depreciation table for the relinquished MACRS property, the taxpayer may use the appropriate table for the depreciable exchanged basis of the replacement MACRS property. If a taxpayer decides not to use the table for the depreciable exchanged basis of the replacement MACRS property, the depreciation allowance for this property for the year of replacement and subsequent taxable years is determined under paragraph (c) of this section. If a taxpayer decides to use the optional depreciation tables, no depreciation deduction is allowable for MACRS property placed in service by the acquiring taxpayer and subsequently exchanged or involuntarily converted by such taxpayer in the same taxable year, and, if, during the same taxable year, MACRS property is placed in service by the acquiring taxpayer, exchanged or involuntarily converted by such taxpayer, and the replacement MACRS property is disposed of by such taxpayer, no depreciation deduction is allowable for either MACRS property.

(2) *Determination of the depreciation deduction* .—(i) *Relinquished MACRS property* .—In the year of disposition, the depreciation allowance for the relinquished MACRS property is computed by multiplying the unadjusted depreciable basis (less the amount of the additional first year depreciation deduction allowed or allowable, whichever is greater, under section 168(k) or section 1400L(b), as applicable) of the relinquished MACRS property by the annual depreciation rate (expressed as a decimal equivalent) specified in the appropriate table for the recovery year corresponding to the year of disposition. This product is then multiplied by a fraction, the numerator of which is the number of months (including fractions of months) the property is deemed to be placed in service during the year of the exchange or involuntary conversion (taking into account the applicable convention) and the denominator of which is 12. However, if the year of disposition is less than 12 months, the depreciation allowance determined under this paragraph (e)(2)(i) must be adjusted for a short taxable year (for further guidance, for example, see Rev. Proc. 89-15 (1989-1 CB 816) and § 601.601(d)(2)(ii)( *b*) of this chapter).

(ii) *Replacement MACRS property* .—(A) *Determination of the appropriate optional depreciation table* .—If a taxpayer chooses to use the appropriate optional depreciation table for the depreciable exchanged basis, the depreciation allowances for the depreciable exchanged basis beginning in the year of replacement are determined by choosing the optional depreciation table that corresponds to the recovery period, depreciation method, and convention of the replacement MACRS property determined under paragraph (c) of this section.

(B) *Calculating the depreciation deduction for the replacement MACRS property* .—(1) The depreciation deduction for the taxable year is computed by first determining the appropriate recovery year in the table identified under paragraph (e)(2)(ii)(A) of this section. The appropriate recovery year for the year of replacement is the same as the recovery year for the year of disposition, regardless of the taxable year in which the replacement property is acquired. For example, if the recovery year for the year of disposition would have been year 4 in the table that applied before the disposition of the relinquished MACRS property, then the recovery year for the year of replacement is Year 4 in the table identified under paragraph (e)(2)(ii)(A) of this section.

(2) Next, the annual depreciation rate (expressed as a decimal equivalent) for each recovery year is multiplied by a transaction coefficient. The transaction coefficient is the formula (1 / (1 - x)) where x equals the sum of the annual depreciation rates from the table identified under paragraph (e)(2)(ii)(A) of this section (expressed as a decimal equivalent) corresponding to the replacement MACRS property (as determined under paragraph (e)(2)(ii)(A) of this section) for the taxable years beginning with the placed-in-service year of the relinquished MACRS property through the taxable year immediately prior to the year of disposition. The product of the annual depreciation rate and the transaction coefficient is multiplied by the depreciable exchanged basis (taking into account paragraph (e)(2)(i) of this section). In the year of replacement, this product is then multiplied by a fraction, the numerator of which is the number of months (including fractions of months) the property is deemed to be placed in service by the acquiring taxpayer during the year of replacement (taking into account the applicable convention) and the denominator of which is 12. However, if the year of replacement is the year the relinquished MACRS property is placed in service by the acquiring taxpayer, the preceding sentence does not apply. In addition, if the year of replacement is less than 12 months, the depreciation allowance determined under paragraph (e)(2)(ii) of this section must be adjusted for a short taxable year (for further guidance, for example, see Rev. Proc. 89-15 (1989-1 CB 816) and §601.601(d)(2)(ii)(*b*) of this chapter).

(iii) *Unrecovered basis* .—If the replacement MACRS property would have unrecovered depreciable basis after the final recovery year (for example, due to a deferred exchange), the unrecovered basis is an allowable depreciation deduction in the taxable year that corresponds to the final recovery year unless the unrecovered basis is subject to a depreciation limitation such as section 280F.

(3) *Excess basis* .—As provided in paragraph (d)(1) of this section, any excess basis in the replacement MACRS property is treated as property that is placed in service by the acquiring taxpayer at the time of replacement. Thus, if the taxpayer chooses to use the appropriate optional depreciation table for the depreciable excess basis in the replacement MACRS property, the depreciation allowances for the depreciable excess basis are determined by multiplying the depreciable excess basis by the annual depreciation rate (expressed as a decimal equivalent) specified in the appropriate table for each taxable year. The appropriate table for the depreciable excess basis is based on the depreciation method, recovery period, and convention applicable to the depreciable excess basis under section 168 at the time of replacement. However, If the year of replacement is less than 12 months, the depreciation allowance determined under this paragraph (e)(3) must be adjusted for a short taxable year (for further guidance, for example, see Rev. Proc. 89-15 (1989-1 CB 816) and §601.601(d)(2)(ii)(*b*) of this chapter).

(4) *Examples* .—The application of this paragraph (e) is illustrated by the following examples:

*Example 1.* J, a calendar-year taxpayer, acquired 5-year property for $10,000 and placed it in service in January 2001. J uses the optional tables to depreciate the property. J uses the half-year convention and did not make any elections for the property. In December 2003, J exchanges the 5-year property for used 7-year property in a like-kind exchange. Pursuant to paragraph (k)(2)(i) of this section, J decided to apply § 1.168(i)-6 to the exchange of the 5-year property for the 7-year property, the replacement MACRS property. The depreciable exchanged basis of the 7-year property equals the adjusted depreciable basis of the 5-year property at the time of disposition of the relinquished MACRS property, namely $3,840 ($10,000 less $2,000 depreciation in 2001, $3,200 depreciation in 2002, and $960 depreciation in 2003). J must first determine the appropriate optional depreciation table pursuant to paragraph (c) of this section. Since the replacement MACRS property has a longer recovery period and the same depreciation method as the relinquished MACRS property, J uses the optional depreciation table corresponding to a 7-year recovery period, the 200% declining balance method, and the half-year convention (because the 5-year property was depreciated using a half-year convention). Had the replacement MACRS property been placed in service in the same taxable year as the placed-in-service year of the relinquished MACRS property, the depreciation allowance for the replacement MACRS property for the year of replacement would be determined using recovery year 3 of the optional table. The depreciation allowance equals the depreciable exchanged basis ($3,840) multiplied by the annual depreciation rate for the current taxable year (.1749 for recovery year 3) as modified by the transaction coefficient [1 / (1 – (.1429 + .2449))] which equals 1.6335. Thus, J multiplies $3,840, its depreciable exchanged basis in the replacement MACRS property, by the product of .1749 and 1.6335, and then by one-half, to determine the depreciation allowance for 2003, $549. For 2004, J multiples its depreciable exchanged basis in the replacement MACRS property determined at the time of replacement of $3,840 by the product of the modified annual depreciation rate for the current taxable year (.1249 for recovery year 4) and the transaction coefficient (1.6335) to determine its depreciation allowance of $783.

*Example 2.* K, a calendar-year taxpayer, acquired used Asset V for $100,000 and placed it in service in January 1999. K depreciated Asset V under the general depreciation system of section 168(a) by using a 5-year recovery period, the 200-percent declining balance method of depreciation, and the half-year convention. In December 2003, as part of the involuntary conversion, Asset V is involuntarily converted due to an earthquake. In October 2005, K purchases used Asset W with the insurance proceeds from the destruction of Asset V and places Asset W in service to replace Asset V. Pursuant to paragraph (k)(2)(i) of this section, K decided to apply § 1.168(i)-6 to the involuntary conversion of Asset V with the replacement of Asset W, the replacement MACRS property. If Asset W had been placed in service when Asset V was placed in service, it would have been depreciated using a 7-year recovery period, the 200-percent declining balance method, and the half-year convention. K uses the optional depreciation tables to depreciate Asset V and Asset W. For 2003 (recovery year 5 on the optional table), the depreciation deduction for Asset V is $5,760 ((0.1152)($100,000)(1/2)). Thus, the adjusted depreciable basis of Asset V at the time of replacement is $11,520 ($100,000 less $20,000 depreciation in 1999, $32,000 depreciation in 2000, $19,200 depreciation in 2001, $11,520 depreciation in 2002, and $5,760 depreciation in 2003). Under the table that applied to Asset V, the year of disposition was recovery year 5 and the depreciation deduction was determined under the straight line method. The table that applies for Asset W is the table that applies the straight line depreciation method, the half-year convention, and a 7-year recovery period. The appropriate recovery year under this table is recovery year 5. The depreciation deduction for Asset W for 2005 is $1,646 (($11,520)(0.1429)(1/(1- 0.5))(1/2)). Thus, the depreciation deduction for Asset W in 2006 (recovery year 6) is $3,290 ($11,520) (0.1428) (1/(1-0.5)). The depreciation deduction for 2007 (recovery year 7) is $3,292 (($11,520) (.1429) (1/(1-.5))). The depreciation deduction for 2008 (recovery year 8) is $3292 ($11,520 less allowable depreciation for Asset W for 2005 through 2007 ($1,646 + $3,290 + $3,292)).

*Example 3.* L, a calendar-year taxpayer, placed in service used Computer X in January 2002 for $5,000. L depreciated Computer X under the general depreciation system of section 168(a) by using the 200-percent declining balance method of depreciation, a 5-year recovery period, and the half-year convention. Computer X is destroyed in a fire in March 2004. For 2004, the depreciation deduction allowable for Computer X equals $480 ([($5,000) (.1920)] × (1/2)). Thus, the adjusted depreciable basis of Computer X was $1,920 when it was destroyed ($5,000 unadjusted depreciable basis less $1,000 depreciation for 2002, $1,600 depreciation for 2003, and $480 depreciation for 2004). In April 2004, as part of the involuntary conversion, L acquired and placed in service used Computer Y with insurance proceeds received due to the loss of Computer X. Computer Y will be depreciated using the same depreciation method, recovery period, and convention as Computer X. L elected to use the optional depreciation tables to compute the depreciation allowance for Computer X and Computer Y. The depreciation deduction allowable for 2004 for Computer Y equals $384 ([$1,920 × (.1920) (1/(1-.52))] × (1/2)).

(f) *Mid-quarter convention* .—For purposes of applying the 40-percent test under section 168(d) and the regulations under section 168(d), the following rules apply:

(1) *Exchanged basis* .—If, in a taxable year, MACRS property is placed in service by the acquiring taxpayer (but not as a result of a like-kind exchange or involuntary conversion) and—

(i) In the same taxable year, is disposed of by the acquiring taxpayer in a like-kind exchange or an involuntary conversion and replaced by the acquiring taxpayer with replacement MACRS property, the exchanged basis (determined without any adjustments for depreciation deductions during the taxable year) of the replacement MACRS property is taken into account in the year of replacement in the quarter the relinquished MACRS property was placed in service by the acquiring taxpayer; or

(ii) In the same taxable year, is disposed of by the acquiring taxpayer in a like-kind exchange or an involuntary conversion, and in a subsequent taxable year is replaced by the acquiring taxpayer with replacement MACRS property, the exchanged basis (determined without any adjustments for depreciation deductions during the taxable year) of the replacement MACRS property is taken into account in the year of replacement in the quarter the replacement MACRS property was placed in service by the acquiring taxpayer; or

(iii) In a subsequent taxable year, disposed of by the acquiring taxpayer in a like-kind exchange or involuntary conversion, the exchanged basis of the replacement MACRS property is not taken into account in the year of replacement.

(2) *Excess basis* .—Any excess basis is taken into account in the quarter the replacement MACRS property is placed in service by the acquiring taxpayer.

(3) *Depreciable property acquired for nondepreciable property* .—Both the exchanged basis and excess basis of the replacement MACRS property described in paragraph (d)(2)(ii) of this section (depreciable property acquired for nondepreciable property), are taken into account for determining whether the mid-quarter convention applies in the year of replacement.

(g) *Section 179 election* .—In applying the section 179 election, only the excess basis, if any, in the replacement MACRS property is taken into account. If the replacement MACRS property is described in paragraph (d)(2)(ii) of this section (depreciable property acquired for nondepreciable property), only the excess basis in the replacement MACRS property is taken into account.

(h) *Additional first year depreciation deduction* .—See § 1.168(k)-1(f)(5) (for qualified property or 50-percent bonus depreciation property) and § 1.1400L(b)-1(f)(5) (for qualified New York Liberty Zone property). Further, see § 1.168(k)-2(g)(5) for qualified property under section 168(k), as amended by the Tax Cuts and Jobs Act, Public Law 115-97 (131 Stat. 2054 (December 22, 2017)).

(i) *Elections* .—(1) *Election not to apply this section* .—A taxpayer may elect not to apply this section for any MACRS property involved in a like-kind exchange or involuntary conversion. An election under this paragraph (i)(1) applies only to the taxpayer making the election and the election applies to both the relinquished MACRS property and the replacement MACRS property. If an election is made under this paragraph (i)(1), the depreciation allowances for the replacement MACRS property beginning in the year of replacement and for the relinquished MACRS property in the year of disposition are not determined under this section (except as otherwise provided in this paragraph). Instead, for depreciation purposes only, the sum of the exchanged basis and excess basis, if any, in the replacement MACRS property is treated as property placed in service by the taxpayer at the time of replacement and the adjusted depreciable basis of the relinquished MACRS property is treated as being disposed of by the taxpayer at the time of disposition. While the relinquished MACRS property is treated as being disposed of at the time of disposition for depreciation purposes, the election not to apply this section does not affect the application of sections 1031 and 1033 (for example, if a taxpayer does not make the election under this paragraph (i)(1) and does not recognize gain or loss under section 1031, this result would not change if the taxpayer chose to make the election under this paragraph (i)(1)). In addition, the election not to apply this section does not affect the application of sections 1245 and 1250 to the relinquished MACRS property. Paragraphs (c)(5)(i) (determination of depreciation for relinquished MACRS property in the year of disposition), (c)(5)(iii) (rules for deferred transactions), (g) (section 179 election), and (h) (additional first year depreciation deduction) of this section apply to property to which this paragraph (i)(1) applies. See paragraph (j) of this section for the time and manner of making the election under this paragraph (i)(1).

(2) *Election to treat certain replacement property as MACRS property* .—If the tangible depreciable property acquired by a taxpayer in a like-kind exchange or involuntary conversion (the replacement property) replaces tangible depreciable property for which the taxpayer made a valid election under section 168(f)(1) to exclude it from the application of MACRS (the relinquished property), the taxpayer may elect to treat, for depreciation purposes only, the sum of the exchanged basis and excess basis, if any, of the replacement property as MACRS property that is placed in service by the taxpayer at the time of replacement. An election under this paragraph (i)(2) applies only to the taxpayer making the election and the election applies to both the relinquished property and the replacement property. If an election is made under this paragraph (i)(2), the adjusted depreciable basis of the relinquished property is treated as being disposed of by the taxpayer at the time of disposition. Rules similar to those provided in §§ 1.168(i)-6(b)(3) and (4) apply for purposes of determining the time of disposition and time of replacement under this paragraph (i)(2). While the relinquished property is treated as being disposed of at the time of disposition for depreciation purposes, the election under this paragraph (i)(2) does not affect the application of sections 1031 and 1033, and the application of sections 1245 and 1250 to the

relinquished property. If an election is made under this paragraph (i)(2), rules similar to those provided in paragraphs (c)(5)(iii) (rules for deferred transactions), (g) (section 179 election), and (h) (additional first year depreciation deduction) of this section apply to property. Except as provided in paragraph (k)(3)(ii) of this section, a taxpayer makes the election under this paragraph (i)(2) by claiming the depreciation allowance as determined under MACRS for the replacement property on the taxpayer's timely filed (including extensions) original Federal tax return for the placed-in-service year of the replacement property as determined under this paragraph (i)(2).

(j) *Time and manner of making election under paragraph (i)(1) of this section* .—(1) *In general* .—The election provided in paragraph (i)(1) of this section is made separately by each person acquiring replacement MACRS property. The election is made for each member of a consolidated group by the common parent of the group, by the partnership (and not by the partners separately) in the case of a partnership, or by the S corporation (and not by the shareholders separately) in the case of an S corporation. A separate election under paragraph (i)(1) of this section is required for each like-kind exchange or involuntary conversion. The election provided in paragraph (i)(1) of this section must be made within the time and manner provided in paragraph (j)(2) and (3) of this section and may not be made by the taxpayer in any other manner (for example, the election cannot be made through a request under section 446(e) to change the taxpayer's method of accounting), except as provided in paragraph (k)(2) of this section.

(2) *Time for making election* .—The election provided in paragraph (i)(1) of this section must be made by the due date (including extensions) of the taxpayer's Federal tax return for the year of replacement.

(3) *Manner of making election* .—The election provided in paragraph (i)(1) of this section is made in the manner provided for on Form 4562, Depreciation and Amortization, and its instructions. If Form 4562 is revised or renumbered, any reference in this section to that form is treated as a reference to the revised or renumbered form.

(4) *Revocation* .—The election provided in paragraph (i)(1) of this section, once made, may be revoked only with the consent of the Commissioner of Internal Revenue. Such consent will be granted only in extraordinary circumstances. Requests for consent are requests for a letter ruling and must be filed with the Commissioner of Internal Revenue, Washington, DC, 20224. Requests for consent may not be made in any other manner (for example, through a request under section 446(e) to change the taxpayer's method of accounting).

(k) *Effective date* .—(1) *In general* .—Except as provided in paragraphs (k)(3) and (4) of this section, this section applies to a like-kind exchange or an involuntary conversion of MACRS property for which the time of disposition and the time of replacement both occur after February 27, 2004.

(2) *Application to pre-effective date like-kind exchanges and involuntary conversions* .—For a like-kind exchange or an involuntary conversion of MACRS property for which the time of disposition, the time of replacement, or both occur on or before February 27, 2004, a taxpayer may—

(i) Apply the provisions of this section. If a taxpayer's applicable Federal tax return has been filed on or before February 27, 2004, and the taxpayer has treated the replacement MACRS property as acquired, and the relinquished MACRS property as disposed of, in a like-kind exchange or an involuntary conversion, the taxpayer changes its method of accounting for depreciation of the replacement MACRS property and relinquished MACRS property in accordance with this paragraph (k)(2)(i) by following the applicable administrative procedures issued under § 1.446-1(e)(3)(ii) for obtaining the Commissioner's automatic consent to a change in method of accounting (for further guidance, see Rev. Proc. 2002-9 (2002-1 CB 327) and § 601.601(d)(2)(ii)(*b*) of this chapter); or

(ii) Rely on prior guidance issued by the Internal Revenue Service for determining the depreciation deductions of replacement MACRS property and relinquished MACRS property (for further guidance, for example, see Notice 2000-4 (2001-1 CB 313) and § 601.601(d)(2)(ii)(*b*) of this chapter). In relying on such guidance, a taxpayer may use any reasonable, consistent method of determining depreciation in the year of disposition and the year of replacement. If a taxpayer's applicable Federal tax return has been filed on or before February 27, 2004, and the taxpayer has treated the replacement MACRS property as acquired, and the relinquished MACRS property as disposed of, in a like-kind exchange or an involuntary conversion, the taxpayer changes its method of accounting for depreciation of the replacement MACRS property and relinquished MACRS property in accordance with this paragraph (k)(2)(ii) by following the applicable administrative procedures issued under § 1.446-1(e)(3)(ii) for obtaining the Commissioner's automatic consent to a change in method of accounting (for further guidance, see Rev. Proc. 2002-9 (2002-1 CB 327) and § 601.601(d)(2)(ii)(*b*) of this chapter).

(3) *Like-kind exchanges and involuntary conversions where the taxpayer made the election under section 168(f)(1) for the relinquished property*.—(i) *In general*.—If the tangible depreciable property acquired by a taxpayer in a like-kind exchange or involuntary conversion (the replacement property) replaces tangible depreciable property for which the taxpayer made a valid election under section 168(f)(1) to exclude it from the application of MACRS (the relinquished property), paragraph (i)(2) of this section applies to such relinquished property and replacement property for which the time of disposition and the time of replacement (both as determined under paragraph (i)(2) of this section) both occur after February 26, 2007.

(ii) *Application of paragraph (i)(2) of this section to pre-February 26, 2007 like-kind exchanges and involuntary conversions*.—If the tangible depreciable property acquired by a taxpayer in a like-kind exchange or involuntary conversion (the replacement property) replaces tangible depreciable property for which the taxpayer made a valid election under section 168(f)(1) to exclude it from the application of MACRS (the relinquished property), the taxpayer may apply paragraph (i)(2) of this section to the relinquished property and the replacement property for which the time of disposition, the time of replacement (both as determined under paragraph (i)(2) of this section), or both occur on or before February 26, 2007. If the taxpayer wants to apply paragraph (i)(2) of this section and the taxpayer's applicable Federal tax return has been filed on or before February 26, 2007, the taxpayer must change its method of accounting for depreciation of the replacement property and relinquished property in accordance with this paragraph (k)(3)(ii) by following the applicable administrative procedures issued under § 1.446-1(e)(3)(ii) for obtaining the Commissioner's automatic consent to a change in method of accounting (for further guidance, see Rev. Proc. 2002-9 (2002-1 CB 327) and § 601.601(d)(2)(ii)(*b*) of this chapter).

(4) *Qualified property under section 168(k) acquired and placed in service after September 27, 2017*.—(i) *In general*.—The language "1.168(k)-2(g)(5)," in paragraphs (d)(3)(ii)(B) and (E) of this section and the final sentence in paragraphs (d)(4) and (h) of this section apply to a like-kind exchange or an involuntary conversion of MACRS property, which is qualified property under section 168(k)(2), for which the time of replacement occurs on or after September 24, 2019.

(ii) *Early application* .—A taxpayer may choose to apply the language "1.168(k)-2(g)(5)," in paragraphs (d)(3)(ii)(B) and (E) of this section and the final sentence in paragraphs (d)(4) and (h) of this section to a like-kind exchange or an involuntary conversion of MACRS property, which is qualified property under section 168(k)(2), for which the time of replacement occurs on or after September 28, 2017.

(iii) *Early application of regulation project REG-104397-18* .—A taxpayer may rely on the language "1.168(k)-2(f)(5)," in paragraphs (d)(3)(ii)(B) and (E) of this section and the final sentence in paragraphs (d)(4) and (h) of this section in regulation project REG-104397-18 (2018-41 I.R.B. 558) (see §601.601(d)(2)(ii)(*b*) of this chapter) for a like-kind exchange or an involuntary conversion of MACRS property, which is qualified property under section 168(k)(2), for which the time of replacement occurs on or after September 28, 2017, and occurs before September 24, 2019. [Reg. §1.168(i)-6.]

**.01 Historical Comment:** Proposed 3/1/2004. Adopted 2/26/2007 by T.D. 9314. Amended 9/17/2019 by T.D. 9874.

## ¶ 568C

## Reg. §1.168(i)-7

§1.168(i)-7. **Accounting for MACRS property** .—(a) *In general* .—A taxpayer may account for MACRS property (as defined in §1.168(b)-1(a)(2)) by treating each individual asset as an account (a "single asset account" or an "item account") or by combining two or more assets in a single account (a "multiple asset account" or a "pool"). A taxpayer may establish as many accounts for MACRS property as the taxpayer wants. This section does not apply to assets included in general asset accounts. For rules applicable to general asset accounts, see §1.168(i)-1.

(b) *Required use of single asset accounts* .—A taxpayer must account for an asset in a single asset account if the taxpayer uses the asset both in a trade or business or for the production of income and in a personal activity, or if the taxpayer places in service and disposes of the asset during the same taxable year. Also, if general asset account treatment for an asset terminates under §1.168(i)-1(c)(1)(ii)(A), (e)(3)(iii), (e)(3)(v), (e)(3)(vii), (g), or (h)(1), as applicable, the taxpayer must account for the asset in a single asset account beginning in the taxable year in which the general asset account treatment for the asset terminates. If a taxpayer accounts for an asset in a multiple asset account or a pool and the taxpayer disposes of the asset, the taxpayer must account for the asset in a single asset account beginning in the taxable year in which the disposition occurs. See §1.168(i)-8(h)(2)(i). If a taxpayer disposes of a portion of an asset and §1.168(i)-8(d)(1) applies to that disposition, the taxpayer must account for the disposed portion in a single asset account beginning in the taxable year in which the disposition occurs. See §1.168(i)-8(h)(3)(i).

(c) *Establishment of multiple asset accounts or pools* .—(1) *Assets eligible for multiple asset accounts or pools* .—Except as provided in paragraph (b) of this section, assets that are subject to either the general depreciation system of section 168(a) or the alternative depreciation system of section 168(g) may be accounted for in one or more multiple asset accounts or pools.

(2) *Grouping assets in multiple asset accounts or pools* .—(i) *General rules* .—Assets that are eligible to be grouped into a single multiple asset account or pool may be divided into more than one multiple asset account or pool. Each multiple asset account or pool must include only assets that—

(A) Have the same applicable depreciation method;

(B) Have the same applicable recovery period;

(C) Have the same applicable convention; and

(D) Are placed in service by the taxpayer in the same taxable year.

(ii) *Special rules* .—In addition to the general rules in paragraph (c) (2) (i) of this section, the following rules apply when establishing multiple asset accounts or pools—

(A) Assets subject to the mid-quarter convention may only be grouped into a multiple asset account or pool with assets that are placed in service in the same quarter of the taxable year;

(B) Assets subject to the mid-month convention may only be grouped into a multiple asset account or pool with assets that are placed in service in the same month of the taxable year;

(C) Passenger automobiles for which the depreciation allowance is limited under section 280F(a) must be grouped into a separate multiple asset account or pool;

(D) Assets not eligible for any additional first year depreciation deduction (including assets for which the taxpayer elected not to deduct the additional first year depreciation) provided by, for example, section 168(k) through (n), 1400L(b), or 1400N(d), must be grouped into a separate multiple asset account or pool;

(E) Assets eligible for the additional first year depreciation deduction may only be grouped into a multiple asset account or pool with assets for which the taxpayer claimed the same percentage of the additional first year depreciation (for example, 30 percent, 50 percent, or 100 percent);

(F) Except for passenger automobiles described in paragraph (c) (2) (ii) (C) of this section, listed property (as defined in section 280F(d) (4)) must be grouped into a separate multiple asset account or pool;

(G) Assets for which the depreciation allowance for the placed-in-service year is not determined by using an optional depreciation table (for further guidance, see section 8 of Rev. Proc. 87-57, 1987-2 CB 687, 693 (see § 601.601(d) (2) of this chapter)) must be grouped into a separate multiple asset account or pool; and

(H) Mass assets (as defined in § 1.168(i)-8(b) (3)) that are or will be subject to § 1.168(i)-8(g) (2) (iii) (disposed of or converted mass asset is identified by a mortality dispersion table) must be grouped into a separate multiple asset account or pool.

(d) *Cross references* .—See § 1.167(a)-7(c) for the records to be maintained by a taxpayer for each account. In addition, see § 1.168(i)-1(l) (3) for the records to be maintained by a taxpayer for each general asset account.

(e) *Effective/applicability dates* .—(1) *In general* .—This section applies to taxable years beginning on or after January 1, 2014.

(2) *Early application of this section* .—A taxpayer may choose to apply the provisions of this section to taxable years beginning on or after January 1, 2012.

(3) *Early application of regulation project REG-110732-13* .—A taxpayer may rely on the provisions of this section in regulation project REG-110732-13 (2013-43 IRB 404) (see § 601.601(d) (2) of this chapter) for taxable years beginning on or after January 1, 2012. However, a taxpayer may not rely on the provisions of this section in regulation project REG-110732-13 for taxable years beginning on or after January 1, 2014.

(4) *Optional application of TD 9564.* .—A taxpayer may choose to apply § 1.168(i)-7T as contained in 26 CFR part 1 edition revised as of April 1,

2013, to taxable years beginning on or after January 1, 2012. However, a taxpayer may not apply § 1.168(i)-7T as contained in 26 CFR part 1 edition revised as of April 1, 2013, to taxable years beginning on or after January 1, 2014.

(5) *Change in method of accounting* .—A change to comply with this section for depreciable assets placed in service in a taxable year ending on or after December 30, 2003, is a change in method of accounting to which the provisions of section 446(e) and the regulations under section 446(e) apply. A taxpayer also may treat a change to comply with this section for depreciable assets placed in service in a taxable year ending before December 30, 2003, as a change in method of accounting to which the provisions of section 446(e) and the regulations under section 446(e) apply. [Reg. § 1.168(i)-7.]

**.01 Historical Comment:** Adopted 9/13/2013 by T.D. 9636. Amended 8/14/2014 by T.D. 9689 (corrected 12/30/2014).

## ¶ 568D

## Reg. § 1.168(i)-8

§ 1.168(i)-8. **Dispositions of MACRS property.**— (a) *Scope* .—This section provides rules applicable to dispositions of MACRS property (as defined in § 1.168(b)-1(a)(2)) or to depreciable property (as defined in § 1.168(b)-1(a)(1)) that would be MACRS property but for an election made by the taxpayer either to expense all or some of the property's cost under section 179, section 179A, section 179B, section 179C, section 179D, or section 1400I(a)(1), or any similar provision, or to amortize all or some of the property's cost under section 1400I(a)(2) or any similar provision. This section also applies to dispositions described in paragraph (d)(1) of this section of a portion of such property. Except as provided in § 1.168(i)-1(e)(3), this section does not apply to dispositions of assets included in a general asset account. For rules applicable to dispositions of assets included in a general asset account, see § 1.168(i)-1(e).

(b) *Definitions* .—For purposes of this section—

(1) *Building* has the same meaning as that term is defined in § 1.48-1(e)(1).

(2) *Disposition* occurs when ownership of the asset is transferred or when the asset is permanently withdrawn from use either in the taxpayer's trade or business or in the production of income. A disposition includes the sale, exchange, retirement, physical abandonment, or destruction of an asset. A disposition also occurs when an asset is transferred to a supplies, scrap, or similar account, or when a portion of an asset is disposed of as described in paragraph (d)(1) of this section. If a structural component, or a portion thereof, of a building is disposed of in a disposition described in paragraph (d)(1) of this section, a disposition also includes the disposition of such structural component or such portion thereof.

(3) *Mass assets* is a mass or group of individual items of depreciable assets—

(i) That are not necessarily homogenous;

(ii) Each of which is minor in value relative to the total value of the mass or group;

(iii) Numerous in quantity;

(iv) Usually accounted for only on a total dollar or quantity basis;

(v) With respect to which separate identification is impracticable; and

(vi) Placed in service in the same taxable year.

(4) *Portion of an asset* is any part of an asset that is less than the entire asset as determined under paragraph (c)(4) of this section.

(5) *Structural component* has the same meaning as that term is defined in § 1.48-1(e)(2).

(6) *Unadjusted depreciable basis of the multiple asset account or pool* is the sum of the unadjusted depreciable bases (as defined in § 1.168(b)-1(a)(3)) of all assets included in the multiple asset account or pool.

(c) *Special rules* .—(1) *Manner of disposition* .—The manner of disposition (for example, normal retirement, abnormal retirement, ordinary retirement, or extraordinary retirement) is not taken into account in determining whether a disposition occurs or gain or loss is recognized.

(2) *Disposition by transfer to a supplies account* .—If a taxpayer made an election under § 1.162-3(d) to treat the cost of any rotable spare part, temporary spare part, or standby emergency spare part (as defined in § 1.162-3(c)) as a capital expenditure subject to the allowance for depreciation, the taxpayer can dispose of the rotable, temporary, or standby emergency spare part by transferring it to a supplies account only if the taxpayer has obtained the consent of the Commissioner to revoke the § 1.162-3(d) election. If a taxpayer made an election under § 1.162-3T(d) to treat the cost of any material and supply (as defined in § 1.162-3T(c)(1)) as a capital expenditure subject to the allowance for depreciation, the taxpayer can dispose of the material and supply by transferring it to a supplies account only if the taxpayer has obtained the consent of the Commissioner to revoke the § 1.162-3T(d) election. See § 1.162-3(d)(3) for the procedures for revoking a § 1.162-3(d) or a § 1.162-3T(d) election.

(3) *Leasehold improvements* .—This section also applies to—

(i) A lessor of leased property that made an improvement to that property for the lessee of the property, has a depreciable basis in the improvement, and disposes of the improvement, or disposes of a portion of the improvement under paragraph (d)(1) of this section, before or upon the termination of the lease with the lessee. See section 168(i)(8)(B); and

(ii) A lessee of leased property that made an improvement to that property, has a depreciable basis in the improvement, and disposes of the improvement, or disposes of a portion of the improvement under paragraph (d)(1) of this section, before or upon the termination of the lease.

(4) *Determination of asset disposed of* .—(i) *General rules* .—For purposes of applying this section, the facts and circumstances of each disposition are considered in determining what is the appropriate asset disposed of. The asset for disposition purposes may not consist of items placed in service by the taxpayer on different dates, without taking into account the applicable convention. For purposes of determining what is the appropriate asset disposed of, the unit of property determination under § 1.263(a)-3(e) or in published guidance in the Internal Revenue Bulletin (see § 601.601(d)(2) of this chapter) under section 263(a) and the distinct asset determination under § 1.1031(a)-3(a)(4) do not apply.

(ii) *Special rules* .—In addition to the general rules in paragraph (c)(4)(i) of this section, the following rules apply for purposes of applying this section:

(A) Each building, including its structural components, is the asset, except as provided in § 1.1250-1(a)(2)(ii) or in paragraph (c)(4)(ii)(B) or (D) of this section.

(B) If a building has two or more condominium or cooperative units, each condominium or cooperative unit, including its structural components, is the asset, except as provided in § 1.1250-1(a)(2)(ii) or in paragraph (c)(4)(ii)(D) of this section.

(C) If a taxpayer properly includes an item in one of the asset classes 00.11 through 00.4 of Rev. Proc. 87-56 (1987-2 CB 674) (see § 601.601(d)(2) of this chapter) or properly classifies an item in one of the categories under section 168(e)(3), except for a category that includes buildings or structural components (for example, retail motor fuels outlet, qualified leasehold improvement property, qualified restaurant property, and qualified retail improvement property), each item is the asset provided paragraph (c)(4)(ii)(D) of this section does not apply to the item. For example, each desk is the asset, each computer is the asset, and each qualified smart electric meter is the asset.

(D) If the taxpayer places in service an improvement or addition to an asset after the taxpayer placed the asset in service, the improvement or addition and, if applicable, its structural components are a separate asset.

(d) *Disposition of a portion of an asset* .—(1) *In general* .—For purposes of applying this section, a disposition includes a disposition of a portion of an asset as a result of a casualty event described in section 165, a disposition of a portion of an asset for which gain, determined without regard to section 1245 or section 1250, is not recognized in whole or in part under section 1031 or section 1033, a transfer of a portion of an asset in a transaction described in section 168(i)(7)(B), or a sale of a portion of an asset, even if the taxpayer does not make the election under paragraph (d)(2)(i) of this section for that disposed portion. For other transactions, a disposition includes a disposition of a portion of an asset only if the taxpayer makes the election under paragraph (d)(2)(i) of this section for that disposed portion.

(2) *Partial disposition election* .—(i) *In general* .—A taxpayer may make an election under this paragraph (d)(2) to apply this section to a disposition of a portion of an asset. If the asset is properly included in one of the asset classes 00.11 through 00.4 of Rev. Proc. 87-56, a taxpayer may make an election under this paragraph (d)(2) to apply this section to a disposition of a portion of such asset only if the taxpayer classifies the replacement portion of the asset under the same asset class as the disposed portion of the asset.

(ii) *Time and manner for making election* .—(A) *Time for making election* .—Except as provided in paragraph (d)(2)(iii) or (iv) of this section, a taxpayer must make the election specified in paragraph (d)(2)(i) of this section by the due date, including extensions, of the original Federal tax return for the taxable year in which the portion of an asset is disposed of by the taxpayer.

(B) *Manner of making election* .—Except as provided in paragraph (d)(2)(iii) or (iv) of this section, a taxpayer must make the election specified in paragraph (d)(2)(i) of this section by applying the provisions of this section for the taxable year in which the portion of an asset is disposed of by the taxpayer, by reporting the gain, loss, or other deduction on the taxpayer's timely filed, including extensions, original Federal tax return for that taxable year, and, if the asset is properly included in one of the asset classes 00.11 through 00.4 of Rev. Proc. 87-56, by classifying the replacement portion of such asset under the same asset class as the disposed portion of the asset in the taxable year in which the replacement portion is placed in service by the taxpayer. Except as provided in paragraph (d)(2)(iii) or (iv)(B) of this section or except as otherwise expressly provided by other guidance published in the Internal Revenue Bulletin (see § 601.601(d)(2) of this chapter), the election specified in paragraph (d)(2)(i) of this section may not be made through the filing of an application for change in accounting method.

(iii) *Special rule for subsequent Internal Revenue Service adjustment* .—This paragraph (d)(2)(iii) applies when a taxpayer deducted the amount paid or incurred for the replacement of a portion of an asset as a repair under § 1.162-4, the taxpayer did not make the election specified in paragraph (d)(2)(i) of this section for the disposed portion of that asset within the time and in the manner under paragraph (d)(2)(ii) or (iv) of this section, and as a result of an examination of the taxpayer's Federal tax return, the Internal Revenue Service disallows the taxpayer's repair deduction for the amount paid or incurred for the replacement of the portion of that asset and instead capitalizes such amount under § 1.263(a)-2 or § 1.263(a)-3. If this paragraph (d)(2)(iii) applies, the taxpayer may make the election specified in paragraph (d)(2)(i) of this section for the disposition of the portion of the asset to which the Internal Revenue Service's adjustment pertains by filing an application for change in accounting method, provided the asset of which the disposed portion was a part is owned by the taxpayer at the beginning of the year of change (as defined for purposes of section 446(e)).

(iv) *Special rules for 2012 or 2013 returns* .—If, under paragraph (j)(2) of this section, a taxpayer chooses to apply the provisions of this section to a taxable year beginning on or after January 1, 2012, and ending on or before September 19, 2013 (applicable taxable year), and the taxpayer did not make the election specified in paragraph (d)(2)(i) of this section on its timely filed original Federal tax return for the applicable taxable year, including extensions, the taxpayer must make the election specified in paragraph (d)(2)(i) of this section for the applicable taxable year by filing either—

(A) An amended Federal tax return for the applicable taxable year on or before 180 days from the due date including extensions of the taxpayer's Federal tax return for the applicable taxable year, notwithstanding that the taxpayer may not have extended the due date; or

(B) An application for change in accounting method with the taxpayer's timely filed original Federal tax return for the first or second taxable year succeeding the applicable taxable year.

(v) *Revocation* .—A taxpayer may revoke the election specified in paragraph (d)(2)(i) of this section only by filing a request for a private letter ruling and obtaining the Commissioner's consent to revoke the election. The Commissioner may grant a request to revoke this election if the taxpayer acted reasonably and in good faith, and the revocation will not prejudice the interests of the Government. See generally § 301.9100-3 of this chapter. The election specified in paragraph (d)(2)(i) of this section may not be revoked through the filing of an application for change in accounting method.

(e) *Gain or loss on dispositions* .—Solely for purposes of this paragraph (e), the term *asset* is an asset within the scope of this section or the portion of such asset that is disposed of in a disposition described in paragraph (d)(1) of this section. Except as provided by section 280B and § 1.280B-1, the following rules apply when an asset is disposed of during a taxable year:

(1) If an asset is disposed of by sale, exchange, or involuntary conversion, gain or loss must be recognized under the applicable provisions of the Internal Revenue Code.

(2) If an asset is disposed of by physical abandonment, loss must be recognized in the amount of the adjusted depreciable basis (as defined in § 1.168(b)-1(a)(4)) of the asset at the time of the abandonment, taking into account the applicable convention. However, if the abandoned asset is subject to nonrecourse indebtedness, paragraph (e)(1) of this section applies to the asset instead of this paragraph (e)(2). For a loss from physical abandonment to qualify for recognition under this paragraph (e)(2), the taxpayer must intend to discard the asset irrevocably so that the taxpayer will neither use the asset again nor retrieve it for sale, exchange, or other disposition.

(3) If an asset is disposed of other than by sale, exchange, involuntary conversion, physical abandonment, or conversion to personal use (as, for example, when the asset is transferred to a supplies or scrap account), gain is not recognized.

Loss must be recognized in the amount of the excess of the adjusted depreciable basis of the asset at the time of the disposition, taking into account the applicable convention, over the asset's fair market value at the time of the disposition, taking into account the applicable convention.

(f) *Basis of asset disposed of*.—(1) *In general*.—The adjusted basis of an asset disposed of for computing gain or loss is its adjusted depreciable basis at the time of the asset's disposition, as determined under the applicable convention for the asset.

(2) *Assets disposed of are in multiple asset accounts*.—(i) If the taxpayer accounts for the asset disposed of in a multiple asset account or pool and it is impracticable from the taxpayer's records to determine the unadjusted depreciable basis (as defined in § 1.168(b)-1(a)(3)) of the asset disposed of, the taxpayer may use any reasonable method that is consistently applied to all assets in the same multiple asset account or pool for purposes of determining the unadjusted depreciable basis of assets disposed of. Examples of a reasonable method include, but are not limited to, the following:

(A) If the replacement asset is a restoration (as defined in § 1.263(a)-3(k)), and is not a betterment (as defined in § 1.263(a)-3(j)) or an adaptation to a new or different use (as defined in § 1.263(a)-3(l)), discounting the cost of the replacement asset to its placed-in-service year cost using the Producer Price Index for Finished Goods or its successor, the Producer Price Index for Final Demand, or any other index designated by guidance in the Internal Revenue Bulletin (see § 601.601(d)(2) of this chapter) for purposes of this paragraph (f)(2);

(B) A pro rata allocation of the unadjusted depreciable basis of the multiple asset account or pool based on the replacement cost of the disposed asset and the replacement cost of all of the assets in the multiple asset account or pool; and

(C) A study allocating the cost of the asset to its individual components.

(ii) To determine the adjusted depreciable basis of an asset disposed of in a multiple asset account or pool, the depreciation allowable for the asset disposed of is computed by using the depreciation method, recovery period, and convention applicable to the multiple asset account or pool in which the asset disposed of was included and by including the additional first year depreciation deduction claimed for the asset disposed of.

(3) *Disposition of a portion of an asset*.—(i) This paragraph (f)(3) applies only when a taxpayer disposes of a portion of an asset and paragraph (d)(1) of this section applies to that disposition. For computing gain or loss, the adjusted basis of the disposed portion of the asset is the adjusted depreciable basis of that disposed portion at the time of its disposition, as determined under the applicable convention for the asset. If it is impracticable from the taxpayer's records to determine the unadjusted depreciable basis (as defined in § 1.168(b)-1(a)(3)) of the disposed portion of the asset, the taxpayer may use any reasonable method for purposes of determining the unadjusted depreciable basis (as defined in § 1.168(b)-1(a)(3)) of the disposed portion of the asset. If a taxpayer disposes of more than one portion of the same asset and it is impracticable from the taxpayer's records to determine the unadjusted depreciable basis (as defined in § 1.168(b)-1(a)(3)) of the first disposed portion of the asset, the reasonable method used by the taxpayer must be consistently applied to all portions of the same asset for purposes of determining the unadjusted depreciable basis of each disposed portion of the asset. If the asset, a portion of which is disposed of, is in a multiple asset account or pool and it is impracticable from the taxpayer's records to determine the unadjusted depreciable basis (as defined in § 1.168(b)-1(a)(3)) of the disposed portion of the asset, the reasonable method used by the taxpayer must be consistently applied to all assets

in the same multiple asset account or pool for purposes of determining the unadjusted depreciable basis of assets disposed of or any disposed portion of the assets. Examples of a reasonable method include, but are not limited to, the following:

(A) If the replacement portion is a restoration (as defined in § 1.263(a)-3(k)), and is not a betterment (as defined in § 1.263(a)-3(j)) or an adaptation to a new or different use (as defined in § 1.263(a)-3(l)), discounting the cost of the replacement portion of the asset to its placed-in-service year cost using the Producer Price Index for Finished Goods or its successor, the Producer Price Index for Final Demand, or any other index designated by guidance in the Internal Revenue Bulletin (see § 601.601(d)(2) of this chapter) for purposes of this paragraph (f)(3);

(B) A pro rata allocation of the unadjusted depreciable basis of the asset based on the replacement cost of the disposed portion of the asset and the replacement cost of the asset; and

(C) A study allocating the cost of the asset to its individual components.

(ii) To determine the adjusted depreciable basis of the disposed portion of the asset, the depreciation allowable for the disposed portion is computed by using the depreciation method, recovery period, and convention applicable to the asset in which the disposed portion was included and by including the portion of the additional first year depreciation deduction claimed for the asset that is attributable to the disposed portion.

(g) *Identification of asset disposed of*.—(1) *In general*.—Except as provided in paragraph (g)(2) or (3) of this section, a taxpayer must use the specific identification method of accounting to identify which asset is disposed of by the taxpayer. Under this method of accounting, the taxpayer can determine the particular taxable year in which the asset disposed of was placed in service by the taxpayer.

(2) *Asset disposed of is in a multiple asset account*.—If a taxpayer accounts for the asset disposed of in a multiple asset account or pool and the total dispositions of assets with the same recovery period during the taxable year are readily determined from the taxpayer's records, but it is impracticable from the taxpayer's records to determine the particular taxable year in which the asset disposed of was placed in service by the taxpayer, the taxpayer must identify the asset disposed of by using—

(i) A first-in, first-out method of accounting if the unadjusted depreciable basis of the asset disposed of cannot be readily determined from the taxpayer's records. Under this method of accounting, the taxpayer identifies the multiple asset account or pool with the earliest placed-in-service year that has the same recovery period as the asset disposed of and that has assets at the beginning of the taxable year of the disposition, and the taxpayer treats the asset disposed of as being from that multiple asset account or pool;

(ii) A modified first-in, first-out method of accounting if the unadjusted depreciable basis of the asset disposed of can be readily determined from the taxpayer's records. Under this method of accounting, the taxpayer identifies the multiple asset account or pool with the earliest placed-in-service year that has the same recovery period as the asset disposed of and that has assets at the beginning of the taxable year of the disposition with the same unadjusted depreciable basis as the asset disposed of, and the taxpayer treats the asset disposed of as being from that multiple asset account or pool;

(iii) A mortality dispersion table if the asset disposed of is a mass asset. The mortality dispersion table must be based upon an acceptable sampling of the taxpayer's actual disposition experience for mass assets or other acceptable statistical or engineering techniques. To use a mortality dispersion table, the taxpayer must adopt recordkeeping practices consistent with the taxpayer's prior practices and consonant with good accounting and engineering practices; or

(iv) Any other method as the Secretary may designate by publication in the **Federal Register** or in the Internal Revenue Bulletin (see § 601.601(d)(2) of this chapter) on or after September 19, 2013. See paragraph (g)(4) of this section regarding the last-in, first-out method of accounting.

(3) *Disposition of a portion of an asset* .—If a taxpayer disposes of a portion of an asset and paragraph (d)(1) of this section applies to that disposition, but it is impracticable from the taxpayer's records to determine the particular taxable year in which the asset was placed in service, the taxpayer must identify the asset by using any applicable method provided in paragraph (g)(2) of this section, after taking into account paragraph (g)(4) of this section.

(4) *Last-in, first-out method of accounting* .—For purposes of this paragraph (g), a last-in, first-out method of accounting may not be used. Examples of a last-in, first-out method of accounting include the taxpayer identifying the multiple asset account or pool with the most recent placed-in-service year that has the same recovery period as the asset disposed of and that has assets at the beginning of the taxable year of the disposition, and the taxpayer treating the asset disposed of as being from that multiple asset account or pool, or the taxpayer treating the disposed portion of an asset as being from an asset with the most recent placed-in-service year that is the same as the asset of which the disposed portion is a part.

(h) *Accounting for asset disposed of* .—(1) *Depreciation ends* .—Depreciation ends for an asset at the time of the asset's disposition, as determined under the applicable convention for the asset. See § 1.167(a)-10(b). If the asset disposed of is in a single asset account initially or as a result of § 1.168(i)-8(h)(2)(i), § 1.168(i)-8(h)(3)(i), or general asset account treatment for the asset terminated under § 1.168(i)-1(c)(1)(ii)(A), (e)(3)(iii), (e)(3)(v), (e)(3)(vii), (g), or (h)(1), as applicable, the single asset account terminates at the time of the asset's disposition, as determined under the applicable convention for the asset. If a taxpayer disposes of a portion of an asset and paragraph (d)(1) of this section applies to that disposition, depreciation ends for that disposed portion of the asset at the time of the disposition of the disposed portion, as determined under the applicable convention for the asset.

(2) *Asset disposed of in a multiple asset account or pool* .—If the taxpayer accounts for the asset disposed of in a multiple asset account or pool, then—

(i) As of the first day of the taxable year in which the disposition occurs, the asset disposed of is removed from the multiple asset account or pool and is placed into a single asset account. See § 1.168(i)-7(b);

(ii) The unadjusted depreciable basis of the multiple asset account or pool must be reduced by the unadjusted depreciable basis of the asset disposed of as of the first day of the taxable year in which the disposition occurs. See paragraph (f)(2)(i) of this section for determining the unadjusted depreciable basis of the asset disposed of;

(iii) The depreciation reserve of the multiple asset account or pool must be reduced by the greater of the depreciation allowed or allowable for the asset disposed of as of the end of the taxable year immediately preceding the year of disposition. The allowable depreciation is computed by using the depreciation method, recovery period, and convention applicable to the multiple asset account or pool in which the asset disposed of was included and by including the additional first year depreciation deduction claimed for the asset disposed of; and

(iv) In determining the adjusted depreciable basis of the asset disposed of at the time of disposition, taking into account the applicable convention, the depreciation allowable for the asset disposed of is computed by using the depreciation method, recovery period, and convention applicable to the multiple asset account or pool in which the asset disposed of was included and by including the additional first year depreciation deduction claimed for the asset disposed of.

(3) *Disposition of a portion of an asset* .—This paragraph (h)(3) applies only when a taxpayer disposes of a portion of an asset and paragraph (d)(1) of this section applies to that disposition. In this case—

(i) As of the first day of the taxable year in which the disposition occurs, the disposed portion is placed into a single asset account. See §1.168(i)-7(b);

(ii) The unadjusted depreciable basis of the asset must be reduced by the unadjusted depreciable basis of the disposed portion as of the first day of the taxable year in which the disposition occurs. See paragraph (f)(3)(i) of this section for determining the unadjusted depreciable basis of the disposed portion;

(iii) The depreciation reserve of the asset must be reduced by the greater of the depreciation allowed or allowable for the disposed portion as of the end of the taxable year immediately preceding the year of disposition. The allowable depreciation is computed by using the depreciation method, recovery period, and convention applicable to the asset in which the disposed portion was included and by including the portion of the additional first year depreciation deduction claimed for the asset that is attributable to the disposed portion; and

(iv) In determining the adjusted depreciable basis of the disposed portion at the time of disposition, taking into account the applicable convention, the depreciation allowable for the disposed portion is computed by using the depreciation method, recovery period, and convention applicable to the asset in which the disposed portion was included and by including the portion of the additional first year depreciation deduction claimed for the asset that is attributable to the disposed portion.

(i) *Examples* .—The application of this section is illustrated by the following examples:

*Example 1.* A owns an office building with four elevators. A replaces one of the elevators. The elevator is a structural component of the office building. In accordance with paragraph (c)(4)(ii)(A) of this section, the office building, including its structural components, is the asset for disposition purposes. A does not make the partial disposition election provided under paragraph (d)(2) of this section for the elevator. Thus, the retirement of the replaced elevator is not a disposition. As a result, depreciation continues for the cost of the building, including the cost of the retired elevator and the building's other structural components, and A does not recognize a loss for this retired elevator. If A must capitalize the amount paid for the replacement elevator pursuant to §1.263(a)-3, the replacement elevator is a separate asset for disposition purposes pursuant to paragraph (c)(4)(ii)(D) of this section and for depreciation purposes pursuant to section 168(i)(6).

*Example 2.* The facts are the same as in *Example 1,* except A accounts for each structural component of the office building as a separate asset in its fixed asset system. Although A treats each structural component as a separate asset in its records, the office building, including its structural components, is the asset for disposition purposes in accordance with paragraph (c)(4)(ii)(A) of this section. Accordingly, the result is the same as in *Example 1.*

*Example 3.* The facts are the same as in *Example 1,* except A makes the partial disposition election provided under paragraph (d)(2) of this section for the elevator. Although the office building, including its structural components, is the asset for disposition purposes, the result of A making the partial disposition election for the elevator is that the retirement of the replaced elevator is a disposition. Thus, depreciation for the retired elevator ceases at the time of its retirement, taking into account the applicable convention, and A recognizes a loss upon this retirement. Further, A must capitalize the amount paid for the replacement elevator pursuant to § 1.263(a)-3(k)(1)(i), and the replacement elevator is a separate asset for disposition purposes pursuant to paragraph (c)(4)(ii)(D) of this section and for depreciation purposes pursuant to section 168(i)(6).

*Example 4.* B, a calendar-year commercial airline company, owns several aircraft that are used in the commercial carrying of passengers and described in asset class 45.0 of Rev. Proc. 87-56. B replaces the existing engines on one of the aircraft with new engines. Assume each aircraft is a unit of property as determined under § 1.263(a)-3(e)(3) and each engine of an aircraft is a major component or substantial structural part of the aircraft as determined under § 1.263(a)-3(k)(6). Assume also that B treats each aircraft as the asset for disposition purposes in accordance with paragraph (c)(4) of this section. B makes the partial disposition election provided under paragraph (d)(2) of this section for the engines in the aircraft. Although the aircraft is the asset for disposition purposes, the result of B making the partial disposition election for the engines is that the retirement of the replaced engines is a disposition. Thus, depreciation for the retired engines ceases at the time of their retirement, taking into account the applicable convention, and B recognizes a loss upon this retirement. Further, B must capitalize the amount paid for the replacement engines pursuant to § 1.263(a)-3(k)(1)(i), and the replacement engines are a separate asset for disposition purposes pursuant to paragraph (c)(4)(ii)(D) of this section and for depreciation purposes pursuant to section 168(i)(6).

*Example 5.* The facts are the same as in *Example 4*, except B does not make the partial disposition election provided under paragraph (d)(2) of this section for the engines. Thus, the retirement of the replaced engines on one of the aircraft is not a disposition. As a result, depreciation continues for the cost of the aircraft, including the cost of the retired engines, and B does not recognize a loss for these retired engines. If B must capitalize the amount paid for the replacement engines pursuant to § 1.263(a)-3, the replacement engines are a separate asset for disposition purposes pursuant to paragraph (c)(4)(ii)(D) of this section and for depreciation purposes pursuant to section 168(i)(6).

*Example 6.* C, a corporation, owns several trucks that are used in its trade or business and described in asset class 00.241 of Rev. Proc. 87-56. C replaces the engine on one of the trucks with a new engine. Assume each truck is a unit of property as determined under § 1.263(a)-3(e)(3) and each engine is a major component or substantial structural part of the truck as determined under § 1.263(a)-3(k)(6). Because the trucks are described in asset class 00.241 of Rev. Proc. 87-56, C must treat each truck as the asset for disposition purposes. C does not make the partial disposition election provided under paragraph (d)(2) of this section for the engine. Thus, the retirement of the replaced engine on the truck is not a disposition. As a result, depreciation continues for the cost of the truck, including the cost of the retired engine, and C does not recognize a loss for this retired engine. If C must capitalize the amount paid for the replacement engine pursuant to § 1.263(a)-3, the replacement engine is a separate asset for disposition purposes pursuant to paragraph (c)(4)(ii)(D) of this section and for depreciation purposes pursuant to section 168(i)(6).

*Example 7.* D owns a retail building. D replaces 60% of the roof of this building. In accordance with paragraph (c)(4)(ii)(A) of this section, the retail building, including its structural components, is the asset for disposition purposes. Assume D must capitalize the costs incurred for replacing 60% of the roof pursuant to § 1.263(a)-3(k)(1)(vi). D makes the partial disposition election provided under paragraph (d)(2) of this section for the 60% of the replaced roof. Thus, the retirement of 60% of the roof is a disposition. As a result, depreciation for 60% of the roof ceases at the time of its retirement, taking into account the applicable convention, and D recognizes a loss upon this retirement. Further, D must capitalize the amount paid for the 60% of the roof pursuant to § 1.263(a)-3(k)(1)(i) and (vi) and the replacement 60% of the roof is a separate asset for disposition purposes pursuant to paragraph (c)(4)(ii)(D) of this section and for depreciation purposes pursuant to section 168(i)(6).

*Example 8.* (i) The facts are the same as in *Example 7.* Ten years after replacing 60% of the roof, D replaces 55% of the roof of the building. In accordance with paragraph (c)(4)(ii)(A) and (D) of this section, for disposition purposes, the retail building, including its structural components, except the replacement 60% of the roof, is an asset and the replacement 60% of the roof is a separate asset. Assume D must capitalize the costs incurred for replacing 55% of the roof pursuant to § 1.263(a)-3(k)(1)(vi). D makes the partial disposition election provided under paragraph (d)(2) of this section for the 55% of the replaced roof. Thus, the retirement of 55% of the roof is a disposition.

(ii) However, D cannot determine from its records whether the replaced 55% is part of the 60% of the roof replaced ten years ago or whether the replaced 55% includes part or all of the remaining 40% of the original roof. Pursuant to paragraph (g)(3) of this section, D identifies which asset it disposed of by using the first-in, first-out method of accounting. As a result, D disposed of the remaining 40% of the original roof and 25% of the 60% of the roof replaced ten years ago.

(iii) Thus, depreciation for the remaining 40% of the original roof ceases at the time of its retirement, taking into account the applicable convention, and D recognizes a loss upon this retirement. Further, depreciation for 25% of the 60% of the roof replaced ten years ago ceases at the time of its retirement, taking into account the applicable convention, and D recognizes a loss upon this retirement. Also, D must capitalize the amount paid for the 55% of the roof pursuant to § 1.263(a)-3(k)(1)(i) and (vi), and the replacement 55% of the roof is a separate asset for disposition purposes pursuant to paragraph (c)(4)(ii)(D) of this section and for depreciation purposes pursuant to section 168(i)(6).

*Example 9.* (i) On July 1, 2011, E, a calendar-year taxpayer, purchased and placed in service an existing multi-story office building that costs $20,000,000. The cost of each structural component of the building was not separately stated. E accounts for the building and its structural components in its tax and financial accounting records as a single asset with a cost of $20,000,000. E depreciates the building as nonresidential real property and uses the optional depreciation table that corresponds with the general depreciation system, the straight-line method, a 39-year recovery period, and the mid-month convention. As of January 1, 2014, the depreciation reserve for the building is $1,261,000.

(ii) On June 30, 2014, E replaces one of the two elevators in the office building. E did not dispose of any other structural components of this building in 2014 and prior years. E makes the partial disposition election provided under paragraph (d)(2) of this section for this elevator. Although the office building, including its structural components, is the asset for disposition purposes, the result of E making the partial disposition election for the elevator is that the retirement of the replaced elevator is a disposition. Assume the replacement elevator is a restoration under § 1.263(a)-3(k), and not a betterment under § 1.263(a)-3(j)) or an adaptation to a new or different use under § 1.263(a)-3(l)). Because E cannot identify the cost of the elevator from its records and the replacement elevator is a restoration under § 1.263(a)-3(k), E determines the cost of the disposed elevator by discounting the cost of the replacement elevator to its placed-in-service year cost using the Producer Price Index for Final Demand. Using this reasonable method, E determines the cost of the retired elevator by discounting the cost of the replacement elevator to its cost in 2011 (the placed-in-service year) using the Producer Price Index for Final Demand, resulting in $150,000 of the $20,000,000 purchase price for the building to be the cost of the retired elevator. Using the optional depreciation table that corresponds with the general depreciation system, the straightline method, a 39-year recovery period, and the mid-month convention, the depreciation allowed or allowable for the retired elevator as of December 31, 2013, is $9,458.

(iii) For E's 2014 Federal tax return, the loss for the retired elevator is determined as follows. The depreciation allowed or allowable for 2014 for the retired elevator is $1,763 ((unadjusted depreciable basis of $150,000 × depreciation rate of 2.564% for 2014) × 5.5/12 months). Thus, the adjusted depreciable basis of the retired elevator is $138,779 (the adjusted depreciable basis of $140,542 removed from the building cost less the depreciation allowed or allowable of $1,763 for 2014). As a result, E recognizes a loss of $138,779 for the retired elevator in 2014.

(iv) For E's 2014 Federal tax return, the depreciation allowance for the building is computed as follows. As of January 1, 2014, the unadjusted depreciable basis of the building is reduced from $20,000,000 to $19,850,000 ($20,000,000 less the unadjusted depreciable basis of $150,000 for the retired elevator), and the depreciation reserve of the building is reduced from $1,261,000 to $1,251,542 ($1,261,000 less the depreciation allowed or allowable of $9,458 for the retired elevator as of December 31, 2013). Consequently, the depreciation allowance for the building for 2014 is $508,954 ($19,850,000 × depreciation rate of 2.564% for 2014).

(v) E also must capitalize the amount paid for the replacement elevator pursuant to § 1.263(a)-3(k)(1). The replacement elevator is a separate asset for disposition purposes pursuant to paragraph (c)(4)(ii)(D) of this section and for depreciation purposes pursuant to section 168(i)(6).

*Example 10.* (i) Since 2005, F, a calendar year taxpayer, has accounted for items of MACRS property that are mass assets in pools. Each pool includes only the mass assets that have the same depreciation method, recovery period, and convention, and are placed in service by F in the same taxable year. None of the pools are general asset accounts under section 168(i)(4) and the regulations under section 168(i)(4). F identifies any dispositions of these mass assets by specific identification.

(ii) During 2014, F sells 10 items of mass assets with a 5-year recovery period each for $100. Under the specific identification method, F identifies these mass assets as being from the pool established by F in 2012 for mass assets with a 5-year recovery period. Assume F depreciates this pool using the optional depreciation table that corresponds with the general depreciation system, the 200-percent declining balance method, a 5-year recovery period, and the half-year convention. F elected not to deduct the additional first year depreciation provided by section 168(k) for 5-year property placed in service during 2012. As of January 1, 2014, this pool contains 100 similar items of mass assets with a total cost of $25,000 and a total depreciation reserve of $13,000. Because all the items of mass assets in the pool are similar, F allocates the cost and depreciation allowed or allowable for the pool ratably among each item in the pool. This allocation is a reasonable method because all the items of mass assets in the pool are similar. Using this reasonable method, F allocates a cost of $250 ($25,000 × (1/100)) to each disposed of mass asset and depreciation allowed or allowable of $130 ($13,000 × (1/100)) to each disposed of mass asset. The depreciation allowed or allowable in 2014 for each disposed of mass asset is $24 (($250 × 19.2%) / 2). As a result, the adjusted depreciable basis of each disposed of mass asset under section 1011 is $96 ($250 - $130 - $24). Thus, F recognizes a gain of $4 for each disposed of mass asset in 2014, which is subject to section 1245.

(iii) Further, as of January 1, 2014, the unadjusted depreciable basis of the 2012 pool of mass assets with a 5-year recovery period is reduced from $25,000 to $22,500 ($25,000 less the unadjusted depreciable basis of $2,500 for the 10 disposed of items), and the depreciation reserve of this 2012 pool is reduced from $13,000 to $11,700 ($13,000 less the depreciation allowed or allowable of $1,300 for the 10 disposed of items as of December 31, 2013). Consequently, as of January 1, 2014, the 2012 pool of mass assets with a 5-year recovery period has 90 items with a total cost of $22,500 and a depreciation reserve of $11,700. Thus, the depreciation allowance for this pool for 2014 is $4,320 ($22,500 × 19.2%).

*Example 11.* (i) The facts are the same as in *Example 10.* Because of changes in F's recordkeeping in 2015, it is impracticable for F to continue to identify disposed of mass assets using specific identification and to determine the unadjusted depreciable basis of the disposed of mass assets. As a result, F files a Form 3115, Application for Change in Accounting Method, to change to a first-in, first-out method beginning with the taxable year beginning on January 1, 2015, on a modified cut-off basis. See § 1.446-1(e)(2)(ii)(*d*)(*2*)(*vii*). Under the first-in, first-out method, the mass assets disposed of in a taxable year are deemed to be from the pool with the earliest placed-in-service year that has assets as of the beginning of the taxable year of the disposition with the same recovery period as the asset disposed of. The Commissioner of Internal Revenue consents to this change in method of accounting.

(ii) During 2015, F sells 20 items of mass assets with a 5-year recovery period each for $50. As of January 1, 2015, the 2008 pool is the pool with the earliest placed-in-service year for mass assets with a 5-year recovery period, and this pool contains 25 items of mass assets with a total cost of $10,000 and a total depreciation reserve of $10,000. Thus, F allocates a cost of $400 ($10,000 × (1/25)) to each disposed of mass asset and depreciation allowed or allowable of $400 to each disposed of mass asset. As a result, the adjusted depreciable basis of each disposed of mass asset is $0. Thus, F recognizes a gain of $50 for each disposed of mass asset in 2015, which is subject to section 1245.

(iii) Further, as of January 1, 2015, the unadjusted depreciable basis of the 2008 pool of mass assets with a 5-year recovery period is reduced from $10,000 to $2,000 ($10,000 less the unadjusted depreciable basis of $8,000 for the 20 disposed of items ($400 × 20)), and the depreciation reserve of this 2008 pool is reduced from $10,000 to $2,000 ($10,000 less the depreciation allowed or allowable of $8,000 for the 20 disposed of items as of December 31, 2014). Consequently, as of January 1, 2015, the 2008 pool of mass assets with a 5-year recovery period has 5 items with a total cost of $2,000 and a depreciation reserve of $2,000.

(j) *Effective/applicability dates* .—(1) *In general* .—Except as provided in paragraph (j)(5) of this section, this section applies to taxable years beginning on or after January 1, 2014.

(2) *Early application of this section* .—A taxpayer may choose to apply the provisions of this section to taxable years beginning on or after January 1, 2012.

(3) *Early application of regulation project REG-110732-13* .—A taxpayer may rely on the provisions of this section in regulation project REG-110732-13 (2013-43 IRB 404) (see § 601.601(d)(2) of this chapter) for taxable years beginning on or after January 1, 2012. However, a taxpayer may not rely on the provisions of this section in regulation project REG-110732-13 for taxable years beginning on or after January 1, 2014.

(4) *Optional application of TD 9564* .—A taxpayer may choose to apply § 1.168(i)-8T as contained in 26 CFR part 1 edition revised as of April 1, 2014, to taxable years beginning on or after January 1, 2012. However, a taxpayer may not apply § 1.168(i)-8T as contained in 26 CFR part 1 edition revised as of April 1, 2014, to taxable years beginning on or after January 1, 2014.

(5) *Application of paragraph (c)(4)(i)* .—The language "and the distinct asset determination under § 1.1031(a)-3(a)(4) do not apply." in the last sentence

of paragraph (c)(4)(i) of this section applies on or after December 2, 2020. Paragraph (c)(4)(i) of this section as contained in 26 CFR part 1 edition revised as of April 1, 2020, applies before December 2, 2020.

(6) *Change in method of accounting* .—A change to comply with this section for depreciable assets placed in service in a taxable year ending on or after December 30, 2003, is a change in method of accounting to which the provisions of section 446(e) and the regulations under section 446(e) apply. A taxpayer also may treat a change to comply with this section for depreciable assets placed in service in a taxable year ending before December 30, 2003, as a change in method of accounting to which the provisions of section 446(e) and the regulations under section 446(e) apply. This paragraph (j)(5) does not apply to a change to comply with paragraph (d)(2) of this section, except as provided in paragraph (d)(2)(iii) or (iv)(B) of this section or otherwise provided by other guidance published in the Internal Revenue Bulletin (see § 601.601(d)(2) of this chapter). [Reg. § 1.168(i)-8.]

**.01 Historical Comment:** Proposed 9/19/2013. Adopted 8/14/2014 by T.D. 9689 (corrected 12/30/2014). Amended 11/30/2020 by T.D. 9935.

## ¶ 569

## Reg. § 1.168(k)-0

§ 1.168(k)-0. **Table of contents** .—This section lists the major paragraphs contained in § § 1.168(k)-1 and 1.168(k)-2.

(B) Conditions.
(C) Options.
(D) Supply agreements.
(E) Components.
(iii) Self-constructed property.
(A) In general.
(B) When does manufacture, construction, or production begin.
*(1)* In general.
*(2)* Safe harbor.
(C) Components of self-constructed property.
*(1)* Acquired components.
*(2)* Self-constructed components.
(iv) Disqualified transactions.
(A) In general.
(B) Related party defined.
(v) Examples.
(5) Placed-in-service date.
(i) In general.
(ii) Sale-leaseback, syndication, and certain other transactions.
(A) Sale-leaseback transaction.
(B) Syndication transaction and certain other transactions.
(C) Sale-leaseback transaction followed by a syndication transaction and certain other transactions.
(iii) Technical termination of a partnership.
(iv) Section 168(i)(7) transactions.
(v) Example.
(c) Qualified leasehold improvement property.
(1) In general.
(2) Certain improvements not included.
(3) Definitions.
(d) Computation of depreciation deduction for qualified property or 50-percent bonus depreciation property.
(1) Additional first year depreciation deduction.
(i) In general.
(ii) Property having a longer production period.
(iii) Alternative minimum tax.
(2) Otherwise allowable depreciation deduction.
(i) In general.
(ii) Alternative minimum tax.
(3) Examples.
(e) Election not to deduct additional first year depreciation.
(1) In general.
(i) Qualified property.
(ii) 50-percent bonus depreciation property.
(2) Definition of class of property.
(3) Time and manner for making election.
(i) Time for making election.
(ii) Manner of making election.
(4) Special rules for 2000 or 2001 returns.
(5) Failure to make election.
(6) Alternative minimum tax.

(7) Revocation.

(i) In general.

(ii) Automatic 6-month extension.

(f) Special rules.

(1) Property placed in service and disposed of in the same taxable year.

(i) In general.

(ii) Technical termination of a partnership.

(iii) Section 168(i)(7) transactions.

(iv) Examples.

(2) Redetermination of basis.

(i) Increase in basis.

(ii) Decrease in basis.

(iii) Definition.

(iv) Examples.

(3) Section 1245 and 1250 depreciation recapture.

(4) Coordination with section 169.

(5) Like-kind exchanges and involuntary conversions.

(i) Scope.

(ii) Definitions.

(iii) Computation.

(A) In general.

(B) Year of disposition and year of replacement.

(C) Property having a longer production period.

(D) Alternative minimum tax.

(iv) Sale-leasebacks.

(v) Acquired MACRS property or acquired computer software that is acquired and placed in service before disposition of involuntarily converted MACRS property or involuntarily converted computer software.

(A) Time of replacement.

(B) Depreciation of acquired MACRS property or acquired computer software.

(vi) Examples.

(6) Change in use.

(i) Change in use of depreciable property.

(ii) Conversion to personal use.

(iii) Conversion to business or income-producing use.

(A) During the same taxable year.

(B) Subsequent to the acquisition year.

(iv) Depreciable property changes use subsequent to the placed-in-service year.

(v) Examples.

(7) Earnings and profits.

(8) Limitation of amount of depreciation for certain passenger automobiles.

(9) Section 754 election.

(10) Coordination with section 47.

(11) Coordination with section 514(a)(3).

(g) Effective date.

(1) In general.

(2) Technical termination of a partnership or section 168(i)(7) transactions.

(3) Like-kind exchanges and involuntary conversions.
(4) Change in method of accounting.
(i) Special rules for 2000 or 2001 returns.
(ii) Like-kind exchanges and involuntary conversions.
(5) Revisions to paragraphs (b)(3)(ii)(B) and (b)(5)(ii)(B).
(6) Rehabilitation credit.

*§1.168(k)-2 Additional first year depreciation deduction for property acquired and placed in service after September 27, 2017.*

(a) Scope and definitions.
(1) Scope.
(2) Definitions.
(b) Qualified property.
(1) In general.
(2) Description of qualified property.
(i) In general.
(ii) Property not eligible for additional first year depreciation deduction.
(iii) Examples.
(3) Original use or used property acquisition requirements.
(i) In general.
(ii) Original use.
(A) In general.
(B) Conversion to business or income-producing use.
(C) Fractional interests in property.
(iii) Used property acquisition requirements.
(A) In general.
(B) Property was not used by the taxpayer at any time prior to acquisition.
(C) Special rules for a series of related transactions.
(iv) Application to partnerships.
(A) Section 704(c) remedial allocations.
(B) Basis determined under section 732.
(C) Section 734(b) adjustments.
(D) Section 743(b) adjustments.
(v) Application to members of a consolidated group.
(vi) Syndication transaction.
(vii) Examples.
(4) Placed-in-service date.
(i) In general.
(ii) Specified plant.
(iii) Qualified film, television, or live theatrical production.
(A) Qualified film or television production.
(B) Qualified live theatrical production.
(iv) Syndication transaction.
(v) Technical termination of a partnership.
(vi) Section 168(i)(7) transactions.
(5) Acquisition of property.
(i) In general.
(ii) Acquisition date.
(A) In general.

(B) Determination of acquisition date for property acquired pursuant to a written binding contract.

(iii) Definition of binding contract.

(A) In general.

(B) Conditions.

(C) Options.

(D) Letter of intent.

(E) Supply agreements.

(F) Components.

(G) Acquisition of a trade or business or an entity.

(iv) Self-constructed property.

(A) In general.

(B) When does manufacture, construction, or production begin.

(C) Components of self-constructed property.

(v) Determination of acquisition date for property not acquired pursuant to a written binding contract.

(vi) Qualified film, television, or live theatrical production.

(A) Qualified film or television production.

(B) Qualified live theatrical production.

(vii) Specified plant.

(viii) Examples.

(c) Election for components of larger self-constructed property for which the manufacture, construction, or production begins before September 28, 2017.

(1) In general.

(2) Eligible larger self-constructed property.

(i) In general.

(ii) Residential rental property or nonresidential real property.

(iii) Beginning of manufacture, construction, or production.

(iv) Exception.

(3) Eligible components.

(i) In general.

(ii) Acquired components.

(iii) Self-constructed components.

(4) Special rules.

(i) Installation costs.

(ii) Property described in section 168(k)(2)(B).

(5) Computation of additional first year depreciation deduction.

(i) Election is made.

(ii) Election is not made.

(6) Time and manner for making election.

(i) Time for making election.

(ii) Manner of making election.

(7) Revocation of election.

(i) In general.

(ii) Automatic 6-month extension.

(8) Additional procedural guidance.

(9) Examples.

(d) Property described in section 168(k)(2)(B) or (C).

(1) In general.

(2) Definition of binding contract.

(3) Self-constructed property.

(i) In general.
(ii) When does manufacture, construction, or production begin.
(A) In general.
(B) Safe harbor.
(iii) Components of self-constructed property.
(A) Acquired components.
(B) Self-constructed components.
(iv) Determination of acquisition date for property not acquired pursuant to a written binding contract.
(4) Examples.
(e) Computation of depreciation deduction for qualified property.
(1) Additional first year depreciation deduction.
(i) Allowable taxable year.
(ii) Computation.
(iii) Property described in section 168(k)(2)(B).
(iv) Alternative minimum tax.
(A) In general.
(B) Special rules.
(2) Otherwise allowable depreciation deduction.
(i) In general.
(ii) Alternative minimum tax.
(3) Examples.
(f) Elections under section 168(k).
(1) Election not to deduct additional first year depreciation.
(i) In general.
(ii) Definition of class of property.
(iii) Time and manner for making election.
(A) Time for making election.
(B) Manner of making election.
(iv) Failure to make election.
(2) Election to apply section 168(k)(5) for specified plants.
(i) In general.
(ii) Time and manner for making election.
(A) Time for making election.
(B) Manner of making election.
(iii) Failure to make election.
(3) Election for qualified property placed in service during the 2017 taxable year.
(i) In general.
(ii) Time and manner for making election.
(A) Time for making election.
(B) Manner of making election.
(iii) Failure to make election.
(4) Alternative minimum tax.
(5) Revocation of election.
(i) In general.
(ii) Automatic 6-month extension.
(6) Special rules for 2016 and 2017 returns.
(7) Additional procedural guidance.
(g) Special rules.
(1) Property placed in service and disposed of in the same taxable year.

(i) In general.
(ii) Technical termination of a partnership.
(iii) Section 168(i)(7) transactions.
(iv) Examples.
(2) Redetermination of basis.
(i) Increase in basis.
(ii) Decrease in basis.
(iii) Definitions.
(iv) Examples.
(3) Sections 1245 and 1250 depreciation recapture.
(4) Coordination with section 169.
(5) Like-kind exchanges and involuntary conversions.
(i) Scope.
(ii) Definitions.
(iii) Computation.
(A) In general.
(B) Year of disposition and year of replacement.
(C) Property described in section 168(k)(2)(B).
(D) Effect of § 1.168(i)-6(i)(1) election.
(E) Alternative minimum tax.
(iv) Replacement MACRS property or replacement computer software that is acquired and placed in service before disposition of relinquished MACRS property or relinquished computer software.
(v) Examples.
(6) Change in use.
(i) Change in use of MACRS property.
(ii) Conversion to personal use.
(iii) Conversion to business or income-producing use.
(A) During the same taxable year.
(B) Subsequent to the acquisition year.
(iv) Depreciable property changes use subsequent to the placed-in-service year.
(v) Examples.
(7) Earnings and profits.
(8) Limitation of amount of depreciation for certain passenger automobiles.
(9) Coordination with section 47.
(i) In general.
(ii) Example.
(10) Coordination with section 514(a)(3).
(11) Mid-quarter convention.
(h) Applicability dates.
(1) In general.
(2) Applicability of this section for prior taxable years.
(3) Early application of this section and § 1.1502-68.
(i) In general.
(ii) Early application to certain transactions.
(iii) Bound by early application.

[Reg. § 1.168(k)-0.]

**.01 Historical Comment:** Adopted 9/5/2003 by T.D. 9091. Amended 8/28/2006 by T.D. 9283, 9/17/2019 by T.D. 9874 and 11/5/2020 by T.D. 9916.

## ¶ 570

### Reg. § 1.168(k)-1

§ 1.168(k)-1. **Additional first year depreciation deduction .**—(a) *Scope and definitions .*—(1) *Scope .*—This section provides the rules for determining the 30-percent additional first year depreciation deduction allowable under section 168(k)(1) for qualified property and the 50-percent additional first year depreciation deduction allowable under section 168(k)(4) for 50-percent bonus depreciation property.

(2) *Definitions .*—For purposes of section 168(k) and this section, the following definitions apply:

(i) *Depreciable property* is property that is of a character subject to the allowance for depreciation as determined under section 167 and the regulations thereunder.

(ii) *MACRS property* is tangible, depreciable property that is placed in service after December 31, 1986 (or after July 31, 1986, if the taxpayer made an election under section 203(a)(1)(B) of the Tax Reform Act of 1986; 100 Stat. 2143) and subject to section 168, except for property excluded from the application of section 168 as a result of section 168(f) or as a result of a transitional rule.

(iii) *Unadjusted depreciable basis* is the basis of property for purposes of section 1011 without regard to any adjustments described in section 1016(a)(2) and (3). This basis reflects the reduction in basis for the percentage of the taxpayer's use of property for the taxable year other than in the taxpayer's trade or business (or for the production of income), for any portion of the basis the taxpayer properly elects to treat as an expense under section 179 or section 179C, and for any adjustments to basis provided by other provisions of the Internal Revenue Code and the regulations thereunder (other than section 1016(a)(2) and (3)) (for example, a reduction in basis by the amount of the disabled access credit pursuant to section 44(d)(7)). For property subject to a lease, see section 167(c)(2).

(iv) *Adjusted depreciable basis* is the unadjusted depreciable basis of the property, as defined in § 1.168(k)-1(a)(2)(iii), less the adjustments described in section 1016(a)(2) and (3).

(b) *Qualified property or 50-percent bonus depreciation property .*—(1) *In general .*—Qualified property or 50-percent bonus depreciation property is depreciable property that meets all the following requirements in the first taxable year in which the property is subject to depreciation by the taxpayer whether or not depreciation deductions for the property are allowable:

(i) The requirements in § 1.168(k)-1(b)(2) (description of property);

(ii) The requirements in § 1.168(k)-1(b)(3) (original use);

(iii) The requirements in § 1.168(k)-1(b)(4) (acquisition of property); and

(iv) The requirements in § 1.168(k)-1(b)(5) (placed-in-service date).

(2) *Description of qualified property or 50-percent bonus depreciation property .*—(i) *In general .*—Depreciable property will meet the requirements of this paragraph (b)(2) if the property is—

(A) MACRS property (as defined in § 1.168(k)-1(a)(2)(ii)) that has a recovery period of 20 years or less. For purposes of this paragraph (b)(2)(i)(A) and section 168(k)(2)(B)(i)(II) and 168(k)(4)(C), the recovery period is determined in accordance with section 168(c) regardless of any election made by the taxpayer under section 168(g)(7);

(B) Computer software as defined in, and depreciated under, section 167(f)(1) and the regulations thereunder;

(C) Water utility property as defined in section 168(e)(5) and depreciated under section 168; or

(D) Qualified leasehold improvement property as defined in paragraph (c) of this section and depreciated under section 168.

(ii) *Property not eligible for additional first year depreciation deduction* .—(A) *Property that is not qualified property* .—For purposes of the 30-percent additional first year depreciation deduction, depreciable property will not meet the requirements of this paragraph (b)(2) if the property is—

*(1)* Described in section 168(f);

*(2)* Required to be depreciated under the alternative depreciation system of section 168(g) pursuant to section 168(g)(1)(A) through (D) or other provisions of the Internal Revenue Code (for example, property described in section 263A(e)(2)(A) if the taxpayer (or any related person as defined in section 263A(e)(2)(B)) has made an election under section 263A(d)(3), or property described in section 280F(b)(1)).

*(3)* Included in any class of property for which the taxpayer elects not to deduct the 30-percent additional first year depreciation (for further guidance, see paragraph (e) of this section); or

*(4)* Qualified New York Liberty Zone leasehold improvement property as defined in section 1400L(c)(2).

(B) *Property that is not 50-percent bonus depreciation property* .—For purposes of the 50-percent additional first year depreciation deduction, depreciable property will not meet the requirements of this paragraph (b)(2) if the property is—

*(1)* Described in paragraph (b)(2)(ii)(A)( *1*), ( *2*), or ( *4*) of this section; or

*(2)* Included in any class of property for which the taxpayer elects the 30-percent, instead of the 50-percent, additional first year depreciation deduction or elects not to deduct any additional first year depreciation (for further guidance, see paragraph (e) of this section).

(3) *Original use* .—(i) *In general* .—For purposes of the 30-percent additional first year depreciation deduction, depreciable property will meet the requirements of this paragraph (b)(3) if the original use of the property commences with the taxpayer after September 10, 2001. For purposes of the 50-percent additional first year depreciation deduction, depreciable property will meet the requirements of this paragraph (b)(3) if the original use of the property commences with the taxpayer after May 5, 2003. Except as provided in paragraphs (b)(3)(iii) and (iv) of this section, original use means the first use to which the property is put, whether or not that use corresponds to the use of the property by the taxpayer. Thus, additional capital expenditures incurred by a taxpayer to recondition or rebuild property acquired or owned by the taxpayer satisfies the original use requirement. However, the cost of reconditioned or rebuilt property does not satisfy the original use requirement. The question of whether property is reconditioned or rebuilt property is a question of fact. For purposes of this paragraph (b)(3)(i), property that contains used parts will not be treated as reconditioned or rebuilt if the cost of the used parts is not more than 20 percent of the total cost of the property, whether acquired or self-constructed.

(ii) *Conversion to business or income-producing use* .—(A) *Personal use to business or income-producing use* .—If a taxpayer initially acquires new property for personal use and subsequently uses the property in the taxpayer's trade or business or for the taxpayer's production of income, the taxpayer is considered the original user of the property. If a person initially acquires new property for personal use and a taxpayer subsequently acquires the property from the person for use in the taxpayer's trade or business or for the taxpayer's production of income, the taxpayer is not considered the original user of the property.

(B) *Inventory to business or income-producing use* .—If a taxpayer initially acquires new property and holds the property primarily for sale to customers in the ordinary course of the taxpayer's business and subsequently withdraws the property from inventory and uses the property primarily in the taxpayer's trade or business or primarily for the taxpayer's production of income, the taxpayer is considered the original user of the property. If a person initially acquires new property and holds the property primarily for sale to customers in the ordinary course of the person's business and a taxpayer subsequently acquires the property from the person for use primarily in the taxpayer's trade or business or primarily for the taxpayer's production of income, the taxpayer is considered the original user of the property. For purposes of this paragraph (b)(3)(ii)(B), the original use of the property by the taxpayer commences on the date on which the taxpayer uses the property primarily in the taxpayer's trade or business or primarily for the taxpayer's production of income.

(iii) *Sale-leaseback, syndication, and certain other transactions* .—(A) *Sale-leaseback transaction* .—If new property is originally placed in service by a person after September 10, 2001 (for qualified property), or after May 5, 2003 (for 50-percent bonus depreciation property), and is sold to a taxpayer and leased back to the person by the taxpayer within three months after the date the property was originally placed in service by the person, the taxpayer-lessor is considered the original user of the property.

(B) *Syndication transaction and certain other transactions* .—If new property is originally placed in service by a lessor (including by operation of paragraph (b)(5)(ii)(A) of this section) after September 10, 2001 (for qualified property), or after May 5, 2003 (for 50-percent bonus depreciation property), and is sold by the lessor or any subsequent purchaser within three months after the date the property was originally placed in service by the lessor (or, in the case of multiple units of property subject to the same lease, within three months after the date the final unit is placed in service, so long as the period between the time the first unit is placed in service and the time the last unit is placed in service does not exceed 12 months), and the user of the property after the last sale during the three-month period remains the same as when the property was originally placed in service by the lessor, the purchaser of the property in the last sale during the three-month period is considered the original user of the property.

(C) *Sale-leaseback transaction followed by a syndication transaction and certain other transactions* .—If a sale-leaseback transaction that satisfies the requirements in paragraph (b)(3)(iii)(A) of this section is followed by a transaction that satisfies the requirements in paragraph (b)(3)(iii)(B) of this section, the original user of the property is determined in accordance with paragraph (b)(3)(iii)(B) of this section.

(iv) *Fractional interests in property* .—If, in the ordinary course of its business, a taxpayer sells fractional interests in property to third parties unrelated to the taxpayer, each first fractional owner of the property is considered as the original user of its proportionate share of the property. Furthermore, if the taxpayer uses the property before all of the fractional interests of the property are sold but the property continues to be held primarily for sale by the taxpayer, the original use of any fractional interest sold to a third party unrelated to the taxpayer subsequent to the taxpayer's use of the property begins with the first purchaser of that fractional interest. For purposes of this paragraph (b)(3)(iv), persons are not related if they do not have a relationship described in section 267(b) or 707(b) and the regulations thereunder.

(v) *Examples* .—The application of this paragraph (b)(3) is illustrated by the following examples:

*Example 1.* On August 1, 2002, *A* buys from *B* for $20,000 a machine that has been previously used by *B* in *B's* trade or business. On March 1, 2003, *A* makes a $5,000 capital expenditure to recondition the machine. The $20,000 purchase price does not qualify for the additional first year depreciation deduction because the original use requirement of this paragraph (b)(3) is not met. However, the $5,000 expenditure satisfies the original use requirement of this paragraph (b)(3) and, assuming all other requirements are met, qualifies for the 30-percent additional first year depreciation deduction, regardless of whether the $5,000 is added to the basis of the machine or is capitalized as a separate asset.

*Example 2. C*, an automobile dealer, uses some of its automobiles as demonstrators in order to show them to prospective customers. The automobiles that are used as demonstrators by *C* are held by *C* primarily for sale to customers in the ordinary course of its business. On September 1, 2002, *D* buys from *C* an automobile that was previously used as a demonstrator by *C. D* will use the automobile solely for business purposes. The use of the automobile by *C* as a demonstrator does not constitute a "use" for purposes of the original use requirement and, therefore, *D* will be considered the original user of the automobile for purposes of this paragraph (b)(3). Assuming all other requirements are met, *D's* purchase price of the automobile qualifies for the 30-percent additional first year depreciation deduction for *D*, subject to any limitation under section 280F.

*Example 3.* On April 1, 2000, *E* acquires a horse to be used in *E's* thoroughbred racing business. On October 1, 2003, *F* buys the horse from *E* and will use the horse in *F's* horse breeding business. The use of the horse by *E* in its racing business prevents the original use of the horse from commencing with *F*. Thus, *F's* purchase price of the horse does not qualify for the additional first year depreciation deduction.

*Example 4.* In the ordinary course of its business, *G* sells fractional interests in its aircraft to unrelated parties. *G* holds out for sale eight equal fractional interests in an aircraft. On January 1, 2003, *G* sells five of the eight fractional interests in the aircraft to *H*, an unrelated party, and *H* begins to use its proportionate share of the aircraft immediately upon purchase. On June 1, 2003, G sells to I, an unrelated party to G, the remaining unsold 3/8 fractional interests in the aircraft. *H* is considered the original user as to its 5/8 fractional interest in the aircraft and *I* is considered the original user as to its 3/8 fractional interest in the aircraft. Thus, assuming all other requirements are met, *H's* purchase price for its 5/8 fractional interest in the aircraft qualifies for the 30-percent additional first year depreciation deduction and *I's* purchase price for its 3/8 fractional interest in the aircraft qualifies for the 50-percent additional first year depreciation deduction.

*Example 5.* On September 1, 2001, *JJ*, an equipment dealer, buys new tractors that are held by *JJ* primarily for sale to customers in the ordinary course of its business. On October 15, 2001, *JJ* withdraws the tractors from inventory and begins to use the tractors primarily for producing rental income. The holding of the tractors by *JJ* as inventory does not constitute a "use" for purposes of the original use requirement and, therefore, the original use of the tractors commences with *JJ* on October 15, 2001, for purposes of paragraph (b)(3) of this section. However, the tractors are not eligible for the additional first year depreciation deduction because *JJ* acquired the tractors before September 11, 2001.

(4) *Acquisition of property* .—(i) *In general* .—(A) *Qualified property* .— For purposes of the 30-percent additional first year depreciation deduction, depreciable property will meet the requirements of this paragraph (b)(4) if the property is—

*(1)* Acquired by the taxpayer after September 10, 2001, and before January 1, 2005, but only if no written binding contract for the acquisition of the property was in effect before September 11, 2001; or

*(2)* Acquired by the taxpayer pursuant to a written binding contract that was entered into after September 10, 2001, and before January 1, 2005.

(B) *50-percent bonus depreciation property* .—For purposes of the 50-percent additional first year depreciation deduction, depreciable property will meet the requirements of this paragraph (b) (4) if the property is

*(1)* Acquired by the taxpayer after May 5, 2003, and before January 1, 2005, but only if no written binding contract for the acquisition of the property was in effect before May 6, 2003; or

*(2)* Acquired by the taxpayer pursuant to a written binding contract that was entered into after May 5, 2003, and before January 1, 2005.

(ii) *Definition of binding contract* .—(A) *In general* .—A contract is binding only if it is enforceable under State law against the taxpayer or a predecessor, and does not limit damages to a specified amount (for example, by use of a liquidated damages provision). For this purpose, a contractual provision that limits damages to an amount equal to at least 5 percent of the total contract price will not be treated as limiting damages to a specified amount. In determining whether a contract limits damages, the fact that there may be little or no damages because the contract price does not significantly differ from fair market value will not be taken into account. For example, if a taxpayer entered into an irrevocable written contract to purchase an asset for $100 and the contract contained no provision for liquidated damages, the contract is considered binding notwithstanding the fact that the asset had a fair market value of $99 and under local law the seller would only recover the difference in the event the purchaser failed to perform. If the contract provided for a full refund of the purchase price in lieu of any damages allowable by law in the event of breach or cancellation, the contract is not considered binding.

(B) *Conditions* .—A contract is binding even if subject to a condition, as long as the condition is not within the control of either party or a predecessor. A contract will continue to be binding if the parties make insubstantial changes in its terms and conditions or because any term is to be determined by a standard beyond the control of either party. A contract that imposes significant obligations on the taxpayer or a predecessor will be treated as binding notwithstanding the fact that certain terms remain to be negotiated by the parties to the contract.

(C) *Options* .—An option to either acquire or sell property is not a binding contract.

(D) *Supply agreements* .—A binding contract does not include a supply or similar agreement if the amount and design specifications of the property to be purchased have not been specified. The contract will not be a binding contract for the property to be purchased until both the amount and the design specifications are specified. For example, if the provisions of a supply or similar agreement state the design specifications of the property to be purchased, a purchase order under the agreement for a specific number of assets is treated as a binding contract.

(E) *Components* .—A binding contract to acquire one or more components of a larger property will not be treated as a binding contract to acquire the larger property. If a binding contract to acquire the component does not satisfy the requirements of this paragraph (b) (4), the component does not qualify for the 30-percent or 50-percent additional first year depreciation deduction, as applicable.

(iii) *Self-constructed property* .—(A) *In general* .—If a taxpayer manufactures, constructs, or produces property for use by the taxpayer in its trade or business (or for its production of income), the acquisition rules in paragraph (b)(4)(i) of this section are treated as met for qualified property if the taxpayer begins manufacturing, constructing, or producing the property after September 10, 2001, and before January 1, 2005, and for 50-percent bonus depreciation property if the taxpayer begins manufacturing, constructing, or producing the property after May 5, 2003, and before January 1, 2005. Property that is manufactured, constructed, or produced for the taxpayer by another person under a written binding contract (as defined in paragraph (b)(4)(ii) of this section) that is entered into prior to the manufacture, construction, or production of the property for use by the taxpayer in its trade or business (or for its production of income) is considered to be manufactured, constructed, or produced by the taxpayer. If a taxpayer enters into a written binding contract (as defined in paragraph (b)(4)(ii) of this section) after September 10, 2001, and before January 1, 2005, with another person to manufacture, construct, or produce property described in section 168(k)(2)(B) (longer production period property) or section 168(k)(2)(C) (certain aircraft) and the manufacture, construction, or production of this property begins after December 31, 2004, the acquisition rule in paragraph (b)(4)(i)(A)( *2*) or (b)(4)(i)(B)( *2*) of this section is met.

(B) *When does manufacture, construction, or production begin .—(1) In general .—* For purposes of paragraph (b)(4)(iii) of this section, manufacture, construction, or production of property begins when physical work of a significant nature begins. Physical work does not include preliminary activities such as planning or designing, securing financing, exploring, or researching. The determination of when physical work of a significant nature begins depends on the facts and circumstances. For example, if a retail motor fuels outlet or other facility is to be constructed on-site, construction begins when physical work of a significant nature commences at the site; that is, when work begins on the excavation for footings, pouring the pads for the outlet, or the driving of foundation pilings into the ground. Preliminary work, such as clearing a site, test drilling to determine soil condition, or excavation to change the contour of the land (as distinguished from excavation for footings) does not constitute the beginning of construction. However, if a retail motor fuels outlet or other facility is to be assembled on-site from modular units manufactured off-site and delivered to the site where the outlet will be used, manufacturing begins when physical work of a significant nature commences at the off-site location.

*(2) Safe harbor* .—For purposes of paragraph (b)(4)(iii)(B)( *1*) of this section, a taxpayer may choose to determine when physical work of a significant nature begins in accordance with this paragraph (b)(4)(iii)(B)( *2*). Physical work of a significant nature will not be considered to begin before the taxpayer incurs (in the case of an accrual basis taxpayer) or pays (in the case of a cash basis taxpayer) more than 10 percent of the total cost of the property (excluding the cost of any land and preliminary activities such as planning or designing, securing financing, exploring, or researching). When property is manufactured, constructed, or produced for the taxpayer by another person, this safe harbor test must be satisfied by the taxpayer. For example, if a retail motor fuels outlet or other facility is to be constructed for an accrual basis taxpayer by another person for the total cost of $200,000 (excluding the cost of any land and preliminary activities such as planning or designing, securing financing, exploring, or researching), construction is deemed to begin for purposes of this paragraph (b)(4)(iii)(B)( *2*) when the taxpayer has incurred more than 10 percent (more than $20,000) of the total cost of the property. A taxpayer chooses to apply this paragraph (b)(4)(iii)(B)( *2*) by filing an income tax return for the placed-in-service year of the property that

determines when physical work of a significant nature begins consistent with this paragraph (b)(4)(iii)(B)(*2*).

(C) *Components of self-constructed property* .—*(1) Acquired components* .—If a binding contract (as defined in paragraph (b)(4)(ii) of this section) to acquire a component does not satisfy the requirements of paragraph (b)(4)(i) of this section, the component does not qualify for the 30-percent or 50-percent additional first year depreciation deduction, as applicable. A binding contract (as defined in paragraph (b)(4)(ii) of this section) to acquire one or more components of a larger self-constructed property will not preclude the larger self-constructed property from satisfying the acquisition rules in paragraph (b)(4)(iii)(A) of this section. Accordingly, the unadjusted depreciable basis of the larger self-constructed property that is eligible for the 30-percent or 50-percent additional first year depreciation deduction, as applicable (assuming all other requirements are met), must not include the unadjusted depreciable basis of any component that does not satisfy the requirements of paragraph (b)(4)(i) of this section. If the manufacture, construction, or production of the larger self-constructed property begins before September 11, 2001, for qualified property, or before May 6, 2003, for 50-percent bonus depreciation property, the larger self-constructed property and any acquired components related to the larger self-constructed property do not qualify for the 30-percent or 50-percent additional first year depreciation deduction, as applicable. If a binding contract to acquire the component is entered into after September 10, 2001, for qualified property, or after May 5, 2003, for 50-percent bonus depreciation property, and before January 1, 2005, but the manufacture, construction, or production of the larger self-constructed property does not begin before January 1, 2005, the component qualifies for the additional first year depreciation deduction (assuming all other requirements are met) but the larger self-constructed property does not.

*(2) Self-constructed components* .—If the manufacture, construction, or production of a component does not satisfy the requirements of paragraph (b)(4)(iii)(A) of this section, the component does not qualify for the 30-percent or 50-percent additional first year depreciation deduction, as applicable. However, if the manufacture, construction, or production of a component does not satisfy the requirements of paragraph (b)(4)(iii)(A) of this section, but the manufacture, construction, or production of the larger self-constructed property satisfies the requirements of paragraph (b)(4)(iii)(A) of this section, the larger self-constructed property qualifies for the 30-percent or 50-percent additional first year depreciation deduction, as applicable (assuming all other requirements are met) even though the component does not qualify for the 30-percent or 50-percent additional first year depreciation deduction. Accordingly, the unadjusted depreciable basis of the larger self-constructed property that is eligible for the 30-percent or 50-percent additional first year depreciation deduction, as applicable (assuming all other requirements are met), must not include the unadjusted depreciable basis of any component that does not qualify for the 30-percent or 50-percent additional first year depreciation deduction. If the manufacture, construction, or production of the larger self-constructed property began before September 11, 2001, for qualified property, or before May 6, 2003, for 50-percent bonus depreciation property, the larger self-constructed property and any self-constructed components related to the larger self-constructed property do not qualify for the 30-percent or 50-percent additional first year depreciation deduction, as applicable. If the manufacture, construction, or production of a component begins after September 10, 2001, for qualified property, or after May 5, 2003, for 50-percent bonus depreciation property, and before January 1, 2005, but the manufacture, construction, or production of the larger self-constructed property does not begin before January 1, 2005, the component qualifies for the additional first year depreciation deduction (assuming all other requirements are met) but the larger self-constructed property does not.

(iv) *Disqualified transactions* .—(A) *In general* .—Property does not satisfy the requirements of this paragraph (b)(4) if the user of the property as of the date on which the property was originally placed in service (including by operation of paragraphs (b)(5)(ii), (iii), and (iv) of this section), or a related party to the user or to the taxpayer, acquired, or had a written binding contract (as defined in paragraph (b)(4)(ii) of this section) in effect for the acquisition of the property at any time before September 11, 2001 (for qualified property), or before May 6, 2003 (for 50-percent bonus depreciation property). In addition, property manufactured, constructed, or produced for the use by the user of the property or by a related party to the user or to the taxpayer does not satisfy the requirements of this paragraph (b)(4) if the manufacture, construction, or production of the property for the user or the related party began at any time before September 11, 2001 (for qualified property), or before May 6, 2003 (for 50-percent bonus depreciation property).

(B) *Related party defined* .—For purposes of this paragraph (b)(4)(iv), persons are related if they have a relationship specified in section 267(b) or 707(b) and the regulations thereunder.

(v) *Examples* .—The application of this paragraph (b)(4) is illustrated by the following examples:

*Example 1.* On September 1, 2001, *J*, a corporation, entered into a written agreement with *K*, a manufacturer, to purchase 20 new lamps for $100 each within the next two years. Although the agreement specifies the number of lamps to be purchased, the agreement does not specify the design of the lamps to be purchased. Accordingly, the agreement is not a binding contract pursuant to paragraph (b)(4)(ii)(D) of this section.

*Example 2.* Same facts as *Example 1.* On December 1, 2001, *J* placed a purchase order with *K* to purchase 20 new model XPC5 lamps for $100 each for a total amount of $2,000. Because the agreement specifies the number of lamps to be purchased and the purchase order specifies the design of the lamps to be purchased, the purchase order placed by *J* with *K* on December 1, 2001, is a binding contract pursuant to paragraph (b)(4)(ii)(D) of this section. Accordingly, the cost of the 20 lamps qualifies for the 30-percent additional first year depreciation deduction.

*Example 3.* Same facts as *Example 1* except that the written agreement between *J* and *K* is to purchase 100 model XPC5 lamps for $100 each within the next two years. Because this agreement specifies the amount and design of the lamps to be purchased, the agreement is a binding contract pursuant to paragraph (b)(4)(ii)(D) of this section. Accordingly, because the agreement was entered into before September 11, 2001, any lamp acquired by *J* under this contract does not qualify for the additional first year depreciation deduction.

*Example 4.* On September 1, 2001, *L* began constructing an electric generation power plant for its own use. On November 1, 2002, *L* ceases construction of the power plant prior to its completion. Between September 1, 2001, and November 1, 2002, *L* incurred $3,000,000 for the construction of the power plant. On May 6, 2003, *L* resumed construction of the power plant and completed its construction on August 31, 2003. Between May 6, 2003, and August 31, 2003, *L* incurred another $1,600,000 to complete the construction of the power plant and, on September 1, 2003, *L* placed the power plant in service. None of *L's* total expenditures of $4,600,000 qualify for the additional first year depreciation deduction because, pursuant to paragraph (b)(4)(iii)(A) of this section, *L* began constructing the power plant before September 11, 2001.

*Example 5.* Same facts as *Example 4* except that *L* began constructing the electric generation power plant for its own use on October 1, 2001. *L's* total expenditures of $4,600,000 qualify for the additional first year depreciation deduction because, pursuant to paragraph (b)(4)(iii)(A) of this section, *L* began constructing the power plant after September 10, 2001, and placed the power plant in service before January 1, 2005. Accordingly, the additional first year depreciation deduction for the power plant will be $1,380,000, computed as $4,600,000 multiplied by 30 percent.

*Example 6.* On August 1, 2001, *M* entered into a written binding contract to acquire a new turbine. The new turbine is a component part of a new electric generation power plant that is being constructed on *M's* behalf. The construction of the new electric generation power plant commenced in November 2001, and the new electric generation power plant was completed in November 2002. Because *M* entered into a written binding contract to acquire a component part (the new turbine) prior to September 11, 2001, pursuant to paragraph (b)(4)(iii)(C) of this section, the component part does not qualify for the additional first year depreciation deduction. However, pursuant to paragraphs (b)(4)(iii)(A) and (C) of this section, the new plant constructed for *M* will qualify for the 30-percent additional first year depreciation deduction because construction of the new plant began after September 10, 2001, and before May 6, 2003. Accordingly, the unadjusted depreciable basis of the new plant that is eligible for the 30-percent additional first year depreciation deduction must not include the unadjusted depreciable basis of the new turbine.

*Example 7.* Same facts as *Example 6* except that *M* entered into the written binding contract to acquire the new turbine on September 30, 2002, and construction of the new plant commenced on August 1, 2001. Because *M* began construction of the new plant prior to September 11, 2001, pursuant to paragraphs (b)(4)(iii)(A) and (C) of this section, neither the new plant constructed for *M* nor the turbine will qualify for the additional first year depreciation deduction because self-construction of the new plant began prior to September 11, 2001.

*Example 8.* On September 1, 2001, *N* began constructing property for its own use. On October 1, 2001, *N* sold its rights to the property to *O*, a related party under section 267(b). Pursuant to paragraph (b)(4)(iv) of this section, the property is not eligible for the additional first year depreciation deduction because *N* and *O* are related parties and construction of the property by *N* began prior to September 11, 2001.

*Example 9.* On September 1, 2001, *P* entered into a written binding contract to acquire property. On October 1, 2001, *P* sold its rights to the property to *Q*, a related party under section 267(b). Pursuant to paragraph (b)(4)(iv) of this section, the property is not eligible for the additional first year depreciation deduction because *P* and *Q* are related parties and a written binding contract for the acquisition of the property was in effect prior to September 11, 2001.

*Example 10.* Prior to September 11, 2001, *R* began constructing an electric generation power plant for its own use. On May 1, 2003, prior to the completion of the power plant, *R* transferred the rights to own and use this power plant to *S*, an unrelated party, for $6,000,000. Between May 6, 2003, and June 30, 2003, S, a calendar-year taxpayer, began construction, and incurred another $1,200,000 to complete the construction, of the power plant and, on August 1, 2003, S placed the power plant in service. Because *R* and *S* are not related parties, the transaction between *R* and *S* will not be a disqualified transaction pursuant to paragraph (b)(4)(iv) of this section. Accordingly, *S's* total expenditures of $7,200,000 for the power plant qualify for the additional first year depreciation deduction. *S's* additional first year depreciation deduction for the power plant will be $2,400,000, computed as $6,000,000 multiplied by 30 percent, plus $1,200,000 multiplied by 50 percent. The $6,000,000 portion of the total $7,200,000 unadjusted depreciable basis qualifies for the 30-percent additional first year depreciation deduction because that portion of the total unadjusted depreciable basis was acquired by *S* after September 10, 2001, and before May 6, 2003. However, because

*S* began construction to complete the power plant after May 5, 2003, the $1,200,000 portion of the total $7,200,000 unadjusted depreciable basis qualifies for the 50-percent additional first year depreciation deduction.

*Example 11.* On September 1, 2001, *T* acquired and placed in service equipment. On October 15, 2001, *T* sells the equipment to *U*, an unrelated party, and leases the property back from *U* in a sale-leaseback transaction. Pursuant to paragraph (b)(4)(iv) of this section, the equipment does not qualify for the additional first year depreciation deduction because *T*, the user of the equipment, acquired the equipment prior to September 11, 2001. In addition, the sale-leaseback rules in paragraphs (b)(3)(iii)(A) and (b)(5)(ii)(A) of this section do not apply because the equipment was originally placed in service by T before September 11, 2001.

*Example 12.* On July 1, 2001, KK began constructing property for its own use. KK placed this property in service on September 15, 2001. On October 15, 2001, KK sells the property to LL, an unrelated party, and leases the property back from LL in a sale-leaseback transaction. Pursuant to paragraph (b)(4)(iv) of this section, the property does not qualify for the additional first year depreciation deduction because the property was constructed for KK, the user of the property, and that construction began prior to September 11, 2001.

*Example 13.* On June 1, 2004, MM decided to construct property described in section 168(k)(2)(B) for its own use. However, one of the component parts of the property had to be manufactured by another person for MM. On August 15, 2004, MM entered into a written binding contract with NN to acquire this component part of the property for $100,000. The manufacture of the component part commenced on September 1, 2004, and MM received the completed component part on February 1, 2005. The cost of this component part is 9 percent of the total cost of the property to be constructed by MM. MM began constructing the property described in section 168(k)(2)(B) on January 15, 2005, and placed this property (including all component parts) in service on November 1, 2005. Pursuant to paragraph (b)(4)(iii)(C)( *2*) of this section, the self-constructed component part of $100,000 manufactured by NN for MM is eligible for the additional first year depreciation deduction (assuming all other requirements are met) because the manufacturing of the component part began after September 10, 2001, and before January 1, 2005, and the property described in section 168(k)(2)(B), the larger self-constructed property, was placed in service by MM before January 1, 2006. However, pursuant to paragraph (b)(4)(iii)(A) of this section, the cost of the property described in section 168(k)(2)(B) (excluding the cost of the self-constructed component part of $100,000 manufactured by NN for MM) is not eligible for the additional first year depreciation deduction because construction of the property began after December 31, 2004.

*Example 14.* On December 1, 2004, OO entered into a written binding contract (as defined in paragraph (b)(4)(ii) of this section) with PP to manufacture an aircraft described in section 168(k)(2)(C) for use in OO's trade or business. PP begins to manufacture the aircraft on February 1, 2005. OO places the aircraft in service on August 1, 2005. Pursuant to paragraph (b)(4)(iii)(A) of this section, the aircraft meets the requirements of paragraph (b)(4)(i)(B)( *2*) of this section because the aircraft was acquired by OO pursuant to a written binding contract entered into after May 5, 2003, and before January 1, 2005.

(5) *Placed-in-service date* .—(i) *In general* .—Depreciable property will meet the requirements of this paragraph (b)(5) if the property is placed in service by the taxpayer for use in its trade or business or for production of income before January 1, 2005, or, in the case of property described in section 168(k)(2)(B) or (C), is placed in service by the taxpayer for use in its trade or business or for production of income before January 1, 2006 (or placed in service by the taxpayer for use in its trade or business or for production of income before January 1, 2007, in the case of

property described in section 168(k)(2)(B) or (C) to which section 105 of the Gulf Opportunity Zone Act of 2005 (Public Law 109-135, 119 Stat. 2577) applies (for further guidance, see Announcement 2006-29 (2006-19 I.R.B. 879) and §601.601(d)(2)(ii)(*b*) of this chapter)).

(ii) *Sale-leaseback, syndication, and certain other transactions*.—(A) *Sale-leaseback transaction*.—If qualified property is originally placed in service after September 10, 2001, or 50-percent bonus depreciation property is originally placed in service after May 5, 2003, by a person and sold to a taxpayer and leased back to the person by the taxpayer within three months after the date the property was originally placed in service by the person, the property is treated as originally placed in service by the taxpayer-lessor not earlier than the date on which the property is used by the lessee under the leaseback.

(B) *Syndication transaction and certain other transactions*.—If qualified property is originally placed in service after September 10, 2001, or 50-percent bonus depreciation property is originally placed in service after May 5, 2003, by a lessor (including by operation of paragraph (b)(5)(ii)(A) of this section) and is sold by the lessor or any subsequent purchaser within three months after the date the property was originally placed in service by the lessor (or, in the case of multiple units of property subject to the same lease, within three months after the date the final unit is placed in service, so long as the period between the time the first unit is placed in service and the time the last unit is placed in service does not exceed 12 months), and the user of the property after the last sale during this three-month period remains the same as when the property was originally placed in service by the lessor, the property is treated as originally placed in service by the purchaser of the property in the last sale during the three-month period but not earlier than the date of the last sale.

(C) *Sale-leaseback transaction followed by a syndication transaction and certain other transactions*.—If a sale-leaseback transaction that satisfies the requirements in paragraph (b)(5)(ii)(A) of this section is followed by a transaction that satisfies the requirements in paragraph (b)(5)(ii)(B) of this section, the placed-in-service date of the property is determined in accordance with paragraph (b)(5)(ii)(B) of this section.

(iii) *Technical termination of a partnership*.—For purposes of this paragraph (b)(5), in the case of a technical termination of a partnership under section 708(b)(1)(B), qualified property or 50-percent bonus depreciation property placed in service by the terminated partnership during the taxable year of termination is treated as originally placed in service by the new partnership on the date the qualified property or the 50-percent bonus depreciation property is contributed by the terminated partnership to the new partnership.

(iv) *Section 168(i)(7) transactions*.—For purposes of this paragraph (b)(5), if qualified property or 50-percent bonus depreciation property is transferred in a transaction described in section 168(i)(7) in the same taxable year that the qualified property or the 50-percent bonus depreciation property is placed in service by the transferor, the transferred property is treated as originally placed in service on the date the transferor placed in service the qualified property or the 50-percent bonus depreciation property, as applicable. In the case of multiple transfers of qualified property or 50-percent bonus depreciation property in multiple transactions described in section 168(i)(7) in the same taxable year, the placed in service date of the transferred property is deemed to be the date on which the first transferor placed in service the qualified property or the 50-percent bonus depreciation property, as applicable.

(v) *Example* .—The application of this paragraph (b)(5) is illustrated by the following example:

*Example*. On September 15, 2004, QQ acquired and placed in service new equipment. This equipment is not described in section 168(k)(2)(B) or (C). On December 1, 2004, QQ sells the equipment to RR and leases the equipment back from RR in a sale-leaseback transaction. On February 15, 2005, RR sells the equipment to TT subject to the lease with QQ. As of February 15, 2005, QQ is still the user of the equipment. The sale-leaseback transaction of December 1, 2004, between QQ and RR satisfies the requirements of paragraph (b)(5)(ii)(A) of this section. The sale transaction of February 15, 2005, between RR and TT satisfies the requirements of paragraph (b)(5)(ii)(B) of this section. Consequently, pursuant to paragraph (b)(5)(ii)(C) of this section, the equipment is treated as originally placed in service by TT on February 15, 2005. Further, pursuant to paragraph (b)(3)(iii)(C) of this section, TT is considered the original user of the equipment. Accordingly, the equipment is not eligible for the additional first year depreciation deduction.

(c) *Qualified leasehold improvement property* .—(1) *In general* .—For purposes of section 168(k), qualified leasehold improvement property means any improvement, which is section 1250 property, to an interior portion of a building that is nonresidential real property if—

(i) The improvement is made under or pursuant to a lease by the lessee (or any sublessee) of the interior portion, or by the lessor of that interior portion;

(ii) The interior portion of the building is to be occupied exclusively by the lessee (or any sublessee) of that interior portion; and

(iii) The improvement is placed in service more than 3 years after the date the building was first placed in service by any person.

(2) *Certain improvements not included* .—Qualified leasehold improvement property does not include any improvement for which the expenditure is attributable to:

(i) The enlargement of the building;

(ii) Any elevator or escalator;

(iii) Any structural component benefiting a common area; or

(iv) The internal structural framework of the building.

(3) *Definitions* .—For purposes of this paragraph (c), the following definitions apply:

(i) *Building* has the same meaning as that term is defined in § 1.48-1(e)(1).

(ii) *Common area* means any portion of a building that is equally available to all users of the building on the same basis for uses that are incidental to the primary use of the building. For example, stairways, hallways, lobbies, common seating areas, interior and exterior pedestrian walkways and pedestrian bridges, loading docks and areas, and rest rooms generally are treated as common areas if they are used by different lessees of a building.

(iii) *Elevator* and *escalator* have the same meanings as those terms are defined in § 1.48-1(m)(2).

(iv) *Enlargement* has the same meaning as that term is defined in § 1.48-12(c)(10).

(v) *Internal structural framework* has the same meaning as that term is defined in § 1.48-12(b)(3)(i)(D)(iii).

(vi) *Lease* has the same meaning as that term is defined in section 168(h)(7). In addition, a commitment to enter into a lease is treated as a lease, and the parties to the commitment are treated as lessor and lessee. However, a lease between related persons is not considered a lease. For purposes of the preceding sentence, related persons are—

(A) Members of an affiliated group (as defined in section 1504 and the regulations thereunder); and

(B) Persons having a relationship described in section 267(b) and the regulations thereunder. For purposes of applying section 267(b), the language "80 percent or more" is used instead of "more than 50 percent."

(vii) *Nonresidential real property* has the same meaning as that term is defined in section 168(e)(2)(B).

(viii) *Structural component* has the same meaning as that term is defined in § 1.48-1(e)(2).

(d) *Computation of depreciation deduction for qualified property or 50-percent bonus depreciation property* .—(1) *Additional first year depreciation deduction* .—(i) *In general* .—Except as provided in paragraph (f) of this section, the additional first year depreciation deduction is allowable in the first taxable year in which the qualified property or 50-percent bonus depreciation property is placed in service by the taxpayer for use in its trade or business or for the production of income. Except as provided in paragraph (f)(5) of this section, the allowable additional first year depreciation deduction for qualified property is determined by multiplying the unadjusted depreciable basis (as defined in § 1.168(k)-1(a)(2)(iii)) of the qualified property by 30 percent. Except as provided in paragraph (f)(5) of this section, the allowable additional first year depreciation deduction for 50-percent bonus depreciation property is determined by multiplying the unadjusted depreciable basis (as defined in § 1.168(k)-1(a)(2)(iii)) of the 50-percent bonus depreciation property by 50 percent. Except as provided in paragraph (f)(1) of this section, the 30-percent or 50-percent additional first year depreciation deduction is not affected by a taxable year of less than 12 months. See paragraph (f)(1) of this section for qualified property or 50-percent bonus depreciation property placed in service and disposed of in the same taxable year. See paragraph (f)(5) of this section for qualified property or 50-percent bonus depreciation property acquired in a like-kind exchange or as a result of an involuntary conversion.

(ii) *Property having a longer production period* .—For purposes of paragraph (d)(1)(i) of this section, the unadjusted depreciable basis (as defined in § 1.168(k)-1(a)(2)(iii)) of qualified property or 50-percent bonus depreciation property described in section 168(k)(2)(B) is limited to the property's unadjusted depreciable basis attributable to the property's manufacture, construction, or production after September 10, 2001 (for qualified property), or May 5, 2003 (for 50-percent bonus depreciation property), and before January 1, 2005.

(iii) *Alternative minimum tax* .—The 30-percent or 50-percent additional first year depreciation deduction is allowed for alternative minimum tax purposes for the taxable year in which the qualified property or the 50-percent bonus depreciation property is placed in service by the taxpayer. In general, the 30-percent or 50-percent additional first year depreciation deduction for alternative minimum tax purposes is based on the unadjusted depreciable basis of the property for alternative minimum tax purposes. However, see paragraph (f)(5)(iii)(D) of this section for qualified property or 50-percent bonus depreciation property acquired in a like-kind exchange or as a result of an involuntary conversion.

(2) *Otherwise allowable depreciation deduction* .—(i) *In general* .—Before determining the amount otherwise allowable as a depreciation deduction for the qualified property or the 50-percent bonus depreciation property for the placed-in-service year and any subsequent taxable year, the taxpayer must determine the remaining adjusted depreciable basis of the qualified property or the 50-percent bonus depreciation property. This remaining adjusted depreciable basis is equal to

the unadjusted depreciable basis of the qualified property or the 50-percent bonus depreciation property reduced by the amount of the additional first year depreciation allowed or allowable, whichever is greater. The remaining adjusted depreciable basis of the qualified property or the 50-percent bonus depreciation property is then depreciated using the applicable depreciation provisions under the Internal Revenue Code for the qualified property or the 50-percent bonus depreciation property. The remaining adjusted depreciable basis of the qualified property or the 50-percent bonus depreciation property that is MACRS property is also the basis to which the annual depreciation rates in the optional depreciation tables apply (for further guidance, see section 8 of Rev. Proc. 87-57 (1987-2 C.B. 687) and § 601.601(d)(2)(ii)(*b*) of this chapter). The depreciation deduction allowable for the remaining adjusted depreciable basis of the qualified property or the 50-percent bonus depreciation property is affected by a taxable year of less than 12 months.

(ii) *Alternative minimum tax* .—For alternative minimum tax purposes, the depreciation deduction allowable for the remaining adjusted depreciable basis of the qualified property or the 50-percent bonus depreciation property is based on the remaining adjusted depreciable basis for alternative minimum tax purposes. The remaining adjusted depreciable basis of the qualified property or the 50-percent bonus depreciable property for alternative minimum tax purposes is depreciated using the same depreciation method, recovery period (or useful life in the case of computer software), and convention that apply to the qualified property or the 50-percent bonus depreciation property for regular tax purposes.

(3) *Examples* .—This paragraph (d) is illustrated by the following examples:

*Example 1.* On March 1, 2003, *V*, a calendar-year taxpayer, purchased and placed in service qualified property that costs $1 million and is 5-year property under section 168(e). *V* depreciates its 5-year property placed in service in 2003 using the optional depreciation table that corresponds with the general depreciation system, the 200-percent declining balance method, a 5-year recovery period, and the half-year convention. For 2003, *V* is allowed a 30-percent additional first year depreciation deduction of $300,000 (the unadjusted depreciable basis of $1 million multiplied by .30). Next, *V* must reduce the unadjusted depreciable basis of $1 million by the additional first year depreciation deduction of $300,000 to determine the remaining adjusted depreciable basis of $700,000. Then, *V's* depreciation deduction allowable in 2003 for the remaining adjusted depreciable basis of $700,000 is $140,000 (the remaining adjusted depreciable basis of $700,000 multiplied by the annual depreciation rate of .20 for recovery year 1).

*Example 2.* On June 1, 2003, *W*, a calendar-year taxpayer, purchased and placed in service 50-percent bonus depreciation property that costs $126,000. The property qualifies for the expensing election under section 179 and is 5-year property under section 168(e). *W* did not purchase any other section 179 property in 2003. *W* makes the election under section 179 for the property and depreciates its 5-year property placed in service in 2003 using the optional depreciation table that corresponds with the general depreciation system, the 200-percent declining balance method, a 5-year recovery period, and the half-year convention. For 2003, *W* is first allowed a $100,000 deduction under section 179. Next, *W* must reduce the cost of $126,000 by the section 179 deduction of $100,000 to determine the unadjusted depreciable basis of $26,000. Then, for 2003, *W* is allowed a 50-percent additional first year depreciation deduction of $13,000 (the unadjusted depreciable basis of $26,000 multiplied by .50). Next, *W* must reduce the unadjusted depreciable basis of $26,000 by the additional first year depreciation deduction of $13,000 to determine the remaining adjusted depreciable basis of $13,000. Then, *W's* depreciation deduction allowable in 2003 for the remaining adjusted depreciable basis of $13,000 is $2,600 (the remaining adjusted depreciable basis of $13,000 multiplied by the annual depreciation rate of .20 for recovery year 1).

(e) *Election not to deduct additional first year depreciation* .—(1) *In general* .—If a taxpayer makes an election under this paragraph (e), the election applies to all qualified property or 50-percent bonus depreciation property, as applicable, that is in the same class of property and placed in service in the same taxable year. The rules of this paragraph (e) apply to the following elections provided under section 168(k):

(i) *Qualified property* .—A taxpayer may make an election not to deduct the 30-percent additional first year depreciation for any class of property that is qualified property placed in service during the taxable year. If this election is made, no additional first year depreciation deduction is allowable for the property placed in service during the taxable year in the class of property.

(ii) *50-percent bonus depreciation property* .—For any class of property that is 50-percent bonus depreciation property placed in service during the taxable year, a taxpayer may make an election—

(A) To deduct the 30-percent, instead of the 50-percent, additional first year depreciation. If this election is made, the allowable additional first year depreciation deduction is determined as though the class of property is qualified property under section 168(k)(2); or

(B) Not to deduct both the 30-percent and the 50-percent additional first year depreciation. If this election is made, no additional first year depreciation deduction is allowable for the class of property.

(2) *Definition of class of property* .—For purposes of this paragraph (e), the term class of property means:

(i) Except for the property described in paragraphs (e)(2)(ii) and (iv) of this section, each class of property described in section 168(e) (for example, 5-year property);

(ii) Water utility property as defined in section 168(e)(5) and depreciated under section 168;

(iii) Computer software as defined in, and depreciated under, section 167(f)(1) and the regulations thereunder; or

(iv) Qualified leasehold improvement property as defined in paragraph (c) of this section and depreciated under section 168.

(3) *Time and manner for making election* .—(i) *Time for making election* .—Except as provided in paragraph (e)(4) of this section, any election specified in paragraph (e)(1) of this section must be made by the due date (including extensions) of the Federal tax return for the taxable year in which the qualified property or the 50-percent bonus depreciation property, as applicable, is placed in service by the taxpayer.

(ii) *Manner of making election* .—Except as provided in paragraph (e)(4) of this section, any election specified in paragraph (e)(1) of this section must be made in the manner prescribed on Form 4562, "Depreciation and Amortization," and its instructions. The election is made separately by each person owning qualified property or 50-percent bonus depreciation property (for example, for each member of a consolidated group by the common parent of the group, by the partnership, or by the S corporation). If Form 4562 is revised or renumbered, any reference in this section to that form shall be treated as a reference to the revised or renumbered form.

(4) *Special rules for 2000 or 2001 returns* .—For the election specified in paragraph (e)(1)(i) of this section for qualified property placed in service by the

taxpayer during the taxable year that included September 11, 2001, the taxpayer should refer to the guidance provided by the Internal Revenue Service for the time and manner of making this election on the 2000 or 2001 Federal tax return for the taxable year that included September 11, 2001 (for further guidance, see sections 3.03(3) and 4 of Rev. Proc. 2002-33 (2002-1 C.B. 963), Rev. Proc. 2003-50 (2003-29 I.R.B. 119), and § 601.601(d)(2)(ii)(*b*) of this chapter).

(5) *Failure to make election* .—If a taxpayer does not make the applicable election specified in paragraph (e)(1) of this section within the time and in the manner prescribed in paragraph (e)(3) or (4) of this section, the amount of depreciation allowable for that property under section 167(f)(1) or under section 168, as applicable, must be determined for the placed-in-service year and for all subsequent taxable years by taking into account the additional first year depreciation deduction. Thus, any election specified in paragraph (e)(1) of this section shall not be made by the taxpayer in any other manner (for example, the election cannot be made through a request under section 446(e) to change the taxpayer's method of accounting).

(6) *Alternative minimum tax* .—If a taxpayer makes an election specified in paragraph (e)(1) of this section for a class of property, the depreciation adjustments under section 56 and the regulations under section 56 apply to the property to which that election applies for purposes of computing the taxpayer's alternative minimum taxable income.

(7) *Revocation of election* .—(i) *In general* .—Except as provided in paragraph (e)(7)(ii) of this section, an election specified in paragraph (e)(1) of this section, once made, may be revoked only with the written consent of the Commissioner of Internal Revenue. To seek the Commissioner's consent, the taxpayer must submit a request for a letter ruling.

(ii) *Automatic 6-month extension* .—If a taxpayer made an election specified in paragraph (e)(1) of this section for a class of property, an automatic extension of 6 months from the due date of the taxpayer's Federal tax return (excluding extensions) for the placed-in-service year of the class of property is granted to revoke that election, provided the taxpayer timely filed the taxpayer's Federal tax return for the placed-in-service year of the class of property and, within this 6-month extension period, the taxpayer (and all taxpayers whose tax liability would be affected by the election) files an amended Federal tax return for the placed-in-service year of the class of property in a manner that is consistent with the revocation of the election.

(f) *Special rules* .—(1) *Property placed in service and disposed of in the same taxable year* .—(i) *In general* .—Except as provided in paragraphs (f)(1)(ii) and (iii) of this section, the additional first year depreciation deduction is not allowed for qualified property or 50-percent bonus depreciation property placed in service and disposed of during the same taxable year. Also if qualified property or 50-percent bonus depreciation property is placed in service and disposed of during the same taxable year and then reacquired and again placed in service in a subsequent taxable year, the additional first year depreciation deduction is not allowable for the property in the subsequent taxable year.

(ii) *Technical termination of a partnership* .—In the case of a technical termination of a partnership under section 708(b)(1)(B), the additional first year depreciation deduction is allowable for any qualified property or 50-percent bonus depreciation property placed in service by the terminated partnership during the taxable year of termination and contributed by the terminated partnership to the new partnership. The allowable additional first year depreciation deduction for the qualified property or the 50-percent bonus depreciation property shall not be claimed by the terminated partnership but instead shall be claimed by the new partnership for the new partnership's taxable year in which the qualified property or the 50-percent bonus depreciation property was contributed by the terminated partnership to the new partnership. However, if qualified property or 50-percent bonus depreciation property is both placed in service and contributed to a new partnership in a transaction described in section 708(b)(1)(B) by the terminated partnership during the taxable year of termination, and if such property is disposed of by the new partnership in the same taxable year the new partnership received such property from the terminated partnership, then no additional first year depreciation deduction is allowable to either partnership.

(iii) *Section 168(i)(7) transactions* .—If any qualified property or 50-percent bonus depreciation property is transferred in a transaction described in section 168(i)(7) in the same taxable year that the qualified property or the 50-percent bonus depreciation property is placed in service by the transferor, the additional first year depreciation deduction is allowable for the qualified property or the 50-percent bonus depreciation property. The allowable additional first year depreciation deduction for the qualified property or the 50-percent bonus depreciation property for the transferor's taxable year in which the property is placed in service is allocated between the transferor and the transferee on a monthly basis. This allocation shall be made in accordance with the rules in § 1.168(d)-1(b)(7)(ii) for allocating the depreciation deduction between the transferor and the transferee. However, if qualified property or 50-percent bonus depreciation property is both placed in service and transferred in a transaction described in section 168(i)(7) by the transferor during the same taxable year, and if such property is disposed of by the transferee (other than by a transaction described in section 168(i)(7)) during the same taxable year the transferee received such property from the transferor, then no additional first year depreciation deduction is allowable to either party.

(iv) *Examples* .—The application of this paragraph (f)(1) is illustrated by the following examples:

*Example 1.* *X* and *Y* are equal partners in *Partnership XY*, a general partnership. On February 1, 2002, *Partnership XY* purchased and placed in service new equipment at a cost of $30,000. On March 1, 2002, *X* sells its entire 50 percent interest to *Z* in a transfer that terminates the partnership under section 708(b)(1)(B). As a result, terminated *Partnership XY* is deemed to have contributed the equipment to new *Partnership XY*. Pursuant to paragraph (f)(1)(ii) of this section, new *Partnership XY*, not terminated *Partnership XY*, is eligible to claim the 30-percent additional first year depreciation deduction allowable for the equipment for the taxable year 2002 (assuming all other requirements are met).

*Example 2.* On January 5, 2002, *BB* purchased and placed in service new office desks for a total amount of $8,000. On August 20, 2002, *BB* transferred the office desks to *Partnership BC* in a transaction described in section 721. *BB* and *Partnership BC* are calendar-year taxpayers. Because the transaction between *BB* and *Partnership BC* is a transaction described in section 168(i)(7), pursuant to paragraph (f)(1)(iii) of this section the 30-percent additional first year depreciation deduction allowable for the desks is allocated between *BB* and *Partnership BC* in accordance with the rules in § 1.168(d)-1(b)(7)(ii) for allocating the depreciation deduction between the transferor and the transferee. Accordingly, the 30-percent additional first year depreciation deduction allowable for the desks for 2002 of $2,400 (the unadjusted depreciable basis of $8,000 multiplied by .30) is allocated between *BB* and *Partnership BC* based on the number of months that *BB* and *Partnership BC* held the desks in service. Thus, because the desks were held in service by *BB* for 7 of 12 months, which includes the month in which *BB* placed the desks in service but does not include the month in which the desks were transferred, *BB* is allocated $1,400 (7/12 × $2,400 additional first year depreciation deduction). *Partnership BC* is allocated $1,000, the remaining 5/12 of the $2,400 additional first year depreciation deduction allowable for the desks.

(2) *Redetermination of basis* .—If the unadjusted depreciable basis (as defined in § 1.168(k)-1(a)(2)(iii)) of qualified property or 50-percent bonus depreciation property is redetermined (for example, due to contingent purchase price or discharge of indebtedness) before January 1, 2005, or, in the case of property described in section 168(k)(2)(B) or (C), is redetermined before January 1, 2006 (or redetermined before January 1, 2007, in the case of property described in section 168(k)(2)(B) or (C) to which section 105 of the Gulf Opportunity Zone Act of 2005 (Public Law 109-135, 119 Stat. 2577) applies (for further guidance, see Announcement 2006-29 (2006-19 I.R.B. 879) and § 601.601(d)(2)(ii)( *b*) of this chapter)), the additional first year depreciation deduction allowable for the qualified property or the 50-percent bonus depreciation property is redetermined as follows:

(i) *Increase in basis* .—For the taxable year in which an increase in basis of qualified property or 50-percent bonus depreciation property occurs, the taxpayer shall claim an additional first year depreciation deduction for qualified property by multiplying the amount of the increase in basis for this property by 30 percent or, for 50-percent bonus depreciation property, by multiplying the amount of the increase in basis for this property by 50 percent. For purposes of this paragraph (f)(2)(i), the 30-percent additional first year depreciation deduction applies to the increase in basis if the underlying property is qualified property and the 50-percent additional first year depreciation deduction applies to the increase in basis if the underlying property is 50-percent bonus depreciation property. To determine the amount otherwise allowable as a depreciation deduction for the increase in basis of qualified property or 50-percent bonus depreciation property, the amount of the increase in basis of the qualified property or the 50-percent bonus depreciation property must be reduced by the additional first year depreciation deduction allowed or allowable, whichever is greater, for the increase in basis and the remaining increase in basis of—

(A) Qualified property or 50-percent bonus depreciation property (except for computer software described in paragraph (b)(2)(i)(B) of this section) is depreciated over the recovery period of the qualified property or the 50-percent bonus depreciation property, as applicable, remaining as of the beginning of the taxable year in which the increase in basis occurs, and using the same depreciation method and convention applicable to the qualified property or 50-percent bonus depreciation property, as applicable, that applies for the taxable year in which the increase in basis occurs; and

(B) Computer software (as defined in paragraph (b)(2)(i)(B) of this section) that is qualified property or 50-percent bonus depreciation property is depreciated ratably over the remainder of the 36-month period (the useful life under section 167(f)(1)) as of the beginning of the first day of the month in which the increase in basis occurs.

(ii) *Decrease in basis* .—For the taxable year in which a decrease in basis of qualified property or 50-percent bonus depreciation property occurs, the taxpayer shall include in the taxpayer's income the excess additional first year depreciation deduction previously claimed for the qualified property or the 50-percent bonus depreciation property. This excess additional first year depreciation deduction for qualified property is determined by multiplying the amount of the decrease in basis for this property by 30 percent. The excess additional first year depreciation deduction for 50-percent bonus depreciation property is determined by multiplying the amount of the decrease in basis for this property by 50 percent. For purposes of this paragraph (f)(2)(ii), the 30-percent additional first year depreciation deduction applies to the decrease in basis if the underlying property is qualified property and the 50-percent additional first year depreciation deduction applies to the decrease in basis if the underlying property is 50-percent bonus depreciation property. Also, if the taxpayer establishes by adequate records or other sufficient evidence that the taxpayer claimed less than the additional first year depreciation deduction allowable for the qualified property or the 50-percent bonus depreciation property before the decrease in basis or if the taxpayer claimed more than the additional first year depreciation deduction allowable for the qualified property or the 50-percent bonus depreciation property before the decrease in basis, the excess additional first year depreciation deduction is determined by multiplying the amount of the decrease in basis by the additional first year depreciation deduction percentage actually claimed by the taxpayer for the qualified property or the 50-percent bonus depreciation property, as applicable, before the decrease in basis. To determine the amount includible in the taxpayer's income for the excess depreciation previously claimed (other than the additional first year depreciation deduction) resulting from the decrease in basis of the qualified property or the 50-percent bonus depreciation property, the amount of the decrease in basis of the qualified property or the 50-percent bonus depreciation property must be adjusted by the excess additional first year depreciation deduction includible in the taxpayer's income (as determined under this paragraph) and the remaining decrease in basis of—

(A) Qualified property or 50-percent bonus depreciation property (except for computer software described in paragraph (b)(2)(i)(B) of this section) is included in the taxpayer's income over the recovery period of the qualified property or the 50-percent bonus depreciation property, as applicable, remaining as of the beginning of the taxable year in which the decrease in basis occurs, and using the same depreciation method and convention of the qualified property or 50-percent bonus depreciation property, as applicable, that applies in the taxable year in which the decrease in basis occurs; and

(B) Computer software (as defined in paragraph (b)(2)(i)(B) of this section) that is qualified property or 50-percent bonus depreciation property is included in the taxpayer's income ratably over the remainder of the 36-month period (the useful life under section 167(f)(1)) as of the beginning of the first day of the month in which the decrease in basis occurs.

(iii) *Definition* .—Except as otherwise expressly provided by the Internal Revenue Code (for example, section 1017(a)), the regulations under the Internal Revenue Code, or other guidance published in the Internal Revenue Bulletin (see § 601.601(d)(2)(ii)( *b*) of this chapter), for purposes of this paragraph (f)(2)—

(A) An increase in basis occurs in the taxable year an amount is taken into account under section 461; and

(B) A decrease in basis occurs in the taxable year an amount would be taken into account under section 451.

(iv) *Examples* .—The application of this paragraph (f)(2) is illustrated by the following examples:

*Example 1.* (i) On May 15, 2002, *CC*, a cash-basis taxpayer, purchased and placed in service qualified property that is 5-year property at a cost of $200,000. In addition to the $200,000, *CC* agrees to pay the seller 25 percent of the gross profits from the operation of the property in 2002. On May 15, 2003, *CC* paid to the seller an additional $10,000. *CC* depreciates the 5-year property placed in service in 2002 using the optional depreciation table that corresponds with the general depreciation system, the 200-percent declining balance method, a 5-year recovery period, and the half-year convention.

(ii) For 2002, *CC* is allowed a 30-percent additional first year depreciation deduction of $60,000 (the unadjusted depreciable basis of $200,000 multiplied by .30). In addition, *CC's* depreciation deduction for 2002 for the remaining adjusted depreciable basis of $140,000 (the unadjusted depreciable basis of $200,000 reduced by the additional first year depreciation deduction of $60,000) is $28,000 (the remaining adjusted depreciable basis of $140,000 multiplied by the annual depreciation rate of .20 for recovery year 1).

(iii) For 2003, *CC's* depreciation deduction for the remaining adjusted depreciable basis of $140,000 is $44,800 (the remaining adjusted depreciable basis of $140,000 multiplied by the annual depreciation rate of .32 for recovery year 2). In addition, pursuant to paragraph (f)(2)(i) of this section, *CC* is allowed an additional first year depreciation deduction for 2003 for the $10,000 increase in basis of the qualified property. Consequently, *CC* is allowed an additional first year depreciation deduction of $3,000 (the increase in basis of $10,000 multiplied by .30). Also, *CC* is allowed a depreciation deduction for 2003 attributable to the remaining increase in basis of $7,000 (the increase in basis of $10,000 reduced by the additional first year depreciation deduction of $3,000). The depreciation deduction allowable for 2003 attributable to the remaining increase in basis of $7,000 is $3,111 (the remaining increase in basis of $7,000 multiplied by .4444, which is equal to 1/remaining recovery period of 4.5 years at January 1, 2003, multiplied by 2). Accordingly, for 2003, *CC's* total depreciation deduction allowable for the qualified property is $50,911.

*Example 2.* (i) On May 15, 2002, DD, a calendar-year taxpayer, purchased and placed in service qualified property that is 5-year property at a cost of $400,000. To purchase the property, DD borrowed $250,000 from Bank2. On May 15, 2003, Bank2 forgives $50,000 of the indebtedness. DD makes the election provided in section 108(b)(5) to apply any portion of the reduction under section 1017 to the basis of the depreciable property of the taxpayer. DD depreciates the 5-year property placed in service in 2002 using the optional depreciation table that corresponds with the general depreciation system, the 200-percent declining balance method, a 5-year recovery period, and the halfyear convention.

(ii) For 2002, DD is allowed a 30-percent additional first year depreciation deduction of $120,000 (the unadjusted depreciable basis of $400,000 multiplied by .30). In addition, DD's depreciation deduction allowable for 2002 for the remaining adjusted depreciable basis of $280,000 (the unadjusted depreciable basis of $400,000 reduced by the additional first year depreciation deduction of $120,000) is $56,000 (the remaining adjusted depreciable basis of $280,000 multiplied by the annual depreciation rate of .20 for recovery year 1).

(iii) For 2003, DD's deduction for the remaining adjusted depreciable basis of $280,000 is $89,600 (the remaining adjusted depreciable basis of $280,000 multiplied by the annual depreciation rate .32 for recovery year 2). Although Bank2 forgave the indebtedness in 2003, the basis of the property is reduced on January 1, 2004, pursuant to sections 108(b)(5) and 1017(a) under which basis is reduced at the beginning of the taxable year following the taxable year in which the discharge of indebtedness occurs.

(iv) For 2004, DD's deduction for the remaining adjusted depreciable basis of $280,000 is $53,760 (the remaining adjusted depreciable basis of $280,000 multiplied by the annual depreciation rate .192 for recovery year 3). However, pursuant to paragraph (f)(2)(ii) of this section, DD must reduce the amount otherwise allowable as a depreciation deduction for 2004 by the excess depreciation previously claimed for the $50,000 decrease in basis of the qualified property. Consequently, DD must reduce the amount of depreciation otherwise allowable for 2004 by the excess additional first year depreciation of $15,000 (the decrease in basis of $50,000 multiplied by .30). Also, DD must reduce the amount of depreciation otherwise allowable for 2004 by the excess depreciation attributable to the remaining decrease in basis of $35,000 (the decrease in basis of $50,000 reduced by the excess additional first year depreciation of $15,000). The reduction in the amount of depreciation otherwise allowable for 2004 for the remaining decrease in basis of $35,000 is $19,999 (the remaining decrease in basis of $35,000 multiplied by .5714, which is equal to 1/remaining recovery period of 3.5 years at January 1, 2004, multiplied by 2). Accordingly, assuming the qualified property is the only depreciable property owned by DD, for 2004, DD's total depreciation deduction allowable for the qualified property is $18,761 ($53,760 minus $15,000 minus $19,999).

(3) *Section 1245 and 1250 depreciation recapture* .—For purposes of section 1245 and the regulations thereunder, the additional first year depreciation deduction is an amount allowed or allowable for depreciation. Further, for purposes of section 1250(b) and the regulations thereunder, the additional first year depreciation deduction is not a straight line method.

(4) *Coordination with section 169* .—The additional first year depreciation deduction is allowable in the placed-in-service year of a certified pollution control facility (as defined in § 1.169-2(a)) that is qualified property or 50-percent bonus depreciation property, even if the taxpayer makes the election to amortize the certified pollution control facility under section 169 and the regulations thereunder in the certified pollution control facility's placed-in-service year.

(5) *Like-kind exchanges and involuntary conversions* .—(i) *Scope* .—The rules of this paragraph (f)(5) apply to acquired MACRS property or acquired computer software that is qualified property or 50-percent bonus depreciation property at the time of replacement provided the time of replacement is after September 10, 2001, and before January 1, 2005, or, in the case of acquired MACRS property or acquired computer software that is qualified property, or 50-percent bonus depreciation property, described in section 168(k)(2)(B) or (C), the time of replacement is after September 10, 2001, and before January 1, 2006 (or the time of replacement is after September 10, 2001, and before January 1, 2007, in the case of property described in section 168(k)(2)(B) or (C) to which section 105 of the Gulf Opportunity Zone Act of 2005 (Public Law 109-135, 119 Stat. 2577) applies (for further guidance, see Announcement 2006-29 (2006-19 I.R.B. 879) and § 601.601(d)(2)(ii)(*b*) of this chapter)).

(ii) *Definitions* .—For purposes of this paragraph (f)(5), the following definitions apply:

(A) *Acquired MACRS property* is MACRS property in the hands of the acquiring taxpayer that is acquired in a transaction described in section 1031(a), (b), or (c) for other MACRS property or that is acquired in connection with an involuntary conversion of other MACRS property in a transaction to which section 1033 applies.

(B) *Exchanged or involuntarily converted MACRS property* is MACRS property that is transferred by the taxpayer in a transaction described in section 1031(a), (b), or (c), or that is converted as a result of an involuntary conversion to which section 1033 applies.

(C) *Acquired computer software* is computer software (as defined in paragraph (b)(2)(i)(B) of this section) in the hands of the acquiring taxpayer that is acquired in a like-kind exchange under section 1031 or as a result of an involuntary conversion under section 1033.

(D) *Exchanged or involuntarily converted computer software* is computer software (as defined in paragraph (b)(2)(i)(B) of this section) that is transferred by the taxpayer in a like-kind exchange under section 1031 or that is converted as a result of an involuntary conversion under section 1033.

(E) *Time of disposition* is when the disposition of the exchanged or involuntarily converted MACRS property or the exchanged or involuntarily converted computer software, as applicable, takes place.

(F) Except as provided in paragraph (f)(5)(v) of this section, the *time of replacement* is the later of—

*(1)* When the acquired MACRS property or acquired computer software is placed in service; or

*(2)* The time of disposition of the exchanged or involuntarily converted property.

(G) *Carryover basis* is the lesser of:

*(1)* the basis in the acquired MACRS property or acquired computer software, as applicable and as determined under section 1031(d) or 1033(b) and the regulations thereunder; or

*(2)* the adjusted depreciable basis of the exchanged or involuntarily converted MACRS property or the exchanged or involuntarily converted computer software, as applicable.

(H) *Excess basis* is any excess of the basis in the acquired MACRS property or acquired computer software, as applicable and as determined under section 1031(d) or 1033(b) and the regulations thereunder, over the carryover basis as determined under paragraph (f)(5)(ii)(G) of this section.

(I) *Remaining carryover basis* is the carryover basis as determined under paragraph (f)(5)(ii)(G) of this section reduced by—

*(1)* The percentage of the taxpayer's use of property for the taxable year other than in the taxpayer's trade or business (or for the production of income); and

*(2)* Any adjustments to basis provided by other provisions of the Code and the regulations thereunder (including section 1016(a)(2) and (3)) for periods prior to the disposition of the exchanged or involuntarily converted property.

(J) *Remaining excess basis* is the excess basis as determined under paragraph (f)(5)(ii)(H) of this section reduced by—

*(1)* The percentage of the taxpayer's use of property for the taxable year other than in the taxpayer's trade or business (or for the production of income);

*(2)* Any portion of the basis the taxpayer properly elects to treat as an expense under section 179 or section 179C;

*(3)* Any adjustments to basis provided by other provisions of the Code and the regulations thereunder.

(K) *Year of disposition* is the taxable year that includes the time of disposition.

(L) *Year of replacement* is the taxable year that includes the time of replacement.

(iii) *Computation* .—(A) *In general* .—Assuming all other requirements of section 168(k) and this section are met, the remaining carryover basis for the year of replacement and the remaining excess basis, if any, for the year of replacement for the acquired MACRS property or the acquired computer software, as applicable, are eligible for the additional first year depreciation deduction. The 30-percent additional first year depreciation deduction applies to the remaining carryover basis and the remaining excess basis, if any, of the acquired MACRS property or the acquired computer software if the time of replacement is after September 10, 2001, and before May 6, 2003, or if the taxpayer made the election provided in paragraph (e)(1)(ii)(A) of this section. The 50-percent additional first year depreciation deduction applies to the remaining carryover basis and the remaining excess basis, if any, of the acquired MACRS property or the acquired computer software if the time of replacement is after May 5, 2003, and before January 1, 2005, or, in the case of acquired MACRS property or acquired computer software that is 50-percent bonus depreciation property described in section 168(k)(2)(B) or (C), the time of replacement is after May 5, 2003, and before January 1, 2006 (or the time of replacement is after May 5, 2003, and before January

1, 2007, in the case of 50-percent bonus depreciation property described in section 168(k)(2)(B) or (C) to which section 105 of the Gulf Opportunity Zone Act of 2005 (Public Law 109-135, 119 Stat. 2577) applies (for further guidance, see Announcement 2006-29 (2006-19 I.R.B. 879) and §601.601(d)(2)(ii)(*b*) of this chapter)). The additional first year depreciation deduction is computed separately for the remaining carryover basis and the remaining excess basis.

(B) *Year of disposition and year of replacement*.—The additional first year depreciation deduction is allowable for the acquired MACRS property or acquired computer software in the year of replacement. However, the additional first year depreciation deduction is not allowable for the exchanged or involuntarily converted MACRS property or the exchanged or involuntarily converted computer software if the exchanged or involuntarily converted MACRS property or the exchanged or involuntarily converted computer software, as applicable, is placed in service and disposed of in an exchange or involuntary conversion in the same taxable year.

(C) *Property having a longer production period*.—For purposes of paragraph (f)(5)(iii)(A) of this section, the total of the remaining carryover basis and the remaining excess basis, if any, of the acquired MACRS property that is qualified property or 50-percent bonus depreciation property described in section 168(k)(2)(B) is limited to the total of the property's remaining carryover basis and remaining excess basis, if any, attributable to the property's manufacture, construction, or production after September 10, 2001 (for qualified property), or May 5, 2003 (for 50-percent bonus depreciation property), and before January 1, 2005.

(D) *Alternative minimum tax*.—The 30-percent or 50-percent additional first year depreciation deduction is allowed for alternative minimum tax purposes for the year of replacement of acquired MACRS property or acquired computer software that is qualified property or 50-percent bonus depreciation property. The 30-percent or 50-percent additional first year depreciation deduction for alternative minimum tax purposes is based on the remaining carryover basis and the remaining excess basis, if any, of the acquired MACRS property or the acquired computer software for alternative minimum tax purposes.

(iv) *Sale-leaseback transaction*.—For purposes of this paragraph (f)(5), if MACRS property or computer software is sold to a taxpayer and leased back to a person by the taxpayer within three months after the time of disposition of the MACRS property or computer software, as applicable, the time of replacement for this MACRS property or computer software, as applicable, shall not be earlier than the date on which the MACRS property or computer software, as applicable, is used by the lessee under the leaseback.

(v) *Acquired MACRS property or acquired computer software that is acquired and placed in service before disposition of involuntarily converted MACRS property or involuntarily converted computer software*.—If, in an involuntary conversion, a taxpayer acquires and places in service the acquired MACRS property or the acquired computer software before the time of disposition of the involuntarily converted MACRS property or the involuntarily converted computer software and the time of disposition of the involuntarily converted MACRS property or the involuntarily converted computer software is after December 31, 2004, or, in the case of property described in section 168(k)(2)(B) or (C), after December 31, 2005 (or after December 31, 2006, in the case of property described in section 168(k)(2)(B) or (C) to which section 105 of the Gulf Opportunity Zone Act of 2005 (Public Law 109-135, 119 Stat. 2577) applies (for further guidance, see Announcement 2006-29 (2006-19 I.R.B. 879) and §601.601(d)(2)(ii)(*b*) of this chapter)), then—

(A) *Time of replacement* .—The time of replacement for purposes of this paragraph (f)(5) is when the acquired MACRS property or acquired computer software is placed in service by the taxpayer, provided the threat or imminence of requisition or condemnation of the involuntarily converted MACRS property or involuntarily converted computer software existed before January 1, 2005, or, in the case of property described in section 168(k)(2)(B) or (C), existed before January 1, 2006 (or existed before January 1, 2007, in the case of property described in section 168(k)(2)(B) or (C) to which section 105 of the Gulf Opportunity Zone Act of 2005 (Public Law 109-135, 119 Stat. 2577) applies (for further guidance, see Announcement 2006-29 (2006-19 I.R.B. 879) and § 601.601(d)(2)(ii)( *b*) of this chapter)); and

(B) *Depreciation of acquired MACRS property or acquired computer software* .—The taxpayer depreciates the acquired MACRS property or acquired computer software in accordance with paragraph (d) of this section. However, at the time of disposition of the involuntarily converted MACRS property, the taxpayer determines the exchanged basis (as defined in § 1.168(i)-6(b)(7)) and the excess basis (as defined in § 1.168(i)-6(b)(8)) of the acquired MACRS property and begins to depreciate the depreciable exchanged basis (as defined in § 1.168(i)-6(b)(9) of the acquired MACRS property in accordance with § 1.168(i)-6(c). The depreciable excess basis (as defined in § 1.168(i)-6(b)(10)) of the acquired MACRS property continues to be depreciated by the taxpayer in accordance with the first sentence of this paragraph (f)(5)(v)(B). Further, in the year of disposition of the involuntarily converted MACRS property, the taxpayer must include in taxable income the excess of the depreciation deductions allowable, including the additional first year depreciation deduction allowable, on the unadjusted depreciable basis of the acquired MACRS property over the additional first year depreciation deduction that would have been allowable to the taxpayer on the remaining carryover basis of the acquired MACRS property at the time of replacement (as defined in paragraph (f)(5)(v)(A) of this section) plus the depreciation deductions that would have been allowable, including the additional first year depreciation deduction allowable, to the taxpayer on the depreciable excess basis of the acquired MACRS property from the date the acquired MACRS property was placed in service by the taxpayer (taking into account the applicable convention) to the time of disposition of the involuntarily converted MACRS property. Similar rules apply to acquired computer software.

(vi) *Examples* .—The application of this paragraph (f)(5) is illustrated by the following examples:

*Example 1.* (i) In December 2002, EE, a calendar-year corporation, acquired for $200,000 and placed in service Canopy V1, a gas station canopy. Canopy V1 is qualified property under section 168(k)(1) and is 5-year property under section 168(e). EE depreciated Canopy V1 under the general depreciation system of section 168(a) by using the 200-percent declining balance method of depreciation, a 5-year recovery period, and the half-year convention. EE elected to use the optional depreciation tables to compute the depreciation allowance for Canopy V1. On January 1, 2003, Canopy V1 was destroyed in a fire and was no longer usable in EE's business. On June 1, 2003, in an involuntary conversion, EE acquired and placed in service new Canopy W1 with all of the $160,000 of insurance proceeds EE received due to the loss of Canopy V1. Canopy W1 is 50-percent bonus depreciation property under section 168(k)(4) and is 5-year property under section 168(c). Pursuant to paragraph (g)(3)(ii) of this section and § 1.168(i)-6(k)(2)(i), EE decided to apply § 1.168(i)-6 to the involuntary conversion of Canopy V1 with the replacement of Canopy W1, the acquired MACRS property.

(ii) For 2002, EE is allowed a 30-percent additional first year depreciation deduction of $60,000 for Canopy V1 (the unadjusted depreciable basis of

$200,000 multiplied by .30), and a regular MACRS depreciation deduction of $28,000 for Canopy V1 (the remaining adjusted depreciable basis of $140,000 multiplied by the annual depreciation rate of .20 for recovery year 1).

(iii) For 2003, EE is allowed a regular MACRS depreciation deduction of $22,400 for Canopy V1 (the remaining adjusted depreciable basis of $140,000 multiplied by the annual depreciation rate of .32 for recovery year 2 × ½ year).

(iv) Pursuant to paragraph (f)(5)(iii)(A) of this section, the additional first year depreciation deduction allowable for Canopy W1 equals $44,800 (.50 of Canopy W1's remaining carryover basis at the time of replacement of $89,600 (Canopy V1's remaining adjusted depreciable basis of $140,000 minus 2002 regular MACRS depreciation deduction of $28,000 minus 2003 regular MACRS depreciation deduction of $22,400).

*Example 2.* (i) Same facts as in *Example 1*, except EE elected not to deduct the additional first year depreciation for 5-year property placed in service in 2002. EE deducted the additional first year depreciation for 5-year property placed in service in 2003.

(ii) For 2002, EE is allowed a regular MACRS depreciation deduction of $40,000 for Canopy V1 (the unadjusted depreciable basis of $200,000 multiplied by the annual depreciation rate of .20 for recovery year 1).

(iii) For 2003, EE is allowed a regular MACRS depreciation deduction of $32,000 for Canopy V1 (the unadjusted depreciable basis of $200,000 multiplied by the annual depreciation rate of .32 for recovery year 2 × ½ year).

(iv) Pursuant to paragraph (f)(5)(iii)(A) of this section, the additional first year depreciation deduction allowable for Canopy W1 equals $64,000 (.50 of Canopy W1's remaining carryover basis at the time of replacement of $128,000 (Canopy V1's unadjusted depreciable basis of $200,000 minus 2002 regular MACRS depreciation deduction of $40,000 minus 2003 regular MACRS depreciation deduction of $32,000)).

*Example 3.* (i) In December 2001, FF, a calendar-year corporation, acquired for $10,000 and placed in service Computer X2. Computer X2 is qualified property under section 168(k)(1) and is 5-year property under section 168(e). FF depreciated Computer X2 under the general depreciation system of section 168(a) by using the 200-percent declining balance method of depreciation, a 5-year recovery period, and the half-year convention. FF elected to use the optional depreciation tables to compute the depreciation allowance for Computer X2. On January 1, 2002, FF acquired new Computer Y2 by exchanging Computer X2 and $1,000 cash in a like-kind exchange. Computer Y2 is qualified property under section 168(k)(1) and is 5-year property under section 168(e). Pursuant to paragraph (g)(3)(ii) of this section and § 1.168(i)-6(k)(2)(i), FF decided to apply § 1.168(i)-6 to the exchange of Computer X2 for Computer Y2, the acquired MACRS property.

(ii) For 2001, FF is allowed a 30-percent additional first year depreciation deduction of $3,000 for Computer X2 (unadjusted basis of $10,000 multiplied by .30), and a regular MACRS depreciation deduction of $1,400 for Computer X2 (the remaining adjusted depreciable basis of $7,000 multiplied by the annual depreciation rate of .20 for recovery year 1).

(iii) For 2002, FF is allowed a regular MACRS depreciation deduction of $1,120 for Computer X2 (the remaining adjusted depreciable basis of $7,000 multiplied by the annual depreciation rate of .32 for recovery year 2 × ½ year).

(iv) Pursuant to paragraph (f)(5)(iii)(A) of this section, the 30-percent additional first year depreciation deduction for Computer Y2 is allowable for the remaining carryover basis at the time of replacement of $4,480 (Computer X2's unadjusted depreciable basis of $10,000 minus additional first year depreciation deduction allowable of $3,000 minus 2001 regular MACRS depreciation deduction of $1,400 minus 2002 regular MACRS depreciation deduction of $1,120) and for the remaining excess basis at the time of replacement of $1,000 (cash paid for Computer Y2). Thus, the 30-percent additional first year depreciation deduction for the remaining carryover basis at the time of replacement equals $1,344 ($4,480 multiplied by .30) and for the remaining excess basis at the time of replacement equals $300 ($1,000 multiplied by .30), which totals $1,644.

*Example 4.* (i) In September 2002, GG, a June 30 year-end corporation, acquired for $20,000 and placed in service Equipment X3. Equipment X3 is qualified property under section 168(k)(1) and is 5-year property under section 168(e). GG depreciated Equipment X3 under the general depreciation system of section 168(a) by using the 200-percent declining balance method of depreciation, a 5-year recovery period, and the half-year convention. GG elected to use the optional depreciation tables to compute the depreciation allowance for Equipment X3. In December 2002, GG acquired new Equipment Y3 by exchanging Equipment X3 and $5,000 cash in a like-kind exchange. Equipment Y3 is qualified property under section 168(k)(1) and is 5-year property under section 168(e). Pursuant to paragraph (g)(3)(ii) of this section and § 1.168(i)-6(k)(2)(i), GG decided to apply § 1.168(i)-6 to the exchange of Equipment X3 for Equipment Y3, the acquired MACRS property.

(ii) Pursuant to paragraph (f)(5)(iii)(B) of this section, no additional first year depreciation deduction is allowable for Equipment X3 and, pursuant to § 1.168(d)-1T(b)(3)(ii), no regular depreciation deduction is allowable for Equipment X3, for the taxable year ended June 30, 2003.

(iii) Pursuant to paragraph (f)(5)(iii)(A) of this section, the 30-percent additional first year depreciation deduction for Equipment Y3 is allowable for the remaining carryover basis at the time of replacement of $20,000 (Equipment X3's unadjusted depreciable basis of $20,000) and for the remaining excess basis at the time of replacement of $5,000 (cash paid for Equipment Y3). Thus, the 30-percent additional first year depreciation deduction for the remaining carryover basis at the time of replacement equals $6,000 ($20,000 multiplied by .30) and for the remaining excess basis at the time of replacement equals $1,500 ($5,000 multiplied by .30), which totals $7,500.

*Example 5.* (i) Same facts as in *Example 4.* GG depreciated Equipment Y3 under the general depreciation system of section 168(a) by using the 200-percent declining balance method of depreciation, a 5-year recovery period, and the half-year convention. GG elected to use the optional depreciation tables to compute the depreciation allowance for Equipment Y3. On July 1, 2003, GG acquired new Equipment Z1 by exchanging Equipment Y3 in a like-kind exchange. Equipment Z1 is 50-percent bonus depreciation property under section 168(k)(4) and is 5-year property under section 168(e). Pursuant to paragraph (g)(3)(ii) of this section and § 1.168(i)-6(k)(2)(i), GG decided to apply § 1.168(i)-6 to the exchange of Equipment Y3 for Equipment Z1, the acquired MACRS property.

(ii) For the taxable year ending June 30, 2003, the regular MACRS depreciation deduction allowable for the remaining carryover basis at the time of replacement (after taking into account the additional first year depreciation deduction) of Equipment Y3 is $2,800 (the remaining carryover basis at the time of replacement of $20,000 minus the additional first year depreciation deduction of $6,000, multiplied by the annual depreciation rate of .20 for recovery year 1) and for the remaining excess basis at the time of replacement (after taking into account the additional first year depreciation deduction) of Equipment Y3 is $700 (the remaining excess basis at the time of replacement of $5,000 minus the additional first year depreciation deduction of $1,500, multiplied by the annual depreciation rate of .20 for recovery year 1), which totals $3,500.

(iii) For the taxable year ending June 30, 2004, the regular MACRS depreciation deduction allowable for the remaining carryover basis (after taking into account the additional first year depreciation deduction) of Equipment Y3 is $2,240 (the remaining carryover basis at the time of replacement of $20,000 minus the additional first year depreciation deduction of $6,000, multiplied by the annual depreciation rate of .32 for recovery year 2 × ½ year) and for the remaining excess basis (after taking into account the additional first year depreciation deduction) of Equipment Y3 is $560 (the remaining excess basis at the time of replacement of $5,000 minus the additional first year depreciation deduction of $1,500, multiplied by the annual depreciation rate of .32 for recovery year 2 × ½ year), which totals $2,800.

(iv) For the taxable year ending June 30, 2004, pursuant to paragraph (f)(5)(iii)(A) of this section, the 50-percent additional first year depreciation deduction for Equipment Z1 is allowable for the remaining carryover basis at the time of replacement of $11,200 (Equipment Y3's unadjusted depreciable basis of $25,000 minus the total additional first year depreciation deduction of $7,500 minus the total 2003 regular MACRS depreciation deduction of $3,500 minus the total 2004 regular depreciation deduction (taking into account the half-year convention) of $2,800). Thus, the 50-percent additional first year depreciation deduction for the remaining carryover basis at the time of replacement equals $5,600 ($11,200 multiplied by .50).

(6) *Change in use* .—(i) *Change in use of depreciable property* .—The determination of whether the use of depreciable property changes is made in accordance with section 168(i)(5) and regulations thereunder.

(ii) *Conversion to personal use* .—If qualified property or 50-percent bonus depreciation property is converted from business or income-producing use to personal use in the same taxable year in which the property is placed in service by a taxpayer, the additional first year depreciation deduction is not allowable for the property.

(iii) *Conversion to business or income-producing use* .—(A) *During the same taxable year* .—If, during the same taxable year, property is acquired by a taxpayer for personal use and is converted by the taxpayer from personal use to business or income-producing use, the additional first year depreciation deduction is allowable for the property in the taxable year the property is converted to business or income-producing use (assuming all of the requirements in paragraph (b) of this section are met). See paragraph (b)(3)(ii) of this section relating to the original use rules for a conversion of property to business or income-producing use.

(B) *Subsequent to the acquisition year* .—If property is acquired by a taxpayer for personal use and, during a subsequent taxable year, is converted by the taxpayer from personal use to business or income-producing use, the additional first year depreciation deduction is allowable for the property in the taxable year the property is converted to business or income-producing use (assuming all of the requirements in paragraph (b) of this section are met). For purposes of paragraphs (b)(4) and (5) of this section, the property must be acquired by the taxpayer for personal use after September 10, 2001 (for qualified property), or after May 5, 2003 (for 50-percent bonus depreciation property), and converted by the taxpayer from personal use to business or income-producing use by January 1, 2005. See paragraph (b)(3)(ii) of this section relating to the original use rules for a conversion of property to business or income-producing use.

(iv) *Depreciable property changes use subsequent to the placed-in-service year* .—(A) If the use of qualified property or 50-percent bonus depreciation property changes in the hands of the same taxpayer subsequent to the taxable year the qualified property or the 50-percent bonus depreciation property, as applicable, is placed in service and, as a result of the change in use, the property is no longer qualified property or 50-percent bonus depreciation property, as applicable, the additional first year depreciation deduction allowable for the qualified property or the 50-percent bonus depreciation property, as applicable, is not redetermined.

(B) If depreciable property is not qualified property or 50-percent bonus depreciation property in the taxable year the property is placed in service by the taxpayer, the additional first year depreciation deduction is not allowable for the property even if a change in the use of the property subsequent to the taxable year the property is placed in service results in the property being qualified property or 50-percent bonus depreciation property in the taxable year of the change in use.

(v) *Examples* .—The application of this paragraph (f) (6) is illustrated by the following examples:

*Example 1.* (i) On January 1, 2002, *HH*, a calendar year corporation, purchased and placed in service several new computers at a total cost of $100,000. *HH* used these computers within the United States for 3 months in 2002 and then moved and used the computers outside the United States for the remainder of 2002. On January 1, 2003, *HH* permanently returns the computers to the United States for use in its business.

(ii) For 2002, the computers are considered as used predominantly outside the United States in 2002 pursuant to § 1.48-1(g) (1) (i). As a result, the computers are required to be depreciated under the alternative depreciation system of section 168(g). Pursuant to paragraph (b) (2) (ii) (A) ( *2*) of this section, the computers are not qualified property in 2002, the placed-in-service year. Thus, pursuant to (f) (6) (iv) (B) of this section, no additional first year depreciation deduction is allowed for these computers, regardless of the fact that the computers are permanently returned to the United States in 2003.

*Example 2.* (i) On February 8, 2002, *II*, a calendar year corporation, purchased and placed in service new equipment at a cost of $1,000,000 for use in its California plant. The equipment is 5-year property under section 168(e) and is qualified property under section 168(k). *II* depreciates its 5-year property placed in service in 2002 using the optional depreciation table that corresponds with the general depreciation system, the 200-percent declining balance method, a 5-year recovery period, and the half-year convention. On June 4, 2003, due to changes in *II's* business circumstances, *II* permanently moves the equipment to its plant in Mexico.

(ii) For 2002, *II* is allowed a 30-percent additional first year depreciation deduction of $300,000 (the adjusted depreciable basis of $1,000,000 multiplied by .30). In addition, *II's* depreciation deduction allowable in 2002 for the remaining adjusted depreciable basis of $700,000 (the unadjusted depreciable basis of $1,000,000 reduced by the additional first year depreciation deduction of $300,000) is $140,000 (the remaining adjusted depreciable basis of $700,000 multiplied by the annual depreciation rate of .20 for recovery year 1).

(iii) For 2003, the equipment is considered as used predominantly outside the United States pursuant to § 1.48-1(g) (1) (i). As a result of this change in use, the adjusted depreciable basis of $560,000 for the equipment is required to be depreciated under the alternative depreciation system of section 168(g) beginning in 2003. However, the additional first year depreciation deduction of $300,000 allowed for the equipment in 2002 is not redetermined.

(7) *Earnings and profits* .—The additional first year depreciation deduction is not allowable for purposes of computing earnings and profits.

(8) *Limitation of amount of depreciation for certain passenger automobiles* .—For a passenger automobile as defined in section 280F(d) (5), the limitation under section 280F(a) (1) (A) (i) is increased by—

(i) $4,600 for qualified property acquired by a taxpayer after September 10, 2001, and before May 6, 2003; and

(ii) $7,650 for qualified property or 50-percent bonus depreciation property acquired by a taxpayer after May 5, 2003.

(9) *Section 754 election* .—In general, for purposes of section 168(k) any increase in basis of qualified property or 50-percent bonus depreciation property due to a section 754 election is not eligible for the additional first year depreciation deduction. However, if qualified property or 50-percent bonus depreciation property is placed in service by a partnership in the taxable year the partnership terminates under section 708(b)(1)(B), any increase in basis of the qualified property or the 50-percent bonus depreciation property due to a section 754 election is eligible for the additional first year depreciation deduction.

(10) *Coordination with section 47* .—(i) *In general* .—If qualified rehabilitation expenditures (as defined in section 47(c)(2) and § 1.48-12(c)) incurred by a taxpayer with respect to a qualified rehabilitated building (as defined in section 47(c)(1) and § 1.48-12(b)) are qualified property or 50-percent bonus depreciation property, the taxpayer may claim the rehabilitation credit provided by section 47(a) (provided the requirements of section 47 are met)—

(A) With respect to the portion of the basis of the qualified rehabilitated building that is attributable to the qualified rehabilitation expenditures if the taxpayer makes the applicable election under paragraph (e)(1)(i) or (e)(1)(ii)(B) of this section not to deduct any additional first year depreciation for the class of property that includes the qualified rehabilitation expenditures; or

(B) With respect to the portion of the remaining rehabilitated basis of the qualified rehabilitated building that is attributable to the qualified rehabilitation expenditures if the taxpayer claims the additional first year depreciation deduction on the unadjusted depreciable basis (as defined in paragraph (a)(2)(iii) of this section but before the reduction in basis for the amount of the rehabilitation credit) of the qualified rehabilitation expenditures and the taxpayer depreciates the remaining adjusted depreciable basis (as defined in paragraph (d)(2)(i) of this section) of such expenditures using straight line cost recovery in accordance with section 47(c)(2)(B)(i) and § 1.48-12(c)(7)(i). For purposes of this paragraph (f)(10)(i)(B), the remaining rehabilitated basis is equal to the unadjusted depreciable basis (as defined in paragraph (a)(2)(iii) of this section but before the reduction in basis for the amount of the rehabilitation credit) of the qualified rehabilitation expenditures that are qualified property or 50-percent bonus depreciation property reduced by the additional first year depreciation allowed or allowable, whichever is greater.

(ii) *Example* .—The application of this paragraph (f)(10) is illustrated by the following example.

*Example.* (i) Between February 8, 2004, and June 4, 2004, UU, a calendar-year taxpayer, incurred qualified rehabilitation expenditures of $200,000 with respect to a qualified rehabilitated building that is nonresidential real property under section 168(e). These qualified rehabilitation expenditures are 50-percent bonus depreciation property and qualify for the 10-percent rehabilitation credit under section 47(a)(1). UU's basis in the qualified rehabilitated building is zero before incurring the qualified rehabilitation expenditures and UU placed the qualified rehabilitated building in service in July 2004. UU depreciates its nonresidential real property placed in service in 2004 under the general depreciation system of section 168(a) by using the straight line method of depreciation, a 39-year recovery period, and the mid-month convention. UU elected to use the optional depreciation tables to compute the depreciation allowance for its depreciable property placed in service in 2004. Further, for 2004, UU did not make any election under paragraph (e) of this section.

(ii) Because UU did not make any election under paragraph (e) of this section, UU is allowed a 50-percent additional first year depreciation deduction of $100,000 for the qualified rehabilitation expenditures for 2004 (the unadjusted depreciable basis of $200,000 (before reduction in basis for the rehabilitation credit) multiplied by .50). For 2004, UU also is allowed to claim a rehabilitation credit of $10,000 for the remaining rehabilitated basis of $100,000 (the unadjusted depreciable basis (before reduction in basis for the rehabilitation credit) of $200,000 less the additional first year depreciation deduction of $100,000). Further, UU's depreciation deduction for 2004 for the remaining adjusted depreciable basis of $90,000 (the unadjusted depreciable basis (before reduction in basis for the rehabilitation credit) of $200,000 less the additional first year depreciation deduction of $100,000 less the rehabilitation credit of $10,000) is $1,059.30 (the remaining adjusted depreciable basis of $90,000 multiplied by the depreciation rate of .01177 for recovery year 1, placed in service in month 7).

(11) *Coordination with section 514(a)(3)* .—The additional first year depreciation deduction is not allowable for purposes of section 514(a)(3).

(g) *Effective date* .—(1) *In general* .—Except as provided in paragraphs (g)(2), (3), and (5) of this section, this section applies to qualified property under section 168(k)(2) acquired by a taxpayer after September 10, 2001, and to 50-percent bonus depreciation property under section 168(k)(4) acquired by a taxpayer after May 5, 2003.

(2) *Technical termination of a partnership or section 168(i)(7) transactions* .—If qualified property or 50 percent bonus depreciation property is transferred in a technical termination of a partnership under section 708(b)(1)(B) or in a transaction described in section 168(i)(7) for a taxable year ending on or before September 8, 2003, and the additional first year depreciation deduction allowable for the property was not determined in accordance with paragraph (f)(1)(ii) or (iii) of this section, as applicable, the Internal Revenue Service will allow any reasonable method of determining the additional first year depreciation deduction allowable for the property in the year of the transaction that is consistently applied to the property by all parties to the transaction.

(3) *Like-kind exchanges and involuntary conversions* .—(i) If a taxpayer did not claim on a federal tax return for a taxable year ending on or before September 8, 2003, the additional first year depreciation deduction for the remaining carryover basis of qualified property or 50-percent bonus depreciation property acquired in a transaction described in section 1031(a), (b), or (c), or in a transaction to which section 1033 applies and the taxpayer did not make an election not to deduct the additional first year depreciation deduction for the class of property applicable to the remaining carryover basis, the Internal Revenue Service will treat the taxpayer's method of not claiming the additional first year depreciation deduction for the remaining carryover basis as a permissible method of accounting and will treat the amount of the additional first year depreciation deduction allowable for the remaining carryover basis as being equal to zero, provided the taxpayer does not claim the additional first year depreciation deduction for the remaining carryover basis in accordance with paragraph (g)(4)(ii) of this section.

(ii) Paragraphs (f)(5)(ii)(F)(*2*) and (f)(5)(v) of this section apply to a like-kind exchange or an involuntary conversion of MACRS property and computer software for which the time of disposition and the time of replacement both occur after February 27, 2004. For a like-kind exchange or an involuntary conversion of MACRS property for which the time of disposition, the time of replacement, or both occur on or before February 27, 2004, see §1.168(i)-6(k)(2)(ii). For a like-kind exchange or involuntary conversion of computer software for which the time of disposition, the time of replacement, or both occur on or before February 27, 2004, a taxpayer may rely on prior guidance issued by the Internal Revenue Service for determining the depreciation deductions of the acquired computer software and the exchanged or involuntarily converted computer software (for further guidance, see §1.168(k)-1T(f)(5) published in the **Federal Register** on September 8, 2003 (68 FR 53000)). In relying on such guidance, a taxpayer may use any reasonable, consistent method of determining depreciation in the year of disposition and the year of replacement.

(4) *Change in method of accounting* .—(i) *Special rules for 2000 or 2001 returns* .—If a taxpayer did not claim on the Federal tax return for the taxable year that included September 11, 2001, any additional first year depreciation deduction for a class of property that is qualified property and did not make an election not to deduct the additional first year depreciation deduction for that class of property, the taxpayer should refer to the guidance provided by the Internal Revenue Service for the time and manner of claiming the additional first year depreciation deduction for the class of property (for further guidance, see section 4 of Rev. Proc. 2002-33 (2002-1 C.B. 963), Rev. Proc. 2003-50 (2003-29 I.R.B. 119), and §601.601(d)(2)(ii)( *b*) of this chapter).

(ii) *Like-kind exchanges and involuntary conversions* .—If a taxpayer did not claim on a federal tax return for any taxable year ending on or before September 8, 2003, the additional first year depreciation deduction allowable for the remaining carryover basis of qualified property or 50-percent bonus depreciation property acquired in a transaction described in section 1031(a), (b), or (c), or in a transaction to which section 1033 applies and the taxpayer did not make an election not to deduct the additional first year depreciation deduction for the class of property applicable to the remaining carryover basis, the taxpayer may claim the additional first year depreciation deduction allowable for the remaining carryover basis in accordance with paragraph (f)(5) of this section either:

(A) by filing an amended return (or a qualified amended return, if applicable (for further guidance, see Rev. Proc. 94-69 (1994-2 C.B. 804) and §601.601(d)(2)(ii)( *b*) of this chapter)) on or before December 31, 2003, for the year of replacement and any affected subsequent taxable year; or,

(B) by following the applicable administrative procedures issued under §1.446-1(e)(3)(ii) for obtaining the Commissioner's automatic consent to a change in method of accounting (for further guidance, see Rev. Proc. 2002-9 (2002-1 C.B. 327) and §601.601(d)(2)(ii)( *b*) of this chapter).

(5) *Revision to paragraphs (b)(3)(iii)(B) and (b)(5)(ii)(B) of this section* .—The addition of "(or, in the case of multiple units of property subject to the same lease, within three months after the date the final unit is placed in service, so long as the period between the time the first unit is placed in service and the time the last unit is placed in service does not exceed 12 months)" to paragraphs (b)(3)(iii)(B) and (b)(5)(ii)(B) of this section applies to property sold after June 4, 2004.

(6) *Rehabilitation credit* .—If a taxpayer did not claim on a Federal tax return for any taxable year ending on or before September 1, 2006, the rehabilitation credit provided by section 47(a) with respect to the portion of the basis of a qualified rehabilitated building that is attributable to qualified rehabilitation expenditures and the qualified rehabilitation expenditures are qualified property or 50-percent bonus depreciation property, and the taxpayer did not make the applicable election specified in paragraph (e)(1)(i) or (e)(1)(ii)(B) of this section for the class of property that includes the qualified rehabilitation expenditures, the taxpayer may claim the rehabilitation credit for the remaining rehabilitated basis (as defined in paragraph (f)(10)(i)(B) of this section) of the qualified rehabilitated building that is attributable to the qualified rehabilitation expenditures (assuming all the requirements of section 47 are met) in accordance with paragraph (f)(10)(i)(B) of this section by filing an amended Federal tax return for the taxable year for which the

rehabilitation credit is to be claimed. The amended Federal tax return must include the adjustment to the tax liability for the rehabilitation credit and any collateral adjustments to taxable income or to the tax liability (for example, the amount of depreciation allowed or allowable in that taxable year for the qualified rehabilitated building). Such adjustments must also be made on amended Federal tax returns for any affected succeeding taxable years. [Reg. § 1.168(k)-1.]

**.01 Historical Comment:** Adopted 9/5/2003 by T.D. 9091 (corrected 11/7/2003). Amended 2/27/2004 by T.D. 9115 (corrected 4/2/2004), 8/28/2006 by T.D. 9283 and 2/27/2007 by T.D. 9314.

## ¶ 571

## Reg. § 1.168(k)-2

§ 1.168(k)-2. **Additional first year depreciation deduction for property acquired and placed in service after September 27, 2017 .**—(a) *Scope and definitions* .—(1) *Scope* .—This section provides rules for determining the additional first year depreciation deduction allowable under section 168(k) for qualified property acquired and placed in service after September 27, 2017, except as provided in paragraph (c) of this section.

(2) *Definitions* .—For purposes of this section—

(i) *Act* is the Tax Cuts and Jobs Act, Public Law 115-97 (131 Stat. 2054 (December 22, 2017));

(ii) *Applicable percentage* is the percentage provided in section 168(k)(6);

(iii) *Initial live staged performance* is the first commercial exhibition of a production to an audience. However, the term *initial live staged performance* does not include limited exhibition prior to commercial exhibition to general audiences if the limited exhibition is primarily for purposes of publicity, determining the need for further production activity, or raising funds for the completion of production. For example, an initial live staged performance does not include a preview of the production if the preview is primarily to determine the need for further production activity; and

(iv) *Predecessor* includes—

(A) A transferor of an asset to a transferee in a transaction to which section 381(a) applies;

(B) A transferor of the asset to a transferee in a transaction in which the transferee's basis in the asset is determined, in whole or in part, by reference to the basis of the asset in the hands of the transferor;

(C) A partnership that is considered as continuing under section 708(b)(2) and § 1.708-1; or

(D) The decedent in the case of an asset acquired by the estate.

(b) *Qualified property* .—(1) *In general* .—Qualified property is depreciable property, as defined in § 1.168(b)-1(a)(1), that meets all the following requirements in the first taxable year in which the property is subject to depreciation by the taxpayer whether or not depreciation deductions for the property are allowable:

(i) The requirements in § 1.168(k)-2(b)(2) (description of qualified property);

(ii) The requirements in § 1.168(k)-2(b)(3) (original use or used property acquisition requirements);

(iii) The requirements in § 1.168(k)-2(b)(4) (placed-in-service date); and

(iv) The requirements in § 1.168(k)-2(b)(5) (acquisition of property).

(2) *Description of qualified property* .—(i) *In general* .—Depreciable property will meet the requirements of this paragraph (b)(2) if the property is—

(A) MACRS property, as defined in § 1.168(b)-1(a)(2), that has a recovery period of 20 years or less. For purposes of this paragraph (b)(2)(i)(A) and section 168(k)(2)(A)(i)(I), the recovery period is determined in accordance with section 168(c) regardless of any election made by the taxpayer under section 168(g)(7). This paragraph (b)(2)(i)(A) includes the following MACRS property that is acquired by the taxpayer after September 27, 2017, and placed in service by the taxpayer after September 27, 2017, and before January 1, 2018:

*(1)* Qualified leasehold improvement property as defined in section 168(e)(6) as in effect on the day before amendment by section 13204(a)(1) of the Act;

*(2)* Qualified restaurant property, as defined in section 168(e)(7) as in effect on the day before amendment by section 13204(a)(1) of the Act, that is qualified improvement property as defined in § 1.168(b)-1(a)(5)(i)(C) and (a)(5)(ii); and

*(3)* Qualified retail improvement property as defined in section 168(e)(8) as in effect on the day before amendment by section 13204(a)(1) of the Act;

(B) Computer software as defined in, and depreciated under, section 167(f)(1) and § 1.167(a)-14;

(C) Water utility property as defined in section 168(e)(5) and depreciated under section 168;

(D) Qualified improvement property as defined in § 1.168(b)-1(a)(5)(i)(C) and (a)(5)(ii) and depreciated under section 168;

(E) A qualified film or television production, as defined in section 181(d) and § 1.181-3, for which a deduction would have been allowable under section 181 and § § 1.181-1 through 1.181-6 without regard to section 181(a)(2) and (g), § 1.181-1(b)(1)(i) and (ii), and (b)(2)(i), or section 168(k). Only production costs of a qualified film or television production are allowable as a deduction under section 181 and § § 1.181-1 through 1.181-6 without regard, for purposes of section 168(k), to section 181(a)(2) and (g), § 1.181-1(b)(1)(i) and (ii), and (b)(2)(i). The taxpayer that claims the additional first year depreciation deduction under this section for the production costs of a qualified film or television production must be the owner, as defined in § 1.181-1(a)(2), of the qualified film or television production. See § 1.181-1(a)(3) for the definition of production costs;

(F) A qualified live theatrical production, as defined in section 181(e), for which a deduction would have been allowable under section 181 and § § 1.181-1 through 1.181-6 without regard to section 181(a)(2) and (g), § 1.181-1(b)(1)(i) and (ii), and (b)(2)(i), or section 168(k). Only production costs of a qualified live theatrical production are allowable as a deduction under section 181 and § § 1.181-1 through 1.181-6 without regard, for purposes of section 168(k), to section 181(a)(2) and (g), § 1.181-1(b)(1)(i) and (ii), and (b)(2)(i). The taxpayer that claims the additional first year depreciation deduction under this section for the production costs of a qualified live theatrical production must be the owner, as defined in § 1.181-1(a)(2), of the qualified live theatrical production. In applying § 1.181-1(a)(2)(ii) to a person that acquires a finished or partially-finished qualified live theatrical production, such person is treated as an owner of that production, but only if the production is acquired prior to its initial live staged performance. Rules similar to the rules in § 1.181-1(a)(3) for the definition of production costs of a qualified film or television production apply for defining production costs of a qualified live theatrical production; or

(G) A specified plant, as defined in section 168(k)(5)(B), for which the taxpayer has properly made an election to apply section 168(k)(5) for the taxable year in which the specified plant is planted, or grafted to a plant that has already been planted, by the taxpayer in the ordinary course of the taxpayer's farming business, as defined in section 263A(e)(4) (for further guidance, see paragraph (f) of this section).

(ii) *Property not eligible for additional first year depreciation deduction* .—Depreciable property will not meet the requirements of this paragraph (b)(2) if the property is—

(A) Described in section 168(f) (for example, automobiles for which the taxpayer uses the optional business standard mileage rate);

(B) Required to be depreciated under the alternative depreciation system of section 168(g) pursuant to section 168(g)(1)(A), (B), (C), (D), (F), or (G), or other provisions of the Internal Revenue Code (for example, property described in section 263A(e)(2)(A) if the taxpayer or any related person, as defined in section 263A(e)(2)(B), has made an election under section 263A(d)(3), or property described in section 280F(b)(1)). If section 168(h)(6) applies to the property, only the tax-exempt entity's proportionate share of the property, as determined under section 168(h)(6), is treated as tax-exempt use property described in section 168(g)(1)(B) and in this paragraph (b)(2)(ii)(B). This paragraph (b)(2)(ii)(B) does not apply to property for which the adjusted basis is required to be determined using the alternative depreciation system of section 168(g) pursuant to section 250(b)(2)(B) or 951A(d)(3), as applicable, or to property for which the adjusted basis is required to be determined using the alternative depreciation system of section 168(g) for allocating business interest expense between excepted and non-excepted trades or businesses under section 163(j), but only if the property is not required to be depreciated under the alternative depreciation system of section 168(g) pursuant to section 168(g)(1)(A), (B), (C), (D), (F), or (G), or other provisions of the Code, other than section 163(j), 250(b)(2)(B), or 951A(d)(3), as applicable;

(C) Included in any class of property for which the taxpayer elects not to deduct the additional first year depreciation (for further guidance, see paragraph (f) of this section);

(D) A specified plant that is placed in service by the taxpayer during the taxable year and for which the taxpayer made an election to apply section 168(k)(5) for a prior taxable year;

(E) Included in any class of property for which the taxpayer elects to apply section 168(k)(4). This paragraph (b)(2)(ii)(E) applies to property placed in service by the taxpayer in any taxable year beginning before January 1, 2018;

(F) Primarily used in a trade or business described in section 163(j)(7)(A)(iv) and §§1.163(j)-1(b)(15)(i) and 1.163(j)-10(c)(3)(iii)(C)( *3*), and placed in service by the taxpayer in any taxable year beginning after December 31, 2017. For purposes of section 168(k)(9)(A) and this paragraph (b)(2)(ii)(F), the term *primarily used* has the same meaning as that term is used in §1.167(a)-11(b)(4)(iii)( *b*) and (e)(3)(iii) for classifying property. This paragraph (b)(2)(ii)(F) does not apply to property that is leased to a lessee's trade or business described in section 163(j)(7)(A)(iv) and §§1.163(j)-1(b)(15)(i) and 1.163(j)-10(c)(3)(iii)(C)( *3*), by a lessor's trade or business that is not described in section 163(j)(7)(A)(iv) and §§1.163(j)-1(b)(15)(i) and 1.163(j)-10(c)(3)(iii)(C)( *3*) for the taxable year; or

(G) Used in a trade or business that has had floor plan financing indebtedness, as defined in section 163(j)(9)(B) and §1.163(j)-1(b)(18), if the floor plan financing interest expense, as defined in section 163(j)(9)(A) and

§ 1.163(j)-1(b)(19), related to such indebtedness is taken into account under section 163(j)(1)(C) for the taxable year. Such property also must be placed in service by the taxpayer in any taxable year beginning after December 31, 2017. Solely for purposes of section 168(k)(9)(B) and this paragraph (b)(2)(ii)(G), floor plan financing interest expense is taken into account for the taxable year by a trade or business that has had floor plan financing indebtedness only if the business interest expense, as defined in section 163(j)(5) and § 1.163(j)-1(b)(3), of the trade or business for the taxable year (which includes floor plan financing interest expense) exceeds the sum of the amounts calculated under section 163(j)(1)(A) and (B) for the trade or business for the taxable year. If the trade or business has taken floor plan financing interest expense into account pursuant to this paragraph (b)(2)(ii)(G) for a taxable year, this paragraph (b)(2)(ii)(G) applies to any property placed in service by that trade or business in that taxable year. This paragraph (b)(2)(ii)(G) does not apply to property that is leased to a lessee's trade or business that has had floor plan financing indebtedness, by a lessor's trade or business that has not had floor plan financing indebtedness during the taxable year or that has had floor plan financing indebtedness but did not take into account floor plan financing interest expense for the taxable year pursuant to this paragraph (b)(2)(ii)(G).

(iii) *Examples* .—The application of this paragraph (b)(2) is illustrated by the following examples. Unless the facts specifically indicate otherwise, assume that the parties are not related within the meaning of section 179(d)(2)(A) or (B) and § 1.179-4(c), and are not described in section 163(j)(3):

(A) *Example 1.* On February 8, 2018, *A* finishes the production of a qualified film, as defined in § 1.181-3. On June 4, 2018, *B* acquires this finished production from A. The initial release or broadcast, as defined in § 1.181-1(a)(7), of this qualified film is on July 28, 2018. Because *B* acquired the qualified film before its initial release or broadcast, *B* is treated as the owner of the qualified film for purposes of section 181 and § 1.181-1(a)(2). Assuming all other requirements of this section are met and all requirements of section 181 and §§ 1.181-1 through 1.181-6, other than section 181(a)(2) and (g), and § 1.181-1(b)(1)(i) and (ii), and (b)(2)(i), are met, B's acquisition cost of the qualified film qualifies for the additional first year depreciation deduction under this section.

(B) *Example 2.* The facts are the same as in *Example 1* of paragraph (b)(2)(iii)(A) of this section, except that *B* acquires a limited license or right to release the qualified film in Europe. As a result, *B* is not treated as the owner of the qualified film pursuant to § 1.181-1(a)(2). Accordingly, paragraph (b)(2)(i)(E) of this section is not satisfied, and B's acquisition cost of the license or right does not qualify for the additional first year depreciation deduction.

(C) *Example 3.* *C* owns a film library. All of the films in this film library are completed and have been released or broadcasted. In 2018, *D* buys this film library from *C.* Because *D* acquired the films after their initial release or broadcast, D's acquisition cost of the film library does not qualify for a deduction under section 181. As a result, paragraph (b)(2)(i)(E) of this section is not satisfied, and D's acquisition cost of the film library does not qualify for the additional first year depreciation deduction.

(D) *Example 4.* During 2019, E Corporation, a domestic corporation, acquired new equipment for use in its manufacturing trade or business in Mexico. To determine its qualified business asset investment for purposes of section 250, E Corporation must determine the adjusted basis of the new equipment using the alternative depreciation system of section 168(g) pursuant to sections 250(b)(2)(B) and 951A(d)(3). E Corporation also is required to depreciate the new equipment under the alternative depreciation system of section 168(g) pursuant to section 168(g)(1)(A). As a result, the new equipment does not qualify for the additional first year depreciation deduction pursuant to paragraph (b)(2)(ii)(B) of this section.

(E) *Example 5*. The facts are the same as in *Example 4* of paragraph (b)(2)(iii)(D) of this section, except E Corporation acquired the new equipment for use in its manufacturing trade or business in California. The new equipment is not described in section 168(g)(1)(A), (B), (C), (D), (F), or (G). No other provision of the Internal Revenue Code, other than section 250(b)(2)(B) or 951A(d)(3), requires the new equipment to be depreciated using the alternative depreciation system of section 168(g). To determine its qualified business asset investment for purposes of section 250, E Corporation must determine the adjusted basis of the new equipment using the alternative depreciation system of section 168(g) pursuant to sections 250(b)(2)(B) and 951A(d)(3). Because E Corporation is not required to depreciate the new equipment under the alternative depreciation system of section 168(g), paragraph (b)(2)(ii)(B) of this section does not apply to this new equipment. Assuming all other requirements are met, the new equipment qualifies for the additional first year depreciation deduction under this section.

(F) *Example 6*. In 2019, a financial institution buys new equipment for $1 million and then leases this equipment to a lessee that primarily uses the equipment in a trade or business described in section 163(j)(7)(A)(iv) and §§1.163(j)-1(b)(15)(i) and 1.163(j)-10(c)(3)(iii)(C)(*3*). The financial institution is not described in section 163(j)(7)(A)(iv) and §§1.163(j)-1(b)(15)(i) and 1.163(j)-10(c)(3)(iii)(C)(*3*). As a result, paragraph (b)(2)(ii)(F) of this section does not apply to this new equipment. Assuming all other requirements are met, the financial institution's purchase price of $1 million for the new equipment qualifies for the additional first year depreciation deduction under this section.

(G) *Example 7*. During its taxable year beginning in 2020, *F*, a corporation that is an automobile dealer, buys new computers for $50,000 for use in its trade or business of selling automobiles. For purposes of section 163(j), *F* has the following for 2020: $700 of adjusted taxable income, $40 of business interest income, $400 of business interest expense (which includes $100 of floor plan financing interest expense). The sum of the amounts calculated under section 163(j)(1)(A) and (B) for *F* for 2020 is $390 ($40 + ($700 x 50 percent)). *F*'s business interest expense, which includes floor plan financing interest expense, for 2020 is $400. As a result, *F*'s floor plan financing interest expense is taken into account by *F* for 2020 pursuant to paragraph (b)(2)(ii)(G) of this section. Accordingly, *F*'s purchase price of $50,000 for the computers does not qualify for the additional first year depreciation deduction under this section.

(H) *Example 8*. The facts are the same as in *Example 7* in paragraph (b)(2)(iii)(G) of this section, except *F* buys new computers for $30,000 for use in its trade or business of selling automobiles and, for purposes of section 163(j), *F* has $1,300 of adjusted taxable income. The sum of the amounts calculated under section 163(j)(1)(A) and (B) for *F* for 2020 is $690 ($40 + ($1,300 x 50 percent)). *F*'s business interest expense, which includes floor plan financing interest expense, for 2020 is $400. As a result, *F*'s floor plan financing interest expense is not taken into account by *F* for 2020 pursuant to paragraph (b)(2)(ii)(G) of this section. Assuming all other requirements are met, *F*'s purchase price of $30,000 for the computers qualifies for the additional first year depreciation deduction under this section.

(I) *Example 9*. (*1*) *G*, a calendar-year taxpayer, owns an office building for use in its trade or business and *G* placed in service such building in 2000. In November 2018, *G* made and placed in service an improvement to the inside of such building at a cost of $100,000. In January 2019, *G* entered into a written contract with *H* for *H* to construct an improvement to the inside of the building. In March 2019, *H* completed construction of the improvement at a cost of $750,000 and G placed in service such improvement. Both improvements to the building are section 1250 property and are not described in § 1.168(b)-1(a)(5)(ii).

(*2*) Both the improvement to the office building made by *G* in November 2018 and the improvement to the office building that was constructed by

*H* for *G* in 2019 are improvements made by *G* under § 1.168(b)-1(a)(5)(i)(A). Further, each improvement is made to the inside of the office building, is section 1250 property, and is not described in § 1.168(b)-1(a)(5)(ii). As a result, each improvement meets the definition of qualified improvement property in section 168(e)(6) and § 1.168(b)-1(a)(5)(i)(A) and (a)(5)(ii). Accordingly, each improvement is 15-year property under section 168(e)(3) and is described in § 1.168(k)-2(b)(2)(i)(A). Assuming all other requirements of this section are met, each improvement made by *G* qualifies for the additional first year depreciation deduction for *G* under this section.

(3) *Original use or used property acquisition requirements* .—(i) *In general* .—Depreciable property will meet the requirements of this paragraph (b)(3) if the property meets the original use requirements in paragraph (b)(3)(ii) of this section or if the property meets the used property acquisition requirements in paragraph (b)(3)(iii) of this section.

(ii) *Original use* .—(A) *In general* .—Depreciable property will meet the requirements of this paragraph (b)(3)(ii) if the original use of the property commences with the taxpayer. Except as provided in paragraphs (b)(3)(ii)(B) and (C) of this section, original use means the first use to which the property is put, whether or not that use corresponds to the use of the property by the taxpayer. Additional capital expenditures paid or incurred by a taxpayer to recondition or rebuild property acquired or owned by the taxpayer satisfy the original use requirement. However, the cost of reconditioned or rebuilt property does not satisfy the original use requirement (but may satisfy the used property acquisition requirements in paragraph (b)(3)(iii) of this section). The question of whether property is reconditioned or rebuilt property is a question of fact. For purposes of this paragraph (b)(3)(ii)(A), property that contains used parts will not be treated as reconditioned or rebuilt if the cost of the used parts is not more than 20 percent of the total cost of the property, whether acquired or self-constructed.

(B) *Conversion to business or income-producing use* .—*(1) Personal use to business or income-producing use* .—If a taxpayer initially acquires new property for personal use and subsequently uses the property in the taxpayer's trade or business or for the taxpayer's production of income, the taxpayer is considered the original user of the property. If a person initially acquires new property for personal use and a taxpayer subsequently acquires the property from the person for use in the taxpayer's trade or business or for the taxpayer's production of income, the taxpayer is not considered the original user of the property.

*(2) Inventory to business or income-producing use* .—If a taxpayer initially acquires new property and holds the property primarily for sale to customers in the ordinary course of the taxpayer's business and subsequently withdraws the property from inventory and uses the property primarily in the taxpayer's trade or business or primarily for the taxpayer's production of income, the taxpayer is considered the original user of the property. If a person initially acquires new property and holds the property primarily for sale to customers in the ordinary course of the person's business and a taxpayer subsequently acquires the property from the person for use primarily in the taxpayer's trade or business or primarily for the taxpayer's production of income, the taxpayer is considered the original user of the property. For purposes of this paragraph (b)(3)(ii)(B)( *2*), the original use of the property by the taxpayer commences on the date on which the taxpayer uses the property primarily in the taxpayer's trade or business or primarily for the taxpayer's production of income.

(C) *Fractional interests in property* .—If, in the ordinary course of its business, a taxpayer sells fractional interests in new property to third parties unrelated to the taxpayer, each first fractional owner of the property is considered as the original user of its proportionate share of the property. Furthermore, if the taxpayer uses the property before all of the fractional interests of the property are sold but the property continues to be held primarily for sale by the taxpayer, the original use of any fractional interest sold to a third party unrelated to the taxpayer subsequent to the taxpayer's use of the property begins with the first purchaser of that fractional interest. For purposes of this paragraph (b)(3)(ii)(C), persons are not related if they do not have a relationship described in section 267(b) and § 1.267(b)-1, or section 707(b) and § 1.707-1.

(iii) *Used property acquisition requirements* .—(A) *In general* .— Depreciable property will meet the requirements of this paragraph (b)(3)(iii) if the acquisition of the used property meets the following requirements:

*(1)* Such property was not used by the taxpayer or a predecessor at any time prior to such acquisition;

*(2)* The acquisition of such property meets the requirements of section 179(d)(2)(A), (B), and (C), and § 1.179-4(c)(1)(ii), (iii), and (iv); or § 1.179-4(c)(2) (property is acquired by purchase); and

*(3)* The acquisition of such property meets the requirements of section 179(d)(3) and § 1.179-4(d) (cost of property) (for further guidance regarding like-kind exchanges and involuntary conversions, see paragraph (g)(5) of this section).

(B) *Property was not used by the taxpayer at any time prior to acquisition .—(1)* In *general.* Solely for purposes of paragraph (b)(3)(iii)(A)( *1*) of this section, the property is treated as used by the taxpayer or a predecessor at any time prior to acquisition by the taxpayer or predecessor if the taxpayer or the predecessor had a depreciable interest in the property at any time prior to such acquisition, whether or not the taxpayer or the predecessor claimed depreciation deductions for the property. To determine if the taxpayer or a predecessor had a depreciable interest in the property at any time prior to the acquisition, only the five calendar years immediately prior to the current calendar year in which the property is placed in service by the taxpayer, and the portion of such current calendar year before the placed-in-service date of the property without taking into account the applicable convention, are taken into account (lookback period). If the taxpayer and a predecessor have not been in existence for this entire five-year period, only the number of calendar years the taxpayer and the predecessor have been in existence is taken into account. If either the taxpayer or a predecessor, or both, have not been in existence for the entire lookback period, only the portion of the lookback period during which the taxpayer or a predecessor, or both, as applicable, have been in existence is taken into account to determine if the taxpayer or a predecessor had a depreciable interest in the property at any time prior to the acquisition.

*(2) Taxpayer has a depreciable interest in a portion of the property* .—If a taxpayer initially acquires a depreciable interest in a portion of the property and subsequently acquires a depreciable interest in an additional portion of the same property, such additional depreciable interest is not treated as used by the taxpayer at any time prior to its acquisition by the taxpayer under paragraphs (b)(3)(iii)(A)( *1*) and (b)(3)(iii)(B)( *1*) of this section. This paragraph (b)(3)(iii)(B)( *2*) does not apply if the taxpayer or a predecessor previously had a depreciable interest in the subsequently acquired additional portion. For purposes of this paragraph (b)(3)(iii)(B)( *2*), a portion of the property is considered to be the percentage interest in the property. If a taxpayer holds a depreciable interest in a portion of the property, sells that portion or a part of that portion, and subsequently acquires a depreciable interest in another portion of the same property, the taxpayer will be treated as previously having a depreciable interest in the property

up to the amount of the portion for which the taxpayer held a depreciable interest in the property before the sale.

*(3) Substantial renovation of property* .—If a taxpayer acquires and places in service substantially renovated property and the taxpayer or a predecessor previously had a depreciable interest in the property before it was substantially renovated, the taxpayer's or predecessor's depreciable interest in the property before it was substantially renovated is not taken into account for determining whether the substantially renovated property was used by the taxpayer or a predecessor at any time prior to its acquisition by the taxpayer under paragraphs (b)(3)(iii)(A)( *1*) and (b)(3)(iii)(B)( *1*) of this section. For purposes of this paragraph (b)(3)(iii)(B)( *3*), property is substantially renovated if the cost of the used parts is not more than 20 percent of the total cost of the substantially renovated property, whether acquired or self-constructed.

*(4) De minimis use of property* .—If a taxpayer acquires and places in service property, the taxpayer or a predecessor did not previously have a depreciable interest in the property, the taxpayer disposes of the property to an unrelated party within 90 calendar days after the date the property was originally placed in service by the taxpayer, without taking into account the applicable convention, and the taxpayer reacquires and again places in service the property, then the taxpayer's depreciable interest in the property during that 90-day period is not taken into account for determining whether the property was used by the taxpayer or a predecessor at any time prior to its reacquisition by the taxpayer under paragraphs (b)(3)(iii)(A)( *1*) and (b)(3)(iii)(B)( *1*) of this section. If the taxpayer originally acquired the property before September 28, 2017, as determined under § 1.168(k)-1(b)(4), and the taxpayer reacquires and again places in service the property during the same taxable year the taxpayer disposed of the property to the unrelated party, then this paragraph (b)(3)(iii)(B)( *4*) does not apply. For purposes of this paragraph (b)(3)(iii)(B)( *4*), an *unrelated party* is a person not described in section 179(d)(2)(A) or (B), and § 1.179-4(c)(1)(ii) or (iii) or (c)(2).

(C) *Special rules for a series of related transactions* .—*(1) In general* .—Solely for purposes of paragraph (b)(3)(iii) of this section, each transferee in a series of related transactions tests its relationship under section 179(d)(2)(A) or (B) with the transferor from which the transferee directly acquires the depreciable property (immediate transferor) and with the original transferor of the depreciable property in the series. The transferee is treated as related to the immediate transferor or the original transferor if the relationship exists either when the transferee acquires, or immediately before the first transfer of, the depreciable property in the series. A series of related transactions may include, for example, a transfer of partnership assets followed by a transfer of an interest in the partnership that owned the assets; or a disposition of property and a disposition, directly or indirectly, of the transferor or transferee of the property. For special rules that may apply when the transferor and transferee of the property are members of a consolidated group, as defined in § 1.1502-1(h), see § 1.1502-68.

*(2) Special rules* .—*(i) Property placed in service and disposed of in same taxable year or property not placed in service* .—Any party in a series of related transactions that is neither the original transferor nor the ultimate transferee is disregarded (disregarded party) for purposes of testing the relationships under paragraph (b)(3)(iii)(C)( *1*) of this section if the party places in service and disposes of the depreciable property subject to the series, other than in a transaction described in paragraph (g)(1)(iii) of this section, during the party's same taxable year, or if the party does not place in service the depreciable property subject to the series for use in the party's trade or business or production of income. In either case, the party to which the disregarded party disposed of the

depreciable property tests its relationship with the party from which the disregarded party acquired the depreciable property and with the original transferor of the depreciable property in the series. If the series has consecutive disregarded parties, the party to which the last disregarded party disposed of the depreciable property tests its relationship with the party from which the first disregarded party acquired the depreciable property and with the original transferor of the depreciable property in the series. The rules for testing the relationships in paragraph (b)(3)(iii)(C)( *1*) of this section continue to apply for the other transactions in the series.

*(ii) All section 168(i)(7) transactions*.—This paragraph (b)(3)(iii)(C) does not apply if all transactions in a series of related transactions are described in paragraph (g)(1)(iii) of this section (section 168(i)(7) transactions in which property is transferred in the same taxable year that the property is placed in service by the transferor).

*(iii) One or more section 168(i)(7) transactions*.—Any step in a series of related transactions that is neither the original step nor the ultimate step is disregarded (disregarded step) for purposes of testing the relationships under paragraph (b)(3)(iii)(C)( *1*) of this section if the step is a transaction described in paragraph (g)(1)(iii) of this section. In this case, the relationship is not tested between the transferor and transferee of that transaction. Instead, the relationship is tested between the transferor in the disregarded step and the party to which the transferee in the disregarded step disposed of the depreciable property, the transferee in the disregarded step and the party to which the transferee in the disregarded step disposed of the depreciable property, and the original transferor of the depreciable property in the series and the party to which the transferee in the disregarded step disposed of the depreciable property. If the series has consecutive disregarded steps, the relationship is tested between the transferor in the first disregarded step and the party to which the transferee in the last disregarded step disposed of the depreciable property, the transferee in the last disregarded step and the party to which the transferee in the last disregarded step disposed of the depreciable property, and the original transferor of the depreciable property in the series and the party to which the transferee in the last disregarded step disposed of the depreciable property. The rules for testing the relationships in paragraph (b)(3)(iii)(C)( *1*) of this section continue to apply for the other transactions in the series.

*(iv) Syndication transaction*.—This paragraph (b)(3)(iii)(C) does not apply to a syndication transaction described in paragraph (b)(3)(vi) of this section.

*(v) Certain relationships disregarded*.—If a party acquires depreciable property in a series of related transactions in which the party acquires stock, meeting the requirements of section 1504(a)(2), of a corporation in a fully taxable transaction followed by a liquidation of the acquired corporation under section 331, any relationship created as part of such series of related transactions is disregarded in determining whether any party is related to such acquired corporation for purposes of testing the relationships under paragraph (b)(3)(iii)(C)( *1*) of this section.

*(vi) Transferors that cease to exist for Federal tax purposes*.—Any transferor in a series of related transactions that ceases to exist for Federal tax purposes during the series is deemed, for purposes of testing the relationships under paragraph (b)(3)(iii)(C)( *1*) of this section, to be in existence at the time of any transfer in the series.

*(vii) Newly created party* .—If a transferee in a series of related transactions acquires depreciable property from a transferor that was not in existence immediately prior to the first transfer of such property in such series (new transferor), the transferee tests its relationship with the party from which the new transferor acquired such property and with the original transferor of the depreciable property in the series for purposes of paragraph (b)(3)(iii)(C)( *1*) of this section. If the series has consecutive new transferors, the party to which the last new transferor disposed of the depreciable property tests its relationship with the party from which the first new transferor acquired the depreciable property and with the original transferor of the depreciable property in the series. The rules for testing the relationships in paragraph (b)(3)(iii)(C)( *1*) of this section continue to apply for the other transactions in the series.

*(viii) Application of paragraph (g)(1) of this section* .—Paragraph (g)(1) of this section applies to each step in a series of related transactions.

(iv) *Application to partnerships* .—(A) *Section 704(c) remedial allocations* .—Remedial allocations under section 704(c) do not satisfy the requirements of paragraph (b)(3) of this section. See § 1.704-3(d)(2).

(B) *Basis determined under section 732* .—Any basis of distributed property determined under section 732 does not satisfy the requirements of paragraph (b)(3) of this section.

(C) *Section 734(b) adjustments* .—Any increase in basis of depreciable property under section 734(b) does not satisfy the requirements of paragraph (b)(3) of this section.

(D) *Section 743(b) adjustments* .—*(1) In general* .—For purposes of determining whether the transfer of a partnership interest meets the requirements of paragraph (b)(3)(iii)(A) of this section, each partner is treated as having a depreciable interest in the partner's proportionate share of partnership property. Any increase in basis of depreciable property under section 743(b) satisfies the requirements of paragraph (b)(3)(iii)(A) of this section if—

*(i)* At any time prior to the transfer of the partnership interest that gave rise to such basis increase, neither the transferee partner nor a predecessor of the transferee partner had any depreciable interest in the portion of the property deemed acquired to which the section 743(b) adjustment is allocated under section 755 and § 1.755-1; and

*(ii)* The transfer of the partnership interest that gave rise to such basis increase satisfies the requirements of paragraphs (b)(3)(iii)(A)( *2*) and ( *3*) of this section.

*(2) Relatedness tested at partner level* .—Solely for purposes of paragraph (b)(3)(iv)(D)( *1*)( *ii*) of this section, whether the parties are related or unrelated is determined by comparing the transferor and the transferee of the transferred partnership interest.

(v) *Application to members of a consolidated group* .—For rules applicable to the acquisition of depreciable property by a member of a consolidated group, see § 1.1502-68.

(vi) *Syndication transaction* .—If new property is acquired and placed in service by a lessor, or if used property is acquired and placed in service by a lessor and the lessor or a predecessor did not previously have a depreciable interest in the used property, and the property is sold by the lessor or any subsequent purchaser within three months after the date the property was originally placed in service by the lessor (or, in the case of multiple units of property subject to the same lease, within three months after the date the final unit is placed in service, so long as the period between the time the first unit is placed in service and the time the last unit is placed in service does not exceed 12 months), and the user of the property after the last sale during the three-month period remains the same as when the property was originally placed in service by the lessor, the purchaser of the property in the last sale during the three-month period is considered the taxpayer that acquired the property for purposes of applying paragraphs (b)(3)(ii) and (iii) of this section. The purchaser of the property in the last sale during the three-month period is treated, for purposes of applying paragraph (b)(3) of this section, as—

(A) The original user of the property in this transaction if the lessor acquired and placed in service new property; or

(B) The taxpayer having the depreciable interest in the property in this transaction if the lessor acquired and placed in service used property.

(vii) *Examples* .—The application of this paragraph (b)(3) is illustrated by the following examples. Unless the facts specifically indicate otherwise, assume that the parties are not related within the meaning of section 179(d)(2)(A) or (B) and § 1.179-4(c), no corporation is a member of a consolidated or controlled group, and the parties do not have predecessors:

(A) *Example 1.* ( *1*) On August 1, 2018, *A* buys a new machine for $35,000 from an unrelated party for use in *A*'s trade or business. On July 1, 2020, *B* buys that machine from *A* for $20,000 for use in *B*'s trade or business. On October 1, 2020, *B* makes a $5,000 capital expenditure to recondition the machine. *B* did not have any depreciable interest in the machine before *B* acquired it on July 1, 2020.

( *2*) *A*'s purchase price of $35,000 satisfies the original use requirement of paragraph (b)(3)(ii) of this section and, assuming all other requirements are met, qualifies for the additional first year depreciation deduction under this section.

( *3*) *B*'s purchase price of $20,000 does not satisfy the original use requirement of paragraph (b)(3)(ii) of this section, but it does satisfy the used property acquisition requirements of paragraph (b)(3)(iii) of this section. Assuming all other requirements are met, the $20,000 purchase price qualifies for the additional first year depreciation deduction under this section. Further, *B*'s $5,000 expenditure satisfies the original use requirement of paragraph (b)(3)(ii) of this section and, assuming all other requirements are met, qualifies for the additional first year depreciation deduction under this section, regardless of whether the $5,000 is added to the basis of the machine or is capitalized as a separate asset.

(B) *Example 2. C*, an automobile dealer, uses some of its automobiles as demonstrators in order to show them to prospective customers. The automobiles that are used as demonstrators by *C* are held by *C* primarily for sale to customers in the ordinary course of its business. On November 1, 2017, *D* buys from *C* an automobile that was previously used as a demonstrator by *C*. *D* will use the automobile solely for business purposes. The use of the automobile by *C* as a demonstrator does not constitute a "use" for purposes of the original use requirement and, therefore, *D* will be considered the original user of the automobile for purposes of paragraph (b)(3)(ii) of this section. Assuming all other requirements are met, *D*'s purchase price of the automobile qualifies for the additional first year depreciation deduction for *D* under this section, subject to any limitation under section 280F.

(C) *Example 3.* On April 1, 2015, *E* acquires a horse to be used in *E*'s thoroughbred racing business. On October 1, 2018, F buys the horse from *E* and will use the horse in *F*'s horse breeding business. *F* did not have any depreciable interest in the horse before *F* acquired it on October 1, 2018. The use of the horse by *E* in its racing business prevents *F* from satisfying the original use requirement of paragraph (b)(3)(ii) of this section. However, *F*'s acquisition of the horse satisfies the used property acquisition requirements of paragraph (b)(3)(iii) of this section. Assuming all other requirements are met, *F*'s purchase price of the horse qualifies for the additional first year depreciation deduction for *F* under this section.

(D) *Example 4.* In the ordinary course of its business, *G* sells fractional interests in its aircraft to unrelated parties. *G* holds out for sale eight equal fractional interests in an aircraft. On October 1, 2017, *G* sells five of the eight fractional interests in the aircraft to *H* and *H* begins to use its proportionate share of the aircraft immediately upon purchase. On February 1, 2018, *G* sells to *I* the remaining unsold 3/8 fractional interests in the aircraft. *H* is considered the original user as to its 5/8 fractional interest in the aircraft and *I* is considered the original user as to its 3/8 fractional interest in the aircraft. Thus, assuming all other requirements are met, *H*'s purchase price for its 5/8 fractional interest in the aircraft qualifies for the additional first year depreciation deduction under this section and *I*'s purchase price for its 3/8 fractional interest in the aircraft qualifies for the additional first year depreciation deduction under this section.

(E) *Example 5.* On September 1, 2017, *J*, an equipment dealer, buys new tractors that are held by *J* primarily for sale to customers in the ordinary course of its business. On October 15, 2017, *J* withdraws the tractors from inventory and begins to use the tractors primarily for producing rental income. The holding of the tractors by *J* as inventory does not constitute a "use" for purposes of the original use requirement and, therefore, the original use of the tractors commences with *J* on October 15, 2017, for purposes of paragraph (b)(3)(ii) of this section. However, the tractors are not eligible for the additional first year depreciation deduction under this section because *J* acquired the tractors before September 28, 2017.

(F) *Example 6. K* is in the trade or business of leasing equipment to others. During 2016, *K* buys a new machine (Machine #1) and then leases it to *L* for use in *L*'s trade or business. The lease between *K* and *L* for Machine #1 is a true lease for Federal income tax purposes. During 2018, *L* enters into a written binding contract with *K* to buy Machine #1 at its fair market value on May 15, 2018. *L* did not have any depreciable interest in Machine #1 before *L* acquired it on May 15, 2018. As a result, *L*'s acquisition of Machine #1 satisfies the used property acquisition requirements of paragraph (b)(3)(iii) of this section. Assuming all other requirements are met, *L*'s purchase price of Machine #1 qualifies for the additional first year depreciation deduction for *L* under this section.

(G) *Example 7.* The facts are the same as in *Example 6* of paragraph (b)(3)(vii)(F) of this section, except that *K* and *L* are related parties within the meaning of section 179(d)(2)(A) or (B) and § 1.179-4(c). As a result, *L*'s acquisition of Machine #1 does not satisfy the used property acquisition requirements of paragraph (b)(3)(iii) of this section. Thus, Machine #1 is not eligible for the additional first year depreciation deduction for *L*.

(H) *Example 8.* The facts are the same as in *Example 6* of paragraph (b)(3)(vii)(F) of this section, except *L* incurred capital expenditures of $5,000 to improve Machine #1 on September 5, 2017, and has a depreciable interest in such improvements. *L*'s purchase price of $5,000 for the improvements to Machine #1 satisfies the original use requirement of § 1.168(k)-1(b)(3)(i) and, assuming all other requirements are met, qualifies for the 50-percent additional first year depreciation deduction. Because *L* had a depreciable interest only in the improvements to Machine #1, *L*'s acquisition of Machine #1, excluding *L*'s improvements to such machine, satisfies the used property acquisition requirements of paragraph (b)(3)(iii) of this section. Assuming all other requirements are met, *L*'s unadjusted depreciable basis of Machine #1, excluding the amount of such unadjusted depreciable basis attributable to *L*'s improvements to Machine #1, qualifies for the additional first year depreciation deduction for *L* under this section.

(I) *Example 9.* During 2016, *M* and *N* purchased used equipment for use in their trades or businesses and each own a 50 percent interest in such equipment. Prior to this acquisition, *M* and *N* did not have any depreciable interest in the equipment. Assume this ownership arrangement is not a partnership. During 2018, *N* enters into a written binding contract with *M* to buy *M*'s interest in the equipment. Pursuant to paragraph (b)(3)(iii)(B)(*2*) of this section, *N* is not treated as using *M*'s interest in the equipment prior to *N*'s acquisition of *M*'s interest. As a result, *N*'s acquisition of *M*'s interest in the equipment satisfies the used property acquisition requirements of paragraph (b)(3)(iii) of this section. Assuming all other requirements are met, *N*'s purchase price of *M*'s interest in the equipment qualifies for the additional first year depreciation deduction for *N* under this section.

(J) *Example 10.* The facts are the same as in *Example 9* of paragraph (b)(3)(vii)(I) of this section, except *N* had a 100-percent depreciable interest in the equipment during 2011 through 2015, and *M* purchased from *N* a 50-percent interest in the equipment during 2016. Pursuant to paragraph (b)(3)(iii)(B)(*1*) of this section, the lookback period is 2013 through 2017 to determine if *N* had a depreciable interest in *M*'s 50-percent interest in the equipment *N* acquired from *M* in 2018. Because *N* had a 100-percent depreciable interest in the equipment during 2013 through 2015, *N* had a depreciable interest in *M*'s 50-percent interest in the equipment during the lookback period. As a result, *N*'s acquisition of *M*'s interest in the equipment during 2018 does not satisfy the used property acquisition requirements of paragraphs (b)(3)(iii)(A)(*1*) and (b)(3)(iii)(B)(*1*) of this section. Paragraph (b)(3)(iii)(B)(*2*) of this section does not apply because *N* initially acquired a 100-percent depreciable interest in the equipment. Accordingly, *N*'s purchase price of *M*'s interest in the equipment during 2018 does not qualify for the additional first year depreciation deduction for *N*.

(K) *Example 11.* The facts are the same as in *Example 9* of paragraph (b)(3)(vii)(I) of this section, except *N* had a 100-percent depreciable interest in the equipment only during 2011, and *M* purchased from *N* a 50-percent interest in the equipment during 2012. Pursuant to paragraph (b)(3)(iii)(B)(*1*) of this section, the lookback period is 2013 through 2017 to determine if *N* had a depreciable interest in *M*'s 50-percent interest in the equipment *N* acquired from *M* in 2018. Because *N* had a depreciable interest in only its 50-percent interest in the equipment during this lookback period, *N*'s acquisition of *M*'s interest in the equipment during 2018 satisfies the used property acquisition requirements of paragraphs (b)(3)(iii)(A)(*1*) and (b)(3)(iii)(B)(*1*) of this section. Assuming all other requirements are met, *N*'s purchase price of *M*'s interest in the equipment during 2018 qualifies for the additional first year depreciation deduction for *N* under this section.

(L) *Example 12.* The facts are the same as in *Example 9* of paragraph (b)(3)(vii)(I) of this section, except during 2018, *M* also enters into a written binding contract with *N* to buy *N*'s interest in the equipment. Pursuant to paragraph (b)(3)(iii)(B)(*2*) of this section, both *M* and *N* are treated as previously having a depreciable interest in a 50-percent portion of the equipment. Accordingly, the acquisition by *M* of *N*'s 50-percent interest and the acquisition by *N* of *M*'s 50-percent interest in the equipment during 2018 do not qualify for the additional first year depreciation deduction.

(M) *Example 13.* *O* and *P* form an equal partnership, *OP*, in 2018. *O* contributes cash to *OP*, and *P* contributes equipment to *OP*. *OP*'s basis in the equipment contributed by *P* is determined under section 723. Because *OP*'s basis in such equipment is determined in whole or in part by reference to *P*'s adjusted basis in such equipment, *OP*'s acquisition of such equipment does not satisfy section 179(d)(2)(C) and § 1.179-4(c)(1)(iv) and, thus, does not satisfy the used property acquisition requirements of paragraph (b)(3)(iii) of this section. Accordingly, *OP*'s acquisition of such equipment is not eligible for the additional first year depreciation deduction.

(N) *Example 14.* *Q*, *R*, and *S* form an equal partnership, *QRS*, in 2019. Each partner contributes $100, which *QRS* uses to purchase a retail motor fuels outlet for $300. Assume this retail motor fuels outlet is *QRS*' only property and is qualified property under section 168(k)(2)(A)(i). *QRS* makes an election not to deduct the additional first year depreciation for all qualified property placed in service during 2019. *QRS* has a section 754 election in effect. *QRS* claimed depreciation of $15 for the retail motor fuels outlet for 2019. During 2020, when the retail motor fuels outlet's fair market value is $600, *Q* sells all of its partnership interest to *T* in a fully taxable transaction for $200. *T* never previously had a depreciable interest in the retail motor fuels outlet. *T* takes an outside basis of $200 in the partnership interest previously owned by Q. *T*'s share of the partnership's previously taxed capital is $95. Accordingly, *T*'s section 743(b) adjustment is $105 and is allocated entirely to the retail motor fuels outlet under section 755. Assuming all other requirements are met, *T*'s section 743(b) adjustment qualifies for the additional first year depreciation deduction under this section.

(O) *Example 15.* The facts are the same as in *Example 14* of paragraph (b)(3)(vii)(N) of this section, except that *Q* sells his partnership interest to *U*, a related person within the meaning of section 179(d)(2)(A) or (B) and § 1.179-4(c). *U*'s section 743(b) adjustment does not qualify for the additional first year depreciation deduction.

(P) *Example 16.* The facts are the same as in *Example 14* of paragraph (b)(3)(vii)(N) of this section, except that *Q* dies and his partnership interest is transferred to *V*. *V* takes a basis in *Q*'s partnership interest under section 1014. As a result, section 179(d)(2)(C)(ii) and § 1.179-4(c)(1)(iv) are not satisfied, and *V*'s section 743(b) adjustment does not qualify for the additional first year depreciation deduction.

(Q) *Example 17.* The facts are the same as in *Example 14* of paragraph (b)(3)(vii)(N) of this section, except that *QRS* purchased the retail motor fuels outlet from *T* prior to *T* purchasing *Q*'s partnership interest in *QRS*. *T* had a depreciable interest in such retail motor fuels outlet. Because *T* had a depreciable interest in the retail motor fuels outlet before *T* acquired its interest in *QRS*, *T*'s section 743(b) adjustment does not qualify for the additional first year depreciation deduction.

(R) *Example 18.* ( *1*) *W*, a freight transportation company, acquires and places in service a used aircraft during 2019 (Airplane #1). Prior to this acquisition, *W* never had a depreciable interest in this aircraft. During September 2020, *W* enters into a written binding contract with a third party to renovate Airplane #1. The third party begins to renovate Airplane #1 in October 2020 and delivers the renovated aircraft (Airplane #2) to *W* in February 2021. To renovate Airplane #1, the third party used mostly new parts but also used parts from Airplane #1. The cost of the used parts is not more than 20 percent of the total cost of the renovated airplane, Airplane #2. *W* uses Airplane #2 in its trade or business.

( *2*) Although Airplane #2 contains used parts, the cost of the used parts is not more than 20 percent of the total cost of Airplane #2. As a result, Airplane #2 is not treated as reconditioned or rebuilt property, and *W* is considered the original user of Airplane #2, pursuant to paragraph (b)(3)(ii)(A) of this section. Accordingly, assuming all other requirements are met, the amount paid or incurred by *W* for Airplane #2 qualifies for the additional first year depreciation deduction for *W* under this section.

(S) *Example 19.* ( *1*) *X*, a freight transportation company, acquires and places in service a new aircraft in 2019 (Airplane #1). During 2022, *X* sells Airplane #1 to *AB* and *AB* uses Airplane #1 in its trade or business. Prior to this acquisition, *AB* never had a depreciable interest in Airplane #1. During January 2023, *AB* enters into a written binding contract with a third party to renovate Airplane #1. The third party begins to renovate Airplane #1 in February 2023 and delivers the renovated aircraft (Airplane #2) to *AB* in June 2023. To renovate Airplane #1, the third party used mostly new parts but also used parts from Airplane #1. The cost of the used parts is not more than 20 percent of the total cost of the renovated airplane, Airplane #2. *AB* uses Airplane #2 in its trade or business. During 2025, *AB* sells Airplane #2 to *X* and *X* uses Airplane #2 in its trade or business.

( *2*) With respect to *X*'s purchase of Airplane #1 in 2019, *X* is the original user of this airplane pursuant to paragraph (b)(3)(ii)(A) of this section. Accordingly, assuming all other requirements are met, *X*'s purchase price for Airplane #1 qualifies for the additional first year depreciation deduction for *X* under this section.

( *3*) Because *AB* never had a depreciable interest in Airplane #1 prior to its acquisition in 2022, the requirements of paragraphs (b)(3)(iii)(A)( *1*) and (b)(3)(ii)(B)( *1*) of this section are satisfied. Accordingly, assuming all other requirements are met, *AB*'s purchase price for Airplane #1 qualifies for the additional first year depreciation deduction for *AB* under this section.

( *4*) Although Airplane #2 contains used parts, the cost of the used parts is not more than 20 percent of the total cost of Airplane #2. As a result, Airplane #2 is not treated as reconditioned or rebuilt property, and *AB* is considered the original user of Airplane #2, pursuant to paragraph (b)(3)(ii)(A) of this section. Accordingly, assuming all other requirements are met, the amount paid or incurred by *AB* for Airplane #2 qualifies for the additional first year depreciation deduction for *AB* under this section.

( *5*) With respect to *X*'s purchase of Airplane #2 in 2025, Airplane #2 is substantially renovated property pursuant to paragraph (b)(3)(iii)(B)( *3*) of this section. Also, pursuant to paragraph (b)(3)(iii)(B)( *3*) of this section, *X*'s depreciable interest in Airplane #1 is not taken into account for determining if *X* previously had a depreciable interest in Airplane #2 prior to its acquisition during 2025. As a result, Airplane #2 is not treated as used by *X* at any time before its acquisition of Airplane #2 in 2025 pursuant to paragraph (b)(3)(iii)(B)( *3*) of this section. Accordingly, assuming all other requirements are met, *X*'s purchase price of Airplane #2 qualifies for the additional first year depreciation deduction for *X* under this section.

(T) *Example 20.* In November 2017, AA Corporation purchases a used drill press costing $10,000 and is granted a trade-in allowance of $2,000 on its old drill press. The used drill press is qualified property under section 168(k)(2)(A)(i). The old drill press had a basis of $1,200. Under sections 1012 and 1031(d), the basis of the used drill press is $9,200 ($1,200 basis of old drill press plus cash expended of $8,000). Only $8,000 of the basis of the used drill press satisfies the requirements of section 179(d)(3) and § 1.179-4(d) and, thus, satisfies the used property acquisition requirement of paragraph (b)(3)(iii) of this section. The remaining $1,200 of the basis of the used drill press does not satisfy the requirements of section 179(d)(3) and § 1.179-4(d) because it is determined by reference to the old drill press. Accordingly, assuming all other requirements are met, only $8,000 of the basis of the used drill press is eligible for the additional first year depreciation deduction under this section.

(U) *Example 21.* ( *1*) M Corporation acquires and places in service a used airplane on March 26, 2018. Prior to this acquisition, M Corporation never had a depreciable interest in this airplane. On March 26, 2018, M Corporation also leases the used airplane to N Corporation, an airline company. On May 27, 2018, M Corporation sells to O Corporation the used airplane subject to the lease with N Corporation. M Corporation and O Corporation are related parties within the meaning of section 179(d)(2)(A) or (B) and § 1.179-4(c). As of May 27, 2018, N Corporation is still the lessee of the used airplane. Prior to this acquisition, O Corporation never had a depreciable interest in the used airplane. O Corporation is a calendar-year taxpayer.

(*2*) The sale transaction of May 27, 2018, satisfies the requirements of a syndication transaction described in paragraph (b)(3)(vi) of this section. As a result, O Corporation is considered the taxpayer that acquired the used airplane for purposes of applying the used property acquisition requirements in paragraph (b)(3)(iii) of this section. In applying these rules, the fact that M Corporation and O Corporation are related parties is not taken into account because O Corporation, not M Corporation, is treated as acquiring the used airplane. Also, O Corporation, not M Corporation, is treated as having the depreciable interest in the used airplane. Further, pursuant to paragraph (b)(4)(iv) of this section, the used airplane is treated as originally placed in service by O Corporation on May 27, 2018. Because O Corporation never had a depreciable interest in the used airplane and assuming all other requirements are met, O Corporation's purchase price of the used airplane qualifies for the additional first year depreciation deduction for O Corporation under this section.

(V) *Example 22.* (*1*) The facts are the same as in *Example 21* of paragraph (b)(3)(vii)(U)(*1*) of this section. Additionally, on September 5, 2018, O Corporation sells to P Corporation the used airplane subject to the lease with N Corporation. Prior to this acquisition, P Corporation never had a depreciable interest in the used airplane.

(*2*) Because O Corporation, a calendar-year taxpayer, placed in service and disposed of the used airplane during 2018, the used airplane is not eligible for the additional first year depreciation deduction for O Corporation pursuant to paragraph (g)(1)(i) of this section.

(*3*) Because P Corporation never had a depreciable interest in the used airplane and assuming all other requirements are met, P Corporation's purchase price of the used airplane qualifies for the additional first year depreciation deduction for P Corporation under this section.

(W) *Example 23.* (*1*) The facts are the same as in *Example 21* of paragraph (b)(3)(vii)(U)(*1*) of this section, except M Corporation and O Corporation are not related parties within the meaning of section 179(d)(2)(A) or (B) and § 1.179-4(c). Additionally, on March 26, 2020, O Corporation sells to M Corporation the used airplane subject to the lease with N Corporation.

(*2*) The sale transaction of May 27, 2018, satisfies the requirements of a syndication transaction described in paragraph (b)(3)(vi) of this section. As a result, O Corporation is considered the taxpayer that acquired the used airplane for purposes of applying the used property acquisition requirements in paragraph (b)(3)(iii) of this section. Also, O Corporation, not M Corporation, is treated as having the depreciable interest in the used airplane. Further, pursuant to paragraph (b)(4)(iv) of this section, the used airplane is treated as originally placed in service by O Corporation on May 27, 2018. Because O Corporation never had a depreciable interest in the used airplane before its acquisition in 2018 and assuming all other requirements are met, O Corporation's purchase price of the used airplane qualifies for the additional first year depreciation deduction for O Corporation under this section.

(*3*) Prior to its acquisition of the used airplane on March 26, 2020, M Corporation never had a depreciable interest in the used airplane pursuant to paragraph (b)(3)(vi) of this section. Assuming all other requirements are met, M Corporation's purchase price of the used airplane on March 26, 2020, qualifies for the additional first year depreciation deduction for M Corporation under this section.

(X) *Example 24.* (*1*) J, K, and L are corporations that are unrelated parties within the meaning of section 179(d)(2)(A) or (B) and § 1.179-4(c). None of J, K, or L is a member of a consolidated group. J has a depreciable interest in Equipment #5. During 2018, J sells Equipment #5 to K. During 2020, J merges into

L in a transaction described in section 368(a)(1)(A). In 2021, L acquires Equipment #5 from K.

( *2*) Because J is the predecessor of L, and because J previously had a depreciable interest in Equipment #5, L's acquisition of Equipment #5 does not satisfy paragraphs (b)(3)(iii)(A)( *1*) and (b)(3)(iii)(B)( *1*) of this section. Thus, L's acquisition of Equipment #5 does not satisfy the used property acquisition requirements of paragraph (b)(3)(iii) of this section. Accordingly, L's acquisition of Equipment #5 is not eligible for the additional first year depreciation deduction.

(Y) *Example 25*. ( *1*) *JL* is a fiscal year taxpayer with a taxable year ending June 30. On April 22, 2020, *JL* acquires and places in service a new machine for use in its trade or business. On May 1, 2022, *JL* sells this machine to *JM*, an unrelated party, for use in *JM's* trade or business. *JM* is a fiscal year taxpayer with a taxable year ending March 31. On February 1, 2023, *JL* buys the machine from *JM* and places the machine in service. *JL* uses the machine in its trade or business for the remainder of its taxable year ending June 30, 2023.

( *2*) *JL's* acquisition of the machine on April 22, 2020, satisfies the original use requirement in paragraph (b)(3)(ii) of this section. Assuming all other requirements are met, *JL's* purchase price of the machine qualifies for the additional first year depreciation deduction for *JL* for the taxable year ending June 30, 2020, under this section.

( *3*) *JM* placed in service the machine on May 1, 2022, and disposed of it on February 1, 2023. As a result, *JM* placed in service and disposed of the machine during the same taxable year (*JM's* taxable year beginning April 1, 2022, and ending March 31, 2023). Accordingly, *JM's* acquisition of the machine on May 1, 2022, does not qualify for the additional first year depreciation deduction pursuant to paragraph (g)(1)(i) of this section.

( *4*) Pursuant to paragraph (b)(3)(iii)(B)( *1*) of this section, the lookback period is calendar years 2018 through 2022 and January 1, 2023, through January 31, 2023, to determine if *JL* had a depreciable interest in the machine when *JL* reacquired it on February 1, 2023. As a result, *JL's* depreciable interest in the machine during the period April 22, 2020, to April 30, 2022, is taken into account for determining whether the machine was used by *JL* or a predecessor at any time prior to its reacquisition by *JL* on February 1, 2023. Accordingly, the reacquisition of the machine by *JL* on February 1, 2023, does not qualify for the additional first year depreciation deduction.

(Z) *Example 26*. ( *1*) *EF* has owned and had a depreciable interest in Property since 2012. On January 1, 2016, *EF* contributes assets (not including Property) to existing *Partnership T* in a transaction described in section 721, in exchange for a partnership interest in *Partnership T*, and *Partnership T* placed in service these assets for use in its trade or business. On July 1, 2016, *EF* sells Property to *EG*, a party unrelated to either *EF* or *Partnership T*. On April 1, 2018, *Partnership T* buys Property from *EG* and places it in service for use in its trade or business.

( *2*) *EF* is not *Partnership T's* predecessor with respect to Property within the meaning of paragraph (a)(2)(iv)(B) of this section. Pursuant to paragraph (3)(iii)(B)( *1*) of this section, the lookback period is 2013-2017, plus January through March 2018, to determine if *Partnership T* had a depreciable interest in Property that *Partnership T* acquired on April 1, 2018. *EF* need not be examined in the lookback period to see if *EF* had a depreciable interest in Property, because *EF* is not *Partnership* T's predecessor. Because *Partnership T* did not have a depreciable interest in Property in the lookback period prior to its acquisition of Property on April 1, 2018, *Partnership* T's acquisition of Property on April 1, 2018, satisfies the used property acquisition requirement of paragraph (b)(3)(iii)(B)(1) of this section. Assuming all other requirements of this section are satisfied, *Partnership T's* purchase price of Property qualifies for the additional first year depreciation deduction under this section.

(AA) *Example 27.* ( *1*) The facts are the same as in *Example 26* of paragraph (b)(3)(vii)(Z)(1) of this section, except that on January 1, 2016, *EF's* contribution of assets to *Partnership T* includes Property. On July 1, 2016, *Partnership T* sells Property to *EG*.

( *2*) *Partnership T's* acquisition of Property on January 1, 2016, does not satisfy the original use requirement of § 1.168(k)-1(b)(3) and is not eligible for the additional first year depreciation deduction under section 168(k) as in effect prior to the enactment of the Act.

( *3*) With respect to *Partnership T's* acquisition of Property on April 1, 2018, *EF* is *Partnership T's* predecessor with respect to Property within the meaning of paragraph (a)(2)(iv)(B) of this section. Pursuant to paragraph (b)(3)(iii)(B)(1) of this section, the lookback period is 2013-2017, plus January through March 2018, to determine if *EF* or *Partnership T* had a depreciable interest in Property that *Partnership T* acquired on April 1, 2018. Because *EF* had a depreciable interest in Property from 2013 to 2015 and *Partnership T* had a depreciable interest in Property from January through June 2016, *Partnership T's* acquisition of Property on April 1, 2018, does not satisfy the used property acquisition requirement of paragraph (b)(3)(iii)(B)(1) of this section and is not eligible for the additional first year depreciation deduction.

(BB) *Example 28.* ( *1*) X Corporation has owned and had a depreciable interest in Property since 2012. On January 1, 2015, X Corporation sold Property to *Q*, an unrelated party. Y Corporation is formed July 1, 2015. On January 1, 2016, Y Corporation merges into X Corporation in a transaction described in section 368(a)(1)(A). On April 1, 2018, X Corporation buys Property from *Q* and places it in service for use in its trade or business.

( *2*) Pursuant to paragraph (a)(2)(iv)(A) of this section, Y Corporation is X Corporation's predecessor. Pursuant to paragraph (b)(3)(iii)(B)( *1*) of this section, the lookback period is 2013-2017, plus January through March 2018, to determine if Y Corporation or X Corporation had a depreciable interest in Property that X Corporation acquired on April 1, 2018. Y Corporation did not have a depreciable interest in Property at any time during the lookback period. Because X Corporation had a depreciable interest in Property from 2013 through 2014, X Corporation's acquisition of Property on April 1, 2018, does not satisfy the used property acquisition requirement of paragraph (b)(3)(iii)(B)( *1*) of this section and is not eligible for the additional first year depreciation deduction.

(CC) *Example 29.* ( *1*) Y Corporation has owned and had a depreciable interest in Property since 2012. On January 1, 2015, Y Corporation sells Property to *Q*, an unrelated party. X Corporation is formed on July 1, 2015. On January 1, 2016, Y Corporation merges into X Corporation in a transaction described in section 368(a)(1)(A). On April 1, 2018, X Corporation buys Property from *Q* and places it in service for use in its trade or business.

( *2*) Pursuant to paragraph (a)(2)(iv)(A) of this section, Y Corporation is X Corporation's predecessor. Pursuant to paragraph (b)(3)(iii)(B)( *1*) of this section, the lookback period is 2013-2017, plus January through March 2018, to determine if X Corporation or Y Corporation had a depreciable interest in Property that X Corporation acquired on April 1, 2018. Because Y Corporation had a depreciable interest in Property from 2013 through 2014, X Corporation's acquisition of Property on April 1, 2018, does not satisfy the used property acquisition requirement of paragraph (b)(3)(iii)(B)( *1*) of this section and is not eligible for the additional first year depreciation deduction.

(DD) *Example 30.* ( *1*) On September 5, 2017, *Y*, a calendar-year taxpayer, acquires and places in service a new machine (Machine #1), and begins using Machine #1 in its manufacturing trade or business. On November 1, 2017, *Y* sells Machine #1 to *Z*, then *Z* leases Machine #1 back to *Y* for 4 years, and *Y* continues to use Machine #1 in its manufacturing trade or business. The lease agreement contains a purchase option provision allowing *Y* to buy Machine #1 at the end of the lease term. On November 1, 2021, *Y* exercises the purchase option in the lease agreement and buys Machine #1 from *Z*. The lease between *Y* and *Z* for Machine #1 is a true lease for Federal tax purposes.

( *2*) Because *Y*, a calendar-year taxpayer, placed in service and disposed of Machine #1 during 2017, Machine #1 is not eligible for the additional first year depreciation deduction for *Y* pursuant to § 1.168(k)-1(f)(1)(i).

( *3*) The use of Machine #1 by *Y* prevents *Z* from satisfying the original use requirement of paragraph (b)(3)(ii) of this section. However, *Z*'s acquisition of Machine #1 satisfies the used property acquisition requirements of paragraph (b)(3)(iii) of this section. Assuming all other requirements are met, *Z*'s purchase price of Machine #1 qualifies for the additional first year depreciation deduction for *Z* under this section.

( *4*) During 2017, *Y* sold Machine #1 within 90 calendar days of placing Machine #1 in service originally on September 5, 2017. Pursuant to paragraph (b)(3)(iii)(B)(4) of this section, *Y*'s depreciable interest in Machine #1 during that 90-day period is not taken into account for determining whether Machine #1 was used by *Y* or a predecessor at any time prior to its reacquisition by *Y* on November 1, 2021. Accordingly, assuming all other requirements are met, *Y*'s purchase price of Machine #1 on November 1, 2021, qualifies for the additional first year depreciation deduction for Y under this section.

(EE) *Example 31.* ( *1*) On October 15, 2019, *FA*, a calendar-year taxpayer, buys and places in service a new machine for use in its trade or business. On January 10, 2020, *FA* sells this machine to *FB* for use in *FB's* trade or business. *FB* is a calendar-year taxpayer and is not related to *FA*. On March 30, 2020, *FA* buys the machine from *FB* and places the machine in service. *FA* uses the machine in its trade or business for the remainder of 2020.

( *2*) *FA's* acquisition of the machine on October 15, 2019, satisfies the original use requirement in paragraph (b)(3)(ii) of this section. Assuming all other requirements are met, *FA's* purchase price of the machine qualifies for the additional first year depreciation deduction for *FA* for the 2019 taxable year under this section.

( *3*) Because *FB* placed in service the machine on January 10, 2020, and disposed of it on March 30, 2020, *FB's* acquisition of the machine on January 10, 2020, does not qualify for the additional first year depreciation deduction pursuant to § 1.168(k)-2(g)(1)(i).

( *4*) *FA* sold the machine to *FB* in 2020 and within 90 calendar days of placing the machine in service originally on October 15, 2019. Pursuant to paragraph (b)(3)(iii)(B)(4) of this section, *FA's* depreciable interest in the machine during that 90-day period is not taken into account for determining whether the machine was used by *FA* or a predecessor at any time prior to its reacquisition by *FA* on March 30, 2020. Accordingly, assuming all other requirements are met, *FA's* purchase price of the machine on March 30, 2020, qualifies for the additional first year depreciation deduction for *FA* for the 2020 taxable year under this section.

(FF) *Example 32.* ( *1*) The facts are the same as in *Example 31* of paragraph (b)(3)(vii)(EE)(1) of this section, except that on November 1, 2020, *FB* buys the machine from *FA* and places the machine in service. *FB* uses the machine in its trade or business for the remainder of 2020.

( *2*) Because *FA* placed in service the machine on March 30, 2020, and disposed of it on November 1, 2020, *FA's* reacquisition of the machine on March 30, 2020, does not qualify for the additional first year depreciation deduction pursuant to paragraph (g)(1)(i) of this section.

(*3*) During 2020, *FB* sold the machine to *FA* within 90 calendar days of placing the machine in service originally on January 10, 2020. After *FB* reacquired the machine on November 1, 2020, *FB* did not dispose of the property during the remainder of 2020. Pursuant to paragraph (b)(3)(iii)(B)(*4*) of this section, *FB's* depreciable interest in the machine during that 90-day period is not taken into account for determining whether the machine was used by *FB* or a predecessor at any time prior to its reacquisition by *FB* on November 1, 2020. Accordingly, assuming all other requirements are met, *FB's* purchase price of the machine on November 1, 2020, qualifies for the additional first year depreciation deduction for *FB* under this section.

(GG) *Example 33.* (*1*) The facts are the same as in *Example 32* of paragraph (b)(3)(vii)(FF)(1) of this section, except *FB* sells the machine to *FC*, an unrelated party, on December 31, 2020.

(*2*) Because *FB* placed in service the machine on November 1, 2020, and disposed of it on December 31, 2020, *FB's* reacquisition of the machine on November 1, 2020, does not qualify for the additional first year depreciation deduction pursuant to paragraph (g)(1)(i) of this section.

(*3*) *FC's* acquisition of the machine on December 31, 2020, satisfies the used property acquisition requirement of paragraph (b)(3)(iii)(A)(*2*) of this section. Accordingly, assuming all other requirements of this section are satisfied, *FC's* purchase price of the machine qualifies for the additional first year depreciation deduction under this section.

(HH) *Example 34.* (*1*) In August 2017, *FD*, a calendar-year taxpayer, entered into a written binding contract with *X* for *X* to manufacture a machine for *FD* for use in its trade or business. Before September 28, 2017, *FD* incurred more than 10 percent of the total cost of the machine. On February 8, 2020, *X* delivered the machine to *FD* and *FD* placed in service the machine. The machine is property described in section 168(k)(2)(B) as in effect on the day before the date of the enactment of the Act. *FD's* entire unadjusted depreciable basis of the machine is attributable to the machine's manufacture before January 1, 2020. *FD* uses the safe harbor test in §1.168(k)-1(b)(4)(iii)(B)(*2*) to determine when manufacturing of the machine began. On March 26, 2020, *FD* sells the machine to *FE* for use in *FE's* trade or business. *FE* is a calendar-year taxpayer and is not related to *FD*. On November 7, 2020, *FD* buys the machine from *FE* and places in service the machine. *FD* uses the machine in its trade or business for the remainder of 2020.

(*2*) Because *FD* incurred more than 10 percent of the cost of the machine before September 28, 2017, and *FD* uses the safe harbor test in §1.168(k)-1(b)(4)(iii)(B)(*2*) to determine when the manufacturing of the machine began, *FD* acquired the machine before September 28, 2017. If *FD* had not disposed of the machine on March 26, 2020, the cost of the machine would have qualified for the 30-percent additional first year depreciation deduction pursuant to section 168(k)(8), assuming all requirements are met under section 168(k)(2) as in effect on the day before the date of the enactment of the Act. However, because *FD* placed in service the machine on February 8, 2020, and disposed of it on March 26, 2020, FD's acquisition of the machine on February 8, 2020, does not qualify for the additional first year depreciation deduction pursuant to §1.168(k)-1(f)(1)(i).

(3) Because *FE* placed in service the machine on March 26, 2020, and disposed of it on November 7, 2020, *FE's* acquisition of the machine on March 26, 2020, does not qualify for the additional first year depreciation deduction pursuant to paragraph (g)(1)(i) of this section.

(4) During 2020, *FD* sold the machine to *FE* within 90 calendar days of placing the machine in service originally on February 8, 2020. After *FD* reacquired the machine on November 7, 2020, *FD* did not dispose of the machine during the remainder of 2020. *FD* originally acquired this machine before September 28, 2017. As a result, paragraph (b)(3)(iii)(B)(*4*) of this section does not apply.

Pursuant to paragraph (b)(3)(iii)(B)(*1*) of this section, the lookback period is 2015 through 2019 and January 1, 2020, through November 6, 2020, to determine if *FD* had a depreciable interest in the machine when *FD* reacquired it on November 7, 2020. As a result, *FD's* depreciable interest in the machine during the period February 8, 2020, to March 26, 2020, is taken into account for determining whether the machine was used by *FD* or a predecessor at any time prior to its reacquisition by *FD* on November 7, 2020. Accordingly, the reacquisition of the machine by *FD* on November 7, 2020, does not qualify for the additional first year depreciation deduction.

(II) *Example 35.* (*1*) In a series of related transactions, a father sells a machine to an unrelated individual on December 15, 2019, who sells the machine to the father's daughter on January 2, 2020, for use in the daughter's trade or business. Pursuant to paragraph (b)(3)(iii)(C)(*1*) of this section, a transferee tests its relationship with the transferor from which the transferee directly acquires the depreciable property, and with the original transferor of the depreciable property in the series. The relationship is tested when the transferee acquires, and immediately before the first transfer of, the depreciable property in the series. As a result, the following relationships are tested under section 179(d)(2)(A): the unrelated individual tests its relationship to the father as of December 15, 2019; and the daughter tests her relationship to the unrelated individual as of January 2, 2020, and December 15, 2019, and to the father as of January 2, 2020, and December 15, 2019.

(*2*) Because the individual is not related to the father within the meaning of section 179(d)(2)(A) and § 1.179-4(c)(1)(ii) as of December 15, 2019, the individual's acquisition of the machine satisfies the used property acquisition requirement of paragraph (b)(3)(iii)(A)(*2*) of this section. Accordingly, assuming the unrelated individual placed the machine in service for use in its trade or business in 2019 and all other requirements of this section are satisfied, the unrelated individual's purchase price of the machine qualifies for the additional first year depreciation deduction under this section.

(*3*) The individual and the daughter are not related parties within the meaning of section 179(d)(2)(A) and § 1.179-4(c)(1)(ii) as of January 2, 2020, or December 15, 2019. However, the father and his daughter are related parties within the meaning of section 179(d)(2)(A) and § 1.179-4(c)(1)(ii) as of January 2, 2020, or December 15, 2019. Accordingly, the daughter's acquisition of the machine does not satisfy the used property acquisition requirements of paragraph (b)(3)(iii) of this section and is not eligible for the additional first year depreciation deduction.

(JJ) *Example 36.* (*1*) The facts are the same as in *Example 35* of paragraph (b)(3)(vii)(II)(*1*) of this section, except that instead of selling to an unrelated individual, the father sells the machine to his son on December 15, 2019, who sells the machine to his sister (the father's daughter) on January 2, 2020. Pursuant to paragraph (b)(3)(iii)(C)(*1*) of this section, a transferee tests its relationship with the transferor from which the transferee directly acquires the depreciable property, and with the original transferor of the depreciable property in the series. The relationship is tested when the transferee acquires, and immediately before the first transfer of, the depreciable property in the series. As a result, the following relationships are tested under section 179(d)(2)(A): the son tests his relationship to the father as of December 15, 2019; and the daughter tests her relationship to her brother as of January 2, 2020, and December 15, 2019, and to the father as of January 2, 2020, and December 15, 2019.

(*2*) Because the father and his son are related parties within the meaning of section 179(d)(2)(A) and § 1.179-4(c)(1)(ii) as of December 15, 2019, the son's acquisition of the machine does not satisfy the used property acquisition requirements of paragraph (b)(3)(iii) of this section. Accordingly, the son's acquisition of the machine is not eligible for the additional first year depreciation deduction.

(*3*) The son and his sister are not related parties within the meaning of section 179(d)(2)(A) and § 1.179-4(c)(1)(ii) as of January 2, 2020, or December 15, 2019. However, the father and his daughter are related parties within the meaning of section 179(d)(2)(A) and § 1.179-4(c)(1)(ii) as of January 2, 2020, or December 15, 2019. Accordingly, the daughter's acquisition of the machine does not satisfy the used property acquisition requirements of paragraph (b)(3)(iii) of this section and is not eligible for the additional first year depreciation deduction.

(KK) *Example 37.* (*1*) In June 2018, *BA*, an individual, bought and placed in service a new machine from an unrelated party for use in its trade or business. In a series of related transactions, *BA* sells the machine to *BB* and *BB* places it in service on October 1, 2019, *BB* sells the machine to *BC* and *BC* places it in service on December 1, 2019, and *BC* sells the machine to *BD* and *BD* places it in service on January 2, 2020. *BA* and *BB* are related parties within the meaning of section 179(d)(2)(A) and § 1.179-4(c)(1)(ii). *BB* and *BC* are related parties within the meaning of section 179(d)(2)(B) and § 1.179-4(c)(1)(iii). *BC* and *BD* are not related parties within the meaning of section 179(d)(2)(A) and § 1.179-4(c)(1)(ii), or section 179(d)(2)(B) and § 1.179-4(c)(1)(iii). *BA* is not related to *BC* or to *BD* within the meaning of section 179(d)(2)(A) and § 1.179-4(c)(1)(ii). All parties are calendar-year taxpayers.

(*2*) *BA's* purchase of the machine in June 2018 satisfies the original use requirement of paragraph (b)(3)(ii) of this section and, assuming all other requirements of this section are met, *BA's* purchase price of the machine qualifies for the additional first year depreciation deduction under this section.

(*3*) Pursuant to paragraph (b)(3)(iii)(C)(*1*) of this section, a transferee tests its relationship with the transferor from which the transferee directly acquires the depreciable property, and with the original transferor of the depreciable property in the series. The relationship is tested when the transferee acquires, and immediately before the first transfer of, the depreciable property in the series. However, because *BB* placed in service and disposed of the machine in the same taxable year, *BB* is disregarded pursuant to paragraph (b)(3)(iii)(C)(2)(*i*) of this section. As a result, the following relationships are tested under section 179(d)(2)(A) and (B): *BC* tests its relationship to *BA* as of December 1, 2019, and October 1, 2019; and *BD* tests its relationship to *BC* as of January 2, 2020, and October 1, 2019, and to *BA* as of January 2, 2020, and October 1, 2020.

(*4*) Because *BA* is not related to *BC* within the meaning of section 179(d)(2)(A) and § 1.179-4(c)(1)(ii) as of December 1, 2019, or October 1, 2019, *BC's* acquisition of the machine satisfies the used property acquisition requirement of paragraph (b)(3)(iii)(A)(*2*) of this section. Accordingly, assuming all other requirements of this section are satisfied, *BC's* purchase price of the machine qualifies for the additional first year depreciation deduction under this section.

(*5*) Because *BC* is not related to *BD* and *BA* is not related to *BD* within the meaning of section 179(d)(2)(A) and § 1.179-4(c)(1)(ii), or section 179(d)(2)(B) and § 1.179-4(c)(1)(iii) as of January 2, 2020, or October 1, 2019, *BD's* acquisition of the machine satisfies the used property acquisition requirement of paragraph (b)(3)(iii)(A)(2) of this section. Accordingly, assuming all other requirements of this section are satisfied, *BD's* purchase price of the machine qualifies for the additional first year depreciation deduction under this section.

(LL) *Example 38.* (*1*) In June 2018, *CA*, an individual, bought and placed in service a new machine from an unrelated party for use in his trade or business. In a series of related transactions, *CA* sells the machine to *CB* and *CB* places it in service on September 1, 2019, *CB* transfers the machine to *CC* in a transaction described in paragraph (g)(1)(iii) of this section and *CC* places it in service on November 1, 2019, and *CC* sells the machine to *CD* and *CD* places it in service on January 2, 2020. *CA* and *CB* are not related parties within the meaning of section 179(d)(2)(A) and § 1.179-4(c)(1)(ii). *CB* and *CC* are related parties within the meaning of section 179(d)(2)(B) and § 1.179-4(c)(1)(iii). *CB* and *CD* are related parties within the meaning of section 179(d)(2)(A) and § 1.179-4(c)(1)(ii), or section 179(d)(2)(B) and § 1.179-4(c)(1)(iii). *CC* and *CD* are not related parties within the meaning of section 179(d)(2)(A) and § 1.179-4(c)(1)(ii), or section 179(d)(2)(B) and § 1.179-4(c)(1)(iii). *CA* is not related to *CC* or to *CD* within the meaning of section 179(d)(2)(A) and § 1.179-4(c)(1)(ii). All parties are calendar-year taxpayers.

( *2*) *CA's* purchase of the machine in June 2018 satisfies the original use requirement of paragraph (b)(3)(ii) of this section and, assuming all other requirements of this section are met, *CA's* purchase price of the machine qualifies for the additional first year depreciation deduction under this section.

( *3*) Pursuant to paragraph (b)(3)(iii)(C)( *1*) of this section, a transferee tests its relationship with the transferor from which the transferee directly acquires the depreciable property, and with the original transferor of the depreciable property in the series. The relationship is tested when the transferee acquires, and immediately before the first transfer of, the depreciable property in the series. However, because *CB* placed in service and transferred the machine in the same taxable year in a transaction described in paragraph (g)(1)(iii) of this section, the section 168(i)(7) transaction between *CB* and *CC* is disregarded pursuant to paragraph (b)(3)(iii)(C)(2)(iii) of this section. As a result, the following relationships are tested under section 179(d)(2)(A) and (B): *CB* tests its relationship to *CA* as of September 1, 2019; and *CD* tests its relationship to *CB, CC,* and *CA* as of January 2, 2020, and September 1, 2019.

( *4*) Because *CA* is not related to *CB* within the meaning of section 179(d)(2)(A) and § 1.179-4(c)(1)(ii) as of September 1, 2019, *CB's* acquisition of the machine satisfies the used property acquisition requirement of paragraph (b)(3)(iii)(A)( *2*) of this section. Accordingly, assuming all other requirements of this section are satisfied, *CB's* purchase price of the machine qualifies for the additional first year depreciation deduction under this section. Pursuant to paragraph (g)(1)(iii) of this section, *CB* is allocated 2/12 of its 100-percent additional first year depreciation deduction for the machine, and *CC* is allocated the remaining portion of *CB's* 100-percent additional first year depreciation deduction for the machine.

( *5*) *CC* is not related to *CD* and *CA* is not related to *CD* within the meaning of section 179(d)(2)(A) and § 1.179-4(c)(1)(ii), or section 179(d)(2)(B) and § 1.179-4(c)(1)(iii) as of January 2, 2020, or September 1, 2019. However, *CB* and *CD* are related parties within the meaning of section 179(d)(2)(A) and § 1.179-4(c)(1)(ii), or section 179(d)(2)(B) and § 1.179-4(c)(1)(iii) as of January 2, 2020, or September 1, 2019. Accordingly, *CD's* acquisition of the machine does not satisfy the used property acquisition requirements of paragraph (b)(3)(iii) of this section and is not eligible for the additional first year depreciation deduction.

(MM) *Example 39.* ( *1*) In a series of related transactions, on January 2, 2018, *DA*, a corporation, bought and placed in service a new machine from an unrelated party for use in its trade or business. As part of the same series, *DB* purchases 100 percent of the stock of *DA* on January 2, 2019, and such stock acquisition meets the requirements of section 1504(a)(2). *DB* and *DA* were not related prior to the acquisition within the meaning of section 179(d)(2)(A) and § 1.179-4(c)(1)(ii) or section 179(d)(2)(B) and § 1.179-4(c)(1)(iii). Immediately after acquiring the *DA* stock, and *DB* liquidates *DA* under section 331. In the liquidating distribution, *DB* receives the machine that was acquired by *DA* on January 2, 2018. As part of the same series, on March 1, 2020, *DB* sells the machine to *DC* and *DC* places it in service. Throughout the series, *DC* is not related to *DB* or *DA* within the meaning of section 179(d)(2)(A) and § 1.179-4(c)(1)(ii) or section 179(d)(2)(B) and § 1.179-4(c)(1)(iii).

( *2*) *DA's* purchase of the machine on January 2, 2018, satisfies the original use requirement of paragraph (b)(3)(ii) of this section and, assuming all other requirements of this section are met, *DA's* purchase price of the machine qualifies for the additional first year depreciation deduction under this section.

( *3*) Pursuant to paragraph (b)(3)(iii)(C)(1) of this section, a transferee tests its relationship with the transferor from which the transferee directly acquires the depreciable property, and with the original transferor of the depreciable property in the series. The relationship is tested when the transferee acquires, and immediately before the first transfer of, the depreciable property in the series. Although *DA* is no longer in existence as of the date *DC* acquires the machine, pursuant to paragraph (b)(3)(iii)(C)( *2*)( *vi*) of this section, *DA* is deemed to be in existence at the time of each transfer for purposes of testing relationships under paragraph (b)(3)(iii)(C)( *1*). As a result, the following relationships are tested under section 179(d)(2)(A) and (B): *DB* tests its relationship to *DA* as of January 2, 2019, and January 2, 2018; and *DC* tests its relationship to *DB* and *DA* as of March 1, 2020, and January 2, 2018.

( *4*) Because *DB* acquired the machine in a series of related transactions in which *DB* acquired stock, meeting the requirements of section 1504(a)(2), of *DA* followed by a liquidation of *DA* under section 331, the relationship of *DB* and *DA* created thereof is disregarded for purposes of testing the relationship pursuant to paragraph (b)(3)(iii)(C)( *2*)( *v*) of this section. Therefore, *DA* is not related to *DB* within the meaning of section 179(d)(2)(A) and §1.179-4(c)(1)(ii) or section 179(d)(2)(B) and §1.179-4(c)(1)(iii) as of January 2, 2019, or January 2, 2018, and *DB's* acquisition of the machine satisfies the used property acquisition requirement of paragraph (b)(3)(iii)(A)( *2*) of this section. Accordingly, assuming all other requirements of this section are satisfied, *DB's* depreciable basis of the machine as a result of the liquidation of *DA* qualifies for the additional first year depreciation deduction under this section.

( *5*) Because *DC* is not related to *DB* or *DA* within the meaning of section 179(d)(2)(A) and §1.179-4(c)(1)(ii) or section 179(d)(2)(B) and §1.179-4(c)(1)(iii) as of March 1, 2020, or January 2, 2018, *DC's* acquisition of the machine satisfies the used property acquisition requirements of paragraph (b)(3)(iii)(A)( *2*) of this section. Accordingly, assuming all other requirements of this section are satisfied, *DC's* purchase price of the machine qualifies for the additional first year depreciation deduction.

(NN) *Example 40*. ( *1*) Pursuant to a series of related transactions, on January 2, 2018, *EA* bought and placed in service a new machine from an unrelated party for use in its trade or business. As part of the same series, *EA* sells the machine to *EB* and *EB* places it in service on January 2, 2019. As part of the same series, *EB* sells the machine to *EC* and *EC* places it in service on January 2, 2020. Throughout the series, *EA* is not related to *EB* or *EC* within the meaning of section 179(d)(2)(B) and §1.179-4(c)(1)(iii). *EB* and *EC* were related parties within the meaning of section 179(d)(2)(B) and §1.179-4(c)(1)(iii) until July 1, 2019, at which time, they ceased to be related.

( *2*) *EA's* purchase of the machine on January 2, 2018, satisfies the original use requirement of paragraph (b)(3)(ii) of this section and, assuming all other requirements of this section are met, *EA's* purchase price of the machines qualifies for the additional first year depreciation deduction under this section.

( *3*) Pursuant to paragraph (b)(3)(iii)(C)(1) of this section, a transferee tests its relationship with the transferor from which the transferee directly acquires the depreciable property, and with the original transferor of the depreciable property in the series. The relationship is tested when the transferee acquires, and immediately before the first transfer of, the depreciable property in the series. As a result, the following relationships are tested under section 179(d)(2)(A) and (B): *EB* tests its relationship to *EA* as of January 2, 2019, and January 2, 2018; and *EC* tests its relationship to *EA* and *EB* as of January 2, 2020, and January 2, 2018.

( *4*) Because *EA* is not related to *EB* within the meaning of section 179(d)(2)(B) and §1.179-4(c)(1)(iii) as of January 2, 2019, or January 2, 2018, *EB's* acquisition of the machine satisfies the used property acquisition requirement of paragraph (b)(3)(iii)(A)( *2*) of this section. Accordingly, assuming all other requirements of this section are satisfied, *EB's* purchase price of the machine qualifies for the additional first year depreciation deduction under this section.

( *5*) *EC* and *EA* are not related parties within the meaning of section 179(d)(2)(B) and §1.179-4(c)(1)(iii) as of January 2, 2020, or January 2, 2018. Within the meaning of section 179(d)(2)(B) and §1.179-4(c)(1)(iii), *EC* is not related to *EB* as of January 2, 2020; however, *EC* is related to *EB* as of January 2, 2018. Accordingly, *EC's* acquisition of the machine does not satisfy the used property acquisition requirement of paragraph (b)(3)(iii) of this section and is not eligible for the additional first year depreciation deduction.

(OO) *Example 41.* ( *1*) The facts are the same as in *Example 40* of paragraph (b)(3)(vii)(NN)(1) of this section, except that instead of selling to *EC*, *EB* sells the machine to *EE*, and *EE* places in service on January 2, 2020, and *EE* sells the machine to *EC* and *EC* places in service on January 2, 2021. *EE* was not in existence until July 2019 and is not related to *EA* or *EB*.

( *2*) *EA's* purchase of the machine on January 2, 2018, satisfies the original use requirement of paragraph (b)(3)(ii) of this section and, assuming all other requirements of this section are met, *EA's* purchase price of the machine qualifies for the additional first year depreciation deduction under this section.

( *3*) Pursuant to paragraph (b)(3)(iii)(C)( *1*) of this section, a transferee tests its relationship with the transferor from which the transferee directly acquires the depreciable property, and with the original transferor of the depreciable property in the series. The relationship is tested when the transferee acquires, and immediately before the first transfer of, the depreciable property in the series. However, because *EE* was not in existence immediately prior to the first transfer of the depreciable property in the series, *EC* tests its relationship with *EB* and *EA* pursuant to paragraph (b)(3)(iii)(C)(2)(vii) of this section. As a result, the following relationships are tested under section 179(d)(2)(A) and (B): *EB* tests its relationship to *EA* as of January 2, 2019, and January 2, 2018; *EE* tests its relationship to *EA* and *EB* as of January 2, 2020, and January 2, 2018; and *EC* tests its relationship to *EA* and *EB* as of January 2, 2021, and January 2, 2018.

( *4*) Because *EA* is not related to *EB* within the meaning of section 179(d)(2)(B) and §1.179-4(c)(1)(iii) as of January 2, 2019, or January 2, 2018, *EB's* acquisition of the machine satisfies the used property acquisition requirement of paragraph (b)(3)(iii)(A)( *2*) of this section. Accordingly, assuming all other requirements of this section are satisfied, *EB's* purchase price of the machine qualifies for the additional first year depreciation deduction under this section.

( *5*) Because *EE* is not related to *EA* or *EB* within the meaning of section 179(d)(2)(B) and §1.179-4(c)(1)(iii) as of January 2, 2020, or January 2, 2018, *EE's* acquisition of the machine satisfies the used property acquisition requirement of paragraph (b)(3)(iii)(A)(2) of this section. Accordingly, assuming all other requirements of this section are satisfied, *EE's* purchase price of the machine qualifies for the additional first year depreciation deduction under this section.

( *6*) Within the meaning of section 179(d)(2)(B) and §1.179-4(c)(1)(iii), *EC* is not related to *EA* as of January 2, 2021, or January 2, 2018; however, *EC* is related to *EB* as of January 2, 2018. Accordingly, *EC's* acquisition of the machine does not satisfy the used property acquisition requirement of paragraph (b)(3)(iii) of this section and is not eligible for the additional first year depreciation deduction.

(4) *Placed-in-service date* .—(i) *In general* .—Depreciable property will meet the requirements of this paragraph (b)(4) if the property is placed in service

by the taxpayer for use in its trade or business or for production of income after September 27, 2017; and, except as provided in paragraphs (b)(2)(i)(A) and (D) of this section, before January 1, 2027, or, in the case of property described in section 168(k)(2)(B) or (C), before January 1, 2028.

(ii) *Specified plant* .—If the taxpayer has properly made an election to apply section 168(k)(5) for a specified plant, the requirements of this paragraph (b)(4) are satisfied only if the specified plant is planted before January 1, 2027, or is grafted before January 1, 2027, to a plant that has already been planted, by the taxpayer in the ordinary course of the taxpayer's farming business, as defined in section 263A(e)(4).

(iii) *Qualified film, television, or live theatrical production* .—(A) *Qualified film or television production* .—For purposes of this paragraph (b)(4), a qualified film or television production is treated as placed in service at the time of initial release or broadcast as defined under § 1.181-1(a)(7). The taxpayer that places in service a qualified film or television production must be the owner, as defined in § 1.181-1(a)(2), of the qualified film or television production.

(B) *Qualified live theatrical production* .—For purposes of this paragraph (b)(4), a qualified live theatrical production is treated as placed in service at the time of the initial live staged performance. The taxpayer that places in service a qualified live theatrical production must be the owner, as defined in paragraph (b)(2)(i)(F) of this section and in § 1.181-1(a)(2), of the qualified live theatrical production.

(iv) *Syndication transaction* .—If new property is acquired and placed in service by a lessor, or if used property is acquired and placed in service by a lessor and the lessor and any predecessor did not previously have a depreciable interest in the used property, and the property is sold by the lessor or any subsequent purchaser within three months after the date the property was originally placed in service by the lessor (or, in the case of multiple units of property subject to the same lease, within three months after the date the final unit is placed in service, so long as the period between the time the first unit is placed in service and the time the last unit is placed in service does not exceed 12 months), and the user of the property after the last sale during this three-month period remains the same as when the property was originally placed in service by the lessor, the property is treated as originally placed in service by the purchaser of the property in the last sale during the three-month period but not earlier than the date of the last sale for purposes of sections 167 and 168, and §§ 1.46-3(d) and 1.167(a)-11(e)(1).

(v) *Technical termination of a partnership* .—For purposes of this paragraph (b)(4), in the case of a technical termination of a partnership under section 708(b)(1)(B) occurring in a taxable year beginning before January 1, 2018, qualified property placed in service by the terminated partnership during the taxable year of termination is treated as originally placed in service by the new partnership on the date the qualified property is contributed by the terminated partnership to the new partnership.

(vi) *Section 168(i)(7) transactions* .—For purposes of this paragraph (b)(4), if qualified property is transferred in a transaction described in section 168(i)(7) in the same taxable year that the qualified property is placed in service by the transferor, the transferred property is treated as originally placed in service on the date the transferor placed in service the qualified property. In the case of multiple transfers of qualified property in multiple transactions described in section 168(i)(7) in the same taxable year, the placed-in-service date of the transferred property is deemed to be the date on which the first transferor placed in service the qualified property.

(5) *Acquisition of property* .—(i) *In general* .—This paragraph (b)(5) provides rules for the acquisition requirements in section 13201(h) of the Act. These rules apply to all property, including self-constructed property or property described in section 168(k)(2)(B) or (C).

(ii) *Acquisition date* .—(A) *In general* .—Except as provided in paragraph (b)(5)(vi) of this section, depreciable property will meet the requirements of this paragraph (b)(5) if the property is acquired by the taxpayer after September 27, 2017, or is acquired by the taxpayer pursuant to a written binding contract entered into by the taxpayer after September 27, 2017. Property that is manufactured, constructed, or produced for the taxpayer by another person under a written binding contract that is entered into prior to the manufacture, construction, or production of the property for use by the taxpayer in its trade or business or for its production of income is not acquired pursuant to a written binding contract but is considered to be self-constructed property under this paragraph (b)(5). For determination of acquisition date, see paragraph (b)(5)(ii)(B) of this section for property acquired pursuant to a written binding contract, paragraph (b)(5)(iv) of this section for self-constructed property, and paragraph (b)(5)(v) of this section for property not acquired pursuant to a written binding contract.

(B) *Determination of acquisition date for property acquired pursuant to a written binding contract* .—Except as provided in paragraphs (b)(5)(vi) and (vii) of this section, the acquisition date of property that the taxpayer acquired pursuant to a written binding contract is the later of—

*(1)* The date on which the contract was entered into;

*(2)* The date on which the contract is enforceable under State law;

*(3)* If the contract has one or more cancellation periods, the date on which all cancellation periods end. For purposes of this paragraph (b)(5)(ii)(B)( *3*), a cancellation period is the number of days stated in the contract for any party to cancel the contract without penalty; or

*(4)* If the contract has one or more contingency clauses, the date on which all conditions subject to such clauses are satisfied. For purposes of this paragraph (b)(5)(ii)(B)( *4*), a contingency clause is one that provides for a condition (or conditions) or action (or actions) that is within the control of any party or a predecessor.

(iii) *Definition of binding contract* .—(A) *In general* .—Except as provided in paragraph (b)(5)(iii)(G) of this section, a contract is binding only if it is enforceable under State law against the taxpayer or a predecessor, and does not limit damages to a specified amount (for example, by use of a liquidated damages provision). For this purpose, any contractual provision that limits damages to an amount equal to at least 5 percent of the total contract price will not be treated as limiting damages to a specified amount. If a contract has multiple provisions that limit damages, only the provision with the highest damages is taken into account in determining whether the contract limits damages. Also, in determining whether a contract limits damages, the fact that there may be little or no damages because the contract price does not significantly differ from fair market value will not be taken into account. For example, if a taxpayer entered into an irrevocable written contract to purchase an asset for $100 and the contract did not contain a provision for liquidated damages, the contract is considered binding notwithstanding the fact that the asset had a fair market value of $99 and under local law the seller would only recover the difference in the event the purchaser failed to perform. If the contract provided for a full refund of the purchase price in lieu of any damages allowable by law in the event of breach or cancellation, the contract is not considered binding.

(B) *Conditions* .—Except as provided in paragraph (b)(5)(iii)(G) of this section, a contract is binding even if subject to a condition, as long as the condition is not within the control of either party or a predecessor. A contract will continue to be binding if the parties make insubstantial changes in its terms and conditions or if any term is to be determined by a standard beyond the control of either party. A contract that imposes significant obligations on the taxpayer or a predecessor will be treated as binding notwithstanding the fact that certain terms remain to be negotiated by the parties to the contract.

(C) *Options* .—An option to either acquire or sell property is not a binding contract.

(D) *Letter of intent* .—A letter of intent for an acquisition is not a binding contract.

(E) *Supply agreements* .—A binding contract does not include a supply or similar agreement if the amount and design specifications of the property to be purchased have not been specified. The contract will not be a binding contract for the property to be purchased until both the amount and the design specifications are specified. For example, if the provisions of a supply or similar agreement state the design specifications of the property to be purchased, a purchase order under the agreement for a specific number of assets is treated as a binding contract.

(F) *Components* .—A binding contract to acquire one or more components of a larger property will not be treated as a binding contract to acquire the larger property. If a binding contract to acquire the component does not satisfy the requirements of this paragraph (b)(5), the component does not qualify for the additional first year depreciation deduction under this section.

(G) *Acquisition of a trade or business or an entity* .—A contract to acquire all or substantially all of the assets of a trade or business or to acquire an entity (for example, a corporation, a partnership, or a limited liability company) is binding if it is enforceable under State law against the parties to the contract. The presence of a condition outside the control of the parties, including, for example, regulatory agency approval, will not prevent the contract from being a binding contract. Further, the fact that insubstantial terms remain to be negotiated by the parties to the contract, or that customary conditions remain to be satisfied, does not prevent the contract from being a binding contract. This paragraph (b)(5)(iii)(G) also applies to a contract for the sale of the stock of a corporation that is treated as an asset sale as a result of an election under section 338 or under section 336(e) made for a disposition described in § 1.336-2(b)(1).

(iv) *Self-constructed property* .—(A) *In general* .—If a taxpayer manufactures, constructs, or produces property for use by the taxpayer in its trade or business or for its production of income, the acquisition rules in paragraph (b)(5)(ii) of this section are treated as met for the property if the taxpayer begins manufacturing, constructing, or producing the property after September 27, 2017. Property that is manufactured, constructed, or produced for the taxpayer by another person under a written binding contract, as defined in paragraph (b)(5)(iii) of this section, that is entered into prior to the manufacture, construction, or production of the property for use by the taxpayer in its trade or business or for its production of income is considered to be manufactured, constructed, or produced by the taxpayer. If a taxpayer enters into a written binding contract, as defined in paragraph (b)(5)(iii) of this section, before September 28, 2017, with another person to manufacture, construct, or produce property and the manufacture, construction, or production of this property begins after September 27, 2017, the acquisition rules in paragraph (b)(5)(ii) of this section are met.

(B) *When does manufacture, construction, or production begin .—(1) In general .—* For purposes of paragraph (b)(5)(iv)(A) of this section, manufacture, construction, or production of property begins when physical work of a significant nature begins. Physical work does not include preliminary activities such as planning or designing, securing financing, exploring, or researching. The determination of when physical work of a significant nature begins depends on the facts and circumstances. For example, if a retail motor fuels outlet is to be constructed on-site, construction begins when physical work of a significant nature commences at the site; that is, when work begins on the excavation for footings, pouring the pads for the outlet, or the driving of foundation pilings into the ground. Preliminary work, such as clearing a site, test drilling to determine soil condition, or excavation to change the contour of the land (as distinguished from excavation for footings) does not constitute the beginning of construction. However, if a retail motor fuels outlet is to be assembled on-site from modular units manufactured off-site and delivered to the site where the outlet will be used, manufacturing begins when physical work of a significant nature commences at the off-site location.

*(2) Safe harbor .*—For purposes of paragraph (b)(5)(iv)(B)( *1*) of this section, a taxpayer may choose to determine when physical work of a significant nature begins in accordance with this paragraph (b)(5)(iv)(B)( *2*). Physical work of a significant nature will be considered to begin at the time the taxpayer incurs (in the case of an accrual basis taxpayer) or pays (in the case of a cash basis taxpayer) more than 10 percent of the total cost of the property, excluding the cost of any land and preliminary activities such as planning or designing, securing financing, exploring, or researching. When property is manufactured, constructed, or produced for the taxpayer by another person, this safe harbor test must be satisfied by the taxpayer. For example, if a retail motor fuels outlet or other facility is to be constructed for an accrual basis taxpayer by another person for the total cost of $200,000, excluding the cost of any land and preliminary activities such as planning or designing, securing financing, exploring, or researching, construction is deemed to begin for purposes of this paragraph (b)(5)(iv)(B)( *2*) when the taxpayer has incurred more than 10 percent (more than $20,000) of the total cost of the property. A taxpayer chooses to apply this paragraph (b)(5)(iv)(B)( *2*) by filing a Federal income tax return for the placed-in-service year of the property that determines when physical work of a significant nature begins consistent with this paragraph (b)(5)(iv)(B)( *2*).

(C) *Components of self-constructed property .—(1) Acquired components .*—If a binding contract, as defined in paragraph (b)(5)(iii) of this section, to acquire a component does not satisfy the requirements of paragraph (b)(5)(ii) of this section, the component does not qualify for the additional first year depreciation deduction under this section. A binding contract described in the preceding sentence to acquire one or more components of a larger self-constructed property will not preclude the larger self-constructed property from satisfying the acquisition rules in paragraph (b)(5)(iv)(A) of this section. Accordingly, the unadjusted depreciable basis of the larger self-constructed property that is eligible for the additional first year depreciation deduction under this section, assuming all other requirements are met, must not include the unadjusted depreciable basis of any component that does not satisfy the requirements of paragraph (b)(5)(ii) of this section. If the manufacture, construction, or production of the larger self-constructed property begins before September 28, 2017, the larger self-constructed property and any acquired components related to the larger self-constructed property do not qualify for the additional first year depreciation deduction under this section. If a binding contract to acquire the component is entered into after

September 27, 2017, but the manufacture, construction, or production of the larger self-constructed property does not begin before January 1, 2027, the component qualifies for the additional first year depreciation deduction under this section, assuming all other requirements are met, but the larger self-constructed property does not, except as provided in paragraph (c) of this section.

(2) *Self-constructed components* .—If the manufacture, construction, or production of a component does not satisfy the requirements of this paragraph (b) (5) (iv), the component does not qualify for the additional first year depreciation deduction under this section. However, if the manufacture, construction, or production of a component does not satisfy the requirements of this paragraph (b) (5) (iv), but the manufacture, construction, or production of the larger self-constructed property satisfies the requirements of this paragraph (b) (5) (iv), the larger self-constructed property qualifies for the additional first year depreciation deduction under this section, assuming all other requirements are met, even though the component does not qualify for the additional first year depreciation deduction under this section. Accordingly, the unadjusted depreciable basis of the larger self-constructed property that is eligible for the additional first year depreciation deduction under this section, assuming all other requirements are met, must not include the unadjusted depreciable basis of any component that does not qualify for the additional first year depreciation deduction under this section. If the manufacture, construction, or production of the larger self-constructed property began before September 28, 2017, the larger self-constructed property and any self-constructed components related to the larger self-constructed property do not qualify for the additional first year depreciation deduction under this section. If the manufacture, construction, or production of a component begins after September 27, 2017, but the manufacture, construction, or production of the larger self-constructed property does not begin before January 1, 2027, the component qualifies for the additional first year depreciation deduction under this section, assuming all other requirements are met, but the larger self-constructed property does not, except as provided in paragraph (c) of this section.

(v) *Determination of acquisition date for property not acquired pursuant to a written binding contract* .—Except as provided in paragraphs (b) (5) (iv), (vi), and (vii) of this section, the acquisition date of property that the taxpayer acquires pursuant to a contract that does not meet the definition of a written binding contract in paragraph (b) (5) (iii) of this section, is the date on which the taxpayer paid, in the case of a cash basis taxpayer, or incurred, in the case of an accrual basis taxpayer, more than 10 percent of the total cost of the property, excluding the cost of any land and preliminary activities such as planning and designing, securing financing, exploring, or researching. The preceding sentence also applies to property that is manufactured, constructed, or produced for the taxpayer by another person under a written contract that does not meet the definition of a binding contract in paragraph (b) (5) (iii) of this section, and that is entered into prior to the manufacture, construction, or production of the property for use by the taxpayer in its trade or business or for its production of income. This paragraph (b) (5) (v) does not apply to an acquisition described in paragraph (b) (5) (iii) (G) of this section.

(vi) *Qualified film, television, or live theatrical production* .—(A) *Qualified film or television production* .—For purposes of section 13201 (h) (1) (A) of the Act, a qualified film or television production is treated as acquired on the date principal photography commences.

(B) *Qualified live theatrical production* .—For purposes of section 13201 (h) (1) (A) of the Act, a qualified live theatrical production is treated as acquired on the date when all of the necessary elements for producing the live theatrical production are secured. These elements may include a script, financing, actors, set, scenic and costume designs, advertising agents, music, and lighting.

(vii) *Specified plant*.—If the taxpayer has properly made an election to apply section 168(k)(5) for a specified plant, the requirements of this paragraph (b)(5) are satisfied if the specified plant is planted after September 27, 2017, or is grafted after September 27, 2017, to a plant that has already been planted, by the taxpayer in the ordinary course of the taxpayer's farming business, as defined in section 263A(e)(4).

(viii) *Examples*.—The application of this paragraph (b)(5) is illustrated by the following examples. Unless the facts specifically indicate otherwise, assume that the parties are not related within the meaning of section 179(d)(2)(A) or (B) and § 1.179-4(c), paragraph (c) of this section does not apply, and the parties do not have predecessors:

(A) *Example 1.* On September 1, 2017, *BB*, a corporation, entered into a written agreement with *CC*, a manufacturer, to purchase 20 new lamps for $100 each within the next two years. Although the agreement specifies the number of lamps to be purchased, the agreement does not specify the design of the lamps to be purchased. Accordingly, the agreement is not a binding contract pursuant to paragraph (b)(5)(iii)(E) of this section.

(B) *Example 2.* The facts are the same as in *Example 1* of paragraph (b)(5)(viii)(A) of this section. On December 1, 2017, *BB* placed a purchase order with *CC* to purchase 20 new model XPC5 lamps for $100 each for a total amount of $2,000. Because the agreement specifies the number of lamps to be purchased and the purchase order specifies the design of the lamps to be purchased, the purchase order placed by *BB* with *CC* on December 1, 2017, is a binding contract pursuant to paragraph (b)(5)(iii)(E) of this section. Accordingly, assuming all other requirements are met, the cost of the 20 lamps qualifies for the 100-percent additional first year depreciation deduction.

(C) *Example 3.* The facts are the same as in *Example 1* of paragraph (b)(5)(viii)(A) of this section, except that the written agreement between *BB* and *CC* is to purchase 100 model XPC5 lamps for $100 each within the next two years. Because this agreement specifies the amount and design of the lamps to be purchased, the agreement is a binding contract pursuant to paragraph (b)(5)(iii)(E) of this section. However, because the agreement was entered into before September 28, 2017, no lamp acquired by *BB* under this contract qualifies for the 100-percent additional first year depreciation deduction.

(D) *Example 4.* On September 1, 2017, *DD* began constructing a retail motor fuels outlet for its own use. On November 1, 2018, *DD* ceases construction of the retail motor fuels outlet prior to its completion. Between September 1, 2017, and November 1, 2018, *DD* incurred $3,000,000 of expenditures for the construction of the retail motor fuels outlet. On May 1, 2019, *DD* resumed construction of the retail motor fuels outlet and completed its construction on August 31, 2019. Between May 1, 2019, and August 31, 2019, *DD* incurred another $1,600,000 of expenditures to complete the construction of the retail motor fuels outlet and, on September 1, 2019, *DD* placed the retail motor fuels outlet in service. None of *DD*'s total expenditures of $4,600,000 qualify for the 100-percent additional first year depreciation deduction because, pursuant to paragraph (b)(5)(iv)(A) of this section, *DD* began constructing the retail motor fuels outlet before September 28, 2017.

(E) *Example 5.* The facts are the same as in *Example 4* of paragraph (b)(5)(viii)(D) of this section except that *DD* began constructing the retail motor fuels outlet for its own use on October 1, 2017, and *DD* incurred the $3,000,000 between October 1, 2017, and November 1, 2018. *DD*'s total expenditures of $4,600,000 qualify for the 100-percent additional first year depreciation deduction because, pursuant to paragraph (b)(5)(iv)(A) of this section, *DD* began constructing the retail motor fuels outlet after September 27, 2017, and *DD* placed the retail motor fuels outlet in service on September 1, 2019. Accordingly, assuming all other requirements are met, the additional first year depreciation deduction for the retail motor fuels outlet will be $4,600,000, computed as $4,600,000 multiplied by 100 percent.

(F) *Example 6.* On August 15, 2017, *EE*, an accrual basis taxpayer, entered into a written binding contract with *FF* to manufacture an aircraft described in section 168(k)(2)(C) for use in *EE*'s trade or business. *FF* begins to manufacture the aircraft on October 1, 2017. The completed aircraft is delivered to *EE* on February 15, 2018, at which time *EE* incurred the total cost of the aircraft. *EE* places the aircraft in service on March 1, 2018. Pursuant to paragraphs (b)(5)(ii)(A) and (b)(5)(iv)(A) of this section, the aircraft is considered to be manufactured by *EE*. Because *EE* began manufacturing the aircraft after September 27, 2017, the aircraft qualifies for the 100-percent additional first year depreciation deduction, assuming all other requirements are met.

(G) *Example 7.* On June 1, 2017, *HH* entered into a written binding contract with GG to acquire a new component part of property that is being constructed by *HH* for its own use in its trade or business. *HH* commenced construction of the property in November 2017, and placed the property in service in November 2018. Because *HH* entered into a written binding contract to acquire a component part prior to September 28, 2017, pursuant to paragraphs (b)(5)(ii) and (b)(5)(iv)(C)( *1*) of this section, the component part does not qualify for the 100-percent additional first year depreciation deduction. However, pursuant to paragraphs (b)(5)(iv)(A) and (b)(5)(iv)(C)( *1*) of this section, the property constructed by *HH* will qualify for the 100-percent additional first year depreciation deduction, because construction of the property began after September 27, 2017, assuming all other requirements are met. Accordingly, the unadjusted depreciable basis of the property that is eligible for the 100-percent additional first year depreciation deduction must not include the unadjusted depreciable basis of the component part.

(H) *Example 8.* The facts are the same as in *Example 7* of paragraph (b)(5)(viii)(G) of this section except that *HH* entered into the written binding contract with GG to acquire the new component part on September 30, 2017, and *HH* commenced construction of the property on August 1, 2017. Pursuant to paragraphs (b)(5)(iv)(A) and (C) of this section, neither the property constructed by *HH* nor the component part will qualify for the 100-percent additional first year depreciation deduction, because *HH* began construction of the property prior to September 28, 2017.

(I) *Example 9.* On September 1, 2017, II acquired and placed in service equipment. On January 15, 2018, II sells the equipment to *JJ* and leases the property back from *JJ* in a sale-leaseback transaction. Pursuant to paragraph (b)(5)(ii) of this section, II's cost of the equipment does not qualify for the 100-percent additional first year depreciation deduction because II acquired the equipment prior to September 28, 2017. However, *JJ* acquired used equipment from an unrelated party after September 27, 2017, and, assuming all other requirements are met, *JJ*'s cost of the used equipment qualifies for the 100-percent additional first year depreciation deduction for *JJ*.

(J) *Example 10.* On July 1, 2017, *KK* began constructing property for its own use in its trade or business. *KK* placed this property in service on September 15, 2017. On January 15, 2018, *KK* sells the property to *LL* and leases the property back from *LL* in a sale-leaseback transaction. Pursuant to paragraph (b)(5)(iv) of this section, *KK*'s cost of the property does not qualify for the 100-percent additional first year depreciation deduction because *KK* began construction of the property prior to September 28, 2017. However, *LL* acquired used property from an unrelated party after September 27, 2017, and, assuming all other requirements are met, *LL*'s cost of the used property qualifies for the 100-percent additional first year depreciation deduction for *LL*.

(K) *Example 11. MM*, a calendar year taxpayer, is engaged in a trade or business described in section 163(j)(7)(A)(iv). In December 2018, *MM* began constructing a new electric generation power plant for its own use. *MM* placed in service this new power plant, including all component parts, in 2020. Even though *MM* began constructing the power plant after September 27, 2017, none of *MM*'s total expenditures of the power plant qualify for the additional first year depreciation deduction under this section because, pursuant to paragraph (b)(2)(ii)(F) of this section, the power plant is property that is primarily used in a trade or business described in section 163(j)(7)(A)(iv) and the power plant was placed in service in *MM*'s taxable year beginning after 2017.

(c) *Election for components of larger self-constructed property for which the manufacture, construction, or production begins before September 28, 2017* .—(1) *In general* .—A taxpayer may elect to treat any acquired or self-constructed component, as described in paragraph (c)(3) of this section, of the larger self-constructed property, as described in paragraph (c)(2) of this section, as being eligible for the additional first year depreciation deduction under this section, assuming all requirements of section 168(k) and this section are met. The taxpayer may make this election for one or more such components.

(2) *Eligible larger self-constructed property* .—(i) *In general* .—Solely for purposes of this paragraph (c), a larger self-constructed property is property that is manufactured, constructed, or produced by the taxpayer for its own use in its trade or business or production of income. Solely for purposes of this paragraph (c), property that is manufactured, constructed, or produced for the taxpayer by another person under a written binding contract, as defined in paragraph (b)(5)(iii) of this section, or under a written contract that does not meet the definition of a binding contract in paragraph (b)(5)(iii) of this section, that is entered into prior to the manufacture, construction, or production of the property for use by the taxpayer in its trade or business or production of income is considered to be manufactured, constructed, or produced by the taxpayer. Except as provided in paragraph (c)(2)(iv) of this section, such larger self-constructed property must be property—

(A) That is described in paragraph (b)(2)(i)(A), (B), (C), or (D) of this section. Solely for purposes of the preceding sentence, the requirement that property has to be acquired after September 27, 2017, is disregarded;

(B) That meets the requirements under paragraph (b) of this section, determined without regard to the acquisition date requirement in paragraph (b)(5) of this section; and

(C) For which the taxpayer begins the manufacture, construction, or production before September 28, 2017.

(ii) *Residential rental property or nonresidential real property* .—If the taxpayer constructs, manufactures, or produces residential rental property or nonresidential real property, as defined in section 168(e)(2), or an improvement to such property, for use in its trade or business or production of income, all property that is constructed, manufactured, or produced as part of such residential rental property, nonresidential real property, or improvement, as applicable, and that is described in paragraph (c)(2)(i)(A) of this section is the larger self-constructed property for purposes of applying the rules in this paragraph (c).

(iii) *Beginning of manufacturing, construction, or production* .—Solely for purposes of paragraph (c)(2)(i)(C) of this section, the determination of when manufacture, construction, or production of the larger self-constructed property begins is made in accordance with the rules in paragraph (b)(5)(iv)(B) of this section if the larger self-constructed property is manufactured, constructed, or produced by the taxpayer for its own use in its trade or business or production of income, or is manufactured, constructed, or produced for the taxpayer by another person under a written binding contract, as defined in paragraph (b)(5)(iii) of this section, that is entered into prior to the manufacture, construction, or production of the property for use by the taxpayer in its trade or business or production of income. If the larger self-constructed property is manufactured, constructed, or produced for the taxpayer by another person under a written contract that does not meet the definition of a binding contract in paragraph (b)(5)(iii) of this section, that is entered into prior to the manufacture, construction, or production of the property for use by the taxpayer in its trade or business or production of income, the determination of when manufacture, construction, or production of the larger self-constructed property begins is made in accordance with the rules in paragraph (b)(5)(v) of this section. If the taxpayer enters into a written binding contract, as defined in paragraph (b)(5)(iii) of this section, before September 28, 2017, with another person to manufacture, construct, or produce the larger self-constructed property and the manufacture, construction, or production of this property begins after September 27, 2017, as determined under paragraph (b)(5)(iv)(B) of this section, this paragraph (c) does not apply. If the taxpayer enters into a written contract that does not meet the definition of a binding contract in paragraph (b)(5)(iii) of this section before September 28, 2017, with another person to manufacture, construct, or produce the larger self-constructed property and the manufacture, construction, or production of this property begins after September 27, 2017, as determined under paragraph (b)(5)(v) of this section, this paragraph (c) does not apply.

(iv) *Exception* .—This paragraph (c) does not apply to any larger self-constructed property that is included in a class of property for which the taxpayer made an election under section 168(k)(7) (formerly section 168(k)(2)(D)(iii)) not to deduct the additional first year depreciation deduction.

(3) *Eligible components* .—(i) *In general* .—Solely for purposes of this paragraph (c), a component of the larger self-constructed property, as described in paragraph (c)(2) of this section, must be qualified property under section 168(k)(2) and paragraph (b) of this section. Solely for purposes of the preceding sentence, a component will satisfy the acquisition date requirement in paragraph (b)(5) of this section if it satisfies the requirements in paragraph (c)(3)(ii) or (iii) of this section, as applicable.

(ii) *Acquired components* .—If a component of the larger self-constructed property is acquired pursuant to a written binding contract, as defined in paragraph (b)(5)(iii) of this section, the component must be acquired by the taxpayer after September 27, 2017, as determined under the rules in paragraph (b)(5)(ii)(B) of this section. If a component of the larger self-constructed property is acquired pursuant to a written contract that does not meet the definition of a binding contract in paragraph (b)(5)(iii) of this section, the component must be acquired by the taxpayer after September 27, 2017, as determined under the rules in paragraph (b)(5)(v) of this section.

(iii) *Self-constructed components* .—The manufacture, construction, or production of a component of a larger self-constructed property must begin after September 27, 2017. The determination of when manufacture, construction, or production of the component begins is made in accordance with the rules in—

(A) Paragraph (b)(5)(iv)(B) of this section if the component is manufactured, constructed, or produced by the taxpayer for its own use in its trade or business or for its production of income, or is manufactured, constructed, or produced for the taxpayer by another person under a written binding contract, as defined in paragraph (b)(5)(iii) of this section, that is entered into prior to the manufacture, construction, or production of the component for use by the taxpayer in its trade or business or for its production of income; or

(B) (B) Paragraph (b)(5)(v) of this section if the component is manufactured, constructed, or produced for the taxpayer by another person under a written contract that does not meet the definition of a binding contract in paragraph (b)(5)(iii) of this section, that is entered into prior to the manufacture, construction, or production of the component for use by the taxpayer in its trade or business or for its production of income.

(4) *Special rules* .—(i) *Installation costs* .—If the taxpayer pays, in the case of a cash basis taxpayer, or incurs, in the case of an accrual basis taxpayer, costs, including labor costs, to install a component of the larger self-constructed property, as described in paragraph (c)(2) of this section, such costs are eligible for the additional first year depreciation under this section, assuming all requirements are met, only if the component being installed meets the requirements in paragraph (c)(3) of this section.

(ii) *Property described in section 168(k)(2)(B)* .—The rules in paragraph (e)(1)(iii) of this section apply for determining the unadjusted depreciable basis, as defined in §1.168(b)-1(a)(3), of larger self-constructed property described in paragraph (c)(2) of this section and in section 168(k)(2)(B).

(5) *Computation of additional first year depreciation deduction* .—(i) *Election is made* .—Before determining the allowable additional first year depreciation deduction for the larger self-constructed property, as described in paragraph (c)(2) of this section, for which the taxpayer makes the election specified in this paragraph (c) for one or more components of such property, the taxpayer must determine the portion of the unadjusted depreciable basis, as defined in §1.168(b)-1(a)(3), of the larger self-constructed property, including all components, attributable to the component that meets the requirements of paragraphs (c)(3) and (c)(4)(i) of this section (component basis). The additional first year depreciation deduction for the component basis is determined by multiplying such component basis by the applicable percentage for the placed-in-service year of the larger self-constructed property. The additional first year depreciation deduction, if any, for the remaining unadjusted depreciable basis of the larger self-constructed property, as described in paragraph (c)(2) of this section, is determined under section 168(k), as in effect on the day before the date of the enactment of the Act, and section 168(k)(8). For purposes of this paragraph (c), the remaining unadjusted depreciable basis of the larger self-constructed property is equal to the unadjusted depreciable basis, as defined in §1.168(b)-1(a)(3), of the larger self-constructed property, including all components, reduced by the sum of the component basis of the components for which the taxpayer makes the election specified in this paragraph (c).

(ii) *Election is not made* .—If the taxpayer does not make the election specified in this paragraph (c), the additional first year depreciation deduction, if any, for the larger self-constructed property, including all components, is determined under section 168(k), as in effect on the day before the date of the enactment of the Act, and section 168(k)(8).

(6) *Time and manner for making election* .—(i) *Time for making election* .—The election specified in this paragraph (c) must be made by the due date, including extensions, of the Federal tax return for the taxable year in which the taxpayer placed in service the larger self-constructed property.

(ii) *Manner of making election* .—The election specified in this paragraph (c) must be made by attaching a statement to such return indicating that the taxpayer is making the election provided in this paragraph (c) and whether the taxpayer is making the election for all or some of the components described in paragraph (c)(3) of this section. The election is made separately by each person owning qualified property (for example, for each member of a consolidated group by the agent for the group (within the meaning of § 1.1502-77(a) and (c)), by the partnership (including a lower-tier partnership), or by the S corporation).

(7) *Revocation of election* .—(i) *In general* .—Except as provided in paragraph (c)(7)(ii) of this section, the election specified in this paragraph (c), once made, may be revoked only by filing a request for a private letter ruling and obtaining the Commissioner of Internal Revenue's written consent to revoke the election. The Commissioner may grant a request to revoke the election if the taxpayer acted reasonably and in good faith, and the revocation will not prejudice the interests of the Government. See generally § 301.9100-3 of this chapter. The election specified in this paragraph (c) may not be revoked through a request under section 446(e) to change the taxpayer's method of accounting.

(ii) *Automatic 6-month extension* .—If a taxpayer made the election specified in this paragraph (c), an automatic extension of 6 months from the due date of the taxpayer's Federal tax return, excluding extensions, for the placed-in-service year of the larger self-constructed property is granted to revoke that election, provided the taxpayer timely filed the taxpayer's Federal tax return for that placed-in-service year and, within this 6-month extension period, the taxpayer, and all taxpayers whose tax liability would be affected by the election, file an amended Federal tax return for the placed-in-service year in a manner that is consistent with the revocation of the election.

(8) *Additional procedural guidance* .—The IRS may publish procedural guidance in the Internal Revenue Bulletin (see § 601.601(d)(2)(ii)( *b*) of this chapter) that provides alternative procedures for complying with paragraph (c)(6) or (c)(7)(i) of this section.

(9) *Examples* .—The application of this paragraph (c) is illustrated by the following examples. Unless the facts specifically indicate otherwise, assume that the larger self-constructed property is described in paragraph (c)(2) of this section, the components that are acquired or self-constructed after September 27, 2017, are described in paragraph (c)(3) of this section, the taxpayer is an accrual basis taxpayer, and none of the costs paid or incurred after September 27, 2017, are for the installation of components that do not meet the requirements of paragraph (c)(3) of this section.

(i) *Example 1* .—(A) *BC*, a calendar year taxpayer, is engaged in a trade or business described in section 163(j)(7)(A)(iv) and §§ 1.163(j)-1(b)(15)(i) and 1.163(j)-10(c)(3)(iii)(C)( *3*). In December 2015, *BC* decided to construct an electric generation power plant for its own use. This plant is property described in section 168(k)(2)(B) as in effect on the day before the date of the enactment of the Act. However, the turbine for the plant had to be manufactured by another person for *BC*. In January 2016, *BC* entered into a written binding contract with *CD* to acquire the turbine. *BC* received the completed turbine in August 2017 at which time *BC* incurred the cost of the turbine. The cost of the turbine is 11 percent of the total cost of the electric generation power plant to be constructed by *BC*. *BC* began constructing the electric generation power plant in October 2017 and placed in service this new power plant, including all component parts, in 2020.

(B) The larger self-constructed property is the electric generation power plant to be constructed by *BC*. For determining if the construction of this power plant begins before September 28, 2017, paragraph (b)(5)(iv)(B) of this section provides that manufacture, construction, or production of property begins when physical work of a significant nature begins. *BC* uses the safe harbor test in paragraph (b)(5)(iv)(B)( *2*) of this section to determine when physical work of a significant nature begins for the electric generation power plant. Because the turbine that was manufactured by *CD* for *BC* is more than 10 percent of the total cost of the electric generation power plant, physical work of a significant nature for this plant began before September 28, 2017.

(C) The power plant is described in section 168(k)(9)(A) and paragraph (b)(2)(ii)(F) of this section and, therefore, is not larger self-constructed property eligible for the election pursuant to paragraph (c)(2)(i)(B) of this section. Accordingly, none of *BC's* expenditures for components of the power plant that are acquired or self-constructed after September 27, 2017, are eligible for the election specified in this paragraph (c). Assuming all requirements are met under section 168(k)(2) as in effect on the day before the date of the enactment of the Act, the unadjusted depreciable basis of the power plant, including all components, attributable to its construction before January 1, 2020, is eligible for the 30-percent additional first year depreciation deduction pursuant to section 168(k)(8).

(ii) *Example 2*.—(A) In August 2017, *BD*, a calendar-year taxpayer, entered into a written binding contract with *CE* for *CE* to manufacture a locomotive for *BD* for use in its trade or business. Before September 28, 2017, *BD* acquired or self-constructed components of the locomotive. These components cost $500,000, which is more than 10 percent of the total cost of the locomotive, and *BD* incurred such costs before September 28, 2017. After September 27, 2017, *BD* acquired or self-constructed components of the locomotive and these components cost $4,000,000. In February 2019, *CE* delivered the locomotive to *BD* and *BD* placed in service the locomotive. The total cost of the locomotive is $4,500,000. The locomotive is property described in section 168(k)(2)(B) as in effect on the day before the date of the enactment of the Act. On its timely filed Federal income tax return for 2019, *BD* made the election specified in this paragraph (c).

(B) The larger self-constructed property is the locomotive being manufactured by *CE* for *BD*. For determining if the manufacturing of this locomotive begins before September 28, 2017, paragraph (b)(5)(iv)(B) of this section provides that manufacture, construction, or production of property begins when physical work of a significant nature begins. *BD* uses the safe harbor test in paragraph (b)(5)(iv)(B)(*2*) of this section to determine when physical work of a significant nature begins for the locomotive. Because *BD* had incurred more than 10 percent of the total cost of the locomotive before September 28, 2017, physical work of a significant nature for this locomotive began before September 28, 2017.

(C) Because *BD* made the election specified in this paragraph (c), the cost of $4,000,000 for the locomotive's components acquired or self-constructed after September 27, 2017, qualifies for the 100-percent additional first year depreciation deduction under this section, assuming all other requirements are met. The remaining cost of the locomotive is $500,000 and such amount qualifies for the 40-percent additional first year depreciation deduction pursuant to section 168(k)(8), assuming all other requirements in section 168(k) as in effect on the day before the date of the enactment of the Act are met.

(iii) *Example 3*.—(A) In February 2016, *BF*, a calendar-year taxpayer, entered into a written binding contract with *CG* for *CG* to manufacture a vessel for *BF* for use in its trade or business. Before September 28, 2017, *BF* acquired or self-constructed components for the vessel. These components cost $30,000,000, which is more than 10 percent of the total cost of the vessel, and *BF* incurred such costs before September 28, 2017. After September 27, 2017, *BF* acquired or self-constructed components for the vessel and these components cost $15,000,000. In February 2021, *CG* delivered the vessel to *BF* and *BF* placed in service the vessel. The vessel is property described in section 168(k)(2)(B) as in effect on the day before the date of the enactment of the Act. The total cost of the vessel is

$45,000,000. On its timely filed Federal income tax return for 2021, *BF* made the election specified in this paragraph (c).

(B) The larger self-constructed property is the vessel being manufactured by *CG* for *BF*. For determining if the manufacturing of this vessel begins before September 28, 2017, paragraph (b)(5)(iv)(B) of this section provides that manufacture, construction, or production of property begins when physical work of a significant nature begins. *BF* uses the safe harbor test in paragraph (b)(5)(iv)(B)(*2*) of this section to determine when physical work of a significant nature begins for the vessel. Because *BF* had incurred more than 10 percent of the total cost of the vessel before September 28, 2017, physical work of a significant nature for this vessel began before September 28, 2017.

(C) Because *BF* made the election specified in this paragraph (c), the cost of $15,000,000 for the vessel's components acquired or self-constructed after September 27, 2017, qualifies for the 100-percent additional first year depreciation deduction under this section, assuming all other requirements are met. Pursuant to section 168(k)(8) and because *BF* placed in service the vessel after 2020, none of the remaining cost of the vessel is eligible for any additional first year depreciation deduction under section 168(k) and this section nor under section 168(k) as in effect on the day before the date of the enactment of the Act.

(iv) *Example 4*.—(A) In March 2017, *BG*, a calendar year taxpayer, entered into a written contract with *CH* for *CH* to construct a building for *BG* to use in its retail business. This written contract does not meet the definition of a binding contract in paragraph (b)(5)(iii) of this section. In September 2019, the construction of the building was completed and placed in service by *BG*. The total cost is $10,000,000. Of this amount, $3,000,000 is the total cost for all section 1245 properties constructed as part of the building, and $7,000,000 is for the building. Under section 168(e), section 1245 properties in the total amount of $2,400,000 are 5-year property and in the total amount of $600,000 are 7-year property. The building is nonresidential real property under section 168(e). Before September 28, 2017, *BG* acquired or self-constructed certain components and the total cost of these components is $500,000 for the section 1245 properties and $3,000,000 for the building. *BG* incurred these costs before September 28, 2017. After September 27, 2017, BG acquired or self-constructed the remaining components of the section 1245 properties and these components cost $2,500,000. BG incurred these costs of $2,500,000 after September 27, 2017. On its timely filed Federal income tax return for 2019, *BG* made the election specified in this paragraph (c).

(B) All section 1245 properties are constructed as part of the construction of the building and are described in paragraph (b)(2)(i)(A) of this section. The building is not described in paragraph (b)(2)(i)(A), (B), (C), or (D) of this section. As a result, under paragraph (c)(2)(ii) of this section, the larger self-constructed property is all section 1245 properties with a total cost of $3,000,000. For determining if the construction of these section 1245 properties begins before September 28, 2017, paragraph (b)(5)(v) of this section provides that manufacture, construction, or production of property begins when the taxpayer incurs more than 10 percent of the total cost of the property. Because *BG* incurred more than 10 percent of the total cost of the section 1245 properties before September 28, 2017, construction of the section 1245 properties began before September 28, 2017.

(C) Because *BG* made the election specified in this paragraph (c), the cost of $2,500,000 for the section 1245 components acquired or self-constructed by *BG* after September 27, 2017, qualifies for the 100-percent additional first year depreciation deduction under this section, assuming all other requirements are met. The remaining cost of the section 1245 components is $500,000 and such amount qualifies for the 30-percent additional first year depreciation deduction pursuant to section 168(k)(8), assuming all other requirements in section 168(k), as in effect on the day before the date of the enactment of the Act, are met. Because the building is not qualified property under section 168(k), as in effect on the day before the date of the enactment of the Act, none of the cost of $7,000,000 for the building is eligible for any additional first year depreciation deduction under section 168(k) and this section or under section 168(k), as in effect on the day before the date of the enactment of the Act.

(d) *Property described in section 168(k)(2)(B) or (C)* .—(1) *In general* .— Property described in section 168(k)(2)(B) or (C) will meet the acquisition requirements of section 168(k)(2)(B)(i)(III) or (k)(2)(C)(i) if the property is acquired by the taxpayer before January 1, 2027, or acquired by the taxpayer pursuant to a written binding contract that is entered into before January 1, 2027. Property described in section 168(k)(2)(B) or (C), including its components, also must meet the acquisition requirement in section 13201(h)(1)(A) of the Act (for further guidance, see paragraph (b)(5) of this section).

(2) *Definition of binding contract* .—For purposes of this paragraph (d), the rules in paragraph (b)(5)(iii) of this section for a binding contract apply.

(3) *Self-constructed property* .—(i) *In general* .—If a taxpayer manufactures, constructs, or produces property for use by the taxpayer in its trade or business or for its production of income, the acquisition rules in paragraph (d)(1) of this section are treated as met for the property if the taxpayer begins manufacturing, constructing, or producing the property before January 1, 2027. Property that is manufactured, constructed, or produced for the taxpayer by another person under a written binding contract, as defined in paragraph (b)(5)(iii) of this section, that is entered into prior to the manufacture, construction, or production of the property for use by the taxpayer in its trade or business or for its production of income is considered to be manufactured, constructed, or produced by the taxpayer. If a taxpayer enters into a written binding contract, as defined in paragraph (b)(5)(iii) of this section, before January 1, 2027, with another person to manufacture, construct, or produce property described in section 168(k)(2)(B) or (C) and the manufacture, construction, or production of this property begins after December 31, 2026, the acquisition rule in paragraph (d)(1) of this section is met.

(ii) *When does manufacture, construction, or production begin* .—(A) *In general* .— For purposes of this paragraph (d)(3), manufacture, construction, or production of property begins when physical work of a significant nature begins. Physical work does not include preliminary activities such as planning or designing, securing financing, exploring, or researching. The determination of when physical work of a significant nature begins depends on the facts and circumstances. For example, if a retail motor fuels outlet is to be constructed on-site, construction begins when physical work of a significant nature commences at the site; that is, when work begins on the excavation for footings, pouring the pads for the outlet, or the driving of foundation pilings into the ground. Preliminary work, such as clearing a site, test drilling to determine soil condition, or excavation to change the contour of the land (as distinguished from excavation for footings) does not constitute the beginning of construction. However, if a retail motor fuels outlet is to be assembled on-site from modular units manufactured off-site and delivered to the site where the outlet will be used, manufacturing begins when physical work of a significant nature commences at the off-site location.

(B) *Safe harbor* .—For purposes of paragraph (d)(3)(ii)(A) of this section, a taxpayer may choose to determine when physical work of a significant nature begins in accordance with this paragraph (d)(3)(ii)(B). Physical work of a significant nature will be considered to begin at the time the taxpayer incurs (in the case of an accrual basis taxpayer) or pays (in the case of a cash basis taxpayer) more than 10 percent of the total cost of the property, excluding the cost of any land and preliminary activities such as planning or designing, securing financing, exploring, or researching. When property is manufactured, constructed, or produced for the taxpayer by another person, this safe harbor test must be satisfied by the taxpayer. For example, if a retail motor fuels outlet is to be constructed for an accrual basis taxpayer by another person for the total cost of $200,000, excluding the cost of any land and preliminary activities such as planning or designing, securing financing, exploring, or researching, construction is deemed to begin for purposes of this paragraph (d)(3)(ii)(B) when the taxpayer has incurred more than 10 percent (more than $20,000) of the total cost of the property. A taxpayer chooses to apply this paragraph (d)(3)(ii)(B) by filing a Federal income tax return for the placed-in-service year of the property that determines when physical work of a significant nature begins consistent with this paragraph (d)(3)(ii)(B).

(iii) *Components of self-constructed property* .—(A) *Acquired components* .—If a binding contract, as defined in paragraph (b)(5)(iii) of this section, to acquire a component does not satisfy the requirements of paragraph (d)(1) of this section, the component does not qualify for the additional first year depreciation deduction under this section. A binding contract described in the preceding sentence to acquire one or more components of a larger self-constructed property will not preclude the larger self-constructed property from satisfying the acquisition rules in paragraph (d)(3)(i) of this section. Accordingly, the unadjusted depreciable basis of the larger self-constructed property that is eligible for the additional first year depreciation deduction under this section, assuming all other requirements are met, must not include the unadjusted depreciable basis of any component that does not satisfy the requirements of paragraph (d)(1) of this section. If a binding contract to acquire the component is entered into before January 1, 2027, but the manufacture, construction, or production of the larger self-constructed property does not begin before January 1, 2027, the component qualifies for the additional first year depreciation deduction under this section, assuming all other requirements are met, but the larger self-constructed property does not.

(B) *Self-constructed components* .—If the manufacture, construction, or production of a component by the taxpayer does not satisfy the requirements of paragraph (d)(3)(i) of this section, the component does not qualify for the additional first year depreciation deduction under this section. However, if the manufacture, construction, or production of a component does not satisfy the requirements of paragraph (d)(3)(i) of this section, but the manufacture, construction, or production of the larger self-constructed property satisfies the requirements of paragraph (d)(3)(i) of this section, the larger self-constructed property qualifies for the additional first year depreciation deduction under this section, assuming all other requirements are met, even though the component does not qualify for the additional first year depreciation deduction under this section. Accordingly, the unadjusted depreciable basis of the larger self-constructed property that is eligible for the additional first year depreciation deduction under this section, assuming all other requirements are met, must not include the unadjusted depreciable basis of any component that does not qualify for the additional first year depreciation deduction under this section. If the manufacture, construction, or production of a component begins before January 1, 2027, but the manufacture, construction, or production of the larger self-constructed property does not begin before January 1, 2027, the component qualifies for the additional first year depreciation deduction under this section, assuming all other requirements are met, but the larger self-constructed property does not.

(iv) *Determination of acquisition date for property not acquired pursuant to a written binding contract* .—For purposes of the acquisition rules in paragraph (d)(1) of this section, the following property is acquired by the taxpayer before January 1, 2027, if the taxpayer paid, in the case of a cash basis taxpayer, or incurred, in the case of an accrual basis taxpayer, more than 10 percent of the total cost of the property before January 1, 2027, excluding the cost of any land and preliminary activities such as planning and designing, securing financing, exploring, or researching:

(A) Property that the taxpayer acquires pursuant to a contract that does not meet the definition of a written binding contract in paragraph (b)(5)(iii) of this section; or

(B) Property that is manufactured, constructed, or produced for the taxpayer by another person under a written contract that does not meet the definition of a binding contract in paragraph (b)(5)(iii) of this section, and that is entered into prior to the manufacture, construction, or production of the property for use by the taxpayer in its trade or business or production of income.

(4) *Examples* .—The application of this paragraph (d) is illustrated by the following examples:

(A) *Example 1.* ( *1*) On June 1, 2016, *NN* decided to construct property described in section 168(k)(2)(B) for its own use. However, one of the component parts of the property had to be manufactured by another person for *NN*. On August 15, 2016, *NN* entered into a written binding contract with *OO* to acquire this component part of the property for $100,000. *OO* began manufacturing the component part on November 1, 2016, and delivered the completed component part to *NN* on September 1, 2017, at which time *NN* incurred $100,000 for the cost of the component. The cost of this component part is 9 percent of the total cost of the property to be constructed by *NN*. *NN* did not incur any other cost of the property to be constructed before *NN* began construction. *NN* began constructing the property described in section 168(k)(2)(B) on October 15, 2017, and placed in service this property, including all component parts, on November 1, 2020. *NN* uses the safe harbor test in paragraph (d)(3)(ii)(B) of this section to determine when physical work of a significant nature begins for the property described in section 168(k)(2)(B).

( *2*) Because the component part of $100,000 that was manufactured by *OO* for *NN* is not more than 10 percent of the total cost of the property described in section 168(k)(2)(B), physical work of a significant nature for the property described in section 168(k)(2)(B) did not begin before September 28, 2017.

( *3*) Pursuant to paragraphs (b)(5)(iv)(C)( *2*) and (d)(1) of this section, the self-constructed component part of $100,000 manufactured by *OO* for *NN* is not eligible for the 100-percent additional first year depreciation deduction because the manufacturing of such component part began before September 28, 2017. However, pursuant to paragraph (d)(3)(i) of this section, the cost of the property described in section 168(k)(2)(B), excluding the cost of the component part of $100,000 manufactured by *OO* for *NN*, is eligible for the 100-percent additional first year depreciation deduction, assuming all other requirements are met, because construction of the property began after September 27, 2017, and before January 1, 2027, and the property described in section 168(k)(2)(B) was placed in service by *NN* during 2020.

(B) *Example 2.* ( *1*) On June 1, 2026, *PP* decided to construct property described in section 168(k)(2)(B) for its own use. However, one of the component parts of the property had to be manufactured by another person for *PP*. On August 15, 2026, *PP* entered into a written binding contract with *XP* to acquire this component part of the property for $100,000. *XP* began manufacturing the component part on September 1, 2026, and delivered the completed component part to *PP* on February 1, 2027, at which time *PP* incurred $100,000 for the cost of the component. The cost of this component part is 9 percent of the total cost of the property to be constructed by *PP*. *PP* did not incur any other cost of the property to be constructed before *PP* began construction. *PP* began constructing the property described in section 168(k)(2)(B) on January 15, 2027, and placed this property, including all component parts, in service on November 1, 2027.

(*2*) Pursuant to paragraph (d)(3)(iii)(B) of this section, the self-constructed component part of $100,000 manufactured by *XP* for *PP* is eligible for the additional first year depreciation deduction under this section, assuming all other requirements are met, because the manufacturing of the component part began before January 1, 2027, and the property described in section 168(k)(2)(B), the larger self-constructed property, was placed in service by *PP* before January 1, 2028. However, pursuant to paragraph (d)(3)(i) of this section, the cost of the property described in section 168(k)(2)(B), excluding the cost of the self-constructed component part of $100,000 manufactured by *XP* for *PP*, is not eligible for the additional first year depreciation deduction under this section because construction of the property began after December 31, 2026.

(C) *Example 3.* On December 1, 2026, *QQ* entered into a written binding contract, as defined in paragraph (b)(5)(iii) of this section, with *RR* to manufacture an aircraft described in section 168(k)(2)(C) for use in *QQ*'s trade or business. *RR* begins to manufacture the aircraft on February 1, 2027. *QQ* places the aircraft in service on August 1, 2027. Pursuant to paragraph (d)(3)(i) of this section, the aircraft meets the requirements of paragraph (d)(1) of this section because the aircraft was acquired by *QQ* pursuant to a written binding contract entered into before January 1, 2027. Further, the aircraft was placed in service by *QQ* before January 1, 2028. Thus, assuming all other requirements are met, *QQ*'s cost of the aircraft is eligible for the additional first year depreciation deduction under this section.

(e) *Computation of depreciation deduction for qualified property* .—(1) *Additional first year depreciation deduction* .—(i) *Allowable taxable year* .—The additional first year depreciation deduction is allowable—

(A) Except as provided in paragraph (e)(1)(i)(B) or (g) of this section, in the taxable year in which the qualified property is placed in service by the taxpayer for use in its trade or business or for the production of income; or

(B) In the taxable year in which the specified plant is planted, or grafted to a plant that has already been planted, by the taxpayer in the ordinary course of the taxpayer's farming business, as defined in section 263A(e)(4), if the taxpayer properly made the election to apply section 168(k)(5) (for further guidance, see paragraph (f) of this section).

(ii) *Computation* .—Except as provided in paragraph (g)(5) of this section, the allowable additional first year depreciation deduction for qualified property is determined by multiplying the unadjusted depreciable basis, as defined in § 1.168(b)-1(a)(3), of the qualified property by the applicable percentage. Except as provided in paragraph (g)(1) of this section, the additional first year depreciation deduction is not affected by a taxable year of less than 12 months. See paragraph (g)(1) of this section for qualified property placed in service or planted or grafted, as applicable, and disposed of during the same taxable year. See paragraph (g)(5) of this section for qualified property acquired in a like-kind exchange or as a result of an involuntary conversion.

(iii) *Property described in section 168(k)(2)(B)* .—For purposes of paragraph (e)(1)(ii) of this section, the unadjusted depreciable basis, as defined in § 1.168(b)-1(a)(3), of qualified property described in section 168(k)(2)(B) is limited to the property's unadjusted depreciable basis attributable to the property's manufacture, construction, or production before January 1, 2027. The amounts of unadjusted depreciable basis attributable to the property's manufacture, construction, or production before January 1, 2027, are referred to as "progress expenditures." Rules similar to the rules in section 4.02(1)(b) of Notice 2007-36 (2007-17 I.R.B. 1000) (see § 601.601(d)(2)(ii)(*b*) of this chapter) apply for determining progress expenditures, regardless of whether the property is manufactured, constructed, or produced for the taxpayer by another person under a written binding contract, as defined in paragraph (b)(5)(iii) of this section, or under a written contract that does not meet the definition of a binding contract in paragraph (b)(5)(iii) of this section. The IRS may publish procedural guidance in the Internal Revenue Bulletin (see § 601.601(d)(2)(ii)(*b*) of this chapter) that provides alternative procedures forcomplying with this paragraph (e)(1)(iii).

(iv) *Alternative minimum tax* .—(A) *In general* .—The additional first year depreciation deduction is allowable for alternative minimum tax purposes—

*(1)* Except as provided in paragraph (e)(1)(iv)(A)(*2*) of this section, in the taxable year in which the qualified property is placed in service by the taxpayer; or

*(2)* In the taxable year in which a specified plant is planted by the taxpayer, or grafted by the taxpayer to a plant that was previously planted, if the taxpayer properly made the election to apply section 168(k)(5) (for further guidance, see paragraph (f) of this section).

(B) *Special rules* .—In general, the additional first year depreciation deduction for alternative minimum tax purposes is based on the unadjusted depreciable basis of the property for alternative minimum tax purposes. However, see paragraph (g)(5)(iii)(E) of this section for qualified property acquired in a like-kind exchange or as a result of an involuntary conversion.

(2) *Otherwise allowable depreciation deduction* .—(i) *In general* .—Before determining the amount otherwise allowable as a depreciation deduction for the qualified property for the placed-in-service year and any subsequent taxable year, the taxpayer must determine the remaining adjusted depreciable basis of the qualified property. This remaining adjusted depreciable basis is equal to the unadjusted depreciable basis, as defined in § 1.168(b)-1(a)(3), of the qualified property reduced by the amount of the additional first year depreciation allowed or allowable, whichever is greater. The remaining adjusted depreciable basis of the qualified property is then depreciated using the applicable depreciation provisions under the Internal Revenue Code for the qualified property. The remaining adjusted depreciable basis of the qualified property that is MACRS property is also the basis to which the annual depreciation rates in the optional depreciation tables apply (for further guidance, see section 8 of Rev. Proc. 87-57 (1987-2 C.B. 687) and § 601.601(d)(2)(ii)(*b*) of this chapter). The depreciation deduction allowable for the remaining adjusted depreciable basis of the qualified property is affected by a taxable year of less than 12 months.

(ii) *Alternative minimum tax* .—For alternative minimum tax purposes, the depreciation deduction allowable for the remaining adjusted depreciable basis of the qualified property is based on the remaining adjusted depreciable basis for alternative minimum tax purposes. The remaining adjusted depreciable basis of the qualified property for alternative minimum tax purposes is depreciated using the same depreciation method, recovery period (or useful life in the case of computer software), and convention that apply to the qualified property for regular tax purposes.

(3) *Examples* .—This paragraph (e) is illustrated by the following examples:

(i) *Example 1.* On March 1, 2023, *SS,* a calendar-year taxpayer, purchased and placed in service qualified property that costs $1 million and is 5-year property under section 168(e). *SS* depreciates its 5-year property placed in service in 2023 using the optional depreciation table that corresponds with the general depreciation system, the 200-percent declining balance method, a 5-year recovery period, and the half-year convention. For 2023, *SS* is allowed an 80-percent additional first year depreciation deduction of $800,000 (the unadjusted depreciable basis of $1 million multiplied by 0.80). Next, *SS* must reduce the unadjusted depreciable basis of $1 million by the additional first year depreciation deduction of $800,000 to determine the remaining adjusted depreciable basis of $200,000. Then, *SS'* depreciation deduction allowable in 2023 for the remaining adjusted depreciable basis of $200,000 is $40,000 (the remaining adjusted depreciable basis of $200,000 multiplied by the annual depreciation rate of 0.20 for recovery year 1).

(ii) *Example 2.* On June 1, 2023, *TT*, a calendar-year taxpayer, purchased and placed in service qualified property that costs $1,500,000. The property qualifies for the expensing election under section 179 and is 5-year property under section 168(e). *TT* did not purchase any other section 179 property in 2023. *TT* makes the election under section 179 for the property and depreciates its 5-year property placed in service in 2023 using the optional depreciation table that corresponds with the general depreciation system, the 200-percent declining balance method, a 5-year recovery period, and the half-year convention. Assume the maximum section 179 deduction for 2023 is $1,000,000. For 2023, *TT* is first allowed a $1,000,000 deduction under section 179. Next, *TT* must reduce the cost of $1,500,000 by the section 179 deduction of $1,000,000 to determine the unadjusted depreciable basis of $500,000. Then, for 2023, *TT* is allowed an 80-percent additional first year depreciation deduction of $400,000 (the unadjusted depreciable basis of $500,000 multiplied by 0.80). Next, *TT* must reduce the unadjusted depreciable basis of $500,000 by the additional first year depreciation deduction of $400,000 to determine the remaining adjusted depreciable basis of $100,000. Then, *TT*'s depreciation deduction allowable in 2023 for the remaining adjusted depreciable basis of $100,000 is $20,000 (the remaining adjusted depreciable basis of $100,000 multiplied by the annual depreciation rate of 0.20 for recovery year 1).

(f) *Elections under section 168(k)*.—(1) *Election not to deduct additional first year depreciation*.—(i) *In general*.—A taxpayer may make an election not to deduct the additional first year depreciation for any class of property that is qualified property placed in service during the taxable year. If this election is made, the election applies to all qualified property that is in the same class of property and placed in service in the same taxable year, and no additional first year depreciation deduction is allowable for the property placed in service during the taxable year in the class of property, except as provided in § 1.743-1(j)(4)(i)(B)(*1*).

(ii) *Definition of class of property*.—For purposes of this paragraph (f)(1), the term *class of property* means:

(A) Except for the property described in paragraphs (f)(1)(ii)(B) and (D), and (f)(2) of this section, each class of property described in section 168(e) (for example, 5-year property);

(B) Water utility property as defined in section 168(e)(5) and depreciated under section 168;

(C) Computer software as defined in, and depreciated under, section 167(f)(1) and § 1.167(a)-14(b);

(D) Qualified improvement property as defined in § 1.168(b)-1(a)(5)(i)(C) and (a)(5)(ii) (acquired by the taxpayer after September 27, 2017, and placed in service by the taxpayer after September 27, 2017, and before January 1, 2018), and depreciated under section 168;

(E) Each separate production, as defined in § 1.181-3(b), of a qualified film or television production;

(F) Each separate production, as defined in section 181(e)(2), of a qualified live theatrical production; or

(G) Each partner's basis adjustment in partnership assets under section 743(b) for each class of property described in paragraphs (f)(1)(ii)(A) through (F), and (f)(2) of this section (for further guidance, see §1.743-1(j)(4)(i)(B)(*1*)).

(iii) *Time and manner for making election* .—(A) *Time for making election* .—Except as provided in paragraph (f)(6) of this section, any election specified in paragraph (f)(1)(i) of this section must be made by the due date, including extensions, of the Federal tax return for the taxable year in which the qualified property is placed in service by the taxpayer.

(B) *Manner of making election* .—Except as provided in paragraph (f)(6) of this section, any election specified in paragraph (f)(1)(i) of this section must be made in the manner prescribed on Form 4562, "Depreciation and Amortization," and its instructions. The election is made separately by each person owning qualified property (for example, for each member of a consolidated group by the common parent of the group, by the partnership (including a lower-tier partnership; also including basis adjustments in the partnership assets under section 743(b)), or by the S corporation). If Form 4562 is revised or renumbered, any reference in this section to that form shall be treated as a reference to the revised or renumbered form.

(iv) *Failure to make election* .—If a taxpayer does not make the election specified in paragraph (f)(1)(i) of this section within the time and in the manner prescribed in paragraph (f)(1)(iii) of this section, the amount of depreciation allowable for that property under section 167 or 168, as applicable, must be determined for the placed-in-service year and for all subsequent taxable years by taking into account the additional first year depreciation deduction. Thus, any election specified in paragraph (f)(1)(i) of this section shall not be made by the taxpayer in any other manner (for example, the election cannot be made through a request under section 446(e) to change the taxpayer's method of accounting).

(2) *Election to apply section 168(k)(5) for specified plants* .—(i) *In general* .—A taxpayer may make an election to apply section 168(k)(5) to one or more specified plants that are planted, or grafted to a plant that has already been planted, by the taxpayer in the ordinary course of the taxpayer's farming business, as defined in section 263A(e)(4). If this election is made for a specified plant, such plant is not treated as qualified property under section 168(k) and this section in its placed-in-service year.

(ii) *Time and manner for making election* .—(A) *Time for making election* .—Except as provided in paragraph (f)(6) of this section, any election specified in paragraph (f)(2)(i) of this section must be made by the due date, including extensions, of the Federal tax return for the taxable year in which the taxpayer planted or grafted the specified plant to which the election applies.

(B) *Manner of making election* .—Except as provided in paragraph (f)(6) of this section, any election specified in paragraph (f)(2)(i) of this section must be made in the manner prescribed on Form 4562, "Depreciation and Amortization," and its instructions. The election is made separately by each person owning specified plants (for example, for each member of a consolidated group by the common parent of the group, by the partnership (including a lower-tier partnership), or by the S corporation). If Form 4562 is revised or renumbered, any reference in this section to that form shall be treated as a reference to the revised or renumbered form.

(iii) *Failure to make election* .—If a taxpayer does not make the election specified in paragraph (f)(2)(i) of this section for a specified plant within the time and in the manner prescribed in paragraph (f)(2)(ii) of this section, the specified plant is treated as qualified property under section 168(k), assuming all requirements are met, in the taxable year in which such plant is placed in service by the taxpayer. Thus, any election specified in paragraph (f)(2)(i) of this section shall not be made by the taxpayer in any other manner (for example, the election cannot be made through a request under section 446(e) to change the taxpayer's method of accounting).

(3) *Election for qualified property placed in service during the 2017 taxable year*.—(i) *In general*.—A taxpayer may make an election to deduct 50 percent, instead of 100 percent, additional first year depreciation for all qualified property acquired after September 27, 2017, by the taxpayer and placed in service by the taxpayer during its taxable year that includes September 28, 2017. If a taxpayer makes an election to apply section 168(k)(5) for its taxable year that includes September 28, 2017, the taxpayer also may make an election to deduct 50 percent, instead of 100 percent, additional first year depreciation for all specified plants that are planted, or grafted to a plant that has already been planted, after September 27, 2017, by the taxpayer in the ordinary course of the taxpayer's farming business during such taxable year.

(ii) *Time and manner for making election*.—(A) *Time for making election*.—Except as provided in paragraph (f)(6) of this section, any election specified in paragraph (f)(3)(i) of this section must be made by the due date, including extensions, of the Federal tax return for the taxpayer's taxable year that includes September 28, 2017.

(B) *Manner of making election*.—Except as provided in paragraph (f)(6) of this section, any election specified in paragraph (f)(3)(i) of this section must be made in the manner prescribed on the 2017 Form 4562, "Depreciation and Amortization," and its instructions. The election is made separately by each person owning qualified property (for example, for each member of a consolidated group by the common parent of the group, by the partnership (including a lower-tier partnership), or by the S corporation).

(iii) *Failure to make election*.—If a taxpayer does not make the election specified in paragraph (f)(3)(i) of this section within the time and in the manner prescribed in paragraph (f)(3)(ii) of this section, the amount of depreciation allowable for qualified property under section 167 or 168, as applicable, acquired and placed in service, or planted or grafted, as applicable, by the taxpayer after September 27, 2017, must be determined for the taxable year that includes September 28, 2017, and for all subsequent taxable years by taking into account the 100-percent additional first year depreciation deduction, unless the taxpayer makes the election specified in paragraph (f)(1)(i) of this section within the time and in the manner prescribed in paragraph (f)(1)(iii) of this section for the class of property in which the qualified property is included. Thus, any election specified in paragraph (f)(3)(i) of this section shall not be made by the taxpayer in any other manner (for example, the election cannot be made through a request under section 446(e) to change the taxpayer's method of accounting).

(4) *Alternative minimum tax*.—If a taxpayer makes an election specified in paragraph (f)(1) of this section for a class of property or in paragraph (f)(2) of this section for a specified plant, the depreciation adjustments under section 56 and the regulations in this part under section 56 do not apply to the property or specified plant, as applicable, to which that election applies for purposes of computing the taxpayer's alternative minimum taxable income. If a taxpayer makes an election specified in paragraph (f)(3) of this section for all qualified property, see paragraphs (e)(1)(iv) and (e)(2)(ii) of this section.

(5) *Revocation of election* .—(i) *In general* .—Except as provided in paragraphs (f)(5)(ii) and (f)(6) of this section, an election specified in this paragraph (f), once made, may be revoked only by filing a request for a private letter ruling and obtaining the Commissioner of Internal Revenue's written consent to revoke the election. The Commissioner may grant a request to revoke the election if the taxpayer acted reasonably and in good faith, and the revocation will not prejudice the interests of the Government. See generally §301.9100-3 of this chapter. An election specified in this paragraph (f) may not be revoked through a request under section 446(e) to change the taxpayer's method of accounting.

(ii) *Automatic 6-month extension* .—If a taxpayer made an election specified in this paragraph (f), an automatic extension of 6 months from the due date of the taxpayer's Federal tax return, excluding extensions, for the placed-in-service year or the taxable year in which the specified plant is planted or grafted, as applicable, is granted to revoke that election, provided the taxpayer timely filed the taxpayer's Federal tax return for the placed-in-service year or the taxable year in which the specified plant is planted or grafted, as applicable, and, within this 6-month extension period, the taxpayer, and all taxpayers whose tax liability would be affected by the election, file an amended Federal tax return for the placed-in-service year or the taxable year in which the specified plant is planted or grafted, as applicable, in a manner that is consistent with the revocation of the election.

(6) *Special rules for 2016 and 2017 returns* .—For an election specified in this paragraph (f) for qualified property placed in service, or for a specified plant that is planted, or grafted to a plant that has already been planted, by the taxpayer during its taxable year that included September 28, 2017, the taxpayer should refer to Rev. Proc. 2019-33 (2019-34 I.R.B. 662) (see §601.601(d)(2)(ii)( *b*)of this chapter) for the time and manner of making the election on the 2016 or 2017 Federal tax return.

(7) *Additional procedural guidance* .—The IRS may publish procedural guidance in the Internal Revenue Bulletin (see §601.601(d)(2)(ii)( *b*) of this chapter) that provides alternative procedures for complying with paragraph (f)(1)(iii), (f)(1)(iv), (f)(2)(ii), (f)(2)(iii), (f)(3)(ii), (f)(3)(iii), or (f)(5)(i) of this section.

(g) *Special rules* .—(1) *Property placed in service and disposed of in the same taxable year* .—(i) *In general* .—Except as provided in paragraphs (g)(1)(ii) and (iii) and by the application of paragraph (b)(3)(iii)(B)( *4*) of this section, the additional first year depreciation deduction is not allowed for qualified property placed in service or planted or grafted, as applicable, and disposed of during the same taxable year. If a partnership interest is acquired and disposed of during the same taxable year, the additional first year depreciation deduction is not allowed for any section 743(b) adjustment arising from the initial acquisition. Also, if qualified property is placed in service and disposed of during the same taxable year and then reacquired and again placed in service in a subsequent taxable year, the additional first year depreciation deduction is not allowable for the property in the subsequent taxable year, except as otherwise provided by the application of paragraph (b)(3)(iii)(B) of this section.

(ii) *Technical termination of a partnership* .—In the case of a technical termination of a partnership under section 708(b)(1)(B) in a taxable year beginning before January 1, 2018, the additional first year depreciation deduction is allowable for any qualified property placed in service or planted or grafted, as applicable, by the terminated partnership during the taxable year of termination and contributed by the terminated partnership to the new partnership. The allowable additional first year depreciation deduction for the qualified property shall not be claimed by the terminated partnership but instead shall be claimed by the new partnership for the new partnership's taxable year in which the qualified property was contributed by the terminated partnership to the new partnership. However, if qualified property is both placed in service or planted or grafted, as applicable, and contributed to a new partnership in a transaction described in section 708(b)(1)(B) by the terminated partnership during the taxable year of termination, and if such property is disposed of by the new partnership in the same taxable year the new partnership received such property from the terminated partnership, then no additional first year depreciation deduction is allowable to either partnership.

(iii) *Section 168(i)(7) transactions* .—If any qualified property is transferred in a transaction described in section 168(i)(7) in the same taxable year that the qualified property is placed in service or planted or grafted, as applicable, by the transferor, the additional first year depreciation deduction is allowable for the qualified property. If a partnership interest is purchased and transferred in a transaction described in section 168(i)(7) in the same taxable year, the additional first year depreciation deduction is allowable for any section 743(b) adjustment that arises from the initial acquisition with respect to qualified property held by the partnership, provided the requirements of paragraph (b)(3)(iv)(D) of this section and all other requirements of section 168(k) and this section are satisfied. The allowable additional first year depreciation deduction for the qualified property for the transferor's taxable year in which the property is placed in service or planted or grafted, as applicable, is allocated between the transferor and the transferee on a monthly basis. The allowable additional first year depreciation deduction for a section 743(b) adjustment with respect to qualified property held by the partnership is allocated between the transferor and the transferee on a monthly basis notwithstanding that under §1.743-1(f) a transferee's section 743(b) adjustment is determined without regard to a transferors section 743(b) adjustment. These allocations shall be made in accordance with the rules in §1.168(d)-1(b)(7)(ii) for allocating the depreciation deduction between the transferor and the transferee. However, solely for purposes of this section, if the qualified property is transferred in a section 721(a) transaction to a partnership that has as a partner a person, other than the transferor, who previously had a depreciable interest in the qualified property, in the same taxable year that the qualified property is acquired or planted or grafted, as applicable, by the transferor, the qualified property is deemed to be placed in service or planted or grafted, as applicable, by the transferor during that taxable year, and the allowable additional first year depreciation deduction is allocated entirely to the transferor and not to the partnership. Additionally, if qualified property is both placed in service or planted or grafted, as applicable, and transferred in a transaction described in section 168(i)(7) by the transferor during the same taxable year, and if such property is disposed of by the transferee, other than by a transaction described in section 168(i)(7), during the same taxable year the transferee received such property from the transferor, then no additional first year depreciation deduction is allowable to either party.

(iv) *Examples* .—The application of this paragraph (g)(1) is illustrated by the following examples:

(A) *Example 1. UU* and *VV* are equal partners in *Partnership JL*, a general partnership. *Partnership JL* is a calendar-year taxpayer. On October 1, 2017, *Partnership JL* purchased and placed in service qualified property at a cost of $30,000. On November 1, 2017, *UU* sells its entire 50 percent interest to *WW* in a transfer that terminates the partnership under section 708(b)(1)(B). As a result, terminated *Partnership JL* is deemed to have contributed the qualified property to new *Partnership JL*. Pursuant to paragraph (g)(1)(ii) of this section, new *Partnership JL*, not terminated *Partnership JL*, is eligible to claim the 100-percent additional first year depreciation deduction allowable for the qualified property for the taxable year 2017, assuming all other requirements are met.

(B) *Example 2.* On January 5, 2018, XX purchased and placed in service qualified property for a total amount of $9,000. On August 20, 2018, *XX* transferred this qualified property to *Partnership BC* in a transaction described in section 721(a). No other partner of *Partnership BC* has ever had a depreciable interest in the qualified property. *XX* and *Partnership BC* are calendar-year taxpayers. Because the transaction between XX and *Partnership BC* is a transaction described in section 168(i)(7), pursuant to paragraph (g)(1)(iii) of this section, the 100-percent additional first year depreciation deduction allowable for the qualified property is allocated between XX and *Partnership BC* in accordance with the rules in § 1.168(d)-1(b)(7)(ii) for allocating the depreciation deduction between the transferor and the transferee. Accordingly, the 100-percent additional first year depreciation deduction allowable of $9,000 for the qualified property for 2018 is allocated between *XX* and *Partnership BC* based on the number of months that *XX* and *Partnership BC* held the qualified property in service during 2018. Thus, because the qualified property was held in service by *XX* for 7 of 12 months, which includes the month in which XX placed the qualified property in service but does not include the month in which the qualified property was transferred, XX is allocated $5,250 ( 7/12 × $9,000 additional first year depreciation deduction). *Partnership BC* is allocated $3,750, the remaining 5/12 of the $9,000 additional first year depreciation deduction allowable for the qualified property.

(2) *Redetermination of basis* .—If the unadjusted depreciable basis, as defined in § 1.168(b)-1(a)(3), of qualified property is redetermined (for example, due to contingent purchase price or discharge of indebtedness) before January 1, 2027, or in the case of property described in section 168(k)(2)(B) or (C), is redetermined before January 1, 2028, the additional first year depreciation deduction allowable for the qualified property is redetermined as follows:

(i) *Increase in basis* .—For the taxable year in which an increase in basis of qualified property occurs, the taxpayer shall claim an additional first year depreciation deduction for qualified property by multiplying the amount of the increase in basis for this property by the applicable percentage for the taxable year in which the underlying property was placed in service by the taxpayer. For purposes of this paragraph (g)(2)(i), the additional first year depreciation deduction applies to the increase in basis only if the underlying property is qualified property. To determine the amount otherwise allowable as a depreciation deduction for the increase in basis of qualified property, the amount of the increase in basis of the qualified property must be reduced by the additional first year depreciation deduction allowed or allowable, whichever is greater, for the increase in basis and the remaining increase in basis of—

(A) Qualified property, except for computer software described in paragraph (b)(2)(i)(B) of this section, a qualified film or television production described in paragraph (b)(2)(i)(E) of this section, or a qualified live theatrical production described in paragraph (b)(2)(i)(F) of this section, is depreciated over the recovery period of the qualified property remaining as of the beginning of the taxable year in which the increase in basis occurs, and using the same depreciation method and convention applicable to the qualified property that applies for the taxable year in which the increase in basis occurs; and

(B) Computer software, as defined in paragraph (b)(2)(i)(B) of this section, that is qualified property is depreciated ratably over the remainder of the 36-month period, the useful life under section 167(f)(1), as of the beginning of the first day of the month in which the increase in basis occurs.

(ii) *Decrease in basis* .—For the taxable year in which a decrease in basis of qualified property occurs, the taxpayer shall reduce the total amount otherwise allowable as a depreciation deduction for all of the taxpayer's depreciable property by the excess additional first year depreciation deduction previously claimed for the qualified property. If, for such taxable year, the excess additional first year depreciation deduction exceeds the total amount otherwise allowable as a depreciation deduction for all of the taxpayer's depreciable property, the taxpayer shall take into account a negative depreciation deduction in computing taxable income. The excess additional first year depreciation deduction for qualified property is determined by multiplying the amount of the decrease in basis for this property by the applicable percentage for the taxable year in which the underlying property was placed in service by the taxpayer. For purposes of this paragraph (g)(2)(ii), the additional first year depreciation deduction applies to the decrease in basis only if the underlying property is qualified property. Also, if the taxpayer establishes by adequate records or other sufficient evidence that the taxpayer claimed less than the additional first year depreciation deduction allowable for the qualified property before the decrease in basis, or if the taxpayer claimed more than the additional first year depreciation deduction allowable for the qualified property before the decrease in basis, the excess additional first year depreciation deduction is determined by multiplying the amount of the decrease in basis by the additional first year depreciation deduction percentage actually claimed by the taxpayer for the qualified property before the decrease in basis. To determine the amount to reduce the total amount otherwise allowable as a depreciation deduction for all of the taxpayer's depreciable property for the excess depreciation previously claimed, other than the additional first year depreciation deduction, resulting from the decrease in basis of the qualified property, the amount of the decrease in basis of the qualified property must be adjusted by the excess additional first year depreciation deduction that reduced the total amount otherwise allowable as a depreciation deduction, as determined under this paragraph (g)(2)(ii), and the remaining decrease in basis of—

(A) Qualified property, except for computer software described in paragraph (b)(2)(i)(B) of this section, a qualified film or television production described in paragraph (b)(2)(i)(E) of this section, or a qualified live theatrical production described in paragraph (b)(2)(i)(F) of this section, reduces the amount otherwise allowable as a depreciation deduction over the recovery period of the qualified property remaining as of the beginning of the taxable year in which the decrease in basis occurs, and using the same depreciation method and convention of the qualified property that applies in the taxable year in which the decrease in basis occurs. If, for any taxable year, the reduction to the amount otherwise allowable as a depreciation deduction, as determined under this paragraph (g)(2)(ii)(A), exceeds the total amount otherwise allowable as a depreciation deduction for all of the taxpayer's depreciable property, the taxpayer shall take into account a negative depreciation deduction in computing taxable income; and

(B) Computer software, as defined in paragraph (b)(2)(i)(B) of this section, that is qualified property reduces the amount otherwise allowable as a depreciation deduction over the remainder of the 36-month period, the useful life under section 167(f)(1), as of the beginning of the first day of the month in which the decrease in basis occurs. If, for any taxable year, the reduction to the amount otherwise allowable as a depreciation deduction, as determined under this paragraph (g)(2)(ii)(B), exceeds the total amount otherwise allowable as a depreciation deduction for all of the taxpayer's depreciable property, the taxpayer shall take into account a negative depreciation deduction in computing taxable income.

(iii) *Definitions* .—Except as otherwise expressly provided by the Internal Revenue Code (for example, section 1017(a)), the regulations under the Internal Revenue Code, or other guidance published in the Internal Revenue Bulletin for purposes of this paragraph (g)(2)—

(A) An increase in basis occurs in the taxable year an amount is taken into account under section 461; and

(B) A decrease in basis occurs in the taxable year an amount would be taken into account under section 451.

(iv) *Examples* .—The application of this paragraph (g)(2) is illustrated by the following examples:

(A) *Example 1.* ( *1*) On May 15, 2023, *YY*, a cash-basis taxpayer, purchased and placed in service qualified property that is 5-year property at a cost of $200,000. In addition to the $200,000, *YY* agrees to pay the seller 25 percent of the gross profits from the operation of the property in 2023. On May 15, 2024, *YY* paid to the seller an additional $10,000. *YY* depreciates the 5-year property placed in service in 2023 using the optional depreciation table that corresponds with the general depreciation system, the 200-percent declining balance method, a 5-year recovery period, and the half-year convention.

( *2*) For 2023, *YY* is allowed an 80-percent additional first year depreciation deduction of $160,000 (the unadjusted depreciable basis of $200,000 multiplied by 0.80). In addition, *YY*'s depreciation deduction for 2023 for the remaining adjusted depreciable basis of $40,000 (the unadjusted depreciable basis of $200,000 reduced by the additional first year depreciation deduction of $160,000) is $8,000 (the remaining adjusted depreciable basis of $40,000 multiplied by the annual depreciation rate of 0.20 for recovery year 1).

( *3*) For 2024, *YY*'s depreciation deduction for the remaining adjusted depreciable basis of $40,000 is $12,800 (the remaining adjusted depreciable basis of $40,000 multiplied by the annual depreciation rate of 0.32 for recovery year 2). In addition, pursuant to paragraph (g)(2)(i) of this section, *YY* is allowed an additional first year depreciation deduction for 2024 for the $10,000 increase in basis of the qualified property. Consequently, *YY* is allowed an additional first year depreciation deduction of $8,000 (the increase in basis of $10,000 multiplied by 0.80, the applicable percentage for 2023). Also, *YY* is allowed a depreciation deduction for 2024 attributable to the remaining increase in basis of $2,000 (the increase in basis of $10,000 reduced by the additional first year depreciation deduction of $8,000). The depreciation deduction allowable for 2024 attributable to the remaining increase in basis of $2,000 is $889 (the remaining increase in basis of $2,000 multiplied by 0.4444, which is equal to 1/remaining recovery period of 4.5 years at January 1, 2024, multiplied by 2). Accordingly, for 2024, *YY*'s total depreciation deduction allowable for the qualified property is $21,689 ($12,800 plus $8,000 plus $889).

(B) *Example 2.* ( *1*) On May 15, 2023, *ZZ*, a calendar-year taxpayer, purchased and placed in service qualified property that is 5-year property at a cost of $400,000. To purchase the property, *ZZ* borrowed $250,000 from Bank1. On May 15, 2024, Bank1 forgives $50,000 of the indebtedness. *ZZ* makes the election provided in section 108(b)(5) to apply any portion of the reduction under section 1017 to the basis of the depreciable property of the taxpayer. *ZZ* depreciates the 5-year property placed in service in 2023 using the optional depreciation table that corresponds with the general depreciation system, the 200-percent declining balance method, a 5-year recovery period, and the half-year convention.

( *2*) For 2023, *ZZ* is allowed an 80-percent additional first year depreciation deduction of $320,000 (the unadjusted depreciable basis of $400,000 multiplied by 0.80). In addition, *ZZ*'s depreciation deduction allowable for 2023 for the remaining adjusted depreciable basis of $80,000 (the unadjusted depreciable basis of $400,000 reduced by the additional first year depreciation deduction of $320,000) is $16,000 (the remaining adjusted depreciable basis of $80,000 multiplied by the annual depreciation rate of 0.20 for recovery year 1).

( *3*) For 2024, *ZZ*'s deduction for the remaining adjusted depreciable basis of $80,000 is $25,600 (the remaining adjusted depreciable basis of $80,000 multiplied by the annual depreciation rate 0.32 for recovery year 2). Although Bank1 forgave the indebtedness in 2024, the basis of the property is reduced on

January 1, 2025, pursuant to sections 108(b)(5) and 1017(a) under which basis is reduced at the beginning of the taxable year following the taxable year in which the discharge of indebtedness occurs.

(*4*) For 2025, *ZZ*'s deduction for the remaining adjusted depreciable basis of $80,000 is $15,360 (the remaining adjusted depreciable basis of $80,000 multiplied by the annual depreciation rate 0.192 for recovery year 3). However, pursuant to paragraph (g)(2)(ii) of this section, *ZZ* must reduce the amount otherwise allowable as a depreciation deduction for 2025 by the excess depreciation previously claimed for the $50,000 decrease in basis of the qualified property. Consequently, *ZZ* must reduce the amount of depreciation otherwise allowable for 2025 by the excess additional first year depreciation of $40,000 (the decrease in basis of $50,000 multiplied by 0.80, the applicable percentage for 2023). Also, *ZZ* must reduce the amount of depreciation otherwise allowable for 2025 by the excess depreciation attributable to the remaining decrease in basis of $10,000 (the decrease in basis of $50,000 reduced by the excess additional first year depreciation of $40,000). The reduction in the amount of depreciation otherwise allowable for 2025 for the remaining decrease in basis of $10,000 is $5,714 (the remaining decrease in basis of $10,000 multiplied by 0.5714, which is equal to (1/remaining recovery period of 3.5 years at January 1, 2025, multiplied by 2). Accordingly, assuming the qualified property is the only depreciable property owned by *ZZ*, for 2025, *ZZ* has a negative depreciation deduction for the qualified property of $30,354 ($15,360 minus $40,000 minus $5,714).

(3) *Sections 1245 and 1250 depreciation recapture* .—For purposes of section 1245 and §§1.1245-1 through -6, the additional first year depreciation deduction is an amount allowed or allowable for depreciation. Further, for purposes of section 1250(b) and §1.1250-2, the additional first year depreciation deduction is not a straight line method.

(4) *Coordination with section 169* .—The additional first year depreciation deduction is allowable in the placed-in-service year of a certified pollution control facility, as defined in §1.169-2(a), that is qualified property even if the taxpayer makes the election to amortize the certified pollution control facility under section 169 and §§1.169-1 through -4 in the certified pollution control facility's placed-in-service year.

(5) *Like-kind exchanges and involuntary conversions* .—(i) *Scope* .—The rules of this paragraph (g)(5) apply to replacement MACRS property or replacement computer software that is qualified property at the time of replacement provided the time of replacement is after September 27, 2017, and before January 1, 2027; or, in the case of replacement MACRS property or replacement computer software that is qualified property described in section 168(k)(2)(B) or (C), the time of replacement is after September 27, 2017, and before January 1, 2028.

(ii) *Definitions* .—For purposes of this paragraph (g)(5), the following definitions apply:

(A) *Replacement MACRS property* has the same meaning as that term is defined in §1.168(i)-6(b)(1).

(B) *Relinquished MACRS property* has the same meaning as that term is defined in §1.168(i)-6(b)(2).

(C) *Replacement computer software* is computer software, as defined in paragraph (b)(2)(i)(B) of this section, in the hands of the acquiring taxpayer that is acquired for other computer software in a like-kind exchange or in an involuntary conversion.

(D) *Relinquished computer software* is computer software that is transferred by the taxpayer in a like-kind exchange or in an involuntary conversion.

(E) *Time of disposition* has the same meaning as that term is defined in § 1.168(i)-6(b)(3) for relinquished MACRS property. For relinquished computer software, *time of disposition* is when the disposition of the relinquished computer software takes place under the convention determined under § 1.167(a)-14(b).

(F) Except as provided in paragraph (g)(5)(iv) of this section, the *time of replacement* has the same meaning as that term is defined in § 1.168(i)-6(b)(4) for replacement MACRS property. For replacement computer software, the *time of replacement* is, except as provided in paragraph (g)(5)(iv) of this section, the later of—

*(1)* When the replacement computer software is placed in service under the convention determined under § 1.167(a)-14(b); or

*(2)* The time of disposition of the relinquished property.

(G) *Exchanged basis* has the same meaning as that term is defined in § 1.168(i)-6(b)(7) for MACRS property, as defined in § 1.168(b)-1(a)(2). For computer software, the *exchanged basis* is determined after the amortization deductions for the year of disposition are determined under § 1.167(a)-14(b) and is the lesser of—

*(1)* The basis in the replacement computer software, as determined under section 1031(d) and § 1.1031(d)-1, 1.1031(d)-2, 1.1031(j)-1, or 1.1031(k)-1; or section 1033(b) and § 1.1033(b)-1; or

*(2)* The adjusted depreciable basis of the relinquished computer software.

(H) *Excess basis* has the same meaning as that term is defined in § 1.168(i)-6(b)(8) for replacement MACRS property. For replacement computer software, the *excess basis* is any excess of the basis in the replacement computer software, as determined under section 1031(d) and § 1.1031(d)-1, 1.1031(d)-2, 1.1031(j)-1, or 1.1031(k)-1; or section 1033(b) and § 1.1033(b)-1, over the exchanged basis as determined under paragraph (g)(5)(ii)(G) of this section.

(I) *Remaining exchanged basis* is the exchanged basis as determined under paragraph (g)(5)(ii)(G) of this section reduced by—

*(1)* The percentage of such basis attributable to the taxpayer's use of property for the taxable year other than in the taxpayer's trade or business or for the production of income; and

*(2)* Any adjustments to basis provided by other provisions of the Code and the regulations under the Code (including section 1016(a)(2) and (3)) for periods prior to the disposition of the relinquished property.

(J) *Remaining excess basis* is the excess basis as determined under paragraph (g)(5)(ii)(H) of this section reduced by—

*(1)* The percentage of such basis attributable to the taxpayer's use of property for the taxable year other than in the taxpayer's trade or business or for the production of income;

*(2)* Any portion of the basis the taxpayer properly elects to treat as an expense under section 179 or 179C; and

*(3)* Any adjustments to basis provided by other provisions of the Code and the regulations under the Code.

(K) *Year of disposition* has the same meaning as that term is defined in § 1.168(i)-6(b)(5).

(L) *Year of replacement* has the same meaning as that term is defined in § 1.168(i)-6(b)(6).

(M) *Like-kind exchange* has the same meaning as that term is defined in § 1.168(i)-6(b)(11).

(N) *Involuntary conversion* has the same meaning as that term is defined in § 1.168(i)-6(b)(12).

(iii) *Computation* .—(A) *In general* .—If the replacement MACRS property or the replacement computer software, as applicable, meets the original use requirement in paragraph (b)(3)(ii) of this section and all other requirements of section 168(k) and this section, the remaining exchanged basis for the year of replacement and the remaining excess basis, if any, for the year of replacement for the replacement MACRS property or the replacement computer software, as applicable, are eligible for the additional first year depreciation deduction under this section. If the replacement MACRS property or the replacement computer software, as applicable, meets the used property acquisition requirements in paragraph (b)(3)(iii) of this section and all other requirements of section 168(k) and this section, only the remaining excess basis for the year of replacement for the replacement MACRS property or the replacement computer software, as applicable, is eligible for the additional first year depreciation deduction under this section. See paragraph (b)(3)(iii)(A)( *3*) of this section. The additional first year depreciation deduction applies to the remaining exchanged basis and any remaining excess basis, as applicable, of the replacement MACRS property or the replacement computer software, as applicable, if the time of replacement is after September 27, 2017, and before January 1, 2027; or, in the case of replacement MACRS property or replacement computer software, as applicable, described in section 168(k)(2)(B) or (C), the time of replacement is after September 27, 2017, and before January 1, 2028. The additional first year depreciation deduction is computed separately for the remaining exchanged basis and any remaining excess basis, as applicable.

(B) *Year of disposition and year of replacement* .—The additional first year depreciation deduction is allowable for the replacement MACRS property or replacement computer software in the year of replacement. However, the additional first year depreciation deduction is not allowable for the relinquished MACRS property or the relinquished computer software, as applicable, if the relinquished MACRS property or the relinquished computer software, as applicable, is placed in service and disposed of in a like-kind exchange or in an involuntary conversion in the same taxable year.

(C) *Property described in section 168(k)(2)(B)* .—For purposes of paragraph (g)(5)(iii)(A) of this section, the total of the remaining exchanged basis and the remaining excess basis, if any, of the replacement MACRS property that is qualified property described in section 168(k)(2)(B) and meets the original use requirement in paragraph (b)(3)(ii) of this section is limited to the total of the property's remaining exchanged basis and remaining excess basis, if any, attributable to the property's manufacture, construction, or production after September 27, 2017, and before January 1, 2027. For purposes of paragraph (g)(5)(iii)(A) of this section, the remaining excess basis, if any, of the replacement MACRS property that is qualified property described in section 168(k)(2)(B) and meets the used property acquisition requirements in paragraph (b)(3)(iii) of this section is limited to the property's remaining excess basis, if any, attributable to the property's manufacture, construction, or production after September 27, 2017, and before January 1, 2027.

(D) *Effect of § 1.168(i)-6(i)(1) election* .—If a taxpayer properly makes the election under § 1.168(i)-6(i)(1) not to apply § 1.168(i)-6 for any MACRS property, as defined in § 1.168(b)-1(a)(2), involved in a like-kind exchange or involuntary conversion, then:

*(1)* If the replacement MACRS property meets the original use requirement in paragraph (b)(3)(ii) of this section and all other requirements of section 168(k) and this section, the total of the exchanged basis, as defined in § 1.168(i)-6(b)(7), and the excess basis, as defined in § 1.168(i)-6(b)(8), if any, in the replacement MACRS property is eligible for the additional first year depreciation deduction under this section; or

*(2)* If the replacement MACRS property meets the used property acquisition requirements in paragraph (b)(3)(iii) of this section and all other requirements of section 168(k) and this section, only the excess basis, as defined in § 1.168(i)-6(b)(8), if any, in the replacement MACRS property is eligible for the additional first year depreciation deduction under this section.

(E) *Alternative minimum tax* .—The additional first year depreciation deduction is allowed for alternative minimum tax purposes for the year of replacement of replacement MACRS property or replacement computer software, as applicable, that is qualified property. If the replacement MACRS property or the replacement computer software, as applicable, meets the original use requirement in paragraph (b)(3)(ii) of this section and all other requirements of section 168(k) and this section, the additional first year depreciation deduction for alternative minimum tax purposes is based on the remaining exchanged basis and the remaining excess basis, if any, of the replacement MACRS property or the replacement computer software, as applicable, for alternative minimum tax purposes. If the replacement MACRS property or the replacement computer software, as applicable, meets the used property acquisition requirements in paragraph (b)(3)(iii) of this section and all other requirements of section 168(k) and this section, the additional first year depreciation deduction for alternative minimum tax purposes is based on the remaining excess basis, if any, of the replacement MACRS property or the replacement computer software, as applicable, for alternative minimum tax purposes.

(iv) *Replacement MACRS property or replacement computer software that is acquired and placed in service before disposition of relinquished MACRS property or relinquished computer software* .—If, in an involuntary conversion, a taxpayer acquires and places in service the replacement MACRS property or the replacement computer software, as applicable, before the time of disposition of the involuntarily converted MACRS property or the involuntarily converted computer software, as applicable; and the time of disposition of the involuntarily converted MACRS property or the involuntarily converted computer software, as applicable, is after December 31, 2026, or, in the case of property described in service 168(k)(2)(B) or (C), after December 31, 2027, then—

(A) The time of replacement for purposes of this paragraph (g)(5) is when the replacement MACRS property or replacement computer software, as applicable, is placed in service by the taxpayer, provided the threat or imminence of requisition or condemnation of the involuntarily converted MACRS property or involuntarily converted computer software, as applicable, existed before January 1, 2027, or, in the case of property described in section 168(k)(2)(B) or (C), existed before January 1, 2028; and

(B) The taxpayer depreciates the replacement MACRS property or replacement computer software, as applicable, in accordance with paragraph (e) of this section. However, at the time of disposition of the involuntarily converted MACRS property, the taxpayer determines the exchanged basis, as defined in § 1.168(i)-6(b)(7), and the excess basis, as defined in § 1.168(i)-6(b)(8), of the replacement MACRS property and begins to depreciate the depreciable exchanged basis, as defined in § 1.168(i)-6(b)(9), of the replacement MACRS property in accordance with § 1.168(i)-6(c). The depreciable excess basis, as defined in § 1.168(i)-6(b)(10), of the replacement MACRS property continues to be depreciated by the taxpayer in accordance with the first sentence of this paragraph (g)(5)(iv)(B). Further, in the year of disposition of the involuntarily converted MACRS property, the taxpayer must include in taxable income the excess of the depreciation deductions allowable, including the additional first year depreciation deduction allowable, on the unadjusted depreciable basis of the replacement MACRS property over the additional first year depreciation deduction that would have been allowable to the taxpayer on the remaining exchanged basis of the replacement MACRS property at the time of replacement, as defined in paragraph (g)(5)(iv)(A) of this section, plus the depreciation deductions that would have been allowable, including the additional first year depreciation deduction allowable, to the taxpayer on the depreciable excess basis of the replacement MACRS property from the date the replacement MACRS property was placed in service by the taxpayer, taking into account the applicable convention, to the time of disposition of the involuntarily converted MACRS property. Similar rules apply to replacement computer software.

(v) *Examples* .—The application of this paragraph (g)(5) is illustrated by the following examples:

(A) *Example 1.* ( *1*) In April 2016, *CSK*, a calendar-year corporation, acquired for $200,000 and placed in service Canopy V1, a gas station canopy. Canopy V1 is qualified property under section 168(k)(2), as in effect on the day before amendment by the Act, and is 5-year property under section 168(e). *CSK* depreciated Canopy V1 under the general depreciation system of section 168(a) by using the 200-percent declining balance method of depreciation, a 5-year recovery period, and the half-year convention. *CSK* elected to use the optional depreciation tables to compute the depreciation allowance for Canopy V1. In November 2017, Canopy V1 was destroyed in a fire and was no longer usable in *CSK*'s business. In December 2017, in an involuntary conversion, *CSK* acquired and placed in service Canopy W1 with all of the $160,000 of insurance proceeds *CSK* received due to the loss of Canopy V1. Canopy W1 is qualified property under section 168(k)(2) and this section, and is 5-year property under section 168(e). Canopy W1 also meets the original use requirement in paragraph (b)(3)(ii) of this section. *CSK* did not make the election under § 1.168(i)-6(i)(1).

( *2*) For 2016, *CSK* is allowed a 50-percent additional first year depreciation deduction of $100,000 for Canopy V1 (the unadjusted depreciable basis of $200,000 multiplied by 0.50), and a regular MACRS depreciation deduction of $20,000 for Canopy V1 (the remaining adjusted depreciable basis of $100,000 multiplied by the annual depreciation rate of 0.20 for recovery year 1).

( *3*) For 2017, *CSK* is allowed a regular MACRS depreciation deduction of $16,000 for Canopy V1 (the remaining adjusted depreciable basis of $100,000 multiplied by the annual depreciation rate of 0.32 for recovery year 2 × ½ year).

( *4*) Pursuant to paragraph (g)(5)(iii)(A) of this section, the additional first year depreciation deduction allowable for Canopy W1 for 2017 equals $64,000 (100 percent of Canopy W1's remaining exchanged basis at the time of replacement of $64,000 (Canopy V1's remaining adjusted depreciable basis of $100,000 minus 2016 regular MACRS depreciation deduction of $20,000 minus 2017 regular MACRS depreciation deduction of $16,000)).

(B) *Example 2.* ( *1*) The facts are the same as in *Example 1* of paragraph (g)(5)(v)(A)( *1*) of this section, except *CSK* elected not to deduct the additional first year depreciation for 5-year property placed in service in 2016. *CSK* deducted the additional first year depreciation for 5-year property placed in service in 2017.

( *2*) For 2016, *CSK* is allowed a regular MACRS depreciation deduction of $40,000 for Canopy V1 (the unadjusted depreciable basis of $200,000 multiplied by the annual depreciation rate of 0.20 for recovery year 1).

( *3*) For 2017, *CSK* is allowed a regular MACRS depreciation deduction of $32,000 for Canopy V1 (the unadjusted depreciable basis of $200,000 multiplied by the annual depreciation rate of 0.32 for recovery year 2 × ½ year).

( *4*) Pursuant to paragraph (g)(5)(iii)(A) of this section, the additional first year depreciation deduction allowable for Canopy W1 for 2017 equals $128,000 (100 percent of Canopy W1's remaining exchanged basis at the time of replacement of $128,000 (Canopy V1's unadjusted depreciable basis of $200,000 minus 2016 regular MACRS depreciation deduction of $40,000 minus 2017 regular MACRS depreciation deduction of $32,000)).

(C) *Example 3.* The facts are the same as in *Example 1* of paragraph (g) (5) (v) (A) ( *1*) of this section, except Canopy W1 meets the used property acquisition requirements in paragraph (b) (3) (iii) of this section. Because the remaining excess basis of Canopy W1 is zero, *CSK* is not allowed any additional first year depreciation for Canopy W1 pursuant to paragraph (g) (5) (iii) (A) of this section.

(D) *Example 4.* ( *1*) In December 2016, *AB*, a calendar-year corporation, acquired for $10,000 and placed in service Computer X2. Computer X2 is qualified property under section 168(k) (2), as in effect on the day before amendment by the Act, and is 5-year property under section 168(e). *AB* depreciated Computer X2 under the general depreciation system of section 168(a) by using the 200-percent declining balance method of depreciation, a 5-year recovery period, and the half-year convention. *AB* elected to use the optional depreciation tables to compute the depreciation allowance for Computer X2. In November 2017, *AB* acquired Computer Y2 by exchanging Computer X2 and $1,000 cash in a like-kind exchange. Computer Y2 is qualified property under section 168(k) (2) and this section, and is 5-year property under section 168(e). Computer Y2 also meets the original use requirement in paragraph (b) (3) (ii) of this section. *AB* did not make the election under § 1.168(i)-6(i) (1).

( *2*) For 2016, *AB* is allowed a 50-percent additional first year depreciation deduction of $5,000 for Computer X2 (unadjusted basis of $10,000 multiplied by 0.50), and a regular MACRS depreciation deduction of $1,000 for Computer X2 (the remaining adjusted depreciable basis of $5,000 multiplied by the annual depreciation rate of 0.20 for recovery year 1).

( *3*) For 2017, *AB* is allowed a regular MACRS depreciation deduction of $800 for Computer X2 (the remaining adjusted depreciable basis of $5,000 multiplied by the annual depreciation rate of 0.32 for recovery year 2 × ½ year).

( *4*) Pursuant to paragraph (g) (5) (iii) (A) of this section, the 100-percent additional first year depreciation deduction for Computer Y2 for 2017 is allowable for the remaining exchanged basis at the time of replacement of $3,200 (Computer X2's unadjusted depreciable basis of $10,000 minus additional first year depreciation deduction allowable of $5,000 minus the 2016 regular MACRS depreciation deduction of $1,000 minus the 2017 regular MACRS depreciation deduction of $800) and for the remaining excess basis at the time of replacement of $1,000 (cash paid for Computer Y2). Thus, the 100-percent additional first year depreciation deduction allowable for Computer Y2 totals $4,200 for 2017.

(E) *Example 5.* ( *1*) In July 2017, *BC*, a calendar-year corporation, acquired for $20,000 and placed in service Equipment X3. Equipment X3 is qualified property under section 168(k) (2), as in effect on the day before amendment by the Act, and is 5-year property under section 168(e). *BC* depreciated Equipment X3 under the general depreciation system of section 168(a) by using the 200-percent declining balance method of depreciation, a 5-year recovery period, and the half-year convention. *BC* elected to use the optional depreciation tables to compute the depreciation allowance for Equipment X3. In December 2017, *BC* acquired Equipment Y3 by exchanging Equipment X3 and $5,000 cash in a like-kind exchange. Equipment Y3 is qualified property under section 168(k) (2) and this section, and is 5-year property under section 168(e). Equipment Y3 also meets the used property acquisition requirements in paragraph (b) (3) (iii) of this section. *BC* did not make the election under § 1.168(i)-6(i) (1).

( *2*) Pursuant to § 1.168(k)-1(f) (5) (iii) (B), no additional first year depreciation deduction is allowable for Equipment X3 and, pursuant to

§ 1.168(d)-1(b)(3)(ii), no regular depreciation deduction is allowable for Equipment X3, for 2017.

(*3*) Pursuant to paragraph (g)(5)(iii)(A) of this section, no additional first year depreciation deduction is allowable for Equipment Y3's remaining exchanged basis at the time of replacement of $20,000 (Equipment X3's unadjusted depreciable basis of $20,000). However, pursuant to paragraph (g)(5)(iii)(A) of this section, the 100-percent additional first year depreciation deduction is allowable for Equipment Y3's remaining excess basis at the time of replacement of $5,000 (cash paid for Equipment Y3). Thus, the 100-percent additional first year depreciation deduction allowable for Equipment Y3 is $5,000 for 2017.

(F) *Example 6.* (*1*) The facts are the same as in *Example 5* of paragraph (g)(5)(v)(E)(*1*) of this section, except *BC* properly makes the election under § 1.168(i)-6(i)(1) not to apply § 1.168(i)-6 to Equipment X3 and Equipment Y3.

(*2*) Pursuant to § 1.168(k)-1(f)(5)(iii)(B), no additional first year depreciation deduction is allowable for Equipment X3 and, pursuant to § 1.168(d)-1(b)(3)(ii), no regular depreciation deduction is allowable for Equipment X3, for 2017.

(*3*) Pursuant to § 1.168(i)-6(i)(1), *BC* is treated as placing Equipment Y3 in service in December 2017 with a basis of $25,000 (the total of the exchanged basis of $20,000 and the excess basis of $5,000). However, pursuant to paragraph (g)(5)(iii)(D)(*2*) of this section, the 100-percent additional first year depreciation deduction is allowable only for Equipment Y3's excess basis at the time of replacement of $5,000 (cash paid for Equipment Y3). Thus, the 100-percent additional first year depreciation deduction allowable for Equipment Y3 is $5,000 for 2017.

(6) *Change in use*.—(i) *Change in use of MACRS property*.—The determination of whether the use of MACRS property, as defined in § 1.168(b)-1(a)(2), changes is made in accordance with section 168(i)(5) and § 1.168(i)-4.

(ii) *Conversion to personal use*.—If qualified property is converted from business or income-producing use to personal use in the same taxable year in which the property is placed in service by a taxpayer, the additional first year depreciation deduction is not allowable for the property.

(iii) *Conversion to business or income-producing use*.—(A) *During the same taxable year*.—If, during the same taxable year, property is acquired by a taxpayer for personal use and is converted by the taxpayer from personal use to business or income-producing use, the additional first year depreciation deduction is allowable for the property in the taxable year the property is converted to business or income-producing use, assuming all of the requirements in paragraph (b) of this section are met. See paragraph (b)(3)(ii) of this section relating to the original use rules for a conversion of property to business or income-producing use. See § 1.168(i)-4(b)(1) for determining the depreciable basis of the property at the time of conversion to business or income-producing use.

(B) *Subsequent to the acquisition year*.—If property is acquired by a taxpayer for personal use and, during a subsequent taxable year, is converted by the taxpayer from personal use to business or income-producing use, the additional first year depreciation deduction is allowable for the property in the taxable year the property is converted to business or income-producing use, assuming all of the requirements in paragraph (b) of this section are met. For purposes of paragraphs (b)(4) and (5) of this section, the property must be acquired by the taxpayer for personal use after September 27, 2017, and converted by the taxpayer from personal use to business or income-producing use by January 1, 2027. See paragraph (b)(3)(ii) of this section relating to the original use rules for a conversion of property to business or income-producing use. See § 1.168(i)-4(b)(1) for determining the depreciable basis of the property at the time of conversion to business or income-producing use.

(iv) *Depreciable property changes use subsequent to the placed-in-service year*.—(A) If the use of qualified property changes in the hands of the same taxpayer subsequent to the taxable year the qualified property is placed in service and, as a result of the change in use, the property is no longer qualified property, the additional first year depreciation deduction allowable for the qualified property is not redetermined.

(B) If depreciable property is not qualified property in the taxable year the property is placed in service by the taxpayer, the additional first year depreciation deduction is not allowable for the property even if a change in the use of the property subsequent to the taxable year the property is placed in service results in the property being qualified property in the taxable year of the change in use.

(v) *Examples*.—The application of this paragraph (g)(6) is illustrated by the following examples:

(A) *Example 1*. (*1*) On January 1, 2019, *FFF*, a calendar year corporation, purchased and placed in service several new computers at a total cost of $100,000. *FFF* used these computers within the United States for 3 months in 2019 and then moved and used the computers outside the United States for the remainder of 2019. On January 1, 2020, *FFF* permanently returns the computers to the United States for use in its business.

(*2*) For 2019, the computers are considered as used predominantly outside the United States in 2019 pursuant to § 1.48-1(g)(1)(i). As a result, the computers are required to be depreciated under the alternative depreciation system of section 168(g). Pursuant to paragraph (b)(2)(ii)(B) of this section, the computers are not qualified property in 2019, the placed-in-service year. Thus, pursuant to paragraph (g)(6)(iv)(B) of this section, no additional first year depreciation deduction is allowed for these computers, regardless of the fact that the computers are permanently returned to the United States in 2020.

(B) *Example 2*. (*1*) On February 8, 2023, *GGG*, a calendar year corporation, purchased and placed in service new equipment at a cost of $1,000,000 for use in its California plant. The equipment is 5-year property under section 168(e) and is qualified property under section 168(k). *GGG* depreciates its 5-year property placed in service in 2023 using the optional depreciation table that corresponds with the general depreciation system, the 200-percent declining balance method, a 5-year recovery period, and the half-year convention. On June 4, 2024, due to changes in *GGG*'s business circumstances, *GGG* permanently moves the equipment to its plant in Mexico.

(*2*) For 2023, *GGG* is allowed an 80-percent additional first year depreciation deduction of $800,000 (the adjusted depreciable basis of $1,000,000 multiplied by 0.80). In addition, *GGG*'s depreciation deduction allowable in 2023 for the remaining adjusted depreciable basis of $200,000 (the unadjusted depreciable basis of $1,000,000 reduced by the additional first year depreciation deduction of $800,000) is $40,000 (the remaining adjusted depreciable basis of $200,000 multiplied by the annual depreciation rate of 0.20 for recovery year 1).

(*3*) For 2024, the equipment is considered as used predominantly outside the United States pursuant to § 1.48-1(g)(1)(i). As a result of this change in use, the adjusted depreciable basis of $160,000 for the equipment is required to be depreciated under the alternative depreciation system of section 168(g) beginning in 2024. However, the additional first year depreciation deduction of $800,000 allowed for the equipment in 2023 is not redetermined.

(7) *Earnings and profits* .—The additional first year depreciation deduction is not allowable for purposes of computing earnings and profits.

(8) *Limitation of amount of depreciation for certain passenger automobiles* .—For a passenger automobile as defined in section 280F(d)(5), the limitation under section 280F(a)(1)(A)(i) is increased by $8,000 for qualified property acquired and placed in service by a taxpayer after September 27, 2017.

(9) *Coordination with section 47* .—(i) *In general* .—If qualified rehabilitation expenditures, as defined in section 47(c)(2) and § 1.48-12(c), incurred by a taxpayer with respect to a qualified rehabilitated building, as defined in section 47(c)(1) and § 1.48-12(b), are qualified property, the taxpayer may claim the rehabilitation credit provided by section 47(a), provided the requirements of section 47 are met—

(A) With respect to the portion of the basis of the qualified rehabilitated building that is attributable to the qualified rehabilitation expenditures if the taxpayer makes the applicable election under paragraph (f)(1)(i) of this section not to deduct any additional first year depreciation for the class of property that includes the qualified rehabilitation expenditures; or

(B) With respect to the portion of the remaining rehabilitated basis of the qualified rehabilitated building that is attributable to the qualified rehabilitation expenditures if the taxpayer claims the additional first year depreciation deduction on the unadjusted depreciable basis, as defined in § 1.168(b)-1(a)(3) but before the reduction in basis for the amount of the rehabilitation credit, of the qualified rehabilitation expenditures; and the taxpayer depreciates the remaining adjusted depreciable basis, as defined in paragraph (e)(2)(i) of this section, of such expenditures using straight line cost recovery in accordance with section 47(c)(2)(B)(i) and § 1.48-12(c)(7)(i). For purposes of this paragraph (g)(9)(i)(B), the remaining rehabilitated basis is equal to the unadjusted depreciable basis, as defined in § 1.168(b)-1(a)(3) but before the reduction in basis for the amount of the rehabilitation credit, of the qualified rehabilitation expenditures that are qualified property reduced by the additional first year depreciation allowed or allowable, whichever is greater.

(ii) *Example* .—The application of this paragraph (g)(9) is illustrated by the following example:

(A) Between February 8, 2023, and June 4, 2023, *JM*, a calendar-year taxpayer, incurred qualified rehabilitation expenditures of $200,000 with respect to a qualified rehabilitated building that is nonresidential real property under section 168(e). These qualified rehabilitation expenditures are qualified property and qualify for the 20-percent rehabilitation credit under section 47(a)(1). *JM*'s basis in the qualified rehabilitated building is zero before incurring the qualified rehabilitation expenditures and *JM* placed the qualified rehabilitated building in service in July 2023. *JM* depreciates its nonresidential real property placed in service in 2023 under the general depreciation system of section 168(a) by using the straight line method of depreciation, a 39-year recovery period, and the mid-month convention. *JM* elected to use the optional depreciation tables to compute the depreciation allowance for its depreciable property placed in service in 2023. Further, for 2023, *JM* did not make any election under paragraph (f) of this section.

(B) Because *JM* did not make any election under paragraph (f) of this section, *JM* is allowed an 80-percent additional first year depreciation deduction of $160,000 for the qualified rehabilitation expenditures for 2023 (the unadjusted depreciable basis of $200,000 (before reduction in basis for the rehabilitation credit) multiplied by 0.80). *JM* also is allowed to claim a rehabilitation credit of $8,000 for the remaining rehabilitated basis of $40,000 (the unadjusted depreciable basis (before reduction in basis for the rehabilitation credit) of $200,000 less the additional first year depreciation deduction of $160,000, multiplied by 0.20 to calculate the rehabilitation credit). For 2023, the ratable share of the rehabilitation credit of $8,000 is $1,600. Further, *JM*'s depreciation deduction for 2023 for the remaining adjusted depreciable basis of $32,000 (the unadjusted depreciable basis (before reduction in basis for the rehabilitation credit) of $200,000 less the additional first year depreciation deduction of $160,000 less the rehabilitation credit of $8,000) is $376.64 (the remaining adjusted depreciable basis of $32,000 multiplied by the depreciation rate of 0.01177 for recovery year 1, placed in service in month 7).

(10) *Coordination with section 514(a)(3)* .—The additional first year depreciation deduction is not allowable for purposes of section 514(a)(3).

(11) *Mid-quarter convention* .—In determining whether the mid-quarter convention applies for a taxable year under section 168(d)(3) and § 1.168(d)-1, the depreciable basis, as defined in § 1.168(d)-1(b)(4), for the taxable year the qualified property is placed in service by the taxpayer is not reduced by the allowed or allowable additional first year depreciation deduction for that taxable year. See § 1.168(d)-1(b)(4).

(h) *Applicability dates* .—(1) *In general* .—Except as provided in paragraphs (h)(2) and (3) of this section, this section applies to—

(i) Depreciable property acquired after September 27, 2017, by the taxpayer and placed in service by the taxpayer during or after the taxpayer's taxable year that begins on or after January 1, 2021;

(ii) A specified plant for which the taxpayer properly made an election to apply section 168(k)(5) and that is planted, or grafted to a plant that was previously planted, by the taxpayer during or after the taxpayer's taxable year that begins on or after January 1, 2021; and

(iii) Components acquired or self-constructed after September 27, 2017, of larger self-constructed property described in paragraph (c)(2) of this section and placed in service by the taxpayer during or after the taxpayer's taxable year that begins on or after January 1, 2021.

(2) *Applicability of this section for prior taxable years* .—For taxable years beginning before January 1, 2021, see § 1.168(k)-2 as contained in 26 CFR part 1, revised as of April 1, 2020.

(3) *Early application of this section and § 1.1502-68* .—(i) *In general* .—Subject to paragraphs (h)(3)(ii) and (iii) of this section, and provided that all members of a consolidated group consistently apply the same set of rules, a taxpayer may choose to apply both the rules of this section and the rules of § 1.1502-68 (to the extent relevant), in their entirety and in a consistent manner, to—

(A) Depreciable property acquired after September 27, 2017, by the taxpayer and placed in service by the taxpayer during a taxable year ending on or after September 28, 2017;

(B) A specified plant for which the taxpayer properly made an election to apply section 168(k)(5) and that is planted, or grafted to a plant that was previously planted, after September 27, 2017, by the taxpayer during a taxable year ending on or after September 28, 2017; and

(C) Components acquired or self-constructed after September 27, 2017, of larger self-constructed property described in paragraph (c)(2) of this section and placed in service by the taxpayer during a taxable year ending on or after September 28, 2017.

(ii) *Early application to certain transactions* .—In the case of property described in § 1.1502-68(e)(2)(i) that is acquired in a transaction that satisfies the requirements of § 1.1502-68(c)(1)(ii) or (c)(2)(ii), the taxpayer may apply the rules of this section and the rules of § 1.1502-68 (to the extent relevant), in their entirety and in a consistent manner, to such property only if those rules are applied, in their entirety and in a consistent manner, by all parties to the transaction, including the transferor member, the transferee member, and the target, as applicable, and the consolidated groups of which they are members, for the taxable year(s) in which the transaction occurs and the taxable year(s) that includes the day after the deconsolidation date, as defined in § 1.1502-68(a)(2)(iii).

(iii) *Bound by early application* .—Once a taxpayer applies the rules of this section and the rules of § 1.1502-68 (to the extent relevant), in their entirety, for a taxable year, the taxpayer must continue to apply the rules of this section and the rules of § 1.1502-68 (to the extent relevant), in their entirety, for the taxpayer's subsequent taxable years. [Reg. § 1.168(k)-2.]

**.01 Historical Comment:** Adopted 9/17/2019 by T.D. 9874. Amended 11/5/2020 by T.D. 9916. Reg. § 168(k)-2 does not reflect P.L. 116-136 (2020). See ¶ 12,250.018 (P.L. 116-136).

# Code Sec. 179 Expensing Regulations

¶ 576

## Reg. § 1.179-0

§ 1.179-0. **Table of contents for section 179 expensing rules.**

This section lists captioned paragraphs contained in §§ 1.179-1 through 1.179-6.

(5) Joint returns.
(i) In general.
(ii) Joint returns filed after separate returns.
(iii) Example.
(6) Married individuals filing separately.
(i) In general.
(ii) Example.
(7) Component members of a controlled group.
(i) In general.
(ii) Statement to be filed.
(iii) Revocation.
(c) Taxable income limitation.
(1) In general.
(2) Application to partnerships and partners.
(i) In general.
(ii) Taxable year.
(iii) Example.
(iv) Taxable income of a partnership.
(v) Partner's share of partnership taxable income.
(3) S corporations and S corporation shareholders.
(i) In general.
(ii) Taxable income of an S corporation.
(iii) Shareholder's share of S corporation taxable income.
(4) Taxable income of a corporation other than an S corporation.
(5) Ordering rule for certain circular problems.
(i) In general.
(ii) Example.
(6) Active conduct by the taxpayer of a trade or business.
(i) Trade or business.
(ii) Active conduct.
(iii) Example.
(iv) Employees.
(7) Joint returns.
(i) In general.
(ii) Joint returns filed after separate returns.
(8) Married individuals filing separately.
(d) Examples.

*§ 1.179-3 Carryover of disallowed deduction.*

(a) In general.
(b) Deduction of carryover of disallowed deduction.
(1) In general.
(2) Cross references.
(c) Unused section 179 expense allowance.
(d) Example.
(e) Recordkeeping requirement and ordering rule.
(f) Dispositions and other transfers of section 179 property.
(1) In general.
(2) Recapture under section 179(d)(10).
(g) Special rules for partnerships and S corporations.
(1) In general.

(2) Basis adjustment.

(3) Dispositions and other transfers of section 179 property by a partnership or an S corporation.

(4) Example.

(h) Special rules for partners and S corporation shareholders.

(1) In general.

(2) Dispositions and other transfers of a partner's interest in a partnership or a shareholder's interest in an S corporation.

(3) Examples.

*§ 1.179-4 Definitions.*

(a) Section 179 property.

(b) Section 38 property.

(c) Purchase.

(d) Cost.

(e) Placed in service.

(f) Controlled group of corporations and component member of controlled group.

*§ 1.179-5 Time and manner of making election.*

(a) Election.

(b) Revocation.

(c) Section 179 property placed in service by the taxpayer in a taxable year beginning after 2002 and before 2008.

(d) Election or revocation must not be made in any other manner.

*§ 1.179-6 Effective dates.*

(a) In general.

(b) Section 179 property placed in service by the taxpayer in a taxable year beginning after 2002 and before 2008.

(c) Application of § 1.179-5(d).

[Reg. § 1.179-0.]

**.01 Historical Comment:** Proposed 3/28/91. Adopted 12/23/92 by T.D. 8455. Amended 8/3/2004 by T.D. 9146 and 7/12/2005 by T.D. 9209.

## ¶ 577

## Reg. § 1.179-1

§ 1.179-1. **Election to expense certain depreciable assets.**— (a) *In general* .—Section 179(a) allows a taxpayer to elect to expense the cost (as defined in § 1.179-4(d)), or a portion of the cost, of section 179 property (as defined in § 1.179-4(a)) for the taxable year in which the property is placed in service (as defined in § 1.179-4(e)). The election is not available for trusts, estates, and certain noncorporate lessors. See paragraph (i)(2) of this section for rules concerning noncorporate lessors. However, section 179(b) provides certain limitations on the amount that a taxpayer may elect to expense in any one taxable year. See § § 1.179-2 and 1.179-3 for rules relating to the dollar and taxable income limitations and the carryover of disallowed deduction rules. For rules describing the time and manner of making an election under section 179, see § 1.179-5. For the effective date, see § 1.179-6.

(b) *Cost subject to expense* .—The expense deduction under section 179 is allowed for the entire cost or a portion of the cost of one or more items of section 179 property. This expense deduction is subject to the limitations of section 179(b) and § 1.179-2. The taxpayer may select the properties that are subject to the election as well as the portion of each property's cost to expense.

(c) *Proration not required* .—(1) *In general* .—The expense deduction under section 179 is determined without any proration based on—

(i) The period of time the section 179 property has been in service during the taxable year; or

(ii) The length of the taxable year in which the property is placed in service.

(2) *Example* .—The following example illustrates the provisions of paragraph (c)(1) of this section.

*Example.* On December 1, 1991, X, a calendar-year corporation, purchases and places in service section 179 property costing $20,000. For the taxable year ending December 31, 1991, X may elect to claim a section 179 expense deduction on the property (subject to the limitations imposed under section 179(b)) without proration of its cost for the number of days in 1991 during which the property was in service.

(d) *Partial business use* .—(1) *In general* .—If a taxpayer uses section 179 property for trade or business as well as other purposes, the portion of the cost of the property attributable to the trade or business use is eligible for expensing under section 179 provided that more than 50 percent of the property's use in the taxable year is for trade or business purposes. The limitations of section 179(b) and § 1.179-2 are applied to the portion of the cost attributable to the trade or business use.

(2) *Example* .—The following example illustrates the provisions of paragraph (d)(1) of this section.

*Example.* A purchases section 179 property costing $10,000 in 1991 for which 80 percent of its use will be in A's trade or business. The cost of the property adjusted to reflect the business use of the property is $8,000 (80 percent × $10,000). Thus, A may elect to expense up to $8,000 of the cost of the property (subject to the limitations imposed under section 179(b) and § 1.179-2).

(3) *Additional rules that may apply* .—If a section 179 election is made for "listed property" within the meaning of section 280F(d)(4) and there is personal use of the property, section 280F (d)(1), which provides rules that coordinate section 179 with the section 280F limitation on the amount of depreciation, may apply. If section 179 property is no longer predominantly used in the taxpayer's trade or business, paragraphs (e)(1) through (4) of this section, relating to recapture of the section 179 deduction, may apply.

(e) *Change in use; recapture* .—(1) *In general* .—If a taxpayer's section 179 property is not used predominantly in a trade or business of the taxpayer at any time before the end of the property's recovery period, the taxpayer must recapture in the taxable year in which the section 179 property is not used predominantly in a trade or business any benefit derived from expensing such property. The benefit derived from expensing the property is equal to the excess of the amount expensed under this section over the total amount that would have been allowable for prior taxable years and the taxable year of recapture as a deduction under section 168 (had section 179 not been elected) for the portion of the cost of the property to which the expensing relates (regardless of whether such excess reduced the taxpayer's tax liability). For purposes of the preceding sentence, (i) the "amount expensed under this section" shall not include any amount that was not allowed as a deduction to a taxpayer because the taxpayer's aggregate amount of allowable section 179 expenses exceeded the section 179(b) dollar limitation, and (ii) in the case of an individual who does not elect to itemize deductions under section 63(g) in the taxable year of recapture, the amount allowable as a deduction under section

168 in the taxable year of recapture shall be determined by treating property used in the production of income other than rents or royalties as being property used for personal purposes. The amount to be recaptured shall be treated as ordinary income for the taxable year in which the property is no longer used predominantly in a trade or business of the taxpayer. For taxable years following the year of recapture, the taxpayer's deductions under section 168(a) shall be determined as if no section 179 election with respect to the property had been made. However, see section 280F(d)(1) relating to the coordination of section 179 with the limitation on the amount of depreciation for luxury automobiles and where certain property is used for personal purposes. If the recapture rules of both section 280F(b)(2) and this paragraph (c)(1) apply to an item of section 179 property, the amount of recapture for such property shall be determined only under the rules of section 280F(b)(2).

(2) *Predominant use* .—Property will be treated as not used predominantly in a trade or business of the taxpayer if 50 percent or more of the use of such property during any taxable year within the recapture period is for a use other than in a trade or business of the taxpayer. If during any taxable year of the recapture period the taxpayer disposes of the property (other than in a disposition to which section 1245(a) applies) or ceases to use the property in a trade or business in a manner that had the taxpayer claimed a credit under section 38 for such property such disposition or cessation in use would cause recapture under section 47, the property will be treated as not used in a trade or business of the taxpayer. However, for purposes of applying the recapture rules of section 47 pursuant to the preceding sentence, converting the use of the property from use in a trade or business to use in the production of income will be treated as a conversion to personal use.

(3) *Basis; application with section 1245* .—The basis of property with respect to which there is recapture under paragraph (e)(1) of this section shall be increased immediately before the event resulting in such recapture by the amount recaptured. If section 1245(a) applies to a disposition of property, there is no recapture under paragraph (e)(1) of this section.

(4) *Carryover of disallowed deduction* .—See § 1.179-3 for rules on applying the recapture provisions of this paragraph (e) when a taxpayer has a carryover of disallowed deduction.

(5) *Example* .—The following example illustrates the provisions of paragraphs (e)(1) through (e)(4) of this section.

*Example.* A, a calendar-year taxpayer, purchases and places in service on January 1, 1991, section 179 property costing $15,000. The property is 5-year property for section 168 purposes and is the only item of depreciable property placed in service by A during 1991. A properly elects to expense $10,000 of the cost and elects under section 168(b)(5) to depreciate the remaining cost under the straight-line method. On January 1, 1992, A converts the property from use in A's business to use for the production of income, and A uses the property in the latter capacity for the entire year. A elects to itemize deductions for 1992. Because the property was not predominantly used in A's trade or business in 1992, A must recapture any benefit derived from expensing the property under section 179. Had A not elected to expense the $10,000 in 1991, A would have been entitled to deduct, under section 168, 10 percent of the $10,000 in 1991, and 20 percent of the $10,000 in 1992. Therefore, A must include $7,000 in ordinary income for the 1992 taxable year, the excess of $10,000 (the section 179 expense amount) over $3,000 (30 percent of $10,000).

(f) *Basis*.—(1) *In general*.—A taxpayer who elects to expense under section 179 must reduce the depreciable basis of the section 179 property by the amount of the section 179 expense deduction.

(2) *Special rules for partnerships and S corporations*.—Generally the basis of a partnership or S corporation's section 179 property must be reduced to reflect the amount of section 179 expense elected by the partnership or S corporation. This reduction must be made in the basis of partnership or S corporation property even if the limitations of section 179(b) and § 1.179-2 prevent a partner in a partnership or a shareholder in an S corporation from deducting all or a portion of the amount of the section 179 expense allocated by the partnership or S corporation. See § 1.179-3 for rules on applying the basis provisions of this paragraph (f) when a person has a carryover of disallowed deduction.

(3) *Special rules with respect to trusts and estates which are partners or S corporation shareholders*.—Since the section 179 election is not available for trusts or estates, a partner or S corporation shareholder that is a trust or estate, may not deduct its allocable share of the section 179 expense elected by the partnership or S corporation. The partnership or S corporation's basis in section 179 property shall not be reduced to reflect any portion of the section 179 expense that is allocable to the trust or estate. Accordingly, the partnership or S corporation may claim a depreciation deduction under section 168 or a section 38 credit (if available) with respect to any depreciable basis resulting from the trust or estate's inability to claim its allocable portion of the section 179 expense.

(g) *Disallowance of the section 38 credit*.—If a taxpayer elects to expense under section 179, no section 38 credit is allowable for the portion of the cost expensed. In addition, no section 38 credit shall be allowed under section 48(d) to a lessee of property for the portion of the cost of the property that the lessor expensed under section 179.

(h) *Partnerships and S corporations*.—(1) *In general*.—In the case of property purchased and placed in service by a partnership or an S corporation, the determination of whether the property is section 179 property is made at the partnership or S corporation level. The election to expense the cost of section 179 property is made by the partnership or the S corporation. See sections 703(b), 1363(c), 6221, 6231(a)(3), 6241, and 6245.

(2) *Example*.—The following example illustrates the provisions of paragraph (h)(1) of this section.

*Example*. A owns certain residential rental property as an investment. A and others form ABC partnership whose function is to rent and manage such property. A and ABC partnership file their income tax returns on a calendar-year basis. In 1991, ABC partnership purchases and places in service office furniture costing $20,000 to be used in the active conduct of ABC's business. Although the office furniture is used with respect to an investment activity of A, the furniture is being used in the active conduct of ABC's trade or business. Therefore, because the determination of whether property is section 179 property is made at the partnership level, the office furniture is section 179 property and ABC may elect to expense a portion of its cost under section 179.

(i) *Leasing of section 179 property*.—(1) *In general*.—A lessor of section 179 property who is treated as the owner of the property for Federal tax purposes will be entitled to the section 179 expense deduction if the requirements of section 179 and the regulations thereunder are met. These requirements will not be met if the lessor merely holds the property for the production of income. For certain leases entered prior to January 1, 1984, the safe harbor provisions of section 168(f)(8) apply in determining whether an agreement is treated as a lease for Federal tax purposes.

(2) *Noncorporate lessor* .—In determining the class of taxpayers (other than an estate or trust) for which section 179 is applicable, section 179(d)(5) provides that if a taxpayer is a noncorporate lessor ( *i.e.*, a person who is not a corporation and is a lessor), the taxpayer shall not be entitled to claim a section 179 expense for section 179 property purchased and leased by the taxpayer unless the taxpayer has satisfied all of the requirements of section 179(d)(5)(A) or (B).

(j) *Application of sections 263 and 263A* .—Under section 263(a)(1)(G), expenditures for which a deduction is allowed under section 179 and this section are excluded from capitalization under section 263(a). Under this paragraph (j), amounts allowed as a deduction under section 179 and this section are excluded from the application of the uniform capitalization rules of section 263A.

(k) *Cross references* .—See section 453(i) and the regulations thereunder with respect to installment sales of section 179 property. See section 263(a)(1)(H) and the regulations thereunder with respect to capitalizing section 179 property. [Reg. § 1.179-1.]

**.01 Historical Comment:** Proposed 9/26/85. Adopted 1/5/87 by T.D. 8121. Amended 12/23/92 by T.D. 8455.

## ¶ 578

## Reg. § 1.179-2

§ 1.179-2. **Limitations on amount subject to section 179 election.**— (a) *In general* .—Sections 179(b)(1) and (2) limit the aggregate cost of section 179 property that a taxpayer may elect to expense under section 179 for any one taxable year (dollar limitation). See paragraph (b) of this section. Section 179(b)(3)(A) limits the aggregate cost of section 179 property that a taxpayer may deduct in any taxable year (taxable income limitation). See paragraph (c) of this section. Any cost that is elected to be expensed but that is not currently deductible because of the taxable income limitation may be carried forward to the next taxable year (carryover of disallowed deduction). See § 1.179-3 for rules relating to carryovers of disallowed deductions. See also sections 280F(a), (b), and (d)(1) relating to the coordination of section 179 with the limitations on the amount of depreciation for luxury automobiles and other listed property. The dollar and taxable income limitations apply to each taxpayer and not to each trade or business in which the taxpayer has an interest.

(b) *Dollar limitation* .—(1) *In general* .—The aggregate cost of section 179 property that a taxpayer may elect to expense under section 179 for any taxable year beginning in 2003 and thereafter is $25,000 ($100,000 in the case of taxable years beginning after 2002 and before 2008 under section 179(b)(1), indexed annually for inflation under section 179(b)(5) for taxable years beginning after 2003 and before 2008), reduced (but not below zero) by the amount of any excess section 179 property (described in paragraph (b)(2) of this section) placed in service during the taxable year.

(2) *Excess section 179 property* .—The amount of any excess section 179 property for a taxable year equals the excess (if any) of—

(i) The cost of section 179 property placed in service by the taxpayer in the taxable year; over

(ii) $200,000 ($400,000 in the case of taxable years beginning after 2002 and before 2008 under section 179(b)(2), indexed annually for inflation under section 179(b)(5) for taxable years beginning after 2003 and before 2008).

(3) *Application to partnerships* .—(i) *In general* .—The dollar limitation of this paragraph (b) applies to the partnership as well as to each partner. In applying the dollar limitation to a taxpayer that is a partner in one or more partnerships, the partner's share of section 179 expenses allocated to the partner from each partnership is aggregated with any nonpartnership section 179 expenses of the taxpayer for the taxable year. However, in determining the excess section 179 property placed in service by a partner in a taxable year, the cost of section 179 property placed in service by the partnership is not attributed to any partner.

(ii) *Example* .—The following example illustrates the provisions of paragraph (b) (3) (i) of this section.

*Example.* During 1991, CD, a calendar-year partnership, purchases and places in service section 179 property costing $150,000 and elects under section 179(c) and § 1.179-5 to expense $10,000 of the cost of that property. CD properly allocates to C, a calendar-year taxpayer and a partner in CD, $5,000 of section 179 expenses (C's distributive share of CD's section 179 expenses for 1991). In applying the dollar limitation to C for 1991, C must include the $5,000 of section 179 expenses allocated from CD. However, in determining the amount of any excess section 179 property C placed in service during 1991, C does not include any of the cost of section 179 property placed in service by CD, including the $5,000 of cost represented by the $5,000 of section 179 expenses allocated to C by the partnership.

(iii) *Partner's share of section 179 expenses* .—Section 704 and the regulations thereunder govern the determination of a partner's share of a partnership's section 179 expenses for any taxable year. However, no allocation among partners of the section 179 expenses may be modified after the due date of the partnership return (without regard to extensions of time) for the taxable year for which the election under section 179 is made.

(iv) *Taxable year* .—If the taxable years of a partner and the partnership do not coincide, then for purposes of section 179, the amount of the partnership's section 179 expenses attributable to a partner for a taxable year is determined under section 706 and the regulations thereunder (generally the partner's distributive share of partnership section 179 expenses for the partnership year that ends with or within the partner's taxable year).

(v) *Example* .—The following example illustrates the provisions of paragraph (b) (3) (iv) of this section.

*Example.* AB partnership has a taxable year ending January 31. A, a partner of AB, has a taxable year ending December 31. AB purchases and places in service section 179 property on March 10, 1991, and elects to expense a portion of the cost of that property under section 179. Under section 706 and § 1.706-1(a) (1), A will be unable to claim A's distributive share of any of AB's section 179 expenses attributable to the property placed in service on March 10, 1991, until A's taxable year ending December 31, 1992.

(4) *S Corporations* .—Rules similar to those contained in paragraph (b) (3) of this section apply in the case of S corporations (as defined in section 1361(a)) and their shareholders. Each shareholder's share of the section 179 expenses of an S corporation is determined under section 1366.

(5) *Joint returns* .—(i) *In general* .—A husband and wife who file a joint income tax return under section 6013(a) are treated as one taxpayer in determining the amount of the dollar limitation under paragraph (b) (1) of this section, regardless of which spouse purchased the property or placed it in service.

(ii) *Joint returns filed after separate returns* .—In the case of a husband and wife who elect under section 6013(b) to file a joint income tax return for a taxable year after the time prescribed by law for filing the return for such taxable year has expired, the dollar limitation under paragraph (b)(1) of this section is the lesser of—

(A) The dollar limitation (as determined under paragraph (b)(5)(i) of this section); or

(B) The aggregate cost of section 179 property elected to be expensed by the husband and wife on their separate returns.

(iii) *Example* .—The following example illustrates the provisions of paragraph (b)(5)(ii) of this section.

*Example.* During 1991, Mr. and Mrs. B, both calendar-year taxpayers, purchase and place in service section 179 property costing $100,000. On their separate returns for 1991, Mr. B elects to expense $3,000 of section 179 property as an expense and Mrs. B elects to expense $4,000. After the due date of the return they elect under section 6013(b) to file a joint income tax return for 1991. The dollar limitation for their joint income tax return is $7,000, the lesser of the dollar limitation ($10,000) or the aggregate cost elected to be expensed under section 179 on their separate returns ($3,000 elected by Mr. B plus $4,000 elected by Mrs. B, or $7,000).

(6) *Married individuals filing separately* .—(i) *In general* .—In the case of an individual who is married but files a separate income tax return for a taxable year, the dollar limitation of this paragraph (b) for such taxable year is the amount that would be determined under paragraph (b)(5)(i) of this section if the individual filed a joint income tax return under section 6013(a) multiplied by either the percentage elected by the individual under this paragraph (b)(6) or 50 percent. The election in the preceding sentence is made in accordance with the requirements of section 179(c) and §1.179-5. However, the amount determined under paragraph (b)(5)(i) of this section must be multiplied by 50 percent if either the individual or the individual's spouse does not elect a percentage under this paragraph (b)(6) or the sum of the percentages elected by the individual and the individual's spouse does not equal 100 percent. For purposes of this paragraph (b)(6), marital status is determined under section 7703 and the regulations thereunder.

(ii) *Example* .—The following example illustrates the provisions of paragraph (b)(6)(i) of this section.

*Example.* Mr. and Mrs. D, both calendar-year taxpayers, file separate income tax returns for 1991. During 1991, Mr. D places $195,000 of section 179 property in service and Mrs. D places $9,000 of section 179 property in service. Neither of them elects a percentage under paragraph (b)(6)(i) of this section. The 1991 dollar limitation for both Mr. D and Mrs. D is determined by multiplying by 50 percent the dollar limitation that would apply had they filed a joint income tax return. Had Mr. and Mrs. D filed a joint return for 1991, the dollar limitation would have been $6,000, $10,000 reduced by the excess section 179 property they placed in service during 1991 ($195,000 placed in service by Mr. D plus $9,000 placed in service by Mrs. D less $200,000, or $4,000). Thus, the 1991 dollar limitation for Mr. and Mrs. D is $3,000 each ($6,000 multiplied by 50 percent).

(7) *Component members of a controlled group* .—(i) *In general* .—Component members of a controlled group (as defined in §1.179-4(f)) on a December 31 are treated as one taxpayer in applying the dollar limitation of sections 179(b)(1) and (2) and this paragraph (b). The expense deduction may be taken by any one component member or allocated (for the taxable year of each member that includes that December 31) among the several members in any manner. Any

allocation of the expense deduction must be pursuant to an allocation by the common parent corporation if a consolidated return is filed for all component members of the group, or in accordance with an agreement entered into by the members of the group if separate returns are filed. If a consolidated return is filed by some component members of the group and separate returns are filed by other component members, the common parent of the group filing the consolidated return must enter into an agreement with those members that do not join in filing the consolidated return allocating the amount between the group filing the consolidated return and the other component members of the controlled group that do not join in filing the consolidated return. The amount of the expense allocated to any component member, however, may not exceed the cost of section 179 property actually purchased and placed in service by the member in the taxable year. If the component members have different taxable years, the term "taxable year" in sections 179(b)(1) and (2) means the taxable year of the member whose taxable year begins on the earliest date.

(ii) *Statement to be filed* .—If a consolidated return is filed, the common parent corporation must file a separate statement attached to the income tax return on which the election is made to claim an expense deduction under section 179. See § 1.179-5. If separate returns are filed by some or all component members of the group, each component member not included in a consolidated return must file a separate statement attached to the income tax return on which an election is made to claim a deduction under section 179. The statement must include the name, address, employer identification number, and the taxable year of each component member of the controlled group, a copy of the allocation agreement signed by persons duly authorized to act on behalf of the component members, and a description of the manner in which the deduction under section 179 has been divided among the component members.

(iii) *Revocation* .—If a consolidated return is filed for all component members of the group, an allocation among such members of the expense deduction under section 179 may not be revoked after the due date of the return (including extensions of time) of the common parent corporation for the taxable year for which an election to take an expense deduction is made. If some or all of the component members of the controlled group file separate returns for taxable years including a particular December 31 for which an election to take the expense deduction is made, the allocation as to all members of the group may not be revoked after the due date of the return (including extensions of time) of the component member of the controlled group whose taxable year that includes such December 31 ends on the latest date.

(c) *Taxable income limitation* .—(1) *In general* .—The aggregate cost of section 179 property elected to be expensed under section 179 that may be deducted for any taxable year may not exceed the aggregate amount of taxable income of the taxpayer for such taxable year that is derived from the active conduct by the taxpayer of any trade or business during the taxable year. For purposes of section 179(b)(3) and this paragraph (c), the aggregate amount of taxable income derived from the active conduct by an individual, a partnership, or an S corporation of any trade or business is computed by aggregating the net income (or loss) from all of the trades or businesses actively conducted by the individual, partnership, or S corporation during the taxable year. Items of income that are derived from the active conduct of a trade or business include section 1231 gains (or losses) from the trade or business and interest from working capital of the trade or business. Taxable income derived from the active conduct of a trade or business is computed without regard to the deduction allowable under section 179, any section 164(f) deduction, any net operating loss carryback or carryforward, and deductions suspended under any section of the Code. See paragraph (c)(6) of this section for rules on determining whether a taxpayer is engaged in the active conduct of a trade or business for this purpose.

(2) *Application to partnerships and partners* .—(i) *In general* .—The taxable income limitation of this paragraph (c) applies to the partnership as well as to each partner. Thus, the partnership may not allocate to its partners as a section 179 expense deduction for any taxable year more than the partnership's taxable income limitation for that taxable year, and a partner may not deduct as a section 179 expense deduction for any taxable year more than the partner's taxable income limitation for that taxable year.

(ii) *Taxable year* .—If the taxable year of a partner and the partnership do not coincide, then for purposes of section 179, the amount of the partnership's taxable income attributable to a partner for a taxable year is determined under section 706 and the regulations thereunder (generally the partner's distributive share of partnership taxable income for the partnership year that ends with or within the partner's taxable year).

(iii) *Example* .—The following example illustrates the provisions of paragraph (c)(2)(ii) of this section.

*Example.* AB partnership has a taxable year ending January 31. A, a partner of AB, has a taxable year ending December 31. For AB's taxable year ending January 31, 1992, AB has taxable income from the active conduct of its trade or business of $100,000, $90,000 of which was earned during 1991. Under section 706 and § 1.706-1(a)(1), A includes A's entire share of partnership taxable income in computing A's taxable income limitation for A's taxable year ending December 31, 1992.

(iv) *Taxable income of a partnership* .—The taxable income (or loss) derived from the active conduct by a partnership of any trade or business is computed by aggregating the net income (or loss) from all of the trades or businesses actively conducted by the partnership during the taxable year. The net income (or loss) from a trade or business actively conducted by the partnership is determined by taking into account the aggregate amount of the partnership's items described in section 702(a) (other than credits, tax-exempt income, and guaranteed payments under section 707(c)) derived from that trade or business. For purposes of determining the aggregate amount of partnership items, deductions and losses are treated as negative income. Any limitation on the amount of a partnership item described in section 702(a) which may be taken into account for purposes of computing the taxable income of a partner shall be disregarded in computing the taxable income of the partnership.

(v) *Partner's share of partnership taxable income* .—A taxpayer who is a partner in a partnership and is engaged in the active conduct of at least one of the partnership's trades or businesses includes as taxable income derived from the active conduct of a trade or business the amount of the taxpayer's allocable share of taxable income derived from the active conduct by the partnership of any trade or business (as determined under paragraph (c)(2)(iv) of this section).

(3) *S corporations and S corporation shareholders* .—(i) *In general* .—Rules similar to those contained in paragraphs (c)(2)(i) and (ii) of this section apply in the case of S corporations (as defined in section 1361(a)) and their shareholders. Each shareholder's share of the taxable income of an S corporation is determined under section 1366.

(ii) *Taxable income of an S corporation* .—The taxable income (or loss) derived from the active conduct by an S corporation of any trade or business is computed by aggregating the net income (or loss) from all of the trades or businesses actively conducted by the S corporation during the taxable year. The net income (or loss) from a trade or business actively conducted by an S corporation is determined by taking into account the aggregate amount of the S corporation's items described in section 1366(a) (other than credits, tax-exempt income, and deductions for compensation paid to an S corporation's shareholder-employees) derived from that trade or business. For purposes of determining the aggregate amount of S corporation items, deductions and losses are treated as negative income. Any limitation on the amount of an S corporation item described in section 1366(a) which may be taken into account for purposes of computing the taxable income of a shareholder shall be disregarded in computing the taxable income of the S corporation.

(iii) *Shareholder's share of S corporation taxable income* .—Rules similar to those contained in paragraph (c)(2)(v) and (c)(6)(ii) of this section apply to a taxpayer who is a shareholder in an S corporation and is engaged in the active conduct of the S corporation's trades or businesses.

(4) *Taxable income of a corporation other than an S corporation* .—The aggregate amount of taxable income derived from the active conduct by a corporation other than an S corporation of any trade or business is the amount of the corporation's taxable income before deducting its net operating loss deduction and special deductions (as reported on the corporation's income tax return), adjusted to reflect those items of income or deduction included in that amount that were not derived by the corporation from a trade or business actively conducted by the corporation during the taxable year.

(5) *Ordering rule for certain circular problems* .—(i) *In general* .—A taxpayer who elects to expense the cost of section 179 property (the deduction of which is subject to the taxable income limitation) also may have to apply another Internal Revenue Code section that has a limitation based on the taxpayer's taxable income. Except as provided in paragraph (c)(1) of this section, this section provides rules for applying the taxable income limitation under section 179 in such a case. First, taxable income is computed for the other section of the Internal Revenue Code. In computing the taxable income of the taxpayer for the other section of the Internal Revenue Code, the taxpayer's section 179 deduction is computed by assuming that the taxpayer's taxable income is determined without regard to the deduction under the other Internal Revenue Code section. Next, after reducing taxable income by the amount of the section 179 deduction so computed, a hypothetical amount of deduction is determined for the other section of the Internal Revenue Code. The taxable income limitation of the taxpayer under section 179(b)(3) and this paragraph (c) then is computed by including that hypothetical amount in determining taxable income.

(ii) *Example* .—The following example illustrates the ordering rule described in paragraph (c)(5)(i) of this section.

*Example.* X, a calendar-year corporation, elects to expense $10,000 of the cost of section 179 property purchased and placed in service during 1991. Assume X's dollar limitation is $10,000. X also gives a charitable contribution of $5,000 during the taxable year. X's taxable income for purposes of both sections 179 and 170(b)(2), but without regard to any deduction allowable under either section 179 or section 170, is $11,000. In determining X's taxable income limitation under section 179(b)(3) and this paragraph (c), X must first compute its section 170 deduction. However, section 170(b)(2) limits X's charitable contribution to 10 percent of its taxable income determined by taking into account its section 179 deduction. Paragraph (c)(5)(i) of this section provides that in determining X's section 179 deduction for 1991, X first computes a hypothetical section 170 deduction by assuming that its section 179 deduction is not affected by the section 170 deduction. Thus, in computing X's hypothetical section 170 deduction, X's taxable income limitation under section 179 is $11,000 and its section 179 deduction is $10,000. X's hypothetical section 170 deduction is $100 (10 percent of $1,000 ($11,000 less $10,000 section 179 deduction)). X's taxable income limitation for section 179 purposes is then computed by deducting the hypothetical charitable contribution of $100 for 1991. Thus, X's section 179 taxable income limitation is $10,900 ($11,000 less hypothetical $100 section 170 deduction), and its section 179 deduction for 1991 is $10,000. X's section 179 deduction so calculated applies for all purposes of the Code, including the computation of its actual section 170 deduction.

(6) *Active conduct by the taxpayer of a trade or business* .—(i) *Trade or business* .—For purposes of this section and § 1.179-4(a), the term "trade or business" has the same meaning as in section 162 and the regulations thereunder. Thus, property held merely for the production of income or used in an activity not engaged in for profit (as described in section 183) does not qualify as section 179 property and taxable income derived from property held for the production of income or from an activity not engaged in for profit is not taken into account in determining the taxable income limitation.

(ii) *Active conduct* .—For purposes of this section, the determination of whether a trade or business is actively conducted by the taxpayer is to be made from all the facts and circumstances and is to be applied in light of the purpose of the active conduct requirement of section 179(b)(3)(A). In the context of section 179, the purpose of the active conduct requirement is to prevent a passive investor in a trade or business from deducting section 179 expenses against taxable income derived from that trade or business. Consistent with this purpose, a taxpayer generally is considered to actively conduct a trade or business if the taxpayer meaningfully participates in the management or operations of the trade or business. Generally, a partner is considered to actively conduct a trade or business of the partnership if the partner meaningfully participates in the management or operations of the trade or business. A mere passive investor in a trade or business does not actively conduct the trade or business.

(iii) *Example* .—The following example illustrates the provisions of paragraph (c)(6)(ii) of this section.

*Example.* A owns a salon as a sole proprietorship and employs B to operate it. A periodically meets with B to review developments relating to the business. A also approves the salon's annual budget that is prepared by B. B performs all the necessary operating functions, including hiring beauticians, acquiring the necessary beauty supplies, and writing the checks to pay all bills and the beauticians' salaries. In 1991, B purchased, as provided for in the salon's annual budget, equipment costing $9,500 for use in the active conduct of the salon. There were no other purchases of section 179 property during 1991. A's net income from the salon, before any section 179 deduction, totaled $8,000. A also is a partner in PRS, a calendar-year partnership, which owns a grocery store. C, a partner in PRS, runs the grocery store for the partnership, making all the management and operating decisions. PRS did not purchase any section 179 property during 1991. A's allocable share of partnership net income was $6,000. Based on the facts and circumstances, A meaningfully participates in the management of the salon. However, A does not meaningfully participate in the management or operations of the trade or business of PRS. Under section 179(b)(3)(A) and this paragraph (c), A's aggregate taxable income derived from the active conduct by A of any trade or business is $8,000, the net income from the salon.

(iv) *Employees* .—For purposes of this section, employees are considered to be engaged in the active conduct of the trade or business of their employment. Thus, wages, salaries, tips, and other compensation (not reduced by unreimbursed employee business expenses) derived by a taxpayer as an employee are included in the aggregate amount of taxable income of the taxpayer under paragraph (c)(1) of this section.

(7) *Joint returns* .—(i) *In general* .—The taxable income limitation of this paragraph (c) is applied to a husband and wife who file a joint income tax return under section 6013(a) by aggregating the taxable income of each spouse (as determined under paragraph (c)(1) of this section).

(ii) *Joint returns filed after separate returns* .—In the case of a husband and wife who elect under section 6013(b) to file a joint income tax return for a taxable year after the time prescribed by law for filing the return for such taxable year, the taxable income limitation of this paragraph (c) for the taxable year for which the joint return is filed is determined under paragraph (c)(7)(i) of this section.

(8) *Married individuals filing separately* .—In the case of an individual who is married but files a separate tax return for a taxable year, the taxable income limitation for that individual is determined under paragraph (c)(1) of this section by treating the husband and wife as separate taxpayers.

(d) *Examples* .—The following examples illustrate the provisions of paragraphs (b) and (c) of this section.

*Example 1.* (i) During 1991, PRS, a calendar-year partnership, purchases and places in service $50,000 of section 179 property. The taxable income of PRS derived from the active conduct of all its trades or businesses (as determined under paragraph (c)(1) of this section) is $8,000.

(ii) Under the dollar limitation of paragraph (b) of this section, PRS may elect to expense $10,000 of the cost of section 179 property purchased in 1991. Assume PRS elects under section 179(c) and § 1.179-5 to expense $10,000 of the cost of section 179 property purchased in 1991.

(iii) Under the taxable income limitation of paragraph (c) of this section, PRS may allocate to its partners as a deduction only $8,000 of the cost of section 179 property in 1991. Under section 179(b)(3)(B) and § 1.179-3(a), PRS may carry forward the remaining $2,000 it elected to expense, which would have been deductible under section 179(a) for 1991 absent the taxable income limitation.

*Example 2.* (i) The facts are the same as in *Example 1,* except that on December 31, 1991, PRS allocates to A, a calendar-year taxpayer and a partner in PRS, $7,000 of section 179 expenses and $2,000 of taxable income. A was engaged in the active conduct of a trade or business of PRS during 1991.

(ii) In addition to being a partner in PRS, A conducts a business as a sole proprietor. During 1991, A purchases and places in service $201,000 of section 179 property in connection with the sole proprietorship. A's 1991 taxable income derived from the active conduct of this business is $6,000.

(iii) Under the dollar limitation, A may elect to expense only $9,000 of the cost of section 179 property purchased in 1991, the $10,000 limit reduced by $1,000 (the amount by which the cost of section 179 property placed in service during 1991 ($201,000) exceeds $200,000). Under paragraph (b)(3)(i) of this section, the $7,000 of section 179 expenses allocated from PRS is subject to the $9,000 limit. Assume that A elects to expense $2,000 of the cost of section 179 property purchased by A's sole proprietorship in 1991. Thus, A has elected to expense under section 179 an amount equal to the dollar limitation for 1991 ($2,000 elected to be expensed by A's sole proprietorship plus $7,000, the amount of PRS's section 179 expenses allocated to A in 1991).

(iv) Under the taxable income limitation, A may only deduct $8,000 of the cost of section 179 property elected to be expensed in 1991, the aggregate taxable income derived from the active conduct of A's trades or businesses in 1991 ($2,000 from PRS and $6,000 from A's sole proprietorship). The entire $2,000 of taxable income allocated from PRS is included by A as taxable income derived from the active conduct by A of a trade or business because it was derived from the active conduct of a trade or business by PRS and A was engaged in the active conduct of a trade or business of PRS during 1991. Under section 179(b)(3)(B) and § 1.179-3(a), A may carry forward the remaining $1,000 A elected to expense, which would have been deductible under section 179(a) for 1991 absent the taxable income limitation. [Reg. § 1.179-2.]

**.01 Historical Comment:** Proposed 9/26/85. Adopted 1/5/87 by T.D. 8121. Amended 12/23/92 by T.D. 8455, 8/3/2004 by T.D. 9146 and 7/12/2005 by T.D. 9209.

## ¶ 579

## Reg. § 1.179-3

§ 1.179-3. **Carryover of disallowed deduction.**— (a) *In general* .—Under section 179(b)(3)(B), a taxpayer may carry forward for an unlimited number of years the amount of any cost of section 179 property elected to be expensed in a taxable year but disallowed as a deduction in that taxable year because of the taxable income limitation of section 179(b)(3)(A) and § 1.179-2(c) ( "carryover of disallowed deduction"). This carryover of disallowed deduction may be deducted under section 179(a) and § 1.179-1(a) in a future taxable year as provided in paragraph (b) of this section.

(b) *Deduction of carryover of disallowed deduction* .—(1) *In general* .—The amount allowable as a deduction under section 179(a) and § 1.179-1(a) for any taxable year is increased by the lesser of—

(i) The aggregate amount disallowed under section 179(b)(3)(A) and § 1.179-2(c) for all prior taxable years (to the extent not previously allowed as a deduction by reason of this section); or

(ii) The amount of any unused section 179 expense allowance for the taxable year (as described in paragraph (c) of this section).

(2) *Cross references* .—See paragraph (f) of this section for rules that apply when a taxpayer disposes of or otherwise transfers section 179 property for which a carryover of disallowed deduction is outstanding. See paragraph (g) of this section for special rules that apply to partnerships and S corporations and paragraph (h) of this section for special rules that apply to partners and S corporation shareholders.

(c) *Unused section 179 expense allowance* .—The amount of any unused section 179 expense allowance for a taxable year equals the excess (if any) of—

(1) The maximum cost of section 179 property that the taxpayer may deduct under section 179 and § 1.179-1 for the taxable year after applying the limitations of section 179(b) and § 1.179-2; over

(2) The amount of section 179 property that the taxpayer actually elected to expense under section 179 and § 1.179-1(a) for the taxable year.

(d) *Example* .—The following example illustrates the provisions of paragraphs (b) and (c) of this section.

*Example.* A, a calendar-year taxpayer, has a $3,000 carryover of disallowed deduction for an item of section 179 property purchased and placed in service in 1991. In 1992, A purchases and places in service an item of section 179 property costing $25,000. A's 1992 taxable income from the active conduct of all A's trades or businesses is $100,000. A elects, under section 179(c) and § 1.179-5, to expense $8,000 of the cost of the item of section 179 property purchased in 1992. Under paragraph (b) of this section, A may deduct $2,000 of A's carryover of disallowed deduction from 1991 (the lesser of A's total outstanding carryover of disallowed deductions ($3,000), or the amount of any unused section 179 expense allowance for 1992 ($10,000 limit less $8,000 elected to be expensed, or $2,000)). For 1993, A has a $1,000 carryover of disallowed deduction for the item of section 179 property purchased and placed in service in 1991.

(e) *Recordkeeping requirement and ordering rule* .—The properties and the apportionment of cost that will be subject to a carryover of disallowed deduction are selected by the taxpayer in the year the properties are placed in service. This selection must be evidenced on the taxpayer's books and records and be applied consistently in subsequent years. If no selection is made, the total carryover of disallowed deduction is apportioned equally over the items of section 179 property elected to be expensed for the taxable year. For this purpose, the taxpayer treats any section 179 expense amount allocated from a partnership (or an S corporation) for a taxable year as one item of section 179 property. If the taxpayer is allowed to deduct a portion of the total carryover of disallowed deduction under paragraph (b) of this section, the taxpayer must deduct the cost of section 179 property carried forward from the earliest taxable year.

(f) *Dispositions and other transfers of section 179 property* .—(1) *In general* .—Upon a sale or other disposition of section 179 property, or a transfer of section 179 property in a transaction in which gain or loss is not recognized in whole or in part (including transfers at death), immediately before the transfer the adjusted basis of the section 179 property is increased by the amount of any outstanding carryover of disallowed deduction with respect to the property. This carryover of disallowed deduction is not available as a deduction to the transferor or the transferee of the section 179 property.

(2) *Recapture under section 179(d)(10)* .—Under § 1.179-1(e), if a taxpayer's section 179 property is subject to recapture under section 179(d)(10), the taxpayer must recapture the benefit derived from expensing the property. Upon recapture, any outstanding carryover of disallowed deduction with respect to the property is no longer available for expensing. In determining the amount subject to recapture under section 179(d)(10) and § 1.179-1(e), any outstanding carryover of disallowed deduction with respect to that property is not treated as an amount expensed under section 179.

(g) *Special rules for partnerships and S corporations* .—(1) *In general* .—Under section 179(d)(8) and § 1.179-2(c), the taxable income limitation applies at the partnership level as well as at the partner level. Therefore, a partnership may have a carryover of disallowed deduction with respect to the cost of its section 179 property. Similar rules apply to S corporations. This paragraph (g) provides special rules that apply when a partnership or an S corporation has a carryover of disallowed deduction.

(2) *Basis adjustment* .—Under § 1.179-1(f)(2), the basis of a partnership's section 179 property must be reduced to reflect the amount of section 179 expense elected by the partnership. This reduction must be made for the taxable year for which the election is made even if the section 179 expense amount, or a

portion thereof, must be carried forward by the partnership. Similar rules apply to S corporations.

(3) *Dispositions and other transfers of section 179 property by a partnership or an S corporation* .—The provisions of paragraph (f) of this section apply in determining the treatment of any outstanding carryover of disallowed deduction with respect to section 179 property disposed of, or transferred in a nonrecognition transaction, by a partnership or an S corporation.

(4) *Example* .—The following example illustrates the provisions of this paragraph (g).

*Example.* ABC, a calendar-year partnership, owns and operates a restaurant business. During 1992, ABC purchases and places in service two items of section 179 property—a cash register costing $4,000 and office furniture costing $6,000. ABC elects to expense under section 179(c) the full cost of the cash register and the office furniture. For 1992, ABC has $6,000 of taxable income derived from the active conduct of its restaurant business. Therefore, ABC may deduct only $6,000 of section 179 expenses and must carry forward the remaining $4,000 of section 179 expenses at the partnership level. ABC must reduce the adjusted basis of the section 179 property by the full amount elected to be expensed. However, ABC may not allocate to its partners any portion of the carryover of disallowed deduction until ABC is able to deduct it under paragraph (b) of this section.

(h) *Special rules for partners and S corporation shareholders* .—(1) *In general* .—Under section 179(d)(8) and § 1.179-2(c), a partner may have a carryover of disallowed deduction with respect to the cost of section 179 property elected to be expensed by the partnership and allocated to the partner. A partner who is allocated section 179 expenses from a partnership must reduce the basis of his or her partnership interest by the full amount allocated regardless of whether the partner may deduct for the taxable year the allocated section 179 expenses or is required to carry forward all or a portion of the expenses. Similar rules apply to S corporation shareholders.

(2) *Dispositions and other transfers of a partner's interest in a partnership or a shareholder's interest in an S corporation* .—A partner who disposes of a partnership interest, or transfers a partnership interest in a transaction in which gain or loss is not recognized in whole or in part (including transfers of a partnership interest at death), may have an outstanding carryover of disallowed deduction of section 179 expenses allocated from the partnership. In such a case, immediately before the transfer the partner's basis in the partnership interest is increased by the amount of the partner's outstanding carryover of disallowed deduction with respect to the partnership interest. This carryover of disallowed deduction is not available as a deduction to the transferor or transferee partner of the section 179 property. Similar rules apply to S corporation shareholders.

(3) *Examples* .—The following examples illustrate the provisions of this paragraph (h).

*Example 1.* (i) G is a general partner in GD, a calendar-year partnership, and is engaged in the active conduct of GD's business. During 1991, GD purchases and places section 179 property in service and elects to expense a portion of the cost of the property under section 179. GD allocates $2,500 of section 179 expenses and $15,000 of taxable income (determined without regard to the section 179 deduction) to G. The income was derived from the active conduct by GD of a trade or business.

(ii) In addition to being a partner in GD, G conducts a business as a sole proprietor. During 1991, G purchases and places in service office equipment costing $25,000 and a computer costing $10,000 in connection with the sole proprietorship. G elects under section 179(c) and § 1.179-5 to expense $7,500 of the cost of the office equipment. G has a taxable loss (determined without regard to the section 179 deduction) derived from the active conduct of this business of $12,500.

(iii) G has no other taxable income (or loss) derived from the active conduct of a trade or business during 1991. G's taxable income limitation for 1991 is $2,500 ($15,000 taxable income allocated from GD less $12,500 taxable loss from the sole proprietorship). Therefore, G may deduct during 1991 only $2,500 of the $10,000 of section 179 expenses. G notes on the appropriate books and records that G expenses the $2,500 of section 179 expenses allocated from GD and carries forward the $7,500 of section 179 expenses with respect to the office equipment purchased by G's sole proprietorship.

(iv) On January 1, 1992, G sells the office equipment G's sole proprietorship purchased and placed in service in 1991. Under paragraph (f) of this section, immediately before the sale G increases the adjusted basis of the office equipment by $7,500, the amount of the outstanding carryover of disallowed deduction with respect to the office equipment.

*Example 2.* (i) Assume the same facts as in *Example 1*, except that G notes on the appropriate books and records that G expenses $2,500 of section 179 expenses relating to G's sole proprietorship and carries forward the remaining $5,000 of section 179 expenses relating to G's sole proprietorship and $2,500 of section 179 expenses allocated from GD.

(ii) On January 1, 1992, G sells G's partnership interest to A. Under paragraph (h)(2) of this section, immediately before the sale G increases the adjusted basis of G's partnership interest by $2,500, the amount of the outstanding carryover of disallowed deduction with respect to the partnership interest. [Reg. § 1.179-3.]

**.01 Historical Comment:** Adopted 12/23/92 by T.D. 8455.

## ¶ 580

## Reg. § 1.179-4

§ 1.179-4. **Definitions.**—The following definitions apply for purposes of section 179 and § § 1.179-1 through 1.179-6:

(a) *Section 179 property* .—The term *section 179 property* means any tangible property described in section 179(d)(1) that is acquired by purchase for use in the active conduct of the taxpayer's trade or business (as described in § 1.179-2(c)(6)). For taxable years beginning after 2002 and before 2008, the term *section 179 property* includes computer software described in section 179(d)(1) that is placed in service by the taxpayer in a taxable year beginning after 2002 and before 2008 and is acquired by purchase for use in the active conduct of the taxpayer's trade or business (as described in § 1.179-2(c)(6)). For purposes of this paragraph (a), the term *trade or business* has the same meaning as in section 162 and the regulations under section 162.

(b) *Section 38 property* .—The term "section 38 property" shall have the same meaning assigned to it in section 48(a) and the regulations thereunder.

(c) *Purchase* .— (1)(i) Except as otherwise provided in paragraph (d)(2) of this section, the term "purchase" means any acquisition of the property, but only if all the requirements of paragraphs (d)(1)(ii), (iii), and (iv) of this section are satisfied.

(ii) Property is not acquired by purchase if it is acquired from a person whose relationship to the person acquiring it would result in the disallowance of losses under section 267 or 707(b). The property is considered not acquired by purchase only to the extent that losses would be disallowed under section 267 or

707(b). Thus, for example, if property is purchased by a husband and wife jointly from the husband's father, the property will be treated as not acquired by purchase only to the extent of the husband's interest in the property. However, in applying the rules of section 267(b) and (c) for this purpose, section 267(c)(4) shall be treated as providing that the family of an individual will include only his spouse, ancestors, and lineal descendants. For example, a purchase of property from a corporation by a taxpayer who owns, directly or indirectly, more than 50 percent in value of the outstanding stock of such corporation does not qualify as a purchase under section 179(d)(2); nor does the purchase of property by a husband from his wife. However, the purchase of section 179 property by a taxpayer from his brother or sister does qualify as a purchase for purposes of section 179(d)(2).

(iii) The property is not acquired by purchase if acquired from a component member of a controlled group of corporations (as defined in paragraph (g) of this section) by another component member of the same group.

(iv) The property is not acquired by purchase if the basis of the property in the hands of the person acquiring it is determined in whole or in part by reference to the adjusted basis of such property in the hands of the person from whom acquired, is determined under section 1014(a), relating to property acquired from a decedent, or is determined under section 1022, relating to property acquired from certain decedents who died in 2010. For example, property acquired by gift or bequest does not qualify as property acquired by purchase for purposes of section 179(d)(2); nor does property received in a corporate distribution the basis of which is determined under section 301(d)(2)(B), property acquired by a corporation in a transaction to which section 351 applies, property acquired by a partnership through contribution (section 723), or property received in a partnership distribution which has a carryover basis under section 732(a)(1).

(2) Property deemed to have been acquired by a new target corporation as a result of a section 338 election (relating to certain stock purchases treated as asset acquisitions) or a section 336(e) election (relating to certain stock dispositions treated as asset transfers) made for a disposition described in § 1.336-2(b)(1) will be considered acquired by purchase.

(d) *Cost* .—The cost of section 179 property does not include so much of the basis of such property as is determined by reference to the basis of other property held at any time by the taxpayer. For example, X Corporation purchases a new drill press costing $10,000 in November 1984 which qualifies as section 179 property, and is granted a trade-in allowance of $2,000 on its old drill press. The old drill press had a basis of $1,200. Under the provisions of sections 1012 and 1031(d), the basis of the new drill press is $9,200 ($1,200 basis of old drill press plus cash expended of $8,000). However, only $8,000 of the basis of the new drill press qualifies as cost for purposes of the section 179 expense deduction; the remaining $1,200 is not part of the cost because it is determined by reference to the basis of the old drill press.

(e) *Placed in service* .—The term "placed in service" means the time that property is first placed by the taxpayer in a condition or state of readiness and availability for a specifically assigned function, whether for use in a trade or business, for the production of income, in a tax-exempt activity, or in a personal activity. See § 1.46-3(d)(2) for examples regarding when property shall be considered in a condition or state of readiness and availability for a specifically assigned function.

(f) *Controlled group of corporations and component member of controlled group* .—The terms "controlled group of corporations" and "component member" of a controlled group of corporations shall have the same meaning assigned to those terms in section 1563(a) and (b), except that the phrase "more than 50 percent" shall be substituted for the phrase "at least 80 percent" each place it appears in section 1563(a)(1). [Reg. § 1.179-4.]

**.01 Historical Comment:** Proposed 9/26/85. Adopted 1/5/87 by T.D. 8121. Amended 12/23/92 by T.D. 8455, 8/3/2004 by T.D. 9146, 7/12/2005 by T.D. 9209, 1/18/2017 by T.D. 9811 and 9/17/2019 by T.D. 9874.

## ¶ 581

## Reg. § 1.179-5

§ 1.179-5. **Time and manner of making election.**— (a) *Election* .—A separate election must be made for each taxable year in which a section 179 expense deduction is claimed with respect to section 179 property. The election under section 179 and § 1.179-1 to claim a section 179 expense deduction for section 179 property shall be made on the taxpayer's first income tax return for the taxable year to which the election applies (whether or not the return is timely) or on an amended return filed within the time prescribed by law (including extensions) for filing the return for such taxable year. The election shall be made by showing as a separate item on the taxpayer's income tax return the following items:

(1) The total section 179 expense deduction claimed with respect to all section 179 property selected; and

(2) The portion of that deduction allocable to each specific item.

The person shall maintain records which permit specific identification of each piece of section 179 property and reflect how and from whom such property was acquired and when such property was placed in service. However, for this purpose a partner (or an S corporation shareholder) treats partnership (or S corporation) section 179 property for which section 179 expenses are allocated from a partnership (or an S corporation) as one item of section 179 property. The election to claim a section 179 expense deduction under this section, with respect to any property, is irrevocable and will be binding on the taxpayer with respect to such property for the taxable year for which the election is made and for all subsequent taxable years, unless the Commissioner consents to the revocation of the election. Similarly, the selection of section 179 property by the taxpayer to be subject to the expense deduction and apportionment scheme must be adhered to in computing the taxpayer's taxable income for the taxable year for which the election is made and for all subsequent taxable years, unless consent to change is given by the Commissioner.

(b) *Revocation* .—Any election made under section 179, and any specification contained in such election, may not be revoked except with the consent of the Commissioner. Such consent will be granted only in extraordinary circumstances. Requests for consent must be filed with the Commissioner of Internal Revenue, Washington, D.C., 20224. The request must include the name, address, and taxpayer identification number of the taxpayer and must be signed by the taxpayer or his duly authorized representative. It must be accompanied by a statement showing the year and property involved, and must set forth in detail the reasons for the request.

(c) *Section 179 property placed in service by the taxpayer in a taxable year beginning after 2002 and before 2008* .—(1) *In general* .—For any taxable year beginning after 2002 and before 2008, a taxpayer is permitted to make or revoke an election under section 179 without the consent of the Commissioner on an amended Federal tax return for that taxable year. This amended return must be filed within the time prescribed by law for filing an amended return for such taxable year.

(2) *Election* .—(i) *In general* .—For any taxable year beginning after 2002 and before 2008, a taxpayer is permitted to make an election under section 179 on an amended Federal tax return for that taxable year without the consent of the

Commissioner. Thus, the election under section 179 and § 1.179-1 to claim a section 179 expense deduction for section 179 property may be made on an amended Federal tax return for the taxable year to which the election applies. The amended Federal tax return must include the adjustment to taxable income for the section 179 election and any collateral adjustments to taxable income or to the tax liability (for example, the amount of depreciation allowed or allowable in that taxable year for the item of section 179 property to which the election pertains). Such adjustments must also be made on amended Federal tax returns for any affected succeeding taxable years.

(ii) *Specifications of elections* .—Any election under section 179 must specify the items of section 179 property and the portion of the cost of each such item to be taken into account under section 179(a). Any election under section 179 must comply with the specification requirements of section 179(c)(1)(A), § 1.179-1(b), and § 1.179-5(a). If a taxpayer elects to expense only a portion of the cost basis of an item of section 179 property for a taxable year beginning after 2002 and before 2008 (or did not elect to expense any portion of the cost basis of the item of section 179 property), the taxpayer is permitted to file an amended Federal tax return for that particular taxable year and increase the portion of the cost of the item of section 179 property to be taken into account under section 179(a) (or elect to expense any portion of the cost basis of the item of section 179 property if no prior election was made) without the consent of the Commissioner. Any such increase in the amount expensed under section 179 is not deemed to be a revocation of the prior election for that particular taxable year.

(3) *Revocation* .—(i) *In general* .—Section 179(c)(2) permits the revocation of an entire election or specification, or a portion of the selected dollar amount of a specification. The term *specification* in section 179(c)(2) refers to both the selected specific item of section 179 property subject to a section 179 election and the selected dollar amount allocable to the specific item of section 179 property. Any portion of the cost basis of an item of section 179 property subject to an election under section 179 for a taxable year beginning after 2002 and before 2008 may be revoked by the taxpayer without the consent of the Commissioner by filing an amended Federal tax return for that particular taxable year. The amended Federal tax return must include the adjustment to taxable income for the section 179 revocation and any collateral adjustments to taxable income or to the tax liability (for example, allowable depreciation in that taxable year for the item of section 179 property to which the revocation pertains). Such adjustments must also be made on amended Federal tax returns for any affected succeeding taxable years. Reducing or eliminating a specified dollar amount for any item of section 179 property with respect to any taxable year beginning after 2002 and before 2008 results in a revocation of that specified dollar amount.

(ii) *Effect of revocation* .—Such revocation, once made, shall be irrevocable. If the selected dollar amount reflects the entire cost of the item of section 179 property subject to the section 179 election, a revocation of the entire selected dollar amount is treated as a revocation of the section 179 election for that item of section 179 property and the taxpayer is unable to make a new section 179 election with respect to that item of property. If the selected dollar amount is a portion of the cost of the item of section 179 property, revocation of a selected dollar amount shall be treated as a revocation of only that selected dollar amount. The revoked dollars cannot be the subject of a new section 179 election for the same item of property.

(4) *Examples* .—The following examples illustrate the rules of this paragraph (c):

*Example 1.* Taxpayer, a sole proprietor, owns and operates a jewelry store. During 2003, Taxpayer purchased and placed in service two items of section 179 property — a cash register costing $4,000 (5-year MACRS property) and office furniture costing $10,000 (7-year MACRS property). On his 2003 Federal tax return filed on April 15, 2004, Taxpayer elected to expense under section 179 the full cost of the cash register and, with respect to the office furniture, claimed the depreciation allowable. In November 2004, Taxpayer determines it would have been more advantageous to have made an election under section 179 to expense the full cost of the office furniture rather than the cash register. Pursuant to paragraph (c)(1) of this section, Taxpayer is permitted to file an amended Federal tax return for 2003 revoking the section 179 election for the cash register, claiming the depreciation allowable in 2003 for the cash register, and making an election to expense under section 179 the cost of the office furniture. The amended return must include an adjustment for the depreciation previously claimed in 2003 for the office furniture, an adjustment for the depreciation allowable in 2003 for the cash register, and any other collateral adjustments to taxable income or to the tax liability. In addition, once Taxpayer revokes the section 179 election for the entire cost basis of the cash register, Taxpayer can no longer expense under section 179 any portion of the cost of the cash register.

*Example 2.* Taxpayer, a sole proprietor, owns and operates a machine shop that does specialized repair work on industrial equipment. During 2003, Taxpayer purchased and placed in service one item of section 179 property—a milling machine costing $135,000. On Taxpayer's 2003 Federal tax return filed on April 15, 2004, Taxpayer elected to expense under section 179 $5,000 of the cost of the milling machine and claimed allowable depreciation on the remaining cost. Subsequently, Taxpayer determines it would have been to Taxpayer's advantage to have elected to expense $100,000 of the cost of the milling machine on Taxpayer's 2003 Federal tax return. In November 2004, Taxpayer files an amended Federal tax return for 2003, increasing the amount of the cost of the milling machine that is to be taken into account under section 179(a) to $100,000, decreasing the depreciation allowable in 2003 for the milling machine, and making any other collateral adjustments to taxable income or to the tax liability. Pursuant to paragraph (c)(2)(ii) of this section, increasing the amount of the cost of the milling machine to be taken into account under section 179(a) supplements the portion of the cost of the milling machine that was already taken into account by the original section 179 election made on the 2003 Federal tax return and no revocation of any specification with respect to the milling machine has occurred.

*Example 3.* Taxpayer, a sole proprietor, owns and operates a real estate brokerage business located in a rented storefront office. During 2003, Taxpayer purchases and places in service two items of section 179 property—a laptop computer costing $2,500 and a desktop computer costing $1,500. On Taxpayer's 2003 Federal tax return filed on April 15, 2004, Taxpayer elected to expense under section 179 the full cost of the laptop computer and the full cost of the desktop computer. Subsequently, Taxpayer determines it would have been to Taxpayer's advantage to have originally elected to expense under section 179 only $1,500 of the cost of the laptop computer on Taxpayer's 2003 Federal tax return. In November 2004, Taxpayer files an amended Federal tax return for 2003 reducing the amount of the cost of the laptop computer that was taken into account under section 179(a) to $1,500, claiming the depreciation allowable in 2003 on the remaining cost of $1,000 for that item, and making any other collateral adjustments to taxable income or to the tax liability. Pursuant to paragraph (c)(3)(ii) of this section, the $1,000 reduction represents a revocation of a portion of the selected dollar amount and no portion of those revoked dollars may be the subject of a new section 179 election for the laptop computer.

*Example 4.* Taxpayer, a sole proprietor, owns and operates a furniture making business. During 2003, Taxpayer purchases and places in service one item of section 179 property—an industrial-grade cabinet table saw costing $5,000. On Taxpayer's 2003 Federal tax return filed on April 15, 2004, Taxpayer elected to expense under section 179 $3,000 of the cost of the saw and, with respect to the remaining $2,000 of the cost of the saw, claimed the depreciation allowable. In November 2004, Taxpayer files an amended Federal tax return for 2003 revoking the selected $3,000 amount for the saw, claiming the depreciation allowable in 2003 on the $3,000 cost of the saw, and making any other collateral adjustments to taxable income or to the tax liability. Subsequently, in December 2004, Taxpayer files a second amended Federal tax return for 2003 selecting a new dollar amount of $2,000 for the saw, including an adjustment for the depreciation previously claimed in 2003 on the $2,000, and making any other collateral adjustments to taxable income or to the tax liability. Pursuant to paragraph (c)(2)(ii) of this section, Taxpayer is permitted to select a new selected dollar amount to expense under section 179 encompassing all or a part of the initially non-elected portion of the cost of the elected item of section 179 property. However, no portion of the revoked $3,000 may be the subject of a new section 179 dollar amount selection for the saw. In December 2005, Taxpayer files a third amended Federal tax return for 2003 revoking the entire selected $2,000 amount with respect to the saw, claiming the depreciation allowable in 2003 for the $2,000, and making any other collateral adjustments to taxable income or to the tax liability. Because Taxpayer elected to expense, and subsequently revoke, the entire cost basis of the saw, the section 179 election for the saw has been revoked and Taxpayer is unable to make a new section 179 election with respect to the saw.

(d) *Election or revocation must not be made in any other manner* .—Any election or revocation specified in this section must be made in the manner prescribed in paragraphs (a), (b), and (c) of this section. Thus, this election or revocation must not be made by the taxpayer in any other manner (for example, an election or a revocation of an election cannot be made through a request under section 446(e) to change the taxpayer's method of accounting), except as otherwise expressly provided by the Internal Revenue Code, the regulations under the Code, or other guidance published in the Internal Revenue Bulletin. [Reg. § 1.179-5.]

**.01 Historical Comment:** Proposed 9/26/85. Adopted 1/5/87 by T.D. 8121. Amended 12/23/92 by T.D. 8455, 8/3/2004 by T.D. 9146 and 7/12/2005 by T.D. 9209.

## ¶ 582

## Reg. § 1.179-6

§ 1.179-6. **Effective/applicability dates.**— (a) *In general* .—Except as provided in paragraphs (b), (c), and (d) of this section, the provisions of § § 1.179-1 through 1.179-5 apply for property placed in service by the taxpayer in taxable years ending after January 25, 1993. However, a taxpayer may apply the provisions of § § 1.179-1 through 1.179-5 to property placed in service by the taxpayer after December 31, 1986, in taxable years ending on or before January 25, 1993. Otherwise, for property placed in service by the taxpayer after December 31, 1986, in taxable years ending on or before January 25, 1993, the final regulations under section 179 as in effect for the year the property was placed in service apply, except to the extent modified by the changes made to section 179 by the Tax Reform Act of 1986 (100 Stat. 2085), the Technical and Miscellaneous Revenue Act of 1988 (102 Stat. 3342) and the Revenue Reconciliation Act of 1990 (104 Stat. 1388-400). For that property, a taxpayer may apply any reasonable method that clearly reflects income in applying the changes to section 179, provided the taxpayer consistently applies the method to the property.

(b) *Section 179 property placed in service by the taxpayer in a taxable year beginning after 2002 and before 2008* .—The provisions of § 1.179-2(b)(1) and (b)(2)(ii), the second sentence of § 1.179-4(a), and the provisions of § 1.179-5(c), reflecting changes made to section 179 by the Jobs and Growth Tax Relief Reconciliation Act of 2003 (117 Stat. 752) and the American Jobs Creation Act of 2004 (118 Stat. 1418), apply for property placed in service in taxable years beginning after 2002 and before 2008.

(c) *Application of § 1.179-5(d)* .—Section 1.179-5(d) applies on or after July 12, 2005.

(d) *Application of § 1.179-4(c)(1)(iv)* .—The provisions of § 1.179-4(c)(1)(iv) relating to section 1022 are effective on and after January 19, 2017.

(e) *Application of § 1.179-4(c)(2)* .—(1) *In general* .—Except as provided in paragraphs (e)(2) and (3) of this section, the provisions of § 1.179-4(c)(2) relating to section 336(e) are applicable on or after September 24, 2019.

(2) *Early application of § 1.179-4(c)(2)* .—A taxpayer may choose to apply the provisions of § 1.179-4(c)(2) relating to section 336(e) for the taxpayer's taxable years ending on or after September 28, 2017.

(3) *Early application of regulation project REG-104397-18* .—A taxpayer may rely on the provisions of § 1.179-4(c)(2) relating to section 336(e) in regulation project REG-104397-18 (2018-41 I.R.B. 558) (see § 601.601(d)(2)(ii)(b)of this chapter) for the taxpayer's taxable years ending on or after September 28, 2017, and ending before September 24, 2019. [Reg. § 1.179-6.]

**.01 Historical Comment:** Adopted 8/3/2004 by T.D. 9146. Amended and redesignated 7/12/2005 by T.D. 9209, 1/18/2017 by T.D. 9811 and 9/17/2019 by T.D. 9874.

# Quick Reference Tables—Vehicles With GVWR Exceeding 6,000 Pounds and Trucks With Bed Length Less Than 6 Feet

Trucks (including SUVs that are considered trucks) and vans with a gross vehicle weight rating (GVWR) greater than 6,000 pounds are not subject to the annual depreciation limitations applicable to passenger automobiles. See ¶ 200.

Effective for vehicles placed in service after October 22, 2004 and that are not subject to the caps, the Code Sec. 179 expensing allowance is limited to $25,000, as adjusted for inflation after 2018 ($27,000 in 2022, $26,200 in 2021, and $25,900 in 2020) in the case of (1) an SUV, (2) a van that does not seat more than 9 persons behind the passenger seat, and (3) a truck with an interior cargo bed length less than 6 feet. Most cargo vans are exempt from the $25,000 limit. See, below.

Table I below lists trucks in excess of 6,000 GVWR.

Table II below lists SUVs in excess of 6,000 GVWR.

Table III below lists vans in excess of 6,000 GVWR.

Table IV below lists trucks in excess of 6,000 GVWR with an interior bed length under 6 feet.

***Requirement that SUVs must be built on truck chassis to be considered truck has changed.*** In Rev. Proc. 2003-75, the IRS announced a separate set of depreciation limitations for trucks or vans which do not weigh more than 6,000 pounds. Within this Revenue Procedure, the IRS defined a vehicle as a truck or van only if it is built on a "truck chassis." SUVs and vans that are built on a car chassis, therefore, did not fall within this definition.

Although Rev. Proc. 2003-75 (Section 2.01) states that the definition applies "for purposes of this revenue procedure," the IRS used the same definition in the instructions to Form 4562 and in IRS Publication 463 in the context of determining whether an SUV with a GVWR in excess of 6000 pounds is a truck or a van. By extending the definition in this manner, the IRS seemed to imply that SUVs and vans built on a car chassis (i.e., unibody) were not eligible for the exemption from the annual depreciation caps under the luxury car rules.

In its update of the depreciation caps for 2008 (Rev. Proc. 2008-22) the language defining an SUV built on a truck chassis as a truck was dropped. CCH contacted the IRS and was told informally that this definition was intended as a safe harbor and not to exclude unibody vehicles from truck classification. IRS Publications and Form instructions have now been revised to eliminate any implication that an SUV categorization as a truck is based solely on its platform type. According to the IRS, the determination of whether an SUV is a truck should be based on the manufacturer's classification of the vehicle in accordance with applicable Department of Transportation Standards.

Unfortunately, the Department of Transportation appears to provide several definitions of a truck for various purposes. The question then arises: Which definition should apply for purposes of the Code Sec. 280F depreciation caps?

The best answer may be to use the definition of a truck that applies for purposes of the gas guzzler tax under Code Sec. 4064. First, consistent definitions of the same term should be used within the Internal Revenue Code whenever possible. More importantly, however, Code Sec. 4064(b)(1); and Code Sec. 280F(d)(5) share an essentially common definition of the term passenger automobiles, which is also included in the regulations at Reg. §1.280F-6(c) and Reg. §48.4064-1(b)(3). The gas guzzler tax does not apply to nonpassenger automobiles, which includes light trucks. Reg. §48.4064-1(b)(3)(iv) states that the definition of a light truck for gas guzzler tax purposes is contained at 49 CFR 523.5 (1978).

Those regulations, which are issued by the National Highway Traffic Safety Administration (an agency of the DOT) in connection with CAFÉ (Corporate Average Fuel Economy) standards define a light truck as a four-wheel vehicle that is designed for off-road operation (has four-wheel drive or is more than 6,000 lbs. GVWR and has physical features consistent with those of a truck); or that is designed to perform at least one of the following functions: (1) transport more than 10 people; (2) provide temporary living quarters; (3) transport property in an open bed; (4) permit greater cargo-carrying capacity than passenger-carrying volume; or (5) can be converted to an open bed vehicle by removal of rear seats to form a flat continuous floor with the use of simple tools.

Applying this definition, virtually every, if not all, heavy SUVs qualify as light trucks exempt from the gas guzzler tax. Annual lists of vehicles subject to the gas guzzler tax are located on the Environmental Protection Agency's website at http://www.epa.gov/fueleconomy/guzzler/index.htm

Given the absence of any specific IRS definition of a truck for purposes of Code Sec. 280F (despite the specific regulatory authority granted in Code Sec. 280F(d)(5)(B)(iii)), it seems unlikely that the IRS would retroactively apply any definition that it may ultimately adopt. Thus, it appears reasonable to claim exemption from the depreciation caps if the manufacturer has or is entitled to categorize an SUV in excess of 6,000 GVWR as a light truck for purposes of the gas guzzler tax.

*Code Section 179 limitation on heavy SUVs, heavy trucks with a cargo bed under 6 feet in length, and certain heavy vans placed in service after October 22, 2004.* Effective for vehicles placed in service after October 22, 2004, the maximum Code Sec. 179 expense allowance that may be claimed on a "sport utility vehicle" that is exempt from the luxury car depreciation caps is limited to $25,000 (Code Sec. 179(b)(6), as added by the American Jobs Creation Act of 2004). The rate is inflation-adjusted for tax years beginning after 2018. The inflation-adjusted amount for tax years beginning in 2022 is $27,000 (Rev. Proc. 2021-45), $26,200 in 2021 (Rev. Proc. 2020-45), $25,900 in 2020 (Rev. Proc. 2019-44), and 2019 is $25,500 (Rev. Proc. 2018-57).

The term sport utility vehicle is defined as any 4-wheeled vehicle that is primarily designed or which can be used to carry passengers over public streets, roads, or highways, which is not subject to the depreciation limitations, and which is rated at not more than 14,000 pounds gross vehicle weight. Because this definition is broad enough to encompass most trucks, an exception is made for vehicles which have an open cargo area of at least 6 feet in interior length or a capped cargo area of that length if the cargo area was designed for use as an open area and is not readily accessible directly from the passenger compartment.

The definition of a sport utility vehicle also encompasses vans. Exceptions, however, are made for a vehicle (1) designed to have a seating capacity of more than 9 passengers behind the driver's seat (i.e., certain large commuter vans) or (2) which has an integral enclosure, fully enclosing the driver compartment, does not have seating behind the driver's seat and has no body section protruding more than

30 inches ahead of the leading edge of the windshield (i.e. certain cargo vans). See ¶ 201 for additional details.

*GVWR defined.* Gross Vehicle Weight Rating is the maximum allowable weight of a fully loaded vehicle (i.e., weight of vehicle, including vehicle options, passengers, cargo, gas, oil, coolant etc.). Generally, the GVWR is equal to the sum of the vehicle's curb weight and payload capacity. The gross vehicle weight rating is located on the vehicle's Safety Compliance Certification Label, which is generally located on the left front door lock facing or the door latch post pillar.

*Unofficial Tables.* These tables were compiled by the Editors primarily from information obtained at cars.com and at carsdirect.com and do not necessarily include all qualifying vehicles. Tables I, II, and III only list model years 2002-2022. Table IV only lists model years 2004-2022.

*Taxpayers should always independently verify the GVWR, chassis construction, and bed length of a truck before making any purchase or claiming exemption from the depreciation limitations.*

# TABLE I — TRUCKS WITH GVWR IN EXCESS of 6,000 LBS.

**Cadillac trucks in excess of 6,000 pounds**

Escalade EXT (2002 - 2013) (beds under 6', see Table IV)

**Chevrolet trucks in excess of 6,000 pounds**

Avalanche (2002-2013) (beds under 6', see Table IV)

Silverado (2002-2022) (certain beds under 6', see Table IV)

SSR (2002-2006) (beds under 6', see Table IV) (discontinued in 2007)

**Dodge trucks in excess of 6,000 pounds**

Dakota (certain trims) (certain beds under 6', see Table IV)

2002—All quad cabs

2003—All quad cabs and all club cabs (4x2 and 4x4)

2004—All quad cabs and all 4x4 club cabs

2005-2008—All quad cabs and all club cabs

2009-2011—All trims

Ram (2002-2011) (certain crew cab beds under 6', see Table IV)

See "Ram trucks in excess of 6,000 pounds" for post-2011 Ram models.

**Ford trucks in excess of 6,000 pounds**

F-150 (2002-2022) (certain beds under 6', see Table IV)

F-250 (2002-2022)

F-350 (2002-2022)

F-450 (2008-2022)

Ranger (2019 - 2022)

**GMC trucks in excess of 6,000 pounds**

Hummer EV (2022) (see Hummer trucks for earlier years)

Sierra 1500, 2500, 3500 (2002-2022) (certain Sierra 1500 beds under 6', see Table IV)

**Honda trucks in excess of 6,000 pounds**

Ridgeline (2017 - 2021 AWD; 2006-2014 FWD and AWD) (bed under 6') (discontinued in 2015 and 2016)

**Hummer trucks in excess of 6,000 pounds**

H2 SUT (2005-2010) (bed under 6')

H3T SUT (2009 - 2010) (bed under 6')

**Jeep trucks in excess of 6,000 pounds**

Gladiator (2020 - 2022) (bed under 6')

**Lincoln trucks in excess of 6,000 pounds**

Blackwood Pickup (2002)

Mark LT (2006-2008) (bed under 6', see Table IV) (discontinued)

**Mitsubishi trucks in excess of 6,000 pounds**

Raider (2006–2009) (discontinued) (certain beds under 6', see Table IV)

**Nissan trucks in excess of 6,000 pounds**

Frontier (2022) (certain beds under 6', see Table IV)

Titan (2004–2021) (certain beds under 6', see Table IV)

**Ram trucks in excess of 6,000 pounds**

Ram 1500, 2500, 3500 (2012 - 2022) (certain beds under 6', see Table IV) (see Dodge trucks for earlier years)

**Toyota trucks in excess of 6,000 pounds**

Tundra (certain trims over 6,000 GVWR) (certain beds under 6', see Table IV)

2007 - 2021—All trims over 6,000 GVWR (certain beds under 6', see Table IV)

2005 and 2006—All trims over 6,000 GVWR except: (1) Base V-6 2 dr. 4x2 Regular Cab and (2) SR5 V-6 4 dr. 4x2 A6ccess Cab

2004—All trims over 6,000 GVWR except (1) trims with Access Cab Stepside (however, some websites report a GVWR of 6010), (2) Base 2dr 4x2 regular cab, (3) SR5 V-6 4dr 4x2 Access Cab (V-8 version qualifies), and (4) SR5 V6 4dr 4x4 Access Cab* (GVW is exactly 6,000 pounds (V-8 version qualifies))

2003—All trims over 6,000 GVWR except (1) Base 2dr 4x2 Regular Cab, (2) SR5 V-6 4dr 4x2 Access Cab (V8 version qualifies), and (3) SR5 V6 4dr 4x4 Access Cab* (GVW is exactly 6,000 pounds (V-8 version qualifies))

2002—All trims over 6,000 GVWR except (1) Base 2dr 4x2 Regular Cab, (2) SR5 V-6 4dr 4x2 Access Cab (V-8 version qualifies), and (3) SR5 V-6 4dr 4x4 Access Cab* (GVW is exactly 6,000 lbs (V-8 version qualifies))

**A vehicle must have a GVWR in excess of 6,000 pounds to qualify for exemption from caps.*

# *TABLE II — SUVS AND CROSSOVERS IN EXCESS OF 6,000 LBS. GVWR*

**Aston Martin suvs in excess of 6,000 pounds**

DBX (2022)

**Audi suvs in excess of 6,000 pounds**

e-tron (2022)

Q7 (2015 - 2022)

Q8 (2019 - 2022)

**Bentley suvs in excess of 6,000 pounds**

Bentayga (2017-2022)

**BMW suvs in excess of 6,000 pounds**

X5 (2002-2022)

X6 (2008-2022)

X7 (2019 - 2022)

**Buick suvs in excess of 6,000 pounds**

Enclave (2008-2022)

**Cadillac suvs in excess of 6,000 pounds**

Escalade (2002-2022)

SRX (2004-2009)

XT5 (2017-2022) (GVWR 6001 lbs.)

XT6 (2020 - 2022) (GVWR 6001 lbs.)

**Chevrolet suvs in excess of 6,000 pounds**

Blazer (2019 - 2022) (GVWR 6001 lbs.)

Suburban 1500, 2500 (2002-2022)

Tahoe (2002-2022)

TrailBlazer Ext (2002-2006)

TrailBlazer SS (2007–2009) (discontinued)

Traverse (2009-2022)

**Chrysler suvs in excess of 6,000 pounds**

Aspen (2007 - 2009) (discontinued)

**Dodge suvs in excess of 6,000 pounds**

Durango (2011-2022; 2004-2009)

**Ford suvs in excess of 6,000 pounds**

Excursion (2002-2005) (discontinued)

Expedition (2002-2022)

Explorer (2006-2021)

Explorer Sport Trac (2007–2010) (discontinued)

Flex AWD (2009 - 2019) (discontinued)

Genesis (2021) (discontinued)

**GMC suvs in excess of 6,000 pounds**

Acadia (2007–2022) (GVWR 6001 lbs.)

Envoy XL (2002-2006)

Envoy XUV (2004, 2005) (discontinued)

Envoy Denali (2005-2009) (discontinued)

Hummer EV (2022)

Yukon (2002-2022)

**Honda suvs in excess of 6,000 pounds**

Pilot 4x4 (2009 - 2015)

**Hummer suvs in excess of 6,000 pounds**

Hummer H1 (2003-2006) (discontinued)

Hummer H2 (2003-2010) (discontinued)

Hummer H3 (2008-2010 (6,001 lbs)) (discontinued) (2006-2007 models *do not* exceed 6,000 GVWR)

**Infiniti suvs in excess of 6,000 pounds**

QX56 (2005-2013) (discontinued)

QX80 (2014-2022)

**Isuzu suvs in excess of 6,000 pounds**

Ascender (2003 all models, 2004 - 2006 (7-passenger models), no 2007/2008 models qualify)

**Jeep suvs in excess of 6,000 pounds**

Grand Cherokee (2011- 2022) (all trims)

Grand Cherokee (2009-2010) (all trims other than Limited and Laredo)

Grand Cherokee (2005-2008) (all trims other than Laredo)

Grand Wagoneer (2021- 2022) (all trims)

Commander (2006-2010) (discontinued)

**Kia suvs in excess of 6,000 pounds**

Borrego (certain EX V6 and EX V8 trims exceed 6,000 lbs.) (2009) (discontinued)

**Land Rover suvs in excess of 6,000 pounds**

Defender (2022)

Discovery (2017-2022; 2002-2004)

LR3 (2005-2009)

LR4 (2010-2016)

Range Rover (2002-2022)

Range Rover Sport (2006-2022)

**Lexus suvs in excess of 6,000 pounds**

GX460 (2010-2022)

GX470 (2004-2009) (discontinued)

(2003 GX470 does not qualify per manufacturer's recall)

LX470 (2002-2007)

LX570 (2008-2021)

LX600 (2022)

**Lincoln suvs in excess of 6,000 pounds**

Aviator (2020 - 2022) (2003-2005)

MKT AWD (2013 - 2020) (discontinued)

MKT (2010 - 2012)

Navigator (2002-2022)

**Maserati suvs in excess of 6,000 pounds**

Levante (2018 - 2022)

**Mazda suvs in excess of 6,000 pounds**

CX-9 (certain trims)

Touring AWD (2007-2010)

Grand Touring AWD (2007-2010)

Sport AWD (2007-2010)

**Mercedes-Benz suvs in excess of 6,000 pounds**

G55 (2004-2005; 2007–2012) (discontinued)

G63 (2013-2021)

G65 (2016-2018)

G500 (2002-2008)

G550 (2009-2022)

GL63 (2013-2017)

GL320 (2007-2010)

GL350 (2010-2016)

GL450 (2007-2016)

GL550 (2008-2016)

GLE 43 AMG (2017-2019)

GLE 53 AMG (2022)

GLE 63 AMG (2016-2021)

GLE 300d (2016-2017)

GLE 350 (2016-2022)

GLE 400 (2016-2019)

GLE 450 (2020 - 2022) (2016)

GLE 550e (2016-2018)

GLS 63 (2017-2021)

GLS 350d (2017)

GLS 450 (2017-2022)

GLS 550 (2017-2019)

GLS 580 (2020 - 2021)

GLS 600 (2021)

ML55 (2002-2003)

ML63 (2007-2015)

ML320 (2002-2003) (2007-2009) (discontinued)

ML350 (2003-2015)

ML 400 (2015) (discontinued in 2016)

ML450 (2010-2011) (discontinued)

ML500 (2002-2007)

ML550 (2008-2014) (discontinued)

R63 (2007)

R320 (2007–2009)

R350 (2006-2012)

R500 (2006-2007)

**Mercury suvs in excess of 6,000 pounds**

Mountaineer (2006-2010) (discontinued)

**Mitsubishi suvs in excess of 6,000 pounds**

Montero (2003-2005) (2002 and 2006 models have GVWR less than 6,000)

Montero Sport does not qualify

**Nissan suvs in excess of 6,000 pounds**

Armada (2005-2022; 2005-2015)

Pathfinder (2009-2012) (all 4x4 trims exceed 6,000 pounds)

Pathfinder (2008) (all 4x4, SE V8 4x2, and LE V8 4x2 trims exceed 6,000 pounds)

Pathfinder Armada (2004)

**Porsche suvs in excess of 6,000 pounds**

Cayenne (2003-2022)

**Saab suvs in excess of 6,000 pounds**

9-7x (2005-2009) (discontinued)

**Saturn suvs in excess of 6,000 pounds**

Outlook (2007-2009) (discontinued)

**Subaru suvs in excess of 6,000 pounds**

Ascent (2019 - 2022)

**Tesla suvs in excess of 6,000 pounds**

Model X (2016-2022)

**Toyota suvs in excess of 6,000 pounds**

4Runner

- 2010-2022 all trims
- 2005-2009—SR5 Sport V8 4x4; SR5 V8 4x4; Limited V8 4x4

Land Cruiser (2002-2022)

Sequoia (2002-2022)

**Volkswagen suvs in excess of 6,000 pounds**

Touareg (2004-2017) (discontinued)

**Volvo suvs in excess of 6,000 pounds**

XC90 (certain trims)

- 2003—T6 A SR AWD
- 2004—2.5 TA AWD and T6 A AWD
- 2005-2009—all V8 trims and certain other trims
- 2010-2014—all trims

# *TABLE III — VANS IN EXCESS OF 6,000 LBS GVWR*

**Chevrolet vans in excess of 6,000 pounds**

Astro (certain passenger trims listed below)

- 2002—LS all-wheel drive passenger van
- 2002, 2003, 2004, 2005—LT with 1SE all wheel drive passenger van
- 2003, 2004, 2005—Base all-wheel drive passenger van
- 2003, 2004, 2005—LS with 1SC all wheel drive passenger van

Express (2002-2022)

**Chrysler vans in excess of 6,000 pounds**

Pacifica (2017 - 2022)

Voyager (2020 - 2021)

**Dodge vans in excess of 6,000 pounds**

Grand Caravan (2012 - 2020) (discontinued)

Ram Van (1500, 2500, 3500) (2002-2003)

Ram Wagon Van (1500, 2500, 3500) (2002)

Sprinter Van (2500, 3500) (2003-2009) (discontinued)

**Ford vans in excess of 6,000 pounds**

Econoline (E Series) (discontinued)

- E-150 (2002-2014)
- E-250 (2002-2014)
- E-350 (2002-2014)

Transit

- 150 (2015-2022)
- 250 (2015-2022)
- 350 (2015-2022)
- Transit Connect less than 6,000 pounds

**GMC vans in excess of 6,000 pounds**

Safari (certain trims)

- SLE AWD passenger van (2002)
- SLT with 1SE AWD passenger van (2002)
- Base AWD passenger van (2003-2005)
- SLE with 1SC AWD passenger van (2003-2005)
- SLT with 1SE AWD passenger van (2003-2005)

Savana 1500 (2009-2014)

Savana 2500 (2010-2022)

Savana 3500 (2010-2022)

Savana (2002-2008)

**Honda vans in excess of 6,000 pounds**

Odyssey (2011 - 2022)

**Mercedes Benz vans in excess of 6,000 pounds**

Metris (2016 - 2022)

Sprinter (2010 - 2022)

**Nissan vans in excess of 6,000 pounds**

NV 1500, 2500, 3500 (2012-2021) (discontinued)

**Ram vans in excess of 6,000 pounds**

Cargo Tradesman (2012-2015) (discontinued)

Promaster (2014-2022)

Promaster City is less than 6,000 pounds

# TABLE IV — TRUCKS IN EXCESS OF 6,000 LBS GVWR WITH BED LENGTH UNDER 6 FT. (Code Sec. 179 Expensing Limit Applies)

**Cadillac trucks with short beds**

Escalade EXT (2004-2013)

**Chevrolet trucks with short bed**

Avalanche (2004-2013)

SSR (2004-2006) (discontinued)

Silverado 1500 (certain crew cabs) (2014-2022)

Silverado 1500 (crew cabs) (2010-2013)

Silverado 1500 (certain crew cabs and certain extended cabs) (2006-2009)

Silverado 1500 (crew cabs) (2004-2005)

**Dodge trucks with short bed**

Dakota Quad Cabs (2004-2008) (discontinued)

Dakota Crew Cabs (2009-2011) (discontinued)

Ram 1500 (certain crew cabs) (2010-2011) (see Ram trucks for post-2011 years)

Ram 1500 (certain trims) (2004-2009)

**Ford trucks with short beds**

Explorer Trac (2007-2010) (discontinued)

F-150 (short-bed trims) (2004-2022)

Maverick (2004-2022)

Ranger trucks (2019 - 2022) (certain trims)

**GMC trucks with short beds**

Canyon certain crew cabs (2022)

Sierra 1500 certain crew cabs (2014-2022)

Sierra 1500 crew cabs (2004-2013)

Sierra Classic 1500 crew cabs (2007)

Sierra 1500 extended cabs with 5.75 foot box (2006-2009)

Sierra Classic 1500 extended cabs with 5.75 foot box (2007)

Sierra 1500 Denali certain crew cabs (2014 - 2018)

Sierra 1500 Denali (2005-2013)

**Honda trucks with short bed**

Ridgeline (2017-2022; 2006-2014 FWD and AWD)

**Hummer trucks with short bed**

H2 SUT (2005-2010) (discontinued)

H3T (2009-2010) (discontinued)

**Jeep**

Gladiator (2020 - 2022)

**Lincoln trucks with short bed**

Mark LT (2006-2008) (discontinued)

**Mitsubishi trucks with short bed**

Raider Double Cabs (2006-2009) (discontinued)

**Nissan trucks with short bed**

Frontier (certain crew cabs) (2022)

Titan (certain crew cabs) (2008-2021)

Titan Crew Cabs (all trims) (2004-2007)

**RAM trucks with short bed**

Ram 1500 (certain crew cabs) (2012-2022)

**Toyota trucks with short bed**

Tundra Crew Cabs (2007-2022)

***Primary source of information: http://www.carsdirect.com and http://cars.com***

# Quick Reference Table—State Corporate Depreciation Conformity

Code Sec. 167 allows a deduction from federal taxable income for the exhaustion, wear and tear of property used in a trade or business, or of property held for the production of income. Under the Modified Accelerated Cost Recovery System (MACRS) and the Accelerated Cost Recovery System (ACRS) of Code Sec. 168, the cost or other basis of an asset is generally recovered over a specific recovery period. MACRS applies to tangible property generally placed in service after 1986 and the Accelerated Cost Recovery System (ACRS) applies to property placed in service after 1980 and before 1987.

This Multistate Quick Answer Chart from the CCH State Tax Library shows the tax treatment by each state and the District of Columbia of federal depreciation under Code Sec. 167, and Code Sec. 168, including bonus depreciation (Code Sec. 168(k)) *for corporations*. In certain cases, tax treatment for individuals will differ. Many states follow federal depreciation rules, but require adjustments to taxable income for bonus depreciation.

This Multistate Quick Answer Chart from the CCH State Tax Library is located in the IntelliConnect browse tree under "State Tax" - "Practice Aids" - "MultiState Quick Answer Charts" - "Quick Answer Charts" - "Corporation Income Tax Quick Answer Charts" - "Regular and Bonus Depreciation /IRS 167/IRC168."

This chart is based on the chart as it appeared on IntelliConnect on December 20, 2021. Check the IntellConnect version for additional updates.

| State | Corporate Answer | Comments |
|---|---|---|
| Alabama | No adjustments to federal deduction required for tax years before and after 2008.<br>Addition required for federal bonus depreciation claimed in tax year 2008. | See CCH Alabama State Tax Law Reporter ¶ 10-670 |
| Alaska | Addition by oil and gas producers and pipelines required for federal deduction. Subtraction by oil and gas producers and pipelines allowed for depreciation based on federal provisions in effect on June 30, 1981, or financial statement depreciation. No other adjustments for federal deduction, including bonus depreciation, required. | See CCH Alaska State Law Reporter ¶ 10-510, ¶ 10-525, ¶ 10-600 |
| Arizona | Addition required for federal deduction, including bonus depreciation. Subtraction allowed for depreciation computed as if bonus depreciation had not been elected for federal purposes. | See CCH Arizona State Law Tax Reporter ¶ 10-670, ¶ 10-900 |

| State | Corporate Answer | Comments |
|---|---|---|
| Arkansas | Subtraction allowed for depreciation computed using federal provisions in effect on January 1, 2019, without regard to bonus depreciation, for property purchased in tax years beginning after 2014.<br>Subtraction allowed for depreciation computed using federal provisions in effect on January 1, 2017, without regard to bonus depreciation, for property purchased in tax years beginning after 2014.<br>Subtraction allowed for depreciation computed using federal provisions in effect on January 1, 2015, without regard to bonus depreciation, for property purchased in tax years beginning after 2013 and before 2015.<br>Subtraction allowed for depreciation computed using federal provisions in effect on January 2, 2013, without regard to bonus depreciation for property purchased in tax years beginning after 2011 and before 2014.<br>Subtraction allowed for depreciation computing using federal provisions in effect on January 1, 2009, without regard to bonus depreciation, for property purchased in tax years beginning after 2008 and before 2012. | See CCH Arkansas State Tax Reporter ¶ 10-670, ¶ 10-900 |
| California | Addition required if federal deduction exceeds allowable state deduction due to state differences, including:<br>• federal bonus depreciation;<br>• accelerated depreciation under ACRS and MACRS recovery systems.<br>Subtraction allowed if state deduction exceeds federal deduction due to state differences, including:<br>• depreciation computed using pre-1981 federal provisions; and<br>• additional first-year depreciation under state provisions. | Adjustments computed on Form 3885.<br>See CCH California State Tax Reporter ¶ 10-670, ¶ 10-900 |
| Colorado | No adjustments to federal deduction, including bonus depreciation, required. | See CCH Colorado State Tax Reporter ¶ 10-515, ¶ 10-600 |
| Connecticut | Addition required for federal bonus depreciation.<br>Subtraction allowed for depreciation computed without regard to federal bonus depreciation. | Subtraction adjustment computed on Form CT-1120 ATT.<br>See CCH Connecticut State Tax Reporter ¶ 10-670, ¶ 10-900 |
| Delaware | No adjustments to federal deduction, including bonus depreciation, required. | See CCH Delaware State Tax Reporter ¶ 10-510, ¶ 10-600 |
| District of Columbia | Subtraction allowed for depreciation computed without regard to federal bonus depreciation. | Federal depreciation form and statement showing computation must be attached to state return.<br>See CCH District of Columbia Tax Reporter ¶ 10-900 |

| State | Corporate Answer | Comments |
|---|---|---|
| Florida | Addition required for:<br>• federal bonus depreciation claimed for property placed in service beginning after 2007 and before 2027; and<br>• federal depreciation claimed for qualified improvement property placed in service on or after January 1, 2018.<br>Subtraction allowed equal to 1/7 of addback amount in first and succeeding six tax years. | See CCH Florida State Tax Reporter ¶ 10-670, ¶ 10-900 |
| Georgia | Addition required for amount of federal deduction, including bonus depreciation.<br>Subtraction allowed for depreciation computed on a separate basis using Form 4562 without regard to federal bonus depreciation, as well as special depreciation and shortened recovery periods for certain property: | Federal and state depreciation forms must be attached to state return.<br>See CCH Georgia State Tax Reporter ¶ 10-670, ¶ 10-900 |
| Hawaii | Addition required for federal deduction relating to:<br>• federal bonus depreciation;<br>• depreciation of property on Native American Indian reservations.<br>Subtraction allowed using federal guidelines in effect before federal bonus depreciation provisions. | Adjustment computed by completing federal depreciation form. Federal form and any worksheet showing computation of adjustments must be attached to state return.<br>See CCH Hawaii State Tax Reporter ¶ 10-670, ¶ 10-900 |
| Idaho | Addition required for tax years before 2008 and after 2009 if federal deduction exceeds allowable state deduction due to federal bonus depreciation.<br>Subtraction allowed for tax years before 2008 and after 2009 if federal deduction computed without regard to bonus depreciation is less than allowable state deduction.<br>No adjustments to federal deduction, including bonus depreciation, required for tax years after 2007 and before 2010. | Adjustment computed by completing and attaching federal depreciation form or detailed computation.<br>See CCH Idaho State Tax Reporter ¶ 10-670, ¶ 10-900 |
| Illinois | Addition required for federal bonus depreciation, including 100% bonus depreciation for tax years ending on or after December 31, 2021.<br>Subtraction may be claimed for a portion of federal bonus depreciation:<br>• the last tax year federal regular depreciation is claimed on the property; or<br>• when the taxpayer sells, transfers, abandons, or otherwise disposes of the property.<br>Subtraction adjustment is equal to:<br>• 42.9% of federal depreciation for which 30% or 50% federal bonus depreciation was claimed in tax years beginning after 2001 and ending on or before December 31, 2005; and<br>• 100% of depreciation on property for which 50% bonus depreciation was claimed in tax years beginning after December 31, 2005. | Adjustments computed on Form IL-4562, which must be attached to state return.<br>See CCH Illinois State Tax Reporter ¶ 10-670, ¶ 10-900 |

| State | Corporate Answer | Comments |
| --- | --- | --- |
| Indiana | Addition required for federal bonus depreciation.<br>Subtraction allowed for depreciation computed without regard to bonus depreciation. | See CCH Indiana State Tax Reporter ¶ 10-670, ¶ 10-900 |
| Iowa | No adjustment for federal deduction required for tax years after 2020.<br>Tax years before 2021:<br>Addition required for federal bonus depreciation. Subtraction was allowed for depreciation computed without regard to bonus depreciation. | Adjustment computed on Schedule IA 4562A.<br>See CCH Iowa State Tax Reporter ¶ 10-670, ¶ 10-900 |
| Kansas | Addition required for federal depreciation of (1) buildings or facilities for which state disabled access credit is claimed, and (2) the following types of property if state amortization deduction is claimed:<br>• oil refineries;<br>• oil or natural gas pipelines;<br>• integrated coal or coke gasification nitrogen fertilizer plants;<br>• biomass-to-energy plants;<br>• renewable electric cogeneration facilities;<br>• waste heat utilization systems at an electric generation facility;<br>• biofuel storage and blending equipment;<br>• carbon dioxide capture, sequestration or utilization machinery and equipment.<br>No other adjustments to federal deduction, including bonus depreciation, required. | See CCH Kansas State Tax Reporter ¶ 10-670, ¶ 10-895 |
| Kentucky | Addition required for federal bonus depreciation<br>Subtraction allowed for depreciation using federal provisions in effect on December 31, 2001. | Adjustment computed by converting federal form and attaching to state return.<br>See CCH Kentucky State Tax Reporter ¶ 10-670, ¶ 10-900 |
| Louisiana | No adjustments to federal deduction, including bonus depreciation, required. | See CCH Louisiana State Tax Reporter ¶ 10-510, ¶ 10-600 |

| State | Corporate Answer | Comments |
|---|---|---|
| Maine | Addition to federal tax base required equal to:<br>• net increase in depreciation attributable to federal bonus depreciation on property placed in service in 2013 tax year and thereafter for which a capital investment credit is claimed;<br>• federal bonus depreciation on property placed in service in 2011 and 2012 tax years for which a capital investment credit is claimed;<br>• net increase in depreciation attributable to federal bonus depreciation on property placed in service in 2011 tax year and thereafter for which a capital investment credit is not claimed; and<br>• net increase in depreciation attributable to federal bonus depreciation on property placed in service in 2008 to 2010 tax years.<br>Subtraction from federal tax based required equal to:<br>• depreciation computed as though bonus depreciation had not been claimed on property placed in service in 2011 tax year and thereafter for which a capital investment credit is not claimed;<br>• depreciation computed as though bonus depreciation had not been claimed on property placed in service in 2008 to 2010 tax years;<br>• 5% of addition modification for property placed in service in 2003 to 2005 tax years beginning in tax year following year property was placed in service, with remaining 95% of modification recovered evenly over remainder of asset's life beginning in year 3; and<br>• equal amounts of addition modification for property placed in service in 2002 tax year over remainder of asset's life beginning in 2004 tax year. | Capital investment credit allowed equal to:<br>• 1.2% of net increase in depreciation deduction reported as addition to income for 2020 tax year and thereafter, excluding certain utility and telecommunications property;<br>• 9% of net increase in depreciation deduction reported as addition to income for 2013 through 2019 tax years, excluding certain utility and telecommunications property; and<br>• 10% of federal bonus depreciation claimed on property placed in service for tax years 2011 and 2012, excluding certain utility and telecommunications property.<br>See CCH Maine State Tax Reporter ¶ 10-670, ¶ 10-900<br>We recommend you reference cited authority for more information |
| Maryland | After 2018, addition required if federal deduction exceeds allowable state deduction due to decoupling from federal bonus depreciation, except for certain manufacturing businesses.<br>Before 2019, addition required if federal deduction exceeds allowable state deduction due to decoupling from federal bonus depreciation and higher depreciation deduction for certain heavy duty SUV's.<br>Subtraction allowed if state deduction exceeds federal deduction. | Adjustments computed on Form 500 DM.<br>We recommend you reference cited authority for more information.<br><br>See CCH Maryland State Tax Reporter ¶ 10-670, ¶ 10-900 |
| Massachusetts | Addition required for federal bonus depreciation. | See CCH Massachusetts State Tax Reporter ¶ 10-670 |

| State | Corporate Answer | Comments |
|---|---|---|
| Michigan | Addition required for federal bonus depreciation. | Tax years after 2008 and before 2011:<br>MBT credit is available for portion of denied federal bonus depreciation deduction.<br>We recommend you reference cited authority for more information.<br>See CCH Michigan State Tax Reporter ¶ 10-515, ¶ 10-670 |
| Minnesota | Addition required for 80% of federal bonus depreciation.<br>Subtraction allowed for amount of addition adjustment over five following tax years.<br>State does not conform to federal bonus depreciation changes made by the Tax Cuts and Jobs Act. | See CCH Minnesota State Tax Reporter ¶ 10-670, ¶ 10-900 |
| Mississippi | Addition required for federal bonus depreciation.<br>Subtraction allowed by computing depreciation without regard to bonus depreciation. | Adjustments computed by converting federal depreciation form.<br>We recommend you reference cited authority for more information.<br>See CCH Mississippi State Tax Reporter ¶ 10-670, ¶ 10-900 |
| Missouri | Addition required for 30% federal bonus depreciation on property purchased between July 1, 2002 and June 30, 2003.<br>Subtraction allowed for depreciation on property purchased between July 1, 2002 and June 30, 2003 computed without regard to 30% bonus depreciation.<br>No other adjustments required. | See CCH Missouri State Tax Reporter ¶ 10-670, ¶ 10-900 |
| Montana | No adjustments to federal deduction, including federal bonus depreciation, required. | See CCH Montana State Tax Reporter ¶ 10-515, ¶ 10-670 |
| Nebraska | Subtraction from federal tax base allowed beginning on or after January 1, 2006, and in each of the four following taxable years, for 20% of the total amount of bonus depreciation that was required as an addition adjustment for tax years 2003 through 2005. | Adjustment computed on separate schedule that must be attached to state return.<br>We recommend you reference cited authority for more information.<br>See CCH Nebraska State Tax Reporter ¶ 10-670, ¶ 10-900 |
| Nevada | N/A because state does not tax general business corporation income | See CCH Nevada State Tax Reporter ¶ 10-001 |
| New Hampshire | Addition required for federal bonus depreciation.<br>Subtraction allowed for depreciation computed using federal provisions in effect on December 31, 2015, without regard to bonus depreciation, effective for taxable periods after 2016. | See CCH New Hampshire State Tax Reporter ¶ 10-670, ¶ 10-900.<br>We recommend you reference cited authority for more information. |

| State | Corporate Answer | Comments |
|---|---|---|
| New Jersey | Subtraction allowed after recomputing depreciation without regard to federal deduction relating to:<br>• federal bonus depreciation;<br>• accelerated depreciation on property placed in service on or after 1981 and prior to July 7, 1993;<br>• depreciation of safe harbor lease property; and<br>• depreciation attributable to partnership interests. | Adjustment computed on Form CBT-100, Schedule S.<br>See CCH New Jersey State Tax Reporter ¶ 10-670, ¶ 10-900 |
| New Mexico | No adjustments to federal deduction, including bonus depreciation, required. | See CCH New Mexico State Tax Reporter ¶ 10-515, ¶ 10-600, ¶ 10-800 |
| New York | Addition required for federal deduction relating to:<br>• federal bonus depreciation on property, except qualified resurgence zone and New York Liberty Zone property, placed in service on or after June 1, 2003 in tax periods beginning after 2002;<br>• depreciation of safe harbor lease property;<br>• accelerated depreciation on property placed in service either in or outside the state after 1980 in tax periods beginning before 1985; and<br>• accelerated depreciation on property placed in service outside the state in tax periods beginning after 1984 and before 1994, if an election was made to continue using depreciation under IRC § 167.<br>Subtraction allowed for depreciation computed without regard to disallowed federal provisions. | Adjustment computed on Form CT-399.<br>See CCH New York State Tax Reporter ¶ 10-670, ¶ 10-900 |
| North Carolina | Addition required equal to 85% of federal bonus depreciation.<br>Subtraction allowed for 20% of addback over next five years. | Addition also required for depreciation on a utility plant acquired by a natural gas local distribution company.<br>We recommend you reference cited authority for more information.<br>See CCH North Carolina State Tax Reporter ¶ 10-670, ¶ 10-900 |
| North Dakota | Addition required for federal deduction relating to:<br>• accelerated depreciation on property placed in service in 1981 and 1982; and<br>• depreciation of safe harbor lease property.<br>No other adjustments to federal deduction, including bonus depreciation, required. | See CCH North Dakota State Tax Reporter ¶ 10-670, ¶ 10-900 |
| Ohio | Commercial Activity Tax (CAT)<br>No adjustment required because CAT is not considered an income tax and is not tied to federal income tax base. | See CCH Ohio State Tax Reporter ¶ 14-140 |

| State | Corporate Answer | Comments |
|---|---|---|
| Oklahoma | Addition required for federal deduction relating to:<br>• 80% of amount of bonus depreciation for assets placed in service after December 31, 2007, and before January 1, 2010;<br>• 80% of amount of bonus depreciation for assets placed in service after September 10, 2001, and before September 11, 2004;<br>• depreciation of refinery property located in the state if an election was made to expense 100% of cost.<br>Subtraction allowed for 25% of bonus depreciation addition adjustment over following four tax years.<br>No adjustment to federal deduction, including bonus depreciation, required for tax years after 2010. | Certification report for refinery expense election must be enclosed with state return.<br>See CCH Oklahoma State Tax Reporter ¶ 10-670, ¶ 10-900 |
| Oregon | Addition required for federal deduction relating to:<br>• federal bonus depreciation after 2008 and before 2011;<br>• accelerated depreciation in tax years prior to 2009 on property placed into service on or after January 1, 1981 and before January 1, 1985; and<br>• depreciation of safe harbor lease property in tax years prior to 2009.<br>Subtraction allowed if state deduction exceeds federal deduction due to state differences in depreciable basis of property, including differences relating to the disallowance of federal bonus depreciation and enhanced IRC § 179 expense deduction limits for 2009 and 2010 tax years. | Adjustment is computed on Depreciation Schedule for Individuals, Partnerships, Corporations, and Fiduciaries.<br>We recommend you reference cited authority for more information.<br>See CCH New Oregon State Tax Reporter ¶ 10-670, ¶ 10-900 |
| Pennsylvania | Addition required for:<br>• 50% federal bonus depreciation; and,<br>• 100% bonus depreciation for property placed in service after September 27, 2017<br>Subtraction allowed for property placed in service after September 27, 2017 equal to federal depreciation determined under:<br>• IRC Sec. 167; and<br>• IRC Sec. 168, except IRC Sec. 168(k) does not apply.<br>Subtraction allowed in current and subsequent tax years for property placed in service before September 28, 2017 equal to 3/7 of 50% bonus depreciation addition adjustment. | Adjustments computed on Schedule C-3 of corporate tax report.<br>• no addition required for 100% bonus depreciation for property acquired after September 8, 2010 and placed in service before 2012<br>We recommend you reference cited authority for more information. See CCH Pennsylvania State Tax Reporter ¶ 10-670, ¶ 10-900 |
| Rhode Island | Addition required for federal bonus depreciation. | See CCH Rhode Island State Tax Reporter ¶ 10-670, ¶ 10-900 |
| South Carolina | Addition required if federal deduction exceeds allowable state deduction due to decoupling from federal bonus depreciation provisions.<br>Subtraction allowed if state deduction exceeds federal deduction. | Schedule showing computation of differences must be attached to state return.<br>See CCH South Carolina State Tax Reporter ¶ 10-670, ¶ 10-900 |

| State | Corporate Answer | Comments |
|---|---|---|
| South Dakota | N/A, because state does not tax general business corporation income. | See CCH South Dakota State Tax Reporter ¶ 14-001 |
| Tennessee | Addition required for federal deduction relating to:<br>• federal bonus depreciation; and<br>• depreciation of safe harbor lease property. | See CCH Tennessee State Tax Reporter ¶ 10-670, ¶ 10-900 |
| Texas | Federal bonus depreciation is not includable in franchise tax depreciation. If federal bonus depreciation is claimed, franchise tax depreciation must be recomputed using an appropriate federal depreciation method in effect for the federal tax year beginning January 1, 2007. | See CCH Texas State Tax Reporter ¶ 10-670, ¶ 10-900 |
| Utah | Addition required for depreciation by purchaser-lessors of safe harbor lease property.<br>Subtraction allowed for depreciation by seller-lessees of safe harbor lease property.<br>No other adjustments to federal deduction, including federal bonus depreciation, required. | See CCH Utah State Tax Reporter ¶ 10-670, ¶ 10-900 |
| Vermont | Addition required for federal bonus depreciation. | See CCH Vermont State Tax Reporter ¶ 10-670 |
| Virginia | Addition to federal tax base required if federal deduction recomputed without regard to bonus depreciation exceeds allowable state deduction.<br>Subtraction allowed if state deduction exceeds federal deduction. | State generally decouples with provisions of the Tax Cuts and Jobs Act after 2017.<br>We recommend you reference cited authority for more information.<br>See CCH Virginia State Tax Reporter ¶ 10-670, ¶ 10-900 |
| Washington | N/A, because state does not tax general business corporation income. | See CCH Washington State Tax Reporter ¶ 10-001 |
| West Virginia | Addition required for federal depreciation of certain water and air pollution control facilities if election was made to expense costs.<br>No other adjustments to federal deduction, including bonus depreciation, required. | See CCH West Virginia State Tax Reporter ¶ 10-670 |

| State | Corporate Answer | Comments |
|---|---|---|
| Wisconsin | Addition required if federal deduction exceeds allowable state deduction due to state differences, including:<br>• federal bonus depreciation;<br>• depreciation of safe harbor lease property for taxable years beginning before 2014; and<br>• depreciation for taxable years beginning before 2014 of certain assets placed in service before 1987.<br>Adjustment allowed for tax years equal to 20% of the difference between the combined federal basis of all depreciated or amortized assets (as of the last day of the taxable year beginning in 2013) over the combined state adjusted basis of those assets beginning in the first taxable year after 2013 and each of the next four taxable years.<br>Subtraction allowed for tax years beginning before 2014 equal to excess of state deduction over federal deduction using federal depreciation provisions in effect on December 31, 2000. | We recommend you reference cited authority for more information.<br>See CCH Wisconsin State Tax Reporter ¶ 10-670, ¶ 10-900 |
| Wyoming | N/A, because state does not tax general business corporation income. | See CCH Washington State Tax Reporter ¶ 10-001 |

# Quick Reference Tables—Cost Segregation Matrixes for Casinos, Restaurants, Retail Stores, and Auto Dealerships

*The following four tables reproduced below are taken from the IRS's "Audit Technique Guide for Cost Segregation," revision date October 2016. A fifth table for the motor vehicle manufacturing industry and a sixth table for the pharmaceutical industry are not reproduced but can be found in the audit guide. The motor vehicle manufacturing table was also reproduced in the 2018 CCH U.S. Master Depreciation Guide, published in December 2017. The audit guide provides more than 100 pages of information on cost segregation, including the tables reproduced below. The general purpose of each table is to distinguish between the structural components of a building (section 1250 property which is depreciable over 39-years) and section 1245 components of a building which can be depreciated over a shorter period of time under the cost segregation rules described beginning at ¶ 127. In addition, section 1245 property may be able to qualify for expensing under section 179 and the bonus depreciation deduction.*

Note that the depreciation period provided in the tables for section 1245 property is based upon its proper Asset Class in Rev. Proc. 87-56, which in turn generally depends upon the type of activity in which the property is used. For example, section 1245 property used in the casino/theatre area of a casino complex is generally classified as MACRS 7-year property (Asset Class 79.0 of Rev. Proc. 87-56 dealing with assets used in the recreation industry). However, most assets used outside of the casino/theatre area are classified as MACRS 5-year property (Asset Class 57.0, relating to assets used in the distributive trades and services). See ¶ 104 for a discussion of this very important asset class which includes retail and wholesale trades and trades primarily involving the provision of personal or professional services. Most section 1245 property used in a restaurant falls within this category, as does most section 1245 property used in retail stores and by the pharmaceutical industry.

If an asset cannot be properly assigned to a particular asset class in Rev. Proc. 87-56 or is otherwise not assigned a specific recovery period by Code Sec. 168, then it is considered an asset without a class life and is assigned a 7-year MACRS recovery period under a default rule (Code Sec. 168(e)(3)(C)(v)). The types of section 1245 assets assigned a 7-year recovery period as property without a class life appear in these tables are "generic" assets that are not used directly in connection with any particular activity or machinery (e.g., decorative lighting and decorative molding, wall coverings, and window treatments). Note that these same items when located in a retail store or restaurant are assigned a 5-year recovery period by the tables (Asset Class 57.0 relating to assets used in wholesale and retail trade) rather than a 7-year recovery period. One reason for Asset Class 57.0 classification is that the appearance of the interior and exterior of the building is directly linked to the success of the retail store or restaurant. That is to say, the decorative molding and lighting, and wall coverings etc. are actually considered used in a retail trade or business within the meaning of Asset Class 57.0).

For a detailed discussion on the manner in which an asset's recovery period is determined, see ¶ 190 and ¶ 191.

The following recent legislation may affect the applicable depreciation period shown in the tables below and is not fully reflected in those tables.

*15-year recovery period for restaurant buildings and interior structural improvements.* Restaurant buildings placed in service after 2008 and before 2018 are depreciable as section 1250 15-year property using the straight-line method. Improvements to the interior of a restaurant that are structural components are similarly depreciated if placed in service after October 22, 2004 and before 2018. An improvement to a restaurant will no longer need to be made to a building that is at least three years old provided that the improvement is placed in service after 2008. See ¶ 110.

*15-year recovery period for qualified retail improvement property.* A qualified interior improvement to a building used for a retail business is depreciated under MACRS over 15 years using the straight-line method if the improvement is placed in service in after 2008 and before 2018 and the building is at least three years old when the improvement is placed in service (Code Sec. 168(e)(8), stricken by P.L. 115-97). See ¶ 126.

*15-year recovery period for qualified leasehold improvements.* Qualified leasehold improvement property placed in service after October 22, 2004 and before 2018 is depreciated over a 15-year recovery period using the straight-line method. Qualified leasehold improvement property is any improvement to an interior portion of nonresidential real property if the following requirements are satisfied: (1) the improvement is made under or pursuant to a lease by the lessee, any sublessee, or the lessor (a commitment to enter into a lease is treated as a lease for this purpose); (2) the lease is not between related persons; (3) the building (or portion that the improvement is made to) is occupied exclusively by the lessee or sublessee; (4) the improvement is section 1250 property (i.e., a structural component); and (5) the improvement is placed into service more than 3 years after the date that the building was first placed into service (Code Sec. 168(e)(3)(E)(iv), stricken by P.L. 115-97). The improvements must be made to the interior portion of nonresidential real property. See ¶ 126.

*Bonus depreciation.* Bonus depreciation may be claimed on qualified leasehold improvements placed in service before 2016. If a qualified retail improvement or qualified restaurant improvement also meets the definition of a qualified leasehold improvement bonus depreciation may be claimed (Rev. Proc. 2011-26). Effective for property placed in service after 2015 qualified improvement property qualifies for bonus depreciation. See ¶ 127D.

[Full Text IRS Document.—Editor.]

**Cost Segregation ATG - Chapter 7.1 Industry Specific Guidance - Casinos**

*Chapter 6.8 / Table of Contents / Chapter 7.2*

**Field Directive on Asset Class and Depreciation for Casino Construction Costs**

LMSB-04-0706-005

July 11, 2006

MEMORANDUM FOR INDUSTRY DIRECTORS, LMSB DIRECTOR, FIELD SPECIALISTS, LMSB DIRECTOR, PREFILING AND TECHNICAL GUIDANCE, LMSB DIVISION COUNSEL, LMSB DIRECTOR, COMPLIANCE, SBSE

| | |
|---|---|
| FROM: | JoAnn Bank /s/ JoAnn G. Bank Acting Industry Director, Communications, Technology & Media |
| SUBJECT: | Field Directive on Asset Class and Depreciation for Casino Construction Costs |

## INTRODUCTION

This memorandum is intended to provide direction to effectively utilize resources in the classification and examination of a taxpayer who is recovering construction costs through depreciation of tangible property used in connection with a hotel/casino property.

## RECOMMENDATIONS

The matrix included in this document contains recommendations for the categorization and lives of various hotel/casino assets. If the taxpayer's tax return position for these assets is consistent with these recommendations, no adjustments should be made to categorizations and lives. If the taxpayer reports assets differently, then adjustments should be considered.

## EFFECT ON OTHER GUIDANCE

This directive should be applied in the context of other applicable depreciation principles. For example, normal examination procedures should be followed to determine whether all appropriate costs, including IRC § 263A expenses, have been associated with a particular asset. Examiners are encouraged to exercise their professional judgment when developing and resolving factual issues.

This memorandum is not an official pronouncement of the law or the Service's position and cannot be used, cited, or relied upon as such.

## CONTACTS

If you have any questions, please have a member of your staff contact Eric Lacher, Gaming Industry Technical Advisor, at (702) 868-5262 (*Eric.A.Lacher2@irs.gov*).

Attachments

cc: Commissioner, LMSB

Deputy Commissioner, LMSB

Director, Performance, Quality and Audit Assistance

### LMSB Directive on Cost Segregation in the Gaming Industry

This matrix, which is part of the Cost Segregation Audit Techniques Guide, is intended to provide direction to effectively utilize resources in the classification and examination of property used in the operation of a casino/hotel property. General fact patterns specific to this industry have been considered in the classification of these assets and may not be applicable to other industries. Similarly, asset classification guidance issued for other industries is based on the general fact pattern for that industry and may not be applicable to a casino/hotel business situation. For example, for asset classification of restaurants located within a casino, refer to the industry directive for restaurants. For examination techniques and historical background related to this issue, refer to the Cost Segregation Audit Techniques Guide.

**NOTE:** In the case of certain leasehold improvement property, the classifications in this directive are superseded to the extent that the American Jobs Creation Act of 2004 modifies IRC Section 168. Thus, a 15-year straight line recovery period should replace the recovery period shown in the following matrix if the asset is "qualified leasehold improvement property" (as defined in IRC Section 168(e)(6)) placed in service by the taxpayer after 10/22/04 and before 1/1/18.

| ASSET | DESCRIPTION | PROPERTY TYPE | RECOVERY PERIOD |
|---|---|---|---|
| Ceilings | Dropped or lowered ceilings with decorative finishes (such as ornamental polished gold and copper metal panels suspended from the finished ceiling or glued to soffits or lowered drywall ceiling systems). The suspension grids are hung by hanger wires from hooks or eyes set in the floor above or bottom of the roof, and attached to walls with nails or screws. Components such as lighting fixtures and air conditioning registers are placed on the grid. The ceilings conceal plumbing, wiring, sprinkler systems and air conditioning ducts. Includes grid systems where the actual building ceiling above the suspended ceiling can be seen. The actual building ceiling is generally painted a dark color so as to hide the various conduit, wires, and mechanical systems hanging from it. | § 1250 | 39 years (40 years for purposes of § 168 (g)) |
| Doors and Door Locks | Interior and exterior doors, regardless of decoration, including but not limited to, double opening doors, overhead doors, revolving doors, entrance security gates, roll-up or sliding wire mesh or steel grills and gates, and door hardware (such as doorknobs, closers, kick plates, hinges, locks, automatic openers, etc.). Includes hotel guest room computerized door locks. Includes encoders, computers, and other associated hardware of the computerized lock system. | § 1250 | 39 years (40 years for purposes of § 168 (g)) |
| | Special lightweight, double action doors installed to prevent accidents in a heavily trafficked area ("Eliason"-type door). For example, flexible doors, clear curtains, or strip curtains used between stock areas and selling areas. | § 1245 | 5 years (57.0 Distributive Trades and Services) |

| ASSET | DESCRIPTION | PROPERTY TYPE | RECOVERY PERIOD |
|---|---|---|---|
| Electrical Hook-ups (includes duplex, fourplex, junction box, conduit/ wiring and allocation of panels) | Includes electrical outlets of general applicability and accessibility located in *Accounting and Administrative Offices, Ballrooms, "Back of House" areas, Pre-function areas, and Support areas* (such as shop areas, engineering and construction offices). Includes but is not limited to outlets connected to copy machines, fax machines, personal computers, break rooms, coffee rooms, lounges, etc. | § 1250 | 39 years (40 years for purposes of § 168 (g)) |
| | Includes electrical outlets located in hotel guest rooms and guest bathrooms of general applicability and accessibility (includes bathroom GFI outlet). | § 1250 | 39 years (40 years for purposes of § 168 (g)) |
| | Includes electrical outlets specifically associated to particular items of machinery and equipment located in the Casino area. Includes ATM machines, slot machines, and other gaming related equipment. Also includes all electrical hook-ups associated with the activities described in Asset Class 79.0 of Rev. Proc. 87-56, *1987-2 CB 674*, such as Theater and Showroom. | § 1245 | 7 years (79.0 Recreation) |
| | Includes electrical outlets specifically associated to a particular item of machinery or equipment located in *Conference Rooms, Guest Rooms, Public Facility areas, Meeting Rooms, and Support Areas*, but not in the Casino/Theater area. Examples include equipment in Exercise rooms, ice machines, vending machines, audio visual equipment, televisions (and the riser conduit and wiring), garbage disposals, refrigerators, and workbenches. | § 1245 | 5 years (57.0 Distributive Trades and Services) |
| Exit Signs | Signs posted along exit routes that indicate the direction of travel to the nearest exit. These signs typically read "EXIT" and may have distinctive colors, illumination, or arrows indicating the direction to the exit. | § 1250 | 39 years (40 years for purposes of § 168 (g)) |
| Facades - Exterior | Decorative exterior wall covering of the hotel/casino complex to help create the theme for the hotel/ casino complex. Generally consists of a synthetic plaster, or stucco, that is cemented, or in some cases, bolted on in the form of a panel, to the frames of the exterior walls of the buildings. | § 1250 | 39 years (40 years for purposes of § 168 (g)) |

| ASSET | DESCRIPTION | | PROPERTY TYPE | RECOVERY PERIOD |
|---|---|---|---|---|
| Facades - Interior | Interior Columns | Includes finishes on interior columns that are affixed with permanent adhesive or nailed or screwed in place. Examples include marble tile, millwork and other coverings cemented, mudded, or grouted to the column. | § 1250 | 39 years (40 years for purposes of § 168 (g)) |
| | | Includes finishes on interior columns that are not permanently attached and not intended to be permanent. Located in the Casino area. Also includes interior columns associated with the activities described in Asset Class 79.0 of Rev. Proc. 87-56, such as Theater and Showroom. | § 1245 | 7 years (79.0 Recreation) |
| | | Includes finishes on interior columns that are not permanently attached and not intended to be permanent. Not located in the Casino/Theater area. | § 1245 | 5 years (57.0 Distributive Trades and Services) |

| ASSET | DESCRIPTION | | PROPERTY TYPE | RECOVERY PERIOD |
|---|---|---|---|---|
| | False Balcony | Finishes generally made of millwork or wrought iron (forged balconies and gates) and located in the Casino area. Also includes false balconies associated with the activities described in Asset Class 79.0 of Rev. Proc. 87-56, such as Theater and Showroom. | § 1245 | 7 years (79.0 Recreation) |
| | | Finishes generally made of millwork or wrought iron (forged balconies and gates). Not located in the Casino/Theater area. | § 1245 | 5 years (57.0 Distributive Trades and Services) |
| | Storefronts | Includes the framework, sheetrock, or any other component that comprises the framing of the storefront walls. | § 1250 | 39 years (40 years for purposes of § 168 (g)) |
| | | Includes storefronts made primarily of synthetic materials (foam, fiberglass, cast stone, or glass reinforced concrete) that are affixed with permanent adhesive or nailed or screwed in place. Also includes costs relating to the exposed millwork, trim molding and lining around doors, windows, and baseboards. See also **Wall Coverings and Millwork.** | § 1250 | 39 years (40 years for purposes of § 168 (g)) |

| ASSET | DESCRIPTION | | PROPERTY TYPE | RECOVERY PERIOD |
|---|---|---|---|---|
| Facades - Interior (continued) | Storefronts (continued) | Includes false storefronts made primarily of synthetic materials (foam, fiberglass, cast stone, or glass reinforced concrete) that are not permanently attached and not intended to be permanent. Located in the Casino area. Also includes storefronts associated with the activities described in Asset Class 79.0 of Rev. Proc. 87-56, such as Theater and Showroom. | § 1245 | 7 years (79.0 Recreation) |
| | | Includes false storefronts made primarily of synthetic materials (foam, fiberglass, cast stone, or glass reinforced concrete) that are not permanently attached and not intended to be permanent. Not located in the Casino/Theater area. | § 1245 | 5 years (57.0 Distributive Trades and Services) |
| | Painted Ceilings | Includes painted ceilings applied with spray guns and brushes (regardless of theme or design). | § 1250 | 39 years (40 years for purposes of § 168 (g)) |
| | | Includes *custom* painted ceilings designed on computers, transferred to canvases, and hand-painted with acrylics (fire-retardant materials). | § 1250 | 39 years (40 years for purposes of § 168 (g)) |

| ASSET | DESCRIPTION | | PROPERTY TYPE | RECOVERY PERIOD |
|---|---|---|---|---|
| | | Includes painted ceilings designed on computers, transferred to canvases, and hand-painted with acrylics that are not permanently attached and not intended to be permanent and located in the Casino area. Also includes painted ceilings that are not permanently attached associated with the activities described in Asset Class 79.0 of Rev. Proc. 87-56, such as Theater and Showroom. | § 1245 | 7 years (79.0 Recreation) |
| | | Includes painted ceilings designed on computers, transferred to canvases, and hand-painted with acrylics that are not permanently attached and not intended to be permanent. Not located in the Casino/Theater area. | § 1245 | 5 years (57.0 Distributive Trades and Services) |

| ASSET | DESCRIPTION | | PROPERTY TYPE | RECOVERY PERIOD |
|---|---|---|---|---|
| Facades - Interior (continued) | Rockscape | Includes rock finishes made of synthetic materials (such as interior fountains containing waterproofed liners and molded rockscape features) and decorative stonework embedded in walls that are an integral part of a buildings structural shell. Includes non-load bearing rockscape and decorative stonework embedded in walls (regardless of height) that divide or create rooms or provide traffic control where the rockscape and stonework cannot be 1) readily removed and remain in substantially the same condition after removal as before, or 2) moved and reused, stored or sold in its entirety. | § 1250 | 39 years (40 years for purposes of § 168 (g)) |
| | | Includes rockscape and decorative stonework that do not function as part of the building and would be considered as non-structural theme elements that function merely as ornamentation. | § 1245 | 5 years (57.0 Distributive Trades and Services) |

| ASSET | DESCRIPTION | PROPERTY TYPE | RECOVERY PERIOD |
|---|---|---|---|
| Fire Protection & Alarm Systems | Includes sensing devices, computer controls, sprinkler heads, piping or plumbing, pumps, visual and audible alarms, alarm control panels, heat and smoke detection devices, fire escapes, fire doors, emergency exit lighting and signage, and wall mounted fire extinguishers necessary for the protection of the building. | § 1250 | 39 years (40 years for purposes of § 168 (g) |
| Fire Protection Equipment | Includes special fire detection or suppression systems directly associated with a piece of equipment. For example a fire extinguisher designed and used for protection against a particular hazard created by the business activity. | § 1245 | 5 years (57.0 Distributive Trades and Services) |
| Floor Covering | Includes floor covering that is affixed with permanent adhesive or nailed or screwed in place. Examples include ceramic or quarry tile, marble, paving brick, most vinyl coverings and other coverings cemented, mudded, or grouted to the floor; epoxy or sealers; and wood flooring. | § 1250 | 39 years (40 years for purposes of § 168 (g)) |
| | Includes floor covering that is not permanently attached and not intended to be permanent, such as vinyl composition tile (VCT) installed with strippable adhesive, sheet vinyl, and carpeting, and located in the Casino area. Also includes floor covering that is not permanently attached associated with the activities described in Asset Class 79.0 of Rev. Proc. 87-56, such as Theater and Showroom. | § 1245 | 7 years (79.0 Recreation) |
| Floor Covering (continued) | Includes floor covering that is not permanently attached and not intended to be permanent, such as vinyl composition tile (VCT) installed with strippable adhesive, sheet vinyl, and carpeting, but not located in the Casino/Theater area. | § 1245 | 5 years (57.0 Distributive Trades and Services) |
| Floors | Includes concrete slabs and other floor systems. Floors include special treatments applied to or otherwise a permanent part of the floor. For example "super flat" finish, sloped drainage basins, raised perimeter, serving line curb, or cooler, freezer and garbage room floors. | § 1250 | 39 years (40 years for purposes of § 168 (g)) |
| Furniture-Guest Room | Includes furniture unique to guest rooms and distinguishable from office furniture. For example, beds, dressers, armoires, and night-tables. See also **Furniture-Office**. | § 1245 | 5 years (57.0 Distributive Trades and Services) |

| ASSET | DESCRIPTION | PROPERTY TYPE | RECOVERY PERIOD |
|---|---|---|---|
| Furniture-Office (includes Communication Equipment and Hook-ups) | Includes desk, chair, credenza, file cabinet, table (whether located in *Administrative Areas or Guest Rooms*) and other furniture such as workstations. Also includes communication equipment and related hook-ups. | § 1245 | 7 years (00.11 Office Furniture and Fixtures) |
| Generators | Emergency power generators for building related operations (emergency/safety systems). | § 1250 | 39 years (40 years for purposes of § 168 (g)) |
| | Depreciable assets, whether such assets are section 1245 property or 1250 property, used in the production and/or distribution of electricity with rated total capacity in excess of 500 Kilowatts and/or assets used in the production and/or distribution of steam with rated total capacity in excess of 12,500 pounds per hour for use by the taxpayer in its industrial manufacturing process or plant activity and not ordinarily available for sale to others. Does not include buildings and structural components as defined in section 1.48-1(e) of the regulations. See **Asset Class 00.4 (Rev. Proc. 87-56)**. Note* asset class 00.4 includes both section 1245 and 1250 property per Rev. Proc. 87-56. | See Note* | 15 years (00.4 Industrial Steam and Electric Generation and/or Distribution Systems) |
| | Emergency power generators for casino operations. (See **Cost Segregation Audit Techniques Guide** for allocation examples) | § 1245 | 7 years (79.0 Recreation) |
| Kitchen Equipment Hook-ups | Encompasses the electrical distribution system of the kitchen. Refer to the industry directive for **Restaurants - Kitchen Equipment Hook-up.** | § 1245 | 5 years (57.0 Distributive Trades and Services) |
| Light Fixtures - Interior | Includes lighting such as recessed and lay-in lighting, night lighting, and exit lighting, as well as decorative lighting fixtures that provide substantially all the artificial illumination (*primary* source of lighting). Includes guest room lighting, wall sconces (bathroom, guest room, and hallway), hallway chandeliers, and all electrical connections associated with these fixtures, such as power junction boxes, riser conduit, and wiring. | § 1250 | 39 years (40 years for purposes of § 168 (g)) |

| ASSET | DESCRIPTION | PROPERTY TYPE | RECOVERY PERIOD |
|---|---|---|---|
| | Includes decorative light fixtures such as chandeliers, wall sconces, down lighting, neon lighting, column lights which are decorative in nature and not necessary for the operation of the building and located in the Casino area plus cost of all wiring and electrical connections associated with these fixtures. Also includes all decorative lighting fixtures associated with the activities described in Asset Class 79.0 of Rev. Proc. 87-56, such as Theater and Showroom. | § 1245 | 7 years (79.0 Recreation) |
| | Includes decorative light fixtures, such as neon lights, table lamps, or track lighting, which are decorative in nature and not necessary for the operation of the building and not located in the Casino/Theater area. In other words, if the decorative lighting were turned off, the other sources of lighting would provide sufficient light for operation of the building. If the decorative lighting is the *primary* source of lighting, then it is section 1250 property. | § 1245 | 5 years (57.0 Distributive Trades and Services) |
| Light Fixtures - Exterior | Exterior lighting (whether decorative or not) to the extent that the lighting relates to the maintenance or operation of the building. This category includes building mounted lighting to illuminate walkways, entrances, parking, etc. | § 1250 | 39 years (40 years for purposes of § 168 (g)) |
| | Pole mounted or freestanding outdoor lighting system to illuminate sidewalks, parking or recreation areas. See also **Poles & Pylons**. Note* asset class 00.3 Land improvements includes both section 1245 and 1250 property per Rev. Proc. 87-56. | See Note* | 15 years (00.3 Land Improvement) |
| | Removable plant grow lights or removable lighting that highlights *only* the landscaping or building exterior (but not parking areas or walkways) and does not relate to the maintenance or operation of the building. | § 1245 | 5 years (57.0 Distributive Trades and Services) |
| Loading Dock | Includes bumpers, permanently installed dock levelers, plates, seals, lights, canopies, and overhead doors used in the receiving and shipping of merchandise. | § 1250 | 39 years (40 years for purposes of § 168 (g)) |
| | Includes items such as compactors, conveyors, hoists and/or balers. | § 1245 | 5 years (57.0 Distributive Trades and Services) |

| ASSET | DESCRIPTION | PROPERTY TYPE | RECOVERY PERIOD |
|---|---|---|---|
| Millwork - General Building or Structural | Includes millwork that is made of finished wood for example, doors and frames, window frames, sashes, porch work, mantels, panel work, stairways, and special woodwork. Includes pre-built wooden items brought to the site for installation and items constructed on site such as restroom cabinets, door jambs, moldings, trim, etc. | § 1250 | 39 years (40 years for purposes of § 168 (g)) |
| | Corner Guards and Wall Guards (includes guards made of stainless steel, e.g., diamond plate) | § 1250 | 39 years (40 years for purposes of § 168 (g)) |
| Millwork - Decorative | Includes decorative finish carpentry in a Casino area. Examples include detailed crown moldings, lattice work placed over finished walls or ceilings, and cabinets. The decorative millwork serves to enhance the overall décor of the Casino area and is not related to the operation of the building. Cabinets and counters in a restroom are excluded from this category; see **Restroom Accessories.** Also includes decorative millwork associated with the activities described in Asset Class 79.0 of Rev. Proc. 87-56, such as Theater and Showroom. | § 1245 | 7 years (79.0 Recreation) |
| | Includes decorative finish carpentry in the *hotel and retail* areas. Examples include detailed crown moldings, lattice work placed over finished walls or ceilings, and cabinets. The decorative millwork serves to enhance the overall décor of the hotel and retail areas and is not related to the operation of the building. Cabinets and counters in a restroom are excluded from this category; see **Restroom Accessories.** | § 1245 | 5 years (57.0 Distributive Trades and Services) |
| Poles & Pylons | Light poles for parking areas and other poles poured in concrete footings or bolt-mounted for signage, flags, etc. Note* asset class 00.3 Land improvements includes both section 1245 and 1250 property per Rev. Proc. 87-56. See also **Pylon Sign - Exterior** and **Light Fixtures - Exterior**. | See Note* | 15 years (00.3 Land Improvement) |
| Pools & Pool Equipment | Includes swimming pools and pool equipment (and spas attached to the swimming pools) that are contained within, on, or attached to a building. | § 1250 | 39 years (40 years for purposes of § 168 (g)) |

| ASSET | DESCRIPTION | PROPERTY TYPE | RECOVERY PERIOD |
|---|---|---|---|
| | Includes exterior swimming pools and pool equipment (and spas attached to the swimming pools) that are built on land. Note* asset class 00.3 Land improvements includes both section 1245 and 1250 property per Rev. Proc. 87-56. | See Note* | 15 years (00.3 Land Improvement) |
| Pylon Sign - Exterior | Pylons made of concrete, brick, wood frame, stucco, or similar materials usually set in the ground or on a concrete foundation, and usually used for signage. Note* asset class 00.3 Land improvements includes both section 1245 and 1250 property per Rev. Proc. 87-56. See also **Poles & Pylons** | See Note* | 15 years (00.3 Land Improvement) |
| | Includes only the sign face and/or message screen and related components. | § 1245 | 5 years (57.0 Distributive Trades and Services) |
| Restroom Accessories | Includes paper towel dispensers, electric hand dryers, towel racks or holders, cup dispensers, purse shelves, toilet paper holders, soap dispensers or holders, lotion dispensers, sanitary napkin dispensers and waste receptacles, coat hooks, handrails, grab bars, mirrors, shelves, vanity cabinets, counters and ashtrays and other items generally found in public restrooms that are built into or mounted on walls or partitions. | § 1250 | 39 years (40 years for purposes of § 168 (g)) |
| Restroom Partitions | Includes shop made and standard manufacture toilet partitions, typically metal, but may be plastic or other materials. | § 1250 | 39 years (40 years for purposes of § 168 (g)) |
| Security Equipment | Includes security equipment for the protection of the building and its contents, including the building exterior and grounds, from theft or vandalism and protection of employees and guests from assault. Examples include security cameras, recorders, monitors and related equipment (including those located in the elevator and elevator lobbies); building exterior and interior motion detectors; security lighting; alarm systems; security systems and related junction boxes, wiring, and conduit). | § 1250 | 39 years (40 years for purposes of § 168 (g) |

| ASSET | DESCRIPTION | PROPERTY TYPE | RECOVERY PERIOD |
|---|---|---|---|
| Security Equipment (continued) | Includes surveillance cameras, recorders, monitors and related equipment, the primary purpose of which is to surveil gaming activities and to minimize theft in the Casino area. Also includes surveillance equipment associated with the activities described in Asset Class 79.0 of Rev. Proc. 87-56, such as Theater and Showroom. | § 1245 | 7 years (79.0 Recreation) |
| | Includes electronic article surveillance systems including surveillance cameras, recorders, monitors and related equipment, the primary purpose of which is to minimize theft in the *retail* areas. Does not include the Casino/ Theater area. | § 1245 | 5 years (57.0 Distributive Trades and Services) |
| Signs | Exit signs, restroom identifiers, room numbers, and other signs relating to the operation or maintenance of a building. See also **Exit Signs**. | § 1250 | 39 years (40 years for purposes of § 168 (g)) |
| | Includes interior signs used to display gaming related activities such as keno, slots, video poker, etc. Also includes interior signs associated with the activities described in Asset Class 79.0 of Rev. Proc. 87-56, such as Theater and Showroom. | § 1245 | 7 years (79.0 Recreation) |
| | Includes interior signs used to display directories of names or indicate the location of business functions and departments, (registration desk, buffet, retail shops, etc), but not associated with the Casino/Theater activities. Not related to the operation or maintenance of a building. Also includes exterior signs used to display names, symbols, directions, etc. For pylon signs, includes only the sign face and related dedicated wiring. See also **Pylon Sign - Exterior**. | § 1245 | 5 years (57.0 Distributive Trades and Services) |

| ASSET | DESCRIPTION | PROPERTY TYPE | RECOVERY PERIOD |
|---|---|---|---|
| Site Grading & Excavation | Nondepreciable land preparation costs, in general, include the one time cost of demolition, clearing and grubbing, blasting, site stripping, fill or excavation, dewatering, and grading to allow development of land. Clearing and grubbing is the removal of debris, brush, trees, etc. from the site. Stripping is the removal of the topsoil to provide a stable surface for site and building improvements. The grading of land involves moving soil for the purpose of producing a more level surface to allow development of the land. These costs would not have to be incurred again if the building was repaired, rebuilt, or even torn down and replaced with some other type of building. | | Land |
| Site Grading & Excavation (continued) | Clearing, grading, excavating and removal costs directly associated with the construction of buildings and building components are part of the cost of construction of the building and depreciated over the life of the building. | § 1250 | 39 years (40 years for purposes of § 168 (g)) |
| | Clearing, grading, excavating and removal costs directly associated with the construction of sidewalks, parking areas, roadways and other depreciable land improvements are part of the cost of construction of the improvements and depreciated over the life of the associated asset. Note* asset class 00.3 Land improvements includes both section 1245 and 1250 property per Rev. Proc. 87-56. | See Note* | 15 years (00.3 Land Improvement) |
| Site Utilities | Systems that are used to distribute utility services from the property line to the casino complex. Includes water, sanitary sewers, gas and electrical services. | § 1250 | 39 years (40 years for purposes of § 168 (g) |
| | Storm Piping (for draining the site of rainwater). Note* asset class 00.3 Land improvements includes both section 1245 and 1250 property per Rev. Proc. 87-56. | See Note* | 15 years (00.3 Land Improvement) |

| ASSET | DESCRIPTION | PROPERTY TYPE | RECOVERY PERIOD |
|---|---|---|---|
| Site Work | Site work includes curbing, paving, general site improvements, fencing, landscaping, roads, sewers, sidewalks, site drainage and all other site improvements not directly related to the building. Note* asset class 00.3 Land improvements includes both section 1245 and 1250 property per Rev. Proc. 87-56. See **Site Utilities** for sanitary sewers. | See Note* | 15 years (00.3 Land Improvement) |
| Spa Hook-ups | Includes Jacuzzi, Whirlpools, and bathtubs located in Guest Rooms and Suites. | § 1250 | 39 years (40 years for purposes of § 168 (g)) |
| | Includes Jacuzzi and Whirlpools located in the *Hotel Spa/Fitness Center*. Does not include spa hook-ups that may be associated with swimming pools or pool equipment. See also **Pools & Pool Equipment**. | § 1245 | 5 years (57.0 Distributive Trades and Services) |
| Wall Coverings | Includes interior and exterior paint; ceramic or quarry tile, marble, stone, brick and other finishes affixed with mortar, cement or grout; paneling, wainscoting and other wood finishes affixed with nails, screws or permanent adhesives; and sanitary kitchen wall panels such as fiberglass, stainless steel and plastic wall panels. | § 1250 | 39 years (40 years for purposes of § 168 (g)) |

| ASSET | DESCRIPTION | PROPERTY TYPE | RECOVERY PERIOD |
|---|---|---|---|
| Wall Coverings (continued) | Includes strippable wall paper and vinyl that causes no damage to the underlying wall or wall surface and located in the Casino area. For purposes of this directive, such wallpaper is considered not permanently attached or intended to be permanent. Also includes strippable wall coverings associated with the activities described in Asset Class 79.0 of Rev. Proc. 87-56, such as Theater and Showroom. | § 1245 | 7 years (79.0 Recreation) |
| | Includes strippable wall paper and vinyl that causes no damage to the underlying wall or wall surface and located in the *hotel and retail* areas. For purposes of this directive, such wallpaper is considered not permanently attached or intended to be permanent. | § 1245 | 5 years (57.0 Distributive Trades and Services) |

## Cost Segregation Guide - Chapter 7.2 Industry Specific Guidance - Restaurants

*Chapter 7.1 / Table of Contents / Chapter 7.3*

**INDUSTRY SPECIFIC GUIDANCE - CHAPTER 7.2 - RESTAURANTS**

DEPARTMENT OF THE TREASURY

INTERNAL REVENUE SERVICE

WASHINGTON, D.C. 20224

Large and Mid-Size

Business Division

December 27, 2004

**MEMORANDUM FOR**

**INDUSTRY DIRECTORS**

**DIRECTORS, FIELD OPERATIONS**

**DIRECTOR, FIELD SPECIALISTS**

**DIRECTOR, PREFILING AND TECHNICAL GUIDANCE**

**DIRECTOR OF COMPLIANCE, SBSE**

**FROM:** /s/ Henry V. Singleton

Industry Director

/s/ Steve Burgess

Director, Examination, SBSE

**SUBJECT:** Field Directive on the Planning and Examination of Cost Segregation Issues in the Restaurant Industry

## Introduction

**This memorandum is intended to provide direction to effectively utilize resources in the classification and examination of a taxpayer who is recovering costs through depreciation of tangible property used in the operation of a restaurant business. This LMSB Directive is not an official pronouncement of the law or the position of the Service and cannot be used, cited or relied upon as such.**

The American Jobs Creation Act of 2004, enacted October 22, 2004, modifies I.R.C. § 168. This development has been incorporated into the guidelines through the notc to Exhibit A. In addition, this directive has been modified in content and format to conform to the Field Directive issued for the retail industry on December 16, 2004.

## Background

The crux of cost segregation is determining whether an asset is I.R.C. § 1245 property (shorter cost recovery period property, 5 or 7 years) or § 1250 property (longer cost recovery period property, 39, 31.5 or 15 years). The most common example of § 1245 property is depreciable personal property, such as equipment. The most common examples of § 1250 property are buildings and building components, which generally are not § 1245 property. [1]

The difference in recovery periods has placed the Internal Revenue Service and taxpayers in adversarial positions in determining whether an asset is § 1245 or § 1250 property. Frequently, this causes the excessive expenditure of examination resources. The Director for the Retailers, Food, Pharmaceuticals and Healthcare Industry chartered a working group to address the most efficient way to approach cost segregation issues specific to the restaurant industry. The group produced the attached matrix and related definitions as a tool to reduce unnecessary disputes and foster consistent audit treatment.

## Planning and Examination Guidance

Attached Exhibit A is a matrix recommending the categorization and general depreciation system recovery period of various restaurant assets. (For recovery periods under IRC § 168(g) alternative depreciation system see Revenue Procedure 87-56, 1987-2 CB 674.) If the taxpayer's tax return position for these assets is consistent with the recommendations in Exhibit A, examiners should not make adjustments to categorization and lives. If the taxpayer reports assets differently, then adjustments should be considered. The Industry intends to update Exhibit A regularly.

See the Cost Segregation Audit Techniques Guide for additional guidance. See also Revenue Procedure 2002-12, I.R.B. 2002-3, 374 (Jan. 07, 2002), for the proper treatment of smallwares.

If you have any questions, please contact Philip J. Hofmann Technical Advisor, Food at (316) 352-7434, or Ardell Mueller, Senior Program Analyst, Retailers Food, Pharmaceuticals and Healthcare Industry at (630) 493-5946.

Attachments: Exhibit A

LMSB DIRECTIVE ON COST SEGREGATION IN THE RESTAURANT INDUSTRY

EXHIBIT A

**NOTE:** In the case of certain leasehold improvements and restaurant property, the classifications in this directive are superseded to the extent that the American Jobs Creation Act of 2004 modifies IRC Section 168. Thus, a 15-year straight line recovery period should replace the recovery period shown in the following matrix if the asset is "qualified leasehold improvement property" (as defined in IRC Section 168(e)(6)) or "qualified restaurant property" (as defined in IRC Section 168(e)(7)) placed in service by the taxpayer after October 22, 2004 and before January 1, 2008. [The 15-year recovery period expired effective for property placed in service after 2017—CCH.]

[1] I.R.C. Section 1245 can apply to certain qualified recovery nonresidential real estate placed in service after 1980 and before 1987. See I.R.C. Section 1245(a)(5).

| Asset | Description | Property Type | Recovery Period |
|---|---|---|---|
| **Beverage Equipment** | Equipment for storage and preparation of beverages and beverage delivery systems. Beverage equipment includes the refrigerators, coolers, dispensing systems, and the dedicated electrical, tubing or piping for such equipment. The dispensing system may be gravity, pump or gas driven. | 1245 | 57.0 Distributive Trades and Services — 5 Years |
| **Canopies & Awnings** | Readily removable overhang or covering, often of canvas or plastic, used to provide shade or cover over a storefront, window, or door; or used inside a structure to identify a particular area. Examples include applications over an exterior door or window, or attached to interior walls or suspended from ceilings to identify a buffet line or bar area of the restaurant. Does not include canopies that are an integral part of a building's structural shell, such as in the casino industry, or over docks. | 1245 | 57.0 Distributive Trades and Services — 5 Years |
| **Ceilings** | Includes all interior ceilings regardless of finish or décor, e.g. drywall or plaster ceilings, acoustic ceilings, suspended ceilings (including all hangers, frames, grids, and tiles or panels), decorative metal or tin finishes, kitchen plastic panels, decorative panels, etc. | 1250 | Building or Building Component - 39 Years |
| **Computers** | Processors (CPU), direct access storage device (DASD), tape drives, desktop and laptop computers, CRT, terminals, monitors, printers, and other peripheral equipment. Excludes Point of Sale (POS) systems and computers that are an integral part of other equipment (e.g., fire detection, heating, cooling, or energy management systems, etc.). | 1245 | 00.12 Information Systems - 5 Years |

| Asset | Description | Property Type | Recovery Period |
|---|---|---|---|
| **Concrete Foundations & Footings** | Includes formwork, reinforcement, concrete block, and pre-cast or cast-in-place work related to foundations and footings necessary for the proper setting of the building. | 1250 | Building or Building Component - 39 Years |
| | Foundations or footings for signs, light poles, canopies and other land improvements (except buildings). | 1250 | 00.3 Land Improvements - 15 Years |
| **Data Handling Equipment** | Includes adding and accounting machines, calculators, copiers and duplicating machines. Excludes computers and computer peripheral equipment, see **Computers**. | 1245 | 00.13 Data Handling Equipment, except Computers - 5 Years |
| **Doors** | Interior and exterior doors, regardless of decoration, including but not limited to, double opening doors, overhead doors, revolving doors, mall entrance security gates, roll-up or sliding wire mesh or steel grills and gates, and door hardware (such as doorknobs, closers, kick plates, hinges, locks, automatic openers, etc.). | 1250 | Building or Building Component - 39 Years |
| | Special lightweight, double action doors installed to prevent accidents in a heavily trafficked area. For example, Eliason doors providing easy access between the kitchen and dining areas. | 1245 | 57.0 Distributive Trades and Services - 5 Years |
| **Doors - Air Curtains** | Air doors or curtains are air systems located above doors and windows that circulate air to stabilize environments and save energy by minimizing the heated/air conditioned air loss through open doorways and windows. They also effectively repel flying insects, dust, and pollutants. | 1250 | Building or Building Component - 39 Years |
| **Drive-Through Equipment** | Drive-through equipment includes order taking, food delivery and payment processing systems whether mechanical or electronic. Excludes building elements such as doors, bays, or windows. See also **Walls - Exterior**, and **Windows** for drive-through bays and windows. | 1245 | 57.0 Distributive Trades and Services — 5 Years |
| **Electrical** | Includes all components of the building electrical system used in the operation or maintenance of the building or necessary to provide general building services such as electrical outlets of general applicability and accessibility, lighting, heating, ventilation, air conditioning and electrical wiring. See also **Kitchen Equipment Hook-ups.** | 1250 | Building or Building Component - 39 Years |

| Asset | Description | Property Type | Recovery Period |
|---|---|---|---|
| | Special electrical connections which are necessary to and used directly with a specific item of machinery or equipment or connections between specific items of individual machinery or equipment; such as dedicated electrical outlets, wiring, conduit, and circuit breakers by which machinery and equipment is connected to the electrical distribution system. Does not include electrical outlets of general applicability and accessibility. See Chapter 5 of the Cost Segregation Audit Techniques Guide for allocation examples. | 1245 | 57.0 Distributive Trades and Services — 5 Years |
| **Elevators & Escalators** | Elevators and escalators, which include handrails and smoke baffles, are permanently affixed to the building and intended to remain in place. They relate to the operation or maintenance of the building and are structural components. | 1250 | Building or Building Component - 39 Years |
| **Equipment Installation** | Expenses incurred in the installation of furnishings and restaurant equipment. Some examples include booths, tables, counters and interior theme décor. | 1245 | 57.0 Distributive Trades and Services — 5 Years |
| **Exit Signs** | Signs posted along exit routes that indicate the direction of travel to the nearest exit. These signs typically read "EXIT" and may have distinctive colors, illumination, or arrows indicating the direction to the exit. | 1250 | Building or Building Component - 39 Years |
| **Fire Protection & Alarm Systems** | Includes sensing devices, computer controls, sprinkler heads, piping or plumbing, pumps, visual and audible alarms, alarm control panels, heat and smoke detection devices, fire escapes, fire doors, emergency exit lighting and signage, and wall mounted fire extinguishers necessary for the protection of the building. | 1250 | Building or Building Component - 39 Years |
| **Fire Protection Equipment** | Includes special fire detection or suppression systems located in equipment hoods or directly associated with a piece of equipment. For example, a fire extinguisher designed and used for protection against a particular hazard created by the business activity. | 1245 | 57.0 Distributive Trades and Services — 5 Years |
| **Fireplaces** | Includes masonry and gas fireplaces, flues, chimneys and other components of built-in fireplaces. | 1250 | Building or Building Component - 39 Years |

| Asset | Description | Property Type | Recovery Period |
|---|---|---|---|
| **Floor Coverings** | Floor covering affixed with permanent adhesive, nailed, or screwed in place. Examples include ceramic or quarry tile, marble, paving brick, and other coverings cemented, mudded, or grouted to the floor; epoxy or sealers; and wood flooring. | 1250 | Building or Building Component - 39 Years |
| | Floor covering that is installed by means of strippable adhesives. For the restaurant industry, all carpeting will be treated as not permanently attached and not intended to be permanent. Excludes rugs or tapestries that are considered artwork and do not suffer wear and tear (e.g. Persian rugs that may appreciate are considered artwork). | 1245 | 57.0 Distributive Trades and Services — 5 Years |
| **Floors** | Includes concrete slabs and other floor systems. Floors include special treatments applied to or otherwise a permanent part of the floor. For example, "superflat" finish, sloped drainage basins, raised perimeter, serving line curb, or cooler, freezer and garbage room floors. | 1250 | Building or Building Component - 39 Years |
| **Food Storage & Preparation Equipment** | Food storage, cleaning, preparation, and delivery systems including all machinery, equipment, furniture and fixtures used to process food items from storage through delivery to the customer. | 1245 | 57.0 Distributive Trades and Services — 5 Years |
| **Heating Ventilating & Air Conditioning (HVAC)** | Includes all components of a central heating, ventilating and air conditioning system not specifically identified elsewhere. HVAC systems that are installed not only to meet the temperature and humidity requirements of machinery, but are also installed for additional significant purposes, such as customer comfort and ventilation, are building components. | 1250 | Building or Building Component - 39 Years |

| Asset | Description | Property Type | Recovery Period |
|---|---|---|---|
| | Only separate kitchen HVAC units that meet the sole justification test are included (i.e., machinery the sole justification for the installation of which is the fact that such machinery is required to meet temperature or humidity requirements which are essential for the operation of other machinery or the processing of materials or foodstuffs.) Kitchen HVAC may meet the sole justification test even though it incidentally provides for the comfort of employees, or serves, to an insubstantial degree, areas where such temperature or humidity requirements are not essential. Includes refrigeration units, condensers, compressors, accumulators, coolers, pumps, connecting pipes, and wiring for the mechanical equipment for climate controlled rooms such as walk-in freezers and coolers. Allocation of HVAC is not appropriate. | 1245 | 57.0 Distributive Trades and Services — 5 Years |
| **Kitchen Equipment Hook-ups** | Includes separate water lines from the incoming water main to equipment (such as steam trays, cooking vessels, or ice machines), gas lines from the building's main gas line to equipment (such as fryers or ovens), and special drain lines from equipment (such as refrigerator or dishwasher) to the drain. Also includes ventilation system or kitchen air makeup unit solely to maintain specific ventilation requirements essential for operation of kitchen equipment, equipment exhaust hoods, and electric outlets and conduit extending back to the circuit box to provide a localized power source for specialized equipment. For example, a dishwasher requires electric and plumbing hook-ups, electrical from the dishwasher to the source of electricity (such as an outlet or junction box), and plumbing to connect the dishwasher to the water line and the drain. Excludes outlets of general applicability and accessibility or kitchen hand sink plumbing; see also **Electrical, HVAC,** and **Plumbing**. | 1245 | 57.0 Distributive Trades and Services — 5 Years |
| **·Light Fixtures - Interior** | Includes lighting such as recessed and lay-in lighting, night lighting, and exit lighting, as well as decorative lighting fixtures that provide substantially all the artificial illumination in the building or along building walkways. For emergency and exit lighting, see **Fire Protection & Alarm Systems**. | 1250 | Building or Building Component - 39 Years |

| Asset | Description | Property Type | Recovery Period |
|---|---|---|---|
| | Decorative light fixtures are light fixtures, such as neon lights or track lighting, which are decorative in nature and not necessary for the operation of the building. In other words, if the decorative lighting were turned off, the other sources of lighting would provide sufficient light for operation of the building. If the decorative lighting is the *primary* source of lighting, then it is section 1250 property. | 1245 | 57.0 Distributive Trades and Services - 5 Years |
| **-Light Fixtures - Exterior** | Exterior lighting whether decorative or not is considered section 1250 property to the extent that the lighting relates to the maintenance or operation of the building. Includes building mounted lighting to illuminate walkways, entrances, parking, etc. | 1250 | Building or Building Component - 39 Years |
| | Pole mounted or freestanding outdoor lighting system to illuminate sidewalks, parking or recreation areas. See also **Poles & Pylons**. Note* asset class 00.3 Land improvements includes both section 1245 and 1250 property per Rev. Proc. 87-56. | See Note* | 00.3 Land Improvements - 15 Years |
| | Plant grow lights or lighting that highlights *only* the landscaping or building exterior (but not parking areas or walkways) does not relate to the maintenance or operation of the building. | 1245 | 57.0 Distributive Trades and Services — 5 Years |
| **Millwork - Decorative** | Decorative millwork is the decorative finish carpentry in the restaurant. Examples include detailed crown moldings, lattice work placed over finished walls or ceilings, cabinets and counters. The decorative millwork serves to enhance the overall theme of the restaurant and is not related to the operation of the building. Excludes cabinets and counters in a restroom; see **Restroom Accessories**. | 1245 | 57.0 Distributive Trades and Services — 5 Years |
| **Millwork - General Building or Structural** | General millwork is all building materials made of finished wood (e.g., doors and frames, window frames, sashes, porch work, mantels, panel work, stairways, and special woodwork). Includes pre-built wooden items brought to the site for installation and items constructed on site such as restroom cabinets, door jambs, moldings, trim, etc. | 1250 | Building or Building Component - 39 Years |

| Asset | Description | Property Type | Recovery Period |
|---|---|---|---|
| **Office Furnishings** | Includes desk, chair, credenza, file cabinet, table, or other furniture such as workstations. Also includes telephone equipment, fax machines, and other communications equipment. Does not include communications equipment included in other asset classes in Rev. Proc. 87-56. | 1245 | 00.11 Office Furniture, Fixtures, and Equipment - 7 Years |
| **Parking Lots** | Grade level surface parking area usually constructed of asphalt, brick, concrete, stone or similar material. Category includes bumper blocks, curb cuts, curb work, striping, landscape islands, perimeter fences, and sidewalks. | 1250 | 00.3 Land Improvements -15 Years |
| **Plumbing** | All piping, drains, sprinkler mains, valves, sprinkler heads, water flow switches, restroom plumbing fixtures (e.g. toilets) and piping, kitchen hand sinks, electric water coolers, and all other components of a building plumbing system (water or gas) not specifically identified elsewhere. Excludes water or gas connections directly to appliances or kitchen drainage and kitchen hot water heater; see **Kitchen Equipment Hook-ups**. | 1250 | Building or Building Component - 39 Years |
| | Includes water, gas, or refrigerant hook-ups directly connected to appliances or equipment, eyewash stations, kitchen drainage, and kitchen hot water heater. For example, a dishwasher would require special water hook-up. | 1245 | 57.0 Distributive Trades and Services — 5 Years |
| **Point of Sale (POS) Systems** | A register or terminal based data collection system used to control and record all sales. Includes cash registers, computerized sales systems, and related peripheral equipment. See also **Electrical** for hook-ups. | 1245 | 57.0 Distributive Trades and Services — 5 Years |
| **Poles & Pylons** | Light poles for parking areas and other poles poured in concrete footings or bolt-mounted for signage, flags, etc. Note* asset class 00.3 Land Improvements includes both section 1245 and 1250 property per Rev. Proc. 87-56. | See Note* | 00.3 Land Improvements - 15 Years |
| **Restaurant Décor Accessories** | Decorative mobile props such as playground equipment, potted plants, hanging mirrors, ceiling fans, and theme related props (such as coat of arms, sporting equipment or memorabilia, artifacts, pictures, plaques, etc., excluding non-depreciable artwork, antiques or collectibles). | 1245 | 57.0 Distributive Trades and Services — 5 Years |

| Asset | Description | Property Type | Recovery Period |
|---|---|---|---|
| **Restaurant Furniture** | Includes furniture unique to restaurants and distinguishable from office furniture. For example, a high stool in a bar, dining room table and chairs, booths, lockers, or benches. See also **Office Furnishings**. | 1245 | 57.0 Distributive Trades and Services — 5 Years |
| **Restaurant Non-structural Theme Elements** | Interior non-load bearing decorative structures. These are items that do not function as part of the building and are not integrated with building elements such as wiring, plumbing or ventilation. For example a model castle constructed of gypsum board or plaster and wood studs would be considered a non-structural theme element that functions merely as ornamentation. Excludes a half wall whose function is to provide traffic control or space subdivision, see **Walls -Interior Partitions**. Excludes decorative ceilings, see **Ceilings**. | 1245 | 57.0 Distributive Trades and Services — 5 Years |
| **Restroom Accessories** | Includes paper towel dispensers, electric hand dryers, towel racks or holders, cup dispensers, purse shelves, toilet paper holders, soap dispensers or holders, lotion dispensers, sanitary napkin dispensers and waste receptacles, coat hooks, grab bars, mirrors, shelves, vanity cabinets, counters, ashtrays, baby changing stations, and other items generally found in public restrooms that are built into or mounted on walls or partitions. | 1250 | Building or Building Component - 39 Years |
| **Restroom Partitions** | Includes shop made and standard manufacture toilet partitions, typically metal, but may be plastic or other materials. | 1250 | Building or Building Component - 39 Years |
| **Roof** | All elements of the roof including but not limited to joists, rafters, deck, shingles, vapor barrier, skylights, trusses, girders and gutters. Determination of whether decorative elements of a roof (e.g. false dormers, mansard) constitute structural building components depends on their integration with the overall roof not their load bearing capacity. If removal of the decorative element results in the direct exposure of building components to water, snow, wind, or moisture damage, or if the decorative element houses lighting fixtures, wiring, or other structural components, then the decorative elements are part of the overall roof system and are structural components of the building. | 1250 | Building or Building Component - 39 Years |

| Asset | Description | Property Type | Recovery Period |
|---|---|---|---|
| **Security Systems** | Includes security equipment for the protection of the building (and its contents) from burglary or vandalism and protection of employees from assault. Examples include window and door locks; card key access systems; keyless entry systems; security cameras, recorders, monitors and related equipment; perimeter and interior building motion detectors; security lighting; alarm systems; and security system wiring and conduit. | 1250 | Building or Building Component - 39 Years |
| **Signs** | Exit signs, restroom identifiers and other signs relating to the operation or maintenance of a building. | 1250 | Building or Building Component - 39 Years |
| | Interior and Exterior Signs used for menu display or theme identity. For pylon signs, includes only sign face. See also **Poles & Pylons**. | 1245 | 57.0 Distributive Trades and Services — 5 Years |
| **Site Preparation, Grading, & Excavation** | In general, land preparation costs include one time cost of clearing and grubbing, site stripping, fill or excavation, and grading to allow development of land. Clearing and grubbing is the removal of debris, brush, trees, etc. from the site. Stripping is the removal of the topsoil to provide a stable surface for site and building improvements. The grading of land involves moving soil to produce a more level surface to allow development of the land. | | Land |
| | Clearing, grading, excavating and removal costs directly associated with the construction of buildings and building components are part of the cost of construction of the building. | 1250 | Building or Building Component - 39 Years |
| | Clearing, grading, excavating and removal costs directly associated with the construction of sidewalks, parking areas, roadways and other depreciable land improvements are part of the cost of construction of the improvements. | 1250 | 00.3 Land Improvements - 15 Years |
| **Site Utilities** | Site utilities are the systems that are used to distribute utility services from the property line to the restaurant building. Includes water, sanitary sewer, gas, and electrical services. | 1250 | Building or Building Component - 39 Years |

| Asset | Description | Property Type | Recovery Period |
|---|---|---|---|
| **Site Work** | Site work includes curbing, paving, general site improvements, fencing, landscaping, roads, sewers, sidewalks, site drainage and all other site improvements not directly related to the building. For sanitary sewers, see **Site Utilities**. | 1250 | 00.3 Land Improvements - 15 Years |
| **Sound Systems** | Equipment and apparatus, including wiring, used to provide amplified music or sound. For example, public address by way of paging a customer or background music. Excludes applications linked to fire protection and alarm systems. | 1245 | 57.0 Distributive Trades and Services — 5 Years |
| **Stonework** | Exterior decorative stonework embedded in half walls, such as patio half walls, that are an integral part of a building's structural shell. Such half walls relate to the operation or maintenance of the building. | 1250 | Building or Building Component - 39 Years |
| | Includes patio stonework imbedded in the ground or applied to exterior half walls that are not an integral part of the building's structural shell. | 1250 | 00.3 Land Improvements - 15 Years |
| **Trash Enclosures** | Enclosures for waste receptacles that are attached to the building. Typically constructed of the same materials as the building shell with either interior or exterior access. These trash enclosures are an integral part of the building shell and cannot be moved without damage to the underlying building. | 1250 | Building or Building Component - 39 Years |
| | Freestanding enclosures for waste receptacles, typically constructed on a concrete pad with its posts set in the concrete. Serves both safety and decorative functions. | 1250 | 00.3 Land Improvements - 15 Years |
| **Upholstery** | Any material used in the coverage and protection of furnishings. | 1245 | 57.0 Distributive Trades and Services — 5 Years |
| **Wall Coverings** | Includes interior and exterior paint; ceramic or quarry tile, marble, stone, brick and other finishes affixed with mortar, cement or grout; paneling, wainscoting and other wood finishes affixed with nails, screws or permanent adhesives; and sanitary kitchen wall panels such as Fiberglass Reinforced Plastic (FRP), stainless steel or plastic wall panels. | 1250 | Building or Building Component - 39 Years |

| Asset | Description | Property Type | Recovery Period |
|---|---|---|---|
| | Strippable wallpaper that causes no damage to the underlying wall or wall surface. | 1245 | 57.0 Distributive Trades and Services — 5 Years |
| **Walls - Exterior** | Includes all exterior walls and building support regardless of construction materials. Exterior walls may include columns, posts, beams, girders, curtain walls, tilt up panels, studs, framing, sheetrock, insulation, windows, doors, exterior façade, brick, masonry, etc. Also includes drive-through bay, windows, and doors. | 1250 | Building or Building Component - 39 Years |
| **Walls - Interior Partitions** | Includes all load bearing interior partitions regardless of construction. Also includes non-load bearing partitions regardless of height (typically constructed of studs and sheetrock or other materials) that divide or create rooms or provide traffic control. Includes rough carpentry and plaster, dry wall or gypsum board, and other finishes. | 1250 | Building or Building Component - 39 Years |
| | Interior walls where the partition can be 1) readily removed and remain in substantially the same condition after removal as before, or 2) moved and reused, stored or sold in its entirety. | 1245 | 57.0 Distributive Trades and Services — 5 Years |
| **Windows** | Exterior windows, including store front windows, drive-through service and carousel windows, and vestibule. | 1250 | Building or Building Component - 39 Years |
| **Window Treatments** | Window treatments such as drapes, curtains, louvers, blinds, post construction tinting or interior decorative theme décor that are readily removable. | 1245 | 57.0 Distributive Trades and Services — 5 Years |

## Cost Segregation ATG - Chapter 7.3 Industry Specific Guidance - Retail Industries

*Chapter 7.2 / Table of Contents / Chapter 7.4*

**INDUSTRY SPECIFIC GUIDANCE - CHAPTER 7.3 - RETAIL INDUSTRIES**

December 16, 2004

Department of the Treasury

Internal Revenue Service

Washington, D.C. 20224

**MEMORANDUM FOR**

**INDUSTRY DIRECTORS, LMSB**

**DIRECTORS, FIELD OPERATIONS**

**DIRECTOR, FIELD SPECIALISTS**

**DIRECTOR, PREFILING AND TECHNICAL GUIDANCE**

**AREA DIRECTORS, SBSE**

**FROM:** /s/ Henry V. Singleton

Industry Director Retailers, Food, Pharmaceuticals & Healthcare

/s/ Steve Burgess

Director, Examination, SBSE

**SUBJECT:** Field Directive on the Planning and Examination of Cost Segregation Issues in the Retail Industry

**INTRODUCTION**

**This memorandum is intended to provide direction to effectively utilize resources in the classification and examination of a taxpayer who is recovering costs through depreciation of tangible property used in the operation of a retail business. This Directive is not an official pronouncement of the law or the position of the Service and cannot be used, cited or relied upon as such.**

**BACKGROUND**

The crux of cost segregation is determining whether an asset is I.R.C. § 1245 property (shorter cost recovery period property, 5 or 7 years) or § 1250 property (longer cost recovery period property, 39, 31.5 or 15 years). The most common example of § 1245 property is depreciable personal property, such as equipment. The most common examples of § 1250 property are buildings and building components, which generally are not § 1245 property.

The difference in recovery periods has placed the Internal Revenue Service and taxpayers in adversarial positions in determining whether an asset is § 1245 or § 1250 property. Frequently, this causes the excessive expenditure of examination resources. The Director for the Retailers, Food, Pharmaceuticals and Healthcare Industry chartered a working group to address the most efficient way to approach cost segregation issues specific to the retail industry. The group produced the attached matrix and related definitions as a tool to reduce unnecessary disputes and foster consistent audit treatment.

**PLANNING AND EXAMINATION GUIDANCE**

Attached Retail Exhibit A is a matrix recommending the categorization and general depreciation system recovery period of various retail assets. (For recovery periods under IRC § 168(g) alternative depreciation system, see Revenue Procedure 87-56, 1987-2 CB 674). If the taxpayer's tax return position for these assets is consistent with the recommendations in Retail Exhibit A, examiners should not make adjustments to categorization and lives. If the taxpayer reports assets differently, then adjustments should be considered. The Industry intends to update Retail Exhibit A regularly.

See also the Cost Segregation Audit Techniques Guide.

If you have any questions, please contact either David Moser, Technical Advisor, Retail at 636-940-6226, Bernie Crinigan, Engineering & Valuation Group Manager at 415-522-6188, Milton Pagan, SBSE Senior Program Analyst at 619-615-9583, or Ardell Mueller, Senior Program Analyst, Retailers Food, Pharmaceuticals and Healthcare Industry at 630-493-5946.

Attachments: Exhibit A

This matrix, which is part of the Cost Segregation Audit Techniques Guide, is intended to provide direction to effectively utilize resources in the classification and examination of property used in the operation of a retail business such as a department or grocery store. General fact patterns specific to this industry have been considered in the classification of these assets and may not be applicable to other industries. Similarly, asset classification guidance issued for other industries is based on the general fact pattern for that industry and may not be applicable to a retail business situation. For example, for asset classification of restaurants located within a retail store, refer to the industry directive for restaurants. For examination techniques and historical background related to this issue, refer to the Cost Segregation Audit Techniques Guide.

**NOTE**: In the case of certain leasehold improvement property, the classifications in this directive are superseded to the extent that the American Jobs Creation Act of 2004 modifies IRC Section 168. Thus, a 15-year straight line recovery period should replace the recovery period shown in the following matrix if the asset is "qualified leasehold improvement property" (as defined in IRC Section 168(e)(6)) placed in service by the taxpayer after 10/22/04 and before 01/01/08. [The 15-year recovery period expired effective for property placed in service after 2017t—CCH.]

| Asset | Description | Property Type | Recovery Period |
|---|---|---|---|
| Awnings & Canopies | Readily removable overhang or covering, often of canvas or plastic, used to provide shade or cover over a storefront, window, or door; or used inside a structure to identify a particular department or selling area. Examples include applications over an exterior door or window, or attached to interior walls or suspended from ceilings for bakery, deli, floral, meat, or produce departments. Also includes canopies designed to protect customers and gasoline fueling equipment from weather conditions and to act as advertising displays that are anchored with bolts and are not attached to buildings or other structures. Does not include canopies that are an integral part of a building's structural shell, such as in the casino industry, or over docks. See also **Concrete Foundations & Footings** and **Loading Docks**. | 1245 | 57.0 Distributive Trades and Services — 5 Years |
| Beverage Equipment | Equipment for storage and preparation of beverages and beverage delivery systems. Beverage equipment includes the refrigerators, coolers, dispensing systems, and the dedicated electrical, tubing or piping for such equipment. The dispensing system may be gravity, pump or gas driven. See also **Refrigerated Structures**. | 1245 | 57.0 Distributive Trades and Services — 5 Years |

| Asset | Description | Property Type | Recovery Period |
|---|---|---|---|
| Ceilings | Includes all interior ceilings regardless of finish or décor; e.g. drywall or plaster ceilings, acoustic ceilings, suspended ceilings (including hangers, frames, grids and tiles or panels), decorative metal or tin finishes, plastic panels, decorative panels, etc. See also **Awnings & Canopies, Millwork - Decorative** and **Millwork - General Building or Structural**. | 1250 | Building or Building Component - 39 Years |
| Computers | Processors (CPU), direct access storage device (DASD), tape drives, desktop and laptop computers, CRT, terminals, monitors, printers, and other peripheral equipment. Excludes Point of Sale (POS) systems and computers that are an integral part of other equipment (e.g. fire detection, heating, cooling, or energy management systems, etc.). | 1245 | 00.12 Information Systems - 5 Years |
| Concrete Foundations & Footings | Includes formwork, reinforcement, concrete block, and pre-cast or cast-in-place work related to foundations and footings necessary for the proper setting of the building. | 1250 | Building or Building Component - 39 Years |
| | Foundations or footings for signs, light poles, and other land improvements (except buildings). | 1250 | 00.3 Land Improvements - 15 Years |
| | The supporting concrete footings used to anchor gasoline pump canopies are inherently permanent structures and are classified as land improvements. | 1250 | 57.1 Distributive Trades and Services - 15 years |
| Data Handling Equipment | Includes adding and accounting machines, calculators, copiers, and duplicating machines. Excludes computers and computer peripheral equipment, see **Computers**. | 1245 | 00.13 Data Handling Equipment, except Computers - 5 Years |
| Doors | Interior and exterior doors, regardless of decoration, including but not limited to, double opening doors, overhead doors, revolving doors, mall entrance security gates, roll-up or sliding wire mesh or steel grills and gates, and door hardware (such as doorknobs, closers, kick plates, hinges, locks, automatic openers, etc.). | 1250 | Building or Building Component - 39 Years |
| | Special lightweight, double action doors installed to prevent accidents in a heavily trafficked area. For example, flexlble doors, or clear or strip curtains used between stock and selling areas. | 1245 | 57.0 Distributive Trades and Services - 5 Years |

| Asset | Description | Property Type | Recovery Period |
| --- | --- | --- | --- |
| Doors - Air Curtains | Air doors or curtains are air systems located above doors and windows that circulate air to stabilize environments and save energy by minimizing the heated/air conditioned air loss through open doorways and windows. They also effectively repel flying insects, dust, and pollutants. | 1250 | Building or Building Component - 39 Years |
| Drive-Through Equipment | Drive-through equipment includes order taking, merchandise delivery, and payment processing systems whether mechanical or electronic. Excludes building elements such as doors, bays, or windows. See also **Walls - Exterior**, and **Windows** for drive-through bays and windows. | 1245 | 57.0 Distributive Trades and Services — 5 Years |
| Electrical | Includes all components of the building electrical system used in the operation or maintenance of the building or necessary to provide general building services such as electrical outlets of general applicability and accessibility, lighting, heating, ventilation, air conditioning, and electrical wiring. | 1250 | Building or Building Component - 39 Years |
| | Special electrical connections which are necessary to and used directly with a specific item of machinery or equipment or connections between specific items of individual machinery or equipment; such as dedicated electrical outlets, wiring, conduit, and circuit breakers by which machinery and equipment is connected to the electrical distribution system. Does not include electrical outlets of general applicability and accessibility. See Chapter 5 of the Cost Segregation Audit Techniques Guide for allocation examples. | 1245 | 57.0 Distributive Trades and Services — 5 Years |
| Elevators and Escalators | Elevators and escalators, which include handrails and smoke baffles, are permanently affixed to the building and intended to remain in place. They relate to the operation or maintenance of the building and are structural components. | 1250 | Building or Building Component - 39 Years |

| Asset | Description | Property Type | Recovery Period |
|---|---|---|---|
| Energy Management Systems | Energy management systems control all energy-using systems in a building, automatically checking occupancy schedules, reading temperatures, and re-circuiting light levels, causing all heating, cooling and lighting equipment to operate so as to minimize energy costs. Includes, for example, detection devices such as smoke, motion and infrared devices, photocells, foil and contact switches, pressure switches, proximity alarms, sensors, alarm transmitting controls, data gathering panels, demand controllers, thermostats, computer controls, outside air economizers, occupancy sensors, electronic ballasts, and all related wiring and conduit. May also provide for fire and burglary protection. | 1250 | Building or Building Component - 39 Years |
| Exit Signs | Signs posted along exit routes that indicate the direction of travel to the nearest exit. These signs typically read "EXIT" and may have distinctive colors, illumination, or arrows indicating the direction to the exit. | 1250 | Building or Building Component - 39 Years |
| Fire Protection & Alarm Systems | Includes sensing devices, computer controls, sprinkler heads, piping or plumbing, pumps, visual and audible alarms, alarm control panels, heat and smoke detection devices, fire escapes, fire doors, emergency exit lighting and signage, and wall mounted fire extinguishers necessary for the protection of the building. | 1250 | Building or Building Component - 39 Years |
| Fire Protection Equipment | Includes special fire detection or suppression systems directly associated with a piece of equipment. For example a fire extinguisher designed and used for protection against a particular hazard created by the business activity. | 1245 | 57.0 Distributive Trades and Services — 5 Years |
| Floor Coverings | Floor covering affixed with permanent adhesive, nailed, or screwed in place. Examples include ceramic or quarry tile, marble, paving brick, and other coverings cemented, mudded, or grouted to the floor; epoxy or sealers; and wood flooring. | 1250 | Building or Building Component - 39 Years |

| Asset | Description | Property Type | Recovery Period |
|---|---|---|---|
| | Floor covering that is installed by means of strippable adhesives. For the retail industry, all vinyl composition tile (VCT), sheet vinyl, and carpeting will be treated as not permanently attached and not intended to be permanent. Also includes flooring that is frequently moved and reused to create a department theme or seasonal display. | 1245 | 57.0 Distributive Trades and Services — 5 Years |
| Floors | Includes concrete slabs and other floor systems. Floors include special treatments applied to or otherwise a permanent part of the floor. For example "super flat" finish, sloped drainage basins, raised perimeter, serving line curb, or cooler, freezer and garbage room floors. | 1250 | Building or Building Component - 39 Years |
| Heating, Ventilating & Air Conditioning (HVAC) | Includes all components of a central heating, ventilating and air conditioning system not specifically identified elsewhere. HVAC systems that are installed not only to meet the temperature and humidity requirements of machinery, but are also installed for additional significant purposes, such as customer comfort and ventilation, are building components. | 1250 | Building or Building Component - 39 Years |
| | Only separate HVAC units that meet the sole justification test are included (i.e., machinery the sole justification for the installation of which is the fact that such machinery is required to meet temperature or humidity requirements which are essential for the operation of other machinery or the processing of materials or foodstuffs.) HVAC may meet the sole justification test even though it incidentally provides for the comfort of employees, or serves, to an insubstantial degree, areas where such temperature or humidity requirements are not essential. Includes refrigeration units, condensers, compressors, accumulators, coolers, pumps, connecting pipes, and wiring for the mechanical equipment for climate controlled rooms, walk-in freezers, coolers, humidors and ripening rooms. Allocation of HVAC is not appropriate. See also **Refrigerated Structures, Refrigeration Equipment,** and **Ripening Rooms**. | 1245 | 57.0 Distributive Trades and Services — 5 Years |

| Asset | Description | Property Type | Recovery Period |
|---|---|---|---|
| Kiosks | A small retail outlet, often prefabricated, which acts like a fixed retail outlet yet is not permanent. Kiosks may be used to retail merchandise such as newspapers and magazines, film and digital images, and food and beverages. Kiosks are also present in shopping centers or malls where they function as temporary or portable retail outlets for a variety of merchandise. | 1245 | 57.0 Distributive Trades and Services - 5 Years |
| Light Fixtures - Interior | Includes lighting such as recessed and lay-in lighting, night lighting, and exit lighting, as well as decorative lighting fixtures that provide substantially all the artificial illumination in the building or along building walkways. For emergency and exit lighting, see **Fire Protection & Alarm Systems.** | 1250 | Building or Building Component - 39 Years |
| | Decorative light fixtures are light fixtures, such as neon lights or track lighting, which are decorative in nature and not necessary for the operation of the building. In other words, if the decorative lighting were turned off, the other sources of lighting would provide sufficient light for operation of the building. If the decorative lighting is the *primary* source of lighting, then it is section 1250 property. | 1245 | 57.0 Distributive Trades and Services - 5 Years |
| Light Fixtures - Exterior | Exterior lighting whether decorative or not is considered section 1250 property to the extent that the lighting relates to the maintenance or operation of the building. This category includes building mounted lighting to illuminate walkways, entrances, parking, etc. | 1250 | Building or Building Component - 39 Years |
| | Pole mounted or freestanding outdoor lighting system to illuminate sidewalks, parking or recreation areas. See also **Poles & Pylons**. Note* asset class 00.3 Land improvements includes both section 1245 and 1250 property per Rev. Proc. 87-56. | See Note* | 00.3 Land Improvements - 15 Years |
| | Plant grow lights or lighting that highlights *only* the landscaping or building exterior (but not parking areas or walkways) does not relate to the maintenance or operation of the building. | 1245 | 57.0 Distributive Trades and Services — 5 Years |
| Loading Docks | Includes bumpers, permanently installed dock levelers, plates, seals, lights, canopies, and overhead doors used in the receiving and shipping of merchandise. | 1250 | Building or Building Component - 39 Years |

| Asset | Description | Property Type | Recovery Period |
|---|---|---|---|
| | Includes items such as compactors, conveyors, hoists and balers. | 1245 | 57.0 Distributive Trades and Services — 5 Years |
| Millwork - Decorative | Decorative millwork is the decorative finish carpentry in a retail selling area. Examples include detailed crown moldings, lattice work placed over finished walls or ceilings, cabinets, cashwraps, counters and toppers. The decorative millwork serves to enhance the overall décor of the retail store and is not related to the operation of the building. Cabinets and counters in a restroom are excluded from this category; see **Restroom Accessories**. | 1245 | 57.0 Distributive Trades and Services — 5 Years |
| Millwork - General Building or Structural | General millwork is all building materials made of finished wood (e.g., doors and frames, window frames, sashes, porch work, mantels, panel work, stairways, and special woodwork). Includes pre-built wooden items brought to the site for installation and items constructed on site such as restroom cabinets, door jambs, moldings, trim, etc. | 1250 | Building or Building Component - 39 Years |
| Office Furnishings | Includes desk, chair, credenza, file cabinet, table or other furniture such as workstations. Also includes telephone equipment, fax machines, and other communications equipment. Does not include communications equipment included in other asset classes in Rev. Proc. 87-56. | 1245 | 00.11 Office Furniture, Fixtures, and Equipment - 7 Years |
| Parking Lots | Grade level surface parking area usually constructed of asphalt, brick, concrete, stone or similar material. Category includes bumper blocks, curb cuts, curb work, striping, landscape islands, perimeter fences, and sidewalks. | 1250 | 00.3 Land Improvements - 15 Years |
| Parking Structures | Any structure or edifice the purpose of which is to provide parking space. Includes, for example, garages, parking ramps, or other parking structures. | 1250 | Building or Building Component - 39 Years |
| Plumbing | All piping, drains, sprinkler mains, valves, sprinkler heads, water flow switches, restroom plumbing fixtures (e.g. toilets) and piping, kitchen hand sinks, electric water coolers, and all other components of a building plumbing system (water or gas) not specifically identified elsewhere. | 1250 | Building or Building Component - 39 Years |

| Asset | Description | Property Type | Recovery Period |
|---|---|---|---|
| | Includes water, gas, or refrigerant hook-ups directly connected to appliances or equipment, eyewash stations, kitchen drainage, and kitchen hot water heater. For example, a hair salon in a retail outlet would require special hair washing sinks and water hook-up for the sinks. | 1245 | 57.0 Distributive Trades and Services — 5 Years |
| Point of Sale (POS) Systems | A register or terminal based data collection system used to control and record all sales (cash, charge, COD, gift cards, layaway, etc.) at the point of sale. Includes cash registers, computerized sales systems and related peripheral equipment, satellite systems, scanners, and wands. See also **Electrical** for hook-ups. | 1245 | 57.0 Distributive Trades and Services — 5 Years |
| Poles & Pylons | Light poles for parking areas and other poles poured in concrete footings or bolt-mounted for signage, flags, etc. Note* asset class 00.3 Land improvements includes both section 1245 and 1250 property per Rev. Proc. 87-56. See also **Signs** and **Light Fixtures - Exterior**. | See Note* | 00.3 Land Improvements - 15 Years |
| Refrigeration Equipment | Includes refrigeration units, condensers, compressors, accumulators, coolers, pumps, connecting pipes, and associated wiring. Refrigeration equipment is commonly found in climate controlled rooms, walk-in freezers, coolers, humidors, and ripening rooms. | 1245 | 57.0 Distributive Trades and Services — 5 Years |
| Refrigerated Structures | Includes structural components such as walls, floors, ceilings, and insulation to construct a climate controlled structure, room or facility such as a cold storage warehouse, walk-in freezer, cooler, garbage room, or humidor. See also **Refrigeration Equipment**. | 1250 | Building or Building Component - 39 Years |
| | A portable structure installed inside the building, consisting of prefabricated panels mounted on a movable framework. Portable structures are designed to be able to be disassembled and moved. See also **Refrigeration Equipment**. | 1245 | 57.0 Distributive Trades and Services — 5 Years |
| Restaurant - In Store | See Restaurant Industry Directive. For retail situations that include a restaurant or other food preparation property within a store, such as a deli or snack bar, the facts are similar to those considered in the industry directive on restaurants and that directive may be relied upon for asset classification. | | |

| Asset | Description | Property Type | Recovery Period |
|---|---|---|---|
| Restroom Accessories | Includes paper towel dispensers, electric hand dryers, towel racks or holders, cup dispensers, purse shelves, toilet paper holders, soap dispensers or holders, lotion dispensers, sanitary napkin dispensers and waste receptacles, coat hooks, handrails, grab bars, mirrors, shelves, vanity cabinets, counters, ashtrays, baby changing stations, and other items generally found in public restrooms that are built into or mounted on walls or partitions. | 1250 | Building or Building Component - 39 Years |
| Restroom Partitions | Includes shop made and standard manufacture toilet partitions, typically metal, but may be plastic or other materials. | 1250 | Building or Building Component - 39 Years |
| Retail Accessories | Accessories used to better display merchandise that are not held for sale. Includes assets such as audio/ video display devices, artwork (if depreciable), holiday decorations, lamps, mirrors, pictures, plaques, potted plants, and decorative mobile props (such as coat of arms, sporting equipment or memorabilia, etc., excluding non-depreciable art, antiques or collectibles). | 1245 | 57.0 Distributive Trades and Services — 5 Years |
| Retail Conveying Equipment | Includes assets such as belt or roller conveyors and pneumatic tube systems used to distribute retail merchandise. | 1245 | 57.0 Distributive Trades and Services — 5 Years |
| Retail Equipment | Includes assets such as sewing machines, tackers, ironing equipment, pressing tables, steam presses, pinning machines, price mark guns, marking machines, work benches, power tools, check writers, endorsing machines, paper cutters, perforators, postage meters, money sorters, coin counting and dispensing equipment, and shopping carts. | 1245 | 57.0 Distributive Trades and Services — 5 Years |
| Retail Fixtures | Includes assets such as back cases or islands, cabinets, cubes, deli cases, end caps, floor stands, garment racks, gondolas, grid systems, mannequins, refrigerator/ freezer cases, shelving, sign holders or stands, show cases, wall display units and other retail fixtures (such as dressing or fitting room partitions) needed in the business operation that are not a building component. | 1245 | 57.0 Distributive Trades and Services — 5 Years |

| Asset | Description | Property Type | Recovery Period |
|---|---|---|---|
| Retail Furniture | Includes furniture unique to retail stores and distinguishable from office furniture. For example, a high stool in a cosmetic department, a shoe department footstool, a hair salon barber chair, or a bench outside a dressing room. See also **Office Furnishings**. | 1245 | 57.0 Distributive Trades and Services — 5 Years |
| Ripening Rooms | Special enclosed equipment boxes used to ripen produce by circulating special gases. The rooms are large boxes with special doors and large airplane-type propellers, which circulate the gases used to ripen the produce. The boxes are housed within a distribution center warehouse. These specialized facilities are considered to be part of the retail distribution equipment because they have a special retail purpose and can not be used for any other purpose. The boxes are not a part of the building structure. | 1245 | 57.0 Distributive Trades and Services — 5 Years |
| Roof | All elements of the roof including but not limited to joists, rafters, deck, shingles, vapor barrier, skylights, trusses, girders, and gutters. Determination of whether decorative elements of a roof (e.g. false dormers, mansard) constitute structural building components depends on their integration with the overall roof, not their load bearing capacity. If removal of the decorative element results in the direct exposure of building components to water, snow, wind, or moisture damage, or if the decorative element houses lighting fixtures, wiring, or other structural components, then the decorative elements are part of the overall roof system and are structural components of the building. | 1250 | Building or Building Component - 39 Years |
| Security Systems | Includes security equipment for the protection of the building (and its contents) from burglary or vandalism and protection of employees from assault. Examples include window and door locks; card key access systems; keyless entry systems; security cameras, recorders, monitors and related equipment; perimeter and interior building motion detectors; security lighting; alarm systems; and security system wiring and conduit. | 1250 | Building or Building Component — 39 Years |

| Asset | Description | Property Type | Recovery Period |
|---|---|---|---|
| | Electronic article surveillance systems including electronic gates, surveillance cameras, recorders, monitors and related equipment, the primary purpose of which is to minimize merchandise shrinkage due to theft. Also includes teller-style pass-through windows, security booths, and bulletproof enclosures generally located in the cash office and customer service areas. | 1245 | 57.0 Distributive Trades and Services — 5 Years |
| Signs | Exit signs, restroom identifiers, room numbers, and other signs relating to the operation or maintenance of a building. | 1250 | Building or Building Component - 39 Years |
| | Interior and exterior signs used for display or theme identity. For example, interior signs to identify departments or exterior signs to display trade names or trade symbols. For pylon signs, includes only sign face. See also **Poles & Pylons**. | 1245 | 57.0 Distributive Trades and Services — 5 Years |
| Site Preparation, Grading & Excavation | In general, land preparation costs include the one time cost of clearing and grubbing, site stripping, fill or excavation, and grading to allow development of land. Clearing and grubbing is the removal of debris, brush, trees, etc. from the site. Stripping is the removal of the topsoil to provide a stable surface for site and building improvements. The grading of land involves moving soil for the purpose of producing a more level surface to allow development of the land. | | Land |
| | Clearing, grading, excavating and removal costs directly associated with the construction of buildings and building components are part of the cost of construction of the building and depreciated over the life of the building. | 1250 | Building or Building Component - 39 Years |
| | Clearing, grading, excavating and removal costs directly associated with the construction of sidewalks, parking areas, roadways and other depreciable land improvements are part of the cost of construction of the improvements and depreciated over the life of the associated asset. | 1250 | 00.3 Land Improvements - 15 Years |
| Site Utilities | Site utilities are the systems that are used to distribute utility services from the property line to the retail building. Includes water, sanitary sewer, gas and electrical services. | 1250 | Building or Building Component - 39 Years |

| Asset | Description | Property Type | Recovery Period |
|---|---|---|---|
| Site Work | Site work includes curbing, paving, general site improvements, fencing, landscaping, roads, sewers, sidewalks, site drainage and all other site improvements not directly related to the building. For sanitary sewers, see **Site Utilities**. | 1250 | 00.3 Land Improvements - 15 Years |
| Sound Systems | Equipment and apparatus, including wiring, used to provide amplified sound or music. For example, public address by way of paging a customer or background music. Excludes applications linked to fire protection and alarm systems. | 1245 | 57.0 Distributive Trades and Services — 5 Years |
| Trash Enclosures | Enclosures for waste receptacles that are attached to the building. Typically constructed of the same materials as the building shell with either interior or exterior access. These trash enclosures are an integral part of the building shell and cannot be moved without damage to the underlying building. | 1250 | Building or Building Component - 39 Years |
| | Freestanding enclosures for waste receptacles, typically constructed on a concrete pad with its posts set in the concrete. Serves both safety and decorative functions. | 1250 | 00.3 Land Improvements - 15 Years |
| Wall Coverings | Includes interior and exterior paint; ceramic or quarry tile, marble, stone, brick and other finishes affixed with mortar, cement or grout; paneling, wainscoting and other wood finishes affixed with nails, screws or permanent adhesives; and sanitary kitchen wall panels such as fiberglass, stainless steel and plastic wall panels. | 1250 | Building or Building Component - 39 Years |
| | Strippable wallpaper that causes no damage to the underlying wall or wall surface. | 1245 | 57.0 Distributive Trades and Services — 5 Years |
| Walls - Exterior | Includes all exterior walls and building support regardless of construction materials. Exterior walls may include columns, posts, beams, girders, curtain walls, tilt up panels, studs, framing, sheetrock, insulation, windows, doors, exterior façade, brick, masonry, etc. Also includes drive-through bay, windows, and doors. | 1250 | Building or Building Component - 39 Years |

| Asset | Description | Property Type | Recovery Period |
|---|---|---|---|
| Walls - Interior Partitions | Includes all load bearing interior partitions regardless of construction. Also includes non-load bearing partitions regardless of height (typically constructed of studs and sheetrock or other materials) that divide or create rooms or provide traffic control. Includes rough carpentry and plaster, dry wall or gypsum board, and other finishes. | 1250 | Building or Building Component - 39 Years |
| | Interior walls for merchandise display where the partition can be 1) readily removed and remain in substantially the same condition after removal as before, or 2) moved and reused, stored, or sold in their entirety. | 1245 | 57.0 Distributive Trades and Services — 5 Years |
| Windows | Exterior windows, including store front windows, drive-through service and carousel windows, and vestibule. | 1250 | Building or Building Component - 39 Years |
| Window Treatments | Window treatments such as drapes, curtains, louver, blinds, post construction tinting and interior decorative theme décor which are readily removable. | 1245 | 57.0 Distributive Trades and Services — 5 Years |

## Cost Segregation Audit Techniques Guide - Chapter 7.4 - Industry Specific Guidance - Pharmaceutical and Biotechnology

The asset matrix for Pharmaceutical and Biotechnology is not reproduced. However, it is located in the IRS Audit Guide for Cost Segregation—CCH.

## Cost Segregation Audit Techniques Guide - Chapter 7.5 - Industry Specific Guidance - Auto Dealership Industry

***Note***: Each chapter in this Audit Techniques Guide can be printed individually. Please follow the links at the beginning or end of this chapter to return to either the previous chapter or the Table of Contents or to proceed to the next chapter.

*Chapter 7.4 / Table of Contents / Chapter 7.6*

LMSB Control No. 4-0208-006

Impacted IRM 4.51.5

February 25, 2008

MEMORANDUM FOR LMSB INDUSTRY DIRECTORS DIRECTOR, PREFILING AND TECHNICAL GUIDANCE DIRECTOR, FIELD SPECIALISTS DIRECTOR, INTERNALTIONAL COMPLICANCE LMSB AREA COUNSEL

FROM: /s/ Charlie Brantley<br>Industry Director<br>Heavy Manufacturing and Transportation

SUBJECT: Field Directive on the Planning and Examination of Cost Segregation Issues in the Auto Dealership Industry

This Directive is intended to provide technical guidance to effectively reduce exam time and taxpayer burden. The matrix contained in attachment A is a new chapter in the Cost Segregation Audit Technique Guide. This matrix will provide assistance to agents in the classification and examination of a taxpayer who is recovering costs through depreciation of tangible property used in the Auto Dealership Industry.

**Background**

The crux of cost segregation is determining whether an asset is I.R.C. § 1245 property (shorter cost recovery period property) or § 1250 property (longer cost recovery period property). The most common example of § 1245 property is depreciable personal property, such as equipment. The most common examples of § 1250 property are buildings and building components, which generally are not § 1245 property.[1]

The difference in recovery periods has placed the Internal Revenue Service and taxpayers in adversarial positions in determining whether an asset is § 1245 or § 1250 property. Frequently, this causes the excessive expenditure of examination resources. The Director for the Heavy Manufacturing and Transportation Industry chartered a working group to address the most efficient way to approach cost segregation issues specific to the Auto Dealership Industry. The group produced the attached matrix and related definitions as a tool to reduce unnecessary disputes and foster consistent audit treatment.

**Issue Tracking**

UIL Code 168-20-00 Classification of Property.

**Planning and Examination Risk Analysis**

The Auto Dealership Industry Matrix recommending the categorization and general depreciation system recovery period of various assets is attached as Exhibit A. (for recovery periods under IRC § 168(g) alternative depreciation system, see Revenue Procedure 87-56, 1987-2 CB 674). If the taxpayer's tax return position for these assets is consistent with the recommendations in Auto Dealership Matrix (Exhibit A), examiners should not make adjustments to categorization and recovery periods. If the taxpayer reports assets differently, then adjustments should be considered.

Please consider the Cost Segregation Audit Techniques Guide in its entirety. Refer especially to Appendix Chapter 6.3, which provides examples and general rules for asset classification.

**Internal Communications**

Questions regarding the development of the Cost Segregation issue for Auto Dealerships should be addressed to the Motor Vehicle - Retail; Technical Advisor Team.

**This LMSB Directive is not an official pronouncement of the law or the position of the Service and cannot be used, cited or relied upon as such.**

Attachment: Exhibit A

Attachment

---

[1] I.R.C. § 1245 can apply to certain qualified recovery nonresidential real estate placed in service after 1980 and before 1987. *See* I.R.C. § 1245(a)(5).

## LMSB DIRECTIVE ON COST SEGREGATION IN THE AUTO DEALERSHIP INDUSTRY

### EXHIBIT A

This matrix, which is part of the Cost Segregation Audit Techniques Guide, is intended to provide direction to effectively utilize resources in the classification and examination of property used in the operation of an Auto Dealership. General fact patterns specific to this industry have been considered in the classification of these assets and may not be applicable to other industries. Similarly, asset classification guidance issued for other industries is based on the general fact pattern for that industry and may not be applicable to an Auto Dealership situation. For examination techniques and historical background related to this issue, refer to the Cost Segregation Audit Techniques Guide.

**NOTE**: In the case of certain leasehold improvement property, the classifications in this directive are superseded to the extent that the American Jobs Creation Act of 2004 modifies IRC Section 168. Thus, a 15-year straight line recovery period should replace the recovery period shown in the following matrix if the asset is "qualified leasehold improvement property" (as defined in IRC Section 168(e)(6)) placed in service by the taxpayer after 10/22/04 and before 1/1/08. [The 15-year recovery period expired effective for property placed in service after 2017—CCH.]

| Asset | Description | Property Type | Recovery Period |
|---|---|---|---|
| Awnings & Canopies | Readily removable overhang or covering, often of canvas or plastic, used to provide shade or cover over a storefront, a window, or a door; or used inside a structure to identify a particular department or selling area. Also includes canopies designed to protect employees and gasoline fueling equipment from weather conditions and to act as advertising displays that are anchored with bolts and are not attached to buildings or other structures. Does not include permanent canopies that are an integral part of a building's structural shell, such as porte-cochere (covered entrances for vehicle drive-up) and porticos (covered porches), or over docks. See also **Concrete Foundations & Footings, Loading Docks,** and **Signs**. | 1245 | 57.0 Distributive Trades and Services — 5 Years |

| Asset | Description | Property Type | Recovery Period |
|---|---|---|---|
| Bollards & Guardrails | Bollards (heavy steel posts generally filled with concrete) and Guardrails mounted in a concrete foundation or sturdily affixed to the ground so as to create a protective barrier around areas of the building vulnerable to vehicle traffic such as Service Bay doors, glass storefront partitions, doors, door frames, HVAC components, building corners, etc. Bollards and Guardrails can be located inside or outside the building are permanently attached and are intended to be permanent. (Placement to protect the building). | 1250 | Building or Building Component - 39 Years |
| | Bollards (heavy steel posts generally filled with concrete) and Guardrails mounted in the ground or concrete to protect machinery and equipment from vehicular damage, or to prevent vehicles from trespassing onto specific areas. Placement to protect land improvements and non-building items such as signs, sign poles, flagpoles, trees, as well as inventories of autos and trucks. Bollard and Guardrails are permanently attached and intended to be permanent. **Note* asset class 00.3 Land improvements includes both section 1245 and 1250 property per Rev. Proc. 87-56.** | *See Note** | 00.3 Land Improvements - 15 Years |
| Bollards & Guardrails | Bollards (heavy steel posts) and Guardrails, not permanently attached and not intended to be permanent, placed near machinery and equipment inside buildings that can be damaged by vehicular traffic. Bollards and Guardrails withstand vehicular impact and protect personal property items such as: forklift recharging stations, service write-up station, hazardous material storage racks, service department air compressors, etc. | 1245 | 57.0 Distributive Trades and Services — 5 Years |

| Asset | Description | Property Type | Recovery Period |
|---|---|---|---|
| Cabinetry | Includes cabinets and counters constructed or installed within buildings that relate to the general operation and maintenance of the building. For example, cabinets and counters used to house or enclose electrical equipment, plumbing components, sinks, fire protection systems, and other structural elements of a building which are designed to remain in place. Includes counters and cabinets in restrooms,**Employee Break Areas, Employee Coffee Bars, and Office Areas**. See also **Restroom Accessories.** | 1250 | Building or Building Component - 39 Years |
| | Includes cabinets and counters related to the retail activity and not related to the operation and maintenance of the building. For example: retail counters and cabinets, display shelving and cabinets, customer reception counter,**Customer Lounge Area** cabinets and counters,**Sales Area** cabinets and counters, parts counters, etc. See also **Retail Fixtures** and **Office Furniture.** | 1245 | 57.0 Distributive Trades and Services — 5 Years |
| Computers | Processors (CPU), direct access storage device (DASD), tape drives, desktop and laptop computers, CRT, terminals, monitors, printers, and other peripheral equipment. Excludes Point of Sale (POS) systems and computers that are an integral part of other equipment (e.g. fire detection, heating, cooling, or energy management systems, etc.). See also **Point of Sale (POS) Systems.** | 1245 | 00.12 Information Systems - 5 Years |
| Concrete Foundations & Footings | Foundations and footings necessary for the proper setting of the building. Excavation and backfill for building foundations. Excavation and backfill for special equipment foundations where contained within the footprint of the building. Includes formwork, reinforcement, concrete block, and pre-cast or cast-in-place work. | 1250 | Building or Building Component - 39 Years |
| | Foundations or footings for signs, light poles, and other land improvements (except buildings). Includes excavation, backfill, formwork, reinforcement, concrete block, and pre-cast or cast-in-place work. **Note* asset class 00.3 Land improvements includes both section 1245 and 1250 property per Rev. Proc. 87-56.** | See**Note*** | 00.3 Land Improvements - 15 Years |

| Asset | Description | Property Type | Recovery Period |
|---|---|---|---|
| Concrete Foundations & Footings | A foundation, pad, or footing for machinery or equipment that is so specially designed that it is in essence a part of the machinery or equipment. Any function as a building component must be strictly incidental to the function as an essential part of the item of machinery or equipment that necessitated the special design of the foundation. Increased thickness of the building's slab alone is not sufficient to show that the foundation, pad, or footing is so specially designed that it is in essence a part of the machinery or equipment it supports. Excavation and backfill are not included where the foundation, pad, or footing is contained within the footprint of the building. Includes formwork, reinforcement, concrete block, and pre-cast or cast-in-place work. | 1245 | 57.0 Distributive Trades and Services - 5 Years |
| Data Handling Equipment | Includes adding and accounting machines, calculators, copiers, and duplicating machines. Excludes computers and computer peripheral equipment. | 1245 | 00.13 Data Handling Equipment, except Computers - 5 Years |
| Doors | Interior and exterior doors, regardless of decoration, including but not limited to, double opening doors, fire doors and fire containment safety doors, overhead and roll-up doors, revolving doors, roll-up or sliding wire mesh or steel grills,**Service Bay** doors, and related door hardware (such as doorknobs, closers, kick plates, hinges, locks, automatic openers, computerized door locks, etc.). See also **Millwork.** | 1250 | Building or Building Component - 39 Years |
| | Special lightweight, double action doors installed to prevent accidents in a heavily trafficked area. For example, flexible doors, or clear or strip curtains used between stock and selling areas. | 1245 | 57.0 Distributive Trades and Services - 5 Years |

| Asset | Description | Property Type | Recovery Period |
|---|---|---|---|
| Electrical | Includes all components of the building electrical system used in the operation or maintenance of the building or necessary to provide general building services such as electrical outlets of general applicability and accessibility, lighting, heating, ventilation, air conditioning, and electrical wiring. Includes but is not limited to general purpose outlets connected to copy machines, fax machines, personal computers, and general purpose outlets in the**Break Rooms, Coffee Rooms, Lounges**, etc. | 1250 | Building or Building Component - 39 Years |
| Electrical | Includes electrical outlets specifically associated to a particular item of machinery or equipment located in the**Service Department, Body Shop, and Showroom**. Special electrical connections which are necessary to and used directly with a specific item of machinery or equipment or connections between specific items of individual machinery or equipment; such as dedicated electrical outlets, wiring, conduit, and circuit breakers by which machinery and equipment is connected to the electrical distribution system. Does not include electrical outlets of general applicability and accessibility. See Chapter 5 of the Cost Segregation Audit Techniques Guide for allocation examples.<br>Examples include: Dedicated electrical service to lifts, jacks and *Service Bay* equipment; paint booths; car washes; oil change stations; frame straightening equipment and**Body Shop** equipment. Also includes dedicated electrical to**Customer Areas**, such as suspended television monitors. | 1245 | 57.0 Distributive Trades and Services — 5 Years |
| Elevators and Escalators | Elevators and escalators, which include handrails and smoke baffles, are permanently affixed to the building and intended to remain in place. They relate to the operation or maintenance of the building and are structural components. Includes elevators to move autos in multi-story dealerships. | 1250 | Building or Building Component - 39 Years |

| Asset | Description | Property Type | Recovery Period |
|---|---|---|---|
| Energy Management Systems | Energy management systems control all energy-using systems in a building, automatically checking occupancy schedules, reading temperatures, and re-circuiting light levels, causing all heating, cooling and lighting equipment to operate so as to minimize energy costs. Includes, for example, detection devices such as smoke, motion and infrared devices, photocells, foil and contact switches, pressure switches, proximity alarms, sensors, alarm transmitting controls, data gathering panels, demand controllers, thermostats, computer controls, outside air economizers, occupancy sensors, electronic ballasts, and all related wiring and conduit. May also provide for fire and burglary protection. | 1250 | Building or Building Component - 39 Years |
| Exit Signs | Signs posted along exit routes within buildings that indicate the direction of travel to the nearest exit. These signs typically read "EXIT" and may have distinctive colors, illumination, or arrows indicating the direction to the exit. | 1250 | Building or Building Component - 39 Years |
| Fire Protection & Alarm Systems | Includes sensing devices, computer controls, sprinkler heads, piping or plumbing, pumps, visual and audible alarms, alarm control panels, heat and smoke detection devices, fire escapes, fire doors, emergency lighting and signage, and wall mounted fire extinguishers necessary for the protection of the building. | 1250 | Building or Building Component - 39 Years |
| Fire Protection Equipment | Includes special fire detection or suppression systems directly associated with a piece of equipment and designed and used for protection against a particular hazard created by the business activity (such as in the **Body Shop**). | 1245 | 57.0 Distributive Trades and Services — 5 Years |
| Floor Coverings | Floor covering affixed with permanent adhesive, nailed, or screwed in place. Examples include ceramic or quarry tile, marble, paving brick, and other coverings cemented, mudded, or grouted to the floor; epoxy or sealers; and wood flooring. | 1250 | Building or Building Component - 39 Years |
| | Floor covering that is installed by means of strippable adhesives. For the auto dealership industry, all vinyl composition tile (VCT), sheet vinyl, and carpeting will be treated as not permanently attached and not intended to be permanent. | 1245 | 57.0 Distributive Trades and Services — 5 Years |

| Asset | Description | Property Type | Recovery Period |
|---|---|---|---|
| Floors | Includes concrete slabs and other floor systems. Floors include special treatments applied to or otherwise a permanent part of the floor. For example, reflective flooring, express lube and reconditioning area floors, and epoxy floor paint or sealant applied directly to the concrete slab to keep a sealed, water and oil resistant, easy-to-clean surface. See also **Floor Coverings.** | 1250 | Building or Building Component - 39 Years |
| Floor Pits & Trenches | Work areas built at a lower level than the garage floor to allow technicians to stand beneath the vehicles while working. These floor pits allow the technician to service a vehicle from below (for example, to change automotive oil, radiator and transmission fluids). Work areas include pits and trenches with concrete floors and walls with overhead access to vehicles. Some of these floor pits resemble full basements allowing multiple technicians access to vehicles above. | 1250 | Building or Building Component - 39 Years |
| | Equipment included in the floor pits & trenches such as lifts, trays, and piping for supply fluid systems; waste fluid recovery and containment systems; and automotive fluid waste tanks. | 1245 | 57.0 Distributive Trades and Services — 5 Years |
| Heating, Ventilating & Air Conditioning (HVAC) | Includes all components of a central heating, ventilating and air conditioning system not specifically identified elsewhere. HVAC systems that are installed not only to meet the temperature and humidity requirements of machinery, but are also installed for additional significant purposes, such as customer comfort and ventilation, are building components. | 1250 | Building or Building Component - 39 Years |
| | Only separate HVAC units that meet the sole justification test are included (i.e., machinery the sole justification for the installation of which is the fact that such machinery is required to meet temperature or humidity requirements which are essential for the operation of other machinery or the processing of materials or paint). For example, special ventilation for paint booths;**Body Shop and Service Area** exhaust removal systems. Allocation of HVAC is not appropriate. | 1245 | 57.0 Distributive Trades and Services — 5 Years |

| Asset | Description | Property Type | Recovery Period |
|---|---|---|---|
| Inventory Display Equipment | Includes inventory displays that are permanently added to the land. Examples include concrete ramps and pedestals, and exterior "turntable" displays that are permanently affixed, etc. **Note* asset class 00.3 Land improvements includes both section 1245 and 1250 property per Rev. Proc. 87-56.** | **See Note*** | 00.3 Land Improvements - 15 Years |
| | Includes inventory displays that are not permanently added to the land and intended to be moved. Examples include metal ramps, portable "turntable" displays, etc. | 1245 | 57.0 Distributive Trades and Services — 5 Years |
| Landscaping & Shrubbery | Landscaping that will not be replaced contemporaneously with a related depreciable asset or that will not be destroyed when the related depreciable asset is replaced. Examples include landscaping, shrubbery, trees, plant foliage, or sod placed around the perimeter of the tract of land. | | Land |
| | Landscaping that will be replaced contemporaneously with a related depreciable asset or that will be destroyed when the related depreciable asset is replaced. Examples include depreciable landscaping, shrubbery, trees, plant foliage, or sod placed around the parking lot in outdoor**Sales Area**. Includes associated irrigation systems (sprinkler systems). **Note* asset class 00.3 Land improvements includes both section 1245 and 1250 property per Rev. Proc. 87-56.** | **See Note*** | 00.3 Land Improvements - 15 Years |
| Light Fixtures - Interior | Includes lighting such as recessed and lay-in lighting, night lighting, and exit lighting, as well as decorative lighting fixtures that provide substantially all the artificial illumination in the building or along building walkways. For emergency and exit lighting, see **Fire Protection & Alarm Systems.** | 1250 | Building or Building Component - 39 Years |

| Asset | Description | Property Type | Recovery Period |
|---|---|---|---|
| | Special display lighting specifically for highlighting automobiles in the**Showroom**, or highlighting displays of merchandise, decorative lighting, and specific task lighting in the service area. Decorative light fixtures are light fixtures, such as neon lights or track lighting, which are decorative in nature and not necessary for the operation of the building. If the decorative or task lighting were turned off, the other sources of lighting would provide sufficient light for operation of the building. If the decorative or task lighting is the**primary** source of lighting, then it is section 1250 property. | 1245 | 57.0 Distributive Trades and Services - 5 Years |
| Light Fixtures - Exterior | Exterior lighting is considered section 1250 property to the extent that the lighting relates to the maintenance or operation of the building. This category includes building mounted lighting to illuminate walkways, entrances, parking, etc. (whether decorative or not). | 1250 | Building or Building Component - 39 Years |
| | Pole mounted or freestanding outdoor lighting system to illuminate sidewalks,**Employee Parking Area, Customer Parking Area, and Product Display Parking Areas.** See also **Poles. Note* asset class 00.3 Land improvements includes both section 1245 and 1250 property per Rev. Proc. 87-56. The Revenue Procedure establishes two broad categories of depreciable assets: (1) asset classes 00.11 through 00.4 that consist of specific assets used in all business activities; and (2) asset classes 01.1 through 80.0 that consist of assets used in specific business activities. An asset described in both an asset and an activity category is classified in the asset category.** | **See Note*** | 00.3 Land Improvements - 15 Years |
| | Exterior lighting that highlights the merchandise and building exterior, for example a floodlight, spotlight, and uplighting which do not illuminate parking areas or walkways. Does not include the pole mounted lighting systems used to illuminate**Employee Parking Area, Customer Parking Area, and Product Display Parking Areas**. See also **Poles**. | 1245 | 57.0 Distributive Trades and Services — 5 Years |

| Asset | Description | Property Type | Recovery Period |
|---|---|---|---|
| Loading Docks | Includes bumpers, permanently installed dock levelers, plates, seals, lights, canopies, and overhead doors used in the receiving and shipping of merchandise. See also **Awnings & Canopies**. | 1250 | Building or Building Component - 39 Years |
| | Includes equipment such as compactors, conveyors, hoists and balers. | 1245 | 57.0 Distributive Trades and Services — 5 Years |
| Machinery & Equipment | Tangible personal property not covered elsewhere, which is in the nature of machinery or equipment. Includes, for example, machinery and equipment located in the**Body Shop, Parts Department and Service Departments** such as paint booths; exhaust systems; air compressors; pneumatic tools systems (including support equipment such as piping and related pumps); tanks and related pumps; automotive fluid and waste fluid recovery systems; above-ground lifts; car wash systems, etc. Does not include structural components of a building or other inherently permanent structure. See also **Concrete Foundation & Footings; Electrical;** and **Plumbing.** | 1245 | 57.0 Distributive Trades and Services — 5 Years |
| Millwork | General millwork is all building materials made of finished wood (e.g., doors and frames, window frames, sashes, porch work, mantels, panel work, stairways, and special woodwork). Includes pre-built wooden items brought to the site for installation and items constructed on site such as restroom cabinets, door jambs, moldings, trim, etc. | 1250 | Building or Building Component - 39 Years |
| | Decorative millwork is the decorative finish carpentry in the building. Examples include detailed crown moldings, lattice work placed over finished walls or ceilings, and merchandise display cabinets. The decorative millwork serves to enhance the overall décor of the dealership and is not related to the operation of the building. Cabinets and counters in the restroom are excluded from this category. See also **Cabinetry** and **Restroom Accessories**. | 1245 | 57.0 Distributive Trades and Services — 5 Years |

| Asset | Description | Property Type | Recovery Period |
|---|---|---|---|
| Office - Furniture (includes Communication Equipment and Hook-ups) | Includes desks, chairs, cashiers safes, credenzas, file cabinets, tables (or other furniture such as workstations and the**Sales Manager's office tower)** and shelving, including cost of shelves in record storage room. Also includes telephone equipment, fax machines, and other communications equipment. Does not include communications equipment included in other asset classes in Rev. Proc. 87-56. | 1245 | 00.11 Office Furniture, Fixtures, and Equipment - 7 Years |
| Parking Lots | Depreciable improvements directly to or added to land, whether such improvements are section 1245 or 1250. Grade level surface parking and base area usually constructed of asphalt, brick, concrete, stone or similar material. Also includes bumper blocks, curb cuts, curb work, striping, concrete landscape islands, gates, fences, truck parking ramps and staging areas, and traffic control systems (such as traffic lights and detectors, card readers, parking equipment, etc.). Includes*Employee* **Parking, Customer Parking, and New and Used Vehicle Parking Areas. Note* asset class 00.3 Land improvements includes both section 1245 and 1250 property per Rev. Proc. 87-56. The Revenue Procedure establishes two broad categories of depreciable assets: (1) asset classes 00.11 through 00.4 that consist of specific assets used in all business activities; and (2) asset classes 01.1 through 80.0 that consist of assets used in specific business activities. An asset described in both an asset and an activity category is classified in the asset category.** | **See Note*** | 00.3 Land Improvements - 15 Years |
| Parking Structures | Any structure or edifice the purpose of which is to provide parking space. Includes, for example, garages, parking ramps, or other parking structures. | 1250 | Building or Building Component - 39 Years |
| Plumbing | All piping, drains, sprinkler mains, valves, sprinkler heads, water flow switches, restroom plumbing fixtures (e.g. toilets) and piping, sinks, electric water coolers, and all other components of a building plumbing system (water or gas) not specifically identified elsewhere. Includes floor drains which ultimately lead to the municipal sewer system or site septic system. | 1250 | Building or Building Component - 39 Years |

| Asset | Description | Property Type | Recovery Period |
|---|---|---|---|
| | Special plumbing connections which are necessary to and used directly with a specific item of machinery or equipment or connections between specific items of individual machinery or equipment. Includes dedicated piping, valves, and hook-ups by which machinery and equipment is connected to the building or other inherently permanent structure's plumbing distribution system(s). Example includes plumbing hook-ups to the car wash system. Does not include plumbing hook-ups of general applicability and accessibility. See also **Floor Pits & Trenches**. | 1245 | 57.0 Distributive Trades and Services — 5 Years |
| Point of Sale (POS) Systems | A register or terminal based data collection system used to control and record all sales (cash, charge, COD, gift cards, layaway, etc.) at the point of sale. Includes cash registers, computerized sales systems and related peripheral equipment, satellite systems, scanners, and wands. See also **Electrical** for hook-ups. | 1245 | 57.0 Distributive Trades and Services — 5 Years |
| Poles | Light poles for parking areas and other poles poured in concrete footings or bolt-mounted for signage, flags, etc. **Note* asset class 00.3 Land improvements includes both section 1245 and 1250 property per Rev. Proc. 87-56.** See also **Bollards & Guardrails; Signs;** and **Light Fixtures - Exterior**. | **See Note*** | 00.3 Land Improvements - 15 Years |
| Premise (Pylon) Sign - Exterior | Pylons made of concrete, brick, wood frame, stucco, or similar materials usually set in the ground or on a concrete foundation, and usually used for signage.**Note* asset class 00.3 Land improvements includes both section 1245 and 1250 property per Rev. Proc. 87-56**. See also **Poles.** | **See Note*** | 00.3 Land Improvements - 15 Years |
| | Includes only the sign face and/or message screen and related components. Includes brand displays and dealership brand image enhancements. | 1245 | 57.0 Distributive Trades and Services — 5 Years |

| Asset | Description | Property Type | Recovery Period |
|---|---|---|---|
| Restroom Accessories | Includes paper towel dispensers, electric hand dryers, towel racks or holders, cup dispensers, purse shelves, toilet paper holders, soap dispensers or holders, lotion dispensers, sanitary napkin dispensers and waste receptacles, coat hooks, handrails, grab bars, mirrors, shelves, vanity cabinets, counters, ashtrays, baby changing stations, and other items generally found in public restrooms that are built into or mounted on walls or partitions. | 1250 | Building or Building Component - 39 Years |
| Restroom Partitions | Includes shop made and standard manufacture toilet partitions, typically metal, but may be plastic, sheetrock, wall board, or other materials. | 1250 | Building or Building Component - 39 Years |
| Retail Accessories | Accessories used to better display merchandise, advertising, and brochures that are not held for sale. Includes assets such as audio/video display devices, graphic rear projection displays, artwork (if depreciable),**Showroom** displays, decorative mobile props, holiday decorations, lamps, mirrors, pictures, plaques, potted plants, and props (such as sporting equipment or memorabilia, etc.). Does not include non-depreciable art, antiques, or collectibles). | 1245 | 57.0 Distributive Trades and Services — 5 Years |
| Retail Fixtures | Includes assets such as the retail counter space within the**Body Shop**, shelving to store parts and supplies, mechanical retrieval system or equipment for parts and supplies, clocks, including time clocks, counter space related to the**Parts Department**, including retail counter space and cashier, etc., shelving systems, shelf racks in the**Service Department** tool room, counter space within the**Service Department**(including dispatcher counter and parts counter for technicians) and other dealership fixtures needed in the business operation that are not a building component. Also includes fixtures and shelving for vehicle brand clothing and accessory**Retail Shop**, children's**Play Area** improvements for customers, fixtures for inventory information centers, and express lube after care business fixtures. | 1245 | 57.0 Distributive Trades and Services — 5 Years |

| Asset | Description | Property Type | Recovery Period |
|---|---|---|---|
| Roof | All elements of the roof including but not limited to joists, rafters, deck, shingles, vapor barrier, skylights, trusses, girders, and gutters. Determination of whether decorative elements of a roof (e.g. false dormers, mansard) constitute structural building components depends on their integration with the overall roof, not their load bearing capacity. If removal of the decorative element results in the direct exposure of building components to water, snow, wind, or moisture damage, or if the decorative element houses lighting fixtures, wiring, or other structural components, then the decorative elements are part of the overall roof system and are structural components of the building. | 1250 | Building or Building Component - 39 Years |
| Security Systems | Includes security equipment for the protection of the building (and its contents) from burglary or vandalism and protection of employees from assault. Examples include window and door locks; card key access systems; keyless entry systems; security cameras, recorders, monitors and related equipment; perimeter and interior building motion detectors; security lighting; alarm systems; and security system wiring and conduit. | 1250 | Building or Building Component — 39 Years |
| | Electronic surveillance systems used to track and monitor tangible items, e.g., devices used to protect New and Used automobile inventory. Includes scanners, electronic gates, surveillance cameras, recorders, monitors and related equipment. | 1245 | 57.0 Distributive Trades and Services — 5 Years |
| Sidewalks & Curbs | Depreciable improvements directly to or added to land, whether such improvements are section 1245 or 1250. Sidewalks and curbs are usually constructed of concrete, asphalt, stone or similar material. **Note* asset class 00.3 Land improvements includes both section 1245 and 1250 property per Rev. Proc. 87-56.** | **See Note*** | 00.3 Land Improvements - 15 Years |
| Signs | Exit signs, restroom identifiers, room numbers, and other signs relating to the operation or maintenance of a building. See also **Exit Signs.** | 1250 | Building or Building Component - 39 Years |

| Asset | Description | Property Type | Recovery Period |
|---|---|---|---|
| | Interior and exterior signs used to display brand or theme identity. For example, interior signs to identify departments or exterior signs to display trade names or trade symbols. For pylon signs, includes only sign face. See also **Poles** and **Premise (Pylon) Sign - Exterior**. | 1245 | 57.0 Distributive Trades and Services — 5 Years |
| *Site Preparation Grading & Excavation* | In general, land preparation costs include the one time cost of clearing and grubbing, site stripping, mucking, and fill or excavation to allow development of land. Clearing and grubbing is the removal of debris, brush, trees, etc. from the site. Stripping is the removal of the topsoil to provide a stable surface for site and building improvements. Mucking is the removal of unstable soils and materials to insure a solid base for intended improvements. The grading of land involves moving soil for the purpose of producing a more level surface to allow development of the land. | | Land |
| | Clearing, grading, excavating and removal costs directly associated with the construction of buildings and building components are part of the cost of construction of the building and depreciated over the life of the building. This includes building the showroom facility on a mound foundation for higher visibility and enhanced visual impact for the dealership building. | 1250 | Building or Building Component - 39 Years |
| | Clearing, grading, excavating and removal costs directly associated with the construction of sidewalks, parking areas, roadways and other depreciable land improvements are part of the cost of construction of the improvements and depreciated over the life of the associated asset. **Note* asset class 00.3 Land improvements includes both section 1245 and 1250 property per Rev. Proc. 87-56.** | **See Note*** | 00.3 Land Improvements - 15 Years |
| Site Utilities | Site utilities are the systems that are used to distribute utility services from the property line to the building. Includes water, sanitary sewer, gas, electrical services, and data and communication lines. | 1250 | Building or Building Component - 39 Years |

| Asset | Description | Property Type | Recovery Period |
|---|---|---|---|
| Site Work | Site work includes curbing, paving, general site improvements, fencing, depreciable landscaping, roads, sewers, sidewalks, site drainage and all other site improvements, such as storm water retention basins, not directly related to the building. See also **Landscaping & Shrubbery**. For sanitary sewers, see **Site Utilities**. Does not include land preparation costs, see also **Site Preparation Grading & Excavation.** **Note* asset class 00.3 Land improvements includes both section 1245 and 1250 property per Rev. Proc. 87-56.** | **See Note*** | 00.3 Land Improvements - 15 Years |
| Sound Systems | Equipment and apparatus, including wiring, used to provide amplified sound or music. For example, public address by way of paging a customer or employee. Excludes applications linked to fire protection and alarm systems. | 1245 | 57.0 Distributive Trades and Services — 5 Years |
| Trash Enclosures | Enclosures for waste receptacles that are attached to the building. Typically constructed of the same materials as the building shell with either interior or exterior access. These trash enclosures are an integral part of the building shell and cannot be moved without damage to the underlying building. | 1250 | Building or Building Component - 39 Years |
| | Freestanding enclosures for waste receptacles, typically constructed on a concrete pad with its posts set in the concrete. Serves both safety and decorative functions. **Note* asset class 00.3 Land improvements includes both section 1245 and 1250 property per Rev. Proc. 87-56.** | **See Note*** | 00.3 Land Improvements - 15 Years |
| Wall Coverings | Includes interior and exterior paint; ceramic or quarry tile, marble, stone, brick and other finishes affixed with mortar, cement or grout; paneling, wainscoting and other wood finishes affixed with nails, screws or permanent adhesives; and wall panels such as fiberglass, stainless steel and plastic wall panels. | 1250 | Building or Building Component - 39 Years |
| | Strippable wallpaper that causes no damage to the underlying wall or wall surface. | 1245 | 57.0 Distributive Trades and Services — 5 Years |

| Asset | Description | Property Type | Recovery Period |
|---|---|---|---|
| Walls - Exterior | Includes all exterior walls and building support regardless of construction materials. Exterior walls may include columns, posts, beams, girders, curtain walls, tilt up panels, studs, framing, sheetrock, insulation, windows, doors, exterior façade, brick, masonry, etc. Also includes drive-through bay, windows, and doors. | 1250 | Building or Building Component - 39 Years |
| Walls - Interior Partitions | Includes all load bearing interior partitions regardless of construction. Also includes non-load bearing partitions regardless of height (typically constructed of studs and sheetrock or other materials) that divide or create rooms or provide traffic control. Includes rough carpentry and plaster, dry wall or gypsum board, and other finishes. | 1250 | Building or Building Component - 39 Years |
| Walls - Interior Partitions | Interior walls where the partition can be 1) readily removed and remain in substantially the same condition after removal as before, or 2) intended to be moved and reused, stored, or sold in their entirety. | 1245 | 57.0 Distributive Trades and Services — 5 Years |
| Windows | Exterior windows, including store front windows, and exterior glass partitions. Includes interior glass partitions from floor to ceiling or as a part of an interior wall. | 1250 | Building or Building Component - 39 Years |
| Window Treatments | Window treatments such as drapes, curtains, louver, blinds, post construction tinting and interior decorative theme décor which are readily removable. | 1245 | 57.0 Distributive Trades and Services — 5 Years |

# Quick Reference Tables—Functional Allocation Approach to Allocation of Building's Electrical Distribution System

**Cost Segregation ATG - Chapter 8.1 Functional Allocation Approach to Allocation of Building's Electrical Distribution System**

*Table of Contents*



**Introduction**

This chapter provides procedures for the proper allocation of a building's electrical distribution system (EDS) in connection with a cost segregation study. In order to properly identify, separate and allocate the costs of a building's overall EDS, various sources of information are relied on such as engineering design practices and terminology, case law, and IRS guidance.

The method discussed herein, the functional allocation approach, has been developed over decades by various courts. See Section III, Legal Background.

Although this chapter utilizes/references the functional allocation approach, a taxpayer may use other methods to reasonably allocate a building's EDS to § 1245 property or § 1250 property. If a taxpayer properly uses the functional allocation approach outlined within this chapter to allocate the costs associated with a building's EDS, the allocation should not be challenged and no adjustments to categorization and lives of the various components of the EDS are necessary.

If the taxpayer either purports to follow the functional allocation method, but its method differs from that outlined within this chapter, or allocates the costs of its EDS under a method other than the functional allocation method, the Examiner should risk assess the position and determine if further examination is warranted. In such case, advice from an Engineer should be requested.

**Note 1.1:** Examiners should carefully consider the extent to which a detailed examination of this issue is viable without engineering support.

**Definitions and Illustration of a Building's Overall Electrical System**

The following definitions were derived from published court decisions with some additional industry terms for clarification.

**Connected Load** - an Industry term used for the actual power required by the specific circuit to safely operate the attached end-use equipment. This is the unfactored load of the branch circuit but is the load to which the Demand Factor is applied to get the Demand Load. See Section IV of this Chapter.

**Demand Load** - an Industry term used for the factored load for the design of the overall electrical system of a building. The demand factors used are applied to the EDS portions of the electrical system (NEC Article 220) and are a key part in the design and cost of a building's EDS. See Section IV of this Chapter.

**Functional Allocation Approach** - term coined by courts to describe how a building's EDS is allocated proportionally by electrical Demand Load to the various items served. This approach was first utilized in the case of *Scott Paper v. Commissioner*, 74 T.C. 137 (1980) to allocate the EDS between § 1245 property and § 1250 property.

**Overall Electrical System** - the entire electrical system of a building that includes the Primary EDS, the Secondary EDS, and the branch circuits including the wires that provide the connections to the end-use equipment "hook-ups."

The following terms are for the various portions of a building's overall electrical system, defined below and shown on Figure 2.1:

**Primary EDS** - the electrical equipment that receives the electrical service from the outside source (power utility company) to the main distribution panels (MDPs) and transformers (also known as "switchgear" on large building projects), that deliver power at the correct voltages to the secondary EDS. This includes large feeder circuits, power service entrance equipment, transformers, and conduit. In some instances, motor control centers, power transfer switches and meters are included.

**Secondary EDS** -the electrical equipment that brings the electrical power from the MDP to the local distribution panels that feed the branch circuits. There are typically several distribution panels in a building facility, each one constituting a part of the secondary EDS for its specific function or location. (There are two separate systems shown in the Figure 2.1, L1 - "Lighting" and P1- "Power.") This includes feeder circuits leading from the MDP to the secondary distribution panels and any transformers in between. It also includes subpanels, whose power is fed from a secondary distribution panel, for servicing specific equipment in areas such as kitchens, laundry rooms or even specialty lighting panels.

For small buildings, the power from the electrical utility generally feeds directly to a main electrical panel instead of an MDP or transformer, thus eliminating the primary and secondary designation. In any case, the EDS should be allocated in the same manner, by design load of the end-user equipment as defined below.

**Branch Circuits** - the electrical connections between a distribution or subpanel and the final electrical device. This includes wire and conduit, junction boxes, wall switches, cut-off switches, duplex outlets (receptacles), quad outlets, specific NEMA outlets (alternate plug configurations), and special connections to lights, appliances, and end-use equipment. Branch circuits are not part of the building EDS.

**Hook-Ups** - the labor and materials necessary to make an electrical connection from the power source to the end-use equipment. This could be as simple as the act of plugging an electrical plug into an electrical outlet, or a more complex task like "hard wiring" appliance motors to junction boxes (j-boxes) or connecting light fixtures with flexible conduit and wiring to a j-box connected to a three-way electrical on/off switch. Hook-ups are not part of the building EDS.

**End-use equipment "consumptive devices"** -the actual equipment, machinery, or appliances to which the overall electrical system provides power. This could include process equipment (such as manufacturing machinery), building equipment (such as lighting, HVAC and outlets for general accessibility), or other personal property (such as computers, printers, ovens, lamps etc.). This equipment is not part of the building EDS.

**Note 2.1:**

**Risk Analysis Item** - Some buildings and facilities may not have a substantial amount of cost in the EDS, such as in a renovation of an existing building. Therefore, a risk assessment should always be made to see if the project warrants such in-depth analysis.

*Figure 2.1 Illustration of a Building's Electrical Distribution System (EDS)* (pdf)

**Legal Background**

This section provides a brief overview of the legal principles involved in understanding the functional allocation approach of EDS to § 1245 and § 1250 property.

Tangible property can be divided into "§ 1250 property" and "§ 1245 property" under the Internal Revenue Code (IRC). "§ 1250 property" is any real property, other than § 1245 property, which is, or has been, of a character subject to the allowance for depreciation provided in § 167. "§ 1245 property" includes any property that is of a character subject to the allowance for depreciation under § 167 and is, among other things, either personal property or other tangible property (not including a building or its structural components) used as an integral part of certain specified activities. The regulations under § § 1250 and 1245 reference the regulations under former § 48 (pertaining to the Investment Tax Credit (ITC), which was eliminated in 1990) for definitions of the terms "tangible personal property," "other tangible property," "building," and "structural components" (Treas. Reg. § 1.48-1).

The depreciation deduction provided by § 167 for tangible property placed in service after 1986 generally is determined under § 168, the Modified Accelerated Cost Recovery System (MACRS). Courts have determined that the tests developed to ascertain whether property constituted tangible personal property for purposes of ITC equally are applicable to decide whether the property constitutes tangible personal property for purposes of MACRS. Accordingly, to the extent a property item would have qualified as tangible personal property for ITC that property also will qualify as tangible personal property for purposes of MACRS.

In *Scott Paper Co. v. Commissioner*, 74 T.C. 137 (1980), the court allowed an allocation of a paper plant facility's overall electrical systems between: 1) property qualifying for the ITC because it was or related to tangible personal property (i.e., § 1245 property), or 2) property not qualifying for the ITC because it was related to the operation or maintenance of a building (i.e., § 1250 property). The allocation was based on the power demand or design "load" (expressed in kilo-Volt amperes or kVA) of the machinery and equipment for which it was designed. Thus, the power demand of the end-user machinery and equipment forms the basis for the functional allocation approach.

It should be noted that the Fourth Circuit rejected the functional allocation approach in *A.C. Monk and Co., Inc. v. United States*, 686 F.2d 1058 (4th Cir. 1982), and held that the proper approach was to determine whether the electrical system had more general uses than simply operating specific items of machinery. Thus, if the wiring and other components of the electrical system could be reasonably adapted to more general uses, they were structural components of the building. It should also be noted that the Federal Claims Court takes a third approach in determining whether any portion of the EDS is allocable to § 1245 property. In *Boddie-Noell Enterprises, Inc. v. United States*, 36 Fed. Cl. 722, 740-1 (1996), aff'd without opinion by 132 F.3d 54 (Fed. Cl. 1997), the court took the approach that since "electric wiring and lighting fixtures" are explicitly mentioned as in § 1.48-1(e)(2) as structural components, no portion of the EDS is allocable to § 1245 property. These alternate approaches, however, have not been followed by other courts.

In *Illinois Cereal Mills, Inc. v. Commissioner*, 789 F.2d 1234 (7th Cir. 1986), the Seventh Circuit affirmed the opinion of the Tax Court and its use of the functional allocation approach. The U.S. Supreme Court denied certiorari in *Illinois Cereal Mills, Inc. v. Commissioner* 479 U.S. 995 (1986), concerning the different methodologies in the two Circuit Courts. Therefore, the conflicting opinions of the Seventh Circuit for *Illinois Cereal Mills* and the Fourth Circuit for *A.C. Monk* remain intact.

In *Morrison, Inc. v. Commissioner*, T.C. Memo 1986-129, the court dealt in part with the primary EDS of cafeteria buildings. The court allowed a portion of the primary electric as tangible personal property for purposes of the ITC. In its findings, the Tax Court again followed the functional allocation approach it espoused in *Scott Paper*. On appeal, *Morrison, Inc. v. Commissioner*, 891 F.2d 857 (11th Cir. 1990), the Circuit Court concluded that the Tax Court correctly used the "functional allocation approach" and held as follows, at 863:

First, we accept Morrison's argument that taxpayers can claim investment tax credit on a percentage basis. In this regard, we adopt the reasoning in *Illinois Cereal* and reject the reasoning in *Monk*. . . . Second, we adopt the Tax Court's method of focusing on the ultimate use of electricity distributed by Morrison's primary electrical systems. . . . Third, the Tax Court's method is consistent with the investment tax credit's purpose.

Subsequent to the Eleventh Circuit's opinion in *Morrison*, in 1991 the IRS revised an AOD on *Illinois Cereal Mills*, AOD 1991-019. In the AOD, the Commissioner stated:

In view of the Eleventh Circuit's rejection of the *Monk* standard in favor of the functional allocation method approved by the Seventh Circuit in *Illinois Cereal*, and the Supreme Court's rejection of the government's petition for certiorari in *Illinois Cereal*, further litigation of this issue is not warranted. Accordingly, the IRS will not challenge the functional allocation approach set forth in *Scott Paper* to determine the eligibility of electrical systems of a building to qualify as § 38 property.

In *Hospital Corporation of America v. Commissioner*, 109 T.C. 21 (1997), the court found that the standards for determining the categorization of property under ACRS and MACRS were the same as for the ITC, at 55:

We conclude that the tests developed to ascertain whether property constituted tangible personal property for purposes of ITC equally are applicable to decide whether the property constitutes tangible personal property for purposes of MACRS. Accordingly, we conclude that, to the extent a disputed property item would have qualified as tangible personal property for ITC, that property also will qualify as tangible personal property for purposes of ACRS and MACRS.

Next, the court in *HCA* found that the functional allocation approach was proper for the primary and secondary electric systems, at 63-64. Subsequently, the IRS issued an Action on Decision for *HCA*, 1999-008 (August 30, 1999), in which the IRS acquiesced in the court's decision to the extent that it held that the tests developed under prior law for ITC purposes could be used to distinguish § 1245 property from § 1250 property for depreciation purposes. However, the IRS did not agree with the conclusions reached by the court with respect to the various items of property at issue in the case.

**Functional Allocation - Illustration**

**Step 1** of the audit, as outlined in *Scott Paper*, is to determine whether the components of the EDS are inherently permanent structures by applying the six-factor *Whiteco* test. See *Whiteco Industries, Inc. v. Commissioner*, 65 T.C. 664 (1975). Accordingly, one needs to determine whether each component constitutes "tangible personal property" or "other tangible property," rather than a "building," or a "structural component." See *Morrison*, 891 F.2d at 860-861.

**Step 2** of the audit is to determine if the EDS serves the operation and maintenance of a building or if it serves to supply power for the taxpayer's tangible personal property or other tangible property. It is possible that the EDS, or certain components thereof, may serve both purposes.

**Step 3** of the audit is to utilize the functional allocation approach as illustrated below. All of the types of property served by the EDS must be analyzed and their costs should be allocated proportionally by electrical demand load to the various items served. The building's electrical design plans must be studied to perform this step.

**Step 4** of the audit is to record and tally the electrical demand load for every item of § 1245 property as well as every item of § 1250 property. Once the entire electrical demand load is totaled, the proportion of § 1245 property versus § 1250 property of the EDS can be determined.

Please note that there are vast differences in the physical characteristics and engineering design criteria between a large manufacturing plant and a public building such as an office building, retail store, or restaurant.

**NOTE 4.1:** It is highly advised to verify the total cost of the EDS before applying resources and personnel to perform the following tasks. In certain instances, the total costs of the system may not warrant significant resources allocated to such an in-depth analysis.

**NOTE 4.2:** The electrical drawings or "Plans" of the building contain vital information for this approach. The electrical panel schedules and the "Electrical Load Summary" or "Calculation" (per the National Electric Code (NEC)) are required to be included in the electrical drawings and should be used as source documents for all calculations. All Watts or volt-amps should reconcile to the totals shown on the calculation or panels.

It is NOT appropriate to use a residual method to analyze the loads of the building. It is highly recommended that a qualified and knowledgeable person, such as an Engineer, perform the analysis.

**A. Load Analysis Located on Electrical Plans:**

Generally, there is a table included on the plans for a building facility that will provide the total amount of power intended to be used by the facility. This table shows the load requirements of National Electric Code (NEC) Article 220 "Branch-Circuit, Feeder, and Service Calculations" and is referred to in the industry as the "Electrical Load Calculation." The city or municipality typically requires this calculation in the plan review stage before the project is approved for construction by the city. The building contractor typically cannot begin construction without this information.

This table serves many functions: 1) it lets the municipality know the amount of power the facility is intended to use in order for the proper permits and fees to be set on a project; 2) the local power company must be aware of the power consumption of the facility to know how, or if, it will affect the local power grid thereby getting sufficient time to make the proper preparations, if needed; and 3) the designers of the electrical system of the facility and the electrical Engineers use this information to properly size the necessary equipment so the capacity of the system is adequate to provide for the power requirements of the building and also the required fire code and safety standards.

The Electrical Load Schedule or Calculation is typically located with the electrical drawings of the building's plans or "Blueprints" as commonly known. Usually it is on or close to the "One-Line Diagram" of the entire building's power system or is included on the Electrical Panel Schedules. The following table shows an example of an electrical load calculation for a large supermarket with a restaurant, bakery, deli, and other areas.

**Table 4.1:**

**Electrical Load Calculation**

**Large Supermarket**

| Load Description | Connect Watts | Demand Factor | Demand Load |
|---|---|---|---|
| Heating and Air Conditioning (HVAC) | 1,320,000 | 100% | 1,320,000 |
| Refrigerator & Freezer Equipment | 700,000 | 100% | 700,000 |
| Lunch Counter/Restaurant | 125,000 | 50% | 62,500 |
| Customer Service and Office | 105,000 | 70% | 73,500 |
| Interior Lighting | 85,000 | 100% | 85,000 |
| Bakery/Deli Department | 120,000 | 50% | 60,000 |
| Generator Back-Up Emerg. Power | 55,000 | 100% | 55,000 |
| Display Signs/Exterior Lighting | 46,000 | 100% | 46,000 |
| Cardboard Balers | 51,000 | 100% | 51,000 |
| Misc. Backroom Items | 60,000 | 70% | 42,000 |
| Meat Cutting Department (Butcher) | 50,000 | 70% | 35,000 |
| Trash Compactors | 21,000 | 100% | 21,000 |
| Cash Registers | 15,000 | 80% | 12,000 |
| Rolling Refrigerated Cases (Floor Receptacles) | 4,000 | 20% | 800 |
| **Totals** | **2,757,000** | | **2,563,800** |

This schedule shows the "Connected" Watts which is the power required if the item were to run at 100% capacity. The "Demand Factor" is a diversity factor applied to the power usage of that equipment for the design of the feeders and other parts of the EDS. The NEC Article 220 provides guideline Demand Factors (diversity factors or percentages) that are to be used as a minimum for calculating a demand load on the feeders and service of a building, or the EDS (see Note 4.2a.). All states and municipalities in the U.S. have adopted some version of the NEC as the minimum requirement for electrical construction in their region.

In the electrical design industry, "Demand Load" means the factored load for the design of the overall electrical system. In general, the items that require full

100% demand load are the dedicated pieces of equipment that are: 1) necessary to operate at all times, at near full capacity during operation; or 2) required by the NEC to be designed at full capacity. The lower "demand" percentages are placed on non-crucial equipment that may only be turned on part of the time during the operation of the facility. For example, not every outlet in a building will have equipment plugged into it at all times, or there may be equipment plugged in but turned off, and there may also be many outlets that remain entirely unused. The NEC specifies a minimum Demand Factor to be applied, about 50-70%, which is intended to approximate real-world scenarios, but still allow for safe operation of the entire system.

**NOTE 4.2a:** These Demand Factors are not used for designing the branch circuits which must comply with the required circuit design in NEC Article 220 Part I. However, the Demand Factors are applied to feeders and service (EDS) under specific NEC tables and rules as covered in NEC Article 220 Parts II, III, and IV.

The total demand load determines the size and type of electrical power service required to supply the facility. This information is also used to specify the proper sizes of the electrical equipment; conductors (wires), circuit breakers, transformers, switchgear, capacitors, conduit, etc., so the system will work safely during peak operating hours of the facility. The size of the equipment directly affects the cost of the equipment installed, and is the primary focus of the proper basis of § 1245 property in the functional allocation approach.

**NOTE 4.3:**

An energy usage study, measured in kilowatt-hours (kWh), which is performed for energy efficiency purposes by measuring the amount of energy used within a specified period, is a completely different study from the demand load analysis performed when designing and sizing building electrical equipment. The energy efficiency study should **not** be used as part of the functional allocation approach.

### B. Watts versus Volt-Amperes - Power Factor

The load calculation in *Scott Paper* is illustrated with units of kilovolt-amperes (kVA). The typical electrical load schedule for a building may be seen with units in kVA or in kilowatts (kW), or both.

The difference is something called a power factor. The kilowatts can be easily converted to kVA by the simple formula:

Kilowatts = kilovolt-Amperes X Power Factor,

Or simply:

kW = kVA x pf

For the purposes of this chapter, the power factors will be assumed to equal "1"; therefore kW will equal kVA.

Accordingly, an analysis of a building's EDS using units in kVA or in kW will yield the same results. However, the units may not be mixed and one must be consistent with the unit used.

### C. Item Cost versus Electrical Load

The costs of the individual portions of the building overall electrical system are usually addressed in the cost segregation study. These costs are either estimated using costing data or are taken directly from general or electrical contractor payment records.

The costs of the individual branch circuits for the end-use equipment are usually addressed in the detailed estimate of the cost segregation study. The circuits to the qualified § 1245 property are typically identified and are allocated to that property.

The total costs of the entire building's EDS, including all the transformers, panels, subpanels, feeder circuits, etc., must be distinguished in the cost segregation study and must reconcile with the amount actually paid by the taxpayer for the corresponding electrical system.

The functional allocation approach uses the electrical loads, not the costs of the specified circuits, to determine the proper portion of the EDS that is allocable to § 1245 property.

As an example, for the supermarket electrical load calculation in Table 4.1, the cost segregation study shows $2,500,000 in costs for the entire electrical contract for the project. This is verified on the Taxpayer's cost records for the construction project. A study of the individual items in the Electrical Contract reveal that the primary EDS costs are $500,000, the secondary EDS costs are $500,000, the branch circuits are $1.1 million, and the various hook-ups to the end-use equipment are $400,000.

The cost that will be involved in the functional allocation is the $1,000,000 for the combined primary and secondary distribution system costs. The asset classification of the remaining $1.5 million of the electrical contract consisting of branch circuit and equipment hook-up costs identified in the cost segregation study follow the same recovery period as the dedicated end-use equipment or as the building if they relate to the operation thereof.

### D. Example 1 - Large Supermarket

**Steps 1 and 2.** Using the electrical load calculation in Table 4.1, the field examination of the grocery store facility and an end-use analysis from the information on the electrical plans for the building show the following facts:

1. The exhaust fans for the kitchen pull 100,000 of the Connected Watts of the HVAC's total 1,320,000 Connected Watts. Therefore, the HVAC load must be split between § 1245 and § 1250 property.

2. The Refrigerator & Freezer Compressors were found to qualify as § 1245 property, as well as the Display Signs/Exterior Lighting, Cardboard Balers, Trash Compactors and Cash Registers. These loads do not need to be split; they are all for § 1245 property.

3. For the Lunch Counter/Restaurant, only 35,000 of the 125,000 Connected Watts are dedicated to qualifying § 1245 property. The remainder are for general use and do not qualify as § 1245 property. The Lunch Counter/Restaurant load should be split between § 1245 and § 1250 property.

4. The Customer Service/Office end-use equipment was all found to be electrical outlets for general use and accessibility and should remain as § 1250 property. The Interior Lighting, Generator, and Backroom electrical were all found to be for § 1250 property as well. These loads do not need to be split, they are all for § 1250 property.

5. In the meat cutting department, 30,000 of the 50,000 total Watts were found to be for dedicated § 1245 equipment, the remainder are for electrical outlets of general use and do not qualify as § 1245 property. This item load should be split between § 1245 and § 1250 property.

6. The circuits for the floor outlets labeled as "Rolling Refr. Cases" served also for regular maintenance equipment such as floor polishers, and vacuums. The IRS and the Taxpayer agree that this item should be split 50/50 as § 1245 and § 1250 property. Therefore, this item load should be split between § 1245 and § 1250 property.

**Step 3.** Table 4.2, below, shows the resulting Personal Property/Real Property split for each line item on the Load Calculation of Table 4.1. The functional allocation calculation concentrates on the demand loads. Therefore, the connected loads should be multiplied by the corresponding Demand Factor to achieve the Demand Watts. The total Demand for this project is 2,563,800 Watts.

Each line item is allocated to either Personal Property (§ 1245 property) or Real Property (§ 1250 property) based on their qualifying demand loads. The line items that required splitting and allocation between personal property and real property are shown on Table 4.2 with the § 1245 property in italics. The Load % shown on the table is the items portion of the total 2,563,800 Demand Watts.

Taking the HVAC as an example, the total Connected Watts is 1,320,000 with a Demand Factor of 100%. The 100,000 Watts for the kitchen exhaust fans is separated as qualified § 1245 personal property and the remaining 1,220,000 Watts is for § 1250 real property.

These are both proportioned to the total Demand Watts to calculate their percent allocation:

**Load % for 1250 HVAC;**

Demand Watts HVAC/Total Demand Watts Building = 1,220,000 ÷ 2,563,800 = 47.6%

**Load % for Kitchen Equipment;**

Demand Watts Kt. Equip/Tot. Demand Watts Building = 100,000 ÷ 2,563,800 = 3.9%

Each line item on the Load Calculation is allocated according to the facts and circumstances found in the examination. The results are shown on Table 4.2.

**Step 4.** Each load line item was examined and the demand load for the § 1245 property was separated from the demand load for the § 1250 property. The segregated totals are shown on the bottom of Table 4.2. The total portion of the electrical load determined to be for the § 1245 property is 38.4%.

Applying this percentage to the total cost of the building primary and secondary EDS, $1,000,000, yields the correct basis of the § 1245 portion of the EDS:

| Cost of Electrical Distribution System | X | Percent as Personal Property | = | Basis of Personal Property, Electrical Dist. Syst. |
|---|---|---|---|---|
| $1,000,000 | X | 38.4% | = | $384,000 |

The remaining EDS costs, 61.6% or $616,000 would be allocated to § 1250 property.

Therefore, the functional allocation of the building's EDS yields:

§ 1245 Property $384,000 + § 1250 Property $616,000 = Total Cost Elect. Dist. System $1,000,000

These totals are then added to the results of the branch circuit and equipment hook up allocation to get the total § 1245 and 1250 allocation of the entire electrical portion of the building project.

Table 4.2 - 1250/1245 Analysis of Large Supermarket

| Load Description | Connected Watts | Demand Factor | Demand Watts | Load % | Personal Property | Real Property |
|---|---|---|---|---|---|---|
| **Heat, Vent., & Air Cond. (HVAC)** | **1,220,000** | **100%** | **1,220,000** | **47.6%** | | **47.6%** |
| Kitchen Exhaust Fan | 100,000 | 100% | 100,000 | 3.9% | 3.9% | |
| **Refrigerator & Freezer Equip. - Compressors** | **700,000** | **100%** | **700,000** | **27.3%** | **27.3%** | |
| Lunch Counter/ Restaurant | 90,000 | 50% | 45,000 | 1.8% | | 1.8% |
| Dedicated Circuits to Kitchen Equip. | 35,000 | 50% | 17,500 | 0.7% | 0.7% | |
| **Customer Service/Office** | **105,000** | **70%** | **73,500** | **2.9%** | | **2.9%** |
| Dedicated Circuits to Office Equip. | - | 70% | - | 0.0% | 0.0% | |
| **Interior Lighting** | **85,000** | **100%** | **85,000** | **3.3%** | | **3.3%** |
| **Bakery/Deli Department** | **90,000** | **50%** | **45,000** | **1.8%** | | **1.8%** |
| Dedicated Circuits to Deli Equip. | 30,000 | 50% | 15,000 | 0.6% | 0.6% | |
| **Generator Back-Up Emerg. Power** | **55,000** | **100%** | **55,000** | **2.1%** | | **2.1%** |
| **Display Signs/ Ext. Lighting** | **46,000** | **100%** | **46,000** | **1.8%** | **1.8%** | |
| **Cardboard Balers** | **51,000** | **100%** | **51,000** | **2.0%** | **2.0%** | |
| **Misc. Backroom Items** | **60,000** | **70%** | **42,000** | **1.6%** | | **1.6%** |
| **Meat Cutting/ Seafood Dept.** | **20,000** | **70%** | **14,000** | **0.5%** | | **0.5%** |
| Dedicated Circuits to Meat Equip. | 30,000 | 70% | 21,000 | 0.8% | 0.8% | |
| **Trash Compactors** | **21,000** | **100%** | **21,000** | **0.8%** | **0.8%** | |

| Load Description | Connected Watts | Demand Factor | Demand Watts | Load % | Personal Property | Real Property |
|---|---|---|---|---|---|---|
| **Cash Registers** | **15,000** | **80%** | **12,000** | **0.5%** | **0.5%** | |
| **Rolling Refr. Floor Recpts.** | **2,000** | **20%** | **400** | **0.01%** | | **0.01%** |
| Dedicated Receptacles - 1245 | 2,000 | 20% | 400 | 0.01% | 0.01% | |
| **Totals** | **2,757,000** | | **2,563,800** | **100.00%** | **38.4%** | **61.6%** |

## E. Asset Classification for § 1245 property portion of the EDS

Once the functional allocation of the EDS is complete, you will need to determine the depreciation deduction for the § 1245 property portion of the EDS. The depreciation deduction for tangible property placed in service after 1986 generally is determined under § 168 using a prescribed depreciation method, recovery period, and convention. The applicable recovery period is determined by reference to class life or by statute.

Revenue Procedure 87-56, 1987-2 C.B. 674, sets forth the class lives of property that are necessary to compute the depreciation allowances under § 168. The revenue procedure establishes two broad categories of depreciable assets: 1) asset classes 00.11 through 00.4 that consist of specific assets used in all business activities; and 2) asset classes 01.1 through 80.0 that consist of assets used in specific business activities. The same item of depreciable property can be described in both an asset category (asset classes 00.11 through 00.4) and an activity class (asset classes 01.1 through 80.0), in which case the item is classified in the asset category. See *Norwest Corp. & Subs. v. Commissioner*, 111 T.C. 105 (1998) (items described in both an asset and an activity category should be placed in the asset category).

If a particular asset is used in more than one activity, the cost of the asset is not allocated between the two activities. Rather, the total cost of the asset will be classified according to the activity in which the asset is primarily used, regardless of whether the activity is insubstantial in relation to all the taxpayer's activities. For example, if a taxpayer operates a hotel/casino, decorative lighting used in the casino area would be classified in activity class 79.0, Recreation, with a 7-year recovery period whereas decorative lighting used in the hotel lobby area would be classified in activity class 57.0, Distributive Trades and Services, with a 5-year recovery period. Also, for depreciation purposes, the lessor of assets generally classifies such assets according to the activity they are primarily used in by the lessee.

### Summary

The Courts have accepted the functional allocation approach and have used it in different types of buildings. The appropriate application of this approach is complex and labor intensive. It entails:

Determining the proper cost of the specific parts of the overall EDS, includes the hook-ups, branch circuits, various sections of the secondary EDS, and the primary EDS, analyzing the over-all electrical demand load for the building, and allocating the primary and secondary EDS to § 1245 and § 1250 appropriately.

The costs of the hook-ups and branch circuits that service building related items, such as HVAC, power outlets for general use, lighting, and other building services, should be recovered over the recovery period of the building. The costs of the hook-ups and branch circuits that supply power to dedicated machinery and equipment used as an integral part of the taxpayer's business should be recovered over the appropriate recovery periods of the equipment that they serve based on § 168 and Rev. Proc. 87-56.

The primary and secondary EDS components of a building or other inherently permanent structure used in the operation or maintenance of the building or necessary to provide general building services (such as lighting, heating, ventilation, air conditioning, etc.), including electrical outlets of general applicability and accessibility, are § 1250 property and are recovered over the same recovery period as the building.

Examiners are encouraged to risk assess the taxpayer's EDS allocation using the analyses discussed in this chapter to verify that the claimed functional allocation method is applied correctly and that it yields the appropriate percentage for § 1245 property portion of the EDS of the building.

If the taxpayer uses a correct functional allocation approach as illustrated in this Chapter to define which parts of a building's primary and secondary EDS were designed to service § 1245 property, the Examiner should not challenge the use of the functional allocation approach.

# Quick Reference Table—Recovery Periods for Various Assets and Activities

The table below, although not exhaustive, lists the recovery periods for many depreciable assets under MACRS. Cross references are provided to the applicable CCH discussion in this guide.

*How to determine the depreciation period.* The principals involved in determining the depreciation period of an asset are described in detail at ¶ 190.

See also ¶ 191 for a comprehensive list of asset classes and recovery periods provided by the IRS in Rev. Proc. 87-56.

*Building components.* See (1) ¶ 127A for lists of components of buildings that may be depreciated under the cost segregation rules as over shortened recovery periods that usually depend upon the business activity that the building is used in and (2) the cost segregation tables that immediately precede this quick reference table.

*Additions and improvements to buildings.* See ¶ 126.

*Land improvements.* Land improvements are generally depreciated over 15 years unless otherwise provided in Rev. Proc. 87-56. See ¶ 5, ¶ 110, ¶ 127C, and the immediately preceding quick reference cost segregation table for building components.

*Farm assets.* An additional rapid finder table showing the recovery period of farm assets is at ¶ 118.

*Assets used in retail or wholesale trade or business and by personal and professional service providers.* If an asset is used in the provision of personal or professional services or in a wholesale or retail trade or business that asset is classified as five-year property (Asset Class 57.0) unless it is a specifically described asset in Table B-1 of Rev. Proc. 87-56 (Asset Classes 00.11 through 00.4 at ¶ 191). See ¶ 104 for a detailed discussion, including the types of businesses and professions that are covered by this rule.

| | *Recovery Period* | |
|---|---|---|
| *Type of Asset/Activity* | *MACRS* | *Alt. MACRS* |
| Accountant | See ¶ 104 | |
| Adding machine (¶ 104) | 5 | 6 |
| Aerospace products, assets used in manufacture and assembly of | 7 | 10 |
| Additions and improvements | See ¶ 126 | |
| Agricultural structures, single purpose, post-1988 property (¶ 106) | 10 | 15 |
| Agricultural structures, single purpose, pre-1989 property (¶ 106) | 7 | 15 |
| Agriculture, assets used in (¶ 106, ¶ 118) | 7 | 10 |
| . equipment | | |
| . fences | | |
| . grain bins | | |
| . machinery | | |
| Air conditioning | See ¶ 127A | |

| Type of Asset/Activity | Recovery Period: MACRS | Recovery Period: Alt. MACRS |
|---|---|---|
| Air filtration systems | See ¶ 127A | |
| Airplanes, used in commercial or contract carrying of passengers (¶ 106) | 7 | 12 |
| Airplane hangar | See ¶ 127C | |
| Airplanes, not used in commercial or contract carrying of passengers (¶ 104) | 5 | 6 |
| Apparel, assets used in production of (¶ 191) | 5 | 9 |
| Appliances, apartment | See ¶ 104 | |
| Architect | See ¶ 104 | |
| Art supplies, assets used in production of (¶ 191) | 7 | 12 |
| Artwork | See ¶ 3 | |
| Barber shop | See ¶ 104 | |
| Barges, not used in marine construction (¶ 108) | 10 | 18 |
| Barns | See ¶ 112 | |
| Beauty shop | See ¶ 104 | |
| Bed and breakfasts | See ¶ 125 | |
| Bee keeping | See ¶ 106 | |
| Billboards, signs | See ¶ 110, ¶ 127A | |
| Boats or vessels | See ¶ 108 | |
| Bobcats | See ¶ 125 | |
| Bowling alleys, assets used in (¶ 106) | 7 | 10 |
| Breast implants | See ¶ 125 | |
| Brooms, assets used in production of (¶ 191) | 7 | 12 |
| Buildings | See ¶ 127, ¶ 127C | |
| Buses (¶ 104) | 5 | 9 |
| Calculators (¶ 104) | 5 | 6 |
| Carpets | See ¶ 127A | |
| Car wash buildings (¶ 110) | 15 | 20 |
| Carpeting | See ¶ 104, ¶ 127A | |
| Carpets, assets used in manufacture of (¶ 191) | 5 | 9 |
| Cars (¶ 104) | 5 | 5 |
| Cars, show cars, antiques, exotics | See ¶ 125 | |
| Cash register | See ¶ 191 | |
| Casinos | See ¶ 106 | |
| Cattle, breeding or dairy (¶ 104, ¶ 118) | 5 | 7 |
| Ceilings | See ¶ 127A | |
| Cement, assets used in producing (¶ 110) | 15 | 20 |
| Cell phone (¶ 106) | 7 | 10 |
| Cellular phone companies | See ¶ 125 | |
| Chemicals, assets used in manufacture of (¶ 191) | 5 | 9.5 |
| Clay products, assets used in manufacture of (¶ 191) | 7 | 15 |
| Coin operated dispensing machines (¶ 104) | 5 | 9 |
| Communications equipment not in other classes (¶ 106) | 7 | 10 |
| Computer peripheral equipment (¶ 105) | 5 | 5 |
| . card punches | | |
| . card readers | | |
| . card sorters | | |
| . data entry devices | | |
| . disc drives, packs, files | | |

| Type of Asset/Activity | Recovery Period MACRS | Alt. MACRS |
|---|---|---|
| . keypunches | | |
| . magnetic tape feeds | | |
| . mass storage units | | |
| . optical character readers | | |
| . paper tape equipment | | |
| . printers, high speed | | |
| . tape cassettes | | |
| . teleprinters | | |
| . terminals | | |
| Computer software | See ¶ 48, ¶ 102 | |
| Computers (¶ 104) | 5 | 5 |
| Concert halls, assets used in (¶ 106) | 7 | 10 |
| Concrete trucks (¶ 104) | 5 | 6 |
| Condominiums | See ¶ 114 | |
| Construction, assets used in (¶ 104) | 5 | 6 |
| Containers | See ¶ 5 | |
| Convenience store | See ¶ 110 | |
| Copiers (¶ 104) | 5 | 6 |
| Cotton ginning, assets used in (¶ 191) | 7 | 12 |
| Dam | See ¶ 110 | |
| Dental supplies, assets used in manufacture of (¶ 191) | 5 | 9 |
| Dentist | See ¶ 104 | |
| Desks (¶ 106) | 7 | 10 |
| Distribution center | See ¶ 104 | |
| Doctor | See ¶ 104 | |
| Doors | See ¶ 127A | |
| Dry cleaning | See ¶ 104 | |
| Dump truck (¶ 104) | 5 | 6 |
| Duplicating equipment (¶ 104) | 5 | 6 |
| Electric utility steam production plants (¶ 191) | 20 | 28 |
| Electrical and non-electrical machinery, assets used to manufacture or rebuild (¶ 191) | 3 | 3 |
| Electrical distribution system | See ¶ 127 | |
| Electronic components, assets used in manufacture of electronic communication, computation, instrumentation and control systems (¶ 191) | 7 | 10 |
| Electronic systems, assets used in manufacture of electronic communication, computation, instrumentation and control systems (¶ 191) | 5 | 6 |
| Elevators and escalators | See ¶ 114, ¶ 116 | |
| Energy maintenance system | See ¶ 127A | |
| Energy property (¶ 104) | 5 | |
| . geothermal | | |
| . ocean thermal | | |
| . solar | | |
| . wind | | |
| Engineer | See ¶ 104 | |
| Environmental cleanup costs | See ¶ 5 | |
| Ethanol plants | See ¶ 106 | |
| Exterior building ornamentation, facades, balconies | See ¶ 127A | |

| Type of Asset/Activity | Recovery Period MACRS | Alt. MACRS |
|---|---|---|
| Fabric, woven, assets used in production of (¶ 191) | 7 | 11 |
| Farm buildings and property | See ¶ 118 | |
| Fax machines (¶ 106) | 7 | 10 |
| Fences (nonagricultural) (¶ 110) | 15 | 20 |
| Fences (agricultural) (¶ 118) | 7 | 10 |
| Files, office (¶ 106) | 7 | 10 |
| Fire and burglary protection | See ¶ 104 and ¶ 127A | |
| Fishing vessels (¶ 106) | 7 | 12 |
| Fixtures, office (¶ 106) | 7 | 10 |
| Floor coverings | See ¶ 127A | |
| Floors, raised floors and concrete floors | See ¶ 127A | |
| Food and kindred products, manufacturing not otherwise specified (¶ 191) | 7 | 12 |
| Food and beverage manufacturing, special handling devices (¶ 191) | 3 | 4 |
| . fish processing equipment | | |
| .. baskets | | |
| .. boxes | | |
| .. carts | | |
| .. flaking trays | | |
| . palletized containers | | |
| . returnable pallets | | |
| Fork lifts | See ¶ 125 | |
| Furniture, apartment (¶ 104) | 5 | 9 |
| Furniture, assets used in production of | 7 | 10 |
| Furniture, office (¶ 106) | 7 | 10 |
| Furniture rental | See ¶ 104 | |
| Gaming equipment, slots etc. (¶ 106) | 7 | 10 |
| Gasoline station | See ¶ 110, ¶ 125 | |
| Gas production plants of gas utilities (¶ 191) | 20 | 30 |
| Gathering systems, oil and gas | See ¶ 106 | |
| Generators, emergency | See ¶ 127A | |
| Geothermal energy property (¶ 104) | 5 | |
| Glass products, assets used in production of (¶ 191) | 7 | 14 |
| Glass products, manufacture of, special tools (¶ 191) | 3 | 2.5 |
| . molds | | |
| . pallets | | |
| . patterns | | |
| . specialty transfer and shipping devices | | |
| . steel racks | | |
| Goats, breeding (¶ 118) | 5 | 5 |
| Golf course | See ¶ 5 | |
| Grading | See ¶ 5 | |
| Grain and grain mill products, assets used in production of (¶ 191) | 10 | 17 |
| Greenhouses (¶ 108, ¶ 118) | 10 | 15 |
| Gym equipment | See ¶ 125 | |
| Handrails | See ¶ 127A | |
| Hangar | See ¶ 108 | |
| Helicopters (¶ 104) | 5 | 6 |

| *Type of Asset/Activity* | *Recovery Period* *MACRS* | *Alt. MACRS* |
|---|---|---|
| Hogs, breeding (¶ 102, ¶ 118) | 3 | 3 |
| Home office | See ¶ 116 | |
| Horses | See ¶ 102, ¶ 106, ¶ 118 | |
| Hotels | See ¶ 104 | |
| HVAC | See ¶ 127A | |
| Horticultural structures, single purpose (¶ 118) | 10 | 15 |
| Indian reservation property | See ¶ 124 | |
| Irrigation system | See ¶ 118 | |
| Jewelry, assets used in production of (¶ 191) | 7 | 12 |
| Keycard locking system | See ¶ 127A | |
| Knitted goods, laces, assets used in manufacture of (¶ 191) | 5 | 7.5 |
| Land improvements (¶ 5, ¶ 110, ¶ 127C) | 15 | 20 |
| . bridges | | |
| . canals | | |
| . drainage facilities | | |
| . fences | | |
| . landscaping | | |
| . parking lots | | |
| . radio and television towers | | |
| . roads | | |
| . sewers (non-municipal) | | |
| . sidewalks | | |
| . shrubbery, trees | | |
| . waterways | | |
| . wells (water) | | |
| . wharves and docks | | |
| Land preparation costs | See ¶ 5, ¶ 110 | |
| Landscaping (¶ 5, ¶ 110) | 15 | 20 |
| Laundry | See ¶ 104 | |
| Lawyer | See ¶ 104 | |
| Leather and leather products, assets used in manufacture of (¶ 191) | 7 | 11 |
| Leasehold improvements | See ¶ 126 | |
| Library | See ¶ 104 | |
| Lighting, interior and exterior | See ¶ 127A | |
| Limousine (¶ 104) | 5 | 6 |
| Livestock | See ¶ 118 | |
| Logging machinery and equipment (¶ 104) | 5 | 6 |
| Lottery terminals (¶ 106) | 7 | 10 |
| Low-income housing (¶ 114) | 27.5 | 40 |
| Manufactured homes, residential (¶ 114) | 27.5 | 40 |
| Manufacturing equipment, semi-conductor (¶ 104) | 5 | 5 |
| Medical equipment | See ¶ 104 | |
| Medical supplies, assets used in manufacture of (¶ 191) | 5 | 9 |
| Miniature golf course, assets used in (¶ 106) | 7 | 10 |
| Mining, assets used in mining and quarrying of minerals and milling and other primary preparation of such materials (¶ 191) | 7 | 10 |

| Type of Asset/Activity | Recovery Period MACRS | Alt. MACRS |
|---|---|---|
| Mobile homes parks | See ¶ 5 | |
| Mobile homes | See ¶ 127 | |
| Molding, millwork, trim, finish carpentry, paneling | See ¶ 127A | |
| Mortuary | See ¶ 104 | |
| Motels | See ¶ 104 | |
| Motor homes | See ¶ 104, ¶ 302 | |
| Motion picture films and tapes, assets used in production of (¶ 191) | 7 | 12 |
| Motor transport (freight and passengers) (¶ 104) | 5 | 8 |
| Motor vehicles, assets used in manufacture and assembly of (¶ 191) | 7 | 12 |
| Motor vehicles, manufacture of—special tools (¶ 191) | 3 | 3 |
| . dies | | |
| . fixtures | | |
| . gauges | | |
| . jigs | | |
| . molds | | |
| . patterns | | |
| Musical instruments, assets used in production of | 7 | 12 |
| Musical instruments (¶ 3, ¶ 104)) | 5 | 9 |
| Nonresidential real property (¶ 116) | 39 | 40 |
| Nurseries | See ¶ 118 | |
| Nursing home | See ¶ 114 | |
| Ocean thermal energy property (¶ 104) | 5 | |
| Office equipment (¶ 106) | 7 | 10 |
| Office furniture, fixtures (¶ 106) | 7 | 10 |
| Office supplies, assets used in production of (¶ 191) | 7 | 12 |
| Ore trucks (¶ 104) | 5 | 6 |
| Parking buildings (open air) (¶ 127C | 39 | 40 |
| Parking lots (¶ 5, ¶ 110) | 15 | 20 |
| Partitions and walls | See ¶ 127A | |
| Picnic table (¶ 110) | 15 | 20 |
| Pens, assets used in production of (¶ 191) | 7 | 12 |
| Photographic studio | See ¶ 104 | |
| Pipeline transportation assets (¶ 106) | 15 | 22 |
| Plastic products, finished, assets used in manufacture of (¶ 191) | 7 | 11 |
| Plastic products, finished, manufacture of—special tools (¶ 191) | 3 | 3.5 |
| . dies | | |
| . fixtures | | |
| . gauges | | |
| . jigs | | |
| . molds | | |
| . patterns | | |
| . specialty transfer and shipping devices | | |
| Playground equipment | See ¶ 5 | |
| Plumbing and wiring | See ¶ 127A | |
| Pool halls, assets used in (¶ 106) | 7 | 10 |
| Precious metals (¶ 125) | 7 | 11 |
| Printing, assets used in (¶ 191) | 7 | 11 |

| *Type of Asset/Activity* | *Recovery Period* *MACRS* | *Alt. MACRS* |
|---|---|---|
| Professional service provider, assets used by | see ¶ 104 | |
| Projector (overhead) (¶ 106) | 7 | 10 |
| Public utility property | | |
| . electric utility steam production plants (¶ 191) | 5 | 5 |
| . gas utility manufactured gas production plants (¶ 191) | 20 | 30 |
| . telephone distribution plants (¶ 110) | 15 | 24 |
| Publishing, assets used in (¶ 191) | 7 | 11 |
| Race cars (¶ 104) | 7 | 10 |
| Race tracks (¶ 110) | 15 | 20 |
| Railroad assets | See ¶ 106 | |
| Recreation, assets used in | See ¶ 106 | |
| Recreational vehicles (RV) | | |
| . actual unloaded weights of less than 13,000 pounds (¶ 104, ¶ 114, ¶ 302) | 5 | 5 |
| . actual unloaded weights of 13,000 pounds or more (¶ 104, ¶ 114, ¶ 302) | 5 | 6 |
| Rent-to-own property (¶ 102) | 3 | 4 |
| Research and experimentation property (¶ 104) | 5 | |
| Residential rental property (¶ 114) | 27.5 | 40 |
| Restaurant buildings and improvements | See ¶ 110 | |
| Restrooms | See ¶ 127A | |
| Retail improvement property | See ¶ 126 | |
| Roads | See ¶ 5, ¶ 110 | |
| Roofs | See ¶ 125 | |
| Rotable spare parts | See ¶ 125 | |
| Rubber products, assets used in production of (¶ 191) | 7 | 14 |
| Rubber products, manufacture of special tools (¶ 191) | 3 | 4 |
| . jigs and dies | | |
| .. lasts, mandrels, molds, patterns | | |
| . specialty containers | | |
| .. pallets, shells, tire molds | | |
| Safes, office (¶ 106) | 7 | 10 |
| Samples (¶ 125) | 7 | 10 |
| Sawmills | See ¶ 104 | |
| Security systems | See ¶ 127A | |
| Septic system | See ¶ 127A | |
| Service station | See ¶ 110 | |
| Sewer tap fees | See ¶ 70 | |
| Sewers, municipal (¶ 113) | 25 | 50 |
| Shed | See ¶ 127C | |
| Sheep, breeding (¶ 118) | 5 | 5 |
| Ship- and boat-building machinery, assets used in manufacture and repair of ships (¶ 191) | 7 | 12 |
| Ships, not used in marine construction (¶ 108) | 10 | 18 |
| Shop equipment | See ¶ 125 | |
| Signs, billboards, scoreboards | See ¶ 127A | |
| Site utilities | See ¶ 127A | |
| Slot machines (¶ 106) | 7 | 10 |
| Small power production facilities, biomass properties (¶ 104) | 5 | |

| Type of Asset/Activity | Recovery Period MACRS | Alt. MACRS |
|---|---|---|
| Smallwares of restaurants and taverns | See ¶ 125 | |
| Smart electric meters | See ¶ 125 | |
| Sod | See ¶ 5 | |
| Software | See ¶ 48, ¶ 102 | |
| Solar energy property, including solar panels (¶ 104) | 5 | |
| Sporting goods, assets used in production of (¶ 191) | 7 | 12 |
| Storage sheds | See ¶ 127C | |
| Street lights | See ¶ 112 | |
| Structural components of buildings | See ¶ 127 | |
| Swimming pool | See ¶ 127A | |
| Sugar and sugar products, assets used in production of (¶ 191) | 10 | 18 |
| Taxis (¶ 104) | 5 | 5 |
| Technological equipment (¶ 104) | 5 | 5 |
| . computers & peripheral equipment | | |
| . high technology medical equipment | | |
| . high technology telephone station equipment installed on customer's premises | | |
| Telephone, central office switching equipment (¶ 110) | 15 | 18 |
| Telephone, central office switching equipment, computer based (¶ 104) | 5 | 9.5 |
| Telephone distribution plants (¶ 110) | 15 | 24 |
| Television films and tapes, assets used in production of (¶ 191) | 7 | 12 |
| Textile products, dyeing, finishing & packaging (¶ 191) | 5 | 9 |
| Theaters, assets used in (¶ 106) | 7 | 10 |
| Theme park structures (¶ 106) | 7 | 12.5 |
| Thread, assets used in production of (¶ 191) | 7 | 11 |
| Timber cutting, equipment used in (¶ 191) | 5 | 6 |
| Tires and tubes | See ¶ 125 | |
| Tobacco and tobacco products, assets used in production of cigarettes, cigars, etc.(¶ 191) | 7 | 15 |
| Tobacco barns | See ¶ 127C | |
| Tools | See ¶ 125 | |
| Toys, assets used in production of (¶ 191) | 7 | 12 |
| Tractor units, over-the-road use (¶ 102) | 3 | 4 |
| Trailer-mounted containers (¶ 104) | 5 | 6 |
| Trailers (¶ 104, ¶ 114, ¶ 127C) | 5 | 6 |
| Transportation equipment | | |
| . air, passenger (¶ 106) | 7 | 12 |
| . motor transport, freight (¶ 191) | 5 | 8 |
| . motor transport, passengers (¶ 191) | 5 | 8 |
| . water, passenger and freight (¶ 110) | 15 | 20 |
| Trees and vines (orchards and vineyards) | See ¶ 108 | |
| Trees, fruit or nut bearing, post-1988 (¶ 108) | 10 | 20 |
| Trellis | See ¶ 118 | |
| Trucks | | |
| . heavy general purpose (¶ 102, ¶ 104) | 5 | 6 |
| .. concrete ready-mix trucks | | |

| Type of Asset/Activity | Recovery Period MACRS | Alt. MACRS |
|---|---|---|
| .. ore trucks | | |
| .. over-the-road trucks, actual unloaded weight 13,000 | | |
| . light general purpose, actual unloaded weight less than 13,000 pounds (¶ 102, ¶ 104) | 5 | 5 |
| Tugs, not used in marine construction (¶ 108) | 10 | 18 |
| Tuxedo rental (¶ 104) | 5 | 9 |
| Typewriters (¶ 104) | 5 | 6 |
| Uniforms | See ¶ 125 | |
| Vacation homes | See ¶ 114 | |
| Vegetable oils and products, assets used in manufacture of (¶ 191) | 10 | 18 |
| Vessels and barges | See ¶ 108 | |
| Veterinarians | See ¶ 104 | |
| Video cassettes | See ¶ 140 | |
| Vines, fruit or nut bearing, post-1988 (¶ 108) | 10 | 20 |
| Wall paper and wall coverings | See ¶ 127A | |
| Walls and partitions | See ¶ 127A | |
| Warehouse (¶ 127C) | 10 | 20 |
| Wastewater treatment plant, municipal (¶ 110) | 15 | 24 |
| Water heaters and water softeners | See ¶ 127A | |
| Water utility property (¶ 113) | 25 | 50 |
| Web site | See ¶ 125 | |
| Wells (water) (¶ 118) | 15 | 20 |
| Wind energy property (¶ 104) | 5 | |
| Wiring and plumbing | See ¶ 127A | |
| Wood products, assets used in production of (¶ 191) | 7 | 10 |
| Yachts (¶ 108) | 10 | 18 |
| Yarn, assets used in production of (¶ 191) | 7 | 11 |
| Zoning variation | See ¶ 125 | |

The table above generally does not list structural components of buildings or items affixed or attached to the interior or exterior of a building which are considered personal property, separately depreciable from the building. The classification of property as personal or real (i.e., a structural component) is often unclear and remains the subject of much controversy. See ¶ 127 and ¶ 127A for a detailed discussion.

Structural components (if related to operation and maintenance of building) (¶ 127 and ¶ 127A):

- Acoustical ceilings
- Bathtubs
- Boilers
- Ceilings
- Central air conditioning and heating (including motors, compressors, pipes, and ducts)
- Chimneys
- Doors
- Electrical systems
- Elevators
- Escalators
- Mechanical service systems
- Paneling
- Partitions (not movable)
- Plumbing
- Plumbing fixtures
- Raised floor
- Roofs
- Siding
- Sinks
- Sprinkler system

- Fire escapes
- Floors
- Hot water heaters
- HVAC units
- Keycard door locking system
- Lighting fixtures
- Stairs
- Tiling
- Walls
- Windows
- Wiring

Personal property:

- Carpeting (removable)
- Display racks and shelves
- Electrical and wiring allocable to machinery and equipment
- Eliason doors
- Folding wall partitions
- Gasoline pumps
- Grocery counters
- Hydraulic car lifts
- Kitchen hoods and exhaust systems
- Kitchen steam lines
- Kitchen water piping
- Neon and other signs
- Partitions (movable)
- Plumbing connections for equipment
- Plumbing for x-ray machines
- Printing presses
- Production machinery
- Refrigerators
- Telephone and communications wiring and equipment
- Testing equipment
- Transportation and office equipment
- Vending machines
- Vinyl wall and floor coverings (removable)

# Case Table

## A



## B



## C



## D



## E



## F



## G

# Finding Lists

## Announcements



## General Counsel Memoranda



## IRS Letter Rulings and Memorandums

## Notices



## Revenue Procedures

## Revenue Rulings

# Topical Index

***Also refer to the quick reference guide on page 1391 immediately preceding the case table for depreciation periods of particular assets or assets used in particular business activities. The quick reference guide also includes cross references to related explanations.***

***All references are to paragraph (¶) numbers.***

## A

## D

## T